lonely planet



# Africa

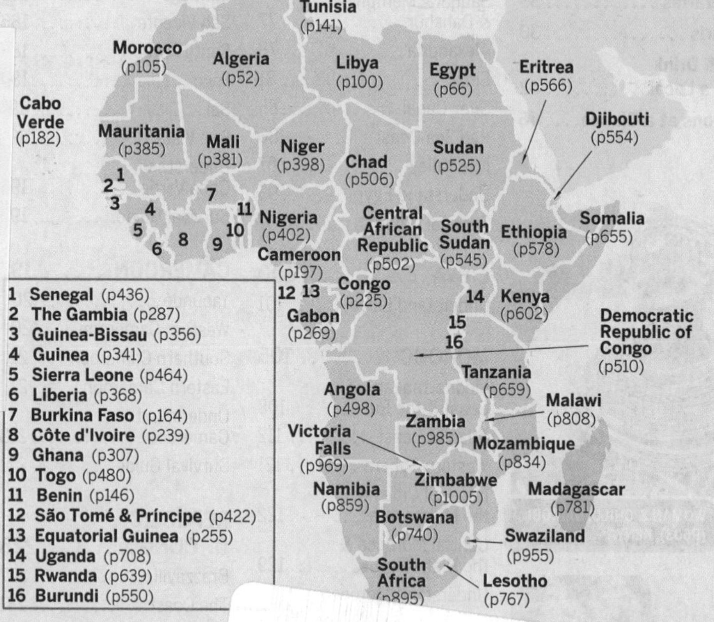






Brett Atkinson, ... an-Bernard Carillet, Paul Clam... y Fitzpatrick, Michael Grosberg, Trent Holden, Jess... en Lioy, Nana Luckham, Vesna Maric, Tom Masters, Virginia Maxwell, Lorna Parkes, Helen Ranger, Brendan Sainsbury, Caroline Sieg, Helena Smith, Regis St Louis, Paul Stiles

## PLAN YOUR TRIP



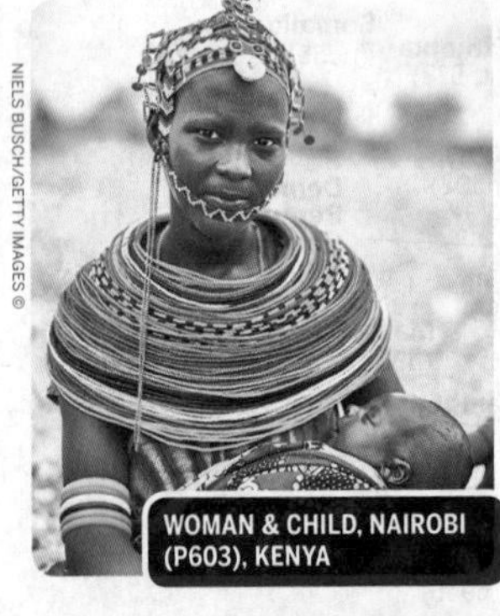
WOMAN & CHILD, NAIROBI (P603), KENYA

LOCAL MOROCCAN DISHES (P138)



## ON THE ROAD

# Contents

# Contents

## ON THE ROAD

# Contents

## UNDERSTAND



## SURVIVAL GUIDE



## SPECIAL FEATURES

# Welcome to Africa

*Africa. There's nowhere like it on the planet for wildlife, wild lands and rich traditions that endure. Prepare to fall in love.*

## Natural Beauty

Whether you're a wide-eyed first-timer or a frequent visitor, Africa cannot fail to get under your skin. The canvas upon which the continent's epic story is written is itself astonishing, and reason enough to visit. From the tropical rainforests and glorious tropical coastline of Central Africa to the rippling dunes of the Namib, from the signature savannah of the Serengeti to jagged mountains, green-tinged highlands and deep canyons that mark the Great Rift Valley's continental traverse – wherever you find yourself on this big, beautiful continent, Africa has few peers when it comes to natural beauty.

## Ancient Africa

On this continent where human beings first came into existence, customs, traditions and ancient rites tie Africans to generations and ancestors past and to the collective memory of myriad people. In many rural areas it can feel as though the modern world might never have happened, and they are all the better for it, and old ways of doing things – with a certain grace and civility, hospitality and a community spirit – survive. There are time-honoured ceremonies, music that dates back to the days of Africa's golden empires, and masks that tell stories of spirit worlds never lost. Welcome to Old Africa.

## New Africa

The past retains its hold over the lives of many Africans, but just as many have embraced the future, bringing creativity and sophistication to the continent's cities and urban centres. Sometimes this New Africa is expressed in a creative-conservation search for solutions to the continent's environmental problems, or in an eagerness to break free of the restrictive chains of the past and transform the traveller experience. But just as often, modern Africans are taking all that is new and fusing it onto the best of the old.

## Wildlife Bonanza

A Noah's ark of wildlife brings Africa's landscapes to life, with a tangible and sometimes profoundly mysterious presence that adds so much personality to the African wild. So many of the great beasts, including elephants, hippos and lions, call Africa home. Going on safari may be something of a travel cliché, but we're yet to find a traveller who has watched the wildlife world in motion in the Masai Mara, watched the epic battles between predator and prey in the Okavango Delta, or communed with gorillas and surfing hippos in Gabon and has not been reduced to an ecstatic state of childlike wonder.

## Why I Love Africa

By Anthony Ham, Writer

Africa is for me a place of the soul. It is the wildlife, the great deserts and the savannah plains that speak of eternity, and the people who bring such warmth to the experience. It is the Serengeti and the Sahara, Etosha and Amboseli National Parks, the Namib Desert and the forests of Madagascar. It is drawing near to a black-maned lion in the Kalahari, or watching the hyenas stream across the plains of Liuwa Plain National Park, or sleeping in a luxury lodge or remote wilderness campsite and staring up at the stars in utter, blissful silence.

**For more about our writers, see p1120**

Above: Maasai warriors, Masai Mara National Reserve (p620)

# Africa

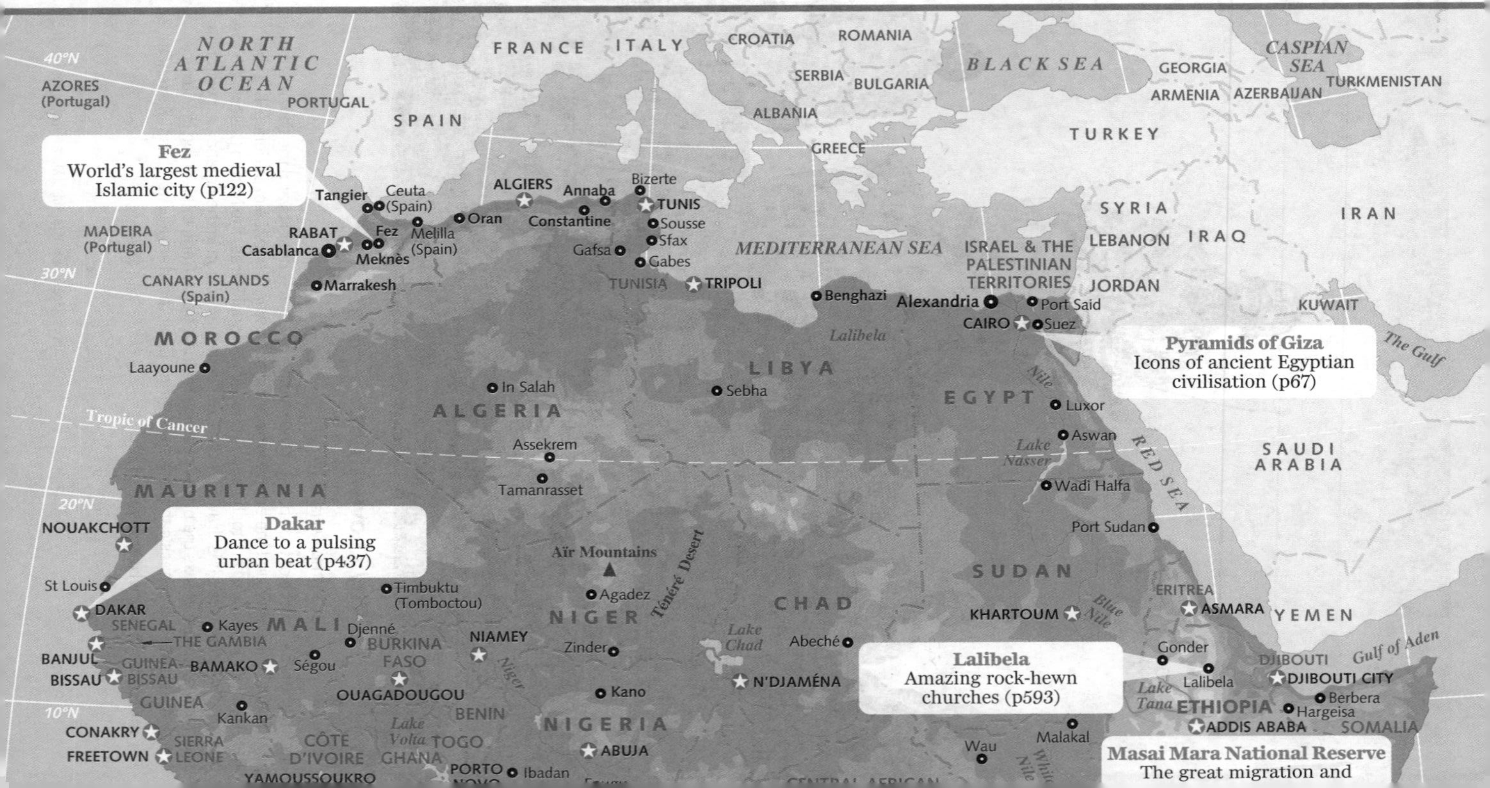

0 — 1000 km
0 — 500 miles

**Fez**
World's largest medieval Islamic city (p122)

**Pyramids of Giza**
Icons of ancient Egyptian civilisation (p67)

**Dakar**
Dance to a pulsing urban beat (p437)

**Lalibela**
Amazing rock-hewn churches (p593)

**Masai Mara National Reserve**
The great migration and

NORTH ATLANTIC OCEAN
AZORES (Portugal)
MADEIRA (Portugal)
CANARY ISLANDS (Spain)
PORTUGAL
SPAIN
FRANCE
ITALY
CROATIA
ROMANIA
SERBIA
BULGARIA
ALBANIA
GREECE
BLACK SEA
GEORGIA
ARMENIA
AZERBAIJAN
CASPIAN SEA
TURKMENISTAN
TURKEY
SYRIA
LEBANON
IRAQ
IRAN
ISRAEL & THE PALESTINIAN TERRITORIES
JORDAN
KUWAIT
The Gulf
SAUDI ARABIA
YEMEN
Gulf of Aden
MEDITERRANEAN SEA
RED SEA
Tangier
Ceuta (Spain)
Melilla (Spain)
Oran
ALGIERS
Annaba
Constantine
Bizerte
TUNIS
Sousse
Sfax
Gafsa
Gabes
TUNISIA
TRIPOLI
Benghazi
Alexandria
Port Said
CAIRO
Suez
RABAT
Fez
Casablanca
Meknès
Marrakesh
MOROCCO
Laayoune
In Salah
ALGERIA
Sebha
LIBYA
Lalibela
EGYPT
Nile
Luxor
Aswan
Lake Nasser
Wadi Halfa
Tropic of Cancer
Assekrem
Tamanrasset
MAURITANIA
NOUAKCHOTT
Port Sudan
SUDAN
Aïr Mountains
Ténéré Desert
St Louis
DAKAR
SENEGAL
Timbuktu (Tombouctou)
Agadez
NIGER
CHAD
ERITREA
ASMARA
KHARTOUM
Blue Nile
Kayes
MALI
Djenné
THE GAMBIA
BANJUL
GUINEA-BISSAU
BISSAU
BAMAKO
Ségou
BURKINA FASO
NIAMEY
Niger
Zinder
Lake Chad
Abeché
Gonder
Lalibela
DJIBOUTI
DJIBOUTI CITY
Berbera
Hargeisa
OUAGADOUGOU
N'DJAMÉNA
Kano
Lake Tana
ETHIOPIA
ADDIS ABABA
SOMALIA
GUINEA
Kankan
BENIN
NIGERIA
Malakal
CONAKRY
SIERRA LEONE
FREETOWN
CÔTE D'IVOIRE
Lake Volta
TOGO
GHANA
ABUJA
Wau
White Nile
YAMOUSSOUKRO
PORTO NOVO
Ibadan
40°N
30°N
20°N
10°N

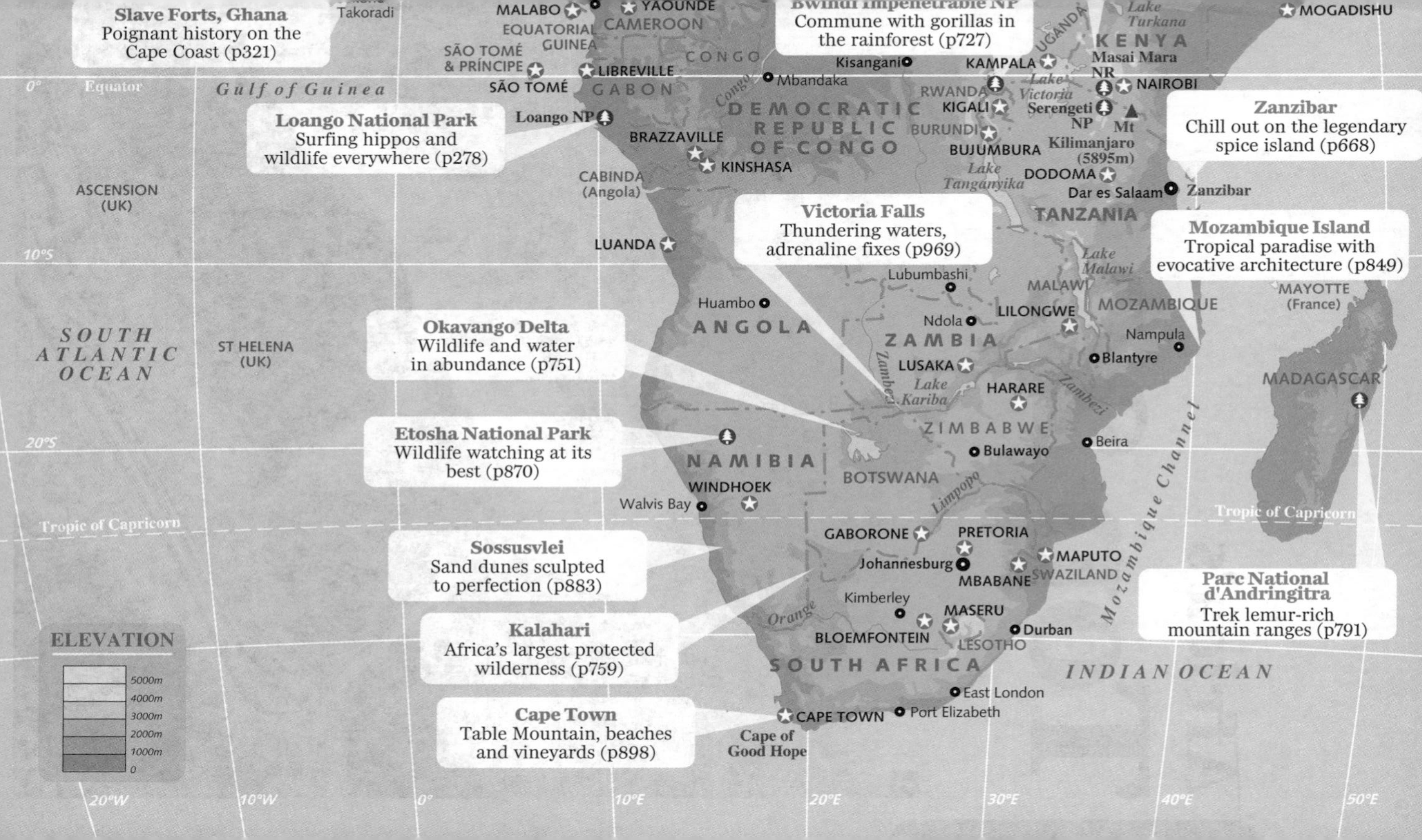

Slave Forts, Ghana
Poignant history on the Cape Coast (p321)
Bwindi Impenetrable NP
Commune with gorillas in the rainforest (p727)
Zanzibar
Chill out on the legendary spice island (p668)
Loango National Park
Surfing hippos and wildlife everywhere (p278)
Victoria Falls
Thundering waters, adrenaline fixes (p969)
Mozambique Island
Tropical paradise with evocative architecture (p849)
Okavango Delta
Wildlife and water in abundance (p751)
Etosha National Park
Wildlife watching at its best (p870)
Sossusvlei
Sand dunes sculpted to perfection (p883)
Kalahari
Africa's largest protected wilderness (p759)
Cape Town
Table Mountain, beaches and vineyards (p898)
Parc National d'Andringitra
Trek lemur-rich mountain ranges (p791)
Takoradi
MALABO
YAOUNDE
MOGADISHU
EQUATORIAL GUINEA
CAMEROON
SÃO TOMÉ & PRÍNCIPE
LIBREVILLE
SÃO TOMÉ
CONGO
GABON
Gulf of Guinea
Equator
0°
Loango NP
BRAZZAVILLE
KINSHASA
CABINDA (Angola)
ASCENSION (UK)
LUANDA
10°S
Kisangani
Mbandaka
Congo
DEMOCRATIC REPUBLIC OF CONGO
UGANDA
KAMPALA
RWANDA
KIGALI
BURUNDI
BUJUMBURA
Lake Tanganyika
Lake Victoria
Lake Turkana
KENYA
Masai Mara NR
NAIROBI
Serengeti NP
Mt Kilimanjaro (5895m)
DODOMA
Dar es Salaam
Zanzibar
TANZANIA
Lake Malawi
MALAWI
LILONGWE
MOZAMBIQUE
MAYOTTE (France)
Nampula
Blantyre
MADAGASCAR
Lubumbashi
Huambo
ANGOLA
Ndola
ZAMBIA
LUSAKA
Zambezi
Lake Kariba
HARARE
ZIMBABWE
Bulawayo
Beira
Mozambique Channel
SOUTH ATLANTIC OCEAN
ST HELENA (UK)
20°S
NAMIBIA
BOTSWANA
Limpopo
WINDHOEK
Walvis Bay
Tropic of Capricorn
GABORONE
PRETORIA
Johannesburg
MBABANE
MAPUTO
SWAZILAND
Kimberley
MASERU
Orange
BLOEMFONTEIN
LESOTHO
Durban
SOUTH AFRICA
INDIAN OCEAN
East London
Port Elizabeth
CAPE TOWN
Cape of Good Hope
ELEVATION
5000m
4000m
3000m
2000m
1000m
0
20°W
10°W
0°
10°E
20°E
30°E
40°E
50°E

# Africa's Top 20

1

## Victoria Falls, Zambia & Zimbabwe

**1** The mighty Victoria Falls (p969) is worth crossing the continent for, whether it's to laze in the aptly named Devil's Pool (take the precarious walk, literally out across the top of the falls to this natural infinity pool, to see what we mean) or to get active with all manner of adventures from white-water rafting to bungee jumping within sight and sound of the falls, known locally as 'the smoke that thunders'. It's a beautiful, beautiful place, not to mention one of the most awe-inspiring sights on the continent.

## Pyramids of Giza, Egypt

**2** The last of the seven wonders of the ancient world stands right on the edge of Cairo, as if guarding the desert from the city's creeping urban sprawl. You may have seen the images a thousand times beforehand but nothing beats your first face-to-face meeting with the impeccable geometry and sheer bulk of this mammoth funerary complex (p67). Battered by the passing of time, from the Sphinx' chipped nose to the graffiti of past explorers, these age-old structures have not lost their ability to awe.

VADIM PETRAKOV/SHUTTERSTOCK ©

2

SCULPIES/SHUTTERSTOCK ©

MICHAEL HEFFERNAN/LONELY PLANET ©

## Medinas, Morocco

**3** Ancient meets modern in the medinas (old, walled city-centres) of Morocco, and those of Fez and Marrakesh sit at the top of any traveller's list. Narrow alleys hide centuries-old riads restored into fabulous guesthouses, while the delivery man outside unloads his donkeys while chatting on his mobile phone. Fez (p122) is the oldest of the two, with celebrated mosques and the longest and most-winding streets, while in Marrakesh all paths seem to converge on the Djemaa el-Fna square (p130), which springs to life daily with 1001 nights' worth of attractions.

## Mozambique Island, Mozambique

**4** There are no crowds and few vehicles, but Mozambique Island (p849) is hardly silent. Echoes of its past mix with the squawking of chickens, the sounds of children playing and the calls of the muezzin to remind you that the island is still very much alive. Wander along cobbled streets, past graceful *praças* (plazas) rimmed by once-grand churches and stately colonial-era buildings. This Unesco World Heritage Site, with its time-warp atmosphere and backdrop of turquoise seas, is a Mozambique highlight, and not to be missed.

## Lalibela, Ethiopia

**5** Follow a white-robed pilgrim down a dark passageway, hear the hypnotic thud of a muffled drumbeat, smell the sweet aroma of incense and emerge into a sliver of daylight just in time to see a priest in royal robes, holding a cross of silver, enter a church carved into and out of the rust-red rock. Lalibela (p593) is a place of pilgrimage where the buildings are frozen in stone and the soul is alive with the rites and awe of Christianity at its most ancient and unbending.
Bet Giyorgis (p593)

## Stone Town in Zanzibar, Tanzania

6 Whether it's your first visit or your 50th, Zanzibar's Stone Town (p668) never loses its touch of the exotic. First you'll see the skyline, with the spires of St Joseph's Cathedral and the Old Fort. Then wander through narrow alleyways that reveal surprises at every turn. Linger at dusty shops scented with cloves; watch as *kanzu*-clad men play the board game *bao;* admire intricate henna designs on the hands of women. Island rhythms quickly take over as mainland life slips away.

## Dakar, Senegal

7 Hit West Africa's trendiest nightlife venues and swing your hips to *mbalax*, the mix of Cuban beats and traditional drumming that forms the heart and soul of the Senegalese music scene. Relax with a lazy day at the beach and feast on fresh-off-the-boat seafood, or explore the workshops of Senegal's most promising artists at the Village des Arts. Finally, climb up one of Dakar's 'breasts' to contemplate the controversial, socialist-style African Renaissance Monument and take in sweeping views across the city (p437).

6

7

## Etosha National Park, Namibia

8 There are few places in Southern Africa that can compete with the wildlife prospects in extraordinary Etosha National Park (p870). A network of water holes dispersed among the bush and grasslands surrounding the pan – a blindingly white, flat, saline desert that stretches into the horizon – attracts enormous congregations of animals. A single water hole can render thousands of sightings over the course of a day – Etosha is simply one of the best places on the planet for watching wildlife. Zebras

## Kalahari, Botswana

9 There is something about the Kalahari (p759). Perhaps it owes its unmistakable gravitas to its sheer vastness; Africa's largest protected wilderness area is a place where the San inhabitants once roamed free and still guide travellers out onto their ancestral lands. The presence of black-maned Kalahari lions doesn't hurt either. Whatever the reason, this is not your average desert; it's home to ancient river valleys, light woodland and surprising concentrations of wildlife around its network of salt pans. And then there is the silence of the Kalahari night... Red hartebeest

## Masai Mara Wildlife, Kenya

**10** The sweeping savannah of the Masai Mara (p620), studded with acacia trees and cut through by the occasional red-dirt road, is the perfect theatre for the world's most spectacular display of wildlife. Gangly giraffes, ambling elephant herds and skittish zebras are just some of sights you're pretty much guaranteed to see. The drama is at its most intense in July and/or August, the start of the tragicomic wildebeest migration, when vast numbers of the hapless animals fall prey to rushing rivers, pacing lions and scavenging hyenas. Silhouette of a wildebeest and acacia tree

## Gorilla Tracking

**11** It's one of the most thrilling wildlife encounters on the planet; nothing can really prepare you for that first moment as you stand just metres from a family of mountain gorillas. It's an utterly humbling experience – particularly that first glimpse of the silverback, whose sheer size and presence will leave you in awe. Or the glee as you watch adorable fuzzy-black babies clowning about. The term 'once in a lifetime' is often bandied about, but gorilla tracking in Uganda's Bwindi (p727), Rwanda or DRC is a genuine one that you'll cherish forever. Gorilla in Volcanoes National Park (p647), Rwanda

MICHAELJUNG/SHUTTERSTOCK ©

## Cape Town, South Africa

**12** Sitting in the continent's southwest corner, Cape Town (p898) is one of those places that travellers don't want to leave. The city is heavily peppered with fine restaurants, theatres, museums and galleries; the suburbs boast encounters with penguins, seals and baboons. The coast caters to beachgoers, surfers and photographers with its white-sand beaches and craggy ocean-sprayed cliffs. And sitting amid it all is the ever-visible form of Table Mountain, a hub for adventure activities including hiking, climbing, mountain biking and abseiling.

## Parc National d'Andringitra, Madagascar

**13** With more than 100km of trails, a majestic mountain range, three challenging peaks and epic landscapes, this national park (p791) is a trekker's paradise. Walkers will be rewarded with a dip in natural swimming pools and wonderful accommodation. You could also spend a couple of nights under the stars: the park office rents out everything you need to mount your very own expedition, from guides to cooks, porters and even camping equipment. Just don't forget a warm sleeping bag.

## Lake Malawi & Likoma Island, Malawi

**14** This emerald jewel in Malawi's crown is fringed by golden beaches and offers travellers an underwater palace to swim among brilliantly coloured chiclid fish. On this 'interior sea', is a hidden idyll straight from a Bond movie: Likoma Island (p819). With its towering cathedral, the country's finest backpacker hostel and one of Africa's most chichi boutique hotels, Likoma is the ultimate escape. Think turquoise coves, scuba diving, candlelit beach dinners and rock-carved rooms...and you're halfway there.

## Slave Forts, Ghana

**15** No matter how well versed you are with the history of the slave trade, nothing can prepare you for the experience of visiting Ghana's slave forts (p321). Standing in the damp dungeons or being shut in the pitch-black punishment cells will chill your blood, and the wreaths and messages left by those whose forebears went through the ordeal are poignant. Cape Coast Castle and St George's Castle are the two largest and best-preserved forts, but there are many smaller ones along the coast too, which tell the same sorry tale. Cape Coast Castle (p321)

FELIX LIPOV/SHUTTERSTOCK ©

## South Luangwa National Park, Zambia

**16** Strolling through the bush single file with a rifle-carrying scout in the lead, there are no Land Rover engine sounds, no obstructed sight lines and no barrier between you and the wildlife, both predator and prey. Animals scurry in the underbrush upon your approach, which means the focus is on the little things, including a *CSI*-like investigation of animal dung. Even simply sitting under a tree looking over a plain filled with grazers is an opportunity for a quasi-meditative immersion in the park (p993).
Hippo yawning

## Loango National Park, Gabon

**17** Of Gabon's myriad spectacular national parks, Loango (p278) is undoubtedly the most impressive. Heaving with elephants, hippos, gorillas, buffaloes, monkeys and crocodiles, Loango offers long journeys through island-studded lagoons, nature hikes through virgin rainforest and lonely walks along empty beaches. Whether you visit the eye-wateringly expensive safari lodges, or choose a far cheaper DIY approach, the impressive wildlife, the vast Eden-like empty spaces and the charming locals will be the same.

16

17

TORSTEN KAROCK/GETTY IMAGES ©

ILONDE VAN HOOLWERFF/500PX ©

## Sossusvlei, Namibia

**18** The towering red dunes of Sossusvlei (p883) rank among the most beautiful desert landscapes on earth. They're also one of the more improbable: the sands originated in the Kalahari millions of years ago and are now reclaiming land from the sea. The valley is dotted by hulking dunes, and interspersed with unearthly, dry *vleis* (low, open landscapes). Clambering up the face of these constantly moving giants is a uniquely Namibian experience, and as you survey the sand sea that surrounds you, you'll feel as though time itself has slowed.

## Okavango Delta, Botswana

**19** The Okavango (p751) in Botswana is an astonishing, beautiful and wild place. Home to wildlife spectacles of rare power and drama, the delta changes with the seasons as floodwaters ebb and flow, creating islands, river channels and pathways for animals that move this way and that at the waters' behest. No visit to the delta is complete without drifting in a traditional *mokoro* (dugout canoe). Exclusive and remote lodges are an Okavango speciality, and self-drivers can find outstanding campsites in the heart of the Okavango's Moremi Game Reserve.

## South Africa's Winelands

**20** Whitewashed Cape Dutch architecture dots an endlessly photogenic landscape of rolling hills and vines in neat rows. The Winelands (p910) is the quintessential Cape, where world-class wines are the icing on the proverbial cake. Stellenbosch, Franschhoek and Paarl, the area's holy trinity of wine-tasting towns, host some of the southern hemisphere's oldest, largest and prettiest wine estates. But this is not the only wine region – head to Tulbagh for sparkling wines, the heights of the Cederberg for crisp sauvignon blancs, and Rte 62 for robust reds and port.

# Need to Know

For more information, see Survival Guide (p1061)

### Currency

More than 25 different currencies. US dollar ($) most readily recognised international currency; euro (€) and UK pound (£) also accepted

### Language

Arabic, English, French, Portuguese and thousands of African languages

### Mobile Phones

Buy local SIM cards to access local mobile networks cheaply.

### Money

ATMs are increasingly common but don't rely on them or being able to pay by credit card; always carry sufficient cash.

### Time

Four times zones from UTC (former GMT) in the west to UTC plus three hours in the east.

### Visas

For short trips sort out visas before leaving home; for longer ones, arrange as you go. In some countries they're available at borders, others not.

## When to Go

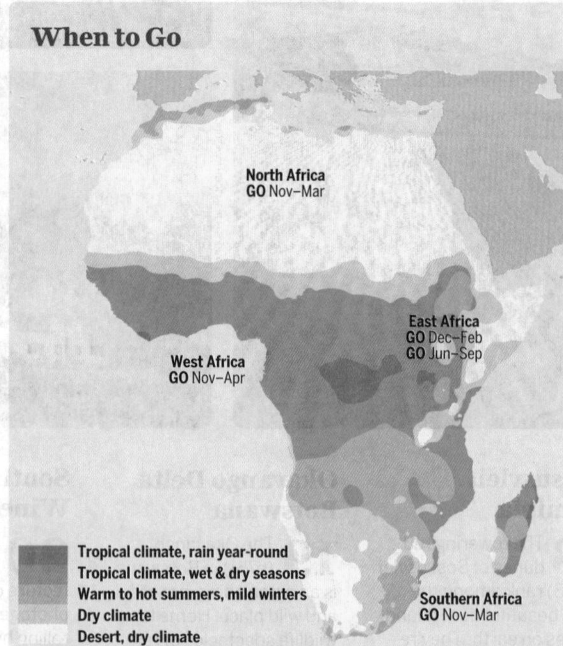


### High Season

➡ **North Africa** Nov–Mar is the coolest period.

➡ **Central Africa** Jun–Sep is the dry time.

➡ **East Africa** Dec–Feb and Jun–Sep are the two main dry seasons.

➡ **West Africa** Nov–Apr is the dry season.

➡ **Southern Africa** Nov–Mar, but rain can continue until Dec in South Africa.

### Shoulder

➡ **North Africa** Apr, May, Sep and Oct.

➡ **Central, West & Southern Africa** Oct and May.

➡ **East Africa** Mar and Oct.

### Low Season

➡ **North & West Africa** Jun–Aug.

➡ **Central Africa** Nov–Apr.

➡ **East Africa** Apr, May and Nov.

➡ **Southern Africa** Jun–Sep; great for wildlife watching.

## Useful Websites

**Lonely Planet** (www.lonelyplanet.com/africa) Destination information, hotel bookings, traveller forum and more.

**Safari Bookings** (www.safaribookings.com) Fantastic resource for booking your safari, with expert and traveller reviews.

**Expert Africa** (www.expertafrica.com) A tour operator with extensive online coverage of the region.

**Travel Africa** (www.travelafricamag.com) Features articles on every corner of the continent and a useful 'safari planner'.

**Africa Geographic** (www.africageographic.com) Nature-focused Africa online mag with good wildlife and birdwatching info.

**BBC News** (www.bbcnews.com/africa) Good for up-to-the-minute news from Africa.

## Exchange Rates

For exchange rates, see individual country chapters and www.xe.com.

## Daily Costs

### Budget: Less than US$100

- Dorm bed: US$10–20
- Double room in a budget hotel: up to US$75
- Meal at cheap hotel or street stall: less than US$5

### Midrange: US$100–250

- Double room in a midrange hotel: US$75–200
- Lunch or dinner in a midrange restaurant: US$20
- Car hire: from $30 per day

### Top End: More than US$250

- Safari-lodge or top-end hotel room: at least US$200
- Guided safari or 4WD rental: from US$150 per day
- Meal at a top restaurant with wine: US$50–100

## Arriving in Africa

**Cairo International Airport** (p1073) Buses E£4, every 20 minutes 7am to midnight, up to two hours to central Cairo; taxi around E£120 to E£150.

**Léopold Sédar Senghor International Airport** (p1073) (Senegal) No public transport; taxis outside arrivals hall cost CFA5000 to city centre.

**Jomo Kenyatta International Airport** (p1073) (Nairobi) Recommended to take taxi (KSh2000 to KSh2500, but bargain hard) to centre of Nairobi (up to one hour).

**OR Tambo International Airport** (p1073) (Johannesburg) Taxi R400 to central Jo'burg; trains (R145) and bus shuttle (400) to downtown (one hour).

## Getting Around

In Africa, the journey is very often the destination. There's everything from impossibly crowded minibus services along rutted roads to international-standard airlines between major cities.

**Air** Major capitals are reasonably well connected by flights within Africa; smaller capitals may require inconvenient connections.

**Bus & Bush Taxi** Often the only option in rural areas, bush or shared taxis leave when full; buses connect major cities.

**Car & 4WD** Reasonable road infrastructure connects major cities; roads deteriorate elsewhere, and are sometimes impassable after rains so 4WD is often required.

**Train** Trains operate in West Africa and South Africa with limited services elsewhere and very few cross-border operations.

For much more on **getting around**, see p1074.

# First Time Africa

For more information, see Survival Guide (p1061)

## Checklist

- Ensure your passport is valid for at least six months and has plenty of free pages for stamp-happy officials.
- Inform your debit-/credit-card company that you're heading away.
- Arrange travel insurance.
- Leave time for researching visas and making visa applications.
- Arrange vaccinations well before departure.
- Ensure you have a yellow-fever certificate.

## What to Pack

- Mosquito repellent, net and malaria medicine
- Neutral-coloured clothing for safari
- Sunscreen
- Torch (flashlight)
- Wind- and waterproof jacket
- Yellow-fever vaccination certificate
- Spare camera batteries and memory cards
- Photocopies of important documents
- Water purifier

## Top Tips for Your Trip

- Book months ahead if you're travelling here during high season, especially during Christmas and European summer holidays.
- Distances can be long – plan your trip to see a few places well instead of trying to see everything and ending up spending all your trip driving.
- Consider taking an off-road introductory driving course before setting out.
- If driving, fill up with fuel at every available opportunity – you never quite know when supplies will run out, and off-road driving uses up much more fuel than you might think.
- Wildlife seasons are quite specific and vary significantly across the region.
- In the main safari areas, book your luxury lodge, tented camp, or self-drive campsite many months in advance for peak periods.
- Book months ahead also for your 4WD rental vehicle, particularly in Southern Africa.
- At many luxury lodges or tented camps, laundry is usually included, so no need for a really full suitcase.

## Sleeping

Lodges usually need to be booked far in advance; hotels and hostels should be reserved during high season.

- **Lodges & Tented Camps** A speciality in Southern and East Africa; often in remote wildlife-rich areas, they offer an all-inclusive experience.
- **Camping** Southern Africa has the best campsites, from wilderness sites with no facilities to well-provisioned camping grounds. Less common elsewhere.
- **Hotels** From cheap and cheerful to high-end international chains. More often it's a simple, uninspiring place and the only game in town.
- **Guesthouses & B&Bs** A handful but quite country-specific (South Africa and Burkina Faso, for example).
- **Hostels** Plenty from Nairobi to Cape Town.

## What to Wear

Africans generally expect visitors to dress neatly and respectfully, so loose-fitting, light casual wear is the recommended minimum; avoid dirty, torn or overly revealing clothes. At least one nice set of clothes (eg a button-up shirt for men) or two is a good idea for nicer restaurants and hotels. Out in the bush, light neutral tones are recommended. In rural and/or predominantly Muslim areas, clothes that cover most exposed skin are recommended; a scarf of some description is worth carrying by women so that you can cover your head when visiting mosques; it can also be useful for keeping wind-blown sand at bay in drier areas.

## Bargaining

In many parts of Africa, especially in markets and/or craft and curio stalls, items are worth whatever the seller can get. Once you get the hang of bargaining, it's all part of the fun. Hagglers are rarely trying to rip you off, so there's no point getting cross. Decide what price you're prepared to pay and if you can't get it, decline politely and move on.

## Tipping

Tipping varies across the continent, but as a general rule the following applies:

➡ **Hotels & Restaurants** Usually expected in top-end hotels and restaurants, very rarely in cheaper places.

➡ **Safari Lodges** Count on US$10 per guest per day, plus more for guides.

➡ **Taxis** Rounding up is usually sufficient.

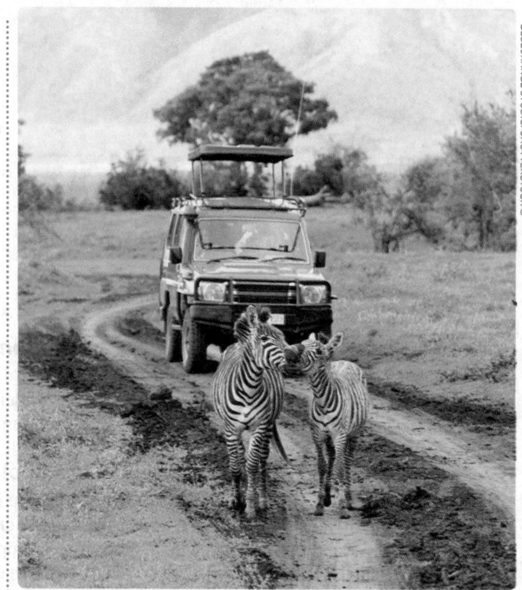



Safari, Ngorongoro Crater (p693), Tanzania

## Etiquette

Although things vary greatly, social mores remain generally conservative. Even so, Africans are usually relaxed in their dealings with foreign travellers; good manners and acting politely and modestly are key to avoiding offence.

➡ Greetings are always important. Even if you're in a hurry, greet people you meet, ask how they are, how their day is going and so on.

➡ Treat elders and those in positions of authority with deference and respect.

➡ If in a frustrating situation, be patient, friendly and considerate. A confrontational attitude can easily inflame the situation and offend local sensibilities.

➡ Always ask permission to photograph people.

➡ Avoid vocal criticism of the government or country; the former could get your friends in trouble and many Africans take the latter personally.

➡ When receiving a gift, accept it with both hands, sometimes with a slight bow.

➡ Be respectful of Islamic traditions and don't wear revealing clothing.

# What's New

### Soweto

With cool cafes and hip restaurants popping up, Soweto is becoming much more than a spot for a simple day trip from Johannesburg. (p937)

### Caprivi Wildlife

Namibia's Caprivi Strip is definitely a safari destination to watch, with lions, wild dogs and other charismatic megafauna returning in small but significant numbers; try Bwabwata National Park. (p873)

### Boutique Booze

There are now nearly 200 microbreweries across South Africa's nine provinces, but it's not all about beer. Cider-makers, gin distilleries and even craft-soft-drinks producers are opening around the country.

### Okonjima Nature Reserve

Okonjima Nature Reserve in central Namibia has been there a while, but a shift in focus by AfriCats has transformed it into a major big-cat attraction. (p868)

### Elephants on the Move

The logistical challenges of moving over 500 elephants from Malawi's overcrowded Liwonde and Majete to Nkhotakota Wildlife Reserve are massive. The results are fantastic. (p821)

### Rhino expansion

News from the world of rhinos has been relentlessly bad, but there's some good news: the Okavango Delta's (p751) reintroduced rhino population is growing and increasingly sighted, while the new Lusaka National Park (p988) has white rhinos, too.

### Parc National d'Odzala

Republic of Congo's showcase national park has undergone a facelift with luxury camps and improved infrastructure. (p233)

### Ouaga Cool

Ouagadougou has been one of West Africa's coolest cities for some time now, but given recent political turmoil and other challenges, the ongoing transformation is remarkable. (p165)

### Príncipe

The island of Príncipe is about to take off, and why not? This unspoilt island has a spectacular lost-world ambience with good accommodation and an international airport. (p431)

### Ponte Kassuende

In November 2014 the Ponte Kassuende was inaugurated in Tete, Mozambique. Three years in the making, this modern road bridge over the Zambezi River has eased local congestion and cut journey times between Zimbabwe and Malawi.

For more recommendations and reviews, see lonelyplanet.com/africa.

# If You Like...

## Beaches & Islands

The rigours of travelling in Africa mean that many visitors looking for a break from life on the road end up on a beach or island. And what beaches and islands!

**Zanzibar** The very name conjures up a spicy heaven of perfume plantations, endless white beaches and whispering palm trees. (p668)

**Príncipe** World-class beaches in a blissfully remote setting, including gorgeous Praia Banana and Baia das Agulhas. (p431)

**Watamu** Seven kilometres of unspoilt beach with a lovely fishing village nearby. (p628)

**Pemba** Lovely white-sand coves with plenty of space to spread your towel. (p679)

**Lake Malawi** Soft sand fringes the shore of this turquoise lake lined with reggae bars. (p820)

**Tofo** A long arc of white sand with azure waters, plus surfing and diving with manta rays. (p843)

**Isla Corisco** Beaches here are the stuff of dreams: pure white sands, swaying palms and azure sea. (p263)

**Mayumba National Park** Bodysurfing the waves while watching humpback whales breach in the distance. (p279)

**Akwidaa & Cape Three Points** Sweeping beaches; trips through plantations and mangroves; and, in season, turtles nesting in the sand. (p327)

**Cap Skirring** The coastal jewel of Casamance, with some of Senegal's loveliest beaches. (p457)

## Watching Wildlife

Some of the best wildlife viewing on the continent – nay, on the planet! – is at your fingertips. Unique opportunities abound while on safari.

**Masai Mara National Reserve** Arguably the best place to spot cheetahs, leopards and lions and much more, especially from July to October. (p620)

**Serengeti National Park** Even if you're not here for the migration, the Seronera River is big-cat central. (p694)

**Chobe Riverfront** Africa's largest elephants draw near to the water's edge with predators prowling nearby. (p749)

**Etosha National Park** Incredible wildlife viewing with animals crowding around easily seen water holes. (p870)

**Kruger National Park** South Africa's famous park has 5000 rhinos alone, and landscapes from woodland to mopane-veld. (p943)

**Mana Pools National Park** For the wild at heart – you're almost guaranteed to see lions; unguided walks allowed. (p1014)

**South Luangwa National Park** Abundant wildlife, wonderful scenery and walking safaris. (p993)

**Parc National Andasibe Mantadia** Madagascar's largest lemur, the *indri*, is easily seen – and heard! – here. (p797)

**Loango National Park** Elephants on the beach, surfing hippos and habituated gorillas – what a place! (p278)

## Music

In Africa music is more than a way of life. It is a force. Get ready to feel it at these rhythmic destinations.

**Dakar** Get down to Senegal's *mbalax*, a blend of Cuban sounds and traditional drum beats. (p437)

**Conakry** One of West Africa's most important musical cities, with numerous live venues. (p342)

**New Afrika Shrine** Fela Kuti's family keep his name alive at Lagos' earthiest club. (p408)

**Harare** Zimbabwe's capital has a rockin' music scene and the Harare International Festival of Arts. (p1007)

**Jazz à Ouaga** Afrobeat, soul and blues influence jazz in the Burkinabé capital. (p165)

**Cape Town** Groove at musical events from November through March, including an international jazz festival. (p898)

**Stone Town** Visit Zanzibar for its five-day Sauti za Busara Swahili Music Festival in February. (p668)

**Essaouira** Visit this laid-back Moroccan resort in June for its Gnaoua and World Music Festival. (p119)

**Abidjan** Hit the bars and dance floors and experience the crazy upbeat sound of *coupé-décalé*. (p240)

**Saint-Louis** This charming French-colonial settlement in Senegal hosts an international jazz festival in May. (p451)

## World Heritage Sites

Among the 129 Unesco World Heritage Sites of Africa, well over half are cultural or mixed, representing both natural and cultural factors.

**Pyramids of Giza** The last remaining wonder of the ancient world. (p67)

**Okavango Delta** One of the most beautiful and biodiverse corners of the continent. (p751)

**Lalibela** A mind-blowing maze of Unesco World Heritage–listed rock-hewn churches. (p593)

**Elmina** Ghana's slave castles and one of the oldest European structures in sub-Saharan Africa. (p324)

**Aksum** Ponder the mysteries of the one-time home of the Queen of Sheba. (p589)

**Medina of Fez** One of the most magical urban spaces in Africa, with ancient, tangled lanes. (p122)

**Namib Sand Sea** The desert of childhood imaginings, with

**Top**: Fez medina (p122), Morocco

**Bottom**: Amboseli National Park (p629), Kenya, against the backdrop of Mt Kilimanjaro

perfectly sculpted sand dunes. (p883)

**Serengeti National Park** One of the best places on the planet to watch wildlife. (p694)

**Robben Island** Nelson Mandela's former prison and cultural touchstone of a continent. (p898)

## Adventure Activities

Many travellers are drawn to Africa by the lure of high-adrenaline thrills. If you're among them, you'll want to make a beeline for these locations.

**Victoria Falls** Adrenaline activities at both the Zambian and Zimbabwean sides of the 'smoke that thunders'. (p969)

**Swakopmund** World-famous for its sweaty and breathless opportunities, from sand-dune surfing to skydiving. (p878)

**Jinja** The source of the Nile, with white-water rafting, kayaking, mountain biking and quad bikes. (p719)

**Dahab** Chic-*and*-hippie Egyptian resort that's a prime base for Red Sea diving and snorkelling. (p81)

**Orange River** Canoe and white-water raft through spectacular canyons along the Nambia–South Africa border. (p946)

**Semonkong** Plunge 204m down Lesotho's Maletsunyane Falls, on the longest commercially operated single-drop abseil. (p775)

**Great Usutu River** White-water rafting in Swaziland including Grade IV rapids not for the faint-hearted. (p965)

## Inspiring Landscapes

Africa has few peers when it comes to natural beauty, encompassing everything from the shifting dunes of the Sahara to the steamy rainforests of the Congo.

**Masai Mara National Reserve** Backed by the spectacular Siria Escarpment and breathtaking year-round. (p620)

**Fish River Canyon** This epic tear in Africa's fabric is often called 'Africa's Grand Canyon'. (p885)

**Sani Pass** This 2865m road pass affords spectacular views across the southern Drakensberg. (p774)

**Mt Kilimanjaro** Hiking up the continent's highest peak is an experience never forgotten. (p685)

**Okavango Delta** Take in the lush, watery scenery from a *mokoro*, a traditional dugout canoe. (p751)

**Ngorongoro Conservation Area** Perfectly formed crater, lost world of wildlife and exceptionally beautiful landforms. (p693)

**Danakil Depression** Unique in the world, the sub-sea-level volcanic landscape here is eerily beautiful (p588)

**Simien Mountains National Park** Huge cliffs, oddly formed mountains and unusual Afro-alpine habitat. (p589)

**Parc National d'Odzala** Astonishing wilderness with elephants and gorillas deep in the Congo rainforest. (p233)

## Trekking & Mountains

As befitting a continent where humankind first walked out of the jungle, there are world-class hiking trails all across Africa, plus mountains so high they are capped by glaciers.

**Mt Meru** In Arusha National Park, this peak offers some lovely hiking. (p691)

**Mt Kenya** Africa's second-highest mountain crowns some wonderful hiking country and provides superb views. (p613)

**Rwenzori Mountains National Park** Uganda's fabled Mountains of the Moon feature snow and glaciers and a lack of other climbers. (p725)

**High Atlas** Tread steep paths past flat-roofed, earthen Berber villages, terraced gardens and walnut groves in this beautiful part of Morocco. (p129)

**Simien Mountains National Park** This very popular park holds some of the most stunning mountain scenery in Africa and trekking is easily organised. (p589)

**Drakensberg** From day hikes to weeklong treks, South Africa's dramatic Drakensberg creates happy hikers. (p926)

**Fish River Canyon** The best way to get a feel for this massive gash in the earth is to embark on a five-day hike along the valley floor. (p885)

**Waterberg Plateau Park** Four-day guided and unguided trails are available through some pristine wilderness landscape. (p869)

# Month by Month

**TOP EVENTS**

**Cape Town Minstrel Carnival**, January

**Fespaco**, February/March

**Saint-Louis Jazz Festival**, May

**Festival of the Dhow Countries**, July

**AfrikaBurn**, April

## January

**High season across most of Africa, particularly sub-Saharan Africa. The northern-hemisphere winter is also cooler in North and West Africa; one downside can be the early arrival of the dust-laden harmattan winds.**

### Cape Town Minstrel Carnival

Called the Kaapse Klopse in Afrikaans, the Mother City's equivalent of Mardis Gras runs throughout the month. The big parade on 2 January sees thousands take to the street in satin- and sequin-bedecked costumes. (p908)

### Voodoo Festival

Held on 10 January across Benin; the celebrations in the voodoo heartland around Ouidah are the largest and most exuberant.

### Timkat

Ethiopa's most important Christian festival is this celebration of Epiphany on 19 January involving elaborate costumed processions and ritual. (p587)

## February

**Relatively cool, dry weather in North, East and West Africa makes for good hiking and it's the last month where you would sensibly head into the Sahel (a semiarid region that stretches from Mauritania, the Gambia and Senegal to Chad). Rains, high temperatures and good birding in Southern Africa.**

### Buganu (Marula) Festival

One of Swaziland's most popular 'first fruits' harvest festivals, Buganu celebrates the marvellous marula. Throughout this month and March women make *buganu* (marula wine), men drink the results and everyone celebrates. Swazi royals attend the three-day ceremony.

### Hands-On Harvest

The wine-producing region of Robertson, South Africa, celebrates the first of its five annual festivals (www.handsonharvest.com). Budding vintners can help with the harvest and sample the results.

### Sauti za Busara

Zanzibar gets even more rhythm than usual with the three-day Sauti za Busara. Swahili songs from every era fill the night, and dance troupes take over the stages of Stone Town and elsewhere on the island. (p669)

### Wildebeest Births

The annual wildebeest migration midyear may grab the headlines, but the species' great calving, a similarly epic yet also heartwarming sight, occurs in February in Tanzania's Serengeti National Park, with approximately 500,000 births occuring in a three-week period.

### Marrakech Biennale

Held on even-numbered years, the Marrakech Biennale is the city's foray into both high and popular artistic culture, with everything from public art displays to chin-scratching conceptual installations. (p132)

**Top**: Timkat (p587), Ethiopia

**Bottom**: Parade participant, Cape Town Minstrel Carnival (p908), South Africa

### Carnival

West Africa's former Portuguese colonies celebrate Carnival (sometimes spelt Carnaval) with infectious zeal. Bissau – with its Latin-style street festival of masks, parties and parades – or Mozambique are the places to be; Porto Novo in Benin also gets into the spirit. Usually in February, but sometimes January, sometimes March.

### Mask Festivals

Held in villages in western Côte d'Ivoire, the region's most significant mask festival (Fêtes des Masques) brings together a great variety of masks and dances from the area.

### Fespaco

Africa's premier film festival is held in February or March in Ouagadougou in Burkina Faso in odd years. Cinemas across the city screen African films, and there's a prestigious awards ceremony. (p165)

## March

**While temperatures are warming up in North and West Africa, the harmattan winds are blowing in Southern and some of East Africa. It's beginning to cool down as the season moves to autumn.**

### Cape Town Cycle Tour

Held in mid-March, this spin around the Cape Peninsula is the world's largest timed cycling event (www.capetowncycletour.com), attracting more than 30,000 contestants from serious racers to costumed Capetonians.

### Infecting the City

Cape Town's squares, fountains, museums and theatres are the venues for this innovative performing-arts festival (http://infectingthecity.com) featuring artists from across the continent.

### Kilimanjaro Marathon

Runners can take part in the full marathon, half marathon or fun runs around the base of the great Tanzanian mountain. The entire race (www.kilimanjaromarathon.com) is held between 830m and 1150m above sea level, on good tarred roads.

### Marathon des Sables

Starting and finishing in Morocco's movie town, Ouarzazate, the Saharan ultramarathon (www.marathondessables.com) is an epic. The gruelling six-day challenge, held in March or April, crosses 243km of desert. Water is provided.

### Enjando Street Festival

The Namibian capital's biggest street party, also known as Mbapira, occurs in March every year. It's also a good excuse for people to dress in extravagant ethnic clothes that bring the streets to life. (p862)

### Maitisong Festival

Botswana's largest performing-arts festival is held annually over seven days from mid-March to early April in Gaborone. The festival features an outdoor program of music, theatre, film and dance, with top performing artists from around Africa. (p741)

## April

**Much of the Sahel is too hot for comfort and the harmattan is a staple throughout the month. The humidity along the West African coast and hinterland gets uncomfortable as temperatures drop in Southern Africa.**

### AfrikaBurn

Inspired by the USA's Burning Man event, this is both a subcultural blowout and a survivalist challenge (www.afrikaburn.com). Art installations and themed camps turn a corner of the South Africa's Karoo into a surreal experience even without mind-altering substances.

### Jazz à Ouaga

An established fixture on West Africa's musical circuit, this fine festival traverses jazz, Afrobeat, soul and blues with some respected regional names in attendance. (p165)

### Festival of Sufi Culture

Fez' festival hosts events including films and lectures, and concerts with Sufi musicians from around the world. The setting is the Andalusian-style garden of a museum, which is housed in a 19th-century summer palace.

## May

**Avoid the northern and western desert and coastal areas unless you favour extreme heat and humidity. Rains should be easing in green-as-green East and Southern Africa.**

### Harare International Festival of Arts

A not-to-be-missed event in Zimbabwe, Harare International Festival of Arts features local and international performers in opera, jazz, classical music, funk, theatre and dance. (p1007)

### Festival Azgo

This Maputo-based extravaganza (www.azgofestival.com) has become Mozambique's largest arts and culture festival, featuring artists from Mozambique as well as elsewhere in the region.

### Art Bienale

In even years in May, Dakar hosts the Dak'Art Biennale, which is easily West Africa's premier arts festival. In addition to the main exhibitions, there's some fabulous fringe stuff happening. (p441)

### Saint-Louis Jazz Festival

Hands down the most internationally renowned festival in West Africa, this Senegal festival attracts major performers to this sexy, Unesco Heritage–designated colonial town. (p453)

## June

**The rains are underway in West Africa. Morocco and other North African countries start to see the annual influx of summer visitors from Europe. High season, with great weather and growing crowds, in Southern Africa.**

### Lake Turkana Cultural Festival

One of Kenya's biggest cultural events, this festival focuses on the tribal groups that inhabit Northern Kenya, among them the El Molo, the Samburu, the Pokot and the Turkana. (www.laketurkanaculturalfestival.com)

### Festival of World Sacred Music

Fez' successful world-music festival has hosted everyone from Youssou N'Dour to Bjork. Equally impressive are the concerts by Moroccan *tariqas* (Sufi orders); fringe events include exhibitions, films and talks. May be held in May depending on Ramadan dates. (p125)

### Gnaoua & World Music Festival

A passionate celebration held in Essaouira in late June, with concerts featuring international, national and local performers, and art exhibitions. A great chance to hear some bluesy Gnaoua. (p119)

## July

**Rain is heavy south of the Sahara – it's a good time for a travel bargain in South Africa, for example. In Morocco, Europeans flood the country; accommodation can be pricey and scarce. High-season peak in Southern Africa.**

### National Arts Festival

Feel South Africa's creative pulse at its premier arts festival (www.nationalartsfestival.co.za), held in Grahamstown in early July.

### Festival of the Dhow Countries

The Zanzibar International Film Festival is the centrepiece of this two-week jamboree of arts and culture that can sometimes kick off at the end of June. (p669)

### Lesotho Ski Season

That's right, skiing in Southern Africa. Lesotho's peaks and passes receive snow in winter – particularly around Oxbow where a ski slope makes the most of snowfall. It all happens at Afriski Mountain Resort (www.afriski.net).

### Oyster Festival

Travel to the South African Garden Route resort of Knysna to indulge in a 10-day oyster orgy (www.oysterfestival.co.za). Events include the Knysna Forest Marathon.

### East Africa Migration

Wildebeest cross the Mara River en masse, passing from Tanzania's Serengeti National Park to Kenya's Masai Mara National Reserve, with predators following in their wake. It's one cliché that just happens to be true: this is the greatest wildlife show on earth.

### Marrakech Festival of Popular Arts

This street-theatre festival is a typically colourful Marrakshi event, highlighting the best of Moroccan traditional and popular culture. Djemaa el-Fna is even more anarchic than usual during the opening-night parade, featuring 500-plus performers.

## August

**Rains and humidity make travel difficult in West and East Africa. The peak of Southern Africa's high season, with Europeans escaping their winter in Botswana, Namibia and elsewhere.**

### Panafest

Ghana's Cape Coast hosts the biennial Pan-African Historical Theatre Festival (Panafest) with a focus on African contemporary and traditional arts, including music, dance, fashion and theatre. Its centrepiece is a moving candlelit emancipation ceremony to honour African slaves.

### Umhlanga Dance

A showcase of potential wives for the king: marriageable young Swazi women journey from all over the kingdom, carrying reeds, to help repair the queen mother's home around August or September (dates vary). (p961)

### Camel Racing

Maralal's Yare Camel Cup in northern Kenya is at once serious camel racing and a chance to join the fun. It's a huge event.

## September

**The wet weather is beginning to ease in East and West Africa while Southern Africa moves out of winter towards spring – look out for brilliant displays of wildflowers in South Africa's Northern and Western Cape regions.**

### Hermanus Whale Festival

One of the world's best land-based whale-watching destinations is the town of Hermanus, 122km east of Cape Town – visit during this annual September/October 'enviro-arts festival' (www.whalefestival.co.za).

### Meskel

Starting on 27 September, this two-day festival is the most colourful after Timkat. Bonfires are built, topped by a cross to which flowers, most commonly the Meskel daisy, are tied. Priests don their full regalia. Addis Ababa, Gonder and Aksum are good places to be. (p587)

### Lake of Stars Music Festival

'Glastonbury on the beach': this brilliant three-day Malawian festival bubbles with stellar UK and African bands, and a host of celebrated global DJs. Money raised goes towards the Children in the Wilderness charity. (p830)

### Ashanti Festivals

Coinciding with the yam-harvest season, the Adae Kese Festival in Ghana celebrates the glorious Ashanti past and involves ritual purifications of the ancestral burial shrines.

## October

**Clear, post-rain skies make for good visibility and the high-season crowds have yet to arrive across much of the continent. Temperatures can be decidedly chilly in Morocco, especially in the High Atlas. Rains on the way in the south.**

### Felabration

The weeklong celebration of Afrobeat-legend Fela Kuti in October in Lagos takes place around the great man's birthday on the 15th. Concerts, theatre pieces and exhibitions, culminating in a free gig at the Shrine.

### Oktoberfest

Windhoek in Namibia stages its own Oktoberfest – an orgy of food, drink and merrymaking in an event that showcases the best in German beer, usually drunk at tables set up inside large marquees. There's plenty of traditional German dress on display too. (p862)

### Gorilla Tracking

Although the dry-season months of June to September are the prime months for gorilla tracking in Uganda, the short (and not-so-disruptive) rains in October and November see permit prices drop; permits are also much easier to obtain.

## November

**The beginning of the month can be a quiet time to travel across the continent. Rains in the south and East Africa. Nighttime temperatures in desert regions drop close to zero.**

### Kirstenbosch Summer Sunset Concerts

Summer music festivals take place in stunning settings nationwide. In South Africa's Western Cape province, the choice includes the Kirstenbosch Summer Sunset Concerts in Cape Town's botanic gardens. (p908)

### East African Safari Rally

This classic car rally (www.eastafricansafarirally.com) held in late November is more than 50 years old, and there's more than a whiff of colonial atmosphere about it. The rally traverses Kenya, Tanzania and Uganda and is open only to pre-1971 vehicles.

### Maulid Festival

A huge celebration in Lamu, Kenya, this annual four-day celebration (www.lamu.org/maulid-celebration.html) of the Prophet Mohammed's birthday falls in October/November in 2018, 2019 and 2020.

### Festival of Maryam Zion

This vibrant festival is held in Aksum, Ethiopia. Thousands of pilgrims head towards Aksum ahead of the event, which begins on 30 November. (p590)

## December

**High season is very much underway south of the Sahara, and accommodation should be booked months in advance; beach areas are particularly busy with sun-starved Europeans. Weather is mild and dry.**

### Marrakesh International Film Festival

This event (www.festival-marrakech.info/en) lives up to its name, with stars from Hollywood to Bollywood jetting in to walk the red carpet.

# Itineraries

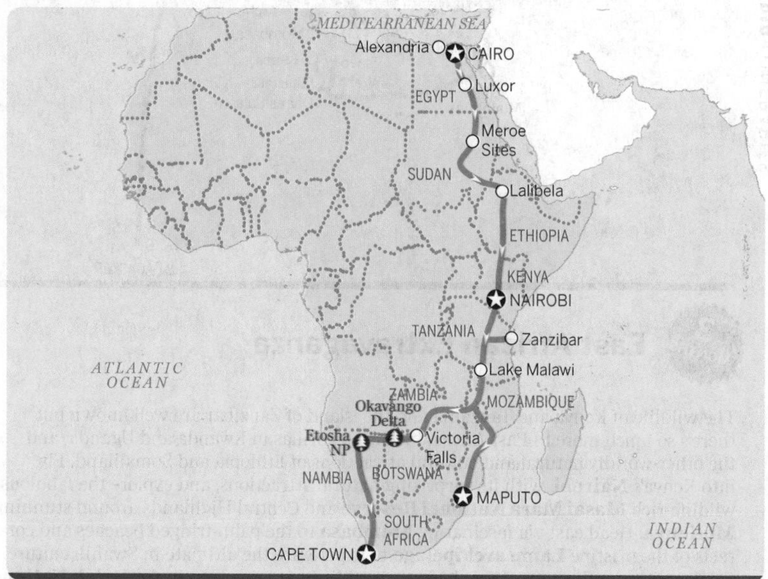

## Cairo to Cape Town

Who says you need a year to travel the length of Africa? The Cairo to Cape Town route can easily be tailored to a shorter time frame. Start off with a visual bang at the pyramids in **Cairo**, then head to the Mediterrenean coast to sample the colonial grandeur and period cafes of **Alexandria**. Return to Cairo and take the overnight train to **Luxor**, where you can explore the temples and tombs of ancient Egypt.

Continue south across Lake Nasser into Sudan, where the glorious Meroe sites and the rest of northern Sudan are the highlights. Ethiopia has some exceptional sites, especially **Lalibela**, before you journey down to **Nairobi**.

The wildlife-sprinkled plains of Kenya and Tanzania form the centrepiece of many classic African journeys; afterwards, recharge your batteries by chilling out on **Zanzibar** or on the shores of beautiful **Lake Malawi**. Detour into Mozambique, where you shouldn't miss dynamic **Maputo**. Track back to Zambia to experience breathtaking **Victoria Falls**. From here, there's spectacular wildlife territory in Botswana's **Okavango Delta** and Namibia's **Etosha National Park**, before reaching stunning **Cape Town**, South Africa, practically the continent's southern tip.

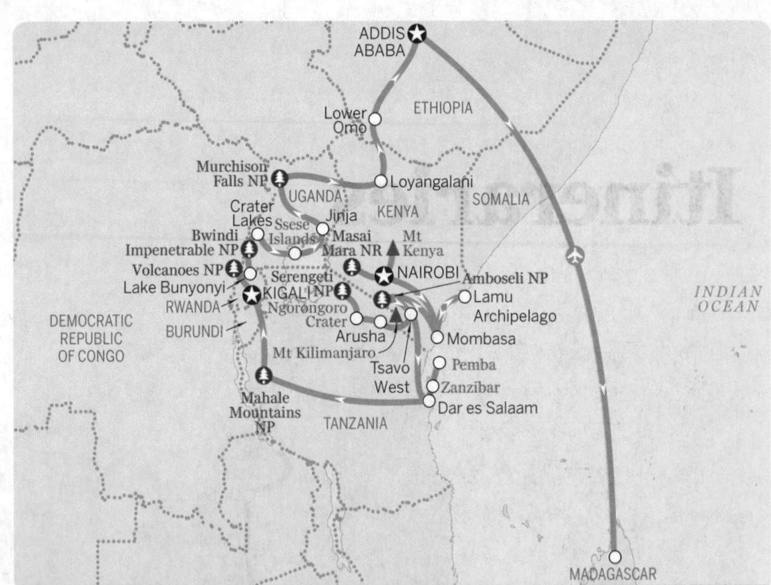

## East African Extravaganza

The wildlife of Kenya and Tanzania and the island of Zanzibar are well known but there's so much more to East Africa, including gorillas in Rwanda and Uganda, and the other-worldly natural and cultural attractions of Ethiopia and Somaliland. Fly into Kenya's **Nairobi**, with its surprising natural attractions, and explore the fabulous wildlife-rich **Masai Mara National Reserve** and Central Highlands around stunning **Mt Kenya**. Head east via fascinating **Mombasa** to the palm-fringed beaches and coral reefs of the pristine **Lamu archipelago** to experience the ultimate in Swahili culture. On your way south, stop off for elephants and Kilimanjaro views in **Amboseli National Park** and the wild country of **Tsavo West**.

Cross the border into Tanzania, where your first stop is **Arusha**, from where you can arrange 4WD safaris to the other-worldly **Ngorongoro crater** or wildlife-watching in **Serengeti National Park**, and trekking trips up **Mt Kilimanjaro**. From intriguing **Dar es Salaam**, follow the crowds to the Spice Island of **Zanzibar** then shake them off by heading to **Pemba**, an intriguing island further north. Return to Dar es Salaam then head west to spend time hanging with wild chimpanzees in **Mahale Mountains National Park**.

Walk across the Kagera River Bridge to Rusumu in Rwanda, where you can catch a minibus to **Kigali**. This attractive city is worth seeing before striking out for **Volcanoes National Park**, where you can hike in search of silverback gorillas. Cross into western Uganda, stopping off at stunning **Lake Bunyonyi**, before searching for mountain gorillas in **Bwindi Impenetrable National Park**. Also possible is the chance to kick back for a few days at the **Crater Lakes** or **Ssese Islands**, or go white-water rafting at **Jinja**; in the north, **Murchison Falls National Park** is a gem.

From Uganda travel east back into Kenya to remote **Loyangalani**, home to unforgettable tribes and the jade-coloured Lake Turkana. From here, cross the border north into Ethiopia. In Ethiopia's south, the **Lower Omo Valley** is one of East Africa's most underrated wilderness areas. Continue north to **Addis Ababa**, an engaging city with good museums and great food, then fly out to **Madagascar** to explore one of Africa's most pristine and remote environments, rich in wildlife (including lemurs and great birding) and adventure.

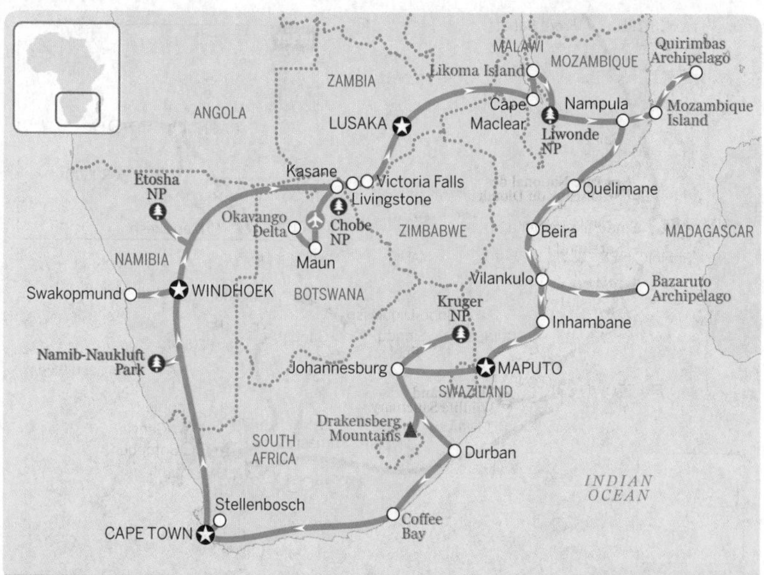

## Southern Africa Smorgasbord

This itinerary – ideal for Africa novices – takes in nine countries and the best Southern Africa has to offer. Most places are easily accessible, English is widely spoken and the countries are well set up for foreign visitors.

Start in South Africa's mother city, vibrant **Cape Town**, where you can stand on top of Table Mountain, sleep off your jet lag on stunning beaches and party into the night on Long St. Also squeeze in a trip to the Winelands: **Stellenbosch** is a good choice. Head north into Namibia to take in the endless sand dunes of **Namib-Naukluft Park**, well-heeled **Windhoek** with its German colonial heritage, and the high-adrenaline activities of **Swakopmund**. Continue north to **Etosha National Park**, then east along the Caprivi Strip to **Kasane**, the gateway to Botswana's **Chobe National Park** and its amazing concentration of elephants. Fly to **Maun** for a few days poling through the swampy maze of the **Okavango Delta**. Back in Kasane, it's a short hop into Zambia's **Livingstone**, for some high-speed thrills and the spectacular **Victoria Falls**.

Zambia's capital **Lusaka** might not be a looker but its bar and clubbing scene is lively and you'll need to pass through en route to Malawi. From Lilongwe head south to **Liwonde National Park** for elephant and hippo spotting. The white beaches and clear waters of Lake Malawi beckon – experience them at **Cape Maclear** and blissful **Likoma Island**.

Once across the border in Mozambique, take the train from Cuamba to **Nampula**, the jumping-off point for trips to the unforgettable **Mozambique Island**. Take a trip to the lost-in-time **Quirimbas Archipelago** then head south via the sleepy towns of **Quelimane**, **Beira** and **Vilankulo** for the **Bazaruto Archipelago**, and **Inhambane**. Next stop is beguiling **Maputo** for a fiesta of seafood and caipirinhas. Drop into Swaziland en route to **Johannesburg**, South Africa's hustling, bustling commercial capital. From here you can head to **Kruger National Park**, or venture south to the **Drakensberg Mountains** for great hiking – even across the border into Lesotho. Drop back down to tropical **Durban**, a good base for exploring Zululand. On the Wild Coast pause at beautiful **Coffee Bay** before making your way back to **Cape Town**.

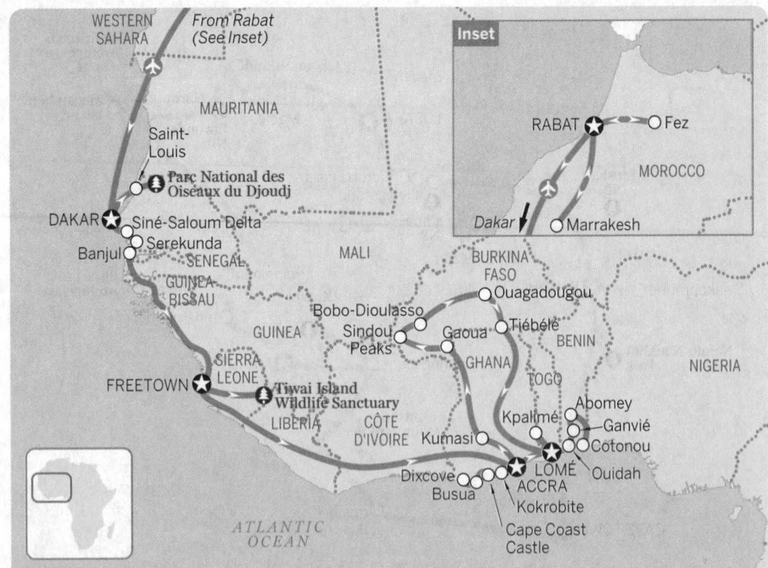

## 6 WEEKS Morocco to Benin

From the cusp of Europe in Morocco to the palm-fringed semi-tropics around Cotonou, West Africa's Atlantic coastline, is one of the most varied and beautiful coastal areas in Africa. Begin in **Rabat**, a quintessentially modern Moroccan city, then make your way to **Fez**, Morocco's most evocative medieval medina, and then on to **Marrakesh**, with its palpable sense of the exotic. After a week or so in Morocco, fly down to Senegal's capital **Dakar**, with its African sophistication and role as regional air hub. To the north, **Saint-Louis** is like stepping back into pre-colonial Africa. Other Senegalese excursions include enjoying some of Africa's best birdwatching in the **Parc National des Oiseaux du Djoudj** and drifting through the **Siné-Saloum Delta**. You could easily spend a week or more exploring it all, before heading south to The Gambia, which may be small, but its beaches, especially those around **Serekunda**, make a good (English-speaking) rest stop for taking time out from the African road. From sleepy **Banjul**, consider flying to **Freetown** in Sierra Leone – the nearby beaches are beautiful and utterly undeveloped. Attractions such as **Tiwai Island Wildlife Sanctuary**, with its fabulous wildlife concentrations, should not be missed.

With three weeks under your belt, you could continue along the coast through Liberia and Côte d'Ivoire, but most travellers fly over them to agreeable **Accra** in Ghana. From there excursions to the old coastal forts, **Cape Coast Castle** and stunning beaches at **Kokrobite**, **Busua** and **Dixcove** never disappoint. Don't fail to detour north to **Kumasi** in the Ashanti heartland, then loop up and into Burkina Faso, through **Gaoua**, the heart of culture-rich Lobi country, and to the dramatic **Sindou Peaks** (great for hiking) en route to soulful **Bobo-Dioulasso**. Make your way to buzzing **Ouagadougou** then south to the painted houses of **Tiébélé**.

After two weeks in Ghana and Burkina Faso, continue on to the markets and museum of Togo's **Lomé**, and don't miss an inland hiking detour around **Kpalimé**. Not far away is Benin, with **Ouidah** (the evocative former slaving port and home of voodoo), the history-rich town of **Abomey** and the stilt-villages of **Ganvié** filling up your final week. **Cotonou** has all the steamy appeal of the tropics and is a fine place to rest at journey's end.

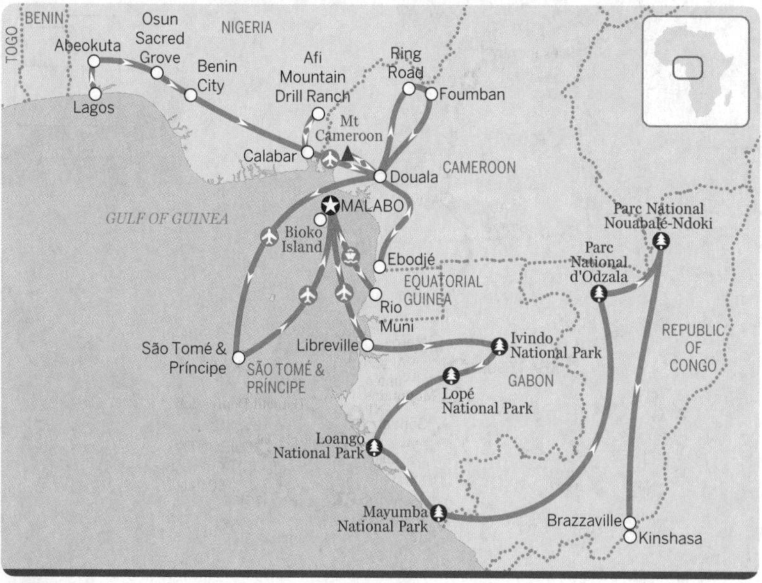

## Gulf of Guinea & Congo

Nigeria is one of those destinations that suffers from bad press, although most visitors will encounter nothing but warmth and humour in their interactions with Nigerians.

**Lagos** may be in-your-face, high-volume and logistically confronting, but it's also Africa's most energetic city, awash with pulsating nightlife, clamorous markets and a resurgent arts scene. Historic **Abeokuta** with its Yoruba shrines and sacred rock, **Osun Sacred Grove** and the Oba's Palace in **Benin City** are worthwhile stopovers en route to **Calabar**, which is likeable for its old colonial buildings, fish market and lovely setting. Close to Calabar, don't miss **Afi Mountain Drill Ranch**, the focus of an outstanding primate project. Count on 10 days in Nigeria.

From here fly east to steamy **Douala** in Cameroon, a regional air hub and important cultural centre. After longish detours to see the sea turtles at **Ebodjé** and to climb **Mt Cameroon**, West Africa's highest peak, head for Bamenda, which serves as a gateway to the villages of the **Ring Road**, a deeply traditional area of Cameroon that feels untouched by time; Bafut is one of our favourite villages in the region. Later, head for **Foumban** for a slice of traditional West Africa, and a fascinating vision of the town's ancient and still-active sultanate. A week in Cameroon should give you a taste of the country's riches.

Return to Douala then fly out to **São Tomé & Príncipe**, one of West Africa's most beautiful destinations and an emerging ecotourism hot spot. From São Tomé, fly into **Malabo** in Equatorial Guinea, obtain a tourist permit and set out to see the colonial architecture, rainforest and wildlife on **Bioko Island**, and the fabulous beaches and national parks on the mainland, **Rio Muni**. Return to Malabo and fly (Equatorial Guinea's land borders are not open to foreigners) to **Libreville** in Gabon. Gabon's national parks are the stuff of legend – spend as much time as you have (at least a week) in **Ivindo**, **Lopé**, **Loango** and **Mayumba** National Parks. Cross into Republic of Congo for more fabulous wildlife watching at **Parc National d'Odzala** and **Parc National Nouabalé-Ndoki** before watching the sun set over the Congo River in **Brazzaville**. You've just enough time left to cross the river to **Kinshasa**, the roiling, music-rich capital of the Democratic Republic of Congo.

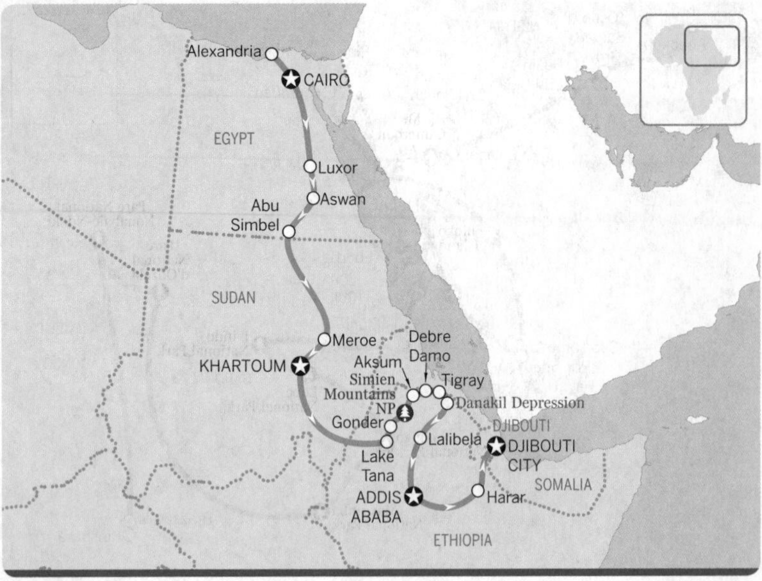

## Cairo to the Horn

One of the few ways left to combine North Africa with the East, this route takes in the best of Egypt, then crosses Sudan en route to Ethiopia and the Horn.

Begin in **Cairo** – not for nothing is this rambunctious yet beguiling city known as the Mother of the World. Visit the museums, cruise the Nile, dive into the old city and its mosques and don't miss the Egyptian Museum. Head north for a visit to **Alexandria**, a sophisticated Mediterranean city steeped in history, then return to Cairo for your train journey south to **Luxor**, home to some of the greatest relics from ancient Egypt. Jump on a felucca and sail down to **Aswan** – one of Africa's most soulful river journeys.

From Aswan, head south, stopping at the glorious and grand rock-hewn monument of **Abu Simbel** on your way into Sudan and the fabulous pyramids of **Meroe**. Keep going south until you reach **Khartoum** – the confluence of the Blue and White Niles and the bazaar at Omdurman are fine introductions to the city.

Cross into Ethiopia and begin your exploration of this fascinating country at Bahir Dar and the **Lake Tana Monasteries**. From here, make for **Gonder** with its ancient fortress, great coffee and church with extraordinary murals. Next it's the **Simien Mountains**, home to fabulous scenery and equally fabulous trekking. The road from here is one of Africa's most precipitous, so enjoy the views on your way to **Aksum**, Ethiopia's holiest city and epicentre of the Ethiopian Orthodox faith. Climb the cliff to the church at **Debre Damo**, climb a mountain or two in search of the splendid rock-hewn churches of **Tigray**, then continue to Mekele, your gateway to the weird-and-wonderful **Danakil Depression**. Return to Mekele, then track south **Lalibela**, home to simply astonishing rock-cut churches and filled with pilgrims. **Addis Ababa** is next on your itinerary and it's an intriguing city worth a few days of your time – take a food tour while you're here.

Next stop, **Harar**, with a feel utterly unlike anywhere else in the country, not to mention hyenas. Then it's to **Djibouti**, the Horn, and your first sight of the sea in quite a while...

# Plan Your Trip
# Safaris

Africa's unique wildlife and landscapes make for a magical safari experience. But making the most of this dream journey into the African wilds requires careful planning – here's where we show you how.

## Where to Go

### East Africa

From the spectacular wildebeest migrations across the Masai Mara to the elephants of Amboseli, from the millions of flamingos in the Rift Valley Lakes to the gorillas of Bwindi Impenetrable National Park, East Africa offers an amazing range of safari opportunities. However, don't be tempted to fit too much into your itinerary. Distances between parks in East Africa are great, and moving too quickly from park to park is likely to leave you tired and unsatisfied. Instead, try to stay at just one or two parks, exploring them in depth and taking advantage of nearby cultural and walking opportunities.

### Southern Africa

If you thought that East Africa was safari wonderland, prepare yourself for an equally enticing sweetie shop in Southern Africa. South Africa alone has close to 600 national parks and reserves, many featuring wildlife, although others are primarily wilderness sanctuaries or hiking areas. Elsewhere both Botswana's Chobe National Park and Namibia's Etosha National Park have good populations of iconic species plus excellent birdwatching. If you make it across to Madagascar, look for the endangered lemur, the Indri, in Parc National d'Andasibe.

## Best Safaris

**West Africa**

Parc National de la Pendjari (Benin)

Mole National Park (Ghana)

Loango National Park (Gabon)

Parc National d'Odzala (Republic of Congo)

Parc National Nouabalé-Ndoki (Republic of Congo)

**Central Africa**

Parc National Des Virunga (DRC)

Parc National de Kahuzi-Biéga (DRC)

Lola Ya Bonobo Sanctuary (DRC)

**East Africa**

Masai Mara National Reserve (Kenya)

Serengeti National Park (Tanzania)

Ngorongoro Conservation Area (Tanzania)

Bwindi Impenetrable National Park (Uganda)

Amboseli National Park (Kenya)

Kibale Forest National Park (Uganda)

Simien Mountains National Park (Ethiopia)

**Southern Africa**

Chobe National Park (Botswana)

Etosha National Park (Namibia)

South Luangawa National Park (Zambia)

Kruger National Park (South Africa)

Kgalagadi Transfrontier Park (South Africa & Botswana)

### West Africa

West Africa is an underrated wildlife destination and its little-known national parks host more African megafauna than they do tourists.

Benin's Parc National de la Pendjari is one of the region's best parks with lions, leopards, elephants and hippos. The same can be said for the Benin–Niger cross-border Parc Regional du W. Ghana's Mole National Park, with 94 mammal species, including elephants, baboons and antelopes, is that country's conservation showpiece.

The Gambia offers the compact Abuko Nature Reserve, home to crocodiles and hundreds of bird species. Senegal's Parc National des Oiseaux du Djoudj and Mauritania's Parc National du Banc D'Arguin are among the best birding sites in the world for migratory species.

But it's down in the southwest where things really get exciting. Gabon is the region's star ecotourism destination with 10% of its territory locked away in national parks. You'll find habituated lowland gorillas in Gabon and the Republic of Congo. Equatorial Guinea is a largely uncharted paradise, while Gabon and São Tomé & Príncipe are brilliant for whales and sea turtles.

## When to Go

Much of East and Southern Africa offer exceptional wildlife viewing year-round. That said, wildlife is generally easier to spot during the dry season when waterholes become a focus for activity. In Southern Africa, the rainy season (November to March) is good for birds but getting around the Okavango Delta is more difficult. This is also when visitor numbers and prices will be highest – something to bear in mind when weighing up costs and scheduling. West Africa's best time for wildlife is generally from November to March, while Central Africa is similar.

Wildlife usually disperses during the wet season and denser vegetation can make observation more difficult, but you may be rewarded with viewings of behaviour such as breeding activity without the tourist crowds.

## Types of Safari

### DIY Safaris

When it comes to safaris, doing things yourself (taking the bus, renting your own 4WD, using your own tent, carrying your own food) is rarely cheaper, and is a lot more complicated. Public transport rarely goes into parks, and even if it does, you still need to rent a vehicle or arrange lifts to tour the park itself. And the main expense – park entry fees – has to be paid however you get there.

However, in some countries there's less of an organised safari set-up, and the usual way of doing things is to get to the park under your own steam, stay at a lodge or campsite (either inside the park, or just outside to save on park fees), then arrange activities on the spot to suit your budget and interest.

You can join walking safaris, wildlife-viewing drives, boat trips or visits to nearby villages – all normally for a half or full day, although longer options may also be available. National parks where this is possible include Liwonde (Malawi), Kruger (South Africa), Gorongosa (Mozambique) and South Luangwa (Zambia). Doing things this way can cost more than fully organised trips, but generally you're paying for a more exclusive experience.

Many parks in Southern Africa, especially in Botswana and Namibia, cater to both luxury lodges (usually fly-in safaris) and self-drive 4WD safaris.

### Organised Safaris

Vast distances – some parks are bigger than small nations – and the unpredictable nature of large animals usually mean you need a vehicle to visit the national parks, often a 4WD, and a knowledgable guide. The obvious solution is to join an organised safari. There are options to suit all budgets, starting from around US$150 per day for a basic all-inclusive experience.

If you want to team up and share the costs of a safari, companies in Nairobi (Kenya), Arusha (Tanzania) and Kampala (Uganda) will help you find other travellers. Some have regular departures where you can just rock up, pay and head for the wilds the next day. Many safari companies also take (and most prefer) bookings in advance, especially at the top end of the market.

One factor that can make or break a safari is the driver. A good driver is a guide too, and can turn even the most mundane trip into a fascinating one; a driver's experience in spotting animals and understanding their behaviour is paramount. A bad driver does just that – drive. Always try to meet your driver-guide before booking a safari, to gauge their level of knowledge and enthusiasm.

If you're offered a ridiculously cheap deal by a safari company, think again. Anything less than the norm may compromise in quality – vehicles break down, food is substandard, park fees are dodged or fuel is skimped on, meaning your driver won't take detours in search of animals. At the higher end of the price spectrum, ambience, safari style and the operator's overall focus are important considerations.

The best way to avoid the sharks and find good guides is to get advice from other travellers who've recently returned from a safari, so do your research online beforehand and ask around once you arrive in Africa. Also check to see if an operator is a member of a professional association or regulatory body such as the Kenyan Association of Tour Operators (KATO; www.katokenya.org) or the Tanzanian Association of Tour Operators (TATO; www.tatotz.org).

## Mobile Safaris

Many visitors to Southern Africa will experience some sort of organised mobile safari – ranging from an all-hands-on-deck 'participation safari', where you might be expected to chip in with camp chores and supply your own sleeping bag and drinks, all the way up to top-class, privately guided trips.

As trips at the lower end of the budget scale can vary enormously in quality, it pays to canvass opinion for good local operators. This can be done on Lonely Planet's Thorn Tree forum (lonelyplanet.com/thorntree) or by chatting to other travellers on the ground. Failing this, don't hesitate to ask lots of questions of your tour operator and make your priorities and budget clear from the start.

For those booking through overseas tour operators, try to give as much notice as possible, especially if you want to travel in the high season. This will give you a better chance of booking the camps and lodges of your choice.

### TIPPING

Guides and drivers of safari vehicles will expect a tip, especially if you've spent a number of days under their care. Most safari companies suggest the following as a rule of thumb:

- guides/drivers – US$10 per person per day
- *mokoro* (dugout canoe) trackers and polers – US$5 per person per day
- camp or lodge staff – US$10 per guest per day (usually placed in a communal box)
- transfer drivers and porters – US$3

## Fly-In Safaris

Taking off in a little six-seater aircraft to nip across to the next remote safari camp or designer lodge means you'll be able to maximise your time and cover a selection of parks and reserves to give yourself an idea of the fantastic variety of landscapes on offer.

The biggest temptation will be to cram too much into your itinerary, leaving you rushing from place to place. It's always better to give yourself at least three days in each camp or lodge in order to really avail yourself of the various activities on offer.

While a fly-in safari is never cheap, they are all-inclusive and what you pay should cover the cost of your flight transfers as well as meals, drinks and activities in each camp. Obviously, this all takes some planning and the earlier you can book a fly-in safari the better – many operators advise on at least six to eight months' notice if you want to pick and choose where you stay.

Fly-in safaris are particularly popular and sometimes a necessity in the Okavango Delta region of Botswana. Given the country's profile as a top-end safari destination, many tour operators specialise in fly-in safaris or include a fly-in element in their itineraries.

# Resources

**Safari Bookings** (www.safaribookings.com) Fantastic resource for booking your safari with expert and traveller reviews.

**Good Safari Guide** (www.goodsafariguide) An independent online resource with a focus on luxury lodges and tented camps.

Food stall, Djemaa El-Fna (p133), Moroc

## Plan Your Trip

# Eat & Drink Like a Local

Whether it's a group of Kenyans gathering in a nyama choma (barbecued meat) shop to consume hunks of grilled meat, or Ghanaians dipping balls of fufu (pounded yam or cassava with a dough-like consistency) into a steaming communal bowl of stew, there are two things all Africans have in common – they love to eat and it's almost always a social event. African food is generally bold and colourful, with rich, earthy textures and strong, spicy undertones.

## Best Places to Eat

**Test Kitchen (p907)**
Cape Town institution and often described as Africa's best.

**Four Sisters (p588)**
Fabulous Ethiopian banquets with a coffee ceremony thrown in.

**La Canne d'Or (p173)**
Franco-African fusion with fine service and stunning setting in Bobo-Dioulasso.

**La Table by Madada (p120)**
Morocco's wonderful cuisine by the sea at Essaouira.

**Djemaa El-Fna Food Stalls (p133)**
The food is marvellous, the Marrakesh atmosphere unlike anywhere else.

## Staples & Specialities

Each region has its own key staples. In East and Southern Africa, the base for many local meals is a stiff dough made from maize flour, called – among other things – *ugali, sadza, pap* and *nshima*. In West Africa millet is also common, and served in a similar way, while staples nearer the coast are root crops such as yam or cassava (*manioc* in French), served as a near-solid glob called *fufu*.

In North Africa, bread forms a major part of the meal, while all over Africa rice is an alternative to the local specialities. In some countries, plantain (green banana) is also common, either fried, cooked solid or pounded into *fufu*. A sauce of meat, fish, beans or vegetables is then added to the carbo base. If you're eating local-style, you grab a portion of bread or dough or pancake (with your right hand, please!), dip it in the communal pot of sauce and sit back, beaming contentedly, to eat it.

## Habits & Customs

- In Islamic countries, food is always eaten, passed and touched with the right hand only (the left hand is reserved for washing your bottom, and the two are understandably kept separate).
- Water in a basin is usually brought to wash your hands before you start eating – hold your hands out and allow the person who brings it to pour it over, then shake your hands dry.
- It's customary in some parts of Africa for women and men to eat separately, with the women eating second after they've served the food.
- In some countries, lunch, rather than dinner, is the main meal of the day, and everything stops for a couple of hours while a hot meal is cooked, prepared and consumed.

## Where to Eat & Drink

### Food Stalls & Street Food

Most African towns have a shack-like stall or 10 serving up cheap local staples. Furniture is usually limited to a rough bench and a couple of upturned boxes, and hygiene is rarely a prime concern. However, this is the place to save money and meet the locals. Seek out these no-frills joints at bus stations or markets. Lighter snacks include nuts sold in twists of newspaper, hard-boiled eggs (popular for long bus journeys), meat kebabs, or, in some places, more exotic fare such as fried caterpillars or baobab fruits. Street food is served on a stick, wrapped in paper, or in a plastic bag.

### Restaurants

Most towns have cheap cafes and restaurants where you can buy traditional meals, as well as smarter restaurants with facilities such as tablecloths, waiters and menus. If you're eating in cheaper places, you can expect to be served the same food as the locals, but more upmarket, tourist-oriented establishments serve up more familiar fare, from the ubiquitous chicken and chips to pizzas, pasta dishes and toasted sandwiches.

Colonial influences remain important: you can expect croissants for breakfast in Dakar, and Portuguese custard tarts in the bakeries of Mozambique. Africa also has its share of world-class dining, with the best restaurants brilliantly fusing African culinary traditions with those of the rest of the world. Less impressively, even smaller towns are now succumbing to the fast-food craze, with greasy burger and chicken joints springing up frequently.

## Celebrations

In much of Africa, a celebration, be it a wedding, a coming-of-age ceremony or even a funeral, is an excuse to stuff yourself until your eyes pop out. In non-Islamic countries, this eating-fest could well be accompanied by a lot of drinking. Celebration food of course varies widely from country to country, but vegetarians beware – many feasts involve goats, sheep, cows or chickens being slaughtered and added to the pot.

If you're lucky enough to be invited to a celebration while you're in Africa, it's polite to bring something (litre bottles of fizzy drink often go down well), but be prepared for a lot of hanging around – nothing happens in a hurry. The accepted wisdom is that it's considered very rude to refuse any food you're offered, but in practice it's probably perfectly acceptable to decline something politely if you really don't want to eat it, as long as you eat something else with gusto!

Tea, Morocco

## Vegetarians & Vegans

Many Africans may think a meal is incomplete unless half of it once lived and breathed, but across Africa many cheap restaurants serve rice and beans and other meals suitable for vegans simply because it's all the locals can afford. For vegetarians, eggs are usually easy to find – expect to eat an awful lot of egg and chips – and, for pescetarians, fish is available nearer

### TASTES LIKE CHICKEN

In many parts of Africa you'll find the locals chomping with gusto on some unusual foods. Here are some of the continent's more adventurous snacks:

**Giant cane rat** About the size of a rabbit, this ratlike creature frequently turns up in West African stews and markets, where it's roasted over coals and sold on skewers. In some areas it is also known as a 'baby grasscutter' or by the misnomer 'agouti'.

**Land snails** Described as having a texture like 'stubborn rubber', giant land snails are eaten in parts of Nigeria.

**Mopane worms** These are actually not worms but caterpillars – the emperor moth's green and blue larvae, which make their home in the mopane trees of Southern Africa. These protein-rich critters are boiled and then dried in the sun before being eaten.

Street food in Stone Town (p668), Zanzibar

the coast. Be aware that in many places chicken is usually not regarded as meat, while even the simplest vegetable sauce may have a bit of animal fat thrown in. Expect to meet with bemusement when you announce that you don't eat meat – the idea of voluntarily giving up something that's seen as an aspirational luxury is hard to understand for many people.

## Drinks

Tea and coffee are the standard drinks, and countries seem to follow the flavours of their former colonisers. In (formerly British) East Africa, tea and coffee tends to be weak, grey and milky. In much of (formerly French) West Africa, tea is usually served black, while the coffee from roadside stalls contains enough sugar and sweetened condensed milk to keep you fully charged for hours. In North Africa and some Sahel countries (the Sahel is a semiarid region, which stretches from Mauritania, the Gambia and Senegal to Chad), mint tea and strong Arab-style coffee are the local hot beverages of choice. Other variations include chai or coffee spiced up with lemon grass or cardamom in East Africa, or flavoured with a woody leaf called *kinkiliba* in West Africa.

International soft drinks are widely available, while many countries have their own brands that are cheaper. You can also get locally made soft drinks and fruit juices, sold in plastic bags, or frozen into 'ice-sticks', but avoid these if you're worried about your stomach, as the water they're made from is usually unpurified. Alcohol allegedly kills the bugs…

In bars, you can buy local or imported beer in bottles. Excellent wines and liqueurs, from South Africa or further afield, may be available in more upmarket establishments. Traditional beer is made from millet or maize, and drunk from huge communal pots with great ceremony at special events, and with less pomp in everyday situations.

West Africa's most popular brew is palm wine. The tree is tapped and the sap comes out mildly fermented. In other parts of the continent, alcohol is made using bananas, pineapples or other fruit, sometimes fermented overnight. This homemade alcohol is often outrageously strong, can lead to blindness or mental illness, and is often illegal in some places. You have been warned!

# Regions at a Glance

Split from the rest of Africa by the Sahara, North Africa is the continent's bridge between Europe and the Middle East. West Africa is home to signature African landscapes and inhabited by an astonishing diversity of people who hold fast to their traditions.

Hot, steamy and precarious, Central Africa is the continent's proverbial 'dark heart' but also a land rich in virgin jungle, fabled rivers and amazing wildlife. East Africa plays host to profound cultural riches and overwhelming natural splendour, as well as people who have remained resilient to tragic conflict.

Southern Africa has some of the continent's most accessible wilderness and dynamic cities, the playgrounds in which to experience a multitude of adventures.

## North Africa

History
Landscapes
Islamic Culture

### Ancient Civilisations

The glories of ancient Egypt are the most famous, but extraordinary Roman and Greek cities and other cities of Mediterranean antiquity are found all along the North African coast.

### The Sahara Desert

The Sahara is the stuff of dreams, and while much of it is off limits, accessible desert expeditions are possible in Egypt and Morocco. In the last, you can drop down from the epic Atlas Mountains into the dunes that stretch deep into Africa.

### The Beauty of Islam

Whether in Marrakesh, Fez, Algiers or Cairo, you'll find yourself surrounded by the best of Arab-Islamic culture, from the soaring mosques and exquisite architecture to the warm hospitality for which the region is famous.

p51

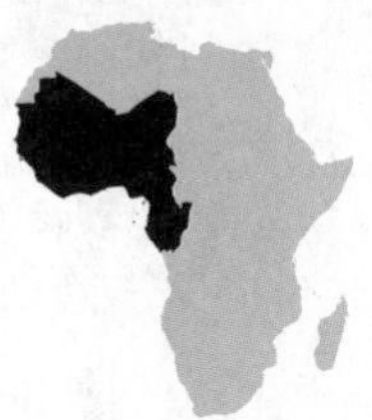

## West Africa

**Landscapes**
**Music & Tradition**
**Diversity**

### Tropical Coast

West Africa's allure will take hold amid the verdant rainforests of Cameroon, Congo, Equatorial Guinea and Gabon, or while contemplating an Atlantic sunset alongside swaying palm trees.

### African Rhythms

Extraordinarily rich musical traditions animate this epic landscape, from the live-music scene in Dakar and Conakry to the masks and stilt dancing of the Dans in Côte d'Ivoire. The region's artistic traditions (the woodcarvings here are Africa's best) provide a wonderful link to the past.

### New Frontiers

West Africa's appeal resides in its isolation, being one of the least-known corners of the continent. Emerging destinations such as Sierra Leone, Benin and Burkina Faso sit easily alongside the better-known attractions such as the beaches of The Gambia.

p145

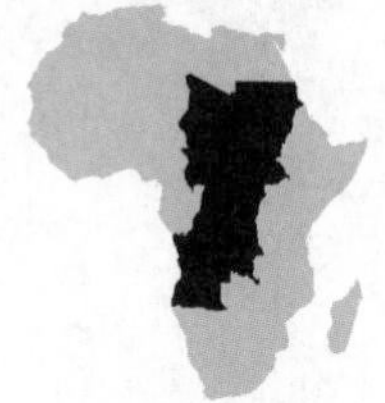

## Central Africa

**Adventure**
**Wildlife**
**Landscapes**

### Off the Map

Just coming here can be an adventure. While it would be wrong to paint Central Africa as an oasis of peace, much of the region can now be visited and destinations such as the DRC are opening up to intrepid travellers.

### Gorillas & Bonobos

Wildlife wedded to extraordinary natural beauty is the region's trump card. In the DRC there are national parks where you can see gorillas and a sanctuary for rare bonobo primates.

### Rivers & Forests

The dense rainforests of the Congo Basin and Africa's second-longest river define this remote region as rich in beauty as in biodiversity. This is the Africa you imagined when you dreamed of the continent's tropical heart.

p497

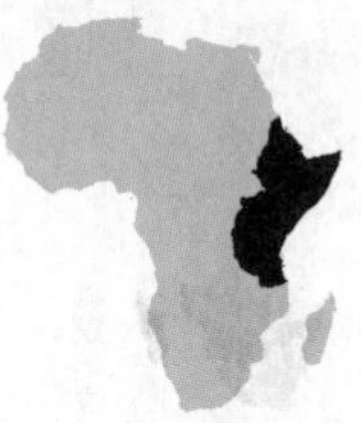

## East Africa

**Architecture**
**Landscapes**
**Wildlife**

### Architecture as Art

On the islands of Zanzibar and Lamu, cities of hewn coral pay tribute to once-vast trading empires that stretched along the coastline and deep into the interior. Ethiopia's rock churches and ruined palaces are poignant reminders of treasures won and lost.

### Africa's Highs & Lows

East Africa is home to Africa's largest lake, deepest point, swathes of primate-rich equatorial rainforest and some of the world's greatest wildlife parks. Up in the heavens the summits of Mt Kilimanjaro and Mt Kenya beckon to be climbed.

### Primates, Predators & Prey

East Africa has fabulous wildlife. Witness the annual wildebeest migration between the Serengeti and Masai Mara. Penetrate Uganda's Bwindi Impenetrable National Park to encounter mountain gorillas or the Mahale Mountains National Park to hang with chimpanzees.

p549

## Southern Africa

**Wildlife & Landscapes**
**Adventure Activities**
**Relaxation**

### Wildlife Central

This corner has some of Africa's most accessible wilderness – an astonishing variety and density of wildlife, dreamy landscapes and world-class natural features like thundering Victoria Falls. Botswana offers the wildlife-rich, water-soaked Okavango Delta, Zambia's majestic national parks – the list goes on and on.

### Adventure Activities

Southern Africa will fill the part of your heart that yearns for adventure. Want to bungee jump? No problem. Fly over mighty Victoria Falls? Absolutely. White-water raft raging rapids? Of course!

### African Chill

The region's ambient rhythm swoons visitors into a blissful stupor. Change down a gear and relax on Mozambique's uncrowded beaches and romantic offshore islands, or Botswana's remote luxury lodges, or join locals for a drink at a South African *shebeen* (informal drinking establishment)...

**p739**

# On the Road

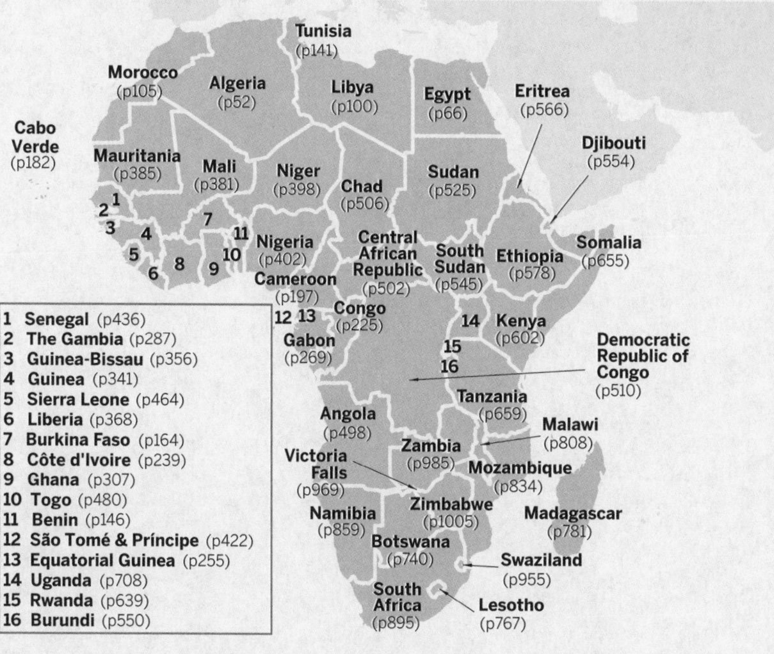

Tunisia
(p141)
Morocco
(p105)
Algeria
(p52)
Libya
(p100)
Egypt
(p66)
Eritrea
(p566)
Cabo
Verde
(p182)
Djibouti
(p554)
Mauritania
(p385)
Mali
(p381)
Niger
(p398)
Sudan
(p525)
Chad
(p506)
Nigeria
(p402)
Central
African
Republic
(p502)
South
Sudan
(p545)
Ethiopia
(p578)
Somalia
(p655)
Cameroon
(p197)
Congo
(p225)
Kenya
(p602)
Gabon
(p269)
Democratic
Republic of
Congo
(p510)
Tanzania
(p659)
Angola
(p498)
Malawi
(p808)
Zambia
(p985)
Victoria
Falls
(p969)
Mozambique
(p834)
Namibia
(p859)
Zimbabwe
(p1005)
Madagascar
(p781)
Botswana
(p740)
Swaziland
(p955)
South
Africa
(p895)
Lesotho
(p767)
1 Senegal (p436)
2 The Gambia (p287)
3 Guinea-Bissau (p356)
4 Guinea (p341)
5 Sierra Leone (p464)
6 Liberia (p368)
7 Burkina Faso (p164)
8 Côte d'Ivoire (p239)
9 Ghana (p307)
10 Togo (p480)
11 Benin (p146)
12 São Tomé & Príncipe (p422)
13 Equatorial Guinea (p255)
14 Uganda (p708)
15 Rwanda (p639)
16 Burundi (p550)

# North Africa

CURIOSO/SHUTTERSTOCK ©

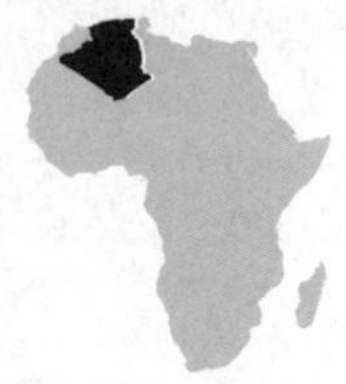

# Algeria

POP 40.7 MILLION / ☎213

## Includes ➡



## Best Places to Eat

- ➡ Le Caïd (p57)
- ➡ Cafe-Restaurant El Salam (p56)
- ➡ Café Tontonville (p57)

## Best Places to Sleep

- ➡ ST Hotel (p56)
- ➡ Hôtel el-Djazaïr (p56)
- ➡ Hôtel des Princes (p59)

## Why Go?

Africa's largest country lies just a short hop from Europe. The north, with its snow-flecked mountains and stunning coastline, is home to urbane and charismatic cities such as Algiers and Constantine, as well as some of the most magnificent Roman sites in existence including Timgad and Djemila, both vast, perfectly preserved Roman towns with barely another tourist in sight.

Algeria's other big draw is its extraordinary Saharan region. Whether it's a glimpse of the sand seas that surround Timimoun, or the burnt-red mountains of the far south, these are the desert landscapes of legend.

But, for all its peach-coloured dunes and grand ruins, it's perhaps the Algerians themselves, who welcome visitors with warmth and curiosity, that are the real highlight of this nation. For accessible adventure and a complex, enthralling cultural odyssey, head for Algeria.

## When to Go

### Algiers

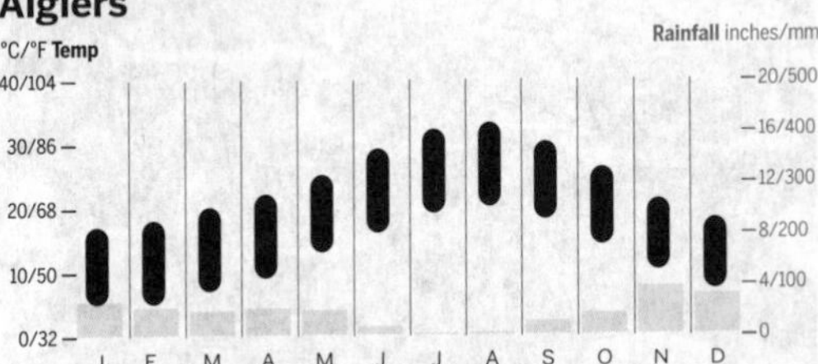


**Nov–Apr** Less ferocious temperatures mean high season in the Sahara (the autumn date harvest is a bonus).

**Mar–Jul** The north literally blossoms in the spring; warm, dry days are perfect for exploring Roman sites.

**Aug** It's very hot throughout the country and the beaches are busy with local tourists. Avoid the Sahara.

# ALGIERS

POP 3.4 MILLION / ☎021

Algiers (Al-Jazaïr) never fails to make an impression. This is a city of rare beauty and of thrilling, disorientating and sometimes brutal contrast. The country's turbulent history is writ large in the city's richly textured architecture: wide French-built boulevards and elegant apartments and villas, Socialist-era monuments and public buildings, and an enduring Islamic heart secreted in the steep, hillside Casbah. Labyrinthine streets spill down to the yawning big blue of the Bay of Algiers, sea and sky and green ravines glimpsed at every step. Though people often spend just enough time in Algiers to organise an onward journey, it's a fascinating place well worth at least a couple of days' exploration.

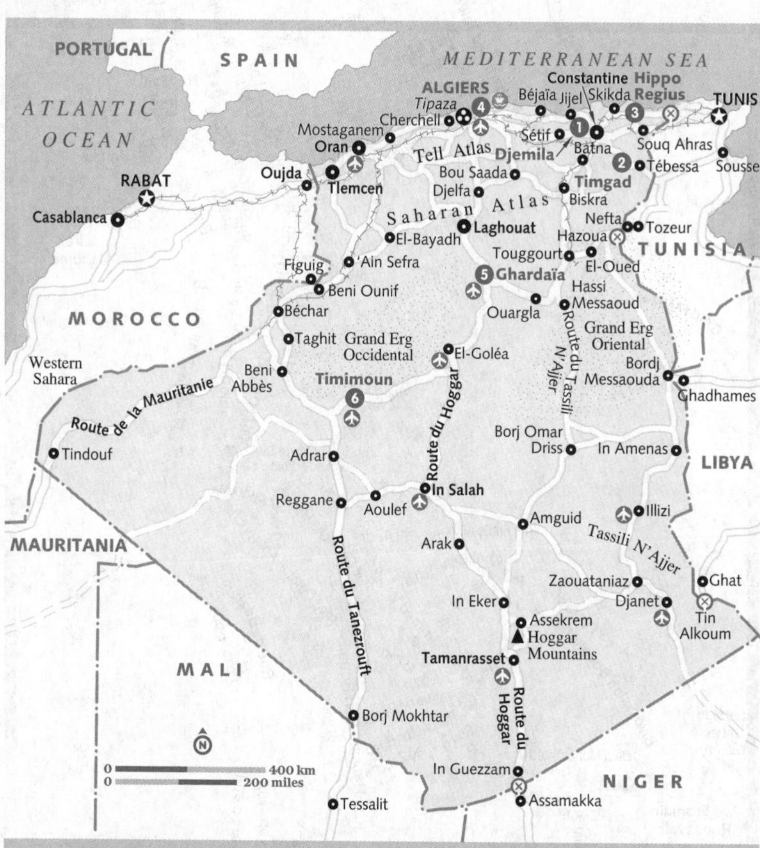


## Algeria Highlights

1. **Djemila** (p58) Listening out for the ghostly footsteps of Roman legionnaires in this beautiful ruined town.
2. **Timgad** (p58) Standing atop the theatre and surveying the ruined grandeur of this vast Roman city.
3. **Hippo Regius** (p58) Picnicking among the flowers surrounded by the tapering columns of the Roman city.
4. **Algiers** (p53) Experiencing 'la Blanche', where modern, traditional and colonial-era Algeria meet.
5. **Ghardaïa** (p60), Bargaining for a carpet, peeking at a medieval town and then swimming in the shade of date palms.
6. **Timimoun** (p59) Striking out into the dunes of the Grand Erg Occidental from this red oasis.

## Algiers

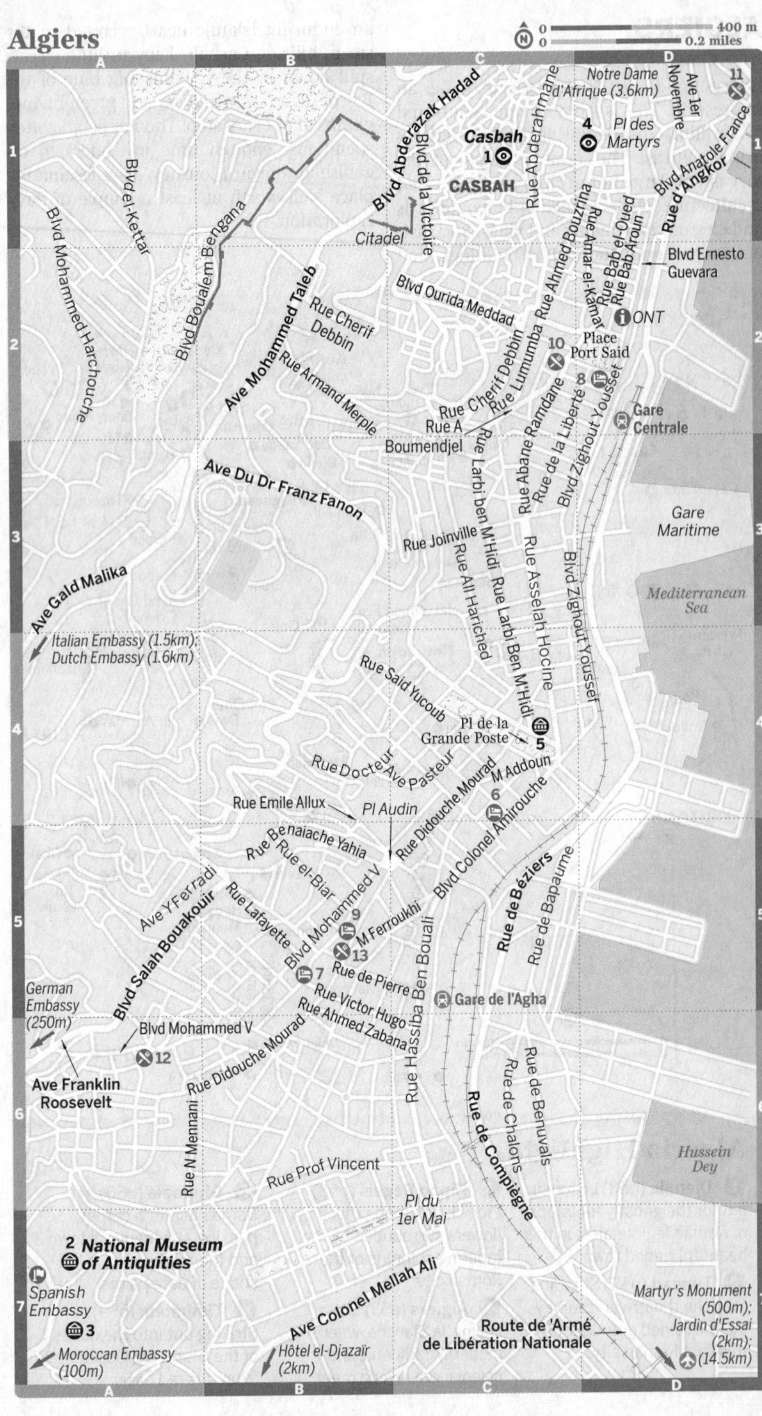
0 400 m
0 0.2 miles
A
B
C
D
1
2
3
4
5
6
7
Casbah
1
CASBAH
4
Pl des Martyrs
Notre Dame d'Afrique (3.6km)
11
Ave 1er Novembre
Blvd Anatole France
Rue d'Angkor
Blvd Abderazak Hadad
Blvd de la Victoire
Citadel
Rue Abderahmane
Blvd el-Kettar
Blvd Mohammed Harchouche
Blvd Boualem Bengana
Ave Mohammed Taleb
Rue Cherif Debbin
Rue Armand Merple
Blvd Ourida Meddad
Rue Ahmed Bouzrina
Rue Amar el-Kamar
Rue Bab el-Oued
Rue Bab Aroun
Blvd Ernesto Guevara
ONT
10
Place Port Said
8
Rue Cherif Debbin
Rue Lumumba
Rue A Boumendjel
Rue Abane Ramdane
Rue de la Liberté
Blvd Zighout Youssef
Gare Centrale
Ave Du Dr Franz Fanon
Rue Larbi ben M'Hidi
Rue Joinville
Rue Ali Hariched
Rue Larbi Ben M'Hidi
Rue Asselah Hocine
Blvd Zighout Youssef
Gare Maritime
Mediterranean Sea
Ave Gald Malika
Italian Embassy (1.5km); Dutch Embassy (1.6km)
Rue Said Yucoub
Pl de la Grande Poste
5
Rue Docteur
Ave Pasteur
M Addoun
6
Rue Didouche Mourad
Blvd Colonel Amirouche
Rue Emile Allux
Pl Audin
Rue Benaiache Yahia
Rue el-Biar
Ave Y Ferradi
Blvd Salah Bouakouir
Rue Lafayette
Blvd Mohammed V
9
M Ferroukhi
13
7
Rue de Pierre
Rue Victor Hugo
Rue Ahmed Zabana
Blvd Hassiba Ben Bouali
Rue de Béziers
Rue de Bapaume
Gare de l'Agha
German Embassy (250m)
Blvd Mohammed V
12
Ave Franklin Roosevelt
Rue Didouche Mourad
Rue N Mennani
Rue de Chalons
Rue de Benuvals
Rue de Compiègne
Hussein Dey
Rue Prof Vincent
Pl du 1er Mai
2 National Museum of Antiquities
Spanish Embassy
3
Moroccan Embassy (100m)
Ave Colonel Mellah Ali
Hôtel el-Djazaïr (2km)
Route de 'Armé de Libération Nationale
Martyr's Monument (500m); Jardin d'Essai (2km); (14.5km)

## Algiers

**Top Sights**



**Sights**



**Sleeping**



**Eating**



**Drinking & Nightlife**



## Sights

Much of the enjoyment to be had in Algiers comes from clambering up its steep streets, strolling in the parks and taking in *those* views. That said, there are a number of sights and interesting museums to easily fill a few days.

### ★Casbah — AREA

The heart of the city is its ancient Casbah, a steep and narrow maze of streets just west of the Pl des Martyrs. There are several magnificent Ottoman palaces to explore here, most concentrated around the **Djemaa Ketchoua** (rue Hadj Omar) at the end of Rue Ahmed Bouzrina; the finest is the Dar Hassan Pacha.

### ★National Museum of Antiquities — MUSEUM

(☎021 681129; www.musee-antiquites.art.dz; 177 Blvd Krim Belkacem; DA100; ⏲9am-5pm Sun-Thu, 10am-noon & 2-4.30pm Fri, 9am-4.30pm Sat) The richness of Algeria's heritage is brought home in this museum. The collection of antiquities is drawn from sites around the city and throughout Algeria. Among the early works are fine ivory carvings and large, totemic Libyan-period warriors on horseback. There is sculpture from Cherchell and mosaics from Tipaza, a room of bronzes including a wonderful fragment of a horse's leg and hoof, and an extraordinary 3rd-century figure of a chubby child holding an eagle to its chest.

### Dar Hassan Pacha — HISTORIC SITE

(☎021439229; rue Hadj Omar; DA140; ⏲9am-4pm Sat-Thu) Carrying the name of its original owner, Dar Hassan Pacha, this is one of the city's grandest mansions. The building now houses a collection of illuminated manuscripts and contemporary calligraphy by artists from across North Africa and the Middle East.

### Bardo Museum of Prehistory & Ethnography — MUSEUM

(☎021 747641; www.musee-bardo.art.dz; 3 Ave FD Roosevelt; DA200; ⏲9am-5pm Sat-Thu) The Bardo, which focuses on the prehistory of Algeria, is one of the best museums in Algiers. The collection is well-displayed with videos, models and excellent diagrams and information panels (in French) that reveal how the climate and environment of the region have changed over the eons and how that has affected human and wildlife development. There are lots of fossils, neolithic pottery, rock carvings and examples of Neanderthal paintings from the Sahara.

### Grande Poste — HISTORIC BUILDING

(Pl de la Grande Poste) Algier's beloved main post office is an unmissable piece of living history, a fine example of French-designed, early 20th-century Moorish architecture. Look out for what is possibly the world's most exquisitely decorated post box near the entrance. At the time of research it was closed to visitors and in the process of being converted into a museum; it's expected to reopen in 2018.

### Jardin d'Essai — GARDENS

(www.jardindessai.com; Rue Belouizdid, El-Hamma; DA100; ⏲9am-7pm Jun-Sep, to 5pm Oct-May) These bayside botanical gardens date to the first years of French occupation and today they are a sprawling natural hothouse. It's a place of outstanding beauty with avenues of palms and stands of exotic trees. To escape here from the city centre take the metro to the Jardin d'Essai stop.

## Sleeping

City accommodation can be hard to find (book well ahead) and is seldom good value. Budget hotels cluster around Pl Port Said on the edge of the Casbah, though they're not for the faint-hearted.

### Hotel Djurdjura — HOTEL $

(☎021 635455; 6 rue Lounés Merar; s/d/tw DA2400/2600/3000; ❄) A very basic, bare-bones hotel for an equally bare-bones price. The rooms have saggy beds and bathrooms

WORTH A TRIP

## TIPAZA

**Tipasa Archaeological Park** (rue du Musée; DA80; ⏲9am-7pm May-Sep, to 5pm Oct-Apr) The founders of Tipasa (as Tipaza was known during the Roman era) obviously had an eye for aesthetics. The town rolls gently downhill through pine trees to a small beach and a blue silvered sea. It's this natural beauty, as much as the honey-toned sandstone walls, the amphitheatre where naval battles were re-enacted and the remnants of markets where fish were gutted and sold, that really makes Tipasa stand out as one of North Africa's finest Roman sites.

**Tipaza Museum** (☎024 477 543; rue du Musée; DA60; ⏲9am-7pm May-Sep, to 5pm Oct-Apr) This small museum has some fine funerary stele showing warriors on horseback and, the show-stopper of the collection, a mosaic of captives, which at its centre depicts parents and their son bound in ropes. Around the mosaics border are the heads of various Africans. The museum also contains some finely carved sarcophagi and some exquisite 1st- to 3rd-century AD glass objects.

### Getting There & Away

Around about every half-hour buses travelling between Algiers (DA100, 1½ hours) and Cherchell (DA40, 30 minutes) pass by Tipaza.

with squat toilets with the shower heads interestingly positioned directly above said toilet. On the plus side it's very central and the little balconies have street-life views.

**Hôtel Terminus** HOTEL $
(☎021 737817; 2 Rue Rachid Ksentini; r DA1400-4500; ❄📶) Excellently located in the heart of the city, the Terminus is just moments from the train station. Rooms come in a bewildering array of styles and prices and vary enormously from windowless boxes with grim shared facilities to rooms with sea views and private bathrooms.

**Hôtel Suisse** HISTORIC HOTEL $$
(☎021 631009; www.hotelsuisse-dz.com; 6 rue Lt Boulhat; s/d DA6500/8200; ❄📶) Okay, so it's a little run down and the hot water comes and goes, but the Suisse makes up for all that with bucket loads of 1930s period charm. There are arched doorways, a clanky old leather-lined elevator and a time warp **bar** (⏲10am-midnight Sat-Thu) with bottles of whisky gathering dust on the shelves. The side-street location keeps things quiet.

**ST Hotel** HOTEL $$
(☎021 638065; www.tourisme-hotel.dz; 4 Rue Mikideche Mouloud; s/d/tw DA8200/10,200/9500; ❄📶) A great find on a side street in the centre of town (although road noise can still drift into your dreams). This is a well-run and friendly hotel where the rooms are generous in size and painted in all manner of brash colours. Some have small balconies. Breakfast is served in a sun-filled top-floor room.

**Hôtel el-Djazaïr** HISTORIC HOTEL $$$
(Hôtel St George; ☎023 481164; www.chaineeld-jazair.com; 24 Ave Souidani Boudjemma; s/d from DA26,500/30,500; ❄@🏊) Kipling, Gide, Churchill and Eisenhower all stayed in this gracious place, locally known as the St George. It's lost some of its dusty ambience to recent renovations, but gained a smart, business outlook and a lot more comfort. The real draws, though, are the location, lavish public areas and heritage gardens. There are four restaurants, a bar and a pool.

## Eating & Drinking

There's no shortage of cheap fast food around town and excellent bread and pastries from ubiquitous bakeries. Good seafood restaurants can be found along the Rampe de la Pêcherie near the port, as well as in the beach suburbs to the west.

Algiers is not a hard place to find a drink, though bars here aren't always a pleasant experience. Try the top-end or historic hotels for a bar with more class or character. On Friday (the Islamic Holy day) it can be hard to find a drink at all outside of the hotels.

★ **Cafe-Restaurant El Salam** ALGERIAN $
(☎055 0056252; rue de la Marin; mains DA400-500; ⏲6am-4pm Sat-Thu) A handy place to eat when exploring the Casbah district, this cheap locals favourite serves traditional home cooking that can be hard to find elsewhere. Try the grilled sardines, various kebabs and, if you're feeling game, the sheep brain in a tomato sauce. Wash it all down

with the delicious homemade lime juice. Before 10am only coffee and breakfast is served.

**Oriental Restaurant** MIDDLE EASTERN $
(☎055 1118300; rue Didouche Mourad; mains DA400-600; ⏰10am-11pm Sat-Thu, 3-11pm Fri) A fast, fun, noisy and busy Palestinian restaurant with a calling card of succulent dripping *shawarma* (doner kebab) and plates of mezze loaded with hummus, olives and falafels.

**Café Tontonville** CAFE $$
(☎021 748661; 7 Pl Port Said; mains DA500-900; ⏰restaurant 8am-5pm Sat-Thu, cafe 5am-10pm) This Algiers institution is a great place for breakfast and coffee on the ever-busy terrace of the cafe. Around the back is the restaurant serving grilled meat and fish dishes as well as thin-crust pizza.

★**Le Caïd** ALGERIAN $$$
(☎021 631357; 79 bis Blvd Mohamed V; meals around DA24,000; ⏰11am-3pm & 6pm-midnight) This classy, intimate and laid-back restaurant is perhaps the best place in Algiers to eat gourmet versions of local classics. It's best known for its *mechoui,* delicious slow roasted lamb on the bone. It also does salads and, on Wednesday and Thursday, a rich paella. There's a small list of Algerian wines, and live music upstairs (jazz on Wednesday and Thursday and classical Algerian on Friday).

## ℹ Information

There are banks all over the city centre and most now have ATMs that work with foreign cards. You can also try the airport or the reception area of one of the five-star hotels.

ONT (p64) is an enthusiastic, if not wildly helpful, tourist office.

## ℹ Getting There & Away

### AIR

Houari Boumediene Airport (p64), the country's biggest and busiest airport, is located a very congested 17km southeast of the city. The domestic and international terminals are a short walk apart.

There are frequent airport buses into town (bus number 110; DA50), but it's simpler to take a private taxi (DA600 to DA800 on the street, DA1200 to DA1500 through a hotel).

### BUS

The main intercity bus station is east of the city centre on the road to the airport. The bus station is very well organised with a central booking office and TV screens displaying upcoming departures and parking bay numbers.

Buses go frequently to Annaba (DA1060; eight hours), Constantine (DA770, six hours), Ghardaïa (DA1050), Oran (DA770, six hours), Sétif (DA530, five hours), Timimoun (DA1940, 20 hours) and Tlemcen (DA1040, eight hours).

### TRAIN

Trains are run by SNTF (p65). East-bound trains run out of **Gare Centrale** (☎021 711510; rue d'Angkor), beside the Gare Maritime, and west-bound services depart from **Gare de l'Agha** (☎021 636525; off rue Hassiba ben Bouali). Both stations are very central.

Trains run once daily to Constantine (from DA985, 6½ hours) and Oran (from DA900, five hours) and twice daily from Sétif (from DA645, four hours), among other destinations.

## ℹ Getting Around

Taxis can be hired by you alone, or shared. Drivers can be found outside the larger central hotels. If you want to book a taxi pick up, ask for recommended drivers at your hotel. Short trips across town should not cost more than DA500, though prices are higher between 9pm and 5am. A taxi from the city centre to the main bus station will cost around DA300 to DA400.

# NORTHERN ALGERIA

Northern Algeria's various urban hubs make fascinating destinations for adventurous city lovers. Oran is a port city with extraordinary 20th-century architecture and an easy Mediterranean vibe. Inland, there's medieval Tlemcen, former Islamic capital and with some of the more impressive buildings in the country. On the east coast, Annaba possesses a pretty, seaside melancholy and has a significant Roman site, Hippo Regius (p58), the home of Christian church father St Augustine. Constantine, a bustling inland city, is known for its spectacularly spanned gorges and large student population.

The stand-out attractions of the north, however, are the Roman cities of Tipaza, a short day trip from Algiers, and Djemila and Timgad, two of the most breathtaking and best-preserved Roman cities in the world. A visit to these two sites is more akin to pilgrimage than mere sightseeing.

## Constantine

POP 465,000 / ☎031

Constantine, Algeria's third city, is one of the grand urban spectacles of Algeria, made by nature but embellished by man. Over time, the Oued Rhumel (Rhumel River) carved

DON'T MISS

## ROMAN SITES

Djemila, Timgad and Hippo Regis can be visited on a day trip from Constantine.

**Djemila** (DA80; ⌚8am-8pm Apr-Sep, to 5pm Oct-Mar) The spectacular ruined Roman town of Djemila (or Cuicul as it was then known) is small enough to breeze around in half a day. But spend longer here, linger in the temples and markets, stroll through the bath chambers, or just lie down in the shade of villa walls and conjure up the sounds and sensations of those long gone days; one of the world's great archaeological sites will come alive.

**Timgad** (DA200; ⌚9am-6pm Apr-Sep, to 5pm Oct-Mar) One of the finest Roman sites in existence, the ruins of Timgad stretch almost as far as the eye can see over a plain that in winter is cold and desolate and in summer hot and tinder-dry. Its perfect preservation has made it a Unesco World Heritage Site – take the time to walk around slowly, inhabit the place and Timgad will spring to life.

**Hippo Regius** (adult DA60; ⌚8am-7pm May-Sep, to 5pm Oct-Apr) The vast ruins of the ancient Roman city of Hippo Regius, also known as Hippone, are among the most evocative in Algeria, stretched across a rolling site, full of flowers, rosemary, olive trees, birds and sheep, and overlooked by the imposing, colonial-era **Basilica de Saint Augustine** (⌚9-11.30am & 2.30-4.30pm Mon-Thu, 2.30-4.30pm Fri, 11-11.30am & 2.30-4.30pm Sun).

out a deep, and almost circular, gorge around an outcrop of rock, creating a natural fortress that was already occupied in Neolithic times. Since then, Constantine has always been a city of political, cultural and economic significance.

Despite this epic history and setting, actual tourist sites are remarkably thin on the ground – the real pleasure of a visit here is all in the atmosphere.

## Sights

Constantine might have long since burst out and over its mountain fortress, but most sights of interest are crammed in and around the narrow, bustling streets of this area.

### ★National Museum Cirta — MUSEUM

(blvd de la Liberté; DA200; ⌚9am-noon & 1-4.30pm Sat-Thu, 2-4.30pm Fri) Highlighting the numerous finds from excavations in and around Constantine and nearby Tiddis, there are some stunning pieces in this museum. The highlights include a seated terracotta figure from a 2nd-century BC tomb and an exquisite marble bust of a woman known as the 'beauty of Djemila'. Also worth finding is the beautifully cast bronze sculpture of winged 'Victory of Constantine', found by soldiers while excavating the streets of the Casbah in 1855.

### ★Tiddis — ROMAN SITE

(DA80; ⌚8am-7pm May-Sept, to 5pm Oct-Apr) Hovering on a barren mountain slope, some 30km from Constantine, the ruined Roman town of Tiddis is perhaps the most impressively situated of all Algeria's Roman sites. However, the ruins themselves are fairly weather beaten and cannot compare with some of the more famous Roman cities around these parts.

### Palace of Ahmed Bey — PALACE

(Musée National des Arts et Expressions Culturelles Traditionelles; place Si-El Haoues; DA80; ⌚9am-noon & 1-4pm Sat-Thu) The palace of Hajj Ahmed, the bey or ruler of Constantine from 1826, is one of the finest Ottoman-era buildings in the country. With a series of courtyards surrounded by tiled arcades, it is filled with gardens of palm and orange trees, and decorated with Tunisian and French tiles and murals depicting Ahmed's pilgrimage to Mecca.

### Mellah Slimane Bridge & Elevator — BRIDGE

(elevator DA5; ⌚elevator 7am-6pm Sat-Thu, 9am-12.30pm Fri) Of all the dramatic bridges that cross the Oued Rhumel, none is as exciting to walk across as the Mellah Slimane Bridge, some 100m above the water. Stretching 125m long and a mere 2.5m wide, it joins the train station with the centre of the old town and, vertigo sufferers will be delighted to hear, you can feel it wobble as you cross. An elevator carries you down to it from the old town.

### Sidi M'Cid Bridge — BRIDGE

The Sidi M'Cid Bridge, also known as the Suspended Bridge, is Constantine's iconic monument, its image defining the city. It is a 164m-long suspension bridge, opened to traffic in April 1912. The bridge links the Casbah to the slopes of Sidi M'Cid hill. Views of town and the gorge, 175m below, are stunning.

## Sleeping & Eating

Constantine has several international chain hotels, but sadly there's a distinct dearth of decent independent hotels. The historic **Citra Hotel** is expected to re-open in 2018.

There are very few restaurants but fast food and kebab places can be found throughout the city (try rue Abane Ramdane in the town centre for particularly rich pickings).

**★Hôtel des Princes** HISTORIC HOTEL $
(☎031 912625; http://hoteldesprinces.wix.com/hotel-des-princes; 29 rue Abane Ramdane; s/d from DA4000/4500; ❄📶) Dating from 1935 and still retaining much of its period charm, this immaculately presented, family-run hotel has ornate gold-and-white carved plaster ceilings, faded buttercup-yellow window shutters, drooping lamp shades and an atrium filled with leafy house plants. You'd be hard pushed to find a hotel elsewhere in Algeria with this much character for such a reasonable price.

**Ibis Hotel** HOTEL $$
(☎031 992000; www.ibis.com; Place Hadj Ali; r from DA7500; P❄📶) With a plumb position right in the centre of Constantine, this well-priced chain hotel is easily the most popular place to stay for visiting Algerians and foreigners. As is normal with Ibis hotels, everything runs smoothly, cleanliness is all important, the rooms are well insulated and sound-proofed, and there's good wi-fi and fast service.

**Restaurant le Concorde** ALGERIAN $
(rue Abane Ramdane; mains DA300-500; ⏰11am-3pm & 5.30-9.30pm) The travel-mad owner of this restaurant will fill you up with steaks, lentil soup and the local speciality of *chachoukha* (think: chopped pasta with a tomato sauce and green pepper). He may shut up shop unexpectedly and head off on an adventure, but we're sure you'll understand his need!

## Getting There & Away

### AIR

Constantine's **Mohamed Boudiaf International Airport** (☎031 810101; www.elmatar.com; Bellahreche) has a few international flights to France and numerous daily flights to Algiers.

### BUS

The bus station (off N5) is a couple of kilometres south of the town centre and Casbah. Buses leave roughly every hour for Algiers (DA760, six hours), Annaba (DA280, four hours), Batna (DA220, three hours) and Setif (DA200, three hours). A taxi from the city centre to the bus station costs DA200.

### TRAIN

Constantine's train station (rue Kouicem Abdelhamid) is a slightly scary walk across a wobbly bridge from the Casbah. There's a nightly train to Annaba but it leaves at the uncivilised time of 2.50am (from DA245, 2½ hours). A daily train heads to Algiers (from DA985, 6½ hours) at 6.40am and twice daily trains serve Batna (DA250, 1½ hours) and Setif (from DA335, 2½ hours).

# CENTRAL ALGERIA

In the mysterious, picturesque M'zab Valley, life goes on much as it has for centuries (give or take the odd game of football).

Southwest, deep into the sand seas of the Grand Erg Occidental, is Timimoun, an oasis town with evocative red architecture, a unique ethnic mix and easy access to gob-smacking desert scenery.

WORTH A TRIP

### TIMIMOUN

The largest oasis in the Grand Erg Occidental, this dusty desert city is an enchanting place. It's characteristic architecture, red-mud buildings studded with spikes, hints at sub-Saharan Africa. Its location, at the edge of an escarpment, makes for breathtaking views across a salt lake and out to the dunes beyond. The main street bustles in the morning and evening; the locals are a diverse mix that includes Haratines, Berbers and the descendants of Malian merchants and slaves.

Timimoun makes a good base for the **Sebkha Circuit**, a 75km to 90km loop that takes in the Saharan dunes of popular imagination, as well as the salt lake, crumbling hilltop ksars and deep red caves. You can arrange a car and driver with the tourist office in the commune office near the market, or ask your hotel.

There is a helpful **tourist office** (☎049 904080; Place de l'Indépendance; ⏰8am-4pm Sun-Thu) in Timimoun.

## Ghardaïa

POP 356,000 / ☎029

In the river valley of the Oued M'Zab, in a long valley on the edge of the Sahara, is a cluster of five towns: Ghardaïa, Melika, Beni Isguen, Bou Noura and El-Atteuf. Often referred to collectively as Ghardaïa, the once distinct villages are gradually sprawling together, but retain separate identities.

The M'Zab is home to a conservative Muslim sect known as the *Ibadites,* who broke from mainstream Islam some 900 years ago. This is, some say, a country unto itself, with ancient, unchanging social codes. The traditional white *haik* (a head-to-toe wool wrap) is worn by most women, who cover their entire face, exposing only one eye. Men sport extravagantly pleated baggy trousers called *saroual loubia*. While locals here can be reserved, it's a friendly and surprisingly laid-back place. The area is justifiably famous for its carpets – head for Ghardaïa's market square for a good selection.

The best accommodation is in and around Beni Isguen. Most guesthouses provide dinner, and there are fast-food shops aplenty in downtown Ghardaïa

Air Algérie (p65) flies here from Algiers (one hour, daily) and Tamanrasset (2½ hours, one weekly). Regular buses run from Ghardaïa to Algiers and to Tamanrasset.

# UNDERSTAND ALGERIA

## Algeria Today

In July 2012 Algeria celebrated the 50th anniversary of its independence, and the end of what is considered one of the most brutal of the 20th century's wars of decolonisation. Parliamentary elections held earlier in May of the same year had replicated the results of 2004 and 2009 with the Front de Libération Nationale (FLN; National Liberation Front) once again winning a majority.

Since the horrors of the *décennie noir*, the civil war of the 1990s, the country has enjoyed a period of peace, but oil- and gas-fuelled prosperity has failed to trickle down. People took to the streets during January 2011, protesting, like their Tunisian neighbours, about painfully high unemployment, housing shortages and the spiraling cost of living. But this dissent was soon calmed; many Algerians suggesting they are just too haunted by the past to stomach the possibility of a return to violence.

In presidential elections in April 2014, 77-year-old President Abdelaziz Bouteflika won a fourth term in office. Elections were condemned as 'flawed' by opposition parties. Since then, Bouteflika' health has become increasingly frail, however, and with no obvious successor many Algerians wonder who – or what – will eventually replace him.

## History

### The Barbary Coast

By the late 1600s, Algeria was a military republic, ruled by locally appointed officers, with Istanbul-anointed pashas (governors) retaining only a symbolic role.

The country was, of course, better known to Europeans as the Barbary (a corruption of Berber) Coast, an anarchic place where fearsome pirates preyed on Christian – and in particular, Catholic – shipping. Mediterranean piracy took off during the Holy Wars, and a few centuries later it had become the mainstay of North Africa's economy. Khayr al-Din, also known as Barbarossa, the first regent of Algiers, at one point held no fewer than 25,000 Christians captive in the city.

Algerian attacks on US shipping led to the two Barbary Wars, and the eventual defeat of the Algerian fleet off Algiers in 1815.

### French Rule

Northern Algeria was mostly under French control by 1834 but resistance continued, led by Emir Abdelkader, ruler of western and central Algeria and the great hero of Algeria's nationalist movement. His armies held off the French for almost six years before they were defeated near Oujda in 1844. Abdelkader himself finally surrendered in 1846 and spent the rest of his life in exile.

French Algeria was not a colony, rather its three departements were constitutionally part of France. The French rebuilt Algeria in France's image and distributed large parts of prime farming land to European settlers (known as *colons* and later *pied-noirs*) who arrived from Italy, Malta, Spain and Portugal, as well as France. Algerians could become citizens if they renounced Islam and Islamic law, something very few did, otherwise they remained 'subjects' with severely limited rights. By 1960, the population consisted of around nine million 'Muslims' and a million 'Algerians' – Europeans.

## Revolution & Independence

Algeria's war of independence, led by the newly formed Front de Libération Nationale (FLN; National Liberation Front), began on 31 October 1954 in Batna, east of Algiers. The French military, the FLN and the *pied-noirs* all committed atrocities, with the use of torture routine. It's estimated that between 700,000 and 1.5 million lives were lost over seven years. President Charles de Gaulle, convinced of the impossibility of continued French rule, agreed to a referendum on independence in March 1962. The result was nearly unanimous, with most *pied-noirs* either abstaining or long departed. Independence was declared on 5 July 1962. By August, around 900,000 *pied-noirs* and *harkis* (Algerians who worked with the French) had left for France.

FLN candidate Ahmed ben Bella became Algeria's first president. He pledged to create a 'revolutionary Arab-Islamic state based on the principles of socialism and collective leadership at home and anti-imperialism abroad'. He was soon overthrown by former colleague Colonel Houari Boumédienne, who effectively returned the country to military rule in 1965.

Boumédienne died in December 1978 and the FLN replaced him with the slightly more moderate Colonel Chadli Benjedid, who was re-elected in 1984 and 1989. In October 1988, thousands of people took to the streets in protest against austerity measures and food shortages. The army was called in to restore order, and between 100 and 600 people were killed.

The extent of the opposition became clear at local government elections held in early 1990, with landslide victories for the previously outlawed fundamentalist group Front Islamique du Salut (FIS; Islamic Salvation Front).

The initial round of Algeria's first multiparty parliamentary elections, held in December 1991, produced another landslide win for the FIS. Chadli's apparent acceptance of this prompted the army to step in, replacing him with a five-person Haut Conseil d'Etat (HCE; High Council of State) headed by Mohammed Boudiaf, a hero of the Algerian revolution. The second round of elections was cancelled, and FIS leaders Abbas Madani and Ali Belhadj were arrested, while others fled into exile.

## Civil War

Boudiaf lasted six months before he was assassinated amid signs of a growing guerrilla offensive led by the Groupe Islamique Armé (GIA; Armed Islamic Group). He was replaced by former FLN hardliner Ali Kafi, who oversaw the country's rapid descent into civil war before he was replaced by a retired general, Liamine Zéroual. Zéroual attempted to defuse the situation by holding fresh elections in 1995, but Islamic parties were barred from the poll and Zéroual's sweeping victory came amid widespread claims of fraud.

Hopes for peace went unfulfilled; the war became even more remorseless, with Amnesty International accusing both sides of massacres. The GIA, angered by French aid to the government, extended the war to French soil with a series of bombings and hijackings.

Eventually, government security forces began to gain the upper hand, and at the beginning of 1999 Zéroual announced that he would be stepping down. New elections held in April that year resulted in a controversial victory for the establishment candidate Abdelaziz Bouteflika.

Bouteflika moved quickly to establish his legitimacy by calling a referendum on a plan to offer amnesty to the rebels. War-weary Algerians responded overwhelmingly with a 98% 'yes' vote, and by the end of 1999 many groups had responded and laid down their weapons. The exact number of those killed in the war will likely never be known and estimates vary from 44,000 to 200,000.

# People

The majority of Algerians are ethnically Arab-Berber and live in the north of the country. Berber traditions are best preserved in the Kabylie, east of Algiers, where people speak the Berber tongue, Tamazight, as their first language. The Tuareg people of the Sahara are also Berbers, and speak Tamashek. In 2016 Berber was, for the first time in the modern age, made one of the official languages of Algeria.

An estimated 99% of Algeria's population are Sunni Muslims, along with the Ibadis of the Mzeb Valley, and small numbers of Christians and Jews. While Islam is part of everyday life in Algeria, alcohol is available in a few bars and upmarket restaurants and not all women wear hijab.

## Cuisine

Algerians are generally big carnivores and meat in some form or another (normally grilled) is the centrepiece of most meals. It's often eaten with bread and fresh or pickled vegetables. Along the coast superb seafood is widely available and thick, filling, slightly spiced soups are common everywhere. In the north there's plenty of delicious fresh fruit (don't miss the winter oranges – delicious!) while in the south dates are king.

## Music

Algeria's most well-known cultural export is raï, a musical hybrid that was spawned in the clubs of colonial-era Oran and flourished as protest pop fusion in the 1970s and '80s. Initially suppressed by the Boumédienne government, it was, ironically, the popularity of raï in France that ended its censorship. Early greats include the Algerian James Brown, Boutaïba S'ghir, sweet, soulful Belkacem Bouteldja and the lyrical and sensual Chiekha Remiti. The celebrity status of Khaled, Rachid Taha and Faudel was cemented in the legendary concert 1, 2, 3 Soleils in Paris in 1998; the live album is a good place to start for raï neophytes.

# SURVIVAL GUIDE

## 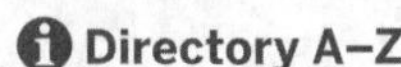 Directory A–Z

### ACCOMMODATION

Algerian towns normally have a good selection of hotels in the budget and midrange categories with comfortable rooms, hot-water bathrooms and wi-fi being the norm (although the very cheapest places can be rough around the edges). However, in most cases hotels are merely functional and finding hotels with a bit of character is rare. Genuine top-end hotels are limited to big northern cities.

### ELECTRICITY

**220V** European-style two-pin plugs

### EMBASSIES & CONSULATES

Diplomatic missions in Algiers include:

**British Embassy** (0770 085000; www.ukinalgeria.fco.gov.uk; 3 Chemin Slimane, Hydra; 9am-12.30pm Mon-Thu)

**Canadian Embassy** (0770 083000; www.voyage.gc.ca; 18 Rue Mustapha Khalef, Ben Aknoun; 8.30am-4pm Sun-Wed, 8am-2pm Thu) Also provides consular assistance to Australians.

**Dutch Embassy** (021 922829; http://algerije.nlambassade.org; 23/27 Chemin Bachir El-Ibrahimi, El-Biar; 8am-4.30pm Sun-Wed, to 2pm Thu)

**French Embassy** (021 981717; www.ambafrance-dz.org; 25 Chemin Gadouche, Hydra; 8am-4.30pm Sun-Thu)

**German Embassy** (021 741941; www.algier.diplo.de; 165 Chemin Sfindja; 8.30am-4.30pm Mon-Wed, to 1.30pm Thu)

**Italian Embassy** (021 922330; www.ambalgeri.esteri.it; 18 Rue Mohammed Ouidir, El-Biar; 9am-noon Sun-Thu)

**Malian Embassy** (021 547214; Cité DNC, Villa No 15, Chemin Kara, Hydra; 9am-3pm Sun-Thu)

**Moroccan Embassy** (021 605707; 8 Rue Abdulkader Azil, El-Mouradia; 9am-3pm Sun-Thu)

**Nigerien Embassy** (021- 691083; Rue 3, Paradou, Hydra; 9am-4pm Sun-Thu)

**Spanish Embassy** (021 92239786; www.exteriores.gob.es/Embajadas/ARGEL; 3 Chemin Ziryab; 8am-3.30pm Sun-Thu)

**Tunisian Embassy** (021 691388; 11 Rue du Bois de Boulogne, Hydra; 9am-3pm Sun-Thu)

**US Embassy** (0770 082000; http://algiers.usembassy.gov; 5 Chemin Cheikh Ibrahimi, El-Biar; 9am-4pm Sun-Thu)

### EMERGENCY & IMPORTANT NUMBERS

| | |
|---|---|
| Ambulance | 213 |
| Fire | 14 |
| Police | 17 |
| Tourist police | 1548 |

### INTERNET ACCESS

Wi-fi is common in the north and is standard in all but the very cheapest hotels. Internet cafe prices are reasonable (no more than DA150 per hour). Whichever way you get online, don't expect browsing speeds to be very fast and in the early evening the system can almost give up completely.

### LGBTIQ TRAVELLERS

Homosexual sex is illegal for both men and women in Algeria, and it incurs a maximum penalty of three years in jail and a stiff fine. You're unlikely to have any problems as a tourist, but discretion is advised.

## MONEY

ATMs are widespread in all larger towns. Credit cards can be used only in big hotels and at car-rental companies. You'll need dinars for day-to-day expenses, but businesses catering to tourists (hotels, airlines, tour companies etc) will often accept Euros.

### Exchange Rates

| | | |
|---|---|---|
| Australia | A$1 | DA79 |
| Canada | C$1 | DA81 |
| Japan | ¥100 | DA94 |
| NZ | NZ$1 | DA76 |
| Euro | €1 | DA116 |
| UK | UK£1 | DA135 |
| US | US$1 | DA110 |

For current exchange rates, see www.xe.com.

### Black Market

The black-market exchange rate is significantly better than what you'll get at banks. Ask locals where you can change money, but if you choose to use it, be aware that you're breaking the law, with all the risks that entails. You can only change dinars back to Euros or dollars unofficially.

## OPENING HOURS

As an Islamic nation, a day of rest on Friday is almost universally observed. Some businesses and most shops are open for half a day on Saturday. In the south, expect long afternoon siestas through the hotter parts of the year.

**Banks** 8.30am–4.30pm Sunday to Thursday

**Government offices** 8am–4pm Sunday to Thursday

**Restaurants** noon–2pm and 7–10pm

**Shops** 8.30am–4.30pm Saturday to Thursday

## PUBLIC HOLIDAYS

Algeria observes Islamic holidays (the dates of which change each year in line with the lunar calendar) as well as the following national holidays:

**Labour Day** 1 May

**Revolutionary Readjustment (1965)** 19 June

**Independence Day** 5 July

**National Day (Revolution Day)** 1 November

## SAFE TRAVEL

Algeria has improved in safety immensely in recent years and for much of the country there are no significant safety issues. However, the lack of foreign visitors means that you will stand out in a crowd and so it still pays to exercise caution.

### PRICE RANGES

The following price ranges refer to a double room with bathroom. Unless otherwise stated, breakfast is included in the price. Prices are based on official bank exchange rates.

**€** less than €50

**€€** €50–€100

**€€€** more than €100

The following price ranges refer to a main course. Prices are based on official bank exchange rates.

**€** less than €5

**€€** €5–€10

**€€€** more than €10

- Check the current local advisories when travelling to the northwest Kabylie region, a short way east of Algiers, where the threat of kidnap is very real. At the time of research most foreign governments were continuing to warn their citizens against all but essential travel to this region.
- Avoid driving anywhere in the countryside after dark. Hold ups are not unheard of.
- It's illegal to visit the Saharan regions without an officially accredited guide. Many times you will also be provided with an armed police escort.
- Militant Islamic groups are active in parts of the Sahara as are smugglers and there are incidents of banditry in some parts. Most foreign governments advice their citizens to avoid all travel to large parts of the south including anywhere within 400km of the borders with Mali, Mauritania and Niger.
- Many *pistes* around Tamanrasset and Djanet remain closed for the security reasons outlined above.
- Carry your passport/ID card with you at all times.

## TELEPHONE

International phone calls can be made from any of the public Taxiphone offices found in most towns.

### Mobile Phones

The mobile phone service in Algeria is good and there's 4G reception in most bigger towns. In the southern desert regions there are vast areas away from the towns without any phone signal.

SIM cards from local carriers – Nedjma, Djezzy and Mobilis – are cheap and readily available and top-up cards are available on seemingly every street corner. You will need a copy of your passport in order to buy a SIM card.

## TIME

Algeria is on Central European Time (GMT/UTC plus one hour) and there's no daylight saving.

## TOURIST INFORMATION

Tourist offices can be found in many larger towns as well as in more tourist-orientated villages and tourist sites. They are normally pretty helpful although can be a little lacking in actual information. The Algiers office of the state-run travel agency **ONT** (Office National du Tourisme; ☎021 438060; www.ont.dz; 2 Rue Kerrar; ⊗8am-4.30pm Sat-Thu) organises excursions.

## VISAS

Everyone except nationals of Morocco, Tunisia and Malaysia needs a visa, and getting one can be a frustrating experience. Visas are not available on arrival.

### Obtaining a Visa

The exact list of papers you will be required to submit alongside the visa application depends upon your nationality and the embassy or consulate you're applying through. For tourist visas, though, you will always require an 'invitation' to visit the country from an Algerian contact or tourist agency. This can take the form of a signed and stamped letter from a local or international tour operator confirming a booking on an organised tour of Algeria. This letter will need to include a list of places to be visited in Algeria, complete with dates. If you're travelling independently then you will need to provide hotel bookings certified by the local authorities in Algeria (normally the town hall where the hotel is located). Actually getting these certified bookings is no easy task as many cheaper hotels don't respond to emails. If you're on an organised tour then hotel bookings aren't always required, or if they are and you're booking your own hotels, then you normally don't need to have the booking certified by local authorities. Most embassies also require proof of flight bookings, travel insurance, proof of employment and/or proof of sufficient funds for the duration of your stay in Algeria.

Currently applications can only be made from your own country of residence. Citizens and residents of France have to apply at their nearest Algerian consulate (there are around a dozen consulates in France) and exact requirements vary on a consulate by consulate basis.

A 30-day visa costs anywhere between US$50 and US$110, depending on the embassy and your nationality. Allow plenty of time for your application to be issued. Waits of up to eight weeks are not unknown if you're planning on heading to the southern desert regions. Almost all Algerian embassies take at least two weeks to process the visas and there are no fast track services. For people applying through regional consulates in France the processing time can sometimes be quicker.

### Passports

A valid passport with at least six months left before expiry is required by all visitors. Nationals of Israel are not allowed into the country, and if you have a stamp in your passport from Israel your application may be rejected.

## WOMEN TRAVELLERS

A solo female traveller in Algeria will usually garner a lot of attention, both positive and negative. Being asked a zillion times a day whether you're married and have children and why you're travelling alone is not unusual. It's wise to have some stock answers and perhaps an imaginary husband. While this attention can be tiring it also has some advantages and doors will open to you that would likely never open to a solo male traveller. A foreign women travelling alone will likely find herself with constant invitations by local women to join them in whatever it is they're doing.

How you dress will have a big impact on how people perceive and approach you. Dress conservatively with long skirts and long sleeves. A head scarf isn't required although in the south it could be worth wearing as much for the sun protection as for the modesty value.

In cases where you are subjected to unwanted come-ons and suggestive lines, trying to ignore them is one possibility. If that doesn't work, it's a good idea to turn to other people (men or women) for help. They will almost certainly come down like a tonne of bricks on the perpetrator.

One of the more awkward situations a woman travelling alone might have is if she hires a guide. Most will be completely honest and trustworthy, others might have more romantic ideas. Use your own judgement when hiring a guide, even if it's only for an hour or so.

# ℹ Getting There & Away

## AIR

**Houari Boumediene Airport** (☎021 509191; www.elmatar.com/aeroport-alger-houari-boumediene; Chemin de Wilaya, Beaulieu), 17km southeast of Algiers, is the country's biggest and busiest international airport and is served by numerous international airlines. In 2018 a new terminal is expected to open.

## LAND

Algeria shares land borders with six other countries, but don't get excited by a potential overland adventure – all but the Tunisian border are closed and/or dangerous for overland travel.

### Tunisia

There are several border-crossing points between Tunisia and Algeria, and these are currently the only way for overlanders to enter or depart Algeria. The more southerly, desert border crossings are generally considered unsafe. North coast crossings are fine and include those from El Kala to Tabarka or inland to Babouch near Ain Draham. Allow a couple of hours to get through formalities and customs on these border crossings. Share taxis run between Annaba and El Kala (the nearest town to the Algerian–Tunisia border on the Algeria side) and the actual border.

### Tours

Due to visa complications and strict travel restrictions in the desert regions, most people end up signing up to an organised tour. If the thought of an organised tour makes you break out in a cold sweat, don't worry – tours can consist of just you and your guide/driver and most companies allow you to customise your tour and select your own accommodation and pace of travel.

To travel in the Sahara it's obligatory to use the services of a tour company.

The following are all recommended.

**Akaoka** (www.akaoka.com) French-run and -based agency specialising in 4WD Saharan tours.

**Algerie Tours** (www.algerie-tours.com) This French-based tour company offers a wide array of set tours taking in the northern Roman sites, southern desert scapes or a combination of the two.

**Bachir Hafach** (http://touaregbachir.blogspot.fr) This English-speaking Toureg guide is based in Djanet but can also organise circuits from Tamanrasset.

**Expert Algeria** (☎0554 780995; www.expertalgeria.com) A very professional and reliable company that operates throughout the country and specialises in the English-speaking market. It offers tailored tours and uses only the very best specialist guides to the historical sites in the north.

**Tim Missaw Tours** (☎029 324410; http://timmissawtours.e-monsite.com; Tamanrasset) This long-established company organises desert tours and has its own accommodation.

**Waléne Voyages** (☎029 312329; http://walenevoyages.com; Tamanrasset) Organises 4WD and camel trekking to Asskrem and the Hoggar.

### SEA

It's possible to arrive in Algeria by ferry from Europe, though it's far from the cheapest option.

**Algérie Ferries** (☎021 635388; http://algerieferries.dz) Connects Algiers, Annaba, Bejaia, Oran and Skikda to Marseille (Marseille–Algiers two to three times weekly), and Oran and Alicante (once or twice a week). It also operates occasional boats between Valencia (Spain) and Mostaghanem (near Oran) and Genoa (Italy) and Skikda. Tickets between Algiers and Marseille with Algérie Ferries cost between DA7400 for a seat, upwards to DA20,000 for cabins.

**Corsica Linea** (☎France + 33 (0) 825 888088; www.corsicalinea.com) This French company operates ferry services between Marseille and Algiers (from DA25,000 for a seat) once a week, considerably more expensive than Algérie Ferries.

The voyage to Marseille takes about 20 hours, and to Alicante 10 hours. Expect long waits on disembarkation if travelling with a car.

## Getting Around

As Africa's largest country distances can be vast in Algeria and journey times very long. This is especially true in the southern desert regions where hundreds of kilometres of burning sand and rock can separate even quite minor settlements. In the northern part of the country, where most people live, the transport network is much more comprehensive and road, rail and air links are generally good.

### AIR

**Air Algérie** (☎021 986363; https://airalgerie.dz) Offers extensive and reasonably priced domestic services, including flights to Tamanrasset and Ghardaïa. Its safety record is generally pretty good and flights are fairly punctual.

**Tassili Airlines** (☎021 737800; www.tassiliairlines.aero) Has an extensive domestic network linking most big northern cities with each other and Algiers with southern desert cities. For long-distance north–south travel, going by plane is by far the most comfortable, and safest, way to travel.

### BUS

Long-distance buses are run by various regional companies and are usually reasonably comfortable. Routes go as far south as Tamanrasset. Try to buy your ticket at least a day ahead: less frequently serviced Saharan routes sell out. Bus service in the north is extensive and reaches most towns. Getting to archaeological sites by bus, however, can sometimes be difficult.

### TRAIN

**SNTF** (Société Nationale des Transports Ferroviaires; www.sntf.dz) trains run from Algiers along the eastern line to Bejaia, Constantine and Annaba (seven to 10 hours) and along the western line to Oran (four to six hours) and from there to Tlemcen (2½ hours). Additional lines run south from Oran to Béchar and from Constantine to Touggourt.

The trains are fairly modern and are generally punctual and at least as fast as road travel.

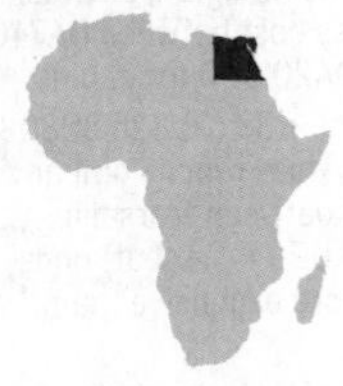

# Egypt

POP 94.7 MILLION / ☎20

### Includes ➡



## Best Places to Eat

- ➡ Kadoura (p79)
- ➡ Abu Tarek (p72)
- ➡ Sofra (p90)
- ➡ Panorama Restaurant & Bar (p94)
- ➡ Citadel View (p73)

## Best Places to Sleep

- ➡ Pension Roma (p72)
- ➡ Hotel Longchamps (p72)
- ➡ Beit Sabée (p90)
- ➡ Steigenberger Cecil Hotel (p79)
- ➡ Eldorado (p82)

## Why Go?

Herodotus let the cat out of the bag in the 5th century BC, leaving the door open for over a millennium of conquerors and adventurers to gawp, graffiti and pilfer Egypt's mammoth racks of Pharaonic rubble. Today it may be 'gawping only' allowed, but these ancient monuments still inspire the same reverence in travellers as they have for centuries. Walk away from the click of a million camera shutters for a minute though and you'll discover Egypt isn't just mummies and colossal columns. Sink into a meditative stupor of (hookah) smoking in a cafe. Bed down on a desert dune. Watch the sun rise over the palm-tree-fringed Nile banks. Stand streetside when the call to prayer wafts over the nightmare symphony of car horns.

Modern Egypt can frustrate and confound but it enchants in equal measure. The temples, tombs and pyramids will still be there when you get back to them; basking in their sheer awesomeness as they have done since time immemorial.

## When to Go

### Cairo

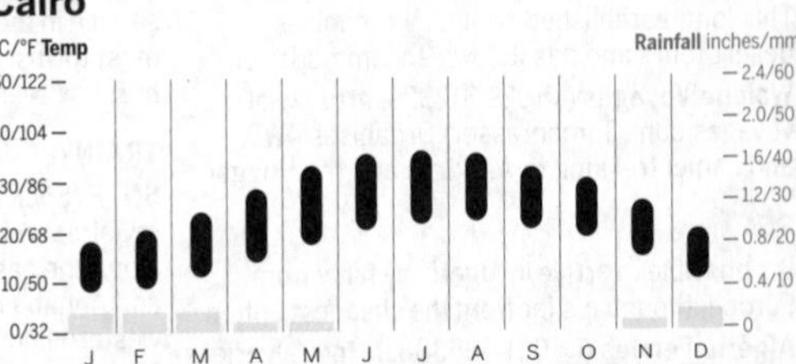


**Mar–Apr** Dust off your explorer hat and head into the Western Desert while temperatures stay mild.

**Jul–Sep** Summer's furnace sizzles but underwater conditions are perfect for Red Sea diving.

**Oct–Nov** In Upper Egypt, the gorgeous painterly light makes a Nile journey a photographer's dream.

# CAIRO

POP 22 MILLION / ☎ 02

The urban buzz felt in this extraordinary city is a product of 22-or-so million inhabitants simultaneously crushing the city's infrastructure under their collective weight and lifting its spirit up with their exceptional charm and humour. One taxi ride can pass resplendent mosques, grand avenues, and 19th-century palaces, with a far away view of the pyramids of Giza. A caked-on layer of beige sand unifies the mix of eras and styles.

But, Cairo's crowds make Manhattan look like a ghost town, papyrus sellers and would-be guides hound you at every turn, and your snot will run black from the smog. It's a small price to pay to tap into the energy of the place Egyptians call Umm ad-Dunya – the Mother of the World.

Blow your nose, crack a joke and look through the dirt to see the city's true colours. If you love Cairo, it will definitely love you back.

## Sights

**★Pyramids of Giza** ARCHAEOLOGICAL SITE

(adult/student E£80/40; ⏲8am-4pm) The last remaining wonder of the ancient world; for nearly 4000 years, the extraordinary shape, impeccable geometry and sheer bulk of the Giza Pyramids have invited the obvious questions: 'How were we built, and why?' Centuries of research have given us parts of the answer. Built as massive tombs on the orders of the pharaohs, they were constructed by teams of workers tens-of-thousands strong.

Today they stand as an awe-inspiring tribute to the might, organisation and achievements of ancient Egypt.

**Sphinx** ARCHAEOLOGICAL SITE

Known in Arabic as Abu al-Hol (Father of Terror), this sculpture of a man with the haunches of a lion was dubbed the Sphinx by the ancient Greeks because it resembled their mythical winged monster who set riddles and killed anyone unable to answer them. A geological survey has shown that it was most likely carved from the bedrock at the bottom of the causeway, during this Khafre's reign, so it probably portrays his features.

**★Egyptian Museum** MUSEUM

(Map p74; ☎02-2579 6948; www.egyptianmuseumcairo.org; Midan Tahrir, Downtown; adult/student E£75/35, entry after 5.30pm E£120/60, mummy room E£100/75, after 5.30pm E£150/75, photography ticket E£50; ⏲9am-9pm Sun-Thu, to 4pm Sat-Fri; Ⓜ Sadat) One of the world's most important collections of ancient artefacts, the Egyptian Museum takes pride of place in Downtown Cairo, on the north side of Midan Tahrir. Inside the great domed, oddly pinkish building, the glittering treasures of Tutankhamun and other great pharaohs lie alongside the grave goods, mummies, jewellery, eating bowls and toys of Egyptians whose names are lost to history.

To walk around the museum is to embark on an adventure through time.

**★Khan al-Khalili** MARKET

(Map p70; off Sharia al-Azhar & al-Gamaliyya) The skinny lanes of Khan al-Khalili are basically a medieval-style mall. This agglomeration of shops – many arranged around small courtyards – stock everything from soap powder to semiprecious stones, not to mention toy camels and alabaster pyramids. It's open from early morning to sundown (except Friday morning and Sunday), although many shops are open as long as there are customers, even on Sunday.

**★Al-Azhar Mosque** MOSQUE

(Gami' al-Azhar; Map p70; Sharia al-Azhar; ⏲24hr) FREE Founded in AD 970 as the centrepiece of the newly created Fatimid city, Al-Azhar is one of Cairo's earlier mosques, and its sheikh is considered the highest theological authority for Egyptian Muslims. The building is a harmonious blend of architectural styles, the result of numerous enlargements over 1000 years. The tomb chamber, located through a doorway on the left just inside the entrance, has a beautiful mihrab (a niche indicating the direction of Mecca) and should not be missed.

**★Mosque-Madrassa of Sultan Hassan** MOSQUE

(Map p70; Midan Salah ad-Din; combo ticket with Mosque of ar-Rifa'i E£40; ⏲8am-4.30pm) Massive yet elegant, this great structure is regarded as the finest piece of early-Mamluk architecture in Cairo. It was built between 1356 and 1363 by Sultan Hassan, a grandson of Sultan Qalaun; he took the throne at the age of 13, was deposed and reinstated no less than three times, then assassinated shortly before the mosque was completed. Beyond the striking, recessed entrance, a dark passage leads into a peaceful courtyard surrounded by soaring walls.

**★Coptic Museum** MUSEUM

(Map p70; ☎02-2363 9742; www.coptic-cairo.com/museum; 3 Sharia Mar Girgis; adult/student E£60/30, audio guide E£10; ⏲9am-4pm; Ⓜ Mar Girgis) This museum, founded in 1908, houses Coptic art from the earliest days of

# Egypt Highlights

**1 Luxor** (p87) Overloading on tombs and temples in ancient Thebes.

**2 Pyramids of Giza** (p67) Visiting the ancient wonder; still as iconic today.

**3 Cairo** (p67) Immersing yourself in the chaotic, confounding heartbeat of the nation.

**4 Temples of Abu Simbel** (p95) Exploring the temple to out-temple them all.

**5 Aswan** (p92) Embracing sunset felucca trips and Nubian culture.

**6 Ras Mohammed National Park** (p84) Venturing offshore to a fantasia of coral reefs and ghostly shipwrecks.

**7 Alexandria** (p78) Soaking up crumbling 19th-century grandeur along the Corniche.

**8 Dahab** (p81) Relaxing at laidback beach breaks with superb diving.

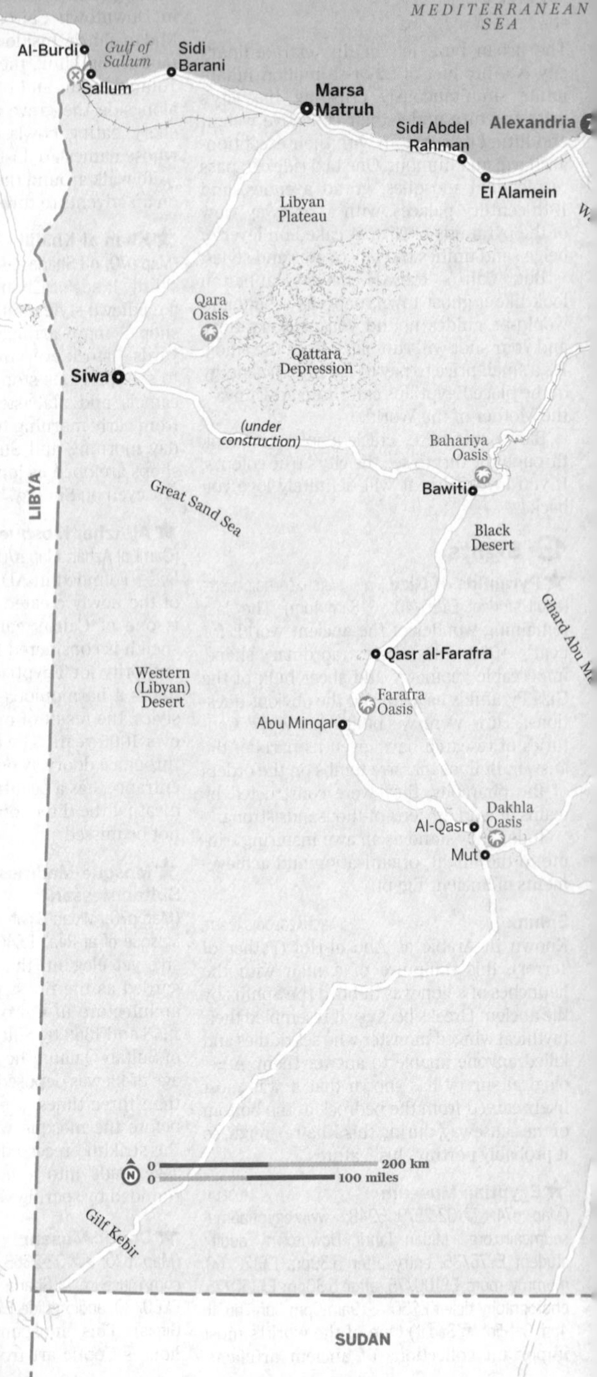

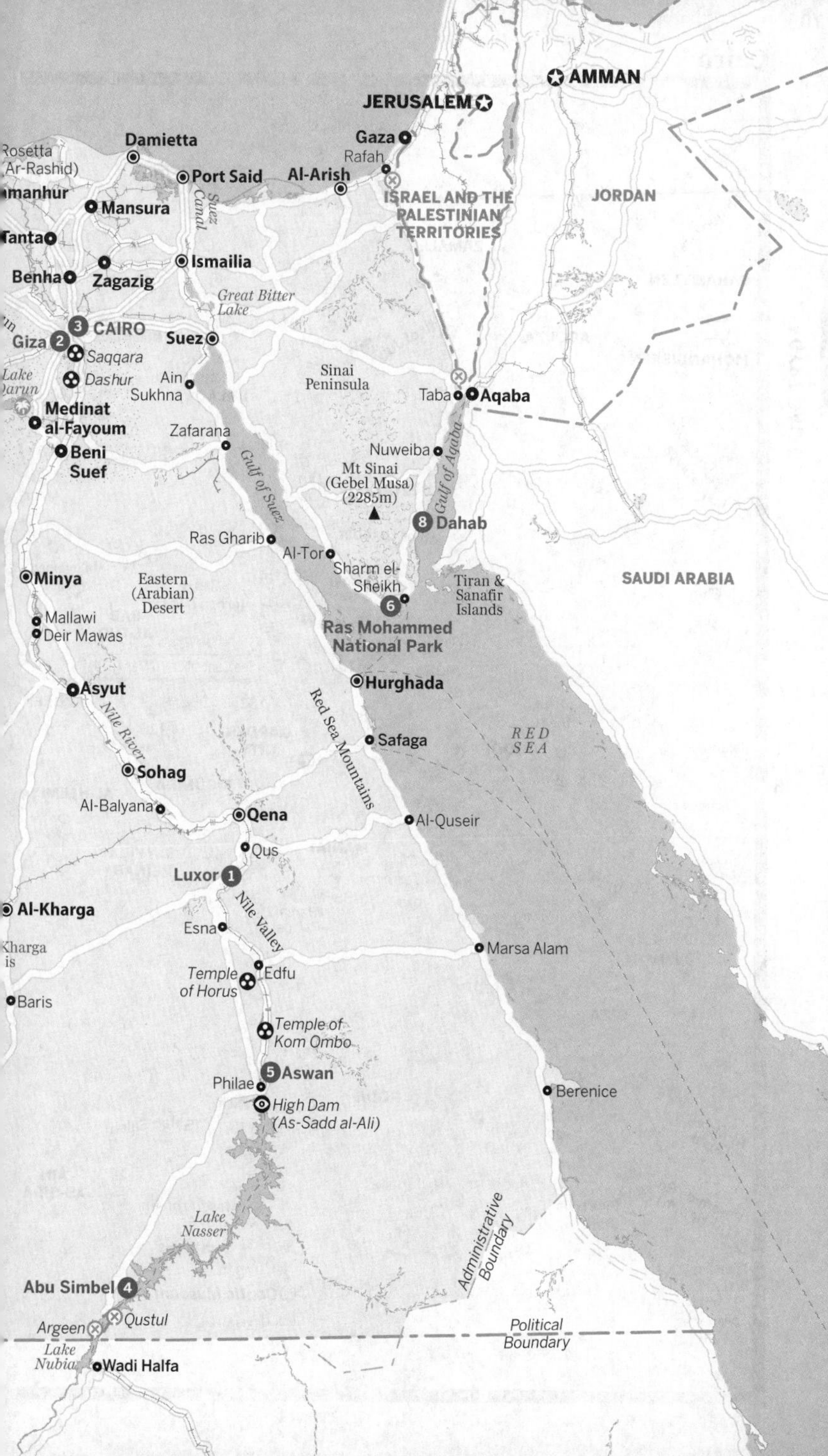

AMMAN
JERUSALEM
Gaza
Rafah
Damietta
Rosetta (Ar-Rashid)
Port Said
Al-Arish
ISRAEL AND THE PALESTINIAN TERRITORIES
JORDAN
Mansura
Suez Canal
Tanta
Ismailia
Benha
Zagazig
Great Bitter Lake
3 CAIRO
Giza 2
Suez
Saqqara
Dashur
Sinai Peninsula
Ain Sukhna
Taba
Aqaba
Medinat al-Fayoum
Zafarana
Beni Suef
Nuweiba
Gulf of Aqaba
Gulf of Suez
Mt Sinai (Gebel Musa) (2285m)
8 Dahab
Ras Gharib
Al-Tor
Sharm el-Sheikh
Tiran & Sanafir Islands
SAUDI ARABIA
Minya
Eastern (Arabian) Desert
6
Mallawi
Deir Mawas
Ras Mohammed National Park
Hurghada
Asyut
Red Sea Mountains
Nile River
Safaga
RED SEA
Sohag
Al-Balyana
Qena
Al-Quseir
Qus
Luxor 1
Al-Kharga
Nile Valley
Esna
Marsa Alam
Temple of Horus
Edfu
Baris
Temple of Kom Ombo
5 Aswan
Philae
Berenice
High Dam (As-Sadd al-Ali)
Lake Nasser
Administrative Boundary
Abu Simbel 4
Qustul
Argeen
Political Boundary
Lake Nubia
Wadi Halfa

# Cairo

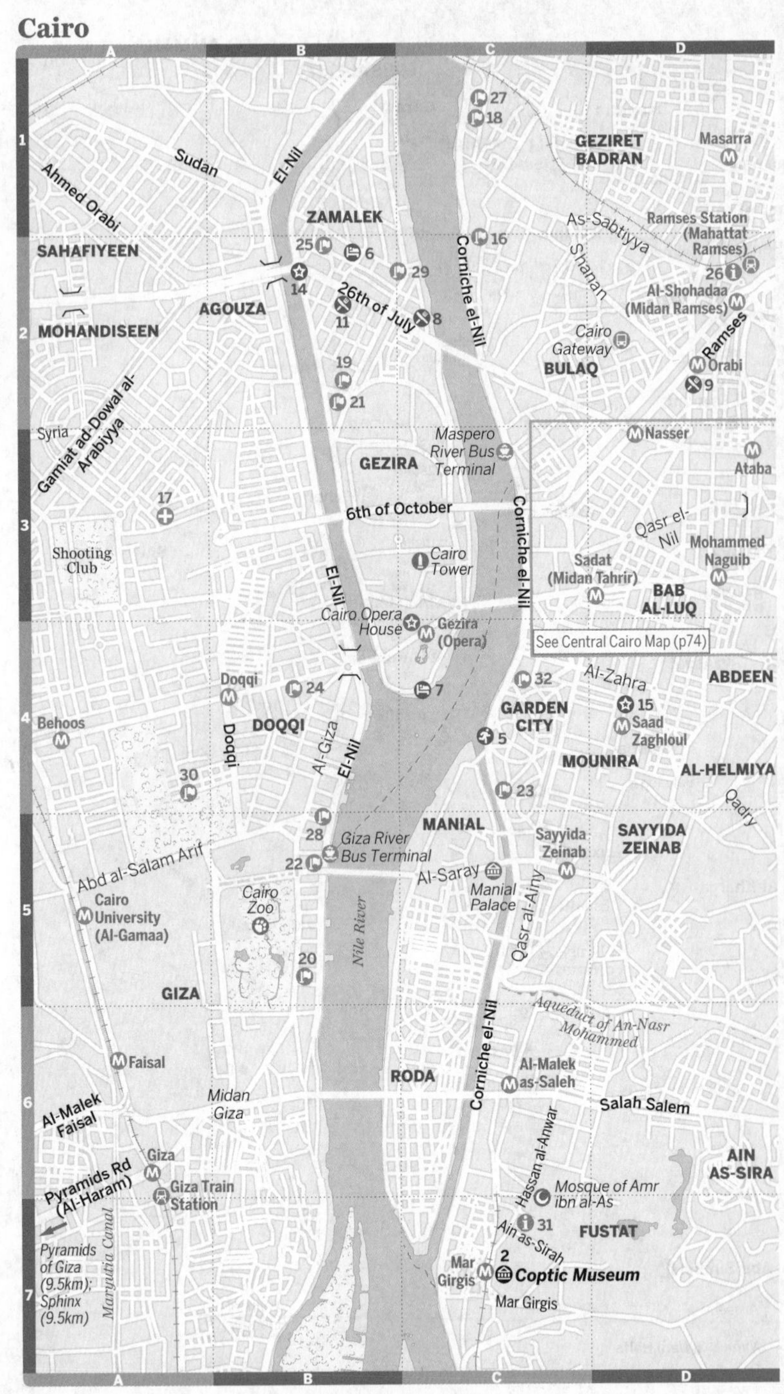


EGYPT CAIRO

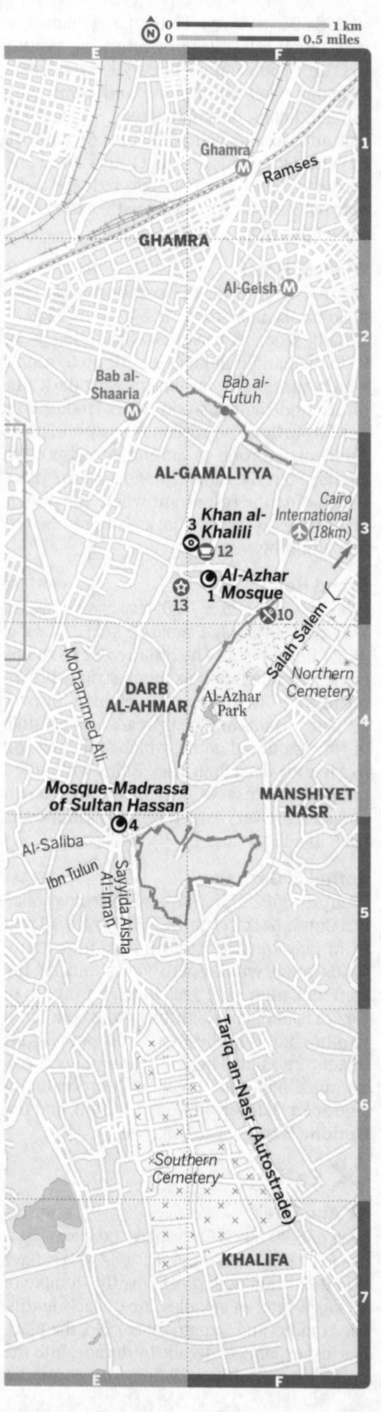


## Cairo

**Top Sights**

1 Al-Azhar Mosque ........ F3
2 Coptic Museum ........ C7
3 Khan al-Khalili ........ F3
4 Mosque-Madrassa of Sultan Hassan ........ E5

**Activities, Courses & Tours**

5 Dok Dok Landing Stage ........ C4

**Sleeping**

6 Hotel Longchamps ........ B2
7 Sofitel El Gezirah ........ C4

**Eating**

8 Abou El Sid ........ C2
9 At-Tabei Ad-Dumyati ........ D2
10 Citadel View ........ F3
11 Zööba ........ B2

**Drinking & Nightlife**

Buddha Bar ........ (see 7)
12 Fishawi's ........ F3

**Entertainment**

13 Al-Tannoura Egyptian Heritage Dance Troupe ........ E3
14 El Sawy Culture Wheel ........ B2
15 Makan ........ D4

**Information**

16 Australian Embassy ........ C2
17 Badran Hospital ........ A3
18 Canadian Embassy ........ C1
19 Dutch Embassy ........ B2
20 French Embassy ........ B5
21 German Embassy ........ B2
Irish Embassy ........ (see 19)
22 Israeli Embassy ........ B5
23 Italian Embassy ........ C4
24 Jordanian Embassy ........ B4
25 Lebanese Embassy ........ B2
26 Ministry of Tourism ........ D2
27 New Zealand Embassy ........ C1
28 Saudi Arabian Embassy ........ B5
29 Spanish Embassy ........ C2
30 Sudanese Embassy ........ A4
31 Tourist Information ........ C7
Turkish Embassy ........ (see 15)
32 UK Embassy ........ C4

Christianity in Egypt right through to early Islam. It is a beautiful place, as much for the elaborate woodcarving in all the galleries as for the treasures they contain. These include sculpture that shows obvious continuity from the Ptolemaic period, rich textiles and whole walls of monastery frescoes. Allow at least a couple of hours to explore the 1200 or so pieces on display.

## Activities

**Dok Dok Landing Stage** BOATING

(Map p70; Corniche el-Nil) One of the most pleasant things to do on a warm day is to go out on a felucca, Egypt's ancient broad-sail boat, with a supply of beer and a small picnic, just as sunset approaches. Because it's near a wider spot in the river, this is the best place for hiring a felucca (it's opposite the Four Seasons hotel).

## Sleeping

**★Pension Roma** PENSION $

(Map p74; ☎02-2391 1088; www.pensionroma.com.eg; 4th fl, 169 Sharia Mohammed Farid, Downtown; d E£220-285, tr E£295-392, without bathroom s E£105-165, d E£170-249, tr E£240-346; ) Run by a French-Egyptian woman with impeccable standards, the Roma brings dignity, even elegance, to the budget-travel scene. Staff are genuinely friendly and welcoming and the towering ceilings, antique furniture and filmy white curtains create a feeling of timeless calm. Most rooms share toilets, though many have showers. Rooms in the new extension have en suite bathrooms and air-con, and are quieter.

**Travelers House Hotel** HOSTEL $

(Map p74; ☎02-2396 4362; travelershousehotel@yahoo.com; 4th fl, 43 Sharia Sherif, Downtown; s/d/tr E£200/280/320, s/d without bathroom E£170/230; ) With only five rooms (three with private bathroom), this place is a cosy budget traveller choice. All rooms are large, high-ceilinged, very simple and clean. There's a cute lounge to hang out in, scattered with kitsch Egyptian souvenirs, and with a dinky balcony where you can overlook the madness of Sharia 26th of July from above. Breakfast is an extra E£10.

**Bella Luna Hotel** HOSTEL $

(Map p74; ☎02-2393 8139; www.hotellunacairo.com; 3rd fl, 27 Sharia Talaat Harb, Downtown; s/d/tr/q E£220/320/400/480; ) Modern, backpacker-friendly Bella Luna offers great value for money with bright, large rooms decked out in soothing pastel-coloured combos, all with small but clean bathrooms. The fastidious owner has provided many small comforts such as bedside lamps and bathmats. For those watching their pennies, there are also cheaper, slightly aged rooms upstairs (5th floor) in their older 'Luna Hostel'.

**★Hotel Longchamps** BOUTIQUE HOTEL $$

(Map p70; ☎02-2735 2311; www.hotellongchamps.com; 5th fl, 21 Sharia Ismail Mohammed, Zamalek; r US$84-96; ) Hotel Longchamps is very much a favourite of returning visitors to Cairo. The comfortable, stylish rooms are spacious, well maintained and come with full mod-cons of a flat-screen TV, a minibar, and, lo and behold, kettles (a rarity in Egypt). Bathrooms are generously sized and modern. The greenery-covered, peaceful rear balcony, where guests gather to chat at sunset, is a major bonus.

**Windsor Hotel** HISTORIC HOTEL $$

(Map p74; ☎02-2591 5810; www.windsorcairo.com; 19 Sharia Alfy, Downtown; s US$46-62, d US$58-74, s/d with shower & hand basin US$37/46; ) Ride the hand-cranked elevator up to rooms which ooze old-timer charm with dark furniture and scuffed wood floors (room 25 is our favourite). The air-con is noisy and management is prone to adding surprise extra charges, but the faded romance of the place – including the restaurant where the dinner bell chimes every evening at 7.30pm – is nostalgia buff heaven.

**Grand Hotel** HOTEL $$

(Map p74; ☎02-2575 7700; grandhotel@link.net; 17 Sharia 26th of July, Downtown; s/d E£500/666; ) Retro-tastic. The hundred or so rooms come crammed with as much stripey brown furniture – to match the fetching brown-striped curtains and bedspreads – as possible in this grand old dame, which still clings on to a few art-deco flourishes. Shiny white-tiled bathrooms are a wonderful modern touch and staff are very sweet. Entry is around the back in a tiny plaza.

**Sofitel El Gezirah** HOTEL $$$

(Map p70; ☎02-2737 3737; www.sofitel.com; Sharia al-Orman, Gezira; r from US$130; ) Tired from long travels? Rest up here in a sumptuous room with superb views and let the staff look after you. This hotel, on the tip of Gezira island, is delightfully quiet compared to other hotels in the area, but it can be hard to get a cab out. There are several good restaurants, including excellent Moroccan cuisine at **La Palmeraie** (3pm to 3am), and the **Buddha Bar** (5pm-2am).

## Eating

**★Abu Tarek** EGYPTIAN $

(Map p74; 40 Sharia Champollion, Downtown; kushari E£10-20; 8am-midnight; ) 'We have no other branches!' proclaims this temple of *kushari* (mix of noodles, rice, black lentils, fried onions and tomato sauce). No, the place has just expanded, decade by decade, into the upper storeys of its building, and continues to hold on to Cairo's unofficial 'Best Kushari' title. Eat in, rather than takeaway, to check out the elaborate decor upstairs.

**★Zööba** EGYPTIAN $

(Map p70; ☎16082; www.facebook.com/Zooba Eats; Sharia 26th of July, Zamalek; dishes E£3.50-38.50; ⏰8am-1am) This small restaurant serves up Egyptian street food with gourmet twists; fresh juices, whole-wheat *kushari* and fabulous salads. The delicious dishes can be taken away – ideal for a picnic. Keep space for the mouth-watering desserts like rice pudding with sweet potatoes and cinnamon. All is served at a zinc-clad table in the funkiest and most eclectic of decors.

**At-Tabei Ad-Dumyati** EGYPTIAN $

(Map p70; ☎02-2579 7533; 31 Sharia Orabi, Downtown; ta'amiyya, shwarma & sandwiches E£2-21, dishes E£2-37; ⏰7am-1am; ❄✍) The takeaway section out front does a roaring trade in shwarma and ta'amiyya (an Egyptian variant of felafel), while out the back is a peaceful sit-down canteen that attracts families and offers some of the cheapest meals in Cairo, with a popular salad bar and friendly waiters. Pick your salads, eat some fuul (fava-bean paste) or tuck into Alexandrian-style liver.

**Abou El Sid** EGYPTIAN $$

(Map p70; ☎02-2735 9640; www.abouelsid.com; 157 Sharia 26th of July, Zamalek; mezze E£15-47, mains E£37-90; ⏰noon-2am) Cairo's first hipster Egyptian restaurant (and now a national franchise), Abou El Sid is as popular with tourists as it is with upper-class natives. You can get better *molokhiyya* (garlicky leaf soup) elsewhere, but here you wash it down with a wine or beer and lounge on kitschy gilt 'Louis Farouk' furniture.

**Citadel View** MIDDLE EASTERN $$

(Map p70; ☎02-2510 9151; Al-Azhar Park; mains E£42-130; ⏰noon-midnight; ✍) Eating at this gorgeous restaurant in Al-Azhar Park – on a vast multilevel terrace, with the whole city sprawled below – feels great. Fortunately the prices are not so stratospheric and the food is good, with dishes like spicy sausage with pomegranate syrup and grilled fish with tahini. On Friday, only a buffet (E£150) is on offer. No alcohol.

**Café Riche** EGYPTIAN $$

(Map p74; ☎02-2392 9793; 17 Sharia Talaat Harb, Downtown; mezze E£8-25, mains E£25-70; ⏰10am-midnight; ✍) This narrow restaurant, allegedly the oldest in Cairo, was the favoured drinking spot of the intelligentsia. A certain old guard still sits under the ceiling fans, along with tourists who like the historical ambience. It's a reliable and nostalgic spot to enjoy a cold beer (E£35) and a meal of slightly Frenchified Egyptian dishes.

## Drinking & Nightlife

**Fishawi's** COFFEE

(Map p70; Khan al-Khalili; ⏰24hr, during Ramadan 5pm-3am) Probably the oldest ahwa (coffeehouse) in the city, and certainly the most celebrated, Fishawi's has been a great place to watch the world go by since 1773. Despite being swamped by foreign tourists and equally wide-eyed out-of-town Egyptians, it is a regular ahwa, serving up *shai* (tea) and sheesha to stallholders and shoppers alike. Prices vary so confirm with your waiter.

**Eish + Malh** CAFE

(Map p74; ☎010 9874 4014; 20 Sharia Adly, Downtown; ⏰8am-midnight; 📶) This spacious, high-ceilinged cafe, with its original arched windows framed by floor-to-ceiling city scenes, is a favoured hang-out for hip, young Cairenes. It also does the best flat white in Downtown, as well as other espresso-based coffees, and a selection of loose-leaf teas. There's a decent menu of pasta and pizza, and good ice cream, for when you're peckish.

## ☆ Entertainment

**★Makan** TRADITIONAL MUSIC

(Map p70; ☎02-2792 0878; http://egyptmusic.org; 1 Sharia Saad Zaghloul, Mounira; Ⓜ Saad Zaghloul) The Egyptian Centre for Culture & Art runs this intimate space dedicated to folk music. Don't miss the traditional women's *zar*, a sort of musical trance and healing ritual (Wednesday, 8pm; E£30, advance booking advised). Tuesday has various performances of folk music, often an Egyptian-Sudanese jam session. To find the space, walk north on Sharia Mansour from Saad Zaghloul metro.

**El Sawy Culture Wheel** LIVE MUSIC

(El Sakia; Map p70; ☎02-2736 8881; www.culturewheel.com; Sharia 26th of July, Zamalek; ⏰8am-midnight) The most popular young Egyptian rock and jazz bands play at this lively and very active complex of a dozen performance spaces and galleries tucked under a bridge overpass. The main entrance is on the south side of 26th of July; there's a nice outdoor cafe by the Nile too.

**Al-Tannoura Egyptian Heritage Dance Troupe** DANCE

(Map p70; ☎02-2512 1735; Wikala of Al-Ghouri, Sharia Mohammed Abduh, Islamic Cairo, off Sharia al-Azhar; ⏰performances at 8pm Mon, Wed & Sat)

# Central Cairo

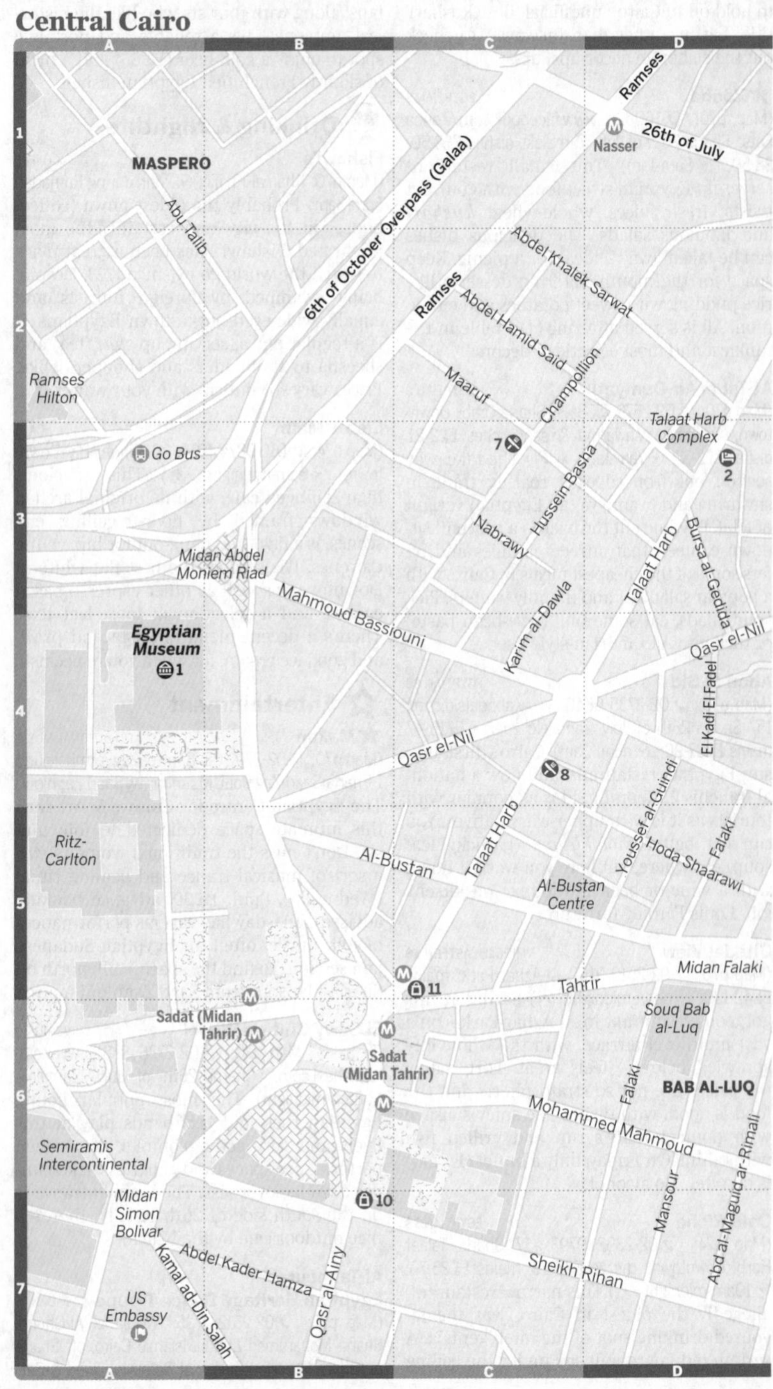

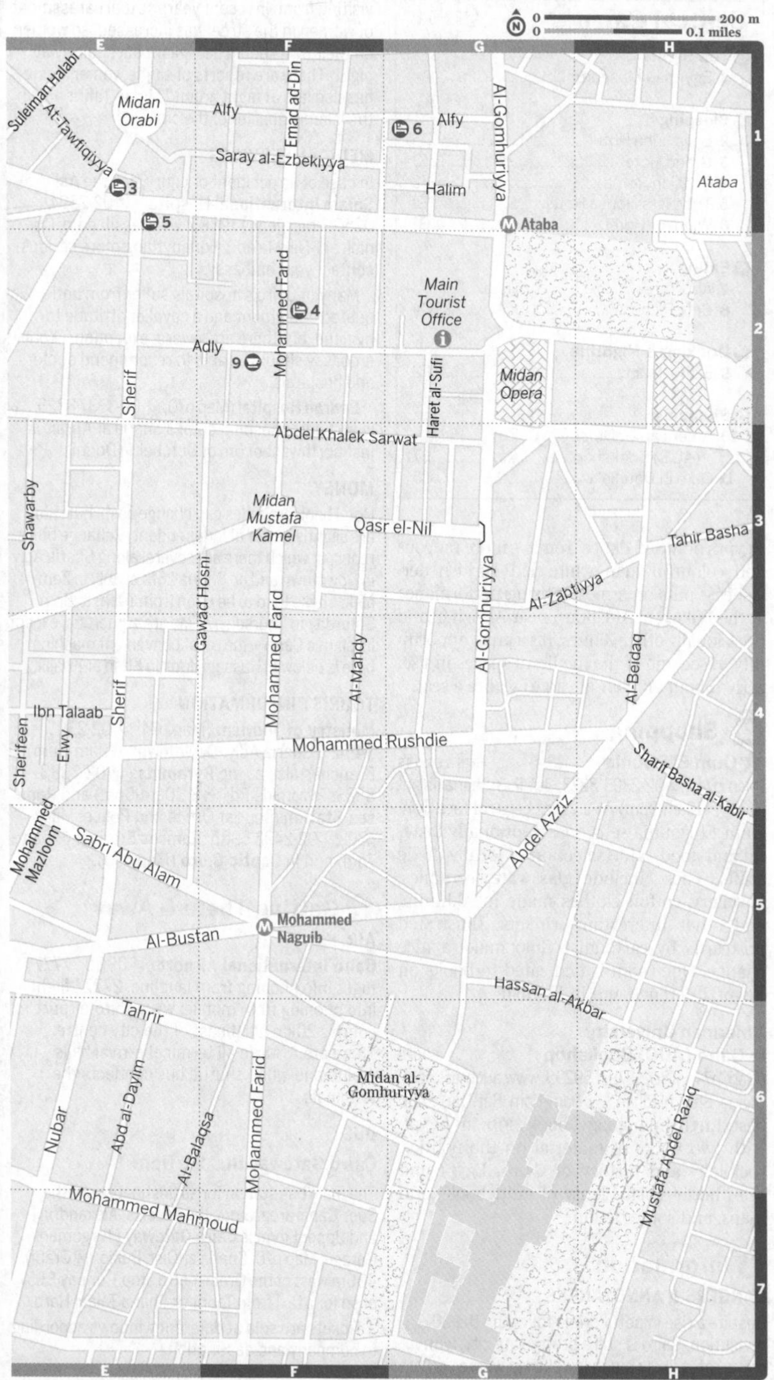
0 200 m
0 0.1 miles
E
F
G
H
1
2
3
4
5
6
7
Suleiman Halabi
Midan Orabi
At-Tawfiqiyya
Alfy
Emad ad-Din
Saray al-Ezbekiyya
6
Alfy
Al-Gomhuriyya
Halim
Ataba
3
5
Ataba
Main Tourist Office
4
Mohammed Farid
Adly
9
Sherif
Haret al-Sufi
Midan Opera
Abdel Khalek Sarwat
Shawarby
Midan Mustafa Kamel
Qasr el-Nil
Tahir Basha
Gawad Hosni
Mohammed Farid
Al-Zabtiyya
Al-Gomhuriyya
Al-Mahdy
Al-Beidaq
Ibn Talaab
Sherif
Sherifeen
Elwy
Mohammed Rushdie
Sharif Basha al-Kabir
Abdel Azziz
Mohammed Mazloom
Sabri Abu Alam
Mohammed Naguib
Al-Bustan
Hassan al-Akbar
Tahrir
Midan al-Gomhuriyya
Nubar
Abd al-Dayim
Al-Balaqsa
Mohammed Farid
Mustafa Abdel Raziq
Mohammed Mahmoud

## Central Cairo

**Top Sights**
1 Egyptian Museum ... A4

**Sleeping**
2 Bella Luna Hotel ... D3
3 Grand Hotel ... E1
4 Pension Roma ... F2
5 Travelers House Hotel ... E1
6 Windsor Hotel ... G1

**Eating**
7 Abu Tarek ... C3
8 Café Riche ... C4

**Drinking & Nightlife**
9 Eish + Malh ... F2

**Shopping**
10 American University in Cairo (AUC) Bookshop ... B7
11 Oum El Dounia ... C5

Egypt's only Sufi dance troupe – more raucous and colourful than white-clad Turkish dervishes – puts on a mesmerising performance at the Wikala of Al-Ghouri near Al-Azhar, and occasionally other venues. It's a great opportunity to see one of the medieval spaces in use; arrive about an hour ahead to secure a seat.

## Shopping

**★Oum El Dounia** ARTS & CRAFTS
(Map p74; ☎02-2393 8273; 1st fl, 3 Sharia Talaat Harb; ⏰10am-9pm) At a great central location, Oum El Dounia sells an exceptionally tasteful and good-value selection of locally made crafts. These include glassware, ceramics, jewellery, cotton clothes made in Akhmim, and other interesting trinkets. Illustrated postcards by cartoonist Golo make a nice change. One room is dedicated to books on Egypt, in French and in English.

**American University in Cairo (AUC) Bookshop** BOOKS
(Map p74; ☎02-2797 5929; www.aucpress.com; Sharia Sheikh Rihan; ⏰9am-6pm Sat-Thu) The best English-language bookshop in Egypt, with two floors of material on the politics, sociology and history of Cairo, Egypt and the Middle East. Plenty of guidebooks and maps, and some fiction.

## Information

### DANGERS & ANNOYANCES

Despite a rise in petty crime following the 2011 revolution, Cairo is still a pretty safe city, with crime rates likely much lower than where you're visiting from. In recent years sexual harassment of women in the street has increased, so women on their own should be vigilant particularly at night. There are reports of single women being hassled late at night around Midan Tahrir and in the Islamic quarter of the city.

### MEDICAL SERVICES

In case of an accident or injury, call the **As-Salam International Hospital** (☎02-2524 0250, emergency 19885; www.assih.com; Corniche el-Nil, Ma'adi). For anything more serious, contact your embassy.

Many of Cairo's hospitals suffer from antiquated equipment and a cavalier attitude to hygiene, but there are several exceptions. Your embassy should be able to recommend doctors and hospitals.

**Badran Hospital** (Map p70; ☎02-3337 8823; www.badranhospital.com; 3 Sharia al-Ahrar) is just northwest of 6th of October in Doqqi.

### MONEY

Hotel bank branches can change cash, but rates are slightly better at independent exchange bureaus, of which there are several along Sharia Adly in Downtown and on Sharia 26th of July in Zamalek. These tend to be open from 10am to 8pm Saturday to Thursday. ATMs are numerous, except in Islamic Cairo – the most convenient machine here is below El Hussein hotel in Khan al-Khalili.

### TOURIST INFORMATION

**Ministry of Tourism** (Map p74; ☎02-2391 3454; 5 Sharia Adly, Downtown; ⏰9am-6pm) Branches also at the **Pyramids** (☎02-3383 8823; Pyramids Rd; ⏰8.30am-5pm) and **Ramses Station** (Tourist Office and Police; Map p70; ☎02-2492 5985; Ramses Station; ⏰9am-7pm) and in **Coptic Cairo** (Map p70).

## Getting There & Away

### AIR

**Cairo International Airport** (☎0900 77777 flight info phoning from landline, 27777 flight info phoning from mobile; www.cairo-airport.com) is 20km northeast of the city centre. There are ATMs in all terminal arrival halls. A blue-and-white shuttle bus connects the terminals.

### BUS

#### Cairo Gateway Bus Station

The main bus station for all destinations in the Suez Canal area, Sinai, the deserts, Alexandria and Upper Egypt is **Cairo Gateway** (Turgoman Garage; Map p70; Sharia al-Gisr, Bulaq; Ⓜ Orabi), 400m west of the Orabi metro stop – or pay E£5 or so for a taxi from Tahrir or Sharia Talaat Harb.

Tickets are sold at different windows according to company and destination.

**East Delta Travel Co** (02-2419 8533), for Suez and Sinai, and **Super Jet** (02-2290 9017, 02-3572 5032), for Hurghada, Luxor and Sharm el-Sheikh, are to the right. **West & Mid Delta Bus Co** (02-2432 0049; http://westmidbus-eg.com), for Alexandria, Marsa Matruh and Siwa, and **Upper Egypt Travel Co** (02-2576 0261), for Western Desert oases and Luxor (though for the latter the train is better), are to the left.

It is advisable to book most tickets in advance, particularly for popular routes such as Sinai, Alexandria and Marsa Matruh in summer.

Student discounts are not offered on bus tickets.

There are also bus services to Libya, Israel and Jordan.

### Go Bus Station

**Go Bus** (Map p74; 19567; www.gobus-eg.com; Midan Abdel Moniem Riad, Downtown) runs regular buses to Alexandria, Hurghada and Sharm el-Sheikh and several towns in Middle Egypt. They have also recently started up a direct service to Dahab. Buses come in a baffling array of service classes with the higher-priced buses offering bigger seats, wi-fi and a free snack. Sample ticket prices to Hurghada: Economic/Deluxe/Elite, E£85/105/220. Tickets – and even specific seats – can be booked online.

Services depart/arrive from their Tahrir office on Midan Abdel Moniem Riad (behind the Egyptian Museum, opposite the Ramses Hilton).

### TRAIN

Trains to Alexandria, Upper Egypt and major towns in the Delta are the most efficient and comfortable. Train travel to smaller towns is recommended for rail-fans only, as it's often quite slow and scruffy.

**Ramses Station** (Mahattat Ramses; 02-2575 3555; Midan Ramses, Downtown; M Al-Shohadaa) is Cairo's main train station. It has a left luggage office, a post office, ATMs and a tourist information office.

# SAQQARA, MEMPHIS & DAHSHUR

Although most tourists associate Egypt with the Pyramids of Giza, there are known to be at least 118 ancient pyramids scattered around the country, with more being discovered every few years or so. The majority of these monuments are spread out along the desert between the Giza Plateau and the semi-oasis of Al-Fayoum. They include the must-see Step Pyramid of Zoser at Saqqara and the Red Pyramid and Bent Pyramid of Dahshur. These three pyramids represent the formative steps of architecture that reached fruition in the Great Pyramid of Khufu (Cheops).

## Sights

At **Saqqara** (adult/student E£80/40, parking E£2; 8am-4pm, to 3pm during Ramadan) you'll find a massive necropolis strewn with pyramids, temples and tombs where pharaohs, generals and sacred animals were interred. The star attraction is the Step Pyramid of Zoser, the world's oldest stone monument; the interior is closed due to restoration works. The stunning decoration inside the Pyramid of Unas, Mastaba of Ti and Tomb of Kagemni are three more reasons to visit this huge site. And don't miss the small but wonderfully curated Imhotep Museum at the site entrance.

### ★ Imhotep Museum — MUSEUM

In the complex at the entrance to the Saqqara site is this beautiful collection of some of the best finds from Saqqara, and one of the finest small museums in Egypt. It is framed as a tribute to the architect Imhotep, who served Pharaoh Zoser and is credited with creating ancient Egypt's first comprehensive vision of stone architecture (he also happens to be considered the world's first physician). His solid wood coffin is on display in one room.

### ★ Mastaba of Ti — TOMB

The Mastaba of Ti was discovered by Auguste Mariette in 1865. It is perhaps the grandest and most detailed private tomb at Saqqara, and one of our main sources of knowledge about life in Old Kingdom Egypt. Its owner, Ti, was overseer of the Abu Sir pyramids and sun temples (among other things) during the 5th dynasty. In fact, the superb quality of his tomb is in keeping with his nickname, Ti the Rich. This is Old Kingdom art at its best.

### Step Pyramid of Zoser — MONUMENT

In the year 2650 BC Pharaoh Zoser (2667–2648 BC) asked his chief architect, Imhotep (later deified), to build him a Step Pyramid. This is the world's earliest stone monument, and its significance cannot be overstated. The Step Pyramid is surrounded by a vast funerary complex, enclosed by a 1645m-long panelled limestone wall, and covers 15 hectares. Part of the enclosure wall survives today, and a section near the entrance was restored to its original 10m height.

### Dahshur — ARCHAEOLOGICAL SITE

(adult/student E£40/20, parking E£2; 8am-4pm, to 3pm during Ramadan) Ten kilometres south of Saqqara is a 3.5km-long field of pyramids. The two most striking are the **Red Pyramid** (North Pyramid), with its narrow 63m-long passage down into the antechamber, and the **Bent Pyramid**, the interior of which is closed to visitors. Both were built by Pharaoh Sneferu (2613-2589 BC), father of Khufu.

### Getting There & Away

Due to extremely limited public transport options, this area is typically visited as part of an organised tour, or with a private taxi from Cairo hired for the day (about E£320 to E£400, plus parking at each site). Moreover, the sites of Saqqara and Dahshur are quite vast, and it's an asset to have a car to drive you around them.



## ALEXANDRIA

POP 4.1 MILLION / ☎03

Founded by Alexander the Great, once the seat of Queen Cleopatra, Alexandria is the stuff legends are made of. Alas, fate dealt the city a spate of cruel blows and today there is little left of the once lauded ancient metropolis.

The 19th century kick-started a cosmopolitan renaissance when Alexandria became one of the Mediterranean's key commercial hubs, bringing the city a swaggering fame. This revival was cut short in the 1950s by President Nasser's nationalism. Alexandria, however, is a champion survivor. Today the modern library of Alexandria sits amid faded remnants of the once grand seafront Corniche as a symbol of the city's latest revival as Egypt's cultural capital.

For many visitors, Alexandria remains a city of ambience rather than sights. This is the ideal place to spend time sipping coffee in old-world cafes and meandering the harbour area, gazing up at belle époque architecture and pondering the ghosts of the past.

### Sights

**★Bibliotheca Alexandrina** MUSEUM
(☎03-483 9999; www.bibalex.org; Al-Corniche, Shatby; adult/student E£70/35; ⏲11am-7pm Sun-Thu, noon-4pm Sat) Alexandria's ancient library was one of the greatest of all classical institutions, and while replacing it might seem a Herculean task, the new Bibliotheca Alexandrina manages it with aplomb. Opened in 2002, this impressive piece of modern architecture is a deliberate attempt to rekindle the brilliance of the original centre of learning and culture. The complex has become one of Egypt's major cultural venues and a stage for numerous international performers, and is home to a collection of brilliant museums.

**★Alexandria National Museum** MUSEUM
(110 Sharia Tariq al-Horreyya; adult/student E£40/25; ⏲9am-4.30pm) This excellent museum sets a high benchmark for summing up Alexandria's past. Housed in a beautifully restored Italianate villa, the small but thoughtfully selected and well-labelled collection does a sterling job of relating the city's history from antiquity until the modern period.

**Catacombs of Kom ash-Shuqqafa** ARCHAEOLOGICAL SITE
(Carmous; adult/student E£40/25; ⏲9am-5pm) Discovered accidentally in 1900 when a donkey disappeared through the ground, these catacombs are the largest known Roman burial site in Egypt and one of the last major works of construction dedicated to the religion of ancient Egypt.

**Fort Qaitbey** FORT
(Eastern Harbour; adult/student E£30/15; ⏲9am-4pm) The Eastern Harbour is dominated by the bulky walls of Fort Qaitbey, built on a narrow peninsula over the remains of the legendary Pharos lighthouse by the Mamluk sultan Qaitbey in 1480. Finely restored, there are a warren of rooms to explore, and the walk here is just as rewarding. From Midan Ramla it's a 30-to-45-minute stroll along the Corniche with spectacular harbour views along the way.

### Sleeping

**Hotel Union** HOTEL $
(☎03-480 7312; 5th fl, 164 Al-Corniche; s/d sea view E£175/205, s/d E£155/185; 📶) Get a seafront room and those princely views of the Med from the balcony are yours for a pauper's budget. The Union is Alexandria's safest, most solid budget option; always bustling with a mix of Egyptian holidaymakers and foreign travellers. The simple rooms are decently maintained and clean, and the staff is a cheerful lot even if the service can be hilariously haphazard.

**Alex Otel** HOTEL $$
(Alexander the Great Hotel; ☎03-487 0081, 012 2560 3476; 5 Sharia Oskofia; s/d E£350/450; ❄📶) In a quiet position – beside St Katherine School – the Alex Otel may have no grand harbour views but its squeaky-clean rooms are a breath of fresh air compared to most of Alexandria's hotels. Here you get bright and breezy contemporary style thanks to lashings of white paint, Islamic design art prints on the walls, new furniture, modern bathrooms and even in-room kettles.

**★Steigenberger Cecil Hotel** HISTORIC HOTEL $$$
(☎03-487 7173; www.steigenberger.com; 16 Midan Saad Zaghloul; s/d sea view US$135/143, s/d US$120/135; ❄📶) The historic Cecil Hotel is a true Alexandria legend, though a series of refits over the years have unfortunately erased most of the days-gone-by lustre from when Durrell and Churchill propped up the famous bar here. Rooms are elegantly attired in red and cream. Bag a seafront one to make the most of the sweeping views over the Eastern Harbour.

## Eating

**★Mohammed Ahmed** EGYPTIAN $
(☎03-483 3576; 17 Sharia Shakor Pasha; dishes E£2-12; ⌚24hr; 📝) Looking for us at lunchtime in Alex? We're usually scoffing fuul and falafel here. Mohammed Ahmed is the undisputed king of spectacularly good and cheap Egyptian standards. Select your fuul (we recommend *iskandarani*), add some falafel, choose a few accompanying salads and let the feasting begin.

**Taverna** EGYPTIAN $
(☎03-487 8591; Mahattat Ramla; mains E£8-35; ⌚7am-1am; 📝) This bustling joint serves some of the best shawarma in town plus excellent hand-thrown sweet or savoury *fiteer* (Egyptian flaky pizza). Can't choose? Order the shawarma *fiteer* for an Egyptian fast-food double-up. Don't miss watching the *fiteer* chef showing off his craft; he could give any Italian a run for their money with his dough-stretching skills. Eat in or takeaway.

**★Kadoura** SEAFOOD $$
(☎03-480 0405; 33 Sharia Bairam at-Tonsi; mains E£35-80; ⌚noon-midnight) Pronounced 'Adora', this is one of Alexandria's most authentic fish restaurants, where food is served at tables in the narrow street. Pick your fish from a huge ice-packed selection, usually including sea bass, red and grey mullet, bluefish, sole, squid, crab and prawns. A selection of mezze is served with all orders (don't hope for a menu).

**La Varanda** EUROPEAN $$
(☎03-486 1432; 46 Sharia Saad Zaghloul; mains E£25-60; ⌚11am-midnight; 📶) Next door to famous tea room Delices, and run by the same people, La Varanda is a cosy place that specialises in Greek and French cuisine with steaks, good meatball dishes and *yuvetsi* (Greek pasta) on the menu. Dessert is taken care of by Delices' mammoth patisserie selection. Beer and Egyptian wine are served.

## Drinking & Nightlife

**★Delices** CAFE
(46 Sharia Saad Zaghloul; ⌚9am-late; 📶) This old tea room has been in business since 1922 and is *the* place to come for tea and cake (E£16 to E£20). Although much of its original grandeur has been scrubbed away, its high-ceilinged halls still exude a sense of old world atmosphere. The patisserie here once supplied Egypt's royalty and the cafe was a favourite haunt of Allied soldiers during WWII.

**★Selsela Cafe** CAFE
(Chatby Beach, Al-Corniche; ⌚approx 10am-late) At this fantastic cafe across from the Bibliotheca Alexandrina you can sip tea and smoke sheesha to the sound of waves rolling in, and smell sea air instead of petrol fumes (yay). Directly on the water, it has rustic palm-frond-shaded tables replete with twinkling coloured lights, set on a small curving beach where you can hardly hear the traffic.

## Shopping

**Souq District** MARKET
At the western end of Midan Tahrir, the battered, grand architecture switches scale to something more intimate as you enter the city's main souq district. It's one long, heaving bustle of produce, fish and meat stalls, bakeries, cafes and sundry shops selling every imaginable household item. This is a great area to check out at night.

**Attareen Antique Market** ANTIQUES
(⌚10am-late) Antique collectors will have a blast diving through the confusion of backstreets and alleys of this antique market. Many items found their way here after the European upper class was forced en masse to make a hasty departure from Egypt following the 1952 revolution.

## Information

**Mahattat Misr Tourist Office** (☎392 5985; Platform 1, Misr Train Station; ⌚8.30am-6pm) The staff is eager to help, even if they don't have much actual information.

**Main Tourist Office** (☎03-485 1556; Midan Saad Zaghloul; ⌚8.30am-6pm) Hands out a good brochure (with map) of Alexandria sights and has friendly staff.

## Getting There & Away

### AIR

**Burg al-Arab Airport** (☎03-459 1484; http://borg-el-arab.airport-authority.com), about 45km southwest of Alexandria, handles all

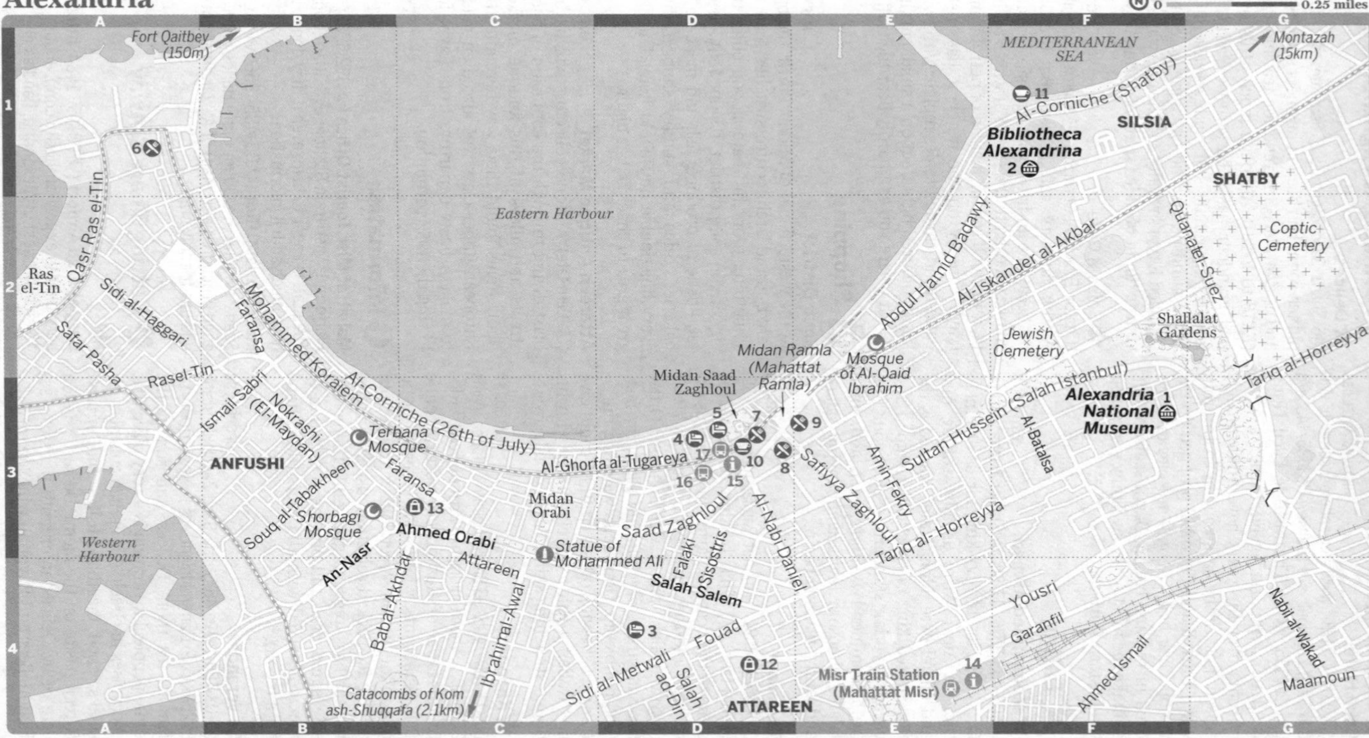
Alexandria
0 500 m
0 0.25 miles
Fort Qaitbey (150m)
Montazah (15km)
MEDITERRANEAN SEA
Eastern Harbour
Western Harbour
Ras el-Tin
Qasr Ras el-Tin
Sidi al-Haggari
Safar Pasha
Rasel-Tin
Faransa
Mohammed Koraiem
Al-Corniche (26th of July)
Ismail Sabri
Nokrashi (El-Maydan)
ANFUSHI
Terbana Mosque
Souq al-Tabakheen
Shorbagi Mosque
Faransa
13
Ahmed Orabi
An-Nasr
Babal-Akhdar
Attareen
Ibrahimal-Awal
Catacombs of Kom ash-Shuqqafa (2.1km)
Midan Orabi
Statue of Mohammed Ali
Al-Ghorfa al-Tugareya
Saad Zaghloul
Falaki
Sisostris
Salah Salem
Al-Nabi Daniel
3
Fouad
Sidi al-Metwali
Salah ad-Din
12
ATTAREEN
Midan Saad Zaghloul
Midan Ramla (Mahattat Ramla)
4
5
7
9
8
10
15
16
17
6
Safiyya Zaghloul
Amin Fekry
Tariq al-Horreyya
Misr Train Station (Mahattat Misr)
14
Mosque of Al-Qaid Ibrahim
Abdul Hamid Badawy
Al-Iskander al-Akbar
Jewish Cemetery
Sultan Hussein (Salah Istanbul)
Al-Batalsa
Alexandria National Museum
1
Yousri
Garanfil
Ahmed Ismail
11
Al-Corniche (Shatby)
SILSIA
Bibliotheca Alexandrina
2
SHATBY
Quanatel-Suez
Coptic Cemetery
Shallalat Gardens
Tariq al-Horreyya
Nabil al-Wakad
Maamoun

## Alexandria

**Top Sights**
1 Alexandria National Museum ........ F3
2 Bibliotheca Alexandrina ........ F1

**Sleeping**
3 Alex Otel ........ D4
4 Hotel Union ........ D3
5 Steigenberger Cecil Hotel ........ D3

**Eating**
6 Kadoura ........ A1
7 La Varanda ........ D3
8 Mohammed Ahmed ........ D3
9 Taverna ........ E3

**Drinking & Nightlife**
10 Delices ........ D3
11 Selsela Cafe ........ F1

**Shopping**
12 Attareen Antique Market ........ D4
13 Souq District ........ C3

**Information**
14 Mahattat Misr Tourist Office ........ E4
15 Main Tourist Office ........ D3

**Transport**
16 Go Bus Ticket Office ........ D3
17 West & Mid Delta Bus Co ........ D3

international and domestic flights in and out of the city. Most services are to/from the Arabian Peninsula and North African destinations.

Smaller **Nouzha Airport** (03-425 0527), 7km southeast, has been shut for renovation since 2011. When it reopens, it's likely that domestic flights will be re-routed there.

### BUS

The main bus station is **Al-Mo'af al-Gedid Bus Station** (New Garage; Moharrem Bey). It's several kilometres south of Midan Saad Zaghloul; to get there either catch a microbus from Misr Train Station (E£2) or grab a taxi from the city centre (E£25).

The main companies operating from here are **West & Mid Delta Bus Co** (03-480 9685; Midan Saad Zaghloul; 9am-7pm) and **Super Jet** (03-543 5222; Sidi Gaber Train Station; 8am-10pm); both have central city booking offices, though Super Jet's is inconveniently in Sidi Gaber.

**Go Bus** (www.go-bus.com; Moharrem Bey) services leave from a separate terminal close by Al-Mo'af al-Gedid. Their ticket booking **office** (Sharia Mohammed Talaat Noeman) is near Midan Saad Zaghloul.

### TRAIN

There are two train stations in Alexandria. The main terminal is **Misr Train Station** (Mahattat Misr; 03-426 3207; https://enr.gov.eg; Sharia al-Nabi Daniel), about 1km south of Midan Ramla. **Sidi Gaber Train Station** (Mahattat Sidi Gaber; 03-426 3953) serves the eastern suburbs. Trains from Cairo stop at Sidi Gaber first and most locals get off here, but if you're going to the city centre around Midan Saad Zaghloul, make sure you stay on until Misr Train Station.

At Misr Train Station, 1st- and 2nd-class tickets to Cairo are sold at the ticket office along platform 1; 2nd- and 3rd- class tickets to destinations other than Cairo are purchased in the front hall.

If you're getting a taxi from the station, it's advisable to bypass the drivers lurking outside the entrance as they're renowned for overcharging new arrivals – instead walk out on to the street and flag one down.

# SINAI

## Dahab

POP 7494 / 069

Low-key, laid-back and low-rise, Dahab is the Middle East's prime beach resort for independent travellers. The startling transformation from dusty Bedouin outpost to spruced-up tourist village is not without its detractors, who reminisce fondly of the days when beach bums dossed in basic huts by the shore. But for all the starry-eyed memories, there are plenty of pluses that have come with prosperity. Diving is now a much safer and more organised activity thanks to better regulation of operators; and the town is cleaner and more family-friendly, offering accommodation choices for everyone rather than just hardened backpackers.

This is the one town in South Sinai where independent travellers are the rule rather than the exception and Dahab's growth has not destroyed its budget-traveller roots. Reeled in by its mellow ambience, many travellers plan a few nights here and instead stay for weeks.

### Sights

**★Blue Hole** DIVE SITE

Carved into a reef just offshore, 8km north of Dahab, is Egypt's most infamous dive site. The Blue Hole is a gaping sinkhole that drops straight down – some say as deep as

130m. Exploring the deeper depths should be left to experienced technical divers. There's plenty to discover close to the surface. The outer lip is full of marine life, and a reasonable plunge into the hole itself is somewhat akin to skydiving. Depth: 7m to 27m. Rating: intermediate. Access: shore.

## Activities

**Red Sea Relax Dive Centre** DIVING
(069-364 1309; www.red-sea-relax.com; Red Sea Relax Hotel, Waterfront Promenade, Masbat; per shore/night dive from US$18/24, 1 day, 2/3 dives US$76/89) Long-standing five-star PADI centre with an excellent reputation. Highly recommended for PADI learn-to-dive courses. AIDA free-diving courses also available.

**Poseidon Divers** DIVING
(069-364 0091; www.poseidondivers.com; Waterfront Promenade, Crazy Camel Camp, Mashraba; 1 day, 2 dives €44) Award-winning PADI centre that consistently gets recommended by travellers.

**Nesima Dive Centre** DIVING
(069-364 0320; www.nesima-resort.com; Nesima Resort, Sharia Tawfik al-Hakim, Mashraba; 1/2 dives €28/55) A reputable club owned by local environmental activist and veteran diver Sherif Ebeid.

## Sleeping

**Ghazala Hotel** HOTEL $
(069-364 2414, 010 0117 5869; www.ghazaladahab.com; Waterfront Promenade, Mashraba; s/d/tr E£130/200/300; ) Ghazala's cute white-domed rooms rim a narrow courtyard set with colourful mosaic tiles. There's a level of spic-and-span cleanliness here that punches well above most of Dahab's budget scene, although we're personally not fans of the 'funny' signs posted around the place. It's located right at the southern end of the shorefront promenade, so may be too quiet for some.

★**Eldorado** BOUTIQUE HOTEL $$
(012 2759 3235, 069-365 2157; www.eldoradodahab.com; Sharia el-Melal, Assalah; s/d €30/50, without bathroom €20/35; ) This intimate, Italian-owned hotel oozes chic, easygoing beach style. The colourful cabana-type rooms host big beds, painted wood panels and cheerful lemon detailing, plus modern bathrooms and exceptional levels of brushed-up maintenance. Even better, there's a proper patch of sandy beach out front, which is immaculately cared for and comes complete with beckoning sun loungers and shaded seating.

**Nesima Resort** RESORT $$
(069-364 0320; www.nesima-resort.com; Sharia Tawfik al-Hakim, Mashraba; s/d E£250/350, sea-view r E£500; ) A lovely compromise if you want resort living without being isolated from town. Set amid a mature garden of blooming bougainvillea, Nesima's cosy (read: small) brick cottages have domed ceilings and cute terraces. Upgrade to a sea-view room, rimming the pool, to sit on your terrace looking out to the Red Sea.

## Eating

★**Ralph's German Bakery** CAFE $
(Sharia al-Fanar, Masbat; pastries E£6-18, sandwiches & breakfasts E£33-60; 7am-6pm; ) Everybody in Dahab ends up at Ralph's at some point. Single-handedly raising the bar for coffee in town, this place is caffeine heaven and also Dahab's top stop for breakfast. People who have the willpower to not add one of the delectable Danish pastries on to their order are doing better than us.

★**Lakhbatita** ITALIAN $$
(Waterfront Promenade, Mashraba; dishes E£65-120; 6-11.30pm; ) We adore Lakhbatita's eccentric decoration, friendly service and serene ambience, all of which bring a touch of Italian flair to Dahab. The small menu of homemade pasta dishes, many featuring seafood, is a cut above what's served up elsewhere. Try the mushroom ravioli or the garlic and chilli prawns. No alcohol served but diners are welcome to bring their own.

**Ali Baba** INTERNATIONAL $$$
(Waterfront Promenade, Masbat; mains E£87-193; 10am-late; ) One of the most popular restaurants along the waterfront strip for good reason: this place adds flair to its seafood selection with some inspired menu choices. Great service, comfy sofas to lounge on, stylish lanterns and twinkly fairy lights add to the relaxed seaside ambience. All meals come with a mezze selection to start with.

## Information

### DANGERS & ANNOYANCES

After the Dahab suicide bombing of April 2006 (which killed 23 people and injured dozens), the government pumped up security within Dahab and the town hasn't been targeted since. Dahab's location, however, within the greater South Sinai region, does mean that many government travel advisories currently warn against visiting.

### MONEY

There are plenty of stand-alone ATMs scattered along the waterfront.

**Banque du Caire** (Sharia al-Mashraba, Mashraba; ⏲8.30am-2pm Sun-Thu) Has an ATM.

**National Bank of Egypt** (Sharia Tawfik al-Hakim, Mashraba; ⏲8.30am-2pm Sun-Thu) Has an ATM.

### Getting There & Away

#### BUS

The **East Delta bus station** (☎069-364 1808) is in Dahab City, well southwest of the centre of the action. East Delta has a **ticket office** (Peace Rd; ⏲9am-6pm) in Masbat. Some buses will pick up passengers from here; ask when booking. Departure times change frequently so always check a day beforehand.

**Go Bus** (www.gobus-eg.com) had just started up a direct Dahab–Cairo service when we were last in town.

#### TAXI

Taxi drivers around town charge around E£150 to Sharm el-Sheikh and E£250 to St Katherine.

## Sharm el-Sheikh & Na'ama Bay

POP 38,480 / ☎069

The southern coast of the Gulf of Aqaba, between Tiran Island and Ras Mohammed National Park, features some of the world's most amazing underwater scenery. In a prime position on the coast, incorporating the two adjacent coves of Na'ama Bay and Sharm al-Maya, is the purpose-built resort of Sharm el-Sheikh, a tourism boom-town devoted to sun-and-sea holidays. Many independent travellers prefer the low-key and more backpacker-friendly town of Dahab.

### Activities

**Oona's Dive Club** DIVING
(☎069-360 0561; www.oonasdiveclub.com; Oona's Hotel, Na'ama Bay Promenade, Na'ama Bay; 1-day, 2 dives €70, snorkelling boat trips €35) Recommendable for their friendly and professional instructors. Oona's offers good-value one-week dive and hotel packages for €320 (three-days' diving), €420 (five-days' diving) and €468 (six-days' diving).

**Sinai Divers** DIVING
(☎069-360 0697; www.sinaidivers.com; Ghazala Beach Hotel, Na'ama Bay Promenade, Na'ama Bay; 1-day, 2 dives €65, 1-day snorkelling boat trips €25) Based at the Ghazala Beach Hotel, this is one of Sharm el-Sheikh's most established dive centres.

**Camel Dive Club** DIVING
(☎069-360 0700; www.cameldive.com; Camel Hotel, King of Bahrain St, Na'ama Bay; 1-day, 2 dives shore/boat €50/70, snorkelling boat trips €38) This highly professional and respected club is owned by Sinai diver Hisham Gabr. As well as being a 5-Star PADI Instructor Development Centre, it is fully fitted out for wheelchair access and holds a PADI Accessibility Award.

### Sleeping

**★Camel Hotel** HOTEL $$
(☎069-360 0700; www.cameldive.com; King of Bahrain St, Na'ama Bay; s €36-42, d €42-48, tr €56-63; ) Attached to the highly reputable dive centre of the same name, Camel Hotel is the smart choice to stay at if diving is your main agenda. Despite being in the heart of Na'ama Bay, the spacious, modern rooms, set around a lovely courtyard pool area, are gloriously quiet (thanks to soundproof windows).

**Oonas Hotel** HOTEL $$
(☎069-360 0581; www.oonasdiveclub.com; Na'ama Bay; s/d/ste €45/60/140; ) The good-size rooms at this combo dive centre and hotel may be a tad plain, but they come with excellent facilities (kettle, fridge and satellite TV) and balconies. The dive centre here comes highly recommended and accommodation is cheaper if booked as part of a dive package. Their beach (shared with the neighbouring resort) is a stone's throw away.

**Mövenpick Sharm el-Sheikh** RESORT $$$
(☎069-360 0081; www.movenpick.com; Peace Rd, Na'ama Bay; r from US$133; ) Dominating Na'ama Bay's northern cliff, this whitewashed hotel terraces majestically down towards the sea like a Sultan's palace. Standard rooms are surprisingly dull for the price but the views and facilities (five private beaches, spa, pool and on-site horse stables) are five-star. Unlike most of Sharm's megaresorts, here you have an easy stroll into Na'ama Bay.

### Eating

**El-Masrien** EGYPTIAN $
(King of Bahrain St, Sharm Old Market, Sharm al-Maya; dishes E£7-80; ⏲noon-late; ) This old-fashioned restaurant is our top dining spot in Sharm Old Market. There's a huge range of kebabs but also plenty of gutsy flavoured *tagens* (stews cooked in a deep clay-pot), and typical Egyptian vegetarian dishes from which you can make a cheap and tasty mezze spread. Local Egyptian holidaymakers flock here in the evening.

DON'T MISS

## RAS MOHAMMED NATIONAL PARK

About 20km west of Sharm el-Sheikh lies the headland of Ras Mohammed National Park, named by local fishers for a cliff that resembles a man's profile. The waters surrounding the peninsula are considered the jewel in the crown of the Red Sea. The park is visited annually by more than 50,000 visitors, enticed by the prospect of marvelling at some of the world's most spectacular coral-reef ecosystems, including a profusion of coral species and teeming marine life.

Those planning to dive here need to arrive via a boat tour or a liveaboard, both of which typically depart from Sharm el-Sheikh or Dahab.

If arriving at the park by private car, you can follow the network of (colour-coded) tracks to a variety of wilderness beaches for snorkelling on the offshore reefs – bring your own snorkelling equipment.

Ras Mohammed's **visitors centre** (⌚10am-4pm) is clearly marked on the park's main access road in an area known as Marsa Ghoslane. Maps are usually available here.



**★Fares Seafood** SEAFOOD **$$**
(☎069-366 3076; City Council St, Hadaba; mains E£35-100; ⌚noon-1am; ❄) Always crowded with locals, Fares is a Sharm el-Sheikh institution for good-value seafood. Order fish priced by weight or choose from one of the pasta or *tagen* options on the menu. We're pretty partial to the mixed *tagen* of calamari and shrimp. There's another **branch** (☎069-366 4270; Sharm al-Maya; mains E£35-100; ⌚11am-1am; ❄) at Sharm Old Market.

**Pomodoro** ITALIAN **$$**
(King of Bahrain St, Na'ama Bay; pizza & pasta E£60-80, other mains E£130-249; ⌚11am-midnight; ❄📶) Hands down the best pizza in the Sinai. A great spot for casual dining, Pomodoro has a modern, buzzy, friendly vibe and a menu stuffed with pasta and a fair whack of seafood, but its thin-crust pizzas are the serious winner here. Try the house special pizza with olives, lip-smacking tomato sauce, mozzarella, rocket and generous lashings of Parmesan.

## Drinking & Nightlife

**★Farsha Cafe** CAFE
(Sharia el-Bahr, Ras Um Sid; ⌚11am-late; 📶) All nooks and crannies, floor cushions, Bedouin tents and swinging lamps, Farsha is the kind of place that travellers come to for a coffee and find themselves lingering at four drinks and a sheesha pipe later. Great for a lazy day full of lounging or a night of chilled-out music and cocktails.

## Information

### DANGERS & ANNOYANCES

Serious security concerns regarding Sharm el-Sheikh's airport were raised in the aftermath of the downing of Russian Metrojet Flight 9268 in October 2015, which disintegrated mid-air shortly after take off from Sharm el-Sheikh, killing all 224 aboard. A bomb is widely thought to be the cause of the crash. International direct flights into Sharm el-Sheikh were suspended afterwards, and currently most European countries have yet to lift the suspension.

Sharm el-Sheikh town itself, though, is generally considered a safe destination.

### MONEY

There are copious ATMs in Na'ama Bay, including several in and around Sharia Sultan Qabos. All the larger hotels also have ATMs in their lobbies. Otherwise, all the major banks have branches in Hadaba. Sharm hotels, and many businesses, accept British pounds, euros and US dollars as payment as well as Egyptian pounds.

**Banque du Caire** (Bank St, Hadaba; ⌚8.30am-2.30pm Sun-Thu) Has an ATM.

**HSBC** (☎069-360 0614; Na'ama Centre, Na'ama Bay; ⌚8.30am-2.30pm Sun-Thu) Has an ATM.

**National Bank of Egypt** (Bank St, Hadaba; ⌚8.30am-2.30pm Sun-Thu) Also has a branch in **Na'ama Bay** (Na'ama Centre, Na'ama Bay; ⌚8.30am-2pm Sun-Thu).

**Travel Choice** (☎096-360 1808; www.travelchoiceegypt.com; Gafy Mall, Peace Rd, Na'ama Bay; ⌚9am-2pm & 6-8pm) Just west of Sinai Star Hotel.

**Western Union** (☎069-364 0466; Rosetta Hotel, Na'ama Bay; ⌚8.30am-2pm & 6-10pm Sat-Thu, 3-10pm Fri)

## Getting There & Away

### AIR

**Sharm el-Sheikh International Airport** (☎069-362 3304; www.sharm-el-sheikh.airport-authority.com; Peace Rd) is Sinai's major travel hub. After the crash of Metrojet Flight 9268, all European airlines suspended flights in and out of Sharm el-Sheikh Airport. Currently, the only European Airline that has restarted direct flights to Sharm from Europe is German budget airline Germania (www.flygermania.com).

For now, to travel to Sharm by air you'll usually have transit through Cairo. Egypt Air (www.egyptair.com) has several flights to and from Cairo per day.

### BOAT

The **La Pespes high-speed catamaran ferry service** (☎ 012 1014 4000, 012 2449 5592; High Jet Office, Peace Rd, Sharm al-Maya; ⊙ 10am-10pm) operates between Sharm el-Sheikh and Hurghada three times per week. The journey takes 2½ hours.

### BUS

The **taxi station** (☎ 069-366 1622), just behind the East Delta station, has ticket offices and is the main bus arrival/departure point for Super Jet and Go Bus (www.go-bus.com) services. A taxi from here to Na'ama Bay shouldn't cost more than E£15.

# SUEZ CANAL

## Port Said

POP 678,564 / ☎ 066

In its late-19th-century raffish heyday, Port Said was Egypt's city of vice and sin. The boozing seafarers and packed brothels may have long since been scrubbed away, but this louche period is evoked still in the waterfront's muddle of once grand architecture slowly going to seed. While the yesteryear allure of the centre is enough to prompt a visit, the main attraction, and the reason for the town's establishment, is the Suez Canal. The raised pedestrian-only boardwalk running along the waterfront provides up-close views over the canal's northern entry point.

### Sleeping

**New Continental** HOTEL $

(☎ 066-322 5024; 30 Sharia al-Gomhuriyya; s/d E£200/305; ❄) Your best budget bet in Port Said. Friendly management makes this typical Egyptian cheapie stand out from the crowd. Light-filled rooms have teensy balconies and come in a range of sizes, so ask to see a few. All come with TV and an astounding clutter of furniture.

**Resta Port Said Hotel** HOTEL $$$

(☎ 066-320 0511; www.restahotels.com; off Sharia Palestine; s/d US$120/150; P ❄ 📶 ≋) Not as posh as it likes to think it is and ridiculously overpriced, but the Resta is about as snazzy as Port Said gets. The pool area has views out to the canal, while the business-style rooms are well sized and comfortable enough. Ask for a room overlooking the canal.

### Eating

**★ El Borg** SEAFOOD $$

(☎ 066-332 3442; Beach Plaza, off Sharia Atef as-Sadat; mains E£30-80; ⊙ 10am-3am) This massive Port Said institution is always buzzing with families on a night out. There's a small menu of grills for when you don't feel like fish, but the good-value fresh seafood is really what the crowds flock here for. Eat on the shorefront terrace in the evening for superb beach promenade people-watching.

**Pizza Pino** ITALIAN $$

(Sharia al-Gomhuriyya; mains E£30-70; ⊙ noon-11pm; ❄) This art deco–style bistro has plenty of cosy appeal and attentive staff. Pizza Pino is a local favourite for its hearty portions of pasta, good pizzas and decently priced grills. If only the background music didn't make you feel like you're stuck in an elevator with Kenny G.

### Information

#### MONEY

Most banks and important services are on Sharia al-Gomhuriyya, two blocks inland from the canal. Both of the following have an ATM:

**Bank of Alexandria** (Sharia al-Gomhuriyya; ⊙ 8.30am-2pm Sun-Thu)

**National Bank of Egypt** (Sharia al-Gomhuriyya; ⊙ 8.30am-2.30pm Sun-Thu)

#### TOURIST INFORMATION

**Tourist Office** (☎ 066-323 5289; 8 Sharia Palestine; ⊙ 10am-7pm Sat-Thu) After the enthusiastic staff has gotten over the shock of a foreign tourist walking into the office, they can give out a good map of town.

#### BUSES FROM PORT SAID

| DESTINATION | PRICE | DURATION | TIME/COMPANY |
|---|---|---|---|
| Alexandria | E£35 | 4-5hr | 7am, 11am, 2pm, 6pm & 8pm (East Delta); 4.30pm (Super Jet) |
| Cairo | E£30 | 4hr | hourly (East Delta); every two hours (Super Jet) |
| Ismailia | E£15 | 1-1½hr | hourly 6-11am & 2-6pm (East Delta) |
| Suez | E£25 | 2½hr | 6am, 10am, 2pm & 4pm (East Delta) |

## Getting There & Away

The bus station is about 3km from the town centre at the beginning of the road to Cairo (about E£10 in a taxi). Both **Super Jet** (☎066-372 1779) and **East Delta Travel Co** (☎066-372 9883) operate buses from the station.

# RED SEA COAST

## Hurghada

POP 160,901 / ☎065

Plucked from obscurity during the early days of the Red Sea's tourism drive, the fishing village of Hurghada has long since morphed into today's dense band of concrete that marches along the coastline for more than 20km. In recent years Hurghada's star has largely lost its lustre with an influx of package holiday-makers, while independent travellers prefer to press on to Dahab.

### Activities

**Aquanaut Blue Heaven** DIVING
(☎012 2248 0463; www.aquanautclub.com; Hurghada Marina, Sigala; 1 day, 2 dives €45; ⊙9am-4pm) Long-standing Hurghada dive centre, located off Sharia Sheraton, Sigala.

**Subex** DIVING
(☎065-354 7593; www.subex.org; Ad-Dahar; 6-dive packages €170) This well-known Swiss outfit is known for its professionalism.

**Jasmin Diving Centre** DIVING
(☎346 0334; www.jasmin-diving.com; Grand Seas Resort Hostmark, Resort Strip; 3-day, 6-dive packages €159) This centre has an excellent reputation and was a founding member of Hurghada Environmental Protection & Conservation Association (HEPCA).

### Sleeping

**Luxor Hotel** HOTEL $
(☎065-354 2877; www.luxorhotel-eg.com; Sharia Mustafa, Ad-Dahar; s/d/tr with air-con E£120/200/270; ❄📶) This small hotel, run by friendly Said, has good-sized, clean doubles and triples, all home to drab furnishings but with surprisingly good facilities for the price tag. If you're solo, upgrade yourself from a single room, as they're a bit poky and dark.

**Hurghada Marriott Beach Resort** RESORT $$
(☎065-344 6950; www.marriott.com; Resort Strip; r from €40; P⊖❄@📶≋) Within walking distance of the resort strip's nightlife and restaurants, the well-kept rooms here are spacious, light-filled and all come with balcony. Some may be disappointed by the small beach area, but if you want full facilities and the freedom to pick and choose where to eat, it's a great choice.

### Eating

**Gad** EGYPTIAN $
(Sharia Sheraton, Sigala; shawarma E£6-12, mains E£15-46; ⊙10am-late; 🖉) If you're looking for cheap, filling and tasty Egyptian staples, you can't go wrong with Egypt's favourite fast-food restaurant. The menu covers everything from falafel and shawarma to *fiteer* (flaky pizza) and full kebab meals. There's another **branch** (Sharia an-Nasr) in Ad-Dahar.

**Nubian Cafe** EGYPTIAN $$
(Hurghada Marina Promenade, Sigala; mains E£25-70; ⊙noon-10pm; 🖉) In a town where international food rules, it's nice to see someone taking a stand for Egyptian cuisine. The Nubian Cafe does flavoursome *tagens*; good mezze, including a scrumptious *baba ghanoog* (purée of grilled aubergines); and meaty grills. There's plenty here for vegetarians, too.

### Getting There & Away

**AIR**

**Hurghada Airport** (☎065-346 2722; Main Hwy), near the resort strip, receives plenty of (mostly charter) flights direct from European destinations.

EgyptAir (www.egyptair.com) has several daily flights to Cairo. Prices fluctuate greatly, but tickets can be as low as E£700.

**BOAT**

The high-speed catamaran ferry service between Hurghada and Sharm el-Sheikh is operated by **La Pespes** (www.lapespes.com). Boats leave at 8am on Sunday, Tuesday and Thursday (2½ hrs, adult/child US$40/30) from Hurghada Tourist Port in Sigala. You must be at the port 1½ hours before departure and have your passport on hand for identification.

Tickets can be purchased in advance from the **La Pespes ticket office** (☎012 1014 2000; www.lapespes.com; High Jet Office, Midan Aka, Sharia an-Nasr, Sigala; ⊙10am-10pm). Many travel agents and hotels in Hurghada can also book the tickets for you.

**BUS**

Hurghada doesn't have a central bus station. Instead, the major companies, including **Upper Egypt Bus Co** (☎065-354 7582; off Sharia an-Nasr, Ad-Dahar), **Super Jet** (☎065-355 3499; Sharia an-Nasr, Ad-Dahar) and **Go Bus** (www.gobus-eg.com; Sharia an-Nasr, Ad-Dahar), all arrive and depart from their own separate stations, which are strung out along Sharia An-Nasr in Ad-Dahar. Go Bus has a handy **ticket booking office** (Sharia Sheraton, Sigala; ⏲10am-10pm) in Sigala. Super Jet tends to run the most comfortable and quickest bus service to Luxor. Schedules change randomly, so check timings when booking.

# NILE VALLEY

## Luxor

POP 484,132 / ☎095

Luxor is often called the world's greatest open-air museum, but that comes nowhere near describing this extraordinary place. Nothing in the world compares to the scale and grandeur of the monuments that have survived from ancient Thebes. The setting, too, is breathtakingly beautiful, with the Nile flowing between the modern city and west-bank necropolis, backed by the enigmatic Theban escarpment.

### Sights

#### East Bank

**★Karnak** TEMPLE
(☎095-238 0270; Sharia Maabad al-Karnak; adult/student E£80/40; ⏲6am-6pm; P) Karnak is an extraordinary complex of sanctuaries, kiosks, pylons and obelisks dedicated to the Theban triad but also to the greater glory of pharaohs. The site covers over 2 sq km; it's large enough to contain about 10 cathedrals. At its heart is the Temple of Amun, the earthly 'home' of the local god. Built, added to, dismantled, restored, enlarged and decorated over nearly 1500 years, Karnak was the most important place of worship in Egypt during the New Kingdom.

**★Luxor Museum** MUSEUM
(Corniche an-Nil; adult/student E£100/50; ⏲9am-2pm & 5-9pm) This museum has a well-chosen and brilliantly displayed and explained collection of antiquities dating from the end of the Old Kingdom right through to the Mamluk period, mostly gathered from the Theban temples and necropolis. The ticket price puts off many, but don't let that stop you: this is one of the most rewarding sights in Luxor.

**Luxor Temple** TEMPLE
(☎095-237 2408; Corniche an-Nil; adult/student E£60/30; ⏲6am-9pm) Largely built by the New Kingdom pharaohs Amenhotep III (1390–1352 BC) and Ramses II (1279–1213 BC), this temple is a strikingly graceful monument in the heart of the modern town. Also known as the Southern Sanctuary, it was largely built for the Opet celebrations, when the statues of Amun, Mut and Khonsu were brought from Karnak, along the Avenue of Sphinxes, and reunited here during the inundation.

#### West Bank

**★Valley of the Kings** TOMB
(Wadi Biban al-Muluk; www.thebanmappingproject.com; adult/student for 3 tombs E£100/50, additional tickets req for Ramses VI E£50/30, Ay E£30/15, Seti I E£1000 & Tutankhamun E£100/50; ⏲6am-4pm) The west bank of Luxor had been the site of royal burials since around 2100 BC, but it was the pharaohs of the New Kingdom period (1550–1069 BC) who chose this isolated valley dominated by the pyramid-shaped mountain peak of Al-Qurn (The Horn). Once called the Great Necropolis of Millions of Years of Pharaoh, or the Place of Truth, the Valley of the Kings has 63 magnificent royal tombs, each quite different from the other.

**Memorial Temple of Hatshepsut** TEMPLE
(Deir al-Bahri; adult/student E£50/25; ⏲6am-5pm) At Deir al-Bahri, the eyes first focus on the rugged limestone cliffs that rise nearly 300m above the desert plain, only to realise that at the foot of all this immense beauty lies a monument even more extraordinary, the dazzling Temple of Hatshepsut. The almost-modern-looking temple blends in beautifully with the cliffs from which it is partly cut. Most of what you see has been painstakingly reconstructed.

**★Medinat Habu** TEMPLE
(adult/student E£40/20; ⏲6am-5pm) Ramses III's magnificent memorial temple of Medinat Habu, fronted by sleepy Kom Lolah village and backed by the Theban mountains, is perhaps one of the west bank's most underrated sites. This was one of the first places in Thebes closely associated with the local god Amun. At its height, Medinat Habu contained temples, storage rooms, workshops, administrative buildings, a royal palace and accommodation for priests and officials. It was the centre of the economic life of Thebes for centuries.

**Valley of the Queens** TOMB
(Biban al-Harim; adult/student E£50/25, additional ticket req for Nefertari E£1000; ⏲6am-5pm) At the southern end of the Theban hillside, the Valley of the Queens contains at least 75 tombs that belonged to queens of the 19th and 20th dynasties as well as to other members of the royal families, including princesses and the Ramesside princes. Four

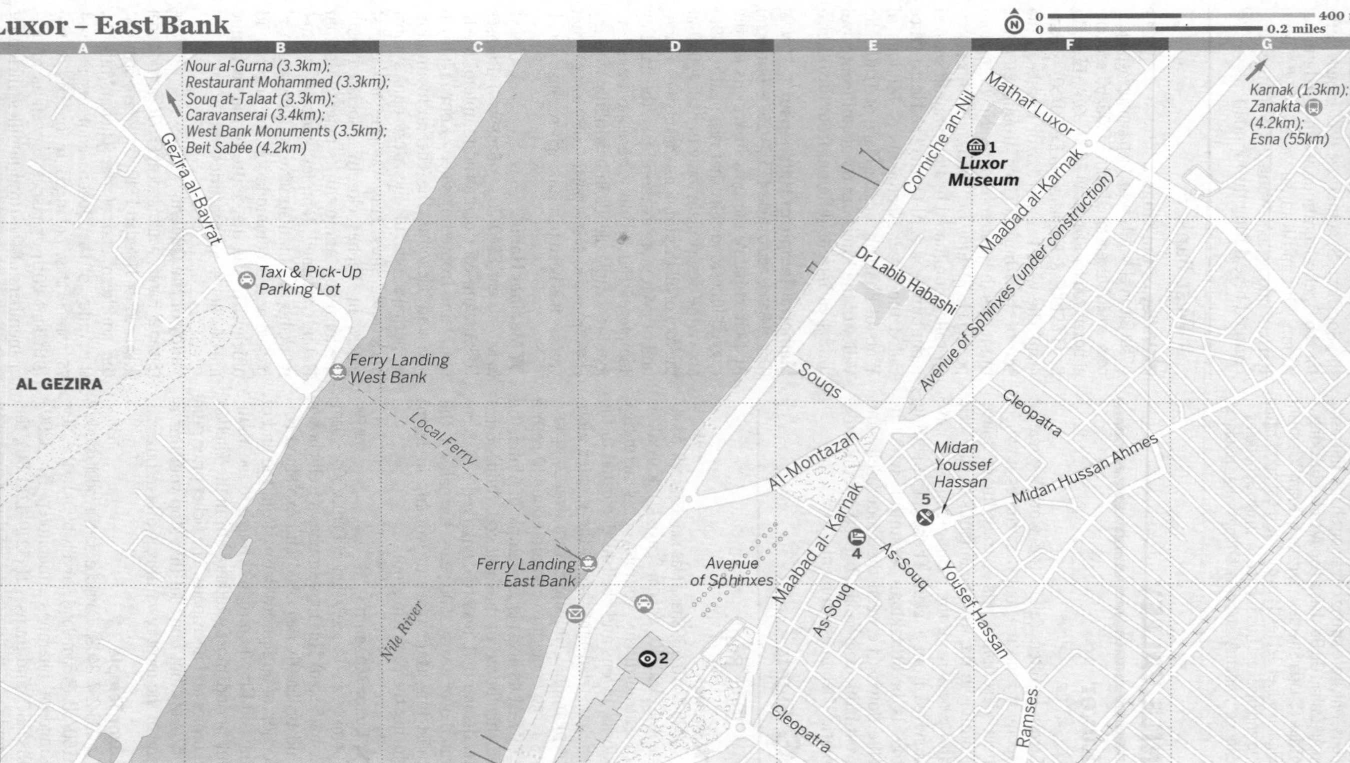

Luxor – East Bank
400 m
0.2 miles
Nour al-Gurna (3.3km); Restaurant Mohammed (3.3km); Souq at-Talaat (3.3km); Caravanserai (3.4km); West Bank Monuments (3.5km); Beit Sabée (4.2km)
Karnak (1.3km); Zanakta (4.2km); Esna (55km)
Gezira al-Bayrat
Taxi & Pick-Up Parking Lot
AL GEZIRA
Ferry Landing West Bank
Local Ferry
Ferry Landing East Bank
Nile River
Corniche an-Nil
Mathaf Luxor
1 Luxor Museum
Maabad al-Karnak
Avenue of Sphinxes (under construction)
Dr Labib Habashi
Souqs
Cleopatra
Al-Montazah
Midan Youssef Hassan
5
Midan Hussan Ahmes
Maabad al- Karnak
4
As-Souq
Yousef Hassan
Avenue of Sphinxes
As-Souq
2
Cleopatra
Ramses

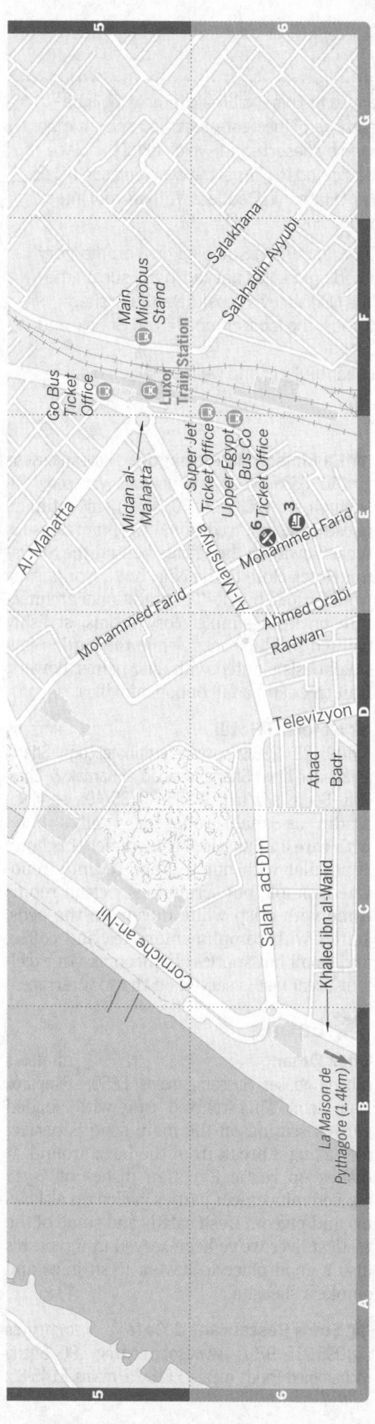


# Luxor – East Bank

**Top Sights**
1 Luxor Museum ....................................F1

**Sights**
2 Luxor Temple .................................. D4

**Activities, Courses & Tours**
Aladin Tours ..............................(see 4)

**Sleeping**
3 Boomerang Hotel...............................E6
4 Nefertiti Hotel...................................E3

**Eating**
As-Sahaby Lane ..........................(see 4)
5 Chez Omar..........................................E3
6 Sofra Restaurant & Café....................E6

of the tombs are open for viewing. The most famous of these, the tomb of Nefertari, was only reopened to the public in late 2016.

**Tombs of the Nobles** TOMB
(adult/student Khonsu, Userhet & Benia E£20/10, Menna, Nakht & Amenenope E£30/15, Ramose, Userhet & Khaemhet E£40/20, Sennofer & Rekhmire E£30/15, Neferronpet, Dhutmosi & Nefersekheru E£30/15; 6am-5pm) The tombs in this area are some of the best, but least visited, attractions on the west bank. Nestled in the foothills opposite the Ramesseum are more than 400 tombs belonging to nobles from the 6th dynasty to the Graeco-Roman period. The tombs that are open to the public are divided into groups and each requires a separate ticket from the **Antiquities Inspectorate ticket office** (main road, 3km inland from ferry landing; 6am-5pm) near Medinat Habu.

**Colossi of Memnon** MONUMENT
FREE The two faceless Colossi of Memnon, originally representing Pharaoh Amenhotep III, rising about 18m from the plain, are the first monuments tourists see when they visit the west bank. The magnificent colossi, each cut from a single block of stone and weighing 1000 tonnes, were already a great tourist attraction during Graeco-Roman times, when the statues were attributed to Memnon, the legendary African king who was slain by Achilles during the Trojan War.

## Tours

**Aladin Tours** CULTURAL
(010 0601 6132, 095-237 2386; www.nefertitihotel.com/tours; Nefertiti Hotel, Sharia as-Sahbi; 10am-6pm) This very helpful travel agency, run by the young, energetic Aladin,

WORTH A TRIP

## SIGHTS AROUND LUXOR

**Temple of Horus** (adult/student E£60/30; ⏲7am-7pm) This Ptolemaic temple, built between 237 and 57 BC, is Edfu's star attraction, and one of the best-preserved ancient monuments in Egypt, and perhaps the world. Preserved by desert sand, which filled the place after the pagan cult was banned, the temple is dedicated to Horus, the avenging son of Isis and Osiris. It is very similar in style to the Temple of Hathor in Dendera. With its roof intact, it is also one of the most atmospheric of ancient buildings.

**Temple of Kom Ombo** (adult/student E£40/20; ⏲7am-7pm) Standing on a promontory at a bend in the Nile, where in ancient times sacred crocodiles basked in the sun on the riverbank, is the Temple of Kom Ombo, one of the Nile Valley's most beautifully sited temples. Unique in Egypt, it is dedicated to two gods; the local crocodile god Sobek, and Haroeris (from har-wer), meaning Horus the Elder.

Also on site is the Crocodile Museum with a beautifully lit and well-explained display of crocodile mummies and inscriptions.

organises sightseeing tours in Luxor and around as well as in the Western Desert, plus boat trips and ferry tickets to Sinai.

## Sleeping

**★Boomerang Hotel** HOSTEL $
(Bob Marley Peace Hotel; ☎095-228 0981; www.boomerangluxor.com; Sharia Mohammed Farid; dm E£75, s/d E£170/300, without bathroom E£120/200; ❄📶) The east bank's best-run budget digs, the Boomerang offers great facilities on a backpacker budget. Rooms and dorm are squeaky clean (private rooms with en suite are surprisingly spacious), there's a cushion-scattered roof terrace, tour booking, Aussie BBQ, free wi-fi and just about everything else you could need. It's also an easy walk with a pack from Luxor Train Station.

**Nour al-Gurna** GUESTHOUSE $
(☎0100 129 5812, 095-231 1430; www.nourelgournahotel.com; Old Gurna; s/d/tr €15/25/30) Set in a palm grove, easy strolling distance to Medinat Habu and the Ramesseum, Nour al-Gurna has large mud-brick rooms, with fans, mosquito nets, small stereos, locally made furniture, tiled bathrooms and *jireed* (palm-thatch) ceilings. Romantic and original, with friendly management, this is a tranquil and intimate guesthouse, very conveniently located for visiting the west bank's monuments.

**★Beit Sabée** BOUTIQUE HOTEL $$
(☎011 1837 5604; www.beitsabee.com; Bairat; d €40-100; 🚭❄📶) Set in a traditional-style, two-storey, mud-brick house, Beit Sabée has appeared in design magazines for its cool use of Nubian colours and local furnishings with a twist. Near the farms around Medinat Habu, it offers chic rooms, a closer contact with rural Egypt and fabulous views of the desert and Medinat Habu from the rooftop.

**★La Maison de Pythagore** GUESTHOUSE $$
(☎010 0535 0532; www.louxor-egypte.com; Al-Awamiya; s/d/tr €35/50/60; ❄📶) This intimate guesthouse in a traditional Egyptian house is tucked away in the village behind the Sheraton Hotel, close to the Nile, but a world away from Luxor's hustle. The traditional architecture encloses simple, cosy rooms, stylishly painted in blue tones, while the garden is a small oasis planted with date palms, flowers, fruit trees and a fall of bougainvillea.

**★Nefertiti Hotel** HOTEL $$
(☎095-237 2386; www.nefertitihotel.com; Sharia as-Sahabi, btwn Sharia Maabad al-Karnak & Sharia as-Souq; s/d/tr/f US$25/30/35/40; 🚭❄📶) Aladin as-Sahabi runs his family's hotel with care and passion. No wonder this hotel is popular with our readers: recently renovated, simple but scrupulously clean rooms come with crisp white duvets on the beds, kettles with complimentary tea and coffee, and small but spotless bathrooms. An excellent breakfast is served on the roof terrace.

## Eating

**Chez Omar** EGYPTIAN $
(Sharia Yousef Hassan; mains E£50; ⏲approx 11am-11pm) This relaxed cafe with shaded garden seating off the main souq is perfect for taking a break from the buzz around. It dishes up rustic Egyptian dishes of *kofta* (spiced mincemeat patties grilled on a skewer) and pigeon, fresh salads and some of the tastiest liver we've been served in Egypt. It's also a good place to have a fresh juice and smoke a sheesha.

**★Sofra Restaurant & Café** EGYPTIAN $$
(☎095-235 9752; www.sofra.com.eg; 90 Sharia Mohammed Farid; mezze E£16-25, mains E£45-85;

11am-midnight) Sofra remains our favourite restaurant in Luxor. Both the intimate salons and the spacious rooftop terrace of this 1930s house are stylishly decorated. The menu features excellent mezze and well-executed traditional Egyptian classics such as stuffed pigeon and excellent duck. With friendly staff and sheesha to finish, the place is a real treat.

**As-Sahaby Lane** EGYPTIAN **$$**
(095-236 5509; www.nefertitihotel.com/sahabi.htm; Sharia as-Sahaby, off Sharia as-Souq; dishes E£13-150; 9am-11.30pm) This easy-going al fresco restaurant, adjoining the Nefertiti Hotel, takes over the alleyway running between the souq and the street to the Karnak temples. Fresh and well-prepared Egyptian standards like *fiteer* and *tagen* are served alongside good pizzas and salads, and more adventurous dishes such as camel with couscous.

**Restaurant Mohammed** EGYPTIAN **$$**
(012 0325 1307; Kom Lolah; set meals E£75-80; approx 10am-late) Mohammed's is a blast of old-time Luxor, a simple, family-run restaurant attached to the owner's mud-brick house, where charming Mohammed Abdel Lahi serves with his son Azab, while his wife cooks. The small menu includes meat grills, delicious chicken and duck as well as stuffed pigeon, a local speciality. Stella beer and Egyptian wine are available.

## Entertainment

**Karnak Sound & Light Show** SHOW
(02-3385 7320; www.soundandlight.com.eg; E£100, video camera E£35; shows at 7pm, 8pm & 9pm in winter, at 8pm, 9pm & 10pm in summer) This kitsch sound and light show is a 1½-hour Hollywood-style extravaganza that recounts the history of Thebes and the lives of the many pharaohs who built here in honour of Amun. It's worth a visit particularly for a chance to walk through the beautifully lit temple at night. Sessions are in different languages – check the website to see what's on.

## Shopping

★**Caravanserai** ARTS & CRAFTS
(012 2327 8771; www.caravanserailuxor.com; Kom Lolah; 8am-10pm) This delightful treasure trove of Egyptian crafts, near Medinat Habu on the west bank, is run by friendly Khairy and his family. Inside you'll find beautiful pottery from the Western Oases, Siwan embroideries, a colourful selection of handwoven scarves, amazing appliqué bags and many other crafts that can be found almost nowhere else in Egypt. All at highly reasonable prices.

**Souq at-Talaat** MARKET
(Tue mornings) The wonderful weekly market Souq at-Talaat, in Taref, is held opposite the Temple of Seti I.

## Getting There & Around

### AIR

**Luxor Airport** (095-232 4455) is 7km east of central Luxor. EgyptAir (www.egyptair.com) operates regular flights to Cairo from around E£620.

#### To/From the Airport

There is no official price for taxis from Luxor airport into town, so the drivers set their prices, often at about E£70 to E£100 or more. If you want peace of mind ask the hotel to arrange your transfer. There is no bus between the airport and the town.

### BUS

**Upper Egypt Bus Co** (095-237 2118, 095-232 3218; Midan al-Mahatta; 7am-10pm) and **Super Jet** (095-236 7732; Midan al-Mahatta; 8am-10pm) have ticket offices just south of the train station. The **Go Bus office** (www.gobus-eg.com; Sharia Ramses) is just to the north. Most bus services leave from outside of the respective ticket office; check when booking. Otherwise, for some Upper Egypt Bus Co services, the **Zanakta bus station** (012 8436 663) is out of town on the road to the airport – about 1km before it. A taxi from downtown Luxor to the bus station costs between E£25 and E£35.

Microbuses are often the quickest and easiest way to get about in Luxor. They ply fixed routes and will stop whenever flagged down. Just shout your destination to the driver and if he's going that way he'll stop and pick you up. To get to the Karnak temples, take a microbus from the **main microbus stand** directly behind Luxor Train Station, or from behind Luxor Temple, for E£1. Other routes run inside the town.

### FELUCCA

You can't take a felucca from Luxor to Aswan; most feluccas leave from Esna because of the Esna Lock. But unless you have a strong wind, it can take days to go more than a few kilometres in this direction. We recommend taking a felucca downstream from Aswan.

### TRAIN

The train is the most comfortable and easiest way to travel to Aswan and Cairo. The Watania Sleeping Train (www.wataniasleepingtrains.com) has a ticket booking office inside the station.

# Aswan

POP 266,013 / 097

On the northern end of the First Cataract, marking ancient Egypt's southern frontier, Aswan has always been of great strategic importance. Today, slow and laid-back, it is the perfect place to linger for a few days and recover from the rigours of travelling.

## Sights

**★Ruins of Abu** ARCHAEOLOGICAL SITE
(Elephantine Island; adult/student E£35/15; 8am-5pm) The evocative ruins of ancient Abu and the Aswan Museum (closed for renovation) lie at Elephantine Island's southern tip. Numbered plaques and reconstructed buildings mark the island's long history from around 3000 BC to the 14th century AD. The largest structure on-site is the partially reconstructed Temple of Khnum (plaque numbers 6, 12 and 13). Built in honour of the god of inundation during the Old Kingdom, it was used for more than 1500 years before being extensively rebuilt in Ptolemaic times.

**★Nubia Museum** MUSEUM
(Sharia el Fanadek; adult/student E£60/30; 9am-1pm & 4-9pm winter, 6-10pm summer) This little-visited museum, opposite Basma Hotel, is a treat, showcasing the history, art and culture of Nubia. Established in 1997, in cooperation with Unesco, the museum is a reminder of what was lost beneath Lake Nasser. Exhibits are beautifully displayed, and clearly written explanations take you from 4500 BC through to the present day.

**Sharia as-Souq** MARKET
(Sharia as-Souq) Starting from the southern end, Sharia as-Souq appears very much like the tourist bazaars all over Egypt, with slightly less persistent traders than elsewhere in the country trying to lure passers-by into their shops to buy scarves, perfume, spice and roughly carved copies of Pharaonic statues. But a closer look reveals more exotic elements. Traders sell Nubian talismans for good luck, colourful Nubian baskets and skullcaps, Sudanese swords, African masks, and enormous stuffed crocodiles and desert creatures.

**Elephantine Island** ISLAND
Elephantine Island lies opposite central Aswan, just north of the First Cataract. The island's southern end comprises the site of ancient Abu. Its name meant both 'elephant' and 'ivory' in ancient Egyptian, a reminder of the important role the island once played in the ivory trade. The island's Nubian villages of **Siou** and **Koti** make a surprising counterpoint to the bustle of the city across the water. A recent building boom has changed the nature of the island, but it remains calm and essentially rural.

**Monastery of St Simeon** MONASTERY
(Deir Amba Samaan; West Bank; adult/student E£30/15; 8am-4pm) The fortresslike 7th-century Monastery of St Simeon was first dedicated to the local saint Anba Hedra, who renounced the world on his wedding day. It was rebuilt in the 10th century and dedicated to St Simeon. From here the monks travelled into Nubia, in the hope of converting the Nubians to Christianity. To get there, take a private boat across the Nile then walk up the (mostly paved) desert track, or hire a camel to take you up.

## Sleeping

**★Baaba Dool** GUESTHOUSE $
(010 0497 2608; Siou, Elephantine Island; r without bathroom per person €10) A great place to unwind for a few days. The rooms in this mud-brick house are painted in Nubian style, decorated with colourful carpets and local crafts, and have superb views over the Nile and the botanical gardens. Rooms are basic but clean and there are shared hot showers. Mustapha can arrange meals. Book ahead.

**★Philae Hotel** HOTEL $$
(097-246 5090, 011 1901 1995; philaehotel@gmail.com; Corniche an-Nil; s/d/tr/ste US$70/80/105/120; ) By far the best midrange hotel in town. The Philae's modern, minimalist-style rooms are decorated in fabrics with Arabic calligraphy and elegant local furnishings. The hotel restaurant serves mainly vegetarian organic food from its own gardens, and at very reasonable prices for the quality (mains from E£55 to E£70). It's no longer a secret, so book ahead.

**Bet el-Kerem** GUESTHOUSE $$
(012 384 2218, 012 391 1052; www.betelkerem.com; Gharb Aswan, West Bank; d €35, without bathroom €30; ) This modern hotel on the west side of the Nile overlooking the desert and the Tomb of the Nobles is a great find, offering nine quiet, clean and comfortable rooms. The hotel boasts a wonderful rooftop terrace, and the staff is both friendly and proud to be Nubian.

**Marhaba Palace Hotel** HOTEL $$
(097-233 0102; www.marhaba-aswan.com; Corniche an-Nil; s/d city view US$35/60, Nile view US$50/70; ) The homely Marhaba has sparkling clean, cosy rooms with comfortable beds, sumptuous bathrooms (for this price range) and satellite TV. Bright, welcoming and well-run, it overlooks a park on the Corniche and has two restaurants, friendly staff and a roof terrace with excellent Nile views. Grab a room with a balcony if you can.

## Aswan

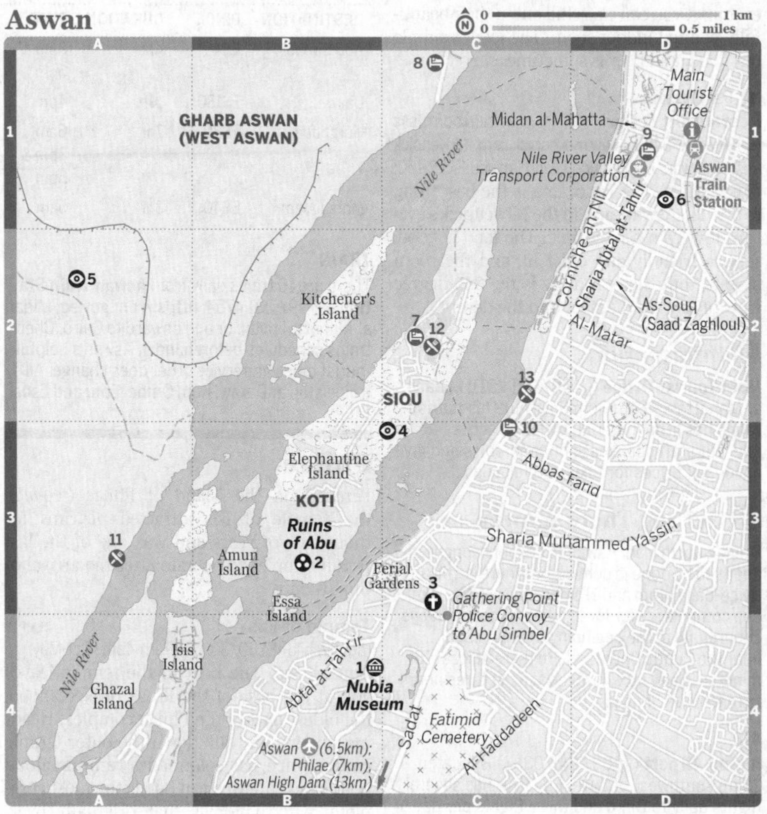




### Aswan

**Top Sights**

| | |
|---|---|
| 1 Nubia Museum | B4 |
| 2 Ruins of Abu | B3 |

**Sights**

| | |
|---|---|
| 3 Coptic Cathedral | C3 |
| 4 Elephantine Island | C3 |
| 5 Monastery of St Simeon | A2 |
| 6 Sharia as-Souq | D1 |

**Sleeping**

| | |
|---|---|
| 7 Baaba Dool | C2 |
| 8 Bet el-Kerem | C1 |
| 9 Marhaba Palace Hotel | D1 |
| 10 Philae Hotel | C3 |

**Eating**

| | |
|---|---|
| 11 Nubian Beach | A3 |
| 12 Panorama Restaurant & Bar | C2 |
| 13 Salah Ad-Din | C2 |

## Eating

**Salah Ad-Din** INTERNATIONAL $

(097-231 0361; Corniche an-Nil; mains E£25-50; noon-late) One of the best of the Nile-side restaurants, with several terraces and a freezing air-con dining room. The menu has Egyptian, Nubian and international dishes, a notch better than most restaurants in Aswan. The service is efficient and the beers (E£20) are cold. There is also a terrace on which to smoke a sheesha.

**Nubian Beach** EGYPTIAN $$

(West Bank; set menu per person E£65) Nubian cafe-restaurant set in a quiet garden on the west bank of the Nile, against the backdrop of a towering sand dune and near a popular swimming spot. When it's too hot or on colder evenings, you can also chill out in their beautifully painted indoor room. The food is simple but good, and beer is sometimes served.

**★ Panorama Restaurant & Bar** INTERNATIONAL **$$$**
(☎ 097-230 3455; www.movenpick.com; Mövenpick Resort Aswan, Elephantine Island; mains E£90-160; ⏲ noon-11pm) The Panorama is the best thing to open in Aswan, and in the Mövenpick's eyesore tower, in a long time. The food is good, service friendly and efficient, and the room elegant; but the real draw is the 360-degree view of Aswan, the river and the desert.

## ℹ Information

**Main Tourist Office** (☎ 097-231 2811; Midan al-Mahatta; ⏲ 8am-3pm Sat-Thu) This tourist office has little material, and little access to any, but staff can advise on timetables and give an idea of prices for taxis and feluccas.

## ℹ Getting There & Away

Driving north from Aswan to Luxor no longer needs to be done in convoy, but there is still a twice-daily (4am and 11am) convoy to Abu Simbel, compulsory for foreigners. **Armed convoys** congregate at the beginning of Sharia Sadat, near the Coptic Cathedral. Be there at least 15 minutes in advance. It takes at least three hours to reach Abu Simbel.

### AIR

**Aswan Airport** (☎ 097-248 0333) is located 25km southwest of town. EgyptAir has several flights daily to Cairo and three flights per day to Abu Simbel, Sunday to Thursday.

### BOAT

Aswan is the most popular starting point for Nile cruises. It's also the best place to arrange an overnight or multiday felucca trip.

#### Wadi Halfa Ferry to Sudan

The ferry to Wadi Halfa in Sudan (1st/2nd class E£520/380) leaves every Sunday and Wednesday. Purchase tickets in advance from the **Nile River Valley Transport Corporation** (☎ 097-244 0384, 011 8316 0926; ⏲ 8am-2pm Sat-Thu), in the shopping arcade behind the tourist police office. The journey is supposed to take 16 hours but usually takes considerably longer.

With buses now running to Wadi Halfa, many travellers prefer to take the land route.

Although the ferry generally doesn't leave until early afternoon, you should be at the port by 8.30am. You can get to the port by train.

### BUS

The bus station is 3.5km north of the train station. Services are run by Upper Egypt Bus Co. A taxi there will cost E£15, or it's E£1 in a microbus from downtown.

| DESTINATION | PRICE | DURATION | TIME |
|---|---|---|---|
| Abu Simbel | E£40 | 4hr | 8am & 5pm |
| Cairo | E£130 | 14hr | 4pm |
| Hurghada | E£80 | 7hr | 6am, 3pm & 5pm |
| Marsa Alam | E£40 | 3hr | 5am |

### TRAIN

There are 10 trains daily from **Aswan Train Station** (☎ 097-231 4754; https://enr.gov.eg; Midan al-Mahatta) to Luxor and onward to Cairo. Check trains schedules beforehand at Aswan's helpful tourist office as service order does change. All trains stop at Daraw, Kom Ombo, Edfu and Esna.

# Philae

Perched on the island of Philae (fee-*leh*), the Temple of Isis attracted pilgrims for thousands of years and was one of the last pagan temples to operate after the arrival of Christianity.

**Temple of Isis** TEMPLE
(adult/child E£60/30; ⏲ 7am-4pm Oct-May, to 5pm Jun-Sep) The boat to the temple leaves you at the base of the Kiosk of Nectanebo, the oldest part of the Philae complex. Heading north, you walk down the outer temple court, which has colonnades running along both sides; the western one is the most complete, with windows that originally overlooked the island of Bigga. At the end is the entrance of the Temple of Isis, marked by the 18m-high towers of the first pylon with reliefs of Ptolemy XII Neos Dionysos smiting enemies.

**Sound & Light Show** SHOW
(www.soundandlight.com.eg; adult/child E£70/50; ⏲ shows 6.30pm, 7.45pm & 8.45pm Oct-May, 7pm, 8.15pm & 9.30pm Jun-Sep) Although the commentary is predictably cheesy, you really can't beat strolling through Philae's temple at night. Show times, with commentary in alternate languages depending on schedule, have a habit of changing, so it's best to double-check the timetable with the Aswan tourist office.

## ℹ Getting There & Away

Combo-tours of Philae and the Aswan High Dam, including guide, can be arranged by most hotels and travel agencies in Aswan, for around E£150 per person. The return taxi fare is about E£60.

# Abu Simbel

☎097

Laid-back and quiet, the town of Abu Simbel lies 280km south of Aswan and only 40km north of the Sudanese border. Few tourists linger more than the few hours needed to visit the colossal temples for which it is famous. But anyone interested in Lake Nasser, in seeing the temples without the crowds, in wandering around a small nontouristy Nubian town without a police escort, or in listening to Nubian music might choose to hang around for a day or two.

## Sights

**Temples of Abu Simbel** TEMPLE
(adult/student incl guide fee E£115/63.50; ⏲6am-5pm Oct-Apr, to 6pm May-Sep) Overlooking Lake Nasser, the Great Temple of Ramses II and the Temple of Hathor, which together make up the Temples of Abu Simbel, are among the most famous and spectacular monuments in Egypt. In a modern marvel of engineering, which matches Ramses II's original construction for sheer audacity, the temple complex was saved from being swallowed by rising waters and lost forever after the building of the High Dam, by being moved lock, stock and barrel to the position it sits upon today.

**Great Temple of Ramses II** TEMPLE
Carved out of the mountain on the west bank of the Nile between 1274 and 1244 BC, this main temple of the Abu Simbel complex was as much dedicated to the deified Ramses II himself as to Ra-Horakhty, Amun and Ptah. The four colossal statues of the pharaoh, which front the temple, are like gigantic sentinels watching over the incoming traffic from the south, undoubtedly designed as a warning of the strength of the pharaoh.

## Sleeping

**Abu Simbel Village** HOTEL $
(☎097-340 0092; s/d E£80/100; ❄) The only reason to recommend the Abu Simbel Village is its price: its basic, vaulted rooms are tired and not always clean, but it is the cheapest option for staying in Abu Simbel, which you have to do if you want to get to the temples at dawn or see the Sound & Light Show. Take meals in town.

★**Eskaleh** GUESTHOUSE $$
(☎097-340 1288, 012 2368 0521; www.eskaleh.net; d €60-70; ❄@📶) Part Nubian cultural centre with a library dedicated to Nubian history, part ecolodge in a traditional mud-brick house, Eskaleh is by far the most interesting place to stay or eat in Abu Simbel. It's also a destination in its own right and a perfect base for a visit to the temples. It's known locally as the Nubian house (Beit an-Nubi).

## Entertainment

**Sound & Light Show** SHOW
(www.soundandlight.com.eg; adult/child E£100/50; ⏲shows 6.30pm & 7.30pm Oct-Apr, 7.30pm May-Sep) A sound-and-light show is performed nightly at Abu Simbel. Headphones are provided, allowing visitors to listen to the commentary in various languages. While the text is flowery and forgettable, the laser show projected on to the temples is stunning and well worth the detour. Shows are only held with a minimum of 10 spectators.

## Getting There & Away

The vast majority of visitors to Abu Simbel come here on an organised tour from Aswan. All the hotels, cruise ships and travel agencies in Aswan can arrange tours. Budget trips – which basically just include return transport with two hours at the site – start from about E£140.

# UNDERSTAND EGYPT

## Egypt Today

Egypt was long seen as the land of eternity, where nothing ever changed. That image has been shattered by recent events, but some things remain: Egypt's location, its huge population and its control of the Suez Canal ensure that it is still a major player in the region. Even with the turmoil following the downfall of two presidents in as many years, it still enjoys great prestige in diplomacy, the arts and as a moderate Islamic country.

### After Mubarak

In the aftermath of the 'Arab Spring', Egypt continues to be shaken by internal strife as it struggles to define its identity as a moderate, pluralistic yet overwhelmingly Islamic country. Whatever might come in the following years, it is hard to overstate the significance of the fall of the old regime. When interim president Adli Mansour handed over to Sisi in June 2014, it was the first time an incumbent Egyptian president had ever relinquished power. Sisi's rule so far, though, has struggled to address Egypt's political and economic instability. Mass poverty, poor education, growing sectarian conflict, the Israeli-Palestinian deadlock and economic turmoil are all, to some degree, interconnected, and none of them can be resolved easily. Steps in 2016 to devalue the Egyptian pound and slash subsidies, in order to secure a US$12-billion loan from the IMF and stimulate the economy, have, in the short term, resulted in sky-rocketing prices that have hit the poorest segments of Egyptian society the hardest.

The role of the armed forces, one of the taboo subjects under Mubarak, has become one of the main bones of contention in post-revolution Egypt. But with a former defence minister and field marshal as president, the independence and power of the armed forces remains unchallenged as yet. The continuing crackdown on journalists and political opponents also hampers efforts to fully confront this and Egypt's other controversial issues.

It remains to be seen whether the new regime will allow the sort of independent, open government that is needed to address the country's problems.

# History

## Old, Middle & New Kingdoms

Ancient Egyptian history comprises three principal kingdoms. The pyramids date from the Old Kingdom (2670–2150 BC), when lively trade made ambitious building projects possible. Ruling from the nearby capital of Memphis, Pharaoh Zoser and his chief architect, Imhotep, built the pyramid at Saqqara. Subsequent pharaohs constructed ever larger temples and pyramids, which eventually culminated in the mighty pyramids of Giza, built for Cheops, Chephren and Mycerinus.

The Middle Kingdom (2056–1650 BC) was marked by the rise of a new and illustrious capital at Thebes (Luxor). It was during the period of the New Kingdom (1550–1076 BC), however, that ancient Egyptian culture blossomed. Wonders such as the Temple of Karnak and the West Bank tombs were the visible expression of a rich culture that established Egypt, under the great dynasties of Tuthmosis and Ramses, as the greatest regional power.

## From Alexander to Sadat

From the year 1184 BC, Egypt disintegrated into local principalities, and it wasn't until Alexander the Great arrived in the 4th century BC that the country was reunited. For the next 300 years, Egypt was ruled from Alexandria by the descendants of his general, Ptolemy.

The Romans arrived in 31 BC, leaving behind little to show for their occupation except the introduction of Christianity in AD 2. In AD 640, Arab armies brought Islam to Egypt. With it came a cultural revival and the foundation of Cairo in AD 969 by the Fatimid dynasty. The arts and sciences flourished, and trade brought much wealth into the country. But the Turks found the prize irresistible, and in the early 16th century, Egypt became part of the Ottoman Empire.

The French followed suit during the 19th century under Napoleon, and then the British made Egypt a protectorate during WWI. After nearly 2000 years of colonisation, revolution resulted in self-rule in 1952.

Gamal Abdel Nasser became Egypt's first president in 1956, and established his authority by buying out French and British claims to the Suez Canal. He did, however, lose the 1967 war with Israel. His successor, Anwar Sadat, who came to power in 1970, concluded the second war with Israel with the controversial 1978 Camp David Accords. Widely blamed for betraying pan-Arabist principles, Sadat was assassinated by a member of the extremist organisation Islamic Jihad in 1981.

## The Mubarak Era

Sadat's successor, Hosni Mubarak, retaliated against the extremists, declaring a state of emergency that continued throughout his presidency. Although Mubarak was canny in rehabilitating Egypt's relations with Arab states, harsh socio-economic domestic conditions, continual government crackdowns on legitimate opposition and abuses by Mubarak's security forces meant his rule was marked by violence. During the 1990s Egyptian Islamist extremist groups began to target tourism, the state's most valuable source of income, in their campaign to overthrow the government. This culminated in the massacre of 58 holidaymakers at the Funerary Temple of Hatshepsut in 1997. The following decade saw further bombings in the Sinai holiday centres of Taba, Sharm el-Sheikh and Dahab, resulting in multiple deaths and a serious decline in tourism.

Mubarak introduced some minor democratic measures in 2005, but with Egypt's economy in turmoil and with an evergrowing population and rising unemployment, this wasn't enough to stop the tide of disenchantment with his regime.

## People

Egypt has the third-highest population in Africa. Growing at a rate of 2% annually, it places enormous strain on infrastructure and the national economy. Unemployment is officially 12%; unofficially, it's much higher. About 90% of Egypt's population is Muslim, with Coptic Christians being the largest minority.

## Cuisine

Egyptian food is good, fresh, honest peasant fare that packs an occasional sensational punch. Pulses feature large on the menu, and come cooked in a stew, as a soup or fried in patties as falafel. Meat is increasingly becoming a luxury, but if they can afford it Egyptians love their kebabs and *kofta*. Lamb and chicken are the most common meats. There's plenty of coastline to reel in the fruits of the Mediterranean and Red Seas, although much fish also comes from the Nile.

# SURVIVAL GUIDE

## Directory A–Z

### ACCOMMODATION

It's generally only necessary to book your accommodation in advance if you are planning to visit during the Christmas, Easter and half-term school holidays.

**Hotels** Range from dusty fleapits to deluxe accommodation in the larger cities and resorts. In smaller towns accommodation is mostly limited to basic options.

**B&Bs** Less common in Egypt, and places that call themselves that are often small family-run one- or two-star hotels.

**Camping** Only recommended in Sinai, when the situation there calms down.

### ELECTRICITY

Electricity has become increasingly unreliable since 2011 and everywhere in Egypt, including central Cairo, suffers regular, usually daily, outages.

### EMBASSIES & CONSULATES

Embassies are in Cairo.

**Australian Embassy** (Map p70; 02-2770 6600; www.egypt.embassy.gov.au; 11th fl, World Trade Centre, 1191 Corniche el-Nil, Cairo; 8am-4.15pm Sun-Wed, to 1.30pm Thu)

**Canadian Embassy** (Map p70; 02-2461 2200; www.canadainternational.gc.ca/egypt-egypte; 18th fl, South Tower, Nile City Towers, 2005 Corniche el-Nil, Cairo; 8am-4.30pm Sun-Wed, to 1.30pm Thu)

**Dutch Embassy** (Map p70; 02-2739 5500; http://egypt.nlembassy.org; 18 Sharia Hassan Sabry, Zamalek, Cairo; 8am-5pm Sun-Thu)

**French Embassy** (Map p70; 02-3567 3200; www.ambafrance-eg.org; 29 Sharia Charles de Gaulle, Giza, Cairo; 9.30am-5pm Sun-Thu)

**German Embassy** (Map p70; 02-2728 2000; www.kairo.diplo.de; 2 Sharia Berlin, off Sharia Hassan Sabry, Zamalek, Cairo; 8am-3pm Sun-Thu)

**Irish Embassy** (Map p70; 02-2728 7100; www.dfa.ie/irish-embassy/egypt/; 18 Sharia Hassan Sabry, Zamalek, Cairo; 9am-3pm Sun-Thu)

**Israeli Embassy** (Map p70; 02-2359 7304; http://embassies.gov.il; 6 Sharia Ibn Malek, Giza, Cairo; 9am-4pm Sun-Thu)

**Italian Embassy** (Map p70; 02-2794 3194; www.ambilcairo.esteri.it; 15 Sharia Abd al-Rahman Fahmy, Garden City, Cairo; 9am-3.30pm Sun-Thu)

**Jordanian Embassy** (Map p70; 02-3749 9912, 02-3748 5566; 6 Sharia Gohainy, Doqqi, Cairo; 9am-3pm Mon-Thu)

**Lebanese Embassy** (Map p70; 02-2738 2823; 22 Sharia Mansour Mohammed, Zamalek, Cairo; 9.30am-12pm Sat-Thu)

**New Zealand Embassy** (Map p70; 02-2461 6000; www.mfat.govt.nz; Level 8, North Tower, Nile City Towers, 2005 Corniche el-Nil, Cairo; 9am-3pm Sun-Thu)

**Saudi Arabian Embassy** (Map p70; 02-3762 5000; http://embassies.mofa.gov.sa; 2 Sharia al-Yaman, Giza, Cairo; 9am-4pm Sun-Thu)

**South Sudanese Embassy** (02-2358 6513; www.erssegypt.com; 53 Sharia El Nadi, Maadi; 9am-3pm Sun-Thu)

**Spanish Embassy** (Map p70; 02-2735 6462; www.exteriores.gob.es; 41 Sharia Ismail Mohammed, Zamalek, Cairo; 8am-3.30pm Sun-Thu)

### ASWAN HIGH DAM

Egypt's modern example of construction on a monumental scale, the controversial **Aswan High Dam** (As-Sadd al-Ali; adult/child E£20/10), 13km south of Aswan, contains 18 times the amount of material used in the Great Pyramid of Khufu and it created Lake Nasser, the world's largest artificial lake.

Most people visit the High Dam as part of an organised trip to sights south of Aswan. A visit here is often included with Philae Temple, but can also be combined with a trip to the Temple of Kalabsha.

**Sudanese Embassy** (Map p70; ☎02-3748 5648; 3 Sharia Ahmed Ali al-Shatouri, Doqqi, Cairo; ⏰9am-4pm Sun-Thu)

**Turkish Embassy** (Map p70; ☎02-2797 8410; http://cairo.emb.mfa.gov.tr; 25 Sharia Falaki, Mounira, Cairo; ⏰9am-1pm & 1.30-5.30pm Sun-Thu)

**UK Embassy** (Map p70; ☎02-2791 6000; www.ukinegypt.fco.gov.uk; 7 Sharia Ahmed Ragheb, Garden City, Cairo; ⏰8am-3.30pm Sun-Wed, to 2pm Thu)

**US Embassy** (Map p74; ☎02-2797 3300; https://eg.usembassy.gov/; 5 Sharia Tawfiq Diab, Garden City, Cairo; ⏰9am-4pm Sun-Thu)

## INTERNET ACCESS

Free wi-fi is widely available in hotels throughout Egypt, though it's not always fast and often doesn't reach all the guest rooms. Many cafes in Cairo, and tourist centres such as Luxor and Dahab, also have free wi-fi.

Internet cafes are common, if not rampant; rates are usually between E£5 and E£10 per hour.

## LGBTIQ TRAVELLERS

Egypt is a conservative society that increasingly condemns homosexuality. Although homosexuality is technically not a crime in Egypt, gay men can be prosecuted using debauchery and public morals laws with prison terms of up to 17 years.

As long as common sense discretion is used and public displays of affection are avoided, foreign gay or lesbian couples should have no issues. Most midrange and top-end accommodation will have no problem with a same-sex couple requesting a double bed but it's advisable to steer clear of the very budget end of the accommodation market, particularly in nontouristy towns.

Lesbian travellers are unlikely to encounter any problems in the country. For the majority of Egyptians, lesbianism is unfathomable and most would declare that there is no such thing as an Egyptian lesbian. Gay male travellers should also be aware that signals in Egypt can be ambiguous; Egyptian men routinely hold hands, link arms and kiss each other on the cheek in greeting.

## MONEY

ATMs are widely available. Credit cards are only accepted at higher-end businesses. There is a major shortage of small change; large bills can be difficult to break.

### Exchange Rates

| | | |
|---|---|---|
| Australia | A$1 | E£12 |
| Canada | C$1 | E£12 |
| Europe | €1 | E£16.6 |
| Israel | 1NIS | E£4.2 |
| Japan | ¥100 | E£14 |
| Jordan | JD1 | E£22.2 |
| New Zealand | NZ$1 | E£11.3 |
| UK | £1 | E£19.6 |
| USA | US$1 | E£15.7 |

For current exchange rates see www.xe.com.

## OPENING HOURS

The weekend is Friday and Saturday; some businesses close Sunday. During Ramadan, offices, museums and tourist sites keep shorter hours.

**Banks** 8.30am–2.30pm Sunday to Thursday

**Bars and clubs** Early evening until 3am, often later (particularly in Cairo)

**Cafes** 7am–1am

**Government offices** 8am–2pm Sunday to Thursday; tourist offices are generally open longer

**Post offices** 8.30am–2pm Saturday to Thursday

**Private offices** 10am–2pm and 4pm–9pm Saturday to Thursday

**Restaurants** Noon–midnight

**Shops** 9am–1pm and 5pm–10pm June to September, 10am–6pm October to May; in Cairo shops generally open 10am–11pm

## PUBLIC HOLIDAYS

Businesses and government offices also close on major Islamic holidays.

**New Year's Day** 1 January

**Coptic Christmas** 7 January

**January 25 Revolution Day** 25 January

**Sham an-Nessim** The first Monday after Coptic Easter (March/April)

**Sinai Liberation Day** 25 April

**May Day** 1 May

**Revolution Day** 23 July

**Armed Forces Day** 6 October

## TIME

Egypt is two hours ahead of GMT/UTC.

## TOURIST INFORMATION

The Egyptian Tourist Authority (www.egypt.travel) has offices throughout the country. Individual office staff members may be helpful, but often they're just doling out rather dated maps and brochures. The smaller towns and oases tend to have better offices than the big cities. In short, don't rely on these tourist offices, but don't rule them out either.

## VISAS

Visas are required for all foreigners visiting Egypt, excepting nationals of certain Arab countries. Many nationalities can purchase a visa on arrival including all EU, Australian, Canadian, Japanese, New Zealander and US passport holders.

➡ Tourist visas purchased on arrival cost US$25 and are valid for 30 days. The visa can be purchased in US dollars, euros or British pounds.

➡ If you want more time or a multiple-entry visa, apply in advance or get an extension with multiple-entry once in Egypt.

➡ If you are arriving by ferry from Jordan into Nuweiba, visas are available at Nuweiba port. Entering from Eilat in Israel, through the Taba land border, the free Sinai-only entry stamp is normally issued. Alternatively, apply in advance at the Egyptian Embassy in Tel Aviv or the consulate in Eilat.

### WOMEN TRAVELLERS

Lots of women travel solo in Egypt and most have a great time in the country. Travelling alone as a female though is unfathomable to many Egyptians so expect a lot of attention. Some of this is welcome; as a lone female you're more likely, than a single male or travelling couple, to be befriended by families and local women and garner invites to people's houses. Unfortunately though, you're also more likely to encounter some unwelcome attention as well.

Egypt has a bad reputation for sexual harassment. For the most part, this comes in the form of wearying amounts of cat-calling, declarations of love, leering or being followed down the street, and minor groping in crowds or closed-in spaces such as buses or taxis. Attitudes are slowly changing. Sexual harassment was made a criminal offence in Egypt in June 2014.

## PRICE RANGES

The following price ranges refer to a double room, with breakfast included, in high season (November to February), including taxes.

**$** less than E£400 (US$25)

**$$** E£400–1600 (US$25–100)

**$$$** more than E£1600 (US$100)

The following price categories are for a typical main dish.

**$** less than E£50 (US$3)

**$$** E£50–80 (US$3–5)

**$$$** more than E£80 (US$5)

## Getting There & Away

### AIR

**EgyptAir** (www.egyptair.com.eg) is the national carrier.

**Cairo International Airport** (p1073) Egypt's main entry point, served by most international carriers.

**Burg al-Arab Airport** (p79) Alexandria's airport mostly receives flights from Middle Eastern and North African cities.

**Hurghada Airport** (p86) Receives mainly charter international flights.

**Luxor Airport** (p91) Very few international direct flights; EgyptAir flies direct from London Heathrow.

### LAND

#### Israel & the Palestinian Territories

The Taba border is the main entry/exit point between Egypt and Israel. Technically only the free Sinai-only entry stamp is issued here and full Egyptian visas have to bought in advance. In reality, a full Egyptian visa can be purchased here after paying an extra fee to a local Taba travel agency. Departure tax from Israel is 101NIS. Departure tax from Egypt is E£75. Entry procedures can be slightly shambolic on the Egyptian side.

#### Sudan

The two land border crossings between Egypt and Sudan reopened in 2014 and a number of Sudanese bus companies now operate Aswan–Wadi Halfa–Khartoum services. The Qustul border crossing is the border most commonly used.

From Aswan, buses drive to Abu Simbel and cross Lake Nasser on a vehicle ferry (one hour) to Qustul, from where it's a short drive (15 minutes) to the border. After all border formalities are finalised the bus carries on to Wadi Halfa and then onward to Khartoum.

If travelling to Sudan, you need to purchase your Sudanese visa beforehand in either Cairo or Aswan. Travelling north from Sudan into Egypt, Egyptian visas are issued at the border. Egyptian departure tax is E£50.

### SEA

AB Maritime (www.abmaritime.com.jo) runs both a daily fast and slow passenger ferry connecting Nuweiba in Egypt and Aqaba in Jordan. The service is noted for its delays. Both Egyptian and Jordanian visas are available on arrival.

## Getting Around

Transport in Egypt is fairly efficient and very reasonably priced. Be aware that due to security concerns, some areas and transport modes are off limits to foreign travellers.

**Air** Most domestic flights go through Cairo. When using EgyptAir's website, switch your home location to Egypt to get the cheapest domestic fares.

**Train** The most comfortable option for travelling to Alexandria, Luxor and Aswan. The two classes of trains – Spanish and the more expensive Special – both have air-con 1st- and 2nd-class seats.

**Bus** There are frequent buses between Egyptian cities. Buses are comfortable and reliable. Book in advance.

**Car** It is not advisable to drive in Cairo, but cars with driver are readily available and reasonably priced.

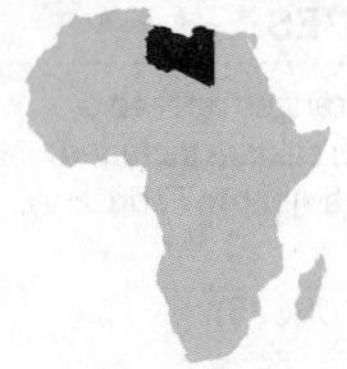

# Libya

**Includes ➡**



## Fast Facts

**Capital** Tripoli

**Population** 6.54 million

**Languages** Arabic, Berber

**Area** 1.759 million sq km

**Currency** Libyan dinar (LD)

## Ancient Ruins & Saharan Sand

Libya is an ancient crossroads of civilisations that bequeathed to the Libyan coast some of the finest Roman and Greek ruins in existence, among them Leptis Magna, Cyrene and Sabratha. Libya also has some of the most beautiful corners of the Sahara Desert, from seas of sand the size of Switzerland and sheltering palm-fringed lakes (the Ubari Sand Sea) to remote massifs adorned with prehistoric rock art (the Jebel Acacus), labyrinthine caravan towns (Ghadames) and an isolated black-as-black volcano (Wawa al-Namus) in the desert's heart.

The upheaval caused by Libya's revolution in 2011 and 2012 continues and the whole country remains off-limits to travellers with chronic instability and ongoing conflict.

## Libya at a Glance

**Leptis Magna** One of the world's best-preserved Roman cities looks out across the Mediterranean.

**Tripoli** An atmospheric whitewashed medina and a world-class museum.

**Ghadames** The Sahara's most enchanting oasis town with a labyrinth of covered passageways shadowed by palm gardens.

**Cyrene** This extraordinary ancient city has some of North Africa's finest monuments to Ancient Greece.

**Jebel Acacus** A jagged Saharan massif with 12,000-year-old rock art, Tuareg inhabitants and extraordinary scenery.

**Ubari Lakes** Idyllic lakes surrounded by exquisite sand dunes in one of the world's largest and most beautiful sand seas.

**Waw al Namus** A black-sand volcano sheltering multicoloured lakes and otherworldly scenery.

# UNDERSTAND LIBYA

## Libya Today

Libya is a country awakening from a nightmare, but it's not over yet. Qaddafi may no longer rule over the country, but the country is deeply divided, not in two, but rather into as many fiefdoms as there are armed militias. It's difficult to see from where true peace will come, but if the number of Libyans who turn out to vote is any indication, they haven't quite given up hope yet.

In the west, militias from Zintan and Misrata each control large swathes of territory and refuse to recognise the elected governments. In the east, around Benghazi, renegade General Khalifa Haftar battles militant Islamists in a devastating turf war that has destroyed large parts of Libya's second city. Into the power vacuum has stepped the so-called Islamic State, including many battle-hardened veterans of the war in Syria and Iraq; for a time they controlled Derna and Sirt. And all the while, rival governments – one in Tripoli backed by the UN as a unity government, one in Tobruk voted to power in earlier elections – claim to be the rightful administration. In the short term, Libya's future looks bleak. The path to a peaceful future is a complicated one that must resolve or remove at least two major roadblocks: the ongoing power of armed militias and the difficulties of the government – whoever that may be – in asserting effective control over the country.

**WARNING**

There is nowhere in Libya that is currently considered safe to travel. Terrorist attacks and the threat of kidnapping remain extremely high across the country. Although fighting is not constant everywhere, car bombings and the escalation of tensions into outright military conflict are a serious risk.

## History

### The Great Civilisations of Antiquity

From 700 BC, Lebdah (Leptis Magna), Oea (Tripoli) and Sabratha formed some of the links in a chain of safe Phoenician (Punic) ports stretching from the Levant around to Spain. Traces of the Phoenician presence in Libya remain at Sabratha and Leptis Magna.

On the advice of the Oracle of Delphi, in 631 BC Greek settlers established the city of Cyrene in the east of Libya. Within 200 years the Greeks had built four more cities of splendour as part of the Pentapolis (Five Cities), which included Apollonia. But with Greek influence on the wane, the last Greek ruler, Ptolemy Apion, finally bequeathed the region of Cyrenaica to Rome in 75 BC.

Meanwhile, the fall of the Punic capital at Carthage (in Tunisia) prompted Julius Caesar to formally annex Tripolitania in 46 BC. The Pax Romana saw Tripolitania and Cyrenaica become prosperous Roman provinces. Such was Libya's importance that a Libyan, Septimius Severus, became Rome's emperor (r AD 193–211).

### Islamic Libya

By AD 643, Tripoli and Cyrenaica had fallen to the armies of Islam. From 800, the Abbasid-appointed emirs of the Aghlabid dynasty repaired Roman irrigation systems, restoring order and bringing a measure of prosperity to the region, while the mass migration of two tribes – the Bani Salim and Bani Hilal – from the Arabian Peninsula forever changed Libya's demographics. The Berber tribespeople were displaced from their traditional lands and the new settlers cemented the cultural and linguistic Arabisation of the region.

After centuries of rule by local and other North African Islamic dynasties, the Ottomans occupied Tripoli in 1551. The soldiers sent by the sultan to support the Ottoman pasha (governor) grew powerful and cavalry officer Ahmed Karamanli seized power in 1711. His Karamanli dynasty would last 124 years. The Ottoman Turks finally reined in their erstwhile protégés in 1835 and resumed direct control over much of Libya.

On 3 October 1911 the Italians attacked Tripoli, claiming to be liberating Libya from Ottoman rule. During almost three decades of brutal Italian rule, a quarter of Libya's population died as a result of the occupation, whether from direct military attacks, starvation or forced migration.

With the onset of WWII, devastating fighting broke out in the area around Tobruk. By January 1943, Tripoli was in British hands and by February the last German and Italian soldiers were driven from Libya.

# Libya

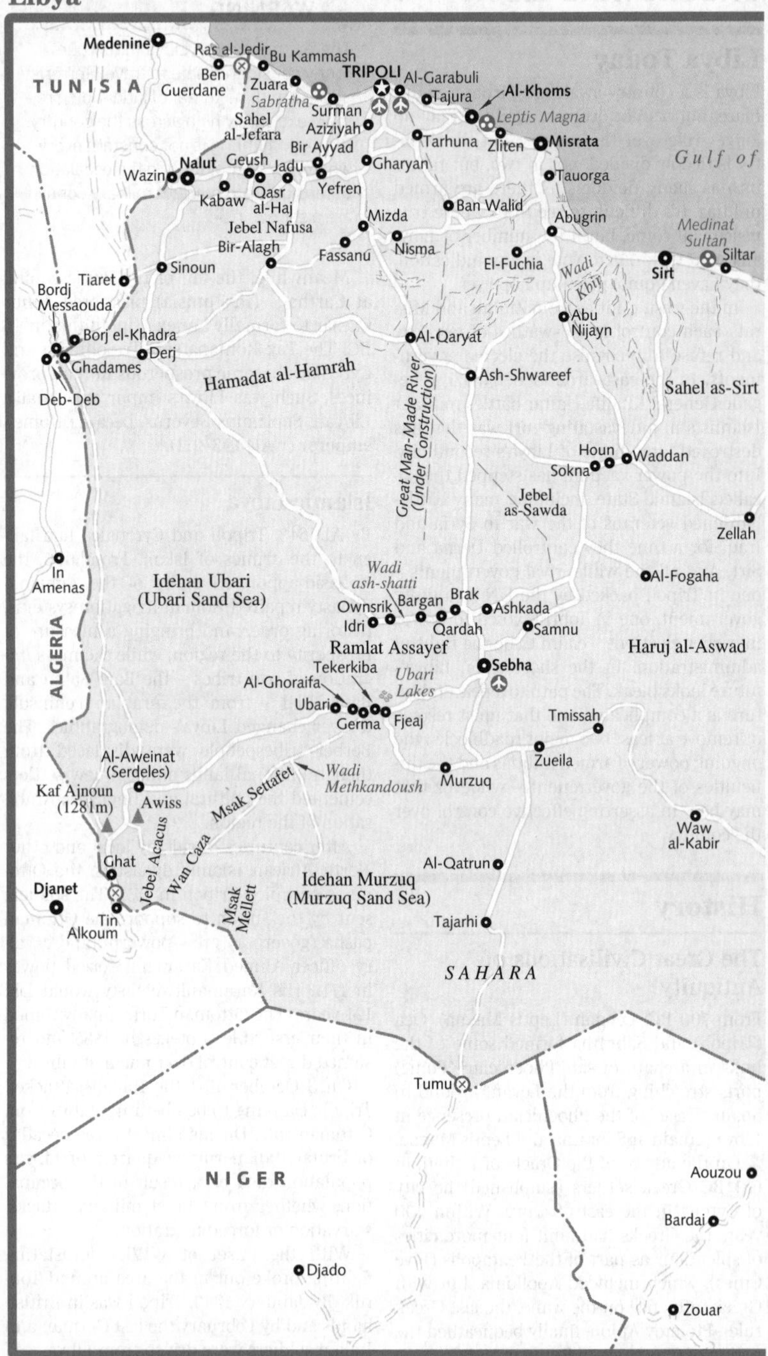
Medenine
Ras al-Jedir
Bu Kammash
Ben Guerdane
TUNISIA
Zuara
Sabratha
TRIPOLI
Al-Garabuli
Tajura
Al-Khoms
Leptis Magna
Surman
Sahel al-Jefara
Aziziyah
Tarhuna
Zliten
Misrata
Gulf of
Bir Ayyad
Nalut
Geush
Jadu
Gharyan
Wazin
Qasr al-Haj
Yefren
Kabaw
Tauorga
Ban Walid
Abugrin
Jebel Nafusa
Mizda
Medinat Sultan
Bir-Alagh
Fassanu
Nisma
El-Fuchia
Sirt
Siltar
Sinoun
Wadi Kbir
Tiaret
Bordj Messaouda
Abu Nijayn
Borj el-Khadra
Al-Qaryat
Derj
Ghadames
Hamadat al-Hamrah
Ash-Shwareef
Deb-Deb
Sahel as-Sirt
LIBYA
Great Man-Made River (Under Construction)
Houn
Waddan
Sokna
Jebel as-Sawda
Zellah
In Amenas
Idehan Ubari (Ubari Sand Sea)
Wadi ash-shatti
Al-Fogaha
Brak
Ownsrik
Bargan
Ashkada
Idri
Qardah
Samnu
ALGERIA
Ramlat Assayef
Haruj al-Aswad
Tekerkiba
Sebha
Al-Ghoraifa
Ubari Lakes
Ubari
Germa
Fjeaj
Tmissah
Zueila
Al-Aweinat (Serdeles)
Wadi Methkandoush
Murzuq
Kaf Ajnoun (1281m)
Awiss
Msak Settafet
Waw al-Kabir
Jebel Acacus
Ghat
Wan Caza
Al-Qatrun
Djanet
Idehan Murzuq (Murzuq Sand Sea)
Msak Mellett
Tin Alkoum
Tajarhi
SAHARA
Tumu
NIGER
Aouzou
Bardai
Djado
Zouar

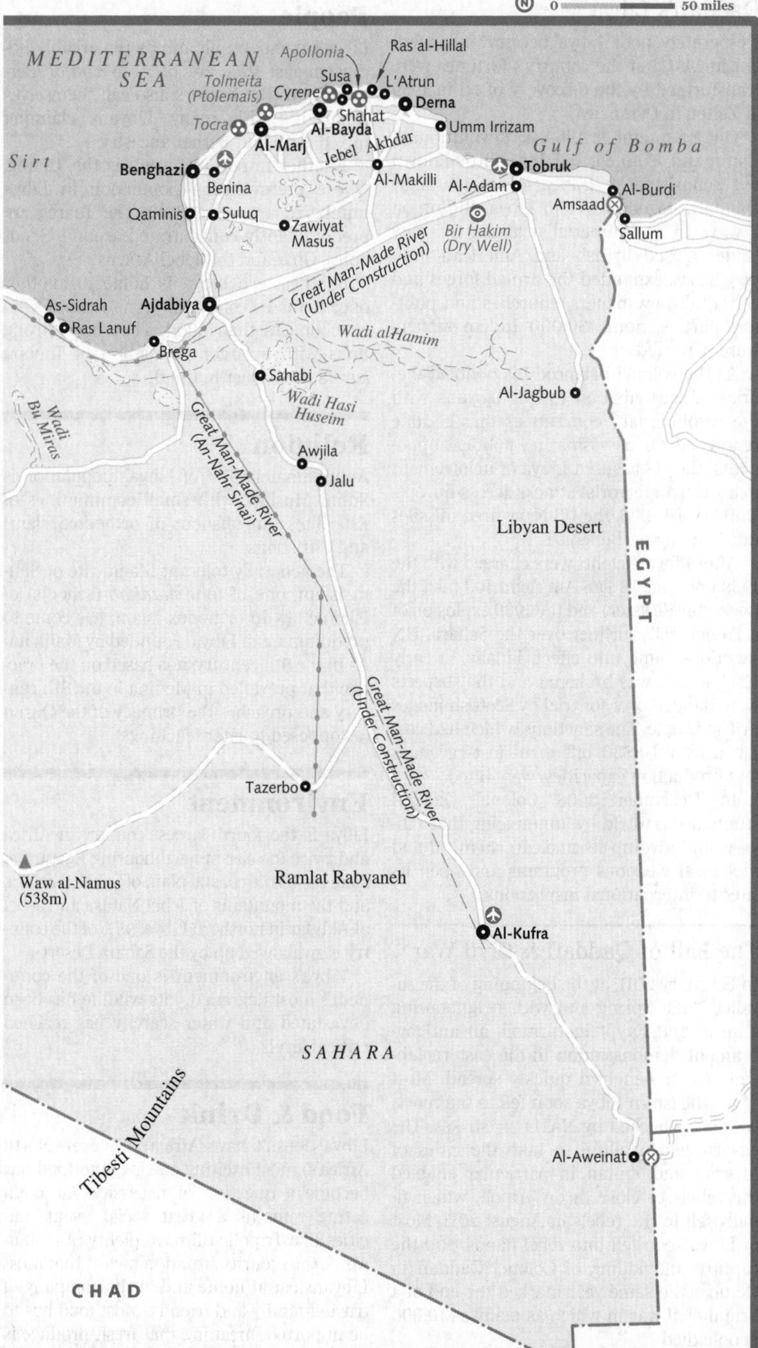
0 100 km
0 50 miles
MEDITERRANEAN SEA
Apollonia
Ras al-Hillal
Tolmeita (Ptolemais)
Susa
L'Atrun
Cyrene
Shahat
Derna
Tocra
Al-Marj
Al-Bayda
Umm Irrizam
Gulf of Bomba
Jebel Akhdar
Sirt
Benghazi
Benina
Tobruk
Al-Makilli
Al-Adam
Al-Burdi
Amsaad
Sallum
Qaminis
Suluq
Zawiyat Masus
Bir Hakim (Dry Well)
Great Man-Made River (Under Construction)
As-Sidrah
Ajdabiya
Ras Lanuf
Brega
Wadi al Hamim
Sahabi
Wadi Hasi Huseim
Wadi Bu Miras
Al-Jagbub
LIBYA
Great Man-Made River (An-Nahr Sinai)
Awjila
Jalu
Libyan Desert
EGYPT
Great Man-Made River (Under Construction)
Tazerbo
Waw al-Namus (538m)
Ramlat Rabyaneh
Al-Kufra
SAHARA
Tibesti Mountains
Al-Aweinat
CHAD

## Qaddafi's Libya

Desperately poor Libya became independent in 1951, but the country's fortunes were transformed by the discovery of oil in 1959 at Zelten in Cyrenaica.

On 1 September 1969, a Revolutionary Command Council, led by a little-known but charismatic 27-year-old Muammar Qaddafi, seized power in Libya. Riding on a wave of anti-imperialist anger, the new leader closed British and American military bases, expanded the armed forces and closed all newspapers, churches and political parties. Some 30,000 Italian settlers were deported.

As the colonel balanced his political theories of participation for all Libyans with the revolutionary committees that became renowned for assassinating political opponents, the US accused Libya of involvement in a string of terrorist attacks across Europe. On 15 April 1986, the US Navy fired missiles into Tripoli and Benghazi.

After Libyan agents were charged with the 1988 bombing of Pan Am flight 103 (aka the Lockerbie disaster) and the 1989 explosion of a French UTA airliner over the Sahara, UN sanctions came into effect. Finally, in early 1999, a deal was brokered and the suspects were handed over for trial by Scottish judges in The Hague. The sanctions, which had cost Libya over US$30 billion in lost revenues and production capacities, were lifted.

In December 2003 Colonel Qaddafi stunned the world by announcing that Libya would give up its nuclear, chemical and biological weapons programs and open its sites to international inspections.

## The Fall of Qaddafi & Civil War

In February 2011, at the beginning of the so-called Arab Spring and with neighbouring Tunisia and Egypt in turmoil, an antigovernment demonstration in the eastern Libyan city of Benghazi quickly spread. Most of northeastern Libya soon fell to the rebels who were backed by NATO air strikes. The government's failure to take the cities of Misrata and Zintan in particular enabled the rebels to close in on Tripoli, which finally fell to the rebels in August 2011. Most of Libya soon fell into rebel hands, and the capture and killing of Colonel Qaddafi in October the same year marked the end of a brutal civil war in which as many as 10,000 people died.

# People

Libya's demographic mix is remarkably homogeneous: 97% are of Arab and/or Berber origin (the Berbers also call themselves Amazigh), with many Libyans claiming mixed Arab and Berber ancestry.

Another important group is the Tuareg, whose prerevolution population in Libya numbered around 50,000. The Tuareg are predominantly concentrated around Ghadames, Ghat and the Jebel Acacus.

Southeastern Libya is home to another once-nomadic community: the Toubou, who number less than 3000. They have strong links with a larger population of Toubou across the border in Chad.

# Religion

Approximately 97% of Libya's population is Sunni Muslim, with small communities of Kharijites (an offshoot of orthodox Islam) and Christians.

The generally tolerant Maliki rite of Sunni Islam, one of four *madhab* (schools) of Islamic law in orthodox Islam, has come to predominate in Libya. Founded by Malik ibn As in the 8th century, it is based on the practice that prevailed in Medina in the 8th century and preaches the primacy of the Quran (as opposed to later teachings).

# Environment

Libya is the fourth-largest country in Africa and twice the size of neighbouring Egypt. Despite the fertile coastal plain of Sahel al-Jefara, and the mountains of Jebel Nafusa and Jebel al-Akhdar in northern Libya, 95% of the country is swallowed up by the Sahara Desert.

Libya's environment is one of the continent's most degraded – its wildlife has been devastated and water scarcity has reached critical levels.

# Food & Drink

Libya doesn't have Africa's (or even North Africa's) most exciting cuisine, and food has become a question of necessity. Although eating remains a great social event and cities like Tripoli still have plenty of restaurants, the security situation means that most Libyans eat at home and in the company of trusted family and friends. Most food has to be imported, meaning that fresh produce is not always easy to find.

# Morocco

POP 33,655,800 / ☎212

## Includes ➡



## Best Places to Eat

- La Table by Madada (p120)
- Restaurant Brasserie La Bavaroise (p117)
- Djemaa El-Fna Food Stalls (p133)
- Ruined Garden (p126)

## Best Places to Sleep

- Le Gallia (p132)
- Riad Azoulay (p133)
- Riad Bledna (p132)
- Dar Nour (p109)

## Why Go?

For many travellers Morocco might be just a short hop by budget airline, or by ferry from Spain, but culturally it's a much further distance to travel. On arrival, the regular certainties of Europe are swept away by the full technicolour arrival of Africa and Islam. It's a complete sensory overload.

Tangier – that faded libertine on the coast – has traditionally been a first port of call, but the winds quickly blow you along the coast to cosmopolitan, movie-star-famous Casablanca and the whitewashed fishing-port gem Essaouira. Inland the great imperial cities of Marrakesh and Fez attract visitors in droves; the winding streets of their ancient medinas hold enough surprises to fill a dozen repeat trips. If you really want to escape from everything, Morocco still has a couple of trump cards. The High Atlas Mountains seem custom-made for hiking, with endless trails between Berber villages, and North Africa's highest peak to conquer.

Morocco can feel like another world, but you don't need a magic carpet to get there.

## When to Go

### Marrakesh

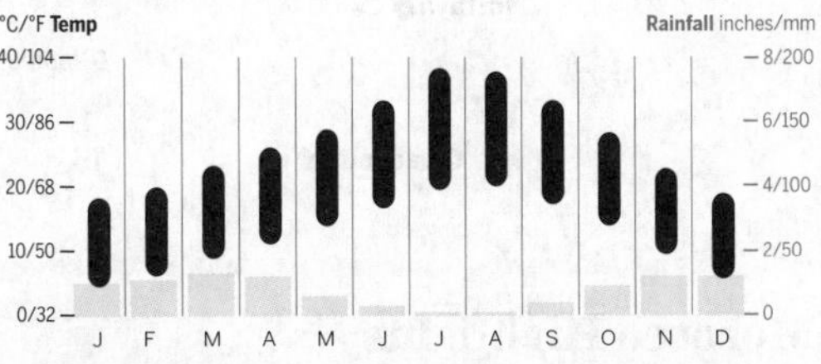


**Nov–Mar** Marrakesh and the south are popular at Christmas and New Year; the north can be wet.

**Apr & Oct** Spring sandstorms in the Sahara and persistent rain in the north; popular elsewhere.

**May–Sep** Discounts in accommodation and souqs. Prices can be high on the coast, where it's shoulder season.

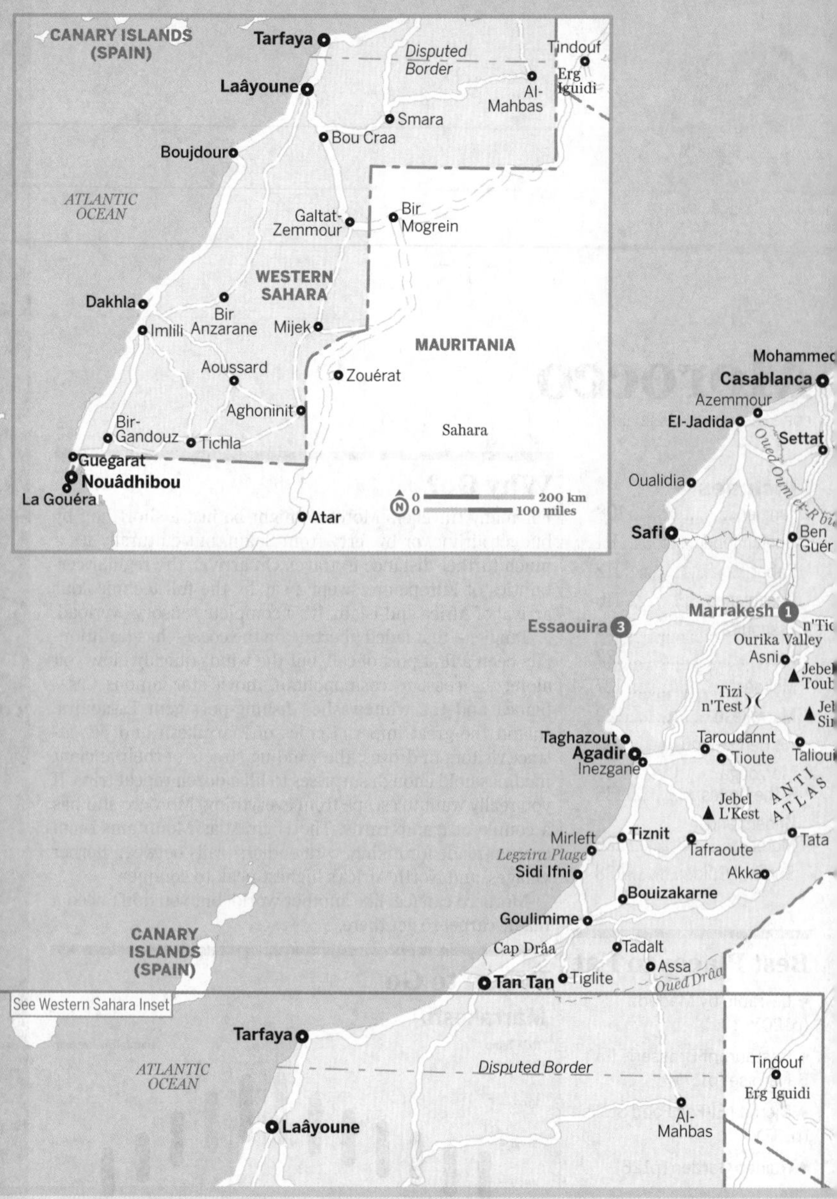


# Morocco Highlights

1 **Djemaa el-Fna** (p130) Witnessing the endless spectacle of Morocco's most dynamic city, Marrakesh.

2 **Fez** (p122) Losing yourself in the mazelike charms of this medieval city, replete with sights, sounds and smells.

3 **Essaouira** (p119) Lazing by the sea in Morocco's coolest and most evocative resort.

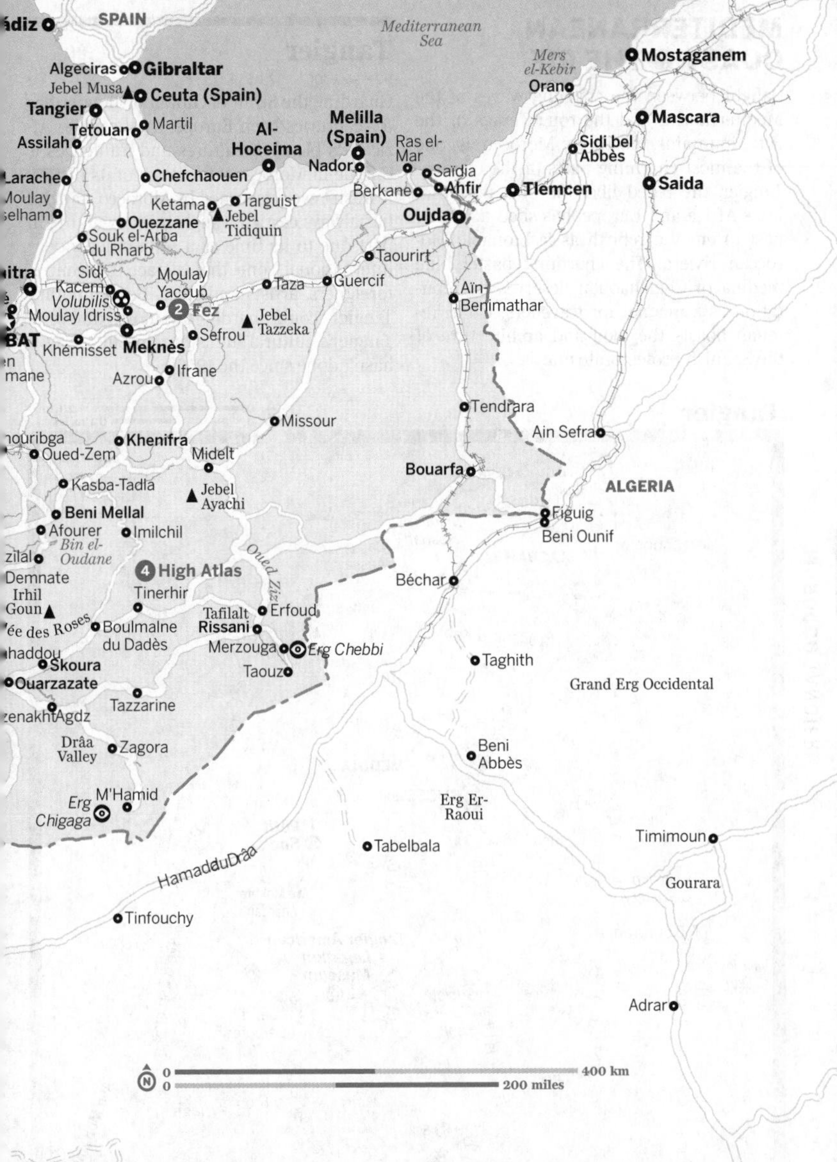


**4 High Atlas** (p129)
Trekking deep into a world of stunning scenery and isolated Berber villages.

# MEDITERRANEAN COAST & THE RIF

Caught between the crashing waves of the Mediterranean and the rough crags of the Rif Mountains, northern Morocco is one of the most charming parts of the country. Tangier, the faded libertine of a port that links Africa and Europe, has shed its shady past to enjoy a rebirth as fashionable Moroccan riviera. The charming pastel blue medina of Chefchaouen deserves its reputation as a magnet for travellers, while Tetouan boasts the food and architecture of the Spanish protectorate era.

## Tangier

POP 950,000 / 0539

Guarding the Strait of Gibraltar, Tangier has for centuries been Europes's gateway to Africa. Its blend of cultures and influences is unique in Morocco – for much of its history it wasn't even governed by Morocco. Tangier has always carried a slightly seedy allure, in part due to its time as a semi-independent international zone that attracted eccentric foreigners, artists and spies. Contemporary Tangier could hardly be more different. Tangier's cultural life is buzzing in a way it hasn't done since the 1950s.

### Tangier

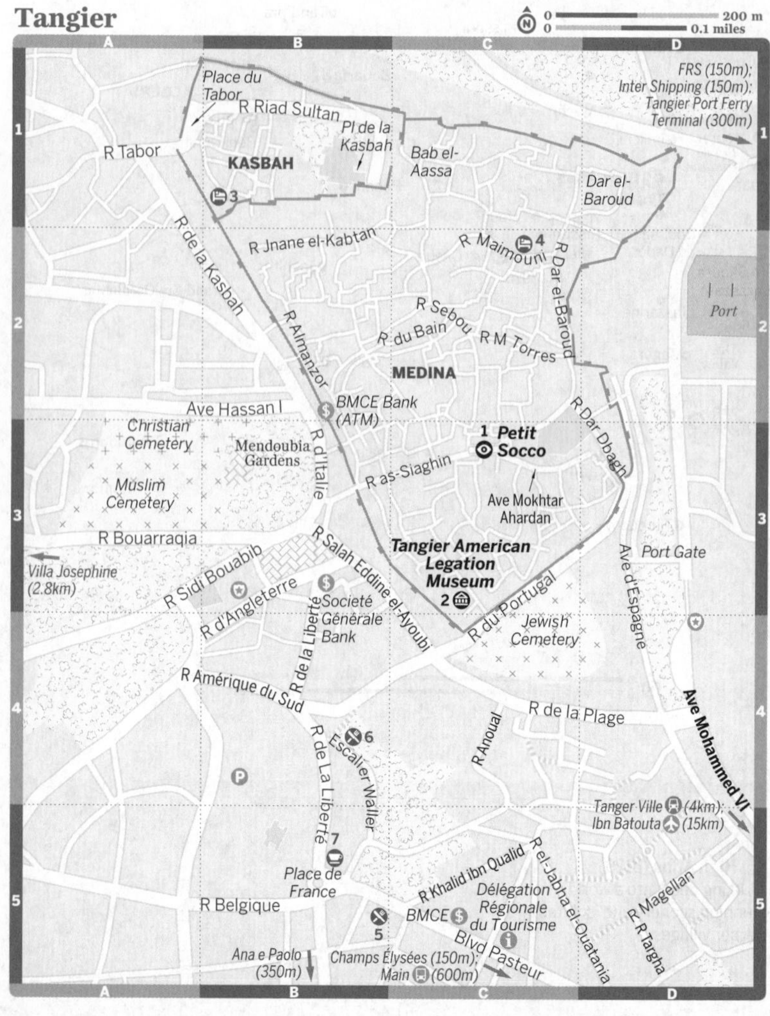

## Sights

**★ Medina** AREA

The medina, Tangier's top attraction, is a labyrinth of alleyways both commercial and residential. It's contained by the walls of a 15th-century Portuguese fortress, although most buildings are actually relatively young for a Moroccan medina. Clean and well lit as medinas go, the place is full of travellers' treasures, from glimpses of traditional living, to the more material rewards of the souqs.

**★ Tangier American Legation Museum** MUSEUM

(☎0539 93 53 17; www.legation.org; 8 Rue D'Amerique; Dh20, guided tour Dh50; ⏲10am-5pm Mon-Fri, 10am-3pm Sat) FREE This museum, in an elegant five-storey mansion, is a must-see: Morocco was the first country to recognise the fledgling United States, in 1777, and this was the first piece of American real estate abroad, as well as the only US National Historic Landmark on foreign soil.

**★ Petit Socco** SQUARE

(Souq Dakhel) Officially named Pl Souq ad-Dakhil, this was once the most notorious crossroads of Tangier, the site of drug deals and all forms of prostitution. Today the facades are freshly painted, tourists abound and it's a wonderful square for people-watching over a mint tea.

## Festivals & Events

**TANJAzz** MUSIC

(www.tanjazz.org; Tangier; ⏲Sep) This ever-popular festival with a good reputation for attracting leading names, has been running for over 17 years and hosts concerts by local and international jazz musicians.

### Tangier

**Top Sights**



**Sleeping**



**Eating**



**Drinking & Nightlife**



## Sleeping

**★ Melting Pot Hostel** HOSTEL $

(☎0539 33 15 08; www.meltingpothostels.com/tanger; 3 Rue Tsouli; dm Dh130, d Dh330; 📶) This bright and cheerful hostel is a perfect backpacker's hub, with a big, clean kitchen and plenty of chill-out space, including a roof terrace with terrific views. Shared facilities are clean and the staff very friendly and helpful. It's a short walk from Petit Socco or, if you're walking up from the port, the Hotel Continental.

**★ Dar Nour** GUESTHOUSE $$

(☎0662 11 27 24; www.darnour.com; 20 Rue Gourna, Kasbah; d/ste incl breakfast from Dh720/1300; 📶) This peppermint-walled guesthouse has no central courtyard, rooms here instead branch off two winding staircases, creating a maze of rooms and salons, each more romantic than the last. Rooms are stylishly decorated with objets d'art and packed with books, creating a relaxed and homely atmosphere, while bathrooms are *tadelakt* (polished plaster). Some rooms have a private terrace.

**★ Villa Josephine** HERITAGE HOTEL $$$

(☎0539 33 45 35; www.villajosephine-tanger.com; r Dh3600-7600; P📶🏊) A mansion or a palace? It's hard to decide at this restored 1920s residence, once a summer retreat for Moroccan royalty and partying European diplomats. Everything about the 10 rooms here is sumptuous, from the period decor to the up-to-the-minute amenities and service. All have balconies or terraces looking out to sea.

## Eating

**Champs Élysées** CAFE $

(6 Ave Mohammed V; breakfast from Dh25; ⏲6am-10pm) This enormous cafe-in-the-round is high on opulence, with a huge central chandelier and red velour upholstery. Great sticky pastries.

**La Giralda** CAFE $

(☎0539 37 04 07; 1st fl, 5 Blvd Pasteur; breakfast from Dh25; ⏲7am-midnight; ❄) The young and beautiful adore this grand cafe overlooking the Terrasse des Paresseux, with its sumptuous, Egyptian-influenced decor and intricately carved ceiling. Huge windows give great sea views. A light menu of crêpes and paninis make it a good lunch stop, too.

**★ Ana e Paolo** ITALIAN $$

(☎0539 94 46 17; 77 Rue Prince Héretier; mains from Dh85; ⏲noon–3pm & 7.30–11pm, closed Sun) This is a genuine, family-run Italian bistro with Venetian owners; it feels like you've been invited for Sunday dinner. Expect a highly international crowd, lots of cross-table conversations about the events of the day, and wholesome food, including excellent charcuterie and pizzas, homemade pastas, meat and fish.

**★Populaire Saveur de Poisson** SEAFOOD $$$

(☎0539 33 63 26; 2 Escalier Waller; fixed-price menu Dh200; ⏰1–5pm & 8–11pm, closed Fri) This charming seafood restaurant offers an excellent, filling set menu in rustic surroundings. The owner serves a four-course meal of fish soup followed by inventive plates of fresh catch, olives and various fresh breads, all of it washed down with a homemade juice cocktail made from a dozen fruits. Dessert is honey and almonds. Not just a meal, a whole experience.

## Drinking & Nightlife

**★Gran Café de Paris** CAFE

(Pl de France; ⏰6am-10.30pm) Gravity weighs upon the grand letters of the Gran Café de Paris, reminding us of its age at the crossroads of Tangier. Facing the Pl de France since 1927, this is the most famous of the coffee establishments along Blvd Pasteur, most recently used as a setting in *The Bourne Ultimatum*. In the past it was a prime gathering spot for the Tangier literati.

## Information

### DANGERS & ANNOYANCES

As in any big city, it's best to stick to the beaten path at all times, and to take taxis point to point at night. Solo women may be subject to being hassled after about 10pm, and should avoid the port area after dark. If you have a serious problem and need help from the authorities, contact the **Brigade Touristique** (Tourist Police; ☎177; Ave Mohammed VI, Tangier Port).

### MONEY

Blvds Pasteur and Mohammed V are lined with numerous banks with ATMs and *bureau de change* counters. Outside of working hours, try the exchange bureaus in the big hotels.

### TOURIST INFORMATION

**Délégation Régionale du Tourisme** (☎0539 94 80 50; 29 Blvd Pasteur; ⏰9am-1pm & 3-6pm Mon-Fri) The recent investment in tourism infrastructure hasn't made it here. Some verbal help, but no printed material. The Hotel de Paris across the road has lots of brochures and staff are willing to help.

## Getting There & Away

### AIR

The **Ibn Batouta International Airport** (☎0539 39 37 20) is 15km southwest of the city centre. It attracts a number of budget airlines (including easyJet, RyanAir and Air Arabia) as well as Iberia and Royal Air Maroc. Check the internet for the latest service providers and schedules, as these are constantly changing.

### BOAT

Tangier effectively has two ports: **Tangier Port** (in the city) and the newer Tanger Med terminal, 48km east along the coast.

From Tangier Port there are fast catamaran ferries run by **FRS** (www.frs.es) and **Inter Shipping** (www.intershipping.es) to Tarifa (Dh350, 40 minutes). There are more than a dozen sailings a day, with the ferry companies leaving on alternate hours.

Services from Tanger Med are primarily to Algeciras. A shuttle bus (Dh25) leaves Tanger Med every hour on the hour for the Tangier bus station, taking 45 minutes.

### BUS

CTM buses depart from the **main bus station** (gare routière; ☎0539 94 69 28; Pl Jamaa el-Arabia), about 2km to the south of the city centre by the Syrian mosque – the distinctly un-Moroccan-looking minarets are a useful nearby landmark. Destinations include the following:

| DESTINATION | COST (DH) | DURATION (HR) |
|---|---|---|
| Casablanca | 150 | 5½ |
| Chefchaouen | 50 | 3 |
| Fez | 125 | 6 |
| Marrakesh | 250 | 10 |
| Meknès | 100 | 5 |
| Rabat | 115 | 4 |
| Tetouan | 25 | 1 |

Cheaper bus companies also operate from the main bus station. There are regular departures for all the destinations listed for CTM, plus services to Al-Hoceima (Dh105, 10 hours) and Fnideq (Dh25, 1½ hours) – a small town 3km from the Ceuta border. A metered petit taxi to/from the town centre is around Dh10.

The main bus station has a **left-luggage facility** (per item per 24hr Dh5-7; ⏰5am-1am).

### TRAIN

Tanger Ville is a hassle-free train station, though under massive remodelling. Trains depart throughout the day for Meknès (Dh90), Fez (Dh111), Rabat (Dh101), Casablanca (Dh132) and Marrakesh (Dh 216).

# Chefchaouen

POP 42,800

Beautifully perched beneath the raw peaks of the Rif, Chefchaouen is one of the prettiest towns in Morocco, an artsy, blue-washed mountain village that feels like its own world. While tourism has definitely taken hold, the balance between ease and authenticity is just right. The old medina is a delight of Moroccan and Andalucian influence with red-tiled roofs, bright-blue buildings and narrow lanes converging on a delightful square.

## Sights

Chefchaouen's **medina** is one of the loveliest in Morocco. Small and uncrowded, it's easy to explore, with enough winding paths to keep you diverted, but compact enough that you'll never get too lost. Most of the buildings are painted a blinding blue-white, giving them a clean, fresh look, while terracotta tiles add an Andalucian flavour.

The heart of the medina is the shady, cobbled **Plaza Uta el-Hammam**. The plaza is dominated by the red-hued walls of the kasbah and the adjacent **Grande Mosquée**. The **kasbah** (☎0539 98 63 43; museum & gallery Dh10; ⏰9am-1pm & 3-6.30pm Wed, Thu & Sat-Mon, 9am-noon & 3-6.30pm Fri) contains a lovely garden, an **ethnographic museum** (museum & gallery Dh10; ⏰9am-1pm & 3-6.30pm Wed, Thu & Sat-Mon, 9am-noon & 3-6.30pm Fri), and an art gallery.

Looking east, you'll easily spot the so-called **Spanish mosque** on a hilltop not far from the medina. It's a pleasant walk along clear paths and well worth the effort. Start at the waterfall **Ras el-Maa**, just beyond the far northeastern gate of the medina. Continuing over the bridge, you can walk to the Spanish mosque following the hillside path. The mosque was built by the Spanish in the 1920s, but never used.

## Sleeping

★**Dar Baraka** GUESTHOUSE $

(☎0614 68 24 80; www.riad-baraka.com; 12 Derb Ben Yacoub; d with/without bathroom Dh275/Dh220, dm Dh100; 📶) English-owned Dar Baraka is a bright and cheery place to rest your backpack. The rooms are comfortable and share spotless facilities, and there's a convivial terrace with good views for meeting fellow travellers. There are a handful of private rooms or dorms for four, with bunk beds. Map murals help orientate yourself in the medina.

★**Casa Perleta** GUESTHOUSE $$

(☎0539 98 89 79; www.casaperleta.com; Bab Souq; d incl breakfast Dh500-900; 📶) This lovely house offers rooms sleeping two or three, and one suite for four. It's full of wonderful local fabrics and furniture and white walls that soothe after the blue medina. The cosy sitting room has a fireplace for chilly nights, and there's central heating in all rooms. Topping it off is a terrace with great views.

## Eating

**La Lampe Magique** MOROCCAN $

(Rue Targhi; mains from Dh45, set menu Dh100; ⏰11am-10pm) This magical favourite overlooking Plaza Uta el-Hammam serves delicious Moroccan staples in a grand setting. Three bright-blue floors include a laid-back lounge, a more formal dining area and a rooftop terrace. The menu – featuring favourites such as lamb tajine with prunes and some great cooked salads – is much better than average, and the ambience is relaxed.

★**Auberge Dardara Restaurant** MOROCCAN $$

(☎0661 15 05 03, 0539 70 70 07; www.dardara.ma; Rte Nationale 2; menu Dh120; ⏰lunch & dinner) This is the best restaurant in the area, and worth the 10-minute drive from town (to Bab Taza, Dh5). The Tangerine owner uses only the freshest ingredients from the garden, bakes his own bread and makes his own olive oil and goat's cheese. Try the superb salads, the venison cooked with dried figs or the succulent rabbit with quince.

## Information

There is a useful **pharmacy** (☎0539 98 61 58; Ave Moulay Driss; ⏰8am-6pm Mon-Sat) on Ave Moulay Driss.

**Banque Populaire** (Ave Hassan II, near Bab el-Ain; ⏰8.45am-6pm Mon-Thu, 8.45am-noon Sat) Bank with ATM and money-changing facilities.

**Post Office** (Ave Hassan II; ⏰8am-4pm Mon-Fri, 8-11am Sat)

## Getting There & Away

Bus services from Chefchaouen originate elsewhere, so are often full on arrival. Buy the ticket for your onward journey on arrival in Chefchaouen to secure a seat. The **bus station** (☎0539 98 76 69) is 1.5km southwest of the town centre at the far end of Ave Mohammed V (Dh10 in a petit taxi from Pl el-Majzen). CTM and all other buses use the same station.

## Chefchaouen

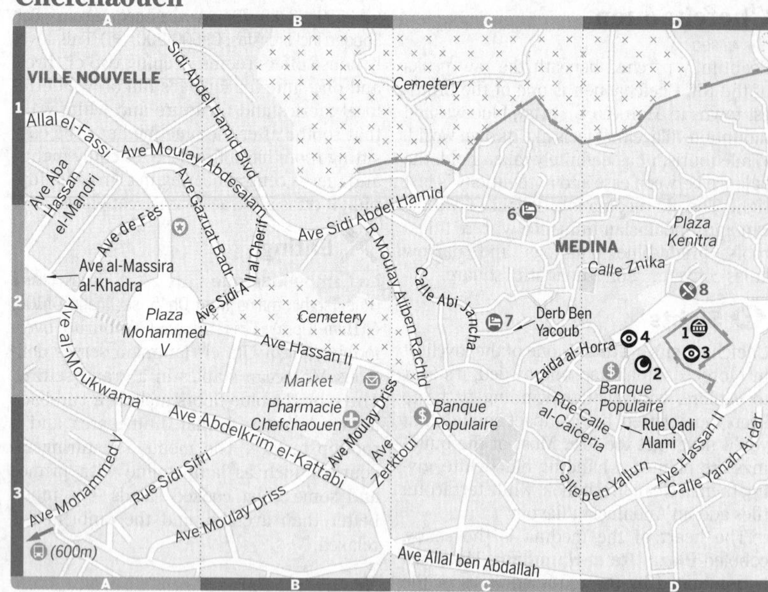


CTM serves the following destinations.

| DESTINATION | COST (DH) | DURATION (HR) |
|---|---|---|
| Casablanca | 140 | 6 |
| Fez | 75 | 4 |
| Nador | 120 | 11½ |
| Rabat | 100 | 4½ |
| Tangier | 45 | 3 |

Other companies run a number of cheaper services to the same destinations, including a daily departure for Oued Laou (Dh32, 1½ hours).

# ATLANTIC COAST

This windswept coast is home to Morocco's cultured capital, Rabat, and its economic hub, Casablanca. The region is bookended by Asilah and Essaouira, famed for their medinas and surrounding beaches.

## Rabat

POP 565,000

Morocco's political and administrative capital may be short on top-drawer tourist attractions, but it compensates with plenty of charm. The ville nouvelle's palm-lined boulevards are clean, well kept and relatively free of traffic – a blessed relief for those who have spent time in Casablanca. There's a clean central beach, an intact and evocative kasbah, and an attractive walled medina that is far less touristy than those in other large cities. All in all, the city is a good choice for a short sojourn.

### Sights

**Rabat Medina** AREA

(Medina Rabat, Bab Chellah) When the French arrived in the early 20th century, this walled medina by the sea was the full extent of the city. Built on an orderly grid in the 17th century, it is small enough to be easily explored in half a day, but large enough to make getting lost inevitable. The main market street is Rue Souika, with local shopping on its western stretch and shops geared largely to tourists in the covered **Souq as-Sebbat** (Bab Chellah) to its east.

**Kasbah les Oudaias** FORTRESS

(Rue Jamaa; Bab Chellah) Rabat's historic citadel occupies the site of the original *ribat* (fortress-monastery) that gave the city its name. Predominately residential, its narrow streets are lined with whitewashed houses –

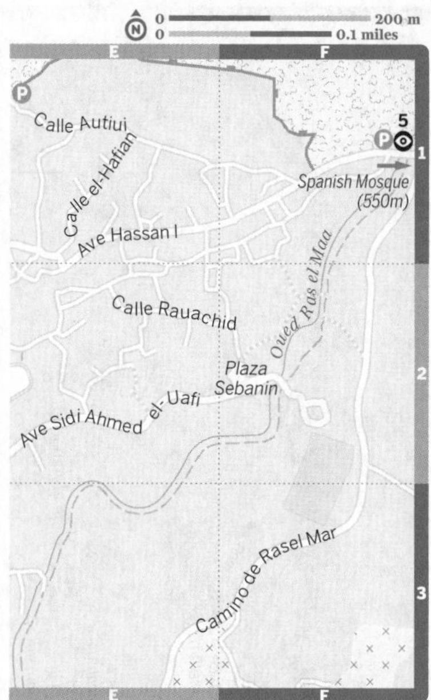


## Chefchaouen

**Sights**

1 Ethnographic Museum........D2
2 Grande Mosquée........D2
3 Kasbah........D2
4 Plaza Uta el-Hammam........D2
5 Ras el-Maa........F1

**Sleeping**

6 Casa Perleta........C2
7 Dar Baraka........C2

**Eating**

8 La Lampe Magique........D2

most of which were built by Muslim refugees from Spain. There are scenic views over the river and ocean from the highest point of the **Plateforme du Sémaphore** (Signal Platform; Kasbah les Oudaias; Bab Chellah), and the attractive **Andalusian Gardens** (sunrise-sunset; Bab Chellah) at its southern edge are a popular relaxation and meeting point for locals.

**Chellah** HISTORIC SITE

(cnr Ave Yacoub al-Mansour & Blvd Moussa ibn Nassair; adult/child under 12yr Dh10/3; 8.30am-5.30pm) The Phoenicians were the first to settle on this sloping site above the Bou Regreg river, and the Romans took control in about AD 40, renaming the settlement Sala Colonia. Scattered stones from their city remain, but give little idea of its size or form. Abandoned in 1154, it lay deserted until the 14th century, when Merenid sultan Abou al-Hassan Ali built a necropolis on top of the Roman site and surrounded it with the defensive wall that stands today.

## Sleeping

**★Riad Meftaha** B&B $

(0537 72 14 06; www.riad-meftaha.com; 15 Rue Iran, Quartier Marassa Océan; d/tr/ste incl breakfast Dh575/640/660; Bab El Had, Medina Rabat) Owner Franck and his sidekick Khadija are friendly and helpful hosts, making this quiet riad just outside Bab Laalou an excellent choice. The building is modern and not particularly attractive, but rooms are pleasantly decorated. The pick of the bunch is undoubtedly the terrace suite. Note that double rooms lack air-conditioning; all have satellite TV. Breakfast is generous.

**★Le Piétri Urban Hotel** HOTEL $$

(0537 70 78 20; www.lepietri.com; 4 Rue Tobrouk, Ville Nouvelle; incl breakfast s Dh760-1020, d Dh860-1120, ste Dh1300; @; Mohammed V/Gare de Rabat) If only all midrange hotels in Morocco lived up to the standard set by this impressive business hotel! On offer are reasonable prices, a central location, helpful bilingual staff and 35 spacious and bright rooms with good beds, satellite TV, work desk and double-glazed windows. There's also an excellent restaurant, **Le Bistro du Pietri** (mains Dh140-170; noon-3pm Mon-Fri, 7-11pm daily; ), where live jazz is performed on weekends.

**★L'Alcazar** BOUTIQUE HOTEL $$$

(0537 73 69 06; www.lalcazar.com; 4 Impasse Ben Abdellah, off Ave Laalou, Medina; r Dh1000-3500; P; Medina Rabat) Rabat's most stylish hotel is entered through a royal-blue doorway at the end of a dead-end lane near Bab Laalou. A chic French-style adaptation of a traditional riad, the hotel offers eight extremely comfortable rooms, a charming central dining area and a multitiered rooftop terrace with expansive medina views. Amenities are top quality, breakfast is delicious and service is friendly.

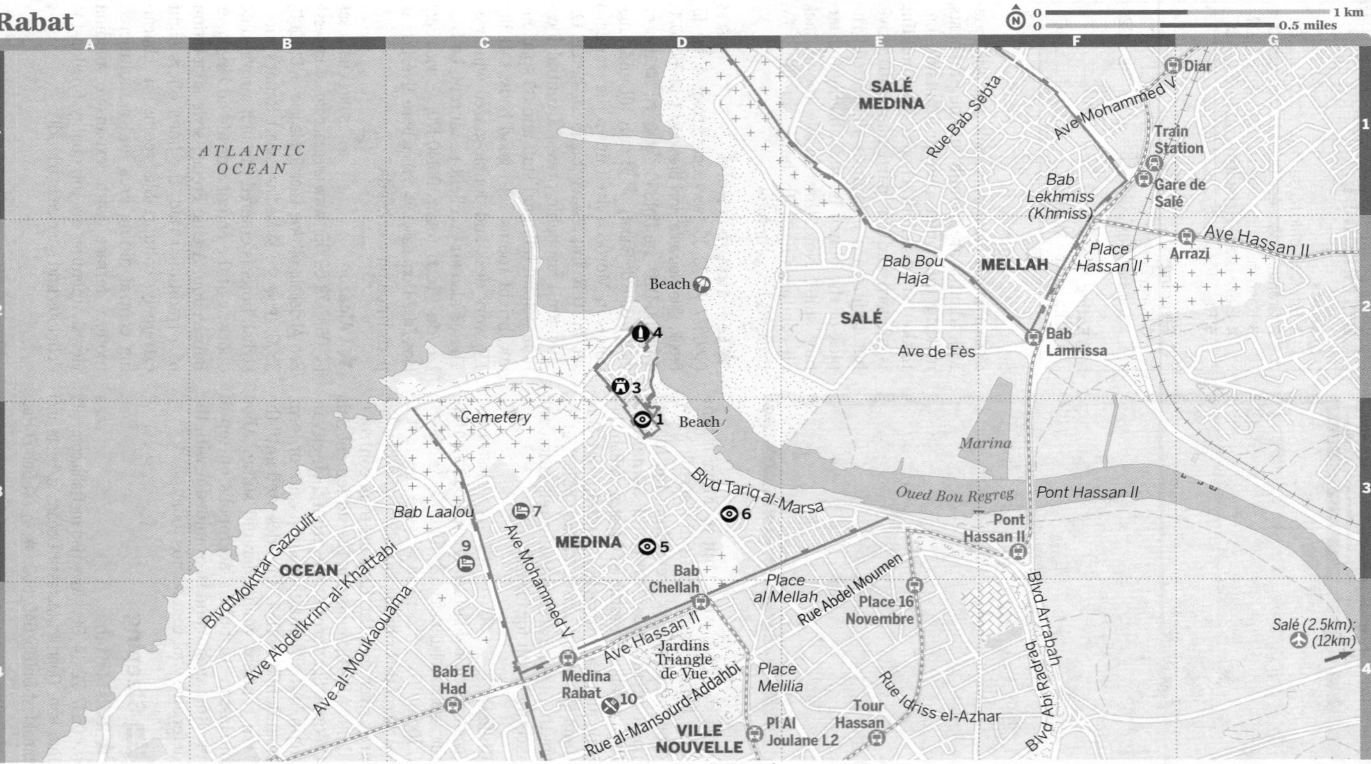
Rabat
0 1 km
0 0.5 miles
A B C D E F G
1 2 3 4
ATLANTIC OCEAN
SALÉ MEDINA
Rue Bab Sebta
Ave Mohammed V
Diar
Train Station
Gare de Salé
Bab Lekhmiss (Khmiss)
Ave Hassan II
Arrazi
Place Hassan II
MELLAH
Bab Bou Haja
SALÉ
Beach
4
3
1
Beach
Ave de Fès
Bab Lamrissa
Cemetery
Marina
Oued Bou Regreg
Pont Hassan II
Pont Hassan II
Blvd Tariq al-Marsa
6
Bab Laalou
7
MEDINA
5
9
OCEAN
BlvdMokhtar Gazoulit
Ave Abdelkrim al-Khattabi
Ave al-Moukaouama
Ave Mohammed V
Bab Chellah
Place al Mellah
Rue Abdel Moumen
Place 16 Novembre
Blvd Arrabah
Blvd Abi Radraq
Salé (2.5km); (12km)
Ave Hassan II
Jardins Triangle de Vue
Place Melilia
Rue Idriss el-Azhar
Tour Hassan
Bab El Had
Medina Rabat
10
Rue al-Mansour-Addahbi
VILLE NOUVELLE
Pl Al Joulane L2

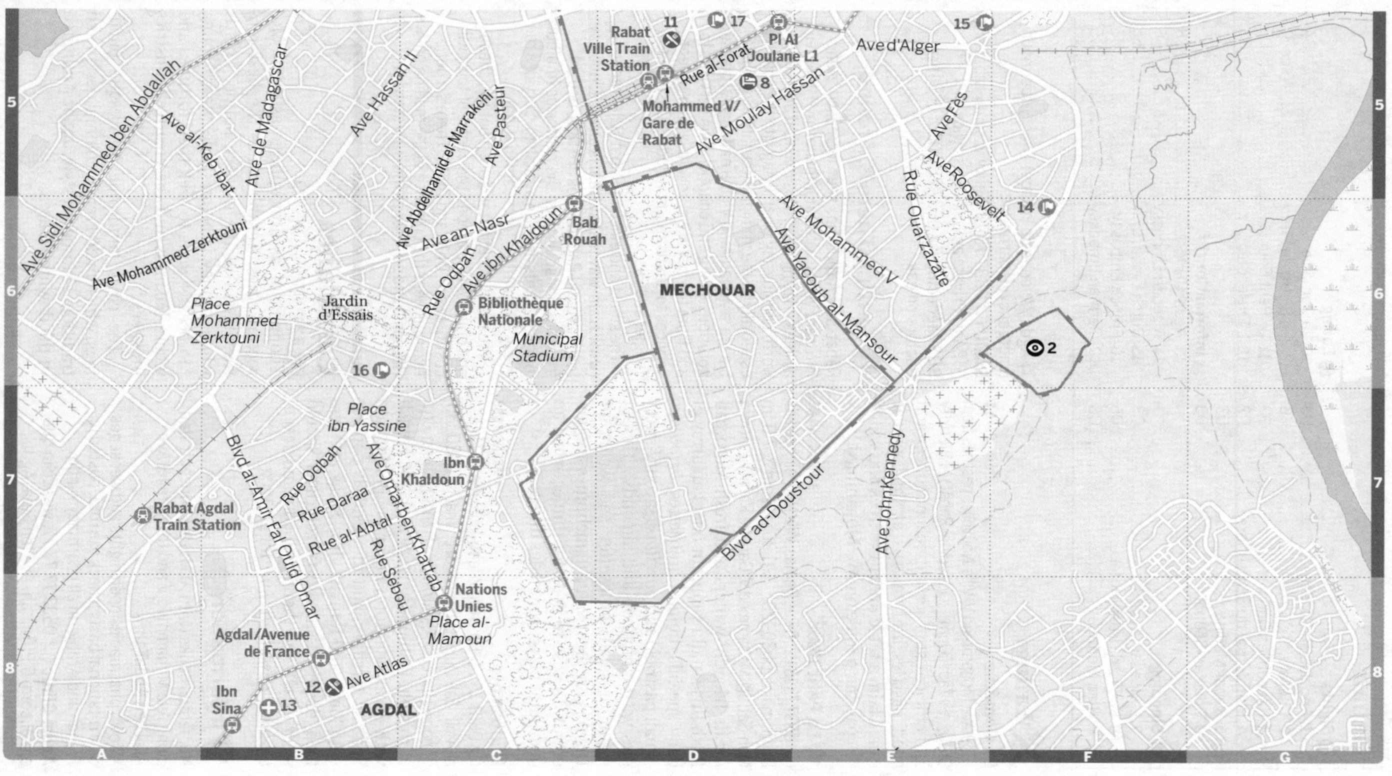

Rabat Ville Train Station
11
17
Pl Al Joulane L1
15
Ave d'Alger
Rue al-Forat
8
Mohammed V/ Gare de Rabat
Ave Moulay Hassan
Ave Fes
Ave Roosevelt
Rue Ouarzazate
14
Ave Sidi Mohammed ben Abdallah
Ave al-Keb ibat
Ave de Madagascar
Ave Hassan II
Ave Abdelhamid el-Marrakchi
Ave Pasteur
Ave an-Nasr
Ave ibn Khaldoun
Bab Rouah
Ave Mohammed Zerktouni
Rue Oqbah
MECHOUAR
Ave Mohammed V
Ave Yacoub al-Mansour
2
Place Mohammed Zerktouni
Jardin d'Essais
Bibliothèque Nationale
Municipal Stadium
16
Place ibn Yassine
Ibn Khaldoun
Blvd al-Amir Fal Ould Omar
Rue Oqbah
Rue Daraa
Rue al-Abtal
Ave Omar ben Khattab
Rue Sebou
Rabat Agdal Train Station
Blvd ad-Doustour
Ave John Kennedy
Nations Unies
Place al-Mamoun
Agdal/Avenue de France
Ave Atlas
12
Ibn Sina
13
AGDAL
A
B
C
D
E
F
G
5
6
7
8

## Rabat

**Sights**

1 Andalusian Gardens ........ D3
2 Chellah ........ F6
3 Kasbah les Oudaias ........ D2
4 Plateforme du Sémaphore ........ D2
5 Rabat Medina ........ D3
6 Souq as-Sebbat ........ D3

**Sleeping**

7 L'Alcazar ........ C3
8 Le Piétri Urban Hotel ........ D5
9 Riad Meftaha ........ C3

**Eating**

10 La Comédie ........ D4
Le Bistro du Pietri ........ (see 8)
11 Le Petit Beur ........ D5
12 L'Entrecôte ........ B8

**Information**

13 Agdal Clinic ........ B8
14 Algerian Embassy ........ F6
15 Dutch Embassy ........ E5
16 French Embassy ........ B6
17 German Embassy ........ D5

### Eating

**La Comédie** CAFE $
(269 Ave Mohammed V, Ville Nouvelle; pastries from Dh10; 7am-10pm; Medina Rabat) Friendly and efficient staff serve excellent coffees and good pastries and gateaux at this popular cafe. Claim a table under the trees and watch the passing parade on Ave Mohammed V.

★ **Le Petit Beur** MOROCCAN $$
(0537 73 13 22; 8 Rue Damas, Ville Nouvelle; salads Dh45, mains Dh80-120; 11.30am-2pm & 7-11pm Mon-Sat; Mohammed V/Gare de Rabat) Known for its friendly waiters and fresh Moroccan food, this small restaurant offers an array of daily specials, tajines, brochettes, *briouates* (small pastries) and *pastillas* (savoury-sweet pies with cinnamon and almonds). The set menu of salad, brochettes and water for Dh90 is excellent value. Lunchtimes are quiet but it's wise to book for dinner, when an oud (lute) player serenades diners.

**L'Entrecôte** FRENCH $$$
(0661 15 59 59; http://lentrecote.ma/; 74 Blvd al-Amir Fal Ould Omar, Agdal; mains Dh80-180; noon-11pm; Agdal/Ave de France) The menu at this old-fashioned eatery is classic French with occasional forays over the border into Spanish territory, and the result is popular with locals and tourists alike. Steak and seafood dishes dominate (vegetarians should steer clear), and there's a good value deal of a *plat et dessert du jour* for Dh120.

### Information

Numerous banks (with ATMs) are concentrated along Ave Mohammed V and the parallel Ave Allal ben Abdallah.

Town pharmacies open nights and weekends on a rotational basis; check the rota, posted in French and Arabic, in all pharmacy windows.

**Agdal Clinic** (0537 77 77 77; www.clinique-agdal.com; 6 Pl Talhah, Ave Ibn Sina, Agdal; Agdal/Avenue de France) Twenty-four hour emergency department.

**SAMU** (0537 73 73 73; www.samu-rabat.org; 24hr) Private ambulance service.

**SOS Médecins** (0537 20 2020; 24hr) Doctors on call.

### Getting There & Around

Rabat-Salé Airport has seen increased traffic in recent years, with a number of international airlines arriving here. This makes it an option worth considering when flying into the country, especially as the immigration queues at Casablanca's Mohammed V International Airport are notoriously long and chaotic. Train services to and from the city are excellent, with frequent services to destinations including Casablanca, Tangier and Fez.

The smart and efficient Rabat-Salé tramway (www.tram-way.ma) system is an excellent way to get around Rabat. Fares are Dh6, bought from ticket machines on the platforms (multiple journey tickets are also available). Services run every 20 minutes, from 6am to 10pm.

Rabat's blue petits taxis are plentiful, cheap and quick. A ride around the centre of town will cost between Dh15 and Dh30. There's a petit-taxi rank near the entrance of the medina on Ave Hassan II and another at the train station.

## Casablanca

POP 3.34 MILLION / 0522

Though not as atmospheric as other Moroccan cities, Casablanca is the best representation of the modern nation. This is where money is being made, where young Moroccans come to seek their fortunes and where business and the creative industries prosper.

The city's handsome Mauresque buildings, which meld French-colonial design and traditional Moroccan style, are best admired in the downtown area.

## Sights

### ★Hassan II Mosque
MOSQUE

(Blvd Sidi Mohammed ben Abdallah; guided tours adult/student/child 4-12yr Dh120/60/30; ⏲tours 9am, 10am, 11am, 3pm & 4pm Sat-Fri, plus noon Sat-Thu) This flamboyant building was built at enormous expense to commemorate the former king's 60th birthday. Set on an outcrop jutting over the ocean and with a 210m-tall minaret that serves as the city's major landmark, it is a showcase of the very best Moroccan artisanship: hand-carved stone and wood, intricate marble flooring and inlay, gilded cedar ceilings and exquisite *zellij* (colourful ceramic tiling) abound. Multilanguage guided tours of the interior are conducted outside prayer times for modestly clad visitors.

### Moroccan Jewish Museum
MUSEUM

(☎0522 99 49 40; www.casajewishmuseum.com; 81 Rue Chasseur Jules Gros, Quartier Oasis; Dh50; ⏲10am-5pm Mon-Fri, 11am-3pm Sun; 🚊Gare de l'Oasis) The only Jewish museum in the Arab-speaking world, this institution is set in an attractive garden villa that once functioned as a Jewish orphanage. It traces the 2000-year history of Jews in Morocco, focusing on Casablanca's Jewish community (most of the country's Jews live here). The thoughtfully curated and well labelled collection includes ornate clothing, traditional tools and ritual objects. Photographs usually feature in the temporary exhibition space, and there's a reconstructed 1930s synagogue from Larache in an adjoining room.

## Sleeping

### Hotel Guynemer
HOTEL $

(☎0522 27 57 64; hotelguynemer@yahoo.com; 2 Rue Mohammed Belloul; s/d incl breakfast Dh350/450, ste s/d incl breakfast Dh450/650; ❄📶; 🚊Place Mohammed V) Friendly and well priced, the Guynemer has recently undergone a major renovation, but the owners have ensured that many of the building's original features have been retained. Regular rooms are comfortable but slightly cramped (especially the bathrooms); suite rooms are well sized. All have double-glazed windows, satellite TV and good beds. Parking costs Dh10 per 24 hours.

### Hôtel les Saisons
HOTEL $$

(☎0522 49 09 01; www.hotellessaisonsmaroc.ma; 19 Rue el-Oraïbi Jilali; s/d/ste incl breakfast Dh950/1150/1450; ❄📶; 🚊Place Nations Unies) This small and efficiently run modern hotel near Casa Port train station offers clean and comfortable rooms, a decent breakfast and an in-house restaurant serving alcohol.

### ★Hôtel Le 135
HOTEL $$$

(☎0522 27 91 12; www.le135hotel.com; 135 Ave Hassan II; s/d/tr Dh1400/1800/1900; P❄📶; 🚊Avenue Hassan II) Good upper-midrange accommodation choices are few and far between in Casablanca, so the 2016 opening of this 10-room hotel opposite the Parc de la Ligue Arabe was greeted with acclaim by regular visitors to the city. Huge, light-filled rooms are exceptionally well appointed (top-quality bed, satellite TV, bathtub and shower). Breakfast costs Dh100 per person and parking Dh35 per night.

## Eating

### ★Pâtisserie Bennis Habous
BAKERY $

(☎0522 30 30 25; 2 Rue Fkih el-Gabbas, Quartier Habous; pastries Dh5; ⏲8am-9pm) Secreted in a lane in the Souq Habous, this famous patisserie deserves a dedicated visit. Make your choice of traditional Maghribi pastries such as *cornes de gazelle* (gazelle horns; pastries filled with a paste of almond and orange water) or *akda aux amandes* (almond macaroons), then head to nearby Cafe Imperial to order a coffee and scoff your bounty.

### Marché Central
MARKET $

(meals from Dh40; ⏲9am-6pm; 🚊Marché Central) The Marché Central is a great place to go for lunch – busy tables from a dozen simple eateries are crammed with diners feasting on huge platters of fish, grilled vegetables, bread, salads and seafood soup. Cheap, filling and perfect for people-watching.

### ★Restaurant du Port de Pêche
SEAFOOD $$

(☎0522 31 85 61; Le Port de Pêche; mains Dh90-135; ⏲noon-2.30pm & 7-10.30pm) Packed to the gills at lunch and dinner, this tried and trusted restaurant on the upstairs floor of a building in the middle of Casablanca's port serves the city's freshest and best seafood. Fish can be enjoyed fried or grilled, plain or meunière, and there are oysters and other shellfish on offer. Note that smokers on nearby tables are inevitable.

### ★Restaurant Brasserie La Bavaroise
FRENCH $$$

(☎0522 31 17 60; www.bavaroise.ma; 133 Rue Allah ben Abdellah; mains Dh160-230; ⏲noon-10.30pm Mon-Fri, 7-10.30pm Sat; ❄; 🚊Marché Central) Located in a dishevelled street behind the Marché Centrale, La Bavaroise has been serving an ultraloyal local clientele since 1968 and shows no sign of losing its popularity. The speciality is grass-fed beef from the Atlas served in the form of steak with

## Central Casablanca

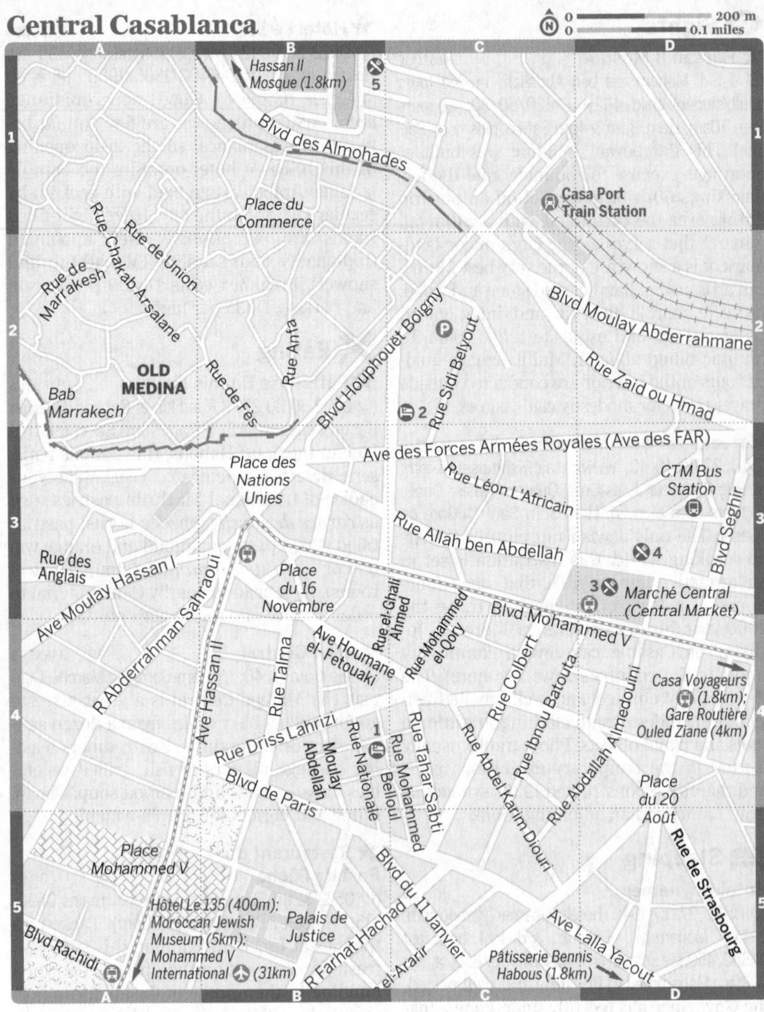


### Central Casablanca

**Sleeping**
1 Hotel Guynemer ........ B4
2 Hôtel les Saisons ........ C2

**Eating**
3 Marché Central ........ D3
4 Restaurant Brasserie La Bavaroise ........ D3
5 Restaurant du Port de Pêche ........ B1

pommes frites, green salad and French-style sauces. Other highlights include oysters from Dakhla and decadent desserts.

## Getting There & Away

### AIR

Casablanca's **Mohammed V International Airport** (www.onda.ma) is 30km southeast of the city on the Marrakesh road. Regular flights leave from here for most countries in Western Europe, as well as to West Africa, Algeria, Tunisia, Egypt, the Middle East and North America. Internally, the vast majority of Royal Air Maroc's (RAM) flights go via Casablanca, so you can get to many destinations in Morocco directly from the city.

### BUS

**CTM bus station** (0522 54 10 10; www.ctm.ma; 23 Rue Léon L'Africain; Marché Central)

Destinations include seven daily services (Dh110, 7¼ hours) and one premium service (Dh270, 6¾ hours) to Agadir; four services to Essaouira (Dh140, 7¼ hours); and seven daily services (Dh85, 7¼ hours) and one premium service (Dh120, four hours) to Marrakesh.

### TRAIN

Casa Port train station is located a few hundred metres northeast of Pl des Nations Unies, in the port precinct. This is the station for trains to/from Rabat (1st/2nd class Dh69/37, 70 minutes, every 30 minutes). The train to/from Mohammed V International Airport also starts/ends here.

Long-distance trains to all national destinations except Rabat and Kenitra arrive at and depart from Casa Voyageurs train station.

# Essaouira

POP 77,426 / ☎0524

It is the coastal wind – the beautifully named *alizee*, or *taros* in Berber – that has allowed Essaouira (essa-weera, or es-sweera in Arabic) to retain its traditional culture and character. Known as the 'Wind City of Africa', it attracts plenty of windsurfers between April and November, but the majority of visitors come here in spring and autumn to wander through the spice-scented lanes and palm-lined avenues of the fortified medina; browse the many art galleries and boutiques; relax in some of the country's best hotels; and watch fishing nets being mended and traditional boats being constructed in the hugely atmospheric port.

## Sights & Activities

**★Essaouira Medina** AREA

Essaouira's walled medina dates from the late 18th century and was added to Unesco's World Heritage list in 2001. It is an outstanding and well preserved example of European military architecture in North Africa. For the visitor, the narrow streets, souqs, street vendors, leafy plazas and whitewashed houses with ornate wooden doors make it a wonderful place to stroll. Dramatic, wave-lashed ramparts surround the medina and were famously used in the opening scene of Orson Welles' 1951 film *Othello*.

**Hammam Villa de l'Ô** HAMAM

(☎0524 47 63 75; www.villadelo.com; 3 Rue Mohamed Ben Messaoud, Medina; ⏰by appointment) The in-house spa at hotel Villa de l'Ô has a lovely small hammam where you can enjoy a bath treatment (30-minute bath with *gommage* Dh400, one-hour bath with *gommage* (a scrub down by a hammam attendant) and argan-oil massage Dh550). Also on offer are massages (one hour Dh400) and a variety of beauty treatments. Bookings essential.

## Festivals & Events

**Gnaoua and World Music Festival** MUSIC

(www.festival-gnaoua.net; ⏰late Jun) Essaouira overflows every year for the celebrated Gnaoua and World Music Festival, a four-day extravaganza with concerts staged at venues including the beach and Pl Moulay Hassan.

## Sleeping

**★Hôtel Riad Nakhla** B&B $

(☎tel/fax 0524 47 49 40; www.riadnakhla.com; 12 Rue d'Agadir, Medina; incl breakfasts/tr Dh250/490, d & tw Dh360; 📶) The dark and dingy entrance passageway is unprepossessing, but inside there's a lovely central courtyard surrounded by 16 clean and attractive rooms. All have good beds and satellite TV, some have seating alcoves and a few have sea views. Breakfast is served on the pleasant roof terrace, which has sea views. Ultrafriendly staff and bargain prices seal a great deal.

**★Jack's Apartments & Suites** APARTMENT $$

(Jack's Bohemian Suites; ☎0524 47 55 38; www.jackapartments.com; 1 Pl Moulay Hassan, Medina; r Dh380-850, apt Dh740-1740; 📶) Swiss traveller Jack came to Essaouira to windsurf but ended up marrying a local and opening a business renting apartments and rooms, benefiting fellow travellers in the process. In various locations near Bab Skala, the apartments sleep between two and eight persons and are clean, stylish and extremely well equipped; some have private terraces and others can access a rooftop terrace with sea views.

**★Dar Al-Bahar** B&B $$

(☎0524 47 68 31; www.daralbahar.com; 1 Rue Touahen; incl breakfast d & tw Dh550-825, tr Dh825; 📶) The nine immaculately kept rooms at this lovely guesthouse, under the ramparts near the Skala de la Ville, are simple and stylish, featuring good beds and small bathrooms with colourful tiles. Local art adorns the walls and the views from the roof terrace overlooking the ocean are magnificent.

## Eating

**Restaurant La Découverte** MOROCCAN $

(☎0524 47 31 58; http://essaouira-ladecouverte.com; Rue Houmman El Fatouaki, Medina; mains from Dh50) A small, friendly French-run restaurant, offering a mix of Franco-Moroccan dishes. The *briouates* are particularly good, as are the creamy desserts.

★**Loft** MEDITERRANEAN $$
(☎0524 78 44 62; 5 Rue Hajjali, Medina; mains Dh75-110; ⏲1-4pm & 6-11pm Wed-Mon; 📶) The menu at this tiny eatery near Pl Moulay Hassan changes daily according to what's plentiful and good at the souqs, resulting in food that is fresh and full of flavour. Dishes have Mediterranean accents, but remain predominantly Moroccan – the tajines and couscous are delicious. Decor is retro-funky and the English-speaking waiters are friendly. Alcohol isn't available.

★**La Table by Madada** MEDITERRANEAN $$$
(☎0524 47 55 12; www.latablemadada.com; 7 Rue Youssef el-Fassi, Medina; mains Dh100-220; ⏲7-10.30pm Fri-Wed; ❄📶) Style meets substance at Essaouira's best restaurant, which is housed in an old almond warehouse. The interior is an exhilarating and highly successful meld of traditional Moroccan and modern European, and the menu features contemporary rifts on Moroccan favourites such as tajines and *pastilla*. Fish and seafood dishes dominate. Service is friendly but could do with a polish.

## Information

Essaouira is still mostly a safe, relaxed tourist town, but you should be on your guard in the backstreets of the *mellah* (Jewish quarter) after dark – there are problems with drugs and drinking north of Ave Zerktouni and east of Ave Sidi Mohammed ben Abdallah.

The **tourist office** (☎0524 78 35 32; www.essaouira.com; 10 Rue du Caire, Medina; ⏲8.30am-4.30pm) can offer little assistance. Check www.essaouira.nu for information.

## Getting There & Away

**Aéroport de Mogador** (☎0524 47 67 04; www.onda.ma; Rte d'Agadir), 17km south of the medina, is used by Transavia, flying from Paris, and EasyJet, flying from London Luton.

The **bus station** (Ave Ghazouat) is about 400m northeast of the medina. CTM destinations include Agadir (Dh75, 2¼ hours, three daily), Casablanca (Dh160, seven hours, four daily) and Marrakesh (Dh80, 3½ hours, two daily).

# Agadir

POP 679,000 / ☎548

With a busy port and beach resort sprawling beneath its kasbah, Agadir was completely rebuilt following a devastating earthquake in 1960. It is now the country's premier destination for sun, sand, pubs and pizza. Arching south of the shiny white marina, the sandy beach offers clean water and 300 sunny days a year.

## Sleeping

**Hotel Clichy** HOTEL $
(☎0528 84 42 00; contact@hotelclichy.ma; 48 Ave du President Kennedy; s/d Dh230/270) The rooms certainly aren't as flash as the over-the-top tiled reception, but a recent makeover has definitely resurrected this midrange hotel on the edge of the Nouveau Talborjt neighbourhood. Bathrooms are especially spick and span, and the modern and shiny downstairs terrace cafe is popular with Agadir locals. Ask for a rear room to minimise occasional traffic noise.

★**Atlas Kasbah** BOUTIQUE HOTEL $$
(☎0661 48 85 04; www.atlaskasbah.com; Rte d'Azrarag, Tighanimine El Baz; r/ste incl breakfast from Dh880/1650; 📶🏊) Located on a spectacular hilltop 15km inland from Agadir, the 11 rooms and suites in this Berber-style fortress are the ideal overnight haven after partaking in Atlas Kasbah's busy menu of ecofriendly and cultural activities. Guests can indulge in hammam and massage treatments, learn about Moroccan cuisine and crafts, or go hiking or donkey riding to nearby Berber villages.

★**Paradis Nomade** BOUTIQUE HOTEL $$
(☎0671 12 15 35; www.paradis-nomade.com; Douar Azarag; s/d incl breakfast from Dh405/590, tents per person Dh155; @📶🏊) Located in pleasant rural surroundings around 15km from Agadir, Paradis Nomade combines very impressive suites, smaller but still comfortable rooms, and the option of staying in Berber-style tents. A Berber ambience is also carried through to the best of the rooms, and the garden surroundings are enlivened with a compact swimming pool and a spacious restaurant and bar area.

## Eating

**K Moon** MOROCCAN $
(☎0528 82 47 61; 58 Rue des Oranges; mains Dh25-42; ⏲noon-11pm) Colourful parasols and a sunny outdoor terrace combine at this local spot serving well priced grills – the merguez (spiced sausage) plate for lunch will set you up for an afternoon's exploring of Agadir – and hearty tagines packed with vegetables. If you're hungry and travelling in a small group, push the boat out with the 1kg mixed grill.this museum

**Le P'tit Dôme** MOROCCAN, INTERNATIONAL $$
(☎0528 84 08 05; www.facebook.com/Ptitdome; Blvd du 20 Août; mains Dh80-125; ⏲10am-late) In a line of tourist restaurants, Le P'tit Dôme offers good service, black-and-white decor

and a touch more class than its neighbours. The usual pizza, meat, seafood and Moroccan dishes are served, and the three-course set menu (Dh120) is good value. Outdoor terrace seating provides a pleasant dining environment.

## Information

**Information Booth** (☎0528 83 91 02; www.visitagadir.com; Al-Massira Airport; ⏲24hr)

**ONMT** (Délégation Régionale du Tourisme; ☎0528 84 63 77; www.visitagadir.com; Immeuble Ignouan, Ave Mohammed V; ⏲8.30am-4.30pm Mon-Fri) In the blue building next to DHL; not particularly helpful.

## Getting There & Away

**Al-Massira Airport** (☎0528 83 91 02; www.onda.ma; N10), mainly served by Royal Air Maroc and European charter flights and budget airlines, is 28km southeast of Agadir en route to Taroudannt. Facilities include a post office, bag-wrap service, cafes, souvenir shops and wi-fi hotspots.

**CTM** (☎0528 82 53 41; www.ctm.ma), which has a Nouveau Talborjt ticket office off Pl Lahcen Tamri, has several daily departures to destinations including Casablanca (Dh270, eight hours), Dakhla (Dh395, 20 hours), Essaouira (Dh75, 3½ hours), Marrakesh (Dh110, 3½ hours), Rabat (Dh230, nine hours) and Tangier (Dh340, 13½ hours).

# WESTERN SAHARA

After crossing the rocky and forlorn expanses of the *hammada* (stony desert) south from Tarfaya, the Western Saharan city of Dakhla is an appealingly relaxed destination. A constant feature is the cobalt intensity of the Atlantic Ocean, softened here by palm trees, a pleasant oceanfront esplanade and a shallow island-studded lagoon.

Occasional roadblocks on the fringes of the desert reinforce this is a disputed region, despite what is indicated by the Moroccan flags shifting in tropical breezes.

## Dakhla

POP 106,277 / ☎0528

Established by the Spanish in 1844 and formerly called Villa Cisneros, Dakhla lies just north of the Tropic of Cancer on a sandy peninsula stretching 40km from the main coastline. It's a very lonely 500km drive from Laâyoune (more than 1000km from Agadir) through endless *hammada*, and Dakhla is actually closer to Nouâdhibou (Mauritania) than any Moroccan city.

### Sleeping & Eating

**Hotel Al Baraka** HOTEL **$$**

(☎0528 934 744; hotelalbarakadakhla@gmail.com; Ave Allal Ben Abdellah; s/d incl breakfast Dh550/759, ste Dh850-1000; 📶) Located a short walk from good restaurants, the spacious rooms at the Al Baraka still retain that minty-fresh, just-opened ambience. Big-screen TVs provide access to a planet's worth of satellite services, and a new licensed rooftop restaurant was in the works when we dropped by. Hotel manager Charlie definitely has his pulse on what's going on around town.

**Dakhla Attitude** RESORT **$$$**

(☎0661 835 010; www.dakhla-attitude.ma; Km 30, Dakhla Lagoon; s/d incl full board from Dh1045/1540; 📶) The first of Dakhla's kite-surfing camps has now evolved into an expansive and very comfortable resort with breezy hillside bungalows, an excellent restaurant and a sandy beachfront bar attended by quite possibly the most laid-back dogs in all Morocco. It's a true destination resort with yoga, massage and activities for children, and has a prime location right on the lagoon.

### Getting There & Away

**AIR**

**Dakhla Airport** (☎0528 93 06 30; www.onda.ma) Located a short 2.5km drive north of the waterfront. A shared taxi from the airport to central hotels costs Dh15.

**Royal Air Maroc** (RAM; ☎0528 89 70 49; www.royalairmaroc.com) Regular flights to/from Casablanca and Agadir, and to Las Palmas on Gran Canaria (Tuesday only).

**BUS**

**CTM** (☎0528 89 81 66; Blvd 4 Mars) and **Supratours** (Ave Mohammed V) both have offices in the centre. Book ahead for popular daily services to: Agadir (Dh395, 20 hours), Laâyoune (Dh175, 8½ hours), Marrakesh (Dh490, 23 hours) and Tan Tan (Dh300, 13½ hours). These fares and durations are for CTM buses.

For onward travel south to Mauritania, Supratours runs daily services leaving Dakhla at 8.30am and 7.30pm (Dh160) south to Gargarate, around 5km north of the border. At the border, Mauritanian taxi drivers will want around Dh200 per person to drive you through the border and a further 25km into Mauritania for onward transport.

# IMPERIAL CITIES & THE MIDDLE ATLAS

Several important cities have taken root here, including ancient Fez, Meknès and the Roman city of Volubilis. Heading south, the low-rise Middle Atlas mountains come into play. Oak and cedar forests create refreshing pockets of woodland and easy hiking terrain, connecting the dots between Berber hill towns and villages.

## Fez

POP 1.15 MILLION / ☎0535

An ancient breeding ground for scholars and artisans, imams and gourmands – Fez is a supremely self-confident city with a historical and cultural lineage that beguiles visitors. And there is something intangibly raw about a place where 70,000 people still choose to live in the maelstrom of a medina so dark, dense and dilapidated that it remains the world's largest car-free urban area. In the **Medina (Fès el-Bali)** donkeys cart goods down the warren of alleyways as they have done since medieval times, and ruinous pockets loom around every corner, though a government drive to restore the medina to its former glory is spurring changes.

### Sights

#### Medina (Fès el-Bali)

The major sights are really only a small part of the charm of the medina. It pays to do a little random exploration, and simply follow your nose or ears to discover the most unexpected charms of Fez' nature. Everywhere, listen out for the call to prayer or the mule driver's cry *'balak!'* ('look out!') to warn of the approach of a heavily laden pack animal.

Navigation can be confusing and getting lost at some stage is a certainty, but look at this as part of the adventure. A handy tip is to note the 'main' streets that eventually lead to a gate or landmark – just follow the general flow of people.

**★Chaouwara Tanneries** WORKSHOP

(Map p124; Derb Chaouwara, Blida) The Chaouwara tanneries are one of the city's most iconic sights (and smells), offering a unique window into the pungent, natural process of producing world-class leather using methods that have changed little since medieval times. In 2015–16 it underwent a year-long restoration to spruce up the crumbling environs surrounding the pits, including the viewing terraces, but fear not – the tanneries' atmosphere remains intact. Try to get here in the morning when the pits are awash with coloured dye. Heading east or northeast from Pl as-Seffarine, you'll soon pick up the unmistakable waft of skin and dye that will guide you into the heart of the leather district. Beware the persistent touts, who will pounce on you as soon as you get within sniffing distance of the streets surrounding the tanneries: it is completely unnecessary to hire one and if you let a tout lead you into a shop, you'll pay more for anything you happen to buy there, to pay for his commission.

**★Medersa Bou Inania** ISLAMIC SITE

(Map p124; Talaa Kebira; Dh20; ⏲9am-5pm, closed during prayers) A short walk down Talaa Kebira from Bab Bou Jeloud, the Medersa Bou Inania is the finest of Fez' theological colleges. It was built by the Merenid sultan Bou Inan between 1351 and 1357, and has been impressively restored with elaborate *zellij* (tiles) and carved plaster, beautiful cedar *mashrabiyyas* (lattice screens) and massive brass entrance doors. Whereas most *medersas* just have a simple prayer hall, the Bou Inania is unusual in that it hosts a complete mosque.

**★Nejjarine Museum of Wooden Arts & Crafts** MUSEUM

(Map p124; ☎0535 74 05 80; Pl an-Nejjarine; Dh20; ⏲10am-5pm) This museum is in a wonderfully restored *fondouq* (rooming house) – a caravanserai for travelling merchants who stored and sold their goods below and took lodgings on the floors above. Centred on a courtyard, the rooms are given over to displays of traditional artefacts of craftsmen's tools, chunky prayer beads and Berber locks, chests and musical instruments. Everything is beautifully presented, although the stunning building gives the exhibits a run for their money. The rooftop cafe has great views over the medina. Photography is forbidden.

**★Medersa el-Attarine** ISLAMIC SITE

(Map p124; Dh20; ⏲9am-5pm) Founded by Abu Said in 1325 in the heart of the medina, the Attarine was designed as an annexe to the nearby Kairaouine. The central courtyard displays the traditional patterns of Merenid artisanship. Onyx columns flank the mihrab. Slightly smaller than the Medersa Bou Inania, it has been sensitively restored.

**Kairaouine Mosque & University** MOSQUE

(Map p124) One of Africa's largest mosques and possibly the oldest university in the world, this complex is the spiritual heart of

## Fez

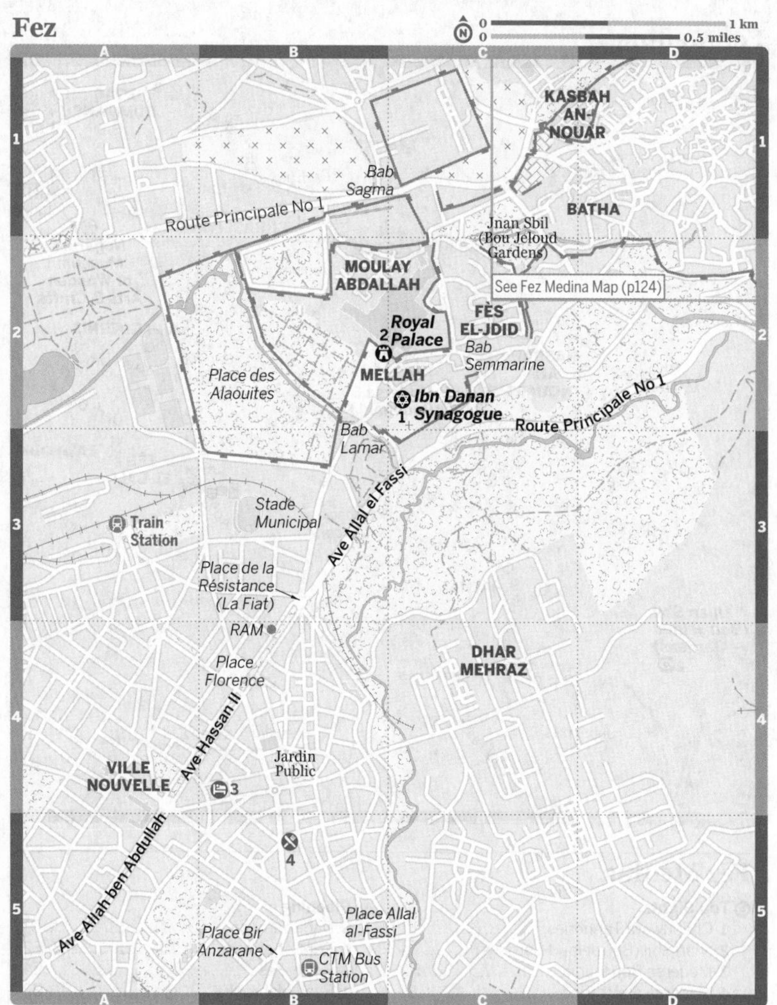




Fez and Morocco itself. It's so large that it can be difficult to actually see: over the centuries the streets and houses of the Kairaouine quarter have encroached on the building so much they disguise its true shape. Non-Muslims cannot enter, but the university library has recently been impressively restored and opened to the public in 2016.

### Fez

**Top Sights**

1 Ibn Danan Synagogue .......... C2
2 Royal Palace .......... B2

**Sleeping**

3 Hôtel Splendid .......... B4

**Eating**

4 Restaurant Marrakech .......... B5

## Fez el-Jdid (New Fez)

Only in a city as old as Fez could you find a district dubbed 'New' because it's only 700 years old. The paranoid Merenid sultan Abu Yusuf Yacoub (1258–86) purpose-built the quarter, packing it with his Syrian mercenary guards and seeking to isolate himself from his subjects. Even today almost half of the area is given over to the grounds of

## Fez Medina

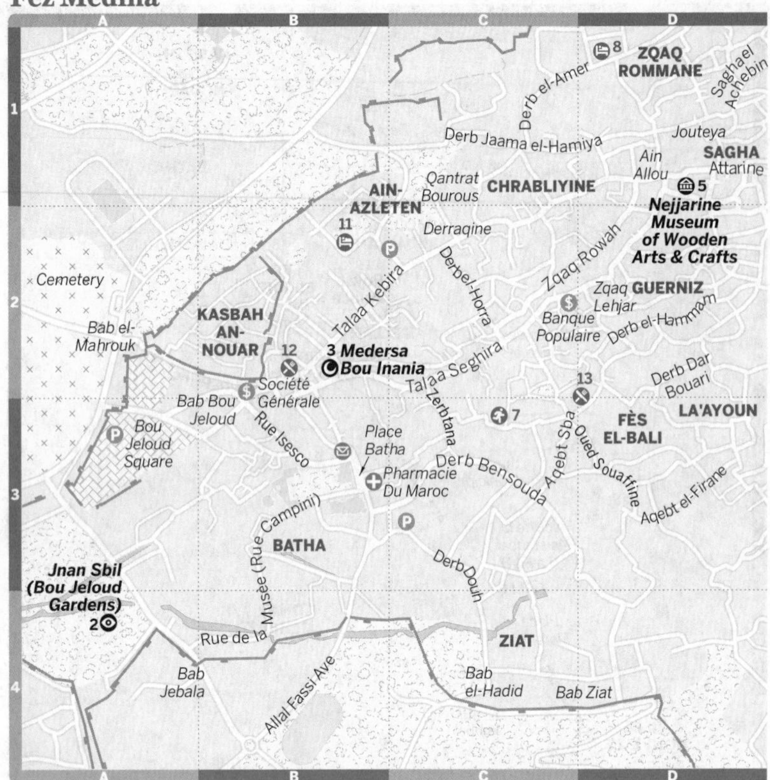


## Fez Medina

**Top Sights**

1 Chaouwara Tanneries ........ E1
2 Jnan Sbil (Bou Jeloud Gardens) ........ A4
3 Medersa Bou Inania ........ B2
4 Medersa el-Attarine ........ E1
5 Nejjarine Museum of Wooden Arts & Crafts ........ D1

**Sights**

6 Kairaouine Mosque & University ........ E2

**Activities, Courses & Tours**

7 Riad Fès ........ C3

**Sleeping**

8 Dar Roumana ........ D1
9 Dar Seffarine ........ E2
10 Funky Fes ........ E4
11 Ryad Mabrouka ........ B2

**Eating**

12 B'sara Stalls ........ B2
Restaurant Dar Roumana ........ (see 8)
13 Ruined Garden ........ D2

**Drinking & Nightlife**

14 Abdullah's ........ E2
Riad Fès ........ (see 7)

the **Royal Palace** (Dar el-Makhzen; Map p123; Pl des Alaouites). Its other main legacy is the architectural evidence of its early Jewish inhabitants and the fascinating **Ibn Danan Synagogue** (Map p123; off Derb Taquriri; donations welcome; ⌚9am-8pm). Halfway between the *mellah* (Jewish quarter) and Bab Bou Jeloud, **Jnan Sbil** (Bou Jeloud Gardens; Map p124; Ave Moulay Hassan; ⌚8am-7pm) are a breath of fresh air after the intensity of Fez' medina and is a good spot to take a break. The main entrance is on Ave Moulay Hassan, but there's another at the opposite end of the park.

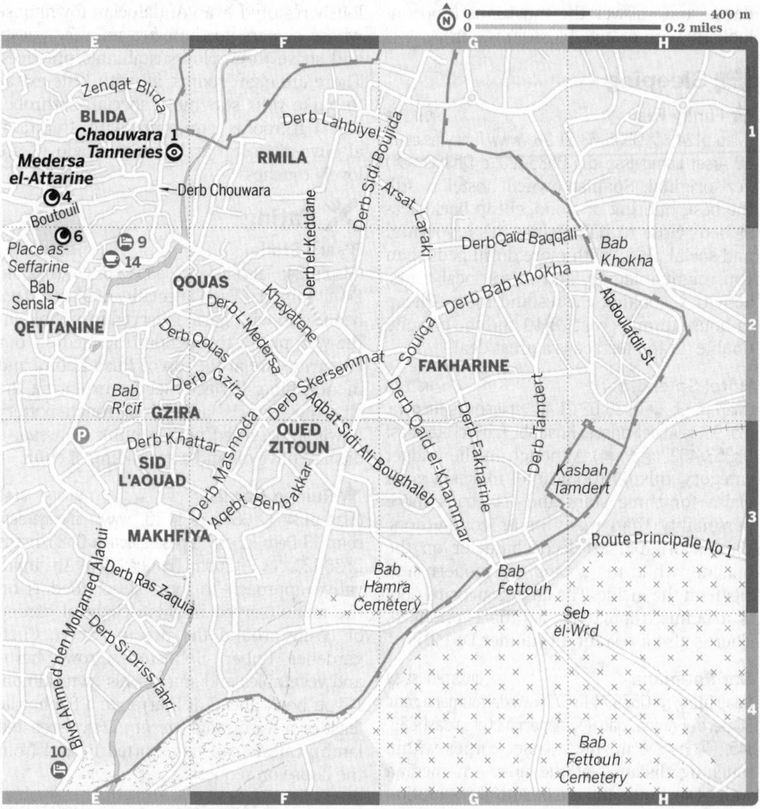

0 400 m
0 0.2 miles
E F G H
1 2 3 4
Zenqat Blida
BLIDA
Chaouwara Tanneries 1
Medersa el-Attarine 4
Boutouil 6
Place as-Seffarine
9
14
Bab Sensla
QETTANINE
RMILA
Derb Lahbiyel
Derb Sidi Boujida
Arsat Laraki
Derb Chouwara
Derb el-Keddane
QOUAS
Derb L'Medersa
Khayatene
Derb Qouas
Derb Gzira
Bab R'cif
GZIRA
Derb Khattar
SID L'AOUAD
Derb Masmoda
Derb Skersemmat
OUED ZITOUN
Aqbat Sidi Ali Boughaleb
'Aqebt Benbakkar
MAKHFIYA
Derb Ras Zaquia
Derb Si Driss Tahri
Blvd Ahmed ben Mohamed Alaoui
10
Derb Qaïd Baqqali
Bab Khokha
Derb Bab Khokha
Souïqa
Abdoulafdil St
FAKHARINE
Derb Qaid el-Khammar
Derb Fakharine
Derb Tamdert
Kasbah Tamdert
Route Principale No 1
Bab Hamra Cemetery
Bab Fettouh
Seb el-Wrd
Bab Fettouh Cemetery

## Ville Nouvelle

Compared to the sensory overload provided by the medina, the ville nouvelle can seem as if there's less going on. But for most Fassis, this is where it's at and, far more interesting and progressive than crumbling Fès el-Bali. In the past few years, huge amounts of money have been poured into the area, the benefits of which can best be seen along the long boulevard of Ave Hassan II, with its manicured lawns, palm trees, flower beds and fountains. This is the 'real' Morocco as much as any donkey-packed lane in the old city.

## Activities

**Riad Fès** HAMAM
(Map p124; ☎0535 94 76 10; www.riadfes.com; Derb Zerbtana; hamam from Dh350; ⏰noon-8pm) Recent renovations at swanky Riad Fès have devoured an adjoining house to create a new hamam area spectacularly situated around a riad patio. Another addition has enabled the hotel to build a beautiful enlarged pool.

## Festivals & Events

**Fès Festival of World Sacred Music** MUSIC
(☎0535 74 05 35; www.fesfestival.com; Fez; ⏰May/Jun) This festival brings together music groups and artists from all corners of the globe, and it has become one of the most successful world music festivals around. Based on the idea that music can engender harmony between different cultures, the festival has attracted big international stars such as Ravi Shankar, Bjork and Patti Smith.

**Moussem of Moulay Idriss II** RELIGIOUS
(⏰varies) Fez' biggest religious festival is also one of the country's largest. The *moussem* (festival in honour of a saint) of the city's founder, Moulay Idriss, draws huge crowds. Local artisans create special tributes and there's a huge procession through the medina. Traditional music is played and followers

dance and shower the musicians (and onlookers) with orange-blossom water.

## Sleeping

**★ Funky Fes** HOSTEL $
(Map p124; ☎0535 63 31 96; www.funkyfes.com; 60 Arset Lamdelssi; dm Dh85-120, d Dh300; ) Fez' original, Spanish-owned hostel is still the best, offering up good, cheap backpacker beds close to Bab el-Jdid. It's a youthful and social place, with more dorm beds than you might imagine, and offers local tours, activities, cooking classes and more. Cheap in-house dinners cost Dh40 and the en suite double on the terrace is a great deal.

**Hôtel Splendid** HOTEL $
(Map p123; ☎0535 62 21 48; splendidf@menara.ma; 9 Rue Abdelkarim el-Khattabi; s/d incl breakfast Dh353/432; ) Although in the budget category, this 69-room hotel makes a good claim for three stars and has bags more personality than many of its competitors. There's original art-deco character on the outside, while the rooms are modern and clean on the inside. The large courtyard pool is a bonus, though it's a little overlooked. There's also a restaurant (dinner Dh150).

**Dar Roumana** GUESTHOUSE $$
(Map p124; ☎0535 74 16 37; www.darroumana.com; 30 Derb el-Amer, Zqaq Roumane; r incl breakfast €85-145; ) Occupying a quiet corner within touching distance of the northern medina walls, Dar Roumana is a beautiful restoration job with hard-to-beat views from its roof terrace. Uncommonly, three of the rooms have wonderful baths (one a roll-top) and a couple of the rooms have external-facing windows. Push the boat out for the Yasmina suite, with its four-poster bed and leafy balcony.

**Dar Seffarine** GUESTHOUSE $$
(Map p124; ☎0671 11 35 28; www.darseffarine.com; 14 Derb Sbaalouyat, R'cif; incl breakfast r from €75, ste €110-130; ) A short walk from Pl Seffarine, this classy *dar* (small house) stands on high ground, meaning it's filled with light and blessed with plenty of external-facing windows – the lovely roof terrace towers over much of the rest of the medina. Its owner is an Iraqi architect and graphic designer whose talents are reflected in the understated room interiors. Dinner (Dh200) and alcohol can be served in-house.

**★ Ryad Mabrouka** GUESTHOUSE $$$
(Map p124; ☎0535 63 63 45; www.ryadmabrouka.com; 25 Derb el-Mitter, Ain-Azleten; incl breakfast d Dh1150-1450, ste Dh1300-2000; ) An old favourite, Mabrouka is a large, meticulously restored Arab-Andalucian townhouse whose owners go the extra mile for guests and strive to employ sustainable practices. There are eight rooms, all with little extras to make your stay more special: bathrobes and bathrooms equipped with traditional olive-pitt soap and scrubbing gloves are lovely touches.

## Eating

**B'sara Stalls** MOROCCAN $
(Map p124; Talaa Kebira; soup Dh6; 7am-2pm) Don't miss the Fassi speciality of *b'sara* (fava bean soup with garlic). Served from hole-in-the-wall places throughout the medina, our favourites are at the top of Talaa Kebira and in Achebine. Perfect fuel for exploring the city, the soup is ladled into rough pottery bowls and served with a hunk of bread, a dash of olive oil and a sprinkling of chilli.

**★ Ruined Garden** MOROCCAN $$
(Map p124; ☎0649 19 14 10; www.ruinedgarden.com; 13 Derb Idrissi; tapas selection Dh85, mains Dh80-120; 1-9.30pm Thu-Tue; ) An innovative approach to local street food is on the menu, served in this delightful garden or cosily around the fire in winter. Chef-gardener Robert Johnstone grows herbs and vegetables and smokes his own salmon. If you book ahead, it'll arrange a Sephardic feast or a traditional *mechoui* (slow-roasted lamb). Guests can be escorted to and from the house on request.

**Restaurant Marrakech** MOROCCAN $$
(Map p123; ☎0535 93 08 76; 11 Rue Omar el-Mokhtar; mains from Dh79; noon-3pm & 6pm-late; ) Hidden behind thick wooden doors, this restaurant exudes more charm than just about any other food stop in the ville nouvelle. Red *tadelakt* walls and dark furniture, with a cushion-strewn salon at the back, add ambience, while the menu offers some interesting variations on the usual Moroccan fare.

**★ Restaurant Dar Roumana** MEDITERRANEAN $$$
(Map p124; ☎0660 29 04 04, 0535 74 16 37; 30 Derb el-Amer, Zqaq Roumane; 2/3 courses Dh275/350; 7-9pm Tue-Sun; ) Dining at Dar Roumana is a white-linen affair with fine service and fine food, and its gorgeous courtyard creates an atmospheric dining spot. French chef Vincent Bonnin's menu makes the best of local Moroccan produce while celebrating Mediterranean flavours. There are innovative salads and excellent fish and meat dishes, and vegetarians are well catered for (notify in advance). Alcohol is served.

## Drinking & Nightlife

**★Abdullah's** CAFE

(Map p124; Rue Lmachatine; ⌚8am-8pm Sat-Thu) There's something a bit special about Abdullah's nook-in-the-wall tea shop, and it's not just the owner's beaming smile and *zellij*-decorated counter piled high with fresh herbs to pop in your brew. Abdullah swears by the water he uses to make his teas (featuring not just mint, but also herbs such as absinthe): it comes straight from the holy Kairaouine complex. A blessed infusion, indeed.

**★Riad Fès** BAR

(Map p124; www.riadfes.com; 5 Derb ben Slimane, Zerbtana; ⌚10am-midnight) You're spoilt for choice at Riad Fès, without doubt the classiest place for a drink in the whole city. Its courtyard Alcazar bar is a delight, with stucco columns that catch the light reflected off the central ornamental pool. The riad also now has a wine bar next to the new swimming pool, and an ultra-modern Sky Bar peeping over the medina rooftops.

## Information

### DANGERS & ANNOYANCES

- It's not really safe to walk on your own in the medina late at night, especially for women.
- Knife-point robberies are not unknown.
- Hotels and many restaurants are usually happy to provide an escort on request if you're out late.
- Fez has long been notorious for its *faux guides* (unofficial guides) and carpet-shop hustlers, all after their slice of the tourist dirham.

### MEDICAL SERVICES

**Clinique al-Kawtar** (☎0535 61 19 00; Ave Mohamed el-Fassi, Route d'Immouzzer) Large modern hospital in the ville nouvelle, just off the main road to the airport.

**Pharmacie Du Maroc** (Map p124; Pl Batha; ⌚8.30am-12.30pm & 3-7.30pm Nov-Apr, 9am-1pm & 3.30-8pm May-Oct) An easily accessible modern pharmacy in the medina.

### MONEY

There are plenty of banks (with ATMs) in the ville nouvelle along Blvd Mohammed V. In the medina there is an ATM at the Batha Post Office and at banks around Place R'cif, as well as these useful spots:

**Banque Populaire** (Map p124; Talaa Seghira; ⌚8.15am-3.45pm Mon-Fri)

**Société Générale** (Map p124; Bab Bou Jeloud; ⌚9.15am-5.15pm Mon-Thu, 8.15-11.45am Fri, 9.15-12.45pm Sat)

## Getting There & Away

### AIR

**Fes-Saïss Airport** (☎0535 67 47 12) is 15km south of the city and has recently been expanded with a swanky new hall, though at the time of writing it had yet to open. **RAM** (Map p123; ☎0535 94 85 51; 54 Ave Hassan II) operates daily flights to Casablanca, as well as connections to Europe.

### BUS

**CTM** (Map p123; ☎0800 09 00 30; www.ctm.ma) runs 16 buses a day to Casablanca (Dh90, 4½ hours) via Rabat (Dh75, three hours) between 1.30am and 7.15pm, plus one other premium bus to Rabat only at 9.30pm (Dh100). Buses to Meknès (Dh25, one hour) run 24 hours a day but departure times are irregular. There are seven buses a day to Marrakesh (Dh165 to Dh175, 9½ hours) between 6.30am and 8pm, plus a quicker premium bus departing at 9.30pm (Dh225). Heading north and east, there are six buses for Tangier (Dh110, six to seven hours) and three for Chefchaouen (Dh75, four hours).

### TRAIN

Trains depart almost hourly between 1.30am and 8.40pm to Casablanca (Dh116, four hours), via Rabat (Dh127, three hours) and Meknès (Dh30, 30 minutes). Eight trains go to Marrakesh (Dh206, eight hours) and four go direct to Tangier (Dh164, five hours) – two more go via Sidi Kacem.

# Meknès

POP 835,695 / ☎0535

Quieter and smaller than Fez, Meknès feels rather overshadowed and receives fewer visitors than it should. It's more laid-back with less hassle, yet still has all the winding narrow medina streets and grand buildings that it warrants as an imperial city and one-time home of the Moroccan sultanate.

## Sights

**★Heri es-Souani** RUINS

(Dh10; ⌚9am-noon & 3-6.30pm) Nearly 2km southeast of Moulay Ismail's mausoleum, the king's immense granaries and stables, Heri es-Souani, were ingeniously designed. Tiny ceiling windows, massive walls and a system of underfloor water channels kept the temperatures cool and air circulating. Incredibly the building provided stabling and food for 12,000 horses, and Moulay Ismail regarded it as one of his finest architectural projects.

**★Place el-Hedim** SQUARE

The heart of the Meknès medina is Pl el-Hedim, the large square facing Bab el-Mansour. Before Moulay Ismail swept

## Meknès

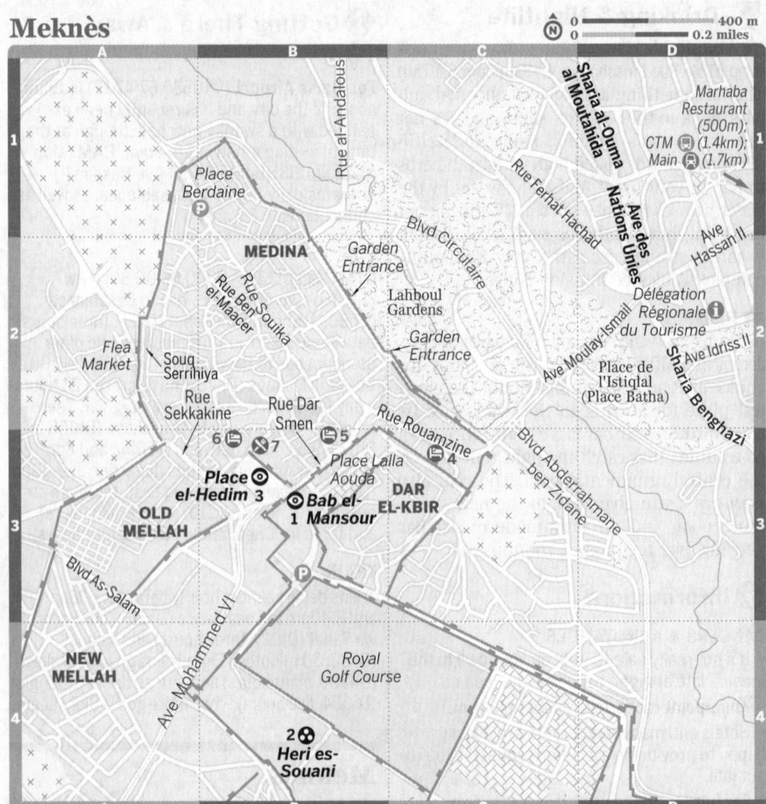


### Meknès

**Top Sights**

| | | |
|---|---|---|
| 1 | Bab el-Mansour | B3 |
| 2 | Heri es-Souani | B4 |
| 3 | Place el-Hedim | B3 |

**Sleeping**

| | | |
|---|---|---|
| 4 | Hôtel Maroc | C3 |
| 5 | Riad d'Or | B3 |
| 6 | Ryad Bahia | B3 |

**Eating**

| | | |
|---|---|---|
| 7 | Restaurant Yahala | B3 |
| | Ryad Bahia | (see 6) |

through town, a kasbah stood on this spot, but once the *bab* (gate) was erected the king ordered for it to be demolished in favour of a broad plaza from which the gate could be better admired. Originally used for royal announcements and public executions, it's a good place to sit and watch the world go by.

The focus of Pl el-Hedim is the huge gate of **Bab el-Mansour**, the grandest of all imperial Moroccan gateways.

## Festivals & Events

**Moussem of Sidi ben Aïssa** RELIGIOUS

One of the largest *moussems* in Morocco takes place on the eve of Moulid at Meknès' Mausoleum of Sidi ben Aïssa, outside the medina walls, in celebration of the Aïssawa Sufi brotherhood. It's a busy and popular festival with *fantasias* (musket-firing cavalry charge), fairs, singing and dancing. The dates change each year as they're fixed by the Islamic lunar calendar.

## Sleeping

**Hôtel Maroc** HOTEL $

(☎0535 53 00 75; 7 Rue Rouamzine; per person Dh100, roof terrace Dh50) A perennially popular shoestring option, the Maroc has the edge on location as it's just a five-minute walk from the medina, Bab el-Mansour and

Pl el-Hedim. Friendly and quiet, rooms (with sinks) are simple, and the shared bathrooms are clean. For a 50% discount you can sleep on a mattress on the roof terrace, surrounded by pot plants and washing.

★ **Ryad Bahia** GUESTHOUSE **$$**
(☎0661 81 52 37, 0535 55 45 41; www.ryad-bahia.com; Tiberbarine; s/d incl breakfast from Dh400/650; ❄📶) This charming riad, a converted family home, is just a stone's throw from Pl el-Hedim. The main entrance opens onto a cavernous courtyard, which also hosts a great **restaurant** (mains from Dh90, set menus Dh160-190; ⊙noon-3pm & 7-10pm; 📶). Rooms are pretty and carefully restored, and the owners (keen travellers themselves) are eager to swap travel stories as well as guide guests in the medina; Bouchra is a licensed (female!) guide.

**Riad d'Or** GUESTHOUSE **$$**
(☎0641 07 86 25; www.riaddor.com; 17 Derb el-Anboub; r/ste €50/80; ❄📶🏊) This labyrinthine riad is spread over two townhouses. The mix of traditional and modern-styled rooms caters to all tastes. Many can sleep four or more people and have sitting areas, and provide outstanding value for money. The biggest surprise is hidden on one of the roof terraces: a larger-than-average swimming pool.

## Eating

**Marhaba Restaurant** MOROCCAN **$**
(23 Ave Mohammed V; mains from Dh25; ⊙noon-10pm; 📶) This retro canteen-style place – the essence of cheap and cheerful – is hugely popular. At lunchtime, go for the freshly grilled meats. Later in the day do as everyone else does and fill up on a bowl of *harira* (lentil soup) and a plate of *maâkouda* (potato fritters) with bread and hard-boiled eggs (served from 4pm) – and get change from Dh15.

**Restaurant Yahala** MOROCCAN **$$**
(☎0649 98 88 16; restaurant.yahala@gmail.com; 10 Rue Sidi Amar Bouaouda; mains Dh60-95; 📶) There's a nice atmosphere at this petite restaurant, where chatter wafts down from the family kitchen. Everything in the white stuccoed dining salon is bright, clean and modern, though lacking in natural light, and the Moroccan dishes are cooked fresh to order.

## Information

**Délégation Régionale du Tourisme** (☎0535 52 44 26, 0535 51 60 22; Pl de l'Istiqlal; ⊙8.30am-4.30pm Mon-Fri, 8-11.30am Sat) Meknes' main tourist office is in the ville nouvelle, but it doesn't keep to its advertised opening hours.

WORTH A TRIP

### VOLUBILIS

The best-preserved archaeological site in Morocco is the Roman ruins of **Volubilis** (adult/child Dh10/3; ⊙8.30am-sunset), about 33km north of Meknès. Volubilis can easily be combined with the nearby hill town of **Moulay Idriss** to make a fantastic day trip from Meknès. A half-day outing by grand taxi from Meknès will cost around Dh350, with a couple of hours at the site and a stop at Moulay Idriss. A cheaper alternative is to take a shared grand taxi from near Meknès's Institut Français to Moulay Idriss (Dh10) then hire a grand taxi to take you to Volubils (Dh30, one way).

## Getting There & Away

From the **CTM bus station** (☎0522 43 82 82; Ave des FAR), departures include Casablanca (Dh85, three to four hours, seven daily), some of which go via Rabat (Dh55, two hours, eight daily), as well as Fez (Dh25, one hour, 17 daily) and Marrakesh (Dh165, seven to eight hours, twice daily) and Tangier (Dh90 to Dh100, five hours, four daily).

There are trains to Fez (Dh32, 45 minutes, hourly), Casablanca (Dh143, three to 3½ hours, 19 daily) via Rabat (Dh95, two to three hours), and to Marrakesh (Dh280, seven hours, eight daily). For Tangier, there are four direct trains a day (Dh90, four to five hours) and two night trains that involve a change at Sidi Kacem.

# CENTRAL MOROCCO & THE HIGH ATLAS

Marrakesh is the queen bee of Moroccan tourism but look beyond it and you'll find great trekking in the dramatic High Atlas, and spectacular valleys and gorges that lead to the vast and empty sands of the Saharan dunes.

## Marrakesh

POP 1.32 MILLION / ☎0524

Marrakesh grew rich on the camel caravans threading their way across the desert, although these days it's cheap flights from Europe bringing tourists to spend their money in the souqs that fatten the city's coffers. But Marrakesh's old heart still beats strongly enough, from the time-worn ramparts that ring the city to the nightly spectacle of the Djemaa el-Fna that leaps from the pages of the 1001 Nights on the edge of the labyrinthine medina.

# Marrakesh

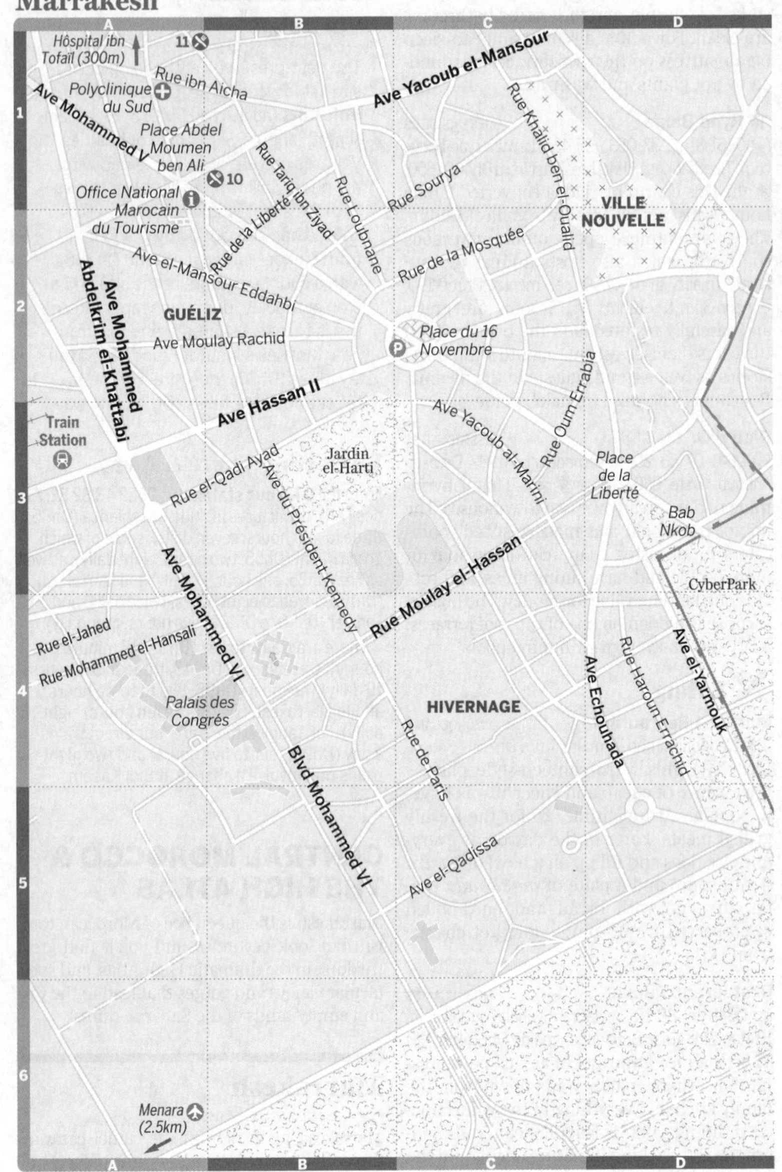




## Sights

**★Djemaa el-Fna** SQUARE

(off Pl de Foucauld) Think of it as live-action channel-surfing: everywhere you look in the Djemaa el-Fna, Marrakesh's main square, you'll discover drama in progress. The hoopla and *halqa* (street theatre) has been nonstop here ever since this plaza was the site of public executions around AD 1050 – hence its name, which means 'assembly of the dead'. By midmorning the soundtrack of snake-charmer flutes has already begun, but

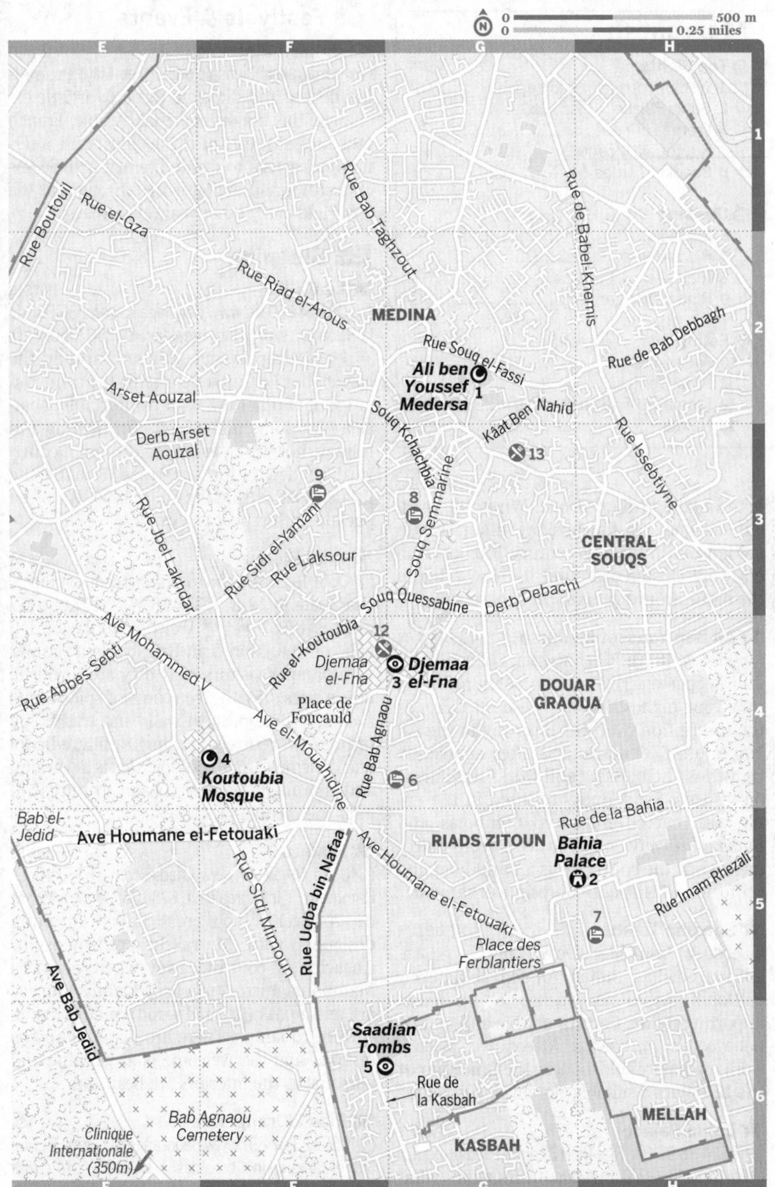




the show doesn't kick off until sunset when restaurants fire up their grills, cueing musicians to tune up their instruments.

★**Koutoubia Mosque** MOSQUE
(cnr Rue el-Koutoubia & Ave Mohammed V; ⏲closed to non-Muslims) Five times a day, one voice rises above the Djemaa din as the muezzin calls the faithful to prayer from the Koutoubia Mosque minaret. Excavations confirm a Marrakshi legend: the original mosque, built by Almoravid architects, wasn't properly aligned with Mecca, so the pious Almohads levelled

## Marrakesh

**Top Sights**

1 Ali ben Youssef Medersa ........ G2
2 Bahia Palace ........ H5
3 Djemaa el-Fna ........ G4
4 Koutoubia Mosque ........ F4
5 Saadian Tombs ........ F6

**Sleeping**

6 Le Gallia ........ G4
7 Riad Azoulay ........ H5
8 Riad Le J ........ G3
9 Riad L'Orangeraie ........ F3

**Eating**

10 Al Fassia ........ B1
11 Amal Center ........ A1
12 Djemaa El-Fna Food Stalls ........ F4
13 Naima ........ G3

it to build a realigned one. When the present mosque was finished by Sultan Yacoub el-Mansour in the 12th century, 100 booksellers were clustered around its base – hence the name, from *kutubiyyin* (booksellers).

**★Ali ben Youssef Medersa** ISLAMIC SITE
(☎0524 44 18 93; Pl ben Youssef; Dh20; ⊙9am-7pm, to 6pm winter) 'You who enter my door, may your highest hopes be exceeded', reads the inscription over the entryway to the Ali ben Youssef Medersa, and after almost six centuries, the blessing still works its charms on visitors. Sight lines are lifted in the entry with carved Atlas cedar cupolas and *mashrabiyya* (wooden-lattice screen) balconies, while the courtyard is a mind-boggling profusion of Hispano-Moresque ornament.

**★Saadian Tombs** HISTORIC SITE
(Rue de la Kasbah; adult/child Dh10/3; ⊙9am-4.45pm) Saadian Sultan Ahmed al-Mansour ed-Dahbi spared no expense on his tomb, importing Italian Carrara marble and gilding honeycomb *muqarnas* (decorative plasterwork) with pure gold to make the **Chamber of the 12 Pillars** a suitably glorious mausoleum.

**★Bahia Palace** PALACE
(☎0524 38 95 64; Rue Riad Zitoun el-Jedid; adult/child Dh10/3; ⊙9am-4.30pm) Imagine what you could build with Morocco's top artisans at your service for 14 years, and here you have it. The salons of both the **petit riad** and **grand riad** host intricate marquetry and *zouak* (painted wood) ceilings while the vast **grand courtyard**, trimmed in jaunty blue and yellow, leads to the **Room of Honour**, with a spectacular cedar ceiling.

## Festivals & Events

**Marrakech Biennale** ART
(www.marrakechbiennale.org; ⊙Feb-May) Promoting debate and dialogue through artistic exchange, this major trilingual (Arabic, French and English) festival invites local and international artists to create literary, artistic, architectural and digital works throughout the city. Held every other year (even years).

## Sleeping

**★Le Gallia** HOTEL $
(☎0524 44 59 13; www.hotellegallia.com; 30 Rue de la Recette; s/d/tr incl breakfast Dh350/550/850; ❄📶) Madcap Djemaa el-Fna is around the corner, but Le Gallia maintains the calm and grace of another era with comfortable, neat-as-a-pin rooms, all with air-con, heating and reliable hot water, arranged around a courtyard shaded by orange trees. Run by the French Galland family since 1929, it's often packed with repeat visitors.

**★Riad Bledna** GUESTHOUSE $$
(☎0661 18 20 90; www.riadbledna.com; off Rte de Ouarzazate, Km19, N 31°35'46.8, W 7°52'28.5; d incl breakfast €70; P🏊) 🌿 Welcome to the garden villa of the Moroccan-British Nour family, who pamper visitors as if they are favourite house guests. With five rooms of spice-toned *tadelakt* (lime plaster) walls and traditional *tataoui* (woven reed) ceilings, a filtered pool and delicious home cooking, this is a peaceful and thoroughly homey cocoon to retreat to after the medina hustle.

**★Riad Le J** B&B $$
(☎0524 39 17 87; www.riadlej.com; 67 Derb el-Hammam; r incl breakfast €75-105; ❄📶) What do you get if you cross Italian furniture designers with Marrakshi craftsmanship? An achingly cool hideaway where art deco Mamounia mirrors meet silk kaftans hung as art, and *zouak* (painted wood) ceilings merge with retro lamps. There are just four rooms on offer and the welcome is as genuine and personal as the interiors are beautiful.

**★Riad L'Orangeraie** B&B $$$
(☎0661 23 87 89; www.riadorangeraie.com; 61 Rue Sidi el-Yamani; incl breakfast r €140-150, ste €180; ❄📶🏊) From Moroccan sweets and fresh flowers in your room to top-notch, personal service provided by owner Cyril and manager Ismail, Riad L'Orangeraie gets all the finer details right. Amply proportioned rooms come with bathrooms of perfectly buffed *tadelakt* walls and massaging showers (the best in town), while the courtyard rimmed by cosy sitting alcoves leads out to a generous pool.

★**Riad Azoulay** B&B $$$

(☎0524 38 37 29; www.riad-azoulay.com; 3 Derb Jamaa Kebir; incl breakfast d €100-130, ste from €170; ) The restoration of this 300-year-old mansion, once home to the wealthy Azoulay family, who served as advisors to the royal family, was a labour of love for owner Sandro. The result is a haven of casual luxury where original cedar ceilings and plasterwork decor sit comfortably alongside modern art, painted-wood antique furniture and sumptuously coloured kilims.

## Eating

★**Amal Center** MOROCCAN $

(☎0524 44 68 96; amalnonprofit.org; cnr Rues Allal ben Ahmad & Ibn Sina; mains Dh50-60; ⊙noon-4pm) Do good while eating delicious food – double bonus. The Amal Center supports and trains disadvantaged Moroccan women in restaurant skills and you get to feast on their flavours. So many Marrakesh restaurants reflect poorly on local cuisine, but here you get the real home-cooking deal. On our last visit we had the best fish tajine we've ever tasted in Morocco.

**Djemaa El-Fna Food Stalls** MOROCCAN $

(mains Dh30-50; ⊙sunset-1am) Grilled meat and tajines as far as the eye can see! Plus Moroccan specialities of snail soup, sheep's brains and skewered hearts for the more adventurous gourmet. Eating amid the mayhem of the Djemaa food stalls at least once in your trip is not to be missed. Always go for the busiest stalls as they'll have the freshest meat.

**Naima** MOROCCAN $$

(Derb Sidi Ishak; meals Dh100; ⊙11am-10pm) If you want to eat couscous prepared by a proper Marrakshi mamma then Naima is the place to be. Squeeze into the tiny dining room, order either tajine or couscous (there's no menu) and settle back with a mint tea as the women get cooking. Bring your appetite – this is family-style Moroccan food and the portions are huge.

★**Al Fassia** MOROCCAN $$$

(☎0524 43 40 60; www.alfassia.com; 55 Blvd Mohammed Zerktouni; mains Dh110-175; ⊙noon-2.30pm & 7.30-11pm Wed-Mon) In business since 1987, this stalwart of the Marrakesh dining scene is still one of the best. Meals begin with a bang with complimentary 12-dish *mezze* (salads), while Moroccan mains of chicken tajine or caramelised pumpkin and lamb tajine with almonds and eggs – served by an all-female waiter crew – show how the classics should be done. Reservations essential.

## Information

### DANGERS & ANNOYANCES

Marrakesh is, in general, a safe city.

- Pickpockets work on Djemaa el-Fna and, to a lesser extent, around the medina. Carry only the minimum amount of cash necessary.
- Be particularly vigilant if walking around the medina at night.
- Hustlers and unofficial guides hang around the medina. They can be persistent and sometimes unpleasant. Maintain your good humour and be polite when declining offers of help.

### MEDICAL SERVICES

**Clinique Internationale** (☎0524 36 95 95; www.clinique-internationale-marrakech.com; Bab Ighli, off Av Guemassa) Recommended central private hospital.

**Hôspital ibn Tofaïl** (Rue Abdelouahab Derraq; ⊙0524 43 92 74) Public hospital.

**Polyclinique du Sud** (☎0524 44 79 99; 2 Rue de Yougoslavie; ⊙24hr) Well regarded private hospital in Guéliz.

### TOURIST INFORMATION

**Office National Marocain du Tourisme** (ONMT; ☎0524 43 61 79; Pl Abdel Moumen ben Ali, Guéliz; ⊙8.30am-noon & 2.30-8pm Mon-Thu, 8.30-11.30am & 3-6.30pm Fri) Offers pamphlets but little in the way of actual information.

## Getting There & Away

### AIR

**Royal Air Maroc** (RAM; ☎0890 00 08 00; www.royalairmaroc.com) has several flights daily to and from Casablanca (one way from around Dh800, 55 minutes).

### BUS

| DESTINATION | PRICE (DH) | DURATION (HR) | FREQUENCY (DAILY) |
|---|---|---|---|
| Agadir | 120/150 regular/ premium | 3½-4 | 17 |
| Casablanca | 90/130 regular/ premium | 3½ | 15 |
| Er-Rachidia | 180 | 10 | 1 |
| Essaouira | 80 | 3½ | 2 |
| Fez | 185-190 | 8-9 | 6 |
| Laâyoune | 350 | 14-15½ | 7 |
| Ouarzazate | 90 | 4½ | 5 |
| Tan Tan | 225 | 9 | 8 |
| Tiznit | 140-150 | 5½ | 8 |
| Zagora | 155 | 7½ | 2 |

TRAIN

| DESTINATION | PRICE (DH) 2ND/1ST CLASS | DURATION (HR) | FRE-QUENCY (DAILY) |
|---|---|---|---|
| Casablanca | 95/148 | 3¼ | 9 |
| Fez | 206/311 | 7½ | 8 |
| Meknèz | 184/280 | 6¾ | 8 |
| Rabat | 127/195 | 4¼ | 9 |
| Safi | 69/103 | 3¼ | 2 |
| Tangier | 216/327 | 9¾ | 7 |

The last Tangier train travels overnight. Sleeping-car compartment tickets cost Dh370; book at least two days in advance.

# Drâa Valley

From Ouarzazate the N9 plunges southeast into the Drâa Valley, formed by a narrow ribbon of water from the High Atlas that occasionally emerges triumphantly in lush oases.

## M'hamid

POP 3000

Once it was a lonesome oasis, but these days M'Hamid is a wallflower no more. Border tensions between Algeria, Morocco and the Polisario had isolated this caravan stop until the 1990s, when accords allowed M'Hamid to start hosting visitors again. From here, it doesn't take long to reach the dunes, but to be enveloped by large dunes, you'll have to head out across the *reg* (hard-packed rocky desert) by dromedary or 4WD.

### Sights

**★Erg Chigaga** DUNES

The star attraction is the misnamed Erg Chigaga, not a single dune *(erg)* but an awesome stretch of golden sand sea some 56km southwest of M'Hamid. It is the largest sand sea in Morocco, snaking along the horizon for 40km and bordered to the north and south by mountain ridges. The best way to reach them is in classic movie style: by camel, which takes five days or a week (from Dh500 to Dh600 per day) round-trip.

### Tours

**★Sahara Services** OUTDOORS

(☎0661 77 67 66; www.saharaservices.info; per person from €75) Far and away the most professional outfit operating in M'Hamid, Sahara Services offers memorable, all-inclusive desert trips via camel and 4WD, including overnights to an encampment of handsomely set Berber tents in Erg Chigaga. You'll dine well here, enjoy fireside music and watch the night sky light up with stars before falling asleep on a comfy bed surrounded by a sea of silence.

### Sleeping & Eating

**Auberge Kasbah Dar Sahara** GUESTHOUSE $

(☎0667 85 33 17; http://darsaharatour.com; s/d/q Dh150/200/400; P 📶) A big draw for budget travellers, this small, very welcoming place has rustic rooms with shared facilities and relaxing common areas, and outdoor space where you can unwind and contemplate the peace of the desert. To get there, head all the way through town and look for the sign leading up to the left.

**Dar Sidi Bounou** GUESTHOUSE $$$

(☎0677 29 13 10; www.darsidibounou.com; s/d incl half-board Dh460/810, Berber tent per person incl half-board Dh350; P 📶) A desert dream: dunes in the backyard, sand hamams, Saharawi music jam sessions and *mechoui* feasts on starry terraces. Retreat to Berber tents and mudbrick huts that sleep six to eight, sleep on the roof, or curl up between crisp cotton sheets in the main house.

### Getting There & Away

A daily 6am CTM bus leaves M'Hamid (listed online as Lamhamid Ghozlane) for Zagora (Dh35, 1½ hours), Ouarzazate (Dh80, five hours) and Marrakesh (Dh160, 10 hours). Local buses and taxis leave for Zagora (Dh35) throughout the day. Buses and taxis all depart from the main square in M'Hamid.

## Zagora

POP 36,000

The original, iconic 'Tombouctou, 52 jours' (Timbuktu, 52 days) sign, featuring a nomad with a smirking camel, may have been swept away in an inexplicable government beautification scheme, but Zagora's fame as a desert outpost remains indelible. The Saadians launched their expedition to conquer Timbuktu here in 1591, and desert caravans passing through Zagora gave this spot cosmopolitan character. These days Zagora remains a trading post and meeting place, hosting a regional souq on Wednesday and Sunday and putting on a variety of festivals.

### Sleeping

**★Auberge Restaurant Chez Ali** INN $

(☎0524 84 62 58; http://chezali.net; Ave de l'Atlas Zaouiate El Baraka; d incl breakfast Dh200-300, without bathroom Dh70-90; P ❄ 📶 ≋) The peacocks stalking the pool can't be bothered, but otherwise the welcome here is enthusiastic. Skylit upstairs rooms have simple pine furnishings, bathrooms and air-con, and 'traditional' rooms have mattresses on carpets and shared bathrooms. Enjoy fantastic Berber meals (Dh100) and overnight trips run by English-speaking guides Mohamed and Yusuf.

**Kasbah Ziwana** GUESTHOUSE **$$**
(☎0667 69 06 02; www.kasbah-ziwana-zagora.com; s/d incl half-board Dh300/600; ❄) Next to the Musée des Arts in Tissergat, 8km north of Zagora, the Kasbah Ziwana is made of native materials, and has attractively furnished rooms. Relax in the peaceful inner courtyard or on the roof terrace, and get loads of local insight from the kindhearted host Mustapha, a desert guide with many years of experience.

★ **Riad Dar Sofian** GUESTHOUSE **$$$**
(☎0524 84 73 19; www.riaddarsofian.com; Rte de Nakhla, Amezrou; s/d/tr incl breakfast Dh680/880/1100, tents Dh220; P ❄ 📶 ≋) Dar Sofian is a stunning desert oasis. The fabulous pisé (rammed earth or clay) edifice was constructed by a team from Skoura, while Fassi craftsmen executed the acres of tilework inside. The decor is a successful take on contemporary Moroccan with a mix of modern beds and bathrooms, antique furnishings and traditional detailing.

## Information

**Banque Populaire** (Blvd Mohammed V) Stock up on cash at one of the last ATMs you'll find before you hit the Sahara.

**BMCE** (Blvd Mohammed V) ATM.

## Getting There & Away

Zagora has a small airport, southwest of town off the N12, that has two weekly flights (Monday and Wednesday) from Casablanca with Royal Air Maroc (www.royalairmaroc.com).

**Supratours** (☎0524 84 76 88; Blvd Mohammed V), near the Banque Populaire, offers a daily 6am bus to Marrakesh (Dh135, 7½ hours) and Ouarzazate (Dh50, 2¾ hours). There is also a daily **CTM** (☎0524 84 73 27; Blvd Mohammed V) bus to M'Hamid (Dh35, 2¾ hours) and three daily CTM buses to Ouarzazate (Dh55, three hours), two of which continue to Marrakesh (Dh135, 8½ hours).

# Aït Benhaddou

POP 4200

**Ksar Aït Benhaddou** is a Unesco-protected red mudbrick ksar (fort) 32km from Ouarzazate. With the help of some Hollywood touch-ups, it seems frozen in time, still resembling its days in the 11th century as an Almoravid caravanserai. Movie buffs may recognise it from *Lawrence of Arabia*, *Jesus of Nazareth* (for which much of Aït Benhaddou was rebuilt), *Jewel of the Nile* (note the Egyptian towers) and *Gladiator*. A less retouched kasbah can be found 6km north along the tarmac from Aït Benhaddou: the Tamdaght kasbah, a crumbling Glaoui fortification topped by storks' nests.

## Sleeping

**Kasbah du Jardin** HOTEL **$**
(☎0524 88 80 19; www.kasbahdujardin.com; campsite Dh50-70, d Dh250-400; ❄ 📶 ≋) Near the western entrance to town, the friendly Kasbah du Jardin has decent, nicely equipped rooms set around a sparkling pool – book an upstairs one for better views. You can also pitch a tent here, but there's not much shade.

**Etoile Filante d'Or** GUESTHOUSE **$$**
(☎0524 890322; www.etoilefilantedor.com; d incl breakfast from €35; ❄ 📶) Moonlit desert nights on the Etoile's roof terrace lure guests out of 17 spacious rooms for movie-script-inspiring *ksar* views. Guest rooms feature traditional touches such as *tataoui* ceilings and Berber blankets. The guesthouse also has an inviting restaurant where you can enjoy Moroccan and European fare (three-course dinner Dh100) and a full bar. Nadia, the welcoming host, can arrange camel rides, mountain biking and other excursions.

**Dar L'Haja** GUESTHOUSE **$$**
(☎0652 03 38 25; www.elhaja-aitbenhaddou.com; s/d Dh350/600) Fuel those Lawrence of Arabia fantasies by overnighting inside the *ksar*. Set along the steps leading through the old fortified village, this guesthouse offers amazing views from the terrace, and the comfortably furnished rooms are nicely maintained.

## Eating

**Cafe-Restaurant Amlalte** MOROCCAN **$**
(mains around Dh40; ⊙noon-9pm) Just before the footbridge across to the *ksar*, this laid-back eatery serves up an unsurprising selection of soups, salads, tagines and couscous. The best reason to come here is for the views from the terrace.

**Chez Brahim** MOROCCAN **$$**
(☎0671 81 63 12; meals Dh100; ⊙10am-9pm; 📶) Sure, there are other tajines in town, but only Brahim's improve international

relations: the chef-owner has a letter from Hilary Rodham Clinton thanking him for a meal in her First Lady days. The set menu includes salads, tajine and dessert in a pisé-walled salon with *ksar* views.

### Getting There & Away

To get here from Ouarzazate take the main road towards Marrakesh to the signposted turn-off (22km); Aït Benhaddou is another 9km down a bitumen road. Cycling from Ouarzazate takes three hours.

Grands taxis run from outside Ouarzazate bus station when full (Dh20 per person) and from the turn-off (around Dh5 per person or Dh30 for the whole vehicle). Minibuses run from Tamdaght to Ouarzazate in the morning when full.

## Merzouga & the Dunes

POP 4100

When a wealthy family refused hospitality to a poor woman and her son, God was offended, and buried them under the mounds of sand called Erg Chebbi. So goes the legend of the dunes rising majestically above the twin villages of Merzouga and Hassi Labied, which for many travellers fulfill Morocco's promise as a dream desert destination. But Erg Chebbi's beauty coupled with Merzouga's accessibility has its price. Paved roads across the Middle Atlas from Midelt and east from Ouarzazate mean that desert tourism is booming. In high season, coaches and convoys of 4WDs churn up huge dust clouds as they race across the *hammada* in time for sunset camel rides, and purists lament the encroachment of hotels flanking the western fringes of the dunes – although there's no denying the spectacular dune views from rooms and terraces.

### Sights

**★Erg Chebbi** DUNES

Shape-shifting over 28km from north to south and reaching heights of 160m, Erg Chebbi may be modest compared with the great sand seas of Algeria, Libya and Namibia, but it is extraordinarily scenic. The rose gold dunes rise dramatically above a pancake-flat, black hammada and glow stunning shades of orange, pink and purple as the afternoon sun descends.

### Sleeping & Eating

**Chez Youssef** GUESTHOUSE $

(0666 36 71 74; www.chezyoussef.com; Merzouga Village; d/tr incl breakfast Dh330/440, s/d/tr incl half-board Dh275/510/710; ) Youssef's simple pisé home offers four rooms arranged around a tiny courtyard shaded by a single palm. The oasis-inspired decor is sparing, but beds are firm, linens are spotlessly clean and food home-cooked. Your host offers good-value camel treks and overnights in a peaceful camp far from the crowds (Dh450 per person).

**Kasbah Kanz Erremal** HOTEL $$

(0535 57 84 82; www.kanzerremal.com; N 31°07.765, W 004°00.769; d/tr/q incl breakfast Dh480/720/950; ) Eschewing the rustic vibe of many other Merzouga hotels, Kanz Erremal favours understated stylish decor. Cushioned banquets line the airy, central courtyard while rooms with desert views are swathed in cool, white linens and gauzy curtains. Best of all is the wide terrace that overlooks the sand and a sleek infinity pool with dreamy dune views.

**★Ali & Sara's Desert Palace** CAMPGROUND $$$

(0668 95 01 44; thedesertpalace@hotmail.com; per person incl full board Dh975; ) Make friends with Romeo, George and Casanova – no, they aren't local lads trying it on, but your trusty dromedaries – as you head out from Merzouga for a trip of a lifetime. Husband-and-wife team, Ali and Sara, have spent four years crafting a personalised experience that gets rave reviews.

### Getting There & Away

The N13 runs from Rissani to Merzouga, and the *piste* from Erfoud will probably be sealed in the next few years. That said, most hotels are some distance from the road on *pistes* marked with signs. If you're driving a standard rental car, don't head off-road as you'll likely get stuck in the sand. Minibuses will pick up or drop off in Hassi Labied – your hotel can make arrangements. Minivans run from Merzouga between 7.30am and 9.30am in high season.

# UNDERSTAND MOROCCO

## Morocco Today

Morocco in the early 21st century is a confident country, increasingly sure of its role as a stable link between Europe, Africa and the Arab world, and a place that welcomes tourists and investors alike. It sailed through the Arab Spring unscathed, and while the perennial question of Western Sahara shows no sign of resolution, the nation is taking big steps to cement its role as a regional player, and a leader in renewable energy and responses to climate change

# History

## Berbers & Romans

Morocco's first-known inhabitants were Near Eastern nomads who may have been distant cousins of the ancient Egyptians. Phoenicians appear to have arrived around 800 BC. When the Romans arrived in the 4th century BC, they called the expanse of Morocco and western Algeria 'Mauretania' and the indigenous people 'Berbers', meaning 'barbarians'.

In the 1st century AD, the Romans built up Volubilis into a city of 20,000 (mostly Berber) people, but emperor Caligula declared the end of Berber autonomy in North Africa in AD 40. However, Berber rebellions in the Rif and the Atlas ultimately succeeded through a campaign of near-constant harassment. As Rome slipped into decline, the Berbers harried and hassled any army that dared to invade, to the point where the Berbers were free to do as they pleased.

## Islamic Dynasties

In the second half of the 7th century, the soldiers of the Prophet Mohammed set forth from the Arabian Peninsula. Within a century, nearly all the Berber tribes of North Africa had embraced Islam, although local tribes developed their own brand of Islamic Shi'ism, which sparked rebellion against the eastern Arabs.

By 829, local elites had established an Idrissid state, with its capital at Fez, dominating Morocco. Thus commenced a cycle of rising and falling Islamic dynasties, which included the Almoravids (1062–1147), who built their capital at Marrakesh; the Almohads (1147–1269), famous for building the Koutoubia Mosque; the Merenids (1269–1465), known for their exquisite mosques and *madrassas* (Quranic schools), especially in Fez; the Saadians (1524–1659), responsible for the Palais el-Badi in Marrakesh; and the Alawites (1659–present), who left their greatest monuments in Meknès.

France took control in 1912, making its capital at Rabat and handing Spain a token zone in the north. Opposition from Berber mountain tribes continued to simmer away and moved into political channels with the development of the Istiqlal (independence) party. Sultan Mohammed V proved vocally supportive of movements opposing colonial rule and was exiled for his pains.

## Morocco Since Independence

France allowed Mohammed V to return from exile in 1955, and Morocco successfully negotiated its independence from France and Spain in 1956. When Mohammed V died in 1961, King Hassan II became the leader of the new nation. Hassan II consolidated power by cracking down on dissent and suspending parliament for a decade.

With heavy borrowing and an ever-expanding bureaucracy, Morocco was deeply in debt by the1970s. In 1973 the phosphate industry in the Spanish Sahara started to boom. Morocco staked its claim to the area with the 350,000-strong Green March into Western Sahara in 1975. It settled the area with Moroccans while greatly unsettling indigenous Sahrawi people agitating for self-determination. The UN brokered a cease-fire in 1991, but the promised referendum, in which the Sahrawis could choose between independence and integration with Morocco, has yet to materialise, and Western Sahara's status remains undecided in international law.

However, the growing gap between the rich and the poor ensured that dissent against the regime was widespread. Protests against price rises in 1981 prompted a government crackdown, but sustained pressure from human-rights activists achieved unprecedented results in 1991, when Hassan II founded the Truth and Reconciliation Commission to investigate human-rights abuses that occurred during his own reign – a first for a king.

# People

Morocco's population is of mixed Arab-Berber descent. The population is young, growing and increasingly urbanised. Nearly 60% of Moroccans live in cities and the median age is just 25 years and decreasing – two trends that present the country with clear social and economic challenges.

Emigration to France, Israel and the US has reduced Morocco's once-robust Jewish community to approximately 7000 from a high of around 300,000 in 1948. The Jewish communities that once inhabited the historic *mellahs* (Jewish quarters) of Fez, Marrakesh, Essaouira and Meknès have largely relocated to Casablanca.

## Cuisine

The food you find in Morocco is likely to be fresh, locally grown and homemade, rather than shipped in, microwaved and served semithawed. Most Moroccan ingredients are cultivated in small quantities the old-fashioned way, without GMOs (genetically modified organisms), chemical fertilisers, pesticides or even mechanisation. These technologies are far too costly an investment for the average small-scale Moroccan farmer, as is organic certification and labelling – so though you may not see a label on it to this effect, much of the Moroccan produce you'll find in food markets is chemical- and GMO-free.

# SURVIVAL GUIDE

## Directory A–Z

### ACCOMMODATION

A wide range of accommodation options is available in Morocco. In our listings, the official, government-assigned rates (including taxes) are quoted, although these are intended as a guide only. The country is famous for its riads (traditional medina houses converted into boutique guesthouses). Hotels range from the most basic to the glitziest, while camping is mostly restricted to trekkers.

#### PRICE RANGES

The following price ranges refer to the cost of a double room in high season (November to April). Unless otherwise mentioned, prices exclude breakfast.

**€** less than Dh400

**€€** Dh400–Dh800

**€€€** more than Dh800

Exceptions to these price ranges are Casablanca, Essaouira, Fez, Marrakesh, Rabat and Tangier. For these places, the following price ranges apply:

**€** less than Dh600

**€€** Dh600–Dh1200

**€€€** more than Dh1200

The following price ranges refer to a standard main course.

**$** less than Dh70

**$$** Dh70–Dh150

**$$$** more than Dh150

### ACTIVITIES

Hike in North Africa's best mountain ranges, trek by camel into the sand dunes of the Sahara, surf along its beaches – and after you're done, scrub off your exertions at a traditional hamam.

### DANGERS & ANNOYANCES

Morocco is a pretty safe country that can be navigated with a bit of common sense, but there are a few things to be aware of:

- getting lost in winding medina streets
- getting hassled by unofficial guides (known as 'faux guides')
- the widespread use of marijuana *(kif)*, which is grown in Morocco.

### EMBASSIES & CONSULATES

The Moroccan Ministry of Foreign Affairs and Cooperation (www.diplomatie.ma/en) has a list of embassies and consulates in Morocco. Most embassies and diplomatic representation are in Rabat, and open from about 9am until noon Monday to Friday. Rabat embassies include the following:

**Algerian Embassy** (☎0537 66 15 74; algerabat@iam.net.ma; 46-48 Ave Tariq ibn Zayid, Quartier Hassan; 🚊Tour Hassan) Also has a consulate-general in Casablanca and consulate in Oujda.

**Canadian Embassy** (☎0537 54 49 49; www.canadainternational.gc.ca/morocco-maroc; 66 Mehdi Ben Barka Ave, Souissi; ⏰8am-4.30pm Mon-Thu, to 1.30pm Fri) Also provides consular assistance to Australians.

**Dutch Embassy** (☎0537 21 96 00; http://marokko.nlambassade.org; 40 Rue de Tunis, Quartier Hassan; 🚊Tour Hassan) Also has a consulate-general in Casablanca.

**French Embassy** (☎0537 67 87 00; www.consulfrance-ma.org; 1 Rue Aguelmane Sidi Ali, Agdal; ⏰8.30am-1.45pm Mon-Fri; 🚊Bibliotèque Nationale) Also has consulates in Agadir, Casablanca, Fez, Marrakesh, Rabat and Tangier.

**German Embassy** (☎0537 21 86 00; www.rabat.diplo.de; 7 Rue Madnine, Ville Nouvelle; ⏰9am-noon Mon-Fri; 🚊Place al-Joulane) Also has a consulate in Rabat and honorary consulates in Agadir and Casablanca.

**Mauritanian Embassy** (☎0537 65 66 78; 6 Rue Thami Lamdaouar, Soussi)

**Spanish Embassy** (☎0537 63 39 00; www.exteriores.gob.es/embajadas/rabat; Rue Ain Khalouiya, Souissi; ⏰8.30am-4.30pm Mon-Fri) Also has consulates-general in Agadir, Casablanca, Larache, Nador, Rabat, Tangier and Tetouan.

**UK Embassy** (☎0537 63 33 33; www.gov.uk; 28 Ave S.A.R. Sidi Mohammed, Souissi; ⏰8am-4.15pm Mon-Thu, to 1pm Fri) Also has honorary consulates in Agadir, Marrakesh and Tangier.

**US Embassy** (☎0522 64 20 99; http://rabat.usembassy.gov; Km 5.7, Ave Mohamed VI, Souissi; ⏰8am-5pm Mon-Fri) Also has a consulate-general in Casablanca.

Australia, New Zealand and Ireland do not have embassies in Morocco.

### INTERNET ACCESS

- Moroccan internet cafes are common, efficient and cheap (Dh5 to Dh10 per hour), usually with reasonable connection speeds.
- Two irritants for many travellers are the widespread French and Arabic (nonqwerty) keyboards, and Moroccan men's common use of internet cafes to view pornographic websites and similar.
- Wi-fi is widely available in midrange and top-end accommodation and in many of the better budget options. It is becoming more widespread in destinations that host lots of foreigners.
- If you're bringing a laptop, check the power-supply voltage and bring a universal adapter. USB modems are widely available from mobile-phone shops, and cost around Dh100 for one month's internet access. Buy them at a phone shop from Maroc Telecom, Meditel or Inwi (ID is required).

### LGBTIQ TRAVELLERS

Homosexual acts (including kissing) are illegal in Morocco, and carry a potential jail term of up to three years and/or a fine. Moroccan authorities have recently shown an increased tendency to prosecute. For travellers, discretion is the key in most places. Avoid public displays of affection.

Some towns are more gay-friendly than others, with Marrakesh winning the prize, followed by Tangier. However, there are are no dedicated gay destinations; nightlife in the bigger cities has become increasingly discreet in recent years.

Lesbians shouldn't encounter any problems, though it's commonly believed by Moroccans that there are no lesbians in their country.

### MONEY

ATMS are widely available. Credit cards are accepted in most midrange hotels and above, and at top-end restaurants.

#### Exchange Rates

| | | |
|---|---|---|
| Australia | A$1 | Dh7.36 |
| Canada | C$1 | Dh7.18 |
| Europe | €1 | Dh10.94 |
| Japan | Y100 | Dh9.57 |
| Mauritania | UM100 | Dh2.71 |
| New Zealand | NZ$1 | Dh7.07 |
| UK | UK$1 | Dh12.16 |
| USA | US$1 | Dh9.70 |

For current exchange rates, see www.xe.com.

### OPENING HOURS

Morocco keeps the Western working week, but some businesses may close early/completely on the Muslim prayer day or Friday. Exact opening hours may vary.

**Banks** 8.30am to 6.30pm Monday to Friday
**Bars** 4pm till late
**Government offices** 8.30am to 6.30pm Monday to Friday
**Post offices** 8.30am to 4.30pm Monday to Friday
**Restaurants** noon to 3pm and 7pm to 10pm (cafes generally open earlier and close later)
**Shops** 9am to 12.30pm and 2.30pm to 8pm Monday to Saturday (often closed longer at noon for prayer)

Work hours may be severely truncated during Ramadan.

### PUBLIC HOLIDAYS

Banks, post offices and most shops shut on the main public holidays, although transport still runs.

**New Year's Day** 1 January
**Independence Manifesto** 11 January
**Labour Day** 1 May
**Feast of the Throne** 30 July
**Allegiance of Oued Eddahab** 14 August
**Anniversary of the King's and People's Revolution** 20 August
**Young People's Day** 21 August
**Anniversary of the Green March** 6 November
**Independence Day** 18 November

### TELEPHONE

- Morocco has three GSM mobile-phone networks: Méditel (www.meditelecom.ma), Maroc Telecom (www.iam.ma) and Inwi (www.inwi.ma).
- Coverage is generally excellent, apart from in the mountains and deserts. 4G is available in most cities and many towns. If your mobile phone is unlocked, buying a prepaid mobile SIM card will likely be cheaper than using your phone on roaming.

### TIME

Standard Moroccan time is on GMT/UTC.

**Daylight saving** runs from the end of March to the end of October. The exception is during Ramadan, when Morocco reverts to GMT, but it goes back again to daylight saving afterwards.

### TOURIST INFORMATION

Some cities and larger towns have tourist offices, which are normally repositories of brochures run by uninformed staff and, as such, usually best avoided. Often the receptionist in your hotel or another local will be more helpful than such bureaus. The Moroccan National Tourist Office (www.visitmorocco.com) runs most tourist offices.

### VISAS

- Holders of UK, EU, US, Canadian, Australian and New Zealand passports may remain in the country for 90 days on entry.
- In all cases, your passport must be valid for at least six months beyond your date of entry.

- Nationals of Israel and many Sub-Saharan African countries (including South Africa) must apply in advance for a three-month visa (single/double entry about US$30/50).
- Applications are normally processed in 48 hours.
- You need three passport photos.
- In Morocco's neighbouring countries, there is a Moroccan embassy in Madrid (Spain) and consulates-general in locations including Algeciras; an embassy in Nouakchott (Mauritania) and a consulate-general in Nouâdhibou; and diplomatic missions in Algeria including an embassy in Algiers.
- Further information, including a list of Morocco's diplomatic missions, is available from the Moroccan Ministry of Foreign Affairs and Cooperation (www.diplomatie.ma/en).
- As visa requirements change, it's a good idea to check with the Moroccan mission in your country or a reputable travel agency before travelling.

### WOMEN TRAVELLERS

- Prior to marriage, many Moroccan men have little opportunity to meet and get to know women outside their family – a major reason why Western women receive so much attention.
- Frequent unwanted looks and comments can come as something of shock to first-time visitors and the constant attention can be extremely wearing.
- Some women choose to develop a thick skin and ignore the hassle and it's worth keeping in mind that low-level harassment rarely goes any further.
- A benefit is that, unlike male travellers, you'll have opportunities to meet local women.

## Getting There & Away

### AIR

Royal Air Maroc (p133) is Morocco's national carrier. For information about Moroccan airports, visit the website of Office National des Aéroports (www.onda.ma). Casablanca's Mohammed V International Airport is the country's main gateway, followed by Menara airport (Marrakesh). Other important airports include Fes–Saïss (Fez), Ibn Batouta International (Tangier), as well as Ouazazarte, Agadir, Essaouira, Oujda and Nador.

### LAND

#### Border Crossings

- **Algeria** This border remains closed. Algeria is reluctant to reopen it until the status of the Western Sahara is resolved – don't hold your breath.
- **Mauritania** The only crossing is in the Western Sahara between Dakhla (Morocco) and Nouâdhibou (Mauritania). Check both Western Sahara and Mauritania safety advice before travelling.
- **Spain** You can cross to mainland Spain via the Spanish enclaves of Ceuta and Melilla in northern Morocco.

### SEA

There are extensive ferry links between northern Morocco and southern Europe, the most popular of which is Algeciras (Spain) to Tangier. Ferries to Tangier now dock at Tanger Med terminal, except for those from Tarifa, 40km from Tangier.

From southern Spain and northern Morocco, you can just turn up at the dock and buy a ticket for the next ferry, but book in advance online during high season (mid-June to mid-September, Christmas, New Year and Easter).

## Getting Around

### AIR

- National carrier Royal Air Maroc (p133) is the main domestic airline. All flights are via its hub at Mohammed V International Airport, Casablanca.
- RAM serves Tangier, Nador, Oujda, Fez, Er-Rachidia, Marrakesh, Essaouira, Agadir, Laâyoune and Dakhla.
- Flying is relatively expensive but may be worth it if you are pushed for time. The 2¼-hour flight from Casablanca to Dakhla costs from Dh980, compared with Dh600 for a 1st-class seat on the 32-hour CTM bus journey.
- You can buy tickets online and at RAM offices and travel agencies.
- English is spoken at RAM's call centre.

### BUS

Buses are the cheapest and most efficient way to travel around the country. They are generally safe, although drivers sometimes leave a little to be desired. Most cities and towns have a single central bus station (gare routière), but Supratours and CTM often maintain separate terminals, and often have offices outside the station. Occasionally, there are secondary stations for a limited number of local destinations.

Where possible, and especially if services are infrequent or don't originate in the place you want to leave, book ahead for CTM and Supratours buses.

### TRAIN

Morocco's excellent train network is one of Africa's best, linking most of the main centres. Trains are reasonably priced and preferable to buses where available. Trains are comfortable, fast and generally run to their timetables. The ONCF (Office National des Chemins de Fer; www.oncf.ma) runs the network.

There are two main lines: Tangier down to Marrakesh via Rabat and Casablanca; and Oujda or Nador in the northeast down to Marrakesh, passing Fez and Meknès before joining the line from Tangier at Sidi Kacem.

A high-speed (TGV) line to link Tangier, Rabat and Casablanca is due to open in July 2018.

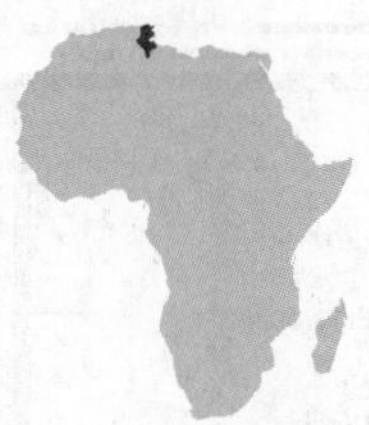

# Tunisia

POP 11.135 MILLION / ☎216

**Includes ➡**



## Fast Facts

**Capital** Tunis

**Population** 11.14 million

**Language** Arabic

**Area** 163,610 sq km

**Currency** Tunisian dinar (TD)

## Sand, Sea & Ancient Sites

It may be but a slim wedge of North Africa's vast horizontal expanse, but Tunisia has enough history and diverse natural beauty to pack a country many times its size. With a balmy, sand-fringed Mediterranean coast, scented with jasmine and sea breezes, and where the fish on your plate is always fresh, Tunisia has in the past been prime territory for a straightforward sun-sand-and-sea holiday. It's also a destination with distinct cultures and incredible extremes of landscape – forested coastlines along the coast, and Saharan sand seas in the south.

Sadly, there have been a number of terrorist attacks in Tunisia is recent years and most Western governments were advising against travel to the country at the time of writing.

## Tunisia at a Glance

**Tunis** This cosmopolitan Mediterranean city has a fascinating medina, museum and cultural events.

**Mahdia** Small-town charm on the coast.

**Jerba** This island has near-perfect beaches and a fascinating cultural mix.

**Carthage** The modern appearance of these low-slung ruins belies a history as one of the greatest cities of the Ancient World.

**Dougga** Extraordinarily well-preserved Roman ruins and sublime views.

**El Jem** One of the finest extant coliseums from the Ancient Roman times, with fabulous mosaics also in situ.

**Midès Gorge** One of Tunisia's most dramatic natural rock formations.

# Tunisia

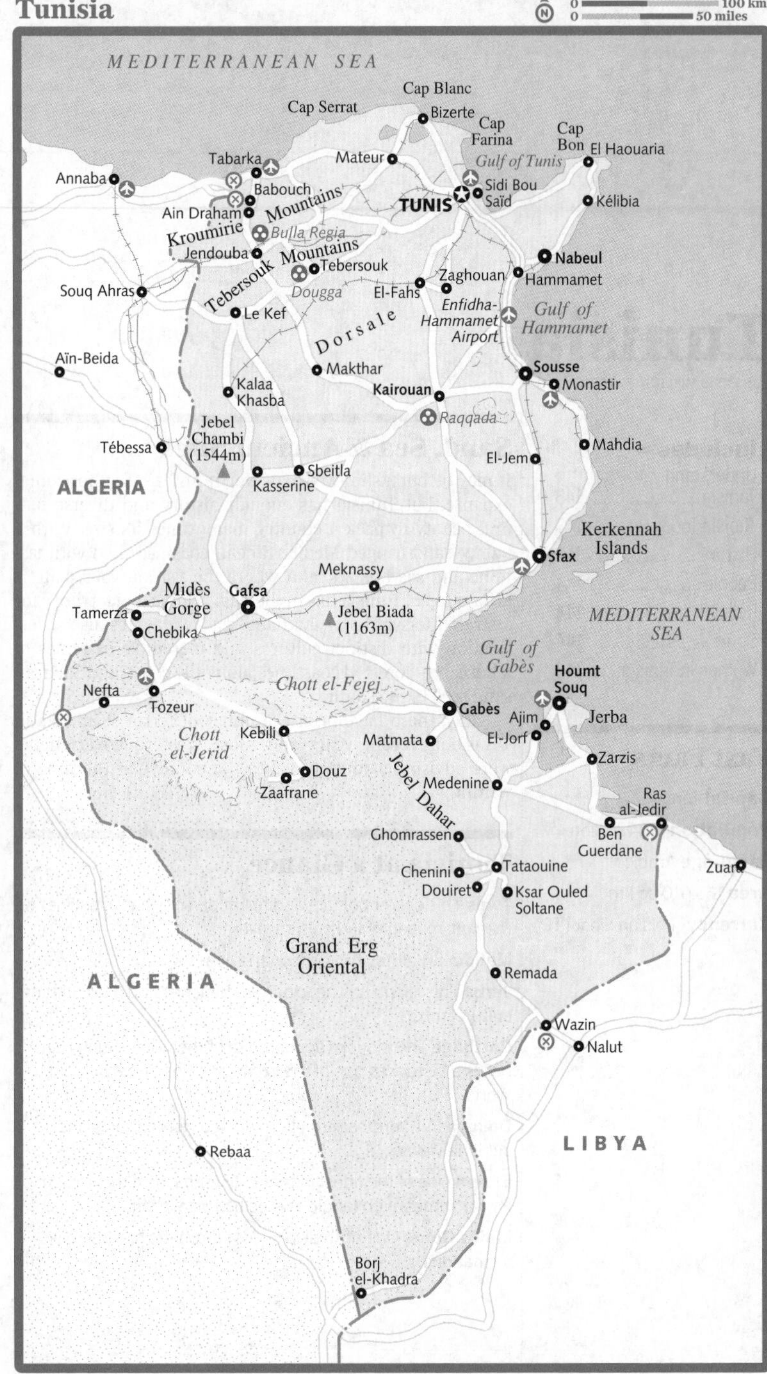
0 100 km
0 50 miles
MEDITERRANEAN SEA
Cap Blanc
Cap Serrat
Bizerte
Cap Farina
Cap Bon
El Haouaria
Gulf of Tunis
Tabarka
Mateur
Annaba
Babouch
Sidi Bou Saïd
TUNIS
Kélibia
Ain Draham
Kroumirie Mountains
Bulla Regia
Jendouba
Tebersouk Mountains
Tebersouk
Nabeul
Zaghouan
Hammamet
Souq Ahras
Dougga
El-Fahs
Enfidha-Hammamet Airport
Gulf of Hammamet
Le Kef
Dorsale
Aïn-Beida
Makthar
Sousse
Monastir
Kalaa Khasba
Kairouan
Raqqada
Jebel Chambi (1544m)
Mahdia
Tébessa
El-Jem
Sbeitla
Kasserine
ALGERIA
Kerkennah Islands
Sfax
Meknassy
Midès Gorge
Gafsa
Tamerza
Jebel Biada (1163m)
MEDITERRANEAN SEA
Chebika
Gulf of Gabès
Houmt Souq
Chott el-Fejej
Nefta
Tozeur
Gabès
Ajim
Jerba
Chott el-Jerid
Kebili
Matmata
El-Jorf
Zarzis
Douz
Zaafrane
Jebel Dahar
Medenine
Ras al-Jedir
Ghomrassen
Ben Guerdane
Chenini
Tataouine
Zuara
Douiret
Ksar Ouled Soltane
Grand Erg Oriental
ALGERIA
Remada
Wazin
Nalut
LIBYA
Rebaa
Borj el-Khadra
TUNISIA

# UNDERSTAND TUNISIA

## Tunisia Today

Of all the countries that experienced massive upheaval during the Arab Spring, it's the one that started it all that has fared best. Yes, Tunisia's tourism industry is in freefall, its economy is struggling partly as a result and terrorism remains a constant threat. And yes, Tunisia has had a rough few years with political turmoil, assassinations and a society deeply divided between conservatives and liberals. But it also remains the only country of the four major Arab Spring protagonists – Tunisia, Egypt, Libya and Syria – still managing to meaningfully address the major issues facing the country through the ballot box and peaceful political debate.

**WARNING**

In 2015, terrorist attacks on Bardo National Museum and a beach resort at Sousse killed at least 60 people, with foreign tourists a particular target. At the time of writing, most Western governments were advising against all but essential travel to Tunisia, and against all travel to border areas with Libya, southern desert regions, border crossings with Algeria and the Chaambi Mountains National Park area.

## History

### Empire Strikes Back

The Phoenicians set their sights on Tunisia around 800 BC, and their capital Carthage – today a suburb of Tunis – was the main power in the western Mediterranean by the 6th century BC. The burgeoning Roman Empire became uneasy with a nation of such mercantile genius and mercenary strength on its doorstep, and 128 years of conflict – including the three Punic Wars – ensued. The legendary general of Carthage, Hannibal, invaded Italy in 216 BC, but the Romans finally triumphed. Roman Tunisia boomed in the 1st century AD, as sights such as Dougga and El-Jem attest.

In the 7th century, Arabs arrived from the east, bringing Islam. Various Arab dynasties ruled Tunisia until the 16th century. After fending off the Spanish Reconquistas, Tunisia became an outpost of the Ottoman Empire. France began its colonial push into the region in the 19th century. Establishing their rule in 1881, the French spent the next 50 years attempting to reinvent Tunisia as an outpost of Europe.

### Bourguiba & Ben

Tunisia was granted full independence from France and became a republic in 1956, a relatively peaceful process that saw exiled lawyer Habib Bourguiba returning to become the first president. He swore to eradicate poverty and separate politics from religion, while 'righting all the wrongs done to women'. Bourguiba gave Tunisia a secular state, championed women's rights, and introduced free education and heath care. As the years wore on, however, he wasn't too keen to give up power. His increasingly erratic and autocratic behaviour led to a bloodless coup in 1987. His successor, Zine el-Abidine Ben Ali, continued down a similar, if far less radical, road. Unfortunately, he too had an aversion to retirement. An appalling human-rights record and his zeal for feathering his extended family's nest was to prove his undoing.

### The Arab Spring

On 17 December 2010, a young Tunisian street trader in the provincial Tunisian town of Sidi Bouzid, Mohamed Bouazizi, set fire to himself in protest at his treatment at the hands of the police and local authorities. He died 18 days later, but his desperate act of self-immolation set off a wave of protests and regime change across the region and the wider Arab World.

Local protests in Tunisia went national, calling for political and economic reforms. It was an unstoppable tide and it forced President Zine el-Abidine Ben Ali and his family to flee into exile, in Saudi Arabia, where they remain to this day. In October 2011, just 10 months after Mohamed Bouazizi committed suicide, the Ennahda Islamist Party won the largest number of seats in national elections, although fell short of a parliamentary majority. In the months that followed, fundamentalist attacks on sellers of alcohol and art exhibitions prompted many to fear that Tunisia was in danger of falling under the sway of those who advocate a strict interpretation of Islam. The killing of two opposition politicians in the months and years that followed only deepened such concerns.

The political pendulum shifted back in favour of secular parties with the 2014 elections, but three terrorist attacks in 2015 – including two targeting foreign tourists in Tunis and Sousse – and ongoing concerns about fundamentalist Islamist activity, particularly in the south and in border regions, cast a pall over the country's future.

## People

After 14 centuries of intermarriage, the indigenous Berbers and later-on-the-scene Arabs are thoroughly entwined (some Turkish, Andalusian, Italian, French or sub-Saharan ancestry is also not uncommon). Unlike Morocco or Algeria, few Berbers still speak their own languages, and distinct Berber culture lives on only on the northern fringe of the Sahara and in Jerba. Tunisia has a very young population, though recent government family-planning programs have slowed the growth rate to under 1%.

## Religion

Tunisia is 98% Muslim, and Islam is the state religion. Jews and Christians make up the other 2%. Most Tunisian Muslims are Sunnis and belong to the Malekite school of Quranic interpretation, which leans towards a less rigid application and interpretation of the holy text. There are also small numbers of Ibadis, based on the island of Jerba, and Sufis, the ecstatic, mystical branch of Islam that has a strong following in the Berber south.

## Sport

Football (soccer) is the sport closest to Tunisian hearts. The Tunisian national team, nicknamed Les Aigles de Carthage (the Carthage Eagles; www.ftf.org.tn), is one of the strongest in Africa, qualifying for the World Cup finals in 1978, 1998, 2002 and 2006 (though so far they've only made it to the first round). Tunisia hosted the 2004 African Cup of Nations and the country erupted in delight when they won the tournament (2–1 against old enemies Morocco).

Tunisian club teams are also among the best on the continent, with Espérance Sportive de Tunisie (Tunis) and Étoile Sportif du Sahel (Sousse) regularly reaching the final of the continent-wide club competitions. These two clubs routinely dominate the domestic competition. Club allegiances, especially in Tunis, tend to run along class lines.

## Women in Tunisia

One of the many titles that Habib Bourguiba, Tunisia's first president, awarded to himself during his reign was 'the Liberator of Women' – it's even on his tombstone. Bourguiba's 1956 Personal Status Code guaranteed women full citizenship, banned polygamy and ended divorce by renunciation. It also placed restrictions on the tradition of arranged marriages, setting a minimum marriage age of 17 for girls and giving them the right to refuse a proposed marriage.

The code has since been regularly updated, most recently in 2005 and 2006, with women's custodial rights and rights to housing on divorce further safeguarded, as well as the addition of policies that enable women to return to work after childbirth at half-time on two-thirds of their salary, as well as retaining full social-security and retirement benefits.

Bourguiba regarded the hijab worn by Muslim women as demeaning and called it an 'odious rag'. He banned it from schools in 1981 in the hope that he could 'phase it out'. But in 2007, the courts found in favour of a teacher who had been stood down from her job for continuing to wear the hijab at work.

While the Personal Status Code formed the very cornerstone of the independence movement, and 50 years of ongoing commitment to it has seen women significantly represented in professions (outnumbering men in both secondary and higher education), real change has been slow. Women often feel split between a society that encourages them to be professionally ambitious and the highly traditional values of families that still believe marriage and motherhood are a woman's ultimate destiny.

And the situation has in some ways become more complicated since the overthrow of Ben Ali. The rise of Islamist parties has seen women's rights increasingly a defining issue in the struggle for supremacy between liberals and conservatives in the new Tunisia. In the end, under the new constitution adopted in 2014, 'the state commits to protect women's established rights and works to strengthen and develop those rights', and guarantees 'equality of opportunities between women and men to have access to all levels of responsibility and in all domains'.

# West Africa

WORLD TREK PHOTOGRAPHY/500PX

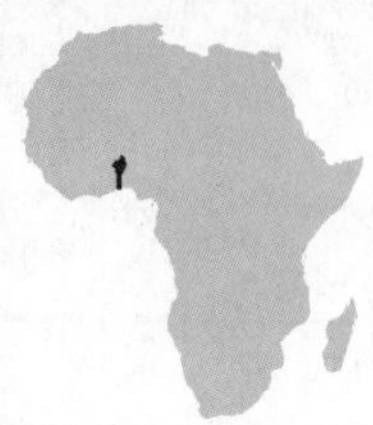

# Benin

229 / POP 9.6 MILLION

### Includes ➡



## Best Places to Eat

- ➡ Chez Delphano (p157)
- ➡ Saveurs d'Afrique (p155)
- ➡ L'Atelier (p149)
- ➡ Bab's Dock (p152)

## Best Places to Sleep

- ➡ La Guesthouse (p148)
- ➡ Maison Rouge (p148)
- ➡ Auberge Le Jardin Secret – Chez Pascal (p154)
- ➡ Pendjari Lodge (p158)
- ➡ Hôtel Chez Théo (p156)

## Why Go?

The birthplace of voodoo and a pivotal platform of the slave trade for nearly three centuries, Benin is steeped in a rich and complex history still very much in evidence today.

A visit to this small, club-shaped nation could therefore not be complete without learning about spirits and fetishes and the Afro-Brazilian heritage of Ouidah, Abomey and Porto Novo.

But Benin will also wow visitors with its palm-fringed beach idyll of the Atlantic coast, the rugged scenery of the north and the Parc National de la Pendjari, one of the best wildlife parks in West Africa. Lions, cheetahs, leopards, elephants and hundreds of other species thrive here.

In fact, Benin is wonderfully tourist friendly. There are good roads, a wide range of accommodation options and ecotourism initiatives that offer the chance to delve into Beninese life. Now is an ideal time to go: the country sits on the cusp of discovery.

## When to Go

### Cotonou

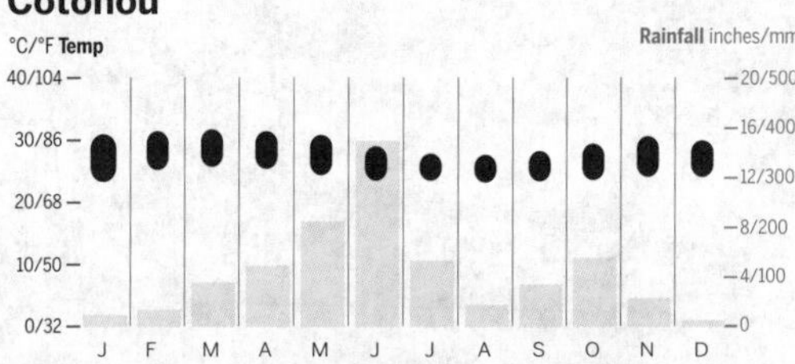


**Nov–Feb** Warm and dry. Wildlife-watching at its prime. Ouidah Voodoo Festival in January.

**Mar–May** The hottest period, after the harmattan lifts. Some rains in the south.

**Jun–Oct** Usually wet and uncomfortably humid; dry spell mid-July to mid-September in the south.

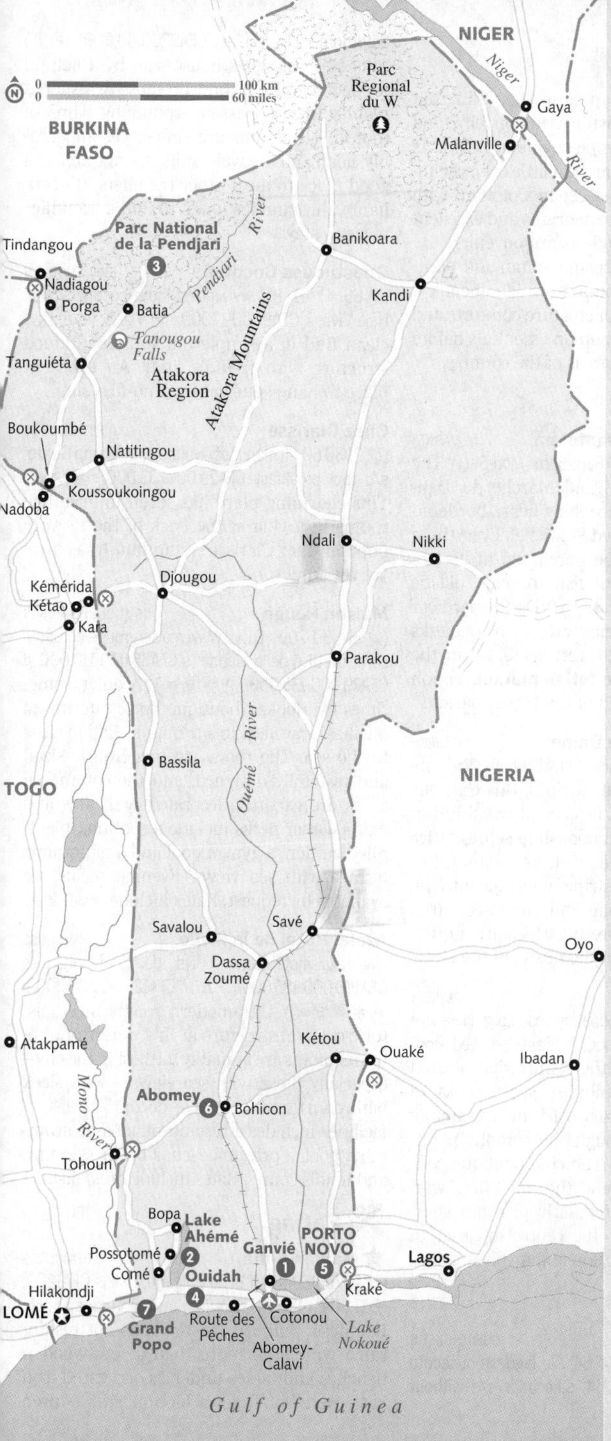


# Benin Highlights

1. **Ganvié** (p153) Spending a night at this lakeside stilt village while while peering out over sublime lake life.
2. **Lake Ahémé** (p156) Learning traditional fishing techniques and taking a dip at lake's shores.
3. **Parc National de la Pendjari** (p158) Spotting lions, cheetahs, elephants and more in one of West Africa's best wildlife parks.
4. **Zinzou Foundation Museum** (p154) Pondering contemporary African Art at this remarkable museum.
5. **Porto Novo** (p152) Discovering Benin's mellow capital, with its Afro-Brazilian heritage.
6. **Abomey** (p156) Visiting the ruined palaces and temples of the kings of Dahomey.
7. **Grand Popo** (p155) Putting your bags down at this lovely beach town and relaxing on Benin's beautiful palm-fringed coast.

# COTONOU

☎21 / POP 970,000

Cotonou is Benin's capital in everything but name: a vibrant, bustling, full-on city, and very much the economic engine of Benin. As a first port of call, it can be a little overwhelming, but life can be sweet in Cotonou, with good nightlife, great restaurants and excellent shopping (ideal for end-of-trip souvenirs).

It's also the most cosmopolitan and Western place in the country, which means a slightly higher level of creature comforts and a good place to stock up on essentials before venturing into rural areas of the country.

## Sights

**Grand Marché de Dantokpa** MARKET

(north of Jonquet; ⏲8am-5pm Mon-Sat) The seemingly endless Grand Marché du Dantokpa is Cotonou's throbbing heart, bordered by the lagoon and Blvd St Michel. Everything under the sun can be purchased in its labyrinthine lanes, from fish to soap, plastic sandals to goats, pirated DVDs to spare car parts. More traditional fare, such as batiks and Dutch wax cloth, can be found in the market building. The **fetish market** section is at the northern end of the larger market.

**Cathedral de Notre Dame** CHURCH

(Ave Clozel, by the Ancien Pont Bridge) With its vibrant red and white stripes, this Catholic cathedral is not just a place of worship but also home to a small bookshop selling titles by regional writers as well as a handful of academic texts. The stripes continue into the inside with sandstone and cream-coloured arches. Beyond its pretty stripes, it's a quiet and cool escape from the bustle of the city.

**Fondation Zinsou** GALLERY

(☎21 30 99 92; www.fondationzinsou.org; Haie Vive District, near the Carrefour; ⏲10am-7pm Wed-Mon) FREE Named after the family that started it, this fantastic exhibition space seeks to promote contemporary African art among Beninese people through photography, paintings and sculptures. The chic boutique sells beautiful art books and the cafe offers wi-fi access. The gallery regularly provides shuttles from schools to the centre in order to promote art appreciation and involvement.

## Sleeping

★**La Guesthouse** GUESTHOUSE $

(☎99 36 80 09, 67 34 64 77; laguesthousecotonou@gmail.com; Rue 214, Sikécodji; s/d without bathroom incl breakfast CFA9200/13,000; P 📶) This adorable guesthouse, run by a helpful French couple, is one of those whispered secrets that is passed around by word of mouth. The rooms are simple yet impeccably clean and the welcoming lounge area is a good place to meet other travellers. It's brilliant value, and it's tough to find a friendlier place to stay.

**Guesthouse Cocotiers** GUESTHOUSE $

(☎66 41 61 17; www.guesthouse-cocotiers.com; Haie Vive; r CFA9000-17,000; P 📶) A squeaky-clean find in a simple but well-maintained structure with friendly staff. An excellent place to hang your hat for a no-fuss stay.

**Chez Clarisse** GUESTHOUSE $$

(☎21 30 60 14; clarishot@yahoo.com; Camp Guézo; s/d incl breakfast CFA29,000/33,000; ❄ 📶 🏊) This charming place has seven immaculate rooms in a villa at the back of the its very popular Chez Clarisse restaurant. It's central yet very quiet.

**Maison Rouge** BOUTIQUE HOTEL $$$

(☎21 30 09 01; www.maison-rouge-cotonou.com; off Blvd de la Marina; s CFA65,000-110,000, d CFA79,000-135,000; P ❄ 📶 🏊) A quiet, sometimes overlooked boutique hotel catering to business travellers in a tranquil location close to the sea. The rooms are generously sized and tastefully designed, and the communal areas are expertly decorated with arts and crafts. Other perks include a soothing plant-filled garden, a gym, a pool and a panoramic terrace with sea views. Evening meals are available by request. Rates include breakfast.

**Azalai Hotel de la Plage** HOTEL $$$

(www.azalaihotels.com; Blvd de la Marina; s CFA109,000-185,000, d CFA125,000-200,000; P ❄ @ 📶 🏊) Ultramodern rooms meet historic colonial structure at this waterfront hotel. Its rooms are arguably the best in the city – especially those with sea views – with sleek bathrooms and attractive decor. The list of facilities includes a restaurant, a bar, a swimming pool, a private beach, a business centre and tennis courts. Rates include breakfast.

## Eating

★**Maman Aimé** BENINESE $

(☎97 64 16 49; off Pl de Bulgarie; mains CFA1200; ⏲11.30am-10pm) This is a super atmospheric Beninese *maquis* (rustic open-air restaurant) with little more than a few wooden benches and tables under a corrugated iron roof. Here you'll get a blob of *pâte* (starch staple, often made from millet, corn, plantains, manioc or yams) and ladle of sauce for next to nothin'. And yes, you'll eat with your fingers. There's no signboard; it's in a *von* (alleyway) off Pl de Bulgarie.

**Chez Maman Bénin** AFRICAN **$**
(☎21 32 33 38; Rue 201A; meals CFA1000-3000; ⏲11.30am-11pm) This long-standing no-frills canteen off Blvd St Michel has a large selection of West African dishes. There's no decor except for a couple of blaring TVs showing the latest football action.

★**Chez Clarisse** FRENCH **$$**
(☎21 30 60 14; Camp Guézo; mains CFA3000-15,000; ⏲8am-10pm) This small French restaurant, in a pretty residential area next to the US embassy, is a perennial favourite that churns out excellent French and local specialties, such as fish with moyo sauce, as well as pancakes and sandwiches.

★**L'Atelier** FRENCH **$$$**
(☎21 30 17 04; Cadjéhoun; mains CFA8000-19,000; ⏲11am-11pm Mon-Sat) Considered by some connoisseurs to be one of the most refined restaurants in town, with excellent French and fusion cuisine, and an ambience that's as optimal for business lunches as it is for a romantic evening out.

## Drinking & Nightlife

Haie Vive is a lively, safe area by night, with many of the city's best bars and restaurants. There are also plenty of unpretentious bars and *buvettes* (small cafes that double as drinking places) in the Jonquet area and around Stade de l'Amitié.

★**Buvette** BAR
(Carrefour de Cadjéhoun; ⏲3pm or 4pm-late) This place with no name is brilliant for sundowners. Tables spill out of nowhere as soon as darkness falls and there is often live music.

★**Le Livingstone** BAR
(☎21 30 27 58; Haie Vive; ⏲11am-late) One of the most atmospheric spots for a drink is the terrace of this pub in Haie Vive, which serves as one of the biggest expat hangouts in town.

## Shopping

**Centre de Promotion de l'Artisanat** ARTS & CRAFTS
(Blvd St Michel; ⏲9am-6pm) Here you'll find woodcarvings, bronzes, batiks, leather goods, jewellery and appliqué banners.

### ARRIVING IN COTONOU

Upon arrival at Aéroport International de Cotonou Cadjéhoun (p162), porters wearing blue uniforms will surround you. It's best to pay one for safe transfer of your luggage and a seamless transfer (past the aggressive touts and rampant thieves) to the taxi stand (tip them about CFA1500 to CFA2000). Taxis are the best way to get to the the city and cost around CFA3000 to CFA6000 to the centre (depending on your negotiating skills).

## Information

### DANGERS & ANNOYANCES

The biggest danger in Cotonou is the traffic – the reckless *zemi-johns* (or *zems*, motorcycle taxis) in particular. They're unavoidable, however, so always make sure that the driver agrees to drive slowly *(aller doucement)* before hopping on.

The Jonquet, the beach and the port area all have their fair share of undesirables: don't walk alone at night and watch your bag at traffic lights if you're on a *zem*.

### INTERNET ACCESS

Ave Clozel, Blvd Steinmetz and Rue des Cheminots have the most internet cafes.

**Cyber Océane** (☎21 30 69 41; Haie Vive; per hr CFA500; ⏲9am-10pm)

**Star Navigation** (☎21 31 81 28; off Blvd Steinmetz; per hr CFA700; ⏲8am-10pm) Perhaps country's fastest internet connections.

### MEDICAL SERVICES

There are numerous pharmacies around town.

**Pharmacie Jonquet** (☎21 31 20 80; Rue des Cheminots; ⏲24hr) Open seven days a week.

**Polyclinique les Cocotiers** (☎21 30 14 20; Rue 373, Cadjéhoun) A private clinic at Carrefour de Cadjéhoun; also has a dentist.

### MONEY

All banks change cash. There are plenty of ATMs, most of which accept Visa.

**Banque Atlantique** (Blvd St Michel; ⏲8am-5pm Mon-Fri, 9am-12.30pm Sat) Temperamental MasterCard and Visa ATM.

**Trinity Forex** (Bureau de Change Forex Bureau; ☎21 31 79 38; Ave van Vollenhoven; ⏲8am-6.30pm Mon-Fri, 8am-2pm Sat) Changes US dollars, euros, Swiss francs and British pounds.

### POST

**Main Post Office** (off Ave Clozel; ⏲7am-7pm Mon-Fri, 8am-11.30am Sat)

## Cotonou

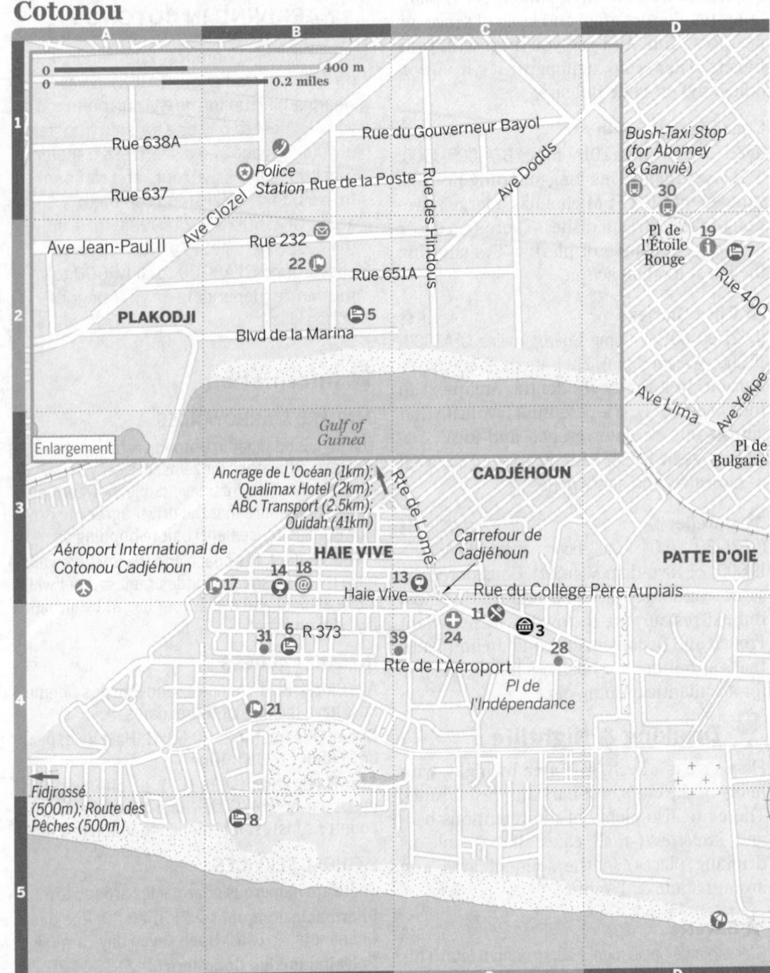


### TELEPHONE

**Telecom (OPT) Building** (Ave Clozel; ⏲7.30am-7pm Mon-Sat, 9am-1pm Sun) You can make overseas telephone calls and send faxes.

### TOURIST INFORMATION

**Direction du Tourisme et de l'Hôtellerie** (☎21 32 68 24; Pl de l'Étoile Rouge; ⏲8am-12.30pm & 3-6.30pm Mon-Fri) Inconveniently located out of the city centre, behind Pharmacie de l'Étoile Rouge; of limited use.

## Getting There & Away

### BUSH TAXI & BUS

Cotonou has a confusingly large number of stations for minibuses, buses and bush taxis. It's easiest to ask a taxi or a *zemi-john* to take you to the right one.

**Gare Jonquet** (Rue des Cheminots), just west of Blvd Steinmetz, services western destinations such as Grand Popo (CFA4000, two hours).

Bush taxis for Porto Novo (CFA500 to CFA700, 45 minutes) leave from **Gare du Dantokpa** (Ave de la Paix) at the new bridge; those to Calavi-Kpota (for Ganvié; CFA500, 25 minutes),

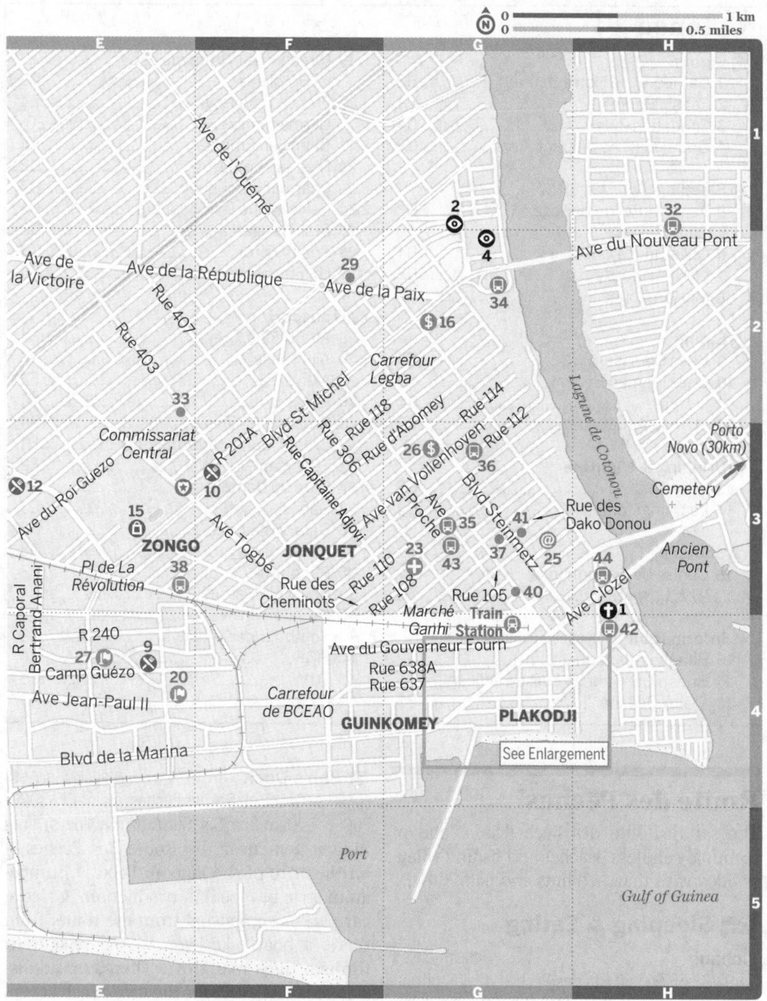


Ouidah (CFA1000) and Abomey (CFA3100, two hours) leave **north of Stade de l'Amitié**. **Gare Missébo** (Ave van Vollenhoven) services Abomey (CFA2500).

For more-distant destinations, such as Natitingou, take the bus. The most reliable company at the time of writing was **ATT** (☎95 95 34 18; Pl de l'Étoile Rouge), with daily services for Natitingou (CFA85600).

There are also additional national and international services with **ABC Transport** (☎66 56 45 15; Stade de l'Amitié), **Cross Country International** (☎66 99 92 41; Ave du Nouveau Pont), **Rimbo-RTV** (☎95 23 24 82; Zongo), **STIF** (☎97 98 11 80; off Ave Clozel), **TCV** (☎97 60 39 68; Rue 108) and **UTB** (☎95 42 71 20; Ave Clozel).

## Getting Around

A *zemi-john* will whiz you around town for CFA100 to CFA500, depending on the distance.

Fares in shared taxis are CFA150 to CFA400.

# SOUTHERN BENIN

Benin's south is an enticing but intriguing mix of heavenly shores, lush lagoons and momentous history.

## Cotonou

**Sights**
1 Cathedral de Notre Dame ........ H3
2 Fetish Market ........ G1
3 Fondation Zinsou ........ C4
4 Grand Marché de Dantokpa ........ G2

**Sleeping**
5 Azalai Hotel de la Plage ........ B2
Chez Clarisse ........ (see 9)
6 Guesthouse Cocotiers ........ B4
7 La Guesthouse ........ D2
8 Maison Rouge ........ B5

**Eating**
9 Chez Clarisse ........ E4
10 Chez Maman Bénin ........ F3
11 L'Atelier ........ C4
12 Maman Aimé ........ E3

**Drinking & Nightlife**
13 Buvette ........ C3
14 Le Livingstone ........ B3

**Shopping**
15 Centre de Promotion de l'Artisanat ........ E3

**Information**
16 Banque Atlantique ........ G2
17 British Community Liaison Officer ........ B3
18 Cyber Océane ........ B3
19 Direction du Tourisme et de l'Hôtellerie ........ D2
20 French Embassy ........ E4
German Embassy ........ (see 20)
21 Ghanaian Embassy ........ B4
22 Nigerian Embassy ........ B2
23 Pharmacie Jonquet ........ G3
24 Polyclinique les Cocotiers ........ C4
25 Star Navigation ........ G3
26 Trinity Forex ........ G3
27 US Embassy ........ E4

**Transport**
28 Air Burkina ........ C4
Air France ........ (see 6)
29 Asky ........ F2
30 ATT ........ D1
31 Brussels Airlines ........ B4
32 Cross Country International ........ H1
33 Ethiopian Airlines ........ E2
34 Gare du Dantokpa ........ G2
35 Gare Jonquet ........ G3
36 Gare Missébo ........ G3
37 Kenya Airways ........ G3
38 Rimbo-RTV ........ E3
39 Royal Air Maroc ........ C4
40 Senegal Airlines ........ G3
41 South African Airways ........ G3
42 STIF ........ H4
43 TCV ........ G3
44 UTB ........ H3

# Route des Pêches

The sandy Route des Pêches is a land of seemingly endless beaches and fishing villages filled with thatched huts and palm groves.

## Sleeping & Eating

**Tichani** GUESTHOUSE $
(97 88 65 60; off Rte des Pêches; r with fan/air-con incl breakfast CFA12,000/18,000; ) This well-run guesthouse scores high points with its location – it's only 300m away from the beach in a peaceful area. The six sun-soaked rooms are neat and tidy, the flower-filled garden is a great spot to decompress and the views of the sea from the rooftop terrace are nothing short of charming. Meals can be arranged (from CFA3000).

**Wado** SEAFOOD $$
(97 68 53 18; Rte des Pêches; mains CFA3500-3900, seafood platters CFA27,000; lunch & dinner Sat & Sun) This eatery overlooking the beach has garnered high praise for its ultra-fresh fish and seafood platters.

★ **Bab's Dock** EUROPEAN, BAR $$$
(97 97 01 00; off Rte des Pêches; mains CFA3000-7000; 10am-8pm Sat, Sun & bank holidays) This hidden gem near the Route des Pêches is on the edge of the lagoon. Food is European in style but local in production. A secure car park is signposted from the route; from there, a boat takes you to the restaurant through thick mangrove. There's an admission fee (CFA2500) for the day, which covers the car park and boat trip.

## Getting There & Away

The best way to reach this area is by taxi. From Cotonou centre it costs around CFA500 to CFA600. From Ouidah, expect to pay CFA100 to CFA300.

# Porto Novo

POP 262,000

Nestling on the shores of Lake Nokoué, Porto Novo is Benin's unlikely capital. Its leafy streets, wonderful colonial architecture, unperturbed pace and interesting museums are in striking contrast to full-on Cotonou.

DON'T MISS

## GANVIÉ

The main attraction in Ganvié is the **stilt village**, where roughly 24,000 Tofinu people live in bamboo huts on stilts. The village extends several kilometres out on Lake Nokoué.

This stilt village was created to protect the Tofinu people from slave hunters. It has become part of their culture and way of life. The teetering houses, schools, churches and other structures form a ramshackle village. The villagers live almost exclusively from fishing.

The best way to get to Ganvié is via Cotonou. Take a taxi from Pl de l'Étoile Rouge or Stade de l'Amitié to Calavi-Kpota (CFA700, 25 minutes). The embarkation point is 800m downhill (take a *zem*). If you opt for a tour, head to the people standing at the tour counters at Stade de l'Amitié. Return fares to Ganvié in a regular/motorised pirogue are CFA9000/11,500 per person, or CFA6300/8200 each for two to four people, including tour and pirogue transport. Prices generally include a circuit of the village with stop-offs. The trip takes about 2½ hours. You can also hire a guide.



The Portuguese named the city after Porto when they established a slave-trading post here in the 16th century.

## Sights

**★Centre Songhai** GARDENS
(☎20 24 68 81; www.songhai.org; Rte de Pobè; guided tours CFA500; ⏲guided tours 8.30am, 10.30am, noon, 3.30pm & 5pm Mon-Sat) The Centre Songhai is a major research, teaching and production centre in sustainable farming. There are one-hour guided tours to visit the plantations and workshops. You can also buy the centre's produce – anything from fresh quail eggs to biscuits and preserves. Songhai is about 1km north of town. Every *zem* knows where it is.

**Musée Honmé** MUSEUM
(☎20 21 35 66; Rue Toffa; CFA1000; ⏲9am-noon & 3.30-6pm) This museum is housed in the walled palace of King Toffa, who signed the first treaty with the French in 1863. It focuses on the *alounloun* musical instrument, a long piece with a sliding metal ring, the key element in the local Porto Novo *adjogan* music. The museum traces the instrument's symbolism as a sound that echoed the king's strength.

**Musée Ethnographique de Porto Novo** MUSEUM
(☎20 21 25 54; Ave 6; CFA1000; ⏲9am-6pm, closed 1 May & 1 Jan) Housed in a pretty colonial building, this museum is well worth a gander. The top floor is organised thematically around birth, life and death, with everything from costumes to carved drums. Downstairs there's an impressive display of ceremonial masks.

## Sleeping & Eating

**Centre Songhai** HOTEL $
(☎20 24 68 81; www.songhai.org; Rte de Pobè; r with fan CFA5500-7500, with air-con CFA12,500-15,500, ste CFA30,000-50,000; P❄@☕) Built to accommodate its numerous visitors, the 70 rooms at Centre Songhai are spartan but clean. Fan rooms have a shower cubicle but shared toilets; the more-expensive air-con rooms have a private bathroom (with hot water) but are still very good value. The centre has two good restaurants: a cheap African open-air *maquis* (mains CFA1200) and a more upmarket restaurant (mains CFA2500 to CFA3500).

**Hôtel Beaurivage** HOTEL $$
(☎20 21 23 99; Blvd Lagunaire; r CFA15,500-25,500; ❄) Tired but spacious rooms (and new beds, finally!) with the town's best lagoon views and a wonderful terrace bar and restaurant. Even if you don't sleep here, you should definitely come for sundowners.

**Java Promo** AFRICAN, FRENCH $
(☎66 96 68 78; Pl du Gouvernement; meals CFA1600-4200; ⏲8am-9pm) No one seems to remember a time before Java Promo. Hidden behind the aquamarine shutters of a crumbling colonial building and shielded from the sun by a big *paillote* (straw awning), this is a popular haunt for an omelette at brekkie or rustic European meals for lunch.

## Information

Porto Novo has several banks with ATMs that accept Visa.

**Bank of Africa** (Ave Liotard; ⏲8am-4pm Mon-Fri) Changes money.

**County Hospital De L'ouémé** (☎97 09 25 14)

**Tourist Office** (☎97 02 52 29; www.porto-novo.org; Pl Bayol; ⊙9am-1pm & 3-6pm Mon-Fri) Has a few brochures and can help with finding guides. Near the cathedral.

## Getting There & Away

Plenty of minibuses and bush taxis leave for Cotonou (minibus/bush taxi CFA6500/900, 45 minutes) from Carrefour Catchi and in front of Ouando mosque. To Abomey from Porto Novo is CFA3800. ATT buses that ply the Cotonou–Natitingou route also stop in front of Ouando mosque (CFA7900 for Natitingou) and at the Gare Routière.

For Nigeria, you can get a taxi to the border point in Kraké (CFA900, 30 minutes), but you'll have to change there to go on to Lagos.



# Ouidah

POP 86,500

Ouidah is a relaxed and relatively prosperous beach town with sweeping expanses of golden sand to laze upon. It's also a must-see for anyone interested in voodoo (it's considered the voodoo capital of Benin), Benin's history of slavery or its Brazilian heritage. From the 17th to the late 19th centuries, captured countrymen from across West Africa left Ouidah for the Americas.

DON'T MISS

### VOODOO DAY

*Vodou* (voodoo) got its current name in Haiti and Cuba, where the religion arrived with Fon and Ewe slaves from the Dahomey Kingdom and mixed with Catholicism. It means 'the hidden' or 'the mystery'. Traditional priests are consulted for their power to communicate with particular spirits and seek intercession with them. This communication is achieved through spirit possession and ritual that often involves a gift or 'sacrifice' of palm wine, chickens or goats.

Voodoo was formally recognised as a religion by the Beninese authorities in February 1996. Since then, 10 January, Voodoo Day, has been a bank holiday, with celebrations all over the country. Those in Ouidah, voodoo's historic centre, are among the best and most colourful, with endless singing, dancing, beating of drums and drinking.

## Sights

★**Zinzou Foundation Museum** MUSEUM
(☎21 34 11 54; http://fondationzinsou.org; Rue des Missions; ⊙9am-7pm Wed-Sun, 1-7pm Tue) FREE This museum of contemporary African art, housed in a stunning 1920s Afro-Brazilian villa, displays paintings and sculptures as well as light, video and sound installations. It's a classy affair, run by the Zinzou foundation out of Cotonou, a respectable organisation with a strong history of supporting Beninese artists. Most guides speak at least passable English.

**Route des Esclaves** MEMORIAL
(Route of the Slaves; museum CFA1200; ⊙museum 10am-5pm) The Route of the Slaves includes the slave auction plaza, the Tree of Forgetfulness (where slaves were branded with their owners' symbols and, to make them forget where they came from, forced to walk around the tree in circles) and the Tree of Return, another tree the slaves often circled with the belief that their souls would return home after death. There is a poignant memorial on the beach, **Gate of No Return**, with a bas-relief depicting slaves in chains.

**Musée d'Histoire de Ouidah** MUSEUM
(☎21 34 10 21; www.museeouidah.org; Rue van Vollenhoven; CFA1000; ⊙8am-12.30pm & 3-6pm Mon-Fri, 9am-6pm Sat & Sun) Ouidah's main site is its Musée d'Histoire de Ouidah, housed in the beautiful Fortaleza São João Batista, a Portuguese fort built in 1721. It retraces the town's slave-trading history and explores the links between Benin, Brazil and the Caribbean.

**Python Temple** TEMPLE
(off Rue F Colombani; admission CFA1000, photos CFA5000; ⊙9am-6.30pm) Those interested in voodoo could visit the python temple, home to some 60 sleepy snakes. The guide explains some of the beliefs and ceremonies associated with the temple.

## Sleeping

★**Auberge Le Jardin Secret – Chez Pascal** GUESTHOUSE $
(☎96 66 90 14; www.lejardinsecretouidah.net; near Radio Kpassé; r CFA12,000-15,000; P) An atmosphere of dreamlike tranquility wafts over this well-organised guesthouse tucked away in a side *von* in a quiet neighbourhood. The neatly tended garden has places to lounge; the six rooms, though not luxuri-

ous are crisp and spruce; and there's an on-site restaurant (meals from CFA2500). Bike hire is available.

**Casa Del Papa** RESORT $$$

(☎95 95 39 04; www.casadelpapa.com; Ouidah Plage; d incl breakfast CFA37,500-68,000; P ❄ ≈) Squeezed between the ocean and the lagoon, Casa Del Papa is the closest thing to an exclusive resort you'll find on the coast. It features a host of facilities and amenities, including three pools, a volleyball court, two bars and a restaurant overlooking the beach. There are numerous activities on offer as well as excursions across the lagoon and to nearby villages.

## Eating

**Restaurant d'Amicale** AFRICAN $

(by the Catholic church; mains CFA1000-3000; ⏲10am-11.30pm) This colourful, friendly spot serves a mix of sandwiches and pizzas, fresh salads and *attiéké* (a dish from Côte d'Ivoire made with cassava, beans, fish, plantains and pasta). It's a spacious spot with shaded tables and an interior with fans so strong they'll quickly cool your food down.

**Côté Pêche** SEAFOOD $$

(☎96 82 27 03, 97 46 43 79; Rte des Esclaves; mains CFA3400-4500; ⏲7.30am-9pm) Fish lovers, you'll find nirvana here: Côté Pêche has a wide assortment of fish delivered daily from the harbour, including barracuda and grouper. The menu also features meat dishes, pasta, salads and sandwiches. The owners have three rooms for rent (CFA7000). It's at the beginning of Rte des Esclaves.

## Information

**Continental Bank Bénin** (☎21 34 14 32; Pl du Marché; ⏲8.30am-noon & 3-6pm Mon-Fri) Changes cash.

**Tourist Office** (☎21 19 35 11, 97 87 80 93; ouidah_tourisme@yahoo.fr; ⏲8.30am-6.30pm) Has various brochures and can arrange cultural tours. Ask for Modeste Zinsou. Near the post office.

**UBA** The only bank with an ATM (Visa only).

## Getting There & Away

Ouidah is 42km west of Cotonou. From Carrefour Gbena, north of town, you can catch shared taxis to Cotonou (CFA1200, one hour), Grand Popo (CFA1700, one hour) and the Hilakondji border (CFA1800, 1½ hours).

WORTH A TRIP

### ADJARA

Adjara is famous for its market, one of the most colourful in Benin. Held every fourth day, it's stocked with fetishes, grigri charms, unique blue-and-white tie-dyed cloth, some of the best pottery in Benin, and tam-tams and other musical instruments. You'll also see blacksmiths at work.

**Chez Houssou** (Adjara; mains CFA1500; ⏲11am-3pm) is an unpretentious *maquis* (open-air restaurant), with no more than a couple of wooden benches, famous for one thing and one thing only: *porc grillé sauce sang* (grilled pork cooked in a blood sauce). Houssou cuts morsels of pork, puts them in a mudbrick oven, then serves them on a small plate – it can't get more authentic than that.

From Porto Novo, a *zem* ride shouldn't cost more than CFA900.

# Grand Popo

POP 9000

Grand Popo is a wonderful beach town in which to spend a few tranquil days. The village has plenty going on at the weekend, when Cotonou residents come to decompress.

On the main road through the village, **Villa Karo** (☎94 20 31 20; ⏲gallery 8am-noon & 4-6pm Mon-Fri, 8-11am Sat) is a small gallery with great exhibitions focusing on local art.

Run by two local guides, **GG Tours** (☎95 85 74 40; Azango Maison) organises excursions on the Mono River or to the Bouche du Roy, where the river meets the ocean. Trips on the river last about two hours (CFA6000 per person). Trips to the Bouche du Roy cost CFA50,000: you need a motorised boat, which fits up to eight people; the trip lasts about six hours.

## Sleeping & Eating

★ **Saveurs d'Afrique** BUNGALOW $

(☎66 69 69 80, 97 89 28 19; www.saveursdafrique.net; bungalows CFA17,000; P) Looking for a night at some place extra-special? Make a beeline for this lovely property, the pride and joy of affable Mathieu Yélomé, a young Beninese chef. The six units borrow from

African traditional designs and are embellished with various artistic touches.

Food is a big thing here; the range of daily specials (around CFA600) on offer – mostly French-influenced dishes prepared with local ingredients – is well priced and filled with subtle flavours. Near the beach.

**Lion Bar** GUESTHOUSE $
(☎95 42 05 17; kabla_gildas@yahoo.fr; campsite per person CFA5500, r without bathroom CFA5000-7000) Down a track from the main street, you'll easily find this reggae land by following Bob Marley's languorous beats. It's the hideout of choice for Cotonou's expat beatniks, and oozes peace and love: cocktails flow at all hours of the day and night, rooms are spartan yet funky and the shared facilities surprisingly clean.

**Awalé Plage** RESORT $$
(☎22 43 01 17; www.hotel-benin-awaleplage.com; Rte du Togo; r CFA37,000, bungalows with fan/air-con CFA27,500/32,500; P ❄ ≋ ≈) A great place to recharge the batteries, Awalé Plage's most notable features are its excellent service, beachfront setting, beautiful gardens awash with tropical trees, large swimming pool and well-maintained bungalows. There is an excellent beach bar and the on-site restaurant (mains CFA2600 to CFA6500) prepares delectable French-inspired dishes with a tropical twist.

**Auberge de Grand Popo** HOTEL $$
(☎22 43 00 47; www.voyageurbenin.com; d CFA17,500-28,000; P) Right by the beach, this place oozes colonial charm and serves divine cuisine in its attractive terrace restaurant (menus CFA8500).

### ℹ Getting There & Away

From Cotonou, take a bush taxi from Gare Jonquet, Stade de l'Amitié or Pl de l'Étoile Rouge (CFA3500, two hours) and have it drop you off at the Grand Popo junction on the main coastal highway, 20km east of the Togo border crossing at Hilakondji. The beach and village are 3.5km off the main road and are easily accessible via *zemi-john* (CFA280).

## Possotomé & Lake Ahémé

The fertile shores of Lake Ahémé are a wonderful place to spend a few days, particularly around lively Possotomé, the area's biggest village. It's possible to swim in the lake, which makes for a great way to cool down, or explore the area's wildlife.

### Activities

Learn traditional fishing techniques, meet craftspeople at work or go on a fascinating two-hour botanic journey to hear about local plants and their medicinal properties. There are half a dozen thematic circuits to choose from (from two hours to day trips, CFA4800 to CFA17,000), all run by delightful local guides.

**Eco-Bénin** ADVENTURE SPORTS
(www.ecobenin.org) Various trips and excursions are offered by this local tour operator.

### Sleeping & Eating

**Gîte de Possotomé** GUESTHOUSE $
(☎67 19 58 37, 94 38 80 34; www.ecobenin.org; s without bathroom CFA5700-6000, d without bathroom CFA7000-8500, s/d CFA9500/15,000; P ≋) Embedded in a manicured tropical garden, this well-run venture has eight impeccable rooms with salubrious bathrooms. It's not on the lakeshore, but the congenial atmosphere more than makes up for this. The ethos here is laid-back, ecological and activity-oriented – various tours can be arranged.

**Hôtel Chez Théo** RESORT $$
(☎96 44 47 88, 95 05 53 15; www.chez-theo.com; r CFA18,000-23,000, bungalows CFA36,000; P ❄ ≋) In a stunning lakeside location, Chez Théo is guaranteed to help you switch to 'relax' mode. A path through a garden bursting with all sorts of exotic trees leads to a great bar-restaurant (mains from CFA4200) on a stilt platform with cracking views. Rooms are far from fancy but are kept scrupulously clean. All kinds of tours can be organised.

### ℹ Getting There & Away

Taxis that ply the Cotonou–Hilakondji (or Comé) route will generally drop you off at the Comé turn-off (CFA2700), from where the only option to Possotomé is a *zemi-john* (CFA1500).

## Abomey

POP 124,500

If you're looking to immerse yourself in ancient Beninese history, one of the best places to start is Abomey. The name is mythical, and not without reason: Abomey, 144km northwest of Cotonou, was the capital of the fierce Dahomey kingdom and a force colonial powers had to reckon with for centuries. Its winding lanes dotted with palaces and temples, Abomey is shrouded with a palpable historical aura and filled with character.

## Sights

**Musée Historique d'Abomey** MUSEUM

(22 50 03 14; www.epa-prema.net/abomey; adult/child CFA1500/1000; 9am-6pm) Abomey's main and seriously impressive attraction (and a World Heritage site since 1985), this sprawling museum is housed in two palaces, those of the ancient kings Ghézo and Glélé. The museum displays royal thrones and tapestries, human skulls that were once used as musical instruments, fetish items and Ghézo's throne, mounted on four real skulls of vanquished enemies.

## Sleeping & Eating

**A La Lune – Chez Monique** GUESTHOUSE $

(22 50 01 68; north of Rond-Point de la Préfecture; r CFA7600-9200; P) You'll love the exotic garden, complete with antelopes, crocodiles, tortoises, monkeys, flower bushes and huge wood carvings. Accommodation-wise, it's a bit less overwhelming, with no-frills, yet spacious, rooms. The on-site restaurant is average; opt for a contemplative drink in the garden instead.

**Auberge d'Abomey** GUESTHOUSE $$

(97 89 87 25, 95 82 80 28; www.voyageurbenin.com; Rond-Point de la Préfecture; s/d with fan CFA13,500/15,000, with air-con CFA19,000/25,500; ) This reliable option off the main roundabout is a small, rustic hotel with a colonial feel and just a handful of spare rooms. It gets high marks from travellers for its relaxing garden full of mango trees and its on-site restaurant (menus from CFA8500). Staff can organise various excursions.

★ **Chez Delphano** BENINESE $

(93 64 02 40; mains CFA800-1900; 8am-10pm) This delightful *maquis* is a winner. Marguerite prepares exquisite Beninese cuisine in a jovial atmosphere. She also prepares crêpes in the morning, with freshly ground coffee and a mountain of fruit. Yum! Chez Delphano is north of Rond-Point de la Préfecture.

## Information

**Tourist Office** (94 14 67 30, 95 79 09 45; near the Rond-Point de la Préfecture.; 9am-1pm & 3-6pm Mon-Fri, 9am-4pm Sat) Has some interesting brochures and can provide information about Abomey's main sights. It also keeps a list of accredited guides (some of whom speak English) and can arrange guided tours.

DON'T MISS

### THE ROUTE OF KINGS

The tourist office runs excellent cultural tours focusing on Abomey's rich architectural heritage. They last about two hours and cost CFA3000 per person (not including *zem* rental). There are some 10 sites to be seen, all of which have an air of faded majesty about their crumbling walls. Highlights include Palais Akaba, Place de Goho, Palais Ghézo, Palais de Glélé, Temple Hwemu, Temple Zéwa and Palais Agonglo – the best-kept of Abomey's nine palaces.

## Getting There & Away

Plenty of bush taxis depart from Cotonou (CFA3800, three hours), sometimes with a connection at Bohicon. *Zemi-johns* (CFA1200) frequently run between Abomey and Bohicon.

Most **Confort Lines** (21 32 58 15) and **Inter City Lines** (21 00 85 54) buses (between Cotonou and Natitingou) stop in Bohicon on the way, but be sure to verify this with the driver.

# NORTHERN BENIN

Northern Benin's arid, mountainous landscape is a world away from the south's beaches and lagoons but all the more attractive for it. It's all about the natural heritage, with one fantastic wildlife park and a mountain range. It is also ethnically more diverse than the south, and Islam is the main religion.

## The Atakora Region

This fantastic trekking destination is famous for its scrubby, rugged and rocky mountain range full of red *piste* (rough track), bucolic corn fields and huge baobab trees, as well as lively markets where *tchoukoutou* (sorghum beer) flows. It's also home to Parc National de la Pendjari, one of West Africa's most respected wildlife parks.

## Activities

**Perle de l'Atakora** WALKING

(Pearl of the Atakora; 97 44 28 61; www.ecobenin.org/koussoukoingou) The ecotourism

### CROSSING INTO TOGO

If you cross into Togo from Boukoumbé, make sure you get your passport stamped at the *gendarmerie* (police station) at Boukoumbé as there is no border checkpoint.

association Perle de l'Atakora offers guided walks around Koussoukoingou (CFA2000 to CFA3500 for 2½ to 3½ hours) taking in local sights such as the famous *tata* houses (fort-like huts with clay turrets and thatched spires). You can arrange to spend the night at a *tata* (CFA8000 per person including breakfast and dinner, without bathroom).

## Sleeping

**Ecolodge La Perle de l'Atakora** GUESTHOUSE **$**
(☎67 46 78 01, 97 35 02 86; www.ecobenin.org; Koussoukoingou; r without bathroom CFA8000; P) We can't think of a better place for immersion in local culture. This modern-ish *tata* house features five rooms that are tidy, functional and well priced, and a well-scrubbed ablution block. Hearty meals too. It's run by Ecobenin, which offers high-quality ecotours in the area. Bikes are also available. Rooms include breakfast and dinner.

**Tata Touristique Koubetti Victor** GUESTHOUSE **$**
(☎97 35 29 24, 94 68 75 49; Boukombé; r without bathroom CFA6000; P 📶) This is a wonderfully laid-back Boukombé haven, with a leafy courtyard, a chilled-out ambience and tasty meals. Rooms occupy a large *tata* house. It's basic but clean and high on character. Joséphine and her daughter Valérie can organise village visits, cultural tours and dance classes. Pick-ups from Natitingou can also be arranged.

## Getting There & Away

It's best to get to the Atakora with your own transport, but a few bush taxis do ply the dusty trail between Nati, Koussoukoingou and Boukoumbé (CFA2500, roughly two hours), where you can cross into Togo. Otherwise, *zemi-johns* (about CFA7000, three hours) will take you, but be prepared for a dusty and tiring ride.

# Parc National de la Pendjari

Set amid the majestic landscape of the Atakora's rugged cliffs and wooded savannah, this 2750-sq-km **park** (Pendjari National Park; www.pendjari.net; 1/2/3 days per person CFA10,000/20,000/25,000, per vehicle CFA3000, 'A' guides per day CFA10,000; ⏰6am-5pm) is home to lions, cheetahs, leopards, elephants, baboons, hippos, myriad birds (it's estimated 300 to 350 varieties live here) and countless antelope – it's undoubtedly one of the West Africa's top wildlife destinations.

## Activities

With big cats, elephants, antelope, hippos and other iconic wildlife, the park is ripe for wildlife viewing. The best viewing time for sighting animals is near the end of the dry season (November to February), when animals start to hover around waterholes. To maximise your chances, use an accredited grade 'A' guide. The list of accredited guides can be found on the park's website, at park entrances and in Nati's better hotels. The 'A' guides have the most in-depth knowledge and several years of experience in the park, and they can be trusted to handle the terrain and conduct a tour that is both informative and safe.

## Sleeping

★**Pendjari Lodge** LODGE **$$**
(☎in France 336 68 42 73 43; www.pendjari-lodge.com; tents CFA34,000-37,000; ⏰Nov-Jul; P 📶) A lovely place in a beautiful setting on a small hill (views!), Pendjari Lodge mixes old-style safari ambience with nouveau bush chic. It sports a handful of luxury, semipermanent tents and a large dining area and lounge with wooden decks overlooking a valley. One quibble: the menu (set menus from CFA6000) is a bit limited but does the trick after a hot day out and about.

**Hôtel de la Pendjari** HOTEL **$$**
(☎23 82 11 24; http://hoteltatasomba.5web5.com; r CFA27,000-30,000; ⏰Dec-May; P ❄ 🏊) Although it's starting to fray around the edges, this establishment offers spacious, utilitarian rooms with good bedding, and its location at the heart of the park is hard to beat. If you're watching your money, opt for the spartan bungalows. There's an on-site restaurant (meals CFA6500) and bar with decent Beninese fare and cold-ish beers.

# UNDERSTAND BENIN

## Benin Today

Benin is one of the more stable countries in West Africa, although things are not all that rosy. The current president, Patrice Talon, has been in office since 2016. He has pledged to overhaul and reform the current constitution, improve relations with France, reduce the maximum presidential term to five years and reduce internal government corruption. He inherits a country with a recent history of corruption scandals and a distrustful public, with the majority living below the poverty line.

## History

More than 350 years ago the area now known as Benin was split into numerous principalities. Akaba of Abomey conquered his neighbouring ruler Dan and called the new kingdom Dan-Homey, later shortened to Dahomey by French colonisers. By 1727, Dahomey spread from Abomey down to Ouidah and Cotonou and into parts of modern Togo. The kingdoms of Nikki, Djougou and Parakou were still powerful in the north, as was the Kingdom of Toffa in Porto-Novo.

Each king pledged to leave his successor more land than he inherited, achieved by waging war with his neighbours. They grew rich by selling slaves to the European traders, notably the Portuguese, who established trading posts in Porto Novo, Ouidah and along the coast. For more than a century, an average of 10,000 slaves per year were shipped to the Americas. Southern Dahomey was dubbed the Slave Coast.

Following colonisation by the French, great progress was made in education, and many Dahomeyans were employed as government advisers throughout French West Africa.

### Independence & le Folklore

When Dahomey became independent in 1960, other former French colonies started deporting their Dahomeyan populations. Back home without work, they were the root of a highly unstable political situation. Three years after independence, following the example of neighbouring Togo, the Dahomeyan military staged a coup.

During the next decade Dahomey saw four military coups, nine changes of government and five changes of constitution: what the Dahomeyans called, in jest, *le folklore*.

### Revolution

In 1972 a group of officers led by Lieutenant Colonel Mathieu Kérékou seized power in a coup, then embraced Marxist-Leninist ideology and aligned the country with superpowers such as China. To emphasise the break from the past, Kérékou changed the flag and renamed the country Benin. He informed his people of the change by radio on 13 November 1975.

The government established Marxist infrastructure, which included implementing collective farms. However, the economy became a shambles, and there were ethnic tensions between the president, a Natitingou-born northerner, and the Yoruba population in the south. There were six attempted coups in one year alone.

In December 1989, as a condition of French financial support, Kérékou ditched Marxism and held a conference to draft a new constitution. The delegates engineered a coup, forming a new cabinet under Nicéphore Soglo.

Soglo won the first free multiparty elections, held in March 1991, but his autocracy, nepotism and austere economic measures – following the devaluation of the CFA franc – came under fire. Kérékou was voted back into power in March 1996. Kérékou's second and final five-year term in office finished with the presidential elections in March 2006, bringing an end to his 33 years at the top.

## People of Benin

There is an array of different ethnic groups within Benin's narrow borders, although three of them account for nearly 60% of the population: Fon, Adja and Yoruba. The Adja people live near the border of Benin and Togo and are primarily farmers. The Fon and the Yoruba both migrated from Nigeria and occupy the southern and mideastern zones of Benin.

The Bariba and the Betamaribé, who make up 9% and 8% of the population respectively, live in the northern half of the country and have traditionally been very

### THE SOMBA

Commonly referred to as the Somba, the Betamaribé people are concentrated to the southwest of Natitingou in the plains of Boukoumbé on the Togo border. What's most fascinating about the Betamaribé is their *tata somba* houses – fort-like huts with clay turrets and thatched spires. The ground floor of a house is mostly reserved for livestock. A stepladder leads from the kitchen to the roof terrace, where there are sleeping quarters and grain stores.

The Betamaribé's principal religion is animism – as seen in the rags and bottles they hang from the trees. Once famous for their nudity, they began wearing clothes in the 1970s.

protective of their cultures and distant towards southern people.

The nomadic Fula (also called Fulani or Peul), found widely across West Africa, live primarily in the north and comprise 6% of the population.

Despite the underlying tensions between the southern and northern regions, the various groups live in relative harmony and have intermarried.

## Religion

Some 40% of the population is Christian and 25% Muslim, but most people practise voodoo, whatever their religion. The practice mixed with Catholicism in the Americas, to where the Dahomeyan slaves took it and their Afro-Brazilian descendants brought it back. Christian missionaries also won over Dahomeyans by fusing their creed with voodoo.

## The Arts

Under the Dahomeyan kings, richly coloured appliqué banners were used to depict the rulers' past and present glories. With their bright, cloth-cut figures, the banners are still being made, particularly in Abomey.

Benin has a substantial Afro-Brazilian architectural heritage, best preserved in Porto Novo and Ouidah – there are plenty of hidden gems to seek out in the streets. The Lake Nokoué stilt villages, especially Ganvié, and the *tata somba* houses around Natitingou, are remarkable examples of traditional architecture.

The *cire perdue* (lost wax) method used to make the famous Benin bronzes originates from Benin City, which lies in present-day Nigeria. However, the method spread west and the figures can be bought throughout Benin itself.

If you're into music, you'll love Angélique Kidjo, a major international star and Benin's most famous recording artist. Born in Ouidah in 1960 to a choreographer and a musician with Portuguese and English ancestry, Kidjo is a world musician in the true, boundary-busting sense of the phrase. Her music is inspired by the links between Africa and Latin America and the fusion of cultures. Check out www.kidjo.com for more information about her career. Other well-known Beninese artists include Gnonnas Pedro, Nel Oliver and Yelouassi Adolphe, and the bands Orchestre Poly-Rythmo and Disc Afrique.

## Food & Drink

Beninese grub is unquestionably among the best in West Africa and is very similar to Togolese food, the main differences being the names: *fufu* (a starchy staple from ground plantain or cassava) is generally called *igname pilé* here, and *djenkoumé* (a savoury cornmeal and tomato cake) is called *pâte rouge,* for example. In southern Benin, fish is a highlight of local cuisine. It's usually barracuda, dorado or grouper, and is usually served grilled or fried.

## Environment

Sandwiched between Nigeria and Togo, Benin is 700km long and 120km across in the south, widening to about 300km in the north. Most of the coastal plain is a sand bar that blocks the seaward flow of several rivers. As a result, there are lagoons a few kilometres inland all along the coast, which is being eroded by the strong ocean currents. Inland is a densely forested plateau and, in the far northwest, the Atakora Mountains.

Wildlife thrives in Parc National de la Pendjari, with elephants and several feline species.

Deforestation and desertification are major issues because of the logging of valuable wood, such as teak.

# SURVIVAL GUIDE

## Directory A–Z

### ACCOMMODATION

Benin has accommodation to suit every budget – from beach resorts to guesthouses. Swanky hotels are confined to Cotonou and, to a lesser extent, Ouidah and Natitingou. Most have restaurants and bars, offer wi-fi service and have air-con.

### DANGERS & ANNOYANCES

- Cotonou has its fair share of traffic accidents and muggings, so be careful. In Ouidah, avoid the roads to and along the coast at any time of day.
- Children, and sometimes also adults, will shout '*Yovo! Yovo!*' (meaning 'white person') ad nauseam. It's normally harmless, but tiresome.
- The beaches along the coast are not safe for swimming because of strong currents. Stick to hotel swimming pools or the lagoon.

### EMBASSIES & CONSULATES

**British Community Liaison Officer** (☎21 30 32 65; www.fco.gov.uk; Haie Vive, Cotonou; ⏲10am-4pm Mon-Fri) Officially, British nationals must deal with the British Deputy High Commission in Lagos (Nigeria). However, the Community Liaison Officer for the British community in Benin, based at the English International School, can be of some help.

**French Embassy** (☎21 36 55 33; www.ambafrance-bj.org; Ave Jean-Paul II; ⏲11am-4pm Mon-Thu)

**German Embassy** (☎21 31 29 67; www.cotonou.diplo.de; Ave Jean-Paul II)

**Ghanaian Embassy** (☎21 30 07 46; off Blvd de la Marina, Cotonou)

**Nigerian Embassy** (☎21 31 56 65; off Blvd de la Marina, Cotonou)

**US Embassy** (☎21 30 06 50; cotonou.usembassy.gov; Rue Caporal Bernard Anani)

### EMERGENCY & IMPORTANT NUMBERS

| | |
|---|---|
| Benin's country code | ☎229 |
| Police | ☎117 |
| Ambulance | ☎112 |
| Fire | ☎118 |

### INTERNET ACCESS

In towns and cities, complimentary wi-fi is available in almost every midrange and top-end hotel.

Internet cafes are plentiful in towns and cities. Connection speeds vary from pretty good to acceptable.

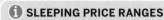

> **SLEEPING PRICE RANGES**
>
> The following price ranges refer to a double room with bathroom and air-con.
>
> **$** less than CFA16,000
>
> **$$** CFA16,000–40,000
>
> **$$$** more than CFA40,000

### LGBTIQ TRAVELLERS

While homosexuality is technically legal in Benin, it is a conservative country and gay and lesbian travellers should avoid making their sexual orientation known.

### MONEY

The currency in Benin is the West African CFA franc. The best foreign currency to carry is euros, which are easily exchanged at banks, hotels or bureaux de change.

#### Exchange Rates

| | | |
|---|---|---|
| Australia | A$1 | CFA452 |
| Canada | C$1 | CFA440 |
| Europe | €1 | CFA656 |
| Japan | ¥100 | CFA538 |
| New Zealand | NZ$1 | CFA415 |
| United Kingdom | £1 | CFA774 |
| United States | US$ | CFA600 |

For current exchange rates, see www.xe.com.

#### Tipping

Tipping is generally not necessary except at upmarket restaurants, where around 10% extra should be given for good service.

### OPENING HOURS

**Banks** 8am to 12.30pm and 3pm to 6.30pm Monday to Friday, 9am to 1pm Saturday. Some banks are open through lunchtime.

**Bars** Late morning until the last customers leave (late); nightclubs generally go from 10pm into the wee hours.

**Restaurants** Lunch 11.30am to 2.30pm, dinner 6.30pm to 10.30pm.

**Shops & businesses** 8am to noon and 3pm to 7pm Monday to Saturday.

### PUBLIC HOLIDAYS

In addition to Muslim holidays, Benin celebrates the following days:

**New Year's Day** 1 January

**Vodoun** 10 January

**Easter Monday** March/April

**Labour Day** 1 May

**Ascension Thursday** May

### EATING PRICE RANGES

The following price ranges refer to a main course.

**$** less than CFA2000

**$$** CFA2000–4000

**$$$** more than CFA4000

**Pentecost Monday** May
**Independence Day** 1 August
**Assumption** 15 August
**Armed Forces Day** 26 October
**All Saints' Day** 1 November
**Christmas** 25 December

### TELEPHONE

Depending on which mobile network you use at home, your phone may or may not work while in Benin – ask your mobile network provider. However, local mobile phone coverage is excellent and fairly cheap. Local networks include Moov and MTN. You can buy a local SIM card (CFA1500). Top-up vouchers are readily available.

### TOURIST INFORMATION

There are tourist offices in Cotonou, Abomey, Ouidah and Porto Novo. The **Benin Tourism** (www.benin-tourisme.com) website is another source of information.

### VISAS

Local authorities have done a couple of U-turns on visa policies in recent years, with the latest turn meaning that visas were not obtainable at the border or upon arrival at the airport. Be sure to get your visa from a Beninese embassy before travelling. Allow €50 for a one-month single-entry visa.
Visa des Pays de l'Entente (p451) are not available in Benin.

### PRACTICALITIES

**Electricity** Supply is 220V and plugs are of the European two-round-pin variety. Network cuts are frequent.

**Newspapers** Cotonou's daily newspapers include La Nation and Le Matinal.

**Radio** The state-owned ORTB broadcasts on the radio in French and local languages.

**Weights & measures** Benin uses the metric system.

For onward travel, the following embassies deliver visas:

**Burkina Faso** No diplomatic representation in Benin – contact the French consulate.

**Niger** The embassy in Cotonou issues 30-day visas. They cost CFA23,500 and you'll need two photos. Allow three to four working days. You cannot get visas at the border.

**Nigeria** The Nigerian embassy only issues transit visas to travellers with a Nigerian embassy in their home country (there is no need to contact the embassy in your home country beforehand). You need two photos, along with photocopies of your passport and, if you have one, your ticket for onward travel from Nigeria. Fees vary according to nationality. Visas are normally issued on the same day.

**Togo** Seven-day visas (CFA10,000) are issued at the border. If crossing the border at Nadoba (coming from Boukombé), head to Kara where the Direction Régionale de la Documentation Nationale issues 30-day multiple-entry visas (CFA10,000, four photos).

### WOMEN TRAVELLERS

Beninese men can give women travellers a lot of unwanted attention. Particularly unnerving are military and other officials using their power to get more of your company than is strictly necessary. Always stay polite but firm and make sure you have a good 'husband story'.

## Getting There & Away

### AIR

The **Aéroport International de Cotonou Cadjéhoun** (www.aeroport-cotonou.com) is Benin's main gateway.

The main international carriers are **Air France** (www.airfrance.com; Rte de l'Aéroport), **Royal Air Maroc** (☎21 30 86 04; www.royalairmaroc.com; Rte de l'Aéroport), **Brussels Airlines** (☎21 30 16 82; www.brusselsairlines.com; Rte de l'Aéroport) and **Ethiopian Airlines** (☎21 32 71 61; www.flyethiopian.com; Rue 403), which offer direct flights to France, Morocco, Belgium and Ethiopia respectively, and connecting flights to the rest of the world.

Other major airlines include **Asky** (☎21 32 54 18; www.flyasky.com; Ave de la Paix), which flies to major capitals in West and Central Africa via Lomé; **South African Airways** (www.flysaa.com; Blvd Steinmetz), which flies to Johannesburg (South Africa); **Kenya Airways** (☎21 31 63 71; www.kenya-airways.com; Blvd Steinmetz), which flies to Nairobi (Kenya) and Ouagadougou (Burkina Faso); **Air Burkina** (www.air-burkina.com; Rte de l'Aéroport), which serves Ouagadougou (Burkina Faso) and Abidjan (Côte d'Ivoire); and **Senegal Airlines** (☎21 31 76 51; www.senegalairlines.aero; Ave Steinmetz), which flies to

Dakar (Senegal) and Abidjan (Côte d'Ivoire). All airlines have offices in Cotonou.

### LAND

#### Burkina Faso

From Tanguiéta in northwestern Benin, you can find bush taxis to Nadiagou, on the Burkina side of the border north of Porga, from where you can find services to Ouagadougou. There's also a daily bus from Tanguiéta to Ouagadougou.

TCV (p151) bus services go two times a week between Cotonou and Bobo Dioulasso via Ouagadougou (CFA19,000, 18 hours).

#### Niger

From Malanville in northeastern Benin, a *zemi-john* (motorcycle taxi) or shared taxi can take you across the Niger River to Gaya in Niger.

From Cotonou, Rimbo-RTV (p151) has daily services to Niamey (CFA24,000, 18 hours).

#### Nigeria

ABC Transport (p151) operates a daily Lagos–Accra bus service, which stops in Cotonou (CFA12,000 to CFA14,000, four hours). Add another CFA6000 for the *convoyeur* (the middleman who'll handle and facilitate formalities at the border).

There are no direct taxis to Lagos from Porto Novo, so you'll have to change at the Kraké–Seme border (CFA1000, 30 minutes). Make sure you have some naira to pay for your journey on the other side.

#### Togo

Cotonou and Lomé are connected by frequent bush taxis (CFA6500, three hours), which regularly leave the Gare Jonquet in Cotonou for Lomé. Alternatively, pick up a taxi to the border point at Hilakondji and grab another taxi on the Togolese side of the border.

Various bus companies, including STIF (p151), **CTS** (☎ 99 27 83 32; Blvd du 13 Janvier (Blvd Circulaire)) and UTB (p151), also regularly service the Cotonou–Lomé–Accra–Abidjan route (CFA5000 for Lomé, four hours).

Other crossings are at Kétao–Ouaké, on the Kara–Djougou road, and between Nadoba in Togo and Boukoumbé in Benin along a good track. The latter crossing takes you through spectacular countryside but has little public transport except on Wednesdays, Nadoba market day.

## ℹ Getting Around

### BUS

Buses are the most reliable and comfortable way to get around, especially between cities in southern Benin and Natitingou to the north. ATT (p151) and Confort Lines (p157) buses are better maintained and more reliable than those of other companies. They also have air-con.

Buses almost always operate with guaranteed seating and fixed departure times; arrive early or book the day before to ensure you have a seat on your preferred service.

### CAR & MOTORCYCLE

Roads are in relatively good condition throughout Benin except the Cotonou–Bohicon road, which is appalling. It has been scheduled for resurfacing for years, but little progress has been made.

Hiring a car with a driver is a good option if you're short on time. Travel agencies and tour operators in Cotonou can organise 4WD hire for about CFA50,000 per day (with driver). For a regular vehicle, you'll pay about CFA20,000 per day. Fuel is extra.

If you're driving, you need an International Driving Permit. A litre of petrol cost around CFA600 at the time of research. Petrol stations are easy to find throughout the country.

### LOCAL TRANSPORT

#### Bush Taxi

Bush taxis, generally beaten-up old vehicles, cover outlying communities that large buses don't serve, but also run between major towns and cities. There is sometimes a surcharge for luggage. Most leave from the *gares routières*; morning is the best time to find them.

#### Zemi-Johns

The omnipresence of *zems* (*zemi-johns;* motorbike taxis) has translated into the near disappearance of car taxis for short journeys. While they are by far the fastest and most convenient way of getting around, they are dangerous: most drive like lunatics and helmets are not available.

*Zem* drivers wear numbered yellow shirts in Cotonou (various colours in other towns). Hail them just as you would a taxi, and be sure to agree on a price before the journey. The typical fare is from CFA200 to CFA350 for trips within a town. They are also an easy way to get to remote villages where public transport is infrequent.

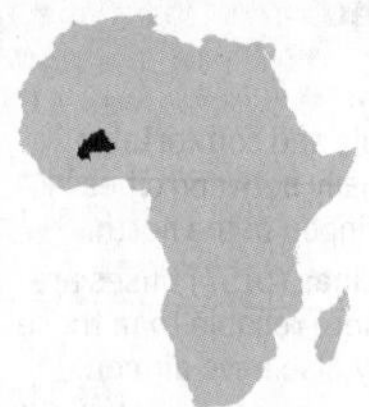

# Burkina Faso

☎226 / POP 18.5 MILLION

**Includes ➡**



## Best Places to Eat

- La Canne d'Or (p173)
- Le Calypso (p174)
- Maquis Aboussouan (p168)
- Le Verdoyant (p169)
- Chez Haregua (p169)

## Best Places to Sleep

- Villa Bobo (p171)
- Auberge Kunkolo (p176)
- Le Calypso (p174)
- Les Jardins de Koulouba (p165)
- Ranch de Nazinga (p176)

## Why Go?

Burkina should be on everyone's travel list – it may not have many big-ticket attractions, but the warmth of its welcome and the friendliness of the Burkinabé people is unique. Wherever you go you'll be greeted with a memorable *bonne arrivée* ('welcome') and a handshake.

There's also the lively cultural scene. The capital, Ouagadougou, and Bobo-Dioulasso, Burkina's two largest and gloriously named cities, are famous for their musical traditions and beautiful handicrafts. Throw in Fespaco, Africa's premier film festival (held in Ouaga every odd-numbered year), and there's enough to engage your mind and senses for a couple of weeks or so.

Tourism infrastructure is fairly limited, but the true gems of Burkina Faso are in the remoter areas, outside of the cities: the enchanting beauty of the landscapes – from rolling savannah and surprising geology to the mesmerising painted houses at Tiébélé – and the unique culture and genuine hospitality of the Burkinabé.

## When to Go

### Ouagadougou

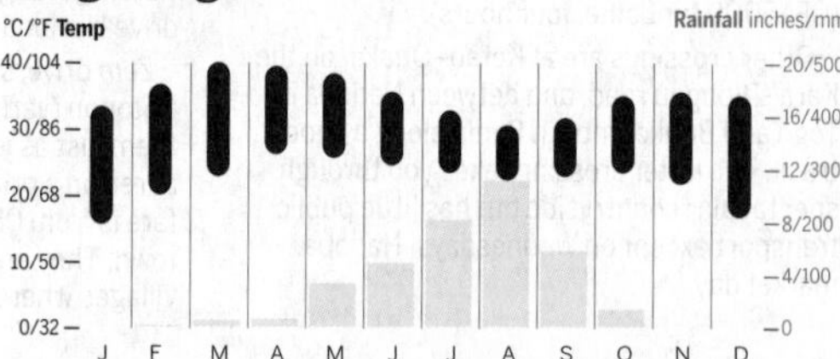


**Jan–Mar** Perfect wildlife-viewing time; dusty harmattan winds can produce hazy skies.

**Apr–Sep** Hot season (April to May) best avoided; rainy season (June to September) difficult for transport.

**Oct–Dec** A lovely time of year, with green landscapes and pleasant temperatures.

# OUAGADOUGOU

POP 1.4 MILLION

Ouaga, as it's affectionately dubbed, is a thriving, eclectic arts hub, with dance and concert venues, live bands, theatre companies, a busy festival schedule and beautiful handicrafts. Its streets are a busy, dusty mix of concrete and red roads, thousands of mopeds, street-peddlers and general, exuberant life that more than makes up for the capital's lack of major sights.

## Sights

**Moro-Naba Palace** PALACE
(Ave Moro-Naba) FREE On Fridays at 7am the Moro-Naba of Ouagadougou – emperor of the Mossi and the most powerful traditional chief in Burkina Faso – presides over the **Moro-Naba Ceremony** at the palace. It's a formal ritual that lasts only about 15 minutes. Travellers are welcome to attend, but photos are not permitted.

**National Museum** MUSEUM
(25 39 19 34; Blvd Charles de Gaulle; CFA1000; 9am-12.30pm & 3-5.30pm Tue-Sat) The national museum, almost 4km east of the city centre, has displays of the various masks, ancestral statues and traditional costumes of Burkina Faso's major ethnic groups.

**Musée de la Musique** MUSEUM
(Ave d'Oubritenga; CFA1000; 9am-4pm Tue-Sat, by appt Sun) You don't need to be into music to enjoy this excellent museum: the Burkinabé live and breathe music and a visit to the museum serves as a great introduction to Burkinabé culture. The new building is a traditional adobe structure that gives the place a special atmosphere in which to soak up local music history.

## Festivals & Events

★**Fespaco** FILM
(Festival Pan-Africain du Cinéma de Ouagadougou; www.fespaco.bf; Feb-Mar) Going strong since 1969, this world-renowned biennial festival (held in odd-numbered years) sees African films competing for the prestigious Étalon d'Or de Yennenga – Fespaco's equivalent of the Oscars.

**Jazz à Ouaga** MUSIC
(www.jazz-ouaga.org; Apr-May) A well-established music festival bringing out the Afrobeat, soul and blues influence in jazz.

**SIAO** ART
(Salon International de l'Artisanat de Ouagadougou; www.siao.bf; Blvd des Tensoba; Oct) Biennial trade fair (held in even-numbered years) of reference for the arts and crafts sector in Africa – and a godsend for gem-hunting visitors.

## Sleeping

★**Les Jardins de Koulouba** GUESTHOUSE $
(25 30 25 81; www.jardins-koulouba.fr; r with air-con CFA25,000, with fan & without bathroom CFA15,000; ) A wonderfully decorated patio and a lush tropical garden, African art, spacious rooms, a fantastic location, a pool and a relaxed vibe make this lovely guesthouse one of the best in Ouaga.

★**Le Pavillon Vert** HOSTEL $
(25 31 06 11; www.hotel-pavillonvert.com; Ave de la Liberté; s/d with fan CFA12,500/13,500, with air-con CFA17,000/18,000, with fan & without bathroom CFA8000/8500; ) The stalwart 'PV' is the best backpackers' spot in Ouaga. It has competitive prices, a lively bar and restaurant, a gorgeous plant-filled garden and an assortment of well-kept rooms for all budgets. It's run by the same management as the excellent Couleurs d'Afrique (p170) travel agency and the **Hotel de la Liberte** (25 33 23 63; www.hotel-liberte.com; Avenue de la Liberté; s/d CFA17,500/20,000; ).

**Villa Yiri Suma** GUESTHOUSE $
(25 30 54 82; www.yirisuma.com; 428 Ave du Petit Maurice Yameogo; d CFA21,000-28,000; ) Yiri Suma is all about art: Lucien, the owner, is passionate about African art and likes nothing better than to share his passion with guests via displaying contemporary Burkinabé works in the courtyard. The villa regularly houses exhibitions and cultural events, and the five spotless rooms enjoy their own contemporary decor and unique works.

**Chez Giuliana** GUESTHOUSE $
(25 36 33 97; www.chezgiuliana.com; Rue Lamine Gueye, Quartier 1200 Logements; s/d without bathroom CFA16,000/20,000, with bathroom CFA20,000/24,000; ) This bustling Italian guesthouse is a perennial favourite among aid workers: the welcome is as colourful as the rooms and the roof terrace is simply awesome for sundowners. It's about 3km outside the centre, near the Maternité Sainte Camille hospital. Rates include breakfast.

**Auberge Le Karité Bleu** B&B $$
(25 36 90 46; www.karitebleu.com; 214 Blvd de l'Onatel, Zone du Bois; d CFA28,000-47,000; ) In a residential neighbourhood, this adorable B&B offers eight spiffy rooms decorated

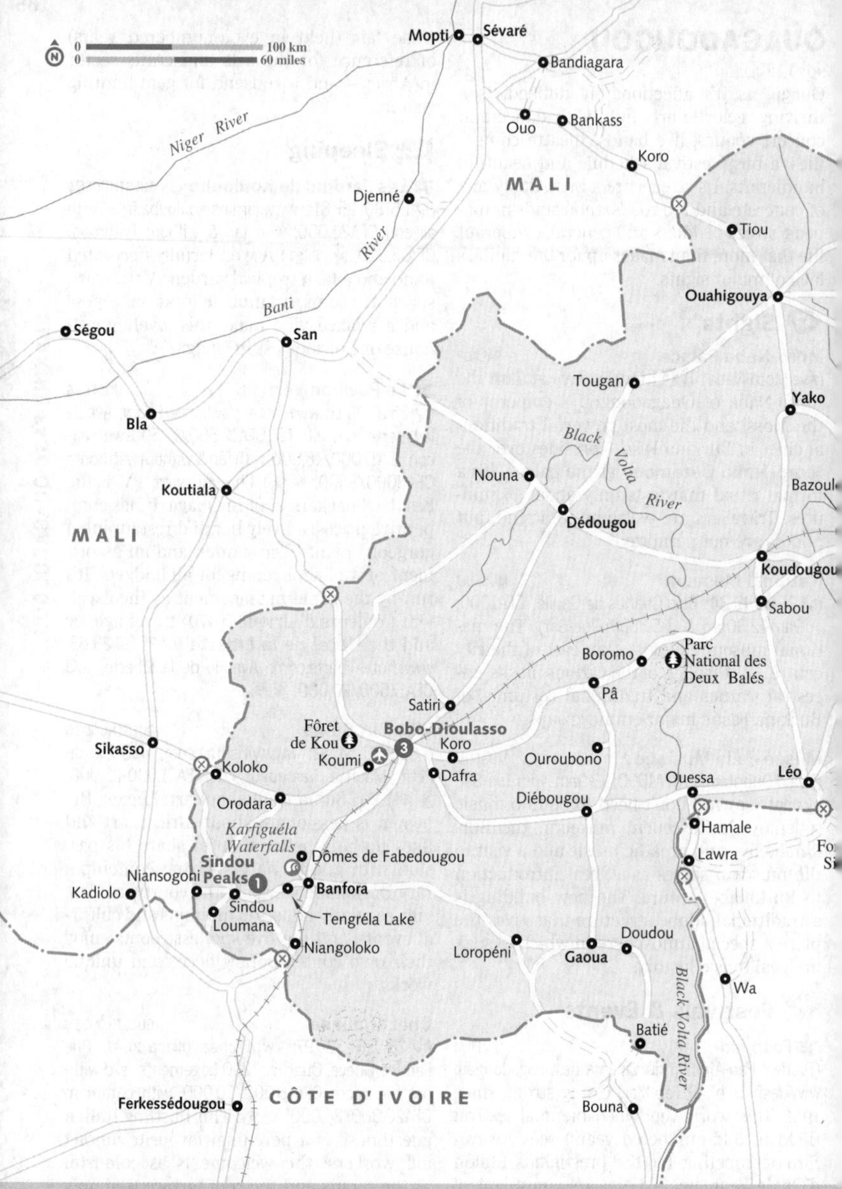


## Burkina Faso Highlights

**1 Sindou Peaks** (p175) Wandering amid other-worldly rock formations and Burkina's lush landscapes.

**2 Cour Royale** (p176) Marvelling over the meaning and originality of Kassena houses at Tiébélé.

**3 Live music** (p173) Sipping beers to the sound of Bobo-Dioulasso's fantastic musicians.

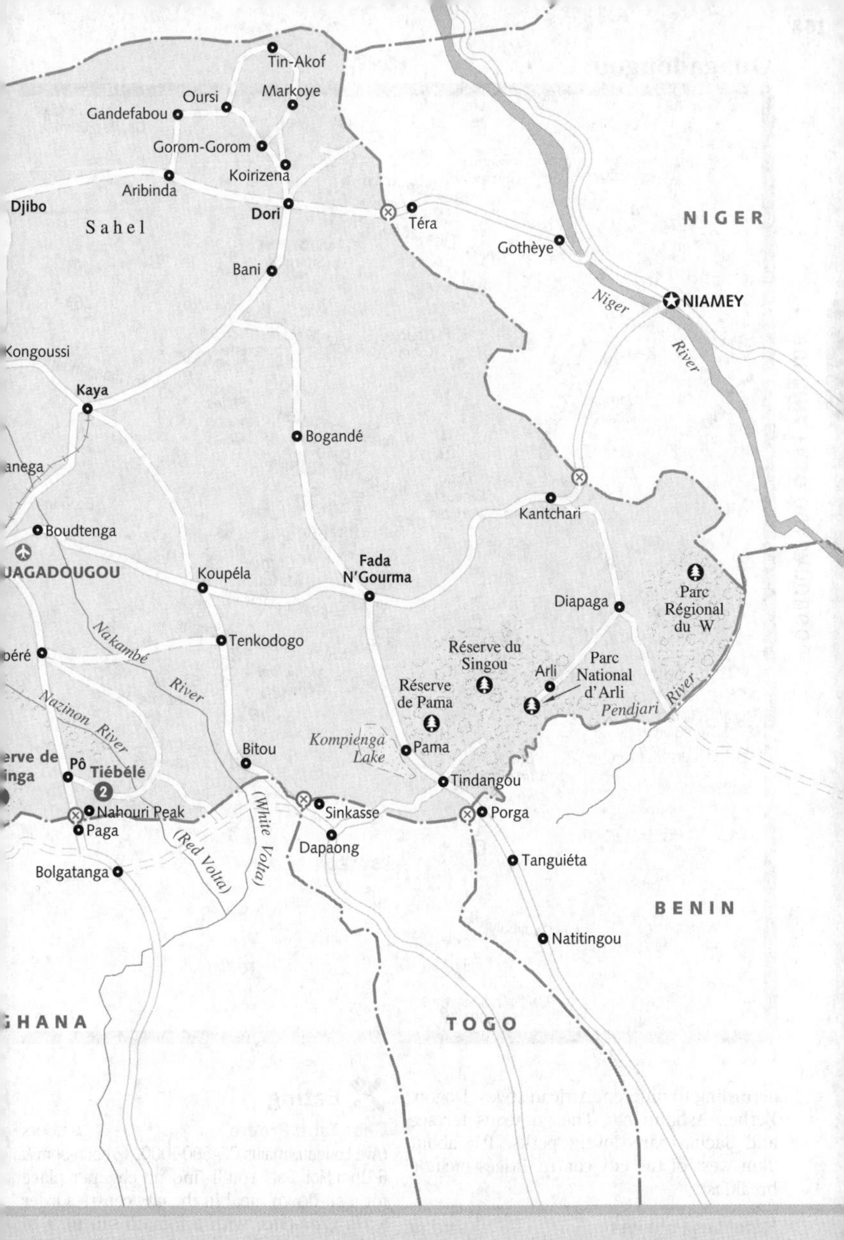


4 **Réserve de Nazinga** (p176) Coming face-to-face with the elephants, alligators and antelope at Burkina's favourite national park.

5 **Festivals** (p165) Joining in one of the fabulous Ouagadougou festivals and soaking up the atmosphere.

## Ouagadougou

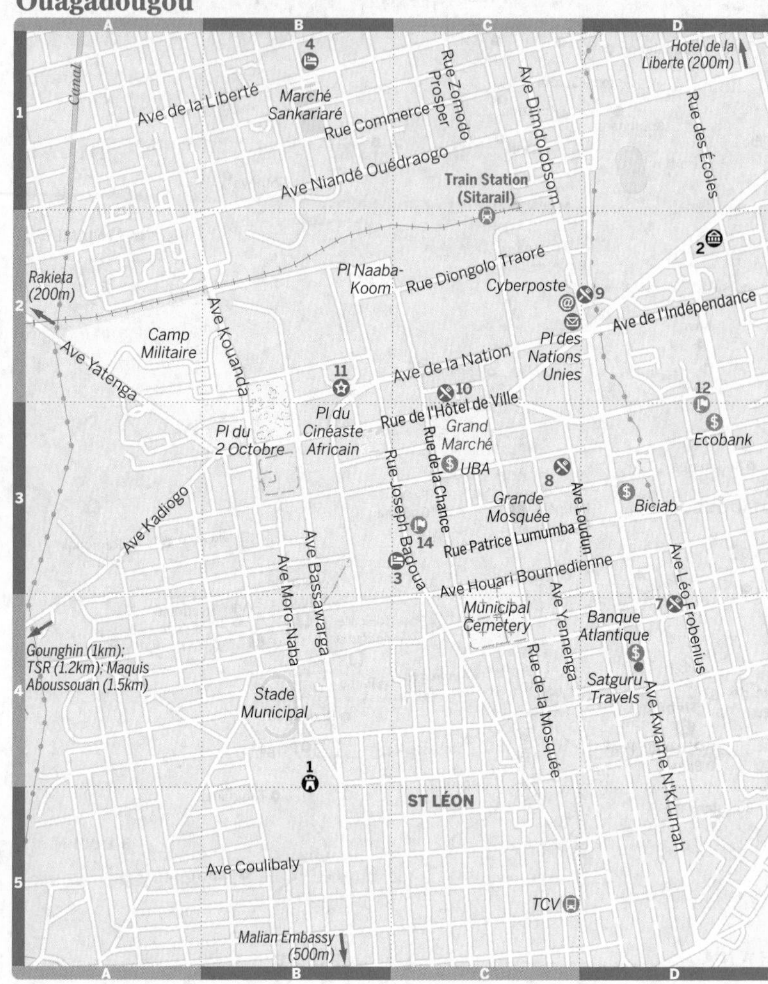




according to different African styles: Dogon, Berber, Ashanti etc. The gorgeous terrace and Jacuzzi are lovely perks. It's about 2km west of the city centre. Prices include breakfast.

**Hôtel Les Palmiers** HOTEL **$$**
(☎25 33 33 30; www.hotellespalmiers.net; Rue Joseph Badoua; d CFA35,000-45,000; ❄📶🏊) Les Palmiers is an oasis blending African touches with European levels of comfort. The rooms are arranged around a leafy compound and embellished with local decorations. The garden, pool and terrace provide the finishing touches.

### Eating

**Chez Tanti Propre** AFRICAN **$**
(Ave Loudun; mains CFA500-1000; ⏰noon-3pm & 6-11pm Mon-Sat) You'll find no cheaper place for a sit-down meal in the city centre. Order a *riz gras* (rice with a tomato sauce), a *tô* (millet- or sorghum-based *pâte)* or an *alloco* (fried plantain) prepared grandma-style. Perfect for a quick bite at lunchtime.

★**Maquis Aboussouan** AFRICAN **$$**
(☎25 34 27 20; Rue Simon Compaoré; mains CFA2500-5000; ⏰11am-11pm Tue-Sun; ❄) This upmarket *maquis* (rustic, open-air restau-

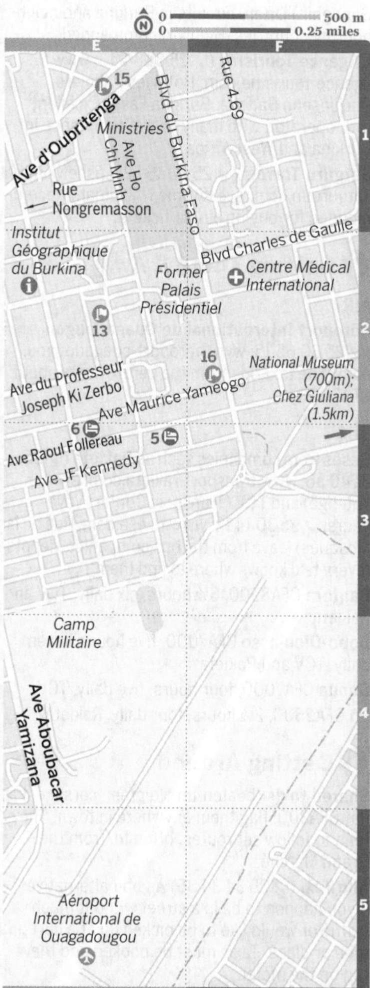


rant) is the place to enjoy Burkinabé and Ivoirian staples such as *poulet kedjenou* (slow-cooked chicken with peppers and tomatoes) or *attiéké* (grated cassava). The ample, lively courtyard is filled with regular locals and is great for soaking up the atmosphere.

**★Le Verdoyant** PIZZA, ITALIAN $$
(☎25 31 54 07; Ave Dimdolobsom; mains CFA4000-6000; ⏲noon-2.30pm & 6.30-11pm Thu-Tue) A favourite haunt of expats, the ultracentral Le Verdoyant is famous for its pasta, wood-fired pizzas and ice creams. Note that the mosquitoes are ferocious at night.

## Ouagadougou

**Sights**
1 Moro-Naba Palace B4
2 Musée de la Musique D2

**Sleeping**
3 Hôtel Les Palmiers C3
4 Le Pavillon Vert B1
5 Les Jardins de Koulouba E3
6 Villa Yiri Suma E3

**Eating**
7 Chez Haregua D4
8 Chez Tanti Propre C3
9 Le Verdoyant D2
10 L'Eau Vive C2

**Entertainment**
11 Institut Français B2

**Information**
12 Canadian Embassy D3
13 French Embassy E2
14 German Embassy C3
15 Ghanaian Embassy E1
16 Ivorian Embassy F2
L'Agence Tourisme (see 3)

**Espace Gondwana** FUSION $$
(☎50 36 11 24; www.africartisanat.com; Rue du Dr Balla Moussa Traoré, Zone du Bois; mains CFA4000-9000; ⏲6-11pm; ❄📶) Espace Gondwana sports sensational decor, with four dining rooms richly adorned with masks and traditional furniture. The food impresses, too, with an imaginative menu that runs the gamut from frogs' legs and fish dishes to grilled meats and salads.

**L'Eau Vive** FRENCH $$
(Rue de l'Hôtel de Ville; mains CFA2000-7000; ⏲noon-2.30pm & 7-10pm; ❄📶) This Ouagadougou institution is run by an order of nuns and promises an air-conditioned haven from the clamour outside; there's also a garden dining area out the back. French staples are served, and 'Ave Maria' is sung at 9.30pm every night. There is a sister (excuse the pun) restaurant in Bobo (p173).

**★Chez Haregua** ETHIOPIAN $$$
(☎25 50 52 38; chezharegua@gmail.com; Ave Léo Frobenus; mains CFA6000-10,000; ❄) If you want to give your taste buds a sensuous treat, go for this Ethiopian choice – the excellent *alicha doro* (turmeric chicken) is served with the traditional, pancake-like injera bread and eaten by hand. The staff is super-friendly and the service excellent. Highly recommended.

## Entertainment

**Institut Français** ARTS CENTRE

(Ave de la Nation) The French cultural centre has one of the best line-ups of Burkinabé and West African musicians, theatre directors, cinema and visual artists.

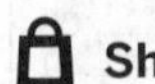

## Shopping

**★Village Artisanal de Ouaga** GIFTS & SOUVENIRS

(☎25 37 14 83; Blvd Tengsoba; ⏰7am-7pm) A government-run cooperative with a wide range of crafts, ideal for souvenir-shopping without the hard sell. If you're not a fan of bargaining to death and want to find real local handicrafts, this is the place to go. Note that Blvd Tengsoba is also known as Blvd Circulaire.

## Information

### DANGERS & ANNOYANCES

Ouagadougou is one of the safer cities in the region, but avoid walking around alone at night. Bag snatching is a problem – don't carry valuables with you.

### INTERNET ACCESS

**Cyberposte** (off Ave de la Nation; per hr CFA500; ⏰8am-8pm Mon-Sat) Also offers printing and scanning services.

### MEDICAL SERVICES

**Centre Médical International** (☎70 20 00 00, 50 30 66 07; Rue Nazi Boni, Koulouba; ⏰24hr) In the Koulouba neighbourhood, west of the centre.

### MONEY

There are numerous banks around town, most with ATM.

**Banque Atlantique** (Ave Kwame N'Krumah; ⏰9am-2pm)

**Biciab** (Ave Kwame N'Krumah; ⏰7-11am & 3.30-5pm Mon-Fri) Efficient exchange office with a Biciab ATM (Visa only). There are also two other Bicicab ATMs in the centre, at Ave Yennenga and Ave Loudun.

**Ecobank** (Rue Maurice Bishop; ⏰7-11am & 3.30-5pm)

**UBA** (Rue de la Chance; ⏰9am-2pm)

### TOURIST INFORMATION

**Institut Géographique du Burkina** (Ave de l'Indépendance) Maps and general info on the country are available here.

### TRAVEL AGENCIES

**Couleurs d'Afrique** (☎25 31 06 11; www.couleurs-afrique.com; Ave de l'Olympisme, Gounghin) Offers circuits in Burkina and neighbouring countries. Highly recommended.

**L'Agence Tourisme** (☎25 31 84 43; www.agence-tourisme.com; Hôtel les Palmiers, Rue Joseph Badoua, Burkina Faso) Excellent tour operator, with many years' experience in Burkina and West Africa.

**Satguru Travels** (☎25 30 16 52; cpshewkani@satguruun.com; Ave Kwame N'Krumah) Recommended for buying airline tickets.

## Getting There & Away

### AIR

**Aéroport International de Ouagadougou** (☎25 30 65 15; www.aeroport-ouagadougou.com) The taxi ride from the centre costs about CFA3000.

### BUS

Buses from companies such as **Rakieta** (☎25 31 40 56; www.transport-rakieta.com; Ave Yatenga) and **TCV** (Transport Confort Voyageurs; ☎25 30 14 12; www.tcv-sa.com; Rue de la Mosquée) leave from the bus companies' depots (every taxi knows where to find them).

**Banfora** CFA8500, 6½ hours, six daily, TCV and Rakieta

**Bobo-Dioulasso** CFA7000, five hours, seven daily, TCV and Rakieta

**Gaoua** CFA7000, four hours, five daily, TCV

**Pô** CFA2500, 2½ hours, four daily, Rakieta

## Getting Around

**Shared taxis** (beaten-up old green cars) cost a flat CFA300; flag them anywhere in town. They tend to follow set routes, often to/from the Grand Marché.

**Allo Taxi** (☎25 34 34 35) A good alternative if you happen to be in a street without much traffic or would like to be picked up at a certain time or place. Taxis must be booked and they run on the meter.

# THE SOUTHWEST

Southwestern Burkina Faso ticks all the right boxes, with a heavy mix of natural and cultural sights vying for your attention.

## Bobo-Dioulasso

POP 490,000

Bobo-Dioulasso – or Bobo, as it's widely known – may be Burkina Faso's second-largest city, but it has small-town charm. Its tree-lined streets exude a languid, semitropical atmosphere that makes it a favourite rest stop for travellers.

You'll have plenty to do during the day in and around the city – hire a moped to see the surrounding sights – but save some energy for night time to enjoy Bobo's thriving live-music scene and excellent restaurants.

## Sights

**Grande Mosquée** MOSQUE

(CFA1000) Built in 1893, this mosque is an outstanding example of Sahel-style mud architecture, with conical towers and wooden struts (which both support the structure and act as scaffolding during replastering efforts). Visits take you inside the building and onto the roof terrace, where you'll get a different perspective of the towers.

**Koro** VILLAGE

(CFA1000) Perched on the hillside, Koro's houses – built amid rock formations – are unique in the area, and there are fine panoramic views over the countryside from the top of the village. Koro is 13km east of Bobo, off the main Ouagadougou road.

**Kibidwé** AREA

(CFA1000) Bobo's historical centre is a thriving neighbourhood. Little has changed over the centuries in terms of organisation: Muslims, *griots* (traditional musicians, storytellers or praise singers), blacksmiths and 'nobles' (farmers) still live in their respective quarters but happily trade services and drink at the same *chopolo* (millet beer) bars.

Guided tours are not official, but unavoidable in practice – allow CFA2000 to CFA3000. They offer a great insight into local life, although the compulsory stops at craft shops are tedious.

**Grand Marché** MARKET

(Rue du Commerce, Harndalaye) Bobo-Dioulasso's centrepiece, the expansive Grand Marché, is hugely enjoyable and atmospheric, and a wonderful (and largely hassle-free) place to experience a typical African city market. The market spills over onto the surrounding streets in a chaos of mopeds, wandering traders and general clamour, which together provide a lively counterpoint to Bobo's otherwise tranquil streets.

**Koumi** VILLAGE

(CFA1000) The village of Koumi, on the Bobo–Orodara road (6km south of Kou), is well-known for its ochre-coloured adobe houses. Villagers run informative **guided tours** (CFA1000) touching on animist beliefs, architecture and local life.

### FÊTE DES MASQUES

In the Bobo-Dioulasso region, whenever there's a major funeral, it's accompanied by a late-night *fête des masques* (festival of masks).

Masked men dance to an orchestra of flute-like instruments and narrow drums beaten with curved canes. Each dancer, representing a different spirit, performs in turn – leaping, waving sticks and looking for evil spirits that might prevent the deceased from going to paradise.

As the celebrations continue, dancers become increasingly wild, performing acrobatic feats and waving their heads backwards and forwards until they catch someone and strike them. The victim, however, must not complain.

## Sleeping

★ **Villa Rose** GUESTHOUSE $

(20 97 67 58; www.villarosebobodioulasso.com; Ave Philiippe Zinda Kaboré, Koko; s/d with fan CFA13,000/14,000, with air-con CFA16,500/17,500; ) This lovely guesthouse, run by Dutch-Burkinabé couple Franca and Moctar, sits in the leafy neighbourhood of Koko, east of the centre, just off the main street. The fourteen rooms are impeccable, combining a minimalist decor and Burkinabé arts and crafts. The massive courtyard garden is the hotel's centrepiece, and a beautiful place to relax.

★ **Villa Bobo** B&B $

(20 98 54 16; www.villabobo.com; No 292 Rue 35, Secteur 4, Koko; s/d with fan CFA12,000/15,000, with air-con CFA16,500/19,000; P) With its four zealously maintained rooms, prim bathrooms, atmospheric veranda, colourful garden and pool, Villa Bobo is a delight. Xavier, the French owner, speaks English and can arrange excursions in the area, and you can hire scooters (CFA5000 per day).

**Entente Hôtel** HOTEL $

(20 97 12 05; sopresbobo@yahoo.fr; Rue du Commerce; s/d with fan CFA9300/12,600, s/d/tr with air-con CFA12,300/20,600/27,900; ) One of the few central establishments in Bobo, Entente has clean, tidy rooms. The fan rooms are rather small for the price, but there is

## Bobo-Dioulasso

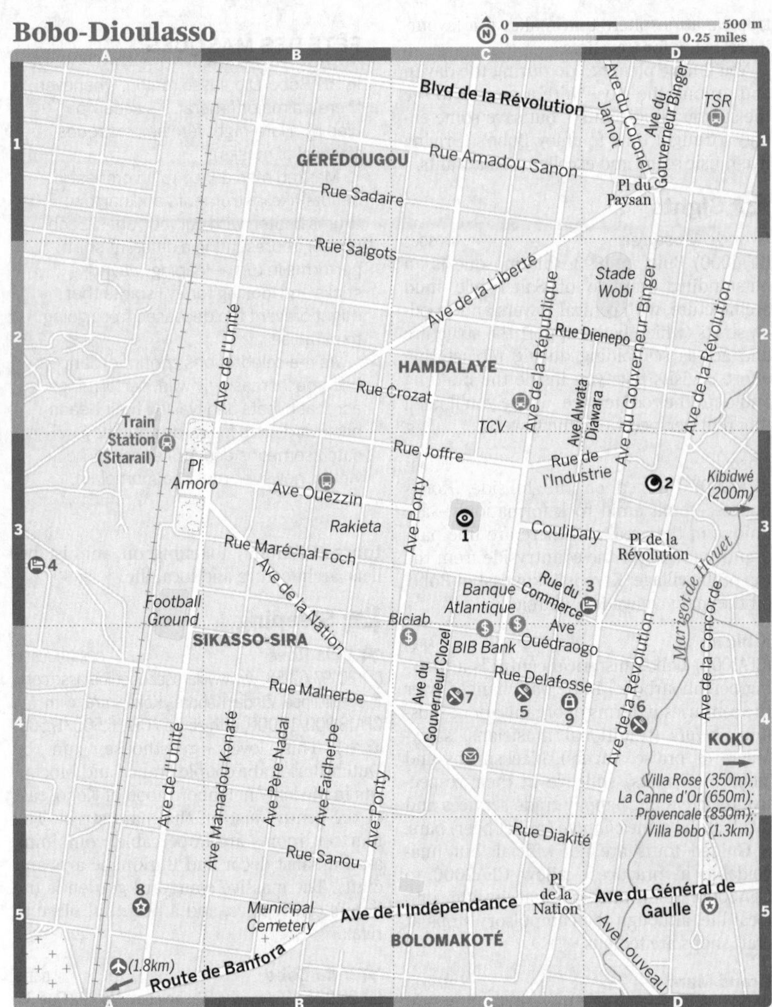


plenty of space to hang out in the pleasant courtyard.

**Les 2 Palmiers** HOTEL **$$**
(☎20 97 27 59; www.hotelles2palmiers.com; off Rue Malherbe; d CFA37,500-41,500; ❄📶) In a quiet street, this excellent option gets an A+ for its spotless rooms embellished with African crafts. The on-site restaurant is hailed as one of the best in Bobo.

## Eating

**Restaurant Dankin** AFRICAN **$**
(☎20 98 28 42; Rue Malherbe; mains CFA1000-4000; ⏲7am-3pm & 6-11pm; 📶) Sister restaurant to Mandé, Dankin serves a loyal base of local customers, who come for the simple West African dishes – *riz gras* or *riz arachide* (rice with a peanut sauce) – delicious fresh juices and Brakina beer. The atmosphere is always lively, and the service jovial.

**Mandé** AFRICAN **$**
(Ave de la Révolution; mains CFA1000-4000; ⏲7am-3pm & 6-11pm; ❄📶) With an open-air terrace, great prices and a wide-ranging menu specialising in African dishes, Mandé is an excellent deal. If you just eat *riz sauce* (rice with sauce) or couscous and drink tamarind juice, you'll be well fed for around

## Bobo-Dioulasso

**Sights**
1 Grand Marché ... C3
2 Grande Mosquée ... D3

**Sleeping**
3 Entente Hôtel ... D3
4 Les 2 Palmiers ... A3

**Eating**
5 L'Eau Vive ... C4
6 Mandé ... D4
7 Restaurant Dankin ... C4

**Entertainment**
8 Le Bois d'Ébène ... A5

**Shopping**
9 Gafreh ... C4

CFA1500. Its owners also run nearby Restaurant Dankin.

★ **La Canne d'Or** FUSION $$
(☎20 98 15 96; Ave Philippe Zinda Kaboré; mains CFA4000-6000; ⏲11.30am-2.30pm & 6.30-10pm Tue-Sun) This villa-style eatery, with its African decor and riot of fairy lights, serves French fare with an African twist. House faves include frogs' legs and a great grill selection (kebabs, steak, Nile perch etc). Service is stellar.

**L'Eau Vive** FRENCH $$
(Rue Delafosse; mains CFA2500-6000; ⏲noon-2.30pm & 6.30-10pm Mon-Sat; ❄📶) L'Eau Vive offers imaginative French cooking and a varied menu. Try the fresh mango juice – it's absolutely delightful. It's the sister venue of the restaurant of the same name in Ouagadougou, and is also run by nuns.

### Drinking & Entertainment

**Provencale** CLUB
(Ave Phililippe Zinda Kaboré, Koko; ⏲11am-late) Come and shake your stuff to *coupé-décalé* (Ivoirian beats) and other Afro-beats at the funky Provencale. The Sunday matinée is particularly popular.

**Le Bois d'Ébène** LIVE MUSIC
(Ave de l'Unité; ⏲noon-late) One of the best venues in town for live music. Local bands come to play Afrobeat and there's always lots of dancing. Concerts held Thursday to Sunday.

### Shopping

★ **Gafreh** FASHION & ACCESSORIES
(www.gafreh.org; Rue Delafosse; ⏲7am-7pm Mon-Sat) This brilliant initiative, a women's cooperative, recycles the millions of black sachets handed out with purchases across Burkina into chic handbags, wallets and other accessories. Check out their factory outlet in Koko: ask someone at this location to take you there for the full range of their products.

### Information

Most banks are in the centre, and have ATMs.

**Banque Atlantique** (Ave de la République; ⏲8.30am-5.30pm)
**BIB Bank** (Ave Ouédraogo; ⏲9am-2pm)
**Biciab** (Ave Ouédraogo; ⏲9am-2pm)
**Main Post Office** (Ave de la Republique; ⏲9am-4pm)

### Getting There & Away

Bus services, such as those of **Rakieta** (☎20 97 18 91; www.transport-rakieta.com; Ave Ouezzin), **TCV** (Transport Confort Voyageurs; ☎20 97 75 75; www.tcv-sa.com; Rue Crozat) and **TSR** (Transport Sana Rasmane; ☎25 34 25 24; Blvd de la Revolution), leave from each company's depot.

**Banfora** CFA1500, 1½ hours, eight daily, TCV and Rakieta
**Gaoua** CFA5000, 2½ hours, two to three daily, TSR
**Ouagadougou** CFA7000, five hours, seven daily, TCV and Rakieta

### Getting Around

Standard taxi fare for a shared cab ride in town is CFA300.

**Ismael Sawadogo** (☎76 45 85 71) is a delightful and very reliable taxi driver (as well as a professional storyteller!). He can arrange anything from early morning pick-ups for bus services to day trips around Bobo.

## Banfora

POP 76,000

Banfora is a sleepy town in its eponymous region, one of the most beautiful areas in Burkina Faso. It makes an ideal base for exploring the lush surrounding countryside: scaling up the magnificent Dômes de Fabedougou and taking a dip in the Karfiguéla Falls are experiences that are bound to stay with you for years, and a boat ride on Tengréla Lake is the perfect way to spot hippos.

The town itself has a lively **Sunday market**, with plenty of goods from nearby Côte d'Ivoire – heaps of bananas, pineapples and great ceramics and textiles.

WORTH A TRIP

### LA MARE AUX POISSONS SACRÉS & KORO

The sacred fish pond of **Dafra**, around 6km southeast of Bobo, is an important animist site: local people come here to solicit spirits by sacrificing chickens and feeding them to the fish. It is a fairly grisly sight, with chicken bones and feathers everywhere; the 30-minute walk from the nearest parking spot to the pond is truly stunning, however, with arresting rock formations and gorgeous savannah landscapes. A taxi there and back from Bobo-Dioulasso will cost around CFA10,000 (be aware that the track is atrocious).

You can easily follow on from Dafra to the village of Koro (p171) for some beautiful views of the area.

## Sights & Activities

**Dômes de Fabedougou** LANDMARK
(CFA1000) These limestone formations were sculpted into quirky domelike shapes over millennia by water and erosion – an arresting sight. They're found 3km north of the Karfiguéla Waterfalls (off the N2 road to Bobo). Don't miss it.

**Karfiguéla Waterfalls** WATERFALL
(Cascades de Karfiguéla; CFA1000) The Karfiguéla Waterfalls, where you can take a dip in the lovely natural pools on the upper section, are at their best during and just after the rainy season. Unfortunately, the dirt tracks leading to the falls via a magnificent avenue of mango trees can be impassable at these times. But if the track is open (you'll have to ask around), it's worth the journey. The site is some 11km northwest of Banfora.

**Tengréla Lake** WILDLIFE, CANOEING
(CFA2000) Just 7km west of Banfora, Tengréla Lake is home to a variety of birdlife; if you're lucky, you'll even see hippos (especially from January to April). The admission price includes a guided pirogue (traditional canoe) trip.

## Sleeping & Eating

**★Le Calypso** LODGE $
(☎70 74 14 83, 20 91 02 29; famille_houitte@yahoo.fr; Rte de Bobo-Dioulasso; r with fan/air-con CFA9500/16,000; ❄📶) Le Calypso's lovely rooms combine traditional adobe architecture with modern comforts and impeccable cleanliness. The huts are arranged around a beautiful garden. It's about 1km outside of town on the road to Bobo.

**Campement Farafina** HUT $
(☎26 24 46 21; http://farafinaclub.free.fr; Tengréla Lake; huts without bathroom CFA4000) Want to laze a few days at Tengréla Lake? Park your backpack here – it's a five-minute walk from the lake. Facilities are very basic (bucket shower, mud huts without fan) but the owner, Solo, is an adept musician and a fantastic host.

**Hôtel La Canne à Sucre** HOTEL $$
(☎20 91 01 07; www.banfora.com; off Rue de la Poste; d with fan from CFA8500, with air-con CFA15,000-35,000, 4-bed apt CFA49,000; ❄📶🏊) Beautiful rooms are kitted out with African woodcarvings and cloth and the leafy garden feels like heaven after a tiring day. The apartments (located across the road) are ideal for groups and have exclusive use of the pool. The restaurant is the fanciest in town, and perfect for a treat (mains CFA3000 to CFA5000).

**McDonald** BURGERS, AFRICAN $
(off Rue de la Préfecture; mains CFA1500-3000; ⏲11am-10pm Thu-Tue) This cool den off the main drag boasts an inviting covered terrace and a vividly decorated interior. It churns out a good range of satisfying dishes, including its famous *hamburger frites* (burger with fries) and the standard West African staples.

**★Le Calypso** EUROPEAN, AFRICAN $$
(☎20 91 02 29; off Rue de la Poste; mains around CFA3000; ⏲11.30am-11pm; 📶) Run by the same jovial Franco-Burkinabé family as Le Calypso hotel, this popular restaurant is a wonderful place for tasty, slow-cooked fish, marinated steak and pizzas. The homemade juices are highly recommended.

## Information

There are Visa ATMs at **Banque Atlantique** (Rte de la Côte d'Ivoire) and **Ecobank** (Rte de la Côte d'Ivoire).

## Getting There & Away

**Rakieta** (☎20 91 03 81; www.transport-rakieta.com; Rue de la Poste) and **TCV** (Transport Confort Voyageurs; ☎75 79 13 08; www.tcv-sa.com; Rue de la Poste) have regular departures for Bobo-Dioulasso (CFA1500, 1½ hours, eight daily) and Ouaga (CFA8500, 6½ hours, six daily), and one daily service each to Bouaké in Côte d'Ivoire (CFA11,500, 10 hours).

The road to Gaoua is in bad condition and is serviced only by taxi-brousse (bush taxi; CFA5000, four to five hours). Pick them up at the **gare routière** (bus station; Rte de Bobo-Dioulasso). Otherwise go by bus via Bobo.

# Sindou Peaks

**Sindou Peaks** (Pics de Sindou; CFA1000) are one of Burkina's most unforgettable sights. Millions of years ago, these brown, sandy cones were underwater, and they've been shaped by the elements ever since. It's a great place for light hiking and exploring the different formations. A sunrise and a breakfast here promise a magical experience.

## Activities

**Association Djiguiya** HIKING
(☎76 08 46 60; www.djiguiya.org; Sindou) Run by the brilliant Tiémoko Ouattara, this organisation promotes responsible travel and offers a range of services to travellers: anything from half-day walks, moped and cycling tours to cultural activities, homestays and even multi-day treks in Sénoufo country, featuring a sunrise breakfast among the Sindou Peaks.

## Sleeping

**Campement Soutrala** HUT $
(☎76 08 46 60; Sindou; huts without bathroom CFA5000) In Sindou, and run by Association Djiguiya (p175), this friendly *campement* (guesthouse) has basic huts with open-air showers; they also have electricity. Meals must be ordered two hours in advance (mains CFA600 to CFA6000). It's a good base if you'd like to spend time in the area rather than visit on a day trip from Banfora.

## Getting There & Away

There are a few taxis-brousses (bush taxis) plying the asphalted road between Sindou and Banfora every day. Consider chartering a taxi for the day (CFA25,000).

Coming from Banfora, the main gateway is located about 1km before the entrance to the town of Sindou.

# Gaoua & Lobi Country

The small town of Gaoua (population 31,000) is a good base for exploring Lobi country, an area that's culturally distinct from the traditions found in the rest of the country. There's a vibrant **Sunday market**, but the town's unique selling point is its excellent ethnological museum, Musée de Poni.

## Sights

**Musée de Poni** MUSEUM
(www.musee-gaoua.gov.bf; Gaoua; CFA2000; ⌚8am-12.30pm & 3-6pm Tue-Sun) This excellent ethnological museum contains full-scale reproductions of Lobi and Gan compounds, as well as a wide range of photographs and artefacts. The guides really know their stuff, too; Golane Oumar is particularly recommended.

## Sleeping & Eating

**Hôtel Hala** HOTEL $
(☎20 90 01 21; www.hotelhala.com; Gaoua; s/d with fan CFA13,000/15,000, with air-con CFA23,000/27,500; ❄📶) This is, all told, Gaoua's best option; service is glacial and the rooms are nothing to write home about but the compound is very pleasant. It has a handy location between town and the bus station and the wi-fi works. It also has the only decent restaurant in town, serving grilled meat and a few Lebanese specials (mains CFA2000 to CFA5000).

**Maison Madeleine Père** GUESTHOUSE $
(☎20 90 03 41; Gaoua; s/d CFA6000/8000) Run by nuns, this quiet establishment in a monastery southwest of the city centre has impeccable rooms in pretty grounds. The biggest downsides are that it doesn't serve meals and that it's a bit out of the way. To find it, ask in the centre of town; most people will know it.

**Le Flamboyant** AFRICAN $
(Gaoua; mains CFA800-2000; ⌚10am-10pm) One of the town's better *maquis*, right in the centre of town; expect the usual rice or *tô* (millet- or sorghum-based *pâte*) with sauce.

## Information

For internet, head to the women-run **Association Pour la Promotion Féminine de Gaoua** (Gaoua; ⌚7.30am-6pm Mon-Fri) in the centre of Gaoua. Also, Hôtel Hala has wi-fi, which you can use in the bar/restaurant.

There are a couple of ATMs (Visa only) in town.

## Getting There & Around

The *gare routière* is 2km out of town. You'll find bus services to Bobo-Dioulasso (CFA5000, 2½ hours, two to three daily) and Ouagadougou (CFA7000, four hours, five daily).

Direct services to Banfora are by taxi-brousse only (CFA5000, four to five hours); it's best to go to Bobo and find onward connections.

To get around Lobi country, charter a taxi in Gaoua; prices should start around CFA25,000, depending on how far you want to go.

# THE SOUTH

The beauty of southern Burkina is a highlight of any trip to the country; it's also one of Burkina's most accessible corners.

## Réserve de Nazinga

The 97,000-hectare **Réserve de Nazinga** (☎72 66 47 95; CFA10,000, vehicle entry CFA1000, guide fee CFA5000; ⏲6am-6pm), about 40km southwest of Pô near the Ghanaian border, has become a highlight on many a wildlife-lover's itinerary, with antelope, monkeys, warthogs, crocodiles and plenty of birds. Elephants are the stars of the show. The best time to see them is December to April, though your chances are pretty good year-round.

At the heart of Nazinga, **Ranch de Nazinga** (☎72 66 47 95; nazingaranch@yahoo.fr; r CFA10,000, bungalows CFA25,000) has an exceptional location right by the reserve's biggest watering hole. Accommodation is a little lacklustre but the restaurant churns out tasty meals (mains CFA1000 to CFA3000) and the setting is unrivalled – you'll see animals regularly roaming among the bungalows.

You will need your own vehicle to access the reserve and go on wildlife drives. The travel agencies in Ouaga are your best bet.

## Tiébélé & Kassena Country

Set in the heart of the green and low-lying Kassena country, Tiébélé, 40km east of Pô on a dirt track, is famous for its *sukhala* – colourful, windowless traditional houses. Painted by women in geometrical patterns of red, black and white guinea-fowl feathers, the houses offer an antidote to the monochrome mudbrick villages found elsewhere in Burkina Faso.

More than 450 people live in Tiébélé's royal court, the **Cour Royale** (Tiébélé; CFA2000, guide fee CFA3000; ⏲8am-5.30pm), a large compound of typical *sukhalas*, or traditional painted houses. Children live with their grandparents in octagonal huts, couples live in rectangular huts and single people in round ones. Painting is generally done in February/March, after the harvest. Each drawing, whether geometrical or illustrative, has a meaning (fertility, afterlife, wisdom etc).

At nearly 800m, the cone-shape **Nahouri Peak** (CFA1000) is the tallest structure for miles around: the steep climb to its summit guarantees 360 degrees of uninterrupted savannah views. You'll have to hire a guide (CFA500) from Nahouri village, at the foot of the peak. The drive from Tiébélé will take one to 1½ hours (depending on the season), on a rough road.

**Auberge Kunkolo** (☎50 36 97 38, 76 53 44 55; Tiébélé; huts without bathroom CFA5000), a lovely guesthouse with impeccable Kassena-style huts and beautiful garden, is the best place to stay in the area, and one of Burkina's most atmospheric settings. Simple huts with fans and outdoor showers make up the accommodation, but the starlit skies above are magical. It's just 200m from the

### LOBI TRADITIONS

Lobi traditions are some of the best preserved in West Africa. For travellers, the most obvious is the architecture of rural Lobi homes. The mudbrick compounds are rectangular and walls have only small slits for windows, for defensive purposes. In the old days, polygamous men built a bedroom for each of their wives.

The Lobi are also known for their cultural rituals. For example, the *dyoro* initiation rites, which take place every seven years, are still widely observed. As part of this important rite of passage, young men and women are tested on their stamina and skills; they also learn about sexual mores, the clan's history and the dos and don'ts of their culture.

The best way to explore Lobi heritage is to hire a guide in Gaoua (ask at Hôtel Hala). Visits will take in villages such as **Sansana** and **Doudou**, where you can admire different architectural styles and crafts (pottery, basket-weaving, sculpture). Doudou is famed for its artisanal gold-mining, which is the prerogative of women, and its market (held every five days).

chief's compound in Tiébélé. Simple meals (CFA1000) are also served.

### Getting There & Away

There is one direct bus from Ouaga to Tiébélé (and back) on Tuesdays, Fridays and Sundays (CFA3000, 3½ hours).

If you don't have your own vehicle, you can easily rent mopeds in Tiébélé for CFA4000 to CFA6000 per day.

# UNDERSTAND BURKINA FASO

## Burkina Faso Today

In November 2015 former prime minister Roch Marc Christian Kaboré, a French-educated banker who identifies as a social democrat, became president. His platform aimed to reduce youth unemployment and to improve education and health care, with free health care provided for children under six.

But Burkina's relative stability was profoundly shaken in January 2016, when Islamist militants attacked a hotel and cafe in Ouagadougou. Twenty-nine people died, several of them foreigners. This has affected the rate of visitors to the country, leading to closures of businesses dependent on tourism.

Burkina ranks 181st out of 187 countries on the UN's Human Development Index. The economy remains overly reliant on cotton exports, and a recent gold rush – which has seen a huge increase in illegal mining – has increased the country's exposure to market fluctuations. Socially, Burkina's biggest challenges are to improve access to education (the child literacy rate remains under 30%) and address chronic food insecurity.

## History

### The Mossi & the French

Little is known about Burkina Faso's early history, though archaeological finds suggest that the country was populated as far back as the Stone Age. Its modern history starts with the Mossi peoples (now almost half of Burkina Faso's population), who moved westward from settlements near the Niger River in the 13th century; they founded their first kingdom in what is now Ouagadougou. Three more Mossi states were subsequently established in other parts of the country, all paying homage to Ouagadougou, the strongest. The government of each of the Mossi states was highly organised, with ministers, courts and a cavalry known for its devastating attacks against the Muslim empires in Mali.

During the colonial scramble for Africa in the second half of the 19th century, the French exploited rivalries between the different Mossi kingdoms and established their sway over the region. At first the former Mossi states were assimilated into the Colonie du Haut Sénégal-Niger. Then, in 1919, the area was hived off for administrative expedience as a separate colony, Haute Volta (Upper Volta).

### Thomas Sankara

World War II brought about profound changes in France's relationship with its colonies. The Mossi, like numerous other people in Africa, started challenging the colonial hegemony. The Upper Volta became a state in 1947; in 1956, France agreed to give its colonies their own governments, with independence quickly following in 1960.

Following independence, dreams of freedom and prosperity quickly evaporated. Between 1960 and 1983, the country experienced six coups and counter-coups and the economy stagnated. Then in 1983, Captain Thomas Sankara, an ambitious young left-wing military star, seized power.

Over the next four years 'Thom Sank' (as he was popularly known) recast the country. He changed its name to Burkina Faso (meaning 'Land of the Incorruptible'), restructured the economy to promote self-reliance in rural areas and tackled corruption with rare zeal. He was ahead of his time, promoting women's rights and standing up against Western paradigms on aid and development. But his authoritarian grip on power and intolerance towards those who didn't share his ideals were to be his downfall: in late 1987 a group of junior officers seized power and Sankara was killed.

### The Compaoré Years

The new junta was headed by Captain Blaise Compaoré, Sankara's former friend and co-revolutionary. In late 1991 Compaoré was elected president. But as the sole candidate – with low voter turnout and the assassination of Clément Ouédraogo, the leading opposition figure, a couple of weeks later – his legitimacy remained weak.

In a bid to mark a clear break with Sankara, Compaoré immediately orchestrated a U-turn on the economy, overturning nationalisation and bringing the country back to the IMF fold. He was reelected three times, in 1998, 2005 and 2010, each time with more than 80% of the vote. In July 2013, thousands of demonstrators took to the streets over plans to create a senate; they continued to demonstrate into the following year in opposition to possible plans by President Compaoré to extend his rule. The revolt culminated with a mass uprising in October 2014, driving Compaoré out of office and leading to the establishment of a provisional government.

## People of Burkina Faso

Burkina Faso, which occupies an area about half the size of France, is extremely diverse, with its 18.5 million people scattered among some 60 ethnic groups. The largest of these is the Mossi, who are primarily concentrated in the central plateau area.

Important groups in the south include the Bobo, Senoufo, Lobi and Gourounsi. In the Sahel areas of the north are the Hausa, Fula, Bella and Tuareg.

## Religion

An old local joke says that 50% of Burkinabés are Muslim, 50% are Christian – and 100% are animist. In reality, the actual percentages for Islam and Christianity are about 60% and 23%, respectively, but most people do retain traditional beliefs.

The remaining are animists, who have not been converted or adopted Christianity or Islam. This traditional religion attributes a living soul to plants, inanimate objects and natural phenomena, and involves ritual sacrifice of animals (such as chickens or cattle) to ancestors.

## The Arts

Burkina Faso has a vibrant contemporary arts and crafts scene: painting, sculpture, woodcarving, bronze and brass metalwork and textiles are all represented. Artistic works are exhibited in Ouagadougou's galleries, cultural centres and collective workshops.

The Burkinabés live and breathe music: it's the mainstay of traditional celebrations, with djembe (drum), balafon (a kind of xylophone) and flute the main instruments. Modern musicians draw on traditional influences from home and the rest of the continent, especially Mali, Congo and Côte d'Ivoire, as well as Jamaican reggae, jazz, rock and rap.

Burkina Faso also has a thriving film industry that receives considerable stimulation from the biennial Fespaco film festival (p165). Two Burkinabé filmmakers who have won prizes and developed international reputations are Idrissa Ouédraogo, who won the 1990 Grand Prix at Cannes for *Tilä*, and Gaston Kaboré, whose film *Buud Yam* was the 1997 winner of the Étalon d'Or.

## Food & Drink

Burkinabé food is largely influenced by Senegalese and Ivoirian cuisines. Sauces, especially *arachide* (peanut) or *graine* (a hot sauce made with palm nuts), are the mainstay and are always served with a starch, usually rice (called *riz sauce* or *riz gras*) or the Burkinabé staple, *tô*, a millet- or sorghum-based *pâte* (a pounded, dough-like substance). The Ivoirian *attiéké* (grated cassava), *aloco* (plantain fried with chilli in palm oil) and *kedjenou* (simmered chicken or fish with vegetables) are also commonly found.

Grilled dishes of chicken, mutton, beef, guinea fowl, fish (especially Nile perch, known locally as *capitaine*) and agouti (a large rodent) also feature on the menu. In the Sahel, couscous is widely available.

Castel, Flag, Brakina, Beaufort and So.b.bra are popular and palatable brands of beer; more adventurous – and potent – is *dolo* (millet beer). Locally produced juices include *bissap* (hibiscus), *gingembre* (ginger), tamarind and mango; soft drinks are available everywhere, too.

Lafi is the most reliable brand of bottled water. Avoid the water sold in small plastic bags, since it's often tap water.

## Environment

Landlocked Burkina Faso's terrain ranges from the harsh desert and semidesert of the north to the woodland and savannah of the green southwest. Around Banfora, rainfall is heavier and forests thrive alongside irrigated sugar-cane and rice fields; it's here that most of Burkina Faso's meagre 13% of arable land is found. The country's dominant feature, however, is the vast central laterite plateau of the Sahel, where hardy trees and bushes thrive.

Burkina's former name, Haute Volta (Upper Volta), referred to its three major rivers – the Black, White and Red Voltas, known today as the Mouhoun, Nakambé and Nazinon Rivers. All flow into the world's second-largest artificial lake, Lake Volta, in Ghana.

# SURVIVAL GUIDE

## Directory A–Z

### ACCOMMODATION

Ouagadougou, Bobo-Dioulasso and Banfora have a good range of accommodation, including charming B&Bs. In more remote areas, *campements* (basic mud huts with bucket showers and no electricity) are usually the only option but can be very atmospheric.

### DANGERS & ANNOYANCES

Burkina Faso is one of the safest countries in West Africa. Crime isn't unknown, particularly around big markets and *gares routières* (transport stations), but it's usually confined to petty theft and pickpocketing. Wear a money belt and don't flash cash or valuables in public. Solo women might get some hassle, but a simple *bonne journée* ('have a good day') should suffice in warding off unwanted attention.

### EMBASSIES & CONSULATES

The following embassies are based in Ouagadougou:

**Canadian Embassy** (☎25 31 18 94; www.canadainternational.gc.ca/burkinafaso; 316 Ave du Professeur Joseph Ki Zerbo; ⏰8.30am-noon Mon-Fri & 2-4pm Mon-Thu) Also offers diplomatic help to Australian citizens.

**French Embassy** (☎25 49 66 66; www.ambafrance-bf.org; Ave du Trésor; ⏰8-11.30am Mon, Wed & Thu)

**German Embassy** (☎25 30 67 31; www.ouagadougou.diplo.de; Rue Joseph Badoua; ⏰9-11am Mon-Fri)

**Ghanaian Embassy** (☎25 30 76 35; embagna@fasonet.bf; Ave d'Oubritenga; ⏰8am-2pm)

**Ivoirian Embassy** (☎25 31 82 28; cnr Ave Maurice Yameogo & Ave du Burkina Faso)

**US Embassy** (☎25 49 53 00; http://ouagadougou.usembassy.gov; Rue 15.873, Secteur 15, Ouagadougou; ⏰7.30am-5pm Mon-Thu, to 12.30pm Fri)

British citizens should contact the **British High Commission** (☎030-2213250; www.ukinghana.fco.gov.uk; Julius Nyerere Link, off Gamel Abdul Nasser Ave; ⏰9.30-11.30am Mon-Thu, 8.30-10.30am Fri) in Accra, Ghana.

### SLEEPING PRICE RANGES

The following price ranges refer to a double room with bathroom during high season. Breakfast is not included in the price unless noted.

**$** less than CFA30,000

**$$** CFA30,000–90,000

**$$$** more than CFA90,000

### EMERGENCY & IMPORTANT NUMBERS

| | |
|---|---|
| Ambulance | ☎112 |
| Burkina Faso's country code | ☎226 |
| Fire | ☎18 |
| International access code | ☎00 |
| Police | ☎17 |

### INTERNET ACCESS

Wi-fi is available in most midrange and top-end hotels and restaurants in towns and cities. Internet cafes are plentiful there, too – the post office is usually a good bet – but nonexistent in more remote areas.

### LGBTIQ TRAVELLERS

Homosexuality is not illegal in Burkina Faso, but any sexual behaviour that goes against 'good morals' is punishable by law. Local attitudes are highly conservative and utmost discretion is advisable. Public displays of affection between same-sex (and even opposite-sex) couples should be avoided. There are no openly gay or lesbian bars or clubs in Burkina.

### MONEY

**ATMs** There are numerous Visa ATMs in every city; the only bank to accept MasterCard is Banque Atlantique (in Ouaga, Bobo and Banfora only).

### PRACTICALITIES

**Electricity** The power supply is 220V. Plugs are of the European two-round-pin variety.

**Newspapers & magazines** International versions of French- and (a few) English-language publications are available in Ouagadougou and Bobo-Dioulasso.

**Radio** BBC World Service is on 99.2FM in Ouagadougou. For a French-language service, tune in to RFI on 94.0FM.

**Weights & measures** The metric system is used.

### EATING PRICE RANGES

The following price ranges refer to the cost of a main dish.

**$** less than CFA3000

**$$** CFA3000–6000

**$$$** more than CFA6000

**Cash** Burkina Faso uses the West African franc (CFA). The bank notes come in 500, 1000, 2000, 5000 and 10,000; coins are split into 1, 5, 10, 25, 50, 100, 200, 250 and 500 francs.

**Changing money** The best foreign currency to carry is euros, which are easily exchanged at any bank, hotel or bureau de change.

**Credit cards** Payments by credit card are rarely accepted and are subject to a 5% surcharge.

**Tipping** There are no strict rules about tipping in Burkina Faso. Tipping in a *maquis* (rustic restaurant), or if you've bargained a taxi fare, is not done. More upmarket restaurants are accustomed to receiving tips, though it remains very much at your discretion.

### Exchange Rates

| | | |
|---|---|---|
| Australia | A$1 | CFA452 |
| Canada | C$1 | CFA440 |
| Europe | €1 | CFA656 |
| Japan | ¥100 | CFA538 |
| NZ | NZ$1 | CFA415 |
| UK | UK£1 | CFA774 |
| US | US$1 | CFA600 |

For current exchange rates, see www.xe.com.

### OPENING HOURS

**Banks** Typically open 9am to 2pm, Monday to Friday.

**Bars & clubs** Normally open from late morning until the last customers leave (late); nightclubs generally open from 9pm into the wee hours.

**Restaurants** Lunch is served from 11.30am to 2.30pm, dinner 6.30pm to 10.30pm.

**Shops & businesses** Usually 8am to noon and 3pm to 6pm, Monday to Friday, as well as 9am to 1pm on Saturday.

### POST

Sonapost is Burkina's national postal service. The main **post office** (Ave de la Liberte; ⏲7.30am-noon & 3.30-5pm Mon-Fri, 8am-noon Sat) branch in Ouagadougou is on Avenue de la Liberté.

### PUBLIC HOLIDAYS

Burkina Faso also celebrates Islamic holidays, including **Eid al-Fitr** and **Eid al-Adha**, the dates of which change each year.

**New Year's Day** 1 January

**Revolution Day** 3 January

**Women's Day** 8 March

**Easter Monday** March/April

**Labour Day** 1 May

**Ascension Day** 40 days after Easter

**National Day** 5 August

**Assumption** 15 August

**All Saints' Day** 1 November

**Republic Day** 11 December

**Christmas Day** 25 December

### TELEPHONE

- Landline phone numbers here start with 2, while mobile numbers begin with 7.
- Telephone cards for international calls are expensive; using a VoIP service (such as Skype) is a better bet.

### TOURIST INFORMATION

**Couleurs d'Afrique** (p170) In the Ouagadougou neighbourhood of Gounghin.

**L'Agence Tourisme** (p170) In Hôtel les Palmiers, Ouagadougou.

## Getting There & Away

### AIR

Tiny **Aéroport International de Ouagadougou** (p170) is Burkina's main gateway.

The main international carriers are **Air France** (www.airfrance.com) and **Royal Air Maroc** (www.royalairmaroc.com), which offer direct flights to France and Morocco and connecting flights to the rest of the world.

**Air Burkina** (www.air-burkina.com), the national carrier, flies to Paris (France) as well as regional destinations including Accra (Ghana), Abidjan (Côte d'Ivoire), Bamako (Mali), Cotonou (Benin), Dakar (Senegal) and Lomé (Togo).

### LAND

#### Benin

TSR (p173) has a twice-weekly bus service from Ouagadougou to Cotonou (CFA21,000, 24 hours), while TCV has a weekly departure (on Sunday).

The alternative is to take a bus to Fada N'Gourma (CFA4500, five hours), where taxis-brousses and minibuses wait for customers – sometimes all day, as transport to the border (CFA4000) is scarce and fills up slowly.

#### Côte d'Ivoire

**Sitarail** (☎25 31 07 39) passenger-train services between Burkina Faso and Côte d'Ivoire

## INTERNATIONAL BUSES

| DESTINATION | FARE (CFA) | DURATION (HR) | FREQUENCY | COMPANY | DEPARTS |
|---|---|---|---|---|---|
| Abidjan (Côte d'Ivoire) | 27,000 | 36 | daily | TCV, Rakieta | Ouagadougou |
| Bamako (Mali) | 17,000 | 17 | daily | TCV | Bobo |
| Bouaké (Côte d'Ivoire) | 17,000 | 20 | daily | TCV, Rakieta | Bobo |
| Cotonou (Benin) | 21,000 | 24 | twice weekly | TCV, TSR | Ouagadougou |
| Kumasi (Ghana) | 10,000 | 11 | daily | TCV | Ouagadougou |
| Lagos (Nigeria) | 38,000 | 36 | weekly | TCV | Ouagadougou |
| Lomé (Togo) | 18,000 | 24 | twice weekly | TCV, TSR | Ouagadougou |
| Niamey (Niger) | 11,000 | 8-10 | daily | TCV | Ouagadougou |

(three weekly) have resumed, but it's a long, tiring journey to Abidjan (at least 36 hours, possibly more). Get an update while in Bobo before setting off.

TCV has a daily bus service to Bouaké from Bobo-Dioulasso (CFA17,000, 20 hours) and Abidjan (CFA27,000, 36 hours). You can also take one of Rakieta's two daily buses from Banfora (CFA900, one hour) to Niangoloko, from where onward transport may be possible.

### Ghana

TCV has a daily service from Ouagadougou to Kumasi (CFA10,000, 11 hours).

The other frequently used border crossing is at Hamale (Ghana), near Ouessa in the southwest of Burkina Faso. Coming from Ghana, you may have to stay at Hamale's cheap hotel and catch a bus to Bobo-Dioulasso the next morning. From Bobo-Dioulasso, Rakieta has two buses per day (at 8am and 2.30pm) to Hamale (CFA4500) that pass through Banfora en route.

### Mali

Almost every bus company in Bobo-Dioulasso offers a daily service to Bamako (CFA17,000, 17 hours).

### Niger

TCV operates a daily bus service between Ouagadougou and Niamey, via Fada N'Gourma (CFA11,000, eight to 10 hours).

### Togo

TSR has twice-weekly bus services from Ouagadougou to Lomé (CFA18,000, 24 hours), while TCV has weekly departures.

## Getting Around

### AIR

**Air Burkina** (www.air-burkina.com) has two flights per week between Ouagadougou and Bobo-Dioulasso (CFA55,000).

### BUS

Buses are the most reliable and comfortable way to get around the country. They almost always operate with guaranteed seating and fixed departure times; arrive early or book the day before to ensure you have a seat on your preferred service.

TCV (p170) and Rakieta (p170) buses are better maintained and more reliable than those of other companies; they also have air-con.

### TAXIS-BROUSSES

Taxis-brousses (bush taxis) are generally beaten-up old vehicles that cover routes to outlying communities that large buses don't serve. Most leave from the *gares routières* (bus stations); morning is the best time to find them. There are more-or-less fixed prices, starting from CFA1000, that local people share. You can bargain if you're hiring one alone.

### CAR & MOTORCYCLE

Travel agencies in Ouagadougou can organise 4WD rental (with a driver) for about CFA60,000 per day.

In rural areas, mopeds are ideal on unsealed roads and readily available for CFA5000 per day (not including fuel).

### TRAIN

There are Sitarail trains between Ouaga and Bobo, but they can take up to 10 hours and are highly unreliable.

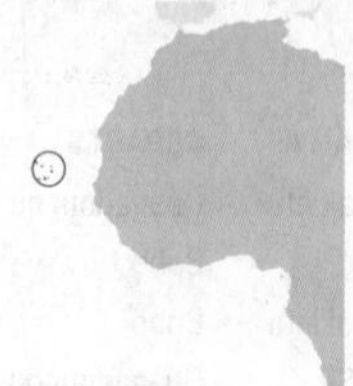

# Cabo Verde

238 / POP 553,000

**Includes ➡**



## Best Places to Eat

- Casa Cafe Mindelo (p188)
- Maracujá (p184)
- Pipi's (p190)

## Best Places to Sleep

- Jardim do Vinho (p184)
- Kira's (p187)
- Casa Colonial (p187)

## Why Go?

Jutting up from the Atlantic, some 500km west of Senegal, this stunning island chain has a captivating blend of mountains, beaches and peaceful seaside villages. On Santo Antão, craggy peaks hide piercing green valleys of flowers and sugar cane, ideal for epic hikes. São Vicente is home to the cultural capital of the islands, Mindelo, which throbs with bars and music clubs. On Sal and Maio, undulating windswept dunes merge with indigo-blue seas on unspoilt beaches of powdery white sand. Meanwhile far-flung Fogo and Brava in the southwest offer their own enchantments, from surreal volcanic landscapes to sparkling bays framed by towering peaks. Throw in the constant beat of music that Cabo Verde is famed for and the renowned *morabeza* (Creole for hospitality) of its people and you'll see why many have come – and never left.

## When to Go

### Santiago

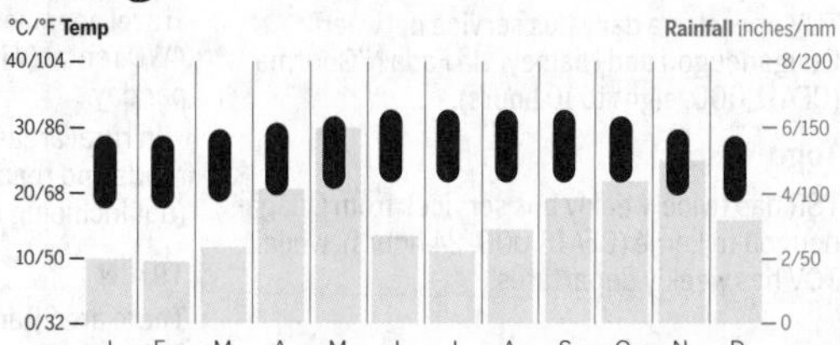


**Aug–Oct** So-called rainy season; very hot, and weeks can go by without a downpour.

**Dec–Apr** Best time for surfing. Whale watching February to May.

**Jun–Oct** Turtle-watching season.

# SANTIAGO

POP 266,000

Santiago, the largest island of the archipelago and the first to be settled, has a little bit of all the other islands. It has the sandy beaches, the desert plains, the verdant valleys and the mountainous interior as well as the capital, Praia. All this makes it a worthy stop on your Cabo Verdean rambles.

## Getting There & Away

### AIR

Praia's airport is, together with Sal's, the main air hub for the islands. **TACV** (Rua Serpa Pinto; 8am-5pm Mon-Fri) has daily flights to Boa Vista, Fogo (São Filipe), Sal and São Vicente (Mindelo), three flights weekly to Maio and four weekly (via Sal or São Vicente) to São Nicolau. **TAP** (2615826; www.flytap.com; Praia International Airport) has one to two flights daily connecting Lisbon with Praia.

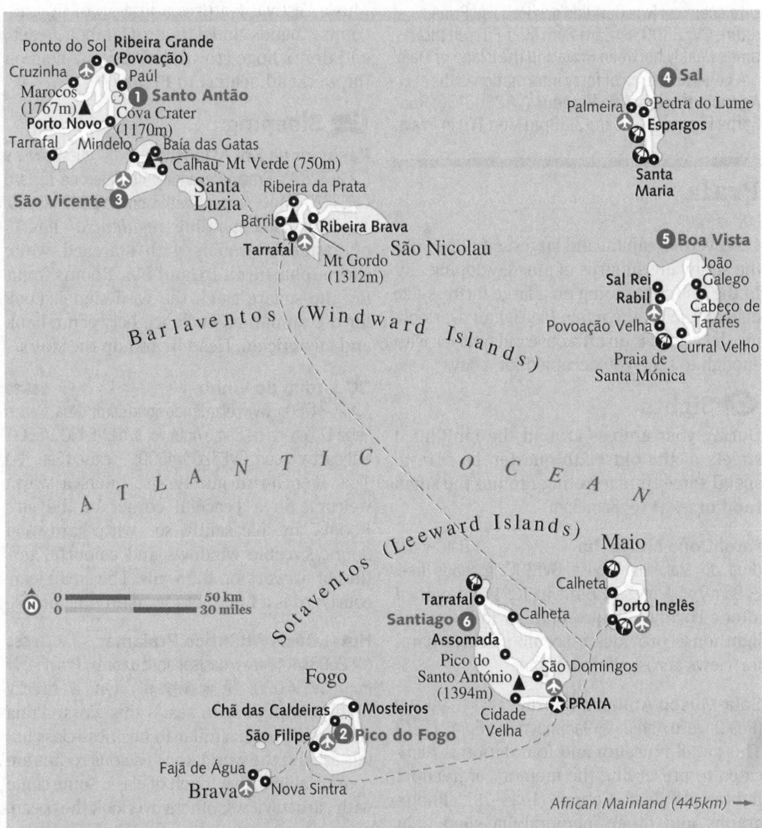


## Cabo Verde Highlights

1 **Santo Antão** (p189) Hiking the misty pine-clad ridges, the canyons and the valleys of Cabo Verde's most spectacular island.

2 **Pico do Fogo** (p190) Admiring the views from the summit of a stunning, active volcano.

3 **São Vicente** (p186) Following the sounds of *morna* and *coladeira* around music-loving seaside towns.

4 **Sal** (p191) Riding the giant waves in one of the finest destinations in the archipelago for windsurfing.

5 **Boa Vista** (p191) Relaxing on the beach and feasting on seafood at this wondrously laid-back island.

6 **Santiago** (p183) Exploring the colonial ruins of the Cidade Velha followed by seaside drinks and dancing in nearby Praia.

BOAT

**Fast Ferry** (☎2617552; www.cvfastferry.com; Av Andrade Corvo 35; ⊙8am-6pm Mon-Fri, 8.30am-12.30pm Sat) departs Praia several times per week for Fogo (3½ hours, CVE3350) and on to Brava (40 minutes, CVE3750). Fast Ferry also goes to São Vicente via São Nicolau, but these run irregularly (only twice a month), and the boats can often be delayed by many hours (or even days). Purchase tickets from the office in the Platô (city centre) or from the port.

Ferries operated by **Polar** (☎2615223; polarp@cvtelecom.cv; Rua Candido dos Reis 6A, Praia; return CVE3800; ⊙8am-2pm Mon-Fri) run three times weekly between Praia and the island of Maio.

A general source of ferry information is the **Agencia Nacional de Viagens** (☎2603100; Rua Serpa Pinto 58; ⊙8am-3.30pm Mon-Fri) in Praia.



# Praia

POP 134,000

Cabo Verde's capital and largest city, Praia has the sprawling suburbs of any developing city. In the centre, standing on a large fortress-like plateau (hence the name Platô) and overlooking the ocean, is an attractive old quarter with enough to keep you occupied for a day.

## Sights

During your ambles around the multihued streets of the old Platô quarter, be sure to spend some time ferreting around the small **food market** (⊙8am-5pm).

**Farol Dona Maria Pia** LIGHTHOUSE

(Rua do Mar; lighthouse CVE100, grounds free; ⊙9am-7pm Mon-Sat) Built in 1881 and named after a Portuguese queen, this wind-battered lighthouse provides a scenic vantage point for views across the coastline.

**Sala-Museu Amilcar Cabral** MUSEUM

(Rua Dr Julio Abreu; ⊙9am-noon & 3-6pm) FREE This small museum and foundation is dedicated to preserving the memory of freedom fighter Amilcar Cabral (1924–73). Photographs and other memorabilia shed light on one of West Africa's great visionaries. An intellectual, poet, engineer, revolutionary and diplomat, Cabral helped lead an independence movement for Cabo Verde and Guinea-Bissau – he was assassinated in 1973.

## Tours

**CaboNed** HIKING

(☎9210488; www.caboned.com; excursions from CVE3200) Great day-trip options on Santiago, including hikes, photo safaris and explorations of the interior. Book by email or phone.

## Festivals & Events

**Atlantic Music Expo** MUSIC

(www.atlanticmusicexpo.com; ⊙Apr) Over four days in April, this big music bash always offers a good time, with a line-up of performers from Cabo Verde, Africa, Europe and beyond. There's also a good street market. It happens just before the big Kriol Jazz Festival.

**Gamboa Music Festival** MUSIC

(www.festivalgamboa.com; ⊙May) The Gamboa Music Festival features a line-up of up-and-coming bands and DJs on Gamboa Beach, and draws huge crowds. It's usually held on the weekend nearest to 19 May.

## Sleeping

**Residencial Sol Atlántico** GUESTHOUSE $

(☎2612872; Praça Alexandre Albuquérque 13; s/d CVE3220/4440, without bathroom CVE2520/3740; ❄) This long-standing *residencial* has 15 old-fashioned rooms with starched white sheets, blue furniture and TVs. Rooms fronting the square catch the wi-fi signal. Look for the unmarked entrance between a bank and an optician. Head in and up the stairs.

★ **Jardim do Vinho** B&B $$

(☎2624760; www.ojardimdovinho.com; Rua Carlos Veiga 17, Achada de Santo António; s/d CVE4300/5600, without bathroom CVE3200/4500; ⊙closed Sep; 📶) This French-run guesthouse offers a warm welcome in a peaceful corner of the city. Rooms are pleasantly set with hardwood floors, sizeable windows and colourful textiles or artwork on the walls. The small leafy courtyard is a fine spot for an evening drink.

**Hotel Oásis Atlântico Praiamar** HOTEL $$$

(☎2608440; www.oasisatlantico.com; Prainha; r from CVE14,000; P❄@📶🏊) On a breezy bluff pointing out to sea is this glossy Praia address. Though similar to business-class hotels around the world, the spacious rooms are comfortable with a touch of class. Some come with garden views; others overlook the ocean.

## Eating & Drinking

**Mirage** CAFE $

(Av Jorge Barbosa, Quebra-Canela; mains around CVE500; ⊙9.30am-1.30am; 📶) For dining and drinking with a view, Mirage serves up pizza, sandwiches, salads and cocktails from the open-air terrace at Praia Shopping.

★ **Maracujá** FUSION $$

(☎9138854; Rua 19 de Maio, Chã d'Areia; mains CVE550-950; ⊙10am-11pm Tue-Sun) Inés, who spent 40 years in France, brings a touch

# Praia

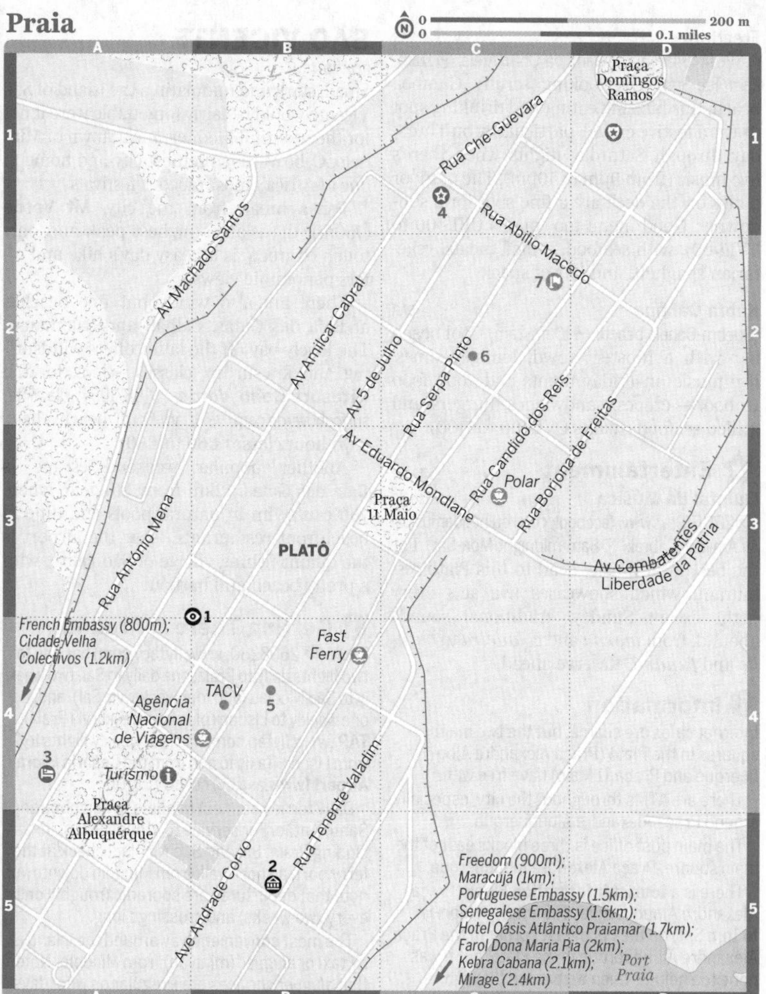


of Europe to her cooking in this cheery cafe across the road from Gamboa beach. Market-fresh ingredients play a starring role in zesty salads, grilled octopus, seafood spaghetti, and crepes with seasonal vegetables. Great daily lunch specials (around CVE450).

**Churrasqueira Dragoeiro** BARBECUE **$$**
(☎2624767; Rua da UCCLA, Achada de Santo António; mains CVE600-1200; ⏲noon-5pm & 6.30pm-1am) Follow the scent of barbecue pluming overhead at this famous, open-sided grill-house. It's a very casual spot that draws a mix of locals and tourists, who chatter away over drinks and sizzling plates of char-grilled chicken, tuna or pork skewers.

## Praia

**Sights**
1 Mercado de Sucupira ........ B3
2 Sala-Museu Amilcar Cabral ........ B5

**Sleeping**
3 Residencial Sol Atlántico ........ A4

**Entertainment**
4 Quintal da Música ........ C1

**Information**
5 Direcção de Emigração e Fronteiras ........ B4
6 Girassol Tours ........ C2
7 US Embassy ........ C2

**Freedom** BAR
(☎2614454; Praia de Gamboa, Chã d'Areia; ⏲11am-2am Tue-Sun) Overlooking scruffy Gamboa beach, this buzzing eating and drinking spot draws a festive crowd, particularly on Thursday through Saturday nights when there's live music (from 9pm or 10pm). The outdoor tables on the deck are a fine spot for a sundowner. Good menu too (mains CVE400 to CVE900), with seafood, grilled meats, vegetarian spaghetti and lots of snacks.

**Kebra Cabana** BAR
(Quebra-Canela beach; ⏲10am-2am) Cool beach bar with a hipster crowd, loungey tunes, live music on Friday nights and good food to boot – crêpes, sandwiches, burgers and grilled seafood (mains CVE400 to 1100).

## ☆ Entertainment

**Quintal da Música** LIVE MUSIC
(☎2611679; www.facebook.com/quintaldamusica; Av Amilcar Cabral; ⏲8am-midnight Mon-Sat) For the best local music, head to this Platô restaurant, which showcases live acts every night except Sunday. Traditional sounds abound, from *morna* and *coladeira* to *batuko* and *funaná*. Reserve ahead.

## ℹ Information

Internet cafes are scarce, but the two main squares in the Platô (Praça Alexandre Albuquérque and Praça 11 Maio) have free wi-fi.

There are ATMs throughout the city, especially around Praça Alexandre Albuquérque.

The main post office is three blocks east of the main square, Praça Alexandre Albuquerque.

There is a **tourist information kiosk** (Praça Alexandre Albuquerque; ⏲9am-6pm Mon-Fri, to 1pm Sat) on the northeast corner of the Praça Alexandre Albuquerque in the Platô, but it was none too helpful when we passed through.

Travel agency **Girassol Tours** (☎2614178; www.girassol.cv; Rua Serpo Pinto 46; ⏲8am-6pm Mon-Fri, to noon Sat) sells plane tickets and offers tours of Santiago and car rental.

## ℹ Getting There & Around

A taxi from the airport to Platô (5km) costs around CVE1000. There's no regular bus service.

Small Transcor buses connect Platô with all sections of the city; short journeys cost from CVE50. Destinations are marked on the windshields.

Cream-coloured taxis are plentiful and inexpensive – you can go from Platô to Achada de Santo António, for example, for about CVE200. Note that fares go up after 8pm. You can rent a taxi for the day for an island tour for around CVE9000.

It is best to move around Praia by taxi at night, no matter what the distance, as crime has been on the rise, especially in Achada de Santo António.

# SÃO VICENTE

POP 79,400

Small, stark and undulating, the island of São Vicente would be fairly forgettable were it not for the beautiful Mediterranean town of Mindelo, Cabo Verde's prettiest city and home to one of Africa's most raucous festivals.

For a break from the city, **Mt Verde** (750m), the island's highest peak and only touch of green, is an easy day's hike and offers panoramic views.

There are also windy but fine beaches at Baía das Gatas, Calhau and Salamansa. The lovely bay off the latter offers windsurfing and kitesurfing classes – look for the **Kitesurf Cabo Verde** (☎9871954; ola@kitesurfcaboverde.com; ⏲10am-6pm) beach shack (two-hour classes €60 to €80).

Another popular weekend escape is Baía das Gatas, 12km from Mindelo, where you can swim in natural pools and dine in beachfront restaurants. Near the airport is the quaint fishing village of São Pedro, with a pretty beach and harbour.

## ℹ Getting There & Around

**TACV** (☎2608260; www.flytacv.com) has one to two flights daily to Praia, one daily to Sal, two weekly to São Nicolau (and four weekly via Sal), and one weekly to Lisbon (plus four weekly via Praia). **TAP** (www.flytap.com) has four weekly flights to/from Lisbon. Taxis to and from the **Cesária Évora Airport** (www.asa.cv) cost CVE1000.

Daily ferries connect Mindelo to neighbouring Santo Antão. For service to other islands, including Praia, Sal and São Nicolau, check at the ferry port, a short walk from Mindelo downtown; note that departures are sporadic (roughly once every two weeks) and crossings long.

The most convenient way around the island is by taxi or *aluguer* (minivan) from Mindelo. Note that *aluguer* services are irregular on weekdays and can involve long waits.

## Mindelo

POP 72,000

Set around a moon-shaped port and ringed by mountains, Mindelo is Cabo Verde's answer to the Riviera, complete with cobblestone streets, candy-coloured colonial buildings and yachts bobbing in the harbour. Around a bend is the country's deepest industrial port, which in the late 19th century was a key coaling station for British ships and remains the source of the city's relative prosperity.

Mindelo has long been the country's cultural centre, producing more than its share of poets and musicians. It's a fine place to hear *morna* while downing *grogue* (a rum-like drink).

DON'T MISS

## CREOLE CARNIVAL

There's nothing like Mindelo's Mardi Gras (February or March) anywhere else in Africa. Taking the best African beats and mixing it up with a healthy dose of Latin style and Brazilian sex appeal, the result is a sultry, raunchy party you'll never forget. Preparations begin several months in advance, and on Sunday you can see the various groups practising for the procession. The saucy costumes, however, are worn only on Mardi Gras Tuesday. The weekend just prior to this sees a number of lesser processions and street parties, while on the Monday afternoon the whole city goes crazy as a huge street party takes place and people dress up in 'lesser costumes'. The Tuesday itself is a much more organised affair and after the procession has wound around the city a couple of times everyone seems to magically disappear.

If you want to be a part of it, plan accordingly, as all flights and accommodation are booked up way in advance. If you can't make it to Mindelo then head to São Nicolau, which puts on a fabulous, nontouristy affair. Fogo (p189) puts on a pretty good show as well.

## Sights

Mindelo's colonial heart is centred on Rua da Libertad d'Africa, also known as Rua de Lisboa, which runs from the oceanfront to **Palácio do Povo** (Av Baltazar Lopes da Silva; CVE200; 9am-1pm & 3-6pm Tue-Sat) and an exhibition dedicated to Cesária Évora.

Heading about 1km north via the coastal road, Avenida Marginal, you'll reach **Prainha Laginha**, the pleasant town beach. It may be ringed by industrial-looking silos, but its waters are clean and crystal clear.

**Museu do Mar** MUSEUM
(Av Marginal; CVE100; 9am-6pm Mon-Fri, 9.30am-12.30pm Sat) Inside the Torre de Belém, Mindelo's most intriguing museum gives an overview of São Vicente's history, from the island's role in the triangular trade to whaling in the late 19th century. Displays from shipwrecks reveal intriguing finds like 200-year-old bottles of port wine and massive elephant tusks (a jaw-dropping 820 tusks were logged on the 1743 wreck of the *Princess Louisa*).

**Fish Market** MARKET
(Av Marginal; 7am-3pm) The city's photogenic fish market lies just beyond Torre de Belém, with a jetty right behind it where fishermen unload their daily catch.

## Activities

**Dive Tribe** DIVING
(9829498; www.dive-tribe.com; Av Marginal; 1 dive with equipment €55, open-water course €420) This professionally run outfit offers a wide range of diving packages around São Vicente. There are over 50 dive sites in the area, including wreck-diving opportunities. It offers instruction for beginners as well. It's located below Dokas restaurant just south of the port.

**Sabura Adventures** ADVENTURE SPORTS
(9775681; www.sabura-adventures.com; Av Marginal) Based out of Nautilus (p188), this outfit offers surf lessons (two hours €48) and gear hire. It also offers horse riding (€35 per hour) and snorkelling trips (€30 per person).

## Sleeping

**Simabo** HOSTEL $
(2312465; www.simabo.org; Av Rendall Leite 13; r per person CVE1500) A top choice for animal lovers, Simabo is a budget-friendly guesthouse and rescue shelter for abandoned dogs and cats. Lodging is clean but simple, with shared (cold-water) facilities for its four rooms. Opportunities for volunteers too.

★**Kira's** BOUTIQUE HOTEL $$
(2300274; www.kirashotel.com; Rua de Argélia 24; s CVE7400-9600, d CVE9100-11,300) In a pretty yellow building near Praça Amilcar Cabral, Kira's earns rave reviews for its well-equipped, handsome rooms, and kind-hearted multilingual staff. Each of the guestrooms is named after an island – forest-green Santo Antão evokes its lush peaks, while powder-blue Maio calls to mind its gently lapping seas.

★**Casa Colonial** GUESTHOUSE $$
(9995350; www.casacolonial.info; Rua 24 de Setembro; s/d CVE7200/8300) A boutique British-owned guesthouse on a quiet street, Casa Colonial sits inside a beautifully restored colonial building. Rooms are spacious with tall ceilings, dark wood floors and period details. Perks include a small patio with a plunge pool where breakfast is served, and free wi-fi.

**Prassa** BOUTIQUE HOTEL $$$
(2300809; www.prassa3hotel.com; Praça Amilcar Cabral 3; s/d from CVE8700/9900) Prassa has attractively set rooms with eye-catching

wallpaper, suede furniture, shag carpets and an ultra-modern vibe. It has a good restaurant and tapas bar on the ground floor.

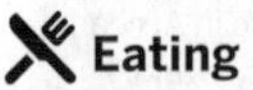

## Eating

**La Pergola** CAFETERIA $$

(Rua Santo António, Alliance Française; mains CVE550-700; 8am-7pm Mon-Fri, 8am-2pm Sat; ) This cosy cafe, under a straw roof inside the courtyard of the Alliance Française, has delicious salads, pasta and mixed seafood plates, plus tempting cakes and pastries. It's also a fine anytime spot for coffee or a glass of Fogo wine.

**Nautilus** INTERNATIONAL $$

(Av Marginal; mains CVE650-1650; 9am-2am; ) Near the waterfront, Nautilus has an open-air courtyard with a sizzling grill where you can get tasty plates of char-grilled tuna, grouper, octopus, chicken and filet mignon, along with *cachupa, arroz de marisco* (seafood rice) and other hits. The daily lunch special is a deal at CVE490. There's live music Friday through Sunday nights.

★**Casa Cafe Mindelo** BISTRO $$$

(2313735; www.casacafemindelo.com; Rua Governador Calheiros 6; mains CVE1300-2500, lunch specials CVE400-500; 7am-11pm) Near the waterfront, this buzzing place serves up some of the best cooking in town amid chunky wooden tables and industrial light fixtures, with traditional artwork adorning the walls. The chalkboard menu lists changing specials like pasta with lobster, mussels in white wine, and Portuguese-style seafood stew, and there's live music nightly (from 8pm).

## Drinking & Nightlife

**ZeroPointArt** WINE BAR

(2312525; www.zeropointart.org; Rua Unidade Africana 62; 10am-12.30pm & 6pm-midnight Mon, Wed & Thu, 8pm-2am Fri & Sat, 8pm-midnight Sun) Gallery space downstairs and a chilled wine bar upstairs, with lots of contemporary artwork, dark ambient lighting and cool music. A good place for a low-key night out, over wine and tapas-style snacks. It has live music and other events (like film screenings) from time to time. Stop in to see what's on.

**Jazzy Bird** BAR

(Av Baltazar Lopes da Silva; 6pm-1am Mon-Sat) Known to locals as Vou, after the friendly owner, this cool little basement bar plastered with old jazz posters attracts an older crowd. Big-name local musicians play jazz late on Friday nights.

## ☆ Entertainment

**Casa da Morna** LIVE MUSIC

(Av Marginal; 8.30-11pm Fri & Sat) On the waterfront, this breezy top-floor restaurant draws a good mix of talent to its live concerts on Friday and Saturday nights. It has a tropical vibe and the usual array of seafood dishes (mains CVE850 to CVE1100).

## Information

There's free wi-fi on Praça Amilcar Cabral, although the signal is finicky.

### MEDICAL SERVICES

**Hospital Baptista de Sousa** (2311879; Rua Domingos Ramos)

### MONEY

The city centre has several banks with ATMs. There's also a handy ATM at the port.

**Banco Comercial do Atlântico** (Rua da Libertad d'Africa)

**Caixa Económica** (Av 5 de Julho)

### POLICE

**Police Station** (Av Marginal) Near the fish market.

### POST

**Post Office** (Rua Cristiano Barcelos; 9am-4pm Mon-Fri) Near the main plaza.

### TOURIST INFORMATION

**Tourist Info** (9110016; www.cabocontact.com; 8.30am-12.30pm & 2.30-6.30pm Mon-Fri, 9am-1pm Sat) This kiosk near the harbour offers info on attractions and books activities and tours. São Vicente maps available for CVE220.

### TRAVEL AGENCIES

**Barracuda Tours** (2325591; www.barracudatours.com; Av Baltazar Lopes da Silva 54; 8am-12.30pm & 2.30-6pm Mon-Fri, 9am-1pm Sat) A full-service travel agency that can book flights, car rentals, accommodation and tours.

## Getting There & Around

Mindelo has flight connections to the islands of Santiago and Sal, and a daily ferry to Santo Antão. **TACV** (www.flytacv.com; Av 5 de Julho) has an office in the town centre.

The most convenient way around the island is by taxi from Mindelo, including trips to Monte Verde (CVE1000), Calhau (CVE1200), Baía das Gatas (CVE1000) and Salamansa (CVE1000).

Official taxis are generally safe and easy to find in Mindelo. In the city centre, expect to pay CVE150 to CVE170 for a ride. After 8pm, the fare goes up to CVE200. *Alugueres* (minivans) to Baia das Gatas (CVE100), Salamansa (CVE100) and Calhau (CVE150) leave from Praça Estrela in the morning (around 10am) and afternoon (around 4pm) when full. Note that service is irregular on weekdays and can involve long waits.

## SANTO ANTÃO

POP 47,500

For many people the main reason for visiting Cabo Verde is the spectacular island of Santo Antão. This dizzyingly vertical isle, ruptured by canyons, gorges and valleys, offers some of the most amazing hiking in West Africa.

### Hiking Santo Antão

Dramatic canyons, cloud-soaked peaks and vertigo-inspiring drops all help to make Santo Antão a hiker's paradise. Walks here cover all ranges of abilities, from gentle hour-long valley hikes to strenuous ascents only for the fittest. If you're intending to do some serious hiking, get hold of the Goldstadt Wanderkarte hiking map. You may also consider hiring a local guide; prices depend on the hike and whether the guide speaks English, but rates are about CVE4000.

Many of the hikes begin or end on the trans-island road. From here you can hitch a ride on a passing *aluguer* (minibus), or arrange for a taxi to wait for you ahead of time.

The classic hike is from the Cova crater (1170m), with its fascinating patchwork of farms, down to the stunning Valé do Paúl. The steep downhill route, which can get dangerously slippery, passes through lush mountainside, verdant stands of bananas and fields of sugarcane, down to the country road leading to the coastal town of Vila das Pombas.

An easier hike is along the coastal track from Ponta do Sol to Fontainhas. This hour-long walk takes you along a narrow path carved out of the cliff face, which in places is really high and steep. At the end, the village of Fontainhas clings like a spider to a little ridge high above its fertile valley and a small, rocky cove. From Fontainhas, you can continue the marvellous clifftop walk all the way to Cruzinha (another four hours).

### Getting There & Around

Currently, two ferry companies offer daily services between Mindelo and Porto Novo in Santo Antão. The *Mar d'Canal* leaves Mindelo at 8am, returning at 10am. It leaves Mindelo again at 3pm (except on Sunday, when there's only the morning departure), returning at 5pm. The *Inter-Ilhas* has a similar schedule, leaving an hour earlier (departing Mindelo at 7am and 2pm, returning at 9am and 4pm). The trip on either boat costs CVE800 and lasts just under one hour. Buy tickets 30 minutes before departure (or the day before) at the ferry-dock offices on both islands.

If you want to see a lot of the island in a single day, your best bet is to hire your own *aluguer*, though expect to pay around CVE9000 for a full day around the east side of the island. Alternatively, you can join locals on an *aluguer* headed towards Ribeira Grande and Ponta do Sol (CVE500, 45 minutes). Note that *alugueres* use the new faster coastal road; if you want to travel along the scenic mountain road, be prepared to negotiate with the driver and dish out extra.

## FOGO

POP 38,000

Whether you're being tossed and turned in the heavy seas during the boat ride from Praia or thrown about by unpredictable winds and turbulence in the small prop plane, the drama of Fogo begins long before you set foot on this island's volcanic soils. The island of Fire (Fogo translates as fire) consists of a single, giant black volcano, at 2829m Cabo Verde's highest peak, which dominates every view. It burst back to life with a large eruption in late 2014.

**TACV** (☎2608260; www.flytacv.com) has one to two daily flights to/from Praia, which last 30 minutes. A taxi from the airport into São Filipe (2km) costs CVE300. Boats arrive at the port 3km from town (taxis charge CVE400). The port looks like a giant construction site.

## São Filipe

POP 23,000

Set commandingly atop the cliffs like the nest of a seabird, São Filipe is a town of grace, charm, immaculate Portuguese houses, and plazas full of flowers and sleepy benches. Below, at the base of the cliffs, lies a beach of jet-black sand and evil, dumping waves; beyond, tantalising on the horizon, squats the island of Brava. All this makes São Filipe one of the most compelling and charming towns in Cabo Verde. Note that strong currents make the town beach unsafe for swimming, especially in winter.

### Sights

**Casa da Memoria** MUSEUM
(☎2812765; www.casadamemoria.com.cv; Praça da Igreja; donations accepted; ⊙10am-noon Wed-Fri or by apartment) FREE Set in an 1820s house, this delightful little cultural space illustrates what life was like in Fogo over the past two centuries, via a collection of ceramics, photographs, decorative objects and household items.

**Dja'r Fogo** GALLERY
(☎9919713; djarfogo-agnelo@hotmail.com; ⊙9am-12.30pm & 3-6pm Mon-Fri, 9am-12.30pm Sat) A must-stop for those interested in history, culture and coffee, Dja'r Fogo serves as art gallery,

cafe, information point and launch pad for informal trips around the island. It's also the best place to taste artisanal Fogo coffee; the owner's family has had a coffee plantation since 1874, and six generations later he still roasts and packages it into neat cotton bags.

## Sleeping

**Pousada Belavista** GUESTHOUSE $
(2811734; www.bela-vista.net; s/d from CVE2800/3800; ) An understated, impeccably run hotel built around an old colonial home and a new adjacent building. Rooms, some with ocean views, are well furnished if a little stuffy, and breakfasts are hearty. Balcony rooms are brightest, though a little noisy.

**Colonial Guest House** GUESTHOUSE $$
(9914566; Rua do Câmara Municipal; s/d from CVE6100/9100; ) This gorgeously renovated colonial mansion houses the town's nicest place to stay. Rooms have antique furniture and wooden floors; some have terraces with ocean views. On the downside, some rooms lack bathrooms (though every room has its own private bathroom in the corridor).

**Tortuga B&B** GUESTHOUSE $$
(9941512; www.tortuga-fogo.eu; s/d CVE4500/6100) This heavenly little beach hideaway is a 10-minute drive or a 30-minute walk along the beach from town. The live-in owners take good care of their guests, who stay in one of four stylish rooms with an earthy look or the straw bungalow in the garden. Think hammocks between palm trees, the sound of crashing waves, a beach at your doorstep…

## Eating

**Maria Augusta Bakery** BAKERY $
(Praça Igreja; snacks from CVE20; 7am-7pm Mon-Sat, to noon Sun) The friendly Maria Augusta churns out delicious bread and pastries from the giant wood-burning oven inside what looks like a garage. Look for an orange building on the edge of the sea near the church. Stock up on *pudim de queijo* (sweet goat-cheese tarts), coconut biscuits and marmalade-filled doughnuts.

★**Pipi's** INTERNATIONAL $$
(2814156; Rua do Câmara Municipal; 11am-3pm & 6-11pm Mon-Sat, 6-11pm Sun) Overlooking a small plaza, Pipi's fires up some of the best cooking in Fogo. Senegalese-style *maffé* (a peanut sauce) with grilled tuna or chicken is first-rate, along with fish stew and spaghetti with shrimp. There's also lighter fare like crêpes, sandwiches and pumpkin ice cream.

**Calerom** CABO VERDEAN $$
(2813267; mains CVE800-1400; noon-11pm Mon-Fri, to late Sat) Calerom's courtyard makes a laid-back setting for grilled meat and seafood dishes. It draws locals on game days as well as on Saturday nights, when there's live music from 10.30pm onward.

**Tortuga** SEAFOOD $$
(9941512; www.tortuga-fogo.eu; 3-course dinner CVE1800, lunch mains CVE700-1000; noon-2pm & 7.30-10pm) For a special meal, make dinner reservations at Tortuga B&B, where Italian owner Roberto cooks up innovative seafood dishes based on his father's old recipes, prepared using local ingredients and homemade products; wash it all down with the top-quality aged *grogue* from Brava.

## Information

The main plaza has free wi-fi, although with a spotty signal. There are several banks with ATMs around the centre.

Well-run **Qualitur** (2811089; www.qualitur.cv; Praça 4 de Setembro; 8am-1pm & 2-5pm Mon-Fri, 8am-noon Sat) offers island tours and trekking excursions, books plane and ferry tickets and can arrange hire cars. Its most popular outing is a full-day excursion to Chã das Caldeiras, visiting the settlement still rebuilding after the 2014 eruption.

Based out of Colonial Guest House, **Zebra Travel** (9194566; www.zebratravel.net; Rua do Câmara Municipal; 8am-5pm Mon-Fri, 9am-noon Sat) offers guided volcano climbs and day trips to the crater.

# Chã das Caldeiras

The conical 2829m-high **Pico do Fogo** volcano, shrouded in black cinder, rises dramatically out of the floor of an ancient crater known as Chã das Caldeiras ('Chã'). Bound by a half-circle of precipitous cliffs, Chã was born when, sometime in the last 100,000 years, some 300 cubic km of the island collapsed and slid into the sea to the east. The main cone has been inactive for more than 200 years, though there have been regular eruptions in Chã. The latest, in 2014–15, devastated the villages of Portela and Bangaeira. Today a new settlement is rising atop the ashes of half-buried houses, but no one refers to it by either of the old village names. Instead, most people call the new village simply (and somewhat confusingly since it's also the name of the surrounding area) Chã das Caldeiras.

A few kilometres outside the village (en route to São Filipe), stop into state-of-the-art **Chã Vinho do Fogo** (2821533; agrocoopcha@gmail.com) winery. It's a recent rebuild of the original, which was destroyed by the eruption of 2014–15 and vines are actually grown in the volcanic ash of the crater.

Locals provide dozens of guestrooms for visitors in Chã. Keep in mind that power is available only by generator a few hours a night, many places lack hot water and there's no wi-fi. Prices are fairly standard: CVE3500 to CVE4000 for a double (CVE2500 for a single) including breakfast. Recommended options include **Casa Alcindo & Laetitia** (☎9921409; alcindo6@gmail.com; s/d CVE2500/3500) and **Casa Lavra Cicilio** (☎9882127; casadelavrafogo@hotmail.com; s/d/tr CVE2500/3500/4200).

If you're staying overnight, don't miss the nightly live-music performance (around 6pm) at **Casa Ramiro** (noon-11pm), a grocery store where you can try local goat cheese and homemade manecon wine.

### Getting There & Away

*Colectivos* run from São Filipe (near the market) to Chã das Caldeiras; these depart in the afternoon and return the following morning around 6am (confirm return times wherever you lodge for the night). Fare for the two-hour ride is CVE1000.

You can also get here on a tour offered by Qualitur (p190) and Zebra Travel (p190). These don't allow much time to wander around Chã, however.

## SAL

POP 26,000

Though flat, desolate and overdeveloped, Sal boasts more tourists than any other island. They fall into three categories: the package-holiday crowd, hard-core windsurfers and those in transit to more interesting islands. If you don't mind the heavy tourist crowds, Sal has a fine restaurant scene, plenty of nightlife and some lovely beaches where you can unwind and enjoy some water sports.

The largest town is Espargos, right next to the international airport, but most people stay near the pretty beach in Santa Maria, 18km to the south.

The great attraction in Sal is the surreal, lunarlike **Pedra do Lume** (CVE550; 9am-5.45pm), an ancient volcano, where seawater is transformed into shimmering salt beds. You can see the old salt extraction machinery of the 1805 plant; float in the medicinal salt water; have a massage, salt scrub or mud treatment at the small Salinas Relax spa; and have a meal at the restaurant.

Other points of interest include the fish market in **Palmeira**, the gorgeous **Igrejinha beach** at the eastern end of Santa Maria and the **Buracona** natural swimming pool (time your visit for noon to see the Blue Eye, a natural light effect in a small underground pool).

The airport has an ATM, a bureau de change, free (but rarely working) wi-fi and a tourist info booth.

### Getting There & Around

**TACV** (☎2411305; www.flytacv.com) has several flights daily to/from Praia, five weekly to São Vicente, five weekly to Boa Vista and three weekly to São Nicolau.

There are currently no regular inter-island ferries at Sal. The port is at Palmeira, about 4km northwest of Espargos.

Minibuses ply the road between Santa Maria and Espargos (CVE100, 25 minutes); all stop on the main road just in front of the airport. Taxis from the airport to Santa Maria charge CVE1000 during the day and CVE1200 at night.

## BOA VISTA

POP 12,000

With its feathery lines of peachy dunes, stark plains and scanty oases, the island of Boa Vista looks as if a chunk of the Sahara somehow broke off the side of Africa and floated out to the middle of the Atlantic. Though the island offers some fantastic if wind-blown beaches, incredible windsurfing, the pretty little town of Sal Rei and an ever-increasing number of resorts and hotels, it's this desert interior that is the best reason for venturing out here. Be ready for some rough off-roading, as most of Boa Vista's roads are treacherous.

### Sights & Activities

A short stroll south of the Sal Rei town centre, the turquoise waters and and white sands of **Praia de Estoril** make a fine setting for a day out. A handful of beach bars serve up seafood, snacks and plenty of drinks, with tables and lounge chairs on the sand. Several places here hire out gear – stand-up paddleboards, surfboards, kayaks – and give lessons in surfing, kitesurfing, windsurfing and sailing.

The **Centro de Artes e Cultura** (☎2519690; Sal Rei; 9am-5pm Mon-Fri) is a new arts centre that hosts a wide range of events, from art and photography exhibitions to concerts and African craft shows. The centre is a 10-minute walk northeast (inland) from Sal Rei's main plaza.

In addition to Praia de Estoril and the arts centre, there's the long and beautiful **Praia de Santa Mónica** on the island's southern coast and the beaches of **Curralinho** and **Varandinha**. It's worth whizzing through the village of **Povoaçao Velha**, the **Viana Desert** – great on a full-moon night; Migrante Guesthouse offers tours – and the oasis town of **Rabil**.

While you can't take in all these sights in one day, two days is more than enough to see the entire island. Several agencies offer excursions, including **Sabura Center** (☎2511933; saburacenter@ymail.com; Sal Rei; half-/full-day tour per person from €25/37), but **Naturalia** (☎2511558; www.naturaliaecotours.com; Largo Santa Isabel) is the best and most environmentally sensitive.

Turtle-watching tours in season (July to October) cost €50 per person with Naturalia and typically depart around 7.30pm, returning around 1am. Naturalia also offers whale-watching trips (€65 per person for a half day) between February and May and arranges snorkelling trips to Baía das Gatas, where you swim among rich coral and nurse sharks.



## Sleeping

**La Boaventura** HOSTEL $
(☎9509167; www.laboaventura.com; Av dos Pescadores, Sal Rei; dm €10, r €25-55; ) La Boaventura has simply furnished dorms and guestrooms – all with private bathrooms and some with sea views – set around a vine-fringed courtyard. The real draw, though, is the low-lit cafe/lounge, where you can meet other travellers or use wi-fi over drinks. This hostel is popular: book well ahead.

★ **Migrante Guesthouse** GUESTHOUSE $$
(☎2511143; www.migrante-guesthouse.com; Av Amilcar Cabral, Sal Rei; s/d from CVE7700/9900; ) The gorgeous Migrante has four rooms set around a colourful courtyard with a giant palm tree. Each room has dark-wood floors, big soft beds and black-and-white portraits hanging on the white walls, which give an arty feel. The downstairs cafe is lovely too. Rates include airport transfers.

**Spinguera Eco Lodge** LODGE $$$
(☎2511941; www.spinguera.com; s/d CVE17,000/26,000; P) Boa Vista's most magical hideaway is an abandoned fishing village converted into a stunning ecolodge by the artist owner. Inside whitewashed cottages, stylish and minimalist rooms showcase reclaimed wood and clay floors, and ocean views. The restaurant serves delectable food and there's a walkway down to your own little beach. A stay here is a splurge but a worthy one. It's about 18km northeast of Sal Rei.

## Eating

★ **Beramar** FUSION $$
(☎9746514; Av dos Pescadores, Sal Rei; small/large plates CVE600/1100; noon-2pm & 7-10pm Mon-Fri, 7-10pm Sun, closed May-Sep) With a talented Milanese chef at the helm, Beramar showcases high-quality local ingredients with creative accents in its dishes, which are ideal for sharing. Think crunchy risotto with goat cheese, pork ribs with lentil and apple, wahoo curry and char-grilled vegetables. It's near the waterfront, south of Sal Rei's plaza.

**Blue Marlin** SEAFOOD $$
(mains CVE800-1300; noon-3pm & 7-10pm) On Sal Rei's main square, this tiny restaurant with chequered tablecloths and graffiti-covered walls serves some of the island's best seafood. Start off with an appetiser of smoked fish or grilled goat cheese, then opt for grilled tuna or seafood pasta. Good Portuguese wines by the glass. Book in advance.

★ **Fado Crioula** FUSION $$$
(☎9314703; www.facebook.com/FadoCrioula8; Sal Rei; mains around CVE1400; 9am-10pm Mon-Thu, to 11pm Sun; ) This creative, art-filled space serves up market-fresh fare that changes daily: expect delightful salads, creative appetisers and a fresh-grilled fish of the day. Fado Crioula hosts jam sessions, film screenings, art exhibitions, language exchanges and other events. It's set on a breezy perch, with views over the coastline.

## Drinking & Nightlife

**Caffè del Porto** CAFE
(Sal Rei; noon-10pm) Near the Sal Rei waterfront, a few blocks from the plaza, this place with outdoor tables makes a fine spot for a sundowner. You can also order food (seafood, pizza, kebabs), watch televised football matches and catch live music from time to time.

**Wakan Bar** CAFE
(Sal Rei; 1-11pm Mon-Sat) Adorable little blue-and-white shack with a boat shape, right by the fishing boats on Praia de Diante. Expect no less than 70 cocktail varieties, nice snacks, good Italian coffee and a good happy hour.

## Information

The plaza has free wi-fi. There are several banks with ATMs around the plaza.

## Getting There & Around

**TACV** (☎2412401; www.flytacv.com) has six weekly flights to Praia (one hour) and five weekly to Sal (15 minutes). Irregular ferries sail to/from Boa Vista, Praia and Sal, but they are so sporadic you may lose many days waiting for one.

*Alugueres* (from CVE200) ply the island's roads, but they're scarce. Taxis are readily available; the short hop from the airport to Sal Rei costs CVE700.

Bikes and scooters are available from **Let's Go** (☎29773000; Av 4 de Julho, Sal Rei; ⏰10am-12.30pm & 4-6pm Mon-Sat), on the main road before reaching the plaza.

# UNDERSTAND CABO VERDE

## Cabo Verde Today

Cabo Verde is one of West Africa's most stable nations, both politically and economically. In many areas it tops the charts in comparison to other parts of Africa – and the developing world. It has a high literacy rate of 88% (and over 97% among school-age children), an active and relatively free press, a declining poverty rate and one of the highest living standards in West Africa. In fact, a little over a decade ago it became one of the few countries to 'graduate' out of its ranking among the world's 50 least developed nations according to the UN. This in spite of a lack of natural resources – and even adequate water supplies. Today tourism, which accounts for over 25% of GDP, is helping to fuel the growth. Though the global financial crisis of 2008–9 had an impact, GDP growth has been on the rise in the last few years, and is expected to reach 4% in 2017 – a healthy figure, though still below the boom years.

In 2016 Cabo Verde re-elected its popular president, Jorge Carlos Fonseca, to a second term. Despite the nation's solid economic performance, big challenges remain: taming the public debt (over 115% of GDP), lowering the unemployment rate (over 12%) and grappling with crumbling infrastructure spread over nine inhabited islands.

## History

### Slavery, Drought & Neglect

When Portuguese mariners discovered the archipelago in 1456, the islands that would become known as Cabo Verde were uninhabited but fertile enough to attract the first group of settlers six years later. They founded Ribeira Grande (now Cidade Velha), the first European town in the tropics, on the island of Santiago. To work the land, settlers almost immediately began to import slaves from the West African coast. The islands' remote yet strategic position made them a perfect clearing house and victualling station for the transatlantic slave trade.

Cabo Verde's first recorded drought occurred in 1747; from that date droughts became ever more common and, in the century from 1773, three droughts killed some 100,000 people. This cycle lasted well into the 20th century. At the same time, the island's economic clout fell as Britain, France and the Netherlands challenged Portugal's control over the slave trade. As a result, Lisbon invested little in Cabo Verde. To escape hunger, many men left the islands, principally to work as hired hands on American whaling ships. Even today, Cabo Verdean communities along the New England coast in the US rival the population of Cabo Verde itself.

### Independence from Portugal

Africans in Cabo Verde's mostly mixed-race population tended to fare better than in other Portuguese colonies. Beginning in the mid-19th century, a privileged few received an education, many going on to help administer mainland colonies. By independence 25% of the population could read (compared with 5% in Guinea-Bissau).

In 1956 Cabo Verdean intellectual Amilcar Cabral (born in Guinea-Bissau) founded the Marxist-inspired Partido Africano da Independência da Guiné e Cabo Verde (PAIGC), later renamed the Partido Africano da Independência de Cabo Verde (PAICV).

As other European powers were relinquishing their colonies, Portugal's right-wing dictator, António de Oliveira Salazar, propped up his regime with dreams of colonial greatness. From the early 1960s, one of Africa's longest wars of independence ensued. However, most of the fighting took place in Guinea-Bissau rather than Cabo Verde, and indeed many middle-class Cabo Verdeans remained lukewarm about independence.

Eventually Portugal's war became an international scandal and led to a nonviolent end to its dictatorship in 1974, with Cabo Verde gaining full independence a year later.

### Cabo Verde Since Independence

On gaining power, the PAICV created a one-party state but also instituted a remarkably successful health and education program. Drought and food-aid dependence remained a serious issue in a country that produces only about 20% of its food supply.

By the late 1980s there were increasing calls for a multiparty democracy, and in 1990 the PAICV acquiesced, allowing lawyer Carlos Veiga to found the Movimento para a Democracia (MpD). With a centre-right policy of political

**PRICE RANGES**

The following price ranges refer to a double room with bathroom:

**$** less than CVE4500

**$$** CVE4500-9000

**$$$** more than CVE9000

The following price ranges refer to a main course:

**$** less than CVE700

**$$** CVE700-1200

**$$$** more than CVE1200

and economic liberalisation, the MpD swept to power in the 1991 elections. Privatisation and foreign investment brought only slow results, and in 2001 the PAICV reclaimed power and Pedro Pires became president.

## Culture

Cabo Verde boasts by far the highest GDP per capita (US$3900) in West Africa. The country's literacy rate of 88% is also the highest in the region. Virtually all children of primary-school age attend school, though attendance at secondary schools is considerably lower. Opportunities for pursuing higher education have improved markedly in the past decade. The islands have some 10 postsecondary educational institutes, with several key universities in Praia and Mindelo.

## Food

While Cabo Verdean cuisine may include Portuguese niceties such as imported olives and Alentejo wines, it's built on a firm African base, with *milho* (corn) and *feijão* (beans) the ubiquitous staples. Thanks to the large number of Italian tourists and expats, good pizza and pasta dishes are available in even the most out-of-the-way places.

## People

Based on the UN's *Africa Human Development Report 2012,* Cabo Verde comes out on top in West Africa. From 1975 to 2016, life expectancy leapt from 46 years to 73 years, far higher than the sub-Saharan African average. The country also has one of the lowest population-growth rates in the region. It's the only country in West Africa with a population of primarily mixed European and African descent. About 40% of the population lives on Santiago – mainly around the capital, Praia. The rest live largely in small towns clustered in the agriculturally productive valleys.

## Religion

The vast majority of Cabo Verdeans are Roman Catholic. Evangelical Protestantism is making inroads thanks to the influence of Cabo Verdean expats returning from the US. Traces of African animism remain in the beliefs of even devout Christians.

## Music

Much of Cabo Verdean music evolved as a form of protest against slavery and other types of oppression. Today, two kinds of song dominate traditional Cabo Verdean music: *mornas* and *coladeiras,* both built on the sounds of stringed instruments like the fiddle and guitar. As the name suggests, *mornas* (melodic, melancholic music) are mournful songs of *sodade* – an unquenchable longing, often for home. With faster, more upbeat rhythms, *coladeiras,* in contrast, tend to be romantic love songs or else more active expressions of protest. Another popular style is *funaná,* built on fast-paced, Latin-influenced rhythms and underpinned by the accordion. The most African of music and dance styles is *batuko,* with lots of drumming and call-and-response chanting.

## Environment

Cabo Verde consists of 10 major islands (nine of them inhabited) and five islets, all of volcanic origin. All are arid or semiarid, but the mountainous islands of Brava, Santiago, Fogo, Santo Antão and São Nicolau – all with peaks over 1000m – catch enough moisture to support grasslands as well as fairly intensive agriculture. Still, only 20% of the total land mass is arable. Maio, Boa Vista and Sal are flatter and almost entirely arid, with long, sandy beaches and desert-like interiors.

Cabo Verde has less fauna than just about anywhere in Africa. Birdlife is a little richer (around 75 species), and includes a good number of endemics (38 species). The frigate bird and the extremely rare razo lark are much sought after by twitchers.

Humpback whales breed in these waters; the peak is March and April. Five endangered species of turtle visit the islands on their way across the Atlantic. Cabo Verde also has the world's third-largest loggerhead turtle nesting population. Nesting takes place from June to October.

# SURVIVAL GUIDE

## Directory A–Z

### ACCOMMODATION

By West African standards, accommodation is expensive in Cabo Verde, especially on Sal and Boa Vista, and in Praia, where prices are around 30% higher than in the rest of the country.

There are no campsites in Cabo Verde, but camping on remote beaches, and on Santa Luzia, is possible and generally safe (except on Sal, Boa Vista and Santiago).

### CHILDREN

Travel in Cabo Verde can be a great experience for kids. There are gorgeous beaches for fun days in the sun, eerie volcanic landscapes and great walks (including short rambles) amid lush valleys and towering peaks.

### DANGERS & ANNOYANCES

Violent crime is a threat in Praia, where it's highly advisable to take taxis at night, no matter where and how far you're going. Take caution in Mindelo, too, where pickpocketing and muggings are not uncommon.

Some hiking trails have become sites of banditry in recent years, as on Boa Vista and around Tarrafal on Santiago; always ask locals before you set out.

The rest of Cabo Verde is very safe, though petty crime like pickpocketing is always a possibility.

### ELECTRICITY

Cabo Verde uses 220V and plugs are European-style twin-pronged.

### EMBASSIES & CONSULATES

**French Embassy** (☎2604535; www.ambafrance-cv.org; Quartier de Prainha, Praia; ⏰8am-5.30pm Mon-Thu, to 1pm Fri)
**Portuguese Consulate** (☎2323130; Av 5 de Julho; ⏰8.30-11.30am Mon-Fri)
**Portuguese Embassy** (☎2626097; www.praia.embaixadaportugal.mne.pt; Av da OUA, Achada de Santo António; ⏰9am-1pm & 3-6pm Mon-Fri)
**Senegalese Embassy** (☎2615621; www.gouv.sn; Rua Dr Manuel Duarte)
**US Embassy** (☎2608900; http://praia.usembassy.gov; Rua Abilio Macedo 6; ⏰8am-5pm Mon-Fri)

### EMERGENCY NUMBERS

For **fire**, **medical** and **police** services, call ☎112.

### INTERNET ACCESS

Internet cafes are a rare breed in a country with a growing number of smartphone users, but the main town squares on all major islands in Cabo Verde have free wi-fi. Note that some hotels, even the upmarket ones, charge for wi-fi.

### LGBTIQ TRAVELLERS

Cabo Verde has less of the homophobia and open discrimination encountered in other parts of West Africa. Homosexual acts were decriminalised in 2004, and although the LGBTIQ community is largely underground, the islands are fairly tolerant. The most gay-friendly destinations in the archipelago are Santa Maria (Sal) and Mindelo (São Vicente). Mindelo even hosts an annual Gay Pride parade (late June), which first kicked off in 2013.

### MONEY

- The unit of currency is the Cabo Verde escudo (CVE), divided into 100 centavos. It is a stable currency, pegged to the euro. Most businesses also accept euros.
- Most banks change travellers cheques and cash (except the West African CFA), and have ATMs.
- Most ATMs accept bank cards and Visa, but the daily withdrawal limit is CVE20,000.
- It's common to tip at restaurants, typically around 5% to 10% of the bill.
- Credit cards are not widely accepted (Visa preferable). If accepted, there's typically a 3% to 5% commission for credit-card payments.

**EXCHANGE RATES**

| | | |
|---|---|---|
| Australia | A$1 | CVE76 |
| Canada | C$1 | CVE74 |
| Eurozone | €1 | CVE110 |
| Japan | ¥100 | CVE91 |
| New Zealand | NZ$1 | CVE70 |
| UK | UK£1 | CVE131 |
| USA | US$ | CVE104 |

### OPENING HOURS

Note that for hours posted on shop windows, days are often numbered according to the Portuguese system from 1º to 7º (1º is Sunday, 7º is Saturday).

**Banks** From 8am to 3pm Monday to Friday.
**Businesses** Generally 8am to noon and 3pm to 6pm Monday to Friday, and 8am to noon or 1pm Saturday.
**Restaurants** Mostly open from around noon to 3pm and 7pm to 10pm.

### POST

The postal service is cheap, reliable and reasonably quick. Correios (post offices) are generally open 8am to 3pm Monday to Friday, with additional Saturday morning hours in Praia and Mindelo.

### PUBLIC HOLIDAYS

**New Year's Day** 1 January
**National Heroes' Day** 20 January
**Labour Day** 1 May
**Independence Day** 5 July

**Assumption Day** 15 August
**All Saints' Day** 1 November
**Immaculate Conception** 8 December
**Christmas Day** 25 December

### TELEPHONE

Every number for a fixed telephone line in Cabo Verde has seven digits; all landlines start with '2'.

➡ Don't expect to rely on public telephones. Most are gone or don't work.

➡ Mobile-phone reception is excellent, and numbers are seven digits long.

➡ If bringing a phone from home with roaming facilities, it will connect automatically.

➡ Local SIM cards (from CVE100) are available at all mobile phone offices and will work with unlocked phones.

### TOURIST INFORMATION

Do your planning in advance of your trip to Cabo Verde. On the islands, tourist information is limited. Mindelo (São Vicente), Santa Maria (Sal) and Tarrafal (Santiago) all have helpful info kiosks. Elsewhere the best source of information is often the guesthouse where you stay. You can get an overview of the islands at the country's tourism website, www.turismo.cv.

### VISAS

The one-month tourist visa for Cabo Verde is available on arrival at the airports and at the ports of Praia and Sal. The €25 fee is payable in euros only – it helps to bring the exact money.

Technically, there's a fine of CVE15,000 if you let your Cabo Verdean visa expire; in reality, if you're only a little over nobody is likely to care.

For an extension you need, in theory, to fill in a form, supply a photo and lodge the application at the **Direcção de Emigração e Fronteiras** (☎2611845; Rua Serpa Pinto, Praia; ⏰9am-4pm Mon-Fri); in reality, staff members here are likely to be highly confused if you turn up requesting an extension!

### VOLUNTEERING

It's helpful to have some Portuguese or, better yet, Crioulo (Creole) skills before approaching volunteer organisations. SOS Tartarugas (www.sostartarugas.org) accepts volunteers for conservation programs on Sal, Boa Vista and Maio.

## ℹ Getting There & Away

Most international flights land on Sal or Santiago, though there are also international flights arriving in Boa Vista and São Vicente.

### AIR

International flights arrive at the following airports:

**Aeroporto Internacional Amílcar Cabral, Sal** (www.asa.cv/aeroportos/aeroporto-internacional-amilcar-cabral)
**Aeroporto Internacional da Praia Nelson Mandela, Santiago** (www.asa.cv/aeroportos/aeroporto-da-praia)
**Aeroporto Internacional da Boa Vista Aristides Pereira, Boa Vista** (www.asa.cv/aeroportos/aeroporto-da-boavista)
**Aeroporto Internacional Césaria Évora, São Vicente** (www.asa.cv/aeroportos/aeroporto-internacional-cesaria-evora)

TACV (https://flytacv.com) is the national carrier of Cabo Verde and connects the islands with Lisbon (Portugal), Dakar (Senegal), Bissau (Guinea-Bissau), Providence (USA), Amsterdam, Fortaleza (Brazil) and Paris (France). TACV also offers inter-island flights.

Other airlines include TAP (p183) and the various charter airlines that fly to Sal and Boa Vista from the UK, Germany and Italy.

## ℹ Getting Around

### AIR

**TACV** (https://flytacv.com) serves seven of the nine inhabited islands of Cabo Verde, except Brava and Santo Antão. You can purchase tickets at travel agents or online, and it's wise to book in advance as flights can fill up in peak season.

Inter-island flights are generally not expensive. Fares with tax range from CVE4300 (Praia to Maio, 20 minutes, twice weekly) to CVE8600 (Praia to São Vicente; 55 minutes, one to two daily).

Newly launched at time of research, **Binter Canarias** (www.bintercanarias.com) offers inter-island flights around Cabo Verde.

### BOAT

The only reliable scheduled ferry services in Cabo Verde are between Praia, Brava and Fogo; Praia and Maio; and Mindelo (São Vicente) and Santo Antão. There's less frequent service (twice monthly) from Praia to São Vicente via São Nicolau.

Seas can be rough and the crossings rocky, especially during winter months.

There are cafes on board the bigger boats, but it's always a good idea to bring a reserve of water and snacks.

### CAR & MOTORCYCLE

You can rent cars on many Cabo Verdean islands, but the only three that make the expense worth it are Santiago, Boa Vista and possibly Fogo. Cars cost from CVE5000 per day, including tax and insurance.

Consider a 4WD, especially on Boa Vista, as conditions are rough once you're off the few main roads.

### MINIBUS

Ranging from comfortable vans to pick-up trucks with narrow wooden benches, minibuses – known as colectivos or *alugueres* – provide connections between even relatively small towns on most islands.

### TAXIS

Taxis are generally plentiful in Cabo Verde, with round-town fares rarely topping CVE300. Airport runs and excursions are more costly.

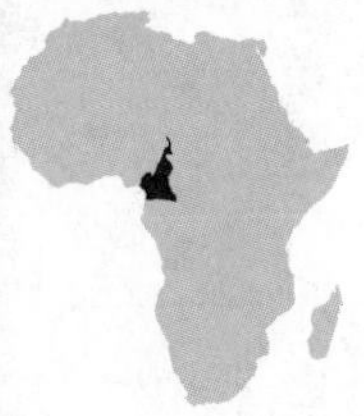

# Cameroon

☎237 / POP 24.4 MILLION

**Includes ➜**



## Why Go?

Cameroon is Africa's throbbing heart, a crazed, sultry mosaic of active volcanoes, white-sand beaches, thick rainforest and magnificent parched landscapes broken up by the bizarre rock formations of the Sahel. With both Francophone and Anglophone regions, not to mention some 250 local languages, the country is a vast ethnic and linguistic jigsaw, yet one that, in contrast to so many of its neighbours, enjoys a great deal of stability.

With reasonable road infrastructure, travel is a lot easier here than in many parts of Africa. Still, you'll miss none of those indicators that you're in the middle of this fascinating continent: everyone seems to be carrying something on their heads, *makossa* music sets the rhythm, the street smells like roasting plantains and African bliss is just a piece of grilled fish and a sweating beer away.

## Best Places to Eat

➜ Saga African Restaurant (p207)

➜ Iya (p208)

➜ La Fourchette (p207)

➜ La Paillote (p201)

## Best Places to Sleep

➜ Foyer du Marin (p205)

➜ Bird Watchers' Club (p209)

➜ Hotel Ilomba (p216)

➜ Hotel Akwa Palace (p206)

## When to Go

**Yaoundé**

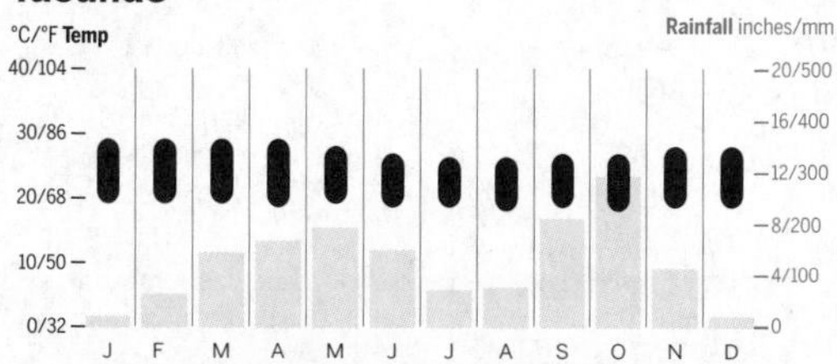


**Nov–Feb** High season; dry but not too hot.

**Mar & Oct** Light rains in the grasslands in March. In the north temperatures can reach 40°C.

**Apr–Oct** Intense rainfall; road travel is slow, muddy and at times impossible.

# Cameroon Highlights

1. **Ring Road** (p213) Exploring stunning verdant scenery, picturesque villages and rushing rivers in the region around Bamenda.

2. **Village des Artisans** (p215) Shopping for flamboyant bronze and beaded crafts in the attractive Islamic town of Foumban.

3. **Mt Cameroon** (p208) Donning your hiking boots to climb the mist-shrouded slopes of West Africa's highest peak.

4. **Limbe** (p209) Taking in the charming scenery, volcanic sand beaches and laid-back vibe at Cameroon's most enjoyable seaside town.

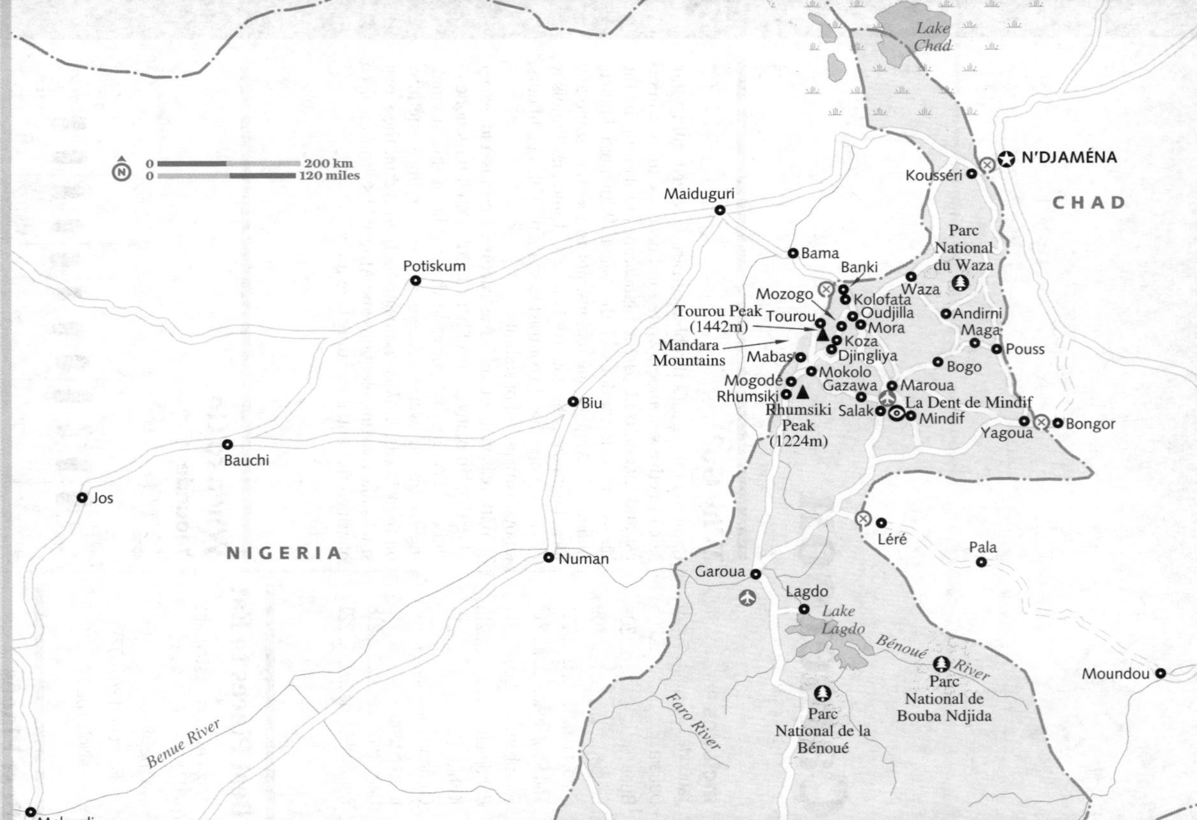

**5 Yaoundé** (p200)
Checking out art deco and Independence architecture as well as esoteric museums in the country's capital.

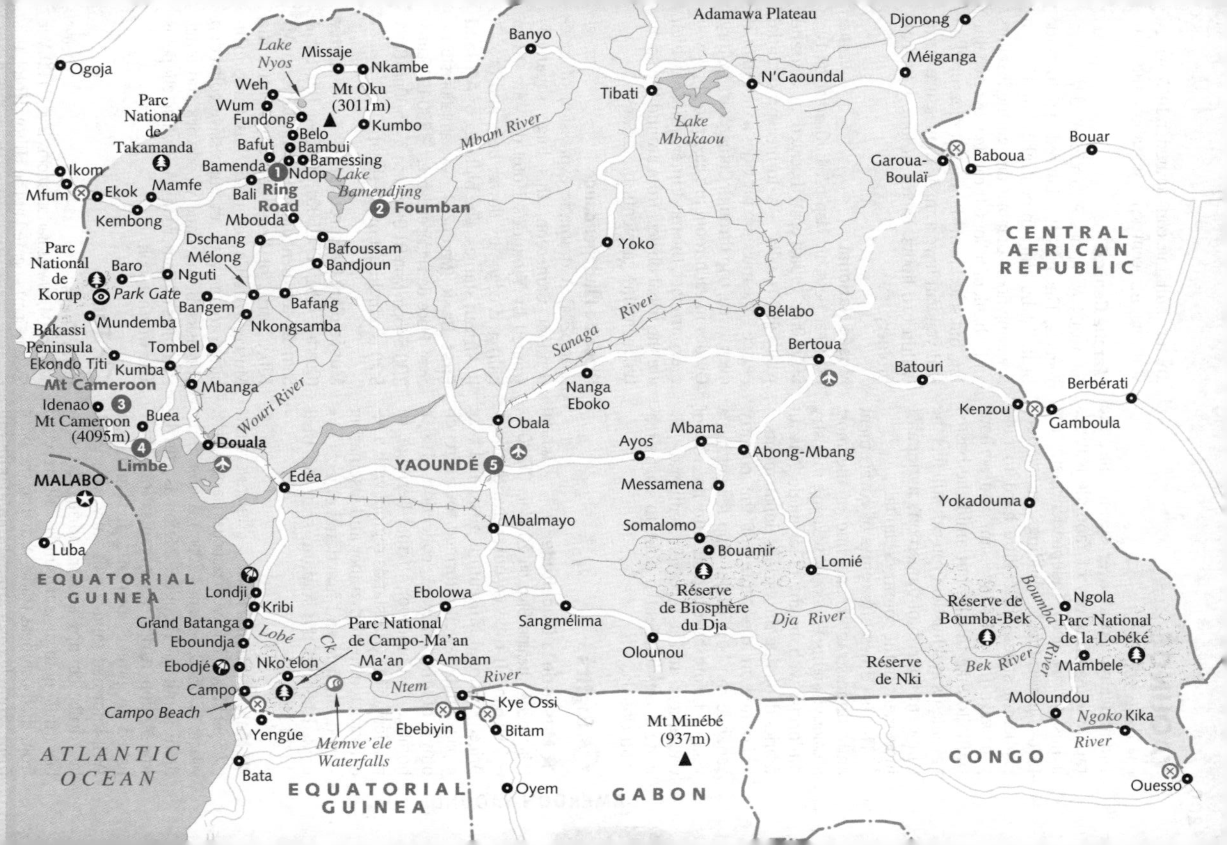

# YAOUNDÉ

POP 3 MILLION

Dramatically spread over seven hills, the rapidly expanding city of Yaoundé features a host of art deco, independence-era and 1970s government buildings in various exuberant styles. It's a little hard to raise your gaze from the incessant and perilous traffic to take this in, but amid the busted pavements and hustlers you can still feel the confident flourish of Cameroon's nationalist movement in the country's capital.

This is Cameroon's centre of government and administration, and one of the most attractive sights is people wearing ministry uniforms, with bright tailor-made African fabrics depicting the various departments.

Located in the centre of the country, Yaoundé can be a useful stop for getting a visa or before heading off into the rest of Cameroon, and a relatively temperate climate makes it a gentler place to start a trip than Douala.

## Sights

**★Musée de la Blackitude** MUSEUM
(Map p204; behind Blvd du 20 Mai; CFA2000; 9am-6pm) If time is short, give the overpriced National Museum a miss, and take a passionately well-informed tour (French only) of this private collection. It's a homage to Cameroon's tribal heritage, in particular the Grasslands region, with a reconstructed royal chamber and fascinating sacred, musical and functional objects. It's tucked behind the stadium seats on Blvd du 20 Mai.

**★Mefou National Park** NATURE RESERVE
(6 99 51 30 73; www.apeactionafrica.org; Metet village; CFA7500; 9am-4.30pm) A 45-minute drive south of Yaoundé, Mefou is run by Ape Action Africa, an organisation established to protect primates in Cameroon. Well-informed guides will show you gorillas, drills, chimps and mandrills living in beautiful natural surrounds, all rescued from the bushmeat trade. A taxi to the park from Yaoundé costs around CFA50,000; call ahead if it's rainy to check if the park's open.

**Nôtre Dame Cathedral** CATHEDRAL
(Our Lady of Victories; Map p204; Ave Monseigneur Vogt; 8am-6pm) The honking of Yaoundé's traffic merges with the sound of prayer and song at Nôtre Dame Cathedral. It's a bold triangular building, consecrated in 1955, with a stunning Afrocentric mosaic above the altar.

**Marché Central** MARKET
(Map p204; Ave Ahidjo; 7am-7pm Wed-Mon, 1pm-7pm Tue) The market is housed in a dramatic brutalist building in central Yaoundé, with towering floors of fabric and garment sellers and a bank of tailors. It can feel overwhelming, but select some fabric, get measured up and you can have a made-to-measure outfit within two hours. Factor in longer for embroidery.

**Musée National** MUSEUM
(National Museum; Map p204; Quartier du Lac; CFA10,000; 9am-6pm) Located in a grand white 1930s villa – a former presidential palace – the museum provides a thorough, if overpriced, trip through Cameroon's history. Guides in each room are eager to show you every artefact, the most interesting of which are the tribal objects from around the country, including garments and drums.

**Place de l'Indépendance** SQUARE
(Map p204) A dramatic expression of independent Cameroon, this huge square is fronted by Yaoundé's Hôtel de Ville (town hall) and edged by flower beds and proudly African statues. The building of **Afriland First Bank** (Map p204; www.afrilandfirstbank.com; Place de l'Indépendance; 7.30-11.45am & 2.30-5.45pm Mon-Fri, 9am-noon & 4-5.30pm Sat & Sun) is a highlight of the square.

**Musée d'Art Camerounais** MUSEUM
(Quartier Fébé; CFA1500; 3-6pm Thu, Sat & Sun) At the Benedictine monastery on Mt Fébé, north of Yaoundé's city centre, the Musée d'Art Camerounais has three exhibition rooms with an impressive collection of masks, bronze- and woodwork and other examples of Cameroonian art. The chapel is also worth a look.

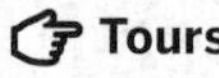

## Tours

**Safar Tours** TOURS
(Map p204; www.safartours.com; Blvd du 20 Mai; 9am-6pm) Located at the Hilton Hotel, this tour operator organises packaged and special interest tours.

## Sleeping

**Foyer International de l'Église Presbytérienne** HOSTEL $
(Map p202; 2 99 85 23 76; off Rue Joseph Essono Balla; tent/dm/s/d CFA2000/5000/8000/10,000; P) This 100-year-old building has two fairly

uninviting private rooms and two eight-bed dorms, all of which share the same very basic bathrooms. Campers can set up their own tents in the garden where there's a bonfire pit. From the main road, walk to the right of the water towers, and it's in the second brick house on your left.

**Ideal Hotel** HOTEL $

(Map p202; ☎2 22 66 95 37; idealhotel72@yahoo.fr; Carrefour Nlongkak; d CFA8000-10,000, apt CFA15,000; P) Rooms here are decent enough for the low price, though there's no hot water and rooms are fan cooled. Balconies in some make up for a general lack of light (plus you get Yaoundé smog for free). If you're visa-hunting, this is well located for embassies.

**Central Hotel** HOTEL $$

(Map p204; ☎2 22 22 65 98; Quartier des Ministères; d CFA32,000; P ❄) Central indeed, but miraculously tucked away from Yaoundé traffic in a spacious courtyard garden in the ministerial district. Rooms are threadbare but clean with large balconies: this old-fashioned and modestly welcoming place is one of the city's best bargains. Have something to eat or sink a beer at the pavilion restaurant opposite.

**Prestige Hotel** HOTEL $$

(Map p202; ☎2 22 31 82 52; Ave Charles Atangana; d CFA22,000; ❄ 📶) This sprawling and rather raucous hotel has good-value rooms and is handily located for buses from Yaoundé to Douala. Rooms are on the small side, but they're fairly clean and secure, and many have balconies. There's a popular bar and restaurant on the site, too, but also lots of traffic noise.

**Tou'ngou Hotel** HOTEL $$

(Map p202; ☎2 22 20 10 25; www.toungouhotel.com; Rue Onembele Nkou; s/d/ste incl breakfast CFA23,000/30,000/45,000; P ❄ 📶) One of Yaoundé's better-value midrange hotels, the Tou'ngou is a relatively smart and popular option. The rooms are comfortable and clean, the location is central and there's a good restaurant with a dramatic terrace view. It's best to book ahead.

**Merina Hotel** HOTEL $$$

(Map p204; ☎6 55 09 94 98; hotelmerina@cameroun-plus.com; Ave Ahidjo; s & d CFA38,000-45,000; P ❄ 📶 🏊) Located right in the heart of Yaoundé, the smart Merina has a fancy orchid-strewn lobby, modern and comfortable rooms and good service. Other perks include a free airport-shuttle service and small pool.

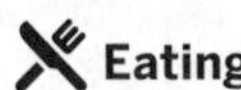

## Eating

Around Carrefours Bastos and Nlongkak there are grills serving brochettes (kebabs) throughout the day. On Place de l'Indépendance, you can get delicious grilled fish with chilli or peanut sauce from CFA1000. Yaoundé excels at bustling patisseries, and there are several decent eating places.

**Calafatas** PATISSERIE $

(Map p204; ☎2 22 23 17 29; www.calafatas.com; Rue de Nachtigal; baked goods CFA200-2000) Concealed in a synthetic wooden cabin but founded way back in 1935, this is Yaoundé's best bakery, selling scrumptious madeleines, palmiers and croissants.

**Le Sintra** INTERNATIONAL $

(Map p204; Ave Kennedy; dishes CFA3000-5000; ⏰6am-11pm Mon-Sat) With a friendly welcome, a faint whiff of colonial atmosphere and a pleasant screened terrace in the heart of Yaoundé, La Sintra does a full breakfast menu, Italian and Cameroonian cuisine, as well as delicious French dishes such as *crevettes à la provençale* (shrimps cooked in garlic).

**Patisserie Select Plus** BAKERY $

(Map p204; Ave Monseigneur Vogt; baked goods CFA200-1500; ⏰24hr) This bustling bakery near Yaoundé's cathedral sells a delicious line of freshly baked croissants, *beignets* (pastries) and sandwiches which you can consume at stand-up tables by the window. Other treats include pizzas, burgers and coffee to go.

**Le Biniou** CRÊPES $

(Map p204; ☎6 99 50 31 68; off Pl de l'Indépendance; pancakes CFA3800; ⏰10am-midnight Mon-Fri & Sun) Well located near the Afriland First Bank (p200), in a gated enclosure with a terrace enclosed by greenery. Sweet and savoury pancakes are a speciality, as well as Cameroonian meat and fish dishes.

★ **La Paillote** VIETNAMESE $$

(Map p202; Rue Joseph Essono Balla; mains CFA3500-6000; ⏰noon-2pm & 7-10pm; ❄ 🖉) This stylish Vietnamese restaurant has a charming shaded terrace and a smart dining room inside, both of which attract a loyal crowd of Yaoundé expats. The dishes are delicious and service is excellent. The iced coffee and spring rolls are a treat.

**Istanbul** TURKISH $$

(Map p202; Rue Joseph Mballa Eloumden; mains CFA4500; ⏰8am-11pm; ❄ 🖉) Fresh and

# Yaoundé

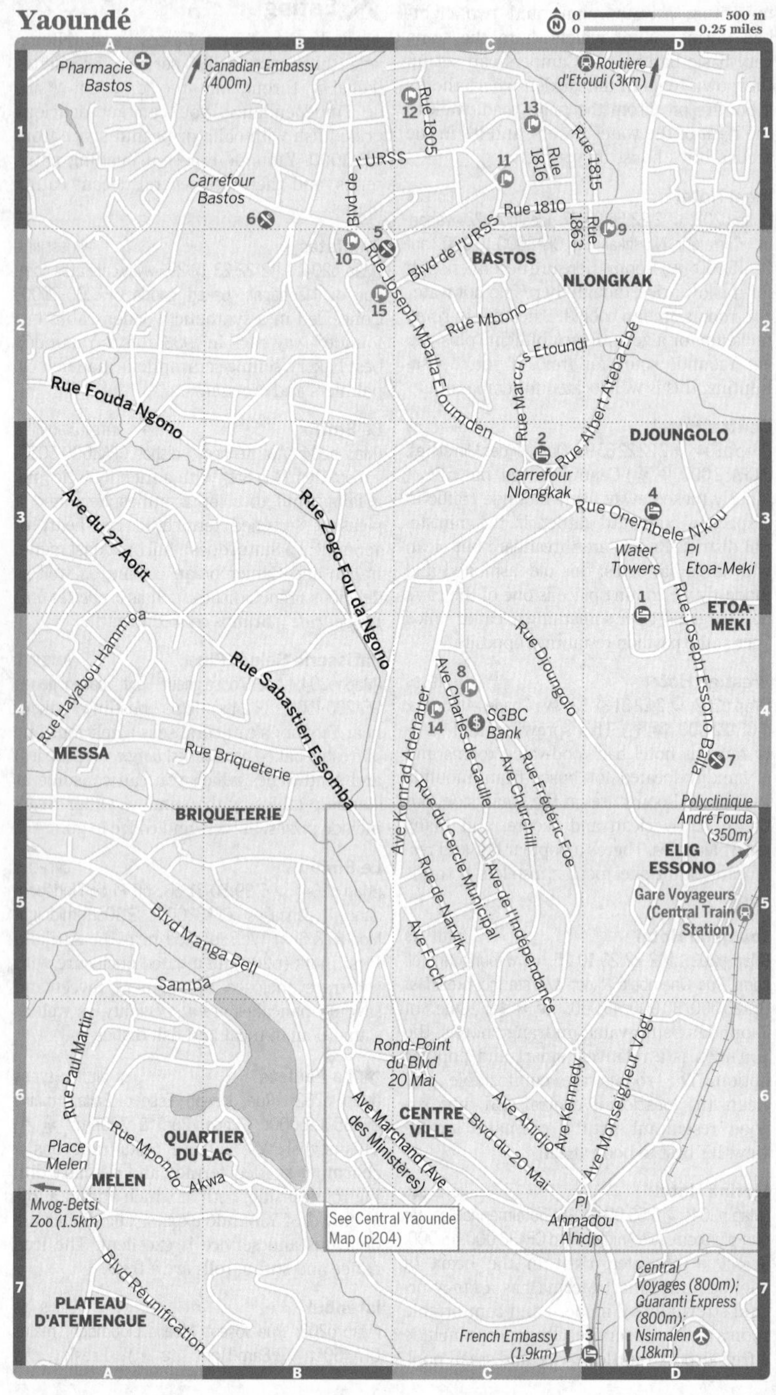

0 500 m
0 0.25 miles
Pharmacie Bastos
Canadian Embassy (400m)
Routière d'Etoudi (3km)
Rue 1805
Rue 1816
Rue 1815
Rue 1810
Rue 1863
Blvd de l'URSS
Carrefour Bastos
Rue Joseph Mballa Eloumden
BASTOS
NLONGKAK
Rue Mbono
Rue Marcus Etoundi
Rue Albert Ateba Ébé
Rue Fouda Ngono
DJOUNGOLO
Carrefour Nlongkak
Rue Onembele N'kou
Water Towers
Pl Etoa-Meki
ETOA-MEKI
Ave du 27 Août
Rue Zogo Fou da Ngono
Rue Djoungolo
Rue Joseph Essono Balla
Rue Hayabou Hammoa
Rue Sabastien Essomba
Ave Charles de Gaulle
SGBC Bank
Ave Konrad Adenauer
Rue Frédéric Foe
Ave Churchill
MESSA
Rue Briqueterie
BRIQUETERIE
Rue du Cercle Municipal
Polyclinique André Fouda (350m)
ELIG ESSONO
Gare Voyageurs (Central Train Station)
Rue de Narvik
Ave de l'Indépendance
Ave Foch
Blvd Manga Bell
Samba
Rond-Point du Blvd 20 Mai
Rue Paul Martin
Ave Monseigneur Vogt
Ave Kennedy
Ave Ahidjo
CENTRE VILLE
Blvd du 20 Mai
Ave Marchand (Ave des Ministères)
QUARTIER DU LAC
Rue Mpondo Akwa
Place Melen
MELEN
Mvog-Betsi Zoo (1.5km)
Pl Ahmadou Ahidjo
See Central Yaounde Map (p204)
Central Voyages (800m); Guaranti Express (800m); Nsimalen (18km)
Blvd Réunification
PLATEAU D'ATEMENGUE
French Embassy (1.9km)

## Yaoundé

**Sleeping**
1 Foyer International de l'Église Presbytérienne........D3
2 Ideal Hotel........C3
3 Prestige Hotel........D7
4 Tou'ngou Hotel........D3

**Eating**
5 Chez Wou........B2
6 Istanbul........B1
7 La Paillote........D4

**Information**
8 British High Commission........C4
9 Central African Republic Embassy........D1
10 Chadian Embassy........B2
11 Congolese Embassy........C1
12 Equatorial Guinean Embassy........C1
13 Gabonese Embassy........C1
14 German Consulate........C4
15 Nigerian Embassy........B2

well-prepared Turkish food is served up swiftly at this smart terrace restaurant (with an even smarter inside dining room complete with white tablecloths and silver service). Takeaway is available.

**Chez Wou** CHINESE **$$**
(Map p202; Rue Joseph Mballa Eloumden; mains from CFA4500; noon-3.30pm & 6-11pm) One of Yaoundé's older Chinese restaurants, this one has nice tables set under a wide porch, and a comprehensive menu. It's good if you're ready for a change from Cameroonian food: try the ginger-and-garlic prawns.

## ☆ Entertainment

**★Institut Français** ARTS CENTRE
(Map p204; 2 22 22 09 44; www.ifcameroun.com/category/yaounde; 140 Ave du Président Ahmadou Ahidjo; 8.30am-1pm & 3-6pm Mon-Fri plus evening events; ) With a hip, graffitied exterior and a culturally buzzing interior, this is a relaxed spot to catch a film or music event, see an exhibition or have a drink or food at the in-house Café de France. There's a good library of French titles to browse.

## Information

### DANGERS & ANNOYANCES

Western visitors in Yaoundé are conspicuous, and muggings happen, though you'll be the object of lots of friendly attention, too. Daytime is generally fine, but take taxis at night and be particularly wary around the Marché Central and tourist hotels.

### INTERNET ACCESS

Your best bet for internet in Yaoundé is the smarter hotels and restaurants for a wireless connection. Try also **Cometé Internet** (Map p204; Rue de Narvik; 8pm-6pm).

### MEDICAL SERVICES

**Pharmacie Bastos** (Map p202; 2 22 20 65 55; Carrefour Bastos; 8am-6pm) Well-stocked pharmacy.

**Polyclinique André Fouda** (2 22 23 30 38; Route De Ngousso; 8am-6pm) For medical emergencies; in Elig Essono, southeast of Carrefour Nlongkak.

### MONEY

There are ATMs at most of the major banks in Yaoundé. As always in Cameroon, travellers cheques are problematic to change in banks – try the banks around the cathedral.

**Bicec Bank** (Map p204; Ave Ahidjo; 8am-3.30pm Mon-Fri) Has an ATM.

**Express Exchange** (Map p204; Ave Kennedy; 8.30pm-6pm Mon-Sat) For money changing.

**SCB** (Map p204; near Place Ahmadou Ahidjo; 8.30am-3.30pm Mon-Fri) Money exchange and ATM.

**SGBC Bank** (Map p202; Ave Charles de Gaulle; 8am–3.30pm Mon–Fri) Has an ATM.

**Standard Chartered Bank** (Map p204; Ave de l'Indépendance; 8am–3pm Mon–Fri) Has an ATM.

### POST

**Central Post Office** (Map p204; Pl Ahmadou Ahidjo; 7.30am-3.30pm Mon-Fri, 7.30am-noon Sat)

## Getting There & Away

### AIR

Yaoundé's airport is Yaoundé Nsimalen International Airport, although far more international services go to and from Douala. Internal flights with **Camair-Co** (2 33 50 55 00; www.camair-co.cm) connect Yaoundé to Douala daily (CFA45,000, 45 minutes) and other cities.

### BUS

There are buses between Yaoundé and all major cities in Cameroon. Buses leave from their companies' offices, spread out on the outskirts of town. For Douala (CFA3000 to CFA6000, three to four hours, three to five daily), **Central Voyages** (2 22 30 39 94; Carrefour Coron, Mvog-Mbi; 6am-10pm) and **Guaranti Express** (6 77 08 41 08; Blvd de l'Oua, Quartier Nsam; 6am-10pm) are recommended. Guaranti Express is also recommended for travel to

## Central Yaoundé

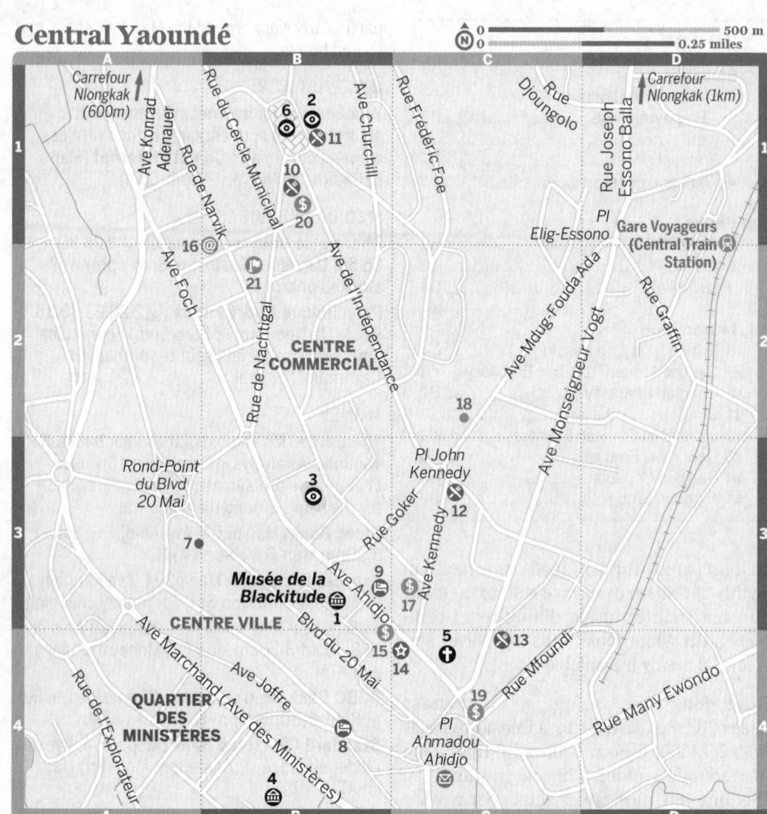


Limbe (CFA5000, five hours, three to four daily), Bamenda (CFA5000, six hours, two daily), Bafoussam (CFA2500, three hours, two daily) and Kumba (CFA4000, four hours, two daily).

Otherwise, all agency and nonagency buses for Kribi, Bertoua, Batouri, Ebolowa, Limbe and Buea depart from Blvd de l'Ocam, about 3km south of Pl Ahmadou Ahidjo (direct taxi drivers to Agences de Mvan; fare is around CFA1000).

Transport to Bafoussam, Bamenda and points north departs from Gare Routière d'Etoudi, 5km north of Centre Ville. Taxi fare there costs around CFA1500.

### TRAIN

There are also two daily services between Yaoundé and Douala (1st/2nd class CFA9000/3600), though these are used much less frequently, as buses are cheaper, faster and more convenient. A major derailment in 2016 caused many deaths, so travel on the service can't be recommended at this time.

### Getting Around

Shared taxis and *moto-taxis* (motorbike taxis) are the only public-transport option in Yaoundé. Fares are CFA200 per place for short- to medium-length rides. A private taxi to Nsimalen airport from central Yaoundé should cost CFA4000 to CFA6000 (40 minutes).

# WESTERN CAMEROON

Imagine Africa: wormy red tracks and vegetation so intensely green you can almost taste the colour. This image comes alive in Western Cameroon. The country's economic heart intermittently beats in Douala, and from here it's a short hop to the haze and laze of beach towns like Limbe and the savannah-carpeted slopes of the magnificent Mountain of Thunder – Mt Cameroon. In the Anglophone northwest you can slip between

### Central Yaoundé

**Top Sights**
1 Musée de la Blackitude ........ B3

**Sights**
2 Afriland First Bank ........ B1
3 Marché Central ........ B3
4 Musée National ........ B4
5 Nôtre Dame Cathedral ........ C4
6 Place de l'Indépendance ........ B1

**Activities, Courses & Tours**
7 Safar Tours ........ A3

**Sleeping**
8 Central Hotel ........ B4
9 Merina Hotel ........ B3

**Eating**
10 Calafatas ........ B1
11 Le Biniou ........ B1
12 Le Sintra ........ C3
13 Patisserie Select Plus ........ C4

**Entertainment**
14 Institut Français ........ C4

**Information**
15 Bicec Bank ........ B4
16 Cometé Internet ........ B2
17 Express Exchange ........ C3
18 Ministry of Immigration ........ C2
19 SCB ........ C4
20 Standard Chartered Bank ........ B1
21 US Embassy ........ B2

sunburnt green hills while exploring a patchwork of secret societies, traditional chiefdoms and some of the country's best arts and crafts, particularly the wooden masks that are so often associated with this continent.

# Douala

POP 2.9 MILLION

Sticky and frenetic, Douala isn't as bad as some say, but it's not likely to be your first choice for a honeymoon, either. By any measurement but political power this is Cameroon's main city. It's the primary air hub and a leading business centre with a major port, and the result is a chaotic hodgepodge. There is some charm in the street life and battered Independence architecture, though, and here you can set your finger on Cameroon's pulse.

## Sights

**Espace Doual'art** MUSEUM
(www.doualart.org; Pl du Gouvernement, Bonanjo; 9am-7pm Mon-Sat) FREE Well worth dropping into if you're nearby in Douala, this contemporary art space hosts changing displays of work from all over Cameroon and the rest of Africa. There's a cafe here too, and it's a good introduction to the city's small art scene.

## Sleeping

**Centre d'Accueil Missionaire** HOSTEL $
(Procure; 2 33 42 27 97; aprocure@yahoo.fr; Rue Franqueville; s CFA10,000, without shower CFA8000, d/tr CFA14,000/18,000; P) Praise be to this Catholic mission in Douala, with its clean if basic upstairs rooms, pleasant veranda and lovely pool. A convenient laundry service and an excellent location seal the deal. You'll be woken by the harmonious sound of hymns from the mission church.

★ **Foyer du Marin** GUESTHOUSE $$
(2 33 42 27 94; Rue Gallieni; s/d/apt CFA27,000/30,000/45,000; P@) Definitely the best-value accommodation in Douala, the German Seaman's Mission is a literal oasis of tranquillity in the city centre. It's set in a gorgeous garden with a pool and terrific views towards the port, the rooms are comfortable and spacious, and the restaurant (p206) serves up delicious poolside food all day long. Book ahead.

**Hotel Majestic** HOTEL $$
(2 33 42 87 34; ngatcherv1@yahoo.fr; Blvd de la Liberté; d CFA25,000; ) You can expect quite a bit of noise at this otherwise good-value hotel; as well as the traffic on Douala's main avenue outside, there's an incredibly loud music shop downstairs blaring out pop music all day. That said, rooms are clean and comfortable, each coming with a fridge, TV and modern bathroom.

**Hotel Beausejour Mirabel** HOTEL $$
(6 50 60 62 57; www.beausejour-mirabel.com; Rue Joffre; d CFA30,000-60,000; ) Centrally located and with very friendly staff, the Beausejour was once quite a smart place, as evidenced by its impressive facade and former rooftop pool. It's fallen on less glamorous times, but the rooms have balconies and are clean and spacious, while downstairs there's wi-fi and a good on-site restaurant, making it one of Douala's best midrange options.

## Douala

A B C D

1 2 3 4 5

Blvd Leclerc
Rue du Prince des Galles
Bicec Bank
Rue Franqueville
Rue Joffre
Rue Sylvani
Rue Alfred Saker
Blvd de la Liberté
AKWA
Wouri River
Rue de Lapeyrère
Rue Pau
Blvd Ahidjo
Main Port
Rue Kitchener
Rue Surcouf
Blvd de Besseké
Rue Joss
Place du Gouvernement
Air France
Hôtel de Ville (City Hall)
BONANJO
Rue Lugard
Rue Tobie Kuoh
Rue French
Rue Pierre Loti
Rue Prince
Rue Koumassi
Ave de Gaulle
Ave des Cocotiers
BALI
Rue Bertaut
Ave Douala Manga Bell
(4.5km)
Bonapriso (1km)

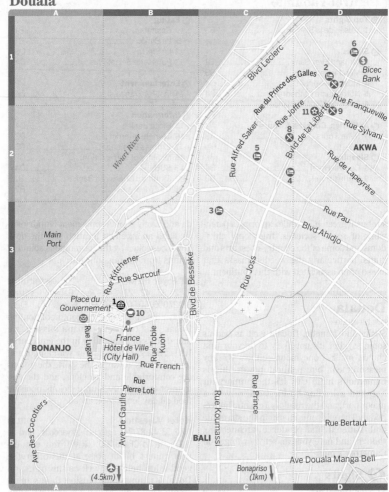

**Hotel Akwa Palace** LUXURY HOTEL $$$

(☎2 33 42 26 01; www.hotel-akwa-palace.com; Blvd de la Liberté; d CFA120,000-180,000; P ❄ @ ≋) If money's not a concern then this is still the best choice in town, if for nothing else than its superb location in the heart of things in Douala. Rooms are plush and stylish, staff are helpful, and the vast swimming pool in the back garden is the best place to forget the chaos outside. The marble- and wood-lined lobby is a good place for a cool drink.

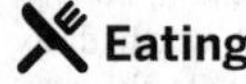

## Eating

**Zepol** BAKERY, EATERY $

(Blvd de la Liberté; baked goods CFA500-4000; ⏲24hr) The best and most stylish takeaway patisserie and *boulangerie* (bakery) in town, founded 1968. The wood-lined interior is decorated with carnival masks. There's also a small supermarket here.

**Foyer du Marin** EUROPEAN $$

(☎2 33 42 27 94; Rue Gallieni; mains CFA4000-8000; ⏲8am-10pm) It's worth making a detour for the nightly grill at this hotel; great kebabs, steaks, chicken, seafood dishes and

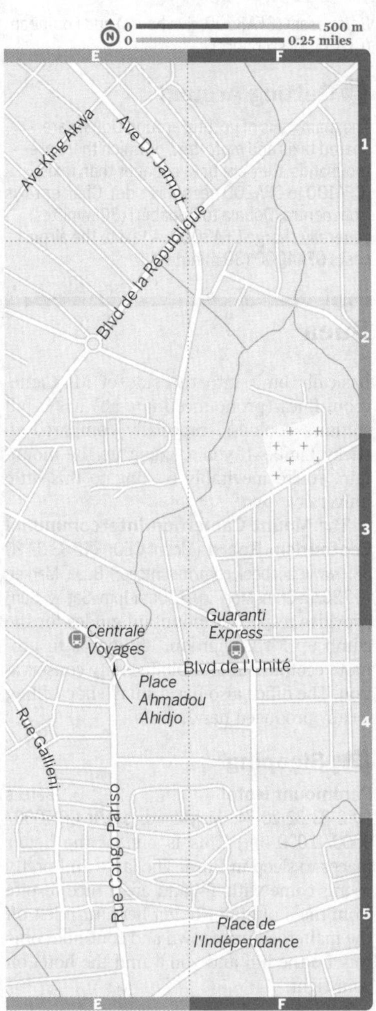


juicy German sausage are all well prepared, and served up by the friendly staff at poolside tables under thatched rondavels. This is also a great drinking spot, with fresh fruit juice as well as beers.

**Saga African Restaurant** AFRICAN **$$**

(Blvd de la Liberté; mains CFA4000-7000; ⏲noon-11pm) Atmospheric and upmarket, the Saga offers an interesting mix of African dishes with some local classics, such as *ndole* (a dish made with bitter leaves similar to spinach and flavoured with smoked fish), plus pizza, Chinese and pasta dishes. It's nicely

## Douala

**Sights**

| | | |
|---|---|---|
| 1 | Espace Doual'art | B4 |

**Sleeping**

| | | |
|---|---|---|
| 2 | Centre d'Accueil Missionaire | D1 |
| 3 | Foyer du Marin | C3 |
| 4 | Hotel Akwa Palace | C2 |
| 5 | Hotel Beausejour Mirabel | C2 |
| 6 | Hotel Majestic | D1 |

**Eating**

| | | |
|---|---|---|
| | Foyer du Marin | (see 3) |
| 7 | La Fourchette | D1 |
| 8 | Saga African Restaurant | C2 |
| 9 | Zepol | D2 |

**Drinking & Nightlife**

| | | |
|---|---|---|
| 10 | Café des Palabres | B4 |

**Entertainment**

| | | |
|---|---|---|
| 11 | Institut Français | D2 |

decked out, with an open-air area at the front and a cool glass-fronted dining room behind.

**★ La Fourchette** INTERNATIONAL **$$$**

(☎2 33 43 26 11; Rue Franqueville; mains CFA7000-18,000; ⏲noon-11pm Mon-Sat) A smart and tasteful option, La Fourchette's menu is out of this world if you're used to the more normal Cameroonian choice of chicken or fish. Here you'll find steak tartare, grilled zebu fillet, goat's-cheese ravioli and stuffed crab, with prices to match. Service is charmingly formal, you should dress to impress and booking ahead is a good idea.

## Drinking & Nightlife

Douala has a lively nightlife scene, though much of it can be inaccessible to visitors without local contacts. The areas of Bonapriso, Bonanjo and Akwa contain the most bars and clubs.

**Café des Palabres** CAFE

(Pl du Gouvernement; mains around CFA8000; ⏲7.30am-11pm Mon-Sat; 📶) Housed inside a 1905 colonial German residence, this charming cafe-restaurant on Bonanjo's main square has a great garden terrace perfect for an evening drink, as well as a cool interior with a full menu and an intellectual vibe. Literary types might like to know this building was identified as 'la Pagode' in Céline's *Journey to the End of the Night*.

## Entertainment

**Institut Français** ARTS CENTRE
(☎6 79 26 33 51; www.ifcameroun.com/category/douala; Blvd de la Liberté; ⊙8am-6pm Mon-Sat, plus evening events) A popular creative space for theatre, dance, movies, debates and workshops. It also runs a Nuit Blanche program, and dance and music festivals. Get a drink or a coffee here, and eat at the Café de France.

## Shopping

★**Marché des Fleurs** MARKET
(Rue Dominique Savio, Bonapriso, entrance opposite Star Land Hotel; ⊙9am–4pm) A huge, atmospheric complex of roofed stalls selling crafts from around Cameroon, but mainly the grasslands region. You can buy wonderful masks, baskets, jewellery, batik clothes and tablecloths. On the airport-road side of the market, large ornamental garden plants are sold in glorious profusion, with cut-flower bouquets lining the Star Land Hotel side.

## Information

Muggings happen: if you'd rather be safe than sorry, after dark it's recommended to take a taxi. Leave valuables in a safe place, and be extra careful around nightspots.

For changing money, try the banks along Blvd de la Liberté, such as **Bicec** (Blvd de la Liberté; ⊙8am–5pm Mon–Fri), or Rue Joss; most have ATMs.

The **Central Post Office** (⊙7.30am–5pm Mon–Fri) is on Rue joss.

## Getting There & Away

Douala has an **international airport** (☎2 33 42 35 77; 10km west of Douala) with links to cities in Cameroon, around the region and to Europe. There's an **Air France office** (1 Pl du Gouvernement; ⊙8am-12.30pm & 3-6pm Mon-Fri, 8am-noon Sat) in town.

Arriving from Limbe by bus, ask to be dropped at Rompoint, which is fairly central.

Buses to Yaoundé (CFA3000 to CFA6000, three to four hours) depart throughout the day from agency offices along Blvd de l'Unité such as **Guaranti Express** (Blvd de la Liberté; ⊙6am-10pm). For buses to Kribi (CFA2000, three hours, four to five daily) use **Centrale Voyages** (Blvd Ahidjo; ⊙6am-10pm).

For other destinations, use the sprawling **Gare Routière Bonabéri** (15km north of Douala, Bonabéri). There are at least five departures daily for destinations including Limbe (CFA3000, 1½ hours), Bamenda (CFA4500, seven hours), Bafoussam (CFA3500, five hours) and Foumban (CFA3500, six hours).

## Getting Around

The main ways of getting around Douala are shared taxis and *moto-taxi*, of which there are thousands; they are both cheaper than taxis (CFA100 to CFA200 per short ride). Charter taxis from central Douala to Bonabéri (30 minutes) generally charge CFA3000. A taxi to the airport costs CFA4000 (30 minutes).

# Buea

POP 95,000

Basically built into the side of Mt Cameroon, Buea (pronounced *boy*-ah) has a hill station's coolness, especially compared to sticky Limbe. If you're going up the mountain, you're inevitably coming to this little university town.

The **Mount Cameroon Intercommunal Ecotourism Board** (Mount CEO; ☎2 33 32 20 38; www.facebook.com/mountceo; Buea Market; ⊙7.30am-5pm Mon-Fri, 7.30am-1pm Sat & Sun) provides respected mountain guides for the climb up Mt Cameroon. Its goal is to promote ecotourism and biodiversity conservation. The office also has a small shop selling locally produced handicrafts.

## Sleeping

**Paramount Hotel** HOTEL $
(☎2 33 32 20 74; Molyko Rd; s/d/tr CFA7000/9000/11,000; P) This is one of the better places to sleep in Buea. The large and pretty rooms come with TV and are a nice respite from the mountain. To get here, turn left off the main road from town and continue some way up the hill and you'll find the hotel on your right.

**Presbyterian Mission** GUESTHOUSE $
(☎2 33 32 23 36; Market Rd; campsites CFA1000, s/d CFA4000/6000, without bathroom CFA3000/5000; P) This church mission is set in attractive gardens and has comfy and spotless rooms, a tidy communal sitting room and cooking facilities. It's up the hill from Buea's police station.

## Eating

★**Iya** FUSION $$
(☎6 65 00 10 00; www.iyabuea.com; former Alliance Franco, Grand Stand; mains CFA3000-6500; ⊙11am-11pm Mon-Sat; P ❄ ☎) A rarity in Cameroon: a stylish restaurant with warm atten-

tive service. The minimal interior has white walls brightened with feathered hats and geometric basketwork from the northwest highlands. The menu is also traditional with a contemporary twist, featuring imaginative reinterpretations of Cameroonian standards. *Ndole* and *kati-kati* (marinated chicken) never looked – or tasted – this good.

### Information

Conveniently, Buea's **Express Exchange** (Molyko Rd) will exchange euros, US dollars and travellers cheques.

### Getting There & Away

From Buea's frenetic bus station at Mile 17, there are regular departures for Limbe (CFA800, 25 minutes), and points north.

## Limbe

POP 88,000

Limbe is a charming place, blessed with a fabulous natural position between the rainforest-swathed foothills of Mt Cameroon and the dramatic Atlantic coastline. Popular with both foreign and Cameroonian tourists, this is a great spot to chill out on the beach for a few days before heading elsewhere.

### Sights

The best of Limbe's beaches are north of town and known by their distance from Limbe. Our favourite is at the village of Batoké at Mile 6, from where the lava flows of one of Mt Cameroon's eruptions are still visible. Head to Bota Road for a shared taxi to the beaches (from CFA500).

Unfortunately, Down Beach in the heart of Limbe is strewn with rubbish.

**Botanical Gardens** GARDENS

(Botanic Garden Rd; admission CFA2000, camera CFA2000, guide CFA2000; 8am-6pm) Limbe's Botanical Gardens, the second oldest in Africa, are the home of, among others, cinnamon, nutmeg, mango, ancient cycads and an unnamed tree that locals describe as 'African Viagra'. There's a small visitors centre and an area with Commonwealth War Graves. Guides aren't required but are recommended as labelling is minimal. Bring bug repellant.

**Limbe Wildlife Centre** ZOO

(www.limbewildlife.org; Bota Rd; CFA3000; 9am-4pm; ) Many zoos in Africa are depressing places, but the Limbe Wildlife Centre is a shining exception. It houses rescued chimpanzees, gorillas, drills and other primates in large enclosures, with lots of interesting information about local conservation issues. Staff are well informed, and are heavily involved in community education.

### Activities

**Bimbia Rainforest & Mangrove Trail** WALKING

(2 77 33 70 14; bbcnaturetrail@yahoo.com; local development fee CFA5000, guide CFA3000) An hour south of Limbe, this trail runs through the only coastal lowland rainforest remaining between Douala and Limbe. An experienced guide will take you on day tours through some rather lovely submerged woods, birdwatching areas and old slave-trading sites. It's CFA15,000 for a taxi-brousse (bush taxi) from Limbe; the trip is cheapest done in a group.

### Sleeping

**Victoria Guest House** GUESTHOUSE $

(2 22 81 62 45; off Makangal St; d CFA9000, with air-con CFA12,000-16,000; ) The best-value budget place in town, the Victoria has clean and well-maintained rooms on the hill above Limbe's main restaurant strip: follow the path up behind the King William Hotel. Nearly all rooms have air-con, but there are a couple of cheaper fan-cooled variants.

★**Bird Watchers' Club** GUESTHOUSE $$

(6 96 83 81 88, 6 75 73 40 86; Limbe Botanical Gardens; d incl breakfast CFA28,000; ) This charmingly secluded and gently welcoming spot on a rocky promontory overlooks the sea. With just two rooms it's a good idea to call ahead and book. You'll be rewarded with spacious accommodation and a great restaurant with superb sea views. Arriving by taxi, steer the driver to Miramar – Bird Watchers' is just up the road.

**Hotel Seme Beach** RESORT $$

(6 77 93 45 50; www.semebeach.com; Mile 11, Rte d'Idenau, Bakingili; r incl breakfast CFA25,000-35,000, ste incl breakfast CFA50,000-100,000; ) Not in Limbe itself, but 18km beyond along the rain-lashed coast, this is a good choice if you want to enjoy the beach and creature comforts. The location is gorgeous, with full frontage onto the beach and views of Equatorial Guinea rising in the distance, while touches such as a freshwater swimming pool and a spa make for great relaxation.

## Limbe

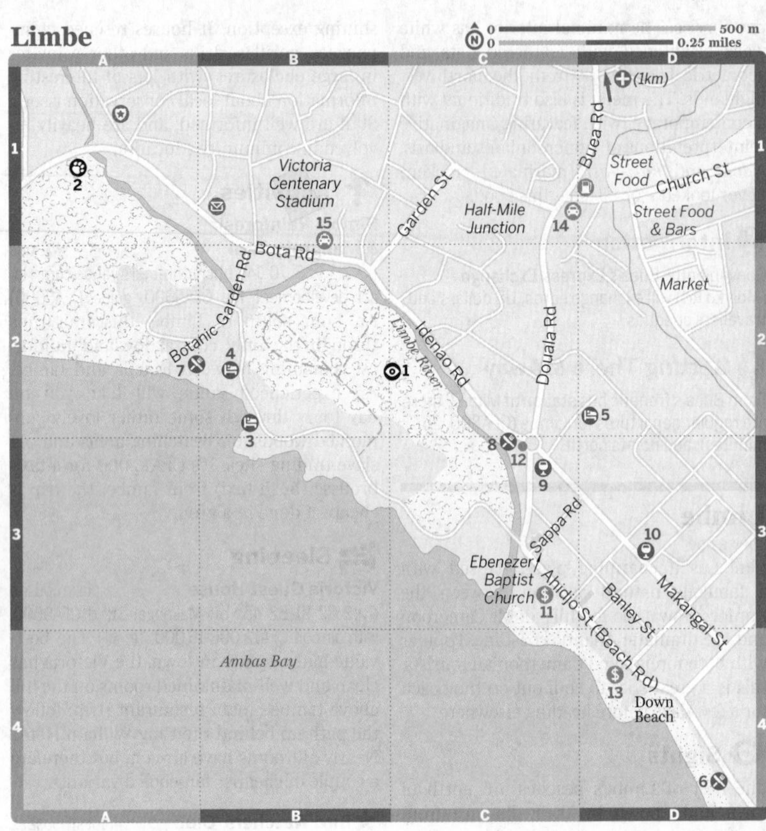




## Limbe

**Sights**

1 Botanical Gardens ........ C2
2 Limbe Wildlife Centre ........ A1

**Sleeping**

3 Bird Watchers' Club ........ B2
4 Park Hotel Miramar ........ B2
5 Victoria Guest House ........ D2

**Eating**

6 Grilled Fish Stalls ........ D4
7 Hot Spot ........ A2
8 Le Moulin ........ C3

**Drinking & Nightlife**

9 Bamboo Lounge ........ C3
10 Ocean Blu ........ D3

**Information**

11 Bicec Bank ........ C3
12 Flora Travel & Tours ........ C3
13 SGBC Bank ........ D4

**Transport**

14 Shared Taxis ........ C1
15 Shared Taxis ........ B1

**Park Hotel Miramar** HOTEL **$$**
(☎2 33 33 29 41; Botanic Garden Rd; d incl breakfast CFA20,500; P ❄ ☜ ≋) While this place has certainly seen better days, its location on a wave-kissed cliff backed by screaming jungle is unbeatable. Accommodation is in cute, if rather dark, *boukarous* (self-contained circular, thatched-mud huts) that abut a restaurant and a decent-sized swimming pool. Book ahead.

## Eating

**Hot Spot** INTERNATIONAL $
(Limbe Botanical Gardens; mains CFA3000-4000; ⏲7.30am-11pm) With hands down the best location in town, overlooking the dramatic coastline and Park Hotel Miramar, this place offers a fairly standard selection of meat grills, shrimp, fish and chicken dishes. The friendly staff, outdoor seating and views make it, though. Get there via the dirt road to the hotels through the gardens and take the middle path after the bridge.

**Le Moulin** INTERNATIONAL $
(Idenao Rd; mains CFA2000-3000; ⏲10am-10pm) Right on the roundabout in the thick of things, Le Moulin is the best eating option in Limbe's town centre. The menu encompasses *ndole*, chicken and beef dishes served up with fresh vegetables, plantains or rice.

**Grilled Fish Stalls** SEAFOOD $
(Down Beach; dishes from CFA1000; ⏲7am-10pm) You'll find this cluster of open-air grills with attached seating where the fishing boats haul up on Limbe's main beach. Soak up your beer with something from the sea that was probably happily unaware it would be your dinner a few minutes before you ordered it.

## Drinking & Nightlife

**Ocean Blu** CLUB
(Makangal St; ⏲10pm–6am) An excellent place to cut loose in Limbe, this is a young vibrant club playing street music, R&B and soul. A lot of posing from funkily dressed locals occurs before the dancing starts around midnight.

**Bamboo Lounge** BAR
(☎6 79 77 92 39; Makangal St, Down Beach; ⏲7pm–7am) Attractively screened with bamboo, this is an upbeat bar hosting DJ nights and live music nights. It serves beers, whiskies and spirits plus barbecued meat and fish dishes.

## Information

Limbe's Ahidjo St has several ATMs; try **Bicec** (Ahidjo St; ⏲8am-3.30pm Mon-Fri) or **SGBC** (Ahidjo St; ⏲8am-4pm Mon-Fri). You'll find the **police station** (opposite Botanic Gardens; ⏲24hr) at the western end of Limbe; the **post office** (Bota Rd; ⏲7.30am-4pm Mon-Sat) is out near the Botanical Gardens.

**Flora Travel & Tours** (☎2 33 33 35 82; www.floratraveltours.com; opposite Total Down-beach; ⏲8am-5pm Mon-Fri) can arrange local tours, hotels and trips up Mt Cameroon.

## Getting There & Away

The main motor park (bus station) is Mile 4, about 6km out of town; shared taxis leave from Douala Rd near the petrol station (around CFA500, 15 minutes). Minibuses and taxis-brousses leave approximately hourly to Buea (CFA800, 25 minutes) and Douala (CFA1500, 70 minutes). From Mile 2, take a bus heading to Yaoundé (CFA5000, five hours, 4-5 daily).

Ferries should travel every Monday and Thursday from Limbe to Calabar in Nigeria (1st/2nd class CFA35,000/45,000, four hours), departing at 2am and returning on Tuesday and Friday at 7am. At the time of writing though, the service was not operating due to problems with the boat. Take your own food and water if you make it on-board.

# Bamenda

POP 275,000

The capital of Northwest Province, Bamenda, is a dusty sprawl that tumbles down a hill at an altitude of more than 1000m. With plenty of traveller amenities, it's a good jumping-off point for exploring the Ring Road (p213) circuit. The colonial Upstation district is the cooler, more residential area of town, while downtown is frenetic and commercial. If you're coming from Douala, you'll see some impressive views of town as you descend the hill. Bamenda has also traditionally been a centre of political opposition to President Biya; rival party the Social Democratic Front (SDF) was founded here.

## Sleeping

**Baptist Mission Resthouse** GUESTHOUSE $
(☎2 75 45 83 39; Finance Junction; dm/s/d CFA4000/9000/13,000, apt CFA50,000; P 📶) This compound on the main road into Bamenda's centre has a bunch of well-maintained rooms, all fan cooled and with mosquito nets and hot water, though some are a little on the small side and rather mildewy. There's a communal kitchen and it's secure and welcoming.

**International Hotel** HOTEL $
(☎2 76 06 70 18; off Commercial Ave; s/d CFA16,000; ❄) Right in the middle of town and convenient for buses, this budget place charges extra for hot water and air-con. Rooms are modern, clean and have reasonable bathrooms as well as balconies

## Bamenda

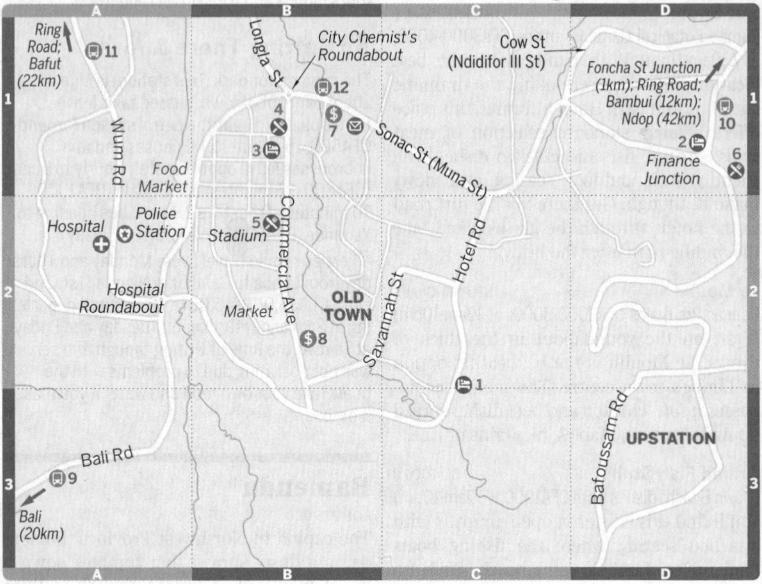

### Bamenda

**Sleeping**

1 Ayaba ... C2
2 Baptist Mission Resthouse ... D1
3 International Hotel ... B1

**Eating**

4 Dreamland Restaurant ... B1
5 Pres Cafe ... B2
6 Super Class Restaurant ... D1

**Information**

7 Express Exchange ... B1
8 SGBC Bank ... B2

**Transport**

9 Bali Motor Park ... A3
10 Nkwen Motor Park ... D1
11 Ntarikon Motor Park ... A1
12 Vatican Express ... B1

offering sweeping views over, er, 'scenic' Bamenda.

**Ayaba** HOTEL **$$**
(☎2 33 02 59 32; Rte N 6, just north of the Catholic University; r CFA30,000; ❄✈) A concrete government-run place in Bamenda with a bold exterior, now in need of renovation. But the restaurant is decent, the staff are friendly and the views from the terrace dramatic. There are tennis courts, too, if you need some exercise.

## Eating

**Dreamland Restaurant** AFRICAN **$**
(Commercial Ave; mains CFA1500-3500; ⌚7am-11pm) Bamenda's Dreamland doesn't look like much from the outside, but inside it's a well-set-out establishment with a large menu. There's a daily lunchtime buffet (CFA3500 per person) and a choice of grills, salads, fish and soups the rest of the time.

**Super Class Restaurant** AFRICAN **$**
(near Finance Junction; mains CFA3000; ⌚7.30am-8pm) This cute little shack in Nkwen Nkwen, Bamenda, with red tablecloths and friendly service, serves up simple Cameroonian fare such as fried chicken and plantains or meat grills with rice.

**Pres Cafe** CAFE **$**
(Commercial Ave, next to the British Council library) Bamenda's Pres Cafe offers rare finds in Cameroon: good local coffee including cappuccino, fresh salads, carrot cake and a wide range of natural juices. It's located by the excellent Fairtrade PresCraft gift shop which sells bronzes, baskets, carvings and jewellery at fixed prices.

## Information

**Express Exchange** (City Chemist's Roundabout; ⏲8am–4pm Mon–Fri) Changes travellers cheques as well as US dollars cash.

**Hospital** (Wum Rd; ⏲24hr) There's a centrally located hospital for medical emergencies.

**Police Station** (Wum Rd; ⏲24hr) Emergency police assistance.

**Post Office** (Sonac Street; ⏲8am–3.30pm Mon–Fri) Send your postcards from here.

**SGBC Bank** (Commercial Ave, Old Town; ⏲7.30–3pm Mon–Fri) ATM.

## Getting There & Away

Most agency offices with buses for destinations to the south are on Sonac St in Bamenda, or try **Vatican Express** (Muna St; ⏲6am-10pm). Destinations include Yaoundé (CFA5000, six hours, four to five daily), Douala (CFA4500, seven hours, four to five daily) and Bafoussam (CFA1500, 90 minutes, six daily). **Nkwen Motor Park** (south end of Nkwen Street; ⏲6am-10pm) has transport to the eastern stretch of the Ring Road, including Ndop (CFA1200, 90 minutes, three daily) and Kumbo (CFA3000, five hours, two to three daily). The west Ring Road is served by **Ntarikon Motor Park** (Wum Rd; ⏲6am-10pm), which runs minibuses to Wum (CFA3000, six hours). Bali and Mamfe transport departs from the **Bali Motor Park** (Bali Rd, 1km south of the centre; ⏲6am-10pm).

# The Ring Road

Cameroon's northwest highlands bear the pretty name 'Grassfields', an appellation too pleasant to really capture the look of this landscape. These aren't gentle fields; they're green and yellow valleys, tall grass, red earth and sharp mountains. Clouds of mist rise, with the wood smoke and dung smoke that mark the villages speckled on this deceptively inviting – but hard and rugged – terrain.

The 367km Ring Road runs a circle around the Grassfields, and if it were in better shape it'd be one of Cameroon's great scenic drives. As it is, get your butt ready for some bumpy, red-earth roads. The pay-off? Mountains dolloped with lakes, cattle loping into the hills and one of the greatest concentrations of fondoms (traditional kingdoms) in Cameroon.

It's worth considering, too, the more manageable small Ring Road route, linking Bamenda, Bafut, Wum, Weh, Fundong, Belo and Bambui. This will take one to two days.

## Sights

**Fon's Palace** PALACE

(Bafut; palace CFA1000, camera CFA1500, museum CFA2000; ⏲10am-4pm Mon-Sat) Just north of Bamenda is the large Tikar community of Bafut, traditionally the most powerful of the Grassfields kingdoms. The *fon*'s (local chief's) palace here is home to the representative of a 700-year-old dynasty and is a fascinating insight into Cameroon's traditional culture.

## Activities

Hiking, cycling and camping are all options for the Ring Road, but always ask the permission of the local chief, and bring some gifts (whisky is a good idea).

## Getting There & Away

Transport links along the Ring Road are extremely slow, crowded and irregular, with minibuses usually leaving very early in the morning. Roads are poor throughout. If you plan to drive this incredibly challenging road, hire a 4WD and don't even think about it in the rainy season.

It's essential to take travel advice in Bamenda before setting out.

# Bafoussam

POP 240,000

The Bamiléké stronghold of Bafoussam is haphazardly built on agriculture money and a refined sense of chaos. But despite its heavy traffic and uninspiring appearance, the town is friendly and has adequate amenities, and you'll have to pass through it on the way to more-enticing Foumban.

## Sleeping & Eating

**Hotel Altitel** HOTEL $$

(☎2 33 44 51 11; www.hotelaltitel.net; Route de Bamenda; d CFA23,000-33,000, ste CFA50,000; P❄📶) Despite the grim brutalist exterior, this is a clean and friendly choice with pleasant en-suite rooms and a good restaurant.

**Residence Sare** HOTEL $$

(☎2 33 44 25 99; Route de Bamenda; d CFA12,500-28,000; ❄📶) On the road towards Bamenda, this hotel is a solid midrange option, with accommodation in green rondavels in a pleasant garden.

**Boulangerie La Paix** BAKERY $

(Rte de Foumban; pastries from CFA150; ⏲8am-10pm) This bakery sells good bread and

### RING ROAD ROUTE

Starting from Bamenda and heading east, you pass Sabga Hill, which rises powerfully above Ndop, then Bamessing, with a handicraft centre and pottery workshop. After that you reach Kumbo, dominated by its Catholic cathedral and *fon*'s (traditional chief's) palace. It's a good place to base yourself, with a nice market. From there you go north to Nkambe and on to Missaje if the road permits.

The road from Missaje to We is just a dirt track and in the rainy season you won't find it; the bridges here are in an ongoing state of collapse. Some travellers continue on foot, sometimes with help from Fula herdsmen. It can take a couple of days to get to We, so bring supplies.

If you hike from Missaje to We, you'll pass Lake Nyos, a volcanic lake that was the site of a natural gas eruption in 1986, which resulted in around 1700 deaths. Continuing south you reach Wum, the biggest town on the west side of the Ring Road. South of Wum the road passes the Metchum Falls, where most shared-taxi drivers will stop to let you take a quick peek or photo.

The last town on the Ring Road (or the first, if you're heading clockwise) is Bafut, traditionally the strongest of the region's kingdoms. The Fon's Palace (p213) is a highlight of the Ring Road and includes a tour of the compound where the *fon*'s large family lives.



sticky sweet treats in the morning, and is a handy general food shop the rest of the day.

## Getting There & Away

Minibuses from Bafoussam to Foumban (CFA800 to CFA1000, one hour, three to four per day) depart from near Carrefour Total, along with shared taxis. Bus agents for Yaoundé (CFA2500 to CFA3000, three hours) and Douala (CFA4000, five hours) have offices along the main road south of the town centre. Transport to Bamenda (CFA1500, 1½ hours) leaves every couple of hours from the Bamenda road, north of the town centre (CFA150 in a shared taxi).

# Foumban

POP 92,000

Foumban has a deep tradition of home-grown arts and its traditional monarchy centred around a sultan, who resides in a palace. The town is plopped architecturally and conceptually between West and North Africa, as if the Sahel and its sharp music, bright robes and Islam – this is the city with most Muslims in the south – were slowly creeping into the eastern corner of Cameroon's West Province.

## Sights

The **Grand Marché** (8am-5pm Sat) is a warren of narrow stalls and alleys, which are great fun to explore; the paths eventually lead to where the **Grande Mosquée** faces the palace.

★**Palais Royal** PALACE
(Sultan's Palace; http://palaisdesroisbamoun.com/; Rue du Palais; admission CFA2000, camera CFA2000; 9am-6pm) The must-see attraction is the sultan's palace, home to the 19th sultan of the Bamoun dynasty. It has a fascinating, well-organised museum providing great historical insight into the region. At the time of writing, the treasures were being transferred to a startling new building symbolically shaped as a serpent and a spider; the palace itself will remain open to visitors.

Constructed in the early 20th century and modelled on German colonial architecture, the palace was built by the remarkable Sultan Njoya, who invented a corn-grinding machine, a script for the Bamun language, and a religion which fused Christianity and Islam. He had 681 wives, which made him well qualified to write his own version of the *Kama Sutra* (look out for it in the museum shop).

Museum artefacts include a ancient feathered cloak worn only for the initiation of each sultan, beaded buffalo masks sported by members of secret societies, documents written using Sultan Njoya's script and a drinking horn made from the skull of one of his enemies.

The palace sits opposite the market and main mosque, the minaret of which can be climbed as part of the palace tour. Palace entrance includes a visit to a nearby ceremonial drum housed in a bamboo hut: it's a huge creation topped with animal hides and carved with a double-headed serpent.

## Festivals & Events

**Nguon tribal festival** CULTURAL

(Dec, every 2 years) A biennial week-long harvest festival which dates back around 600 years; Bamoun culture is celebrated with dance and masquerades.

**Tabaski** RELIGIOUS

Every year at Tabaski, the Islamic holiday of Eid al-Adha, Foumban attracts thousands of pilgrims for an extraordinary blend of Muslim and traditional Bamoun ceremonies, with the sultan playing a key role, parading in his white Cadillac and on horseback. It culminates with horse racing through the town, drumming and dancing.

## Sleeping

**Hotel Complexe Adi** HOTEL $

(2 76 07 95 07; Rue de l'Hotel Beau Regarde; d CFA6000) Look for the giant voodoo statue of a man studded by nails to find Adi's entrance. While the rooms here are clean, they're smallish and very basic (just a bed and a small bathroom), and the bar downstairs gets pretty loud. If there are no rooms available here, try the similar Hotel Beau Regard across the road.

★**Hotel Pekassa de Karché** HOTEL $$

(2 33 26 29 35; hotelpekassadekarche@yahoo.fr; Rte de Bafoussam; s/d without air-con CFA10,000/15,000, d with air-con & balcony CFA25,000, ste CFA40,000; P ❄ @) This friendly hotel decorated with local crafts and fronted by bronze statues is by far the best choice in Foumban. Just 200m from the royal palace, it makes for a pleasant change from the norm in Cameroonian hotels, with smart, clean rooms, well-informed staff and good security. There's a decent on-site restaurant, too (mains CFA2500 to CFA4000).

## Eating

Bars, beer and grilled meat are abundant; Foumban's main street has several cafes, and the hotel restaurants are dependable.

**La Saveur** AFRICAN $

(2 99 95 00 69; main CFA1500) An easy-to-miss upstairs restaurant (near the market on the road to the Catholic mission) with blue-green walls, a mosaic tiled floor, plastic flowers on the tables and bargain food, including a selection of village cuisine: Senegalese rice, *ndole* and *njapche* (another type of green).

## Shopping

★**Village des Artisans** ARTS & CRAFTS

(Rue des Artisans; 10am-2.30pm) South of town, the Village des Artisans seems to produce more handicrafts than the rest of Cameroon combined. Get ready for some bargaining and banter – it's well worth it to explore the fine crafts from this wonderfully artistic region. Feathered hats and beaded staffs are among the collectable items.

## Information

**CPAC bank** (8am-5pm Mon-Fri), south of Foumban's market, may change euros if you're lucky, but it's best to change money in Bafoussam.

Don't wander Foumban at night, not least because of perilous pavements and lack of street lighting.

## Getting There & Away

There are a three to four direct daily buses from Foumban to Yaoundé (CFA3500, five hours) and Douala (CFA3500, six hours); otherwise head for Bafoussam (CFA800 to CFA1000, one hour, four daily) and change there. Bus-agency offices are on the west side of town, about 3km from the Grande Marché (CFA150 in a shared taxi).

Transport between Foumban and Kumbo (CFA3000, around six hours) runs year-round, with journey times varying according to the rains. Although the road is very, very poor, it's easily one of the most beautiful in the country, skirting along the edge of the spectacular Mbam Massif.

# Bandjoun

POP 25,000

The otherwise unremarkable country town of Bandjoun has a remarkable attraction in the form of a huge traditional *chefferie* (chief's compound), its pillars adorned with striking carvings by local artisans.

## Sights

★**Chefferie** HISTORIC BUILDING

(Chief's Compound; www.museumcam.org; just south of Bandjoun; CFA2000; 10am-5pm) Approached via a ceremonial gate, the compound is centred on a hugely impressive bamboo building, its conical thatched roof supported by wooden pillars carved with figures from secret societies, former chiefs, dancers, musicians and even the World Cup–winning Cameroon football team. The interior is out of bounds, but the visitor centre to the left offers an informative tour.

**Bandjoun Station** ARTS CENTRE
(☎6 93 53 79 50; http://bandjounstation.com; BP 52; ⊙10am-6pm) FREE Dramatically decorated with mosaics, this arts centre and workshop boldly announces itself. The centre supports the work of local contemporary artists.

## Sleeping & Eating

**Centre Climatique de Bandjoun** HOTEL $$
(☎2 33 44 67 50; Route National 4; r CFA25,000-35,000; ) This weirdly named country hotel is on the Bafoussam road, where rooms in tin-roofed huts offer TV and wi-fi. There's also a decent restaurant.

## Getting There & Away

Bandjoun is located 3km south of Bafoussam. Your best option for onward travel is to take a shared taxi to Bafoussam (CFA500, 20 minutes), which is a hub for buses.

# SOUTHERN CAMEROON

Southern Cameroon is largely taken up by thick jungle, and there are few large towns or other population centres. However, the coastline is by far Cameroon's best: head to Kribi for great scenery and a relaxed vibe, and continue further down the coast to indulge in a spot of beach exploration and eco-tourism in Parc National de Campo-Ma'an.

## Kribi

POP 64,000

Kribi is home to Cameroon's best beaches: the sand is fine, the water crystal clear, fresh fish is on the menu and cold beer on tap; there are times when Africa hugs you.

However, the biggest port in West Africa has just opened to the north of town, and it remains to be seen what impact this will have on the beaches and forested surroundings of the town.

### Sights

**Chutes de la Lobé** WATERFALL
(8km south of Kribi) The Chutes de la Lobé are an impressive set of waterfalls that empty directly into the sea – it's a beautiful sight. Take a *moto-taxi* (CFA500), or make a trip with Urbain Mandoua, who can arrange a lunch of sole, shrimps and plantains on the beach. The beach itself is idyllic, with log seats and hammocks under the trees.

### Tours

**Urbain Mandoua** OUTDOORS
(☎6 96 20 13 53; urbmand@yahoo.fr) Urbain organises trips in a motorised canoe up the rapidly flowing river from the Chutes de la Lobé to a Pygmy settlement, past a dense tangle of mangrove, bamboo and palms. Bear in mind that some of the Pygmies may not want to meet you, but you can view their huts, shrimp baskets and animal traps.

Wear long-sleeved shirts, trousers and closed shoes, and take mosquito repellent.

### Sleeping

**Hotel Panoramique** HOTEL $
(☎6 70 59 59 48; hotel panoramique@yahoo.fr; Rue du Marché; r CFA6000-15,000; ) This semi-sprawling compound feels like a down-at-heels villa evolved into a low-rent flophouse. Some rooms are good value, but at the cheapest end you're in an ugly annexe with the dust and roaches.

★**Indaba** GUESTHOUSE $$
(☎6 96 52 24 39; http://freeland-kribi.blogspot.co.uk; d CFA30,000-40,000) Indaba offers delightful *boukarous* in a lush garden with banana palms and ferns. There are also four (cheaper) rooms with mosquito nets in the guesthouse itself. There's no pool, but you're a stroll away from the beach. The owners will organise trips to the waterfall, fishing villages and national parks for you.

★**Hotel Ilomba** HOTEL $$
(☎6 99 91 29 23; www.hotelilomba.com; Rte de Campo; d CFA40,000, ste CFA130,000; ) South of Kribi, this is the loveliest and most relaxing hotel in the area. Rooms are in *boukarous*, all well furnished and tastefully decorated. It's also just a short walk to the Chutes de la Lobé and right on a beautiful stretch of beach. The restaurant serves shrimp cooked in coconut milk and other treats.

**Les Gîtes de Kribi** GUESTHOUSE $$
(☎6 75 08 08 45; www.kribiholidays.com; Rte de Campo; r CFA35,000, gîte CFA60,000; ) Ideal for families, the *gîtes* (self-contained

cottages) here are of varying sizes, but all are well equipped and have their own small kitchens. There are also normal rooms in the main building for those not *en famille*. Across the road, a charming beach restaurant serves up fresh fish in high season.

★ **Auberge du Phare** GUESTHOUSE $$$
(☎6 75 64 04 64; off Rte de Campo; d CFA50,000-110,000; P❄📶🏊) Located immediately south of Kribi, this great place has whitewashed terraced rooms splashed with bright colours opening onto the palm-edged pool and beach. Its seafront restaurant is excellent. Turn right on the beach and after 100m you'll see the eponymous 1904 *phare* (lighthouse).

## Eating

**Fish Market** SEAFOOD $
(meals from CFA1000; ⏲10am-5pm Wed & Sat) This market at Kribi's marina grills the day's catch over coals. From crab and lobster to massive barracuda, you'd be hard-pressed to find a better and tastier selection of seafood anywhere in Cameroon.

## ℹ Getting There & Away

Bus agencies have offices on Rue du Marché in the centre of Kribi. Nonagency transport leaves from the main *gare routière* (bus station). Buses for Douala (CFA1800 to CFA2000, three hours) leave throughout the day, along with transport to Campo (CFA2000, three hours) and Yaoundé (CFA3000, 3½ hours).

# Ebolowa

POP 74,000

Ebolowa, capital of Cameroon's Ntem district, is a bustling place built on cocoa wealth, and a possible stopping point en route between Yaoundé and Equatorial Guinea or Gabon. Its main attraction is the artificial Municipal Lake in the centre of town, where there's also a large market.

The basic **Hotel Âne Rouge** (☎2 22 28 34 38; Place Ans 2000; s/d CFA6000/10,000) has a few en-suite rooms with fans, and a pleasant terrace.

The **Florence Hotel** (☎2 22 28 44 04; www.florencehotelebolowa.com; BP 1097; d CFA50,000; P📶🏊) is not cheap and not hugely glamorous, but it is the best option in Ebolowa, and it has a generator to cope with the frequent electricity outages. There's a pool, and the restaurant is the best eating in town.

## ℹ Getting There & Away

During the dry season there's at least one vehicle daily along the rough road between Ebolowa and Kribi (CFA4000, four hours). There are also many buses daily to Yaoundé (CFA3000, three hours). Several vehicles depart in the morning for Ambam (CFA1000, one hour), from where you can find transport towards Ebebiyin (Equatorial Guinea) or Bitam (Gabon).

# Campo

POP 10,000

Taking the road to here from Kribi is half Campo's attraction – it's a hard but rewarding slog through immense rainforest, past Pygmy villages, and with views out to the ocean and fire-spouting petrol platforms shimmering in the west.

For travellers, Campo mainly serves as a jumping-off point for visiting wildlife-rich Parc National de Campo Ma'an, as well as the sea-turtle conservation project in nearby Ebodjé.

Campo is the last Cameroonian town before the Equatorial Guinea border (which theoretically is open, though in practice even with a visa you're unlikely to be allowed to enter EG).

**Parc National de Campo-Ma'an** (CFA5000, vehicle CFA2000, local guide CFA10,000) comprises 7700 sq km of protected biodiverse rainforest, sheltering many wonderful plants and animals, including buffaloes, forest elephants, leopards, gorillas and mandrills. The park is being developed by World Wildlife Fund (WWF) as an ecotourism destination, with canopy walks and river trips available. Because of the difficulty of spotting shy forest animals it's much better to visit with a guide.

Pay your park fee and book a guide at the park HQ in Campo, and aim to get to the park as early as possible.

**Auberge Bon Course** (☎2 74 51 18 83; Campo; CFA5000) is scruffy accommodation with simple meals and very friendly faces – it's found at the Bon Course Supermarché at the main junction in Campo.

## ℹ Getting There & Away

There are daily minibuses between Campo and Kribi (CFA1500, three hours), which also stop at Ebodjé (45 minutes). *Moto-taxis* to Campo Beach (for Equatorial Guinea) cost CFA500 and take 20 minutes. Taxis to Ebodjé (45 minutes) cost CFA500.

## Ebodjé

POP 30,000

Ebodjé, a small fishing village 25km north of Campo, is worth a trip to see the sea-turtle conservation project and eco-tourism site.

**KUDU Cameroun** (☎2 96 22 08 29; per person CFA12,000) offers fantastic turtle walks, where visitors are taken out at night to spot egg-laying turtles. There's no guarantee you'll see any, though some groups see as many as six. Even if you don't see any turtles, the beach is gorgeous, pristine and better than anything in Kribi.

The total fee includes accommodation in a local home, village development fee, meal and tour. A proportion of fees helps locals, many of whom have been trained as guides. For between CFA8000 and CFA115,000 you can arrange local river trips and cultural evenings.

Remember to bring your own water or filter, mosquito net and sleeping sheets as well as good walking shoes.

Taxis between Campo and Ebodjé (45 minutes) cost CFA500.

# EASTERN CAMEROON

Cameroon's remote east is wild and untamed. Populated by Baka people but seldom visited by travellers, it's very much a destination for those with plenty of time and the stamina to back up an appetite for adventure. There's little infrastructure and travel throughout is slow and rugged, with dense green forest and red-laterite earth roads. The rainforest national parks are the main attraction, along with routes into the Central African Republic and Congo.

## Bertoua

POP 218,000

The capital of East Province, administrative hub Bertoua is also a genuine boom town, born of logging and gold-mining. It hasn't got much to excite visitors, but you will find all the facilities lacking elsewhere in the region, including banks and sealed roads. The town has lost its role as a stopping-off spot en route to the Central African Republic because of instability there, but you may just wind up here, at the transition point between Cameroon's forest and grasslands.

### Sleeping

**Hotel Mansa** HOTEL **$$**

(☎2 22 03 92 00; D 30, 1km north of Bertoua; CFA25,000-37,500; P ❄ ☒) Bertoua's best hotel comes complete with an artificial lake, satellite TV and a tennis court. It's definitely worth a splurge if you've been lost in the forest.

### Getting There & Away

Buses to Yaoundé (CFA5000, seven hours, two to three daily), Bélabo (for the train; CFA1000, one hour, four daily) and Garoua-Boulaï (CFA400, four hours, four daily), leave from the *gare routière* near the market.

# UNDERSTAND CAMEROON

## Cameroon Today

Having re-elected presidential strongman Paul Biya in a contentious yet, broadly speaking, free election in 2011, Cameroon has gained a reputation as a relatively stable country. Biya's current seven-year term ends in 2018, with growing pressure on him to stand aside and end his 35-year (and counting) rule. Meanwhile, in the beleaguered north of the country, Cameroonian villagers are struggling to host huge numbers of Nigerian refugees on the run from the Boko Haram insurgency.

For most people though, corruption remains Cameroon's major issue. Paying bribes can be the only way to open a business or access government services and school places. The international anticorruption organisation, Transparency International, consistently ranks Cameroon among the world's most corrupt countries. Until this issue is addressed and genuine political openness permitted, Cameroon will inevitably continue to limp along.

The most spoken-about person in the country is first lady Chantal Biya, who has taken on the mantle of an African Princess Diana. Her love of haute couture, spectacular 'banana' hairdos and high-profile charity work mean she is a staple in the national press.

## History

Parts of what is now Cameroon were divided and ceded between European countries throughout the colonial era until the modern boundaries were established in 1961, creating a part-Anglophone but majority Francophone nation.

## Colonialism to Independence

Portuguese explorers first sailed up the Wouri River in 1472, and named it Rio dos Camarões (River of Prawns). Soon after, Fula pastoral nomads from what is now Nigeria began to migrate overland from the north, forcing the indigenous forest peoples southwards. The Fula migration took on added urgency in the early 17th century as they fled Dutch, Portuguese and British slave traders.

British influence was curtailed in 1884 when Germany signed a treaty with the chiefdoms of Douala and central Bamiléké Plateau. After WWI the German protectorate of Kamerun was carved up between France and Great Britain.

Local revolts in French-controlled Cameroon in the 1950s were suppressed, but the pan-African momentum for throwing off the shackles of colonial rule soon took hold. Self-government was granted in French Cameroon in 1958, quickly followed by independence on 1 January 1960.

## Uniting Cameroon

Ahmadou Ahidjo, leader of one of the independence parties, became president of newly independent French Cameroon, a position he was to hold until his resignation in 1982. Ahidjo ensured his longevity through the cultivation of expedient alliances, brutal repression and wily regional favouritism.

In October 1961 a UN-sponsored referendum in British-mandated northwestern Cameroon split the country in two, with the area around Bamenda opting to join the federal state of Cameroon and the remainder joining Nigeria. In June 1972, the federal structure of two Cameroons (previously French and British) was replaced by the centralised United Republic of Cameroon – a move that is resented to this day by Anglophone Cameroonians, who feel that, as the minority, they have become second-class citizens.

## The Biya Era

In 1982 Ahidjo's hand-picked successor, Paul Biya, distanced himself from his former mentor, but adopted many of Ahidjo's repressive measures, clamping down hard on calls for multiparty democracy. Diversions such as the national football team's stunning performance in the 1990 FIFA World Cup bought him time, but Biya was forced eventually to legalise 25 opposition parties. The first multiparty elections in 25 years were held in 1992 and saw the Cameroonian Democratic People's Movement, led by Biya, hang on to power with the support



### THE BAKA PEOPLE OF SOUTHEAST CAMEROON

With few roads, dense forest and sparse settlements, the southeast of Cameroon is hard for visitors to access. But the area is not empty of human life: it is home to the Baka people, popularly known as Pygmies. These hunter-gatherers maintain a traditional lifestyle in their forest environment, and are notably small, growing to be no taller than 150cm (4ft 11in).

The population of Baka people in the region is hard to estimate, but it is thought to be up to 30,000. The Baka are accomplished hunters, moving with quiet agility through the forest to fell animals such as elephants and antelope with their crossbows and spears. They also collect honey; women fish using wicker baskets, and also gather wild fruit, insects and roots. Baka traditionally wear loin cloths made from beaten bark, and use plant-life to create medicine and poison arrows.

The Baka are semi-nomadic, leaving their rounded leaf-and-branch huts in order to hunt in bands of 20 to 100. They worship spirits of the forest, evoking them in masquerade and dance. Their polyphonic song is akin to yodelling, using sounds rather than words, and women 'drum' river water, slapping it in syncopated rhythms.

Threats to the Baka include the armed poachers involved in the illegal wildlife trade, mining, logging and the transformation of forest into farmland. Their territories are being encroached on, and the way of life is consequently being eroded. You can visit Baka in Cameroon on small-scale tours, though these may well you leave you wondering what the benefit is to you or them.

### WILDLIFE IN SOUTHEAST CAMEROON

With some perseverance it may be possible to visit Cameroon's southeast to explore the wonderful forest wildlife: Lobéké National Park near the (currently unstable) Central African Republic border can be reached either in a 4WD via Bertoua or by chartered plane. The park is rich in animal life, including chimps, forest elephants, red forest buffaloes, leopards and lowland gorillas, plus 215 types of butterflies and more than 300 bird species.

of minority parties. International observers alleged widespread vote-rigging and intimidation; such allegations were repeated in elections in 1999, 2004 and, most recently, in 2011. The next election is set for 2018, amid suppressed dissatisfaction with Biya's long reign.



## Culture

It's hard to pigeonhole more than 250 distinct ethnolinguistic groups divided by colonial languages, Christianity and Islam and an urban-rural split into one identity. The Cameroonian psyche is, ultimately, anything and everything African – diversity is the key.

There's a distinct cultural and political gap between the Francophone and Anglophone parts of Cameroon, albeit one felt predominantly by the Anglophone minority, who complain of discrimination in the workplace and in education (two of the country's eight universities lecture in French only).

A few characteristics do seem shared across Cameroon's divides. Traditional social structures dominate life. Local chiefs (known as *fon* in the west or *lamido* in the north) wield considerable influence; when you are travelling in places that don't receive many tourists, it's polite to announce your presence to them.

Many Cameroonians demonstrate a half-laconic, half-angry sense of frustration with the way their country is run. They are aware that while Cameroon is doing well compared with its neighbours, it could be immeasurably better off if corruption didn't curtail so much potential. Mixed in with this frustration is a resignation ('such is life'), expressed as serenity in good times but simmering rage in bad times.

Meanwhile, the arrival of Chinese immigrants in great numbers – especially in Yaoundé and Douala – is bringing a dash of multiculturalism to this already incredibly multi-ethnic society.

## Arts

Cameroon has produced a few of the region's most celebrated artists: in literature, Mongo Beti deals with the legacies of colonialism; musically, jazz-funk saxophonist Manu Dibango is the country's brightest star.

Woodcarving makes up a significant proportion of traditional arts and crafts. The northwestern highlands are known for their carved masks. These are often representations of animals, and it's believed that the wearers of the masks can transform themselves and take on the animal's characteristics and powers. Cameroon also has some highly detailed bronze- and brasswork, particularly in Tikar areas north and east of Foumban. The areas around Bali and Bamessing (both near Bamenda), and Foumban, are rich in high-quality clay, and some of Cameroon's finest ceramic work originates here, as well as intricate beadwork.

## Sport

Cameroon exploded onto the world's sporting consciousness at the 1990 FIFA World Cup when the national football team, the Indomitable Lions, became the first African side to reach the quarter finals. Football is truly the national obsession. Every other Cameroonian male seems to own a copy of the team's strip; go into any bar and there'll be a match playing on the TV. The country has qualified for the World Cup seven times, amid wild celebrations, and has been garlanded with five Africa Cup of Nations titles, most recently in 2017.

## Food & Drink

Cameroonian cuisine is straightforward and satisfying. The staple dish is some variety of peppery sauce served with starch – usually rice, pasta or *fufu* (mashed yam, corn, plantain or couscous). One of the most popular sauces is *ndole,* made with bitter leaves similar to spinach and flavoured with smoked fish. Grilled meat and fish are eaten in huge quantities, and huge fresh *gambas* (prawns) are a particular delight.

## Environment

Cameroon is geographically diverse. The south is a low-lying coastal plain covered by swaths of equatorial rainforest extending east towards the Congo Basin. Heading north, the sparsely populated Adamawa Plateau divides the country in two. To the plateau's north, the country begins to dry out into a rolling landscape dotted with rocky escarpments that are fringed to the west by the barren Mandara Mountains. That range represents the northern extent of a volcanic chain, now a natural border with Nigeria down to the Atlantic coast, often punctuated by stunning crater lakes. One active volcano remains in Mt Cameroon, at 4095m the highest peak in West Africa.

There is a range of wildlife found in Cameroon, although more exotic species are in remote areas. Elephants stomp and crocodiles glide through the southern and eastern jungles. Of note are several rare primate species, including the Cross River gorilla, mainland drill monkey, chimpanzees and Preuss's red colobus.

Bushmeat (from African wild animals) has traditionally been big business in Cameroon. While there have been crackdowns on the trade both here and abroad (African expats are some of its main consumers), it has not been entirely stamped out.

# SURVIVAL GUIDE

## Directory A–Z

### ACCOMMODATION

Cameroon has a reasonable range of accommodation options, from simple *auberges* (hostels) and dorm beds in religious missions to luxury hotels. Expect to pay around CFA15,000 for a decent single room with bathroom and fan. Most hotels quote prices per room – genuine single and twin rooms are the exception rather than the norm. Rather than seasonal rates, most hotels in Kribi and Limbe generally charge more during holidays and weekends.

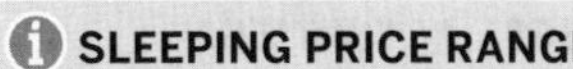

**SLEEPING PRICE RANGES**

**$** less than CFA30,000

**$$** CFA30,000–90,000

**$$$** over CFA90,000

### ACTIVITIES

Hiking is a big drawcard in Cameroon. The two most popular hiking regions are Mt Cameroon (near the coast) and the Mandara Mountains (in the north), the latter currently out of bounds for security reasons. The Ring Road near Bamenda also offers great hiking possibilities, but you'll need to be self-sufficient here.

### CHILDREN

Children will undoubtedly be welcomed with open arms in Cameroon, though you will not find baby-change facilities, and pushing prams on the busted pavements is likely to be a challenge. You often see Cameroonian children on buses, but bear in mind that these are crowded, often hot, and loo breaks are few and far between.

**Limbe Wildlife Centre** (p209) Get your little ones up close to drill monkeys and other primates, saved from the bushmeat trade.

**Mefou National Park** (p200) More appealing rescued primates, including gorillas.

**Kribi's beaches** (p216) Sun, sea and sand on the southwest coast of the country.

### DANGERS & ANNOYANCES

- Douala and Yaoundé both have reputations for petty crime, especially in the crowded central areas.
- Scams and official corruption are a way of life in Cameroon; keep your guard up and maintain a sense of humour.
- It's theoretically a legal requirement to carry your passport with you at all times. In practice, the police rarely target travellers.
- Roads pose a risk, with plenty of badly maintained vehicles driven at punishing speeds.
- The north of Cameroon is out of bounds following Boko Haram's insurgency; check your government's travel advisory for up-to-date information.

### EMBASSIES & CONSULATES

A number of embassies and consulates are located in Yaoundé. Australians and New Zealanders should contact the Canadian High Commission in case of an emergency.

**EATING PRICE RANGES**

An average main-course dish at a restaurant in Cameroon

**$** under CFA5,000

**$$** CFA5,000–10,000

**$$$** over CFA10,000

### BEST ACTIVITIES

**Mt Cameroon** (p208) From hilltop Buea take the three-day hike up this imposing volcano.

**Parc National de Campo-Ma'an** (p217) Enjoy canopy walks and river trips.

**Chutes de la Lobé** (p216) Take the plunge where these wide waterfalls join the sea.

**British High Commission** (Map p202; ☎2 22 22 07 96; bhc.yaounde@fco.gov.uk; Ave Churchill; ⏱8am-4pm Mon-Fri)

**Canadian Embassy** (☎2 22 50 39 00; Les Colonnades Building, New Bastos; ⏱8.30am-2pm Mon-Fri)

**Central African Republic Embassy** (Map p202; ☎2 22 20 51 55; Rue 1863, Bastos; ⏱8.30am-3pm Mon-Fri)

**Chadian Embassy** (Map p202; ☎2 22 60 88 24; Rue Joseph Mballa Eloumden, Bastos; ⏱8am-2pm Mon-Fri)

**Congolese Embassy** (Map p202; ☎2 22 20 51 03; Blvd de l'URSS, Bld 1782, Bastos; ⏱8.30pm-3pm Mon-Fri)

**Equatorial Guinean Embassy** (Map p202; ☎2 22 21 08 04; Rue 1805, Bastos; ⏱9pm-3pm Mon-Fri)

**French Embassy** (☎2 22 22 79 00; Rue Joseph Atemengué, near Pl de la Réunification; ⏱8.30am-4pm Mon-Fri)

**Gabonese Embassy** (Map p202; ☎2 22 20 29 66; Rue 1816, Bastos; ⏱8am-4pm Mon-Fri)

**German Consulate** (Map p202; ☎6 90 69 63 62; Ave Charles de Gaulle, Centre Ville; ⏱8.30am-2pm Mon-Fri)

**Nigerian Embassy** (Map p202; ☎2 22 21 35 09; Rue Joseph Mballa Eloumden, Bastos; ⏱8.30am-3pm Mon-Fri)

**US Embassy** (Map p204; ☎2 22 20 15 00; Ave Rosa Parks, Centre Ville; ⏱7.30am–5pm Mon-Thu, 7.30am-12.30pm Fri)

## EMERGENCY & IMPORTANT NUMBERS

Emergency facilities are severely limited in Cameroon, and these numbers really only apply in big cities. In rural areas, you have to rely on local help.

| | |
|---|---|
| Cameroon's country code | ☎237 |
| Fire | ☎112 |
| Medical assistance | ☎112 |
| Police | ☎112 |

## INTERNET ACCESS

Internet access can be found in any Cameroonian town of a reasonable size. Connections range from OK to awful, and costs average CFA300 to CFA600 per hour. Fancy hotels are the best bet.

## LGBTIQ TRAVELLERS

Homosexuality is illegal in Cameroon and prosecutions have taken place. Sadly it is inadvisable for gay couples to openly express their sexuality.

## MONEY

The currency is the Central African franc (CFA), pegged to both the West African franc and the euro (at an unchanging rate of CFA655.957). Cash is king, especially in remote regions – bring plenty of euros or US dollars.

## ATMs

All Cameroonian towns now have ATMs, tied to the Visa network. It's a good idea to withdraw money during bank hours, as cards can become stuck in the machines and need to be extracted. Banks won't generally offer cash advances on credit cards. Western Union has branches throughout Cameroon for international money transfers.

Banks regularly refuse to change travellers cheques, and charge around 5% commission when they do.

### Changing Money

Moneychangers on the street in Douala and Yaoundé will change money at good rates and without taxes or commission, but there's always an element of risk to such transactions. Express Exchange moneychangers change US dollars as cash; there are branches in many towns across the country.

### Exchange Rates

| | | |
|---|---|---|
| Australia | A$1 | CFA452 |
| Canada | C$1 | CFA440 |
| Europe | €1 | CFA656 |
| Japan | ¥100 | CFA538 |
| New Zealand | NZ$1 | CFA415 |
| UK | UK£1 | CFA774 |
| US | US$1 | CFA600 |

For current exchange rates, see www.xe.com

### Tipping

**Hotels** Tip CFA1000 or so for help with bags.

**Restaurants** For decent service, 10% is customary.

**Taxis** Tips are not expected, but add one for good service.

## OPENING HOURS

**Banks** From 7.30am or 8am to 3.30pm Monday to Friday.

**Businesses** From 7.30am or 8am until 6pm or 6.30pm Monday to Friday, generally with a one- to two-hour break sometime between noon and 3pm. Most are also open from 8am to 1pm (sometimes later) on Saturday.

**Government offices** From 7.30am to 3.30pm Monday to Friday.

## POST

International post is fairly reliable for letters, but international couriers should be preferred for packages – there are branches in all large towns.

## PUBLIC HOLIDAYS

**New Year's Day** 1 January
**Youth Day** 11 February
**Easter** March/April
**Labour Day** 1 May
**National Day** 20 May
**Assumption Day** 15 August
**Christmas Day** 25 December

Islamic holidays are also observed throughout Cameroon; dates change yearly for these.

## TELEPHONE

Cameroon's country code is ☎237. For international calls out, dial ☎00 then the relevant country code.

All Cameroonian telephone numbers have nine digits. Mobile numbers begin with 7, 8 or 9. There are no city area codes in Cameroon – all landline numbers begin with a 2 or 3.

### Mobile Phones

It's easy to buy a SIM card for an unlocked mobile phone to make local calls while in Cameroon. MTN and Orange are the main national networks.

## TOURIST INFORMATION

Formal tourist information is not readily available in Cameroon, though there are some useful small independent agencies and cooperatives which we've listed in the relevant location.

## VISAS

Applications in Europe and the US will require a confirmed flight ticket, a letter of invitation authorised by the Cameroonian police, yellow-fever vaccination certificate and proof of funds (minimum £1000/US$1250). A standard visa is valid for three months.

### Visa Extensions

You can obtain visa extensions at Cameroon's **Ministry of Immigration** (Map p204; ☎2 22 22 24 13; Ave Mdug-Fouda Ada; ⏲8am-4pm Mon-Fri) in Yaoundé, where one photo plus CFA15,000 is required.

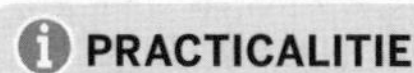

## PRACTICALITIES

**Electricity** Cameroon's electricity supply is 220V and plugs are mostly of the European two-round-pin variety. You'll find a few three-pin sockets in English-speaking areas.

**Newspapers** The *Cameroon Tribune* is the government-owned bilingual paper, which appears daily in French and weekly in English. The weekly bilingual *Le Messager* is the main independent newspaper.

**Radio** Most broadcast programming is government run and in French, through Cameroon Radio-TV Corporation (CRTV). TVs at top-end hotels often have CNN or French news stations.

**Weights & measures** Cameroon uses the metric system.

### Visas for Onward Travel

Visas available in Yaoundé for neighbouring African countries include the following:

**Central African Republic** A one-month visa costs FA55,000 and takes 48 hours to process.

**Congo** A 15-day visa costs CFA50,000, three months costs CFA100,000. A local invitation is required and processing takes 48 hours.

**Equatorial Guinea** Does not generally issue visas to nonresidents or people with an Equatorial Guinean embassy in their home country.

**Gabon** A one-month visa costs CFA50,000; unlike at many Gabonese embassies, a hotel reservation is not required at the Cameroonian office.

**Nigeria** In Yaoundé, a one-month visa costs CFA45,000 to CFA60,000 and takes 48 hours to process, and you'll need a local invitation.

# Getting There & Away

## AIR

The national carrier of Cameroon is Camair-Co (p203), which flies to Libreville (Gabon), N'Djaména (Chad), Brazzaville (Congo), Lagos (Nigeria), Abidjan (Ivory Coast), Cotonou (Benin), Kinshasa (DRC) and Paris.

### Airports & Airlines

Both Yaoundé (p203) and Douala (p208) have international airports linking Cameroon to major cities in Africa and Europe.

Both are served by Camair-Co for internal and regional African flights, and by Air France.

### ARRIVING IN CAMEROON

**Douala International Airport** (p208) Take a licensed taxi to your accommodation. They will be waiting to meet incoming flights but are unmetered, so ask the fee before getting in (around CFA4000, 30 minutes).

**Yaoundé Nsimalen International Airport** (p203) Take a licensed taxi to the centre (around CFA5000, 40 minutes).

#### LAND

Cameroon's borders with neighbouring countries are open, but the border with Congo is sometimes closed, so check in advance. While the border with Equatorial Guinea is theoretically open, in practice you're likely to be refused entry at the land border, even with a visa.

It is not currently safe to travel from Cameroon to Central African Republic or Chad.

#### Equatorial Guinea

The main border crossings into Equatorial Guinea and Gabon are a few kilometres from each other, and are both accessible from Ambam in Cameroon. The road splits here, with the westerly route heading for Ebebiyin and Bata (Equatorial Guinea).

The Cameroon–Equatorial Guinea border at Campo is normally closed.

#### Nigeria

The main crossing point is Ekok, west of Mamfe, where you access Mfum for shared taxis to Calabar (treacherous in the rainy season). The crossing at Banki in the extreme north is inadvisable due to security issues.

#### SEA

A twice-weekly ferry sails from Limbe (Cameroon) to Calabar (Nigeria) on Monday and Thursday, and in the opposite direction every Tuesday and Friday. Boats are dangerous and not recommended; indeed at the time of writing the service wasn't functioning.

## Getting Around

#### AIR

Internal flights in Cameroon are operated by Camair-Co (p203) and connect Douala and Yaoundé to Maroua and Garoua. The hop between Yaoundé and Douala (45 minutes) costs around CFA45,000 one way.

The north and east of Cameroon were inaccessible due to security issues at time of writing, but when operational flights from Douala or Yaoundé to Maroua or Garoua (around 1½ hours) cost around CFA125,000 one way.

#### BUS

*Agences de voyages* (agency buses, running from depots also called *agences*) run along all major and many minor routes in Cameroon. Prices are low and fixed, and on some bus lines you can even reserve a seat. From Yaoundé to Douala it costs anywhere between CFA3000 and CFA6000, depending on the class of bus you take: so-called VIP services have air-conditioning and aren't quite so cramped. However, some drivers are extremely reckless, and bus accidents occur all too frequently.

Taxis-brousses (bush taxis, which are shared private vehicles) are also popular, especially to some more remote destinations.

Note that, while they might be called *agences*, *gares routières* (bus stations) and sometimes motor parks, these are really glorified car parks for buses, that operate all day and far into the night.

#### CAR & MOTORCYCLE

Driving in Cameroon is feasible, with mainly decent roads and little police harassment, though the driving all around you is hair-raising. You can hire cars in all large towns, but there's more choice in Douala and Yaoundé. Car hire is very expensive, however, partly because you'll need a 4WD for most itineraries: this becomes essential in the rainy season. In Douala, try Avis in the Hotel Akwa Palace (p206).

A better option is to hire a car and an experienced local driver, who can negotiate road blocks and potholes on your behalf. Ask at your hotel for suggestions, and expect to pay around CFA100,000 for a full day, including petrol.

#### TRAIN

Cameroon's rail system (Camrail) operates three main lines: Yaoundé to N'Gaoundéré; Yaoundé to Douala; and Douala to Kumba. In 2016 a tragic derailment between Douala and Yaoundé killed 70 passengers and injured many more. Check locally about the current state of train safety.

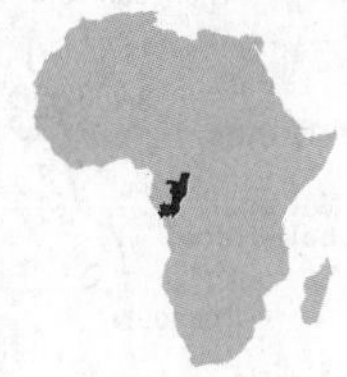

# Republic of Congo

☎242 / POP 4.2 MILLION

**Includes ➡**



## Best Places to Eat

- ➡ Il Pepe Nero (p232)
- ➡ Mami Wata (p227)
- ➡ Restaurant le Nzalangoye (p234)
- ➡ Kactus Restaurant (p232)
- ➡ Nénuphar (p234)

## Best Places to Sleep

- ➡ Ngaga Camp (p233)
- ➡ Malonda Lodge (p232)
- ➡ Mboko Camp (p233)
- ➡ Hotel Hippocampe (p227)
- ➡ Hotel Onanga (p234)

## Why Go?

A land of steamy jungles hiding half the world's lowland gorillas, masses of forest elephants, and hooting, swinging troops of chimpanzees, the Republic of Congo is on the cusp of becoming one of the finest ecotourism destinations in Africa. Boasting three excellent and little-visited national parks where everything from luxurious safaris to bush camping is possible, the main attraction to this alluring slice of West Africa is the raw, untrammelled call of nature. However, Congo-Brazzaville (as it's often called to distinguish it from Democratic Republic of Congo, south of the Congo River) also enjoys a pleasantly laid-back capital city in Brazzaville, some decent beaches on its Atlantic coastline and the warm and welcoming Congolese culture. For those ready to heed the call of the wild – and are not afraid of adventure – the Congo awaits.

## When to Go

### Brazzaville

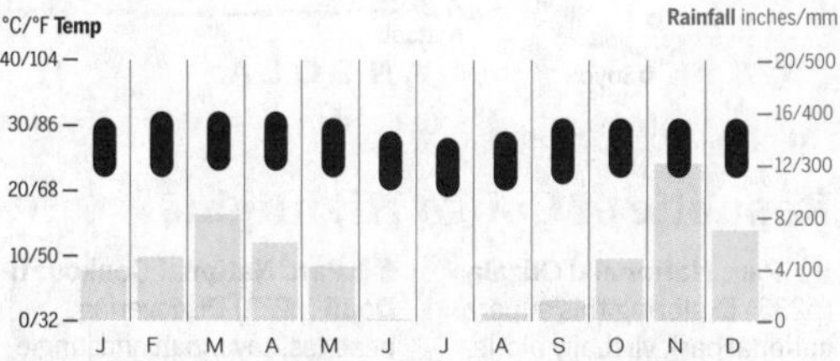


**Jun–Dec** The best overall time to travel in Congo.

**Oct–Jan** The easiest time to see wildlife in the northern forest parks.

**Dec–Feb** Sea turtles nest on beaches of Parc National Conkouati-Douli.

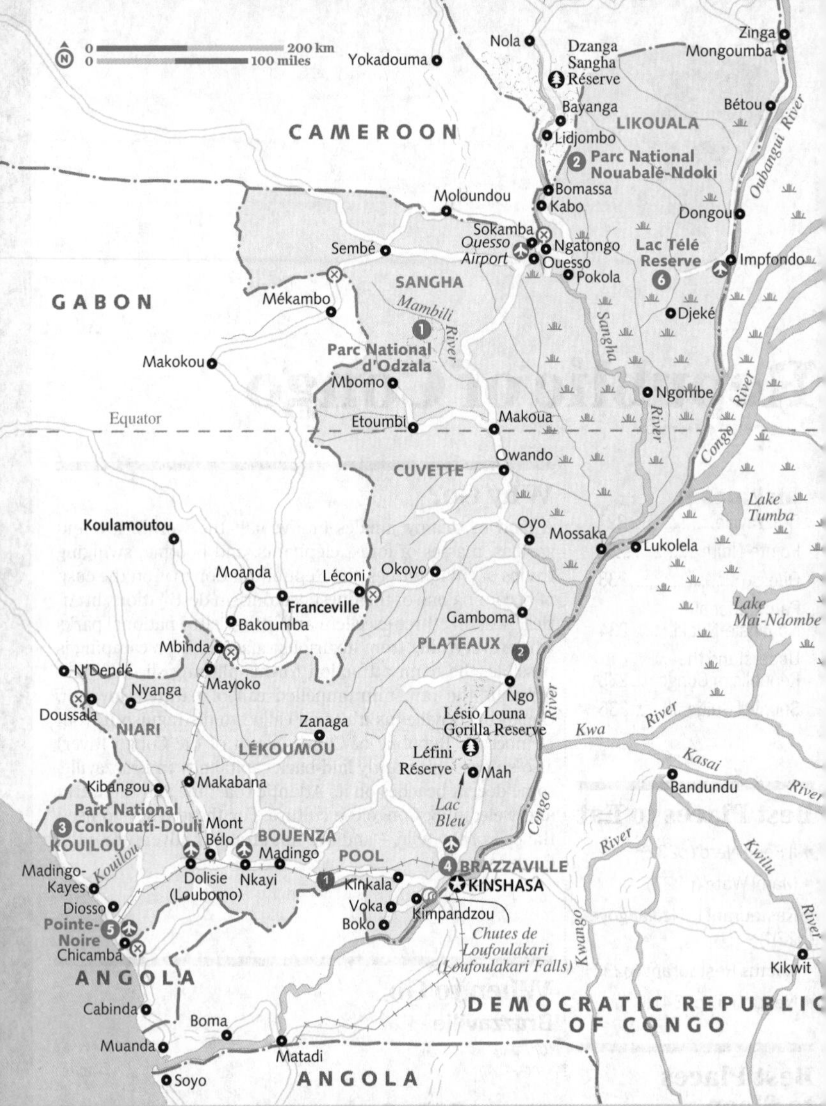


## Republic of Congo Highlights

❶ **Parc National d'Odzala** (p233) Exploring this superb national park virtually alone, with just lowland gorillas, chimpanzees and forest elephants for company.

❷ **Parc National Nouabalé-Ndoki** (p234) Visiting one of Africa's last great wildernesses: an unforgettable experience.

❸ **Parc National Conkouati-Douli** (p231) Discovering beaches, savannah and jungle in this impressively wild national park.

❹ **Brazzaville** (p227) Enjoying this big city's small-town feel on the Congo River and some interesting modernist architecture.

❺ **Pointe-Noire** (p231) Ordering top-notch seafood on the Congolese 'Riviera', then heading to the beach and seeing the lovely gorges in nearby Diosso.

❻ **Lac Télé Reserve** (p235) Getting truly off the beaten path by undertaking a serious expedition to this remote lake.

# BRAZZAVILLE

POP 1.83 MILLION

Founded by Italo-French explorer Pierre Savorgnan de Brazza in 1880 on the Stanley Pool area of the Congo River, 'Brazza' has always been the junior economic partner to Kinshasa (the DRC's capital) which faces it across the immense river. Brazzaville is by far the more laid-back (and safer) town, though it can also feel like a bit of a backwater by comparison.

However, with some attractive modernist architecture, a gorgeous riverside embankment perfect for taking in views of the Congo River and plenty of high-quality eating options, Brazzaville has a lot of charm and character, which makes it a surprisingly pleasant place to while away time between visiting Congo's national parks.

## Sights

**La Corniche** VIEWPOINT

This wonderful modernised embankment is a great place for a stroll, and affords fantastic views over the Congo River to Kinshasa, looming in the distance. La Corniche ends at the massive Pont du 15 août 1960, a brand-new, Chinese-built, cable-stayed bridge connecting central Brazzaville to the presidential palace. The bridge is spectacularly lit up at night.

**Les Rapides** VIEWPOINT

These wide and powerful rapids on the Congo River can be viewed on the outskirts of Brazzaville. Most people observe the rapids from the nearby bar **Site Touristique Les Rapides** (7am-10pm), but the best viewing is at the other end, down the sandy track after the bridge. A taxi from the city centre costs CFA2000, or you can take a minibus to Pont Djoué from next to **Institut Français du Congo** (053929176; www.institutfrancais-congo.com; Rond-Point CCF; 9am-6pm Mon-Sat).

## Sleeping

**SIL Congo** HOTEL $

(055218054; Ave Cardinal Emile Biayenda (Ave Foch); r/apt from CFA12,000/24,000; ) Rooms at this Christian missionary centre are often booked up by long-term renters, but if you can get one, the spacious, clean rooms (some of which have hot-water bathrooms) are some of the best value in the city. There's a 10pm curfew.

★ **Hotel Hippocampe** HOTEL $$

(066686068; www.hippocampebrazza.asia; Rue Behangle; r CFA28,000-38,000; ) Congo's number one travellers' meeting point has clean and comfortable rooms (though try to avoid the smaller, noisier road-facing rooms). Overlanders are welcome to camp for free. The friendly French-Vietnamese owners maintain a really useful travellers' notebook full of tips for onward travel and the location is central and secure. Wi-fi is charged (500MB costs CFA5000).

**Mikhael's Hotel** HOTEL $$$

(053666660; www.mikhaelshotel.com; Ave Nelson Mandela; s/d CFA130,000/140,000; ) Perhaps Brazzaville's most atmospheric top-end property, Mikhael's lobby is decked out in marble and there's local art, sculpture and carvings throughout the hotel. Rooms are sleek, spacious and modern, and there's a good gym, large pool and grand bar. The location is excellent and staff are extremely helpful.

**Radisson Blu M'bamou Palace Hotel** BUSINESS HOTEL $$$

(050506060; www.radissonblu.com/en/hotel-brazzaville; Ave Cabral; r from CFA180,000, ste incl breakfast from CFA260,000; ) Despite its architectural unpleasantness, Brazzaville's only international-standard hotel has a superb location in the centre of town overlooking the Congo River. Sadly the views are not made much of, but otherwise it's a one-stop shop for business travellers, who will appreciate the excellent service, high security, plush (if bland) rooms, gym and pool.

## Eating

**Mian Mian Ju Dao** CHINESE $

(Ave Cabral; mains CFA2000-6000; 8am-5pm) This cheap and cheerful Chinese noodle place in the centre of Brazzaville is a great place for a good-value meal. We recommend the excellent beef noodles. There's no sign in English – look for the Mandarin.

★ **Mami Wata** INTERNATIONAL $$

(La Corniche; mains CFA9000-15,500; noon-11pm) Hands down Brazza's best restaurant, the 'Mermaid' has the best and breeziest river terrace in town, and attracts a wealthy crowd of locals and expats with its Italian- and French-leaning menu. It has an excellent value three-course lunch menu for CFA13,500.

**Ô Sympathic** FRENCH $$

(www.osympathic.com; Rue du Camp; mains CFA8000-12,000; 10am-2.30pm & 6-10pm Mon-Sat; ) About as French as you can get, including a strutting chef who regularly inspects the tables to ensure everyone is

# Brazzaville

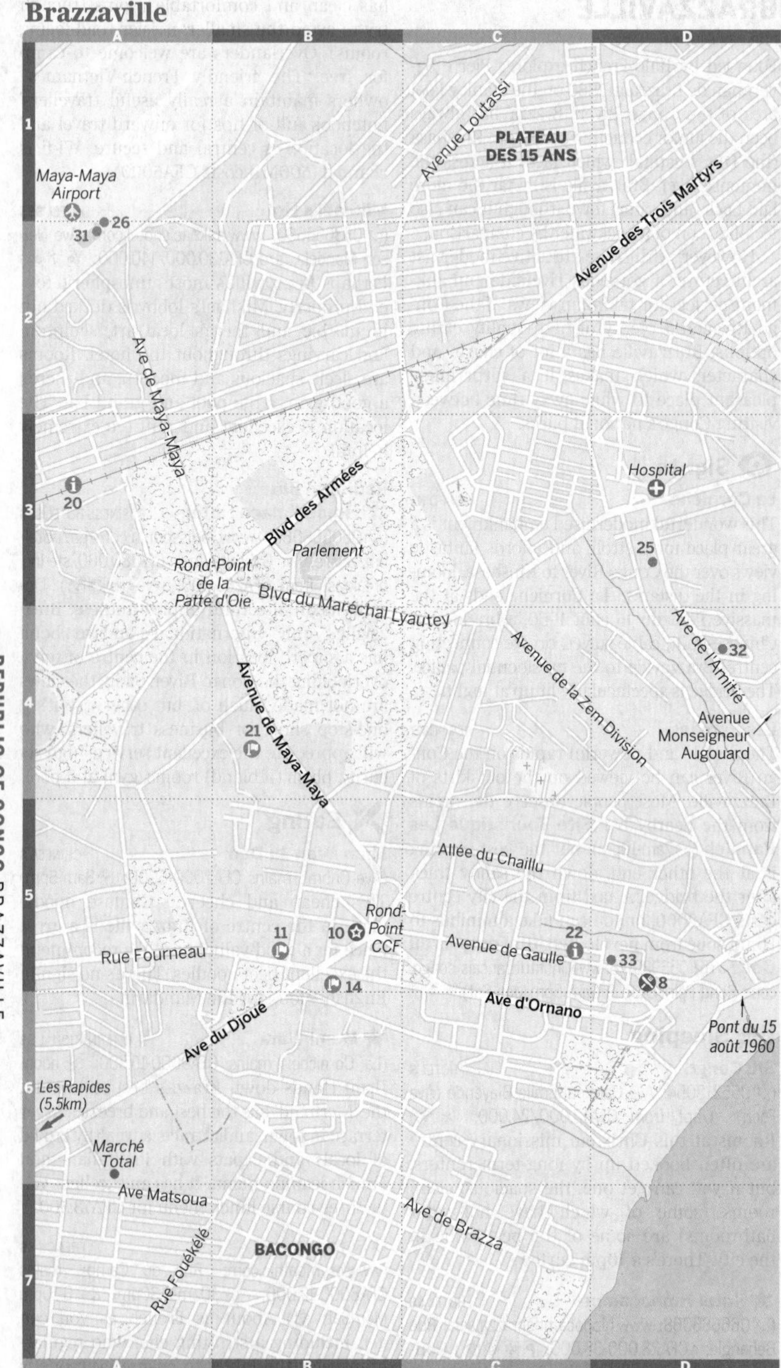

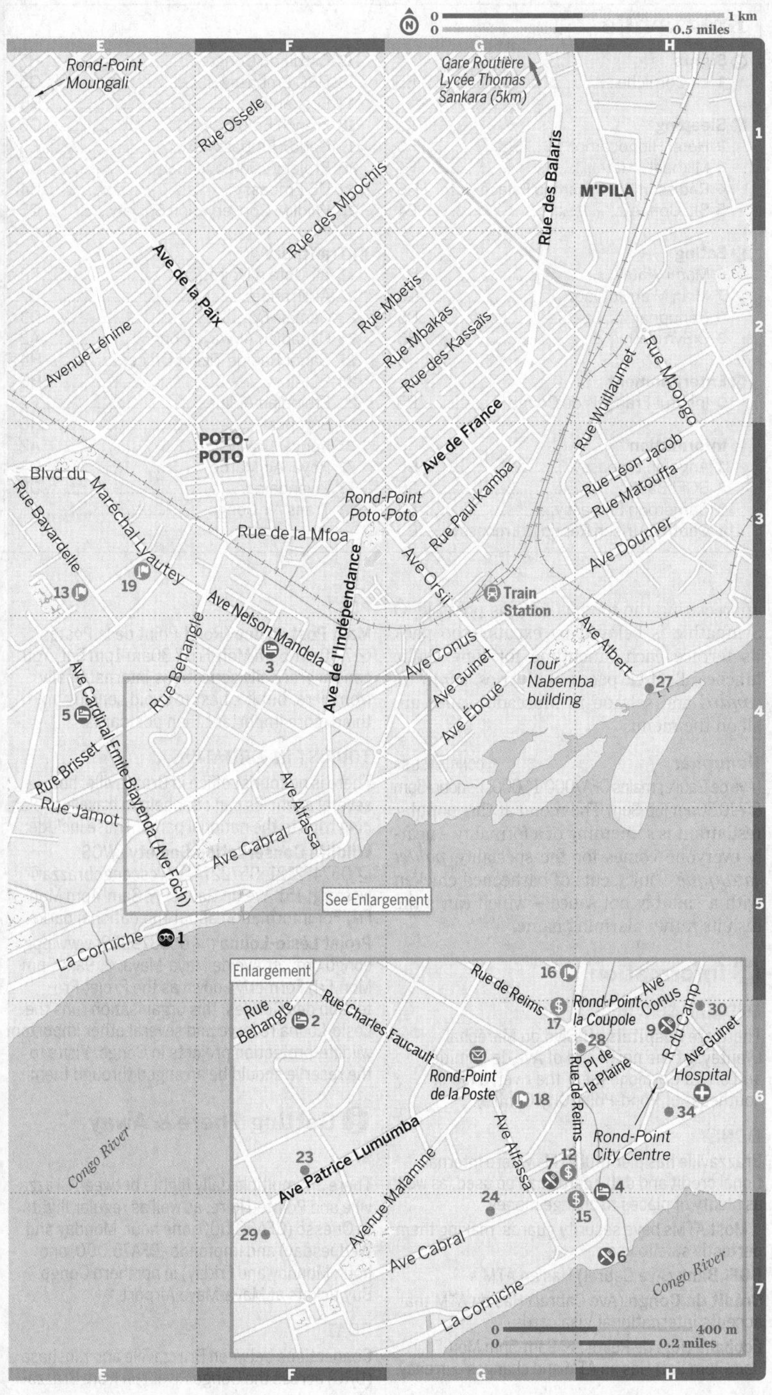
0 1 km
0 0.5 miles
E
F
G
H
1
2
3
4
5
6
7
Rond-Point Moungali
Gare Routière Lycée Thomas Sankara (5km)
Rue Ossele
Rue des Mbochis
Rue des Balaris
M'PILA
Ave de la Paix
Rue Mbetis
Rue Mbakas
Rue des Kassaïs
Avenue Lénine
Rue Wuillaumet
Rue Mbongo
Ave de France
POTO-POTO
Rue Léon Jacob
Rue Matouffa
Blvd du Maréchal Lyautey
Rue Bayardelle
Rond-Point Poto-Poto
Rue Paul Kamba
Rue de la Mfoa
Ave Doumer
Ave de l'Indépendance
Ave Orsii
13
19
Train Station
Ave Nelson Mandela
Rue Behangle
Ave Albert
3
Ave Conus
Ave Guinet
Tour Nabemba building
27
Ave Cardinal Emile Biayenda (Ave Foch)
5
Ave Éboué
Rue Brisset
Ave Alfassa
Rue Jamot
Ave Cabral
See Enlargement
La Corniche
1
Congo River
Enlargement
16
Rue de Reims
Ave Conus
Rue Behangle
2
Rue Charles Faucault
17
Rond-Point la Coupole
R du Camp
30
9
28
Pl de la Plaine
Ave Guinet
Rue de Reims
Rond-Point de la Poste
Hospital
18
34
Ave Alfassa
Rond-Point City Centre
Ave Patrice Lumumba
23
12
7
Avenue Malamine
24
4
15
29
Ave Cabral
6
Congo River
La Corniche
0 400 m
0 0.2 miles

## Brazzaville

**Sights**
1 La Corniche ... E5

**Sleeping**
2 Hotel Hippocampe ... F6
3 Mikhael's Hotel ... F4
4 Radisson Blu M'bamou Palace Hotel ... H6
5 SIL Congo ... E4

**Eating**
6 Mami Wata ... H7
7 Mian Mian Ju Dao ... G6
8 Nénuphar ... D5
9 Ô Sympathic ... H6

**Entertainment**
10 Institut Français du Congo ... B5

**Information**
11 Angolan Embassy ... B5
12 BGFI Bank ... G6
13 Cameroon Embassy ... E3
14 Central African Republic Embassy ... B5
15 Crédit du Congo ... H7
16 DRC Embassy ... G5
17 Ecobank ... G6
18 French Embassy ... G6
19 Gabon Embassy ... E3
20 Projet Lésio-Louna ... A3
21 US Embassy ... B4
22 Wildlife Conservation Society ... C5

**Transport**
23 Air Côte d'Ivoire ... F6
24 Air France ... G7
25 Camair-Co ... D3
26 Canadian Airways Congo ... A2
27 Canot Rapide Ticket Office ... H4
28 EC Air ... H6
29 Ethiopian Airlines ... F7
30 Europcar ... H6
31 Kenya Airways ... A2
32 Royal Air Maroc ... D4
33 Rwandair ... D5
34 Trans Air Congo ... H6

appreciating the food as fully as possible, Ô Sympathic is beloved by expats, who pack its terrace each lunchtime for long Gallic lunches. Beef carpaccio with fries, *confit de canard* and salmon in Muscadet sauce are all on the menu.

**Nénuphar** CONGOLESE **$$**
(Ave de Gaulle; mains CFA7000-14,000; noon-3pm & 7-10.30pm Tue-Sun) The menu at this popular restaurant is something of a formality – nearly everyone comes for the speciality, *poulet satanique* – juicy cuts of barbecued chicken with a suitably hot sauce – which earns the dish its rather alarming name.

## Information

### MEDICAL SERVICES

There are **hospitals** off Blvd du Maréchal Lyautey (at the north end of Ave de l'Amitié) and off La Corniche (near the river, a block southeast of Rond-Point City Centre).

### MONEY

Brazzaville has plentiful ATMs where international credit and debit cards can be used, as well as plenty of places to change money.

Most ATMs have security guards, making them perfectly safe to use.

**BGFI Bank** (Ave Cabral) Has an ATM.

**Crédit du Congo** (Ave Cabral) Has an ATM that accepts international Visa cards.

**Ecobank** (Rue de Reims; 9am-5pm Mon-Fri, 9am-3pm Sat) Has an ATM and changes currency.

### POST

**Main Post Office** (Rond-Point de la Poste; 7.30am-5pm Mon-Fri, 7.30am-1pm Sat) You can theoretically send items internationally from here, but it's best to avoid sending anything more important than postcards.

### TOURIST INFORMATION

There is no tourist office in Brazzaville, but several agencies can offer help to travellers planning trips to the national parks. These include:

**Wildlife Conservation Society** (WCS; 057472121, 057227411; wcscongobrazza@wcs.org; 151 Ave de Gaulle; 8am-4pm Mon-Fri) For information about the national parks.

**Projet Lésio-Louna** (055879999; www.ppgcongo.org; off Ave de Maya-Maya; 9am-5pm Mon-Fri) Formerly known as the Projet Protection des Gorilles, this organisation runs the Lésio-Louna reserve and several other important wildlife-protection projects in Congo. Visits to the reserve should be arranged through them.

## Getting There & Away

### AIR

There are multiple daily flights between Brazzaville and Pointe-Noire, as well as regular flights to Ouesso (CFA60,000, one hour, Monday and Wednesday) and Impfondo (CFA75,000, one hour, Monday and Friday) in northern Congo. Buy tickets at Maya-Maya Airport.

### BOAT

Connections between Brazzaville and Kinshasa (DRC) across the Congo River run from Brazzaville's port, a chaotic and unpleasant place from where multiple **canots rapides** (speedboats; Ave Albert; one way CFA11,000; ⌚7am-3pm Mon-Sat, 8-10am Sun) zip across the water in around 10 minutes, after at least two hours of formalities on each side. The crossing itself costs CFA11,000 per person, but you'll need to spend at least CFA20,000 per person in total, including various fees and downright bribes demanded of you by immigration staff, customs officers and others. It's a good idea to engage one of the protocol guys who hang around outside the ticket office to supervise your passage. Boats run approximately hourly between 7am and 3pm Mon-Sat, and between 8am and midday on Sunday.

#### BUS

The most reliable and comfortable buses are run by Océan du Nord, which has two main depots in the north of the city. For Ouesso (CFA20,000, 14 hours, 7am Monday to Saturday), Makoua (CFA10,000-12,000, nine hours, 7am Monday to Saturday) and Etoumbi (CFA13,000, 11 hours, 7am Tueday, Thursday and Saturday) head to **Agence Océan du Nord** (☎055217678; Ave Marien Ngouabi; ⌚24hrs) on Ave Marien Ngouabi.

If you're heading to Pointe-Noire (CFA15,000, 10 hours) by bus, use the **Agence Océan du Nord Mikalou** (Route Nationale 2, Marché de Mikalou; ⌚24hr) depot. Buses leave daily except Sunday, hourly from 6am to 9am.

All other buses, trucks, and shared and private taxis to the north leave from **Gare Routière Lycée Thomas Sankara** further north on the Route Nationale 2.

#### TRAIN

*The Gazelle* runs between Brazzaville and Pointe-Noire (seat/sleeper CFA22,500/26,000) three times a week in each direction. It leaves Brazzaville's **train station** (Ave Doumer) at 5.40pm on Tuesday, Thursday and Sunday, and officially arrives in Pointe-Noire at 8am the next morning, though delays are very frequent. The return trip from Pointe-Noire departs at 10am Monday, Wednesday and Friday. The service is neither particularly comfortable nor fast, and flying or taking a bus is generally a better option.

### Getting Around

Taxis charge around CFA3000 from Maya-Maya Airport to the centre of town.

Taxis are everywhere in Brazzaville and will sound their horn at the mere sight of a *mzungu* (stranger) on foot. They don't have meters, so be sure to agree on a price before getting in. In general you can expect to pay CFA500 for a short hop, CFA1000 across town, and CFA2000 to the airport and northern bus stations. After dark you're going to have to pay about CFA1000 to CFA2000 to get anywhere. Crowded minibuses (CFA150) are nearly as common as taxis, though they're far less comfortable.

# THE COAST

## Pointe-Noire

POP 650,000

Congo's second-largest city may be rich in oil and SUVs, but otherwise Pointe-Noire is a sprawling and rather unattractive place (despite its seafront location). Here the shanty towns spread for miles, and in places almost abut the walled mansions of the city's petrochemical classes. Due to the large expat community there's a good choice of international eating options, glitzy hotels and lubricious nightclubs, but there's little reason to visit otherwise, though there are a few attractive beaches outside the city. Most travellers will only find themselves here as a stop off if they're heading north to **Parc National Conkouati-Douli** (☎in Brazzaville 057227411; https://programs.wcs.org/congo/; adult CFA10,000, community fee CFA5000).

### Sights

**La Côte Sauvage** BEACH

Pointe-Noire's best and most popular beaches are south of the city and are known locally as 'the wild coast'. There are lots of stalls serving fresh fish and cold beers, as well as plenty of room to escape the crowds. A taxi from Pointe-Noire should be around CFA3000.

**Pointe Indienne** BEACH

This lovely stretch of sandy beach 19km north of Pointe-Noire is a great place for a day trip out of the city. It's popular with locals at weekends, and there are several hotels and restaurants here, though during the week you'll have the place almost entirely to yourself.

**Diosso Gorge** GORGE

Half an hour north of Pointe-Noire, just outside the dusty village of Diosso, this gorge's remarkable scenery tears through the otherwise ordinary landscape between the village and the coast in a blaze of pinks, yellows and oranges. It's quite a sight to behold, and some locals will even offer to guide you on a hike down to the bottom (CFA3000, one hour). A taxi from Pointe-Noire should cost around CFA10,000 to CFA15,000 return.

### Activities

**Rénatura Congo** WILDLIFE-WATCHING

(☎069449999; www.renatura.org; per person CFA10,000; ⌚8am-6pm Mon-Fri, 8am-noon Sat) A turtle protection society that allows

WORTH A TRIP

## LÉSIO LOUNA GORILLA RESERVE

The **Lésio Louna Gorilla Reserve** (☎055879999; www.ppgcongo.org; CFA50,000) is a very important resource in Congo where orphaned gorillas are cared for and eventually released back into the wild. Highlights include seeing the babies in the nursery and watching the adults (who live wild on an island) get fed. You can also swim or just enjoy the peace and quiet at the lovely Lac Bleu, which makes this a relatively easy excursion into the wild from Brazzaville for those unable to travel to the country's remote national parks. Be aware that you'll need to make arrangements at least a week in advance with Projet Lésio-Louna (p230) in Brazzaville in order to process payments before you arrive.

The simple **Iboubikro Guesthouse** (☎055879999; www.ppgcongo.org; r CFA30,000) by the Louna River has eight rooms accommodating a total of 12 people.

Theoretically, if you leave Brazzaville by 5am, a trip to the reserve can all be done as a long day trip, but it's far better to spend a night or two and not to hurry. You need your own wheels for this trip. The road from Brazzaville is generally good, with only a few rough stretches, and the journey takes around 5½ hours. Projet Lésio-Louna can supply you with a car and driver, costing CFA155,000 per day including petrol.

you to accompany its workers on half-day trips to free turtles from fishing nets.

## Sleeping

**Sueco** HOTEL $
(☎055393539; www.suecocongo.org; Ave Moé Telli; s/d without bathroom CFA10,000/15,500, r CFA18,000-30,000; P ) The best budget lodging in the centre, and probably the whole of Pointe-Noire, is Sueco, the Swedish Mission. Curfew is 11pm.

**Migitel** HOTEL $$
(☎055743636; www.congo-hotel-migitel.com; Blvd du Général Charles de Gaulle; s/d/ste CFA48,000/53,000/65,000; ) Has ageing but comfortable rooms at half the price you'd pay on the beach or elsewhere on Blvd de Gaulle. Many have balconies and it's right in the heart of things in Pointe-Noire.

★**Malonda Lodge** LODGE $$$
(☎055575151; www.malondalodge.com; s/d incl breakfast from CFA88,000/95,000; P ) With attractive thatched-roof cottages overlooking a little lagoon and a gorgeous private beach, Malonda Lodge, 18km south of Pointe-Noire, is perhaps the loveliest hotel in Congo, nurtured with great care by owner Grace and her husband Gérard. It's a perfect respite from Pointe-Noire, but can be reached in around 30 minutes from the city.

## Eating

Don't miss the stalls that set up every afternoon and evening at the southern end of La Côte Sauvage (p231), a few kilometres south of the city. Locals flock here for a sunset beer and plate of spicy fried fish (CFA2000).

**Restaurant Gaspard** CONGOLESE $
(Blvd Moe Mokasso; dishes CFA3000; 9am-10.30pm) Excellent barbecued fish and Congolese cuisine makes Restaurant Gaspard a must-visit in Pointe-Noire. Arrive here in good time, as it's fiercely popular and the specials often sell out. It's a fair way out of the city centre – take a cab (CFA2000).

★**Il Pepe Nero** ITALIAN $$
(☎069538383; Ave de l'Emeraude; mains 8000-12,000CFA; noon-2.30pm & 7-10.30pm Thu-Tue; ) Sleek and stylish, with tables scattered across a terrace overlooking a well-kept lawn, this Italian restaurant is one of Pointe-Noire's best and is a favourite for expats who crowd the place at lunch. Dinner is rather quieter, but the traditional Italian home cooking is worth coming for at any time of day.

★**Kactus Restaurant** INTERNATIONAL $$
(Blvd du Général Charles de Gaulle; mains CFA7000-12,000; 8am-11pm; ) This excellent Pointe-Noire institution in the heart of downtown has a large and high-quality menu. Choices run from excellent salads and pasta dishes to a variety of burgers and thin-crust pizzas. Don't miss the show-stopping chocolate mousse.

## Getting There & Away

There are at least eight flights (CFA35,000 to CFA40,000, 45 minutes) a day to Brazzaville with various airlines, as well as flights to Douala (Cameroon) and Paris.

The road from Brazza has now been upgraded and is good, though buses between the coast and capital (CFA15,000) still take around eight hours to do the journey. Océan du Nord, the best bus company, has six departures between 6.30am and 9am each day from its truly chaotic depot.

The third option is the revamped railway to the capital. Smart Chinese-built trains (sleeper/1st/2nd class CFA26,000/22,000/14,300) clatter to Brazza at 10am on Monday, Wednesday and Friday from Pointe-Noire's train station. The trip takes 14 hours, though delays are common.

### Getting Around

Cabs are everywhere in Pointe-Noire. Most taxi trips cost CFA500 to CFA1000, and it's a standard CFA2000 to the airport.

# THE NORTH

## Parc National d'Odzala

This **park** (in Brazzaville 053959600; www.odzala.com; US$20) is easily Congo's most accessible, and is a superb place to visit lowland gorillas and see other West African megafauna in a virtual wilderness. Unlike the other national parks in Congo, Odzala has top-notch (and sadly very expensive) camps and services, and this is the closest you'll get to luxury outside Brazzaville or Pointe-Noire.

Currently the only way to visit Odzala is on an exclusive safari setting out from Brazza, so those on a budget will have to visit another of Congo's national parks.

### Activities

The main Odzala activity is, unsurprisingly, nature-watching. Tours are run by the individual camps, and include the chance to visit one of three habituated gorilla groups at Ngaga Camp. Other activities include boating or kayaking to see elephants at Mboko Camp and just chilling out at the *bai* (watering hole), watching the various animals come for a drink in front of Lango Camp. Birdwatching, nature walks and opportunities to meet the local Baka people can also be arranged.

### Sleeping & Eating

**★Ngaga Camp** LODGE **$$$**
(in Brazzaville 053959600; www.odzala.com/ngaga-camp/; full board per person from US$850; closed 1 Mar-15 Apr; ) The jewel in the crown of the Odzala camps, this magical place is located deep in the rainforest within easy walking distance of two groups of habituated lowland gorillas. The accommodation, in just six entirely secluded rooms, is gorgeous, with beautiful furnishings including a terrace, an unusual copper bathroom and massive, super-comfortable double beds.

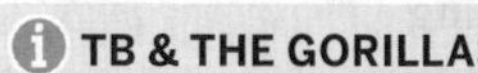

**TB & THE GORILLAS**

Anyone wanting to visit the gorillas at Odzala's Ngaga will need a tuberculosis-free certificate from a doctor, as well as confirmation that they have been vaccinated against measles and polio.

**Lango Camp** CAMPGROUND **$$$**
(in Brazzaville 053959600; www.odzala.com/lango-camp/; full board per person from US$750; closed 1 Mar-15 Apr) A satellite camp of Mboko Camp, Lango has the more enchanting position, overlooking a massive jungle clearing and *bai*, where buffaloes, elephants and many more megafauna are regular visitors. The camp itself is gorgeous, and looks like something from *Swiss Family Robinson*, with raised walkways connecting the stylish wooden cabins, each of which has its own private viewing platform.

**Mboko Camp** LODGE **$$$**
(Brazzaville 053959600; www.odzala.com/mboko-camp/; full board per person from US$750; closed 1 Mar-15 Apr; ) Mboko is an impressive place, set on an open strip of savannah peppered with giant termite hills. The rooms, which are effectively permanent tents, are huge and elegant, with terraces overlooking a rust-coloured stream and every comfort provided. The grand wooden communal area serves meals as hyenas look on from the bush.

### Getting There & Away

Odzala tours begin in Brazzaville, with guests being driven by bus from the capital to the town of Etoumbi (11 hours), where they are met by high-clearance 4WD vehicles for the three- to four-hour journey to one of the camps within the park.

## Ouesso

POP 34,000

Some 800km from Brazzaville, Ouesso (*way*-so) is the capital of Congo's north, a bustling and friendly place that makes for a good contrast to life in Brazza. There's nothing much to see in the town itself, but if you're heading to Parc National Nouabalé-Ndoki (p234) you'll probably spend some time here, and most people find the town pleasant and enjoyable.

## Sleeping

**Nianina Auberge** HOTEL $

(☎069291143; Rue Elapa; r CFA10,000-20,000, ste CFA40,000-50,000; P ❄) The Christmas decorations never come down at this collection of brick cottages in central Ouesso. The interiors are surprisingly colourful and cosy in the better rooms, but extremely basic in the cheapest category.

★ **Hotel Onanga** HOTEL $$

(☎066337272, 055749887; Quartier Mindongo; r CFA45,000-75,000; ❄ 🏊) Formerly the Hotel Mindongo, this is the smartest place in Ouesso, and has a labyrinth of rooms centred on a superb pool complete with sun loungers.

## Eating

**Restaurant Le Nzalangoye** CONGOLESE $

(Ave Marien Ngouabi; mains CFA4000-6000; ⏲8.30am-10pm) This casual place on Ouesso's main drag offers a very high standard of cooking – try the excellent river-fish dishes. There's a pleasant saloon-style dining room with a long bar in it, as well as a shaded terrace outside.

**Nénuphar** CONGOLESE $$

(Rue Inoua; mains CFA5000-10,000; ⏲8am-10pm; ✎) Generally considered the best restaurant in Ouesso, this charming place near the police station is in a side street off the main road. There's a brightly decorated dining room, a patio and a *paillote* (straw awning) to choose from, and the chalkboard menu is a mixture of Congolese cooking and excellent thin-crust pizza. Breakfast is served daily.

## Information

There are now several banks with ATMs accepting international cards along Ouesso's main drag, Ave Marien Ngouabi, as well as a couple of exchange offices.

**Wildlife Conservation Society** (WCS; ☎066642160; www.wcs.org; Ave Marien Ngouabi; ⏲9am-5pm Mon-Fri) The Ouesso office of the WCS is the best source of information about Parc National Nouabalé-Ndoki.

## Getting There & Away

Ouesso has a modern airport with two weekly flights to Brazzaville. **Trans Air Congo** (TAC; ☎066262605; www.flytransaircongo.com; Ave Cabral; ⏲8am-6pm Mon-Sat) flies at 11.30am on Monday (CFA45,000, one hour), while **Canadian Airways Congo** (☎mobile 0220046375; www.canaircongo.com/en/; Maya-Maya Airport; ⏲9am-6pm) flies at 10am Wednesday (CFA50,000, one hour).

**Océan du Nord** (Ave Ngbala) has its depot in the centre of Ouesso, a short distance up the busy shopping street next to the Total petrol station. It has buses to Brazzaville (CFA20,000, 13 hours) that leave at 6am daily except Sunday. These also call at Makoua (CFA10,000, four hours).

## Getting Around

Shared taxis are everywhere in Ouesso and short rides cost from CFA200 – agree on a price before you get in, as foreigners tend to get charged far more. A ride to the airport should cost CFA500.

# PARC NATIONAL NOUABALÉ-NDOKI

A team from *National Geographic* magazine, who visited the fledgling **Parc National Nouabalé-Ndoki** (☎057227411; https://programs.wcs.org/congo; CFA20,000, village development fee per day CFA10,000) in the mid-1990s, called this northern corner of Congo the world's 'Last Eden', and they chose their words wisely. So extraordinary is Nouabalé-Ndoki that in 2012 Unesco declared it a World Heritage Site, as a part of the much larger (7500-sq-km) Sangha Trinational Park, which covers both this park and neighbouring Dzanga Ndoki park in the Central African Republic and Lobéké park in Cameroon.

Visiting Nouabalé-Ndoki is truly one of those 'once in a lifetime' experiences and is as genuine a slice of raw, wild Africa as you will ever encounter.

The swampy forest is home to healthy populations of western lowland gorillas, forest elephants and chimpanzees, and it boasts many natural watering holes (known as *bais*) where masses of elephants and gorillas gather. Viewing platforms have been constructed at Mbeli Bai and Wali Bai. Mbeli is renowned for its elephants, gorillas and sitatunga antelope, and Wali for its buffaloes. If you want to get even closer to the wildlife, Nouabalé-Ndoki also has groups of habituated gorillas (CFA164,000 per person) at Mondika.

Simple rooms at Nouabalé-Ndoki's park headquarters in Bomassa cost CFA32,800 per person including food. At Mondika, camping in permanent tents costs CFA49,200/59,400 per single/double with food included. At Mbeli, accommodation is in bungalows with full board and costs the same. Wali is just a short walk from Bomassa so you can base yourself there. Bookings should be made with the Wildlife Conservation Society (WCS) in Ouesso or Brazzaville (p230) as far in advance as possible.

OFF THE BEATEN TRACK

### LAC TÉLÉ

A journey to the perfect circular form of **Lac Télé** (Lake Télé), hidden away in the unimaginably remote northeast of Congo, is the kind of trip people write books about. It's not just that this lake is surrounded by swamp-forests that remain largely unexplored, nor that are there an estimated 100,000 lowland gorillas inhabiting the area, nor the Pygmy groups living an almost completely traditional lifestyle: local lore has it that Lac Télé is also the home of the Mokèlé-mbèmbé, a large semi-aquatic creature that many believers describe as being similar to a sauropod (a type of long-extinct dinosaur).

To get to Lac Télé you'll need first to take one of the twice-weekly flights from Brazzaville to the river town of Impfondo. Barges also float past Impfondo as they travel between Brazza and Bangui in CAR. From Impfondo a road of sorts runs to little Epéna, after which nothing but unexplored swamp forest stands between you and your goal.

If you're serious about visiting, contact the Wildlife Conservation Society (p230) in Brazzaville and engage a travel agency with experience in the area to assist you with the daunting logistics of this epic expedition!

### Getting There & Away

The easiest way to access Nouabalé-Ndoki from Ouesso is to hire a driver to Bomassa. From Bomassa to Ndoki (the drop-off point for Mondika) WCS charges an eye-watering CFA346,000 for a 4WD to take you on the three-hour journey. On arrival you'll then have to wade through a swamp for 45 minutes and walk through dense jungle for two hours. From Bomassa to Djeké (for Mbeli) a car is CFA65,600.

An even more exciting and scenic way to arrive is by boat. From Ouesso, the park charges CFA328,000 for one to four people for the four-hour trip.

# UNDERSTAND THE REPUBLIC OF CONGO

## Republic of Congo Today

President Denis Sassou N'Guesso won re-election in 2016, guaranteeing him power until at least 2023; the president first came to power in 1979 (ruling until 1992). Sassou, the country's ruler since 1997, controversially held a referendum in 2015 to change the constitution and allow himself to run for a third consecutive term. The investigation of African leaders carried out in France in 2009 revealed that he owned over a hundred properties in France; over 70% of the Congolese population lives on less than US$1 a day.

With 15 years of peace and the brutal civil war of the late 1990s now behind it, Congo has been enjoying a surge of foreign investment. The oil industry is booming, new roads, airports and residential neighbourhoods are being constructed and Chinese-built office towers rise over the skyline of Brazzaville. Corruption among officials and the oil industry is rife, however, and the Congolese economy's heavy reliance on oil revenues substantially contributes to President Denis Sassou N'Guesso's ability to maintain tight control over the country.

## History

People arriving from the east were most likely Congo's first inhabitants. Later several kingdoms of Bantu origin (the Kongo, Loango and Teke among them) arrived and opened trade links across the Congo River basin.

The Portuguese were the first Europeans to arrive on the banks of the Congo River, quickly establishing a slave-trade system with partnering coastal tribes. The French had an early presence here, too, and it was Franco-Italian empire builder Pierre Savorgnan de Brazza who led a major expedition inland in 1875, then five years later charmed local rulers into putting their land on the river's right bank under French control.

### French Rule

The French government made quick work of acquiring Congo's considerable natural resources such as ivory, tropical hardwoods and rubber, as well as using the local population as slave labour. Because of human-rights scandals perpetrated by the companies running the region, the French government was forced to take a greater role in overseeing things, and by 1910 Congo (called Middle Congo) had been formally streamlined into French Equatorial Africa along with Chad,

Gabon and the Central African Republic. Brazzaville was the capital.

Except for initiating construction of the Congo–Ocean Railway (1924–34), the French made few significant changes and locals revolted in protest in 1928. Brazzaville had its moment in the sun when it served as the symbolic capital of Free France between 1940 and 1943. In 1944 genuine reforms such as the abolition of forced labour and the election of local councils were enacted, but ethnic integration was never a colonial priority. Tribal differences continued to fester, and with independence in 1960 the bubbling pot finally boiled over.

### Africa's First Marxist State

Congo's first president, Fulbert Youlou, lasted just three tumultuous years before being deposed in a popular uprising that put Alphonse Massamba-Débat in power. Introducing a one-party state and treading a socialist path, he proved to be equally unpopular and was ousted in a 1968 military coup by Captain Marien Ngouabi. The next year Ngouabi formed the Congolese Worker's Party (PCT) and inaugurated the People's Republic of Congo, ushering in Africa's first Marxist-Leninist state.

After Ngouabi was assassinated in 1977, the PCT appointed Joachim Yhombi-Opango as successor but, charged with 'deviation from party directives' and corruption, he was replaced in 1979 by vice president and defence minister Denis Sassou N'Guesso. Sassou's political survivalism proved to be superior to that of his predecessors (he's currently in power) and his pragmatism got results. Congo forged ties with both capitalist and communist countries and gradually moderated its political course. Following the downfall of the Soviet Union's economy and its subsequent collapse, Sassou agreed to allow multiparty elections in 1992.

### Civil War

Sassou N'Guesso lost the 1992 election to former prime minister Pascal Lissouba, who had been exiled for complicity in the assassination of Ngouabi. Accusations that N'Guesso rigged 1993's parliamentary elections sparked violent unrest between pro-government and opposition militias (both tribally based) until a 1994 ceasefire. Congo fell under full-scale civil war in 1997. Brazzaville was devastated (most of its citizens were forced to flee to the bush for many months) and Sassou's 'Cobra' militia, with the help of Angolan troops, returned him to power.

The coming years saw sporadic fighting, including more attacks on the capital; peace-agreement signings with some rebel groups; the approval of a new constitution in a national referendum; and Sassou winning another election (from which his main rivals, including Lissouba, were barred) in 2002. In 2003 the main rebel group, the 'Ninjas', finally agreed to a peace accord.

In the 2007 parliamentary elections, which were boycotted by Congo's opposition, Sassou's allies won a strong majority. Then, in the presidential vote of 2009, Sassou took 79% of the vote. Both elections were widely criticised by international election observers.

## People & Religion

Of Congo's 16 ethnic groups, the Kongo people predominate, making up nearly half the population. Other key groups include the Sangha (20%), Teke (17%), M'Bochi (12%) and Pygmies (2%). Seventy per cent of the Congolese population lives in Brazzaville, in Pointe-Noire, or along the railroad joining these two cities.

In terms of faith, Congo is divided about half and half between Christian and animist, with a small Muslim minority. No matter the faith, belief in spirits and magic runs deep in Congolese society and many people consult traditional healers and various magic men for advice and medical treatment.

# SURVIVAL GUIDE

## Directory A-Z

### ACCOMMODATION

Accommodation is expensive in Congo, and outside Brazzaville and Pointe-Noire options remain fairly limited, though it's perfectly possible to find clean and safe places to spend the night. While the situation is slowly improving and better hotels are popping up in towns across the country, you can still expect to pay more than you usually would elsewhere in West Africa.

### DANGERS & ANNOYANCES

Travel in Congo is quite safe these days. Brazzaville and Pointe-Noire are typical African cities: trouble-free by day, but best traversed by taxi at night. Power cuts and fuel shortages are common throughout the country, but rarely affect travellers (most hotels have generators and fuel supplies).

While things have become a lot more relaxed in Congo in recent years regarding photography, do not take photographs of any military personnel or police, and it's always worth asking before photographing people in general.

### ELECTRICITY

Congo uses 230V/50Hz; plugs are two-pin Continental Europe style.

### EMBASSIES & CONSULATES

The following countries have diplomatic representation in Brazzaville. France, Belgium and Angola also have consulates in Pointe-Noire.

**Angolan Embassy** (☎055063217; Rue Lucien Fornier; ⏲8am-noon & 2pm-5pm Mon-Tue & Thu-Fri)

**Cameroonian Embassy** (☎040504646; Rue Bayardelle; ⏲9am-4pm Mon-Fri)

**Central African Republic Embassy** (☎0558 22638; Rue Fourneau; ⏲9am-3pm Mon-Fri)

**DRC Embassy** (☎mobile 028913052; Ave de l'Indépendance; ⏲8am-noon Mon-Fri)

**French Embassy** (☎066200303; www.ambafrance-cg.org; Ave Alfassa; ⏲9am-noon & 2pm-5pm Mon-Fri)

**Gabonese Embassy** (☎mobile 022815620; Blvd du Maréchal Lyautey; ⏲8am-3pm Mon-Fri)

**US Embassy** (☎06122000; http://cg.usembassy.gov; Ave de Maya-Maya; ⏲9am-noon & 1-5pm Mon-Fri)

### EMERGENCY & IMPORTANT NUMBERS

Emergency numbers are unreliable in Congo. There is no emergency number for ambulances – take a taxi to the nearest hospital in case of a medical emergency.

**Fire** ☎118

**Police** ☎117

### INTERNET ACCESS

Internet access in Congo is frustratingly slow. Very few hotel wireless networks actually work, and when they do they're incredibly slow. The most reliable internet access can be had through local mobile-phone networks – anybody can register for a SIM card; just go to a mobile provider's office with your passport.

### MONEY

Congo uses the Central African franc (CFA), a stable currency also used by five other countries in the region. It's pegged to the euro at an unchanging rate of CFA655.957. For travellers, euros are the best currency to bring, though you can change US dollars and British pounds in Brazzaville and Pointe-Noire. Banks willing to exchange money are rare outside these cities, but businesses owned by Lebanese and West Africans usually change money, though rates will not be competitive. Whichever currency you bring, make sure your foreign bills are in pristine condition.

Crédit du Congo, Ecobank and BGFI Bank all have ATMs in Brazzaville and Pointe-Noire that accept Visa, MasterCard and Plus cards.

### OPENING HOURS

**Banks** Open around 8am and typically close at 2pm.

### PRICE RANGES

The following price ranges are used in our accommodation reviews and refer to a double room with bathroom. Unless otherwise stated, breakfast is included in the price.

**$** less than CFA30,000

**$$** CFA30,000–60,000

**$$$** more than CFA60,000

The following price ranges are used in our Eating reviews and refer to a main course.

**$** less than CFA6000

**$$** CFA6000–12,000

**$$$** more than CFA12,000

**Offices** Open 8am to 5pm weekdays and until noon on Saturdays. Many close for an hour or two over lunch.

**Restaurants** Open from midday to 2.30pm, and again from 6pm to 10pm.

### PUBLIC HOLIDAYS

Public holidays in Congo:

**New Year's Day** 1 January

**Easter** March/April

**Labour Day** 1 May

**Reconciliation Day** 10 June

**Independence Day** 15 August

**All Saints' Day** 1 November

**Christmas Day** 25 December

### TELEPHONE

Mobile phone numbers in Congo start with ☎05 or ☎06, and they are used by everyone. SIM cards cost very little and can be purchased from one of the major mobile-phone providers, including Airtel and MTN. One of the easiest places to do this is at Maya-Maya Airport in Brazzaville, where there are Airtel offices on both the arrival and departure levels. You'll need your passport to register your SIM card.

### TOURIST INFORMATION

While tourism remains a very low priority for the Congolese government, there are now two tourist information kiosks at Brazzaville's Maya-Maya Airport, with friendly staff who speak a little English and can give out various flyers and free publications.

## Getting There & Away

### AIR

Brazzaville and Pointe-Noire both enjoy international connections to other African countries as well as to Europe.

The only two international airports in Congo are Maya-Maya Airport in Brazzaville and the brand-new Antonio Agostinho Neto International Airport in Pointe-Noire.

In addition to **Air France** (☎ mobile 0222815135; www.airfrance.com; Ave Cabral; ⏲ 9am-6pm Mon-Fri), which offers international and African connections, other international airlines serving Congo include the following:

**Air Côte d'Ivoire** (Ave Patrice Lumumba; ⏲ 9am-5pm Mon-Sat)

**Camair-Co** (☎ 050707374; www.camair-co.cm; Ave de l'Amitié; ⏲ 8am-5pm Mon-Sat)

**EC Air** (☎ 065090509, 065090525; www.flyecair.com; Rond-Point la Coupole) The country's national carrier, based in Brazzaville, though it suspended operations in late 2016 due to debt and it was not clear at the time of writing if it will be resuming services.

**Ethiopian Airlines** (☎ 066712020; www.ethiopianairlines.com; Ave Foch; ⏲ 9am-6pm Mon-Sat)

**Kenya Airways** (☎ 055781538; www.kenya-airways.com; Maya-Maya Airport; ⏲ 9am-noon & 1-5pm Mon-Sat)

**Royal Air Maroc** (☎ 066282828; www.royalairmaroc.com; Ave de l'Amitié; ⏲ 9am-5pm Mon-Thu & Sat)

**Rwandair** (www.rwandair.com; 96 Ave de Gaulle; ⏲ 9am-5pm Mon-Sat)

You must pay CFA1000 departure tax at the airport for domestic flights if you have a paper ticket. For electronic tickets and all international flights, the tax is paid when you buy the ticket.

### LAND

#### Angola

Crossing to Cabinda is possible on good roads, but check the situation carefully before trying it, especially if you are driving your own vehicle. This route has been subject to attacks by militia groups in the past.

#### Cameroon

Travel to Cameroon is slow-going, but possible in the dry season. The best way is to take a boat across the border from Ouesso to Sokamba, then continue through remote southwest Cameroon to Moloundou and Yokadouma. If you're driving, first head southeast of Ouesso to Ngombe, where there's a car ferry over the Sangha River, and then drive to Ngatongo, where another ferry will take you across the border to Sokamba.

#### Central African Republic (CAR)

At the time of writing travel to the CAR is considered unsafe.

#### Gabon

Although it's possible to cross the border at Doussala or Mbinda north of Dolisie (both in Congo), most people heading to Gabon travel between Oyo (Congo) and Franceville via Léconi (Gabon; it's not on the border, but take care of Gabonese immigration formalities here). There's no public transport along most of this route and few lorries, so it can take several days.

## Getting Around

### AIR

Air remains the best way to get around Congo if you're in anything approaching a hurry. Trans Air Congo and Canadian Airways Congo are the two most reliable airlines in Congo.

The main route flown is the hour-long hop between Brazzaville and Pointe-Noire. Other routes link Brazzaville to Ouesso, Impfondo and Dolisie. Except for the Pointe-Noire to Brazzaville route, flight schedules are rarely followed; cancellations and delays are common.

Most internal flights are not bookable online – TAC is a notable exception – so your best bet is purchasing tickets at Maya-Maya Airport.

### BOAT

Boat travel in Congo is slow and extremely uncomfortable, but there's absolutely no better way to see the country and immerse yourself in local culture. The epic barge ride up the Congo and Oubangui Rivers to the remote river-port town of Impfondo is the stuff of travel-writing legend.

### BUS

The vast majority of public transport in Congo is in the form of bush taxis and lorries. Océan du Nord (p231) runs buses across the country's two main roads – from Brazzaville to the coast, and up through the centre of the country to the northern city of Ouesso via Makoua. Bush taxis tend to be a little faster, but far less comfortable and more crowded than the full-size buses. For cross-country travels you can go to Brazzaville's Marché Total to haggle with truck drivers parked on Ave Matsoua.

### CAR & MOTORCYCLE

**Europcar** (☎ 069692222; www.europcar.com; Rue du Camp; ⏲ 9am-6pm Mon-Sat) offers expensive car and 4WD hire, but it's easier and about half the price to charter a taxi with driver for travelling around Brazzaville. The Hotel Hippocampe (p227) can also provide an excellent car and driver for a (relatively) reasonable price.

Hwy 1 to Pointe-Noire has been resurfaced and is now in good condition. Still, even with the improvements it takes a full day's journey from Brazzaville. Hwy 2 to the north of the country is now in good condition all the way to Ouesso.

### TRAIN

Trains run between Brazzaville and Pointe-Noire (standing/seat/sleeper CFA14,300/22,500/26,000) three times a week in each direction. In theory trains leave Brazzaville at 5.40pm on Tuesday, Thursday and Sunday, arriving in Pointe-Noire at 8am the next morning, though delays are very frequent. Return journeys from Pointe-Noire depart at 10am Monday, Wednesday and Friday. Purchase tickets a day ahead.

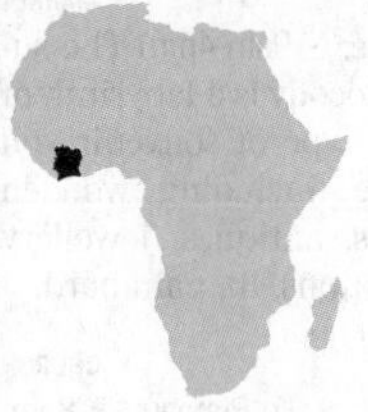

# Côte d'Ivoire

☎225 / POP 23.4 MILLION

**Includes ➡**



## Best Places to Eat

- Bushman Café (p243)
- Le Mechoui (p243)
- Le Nandjelet (p243)
- Aboussouan (p243)
- Allocodrome (p243)

## Best Places to Sleep

- Bushman Café (p240)
- Koral Beach Hotel (p247)
- La Licorne (p240)
- Touraco Ecotel (p250)
- Le Wafou (p241)

## Why Go?

Côte d'Ivoire is a stunner, shingled with starfish-studded sands, palm-tree forests and roads so orange they resemble strips of bronzing powder. This is a true tropical paradise, and a country that is striding towards economic progress – it's a nation that is fast modernising its lifestyle and culture, but managing to do so without losing its identity.

In the south, the Parc National de Taï hides secrets, species and nut-cracking chimps under the boughs of its trees, while the peaks and valleys of Man offer a highland climate, fresh air and fantastic hiking opportunities through tropical forests.

The beach resorts of low-key Assinie and arty Grand Bassam were made for weekend retreats from Abidjan, the capital in all but name, where lagoons wind their way between skyscrapers and cathedral spires pierce the blue heavens.

## When to Go

### Abidjan

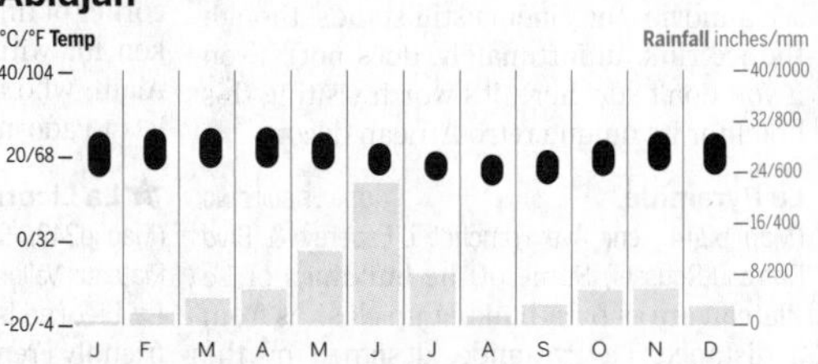


**Nov–May** Dry season and best time to visit; beaches are best during this time.

**May–Jul** Rainy season in the south, along with October to November.

**Oct–Jun** Best time for hiking in the north. Parc National de Taï is best outside wet season.

# ABIDJAN

☎20, 21, 22, 23 / POP 4.5 MILLION

Côte d'Ivoire's economic engine is strapped between lagoons and waterways, overlooking the crested waves of the Atlantic. At first glimpse, you wonder if these shiny skyscrapers can really be West Africa, but once you walk around Abidjan's neighbourhoods, local life comes alive and the city's vibrant tropical mood is revealed.

Abidjan is a challenging city to move around – it's vast and connected by mini-motorways – and you'll have to get in the swing of hailing taxis, negotiating fares and buzzing down the busy roads in order to get from one spot to another. But each neighbourhood's distinct feel gives you an insight into the vast scope of Abidjan's character and contradiction; it's quite common for sharp luxury to exist right next to painful poverty.

Make sure to dip into the markets, street-food stops, art galleries and sleek bars.

## Sights

**★Galerie Cécile Fakhoury** GALLERY

(Map p242; ☎22-446677; www.cecilefakhoury.com; Boulevard Latrille, Cocody; ⏲10am-7pm Tue-Sun) FREE An absolute trove of African contemporary art, this cubical, 600-sq-metre gallery features the best of the continent's artists, from sculpture and painting to photography. Check the website for individual exhibitions or just explore what's on at the time. A real gem of a place.

**Hôtel Ivoire** HISTORIC BUILDING

(Map p242; ☎22-482626; www.sofitel.com; Blvd Hassan II, Blokosso) Every middle-class Abidjani holds a dear memory of Hôtel Ivoire. Built in 1963 by Israeli architect Moshe Mayer, it was *the* place in town to go ice skating and see a movie (the cinema still stands, though the ice rink, unfortunately, does not). Even if you don't stay here, it's worth visiting this hotel for its unique retro African decor.

**La Pyramide** NOTABLE BUILDING

(Map p244; cnr Ave Franchet d'Esperey & Blvd Botreau-Roussel) Some of the buildings of Le Plateau are as breathtaking up close as from a distance. La Pyramide, designed by the Italian architect Rinaldo Olivieri and built between 1970 and 1973, was the first daring structure and is considered a highlight of African modernism in architecture. A concrete pyramid striped horizontally with balconies, it rests upon a gigantic cubic pillar, lifting itself over the city's skyline.

**Marché de Cocody** MARKET

(Map p242; Blvd de France; ⏲9am-4pm) The super lively Marché de Cocody is a labyrinth of stalls that offer every type of souvenir you can possibly imagine, including wooden sculptures and dishes, antiques, jewellery and traditional decorations. Bargain hard.

**Cathedrale St Paul** CHURCH

(Map p242; Blvd Angoulvant, Le Plateau; ⏲8am-7pm) FREE Designed by Italian architect Aldo Spiritom, the Cathedrale St Paul is a bold and innovative modern cathedral. The stained glass is as warm and rich as that inside the Yamoussoukro basilica (p249).

**Musée National** MUSEUM

(Map p242; Blvd Nangul Abrogoua, Le Plateau; CFA2000; ⏲9am-5pm Tue-Sat) The national museum houses a dusty but interesting collection of traditional art and craftwork, including wooden statues and masks, pottery, ivory and bronze.

## Sleeping

**La Nouvelle Pergola** HOTEL $

(Map p242; ☎21-753501; www.hotelnouvellepergola.com; Blvd de Marseille, cnr Rue Pierre et Marie Curie, Zone 4; d CFA30,000; P ❄ 📶 🏊) For reasonable rooms on a budget, La Nouvelle Pergola is an OK bet. There are over 130 rooms in this complex, which includes a pool, a nightclub and wi-fi – though it has none of Côte d'Ivoire's traditional charms.

**★Bushman Café** BOUTIQUE HOTEL $$

(☎88-358508; Riviera 4, Ciad, Cocody; r from CFA60,000; ❄ 🏊) French-Ivoirian couple Alain and Pascale run this fusion of hotel and restaurant, which offers impeccable style, local art and artists, the most exquisite decor, lush rooms and gourmet food. Every corner of this three-storey townhouse is spoken for with antiques and art collected by Alain, who also commissioned Ivoirian artists to adorn the walls.

**★La Licorne** BOUTIQUE HOTEL $$

(Map p242; ☎22-410730; Rue des Jardins, Deux Plateaux Vallons; r CFA65,000-90,000; P ❄ @ 🏊) La Licorne is a pretty boutique hotel run by a friendly French family. Rooms are individually decorated, and there's wi-fi, a bar, a hot tub, a book exchange and a decent restaurant.

**Le Griffon** BOUTIQUE HOTEL $$

(Map p242; ☎22-416622; Rue des Jardins, Deux Plateaux Vallons; r CFA45,000-75,000; ❄ @ 📶 🏊) This boutique hotel offers beautifully deco-

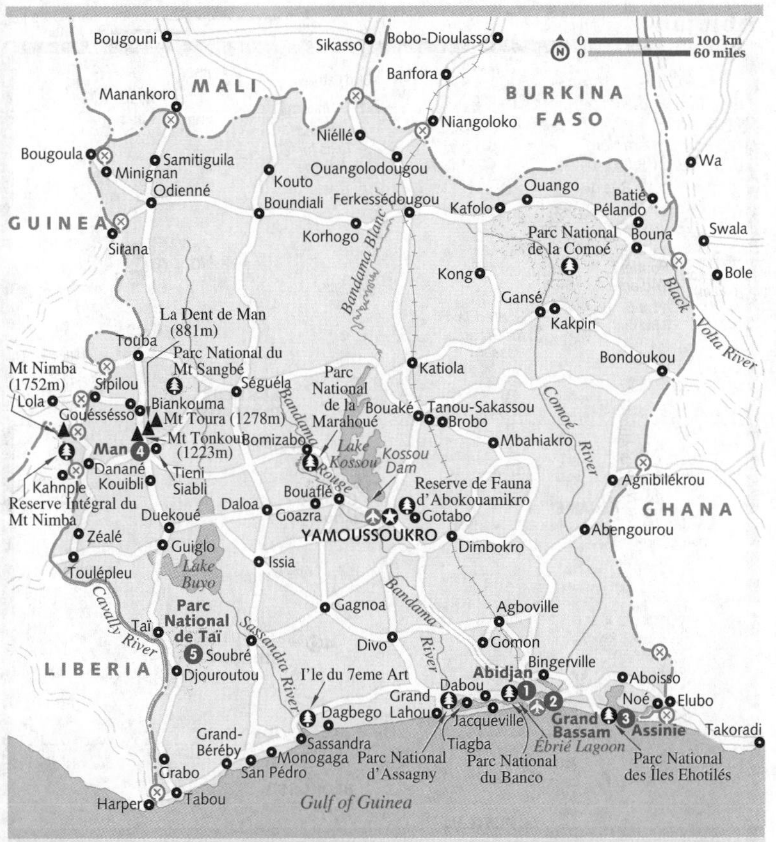


## Côte d'Ivoire Highlights

1. **Abidjan** (p240) Dining on creative Ivoirian dishes, exploring contemporary African art and swaying to the sweet sounds of *coupé-decalé* music in the shadow of the stunning skyline.

2. **Grand Bassam** (p246) Enjoying the relaxed beach vibe and exploring the dilapidating colonial past of Côte d'Ivoire.

3. **Assinie** (p247) Lazing in a pirogue while watching surfers slide to shore, then tucking into fresh seafood under the stars.

4. **Man** (p249) Hiking to the point where three West African countries converge and feasting on the green fields below.

5. **Parc National de Taï** (p250) Exploring the dense rainforest, home to a colony of nut-cracking chimps, and seeing some of the most stunning natural life in Africa.

rated rooms, complete with Ivoirian art and coffee-table books. With friendly staff, great food, wi-fi and a hot tub in the backyard, it's a gem.

**★Le Wafou** BOUTIQUE HOTEL **$$$**
(☎21-256201; www.lewafou.com; Blvd de Marseille, Zone 4; r CFA58,000-110,000, ste CFA150,000-225,000; P ❄ 📶 🏊) If the Flintstones won the lottery and moved to West Africa, they'd live somewhere like this. Set in large grounds, Le Wafou's gorgeous bungalows take cues from traditional Dogon villages in neighbouring Mali. At night you can enjoy great food and wine poolside. A hit with kids, too.

**Le Pullman** HOTEL **$$$**
(Map p244; ☎20-302020; www.sofitel.com; Rue Abdoulaye Fadiga, Le Plateau; r from CFA120,000; P ❄ @ 📶 🏊) A good, upmarket chain hotel.

# Abidjan

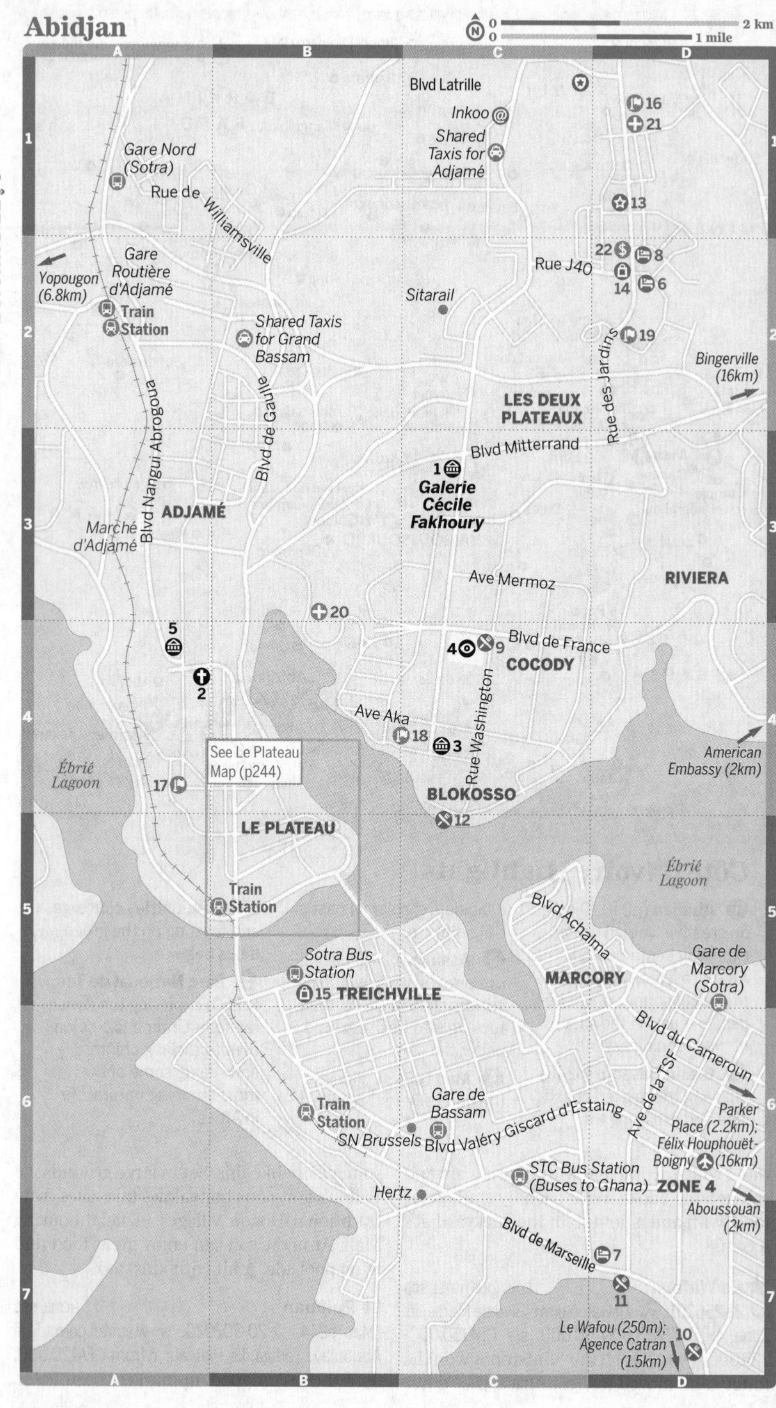

0 2 km
0 1 mile
Blvd Latrille
Inkoo
Shared Taxis for Adjamé
16
21
Gare Nord (Sotra)
Rue de Williamsville
13
22
8
Rue J40
14
6
Yopougon (6.8km)
Gare Routière d'Adjamé
Train Station
Sitarail
Shared Taxis for Grand Bassam
19
Rue des Jardins
Bingerville (16km)
LES DEUX PLATEAUX
Blvd de Gaulle
Blvd Nangui Abrogoua
Blvd Mitterrand
1
Galerie Cécile Fakhoury
ADJAMÉ
Marché d'Adjamé
Ave Mermoz
RIVIERA
20
5
4
9
Blvd de France
COCODY
2
Ave Aka
Rue Washington
18
3
American Embassy (2km)
Ébrié Lagoon
See Le Plateau Map (p244)
17
BLOKOSSO
12
LE PLATEAU
Ébrié Lagoon
Train Station
Blvd Achalma
Sotra Bus Station
15 TREICHVILLE
MARCORY
Gare de Marcory (Sotra)
Blvd du Cameroun
Ave de la TSF
Train Station
Gare de Bassam
Blvd Valéry Giscard d'Estaing
SN Brussels
Parker Place (2.2km); Félix Houphouët-Boigny (16km)
STC Bus Station (Buses to Ghana)
ZONE 4
Hertz
Aboussouan (2km)
Blvd de Marseille
7
11
Le Wafou (250m); Agence Catran (1.5km)
10

## Abidjan

**Top Sights**
1 Galerie Cécile Fakhoury ........ C3

**Sights**
2 Cathedrale St Paul ........ A4
3 Hôtel Ivoire ........ C4
4 Marché de Cocody ........ C4
5 Musée National ........ A4

**Sleeping**
6 La Licorne ........ D2
7 La Nouvelle Pergola ........ D7
8 Le Griffon ........ D2

**Eating**
9 Allocodrome ........ C4
10 Le Marlin Bleu ........ D7
11 Le Mechoui ........ D7
12 Le Nandjelet ........ C5

**Entertainment**
13 L'Acoustic ........ D1

**Shopping**
14 Galerie d'Arts Pluriels ........ D2
15 Marché de Treichville ........ B5

**Information**
16 Beninese Embassy ........ D1
17 Burkinabé Embassy ........ A4
18 German Embassy ........ C4
19 Ghanaian Embassy ........ D2
20 PISAM ........ B3
21 Polyclinique des Deux Plateaux ........ D1
22 SGBCI Bank ........ D2

Plush rooms come equipped with wi-fi and everything you could possibly need.

## Eating

**★Le Nandjelet** AFRICAN $
(Map p242; Blokosso; mains from CFA2000; dinner) Tucked away in Blokosso (opposite the cemetery), this enchanting local spot offers good *kedjenou* (slowly simmered chicken or fish with peppers and tomatoes) and Ivoirian *escargot* (snails). Make a beeline for one of the outdoor tables on the edge of the lagoon – they offer a breathtaking panorama of the Abidjan skyline. Mind that on weekends the music gets very loud.

**Mille Maquis** AFRICAN $
(Map p244; Place de la République) An excellent local strip of *maquis* (rustic open-air restaurants) serving Ivoirian dishes in a jolly, lively atmosphere.

**Allocodrome** AFRICAN $
(Map p242; Rue Washington, Cocody; mains around CFA2000; noon-3pm & 7-11pm) Brochettes (kebabs), beer and beats: this fantastic outdoor spot, with dozens of vendors grilling meats, sizzles until late. Once you arrive you'll be swarmed by different vendors – choose one and surrender to the vibe.

**★Le Mechoui** LEBANESE $$
(Map p242; 21-246893; inside the Athletic Club, Blvd de Marseille, Zone 4; meze from CFA4000; noon-3pm & 7-11pm) In an elegant setting that overlooks the lagoon, Le Mechoui serves fantastic Lebanese food. All the ingredients are fresh, the taste is top-notch, and the choice of the meze is simultaneously authentic and imaginative. Try the lamb tartare, tangy tabbouleh and the classic, creamy hummus – and a serving of hot Lebanese bread. Run by a local Lebanese family.

**★Bushman Café** AFRICAN $$$
(88-358508; Riviera 4; mains from CFA10,000) This rooftop terrace restaurant is number-one for gastronomic delights in Abidjan, drawing locals from across the city to come and dine under the stars. The menu is simple and focused on local flavour, and it's perfect. Try the delicate and fresh fish tartare, or the excellent grilled meat. Properly brewed Ivoirian coffee is served here, too. Do not miss.

**★Aboussouan** AFRICAN $$$
(21-241309; Blvd Giscard-D'Estaing, Treichville; mains from CFA8000; noon-3pm & 7-11pm Tue-Sat; ) Take Côte d'Ivoire's best *maquis* dishes, ask top chefs to prepare them and add fine, innovative touches – that's Aboussouan. Foodie heaven, and there's an excellent wine list too.

**Le Marlin Bleu** SEAFOOD $$$
(Map p242; 21-259727; Blvd de Marseille, Zone 4; mains from CFA15,000) An upmarket, yachting-orientated seafood restaurant (ignore the hotel!) that has fresh fish and luxurious seafood offerings. Popular with the expats. In a kind of compound off Blvd de Marseille.

## Drinking & Entertainment

If there is a city in West Africa to party in, it's Abidjan. There are plenty of parties,

## Le Plateau

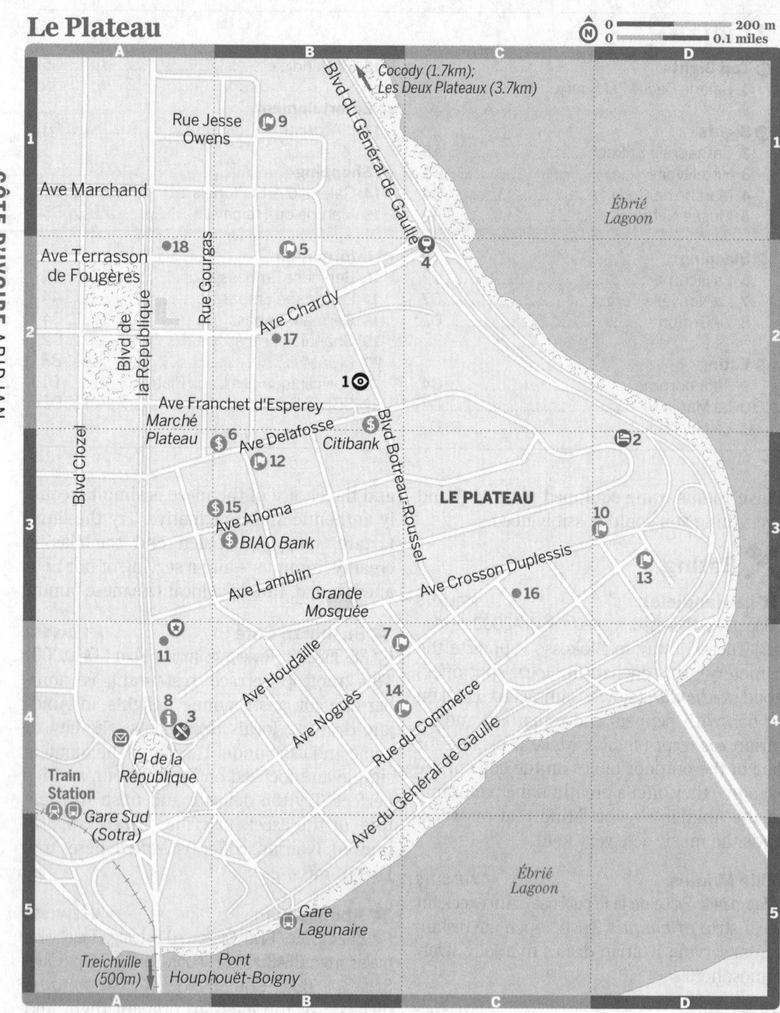


from ordinary *maquis* dancing to sleek DJ parties on rooftops. Note that a lot of the nightclub scene caters to wealthy Ivoirians and expats.

**Bushman Café** ROOFTOP BAR
(☎88-358508; www.facebook.com/africaisafrica; Riviera 4) A wide range of cocktails means you can spend hours choosing between passionfruit cocktails or something with a tamarind twist. There's great music here, and DJ parties, too – check their Facebook page for what's coming up.

**Life Star** CLUB
(Map p244; ☎49-202020; Ave Chardy, Le Plateau; ⏲11pm-6am) A fancy club that attracts wealthy Ivoirians and well-off expats, and anyone who's anyone in Abidjan.

**Parker Place** LIVE MUSIC
(☎05-373459; Rue Paul Langevin, Zone 4; ⏲Tue-Sun) This is Abidjan's most famous reggae bar – Alpha Blondy and Tiken Jah Fakoly played here before they were famous. The bar is still going strong and welcomes live acts most Thursday, Friday and Saturday nights (there's usually a cover charge).

## Le Plateau

**Sights**
1 La Pyramide ... B2

**Sleeping**
2 Le Pullman ... D3

**Eating**
3 Mille Maquis ... A4

**Drinking & Nightlife**
4 Life Star ... C2

**Information**
5 Belgian Embassy ... B2
6 Bicici Bank ... B3
7 Canadian Embassy ... B4
8 Côte d'Ivoire Tourisme ... A4
9 French Embassy ... B1
10 Guinean Embassy ... D3
11 La Sureté Nationale ... A4
12 Liberian Embassy ... B3
13 Malian Embassy ... D3
14 Senegalese Embassy ... C4
15 SGBCI Bank ... B3

**Transport**
16 Air France ... C3
Air Ivoire ... (see 8)
17 Ethiopian Airlines ... B2
Kenya Airways ... (see 18)
18 South African Airways ... A2

**L'Acoustic** LIVE MUSIC
(Map p242; Rue des Jardins, Deux Plateaux) L'Acoustic's stage has held the feet of everyone from hip female vocalists to jazz and big-band ensembles. The place attracts an arty, musical crowd. There's a restaurant for late-night dinners.

## Shopping

**Marché de Treichville** MARKET
(Map p242; Ave Victor Blaka) The Marché de Treichville is an ugly, Chinese-built building, but inside it's African to the core and incredibly well stocked, from food to household products and secondhand clothing. There is little you can't find here.

**Galerie d'Arts Pluriels** ARTS & CRAFTS
(Map p242; ☎22-411506; Centre Commercial Municipal, Rue des Jardins, Deux Plateaux) This fantastic art gallery and shop is run by an Ivoirian art historian. You can view and buy paintings, sculptures and jewellery from all over the continent.

## Information

### INTERNET ACCESS

Most hotels, and a growing number of restaurants and bars, offer wi-fi.

**Inkoo** (Map p242; ☎21-247065; Cap Sud Centre Commercial & Gallerie Sococé, Rue K 125, Deux Plateaux; per 30min CFA500; ⏰9am-8pm) Has speedy connections, a printing centre, phone booths, faxes and scanners.

### MEDICAL SERVICES

**PISAM** (Polyclinique Internationale St Anne-Marie; Map p242; ☎22-483131; www.pisam.ci; Ave Joseph Blohorn, off Blvd de la Corniche, Cocody) Recommended by UN staff. Has a 24-hour intensive care unit.

**Polyclinique des Deux Plateaux** (Map p242; ☎22-413334, 22-414621; www.polycliniquedes2plateaux.com; Rue du Commissariat du 30e Arrondisement, Deux Plateaux) Has good medical services.

The US embassy publishes a list of recommended practitioners on its website at http://abidjan.usembassy.gov.

### MONEY

Euros and dollars can be changed at main branches of banks in Le Plateau. **SGBCI** (Map p244; Ave Anoma, Le Plateau) and **Bicici** (Map p244; Ave Delafosse, Le Plateau) have ATMs that accept Visa, MasterCard and Maestro.

The following banks all have Visa ATMs:

**BIAO Bank** (Map p244; Ave Anoma, Le Plateau)

**Citibank** (Map p244; Ave Delafosse, Le Plateau)

**SGBCI Bank** (Map p242; Rue des Jardins, Deux Plateaux)

### POST

**La Poste** (Map p244; Place de la République, Le Plateau; ⏰7.30am-noon & 2.30-4pm Mon-Fri) Has Western Union service and poste restante.

**ARRIVING IN ABIDJAN**

There is no public transport to or from Félix Houphouët-Boigny International Airport (p246). A taxi to/from Abidjan can cost around CFA5000 to CFA6000, depending on your bargaining skills.

### TOURIST INFORMATION

**Côte d'Ivoire Tourisme** (Map p244; ☎20-251600, 20-251610; Place de la République, Le Plateau; ⏰7.30am-noon & 2.30-4pm Mon-Fri) There's a good map on the wall and the helpful staff will happily shower you with brochures.

## ℹ Getting There & Away

**Félix Houphouët-Boigny International Airport** (Port Bouet Airport; www.aeria-ci.com; Port-Bouët) Takes all of the international air traffic.

**Gare de Bassam** (Map p242; cnr Rue B4 & Blvd Valéry Giscard d'Estaing, Zone 2B) South of Treichville. Bush taxis and minibuses for destinations east along the coast, such as Grand Bassam, Aboisso and Elubo (at the Ghanaian border), stop here.

**Gare Routière d'Adjamé** (Map p242; Ave 13, Adjamé) The main bus station is located some 4km north of Le Plateau, and is quite chaotic. Most UTB and Sotra buses and bush taxis leave from here, and there's frequent transport to all major towns.

Other bus stations here include the following:

**Gare de Marcory (Sotra)** (Map p242; Rue du Taureau, Marcory)

**Gare Lagunaire** (Map p244; Ave du General de Gaulle, Le Plateau)

**Gare Nord (Sotra)** (Map p242; Autoroute d'Abobo, Williamsville)

**Gare Sud (Sotra)** (Map p244; Blvd de la Paix, Le Plateau)

**Sotra Bus Station** (Map p242; ☎21-757100; www.sotra.ci; Ave Christiani, Treichville)

**STC Bus Station** (Map p242; Rue des Carrossiers, Zone 3) For buses to Ghana.

## ℹ Getting Around

*Woro-woro* (shared taxis) cost between CFA300 and CFA800, depending on the length of the journey, and vary in colour according to their function. The yellow taxis work like minibuses, going from one designated spot to another across town; they're usually shared, and do not drop people off to individual destinations.

The red taxis are usually hired just by you (unless you choose to share) and will take you pretty much anywhere within Abidjan. A short hop in a cab from Le Plateau to Zone 4 costs around CFA2000.

**Shared Taxis for Adjamé** (Map p242; Rue K57, Deux Plateaux)

**Shared Taxis for Grand Bassam** (Map p242; Adjamé)

# THE EASTERN BEACHES

## Grand Bassam

☎21

Arty and bathed in faded glory, beachside Bassam was Côte d'Ivoire's French colonial capital until a yellow-fever epidemic broke out in 1896, prompting the French to move their capital to Bingerville. The town, named a Unesco World Heritage Site in 2012, had a glittery image as the top resort in the country until a March 2016 terrorist attack, claimed by al-Qaeda, killed 16 people, many of them foreigners. The town is now safe, but the attack caused a slump in the local tourism industry and Grand Bassam is working hard to recover its flair.

The city is laid out on a long spit of land, with a quiet lagoon on one side and the turbulent Atlantic Ocean on the other. Weekenders fill the beach and enjoy the sun and the sand, but swimming is not advised due to the strong currents – people drown every year, especially tourists.

### Sights & Activities

**Palais de Justice** NOTABLE BUILDING

(Blvd Treich-Laplene) The Palais de Justice should be your first stop on a walk through town. Built in 1910, it was in this building that members of Côte d'Ivoire's PDCI-RDA political group – that of the country's first president, Félix Houphouët-Boigny – were arrested by the French authorities in 1949, in the struggle that preceded the country's independence.

**Nick Amon's Art Gallery** GALLERY

(Blvd Treich-Laplene) One of Côte d'Ivoire's most respected contemporary artists, Amon will greet you with paint-splattered clothing and a warm smile. His canvases start at around CFA50,000; profits go to an organisation that offers art classes to street kids.

**Canoeing** CANOEING

You can take to the waters on a dugout-canoe trip to see traditional crab fishers, mangroves and birdlife. You can make arrangements with local boatmen.

### Festivals & Events

**Fête de l'Abissa** RELIGIOUS

(⏰Oct or Nov) This week-long ceremony honouring the dead offers a great opportunity to witness local traditions.

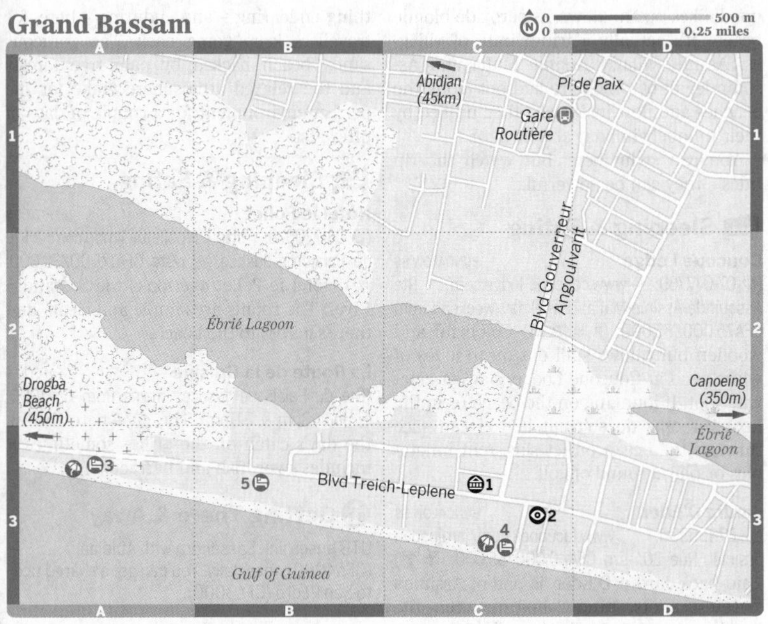


## Grand Bassam

**Sights**

1 Nick Amon's Art Gallery....................C3
2 Palais de Justice.................................C3

**Sleeping**

3 Hôtel Boblin la Mer ...............................A3
4 Koral Beach Hotel..................................C3
5 La Madrague...........................................B3

## Sleeping & Eating

**Hôtel Boblin la Mer** HOTEL $

(☎21-301418; Blvd Treich-Laplene; r with air-con CFA20,000-30,000; P❄📶) Breezy and sun-washed, Boblin la Mer is easily the best value in Bassam. The rooms are decorated with masks and woodcarvings, and breakfast is served on the beach.

★ **Koral Beach Hotel** HOTEL $$

(☎07-239212; koralbeach@yahoo.fr; Blvd Gouverneur Angoulvant/Blvd Treich-Leplene; d from CFA30,000; P❄📶🏊🐾) Run by the wonderful and energetic Cheryl, the KBH has been redecorated to perfection – it's all African wood sculptures and white, pristine walls. The rooms are equally elegant and stylish, with ample beds and featuring local art. The hotel restaurant is good – you can dine overlooking the beach and watching the sunset.

**La Madrague** HOTEL $$

(☎21-301564; www.hotellamadrague.com; Blvd Treich-Laplene; d CFA25,000-40,000; ❄📶🏊) La Madrague taps into Grand Bassam's spirit with its smart, lovingly decorated rooms. There's local art on the walls and Ivoirian cloth swaddling the luxurious beds.

**Drogba Beach** AFRICAN $$

(Blvd Treich-Leplene; mains from CFA3000) A nice and simple *maquis* on the beach, popular with local families at the weekends. Rustic Ivoirian food is served at the simple wooden terrace.

## Getting There & Away

*Woro-woro* (CFA700, 40 minutes) leave from Abidjan's Gare de Bassam. In Bassam, the **gare routière** (bus station) is beside the Place de Paix roundabout, north of the lagoon.

# Assinie

☎21 / POP 16,720

Quiet little Assinie tugs at the heartstrings of overlanders, washed-up surfers and rich weekenders from Abidjan who run their quad bikes up and down its peroxide-blonde beach. It's actually a triumvirate of villages: Assinie village, Assinie Mafia and Assouindé, all of which are laid out along the beaches and flow into each other, unified by their uniquely holiday atmosphere.

You can swim here, but watch the rip tides – they can be powerful.

### Sleeping & Eating

**Coucoue Lodge** BUNGALOW **$$**
(07-077769; www.coucoue-lodge.com; Rte Assouindé-Assinie-Mafia; d weekday/weekend from CFA75,000/85,000; ) Colourful and wooden bungalows spill out on to acres of white sand at Coucoue Lodge, a sweet getaway spot. If lounging on the beach or in the luxury rooms doesn't cut it, you can slice through the ocean on jet skis, rent inflatables or play a round of golf.

**Jardin D'Eden** BUNGALOW **$$**
(07-135300; www.facebook.com/jardineden assinie; Rue 30; s/d CFA40,000/55,000; ) Laid-back Jardin D'Eden is one of Assinie's sweetest spots, sandwiched between the beach and Assinie Mafia. A good bet for a relaxed weekend away with friends, with nice Ivoirian food on offer and cool, calm, clean, comfortable rooms.

**Le Voile Rouge** AFRICAN **$$**
(58-722971; Assinie Mafia; mains from CFA6000; noon-3pm & 6-11pm) A fantastic little place on the waterfront in Assinie Mafia, serving up Ivoirian specialities such as chicken *kedjenou* (slowly simmered chicken or fish with peppers and tomatoes) and grilled prawns. You can swim off the little wooden pier in the afternoons when the tide comes in.

### Getting There & Away

Coming from Grand Bassam or Abidjan, take a *woro-woro* to Samo (CFA2000, 45 minutes). From here you can pick up another car to Assouindé, 15 minutes away. Once there, the rest of the area is accessible by pirogue (traditional canoe) or *woro-woro*.

# THE WEST COAST

## Sassandra

34 / POP 72,220

Sassandra, a low-key beach resort in the far western corner of Côte d'Ivoire, may be a little dog-eared these days but there's something endearing – and enduring – here, for travellers keep going back. The gorgeous sandy beach backed by palm-tree forests and the relaxed atmosphere make for the perfect environment for a couple of days of utter rest.

### Sleeping & Eating

**Hôtel le Pollet** HOTEL **$**
(34-720578; http://lepolletuk.jimdo.com; Rte du Palais de Justice; r/ste CFA17,000/38,000; ) Hôtel le Pollet overlooks the Sassandra River. The rooms are simple and clean, and there's access to the beach.

**La Route de la Cuisine** SEAFOOD **$**
(Rte du Palais de Justice; mains from CFA1000; noon-3pm & 7-11pm) The chef here throws the day's catch on the grill – sometimes it includes swordfish and barracuda.

### Getting There & Away

UTB buses link Sassandra with Abidjan (CFA4000) once daily. You can get a shared taxi to San Pédro (CFA3000).

## San Pédro

34 / POP 631,155

Framed by a strip of soft white sand on one side, and the distant shadows of the fertile Parc National de Taï (p250) on the other, a stop in San Pédro promises a sweet marriage of beach life and forest treks.

West of San Pedro are the balmy beaches of **Grand-Béréby**. It's also the best place to overnight if you're heading overland into Liberia via Tabou and Harper.

### Sleeping & Eating

**Le Cannelle** HOTEL **$**
(34-710539; Blvd Houphouët-Boigny; r CFA25,000; ) Overlooking the waters and with simple and clean rooms, Le Canelle also has a decent **restaurant** on the beach.

**Les Jardins d'Ivoire** HOTEL **$**
(34-713186; Blvd Houphouët-Boigny, Quartier Balmer; r CFA26,000; ) Located in the Balmer area of town, Les Jardins d'Ivoire has a pretty garden, a swimming pool and clean, smart rooms.

### Getting There & Away

UTB buses link San Pédro with Abidjan (CFA5000) once daily. *Woro-woro* go to Grand-Béréby (CFA2500) and east to Sassandra (CFA3000).

For Harper, just across the Liberian border, you can take a shared taxi to Tabou (about CFA4000), then continue on by a combination of road and boat; note that it's not worth attempting in the rainy season.

# THE CENTRE

## Yamoussoukro

30 / POP 281,070

Yamoussoukro (or Yamkro, as it's affectionately dubbed) isn't exactly its country's cultural epicentre, but it is worth a stop here, if only to marvel at the oddity of the capital that was built on the site of former President Félix Houphouët-Boigny's ancestral village. Its basilica, a near-replica of the Vatican's Basilica di San Pietro, is a marvel, its gigantic dome hovering on the flat horizon like a mirage.

The **tourist office** (30-640814; Ave Houphouët-Boigny; 8am-noon & 3-6pm Mon-Fri) arranges Baoulé dancing performances in nearby villages.

### Sights

**Presidential Palace** NOTABLE BUILDING

The presidential palace, where Houphouët-Boigny is now buried, can only be seen from afar, but visitors come to see the **sacred crocodiles** that live in the lake on its southern side. The keeper tosses them some meat around 5pm, touching off an impressive feeding frenzy. Otherwise, the dozens of sleepy reptiles laze away while curious onlookers take photos. But keep your distance: in 2012, a veteran keeper was killed by one of the creatures.

**Basilica** CHURCH

(Basilique Notre-Dame de la Paix; Rte de Daloa; CFA2000; 8am-noon & 2-5.30pm Mon-Sat, 2-5pm Sun) Yamoussoukro's spectacular basilica will leave you wide-eyed. Based on the Basilica of St Peter in the Vatican and designed by Lebanese architect Pierre Fakhoury, it was constructed between 1985 and 1989, with Italian marble and 7000 sq metres of French stained glass specially imported to build it. The nave is a luminous harmony of columns, with a flamboyant altar taking centre stage. There are well-informed English-speaking guides on duty who will take you around the dome and the grounds.

### Sleeping & Eating

**Le Brennus** HOTEL $

(59-127737; www.lebrennus.com; Rte d'Abidjan; r/ste CFA30,000/70,000; ) A good hotel in the centre of town, with simple and clean rooms and efficient service.

**Hôtel Président** HOTEL $$

(30-646464; www.hotelpresident.ci; Rte d'Abidjan; s/d/ste US$65/80/150; ) Yamoussoukro's signature hotel, imposing but faded – the rooms are old, but still swish. There's an 18-hole **golf course**, as well as three restaurants (including a panoramic eatery on the 14th floor), four bars and a nightclub.

**A La Bella Pizza** PIZZA $

(Ave Houphouët-Boigny; mains CFA3500-5000; noon-3pm & 6-11pm) Serves great pastas, crêpes and local fare, as well as its namesake pizzas.

**Maquis le Jardin** AFRICAN $$

(mains CFA3000-5000; noon-3pm & 7-11pm) More upmarket and expensive than the other *maquis* clustered by the lake – the excellent food here makes it worthwhile.

### Getting There & Away

MTT and UTB, whose bus stations are south of town, run buses frequently to Abidjan (CFA4500, 1½ hours); UTB also runs frequently to Bouaké (CFA3800, two hours) and once daily to Man (CFA5000, five hours) and San Pédro (CFA6000, five hours).

# THE NORTH

## Man

33 / POP 188,700

The green, green peaks and valleys of Man are nothing short of magical. Here the air is cooler, the food lighter and the landscapes muddier than in the south. And it's perfect hiking territory. The town itself is a grid of busy streets filled with vendors.

### Sights & Activities

**Silacoro** VILLAGE

This celebrated village is famous for its stilt dancing. It's located around 110km north of Man.

**La Cascade** WATERFALL
(CFA400) The area around Man is known for La Cascade, a crashing waterfall 5km from town that hydrates a bamboo forest. You walk a pretty paved path to reach it. Locals come here to swim and visitors are welcome to join in.

★**Le Dent de Man** HIKING
(guide fee CFA3000) 'The Man's Tooth' sticks out like, well, a tooth, northeast of town. A hike up this steep mountain (881m) starts in the village of **Zoguale** (where you can find a guide), 4km from Man, running through coffee, cocoa and banana plantations. The final stretch requires some serious leg work. Allow at least four hours for the round trip. Bring snacks.

**Mt Tonkoui** HIKING
(guide fee CFA3000) At 1223m, Mt Tonkoui is the second-highest peak in Côte d'Ivoire. The views from the summit are breathtaking and extend to Liberia and Guinea, even during the dusty harmattan winds. The route begins about 18km from Man. You can ask for a guide at your hotel.

## Sleeping & Eating

**Hôtel Amointrin** HOTEL $
(☎33-792670; Rte du Lycée Professionnel; r standard/superior CFA15,000/16,000; ❄) Hôtel Amointrin is probably Man's smartest hotel; the rooms come with hot water and pretty views out over the mountains.

**Hôtel Leveneur** HOTEL $
(☎33-791776; Rue de l'Hôtel Leveneur; r CFA12,000; ❄) The centrally located Hôtel Leveneur has the dishevelled backpacker thing down to a T, though we suspect it's not deliberate.

**Maquis Flamboyant** AFRICAN $
(Rte du Lycée Professionnel; CFA1500) You can find great *attiéké* (grated cassava) – a slightly bitter, couscous-like dish – and brochettes (grilled meat or fish cubes) in this low-key eatery.

**Pâtisserie la Brioche** BAKERY $
(Rue du Commerce; croissants CFA240) A fine place for breakfast or morning coffee.

## Shopping

**Tankari Gallery** ARTS & CRAFTS
(Ave du President Alassane Ouattara; ⏲9am-4pm) You can find West African woodwork here, such as dishes, masks and small wooden sculptures. There is also jewellery and textiles.

## Getting There & Away

You can reach Abidjan by *woro-woro* (CFA8000, seven hours) or UTB bus (CFA7000, eight hours).

Taxis for N'zérékoré in Guinea run via Sipilou (CFA3000, three hours).

# PARC NATIONAL DE TAÏ

There are many places in West Africa that could be dubbed one of the region's 'best-kept secrets', but perhaps none so as much as **Taï** (☎34-722299; www.parcnationaltai.com) FREE, a 5000-sq-km reserve of rainforest so dense that scientists are only just beginning to discover the wealth of flora and fauna that lies within.

Parc National de Taï is one of West Africa's last areas of primary rainforest, and has been a World Heritage Site since 1982. The park is mostly known for its chimpanzees, who famously use tools in their daily activities, but the general wealth of the flora and fauna inside the park is incredible. Besides forest elephants and buffalo, there are at least eleven types of primates, 250 species of birds and 1300 species of plants, more than 50 of which are endemic to the region.

## Activities

Visitors can take **forest hikes** with local rangers, visiting Hana river, Buya lake and **Mt Niénokoué**, where you can stop at the primate research base famous for its nut-cracking chimps.

The **Wild Chimpanzee Foundation** (www.wildchimps.org) is a great source of information on chimp life.

## Sleeping & Eating

**Touraco Ecotel** HUT $
(☎34-722299; www.parcnationaltai.com; huts from CFA10,000) This eco-camp has a mix of thatch-topped round huts with no more than a bed inside them, and a restaurant on the edge of a forest clearing. There are outdoor toilets and showers. You can stay here and explore the park's offerings with the excellent local rangers. Ring ahead.

**Auberge Beau Séjour** GUESTHOUSE
(☎47-971453; Taï; r with fan/air-con CFA6000/12,000; P❄) Simple, clean and minimally furnished rooms in Taï town that are perfect for an overnight stay before you hit the park. There's air-con and en suite bathrooms.

**Le Plein Air** AFRICAN $

(☎47-701637; mains CFA2000-2500) A simple *maquis* (open-air restaurant) in Taï town. You can get the usual grilled chicken or fish with *aloco* (ripe bananas fried with chilli in palm oil) and *attiéké* (grated cassava) or rice with a sauce in a peaceful local setting.

### Getting There & Away

Taï is 213km from San Pédro; it's about a three-hour drive outside the rainy season. If you have your own vehicle, hit the road until you reach the village of Djouroutou, on the west side of the park.

You can also reach Djouroutou from San Pédro via **shuttle** (☎34-722299; CFA4000), but it will take longer and you may have to change cars.

# UNDERSTAND CÔTE D'IVOIRE

## Côte d'Ivoire Today

After the long-delayed presidential elections, Alassane Ouattara took power in 2010. His predecessor, Laurent Gbagbo, had to be forcibly removed from office after refusing to accept defeat. The ensuing violence left 3000 people dead and 500,000 displaced. In November 2011 Gbagbo was extradited to The Hague and charged with war crimes.

Ouattara won a second five-year term in 2015. Economically, Côte d'Ivoire has been one of the best-performing African countries since Ouattara was elected: its GDP grew at an average rate of 8.5% per year between 2012 and 2015.

But while the economy booms, politics remain shaky. Côte d'Ivoire suffered a terrorist attack in March 2016, when an armed group, allegedly Islamist fundamentalists, killed 16 people – both local and foreign – in a beachside resort in Grand Bassam. This has affected tourism, with many hotel owners in Grand Bassam complaining of a dramatic drop in revenue.

January 2017 saw more political instability in the form of military mutiny. Soldiers seized Bouaké and kidnapped the country's defence minister for a short time; there was mild unrest in Abidjan, too. Since the mutiny was reported to be about soldiers' pay, President Ouattara promised salary increases and fired the army and police chiefs, leading the soldiers to withdraw to their barracks.

It is said that many of the soldiers who took part in the mutiny are former rebels who were integrated into the army when Ouattara took power, and that this episode reflects the wider dissatisfaction of the chunk of the population – among them teachers and civil servants – who feel left out of the country's economic boom.

## History

After decades of stability, Côte d'Ivoire's troubles began in September 2002, when troops from the north gained control of much of the country. A truce was short-lived and fighting resumed. France sent in troops to maintain the ceasefire boundaries; meanwhile, tensions from Liberia's war began to spill over the border.

In March 2004 one of numerous peace deals was signed, and Guillaume Soro, formerly the secretary of the New Forces rebel coalition, was named prime minister. UN peacekeepers arrived, but on 4 November President Laurent Gbagbo broke the ceasefire and bombed rebel strongholds, including Bouaké. Two days later, jets struck a French military base, killing nine French peacekeepers. In retaliation, the French destroyed much of the Ivoirian air force's fleet. Government soldiers clashed with peacekeepers, while most French citizens fled, and dozens of Ivoirians died.

A UN resolution backed the president's bid to stay in office until fair elections could be held. In April 2007 French peacekeepers began a staged pull back from the military buffer zone, to be replaced gradually by mixed brigades of government and rebel troops. Gbagbo declared the end of the war and the two sides moved to dismantle the military buffer zone.

In June that year a rocket attack on Prime Minister Soro's plane killed four of his aides, shaking the peace process further. Protests over rising food costs spread through the country. The elections were finally held in 2010.

## Arts & Crafts

The definitive Ivoirian craft is Korhogo cloth, a coarse cotton painted with geometrical designs and fantastical animals. Also prized are Dan masks from the Man region, and

Senoufo wooden statues, masks and traditional musical instruments from the northeast. A fantastic range of contemporary arts can be explored in Abidjan's Galerie Cécile Fakhoury (p240).

## Environment

Côte d'Ivoire used to be covered in dense rainforest, but most of it was cleared during the agricultural boom, and what remains today is under attack from outlawed logging and farming practices.

The country is the world's largest cocoa producer, though much of the production takes place illegally – inside the rainforests, where land is cleared and eventually becomes barren. It is estimated that about 80 percent of the country's forests have disappeared since the 1970s.

Several peaks in the west rise more than 1000m, and a coastal lagoon with a unique ecosystem stretches 300km west from the Ghanaian border. The north is dry scrubland.

# SURVIVAL GUIDE

## Directory A–Z

### ACCOMMODATION

Accommodation in Abidjan is expensive and not always good value for money. Elsewhere in the country, you'll find better deals, but standards of comfort are generally lower.

### ACTIVITIES

Several spots on the coast, most notably Assinie and Dagbego, have decent surfing. Côte d'Ivoire also has a lot to offer birdwatchers, particularly during the (European) winter migration season from December to March. For hiking, head to Man or the beautiful Parc National de Taï.

### SLEEPING PRICE RANGES

The following price ranges refer to a double room with bathroom during high season. Breakfast is not included in the price unless noted.

**$** less than CFA30,000

**$$** CFA30,000–90,000

**$$$** more than CFA90,000

### DANGERS & ANNOYANCES

- Abidjan and other parts of the south are now entirely safe to visit.
- Avoid Bouaké: it's prone to outbreaks of political and military violence.
- If you're heading to the border with Liberia, check with locals first: tensions flare sporadically.
- Take care when walking at night – it's unwise to walk alone outside of well-populated areas.
- Beware of riding in cars without a seatbelt, and in general, if driving – there is a high rate of motor accidents here.
- People drown in the fierce currents and ripping undertow of the Atlantic every year – often strong, overly confident swimmers. Don't swim anywhere the locals won't.

### EMBASSIES & CONSULATES

The following embassies are in Abidjan.

**Belgian Embassy** (Map p244; ☎20-210088, 20-219434; http://cotedivoire.diplomatie.belgium.be; 4th fl, Immeuble Alliance, Ave Terrasson des Fougères 01, Le Plateau; ⏰8-11am Mon-Thu) Also assists Dutch nationals.

**Burkinabé Embassy** (Map p242; ☎20-211501; Ave Terrasson de Fougères, Le Plateau; ⏰8am-noon Mon-Fri) Also has a consulate in Bouaké.

**Canadian Embassy** (Map p244; ☎20-300700; www.canadainternational.gc.ca/cotedivoire; Immeuble Trade Centre, 23 Ave Noguès, Le Plateau; ⏰7.30am-12.30pm & 1.30-4.30pm Mon-Thu, 7.30am-1pm Fri) Also assists Australian nationals.

**French Embassy** (Map p244; ☎20-207500; www.ambafrance-ci.org; 17 Rue Lecoeur, Le Plateau; ⏰8am-4pm Mon-Fri)

**German Embassy** (Map p242; ☎22-442030; www.abidjan.diplo.de; 39 Blvd Hassan II, Cocody; ⏰9am-noon & 2-4pm Mon-Thu, 9am-noon Fri)

**Ghanaian Embassy** (Map p242; ☎22-410288; www.ghanaembassy-ci.org; Rue J95, Deux Plateaux; ⏰8.30am-12.30pm & 2-4pm Mon-Fri)

**Guinean Embassy** (Map p244; ☎20-222520; 3rd fl, Immeuble Crosson Duplessis, Ave Crosson Duplessis, Le Plateau; ⏰8am-noon Mon-Fri)

**Liberian Embassy** (Map p244; ☎20-324636; Immeuble Taleb, Ave Delafosse, Le Plateau; ⏰8am-noon Mon-Thu)

**Malian Embassy** (Map p244; ☎20-311570; Maison du Mali, Rue du Commerce, Le Plateau; ⏰8am-4pm Mon-Fri)

**Senegalese Embassy** (Map p244; ☎20-332876; Immeuble Nabil, off Rue du Commerce, Le Plateau; ⏰8am-2pm Mon-Fri)

## EMERGENCY & IMPORTANT NUMBERS

| | |
|---|---|
| Côte d'Ivoire's country code | 225 |
| International access code | 00 |
| Police | 111 |
| Fire | 180 |
| Medecins Urgence (ambulance) | 07-082626 |
| SOS Medecins (ambulance) | 185 |

## INTERNET ACCESS

Abidjan, and the south, have wi-fi in midrange and upmarket establishments. It's rare to find wi-fi in the north.

## LGBTIQ TRAVELLERS

Same-sex relations are not a crime in Côte d'Ivoire, but there are no legal protections for sexual minorities. Although there are several LGBTIQ organisations (one of them suffered a mob attack in 2014), and a relatively good LGBTIQ scene for the region, there are regular reports of violence based on sexual orientation. Caution and discretion are well advised in public.

## MONEY

ATMs are available in the bigger cities, but take cash if you're going anywhere more remote. Credit cards are accepted in top-end establishments.

### ATMs

Visa ATMs are widespread in Abidjan, Grand Bassam, Yamoussoukro and major towns. Most SGBCI branches have ATMs that accept Visa, MasterCard and sometimes Maestro. There are no banks in Assinie but there is a branch of SGBCI (with an ATM) in Grand Bassam.

### Exchange Rates

| | | |
|---|---|---|
| Australia | A$1 | CFA452 |
| Canada | C$1 | CFA440 |
| Europe | €1 | CFA656 |
| Japan | ¥100 | CFA538 |
| NZ | NZ$1 | CFA415 |
| UK | UK£1 | CFA774 |
| US | US$1 | CFA600 |

For current exchange rates, see www.xe.com.

### Tipping

**Guesthouses** You can tip around CFA500 if the service was very good.

**Hotels** Tipping the cleaning staff is at your discretion, but if you're very happy with the job they did, anything up to CFA1500 is reasonable.

## EATING PRICE RANGES

The following price ranges refer to a main course.

**$** less than CFA3000

**$$** CFA3000–6000

**$$$** more than CFA6000

**Tours** Beyond the guided tour price, if your guide has been excellent, tip them from CFA500 to CFA1000.

**Taxi** Since you'll mostly have to bargain down the price, tipping is not expected.

## OPENING HOURS

**Banks** 8am to 11.30am and 2.30pm to 4.30pm Monday to Friday

**Bars** noon to 11pm

**Cafes** 9am to 6pm

**Clubs** 11pm to 4am

**Government offices** 7.30am to 5.30pm Monday to Friday (with breaks for lunch)

**Restaurants** noon to 3pm (lunch) and 7pm to 11pm (dinner)

**Shops** 8am to 6pm

## POST

La Poste is the country's main postal service. The main **La Poste** branch is in Abidjan (p245).

## PUBLIC HOLIDAYS

**New Year's Day** 1 January

**Labour Day** 1 May

**Independence Day** 7 August

**Fête de la Paix** 15 November

**Christmas** 25 December

## TELEPHONE

If you have a GSM mobile phone, you can buy SIM cards from CFA2500. Street stalls also sell

## PRACTICALITIES

**Electricity** The power supply is 220V. Plugs are of the European two-round-pin variety.

**Newspapers** Among the nearly 20 daily newspapers, all in French, *Soirinfo*, *24 Heures* and *L'Intelligent d'Abidjan* steer an independent course. *Gbich!* is a satirical paper.

**Radio** Jam (99.3FM) and Radio Nostalgie (101.1FM) play hit music. The BBC World Service broadcasts some programs in English on 94.3FM.

top-up vouchers from CFA550. Calls generally cost between CFA25 and CFA150 per minute.

The Orange network is reliable and accessible in most parts of the country, even some rural areas, although it can be expensive.

### TOURIST INFORMATION

Côte d'Ivoire Tourisme (p246) in Abidjan has helpful staff.

### VISAS

Everyone except Ecowas (Economic Community of West African States) nationals must arrange a visa in advance.

Visas can be extended at **La Sureté Nationale** (Map p244; ☎20-320289; www.diplomatie.gouv.ci; Police de l'Air et des Frontières, Immeuble Douane, Blvd de la République, Le Plateau; ⊙8am-noon & 3-5pm Mon-Fri) in Abidjan.

#### Visas for Onward Travel

If you want to travel to several countries in the area, consider the Visa de l'Entente, which allows entry to Côte d'Ivoire, Benin, Burkina Faso, Niger and Togo. This multiple-entry visa is valid for two months and costs €120. Apply for it at the **Beninese Embassy** (Map p242; ☎22-414413, 22-414414; www.ambassadebeninci.com; 09 BP 283, Cocody II; ⊙8-11am Mon-Thu) in Abidjan.

## Getting There & Away

### AIR

**Félix Houphouët-Boigny** (p246) is Côte d'Ivoire's swish international airport, complete with wi-fi access.

Airlines that service Côte d'Ivoire include:

**Air France** (AF; Map p244; ☎20-202424; www.airfrance.com; Immeuble Kharrat, Rue Noguès, Le Plateau)

**Air Ivoire** (VU; Map p244; ☎20-251400, 20-251561; www.airivoire.com; Immeuble Le République, Place de la République, Le Plateau)

**Ethiopian Airlines** (ET; Map p244; ☎20-215284; www.flyethiopian.com; Ave Chardy, Le Plateau)

**Kenya Airways** (KQ; Map p244; ☎20-320767; www.kenya-airways.com; Immeuble Jeceda, Blvd de la République, Le Plateau)

**SN Brussels** (SN; Map p242; ☎27-232345; www.flysn.com; off Blvd Valéry Giscard d'Estaing, Treichville)

**South African Airways** (SA; Map p244; ☎20-218280; www.flysaa.com; Immeuble Jeceda, Blvd de la République, Le Plateau)

### LAND

**Burkina Faso** Passenger train services (at least 36 hours, three times a week) run between Abidjan and Ouagadougou in Burkina Faso. Contact **Sitarail** (Map p242; ☎20-208000, 20-210245).

**Ghana** It will take you about three hours to reach the crossing at Noé from Abidjan. Note that the border shuts at 6pm promptly, accompanied by a fancy flag ceremony.

**Guinea** The most frequently travelled route to Guinea is between Man and N'zérékoré, either through Danané and Nzo or Biankouma and Sipilou. The Liberia–Guinea border closes at 6pm each day.

**Liberia** Minibuses and shared taxis make the quick hop from Danané to the border at Gbé-Nda. A bus takes this route from Abidjan to Monrovia (two days) several times a week. From Monrovia, plan on about three days to cross through Guinea and board a bus for Abidjan.

**Mali** Buses and shared taxis run from Abidjan, Yamoussoukro and Bouaké to Bamako, usually via Ferkessédougou, and Sikasso in Mali. The Mali–Côte d'Ivoire border closes at 6pm each day.

## Getting Around

### AIR

Air Ivoire offers internal flights throughout the country, but prices can be high.

### BUS

The country's large, relatively modern buses are around the same price and are significantly more comfortable than bush taxis or minibuses.

### CAR & MOTORCYCLE

You can hire cars from **Hertz** (Map p242; ☎21-253706; www.hertz.com; 19 Rue Thomas Edison, Marcory Zone 4C) in Abidjan. Road conditions can be bad, and Ivoirian driving is atrocious, so exercise extreme caution when on the road.

### LOCAL TRANSPORT

Shared taxis (ageing Peugeots or covered pick-ups, known as *bâchés*) and minibuses cover major towns and outlying communities not served by the large buses. They leave at all hours of the day, but only when full, so long waits may be required.

### TRAIN

Sitarail offers the romantically named *Bélier* and *Gazelle* trains linking Abidjan with Ferkessédougou (CFA12,000, daily).

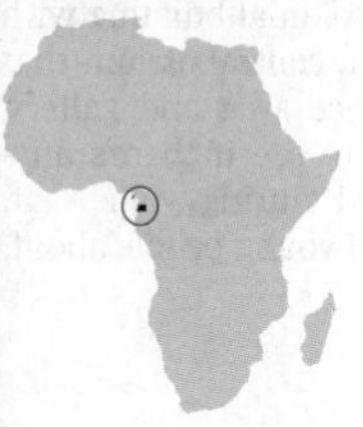

# Equatorial Guinea

240 / POP 1,862,158

**Includes ➡**



## Best Places to Eat

➡ L'Atelier (p259)

➡ La Ferme Beach (p261)

➡ La Luna Complex (p259)

## Best Places to Sleep

➡ Magno Suites (p256)

➡ Apart-Hotel Impala (p256)

➡ Hotel Finisterre San Pedro (p261)

## Why Go?

This is the land of primates with painted faces, soft clouds of butterflies and insects so colourful they belong in the realm of fiction. Yes, Equatorial Guinea has something of a reputation, with a history of failed coups, allegations of corruption, trafficked bushmeat and buckets of oil, but there is plenty to bring you to this country's beautiful black-and-white shores.

The capital, Malabo, boasts fascinating colonial architecture alongside sleek oil company high-rises, yet retains its African flavour with colourful markets and a bustling port. Though the country is currently dripping in oil wealth, many people's taps run dry. Poverty permeates ordinary life, making a trip to Malabo at once hedonistic and heartbreaking.

Beyond Malabo, on Bioko Island, are volcanic views, fishing villages, rainforests full of endangered primates, vibrant birdlife and shores of nesting sea turtles. On the mainland, Rio Mu i's white beaches, forest paths and jungle-scapes await.

## When to Go

**Malabo**

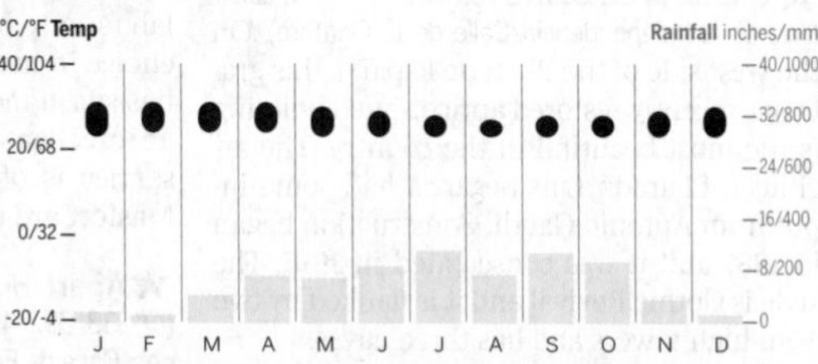


**Jun–Aug** Dry season on the mainland, Rio Muni; more comfortable to travel and roads easier to navigate.

**Dec–Feb** Bioko Island's dry season, although it can rain at any time.

**Nov–Feb** Turtles comes ashore to lay their eggs at Ureca and in the Reserva Natural de Rio Campo.

# BIOKO ISLAND

Bioko Island, rather curiously, sits off the coast of Cameroon rather than the mainland of Equatorial Guinea, and is home to the capital, Malabo. The northern third of the island, Bioko Norte, has a number of small villages along the coast but the further south you go towards Bioko Sur, the thicker the rainforest becomes and stately ceiba trees dot the landscape.

Surrounded by beautiful beaches with either black volcanic or white sands, Bioko has rainforests, woodland, savannah and one volcanic peak, Pico Basile (3012m), usually covered in cloud. While the capital can keep you occupied for a few days, it is worth exploring the southern regions of the island, easily visited on a day trip. Ureca in the far south is the jewel in the crown. Four types of turtles visit from November to February to lay their eggs on the beaches here, and the dense forest around the Luba Crater is home to the primates for which Equatorial Guinea is so well known.

## Malabo

POP 439,070

Malabo is a city of sharp contrasts. To the east is the port and the old city with its splendid cathedral and some interesting colonial architecture. To the west, the city positively gleams with upmarket suburbs sporting elegant villas, smart hotels, government ministries and embassies.

In the heart of it all, the city centre has wide boulevards and modern buildings including a shopping mall featuring upmarket tenants and an array of restaurants and hotels.

### Sights

**★Catedrál de Santa Isabel** CATHEDRAL

(Ave de la Independencia/Calle de 12 Octubre) On the west side of the Plaza de España, this gracious, recently restored apricot-hued building is the most beautiful in the country. The architect, Llairadó Luis Segarra, had some input from Antonio Gaudí. Construction began in 1887 and it was consecrated in 1916. The style is Gothic Revival and it is flanked by two 40m-high towers and has three naves.

**Equatoguinean Cultural Centre** NOTABLE BUILDING

(Centro Cultural Ecuatoguineano; ☎222 110 450, 333 091 032; ccegmalabo@hotmail.com; Ave de la Independencia; ⏰9am-10.30pm Mon-Fri) A bright yellow building on the main street, this centre is a lovely colonial building with large windows. It has a central atrium that serves as a performance area and gallery, and is worth visiting to see if there's anything cultural planned during your visit. There are always lots of young people about, using the free wi-fi.

### Tours

**Ruta 47** TOURS

(☎222 019 786; www.visitguineaecuatorial.com; Hotel Yoly, Calle 3 de Agosto; ⏰8am-6pm) The personable and highly professional Ángel Vañó is a mine of information on Equatorial Guinea. He organises trips (and visa applications) throughout the country.

### Sleeping

**Internet Hostal** HOTEL $

(☎222 126 653; www.facebook.com/Internet-Hostal-548468751952667; Ave de las Naciones Unidas; d CFA20,000, with wi-fi CFA25,000; ❄📶) One of the cheapest options in town, this hotel has large, quiet rooms and is in an excellent location. However, the bathrooms are rather grubby, shower-over-the-toilet affairs. The owner only speaks Chinese so making a reservation in advance is difficult.

**Hotel Yoly & Hermanos** HOTEL $$

(☎333 091 895; www.hotelyolyhermanos.com; d CFA46,000; ❄📶) Hotel Yoly is a good mid-range hotel: the rooms are pleasant and have a fridge, and bathrooms are large. Wi-fi only works in the large, wood-panelled lobby. The location is very good for exploring the old part of the city.

**★Magno Suites** BOUTIQUE HOTEL $$$

(☎333 096 333, Whatsapp 222 755 542; www.magnosuites.com; Carretera del Aeropuerto, Paraíso; d/junior ste/exclusive ste incl breakfast CFA116,000/138,000/275,000; P❄📶🏊) Malabo's only boutique hotel, this is a superb choice in the upmarket suburb of Paraíso. It has swish modern decor, king-size beds and an excellent restaurant. An airport shuttle service is offered free of charge. Visa and MasterCard credit cards are accepted.

**★Apart-Hotel Impala** HOTEL $$$

(☎333 092 492, 222 287 122; www.hotelimpala.net; Calle de Enrique Nvó; s/d CFA50,000/90,000; ❄📶) Don't be put off by the tacky lobby, this place gets better upstairs, and there's a lift. The rooms are very comfortable and have tiny balconies, a fridge and good bathrooms. Staff are friendly and helpful. Be choosy about which room you take: some

## Equatorial Guinea Highlights

**1 Bioko Island** (p256) Going wide-eyed over the strange combination of little villages with Spanish colonial churches, dense rainforest, rare wildlife and oil platforms.

**2 Malabo** (p256) Exploring the colonial architecture, bustling markets and buzzing nightlife of this city of contrasts.

**3 Monte Alen National Park** (p264) Whispering during forest walks in search of gorillas, elephants, chimpanzees and a glorious array of colourful birds and insects.

**4 Ureca** (p260) Watching marine turtles come ashore to lay their eggs from November to January in this region of forests, waterfalls and deserted beaches.

**5 Isla Corisco** (p263) Treading softly on the squeaky-clean sand of this undiscovered paradise isle before the crowds descend.

look out directly onto the Pizza Place terrace next door, and could be noisy.

**Hotel Bahia 2** HOTEL **$$$**
(☎333 096 609; bahia2caracolas@yahoo.com; Calle de los Parques de África, Caracolas; s/d CFA60,000/110,000; P❄📶) The original version of this brand-new hotel used to be situated at the port in central Malabo, but it has relocated to this modern building in the suburb of Caracolas off the airport road. Rooms are nicely decorated and comfortable, and staff are pleasant. It all seems eerily empty, though. The restaurant serves mains from CFA9000.

## Malabo

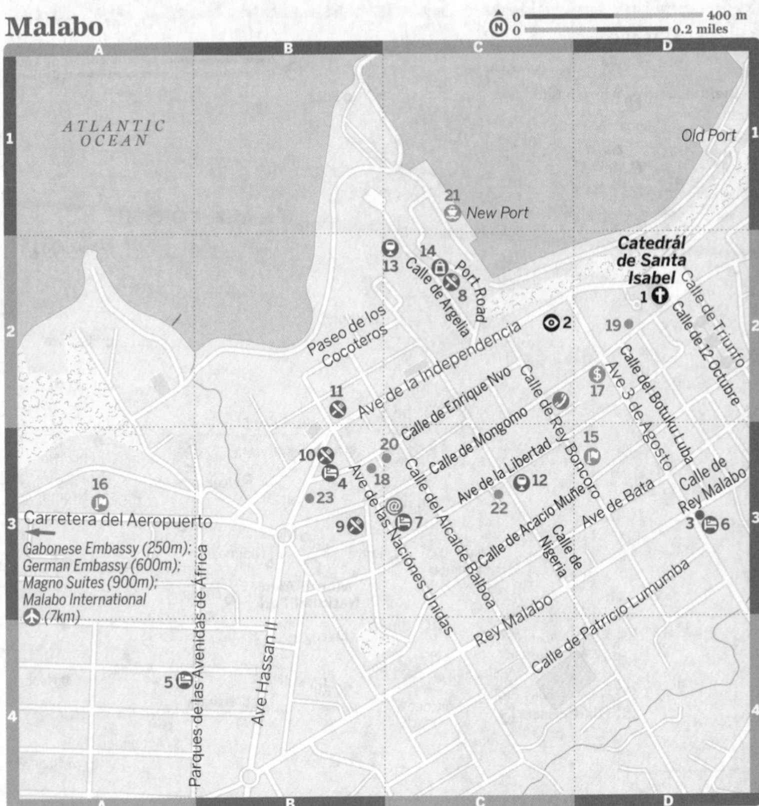


## Malabo

**Top Sights**
1 Catedrál de Santa Isabel .......... D2

**Sights**
2 Equatoguinean Cultural Centre .......... C2

**Activities, Courses & Tours**
3 Ruta 47 .......... D3

**Sleeping**
4 Apart-Hotel Impala .......... B3
5 Hotel Bahia 2 .......... A4
6 Hotel Yoly & Hermanos .......... D3
7 Internet Hostal .......... C3

**Eating**
8 La Luna Complex .......... C2
9 L'Atelier .......... B3
10 Pizza Place .......... B3
11 Restaurant Bidji Binia .......... B2

**Drinking & Nightlife**
12 Aviator Pub & Café .......... C3
13 Bahia Sound Lounge .......... C2
L'Atelier Cabaret Lounge .......... (see 9)

**Shopping**
14 African Crafts .......... C2

**Information**
15 Cameroonian Embassy .......... D3
16 French Embassy .......... A3
17 Pecunia Express .......... D2
18 Satguru Travels & Tours Services .......... B3

**Transport**
19 CEIBA Airlines .......... D2
20 Cronos Airlines .......... C3
Elobey Ferry .......... (see 21)
21 New Port, Malabo .......... C1
22 Punto Azul .......... C3
23 Royal Air Maroc .......... B3

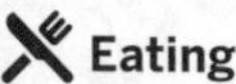

## Eating

There are plenty of restaurants from Senegalese to Italian, Spanish, Lebanese and French. It is worth seeking out those that serve local dishes such as *pepe* soup, giant snails and a local shellfish called *bilolá*. The upmarket hotels often serve buffet lunches on Sundays, while smaller cafes offer tortillas or croissants for breakfast.

**Restaurant Bidji Binia** ITALIAN **$$**
(333 093 878; 359 Ave de la Independencia; pizzas from CFA6500; 8am-noon Mon-Fri, 9am-noon Sat & Sun; ) 'Food like mama makes' is what the name means, and she'd be proud of the pizzas. Pastas and salads are also on offer. There are two levels in the cool interior, and a pleasant terrace at the front. Staff are friendly and this is a popular place with expats. Takeaway is also available.

**Pizza Place** LEBANESE **$$**
(333 093 450; Ave Hassan II; mains from CFA5000; 7am-2am; ) This huge place spreads over several floors, including a lounge with sports screen and a terrace with shisha. There's a wide Lebanese menu with dishes great for sharing and an enormous lunchtime buffet every day for CFA10,000. Wi-fi is intermittent and costs CFA1000 per hour.

**★ L'Atelier** AFRICAN **$$$**
(222 000 030, 555 877 436; Calle Waiso; mains from CFA7000; noon-3.30pm Mon-Wed, noon-2am Thu-Sun; ) All wood, brick and leopard print, this modish restaurant is the place to be seen. There's a bar at the entrance and a cabaret lounge upstairs. The menu features African dishes including giant snails and chicken or fish with chocolate sauce, as well as Cameroonian dishes such as *ndolé* and *follon*. The menu changes weekly.

**La Luna Complex** INTERNATIONAL **$$$**
(333 096 096; www.lalunamalabo.com; Calle de Argelia; mains from CFA7500; 8am-11pm; ) Superb sea views from the wide terrace complement the good food here. The menu is mostly French with a few African options. There's a huge buffet on Sundays (CFA17,000) and a daily happy hour from 5pm to 7pm. You could spend the whole day here, using the pool, too.

## Drinking & Nightlife

**Aviator Pub & Café** PUB
(222 185 534; www.facebook.com/AviatorMalabo; 322 Ave de la Libertad; 9am-3am Mon-Sat; ) The Aviator is a stylish new pub, all dark green walls and some outside seating. There are sports screens, very popular karaoke on Thursdays and live music on Fridays and Saturdays. There's food to soak up the beer: the English owner offers a full English breakfast (CFA4000) and fish and chips (CFA7000). Takeaways are available, too.

**L'Atelier Cabaret Lounge** LOUNGE
(Calle Waiso; 10pm-2am Thu-Sun) Featuring rococo chairs, silver gilt and chandeliers, this 'cabaret lounge' is a great place to sip a cocktail and enjoy live music on weekends. There's no entry fee.

**Bahia Sound Lounge** CLUB
(222 091 538; www.facebook.com/BahiaSoundLounge; Calle de Argelia; 7pm-2am Wed-Sun) There's a great bar here and an open-air dance floor overlooking the sea. It's always popular though entrance and drinks prices are high.

## Shopping

**African crafts** ARTS & CRAFTS
(Luna Complex, Calle Argelia; 10am-10pm) Carved wooden crafts such as figurines and masks are on sale at the entrance to the Luna Complex.

## Information

### INTERNET ACCESS

Many hotels, restaurants and cafes offer free wiifi.

**Cibermax** (Ave de la Naciones Unidas; per hour CFA500; 8am-noon & 4-10pm Mon-Fri, 8am-noon Sat) is a useful internet cafe in a central location.

### MEDICAL SERVICES

**La Paz Hospital** (556 666 156, 556 666 160; www.lapazmalabo.org; Sipopo; 24hr) The top hospital in the country, staffed by Europeans and Israelis. There's a pharmacy and five-star hotel on-site.

### MONEY

Banks and some upmarket hotels will exchange foreign currency.

**Pecunia Express** (Ave 3 de Agosto; 8am-5.30pm Mon-Fri, 10am-2pm Sat) An exchange bureau in the centre of town.

### TRAVEL AGENCIES

**Satguru Travels & Tours Services** (333 090 506, 333 096 326; marketing@satgurutravel.com; Calle de Enrique Nvó; 8am-8pm Mon-Fri, 10am-8pm Sat) An efficient travel agency for booking international and internal flights. It does not offer tours in the country, though.

WORTH A TRIP

## DAY TRIP FROM MALABO

A day trip from Malabo around the northern two-thirds of Bioko Island is well worth taking. Contact a tour operator such as **Ruta 47** (p256) to arrange transport and expect to pay around CFA131,000.

The excellent tarred road with well-tended verges will take you clockwise around the island, passing through small towns and villages. The beautiful Mt Cameroon is visible in the distance as you leave Malabo.

Look out for the pretty yellow **Sagrada Familia Church** (Basakoto) a pretty town with a small lighthouse, a pink church and a large house belonging to the former prime minister. Here the road turns west towards **Moka** and climbs into the central region. You will see huge, stately ceiba trees, the national emblem of Equatorial Guinea. At an elevation of 1000m, Moka is cooler and home to one of the president's palaces complete with two helipads. Continue on to **Luba** on the west coast, which is a good place to stop for lunch. **Arena Blanca** has a lovely yellow-sand beach, clouds of breeding butterflies and a few drinking shacks, all very popular on Sundays. Finally, you'll pass the extension of the university campus, and a striking mosque as you return to Malabo.

## Getting There & Away

### AIR

The easiest way to get from Malabo to Bata is to fly. The local airlines:

**CEIBA Airlines** (ceiba@fly-ceiba.com; Calle de Kenia; 8.30am-5pm Mon-Fri, 9am-4pm Sat)

**Cronos Airlines** (333 090 471; www.cronosair.com; Calle de Enrique Nvó)

**Punto Azul** (222 605 949, 222 111 100; www.flypuntoazul.gq; 8am-4pm Mon-Fri, 8am-noon Sat)

For international flights, **Royal Air Maroc** (333 099 593, 333 099 592; www.royalairmaroc.com; Ave Hassan II; 8am-noon & 4-7pm Mon-Fri) has an office in the centre of town.

### BOAT

There is a ferry service called the **Elobey** (New Port, Malabo; CFA33,000) that runs weekly between Malabo and Bata, departing Friday at 6am and returning on Sunday. It is best to visit the New Port a few days before you intend to leave to try to buy tickets and confirm departure times. Expect to pay around CFA33,000 one way. The journey takes five to 10 hours, depending on the sea and the weather.

## Getting Around

A shared taxi around town costs CFA1000. Expect to pay CFA2000 for longer journeys to the airport or Ministry of Tourism.

## Ureca

POP 2000

This tiny village lies in a spectacular location in the southernmost region of Bioko and is one of the wettest places on earth, receiving some 10,450mm of rain per annum. During the dry season (November to January), turtles come ashore on the beaches at Ureca to lay their eggs. Four types of turtles are represented: Atlantic Green *(Chelonia mydas)*, Leatherback *(Dermochelys coriacea)*, Hawksbill *(Eretmochelys imbricata)* and Olive Ridley *(Lepidochelys olivacea)*. When you're not sunning yourself on the beaches or watching the cycle of life unfold, there are excellent opportunities for hiking in the nearby jungle.

Part of the Bioko Biodiversity Protection Program, **Ureca Nature Center** (www.bioko.org/unc.html; Ureca Village; hikes per person from CFA5000, min charge CFA15,000; 9am-4pm) has three components: an ecotourism program offering comfortable overnight trips aided by local guides, porters, cooks and camp attendants, concentrating on marine turtle ecology, Bioko's diurnal monkeys and visitor responsibility; an Ecoguard Vigilance Point to emphasise sustainable conservation; and the Bioko Artisan Collective shop selling handicrafts made by locals.

If you are taking part in a camp organised through the Moka Wildlife Center they will help you organise transport from Malabo. Otherwise, arrange transport with a tour operator in Malabo as the access road is so steep that you'll need a 4WD vehicle.

# RIO MUNI

From the remote Rio Campo Nature Reserve where turtles come ashore to lay their eggs, to the pristine white sands and azure sea of the beautiful island of Corisco, the coast of mainland Equatorial Guinea is reason enough to visit. Best of all, you'll probably have it to yourself. Venture inland and discover the dense rainforest of the Monte Alen National Park, which teems with animals, including forest elephants, lowland gorillas and chimpanzees.

Bata is the major city, larger even than the capital, Malabo, though a new capital, Oyala, is being constructed in the central region.

## Bata

POP 256,914

Sitting within striking distance of some of the most beautiful (and deserted) stretches of sand on the continent, the city of Bata is the capital and logistical centre of travel in Equatorial Guinea's mainland region of Rio Muni. Besides providing access to the beaches, it also acts as a jumping-off point for ventures into the wilds of Monte Alen National Park.

The city itself, with wide streets and colourful buildings, has a dilapidated colonial charm. Along the beachfront, dusty cranes hover over half-finished hotels and office blocks, acting as poignant reminders of times when oil money and expats flowed in.

### Sleeping

**★Hotel Finisterre San Pedro** HOTEL $

(☎555 612 472, 222 612 473; fassane624@gmail.com; Calle Mbogo Nzogo; d CFA25,000-40,000; ❄📶) Situated behind the Chinese hotel under construction, this Senegalese-owned hotel is bright, clean and well furnished. Some rooms have a bathtub as well as a shower. The cheapest rooms share a bathroom and the largest have fridges. The friendly family also owns the Restaurant Naby next door.

**Hotel Carmen** HOTEL $$

(☎222 677 688; yannismalabo@hotmail.com; Paseo Marítima; d/ste CFA50,000/75,000; P❄📶🏊) While the rooms are fairly plain here, there is a lovely pool by the sea, surrounded by thatched cabanas. There's a restaurant and bar, too. The hotel is on the airport road north of town.

**★Aparthotel Plaza** HOTEL, APARTMENTS $$$

(☎333 080 253; www.hotelplaza.com; Edificio 3 de Agosto; d CFA90,000; ❄📶) Even the standard rooms here are enormous, with a lounge area and good bathroom. It's all dark wood with leather armchairs. There are larger apartments for longer stays, including the Presidential suite at CFA400,000. There are good deals to be had over weekends. The bar is on the ground floor, and the restaurant on the 1st floor (mains from CFA9000).

> **WORTH A TRIP**
>
> **MOKA WILDLIFE CENTER**
>
> The **Moka Wildlife Center** (www.bioko.org; Moka; per person CFA5000 (minimum charge of CFA15,000); ⏱9am-5pm Sat & Sun) belongs to the Bioko Biodiversity Protection Program that has been in operation since 1998. It is involved in education, research and conservation. Since training people to act as guards to patrol the beaches during nesting season, the local market for both turtles and eggs has gradually decreased. They offer various guided hikes around Moka at weekends. Weekday hikes can be arranged by appointment.
>
> Moka can easily be reached from Malabo by shared taxi (CFA2500). It is possible to visit Moka on a day trip from Malabo.

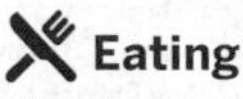

### Eating

**Big Bites** EUROPEAN $

(Calle Jesús Bacale; burgers CFA3500, pizzas CFA5000; ⏱8am-11pm) Lebanese hummus, pizzas, pastas and burgers are on the menu at this friendly place with a large terrace. KFC Big Bites are CFA4000, just don't mention copyright laws.

**Restaurant Naby** AFRICAN $

(☎222 612 473; Calle Mbogo Nzogo; mains CFA4000; ⏱8am-10pm Mon-Sat) Part of the Hotel Finisterre San Pedro, this restaurant is set in a shady terrace and offers good pastries and omelettes for breakfast (but no coffee). There are crêpes, pizzas and salads, but the Senegalese specialities are the best options: *yassa* fish or meat is CFA4000.

**Bar Central** EUROPEAN $$

(☎333 274 307; El Cruce Santy; mains from CFA7000; ⏱7am-11pm; ❄) If you spend any time at all in Bata, you will gravitate to this friendly bar and restaurant. Set on a crossroads, the terrace is surrounded by plants that seem to usher in a welcome cool breeze. There's a wide menu with the usual pizzas, meat and fish. Try the calamari à la Central, dipped in beer batter (CFA10,000).

**★La Ferme Beach** EUROPEAN $$$

(☎222 257 333, 333 08 32 81; Bome Beach, south of Bata; mains from CFA7500; ❄) La Ferme (pronounced Fermay for taxi drivers) is a lovely beach resort about 20 minutes south of Bata port. It has a large terrace, gorgeous pool surrounded by palm trees and spacious restaurant. Fish is the best option here and it couldn't be fresher. The amuse-bouche of tortilla and empanadilla is a nice touch.

**Utonde Beach Club** EUROPEAN **$$$**
(☎555 123 893; Utonde; ⏲11am-2am; P ❄ ☜) This is one of two beach resorts in Utonde and was about to open at the time of our visit. It's very stylish, with thatched umbrellas set around a large pool. Chef Rafi conjures up the usual staples of pizzas, fish and steaks. A great place to escape the city.

## Drinking & Nightlife

**Rolex Discoteca** CLUB
(Calle 3 de Agosto; admission CFA10,000; ⏲10pm-5pm Thu-Sun) The place to be seen in Bata, this place rocks over the weekend with its dark interior, loud music, mirrors and lasers. It's not cheap, though, with its high entrance price and drinks around CFA5000 each. It's next to the Aparthotel Plaza.

**Cervezeria Elik Melen** BAR
(Hotel Elik Melen, Calle 3 de Agosto & Ave Patrice Lumumba; ⏲10am-2am) The 1st-floor terrace at this hotel has sea views, while the bar inside has wood panelling and blasting air-con. It's a convivial place, especially when the football is on TV.

**Bar Estadio** SPORTS BAR
(Calle Mbogo Nzogo; San Miguel beer CFA1500; ⏲noon-midnight) An open-air bar with some sports screens, located next to the old stadium, this is a great place for a beer, especially on match nights.

## Shopping

**African crafts** ARTS & CRAFTS
(Calle Mbogo Nzogo, Bata) This small shack has a range of African souvenirs such as carved wooden figurines, masks and beads.

## Information

### MEDICAL SERVICES

There are plenty of pharmacies in Bata. **Farmacia Afrom** (Calle Mbogo Nzogo, Bata; ⏲9am-4pm Mon-Fri) is well stocked and in a central location.

For medical emergencies, head for the Bata branch of **La Paz Hospital** (☎333 083 515/8, 222 633 344; www.lapazmalabo.org).

### MONEY

Bata has a number of banks. The most central:

**Banco Nacional** (Ave Papa Juan Pablo II, Bata; ⏲8am-2pm Mon-Fri, to noon Sat)

**Ecobank** (Ave de la Naciones Unidas; ⏲9am-5pm Mon-Fri, to 2pm Sat)

**SGBGE** (Ave de la Independencia; ⏲8am-2pm Mon-Fri, to noon Sat)

**Pecunia Express** (☎222 080 807; Ave Papa Juan Pablo II; ⏲8am-5.30pm Mon-Fri, 10am-2pm Sat) For exchanging foreign currency.

### TOURIST INFORMATION

**INDEFOR-AP** (☎222 240 159, 222 561 660; ayetebemme@yahoo.es; Calle Jesús Bacale, Bata; ⏲8am-4pm Mon-Fri) Permits to visit Monte Alen National Park and the coastal parks of Rio Campo and Tika are available here. It has excellent brochures on Monte Alen.

## Getting There & Away

**Bata International Airport** (Paseo Marítimo) has several flights a week to Malabo.

## Getting Around

- Taxis around town cost around CFA500 to CFA1000. Expect to pay more to reach the beach resorts south of the port.
- A taxi to the airport will set you back CFA2000.
- The **taxi rank** (Mercado 5, Colombo) for journeys to towns south of Bata is located at Mercado 5 (5km from the city centre). A private taxi to Mbini takes about an hour, and costs CFA8000 for the whole vehicle, or CFA2000 for one place in a shared taxi. Oliver Rodriguez is a good **private driver** (☎222 581 772) with a 4WD vehicle.

# Rio Campo

POP 1105

Rio Campo is the region in the far northwest of Rio Muni. The tiny village of the same name is separated from Cameroon by the Ntem River. The main reason for visiting this region is to enjoy the Reserva Natural de Rio Campo with its nesting turtles, and the beautiful deserted beaches.

## Sights

**Reserva Natural de Rio Campo** NATURE RESERVE
(Rio Muni; permit per day CFA10,000) This reserve, in the far northwest of Rio Muni spans 335sq km and is a Ramsar Wetland of International Importance. Turtles, hippos and goliath frogs abound. It is managed by INDEFOR-AP in Bata, from whom you can obtain permits to visit.

## Activities

**TOMAGE** WILDLIFE WATCHING

(Tortugas Marinas de Guinea Ecuatorial; ☎222 561 660; www.facebook.com/tortugasguinea/) This is a conservation project situated between Punta Tika and Punta Cuche in the northwest of the Rio Campo reserve. It is managed by INDEFOR-AP in Bata, where permits are available (costing CFA10,000 per day). Between December and February you can see turtles come ashore to lay their eggs. There is also a small eco-museum at Punta Tika.

## Sleeping

Camping on the beach here is the best option. There are some cabins in the nature reserve, but they are not always open – check with INDEFOR-AP when you apply for your permit.

## Eating

**Pescaderia Bar** AFRICAN $

(Rio Campo) One of the only places to eat in Rio Campo, the Pescaderia Bar has snacks and is in the southern part of the town.

## Information

Register your presence at the **Comisario** (Rio Campo Village) when you arrive in the village of Rio Campo. They will want a copy of your passport, visa and tourist permit.

## Getting There & Away

It is best to take your own vehicle so that you can explore more of the reserve than just the village of Rio Campo. If you prefer local transport, a taxi from Mercado 5 in Bata to the village of Rio Campo takes about two hours, and costs CFA12,000 for the whole vehicle.

It is not possible for foreigners to cross the border into Cameroon here.

# Cogo

POP 4693

Cogo (or Kogo) is the jumping-off place for reaching Isla Corisco with its beautiful beaches. It's a small town with a lot of construction going on: the Club Marina & Nautica with a hotel and a marketplace is under construction along the new beachfront corniche.

The tiny Fang village of **Evouat** is worth visiting for its spectacular beach. Standing on the clean sweep of sand, you can see Gabon and the Elobey Islands across the sea. There are dugout canoes on the beach which local people use to catch fish that they smoke for a living. They're a friendly bunch and their wares are tasty.

Evouat lies 8km southwest of Akoga, a small town 13km north of Cogo. Turn southwest at the Somagec cement works and follow a dirt road to the coast.

Cogo is about one hour's drive south of Mbini along a good road. A taxi one way will cost around CFA5000. Alternatively, visit as part of a day trip from Bata.

It's here that locals can cross by pirogue to Gabon. Foreigners can get to Corisco on the **Somagec ferry** (⏲no fixed time, Mon-Sat) free of charge or by pirogue for CFA10,000. A pirogue to Elobey Grande costs about CFA5000. When it's raining, there are a few bars around the jetty to wait in.

# Isla Corisco

POP 3000

For the ultimate getaway with white-sand beaches, warm blue sea and swaying palm trees, look no further than Corisco. And now is the time to go, before the airport becomes operational and plans for a tourist hub take off. For now, swimming and relaxing on the beach are just about the only pastimes.

Known locally as Mandji, this idyllic island is located 44km off Cogo in the Rio Muni estuary. The largest village is Combo on the southwestern side, where you'll find the only hotel. The beach here is excellent, but for that true desert-island feeling, walk to the more remote **Arena Blanca** in the southeast. This is the beautiful beach that dreams are made of, the one that features on Equatorial Guinea's glossy brochures, all white sand, azure sea and palm trees. A five-star hotel is planned for this area.

There is no electricity on the island except that provided by generators, and almost no phone signal.

## Sleeping

**Complejo Turistico Las Islas de Corisco** RESORT $$$

(☎222 274 932, 222 272 737; Combo; d CFA60-70,000; ❄) Currently this is the only place to stay on Corisco and it is in a perfect spot. Rooms have air-con and a fridge though the electricity is turned off at night. Naturally enough, the restaurant specialises in fish, and there's a bar overlooking the sea.

## Getting There & Away

The **Somagec ferry** docks on the northeastern side of the island, so the only way to get to

Combo in the southwest is to walk or hitch a lift with one of the Moroccan truck drivers.

## Monte Alen National Park

The jewel in Equatorial Guinea's crown is **Monte Alen National Park** (☎ office in Bata 222 240 159; ayetebemme@yahoo.es; permits per person per day CFA10,000, guide per day CFA10,000). Covering some 2000 sq km of mountainous rainforest, it's home to forest elephants, western lowland gorillas, chimpanzees, buffalo, crocodiles, leopards and quirky creatures such as goliath frogs.

With no working tourism infrastructure, the park is an adventurer's dream. The best way to experience it is to arrange a camping trip of at least one week, giving you enough time to explore deep into the forest. You will have to organise this yourself as no tour operator in the country offers such trips. However, guides can be found around the park entrance. Permits are available from INDEFOR-AP (p262) in Bata. The Director of Monte Alen, Jesús Mba Mba Ayetebe, has to sign the permit himself, or give his authorisation by phone if he is away.

For a taster, the tour company Ruta 47 (p256) in Malabo offers day trips from Bata including a six-hour hike to the Mosumo Falls.

### ℹ Getting There & Away

The park lies south of Bata along an excellent road. The park centre (which is not in operation), with its hotel, eco-museum and staff accommodation, is 91km from Bata. It's best to hire your own vehicle to get to the park to transport all your equipment, food and water. If, however, you decide to take public transport, head for the taxi rank at Mercado 5 (5km from the city centre) in Colombo, Bata. Expect to pay about CFA12,000 to the park entrance.



# UNDERSTAND EQUATORIAL GUINEA

## Equatorial Guinea Today

Equatorial Guinea exports an annual US$12 billion worth of goods, mostly crude oil, petroleum gas and timber. The World Bank puts per-capita income at US$12,820 (2015). While this is high in comparison with most of the rest of Africa, it has dropped significantly in recent years as the price of oil diminishes (it was US$18,530 in 2013). Profits do not trickle down to most of the population, who linger in appalling poverty while the government generates an oil revenue of about US$8 billion a year. The reduction in the oil price has also meant fewer jobs in the oil industry, tourism and construction. According to the anti-corruption watchdog Transparency International, Equatorial Guinea is one of the most corrupt countries in the world. The group accuses President Obiang of using public money on fancy cars, sleek jets and luxury homes around the world. Obiang, Africa's longest-serving leader, shows no sign of releasing his grip: in 2016 he was voted in for another presidential term, in an election that banned EU monitors and some foreign media. Obiang won, as he predicted he would, gaining 93.5% of the vote.

In November 2011 the government held a referendum proposing changes to the constitution, which it claimed would facilitate democratic reform. However, critics of the changes say that the reforms, which were endorsed by voters, will in fact cement Obiang's position. Presidents are now limited to two terms of seven years in office, of which Obiang has started his second. A vice-presidency was created, the post awarded to Obiang's son, Teodoro Nguema Obiang Mangue, known as Teodorin. He is expected to take his father's place. But Teodorin's expensive tastes – ranging from Paris apartments to Bugattis, Lamborghinis and Ferraris as well as Michael Jackson's sequinned glove – have raised suspicions of money-laundering and accusations of squandering the country's assets: in 2016 the International Criminal Court instigated proceedings against him while France and Switzerland seized assets.

While the official government line is that today's regime offers a much better deal than the horrors of the Macías Nguema years, there is opposition both at home and abroad. In 2014 opposition leaders were granted amnesty and invited by the president to a 'national dialogue'. Participants, including political parties and some independent activists, agreed to several changes relating to elections and political pluralism.

As the price of oil continues to drop and reserves threaten to run dry, Equatorial Guinea will eventually have to diversify, forgo its rigid bureaucracy and allow tourism to flourish as recommended by the government's Horizon 2020 policy. A US$1 billion investment fund was established by the government in 2014 to encourage growth in sectors other than energy.

## History

### The Early Days

Bantu tribes, including the Bubi, came to the mainland in the 12th century from other parts of West and Central Africa. The Bubi are said to have fled to Bioko to escape the Fang, who are believed to have become the dominant ethnic group in the 1600s. Europeans made their first contact on the distant island of Annobón, which was visited by the Portuguese in 1470. In the 18th century, Bioko, Annobón and parts of the mainland were traded to Spain in exchange for regions in Latin America. Bioko subsequently became an important base for slave-trading in the early 19th century and was later a naval base for England, which by then was trying to stop the slave trade. Cocoa plantations were started on the island in the late 19th century, making Malabo Spain's most important possession in equatorial Africa.

Equatorial Guinea attained independence in October 1968 under the presidency of Macías Nguema. Months later, relations with Spain deteriorated rapidly and Nguema's 10-year dictatorship began. Thousands of people were tortured and publicly executed or beaten to death in the forced-labour camps of the mainland. Much of the violence was tribally motivated – the Bubis were particularly sought. By the time Nguema's regime was finally toppled in 1979, only a third of the 300,000 Guineans who lived there at the time of independence remained. In August 1979 Nguema was overthrown by his nephew Teodoro Obiang Nguema, who then ordered his uncle's execution.

### Independence & Coup Attempts

Though it's not far from the warm waters of the Atlantic, the whitewashed prison at Playa Negra (Black Beach) is one of Africa's most notorious hellholes. It's here that South African mercenary Nick du Toit and fellow coup plotter Simon Mann were locked up for their roles in a 2004 attempted coup, an operation that aimed to overthrow President Obiang and install exiled opposition leader Severo Moro in his place. Oil rights were promised to the coup's financiers and plotters, among them Mark Thatcher, the son of former British prime minister Margaret Thatcher. But the coup attempt failed spectacularly: in March 2004 Mann, du Toit and 60 others were arrested when their Boeing jet landed in Harare, Zimbabwe, on a weapons-gathering stop. While du Toit was sent to Black Beach immediately, Mann served four years in jail in Zimbabwe before being extradited to Malabo in 2007, where he was handed a 34-year sentence. President Obiang released Mann, du Toit and other accused prisoners in early 2009, citing good behaviour.

Perhaps hoping to avoid further coup attempts, the president commissioned the building of Oyala, a new capital deep in the central jungle, in 2011. It will house 200,000 people and is expected to be finished in 2020. So far there are six-lane highways, hotels, an airport, shopping centres and the American University of Central Africa.

## People of Equatorial Guinea

On the mainland 80% of the population is Fang, while on Bioko Island the Bubis are the most numerous group, making up about 15% of the total population. Smaller groups, including the Benga, inhabit the other islands.

The majority of the population is Roman Catholic, thanks to 400 years of Spanish occupation, but traditional animist beliefs are strong and are often practiced concurrently.

Traditional rituals and arts including dance are still performed and there's a strong oral tradition, with stories passed down through the generations, often involving the same cast of famous characters such as the grumpy tortoise and the wily monkey.

## Arts & Crafts

Equatorial Guinea shares a similar background in the arts to its neighbours Cameroon and Gabon. Wooden mask-making and traditional sculpture are at the forefront of local crafts, particularly among the Fang ethnic group. Masks are used in celebrations, religious events and funerals. Artisanal jewellery and woven baskets can also be found.

Music and dance play an important part in cultural life. The *balélé* is a Bubi dance usually performed on holidays. The Fang national dance is the *ibanga*, where performers cover themselves in a white powder, while Ndowe *ivanga* dancers paint their faces. Musical accompaniment for these dances

### SLEEPING PRICE RANGES

The following price ranges refer to a double room with bathroom.

**$** less than CFA33,000

**$$** CFA33,000–66,000

**$$$** more than CFA66,000

comprises drums, xylophones and the *mbira* or *sanza*. The Fang are known for their singing tradition, accompanied by the *mvet*, a harp-zither made from a gourd, with up to 15 strings. Most villages have a chorus and drum group where members sing in a call-and-response style. However, there are few places to perform in public, and many artists have left the country to pursue their careers in Spain.

The modern scene is dominated by music from Cameroon, Nigeria and the Democratic Republic of Congo, which you'll hear blasting out from shared taxis. Equatorial Guinea has produced a number of well-known artists such as hip-hop and rapper Jota Mayúscula and the female duo Hijas Del Sol.

## Environment

Both Bioko Island and the mainland hide a wealth of wildlife, most of which is endangered. Rio Muni is home to a hefty wedge of Central African rainforest with gorillas, chimpanzees and forest elephants. It is unknown exactly how many large mammals remain. Large sections of the interior have been set aside as protected areas, including Monte Alen National Park, which covers much of the centre of Rio Muni and offers some amazing hikes. Corrupt logging procedures, deforestation, poaching and the bushmeat trade are still big problems.

Since 1998 conservation staff at the Bioko Biodiversity Protection Program have recorded the number of animals – from monkeys and duikers to wild rats, squirrels and pythons – in meat markets. These tend to be hunted for sale to wealthy locals rather than for subsistence consumption.

### PRACTICALITIES

**Electricity** Equatorial Guinea uses a European-style two-pin 220V AC plug.

**Weights & measures** The metric system is used.

# SURVIVAL GUIDE

## Directory A–Z

### ACCOMMODATION

Malabo and Bata have a reasonable choice of medium and upmarket accommodation options, but few in the budget range. Beyond the cities, you will find pricey beach resorts and basic hotels in small towns. There are no hotels in the Monte Alen National Park or Rio Campo, so camping is the only option.

### DANGERS & ANNOYANCES

- Travelling in Equatorial Guinea is generally safe, including for women on their own.
- Police requests for bribes have lessened and you probably won't be asked for a bribe if all your papers are in order. However, you might occasionally be asked for a 'fanta' (a tip to buy a drink).

### EMBASSIES & CONSULATES

**Cameroonian Embassy** (333 093 473; 37 Calle del Rey Boncoro, Malabo; 8.30am-5pm Mon-Thu, to noon Fri)

**French Embassy** (333 092 005; www.ambafrance-gq.org; Carretera del Aeropuerto, Malabo; 10am-1pm & 3-5pm Mon-Fri)

**Gabonese Consulate** (222 528 048; Pl de Ayuntamiento, Bata; 8.30am-5pm Mon-Thu, to noon Fri)

**Gabonese Embassy** (333 093 180; Paraiso, Malabo; to drop off documents 10am-2pm Mon-Fri, to collect documents 11am-2pm Tue, Wed & Thu)

**German Embassy** (333 093 117; embajada.alemania.malabo@diplo.de; 8.30am-5pm Mon-Thu, to noon Fri)

**US Embassy** (333 095 741; http://malabo.usembassy.gov; Malabo II; 8am-5.30pm Mon-Thu, to noon Fri)

There is no British Embassy in Equatorial Guinea, but in an emergency, consular assistance is available from the British Honorary Consul, David Shaw, in Yaounde, Cameroon.

### EMERGENCY & IMPORTANT NUMBERS

| | |
|---|---|
| Equatorial Guinea's country code | 240 |
| Police | 113 |
| Gendarmería | 114 |
| Fire | 115 |

There is no ambulance service.

### INTERNET ACCESS

The few internet cafes in Equatorial Guinea are found in Malabo. Many hotels, restaurants and cafes offer free wi-fi, though access can

## TOURIST PERMITS

Having a visa for Equatorial Guinea is not sufficient for travelling inside the country. As soon after arrival as possible, you must apply for an Autorización de Turismo (Tourist Permit) at the Ministerio de Turismo (p268) in Malabo II or the **Delegación de Cultura y Turismo** (3rd fl, Banco Nacional, Calle Mbogo Nzogo; ⌚8am-6pm) in Bata. You will be provided with an example of an application letter which must be typed, printed, signed and presented with the CFA15,000 fee and a copy of your passport and visa. Allow at least one day to get the permit. It has to be approved and signed by the Minister of Tourism, but what would happen if he were off sick or on holiday is not clear. In the application letter, it is essential to list everywhere you want to visit. If you are stopped somewhere not on your list, you will be turned away. The tourist permit must be produced along with a copy of your passport and visa whenever you are stopped by police. Take copies of the permit to avoid handing over the precious original. Printing and copying can be done at Cibermax (p259).

When you arrive in a small town or village and intend to stay for a few days, it is advisable to register your presence with the local authority, the Delegado or police station (Comisario). They will require a copy of your passport, visa and tourist permit.

be patchy. Bans on some social media such as Facebook and Twitter are imposed from time to time.

### LGBTIQ TRAVELLERS

While homosexuality is not illegal in Equatorial Guinea, overt displays of affection should be avoided in this conservative Christian country.

### MONEY

The currency is the Central African Franc as used across the region (CFA). It is stable at CFA655 to the euro, and CFA600 to the US dollar.

**ATMs** At all banks in Malabo and Bata, but not elsewhere. They often don't work, only take Visa cards and only give small amounts (usually no more than CFA100,000 per day), meaning frequent trips to the bank.

**Changing Money** You can change euros or US dollars at banks in most towns or bureaux de change such as Pecunia Express (p259) that has branches in both Malabo and Bata.

| | | |
|---|---|---|
| Australia | A$1 | CFA452 |
| Canada | C$1 | CFA440 |
| Europe | €1 | CFA656 |
| Japan | ¥100 | CFA538 |
| NZ | NZ$1 | CFA415 |
| UK | UK£1 | CFA774 |
| US | US$1 | CFA600 |

**Credit Cards** Only in top-end hotels and restaurants. You can't withdraw cash over the counter in banks using your credit card.

**Cash** Cash is king in Equatorial Guinea. Make sure you have plenty of foreign currency to exchange for large purchases such as airline tickets.

**Tipping** Not expected in most restaurants and hotels. However, at those frequented by expats, staff have come to expect a tip. Guides and private drivers also appreciate a tip of around 10%.

### OPENING HOURS

**Shops and offices** 8am to 1pm and 4pm to 7pm Monday to Friday, some are open 8am to 1pm Saturday

**Banks** Hours vary, but usually 8am to 2pm Monday to Friday, 8am to noon Saturday

**Restaurants and cafes** 7am or 9am to 11pm Monday to Saturday

**Clubs** 10pm to 4am Thursday to Saturday

### PUBLIC HOLIDAYS

**New Year's Day** 1 January

**Good Friday** March or April

**Labour Day** 1 May

**Corpus Christi Feast** May or June

**President's Day** 5 June

**Freedom Day** 3 August

**Constitution Day** 15 August

**Independence Day** 12 October

**Feast of the Immaculate Conception** 8 December

**Christmas Day** 25 December

If a public holiday falls on a weekend, the next working day becomes a holiday.

## EATING PRICE RANGES

These price ranges refer to a main course.

**$** less than CFA5000

**$$** CFA5000–7500

**$$$** more than CFA7500

### TELEPHONE

There are no area codes.

Local SIM cards can be used in any unlocked phone. They are available only from **GETESA Central** (cnr Avenida del Rey Bonocoro & Calle de Mongomo; ⏲8am-1pm & 4-7pm Mon-Fri) in Malabo and cost CFA3000. You need to present a copy of your passport and visa, and two photographs. Recharge cards are available everywhere.

### TOURIST INFORMATION

**INDEFOR-AP** (p262) Supplies permits for Monte Alen National Park and Rio Campo in Rio Muni.

**Ministerio de Turismo** (Ministry of Tourism; Ministerios District, Malabo II; ⏲8am-6pm) (Ministry of Tourism) Has a glossy flyer with photographs, but can provide no information (In Malabo).

### VISAS

All nationalities need a visa for Equatorial Guinea except for US residents, who nevertheless still have to complete the form.

Visas for Equatorial Guinea can take some time to obtain. Allow at least three weeks.

## ℹ Getting There & Away

### AIR

The only way to get to Equatorial Guinea is to fly in to Malabo. All land border crossings were closed for non-nationals at the time of writing.

#### Airports & Airlines

**Malabo International Airport** (Santa Isabel Airport; ☎222 091 554; adge@malabo.aero; 9km west of Malabo city centre) lies 9km west of the city centre. At the time of writing, an impressive new airport was being built adjacent. It's a chaotic place; get there at least two hours before your flight.

Check-in for CEIBA flights is in a separate building to boarding. In the main building, there is a cafe, a bank that is only open during banking hours, and an ATM that often does not accept cards. It's worth having euros or dollars in small denominations if you are unable to withdraw cash and have to pay for a taxi in foreign currency (the taxi into town should cost CFA2000).

The following international airlines fly into Malabo:

**Africa's Connection** from São Tomé (www.africas-connection.com)

**Air France** from Paris (www.airfrance.com)

**CEIBA Intercontinental** (Equatorial Guinea's own airline; site under construction at the time of research, but it should eventually be www.fly-ceiba.com)

**Ethiopian Airways** from Addis Ababa (www.ethiopianairlines.com)

**Iberia** from Madrid (www.iberia.com)

**Lufthansa** from Frankfurt (www.lufthansa.com)

**Royal Air Maroc** from Casablanca (www.royalairmaroc.com)

**Bata International Airport** (p262) is also termed 'international', but so far the only international airline flying into Bata is Niger Airlines from Niamey. The airport lies 4km north of the city.

### ℹ ARRIVING IN EQUATORIAL GUINEA

**Malabo International Airport** Taxis into the city (9km) cost CFA2000.

**Bata International Airport** (p262) Taxis wait across the car park and cost CFA2000 into the city.

## ℹ Getting Around

### AIR

Flying is the best option between Malabo and the mainland. There are several national carriers with offices in Malabo and Bata.

### BOAT

The Elobey Ferry (p260) between the New Port in Malabo and Bata plies the waters once a week.

### BUS

In Rio Muni there is an interprovincial bus service, **Kassav Express** (☎222 721 516). However, shared taxis are more comfortable and easier to use.

### CAR & MOTORCYCLE

Roads are excellent in Equatorial Guinea. There are tolls on all roads outside of the cities that cost CFA500 per vehicle.

Car hire is expensive: expect to pay at least CFA70,000 per day, and there's a hefty deposit of around CFA250,000. **Europcar** (☎333 091 902; www.europcar.com/location/equatorial-guinea; Malabo International Airport; ⏲8am-1pm & 4-10pm Mon-Fri, 9am-10pm Sat, 8am-10pm Sun) and **Avis** (☎333 090 769; www.avis.com/en/locations/eq/malabo; Malabo International Airport; ⏲24hr) have offices at Malabo airport. **Autos Litoral** (☎666 591 355, 222 043 518; www.autoslitoral.com; Ibis Hotel, Carreterra del Aeropuerto, Malabo; ⏲9am-8pm Mon-Fri) has a desk at the Ibis Hotel close to the airport and another office in Bata. They provide drivers if required. If you are driving yourself, you will need an International Driving Permit.

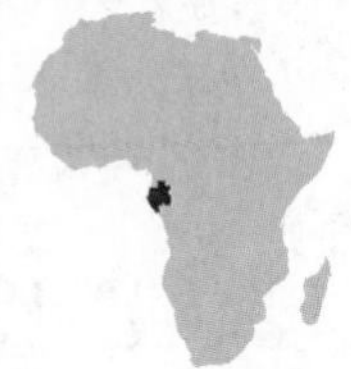

# Gabon

POP 1,738,500 / ☎241

**Includes ➡**



## Best Places to Eat

- ➡ L'Odika (p273)
- ➡ Le Bistrot (p277)
- ➡ La Dolce Vita (p271)
- ➡ Le Voilier (p274)

## Best Places to Sleep

- ➡ Loango Lodge (p279)
- ➡ Pongara Lodge (p276)
- ➡ L'Hôtellerie de l'Hôpital Albert Schweitzer (p280)
- ➡ Le Leet Dorian (p271)

## Why Go?

With an impressive 11.25% of the country proclaimed as national parkland, Gabon offers a spectacular array of wildlife in its dense rainforests and open savannah to enthral nature enthusiasts. Add to that superb white-sand beaches, rushing rivers and ethereal landscapes, and you have an Eden-like travel experience in an unexplored part of Africa.

Gabon is the region's most progressive and traveller-friendly destination, although tourism remains extremely DIY. You'll either have to put yourself into the hands of a travel agency, or negotiate the poor roads, infrequent transport options and the almost total lack of reliable infrastructure yourself. Outside the cosmopolitan Libreville and Port-Gentil, the country's largest cities, Gabon is an undiscovered wonderland not to be missed.

## When to Go

### Libreville

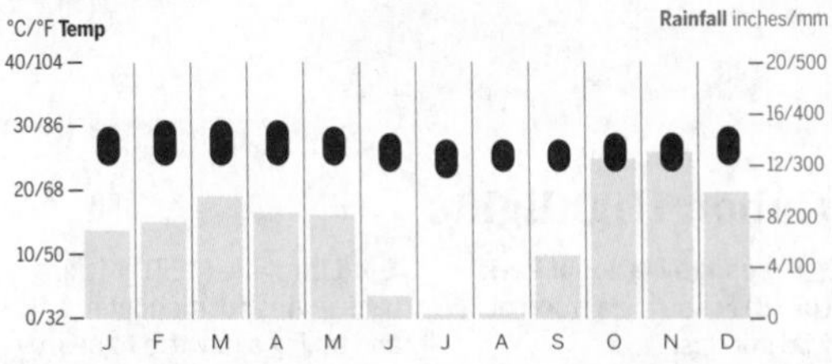


**May–Sep** The dry season makes overland transport faster and wildlife easier to see.

**Jul–Sep** Have a close encounter with a whale swimming off Gabon's coastline.

**Nov–Jan** Spot turtles coming ashore to lay their eggs on the beaches.

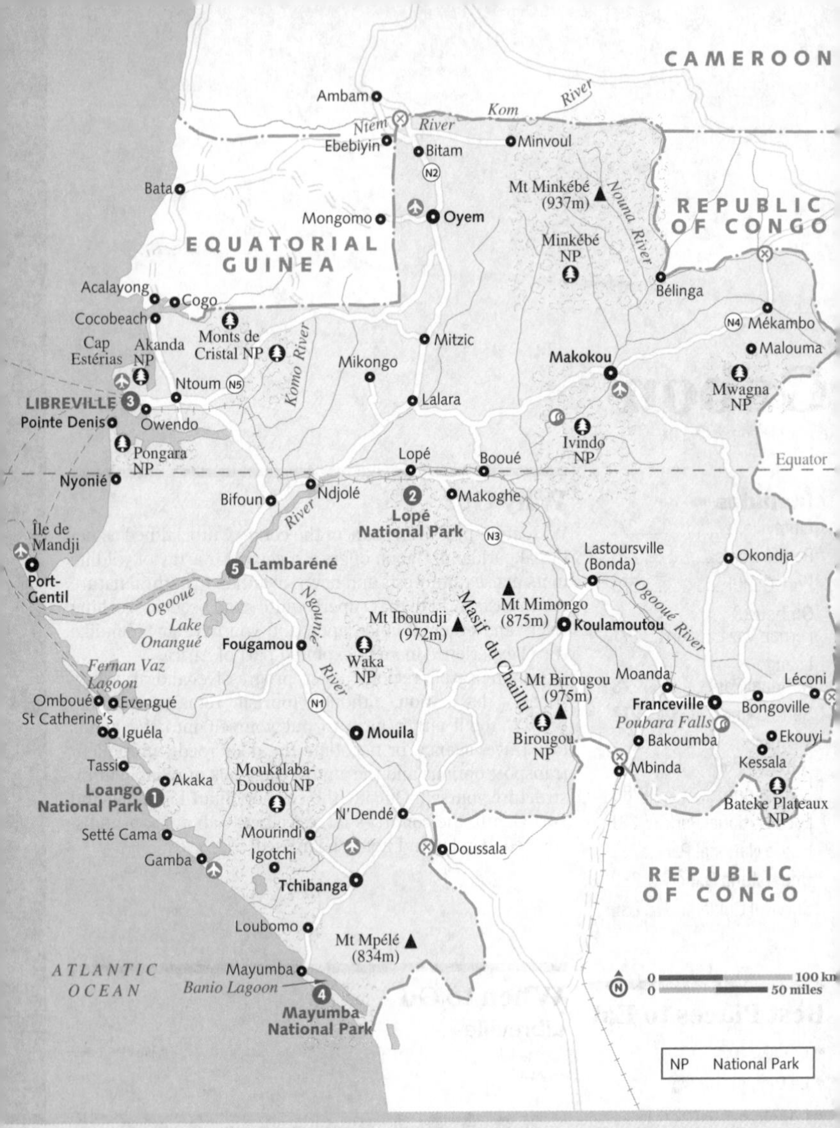

## Gabon Highlights

**1 Loango National Park** (p278) Following a troop of wild gorillas.

**2 Lopé National Park** (p281) Coming across wild elephants amid spectacular scenery.

**3 Libreville** (p271) Kicking back in this cosmopolitan city and taking a day trip to nearby Pointe Denis.

**4 Mayumba National Park** (p279) Bodysurfing the waves while watching humpback whales breach in the distance.

**5 Lambaréné** (p280) Exploring the charming, laid-back town made famous by the Nobel prize-winning Albert Schweitzer.

# LIBREVILLE

POP 582,000

The vibrant, muscular heart of Gabon, Libreville is the largest city and home to over a third of Gabon's population. It's also a city awash in oil money: pavements, clean streets, smart restaurants and vast gated villas are the first impressions of the town. But stay a little longer and you'll easily discover Libreville's essentially African heart: crowded street markets and busy residential areas lie further back from the gleaming coastline.

## Sights & Activities

**Musée Nationale des Arts et Traditions du Gabon** MUSEUM

(National Museum of Art and Tradition; www.gabonart.com; Au Bord de Mer; admission CFA1000, guided tour CFA2000; 10am-5.30pm Tue-Sat) The National Museum of Art and Tradition has exhibitions on tribal crafts and culture, and a great collection of masks and stone carvings. A guided tour (usually only available in French) helps to contextualise a lot of the items on display. Despite the opening hours given, it might not actually be open.

**Ebando** MUSIC, DANCING

(06 25 09 17, 07 81 95 55; www.ebando.org; Rte des Pêcheurs, La Sablière) This NGO is run by the first European *nganga* (traditional healer), Tatayo, and besides Bwiti initiation, offers entertainment at Ebando Village and forest walks that highlight Pygmy culture. It's located 7km north of Libreville airport.

## Sleeping

**Somotel** HOTEL $

(01 76 58 46; Rue Mont Bouët; d incl breakfast CFA27,000-32,000; ) From the French *sommeil* (to sleep), Somotel is just that – a clean and relatively cheap place to crash. It's a bit of a dodgy area, but it's a good-value budget option not far from the centre of town. There are cheaper rooms with noisy, old air-con (CFA22,000 and CFA24,000). There's no wi-fi.

**Tropicana** HOTEL $$

(01 73 15 31; tropicana@inet.ga; Au Bord de Mer; d CFA35-40,000; ) Just across from the airport, all visitors to Libreville are likely to pass through this old favourite set right on the beautiful beach. Rooms are pleasant enough, though quite dark with lots of wood panelling. There are smaller, cheaper rooms next to the car park (twin/double CFA25,000/30,000). Book ahead as many expats from outside Libreville like to stay here.

**Hôtel Le Patio** HOTEL $$

(01 73 47 16; www.hotel-lepatio.com; Rue Pierre Barro; d incl breakfast CFA49,000/55,000, ste CFA90,000; ) This hotel is easily the best-value comfortable option in town: its rooms are spotless, its location is great and there's a charming courtyard that's a joy to relax in. Prices come down if you stay a few days. There's a bar and lounge, and the continental breakfast is substantial. Meals can be ordered in advance.

★ **Le Leet Dorian** BOUTIQUE HOTEL $$$

(07 38 51 84, 07 33 45 45; www.hotelleet-dorian.com; Rue d'Alsace-Lorraine, Quartier Montagne Sainte; d/ste CFA70,000/85,000; ) Definitely the pick of Libreville's hotels, this gorgeous, design-conscious place has individually decorated rooms with Gabonese art on the walls, stylish touches and surprisingly colourful bathrooms. There are also delicious breakfasts (CFA6000), and a restaurant (mains from CFA8500). The price tag isn't small, but it's still far cheaper and more charming than the city's large five-star hotels.

**Le Meridien Re-Ndama** LUXURY HOTEL $$$

(01 79 32 00; www.lemeridienrendama.com; Quartier Glass; d from CFA165,000; ) A full-service hotel with a health club, a beauty salon, a tennis court and a gorgeous pool with an ocean view. It's not particularly central, but if you can afford to stay here then the cost of a taxi into town isn't going to worry you. There are two ATMs in the foyer.

## Eating

**Le Pelisson** CAFE $

(Ave Col Parant; pastries from CFA700, coffee CFA1000; 7am-8pm Mon-Sat) This large place buzzes every day of the week when people drop in for the extensive breakfast menu or lunch (*plat du jour* CFA8000). In operation since 1928, it's a Libreville institution.

**La Dolce Vita** ITALIAN $$

(01 72 42 38; www.facebook.com/ladolcevitalibreville; Port Môle; mains from CFA7000; midday-3pm & 7-11pm Mon-Fri, 12.30-2.30pm & 7-11.30pm Sat & Sun) Ocean views, a great bar, and fabulous seafood, pasta and pizza make this local institution within the bustling passenger port a Libreville favourite. Good specials, friendly staff and huge portions keep people coming back again and again. A lunchtime three-course menu is a reasonable CFA6000. Try the skewered prawns grilled over a wood fire.

# Libreville

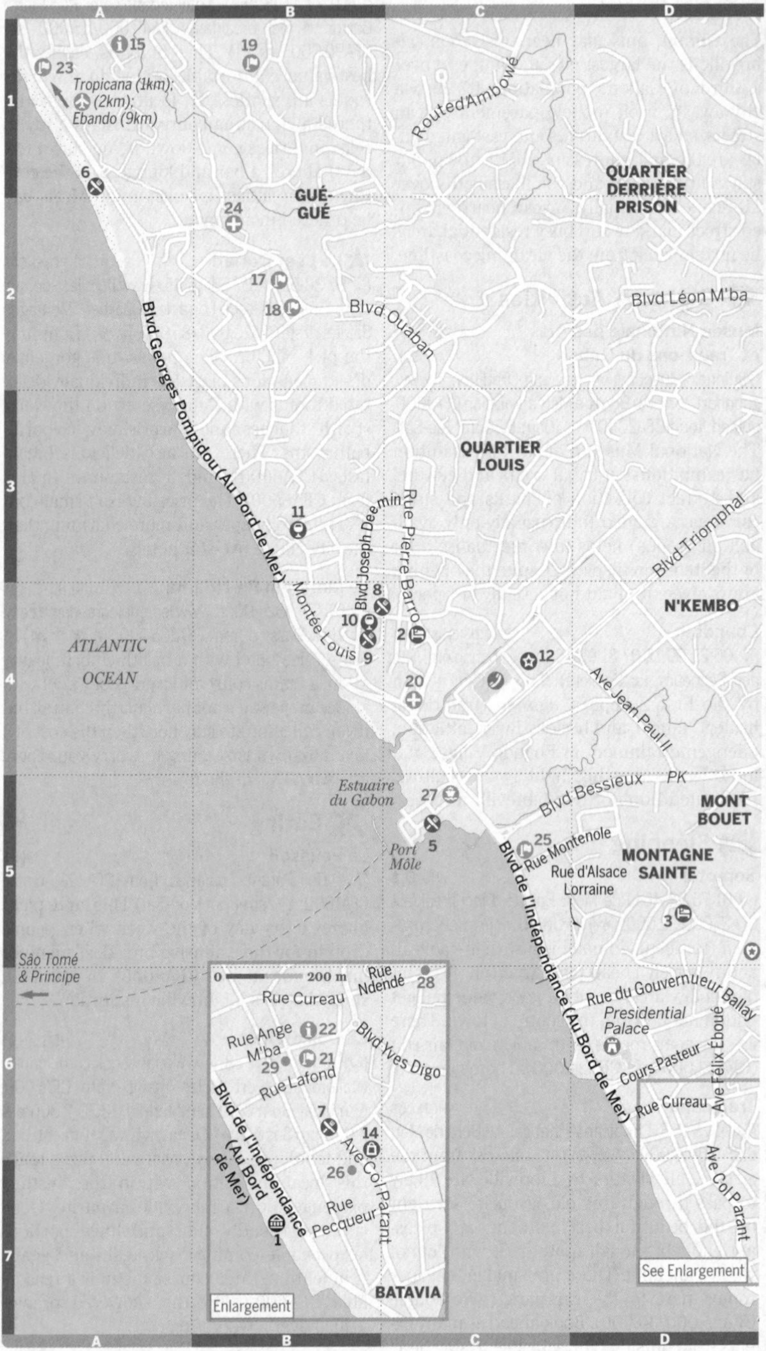

A B C D

1 2 3 4 5 6 7

15
19
23
Tropicana (1km); (2km); Ebando (9km)
Routed'Ambowé
6
QUARTIER DERRIÈRE PRISON
GUÉ-GUÉ
24
17
18
Blvd Ouaban
Blvd Léon M'ba
Blvd Georges Pompidou (Au Bord de Mer)
QUARTIER LOUIS
11
Blvd Joseph Deemin
Rue Pierre Barro
Blvd Triomphal
Montée Louis
8
10
9
2
N'KEMBO
ATLANTIC OCEAN
12
20
Ave Jean Paul II
Estuaire du Gabon
27
Blvd Bessieux
PK
MONT BOUET
5
25
Rue Montenole
Port Môle
MONTAGNE SAINTE
Rue d'Alsace Lorraine
Blvd de l'Indépendance (Au Bord de Mer)
3
São Tomé & Principe
0 200 m
Rue Ndendé
28
Rue Cureau
Rue Ange M'ba
22
21
29
Blvd Yves Digo
Rue Lafond
Rue du Gouvernueur Ballay
Presidential Palace
Ave Félix Éboué
Cours Pasteur
Rue Cureau
Blvd de l'Indépendance (Au Bord de Mer)
7
14
Ave Col Parant
26
Ave Col Parant
Rue Pecqueur
1
BATAVIA
Enlargement
See Enlargement

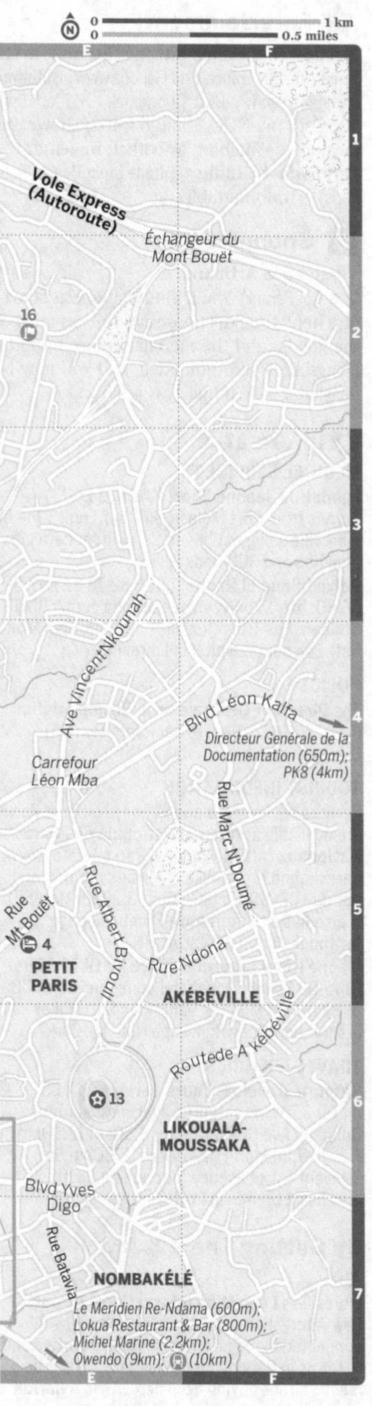


## Libreville

**Sights**

1 Musée Nationale des Arts et Traditions du Gabon ........ B7

**Sleeping**

2 Hôtel Le Patio ........ C4
3 Le Leet Dorian ........ D5
4 Somotel ........ E5

**Eating**

5 La Dolce Vita ........ C5
6 La Voile Rouge ........ A1
7 Le Pelisson ........ B6
8 Le Voilier ........ B4
9 L'Odika ........ B4

**Drinking & Nightlife**

10 MB Club Privé ........ B4
11 New Cotton Club ........ B3

**Entertainment**

12 French Institute ........ C4
13 Omnisport Stadium ........ E6

**Shopping**

14 Village des Artisans ........ B6

**Information**

15 Agence Nationale des Parcs Nationaux ........ A1
16 Cameroon Embassy ........ E2
17 Canadian Consulate ........ B2
18 Congolese Embassy ........ B2
19 Equatorial Guinea Embassy ........ B1
20 Fondation Jeanne Ebori ........ C4
21 French Embassy ........ B6
22 Lopé Hôtel Libreville Office ........ B6
23 Netherlands Consulate ........ A1
24 Polyclinique El Rapha ........ B2
25 São Tomé & Príncipe Embassy ........ C5
26 Satguru Travels & Tours Services ........ B7

**Transport**

27 CNNII ........ C5
28 NRT ........ C6
29 SETRAG ........ B6

**★L'Odika** AFRICAN **$$$**

(☎06 25 34 34, 01 73 69 20; lodika@live.fr; Blvd Joseph Deemin, Quartier Louis; mains from CFA8000; ⏰11am-3pm & 7pm-midnight Wed-Mon; ✎) This lovely colonial-style veranda restaurant in the heart of the Quartier Louis is very attractive. You'll find tempting dishes such as beef *ndolé* (a Cameroonian dish with peanuts, spices and *ndolé* bitter leaves), *colombo du porc* (lightly spiced Mauritian pork dish) or seafood brochettes with *odika* (crushed acacia seed, 'chocolate') sauce. Polished timber floors, fresh flowers and local art on the walls complete the picture.

**Le Voilier** FRENCH **$$$**

(☎05 09 09 06; Galerie Juma, Quartier Louis; mains from CFA12,000; ⊙11am-midnight Mon-Sat) A very smart restaurant, Le Voilier is kitted out like a ship, with wood panelling and brass instruments, and has a small terrace in the front. The food is excellent and there's a good wine list.

**La Voile Rouge** SEAFOOD **$$$**

(☎07 49 79 49; Au Bord de Mer; mains from CFA10,000; ⊙midday-3.30pm daily, 7-11pm Mon-Sat) The most popular of several beachside restaurants along Au Bord de Mer, La Voile Rouge is busiest for Sunday lunch. There are tables inside and on the beach, a cocktail bar, and a menu featuring lots of fish as well as French dishes. Try the grilled tuna (CFA14,000).

## Drinking & Nightlife

If you want to get out and get down, hit the Quartier Louis where there is a host of great drinking spots and clubs that rarely get going before midnight. Check out Blvd Joseph Deemin and the surrounding streets.

**MB Club Privé** CLUB

(☎03 31 36 36; www.mbclubprive.com; Blvd Joseph Deemin, Quartier Louis; ⊙10pm-5am Wed-Sat) Dress up to get in the door here: there's a hugely popular black-and-purple bar, a disco and often live music. The entrance price depends on who's playing, and drinks aren't cheap, as you would expect.

**New Cotton Club** CLUB

(☎04 13 00 00; Montée Quaben; ⊙9pm-3am Tue-Sat) An old Libreville favourite, the Cotton Club attracts a slightly older clientele. It has a great buzz, especially on weekends. There's karaoke on Thursdays.

**Lokua Restaurant & Bar** LIVE MUSIC

(☎06 83 51 83; www.facebook.com/pg/lokualbv; Quartier Glass; ⊙midday-1am Mon-Fri, 5.30pm-2am Sat) It's all about the whisky and roots music at this impeccably dressed bar. There's a live band several times a week with a Louis Armstrong–esque lead singer. A limited bar menu has club sandwiches from CFA6000, while the restaurant has a wider menu and a good wine list.

## ☆ Entertainment

Besides the events at the **French Institute** (Institut Français du Gabon; www.institutfrancais-gabon.com; Blvd Triomphal; ⊙10am-9pm Mon-Sat), the NGO Ebando (p271) showcases local arts. Watching a football match at the **Omnisport Stadium** (Stade Omar Bongo; Petit Paris) is unforgettable.

## Shopping

**Village des Artisans** ARTS & CRAFTS

(Ave Col Parant) You'll find Gabonese souvenirs here, though choose carefully as most of the goods (and the merchants) are imports. Haggling is recommended, and you may be hassled a little if business is slow.

## Information

### MEDICAL SERVICES

**Fondation Jeanne Ebori** (☎01 73 20 12) Across from Port Môle in Quartier Louis. One of Libreville's biggest hospitals, with modern lab facilities and 300 beds.

**Polyclinique El Rapha** (☎06 82 78 51, 07 98 66 60; http://polycliniqueelrapha.com/; Blvd Ouaban, Les Trois Quartiers; ⊙9am-6pm Mon-Sat) The best hospital in Libreville.

### POLICE

The **Directeur Genérale de la Documentation** (☎01 76 24 24; PK5; ⊙8am-3pm Mon-Fri) Extends visas.

### TOURIST INFORMATION

Permits for Pongara and Akanda National Parks are available at **Agence Nationale des Parcs Nationaux** (ANPN; National Parks Board; www.parcsgabon.org; Kalikak; permits per person per day CFA5000; ⊙7.30am-3.30pm Mon-Fri). It also has an informative Facebook page: www.facebook.com/PARCSGABON/.

**Lopé Hôtel Libreville Office** (☎01 72 05 96, 01 77 02 17; www.lopehotel.com; Rue Ange M'Ba; ⊙8am-4pm Mon-Fri, 9am-noon Sat) Makes reservations for within Lopé National Park.

### TRAVEL AGENCIES

**Satguru Travels & Tours Services** (☎05 34 09 33; www.satgurutravel.com; Akiremy Building, Ave Col Parant; ⊙8.30am-12.30pm & 3.30-7pm Mon-Fri, 8.30am-12.30pm Sat) An efficient travel agency for booking flights. It also has a branch in Port-Gentil.

## Getting There & Away

### AIR

Libreville's **Léon M'ba International Airport** (www.adlgabon.com; Au Bord de Mer) is well connected to major African cities, to Europe and to towns in Gabon. Internally there are two domestic airlines flying from here: **Afric Aviation**

(☎ 06 71 71 78; www.africaviation.com; Léon M'ba International Aiport; ⏰ 8.30am-3.30pm Mon-Fri, 8.30am-12.30pm Sat) and **NRT** (National Régionale Transport; ☎ 06 66 90 77, 07 37 22 55; www.nrtgabon.org; Rue Ndendé). NRT flies to Port Gentil, Tchinbanga, Oyem, Mouila, Koulamoutou, Franceville and Makokou. Afric Aviation is based in Port-Gentil, but also has an office in Libreville airport. This airline flies to Franceville, Gamba and Port-Gentil.

### BOAT

There are several passenger boats per week between Port Môle, Libreville and Port-Gentil (CFA20,000, 11 to 12 hours); it's also possible to take cars (CFA120,000 to CFA180,000). Enquire at the **CNNII** (Compagnie Nationale de Navigation Intérieure et internationale; ☎ 07 07 39 45, 01 72 39 28; Port Môle) office at Port Môle in Libreville.

A slow boat from Port Môle to Omboué departs 11am on Friday and returns Monday, stopping at every village along the way on a journey of about 11 hours (CFA20,000).

Boats for the restaurants at Pointe Denis leave from **Michel Marine** (Quartier Glass); boats leave here for La Baie des Tortues Luth (p276) lodge in Pongara National Park too.

### BUS

There are good buses running from PK8 ('peekay weet'), Libreville's transport hub 8km from the centre. These are a better option than the overpacked *taxis-brousses* (bush taxis), minibuses and pick-up trucks. Clearly signposted, behind the pharmacy at PK8, SOGATRA has the following routes:

| DESTINATION | DURATION (HR) | PRICE (CFA) |
|---|---|---|
| Lambaréné | 4 | 4000 |
| Makokou | 7 | 10,000 |
| Mouila | 7 | 8000 |
| Oyem | 7 | 8000 |
| Bitam | 7 | 10,000 |

There are food stalls and an air-conditioned waiting room at the SOGATRA bus station but don't get too comfortable; buses often depart early. Staff manage your luggage and will call you when the bus is ready to leave.

### TRAIN

The Transgabonaise Railway line starts at Owende, 9km south of the city. Book at **SETRAG** (Transgabonais Railway office; ☎ call centre 01 07 80 60; off Rue Lafond; ⏰ 8am-4pm Mon-Fri, 8am-noon Sat) at least two days before travelling as trains are often full. There are two types of train: the *Trans-Ogooué Express* that calls at Ndjolé, Lopé, Booué, Ivindo, Lastoursville, Moanda and Franceville, and the *Equateur* that stops at all stations between Libreville and Franceville.

The *Trans-Ogooué* leaves Libreville at 6.50pm and arrives in Lopé at 1.03am and in Franceville at 6.51am. It runs on Monday, Wednesday and Friday.

There are three classes of seats – VIP, 1st class and 2nd class – but no couchettes. The first two classes are fiercely air-conditioned. There is a restaurant car but it's best to bring your own food.

| TO LOPÉ | 1ST CLASS | 2ND CLASS |
|---|---|---|
| Trans-Ogooué (express) | CFA25,500 | CFA19,500 |
| Equateur (slow) | CFA21,400 | CFA15,000 |

| TO FRANCEVILLE | 1ST CLASS | 2ND CLASS |
|---|---|---|
| Trans-Ogooué (express) | CFA55,800 | CFA41,800 |
| Equateur (slow) | CFA46,800 | CFA32,800 |

You can put a vehicle on the train, too (Libreville to Franceville including one passenger seat CFA259,100).

## Getting Around

A taxi to yourself is called a 'course' and will cost about CFA2000 to CFA5000 per hour. A good private driver with a reliable car is **Alex Binga** (☎ 07 32 40 46, 06 61 69 32). One seat *(une place)* in a shared taxi around town costs CFA300 to CFA500.

# AROUND LIBREVILLE

## Pointe Denis

Pointe Denis is Libreville's weekend bolt hole, just a quick 12km boat ride away though it feels like another planet. Gone are the capital's traffic and crowds, replaced instead by a superb stretch of sand that runs for miles along the peninsula. The beach backs onto the Pongara National Park (p276), and it's lined with fancy weekend houses. If you don't want to spend the night, it's perfectly feasible to come here for the day from Libreville.

Lounge on the beach, enjoy water sports or walk to the Atlantic side of the point to discover miles of empty white sand that is the nesting ground of sea turtles from November to January.

### Sleeping & Eating

**Olando Tchoua La Maringa** CHALET **$$**
(☎ 04 55 63 68, 02 70 26 38; d bungalow or 4-person r CFA50,000; ⏰ Tue-Sun) This fun place offers a diverse medley of entertainment from games tournaments to karaoke, drumming, salsa, making traditional torches and walks in the forest. The wooden bungalows and rooms are comfortably furnished. There are sunshades and loungers on the beach.

You can go on a Saturday or Sunday for CFA50,000, which includes a huge buffet lunch, drinks and one activity, or stay the whole weekend for CFA250,000 per couple. Note it is closed on Mondays.

**Assiga Village** CHALET **$$$**
(☎01 76 33 47, 03 04 48 08; www.facebook.com/villageassiga; 2-person chalet CFA100,000-150,000; ❄📶🏊) White-sand beaches, palm trees and a pool make this an idyllic place to spend the day or stay overnight. The bungalows are large and comfortable and are tastefully decorated with local art. A buffet lunch at weekends costs CFA30,000. A *navette* (passenger boat) from Libreville is CFA15,000.

**River Lodge** LODGE **$$$**
(☎03 30 23 02, 03 20 22 02; http://riverlodgegabon.wixsite.com/islandhotel; Pointe Denis; d weekdays/weekends CFA75,000/95,000; ⏲restaurant Wed-Mon; ❄📶🏊) Modern two-storey wooden cottages look out onto the river or the beach here. It's a dreamy setting with palm trees and a pool. The beach-side restaurant gets good reviews. There are jet skis, quad bikes and paddle boards for hire. The lodge's own *navette* will collect you from Michel Marine (p275; return CFA10,000).

### Getting There & Away

You can reach Pointe Denis from Michel Marine (p275) in Libreville. **Navettes Pointe Denis** (☎06 26 40 77, 05 31 80 80; Michel Marine; return CFA12,000; ⏲9.30am & 4pm Tue-Fri; 10am & 3pm Sat; 9.30am & 10am Sun) has return ferries at the end of both days.

Note that many of the lodges at Pointe Denis have their own boats and will collect and return you as required.

## Pongara National Park

Perhaps the easiest place to get into the wild expanses of Gabon if you're only in the country for a few days, **Pongara National Park** (www.parcsgabon.org; permit per person per day CFA5000) combines forest, savannah and a sweeping expanse of empty beach that backs onto Pointe Denis.

Hippos and crocodiles inhabit the lagoons and beaches, while the mangroves hide a multitude of fish, crabs and frogs. Hundreds of leatherback turtles trundle up the beach to lay their eggs between November and March – this is one of the best places in the world to see them. Out at sea, dolphins and humpback whales visit in the dry season (July to October). In the savannah there are elephants, forest buffaloes, red river hogs and collared mangabeys.

### Activities

**Aventures Sans Frontières** WILDLIFE WATCHING
(ASF; ☎07 54 15 24, 06 60 05 34) This local conservation NGO operates a visitor centre with a sea turtle museum in the Pongara National Park. It organises excursions to see nesting turtles (CFA10,000 per person, November to February), providing a tent on the beach (CFA15,000 per tent for two per day). It also offers walks into the forest (CFA15,000 per person). Boats from Michel Marine can be arranged.

### Sleeping

**La Baie des Tortues Luth** LODGE **$$$**
(☎07 51 05 46, 03 28 64 45; www.baiedestortuesgabon.com; d incl breakfast & transfers CFA200,000; ❄📶🏊) 🍃 With an enviable location miles from anywhere and right on the beach, this lodge has 20 thatched rooms, some elevated for sea views. They are all beautifully appointed, with lovely bathrooms, rain showers and timber floors. There's an excellent restaurant and all vegetables are grown on site. Excursions in the park can be arranged.

**Pongara Lodge** LODGE **$$$**
(☎06 26 33 64, 03 19 26 88; www.pongara-lodge.com; d with full board incl transfers CFA360,000; ❄) 🍃 A remote option on the coast and deep into the park, this excellent lodge has a rustic look and feel, while still being very comfortable and exclusive. As well as a gorgeous beach, there's plenty of scope for nature walks, fishing, and turtle- and whale-watching with a guide organised by the lodge.

### Getting There & Away

You can take a *navette* from Michel Marine (p275) to Pointe Denis (CFA12,000 return).

The lodges have their own boats for transfers to and from Libreville, which are included in the rate. The boat for La Baie des Tortues Luth departs at 9.30am from Michel Marine, and the boat for Pongara Lodge departs from **Club Nautique Barracuda** (Owendo; ⏲9am).

# COASTAL GABON

## Port-Gentil

POP 147,800

Gabon's second city, Port-Gentil has a much more laid-back air about it than Libreville. This is Gabon's industrial and economic engine, and massive oil and gas rigs loom just off the coast. But the city stretches lazily along the beach and has pleasant wide streets and a bustling port. One block back from the corniche, Ave Savorgnan de Brazza has most of the banks, shops and restaurants.

Port-Gentil is a stopping-off point en route to the Fernan Vaz Lagoon and on to Loango National Park. You can also access Lambaréné via boats on the Ogoué River.

## Sleeping

**Hôtel L'Hirondelle** HOTEL **$$**
(☎01 55 17 82; Ave des Douanes; d without/with kitchenette CFA52,000/57,000, studio CFA70,000; P ❄ 📶) Colourful and filled with light, the reception and bar here have lots of interesting local art and sculpture. The rooms are pleasantly appointed, and there are also apartments with one, two or three rooms (CFA95,000/115,000/135,000). Breakfast is CFA7500. There's no sign outside, but it's opposite Hôtel Le Bougainvillier.

**Hôtel Le Bougainvillier** HOTEL **$$**
(☎07 72 14 14; hotel_le_bougainvillier@yahoo.fr; Ave des Douanes; d from CFA35,000; P ❄ 📶) All picked out in bright-red paint, Le Bougainvillier is a favourite in Port-Gentil. The rooms are simply furnished and set around a parking area and garden. The cheapest have old air-con units. Some have a kitchenette (CFA50,000) and there are studio apartments (CFA54,000).

**Chez Jimmy Hôtel** BOUTIQUE HOTEL **$$$**
(☎07 47 54 89, 02 34 77 17; hotelchezjimmy@begoubitia.com; Blvd Léon M'ba, Quartier Sassec; r/ste incl breakfast CFA105,000/191,000; ❄ 📶) This is a chic hotel with Zen-like design – all ochre walls, gravel and sculptural planting in the gardens, and a minimalist look in the rooms. It's very comfortable, and has friendly staff.

## Eating

★**Le Bistrot** FRENCH **$$**
(☎07 15 01 11; www.facebook.com/lebistrotpog/; Ave Savorgnan de Brazza; mains from CFA9000; ⏲9am-11pm; ❄ 📶) Excellent food, funky decor, friendly staff and a lovely garden terrace make this the best find in Port-Gentil. Try the succulent *coupé-coupé* (cubed fillet of beef) or good fresh salads and pasta. Le Bistrot is easy to miss: it's tucked away behind bushes opposite the bright pink-and-white MUG building.

**Café du Wharf** EUROPEAN, AFRICAN **$$**
(☎05 92 82 05; Ave du Gouverneur Chavannes; midsize pizza CFA7000; ⏲7am-10pm; ❄) This is a cavernous place with a large terrace at the front, overlooking the busy Vieux Port (Old Port). And it's an old favourite, serving reasonable pizza of various sizes, fish brochettes, salads and even wild boar in 'chocolate' (*odika,* crushed acacia seeds) sauce. Head here on Sundays for the huge buffet (CFA18,000).

## Information

Be sure to bring plenty of cash or foreign currency to exchange: ATMs at the banks are not reliable and often run out of money, especially towards the end of the month. **BICIG** (Avenue Savorgnan de Brazza), **Ecobank** (Ave Savorgnan de Brazza) and **UGB** (Ave Savorgnan de Brazza) are all on Ave Savorgnan de Brazza.

**Satguru Travels & Tours Services** (☎06 64 65 65; www.satgurutravel.com; Vieux Port; ⏲8.30am-12.30pm & 3.30-7pm Mon-Fri, 8.30am-12.30pm Sat) is a reliable agency for booking flights.

## Getting There & Away

### AIR

The best option is the 30-minute flight from Libreville, offered by all domestic airlines for around CFA95,000.

### BOAT

CNNII (p275) runs boats between Libreville and Vieux Port in Port-Gentil three times a week in both directions. The 11- to 12-hour one-way trip in economy class is CFA20,000 and cars cost CFA120,000 to CFA180,000, depending on size.

A CNNII boat to Omboué departs from Vieux Port every Friday (CFA20,000) for the 11-hour journey, stopping at every village along the way. It returns on Monday. There are quicker boats that stop less often; the journey takes about 5½ hours (CFA10,000).

There are daily boats to and from Lambaréné that take about 7½ hours (CFA15,000).

# Omboué & Fernan Vaz Lagoon

POP 2000

Omboué may be a small port town, but it's the gateway to three great sites: Fernan Vaz Lagoon; Evengué, with its Fernan-Vaz Gorilla rehabilitation project; and, most importantly, Loango National Park (p278).

## Activities

Several excursions can be arranged through the Hôtel Olako (p278). A visit to the **Fernan Vaz Gorilla Project** (Projet Gorille Fernan-Vaz; ☎07 72 54 26, 07 73 86 92; http://gorillasgabon.org/; adult/child CFA20,000/10,000) or to the **Mission**

**Sainte Anne** costs CFA20,000 per person for a group of four. Fishing on the lagoon is very popular, with barracuda, snapper and tarpon. A day's fishing at Olende costs CFA125,000 including the boat; book ahead to reserve equipment or bring your own.

## Sleeping

**Hôtel Olako** HOTEL **$$**
(04 30 67 13; d CFA36,000-46,000, ste CFA61,000; ) With its colonial feel, this charming hotel features plenty of wood panelling. It's tastefully decorated with local photographs and masks. Rooms are comfortable and there's a lounge, a bar, a library and a terrace. Across the road on the lagoon is the large restaurant on stilts over the water. Dinner is CFA15,000.

**Eco-Village d'Enamino** BUNGALOW **$$$**
(07 98 88 34; www.enamino.com; per person per day all inclusive CFA55,675) On the coast 35 minutes south of Omboué by 4WD, this simple, rustic camp has just two bungalows made of local materials, each sleeping four. A great effort is made towards sustainability, using rainwater and solar power, and composting refuse. Accommodation is comfortable and meals feature fish and local oysters. Excursions are arranged into Loango National Park, and there's some world-class fishing.

## Getting There & Around

Boats leave Port-Gentil for the 5½ hour trip to Omboué (CFA10,000).

A slow boat from Port Môle in Libreville to Omboué departs 11am on Friday and returns Monday, stopping at every village along the way on a journey of about 11 hours (CFA20,000).

Omboué is pretty small and easy to traverse on foot, but if you need a taxi there are two in town. It's CFA200 for *une place* (one seat) and CFA500 for the whole vehicle.

### SURFING HIPPOS

Though it hardly seems credible – a fantasy that belongs in the realm of children's novels, unicorns and flying carpets – Gabon's surfing hippos have been making waves around the world since their hobby was outed by conservationist Mike Fay in the 1990s. Unlike human surfers, the two-ton creatures are hardly a picture of grace as they frolic among the waves, but surf they do: wading into the ocean and opening their legs to catch the swell. Despite the hype, however, it's extremely unlikely you'll see hippos partaking – after all, their name comes from the Greek for 'river horse' and in general they prefer freshwater to seawater. Still, who can blame them for seeking a bit of extra excitement?

# Loango National Park

**Loango** (www.parcsgabon.org; per person per day CFA5000) is known justifiably as 'Africa's last Eden'. Here, warm streams criss-cross pockets of thick forest and salty savannah, while vast island-dotted lagoons and miles of white-sand beach provide habitat for all manner of creatures. It's perhaps best known for its legendary surfing hippos, but you'll also find the largest concentration and variety of whales and dolphins in Gabon's waters, elephants wandering the beaches, western lowland gorillas in the forests and an assortment of rare mammals cavorting in the savannah. If your pockets can take it, Loango is one of the best wildlife-watching destinations on the planet.

## Activities

### Gorilla Observation

The **Max Planck Institute of Evolutionary Anthropology** (Loango Gorilla Programme; www.eva.mpg.de/primat/research-groups/chimpanzees/field-sites/loango-ape-project.html; per person CFA300,000), in conjunction with the National Parks Board, offers an enthralling opportunity to observe a group of western lowland gorillas in the wild. Organised through Loango Lodge, you'll be taken by boat (45 minutes) to the sanctuary in the national park forest. Pygmy trackers, who are particularly adept at finding the gorillas, and a guide lead small groups, and the observation lasts about 1½ hours. The gorillas have become habituated to seeing humans. However, the researchers at the institute are working on finding another group of gorillas so that if the first moves on or members disperse, they will have another group to research and show to visitors.

### Other Wildlife

The savannah and forests of Loango contain elephants, buffaloes, gorillas, chimpanzees, sitatungas and other antelopes, and a dazzling array of birds. Both lodges, Gavilo and Loango, have 4WD vehicles to take you on safari.

The northern section of the park is best visited during the rainy season (September to June) when the animals congregate here for the water and food. Elephants can be found on the beaches between January and April.

In the dry season (June to September) the grass and waterholes dry up, and the animals migrate to the southern regions of the park accessed from Setté Cama.

## Sleeping

**★Loango Lodge** LODGE $$$
(07 79 22 07, 04 44 28 76; www.loango-lodge.net; full board per person €325; ) This impressively remote and high-end lodge operated by the National Parks Board is a wonderful option if you want to visit the northern end of the Loango National Park. Comfortable wooden chalets are dotted around a beautiful garden along the lagoon. The central bar and dining room open out onto a wooden deck that stretches into the water and has great views across to the park. The food here is excellent.

**Gavilo Lodge** LODGE $$$
(www.gavilo-iguela.com; full board per person incl excursions & park permit €175; ) The accent here is on fishing: big-game fishing in the estuary and at sea. The lodge has simply furnished chalets set in a garden, and 4WD vehicles for safaris in the park and for transfers.

## Getting There & Away

To access the northern section of the park, you will need to take a boat from Port-Gentil to Omboué (CFA10,000, 5½ hours). From Omboué, there's a rough, unpaved road to the national park that takes about two hours; the lodge you stay at in Loango will organise this transfer for you.

To access the southern section, fly from Libreville or Port-Gentil to Gamba. Once in Gamba, you'll need to take a boat or 4WD to Setté Cama, which is on the park boundary.

There are no roads within the park linking north and south. However, you could walk 18km from Setté Cama to Akaka, where there is a lodge, and then take a boat to Loango Lodge.

# Setté Cama

POP 100

The tiny fishing hamlet of Setté Cama, with its incomparable location on a spit of land between miles of stunning beach and an enormous lagoon packed full of wildlife, is a novel jumping-off point for the wilds of the southern reaches of Loango National Park. Staying here, just outside the park, is a great budget option. You'll find elephants, gorillas, chimpanzees, various antelopes, crocodiles, turtles and superb game fish.

**Case Abietu** GUESTHOUSE $$
(GIC Tourisme 07 33 99 51; gambareservations@yahoo.fr; all-inclusive r per person from CFA65,000) This guesthouse (also known as the Case de Passage) offers six simple but comfortable fan-cooled rooms, a lounge, and a delightful terrace overlooking the lagoon, while the Atlantic beaches are a two-minute walk away. Villagers prepare traditional meals and act as ecoguides in daily park excursions, and the initiative pours money back into the local community.

**Setté Cama Aventure** BUNGALOW $$$
(05 32 06 06, 04 60 92 33; www.settecama-aventure-gabon.com; d from CFA70,000; ) This lodge has five wooden bungalows with six double rooms in a garden set on the lagoon. It attracts game fishermen from all over the world, but there's plenty of wildlife to see, too. Rooms have mosquito nets. There's a library, and the dining room serves excellent fish. Excursions can be arranged.

## Getting There & Away

Gamba, the oil-town transport hub south of Setté Cama, has flights to and from Libreville (around CFA93,500) via Port-Gentil (around CFA110,000), both twice a week. Once in Gamba, you can reach Setté Cama either by boat or 4WD transfer (each lasting around an hour). The hotels in Setté Cama organise this, and the cost is included in the daily rate.

It's a good idea to set up your transfers in advance, as getting stuck in Gamba isn't the best way to experience the wildlife.

To reach Gamba from Mayumba, you'll need to get to Tchibanga first, or walk about 100km along the coast.

# Mayumba National Park

Closer to the Republic of Congo than to Libreville, Mayumba feels like the edge of the earth. This marine **national park** (Eric Augowet, Conservator 07 69 30 92; www.mayumbanationalpark.com; permit per person per day CFA5000) extends 15km out to sea and just 1km inland, encompassing glorious beaches and forest around the Banio Lagoon. Some 550 leatherback turtles – in fact 30% of the world's total – lay their eggs here between November and April. Humpback whales come to mate between June and October, and you'll also see large groups of dolphins, including the rare humpback dolphin. There are elephants and antelopes in the forest. And the land, if you listen to the locals, is hushed by the spirits of ancestors.

To get to the park – and around once you're there – hire a boat (CFA140,000 per day) and an ecoguard (CFA10,000 per two to three people per day) in the small village of Mayumba.

**Mbidia Koukou** HOTEL **$**
(07 31 13 02, 07 38 87 83; d CFA20,000-25,000; ) With sea views, a great beach, comfortable rooms and a full restaurant, this place makes for a good base that doesn't break the bank. It's located at Mayumba airport on the seaward side of the lagoon.

**Likwale Lodge** HOTEL **$$**
(07 96 61 72, 04 50 05 00; www.likwalelodge.com; d from CFA36,000; ) This recently renovated, Kenyan-style beach lodge by the lagoon edge in Mayumba village has expansive gardens, charming chalets and plenty of space to relax in after a hard day's fishing or safari. On offer are a range of excursions with an emphasis on fishing, which include park entry. Expect to pay CFA15,000 to CFA20,000 for meals.



## Getting There & Away

Local airlines do not fly to Mayumba at the moment, but it's worth checking on the ground to see if they've restarted.

However, NRT (p275) has a flight from Libreville to Tchibanga on Monday and Friday (CFA70,000, one hour), from where you can take a *taxi-brousse* to Mayumba on the new tarred road, which takes under two hours.

# CENTRAL GABON

## Lambaréné

POP 38,775

With its glossy lakes, fast-flowing rivers, thick green foliage and ingrained sweetness, Lambaréné feels somehow kind and gentle, as if the profound humanitarian efforts of Nobel winner Albert Schweitzer changed the character of the land. And his legacy is indeed felt everywhere, from the wonderful, still-operational hospital (which Schweitzer founded in 1924 to treat people with leprosy) to the volunteer-staffed lab that researches malaria and other tropical diseases.

### Sights

Explore the area's many serene lakes by pirogue, arranged at the port in town or through the Hotel Ogooué Palace. The bird haven of **Lake Zilé** is closest to Lambaréné and is easily visited in an afternoon, while to the south of town is **Lake Azingo** with its large hippo population – it can be visited on a day trip. The other lakes to the north of the town are more difficult to access and you will need camping equipment if you plan to stay.

**Schweitzer Hospital Museum** MUSEUM
(www.schweitzerlambarene.org; admission CFA2000; 8.30am-5.30pm) Housed in the former hospital building, the museum's guided tour will allow you to view photos, paintings and the impeccably arranged house and artefacts of Schweitzer and his wife. There's also a small zoo, the animals of which include descendants of Schweitzer's beloved pelican Parzival. You're also able to see the graves of Schweitzer, his wife and colleagues.

### Sleeping & Eating

★**L'Hôtellerie de l'Hôpital Albert Schweitzer** GUESTHOUSE **$**
(07 14 16 62; www.schweitzerlambarene.org; Schweitzer Hospital grounds; d with fan/air-con CFA15,000/20,000) Right next to the hospital museum and the river, this is by far the most atmospheric and interesting accommodation in town. Sleek and smart rooms are housed in what used to be the hospital staff's quarters, and in each there's the biography of the room's previous inhabitant. Meals are available if you order ahead.

**Mission Sœurs Bleues de l'Immaculée Conception** GUESTHOUSE **$**
(01 58 10 73, 04 10 84 53; Rte St François; dm/r per person CFA5000/CFA8000) This tranquil little place is staffed by adorable nuns who make you feel as if you've been spirited into *The Sound of Music*. The grounds are gorgeous, there's a kitchen available for use, and the fan-cooled rooms are clean and have mozzie nets.

**SOLF Hôtel Paul Djonguinyo** HOTEL **$$**
(01 58 23 03, 06 61 39 80; d/VIP/ste CFA45,500/60,500/85,000; P) A very pleasant option set on a hill above the town, all rooms at the Paul Djonguinyo are comfortably furnished and have a balcony. It has a good restaurant, too, with an emphasis on fish (menu CFA5000 to CFA8000).

**Hotel Ogooué Palace** LUXURY HOTEL **$$$**
(07 16 28 02; d/ste CFA50,500/150,000; P) This is a smart place with rooms set around the garden, river views and a great pool. It's very popular at weekends; but you'll have the place to yourself during

the week. Rooms have dark-wood furniture, flat-screen TVs, posh bed linen and a terrace. Mosquitoes and flying ants abound in the evenings, so be liberal with the repellent.

### Getting There & Away

**Boat** Leaves the Lambaréné port for Port-Gentil at 7am daily (CFA15,000), arriving at 2.30pm. It's best to buy your ticket at least one day before as the boats are often full. Be at the port at 6am to start queuing, and be prepared to show your passport and visa, and have your bags searched. It's a beautiful journey on the river system with dense rainforest on both banks.

**Bus** More comfortable and cheaper than a shared taxi is the SOGATRA (p275) bus from Libreville's PK8 (four hours, CFA4000). The buses are scheduled to leave at 1pm and 3pm, but can leave earlier. Tell the driver where you are staying and he will drop you at the most convenient place in Lambaréné, or at the **Shell Station** in Quartier Isaac. For the return trip, the buses leave from the Shell Station at 7.30am and 9am.

**Shared taxi** If you beat the Libreville traffic, you can be in Lambaréné within four hours (CFA8000). Shared taxis leave from Le Tribune on the island, a short distance from the port and the bridge to Quartier Isaac known as Pont Isaac. A place in a shared taxi to Ndjolé, from where you pick up the Transgabonaise Railway, costs CFA7000 and takes about three hours.

## Lopé National Park

Smack bang on the equator and framed by the beautiful Ogooué River, **Lopé National Park** (www.parcsgabon.org; permit per person per day CFA5000), a Unesco World Heritage Site, doesn't disappoint. Undulating hills meet savannah and enclaves of rainforest where elephants, buffaloes, gorillas, chimpanzees and the biggest mandrill troops in the world can be found. It's estimated there are three elephants per square kilometre, which would make it the highest concentration on the planet. The rare giant forest warbler, picathartes and seven types of hornbill are some of the more than 400 species of birds. Archaeological treasures include evidence of human activity from the Stone and Iron Ages.

There are vehicle and foot safaris on offer and there's an **ecomuseum** near the park entrance.

### Sights & Activities

Lopé Hôtel offers some wonderful excursions that you can join even if you're not staying at the hotel. They cost CFA30,000 for a full day (two half-day excursions), or CFA20,000 for half a day. Children under 10 are not allowed into the forest or on pirogue trips. Options include the following:

- Walk in the forest to see elephants, apes and antelopes.
- Journey by 4WD into the savannah to see elephants, buffaloes and waterfalls.
- Climb Mont Brazza for fantastic views over the Ogooué River.
- Visit rock art in caves.
- Take a pirogue trip on the Ogooué River.

You can also rent a vehicle (per half/full day CFA75,000/111,000).

### Sleeping

**Motel E. Mbeyi** MOTEL **$$**

(☎04 17 98 32, 07 47 18 18; P ❄) This catchily named place is run by the same management as the Lopé Hôtel, but it's worlds away in style and price. Just a short walk from the train station, the accommodation is made up of pink-painted units with clean, modern bathrooms, wrought-iron beds and freshly painted walls. There's also a cute thatched dining area.

**Lopé Hôtel** HOTEL **$$$**

(☎01 77 02 17, 01 72 05 86; www.lopehotel.com; d incl breakfast from CFA65,000; P ❄ 🛜 🏊) Made up of 30 cottages of varying sizes, the Lopé Hôtel has a superb position overlooking a bend of the Ogooué River surrounded by dramatic hills and thick woods. It's a fairly formal place, and feels quite touristy, being on nearly all Gabon visitors' itineraries, but the accommodation is comfortable and the service friendly.

### Getting There & Away

The train from Libreville takes between six and eight hours, and arrives in the middle of the night.

You can access the park by the RN3 from Libreville. It's 290km from the city.

You can also take a SOGATRA (p275) bus from PK8 in Libreville as far as Ndjole, and then a *taxi-brousse* to the park.

## Ivindo National Park

This dense, tropical 3000-sq-km **national park** (www.ivindo.org; permit per person per day CFA5000) provides visitors with an incredible opportunity to view forest animals undisturbed in their own environment.

Perhaps the *pièce de résistance* of all the Gabonese eco-destinations is **Langoué Baï**, a marshy clearing in the forest where mineral-rich soils and vegetation act as a magnet for large numbers of forest elephants, western lowland gorillas, sitatungas, buffaloes, monkeys and rare bird species. Arrangements to get to the *baï* must be made well in advance through travel agents in Libreville.

The gushing **Kongou Falls** are Gabon's answer to Niagara, with the addition of grey parrots, elephants, gorillas, chimpanzees and red river hogs living in the forest. Access is via pirogue for three to five hours through spectacular rainforest from the village of Loa Loa (17km south of Makokou).

Nearby **Kongou Camp** is run by the NGO Fondation International Gabon Eco-tourisme (FIGET). Visits here to view the waterfalls and wildlife can be arranged through the travel agency Ngondetour (p285). The camp accommodates 14 people in wooden bungalows with shared bathrooms and has a restaurant serving local cuisine.

In the northwest corner of the park, **Mingouli Falls** is a spectacular series of waterfalls on the Ogooué River. Access is by pirogue from the village of Loa Loa, 17km from Makokou. The Mingouli Falls are a further four or five hours by pirogue from the Kongou Falls.

The cheapest way to get to Ivindo from Libreville is to take the train to Booué just west of the park boundary, and then a *taxi-brousse* to Makokou. If self-driving, it's a 650km journey from Libreville to Makokou. There is also a SOGATRA (p275) bus from PK8 in Libreville (CFA10,000, seven hours).

### SACRED RITES OF BWITI

One of three official religions in Gabon (the others being Christianity and Islam), Bwiti is widely practised by both the forest-dwelling tribes and the Fang, and most towns and villages have a temple. It centres on animism and ancestor worship, often including aspects of Christianity. At its heart lies the trance-inducing ingestion of the root bark of the sacred *ibonga* tree, which is used in initiation rites and all other ceremonies, including healing. Practitioners paint their bodies and faces with red and white powder, dress in red, white and black, and wear raffia skirts, animal fur, shells and feathers.

Ceremonies are led by the *N'ganga* (spiritual leader) and are accompanied by dancing and music from drums and *ngombi* (arched harp). They can last several days while the effects of the *ibonga* wear off. Some Westerners have also been initiated.

# UNDERSTAND GABON

## Gabon Today

After the death of his father, Ali Ben Bongo won the 2009 presidential election with just 42% of the vote. With what was reported as a huge turnout, he won again in 2016 by a reported 6000 votes more than his opposition rival, Jean Ping. Ping challenged the result in the Constitutional Court, only to find that a recount confirmed Bongo's win and pushed up the margin by 11,000 votes (or 51% of the votes against Ping's 47%). Riots broke out across the country, injuries and deaths were reported and buildings damaged, but the situation soon returned to a relative calm.

While Bongo introduced some government reforms, his wealth in Gabon's major industries are an ongoing source of controversy.

The boulevards of Libreville are lined with life-size posters of the president – and populist pledges such as doubling the minimum wage, building new social housing and backing changes to the justice system have all kept Ali Bongo's popularity high.

## History

### Of Petroglyphs & Pygmies

Gabon has been inhabited for at least 400,000 years. Some 1200 rock paintings made by iron-working cultures – which razed the forest for agriculture, creating today's savannah – have been found in the area around Lopé National Park. The earliest modern society, the Pygmies, was displaced between the 16th and 18th centuries by migrating peoples from the north, principally the Fang, who came after settling in what is now Cameroon and Equatorial Guinea.

Contact with Europeans, starting with the arrival of the Portuguese in 1472, had a profound effect on tribal structures. British, Dutch and French ships traded for slaves, ivory and tropical woods. The coastal tribes established strong ties with these colonial powers, but the interior tribes defended their lands against European encroachment.

## Libreville & Liberation

The capital, Libreville, was established in 1849 for freed slaves, on an estuary popular with traders. In 1885 the Berlin Conference of European powers recognised French rights in Gabon, which became part of the French Congo and later French Equatorial Africa. The country became self-governing in 1958, and won independence in 1960 under President Léon M'Ba. After M'Ba died in a French hospital in 1967, his vice-president, Albert Bernard Bongo, took power of the nation (changing his name to Omar when he adopted Islam in 1974).

## The Omar Bongo Years

The newly independent nation got off to an extravagant start. As money rolled in from the sale of timber, manganese ore, iron ore, chrome, gold, diamonds and, finally, oil, Gabon's per-capita income soared higher than South Africa's. Relations with France remained tight throughout Bongo's rule.

In 1976 Bongo's government announced a four-year, US$32 billion plan to create a modern transport system, encourage local industry and develop mineral deposits. Few of these projects ever took shape. The government did, however, spend vast sums hosting a summit of the Organization of African Unity in 1977 and (conservative estimates say) US$250 million on the presidential palace.

In 1990, after the country's first real political unrest, Bongo ended more than two decades of one-party rule by legalising the opposition (though subsequent elections were marred by fraud). He died, at the age of 73, in a Spanish hospital in 2009, officially of a heart attack though it's widely believed that he was suffering from cancer. Gabon initially denied the death of the man it couldn't bear to see gone, but two days after the news leaked from Paris, it was confirmed by Libreville. At the funeral in Libreville, France's President Sarkozy was jeered at – many Gabonese felt the relationship with Paris had gone too far.

### THE 'CONSERVATION COUP'

In the late 1990s Mike Fay, of National Geographic and the Wildlife Conservation Society, walked more than 3200km through Central Africa, documenting the stunning natural environment he passed through. The late President Omar Bongo, after seeing the photos of what became known as the 'Megatransect', did the unthinkable: in 2002 he created a 13-park network of protected lands that covered over 11% of the country. Overnight Gabon leapt from having almost no land conserved to having the most in the world. Hailed as a 'conservation coup', the new conservation economy was a wise move by Bongo, who was looking for new sources of revenue.

# Culture

## People

Of the people living in Gabon today, the original forest-dwelling tribes (known as Pygmies) survive only in the remote north of the country, barely keeping their culture intact. Most other people are descendants of the Bantu peoples, and the Fang are still the most numerous. There is also a sizeable French expat community in Libreville and Port-Gentil.

## Religion

Missionary influence is palpable: over 50% of the country counts itself as Christian, though traditional animist beliefs are still strong and beliefs in superstition and witchcraft hold great power over much of the Gabonese population. Interestingly both Presidents Bongo converted to Islam in the 1970s, when African nationalism was all the rage and friendship with Gaddafi was seen as desirable. As a result there are several mosques prominently located in Libreville, despite the Muslim segment of society as a whole being very small.

## Arts & Music

Traditional masks, carvings and *bieri* (ancestral sculpture) using natural materials such as wood, raffia and feathers are found throughout Gabon. Fang masks are prized throughout the world and sold for big bucks at art auctions.

Hip-hop is big in Gabon, and there are plenty of home-grown groups playing on the radio. You'll also find recordings of the sacred music of the Bwiti, which uses, among other extraordinary instruments, harps played with the mouth, as well as brilliant, inspiring Pygmy group recordings.

## Environment

Gabon is a country of astonishing landscapes and biodiversity, much of which is still undiscovered and unexploited. Though almost 75% of the country is covered in dense tropical rainforest, this equatorial country is also full of endless white-sand beaches, savannah, rushing rivers, hidden lagoons, rocky plateaus and canyons, cloud-tipped mountains and *inselbergs* (isolated rock domes overlooking the surrounding forest canopy), all of which are home to an amazing array of flora and fauna.

You're likely to come across gorillas, chimpanzees, mandrills, forest elephants, forest buffaloes, crocodiles, antelopes, hippos, humpback and killer whales, monkeys of all shapes and sizes, leopards, red river hogs, sea turtles and a rainbow of rare birds – to name just a few.

# SURVIVAL GUIDE

##  Directory A-Z

### ACCOMMODATION

Gabon is no bargain destination, and hotels take the biggest bite out of your budget. Many towns have cheap and basic convent hotels – generally your best bet if you're pinching pennies. In remote villages, if you greet the chief and bring a small gift you'll likely be welcome to stay in a hut. Libreville and any form of national park accommodation tends to be universally very expensive by African standards.

### DANGERS & ANNOYANCES

- Treat Libreville like any big city with its fair share of crime. Always carry your passport (or a copy) and a copy of your visa.
- The dreaded *fourous* (tiny insects) will leave red splotches, but won't hurt until a few days into the forest when infernal itchiness ensues. Insect repellent is a must, and calamine lotion will ease the itchiness.
- The terrible roads, drunk drivers and huge trucks carrying unsecured loads of old-growth forest are probably the biggest dangers in the country.

### ELECTRICITY

220v AC, 50Hz (European-style two-round-pin plugs).

### EMBASSIES & CONSULATES

There is no British Embassy in Gabon; in an emergency contact the **British Honorary Consul** (David Harwood; 01 76 22 00; harwood@internetgabon.com; cnr Brossette & ZI Oloumi) in Libreville. Australia, New Zealand and Ireland have no diplomatic presence in Gabon. Countries with diplomatic representation in Libreville include the following:

**Cameroonian Embassy** (01 73 28 00)

**Canadian Consulate** (07 37 02 42; conhon-gab@gmail.com; St-Georges Building, Quartier Kalibak, Pont Gué-Gué)

**Congolese Embassy** (01 73 00 62; Batterie IV)

**Equatorial Guinean Embassy** (01 73 25 23; Haut Gué-Gué)

**French Embassy** (01 79 70 00; Rue Ange M'Ba)

**German Embassy** (01 76 01 88; amb-allemagne@inet.ga; Les Frangipaniers Building, Au Bord de Mer)

**Netherlands Consulate** (01 74 52 82; tchen.ch@iipconsult.com; 6th fl, Immeuble Dumez, 705 Blvd, Au Bord de Mer)

**São Tomé & Príncipe Embassy** (01 72 15 27; Au Bord de Mer)

**US Embassy** (01 45 71 00; https://libreville.usembassy.gov/; Au Bord de Mer, Sablière; 8am-5.15pm Mon-Thu, 8am-2pm Fri)

### EMERGENCY & IMPORTANT NUMBERS

**Ambulance** (1300, 1399)

**Fire** (18)

**Police** (177) In Libreville: 01 76 55 85. In Port-Gentil: 07 36 22 25

### FOOD

Libreville and Port-Gentil have plenty of restaurants serving mostly European food. Look carefully, though, and you'll find some excellent Gabonese flavours, including sauces such as *nyemboué* (crushed palm nuts) or *odika* (crushed acacia seeds, known as 'chocolate') with meat and fish dishes. Fish is plentiful on the coast and tropical fruit abounds. The main side dish is cassava or manioc formed into sticks.

### INTERNET ACCESS

Gabon has good internet connectivity. Most hotels and some cafes and restaurants offer free wi-fi.

### LGBTIQ TRAVELLERS

Homosexuality is not illegal in Gabon; however, overt displays of affection are taboo in this conservative Christian country.

### MONEY

Gabon uses the Central African Franc (CFA) along with other countries in the region.

ATMs in Libreville and Port-Gentil usually only work with Visa cards, although MasterCard sometimes works at branches of UGB. Note that ATMs start to run out of cash on Thursdays as people withdraw money in time for the weekend, particularly at the end of the month. This phenomenon is worse in Port-Gentil than in Libreville.

Cash is king here, so bring plenty with you, and certainly take more than you need everywhere you go outside of Libreville or Port-Gentil, as you won't be able to get more cash outside these cities. There is a national change shortage so ask for small notes wherever possible.

US dollars and euros are the preferred currency for exchange; other currencies are generally not possible to exchange. You can change money at banks and exchange bureaus.

Credit cards are only accepted at top-end hotels, not in restaurants or shops.

### OPENING HOURS

Shops and businesses open early and close for siesta between noon or 1pm and 3pm. Most shops are closed on Sundays, with some banks opening Saturday mornings but not afternoons.

### POST

The postal service is not operational in Gabon.

### PUBLIC HOLIDAYS

As well as Christian holidays, the following are the principal public holidays in Gabon:

**New Year's Day** 1 January

**Renovation Day** 12 March

**Labour Day** 1 May

**Independence Day** 17 August

**All Saints' Day** 1 November

### TELEPHONE

All Gabonese numbers – mobile and landline – have eight digits. There are no area codes. Landlines nationwide begin with ☎01, while numbers beginning with anything else are mobiles. The country code for Gabon is 241.

Mobile phones are used more widely than landlines, although coverage can be very patchy outside of Libreville and Port-Gentil. You can buy a SIM card for an unlocked GSM phone for CFA2000 at **Airtel** (M'bolo Shopping Centre) in Libreville and in other towns. You will need to supply two copies of your passport and visa.

Recharge cards are available pretty much everywhere.

### TOURIST INFORMATION

Travel agencies and conservation organisations tend to have the most up-to-date information on various parts of the country.

**Go To Gabon** (☎07 44 48 57, 07 52 47 47; www.gotogabon.org) is the new government-sponsored initiative grouping all reputable travel agencies in Gabon.

**Ngondetour** (☎WhatsApp number 07 44 48 57; www.ngondetour.com) is the best option for both day trips and longer tours to the national parks of Gabon. There's no office; contact Paul Armand Mombey Indaki through the website or WhatsApp.

### VISAS

Visas are required by all travellers and must be obtained before arrival; they are not available at the airport or at border crossings. Getting a visa for Gabon can be both difficult and expensive. From countries outside Africa it can cost more than US$100. Unless you're flying straight to Libreville from Europe, it may be best to apply for one at the Gabonese embassy in a nearby African country, where it only takes a couple of days and costs around US$60. You will be required to produce a return or onward plane ticket, proof of health insurance and certified proof of accommodation for the first few nights of your trip.

At the Directeur Genérale de la Documentation (p274) you can obtain visa extensions.

### VOLUNTEERING

It is occasionally possible to volunteer with conservation organisations such as the Max Planck Institute of Evolutionary Anthropology (p278) or the Projet Gorille Fernan-Vaz (p277) that work with gorillas and chimpanzees.

### PRICE RANGES

The following price ranges are used in our Sleeping reviews and refer to a double room with bathroom:

**$** less than CFA33,000

**$$** CFA33,000–CFA66,000

**$$$** more than CFA66,000

The following price ranges are used in our Eating reviews and refer to a main course:

**$** less than CFA5000

**$$** CFA5000–CFA9000

**$$$** more than CFA9000

## Getting There & Away

### AIR

Libreville's Léon M'ba International Airport (p274) is currently the only international airport, but Port-Gentil will shortly come on board with a direct link to Paris with Air France. There is no national airline, but Air France, Royal Air Maroc, Lufthansa, Turkish Airlines and South African Airways regularly connect Libreville to Paris, Casablanca, Frankfurt, Istanbul and Johannesburg, respectively.

To neighbouring countries, there are regular flights to Abidjan (Côte d'Ivoire), Addis Ababa (Ethiopia), Brazzaville (Republic of Congo), Cotonou (Benin), Dakar (Senegal), Douala (Cameroon), Kigali (Rwanda), Lagos (Nigeria), Lomé (Togo), Malabo (Equatorial Guinea), Pointe Noire (Congo) and São Tomé (São Tomé and Príncipe).

### LAND

#### Cameroon

Cross at the Ntem River between Bitam (Gabon) and Ambam (Cameroon). From the town of Ebolowa in Cameroon there's a regular bus service to Yaoundé and Douala. Visas can be purchased at the border.

#### Equatorial Guinea

Not possible for foreigners.

#### Republic of Congo

There are crossings at Léconi (Gabon) and Oyo (Republic of Congo). There's no public transport along most of the route and few cargo trucks, so it can take several days and involve more than a few police checkpoints. There's another crossing at N'Dendé (Gabon) and Doussala (Republic of Congo), from where you head to Loubomo to connect with the Pointe-Noire–Brazzaville railway. In the Ivindo National Park, there is a crossing to the Republic of Congo north of Mékambo. Lastly, there's a crossing between Bakoumba (Gabon) and Mbinda (Republic of Congo). Visas must be arranged in advance, and confirmation of a hotel reservation is also required.

## Getting Around

### AIR

Air is by far the easiest way to move around in Gabon, as the roads are not good, distances are long and buses are slow. However, flights aren't cheap or regular. Also be aware that it's perfectly common for flights to leave before their scheduled departure time, so take those two-hour check-ins seriously. Airlines flying internally in Gabon include the reliable Afric Aviation (p274) and NRT (p275).

### BOAT

There are several passenger boats per week between Libreville and Port-Gentil (CFA20,000, 11 to 12 hours) and it's also possible to take cars on this (CFA120,000 to CFA180,000). Enquire at the CNNII (p275) office at Port Môle in Libreville.

A slow boat from Port Môle in Libreville to Omboué departs 11am on Friday and returns Monday, stopping at every village along the way on a journey of about 11 hours (CFA20,000).

Boats from Port-Gentil to Omboué take about 5½ hours (CFA10,000).

There are passenger boats between Lambaréné and Port-Gentil most days in both directions (CFA15,000, about 7½ hours). Check departures and book tickets at the port a few days before travel.

### BUS

SOGATRA (p275) is the state bus company and runs an efficient service between Libreville and most major towns. Most buses are elderly, advertised air-con is usually open windows and seats are hard, but it's cheaper and more comfortable than being cramped in a *taxi-brousse* (bush taxi). Buses are found at the *gare routiere* (bus station) in major towns, and at a central point (for example, a petrol station) in smaller towns.

### CAR

Driving in Gabon is perfectly feasible, but you will need a 4WD during the rainy season. **Europcar** (☎01 74 58 45; www.europcar.com), **Hertz** (☎01 73 20 11; www.hertz.com) and **Avis** (☎01 72 42 51; www.avis.fr) have offices at Léon M'ba International Airport. Expect to pay around CFA140,000 per day. A driver costs CFA35,400 per day around Libreville and Port-Gentil, and CFA76,700 outside these areas.

### LOCAL TRANSPORT

Taxis are found in towns and you can hire the whole vehicle, known as *une course*. Or you can just buy a seat in a shared taxi, known as *une place*. To hail a taxi, indicate to an oncoming taxi that you want to hire it. As he slows down, shout out *une place* and your destination, or a landmark close to it. Taxi fares range from CFA200 to CFA1000 depending on the town you're in and how far you're going. Fares increase at night.

*Taxis-brousses* and *clandos* (minibuses, so-called as they are 'clandestine' or unregistered) congregate at the *gare routiere* (bus station) and leave when full. They are usually dilapidated vehicles crammed full of passengers and operate between towns.

### TRAIN

Gabon's main transport artery is the Transgabonais Railway line, which runs between Owendo (9km south of Libreville) and Franceville. There are four trains a week in each direction and tickets can be bought at the SETRAG office (p275).

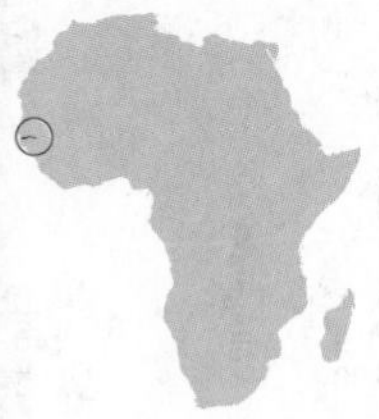

# The Gambia

☎220 / POP 2 MILLION

**Includes ➡**



## Best Places to Eat

- Calypso (p295)
- Sea Shells (p296)
- Butcher's Shop (p295)
- Gida's Garden (p295)
- Ngala Lodge (p294)

## Best Places to Sleep

- Chimpanzee Rehabilitation Project Camp (p301)
- Mandina River Lodge (p298)
- Ngala Lodge (p294)
- Leo's (p299)
- Footsteps Eco Lodge (p299)

## Why Go?

The Gambia may be the smallest country on the continent, but its captivating array of attractions belies its tiny size. Surrounded by Senegal, The Gambia has a mere 80km of coastline, but what a magnificent stretch it encompasses: golden beaches backed by swaying palms and sprinkled with scenic lagoons, sleepy fishing villages and biologically rich coastal reserves.

Of course there's much more to The Gambia than just sun and surf. Its namesake river is teeming with wildlife, including nearly 600 bird species, plus manatees, hippos, crocodiles and troops of wily colobus monkeys. Boat trips and overnights at forest ecolodges reveal some of the great wonders of the hinterland, from a chimpanzee island reserve to the ruins of a 17th-century British fortress. The greatest treasures, though, are the warm-hearted Gambian people, who more than live up to their homeland's moniker of the 'the smiling coast of Africa'.

## When to Go

### Banjul

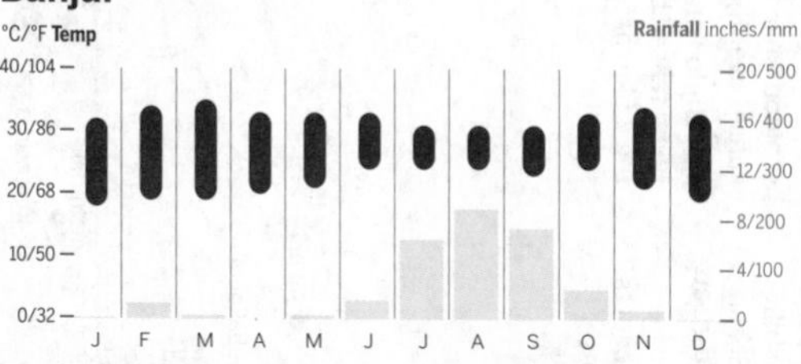


**Nov–Feb** The dry season and the best time to watch wildlife and birds.

**Late Jun–Sep** Rainy season. Many places close but you'll avoid the crowds.

**Oct & Mar–May** Decent weather and ideal for bagging a shoulder-season discount.

# The Gambia Highlights

1 **Chimpanzee Rehabilitation Project** (p301) Boating past river islands where great apes rule.

2 **Atlantic Coast resorts** (p291) Indulging in fresh seafood while watching the sunset over the seaside.

3 **Bijilo Forest Park** (p291) Being teased by monkeys on the 4.5km nature trail.

4 **Abuko Nature Reserve** (p297) Looking out for rare birds and giant crocodiles.

5 **Makasutu Culture Forest** (p297) Sailing along mangrove-lined waterways.

6 **Wide Open Walls** (p298) Checking out the eye-popping murals covering village homes.

7 **National Museum of Albreda** (p300) Contemplating history at the slavery museum.

8 **Sanyang** (p301) Basking on powdery sands along the picturesque beaches.

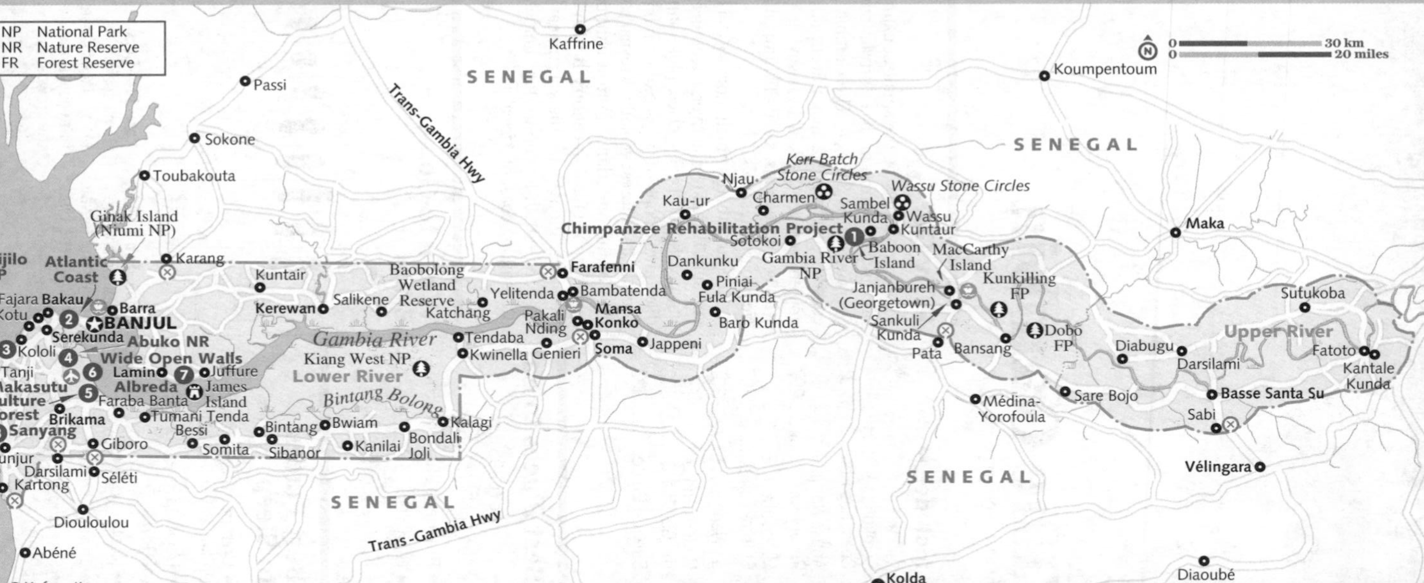

# BANJUL

POP 38,000

It's hard to imagine a more unlikely or consistently ignored capital city than the tiny seaport of Banjul. It sits on an island and sulks, crossed by sand-blown streets and dotted with fading colonial structures. It's also the least-populated capital on the African mainland. And yet, it tempts with a sense of history that the plush seaside resorts lack, and is home to a busy harbour and market that show urban Africa at its best.

## Sights

**★St Joseph's Adult Education & Skills Centre** SCHOOL

(☎4228836; stjskills@qanet.com; Ecowas Ave; ⏰10am-2pm Mon-Thu, to noon Fri) Tucked away inside an ancient Portuguese building, this centre has provided training to disadvantaged women for the last 20 years. Visitors can take a free tour of sewing, crafts and tie-dye classes, and purchase reasonably priced items such as patchwork products, embroidered purses and cute children's clothes at the on-site boutique.

**Albert Market** MARKET

(Russell St; ⏰8am-6pm) Since its founding in the mid-19th century, the Albert Market, an area of frenzied buying, bartering and bargaining, has been Banjul's main hub of activity. This cacophony of Banjul life is intoxicating, with its stalls stacked with shimmering fabrics, hair extensions, shoes, household and electrical wares and the myriad colours and flavours of the fruit and vegetable market.

**Old Town** AREA

West from the ferry terminal towards the wide Ma Cumba Jallow St (Dobson St) is a chaotic assembly of decrepit colonial buildings and Krio-style clapboard houses (steep-roofed structures with wrought-iron balconies and corrugated roofs). It's no coincidence they resemble the inner-city architecture of Freetown in Sierra Leone, as many of them still belong to families who came to Banjul from Freetown, some as early as the 1820s.

**Arch 22** MONUMENT

(Independence Dr; D50; ⏰9am-6pm) This massive 36m-high gateway, built to celebrate the military coup of 22 July 1994, grants excellent views. There's also a cafe and a small museum that enlightens visitors about the coup d'état and houses a few ethnographic exhibitions.

## Activities

**Tanbi Wetland Complex** BIRDWATCHING

The 6.3-sq-km site of the Tanbi Wetland Complex, with its mangroves and creeks, is a great birdwatching area, with Caspian terns, gulls, egrets and several species of wader.

## Sleeping

Not many tourists stay in Banjul as the best hotels are along the coast. There are a few budget guesthouses if the need arises.

**Princess Diana Hotel** HOTEL $

(☎4228715; 30 Independence Dr; r D1200) This is slightly better than most Banjul dosshouses, simply because it has doors that lock plus occasional live music in the bar.

## Eating

Banjul's restaurant scene is a culinary desert and many eateries roll down the blinds before the evening has even started. Around Albert Market you can find several cheap chop shops serving inexpensive plates of rice and sauce.

**Nefertiti Bar & Restaurant** SEAFOOD $

(☎7776600; Marina Pde; mains D300-400; ⏰11am-11pm; 📶) Smack on the beach with a gorgeous view, this laid-back spot serves up local seafood and is a popular location for drinks in the late afternoon and evening.

**Ali Baba Snack Bar** MIDDLE EASTERN $

(☎4224055; Nelson Mandela St; mains D150-250; ⏰9am-7pm Mon-Sat, 10am-5pm Sun) Banjul's main snack bar has a deserved reputation for tasty shwarma (sliced, grilled meat and salad in pita bread) and felafel sandwiches.

## Information

### DANGERS & ANNOYANCES

Albert Market has its share of pickpockets as well as pushy sales people and bumsters, who want to be your friend/guide for the day. The Barra ferry and the ferry terminals are also places to watch out for pickpockets.

### MONEY

**PHB Bank** (☎4428144; 11 Liberation St; ⏰8am-4pm Mon-Thu, to 1.30pm Fri) Has an ATM and changes money.

**Standard Chartered Bank** (☎4222081; Ecowas Ave; ⏰8am-4pm Mon-Thu, to 1.30pm Fri) Withdraw at ATM or change money here.

## Banjul

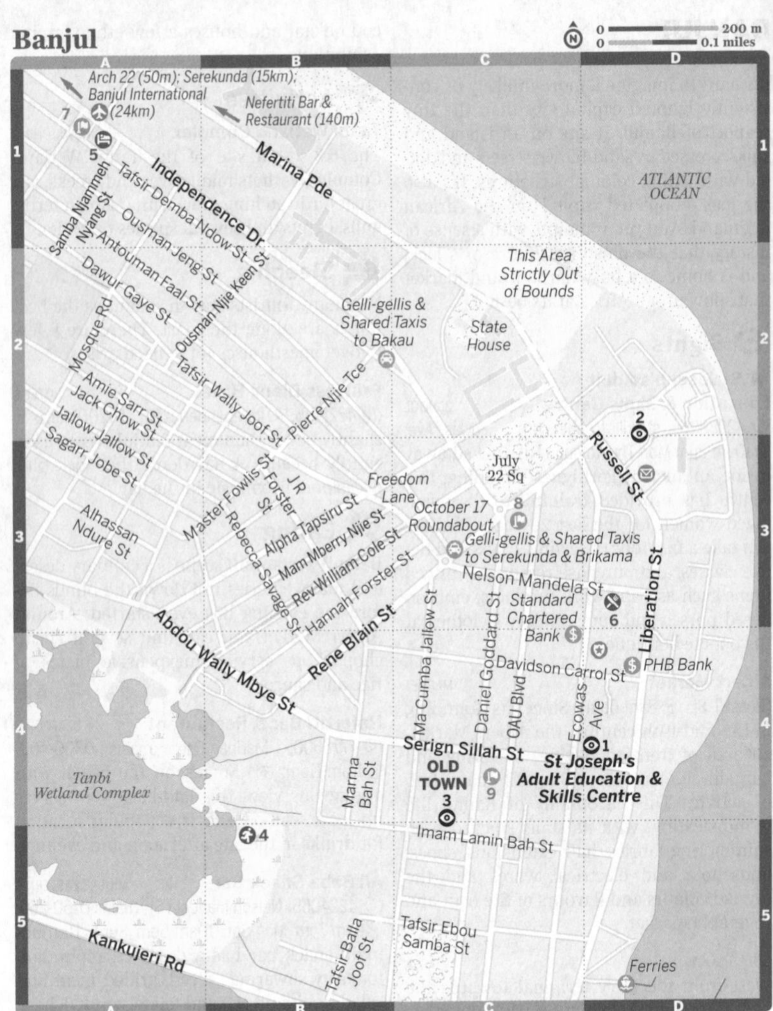


POST

**Main Post Office** (Russell St; ⊙8am-4pm Mon-Sat) Near Albert Market.

### Getting There & Away

**Banjul International Airport** (BLJ; ☎4473000; www.banjulairport.com) is at Yundum, 24km from Banjul city centre and 16km from the Atlantic coast resorts.

**Ferries** (☎4228205; Liberation St; passengers D25, cars D400-500) travel between Banjul and Barra, on the northern bank of the Gambia River. They are supposed to run every two hours from 7am to 9pm and take one hour, though delays and cancellations are frequent.

Gelli-gellis (minibuses) and shared taxis to **Bakau** (Independence Dr) (D15, 45 minutes) and **Serekunda** (D18, one hour) leave from their respective taxi ranks near the National Museum. Note that you might have to pay a bit more for luggage. A private taxi to the coastal resorts will cost around D400 to D500.

### Getting Around

A short ride across Banjul city centre (known as a 'town trip') in a private taxi costs about D40 to D80.

**Banjul**

**Top Sights**
1 St Joseph's Adult Education & Skills Centre ........ D4

**Sights**
2 Albert Market ........ D2
3 Old Town ........ C4

**Activities, Courses & Tours**
4 Tanbi Wetland Complex ........ B5

**Sleeping**
5 Princess Diana Hotel ........ A1

**Eating**
6 Ali Baba Snack Bar ........ D3

**Information**
7 German Embassy ........ A1
8 Guinean Embassy ........ C3
9 Sierra Leonean Embassy ........ C4

# SEREKUNDA & ATLANTIC COAST RESORTS

POP 390,000

Chaotic, splitting-at-the-seams Serekunda is the nation's largest urban centre, and appears to consist of one big, bustling market. The nearby Atlantic Coast resorts of Bakau, Fajara, Kotu Strand and Kololi are where the sun'n'sea tourists flock. This is a great place to spend long days on the beach and late nights on the dance floor.

## Sights

**★Bijilo Forest Park** WILDLIFE RESERVE

(☎7784902; Kololi; D150; ⏰8am-6pm) This small 51-hectare reserve makes for a lovely escape. A series of well-maintained walking trails (ranging from 900m to 1400m) takes you through lush vegetation, gallery forest, low bush and grass, towards the dunes. You'll likely see green vervet, red colobus and patas monkeys – avoid feeding them, as this only encourages them further.

**★Kachikally Crocodile Pool** WILDLIFE RESERVE

(☎7782479; www.kachikally.com; off Salt Matty Rd, Bakau; D100; ⏰7am-7pm) One of The Gambia's most popular tourist attractions is a sacred site for locals. As crocodiles represent the power of fertility in Gambia, women who experience difficulties in conceiving often come here to pray and wash (any child called Kachikally tells of a successful prayer at the pool). The pool and its adjacent nature trail are home to dozens of Nile crocodiles that you can observe basking on the bank.

**Sakura Arts Studio** ARTS CENTRE

(☎9928371; Latrikunda; ⏰10am-5pm) Art lovers should visit Njogu Touray's Sakura Arts Studio for a private viewing of the acclaimed painter's colourful works.

## Activities

**Arch Tours** TOURS

(☎7734941; http://arch-tours.com; Senegambia Strip; excursions from D2500; ⏰9am-8pm) This Gambian-owned outfit receives high marks for its wide range of professionally run excursions and competitive prices. The most popular day trips are the Alex Haley *Roots* cruise and the 4-in-1 tour, taking in markets, Kachikally Crocodile Pool, a school and a remote beach visit. Also goes to Fathala Game Reserve in Senegal.

**Sportsfishing Centre** FISHING

(Denton Bridge) The Sportsfishing Centre is the best place in Serekunda to arrange fishing and pirogue excursions. Various companies are based here, including **African Angler** (☎3086500; www.african-angling.co.uk; Denton Bridge), which runs fishing excursions.

## Tours

**Tilly's Tours** TOURS

(☎7707356; www.tillystours.com; Senegambia Strip, Kololi; half-/full-day excursions from D1400/2400) Small company with responsible tourism products. In addition to many day excursions, Tilly's also offers multiday trips to the highly recommended Chimpanzee Rehabilitation Project in the River Gambia National Park.

**Gambia Experience** TOURS

(☎4461104; www.gambia.co.uk; Senegambia Beach Hotel, Kololi; ⏰9am-5pm) Gambia's biggest tour operator. Does everything from charter flights and all-inclusive holidays to in-country tours.

**Gambia Tours** TOURS

(☎4462602, 4462601; www.gambiatours.gm) Efficient, family-run enterprise.

## Sleeping

**★Luigi's** HOTEL $

(☎9908218; www.luigis.gm; Palma Rima Rd, Kololi; s/d D1400/1700, apt from D2200; ❄📶🏊) This impressive family-run complex has a

# Serekunda & Atlantic Coast Resorts

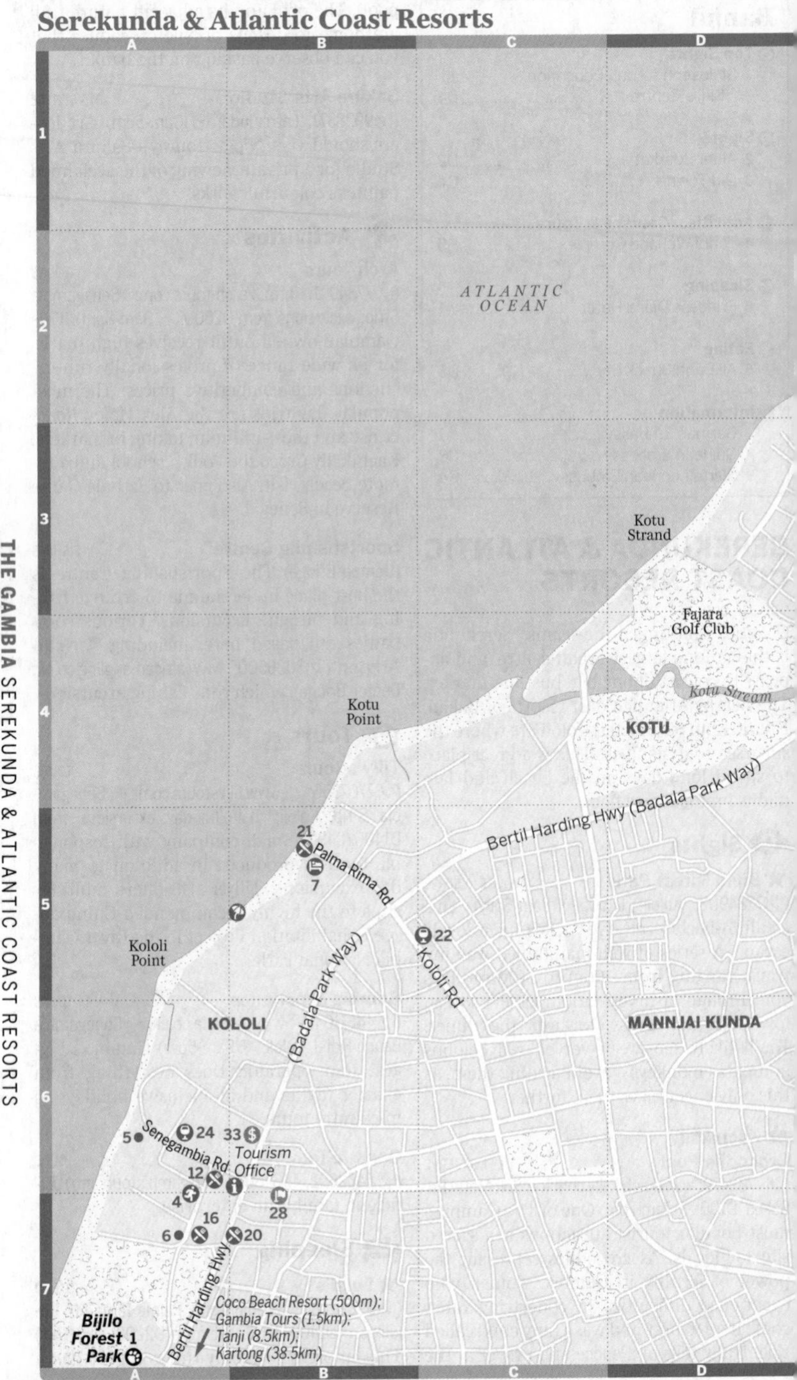

ATLANTIC OCEAN
Kotu Strand
Fajara Golf Club
Kotu Stream
KOTU
Kotu Point
Bertil Harding Hwy (Badala Park Way)
21
Palma Rima Rd
7
22
Kololi Point
(Badala Park Way)
Kololi Rd
KOLOLI
MANNJAI KUNDA
5
24
33
Senegambia Rd
Tourism Office
12
4
28
6
16
20
Bertil Harding Hwy
Coco Beach Resort (500m); Gambia Tours (1.5km); Tanji (8.5km); Kartong (38.5km)
Bijilo Forest Park
1

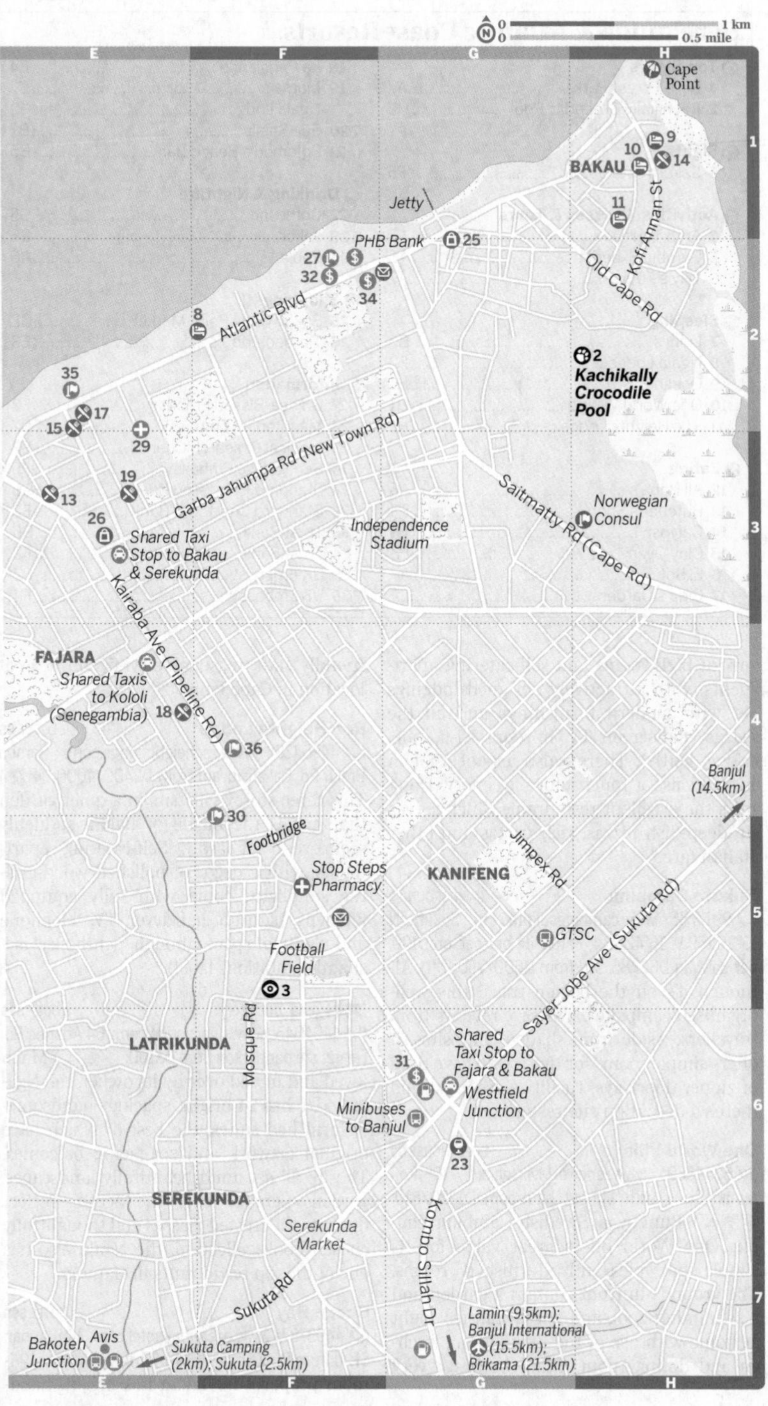
0 1 km
0 0.5 mile
Cape Point
BAKAU
Kofi Annan St
Old Cape Rd
Jetty
PHB Bank
Atlantic Blvd
2
Kachikally Crocodile Pool
Garba Jahumpa Rd (New Town Rd)
Saitmatty Rd (Cape Rd)
Norwegian Consul
Independence Stadium
Shared Taxi Stop to Bakau & Serekunda
Kairaba Ave (Pipeline Rd)
FAJARA
Shared Taxis to Kololi (Senegambia)
Banjul (14.5km)
Footbridge
Stop Steps Pharmacy
KANIFENG
Jimpex Rd
GTSC
Sayer Jobe Ave (Sukuta Rd)
Football Field
3
Mosque Rd
LATRIKUNDA
Shared Taxi Stop to Fajara & Bakau
Westfield Junction
Minibuses to Banjul
SEREKUNDA
Serekunda Market
Kombo Sillah Dr
Sukuta Rd
Bakoteh Junction
Avis
Sukuta Camping (2km); Sukuta (2.5km)
Lamin (9.5km); Banjul International (15.5km); Brikama (21.5km)

## Serekunda & Atlantic Coast Resorts

**Top Sights**
1 Bijilo Forest Park ... A7
2 Kachikally Crocodile Pool ... H2

**Sights**
3 Sakura Arts Studio ... F5

**Activities, Courses & Tours**
4 Arch Tours ... A7
5 Gambia Experience ... A6
6 Tilly's Tours ... A7

**Sleeping**
7 Luigi's ... B5
8 Ngala Lodge ... F2
9 Ocean Bay ... H1
10 One World Village ... H1
11 Roc Heights Lodge ... H1

**Eating**
12 Ali Baba's ... A6
13 Butcher's Shop ... E3
14 Calypso ... H1
15 Clay Oven ... E2
16 El Sol ... A7
17 Gida's Garden ... E2
18 La Parisienne ... E4
19 Mama's ... E3
Ngala Lodge ... (see 8)
20 Sea Shells ... B7
21 Solomon's Beach Bar ... B5

**Drinking & Nightlife**
22 Come Inn ... C5
23 Jokor ... G6
24 Reo's ... A6

**Shopping**
25 Bakau Cape Point Market ... G2
26 Timbooktoo ... E3

**Information**
27 Guinea-Bissau Embassy ... F2
28 Mauritanian Embassy ... B7
29 Medical Research Council ... E2
30 Senegalese Embassy ... F5
31 Standard Chartered Bank ... G6
32 Standard Chartered Bank ... F2
33 Trust Bank ... B6
34 Trust Bank ... F2
35 UK Embassy ... E2
36 US Embassy ... F4

mix of B&B rooms and self-catering apartments, with attractively designed lodgings set with modern furnishings and all the extras (flat-screen TV, in-room wi-fi, safe, fridge, kettle). There's also a pool, though it could use a touch more greenery. Don't miss the excellent restaurant, which serves up deep-dish pizzas, rich pastas and other Italian fare.

**Sukuta Camping** CAMPGROUND **$**
(☎9917786; www.campingsukuta.com; Sukuta, N 13°25,169 W 16°42,934; campsite per person D190, per car/van D60/85, s/d from D600/750; wi-fi) Although it's off the beaten track, this well-organised campsite earns rave reviews from travellers. Aside from shaded campsites, it offers simple rooms for those who have tired of zipper doorways. Facilities are great and there's a decent on-site restaurant.

**One World Village** GUESTHOUSE **$$**
(☎6834569; www.oneworldvillage.eu; 10 Kofi Annan St; r with/without bathroom D1220/810; air-con, wi-fi, pool) Run by a Swedish-Gambian couple, One World offers great value for its simple but pleasantly furnished rooms. The grounds in front contain a garden and a swimming pool, and guests can feel right at home with use of the living room, kitchen and dining room. Other bonuses: very friendly staff, reasonable wi-fi and a great location in Cape Point.

**Roc Heights Lodge** LODGE **$$**
(☎4495428; www.rocheightslodge.com; Samba Breku Rd, Bakau; d/apt from D2400/4000; air-con, wi-fi) This three-storey villa sits in a quiet garden that makes the bustle of Bakau suddenly seem very far away. Self-catering apartments, with a decor of polished wood-and-tile simplicity, come with fully equipped kitchens, bathtub, hairdryer, TV, telephone and plenty of space (though 'penthouse' is a slightly ambitious label).

★ **Ngala Lodge** LODGE **$$$**
(☎4494045; www.ngalalodge.com; 64 Atlantic Rd, Fajara; ste per person from D3100; air-con, @, pool) Much loved and fussed over by its owner, the Ngala Lodge has 24 bright, spacious handsomely furnished suites, the best of which have original artwork and sea-facing balconies. They're all set amid beautifully landscaped gardens perched over the ocean. Perfect down to the frosted glasses and thoughtfully chosen book collection, the Ngala also has one of the top restaurants in Gambia.

**Ocean Bay** HOTEL **$$$**
(☎4495787; www.oceanbayhotel.com; Kofi Annan St; d from D5300; air-con, wi-fi, pool) This massive, 195-room property in Bakau has bright, hand-

somely furnished rooms and suites with all the mod cons – air-con, in-room safe, flat-screen TVs. Pricier rooms have balconies with sea views. The huge pool, exercise room, bar, and restaurant (with a great breakfast buffet) add to the value – though the biggest draw is having the beach right at your (back) door.

## Eating

**La Parisienne** CAFE $
(Karaiba Ave; mains D100-400; 7.30am-midnight; ) Famed for its piping-hot croissants and other bakery items, La Parisienne also serves up great coffee and snacks (pizzas, salads, sandwiches). The terrace is a good spot for a bit of wi-fi.

**Solomon's Beach Bar** SEAFOOD $
( 4460716; Palma Rima Rd, Kololi; mains D200-300; 9am-11pm) At the northern end of Kololi beach, this breezy roundhouse serves excellent grilled fish in a buzzing, youthful atmosphere. As light and sunny as the reggae classics on loop. Grab one of the outdoor tables for prime wave-gazing. There's live music on Thursday nights.

**Ali Baba's** MIDDLE EASTERN $
(Senegambia Strip, Kololi; mains around D300-350; noon-2am) Everyone knows Ali Baba's, so it's as much a useful meeting point as a commendable restaurant. A fast-food joint during the day, it serves dinner with a show in its breezy garden. There's live music most nights, and important football matches on a big screen.

★ **Calypso** INTERNATIONAL $$
( 9920201; off Kofi Annan St, Chez Anne & Fode, Bakau; sandwiches/mains around D350/550; 9am-late daily Nov-Apr, 10am-11pm Sat & Sun May-Oct) Much-loved Calypso serves delicious grilled fish, snacks (such as prawn spring rolls), panini and an African dish of the day, plus a full English breakfast. For peaceful views over the waterfront, head to the upper-level deck or grab one of the private thatched-roof *palapas* (huts) with comfy deckchairs sprinkled around the garden.

**El Sol** MEXICAN $$
( 7149709; www.elsolgambia.com; Senegambia Strip; mains D380-500; 10am-10.30pm Tue-Sun; ) One of the best eateries in the Senegambia area, El Sol spreads a Latin feast, with enchiladas, quesadillas and fajitas, plus a first-rate grilled red snapper, all of which goes down nicely with a few rounds of margaritas or mojitos. It's an upscale spot, with a stylish interior and a few outdoor tables on the covered front deck.

**Gida's Garden** INTERNATIONAL $$
( 3709008; www.facebook.com/pg/gidasgarden; off Atlantic Blvd; mains D300-550; 12.30pm-midnight) This hidden oasis tucked one block south of the Atlantic Blvd is best known for its delectably prepared grilled meats (grilled T-bone, barbecue ribs), though you'll also find a changing array of seafood and excellent desserts. It's a quite the magical and tranquil setting by night, with low-lit tables overlooking the flower-filled gardens. Book ahead.

**Mama's** INTERNATIONAL $$
( 7646452; mains D200-350; 9am-midnight Tue-Sun) Mama's is a long-running institution in Fajara, with a huge menu of satisfying comfort food: brochettes, grilled fish, schnitzel, spaghetti, salads and local specialities like chicken yassa. You can dine alfresco in the garden, which draws a friendly crowd in the evening – particularly for Friday's seafood buffet (D475) and Sunday's roast pork (D450).

**Clay Oven** INDIAN $$
( 4496600; off Atlantic Blvd; mains D400-650; noon-midnight; ) In a converted house surrounded by gardens, the Clay Oven serves up excellent Indian food, with classics like palak paneer, chicken tikka massala and sizzling tandoori grills. On Tuesday, you can try a variety of dishes served tableside for D795 a person.

★ **Butcher's Shop** MOROCCAN $$$
( 4495069; www.thebutchersshop.gm; 130 Kairaba Ave, Fajara; mains lunch D230-500, dinner D385-895; 9am-10pm) Driss, the Moroccan celebrity chef (and TV star), fires up some of the best cooking in The Gambia at this elegant eatery with terrace seating on busy Kairaba Ave. You'll find perfectly grilled fish and juicy steaks, along with global dishes such as rich Moroccan tagines, Italian-style duck confit and high-end comfort classics like fish pie.

**Ngala Lodge** INTERNATIONAL $$$
( 4494045; Atlantic Rd, Fajara; mains D400-900) One of Gambia's most renowned restaurants, this has always been the top address for sumptuous and lovingly presented meals; the service and sea-view setting are impeccable.

### ★Sea Shells
INTERNATIONAL $$$

(☎7760070; Bertil Harding Hwy; ⏲11am-10pm) Despite the unfortunate location on the highway, Sea Shells is well worth a visit for its creative and beautifully prepared dishes. Pop by at lunchtime for fresh vegetable tarts, curried chicken salad, salmon burgers with beetroot chutney and other light fare. At night, the menu shines with coconut-dusted prawns, roast ladyfish with a crab salad, and a famous beef Wellington.

## Drinking & Nightlife

### Reo's
BAR

(www.facebook.com/reosbarandrestaurant; off Senegambia Rd; ⏲10am-late) Reo's is a sleek but welcoming space that ticks all the boxes, with football matches playing on the big screens, a pool table for lazy afternoons, and DJ-fuelled grooves on weekends – plus good pub grub at all hours. There's also a raised deck in front where you can take in the passing street scene.

### Jokor
CLUB

(☎4375690; 13 Kombo Sillah Dr, near Westfield Junction; ⏲10pm-6am Thu-Sat) This nightclub is a raucous local affair, and makes a convincing claim to be the most entertaining club of all. It draws crowds on weekends (after about 11pm), and there's occasionally a live band, usually *mbalax* (percussion-driven, Senegalese dance music) or reggae, on Friday and Saturday. Cool off in the courtyard garden.

### Come Inn
BEER GARDEN

(☎8905724; Palma Rima Junction; ⏲10am-2am; 📶) For a good draught beer and a solid dose of local gossip, there's no better place than this German-style beer garden. There's also a big menu of hearty international fare (mains D200 to D450).

## Shopping

### Timbooktoo
BOOKS

(3 Garba Jahumpa Rd; ⏲10am-7pm; 📶) A delightful bookshop that stocks a good selection of West African titles, plus fiction and children's books. You'll also find a selection of African music CDs, and there's a cafe upstairs.

### Bakau Cape Point Market
ARTS & CRAFTS

(Atlantic Rd; ⏲9am-7pm) A good place to pick up sculptures, batiks and souvenirs is this shaded open-air market on the main road. You can watch the carvers and craft makers in action.

## Information

### DANGERS & ANNOYANCES

Crime rates in Serekunda are low. However, tourists (and especially women) will have to deal with the constant hustling by 'bumsters' (touts). Decline unwanted offers firmly – these guys are hard to shake off. There are also a number of persistent ganja peddlers. Steer clear of the beaches after dark.

### INTERNET ACCESS

Wi-fi connections are increasingly common at restaurants and hotels, where they are typically free for guests. Connections are usually slow. Internet cafes are a dying breed here.

### MEDICAL SERVICES

**Medical Research Council** (MRC; ☎4495446; Fajara) If you find yourself with a potentially serious illness, head for this British-run clinic.

**Stop Steps Pharmacy** (☎4371344; Serekunda; ⏲9am-10pm Mon-Sat) Well stocked; has several branches.

### MONEY

The main banks have ATMs, but withdrawal limits (D5000) makes relying on them impracti-

### BEACHES

The erosion that used to eat its way right up to the hotels has largely been reversed, so that the beaches of Kotu, Kololi and Cape Point are once again wide, sandy and beautiful. Kotu is particularly attractive, with sand and palm trees, beach bars and juice sellers on one side, and an area of lagoons a bit further north, where Kotu Stream cuts into the land (that's where birdwatchers go).

Cape Point, at the northern tip of Bakau, has the calmest beaches. As this is a more residential area, you get less hassle from touts.

Most beaches in this area are relatively safe for swimming, but currents can sometimes be strong. Care should be taken along the beach in Fajara, where there's a strong undertow. Always check conditions before plunging in.

If the Atlantic Ocean and fending off 'bumsters' doesn't appeal, all the major hotels have swimming pools. Most places allow access to nonguests with a meal, a drink or for a fee.

cal. You can also change money at hotels, or at exchange booths around town.

**PHB Bank** (☎4497139; Atlantic Rd, Bakau)

**Standard Chartered Bank** (☎4396102; Kairaba Ave)

**Standard Chartered Bank** (☎4495046; Atlantic Rd)

**Trust Bank** (☎4465303; Wilmon Company Bldg, Badala Park Way)

**Trust Bank** (☎4495486; Atlantic Rd)

#### POST

**Gampost Bakau** (☎8900587; Atlantic Rd, Bakau; ⏲8.30am-4pm Mon-Thu, to noon Fri & Sat) Small, but has a convenient location near the shore.

**Main post office** Off Kairaba Ave, about halfway between Fajara and Serekunda.

#### TOURIST INFORMATION

**Bijilo Forest Park Headquarters** (p291) Park and trail information.

**Tourism Office** (www.visitthegambia.gm; ⏲11am-6pm Mon-Thu) Next to the Senegambia craft market, it doles out info on the region.

### Getting There & Away

For journeys eastward, the new **GTSC** (☎4380000; www.gtsc.gm; Kanifing Depot, off Banjul Serrekunda Hwy) bus is a godsend. Its new, comfy buses make regular scheduled trips between Serekunda and Bassa Santa Su, stopping at key destinations along the way.

There are also bush taxis and gelli-gellis leaving from Westfield Junction. Destinations include Brikama (D30, one hour), Soma (D130, five hours) and Janjanbureh (D230).

For transport heading to the south coast villages of Tanji, Sanyang, Gunjur (D40) and Kartong (D50), take a bush taxi or gelli-gelli from Bakoteh Junction, where Kololi Rd and Sayerrjobe Ave intersect (about 1km west of Karaiba Ave).

#### CAR & MOTORCYCLE

**Avis** (☎4399231; www.avis.com; Banjul International Airport) Handily located at the airport.

**Tippa petrol station** (Bakoteh Junction, Serekunda)

**Petrol Station** (Kombo Sillah Dr)

**Petrol Station** (Kairaba Ave (Pipeline Rd))

### Getting Around

Shared taxis called *six-six* (a short hop costs D15) operate on several routes around the coastal resorts. Shared taxis to Bakau and Serekunda connect Bakau to **Westfield Junction** and Serekunda, passing through **Sabina Junction** near the Timbooktoo bookshop at Fajara. You can also get *six-six* from the traffic-lights junction in Fajara to Senegambia Strip in Kololi and from there to Bakau. Simply flag a taxi down, pay your fare and get off where you want.

For Banjul, there's a minibus stop near Westfield Junction. You can also hire yellow or green taxis (they're more expensive) for trips around town. Rates are negotiable.

# WESTERN GAMBIA

## Abuko Nature Reserve

**Abuko** (Brikama Hwy; adult/child D35/15; ⏲8am-5.30pm) is rare among African wildlife reserves: it's tiny, it's easy to reach and you don't need a car to go in. With amazing diversity of vegetation and animals, this well-managed reserve is one of the region's best bird-watching haunts (more than 250 bird species have been recorded in its environs). Abuko is located about 11km from the Atlantic Coast and makes an easy day's excursion from most lodging near the beach.

The reserve is particularly famous for its Nile crocodiles and other slithering types such as pythons, puff adders, green mambas, spitting cobras and forest cobras.

To get to Abuko, take a private taxi (around D500 to D600) or a minibus headed for Brikama from Banjul (D25) or Serekunda (D18). Most travel agencies and hotels offer organised trips to the reserve.

## Makasutu Culture Forest

Like a snapshot of The Gambia, **Makasutu Culture Forest** (☎9951547; www.mandinalodges.com/makasutu-forest; from D800) bundles the country's array of landscapes into a dazzling 1000-hectare package. The setting is stunning, comprising palm groves, wetlands, mangroves and savannah plains, all inhabited by plenty of animals, including baboons, monitor lizards and hundreds of bird species.

A day in the forest includes a mangrove tour by pirogue; guided walks through a range of habitats, including a palm forest where you can watch palm sap being tapped; a visit to a crafts centre; and demonstrations of traditional dancing. The tours are well organised and run by excellent staff. This is a great day out, especially for families seeking a taste of nature away from the beaches and without the hassle of braving the up-country roads.

## Sights

**★Wide Open Walls** PUBLIC ART
(www.instagram.com/wideopenwalls) Two huge ibex grazing amid swirling waves, a blue tattooed lion, and a lovestruck blacksmith are just a few of the striking images awaiting visitors who stumble upon the village of Kubuneh, located a few kilometres outside of Makasutu Culture Forest. The simple homes of this African settlement have been transformed into a riotous collection of thought-provoking street art, courtesy of a talented group of international artists who have brought a touch of surreal beauty to this corner of West Africa.

## Sleeping

**Mandina River Lodge** LODGE $$$
(in Gambia and international 00 220 3026606, in UK 01489 866 939; www.mandinalodges.com; s/d incl half board from D5000/9000; ) If you feel like a treat, you can stay in the forest at this exclusive and very stunning eco-retreat, an elegant marriage of lavishness and respect for nature.

## Getting There & Away

To get here from the Atlantic Coast, take the GTSC bus (D20, one hour) from Serekunda to Brikama. A private taxi from Brikama costs around D300 (15 minutes).

Any tour outfit in Serekunda can arrange a day-trip, though Gambia Experience (p291) are noted Makasutu specialists.

# Tanji

This petite village is home to the charming Tanji Village Museum, and provides access to the Tanji River Bird Reserve.

## Sights

**Tanji Fish Market** MARKET
Colourful pirogues roll in the waves, women ferry fish elegantly to shore atop their heads, and crowds swarm the beachfront at this charismatic fish market. On show and on sale is everything from smelly sea creatures and colourful peppers to bright flip-flops and clothing. It's busier in the morning, but in the late afternoon it's incredibly photogenic – step inside a smoke house, which preserves masses of *bonga* (shad fish), and you'll see entrancing rays of light cutting through the thick air.

**Tanji River Bird Reserve** WILDLIFE RESERVE
(9919219; entry D35, guide D400; 8am-6pm) The Tanji River Bird Reserve is an area of dunes, lagoons and woodland, and contains Bijol Island, a protected breeding ground for Caspian terns. True to name, the reserve is home to many bird species – over 300 at last count.

**Tanji Village Museum** MUSEUM
(9926618; www.tanjevillagemuseum.com; adult/child D200/50; 9am-5pm) This fascinating cultural museum presents Gambian nature and life scenes by recreating a traditional Mandinka village, where you can peer into huts and learn about craftmaking, traditional music, customs and beliefs, medicinal plants and the local fauna and flora.

There's a lovely mosaic-covered restaurant here (mains around D200) and visitors can overnight in rustic bungalows (per person D500).

## Sleeping

**Tanji Village Museum** BUNGALOW $
(9926618; per person D500) On the grounds of the Tanji Village Museum, guests can get a taste of the simple life by overnighting in a simple bungalow. It's bare-bones but clean, with a bit of light provided by solar panels. The restaurant here (open 9am to 10pm) serves simple plates of roast fish, grilled chicken, seafood kebabs and the like.

**Nyanya's Beach Lodge** LODGE $$
(6134188; Tanji; s/d D700/1200) Nyanya's Beach Lodge has ageing bungalows in a leafy garden on the bank of a Gambia River branch. Although the lodging is basic, it's hard to beat the location just steps from the beach.

## Getting There & Away

To get to Tanji by public transport, catch a bush taxi or gelli-gelli from Bakoteh Junction in Serekunda (D15, 35 minutes).

# Brufut

POP 22,000

Located just to the south of the Atlantic Coast resorts, Brufut has rapidly changed from a tranquil fishing village to a built-up tourist centre – though it's still less hectic than its northern neighbours. The golden sands, backed by palms, are the chief draw here, but there's also some fine birdwatching in the forests to the south.

### Sleeping

**Leo's** BOUTIQUE HOTEL $$$
(☎7212830; http://leos.gm; Brufut Heights 46; s/d D5400/6600, ste for 1/2/3/4 people D6600/7500/8400/9400; ) Perched on a cliff behind Brufut beach, Austrian-run Leo's has five bright, well-appointed rooms and one suite, all attractively furnished. Rooms have sliding glass doors that open onto a shared balcony overlooking the pool with the ocean in the distance. It's a kid-free place, though you might encounter a few families at the excellent on-site restaurant (mains D410 to D730).

**Hibiscus House** B&B $$$
(☎7784552; www.hibiscushousegambia.com; r incl breakfast from D3950; ) Although it's 2km from the beach, this delightful guesthouse in the village has earned many admirers for its warm welcome, great food and sparkling pool surrounded by lush grounds. Staff can help arrange trips to deserted beaches in the south and other excursions.

### Getting There & Away

To get here by public transport take a Tan-Western Gambiaji-bound bush taxi or gelli-gelli from Bakoteh Junction in Serekunda. Note that several hotels in the area are not convenient to public transport (being well off the main road), including Hibiscus House and Leo's.

## Gunjur

POP 17,800

The tranquil fishing village of Gunjur, one of The Gambia's largest fishing centres, lies 10km south of Sanyang. This place is all about fish, guts and nets, though there are some fine opportunities to explore The Gambia's wild side at the avian-rich wetlands of the Bolong Fenyo Community Wildlife Reserve.

The **Bolong Fenyo Community Wildlife Reserve** (www.thegambiawildlife.com) is a 320-hectare reserve encompassing a mix of savanna and wetland habitats, including a freshwater lagoon, and has exceptional birdlife, with some 150 species spotted here

### Sleeping

★**Footsteps Eco Lodge** LODGE $$
(☎7700125; www.footstepsinthegambia.com; s/d D2500/3300, cabins D4200; ⏲closed Jul–mid-Oct; ) This beautiful ecofriendly property on the south coast has nine cheerfully decorated en-suite roundhouses which surround a freshwater swimming pool, along with several more spacious log cabins. Lush forest surrounds the buildings, and it's a pleasant 1km walk down to the beach. There's an excellent restaurant here, with locally sourced produce (including some grown on site).

**Balaba Nature Camp** HUT $$
(☎9919012; www.balabacamp.co.uk; Medina Salaam; r incl full board D2200) Set amid a pristine swath of Gambian forest, this locally run, ecofriendly option has rustic thatched-roof accommodation with mosquito nets and shared toilets and well water for bathing (bucket-and-jug style). With over 100 bird species around, this is a fantastic place for birdwatchers – but obviously not ideal for prima donnas.

### Getting There & Away

To reach this part of the coast by public transit, take a bush taxi or a gelli-gelli that departs from Bakoteh Junction in Serekunda (around D40, 70 minutes).

# LOWER GAMBIA RIVER

## Albreda, Juffureh & Kunta Kinteh Island

When Alex Haley, the American author of *Roots*, traced his origins to Juffureh, the tiny village quickly turned into a popular tourist destination. Together with adjoining Albreda village and Kunta Kinteh Island further offshore, this historical site preserves the memory of the dark legacy of slavery. The entire area was named a Unesco World Heritage site in 2003. Today the area can feel like a bit of a tourist circus, though it still remains a pilgrimage site for Americans with African heritage.

**Fort James** was an important British colonial trading post from 1661 and the departure point of vessels packed with ivory and gold, as well as slave ships. Over subsequent decades, it was the site of numerous skirmishes. Variously held by British, French and Dutch traders, as well as a couple of privateers (pirates), it was completely destroyed at least three times before being finally abandoned in 1829.

WORTH A TRIP

**JANJANBUREH**

Janjanbureh (Georgetown) is a sleepy former colonial administrative centre. It is situated on the northern edge of MacCarthy Island in the Gambia River, and is reached via ferry from either bank. The main reason to come here is to stay in a local lodge and take advantage of the superb birdwatching opportunities. However, a walk around town does reveal a few historic buildings.

There's little in terms of infrastructure – no banks and no hospital. Most visitors come on multiday excursions from the coast, such as those offered by Tilly's Tours (p291) and Arch Tours (p291), with an overnight at Janjanbureh along the way.

The small **National Museum of Albreda** (☎7710276; www.ncac.gm; Albreda; D100; ⊙10am-5pm Mon-Sat) focuses on slavery in The Gambia, with displays detailing the gruesome treatment these human captives suffered. There's also a room dedicated to the *Roots* connection, with photos and memorabilia related to Alex Haley and the subsequent film. Also here is a replica slave ship. Admission includes entrance to Kunta Kinteh Island.

The easiest way to visit Juffureh and Kunta Kinteh Island is with an organised tour. Otherwise, take the ferry to Barra and find a shared (D40) or hire taxi (return D1500, including wait time) to Albreda. Once at Albreda, you'll have to hire a pirogue (from around D800) to get out to Kunta Kinteh Island.

## Baobolong Wetland Reserve & Kiang West National Park

Together, this pair of protected areas straddles the Gambia River and provides habitats for various wildlife, including an array of bird species. A pirogue cruise through the *bolongs* (creeks) and thick mangroves of the Baobolong Wetland Reserve on the north bank is great for birdwatching. On the south bank is the less-accessible Kiang West National Park, which has even more birdlife on show, as well as bushbucks and sitatungas. An easy-to-reach viewpoint, within the boundaries of Kiang West National Park on the south bank, is Toubab Kollon, from where an escarpment follows the river. Its view over woodlands makes a fine spot for watching birds, particularly early in the morning.

Located on the south bank of the Gambia River, **Tendaba Camp** (☎9911088; d from D1000) is well past its prime, with battered lodging and run-down facilities. However, it's one of the best places to arrange excursions in the area, with regular boat trips to the Bao Bolong Wetland Reserve and less frequent excursions to Kiang West National Park.

The easiest way of exploring these parks is by organised tour from Serekunda, usually overnighting at Tendaba Camp. By public transport it's difficult to explore these sights, though you can take a GTSC bus from Serekunda to Kwinella (D90, three hours), and walk or catch a lift for the remaining 6km north to Tendaba Camp.

## BASSE SANTA SU

POP 20,400

With its dusty roads and packed trading stalls, The Gambia's easternmost town almost spills into the scenic river bend that frames it. It's a lively market and border town with a few old Victorian buildings and a feel quite different from the coast – thanks to the influence of Senegalese, Guinean and Malian traders. And while attractions are few, for those seeking an authentic side of The Gambia, well off the beaten track, Basse (as it's usually called) is an intriguing place to explore.

There are plenty of simple chop shops in town and street stalls dolling out belly-filling bowls of *fufu* (a fermented flour dish). The pick of lodging in town, **Basse Guest Inn** (☎7724822; 22 Mansajong St; s/d from D600/800; ❄) is a well-run spot that has clean, modern rooms with nice extras (including a fridge). Meals can be arranged.

Joe's Bar is a fine place for a drink with a riverside setting.

### ℹ Information

Trust Bank and Standard Chartered Bank can change money (no ATMs).

If you haven't found all the necessary immigration officials at the border, you can get your entry stamp from the immigration office in town.

### Getting There & Away

The best way to get here from the Atlantic Coast is aboard one of the GTSC (p297) buses that make the trip regularly (D220 to D260, around eight hours) in the morning (before noon).

Gelli-gellis go to the ferry ramp for Janjanbureh (D100, one hour) and Serekunda (D320, eight hours).

## RIVER GAMBIA NATIONAL PARK

Established in 1978 this lush stretch of riverside covers some 500 hectares of biologically rich forest. Its centrepiece is a group of small islands that are home to the remarkable **Chimpanzee Rehabilitation Project** (CRP; ☎6868826; www.facebook.com/ChimpanzeeRehabilitationProjectCrpInTheGambia).

This project forms the beating heart of River Gambia National Park. Comprised of so-called Baboon Island and several smaller islands, this is one of the most important wildlife sites in The Gambia. Despite the main island's moniker, it is really the kingdom of chimps – over 100 of the primates live across it and three other islands in four separate communities.

No one is allowed to set foot on Baboon Island (including staff), but visitors can see many of the simians during a boat tour around the islands. There's also other wildlife in the area, including hippos, manatees, crocodiles and abundant birdlife, not to mention other primates, such as red colobus monkeys, green vervet monkeys and – yes – even baboons. Knowledgeable guides can share the story of how this reserve came to be, and give insight into the lives and character of the island apes.

At the **Chimpanzee Rehabilitation Project Camp** (☎6868826; baboonislands@gmail.com; s/d incl boat tour & full board £120/220; ⌚Thu-Sun) you can listen to the hoots of the chimpanzees from across the water. Accommodation is decidedly flashpacker, in comfy South African–style safari tents perched on a cliff, with private decks overlooking the river. Prices include a boat tour around the islands, and meals served at the pleasant Waterhouse, which juts over the Gambia River.

If you're travelling on public transport, best to take a GTSC bus from Barra along the north bank and disembark at Kuntaur (D140, four to five hours). By prior arrangement, a CRP boat can pick you up there.

## SANYANG

POP 6300

The beautiful beaches of Sanyang, south of Tujering on the coast, are popular with tour groups. That said, the golden sands feel remarkably untouched, and if it is paradise views that you're after, this is a fine place to add to the itinerary.

### Sleeping

**Kajamor** HOTEL $$
(☎9890035; www.kajamorhotelgambia.com; d from D1500; 📶) This friendly place makes a great base for taking in Sanyang, with simple, reasonably priced accommodation just steps from the sun-kissed beach. There's a good seafood-slinging restaurant on hand and you can arrange excursions. Kajamor draws mostly Spanish travellers.

### Drinking & Nightlife

**Rainbow Beach Bar, Restaurant & Lodge** BAR
(☎9726806; www.rainbow.gm; Sanyang; d from D900, mains from D275; 📶) This place has a perfect location for drinks, though it's often swamped with tour groups all afternoon (between noon and 5pm). Come early or around sunset to enjoy the food and drink without the circus.

### Getting There & Away

Regular gelli-gellis leave from Bakoteh Junction in Serekunda, heading down the coast to Sanyang (D25, one hour) and other stops. Public transport isn't very practical though, as it's still a 2.5km walk from the highway at Sanyang to the beach.

WORTH A TRIP

#### TUJERING

Quirky and wonderful, **Tunbung Arts Village** (☎3524875; Tujering; donations accepted) is a ragged assembly of skewed huts, wildly painted walls and random sculptures that peer out behind walls and from treetops. It's the creative universe of Etu Ndow, a renowned Gambian artist. Sadly, Etu died in 2014, but his nephew Abdoulie continues to keep the memory of his uncle alive.

If you're not coming with your own vehicle, catch a bush taxi or gelli-gellis from Bakoteh Junction in Serekunda (D20, 45 minutes).

## WASSU STONE CIRCLES

This 1200-year-old arrangement of megaliths captures your attention and commands your respect. The stones, weighing several tonnes each, stand between 1m and 2.5m in height. Archaeologists believe the sites may have been used as burial grounds; locals sometimes place a small rock atop the megaliths and make a wish. You'll also find a small historical museum here. The site is about 25km northwest of Janjanbureh, near Kuntaur.

**Kairoh Garden** (☎9830134; www.kairohgarden.com; Kuntaur; r per person from D500) is a riverside spot with simple rooms and a delightful open-sided restaurant overlooking the water. Kairoh means 'peaceful' in Maninka, and it lives up to its name,

Wassu lies off the northbank road. Visit as a side trip while travelling upriver along the north bank, or on a day trip from Janjanbureh.

By public transport, take a GTSC bus from Barra to Wassu (D135). The lodges in Janjanbureh can also arrange trips.



# UNDERSTAND THE GAMBIA

## The Gambia Today

New hope has returned to The Gambia. In a presidential election held in December 2016, former businessman Adama Barrow won a surprise victory over long-time ruler Yahya Jammeh. The momentous event caught many by surprise, not least of all Jammeh himself, a strong-armed leader who, since overthrowing the government in a 1994 coup, had shown little desire to relinquish power. When Jammeh reneged on his promise to accept defeat, the international community intervened, strongly condemning his actions, and several West African nations sent troops into Banjul. In January 2017 Jammeh went into exile (likely in Equatorial Guinea, though his exact whereabouts remain unknown), allegedly absconding with more than US$11 million from state coffers.

President Barrow has ambitious plans, and has taken aim at The Gambia's widespread corruption, starting with his predecessor. Shortly after winning office, Barrow announced plans to establish a truth commission to investigate Jammeh's alleged human rights abuses. Barrow's other pledged goals include creating a free and independent judiciary and laying the foundation for job creation, particularly among the youth. The Gambia certainly faces grave challenges, with nearly 60% of the nation mired in poverty.

## History

Ancient stone circles and burial mounds indicate that this part of West Africa has been inhabited for at least 1500 years. The Empire of Ghana (5th to 11th centuries) extended its influence over the region, and by the 13th century the area had been absorbed into the Empire of Mali. By 1456 the first Portuguese navigators had landed on James Island (now Kunta Kinteh Island), turning it into a strategic trading point.

Built in 1651 by Baltic Germans, the James Island fort was claimed by the British in 1661 but changed hands several times. It was an important collection point for slaves until the abolition of slavery in 1807. New forts were built at Barra and Bathurst (now Banjul), to enforce compliance with the Abolition Act.

The British continued to extend their influence further upstream until the 1820s, when the territory was declared a British protectorate, ruled from Sierra Leone. In 1886 Gambia became a Crown colony.

Gambia became self-governing in 1963, although it took two more years until real independence was achieved. Gambia became The Gambia, Bathurst became Banjul, and David Jawara, leader of the People's Progressive Party, became Prime Minister Dawda Jawara and converted to Islam, while the queen remained head of state.

High groundnut prices and the advent of package tourism led to something of a boom in the 1960s. Jawara consolidated his power, and became president when The Gambia became a fully fledged republic in 1970. The economic slump of the 1980s provoked social unrest. Two coups were hatched, but thwarted with Senegalese assistance. This cooperation led to the 1982 confederation of the two countries under the name of Senegambia, but the union had collapsed by 1989. Meanwhile, corruption increased, economic decline continued and popular discontent rose. In July 1994, Jawara was overthrown in a reportedly bloodless coup led by Lieutenant Yahya Jammeh. After a brief flirtation with military dictatorship, the 30-year-old Jammeh bowed to international pressure, inaugurated a second republic, turned civilian and won the 1996 election comfortably.

## People

With around 115 people per square kilometre, The Gambia has one of the highest population densities in Africa. The strongest concentration of people is around the urbanised zones of the Atlantic Coast. Forty-five per cent of the population is under 14 years old.

The main ethnic groups are the Mandinka (comprising around 34%), the Fula (around 22%) and the Wolof (about 12%). Smaller groups include the Diola – also spelled Jola (11%), the Serer and Manjango. About 96% of the population is Muslim. Christianity is most widespread among the Diola.

## Arts & Craft

The *kora*, Africa's iconic stringed instrument, was created in the region of Gambia and Guinea-Bissau after Malinké groups came here to settle from Mali. Famous *kora* players include Amadou Bansang Jobarteh, Jali Nyama Suso, Dembo Konte and Malamini Jobarteh.

In the 1960s The Gambia was hugely influential in the development of modern West African music. Groups like the Afro-funky Super Eagles and singer Labah Sosse had a huge impact in The Gambia, Senegal and beyond. Today, it's locally brewed reggae and hip-hop that get people moving. Even the president has been seen rubbing shoulders with the world's reggae greats, proud to hear his country nicknamed 'Little Jamaica'.

## Environment

At only 11,295 sq km, The Gambia is mainland Africa's smallest country. It's also the most absurdly shaped one. Its 300km-long territory is almost entirely surrounded by Senegal and dominated by the Gambia River that runs through it. The country is flat, and vegetation consists mainly of savannah woodlands, gallery forests and saline marshes. Six national parks and reserves protect around 4% of the country's landmass. Some of the most interesting ones are Abuko, Kiang West and Gambia River. The Gambia boasts a few large mammals, such as hippos and reintroduced chimps, but most animal lovers are drawn to the hundreds of spectacular bird species that make The Gambia one of the best countries in West Africa for birdwatching. The main environmental issues are deforestation, overfishing and coastal erosion.

# SURVIVAL GUIDE

## Directory A–Z

### ACCOMMODATION

At the Atlantic Coast resorts of Bakau, Fajara, Kotu Strand and Kololi the choice of accommodation ranges from simple hostels to five-star hotels. Upcountry, your options are normally limited to basic guesthouses and hotels.

During the low season (May to October), some places drop their prices by 25% or even 50%. Keep in mind that many places close for several weeks or even months during the low season. It's wise to book ahead.

### CHILDREN

- Start doing your research well in advance. Vaccinations for young ones may require multiple injections spaced a month apart.
- Most travelling parents err on the side of extra caution when it comes to mosquitoes, bringing coils, nets and plenty of spray.
- A pram isn't always handy negotiating the sandy and rutted streets. You may prefer to do as locals do and simply carry your child on your back.
- Once you get over the logistical hurdles, you'll find The Gambia a warm and welcoming place for children. There's plenty to keep kids amused, from days on the beach or at the hotel pool to wildlife-watching on short excursions.

### DANGERS & ANNOYANCES

Serious crime is fairly rare in The Gambia, though muggings and petty theft do occur, particularly around the tourist centres. Avoid walking around alone after dark. Kids will often hassle you for money or tours, but usually this is just a harmless annoyance. Beach boys are another matter.

#### Beach Boys

A beach boy, also referred to as a *sai sai* or bumster, is a womaniser, a smooth operator, a charming hustler, a con man or a dodgy mixture of all of these. These guys are usually young, often good-looking men, who approach women (sometimes bluntly, sometimes with astonishing verbal skills) in towns, nightclubs, bars and particularly on beaches. While some of them

### SLEEPING PRICE RANGES

The following price ranges refer to a double room with bathroom.

**$** less than D1000

**$$** D1000-3000

**$$$** more than D3000

are fairly harmless (just don't get your heart broken), others can pull some pretty sly jobs, involving sexual advances, tricking you out of money or downright stealing.

Use the same yardsticks you would at home before getting involved. It's best to ignore these guys completely. They might respond with verbal abuse, but it's all hot air.

## EMBASSIES & CONSULATES

Several European countries have honorary consuls, including Belgium (at the Kairaba Hotel, Kololi), Denmark, Sweden and Norway (Saitmatty Rd, Bakau).

**German Embassy** (☎221 33 889 4884; www.auswaertiges-amt.de; Ave Pasteur, Dakar, Senegal; ⏲8am-1pm, closed Tue)

**Guinean Embassy** (☎4226862, 909964; 78A Daniel Goddard St, top fl, Banjul; ⏲9am-4pm Mon-Thu, 9am-1pm & 2.30-4pm Fri)

**Guinea-Bissau Embassy** (☎4494884; 78 Atlantic Rd, Bakau; ⏲9am-2pm Mon-Fri, to 1pm Sat)

**Malian Embassy** (☎4228433; 26 Rev William Cole St, Banjul)

**Mauritanian Embassy** (☎4491153; Badala Park Way, Kololi; ⏲8am-4pm Mon-Fri)

**Senegalese Embassy** (☎4373752; www.gouv.sn; off Kairaba Ave, Fajara; ⏲8am-2pm & 2.30-5pm Mon-Thu, to 4pm Fri)

**Sierra Leonean Embassy** (☎4228206; 67 Daniel Goddard St, Banjul; ⏲8.30am-4.30pm Mon-Thu, to 1.30pm Fri)

**UK Embassy** (☎4495134, 4495133; http://ukingambia.fco.gov.uk; 48 Atlantic Rd, Fajara; ⏲9am-noon Mon-Fri)

**US Embassy** (☎4392856, 4375270; http://banjul.usembassy.gov; 92 Kairaba Ave, Fajara; ⏲2-4pm Mon, Wed, Fri)

### EATING PRICE RANGES

The following price ranges are for a main meal.

**$** less than D350

**$$** D350–650

**$$$** more than D650

## EMERGENCY & IMPORTANT NUMBERS

| | |
|---|---|
| The Gambia's country code | ☎220 |
| Ambulance | ☎16 |
| Fire | ☎18 |
| Police | ☎17 |

## INTERNET ACCESS

Wi-fi is common at most hotels and guesthouses, as well as some restaurants. There aren't many internet cafes left in the country.

## LGBTIQ TRAVELLERS

The Gambia is not the place to be out. Open displays of affection can in fact place you in serious danger. Travellers have been arrested in the past for 'propositioning' locals (which included something as harmless as asking where other gay men hang out).

That said, the vast majority of gay travellers who visit The Gambia have no problems. As long as you exercise the utmost caution, there is little to worry about.

## MONEY

The local currency, dalasi (D), fluctuates strongly. It's best to have hard currency (British pounds, euros or US dollars) on hand and exchange it as needed. ATMs exist on the coast, but are not practical.

### ATMs

There are ATMs around the coast, but relying on them is impractical with such low daily withdrawal limits (D5000). There are no ATMs up-country; it's best to chnage all the cash you think you'll need at the coast.

### Changing Money

There aren't any official changing points at the border, just very persistent black-market changers. You'll be fine using CFA, though, until you get to the coast, where changing money is easier. Many hotels can recommend an informal changer, though the rates may be similar to those the banks propose. Many hotels will accept UK pounds sterling.

### Exchange Rates

| | | |
|---|---|---|
| Australia | A$1 | D34 |
| Canada | C$ | D33 |
| Europe | €1 | D50 |
| Japan | ¥100 | D41 |
| New Zealand | NZ$1 | D31 |
| Senegal | CFA100 | D7 |
| UK | £1 | D59 |
| USA | US$1 | D45 |

### Tipping

**Restaurants** Tipping isn't expected at smaller local restaurants; at more touristic places, a 10% tip is fairly common.

**Guides** At many reserves and parks, guides will be available – sometimes even included in the admission price. Regardless, it's always polite to tip the guide. While it's hard to give guidelines, D50 or more per hour is a benchmark.

**Bumsters** Don't tip people who hassle you or harass you for money.

### OPENING HOURS

**Banks** From 1pm to 4pm Monday to Thursday, with lunch break from 1pm to 2.30pm Friday.

**Government offices** From 8am to 3pm or 4pm Monday to Thursday, and from 8am to 12.30pm Friday.

**Restaurants** Lunch from 11am to 2.30pm, dinner from 6pm.

**Shops and businesses** From 8.30am to 1pm and 2.30pm to 5.30pm Monday to Thursday; from 8am until noon Friday and Saturday.

### POST

The postal service is fairly reliable for postcards and letters. For packages, you may want to use a private service such as DHL.

### PUBLIC HOLIDAYS

As well as religious holidays, a few public holidays are observed.

**1 January** New Year's Day

**18 February** Independence Day

**1 May** Workers' Day

**May or June** Eid al Fitr

**July or August** Eid al Adha

**22 July** Revolution Day

**15 August** Assumption

**25 December** Christmas

### TELEPHONE

If you have an unlocked phone, you can purchase inexpensive SIM cards along with talk time and data bundles at service centres around the coast. The only problem: you may have to visit a few shops, as they often run out of SIM cards.

The main mobile providers are Africell, Q Cell and Gamtel.

Coverage is generally good all around the coast, but can be spotty when you head up-country.

### TOURIST INFORMATION

**The Gambia Tourism** (www.visitthegambia.gm) This website has a wealth of information.

**Tourism Office** (⌚11am-6pm Mon-Thu) Located on the Senegambia strip in Kololi.

### TRAVELLERS WITH DISABILITIES

The Gambia can be a challenging place to visit for travellers with disabilities. Badly pockmarked and unpaved roads, broken and missing footpaths, and a general lack of facilities pose the greatest obstacles.

A handful of places along the coast offer accessible rooms, including the following:

**Hibiscus House** (p299)

**Luigi's** (p291)

**Ocean Bayl** (p294)

### VISAS

Visas are not needed for nationals of the UK, Germany, Italy, Australia, Belgium, Canada, Luxembourg, the Netherlands, New Zealand, and Scandinavian and Ecowas countries for stays of up to 90 days.

## Getting There & Away

### AIR

Most people arrive on charter flights with **Gambia Experience** (☎ in UK 01489 866939; www.gambia.co.uk) or **Thomas Cook** (www.thomascookairlines.com). There are a limited number of carriers flying to The Gambia, so it's wise to plan ahead.

#### Airports & Airlines

**Banjul International Airport** (p290) is in Yundum, about 15km southeast of the coast.

Charter flights aside, the only scheduled airlines flying to Gambia are the following:

**Arik** (www.arikair.com) Flies between Accra (Ghana) and Banjul.

**Brussels Airlines** (www.brusselsairlines.com) Flies to Brussels as well as Dakar (Senegal).

**Royal Air Maroc** (www.royalairmaroc.com) Direct flights to Casablanca, Morocco.

**Vueling** (www.vueling.com) Connects to Spain.

### LAND

Minibuses and bush taxis run regularly between Barra and the Senegalese border at Karang (D60, one hour), where you can take care of exit/entrance formalities. From there, hire a taxi

### PRACTICALITIES

**Electricity** 220V. Most plugs have three square pins (the same as the UK); two round pins (same as continental Europe) are also in use

**Newspapers** *The Point* is a daily newspaper published in Bakau.

**Weights & measures** The Gambia uses a mix of the UK imperial system and the metric system.

(or motorbike, which are more prevalent, D15), for 2km further to the bush-taxi garage, where you can catch onward transport to Dakar (D700, six hours) .

To get to southern Senegal (Casamance), minibuses and bush taxis leave from Bakoteh Junction (D220, five hours). Transport also goes from Brikama to Ziguinchor.

At the far-eastern tip of The Gambia, bush taxis run from Basse Santa Su to Vélingara, Senegal (D80, 45 minutes; 27km), and from there bush taxis go to Tambacounda (D90, three hours).

## Getting Around

### BUS

Gambia's new **GTSC bus service** (☎4380000; www.gtsc.gm; Kanifing Depot, off Banjul Serrekunda Hwy) provides much-improved transport up-country, with regular buses travelling along both the south bank and the north bank of the Gambia River.

Along the south bank, buses depart from a depot in Kanifing, about 5km southeast of the coastal resorts. Buses run hourly (from about 6am to 10pm) all the way to Basse Santa Su (D260).

To access points along the north bank, take the ferry from Banjul to Barra and catch one of the five daily buses connecting Barra with Laminkoto (D140), and points in between.

### CAR & MOTORCYCLE

Driving in The Gambia presents the usual challenges of West African road travel: potholes, nonexistent signage and an abundance of pedestrians, slow-moving vehicles and free-roaming livestock. Always take it slow. You'll also have to contend with numerous police/immigration/customs/military checkpoints. Make sure your papers are in order, and don't be surprised if you get hit up for 'tea money' at every stop (D50 is usually a sufficient bribe to avoid lengthy delays with the authorities). Avoid driving at night, as a lack of streetlights ensures a blanket of darkness, and other drivers don't always use their headlights.

#### Driving

Gambians drive on the right-hand side.

#### Hire

A good 4WD is handy once you leave the main highways.

Reliable car-hire companies include **Afriq Cars** (☎3344443; www.afriqcars.com; Senegambia Hwy; ⏰9am-5pm Mon-Thu, to 1pm Fri & Sat) and multinational chains such as Avis (p297).

If you don't want to self-drive, you can usually hire a car and driver for slightly more than you'd pay for a rental. Just make sure you agree on all terms beforehand – whether the cost includes fuel, driver's food and accommodation, any repairs that may arise, etc.

### LOCAL TRANSPORT

To reach the south coast, head to Bakoteh Junction (p297), where you'll find *sept-place* (shared seven-seater) taxis and gelli-gellis (battered, crammed minibuses) that head to the southern villages of Tanji, Sanyang, Gunjur and Kartong.

For north-bank destinations, you'll have to take the ferry from Banjul to Barra, then hop onto a *sept-place* taxi to Kerewan, from where you can change for transport heading further east.

*Sept-place* taxis are by no means a comfy way of travelling; however, they are infinitely better than the gelli-gellis. A few green, government-owned 'express' buses also ply the major roads.

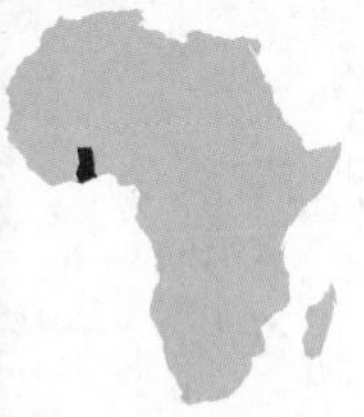

# Ghana

☎ 233 / POP 28 MILLION

## Includes ➡



## Best Places to Eat

- Khana Khazana (p314)
- Baobab Vegetarian Moringa Restaurant (p322)
- View Bar & Grill (p329)
- Asanka Restaurant (p314)
- Santoku Restaurant & Bar (p314)

## Best Places to Sleep

- Escape3points (p327)
- Lou Moon Lodge (p325)
- Four Villages Inn (p329)
- Mountain Paradise (p318)
- Zaina Lodge (p333)

## Why Go?

Hailed as West Africa's golden child, Ghana deserves its place in the sun. One of Africa's great success stories, the country is reaping the benefits of a stable democracy in the form of fast-paced development. And it shows: Ghana is suffused with the most incredible energy.

With its welcoming beaches, gorgeous hinterland, rich culture, vibrant cities, diverse wildlife, easy transport and affable inhabitants, it's no wonder Ghana is sometimes labelled 'Africa for beginners'.

It's easy to come here for a week or a month, but no trip can be complete without a visit to Ghana's coastal forts, poignant reminders of a page of history that defined our modern world.

Travel north and you'll feel like you've arrived in a different country, with a different religion, geography and cultural practices. The beauty is that this diversity exists so harmoniously, a joy to experience and a wonder to behold in uncertain times.

## When to Go

### Accra

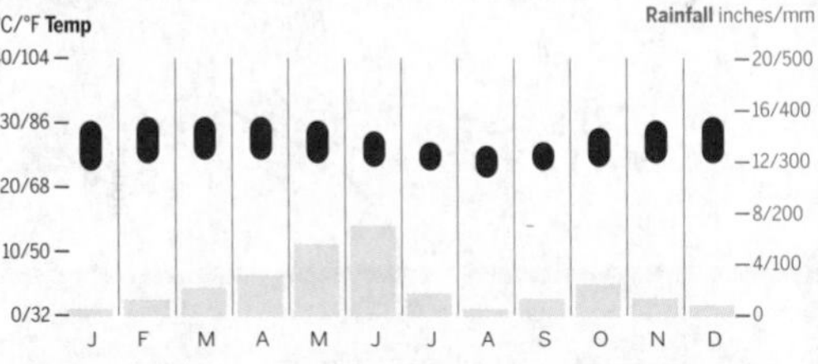


**Apr–Jun** The heaviest of the two rainy seasons (autumn can also be wet).

**Nov–Mar** The dry and easiest season to travel.

**Dec–Apr** Best for wildlife viewing, with good visibility and animals congregating at water holes.

# Ghana Highlights

**1 Cape Coast Castle** (p321) Gaining a chilling insight into the history of the slave trade.

**2 Volta Region** (p318) Hiking, climbing waterfalls and swimming in the former German Togoland, in Ghana's east.

**3 Mole National Park** (p332) Joining a safari for some close-up encounters with herds of elephants.

**4 Kejetia Market** (p327) Shopping till you drop (and getting very lost) in West Africa's biggest market in Kumasi.

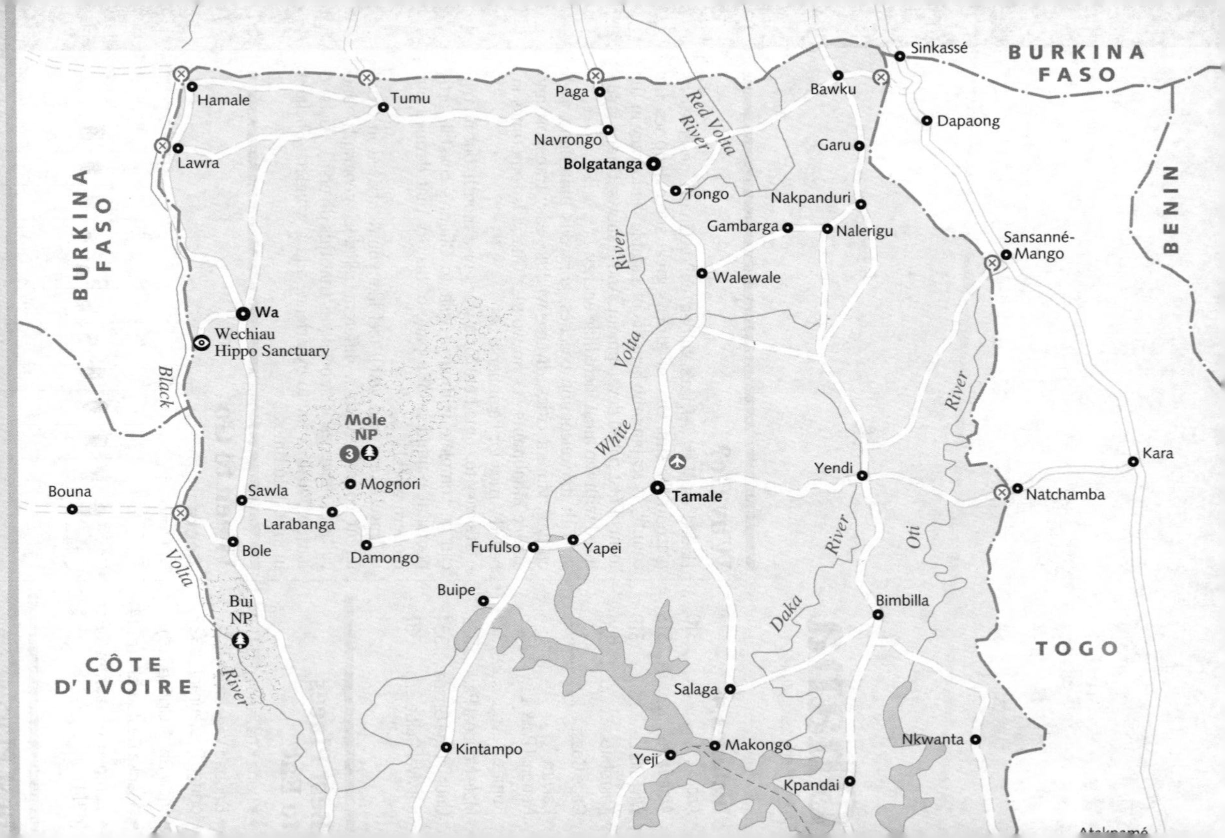

**5 Accra** (p310) Spending a day or two sampling the fine restaurants, nightclubs and city beaches of Ghana's lively capital.

6 **Busua** (p326)
Taking a surf lesson, eating fresh lobster on the beach and chilling out in a beach bar at Ghana's favourite backpacker hangout.

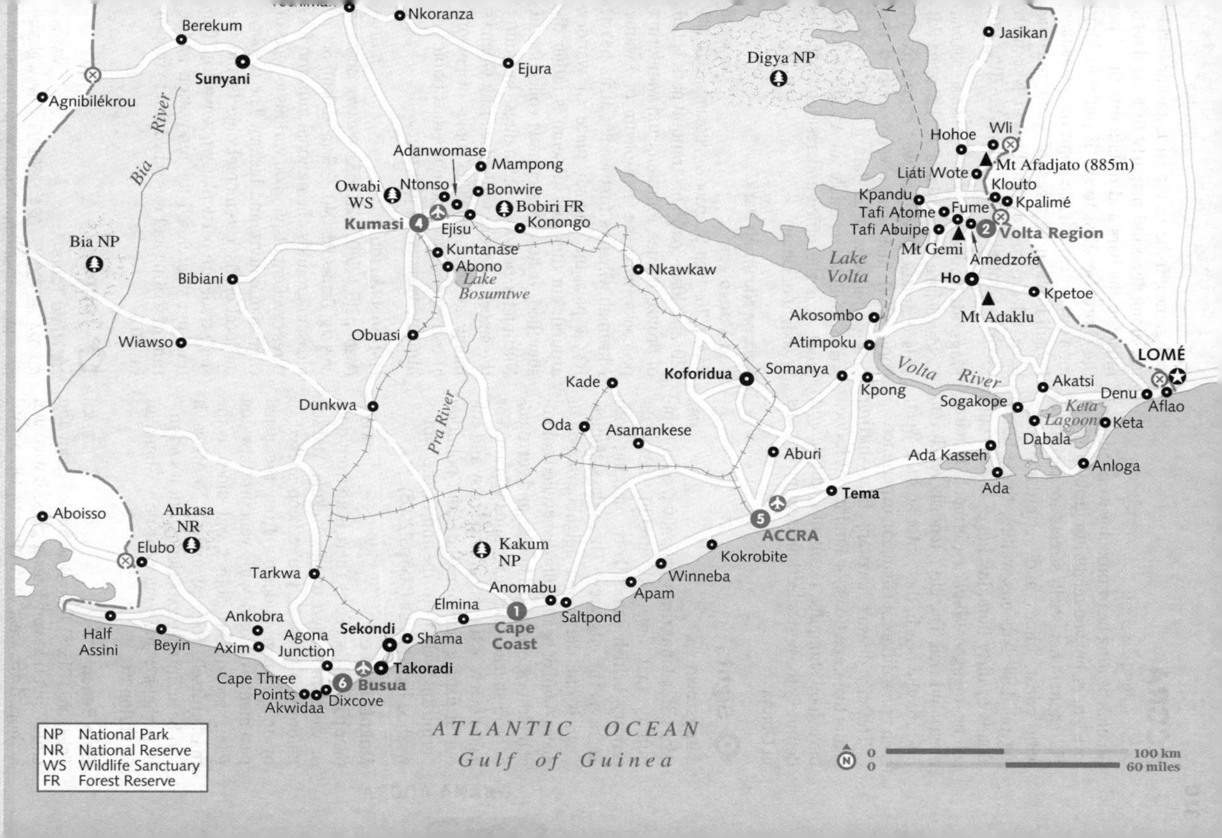

# ACCRA

030 / POP 2.9 MILLION

Ghana's beating heart probably won't inspire love letters, but you might just grow to like it. The capital's hot, sticky streets are perfumed with sweat, fumes and yesterday's cooking oil. Like balloons waiting to be burst, clouds of dirty humidity linger above stalls selling mangoes, *banku* (fermented maize meal) and rice. The city's tendrils reach out towards the beach, the centre and the west, each one a different Ghanaian experience.

The city doesn't have any heavy-hitting sights like Cape Coast or Elmina but it does have good shopping, excellent nightlife and definitely the best selection of eating options in Ghana.

## Sights

**Jamestown** AREA

(Map p312) Jamestown originated as a community that emerged around the 17th-century British James Fort, merging with Accra as the city grew. These days, Jamestown is one the poorer neighbourhoods of Accra – full of beautifully dishevelled colonial buildings, clapboard houses and corrugated iron shacks – but it remains vibrant. For a great view of the city and the busy and colourful fishing harbour (haze and pollution permitting), climb to the top of the white-washed **lighthouse** (Map p312; C5).

**Makola Market** MARKET

(Map p316; 8am-6pm) There is no front door or welcoming sign to the Makola Market. Before you know it, you've been sucked in by the human undertow from the usual pavements clogged with vendors hawking food, secondhand clothes and shoes to the market itself. For new arrivals to Africa, it can be an intense experience, but it's a fun – if, perhaps, a little masochistic – Ghanaian initiation rite.

**Bojo Beach** BEACH

(adult/child C15/5) Bojo Beach is so clean and chilled out that you'd never guess it was such a short drive west of Accra city. On arrival there's a small entrance fee to pay, and you'll then be rowed across a clear strip of water to a pristine strip of beach, where there are sun loungers and refreshments. It's a worthy alternative to hectic Labadi Beach.

**Labadi Beach** BEACH

(admission C5) Come the weekend people flock to Accra's most popular beach to play ball games, frolic in the surf, go horse riding along the sand or party to loud dance music in the bars and restaurants that line the shore. Needless to say, if you're looking for a quieter experience, come on a weekday. Labadi is about 8km east of Accra; to come here, take a tro-tro (minibus) at Nkrumah Circle in Central Accra or along the Ring Rd.

**Flagstaff House** NOTABLE BUILDING

(Golden Jubilee House; Map p312; Liberation Rd) This dramatic structure was completed in 2008 amid huge controversy around the tens of millions of dollars it cost to construct. Built to resemble an Asante Golden Stool, it is the office and residence of the President of Ghana.

**Kwame Nkrumah Park and Mausoleum** MEMORIAL

(Map p316; High St; park & museum adult/child C10/2; 10am-5pm) This tranquil park is full of bronze statues, fountains and wandering peacocks, with the mausoleum of Kwame Nkrumah, Ghana's first leader, at its heart. It's a pleasant enough place to wander around, but the park museum is rather dishevelled. It houses a curious collection of Nkrumah's personal belongings, including the smock he wore while declaring Ghana's independence, as well as copies of personal correspondence and numerous photos of him and various world leaders.

**National Museum** MUSEUM

(Map p316; 030-2221633; www.ghanamuseums.org; Barnes Rd; C40; 9am-4.30pm) Set in pleasant grounds, the national museum features excellent displays on various aspects of Ghanaian culture and history. The displays on local crafts, ceremonial objects and the slave trade are particularly noteworthy. The museum was closed for renovation at the time of writing and was scheduled to reopen in 2017.

## Tours

★**Nima Tours** WALKING

(024 6270095, 024 2561793; www.ghana-nima-tours.yolasite.com; Nima; per person per hour C25) The knowledgeable and affable Charles Sablah offers fun and informative two-hour walking tours of his neighbourhood, one of the most deprived areas of Accra. Tours vary according to the day, time, and what you'd like to do, but could include a stroll around the market, visiting local houses, or listening to a traditional drumming group.

**Jamestown Walking Tours** WALKING
(Map p312; www.jamestownwalkingtours.wordpress.com; Jamestown Lighthouse, High St; C25; ⏲2pm Sat) Jamestown is Accra's oldest suburb, and it has sites that reveal its slavery past, colonial architecture and poor but vibrant fishing community. Joining Jamestown Walking Tours for a Saturday afternoon stroll immerses you in the Ga culture. Visit a family house, taste street food and watch fishers return with their catch. The tours are operated by the Jamestown Community Theatre Centre, a cultural hub helping young people express themselves artistically. Tours start at the lighthouse.

## Sleeping

**Agoo Hostel** HOSTEL $
(Map p312; ☎030-2222726; www.agoohostel.com; C93/5 Keta Close, Nima Residential; dm/d US$17.50/45; P❄📶) A fantastic new addition to Accra's hostel scene, Agoo offers spacious private rooms, squeaky clean dorms with bright yellow bunks and batik bedspreads, and a candy-coloured self-catering kitchen. There's also plenty of lounging space, including a large balcony and a garden. Breakfast is included and home-cooked meals are available on request.

**Somewhere Nice** HOSTEL $
(Map p312; ☎054 3743505; www.hostelaccra.com; 9 Cotton Ave, Kokomlemle; dm/d €10/50; P📶🏊) 🍃 The rooms and dorms at this hostel are very nice indeed. They come with balconies; en-suite bathrooms (with rainfall showers!); and rustic, locally made furniture, much of it recycled. There's also a pool, a garden, and a semi-open-air lounge. The free (excellent) breakfast and filtered drinking water is a bonus.

**Sleepy Hippo Backpacker Hotel** HOSTEL $
(Map p312; ☎026 1113740; www.sleepyhippohotel.com; 38 Duade St, Kokomlemle; dm from US$10, d US$50, with shared bathroom US$30; ❄📶🏊) One of a growing number of Accra backpackers hostels, the Sleepy Hippo has a homely atmosphere and is a good place to meet other travellers. The dorms and rooms are clean and spacious, and there are plenty of spaces to chill out in after a sweaty day on Accra's streets, including a cafe-bar, a roof terrace and a teeny plunge pool.

**Crystal Hostel** GUESTHOUSE $
(☎030-2304634; 27 Akorlu Close, Darkuman; dm/s/d from US$10/18.50/25; 📶) The hosts go out of their way to make travellers welcome at this lovely budget set-up in the quiet suburb of Darkuman. Rooms have private bathrooms, TV and fridges. There's a leafy communal lawn area and a rooftop terrace. Campers can pitch their tents in the garden or on the roof terrace (US$5).

**Urbano Hotel** HOTEL $$
(Map p312; ☎030-2788999, 030-2779688; Oxford St, Osu; s/d/ste US$80/120/160) The rooms may be snug at this new Osu spot, but they're cool, spotless and pretty good value for the area. Plus there's no need to stay in your room when there's a restaurant, a Moroccan-style courtyard, a rooftop lounge and a balcony overlooking the action, all decked out in stylish mid-century replica furniture.

**Chez Delphy** B&B $$
(Map p312; ☎026 2989722, 050 8979778; www.chezdelphy.com; r from US$125; P❄📶) A cosy bolthole close to the bars and restaurants of Labone, Chez Delphy offers welcome respite from the heat and noise of Accra. The rooms are simple but comfortable, there's a peaceful lounge and garden, and excellent dinners are available given advance notice.

**Frankie's Hotel** HOTEL $$
(Map p312; ☎030-2773567; Oxford St, Osu; d/ste from US$100/150; ❄@📶) A good deal, right in the centre of the action. Smart modern rooms come with all the necessary amenities, and there's **Frankie's** (mains C30-50; ⏲7am-midnight; ❄📶) restaurant downstairs if you get hungry. It can be noisy at night, however.

**Paloma** HOTEL $$
(Map p316; ☎030-2231815; www.palomahotel.com; Ring Rd Central; s/d C520/650; P❄@📶) Cool rooms and bungalows with every comfort. The complex includes an excellent restaurant, a sports bar, a garden area and a cocktail bar. The hotel also has a free airport shuttle service.

**La Villa Boutique Hotel** BOUTIQUE HOTEL $$$
(Map p312; ☎030-2730333; www.lavillaghana.com; Nii Saban Atsen Rd, Osu; s/d/apt US$225/255/315; P❄📶) This stylish boutique hotel is very popular and deservedly so – it's brilliantly located in the heart of lively Osu, yet manages to feel serene. The rooms are the epitome of understated chic, and there's a great Italian restaurant, not to mention a small pool.

# Accra

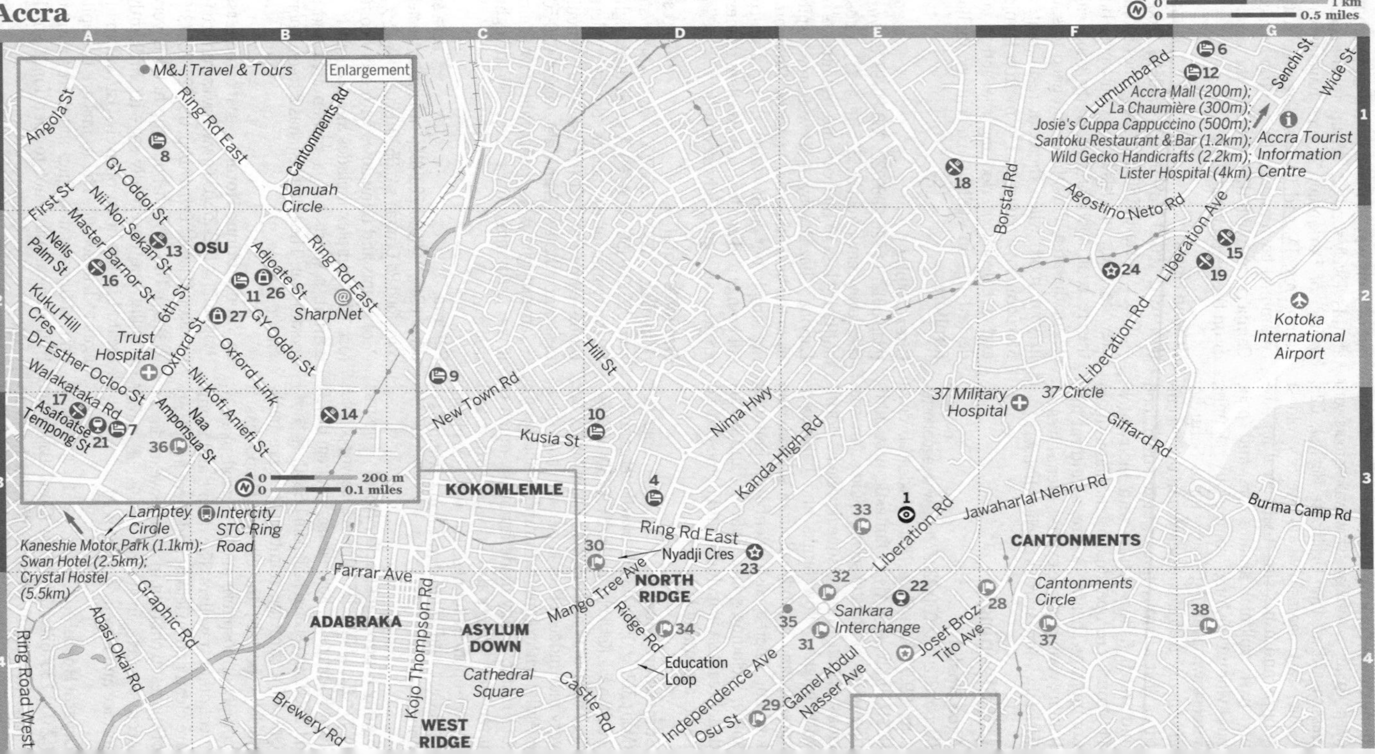
0 1 km
0 0.5 miles
A
B
C
D
E
F
G
1
2
3
4
Enlargement
M&J Travel & Tours
Angola St
Ring Rd East
Cantonments Rd
8
GY Oddoi St
Danuah Circle
First St
Nii Noi Sekan St
13
OSU
Adjoate St
Ring Rd East
Neils Palm St
Master Barnor St
16
11
26
SharpNet
6th St
27
GY Oddoi St
Kuku Hill Cres
Trust Hospital
Oxford St
Oxford Link
Dr Esther Ocloo St
Nii Kofi Aniefi St
Walakataka Rd
17
Asafoatse Tempong St
21
7
Naa Amponsua St
36
14
0 200 m
0 0.1 miles
9
New Town Rd
Hill St
10
Kusia St
Nima Hwy
Kanda High Rd
4
KOKOMLEMLE
Lamptey Circle
Intercity STC Ring Road
Kaneshie Motor Park (1.1km);
Swan Hotel (2.5km);
Crystal Hostel (5.5km)
Ring Rd East
30
Nyadji Cres
23
Farrar Ave
Mango Tree Ave
NORTH RIDGE
Graphic Rd
Abasi Okai Rd
ADABRAKA
Kojo Thompson Rd
ASYLUM DOWN
34
Ridge Rd
Education Loop
Cathedral Square
Castle Rd
Ring Road West
Brewery Rd
WEST RIDGE
Independence Ave
Osu St
29
Gamel Abdul Nasser Ave
6
12
Lumumba Rd
Accra Mall (200m);
La Chaumière (300m);
Josie's Cuppa Cappuccino (500m);
Santoku Restaurant & Bar (1.2km);
Wild Gecko Handicrafts (2.2km);
Lister Hospital (4km)
Accra Tourist Information Centre
Senchi St
Wide St
18
Borstal Rd
Agostino Neto Rd
Liberation Ave
15
24
19
Kotoka International Airport
Liberation Rd
37 Military Hospital
37 Circle
Giffard Rd
Burma Camp Rd
Jawaharlal Nehru Rd
1
33
Liberation Rd
CANTONMENTS
32
22
28
Cantonments Circle
35
Sankara Interchange
31
Josef Broz Tito Ave
38
37

## Accra

**Sights**
- 1 Flagstaff House ........ E3
- 2 Jamestown ........ B6
- 3 Jamestown Lighthouse ........ B6

**Activities, Courses & Tours**
- Jamestown Walking Tours ........ (see 3)

**Sleeping**
- 4 Agoo Hostel ........ D3
- 5 Chez Delphy ........ G6
- 6 Esther's Hotel ........ G1
- 7 Frankie's Hotel ........ A3
- 8 La Villa Boutique Hotel ........ A1
- 9 Sleepy Hippo Backpacker Hotel ........ C2
- 10 Somewhere Nice ........ D3
- 11 Urbano Hotel ........ B2
- 12 Villa Monticello ........ G1

**Eating**
- 13 Buka ........ A2
- 14 Burger & Relish ........ B3
- 15 Café Kwae ........ G2
- 16 Chez Clarisse Mama Africa ........ A2
- 17 Duncan's ........ A3
- Frankie's ........ (see 7)
- 18 Simret ........ E1
- 19 Vida e caffè ........ G2

**Drinking & Nightlife**
- 20 JamesTown Cafe ........ B6
- 21 Republic Bar & Grill ........ A3
- 22 Rockstone's Office ........ E4

**Entertainment**
- 23 +233 ........ D3
- 24 Alliance Française ........ F2

**Shopping**
- 25 Artists Alliance Gallery ........ G6
- 26 Global Mamas ........ B2
- 27 Woodin ........ B2

**Information**
- 28 Australian High Commission ........ F4
- 29 British High Commission ........ D4
- 30 Burkinabé Embassy ........ D3
- 31 Canadian High Commission ........ E4
- 32 Dutch Embassy ........ E4
- 33 French Embassy ........ E3
- 34 German Embassy ........ D4
- 35 Immigration Office ........ E4
- 36 Ivorian Embassy ........ A3
- 37 Togolese Embassy ........ F4
- 38 US Embassy ........ G4

**Villa Monticello** BOUTIQUE HOTEL **$$$**
(Map p312; 030-2773477; www.villamonticello.com; No 1A Mantaka Ave Link, Airport Residential Area; s/d from US$385/435; P ❄ @ 🛜 ≋) Behind the austere khaki concrete facade hides

a sleek boutique hotel. The opulent rooms were designed according to themes – Soho, Coco Chanel, Last Emperor, Out of Africa – and are furnished with exquisite taste.

**Esther's Hotel** BOUTIQUE HOTEL $$$
(Map p312; ☎030-2765751; www.esthers-hotel.com; 4 Volta St, Airport Residential Area; s/d from US$150/180; P❄📶) Long one of Accra's more upscale addresses, Esther's is not as flashy as some of Accra's newer boutique hotels, but for many that's a bonus. It's homely and friendly, with cosy, understated rooms and lovely gardens, complete with wandering peacocks.

## Eating

**★Khana Khazana** SOUTH INDIAN $
(Map p316; ☎057 0656557, 027 5834282; www.khanakhazanagh.com; Kojo Thompson Rd; mains around C20-30; ⏲9am-11pm) Tucked behind a petrol station (Engen Filling Station, next to Avenida Hotel), this outdoor Indian restaurant is a gem – cheap, delicious and with long opening hours. One of the house specialities is the dosa (savoury parcel made of rice flour normally eaten for breakfast). Sunday is thali (set meal) day.

**Café Kwae** CAFE $
(Map p312; ☎020 4004010; www.lovecafekwae.com; ground fl, One Airport Sq, Airport City; cakes C12; ⏲8am-10pm Mon-Fri, from 10am Sat; 📶) Despite Accra's large population, you won't find many real cafes here. That's changing with the recent opening of this cafe inside the extravagant facade of One Airport Sq. Treat yourself with homemade pies, light lunches, a wide variety of teas, freshly ground coffee or cold-pressed juice as you make use of the free wi-fi.

**Duncan's** AFRICAN $
(Map p312; Asafoatse Tempong St, Osu; mains from C15; ⏲10am-11pm) Duncan's is an example of the low-key, outdoor chop bars that manage to get it right. Fresh, grilled fish and simple Ghanaian dishes draw a mixed, appreciative crowd.

**★Buka** AFRICAN $$
(Map p312; ☎030-2782953, 024 4842464; www.thebukarestaurant.com; Nii Noi Sekan St, Osu; mains C16-40; ⏲noon-10pm Mon-Sat, to 7pm Sun; P👪) Ever-popular Buka serves some of the best West African food in Accra, in stylish surroundings to boot. Hearty plates of *jollof rice*, tilapia and groundnut soup are served on a pretty terrace, which fills up with the local office crowd every lunchtime.

**Chez Clarisse Mama Africa** AFRICAN $$
(Map p312; ☎024 2984828; 8th Lane; mains C30; ⏲8am-midnight) You have two choices: tender chicken or whole grilled tilapia topped with onions and tomatoes. The small menu doesn't make this Ivorian favourite any less popular though; this real African food experience includes plastic chairs, eating with your hands and sauces that keep fans coming back. Cutlery available upon request for the less adventurous.

**Simret** ETHIOPIAN $$
(Map p312; ☎050 7408938; www.simret-restaurant.com; Villa Almaz, 7A Roman Rd, Roman Ridge; buffet from C70; ⏲6.30-10pm Tue-Sat; P) The welcome is warm and the authentic Ethiopian food served buffet style at this low-key place. There's a decent selection of veggie options and dinner is finished off with strong Ethiopian coffee and cake.

**Asanka Restaurant** AFRICAN $$
(Map p316; Ring Rd Central; mains C20-50; ⏲9am-9pm) Not to be confused with Asanka Local in Osu, this friendly and rather upmarket joint serves fantastic Ghanaian food, including groundnut soup, *red-red* (bean stew) and grilled tilapia with homemade chilli sauce.

**Burger & Relish** BURGERS $$$
(Map p312; ☎054 0121356; www.burgerandrelish.com; cnr Adjoate & Dadebu Sts; burgers C35-55; ⏲noon-11pm Mon-Wed, noon-1am Thu-Sat, 10.30am-11pm Sun; P❄📶👪) Gourmet burgers have come to Accra in this hip, industrial restaurant, which doubles as a trendy cocktail bar in the evenings, and a family-friendly brunch spot at the weekend. If you can fit anything else in after one of the delicious burgers, there are brownies and ice-cream sundaes. Regular live-music nights here and at sister branch in East Legon.

**Santoku Restaurant & Bar** JAPANESE $$$
(☎054 4311511; www.facebook.com/SantokuAccra; Villaggio Vista, North Airport Rd, East Dzorwulu; mains C60-120; ⏲noon-3pm & 6.30-10.45pm; P❄) Stunning Japanese food, impeccable service and elegant decor make Santoku one of the best restaurants in the country.

**La Chaumière** FRENCH $$$
(☎030-2772408; Liberation Rd, Airport Residential Area; mains C50-90; ⏲12.30-2.30pm & 7-11pm Mon-Fri, 7-11pm Sat; ❄) There's stiff competi-

tion these days, but La Chaumière remains one of Accra's best and fanciest restaurants. It excels in old-school elegance, with soft lighting, polished wooden floors, classical music and delicious French fusion gastronomy. La Chaumière is renowned for its steaks but there is plenty of seafood on the menu too, as well as the odd North African flavour. Bookings essential.

## Drinking & Nightlife

**JamesTown Cafe** BAR
(Map p312; ☎030-2522248; www.facebook.com/Jamestowncafe; High St; ) This stylish architect-owned cafe, bar and music venue sits in a beautifully restored building right in the heart of old Accra, just across from the sea. There's local and international food, great cocktails and live music daily. Once a week, the party spills outside.

**Rockstone's Office** CLUB
(Map p312; Osu Ave Extension; ⏲6pm-late Wed-Sat) Owned by hiplife legend Reggie Rockstone. There's a lounge bar decked out with white leather sofas, an outdoor terrace and regular live music. At the weekend an energetic crowd parties till dawn to hiplife (a highlife/hip-hop hybrid) and hip-hop. It's near the police headquarters, behind the Japanese embassy.

**Republic Bar & Grill** BAR
(Map p312; Asafoatse Tempong St, Osu; ⏲noon-midnight; ) With its bright red walls, black-and-white photos, vintage postcards and outdoor wooden deck, this fab bar wouldn't look out of place in Brooklyn. Here, it delights happening young Ghanaians and expats in equal measure, and is renowned for its innovative cocktails made from local booze such as palm wine. Live music is also fantastic here, with many a highlife giant having turned up to play to exuberant crowds.

## Entertainment

**★+233** LIVE MUSIC
(Map p312; ☎023 3233233; Ring Rd East, North Ridge; ⏲5pm-midnight) This 'Jazz Bar & Grill', as the strapline goes, is probably the best live-music venue in Accra. Bands come from all over the continent and there is a great atmosphere.

**Alliance Française** LIVE MUSIC
(Map p312; ☎050 1287814; www.afaccra.org; Liberation Link, Airport Residential Area; concerts around C20) With several concerts a week (rock, jazz, reggae, hip-hop), exhibitions and various cultural events, the cultural arm of the French embassy is a good bet whenever you're in town.

## Shopping

**★Global Mamas** FASHION & ACCESSORIES
(Map p312; www.globalmamas.org; Adjoate St, Osu; ⏲9am-8pm Mon-Sat, from 1pm Sun) This shop, which stocks pretty dresses, hats, tops, accessories (including lush scented shea butter) and kids clothes in colourful fabrics, is part of a bigger Fair Trade enterprise that promotes sustainable income-generating activities for women. Everything sold here is handmade in Ghana.

**Woodin** CLOTHING
(Map p312; ☎030-2764371; Oxford St; ⏲8am-7pm Mon-Sat, noon-6pm Sun) The place to come for Ghanaian wax print fabrics, Woodin has proved so popular that there are branches throughout Ghana. If you've no time to find a seamstress, there are off-the-peg clothes for men, women and children.

**Artists Alliance Gallery** ART
(Map p312; ☎024 5251404; www.facebook.com/Artists-Alliance-Gallery; Labadi Rd; ⏲9am-5.30pm Mon-Sat, from noon Sun) A well-respected gallery with three neatly organised floors of painting and sculpture by established and up-and-coming Ghanaian artists. Every item has an official, non-negotiable price label, so this popular gallery might not give you the frenetic experience of the city's street markets, but it is a safe bet to find quality items while ensuring a fair amount of the money goes to the artist.

**Centre for National Culture** MARKET
(Arts Centre; Map p316; 28th February Rd; ⏲8am-6pm) A warren of stalls selling arts and crafts, known simply as the Arts Centre, this is the place to shop in Accra. The level of aggressive hassling may make you want to keep your cedis in your pocket but if you have the patience and wherewithal, you can come away with good-quality handicrafts from all over Ghana.

## Information

### DANGERS & ANNOYANCES

Accra is one of Africa's safest cities, with little violent crime against tourists. Bag-snatching and pickpocketing is more common, particularly at markets or bus stations. Avoiding

# Central Accra

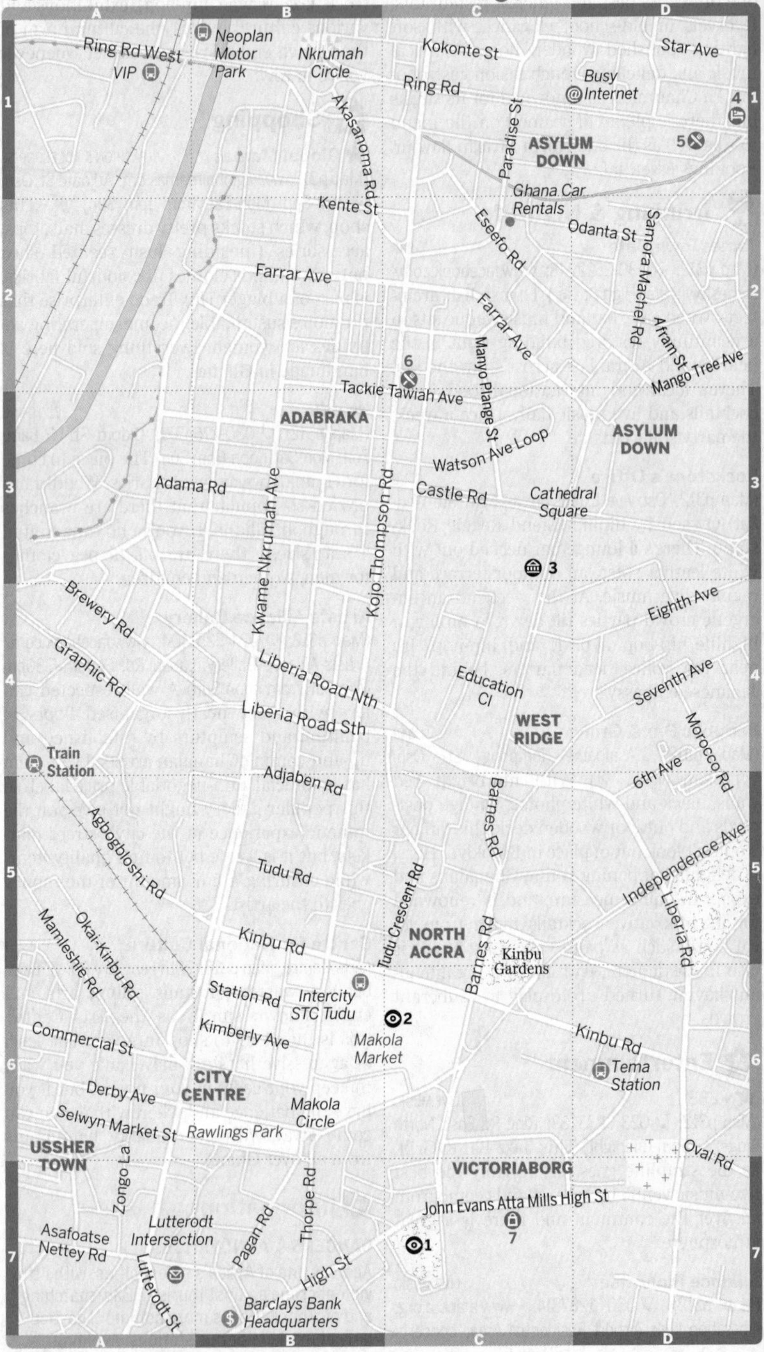

## Central Accra

**Sights**

1 Kwame Nkrumah Park and Mausoleum ........ C7
2 Makola Market ........ C6
3 National Museum ........ C3

**Sleeping**

4 Paloma ........ D1

**Eating**

5 Asanka Restaurant ........ D1
6 Khana Khazana ........ C2

**Shopping**

7 Centre for National Culture ........ C7

carrying obvious bags or valuables can mitigate the risk.

Negotiating the city on foot during daylight hours is generally fine – the greatest risk you'll face is from the traffic or open sewers. Avoid walking around at night, however, which is when (thankfully rare) violent incidents tend to occur.

### INTERNET ACCESS

Most midrange and top-end hotels and guesthouses offer free wi-fi, as do many cafes and restaurants.

**Busy Internet** (Map p316; Ring Rd Central; per hr C7.50; 7am-8pm Mon-Fri, 9am-8pm Sat; ) Fast browsing and printing services.

**SharpNet** (Map p312; Ring Rd East; per hr C3, between midnight & 7am C1.50; 24hr; ) Reliable 24-hour browsing.

**Vida e caffè** (Map p312; 054 0123222; www.vidaecaffe.com; Icon House, Stanbic Heights, North Liberation Link; sandwiches from C20; 7am-7pm) All five branches have speedy wi-fi and good coffee.

### MEDIA

**Time Out Accra** (www.timeoutaccra.com) A fantastic, glossy annual magazine with the low-down on what's hot and what's not in Accra. Great features on Ghana's cultural scene plus a section on day trips. Available in the capital's bookshops and large hotels. For the most up-to-date information, visit its website.

### MEDICAL SERVICES

In addition to the following you can ask your embassy for a list of recommended doctors and specialists. Pharmacies are everywhere.

**Lister Hospital** (030-3409031, 030-3409030; www.listerhospital.com.gh; Airport Hills, Cantonments) Ultramodern hospital. Has lab, pharmacy and emergency services.

**Trust Hospital** (Map p312; 030-2761974/5; www.thetrusthospital.com; Oxford St, Osu) A private hospital with decent general practitioner and lab services.

**37 Military Hospital** (Map p312; Liberation Ave) Large government hospital with a trauma centre and an ICU.

### MONEY

You'll find dozens of banks and ATMs all over town.

**Barclays Bank Headquarters** (Map p316; High St; 8.30am-4.30pm Mon-Fri) Changes cash and travellers cheques; ATM.

### POST

**Main Post Office** (Map p316; Asafoate Nettey Rd; 8am-5pm Mon-Fri, 9am-2pm Sat) In Ussher Town.

### TOURIST INFORMATION

**Accra Tourist Information Centre** (Map p312; 030-2682601; Liberation Rd) This new office provides advice on what's happening in Accra, as well as information about travel throughout the country, and transport and hotel booking services. A restaurant and a small library are planned.

**Ghana Tourism Authority** (Map p312; 030-2682601; www.ghana.travel; Haile Selassie St) Offers advice and information about travel throughout the country.

### TRAVEL AGENCIES

**Abacar Tours** (024 9574691, 030-2223407; www.abacar-tours.com; 39 Bobo St, Tesano) Reputable operator run by a Franco-Ghanaian team, with plenty of options in Ghana and the possibility to extend in neighbouring Togo, Benin and Burkina Faso.

**Easy Track Ghana** (027 6657036; www.easytrackghana.com) Set up by two friends, an American and a Ghanaian, Easy Track has a strong focus on sustainable tourism and runs tours all over the country as well as in the rest of West Africa.

**M&J Travel & Tours** (Map p312; 024 4514824, 030-2773498; www.mandjtravel-ghana.com; Ring Rd East, Osu) Experienced travel agent offering car hire as well as tours throughout Ghana and into neighbouring Togo, Benin and Burkina Faso.

### VISA EXTENSIONS

**Immigration Office** (Map p312; 030-2221667, 030-2224445; off Independence Ave, North Ridge; 8.30am-2pm Mon-Fri) Three-month visa extensions cost C250 and take two weeks to process. You will need two passport photos and a letter of application explaining the reasons for your extension request.

## Getting There & Around

### AIR

**Kotoka International Airport** (Map p312; www.gacl.com.gh), just 5km north of the ring road, is the main international gateway to the country. There are also domestic flights to Kumasi, Takoradi and Tamale.

Allow plenty of time to get to the airport: a one-hour journey is common, two or three hours not unheard of.

A taxi from the airport to the centre should cost around C30.

### BUS

After a couple of problematic years, leading many services to grind to a halt, Intercity STC is back in service, complete with a brand-new fleet of buses. For the moment, however, there are fewer departures than previously. The main **Intercity STC** (Map p312; ☎030-2221912, 030-2221932; http://stc.oyawego.com) bus station and the **VIP** (Map p316; ☎020 8402080) bus station are on Ring Rd West. STC also has another depot in **Tudu** (Map p316).

Services from Accra include:

**Aflao** C22, three hours, one daily, Intercity STC Tudu station

**Bolgatanga** C80, 18 hours, three weekly, Intercity STC Ring Rd station

**Cape Coast** C19, three hours, one daily, Intercity STC Ring Rd station

**Ho** C19, three hours, one daily, Intercity STC Tudu station

**Kumasi** C40, 4½ hours, leave when full, VIP station

**Paga** C95, 20 hours, three weekly, Intercity STC Ring Rd station

**Takoradi** C45, four to five hours, 1pm daily, VIP station

**Takoradi** C27, four hours, one daily, Intercity STC Ring Rd station

**Tamale** C45, 11 hours, one daily, Intercity STC Ring Rd station

**Wa** C85, 14 hours, 3pm daily, VIP station

### LOCAL TRANSPORT

Tro-tros (minibuses or pick-ups) leave from four main motor parks:

**Kaneshie Motor Park** (Kaneshie) Cape Coast (C20, three hours), Takoradi (C25, four to five hours) and other destinations to the west.

**Neoplan Motor Park** (Map p316; Ring Rd West) Kumasi (C30, four hours), Tamale and northern destinations.

**Tema station** (Map p316) Tema (C10, one hour), Ho (C20, three hours), Hohoe (C25, four hours)

**Tudu station** Aflao (C20, three hours), Akosombo (C15, 1¼ hours), Ho (C20, three hours), Hohoe (C25, four hours)

### CAR

**Ghana Car Rentals** (Map p316; ☎026 4264246; www.ghana-car-rentals.com; Odanta St, Asylum Down; saloon car/4WD per day from US$85/100 including driver's expenses) is a reliable company renting vehicles with experienced drivers.

# VOLTA REGION

The Volta region has to be Ghana's most underrated gem. The area is covered in lush, fertile farmland flanked by rocks, and mountains offering beautiful vistas. It is prime hiking territory and has great ecotourism ventures.

## Amedzofe

☎036 / POP 5500

Amedzofe's claim to fame is that, at 750m altitude, it is Ghana's highest settlement. The drive to the village, through the stunning Avatime Hills, is scenic and tortuous; it almost comes as a surprise when Amedzofe suddenly appears around a bend.

The village offers breathtaking vistas, a waterfall, forests, a cool climate and plenty of hiking opportunities. There's a fantastic community-run **visitor centre** (☎054 7297493; www.facebook.com/amedzofe; ⊙8am-5pm) where you can arrange hikes. Popular choices include a 45-minute walk to Amedzofe Falls – the last section is treacherous – and a 30-minute walk to the summit of Mt Gemi (611m), one of the highest mountains in the area, where there is a 3.5m iron cross and stunning views.

### Sleeping

★**Mountain Paradise** GUESTHOUSE $
(☎024 4166226; www.mountainparadise-biakpa.com; Biakpa; campsite C10, d/tw/f C55/80/120, s/d without bathroom C35/45) The nicest place to stay in the area is Biakpa Mountain Paradise, a former government rest home converted into a mountain hideaway near the village of Vane. It's a peaceful place, with a good restaurant that serves home-grown highland coffee. Staff can arrange hikes along the Kulugu River and bike rental.

**Abraerica** HOTEL $
(054 7752361, 020 8132484; www.abraerica.com; Amedzofe; s/d with fan C80/100, d/tw with air-con C120, f C300; P ❄) The rooms in Amedzofe's only hotel are a little uninspiring, but the views – right over Mt Gemi and the hotel's own lawns – are fabulous. There's also a decent restaurant and staff can arrange hiking and mountain-biking tours.

## Getting There & Away

There are tro-tros between Ho and Amedzofe (C6, one hour) daily except on Sundays. It might be quicker to get a tro-tro going from Ho to Hohoe and be dropped off at Vane, getting a share taxi on from there. A private taxi between Ho and Amedzofe will cost C40.

# Tafi Atome & Tafi Abuipe

These two small villages are worthy ecotourism destinations in the region. Tafi Atome has long been known for its monkey sanctuary, while Tafi Abuipe is famed for its kente weaving tradition.

## Sights

**Tafi Atome Monkey Sanctuary** WILDLIFE RESERVE
(024 7877627; tours per person C20) Set up to protect the forest and its inhabitants, the mona monkeys, this community-run sanctuary makes for a fun excursion. The monkeys, revered by the villagers, are habituated and readily come to feed off the hand of visitors. Early in the morning and late in the afternoon, they can be seen roaming the village. Visits to the sanctuary are by tour, arranged at the visitor centre.

**Tafi Abuipe Cultural Centre** CULTURAL CENTRE
(054 2680056; C15) This kente-weaving centre is fun to visit and there's less of a hard-sell than at similar villages in the Ashanti region. You can visit the weaving room, tour the village and have kente-weaving lessons. The kente in this part of Ghana is good value and with a bit of notice, villagers will produce any textile to any measurement and deliver it to where you're staying.

## Sleeping

**Tafi Atome Guesthouse** GUESTHOUSE $
(024 5458170, 024 7877627; r from C50) This basic guesthouse is next to the visitor centre. Simple fan-cooled rooms share a spotless if spartan shower block, and local meals can be prepared given some notice. You will need to call in advance – walk-ins aren't possible.

## Information

**Tafi Atome Visitor Centre** (7am-5pm) The first port of call at Tafi Atome for Monkey Sanctuary tours or to arrange to stay at the guesthouse.

## Getting There & Away

Tafi Atome and Tafi Abuipe lie west off the Ho–Hohoe road, not far from the village of Fume. If you don't have your own transport, you can charter a taxi from Fume for about C20. There is an 8km footpath between Tafi Atome and Tafi Abuipe, that you could either walk or cycle.

# Wli Falls

Ghana's tallest waterfalls, the Wli (pronounced 'vlee') falls stand amid an exquisite landscape of rolling hills, forests and bubbling streams. The falls are most impressive from April to October, when you can hear – and feel – the flow of water thundering down.

It takes about 40 minutes to walk from the Wli Tourist Office to the lower waterfalls (C15) along an easy path. Much more challenging is the hike to the upper falls (C35), which takes about two hours and requires clambering in places. In both cases you'll be required to take a guide, included in the price.

## Activities

**Wli Tourist Office** TOURS
(020 2572400; lower/upper falls per person C15/35; 9am-5pm) Organises guides for walks up to the falls (you won't be allowed up without one).

## Sleeping & Eating

**Big Foot Safari Lodge** LODGE $
(020 8180500, 020 4431744; www.bigfootsafarilodge.com; camping per person US$10, s/d US$40/50; P ❄ ) This place is in a great location, close to the start of the waterfall trail, and has large airy bungalows set in a pretty tropical garden, as well as space for campers.

**Waterfall Lodge at Wli** LODGE $
(054 1359872, 020 5115388; www.ghanacamping.com; camping per person C20, d C75, 2-/4-bed chalet C85/120; P) A serene, friendly and

beautiful place, with views of Wli Falls and the surrounding hills. Huts are simple but comfortable, and there's space for campers. Food is delicious, with Ghanaian and European dishes available. Staff can organise all manner of hikes in the surrounding area. No new arrivals are accepted on Tuesdays.

**Wli Water Heights Hotel** GUESTHOUSE $
(☎020 9119152; www.wliwaterheightshotel.com; d with fan/air-con C100/180, q with fan C180; P) The Wli Water Heights Hotel lacks the atmosphere of some of the more rustic lodges, but it is in a beautiful spot just 500m from the falls. The garden is the perfect place to wind down after a day of trekking.

### Getting There & Away

Wli is right on the border with Togo. Regular tro-tros and shared taxis make the scenic run between Wli and Hohoe (C5, 50 minutes). If you're heading for Togo, the Ghanaian border post is on the eastern side of Wli (turn left at the junction as you enter the village).

# THE COAST

## Kokrobite

☎031 / POP 5000

Endowed with a long stretch of white sand, and just 45 minutes from the capital city, Kokrobite has long been a favourite of backpackers, volunteers and Accra weekenders. While it's not the prettiest or cleanest beach along the coast, it has a fun vibe, an excellent surf school and some great places to stay.

### Activities

**Mr Bright's Surf Shop** SURFING
(☎026 4316053; www.mrbrights.com; group/private lessons per person C60/100) British surfer Brett Davies has moved his surf school down from Busua to Big Milly's in Kokrobite.

### Sleeping & Eating

**Kokrobite Garden** GUESTHOUSE $
(☎054 6392850; www.kokrobitegarden.com; d bungalows with outside/inside bathroom €18/42; P) A quirky collection of bungalows, rooms, and even a vintage caravan sit in tranquil tropical gardens at this relaxed and friendly guesthouse, which is a short stroll from the beach. There's a small pool, a book exchange and a top-notch Italian restaurant (mains C40 to C65).

**Big Milly's Backyard** LODGE $
(☎024 9999330; www.bigmilly.com; camping per person C25, dm C29, r from C69; P @) An eclectic collection of dorms, huts and rooms set in a garden next to the beach, long-standing Big Milly's is popular, fun and sociable. There's a good restaurant (mains C18 to C80), a 24-hour bar and live music at the weekends. It can get noisy, however, so if you're looking for peace and quiet, head elsewhere.

**Dizzy Lizzie's** INTERNATIONAL
(☎020 5600990; mains from C20) This chilled beach-front restaurant a short walk down the sand from Big Milly's serves a mix of international and Ghanaian food. There's live music on Friday nights and drumming on Sundays.

### Information

Security can be an issue here, and there have been reports of muggings on the beach. Ask advice from your guesthouse on where and where not to wander.

### Getting There & Away

Kokrobite is only 25km west of Accra, and a 45-minute drive, though at rush hour the journey can take up to two hours. Tro-tros (C2.50) to Kokrobite go from the western end of Kaneshie Motor Park (p318) in Accra. A taxi from Accra will cost around C80.

## Anomabu

☎033 / POP 14,500

The sands and ribbons of low-key surf are certainly the big draw here, and Anomabu's stunning beaches are among the best in the country. The village has its charms too though, including a historic fort and a number of traditional shrines.

### Sights

The town has a number of *posubans* (the shrines of the city's Asafo companies, ancient fraternities meant to defend the city). Posuban No 6, in the shape of a ship, is one of the largest. To find it, walk west from Fort William for about 50m towards the yellow house. When you see Posuban No 7 on your right, turn left down some steps where you'll find Posuban No 6. Company No 3's *posuban,* which features a whale between two lions, is about 50m from the main road, opposite the Ebeneezer Hotel.

**Fort William** FORT
(C10; ⊙9am-4.30pm Mon-Sat) Now open to the public, this former slave fort hosts lively and fascinating tours, delivered by enthusiastic guides. Having served as a prison from 1962 to 2000, the building itself is in a bad state of repair.

## Sleeping & Eating

**Anomabo Beach Resort** RESORT **$$**
(☎050 1286213, 024 4331731; www.anomabo.com; camping per person US$15, s/d hut US$80/100, s/d hut without bathroom US$60/80; P ❄) Tucked away on a quiet, clean stretch of beach, this collection of huts and cottages, set within a sandy and shady grove of coconut palms, is deservedly popular with weekenders escaping the bustle of Accra. The simple huts are slightly fraying at the edges, but they're clean and spacious, and there are camping pitches and tent rental for those on lower budgets.

The open-air restaurant has gorgeous sea views and serves a mixture of international and Ghanaian dishes, including excellent seafood.

## Getting There & Away

You'll have no problem finding a tro-tro (C2, 15 minutes) to or from Cape Coast along the main road.

# Cape Coast

☎021 / POP 170,000

Forever haunted by the ghosts of the past, Cape Coast is one of Africa's most culturally significant spots. This former European colonial capital, originally named Cabo Corso by the Portuguese, was once the largest slave-trading centre in West Africa. At the height of the slave trade it received a workforce from locations as far away as Niger and Burkina Faso, and slaves were kept locked up in the bowels of Cape Coast's imposing castle. At the shoreline, slaves were herded onto vessels like cattle, irrevocably altering the lives of generations to come.

Today, Cape Coast is an easygoing fishing town with an arty vibe, fanned by salty sea breezes and kissed by peeling waves. Crumbling colonial buildings line the streets, seabirds prowl the beaches and fishermen cast nets where slave ships once sailed. Many travellers use Cape Coast as a base to explore Kakum National Park, Anomabu and even Elmina.

## Sights

As well as Cape Coast Castle, you'll notice the ruins of **Fort William** (adult/student/child C10/7/2), which dates from 1820 and now functions as a lighthouse, and **Fort Victoria** (adult/student/child C10/7/2; ⊙9am-4.30pm), originally built in 1702, on the town's hills but you are advised not to venture to either without a guide because of muggings.

★**Cape Coast Castle** CASTLE
(☎033-2132529; Victoria Rd; adult/student/child C40/30/5; ⊙9am-4.30pm) Cape Coast's imposing, whitewashed castle commands the heart of town, overlooking the sea. Once one of the world's most important slave-holding sites, it provides horrifying insight into the workings of the trade. Staff conduct hour-long tours, during which you'll visit the dark, damp dungeons, where slaves waited for two to 12 weeks, while contemplating rumours that only hinted at their fate. A visit to the dungeons contrasts sharply with the governor's bedroom, blessed with floor-to-ceiling windows and panoramic ocean views.

## Courses

★**Global Mamas** COOKING
(☎054 4323833; www.globalmamas.org; Market St) Set up in 2003 to empower local women by training them to produce and sell handicrafts, this fantastic outfit also organises courses in cooking (US$14), batik (US$18) and drumming and dancing (US$13, minimum two people). Courses last three or four hours and can be organised at short notice (the day before).

## Sleeping

★**Baobab Guesthouse** GUESTHOUSE **$**
(☎054 0436130; www.baobab-children-foundation.de; Commercial St; d/tr/q without bathroom C50/60/70; 📶) All profits from this charming guesthouse go to the Baobab Children Foundation, which runs a school for disadvantaged children. The simple rooms are decked out with bamboo furniture and colourful batik cloth made by the students, and some have views of the ocean or nearby Cape Coast Castle. There is an excellent vegetarian restaurant on site.

## Cape Coast

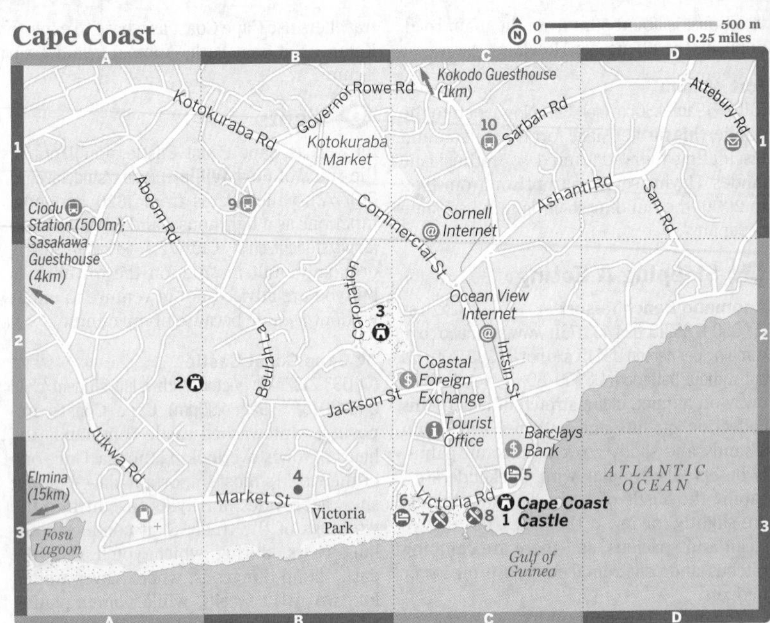




**Sasakawa Guesthouse** GUESTHOUSE $
(☎033-2136871; sasakawa@yahoo.com; University of Cape Coast, Newsite; s/d C80/100; P ❄ wi-fi) Originally built to accommodate Cape Coast University's visiting lecturers, this modern facility on the university's beautiful campus is now open to all. It is an absolute bargain, with wi-fi, satellite TV, air-con and breakfast all included in the price, and it's a great place to meet young Ghanaians. The campus is about 5km out of town, served by a constant stream of taxis.

**Oasis Beach Resort** HOSTEL $
(☎024 5128322, 024 3022594, 024 4089535; www.oasisbeach-ghana.com; seafront, Victoria Park; dm C20, hut C160, deluxe d/f with air-con C270/360, d/tr/q with shared bathroom C100/110/130; P ❄ wi-fi) Like a hip party spot, a night at Oasis is loud, hot and sweaty. Backpackers, volunteers and Cape Coast's beautiful people gravitate towards the beachfront bar and restaurant, which does a good line in sandwiches, salads and cocktails. Staff are very friendly.

**Kokodo Guesthouse** GUESTHOUSE $$
(☎024 4673486, 024 3529191; DeGraft Johnson Rd; r from US$60; P ❄ wi-fi) This gorgeous, modern villa – formerly the house of Barclays Bank's manager – sits atop a bluff in a pretty garden. Rooms are spacious and airy, with gigantic beds. There is a tropical garden and a wonderful restaurant lounge (mains C25). The only drawback is the location, on the outskirts of town.

### Eating

**★Baobab Vegetarian Moringa Restaurant** VEGETARIAN $
(www.baobab-children-foundation.de; ☎054 0436130; Commercial St; sandwiches C11-21, mains C12-24; ⏲7am-8pm; wi-fi ✓) A tiny organic food bar with a wholesome touch, Baobab serves up great veggie stews and curries, black-bread sandwiches and refreshing juices, smoothies and shakes. All this and there's a great sea view too.

**Orange Beach Bar & Restaurant** INTERNATIONAL $
(☎057 6605250; www.facebook.com/orangebeachbarghana; Victoria Rd; mains from C20; ⏲8am-midnight) Sitting on the beach next to Cape Coast Castle, this airy and friendly cafe serves fresh organic juices and smoothies, as well as tasty breakfasts, fish grills and Ghanaian dishes. It's a good place for a party too, with regular beach bonfires and reggae nights.

## Cape Coast

**Top Sights**
1 Cape Coast Castle ........ C3

**Sights**
2 Fort Victoria ........ A2
3 Fort William ........ B2

**Activities, Courses & Tours**
4 Global Mamas ........ B3

**Sleeping**
5 Baobab Guesthouse ........ C3
6 Oasis Beach Resort ........ C3

**Eating**
Baobab Vegetarian Moringa Restaurant ........ (see 5)
7 Orange Beach Bar & Restaurant ........ C3
8 The Castle ........ C3

**Transport**
9 Kotokuraba Station ........ B1
10 Tantri Bus Station ........ C1

**The Castle** AFRICAN $$
(Victoria Rd; mains C20-50; 7am-11pm) Though not as impressive in size as its next-door neighbour (Cape Coast Castle), this wooden bar-restaurant is a charmer. The fare (a mix of Ghanaian and international dishes) is good, though not sensational.

## Information

### INTERNET ACCESS

**Cornell Internet** (Commercial St; per hr C5; 7am-7pm)

**Ocean View Internet** (Commercial St; per hr C5; 7.30am-11pm) Printing, scanning, CD burning.

### MONEY

**Barclays Bank** (Commercial St; 8am-5pm Mon-Fri) Can change travellers cheques and cash; has an ATM.

**Coastal Foreign Exchange** (Jackson St; 8am-4.30pm Mon-Fri, 9am-1pm Sat) A good alternative to the perennially full Barclays for changing cash.

### TOURIST INFORMATION

**Tourist Office** (033-2132062; Heritage House, King St; 8.30am-5pm Mon-Fri) On the 1st floor of Heritage House, a gorgeous colonial building; staff can help with practical information such as transport and directions but little else.

## Getting There & Away

### BUS

The Intercity STC bus station is near the Pedu junction, about 5km northwest of the town centre. Destinations for the moment are just Accra (C25, three hours, one daily) and Takoradi (C10, one hour, one daily). There are several Metro Mass services to and from Cape Coast daily.

### TRO-TRO

Shared taxis and tro-tros (minibuses) to local destinations such as Anomabu (C2, 15 minutes) and Elmina (C2.50, 15 minutes) leave from **Kotokuraba station** (Johnston Rd).

For tro-tros to Accra (C20, three hours) and Kumasi (C30, four hours) head to **Tantri station** (cnr Sarbah Rd & Residential Rd). You can also pick up tro-tros to Accra from the Total petrol station.

**Ciodu station** (Jukwa Rd) serves destinations west of Cape Coast, such as Kakum National Park (C5, 30 minutes) and Takoradi (C8, one hour).

# Kakum National Park

An easy day trip from Cape Coast, **Kakum National Park** (033-2130265, 050 1291683; admission C2, canopy walkway adult/child C50/10; 6am-4pm) is a slice of native rainforest famous for its canopy walk, a series of viewing platforms linked by a string of bouncy suspension bridges 30m above ground. The park is also home to over 300 species of bird, 600 species of butterfly and 40 mammal species, but it can be difficult to see (or hear) any of them, because tours of the walkway are conducted in large groups. It's best to come on a weekday, first thing in the morning or in the late afternoon when there are fewer visitors and you can enjoy the peace of the rainforest.

If you would like to see wildlife, you will need to venture further into the park and make special arrangements with a guide the day before.

While most people will come to Kakum on a day trip from Cape Coast, it is possible to sleep at a campsite (C45) or in a treehouse (C55) inside the forest, though you'll have to be accompanied by a park ranger. Contact the **Kakum National Park Information Centre** (033-2130265, 0501291683; 6am-4pm) for further details.

Kakum is easily accessible by public transport. From Cape Coast, take a tro-tro from Ciodu Station (C5, 30 minutes).

# Elmina

021 / POP 33,500

The enchanting town of Elmina lies on a narrow finger of land between the Atlantic Ocean and Benya Lagoon. Here, the air is salty and the architecture is a charming mix of colonial remnants, elderly *posubans* (shrines) and an imposing historical legacy in the shape of St George's Castle.

The traditional name of Elmina is Anomansa, meaning inexhaustible supply of water. Watching the colourful pirogues pull in and out of the lagoon, breathing in the salty air and listening to the cacophony of shouts at the crowded Mpoben port is like having front-row theatre seats. The vast fish market is also fascinating to wander around, particularly when the day's catch is being unloaded in the afternoon.

## Sights

**St George's Castle** CASTLE

(Elmina Castle; adult/student/child C40/30/50; 9am-5pm) St George's Castle, a Unesco heritage site, was built as a trading post by the Portuguese in 1482, and captured by the Dutch in 1637. It was expanded when slaves replaced gold as the major object of commerce, with storerooms converted into dungeons. The informative tour (included in the entry fee) takes you to the grim dungeons, punishment cells, Door of No Return and the turret room where the British imprisoned the Ashanti king, Prempeh I, for four years.

## Tours

★ **Ghana Ecotours** CULTURAL, WALKING

(024 2176357, 020 8159369; www.ghanaecotours.com; 1st floor, St George's Castle; walking tours per person C30) This sensational outfit offers highly informative walking tours that retrace Elmina's history. Tours take in the local fish market, the town's *posuban*, colonial buildings, small alleyways and great panoramas. It also offers city tours of Cape Coast, as well as nightlife tours of both cities.

## Sleeping & Eating

★ **Stumble Inn** LODGE $

(054 1462733; www.stumbleinnghana.com; dm C20, d C90, d with shared bathroom C70; P ❄) This pretty, ecofriendly haven gets rave reviews from travellers, and rightly so: spotless huts are set beneath palm trees on a gorgeous stretch of beach, there's a fantastic restaurant and bar, and plenty of strategically placed bamboo loungers for enjoying the view to the full (as well as a beach volleyball court and table tennis for the more energetic).

**Coconut Grove Bridge House** HOTEL $$

(026 3000692; www.coconutgrovehotelsghana.com; s/d US$90/125; P ❄ ) Set in a charming old stone building opposite St George's Castle, this is certainly the most atmospheric place to stay in town, even if the rooms are tired and overpriced. The attached restaurant, with a breezy terrace and stunning views, is a bonus.

**Coconut Grove Beach Resort** RESORT $$

(033-2191213; www.coconutgrovehotelsghana.com; village d US$65, resort d from US$120; P ❄ @ ) This beach resort offers a variety of upmarket rooms as well as a pool, a tennis court, a nine-hole golf course and a questionable mini animal sanctuary. Rooms in the resort's extension – called 'The Village' – are more rustic but considerably cheaper, and you still get to enjoy all the fancy facilities. The resort is 3km west of Elmina.

**Almond Tree Guesthouse** B&B $$

(024 4281098, 026 5379798; www.almond3.com; r US$55-75, r with shared bathroom US$35; P ❄ ) It's the hosts' friendly welcome that makes this guesthouse so special. Originally from Jamaica, the family settled in Britain and then here. The rooms, each named after a famous Jamaican, are impeccable and homely, with warm hardwood floors. Some have shared facilities while others enjoy their own little balcony.

**Bridge House** AFRICAN $$

(mains C20-40; 9am-9pm; ❄) With a terrace overlooking the fort and the lagoon, Bridge House is the nicest place to eat in town, and serves huge portions of European and Ghanaian food. It's inside Coconut Grove Bridge House.

## Getting There & Away

From the main taxi and tro-tro station (outside the Wesley Methodist Cathedral) you can get tro-tros to Takoradi (C5, one hour) or passenger taxis to Cape Coast (C2.50, 15 minutes).

# Takoradi

031 / POP 445,000

Takoradi was just a fishing village until it was chosen as Ghana's first deep-water seaport; since then it has prospered. Now feeding on

Ghana's oil industry, Takoradi (or Taadi, as it's known) is growing larger by the day.

There isn't much for visitors here but the town is an important transport hub so you're bound to go through it at some stage.

### Sleeping & Eating

**Petit Palais Guesthouse** GUESTHOUSE $$
(024 4337890; www.petitpalais.com.gh; Beach Rd; d US$120-140, ste US$150-170; P) This superchic boutique hotel, decked out in shades of white and red, is one of the best places to stay in town. There's a pool, a garden and a balcony to chill out on, a homely lounge/kitchen area and excellent food is made to order.

**Planter's Lodge & Spa** BOUTIQUE HOTEL $$$
(031-2199271; www.planterslodge.com; d/ste from C550/790; P@) Originally built to accommodate British Royal Air Force flying officers, this exquisite compound is now a stylish hideaway popular with oil magnates and the Takoradi jet set. The rooms have plenty of old-school colonial elegance and there's a pool, a restaurant and a teashop set in thriving tropical gardens.

**Bocadillos** CAFE $
(7am-7pm Mon-Sat) Perfect for pastries, baguettes, sandwiches and ice cream. Eat on the terrace overlooking the street or in the calm, chic interior.

**Captain Hook's** SEAFOOD $$
(031-2027084; Dixcove Hill; mains from C70; noon-3pm & 6pm-midnight; P) The place to come for huge and delicious platters of fresh seafood. There are steaks and other grills for carnivores. The wood panelling and model ships give the place a seafaring atmosphere.

### Getting There & Away

**Starbow** (www.flystarbow.com) and **Africa World Airlines** (www.flyawa.com.gh) operate two flights a day between Accra and Takoradi (45 minutes; C165). The airport is 1.5 km west of the centre.

**Intercity STC** (http://stc.oyawego.com/) and **Metro Mass** (www.metromass.com) provide daily services to Accra (C25 to C45, five hours).

Tro-tro (minibus or pick-ups) stops are scattered around the main market roundabout. Everyone should be able to direct you. Destinations include Accra (C25, four to five hours), Kumasi (C25, five hours) and Agona Junction (C5, 40 minutes).

## Axim

031 / POP 28,000

Axim is the site of the huge Fort San Antonio, built by the Portuguese in the 16th century. It is also home to some of the country's best beaches and most idyllic resorts. Located 70km from the border with Côte d'Ivoire, Axim is pronounced with a French accent (Akzeem or Azeem).

### Sights

**Fort San Antonio** HISTORIC BUILDING
(adult/child C10/2; 9am-4.30pm) Built in 1515, Fort San Antonio was the second fort constructed by the Portuguese on the Gold Coast, after St George's Castle in Elmina. The entrance fee includes a guided tour, and from the top of the fort, there are spectacular views of the stunning coastline in both directions.

### Sleeping & Eating

**Axim Beach Eco Resort** RESORT $$
(031-7090099, 031-2092397; www.aximbeach.com; budget r/chalet/f bungalow from US$50/80/150; P@) This sprawling resort is the largest in the area – with two restaurants, a pool and a playground – yet it still manages to feel friendly and intimate. The dark red thatch huts are lovely. They're scattered around a lush green hillside that slopes down to a pretty beach, and many have floor-to-ceiling windows to take in the stunning views.

**Ankobra Beach Resort** RESORT $$
(031-2092323; www.ankobrabeachresort.com; budget d/apt US$36/94, r from US$104, chalet from US$142; P) Gorgeous bungalows decorated with African art and textiles are hidden in vibrant tropical gardens along a suitably dreamy stretch of beach. There's also fantastic food, much of it home-grown at the resort.

★**Lou Moon Lodge** LODGE $$$
(020 8241549, 026 4241549; www.lou moon-lodge.com; standard/sea-view d from €75/125, standard/sea-view ste from €100/125; P) Perhaps the loveliest beach resort in the country, Lou Moon sits on a beautiful and private sheltered bay backed by thick forest. Rooms and chalets – all polished plaster, huge windows and crisp white linen – are an exercise in understated chic, and the daily changing menu offers a small

choice of delicious dishes, including kids and veggie options (C45 to C95).

## Getting There & Away

Regular tro-tros (C10, one hour) go from Takoradi to Axim via a smooth, paved road. If coming from the border at Elubo, the journey should take around two hours in a tro-tro.

# Busua

031 / POP 5000

The small village of Busua, some 30km west of Takoradi, is a magnet for volunteers and backpackers, who love coming here to relax on the beach for a few days. There's a sociable vibe, with a number of chilled out bars and cafes in which to while away the hours; and the village has developed a reputation as a surfing hot spot. There are two excellent surf schools here, both offering lessons for absolute beginners.

The downside is the occasional rubbish on the beach, and the rather neglected air in low season.

## Sights & Activities

The stunning village of **Butre** is well worth the 3km walk from Busua. In fact, the walk itself is half the attraction: head east along the beach from Busua for about 2km then veer left along a path to go up a hill. The views of Butre when you reach the summit are a sight to behold, with the ruined Fort Batenstein nestled in palm trees on a bluff, Butre sandwiched between the ocean and the lagoon, and the ocean lapping a long, curvy beach beyond the lagoon. If you want to stay the night, the Green Zion Garden – a tranquil eco-lodge with a vegetarian restaurant – is lovely.

Dixcove (or Dick's Cove, as it was once known) is a large, bustling fishing village, with a very different feel from Busua. Its natural harbour is deep enough for small ships to enter – one of the reasons why the British chose to settle here and built **Fort Metal Cross** in 1696.

Dixcove is just 20 minutes' walk over the headland to the west of Busua. Locals warn against walking the track alone, however, so heed their advice and take a local guide with you (easily arranged by your accommodation).

Run by local surf instructor Peter Ansah, **Ahanta Waves Surf School & Camp** (026 9197812; www.ahantawaves.com) offers fun and professional surf lessons starting from C40 per person. The **Black Star Surf Shop** (055 6267914; www.facebook.com/blackstarsurfshop) rents longboards, shortboards (C20 per hour) and bodyboards (C10). It also runs regular surfing lessons (C40, two hours).

## SLEEPING & EATING

**Green Zion Garden** LODGE $

(020 2949398, 026 4625900; www.greenziongarden.com; Butre; camping per person US$3, 2-/4-person huts US$10/15) Set in flourishing tropical gardens, this tranquil eco-lodge offers rustic, handmade bungalows as well as camping. The vegetarian restaurant (mains C15 to C20) specialises in Indian food, and serves freshly roasted coffee and home-grown lemongrass tea.

**Busua Inn** GUESTHOUSE $$

(020 7373579; www.busuainn.com; d from US$40; P ❄ ) Owners Danielle and Olivier offer four clean, spacious rooms, two of which open out onto a sea-facing balcony. The romantic restaurant has a wooden deck backing right up to the water, and serves tasty French and Senegalese dishes (mains C20 to C50) as well as cocktails and good wine. Just watch out for the light-fingered resident monkey.

★ **Okorye Tree** CAFE $$

(mains C15-50; 7am-9pm) Attached to the Black Star Surf Shop, the Okorye Tree does a roaring trade in pancakes, burgers and great big burritos. Grab a table on the wooden deck, order a frozen margarita and watch the waves break.

**Coconut Dream Bar & Restaurant** INTERNATIONAL $$

(mains C15-40) This rustic, bamboo restaurant is painted in the colours of the Ghanaian flag and has a breezy 1st-floor dining area. At night, benches are placed out in the sand, illuminated by torchlight. Food is the usual mix of Ghanaian and international and it does a nice line in cocktails.

## Information

The only place in town with internet is the **Busua Beach Resort** (031-2093305; gbhghana.net), which has free wi-fi.

There are no banking facilities in Busua (the nearest are in Agona or Takoradi).

### Getting There & Away

Busua is about 12km from the main coastal road between Takoradi and Axim. To get here, get a tro-tro from Takoradi to Agona (C5, 40 minutes) and then a shared taxi to Busua (C2, 15 minutes).

To get to Akwidaa, you'll need to go back to Agona; from Akwidaa to Busua, however, you could stop at Dixcove and then walk from there.

## Akwidaa & Cape Three Points

Akwidaa's unique selling point is its long, pristine, white sandy beach, by far one of the best in Ghana. The village itself isn't as interesting as other settlements on the coast but you can hike in the local forests, explore cocoa and rubber plantations, organise canoe trips through mangroves or visit the windswept Cape Three Points, Ghana's most southern point. In season, you can see turtles on the nearby beaches as well as humpback whales and sperm whales.

### Sleeping

**★Escape3points** LODGE $

(026 7218700; www.escape3points.com; dm €7, chalets €20-35; P ❄ ) Beautiful and ecofriendly, Escape3points is one of the nicest places to stay along the coast. The stilted bungalows are rustic yet stylish. They're handmade from bamboo, raffia, thatch and wood, and are naturally cooled by the sea breezes. Meals are communal and feature food from the organic gardens.

**Ezile Bay Village** LODGE $

(020 7373579, 024 3174860; www.ezilebay.com; dm/hut from US$8/23; P ❄) Simple huts sit among palm trees on this gorgeous stretch of beach. The staff are welcoming and helpful, there's a great restaurant (mains C22 to C50), and the water is clean and a good deal calmer than elsewhere on this stretch of coast, so perfect for swimming.

**Akwidaa Inn** LODGE $

(054 9158469, 024 3628022; www.akwidaainn.com; Dixcove-Akwidaa Old Town Rd; dm from C25, d hut from C100; P ❄) Spacious huts and a dorm sit in plant-filled grounds on a glorious stretch of unspoilt beach. The friendly staff can arrange tours around the region including boating in the mangroves and visiting a rubber plantation.

### Getting There & Away

Akwidaa is about 16km south of the Takoradi–Axim road, and Cape Three Points is a further 6km west. Take a tro-tro from Takoradi to Agona (C6, 40 minutes) and then a tro-tro from Agona to Cape Three Points (90 minutes) or Akwidaa (C6, one hour). The driver can drop you off at your chosen lodge. Tro-tros stop in Dixcove on the way, handy if you want to get to Busua.

If you're driving you'll need a 4WD – the roads are in poor condition.

# THE CENTRE

## Kumasi

032 / POP 1.98 MILLION

Once the capital of the rich and powerful Ashanti kingdom, Ghana's second city is still dripping with Ashanti traditions. Its heart, the huge Kejetia market, throbs like a traditional talking drum and its wares spill into the city so that no matter where you are in Kumasi, it sometimes feels like one enormous marketplace.

Consider staying at Lake Bosumtwe – it's a gorgeous spot just one hour from here – and visiting Kumasi as a day trip.

### Sights & Activities

**★Kejetia Market** MARKET

From afar, the Kejetia Market looks like an alien mothership landed in the centre of Kumasi. Closer up, the rusting tin roofs of this huge market (often cited as the largest in West Africa; there are 11,000 stalls and at least four times as many people working here) look like a circular shanty town. Inside, the throbbing Kejetia is quite disorienting but utterly captivating.

**Prempeh II Jubilee Museum** MUSEUM

(National Cultural Centre; adult/student/child C20/10/5; 10am-4pm Mon-Fri, 6am-6pm Sat) This museum may be small but the personalised tour included with admission is a fascinating introduction to Ashanti culture and history. Among the displays are artefacts relating to the Ashanti king Prempeh II, including the king's war attire, ceremonial clothing, jewellery, protective amulets, personal equipment for bathing and dining, furniture, royal insignia and some fine brass weights for weighing gold. Constructed to resemble an Ashanti chief's house, it has a

## Kumasi

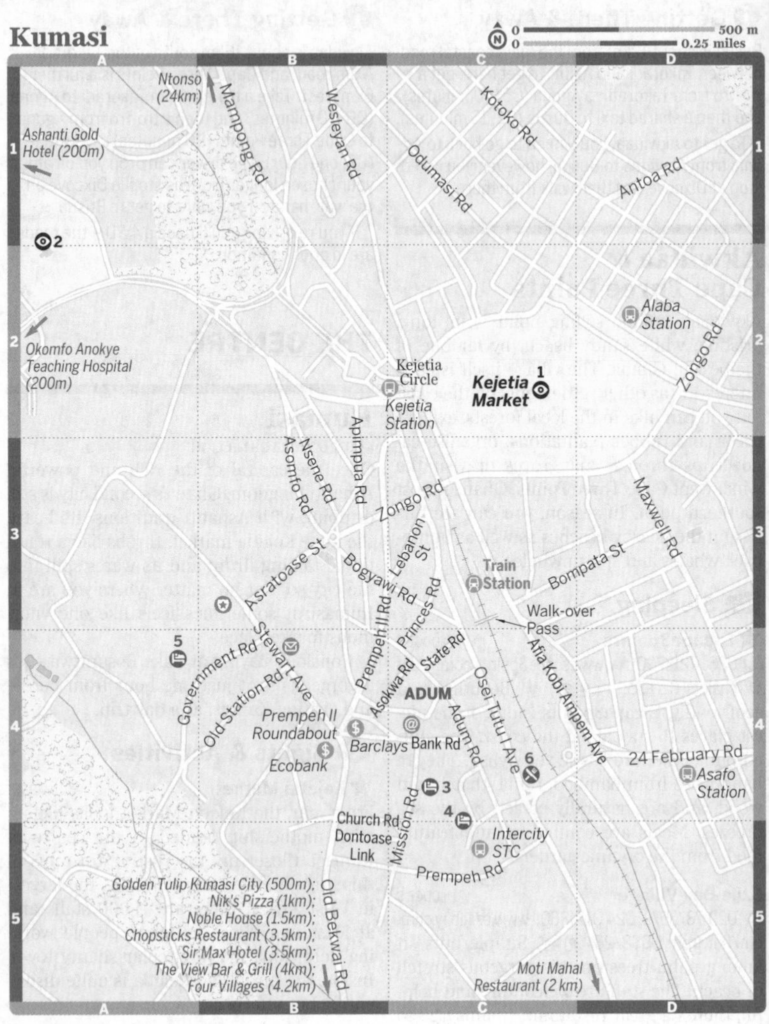


courtyard in front and walls adorned with traditional carved symbols.

**National Cultural Centre** ARTS CENTRE
(⏲9am-6pm) The National Cultural Centre is set within peaceful, shaded grounds and includes craft workshops, where you can see brassworking, woodcarving, pottery making, batik cloth dyeing and kente cloth weaving, as well as a gallery and crafts shop.

**Kumasi Walking Day Tours** WALKING
(☎024 9885370; kwesiannan7@gmail.com) Affable and knowledgeable Ben Kwesi Annan offers excellent walking tours taking in the city's main sights, as well as nightlife tours of Kumasi's pubs and clubs at the weekends.

### Festivals & Events

The Ashanti calendar is divided into nine cycles of 42 days called Adae, which means 'resting place'. Within each Adae, there are two special days of worship, when a celebration is held and no work is done. The most important annual festival is the **Odwira festival**, which marks the last or ninth Adae. The festival features lots of drumming, horn

**Kumasi**

**Top Sights**



**Sights**



**Sleeping**



**Eating**



**Information**



blowing, food offerings and parades of elegantly dressed chiefs. Contact the Ghana Tourist Authority (p330) for exact dates.

## Sleeping

**Daddy's Lodge** GUESTHOUSE $
(032-22022128; www.daddyslodge.com; r from C40; P ❄ 🛜) A two-minute stroll from the STC bus station, this place can't be beat when in comes to convenience, and the simple rooms and dorm aren't too bad either.

**Basel Mission Guesthouse** GUESTHOUSE $
(032-2026966; Mission Rd; d/executive d C80/130, d/tw without bathroom C50; P ❄ 🛜) Set in attractive green grounds, this two-storey guesthouse is a good budget option in central Kumasi, with recently revamped rooms. The building and staff are rather austere and the bathrooms are only just clean.

★ **Four Villages Inn** GUESTHOUSE $$
(032-2022682; www.fourvillages.com; Melcome Rd, Poultry Junction; r incl breakfast US$106; P ❄ @ 🛜) The Ghanaian-Canadian owners have pulled out all the stops at this impressive guesthouse. Each of the four enormous air-conditioned rooms is decorated in a different style, and there's a TV lounge and a tropical garden. Prices exclude the 15% VAT. The knowledgeable hosts can organise Kumasi excursions and tours, including tip-top market tours with their local guide.

**Kumasi Catering Rest House** GUESTHOUSE $$
(032-2026506; kcrhouse@yahoo.com; Government Rd; s/d/ste C200/260/325; P ❄ @ 🛜) Massive, clean rooms with very comfortable beds are set in pretty bungalows in spacious, shady grounds. Some of the rooms and bathrooms are looking rather outdated, however. There's a good restaurant and bar (mains C25 to C50) and a hair salon. It's a short stroll to the centre of town.

**Golden Tulip Kumasi City** HOTEL $$$
(032-2083777; www.goldentulipkumasicity.com; Victoria Opoku-Ware St; r from €160; P ❄ @ 🛜 ≋) Kumasi's plushest hotel has suitably elegant rooms and a host of upscale facilities, tennis court and pool included.

## Eating

**Kentish Kitchen** AFRICAN $
(National Cultural Centre; mains C15-30; 9am-6pm) Set in a pretty garden within the National Cultural Centre, this simple restaurant serves good Ghanaian dishes such as *red-red* (bean stew), *fufu* (fermented cassava, yams, plantain or manioc which is cooked and puréed) and *jollof rice,* as well as a few European choices.

**Sir Max Restaurant** GRILL $$
(Ahodwo; mains C18-50; 7am-11pm; 🛜) Set within the hotel of the same name, Sir Max serves top-quality Lebanese food, including kebabs and mezze platters, on a nice terrace overlooking the hotel pool.

**Vic Baboo's** INTERNATIONAL $$
(Osei Tutu I Ave; mains C20-35; 10am-10pm Mon-Sat, noon-9pm Sun; ❄ 🖉) Vic Baboo's is an institution among travellers and expats. With the biggest menu in town, this place is whatever you want it to be – Indian takeaway, decent burger joint, Lebanese deli or cocktail bar. It has a good selection of vegetarian dishes.

★ **View Bar & Grill** INTERNATIONAL $$$
(024 4668880; www.facebook.com/theviewbarandgrill; 39 Melcom Rd, Ahodwo; mains C20-125; noon-3pm & 6pm-1am; P ❄) Without a doubt the best restaurant in Kumasi. Delicious and beautifully presented food is served up in stylish surroundings, with expansive windows taking in views over the city. The steaks are the stars of the menu, but there are also good chicken, fish and gourmet-burger options. The cocktails are excellent and there are regular DJ parties on the roof terrace.

**Moti Mahal Restaurant** INDIAN $$$
(Top Martins Complex, near Asokwa Flyover; mains C30-70; noon-3pm & 7-11pm; P ❄) One of

WORTH A TRIP

### CLOTH AROUND KUMASI

**Ntonso**, 15km north of Kumasi, is the centre of *adinkra* cloth printing. Adinkra symbols represent concepts and aphorisms; they are traditionally printed on cotton fabric by using a natural brown dye and stamps carved out of calabash. You can see the whole process explained at Ntonso's **Visitor Centre** (☎024 9547110; entry C8; ⏰9am-6pm Mon-Sat) (C8) and even create your own works; strips of fabric are sold for C40 and make a lovely keepsake.

The kente-weaving and cocoa-growing village of **Adanwomase** wins the Palme d'Or of ecotourism in Ghana. Villagers here have put a huge amount of effort into developing fun, informative tours about local culture and artistic traditions. The visitor centre offers two tours: one focusing on kente cloth, and the other on the village itself. There are direct tro-tros (minibuses; C8) from Kejetia station in Kumasi.



the fanciest and best-loved restaurants in Kumasi, Moti Mahal is a formal place serving some of the country's finest Indian cuisine in elegant, fiercely air-conditioned surroundings.

## ℹ Information

### INTERNET ACCESS

Most of the hotels offer free wi-fi.

**Unic Internet** (Bank Rd; per hr C5; ⏰8am-7pm) A good choice.

### MEDICAL SERVICES

Pharmacies are dotted all over town.

**Okomfo Anokye Teaching Hospital** (☎032-2022301; www.kathhsp.org; Bantama Rd) Kumasi's main public hospital with 700-plus beds.

### MONEY

There are half a dozen banks in the centre, all with ATMs and foreign-exchange facilities.

**Barclays** (Prempeh II Roundabout; ⏰8.30am-4.30pm Mon-Fri)

**Ecobank** (Harper Rd)

### TOURIST INFORMATION

**Ghana Tourist Authority** (☎0322-035848; National Cultural Centre; ⏰8am-5pm Mon-Fri) Staff can help arrange guided tours of the city and surrounding villages.

## ℹ Getting There & Away

### AIR

Kumasi airport is on the northeastern outskirts of town, about 2km from the centre. **Africa World Airlines** (www.flyawa.com.gh) and **Starbow** (www.flystarbow.com) both offer regular flights to Accra (one way starts around C260). A taxi from the centre to the airport costs about C20. Allow plenty of time because of the traffic.

### BUS

At the time of research **Intercity STC** (☎020 4314432, 020 4314491) had just starting operating after a period of inaction, though services were subject to cancellation. VIP and VVIP offer a more frequent service, leaving from **Asafo Station** (Asafo). **Metro Mass** operates fill-up-and-go services from its station on the Western bypass.

**Accra** C25, four hours, leaves when full; operated by VIP.

**Ouagadougou, Burkina Faso** C110 + 7,000 CFA, 15 hours, three weekly; operated by STC.

**Takoradi** C30, six hours, once daily; operated by STC.

**Tamale** C45, five hours, once daily; operated by STC.

### TRO-TRO

There are two main motor parks in Kumasi, each with its allocated destinations:

**Alaba station** (Alaba) Wa (C30, six hours), Tamale (C25, five hours)

**Asafo station** Cape Coast (C20, four hours), Accra (C25, four hours), Kunatase (C8, 45 minutes)

## ℹ Getting Around

Local tro-tros around Kumasi depart from **Kejetia station** (Kejetia Circle).

# Lake Bosumtwe & Abono

Formed by a huge meteorite, Lake Bosumtwe (also spelled Bosumtwi) resides in the impact crater. The 86m-deep lake is hugged by lush green hills in which you can hike, cycle and ride horses.

Located 38km southeast of Kumasi, the village of Abono is the gateway to Lake Bosumtwe; it is a popular weekend holiday spot for Kumasi residents, who come here to relax and swim. It's also a sacred site. The Ashanti people believe that their souls come here after death to bid farewell to the god Twi.

Foreign visitors will be charged C5 upon arriving in Abono.

## Activities

**The Green Ranch** HORSE RIDING

(☎020 2917058; Lake Bosumtwe; per hr C55, 10hr tour around lake C500) Enjoy the beauty of the lake and explore traditional villages on horseback, with this excellent, professional company.

## Sleeping & Eating

★**Cocoa Village Guesthouse** GUESTHOUSE $

(☎020 9891228, 020 8612675; www.cocoa-village.com; camping per person €5, dm €8, bungalow from €36; P) Bright and cosy bungalows, some handcrafted using traditional techniques, sit on a beautiful lawn with views down to the lake. A wonderful place to relax for a few days. You'll need a 4WD to negotiate the rough road to get here, or they can arrange a boat transfer from Abono (C50 one-way).

★**Lake Point Guesthouse** LODGE $

(☎024 3452922; Lake Bosumtwe; dm/d/tr C20/60/85; P ❄) Colourful huts and dorms are set on a hillside in dreamy tropical gardens at this sociable lodge. Across the small dirt road at the bottom of the property is a grassy lawn, leading down to a lakeside beach, the jumping-off point for kayaking adventures. The tin-roof bar and restaurant has a delicious daily changing menu (mains C30).

## Getting There & Away

You can sometimes find tro-tros (minibuses) travelling directly between Kumasi and Abono, but it's more likely you'll first need to go to Kuntanase (C8, 45 minutes), a larger town to the west of Abono, and then catch a shared taxi from there (C2, 15 minutes).

# THE NORTH

## Tamale

☎037 / POP 360,000

If the northern region is Ghana's breadbasket, Tamale is its kitchen. If you can take the heat, you'll discover a town with some good food, charm and a whole lot of soul. (If you can't, don't panic: nearby Mole National Park is generally cooler.)

Tamale's population is largely Muslim and there are several interesting mosques around town, notably on Bolgatanga Rd. The **National Culture Centre** (off Salaga Rd) is a lively place, with craft shops and regular dance and music performances.

### Tours

**Grassroot Tours Ghana** TOURS

(☎054 1668682; www.grassroottours.com) Runs excellent tours around the northern region, including to Mole National Park.

### Sleeping

**Clinton Lodge** GUESTHOUSE $

(☎026 2000000; www.clinton-lodge.com; d with fan/air-con & TV C40/80; P ❄ wi-fi) A great-value place that's popular with volunteers and aid workers, Clinton Lodge offers simple rooms with verandas, and good food – both Western and Ghanaian. It's a little bit out of the way, but staff can order taxis for you as well as help arrange trips to Mole National Park and beyond.

**Mash Lodge** HOTEL $

(☎020 6537534; s/d C150/250; P ❄ wi-fi) This solid budget offering has clean and simple rooms with TV, air-con and free wi-fi. There's a decent on-site restaurant or you can pop next door to **Wooden** (☎037-2028943; www.wooden-gh.com; Airport St; mains from around C30; P) for a livelier atmosphere.

**African Dream Hotel** GUESTHOUSE $$

(☎037-2091127, 024 3623179; www.africandreamhotel.com; Bolgatanga Rd; standard/executive d C240/270; P ❄ wi-fi) Set in pretty landscaped gardens complete with wandering chickens, African Dream offers charming, if slightly careworn, rooms as well as a decent restaurant and speedy wi-fi. The location, some 10km out of town, won't be for everyone, but friendly owner Abu Prince offers pick-ups and drop-offs from town and the airport. He can also arrange tours to Mole National Park and northern Ghana.

### Eating

**Chuck's Bar & Restaurant** INTERNATIONAL $$

(☎055 3997379, 055 4819346; Mariam Rd; mains from C35; ⏲5pm-1am Wed-Sat, 11am-midnight Sun) You won't see many locals in here, but as far as expat havens go, this is a good one. A wood-burning pizza oven produces excellent pizzas and the menu also includes pastas, burgers and decadent desserts. There's regular live music and events, and a popular Sunday brunch. The large beer garden is perfect to sink a cold drink or two.

**Luxury Catering Services** AFRICAN **$$**
(☎050 7463655; Jisonayili Rd; mains from C20; Ⓟ) A popular choice serving tasty local and Western food as well as a decent selection of wine and real coffee. The guinea fowl is particularly good.

**Swad Fast Food** INDIAN **$$**
(☎024 4712942, 037-2023588; Gumbihini Rd; mains C18-40; ⊙9am-10pm; Ⓟ) The name might not be a winner, but this place remains as popular as ever. The large garden is dotted with pot plants and visited by the odd wandering goat, and there's a huge menu featuring everything from authentic curries to pizzas to Ghanaian classics.

## ℹ Information

**Barclays** (Salaga Rd; ⊙8.30am-5pm Mon-Fri) Changes cash and travellers cheques; ATM.
**Stanbic** (Salaga Rd; ⊙8.30am-4.30pm Mon-Fri) Changes cash; ATM.
**Tamale Teaching Hospital** (☎037-2022458, 037-2022454; Salaga Rd) The main hospital in northern Ghana, 2km southeast of town.
**Vodaphone** (internet per hr C5; ⊙9am-10pm; 📶) The fastest connection in town (still pretty slow at busy times); it's right next to the towering radio mast near the Intercity STC bus station.

## ℹ Getting There & Away

**AIR**

The airport is about 20km north of town; a private taxi here costs around C40. **Starbow** (www.flystarbow.com) and **Africa World Airlines** (www.flyawa.com.gh) fly between Tamale and Accra from C242 one way.

**BUS & TRO-TRO**

Buses and tro-tros congregate around the Total petrol station and the radio mast in the centre of town. There are regular tro-tros to Bolgatanga (C10, three hours) and Wa (C15, six hours).

**Intercity STC** (www.stc.oyawego.com) buses go to Accra (C70, 12 hours, 6am daily), Kumasi (C40, six hours, 6am daily) and Takoradi (C58, 13 hours, 3pm Tuesday to Saturday). VVIP has a daily service to Accra (C80).

To get to Mole National Park take a tro-tro from the **main bus station** to Wa, and change at either Damongo or Larabanga. There is also a daily **Metro Mass** (www.metromass.com) bus to Wa, that leaves at 5am from the bus station behind the Total petrol station.

## ℹ Getting Around

Motorbikes, tuk-tuks, and share taxis jostle for business around Tamale's streets – a short trip should cost around C2.

# Mole National Park

With its swathes of saffron-coloured savannah, **Mole National Park** (☎027 7564444, 024 4316777; www.molemotelgh.com; adult C40, Ghanaian/foreign car C7/35) offers what must surely be the cheapest safaris in Africa. There are at least 300 species of bird and 94 species of mammal, including African elephants, kob antelopes, buffaloes, baboons and warthogs. Sightings of elephants are common from December to April, and you're guaranteed to see other mammals year-round.

The park headquarters offers excellent walking and driving safaris. You can arrange for an armed ranger to join you in your own 4WD, but you're not allowed to explore the park unaccompanied.

If you tire of elephant spotting, ecotourism venture Mognori Eco Village, on the borders of the park, offers canoe safaris, village tours and the chance to learn about local culture.

## ☞ Tours

**★Mole National Park Headquarters Safaris** SAFARI
(☎024 4316777; www.molemotelgh.com/fsafari.php; walking/jeep/night safaris per person C20/40/60) Two-hour walking safaris and jeep safaris take place daily at 7am and 3.30pm. Night safaris depart at 6pm. You can also rent a safari vehicle for private tours (C80 an hour for the jeep, C10 per person, per hour for the guide). Park rangers are happy to let you pool with other travellers.

**Mognori Eco Village** TOURS, SAFARI
(☎024 9507413, 024 6750646; canoe trip per 1-5 people C40, village tour per person C15, cultural performance per 1-4 people C70) Sitting right on the edge of Mole National Park (about 10km east of the park's visitor centre), the village of Mognori has become a flourishing ecotourism venture. Villagers here offer various activities: canoe safaris on the river, where you'll see monkeys, birds and crocodiles; village tours, on which you'll learn

about shea butter production and traditional medicine; and drumming and dancing performances.

## Sleeping & Eating

**Mole Motel** HOTEL $$
(027 7564444, 024 4316777; www.molemotelgh.com; Mole National Park; dm C60, s/d/tr with fan C80/140/210, s/d with air-con C180/220, bungalow with air-con C300; P) The setting – at the top of an escarpment, with a viewing platform overlooking plains teeming with wildlife – is fantastic. Mole Motel's ugly concrete building is at odds with the natural surroundings, though, and the rooms are underwhelming. There's a small pool and a reasonable restaurant, serving a mix of Ghanaian and international fare (mains C18 to C40).

★ **Zaina Lodge** LODGE $$$
(030-3938736, 054 0111504; www.zainalodge.com; s/d B&B US$180/240, s/d full-board incl game drives US$350/500; P) Luxury Zaina Lodge is a game changer for Mole, and one of the nicest places to stay in all of Ghana. Entrance gates, built in traditional northern mud-and-stick style, give way to a stunning triple-height lobby/lounge with vistas over the saffron savannah – views also shared by the elegant tented rooms, the terrace and the infinity pool.

## Getting There & Away

A charter taxi from Tamale will cost around C400 return. Grassroot Tours Ghana (p331) can take you for the day in a 4WD with a driver for C350 excluding fuel – the advantage being that a park ranger will be able to accompany you in the car, so you won't need to hire a park vehicle.

If coming by public transport from Tamale, you could get a tro-tro headed for Wa, and ask to be dropped at Damongo or Larabanga, from where you can get a taxi or motorbike to the park.

WORTH A TRIP

### LARABANGA

The tiny Muslim village of Larabanga, just 4km from Mole National Park, is most famous for its striking Sudanese-style mud-and-stick mosque, purported to be the oldest of its kind in Ghana. The town itself is hot, dusty and soporific; alleys wrap around traditional mud homes and bedraggled goats roam the streets.

On arrival in Larabanga you'll immediately be approached and asked to pay a visitors fee of C10 per person. Following this you'll be taken to the mosque for a quick tour and history lesson, though you are not allowed to go inside. After the tour you'll be invited to sign a guestbook and make a further donation.

From Tamale, any tro-tro (minibus or pick-up) headed to Wa can drop you at Larabanga. Or you could get the 5am Metro Mass bus from Tamale to Wa, which passes through the town.

# Bolgatanga

039 / POP 66,700

Bolgatanga – usually shortened to Bolga – was once the southernmost point of the ancient trans-Saharan trading route, running through Burkina Faso to Mali. Bolga is laid-back and a fine base to explore the surrounding area – and it's the last stop on the road to Burkina.

## Sights

**Bolgatanga Library** LIBRARY
Built by award-winning American architect J Max Bond Jr, Bolga's library is a stylish piece of 1960s modernist design.

**Chief's Pond** CROCODILE POND
(adult/student C15/10, camera fee C5; P) The pond's reptiles, which are held sacred by the local people, are reputed to be the friendliest in Africa. Local women even do their laundry in the pond while kids frolic in the water. Legend has it that this state of blissful cohabitation goes back to a pact the town's founders made with local crocodiles not to hurt each other. While we're not totally convinced, plenty of visitors do indeed manage to pose with crocs unharmed.

## Festivals & Events

**Bolgatanga International Crafts & Arts Fair** ART
(BICAF; 038-24468; www.facebook.com/Bolgatanga-International-Craft-and-Arts-Fair-BICAF-770519099638046; Dec) Showcases work by artisans from the Upper East region and across Ghana, with a handful of displays from elsewhere on the continent. The four-day event also features live bands.

## Sleeping & Eating

**Premier Lodge** GUESTHOUSE $
(Navrongo Rd; r from C100; P ❄ wi-fi) A good-value guesthouse with spotless (if basic) rooms with air-con and free wi-fi. A decent breakfast is included and home-cooked meals are sometimes available, given advance notice. It's a little out of town, but transport is easy to find.

**Nsamini Guesthouse** GUESTHOUSE $
(☎038-2023403, 027 7316606; off Navrongo Rd; r C60, without bathroom C30; P ❄) A popular choice, this cute courtyard set-up is one of Bolga's best budget buys. Rooms are clean, and Koffi, the affable owner, will make you feel at home. It's up a lane leading off Navrongo Rd.

**Swap Fast Food** INTERNATIONAL $
(☎024 5842397; Navrongo Rd, SSNIT Bldg; mains C20; ⏰10am-9pm; ❄) The outdoor terrace is lovely but if the heat is too much you can always retreat to the air-con dining room. The food is good and varied – the menu includes curries, *jollof rice,* pepper steak, fried noodles – but the service is very slow.

## Information

**Sirius Click Internet Café** (Black Star Hotel, Bazaar Rd; per hr C5; ⏰7.30am-9pm)
**Vodafone Internet Cafe** (Commercial St)

## Getting There & Away

Tro-tros to Tamale (C20, three hours) and Paga (C5, 40 minutes) leave from the motor park off Zuarungu Rd, past the police station.

The Intercity STC bus station is 500m south of the centre, on the road to Tamale. There is a daily service to Kumasi (C45, eight hours) and Accra (C80, 12 hours). The VIP/VVIP station is on Zuarangu Rd, and has a daily service to Tamale, Kumasi and Accra.

WORTH A TRIP

### WECHIAU HIPPO SANCTUARY

The much-hyped **Wechiau Hippo Sanctuary** (www.ghanahippos.com; C20) on the Black Volta River was initiated by local village chiefs in 1999. Hippos can usually be seen from November to March; once the rainy season (April to October) is underway, however, hippos disappear and the site becomes very hard to reach. Activities (C15 per person per hour) include river safaris, birdwatching, village tours and nature walks. Unless you have your own vehicle, you'll need to overnight at the sanctuary.



# THE NORTHWEST

## Wa

☎039 / POP 102,000

The sleepy capital of the Upper Northwest region is home to the Wa Na Palace, a stunning mud-and-stick mosque. There are few attractions otherwise but it has a friendly vibe and is a pleasant place to overnight before or after visiting Wechiau Hippo Sanctuary or to break the journey between Bobo-Dioulasso and Kumasi.

### Sleeping & Eating

**Blue Hill Hotel** GUESTHOUSE $
(☎039-2095525; Wa-Kumasi Rd; r from C150; P ❄) The rooms in this new hotel may look as if they were designed in the 1980s, but they are clean and spacious, with plenty of mod cons. There's also a good restaurant and a small bar.

**Tegbeer Catholic Guesthouse** GUESTHOUSE $
(☎039-2022375; s/d with fan C70/90, with air-con C90/110; P ❄) The Tegbeer Catholic Guesthouse, about 3km north of Wa, is an excellent option with clean, good rooms, a pretty garden and a nice on-site bar-restaurant (mains C15 to C25).

### Getting There & Away

There are regular tro-tros and buses to Wechiau (C5, 90 minutes), Larabanga (C10, 2½ hours) Tamale (C25, five hours), Hamale (C15, three hours). VIP and **Intercity STC** (www.stc.oyawego.com) both have a service to Accra (14 hours) and Kumasi (10 hours).

# UNDERSTAND GHANA

## Ghana Today

Once held up as an example of African growth, Ghana has faltered since 2013. A growing public deficit, high inflation and a weakening currency forced President John Dramani Mahama to turn to the International Monetary Fund (IMF) in 2015 for a bailout as world commodity prices took a nosedive.

While development continues apace in Accra, where wealthier Ghanaians and expats frequent an ever-expanding number of fancy restaurants and hotels, the picture is gloomy for most Ghanaians. Unemployment, public debt and corruption are all high.

The December 2016 presidential elections saw opposition candidate Nana Akufo-Addo beat incumbent Mahama, who conceded peacefully and immediately – a testament to Ghana's strong democratic traditions.

# History

Present-day Ghana has been inhabited since 4000 BC, filled by successive waves of migrants from the north and east. By the 13th century several kingdoms had developed, growing rich from the country's massive gold deposits and gradually expanding south along the Volta River to the coast.

## Power & Conflict

By the 16th century one of the kingdoms, the Ashanti, emerged as the dominant power, taking control of trade routes to the coast. Its capital, Kumasi, became a sophisticated urban centre, with facilities and services equal to those in Europe at the time. And it wasn't long until the Europeans discovered this African kingdom. First the Portuguese came prospecting around the coast; the British, French, Dutch, Swedish and Danish soon followed. They all built forts by the sea and traded slaves, gold and other goods with the Ashanti.

But the slave trade was abolished in the 19th century, and with it went the Ashanti domination. By that time the British had taken over the Gold Coast, as the area had come to be known, and began muscling in on Ashanti turf. This sparked several wars between the two powers, culminating in the British ransacking of Kumasi in 1874. The Gold Coast was soon a British colony.

## Independence & the Nkrumah Years

When Ghana finally won its independence in March 1957, Kwame Nkrumah, who had been the voicve for Ghanaian independence for more than a decade, became the first president of an independent African nation. His speeches, which denounced imperialism and talked about a free, united Africa, made him the darling of the pan-African movement.

But back home Nkrumah was not popular among traditional chiefs and farmers. Factionalism and regional interests created an opposition that Nkrumah tried to contain through repressive laws, and by turning Ghana into a one-party state.

Things were starting to unravel. Nkrumah expanded his personal bodyguard into an entire regiment, while corruption and reckless spending drove the country into serious debt. Nkrumah, seemingly oblivious to his growing unpopularity, made the fatal mistake of going on a state visit to China in 1966. While he was away his regime was toppled in an army coup. Nkrumah died six years later in exile in Guinea.

## The Rawlings Years

By 1979 Ghana was suffering food shortages and people were out on the streets demonstrating against the army fat cats. Enter Jerry Rawlings, a good-looking, charismatic, half-Scottish air-force pilot, who kept cigarettes behind his ear and spoke the language of the people. Nicknamed 'Junior Jesus', Rawlings captured the public's imagination with his calls for corrupt military rulers to be confronted and held accountable for Ghana's problems. The military jailed him for his insubordination, but his fellow junior officers freed him after they staged an uprising. Rawlings' Armed Forces Revolutionary Council (AFRC) then handed over power to a civilian government (after a general election).

The new president, Hilla Limann, was uneasy with Rawlings' huge popularity, and later accused him of trying to subvert constitutional rule. The AFRC toppled him in a coup in 1981, and this time Rawlings stayed in power for the next 15 years. During part of the 1980s, Ghana enjoyed Africa's highest economic growth rates.

## The Democratic Era

By 1992 Rawlings was under worldwide pressure to introduce democracy, so he lifted the 10-year ban on political parties and called a general election. Rawlings won the 1992 elections freely and fairly, with 60% of the vote. In 1996 he repeated this triumph in elections that were again considered free and fair. At much the same time, the appointment of Ghanaian Kofi Annan as UN secretary-general boosted national morale.

After eight years of Rawlings and the NDC (the constitution barred Rawlings from standing for a third term in the 2000 presidential elections), his nominated successor and former vice-president, Professor John Atta Mills, lost to Dr John Kufuor, leader of the well-established New Patriotic Party (NPP). Under the Kufuor administration, primary-school enrolment increased by 25% and many of Ghana's poor were granted access to free health care.

The 2008 election was widely regarded as a test of Ghana's ability to become a modern democracy. Atta Mills won by a slim margin and despite the tensions with NPP competitor Nana Akufo-Addo, the election passed without serious violence. After Atta Mills' unexpected death in July 2012, his vice president, John Dramani Mahama, took the reins, and won the 2012 general election.

## People of Ghana

Ghana's population of 28 million makes it one of the most densely populated countries in West Africa. Of this, population 44% are Akan, a grouping that includes the Ashanti (also called Asante), whose heartland is around Kumasi, and the Fanti, who fish the central coast and farm its hinterland. The Nzema, linguistically close to the Akan, fish and farm in the southwest. Distant migrants from present-day Nigeria, the Ga are the indigenous people of Accra and Tema. The southern Volta region is home to the Ewe.

In the north, the Dagomba heartland is around Tamale and Yendi. Prominent neighbours are the Gonja in the centre, Konkomba and Mamprusi in the far northeast, and, around Navrongo, the Kasena. The Sisala and Lobi inhabit the far northwest.

## Religion

Ghana is a deeply religious country and respect for religion permeates pretty much every aspect of life. You'll come across churches of every imaginable Christian denomination; even the smallest village can have two or three different churches. About 70% of Ghanaians are Christian. Pentecostal and Charismatic denominations are particularly active, as are the mainline Protestant and Catholic churches.

About 15% of the population is Muslim; the majority are in the north, though there are also substantial Muslim minorities in southern cities such as Accra and Kumasi.

Many Ghanaians also have traditional beliefs, notably in spirits and forms of gods who inhabit the natural world. Ancestor veneration is an important part of this tradition. Many people retain traditional beliefs alongside Christian or Muslim beliefs.

## The Arts

### Music

There's no doubt about it, Ghana's got rhythm. Highlife, a mellow mix of big-band jazz, Christian hymns, brass band and sailor sonnets, hit Ghana in the 1920s, and popular recordings include those by ET Mensah, Nana Ampadu and the Sweet Talks. Accra trumpeter ET Mensah formed his first band in the 1930s and went on to be crowned the King of Highlife, later performing with Louis Armstrong in Ghana.

WWII brought American swing to Ghana's shores, prompting the first complex fusion of Western and African music. Hiplife, a hybrid of rhythmic African lyrics poured over imported American hip-hop beats, has now been ruling Ghana since the early 1990s.

Gospel music is also big, as is reggae.

### Textiles

Kente cloth, with its distinctive basketwork pattern in garish colours, is Ghana's signature cloth. Originally worn only by Ashanti royalty, it is still some of the most expensive material in Africa. The cloth can be single-, double- or triple-weaved and the colour and design of the cloth worn are still important indicators of status and clan allegiance.

Kente is woven on treadle looms, by men only, in long thin strips that are sewn together. Its intricate geometric patterns are full of symbolic meaning while its orange-yellow hues indicate wealth.

# SURVIVAL GUIDE

## Directory A–Z

### ACCOMMODATION

If you're looking for a bargain, Ghana probably isn't it – hotels and hostels are generally expensive for what you get, and there are few quality budget options. Budget hotels don't often provide a top sheet, so pack a sleeping liner.

### CHILDREN

Aside from the daily struggle of getting them to swallow malaria tablets, travel with children in Ghana needn't be difficult. There are plenty of child-friendly restaurants in Accra, offering high chairs, kids' menus and even small play areas. Many of the larger hotels and beach resorts have a kids' pool and/or a playground and can provide cots or extra beds for children.

Narrow, uneven pavements and open drains mean that Ghana is not remotely buggy friendly, so bring a sling or infant backpack if you're travelling with a baby or toddler. Nappies are available in supermarkets and general stores throughout Ghana, though designated baby-change facilities are a rarity.

Ghanaian waters are rough, so it's best to stick to splashing in the surf, unless you are lucky enough to be at Lou Moon Lodge (p325), which has a sheltered beach with calm water, perfect for swimming.

### DANGERS & ANNOYANCES

Ghana has proved to be a stable and generally peaceful country. Take care of your valuables on beaches and avoid walking alone at night. If swimming, beware of strong currents; ask locals before diving in.

Bilharzia is present in many of Ghana's freshwater lakes and rivers, so take the necessary precautions, such as applying DEET repellent before going into the water.

### EMBASSIES & CONSULATES

The following are all in Accra.

**Australian High Commission** (Map p312; ☎030-2216400; www.ghana.embassy.gov.au; 2 Second Rangoon Close, Cantonments; ⏰8.30am-3pm Mon-Fri)

**British High Commission** (Map p312; ☎030-2213250; www.ukinghana.fco.gov.uk; Julius Nyerere Link, off Gamel Abdul Nasser Ave; ⏰9.30-11.30am Mon-Thu, 8.30-10.30am Fri)

**Burkinabé Embassy** (Map p312; ☎030-2221988; Nyadji Crescent, Asylum Down)

**Canadian High Commission** (Map p312; ☎030-2211521; www.canadainternational.gc.ca/ghana; 42 Independence Ave, Sankara Interchange; ⏰7.30am-4pm Mon-Thu, to 1pm Fri)

**Dutch Embassy** (Map p312; ☎030-2214350; www.netherlandsworldwide.nl/countries/ghana; 89 Liberation Rd, Ako Adjei Interchange; ⏰9am-4.30pm Mon-Thu, 9am-3pm Fri)

**French Embassy** (Map p312; ☎030-2214550; www.ambafrance-gh.org; Presidential Dr; ⏰8am-noon Mon-Fri)

**German Embassy** (Map p312; ☎030-2211000; www.accra.diplo.de; 6 Kenneth Kaunda Rd, North Ridge)

**Ivorian Embassy** (Map p312; ☎030-774611; Naa Amponsua St, Osu)

**Togolese Embassy** (Map p312; ☎030-2777950; 4th Circular Rd)

**US Embassy** (Map p312; ☎030-2741000; http://ghana.usembassy.gov; 4th Circular Rd)

### SLEEPING PRICE RANGES

The following prices refer to a double room with bathroom. Unless otherwise stated, breakfast is included in the price.

**$** less than US$70

**$$** US$70–150

**$$$** more than US$150

### EMERGENCY & IMPORTANT NUMBERS

| | |
|---|---|
| Ghana's country code | ☎233 |
| Ambulance | ☎193 |
| Fire | ☎192 |
| Police | ☎191 |

### FOOD

Fiery sauces and oily soups are the mainstay of Ghanaian cuisine and are usually served with a starchy staple like rice, *fufu* (cooked and mashed cassava, plantain or yam) or *banku* (fermented maize meal).

Other cuisines, particularly Indian and Chinese, are widely available throughout the country. Accra's ever-evolving dining scene offers everything from top-class sushi to gourmet burgers.

About the most common dish you'll find in Ghana is groundnut stew, a warming, spicy dish cooked with liquefied groundnut paste, ginger and either fish or meat. Palm-nut soup (fashioned from tomatoes, ginger, garlic and chilli pepper, as well as palm nut) takes its bright red colour from palm oil. *Jollof rice* is a spicy dish cooked with a blend of tomatoes and onion and usually served with meat. *Red-red* is a bean stew normally served with fried plantain.

### EATING PRICE RANGES

The following price ranges refer to a main course:

**$** less than C20

**$$** C20–50

**$$$** more than C50

## INTERNET ACCESS

You can get online pretty much anywhere in Ghana these days. Most hotels and many restaurants offer wi-fi, all mobile phone networks have 3G and there are internet cafes in every town and city (connection costs C5 to C10 per hour).

## LGBTIQ TRAVELLERS

Homosexuality is illegal in Ghana and attitudes towards gays and lesbians are for the most part conservative. In many instances same-sex couples will not be allowed to share a room.

## MONEY

**ATMs** Virtually everywhere, with almost all accepting Visa (Stanbic's taking MasterCard and Maestro).

**Changing money** The best currencies to bring are US dollars, UK pounds and euros, in that order. Exchange bureaus are found in most major towns. They give lower exchange rates for small US$ denominations, so pack your $50 and $100 notes.

**Credit cards** Midrange and top-end hotels tend to accept credit cards, but at a surcharge.

**Tipping** Not common in chop houses or cheap eateries, but more expected in upscale venues (a tip of 10% to 15% should suffice). Porters or bag handlers at the airport and bus stations will often expect or ask for a tip. A cedi or two should be fine.

**Travellers cheques** Barclays is the only bank to exchange travellers cheques; there is a maximum of US$250 per transaction.

### Exchange Rates

| | | |
|---|---|---|
| Australia | A$1 | C3 |
| Canada | C$1 | C3.15 |
| Euro zone | €1 | C4.50 |
| Japan | ¥100 | C3.70 |
| New Zealand | NZ$1 | C2.80 |
| US | US$1 | C4.10 |
| UK | UK£1 | C5.30 |

For current exchange rates see www.xe.com.

## OPENING HOURS

**Administrative buildings** 8am to 2pm or so; embassies tend to keep similar hours.

**Banks** 8am to 5pm Monday to Friday; some additionally run until noon on Saturday.

**Markets** 7am to 5pm; in predominately Muslim areas, Friday is quieter; in Christian areas, it's Sunday.

**Shops** 9am to 5pm or 6pm every day except Sunday, when only large stores open.

## POST

Accra's main **post office** (p317) is in Ussher Town, but your post will get to its destination much more quickly if you mail it from Kotoka International Airport.

## PUBLIC HOLIDAYS

**New Year's Day** 1 January

**Independence Day** 6 March

**Good Friday** March/April

**Easter Monday** March/April

**Labour Day** 1 May

**May Bank Holiday** 1st Monday in May

**Africa Unity Day** 25 May

**Republic Day** 1 July

**Founders Day** 21 September

**Christmas Day** 25 December

**Boxing Day** 26 December

Ghana also celebrates Muslim holidays, which change dates every year.

## TELEPHONE

➡ Mobile (cell) phones áre ubiquitous in Ghana and the network coverage is virtually universal and excellent value.

➡ If you have an unlocked phone, SIM cards (C10) can be picked up in shopping centres and communication centres.

➡ MTN, Vodafone, Tigo and Airtel are the main networks; all have 3G.

## TOURIST INFORMATION

As a rule, tourist information is pretty useless in Ghana, with staff working in tourist offices having little understanding of what travellers need. The Ghana Tourism Authority (p317) has an office in Accra, and the brand new Accra Tourist Information Centre (p317) looks like a good bet.

**No Worries Ghana** (www.noworriesghana.com) Published by the North American Women's Association, this guide (both paper and electronic) is more targeted at people moving to rather than travelling to Ghana; nonetheless, the dozens of eating, drinking, and entertainment listings as well as the information on shipping, transport and so on is very useful.

**Touring Ghana** (www.touringghana.com) Ghana's official tourism portal; worth a look for inspiration and general information.

### VISAS

Visas are required by everyone except Ecowas (Economic Community of West African States) nationals. Visas upon arrival are rarely issued.

Though it's technically possible to pick up a visa upon arrival, they only get granted in rare cases so it is highly advisable you get one ahead of travelling. Single-entry three-month visas (US$60) and multiple-entry six-month visas (US$100) are standard. You can get a visa extension at the Immigration Office (p317) in Accra near the Sankara Interchange.

#### Burkina Faso

The embassy (p337) issues visas for three months (C146), usually in 24 hours. You need three photos and a yellow-fever certificate. Three-month tourist visas are also available at the border at Dakola, costing CFA94,000.

#### Côte d'Ivoire

A three-month visa costs €50 and requires a hotel confirmation. See full list of requirements at www.snedai.com.

#### Togo

The embassy (p337) issues visas for one month on the same day. Alternatively, you can get a visa at the border at Aflao (CFA15,000), but it's only valid for seven days and you'll need to extend it in Lomé.

> **PRACTICALITIES**
>
> **Electricity** 230V and three-pin British-style plugs are used. Power cuts are frequent.
>
> **Newspapers** Accra's best dailies are *Daily Graphic* (www.graphic.com.gh) and *Ghanaian Chronicle* (www.thechronicle.com.gh).
>
> **Radio** Local Ghanaian stations include the excellent Joy FM (news and music; 99.7FM), Choice FM (102.3) and Gold FM (90.5). BBC World Service is listened to widely; in Accra it's 101.3FM.
>
> **TV** Ghana's biggest TV stations are GTV, Metro TV and TV3. Satellite TV is available in almost all top-end and many midrange hotels.
>
> **Weights & measures** Ghana uses the metric system.

## Getting There & Away

### AIR

#### Airports & Airlines

- Every major European airline flies to Accra; Emirates now also flies daily to Dubai, opening a host of easy connections to the Asia-Pacific.
- There are direct flights to the US East Coast.
- You'll find plenty of direct flights to other parts of Africa, including South Africa, Kenya, Ethiopia, Egypt, Morocco and most neighbouring West African countries.

A US$50 passenger service charge is included in the price of international flights.

### BORDER CROSSINGS

Ghana has land borders with Côte d'Ivoire to the west, Burkina Faso to the north and west, and Togo to the east. Crossing is generally straightforward. The main border crossings:

**Burkina Faso** Paga–Dakola and Hamale–Ouessa

**Côte d'Ivoire** Elubo–Noe, Sunyani–Agnibilékrou and Bole–Ferkessédougou

**Togo** Aflao–Lomé, Ho–Kpalimé and Wli–Kpalimé

Border crossings are normally open 6am to 6pm. Visas are essential to enter each of these countries.

#### Burkina Faso

- Direct Intercity STC buses run to Ouagadougou from Accra (C150 + CFA1000, 24 hours) and Kumasi (C110 + CFA1000, 18 hours) three times a week.
- From Paga, there are frequent tro-tros (minibuses) to Bolgatanga (C4, 40 minutes); on the Burkina side, you'll find plenty of onward transport to Pô and Ouagadougou.
- From Wa get a tro-tro to Hamale. On the Burkina side, you'll find transport to Diebougou and then Bobo-Dioulasso.

#### Côte d'Ivoire

- Intercity STC buses run daily to Abidjan from Accra (C75 + CFA7000, 12 hours) and Kumasi (C70 + CFA7000).
- Otherwise you'll find tro-tros running between Takoradi and Elubo (three hours), from where you can cross into Côte d'Ivoire and find onward transport to Abidjan.

#### Togo

- The easiest way to cross into Togo is to catch a bus or a tro-tro to Aflao, pass the border on foot (visas CFA15,000) and catch a taxi on the other side to central Lomé.
- Overlanders may prefer to cross at the less hectic Wli border post near Hohoe.

## Getting Around

### AIR

**Starbow Airlines** (www.flystarbow.com) and **Africa World Airlines** (www.flyawa.com.gh) operate domestic flights in Ghana.

### STREET SIGNS & NAME CHANGES

The government is part way through a street-naming project, with the aim of giving every street in Ghana a visible street sign. At the same time, many existing street names are changing. While we have endeavored to mark as many changes as possible, it is likely that more names will have changed by the time you read this.

➡ There are several daily flights from Accra to Kumasi (45 minutes), Takoradi (35 minutes) and Tamale (1¼ hours). They tend to be relatively cheap and a huge time saver when travelling north.

### BUS

➡ Buses are preferable to tro-tros (minibuses) for long journeys as they tend to be more comfortable and reliable.

➡ **Intercity STC** (www.stc.oyawego.com/) is Ghana's main long-haul bus company.

➡ Other relevant bus companies for travellers include **VIP** (www.vipbusgh.com), which runs half-hourly buses between Accra and Kumasi; **VVIP**, which runs north of Accra to Kumasi and Tamale; and **Metro Mass** (www.metromass.com), which runs local services in various parts of the country.

➡ It's wise to book in advance as tickets get snapped up fast on the more popular routes.

➡ Large rucksacks or suitcases are charged a flat fee. Baggage handlers will expect a tip for loading your bags.

### CAR & MOTORCYCLE

➡ Driving is on the right in Ghana.

➡ Most main roads are in pretty good condition, though most secondary roads are unsealed.

➡ You will need an international driver's licence.

➡ Fuel is inexpensive at around C4 per litre.

➡ Hiring a car with a driver is a good option if you're short on time; travel agencies can usually arrange this. Depending on the distance, car and driver experience, factor in anything from US$100 to US$150 per day, plus fuel. Ghana Car Rentals (p318) is an excellent, professional company with reasonably priced vehicles.

### LOCAL TRANSPORT

#### Taxi

➡ Within towns and on some shorter routes between towns, shared taxis are the usual form of transport. They run on fixed routes, along which they stop to pick up and drop off passengers. Fares are generally very cheap (C1 to C2).

➡ Private taxis don't have meters and rates are negotiable. It's best to ask a local in advance for the average cost between two points.

➡ Taxis can be chartered for an agreed period of time, anything from one hour to a day, for a negotiable fee.

➡ Uber officially arrived in Accra in September 2016.

#### Tro-tro

Tro-tro is a catch-all category that embraces any form of public transport that's not a bus or taxi. Generally they're minibuses.

➡ Tro-tros cover all major and many minor routes.

➡ They don't work to a set timetable but leave when full.

➡ Fares are set but may vary on the same route depending on the size and comfort (air-con) of the vehicle.

➡ There is generally an additional luggage fee.

➡ The area where tro-tros and buses congregate is called, interchangeably, lorry park, motor park or station.

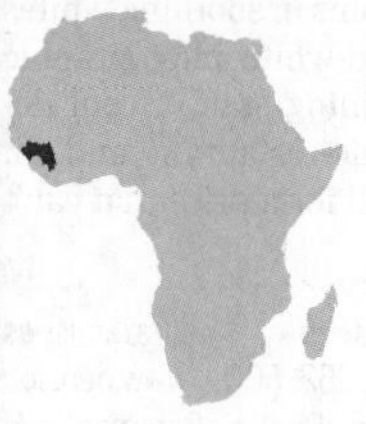

# Guinea

☎224 / POP 11.8 MILLION

**Includes ➡**



## Best Places to Eat

➡ Restaurant Îles des Joies (p345)

➡ Hotel SIB (p348)

➡ Le Sogue Hôtel (p346)

## Best Places to Sleep

➡ Pension Les Palmiers (p342)

➡ Hotel M'lys (p342)

➡ Hotel SIB (p348)

➡ Hôtel Tata (p347)

➡ Le Sogue Hôtel (p346)

## Why Go?

Imagine you're travelling on smooth highways, and then get tempted by a dusty turn-off signed Adventure. Well, that turn-off is Guinea. Little known to most of the world, this is a land of surprising beauty, from the rolling mountain plateau of Fouta Djalon to wide Sahelian lands and thick forests. Overland drivers have long been drawn here for the challenge of steering their vehicles over rocks and washed-out paths. Nature lovers lose themselves on long hikes past plunging waterfalls, proud hills and tiny villages; or by tracking chimpanzees through sticky rainforest. But the best thing about Guinea is that almost nobody else bothers to take this turn-off – meaning you'll likely have the country to yourself.

Devastatingly, the country was caught up in the West Africa Ebola outbreak in 2014. The country was officially declared Ebola-free in June 2016, and related travel restrictions were lifted, meaning now is the time to explore.

## When to Go

### Conakry

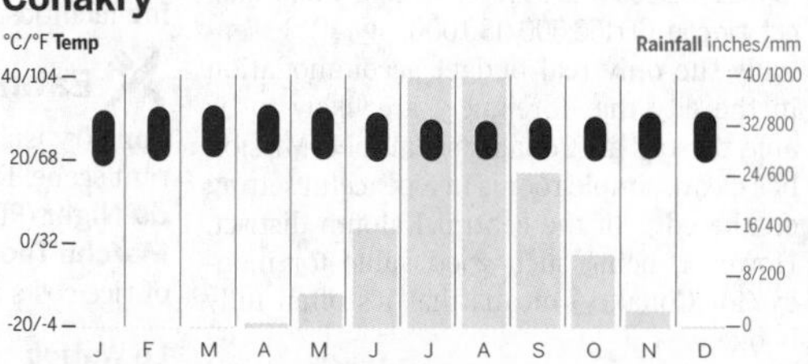


**Nov & Dec** Best time to visit, after the rains and before the dusty harmattan winds.

**Apr** Very hot everywhere and not a pleasant month to travel.

**Jun–Sep** Rainy season. Roads turn into mud rivers and are almost impassable. Avoid!

# CONAKRY

☎4 / POP 1.6 MILLION

Conakry doesn't try to please its guests, and yet, slowly, many are eventually won over by its charms. There aren't many sights in this dusty (and/or muddy, depending on time of year) mess of crumbling buildings, pollution, rubbish and traffic jams, but there is plenty of buzz. From the pungent fishing port of Boulbinet and the street kitchens of Coronthie to the containers-turned-shops of Taouyah, this city goes about its business noisily and with ingenuity, proud and unruffled by the visitor's gaze.

## Sights

**★Centre d'Art Acrobatique Keita Fodeba** CULTURAL CENTRE
(☎624 789059; Dixinn Stadium; ⊙10am-2pm Mon-Fri) FREE The Centre d'Art Acrobatique Keita Fodeba is perhaps the single most amazing experience in Guinea. Every weekday morning scores of acrobats spin, twirl and flip through routines that have made them the envy of circuses the world over. As good as the acrobats are, it's the contortionists who steal the show. When they bend themselves 180 degrees the wrong way you can only wonder if they actually have backbones or if they are in fact jellyfish.

**Musée National** MUSEUM
(7th Blvd, Sandervalia; GFr10,000; ⊙9am-6pm Tue-Fri, 10am-5.30pm Sat & Sun) The Musée National has a modest collection of masks, statues and musical instruments, many of which are used in religious or mystical ceremonies.

## Sleeping

**Maison d'Accueil** HOTEL $
(☎621 752 939; Rte du Niger, Kaloum; r with/without air-con GFr160,000/130,000; P❄) Essentially the only real budget accommodation in the city that foreigners are likely to be able to stay at. Conakry's Catholic Mission has clean, simple rooms in a peaceful setting on the edge of the central Kaloum district. However, being such good value for money (for Conakry) means that it's often fully booked.

**★Hotel M'lys** HOTEL $$
(☎624 299 369; www.hotelmlys.com; Quartier Almamya, Kaloum; r from GFr705,000; ❄📶) This small, central place is turning the Conakry hotel scene on its head. Gone are drowsy overpriced rooms and lacklustre service. In are business smart rooms in soothing whites and browns, back-and-white photographic art, warm and welcoming staff, a cool delicious lipstick-red cafe-restaurant and an outdoor garden bar. All for a price that can't be knocked.

**★Pension Les Palmiers** GUESTHOUSE $$
(Chez Ghussein; ☎622 352 500; www.pensionlespalmiers.com; Rte de Donka, Ratoma; s/d €70/75; P❄📶🏊) The doily-adorned couches, cute living room and caring owners make this one a five-heart guesthouse, if not a five-star hotel, and as such it seems to attract a diverse collection of business people, aid workers and the occasional tourist. The rooms are modern, and polished, with comfortable beds, reliable electricity, internet connections and plenty of hot water.

**★Noom Conakry** DESIGN HOTEL $$$
(☎626 333 333; www.conakry.noomhotels.com; Quartier Ignace Deen, Kaloum; s/d from GFr2,050,000/2,190,000; P❄📶🏊) The brand-new, boat-shaped, Noom Conakry is where the city puts on its most sophisticated face. It's a face that comes with an infinity pool overlooking the ocean, several top-quality bars and restaurants, tree sculpture art and huge black-and-white photos mounted on the walls. And all that's before you've even entered one of the very swish rooms…

**Riviera Royal** HOTEL $$$
(☎664 223 302; www.rivieraroyalhotel.com; off Corniche Nord; r from €156; P❄📶🏊) More affordable than many of the city's top-end hotels, the Riviera Royal has a tropical-garden vibe with rooms in small blocks scattered under the palm trees. There's a huge pool, bar, restaurant, nightclub and various sporting facilities.

## Eating

Conakry isn't blessed with a diverse restaurant scene. For good street food, try **Marché du Niger** (Rte du Niger, Kaloum; ⊙6am-5pm) or **Marché Taouyah** (⊙6am-4pm), where bowls of rice costs around GFr20,000.

**Le Waffou** AFRICAN $
(☎664 337 547; off Rte de Donka, Kipé; mains GFr25,000-40,000; ⊙noon-midnight) You can buy Ivorian *attiéké* (grated cassava) on many a Conakry street corner, but this thatch-roof eatery prepares it fresh and does it better than most. Occasional live bands at weekends.

## Guinea Highlights

**1 Îles de Los** (p346) Stretching out on palm-fringed strands, sipping fresh coconut juice.

**2 Fouta Djalon** (p346) Rambling through the mountains and swimming in the waterfalls of this majestic plateau.

**3 Bossou** (p350) Coming face to face with cheeky, alcohol-drinking chimps during a forest walk.

**4 Conakry** (p342) Hopping through the capital's dubious dives, getting drunk on some of West Africa's best live music.

**5 Dalaba** (p347) Enjoying the endless views and soaking up the colonial ambience.

**6 Parc National du Haut Niger** (p350) Helping a chimp in need and watching for colourful birds in one of West Africa's last tropical dry-forest ecosystems.

**7 Centre d'Art Acrobatique Keita Fodeba** (p342) Bending over backwards in awe while watching some of Africa's best acrobats spin through their routines.

**Le Damier** BAKERY $

(☎655 800 000; www.damier-conakry.com; Rte du Niger, Kaloum; cakes GFr40,000, sandwiches & pizzas GFr60,000, ice cream from GFr15,000; ⏲6.30am-6pm Mon-Sat) Le Damier started over a quarter of a century ago as a simple, French-style patisserie and today still sells by far the most authentically French breads, tarts and croissants in Guinea. It's also diversified into high-class French chocolate and simple sandwiches and pizza-style meals as well as delicious ice creams.

## Conakry

## Conakry

**Top Sights**
1 Centre d'Art Acrobatique Keita Fodeba ........ C2

**Sights**
2 Musée National ........ B2

**Sleeping**
3 Hotel M'lys ........ B1
4 Maison d'Accueil ........ C1
5 Noom Conakry ........ C2
6 Riviera Royal ........ B3

**Eating**
7 Avenue ........ C3
8 Le Damier ........ B1
9 Restaurant Îles des Joies ........ A2

**Drinking & Nightlife**
10 Club Obama ........ A2
11 MLS ........ C3

**Entertainment**
12 Centre Culturel Franco-Guinéen ........ C3
13 Faga Faga Fougou Espace Culturel ........ B4
14 l'Echangeur ........ D1

**Shopping**
15 Marché du Niger ........ B1

**Information**
16 British Embassy ........ C3
17 French Embassy ........ A1
18 German Embassy ........ A1
19 Guinea-Bissau Embassy ........ D1
20 Ivoirian Embassy ........ A1
21 Liberian Embassy ........ D1
22 Malian Embassy ........ C2
23 Senegalese Embassy ........ A2
24 Sierra Leone Embassy ........ D1

**★Restaurant Îles des Joies** SEAFOOD $$
(☎664 385 652; 4th Ave, Kaloum; mains GFr75,000-100,000; ⏰noon-11pm Mon-Sat) Our favourite restaurant in downtown Conakry, this very simple, family-run place is hidden down a dirty side-alley and, at first, looks rather uninviting, but don't fret. The seafood served up here – which is cooked so that it's slightly crunchy on the outside and lush and soft on the inside – is as fresh and delicious as can be.

**Avenue** BURGERS $$
(☎628 682 525; www.avenueconakry.com; Commercial Center Residence 2000, Coléah; mains GFr85,000-105,000; ⏰9am-10.30pm) Classy, expat-popular, American-style diner serving oversized burgers stuffed with cheddar cheese, pickles and salads. It also does fish 'n' chips and pizzas. It's currently one of the 'in' places to eat in Conakry.

## Drinking & Nightlife

**MLS** CLUB
(☎655 888 811; Pl 8 Novembre, Coléah; ⏰6pm-2am Mon-Sat) This very chic place is in a league of its own, subtly styled in polished wood, soft fabrics, spotlighting and handmade furniture. And with a great sound system and good resident and visiting DJs to boot it's got to be one of West Africa's classiest clubs. There's also a casino and lounge bar within the same complex.

**Club Obama** BAR
(Port de Boulbinet, Kaloum; ⏰10am-11pm) Perched on stilts out in the water, this cute thatch-and-wood bar covered in fish skeleton decorations is a great place for a sunset drink. Whether the name will now change to Trump Club remains to be seen…

## Entertainment

Conakry is one of the live-music capitals of West Africa and there are dozens of live-music venues, ranging from down-and-dirty dives to big stadiums and refined cultural centres.

**★Faga Faga Fougou Espace Culturel** CONCERT VENUE
(Corniche Sud, Tumbo; entry from GFr15,000) This is one of the most exciting live-music venues in Conakry. The ocean-side stage hosts a diverse array of local and West African groups performing anything from rap to world music to Afro-funk. The atmosphere is very chilled and welcoming and there are performances most nights, except Sundays. Entry fees vary depending on who is playing.

**★Centre Culturel Franco-Guinéen** ARTS CENTRE
(☎621 904 054; www.ccfg-conakry.org; Pont du 8 Novembre, Tumbo; ⏰8.30am-8pm) French cultural centres in Africa usually put on diverse and exciting events, art-house films, world music concerts and exhibitions, and this one is no exception. As well as a busy cultural calender there's also a library. Closing times vary depending on what events are taking place that evening.

**l'Echangeur** CONCERT VENUE
(☎622 322 390; Rte de Donka, Dixinn II; ⏰11am-2am Mon-Sat) This humble bar looks completely unspectacular, yet it's where many of Guinea's biggest stars jam at the weekend, in a space overflowing with good vibes and cold beer. Bring a few Guinea francs to 'spray' the musicians in thanks for the praises they'll sing. On weekdays it's just a chilled-out bar.

## Information

### DANGERS & ANNOYANCES

Incidents of military aggression and extortion are much rarer than in years past, but they do still happen. Always carry your passport and vaccination certificates with you, especially if you're out on the town after 11pm – *gendarmerie* (police) checkpoints are set up at Pont du 8 Novembre and near the UK embassy (Résidence 2000), and you will usually have to show your papers at night. If everything is in order, you shouldn't have to pay any 'fines', though you might have to discuss this a little with the often intimidating soldiers.

Plenty of pickpockets roam Marché Madina, Marché Niger and Ave de la République.

### MEDICAL SERVICES

Most medical facilities are pretty basic. If something is seriously wrong get yourself to Dakar or home. There are some well-stocked pharmacies along Ave de la République.

**Clinique Pasteur** (5th Blvd, Kaloum; ⏰8.30am-6pm Mon-Sat) Fairly good for malaria tests and minor injuries.

**Hôpital Ambrose Paré** (☎631 401 040; www.cliniqueambroisepare.com; Dixinn) Considered the best in Guinea, though for anything really serious it's still best to get evacuated out of the country.

### MONEY

**Bicigui** (Ave de la République, Kaloum; ⏰8.30am-5pm Mon-Fri, 8.30am-noon Sat)

> **ARRIVING IN CONAKRY**
>
> There's no official public transport to and from Conakry International Airport (p354). Take one of the taxis waiting just beyond the gates. Expect to pay GFr100,000 to Ratoma and GFr200,000 to the city centre during daylight hours and a little more at night. There is no pre-booked taxi service.

This main bank branch claims to change travellers cheques, but doesn't always do so. The 24-hour ATM takes Visa and Mastercard.

## Getting There & Away

Conakry has a number of *gares routières* for share taxis:

**Gare Routière Bambeto** The main station, with daily taxis to Kankan (GFr200,000, two days), Kissidougou (GFr150,000, 1½ days), N'zérékoré (GFr275,000, two days) and Labé (GFr95,000, 10 hours). Internationally, there are daily taxis to Bamako (Mali; GFr300,000, two days), Dakar (Senegal; GFr500,000, three days), Freetown (Sierra Leone; GFr130,000, nine hours) and Monrovia (Liberia; GFr480,000, three days). Taxis to Abidjan (Côte d'Ivoire; GFr650,000, four days) leave twice weekly.

**Gare Routière Madina** Taxis to destinations throughout Guinea. Sample fares include Kankan (GFr200,000, two days), Kissidougou (GFr150,000, 1½ days), N'zérékoré (GFr275,000, two days) and Labé (GFr95,000, 10 hours).

**Gare Routière Matam** (Taxis to southern destinations within Guinea as well as Bissau (Guinea-Bissau; GFr200,000, two days).

## Getting Around

Taxis cost GFr2500 per 3km zone. Minibuses (*magbanas*) are a bit cheaper but much slower.

# Îles de Los

A 30-minute boat ride off Conakry, the Îles de Los are a small huddle of palm-fringed islands that tempt with tropical beach dreams. There are three main islands (and a couple of rocky islets) though only two, Île de Kassa and Île Room, are kitted-out for visitors. All have beautifully forested, bird-filled interiors that reward some gentle exploration. During the dry season (October to May), the islands are a very popular weekend getaway for expats and well-to-do locals escaping Conakry. However, all's not perfect here – debris from the mountains of plastic and other rubbish that utterly blankets the Conakry shoreline drifts across to many of the island beaches in the currents. Even so, a visit here is a hugely welcome relief from the chaos of Conakry.

## Sleeping

There are a couple of places to stay on both Île de Kassa and Île Room, but nothing on the other islands.

★**Le Sogue Hôtel** HOTEL **$$**
(☎657 104 355; lenstonee@aol.com; d GFr700,000) On a short stretch of private white-sand beach (entry for nonguests GFr15,000) that's swept clean every morning, this gorgeous hotel might well be the nicest place to stay in all of Guinea. The rooms are set atop granite boulders in among the trees and are subtly decorated in ocean-blue tones.

## Getting There & Away

Public pirogues head to the islands from Conakry's Port de Boulbinet. It takes about 30 minutes to Île de Kassa, the nearest island. Pirogues leave when full and there's more transport at weekends. Most of the hotels on the islands also organise weekend transfers in faster, safer boats with life jackets.

# FOUTA DJALON

Green rolling hills, balmy temperatures, forest-filled valleys and gushing waterfalls make the Fouta Djalon region one of West Africa's most enchanting corners. But this undulating, kilometre-high plateau isn't just pleasing to the eye, it's also superb hiking country, where experienced local guides can take you exploring along a web of walking trails snaking between interesting villages and impressive natural sites.

# Mamou

Mamou, the gateway to the Fouta Djalon, is a dusty junction town and transport hub perched on a hill just above the scorching plains.

For travellers there's little in the way of attractions but there is every chance you might end up here for a night as you travel between Conakry and the Fouta Djalon or southern parts of Guinea.

## Sleeping & Eating

**Acacia White House** GUESTHOUSE $
(☎655 295 414; road to Dabola; r GFr250,000; P ❄) It's hard to go wrong with this very friendly and helpful family-run guesthouse which has four spotless rooms and 24-hour electricity thanks to a back-up generator.

**Hôtel le Relais de Mamou** HOTEL $
(☎660 315 944; road to Dabola, Quartier Tambassa; r from GFr250,000; P ❄) This impressive and fairly new place offers good-value rooms that are large and bright, with reliable evening electricity and hot showers. Some of the pricier rooms have sofas and desks. Downstairs is a relaxed bar-restaurant.

## Information

There are a couple of banks with ATMs in the town centre.

## Getting There & Away

There are two *gares routières:*

**Conakry Gare Routière** (Conakry Rd) Taxis to Conakry (GFr63,000, eight hours) go from a parking area just to the west of the town centre.

**Gare Routière** (Dalaba Rd) Bush taxis go from the main station at the northern end of town to the following destinations:

**Dabola** GFr45,000, 2½ hours.

**Dalaba** GFr20,000, 1½ hours.

**Faranah** GFr60,000, 2½ hours.

**Kankan** GFr110,000, five hours.

**Kindia** GFr37,000, two hours.

**Labé** GFr45.000, three hours.

# Dalaba

POP 6500

In days past French colonialists would take any opportunity they could get to leave sweaty Conakry behind and decamp to the cool, clear climes of the delightful hill town of Dalaba (altitude 1200m). Today only a couple of dilapidated colonial buildings and one or two hotels redolent in yesteryear atmosphere remain, but the things that first attracted the French to Dalaba – the eternal spring-like climate, the inspiring views down to the lowlands and the fabulous walking – all still entice, and taken together they make Dalaba the most pleasant town in Guinea.

WORTH A TRIP

### FOUTA DJALON HOTELS

The bungalows at **Hôtel Tata** (☎657 926 150; www.hoteltata.com; r GFr250,000; P 📶), with their woven, patterned roofs and colourful bedspreads, are as pretty as the tropical birds that fill the leafy garden each morning. There's a relaxed bar-restaurant with a real wood-fired pizza oven (pizzas from GFr70,000). Camping (GFr100,000) is also available.

**Hôtel Sister** (☎628 176 528; r GFr200,000; P), a Guinean-Welsh–run place on the edge of town, is the exception to Pita's otherwise grotty offering of hotels. Pretty pink rooms have a pleasingly twee look and feel to them, and are set around a large courtyard. There's hot water and 24-hour electricity. Yes, you read that right! Solar panels in the garden ensure its operation (after a while in Guinea you'll understand how wonderful that is!)

## Sights

**Jardins Auguste Chevalier** GARDENS
(GFr20,000; ⏰8am-6pm) Established by a French botanist in 1908 to discover what European and Asian plants would flourish in Guinea, the Jardins Auguste Chevalier offer an enjoyable place to unwind in the shade of huge century-old oaks and forests of bamboo. The gardens are 7km north of Dalaba, just off the Pita road and close to the village of Tinka.

**Chutes de Ditinn** WATERFALL
One of Guinea's tallest – and certainly one of its most beautiful – waterfalls takes a 120m drop straight down off a cliff. Ditinn village is 35km from Dalaba and the falls are 5km further on from the village (a 20-minute walk). A private taxi will charge around GFr150,000 for the round-trip, with waiting time.

**Villa Sili** HISTORIC BUILDING
(GFr10,000) The old French governor's residence, Villa Sili (1936), which was for many years almost on the verge of collapse, has been recently renovated and is a fun place to explore. Look out for the horse statues in the garden. There are no set opening hours but the guardian will, as if by magic, appear and open up for you.

### HIKING THE FOUTA DJALON

With over 16 years' experience in organising hiking adventures in the Fouta Djalon for tourists, as well as researching new routes, **Fouta Trekking** (☎622 912 024; www.foutatrekking.org; one-day trek GFr200,000, overnight trek per person per day €31) has identified the best hikes, cliffs, mountains and waterfalls in the area and developed a number of superb hiking circuits that many people find to be the highlight of their trip to Guinea.

A one man trekking, entertainment and hosting show, **Hassan Bah** (☎622 457 553; guided tour per half-/full-day GFr150,000/250,000) has been leading tours (in French or English) around Doucki for years and nobody who has the good fortune to come into contact with him regrets the encounter. He can organise hikes around the region lasting anything from a half-day to several days.

**Cooperative des Cordonniers** ARTS CENTRE
(7am-7pm) FREE This small cooperative of artisans is one of the best places in Guinea to watch high-quality leather goods such as sandals, wallets and bags being made. And yes, you can add to your baggage by buying a few items.

## Activities

**Pont de Dieu** HIKING
There are many possible walking trails around Dalaba but the most popular half-day hike is to the Pont de Dieu, a series of small waterfalls that pass under a natural rock bridge. The route passes through pine forests, farmland and tiny villages (and even straight through a few family compounds where you'll likely be invited to stop and chat).

There are lots of variations on the route and it can be extended into a full-day hike. Hire a guide through the tourist office.

## Sleeping & Eating

★**Hotel SIB** HISTORIC HOTEL $
(☎625 700 745; r from GFr160,000; P) If this hotel were anywhere else on Earth it would have been converted into a luxury heritage hotel. As it is, this 1930s colonial building, which was originally constructed to house soldiers recuperating from WWII, is a creaky, character-laden place, dripping in yesteryear romance.

**Auberge Seidy II** GUESTHOUSE $
(☎669 418 379; r GFr80,000) Koffi, the English-speaking and ever-laughing owner of the Auberge Seidy II, has created a lovely little guesthouse with clean and well-maintained rooms on the edge of the town, but even better than the rooms are the delicious meals and fun barbecues he puts on for guests. Great value.

**Restaurant Moderne** AFRICAN $
(☎620 306 380; mains GFr10,000-30,000; 8am-10pm) Locals will rightly tell you that this friendly place, which is a proper restaurant rather than just a market stall, is the best place in town to eat. Dishes include rice and peanut sauce, chicken and chips, and spaghetti bolognese.

## Information

The town has a well-established and helpful, privately run **tourist office** (☎657 604 011; 8.30am-noon & 2-5pm Mon-Sat).

## Getting There & Away

Bush taxis go to the following:
**Labé** GFr45,000, 2½ hours.
**Mamou** GFr20,000, one hour.
**Pita** GFr20,000, one hour.

# Mali-Yemberem

POP 5000

The little village of Mali-Yemberem sits on the edge of the spectacular Massif du Tamgué, just before its precipitous drop towards Senegal and the plains far below. Not only is the scenery superb, but at over 1400m, this is the highest, and coolest – sometimes even cold – town in the Fouta. Mali-Yemberem is also famous for Mt Loura (1515m), known as La Dame de Mali, a mountainside resembling a woman's profile.

The incredible landscapes ensure that hiking here is top class – with a guide and time, there are near endless hiking possibilities.

**La Dame de Mali** (The Lady of Mali; guide from GFr70,000) is a curiously shaped mountain outcrop (its real name is Mt Loura) some 7km northeast of the village. There are a number of different walks around the edge of the sheer mountain face. The tourist office in Mali-Yemberem can organise a guide.

**Campement du Mali** (☎for tourist office 628 891 684; hut GFr50,000) consists of two huts (with a third under construction) on the edge of the escarpment close to La Dame de Mali. They are built to mimic traditional thatched village houses and are very basic, with no running water or electricity. But there are plenty of friendly folk around who might cook for you for a negotiable fee!

### Information

**Office du Tourisme** (☎628 891 684; ⊙8am-6pm) Don't get too excited by the name – it's just a shop selling school books and pens – but Sadio Sauaré, the owner, has taken upon himself to promote the surrounding area and help tourists. He can organise guides (half-/full day GFr70,000/100,000) for walks ranging from a half-day to three days. He's also the person to speak to about the Campement du Mali and home stays.

### Getting There & Away

There are reasonably frequent bush taxis between Mali-Yemberem and Labé (GFr47,000). The 'road' is horrendous and in the dry season it can easily take five to seven hours or longer to cover the 140km. In the wet season you could be counting in days.

To Kedougou (Senegal; GFr100,000) the road is equally tortuous but there are daily bush taxis and, if all goes well, you can be there in eight hours. Be aware, however, that it probably won't all go well!

# FOREST REGION

## Kissidougou

POP 103,000

Kissidougou, a large, bustling and colourful market town, serves as the entry to *Guinée forestière* (forest region). Even though it's hard to avoid the temptation to push on south to the forests, it's worth spending a day exploring here.

### Sleeping & Eating

**Hôtel Savanah** HOTEL $

(☎620 962 714; hotelsavanah2014@gmail.com; r from GFr250,000; P ❄) With a wonderfully helpful management who'll go out of their way to please, and quiet, tidy rooms with floral bedsheets, this is as good as it gets in rural Guinea. Hot water comes by the bucket and there's reliable electricity all night.

**Hôtel Fritz** CABIN $$

(Hôtel de la Aeroport; ☎622 525 877; cabins from GFr500,000; P ❄ ≋) Prepare for a very big shock. Impeccable, spacious and tastefully decorated rooms set within individual cabins beside a clean, deep blue swimming pool. Yes you read that right. In fact, this resort-like place is so unexpected you'll most likely start to wonder if you're even in rural Guinea at all.

### Getting There & Away

Bush taxis line up along the road through the centre of town. Taxis go daily to:

**Conakry** GFr140,000,15 hours.

**Faranah** GFr35,000, 2½ hours.

**Gueckedou** GFr35,000, 2½ hours.

**Kankan** GFr75,000, six hours.

**Macenta** GFr75,000, five to six hours.

## N'zérékoré

POP 110,000

N'zérékoré is the major city of southern Guinea and it has all the facilities you might have missed elsewhere in the country. Besides the general buzz and a few markets to keep you happily occupied for a day, it serves as a useful base for nearby forest explorations and chimpanzee encounters.

### Sights

**Centre d'Exposition Artisanal de N'zérékoré** ARTS CENTRE

(⊙8am-6pm Mon-Sat) FREE This modern and impressive arts and handicrafts centre allows you to watch craftspeople carving, weaving, hammering and stitching dyed mudcloth, wooden carvings and raffia bags, among other things. If you're lucky you'll also get to catch some traditional dancing. There are a few statues and carvings on display as museum pieces.

### Sleeping & Eating

**Grand Hôtel de Mont Nimba** HOTEL $

(☎666 559 753; Quartier au Sud; r from GFr300,000; P ❄ ≋) This large place is where all the (many) NGO workers set up base and staff are very used to foreigners. The rooms are spacious and clean but lack much character. There's a decent restaurant (mains around GFr80,000) and a swimming pool - but don't rely on it being full of water.

**Auberge Golo** GUESTHOUSE $
(☎622 601 389; Quartier Telepoulou; r GFr250,000; P ❄) This is a great-value place out on the edge of town. The rooms are actually suites that come with living rooms with sofas and armchairs, a large bedroom with flowery bedspreads, and bathrooms with hot showers. Meals are available with advance notice.

**Mission Catholique** HOTEL $
(☎626 372 955; Quartier Dorota; r GFr100,000; P ❄) The Catholic Mission has simple but tidy rooms with mosquito nets and shared toilets. It's a nice, quiet location downhill behind the church at the eastern end of town. Actually finding someone with the room keys can take time!

### Information

There are several banks in town. The main branches of the Eco Bank and the Bicigui have ATMs that accept foreign cards and give out up to GFr800,000 per transaction.

### Getting There & Away

Bush taxis depart daily from the *gare routière* for:

**Conakry** (GFr180,000, 20 to 22 hours)
**Lola** (GFr10,000-12,000, one hour)
**Macenta** (GFr40,000, four hours)

Allow a full day to travel to Monrovia (Liberia). The road is rough and there's no shortage of checkpoints. Bush taxis go to the border at Diéké (GFr50,000; three hours) where you can walk 2km over the border to Ganta and then get another car to take you deeper into Liberia.

## Bossou

The fragmented forests around the village of Bossou are home to a small troop of eight chimpanzees who can be visited on a chimp-tracking walk organised through the **Institut de Recherche Environnementalde Bossou** (☎622 259 829; chimpanzee tracking GFr500,000, Mt Nimba hike GFr1,000,000). The chimps are very well habituated to humans, so it's almost a given that you will see them – and at very close quarters.

Leering up into the clouds to the east of Bossou is the forest-covered hulk of **Mt Nimba** (guided tour per group GFr1,000,000). At 1752m, this is the highest mountain in Guinea and a Unesco World Heritage Site on account of its unique – and now very threatened – ecology, which includes some endemic amphibians and a sizeable population of chimpanzees. The Institute de Recherche Environnemental de Bossou can organise very long (12 hours without breaks) day hikes to the summit of Mt Nimba.

There's nowhere to stay here. The town of Lola offers the nearest rooms, but the village of N'zérékoré makes for a more enjoyable base.

Biscuits are available from a few little market stalls and shops plus some fruit but that's about the limit.

Bush taxis to/from Lola charge GFr15,000 (one hour). Once in Lola you can change for N'zérékoré (GFr10,000).

## PARC NATIONAL DU HAUT NIGER

Covering some 1200 sq km, the **Parc National du Haut Niger** (per person per day admission/vehicle/camping/guide GFr50,000/100,000/50,000/150,000) is one of West Africa's last significant stands of tropical dry forest and one of the most important protected areas in Guinea. The forest, which is pockmarked with areas of tall grassland savannah and run through by the Niger River, has plenty of wildlife including significant numbers of chimpanzees, buffalo, duikers and waterbuck as well as crocodiles and hippos. You will be very lucky indeed to actually see much wildlife, however, thanks to the dense foliage, a general sense of caution from most of the animals and a near total lack of visitor facilities. Dedicated birders will likely find the forest highly rewarding.

The one place in the Parc National du Haut Niger that you are guaranteed to see large mammals is the **Centre de Conservation pour Chimpanzés** (www.projetprimates.com/chimpanzee-conservation-center; Somoria; GFr50,000). This is a French-run project in which chimpanzees rescued from the exotic animal pet trade are brought here and, over time, reintroduced to the wild. Don't get too excited about seeing wild chimps though, because visits are strictly controlled and the chimps that visitors get to see live in large enclosures.

There is no formal accommodation anywhere within the park. Bring a tent, a guide and a big dollop of adventure.

There's no public transport to the park. You'll need your own set of wheels and they'll need to be able to cope with a lot of mud, bumps and 'roads' that are nothing of the sort.

To get here take the dirt road leading east from Faranah to the village of Sanbaya (Sambonya) via Beindou. The park starts just to the north of the village.

# UNDERSTAND GUINEA

## Guinea Today

The Ebola epidemic that swept the region from 2014 until 2016 and killed 11,310 people began in a village not far from N'zérékoré, after a two-year-old boy became infected after coming into contact with bats.

The virus spread with lightning speed and deadly efficiency through many parts of Guinea, Sierra Leone and Liberia. Airlines cancelled all flights, cross-border road transport was dramatically reduced, international companies repatriated their foreign staff, development projects halted and investment into Guinea trickled away.

The number of people infected with the virus peaked in October 2014 and in June 2016 Guinea was finally declared Ebola free, but the epidemic cost at least 2500 Guineans their lives and had a major impact on the country's already weak economy and development.

Today, the international community is slowly returning to the country, development projects that were put on hold during the epidemic are picking up again, and there is a sense on the streets that Guinea may, finally, be about to enter a brighter future.

## History

Guinea was part of the Empire of Mali, which covered a large part of western Africa between the 13th and 15th centuries; the empire's capital, Niani, is in eastern Guinea. From the mid-1400s Portuguese and other European traders settled Guinea's coastal region, and the country eventually became a French colony in 1891.

The end of French West Africa began with Guinea. In 1958, Sekou Touré was the only West African leader to reject a French offer of membership in a French commonwealth, and instead demanded total independence. French reaction was swift: financial and technical aid was cut off, and there was a massive flight of capital.

Sekou Touré called his new form of state a 'communocracy', a blend of Africanist and communist models. It didn't work; the economy went into a downward spiral, and his growing paranoia triggered a reign of terror.

Days after Touré's death in March 1984, a military coup was staged by a group of colonels, including the barely known, barely educated Lansana Conté, who became president. He introduced austerity measures, and in 1991 bowed to pressure to introduce a multiparty political system. Conté claimed victory in three highly disputed elections. Conté stayed in power until his death in December 2008.

### In the Grip of the Military

Following the death in December 2008 of president Lansana Conté, an army contingent under Captain Moussa Dadis Camara took power in a coup d'état. His initial measures, such as cracking down on Guinean drug rings (Guinea is one of West Africa's hubs of the cocaine trade), and announcing anti-corruption measures and new mining deals (the country is hugely rich in natural resources, owning 30% of the world's bauxite resources), gained him many followers.

However, his announcement in 2009 that he would consider standing in the upcoming elections, and increasing violence committed by members of the army, provoked furious reactions. On 28 September 2009, army elements quashed a large demonstration with extreme violence. A UN commission denounced the events as a crime against humanity, and it is thought that over 150 people were killed. Two months later, Dadis was shot (but not killed) following a dispute with his aide-de-camp Toumba Diakite. A provisional government supervised the transition to civilian rule at the end of 2010.

After half a century in opposition, Alpha Conde, from the Malinke ethnic group, was declared winner in Guinea's first democratic election since independence from France in 1958. However, the vote kindled ethnic tensions. Conde's defeated rival, Cellou Dalein Diallo, is a member of the Fula ethnic group, to which 40% of Guineans belong. Diallo has consistently accused the president of marginalising his constituents, including many Fula.

After many false starts and disputed polls, in October 2015, presidential elections were held and again Conde won, with 58% of the vote. Despite violence and accusations of irregularities, in the post-election report the EU and AU concluded that the process overall was valid and Conde was sworn in for another term in December 2015.

# SURVIVAL GUIDE

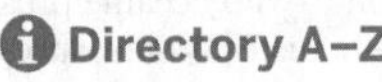

## Directory A–Z

### ACCOMMODATION

Guinea is a country of two tales when it comes to hotels. Conakry has lots of top-end hotels (and ever more are being built), a fair few mid-range hotels and virtually nothing in the budget category. Up-country things are almost totally reversed with almost all hotels being budget or, just about, mid-range and nothing at all in the top-end. Only in Conakry's pricier places can you expect 24-hour electricity.

### DANGERS & ANNOYANCES

- Avoid walking around Conakry and large towns at night due to the threat of muggings.
- Carry your passport and vaccination cards with you at all times.
- Electricity and running water are intermittent even in fairly large towns.

#### Driving & Roads

- Avoid road travel at night. There has been an increase in armed car-jackings.
- There are many police and military road blocks throughout the country and they've long had an unsavoury reputation for demanding bribes. However, in the last couple of years this problem has diminished considerably and many people now get through the country without paying a single bribe.

#### Photography

- Avoid taking photos in Conakry and large towns.
- Never photograph anyone without their express permission (in general people in Guinea do not like having their pictures taken).
- Never point a camera at police, military or anything that could be considered 'sensitive'.

> **SLEEPING PRICE RANGES**
>
> The following price ranges refer to a double room with bathroom (when available). Unless otherwise stated, breakfast is included in the price.
>
> **$** less than GFr450,000
>
> **$$** GFr450,000-900,000
>
> **$$$** more than GFr900,000

### EMBASSIES & CONSULATES

The following are just some of the major embassies found in Conakry:

**French Embassy** (621 000 010; www.ambafrance-gn.org; Ave du Commerce, Kaloum; 8am-noon Mon-Fri)

**German Embassy** (Mobile 621 221 706; www.conakry.diplo.de; Kaloum; 8am-noon Mon-Fri)

**Guinea-Bissau Embassy** (664 271 533; Rte du Donka, Bellevue; 8am-1pm Mon-Fri)

**Ivoirian Embassy** (622 363 485; www.guinee.diplomatie.gouv.ci; Blvd du la République, Kaloum; 7.30am-6pm Mon-Fri)

**Liberian Embassy** (666 144 651; Rte de Donka, Bellevue; 9am-1pm Mon-Fri)

**Malian Embassy** (669 399 403; Camayenne corniche, Dixinn; 7.30am-1pm Mon-Fri)

**Senegalese Embassy** (631 900 202; Villas 41 et 42, Cite des Nations, Boulbinet; 8am-1pm Mon-Fri)

**Sierra Leone Embassy** (631 356 566; Carrefour Bellevue; 9am-1pm Mon-Fri)

**UK Embassy** (631 355 329; www.gov.uk/government/world/organisations/british-embassy-conakry; Villa 1, Residence 2000, Corniche Sud; 8am-4.30pm Mon-Thu, 8am-1pm Fri)

**US Embassy** (655 104 000; https://conakry.usembassy.gov; Koloma; 8.30am-noon Mon-Fri)

### EMERGENCY & IMPORTANT NUMBERS

| | |
|---|---|
| Guinea's country code | 224 |
| International access code | 00 |
| Police | 122 |
| Ambulance | 442-020 |
| Fire | 1717 |

### FOOD

Make no mistake about this. You do not come to Guinea for the food. Even in Conakry proper restaurants are a little thin on the ground and in the interior most towns have next to no proper restaurants. Your diet will normally be limited to a lacklustre hotel restaurant meal or a street stall serving *riz gras* (rice fried in oil and tomato paste and served with fried fish or meat).

### INTERNET ACCESS

Most hotels in Conakry offer (slow) wi-fi nowadays and there are a few internet cafes – but far fewer than in most African capitals. By and large forget using the internet once you head inland, unless you bring your own internet dongle or use your smart phone. There are currently no hotels outside of Conakry offering internet access and very few internet cafes.

### LGBTIQ TRAVELLERS

As in most African countries homosexuality and lesbianism is not just frowned upon but is something that is utterly incomprehensible to the huge majority of Guineans. LGBTIQ travellers in Guinea should be extremely discreet and careful, as situations could quickly become dangerous. Same-sex relations are prohibited by law and can attract prison terms.

### MONEY

- The unit of currency is the Guinea franc (GFr) and it seems to be in a slow but permanent slide against major international currencies.
- The banking system in Guinea has improved recently and some major towns now have ATMs that work with international Visa and Mastercard (the latter though is less likely to be accepted). Most ATMs, however, only allow a very small amount to be withdrawn with each transaction.
- Most travellers continue to bring all the money they might need with them in cash (euros are best, followed by US dollars).
- You can change money inside a bank, with moneychangers on the street in Conakry, or with hotels. There isn't a black market as such, as street moneychangers offer the same rates as banks.
- Guinea is a cash economy. Only the major five-star hotels in Conakry and international airline offices will accept plastic.
- Forget travellers cheques.

#### Exchange Rates

| | | |
|---|---|---|
| Australia | A$1 | GFr6870 |
| Canada | C$1 | GFr6670 |
| Euro zone | €1 | GFr9954 |
| Japan | ¥100 | GFr8160 |
| New Zealand | NZ$1 | GFr6310 |
| UK | UK£1 | GFr11,768 |
| US | US$1 | GFr9125 |
| West Africa CFA | CFA1000 | GFr15,000 |

For current exchange rates, see www.xe.com.

#### Tipping

**Restaurants** In the best restaurants in Conakry a 10% tip is normal. Elsewhere tipping is not expected.

**Tourist guides and drivers** A tip is expected. If you hired a guide or driver for a week expect to tip the equivalent of one extra day's work.

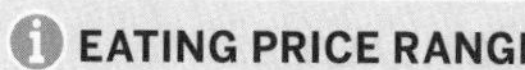

### EATING PRICE RANGES

The following price ranges refer to a main course.

**$** less than GFr45,000

**$$** GFr45,000–90,000

**$$$** more than GFr90,000

### OPENING HOURS

**Banks** 8.30am to 12.30pm & 2.30 to 4.30pm Monday to Thursday, 8.30am to 12.30pm and 2.45 to 4.30pm Friday.

**Businesses and shops** 8am to 6pm Monday to Saturday, except Friday when they might close for an hour to go to the mosque.

**Government offices** 8am to 4.30pm Monday to Thursday and 8am to 1pm Friday.

**Museums** 8am to 5pm Monday to Saturday.

### POST

Guinea's postal service is notoriously unreliable; packages especially often get 'lost'. Postcards should get through; for anything valuable use a private shipping firm.

### PUBLIC HOLIDAYS

**New Years Day** 1 January

**Easter** March/April

**Declaration of the Second Republic** 3 April

**Labour Day** 1 May

**Assumption Day** 15 August

**Independence Day** 2 October

**Christmas Day** 25 December

All major Islamic holidays (dates change each year) are also observed, with Eid al-Fitr being one of the country's biggest holidays.

### TELEPHONE

Mobile phones are ubiquitous in Guinea and service is available in even remote villages. SIM and top-up cards are available from shops and street stalls everywhere and calls and text messages are cheap. In towns 3G service is generally available and you can purchase internet data bundles through the top-up cards.

You will likely be asked to show some form of ID when buying a SIM card, otherwise the process of buying it and getting it all set up is fast and easy.

### TOURIST INFORMATION

There are no tourist information offices. Try the following website:

**Fouta Decouverte** (www.foutadecouverte.over-blog.com) A private tourist information website.

 **PRACTICALITIES**

**Weights & measures** Guinea uses the metric system.

## VISAS

Visas are required by visitors of most nationalities except those of some West African nations.

- Visas are generally easy to get and normally require a return air-ticket, or some other ticket in and out of the country, and a hotel booking for at least the first few days.
- Visas are usually valid for 30 days but can be extended to 90 days without much fuss.
- Visas must be obtained in advance; they are not available at the border.

## VOLUNTEERING

There is very little scope for volunteering in Guinea although the Centre de Conservation pour Chimpanzés (p349) based in the Parc National du Haut Niger (p350) does accept untrained, paying volunteers on six-month stints to work with orphaned chimpanzees. Conditions are very rough.

#  Getting There & Away

## AIR

Guinea's only international airport is **Conakry International Airport** (www.aeroport-conakry.com), 13km from the centre of Conakry. In 2016 the ageing airport was upgraded and it's now fairly fast and efficient to get through the airport.

There is no national airline, though Conakry is served by a small but slowly growing list of international and regional airlines. Regional airlines also connect Conakry with Senegal and Côte d'Ivoire.

Major carriers:

**Air France** (www.airfrance.com)

**Aigle Azur** (www.aigle-azur.com)

**Brussels Airlines** (www.brusselsairlines.com)

**Emirates** (www.emirates.com)

**Royal Air Maroc** (www.royalairmaroc.com)

## BORDER CROSSINGS

### Cote d'Ivoire

The land border between Guinea and Côte d'Ivoire had been closed to overland traffic for some time but it reopened in late 2016. The most frequently travelled route is between Lola and Man via Nzo and Danané. The road is in bad shape and in the rainy season can be close to impassable. There is also a route that goes from Kankan to Odienné via Mandiana, but this is an even remoter and more challenging route that few people use.

### Guinea-Bissau

Most people travelling by bush taxi get to Guinea-Bissau via Labé, Koundara and Gabú. The road is now in good condition except for a dreadful stretch between Gabú and Koundara where it starts to climb up onto the Fouta Djalon plateau. At the time of research crews were busy upgrading that part as well, which means that very soon it will be an easy day by share taxi between Guinea-Bissau and Labé.

A slower alternative route is via Boké to Québo.

### Liberia

There's quite a lot of traffic between Guinea and Liberia. The primary route is from N'zérékoré to Ganta via Diéke. Bush taxis go frequently to the border at Diéké where you can walk across and get a ride to Monrovia.

From Macenta, bush taxis go via Daro to the border and on to Voinjama, although the road is in a bad way.

Another route goes from Lola via Bossou to Yekepa but there's very little traffic on this route (indeed taxi drivers in Lola might instruct you to return to N'zérékore and travel to Liberia from there).

### Mali

Taxis travel directly to Bamako from Kankan, Siguiri and Conakry. The road is sealed and in very good condition from Kankan to Bamako. At the time of research it was considered safe to travel between Guinea and Bamako, but make sure you check the security situation in Mali first.

### Senegal

Taxis to Senegal going via Koundara, the busiest route, stop at Diaoubé, a small town with a huge market, where you can connect to almost anywhere, including Dakar. To get to Koundara most people go from Labé and the road between the two towns is now in generally good shape making it quite an easy run to Senegal. If you get stuck in Koundara there are a couple of very basic hotels. You can also get to Senegal on another route from Labé travelling via Mali-Yemberem and finishing in Kedougou in Senegal, but the route is dreadful all the way from Labé and after rain can be impassable. (When we last travelled this route we saw trucks stuck in potholes where the mud went up as high as the driver's door – and that was at the start of the dry season!)

### Sierra Leone

The road from Freetown to Conakry via Kambla and Parnelap is now sealed and an easy day-long trip. There are several other routes in and out of Sierra Leone, but the roads on these routes are all generally in bad shape and transport far less frequent than the main crossing point.

### CAR & MOTORCYCLE

Travelling overland in your own vehicle or by motorbike is a popular way to arrive in Guinea and, assuming you have all the car ownership, insurance and tax papers in order, presents no major hurdles although you might be asked to pay a bit of money every now and then in order to smooth out 'problems'.

Most of Guinea's border-crossing points are in remote areas with few facilities if you break down en-route to the border. Petrol stations are also unlikely to be found on most roads to the borders. Fill up in the nearest big town.

Most public transport crossing the Guinea borders, or dropping passengers at the borders, takes the form of bush taxis.

## Getting Around

However you do it, getting around Guinea takes time, patience and a passion for potholes...

### AIR

Despite the fact that every town of a reasonable size seems to have an airstrip (and Faranah has a runway that was designed so a Concorde could land there!) there is actually no internal flight network. Nor, indeed, is there a national airline.

### CAR & MOTORCYCLE

If you're driving your own vehicle or a hired vehicle in Guinea, be sure the insurance and registration papers are in perfect order as they will be checked at the police roadblocks many times along the way. All vehicles must carry a warning triangle and police will ask to see this as well. Hiring a car for travel outside of Conakry is usually very expensive (count on US$150 to US$200 per day) and vehicles are hard to come by. One recommended private vehicle owner who rents out a jeep for very reasonable rates is the owner of the website **Fouta Decouverte** (www.foutadecouverte.over-blog.com).

### TAXI-BROUSSE

Normally a battered Peugeot 505 that looks as if a tank has driven over it, these vehicles might be smaller than buses but drivers generally attempt to cram in as many passengers as a bus would take anyway. Whereas in most of West Africa taxis carry seven passengers, here in Guinea they squeeze in nine and then, for good measure, stick a few more on top of the mountain of luggage strapped to the roof. Comfortable, safe and reliable they absolutely are not, but in the right frame of mind they could be described as an 'experience'.

Expect at least one breakdown on even the shortest journey, meaning that any travel times the driver (or we) might give are purely indications on what it should take in an ideal, breakdown and delay-free world. Guinean drivers are extreme risk takers, placing their lives and the lives of their passengers completely in the hands of God, tempting Him with racing in rusty vehicles and overtaking manoeuvres on blind corners. The saving grace is that many times the road is so rutted and torn that drivers cannot go too fast.

Taxis leave when they're full, and most people travel in the morning. You'll always have the quickest getaway around 7am to 8am.

Fares can fluctuate depending on both current fuel prices and demand along that route on any given day. It can also be more expensive if there's a lot of uphill driving to be done as that uses more fuel.

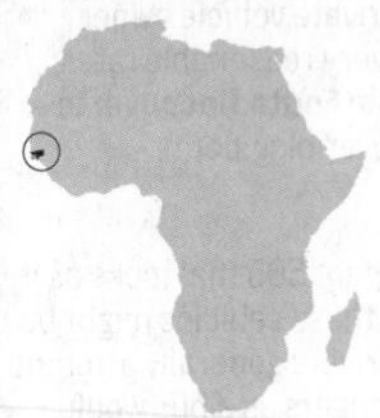

# Guinea-Bissau

☎245 / POP 1.7 MILLION

**Includes ➡**



## Best Places to Eat

➡ Oysters on Quinhámel beach (p362)

➡ O Bistro (p358)

➡ Afrikan Ecolodge Angurman (p361)

## Best Places to Sleep

➡ Ponta Anchaca (p362)

➡ Afrikan Ecolodge Angurman (p361)

➡ Ecocantanhez (p363)

➡ Ledger Plaza Bissau (p357)

➡ Africa Princess (p360)

## Why Go?

Like a microcosm of Africa, this tiny nation contains multitudes – of landscapes, peoples, cultures and plant and animal life. All of it within reach of the capital, Bissau. Faded colonial-era houses sag, from tropical decay and the weight of history. Decades of Portuguese colonisation were followed by a long painful liberation struggle and then cycles of civil war and political chaos.

Despite hardships and poverty, Bissau-Guineans persevere. The jokes, like the music, are loud but tender. The bowls of grilled oysters are served with a sauce spicy enough to give a kick, but not so strong as to mask the bitterness.

The jewel in the country's crown is the labyrinth of tropical islands that make up the Arquipélago dos Bijagós. Long white-sand beaches are lapped by waters brimming with fish. Hippos, monkeys, chimps and buffaloes thrive in protected reserves and hundreds of bird species call its vast mangroves and wetlands home.

## When to Go

### Bissau

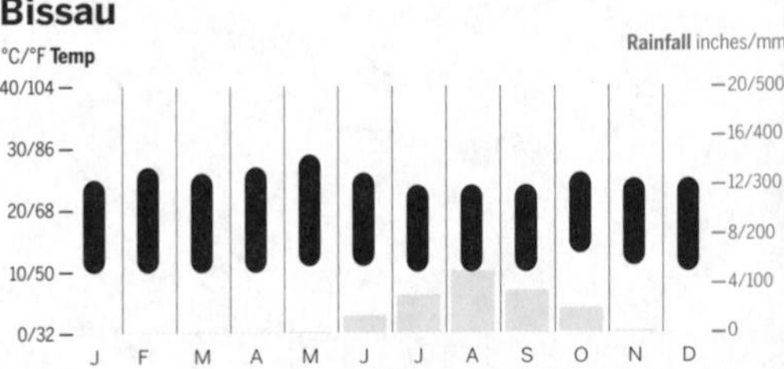


**Dec–Feb** The coolest, driest months, when sea turtles emerge from their nests.

**Mar–Jul** Hot, humid and sweaty; travel with plenty of water and sunscreen.

**Jul–Oct** The rainy season.

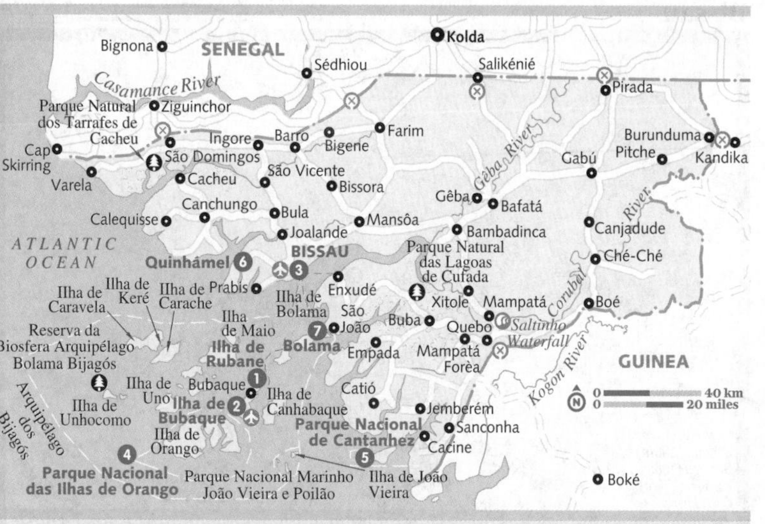


## Guinea-Bissau Highlights

1. **Ilha de Rubane** (p362) Relaxing amid world-class facilities and natural splendour.
2. **Ilha de Bubaque** (p360) Experiencing village life, a short walk from your island getaway.
3. **Bissau Velho** (p357) Tangoing in cobbled streets by candlelight, after a dinner of salty *bacalau* and red wine in the capital.
4. **Parque Nacional das Ilhas de Orango** (p361) Locking eyes with hippos as they emerge from the warm saltwater lagoons.
5. **Parque Nacional de Cantanhez** (p363) Following chimpanzee, elephant and buffalo trails through dense forests.
6. **Quinhámel** (p362) Dipping oysters in hot lime sauce after a day in the water.
7. **Bolama** (p360) Sitting on the steps of the abandoned town hall, with its crumbling Greek-style pillars.

# BISSAU

☎20, 21 / POP 492,000

Built on a low-lying estuary where the Gêba River flows into the Atlantic, apart from the hectic traffic, Bissau is a low-key, unassuming capital. In the early evening, the fading sunlight lends the crumbling colonial facades of Bissau Velho (Old Bissau) a touch of nostalgic glamour. Generators set parts of the town trembling at night, although, street lights or not, people get out of their homes and gather at ramshackle bars.

## Sights

Bissau Velho, a stretch of narrow alleyways and derelict buildings, is 'guarded' by the **Fortaleza d'Amura**. The rebuilt neoclassical **presidential palace** (Praça dos Heróis Nacionais) and brushed-up **Assembleia Ministério da Justiça** (cnr Avs Francisco Mendes & do Brazil) are architectural expressions of the country's hopes for order and democracy.

## Festivals & Events

**Carnaval** CARNIVAL

Bissau and Bubaque's Carnaval are the country's biggest parties. It takes place every year in February or early March during the week leading up to Ash Wednesday and the beginning of Lent. Music, masks, drinking and dancing are the order of the day.

## Sleeping

★**Ledger Plaza Bissau** HOTEL $$

(☎245 955 577007; www.laicohotels.com; Av Combatentes Liberdade da Pátría; r from CFA60,000; ❄@☜≋) Bissau's most luxurious hotel, the Ledger (known to taxi drivers by its former name Lybia Hotel) is where politicians, businesspeople and the small expatriate community congregate – the latter primarily on

## Bissau

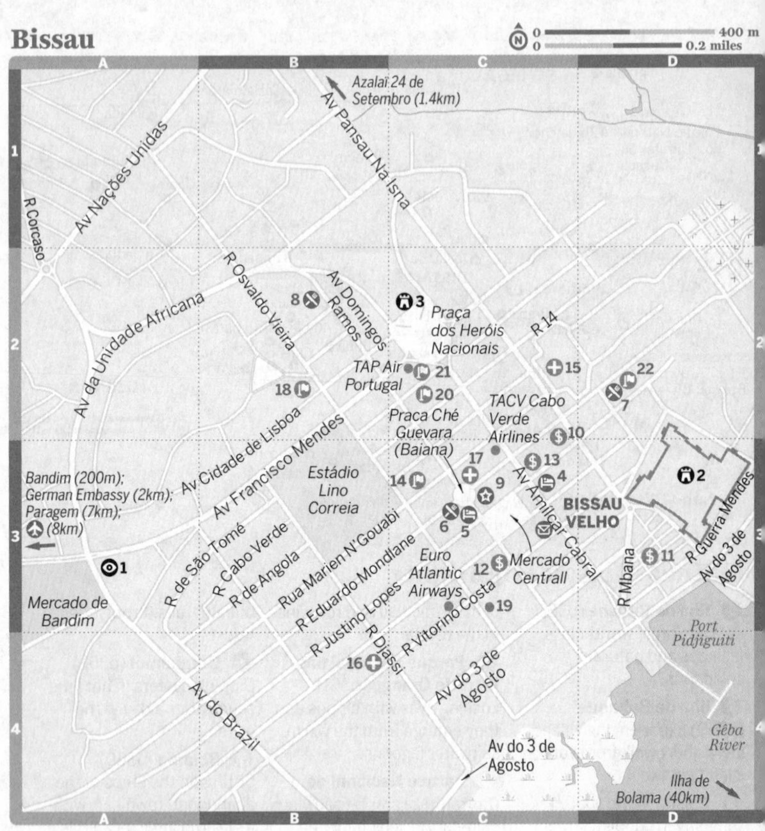




Sundays for a day by the pool and a pricey buffet lunch (CFA20,000). It's efficiently designed with contemporary furnishings and rooms – even the small economy ones are comfortable.

**Coimbra Hotel & Spa** BOUTIQUE HOTEL $$
(☎245 3213467; www.hotel-coimbra-spa.com; Av Amílcar Cabral; r incl breakfast from CFA76,000; ❄@☜) It looks like a hardware store from the street, buit climb the steps from the side entrance to the bougainvillea-fringed terrace and you'll find a lovely oasis in the centre of town. Sparsely furnished rooms are nice enough (shower pressure can be a nuisance), and downstairs houses a spa and restaurant with a good lunch and dinner buffet.

### Eating

**Restaurant Samaritana** AFRICAN $
(Av Domingos Ramos; mains CFA2500; ⊙8am-11pm) It's made from a cut-out container and buzzes with Guineans of all ranks and incomes, all eager to sample Mamadou's reliably delicious meals.

**Kalliste Restaurant** INTERNATIONAL $$
(Praça Ché Guevara; meals from CFA4000; ⊙8am-late) Hotel Kalliste's crumbling poplant-lined courtyard buzzes at night, attracting everyone from tired UN lawyers to politicians, activists, international volunteers and mosquitoes. There's live music most evenings. The pizzas are pretty good, as is the espresso.

**O Bistro** FRENCH $$
(☎245 3206000; Rua Eduardo Mondlane; mains CFA4000; ⊙noon-3pm & 7pm-late; ❄✍) This Belgian-owned spot has all the right ingredients: excellent, reasonably priced mains including good pasta, fresh catches, sautéed vegetables and *crepes au chocolat;* friendly service; a well-stocked bar; and a warm ambience that transcends the air-con. Bring mosquito repellent if you want the big table on the veranda.

## Bissau

**Sights**
1 Assembleia Ministério da justiça .......... A3
2 Fortaleza d'Amura .......... D3
3 Presidential Palace .......... C2

**Sleeping**
4 Coimbra Hotel & Spa .......... C3
5 Hotel Kalliste .......... C3

**Eating**
6 Kalliste Restaurant .......... C3
7 O Bistro .......... D2
8 Restaurant Samaritana .......... B2

**Entertainment**
9 Centre Culturel Franco-Bissao-Guinéen .......... C3

**Information**
10 Banque Atlantique .......... C2
11 BAO .......... D3
12 Casa Cambio Nacional .......... C3
13 Ecobank .......... C3
14 Guinean Embassy .......... C3
15 Hospital Nacional Simão Mendes .......... C2
16 Pharmacia Nur Din .......... B4
17 Policlinica .......... C3
18 Portuguese Embassy .......... B2
19 Satguru .......... C3
20 Senegalese Embassy .......... C2
21 Spanish Embassy .......... C2
22 UK & Netherlands Honorary Consul .......... D2

## Drinking & Nightlife

As far as nightlife goes, your best bet is to head to Praça Che Guevara and wander the surrounding streets. The terrace at the Kalliste Restaurant is a good spot.

## Information

### INTERNET ACCESS

Most accommodation in the city offers wi-fi access.

**Centre Culturel Franco-Bissao-Guinéen** (CCF; ☎245 3206816; Praça Ché Guevera; ⌚9am-10pm Mon-Fri; 📶) Charges CFA2000 per day.

**Hotel Kalliste** (☎245 6765662; kallistebissau@hotmail.com; Praça Ché Guevara) The terrace has wi-fi.

### MEDICAL SERVICES

**Pharmacia Nur Din** (Rua Vitorino Costa) A reasonably well-stocked pharmacy.

**Policlinica** (☎245 3207581; info@policlinica.bissau.com; Praça Ché Guevera) A better option for illnesses than a trip to the hospital.

**Raoul Follerau Hospital** (Av dos Combatentes da Liberdade da Pátria) Probably city and country's best hospital.

**Simão Mendes** (☎245 3212861; Av Pansau Na Isna) Bissau's main hospital in the centre; in a poor state.

### MONEY

**Banque Atlantique** (Av Pansau Na Isna) ATM.

**BAO** (Banco da Africa Occidental; Rua 19 Setembro; ⌚8.30am-3pm) Changes money.

**Casa Cambio Nacional** (Av Domingos Ramos; ⌚hours vary) Changes money at good rates.

**Ecobank** (Av Amílcar Cabral; ⌚7.30am-4.30pm Mon-Fri, 9am-noon Sat) Changes dollars and euros; ATM.

### POST

**Main Post Office** (Av Amílcar Cabral; ⌚8am-6pm Mon-Sat) Housed in a large building built c 1955.

### TOURIST INFORMATION

**Institute for Biodiversity and Protected Areas** (IBAP; ☎245 207106; www.ibapgbissau.org; Av Dom Settimio Arturro Ferrazzetta) Established by the Bissau-Guinean government in 2005, IBAP is charged with managing, protecting and conserving the country's biodiversity and natural ecosystems. Contact for information on visiting any of the country's national parks.

### TRAVEL AGENCIES

**Satguru** (☎245 5994211; www.satgurutravel.com; Rua Osvaldo Vieira) Travel agency that can book any airline, as well as car rentals; shares office (and desk) with ASKY Airlines.

## Getting There & Away

### AIR

There are flights to Bissau's Osvaldo Vieira International Airport (OXB) with TACV Cabo Verde Airlines via Praia/Dakar, Euro Atlantic Airways and **TAP Air Portugal** (TP; ☎245 3201359; www.flytap.com; Praça dos Heróis Nacionais; ⌚9am-5.30pm Mon-Fri) from Lisbon, and Royal Air Maroc from Casablanca.

### BOAT

Reaching the Arquipélago dos Bijagós can be complicated, as the former ferry between the islands and Bissau no longer runs. A replacement ferry was said to be on its way from abroad.

### LAND

Once in Bissau, you can get *sept place* taxis (Peugeot 504s with seven seats) and *transporte misto* buses to just about anywhere in the country at the *gare routière* (bus station), inconveniently located about 10km (CFA1000 by taxi) outside town.

## Getting Around

The airport is 9km from the town centre. A taxi to town should be around CFA3000 (more at night).

Shared taxis – generally blue, well-worn Mercedes – are plentiful and ply all the main routes. Trips cost between CFA250 and CFA1000. Rates for longer routes vary and have to be negotiated.

Blue-yellow *toca-tocas* (minibuses) serve main city routes (for CFA100), including Av de 14 Novembro towards the *paragem* (bus station) and airport.

# ARQUIPÉLAGO DOS BIJAGÓS

The Bijagós islands look like the perfect postcard from paradise. From the skies above, their complexity is fully revealed: islands, creeks, mangroves, islets, sandy bays and more than 20 settlements on 87 islands. Dolphins, hippos, manatees and sea turtles inhabit the waters, and the mangroves are important breeding grounds for migratory birds.

Protected by swift tides, treacherous sandbanks and the Unesco heritage fund, the Bijagós, a matriarchal people, eluded Portuguese control until the 1930s. Their rites and ceremonies remain largely hidden from visitors, conducted far away from the beaches in the heart of the forests.

**Africa Princess** (245 969 283386, in Dakar, Senegal 351 91 722 4936; www.africa-princess.com; 7-day trip per person in double cabin €950; late Sep-late Jul) is the most convenient and comfortable way of seeing the most islands in the Arquipélago dos Bijagós. A large enough group of passengers can customise its own itinerary, but generally visits include Canhabaque and the two national-park areas. Sleeps up to eight in simple and tight cabins on a 15m two-hull catamaran. Solar panels provide most of the power.

Ilha de Bubaque is the gateway to the rest of the Bijagós.

## Ilha de Bolama

POP 21,000

Geographically closer to Bissau than any other island in the Bijagós, eerily beautiful Bolama feels worlds away, both aesthetically and socially. The shores of Bolama town, Portuguese capital of Guinea-Bissau from 1879 to 1943, are awash with crumbling relics that were abandoned after independence. Tree-lined boulevards are mapped out by lamp posts that no longer shine, and the colonial barracks have been recast as a hospital, now – like much of the island – in a dark and desolate state.

The former **town hall**, flanked by Greek style pillars, was built in 1870; these days huge splinters hang like stalactites from its ceilings. The turrets of the once grandiose **Hotel Turismo** sit in an overgrown nest of lianas, 3m-tall weeds and snakes. It's worth walking out to Ofir Beach, around 3km from the town, to see the spooky sweeping **staircase** of a beach hotel that no longer exists.

### Sleeping

**Formaca Pesqueria** HOSTEL $
(245 5286345; Bolama town; r CFA15,000) You can rent a breezy room at the fishing training centre around 200m north of the port. There is electricity, but the rooms do not have fans. Meals can be arranged upon request.

**Hotel Gã-Djau** HOTEL $
(245 955 288717; Bolama town; r CFA13,000) Hotel Gã-Djau is basic, but it's the smartest option. It's a 15-minute walk from the market (ask for directions there). The rooms have fans, but the generator shuts off late at night.

### Getting There & Away

*Canoas* (motor canoes; CFA350) operate three times per week between São João on the mainland and Bolama town. You can also reach Bolama by taking a *sept place* to Buba (three hours), where you can overnight before hiring motorbikes for the journey (three hours, CFA15,000) along rough forest roads to the pirogue at São João.

## Ilha de Bubaque

POP 11,300

A single jetty marks the centre of Bubaque town, the archipelago's largest town and the geographic centre of the Bijagós. It's a ramshackle affair, with a small enclosed market, dirt paths and a few bars and basic shops. If you can't make it to more remote islands, Bubaque, the transport hub of the islands, makes a comfortable place to unwind and a good weekend getaway from Bissau.

## Sleeping

**Casa Dora** HOTEL $
(☎245 969 063585; www.hotelcasadora.yolasite.com; Bubaque town; s/d incl breakfast CFA16,000/22,000; ) Staffed by Dora and her very helpful and service-oriented daughters, the rooms at this budget haunt are fairly basic – little furniture, a fan and concrete walls and floors. In the garden restaurant (meals CFA5000) you get to dig into large platters of seafood in the shade of mango trees.

★ **Kasa Afrikana** LODGE $$
(☎245 7243305; www.kasa-afrikana.com; Bubaque town; per person from CFA40,000; ) Gilles' fishing lodge hits the right ratio of charm to luxury, with comfortable rooms, pretty landscaped grounds, a freshwater swimming pool and excellent food. Come to escape the grind, get closer to nature, fish, visit villages or follow tracks into the Bubaque forest. The only slight downside is that it's located on the inland side of the road along the island's edge.

**Dakosta Island Beach Camp** BUNGALOW $$$
(☎245 969 119999; www.dakostabc.com) Newly opened by Bissau-Guinean-American champion kickboxer Adlino Costa, this camp on Ilha de Bubaque feels worlds away from the relative bustle of town – it's situated at the far southern end of the island. Well-built bungalows are tucked just back from a beautiful white-sand beach. The pièce de résistance is an amazing communal table built from a dugout canoe.

## Getting There & Away

Your choice to/from Bissau is between rough and risky *canoas* (per person CFA2500, six hours) and a speedboat (per four-seater boat CFA150,000 to CFA250,000, 1½ to two hours).

# Ilha de Orango

POP 2500

The heart of **Parque Nacional das Ilhas de Orango** (www.ibapgbissau.org; CFA2000) – several other islands are also part of the park's protected reserve) – Ilha de Orango is the burial site of the Bijagós kings and queens.

WORTH A TRIP

### BIJAGÓS SLEEPING

**Afrikan Ecolodge Angurman**
(☎245 9553077; www.afrikanecolodge.com; Ilha d'Angurman; s/d with full board CFA50,000/66,000) is a true Robinson Crusoe experience, minus the building work. That's been done by Francois, a grizzled, friendly and passionate Frenchman who runs this small out-of-the-way retreat on 50-hectare Angurman Island. Three simple bungalows with cold-water bathrooms and porches front the shoreline. An enormous baobab tree, straight out of Avatar, towers over an idyllic spot where meals are served.

Occupying one half of a tiny islet (Ilha de Keré), **Hotel Keré** (☎245 966 993827; www.bijagos-kere.com; Ilha de Keré; 7 days full board from €750) is an isolated fishing lodge made up of a collection of thatched-roof bungalows – it's ideal for those who like their escapism to come with a little luxury. Prices here are slightly cheaper than those on Ilha de Rubane for a similar experience.

Travellers know it more as the site of Anôr Lagoon, where you can spot rare saltwater hippos – considered sacred, they live in both the sea and freshwater. Local guides (around CFA10,000, plus the park entry fee) lead you on a sandy path through tall grass and swampy wetlands, more reminiscent of the prototypical African savannah than other islands. Be sure to wear shoes you don't mind muddying or sandals with straps, as well as pants you can roll up or shorts. It's a pretty walk, though shade is scarce.

There's a long, beautiful **beach**, basically between the point where the Orango Parque Hotel is located and where you disembark for hippo-spotting walks. No shade, however.

**Orango Parque Hotel** (☎245 955 352446; www.orangohotel.com; r incl full board CFA70,000) is a collection of large and well-kept thatched-roof bungalows atop a hill a short walk up from a beautiful white-sand beach. Food and drinks are served in an outdoor patio area, and there's a small museum with traditional masks and figurines. Well managed and run, it feels remote and far removed from the hustle of Bubaque.

DON'T MISS

**ILHA DE RUBANE**

On the uninhabited island of Ilha de Rubane, you'll find one of Guinea-Bissau's best places to stay.

Superlatives don't do **Ponta Anchaca** (☎245 966 067393, 245 966 394352; www.pontaanchaca.net; s/d with full board from €140/220; ❄📶🏊) justice. Gorgeous. Idyllic. Heavenly. You won't want to leave after disembarking onto a long postcard-perfect white-sand beach. And some guests don't, choosing to buy one of the resort's charming and sophisticated beachfront bungalows. While there's much to do – fishing, kayaking, trips to other islands – it's tempting to simply do nothing for once.

## Ilha João Vieira

This idyllic island is part of the **Parque Nacional Marinho João Vieira e Poilão**, a grouping of four islands (including Mëio, Cavalo and Poilão) in the southeast of the archipelago and one of the most important nesting areas for endangered sea turtles in the Eastern Atlantic. During the main egg-laying season in October and November, the shorelines, especially Mëio and Poilão, can teem with these rare creatures. João Vieira, owned and seasonally inhabited by the Canhabaque people, also houses a guardhouse for the park and its only formal accommodation.

Run by a French couple and situated on a beautiful soft, sandy beach fronting turquoise waters is **Chez Claude** (☎245 955 968677; per person full board CFA51,000; ⏲Dec-May) . It's a modest collection of simple concrete and thatched-roof bungalows and an outdoor eating area. Meals can be provided.

The owner can arrange speedboat pick-up from Bubaque town (around CFA200,000 per boatload).

# THE NORTHWEST

## Quinhámel

POP 3100

Quinhámel, 35km west of Bissau, makes an interesting day or weekend trip. A wide, palm-shaded promenade adds a little grandeur, fittingly as it's the regional capital of the Biombo region and the traditional home of the Papel people. About 2km away, nestled between the mangroves, is a local **beach** popular with families and young people at the weekends.

The region in general is known for its oysters, which are found in nearby mangroves. A few places by the river are picturesque spots to give them a try, as is the restaurant at **Hotel Mar Azu** (☎245 966 197280; r incl lunch CFA40,000; @)l.

## Varela

☎95

Varela's charm lies in its remoteness, and the fact that this means its white-sand, windswept beaches are deserted. This is due to the 45km road from São Domingos being rough, even in a good 4WD. The prettiest beach is **Praia Niquim**, accessible only on foot.

**Aparthotel Chez Hélène** (Chez Fatima; ☎245 5301373; f.cirell.38@gmail.com; d/ste CFA15,000/20,000) consists of nine brightly coloured huts in a pretty garden setting. The thatched-roof huts are lovingly decorated and have fans, mosquito nets and bathrooms. The restaurant offers Italian food and fresh juices (it grows its own tomatoes and passion fruits). Call ahead for information on road conditions. The generator kicks in after dark. Check out the Facebook page for more information.

A *transporte misto* (minibus) leaves every afternoon from São Domingos (CFA3000, 53km), taking around four hours, and returns the following morning. If you're driving by 4WD, plan on at least two hours.

# THE SOUTH

## Parque Natural das Lagoas de Cufada

Sandwiched between the Buba and Corubal Rivers, the 890-sq-km **Parque Natural das Lagoas de Cufada** (www.ibapgbissau.org) is the largest wetlands reserve in Guinea-Bissau. Kayaking across placid waters on an early morning amid twittering birds (there are an estimated 250 species here) makes the effort to get here worthwhile. There's an observation post where you can sit, appreciate the view and tick-off sightings. There are also African buffaloes, gazelles, hyenas, white hippos and crocodiles in the park.

Buses to Bissau, 223km away via asphalt roads, leave early in the morning. It's easier to travel by *sept place* (CFA3500, three hours), though you might have a long wait for the vehicle to fill up. A two-hour drive through the Parque Natural das Lagoas de Cufada – you need a 4WD vehicle – brings you to São João, where you can get a *canoa* to Ilha de Bolama.

## Parque Nacional de Cantanhez

The hardest-to-reach places are often the most beautiful, and so it goes with Parque Nacional de Cantanhez – over 1000 sq km of the country's last rainforest. With a dense web of giant kapok trees, lianas and palm trees (a total of more than 200 plant species), you'll need to get out on a trail to spot elephants, baboons, buffaloes, colobus monkeys, Africa's westernmost troupe of chimpanzees and hundreds of species of birds. In the mangrove and island areas that form part of the protected zone, you'll see plenty of fish, manatees, small hippos and other bird species.

### Sleeping

**Ecocantanhez – Jemberém** BUNGALOW **$**
(www.ecocantanhez.org; s/d/q CFA10,000/15,000/25,000) Ecotourism project designed to encourage sustainable ways of drawing visitors to the Parque Nacional de Cantanhez. Has three thatched-roof bungalows in Jemberém. You can also camp out or park your overland vehicle for the night. Has running cold water and electricity at night.

**Ecocantanhez – Faro Sadjuma** BUNGALOW **$**
(www.ecocantanhez.org; bungalows CFA15,000) Part of the ecotourism project designed to encourage sustainable ways of drawing visitors to the Parque Nacional de Cantanhez, the camp at Faro Sadjuma consists of three bungalows with 24-hour solar-powered electricity. It's surrounded by mango, pineapple and avocado trees.

### Getting There & Away

You'll need time and patience to get to the access point at Jemberém. Only go in the dry season and in a 4WD; dirt tracks turn into rivers in the rainy season.

From Buba to Mampatá Forèa the road is OK. You leave the tarmac for the remaining 70km to Jemberém. No signposts mean the best option is to hire a car or guide from outside the park to direct you.

# UNDERSTAND GUINEA-BISSAU

## Guinea-Bissau Today

A telling fact and microcosm of the country's political instability is that there have been five prime ministers since May 2014. One resigned after 48 hours in office. In late 2016 President José Mário Vaz once again dissolved the government. A new prime minister, Sissoko Embalo, was sworn in. Once again things are in limbo.

Because of the political instability, there's little tourism to speak of, except in the Bijagós. Fishing stocks are said to be hijacked by Chinese boats, and drug-trafficking (while declining) is rampant enough for some to label the country a 'narco-state'. Outside of cashew production, the economy is largely based on international project funding.

## History

In around 1200, when a group of Malinké was led to present-day Guinea-Bissau by a general of Sunjata Keita, the region became an outpost of the Empire of Mali. In 1537, it became a state in its own right – the Kaabu Empire. Gabù became the capital of this small kingdom.

### European Arrival & Colonisation

Portuguese navigators first reached the area around 1450, and established lucrative routes for trading slaves and goods. With the abolition of the slave trade in the 19th century, the Portuguese extended their influence beyond the coast towards the interior in order to continue extracting wealth.

Portuguese Guinea descended into one of the most repressive and exploitative colonial regimes in Africa, particularly when dictator António Salazar came to power in Portugal in 1926.

## War of Liberation

By the early 1960s African colonies were rapidly winning independence, but Salazar refused to relinquish control. The result was a long and bloody war of liberation for Guinea-Bissau and Cape Verde, fought on Guinean soil. Many Guineans were recruited to fight for the Portuguese, essentially pitting brothers against brothers and neighbours against neighbours.

The father of independence was Amílcar Cabral, who in 1956 helped found the Partido Africano da Independência da Guiné e Cabo Verde (PAIGC). In 1961 the PAIGC started arming and mobilising peasants, and within five years controlled half of the country. Cabral was assassinated in Conakry in 1973, but independence had become inevitable. When Salazar's regime fell in 1974, the new Portuguese government recognised the fledgling nation.

## Independence & Instability

Once in power, the PAIGC government was confronted by staggering poverty, lack of education and economic decline. Politically, it wanted a unified Guinea-Bissau and Cape Verde; however, the idea died in 1980 when President Luis Cabral was overthrown in a coup while visiting Cape Verde to negotiate the union. João 'Nino' Vieira, an important military leader in the independence struggle, took over and initially continued the country's socialist policies. In 1986, after a coup attempt, President Vieira reversed course and privatised state enterprises.

Intractable poverty, several coup attempts and growing corruption under Vieira culminated in national strikes in 1997, which spiralled into civil war. Senegal and Guinea became involved in the conflict, sending soldiers in support of government troops loyal to the president. Vieira was killed in a 2009 coup and instability has been endemic ever since, fuelled by deep tensions between the government and the military, which includes ageing officers who fought in the war of independence. The squabble for profits from Bissau's main cash cow – not the humble cashew, but cocaine – is a symptom of these tensions.

### GUINEA-BISSAU WILDLIFE

In the Bijagós archipelago you find rare saltwater hippos, aquatic turtles, dolphins, manatees and sharks. The rainforests of the southeast are the most westerly home of Africa's chimpanzee population. There is also a stunning variety of birds, especially within the coastal wetlands, including cranes and peregrine falcons.

## Constant Inconstancy

In 2012, President Malam Bacai Sanha died from illness, plunging the country into another bout of instability and adding another name to the long list of presidents who have failed to complete a full term in power. A coup d'etat ousted the prime minister and election frontrunner three months later and a transitional government was installed, headed by Manuel Serifo Nhamadjo, who was chosen by West African bloc Ecowas. Nhamadjo's time in power was shaken by coup attempts and attacks, and elections in 2013 were held amid rising tensions between the Balanta and other ethnic groups.

# People

Guinea-Bissau's 1.7 million inhabitants are divided among more than 27 ethnic groups. The two largest are the Balanta (30%) in the coastal and central regions and the Fula (20%) in the east and south. Other groups with significant numbers include the Mankinka, Papel and Manjaco; there are also smaller populations of Beafada, Mancanha, Felupe and Balanta Mane. The offshore islands are mostly inhabited by the Bijagós people. In the last few years, tensions have been growing between the Balanta and other ethnic groups.

About 45% of the people are Muslims and 10% Christians. Animist beliefs remain strong along the coast and in the south.

# Arts & Crafts

Eastern Guinea-Bissau is a centre of kora (a harplike instrument with over 20 strings) playing, being the ancient seat of the Kaabu kingdom, where the instrument was invented. The traditional Guinean beat is gumbé, though contemporary music is mainly influenced by zouk (a style of popular music created in the Caribbean and popular across Africa, with a lilting, sensual beat) from Cape Verde. Besides the reformed Super Mama

Djombo, perhaps the country's most famous band, other contemporary artists include Manecas Costa, Justino Delgado, Dulce Nevas and Rui Sangara. However, the centre of Guinean pop is Lisbon, not Bissau.

# SURVIVAL GUIDE

## Directory A–Z

### ACCOMMODATION

Bissau has a range of accommodation to suit most budgets. However, unless you're paying top dollar, you're unlikely to find anything comfortable and inviting. Conditions are generally more basic elsewhere in the country (the luxury lodges of the Bijagós are an exception). National electricity is severely limited, forcing hoteliers to rely on expensive generator power.

### DANGERS & ANNOYANCES

In Guinea-Bissau periods of calm can be followed by violent flare-ups.

- Attacks and coup attempts rarely wound civilians or visitors.
- Shops, banks, businesses and, more rarely, borders may close during tense periods.
- Even with blackouts and scarce streetlights, you can generally walk most city streets with a modicum of care.
- Depending on weather and the boat, travel to and around the Arquipélago dos Bijagós can be uncomfortable or dangerous.
- Beware of stingrays swimming in the Bijagós.
- There are poisonous green mamba snakes and cobras.
- Land mines from past conflicts are scattered in the following regions: Bafata, Oio, Biombo, Quinara and Tombali. Most have been located and removed.

### EMBASSIES & CONSULATES

All embassies and consulates are in Bissau. The UK and the Netherlands share an **honorary consul** (245 966 622772; mavegro@hotmail.com; Rua Eduardo Mondlane, Supermercardo Mavegro, Bissau). US interests are run out of the embassy in Dakar. The US does have a **Bissau Liaison Office** (245 3256382; Rua Josi Carlos Schwarz, Edificio SITEC, Barrio d'Ajuda) for basic services and hosts a 'virtual' Guinea-Bissau presence at http://guinea-bissau.usvpp.gov.

**French Embassy** (245 3201312; www.ambafrance-gw.org; Av dos Combatentes da Liberdade da Patria, Barrio da Penha)

**German Embassy** (245 443255020; escritorio-bissau@web.de; SITEC Bldg, Barrio d'Ajuda; 9-11am Mon-Fri)

> **SLEEPING PRICE RANGES**
>
> The following price ranges refer to a double room with bathroom.
>
> **$** less than CFA31,000
>
> **$$** CFA31,000–93,000
>
> **$$$** more than CFA93,000

**Guinean Embassy** (245 3201231; ambaguibissau@mae.gov.gn; Rua Marien N'Gouabi; 8.30am-3pm Sat-Thu, to 1pm Fri)

**Portuguese Embassy** (245 3203379; www.consulado-pt-gb.org; Av Cidade de Lisboa; 8am-noon)

**Senegalese Embassy** (245 3212944; Rua General Omar Torrijos, off Praça dos Heróis Nacionais; 8am-noon)

**Spanish Embassy** (245 9667222 46; emb.bissau@maec.es; Praça dos Heróis Nacionais; 8am-noon)

### EMERGENCY & IMPORTANT NUMBERS

| | |
|---|---|
| Guinea-Bissau country code | 245 |
| International access code | 00 |
| Fire | 118 |
| Police | 117 |

### INTERNET ACCESS

Wi-fi is increasingly common in hotels and restaurants in Bissau. Roaming is possible on phones, but connections are generally slow. Outside the capital internet is more scarce. Only a small percentage of Bissau-Guineans are connected to the internet.

### LGBTIQ TRAVELLERS

Bissau-Guinean society is relatively tolerant, though no doubt there are still social taboos against homosexuality that discourage public displays of affection. No laws criminalise sexual orientation, and there are no official discriminatory policies or reports of violence or rights abuses targeting the country's gay and lesbian community.

### MONEY

**ATMs** ATMs that accept international MasterCard and Visa cards can be found at a handful of banks in Bissau, as well as several hotels, including the Malaika and Ledger Plaza. There is also an ATM immediately outside the arrivals hall of the airport in Bissau. Some ATMs work; others don't.

**Cash** The unit of currency is the West African CFA franc. This currency is also used by its neighbours in Senegal, Burkina Faso, Benin, Togo, Mali, Niger and Côte d'Ivoire. CFA stands

### EATING PRICE RANGES

Prices represent the cost of a main dish.

**$** less than CFA3100

**$$** CFA3100–6200

**$$$** more than CFA6200

for 'Communauté Financière d'Afrique' (Financial Community of Africa). It was adopted in 1997 when the country abandoned the Guinea-Bissau peso.

**Changing Money** It's best to change money in Bissau at Ecobank, BAO or Casa Cambio Nacional, one of the moneychangers. You can also ask your hotel, though these tend to have the worst exchange rates. It's probably best to arrive in Guinea-Bissau with a bundle of francs already on hand.

**Credit Cards** MasterCard and Visa are accepted at top-end hotels in Bissau. Cards are mostly useless elsewhere else, including in the Arquipélago dos Bijagós.

**Tipping** You'll often be asked for a *cadeau* (gift), whether you've been helped or not. It's up to you to decide whether it's appropriate in return for services rendered. At top-end hotels, one gratuity for cleaning staff, completely at your discretion. For restaurants, none expected at basic places; upscale, with decent service, 10% to 15%. Loose change is appreciated by taxi drivers. Tips are always expected for guides and drivers, around 10% or more if especially good and for multiday trips.

### Exchange Rates

| | | |
|---|---|---|
| Australia | A$1 | CFA452 |
| Canada | C$1 | CFA440 |
| Euro zone | €1 | CFA656 |
| Japan | ¥100 | CFA538 |
| New Zealand | NZ$1 | CFA415 |
| Switzerland | Sfr1 | CFA605 |
| UK | UK£1 | CFA774 |
| US | US$1 | CFA600 |

For current exchange rates, see www.xe.com.

### Tipping

You'll often be asked for a *cadeau* (gift), whether you've been helped or not. It's up to you to decide whether it's appropriate in return for services rendered.

- **Hotels** At top-end hotels, one gratuity for cleaning staff, completely at your discretion.
- **Restaurants** None expected at basic places; upscale, with decent service, 10% to 15%.
- **Taxis** Loose change appreciated.
- **Guide and driver** Always expected, around 10% or more if especially good and for multiday trips.

## OPENING HOURS

**Banks and government offices** Usually 8am to noon and 2pm to 5pm Monday to Friday, although hours vary.

**Shops** From 8am or 9am until 6pm Monday to Saturday. Some close for lunch.

**Corner grocers** In most towns you can find ones open until 10pm or later.

## POST

The postal service is slow. You're better off posting mail home from Senegal or The Gambia. Post offices generally open Monday to Friday mornings only, but the main post office (p359) in Bissau is open 8am to 6pm Monday to Saturday.

## PUBLIC HOLIDAYS

Islamic feasts, such as Eid al-Fitr (at the end of Ramadan) and Tabaski, are celebrated. Guinea-Bissau also celebrates a number of public holidays.

**New Year's Day** 1 January

**Anniversary of the Death of Amílcar Cabral** 20 January

**Women's Day** 8 March

**Easter** March/April

**Labour Day** 1 May

**Pidjiguiti Day** 3 August

**Independence Day** 24 September

**Christmas Day** 25 December

## TELEPHONE

If you don't have your own mobile telephone, try your hotel or the call centre at the main post office. Guinea-Bissau's country code is ☎245, and its international access code is ☎00.

## TOURIST INFORMATION

There are no functioning official tourism offices in Guinea-Bissau. An unofficial website that might prove useful is www.gbissau.org. But your best bet is asking for information at your accommodation.

## VISAS

According to Guinea-Bissau's Permanent Mission to the UN office in New York City, visas are not issued upon arrival at the airport in Bissau. However, travellers report it's possible to get a visa upon arrival at the airstrip in Bubaque for those flying on a small plane from Cap Skirring or Dakar in Senegal.

The UN office in New York City issues 30-day single-entry visas for US$100; two passport photos are required and the process generally takes three to five days.

Guinea-Bissau's embassies and consulates elsewhere (in Europe, there are embassies in Berlin, Brussels, Madrid, Paris and Lisbon) reportedly can do the same, though the price and time varies.

There is an official government-sponsored website (www.rgb-visa.com) that purports to process visa requests electronically for US$66 (single entry) and US$77 (multiple entry) prior to arrival. Its responsiveness and effectiveness is uneven, to say the least.

### PRACTICALITIES

**Electricity** Supply is 220V and plugs are of the European two-round-pin variety.

**Weights & measures** The metric system is used.

## Getting There & Away

### AIR

Osvaldo Vieira International Airport (p359) is located 9km north west of the centre of Bissau. It's small and has few facilities other than a single cafe. The small airstrip on Ilha de Bubaque services charter flights from Bissau and Cap Skirring and Dakar in Senegal.

Guinea-Bissau does not have its own national carrier. Senegal Airlines was not operating to Guinea-Bissau at the time of research; however, flights could resume in the future. Private planes can also be arranged.

The main airlines flying to Guinea-Bissau:

**ASKY Airlines** (p359)

**Euro Atlantic Airways** (☎245 5361081; www.flyeuroatlantic.pt; Rua Vitorino Costa; ⊙8.30am-5.30pm Mon-Fri) Weekly flights via Lisbon.

**Royal Air Maroc** (☎245 6652000; www.royalairmaroc.com) Via Casablanca. Very early morning arrival and departure times.

**TACV Cabo Verde Airlines** (VR; ☎245 3206087; www.tacv.com; Av Amílcar Cabral; ⊙8.30am-5.30pm Mon-Fri)

**TAP Air Portugal** (p359) Resuming flights in early 2017 after a four-year hiatus. Via Lisbon.

### LAND

#### Guinea

Transport to Guinea (plan on 24 to 48 hours to reach Conakry, depending on road/taxi conditions) leaves from Gabú, crosses the border at Burunduma (Guinea-Bissau) and Kandika (Guinea) and traverses a rough pass through the beautiful Fouta Djalon mountains.

Visas for Guinea can be acquired at its embassy in Bissau. Generally, they take several hours. Have your yellow-fever vaccination card handy for Guinea immigration at the border.

#### Senegal

The busiest crossing point to/from Senegal is at São Domingos, on the main route between Ingore and Ziguinchor. From Ziguinchor's *gare routière* (bus station), it's a three- to four-hour ride on a minibus (CFA3500) to Bissau (around CFA500 extra for luggage).

There are also crossing points between Tanaf and Farim; at Salikénié, just south of Kolda; and near Pirada, north of Gabú on the route to/from Vélingara and Tambacounda.

## Getting Around

### BOAT

The regular ferry linking Bissau to Ilha de Bubaque was not operating at the time of research. A replacement was supposedly on its way. Otherwise, for a fee speedboats from various resorts in the islands are open to nonguests joining if there is a space. *Canoas* (motor canoes) also make the trip; however, these are unreliable, uncomfortable and potentially dangerous. *Canoas* also operate between individual islands.

### SEPT PLACE & TRANSPORTE MISTO

*Sept places* are Peugeot 504 seven-seaters that link the main towns. More common and far less comfortable are large minibuses called *transportes misto* (literally 'mixed transport') or *toca-toca*; most fares are a dirt-cheap CFA100. Before 8am is the best time to get transport.

The main roads between Bissau and Bafatá, Gabú, São Domingos and Buba are all sealed and generally good. Stretches between Buba and Jemberém and São Domingos and Varela are unpaved and in bad condition.

### CAR & MOTORCYCLE

While a few major roadways are paved and in relatively good condition, a 4WD is recommended for most trips. There are few signposts, and animals, chickens, cows, pigs and goats are always a hazard. Your best bet to rent a vehicle in the country is to ask at the Ledger Plaza Bissau (p357), the **Azalaï 24 de Setembro** (☎245 955 803000; www.azalaihotels.com; Av Pansau Na Isna) or a travel agency in Bissau.

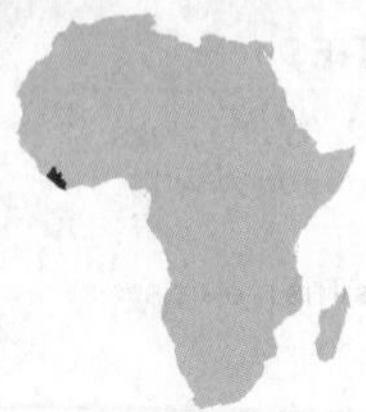

# Liberia

✆231 / POP 4.5 MILLION

**Includes ➡**



## Best Places to Eat

➡ Pak Bat (p376)

➡ Sweet Lips (p372)

➡ Evelyn's (p372)

## Best Places to Sleep

➡ Mamba Point Hotel (p372)

➡ Libassa Eco-Lodge (p374)

➡ Kwepunha Retreat & Villas (p374)

## Why Go?

Liberia, a lush, green, friendly and vibrant land, offers everything from excellent surf spots and shops selling wares by edgy local designers to days spent lolling in a comfy hammock on the edge of the rainforest while listening to tropical birds sing. It's home to one of West Africa's best national parks, and still hangs on to a confident American spirit mixed with West African roots. And despite the ravages of the past, it is a fantastic place to travel, full of hope and energy.

After a decade of dusting themselves off and resuming normal life following their brutal civil war, Liberians experienced another deadly conflict in 2014 – the Ebola virus. While the nation is officially Ebola-free per the WHO, it's struggling economically to recover. With travel restrictions lifted, tourism can play a huge role in this.

## When to Go

### Monrovia

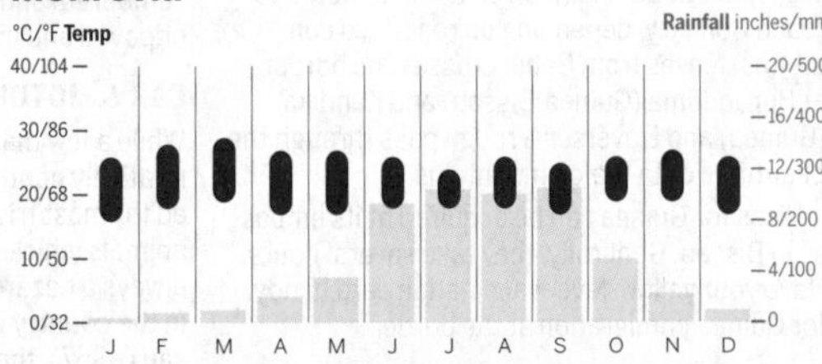


**Dec–Jul** Dry season and the most popular time to visit.

**May–Oct** Rainy season; spectacular stroms and good waves for surfers.

**Oct–Jan** Peak tourist season; prices are at their highest.

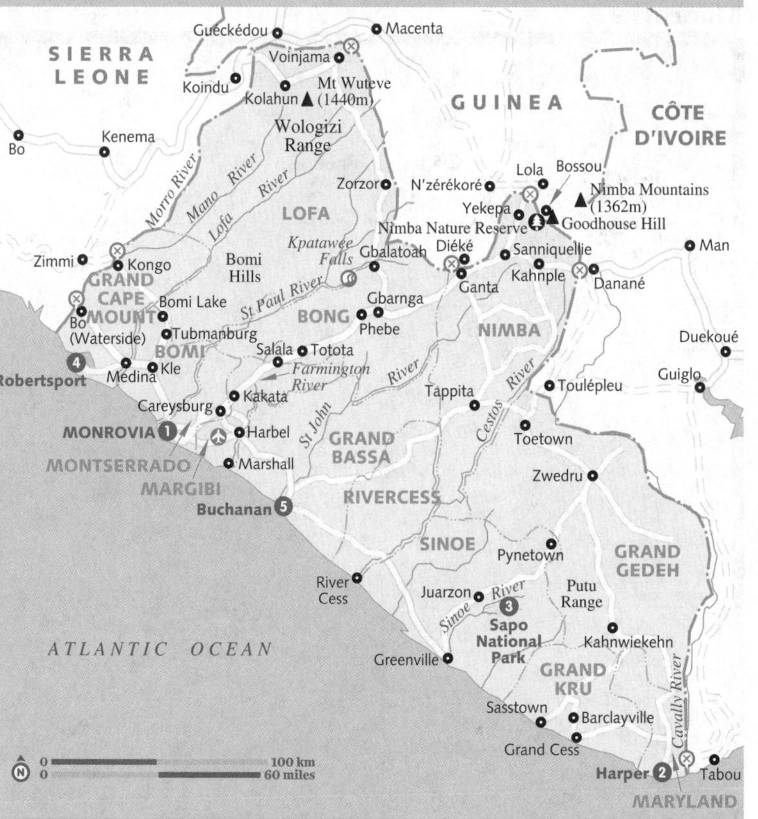




## Liberia Highlights

❶ **Monrovia** (p369) Exploring the relics of Liberia's rich history and the American influence that still shapes the capital.

❷ **Harper** (p376) Hitting the long, bumpy road to this pretty town that's blessed with southern American architecture and an end-of-the-line feel.

❸ **Sapo National Park** (p375) Venturing into the habitat of the endangered pygmy hippo, camping beneath the forest canopy and listening to the sounds of the rainforest.

❹ **Robertsport** (p374) Riding the waves with Liberian surfers, running your hands through the phosphorescent swell and eating fresh lobster in the shade.

❺ **Buchanan** (p374) Camping on the wild and beautiful beaches and relaxing at the port.

# MONROVIA

0880 / POP 1.8 MILLION

Ionrovia has been everything over the decades – a splendid African capital brimming vith elegant stores and faces, a party city nonitored by sheriffs wearing secondhand JS police uniforms, a war zone marred y bullet holes, and a broken-hearted city struggling to climb to its feet after both war and a deadly Ebola outbreak.

Walk along Broad St, Monrovia's main boulevard, and you'll hear the original beat of locally brewed hip-co and the gentle rhythm of Liberian English. You'll see the architectural ghosts of Monrovia's past and the uniformed school children of its future. You'll watch entrepreneurs climb into sleek,

# Monrovia

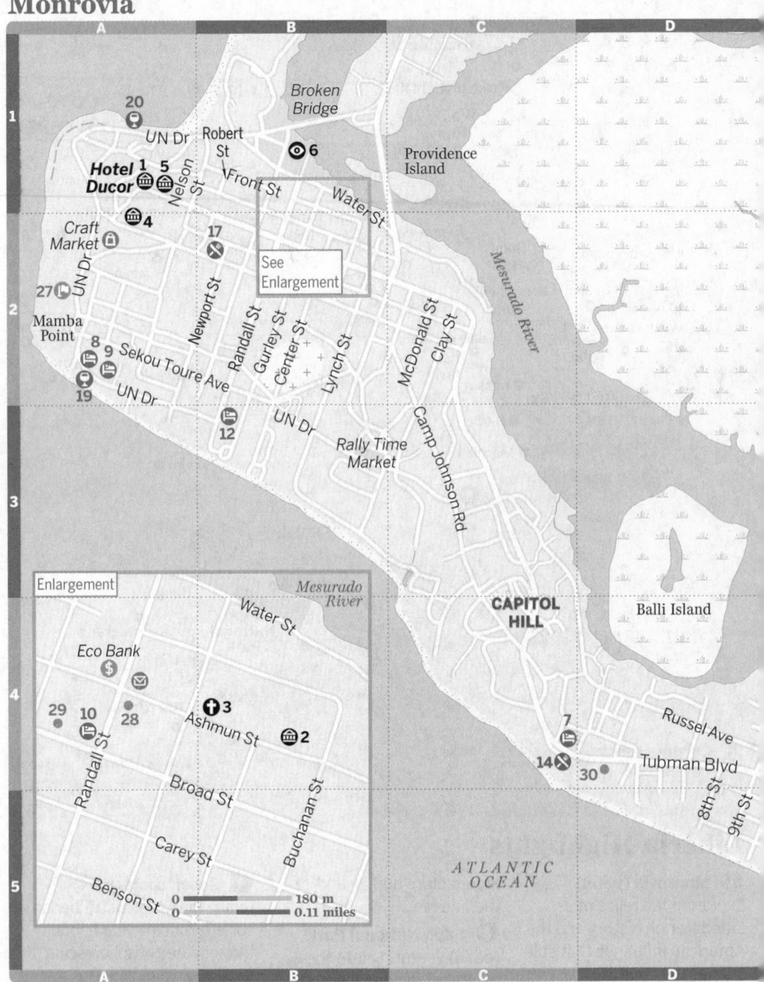




low-slung cars, market men sell coconuts from rusty wheelbarrows, and models sashay in tight jeans and heels. Monrovia has shaken off many of its old epithets and is infused with a new, exciting energy.

## Sights

With the weather on your side and half a day to spare, you can see most of Monrovia's major architectural landmarks on foot. Worthwhile historic buildings include the retro **Rivoli Cinema** (Broad St) and the **EJ Roye building** (Ashmun St), which dominates the skyline and was once home to a spectacular auditorium.

The imposing **Masonic Temple** (Benso St) overlooks the city at the western end c Broad St, in the shadow of the abandone **Hotel Ducor** (Broad St) FREE; this was Wes Africa's finest hotel in the 1970s, where Id Amin swam in the pool and Miriam Makeb sang in the bar.

**Waterside Market** MARKE

(Water St, opposite Providence Island) Chaoti Waterside Market offers almost everythin for sale, including colourful textiles, shoe leather goods and pottery, all with a dose c foul smells and lots of noise. Haggle hard

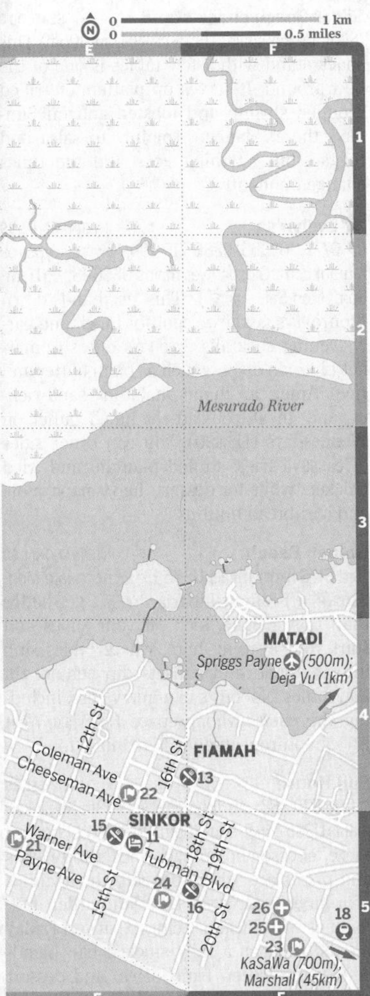


## Monrovia

**Top Sights**
1 Hotel Ducor ... A1

**Sights**
2 EJ Roye Building ... B4
3 First United Methodist Church ... B4
4 Masonic Temple ... A2
5 Rivoli Cinema ... A1
6 Waterside Market ... B1

**Sleeping**
7 Bella Casa ... C4
8 Cape Hotel ... A2
9 Mamba Point Hotel ... A2
10 Palm Hotel ... A4
11 Royal Grand Hotel ... E5
12 St Theresa's Convent ... B3

**Eating**
13 Evelyn's ... F4
14 Golden Beach ... C4
15 Living Room ... E5
16 Sajj House ... F5
17 Sweet Lips ... B2

**Drinking & Nightlife**
18 Deja Vu ... F5
19 Lila Brown's ... A2
20 Tides ... A1

**Information**
21 French Embassy ... E5
22 Ghanaian Embassy ... E4
23 Guinean Embassy ... F5
24 Ivoirian Consulate ... E5
25 JFK Hospital ... F5
26 Lucky Pharmacy ... F5
27 US Embassy ... A2

**Transport**
28 Brussels Airlines ... A4
29 Kenya Airways ... A4
30 Royal Air Maroc ... D4

smile, and embrace raw Monrovia to its fullest.

**Silver Beach** BEACH
This pretty beach is fun and relatively easy to get to, plus it's home to the best beach snack joint in the area. It's located about 15km southeast of Monrovia (a US$12 charter taxi ride).

**First United Methodist Church** CHURCH
(cnr Gurley & Ashmun Sts) You might spot President Ellen Johnson Sirleaf attending a Sunday service here. The church is open to the public.

## Sleeping

**St Theresa's Convent** HOSTEL $
(☎0886 784 276; archdiocesanpastoralcenter@yahoo.com; Randall St; r US$30, without bathroom US$20, ste US$50) Cheap and cheerful St Theresa's has rooms that back onto the convent and religious centre. There's a 10pm curfew.

**Palm Hotel** HOTEL $$
(☎0886 585 959, 0880 425 980; www.palmhotelmonrovia.com; cnr Broad & Randall Sts; s/d incl breakfast from US$115/135; ❄@🛜) Located in the very heart of the city, the Palm is secure, clean and comfortable, with free in-room wi-fi and a great rooftop restaurant. Try to score a room with a balcony.

**Cape Hotel** HOTEL $$

(077 006 633; www.thecapehotelliberia.com; United Nations Dr, Mamba Pt; s/d from US$170/$250, ste or apt from US$400; P ❄ wifi pool) This reasonably priced option features an on-site terrace restaurant, parking and a pool. It's a particularly well-maintained space with a lovely terrace to while away hot afternoons; friendly, helpful staff will provide endless local tips. The smaller 'suites' are really just slightly larger rooms; the larger suites have kitchenettes, and apartments have full kitchens.

**Bella Casa** BOUTIQUE HOTEL $$

(077 692 272, 077 444 110; www.bellacasaliberia.com; cnr 3rd St & Tubman Blvd, Sinkor; d from US$115; P ❄ wifi) A sound midrange boutique-style option, Bella Casa is a short walk from Capitol Hill and the UN building. They might not quite evoke dreams of Italy, but the rooms are comfortable, clean and come with air-con, desks and free wi-fi. The suites are large, with stylish bed linen and a more luxurious touch.

**★Mamba Point Hotel** LUXURY HOTEL $$$

(06 544 544, 06 440 000; www.mambapointhotel.biz; United Nations Dr; r/ste US$240/400; P ❄ wifi pool) Monrovia's finest hotel is an institution. It has 60-plus beautiful rooms, decked out with stylish furnishings and luxurious bathrooms (the suites are divine, with stunning sea views). Staff are top-notch. There's an excellent terrace restaurant, adjacent sushi bar, a casino, a pool, a gym and a cocktail bar.

**Royal Grand Hotel** LUXURY HOTEL $$$

(077-777 788; royalhotelliberia@yahoo.com; cnr 15th St & Tubman Blvd; r from US$260; P ❄ wifi) The Royal is one of the classiest hotels in town. The complex holds plush rooms (including presidential suites from US$890), a coffee shop, a hair salon, an art gallery, an Asian-fusion restaurant and a rooftop cocktail bar. If you want pampering and the closest thing to five-star service in Monrovia, this is it.

## Eating

**Sweet Lips** LIBERIAN $

(Newport St; meals US$1.50-3; 11am-9pm Mon-Sat) This firm favourite is said to serve up the very best Liberian food in town – try the excellent *fufu* (puréed, fermented cassava) and palm butter.

**Silver Beach snack stand** SEAFOOD $

(Silver Beach; mains US$5-15; 11am-10pm) This snack stand with a few tables is one of the best around. It serves up platters of grilled grouper, shrimp and lobster, and on Sundays there's dancing (mainly to salsa and reggae, but anything goes and the tunes change frequently).

**★Evelyn's** INTERNATIONAL $$

(0777 001 155, 0886 710 104; www.evelynsrestaurant.com; Gibson Ave; mains US$6-18; 11am-8pm Mon-Sat; ❄ wifi) This is hands-down Monrovia's favourite spot for lunch and early-evening cocktails. Evelyn's offers upmarket Liberian dishes (such as palm butter and rice), American mains including sandwiches, and an all-you-can-eat lunch buffet on Wednesdays (US$20). You can order sides of cassava fries, stuffed plantain and fried chicken, while for dessert there's papaya pie and cornbread muffins.

**Golden Beach** INTERNATIONAL $$

(3rd St, Sinkor; meals US$5-13; noon-late Mon-Sun; P family) Life in Liberia doesn't get better than this. Exhale, kick off your shoes and start your evening here, where tables sink into the sand and sunsets dip behind gin and tonics. Nobody's in a hurry here, including the chefs, who prepare Liberian/West African, European and Vietnamese food.

**Sajj House** LEBANESE $$

(06 830 888; cnr Tubman Blvd & 18th St, Sinkor; mains US$5-14; 9am-10pm; P wifi menu) Lebanese meze, cheese-and-spinach pies, sandwiches and pizzas are served beneath the awnings of a large traditional Liberian garden hut. Popular with salsa-dancing expats on Friday nights, Sajj has a fully stocked bar, blender (try the frozen fruit juices) and dessert menu, featuring chocolate crêpes. The volume dial turns with the clock.

**Living Room** SUSHI $$

(06 850 333; Royal Grand Hotel, cnr Tubman Blvd & 14th St; sushi US$5-15, mains from US$15; 11am-9pm) Celebrated by expats for its transcendent tuna salad, Monrovia's top sushi bar feels very glamorous with smart leather chairs, sleek black tables and a gleaming sushi counter. Takeaway is available.

## Drinking & Nightlife

**Lila Brown's** BAR

(UN Dr; 5pm-late Mon-Sun; wifi) Lila B's is an elegant duplex bar nestled between the

Mamba Point Hotel and the Atlantic, set in an old colonial home. Downstairs there's a food menu and a party vibe on weekend nights. Climb the wooden staircase for sea views, waiter service and relaxed tables shielded from rainy-season downpours by stylish shower curtains.

**Deja Vu** CLUB
(☎05 555 000; Airfield Short Cut, Sinkor; ⏱10pm-4am Tue-Sat) Join the shimmering, moneyed party people at Liberia's sleekest club, which hosts DJs and regular special nights. No shorts or sandals for men.

**Tides** BAR
(☎0777 666 444; United Nations Dr; ⏱4pm-late Wed-Sun) Wicker armchairs and loveseats line the wide veranda at the oceanfront Tides, where you get views with style. Inside, find the cocktail list scribbled on a blackboard (try the bissap margarita), a pool table and a long bar beneath a safari-lodge ceiling. The kitchen (sandwiches, cassava fries and crispy fried plantain, known as *kelewele*) opens after 4.30pm.

## Shopping

★**KaSaWa** CLOTHING
(☎0886 698 005; 1st St, Sinkor; ⏱10am-6pm Mon-Sat) A fair-trade initiative that brings together designers and producers from Robertsport. The assortment includes colourful bags and clothes. The group often funds local charities – ask what's currently on its radar when you visit.

**Leslie Lumeh** ART
(☎0886 430 483; www.leslielumeh.com) Leslie sells his watercolour and acrylic paintings and is *the* go-to source of info on the Liberian contemporary art scene. He does not have a gallery per se but give him a ring if you want to see his work and he will set something up.

**Craft Market** ARTS & CRAFTS
(⏱10am-6pm) This cluster of craft vendors on the hilltop above the US embassy offers a mix of masks, clothing and other trinkets. It's a good place for bargains.

## Information

### DANGERS & ANNOYANCES

Be careful around Waterside and avoid West Point and most of the beaches in town, for both security and health reasons. Watch your back (and head) if you choose to zip around on the back of a *pen-pen* (motorbike taxi).

### MEDICAL SERVICES

Medical care is limited in Liberia.

**JFK Hospital** (Tubman Blvd, Sinkor) Monrovia's main hospital is fine for basic needs (it can do malaria tests), but should be avoided for more serious matters, unless the hospital's annual flying surgeons are in town.

**Lucky Pharmacy** (Tubman Blvd; ⏱8.30am-late Mon-Sun) Opposite JFK Hospital, this pharmacy is trusted by international organisations and has knowledgeable staff.

**SOS Clinic** (☎0886 841 673; Tubman Blvd, Congo Town) Head here in the first instance if you fall sick; this clinic is the best-equipped in the country, trusted by expats. It's between the YWCA and Total Garage.

### MONEY

**Eco Bank** (Asmun St; ⏱10am-4pm Mon-Fri)

### POST

**Main Post Office** (cnr Randall & Ashmun Sts; ⏱8am-4pm Mon-Fri, to noon Sat)

## Getting There & Away

Flights arrive at **Roberts International Airport** (ROB; Robertsfield), 60km southeast of Monrovia, from where a taxi into the city costs around US$80. There is also the little-used Spriggs Payne Airport (MLW) in Sinkor.

Bush taxis for Robertsport and the Sierra Leone border leave from Duala Motor Park, 9km northeast of the town centre. Transport for most other domestic destinations leaves from the Red Light Motor Park, Monrovia's main motor park, 15km northeast of the centre. Nearby Guinea Motor Park has buses heading to Guinea and Côte d'Ivoire.

# THE COAST

## Marshall

The rural area surrounding Marshall makes for an easy weekend escape from the city. You can camp on the quiet beaches here or see the chimps at Monkey Island.

### Sights

**Monkey Island** ISLAND
(donation US$10-20) This small archipelago is home to chimpanzees that were evacuated from a hepatitis research lab during the war. Enquire in town about the most up-to-date

options for heading there by canoe (US$5 to US$10) – it can be hit or miss, but there will usually be someone around who can take you.

**Firestone Rubber Plantation** PLANTATION
(Harbel) This is the world's largest rubber plantation, which is leased from the government on a controversial 99-year plan. You can view how rubber is processed (not official tours, just ask at the entrance and they will normally oblige), or play a round at the 18-hole golf course. The only way to get here from Marshall is by car. The journey takes roughly an hour.

### Sleeping

★ **Libassa Eco-Lodge** LODGE $$$
(☎0888 555 563, 05 940 930; www.libassa.com; day entry fee US$10, huts US$125, honeymoon ste US$250; P) With pretty, solar-powered huts (named after endangered Liberian species) on the edge of the forest, Libassa makes for a gorgeous weekend retreat near Marshall. Pack your swimsuit: there's a pool, a lagoon and a beach. There's also a lunch buffet run by helpful staff. The 2km stretch of road beyond Kpan Town is rough and only accessible by 4WD (45 minutes from Monrovia, 15 minutes from Marshall).

**RLJ Kendeja** RESORT $$$
(☎0886 219 939; www.rljkendejaresort.com; r from US$205; P) This sleek, dreamy resort is spread across a beach in the environs of the airport. Interlinked walkways take you to the pool, the plush bar and restaurant, and the spa. Sunday brunch is a hit with expat NGO workers and there are romantic getaway deals.

### Getting There & Away

It's a short drive from Roberts International Airport and an hour from Monrovia.

## Robertsport

☎0880 / POP 4100

Framed by gold-spun beaches, phosphorescent waves and a thick mane of forest, this pretty capital of Grand Cape Mount, just a fishing village a few years ago, has largely retained its simple, paradise-found feel. Now, as you emerge from the rust-red roads and wind your way through the old town with its architecture in various states of undress (look out for the stunning scarlet ruins of the defunct Tubman Center of African Culture), you're greeted by surf lodges and body-boarding tourists.

### Sights

**Casava Point** is a beach for ambitious surfers – it heaves towards the shiny granite rocks. **Cotton Trees** has beautiful surf along its shallow sand bar. **Fisherman's Point** is the closest of the surf beaches to town, and is good for beginners.

Destroyed during Liberia's war, the shambles of the **Tubman Center of African Culture**, a former museum and now a ruin, yields a few onlookers. Its draw is to see how the overgrowth keeps gaining ground. Remnants of its bright red colour can still be seen in spots and its grand pillars are still majestic, even in their dilapidated state.

### Sleeping & Eating

★ **Kwepunha Retreat & Villas** GUESTHOUSE $
(☎0888 132 870; www.kwepunha.com; Fisherman's Beach; s/d US$55/90; P) Run by Californian surfers in conjunction with community initiatives, this blue-and-yellow beach house offers pleasant, breezy rooms with wooden four-poster beds. You can join grassroots-style surf retreats here, or book the rooms independently. The house is situated on Fisherman's Beach, where you can tuck into fish tacos and margaritas.

**Nana's Lodge** LODGE $$
(☎086 668 332; Cassava Beach; canvas/wooden bungalows for 2 from US$75/115; P) Robertsport's original eco-lodge, Nana's has 11 bungalows overlooking the beach. The wooden huts are pricier than the canvas ones, but both styles of accommodation come with two comfortable double beds, fans and balconies. The sandy cantina down on the beach is a top sunset spot.

### Getting There & Away

Bush taxis cover the intermittently unpaved 120km route between Robertsport and Monrovia (L$375 to L$400, four to five hours). The same route is possible in 3½ hours via private taxi (US$150) or 4WD (US$200, plus the cost of petrol).

## Buchanan

☎0880 / POP 35,250

Liberia's second port hosts wild, beautiful beaches that are perfect for camping, plus an annual dumboy festival in January: two good reasons to make it here. Pre-Ebola it was on the way up; these days it's still gorgeous but development has ceased. Still, its stunning coast means there is much potential for this place.

### Sleeping & Eating

**Teepro Lodge** LODGE $
(☎0880 961 568; Roberts St, next to the Buchanan Renewables site; r with net & fan US$35) You can sleep at the clean, quiet and reasonably comfortable Teepro Lodge. The staff are extremely friendly and helpful. Should the lodge be full, staff will be happy to advise on beach camping options nearby.

**Sparks Hotel** HOTEL $$
(cnr Gardner & Church Sts; r US$80-110; P ❄ ☎) Although loud and brash, this is still the best choice in town, with functional, spartan rooms. It serves decent Lebanese and African fare (US$13 to US$25), and it is home to a so-so nightclub.

### Information

Be aware of the strong currents if you swim. And it's advisable to hire an overnight security guard if camping on the beach.

### Getting There & Away

Bush taxis ply the route from Monrovia (L$450, three hours) or you can charter a car (US$120 one way) or a 4WD (US$180 plus petrol per day) for the 125km to Buchanan, which is mostly paved.

# THE SOUTHEAST

## Zwedru

☎0880 / POP 24,700

Flanked by thick, lush rainforest that runs along the Côte d'Ivoire border, Zwedru is the capital of Grand Gedeh, one of Liberia's greenest counties. This is the hometown of Samuel Doe, who stole power in a bloody coup in 1980. His mark is still evident in Zwedru, where he installed pavements and was in the process of constructing a house on the edge of town when he was murdered. Many in Grand Gedeh, particularly those who feel forgotten by the Monrovia administration, remain vocal supporters of Doe.

WORTH A TRIP

### MOUNT NIMBA

Beautiful **Mt Nimba** (☎777 397 418; Zortopa; guide for 1 day US$8-15) is Liberia's tallest peak, 1362m above sea level, and you can feasibly climb it if you have a few days on your hands (it's a rewarding way to beat the heat of Monrovia). You can camp along the way if you have your own equipment, hiking along the peaks. Bring a GPS and warm clothing as it can get misty and very cool at night.

The jumping-off point is the curious town of Yekepa, a 10-hour drive from Monrovia and a Truman Show–esque mining town owned by Arcelor Mittal. The road to Mt Nimba is paved for almost three-quarters of the way to the top; you can drive to the peak using a 4WD. The **Noble House Motel** (Yekepa; ☎077 285 158; main road; r from US$22) is the only sleeping option of note in Yekepa.

These days, the best reason to visit is to experience the exceptional primary rainforest of Sapo National Park.

### Sights

**Sapo National Park** NATIONAL PARK
(scnlib2001@yahoo.com) FREE Sapo, Liberia's only national park, is a lush 1808-sq-km tract containing some of West Africa's last remaining primary rainforest. Within it lurk forest elephants, pygmy hippos, chimpanzees, antelopes and other wildlife, although these populations suffered greatly during the war.

### Sleeping

**Munnah Guesthouse** GUESTHOUSE $$
(☎0886 485 288; r from US$40; P) The best place to stay is the Munnah Guesthouse – it's used by NGOs working in the area's Ivoirian refugee camps. The modern, airy rooms have fans.

**Monjue Hotel** HOTEL $$
(☎0880 748 658; r US$50-70; P) A basic hotel that can be noisy at weekends.

### Eating

The main road that runs through town has an assortment of snack bars and one eatery.

**Florida Restaurant** AFRICAN $
(main road; mains US$10-18) This is a popular meeting spot that serves cheap Liberian dishes and European mains.

### Getting There & Away

From Monrovia, Zwedru can be reached by bush taxi for roughly L$800, a private taxi will generally cost around US$500 and a 4WD upwards of US$600 (plus petrol). It's only 200km, but you'll need to allow around nine to 10 hours to get here as the route is long, rough and bumpy.

## Harper

0880 / POP 17,900

Charming, small-town Harper feels like the prize at the end of a long treasure hunt. The capital of the once-autonomous Maryland state, this gem is shingled with decaying ruins that hint at its former grandeur.

### Sights

**Cape Palmas Lighthouse** LIGHTHOUSE
FREE This lighthouse can be climbed for an outstanding panoramic view of the cape. Although no longer functional, it's on a UN base, so get permission first, and don't attempt to scale the small, slippery steps during the rainy season. Don't miss the stunning, palm-lined beach at nearby Fish Town (not to be confused with the larger town of the same name), but take care with the currents if you swim.

**William Tubman mansion** HOUSE
(Maryland Ave) FREE In the early evenings, the soft light gives an eldritch feel to the shell of the presidential mansion of former president William Tubman, who was born in Harper, and the remnants of the Morning Star Masonic Lodge, built by Tubman, himself a Grand Master Freemason.

### Sleeping

**Adina's Guest House** GUESTHOUSE $
(0886 620 005; Maryland Ave; r US$55) Adina's has several basic rooms with fans, but it's a spotless place to rest your head and is arguably the best place to stay in town. Be sure to book as far in advance as possible: this place fills up quick. It's on the main road, next to the church.

**Pastoral Center** HOSTEL $
(Ivory Coast Rd; d US$30-40) The Pastoral Center offers basic dorm beds at low prices – worth it if you are truly on a budget and need a secure place to rest your head.

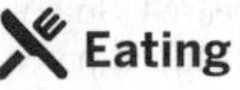

### Eating

**Pak Bat** ASIAN $
(mains US$4-6) There's great South Asian food to be had at Pak Bat, the Pakistani UN peacekeepers' battalion, so long as you're prepared to hang with pretty much only NGO workers.

**Sophie's** LIBERIAN $
(Mechlin St; mains US$5-11) Sophie's offers good potato greens and cassava-leaf stew.

**Jade's** LIBERIAN $$
(cnr Walter & Mechlin Sts; mains US$5-10; 11am-9pm) Jade's (or Sweet Baby, as some locals lovingly call it) serves fish, chicken and rice, as well as sandwiches and pizzas if the delivery truck has brought supplies.

### Getting There & Away

Reachable after two days on some of Liberia's worst road. The drive from Monrovia to Harper can be broken up in Zwedru (10 to 11 hours), from where it's around five to six hours further south. It's inadvisable to attempt this route during the rainy season, even if you're travelling by 4WD.

# UNDERSTAND LIBERIA

## Liberia Today

Liberia's Nobel Peace Prize–winning president, Ellen Johnson Sirleaf, won a second term in power in 2011, after rival party Congress for Democratic Change (CDC) – led by Winston Tubman and former AC Milan footballer George Weah – boycotted the second round of the violence-ridden vote, complaining of fraud. 'Ellen', as she is widely known, enjoys support from a loyal band of Liberians. Others criticise her for being a part of the old set of politicians and accuse her of failing to understand their woes.

Ellen also failed in 2010 to implement the findings of Liberia's Truth and Reconciliation Commission, a post-conflict justice organ that was modelled on South Africa's. The body's final report recommended that the president herself be barred from holding public office for 50 years, after she admitted partially bankrolling former leader Charles Taylor's rebellion that sparked the civil war.

Taylor was sentenced to 50 years behind bars by a UN-backed war crimes tribunal in The Hague in 2011. Many Liberians expressed frustration that Taylor was tried not for his role in the painful Liberian conflict, but for masterminding rebel operations during Sierra Leone's war.

Many middle-class Liberians were excited about the country's new dawn, but for others – particularly those outside Monrovia – the fresh coats of paint and eager investors in the capital did little to heal old wounds.

Today, Liberia is still recovering from the effects of the Ebola virus, which devastated the country economically and ruptured its struggling healthcare system. At time of writing, all eyes were on the 2017 presidential elections and what changes that might bring to a country that is struggling to stay on its feet.

## History

Liberia was ruled along ethnic lines until American abolitionists looking for a place to resettle freed slaves stepped off the boat at Monrovia's Providence Island in 1822. They saw themselves as part of a mission to bring civilisation and Christianity to Africa, but their numbers were soon depleted by tropical diseases and hostile indigenous residents.

The surviving settlers, known as Americo-Liberians, declared an independent republic in 1847, under the mantra 'The Love of Liberty Brought Us Here'. However, citizenship excluded indigenous peoples, and every president until 1980 was of American freed-slave ancestry. For nearly a century, Liberia foundered economically and politically while the indigenous population suffered under forced labour. They were not afforded the right to vote until 1963.

During William Tubman's presidency (1944–71) the tides began to change. Foreign investment flowed into the country, and for several decades Liberia sustained sub-Saharan Africa's highest growth rate. Firestone and other American companies made major investments during this time.

Yet the influx of new money exacerbated existing social inequalities, and hostilities between Americo-Liberians and the indigenous population worsened during the era of William Tolbert, who succeeded Tubman. While the elite continued to live the high life, resentment among other Liberians quietly simmered.

In 2005 Liberia made headlines by electing economist and Nobel Peace Prize-winner Ellen Johnson Sirleaf as Africa's first female head of state. She has been credited with reducing Liberia's debt, maintaining peace and improving infrastructure in the country, but has been criticised for some of the ways she handled the 2014 Ebola outbreak. At the time of writing, she was wrapping up her last year of presidency among multiple contenders for the 2017 presidential election.

From 2014 to 2016 the Ebola virus infected around 10,700 people, killed an estimated 4900 and devastated the economy (the majority of infections occurred in 2014). Liberia was declared Ebola-free in 2015, had several small outbreaks and was then again declared free of the virus in 2016. At the time of writing it was still on the long road to economic and emotional recovery.

## Culture

Liberia remains a country of exceptions. The old inequality hang-ups haven't gone away; you'll notice that Americo-Liberians and returning, educated Liberians often enjoy better treatment than those with indigenous roots. Various initiatives are under way to even things out, but the road to cultural equality is likely to be long.

Regardless of their roots, one thing all Liberians have in common is their devotion to family. Many people you meet will be supporting a dozen others. Religion is also important, with Christian families regularly attending revivals at churches.

The Liberian handshake has Masonic origins and involves a snappy pull-back of the third finger, often accompanied by a wide grin.

## People

The vast majority of Liberians are of indigenous origin, belonging to more than a dozen major tribal groups, including the Kpelle in the centre, the Bassa around Buchanan and the Mandingo (Mandinka) in the north. Americo-Liberians account for barely 5% of the total. There's also an economically powerful Lebanese community in Monrovia.

Close to half of the population are Christians and about 20% are Muslim, with the remainder following traditional religions.

## Arts & Crafts

Liberia has long been famed for its masks, especially those of the Gio in the northeast, including the *gunyege* mask (which shelters a power-giving spirit), and the chimpanzee-like *kagle* mask. The Bassa around Buchanan are renowned for their *gela* masks, which often have elaborately carved coiffures, always with an odd number of plaits.

## Environment

Illegal logging both during and after the conflict has threatened a number of species in Liberia, including the forest elephant, hawk, pygmy hippo (nigh-on impossible to see), manatee and chimpanzee. Liberia's rainforests, which now cover about 40% of the country, comprise a critical part of the Guinean Forests of West Africa Hotspot, an exceptionally biodiverse area stretching across 11 countries in the region.

Liberia's low-lying coastal plain is intersected by marshes, creeks and tidal lagoons, and bisected by at least nine major rivers. Inland is a densely forested plateau rising to low mountains in the northeast. The highest point is Mt Nimba (1362m).

# SURVIVAL GUIDE

## Directory A–Z

### ACCOMMODATION

Accommodation prices in Monrovia are on the high side due to the presence of private companies and NGOs. You can expect to pay top dollar in the capital, comparable to large European or US cities, with a few exceptions. Upcountry, both prices and standards are lower and the range of accommodation options generally cover budget to midrange.

#### SLEEPING PRICE RANGES

The following price ranges refer to a double room.

**$** less than US$50

**$$** US$50–100

**$$$** more than US$100

### DANGERS & ANNOYANCES

- Liberia has some of the strongest rip currents in the world. Check with locals before you swim, never swim alone and learn how to negotiate rip tides before you dip your toes into the ocean.
- The biggest dangers are the roads.
- The security situation is somewhat stable, although it's wise not to walk in Monrovia after dark and be vigilant about staying in secure lodging.
- Exercise caution if using motorbike taxis and don't be afraid to ask the driver to go slow.
- Electric shocks are common in badly wired buildings; wear shoes before plugging in appliances.

### EMERGENCY & IMPORTANT NUMBERS

| | |
|---|---|
| Liberia's country code | ☎231 |
| Emergency (Fire, Police, Ambulance) | ☎911 |

### EMBASSIES & CONSULATES

Canadians and Australians should contact their high commissions in Abidjan, Côte d'Ivoire and Accra, Ghana, respectively.

**French Embassy** (☎031 235 576; German Compound, Congo Town; ⊙11am-3pm Mon-Thu)

**German Embassy** (☎0886 438 365; Tubman Blvd, UNMIL Bldg, Congo Town; ⊙10am-4pm Mon-Fri)

**Ghanaian Embassy** (☎077 016 920; cnr 15th St & Cheesman Ave, Sinkor; ⊙11am-3pm Mon-Fri)

**Guinean Embassy** (☎0886 573 049; Tubman Blvd btwn 23rd & 24th Sts, Sinkor; ⊙10.30am-4pm Mon-Fri)

**Ivoirian Consulate** (☎0886 519 138; Warner Ave btwn 17th & 18th Sts, Sinkor; ⊙10am-4pm Mon-Fri)

**Nigerian Embassy** (☎0886 261 148; Tubman Blvd, Nigeria House, Congo Town; ⊙10am-4pm Mon-Fri)

**Sierra Leonean Embassy** (☎0886 427 404; Tubman Blvd, Congo Town; ⊙10am-3pm Mon-Fri)

**UK Embassy** (☎06 516 973; chalkleyroy@aol.com; United Nations Dr, Clara Town, Bushrod Island; ⊙10am-4pm Mon-Fri) Honorary consul, emergency assistance only; otherwise contact the British High Commission in Freetown, Sierra Leone.

**US Embassy** (☎077 054 826; http://monrovia.usembassy.gov/; United Nations Dr, Mamba Point; ⊙11am-4pm Mon-Fri)

## FOOD

Rice and spicy meat sauces or fish stews are popular Liberian dishes. Palm butter with fish and potato greens are two favourites. Other popular dishes include palava sauce (made with plato leaf, dried fish or meat and palm oil) and *jollof rice* (rice and vegetables with meat or fish). American food is popular in Monrovia. Restaurants in Monrovia are sophisticated and varied; outside the capital, options are more limited.

## INTERNET ACCESS

Internet cafes are popping up more and more, but service (always slow) is limited in rural areas. Wi-fi spaces are increasing (especially in Monrovia). Internet access costs from US$4 to US$6 per hour; wi-fi in hotel lobbies and bars is usually free with a purchase.

## LGBTIQ TRAVELLERS

Homosexual acts in Liberia are punishable by one year in jail, and the idea of making a same-sex relationship a felony crime (punishable with a 10-year prison sentence) has been floated by the government. LBGTIQ campaigners in the country have also been targets of violence. Needless to say, gay travellers need to be extremely cautious travelling here.

## MONEY

The Liberian dollar is tied to the US dollar. When in the country, US dollars are used for anything over approximately US$5. You can pay for anything in US dollars and your change may be in either currency (often a mix of both).

Make sure your US dollars are new (ideally issued after 2000) and in good shape, or risk them being rejected. Counterfeit US dollars is a serious issue, so be sure to closely inspect any bills you receive as change.

Monrovia has ATMs that dispense cash in US dollars. Elsewhere, bring cash. Western Union and Moneygram operate in most towns.

### Exchange Rates

| | | |
|---|---|---|
| Australia | A$1 | US$0.77 |
| Canada | C$ | US$0.76 |
| Euro zone | €1 | US$1.05 |
| Japan | ¥100 | US$0.88 |
| New Zealand | NZ$ | US$0.72 |
| UK | £1 | US$1.25 |

For current exchange rates, see www.xe.com.

### Tipping

**Restaurants** Add 10% for all meals except takeaway.

**Taxis** You don't need to tip taxi drivers, but if you hire a guide or a driver for the day, tip roughly 5%.

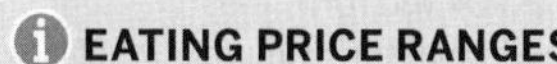

### EATING PRICE RANGES

Price ranges for a main course:

**$** less than US$5

**$$** US$5–15

**$$$** more than US$10

## OPENING HOURS

**Banks** 9am to 4pm Monday to Friday, 9am to noon Saturday.

**Shops** 9am to 6pm Monday to Friday, 9am to 4pm Saturday.

**Businesses** 9am to 5pm Monday to Friday.

## PUBLIC HOLIDAYS

**New Year's Day** 1 January

**Armed Forces Day** 11 February

**Decoration Day** Second Wednesday in March

**JJ Roberts' Birthday** 15 March

**Fast & Prayer Day** 11 April

**National Unification Day** 14 May

**Independence Day** 26 July

**Flag Day** 24 August

**Liberian Thanksgiving Day** First Thursday in November

**Tubman Day** 29 November

**Christmas Day** 25 December

## TELEPHONE

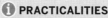

The country code is ☎231.There are no area codes or landlines.

Pick up a Cellcom or Lonestar SIM card from booths on the street for US$6 to US$8.

### PRACTICALITIES

**Electricity** Voltage is 110V. Plugs are a mixture of US-style (two flat pins) and European-style.Grid power is gradually improving in Monrovia, although most hotels and apartment blocks still rely on fuel-heavy generators. Outside of the capital, it's generators all the way.

**Newspapers** There are dozens of national newspapers; among the best-regarded are the *New Dawn*, the *Observer* and *Front Page Africa*.

**Weights & measures** Liberia has been trying to convert to the metric system but the imperial system (feet, yards) is still commonly used.

### TOURIST INFORMATION

There are no formal tourist information offices in the country.

### VISAS

Visas are required by all except nationals of Economic Community of West African States or South Korea. Costs vary depending on where they are procured.

## Getting There & Away

### AIR

**Monrovia Roberts International Airport** (p373) is the main airport in Liberia. Drastic cuts to service were made during the Ebola crisis and, at the time of writing, few airlines served Roberts.

Airlines serving Monrovia:

**Brussels Airlines** (www.brusselsairlines.com; Randall St)

**Kenya Airways** (KQ; ☎ 06 511 522, 06 556 693; www.kenya-airways.com; Broad St, KLM Bldg)

**Royal Air Maroc** (AT; ☎ 06 956 956, 06 951 951; www.royalairmaroc.com; Tubman Blvd)

### LAND

#### Côte d'Ivoire

Border crossings with Côte d'Ivoire are just beyond Sanniquellie towards Danané, and east of Harper, towards Tabou.

From Harper, you must cross the Cavally River by ferry or canoe to reach the Ivoirian border. Plan on two days if you want to reach Abidjan via San Pedro using public transport along this route.

Alternatively, daily bush taxis go from Monrovia to Ganta and Sanniquellie, from where you can continue in stages to Danané and Man (12 to 16 hours).

#### Guinea

For Guinea, the main crossing is just north of Ganta. From just north of Ganta's Public Market you can take a *moto-taxi* (motorcycle taxi) the 2km to the border and walk across. Once in Guinea, there are frequent taxis to N'zérékoré. From Sanniquellie's bush-taxi rank, known as the 'meat packing', there are irregular bush taxis via Yekepa to the Guinean town of Lola (US$6.50). A place in a shared taxi is the same price. A *moto-taxi* (if you can find one!) from Yekepa to the border should cost US$1, after which there are Guinean vehicles to Lola. There is also a border crossing at Voinjama to Macenta via a bad road from Gbarnga (often impassable in the wet season).

#### Sierra Leone

Using a 4WD, you can reach Freetown in about 10 to 12 hours from Monrovia. The main Sierra Leone crossing is at Bo (Waterside). There are frequent daily bush taxis between Monrovia and the Bo (Waterside) border (three hours), from where it's easy to find onward transport to Kenema (six to eight hours in the dry season and 10 to 12 hours in the wet), and then on to Freetown.

## Getting Around

### BUSH TAXI & BUS

Bush taxis go daily from Monrovia to most destinations, including Buchanan, Gbarnga, Ganta, Sanniquellie and the Sierra Leone border, although distant routes are severely restricted during the rainy season. Minivans (called 'buses') also ply most major routes, although they're more crowded and dangerous than bush taxis.

### CAR & MOTORCYCLE

Vehicle rental can be arranged through better hotels from about US$130 per day plus petrol for a 4WD. You can travel by private taxi in Monrovia for US$5 to US$7 per short hop; contact the well-run and trusted network of Guinean taxi drivers, **Alpha** (☎ 0886-600 022), for more information, including on airport pick-ups. Motorbike taxis known as *pen-pens* ply the streets of Monrovia and other cities. In the capital they have a 10pm curfew for a reason; ride with caution.

# Mali

☎223 / POP 14.5 MILLION

**Includes ➡**



## Fast Facts

**Area** 1,240,140 sq km

**Capital** Bamako

**Currency** West African franc (CFA)

**Languages** French, Bambara, Fulfulde, Tamashek, Dogon and Songhai

## Introduction

Like an exquisite sandcastle formed in a harsh desert landscape, Mali is blessed by an extraordinary amount of beauty, wonders, talents and knowledge.

Yet for now, its landscapes, monuments and stories are off-limits, sealed from tourists by a conflict that is threatening the very culture of Mali.

The heart of the nation is Bamako, where Ngoni and Kora musicians play to dancing crowds from all ethnicities, while in the Dogon country villages still cling to the cliffs as they did in ancient times.

Further west, Fula women strap silver jewellery to their ears and their belongings to donkeys, forming caravans worthy of beauty pageants as they march across the *hamada* (dry, dusty scrubland).

And in the northeast, the writings of ancient African civilisations remain locked in the beautiful libraries of Timbuktu, until a new dawn comes for Mali, and they – and it – can be rediscovered by travellers.

## Mali at a Glance

**Dogon Country** A fairytale of rose-coloured villages, big blue skies, sacred crocodiles and sandstone cliffs.

**Djenné** The world's most captivating mudbrick mosque.

**Bamako** The sounds of live music, sprawling markets and motorbikes purring along the banks of the Niger River.

**Timbuktu** Ancient libraries, monuments and texts of wisdom on philosophy and astronomy.

**Segou** Acacia trees, shea butter, pottery and waterside *griots* (prase singers).

**Niger River** The life-blood of Mali and Africa's third-longest river, it bends and twists its way to ancient Sahelian trading kingdoms.

# UNDERSTAND MALI

## Mali Today

Mali's fall from grace in 2012 came as a surprise to many, although not to close watchers of former president Amadou Toumani Touré (commonly referred to as ATT), who was deposed in a coup in April 2012. A band of mutinous soldiers ousted the president and his cabinet in the run-up to elections in which ATT was not planning to stand, claiming the leader was not adequately supporting the under-equipped Malian army against a Tuareg rebellion in the northeast of the country.

Somewhat ironically, the coup only worsened the situation in the northeast, allowing Islamist groups to gain hold of the region. They in turn pushed out the Tuareg groups and went on to install sharia law in the ancient towns of Gao and Timbuktu, destroying ancient monuments, tombs and remnants of history. Seven hundred thousand civilians were forced to flee in 2012 and early 2013, winding up in refugee camps in neighbouring countries as, at the request of the Malian government, French forces and Regional West African Ecowas (Economic Community of West African States) troops launched air raids and ground attacks, successfully and quickly pushing back the Islamists from many of their strongholds. French forces began to draw down in April 2013, and in July of that year they handed over control of military operations to a UN force. At the same time presidential elections were held and won by Ibrahim Boubacar Keïta, but none of this did anything to curtail the instability in the north, and as the French departed, violence increased and Tuareg and rebel groups retook some northern towns.

By mid-2015 the government signed peace agreements with a number of rebel Tuareg groups in exchange for a degree of regional autonomy and the dropping of arrest warrants that had been issued for their leaders. Although this helped to partially improve the security situation in the north, it has done little to halt attacks by Islamic militants on government forces and public places.

The continuing instability is deeply felt by most Malians: many businesses have closed, tourism revenue has dropped dramatically and important sites in Gao and Timbuktu have been destroyed. Sadly, many people feel that it is not only Mali's future that is under threat but also its long-celebrated culture and history.

## History

### The Early Empires

Rock art in the Sahara suggests that northern Mali has been inhabited since 10,000 BC, when the Sahara was fertile and rich in wildlife. By 300 BC, large organised settlements had developed, most notably near Djenné, one of West Africa's oldest cities. By the 6th century AD, the lucrative trans-Saharan trade in gold, salt and slaves had begun, facilitating the rise of West Africa's great empires.

From the 8th to the 16th centuries, Mali formed the centrepiece of the great empires of West African antiquity, most notably the empires of Ghana, Mali and Songhaï. The arrival of European ships along the West African coast from the 15th century, however, broke the monopoly on power of the Sahel kingdoms.

The French arrived in Mali during the mid-19th century. During the French colonial era, Mali was the scene of a handful of major infrastructure projects, including the 1200km Dakar–Bamako train line, which was built with forced labour to enable the export of cheap cash crops, such as rice and cotton. But Mali remained the poor neighbour of Senegal and Côte d'Ivoire.

### Independence & Conflict

Mali became independent in 1960 (for a few months it was federated with Senegal), under the one-party rule of Mali's first president, Modibo Keïta. In 1968, Keïta was overthrown by army officers led by Moussa Traoré. Elections were held in 1979 with Traoré declared the winner.

During the Cold War, Mali was firmly in the Soviet camp. Food shortages were constant, especially during the devastating droughts of 1968–74 and 1980–85. One bright spot came in 1987 when Mali produced its first grain surplus.

The Tuareg are the largest ethnic group in the northern regions of Mali and have long complained of a feeling of marginalisation from the political and economic mainstream. In 1990 this frustration boiled over and the Tuareg rebelion began. The follow-

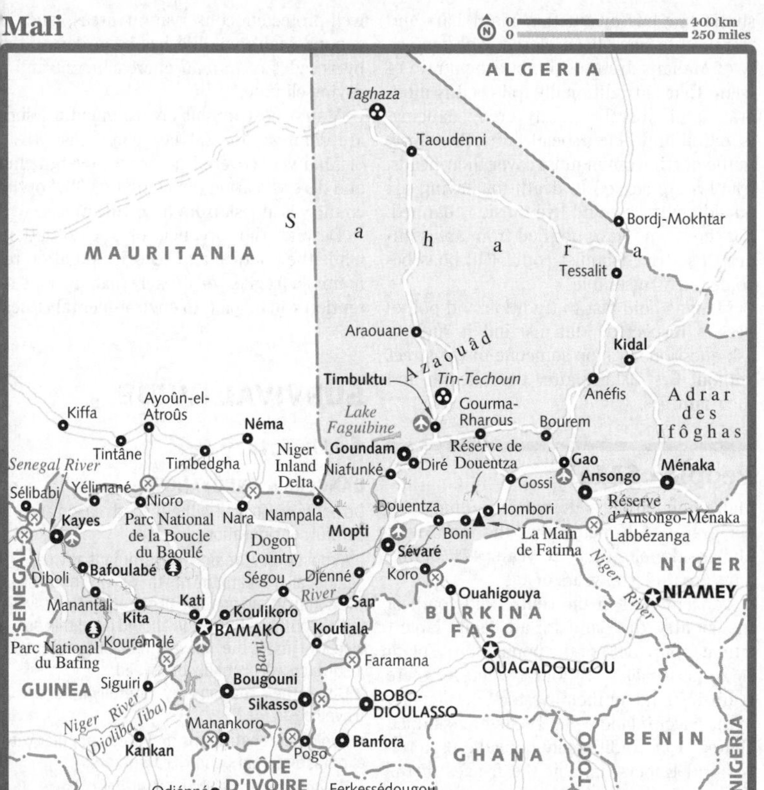


ing year a peaceful pro-democracy demonstration drew machine-gun fire from security forces. Three days of rioting followed, during which 150 people were killed. The unrest finally provoked the army, led by General Amadou Toumani Touré (General ATT as he was known), to seize control from Traoré.

Touré established an interim transitional government and gained considerable respect when he resigned a year later, keeping his promise to hold multiparty elections. But he was rewarded for his patience and elected president in April 2002.

The Tuareg rebellion gained ground in 2007 and was bolstered in 2011 and 2012 by an influx of weapons and unemployed fighters following the Libyan civil war. Islamist fighters, including those linked to Al-Qaeda, gained footing in the northeast soon after, ousting the main Mouvement pour le Liberation d'Azawad (MNLA) Tuareg group and forcing 400,000 civilians to flee the region after harsh sharia law was imposed and ancient monuments destroyed. A transitional government, headed by Dioncounda Traoré, was installed, but deemed too weak to handle the crisis alone. French forces and later Ecowas troops launched air and ground offensives in an attempt to push back the Islamists in January 2013.

## Culture

For the majority of Malians, life continues as usual, although the impact of the conflict weighs heavily on their minds. For those who eke out a living working in shops or businesses, the emphasis is on earning enough to take care of their (large) families on a day-to-day basis. But many have placed long-term plans on hold, as they simply can't predict what the future will bring.

In the northeast of the country, life has changed drastically. The imposition of sharia law has meant that many bars and restaurants have been closed. The majority of Malians are Muslim, but the strain of Islam that is traditionally followed is moderate and liberal – many enjoy dancing, drinking and being social butterflies. Now in the north women must cover their heads, couples are stoned to death for having sex outside marriage and live music is banned. For those who have not fled from areas under this strict Islamist control life has become fairly miserable.

Malians hold fast to tradition and politeness is respected. Malians find it rude to ask questions or stop someone in the street without first asking after their health and their families.

## People of Mali

Mali's population is growing by almost 3% per year, which means that the number of Malians doubles every 20 years; 47% of Malians are under 15 years of age.

Concentrated in the centre and south of the country, the Bambara are Mali's largest ethnic group (34% of the population). Fulani (15%) pastoralists are found wherever there is grazing land for their livestock, particularly in the Niger inland delta. The lighter-skinned Tuareg (1%), traditionally nomadic pastoralists and traders, inhabit the fringes of the Sahara.

Almost 95% of Malians are Muslim, and 2% are Christian. Animist beliefs often overlap with Islamic and Christian practices, especially in rural areas.

## Environment

Mali has four national parks, but for all intents and purposes they're merely parks on paper rather than fully functioning, well-protected conservation areas, and in general Mali's wildlife has been devastated by decades of human encroachment and a drying climate.

Mali's most urgent environmental issues are deforestation (at last count just 10.3% of Mali was covered in forest), overgrazing and desertification (an estimated 98% of the country is at risk from desertification).

Despite the urgency of the situation, while the political and security situation remains so fragile, it's unlikely that any real attention will be paid to environmental issues.

# SURVIVAL GUIDE

## Directory A–Z

### DANGERS & ANNOYANCES

Do not travel in Mali without good reason and careful consideration.

Almost every Western government advises against all travel to the northern two-thirds of the country, and against all but essential travel to the southern third. You should heed this advice. Not just is the risk very real, but your travel insurance will probably be invalid.

- Check the situation very carefully before travelling to Mali.
- Avoid demonstrations and areas popular with expats, diplomats and NGO workers.
- Do not travel anywhere after dark.
- Carry your passport with you at all times.
- Do not try to photograph police, military or sensitive sites.

### VISAS

Despite the troubles within the country Malian tourist visas are being issued with minimal fuss. As long as you have a visa, getting in and out of the country via any of the main southern border crossings is fairly painless. Do not attempt to enter the country via Mauritania, Algeria or Niger.

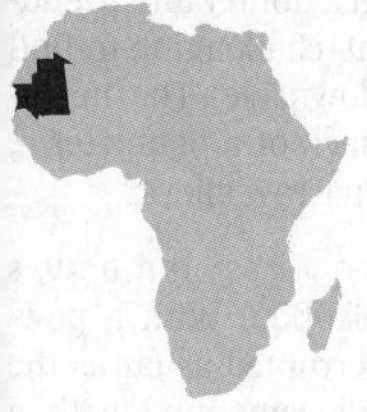

# Mauritania

☎222 / POP 4 MILLION

**Includes ➡**



## Best Places to Eat

➡ La Palmeraie Cafe & Bakery (p387)
➡ Azalaï Hôtel Marhaba (p386)
➡ La Tissayade (p389)

## Best Places to Sleep

➡ Villa Maguela (p391)
➡ Auberge Diaguili (p386)
➡ Maison d'Hôtes Jeloua (p386)
➡ Parc National du Banc d'Arguin (p392)

## Why Go?

Driving through the vast, sun-bleached landscape of Mauritania, you'd be forgiven for expecting to see a tricked-out post-apocalyptic hot rod from *Mad Max: Fury Road* on the horizon. Instead, a solitary, turbaned figure tending a herd of goats tells the story of survival amid millenniums-old geological forces. Mauritania, with one of the world's lowest population densities, is almost equally divided between Moors of Arab-Berber descent and black Africans, a striking cultural combination that is part of its appeal.

There's no doubt that Mauritania has some of the continent's grandest scenery. The Saharan Adrar region, with its World Heritage–listed caravan towns, is currently off-limits for security reasons, but the desert is a constant presence elsewhere, pushing hard up against the Atlantic Coast. Millions of migratory birds winter along the coast at Parc National du Banc d'Arguin, and the expanding capital Nouakchott is where modernity takes root in the desert.

## When to Go

### Nouakchott

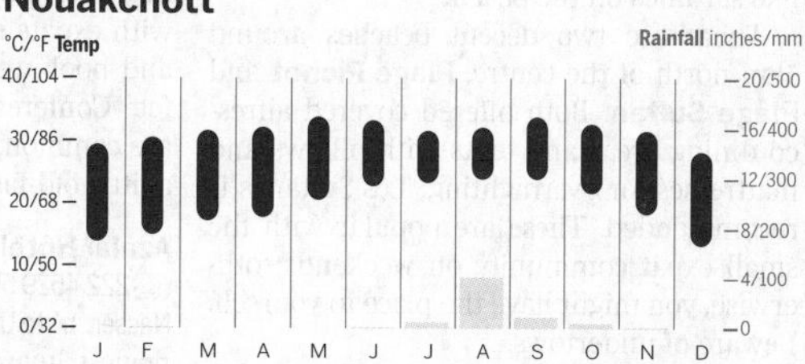


**Nov–Mar** Pleasantly warm for visiting the desert, although nights can be surprisingly cold.

**Jul–Sep** Short rainy season throughout the south; Nouakchott prone to flooding after downpours.

**Mid-Jun–Aug** Mauritanians from the coast head to oases towns to celebrate the date harvest.

# NOUAKCHOTT

☎222 / POP 1 MILLION

Sixty years old, youthful by most standards, Nouakchott mushroomed quickly from a small village to the country's capital and largest city. Near, but not on the coast, building continues apace, even where roads are non-existent. Certainly, they're a strange sight: massive, gated homes plonked down in the desert. The city is unassuming and seemingly unplanned, as if on an overnight caravan stop it was left to grow by accident. Most travellers use it as a staging post before the Adrar, Banc d'Arguin or the next international border.

Nouakchott is sleepily idiosyncratic and you could do worse than spend an afternoon at the gloriously frantic fish market (one of the busiest in West Africa), treat yourself to a comfy hotel or feast in a good restaurant. Laid-back and safe – bliss after the rigours of the desert – the city is chock-a-block with international organisations and geared less to travellers, more to business people.

## Sights

Major landmarks in the centre include the **Grande Mosquée** (Mosquée Saudique; Rue Mamadou Konaté) and the large **Mosquée Marocaine** (Rue de la Mosquée Marocaine), which towers over a bustling market area.

**Port de Pêche** (Fish Market) is Nouakchott's star attraction. Lively and colourful, you'll see hundreds of teams of mostly Wolof and Fula men dragging in heavy fishing nets. Small boys hurry back and forth with trays of fish, which they sort, gut, fillet and lay out on large trestles to dry. The best time to visit is late afternoon, when the fishing boats return. Before or after, it's no less an impressive sight with the pirogues crammed like sardines on the beach.

There are two decent beaches around 5km north of the centre, **Plage Pichot** and **Plage Sultan**. Both offered covered alfresco dining areas and tents with pillows and mattresses for overnighting; Les Sultanes is recommended. These are popular with the small expat community on weekends; otherwise, you might have the place to yourself. Beware of undertows.

## Sleeping

**★Maison d'Hôtes Jeloua** GUESTHOUSE $
(☎222 3636 9450; www.escales-mauritanie.com; r UM10,000-16,000; P❄@🛜) This is a lovely and deservedly popular *maison d'hôtes* (B&B), with a leafy garden, highly recommended restaurant and a homey and friendly vibe. The somewhat challenging-to-find location is the only downside. The neighbourhood streets, for lack of a better term, are wide sandy lots or narrow alleys.

**Les Sultanes** TENTED CAMP $
(☎222 4969 4140; tent UM7000) With a powdery sand beach uninterrupted as far as the eye can see, this small compound with a shady restaurant (mains UM3000) and handful of semi-permanent tent sites is as close to a beach resort as you'll get in Mauritania.

**Auberge Diaguili** GUESTHOUSE $$
(☎222 4646 0003; www.diaguili.com; r incl breakfast UM18,000; ❄🛜) Owners Nadia and Pascal have created a friendly and warm environment, especially good for long-term stays. Rooms are simply furnished; there's a shared kitchen and tastefully designed lounge area.

**Al Khaima City Center** HOTEL $$
(☎222 4524 2222; www.akcc.mr; 10 Rue Mamadou Konaté; r from UM25,000; ❄@🛜) A downtown high-rise of solid value, the Al Khaima has small rooms that are surprisingly stylish, with boutique design elements and comfortable bedding. It's surprising because of the utilitarian lower lobby and lower floors, which include a bank, travel agency, electronics store and other offices. The 10th-floor cafe has unbeatable views of the city from the outdoor terrace.

**Hôtel Monotel Dar el Barka** HOTEL $$$
(☎222 4524 2333; www.monotel-mr.com; Zone des Ambassades; r from UM51,000; ❄@🛜🏊) A large, low-slung complex with tight security near the French embassy, Dar el Barka is one of the more popular business-class hotels in the city. Sundays are especially crowded with expats enjoying the leafy central patio and pool area, and the all-you-can-eat buffet. Conferences, meetings and weddings are common, however room furnishings are a little old-fashioned.

**Azalaï Hôtel Marhaba** HOTEL $$$
(☎222 4529 5051; www.azlaihotels.com; Ave Abdal Nasser; r/ste UM42,000/50,000; ❄@🛜🏊) The newest luxury business-class hotel to open in downtown Nouakchott, the Azlaï is part of a chain of hotels throughout West Africa. More than US$8 million was invested in upgrading what was once a Mercure hotel into a sparkling oasis with a top-flight restaurant and boutique-style rooms.

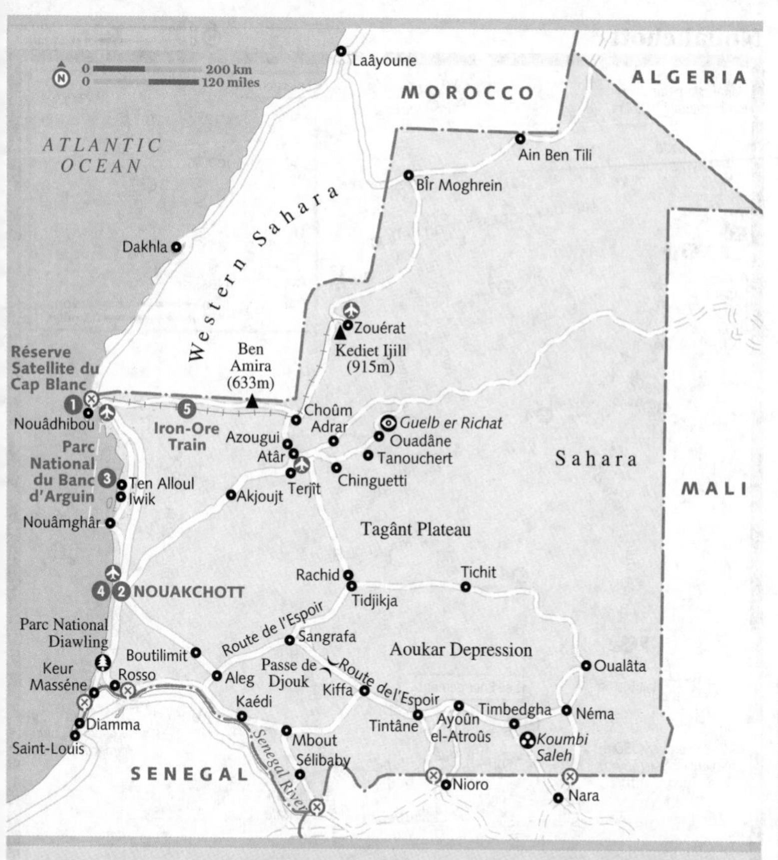


## Mauritania Highlights

1. **Réserve Satellite du Cap Blanc** (p391) Tracking down a rare colony of charismatic Mediterranean monk seals in the country's remote north.
2. **La Tissayade** (p389) Tasting Mauritanian cooking in Nouakchott's best and most atmospheric restaurant.
3. **Parc National du Banc d'Arguin** (p392) Observing vast flocks of birds from a traditional pirogue.
4. **Port de Pêche** (p386) Witnessing the amazing tableau of hundreds of fishing boats returning to the beach just outside Nouakchott.
5. **Iron-ore train** (p390) Hopping on one of the world's longest trains – be ready for the most epic journey of your life!

## Eating

Perhaps the most inviting cluster of restaurants is along Rte des Ambassades, just south of the intersection with Rue de l'Ambassade du Senegal. Another few are grouped around a little further north off Ave Moktar Ould Daddah, just east of the Stade Olympique. Most high-end hotel restaurants are fairly stuffy and unremarkable; the Azalaï Hôtel Marhaba is the exception.

**La Palmeraie Cafe & Bakery** CAFE $
(222 4525 7344; Rue Ahmed Ould Mohamed; sandwiches UM1200; 7am-8pm Sun-Thu, to 11pm Fri; ) Widely considered the best breakfast spot in the city. Enjoy a sit-down meal of crêpes or a set continental breakfast in a contemporary-style dining room, or pick up a croissant and other freshly baked pastries and deserts (gelato as well) to go in bakery

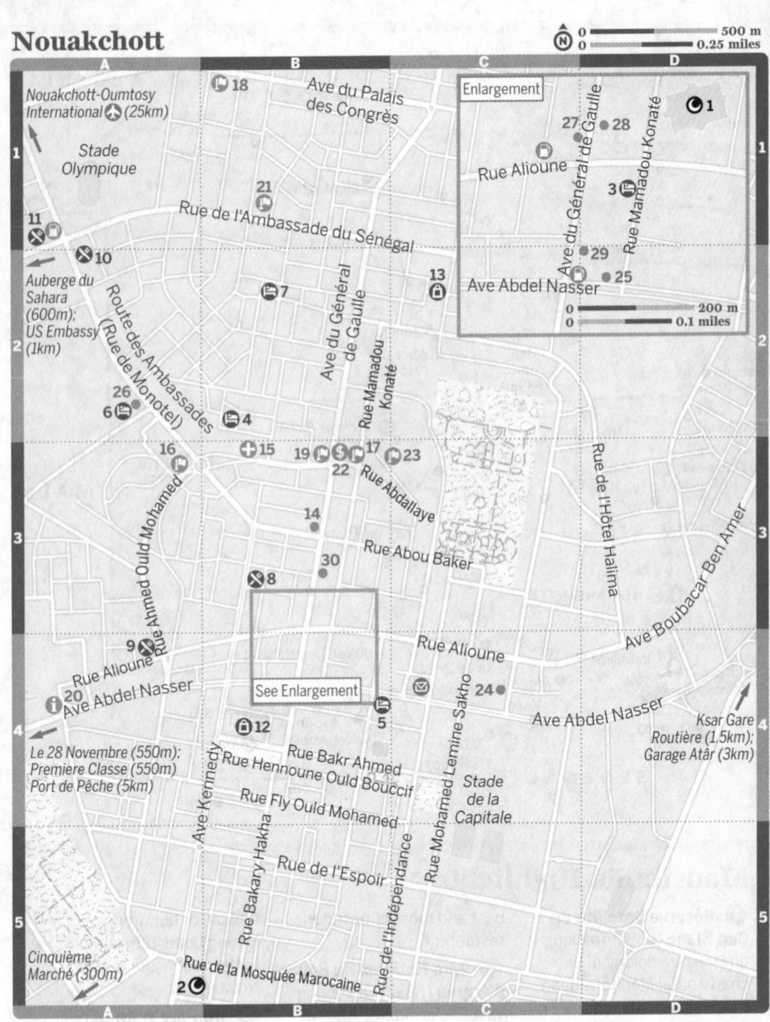




at the front. Other times of day pizzas and sandwiches available.

**Café Tunisie** TUNISIAN $

(Ave Kennedy; set breakfast UM1000; ⏲6.30am-8pm) This cafe is fine for coffee and smoking a water pipe, plus good-value breakfasts – freshly squeezed orange juice, bread, jam, pastries, yoghurt, coffee and a bottle of mineral water. Mains, like *merguez* (spiced sausage) or chicken brochette, come with fries, rice, bread and a salad. Street-front office furniture and couches under tattered awnings make it a good people-watching spot.

**Tafarit** SEAFOOD $$

(mains UM3000; ⏲noon-11pm; 📶) Known for its seafood, which you can hand-pick from a tank (lobster runs around UM6000) in a sunny, slightly tattered dining room. Live music Friday nights adds a lovely, and rare for Nouakchott, soundtrack to your meal.

**Le Manara** LEBANESE $$

(formerly Pizza Lina; Rte des Ambassades; mains from UM2000; ⏲12.30-3.30pm & 7-11pm Tue-Sun; 📶) Known around town, at least within the expat community, as one of the best places for steak in Nouakchott. Also serves some Asian dishes.

## Nouakchott

**Sights**

1 Grande Mosquée ........ D1
2 Mosquée Marocaine ........ A5

**Sleeping**

3 Al Khaima City Center ........ D1
4 Auberge Diaguili ........ B2
5 Azalaï Hôtel Marhaba ........ B4
6 Hôtel Monotel Dar el Barka ........ A2
7 Maison d'Hôtes Jeloua ........ B2

**Eating**

8 Café Tunisie ........ B3
9 La Palmeraie Cafe & Bakery ........ A4
La Tissayade ........ (see 7)
10 Le Manara ........ A2
11 Tafarit ........ A1

**Shopping**

12 Marché Capitale ........ B4
13 Zein Art ........ C2

**Information**

14 Asfaar ........ B3
15 Cabinet Médical Fabienne Cherif ........ B3
Canadian Consulate ........ (see 3)
16 French Embassy ........ A3
17 German Embassy ........ B3
18 Malian Embassy ........ B1
19 Moroccan Embassy ........ B3
20 Parc National du Banc D'Arguin Headquarters ........ A4
PSV Voyages ........ (see 3)
21 Senegalese Embassy ........ B1
22 Societe Generale ........ B3
23 Spanish Embassy ........ C3
24 Sûreté ........ C4

**Transport**

25 Air Algérie ........ D2
26 Air France ........ A2
27 Europcar ........ C1
28 Mauritania Airlines ........ D1
29 Royal Air Maroc ........ D2
Tunis Air ........ (see 8)
30 Turkish Airlines ........ B3

★**La Tissayade** MAURITANIAN $$$
(☎222 3636 9450; Maison d'Hôtes Jeloua; mains UM3000-5000; ) Easily the restaurant with the best atmosphere in the city, La Tissayade is located in the shady front courtyard of Maison d'Hôtes Jeloua. Daily specials like vegetable quiche and a menu of beef, chicken, shrimp and lobster (order 24 hours in advance).

## ☆ Entertainment

**CIMAN** LIVE MUSIC
(Conservatoire International de Musique et des Arts de Nouakchott; ☎222 4685 5161; ciman.nkc@gmail.com) Hosts regular classical and traditional music concerts.

## Shopping

★**Zein Art** ARTS & CRAFTS
(☎222 4651 7465; www.zeinart.com; ⏲3.30-7.30pm Tue-Fri, 10am-7.30pm Sat) A gallery curating the very best work from Mauritanian artists and craftspeople. Periodically hosts exhibitions themed around art and artists in the region.

**Marché Capitale** GIFTS & SOUVENIRS
(Grand Marché; Ave Kennedy) You'll find a bit of everything at Marché Capitale, including brass teapots, silver jewellery, traditional wooden boxes and colourful fabrics.

## Information

### MEDICAL SERVICES

**Bureaux de Change** There are bureaux de change on Ave du Général de Gaulle and on Ave du Gamal Nasser, as well as in the Marché Capitale. Euros, US dollars, CFA and Moroccan dirhams are most easily changed.

**Cabinet Médical Fabienne Sharif** (☎222 4525 1571) English-speaking doctor, recommended by expats.

**Doctor Melhem Hanna** (☎222 4525 2398) Lebanese cardiologist able to handle other general medical issues.

**Le Phare du Désert** (☎222 4644 2421; www.desertmauritanie.com) A reliable tour operator that organises trips throughout the country.

**Main Post Office** (Ave Abdel Nasser; ⏲8am-3pm Mon-Thu, to noon Fri)

**Societe Generale** (Ave du Général de Gaulle) Two branches 100m apart; both have ATMs.

## Getting There & Away

### AIR

The major airlines have offices in Nouakchott. Mauritania Airlines has flights to Nouâdhibou (UM31,000, 45 minutes) daily, except Wednesday.

You can purchase domestic or international air tickets at one of the many travel agencies around town, including **Asfaar** (☎222 4529 0406; asfaar@asfaar.mr; Ave Charles de Gaulle) and **PSV Voyages** (☎222 3630 1342; khattary@amadeus.mr; 2nd fl, Al Khaima City Center).

**Air Algérie** (☎222 529 0922; www.airalgerie.dz; cnr Ave du Général de Gaulle & Ave Abdel Nasser)

**Air France** (☎222 4525 1808; www.airfrance.com; Rte des Ambassades, connected to Monotel Dar El Barka; ⏰8.30am-5pm Mon-Thu, to 1pm Fri)

**Mauritania Airlines** (☎222 4525 4767; www.mauritaniaairlines.mr; Ave du Général du Gaulle)

**Royal Air Maroc** (☎222 4525 3564; www.royalairmaroc.com; Ave du Général de Gaulle)

**Tunis Air** (☎222 525 8762; www.tunisair.com; Ave Kennedy)

**Turkish Airlines** (www.turkishairlines.com; Ave du Général de Gaulle)

#### BUSH TAXIS

For Nouâdhibou (about UM5000, six hours), several companies including **Premiere Classe** (Autoroute Nouadhibou), Le 28 Novembre, Gulf Transport and Prince Voyage, are all clustered together on the N2 (Autoroute Nouâdhibou), just north of the intersection with Ave Gamal Abdel Nasser.

For Rosso (about UM2500, 3½ hours), Garage Rosso is at Carrefour Madrid, a roundabout southeast of the centre.

### ℹ Getting Around

A taxi ride within the centre costs around UM200. It's possible to cover some ground in the centre on foot, however the heat, damaged or non-existent sidewalks and unruly traffic are challenges.

For the Nouakchott-Oumtosy International Airport, 25km north of the city, a convenient shuttle leaves from the Air France office in town to the airport at 6.30pm on Mondays, Wednesdays, Fridays and Sundays (UM2000). Otherwise, a taxi or hotel van should run around UM5000.

**Europcar** (☎222 4430 3241; www.europcar.com; Ave du Général de Gaulle; ⏰8am-6pm Mon-Thu & Sun, 9.30am-12.30pm Fri & Sat) is the only rental vehicle outlet in the city.

# ATLANTIC COAST

## Nouâdhibou

☎222 / POP 118,000

Stretching along the Baie du Lévrier in the middle of a narrow 35km-long peninsula, the fishing port of Nouâdhibou marks the end of the road in many respects. The rail line from the interior ends. The country's northern border is a few kilometres away. Shipwrecks are marooned in the waters south of the city. From the air, the divide with Morocco, mostly empty desert bordering the Atlantic, is stark.

The city itself sprawls north to south; mostly low-slung buildings, paved roads petering out into sandy pathways a few blocks from the main artery. Often bypassed by travellers making a dash to the capital or to the Adrar, its sleepiness is its selling point. North of the centre, the Baie de l'Étoile resembles a mini Banc d'Arugin and a destination for intrepid kitesurfers. Daily life – the call of the muezzin, afternoon football, joggers hugging the coastal road – feels close.



### AN EPIC JOURNEY ON THE IRON-ORE TRAIN

Africa offers some pretty wild train trips, but the train ferrying iron ore from the mines at Zouérat to Nouâdhibou might just be the wildest. One of the longest trains in the world (typically a staggering 2.3km long), when it arrives at the 'station' in Nouâdhibou, a decrepit building in the open desert, a seemingly endless number of ore wagons pass before the passenger carriage at the rear finally appears. The lucky ones – ie most aggressive in a scrum – find a place on one of the two long benches (UM2500); the rest stand or sit on the floor. There are also a dozen 'berths' (UM3000) that are so worn out you can see the springs. It's brutally basic. It's also possible to clamber into the ore cars and travel for free. Impossibly dusty, this is only for the hardcore. Plastic sheets are essential to wrap your bags (and person), plus plenty of warm clothes, as the desert can get fearsomely cold at night, as well as food and drink.

The train leaves Nouâdhibou at around 2pm to 3pm daily. Most travellers get off at Choûm, 12 hours later, where bush taxis wait to take passengers to Atâr, three hours away. In the other direction, the train leaves Zouérat around midday and passes through Atâr at about 5.30pm.

## Sights

**Réserve Satellite du Cap Blanc** WILDLIFE RESERVE
(UM2000; ⏲10am-5pm Tue-Sat) A small nature reserve with an excellent information centre, dedicated to the colony of endangered Mediterranean monk seals *(phoque moin)* that live here. Resembling elephant seals, these grey-skinned animals have been hunted since the 15th century for their valuable skins and oil. The protected colony here of roughly 150 seals is one of the last on earth (less than 500 worldwide). The colony is at the foot of the cliffs; you have a reasonable chance of seeing them swimming offshore.

## Activities

With your own equipment you can enjoy some outdoor activities around Nouâdhibou, including surf fishing on the remote peninsula around Cap Blanc – but security checkpoints can be a hassle. Shallow waters and brisk winds make the bay an excellent spot for kitesurfers. And you can swim near the **Centre de Pêche**, around 12km north of the airport.

## Sleeping

**Bungalow Dauphins** BUNGALOW $
(www.auberge-des-nomades-du-sahara.com; r with full board from UM12,000) Located on an otherwise lonely stretch of road north of the city, this collection of well-designed solar-powered bungalows overlooks the Baie de l'Etoile. Be sure to make a reservation in advance since it's geared towards groups of kitesurfers coming from its sister resort in Dakhla in the Western Sahara and not necessarily independent travellers.

**Camping Baie du Lévrier** HOSTEL $
(☎222 4574 6536; Blvd Médian; s/d UM3000/5000; P) Also known as Chez Ali, this *auberge*-style place has a good location. Rooms are a bit cell-like, and bathroom facilities are shared, but there is a tent to relax in and cooking facilities.

★**Villa Maguela** VILLA $$
(☎222 2295 0820; www.facebook.com/villamaguela; r UM17,000) Easily the nicest place around Nouâdhibou, nay, the nicest place on the entire Mauritanian coast. This simple mud-walled compound is set directly on a magnificent piece of rocky coastline around 3km north of the city. The room design and furnishings are comfortable, if basic, but the wind and lapping waves lulling you to sleep is magnificent.

> WORTH A TRIP
>
> **PARC NATIONAL DIAWLING**
>
> The little-known **Parc National Diawling** (www.pnd.mr; adult UM1200) is a sister to the adjacent Djoudj National Bird Sanctuary in Senegal. It has important mangroves and acacia forest (any bit of greenery comes as a relief), as well as large coastal dunes. Incredibly rich in birdlife – you're also likely to spot monkeys, warthogs and monitor lizards – it's well worth a detour if you have a 4WD. Most people breeze through on their way to Senegal via the border crossing at Diamma. Facilities are almost completely undeveloped.

## Eating

In the centre, you'll find a slew of cheap restaurants along Rue de la Galérie Mahfoud. They're nothing fancy, serving fish and *mafé* (groundnut-based stew) for around UM300 a plate.

**Restaurant Oasis Tunisien** MOROCCAN $
(Blvd Maritime; mains UM1200; wi-fi) Moroccan owned (despite the name), this is a good-value spot for chicken and shwarma served up with fries and a small salad. If you can stand the sun, a few street-front tables are a pleasant spot for people-, and more commonly, vehicle-watching.

**Restaurant La Paillotte** MEDITERRANEAN $$
(☎222 4574 3218; Blvd Maritime; mains UM1500-4000; ⏲noon-3pm & 7-11.30pm, closed Sat) Above-average seafood and more-standard meat and chicken dishes; located inside the Italian-owned Hotel Mauritalia.

## Information

Most of the hotels offer wi-fi, as do some restaurants. A few internet outlets along Blvd Médian double as telephone offices.

There are several bureaux de change along the city's main drag, Blvd Médian, as well as a couple of banks with ATMs.

**Société Générale Mauritanie** (Blvd Médian; ⏲8am-4pm Sun-Thu) ATM open 24 hours.

## Getting There & Away

**Mauritania Airlines** (☎222 4574 4291; www.mauritaniaairlines.mr; Blvd Médian) flies daily (except Wednesday) to Nouakchott (UM31,000, 45 minutes; departure times vary), and three times a week to Casablanca in Morocco and Las Palmas in the Canary Islands (round trip UM161,500). Tickets can be purchased at the airline office or at any one of the handful of travel agencies around town.

There are plenty of minibuses and bush taxis to Nouakchott (UM5000, six hours); the former, of course, are more comfortable and leave from various company offices around the city. Premiere Classe is recommended – best to book a day in advance.

There is a train (p390) that runs from Nouâdhibou to Choûm and Zouérat (UM3000). The train 'station' is about 5km south of town.

## Parc National du Banc d'Arguin

This World Heritage–listed **park** (www.pnba.mr; permit per person per day UM1200) is an important stopover and breeding ground for birds migrating between Europe and southern Africa, and as a result is one of the best birdwatching sites on the entire continent. It extends 200km north from Cape Timiris and 235km south of Nouâdhibou. The ideal way to approach the birds is by traditional fishing boat (UM20,000, plus UM5000 for the guide), best organised from the fishing village of **Iwik**. **Cape Tagarit**, 40km north of Tidra, offers beautiful views and the water is crystal clear.

Permits are issued in the park, or at the **headquarters** (222 425 8541; Ave Abdel Nasser; permits per day UM1200) in Nouakchott; the **park office** (222 574 6744; www.pnba.mr/pnba; Blvd Médian; 8am-4pm Mon-Thu, to noon Fri) in Nouâdhibou is of less help. The Nouakchott office sells a map and guide (English available) with GPS waypoints. There's also a useful map available at the University of Texas website (www.lib.utexas.edu/maps/africa/arguin_map.jpg).

To visit the offshore islands you need to request a special permit from the park office.

### Sleeping & Eating

Inside the park there are official campsites (UM4000/800/12,000 per small/medium/large tent) equipped with traditional tents. Some, located directly on sandy beaches where you can swim, are also wonderful for bonfires and stargazing.

Meals can be ordered at the official campsites.

### Getting There & Away

There's no public transport, so you'll need to hire a 4WD with a knowledgeable driver in Nouakchott (you're less likely to find one in Nouâdhibou), allowing a couple of days for the trip.

# THE ADRAR

The Adrar is the undoubted jewel in Mauritania's crown, but sadly it remains firmly off-limits for security reasons – all Western governments currently advise their nationals against travelling to the Adrar. When it again becomes safe to visit, it's epic Saharan country, and shows the great desert in all its variety: the ancient Saharan towns of Chinguetti and Ouadâne, mighty sand dunes that look sculpted by an artist, vast rocky plateaus and mellow oases fringed with date palms.

# UNDERSTAND MAURITANIA

## Mauritania Today

President Mohamed Ould Abdel Aziz, considered strong in terms of security, has made less progress battling corruption and ensuring Mauritania's rich natural resources accrue to the benefit of all. Despite speculation to the contrary, Aziz, who won re-election to another five-year term in 2014, announced in October 2016 that he would not seek constitutional changes to allow him to run for a third term. Opposition voices – whether in politics or the media – are given little room to breathe in Mauritania.

A prominent blogger, Mohamed Ould Cheikh, was accused of blasphemy and sentenced to death in 2014; and an anti-slavery activist, Biram Ould Dah Ould Abeid, was jailed for 18 months after publicly burning Islamic legal texts purporting to advocate slavery. Abeid turned to politics and was Aziz's primary opposition in the 2014 presidential election. He was jailed again and released in May 2016. The country now looks to 2019, which could mark Mauritania's first transfer of power from one elected president to another.

## History

From the 3rd century AD, the Berbers established trading routes all over the Western Sahara, including in Mauritania. In the 11th century, the Marrakesh-based Islamic Almoravids pushed south and, with the assistance of Mauritanian Berber leaders, destroyed the Empire of Ghana, which covered much of present-day Mauritania. That victory led to the spread of Islam throughout Mauritania and the Western Sahara. The descendants of the Almoravids were finally subjugated by Arabs in 1674.

As colonialism spread throughout Africa in the 19th century, France stationed troops in Mauritania, but it was not until 1904 that, having played one Moorish faction off against another, the French finally managed to make Mauritania a colonial territory. Independence was fairly easily achieved in 1960 because the French wanted to prevent the country from being absorbed by newly independent Morocco. Mokhtar Ould Daddah became Mauritania's first president.

Ould Daddah took a hard line, especially against the (mainly black African) southerners, who were treated like second-class citizens and compelled to fit the Moors' mould. Any opposition was brutally suppressed.

The issue of Western Sahara (Spanish Sahara) finally toppled the government. In 1975 the very sandy Spanish Sahara (a Spanish colony) was divided between Morocco and Mauritania. But the Polisario Front launched a guerrilla war to oust both beneficiaries from the area. Mauritania was incapable, militarily and economically, especially in the midst of terrible droughts, of fighting such a war. A bloodless coup took place in Mauritania in 1978, bringing in a new military government that renounced all territorial claims to the Western Sahara.

Ethnic tensions culminated in bloody riots between the Moors and black Africans in 1989. Around 100,000 Mauritanians were expelled from Senegal and more than 70,000 black Africans were expelled to Senegal, a country most had never known.

Riots over the price of bread in 1995 worsened the political situation. Cosmetic elections were held in 2001; opposing political parties and Islamists were deemed threats to the regime and both were repressed.

The 2000s were marked by more instability until elections in March 2007 saw Sidi Ould Cheikh Abdallahi returned as Mauritania's first democratically elected president. He openly condemned the 'dark years' of the late 1980s, and sought rapprochement with the expelled black Moors – a move that angered the traditional elites and which led, in part, to his overthrow by General Mohamed Ould Abdel Aziz in a coup in August 2008. Despite international condemnation, Aziz's position was consolidated the following year in elections that saw him narrowly returned as president.

## Culture

The extended family, clan or tribe still remains the cornerstone of Mauritanian society, especially with the Moors.

As in many Muslim countries, religion continues to mark the important events of life. Although slavery was declared illegal in 1980, it is reported to still exist and the caste system permeates society's mentality.

Only a third as many women as men are literate and few are involved in commercial activities. Female genital mutilation and forced feeding of young brides are still practised in rural communities. However, Mauritanian women do have the right to divorce and exert it routinely.

## People

Of Mauritania's estimated three million inhabitants, about 60% are Moors of Arab and Berber descent. The Moors of purely Arab descent, called 'Bidan', account for 40% of the population, and hold the levers of political power. The other major group is black Africans, ethnically split into two groups. The Haratin (black Moors), the descendants of people enslaved by the Moors, have assimilated the Moorish culture and speak Hassaniyya, an Arabic dialect. Black Mauritanians living in the south along the Senegal River constitute 40% of the total population and are mostly Fulani or the closely related Tukulor. These groups speak Pulaar (Fula). There are also Soninke and Wolof minorities.

Islam links the country's disparate peoples – more than 99% of the population are Sunni Muslims.

## Arts & Crafts

The traditional music of Mauritania is mostly Arabic in origin, although along its southern border there are influences from the Wolof, Tukulor and Bambara. One of the most popular Mauritanian musicians is Malouma. She has created what is called the 'Saharan blues' and is to Mauritania what Cesária Évora is to Cabo Verde. One of the country's few other internationally known artists was Dimi Mint Abba, who passed away in 2011. Her 1990 album *Khalifa Ould Eide & Dimi Mint Abba: Moorish Music from Mauritania* (Eide was her husband) can be found online. Weddings, raucous and lively affairs, are the best venues to experience Mauritanian music in all its microtonal and often very loud glory. Otherwise, most taxi drivers are happy to pop in a cassette of their favourite tracks.

## Environment

Mauritania is about twice the size of France. About 75%, including Nouakchott, is desert, with huge expanses of flat plains broken by occasional ridges, sand dunes and rocky plateaus, including the Adrar (about 500m high).

The highest peak is Kediet Ijill (915m) near Zouérat. Mauritania has some 700km of shoreline, including the Parc National du Banc d'Arguin, one of the world's major bird-breeding grounds and a Unesco World Heritage Site. The south is mostly flat scrubland.

Major environmental issues are the usual suspects of desertification, overgrazing and pollution. As drought, depleted soil fertility and dusty sandstorms diminish harvests, such as for dates in the Adrar, the rural exodus continues. Overfishing is another concern, with hundreds of tonnes of fish caught every day off the Mauritanian coastline.

# SURVIVAL GUIDE

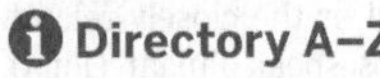

## Directory A–Z

### ACCOMMODATION

There's an expanding number of high-end hotels catering to international business travellers in Nouakchott and, to a much lesser extent, Nouâdhibou and Atâr. In the desert, you'll find numerous basic *auberges* or *campements*. They consist of a series of *tikits* (stone huts) or *khaimas* (tents) that come equipped with mattresses on the floor.

### DANGERS & ANNOYANCES

Mauritania is generally one of the safest countries in Africa, particularly the coastal region from Senegal to Morocco, but the previously popular tourist region of the Adrar was off-limits at time of writing for security reasons.

Other than petty theft, easily preventable through common-sense precautions, and somewhat chaotic driving patterns in Nouakchott, there's little to worry most travellers. In fact, and remarkably so compared to many other countries in the region, you're unlikely to attract any unwanted attention or be hassled when out and about. If anything, one's status as a foreigner and especially as a tourist will only elicit hospitality, warmth and kindness.

#### Travel Warnings

- US and European embassies caution against travel to large swaths of Mauritania, especially areas in the east. These will likely seem hyperbolic and unfair to Mauritanians and expats who know the country well. Of course, warnings should be taken very seriously, but these should be supplemented by up-to-date advice from locals in the area you intend to visit.
- Between late 2007 and 2011, there were a handful of incidents, mostly involving Al-Qaeda in the Islamic Maghreb. The popular Paris–Dakar rally was cancelled in 2008 because of threats against Mauritania by Islamist groups.
- Regional security threats, especially instability in neighbouring Mali, are concerns. Be sure to check the current security situation before travelling to border areas.

### EMBASSIES & CONSULATES

The majority of embassies and consulates have locations in Nouakchott.

**Canadian Consulate** (☎222 4529 2697; www.canadainternational.gc.ca/morocco-maroc; Al Khayma city center, 3rd fl, Rue Mamadou Konaté)

**French Embassy** (☎222 4529 9699; www.ambafrance-mr.org; Rue Ahmed Ould Mohamed)

**German Embassy** (☎222 4529 4075; www.nouakchott.diplo.de; Rue Mamadou Konaté)

**Malian Embassy** (☎222 4525 4081; Ave du Palais des Congress)

**Moroccan Embassy** (☎222 2525 1411; Ave du Général de Gaulle)

**Senegalese Embassy** (☎222 4525 7290; Rue de l'Ambassade du Sénégal)

**Spanish Embassy** (☎222 4529 8650; www.exteriores.gob.es/embajadas/nouakchott; Rue Mamadou Konate)

**US Embassy** (☎222 4525 2660; cnr Autoroute Nouadhibou & Rue Ambassade du Sénégal)

## EMERGENCY & IMPORTANT NUMBERS

| | |
|---|---|
| Mauritania's country code | 222 |
| Police | 17 |
| Fire | 18 |

## FOOD

The desert cuisine of the Moors is rather unmemorable and lacks variety. Dishes are generally bland and limited to rice, mutton, goat, camel or dried fish. With negligible agriculture, fruit and vegetables are imported, and hard to find outside Nouakchott. Mauritanian couscous, similar to the Moroccan variety, is delicious. The cuisine of southern Mauritania, essentially Senegalese, has more variety, spices and even a few vegetables.

## INTERNET ACCESS

You can get online in any reasonably sized town, although outside Nouakchott connection speeds can often be wanting. Expect to pay around UM200 an hour. Top-end and midrange hotels and many restaurants in Nouakchott and Nouâdhibou generally offer free wi-fi.

## LGBTIQ TRAVELLERS

Homosexuality is explicitly illegal in Mauritania. According to religious law, the maximum penalty is death if witnessed by four individuals. For what it's worth, however, there is little evidence of government-sponsored violence or discrimination. Regardless of the legality, Mauritanians are conservative in their attitudes towards gay and lesbian people. In most places, discretion is key and public displays of affection should be avoided, advice that applies to homosexual and heterosexual couples alike.

## MONEY

The unit of currency is the ouguiya (UM). There are plenty of ATMs in Nouakchott and a handful in Nouâdhibou. It's best to take euros or US dollars as back-up.

**Changing money** Only crisp recently issued bills are accepted at bureax de change. Exchange rates at the Nouakchott airport aren't much different than those offered in town. Either way, it's quick and hassle-free with no commissions. Rates at top-end hotels are generally worse.

**Credit cards** Visa and MasterCard, but not Amex, are accepted at top-end hotels and larger businesses.

**Tipping** Leave a gratuity for hotel cleaning staff at your discretion. No tip is expected at basic restaurants; leave between 10% and 15% in more upmarket places. Loose change is appreciated by taxi drivers on short trips. For guides and drivres, tips are always expected; begin around 10%, more for multiday trips or if service has been particularly good.

### SLEEPING PRICE RANGES

The following price ranges refer to a double room with bathroom.

**$** less than UM18,000

**$$** UM18,000–36,000

**$$$** more than UM36,000

### Exchange Rates

| | | |
|---|---|---|
| Australia | A$1 | UM271 |
| Canada | C$1 | UM263 |
| Euro zone | €1 | UM392 |
| Japan | ¥100 | UM322 |
| Morocco | MAD 1 | UM36 |
| New Zealand | NZ$1 | UM285 |
| Senegal | CFA100 | UM60 |
| UK | UK£1 | UM464 |
| US | US$1 | UM359 |

For current exchange rates, see www.xe.com.

## OPENING HOURS

Mauritania is a Muslim country, and for business purposes adheres to the Monday to Friday working week. Friday is the main prayer day, so many businesses have an extended lunch break on Friday afternoon. Many shops are open every day.

Government offices, post offices and banks are usually open 8am to 4pm Monday to Thursday and 8am to 1pm on Friday.

## POST

The headquarters for Mauripost, the company that runs the country's postal service is in Nouakchott. Post is generally slow and unreliable.

## PUBLIC HOLIDAYS

**New Year's Day** 1 January
**National Reunification Day** 26 February
**Workers' Day** 1 May

### WARNING

At the time of writing, travel to the Adrar region of Mauritania and Mauritania's border regions with Mali were considered dangerous. Check the local security situation before considering a trip here.

### EATING PRICE RANGES

The following price ranges refer to a main course.

**$** less than UM1800

**$$** UM1800–3500

**$$$** more than UM3500

**African Liberation Day** 25 May
**Eid al-Fitr** (end of Ramadan) 7 July
**Armed Forces Day** 10 July
**Aid el-Adha** (Feast of Sacrifice) 13 September
**Islamic New Year** 3 October
**Independence Day** 28 November

Mauritania also celebrates other Islamic holidays.

### TELEPHONE

You can make international calls at post offices. The innumerable privately run phone shops in the major cities and towns cost about the same and are open late.

There are no telephone area codes.

A GSM SIM card for the Mauritel, Chinguitell or Mattel networks costs around UM2000 (a SIM with 3G runs around UM3000); a new phone with a pre-installed SIM card should run around UM20,000. Coverage is generally good and the best way of staying connected while travelling.

### TOURIST INFORMATION

The official Ministry of Tourism has two offices, one at the airport in Nouakchott and another in Nouakchott proper, however neither is of much use. Even if open, they're unlikely to have good maps on hand.

### PRACTICALITIES

**Electricity** Current is 220V AC, 50Hz and most electrical plugs are of the European two-pin type.

**Newspapers** For the news (in French), pick up Le Calame or Horizons.

**TV** Mauritania has two state-owned TV stations (TVM and TVM2) with programs in Hassaniyya and French; the five privately owned stations are Elwatania, Chinguitty TV, Sahel TV, El-mourabitoune and Dava. Top-end hotels have satellite TV.

**Weights & measures** Mauritania uses the metric system.

### VISAS

Visas are required for everyone, except nationals of Arab League countries and some African nations.

In countries where Mauritania has no diplomatic representation, including Australia, French embassies often issue visas.

However, visas (US$130) are also issued upon arrival at the airport in Nouakchott, as well as at border crossings from Senegal and Morocco. The process itself, which involves biometric fingerprinting and a photograph, is quick, however the wait can be long, both at the airport and land borders. For the former, de plane as quickly as possible, grab the form and fill it out while you're standing in line.

There's a rumour the visa fee will be reduced substantially in coming years.

One-month visa extensions can be obtained for UM46,000 at the **Sûreté** (☎222 4525 0017; off Ave Abdel Nasser; ⏲8am-3pm Mon-Thu) in Nouakchott.

#### Mali

One-month visas (UM6500) are issued within 24 hours at the embassy in Nouakchott. You need two photos and a passport photocopy.

#### Morocco

Most nationalities do not require visas, and simply get an entry stamp valid for 90 days on arrival. Nationalities that do (mostly Africans, including Mauritanians) must pay around UM9000 and provide two photos and passport photocopies and (according to whim) an air ticket.

#### Senegal

Americans, Australians, Canadians and Europeans do not need a visa to enter Senegal. Its helpful to have a photocopy of your Mauritanian visa page for officials on the Mauritanian side of the border.

### WOMEN TRAVELLERS

Mauritania is a conservative Muslim country, but it is by no means the most extreme in this regard. Women might receive the odd bit of sexual harassment, but it's nothing in comparison with some North African countries. It's wise to dress modestly, covering the upper legs and arms and avoiding shorts or skimpy T-shirts.

## Getting There & Away

### AIR

With its own national carrier and several international airlines flying to Nouakchott, Mauritania is relatively easily accessible by air. Gateways are Paris, Istanbul and Casablanca.

Opened in June 2016, the Nouakchott-Oumtosy International Airport handles most air traffic. It's 25km north of the city, essentially plopped in the middle of the desert. It's polished to a shine, if also mostly empty of facilities. There is a bureau de change and a tourist office with brochures and country maps. Nouâdhibou and Atâr also have small international airports.

### LAND

#### Mali

At the time of writing, the border crossings between Mauritania and Mali were considered off-limits due to the dangerous security situation in the area.

#### Morocco

The trans-Sahara route via Mauritania was once, now less so, a very popular route from North Africa into sub-Saharan Africa. This crosses the internationally disputed territory of Western Sahara, although the border itself is administered by Morocco.

The only border crossing between Morocco/Western Sahara and Mauritania is north of Nouâdhibou. Crossing this border is straightforward, though the process can be painfully slow, and the road is entirely tarred to Nouakchott, except for the 3km no-man's land that separates the two border posts. Note, generally motorcycles are allowed to skip to the head of the car line.

There are direct bush taxis heading north from Nouâdhibou to Dakhla (Western Sahara), but travelling in the opposite direction you'll need to change vehicles at the border. The 425km trip can easily be accomplished in a long day.

#### Senegal

The main border crossing for Senegal is at Rosso (by ferry), but it's also possible to cross by the bridge over a dam at Diamma (Keur Masséne), west of Rosso. The latter is a much calmer and overall prefererable experience, but is only for the dry season.

From Dakar to Nouakchott by public transport usually takes from 11 to 13 hours. At Rosso, most travellers without vehicles cross by pirogue (UM200/CFA500, five minutes) as the ferry crosses only four times daily (free for foot traffic). The border is open from 8.30am to noon and 3pm to 6pm.

Vehicles cost CFA5000. Customs fees are around UM1500 if you're entering Mauritania, CFA2000 for Senegal; keep your paperwork (and vehicle) in good order.

### ARRIVING IN MAURITANIA

**Nouakchott-Oumtosy International Airport** Best to arrange pick-up in advance; via your accommodation is easiest. By the time you're through the potentially long line for visas, taxis are often gone and the parking lot mostly vacant. Otherwise, a few taxis are available for arriving passengers.

**Nouâdhibou International Airport** Few taxis await arriving flights. You can flag one down on the street.

## Getting Around

### AIR

Mauritania Airlines flies daily (except Wednesday) between Nouakchott and Nouâdhibou (UM31,000, 45 minutes), and twice a week via Zouérat (UM39,000, three hours). Tickets can be purchased at the airline's office (p390) in Nouakchott or most travel agencies.

### CAR & MOTORCYCLE

Mauritania's primary road network is mostly good, with tarred roads leading from the border with Western Sahara to Nouakchott, and on to the Senegalese and Malian borders at Rosso and Nioro respectively. Police checkpoints abound.

### MINIBUS & BUSH TAXI

Minibus routes stitch together the main towns and cities linked by tarmac roads. Where tarmac is replaced by *piste*, the bush taxi *(taxi brousse)* – often Mercedes 190s and Peugeot 504s – take over, along with pick-up trucks for the rougher routes.

With long stretches of nothingness, including the route between Nouakchott and Nouâdhibou, basic, gritty rest stops feel like revelations of civilisation. Some, including the petrol station between the two major cities, offer food, including camel sandwiches (UM600).

### TRAIN

The Nouâdhibou–Zouérat train is certainly an epic adventure when the security situation permits, and it is a masochists' dream. It's an iron-ore train with no passenger terminals, but it's become a passenger train for lack of better alternatives. The trip takes 16 to 18 hours, but most travellers get off at Choûm (close to Atâr), 12 hours from Nouâdhibou.

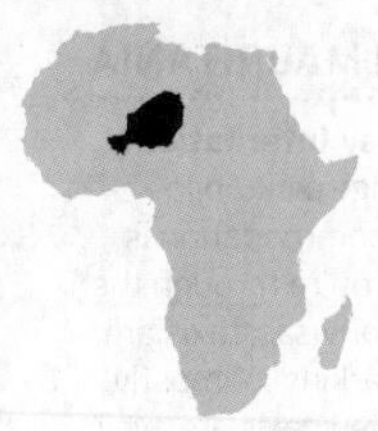

# Niger

☎227 / POP 17.8 MILLION

**Includes ➡**



## Fast Facts

**Area** 1,267,000 sq km

**Capital** Niamey

**Currency** West African franc (CFA)

**Languages Spoken** French, Hausa, Djerma, Fulfulde, Tamashek

## Introduction

Niger rarely makes waves in the international consciousness, and when it does it's invariably for all the wrong reasons: coups, rebellions and famines. But those who have been lucky enough to visit this desert republic normally return with stories of a warm and generous population living in ancient caravan cities at the edge of the Sahara.

In the north, the stark splendour of the Aïr Mountains hides Neolithic rock art and stunning oasis towns. Within the expansive dunes of the Ténéré Desert are dinosaur graveyards and deserted medieval settlements, while to the south is the ancient trans-Saharan trade-route town of Agadez and the sultanate of Zinder.

As good as it all could be, though, the current security situation means that Niger is still largely off limits to travellers. Attacks against foreigners have occurred across the Sahel, and the threat of kidnapping remains high.

## Niger at a Glance

**Agadez** A spiky summit of a majestic mud mosque overlooking town and the Sahara

**Kouré** West Africa's last wild herd of giraffes.

**Zinder** The sultan's palace within the fascinating Birni Quartier of this Hausa city tells of a brutal history.

**Parc Regional du W** Home to lions, crocodiles, monkeys and elephants.

**Ténéré Desert** A sublime section of the mighty Sahara.

**Aïr Mountains** Where camel caravans plod through red sands and past mystical blue rocks.

# Niger

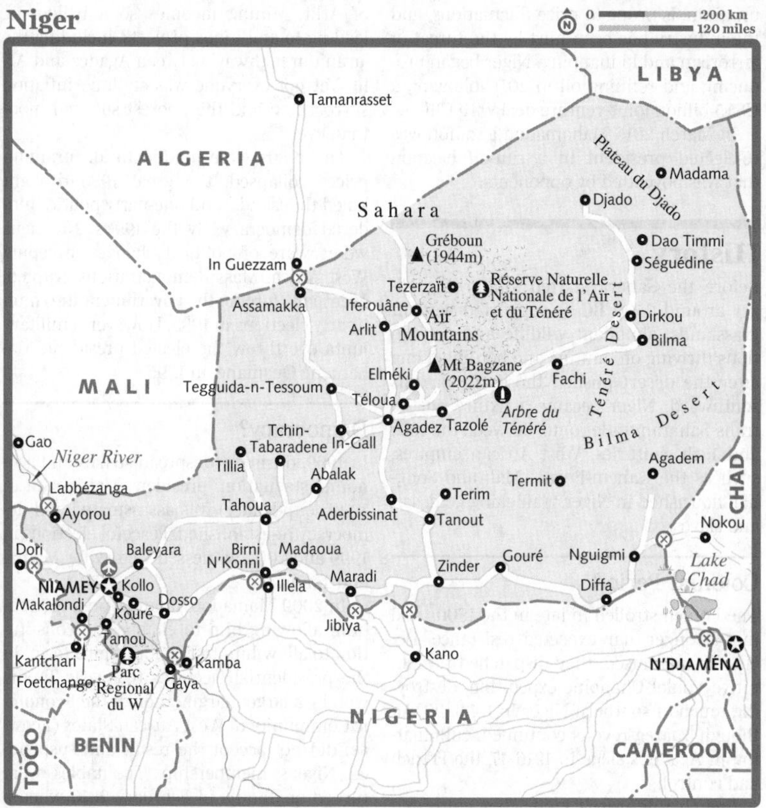




## UNDERSTAND NIGER

### Niger Today

A series of unpleasant events have defined Niger to the outside world in recent years. In 2007 the Tuareg in the north of the country began a rebellion against Niger's government, whom it accused of hoarding proceeds from the region's enormous mineral wealth and failing to meet conditions of previous ceasefires, in a conflict that has reignited at regular intervals since the early 20th century.

A year later Niger again made headlines around the world for less-than-positive reasons when in a landmark case an Economic Community of West African States (Ecowas) court found Niger guilty of failing to protect a young woman from the continued practice of slavery in the country. According to anti-slavery organisations, thousands of people still live in subjugation. In 2014 a man was sentenced to four years in jail on a conviction of slavery. The first such prosecution of its kind.

There have been several high-profile terrorist attacks and kidnappings of tourists and foreign workers over the past few years by groups linked to Al-Qaeda factions operating in the Sahel and Sahara zone. The largest such attack was a coordinated assault by Islamic militants on military and mining sites in the north of the country in 2013. The Islamist takeover of northern Mali in 2012 created a security vacuum and opened up a safe haven for extremists and organised crime groups in the Sahara Desert. But even though terrorist attacks were on the rise in Niger, tens of thousands of refugees flooded into the country from neighbouring conflict zones.

Niger's economy continues to putter and struggle along. The country's main export, uranium, is prone to price fluctuations, and the industry has been hurt by the threat of terrorism and kidnapping. Niger began producing and refining oil in 2011 following a US$5 billion joint-venture deal with China.

In March 2016 Mahamadou Issoufou was re-elected president in a run-off election that was boycotted by opponents.



# History

Before the Sahara started swallowing Niger around 2500 BC, it supported verdant grasslands, abundant wildlife and populations thriving on hunting and herding. Long after the desert pushed those populations southward, Niger became a fixture on the trans-Saharan trade route. Between the 10th and 18th centuries, West African empires, such as the Kanem-Borno, Mali and Songhaï, flourished in Niger, trafficking gold, salt and slaves.

## Colonial Period

The French strolled in late in the 1800s and met stronger-than-expected resistance. Decidedly unamused, they dispatched the punitive Voulet-Chanoîne expedition, destroying much of southern Niger in 1898–99. Although Tuareg revolts continued, culminating in Agadez's siege in 1916–17, the French had control.

French rule wasn't kind. They cultivated the power of traditional chiefs, whose abuses were encouraged as a means of control, and the enforced shift from subsistence farming to high-density cash crops compounded the Sahara's ongoing migration.

In 1958 France offered its West African colonies self-government in a French union or immediate independence. Countless votes disappeared in the ensuing referendum, enabling France to claim that Niger wished to remain within its sphere of influence.

## Independence & Uranium

Maintaining close French ties, Niger's first president, Hamani Diori, ran a repressive one-party state. After surviving several coups, he was overthrown by Lieutenant Colonel Seyni Kountché after food stocks were discovered in ministerial homes during the Sahel drought of 1968–74. Kountché established a military ruling council.

Kountché hit the jackpot in 1968 when uranium was discovered near the town of Arlit. Mining incomes soon ballooned, leading to ambitious projects, including the 'uranium highway' between Agadez and Arlit. Yet not everyone was smiling: inflation skyrocketed and the poorest suffered more than ever.

The 1980s were unkind to all: uranium prices collapsed, the great 1983 drought killed thousands, and one-party politics hindered democracy. By the 1990s, Nigeriens were aware of political changes sweeping West Africa. Mass demonstrations erupted, eventually forcing the government into multiparty elections in 1993. However, a military junta overthrew the elected president, Mahamane Ousmane, in 1996.

## Democracy?

In 1999, during widespread strikes and economic stagnation, president Mainassara (a 1996 coup leader) was assassinated and democracy re-established. Peaceful elections in 1999 and 2004 witnessed victory for Mamadou Tandja.

In 2009 Mamadou Tandja won a referendum allowing him to change the constitution to allow him to run for a third term. In the presidential elections that year Tandja won by a large margin, though the Economic Community of West African States (Ecowas) did not accept the result and suspended Niger's membership. The tables were turned on Tandja in February 2010 when a military coup in Niamey led to his arrest. A year-long military junta ended when veteran opposition leader Mahamadou Issoufou was declared winner of a presidential poll in March 2011.

# Culture

Niger boasts the highest birth rate in the world: in 2015 it was estimated that women have a staggering average of just under seven children each. The population is predicted to reach 21.4 million by 2025.

More than 90% of Nigeriens live in the south, which is dominated by Hausa and Songhaï-Djerma, making up 53% and 21% of Niger's populace respectively. The next largest groups are nomadic Tuareg (11%) and Fulani (6.5%), both in Niger's north, and Kanuri (5.9%), who are located between Zinder and Chad.

Nigeriens are predominantly Muslim (over 80%), with small percentages of Christian urban dwellers. Several rural populations still practise traditional animist religions. Due to the strong influence of Nigeria's Islamic community, some Muslims around the border town of Maradi call for sharia law.

Despite most Nigeriens being devoutly Muslim, the government is steadfastly secular and Islam adopts a more relaxed aura than in nations with similar demographics. Women don't cover their faces, alcohol is quietly consumed and some Tuareg, recognising the harshness of desert life, ignore Ramadan's fast.

While Islam plays an important role in daily life, shaping beliefs and thoughts, little is visible to visitors. The biggest exceptions are *salat* (prayer), when Niger grinds to a halt – buses even break journeys to partake.

Religion aside, survival occupies most people's days. Around 90% make their tenuous living from agriculture and livestock, many surviving on US$1 or less per day. Producing numerous children to help with gruelling workloads is a necessity for many, a fact contributing to population growth. The need for children to work has led to staggering adult illiteracy rates.

Niger's best-known artisans are Tuareg silversmiths, who produce necklaces, striking amulets, ornamental silver daggers and stylised silver crosses, each with intricate filigree designs representing areas boasting Tuareg populations. The most famous cross is the *croix d'Agadez*. To Tuareg, crosses are powerful talismans protecting against ill fortune.

Leatherwork by *artisans du cuir* is well regarded, particularly in Zinder, where traditional items – such as saddlebags, cushions and tasselled pouches – rank alongside attractive modernities like sandals and briefcases.

Beautifully unique to Niger are vibrant *kountas* (Djerma blankets), produced from bright cotton strips.

## Environment

Three quarters of Niger is desert, with the Sahara advancing south 10km a year. The remaining quarter is Sahel, the semi-desert zone south of the Sahara. Notable features include the Niger River (Africa's third-longest), which flows 300km through Niger's southwest; the Aïr Mountains, the dark volcanic formations of which rise over 2000m; and the Ténéré Desert's spectacularly sweeping sand dunes.

Desertification, Niger's greatest environmental problem, is primarily caused by overgrazing and deforestation. Quartz-rich soil also prevents topsoil anchoring, causing erosion.

The southwest's dry savannah woodland hosts one of West Africa's better wildlife parks, Parc Regional du W (although many governments have marked the Niger section of this trans-frontier park as unsafe to visit).

# SURVIVAL GUIDE

## Directory A–Z

### DANGERS & ANNOYANCES

Niger has never had a reputation as a safe and easy place to travel, but today the situation is worse than normal.

Almost every Western government advises against all travel to virtually the entire country. The only exception is for travel to Niamey and a narrow band across the south, and even then most governments advise against all but essential travel.

- Check the situation carefully before travelling to Niger.
- Avoid demonstrations and areas popular with foreign residents.
- Do not travel anywhere after dark.
- Carry your passport with you at all times.
- Do not photograph police, military or sensitive sites.

### VISAS

Should you decide to ignore the advice of most governments and go to Niger anyway, the good news is that tourist visas are not overly hard to come by.

- Visas are available in most neighbouring countries.
- Allow up to two weeks for a visa to be issued.
- Outside West Africa, Niger embassies are few and far between.

# Nigeria

☎234 / POP 186 MILLION

**Includes ➡**



## Best Places to Eat

- ➡ Terra Kulture (p403)
- ➡ Bogobiri House (p403)
- ➡ Indigo (p407)
- ➡ Purple at the Blowfish (p406)

## Best Places to Sleep

- ➡ Bogobiri House (p403)
- ➡ Nike Ambassador Guest House (p414)
- ➡ Wheatbaker (p406)
- ➡ Nordic Villa (p416)

## Why Go?

Nigeria is a pulsating powerhouse: as the most populous nation on the continent – nearly every fifth African is Nigerian – it dominates the region. Recently, though, the boom has shown a few signs of bust: the economy has been hit by the drop in crude oil prices. But Lagos, the main city, is resurgent: with burgeoning tech industries, posh restaurants and clubs, and an exploding arts scene, this megacity is the face of modern Africa.

Outside Gidi (as Lagosians call their city), you may feel as if you're a lone explorer getting a glimpse of the raw edges of the world, immersing yourself in deep and layered cultures. From Yoruba shrines to the slave ports, from the ancient Muslim cities of the north (currently out of bounds for security reasons) to the river deltas, and among stunning natural environments – there are plenty of wonderful antidotes to a sometimes exhausting journey.

## When to Go

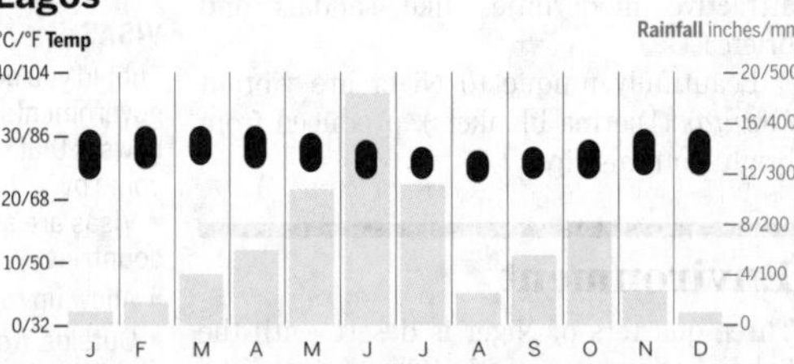


**Nov–Feb** Dry season; many events, such as carnival in Calaba and Felebration in Lagos.

**Apr–Sep** Rainy season; heavy rainfall particularly in the south

**Mar & Oct** Shoulder season; some rain in the south but dry in the north.

# LAGOS

☎01 / POP 21 MILLION

The economic and cultural powerhouse of the country thanks to an influx of oil money, Lagos has an exploding arts and music scene that will keep your *yansh* engaged far past dawn. If you're headed to Nigeria, you'll have no choice but to jump right in.

As well as brilliantly buoyant culture, Lagos has bumper-to-bumper cars, noise and pollution beyond belief, a high crime rate, and maxed-out public utilities. Elevated motorways ringing the island city are jammed with speed freaks and absurd traffic jams ('go-slows') on top, and tin-and-cardboard shacks underneath. It's a divided city, but an undeniably exciting one.

Named after the Portuguese word for lagoon, Lagos has been a Yoruba port, a British political centre and, until 1991, Nigeria's capital.

## Sights

On Lagos Island look out for examples of old Brazilian architecture in the distinctive houses built by former slaves and their descendants who returned from Brazil.

**★Terra Kulture** GALLERY
(Map p410; www.terrakulture.com; Plot 1376 Tiamiyu Savage St, VI) FREE Close to Bar Beach, this welcoming arts centre with a high bamboo roof has a traditional restaurant which is one of the best and most attractive places to eat in town: try the catfish with pounded yam and spicy soup. There's an art gallery, a bookshop with funky crafts, literary readings and events, and a theatre.

**★Nike Art Gallery** GALLERY
(☎0803 4096 656; www.nikeart.com; 3rd Roundabout, Epe Expressway, Lekki; ⏰10am-6pm) FREE One of Nigeria's most important artists, Nike Okundaye, runs this enormous gallery full of contemporary and traditional Nigerian arts. Nike herself is like an incarnation of love and beauty, which is reflected in this astonishing four-storey space. If you're lucky she'll be there and may grace you with a new Yoruba name. There's a small cafe in the grounds.

**★Lekki Conservation Centre** WILDLIFE RESERVE
(☎01 264 2498; www.ncfnigeria.org; Km 19, Lagos-Epe Expressway; N1000; ⏰8.30am-5pm Mon-Sat, 8.30am-noon Sun; 🚌flag down a bus on VI along Maroko Rd) FREE Run by the Nigerian Conservation Foundation, this centre has a huge tract of wetlands set aside for wildlife viewing. Canopy walkways enable you to see monkeys, crocodiles and various birds; early morning is the best time to visit. There is a conservation centre and a library.

**★Kalakuta Republic Museum** MUSEUM
(Map p406; 7 Gbemisola St, Ikeja; N500; ⏰10am-5pm) Legendary musician Fela Kuti's former house and revolutionary headquarters is now a fascinating museum with everything intact from Fela's bedroom to his (very small) underwear. Breath deep and you may even catch a high. And hang around on the rooftop terrace and you might catch a band rehearsal or performance.

**★Lekki Market** MARKET
(Elegushi Market; off Epe Expressway, Lekki) A rich variety of crafts from all around Nigeria and West Africa: this is a brilliant place to wander and look for affordable gifts. You can also buy fabrics and get clothes run up on the spot here.

**African Artists' Foundation** GALLERY
(Map p410; www.africanartists.org; 3b Isiola Oyekan Close, VI; ⏰10am-5pm Mon-Fri, noon-4pm Sat) FREE An organisation supporting young African and international artists with a great gallery of contemporary Nigerian art.

## Sleeping

**Peerage Retreat** HOTEL $
(Map p410; ☎805 633 2902; peerageretreat@yahoo.com; 1 Olabode George St, VI; r N10,000; ❄) The best option for the money on the island, this family-run hotel is clean, friendly and well run. Given the deal, it fills up fast. Just make sure the electricity is working.

**Ritz Hotel** HOTEL $
(Map p408; ☎01 263 0481; King George V Rd; r with fan & without bathroom N2000, with air-con N2900-4000; ❄) The name's a bit of a misnomer, but this hotel is a reasonably decent budget option. Rooms are fine in a grubby 'by the hour' sort of way, but they're secure and management is friendly.

**Hotel Victoria Palace** HOTEL $$
(Map p410; ☎01 262 5901; victoriapalace@gmail.com; 1623 Sake Jojo St; r N14,000; P❄) Basic rooms and friendly staff; a good budget-ish choice on Victoria Island.

**★Bogobiri House** BOUTIQUE HOTEL $$$
(Map p410; ☎706 817 6454; www.bogobiri.com; 9 Maitama Sule St, Ikoyi; r from N50,000; ❄@📶) This charming boutique hotel, beautifully decorated with paintings and sculptures by local artists, serves as the hub of the vibrant

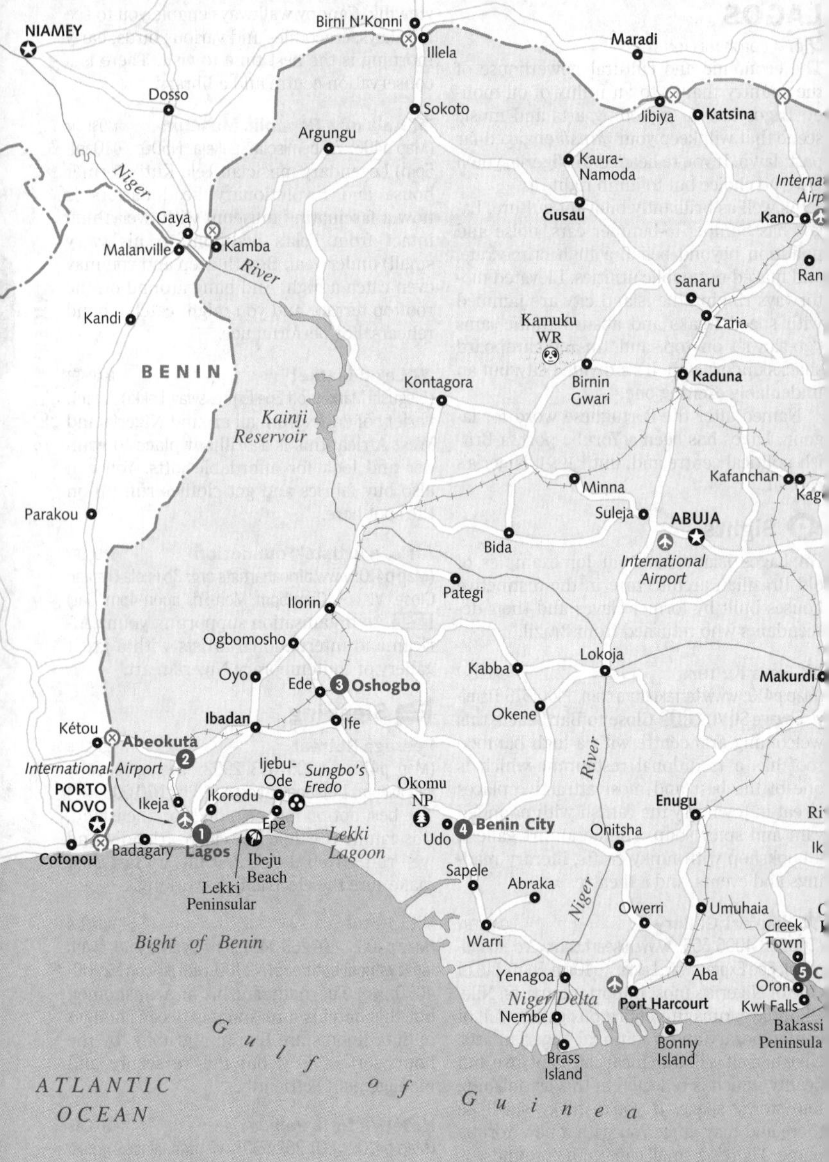


# Nigeria Highlights

❶ **Lagos** (p403) Joining the gold rush of the country's super-confident boom city, and exploring its insatiably lively art and music scene.

❷ **Abeokuta** (p412) Climbing the sacred rock via historic hideouts and shrines, and looking out on the picturesque rooftops from a high vantage point.

❸ **Oshogbo** (p413) Learning about traditional crafts, browsing the impressive galleries and losing yourself on the river bank in the sacred grove.

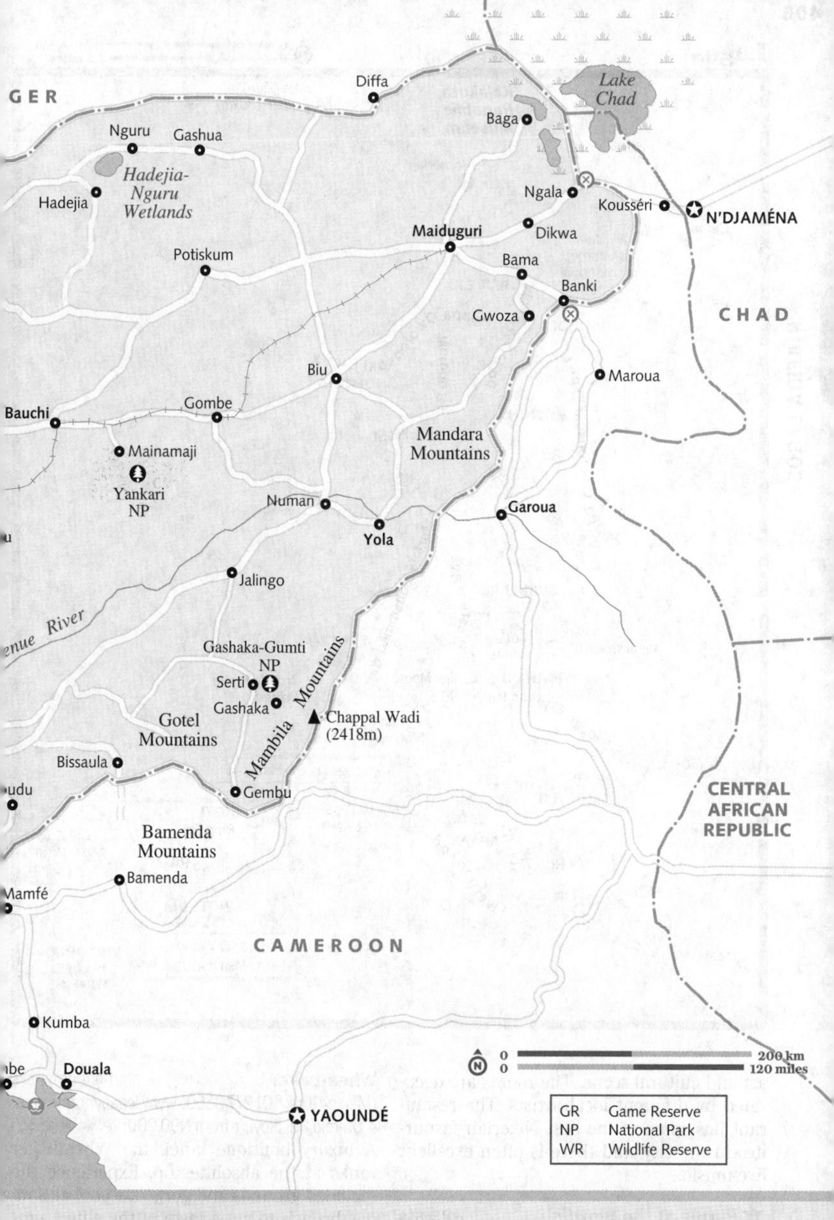


**4 Benin City** (p414) Wandering the Brass Casters St, governed by a secret ancient guild, and catching a flavour of the former glory of the marvellous Benin empire.

**5 Calabar** (p415) Taking in colonial history and cutting-edge conservation in the easygoing old river port.

## Lagos

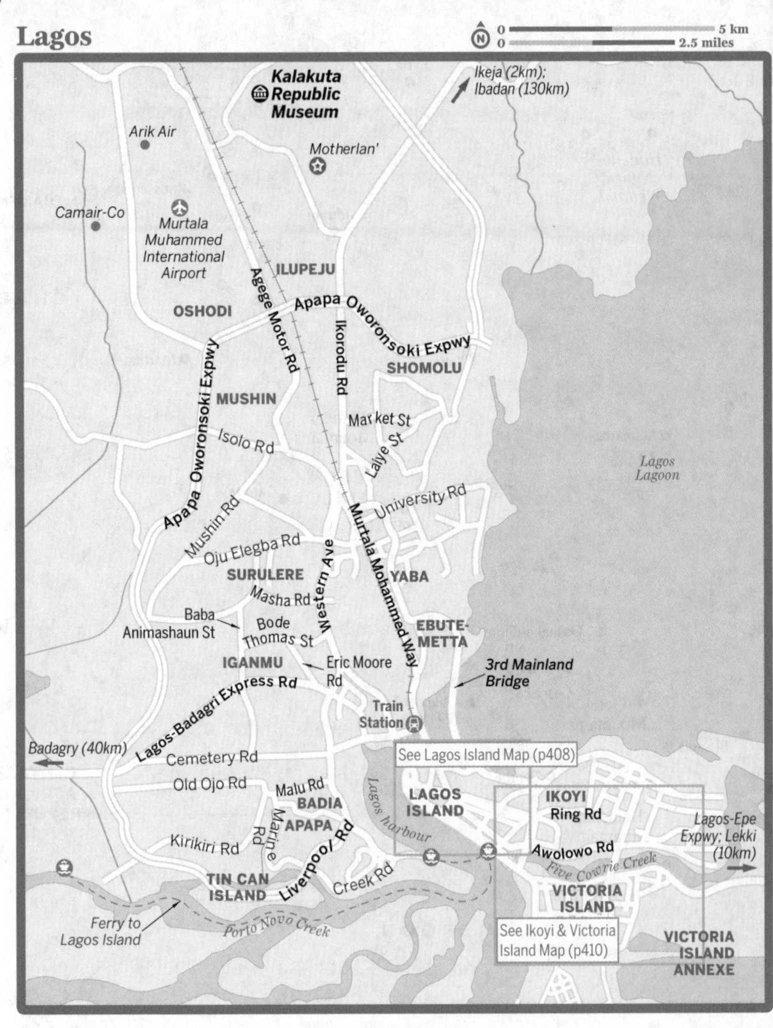


art and cultural scene. The rooms are decorated by different local artists. The restaurant has some of the best Nigerian favourites in the city, and there is often excellent live music.

**★Purple at the Blowfish** HOTEL $$$
(Map p410; ☎01 463 1298; www.theblowfishhotel.com; 17 Oju Olobun Close, VI; r N30,000; ❄📶🏊) Not only a great boutique hotel with classy and comfortable rooms, the Blowfish's restaurant Purple offers nice dining by the pool with Indian, Italian Thai, Lebanese and continental menus.

**Wheatbaker** BOUTIQUE HOTEL $$$
(Map p410; ☎01 277 3560; www.legacyhotels.com; 4 Onitolo Rd, Ikoyi; r from N90,000; P❄@📶🏊) A luxury boutique hotel, the Wheatbaker ranks at the absolute top. Experience the secluded grounds and gorgeous pool at Sunday brunch to get a taste of the elite Lagos lifestyle.

### Eating

Broad St and Campbell St in Lagos Island are good for chop houses and *suya* (Nigerian kebab); the better restaurants are in Ikoyi and Victoria Island. Some of the best places to eat are attached to hotels and cultural centres, such as Bogobiri House, Terra Kulture and Purple at the Blowfish. There are cheap eats at the Bar Beach market.

**Sherlaton** INDIAN $
(Map p410; ☎01 269 1275; 108 Awolowo Rd; mains less than N1500; ⏰noon-3pm & 7-10pm; 🅥) Vegetarians suffer a lot in Nigeria, but this Indian restaurant really comes to the rescue. The Sherlaton is generally considered to be the city's best curry option.

**Ikoyi Hotel Suya** AFRICAN $
(Map p410; Kingsway Rd, Ikoyi Hotel, Ikoyi; suya from N100; ⏰10am-10pm) Lagosians claim the best *suya* in town can be found at the stall outside the Ikoyi Hotel. Not just beef and goat, but chicken, liver and kidney, plus some great fiery *pepe* (pepper) to spice it all up.

**★Indigo** INDIAN $$
(Map p410; ☎0805 235 9793; www.indigolagos.com; 242b Muri Okunola St; mains N1800; ⏰noon-midnight; 🅥) Subtly flavoured Indian food served in a refined atmosphere. There's a picture window onto the traditional clay oven, where fresh bread is baked at high speed. Lots of choice for vegetarians.

**Pizze-Riah** PIZZA $$
(Map p410; 13 Musa Yardua St, VI; pizzas N1500; ⏰noon-11pm) Brick-oven pizza in a lovely outdoor setting, with a play area for kids.

**Cactus** BAKERY $$
(Map p410; Maroko Rd; mains from N1200; ⏰8am-10pm) This place labels itself primarily as a patisserie, but it also serves up proper meals throughout the day. Breakfasts of pancakes or bacon are good, as are the pizzas, and the club sandwiches with salad and chips are simply huge – excellent value at N1800. Giant fresh juices cost N1200.

**Art Cafe** CAFE $$
(Map p410; www.thehomestoresng.com/artcafe; 282 Akin Olugbede St, VI; suya/mains N700/4000; ⏰7.30am-11pm; 📶) A lovely little cafe-pub which also sells arts and crafts. It does good coffee and snacks, and the laid-back arty vibe is a nice contrast to the bland feel of parts of Victoria Island.

**Yellow Chilli** AFRICAN $$
(Map p410; ☎01 280 6876; www.yellowchilling.com; 27 Oju Olubun Close, VI; mains N1500-2500; ⏰noon-midnight; 🅟❄) Well-presented Nigerian dishes in swish surroundings. It's carried off well, with tasty dishes in reasonable portions and good service – a great way to eat your way around the country without leaving your table.

## Drinking & Nightlife

As they say in Lagos, what happens in Gidi stays in Gidi. In other words, Lagos' nightlife is legendary. Be prepared to stay up past dawn. Note that what's hot is constantly changing, and that you have to dig beneath the bling to find the city's earthier venues.

Ask around for the best nights out or check out www.nothingtodoinlagos.com. Bars are best up until midnight, when the clubs and music venues heat up.

**★Bogobiri II/Nimbus** BAR
(Map p410; ☎706 817 6454; www.bogobiri.com; Maitama Sule St, Ikoyi; ⏰8am-11pm) Part of Bogobiri House, this is a lovely place for a drink (and eat) – mellow in the day and happening at night. There's an attached art gallery with works from local artists, and at weekends

### FELA KUTI: MUSIC IS THE WEAPON

The impact of Fela Anikulapo Kuti's music in Nigeria, and worldwide, cannot be overstated. Fela Kuti (1938–97) is Africa's musical genius, the creator of Afrobeat – a genre combining traditional African highlife, jazz, James Brown funk grooves and Latin rhythms into a unique mix that is wholly his own – and a revolutionary. Fela's politically inflammatory songs laid bare the corruption, violence and greed of the ruling regimes in his country and beyond. He was arrested over a hundred times by the Nigerian government, and ultimately 1000 soldiers invaded and destroyed the Kalakuta Republic – Fela's living and performing compound that he shared with his 27 wives – sending nearly all of the inhabitants to the hospital, or worse. Despite the death of his own mother due to the siege, Fela never stopped fighting the powers of imperialism, colonialism, conformity and racism with – as the legend himself put it – music as his weapon. Due to the re-release of his music worldwide and, interestingly, a Broadway musical based on his life, Fela's legacy is enjoying renewed attention and a reinvigorated profile in Nigeria. The Lagos government even donated money to launch the Kalakuta Republic Museum (p403), and Felabration is celebrated for a week each year around his birthday on 15 October.

# Lagos Island

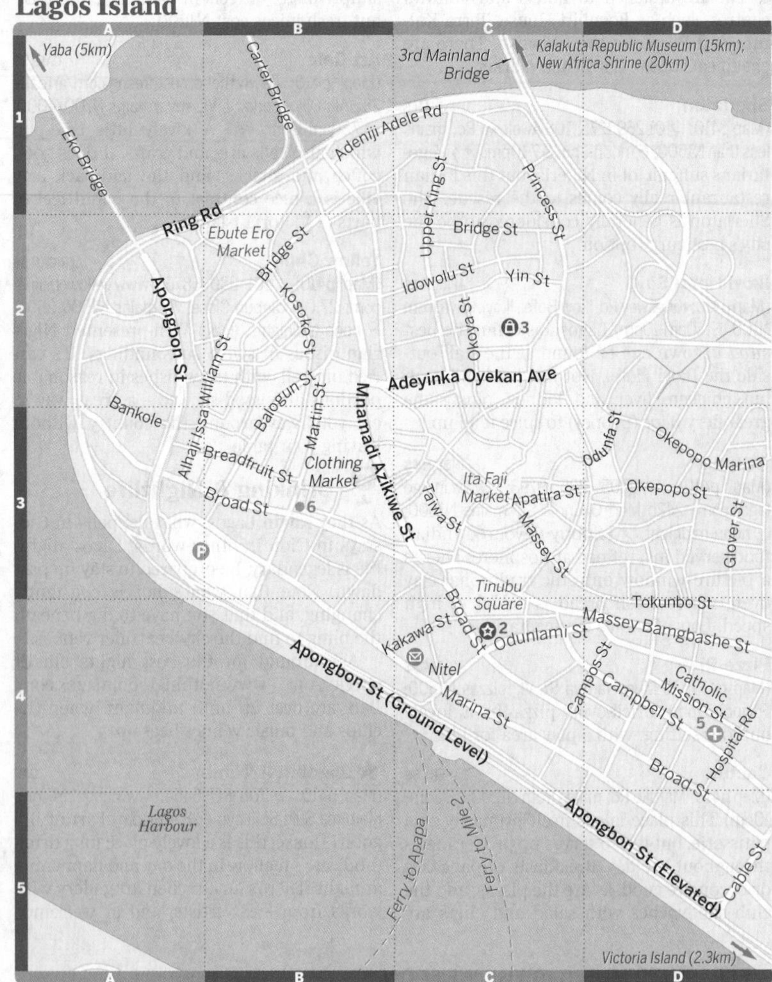


there's live music. At the open mic night on a Thursday you'll hear some astonishing young musicians.

**Elegushi Beach** BAR

Dancing bumper-to-bumper, bottles of the hard stuff – the party does not get better than Elegushi Beach on a Sunday night. Go with a local; there have been robberies. Not for the faint of heart. During the day, pay a fee (N1000) to enjoy the semi-private beach.

**Vapours** BAR

(Map p410; 879 Samuel Manuwa St, VI; ⌚10pm-6am) Starts late, gets good even later. Nigeria's elites, socialites and pop stars come here for the post-party partying. If you get the munchies, head across the street, outside the gate of 1004 Housing Estates, to Chopbox; it's always open.

## ☆ Entertainment

**★New Afrika Shrine** LIVE MUSIC

(Adeleye St, Ikeja; cover charge N500; ⌚6pm-1am Thu-Sun) Just by showing up you'll get a political education, a lesson in shakin' it and a contact high. Though Fela's original Shrine was burnt down, this replacement run by his children is the best show in town. Femi

## Lagos Island

**Sleeping**
1 Ritz Hotel ........ F5

**Entertainment**
2 Freedom Park ........ C4

**Shopping**
3 Jankara Market ........ C2

**Information**
4 Ghanaian High Commission ........ F5
5 St Nicholas Hospital ........ D4

**Transport**
6 Lufthansa ........ B3
7 Obalende Motor Park ........ F4

Kuti plays on Thursdays (free) and Sundays. Fela's most approximate reincarnation Seun Kuti plays the last Saturday of the month.

**Freedom Park** LIVE MUSIC
(Map p408; www.freedomparklagos.com; Old Prison Ground, Broad St, Lagos Island) Formerly the Old Broad Street Prison, a colonial-era instrument of oppression, it has recently been turned into a cultural centere, venue for events and concerts, a museum, a food court and a market. Some of the old prison structures are still standing.

**Motherlan'** LIVE MUSIC
(Map p406; 802 067 8899; 64b Opebi Rd, Ikeja; N1000; Thu-Sun) Owned by renowned mask-wearing musician Lagbaja, this is a big outdoor venue with lots of live music and a robust local following.

## Shopping

**★Jazz Hole** BOOKS
(Map p410; www.glendorabooks.net; 168 Awolowo Road, Ikoyi; 10am-8pm Mon-Sat, 4-8pm Sun) An offspring of the great Glendora Books, Jazz Hole is primarily a book and record store. In this oasis of calm in the mile-a-minute city, sip tea in the lovely cafe and get cultural lessons from the proprietor – ask to see his own book about Abeokuta. Special events and performances in the evenings.

**★Quintessence** ARTS & CRAFTS
(Map p410; 803 327 5401; www.quintessenceltd.com; Plot 13, Block 44, Parkview Estate, off Gerrard Rd; 8am-5pm Mon-Fri, 9am-4pm Sat & Sun) Out in the gated Parkview estate, Quintessence sells artworks and crafts, with an especially good selection of clothes and some antique carvings and artefacts. Some of the colourful and original garments are made here, and there are lovely embroidered Senegalese dresses.

**Jankara Market** MARKET
(Map p408; off Adeyinka Oyekan Ave; 8am-6pm) Jankara Market is the largest market in Lagos and sells everything from tie-dyed cloth, trade beads and jewellery to pirate cassettes, pottery and clothing. There is also a fetishes market where you can buy herbs, traditional medicines and *juju* potions and powders.

## Ikoyi & Victoria Island

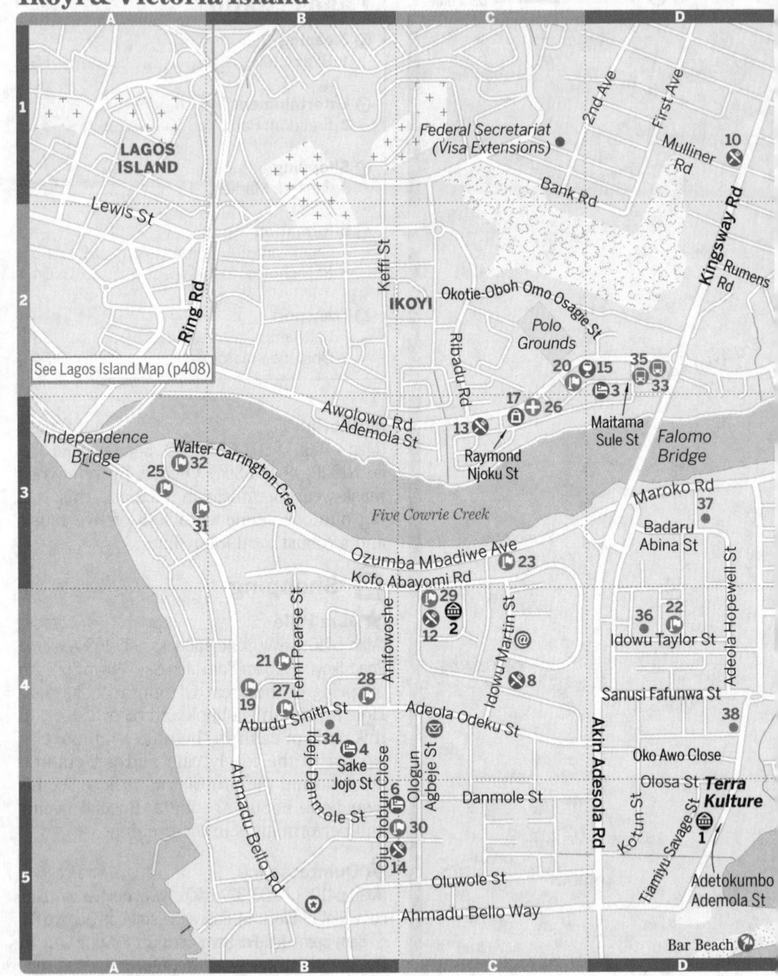


## ℹ Information

### DANGERS & ANNOYANCES

Contrary to popular perception, violent crime has decreased in recent years. Most crime against foreigners targets expats in expensive cars, and travellers are unlikely to encounter any serious problems. Still, never carry more money than is necessary and avoid flaunting valuables and walking outside at night – particularly around hotels and restaurants frequented by foreigners.

### INTERNET ACCESS

Internet cafes are everywhere and cost upwards from N200 per hour. Most upscale restaurants and cafes also have wi-fi.

**Bogobiri House** Have lunch here for a fast connection.

**Cafe Royale** (Map p410; http://royalteas.com.ng/cafe-royal; No 267A, Etim Inyang Cres, VI; ⏲7am-10pm; 📶) Satisfy your sweet tooth and wireless needs at this bakery-restaurant.

**Mega Plaza Internet** (Map p410; Idowu Martin St, Mega Plaza; ⏲10am-6pm)

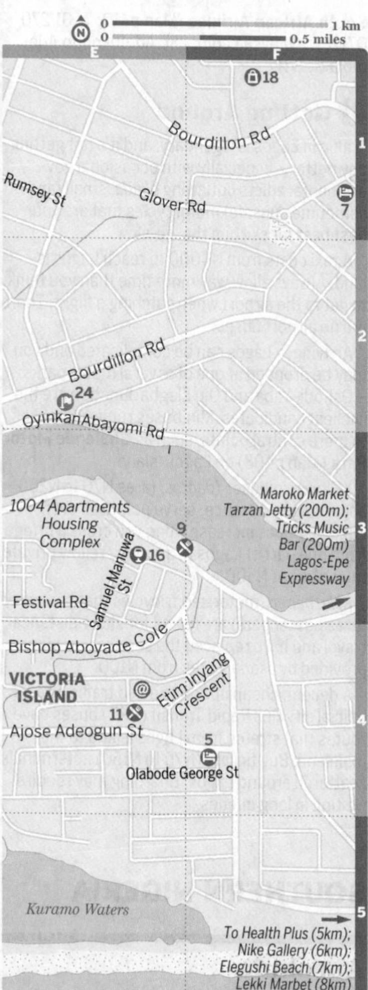


## Ikoyi & Victoria Island

**Top Sights**
1 Terra Kulture .......... D5

**Sights**
2 African Artists' Foundation .......... C4

**Sleeping**
3 Bogobiri House .......... D2
4 Hotel Victoria Palace .......... B4
5 Peerage Retreat .......... F4
6 Purple at the Blowfish .......... B5
7 Wheatbaker .......... F1

**Eating**
8 Art Cafe .......... C4
9 Cactus .......... E3
10 Ikoyi Hotel Suya .......... D1
11 Indigo .......... E4
12 Pizze-Riah .......... C4
13 Sherlaton .......... C3
14 Yellow Chilli .......... B5

**Drinking & Nightlife**
15 Bogobiri II/Nimbus .......... D2
16 Vapours .......... E3

**Shopping**
17 Jazz Hole .......... C3
18 Quintessence .......... F1

**Information**
19 Beninese Embassy .......... B4
20 Burkinabé Embassy .......... C2
21 Cameroonian Embassy .......... B4
22 Canadian Embassy .......... D4
23 Dutch Embassy .......... C3
24 French Embassy .......... E2
25 German Embassy .......... A3
26 Healthplus Integrative Pharmacy .......... C3
27 Ivoirian Embassy .......... B4
28 Nigerien Embassy .......... B4
29 Spanish Embassy .......... C4
30 Togolese Embassy .......... B5
31 UK Embassy .......... A3
32 US Embassy .......... A3

**Transport**
33 ABC Transport .......... D2
34 Air France .......... B4
35 Booking Office .......... D2
36 Ethiopian Airlines .......... D4
37 Kenya Airways .......... D3
KLM .......... (see 37)
38 South African Airlines .......... D4

### MEDICAL SERVICES

**Healthplus Integrative Pharmacy** (Map p410; ☎0802 802 5810; Unit 54, The Palms Shopping Centre, Lekki; ⊙8am-9pm Mon-Sat, 10am-9pm Sun) With branches in Ikeja, Yabo and the airport.

**St Nicholas Hospital** (Map p408; ☎0802 290 8484; www.saintnicholashospital.com; 57 Campbell St) Has a 24-hour emergency clinic.

### MONEY

Find exchange bureaus at Alade Market on the mainland, or outside Federal Palace and Eko Meridien hotels on Victoria Island.

### POST

**Main Post Office** (Map p408; Marina St; ⊙8am-4pm Mon-Sat)

**Post Office** (Map p410; Adeola Odeku St, VI; ⊙8am-4pm Mon-Sat)

### ARRIVING IN LAGOS

**Murtala Muhammed International Airport** Take a licensed taxi to your accommodation; these will be waiting to meet incoming flights. Ask the fee before getting in (30 minutes to one hour depending on traffic; around N6000).

## Getting There & Away

Murtala Muhammed International Airport (MMA1; p421) is the main gateway to Nigeria and is roughly 10km north of Lagos Island. The domestic terminal (MMA2) is 4km away; tickets can be bought on departure or from an agent. Though there are airline offices at the airport and in Lagos, it's best to use a travel agency that can sort your flights all-in-one.

Ojota Motor Park (with Ojota New Motor Park next door), 13km north of Lagos, is the city's main transport hub. Minibuses and bush taxis leaving to all destinations depart from here. Sample fares are Benin City (N3000, four hours), Ibadan (N1000, two hours), Oshogbo (N2500, three hours) and Abuja (N5000, 10 hours).

Mile-2 Motor Park serves destinations east of Lagos, including the Benin border at Seme (N800, 90 minutes). You'll also find a few minibuses going as far north as Ibadan from here.

**ABC Transport** (Map p410; ☎01 740 1010; www.abctransport.com) is a good intercity 'luxury' bus company, serving many major cities, as well as destinations in Benin, Ghana and Togo. The depot is at Jibowu motor park, but there's a useful **booking office** (Map p410; ☎01 740 1010; Awolowo Rd, Block D, Falomo Shopping Centre) inside a shoe shop at Falomo Shopping Centre.

The following airlines fly in and out of Lagos:

**Air France** (Map p410; ☎01 461 0777; www.airfrance.com; Idejo Danmole St)

**Arik Air** (Map p406; ☎01 279 9999; www.arikair.com; Lagos Murtala Muhammed International Airport)

**Camair-Co** (Map p406; ☎01 291 2025; www.camair-co.cm; Murtala Muhammed International Airport)

**Ethiopian Airlines** (Map p410; ☎01 461 1869; www.ethiopianairlines.com; 3 Idowu Tayor St, Victoria Island)

**Kenya Airways** (Map p410; ☎01 271 9433; www.kenya-airways.com; Badaru Abina St, Churchgate Tower)

**KLM** (Map p410; ☎0703 415 3801; www.klm.com; 1 Adeola Odeku St, Sapetro, VI)

**Lufthansa** (Map p408; ☎01 461 2222; www.lufthansa.com; Churchgate Tower, VI)

**South African Airlines** (Map p410; ☎01 270 0712; www.flysaa.com; 28c Adetukonbo Ademola St, VI)

## Getting Around

Traffic in Lagos is legendary, and it's not getting any better – especially with occasional governmental edicts outlawing *okada*, small (and sometimes unsafe) motorcycles that are your best best for skirting the 'go-slow'.

A taxi costs from N4000 to reach Lagos Island. Always allow way more time than you think to get to the airport when catching a flight. There are no airport buses.

Arriving in Lagos can be complicated and you may be dropped at one of several motor parks – Oshodi, Yaba and Oju Elegba Junction are the likeliest candidates. Minibuses run from these to more central points, such as **Obalende Motor Park** (Map p408) on Lagos Island.

Yellow minibuses (*danfos;* fares N70 to N250 according to distance) serve points all over Lagos – prices increase when you cross a bridge from one part of Lagos to another. Yellow private taxis start at N500.

*Keke napep* (motorised tricycles that can carry three passengers) are useful for short-distance travel and have replaced the services previously provided by *okada*. Fares from N100.

A decent, cheap option to avoid traffic, the official city Bus Rapid Transit (BRT) buses have routes that stretch from Lagos Island to the mainland. Buy tickets (N70 to N150) at terminals scattered around Lagos. Boarding may require waiting in long queues.

# SOUTHERN NIGERIA

## Abeokuta

POP 494,700 / ☎35

Abeokuta is a remarkable place, backed by the huge Olumo Rock. Grand but dishevelled Brazilian and Cuban mansions built by returned slaves sit alongside basic shacks with hand-painted signs, historic mosques and churches and the rounded mass of the rocks, creating an unforgettable streetscape.

Abeokuta has its own very strong cultural identity, well known as the birthplace of many famous Nigerians, notably Afrobeat legend Fela Kuti and writer Wole Soyinka, whose autobiography, *Aké,* is a vivid depiction of a childhood spent here.

It's a poor town, unused to visitors except those visiting the rock, and while wandering around is fascinating, you'll feel conspicuous.

## Sights

**Olumo Rock** SHRINE

(off Ijemo Rd; N2500, guide from N1000) The founding site of Abeokuta, famed Olumo Rock has a rich history and great spiritual significance. Hire a guide and climb the rock – at one point it is smooth and quite steep, so go via the steps if you're not confident. You'll see shrines, sacred trees, tribal wartime hideouts, and ultimately, at the top, an astonishing view of the city.

## Sleeping

Most people visit Abeokuta on a day trip from Lagos: accommodation is limited, but the Quarry Imperial Hotel is friendly and comfortable enough, as long as the electricity is functioning.

**Quarry Imperial Hotel** HOTEL $

(811 358 6172; www.quarryimperialhotels.com; 52 Quarry Rd; r N10,100-57,100; ) A grandly named place, built on a weirdly large scale. It's often almost empty, and staff will be delighted to see you. Rooms are large and fairly comfortable, the restaurant is decent and there's even a pool. The electricity and water supplies come and go. Take a motorbike or taxi to the rock.

## Eating

You'll find cheap eating joints throughout the town, and vendors sell snacks around the rock. There's a basic cafe at the foot of the shrine through the entrance gate.

## Getting There & Away

To make the two-hour trip from Lagos take a bush taxi (N300) from Ojota Motor Park. You'll arrive at Kuto Motor Park, where you can hop on an *okada* (N100) or catch a taxi.

# Ibadan

POP 3.3 MILLION / 02

The word sprawling could have been invented to describe Ibadan, now the biggest city in West Africa. You're likely to pass through this major transport junction, but you'll find few formal sites. There's an acclaimed university, and the Gbagi market has an enormous selection of fabric, but otherwise just keep on driving.

**University of Ibadan Guest House** (012 273 9865; Benue Rd, University of Ibadan Campus; r N8000; P) is a bit grimy but on the campus at Nigeria's premier university, with many amenities.

**Kakanfo Inn** (812 094 6333; www.kakanfoinn.com; 1 Nihinlola St, Ring Rd, Ibadan; r N15,000; P) is decent choice, with a pool, a good Indian restaurant and friendly staff. The wi-fi may be theoretical though.

Ibadan's favourite Asian restaurant, **Kabachi Chinese Fusion Bistro** (705 555 0000; Sango Rd, Ventura Mall; mains N2500; 11am-10pm; ) has teppanyaki chefs whipping up meat, fish and veg dishes such as chow mein and Sichuan beef. Great service and attractive decor, with lanterns and oriental screens.

## Getting There & Away

Iwo Rd is Ibadan's major motor park; minibuses run to all points from here, including Lagos (N500, 90 minutes), Abuja (N2000, eight hours) and points north. For Oshogbo (N300, 90 minutes), go to Gate Motor Park in the east of the city.

# Oshogbo

POP 681,600

This very special city has been a traditional centre for Yoruba spirituality and, since the 1950s, the birthplace for much contemporary Nigerian art. The best sight is the Osun Sacred Grove, believed to be the dwelling of Osun, the Yoruba fertility goddess.

## Sights

**★Osun Sacred Grove** FOREST

(Osun Shrine Rd; N200; 10am-6pm) The Sacred Grove is a large area of rainforest on the outskirts of Oshogbo. Within the forest is the beautiful Shrine of Oshuno, the River Goddess. In addition to natural beauty, there are many stunning sculptures by Suzanne Wenger (known locally as Aduni Olosa, the 'Adored One'), an Austrian painter and sculptor who came here in the 1950s.

**Suzanne Wenger's House** CULTURAL CENTRE

(41A Ibokun Rd; by donation) Susanne Wenger's remarkable house sits in the heart of Oshogbo: a tall Gothic place decorated outside with terracotta swirling sculptures, and inside with a mass of wooden votive figures. Sit on one of the fantastical carved chairs at the household shrine (first take your shoes off) and you may hear about Susanne's incredible life from one of her adopted children.

**Nike Centre for Art & Culture** CULTURAL CENTRE

(www.nikeart.com; Old Ede Rd; 9am-5pm) FREE Get your shopping groove on at this fabulous gallery, where you can browse Nike's own paintings, and buy a terrific range of fabrics, batik garments and jewellery.

**Jimoh Buraimoh's African Heritage Gallery** GALLERY
(☎806 797 9333; www.buraimoh.com; 1 Buraimoh St; ⏲9am-5pm) FREE Jimoh pioneered a technique of bead painting – you can see his colourful and dynamic works in the gallery, where he also runs workshops.

## Festivals & Events

**Osun Festival** CULTURAL
(⏲Aug) Thousands descend on Oshogbo in late August for this festival held in honour of the river goddess. Music, dancing and sacrifices form one of the centrepieces of the Yoruba cultural and spiritual year.

## Sleeping & Eating

**★Nike Ambassador Guest House** GUESTHOUSE $
(☎080 340 96656; www.nikeart.com; Ofatedo Rd; r N8000) It's essential to book ahead to stay in this wonderfully tasteful home, decorated with artworks inside and out. It's centred around an internal courtyard, where you can read at low sofas beneath the paintings. Vivid sculptures made from recycled metal dot the garden. You eat breakfast out here with the peacock, and the in-house team can arrange trips and meals.

## Getting There & Away

Okefia Rd is the main motor park. Minibuses leave regularly for Ibadan (N500, 90 minutes) and Lagos (N700, three hours).

WORTH A TRIP

### IE-IFE

Ie-Ife is considered the birthplace of Yoruba civilisation, where people still worship traditional deities at revered spiritual sites. At the 18th-century **Òoni's Palace** (Ile-Ife; around N2000), one of the king's servants will, for a fee, show you the shrine within the palace walls, take you to see Oduduwa's staff, and teach you fantastic Yoruba creation stories including the tale of Moremi the warrior-princess.

To get here, take a bush taxi from Oshogbo (N400, 45 minutes).



# Benin City

POP 1.5 MILLION / ☎052

Benin City, which served as the capital of the Benin kingdom, starting in the 15th century gave rise to one of the first African art forms to be accepted internationally – the Benin brasses (often given the misnomer bronzes). Today the city is the centre of Nigeria's rubber trade, and a sprawling metropolis.

Virtually nothing of the historic city survives: it was destroyed by the British in an epic act of vandalism in 1897. But the culture and the royal family is still deeply venerated here, with the *oba* (king) held in higher esteem than any mere politician.

## Sights

**Brass Casters Street** AREA
(Igun St) On the Unesco-protected Brass Casters St, sculptors reviving the 'lost-wax' sculpture technique can show you their works in progress and sell you one to take home: there are small ornaments as well as hugely impressive figurative statues. The street is governed by an ancient and secretive guild.

**National Museum** MUSEUM
(King's Sq; N100; ⏲9am-6pm) The National Museum has displays of beautiful brasses. There are photographs of pieces which were stolen by the British during the sacking and destruction of the city and are now displayed in the British Museum.

## Festivals & Events

**Igue Festival** CULTURAL
(⏲Dec) Held in Benin City, usually in the first half of December, this festival has traditional dances, a mock battle and a procession to the palace to reaffirm loyalty to the *oba*. It marks the harvest of the first new yams of the season.

## Sleeping & Eating

**Lixborr Hotel** HOTEL $
(☎802 459 1750; Sakowpba Rd; r N12,000; ❄) A popular, well-run place with comfortable rooms though a slightly subterranean murky feel. It's opposite Brass Casters St: look for the giant statue of the Benin woman. The in-house gallery is impressive.

**Hexagon** HOTEL $$
(☎052 941185; www.thehexagonnetwork.com; 2 Golf Course Rd, GRA; r N18,000; P@🛜) Owned by a prince of the Benin royal family, Hexagon has a gallery which displays ancient art works as well as contemporary pieces; the

outdoor Coconut Bar, which serves grilled grub and beer; a nightclub; and 19 rooms. These are spacious, with extremely comfortable beds and good bathrooms. The highlight of a stay here, though, is the excellent live bands at the Coconut Bar.

## Getting There & Away

**Arik Air** (p412) has daily flights from Lagos (N45,000, 40 minutes). Iyaro Motor Park is the main place for minibuses to Lagos (N1600, six hours) and Calabar (N1900, up to 10 hours, depending on the state of the road). Also try the depot next to the Edo-Delta Hotel on Akpakpava Rd, which serves most destinations.

# Calabar

POP 500,000 / ☎087

Tucked into Nigeria's southeastern corner, the capital of Cross River state has a rich history and is well worth a trip. Originally a cluster of Efik settlements, Calabar was once one of Africa's biggest slave ports, and later a major exporter of palm oil. A popular stopover for travellers heading to Cameroon, this tourist-friendly city has a fantastic museum and an excellent primate-conservation centre.

## Sights

★ **Afi Mountain Drill Ranch** WILDLIFE RESERVE

(www.pandrillus.org; green grant N250, guides N1000, car/motorbike N500/250, campsites N2000, huts N6000) The excellent Afi Mountain Drill Ranch near Cross River National Park is one of Nigeria's highlights, with a rainforest canopy walk, close primate encounters and superb accommodation. Its **headquarters** (Pandrillus; ☎0803 5921262; Nsefik Eyo Layout, off Atekong Rd; donations appreciated; ⏰9am-5pm) is in Calabar.

**Slave History Museum** MUSEUM

(☎080 3441 1080; Calabar Marina Resort; ⏰8am-6pm Mon-Fri, noon-6pm Sat & Sun) FREE The museum sits on the site of a 15th-century slave-trading warehouse. Exhibits explore local slave markets, the grim paraphernalia of the trade including shackles and chains, and the variety of currencies used to buy people, such as copper bars, brass bells and flutes.

**Calabar Museum** MUSEUM

(Court Rd; N100; ⏰9am-6pm) Housed in the beautiful 1884 British governor's building overlooking the river, the museum has a fascinating collection covering Calabar's days as the Efik kingdom, the slave and palm-oil trade, and the colonial period.

## Festivals & Events

**Calabar Festival** CULTURAL

(⏰Dec) Calabar hosts a festival throughout December with concerts from national and international stars scheduled closer to Christmas. The highlight of the festival is the cultural masquerade carnival when tens of thousands of costumed revellers descend on the city.

## Sleeping

**Nelbee Executive Guesthouse** GUESTHOUSE $

(☎08 723 2684; Dan Achibong St; r from N3500; P ❄) Close to Watt Market is this handy budget option. Rooms are comfortable, the management is friendly, and there's a terrifically formal dining room.

**Jacaranda Suites** HOTEL $$

(☎08 723 9666; off Atimbo Rd; r from N12,000; P ❄ ≋) Lovely suites, a lively outdoor thatch-roof bar with secluded cabanas, and a restaurant serving Cross River specialities and grilled fish, Jacaranda is an easy choice for high-end sleeping and eating. It was being restored at the time of writing.

**Marian Hotel** HOTEL $$

(☎703 445 2736; www.marianhotels.com; Old Ikang Rd; r N7000-8000; P ❄) The Marian features spacious, tidy and comfortable rooms. It's a little on the dingy side, but the welcome is great and the location ideal.

## Eating & Drinking

Calabar has the usual selection of hotel eating places and chop houses. But you'll find some great street food down at the Marina near the Slave History Museum, and at the Municipal Park.

**Municipal Park** BEER GARDEN

(⏰noon-11pm) Grassy area with a stage for nighttime concerts (free) and thatched cabanas where you can buy beers, smoothies and street food, including fiery baked fish.

## Getting There & Away

Arik Air (p412) flies daily to Lagos and Abuja (for around N55,000).

In theory **Fakoships** (☎0806 9230753) sails every Wednesday and Friday around 7am to Limbe in Cameroon (N6000, seven hours), but at the time of writing the service wasn't running.

The main motor park is tucked between Mary Slessor Ave and Goldie St. Sample minibus fares include Lagos (N3200, 10 hours) and Ikom (for Afi Mountain Drill Ranch; N700, three hours).

WORTH A TRIP

### CREEK TOWN

A day trip to Creek Town is an immersion in the surrounding watery landscape, and the rich history of the area.

Once there, get in touch with **Itaeyo** (☎0803 741 2894), who will show you the prefab colonial buildings and artifacts, traditional architecture and the king's palace (bring booze as a gift for the king). Also learn about the legacy of Scottish missionary Mary Slessor, who ended the traditional practice of killing twins.

You can reach Creek Town by boat (N400) from the wharf on Marina road, leaving around 7am and noon, coming back at 4pm.

# NORTHERN NIGERIA

## Abuja

☎9 / POP 2.7 MILLION

Nigeria's made-to-measure capital, Abuja was founded during the boom years of the 1970s. After the divisive Biafran War, the decision was made to move the capital from Lagos to the ethnically neutral centre of the country. Clean, quiet and with a good electricity supply, sometimes Abuja hardly feels like Nigeria at all. There's not much to do, but it's a good place to catch your breath and do some visa shopping.

**Nike Centre for Art & Culture** (☎080 2313 1067; www.nikeart.com; Km 7.5 Abuja International Airport Rd, Piwoyi Village) FREE is the wondrous Nike gallery's Abuja outpost on the airport road; there are also branches in Lagos, Oshobgo and Ogidi. You can buy artworks and take part in craft workshops, creating tie-dye fabric for example. It's worth asking if they can accommodate you here too.

Abuja has a range of hotels, with mainly upmarket options geared to business people. The city tends to empty at weekends, with people leaving for more exciting destinations, so many hotels offer discounts for Friday and Saturday nights. Hotel restaurants in Abuja are generally reliable if unexciting. It's a good place to seek out Chinese and Indian restaurants if you need some culinary variety.

The **Nordic Villa** (☎809 994 4480; www.thenordicvilla.com; 52 Mike Akhigbe Way; r from N37,000; P ❄ 📶 🏊) is a modern Scandinavian-style guesthouse that feels more like a home, with helpful staff, a calm atmosphere and good internet access. A lovely breakfast is included. It's located near Jabi Lake.

**Wakkis** (☎09 291 1002; www.wakkis.com; 171 Aminu Kano Cres; ⏰noon-midnight; 🌶) is an excellent Indian restaurant in a pointy-roofed brick building: there's a charcoal pit in the open kitchen for cooking up tandoori classics. Good for vegetarians.

### ℹ Getting There & Around

The airport is 40km west of Abuja (N3500 by taxi). Flights depart hourly for Lagos with several airlines (N54,000, one hour). There are also daily flights to Kano and Port Harcourt, as well as flights several times a week to Ibadan, Calabar and Maiduguri.

Jabi Motor Park (also called Utoka) is the main terminus for Abuja. Transport goes to all points from here; sample minibus fares include Kano (N1000, four hours), Jos (N800, three hours), Ibadan (N1500, eight hours) and Lagos (N2600, 10 hours).

*Okadas* have been banned in Abuja but there are plentiful green taxis (around N200 a trip).

# UNDERSTAND NIGERIA

## Nigeria Today

After years of coups and military rule, in 2011 Nigeria elected a democratic leader: President Goodluck Jonathan. In another democracy first for Nigeria, Jonathan conceded defeat to reformed military leader Muhammadu Buhari in 2015 (Buhari was in power in the 1980s, having staged a coup). Buhari has pledged to suppress the jihadist-fuelled violence of northern separatist group Boko Haram, and to combat corruption.

Nigeria's economic growth – due almost entirely to the influx of oil money – has ushered in a time of modernisation and development. But these advances run alongside government mismanagement and corruption. Images of barefoot children hawking fruit alongside slick SUVs are a reminder that new wealth doesn't often trickle down.

## History

### Early Nigeria

Northern and southern Nigeria are essentially two different countries, and their histories reflect this disparity. The first recorded empire to flourish in this part of West Africa was Kanem-Borno around Lake Chad, which grew rich from the trans-Saharan trade routes. Islamic states based in the Hausa cities of Kano, Zaria and Nupe also flourished at this time.

Meanwhile, the southwest developed into a patchwork of small states, often dominated by the Yoruba. The Ijebu kingdom rose in the 10th century and constructed the mysterious earthworks at Sungbo's Eredo. Most famously the Benin kingdom became an important centre of trade and produced some of the finest metal artwork in Africa. In the southeast, the Igbo and other agrarian peoples never developed any centralised empires, instead forming loose confederations.

## Colonial Era

The first contact between Yoruba empires and Europeans was made in the 15th century, when the Portuguese began trading in pepper and, later, slaves. In contrast, the northern Islamic states remained untouched by European influence until well into the 19th century.

In the early 19th century the British took a lead in suppressing slavery along the Niger delta, leading to the annexation of Lagos port – a first colonial toehold. This led to further annexation to thwart the French, who were advancing their territory along the Niger River. By the beginning of the 20th century, British soldiers had advanced as far north as the cities of Kano and Sokoto, where Islamic revivalism had created a rapidly expanding caliphate.

Nigeria was divided in two – the southern, mainly Christian, colony and the northern Islamic protectorate. The British chose to rule indirectly through local kings and chiefs, exacerbating ethnic divisions for political expediency.

## Military Misrule

The ethnic divisions came back to haunt Nigeria when independence came in October 1960. Politics split along ethnic lines, and in 1966 a group of Igbo army officers staged a coup. General Johnson Ironsi took over as head of state. Another coup quickly followed on its heels, along with massacres of Igbos, which in 1967 provoked civil war by secessionist Igbos. The war dragged on for three years. Biafra was blockaded, and by the time its forces capitulated in 1970, up to a million Igbos had died, mainly from starvation.

An oil boom smoothed Nigeria's path to national reconciliation, but as the army jockeyed for political control, the next two decades were marked by a series of military coups, with only a brief democratic interlude in the early 1980s. When General Ibrahim Babangida offered elections in 1993, he annulled them when the result appeared to go against him, only to be toppled in a coup soon after by General Sani Abacha.

Abacha was ruthless, purging the army and locking up intellectuals, unionists and pro-democracy activists. His rule reached a nadir in 1995 with the judicial murder of the Ogoni activist Ken Saro-Wiwa, an act that led to Nigeria's expulsion from the Commonwealth.

Salvation finally came in June 1998, in what Nigerians called the 'coup from heaven'. Aged 54, and worth somewhere between US$2 billion and US$5 billion in stolen government money, Abacha died of a heart attack while in the company of two prostitutes. His successor immediately announced elections and in February 1999 Olusegun Obasanjo, a former military leader and ex-president, was returned as president.

# Culture

With 186 million people, Nigeria has a huge and expanding population. The main ethnic groups are the Yoruba (in the southwest), the Hausa (north) and the Igbo (southeast), each making up around a fifth of the population, followed by the northern Fulani (around 10%). It's thought that up to 500 languages are spoken in Nigeria.

In many towns and villages traditional belief systems remain strong, despite the presence of American-style evangelical mega-churches. The north is predominantly Muslim, but elsewhere you'll find the boundaries between Islam, Christianity and animist beliefs refreshingly fluid.

Chinua Achebe documented the early collision of African religion and Christianity in his ground-breaking novel *Things Fall Apart* (1958). Achebe was Nigeria's most famous author and is still revered for his genius and wisdom; he died in March 2013. Other acclaimed writers from Nigeria include the Nobel Laureate Wole Soyinka, Booker Prize winner Ben Okri *(The Famished Road)* and Chimamanda Ngozi Adichie, who documented the tragedy of the Biafran War in *Half a Yellow Sun*.

Some of Africa's best-known musicians are Nigerian. Two styles have traditionally been dominant – Afrobeat and *juju* – with their respective masters being the late great Fela Kuti and King Sunny Ade.

## Environment

The north touches on the Sahel and is mostly savannah with low hills. Mountains are found only along the Cameroon border in the east, although there is a 1500m-high plateau around Jos in the centre of the country. The coast is an almost unbroken line of sandy beaches and lagoons running back to creeks and mangrove swamps and is very humid most of the year.

An underfunded national parks service does exist, but in practice very little land in Nigeria is effectively protected. The expanding population has contributed to widespread deforestation – 95% of the original forests have been logged. However, the oil industry has caused the greatest number of environmental problems: oil spills and gas flaring have damaged the fishing industry, with little of the industry's wealth trickling down to the local level.



# SURVIVAL GUIDE

## Directory A–Z

### ACCOMMODATION

Hotels in Nigeria are generally reasonable if uninspired. The holy grail is functioning air-con, running water, loo roll and a towel; count yourself lucky if you find all four.

The exception is some expensive and extravagant options in Lagos, and the odd soulful guesthouse.

### CHILDREN

While children will be treated kindly in Nigeria, you may find the practicalities difficult. The broken pavements are very difficult for prams, and public toilets tend to be dire, with no baby-change facilities. Bus journeys are hot and crowded, with few loo breaks.

#### SLEEPING PRICE RANGES

The following price ranges refer to a double room with bathroom. Unless stated, breakfast is not included in the price.

**$** less than N15,000

**$$** N15,000–30,000

**$$$** more than N30,000

Child-friendly sights:

Lekki Conservation Centre (p403) Climb the canopy walkways to get close to the monkeys in this wetland reserve.

Afi Mountain Drill Ranch (p415) Watch drill monkeys and a very lively chimpanzee up close in Calabar.

Osun Sacred Grove (p413) Vervet monkeys scamper through the trees of the grove, but thankfully the snakes and alligators stay well hidden.

### DANGERS & ANNOYANCES

- The most dangerous region is northern Nigeria, where Boko Haram has been waging a low-grade war against the federal government.
- Lagos has a reputation for petty, violent crime, not always undeserved, although it's been on the decline in the past few years.
- You're unlikely to have trouble with large-scale corruption and bribery. Police roadblocks are common, but fines and bribes are paid by the driver. Take care on the major highways into Lagos, where armed robbery is a problem at night.
- Enugu has a reputation for kidnapping schemes, but they're more likely to be after wealthy oil execs than travellers.

### EMERGENCY & IMPORTANT NUMBERS

| | |
|---|---|
| Nigeria's country code | 234 |
| Ambulance | 112 or 199 |
| Fire | 112 or 199 |
| Police | 112 or 199 |

### EMBASSIES & CONSULATES

Some embassies have yet to relocate from Lagos to Abuja.

**Australian Embassy** (09 461 2780; www.nigeria.embassy.gov.au; 48 Aguyi Ironsi St, 5th fl, Oakland Centre, Maitama, Abuja; 8am-4.30pm Mon-Thu, 8am-1pm Fri)

**Beninese Embassy** Abuja (09 413 8424; Yedseram St; 9am-4.30pm Mon-Fri); Lagos (Map p410; 01 261 4411; 4 Abudu Smith St, VI; 9am-11am Mon-Fri)

**Burkinabé Embassy** (Map p410; 01 268 1001; 15 Norman Williams St, Lagos, Ikoyi)

**Cameroonian Embassy** Calabar (087 222782; 21 Ndidan Usang Iso Rd; 9am-3.30pm Mon-Fri); Lagos (Map p410; 01 261 2226; 5 Femi Pearse St, VI; 8am-11am Mon-Fri)

**Canadian Embassy** Abuja (09 461 2900; 13010G, Palm Close, Diplomatic Dr; 8am-4.30pm Mon-Thu, 8am-1.30pm Fri); Lagos (Map p410; 01 271 5650; 4 Anifowoshe St, VI 8am-6pm)

**Dutch Embassy** (Map p410; 01 261 3005; 24 Ozumba Mbadiwe Ave, Lagos, VI; 9am-6pm)

**French Embassy** (Map p410; 01 269 3430; 1 Oyinkan Abayomi Rd, Ikoyi; 8am-2pm Mon-Fri)

**German Embassy** (Map p410; 909 724 9554; 15 Walter Carrington Cres, VI; 8am-6pm)

**Ghanaian Embassy** (Map p408; 01 263 0015; 23 King George V Rd, Lagos Island; 9am-3pm)

**Irish Embassy** (09 462 0611; 11 Negro Cres, off Aminu Kano, Maitama, Abuja; 8am-4.30pm Mon-Thu, 8am-1pm Fri)

**Ivoirian Embassy** (Map p410; 01 261 0963; 5 Abudu Smith St, VI; 9am-2pm)

**Nigerien Embassy** Abuja (09 523 6205; 7 Sangha St, off Mississippi St; 9am-3pm Mon-Fri); Kano (064 64 38 06; 1A Katsina Road; 9am-3pm Mon-Fri); Lagos (Map p410; 01 261 2300; 15 Adeola Odeku St, VI; 9am-2.30pm Mon-Fri)

**Spanish Embassy** (Map p410; 01 261 5215; 21c Kofo Abayomi St, VI; 8am-6pm)

**Togolese Embassy** (Map p410; 01 261 7478; Plot 976, Oju Olobun Cl, VI; 8am-3pm Mon-Fri)

**UK Embassy** Abuja (09 462 2200; www.ukinnigeria.fco.gov.uk; 19 Torrens Close, Mississippi; 8.30am-noon Mon-Thu, 8.30-11am Fri); Lagos (Map p410; 01 261 9531; 11 Walter Carrington Cres, VI; 8.30am-noon Mon-Thu, 8.30-11am Fri)

**US Embassy** Abuja (09 461 4000; http://nigeria.usembassy.gov; Plot 1075, Diplomatic Dr, Central Business District; 8.30am-2pm Mon-Thu, 8.30am-noon Fri); Lagos (Map p410; 01 261 0150; 2 Walter Carrington Cres, VI; 8am-6pm)

## FOOD

Nigerians like their food ('chop') hot and starchy. The classic dish is a fiery pepper stew ('soup') with a little meat or fish and starch – usually pounded yam or cassava (*garri*, *eba*, or slightly sour *fufu*). Another popular dish is *jollof* – peppery rice cooked with palm oil and tomato. Cutlery isn't generally used – yam or cassava soaks up the juices of the stew. Eat only with your right hand.

## INTERNET ACCESS

Decent connections are widespread in major towns, for around N200 per hour. Never use internet banking in a Nigerian cybercafe.

## LGBTIQ TRAVELLERS

Homosexual sex is illegal in Nigeria. The draconian 'Same Sex Marriage Prohibition Bill' permits 14-year prison sentences for those entering into a same-sex marriage, or those witnessing or supporting a same-sex marriage. There are 10-year sentences for those who operate gay clubs and organisations.

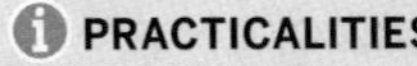

### PRACTICALITIES

**Electricity** Supply is 220V. Plugs are square British three pin, but most hotels have European two-pin adaptors.

**Newspapers** Privately owned English-language daily newspapers include the *Guardian*, *This Day*, the *Punch* and *Vanguard*.

**TV** There are over 30 national and state TV stations, broadcasting in English and all major local languages. South African satellite DSTV is hugely popular.

**Weights & measures** Nigeria uses the metric system.

## MONEY

ATMs are increasingly widespread and many are connected to international systems such as MasterCard or Visa. GTB is the most reliable.

**Cash** The unit of currency is the naira (N).

**Credit cards** Accepted at only a few places; use them with caution. Notify your bank before you use your cards in Nigeria as fraud scams have made it a red-flag country for transactions. For online purchases such as buying internal flights your card may be refused. You may have to ask a trusted local to make the transaction for you, then reimburse them.

**Changing money** Bring higher denomination dollars or pounds for the best exchange rate. There are moneychangers in each town and they are almost always Hausa. Western Union branches are useless unless you have a Nigerian bank account.

**Tipping** For hotels, tip N1000 or so for help with bags. For decent service in restaurants, 10% is customary. Taxi tips are not expected, but add one for good service.

### Exchange Rates

| | | |
|---|---|---|
| Australia | A$1 | N230 |
| Canada | C$1 | N223 |
| Europe | €1 | N333 |
| Japan | ¥100 | N273 |
| New Zealand | NZ$ | N211 |
| UK | UK£1 | N394 |
| US | US$1 | N305 |

For current exchange rates, see www.xe.com.

### WARNING: BOKO HARAM

Between 2009 and 2016, Boko Haram, a jihadist organisation based in the northeast of Nigeria, has been fighting a low-level war against Christian communities and the central government, killing thousands. Known for bombing churches and markets, assassinating police, and motorcycle drive-bys, the group, whose name means 'Western education is sinful' in Hausa, has made travel to northern Nigeria impossible.

Attacks were sporadic and took place in Adawama, Gombe, Yobe, Jigawa and Plateau States, occasionally in an outskirt of Abuja or Jos, with many incidents centred on Maiduguri, the capital of Borno State.

The situation has begun to stabilise after a military campaign directed by President Buhari. But there are now many displaced people and severe food shortages in the north.

At the time of writing the guidance was to avoid northern Nigeria altogether. Read your government's travel advisory and ask locals before attempting to head north.

## OPENING HOURS

General business hours are from 8.30am to 5pm Monday to Friday. Sanitation days are held on the last Saturday of the month – traffic isn't allowed before 10am for street cleaning.

**Banks** 8am to 4pm Monday to Friday.

**Government offices** 7.30am to 3.30pm Monday to Friday

**Shops and supermarkets** 7.30am to 3.30pm Monday to Friday, 7.30 to 1pm Saturday

## POST

Mail sent to or from Nigeria is notoriously slow. Worldwide postcards cost about N80. For parcels, use an international courier like DHL or FedEx, which have offices in most towns.

## PUBLIC HOLIDAYS

**New Year's Day** 1 January

**Easter** March or April

**May Day** 1 May

**National Day** 1 October

**Christmas** 25 December

**Boxing Day** 26 December

Islamic holidays are observed in northern Nigeria.

## TELEPHONE

Nigeria is in love with the mobile phone, and cellular networks are more reliable than landlines. Calls at roadside phone stands are quick and easy to make, costing around N20 per minute inside Nigeria, and around N60 for an international call. Most mobile numbers start with 080.

Having a local SIM card to use in a smart phone is extremely useful. The best service is Etisalat (SIMs cost N300) though MTN has the widest coverage. Street vendors everywhere sell top-up scratch cards.

### EATING PRICE RANGES

The following price ranges refer to a main course.

**$** less than N1500

**$$** N1500–N3000

**$$$** more than N3000

## VISAS

Everyone needs a visa to visit Nigeria, and applications can be quite a process. Three-month visas cost up to US$300, according to nationality.

### Obtaining Visas

Many Nigerian embassies issue visas only to residents and nationals of the country in which the embassy is located, so it's essential to put things in motion well before your trip. Exact requirements vary, but as a rule of thumb, forms are required in triplicate, along with proof of funds to cover your stay, a round-trip air ticket, and possibly confirmed hotel reservations. You also need a letter of invitation from a resident of Nigeria or a business in the country.

If you're travelling overland to Nigeria, the embassy in Accra (Ghana) is consistently rated as the best place in West Africa to apply for a visa, as no letter of introduction is required. The embassy in Niamey (Niger) also claims to issue visas the same way.

### Visa Extensions

Visas can reportedly be extended at the **Federal Secretariat** (Map p410; Forest St; ⌚8am-5pm Mon-Fri) in Lagos, but it's a byzantine process of endless forms, frustration and dash, with no clear sense of success.

### Visas for Onward Travel

**Benin** One-month visas cost around CFA15,000 (CFA, not naira), with two photos, and take 24 hours to issue. The embassy in Lagos carries an uninviting reputation, and unexpected extra fees are not unknown.

**Cameroon** A one-month single-entry visa costs CFA50,000 (CFA, not naira), with two photos, and is issued in a day. As well as Lagos and Abuja, there's a useful consulate in Calabar.

## Getting There & Away

### AIR

The vast majority of flights to Nigeria arrive in Lagos, although there are also international airports in Abuja, Port Harcourt and Kano. Airports are well organised and have official porters, but plenty of touts outside.

Lagos' airport is **Murtala Muhammed International** (Map p406; www.lagosairport.net). Arik Air (p412) operates domestic and some international flights, for example to Douala in Cameroon.

### LAND

#### Benin

The main border crossing is on the Lagos–Cotonou (Benin) highway. Expect requests for bribes. There's a good direct Cotonou–Lagos bus service run by Nigerian bus company **ABC Transport** (☎81 4255 2436, 0805 300 1000; www.abctransport.com). An alternative border crossing is further north at Kétou on the Benin side.

#### Cameroon

The southern border crossing is at Mfum (Nigeria), near Ikom. The road infrastructure collapses pretty much as soon as you cross to Ekok (Cameroon), making this border problematic during the rainy season, so consider taking the Calabar–Limbe ferry instead during the wettest months. However, at the time of writing the ferry was not functioning.

Northern border posts between the two countries were not safe at the time of writing.

### SEA

A ferry sails from Calabar to Limbe every Tuesday and Friday evening (N6000, five hours), returning on Monday and Thursday. It's an overnight trip in each direction. Your passport is collected on boarding and returned at immigration. Try to keep hold of your luggage – if it gets stowed in the hold, you'll be waiting hours to get it back. Note that there are safety issues with the ferry, and at the time of writing it wasn't functioning. Take local advice.

## Getting Around

### AIR

Internal flights are a quick way of getting around Nigeria. Flights start at around N20,000. Most cities are linked by air to Lagos.

The most reliable domestic airline with the best connections is **Arik Air** (p412).

### BUS

Each town has at least one motor park serving as the main transport depot full of minibuses and bush taxis.

Vehicles have signs on their roofs showing their destination, while touts shout out destinations. Minibuses don't run on any schedule but depart when full.

### CAR & MOTORCYCLE

Nigeria's road system veers unpredictably between good and appalling. Accident rates are high, the only real road rule is survival of the fittest and road signage is minimal.

Foreigners driving in Nigeria shouldn't get too much hassle at roadblocks, particularly if your vehicle has foreign plates. If you get asked for dash, a smile and some patience will often defuse the request. It's a legal requirement to wear a seatbelt; not doing so leaves you open to both official and 'unofficial' fines. Petrol stations are everywhere, but fuel shortages are common, causing huge queues and worsening the already terrible traffic. Diesel can sometimes be hard to come by, so keep your tank topped up.

Hiring a good local driver takes a lot of the stress out of car transport: it will cost around N80,000 per day. Ask at your hotel for suggestions.

### LOCAL TRANSPORT

The quickest way to get around town is on the back of a motorcycle-taxi called an *okada* (*achaba* in the north). Because of their general lawlessness, the government has banned *okada* in a few of the major cities, badly affecting traffic and driving up the prices with drivers who are willing to flout the law.

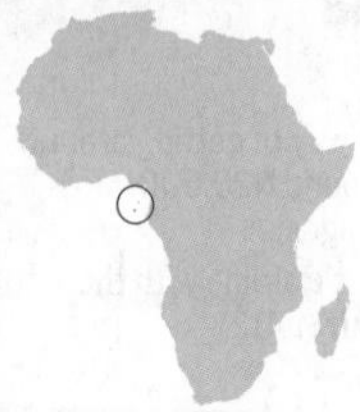

# São Tomé & Príncipe

☎239 / POP 195,000

### Includes ➡



## Best Places to Eat

- ➡ Bom Bom Resort (p432)
- ➡ Papa Figo (p426)
- ➡ 5 Sentidos (p426)
- ➡ Celvas (p427)
- ➡ Roça São João (p429)

## Best Places to Sleep

- ➡ Roça Belo Monte (p432)
- ➡ Mucumbli (p427)
- ➡ Makaira Lodge (p432)
- ➡ Sweet Guest House (p424)
- ➡ Praia Inhame Ecolodge (p429)
- ➡ Bom Bom Resort (p432)

## Why Go?

Floating in the Gulf of Guinea, this two-island nation, Africa's second-smallest, blends natural wonders with a gripping history. Once a vast network of plantations and a centre of global cocoa production, São Tomé & Príncipe (STP) has suffered an economic collapse since independence from Portugal in 1975. In the countryside, squatters inhabit once great mansions; in the capital, historic colonial buildings slowly decay on broken streets. Nevertheless, the country remains amazingly safe and welcoming to visitors, particularly ecotourists, for whom the advancing jungle is a delight. This is particularly true on tidy and unspoiled Príncipe, an island of just 7000 people. A canopy of green broken by spires of primordial rock, Príncipe is a magnificent Lost World, offering fantastic beaches, jungle exploration, snorkelling, fishing, birdwatching and a handful of interesting (if expensive) accommodation options, with minimal tourist pressure. While both islands have their natural rewards, Príncipe should not be missed.

## When to Go

### São Tomé

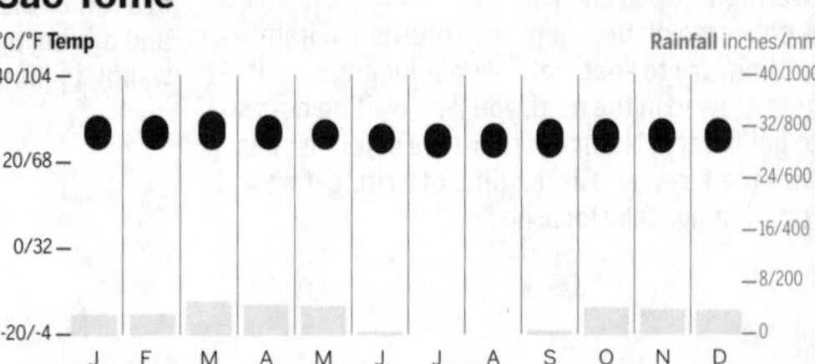


**Jun–Sep** Dry season; ideal for climbing Pico de São Tomé or trekking the Volta a Ilha.

**Oct–May** Rainy season; particularly wet in the southwest.

**Year-round** Temperatures in the high 20s (°C); areas of cloud, rain and sun can be found any time.

## São Tomé & Príncipe Highlights

1. **Baía das Agulhas** (p431) Boating past Príncipe's extraordinary volcanic skyline, a spectacular trip back in time.
2. **Plantation history** Visiting *roças* (plantations) like Roça Agua Izé (p428) for an eye-opening look at a national calamity.
3. **World-class seafood** Eating thick slabs of deep-sea fish at restaurants such as Papa Figo in São Tomé (p426).
4. **Pico de São Tomé** (p430) Climbing the highest peak in the country for an unforgettable jungle adventure.
5. **Praia Banana** (p431) Admiring the golden curves, swaying palms and turquoise waters of a paradise beach – all by yourself.

# SÃO TOMÉ

Ecotourists, listen up: this is an island where nature offers the best rewards. By combining the island's two major ecolodges, Mucumbli in the north and Praia Inhame in the south, you can enjoy the best the island has to offer, including jungle hikes, exploring remote beaches, seeing local wildlife, visiting a *roça* (plantation) or two, and climbing the Pico de São Tomé, all for a very reasonable price. You may also want to splurge on Ilhéu das Rolas, a satellite resort island with exotic twists of its own, including classic tropical beaches.

## São Tomé (City)

POP 53,300

São Tomé city ought to be one of the world's great port towns. It contains an extraordinary collection of colonial buildings, located on a broad curving bay, and is the economic and political hub of the country. Unfortunately STP's long economic decline has devastated its infrastructure. The historic architecture is decaying on every street, the roads are choked with potholes, and the central market is filthy. Even so, stay long enough for a plate of world-class seafood, the city's finest attribute.

### Sights

**★Claudio Corallo Chocolate Factory** FACTORY

(☎222 2236; www.claudiocorallo.com; Ave Marginal 12 de Julho; €4; ⏰tours 4.40pm Mon, Wed & Fri, tickets on sale from 8am) Claudio Corallo is both an extraordinary person and a local institution. For over 40 years this native Italian has pursued an overriding passion for coffee and cocoa in Africa, first in Zaire and later in STP, where he has two plantations and a factory in the capital. The results are on display in this fascinating little tour, which takes you not only through the chocolate production process, but through all the thought and experimentation that went into developing the bean.

**CACAU** CULTURAL CENTRE

(☎994 3810, 222 2625; www.facebook.com/pg/cacau.cultural; Ave Marginal 12 de Julho; ⏰7.30am-11.30pm) The Casa das Artes, Criação, Ambiente e Utopias (House of the Arts, Creativity, Environment and Utopias) is an ambitious attempt to create a true cultural centre in the capital. Located in a huge warehouse, it has various elements: a restaurant/cafe/bar, an exhibition space, a crafts shop, and a stage/movie theater. It can be very quiet however, without a special event going on. See 'Events' on its Facebook page.

**Mercado Grande** MARKET

(Great Market; Ave Geovany & Rua do Municipio; ⏰6am-5.30pm Mon-Sat) Alternately fascinating and repellent, the Mercado Grande is divided into two cavernous and adjacent halls, the Mercado Municipal and the newer, and cleaner, Mercado Novo. They both contain the same goods, mostly food and clothing, which also spill into the street outside, creating a few blocks of densely packed commerce. The spectacle is the point. Photography is not appreciated, so be discreet.

### Activities

**Marapa** WILDLIFE WATCHING

(☎993 3240, 222 2792; www.marapa.org; Largo Bom Despacho; small donation requested) On Monday, Wednesday and Friday in turtle-nesting season (November to February) this marine conservation organisation provides a 5pm briefing, followed by a late night measuring, tagging and collecting eggs on nearby beaches. These are then protected from poachers in a guarded enclosure until they hatch, after which they are released into the sea, a process you can also witness.

**TropicVenture** DIVING

(☎993 4199; www.facebook.com/Divingcentersaotome; ES-1/Airport Rd, Praia Lagarto; 1-tank dive €40; ⏰8am-6pm) Experienced dive master João Santos is an expert on local waters, and books up quickly by word of mouth. Offering various PADI courses, free equipment and two 6m boats, he can craft any diving itinerary for the north of the island. The typical outing is a two-tank dive (three if a night dive is added).

### Sleeping

**★Sweet Guest House** HOTEL $

(☎903 1313, 999 0763; www.sweetguesthouse.com; Vila Dolores; ⏰s/d €45/52, with shared bath €35/42; P❄📶) The budget traveller's salvation, this hotel performs its role perfectly. It feels like a cabin, with a large wooden balcony on the 2nd floor, and panelled rooms. While not in the cheeriest neighborhood, its walled compound has 24-hour security (with parking). One of the few backpacker havens in STP, with an interesting array of global travellers to match.

**Kayla** B&B $

(☎989 8240; kayla.guesthouse@yahoo.com; Rua Palma Carlos, 113B, top floor; s/d incl breakfast

## São Tomé Town

## São Tomé Town

**Top Sights**

1 Claudio Corallo Chocolate Factory .......... A2

**Sights**

2 CACAU .......... D1
3 Mercado Grande .......... B3

**Activities, Courses & Tours**

4 Marapa .......... C1

**Sleeping**

5 Kayla .......... D1
6 Miramar .......... D3
7 Residential Avenida .......... C3
8 Sweet Guest House .......... A4

**Eating**

9 5 Sentidos .......... D2
10 B-24 .......... D2
11 Papa Figo .......... D3
12 Pastelaria Central .......... B3

**Drinking & Nightlife**

13 Pico Mocambo .......... C3

**Shopping**

14 Pica Pau .......... C2

**Information**

15 Banco International de Sao Tomé & Príncipe .......... B3
16 Mistral Voyages .......... A2
17 Navetur .......... B3
18 Tourism Bureau .......... C2

**Transport**

19 Hanna & Silva Rent-a-Car .......... A3
STP Airways .......... (see 18)
20 TAAG .......... A3
21 TAP .......... B3

€35/50; ❄📶) A super option, this family B&B on a quiet residential street near the sea offers three large rooms, each with private bathroom, in a spacious top-floor apartment with a wraparound balcony. The breakfast is a full spread of local fruits, juices, omelettes and more, which you can take on the rooftop. The genial hosts make for a pleasant stay.

**Residential Avenida** HOTEL **$$**
(☎224 1700; ravenida@cstome.net; Ave da Independência; s/d incl breakfast €79/95; ❄📶) This easygoing place is the best midrange option. Spread out on ground level, it has a communal vibe, with a central thatched-roof bar and restaurant (mains €9 to €15; fish is a speciality) and popular TV. There's a nice spread of clean and simple rooms, including triples and two-bedroom suites, but they're a bit dark. English spoken.

**Miramar** HOTEL **$$$**
(☎222 2778; www.pestana.com; Ave Marginal 12 de Julho; s/d incl breakfast €124/130; ❄📶🏊) While older than its nearby flagship sister, the **Pestana São Tomé** (☎224 4500; s/d incl breakfast €195; P❄📶🏊), the Miramar is the better deal. Instead of entering resort-land, you get the feeling of a real hotel rooted in the city, where locals, expats and tourists all mix. A secret bonus: renovated rooms with seaviews can be had for no additional cost (just ask).

**Omali Lodge** RESORT **$$$**
(☎222 2479; www.omalilodge.com; ES1/Airport Rd, Praia Lagarto; s/d incl breakfast €150/200; P❄📶🏊) Striking the right balance between European standards and local ambience, the laid-back Omali is where locals, expats and foreign visitors all meet. Located between the city and the airport, it provides convenient access to either one. Rooms are mildly worn but spacious, and arranged around a large pool set in palms.

## Eating

**B-24** SEAFOOD **$**
(Parque Popular; mains Db100,000-150,000; ⏲7.30am-11pm) The best of the many restaurant shacks lining Parque Popular, this simple thatched hut packs an enormous punch with its fish of the day, as its many patrons reveal.

★**Papa Figo** SEAFOOD, PUB FOOD **$$**
(Ave Kwame Nkrumah; mains Db60,000-250,000; ⏲7am-11.30pm) This charming, well-kept and ever-popular tin-roofed patio restaurant is laid-back in style, but no slouch in the kitchen. Everything on the menu has an interesting new twist. The thick fish steaks are world class: don't miss the barracuda. Tasty sides and special drinks round out a great seafood meal. Pizza and hamburgers also gets a delicious makeover.

★**5 Sentidos** FUSION **$$**
(☎981 8798; Rua da Caixa, 201; mains Db200,000-400,000; ⏲6-11.30pm; 🌶) The 'Five Senses' has rapidly emerged as one of the top gastronomic options in the city. Powered by Lisbon chef João Nunes (formerly of Omali Lodge), it offers an Afro-Portuguese fusion menu with sophisticated meals beautifully presented. Who would expect this cuisine in a terrace walled by packing crates, with a parachute for a ceiling? Reserve on weekends.

**O Pirata** SEAFOOD **$$**
(Estrada de Pantufo; mains Db200,000-250,000; ⏲9am-midnight, to later Fri) Enjoying the best location in the city, the Pirate is little more than a deck perched on a crashing sea wall, facing a rusting shipwreck barely 100m distant. The seafood is excellent, with huge portions. On Friday nights the deck is cleared of tables, and a young crowd arrives after 10pm, forming the hottest club in São Tomé.

## Drinking & Nightlife

★**Pico Mocambo** COCKTAIL BAR
(Ave Amilcar Cabral; ⏲8am-midnight) This delightful rum bar is spread across the grounds of a historic plantation house – STP needs more of this! The bar itself is nestled in the top floor, and strikes just the right note with its plantation shutters and bamboo furniture, not to mention cocktails. Picks up after 9pm.

## Shopping

★**Pica Pau** ARTS & CRAFTS
(Rua de Santo Antonío do Príncipe; ⏲8am-7pm) Looking for a souvenir? This artisans cooperative contains a fantastic collection of wood carvings, by far the best in the city, and more limited jewellery. Various vendors are on hand, and freely interrupt one another for your attention. Be prepared to haggle! Some fine gifts can be had for under €20.

## Information

Moneychangers operate around Praça da Amizade. The Miramar and Pestana São Tomé offer cashback service on credit cards for up to €100 to guests for a 5% fee. **BISTP** (BISTP; ☎224 3105; www.bistp.st; Praça de Independência; ⏲8am-3pm Mon-Fri, to noon Sat) will also offer cashback for a steep €10 fee PLUS 11%

on the transaction, no matter how small it may be. In an emergency, **Navetur** (p425) may be able to help.

**CST** (Ave da Independência; 7am-7pm) Purchase SIM cards and top up your phone here.

**Internet Access** Free wifi is available in the lobby of the Miramar and Pestana São Tomé hotels; you'll need to ask for the code at the restaurant-bar at the Omali, and downtown at **Pastelaria Central** (Rua de Angola; 7am-8pm; ).

**Mistral Voyages** (222 3344; www.mistralvoyages.com; Ave Marginal 12 de Julho; 8am-5pm Mon-Fri) Travel agency with ticketing services.

**Navetur** (222 2122; www.navetur-equatour.st; Rua Viriato da Cruz; 8am-12.30pm & 3-5.30pm Mon-Fri, to noon Sat) Travel agency with ticketing services. The best stop for English speakers, particularly if you are also booking tours through them.

**Post Office** (Ave Marginal 12 de Julho; 7am-noon & 2-5pm Mon-Fri)

**Tourism Bureau** (222 1542; www.turismo.gov.st; Ave Marginal 12 de Julho; 8am-noon & 2-5pm Mon-Fri, to noon Sat) Has an attractive tourist map for €3, but that's about it. No English spoken.

## Getting There & Around

The taxis that depart from the Mercado Grande (p424) head all over the island. Sample shared fares include Santana (Db15,000, 30 minutes), Neves (Db25,000, one hour), São João dos Angolares (Db25,000, one hour) and Porto Alegre (Db30,000, two hours).

**Hanna & Silva Rent-a-Car** (222 6282; www.facebook.com/hannaesilvarentacar; Rua Geovane Caixa; 4-person Suzuki Jimny with full insurance per day €42; 8am-12.30pm & 3-5.30pm Mon-Fri, to 1pm Sat) is a cheerful small company with about 10 vehicles including some inexpensive 4WDs. If Hanna & Silva is out of cars, try **Tortuga Car Rental** (991 1913; tortuga.stp@gmail.com) – the cars are insured, but service is slow, and be very clear about the price.

You can reach anywhere in the city by motorbike taxi, hailed on any street, for Db10,000.

# Northern Coast

The northern coast of São Tomé offers some fine beaches, historic *roças* and one long road, the EN-1. This gets increasingly remote the further you travel upon it, until it disappears completely into the jungle. Here you can pursue numerous activities, including boating the coastline, hiking the Pico de São Tomé, and mountain biking to the road's end, a dramatic journey where the waves crash on one side while the Pico rises on the other.

### ARRIVING IN SÃO TOMÉ

**São Tomé International Airport** Taxis wait for arrivals. A shared ride into the city takes 15 minutes and costs €2 to €3. A private taxi costs €10. Agree on the fee ahead of time. This is the only form of transport available (apart from a motorcycle, if you have no luggage).

One of the island's best beaches, **Praia dos Tamarindos** is a beautiful white crescent facing an emerald sea, with excellent swimming. An easy drive from the capital, it's empty during the week but crowded on weekends. Reaching Guadelupe from the capital, turn right at the monument in the middle of the road, then a further right at the primary school.

**Museo do Mar e da Pesca Artesanal** (Morro Peixe; €2; 8am-6pm Mon-Fri, to 3pm Sat) is a charming marine and fishing museum located in a whitewashed fisherman's shack up on stilts by the water's edge. Created by local marine conservation organisation Marapa (p424), it has some intelligent displays with English signage and is definitely worth a stop. You can also arrange night trips to see nesting turtles here. Located at end of road to Morro Peixe.

## Sleeping & Eating

**★Mucumbli** ECOLODGE **$$**
(990 8736; www.mucumbli.wordpress.com; EN-1, Neves; s/d bungalows incl breakfast €58/68; ) STP's finest ecolodge is situated in a cliffside forest overlooking the sea. Nicely designed wooden bungalows offer plenty of space, light and dreamy views for two to four people. But it's hard to leave the dining area, with its coastal vista, convivial atmosphere and superb food (mains €6 to €12; visitors welcome). This is your launch pad for multiple itineraries, and great value.

**★Celvas** FUSION **$$$**
(223 1093, 993 5849; www.restaurante-celvas.com; EN-1, Guadeloupe; mains Db180,000-400,000; 8.30am-4pm, dinner on reservation only, reserve before 3pm same day) Hidden behind a wall on the main street of Guadeloupe, this restaurant comes as a shockingly good surprise. You'll find two gazebos set in a garden, with tables draped in white

tablecloths. A generous wine selection complements sophisticated meat and fish dishes blending Portuguese and São Toméan flavours. Three garden rooms (singles/doubles €35/47) were also being renovated during research.

## Getting There & Around

A shared taxi from the capital to Mucumbli (one hour) is Db25,000 per seat. You may need to double that for luggage.

If you wish to explore the area on your own you will need to rent a mountain bike (€10 per day) from Mucumbli or bring a rental car from the capital.

# Southern Coast

The southern coast offers diverse attractions, including beach resorts, jungle hikes, diving, and some fine accommodation. These are concentrated in two main areas, near Santana (and hence within range of the capital) and near Porto Alegre, at the southern tip of the island. The entire coast is linked by the EN-2, a 2½-hour drive from end to end. The southern half of this road is particularly pleasant, a jungle drive with little traffic and the awesome sight of Cão Grande, the symbol of São Tomé, rising in the distance. From Porto Alegre a potholed dirt road continues along the coast to a trio of bungalow beach resorts, offering various outdoor activities. As elsewhere, the villages are not the focus of your trip.

**Cão Grande** (Great Canine) is the poster image of São Tomé, and an awesome sight. An enormous tooth of rock 663m high, it is a hardened column of magma, the remains of an ancient volcano whose softer outer shell has long since eroded away. Its diminutive sibling, **Cão Pequeno,** is a phonolite tower best seen from Ilhéu das Rolas.

**Ilhéu de Santana** is an interesting island facing Santana Resort, unique in that a natural tunnel runs straight through the centre of it. Boat trips operated by the Atlantic Diving Center (€8) can get most of the way through before the ceiling lowers too far. You can also snorkel off the island's cliffs, revealing some interesting underwater formations.

### TREKKING VOLTA A ILHA

This two-day trek along the roadless southwestern coast of São Tomé connects the end of the EN-1 to the end of the EN-2. It also includes the island's two best ecolodges, Mucumbli (p427) and Praia Inhame (p429). Those who want to begin in the north should arrange their trek through the former, while those who want to start in the south should organise it through the latter. It is best done in the dry season (June to September), as the wet season makes crossing several ravines difficult.

**Roça Agua Izé** PLANTATION

One of the original 'Big Five' *roças* of São Tomé, this was the plantation that kicked off the cocoa industry in STP, and it still farms the bean, albeit at a much lower production level. If you've seen other *roças* a lap around the buildings will suffice. Otherwise this is a good introduction to the plantation chapter of São Tomé history, assuming you can find a guide on site that speaks your language – a hit-or-miss proposition.

## Activities & Tours

**Atlantic Diving Center** DIVING

(☎224 2400; www.atlanticdivingcenter.com; Club Santana resort; 1-tank dive €45; ⏲8am-1.30pm) STP's best dive center is a very ship-shape operation, offering all PADI courses up to divemaster, with nitrox forthcoming. It reaches about six good dive sites from here on a regular basis. Expect warm clear water, interesting geological formations, and tropical life, although overfishing means that big fish are scarce. Inexpensive boat trips to Ilhéu de Santana are also offered.

**Marapa** ECOTOUR

(☎991 7602; www.marapa.org; EN-2 (Malanza); per person €10) If you have never been in a mangrove swamp, you might find this hour-long trip into one interesting, but pass otherwise. It is fun to canoe up a tropical river, but there is no life to be seen apart from a few mudskippers. Departs from the bridge just south of Malanza. Portuguese only.

## Sleeping

★**Pousada Roça São João** POUSADA $

(☎226 1140; www.facebook.com/rocasaojoao; EN-2, São João dos Angolares; d incl breakfast €35) This budget charmer is the best *roça* to stay in on the island. It's a classic administrator's house, with two stories of wraparound veranda and endless interior rooms (including its famous restaurant) full of books and art. There's lot of places to hang out, including a hammock in the restaurant (grab it!). A herd of ducks guards the entrance.

★**Praia Inhame Ecolodge** ECOLODGE $$
(☎991 6552; www.hotelpraiainhame.com; Praia Inhame; bungalows incl breakfast from €80; ) At the remote southern end of the island, this ecolodge has been a great success due to its excellent management, which pays attention to details. Nicely situated on its own private beach, with a view toward Ilhéu das Rolas, it offers clean wooden bungalows on stilts. The bungalows are of various sizes, with comfy beds and wide decks nestled in the trees.

**Jalé Ecolodge** ECOLODGE $$
(☎222 2792; www.ecolodgejale.com; Praia Jalé; bungalows incl breakfast €45-60) You have reached the end of the road. And that is why you are here. Compared to São Tomé's other ecolodges, Jalé is primitive, with three bungalows, a small restaurant, minimal staff and few activities. What it does have is a long, empty, roaring palm-fringed beach. This is where you come to escape the Feds. Or to see nesting turtles (September to April).

**Praia N'Guembu** BUNGALOW $$
(☎991 3630; Praia N'Guembu; s/d bungalow €40/60) This bungalow resort was about to open during research. It's similar to neighbouring Praia Inhame ecolodge, but with a few disadvantages: the beach is not as protected, the restaurant (menu €15) is a hike up a hill, and the bungalows have tiny decks. It's brand new, however, and nicely furnished.

★**Ondas Divinas** COTTAGE $$$
(☎990 4382; www.facebook.com/casaondasdivinas; Santana; 2-/8-person cottage €130/200; ) STP needs more of this! Trailblazing entrepreneur Yves has built five fantastic beach cottages on a cliff overlooking the sea, with spectacular views from all rooms. A precipitous walkway takes you to the castaway beach below. Arrive with all your groceries, or sign up for the delicious half board (€20), as Yves was a professional chef.

★**Club Santana** RESORT $$$
(☎224 2400; www.clubsantana.com; Praia Messias Alves; s/d bungalows with half board €160/180; ) This resort has a welcome lack of pretension. While its tar-paper roofs resemble a tropical research station, it's so dated it's retro cool, and fits the island perfectly. The 1980s air-conditioned bungalows are spread over a hillside above a beautiful crescent beach, within sight of a fishing village on an attractive cove.

**TREKKING ROÇA CIRCUIT**

Beginning at Roça São João, this easy 2½-hour circuit takes in the neighbouring *dependencias* (satellite plantations) of Roça Soledade and Roça Fraternidade (both in ruins), and follows the beachfront at São João dos Angolares before returning by wading a stream. Along the way you'll catch great views of Pico Maria Fernandez and Cão Grande (p426). Hire a guide (€30 per couple) through Pousada Roça São João (p428).

## Eating

★**Roça São João** FUSION $$
(☎226 1140; EN-2, São João dos Angolares; menu €12; 7am-10pm; ) This well-known restaurant, an ever-popular weekend drive from the capital, occupies a sprawling deck at a classic *roça* administrator's house, with valley views towards the sea. The food is a mélange of European, African and São Toméan tastes, but best when it sticks to creative takes on local fare, be it chicken or fish. The prix fixe menu makes choosing easy.

**Mionga** SEAFOOD $$
(☎226 1140; EN-2, São João dos Angolares; menus €10; 7am-11pm) Located in two colourful waterfront shacks on a swampy peninsula, this is an excellent stop for creative seafood, above and beyond the normal plates of fried fish and banana chips found elsewhere. The only drawback is the flies. Reserve ahead weekends.

## Getting There & Away

Transport is all by shared taxi. A seat from the capital to São João dos Angolares (one hour) costs Db25,000, and to Porto Alegre (two hours) costs Db30,000.

# Ilhéu das Rolas

Ilhéu das Rolas is a small island straddling the equator off the southern tip of São Tomé. It is essentially a resort island, the home of the Pestana Ecuador resort, although there is also a small village in which most of the resort workers live. The island takes about an hour to walk from top to bottom, and two to three hours to circumnavigate, but packs in quite a few attractions, more than enough for a day's adventure. Ideally you should spend a night to get the full experience.

## Sights & Activities

**★Praia Bateria** BEACH
So perfect it stops you in your tracks, this cute little beach is a scallop of sand wedged between long walls of rock. Swimming here is like being in your own private bath. Definitely the couple's first choice, you'll either have it to yourself or you won't want to intrude on someone else.

**★Praia Café** BEACH
In the running for island's best beach, Praia Café is a short walk from the pier, and should not be missed. A beautiful arc of sand, it also offers excellent snorkeling when the waves are calm.

**Costa Norte** DIVING, FISHING
(999 3715; www.costanorte.pt; Pestana Ecuador Resort; 1-/2-tank dive €55/100; 8am-5pm) Although 80% of its business is diving, Costa Norte also offers sport fishing (four/eight hours €375/550), whale and dolphin watching (€40 per hour), and an inexpensive boat trip around Rolas (€25, two-person minimum). It also has an office in the Pestana São Tomé (p426).

## Sleeping

**Pestana Ecuador** RESORT $$$
(226 1195; www.pestana.com; d with full board €255; ) Occupying the northern end of the island, this resort offers spacious duplex cabins of varnished wood with decks in a garden setting, overlooking a massive saltwater pool. There's a nice beach facing São Tomé, and others (like Praia Café) within walking range.

## Getting There & Away

Access to the island is via a ferry run by the Pestana Ecuador resort twice a day. The crossing takes 30 minutes. The ferry departs Ponta Baleia, the peninsula opposite Porto Alegre, at 10.10am and 5.30pm. It departs the resort pier at 9.30am and 4.30pm. The cost is €14 per person round trip. There is also a €6 per person island fee paid upon landing.

Travellers are advised not to try to hire a boat in Porto Alegre to reach Ilhéu das Rolas, as these boats are prone to accidents in the channel.

# Interior

The interior of São Tomé offers the chance to head deep into mountainous jungle along old plantation roads, with some stretches still paved in stone. Cool air, huge trees, roadside waterfalls, alluring vistas and a reflective peacefulness await. The key routes are the EN-3 to Bom Sucesso, and the even better ride to more remote Roça Bombaim.

**Pico de São Tomé** is an impressive peak soaring 2024m above the sea like a great green tooth bleeding mist. You can see it best from the EN-1 as you drive from Neves to Santa Catalina. Or you can reach the summit by making the country's signature climb. **Cascata São Nicolau** is a nice roadside waterfall *(cascata)*, with a bridge across the pool below.

**Roça Monte Café** (museum & tour €4; 8am-4pm Mon-Fri, to 1pm Sat & Sun) is the most pleasant *roça* to visit. A hillside village of plantation houses, it offers a small museum and formal tour of the coffee production process (the arabica variety grows well at this 600m altitude). The tour nicely ties the entire plantation together, including a school with 150 children. Tastings at the small gift shop. English-speaking guide available. The obvious entrance is located on the right about 6km inland from Trindade on the EN-3.

Trekking routes from the interior extend out to the east and west coasts of the island, offering some fine long-distance journeys. Heading east from Roça Bombaim, you can reach Roça Agua-Izé in six hours. Heading west from Bom Succeso, you can reach Roça Ponta Figo via Lagoa Amelia and Pico de São Tomé (p428), a two-day event. Bombaim and Bom Sucesso are further joined by a six-hour trek, with basic accommodations at either end. Guides are generally available at the office at the **Jardim Botânico** (Bom Sucesso; tour €2; 8am-5pm), or book through Navetur (p425). Don't forget your rain gear.

One of the island's better hikes is the hour-long trek from the Jardim Botânico in Bom Sucesso, where you pick up a guide (€20 to €30), to **Lagoa Amelia**. The name notwithstanding, this is no lagoon, but a unique crater filled with water and covered with a thick layer of earth, so that you can walk on it.

## Sleeping

**Pousada Bombaim** POUSADA $
(987 5978; Roça Bombaim; s/d €30/40, full board €54/64) Set in spectacular jungle surroundings in the remote heart of the island, Pousada Bombaim occupies the central plantation house on the otherwise eerily abandoned Roça Bombaim. Unfortunately this classic home with its two-storey verandas has seen better days. What should

be a five star inn is now a hostel with basic rooms, plain food and a widespread lack of maintenance.

**Albergue Bom Sucesso** AGRITURISMO **$**
(Bom Sucesso; d/tr €30/35) The botanical garden in Bom Sucesso offers a few clean and simple en suite rooms with a basic communal kitchen. This is a transit point for several long distance treks, with meals available for €10. Book through Navetur (p425).

## Getting There & Away

While you can reach Bom Sucesso, and possibly Bombaim, by taxi, renting a 4WD for the day is the best option, so you can move around at your own pace. You will also need a guide to not only understand what you are seeing, but to explore a region with no road signs. Guides can be hired through Navetur (p425), or at the Jardim Botânico in Bom Sucesso.

# PRÍNCIPE

POP 7000

Príncipe is in many ways a smaller version of São Tomé, with a port capital in the north, a vast uninhabited forest in the south, and a few *roças* (plantations) sprinkled around. However, due to its much smaller population this island is more unspoiled, feels more remote and is ultimately more attractive. Nature rules here, and beautifully so: an intact canopy covers everything with the exception of the airport and the tiny capital, Santo António, creating an emerald isle accented by fantastic beaches. Raw phonolite towers of various shapes punch through the forest, forming a crazy skyline, and making the entire island feel like Jurassic Park – without the dinosaurs, although there are some interesting endemic species that won't eat you. Recognising this natural patrimony, Unesco made Príncipe a World Biosphere Reserve in 2013. Given recent infrastructure upgrades, including a new international airport, perhaps you should visit sooner rather than later.

Once the subject of a world-famous Bacardi advertisement (you'll remember it when you see it), the picture-perfect tropical beach of **Praia Banana** is located on the grounds of Roça Belo Monte, a 15-minute walk from the front gate. It is first seen from above, at a clifftop *mirador* (overlook; where the ad was shot), before descending to sea level, where you'll find its golden sands.

The spectacular **Baía das Agulhas** (Bay of Spires) is not just Príncipe's top attraction, but STP's as well. It's best seen from the water, where the postcard view of the island's world-class skyline slowly unfolds, including phonolite towers named (for obvious reasons) the Father, the Son and the Grandson, along with Table Mountain. You expect to hear the primordial roar of T-Rex at any moment. If you've flown all this way, you do not want to miss this.

**Praia Macaco** is an excellent swimming beach. It's wonderfully private and isolated, so bring everything you'll need. The best way to find it is to ask the guard at the front gate to Roça Belo Monte; you may also hire a guide here if necessary.

**Praia Boi** is a postcard tropical beach, with turquoise water, swaying palms and no people. You will need to bring your own food, but it is perfect for a picnic. Located around the headland from Praia Macaco, it is accessed by car via a signless complex of rough dirt roads best navigated with local assistance. The guard at the entrance to Roça Belo Monte is a good source of information, and may be able to find you a local guide.

## Activities

Activities including hiking, diving, boat tours, stand-up paddleboarding and quad biking are offered to all comers by the resorts, particularly Bom Bom and Roça Belo Monte. Makaira Lodge is the source for deep-sea fishing. All have guides who speak English.

### Quad Biking

Quad bikes are the perfect way to explore Príncipe, as you can access many of the old plantation roads that interlace the island. Roça Belo Monte offers three-hour quad tours with guide for €40 per person – a bargain.

### Baía das Agulhas Boat Tour

Fully taking in the country's top sight really requires a boat journey, and several resorts offer trips. The best is led by Bom Bom Resort – its three-hour tour costs €150 for the boat (maximum six people). While in the calm bay you can take in the views on a stand-up paddleboard. Or you can dip beneath the waters for some interesting snorkelling among the great variety of fish that inhabit the shoreline.

## Sleeping

**Hotel Rural Abade** POUSADA **$$**
(☎991 6024; www.abadeprincipe.com; Roça Abade; d incl breakfast €70) These basic rooms, some with shared bathroom, in the former administrator's house of Roça Abade are

### TREKKING PORTO REAL TRAIL

In the town of Porto Real, Príncipe's only official self-guided trail has been constructed, a 6km three-hour hike into the forest that ends with a beautiful view. The trailhead is indicated by a big wooden sign, and located to the right of the old hospital ruins, now overrun by jungle. Anyone in the village can direct you.

only a good option if you really want to get away from it all, as they require a significant drive to a remote part of the island. The chief attractions are the low price and the beautiful view of Ilhéu Caroço (Jockey Cap island).

★**Bom Bom Resort** RESORT **$$$**
(☎225 1114; www.bombomprincipe.com; bungalows with pool or garden view and half board s/d €260/320; ) It's hard to find fault with this slice of tropical paradise, for while that term is highly overused, it does apply here. The resort has an extraordinary location encompassing both a coastal peninsula, where the bungalows are, and tiny Bom Bom island, where the bar-restaurant is. The two are connected by a 140m-long wooden bridge flanked by two gorgeous beaches.

★**Roça Belo Monte** POUSADA **$$$**
(☎225 1152; www.belomontehotel.com; s/d incl breakfast €152/235; ) This beautifully renovated and fast-expanding *roça* is the best of its kind in STP. High up on a hill, it affords marvellous views of the coastline from various points, most notably its lovely veranda. There is a great variety of spacious rooms in a quadrangle of outbuildings, the most luxurious being in the main house, as well as several well-appointed cottages.

**Makaira Lodge** TENTED CAMP **$$$**
(☎906 5935; www.makaira-adventure.com; Praia Campanha; s/d/tr with half board €135/165/215) Here lies the great secret of Príncipe lodging. During research Makaira Lodge had just opened, and was putting the finishing touches on its dipping pool. The lodge is brilliantly simple: six high-end safari tents on a beautiful secluded beach. The canvas tents are spacious and furnished with all electrics, private bathrooms and thoughtful design flourishes, beginning with the canopy beds.

## Getting There & Away

The only scheduled transport to or from Príncipe is the twice-daily STP Airways shuttle between Príncipe Airport (PCP) and São Tomé International Airport (TMS). The plane leaves TMS around 9am and returns around 11am. In the afternoon it departs TMS around 4pm and returns around 6pm. The flight lasts around 45 minutes and costs around €150 return.

# Santo António

POP 1500

While it's the island capital, Santo António is just a small grid of unkempt streets scattered with concrete-block buildings. It has an otherwise pretty location astride a river that empties into a narrow bay. The best views of the area are from the yellow hospital at the entrance to the bay. Looking inland affords a dramatic view of Pico Papagaio (Parrot Peak), the island's tallest mountain at 680m. Come here for the island's least expensive accommodation, to top up your phone, change money or mail that postcard.

Your best in-town option, **Complexo Mira Rio** (☎986 9003, 990 6454; gruposalvador51@gmail.com; Rua Martires da Liberdade; s/d €50/70; ⏲6am-10pm; ) is a spick-and-span hotel nicely located opposite the Papagaio River bridge, with a small grocery store downstairs. The rooms are well lit, with comfy mattresses. Best of all there is a nice terrace restaurant overlooking the river, with food cooked to order, including some very generous sandwiches. This is the best place in town to hang out.

If Complexo Mira Rio is full, default to **Residential Palhota** (☎225 1060, 993 8153; hotelpalhota@gmail.com; Ave Martires da Liberdade; s/d €50/70; ). Beaten up but serviceable, it includes the adjacent thatched hut restaurant (menu €10) which is open all day. Book ahead as rooms fill up.

Run by the former chef at Bom Bom resort, the humble **Pastelaria** (☎991 9539; António Segundo II; dinner menu Db100,000; ⏲6-10pm, lunch on request) punches well above its weight. The very clean kitchen turns out a dinner menu each night. Also has a small bar.

Top up your phone at CST, and change money at **BISTP** (Ave Carneiro; ⏲8am-3pm Mon-Fri, to noon Sat). The post office is on Marcelo da Veiga Sq.

There's no public transport in Santo António. Travellers typically arrange transport through their hotel, which can contact informal taxi services. For short trips, flag down a passing motorcycle.

# UNDERSTAND SÃO TOMÉ & PRÍNCIPE

## São Tomé & Príncipe Today

São Toméans face a harsh historical reality: independence has impoverished the country. The elderly will tell you that colonial times may not have been ideal, but at least there was electricity, sanitation, running water and a public bus service.

Deep in the jungle, one comes upon forgotten roads and bridges carefully made of stone, amid cocoa plants gone wild. In the capital, shipwrecks dot the harbour, potholes scar the streets, and scores of once-beautiful colonial homes lie rotting; only one has been restored, with EU funding. Outside the capital, people eke out a living in ramshackle fishing villages, with rudimentary sanitation.

The current prime minister is Patrice Trovoada (son of Miguel Trovoada, the country's first prime minister), who was elected in 2014. With the once-promising search for offshore oil having ground to a halt, the silent question hanging over the people is when the slow, unending decline in their living conditions will finally prompt a revolution. Today 85% of the annual budget consists of foreign aid.

## History

There are essentially two chapters in the history of São Tomé and Príncipe: before 1975, and after 1975. Both are on view everywhere.

Before 1975, STP was one of Portugal's four African colonies. The Portuguese discovered the uninhabited islands in the late 15th century, and transformed them into breadbaskets of tropical agriculture, in two historic waves. The first was based on sugar, powered by slave labour (with freed slaves also part of the social fabric) and lasted for much of the 16th century. Following two centuries of decline, during which the islands became an outpost of the transatlantic slave trade, the 19th century brought two new crops, coffee and cocoa, and extraordinary growth: by the early 20th century São Tomé was one of the world's largest cocoa producers.

The 19th-century agricultural boom transformed STP into an enormous network of plantations, known as *roças* ('clearings'). On São Tomé five major *roças* evolved and over 100 major *dependencias* (satellites), all linked by stone roads and a narrow-gauge rail network that eventually brought crops to the pier for transportation to Europe. The *roças* were towns unto themselves, with a grand administrator's mansion, huge hospitals, warehouses, bean drying sheds, and housing for hundreds of workers and their families. Collectively, they turned STP into one enormously productive farm.

In 1975, all of this changed, and rapidly so, with the independence of STP from Portugal. In 1974, a bloodless coup had restored democracy to Portugal. Tired of fighting costly insurrections in all of its other African colonies, Portugal decided to liberate them all at once. In STP, the effect was immediate. Facing the nationalisation of their property, and fearing for their personal safety, the Portuguese quickly abandoned the entire country, leaving behind a mostly unskilled, illiterate population.

The country first turned to Communism, which lasted 15 years until the fall of the Soviet Union. It remained closely aligned with Angola, Cuba and communist eastern Europe until the demise of the Soviet Union, when São Toméans began to demand multiparty democracy. The first elections were held in 1991. Since then, the islands have experienced a long period of political instability, with several coups and major corruption scandals upending and reinstalling various presidents and prime ministers in a complex soup of events. Neither form of government was able to prevent an economic apocalypse. Without the ability to run the *roças* as profitable businesses, the economic foundation of the entire country collapsed.

## The People

São Toméans consist of *mestiços,* mixed-blood descendants of Portuguese colonists and African slaves; Angolares, reputedly descendants of Angolan slaves who survived a 1540 shipwreck and now earn their livelihood fishing; Forros, descendants of freed slaves; Tongas, the children of *serviçais* (contract labourers from Angola, Mozambique and Cape Verde); and Europeans, primarily Portuguese repatriates, who have started many island businesses.

## Environment

Every country is the product of its environment, but with its far-flung locale, unique topographical features and endemic wildlife,

STP is more so than most. When you step foot here, you'll feel a long way from anywhere. Many of the species that inhabit the islands perilously arrived on natural rafts flushed into the sea from the rivers of West Africa.

# SURVIVAL GUIDE

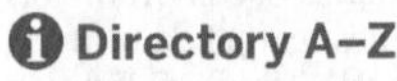

## Directory A–Z

### ACCOMMODATION

STP is top-heavy: budget accommodation of acceptable quality is relatively scarce. Be very careful of accommodation at *roças* (plantations): only a handful – Roça Sao João (p428), Roça Belo Monte (p432), Roça Bombaim (p430) and soon Roça Sundy – offer acceptable accommodation. Most are either abandoned or squatter settlements with squalid conditions.

### DANGERS & ANNOYANCES

São Tomé and Príncipe is an extremely safe destination. However, thefts of personal belongings are common on beaches, particularly those next to villages, where a smartphone is worth an annual salary. The beaches near Morro Peixe, north of São Tomé city, are known for such thefts.

### EMERGENCY & IMPORTANT NUMBERS

| | |
|---|---|
| Country Code | 239 |
| International Access Code | 00 |
| Emergency | 112 |

### INTERNET ACCESS

All major hotels have wi-fi, as do some cafes. When purchasing a SIM, an additional €12 buys you 4GB of web-surfing, and there is coverage virtually everywhere.

### LGBTIQ TRAVELLERS

Homosexuality was decriminalised in 2012. However, there are no lesbian or gay organisations and some social stigma remains. Otherwise the *leve leve* ('easy easy') attitude prevails.

**SLEEPING PRICE RANGES**

The following price ranges refer to a double room with bathroom:

**$** less than €50

**$$** €50–100

**$$$** more than €100

### MONEY

There are no international ATMs, and only certain high-end hotels accept credit cards, with two offering limited cash back (p427), ie they run your credit card for a certain amount and hand it to you in cash. Bringing cash in euros is the best option.

**Cash** Bring cash denominated in euros, as the dollar is increasingly less common. The dobra can only be used in-country, so you must exchange euros for dobras after you arrive, and dobras for euros before you leave.

**Changing money** Foreign exchange is normally done through informal brokers (cheapest) or through a bank or a hotel. Don't be put off when approached by moneychangers on the street in São Tomé city, as this is the normal way of doing business, and entirely legal. Just agree on the rate, use your calculator, and count your money. In Príncipe you must use the bank.

The euro can be used almost anywhere, although you will often receive change in dobras, and only dobras. It is also generally more expensive to spend euros, as one way or another an exchange fee gets added in.

**Tipping** Tipping is not customary, and at the customer's discretion. However, 5% goes a long way locally.

### Exchange Rates

| | | |
|---|---|---|
| Australia | A$1 | Db16,930 |
| Canada | C$1 | Db16,440 |
| Euro zone | €1 | Db24,530 |
| Japan | ¥100 | Db20,110 |
| New Zealand | NZ$1 | Db15,550 |
| UK | £1 | Db28,990 |
| US | $1 | Db22,480 |

For current exchange rates, see www.xe.com.

### OPENING HOURS

**Banks** 8am to 3pm Monday to Friday.

**Bars & Clubs** 10pm to 2am weekends, some during week as well.

**Restaurants** 11am to 3pm and 6 to11pm (generally closed Mondays).

**Shops** 8am to 12.30pm and 2 to 5pm Monday to Friday, 8am to 1pm Saturday (although not all shops observe the siesta).

### POST

The main post offices are in the island capitals, São Tomé city (p425) and **Santo António** (Marcelo da Veiga Sq; 7am-noon & 2-3.30pm Mon-Fri). STP stamps are particularly valued by collectors!

### PUBLIC HOLIDAYS

**New Year's Day** 1 January

**Rei Amador Day** 4 January

**Heroes Day** 3 February
**Labour Day** 1 May
**Independence Day** 12 July
**Agricultural Reform Day** 30 September
**São Tomé Day** 21 December
**Christmas Day** 25 December

### TELEPHONE

Mobile phone coverage is excellent, reaching all developed areas. SIM cards are available from CST (p425) in São Tomé city and **CST** (☎225 1100; Ave Martíres da Liberdade; ⏰7am-noon & 2-7pm Mon-Fri, 7am-7pm Sat) in Santo António (Príncipe) for €3, and work with unlocked phones. Add a few euros of credit for local use, and use wi-fi for international calls. Skype users should check the cost of international pay calls to/from STP, as the fees can be exorbitant.

### TOURIST INFORMATION

There is limited tourist information available on STP. Web surfers will quickly discover that many official websites do not even function, including that of the government's national tourism office. However, a new website, www.turismo.gov.st, is reportedly coming online soon...

The only tourism bureau (p425) in STP is in São Tomé city.

### VISAS

Visas are necessary and a significant headache to obtain. There is an online system (www.smf.st/virtualvisa), but it's known to malfunction for long periods of time.

A 15-day visa is free for citizens from the EU, USA, Canada, and lusophone (Portuguese-speaking) countries, €20 otherwise. A 30-day visa costs €80. Given the problems that may arise in this process, it is best to apply early.

If you book a car rental or hotel booking through the travel agent Navetur (p425), it will sort your visa for you – by far the easiest route. Otherwise you must deal with the closest embassy, of which there are only a few (some offer a mail-in service):

**Africa** Gabon, Angola, Equatorial Guinea, Nigeria
**Asia** Taiwan
**Europe** Lisbon (covers Spain) and Belgium
**USA** New York

## Getting There & Away

### AIR

There are two commercial airports in the country, São Tomé International Airport (TMS) and Príncipe Airport (PCP). At time of research Príncipe's runway had been extended in anticipation of direct international flights but none had yet been scheduled.

From Europe, all flights to TMS originate in Lisbon, with one of two carriers: **TAP** (☎222 2307; www.flytap.com; Rua de Santo António do Príncipe; ⏰24/7), the Portuguese national airline, or **STP Airways** (☎222 1160; www.stpairways.st; Ave Marginal 12 de Julho; ⏰7.30am-4.30pm Mon-Fri, 9am-noon Sat). STP Airways tickets are significantly cheaper than TAP, but do not show up on conventional booking engines. All online ticketing is done via their website.

From Africa, flights to TMS originate from Luanda, Angola with **TAAG** (☎122 2593; www.taag.com; Rua Geovane Caixa; ⏰8am-3pm Mon-Fri); Douala, Cameroon, with **CEIBA** (www.ceibaintercontinental.com); Libreville and Port-Gentil, Gabon, with CEIBA and **Afrijet** (www.flyafrijet.online); Accra, Ghana (TAP); and Malabó, Equatorial Guinea with **Punto Azul** (www.flypuntoazul.gq). TAAG, CEIBA, Afrijet and Punto Azul are all on the European blacklist.

There is a €20 departure tax.

### EATING PRICE RANGES

The following price ranges represent the cost of a main dish:

**$** less than €5

**$$** €5–10

**$$$** more than €10

## Getting Around

### AIR

**STP Airways** (p435) flies back and forth between São Tomé and Príncipe Monday to Saturday (€165, 45 minutes). Seats fill up so book early.

### BOAT

Travellers are advised not to use the intermittent ferry service between the islands. The six-hour, open-ocean voyage is both uncomfortable and dangerous, with two ships having sunk in recent years, one of which capsized in São Tomé harbour due to overloading.

### CAR & MOTORCYCLE

Shared taxis are the most common form of transport, but to ensure a modicum of comfort sit in front and buy two seats. Motorcycle taxis are also used, but for safety reasons you should limit to in-town use, rather than long distance.. Otherwise you will need to rent a car. The only established rental agencies are on São Tomé.

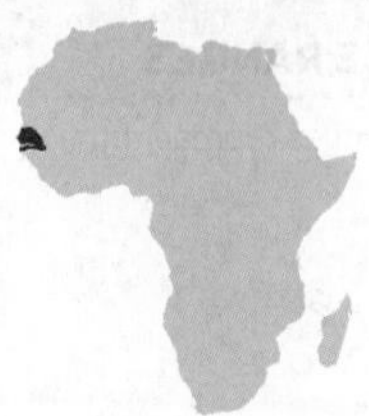

# Senegal

☎221 / POP 14.5 MILLION

### Includes ➡



## Best Places to Eat

- ➡ Le Lagon I (p445)
- ➡ La Kora (p454)
- ➡ La Guingette (p449)
- ➡ Casa-Resto (p459)

## Best Places to Sleep

- ➡ Au Fil du Fleuve (p453)
- ➡ Espace Sobo Badè (p451)
- ➡ Keur Saloum (p451)
- ➡ Lodge des Collines de Niassam (p450)
- ➡ Cisko Centre Culturel (p459)

## Why Go?

Though it's one of West Africa's most stable countries, Senegal is far from dull. Perched on the tip of a peninsula, Dakar the capital, is a dizzying, street-hustler-rich introduction to the country: elegance meets chaos, snarling traffic, vibrant markets and glittering nightlife, while nearby Île de Gorée and the beaches of Yoff and N'Gor tap to slow, lazy beats.

In northern Senegal, the enigmatic capital of Saint-Louis, a Unesco World Heritage Site, tempts with colonial architecture and proximity to scenic national parks. Along the Petite Côte and Cap Skirring, wide strips of beaches beckon and the wide deltas of the Casamance invite mesmerising boat journeys amid astounding biodiversity, including hundreds of bird species.

Whether you want to mingle with the trendsetters of urban Africa or be alone with your thoughts and the sounds of nature, you'll find your place in Senegal.

## When to Go

### Dakar

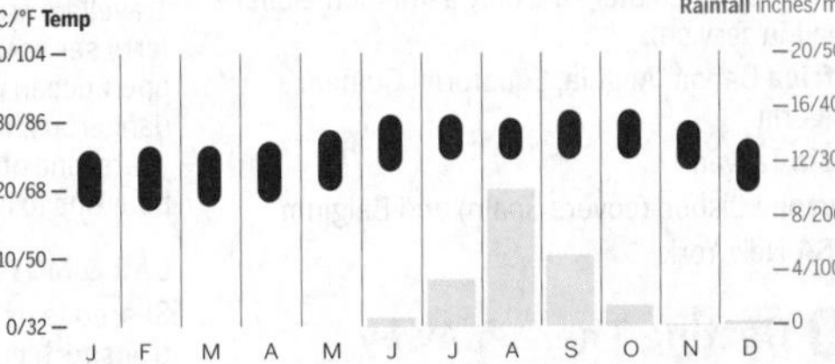


**Nov–Feb** Senegal's main tourist season is dry and cool.

**Dec & Mar–Jun** When most music festivals take place, including the Saint-Louis Jazz Festival.

**Jul–late Sep** Rainy, humid season; some hotels close, others reduce prices by up to 40%.

# DAKAR

POP 1.2 MILLION

Dakar is a city of extremes, where horse-cart drivers chug over swish highways and gleaming SUVs squeeze through tiny sand roads; where elegant ladies dig skinny heels into dusty walkways and suit-clad businessmen kneel down for prayer in the middle of the street. Once a tiny settlement in the south of the Cap Vert peninsula, Dakar now spreads almost across its entire triangle, and keeps growing.

For the traveller, there's much to discover, from peaceful islands just off-shore to vertiginous nightlife dancing to mbalax beats. You can spend your days browsing frenetic markets and taking in the sights of bustling downtown, followed by sunset drinks overlooking the crashing waves. At once both intimidating and deeply alluring, Dakar is a fascinating introduction to Senegal.

## Sights

**★Île de N'Gor** ISLAND

(Map p444) For a quick escape from the frenetic streets of Dakar, head to peaceful Île de N'Gor, a tiny island just off Dakar's north shore. It has a few calm beaches on the bay side, and some legendary surf on the northern coastline. Most visitors just come for the day, to relax on the beaches, stroll the sandy lanes of the village and have lunch in one of the waterside eateries, but there are several appealing guesthouses here as well.

**★Musée Théodore Monod** MUSEUM

(Musée IFAN; Map p442; 33 823 9268; Pl de Soweto, Plateau; adult/child CFA5000/1000; 9am-5pm Tue-Sun) The is one of Senegal's best museums. Exhibitions delve into African art and culture with over 9000 objects on display. Lively displays of masks and traditional dress from across the region (including Mali, Guinea-Bissau, Benin and Nigeria) give an excellent overview of styles without bombarding you with more than you can take in.

**Village des Arts** ARTS CENTRE

(Map p444; 33 835 7160; Rte de Yoff; 9.30am-7pm) FREE An arts tour around Dakar is simply not complete without a visit to this famous art complex, where some of Senegal's most promising and established painters, sculptors and multimedia artists create, shape and display their works in individual studios scattered around a large garden space. There's also an on-site gallery, which exhibits works by artists both home-grown and from abroad.

**Médina** AREA

(Map p440) A bustling popular *quartier* with tiny tailor's shops, a busy **Marché Tilène** (Map p440; Ave Blaise Diagne; 8am-4pm) and streets brimming with life, the Médina was built as a township for the local populace by the French during colonial days. It's the birthplace of Senegalese superstar and current minister of culture Youssou N'Dour. Besides being a very real neighbourhood, where creative ideas and new trends grow between crammed, makeshift homes, it's also home to Dakar's 1664 **Grande Mosquée**, impressive for its sheer size and landmark minaret.

## Activities

Dakar's best beaches are found in the north of the peninsula. **Plage de N'Gor** (Map p444) is often crowded; if so, you're better off catching the frequent pirogues (CFA500) to Île de N'Gor, which has two small beaches.

Dakar has decent waves and a growing surf scene. In Yoff, **Plage de Virage** (Map p444; Yoff) is good; **Plage de Yoff** (Map p444) is rubbish-strewn in parts but waves are strong enough for surfing. Malika Surf Camp (p441), **École Surf Attitude** (Map p444; 77 034 3434; www.senegalsurf.com; Plage des Viviers, Corniche des Almadies; 2hr surf class CFA15,000, 10-class package CFA120,000) and **N'Gor Island Surf Camp** (Map p444; 77 336 9150; www.gosurf.dk; dm/s/d with half-board CFA25,000/50,000/80,000; ) can point out additional surf spots; they also run courses and hire out boards.

**Nautilus Diving** DIVING

(Map p444; 77 637 1422; www.nautilus-diving.com; N'Gor; discovery dives CFA28,000, two dives CFA53,000; 9am-7pm Tue-Sun) Operating out of the Maison Abaka (p442), this professional, French-run outfit offers diving to suit all levels (and courses for those who want to learn). The friendly owners, Hilda and Philippe, also speak English (and some Spanish).

## Tours

**Andaando** (77 793 9432; www.andaando.com; Sicap Mbao 199, Thiaroye) A recommended agency with trips to Saint-Louis, the desert of Lampou, the Casamance

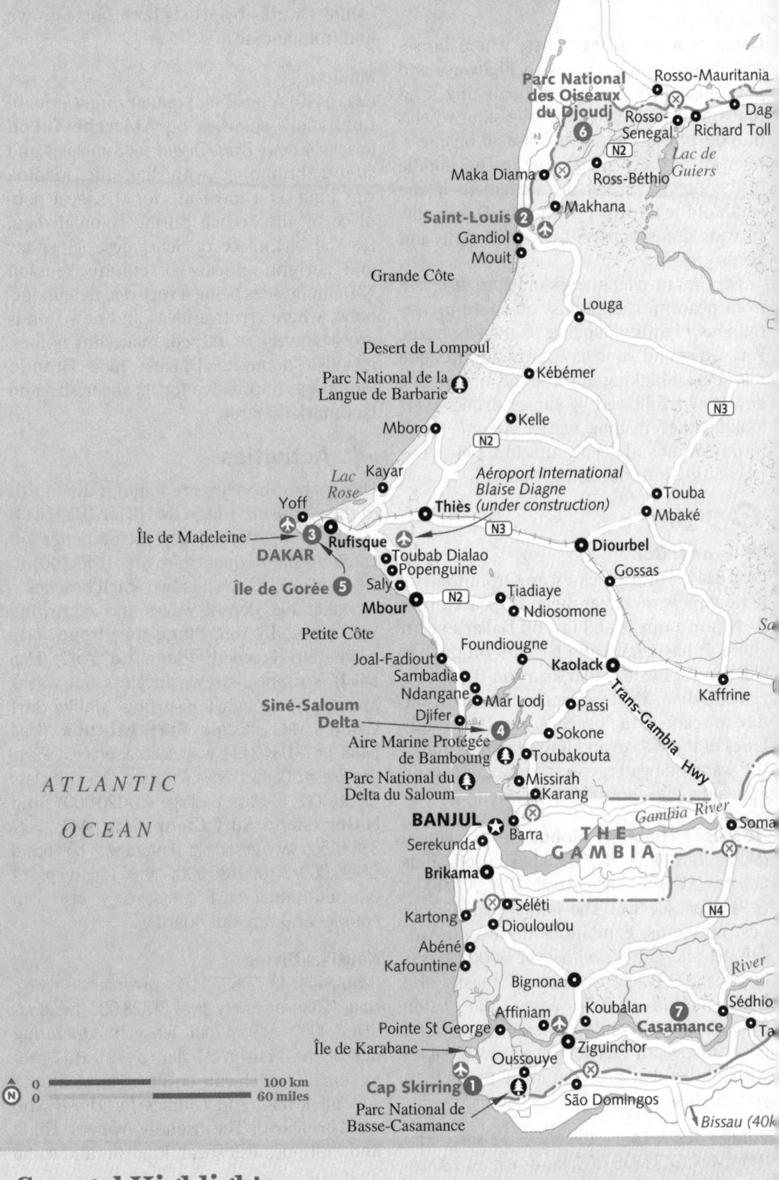


## Senegal Highlights

**1 Cap Skirring** (p457) Weaving your way via tiny villages to Senegal's best beaches and kicking back for a day of doing absolutely nothing.

**2 Saint-Louis** (p451) Wandering the cobblestone streets past colourful French colonial buildings in a Unesco World Heritage Site.

**3 Dakar** (p437) Spending sleepless nights touring the vibrant nightclubs and bars of the capital.

**4 Siné-Saloum Delta** (p449) Gliding through

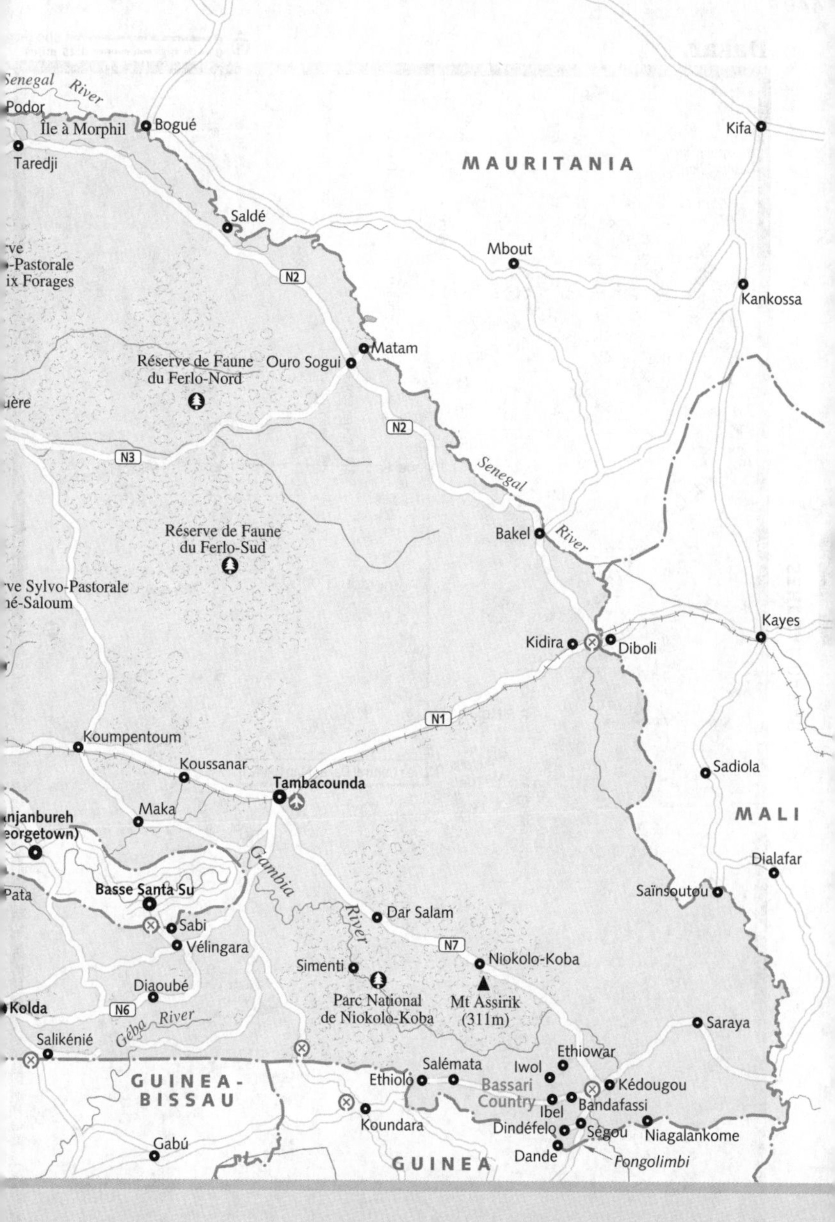


mangroves in a pirogue (traditional motorised canoe).

**5 Île de Gorée** (p448) Contemplating history at Maison des Esclaves and browsing the handiwork of local artists on this peaceful island.

**6 Parc National des Oiseaux du Djoudj** (p454) Spotting flamingos, black-crowned night herons and dozens of other bird species.

**7 Casamance** (p455) Exploring a lush, tropical island or sandy shore.

# Dakar

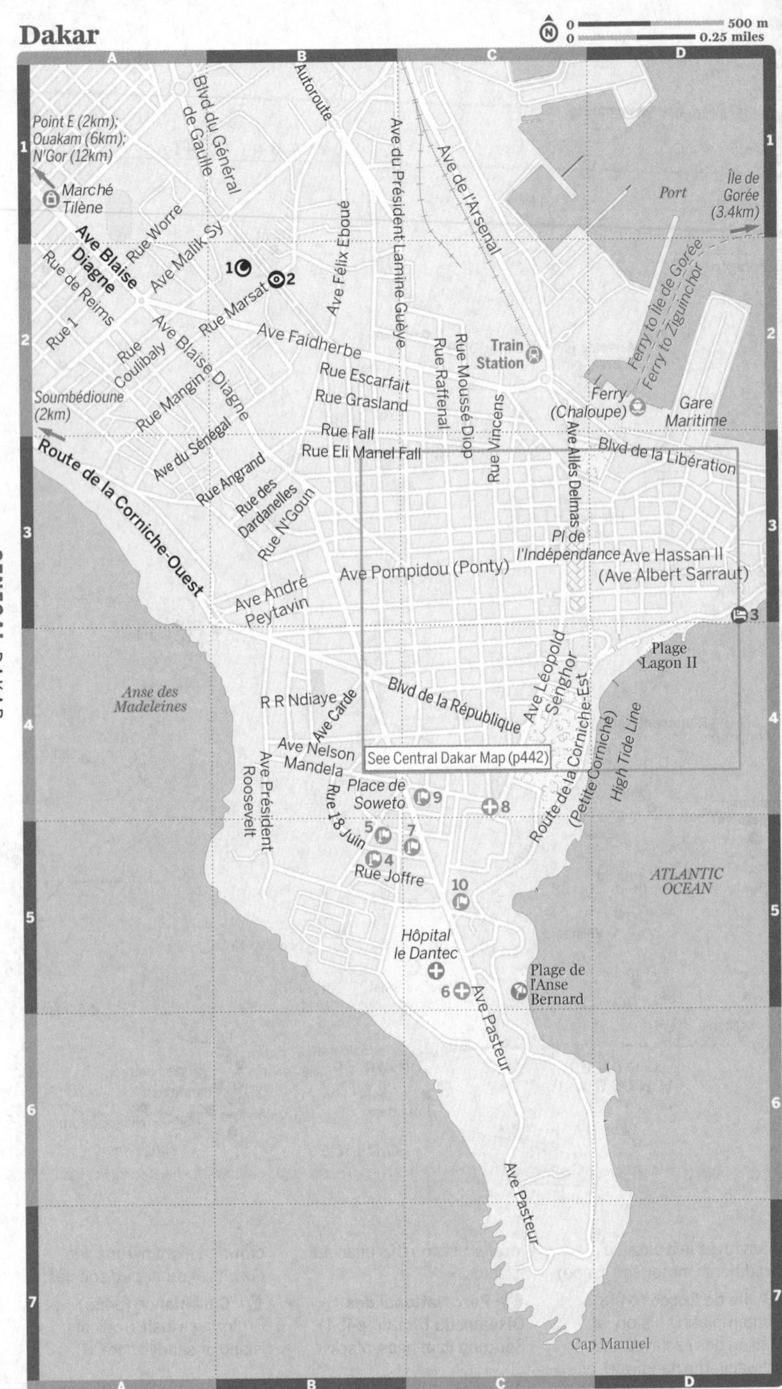

0 500 m
0 0.25 miles
Point E (2km); Ouakam (6km); N'Gor (12km)
Marché Tilène
Blvd du Général de Gaulle
Autoroute
Ave du Président Lamine Guèye
Ave de l'Arsenal
Port
Île de Gorée (3.4km)
Rue Worre
Ave Blaise Diagne
Ave Malik Sy
Rue de Reims
Rue 1
Rue Marsat
Ave Félix Eboué
Ave Faidherbe
Rue Coulibaly
Rue Mangin
Rue Escarfait
Rue Grasland
Rue Raffenal
Rue Moussé Diop
Train Station
Ferry to Île de Gorée
Ferry to Ziguinchor
Soumbédioune (2km)
Ave du Sénégal
Rue Fall
Rue Eli Manel Fall
Rue Vincens
Ferry (Chaloupe)
Gare Maritime
Route de la Corniche-Ouest
Rue Angrand
Rue des Dardanelles
Rue N'Goun
Ave Allés Delmas
Blvd de la Libération
Pl de l'Indépendance
Ave Hassan II (Ave Albert Sarraut)
Ave Pompidou (Ponty)
Ave André Peytavin
Plage Lagon II
Anse des Madeleines
R R Ndiaye
Ave Carde
Blvd de la République
Ave Léopold Senghor
Route de la Corniche-Est (Petite Corniche)
High Tide Line
Ave Nelson Mandela
See Central Dakar Map (p442)
Ave Président Roosevelt
Rue 18 Juin
Place de Soweto
Rue Joffre
ATLANTIC OCEAN
Hôpital le Dantec
Plage de l'Anse Bernard
Ave Pasteur
Cap Manuel

**Dakar**

**Sights**

| | | |
|---|---|---|
| 1 | Grande Mosquée | B2 |
| 2 | Médina | B2 |

**Sleeping**

| | | |
|---|---|---|
| 3 | Le Lagon II | D3 |

**Information**

| | | |
|---|---|---|
| 4 | Cabo Verdean Embassy | B5 |
| 5 | Canadian Embassy | B5 |
| 6 | Clinique du Cap | C5 |
| 7 | German Embassy | C5 |
| 8 | Hôpital Principal | C4 |
| 9 | Spanish Embassy | C4 |
| 10 | UK Embassy | C5 |

and the big national parks, plus day trips around Dakar.

**Boumak NDofféene Diouf** (77 339 7712) English-speaking guide; ask for him at Via Via.

**Nouvelles Frontières** (Map p444; 33 859 4447; www.nfsenegal.com; Lot 1 Mamelles Aviation, Rte des Almadies; 8.30am-6pm Mon-Fri, 9am-12.30pm Sat) Offers a wide range of tours: Lac Rose, Saint-Louis, Parc National de Niokolo-Koba, the Petite Côte and other destinations.

**SenegalStyle** (77 791 5469; SenegalStyle@gmail.com; Cité Africa, Unit 13, Ouest Foire) Offers customised tours (by car or motorbike), plus activities like drumming lessons.

## Festivals & Events

**Dak'Art Biennale** ART
(33 823 0918; www.facebook.com/dakartbiennale; May) Held on even-numbered years, this festival of painting and sculpture is the queen of Dakar's festivals. It drowns the town in colour for the whole of May, with exhibitions all across Dakar. Unmissable.

## Sleeping

**Quicksilver Boardriders Dakar** GUESTHOUSE, HOSTEL $
(Map p444; 78 196 9349; www.quiksilver-boardriders-dakar.com; Rond-point N'Gor, Les Almadies; dm/s/d from CFA10,000/15,000/20,000; ) Tucked behind the Quicksilver shop is this appealing guesthouse, with the hip-but-laid-back vibe you'd expect from the well-known clothing brand. Rooms are clean and well-kept, if minimally furnished, and overlook a lovely patio with a pool and outdoor bar that's great to meet other travellers.

**Malika Surf Camp** GUESTHOUSE $
(Map p444; 77 113 2791; www.surfinsenegal.com; Yoff Plage; r per person with half board from CFA17,000; ) This small, Italian-run place on Yoff beach has a bohemian vibe that draws a mix of surfers, aspiring surfers and those just wanting to enjoy the beach. Rooms are basic, but there's a small courtyard strung with hammocks, and a roof deck where you can sit on a bamboo chair, cold drink in hand, and watch the waves roll in.

**Via Via** GUESTHOUSE $
(Map p444; 33 820 5475; www.viavia.world/en/africa/dakar; Rte des Cimetières, Yoff; s/d CFA17,000/28,000, dm/s/d with shared bathroom CFA9500/12,000/22,000; ) Offers clean, simple rooms with fan and mosquito nets set around a courtyard. The welcoming staff is great here, and in season (November to March) they whip up tasty traditional meals, serve cocktails (a rarity in Yoff) and host monthly events, such as live music and film screenings.

**Keur Diame** HOTEL, HOSTEL $
(Map p444; 33 820 9676; www.aubergekeurdiame.wordpress.com; Cité Djily Mbaye 265, Yoff; s/d CFA21,000/29,000, s/d with shared bathroom CFA15,000/23,000; ) On a peaceful street by the beach, this friendly, Swiss-owned guesthouse offers attractively furnished rooms decorated with touches of African textiles. Three of the seven rooms have ocean views. There's ample space to relax with a roof deck, a courtyard and an indoor dining area with a small lending library.

★**Hôtel du Phare** HOTEL $$
(Map p444; 33 860 3000; www.hotelduphare-dakar.com; 36 Cité des Magistrats, Les Mamelles; r CFA23,000-42,000; ) This attractive and welcoming guesthouse has 10 cheerfully painted rooms, a book-filled lounge, and a restaurant with seats in a small courtyard. The rooftop deck, though, is the best feature, and a fine spot for tapas and sunset cocktails – plus occasional events like film screenings and music jams.

**La Maison d'Italie** GUESTHOUSE $$
(Map p444; 77 572 4306; www.chezcarlahotel.com; Deuxieme Plage, Île de N'Gor; s/d from CFA29,000/40,000; ) A charming guesthouse with five bright, cheerfully painted rooms and a terrace with sea views. The restaurant is also a draw, with a deck perched out over the water and good seafood and Italian plates (mains CFA6000 to CFA9500).

## Central Dakar

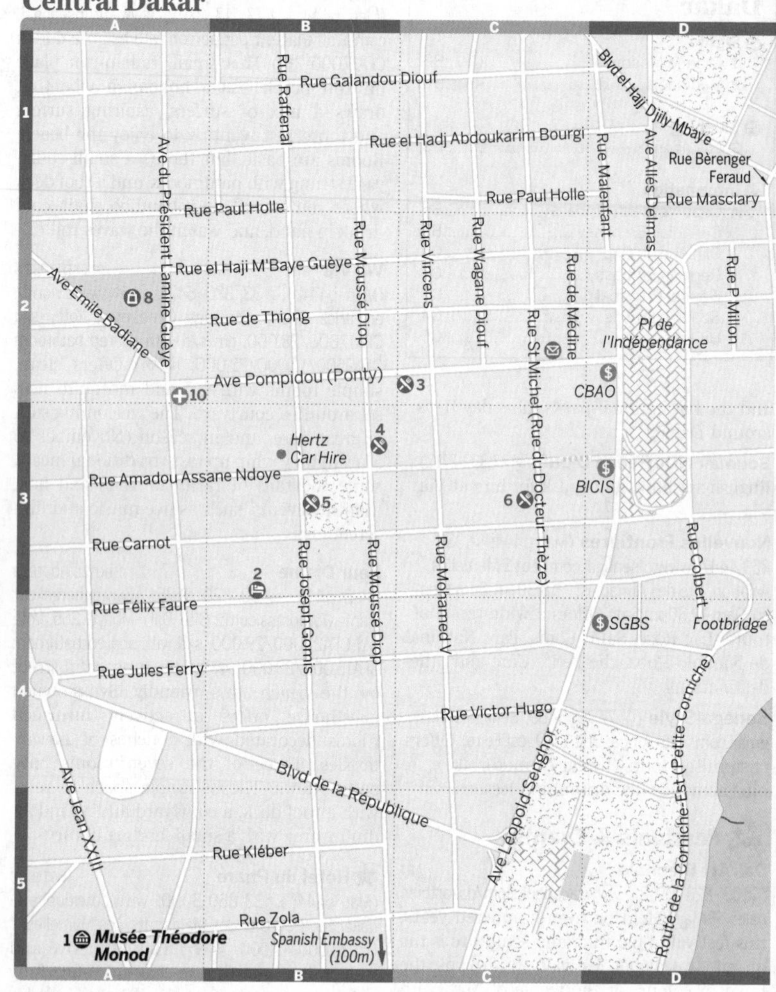


**Fleur de Lys** HOTEL **$$**
(Map p442; ☎33 849 4600; www.hotelfleurdelysdakar.com; 64 Rue Félix Faure; s/d/ste CFA56,000/87,000/120,000; ) This 12-storey hotel offers well-designed rooms and suites with all the essentials, plus extras like rain showers and balconies with views in the pricier chambers. There's a gym, an 11th-floor restaurant with views and a rooftop pool overlooking the city centre.

**La Demeure** GUESTHOUSE **$$**
(Map p444; ☎33 820 7679; www.lademeure-guesthouse.com; off Rte de N'Gor; s CFA50,000-69,000, d CFA59,000-79,000; ) Oozing laid-back elegance, this little guesthouse offers pleasant rooms (all with balconies) in a rambling, well-maintained house filled with a clutch of tasteful art collected by its engaging owner. It boasts a fantastic terrace with views over the greenery and out to the ocean – the perfect spot for a sunset drink from the bar.

**Maison Abaka** HOTEL **$$**
(Map p444; ☎33 820 6486; www.maison-abaka.com; Plage de N'Gor; d CFA40,000-70,000; ) This handsomely designed guest-

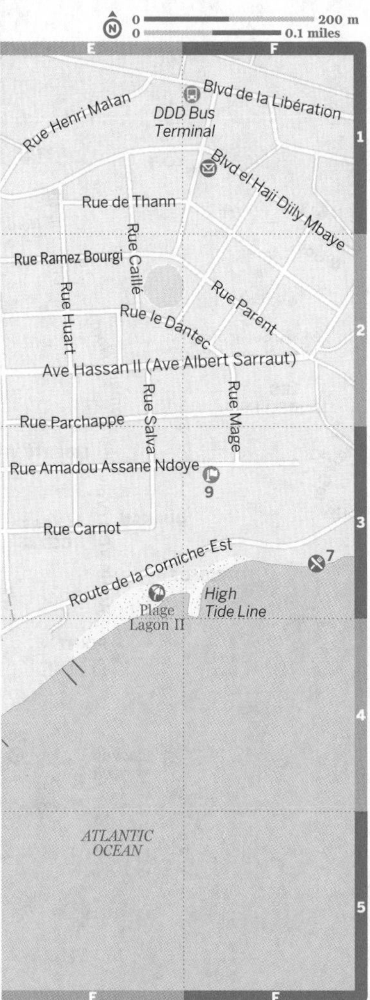


house has airy and lovingly decorated rooms located right behind the beach. The patio is the highlight, with a tiny bar on hand (also good food in the evenings) and small tables that give breezy views over the shore.

**Le Lagon II** HOTEL **$$$**
(Map p440; ☎33 889 2525; www.lelagondakar.com; Rte de la Corniche Est; s/d/ste CFA101,000/112,000/193,000; ❄📶) Tucked along waterfront Corniche Est, this place feels like a nautical hideway, with modern, nicely set rooms, all with balconies perched right over the ocean. After dining next door

## Central Dakar

**Top Sights**
1 Musée Théodore Monod....A5

**Sleeping**
2 Fleur de Lys....B3

**Eating**
3 Ali Baba Snack Bar....C2
4 Chez Loutcha....B3
5 Le Bideew....B3
6 Le Djembé....C3
7 Le Lagon I....F3

**Entertainment**
Institut Français Léopold Sédar Senghor....(see 5)

**Shopping**
8 Marché Sandaga....A2

**Information**
9 French Embassy....F3
10 Pharmacie Guigon....A2

at the good seafood restaurant Le Lagon I, you can drift off to sleep to the sound of waves lapping at the shore.

## Eating

**Le Bideew** INTERNATIONAL **$$**
(Map p442; ☎33 823 1909; 89 Rue Joseph Gomis; mains CFA3500-6000; ⊙10am-11pm Mon-Sat; 🖉) In the cool shade of the garden of the Institut Français Léopold Sédar Senghor, this colourful arts cafe is perfect for a break from the city. The varied menu features vegetable curry, octopus salad, chargrilled pork and creative dishes such as grilled prawns with *bissap* chutney. Sunday brunch is a hit (10am to 2pm).

**Le Djembé** AFRICAN **$$**
(Map p442; ☎33 821 0666; 56 Rue St Michel; dishes CFA2500-5000; ⊙noon-7pm Mon-Sat) A block west of Pl de l'Indépendance, this inviting, colourful eatery is the whispered insider-tip for anyone in search of a filling platter of *thiéboudienne* (rice baked in a thick sauce of fish and vegetables). There's also *poulet yassa* (grilled chicken in onion and lemon sauce), *bissap* juice (a purple drink made from water and hibiscus leaves), lively music and a good mix of locals and expats.

**Ali Baba Snack Bar** FAST FOOD **$$**
(Map p442; ☎33 822 5297; Ave Pompidou; sandwiches around CFA 1700, mains CFA3500-5000; ⊙8am-2am) Dakar's classic fast-food haunt

## Greater Dakar

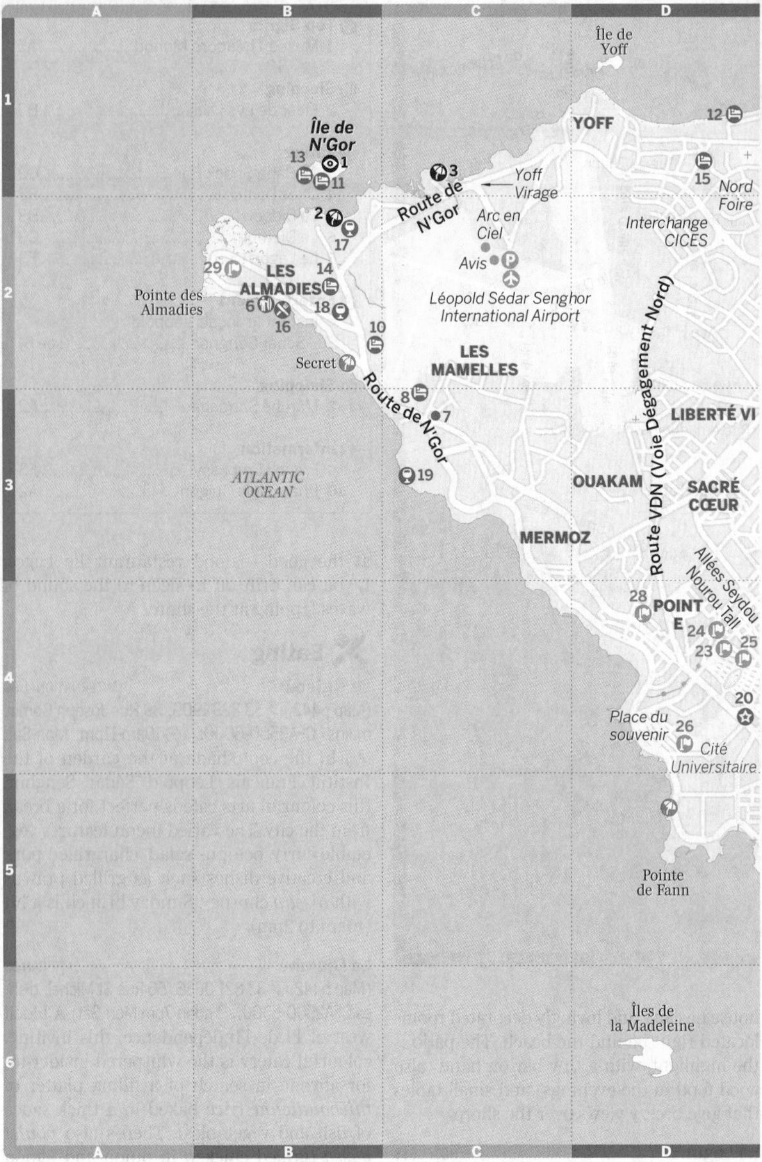

keeps on turning thanks to the undying love of the Senegalese. Serves the whole fast-food range: kebabs, shwarmas and other quick snacks.

**Chez Loutcha** AFRICAN $$

(Map p442; ☎33 821 0302; 101 Rue Moussé Diop; mains CFA4300-7600; ⊙noon-3pm & 7-10pm Mon-Sat) This friendly, always overflowing place serves up huge Senegalese and Cabo Ver-

dean plates to its loyal followers – note that it gets packed at lunch.

**★Le Lagon I** SEAFOOD $$$
(Map p442; ☎33 821 5322; Rte de la Corniche-Est; mains CFA9000-15,000) Perched on stilts over the bay, Le Lagon is one of Dakar's top seafood spots, with a spread of culinary treasures – oysters, sea urchins, chargrilled fish, pastas with mixed seafood. You can dine outside on the breezy waterside deck, or in the classy dining room, amid hanging swordfish, brass sailing instruments and a vintage diving suit.

**Estendera Vivier Beach** INTERNATIONAL $$$
(Map p444; ☎78 459 8181; www.facebook.com/estendera.vivierbeach; mains CFA6000-7500; ⏰10am-11pm Tue-Sun; 👪) A charming little eatery with tables overlooking the crashing waves, Estendera has a small, well-executed menu of seafood, grilled meats and Italian plates. Start off with barracuda carpaccio, then move on to seafood tagliatelle, chicken with porcini mushrooms or oven-baked lasagne.

## Drinking & Nightlife

**★Phare des Mamelles** BAR
(Map p444; ☎77 343 4242; www.pharedesmamelles.com; ⏰7pm-3am Thu-Sat, 10am-3pm Sun) On the hilltop in front of Dakar's iconic lighthouse, this open-air bar draws a dance-loving crowd on Friday nights, when it hosts live music jams. On Saturday nights DJs rule the roost (the cover for either night is CFA5000). At the moment, the Phare is one of the best places to be on a weekend night.

**Bayékou** COCKTAIL BAR
(Map p444; ☎77 631 3888; www.facebook.com/bayekou; Plage de N'Gor; ⏰6pm-1am Tue-Sun) Head upstairs to this stylish, open-sided drinking den near the beach for well-made cocktails, delicious sharing plates (including a tangy red tuna ceviche) and breezy views over the shore. There's also a blackboard menu of well-executed dishes like grilled octopus. It draws a mostly expat crowd. Occasional nights of DJs and live jazz.

**Duplex** CLUB
(Map p444; ☎33 820 9646; Rte de N'Gor; ⏰11pm-5am) One of the anchors of the Dakar club scene, Duplex draws a well-dressed crowd who come to show off their moves on the dance floor. Although it's mostly DJs on rotation here, the occasional live band here takes the stage on Friday or Saturday night.

## Entertainment

**★Institut Français Léopold Sédar Senghor** ARTS CENTRE
(Map p442; ☎33 823 0320; www.institutfrancais-senegal.com; 89 Rue Joseph Gomis) This

## Greater Dakar

**Top Sights**
1 Île de N'Gor ... B1

**Sights**
2 Plage de N'Gor ... B2
3 Plage de Virage ... C1
4 Plage de Yoff ... E1
5 Village des Arts ... E2

**Activities, Courses & Tours**
6 École Surf Attitude ... B2
Nautilus Diving ... (see 2)
7 Nouvelles Frontières ... C3

**Sleeping**
8 Hôtel du Phare ... C3
9 Keur Diame ... E1
10 La Demeure ... B2
11 La Maison d'Italie ... B1
Maison Abaka ... (see 2)
12 Malika Surf Camp ... D1
13 N'Gor Island Surf Camp ... B1
14 Quicksilver Boardriders Dakar ... B2
15 Via Via ... D1

**Eating**
16 Estendera Vivier Beach ... B2

**Drinking & Nightlife**
17 Bayékou ... B2
18 Duplex ... B2
19 Phare des Mamelles ... C3

**Entertainment**
20 Just 4 U ... D4
21 Thiossane ... E4

**Information**
22 Gambian Embassy ... E2
23 Ghanaian Embassy ... D4
Guinea-Bissau Embassy ... (see 23)
24 Guinean Embassy ... D4
25 Ivoirian Embassy ... D4
26 Malian Embassy ... D4
27 Mauritanian Embassy ... E4
28 Moroccan Embassy ... D4
29 US Embassy ... B2

spacious arts centre occupying a whole city block is one of the main hubs of cultural activity in Dakar. It features an open-air stage (a fantastic place to catch a live-music gig), a good cafe, and exhibition and cinema rooms, and also houses a couple of artists' workshops and shops in its vast garden.

**Just 4 U** LIVE MUSIC
(Map p444; ☎77 248 9799; Ave Cheikh Anta Diop; ⏰7pm-3.30am) If you only have time for one live-music venue, don't miss Just 4 U. The small stage of this outdoor restaurant has been graced by the greatest Senegalese and international stars, from jazz to rap to folk and reggae. There's a concert on most nights (best on Thursdays through Saturdays), and you often get to catch the big names. Note that Just 4 U is closed during Ramadan.

**Thiossane** LIVE MUSIC
(Map p444; ☎33 824 7078; Rue 10) Owned by Youssou N'Dour, one of Africa's most notable musicians and Senegal's tourism and culture minister, this legendary club is always packed and jamming to anything from mbalax to international beats. Unfortunately, the schedule can be erratic – phone ahead before heading over.

## Shopping

**Marché Sandaga** MARKET
(Map p442; cnr Ave Pompidou & Ave du Président Lamine Guèye; ⏰9am-5pm) In the endless sprawl of street stalls here you can buy just about anything (as long as no one steals your purse): you'll find tapestries, wood carvings, wildly patterned clothing, beaded jewellery and original paintings, among many other things.

## Information

### DANGERS & ANNOYANCES

- Dakar's notorious street hustlers and hard-to-shake-off traders do a pretty good job of turning any walk around town into mild punishment, particularly for women. Stride purposefully on and throw in a brief *bakhna* ('it's OK') and they'll eventually leave you alone.
- Many of them also double as pickpockets – be particularly vigilant at markets and in town.
- Muggings – often at knifepoint or from passing scooters – are not uncommon. Avoid walking around after dark. Trouble spots include the Petite Corniche (behind the presidential palace), the Rte de la Corniche-Ouest and the beaches.

### MEDICAL SERVICES

Hospitals are understaffed and underequipped; for faster service try a private clinic. Pharmacies are plentiful in Dakar; most are open 8am to

8pm Monday to Saturday and rotate with 24-hour shifts.

**Clinique de Cap** (Map p440; ☎33 889 0202; www.cliniqueducap.com; Ave Pasteur) One of the biggest private medical clinics in Dakar.

**Hôpital le Dantec** (Map p440; ☎33 889 3800; www.hopitaldantec.gouv.sn; 30 Ave Pasteur) A modern, full-service hospital in the Plateau.

**Hôpital Principal** (Map p440; ☎33 839 5050; www.hopitalprincipal.sn; 1 Ave Nelson Mandéla) Main hospital and emergency department.

**Pharmacie Guigon** (Map p442; ☎33 823 0333; 1 Ave du Président Lamine Guèye; 8am-11pm Mon-Sat) One of the best-stocked options.

### MONEY

ATM-equipped banks are never too far away in Dakar. Main branches are at Pl de l'Indépendance.

**BICIS** (Map p442; ☎33 839 0390; Pl de l'Indépendance; 9am-4pm Mon-Thu, to noon Fri)

**CBAO** (Map p442; ☎33 849 9300; Pl de l'Indépendance; 9am-4pm Mon-Thu, to noon Fri)

**SGBS** (Map p444; ☎33 842 5039; Rue de Kaolack; 10am-4pm Mon-Thu, to 1pm Fri)

**SGBS** (Map p442; ☎33 839 5500; 19 Ave Léopold Senghor; 9.30am-4pm Mon-Thu, to noon Fri)

### POST

**Main Post Office** (Map p442; ☎33 839 3400; Blvd el Haji Djily Mbaye; 7am-7pm Mon-Fri, 8am-5pm Sat)

**Post Office** (Map p442; ☎33 839 3400; Ave Pompidou)

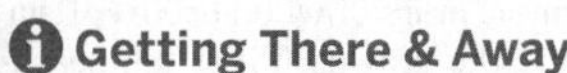

## Getting There & Away

### AIR

**Léopold Sédar Senghor International Airport** (DKR; Map p444; ☎24hr info line 33 869 5050; www.aeroport-dakar.com) is in Yoff. This is likely to be out of service when the new airport, **Aéroport International Blaise Diagne** (www.aibd.sn), opens in Ndiass, 50km southeast of Dakar. The airport is scheduled to open by 2018.

**Arc en Ciel** (Map p444; ☎33 820 2467; www.arcenciel-aviation.com) offers charter fights from Dakar to Bissau and Bubaque in the Arquipélago dos Bijagós.

### BOAT

Three ferries travel between Dakar and Ziguinchor (in the Casamance), with a total of four weekly departures in each direction (Tuesday, Thursday, Friday and Sunday). Buy your ticket in advance from the **office** (COSAMA; Map p444; ☎33 821 2900, 33 821 3434; 1 Blvd de la Libération, Gare Maritime; one-way CFA16,000-31,000) in Dakar's *gare maritime*.

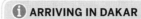

> **ARRIVING IN DAKAR**
>
> **Léopold Sédar Senghor International Airport, Dakar** Book transport through your hotel or guesthouse (which will charge CFA5000 and up to collect you from the airport). Otherwise, taxi touts line up along a fence just outside the airport exit. Pay no more than CFA5000 if going all the way across town to the Plateau, and less if going to Yoff, N'Gor or Les Almadies (in the ballpark of CFA3500).

### BUS & BUSH TAXI

Road transport for long-distance destinations leaves from the **Gare Routière Baux Maraîchers** (☎30 118 4644; Pikine) – a taxi from Place de l'Indépendance should cost around CFA3500. Main destinations include Mbour (CFA2000), Saint-Louis (CFA5000), Karang (at the Gambian border; CFA6000), Tambacounda (CFA10,000) and Ziguinchor (CFA10,000).

While ticket prices are fixed, you'll have to pay extra (and negotiate) over luggage charges, which could be CFA1000 to CFA5000.

### CAR & MOTORCYCLE

**Avis** (Map p444; ☎33 849 7755; www.avis.com; 8am-midnight) Car rental at the airport.

**Hertz** (Map p442; ☎33 889 8181; www.hertz.sn; 64 Rue Joseph Gomis) This rental agency is in the city centre; also has a branch at the airport, and at the hotel Fleur de Lys (p442).

## Getting Around

### BUS

**Dakar Dem Dikk** (www.demdikk.com) buses are a pretty good way of travelling cheaply; fares cost beween CFA150 and CFA300. In downtown, northeast of Place de l'Indépendance is a useful **DDD Bus Terminal** (Map p442; Ave de la Libération).

More frequent but less user-friendly are the white Ndiaga Ndiaye minivans and the iconic blue-yellow *cars rapides*, Dakar's battered, crammed and dangerously driven symbols of identity.

### CAR & MOTORCYCLE

Though he doesn't speak much English, **Adama Ba** (☎77 461 7108) is highly recommended for trips in and around Dakar and around the country; count on about CFA35,000 per day, plus fuel.

### TAXI

Taxis are the easiest way of getting around town. Rates are entirely negotiable. A short hop costs from CFA1000 upwards. Dakar centre to Point E is around CFA1500; it's up to CFA2500 from the centre to N'Gor and Yoff.

# AROUND DAKAR

## Île de Gorée

POP 1300

Ruled in succession by the Portuguese, Dutch, English and French, the historical, Unesco-designated Île de Gorée is enveloped by an almost eerie calm. There are no sealed roads and no cars on this island, just narrow alleyways with trailing bougainvilleas and colonial brick buildings with wrought-iron balconies – it's a living, visual masterpiece.

But Gorée's calm is not so much romantic as meditative, as the ancient, elegant buildings bear witness to the island's role in the Atlantic slave trade. The island is also home to an active artist community with small studios sprinkled around the island.

### Sights

**IFAN Historical Museum** MUSEUM
(Institut Fondamental d'Afrique Noire; 33 822 2003; adult/child CFA500/100; 10am-5pm Tue-Sun) Gives a glimpse of island (and regional) history dating back to the 5th century. Exhibitions cover cultural lore, megalithic sites, key figures in the resistance against European colonisers – and in room 9, the heartbreaking slave trade. Head upstairs for fabulous views of Dakar from the old fortress walls.

### Sleeping & Eating

**Hostellerie du Chevalier de Boufflers** GUESTHOUSE $
(33 822 5364; boufflers@live.fr; r CFA19,000-25,000; ) Set in one of Gorée's classic, elegant old homes, this places is mainly famous for its garden **restaurant** (mains CFA4500 to CFA8000) serving seafood-focused fare, but also offers five tastefully decorated rooms.

**Chez Valerie et Amy** GUESTHOUSE $$
(ASAO; 33 821 8195; www.csao.fr; 7 Rue St Joseph; r CFA15,000-45,000; ) Set in a picturesque Goréen home, this low-key guesthouse has four lovely rooms painted in rich colours and decorated with folk art. There's a **craft shop** below.

**Villa Castel** B&B $$
(77 263 6075; www.villacogelsgoree.com; Rue Castel; s/d/tr CFA35,000/40,000/45,000; ) Guests feel right at home in this charming, Belgian-run guesthouse with attractive rooms opening on to a courtyard garden. The roof deck makes a fine vantage point for sunsets and stargazing.

**L'Amiraute** SEAFOOD $$
(Rue St-Germain; mains CFA4000-6500; 11am-8pm) Escape the crowds filling the beach-side eateries at this peaceful spot just past

### THE SLAVE HOUSE

Île de Gorée was an important trading station during the 18th and 19th centuries, and many merchants built houses in which they would live or work in the upper storey and store their human cargo on the lower floor.

**La Maison des Esclaves** (Slave House; Rue St-Germain; CFA600; 10.30am-noon & 2.30-6.30pm Tue-Sun) is one of the last remaining 18th-century buildings of this type on Gorée. It was built in 1786 and renovated in 1990 with French assistance, with its famous 'doorway to nowhere' opening directly from the storeroom on to the sea.

Walking around the dimly lit dungeons, you can begin to imagine the suffering of the people held here. It is this emotive illustration that really describes La Maison des Esclaves as a whole.

The island's precise status as a slave-trading station is hotly debated. But the number of slaves transported from here isn't what matters in the debate around Gorée. The island and museum stand as a melancholy reminder of the suffering the Atlantic slave trade inflicted on African people.

the Maison des Esclaves. You can sit on the outside terrace overlooking the sea and enjoy decent plates of fresh seafood.

## Getting There & Away

A **ferry** (Liaison Maritime Dakar-Gorée; Map p440; ☎33 849 7961, mobile 78 120 9090; https://lmdg.wordpress.com; Gare Maritime, 21 Blvd de la Libération; adult/child return CFA5200/2700) runs every one or two hours from the *gare maritime* (passenger port) in Dakar to Gorée (20 minutes). Departures are roughly every hour or two from 6.15am (7am Sundays) to after midnight.

# PETITE CÔTE & SINÉ-SALOUM DELTA

The 150km Petite Côte stretches south from Dakar and is one of Senegal's best beach areas. Where the Siné and Saloum Rivers meet the tidal waters of the Atlantic Ocean, the coast is broken into a stunning area of mangrove swamps, lagoons, forests and sand islands, forming part of the magnificent 180-sq-km Siné-Saloum Delta.

## Mbour & Saly

POP 280,000 (COMBINED)

Eighty kilometres south of Dakar, Mbour is the main town on the Petite Côte and the region's most vibrant and important fishing centre. Nearby Saly, with its strip of big ocean-front hotels, is the perfect corner for a beach holiday of soaking up the sun and sipping cocktails.

Mbour's busy, slightly nauseating fish market on the beach, where the catch is immediately gutted and dispatched, is a sight to behold.

### Sights

**Réserve Naturelle Somone** NATURE RESERVE
(Rte Ngaparou-Somone, Somone; CFA1500) This serene 700-hectare reserve is a great spot for seeing some of the avian wildlife along the coast. Pelicans, egrets, herons and flamingos are among the commonly observed species. The best way to see it all is on a short boat trip; from the beach beside the Royal Decameron Baobab, guides ask for about CFA6500 per person (for a roughly one-hour trip), including the CFA1500 admission fee to the reserve.

### Sleeping & Eating

★**Ferme de Saly & Les Amazones** GUESTHOUSE, APARTMENT $$
(☎77 638 4790; www.farmsaly.com; Saly; s/d with half board CFA16,500/33,000, apt per person with half board CFA27,000; ) At this iconic place on the beach you'll find appealing rooms and cottages, great food and a hearty welcome from host Jean-Paul. The lush grounds and sizeable swimming pool make for some leisurely days, though you can also arrange excursions.

**Au Petit Jura** GUESTHOUSE $$
(☎33 957 3767; www.aupetitjura.ch; Saly; d CFA38,000; ) Au Petit Jura is a small, charming, Swiss-run guesthouse located just a short stroll to the beach. Days can be spent lounging poolside, strolling the beach or exploring nearby villages on an excursion offered by the guesthouse. Good meals are available, too.

**Tama Lodge** LODGE $$$
(☎33 957 0040; www.tamalodge.com; Mbour; s/d from CFA80,000/105,000, with half board from CFA95,000/137,000; ) Scattered across a peaceful beachfront property, these nine exquisitely designed bungalows are made of local materials and set with carvings and textiles from across Africa. The open-air thatched-roof restaurant serves up some of the best meals along the coast.

**Le Soleil de Saly** AFRICAN $$
(☎33 958 2865; www.lesoleildesaly.com; Rte de la Somone; mains CFA4000-6000; ⏲noon-11pm) The buzzing new favourite in town has a central location on the main drag and serves up tasty grilled meat and fish dishes, with live music three nights a week (Thursday through Saturday). Owner Mamadou Basse is easy to spot: look for the kind-hearted man in the fedora.

★**La Guingette** FRENCH $$$
(☎77 158 0808; http://laguinguettedesaly.simplesite.com; Saly; mains from CFA6000; ⏲7.30-10pm Thu-Tue & noon-2.30pm Sun) Tucked down a small lane near the entrance to Saly, La Guingette earns rave reviews for its delectable, market-fresh cuisine and its colourful garden setting. Reserve ahead.

### Getting There & Away

There are plenty of transport options heading down the coast, including *sept-place* taxis and minibuses. Things get a little more complicated

WORTH A TRIP

### JOAL-FADIOUT

Joal is a sleepy fishing town at the proverbial end of the road south of Mbour. Nearby mangroves and placid waters lend an air of peace to the settlement. It's also the gateway to Fadiout, a small island made of clam and oyster shells (even the houses, streets and cemeteries!), reached by an impressive wooden bridge. It's dreamy to wander around the island's narrow alleys, admire the shell-world and pop into artisan workshops dotted around.

A guide is required to visit Fadiout; you can find them at the foot of the bridge leading to the island. The going rate is around CFA5000 for a small group.

Minibuses go to/from Mbour (CFA800, one hour) and Palmarin (around CFA1200, 1½ hours). In the morning you can catch an early bus direct to Dakar leaving at 5am or 6am (CFA1500, three hours).



reaching Ndangane and Palmarin, requiring a transfer and waiting time at key transport hubs on the main highway. To get to Toubakouta and Missirah, you'll have to go Kaolack first and transfer from there.

# Palmarin

POP 7200

Palmarin, with its soft lagoons, tall palm groves and labyrinthine creeks, is one of Senegal's most underrated destinations. It's not one community, but rather a string of tiny villages scattered for more than 12km along the coast. The big draw is enjoying a peaceful, relatively empty stretch of beachfront.

## Sleeping

**Sangomar** BUNGALOW $

(☎77 536 4425; moussengomar59@gmail.com; Palmarin Djifer; s/d CFA12,600/21,200, with half-board CFA19,600/31,200, camping per person CFA2500) In the village of Djifer, Sangomar has pleasant bungalows made of native materials that are set amid eucalyptus and palms and front on to a calm beach (which is clean for Djifer, though there are better options further north along the peninsula). The friendly host offers walking or pirogue excursions.

**Djidjack** LODGE $$

(☎33 949 9619; www.djidjack.com; Palmarin Nguedj; bungalow s CFA21,500, d 23,000-33,000, camping per person CFA3500; ) Run by a Swiss couple, welcoming Djidjack has round bungalows with conical thatch ceilings, African artwork and a small terrace. Budget travellers can also camp (mattress and mosquito net provided).

**★Lodge des Collines de Niassam** LODGE $$$

(☎77 639 0639; www.niassam.com; Palmarin Ngallou; with half board s CFA85,000-98,000, d CFA118,000-140,000; ) One of Senegal's most original *campements* lies in a pristine setting on the edge of a lagoon. You can sleep in atmospheric tree houses that cling to the mighty branches of baobabs, in elegant bungalows perched on stilts over the water or in colourful savannah rooms with flower-trimmed terraces.

There's an excellent restaurant, and all manner of tours (and transfers) are available.

## Getting There & Away

Palmarin is most easily reached by minibus from Mbour, via Joal-Fadiout and Sambadia (where you may have to change). The fare from Joal-Fadiout to Sambadia is CFA700 (45 minutes), and from Sambadia to Palmarin it's about CFA500 (30 minutes).

# Toubakouta & Missirah

POP 9000

Toubakouta is a fantastically calm and pretty spot in the south of the Siné-Saloum Delta, and is one of the country's best places for birdwatching. Most guesthouses offer excursions exploring wildlife-filled wetlands, visiting sacred baobabs, and getting a taste of Mandinka village life.

South of Toubakouta, Missirah is the point of entry to the **Parc National du Delta du Saloum** (www.deltadusaloum.com; CFA2000).

For those not heading to wildlife parks in other parts of Africa, the 60-sq-km **Fathala Wildlife Reserve & Lodge** (☎70 986 1993; www.fathala.com; self-drive tour CFA21,000) might be worth adding to your itinerary. This reserve was created in 2006 as a habitat for the western giant eland, and today includes troops of this critically endangered antelope, as well as giraffes, rhinos, warthogs, buffaloes and several monkey species. While it's pricey to visit, it can nevertheless be thrilling to see these animals in the (semi-)wild.

### Sleeping

**Keur Bamboung** GUESTHOUSE $
(77 510 8013; www.oceanium.org; r per person with full board CFA22,000) Managed by local villagers on the island of Sipo, Keur Bamboung sits in a stunning location in the heart of a 68-sq-km protected marine reserve. Things are simple and green, with lodging in wooden bungalows near the water's edge. Phone to arrange pirogue pick-up from Toubakouta; it's a 30-minute boat ride to Keur Bamboung, followed by transfer in a donkey cart.

**Keur Thierry** GUESTHOUSE $
(77 439 8605; www.keurthierry.com; Toubakouta; s/d/tr with fan CFA13,500/17,000/26,000; ) Offers simple, good-value rooms set around a small, shell-strewn courtyard (rooms with air-con cost an extra CFA2500). Thierry has loads of info about the area, and can happily arrange fishing trips and other excursions. The meals here are decent.

★**Keur Saloum** HOTEL $$
(33 948 7715; www.keursaloum.com; Toubakouta; s/d/tr incl breakfast from CFA26,000/38,000/45,000; ) This Belgian-run lodge offers quality accommodation in attractive bungalows, nicely outfitted and set amid lush grounds. But it's all the extras that have earned Keur Saloum such a solid reputation over the years, with a spacious restaurant and deck overlooking the mangroves, an enticing pool and an impressive array of tours.

### Getting There & Around

You can catch *sept-place* taxis heading north or south between Kaolack and Karang. Bank on about CFA2500 one-way to either Kaolack (1½ hours) or Karang (45 minutes).

Taxis-brousses (bush taxis) make infrequent runs between Toubakouta and Missirah (from around CFA500, one hour). A private taxi from Toubakouta to Missirah costs around CFA5000 (45 minutes).

## Toubab Dialao

POP 2500

Located around 55km south of the capital, Toubab Dialao (also spelt Toubab Dialaw) makes for a convenient getaway when *dakarois* need a break from the big city. The beach is the star, a pretty stretch of golden sands backed by low cliffs strung with homes and a few guesthouses. The low-key village has an arty bohemian vibe, with colourfully decorated houses and nights of drumming, dancing and theatre. With classes and activities on offer at one of the coast's most imaginatively designed guesthouses and cultural spaces, it's easy to spend more time here than anticipated enjoying the creative life.

### Sleeping

★**Espace Sobo Badè** GUESTHOUSE $
(33 836 0356; sobobade1@hotmail.com; dm/s/d CFA5000/13,000/22,000; ) Perched over a wave-battered stretch of coastline, Sobo Badè has the wondrous look of a Gaudì creation, with its imaginative brickwork, shell-lined archways, steeply pitched thatched roofs, and mosaic-covered fountains and railings. Haitian-born artist Gerard Chenet (b 1927) is the visionary behind this imaginative space, which has become a magnet for artists, musicians and other creative types.

### Getting There & Away

Collective *sept-place* taxis run from Dakar's *gare routière* (around CFA600 per person, 1½ hours). From the same station, you can also find buses to Toubab Dialaw, though you will likely have to change at Diamniado.

Once the new airport opens, you'll be less than 20km away from the terminal – meaning it'll be faster to come straight here rather than going to Dakar.

# NORTHERN SENEGAL

## Saint-Louis

POP 178,000

With its crumbling colonial architecture, horse-drawn carts and peaceful ambience, West Africa's first French settlement has a unique historical charm – so much so that it's been a Unesco World Heritage Site since 2000. The old town centre sits on an island in the Senegal River, but the city sprawls into Sor on the mainland, and on to the Langue de Barbarie, where you'll find the lively fishing community of Guet N'Dar.

The island is reached via the 500m-long Pont Faidherbe, a feat of 19th-century engineering.

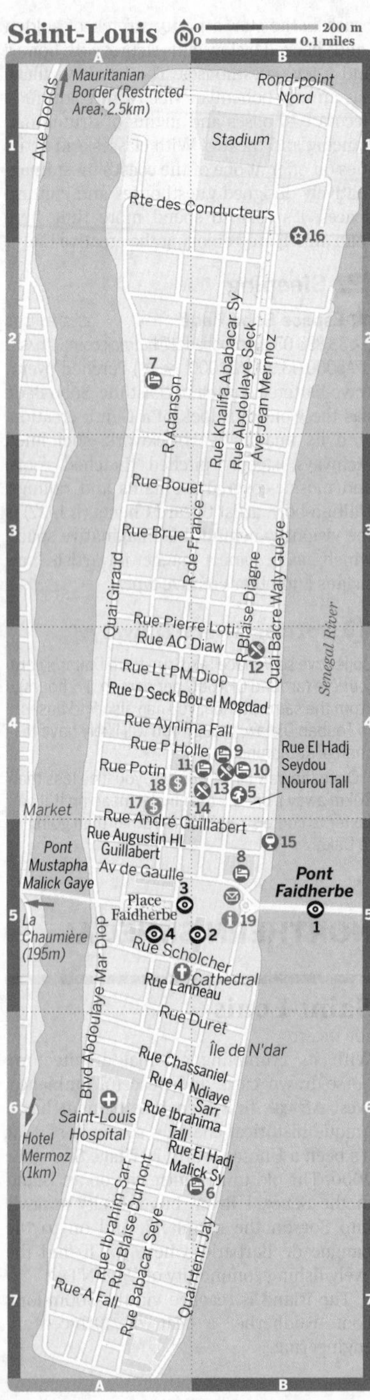


## Saint-Louis

**Top Sights**
1 Pont Faidherbe .......... B5

**Sights**
2 Governor's Palace .......... B5
3 Place Faidherbe .......... A5
4 Rogniat Casernes .......... A5

**Activities, Courses & Tours**
5 Bou El Mogdad .......... B4

**Sleeping**
6 Au Fil du Fleuve .......... B6
7 Cafe des Arts .......... A2
8 Hotel de la Poste .......... B5
9 Jamm .......... B4
10 La Maison Rose .......... B4
11 Siki Hotel .......... B4

**Eating**
12 La Kora .......... B4
13 La Linguère .......... B4
14 Le Reveil .......... B4

**Drinking & Nightlife**
15 Flamingo .......... B5

**Entertainment**
16 Quai des Arts .......... B1

**Information**
17 BICIS .......... A4
18 CBAO .......... A4
Sahel Découverte .......... (see 5)
19 Syndicat d'Initiative .......... B5

## Sights & Activities

**★ Pont Faidherbe** BRIDGE

Transferred to Saint-Louis in 1897, the Pont Faidherbe is the city's most significant landmark. The metal arches of this bridge linking Saint-Louis to the mainland were designed by Gustav Eiffel and originally built to cross the Danube. You'll cross its steel planks when driving into town.

**Parc National de la Langue de Barbarie** NATIONAL PARK

(CFA5000, guide CFA3000; 8am-sunset) This park includes the far southern tip of the Langue de Barbarie peninsula, the estuary of the Senegal River (which contains two small islands) and a section of the mainland on the other side of the estuary. The park covers a total area of 20 sq km, and is home to numerous water birds, swelled from November to April by migrant birds from Europe.

**Place Faidherbe** SQUARE
With its statue of the French governor who led the colonial expansion eastwards and initiated many ambitious infrastructural projects, this square sits adjacent to several intact 19th-century houses, including the **Governor's Palace** (Place Faidherbe), and on its north and south side, former barracks known as the **Rogniat Casernes** (Place Faidherbe). Next to the Governor's Palace, you'll find a lovely 1828 **cathedral** (Rue de l'Eglise; irregular hours) with a neoclassical facade worth admiring.

**Bou El Mogdad** CRUISE
(33 961 5689; www.bouelmogdad.com; Rue Blaise Diagne; 6-day cruise per person from €730) The 52m tourist boat *Bou El Mogdad* sails from Saint-Louis, travelling along the scenic Senegal River en route to Podor with stops and excursions along the way. Departures happen four times a month (twice a month from each direction) from late October to early May. Book through Sahel Découverte (p454).

## Festivals & Events

**Saint-Louis Jazz Festival** MUSIC
(www.saintlouisjazz.org; May) The most internationally renowned festival in West Africa is held annually in early or mid May and attracts jazz greats from around the world. The main event usually happens at the **Quai des Arts** (33 961 5656; Ave Jean Mermoz; 7pm-late) or on an open-air stage in Place Faidherbe, though there are fringe events all over town.

**Les Fanals** CULTURAL
(Dec) Celebrated on one night during the last week of December between Christmas and New Year's Eve, this historic lantern procession has its roots in the lantern-lit marches to midnight Mass once made by the *signares*. Today it evokes Saint-Louisian history and reaffirms the town's unique identity.

## Sleeping

**Zebrabar** BUNGALOW $
(77 638 1862, 33 962 0019; www.zebrabar.net; Mouit; campsites per person CFA5000, s CFA7000-22,000, d CFA13,000-32,000; ) Around 22km south of Saint-Louis, this peaceful spot makes a great base for excursions into the Parc National de la Langue de Barbarie. Accommodation is available in simple huts and spacious bungalows spread across a large terrain. The restaurant with open-air tables is a fine spot for meeting other travellers.

**Cafe des Arts** GUESTHOUSE $
(77 613 8914; Quai Giraud; dm CFA5000, r CFA10,000-15,000) This tiny guesthouse in the north of the island has a handful of simple but brightly painted rooms; the best has a balcony that opens on to the waterfront. There's also a roof deck, but not much shade up top. It's a good value if you're on a budget.

**Hotel de la Poste** HOTEL $$
(33 961 1118; www.hoteldelaposte saintlouis.com; s/d/tr/ste from CFA37,000/44,000/56,000/75,000; ) Step back in time at this elegant 36-room hotel, which first opened its doors back in 1850 and was a favourite with aviator Jean Mermoz and other Aéropostale pilots. Old photos adorn the walls of the dapper guest rooms, and the vintage bar is a great place for a drink.

**Au Fil du Fleuve** GUESTHOUSE $$
(77 379 9534; www.fildufleuve.com; 15 Rue El Hadj Malick Sy; r CFA56,000-62,000; ) In the southern half of Saint-Louis, this grand 19th-century merchant's house has been transformed into a lovely boutique B&B, with three unique rooms, each displaying works by a different African artist, and a lovely courtyard. The friendly host Marie-Caroline has a wealth of information about the island, and serves up fabulous breakfasts (and dinners on request).

**Siki Hotel** BOUTIQUE HOTEL $$
(33 961 6069; www.hotelsenegal.net; Rue Abdoulaye Seck; s/d from CFA35,000/44,000; ) A stylish Spanish-owned option in the centre, Siki Hotel has attractive rooms with wide plank floors and attractive wood furnishings. It's set in the former childhood home of Senegalese boxing champ Battling Siki. There's a first-rate tapas restaurant on the ground floor.

**Jamm** GUESTHOUSE $$
(Chez Yves Lamour; 77 443 4765; www.jamm-saintlouis.com; Rue Paul Holle; s/d incl breakfast CFA56,000/66,000; ) One of Saint-Louis' most beautifully restored houses offers four tiled and brick-walled rooms with ceilings high enough to impress even regular churchgoers. Every tiny decorative detail has been restored with care.

**La Maison Rose** HOTEL $$
(33 938 2222; www.lamaisonrose.net; Rue Blaise Diagne; s/d/ste from CFA54,000/67,000/93,000; ) Old-time elegance meets

contemporary luxuries in one of Saint-Louis' most famous old buildings: every room and suite here is unique, though they all exude a spirit of old-time comfort. The classic furniture and wonderful artworks on display add to the romance.

## Eating

**La Linguère** AFRICAN $

(☎33 961 3949; Rue Blaise Diagne; mains CFA1500-4000; ⊙noon-3.30pm & 7-11pm) A reliable local eatery that serves up tasty *poulet yassa, thiéboudienne* and other Senegalese classics. Friendly service and attention to details (and cleanliness) makes all the difference.

★**La Kora** AFRICAN $$

(Chez Peggy; ☎77 637 1244; www.facebook.com/lakorachezpeggy; 402 Rue Blaise Diagne; mains CFA4000-8500; ⊙11.30am-3pm & 6-11.30pm Mon-Sat, 6-11.30pm Sun) La Kora has earned a stellar reputation for its fabulous cooking, the warm welcome from Peggy (the proprietor) and staff, and the lovely setting – complete with a baobab tree in the vine-trimmed courtyard and a stylish dining room slung with old photos of Saint-Louis. La Kora also hosts occasional concerts.

**Le Reveil** SEAFOOD, AFRICAN $$

(☎77 701 9682; Rue Abdoulaye Seck; mains CFA3000-4000; ⊙10am-6pm & 7-10pm) A friendly, very welcoming restaurant tucked away in the back of the bar Ambuscade, Le Reveil serves up tasty fresh seafood. The *fricassé de la mer* (a kind of mixed seafood plate) and coconut shrimp curry are both first-rate.

## Drinking & Entertainment

**Flamingo** BAR

(☎33 961 1118; Quai Bacre Waly Guèye; ⊙11am-2am) Any night out in this town starts at the pool-adorned riverside bar and restaurant Flamingo. Always packed, it's Saint-Louis' best place for live music – and not a bad place for a meal (mains from CFA5500) around sunset.

**Meyazz Club** LIVE MUSIC

(☎33 916 6451; Route de Khor, Sor; from CFA1000; ⊙8pm-late Wed, 10pm-late Thu-Sat) The best new venue for live music is in Sor – well worth the taxi trip over if a concert is happening. Music is wide-ranging, from African rhythms and mbalax to reggae and global beats, and it draws a well-dressed, dance-loving crowd. In late 2016 the open-air club even hosted its first annual world-music festival, featuring flamenco, Cuban jazz and Afrobeat.

## Information

**BICIS** (☎33 961 1053; Rue de France; ⊙7.45am-12.15pm & 1.40-3.45pm Mon-Thu, 7.45am-1pm & 2.40-3.45pm Fri) Bank.

**CBAO** (☎33 938 2552; Rue Khalifa Ababacar Sy; ⊙8.15am-5.15pm Mon-Fri) Also has a Western Union office.

**Post Office** (Rue du Général de Gaulle; ⊙9am-4pm Mon-Fri) The art-deco building opposite the Hôtel de la Poste.

**Sahel Découverte** (☎33 961 5689; www.saheldecouverte.com; Rue Blaise Diagne; ⊙8.30am-1pm & 3-6pm Mon-Fri, 9am-1pm Sat) Travel agency. Quite simply the best company for exploring the northern region.

**Saint-Louis Hospital** (☎33 938 2400; Blvd Abdoulaye Mar Diop) Has an accident and emergency department.

**Syndicat d'Initiative** (☎33 961 2455; www.saintlouisdusenegal-tourisme.com; Gouvernance; ⊙9am-noon & 2.30-5pm) A haven of regional information with excellent tours.

# Parc National des Oiseaux du Djoudj

With almost 300 species of bird, this 160-sq-km **park** (☎33 961 8621; admission CFA5000 pirogue/car/guide CFA4000/5000/6000; ⊙7am-dusk Nov-Apr) is one of the most important bird sanctuaries in the world. Flamingos, pelicans and waders are most plentiful, and large numbers of migrating birds travel here in November. The lush setting is no less impressive: these vast wetlands comprise lakes, streams, ponds, fords and sandbanks.

The park is best explored by pirogue. Boats trips can be arranged at the park entrance or at the hotels.

The large **Hôtel du Djoudj** (☎33 963 8702; www.hotel-djoudj.com; r CFA31,000; ⊙Nov-May; ❄📶🏊), near the park headquarters, has comfy rooms and a very inviting swimming pool. It offers regular boat trips, and you can also arrange walking excursions and 4WD trips.

The park is 25km off the main road; there's no public transport. You can either negotiate a private taxi from Saint-Louis (from CFA25,000, 90 minutes) or join an organised tour, such as one offered by Sahel Découverte.

# CENTRAL SENEGAL

## Tambacounda

POP 86,000

The junction town Tambacounda is all about dust, sizzling temperatures and lines of traffic heading in all directions. It's a jumping-off point for Mali, Guinea and The Gambia and is a fine place to base yourself to visit the Parc National de Niokolo-Koba. There's not much to the city, and few foreign visitors linger here.

### Sleeping & Eating

**Brasari** GUESTHOUSE **$**

(☎33 981 1102; s/d/tr CFA16,000/22,000/27,000; ❄📶) A welcome addition to Tomba, Brasari is a compact property on the main highway through town, with rooms set in freestanding round buildings. Each has clean African art on the walls and a neat appearance, though there's no hot water. A new restaurant was also in the works when we passed through.

**Oasis Oriental Club** HOTEL **$$**

(☎33 981 1824; Rte de Kaolack; s/d incl breakfast from CFA24,000/29,000, ste CFA45,000-82,000; P❄📶🏊) Try Oasis Oriental Club for some comfort and service. It has attractive rooms set in bungalows surrounding a pool and restaurant. It's outside of town, a few kilometres west of the centre (on the left when arriving from Dakar).

### Getting There & Away

If you're travelling on to Mali, you get your *sept-place* taxi to Kidira (CFA4000, three hours) at Garage Kothiary, on the eastern side of town. Vehicles to other destinations go from the larger *gare routière* four blocks west of the market.

## Parc National de Niokolo-Koba

This biologically rich national park is home to a spectacular array of flora and fauna, with some 350 bird species and 80 mammal species spread across a vast reserve in south-eastern Senegal. Lions, leopards, baboons, hippos and antelope are all found (though not always easily spotted) here. Its terrain encompasses dry savannah, riparian forest and various waterways, including the Gambia River. Sadly, a lack of resources have left the park poorly maintained, so you'll have to anticipate bad access roads and rustic facilities.

The park is inaccessible in the wet months (June to October). The entrance fee gives you access for 24 hours. You get your obligatory guide (CFA10,000) at the entrance gate.

If you want to stay in the national park, **Hotel Sementi** (☎33 984 1136; r from CFA30,000) is your best bet, with lodging in simple rooms and decent thatched-roof bungalows. There's a pleasant terrace with views of the Gambia River, and meals can be arranged.

You will need a vehicle to enter the park. It's best to hire a 4WD (per day around CFA90,000) in Tambacounda. Enquire at the gare routière or at the hotels in the city.

# CASAMANCE

With its lush tropical landscapes watered by the graceful, winding Casamance River, this area seems far from Dakar and its surroundings in every sense. Between the sleepy capital, Ziguinchor, and the wide, sandy beaches of Cap Skirring, the banks of the Casamance River are dotted with tiny, community *campements* that nestle between mangroves and lagoons. You'll find plenty of reason to linger here, whether basking on sandy shorelines, overnighting on forest-covered islands or taking in the beat of traditional villages – all of which are the proud homeland of the fascinating and fiercely independent Diola people.

## Ziguinchor

POP 174,000

With its old houses, tree-lined streets and busy markets, this former colonial centre exudes real atmosphere. It's worth spending a night or two here to feel the pulse of this tropical, mangrove-fringed city before rushing off to the coast.

Ziguinchor is the largest town in southern Senegal, and the main access point for travel in the Casamance region.

### Sights

**Alliance Franco-Sénégalaise** CULTURAL CENTRE

(☎33 991 2823; www.afziguinchor.org; Ave Djignabo; suggested donation CFA1000; ⏲9am-7pm Mon-Sat) This is easily Ziguinchor's most stunning building, a giant *case à impluvium* (a large, round traditional house) decorated with blindingly busy South African Ndebele and Casamance patterns. Inside are exhibitions, a large concert hall (shows take place at least once a week) and a welcoming restaurant and bar (with a weekday lunch special for CFA1000).

## Courses

**Africa Batik** ART
(☎77 653 4936) Offers batik-making courses of varying duration; inquire for rates. You can also browse Mamadou Cherif Diallo's colourful creations for sale – which make brilliant souvenirs to bring home from the Casamance.

## Sleeping

**Le Flamboyant** HOTEL $
(☎33 991 2223; www.casamance.info; Rue de France; r CFA18,000-20,000; ) In a central location, Le Flamboyant offers comfort well above the price you pay. The clean, well-equipped rooms open on to a small flower- and palm-filled courtyard and swimming pool. The decent on-site restaurant and kindly staff add to the value.

**Le Perroquet** GUESTHOUSE $
(☎33 991 2329; www.hotel-le-perroquet.com; Rue du Commerce; s/d CFA11,000/13,000, with view 13,000/15,000) Dozens of yellow-billed storks attract you with their noisy chatter to Zig's favourite budget place. Invest in an upstairs room for the small balconies with river views. The friendly restaurant is a fine spot for early evening drinks.

**Hotel Kadiandoumagne** HOTEL $$
(☎33 938 8000; www.hotel-kadiandoumagne.com; Rue du Commerce; s/d from CFA30,000/38,000; ) Never mind the tongue-twister of a name – this place ticks all the boxes, with attractive, handsomely furnished rooms overlooking the river, an appealing pool and ample outdoor space for lounging, dining and drinking. Good place to book excursions as well.

## Eating

**Le Erobon** AFRICAN $$
(☎33 991 2788; Rue du Commerce; mains CFA2000-4000; 8am-1am) This humble outdoor eatery is highly recommended. You can come here any time of day for grilled fish, carefully spiced and served with a sea view. The ambience is wonderfully relaxed and sometimes includes live music.

**Le Kassa** AFRICAN $$
(☎33 991 1311; Rond-Point Jean-Paul II; mains CFA3000-7500; 8am-1am) Ziguinchor's best-known dining spot has a plant-filled courtyard and classic cooking – the Senegalese dishes are best. The kitchen stays open late and there's live music some nights.

## Information

**CBAO** (Rue de France; 9am-3pm Mon-Fri) Advances on credit cards and ATM.

**French Honorary Consul** (☎33 991 2223; www.ambafrance-sn.org; Rue de France) Across from the hotel Le Flamboyant.

**Guinea-Bissau Consulate** (☎77 512 6497; 8.30am-2pm Mon-Fri) It's hard to find the consulate on your own: take a taxi here (around CFA200).

**Hôpital de la Paix** (☎33 991 9800; Ave Djiniabo Bassene) A new facility that opened in 2015. It's a few kilometres south of the centre.

**Office de Tourisme** (☎77 544 0332; www.casamance-tourisme.sn; Rue du Général de Gaulle; 8am-1pm & 3-6.30pm Mon-Sat Nov-Apr; ) In the town centre, this is one of the best-informed tourism offices in the country. Staff can help arrange village and birdwatching tours and other excursions (even one- or two-week guided trips). You can purchase Casamance maps, and staff have lists of artisans who make and sell handicrafts. Free wi-fi.

**SGBS** (Rue du Général de Gaulle; 9am-4pm Mon-Thu, to 1pm Fri) Change or withdraw money here; there's an ATM.

## Getting There & Around

### AIR

**Groupe Transair** (☎33 865 2565; www.groupetransair.sn) flies twice daily between Dakar and Ziguinchor (one-way/return about CFA65,000/115,000).

**Ziguinchor Airport** (☎33 991 1334) is in the south of the city, about 4.5km south of the waterfront.

### BOAT

There are four weekly departures each way on long, overnight journey between Dakar and Ziguinchor. The voyage takes 14 to 18 hours.

Buy your ticket (CFA16,000 to CFA31,000 one-way) in advance and in person from the *gare maritime* (passenger port). You can also buy tickets through Diambone Voyages based in Ziguinchor – a good option if you're overseas, as ferries can book up.

### SHARED TAXIS & MINIBUS

The *gare routière* is to the east of the city centre. There are frequent *sept-place* taxis to Dakar

## Ziguinchor

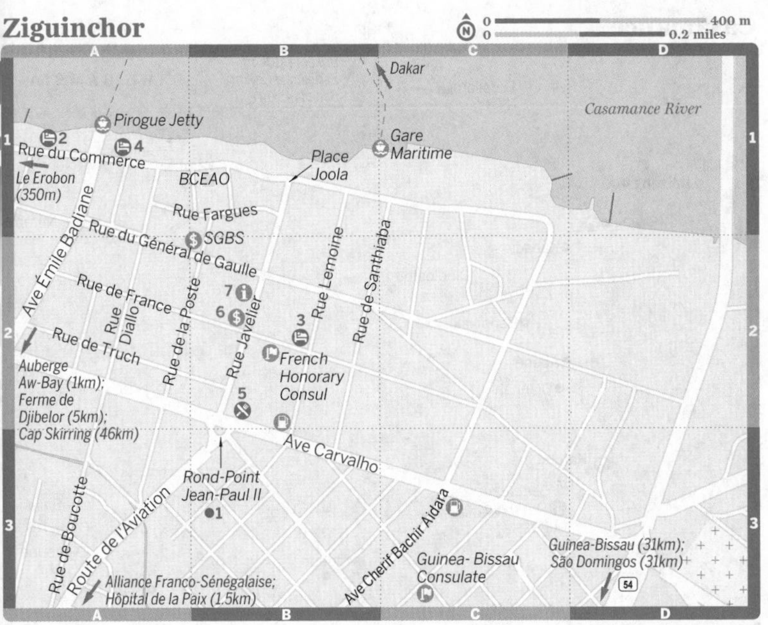


### Ziguinchor

**Activities, Courses & Tours**
1 Africa Batik ....... B3

**Sleeping**
2 Hotel Kadiandoumagne ....... A1
3 Le Flamboyant ....... B2
4 Le Perroquet ....... A1

**Eating**
5 Le Kassa ....... B2

**Information**
6 CBAO ....... B2
7 Office de Tourisme ....... B2

(CFA10,000 plus luggage, minimum 10 hours, 454km) and Cap Skirring (CFA2000, 1¾ hours).

You can also catch a minibus here to Oussouye (CFA1000, one hour).

To get anywhere around town by private taxi costs CFA500 (CFA700 after midnight).

# Cap Skirring

POP 2300

The beaches at Cap Skirring are some of the finest in West Africa – and better still, they're usually empty. While there isn't a lot happening here culturally (aside from weekend nights of live music), Cap Skirring makes a fine base for a few days of unwinding. You can also alternate days on the beach with exploring traditional Diola villages to the east, or opt for some of the many activities on offer, including kayaking and mountain biking.

## Sleeping

**La Tortue Bleue** GUESTHOUSE $

(☎77 635 1399; www.latortuebleue.org; s/d/tr CFA15,000/18,000/24,000; wifi) Guests feel right at home in this delightful, three-room spot run by a Belgian-Senegalese couple. Brightly painted and well-equipped rooms overlook a flower-filled garden, and meals and excursions are available. It's about a 10-minute walk from the beach.

**Le Paradise** HOTEL $

(☎33 993 5129; capskirringparadise@hotmail.fr; r with fan/air-con from CFA15,000/20,000, r with shared bathroom CFA7000; air-con wifi) On the coastal road about 2km south of the village, welcoming Le Paradise has clean, well-maintained rooms – both rustic (in a traditional *case à impluvium)* and comfy (tiled with air-con and sea views). Plus you can organise tours, eat well (mains CFA3500 to CFA5000) and enjoy perfect beach access.

# Casamance

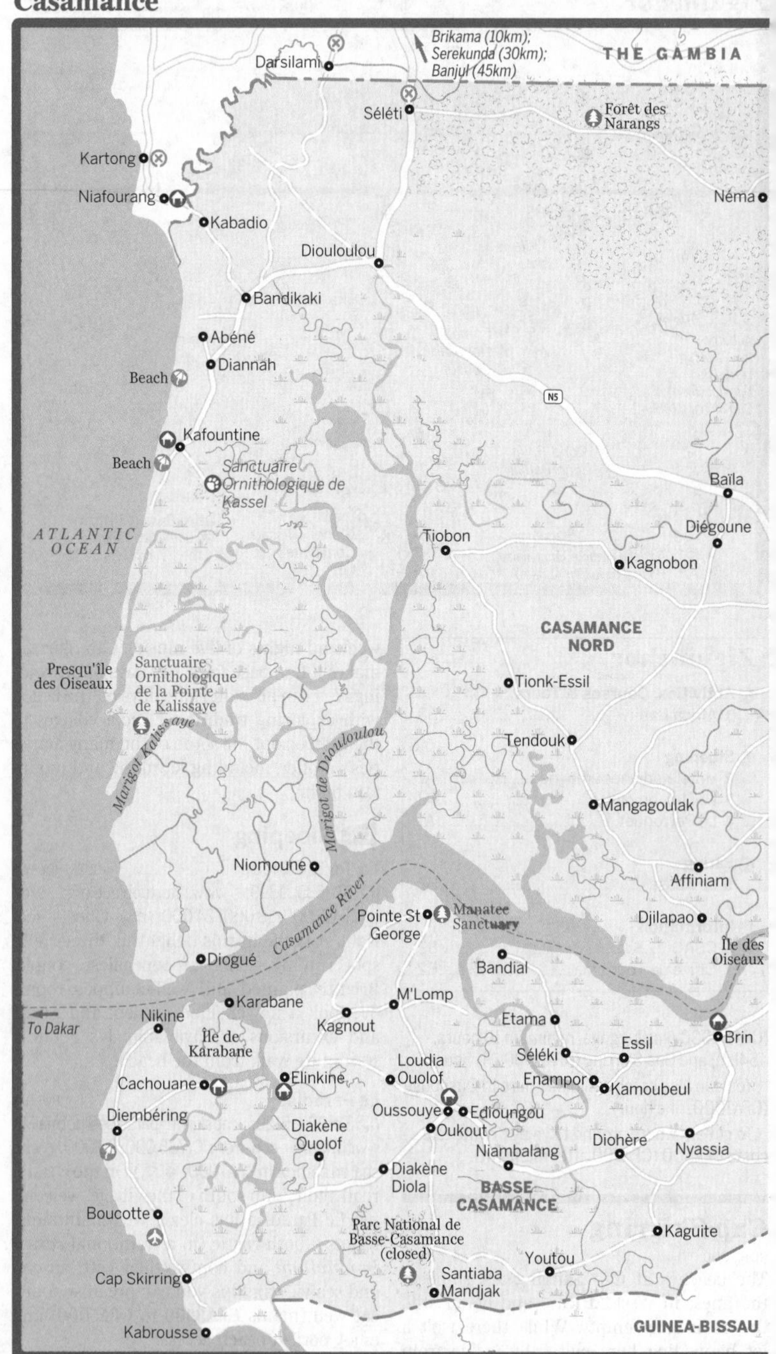

Brikama (10km);
Serekunda (30km);
Banjul (45km)
THE GAMBIA
Darsilami
Séléti
Forêt des Narangs
Kartong
Niafourang
Kabadio
Némа
Diouloulou
Bandikaki
Abéné
Diannah
Beach
N5
Kafountine
Beach
Sanctuaire Ornithologique de Kassel
Baïla
ATLANTIC OCEAN
Tiobon
Diégoune
Kagnobon
CASAMANCE NORD
Presqu'île des Oiseaux
Sanctuaire Ornithologique de la Pointe de Kalissaye
Tionk-Essil
Marigot Kalissaye
Marigot de Diouloulou
Tendouk
Mangagoulak
Niomoune
Affiniam
Casamance River
Pointe St George
Manatee Sanctuary
Djilapao
Île des Oiseaux
Diogué
Bandial
Karabane
M'Lomp
To Dakar
Nikine
Kagnout
Etama
Brin
Île de Karabane
Séléki
Essil
Loudia Ouolof
Cachouane
Elinkine
Enampor
Kamoubeul
Diembéring
Oussouye
Edioungou
Diakène Ouolof
Oukout
Diohère
Nyassia
Niambalang
Diakène Diola
BASSE CASAMANCE
Boucotte
Parc National de Basse-Casamance (closed)
Kaguite
Youtou
Cap Skirring
Santiaba Mandjak
Kabrousse
GUINEA-BISSAU

**Auberge Le Palmier** GUESTHOUSE $
(☎33 993 5109; r CFA11,000-17,000; ) In Cap Skirring village (near the roundabout), the small Auberge Le Palmier is a decent budget bet with clean rooms (but noisy fans), and a good front-terrace restaurant. It's about a 10-minute walk from the beach.

★**Cisko Centre Culturel** HOTEL $$
(☎33 990 3921; www.ciskocentre.com; s/d CFA46,000/62,000, ste CFA114,000-181,000; ) Created by the Senegalese musician Youssouph Cissoko, this sprawling, high-end property is the go-to destination for music lovers, with weekend concerts held on the open-air stage throughout the year. Rooms here are beautifully designed, with African art and textiles, and there are fine places to unwind with a palm-fringed pool (and pool bar) and a good restaurant.

**Kaloa les Palétuviers** HOTEL $$
(☎33 993 0666; www.hotel-kaloa.com; s/d incl breakfast from CFA16,000/30,000; ) This riverside hotel is one of the more upmarket options and sits among lovely mangroves. Decent facilities, with a pool flanked by palms, a pleasant restaurant and a bar that hosts DJ-fuelled dance parties on weekends.

**Villa des Pêcheurs** HOTEL $$
(☎33 993 5253; www.villadespecheurs.com; s/d with full board CFA40,000/62,000; ) An excellent option on the beach. It also has a brilliant restaurant and offers the best fishing expeditions in town.

## Eating

★**Casa-Resto** INTERNATIONAL $$
(☎77 796 2071; mains CFA3500-5000; noon-3pm & 7-11pm) Set on the main road about 400m south of the village roundabout, Casa-Resto may lack the sea views and flashy setting, but it serves up some of the best meals in Cap Skirring. The menu has a bit of everything: good pizzas (made by William at the pizza station out front), seafood spaghetti, juicy steaks and grilled fish.

**Le Biarritz** INTERNATIONAL $$
(mains CFA1500-4000; 10am-late) This much-loved classic serves up reliable plates of pasta with shrimp, grilled fish, sandwiches and ever-flowing drinks. On weekend nights, Le Biarritz embraces its wild side, with DJs (or bands) and dancing – and sometimes stays open till 6am.

**Diaspora** INTERNATIONAL $$
(☎ 33 993 0304; CFA3500-6000; ⊙11am-10pm) Just off the road leading to the beach, Diaspora is an elegant but welcoming setting for nicely prepared crab ravioli, pork cutlets and pizza, as well as grilled seafood. There's live music some nights, too.

**Casa Bambou** FRENCH $$
(mains CFA2500-4000; ⊙10am-11pm) Offers tasty grilled seafood and roast chicken in a cheery, open-sided setting on the main road. The *plat du jour* (daily special) is a steal at CFA1000. Next door the restaurant has a bar-disco that draws a dance-minded crowd on Friday and Saturday nights.

## ℹ Getting There & Away

**Aéroport de Cap Skirring** (☎ 33 993 5194) is served by **Groupe Transair** (p456), which flies twice a week (Fridays and Sundays) between Dakar and Cap Skirring (one-way from around CFA75,000, 45 minutes). There are also charter flights from Paris Orly airport.

Otherwise you can take a *sept-place* taxi (around CFA2000, 1¾ hours) from Ziguinchor.

# UNDERSTAND SENEGAL

## Senegal Today

One of West Africa's most successful democracies, Senegal continues to be a role model for its political stability and steady economic growth. Hoping to further strengthen Senegal against future strongmen, President Macky Sall even championed a referendum in 2016 that curtailed presidential powers, shortening a president's time in office to a maximum of two consecutive terms, and shortening each term from seven to five years. Sall's ambitious economic plan 'Emerging Senegal' has helped spur growth (reaching over 6% annually in both 2015 and 2016), with major investments in infrastructure, tourism and agriculture. Enormous challenges remain, not least creating opportunities for Senegal's least fortunate – over 40% of the population still lives below the poverty line.

## History

Senegal was part of several West African empires, including the Empire of Ghana (8th century), and the Djolof kingdom, in the area between the Senegal River and Dakar (13th and 14th centuries). In the early 16th century Portuguese traders made contact with coastal kingdoms, and became the first in a long line of 'interested' foreigners: soon the British, French and Dutch jostled for control of strategic points for the trade in slaves and goods. In 1659 the French built a trading station at Saint-Louis; the town later became the capital of French West Africa.

Dakar, home to tiny fishing villages, was chosen as capital of the Senegalese territory, and as early as 1848 Senegal had a deputy in the French parliament.

### Independence

In the run-up to independence in 1960, Senegal joined French Sudan (present-day Mali) to form the Mali Federation. It lasted all of two months, and in August 1960, Senegal became a republic. Its first president, Léopold Sédar Senghor, a socialist and poet of international stature, commanded respect in Senegal and abroad. His economic management, however, didn't match his way with words. At the end of 1980, he voluntarily stepped down and was replaced by Abdou Diouf, who soon faced a string of mounting crises.

The 1980s saw the start of an ongoing separatist rebellion in the southern region of Casamance, a three-year diplomatic squabble with Mauritania and rising tensions over the government's economic austerity measures.

In March 2000 the hugely popular opposition leader Abdoulaye Wade won in a free and fair presidential election, thanks to his hope-giving *sopi* (change) campaign. The following year a new constitution was approved, allowing the formation of opposition parties and consolidating the prime minister's role.

Though initially popular, Wade's government wasn't able to lead the country out of economic crisis. The Constitutional Council allowed Wade to run for a highly controversial third term (when already in his mid-80s, no less), but voters rejected him in favor of Macky Sall, who had previously served as prime minister under Wade (from 2004 to 2007).

Macky Sall became president in early 2012, and quickly set about tackling corruption. He also made ambitious plans for new investment in infrastructure, healthcare, agriculture and tourism.

## People & Culture

More than 95% of the population is Muslim, and many of them belong to one of the Sufi brotherhoods that dominate religious life in Senegal. The most important brotherhood is that of the Mourides, founded by Cheikh Amadou Bamba. The marabouts who lead these brotherhoods play a central role in social life and wield enormous political and economic power (possibly the power to make or break the country's leaders).

The dominant ethnic group is the Wolof (39% of the population), whose language is the country's lingua franca. Smaller groups include the Pular (around 27%), the Serer (15%), the Mandinka (4%) and the Diola (4%). Senegal's population is young: just over 40% are under 14 years old.

Senegal has a vast music scene; names such as Youssou N'Dour and Baaba Maal are famous worldwide. The beat that moves the nation is mbalax. Created from a mixture of Cuban music (hugely popular in Senegal in the 1960s) and traditional, fiery *sabar* drumming, mbalax was made famous by Youssou N'Dour in the 1980s.

# SURVIVAL GUIDE

## Directory A-Z

### ACCOMMODATION

Senegal has a very wide range of places to stay, from top-class hotels to bare-bones budget guesthouses. Dakar has the biggest choice, with surfer camps and art-filled boutique guesthouses. If you're after beach getaways, check out Saly and Cap Skirring. Many rural areas, particularly the Casamance, have pleasant *campements* (guest-houses).

### DANGERS & ANNOYANCES

The main concern for visitors is street crime and annoying hustlers in Dakar. Civil unrest in the Casamance is no longer a threat, though it's best to seek out the latest advice before venturing to this southern region.

### EMBASSIES & CONSULATES

The embassies listed are located in Dakar. Most close late morning or early afternoon Monday to Friday, so set off early.

**Bissau-Guinean Embassy** (Map p444; ☎33 850 2574, 33 825 9089; Rue 6, Point E; ⏰8am-12.30pm Mon-Fri) There's a consulate in Ziguinchor (p456).

**Cabo Verdean Embassy** (Map p440; ☎33 860 8408; 3 Rue Mermoz, Plateau)

**Canadian Embassy** (Map p440; ☎33 889 4700; www.canadainternational.gc.ca; Rue Gallieni, Plateau; ⏰8am-12.30pm & 1.15-5pm Mon-Thu, 8am-12.30pm Fri)

**French Embassy** (Map p442; ☎33 839 5100; www.ambafrance-sn.org; 1 Rue Amadou Assane Ndoye, Plateau; ⏰8am-noon Mon-Fri)

**Gambian Embassy** (Map p444; ☎33 820 1198; Villa 128, Cité des Jeunes Cadres, Yoff Toundoup Rya)

**German Embassy** (Map p440; ☎33 889 4884; www.dakar.diplo.de; 20 Ave Pasteur, Plateau; ⏰9am-noon Mon-Fri)

**Ghanaian Embassy** (Map p444; ☎33 869 1990; Rue 6, Point E)

**Guinean Embassy** (Map p444; ☎33 824 8606; Rue de Diourbel, Point E)

**Ivoirian Embassy** (Map p444; ☎33 869 0270; www.ambaci-dakar.org; Allées Seydou Nourou Tall, Point E)

**Malian Embassy** (Map p444; ☎33 824 6250; 23 Rte de la Corniche-Ouest, Point E; ⏰9am-1pm Mon-Fri)

**Mauritanian Embassy** (Map p444; ☎33 823 5344; Mermoz; ⏰8am-2pm Mon-Fri)

**Moroccan Embassy** (Map p444; ☎33 824 3836; Ave Cheikh Anta Diop, Mermoz)

**Spanish Embassy** (Map p440; ☎33 849 2999; www.exteriores.gob.es; 30 Ave Nelson Mandela, Plateau; ⏰9am-2.30pm Mon-Fri)

**UK Embassy** (Map p440; ☎33 823 7392; www.gov.uk/government/world/senegal; 20 Rue du Dr Guillet, Plateau; ⏰8am-4.30pm Mon-Thu, to 12.30pm Fri) One block north of Hôpital le Dantec.

**US Embassy** (Map p444; ☎33 879 4000; www.dakar.usembassy.gov; Rte des Almadies, Les Almadies; ⏰8am-5.30pm Mon-Thu, to 1pm Fri)

### EMERGENCY & IMPORTANT NUMBERS

| | |
|---|---|
| Senegal's country code | ☎221 |
| International access code | ☎00 |
| Ambulance (SOS Médecins) | ☎33 889 1515 |
| Fire | ☎18 |
| Police | ☎17 |

### SLEEPING PRICE RANGES

The following price ranges refer to a double room.

**$** less than CFA30,000

**$$** CFA30,000–90,000

**$$$** more than CFA90,000

## PRACTICALITIES

**Electricity** 220V. Plugs have two round pins (same as continental Europe

**Newspapers** *Le Soleil* (www.lesoleil.sn) is the main daily paper.

**Post** Service is fairly inexpensive, though not entirely reliable. The main post office is in Dakar.

**Television** RTS (www.rts.sn) is Senegal's public broadcasting channel, featuring independent programming (sometimes delving into culture and history).

**Weights & measures** Senegal uses the metric system.

### FOOD

Dakar has a great many restaurants, catering to a wide range of budgets (though prices tend to be higher here than in other parts). Saint-Louis, Saly and Cap Skirring all have a small but vibrant dining scene, but elsewhere, options are sparse, and you'll likely be taking your meals wherever you lodge for the night.

Senegal's national dish is *thiéboudienne* (rice cooked in a thick tomato sauce and served with fried fish and vegetables). Also typical are *poulet yassa* or *poisson yassa* (marinated and grilled chicken or fish) and *mafé* (peanut-based stew).

### INTERNET ACCESS

Internet cafes are a dying breed in Senegal. Free wi-fi is available in many places (particularly in Dakar), and common in most accommodation catering to foreign tourists.

### LGBTIQ TRAVELLERS

In Senegal things feel a little less severe than in neighbouring The Gambia (where gay travellers have been arrested, and the former president promised violence against gays). However, homosexual acts are still illegal in Senegal and can carry a prison sentence of one to five years. Violence and discrimination against gays is a very real threat. Gay travellers need to be extremely cautious travelling here. Being out is simply not an option in Senegal.

## EATING PRICE RANGES

The following price ranges refers to a main course.

**$** less than CFA3000

**$$** CFA3000–6000

**$$$** more than CFA6000

### MONEY

Senegal uses the West African CFA *(SAY-fuh)* franc. All larger towns have banks with ATMs. US dollars and euros are the most easily exchanged currencies.

**Tipping** Not expected at budget eateries; 10% customary at pricier restaurants, though sometimes included in the bill. If you hire a guide or a driver for the day, however, you should plan on tipping (assuming the service wasn't abysmal).

### Exchange Rates

| | | |
|---|---|---|
| Australia | A$1 | CFA452 |
| Canada | C$ | CFA440 |
| Euro zone | €1 | CFA656 |
| The Gambia (Dalasi) | D10 | CFA133 |
| Guinea (Guinean franc) | GF1000 | CFA66 |
| Japan | ¥100 | CFA538 |
| New Zealand | NZ$1 | CFA415 |
| UK | £1 | CFA774 |
| US | US$1 | CFA600 |

### OPENING HOURS

**Banks** 9am to 4pm; a few open Saturday morning.

**Bars** 5pm to 2am.

**Business and government offices** 8.30am to 1pm and 2.30pm to 5pm Monday to Friday.

**Cafes** 8am to 7pm.

**Clubs** 10pm to 5am, mostly Thursday to Saturday.

**Restaurants** Lunch from noon to 2.30pm and dinner from 7pm; many closed on Sunday.

**Shops** 9am to 6pm Monday to Thursday and Saturday, to 1pm Friday; most close on Sunday.

### PUBLIC HOLIDAYS

As well as Islamic religious holidays, Senegal celebrates a few principal public holidays.

**New Year's Day** 1 January

**Independence Day** 4 April

**Workers Day** 1 May

**Assumption** 15 August

### TELEPHONE

➡ Good mobile phone coverage means that most of the public *télécentres* have now closed.

➡ The country code is ☎221. For directory assistance dial ☎1212.

### TOURIST INFORMATION

There isn't much official tourist information available for travellers. One exception is the Office de Tourisme (p456) in Ziguinchor, which is an excellent source of info on the Casamance.

Given the lack of tourism posts (and online info), your best bet is to get local information from your guesthouse or hotel.

### VISAS

Visitors from the EU, USA, Canada, Australia, New Zealand and 80-plus other countries can enter Senegal without a visa for stays of up to 90 days.

## Getting There & Away

### AIR

Dakar is one of Africa's transport hubs, with links across Africa, Europe and America. Dakar's current airport, Léopold Sédar Senghor International Airport (p447), is slated to close once the new airport opens – which might be as early as 2018.

### LAND

#### The Gambia

From Dakar there are *sept-place* taxis south to Karang (CFA7000, six hours, 250km) at the Gambian border, where you connect to Barra and then via ferry to Banjul.

From southern Senegal, *sept-place* taxis run regularly between Ziguinchor and Serekunda (CFA5000, five hours, 145km), and between Kafountine and Brikama (CFA3600, two hours, 60km).

In Eastern Senegal, *sept-place* taxis go from Tambacounda to Vélingara (CFA2500, three hours, 98km), and from there to Basse Santa Su (CFA1500, 50 minutes, 27km).

#### Guinea

Coming from the north, head to Tambacounda, where you can usually find Guinea-bound transport, down through Kalifourou and on to Koundara (Guinea).

If coming from the Casamance, your best bet is by *sept-place* from Diaoubé (Senegal). The enormous market on Wednesday makes it the ideal day to find transport out.

The road is generally in fair shape in Senegal, but deteriorates rapidly when you cross the border.

#### Guinea-Bissau

*Sept-place* taxis leave every morning from Ziguinchor for Bissau (CFA6000, four hours, 147km), via the main border post at São Domingos, and Ingore. The road is sealed and in good condition.

#### Mali

The security situation in Mali remains difficult – check the latest information before visiting. *Sept-place* taxis leave regularly from Tambacounda to Kidira (CFA4000, four hours, 190km), where you cross the border to Diboli in Mali; from Diboli long-distance buses run to Kayes and Bamako.

#### Mauritania

*Sept-place* taxis run regularly from Dakar to the main border point at Rosso (CFA7500, seven hours, 384km), a crowded, hasslesome place, where four daily ferries (free for passengers, CFA5000 for a vehicle) cross to Rosso-Mauritania.

If you have your own wheels, it's less hassle to cross at the Maka Diama dam, 97km southwest of Rosso and just north of Saint-Louis, where the border crossing is swift and largely free of hustlers.

## Getting Around

### AIR

Groupe Transair (p456) flies between Dakar, Ziguinchor and Cap Skirring.

### BOAT

A regular ferry service travels between Dakar and Ziguinchor. There are currently four departures heading in each direction per week (see the latest times and prices on www.cap-skirring.voyage). All are operated by **COSAMA** (☎33 821 3434; info@cosamasn.com).

A regular ferry service travels between Dakar and Île de Gorée. Senegal's other islands can be visited by pirogue, including Île de N'Gor, Mar Lodj and Île de Karabane.

The luxury Bou El Mogdad (p453) travels in the north of the country on six-day voyages between Saint-Louis and Podor along the Senegal River.

### BUS & SEPT-PLACE TAXIS

The quickest (though still uncomfortable) way of getting around the country is by *sept-place* taxi – battered Peugeots that negotiate even the most ragged routes. Slightly cheaper, but infinitely less reliable are the minibuses (Ndiaga Ndiaye or grand car), carrying around 40 people. Vehicles leave from the *gare routière* (transport station) when they're full, and they fill up quickest in the morning, before 8am.

Prices are theoretically fixed, though there's an extra, negotiable charge for luggage (10% to 20% of the bill).

In Dakar, long-distance transports arrive and depart from the Gare Routière Baux Maraîchers (p447) in Pikine.

### CAR & MOTORCYCLE

You can hire vehicles in Senegal (Dakar's airport is the best place for this). To rent a vehicle, you'll need your home licence and, technically, an international drivers licence (though this isn't always asked for).

For less of a headache, you can often hire a car with driver for about the same price as a self-drive (starting from around CFA30,000 per day). Most guesthouses can help arrange this.

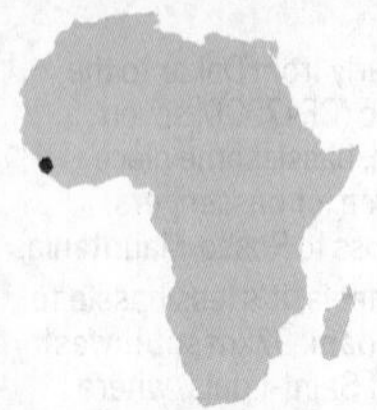

# Sierra Leone

232 / POP 6 MILLION

### Includes ➡



## Why Go?

For the traveller, Sierra Leone is still West Africa's secret beach destination. Sweet sands rise from the soft waters of the Atlantic, with the backdrop dressed in sun-stained hues, rainforest green and the red, red roads of the north.

In Freetown, colourful stilted houses remember the days when freed slaves from the Caribbean were resettled upon these shores. In the north, the Loma Mountains form the highest point west of Cameroon. Further east national parks and rainforest shelter endangered species like the black-and-white colobus monkey and the elusive pygmy hippo.

The scars of Sierra Leone's civil wars had just healed when the 2014–15 Ebola outbreak knocked the country off its feet once again. Tourism can play an important role in helping its recovery, so join the island-hoppers and adventurers, camp in little-visited rainforests and crack open fresh lobster in the shade of skinny palms and rope-strung hammocks.

## Best Places to Eat


➡ Franco's (p472)
➡ Oasis (p469)
➡ Mamba Point Lagoonda (p470)
➡ Tessa's (p469)


## Best Places to Sleep


➡ Freetown Oasis (p468)
➡ Tacugama Sanctuary Lodge (p471)
➡ Rogbonko Village (p473)
➡ Ategbeh Garden (p471)
➡ Cockle Point (p472)


## When to Go

### Freetown

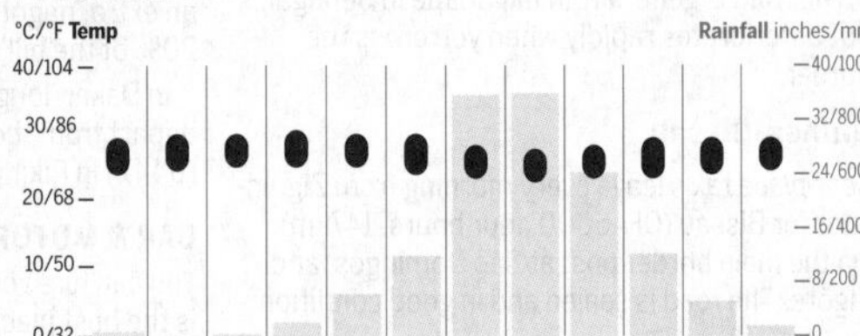


**Nov–Jun** The dry season is marked by mild, dusty harmattan winds in December, January and February.

**April** The average daytime temperature is 32°C.

**Jun–Nov** In the rainy season, spectacular coastal storms mean up to 3200mm of precipitation.

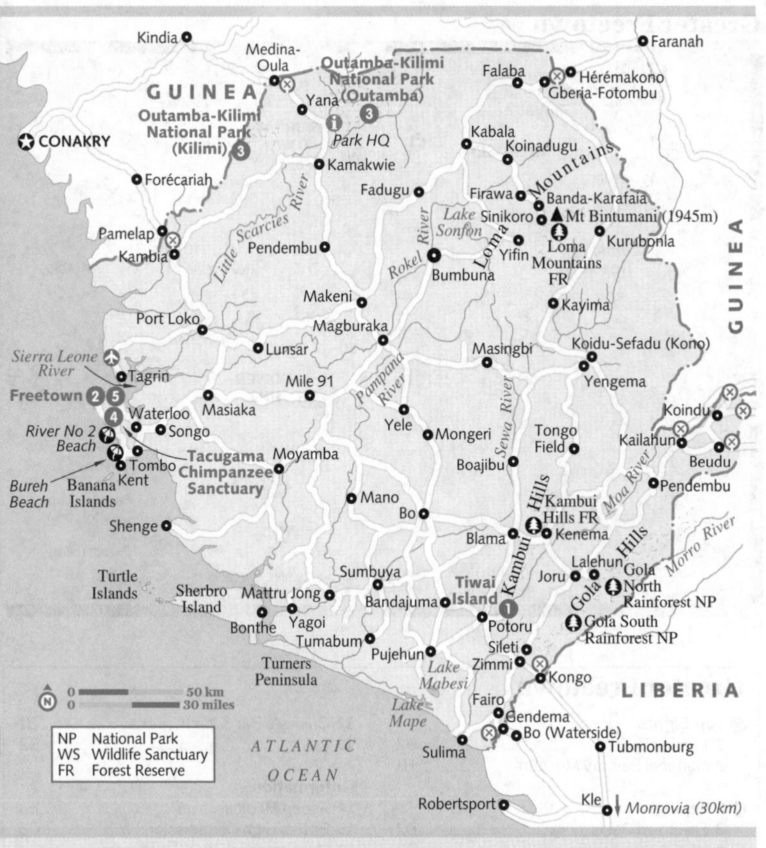


## Sierra Leone Highlights

❶ **Tiwai Island** (p475) Joining a nighttime hike through the forest in search of the elusive pygmy hippo.

❷ **Freetown Peninsula** (p471) Eating barbecued lobster pulled fresh from the sea at one of the peninsula's stunning beaches.

❸ **Outamba-Kilimi National Park** (p474) Gliding down the river by dugout canoe while monkeys and birds chatter in the surrounding forest.

❹ **Tacugama Chimpanzee Sanctuary** (p471) Learning about conservation efforts and viewing chimps playing in their sanctuary home.

❺ **Freetown** (p465) Soaking up the atmosphere: spotting colourful Krio houses, strolling the beach and dancing till dawn at one of the city's energetic clubs.

# FREETOWN

022 / POP 1.1 MILLION

Strung between the mountains and the sea, Sierra Leone's capital is a cheeky, quicksilver city bubbling with energy, colour and charm. One minute it's calm, offering up quiet beaches, friendly Krio chat and warm plates of soup and rice. The next it's frenzied and playing dirty, throwing you into the back of a shared taxi and hurtling you up and down its pretty little hills.

And it might just be the only capital in the world where when you emerge from the airport, blinking after an overnight flight, you find yourself standing on the wooden deck of a port flanked by a backdrop of mountains, beaches and palm trees so idyllic you wonder if it's real. Well it's real, all of it – the chatter and the chaos and the colour and

## Greater Freetown

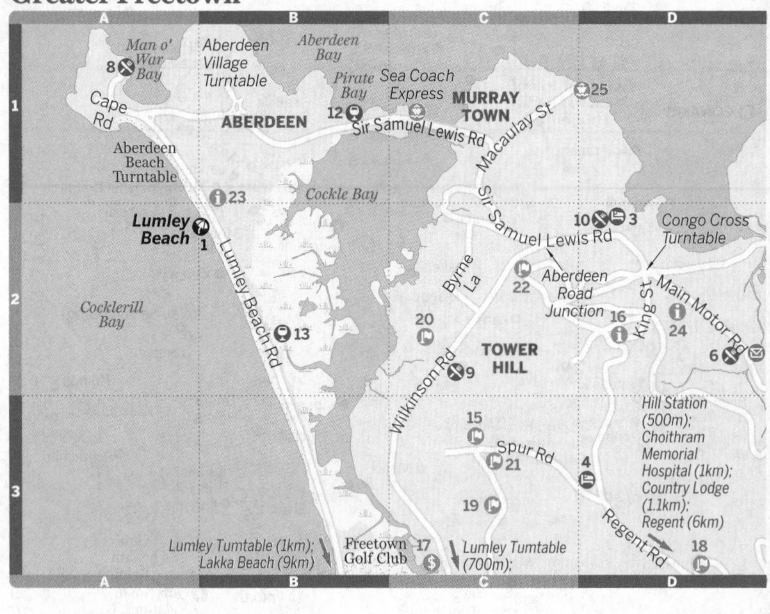


### Greater Freetown

**Top Sights**
1 Lumley Beach ........ B2
2 National Railway Museum ........ H1

**Sleeping**
3 Freetown Oasis ........ D2
4 Hub ........ D3
5 Lacs Villa Guesthouse ........ E3

**Eating**
6 Balmaya Restaurant ........ D2
7 Caribbean Fusion Restaurant ........ E2
8 Mamba Point Lagoonda ........ A1
Oasis ........ (see 3)
9 Senegalese Restaurant ........ C2
10 Tessa's ........ D2

**Drinking & Nightlife**
11 China House ........ E2
12 Quincy's Bar & Nightclub ........ B1
13 Roy's ........ B2

**Information**
14 Aspen Medical ........ E3
15 British High Commission ........ C3
16 Conservation Society of Sierra Leone ........ D2
17 Ecobank ........ C3
18 German Embassy ........ D3
19 Ghanaian High Commission ........ C3
20 Guinean Embassy ........ C2
21 Liberian Embassy ........ C3
22 Malian Consulate ........ C2
23 National Tourist Board ........ B1
24 Visit Sierra Leone ........ D2

**Transport**
25 Sea Bird Express ........ D1

the dirt and the lush lobster dinners and the devastating history of war and Ebola – and those lovely white sands too.

## Sights

**★ National Railway Museum** MUSEUM
(Map p466; ☎077 423575; www.sierraleonerailwaymuseum.com; Cline St; ⏰9.30am-4.30pm Mon-Fri; 👪) FREE You don't have to be a rail fan to enjoy this Clinetown museum, where enthusiastic staff guide you around a surprising collection of restored locomotives, including one commissioned for the Queen of England in 1961. Other attractions include a display of model trains, and fascinating photos of the glory days of the Sierra Leone railway. There's also a small gift shop. Admission is free but donations are encouraged.

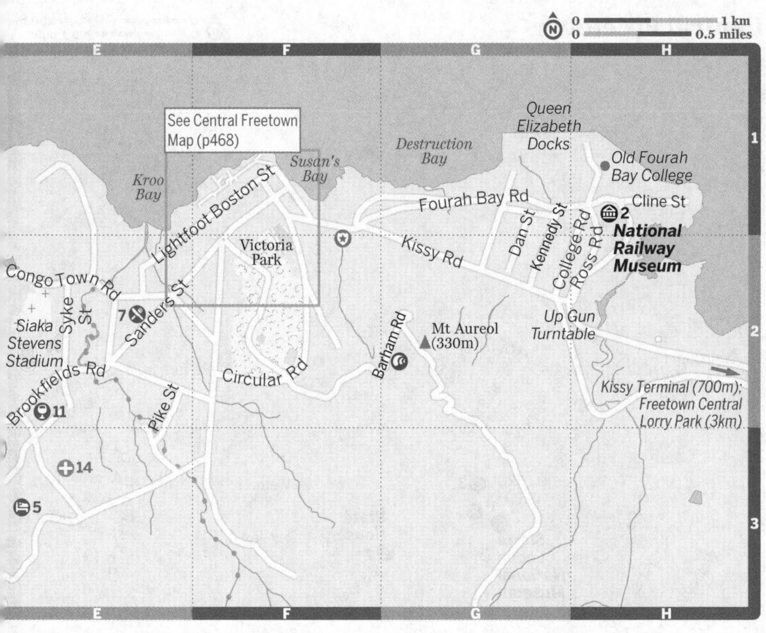


### ★Lumley Beach BEACH

(Map p466) This wide sweep of beach has lost some of its atmosphere since the 2015 demolition of dozens of bamboo and thatch food shacks, and the numerous, ugly construction projects lining the beach road don't add to its appeal. During the week it feels deserted, save for a few joggers pounding the paved beach walkway, but it comes into its own on weekends and public holidays, when Freetown's residents come out to relax and party on the golden sands.

### ★Sierra Leone National Museum MUSEUM

(Map p468; ☎022 223555; Siaka Stevens St; ⏰10.30am-4pm Mon-Fri) FREE There are two galleries inside the Sierra Leone National Museum – one housing a collection of cultural and historical artefacts, including Temne Guerrilla leader Bai Bureh's drum, clothes and sword; and another devoted to temporary exhibitions (at the time of research a fascinating collection of photographs and documents detailing the city's colonial past).

### ★State House HISTORIC BUILDING

(Map p468; Independence Ave) The State House, up on Tower Hill and overlooking the downtown area, is an example of Freetown's old Krio architecture, which features brightly washed buildings and higgledy-piggledy window frames. This building incorporates the bastions and lion gate from Fort Thornton (built at the turn of the 19th century).

### ★Old Fourah Bay College UNIVERSITY

(Map p466; College Rd) Gutted by fire in 1999, only the stone shell of the Old Fourah Bay College remains, but this 1848 building is graceful even in its decay. The World Monuments Fund lists it as one of the world's 100 most-endangered historic sites.

### Cotton Tree GARDENS

(Map p468) Freetown's most famous landmark is the fat Cotton Tree, which looms large over the buildings of central Freetown. Rumoured to be hundreds of years old, it is said to have played a key role in the city's history, when poor black settlers rested in its shadows after landing in Freetown in 1787.

## Sleeping

There's no getting around it – accommodation in Freetown is expensive, and while there are plenty of chic options for those with deep pockets, good-value budget and midrange digs are hard to find. For those looking to make their leones stretch further, home-sharing websites such as Airbnb offer an excellent value alternative.

## Central Freetown

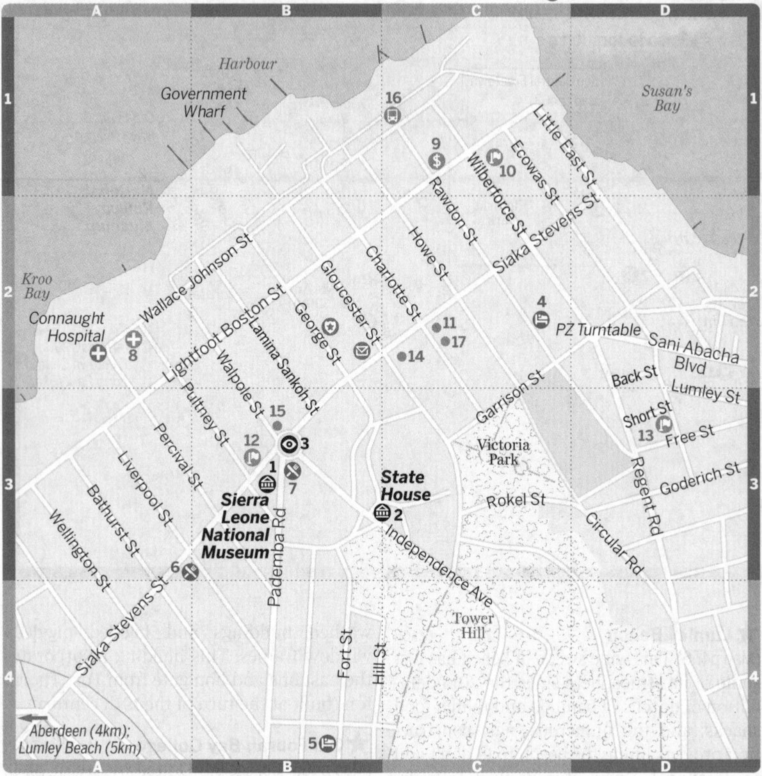

**YMCA** HOSTEL **$**
(Map p468; ☎078 952818; www.sierraleoneymca.org; 32 Fort St; s/d incl breakfast from Le220,000, with shared bathroom Le100,000/150,000; P ❄ ☜) The simple rooms here are the best deal in the city centre. Balconies on each floor provide sweeping views over the city, and there's a restaurant serving hearty local food (Le12,000).

**Hedjazi Hotel** HOTEL **$**
(Map p468; ☎076 601094, 076 790750; 32/24 Rawdon St; s/d Le100,000/150,000; ❄ ☜) Cheap and cheerful is this centrally located budget hotel. Basic rooms have air-con and running water, and there's a guest lounge and wi-fi. As with the neighbouring Sierra International Hotel, this place can get pretty noisy, so ask for a room that faces away from the street.

★ **Freetown Oasis** GUESTHOUSE **$$**
(Map p466; ☎076 605222; 33 Murray Town Rd; P ❄ ☜) Wander down the lane off busy Murray Town Rd to find nine homely, airy rooms in a surprisingly tranquil garden setting, with sea views. There's a wonderful cafe serving healthy meals and fresh fruit smoothies.

**Lacs Villa Guesthouse** GUESTHOUSE **$$**
(Map p466; 9 Cantonment Rd; s/d incl breakfast US$115/138; P ❄ ☜) The location is special – an old colonial house set in pretty green gardens, that seems miles away from the bustle of the city. The rooms in the old building come with high ceilings and polished wood furniture, and are a little more atmospheric than those in the newer annexe.

**Hub** BOUTIQUE HOTEL **$$$**
(Map p466; ☎088 112120; www.thehub-hotel.com; 6 Regent Rd; P ❄ ☜ ≋) This fancy new spot offers plush rooms that wouldn't look out of place in London or New York, as well a pub, a restaurant and an excellent sushi bar. Oh, and not forgetting the rooftop pool, complete with city and beach views.

## Central Freetown

**Top Sights**
1 Sierra Leone National Museum ........... B3
2 State House ........... C3

**Sights**
3 Cotton Tree ........... B3

**Sleeping**
4 Hedjazi Hotel ........... C2
5 YMCA ........... B4

**Eating**
6 D's Bazaar ........... A3
7 Salgus Restaurant ........... B3

**Information**
8 Central Pharmacy ........... A2
9 Ecobank ........... C1
10 Gambian High Commission ........... C1
11 IPC Travel ........... C2
12 Nigerian Embassy ........... B3
13 Senegalese Consulate ........... D3

**Transport**
14 Brussels Airlines ........... C2
15 Kenya Airways ........... B3
16 Main Bus Station ........... C1
17 Royal Air Maroc ........... C2

**Country Lodge** HOTEL $$$
(076 691000; www.countrylodgesl.com; Hill Station; r US$200-320, ste US$350-500; P ❄ @ ☎ ≋) Perched on top of a hill, with stunning views out over the city and the ocean, Country Lodge is one of Freetown's fanciest addresses, popular with everyone from businessmen to VIPs. Rooms are suitably plush, and there's also a pool, gym and tennis court. If you can't afford to stay here, you're welcome to hole up in the excellent restaurant and use the free wi-fi.

## Eating

**Senegalese Restaurant** AFRICAN $
(Map p466; mains Le40,000-50,000; 11am-10pm) Ignore the no-frills interior – this tiny gem serves up delicious West African meals and cold beers. The *yassa* chicken (or fish) is excellent and it even does a nice line in Senegalese deserts.

**Salgus Restaurant** AFRICAN $
(Map p468; 078 664404; cnr Pademba Rd & Independence Ave; 8.30am-7.30pm Mon-Sat; P) A good place for a filling breakfast or to mingle with the lunchtime office crowd. Grills, sandwiches and *jollof rice* (rice and vegetables with meat or fish) are on the menu here, and there's a terrace overlooking the Cotton Tree.

**Balmaya Restaurant** AFRICAN $
(Map p466; 32 Main Motor Rd; mains Le40,000-50,000; 8am-6pm) This is a friendly spot with a lovely terrace overlooking the street. Simple dishes of chicken, fish and rice are served with charm, if not speed.

**Caribbean Fusion Restaurant** CARIBBEAN $
(Map p466; 022 220226; Sanders St; mains Le40,000-60,000; 7am-7.30pm Mon-Sat; ) Krio goes back to its roots at this no-frills Caribbean joint. Written up on the chalkboard outside you'll find a choice of two or three mains a day (perhaps fish curry, jerk chicken or *jollof rice*), as well as a selection of fresh juices and other homemade drinks – it does a mean ginger beer!

**D's Bazaar** AFRICAN $
(Map p468; 077 248759, 076 999993; cnr Liverpool & Siaka Stevens Sts; mains Le15,000-30,000) Both the name and the food beat the decor at this local *plasas* spot. The menu changes daily, according to what's on hand, but you can expect to fill up with sour-sour, cassava leaves or simple rice and fish for less than Le15,000. There's a second branch on Wilkinson Rd.

★**Oasis** RESTAURANT $$
(Map p466; 076 605222; 33 Murray Town Rd, near Boyle Lane; P ❄ ☎ ) This charming little cafe is an oasis indeed. Set in a garden off Murray Town Rd, it feels hundreds of miles away from the chaos of Freetown. Though it's famous for its smoothies, the food here is also excellent and wholesome – think black bean soup, Thai chicken curry and indulgent brownies.

**Tessa's** AFRICAN $$
(Map p466; 076-800085; 13 Wilkinson Rd; mains Le40,000-60,000; 11.30am-10pm; P) Authentic Sierra Leonean dishes such as black-eyed beans with plantain, palm-oil stew, *fufu* (fermented cassava, cooked and puréed) and sour-sour are on the menu here, served by super-friendly staff in either the simple dining room or the garden. There are a few European and Asian menu options too.

**Mamba Point Lagoonda** SEAFOOD $$$
(Map p466; ☎099 100100; 53 Cape Rd, off Aberdeen Rd; P❄🛜) Mamba Point is one of Freetown's most popular (and expensive) restaurants. Come for dinner in the chic dining room, or just to sink a few cocktails and smoke on a shisha pipe on the expansive terrace, which has gorgeous views over Man o' War Bay. On the menu are grilled fish and meats, pastas, and excellent sushi. There's a casino upstairs.

## Drinking & Nightlife

★**Quincy's Bar & Nightclub** CLUB
(Map p466; 63 Sir Samuel Lewis Rd; ⏱2pm-9am) A Freetown institution, Quincy's claims that it shuts 'when the last person leaves', and in their case, it's true. Come the weekend, an exuberant crowd of local posers, government ministers and expats parties well past dawn.

**Roy's** BAR
(Map p466; ☎079 655677; ⏱11am-late) Watch the sun go down and the party people wake up on the expansive split-level terrace at Roy's, a perfect sundowner spot on Lumley Beach. It's hard to find a beef with this place – everyone from backpackers to ministerial employees seems to come here.

**China House** BAR
(Map p466; Youyi Building, cnr Main Motor & Brookfield Rds) Mingle with ministers at China House, strangely located in the compound of the ministerial building. There's regular live music, although you might want to watch who you elbow on your way to the bar.

## ℹ Information

### DANGERS & ANNOYANCES

Freetown has less crime than you'd imagine, but it still makes sense to be cautious and avoid having valuables on display, or walking alone at night. Petty crime is an issue in markets and other crowded areas, and there have been many reports of muggings around Lumley Beach. Don't walk on the beach after dark, and exercise caution on weekdays, when it is almost deserted.

By far the most dangerous creatures in Freetown are not the mosquitoes but the (admittedly cheap) motorbike taxis – take one at your peril and wear a helmet (most drivers carry a spare).

### MEDICAL SERVICES

**Aspen Medical** (Map p466; ☎099 500800, emergencies 099 888000; www.aspenmedicalintl.com)

**Central Pharmacy** (Map p468; ☎076 615503; 30 Wallace Johnson St) Reasonably well-stocked pharmacy.

**Choitram Memorial Hospital** (☎076 980000, emergency 076 888880; www.cmhfreetown.com; Hill Station) Freetown's best hospital.

**Connaught Hospital** (Map p468; ☎076 490595)

### MONEY

There's an exchange bureau at Lungi International Airport with reasonable rates. There's also an ATM just outside the terminal building, which may or may not be working. Forex bureaus are found throughout the city.

Ecobank is located on **Wilkinson Rd** (Map p466; 157 Wilkinson Rd) and **Lightfoot Boston St** (Map p468; Lightfoot Boston St). Other major banks, including UBA and Rokel Commercial

### ARRIVING IN FREETOWN

All international flights land at **Lungi International Airport** (☎099 714421), which is across the water from Freetown. While you can get to the city road, it's a four-hour journey, so it makes much more sense to get a speedboat or ferry.

Speedboats arranged through **Sea Coach Express** (Map p466; ☎033 111118; one-way US$42) take around 30 minutes. They run in coordination with the airport's flight schedule, and drop passengers off at Aberdeen Bridge. Rival company **Sea Bird Express** (Map p466; ☎077 606084; 36 High Broad St, Murray Town; one-way US$42) provides a similar service at a similar price, dropping passengers off at High Broad St in Murray Town.

The ferry service (1st/2nd class Le11,000/5000) leaves from Tagrin Ferry Terminal, a 15-minute taxi or *okada* (motorcycle taxi) ride from the airport. It takes around an hour and drops passengers off at the Kissy Ferry Terminal, in eastern Freetown.

If your flight arrives late at night, you could stay at **Lungi Airport Hotel** (☎076 660055; budget r US$80, standard s/d US$120/140; P❄🛜🏊) and cross over the water in the morning.

Bank, have Visa-card-linked ATMs. There are several ATMs in central Freetown.

### POST

**DHL** (Map p466; ☎099 547672; 30 Main Motor Rd; ⊙8am-6pm Mon-Fri, 9am-5pm Sat)

**Post Office** (Map p468; 27 Siaka Stevens St; ⊙8.30am-4.30pm Mon-Fri) You can send international mail and set up a PO Box.

### TOURIST INFORMATION

**Conservation Society of Sierra Leone** (Map p466; ☎030 522579, 076 633824; www.facebook.com/conservationsl; 14a King St; ⊙9am-5pm Mon-Fri) Helpful for travellers to Sierra Leone's natural reserves, including the Turtle Islands.

**National Tourist Board** (Map p466; ☎025 216362; www.welcometosierraleone.sl; Lumley Beach Rd; ⊙8am-5pm) Government-run, it can provide useful information about travel throughout the country.

### TRAVEL AGENCIES

**IPC Travel** (Map p468; ☎077 444453; info@ipctravel.com; 22 Siaka Stevens St; ⊙8.30am-5.30pm Mon-Fri) Can arrange tours, car hire, flight bookings and airport transfers.

**Visit Sierra Leone** (Map p466; ☎076 877618; www.visitsierraleone.org; 28 Main Motor Rd) A brilliant one-stop shop for tours, information, transport, guides and historical knowledge.

## Getting There & Away

From the **main bus station** (Map p468) at Wallace Johnson St, reasonably well maintained government buses leave for cities including Bo (6am daily, Le20,000), Kenema (6am daily, Le25,000), Makeni (6am daily, Le15,000) and Conakry, in Guinea (6am Monday to Thursday, Le50,000). Shared bush taxis head to the same destinations, stopping at villages and communities along the way. They leave from **Freetown Central Lorry Park** (Bai Bureh Rd) on the far east side of town. Taxis to Conakry park along Free St near Victoria Park Market.

## Getting Around

Shared taxis and *poda-podas* (minibuses) cost Le2000 per short hop and run on fixed routes around town. You can also bargain for a charter taxi (expect to pay around Le20,000 for a short journey, such as Lumley to town).

# FREETOWN PENINSULA

The Freetown Peninsula is the star attraction of Sierra Leone's tourist industry – a deep green interior of mountains and forest, kissed by a dazzling stretch of beaches, each one with its own special appeal. From powdery white sands nudged by a shallow turquoise lagoon, to a saffron bay shaded by palms and studded with boulders, to a wide sweep of thundering waves, perfect for surfing. And just off the tip of the peninsula lie the Banana Islands; an untrammelled hideaway, perfect for snorkelling, fishing and lazy days – or for jumping off an adventure to the storybook Turtle Islands.

## Sights & Activities

**★Tacugama Chimpanzee Sanctuary** WILDLIFE RESERVE
(☎076 611211, 044 625107; www.tacugama.com; adult/child Le100,000/35,000; ⊙tours 10.30am & 4pm, bookings required) In the dense rainforest of Western Area National Park, Sri Lankan founder Bala created Tacugama Chimpanzee Sanctuary, a leafy, waterfall-framed hideaway set up with the purpose of rescuing and rehabilitating endangered primates, and in the process educating humans about one of our closest relatives. The passionate and committed staff offer twice-daily tours of the sanctuary, during which you'll watch rescued chimps frolic in enclosures and spot those who have been released to a larger area in the mountains beyond.

**Bureh Beach Surf Club** SURFING
(☎078 044242, 077 934956; burehbeachsc@gmail.com) Run by a group of locals, with all profits going back into their community, Bureh Beach Surf Club offers board rental (Le60,000 per hour) and beginners surf lessons (Le80,000 for a two-hour lesson) on a beautiful golden beach 90 minutes south of Freetown.

## Sleeping & Eating

**★Ategbeh Garden** GUESTHOUSE $
(☎078 870119; www.ategbehgarden.co.uk; Cambeltown Rd, Waterloo; P ❄) Run by a British-Sierra Leonean couple, this little guesthouse, surrounded by flourishing tropical gardens and local farms, is the perfect antidote to busy Freetown life. The little cabins are calm and cool, with high ceilings, hardwood floors and verandas overlooking the birds and the trees. The food, cooked by your hosts or a local village cook, is wholesome and delicious.

**★Tacugama Sanctuary Lodge** LODGE $$$
(☎044 625107; www.tacugama.com; incl breakfast d US$90-140, 4-person lodges US$180; P)

Near enough to Freetown for an overnight visit, yet deep enough in the mountains to feel as if you're lost in the wilderness, Tacugama is a wonderfully romantic experience. The four cabins, two of which have bedrooms level with the treetops, overlook mist-shrouded forest, so you can fall asleep to the sound of chattering chimps. Rates include a sanctuary tour.

★ **Franco's** ITALIAN $$
(Florence's Resort; ☎076 744406, 077 366366; www.florencesresort.com; 20 Michael St, Sussex Village; mains Le50,000-100,000; ⏰9am-11pm; P 📶 👪) Half an hour from Freetown is Sierra Leone foodie institution Franco's, sprawled on Sussex Beach (beside the lagoon). Run by an Italian–Sierra Leonean couple, this place specialises in seafood and pasta, and is a favourite spot for a long, wine-fuelled Sunday lunch.

## Banana Islands

Dublin (*doo-blin*), Ricketts and Mes-Meheux are the three bananas in this pretty archipelago, hanging from the southern tip of the Freetown Peninsula like a ripe bunch of fruit. The islands were first settled by the Portuguese in the 17th century and were later inhabited by freed slaves from the Caribbean – the descendents of those who live here now.

A private taxi from Freetown to Kent will cost around Le100,000 or you could get a poda poda to Waterloo (Le20,000) and find a shared taxi from there. After paying a Le5000 community 'entry fee', head straight for the port. There you'll receive plenty of offers from young men keen to take you across in a wooden boat (Le100,000). Alternatively, the owners of **Dalton's Banana Guest House** (☎076 278120; www.daltonsbananaguesthouse.com; budget/standard/deluxe Le100,000/250,000/300,000) can organise sea transport (the 30-minute crossing costs Le120,000 per boat one-way).

## River No 2

This beach shot to fame after a Bounty bar ad was filmed here, and the sugary white sands don't disappoint. The popular Sankofa Complex, managed by the local community, organises activities and is home to a popular restaurant and guesthouse. You'll have to pay for the privilege though – there's an entrance fee of Le5000 per person.

### Sleeping

★ **Cockle Point** GUESTHOUSE $
(☎077 073998, 076 687823, 078 717871; www.cocklepoint.com; s/d from US$50/80, tent US$15) A tranquil place with gorgeous views over River No 2, this guesthouse has four lovely thatch-roof bungalows. Two are traditional round huts, and two are split-level with balconies and 1st-floor bedrooms perfectly poised to receive the ocean breezes. The owners also have a couple of tents that they'll happily put up under thatch shelter for those on lower budgets.

**River No 2 Guesthouse** GUESTHOUSE $
(☎078 349941, 088 330597; r incl breakfast Le250,000; P ❄) A community-run spot within the Sankofa Complex that has simple, clean rooms, with beautiful water views.

### Eating

**Africa Point** CAFE $
Just across the river from the Sankofa Complex, Africa Point's wooden tables and sun-loungers make a worthwhile alternative for lunch – with fresh fish and cold beer on the menu.

**Sankofa Complex** INTERNATIONAL $$
(☎088 33059; mains around Le50,000; P) At the relaxed restaurant in the Sankofa Complex you can eat under thatch or on bright-red tables set out on the sand. Food includes lobster, shrimp, barracuda. It's Le20,000 to hire a table and chairs, regardless of how much food you order.

### Getting There & Away

Until the stretch of road between River No 2 and Tokeh Beach is completed, there is limited public transport, and you'll be better off hiring a taxi in Freetown (Le80,000).

## Tokeh Beach

Tokeh Beach is one of the most spectacular beaches on the peninsula, a wide stretch of soft white sand, cradled by palm trees and forested hills. It is the most upmarket destination on the peninsula, and was purportedly popular with European celebs before the war.

### Sleeping & Eating

**Tokeh Beach Resort** HOTEL $$
(☎078 911111; r US$60-180; P❄📶) Tokeh Sands, which has sleek, white rooms with 24-hour power and air-con, opened here in 2013. You can swim out to the old helipad nearby, or kick off your sandals and nap in one of the hammocks strung between the palms while you contemplate your dinner options. There are some basic wooden huts for budget travellers here, but at US$60/80 for a single/double they seem expensive, especially considering that you share a bathroom.

**The Place** HOTEL $$$
(☎099 604002; www.stayattheplace.com; P❄📶🏊) The most luxurious hotel on the peninsula, The Place offers airy bungalows with soaring ceilings, large bathrooms, flat-screen TVs, iPod docks and coffee makers, where you can seal yourself up in an air-conditioned stupor and forget that you're even at the beach. There's also a pricey (and excellent) restaurant and bar, with ground- and 1st-floor terraces overlooking the water.

### Getting There & Away

Get a *poda poda* to Waterloo and from there you can find a share taxi to Tokeh. Tokeh Beach is just around the bend from River No 2 and it's possible to walk between the two at low tide.

## Bunce Island

Once a major trading post for the transatlantic slave trade, Bunce Island lies some 30km up the Sierra Leone River from the ocean. Men, women and children who were kidnapped in the interior were brought to the fort to be traded. Until the British outlawed the industry in 1808, some 30,000 passed through the island and onto slave ships bound for the Americas, many to Georgia and South Carolina. Among those who have been traced back to here are the Gullah families of South Carolina.

Bunce Island is on a tentative list for inclusion as a Unesco World Heritage site, but unlike similar sites in Ghana and Senegal, it sees few visitors, mostly because it's costly and difficult to get to. Its isolation, coupled with the fact that it has never been used for any other purpose – essentially abandoned since the 1800s – makes a visit here feel even more haunting.

Visit Sierra Leone (p471) in Freetown can arrange a trip with a boat and guide for US$260 per group, as can the Sierra Leone National Museum (p467), at a similar price. You could also try hiring a boat yourself from Kissy Ferry Terminal (count on spending around US$200 for a return journey).

Those on lower budgets could try going via Pepel, the nearest village. You could get the public ferry from Kissy Terminal to Tagrin (1st/2nd class Le11,000/5,000), from where Pepel is a 90-minute ride by taxi or *okada*.

# THE NORTH

## Makeni

POP 126,000

Makeni is a good base for exploring the northern highlands, and all of the city's hotels will be able to advise you on getting out into the countryside, including rock-climbing and hiking.

The annual **Sierra Leone Marathon** (www.sierraleonemarathon.com) was set up in 2012. Runners follow a route through the villages and communities surrounding Makeni, raising funds for the charity Street Child (www.streetchild.co.uk). Over 100 international runners travelled to the town for the most recent event in 2016.

### Sleeping

★**St Josephs School for the Hearing Impaired** GUESTHOUSE $
(☎088 509755; Teko Rd; s/d Le150,000/200,000, with shared bathroom Le100,000/200,000; P❄📶) You'll get a warm welcome at St Josephs, by far the nicest place to stay in town. It's set in a beautiful old colonial building, which has a wraparound veranda, and the airy rooms come with high ceilings and splashes of colour from local fabrics. There's also a small dining room where meals are served (lunch/dinner Le30,000/50,000, order in advance). Be sure to tour the well-run school while you're here.

★**Rogbonko Village** GUESTHOUSE $
(☎076 877018; www.rogbonkovillage.com; per person US$20) Experience life in a rural Sierra Leonean village at this excellent, community-run initiative, where guests are invited to take part in daily village life and

WORTH A TRIP

**YORK**

A little Krio village steeped in history, York was settled in the early 1800s by freed slaves starting a new life, including many Royal African Corps (liberated slaves who served Britain in the Napoleonic wars). It's a wonderful place to wander around for an hour or so. The streets are laid out in a grid fashion, and are full of colourful Krio board houses, reminiscent of those found in the southern states of the USA.

sample (or even learn to cook) local country food. The village is beautifully set in native forest, and surrounded by rivers, ripe for exploring.

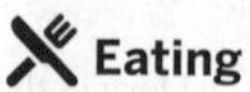

### Eating

**Club House** INTERNATIONAL $$
(mains Le45,000-60,000; 11am-11pm Mon-Fri, 10am-midnight Sat & Sun) Popular with the expat crowd, the place to come for burgers, grills, pizzas and breakfast, or just to drink a cool beer in the courtyard. It's all for a good cause too – profits go towards Street Child Sierra Leone.

**De Rock's** INTERNATIONAL $$
(076 558150; Lunsar Makeni Hwy; 9am-10pm; ) An air-conditioned space above Adnams Supermarket, this restaurant serves grilled meat, burgers, pizza and pasta.

### Getting There & Away

Bush taxis and *poda-podas* run to many destinations, including Freetown (Le25,000, four hours).

## Mt Bintumani

Also known as Loma Mansa, the breathy King of the Mountains, 1945m-high Mt Bintumani is the second-highest peak in West Africa, after Mt Cameroon. The mountain range is rich in highland birds and mammal species, including duikers, colobus monkeys, buffalo, leopards and snakes. And it's well worth the two- to five-day adventure; the spectacular summit looks out over most of West Africa, veiled by soft, cool mist.

Any climbing attempt should be taken seriously, not just because of the difficulty of the climb, but because of the poor condition of the access roads (you might want to stay away during the slippery rainy season!). You'll also need to come prepared with GPS and hiking and camping equipment, as well as adequate provisions for the climb, including plenty of water, and snacks for energy. Hiring a guide/porter who knows the mountain is essential.

Simple accommodation is often available in the villages surrounding Mt Bintumani, or they'll at least find you somewhere in the village to camp. Ask the chief of the village on arrival. On the mountain, camping is the only option, and you'll have to bring all equipment with you.

For Sokurala, you'll have to come via Makeni. Take the road east towards Koidu, then north to Sangbania via Kurubonla. You'll have to leave your car there and walk the final stretch (about an hour) to Sokurala. If coming on public transport, you'll need to get a shared taxi from Makeni to Koidu and from there arrange an *okada* to Sangbania.

To get to Sinekoro, first get to Kabala and then either drive (you'll need a 4WD) or arrange an *okada*. You can reach Yfin from either Kabala or Makeni. If coming from Makeni, head north on the Kabala road, turning right at Binkolo, and following the road past Bumbuna and Alikalia.

## Outamba-Kilimi National Park

About 300km north of Freetown, **Outamba-Kilimi** (Le7500) is a magical place, a mixture of jungle and savannah embedded between two hippo-filled rivers, and home to nine species of primate, pygmy hippo and, reputedly, leopard. While it doesn't match the grandeur of East Africa's parks and reserves, there are more gentle pleasures to be had here, such as searching for elusive forest elephants or gliding down the river listening to the chatter of monkeys and birds in the overhanging trees.

**Safari Village** (079 189718; next to the Kabba ferry; huts US$15; P) is a guesthouse with simple thatch huts and mosquito nets set right next to the river. There's a kitchen for self-catering or meals available on request.

The incongruous **White House** (079 189718; r from US$45; P) built to resemble that well-known building in Washington, DC, has pleasant air-conditioned rooms and a 24-hour bar.

About 15km south of the park's main entrance is the town of Kamakwie, an eight-hour journey from Freetown. Take a bus (Le25,000) or *poda poda* (Le30,000) to Makeni and pick up onward transport there. The cheapest way from Kamakwie to the park is by *okada*.

# THE SOUTH

## Bo

POP 306,000

Sierra Leone's second city is a pleasant place to spend a day or two, dodging the *okadas* that zip about at breakneck speed, or chatting to one of the many students that call this university town their home. There are no must-see attractions here, but it serves as a useful stop-off for travellers heading east to Tiwai Island, or south to Bonthe.

Rooms at the **Sir Milton Hotel** (Kissy Town Rd; s/d Le100,000/120,000; ❄📶) are simple but clean and come equipped with air-conditioning and hot water. The restaurant on the ground floor serves decent plates of grills and rice (mains around Le20,000) and shows football matches on the flat-screen TV.

The fanciest place to stay in Bo is **Doha's Hotel** (☎079 944444; www.dohashotel.net; 103 Towama Rd; s/d Le375,000/525,000; P❄📶≋), where spacious rooms with cool tile floors and wi-fi are set across a series of stupefyingly ugly two-storey villas. There's also a pool (though if the hotel isn't busy, it may not be filled), a bar and a restaurant specialising in Lebanese food.

It's smooth tarmac all the way from Freetown, a journey of three to four hours by either government bus (Le20,000) or *poda poda* (Le25,000). Bush taxis to Freetown (Le25,000) and the Liberian border (Le45,000) depart from Maxwell Khobe Park near the centre. You can also pick up bush taxis to Freetown from the lorry park on the Bo–Freetown highway. The quickest way to Kenema is usually to go out to Shell-Mingo on the highway and jump in a shared taxi there (Le10,000).

## Turtle Islands

This beautiful, remote eight-island archipelago in Sierra Leone's southwest peninsula is made from soft golden sand, thick shavings of palm fronds, the purest turquoise water, and, quite frankly, dreams. Tethered to a traditional way of life, the islands swing to their own rhythms. You can explore most of them with the exception of Hoong, which is a male-only island reserved for rites of passage.

Arrange a fully catered trip through one of the guesthouses on the peninsula. Dalton's Banana Guest House (p472) offers excellent three-day camping trips from Banana Island to the Turtle Islands (a journey of around five hours, depending on the weather) for US$750 per group, including all camping equipment and food (maximum four people).

## Tiwai Island

One of the few remaining tracts of ancient rainforest in West Africa, Tiwai Island, meaning 'Big Island' in the Mende language, is Sierra Leone's most popular and accessible nature reserve. Set on the Moa River, the entire island is run as a conservation research project – known as the Tiwai Island Wildlife Sanctuary. Tiwai covers a mere 12 sq km, but teems with an astonishing range of flora and fauna, and is most famous for its primate population. Although not part of the island, Gola Rainforest National Park shares the same tract of rainforest as Tiwai Island.

### ◉ Sights

**Tiwai Island Wildlife Sanctuary** WILDLIFE RESERVE
(☎076-755146; www.tiwaiisland.org) Sierra Leone's most visited natural reserve is home to over 700 different plant species, 135 bird species (including eight species of hornbill), plus otters and sea turtles. Tiwai is most famous for its primate population – the forests are home to the striking black-and-white Diana monkey as well as chimpanzees. The endangered, elusive pygmy hippopotamus is also a resident here – of the estimated 2000 left in the wild, they are only found in Sierra Leone, Liberia, Guinea and Côte D'Ivoire.

### Activities

For a proper introduction to life on Tiwai Island, take one of the excellent tours, such as guided forest walks (day/night from Le25,000/50,000 per person). If you're keen to do it yourself, there are a few self-guided forest trails.

If you want to spend more time in the area, and experience life in the communities that surround the nature reserve, there's a community-managed initiative called the **Tiwai Heritage Trail** (www.tiwaiheritagetrails.weebly.com). As well as including time on Tiwai Island and/or the Gola Rainforest National Park, multi-day trips follow bush trails and include stays in Mende villages, eating local food and learning about daily village life, culture and history.

## Sleeping

Accommodation is provided either in tents (complete with foam mattresses and bedding) under a thatch canopy (US$30 to US$35), or in a bed at the simple research lodge (US$35). Either way, you'll get clean indoor shared bathrooms and a solid breakfast included in the rate. Drifting to sleep to the sounds of the rainforest makes for an atmospheric stay.

## Getting There & Away

From Bo, take a bus or *poda-poda* to Potoru (Le30,000, about three hours), but be warned that the last section of road is rough and unpaved and can be impassable in the wet season. From Potoru, you'll have to get an *okada* to Kambama, a 30-minute ride via a narrow stretch of road rising up through the forest. Once in Kambama, which sits on the banks of the Moa River, you can cross the river by canoe or speedboat (the journey is included in the Le100,000 entry fee).

If you'd rather have the comfort of an organised excursion, the Environmental Foundation for Africa started running regular weekend trips to Tiwai in November 2016. The trips leave Freetown on Friday mornings (two-/three-night packages US$110/142 per person; see www.tiwaiisland.org for more information).

# Gola Rainforest National Park

Part of the same tract of rainforest as Tiwai Island, the **Gola Rainforest National Park** (076 420218; www.golarainforest.org) is home to an abundance of creatures great and small, from rare, intricately patterned butterflies to lost, lumbering forest elephants having a hard time locating the rest of their species (as in most parts of West Africa, their numbers are critically low). The park runs from Tiwai Island in the south up to the rocky Malema hills in the north. In September 2016, the Liberian side of the rainforest became the Liberian Gola Forest National Park, and together with the Sierra Leonean side becomes a trans-boundary peace park protecting some 1600 sq km.

Almost all visitors tour the park on a pre-arranged package through the **park headquarters** (076 420218; 164 Dama Rd) in Kenema, which include all food, park entry fees, guides and accommodation. Among the 10 packages on offer are camping and canoeing trips (from Le208,000 per person for two days), multiday forest hikes in search of primates and elephants (from Le600,000 per person for a four-day trip), and two-day community stays (from Le147,000 per person). As part of efforts to minimise impact on the park, tours are accompanied by a national park staff member and a community guide.

You can either bed down in a forest campsite (Le30,000 per person; Le15,000 if you bring your own equipment), or in one of three community lodges (Le30,000 per person), each of which has simple rooms with mosquito nets, a clean shared bathroom with running water, and a small lounge. All accommodation must be booked in advance.

Simple local meals, which must be arranged in advance, cost Le10,000 per person per meal.

## Getting There & Away

There are three main entry points to the park: Belebu, Lalehun and Sileti, all accessed via Joru, some 30 km south of Kenema. All roads leading to the park are unpaved and require a 4WD vehicle (the journey should take between two and three hours, depending on which part of the park you are heading to). If you don't have your own wheels, the guys at the office in Kenema can arrange transport for you, or you can make the journey by *okada* (around Le90,000).

# UNDERSTAND SIERRA LEONE

## Sierra Leone Today

In 2013, things were on the up in Sierra Leone. Ernest Bai Koroma had just won a second term in power in an election hailed as a marker of the peaceful postwar era, and the country was poised for an iron ore boom, as well as increased interest in tourism. Then in 2014 the devastating Ebola epidemic hit, freezing much of the country's economy. This was swiftly followed by a crash in the world price of metals and the collapse of two of the country's biggest mining companies, resulting in the loss of tens of thousands of jobs. The country had gone from one of Africa's fastest-growing economies in 2013 to the world's fastest-shrinking economy in 2015.

With Sierra Leone finally declared Ebola-free by the World Health Organization in March 2016, and the government implementing plans to expand agricultural growth, the country is slowly starting to rebuild itself – a revival that will hopefully be bolstered by much needed growth in the tourist industry now that the country is safe to visit once more.

## History

The North American slave trade was effectively launched from Freetown in 1560, and by the 18th century Portuguese and British trading settlements lined the coast. In the late 1700s, freed slaves from places such as Jamaica and Nova Scotia were brought to the new settlement of Freetown. Soon after, Britain abolished slavery and Sierra Leone became a British colony. Many subsequent settlers were liberated from slaving ships intercepted by the British navy and brought here. These people became known as Krios and assumed an English lifestyle, together with an air of superiority.

But things didn't run smoothly in this brave new world. Black and white settlers dabbling in the slave trade, disease, rebellion and attacks by the French were all characteristics of 19th-century Sierra Leone. Most importantly, indigenous people were discriminated against by the British and Krios, and in 1898 a ferocious uprising by the Mende began, ostensibly in opposition to a hut tax.

### Diamonds Are Forever

Independence came in 1961, but the 1960s and 1970s were characterised by coups (once there were three in one year, an all-African record), a shift of power to the indigenous Mende and Temne peoples, and the establishment of a one-party state (which lasted into the 1980s). By the early 1990s, the country was saddled with a shambolic economy and rampant corruption. Then the civil war began.

Foday Sankoh's Revolutionary United Front (RUF) seized large swathes of the country, including Sierra Leone's diamond and gold fields, with looting, robbery, rape, mutilation and summary execution, all tools of the RUF's trade. While their troops plundered to make ends meet, Charles Taylor in Liberia and the RUF's leaders enriched themselves from diamonds smuggled south.

The Sierra Leone government was pretty ineffective and tried using South African mercenaries against the RUF. In 1996, elections were held and Ahmad Tejan Kabbah was declared president, but a year later, after peace talks had brought some hope, the country descended into bloodshed.

### Hopes & Fears

In March 1998, the Economic Community of West African States Monitoring Group (ECOMOG), a Nigerian-led peacekeeping force, retook Freetown and reinstated Kabbah. In January 1999, the RUF and AFRC launched 'Operation No Living Thing'. The ensuing carnage in and around Freetown killed 6000 people and mutilated many more (cutting a limb off was an RUF calling card). A massive UN peacekeeping mission (Unamsil) was deployed. Three hundred UN troops were abducted, but as the RUF closed in on Freetown in mid-2000 the British government deployed 1000 paratroopers and an aircraft carrier to prevent a massacre and shift the balance of power back to Kabbah's government and UN forces. Kabbah was re-elected and the RUF's political wing was soundly defeated.

Unamsil became the largest and most expensive peacekeeping mission in UN history up until that time, and also one of its most effective. The last of the 17,500 soldiers departed in 2005. Peace had won.

The Special Court for Sierra Leone, a UN-backed judicial body charged with investigating war crimes during the conflict, was set up in 2002 and took 10 years for proceedings against more than 15 people to be completed. The court's most famous convictee is Charles Taylor, the former president of next-door Liberia, who received a jail sentence of 50 years in 2012.

## Culture

The two largest of the 18 tribal groups, the Temnes of the north and Mendes of the south, each make up about one-third of the population. Krios, mostly living in Freetown, constitute about 1.5% of the population but a large percentage of the professional class.

About 70% of Sierra Leoneans are Muslim; around 20% Christian; and a further 10% or so are followers of traditional or animist faiths. The majority of Christians live in the south. Sierra Leoneans are very tolerant, and mixed marriages are common.

# SURVIVAL GUIDE

##  Directory A–Z

### ACCOMMODATION

Freetown has a growing number of accommodation choices, although you may have to pay through the roof for 24-hour power, water and internet. Elsewhere in the country, choices are more limited, but you can still find some gems.

### DANGERS & ANNOYANCES

Sierra Leone is generally safe, although the biggest dangers are the roads and the tides, both of which can claim travellers who aren't vigilant about safety. Read up on rip tides before you travel, and be sure to wear a seatbelt whenever possible: driving safety standards aren't always of the highest. Avoid walking on Freetown's beaches alone – you should be fine on the peninsula – and it's best to walk in a group at night. Motorbike taxis are not the safest way to travel, especially in Freetown and other places with smooth roads. Make sure that your driver has a spare helmet.

### EMBASSIES & CONSULATES

Most embassies are located in Freetown.

**British High Commission** (Map p466; ☎076 780713; www.ukinsierraleone.fco.gov.uk; 6 Spur Rd; ⏲8am-4.30pm Mon-Thu, 8am-1pm Fri) Assists French nationals.

**Gambian High Commission** (Map p468; ☎022 225191; 6 Wilberforce St)

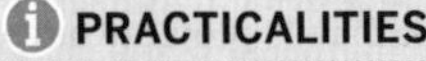

**Electricity** Current is 230V/50Hz. Plugs have three large pins, like the UK.

**Weights & measures** Sierra Leone uses the metric system.

**German Embassy** (Map p466; ☎078 732120; 3 Middle Hill Station; ⏲9am-noon Mon-Fri)

**Ghanaian High Commission** (Map p466; ☎076 100502; www.ghanahighcommission-freetown.sl; 43 Spur Rd)

**Guinean Embassy** (Map p466; ☎022 232584, 022 232469; 6 Carlton Carew Rd)

**Liberian Embassy** (Map p466; ☎022 230991; 2 Spur Rd)

**Malian Consulate** (Map p466; ☎022 231781; 40 Wilkinson Rd)

**Nigerian Embassy** (Map p468; ☎022 224229; 37 Siaka Stevens St)

**Senegalese Consulate** (Map p468; ☎022 222948; 9 Upper East St)

**US Embassy** (☎099 105500; http://freetown.usembassy.gov; Southridge, Hill Station; ⏲8am-5pm Mon-Thu, 8am-12.30pm Fri)

### EMERGENCY & IMPORTANT NUMBERS

| | |
|---|---|
| Sierra Leone's country code | ☎232 |
| Police | ☎999 |
| Ambulance | ☎999 |
| Fire | ☎019 |

### FOOD

Sierra Leone is known for its cuisine, and every town has at least one *cookery* (basic eating house) serving *chop* (meals). Rice is the staple and *plasas* (pounded potato or cassava leaves, cooked with palm oil and often fish or beef) is the most common sauce. Other typical dishes include okra sauce, groundnut stew and pepper soup. Street food, such as fried chicken, roasted corn, chicken kebabs and *fry fry* (simple sandwiches), is easy to find.

### INTERNET ACCESS

Most of the good hotels, and some of the restaurants, offer free wi-fi. Most expats get by with USB pay-as-you-go internet sticks. You can also pick up internet-ready SIM cards for smartphones and tablets.

### LGBTIQ TRAVELLERS

Homosexuality is illegal in Sierra Leone and most gay relationships are carried out in secrecy. Many hotels and guesthouses will refuse to let same-sex couples share a room.

### MONEY

**ATMs** Ecobank and UBA ATMs in Freetown spit out up to Le400,000 per day for those with Visa credit and debit cards. Don't rely on them too heavily, however, as they sometimes don't work. If leaving Freetown (to head down to the peninsula, for example), it pays to take all the cash you think you'll need with you, and then some.

**Changing money** The most easily exchangeable currencies in Sierra Leone are US dollars, UK pounds and euros, in that order. Large denominations get the best rates. Forex bureaus (and street traders, though avoid them unless somebody you trust makes the introduction) invariably offer better rates than banks.

**Credit cards** Not widely accepted in Sierra Leone – you can generally only use them at top end hotels – but some Rokel Commercial Bank branches give cash advances on Visa cards.

**Tipping** At your discretion for hotels; staff at top-end hotels are more like to expect it. Not expected at restaurants, but always welcome. It is common practice to tip guides and drivers at the end of a trip or tour. When visiting a village it's polite to make a cash offering to the local chief.

### Exchange Rates

| | | |
|---|---|---|
| Australia | A$1 | Le5670 |
| Canada | C$1 | Le5500 |
| Euro zone | €1 | Le8200 |
| Japan | ¥100 | Le6800 |
| New Zealand | NZ$1 | Le5200 |
| UK | UK£1 | Le9700 |
| USA | US$1 | Le7525 |
| West African franc | CFA 1US$1 | Le9000 |

### OPENING HOURS

**Banks** Usually 8.30am to 4pm Monday to Friday, with a select few also open 9am to 1pm Saturday.

**General shops and offices** 9am to 5.30pm Monday to Saturday, though some places close at 1pm on Saturday.

### PUBLIC HOLIDAYS

Besides the Islamic and Christian holidays, Sierra Leone celebrates New Year's Day (1 January) and Independence Day (27 April).

### TELEPHONE

SIM and micro-SIM cards are widely available. Airtel and Africell offer 3G coverage and mobile broadband.

### TOURIST INFORMATION

**National Tourist Board** (p471) Might be helpful.

**Visit Sierra Leone** (p471) A great source of pre-departure information.

## Getting There & Away

### AIR

**Brussels Airlines** (Map p468; ☎076 333777; www.brusselsairlines.com; 30 Siaka Stevens St; ⏰9am-5pm Mon-Fri, 10am-noon Sat) serves its hub in Brussels, **Kenya Airways** (Map p468; ☎077 001001; www.kenya-airways.com; 19 Walpole St) flies from Nairobi and Accra; **Royal Air Maroc** (AT; Map p468; ☎022 221015; www.royalairmaroc.com; 19 Charlotte St) flies from London via Casablanca, and Air France flies from Paris via Abidjan. KLM is launching direct fights from Amsterdam to Freetown in 2017.

### LAND

#### Guinea

The main route to Guinea is via Pamelap. Bush taxis from Freetown to Conakry run regularly (Le60,000), and government buses leave central Freetown at 6am Monday to Thursday (Le50,000). The journey usually takes eight to 10 hours.

From Kamakwie to Kindia (Guinea) there's little transport on the Sierra Leone side, where the road is quite bad. Four-wheel drives usually leave Kamakwie every two or three days (Le80,000, eight to 10 hours). Alternatively, hire an *okada* (motorcycle taxi) to the border (they'll ask for around Le150,000), where it's about a 1.5km walk to Madina-Oula in Guinea. Here you might be able to find a bush taxi; if not, an *okada* can take you all the way to Kindia.

#### Liberia

Taxis (Le90,000) and sometimes *poda-podas* (minibuses; Le80,000) depart from Bo and Kenema to the border post at Gendema (taking six to eight hours in the dry season and 10 to 12 hours in the wet), where you walk over to Liberia and continue in one of the frequent taxis to Monrovia.

## Getting Around

### CAR & MOTORCYCLE

Car hire is expensive (starting at around US$100 a day for a car with a driver in Freetown, and at least US$150 to head upcountry, not including the driver's expenses), but don't choose a company only on the price; ask about the terms too. Visit Sierra Leone (p471) and IPC Travel (p471) both hire reliable vehicles with drivers. Another good company is **Sierra Leone Car Hire** (☎076 345687, 077 461316; www.sierraleonecarhire.com).

You could also just charter ('*chatah*') a taxi. In Freetown, you can usually negotiate an hourly rate of Le30,000 per hour.

### LOCAL TRANSPORT

Bush taxis and *poda-podas* (minibuses) link most towns; however, except for departures to and from Freetown and between Bo and Kenema, you'll find that traffic is usually pretty sparse, especially on Sunday. Buses will usually cost a little less, but they are slower.

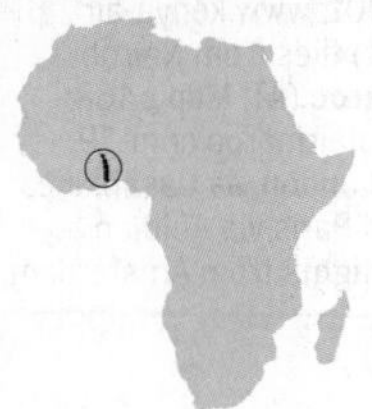


# Togo

☎228 / POP 7.7 MILLION

**Includes ➡**



## Best Places to Eat

- Côté Jardin (p483)
- La Belle Époque (p485)
- Le Fermier (p488)
- Centre Grill (p490)

## Best Places to Sleep

- Chez Alice (p483)
- Côté Sud (p482)
- Hôtel Napoléon Lagune (p483)
- Hôtel Coco Beach (p483)
- La Douceur (p490)

## Why Go?

For those fond of travelling off the beaten track, Togo is a rewarding destination. Its great diversity of landscapes ranges from lakes and palm-fringed beaches along the Atlantic coastline to the rolling forested hills in the centre; heading further north, the mantle of lush forest is replaced by the light-green and yellowy tinges of savannah. It's an excellent playground for hikers – there's no better ecofriendly way to experience the country's savage beauty than on foot.

Another highlight is Togo's melting-pot culture. The fortified compounds of Koutammakou are a reminder that the country's ethnically diverse population didn't always get along, but nowadays voodoo, Muslim, Christian and traditional festivals crowd the calendar and are often colourful celebrations for all. The cherry on top is Lomé, the low-key yet elegant capital, with its large avenues, tasty restaurants and throbbing nightlife – not to mention the splendid beaches on its doorstep.

## When to Go

### Lomé

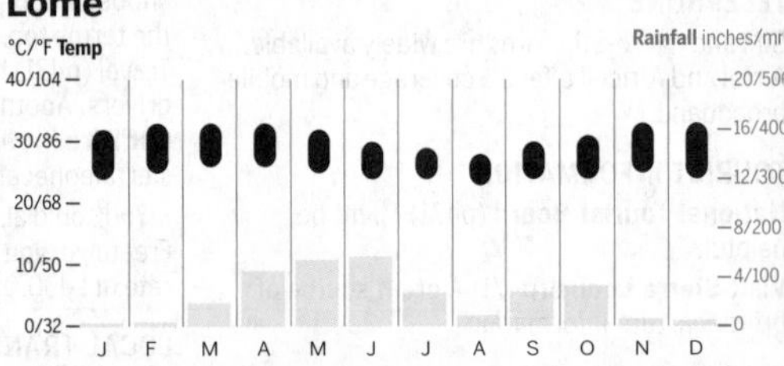


**Mar & Apr** The hottest period throughout the country is best avoided.

**May–Oct** Rainy season; there's a dry spell in the south mid-July to mid-September.

**Nov–Feb** Best time to visit, with pleasant temperatures. Perfect for outdoor activities.

## Togo Highlights

1. **Lomé** (p482) Soaking up the the mellow vibes, jazz clubs and vibrant markets of the coastal capital.
2. **Coco Beach** (p482) Unwinding on this blissful stretch of sand in a hammock while sipping a sundowner.
3. **Lac Togo** (p487) Relaxing on the shores of this serene lake and taking a spin on a pirogue, a traditional local canoe.
4. **Kpalimé** (p487) Hiking in lush forested hills and cooling down with a dip beneath waterfalls.
5. **Parc Sarakawa** (p490) Tracking buffaloes, ostriches and antelope at Togo's most underrated wildlife reserve.
6. **Koutammakou** (p490) Seeking out northern Togo's remote clay-and-straw fortresses, the *tata* compounds.

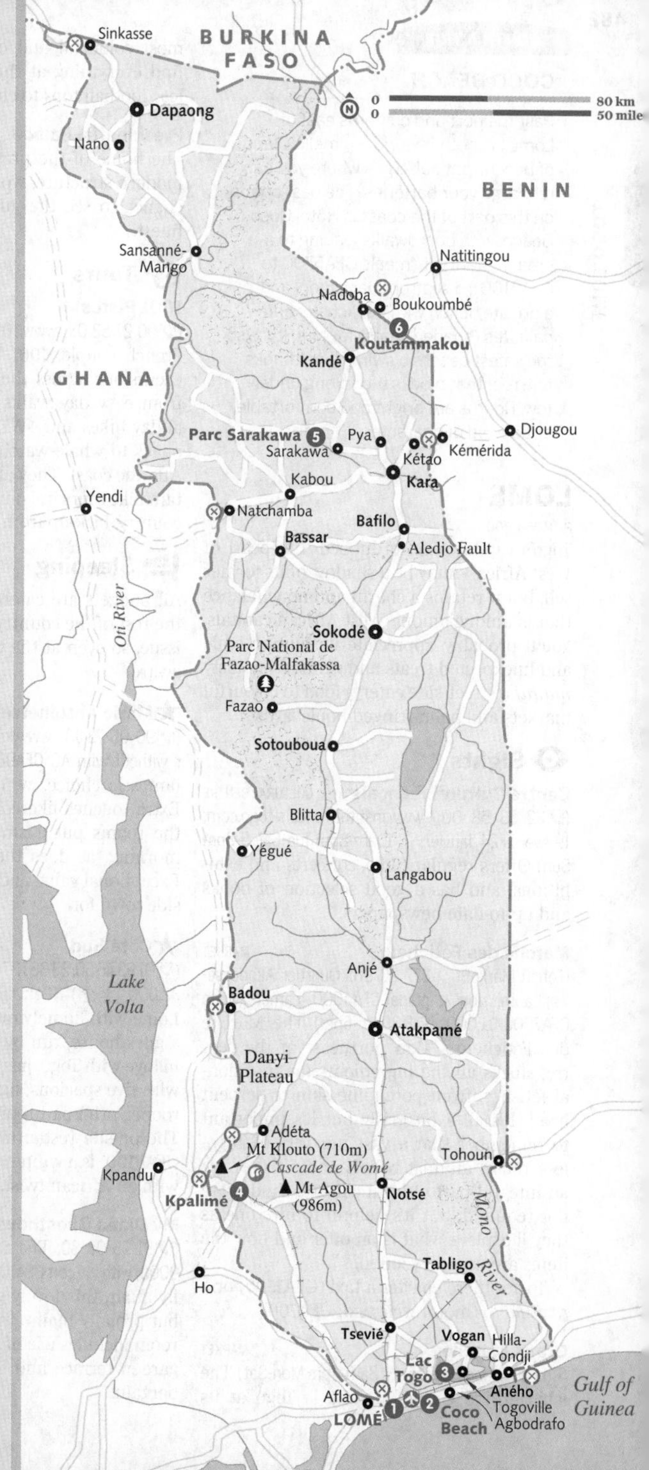

WORTH A TRIP

### COCO BEACH

Past the port and customs east of Lomé is another world – a mellow land of beachfront auberges where you can recharge your batteries. The best option on this part of the coast is Hôtel Coco Beach, with boardwalks leading to a great restaurant (meals CFA5700 to CFA7100), a seafront bar, a pool and a private beach with deckchairs and *paillotes* (shaded seats) for hire. It's also the safest beach to swim from, thanks to a reef that blocks the strong undertow. Rooms are bright and comfortable but devoid of character.

# LOMÉ

POP 754,000

Togo's capital – once dubbed 'the pearl of West Africa' – may be a shadow of its former self, but it retains a charm and nonchalance that is unique among West African capitals. You'll probably appreciate its human scale and unexpected treats and gems: from tasty *maquis* (street-side eatery) food to colourful markets and palm-fringed boulevards.

## Sights

**Centre Culturel Français** CULTURAL CENTRE
(☎22 53 58 00; www.institutfrancais-togo.com; 19 Ave du 24 Janvier; ⏲10am-8pm Tue-Sat, 5-8pm Sun) Offers regular films, concerts and exhibitions, and has a good selection of books and up-to-date newspapers.

**Marché des Féticheurs** MARKET
(Fetish Market; ☎227 20 96; Quartier Akodessewa; admission & guide CFA4000, camera/video CFA7000/11,000; ⏲8.30am-6pm) The Marché des Féticheurs, 4km northeast of the centre, stocks all the ingredients for traditional fetishes, from porcupine skin to serpent head. It's all a bit grisly but it's important to remember that a vast majority of Togolese retain animist beliefs and fetishes are an integral part of local culture. Guides are not required, but it's helpful to hire one as they'll explain what is on offer and how the items are used in voodoo.

To get there charter a taxi (CFA1500) or a *taxi-moto* (motorcycle taxi; CFA700).

**Grand Marché** MARKET
(Rue du Grand Marché; ⏲8am-4pm Mon-Sat) The labyrinthine Grand Marché is Togo at its most colourful and entrepreneurial. You'll find everything at this market, from Togolese football tops to cheap cosmetics.

**Presidential Palace** NOTABLE BUILDING
The home of the president is an imposing modern structure, worth a few pics and the chance to see the guards dressed in their finest.

## Tours

**1001 Pistes** TOURS
(☎90 27 52 03; www.1001pistes.com) Run by a French couple, 1001 Pistes offers excellent excursions across the country. These range from easy day walks from Lomé to several-day hikes and 4WD adventures with bivouacs to whale-watching outings along the Atlantic coast. They also offer guided mountain bike tours in Lomé and elsewhere in the country. Pick-up from your hotel is included.

## Sleeping

All budgets are catered for in Lomé. As in the rest of the country, security is always an issue, so even at the top establishments, be aware.

★**Marie Antoinette** HOTEL $
(☎90 05 73 13; www.kara-tg.com; Blvd 30 Août; r without/with AC CFA9000/12,500; P❄📶) A fantastic choice, with bright clean rooms. Extra touches like colourful wall murals in the rooms put a smile on your face each morning, as does the over-the-top service. Exceptional value and worth being a bit outside town for.

★**Côté Sud** GUESTHOUSE $
(☎91 93 45 50, 23 36 12 70; Rue Nima; r CFA24,000-32,000; ❄📶) Seeking a relaxing cocoon in Lomé with homely qualities? This champ of a guesthouse, run by a Frenchman who fell in love with Togo, has all the key ingredients, with five spacious, light and spick-and-span rooms, prim bathrooms and a small garden. The on-site restaurant (mains CFA3600 to CFA6100) is a winner for tasty French dishes with an African twist.

**My Diana Guesthouse** GUESTHOUSE $
(☎91 25 08 80; Rue des Jonquilles; r CFA6350-9000, with air-con CFA10,000-16,000; ❄) A family affair, this lovely guesthouse is a simple but proudly maintained establishment. The room includes use of the kitchen, a spacious garden terrace and TV lounge. It's a great bargain.

★**Chez Alice** GUESTHOUSE $$
(22 27 91 72; chezalice@hartmann-design.com; Blvd du Mono; campsites per person CFA1600, r CFA24,000-33,000; P) This perennial favourite is run by a friendly and efficient Swiss woman. Rooms in the massive wood structure are spotless and bright; camping is available on the grounds and the owner and the staff know everything about the area and will happily help out travellers. Meals are CFA3500 to CFA5000.

★**Hôtel Napoléon Lagune** HOTEL $$
(22 27 07 32; www.napotogo.com; Route 20 Bé; r CFA42,000-62,000; P) The Napoléon Lagune is not in the centre but its perch on a lively stretch of the Bé lagoon is outstanding. It offers a range of well-equipped (if unspectacular) rooms at reasonable prices. Good service, satellite TV, a plant-filled garden, a small pool and an excellent restaurant (mains CFA3500 to CFA6200) are among the other highlights.

**Hôtel Coco Beach** RESORT $$
(22 71 49 37; www.hotel-togo-cocobeach.com; Coco Beach; s CFA31,000-39,000, d CFA33,000-50,000; P) This breezy, open hotel and grounds is a sweet place to spend a few days. Staff are attentive, the restaurant serves excellent seafood (meals CFA5700 to CFA7100) and a backup generator for the air-con keeps things cool.

**Veronica Guest House** GUESTHOUSE $$
(22 22 69 07; Blvd du Mono; d CFA36,000-55,000; ) This charming 10-room hotel with professional staff, beautiful mahogany fittings and a pint-sized pool is a more Togolese alternative to the chain hotels. Both rooms and common areas are particularly spotless. Although it's on the busy highway, the rooms have thick double-glazing and views across the road to the beach. Meals are available (CFA13,000).

**Hôtel Mercure-Sarakawa** RESORT $$$
(22 27 65 90; www.accorhotels.com; Blvd du Mono; r with city view CFA112,000-119,000, with sea view CFA123,500-135,000; P) Despite its concrete bunker exterior, this is one of West Africa's most exclusive hotels, 3km east of the centre on the coastal road to Benin. Rooms are comfortable, but the Sarakawa's main drawcard is its stunning Olympic-sized swimming pool set in acres of coconut grove. Rates include breakfast.

## Eating

**Nopégali Plage** AFRICAN $
(22 28 06 20; Blvd du 13 Janvier (Blvd Circulaire); mains CFA1500-2000; 8am-10pm) You'll find no cheaper place for a sit-down meal in the centre. It's very much a canteen, but a good one, with friendly service and copious African dishes prepared like your Togolese grandma would make them.

**China Town** CHINESE $
(22 23 00 60; 67 Blvd du 13 Janvier (Blvd Circulaire); meals around CFA7500; noon-10pm Wed-Mon) Welcoming, reliable and in a good location at the Kodjoviakopé end of the Blvd Circulaire, this place offers a great selection of steamed dumplings and meat dishes.

**Brochettes de la Capitale** ARABIC $
(Blvd du 13 Janvier (Blvd Circulaire); kebabs CFA200; 5pm-1am) This Lomé institution is somewhat suffering from its popularity and location on the increasingly polluted Blvd Circulaire, but it's still a cool place to devour lip-smacking kebabs with a beer.

★**Côté Jardin** INTERNATIONAL $$
(Rue d'Assoli; mains CFA3500-7000; 11.30am-10.30pm Tue-Sun) Hands-down the most atmospheric eatery in Lomé, Côté Jardin has an exotic pleasure garden replete with tropical plants and woodcarvings. The supremely relaxing surrounds and eclectic menu make this a winner. Dim lighting contributes to the romantic ambience.

**Big Metro** AFRICAN $$
(Blvd du 13 Janvier (Blvd Circulaire); mains CFA1100-4700; 11.30am-10pm) This little eatery with a pavement terrace is a great spot to catch local vibes and nosh on unpretentious yet tasty African staples. The braised fish of the day is superb.

**Greenfield** PIZZA, INTERNATIONAL $$
(22 21 21 55; Rue Akati; mains CFA4500-6000; 11am-11pm) It's a bit out of the centre of the action, but this great garden bar-restaurant with a French owner has an original decor, with colourful lanterns and funky colonial seats with retro faux-leather cushions. The menu features wood-fired pizzas (evenings only), meat grills, salads and pastas.

**Bena Grill** STEAK $$
(22 21 50 87; Rue du Lac Togo; mains CFA2000-7500; 8am-11pm) A nirvana for carnivores, this cheery restaurant in the market area is lauded for its top-quality meat dishes,

# Lomé

0 – 400 m
0 – 0.2 miles
Rakieta (5km)
US Embassy; Service Immigration Togolaise; Gare d'Agbalépédo
Marché des Féticheurs
Rue Kponvene
Rue Moussons
Ave F Mitterand
Rue Abovey
Le Circus
Ave de la Nouvelle Marche
Ave de la Libération
Blvd Houphouet Boigny
Blvd du 13 Janvier (Blvd Circulaire)
Train Station
Ave Nicolas Grunitsky
Place de l'Indépendance
Place des Martyrs
Ave du 24 Janvier
Rue du Chemin de Fer
Rue Aniko Palako
Rue Kouenou
Blvd Notre Dame des Apôtres
Rue d'Almeida
Rue Litimé
Rue de L'Entente
Blvd du Mono
Veronica Guest House (1.5km); Alt München (2.3km); Hôtel Mercure-Sarakawa (2.5km)
Place du Petit Marché
Rue Koketi
Ave Joseph Strauss
Ave de Nîmes
Eyadéma Omnisports Stadium
Ave Sarakawa
Ave du Golfe
Ave Pompidou
Rue de Kouromé
Rue de la Gare
Rue du Grand Marché
Rue Tokmaké
Rue des Artisans
Rue Sylvanus Olympio
Rue du Lac Togo
Blvd de la Marina (République)
Beach
Ave de Duisberg
Ave Général de Gaulle
Ave de la Présidence
Presidential Palace
Rue des Jonquilles
Rue des Camomilles
KODJOVIAKOPÉ
Route d'Aflao
Blvd de la Marina (République)
Beach
Disused Jetty
Atlantic Ocean (Gulf of Guinea)
Ghanaian border (550m)
1 2 3 4 5 6 7 8 9 10 11 12 13 14 15 16 17 18 19 20 21 22 23 24 25 26 27 28 29 30 31 32 33
A B C D E F G

## Lomé

**Sights**
- 1 Centre Culturel Français ........ D2
- 2 Grand Marché ........ E3

**Sleeping**
- 3 Côté Sud ........ F1
- 4 Hôtel Ibis-le Bénin ........ C3
- 5 My Diana Guesthouse ........ A4

**Eating**
- 6 Bena Grill ........ F2
- 7 Big Metro ........ A3
- 8 Brochettes de la Capitale ........ E1
- 9 China Town ........ B4
- 10 Côté Jardin ........ G2
- 11 La Belle Époque ........ A4
- 12 Le Pêcheur ........ G2
- 13 Nopégali Plage ........ G2

**Drinking & Nightlife**
- 14 Byblos ........ F1
- 15 Le 54 ........ B2

**Entertainment**
- 16 Cotton Club ........ E2
- 17 Le Rézo ........ C1

**Shopping**
- 18 Village Artisanal ........ C1

**Information**
- 19 Banque Atlantique ........ D2
- 20 Direction de la Promotion Touristique ........ F2
- 21 Ecobank ........ E1
- 22 French Embassy ........ C3
- 23 German Embassy ........ A4
- 24 Pharmacie Bel Air ........ D3

**Transport**
- 25 ABC ........ E3
- 26 Air Côte d'Ivoire ........ D3
- 27 Air France ........ A3
- 28 Asky ........ D3
- 29 CTS ........ F1
- 30 Ethiopian Airlines ........ D3
- 31 Gare de Cotonou ........ E3
- 32 NTI ........ F1
- Royal Air Maroc ........ (see 26)
- 33 STIF ........ F3

including a sensational *côte porc grillée* (grilled pork rib). Also serves sandwiches, burgers and salads. It's next to the Marox supermarket.

**★La Belle Époque** FRENCH $$$
(☎22 20 22 40; Hôtel Belle-Vue, Kodjoviakopé; mains CFA9500-18,000; ⊙11am-11:30pm) One of Lomé's finest tables, La Belle Époque – all crisp white tablecloths and dimmed lighting – serves a refined, French-inspired cuisine. You can enjoy your meal in a verdant courtyard or the classy dining room inside.

**Alt München** FRENCH, GERMAN $$$
(☎22 27 63 21; Blvd du Mono; mains CFA6200-11,300; ⊙11am-10pm Thu-Tue) A well-regarded restaurant just east of Hôtel Mercure-Sarakawa, offering a good selection of French and Bavarian specialities, including *jarret de porc* (pork knuckle) and *fondue bourguignonne* (meat fondue). Fish dishes are also available.

**Le Pêcheur** SEAFOOD $$$
(☎91 59 63 50; Blvd du Mono; mains CFA8500-10,500; ⊙11am-3pm Mon-Fri, to 9pm Sat) The name gives it away: this is a fantastic seafood place where you'll enjoy fish fillet *a la plancha* (cooked on a griddle) and skewered *gambas* (prawns). Well worth the splurge – if only it had an outdoor terrace!

### Drinking & Nightlife

Bars and clubs often fuse into one in the capital. Locals dress up when hitting the dance floor and going out for cocktails, so leave your sneakers and casual clothes at home for most dance clubs.

**Le 54** BAR
(☎22 20 62 20; Blvd du 13 Janvier (Blvd Circulaire); ⊙10am-midnight Thu-Sun) A nice blend of exhibition space, affordable craft and jewellery, and a vibrant restaurant-bar. There's great live music Thursday to Sunday, catering for all musical tastes from electronic and house to rap and pop.

**Byblos** CLUB
(Blvd du 13 Janvier (Blvd Circulaire); around CFA7000; ⊙from 10pm Wed-Sun) This trendy nightclub is a favourite haunt of rich young Togolese, with music ranging from electronic to hip hop.

### Entertainment

**Le Rézo** JAZZ
(☎22 20 15 13; 21 Ave de la Nouvelle Marché; ⊙10pm-1am) Inside, it's like a 1980s disco with its blacked-out windows, but Le Rézo is more contemporary than it looks, with giant screens showing Champions League football games, as well as karaoke nights and live jazz on Thursday.

**Cotton Club** JAZZ
(☎90 04 45 70; Ave Augino de Souza; ⊙6pm-late Tue-Sun) This jazz and blues lounge bar is polished, homely and welcoming. Snacks are available.

## Shopping

Head to the stalls of **Rue des Artisans** (⊙7.30am-6pm Mon-Sat) to buy woodcarvings, leather bags and sandals, as well as jewellery from across West Africa – but come with your haggling cap firmly on. It's just off Blvd de la Marina (République), one street west of Rue de la Gare.

**Village Artisanal** GIFTS & SOUVENIRS
(☎22 16 80 70; Ave de la Nouvelle Marché; ⊙9am-5.30pm Mon-Sat) At this easy-going centre you'll see Togolese artisans weaving cloth, carving statues, making baskets and lampshades, sewing leather shoes and constructing cane chairs and tables – all for sale at reasonable, fixed prices.

## Information

### DANGERS & ANNOYANCES

- There are pickpockets around the Rue de Grand Marché and along Rue du Commerce.
- Avoid walking on the beach alone, especially at night – muggings are common.
- There is a very strong undertow along coastal waters, so if you'd like a swim, head for a pool, such as the one available to nonguests at Hôtel Mercure-Sarakawa or **Hôtel Ibis-le Bénin** (☎22 21 24 85; www.ibishotel.com; Blvd de la Marina).

### INTERNET ACCESS

There are numerous internet cafes in Lomé. Expect to pay CFA400 per hour.

### MEDICAL SERVICES

**Centre Hospitalier Universitaire de Tokoin** (☎22 12 50 10; Rte de Kpalimé) The main hospital, 1.5km northwest of the city.

**Pharmacie Bel Air** (☎22 10 32 10; Rue du Commerce; ⊙8am-7pm Mon-Fri, to 1pm Sat) Next to Hôtel du Golfe.

### MONEY

All banks change cash. Banks with ATMs are easy to find in the centre; they accept Visa cards.

**Banque Atlantique** (☎22 20 88 92; Place du Petit Marché; ⊙8am-4pm Mon-Fri, 9am-2pm Sat) is the only place that accepts MasterCard in Togo; it also accepts Visa and has an ATM.

**Ecobank** (☎22 17 11 40; 20 Rue du Commerce) This branch is equipped with Visa cash machines.

### POST

**Post Office** (☎22 13 19 50; Ave de la Libération; ⊙7.30am-5pm Mon-Fri, to 12.30pm Sat) Has an efficient poste-restante service.

### TELEPHONE

Local and international calls can be made from any of the multitude of private telephone agencies around the city.

### TOURIST INFORMATION

**Direction de la Promotion Touristique** (☎22 14 31 30; www.togo-tourisme.com; Rue du Lac Togo) Located in a run-down building near Marox Supermarché. Staff are helpful (if surprised to see tourists), and can give you a reasonable road map of Togo as well as information on traditional festivals, which they are keen to promote.

## Getting There & Away

**Rakieta** (☎90 29 88 04) runs a daily bus service between Lomé and Kara (CFA5900, 6½ hours). It leaves between 7am and 7.30am (or so) from its depot in Atikoumé. Book ahead or arrive early (6am) on the day. This service is a better option than bush taxis.

Bush taxis and minibuses travelling east to Aného (CFA1400, one hour), Lac Togo/Agbodrafo (CFA950, 45 minutes) and to Cotonou (Benin; CFA7400, three hours) leave from **Gare de Cotonou** (Blvd de la Marina), just west of the STIF bus station.

**Gare d'Agbalépédo** (Quartier Agbalépédo), 10km north of central Lomé, serves all northern destinations. Services include Atakpamé (CFA3800, two hours), Dapaong (CFA8900, 10 to 11 hours) and Kara (CFA7900, five hours).

Minibuses to Kpalimé (CFA2000, two hours) leave from **Gare de Kpalimé** (Rue Moyama), 1.5km north of the centre on Rte de Kpalimé.

There are also international services, including to/from Ghana (p496).

## Getting Around

To the airport (5km from central Lomé) the taxi fare is about CFA1900 (but count on CFA2500 from the airport into the city).

Taxis are abundant and have no meters. Fares are from CFA480 for a shared taxi (more after 6pm) and CFA1500 for a private ride. A taxi by the hour should cost CFA3000 if you bargain well.

Zippy little *moto-taxis* (motorcycle taxis) are also popular, if rather dangerous. You should be able to go anywhere in the centre for CFA500 to CFA800.

# SOUTHERN TOGO

The area between Aného, Kpalimé and Atakpamé is one of the most alluring in West Africa, with a combination of superb beaches, a vast lake, forested hills and numerous waterfalls. If you can only visit one area in Togo, this should surely be it.

## Lac Togo

On the southern shores of Lac Togo, part of the inland lagoon that stretches all the way from Lomé to Aného, **Agbodrafo** is a popular weekend getaway for frazzled Lomé residents. Swimming in the lake – which is croc- and bug-free – is blissful. It's also a good place to find a pirogue to **Togoville**, which was the former seat of the Mlapa dynasty and Togo's historical centre of voodoo.

There aren't many places to eat here. Bring your own food or eat at your hotel. East of Agbodrafo, the breezy, resort-like **Hôtel Le Lac**, (☎90 36 28 58; www.hotellelactogo.com; Agbodrafo; r CFA45,000-48,000, bungalows CFA68,000; P ❄ 📶 🏊) on the shores of Lac Togo, is a reliable choice. The renovated rooms are spacious, with private patios and sweeping lake views. There's a good restaurant (mains CFA2800 to CFA6000) overlooking the lake, a swimming pool and a small beach from where you can swim in the lake. Pirogue trips to Togoville (CFA3600) can easily be arranged.

The best route here is from Lomé; from its Gare de Cotonou bush taxis frequently travel along the coastal road to Aného (CFA1200) via Agbodrafo.

## Aného

POP 48,000

All that remains of Aného's days as colonial capital in the late 19th century are its crumbling pastel buildings – a stroll past may have you pondering the echoes of their past residents. Local voodoo practice is also strong, but the real reason to stay here is to use it as a base for visiting Vogan's Friday market, about a half-hour from town.

### Sights

**Vogan Friday Market** MARKET

(⏲8am-5 or 6pm Fri) This is one of the biggest and most colourful markets in Togo, with produce and bric-a-brac and a fun atmosphere. It's great for embracing local culture as well as picking up some fruit and veg.

It's located about 20km northwest of Aného. Taxis (CFA800, 30 minutes) leave from the junction of the coastal road and the highway to Lomé, on the eastern side of town.

### Festivals & Events

Aného plays host to the **Festival des Divinités Noires** (Festival of Black Divinities), which has been held in December each year since 2006. A celebration of voodoo, it features singing, dancing, the beating of drums and parades.

### Sleeping & Eating

There are some simple snack bars around town, but you'll find the quality and service better at hotel restaurants.

**Hôtel Oasis** GUESTHOUSE $

(☎23 31 01 25; Rte de Lomé-Cotonou; d with fan/air-con CFA11,000/17,000; P ❄) An unbeatable location east of the bridge, looking across the lagoon and the beach to the sea. The terrace is a prime place for a sunset drink. Rooms are basic, though – you're paying for the location.

**La Becca Hôtel** HOTEL $

(☎23 31 05 13; Rte de Lomé-Cotonou; r with fan CFA11,000-12,000, with air-con CFA16,500-21,000; P ❄ 📶) The cheap and cheerful La Becca is a good budget option, with smallish yet well-scrubbed rooms. The air-con rooms are significantly better than the fan-cooled units.

### Getting There & Away

From the *gare routière* (bus station), bush taxis and minibuses head to Lomé (CFA1200, one hour), as well as to the Beninese border and Cotonou (CFA2700, 2½ hours).

## Kpalimé

POP 101,500

Kpalimé is only 120km from Lomé, but it feels like another world. Hidden among the forested hills of the cocoa and coffee region, it offers some of Togo's best scenery and hiking and a lovely waterfall. It's also a busy place thanks to its proximity to the Ghanaian border and an important and lively market.

### Sights

**Cascade de Womé** WATERFALL

(Womé Falls; ☎99 01 01 12; Womé; CFA1100; ⏲8am-5pm) One great attraction in the Kpalimé area is these falls, 12km from Kpalimé.

You pay the admission fee to the Association Akatamanso at the entrance of the village of Womé (ask for a receipt); then it's a further 4km to the picnic area near the falls. From there it's a short but steep descent to the waterfalls through lush vegetation. You can swim beneath the falls – bliss!

From Kpalimé, a *moto-taxi* ride to the falls should cost around CFA3600 return, including waiting time.

**Market** MARKET
(⌚8am-6pm Tue & Sat) FREE Local farmers sell their produce here; there's also the usual bric-a-brac of plasticware and clothes. Since it's one of the biggest markets around this area, it's also the place where people meet and chat – offering some great people-watching and a chance to absorb the local culture.

As the location is close to the Ghanaian border, this market has a mix of both Togolese and Ghanaian vendors.

## Tours

**Adetop** TOURS
(☎90 08 88 54, 24 41 08 17; www.adetop-togo.com; Rte de Klouto) A small NGO promoting sustainable tourism, Adetop is based in Kpalimé but runs activities throughout the country. Its main activities are guided tours exploring the culture and heritage of Togo, as well as hiking. It is sensitive to local village culture and does a particularly good job visiting families and arranging meals and homestays with locals.

## Sleeping

**Hôtel Chez Felicia** HOTEL $
(☎22 46 33 49, 90 10 97 77; Rte de Missahoé; r with fan/air-con CFA8000/13,000; P ❄) Off the road to Klouto, the discreet Hôtel Chez Felicia is an excellent bargain. This low-slung building set in verdant surrounds shelters immaculate, bright rooms with back-friendly mattresses, crisply dressed beds and impeccable bathrooms. Meals are CFA2500 to CFA4000.

**Hotel Agbeviade** HOTEL $
(☎24 41 05 11; agbeviade2003@yahoo.fr; Rte de Missahoé, cnr of Rue de Bakula; r with fan CFA10,000, with air-con CFA19,500-22,500; ❄) Off the road to Klouto, the Agbeviade is a safe choice, although the smallish air-con rooms are a bit disappointing for the price. The restaurant's short menu concentrates on European dishes.

**Hôtel Le Geyser** HOTEL $
(☎24 41 04 67; www.hotellegeyser.com; Rte de Missahoé; r CFA15,000-22,000; P ❄ 📶 🏊) This tranquil place is 2km from the centre on the road to Klouto, in a balmy garden setting. Rooms are well tended, functional and airy, and the restaurant (mains CFA3500 to CFA5000) serves good African and European dishes. A real hit is the pool, larger than most others and kept impeccably clean.

**Auberge Vakpo Guest House** GUESTHOUSE $
(☎24 42 56 64, 91 53 17 00; www.vakpoguesthouse.com; Kpodzi; r with fan CFA10,000, with air-con CFA12,500; P ❄ 📶) A well-run little number with a quiet location near the Catholic church, Auberge Vakpo offers neat rooms with good bedding, meticulous bathrooms and a lovely pleasure garden complete with flower bushes, mural frescoes and sculptures. Meals are available for CFA3700. They also organise local excursions.

**Chez Fanny** INN $
(☎24 41 00 99; hotelchezfanny@yahoo.fr; Rte de Lomé; r CFA18,000; P ❄ 📶) This jolly good villa 2km south of town is a homey retreat. The eight rooms are huge and the patio is a lovely spot for relaxing, despite the fact it overlooks the busy Rte de Lomé. The restaurant (mains CFA3000 to CFA6000) is the best in town.

## Eating

★ **Le Fermier** AFRICAN, FRENCH $$
(☎90 02 98 30; mains CFA3000-4000; ⌚11.30am-9pm) For excellent European and African food, try this low-roofed, intimate spot on the northwestern outskirts of town. You can't really go wrong – everything is pretty good – but if you want a recommendation, go for the *fufu* (pounded yam), served in a clay pot.

**Chez Lazare** FRENCH $$
(Rte de Missahoé/Rte de Kusuntu; mains CFA1200-5600; ⌚11am-10pm) Don't be put off by the unappealing concrete walls: Lazare cooks up excellent French specialities – how does a *côte de porc à la dijonnaise* (pork rib in mustard sauce) sound? There's pasta as well. The rooftop terrace is pleasant in the evening.

## Drinking & Nightlife

**Chez Fomen** BAR
(Rue de Bakula; ⌚9am-late) This cheerful, easy-going bar is a fun place for a drink.

DON'T MISS

### HIKING IN THE KPALIMÉ AREA

The heartiest walk is up Togo's highest peak, **Mt Agou** (986m). The path climbs between backyards, through cocoa and coffee plantations and luxuriant forests bristling with life. Small terraced mountain villages pepper the slopes and provide fabulous views of the area – on a clear day, you can see Lake Volta in Ghana. The walk takes four hours' return from the village of Nyogbo. There's also a road to the top, so you can also walk one way and arrange a taxi for a ride back.

It's best to go with a local guide who will show you cool plants and unusual fruit and vegetables, and fill you up on local culture and history. Ask staff at your hotel to recommend the best guides.

Guides can also arrange anything from guided butterfly walks and even overnight village stays, as well as multi-day treks in the area. The area around **Mt Klouto** (710m), 12km northwest of Kpalimé, is another walking heaven, with forested hills, waterfalls and myriad butterflies; early morning is the best time to search for them.

t also shows regular football games and erves food.

**3ar Alokpa** BAR
Rte de Missahoé; ⌚11am-late) A popular bar on he main road, north of the centre.

## Information

3anks with ATMs can be found in the centre.

## Getting There & Away

'he *gare routière* is in the heart of town, two ›locks east of the Shell petrol station. The road ›etween Kpalimé and Atakpamé is the worst 1 the country, which means few taxis from ‹palimé travel further north than Atakpamé CFA2500, four hours) – you'll have to change here for services to Sokodé or Kara.

You can get minibuses direct to Lomé CFA2300, two hours), to the Ghanaian border CFA1000, 40 minutes) and to Ho (Ghana; :FA1650, 1½ hours).

# Atakpamé

OP 85,000

)nce the favourite residence of the German olonial administrators, Atakpamé today is . commercial centre. There are no sights ıere as such, but it makes a pleasant enough ,topover on long journeys.

## Sleeping & Eating

**Hôtel California** HOTEL $
☎23 35 85 44; Rte Internationale; r with fan & hared bathroom CFA3000, with air-con CFA9500-4,000; ❄) Despite being at the back of the 'otal petrol station, this hotel-restaurant s a good surprise, with uncomplicated yet potless rooms, salubrious bathrooms, excellent food (mains CFA1700 to CFA5000) and a friendly welcome. Opt for the air-con rooms, which have en-suite bathrooms and are noticeably better maintained than the fan-cooled units.

**Le Sahélien** AFRICAN $$
(☎24 40 12 44; Rte Internationale; mains CFA1900-6200; ⌚11.30am-9pm) The downstairs *maquis* (an informal, street-side eatery) with its enormous grill and informal atmosphere does a brisk trade with the town's *moto-taxis*. Upstairs is more upmarket, and the roof terrace is a nice spot to catch the evening breeze. It also doubles as a hotel, but the rooms need a freshen up – we recommend staying elsewhere.

## Getting There & Away

Taxis and minibuses leave from the main *gare routière*, south of the centre, to Dapaong (CFA7600, eight hours), Kara (CFA4200, five hours), Kpalimé (CFA2500, four hours) and Lomé (CFA2900, two hours).

There's a secondary *gare routière* next to the market in the centre of town, from where taxis regularly go to Kpalimé (CFA2000).

# NORTHERN TOGO

In the north, Islam takes over from Christianity as the dominant religion and its presence increases the further north you are. Most towns are short on sights, but for those with their own vehicle, or the determination to have a showdown with local bush taxis, fabulous highlights await in the castellated shapes of the Tamberma compounds in Koutammakou.

# Kara

POP 110,000

Laid out by the Germans on a spacious scale, Kara is the relaxed capital of northern Togo and a good base for trips to Koutammakou. Because Gnassingbé Eyadéma, the president of Togo from 1967 to 2005, was from Pya, a Kabye village about 20km to the north, he pumped a lot of money into Kara and the region has remained a political stronghold of the Eyadéma clan. Kara is also the base from which to explore wildlife at Parc Sarakawa.

## Sights

**Parc Sarakawa** WILDLIFE RESERVE

(90 55 49 21; hel228@hotmail.fr; adult/child CFA5000/2500; 8am-5pm) Unpretentious and relaxing, Parc Sarakawa is easily accessed from Kara as a day trip. While its wildlife-watching can't compare with that of the better-known parks in West Africa, this park spreads out over 607 hectares and is home to various species of antelope, buffaloes, ostriches and zebras. **Game drives** (CFA5000) can be arranged at the gate. There are plans to build a lodge within the park in the future.

## Festivals & Events

The area is famous for Evala, a coming-of-age festival held in July. The main event is *la lutte* (wrestling), in which greased-up young men try to topple each other in a series of bouts.

## Sleeping & Eating

★**La Douceur** INN $

(26 60 11 64; douceurkara@yahoo.fr; off Rue de Chaminade; r with fan CFA6000, with air-con CFA9000-12,000; ) Down a dirt track in the stadium's neighbourhood you'll find this cosy bird's nest in a proudly maintained and flowered little compound; rooms are spotless, with simple decor. The well-stocked bar serves the coldest beer in town and the *paillote* (straw awning) restaurant serves fresh, well-prepared food (mains CFA1600 to CFA4000).

**Marie-Antoinette** HOTEL, CAMPGROUND $

(26 60 16 07; http://ma.kara-tg.com; Rte Internationale; camping per person CFA1600, s/d with fan CFA7500/12,500, with air-con CFA15,500/16,500; ) In a pretty house, 3km south of Kara on Rte Internationale, Marie-Antoinette has rooms of varying size and shape. The dearer rooms are spacious, well-organised and come with hot-water bathrooms in good working order; you can also camp in the annexe across the street. One downside is the highway noise. The restaurant cooks up decent meals (CFA2800).

★**Centre Grill** AFRICAN, EUROPEAN $$

(Marox; 90 70 22 33; cnr Rte de Prison & Ave Eyadéma; mains CFA3200-4900; 8am-10pm) An attractive place with a straw roof, wicker light shades and blackboard menus, Centre Grill serves divine Togolese food and good Western dishes. Try its *fufu sauce arachide* with grilled fish or *pâte sorgho* (mashed sorghum), wash the lot down with a cold beer and polish it off with plantain fritters. Great value.

## Getting There & Away

From the main *gare routière*, about 2km south of the town centre, minibuses regularly head north to Kandé (CFA1400) and south to Atakpamé (CFA4700, four hours) and Lomé (CFA4800, seven hours). Taxis heading north to Dapaong (CFA3900, four hours) are scarce – and it's common to have to wait for a half or even a full day for one to fill up.

For buses heading to Lomé, **Rakiéta** (Rue du 23 Septembre) has a daily departure at 7.45am (CFA5800, six hours) from its depot.

To get to the border with Benin via Kétao (CFA700, 45 minutes), get a minibus or bush taxi from **Station du Grand Marché** (Ave Eyadéma), next to the market.

# Koutammakou

Also known as Tamberma Valley after the people who live here, Koutammakou has a unique collection of fortress-like mud houses, founded in the 17th century by people fleeing the slave-grabbing forays of Benin's Dahomeyan kings. Listed as a World Heritage Site by Unesco in 2004, the area is one of the most scenic in the country, with stunning mountain landscapes and intense light.

## Sights

**Tamberma Compound** NOTABLE BUILDING

(Nadoba; CFA1500; roughly 9am-5pm) This is an excellent example of a typical Tamberma compound, called a *tata*. There's a variety of traditional, inhabited *tatas* here, so typically a visit includes a greeting by the head of the compound and then the opportunity to enter a select few homes. Look for the fetish statues out front – they're meant to keep evil spirits away. The compound is about 2km from Nadoba, the area's main village. Purchase tickets at the Accueil et Billetterie office.

### Getting There & Away

To get here turn eastward off the Kara–Dapaong highway in Kandé and follow the track in the direction of Nadoba. The track is in good condition and crosses the valley all the way to Boukoumbé and Natitingou in Benin.

If you don't have your own transport, chartering a *moto-taxi*/taxi for the day (from the centre of town) will cost around CFA7000/26,000.

**TAMBERMA COMPOUNDS**

A typical Tamberma compound, called a *tata,* consists of a series of towers connected by a thick wall with a single entrance chamber, used to trap an enemy and shower them with arrows. The castle-like nature of these extraordinary structures helped ward off invasions by neighbouring tribes – and, in the late 19th century, the Germans.

As in the *tata somba* in nearby Benin, life in a *tata* revolves around an elevated terrace of clay-covered logs, where the inhabitants cook, dry their millet and corn, and spend most of their leisure time.

The Tamberma (the word means 'skilled builders') use only clay, wood and straw for their houses – there are no nails or metal parts. There may be a fetish shrine in front of the compound.

## Dapaong

POP 32,900

This lively little town is a West African melting pot, with the Burkinabé and Ghanaian borders both within 30km. It sits in the middle of Togo's most arid landscape and gets the full force of the dusty harmattan winds between November and February.

### Sleeping & Eating

**Hôtel Le Campement** HOTEL $

(☎90 01 81 06; Rte de la Station de Lomé; r with fan/air-con CFA9800/17,600; P ❄) This is Dapaong's only midrange hotel, but it's a tad overpriced. However, rooms are pleasant and spacious, and the overgrown garden filled with oversized sculptures is a cool place to laze around. The French bar-restaurant is expensive (mains from CFA4200), but the food is very tasty – and the desserts amazing.

**Auberge Idriss** GUESTHOUSE $

(☎27 70 83 49; off Rte Internationale; r with fan & shared bathroom CFA5000, with air-con CFA14,500-18,000; P ❄) A tidy little guesthouse in a quiet neighbourhood 2km north of town. Rooms in the main building are spacious; those in the annexe have shared facilities but are cosier. Rooms with air-con have ensuite bathrooms.

### Getting There & Away

Taxis leave the station on Route de Nasablé for Sinkasse on the Burkinabé border (CFA1400, 40 minutes), from where transport heads to Ouagadougou.

From Station de Lomé on Route Internationale, 2km south of the centre, bush taxis head to Kara (CFA4200, four hours) and Lomé (CFA9000, 12 hours).

## Sokodé

POP 119,000

Sokodé is Togo's second-biggest city – but it certainly doesn't feel like it, with no major sites beyond the odd colonial building. It's the best base for trips to the Parc National de Fazao-Malfakassa, however; head to Fondation Franz Weber's office for more information.

### Sights

**Parc National de Fazao-Malfakassa** NATIONAL PARK

(www.ffw.ch; CFA4000; ⏲10am-5pm Dec-May) This 1920-sq-km national park is one of the most diverse West African parks in terms of landscape, with forest, savannah, rocky cliffs and waterfalls. The park boasts 203 species of bird and many species of mammal, including monkeys, antelope and around 40 somewhat elusive elephants.

The park was run by the Swiss organisation Fondation Franz Weber until 2015 and handed over to the Togolese government, but at the time of writing the park's future was undetermined, as protection from poachers dwindled in 2016 and the delicate fauna of the park was under threat. Visit the website for the most up-to-date information.

## Sleeping & Eating

**Hôtel Essofa** HOTEL $

(☎25 50 09 89; r without/with air-con CFA8500/15,000; ❄) This is one of the better options in Sokodé, with a nice garden and relatively clean rooms. Main meals cost CFA1800.

**Hôtel Ave Kedia** HOTEL $$

(☎25 50 05 34; r without/with air-con CFA9000/16,000; ❄) As it's the only hotel in town with a generator (power cuts are all too frequent here), this is an excellent choice if you want to be assured of a cool escape and restful sleep. Rooms are simple but clean. Meals are CFA2200 to CFA4500.

**Cafeteria 2000** AFRICAN $$

(mains CFA1500-5000; ⏲11am-7pm) If you're not eating at your hotel, try this basic snack bar, where the menu spells out every possible combination of meat and side dish. It's BYO beer.

## Drinking & Nightlife

**Bar Temps en Temps** BAR

(⏲approx 4-11pm) With its massive BBQ and candle-lit tables, this joint doubles as a beer hang-out and a great spot to grab a bite.

## Information

**UTB** Has an ATM (but it often is out of order). They will also exchange euros or US dollars.

## Getting There & Away

You can catch taxis from the *gare routière* (which is one block west of the market, behind the Shell petrol station on Route de Bassar), or on the main square between the market and the mosque.

Minibuses go regularly to Kara (CFA1800, two hours), Atakpamé (CFA3200, four hours) and Lomé (CFA5500, six hours).

# UNDERSTAND TOGO

## Togo Today

Togolese are generally pessimistic about the political outlook for the country. Many believe that the results of the 2010 and 2015 presidential elections, which re-elected Faure Gnassingbé, were corrupted, resulting in protests.

## History

The country was once on the fringes of several great empires and, when the Europeans arrived in the 16th century, this power vacuum allowed the slave-traders to use Togo as a conduit.

Following the abolition of slavery, Germany signed a treaty in Togoville with local king Mlapa. Togoland, as the Germans called their colony, underwent considerable economic development, but the Togolese didn't appreciate the Germans' brutal 'pacification' campaigns. When the Germans surrendered at Kamina – the Allies' first victory in WWI – the Togolese welcomed the British forces.

However, the League of Nations split Togoland between France and Britain – a controversial move that divided the populous Ewe people. Following a 1956 plebiscite, British Togoland was incorporated into the Gold Coast (now Ghana). French Togoland gained full independence in 1960 under the country's first president, Sylvanus Olympio. But his presidency was short-lived. Olympio, an Ewe from the south who appeared to disregard the interests of northerners, was killed by Kabye soldiers in 1963. His replacement was then deposed by Kabye sergeant Gnassingbé Eyadéma. The new leader established a personality cult and became increasingly irrational following a 1974 assassination attempt.

In 1990, France began pressuring Eyadéma to adopt a multiparty system, but he resisted. The following year, after riots, strikes and the deaths of pro-democracy protestors, 28 bodies were dragged from a lagoon and dumped in front of the US embassy, drawing attention to the repression in Togo.

Eyadéma agreed to a conference in 1991, where delegates stripped him of his powers and installed an interim government. However, troops supporting Eyadéma later reinstalled him. Back in power, the general retaliated by postponing planned elections, which prompted strikes in 1992. The strikes paralysed the economy and led to violence, during which 250,000 southerners fled the country.

Eyadéma triumphed his way through ensuing elections throughout the 1990s – elections typically marred by international criticism, opposition boycotts and the killing of rival politicians. Amnesty International made allegations of human rights violations, such as executions and torture, and pressure on the president increased at the same rate that aid from international donors decreased.

Following Eyadéma's death in February 2005, his son, Faure Gnassingbé, seized power in a military coup, then relented and held presidential elections, which he won. Some 500 people were killed in riots in Lomé, amid allegations the elections were fixed.

Faure's Rally of the Togolese People (RPT) party won legislative elections in 2007, the first to be deemed reasonably free and fair by international observers. Opposition parties also won seats in parliament, a political first. Following this milestone, the EU resumed relations with Togo, which had been suspended for 14 years, and dealings with international agencies such as the IMF and the World Bank were restarted.

## People

With about 40 ethnic groups in a population of over six million people, Togo has one of Africa's more heterogeneous populations. The three largest groups are the southern Ewe and Mina, and the northern Kabye; the latter counts President Gnassingbé among its population and is concentrated around Kara.

## Religion

Christianity and Islam are the main religions in Togo (in the south and north, respectively). However, a majority of the population have voodoo beliefs, which are strongest in the southeast.

## Arts & Culture

Batik and wax printing is popular throughout Togo, but the most well-known textile is the Ewe kente cloth, which is less brilliantly coloured than the Ashanti version.

Music and dance play an important part in Togolese daily life. Today, traditional music has fused with contemporary West African, Caribbean and South American sounds, creating a hybrid that includes highlife, reggae and *soukous*. Togo's most famous singing export was Bella Bellow, who, before her death in 1973, ruled the local music scene, toured internationally and released a recording, *Album Souvenir*. Nowadays, King Mensah is Togo's best-known artist, at home and abroad.

The fortified Tamberma compounds in Koutammakou are some of the most striking structures in West Africa.

## Environment

Togo's coastline measures only 56km, but the country stretches inland for over 600km. The coast is tropical; further inland are rolling hills covered with forest, yielding to savannah plains in the north.

There's less wildlife than in neighbouring countries because larger mammals have largely been killed or scared off. Togo's remaining mammals (monkeys, buffaloes and antelope) are limited to the north; crocodiles and hippos are found in some rivers.

The coastline faces serious erosion and pollution problems.

# SURVIVAL GUIDE

## Directory A-Z

### ACCOMMODATION

Togo has a fairly good range of accommodation options, from basic cubicle hotels to upmarket establishments with all mod cons. Unsurprisingly, Lomé has the widest range of hotels. In areas beyond the capital, lodging choices tend to be guesthouses or basic hotels with on-site restaurants; more expensive options usually offer generators and reliable air-con.

### CHILDREN

- Togolese love children. Visitors with tots will find people extra friendly and helpful.
- Nappy-changing tables are available only in high-end restaurants.
- Finding child safety seats, nappies and formula are hit or miss – it's best to bring your own.

**SLEEPING PRICE RANGES**

The following price ranges refer to a double room.

**$** less than CFA30,000

**$$** CFA30,000–50,000

**$$$** more than CFA50,000

### EATING PRICE RANGES

The following price ranges refer to a main course.

**$** less than CFA3000

**$$** CFA3000–6000

**$$$** more than CFA6000

## DANGERS & ANNOYANCES

- Petty theft and muggings are common in Lomé, especially on the beach and near the Grand Marché.
- *Taxi-motos* in the city may be convenient, but they are dangerous.
- Driving in Togo is, to say the least, hair-raising. Take care on the roads, particularly at night.
- The beaches along the coast are not safe for swimming because of strong currents.

## EMBASSIES & CONSULATES

The following embassies are in Lomé:

**French Embassy** (22 23 46 00; www.amba-france-tg.org; Ave du Golfe; 9am-2pm)

**German Embassy** (22 23 32 32; www.lome.diplo.de; Blvd de la Marina; 9am-noon)

**Ghanaian Embassy** (22 21 31 94; ghmfa01@cafe.tg; Rue Moyama, Tokoin; 8am-2pm Mon-Fri)

**US Embassy** (22 61 54 70; http://togo.usembassy.gov; Blvd Eyadéma)

British nationals should contact the **British High Commission** (030-2213250; www.ukinghana.fco.gov.uk; Julius Nyerere Link, off Gamel Abdul Nasser Ave; 9.30-11.30am Mon-Thu, 8.30-10.30am Fri) in Accra (Ghana); the **Australian High Commission** (030-2216400; www.ghana.embassy.gov.au; 2 Second Rangoon Close, Cantonments; 8.30am-3pm Mon-Fri) and **Canadian High Commission** (030-2211521; www.canadainternational.gc.ca/ghana; 42 Independence Ave, Sankara Interchange; 7.30am-4pm Mon-Thu, to 1pm Fri) are also located there. New Zealand citizens should contact the **New Zealand High Commission** (012-435 9000; www.nzembassy.com/south-africa; 125 Middle St, New Muckleneuk, Pretoria) in Pretoria, South Africa.

## EMERGENCY & IMPORTANT NUMBERS

| | |
|---|---|
| Togo's country code | 228 |
| International access code | 00 |
| Ambulance | 8200 |
| Police | 117 |
| Fire | 118 |

## INTERNET ACCESS

In towns and cities, wi-fi is available at almost all midrange and top-end establishments. Internet cafes are easy to find in towns and cities but nonexistent in more remote areas.

## LGBTIQ TRAVELLERS

Togolese society is quite conservative and gay and lesbian travellers should avoid making their sexual orientation known. Homosexual acts are punishable by law.

## MONEY

Togo uses the West African CFA franc. Major towns have Visa ATMs. A few upmarket hotels take credit cards but otherwise cash is king.

**ATMs** You'll find Visa ATMs in major towns. Only Banque Atlantique (p486) in Lomé accepts MasterCard.

**Changing money** The best foreign currency to carry is euros, which are easily exchanged at any bank or hotel.

**Tipping** Not the norm at local restaurants. In upmarket spots, 10% is the usual. Giving 5% to 10% to guides is reasonable.

### Exchange Rates

| | | |
|---|---|---|
| Australia | A$1 | CFA452 |
| Canada | C$1 | CFA440 |
| Euro zone | €1 | CFA656 |
| Japan | ¥100 | CFA538 |
| New Zealand | NZ$1 | CFA415 |
| UK | UK£1 | CFA774 |
| US | US$1 | CFA600 |

For current exchange rates, see www.xe.com.

## OPENING HOURS

**Administrative offices** 7am to noon and 2.30pm to 5.30pm Monday to Friday.

**Banks** 7.45am to 4pm or 5pm Monday to Friday (Many banks are open on Saturdays, too).

**Bars and clubs** around 6pm to late Monday to Saturday.

**Restaurants** 11am to 10pm daily, unless otherwise specified.

**Shops** 7.30am to 12.30pm and 2.30pm to 6pm Monday to Saturday.

## POST

Togo's national postal service is La Poste. Expect long queues.

## PUBLIC HOLIDAYS

Togo also celebrates Islamic holidays, which change dates every year according to the lunar calendar.

**New Year's Day** 1 January

**Meditation Day** 13 January

**Easter** March/April
**National Day** 27 April
**Labour Day** 1 May
**Ascension Day** May
**Pentecost** May/June
**Day of the Martyrs** 21 June
**Assumption Day** 15 August
**All Saints' Day** 1 November
**Christmas Day** 25 December

### TELEPHONE

Landline numbers start with 2, mobile numbers with 9. You can make international calls at the private telephone agencies found in every town.

### TOURIST INFORMATION

Togo's official tourist website (only in French) is at www.togo-tourisme.com.

### TRAVELLERS WITH DISABILITIES

Togo has limited facilities for travellers with disabilities. The capital, Lomé, is slightly better equipped than rural areas. The best bet is to speak to your hotel and ask if you can hire a staff member after-hours for help (eg with lifting), or if they can suggest another trustworthy person.

### VISAS

One-week extendable visas (CFA10,000) are issued at major border crossings with Ghana (Aflao/Lomé), Benin (Hillacondji) and Burkina Faso (Sinkasse), and upon arrival at the airport.

The **Service Immigration Togolaise** (☎25 07 85 60; Ave de la Chance; ⏲8am-4pm Mon-Fri), near the GTA building 8km north of central Lomé, issues 30-day visa extensions in one or two days. They're free when you extend the seven-day visa. Four photos are required.

The Visa des Pays de l'Entente, valid in Côte d'Ivoire, Niger, Benin and Burkina Faso, is available at the Service Immigration Togolaise (p495). Bring two photos, your passport and CFA17,800. It takes 24 to 48 hours to process, but note that the office is closed on weekends.

If you're visiting only a single country, the following embassies deliver visas:

**Benin** A two-week/one-month single-entry visa costs CFA12,000/17,000. You need two photos and photocopies of your passport. It takes one day to process.

**Burkina Faso** Contact the French Embassy in Lomé.

**Ghana** One-month single-entry visas are issued within three days for CFA20,000 and require four photos and a photocopy of your yellow-fever vaccination certificate.

### WOMEN TRAVELLERS

The Togolese are rather conservative when it comes to marriage, so it's incomprehensible to them that women past their 20s might not be married. This will lead to many questions, but it is generally harmless. To avoid attracting any more attention, dress conservatively; if single, wear a fake wedding ring.

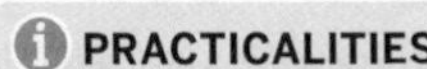

**PRACTICALITIES**

**Electricity** Supply is 220V and plugs are of the European two-round-pin variety.

**Weights & measures** Togo uses the metric system.

## Getting There & Away

### AIR

**Lomé–Tokoin International Airport** (Gnassingbe Eyadema Airport; www.aeroportdelome.com; Ave de la Paix) is 5km northeast of the centre of Lomé. A few major airlines operate in Togo and have offices in Lomé.

The main international carriers are **Air France** (☎22 23 23 23; www.airfrance.com; Immeuble UAT, Blvd du 13 Janvier [Blvd Circulaire]), **Brussels Airlines** (☎22 21 25 25; www.brusselsairlines.com; Ave Joseph Strauss), **Royal Air Maroc** (☎22 23 48 48; www.royalairmaroc.com; Immeuble Taba, Ave Pompidou) and **Ethiopian Airlines** (☎22 21 87 38; www.ethiopianairlines.com; Immeuble Taba, Ave Pompidou), which offer direct flights to France, Belgium, Morocco and Ethiopia respectively, and connecting flights to the rest of the world.

Other major airlines include **Asky** (☎22 23 05 05; www.flyasky.com; Immeuble Taba, Ave Pompidou), which flies to major capitals in West and Central Africa; **Air Burkina** (www.air-burkina.com), with flights to Ouagadougou (Burkina Faso); and **Air Côte d'Ivoire** (☎22 61 18 44; www.aircotedivoire.com; Ave Jean-Paul II), which flies to Abidjan (Côte d'Ivoire).

### LAND

#### Benin

Bush taxis regularly ply the road between Gare de Cotonou in Lomé and Cotonou (Benin; CFA7000, three hours) via Hillacondji (CFA950, one hour), while **ABC** (☎90 07 69 56; Rue Sylvanus Olympio) in Lomé has daily buses to Cotonou (CFA7000, three hours).

The main northern crossing is at Kétao (northeast of Kara). You can also cross at Tohoun (east of Notsé) or Nadoba (in Koutammakou country), arriving in Boukoumbé, but public transport is infrequent.

Note that Beninese visas can be issued at the border.

### Burkina Faso

The best way to get to Ouagadougou from Lomé is by bus (roughly 17 to 20 hours), via Dapaong. **NTI** (☎ 90 19 80 92; Blvd du 13 Janvier [Blvd Circulaire]), **CTS** (☎ 99 27 83 32; Blvd du 13 Janvier [Blvd Circulaire]) and **TCV** (☎ 92 29 48 93; Ave Agustino de Souza) are reliable companies. NTI and CTS have three services weekly (CFA12,800) and TCV has two weekly (CFA16,200); the ride from Lomé to Dapaong takes roughly one to two hours.

From Dapaong, you'll easily find a taxi to Sinkasse (CFA1700, 45 minutes), which straddles the border. From there it's CFA6000 to Ouagadougou by bus. The border is open from 6am to 6pm.

### Ghana

From central Lomé it is only 2km by shared/chartered taxi (CFA600/1750) or *taxi-moto* (CFA500) to the chaotic border crossing (open 6am to 10pm) with Aflao in Ghana. From there, you can cross on foot to pick up minibuses to Accra.

**STIF** (☎ 99 42 72 72; off Blvd de la Marina) runs daily buses between Lomé and Abidjan via Accra (CFA7600, four hours).

There are other crossings from Kpalimé to Ho and Mt Klouto to Kpandu.

## Getting Around

### BUS

Buses are the most reliable way to get around, especially for long-distance trips. Rakiéta (p486) buses are more reliable than those of other companies.

Buses almost always operate with guaranteed seating and fixed departure times.

### CAR & MOTORCYCLE

If you're driving, you will need an International Driving Permit (IDP). Police checkpoints are common throughout the country but rarely nasty or obstructive.

Petrol stations are plentiful in major towns. At time of research, a litre of petrol cost from CFA750 to CFA900.

Cars may be hired at Lomé–Tokoin International Airport.

### LOCAL TRANSPORT

#### Bush Taxis

Togo has an extensive network of dilapidated bush taxis, which can be anything from an old pick-up truck to a normal sedan car or nine- or 15-seat people carriers. Travel is often agonisingly slow, but unfortunately these bush taxis are generally the only way to go from town to town. Fares are fixed-ish.

#### Motorcycle Taxis

You'll find taxis in most cities. *Taxi-motos* (motorcycle taxis) – also called *zemi-johns* – are everywhere. A journey across town costs about CFA200, and more in Lomé. They are also a handy way to get to remote locations in the bush.

Chartering a *taxi-moto* will generally cost CFA2500 to CFA4000 per hour.

# Central Africa

USO/GETTY IMAGES ©

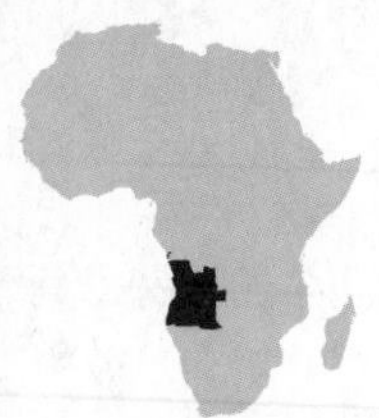

# Angola

POP 25.8 MILLION / ☎ 244

**Includes ➡**



## Fast Facts

**Capital** Luanda

**Population** 25.8 million

**Languages** Portuguese, various Bantu languages

**Area** 1,246,700 sq km

**Currency** Kwanza (Kz)

## Introduction

For most people, Angola is one of Africa's last great travel mysteries. Despite its elemental landscapes and boom-bust oil-dependent economy, the country remains closed off to all but the most adventurous travellers thanks to stringent visa policies, high prices and a history that's been more about war than peace.

It's a shame. Angola has the potential to be one of Africa's dazzling highlights. Lurking within its wild borders lies the continent's second-largest waterfall, scattered remnants of Portuguese colonial history, a handful of emerging national parks, beaches galore and a diverse and unbelievably stoic cross-section of people.

Whether Angola will open up to outsiders any time soon is anyone's guess. The underdeveloped tourist industry has yet to spread it wings and take flight. The sooner the government tackles the country's nagging political issues, the quicker it can emerge from its protracted slumber and show the world what's it's been missing.

## Angola at a Glance

**Kalandula Falls** These massive waterfalls are as spectacular and large as any in Africa, but, as yet, get very few visitors.

**Miradouro de Lua** A magnificent lookout over a canyon of moonlike cliffs that cascade dramatically into the Atlantic Ocean.

**Parque Nacional da Kissama** Angola's most accessible and largest national park has been partly replenished with big fauna.

**Benguela** Angola's cultural capital has colonial architecture, reasonable restaurants and some blissfully quiet Atlantic beaches.

**Lubango** Almost untouched by the war, the highland city of Lubango has busy markets, dramatic volcanic fissures and a giant statue of Christ.

# UNDERSTAND ANGOLA

## Angola Today

Since the end of its debilitating 40-year-long civil war in 2002, Angola has enjoyed an unprecedented period of peace and stability, at least on the political front. Economically, the ride has been a little bumpier. While the Angolan economy has grown – at an average rate of 17% annually in the first six years after 2002 – niggling problems continue to grate, most pressingly, corruption, huge income disparity and a worrying lack of economic diversification.

The country's heavy reliance on oil – which contributes to nearly half of Angola's GDP – came home to roost in 2015 when global oil prices fell from US$100 to US$30 per barrel in little over a year. Reeling from the shock, the value of the Angola kwanza dropped 25% as local prices soared. Suddenly, Angola was facing its biggest economic and humanitarian crisis since the war.

As always, the poor were hit the hardest. Despite a protracted oil boom in the 2000s and 2010s, an estimated one-third of Angolans still live below the poverty line. By early 2016, conditions among the poorest sections of society were said to be as bad as the war years. The situation was exacerbated by a serious yellow-fever outbreak in Luanda coupled with a deadly drought in the south that triggered a crop failure and precipitated the worst food crisis in Angola for a quarter of a century.

Despite the economic turmoil, Angola has logged several small achievements. Landmine clearance continues, aided by humanitarian organisations such as the Halo Trust, while Unita, the one-time belligerent opposition party, appears to have permanently swapped its guns for the ballot box. In 2016 the country's ageing president, Eduardo do Santos (Africa's second-longest



## Angola

**WARNING**

Angola has found it hard to shake off its unsavoury reputation as a hotspot of conflict and civil unrest. But, with the war confined to the history books, there are far more dangerous countries in Africa these days. That's not to say that travel here is straightforward or problem-free. Poverty is still widespread, the transport network is often abysmal, there is almost no tourist infrastructure and crime rates remain high in big cities such as Luanda. To top it all off, the country is prohibitively expensive (Luanda is regularly listed as one of the most expensive cities in the world). Most official travel advice recommends that travellers exercise a high degree of caution in Angola and avoid high-risk areas, such as Cabinda, altogether. Land mines are still a problem in rural areas. Check on your home country's foreign office travel advice website before travelling for current warnings and updates.

Security aside, the main issue thwarting travellers from visiting Angola is visas. Procuring an Angolan visa is a complicated, expensive and long-winded affair with no guaranteed chance of success. Visas fall into nine different categories and most applicants require a 'letter of invitation' from someone in Angola before they can start tackling the rest of the paperwork (all of which must be translated into Portuguese). Do your homework before applying and be prepared for long delays.

serving leader), announced that he would finally step down in 2017, ushering in the opportunity for change under the tutelage of a younger leader.

# History

## The Portuguese Era

In 1483, the Portuguese navigator Diogo Cão first dropped anchor off the shores of northern Angola and unwittingly preempted the start of a conflict that, save for a few intermittent lulls, continued for over half a millennium. The land now known as Angola was, at the time, inhabited by a number of small tribes living in loosely defined kingdoms.

Since the 1390s, the northern third of what is now Angola had been part of the Kingdom of the Kongo, a vast tract of land roughly the size of Greece that made contact with Cão's Portuguese emissaries in the 1480s and quickly adopted their own Africanised version of Catholicism.

Faced with an inevitable conflict against the Portuguese who had established a trading port in Luanda in 1576, the Kongo cleverly exploited European colonial rivalries and allied themselves with the Dutch in the 1620s. For a brief seven years, Angola was a Dutch colony until the Portuguese won it back in 1648.

The more fertile and less threatening lands of Brazil held a far greater attraction for Portugal's colonial farmers and businessmen and Angola became a safe port and a source of slaves. The exact number of African slaves trafficked from Angola to the Americas will never be known, but it probably numbered in the millions (figures of around 10,000 a year were touted as early as the 1620s). The trade was theoretically abolished in Portugal's colonies in 1836, although a system of forced labour continued in Angola until well into the 20th century.

## The Road to Independence

Pro-independence unrest began after WWII and was inflamed in 1961 when colonial authorities began to crush increasingly zealous uprisings by dissidents.

The National Union for Total Independence of Angola (Unita) originally had the support of the Ovimbundu people, but later formed alliances with the Portuguese right wing, the USA and apartheid South Africa.

In 1975 the Portuguese finally granted independence to Angola, following the overthrow of the fascist Salazar government at home. But the colonial withdrawal – a mad scramble involving one of the biggest airlifts in history – was legendary for its ineptitude. Overnight, Luanda's commercial heart was converted into a ghost town and the country lost practically all of its qualified human resources and administrative structure. Problems beckoned.

## The Civil War & Its Aftermath

Angola in 1975 possessed all the essential ingredients for civil war: a weak, uneven infrastructure, low levels of health and education, two feuding sets of tribal elites, and a large slice of unused government oil revenue seemingly up for grabs. As the Moscow-backed MPLA party stepped into the power vacuum left by the Portuguese, other outside influences thickened the plot further: US communist paranoia, Cuba's ambiguous desire for 'world revolution', South African security obsessions and the woefully inadequate process of decolonisation. The stage was set and the civil war began.

In 1991, prompted by the end of the Cold War, a ceasefire agreement was set in place by Cuba, the USA and Angola. But the accord broke down the following year after Unita, having lost a general election deemed free and fair by the UN, returned to war with a new-found ferocity, claiming the poll had been rigged. Almost 200,000 people died between May and October 1993 as Unita took war to the provincial cities, destroying most of the road, rail and communications network in the process.

A revamped 'Lusaka Accord' signed in 1994 and ultimately UN sanctions against Unita diamonds caused Unita's downfall. Its leader Jonas Savimbi – hunted and on the run – was finally killed in a government operation on 22 February 2002.

A new peace accord was signed on 4 April 2002 and – so far – it has held.

# Culture

Angola's cornucopia of ethnic groups is dominated by the Ovimbundu, Ambundu and Bakongo. Local tribal traditions remain strong, though Portuguese has evolved as the national language of choice, particularly among the young. Due to slavery and emigration, much of Angola's cultural legacy has been exported abroad, especially to Brazil. Angolan influence is still evident in samba music, carnival processions, Afro-American religious practices and the combative martial art of capoeira.

The Ovimbundu are Angola's largest 'tribe' making up approximately 40% of the population. Historically, this mainly Christian Bantu group with a strong poetic tradition were agriculturalists and traders based in the country's central southern highlands and along the southern coast. The main Ovimbundu cities today are Benguela and Huambo and this was where Unita drew much of their support during the civil war.

Angola's Kimbundu-speaking Ambundu people make up the country's second-largest tribal group and hail from the lands north of the Kwanza River around Malange and Bengo.

# Environment

Angola's ecology, terrain and climate is extremely diverse, ranging from the rainforests of the Congo River basin in the north to the arid expanses of the Namibe Desert in the south. In between lie savannah grasslands, arid stretches of coastline lapped by the cold Benguela current and high cool mountain plateaus.

The country has a potentially dazzling array of fauna, but animal numbers were severely depleted during the civil war (1975–2002). The Big Five are all found here, though each species is listed as vulnerable or endangered. Angola's most iconic animal is the giant sable, a member of the antelope family that has been adopted as a national symbol. It is currently listed as critically endangered and was only 'rediscovered' in 2004. Total numbers hover at around 100.

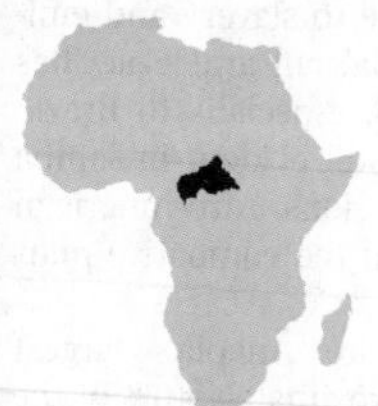

# Central African Republic

POP 4.6 MILLION / ☎236

**Includes ➡**



## Fast Facts

**Capital** Bangui

**Population** 4.6 million

**Languages** French, Sango

**Area** 622,984 sq km

**Currency** Central African franc (CFA)

## Introduction

Central African Republic (CAR) is a country with staggering rare natural beauty and some wonderful wildlife. Not so long ago it was one of the best places in Africa for encounters with huge forest elephants and western lowland gorillas, and the best place in the world, some say, to see butterflies. However, since 2012 political problems and religious-fuelled civil war have made the country completely off limits to travellers for safety reasons, with all Western governments warning against any visits here.

One of the most impoverished and least developed countries on the continent, CAR endured centuries of rapacity from colonisers and then from its own leaders. Yet the people of this plundered nation remain incredibly open and friendly; and their conversations are more full of hope than despair.

## Central African Republic at a Glance

**Dzanga-Sangha Reserve** Western lowland gorillas and elephants inhabit this pocket of virgin rainforest.

**Bangui** A scenic river frontage and the old town's wide colonial boulevards that radiate out from the Point Kilometre Zero monument.

**Bayanga** The Baka (a pygmy tribe) depart for traditional hunts outside the Dzanga-Sangha Reserve from this small village.

**Chutes de Boali** A 50m-high waterfall that bursts to life in the rainy season.

**Bouar** Megalithic stone monuments dot the landscape around this market town.

**Traditional storytelling** Ancient folklore is sung to the music of drums, *ngombi* (harp) and *sanza* (guitar).

# UNDERSTAND CENTRAL AFRICAN REPUBLIC

## Central African Republic Today

Today, with continuing widespread violence throughout the country, the Central African Republic teeters on the edge of the abyss. The recent violence is estimated to have uprooted nearly 1.2 million people and by late 2016 the World Bank estimated that there were still some 384,000 internally displaced people and 467,000 refugees in neighbouring countries. In addition, around 76% of the population continues to live in extreme poverty and around half the population are considered in need of urgent humanitarian assistance. Health facilities within CAR have been devastated by the recent violence with only 55% of health facilities remaining in a functional state.

Economically speaking the situation improved slightly in 2015–16, but that was only in comparison to 2013 when the real GDP of the country fell by 36%, which led to economic collapse.

Perhaps the only bit of good news in the entire mess is that a new constitution has been approved and in February 2016 Faustin-Archange Touadera became the first ever freely elected president in the CAR's history.

## History

Although stone tools provide evidence of human life from 6000 BC, the most notable ancients resided around present-day Bouar some 2500 years ago. Little is known about them, though it must have been a highly organised civilisation because it left behind about 70 groups of megaliths, some weighing three or four tonnes. The country's present cultures most likely arrived in the 15th century, probably fleeing Arab slave traders, but by the 18th century they, too, were sending their captives across the Sahara to markets in Egypt or down the Congo River to the Atlantic Ocean. This industry, which didn't completely end until 1912, decimated entire cultures and largely depopulated the eastern half of the country.

### Colonial Days

France launched into CAR in 1885, finding a shattered society rich in agricultural potential and under the rule of Sudanese-born

## Central African Republic

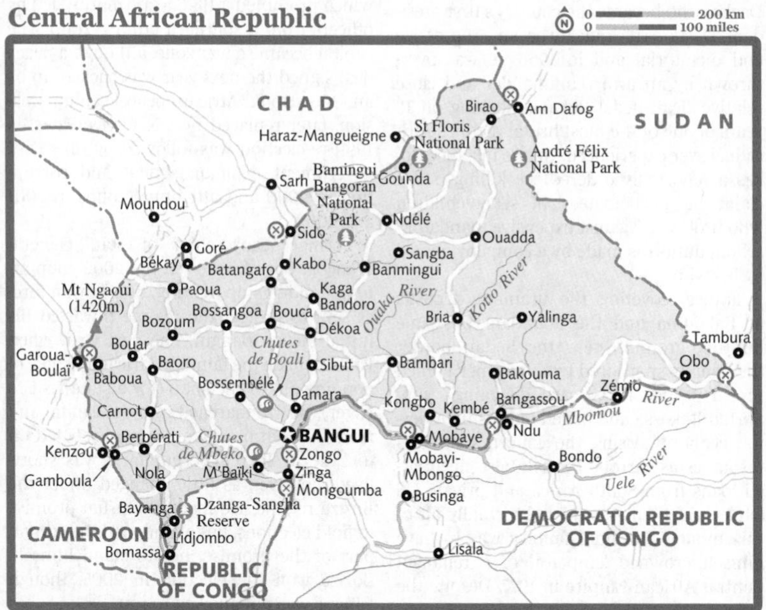

**WARNING**

Tensions remain extremely high across the Central African Republic and the threat of violence is significant – all Western governments advise against all travel to every part of the country.

Sultan Rabah. France killed Rabah in 1900 and soon after consolidated its control of the country, which it divided into 17 parts that were offered to European companies in exchange for a fixed annual payment plus 15% of agricultural profits. Vast cotton, coffee and tobacco plantations were established and worked by an often brutally conscripted local population. The labourers resisted for decades, but opposition was eventually broken through a combination of French military action, famine and severe smallpox epidemics.

The first signs of nationalism sprang up after WWII via Barthélemy Boganda's Mouvement d'Evolution Sociale de l'Afrique Noire (Movement for the Social Evolution of Black Africa). In 1960, a year after Boganda was killed in a suspicious plane crash, his party forced the French to grant independence.

## Bokassa

The leadership was taken over by David Dacko, who became the country's first president. Dacko's rule quickly became repressive and dictatorial and in 1966 he was overthrown by an army commander and close relative, Jean-Bédel Bokassa, kicking off 13 years of one of the most brutal regimes Africa has ever experienced. In one instance Bokassa reportedly ordered the killing (some claim he participated) of schoolchildren who protested against expensive mandatory school uniforms made by a company owned by his wife.

France, coveting the uranium deposits at Bakouma and the abundant big-game hunting grounds near the Sudan border (personally sponsored by the former French president, Valéry Giscard d'Estaing), supported Bokassa and bailed out his floundering economy. Using the country's mineral resources as carrots, Bokassa also negotiated loans from South Africa and private US banks. He then squandered virtually all of this money. His final fantasy was to have himself crowned 'emperor' of a renamed Central African Empire in 1977. Despite the worldwide derision, France helped to fund much of his coronation's price tag of more than US$20 million.

Such excess, together with the out-of-control violence, made Bokassa an embarrassment to his backers. In 1979, France abruptly cut off aid to the 'empire' and, while Bokassa was in Libya seeking still more funds, flew in former president David Dacko together with an undercover French commando squad, special forces and at least 300 French troops. Dacko did no better this time around and was overthrown again in 1981 and replaced by André Kolingba, who in 1986 created a one-party state that was also widely seen as corrupt. At this point Bokassa popped up again, but was promptly convicted of treason, murder and, for good measure, cannibalism, and sentenced to death. This was changed to life imprisonment and he was confined to the palace he'd constructed at Berengo.

## Coups & Chaos

Kolingba's 12 years of absolute rule ended when he was defeated in presidential elections in 1993, held at the insistence of the US and France, and Ange-Félix Patassé became the leader of CAR's first real civilian government. Patassé immediately stacked the government with fellow ethnic group members, which prompted a 1996 army mutiny, led by officers from a southern ethnic group. The capital became a war zone, although a peace deal signed the next year was backed up by an 800-strong African peacekeeping mission, later replaced by UN forces. Patassé's 1999 re-election was followed by riots over government mismanagement and corruption in 2000 and attempted coups in 2001 and 2002.

Former army chief of staff General François Bozizé, who led the 2002 coup attempt, didn't stop fighting after Libyan forces sent to protect the regime thwarted his initial bid on Bangui. The next year, when Patassé made the familiar African mistake of popping out of the shop (for a state visit to Niger), Bozizé marched into the capital and made himself president. Patassé scooted off to exile in Togo. The euphoria was short-lived, however, as little changed under the Bozizé regime. He made the usual promise to hold elections, but abandoned the second part of the promise, not to stand himself. Bozizé won the election in 2005, though Patassé was not allowed to run.

After Bozizé came to power the safety situation in Bangui improved dramatically, as did the economy, but not much changed elsewhere. Fighting continued upcountry, and by the end of 2006 rebel attacks in the northeast and northwest forced some 300,000 people to flee their villages. In June 2008, after most rebel groups signed a peace agreement with the government, fighting slowed down considerably although it didn't stop. A unity government, including leaders of the main rebel groups, kicked off 2009; just a few months later rebel attacks were back on the increase, including by the Lord's Resistance Army (LRA) of neighbouring Uganda, whose insurgency had spread to the wider region.

### From Bad to Worse

By 2010 things were finally starting to look up in CAR with an element of peace arriving in the country. In January 2011 elections were held in which General François Bozizé again won with some 60% of the vote, though the opposition denounced the process as fraudulent. The peace turned out to be paper thin.

In November 2012 a Muslim rebel alliance called New Séléka suddenly overran large, traditionally Muslim regions in the north of the country. By March 2013 it had taken control of much of CAR and marched into Bangui, causing Bozizé to flee. There was an almost total breakdown of law and order, and hundreds of people were killed. After fighting between Christian militia groups (known as anti-Balaka) and New Séléka had led to thousands more deaths, French paratroopers arrived to try and stabilise the situation in December 2013. They were later joined by a UN force. Catherine Samba-Panza took over as interim leader, but the situation remained very volatile with numerous atrocities committed by both sides.

## Culture

Half of Central Africans are Christian, 15% are Muslim and 35% have stuck wholly with traditional animistic convictions; these ancient customs still strongly influence most people's lives, regardless of their principal faith.

CAR encompasses over 80 ethnic groups, which can basically be grouped into riverine, grassland and forest cultures; the latter include the Aka people (pygmies, though they don't like that term; singular is MoAka, plural is BaAka). The Baya-Mandjia and Banda, originating in the western and central savannahs respectively, compose 75% of the population.

Some 70% of the population lives a rural existence, and subsistence agriculture remains the backbone of the economy. The same percentage lives on less than a dollar a day.

While rice and yam, are sometimes available, Central Africans love their cassava, eating it at virtually every meal with a meat, fish or vegetable sauce. Koko, which is a little like eating grass (only it's pretty tasty), is another popular sauce ingredient. Bushmeat, particularly monkey, python and antelope, is also common in markets and even on menus. Forest caterpillars are a popular treat during June. A dash of *piment* (hot sauce) is put on almost everything.

Palm wine is the most popular firewater in the south, while *bili-bili*, a sorghum-based alcohol, predominates in the north. Both are available in Bangui, but beer is king there.

## Environment

CAR, just a tad smaller than France, is landlocked smack bang in the middle of the continent. The country is one immense plateau varying in height mostly between 600m and 700m, tapering down to 350m in the far southwest. The closest thing to a real mountain is Mt Ngaoui, which at 1420m is the highest point in the country.

Though CAR is mostly associated with its tropical rainforest, these are found only in the southwest; sweeping savannahs, interspersed with many rivers, cover most of the country. Poaching is a huge problem and logging is on the increase, which threatens CAR's standing as one of the last great wildlife refuges.

Despite the ongoing security problems, African Parks (www.african-parks.org) have re-established Chinko in the east of the country as a viable reserve. It's home to chimpanzees, elephants, Lord Derby elands and numerous other species. In the southwest of the country the Dzanga-Sangha National Park is one of the most impressive parks in all of Central Africa, with habituated lowland gorillas and masses of forest elephants.

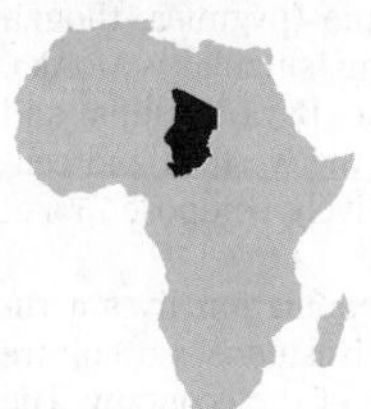

# Chad

POP 13.6 MILLION / ☎235

**Includes ➡**



## Fast Facts

**Capital** N'Djamena

**Population** 13.6 million

**Languages** French, Arabic, more than 120 local languages

**Area** 1,284,000 sq km

**Currency** Central African franc (CFA)

## Introduction

Chad has always been some place where travellers wave goodbye to their comfort zone and say hello to adventure. Even when it is safe to visit, which sadly it is currently not, the art of travel here is demanding in every sense of the word. This, though, is part of the country's allure, an opportunity to break emphatically away from all that you know, and come to a place that promises experiences, good and bad, that happen nowhere else. But if Chad is such a demanding place to travel, why ever bother? Picture sublime oases hiding in the northern deserts, stampeding herds of wildlife running through national parks and deep blues awaiting boats on Lake Chad – put simply, when Chad is accessible it's a country and an experience that can never be forgotten.

## Chad at a Glance

**Zakouma National Park** Big herds of elephants and dazzling birds thrive in one of Central Africa's finest national parks.

**Gaoui** Beautiful painted houses and a fascinating village just minutes from N'Djaména.

**Sarh** A green and pleasant town along the banks of the Chari River.

**Bol** The best place from which to find a boat to head out onto Lake Chad.

**Ennedi** Dramatic desert scenery and rock formations in what is perhaps the most spectacular corner of the Sahara.

**Emi Koussi** Its cratered 3445m summit stands high above the desert that it dominates.

**N'Djaména** A capital city where hippos roam on the banks of the Chari River.

# Chad

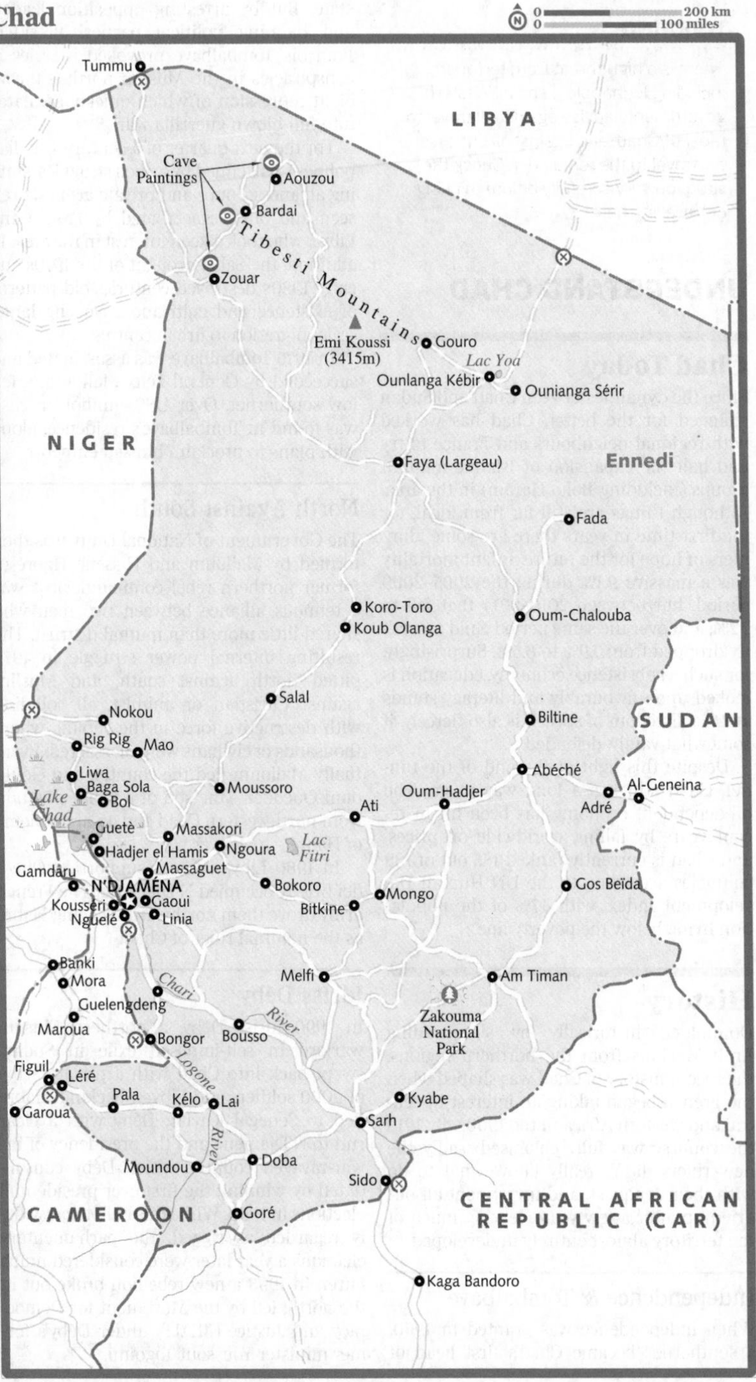

0 — 200 km
0 — 100 miles

LIBYA
Tummu
Cave Paintings
Aouzou
Bardai
Tibesti Mountains
Zouar
Emi Koussi (3415m)
Gouro
Lac Yoa
Ounlanga Kébir
Ounianga Sérir
NIGER
Faya (Largeau)
Ennedi
Fada
Koro-Toro
Koub Olanga
Oum-Chalouba
Salal
Biltine
SUDAN
Nokou
Rig Rig
Mao
Liwa
Baga Sola
Bol
Lake Chad
Moussoro
Abéché
Oum-Hadjer
Al-Geneina
Adré
Ati
Guetè
Hadjer el Hamis
Massakori
Ngoura
Lac Fitri
Massaguet
Gamdaru
N'DJAMÉNA
Kousséri
Gaoui
Nguelé
Linia
Bokoro
Bitkine
Mongo
Gos Beïda
Banki
Mora
Melfi
Am Timan
Chari River
Guelengdeng
Maroua
Zakouma National Park
Bousso
Bongor
Logone River
Figuil
Léré
Garoua
Pala
Kélo
Lai
Kyabe
Sarh
Moundou
Doba
Sido
CAMEROON
Goré
CENTRAL AFRICAN REPUBLIC (CAR)
Kaga Bandoro

CHAD

**WARNING**

There is a high threat from terrorism, including kidnapping, and all Western governments advise against all travel to most of Chad, and against all but essential travel to the remainder. Check the situation very carefully before thinking of travelling here.

# UNDERSTAND CHAD

## Chad Today

Since the dynamic between Chad and Sudan changed for the better, Chad has worked with regional neighbours and France to try and halt the expansion of Islamic militant groups (including Boko Haram) in the area. Although things are still far from ideal, for the first time in years there are some glimmers of hope for the future. Infant mortality was a massive 9.1% during the 2005–2009 period, but between 2010–2014 that fell to 7.2%, and over the same period child mortality dropped from 7.9% to 6.5%. Surprisingly, for such a subsistence economy, education is looked upon favourably and literacy stands at 40%. Freedom of speech is also fiercely, if somewhat vainly, defended.

Despite this light at the end of the tunnel, Chad still has a long way to go. The oil-dependent economy has been hit in recent years by falling worldwide oil prices, and Chad is currently ranked 185 out of 188 countries according to the UN Human Development Index, with 47% of the population living below the poverty line.

## History

Dominated historically by slave-trading Arab Muslims from the northern regions, the recent history of Chad was shaped when the French began taking an interest in central and western Africa in the 1900s. By 1913 the country was fully colonised: sadly the new rulers didn't really know what to do with their conquest, and investment all but dried up after a few years, leaving much of the territory almost entirely undeveloped.

### Independence & Tombalbaye

When independence was granted in 1960, a southerner became Chad's first head of state. But by arresting opposition leaders and banning political parties, President François Tombalbaye provoked a series of conspiracies in the Muslim north – the violent repression of which quickly escalated into full-blown guerrilla war.

For the next quarter of a century, Chadian politics was defined by armed struggles, shifting alliances, coups and private armies, overseen and often exacerbated by France and Libya, who took a keen interest in the area. In addition, the Sahel drought of the 1970s and early 1980s destroyed centuries-old patterns of existence and cultivation, causing large-scale migration to urban centres.

In 1975 Tombalbaye was assassinated and succeeded by General Félix Malloum, a fellow southerner. Over US$1 million in cash was found in Tombalbaye's residence, along with plans to proclaim himself emperor.

### North Against South

The Government of National Unity was then formed by Malloum and Hissène Habré (a former northern rebel commander); it was a tenuous alliance between two men who shared little more than mutual distrust. The resulting internal power struggle in 1979 pitted north against south, and Muslim against Christian or animist, all colliding with destructive force in the capital, where thousands of civilians were massacred. Eventually Malloum fled the country, and Goukouni Oueddei – the son of a tribal chieftain from northwestern Chad and an arch-enemy of Habré – took over.

In 1980 Libyan forces supporting Oueddei briefly occupied N'Djaména. The French army drove them northwards, leaving Habré as the nominal ruler of Chad.

### Idriss Déby

In 1990 Idriss Déby, a northern Muslim warlord in self-imposed exile in Sudan, swept back into Chad with a private army of 2000 soldiers and Libyan backing. Habré fled to Senegal leaving Déby with a clear run to N'Djaména and the presidency of his war-ravaged country, which Déby consolidated by winning the first-ever presidential elections in 1996. While this ballot was widely regarded as rigged, the parliamentary elections a year later were considered much fairer. In 1998 a new rebellion broke out in the north, led by the Movement for Democracy and Justice (MDJT) under Déby's former minister Youssouf Togoïmi.

To nobody's surprise, Déby won the May 2001 presidential elections by a comfortable margin, although results from a quarter of the polling stations had to be cancelled because of irregularities.

Three weeks after a failed 2006 coup and one year after the constitutional two-term presidential limit was overturned, Déby won a presidential election boycotted by the opposition and most citizens. In the April 2011 presidential election, also boycotted by the opposition, Déby was again declared winner.

The fact that Déby's government has not already fallen has much to do with the presence of the French. While the French have never admitted to actual involvement in repelling the rebel attacks of 2006 and 2008, it was reported in the French media that in the 2008 attack France provided logistical support to the government, funnelled weapons to the government via Libya, offered to evacuate Déby to France and sent special forces in to fight the rebels.

### Best Friends Forever?

Chad and Sudan have long been uneasy neighbours, and things took a turn for the worse in 2003 when unrest in Sudan's Darfur region began to spill across the border, along with hundreds of thousands of Sudanese refugees. Chad and Sudan then began accusing each other of backing and harbouring rebels, and the dispute led to the severing of relations in 2006. In the years immediately following this cutting of ties, the Sudanese government was accused of supporting Chadian rebels, who at one point came within a bullet's breeze of seizing N'djaména. Chad was in turn accused of supporting rebels in Sudan. In 2010, however, the two countries agreed to normalise relations and withdraw support for rebel groups operating in each other's territories.

## Culture

The north of Chad is populated by people of Arab descent, as well as nomadic Peul-Fulani and Toubou people. The black Africans are in the majority in the south – the Sara are by far the biggest ethnic group (25% of the population) and have traditionally dominated business and the civil service. The difference between these two broad groups is profound – the Christian (35% of the population) and animist southerners are mostly peasant farmers, tilling fertile land, while the northern Muslims (54%) are desert-dwelling pastoralists.

Most of the crafts you'll see in Chad are imported from Nigeria and Cameroon, though the leatherwork and pottery is usually made locally and many of the large wool rugs come from Abéché and other desert towns.

## Environment

Much of Chad is desert or semidesert and desertification is a serious issue – as is the drying up of Lake Chad. There are fingers of green in the south though, and the small population for the country's size means that there's quite a lot of room to breathe in Chad.

Environmental issues are given little thought in Chad, and across the vast majority of the country wildlife is hounded and poached. But there is one bright spot in an otherwise pretty bleak picture. Thanks to serious government support and funding and expertise from African Parks (www.african-parks.com), Zakouma National Park in the southeast of the country contains large herds of elephants, as well as primates, lions, giraffes, wildebeests, a wide variety of antelopes, and weird and wonderful birdlife.

# Democratic Republic of Congo

POP 81.7 MILLION / ✆243

**Includes ➡**



## Best Places to Eat

- Limoncello (p516)
- Orchids Safari Club Restaurant (p518)
- Le Chalet (p518)
- Patisserie Nouvelle (p511)
- Chez Flore (p511)

## Best Places to Sleep

- Mikeno Lodge (p520)
- Lake Kivu Lodge (p518)
- Elais Hotel (p511)
- Orchids Safari Club (p517)

## Why Go?

Carpeted by huge swathes of rainforest and punctuated by gushing rivers and smoking volcanoes, the Democratic Republic of Congo (DRC, formerly Zaire) is the ultimate African adventure. As much a geographical concept as a fully fledged nation, DRC has experienced one of the saddest chapters in modern history, suffering a brutal 20th century of colonial exploitation, authoritarian madness and what has been dubbed Africa's first 'world war', which finally ended in 2003 with the rise of the Kabila political dynasty.

While real stability remains many years away, the cautious development of DRC's enormous untapped mineral wealth and the presence of the world's largest UN peacekeeping force have bred optimism among its tormented but resilient population. At the same time, a small but fast-growing tourism industry, centred on the incredible Parc National des Virunga, has seen travellers return to what is easily one of Africa's most thrilling – and challenging – destinations.

## When to Go

**Kinchasa**

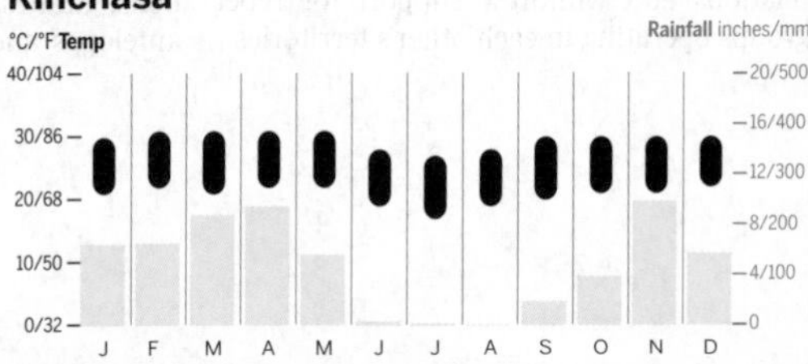


**Dec–Mar** Dry season for the north means slightly easier travel conditions.

**Jan** A good month to have the mountain gorillas totally to yourself.

**Apr–Oct** Dry season for the south and the best time to attempt overland routes across the country.

## KINSHASA

POP 10.1 MILLION

Sub-Saharan Africa's second-largest city, Kin (as locals universally call it) sprawls seemingly forever from the banks of the Congo River to its distant shanty towns. Shot through with chaos, music and a lust for life that is as infectious as it is overwhelming, Kinshasa is a city you experience rather than visit. While it has the same maniacal drivers, dismaying poverty, mounds of trash, terrible air pollution and persistent street hawkers that you've seen in many other African cities, here it's all bigger, faster and louder than you've probably experienced before, and there's no better place for a whirlwind introduction to Congolese life.

### Sights

**★Serpents du Congo** ZOO

(☎0899460477, 0823620634; US$10; ⏱by appointment) This excellent snake farm is located 28km from downtown Kinshasa and makes for a great day out. Owner Franck will gladly show you the poisonous and non-poisonous snakes here, and you even have the opportunity to hold some of the less aggressive ones. It's important to call ahead to reserve an appointment, and also to ensure that Franck gives your driver instructions on how to reach the farm.

**★Musée National de Kinshasa** MUSEUM

(Ave de la Montagne, Mont Ngaliema; US$10; ⏱7.30am-3pm Mon-Fri) This amazing ethnographic archive comprising some 45,000 objects has been waiting patiently for its new home, a US$10 million prestige investment from South Korea currently under construction in the Lingwala area of the city. In the meantime it's possible to visit the small exhibit here, but also to be shown the warehouses where the rest of collection is currently stored. Ask one of the museum employees about doing this – a tip is expected.

**Marché Central** MARKET

(Rue du Marché; ⏱7am–6pm) This one of the largest markets in Central Africa, and is worth visiting for the intrepid. Watch your belongings (better still, bring nothing with you at all) and be sure to go with a local who knows the place.

### Sleeping

**★Hotel Sunnyday** GUESTHOUSE $$

(☎0999906425; www.sunnyday-kinshasa.com; Ave du Col Vangu; studio/r/apt US$150/150/180; ❄📶🏊) This friendly and spotless oasis in Gombe is a great little in-the-know bolthole. Accommodation is divided into rooms, studios (with kitchens) and larger two-room apartments, all arranged around a beautifully kept courtyard and a swimming pool, which make it perfect for kids. There's no restaurant, however.

**★Procure Ste Anne** HOTEL $$

(☎0992330739, 0815183819; propaskin@yahoo.com; Ave Dumi; s/d/tw US$60/70/70; P❄@📶) This quiet colonial-era mansion within a large Catholic compound offers Kinshasa's best value accommodation. Rooms are historic and immaculate with high ceilings and clean bathrooms, and it's safe, central and quiet.

**Elais Hotel** HOTEL $$$

(☎0977384333; www.hotelelais.com/en/kinshasa; 2 Ave Ngongo-Lutete; r/ste US$200/220; P❄📶🏊) This superb place feels like a social club in the heart of downtown Kinshasa. It's an excellent choice for business travellers, who will love their two-room suites that include a minikitchen. A gym, tennis courts, a pool and a popular restaurant complete the scene, and it's unsurprising that it's often a long-term accommodation choice for visitors.

### Eating

**Patisserie Nouvelle** FRENCH $

(www.patisserienouvelle.com; Ave de l'Équateur; sandwiches from US$8; ⏱6.30am-6pm; 📶) A great breakfast choice, this trendy bakery does a range of set breakfasts as well as gorgeous pastries and good coffee. This is the best-located outlet, but the **second one** (Ave Mondjiba) is far more charming and has an outside courtyard.

**Restaurant Al-Dar** LEBANESE $

(Blvd du 30 Juin; mains US$5-10; ⏱7.30am-10pm; ✎) There's a reason why this large, canteen-like Lebanese place is always full to bursting, and that reason is price. The food is classic Lebanese fast food and everyone from smart-suited businessmen to hip hop-styled young locals and exhausted UN workers come to eat here.

**Chez Flore** CONGOLESE $$

(Ave Tombalbaye; mains US$12-20; ⏱midday-11pm) If you're looking for a Congolese restaurant with a local crowd and laid-back vibe, this is it. The friendly staff will explain the large menu, which is in Lingala for the most part, and you can enjoy the enormous portions served at the plastic tables in the garden.

## Democratic Republic of Congo Highlights

**1 Nyiragongo** (p519) Staring down in wonder at the lava lake of this magnificent active volcano is quite simply a once-in-a-lifetime experience.

**2 Parc National des Virunga** (p519) Visiting the habituated mountain gorillas that thrive in the thick forests of Africa's oldest national park.

**3 Lola Ya Bonobo Sanctuary** (p517) Meeting the bonobo, a rare, peace-loving relative of the chimpanzee, at this excellent orphanage.

**4 Kinshasa** (p511) Experiencing the rhythms, colours and chaos of Central Africa's megacity.

**5 Parc National de Kahuzi-Biéga** (p517) Crossing gorgeous Lake Kivu to the friendly town of Bukavu, from where you can explore DRC's most overlooked national park.

**6 Goma** (p518) Seeing Eastern DRC's capital is a fascinating experience – neither volcanic eruptions nor warlords can keep this survivor down!

SOUTH SUDAN
Obo
Juba
Bangassou
Ndu
Garamba National Park
Yei
Aba
Bondo
Niangara
Faradje
Arua
Aru
Isiro
Buta
Opaki Wildlife Reserve
Pakwach
Mahagi
Bumba
River
Lake Albert
Bunia
Mambasa
Epulu
Komanda
River
UGANDA
Kisangani
Beni
Boyoma Falls
Kasindi
Butembo
Ubundu
Lake Edward (Lake Rwitanzige)
Tshuapa
Lubutu
Kayna-Bayonga
Ishasha
Parc National des Virunga
Rutshuru
Congo
Nyiragongo
(3470m)
River
Goma
RWANDA
River
KIGALI
Parc National de Kahuzi-Biéga
Lake Kivu
Kalima
Bukavu
Kindu
Kampene
Uvira
BUJUMBURA
BURUNDI
Kigoma
TANZANIA
Kananga
Kabalo
Kalemie
Congo
Lake Tanganyika
Sankuru
River
River
Kamina
Mpulungu
Lake Mweru
Bukama
River
Parc National de Kundelungu
Luau
Dilolo
Kolwezi
Likasi
Lake Bangweulu
Lubumbashi
Kasumbalesa
Chingola
ZAMBIA
Kitwe
Ndola

## Kinshasa

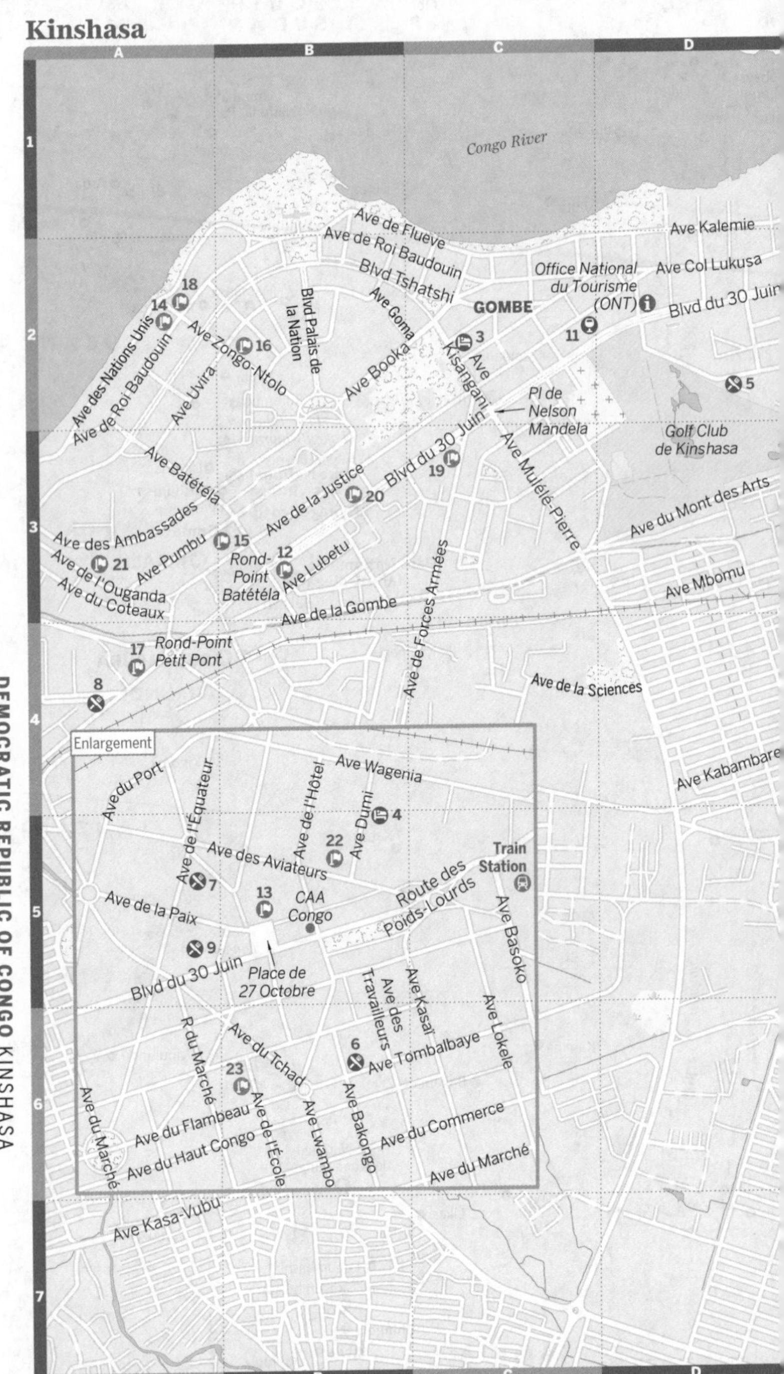

Congo River
Ave de Flueve
Ave de Roi Baudouin
Blvd Tshatshi
Ave Goma
Blvd Palais de la Nation
GOMBE
Office National du Tourisme (ONT)
Ave Kalemie
Ave Col Lukusa
Blvd du 30 Juin
Ave des Nations Unis
Ave de Roi Baudouin
Ave Zongo-Ntolo
Ave Uvira
Ave Booka
Ave Kisangani
Pl de Nelson Mandela
Golf Club de Kinshasa
Ave Batétéla
Ave de la Justice
Blvd du 30 Juin
Ave Mulélé-Pierre
Ave des Ambassades
Ave Pumbu
Rond-Point Batétéla
Ave Lubetu
Ave du Mont des Arts
Ave de l'Ouganda
Ave du Coteaux
Ave de la Gombe
Ave de Forces Armées
Ave Mbomu
Rond-Point Petit Pont
Ave de la Sciences
Ave Kabambare
Enlargement
Ave du Port
Ave de l'Équateur
Ave de l'Hôtel
Ave Wagenia
Ave Dumi
Ave des Aviateurs
Train Station
Ave de la Paix
CAA Congo
Route des Poids-Lourds
Ave Basoko
Blvd du 30 Juin
Place de 27 Octobre
Ave des Travailleurs
Ave Kasaï
Ave Lokele
R du Marché
Ave du Tchad
Ave Tombalbaye
Ave du Marché
Ave du Flambeau
Ave de l'École
Ave Lwambo
Ave Bakongo
Ave du Commerce
Ave du Haut Congo
Ave du Marché
Ave Kasa-Vubu

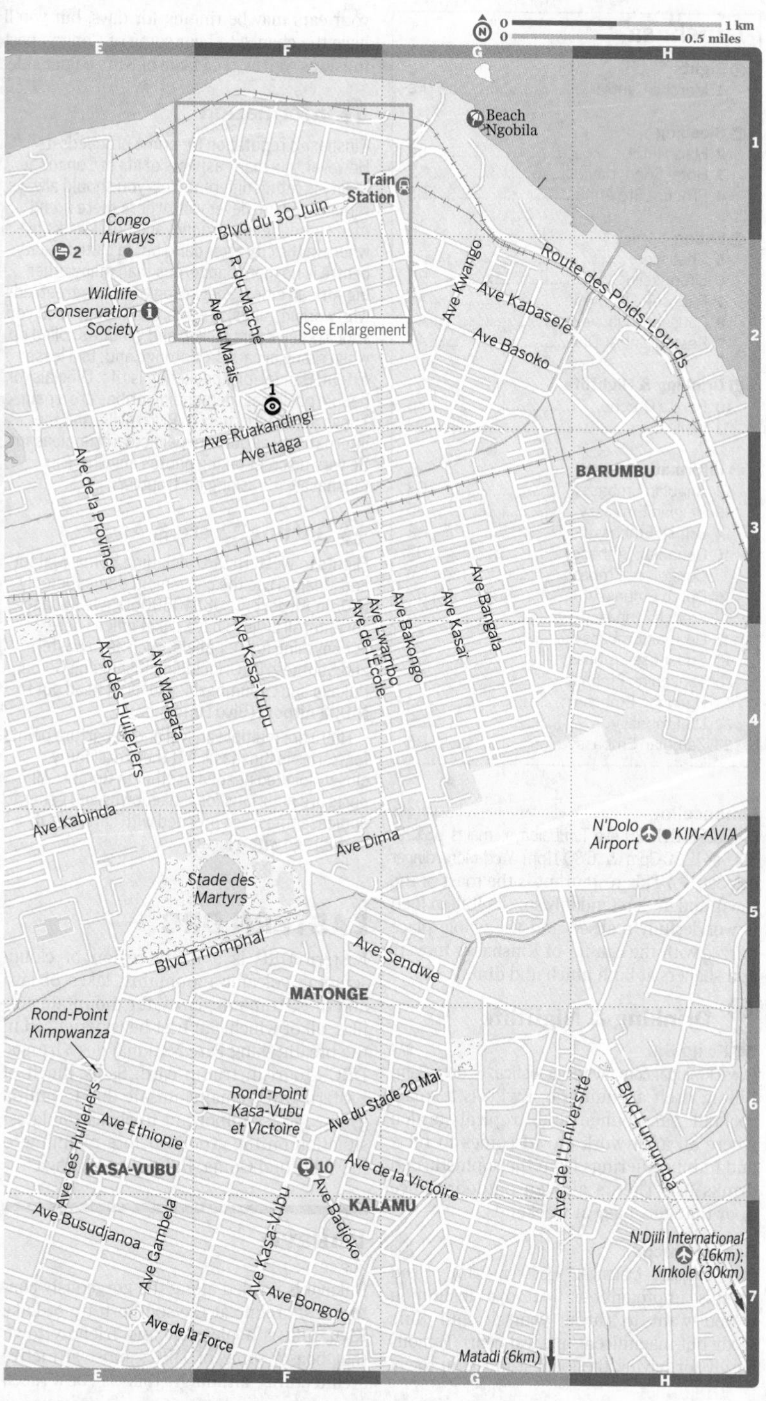

0 1 km
0 0.5 miles
E
F
G
H
Beach Ngobila
Train Station
Congo Airways
2
Wildlife Conservation Society
Blvd du 30 Juin
R du Marché
Ave du Marais
See Enlargement
Ave Kwango
Ave Kabasele
Route des Poids-Lourds
Ave Basoko
1
Ave Ruakandingi
Ave Itaga
BARUMBU
Ave de la Province
Ave Bangala
Ave Kasaï
Ave Bakongo
Ave Lwambo
Ave de l'Ecole
Ave Kasa-Vubu
Ave Wangata
Ave des Huileriers
Ave Kabinda
Ave Dima
N'Dolo Airport
KIN-AVIA
Stade des Martyrs
Blvd Triomphal
Ave Sendwe
MATONGE
Rond-Point Kimpwanza
Rond-Point Kasa-Vubu et Victoire
Ave du Stade 20 Mai
Ave Ethiopie
Ave des Huileriers
KASA-VUBU
10
Ave de la Victoire
Ave Badjoko
KALAMU
Ave de l'Université
Blvd Lumumba
Ave Busudjanoa
Ave Gambela
Ave Kasa-Vubu
Ave Bongolo
Ave de la Force
N'Djili International (16km); Kinkole (30km)
Matadi (6km)
1
2
3
4
5
6
7

## Kinshasa

**Sights**

1 Marché Central ... F2

**Sleeping**

2 Elais Hotel ... E2
3 Hotel Sunnyday ... C2
4 Procure Ste Anne ... B5

**Eating**

5 Chez Flore ... D2
6 Limoncello ... B6
7 Patisserie Nouvelle ... A5
8 Patisserie Nouvelle ... A4
9 Restaurant Al-Dar ... A5

**Drinking & Nightlife**

10 Bar La Crèche ... F6
11 Kwilu Bar ... C2

**Information**

12 Angolan Embassy ... B3
13 Belgian Embassy ... B5
14 British Embassy ... A2
15 Canadian Embassy ... B3
Congolese Embassy ... (see 12)
16 Dutch Embassy ... B2
17 French Embassy ... A4
18 German Embassy ... A2
19 Sudanese Embassy ... C3
20 Tanzanian Embassy ... B3
21 Ugandan Embassy ... A3
22 US Embassy ... B5
23 Zambian Embassy ... B6

**Limoncello** ITALIAN $$$
(0815141111; 20 Ave Tombalbaye; mains US$20-30; 12.30-3pm & 6.30-11pm Wed-Mon, dinner only Sat; ) This restaurant is the toast of the town, and understandably so – its Italian food is wonderfully realised and the whole place buzzes with the chatter of Kinshasa's movers and shakers at both lunch and dinner.

### Drinking & Nightlife

**★Kwilu Bar** BAR
(www.kwilubar.com; Ave de la Justice; 6pm-2am) Billing itself a 'rhumerie', Kwilu is a smart cocktail bar, lounge and tropical garden where an after-work crowd comes to relax and imbibe offerings from the sophisticated drinks list. There's also an outdoor dance floor that gets busy at weekends.

**Bar La Crèche** BAR
(Ave Badjoko, Matonge; 10am–2am) Head to this unpretentious Matonge institution if you want to throw yourself into Kin's seedy-but-magnificent musical heart. Famous locally for having the loudest music in town, your ears may be ringing for days, but you'll have the chance to hear some of Congo's best music as well as get a taste of Kin's edgier side.

### Information

Kinshasa's reputation for crime proceeds it. However, like many aspects of life in Congo the reality is rather different. Yes, you should always remain vigilant, never walk where there aren't many other people around, and don't walk anywhere in the city after dark, but in truth the city centre is no more dangerous than many other big African cities. *Shegue* (aggressive street kids who work in gangs) are a threat, though, and you should keep doors locked and windows rolled up when riding in cars. In Matonge and, to a lesser extent, Bandal, pickpocketing is rife. Officials (or people posing as) demanding bribes are a pain. Those at the ferry port to Brazzaville and the international airport are particularly unpleasant. Be very discreet taking photos anywhere in Kinshasa – it's asking for trouble.

### Getting There & Away

Flights to Western DRC including Boma, Matadi and Muanda use the convenient domestic-only **N'Dolo Airport** (0824060060; Ave Kabasele Joseph); all airlines have ticket offices here. For anything further afield, such as to Eastern and Southern DRC, including Kisangani, Goma, Bukavu and Lubumbashi, you must head out to **N'Djili Airport** (Blvd Lumumba).

There are multiple arrival and departure points for ferries in Kinshasa, but they're all fairly closely located near each other in Gombe. All ports are notorious for shakedowns and general unpleasantness, so proceed with care, and if possible go with a local.

# EASTERN DRC

Eastern DRC is a misty region of cloud-scraping volcanic mountains, lakes of lava and those tranquil giants, the mountain gorillas, all of which can best be experienced in the breathtaking Parc National des Virunga, DRC's tourism trump card. Sadly much of Eastern DRC remains unsafe due to militia groups, so it's important to check the latest situation on the ground before planning to move beyond Goma, Bukavu or Virunga.

## Bukavu

POP 807,000

Bukavu is nestled along the gorgeously contorted shoreline at the southern tip of Lake Kivu, and is a pleasant and friendly town that boasts some of DRC's most attractive architecture, although this is best seen from the water. Bukavu is also the base for visiting the Parc National de Kahuzi-Biéga, Virunga's little-known neighbour, where you can track habituated eastern lowland gorillas (Grauer's gorillas) at relatively low prices.

## Sights

**★Parc National de Kahuzi-Biéga** NATIONAL PARK
(☎ English enquiries 0971300881, French enquiries 0822881012; http://kahuzibiega.wordpress.com) South Kivu's star attraction is this national park, where you can track habituated eastern lowland gorillas (Grauer's gorillas) for just US$400 per person, a relative bargain! The park also contains a chimp orphanage at Lwiro (US$30 per person), where between 40 and 50 chimps are kept in excellent conditions.

**Idjwi Island** ISLAND
Floating out in the middle of Lake Kivu, Idjwi Island is, at 340 sq km, the second-largest lake island in Africa. Isolated from Congo's decades of war, as well as missing out on what little development the mainland has seen, Idjwi is a wonderful place to escape the modern world, enjoy nature and the rich island culture. Lodging is available in small guesthouses and the speedboat between Bukavu and Goma stops here on request.

## Sleeping

**Esperance Guest House** B&B $
(☎ 0999941197; lhenkinbrant@hotmail.com; 8 Ave Pangi, Ibanda; d incl breakfast US$40; wi-fi) There are only two rooms at the friendly little Esperance Guest House – and they both share a bathroom – but everything is kept polished and clean, and a good dinner is available for US$10 extra. Call ahead. Taxi drivers will know the nearby Hotel Horizon.

**★Orchids Safari Club** RESORT $$$
(☎ 0813126467; www.orchids-hotel.com; Ave Lt Dubois; s US$145-190, d US$180-225; P ❄ @ wi-fi) This impressive hotel has gorgeous gardens overlooking the lake and the feel of a colonial-era country club. The rooms are spacious and very well appointed, with private terraces, smart furnishings, comfortable beds and large bathrooms.

**Lodge Co-Co** GUESTHOUSE $$$
(☎ 0993855752; www.lodgecoco.com; Ave Muhumba; s/d US$120/150; wi-fi) This Swiss-run guesthouse is the baby of Carlos, who has been tracking gorillas in the national park for decades. His love for the creatures shines through: each room has his gorilla photographs in them and the corridors are stuffed with local arts and crafts. It's an excellent base for anyone wanting to visit the gorillas with a true expert.

## Eating

**Karibu** CONGOLESE $
(☎ 0993097044; off Ave Muhumba; mains US$5-13; ⌚ 9am-11pm) This fun and friendly bar and restaurant has a decidedly hip feel, with a crowd of locals around the pool table, a garden decorated with empty beer bottles and fairy lights, and a shop selling upcycled clothes with a Congolese touch. The menu

WORTH A TRIP

### SIDE TRIPS FROM KINSHASA

**Chutes du Zongo** A popular day trip from Kinshasa despite the expensive 4WD hire (US$200) necessary to get here, the gorgeous 65m-high Zongo Falls are one of DRC's most spectacular sights. Getting to the viewpoints involves some hiking (bring shoes that you don't mind getting muddy), but watching the water roaring over the precipice into the river below is unforgettable. There's the Seli Safari Resort here, where it's possible to have lunch or overnight. The falls are 130km from Kinshasa, so expect a four-hour journey each way.

**Lola Ya Bonobo Sanctuary** (www.lolayabonobo.org; foreigners US$5; ⌚ 9.30am-4pm Tue-Sun) Ninety minutes west of Kinshasa, just beyond the city's sprawl, this excellent project provides a home for orphaned bonobos. Long thought to be chimpanzees, bonobos are actually a separate species known for being much more peaceful than their cousins. They're also endangered, with only around 50,000 surviving in the wild. Trails here lead around the large, forested enclosures, but the playful bonobos often hang out right at the front, especially in the morning. The sanctuary is 8km off the Matadi road. If you're patient, you can hitch those last 8km off the highway. A hire car with driver from Kinshasa will cost US$100, but in the wet season you'll need a 4WD (US$200).

is of Congolese standards, as well as good pizza. It's in a side street behind the Horizon Hotel.

**★Orchids Safari Club Restaurant** FRENCH $$$
(www.orchids-hotel.com; Ave Lt Dubois; mains US$20-30; ⏲7am-10pm; ❄📶) This smart restaurant inside the Orchids Safari Club (p517) hotel sees a scramble at lunchtime to bag one of its few lake-facing tables, and the views are well worth coming early for. The food is classical French cuisine with a few regional influences and local dishes.

## Getting There & Away

Several boats a day connect Bukavu with Goma. Spend either US$15 on the shadeless, grossly overcrowded deck of a ferry (eight to 10 hours) or splurge US$50 for a *canot rapide* (speedboat; three hours).

Crossing into Rwanda from Bukavu is a cinch – take a taxi to the border (US$5) and then pick up onward transport to Kigali on the other side.

# Goma

POP 1 MILLION

This likeable border town on Lake Kivu is unlike anywhere else in DRC, being home to an enormous UN and NGO presence that gives it an unusually cosmopolitan feel. Having been almost wiped off the map by the eruption of the nearby Nyiragongo volcano in 2002, Goma has done much rebuilding in the past decade and a half, and as a result the city has a surprisingly attractive centre.

People generally visit Goma en route to tracking mountain gorillas, climbing Nyiragongo or trekking the Rwenzori Mountains. The city itself has no proper attractions, but it's a great pre- and post-Virunga hang out, with some excellent sleeping and eating options.

## Activities

**Kivu Travel** TOURS
(☎0992899667, in Belgium +32 495 58 68 07; www.kivutravel.com) A Belgian/Congolese company with an excellent reputation and great connections throughout the east, Kivu Travel has friendly and responsive staff who can help you plan most itineraries.

**Virunga Booking Office** ADVENTURE, TOURS
(☎0991715401; www.visitvirunga.com; Blvd Kanyamulanga; ⏲8.30am-7pm Mon-Fri, 8.30am-12.30pm Sat) While most travellers book their Virunga adventures in advance, this helpful office in the centre of town is the place to come and book tours (including day trips) at the last minute.

## Sleeping

**Caritas Guesthouse** GUESTHOUSE $
(☎081679199; guesthousecaritas@yahoo.fr; off Ave de la Révolution; s/d from US$50/75; 📶) You've got a prime lakeside location here, including some lovely gardens, rooms with balconies and great views and a secure setting. The downside would be the rather basic bathrooms and very unmemorable restaurant.

**Linda Hotel** HOTEL $$
(☎0995487783; www.lindahotelgoma.com; Ave la Corniche; r US$60-80; 📶) It's hard to miss this pink-painted lakeside compound, where a selection of seemingly randomly priced rooms are available. Despite a few eyebrow-raising art choices, rooms are exactly what you need in this price range and include mosquito nets, fridges, balconies and electric fans.

**Lake Kivu Lodge** HOTEL $$$
(☎0971868749; www.lackivulodge.com; Ave de la Paix; r US$130-180; P📶≋) Goma's best hotel is some way out of the city centre, but makes the most of its gorgeous views over the lake. The cheapest rooms are on the small side and the bathrooms are in need of some work, but the standard-plus rooms come with some great extras including espresso machines, private gated terraces and four poster beds.

## Eating

**★Au Bon Pain** BAKERY $$
(Ave Kanyamuhanga; mains US$9-15, sandwiches US$5; ⏲7am-7pm Mon-Sat, 10am-3pm Sun; 📶) The opening of this lifeline marked the beginning of a new era in Goma – and if that sounds like an exaggeration just look at the lovely pastries, the great coffee, the delicious sandwiches or the salads on offer. It's furiously popular at lunchtime, when you may have to wait for a seat.

**★Le Chalet** INTERNATIONAL $$
(Ave de la Paix; mains US$12-18; ⏲11am-midnight 📶) Ten minutes north of Goma's centre by *moto-taxi*, Le Chalet is a tranquil oasis of tropical gardens and calm, lakeside dining. The interesting menu runs beyond the standard meat dishes, and there's also excel-

lent pizza from a wood-fired oven and good set-meal offers. Stick around after lunch for a spot of sunbathing and swimming.

## Information

**BIAC Bank** (off Rond Point des Banques) Reliable ATM accepting international cards.

**Raw Bank** (Blvd Kanyamuhanga) Reliable ATM that accepts Visa and MasterCard.

## Getting There & Away

Goma can be reached on daily flights from Kinshasa on **CAA Congo** (☎0820002776; www.caacongo.com; Goma International Airport) and **Congo Airways** (p524). However, as the Rwandan border is just a couple of kilometres from the city centre, many people cross over from Gisenyi instead. The border crossing is very straight forward, with waiting buses and taxis leaving for Kigali as soon as you cross to the Rwandan side. Taxis wait on the DRC side of the border and will take you to anywhere in Goma for a few dollars.

# Parc National des Virunga

DRC's biggest single draw is this superb national park – the first in Africa – which has been rejuvenated in recent years to offer a superb range of attractions. Trips here are normally focused on visits to the multiple groups of habituated mountain gorillas within the park, as well as to do the magnificent hike to the top of the active Nyiragongo volcano, where you can stare down into a bubbling lava lake in the massive crater below. However, there are many other activities on offer, including chimp treks, mountain climbing and birdwatching. This is Africa's hauntingly beautiful, beating heart and rarely is it possible to recommend somewhere so full heartedly.

## Sights

**★Nyiragongo** VOLCANO

(per person US$300) Perhaps DRC's most magnificent single sight, active volcano Nyiragongo soars above the city of Goma and the surrounding Virunga National Park and sends plumes of smoke into the sky, before becoming a flaming beacon visible for miles around after sundown. The trek to the top is an absolutely unmissable experience, with those who undertake the five-hour climb being rewarded with views into the volcano's explosive lava lake below. Access to the volcano is only via travel agencies in Goma who arrange the trip through the **Virunga National Park** (☎0991715401; www.visitvirunga.org; Blvd Kanya Mulanga).

**Senkwekwe Gorilla Orphanage** WILDLIFE RESERVE

(⌚8am-4pm) Provided you make it back from your gorilla track in a timely fashion, it should be possible to visit the world's only mountain gorilla orphanage, which is integrated into the grounds of the Mikeno Lodge (p520). Named after the silverback who died defending the Rugendo group against gunmen in the infamous 2007 massacre, the orphanage is home to four gorillas, including Ndakasi and Ndeze, both massacre survivors.

## Activities

All activities inside Virunga are run and strictly controlled by the Institut Congolais pour la Conservation de la Nature (p520), who has overall control of Virunga and runs the park from its headquarters at Rumangabo.

### Gorilla Tracking

There are few experiences in the world more memorable than coming face to face with a wild eastern mountain gorilla, and this is one the best places in the world for it.

There are six habituated families in Parc National des Virunga, and you will be assigned a group to visit by the rangers based on how many people are tracking and the current location of each group.

The ideal time to meet a gorilla family is from 10am to 11am (which means a 5.30am departure from Goma).

### Chimpanzee Tracking

Virunga park authorities also offer chimp tracking near the headquarters at Rumangabo (US$100 per person). The habituated group consists of 12 individuals and chances of seeing them are generally excellent. Groups of four people leave Mikeno Lodge at 6am for the tracking and time with the group is limited to one hour. Unlike gorillas, chimps are fast moving, love to climb high into the canopy and are more wary of humans. This means you won't get as close to a wild chimp as you will to a mountain gorilla, but don't let this deter you.

### Climbing Nyiragongo Volcano

Beautiful and brooding, Nyiragongo Volcano is perfectly safe to climb as its serious eruptions can be reliably predicted. Those who do undertake the five-hour climb (US$300 per person) are rewarded with views from the crater's rim, down into the earth's smouldering heart and the world's largest lava lake.

The hike to the rim is just 8km, but takes between four and six hours and is done in five stages. Climbers need to leave by 10am to ensure they reach the top by nightfall – do not be late as you will not be able to climb. Guides and armed security are included with your permit, but consider hiring your own porter (US$12 per day, maximum weight carried 15kg) and cook (US$15 per day) at the small ranger post at the start of the climb. Warm clothing is essential. Accommodation on top, which is included in the permit cost, is in one of the supersimple A-frame shelters built on the crater's rim.

## Sleeping & Eating

All accommodation inside the national park is run by ICCN. Most budget travellers base themselves in Goma and travel up to the park on day trips rather than spend tthe big bucks on the park lodge at Mikeno.

Accommodation within the park works on a full-board system; day trippers should bring a packed lunch and plenty of water.

★**Mikeno Lodge** LODGE $$$
(0991715401; www.mikenolodge.com; s/d & tw incl meals US$316/450; P) Easily the most luxurious and beautifully designed hotel in DRC, Mikeno Lodge is a pampering slice of bliss in the wilds of the Congo jungle. Each of the 12 vast bungalows is made of dark volcanic stone, rich mahogany and beautifully crafted thatched roofs. Inside they boast a cosy lounge, open fire and a bathroom with a stone-lined shower.

**Bukima Camp** TENTED CAMP $$$
(0991715401; www.visitvirunga.org; Bukima; s/d inc meals US$316/450) This magical spot is also the departure point for many of Virunga's gorilla-tracking excursions, which means you'll be able to sleep later by staying here. The campsite consists of eight luxurious tents with their own bathrooms, a large communal dining shelter and some stunning views towards the mountains.

## Information

**Institut Congolais pour la Conservation de la Nature** (ICCN; 0991715401; https://virunga.org/) Virunga National Park, run by ICCN, is your point of contact for arranging everything within the park, including gorilla permits, accommodation, guides, transport, equipment and activities. Its comprehensive website gives full information about all the possibilities in the park, although it's still often easier and faster to book through a travel agency that will deal with ICCN on your behalf.

## Getting There & Away

All transfers within the park are done with a military escort, and convoys to and from Goma (two hours' travel) are common in order to reduce the number of soldiers needed. Transfers are usually included with packages, but can also be ordered directly with ICCN, the national park authorities. Bad roads make journeys long and not particularly comfortable.

# UNDERSTAND DRC

## DRC Today

Despite several years of progress and a relatively high degree of stability following the collapse of the M23 rebellion in 2013, DRC currently finds itself in the grip of a constitutional crisis that threatens to upset the all too fragile status quo. Under the DRC constitution, which sets a two-term limit to the presidency, incumbent president Joseph Kabila was due to step down in December 2016 having completed his second term as president. Rather than amending the constitution to do away with term limits, Kabila managed to persuade the country's electoral commission to postpone the elections due in late 2016 until mid 2018. Popular fury erupted into violence and demonstrations in Kinshasa and other large cities in September 2016.

In the meantime DRC needs effective government more than ever, with massive problems at almost all levels of society – from illiteracy and malnutrition to soaring HIV infection rates, endemic corruption, militia activity and crushing poverty.

## History

### A Tragic Story

The Baka people, formerly known as Pygmies, were probably the first inhabitants of the steaming Congo River Basin, arriving as early as 8000 BC. The Bantu settled most of the Congo by AD1000, bringing agriculture and iron-smelting. Trading goods such as ivory, cloth, pottery, ironware and slaves, the Portuguese made contact 500 years later with a highly developed kingdom known as the Kongo. Kongo royalty became enthusiastic allies, adopting Portuguese names, clothes and customs and converting to Christianity.

In the mid-19th century, Arab traders crossed East Africa to eastern Congo, taking back slaves and ivory. During the same era, Dr David Livingstone opened up the African interior to European exploration. In 1878, Belgium's King Leopold II commissioned explorer Henry Morton Stanley (who found Livingstone in 1871) to return to the Congo. Over the ensuing five years Stanley signed treaties with chiefs on Leopold's behalf, tricking them into handing over their land rights in return for paltry gifts. At the Berlin Conference called by Bismarck in 1884 to carve up Africa, Leopold convinced the Iron Chancellor to declare the Congo a free-trade area and cede it to him. Thereafter, he set about fleecing his Congo Free State of its ivory, copper and rubber. Hideous crimes were committed against the Congolese by Leopold's rubber traders.

## Independence

As Leopold's crimes gradually became public knowledge, the Belgian government took over in 1908. The new Belgians ended forced labour, built schools and roads, and nearly eradicated sleeping sickness, but the Belgians excluded Congolese from roles in the government, and very few Congolese gained college educations.

Gathering pace in the 1950s under charismatic revolutionary Patrice Lumumba, the independence movement finally wrested control from the colonisers on 30 June 1960. Lumumba became prime minister of the new Republic of Congo, but tribalism and personal quests for power quickly erupted, and just a week later the army mutinied. By the end of the year, army chief Joseph Mobutu had seized power, Lumumba had been arrested (and would later be assassinated) and Congo had split into four quasi-independent states. An aggressive intervention by UN and Belgian troops plus several mercenary armies put the country together again by 1965.

Renaming himself Mobutu Sese Seko, and the country Zaire, the new leader embarked on a campaign of 'Africanisation'. Mobutu brought stability to Congo, but he also ruled with an iron fist, quashed opposition and turned corruption and the squandering of state resources into an art form later named kleptocracy. It's estimated he pocketed US$5 billion during his rule.

## Civil War

By the early 1990s Mobutu had driven the country to economic collapse. Not only did schools and hospitals cease to function, but highways were reclaimed by the jungle.

Backing the Hutu perpetrators of the 1994 Rwandan genocide who escaped into Zaire, Mobutu enraged local Tutsis, who, supported enthusiastically by Rwandan and Ugandan troops, started a march across the country in 1996 and easily took Kinshasa in 1997. Mobutu escaped the country, dying of cancer just four months later in Morocco.

Soon after renaming the country the Democratic Republic of Congo, the new leader, Laurent Kabila, a one-time protégé of Che Guevara, dashed any hopes of change by outlawing political opposition. Proving himself every bit as corrupt and repressive as Mobutu.

The DRC's second war (aka 'Africa's World War') started in 1998 when Rwandan and Ugandan troops again entered the country. Kabila was saved by troops from Angola, Zimbabwe, Namibia and other countries, but much of DRC was now under the control of Rwanda and Uganda.

## A New Start

Laurent Kabila was shot by one of his bodyguards in January 2001. He was succeeded by his 29-year-old son Joseph, largely raised in Tanzania, who, to the surprise of nearly everyone, proved to be a competent leader. Kabila the younger welcomed UN troops and presided over a peace agreement that in 2002 paved the way for a transitional government. He also oversaw a new constitution and heeded the advice of the World Bank and IMF, setting the economy back on course. In 2006 Kabila won the DRC's first legitimate elections in over 40 years.

In November 2011 Kabila won another round of presidential and parliamentary elections, but the vote was criticised by foreign observers and the opposition disputes the result. In May 2012 a new rebel group was added to the two-dozen groups already operating in eastern DRC. The M23 rebels were made up of mainly Tutsi fighters who deserted from the Congolese army. The UN accused the group of being backed by Rwanda and Uganda.

## People

Though DRC plays host to more than 250 ethnic groups (and over 700 different languages and dialects), four tribes dominate. The Kongo, Luba, Mongo and Mangbetu-Azande groupings collectively make up 45% of the population. Half the population practises Roman Catholicism, while 20% are Protestant and 10% Muslim. The remaining 20% follow traditional beliefs.

## Cuisine

Congolese cooking is some of Africa's best, and you'll eat well in DRC, though food is expensive by African standards. Typical Congolese dishes include *fufu,* a sticky dough made from cassava flour, and *poulet à la moambé,* chicken served in a sauce made from the outer layer of palm nuts. *Pili pili,* the incredibly hot pepper sauce beloved by the Congolese, is served with nearly everything.

# SURVIVAL GUIDE

##  Directory A–Z

### ACCOMMODATION

Accommodation in DRC is expensive by and large, and both choice and quality are lacking in most places. Real budget accommodation is hard to come by, and where it does exist it's often unpleasant and unsafe. At the US$20 to US$40 level you might get a fan or TV, but running water is still unlikely. Moving into the US$50 to US$100 range and rooms will be much more comfortable. You'll need to spend a minimum of US$100 a night in Kinshasa for a decent midrange hotel.

### ELECTRICITY

220V/50Hz; the European two-pin plug is the most common.

### EMBASSIES & CONSULATES

The following countries have diplomatic representation in Kinshasa.

**Angolan Embassy** (0999906927; 4413 Blvd du 30 Juin; 10am-noon & 2–4pm Mon-Fri)

**Belgian Embassy** (0819700159; http://rd-congo.diplomatie.belgium.be; Pl du 27 Octobre; 7.30am–3pm Mon–Fri)

**British Embassy** (0815566200; http://ukindrc.fco.gov.uk; Ave de Roi Baudouin; 8am–4pm Mon–Thu, 8am–2pm Fri)

**Canadian Embassy** (0996021500; www.congo.gc.ca; 17 Ave Pumbu; 7.30am–noon & 1.30–4pm Mon–Thu, 7.30am–1pm Fri)

**Congo Embassy** (0999909544; Blvd du 30 Juin; 8am–noon Mon–Fri)

**Dutch Embassy** (0996050600; http://drcongo.nlambassade.org; 11 Ave Zongo-Ntolo; 8am–4pm Mon–Fri)

**French Embassy** (0815559999; www.ambafrance-cd.org; 1 Ave du Col Mondjiba; 8am–4pm Mon–Fri)

**German Embassy** (0815561380; www.kinshasa.diplo.de; 82 Ave de Roi Baudouin; 8.30am–3pm Mon–Thu, 8am–noon Fri)

**Sudanese Embassy** (0999937396; Blvd du 30 Juin; 8am–noon & 2–4pm Mon–Thu)

**Tanzanian Embassy** (0815565850; Blvd du 30 Juin; 8am–3pm Mon–Fri)

**Ugandan Embassy** (0810519260; Ave de l'Ouganda; 8am–2pm Mon–Fri)

**US Embassy** (0815560151; http://kinshasa.usembassy.gov; 310 Ave des Aviateurs; 7.30am–5.15pm Mon–Thu, 7.30am–12.30pm Fri)

**Zambian Embassy** (0819999437; Ave de l'École; 8am–noon & 2–4pm Mon–Fri)

### INTERNET ACCESS

Internet access in DRC is frustratingly slow. Very few hotel wireless networks actually work, and when they do they're incredibly slow. The most reliable internet access can be had via local mobile phone networks – anybody can register for a SIM card, just go to a mobile provider's office with your passport.

### LGBTIQ TRAVELLERS

Homosexuality is legal in DRC, but locals tend to be very discreet as homophobia is rife. There is no accessible gay life in the country for travellers, though all the usual apps are used, so it's not difficult to make contacts. Same-sex couples are unlikely to raise eyebrows by sharing a room, but discretion is generally the best way to go.

### MONEY

US dollars are accepted everywhere and moneychangers are omnipresent in DRC's cities. Somewhat reliable, internationally linked ATMs are common in the large cities.

#### Exchange Rates

| COUNTRY | CURRENCY | CDF |
|---|---|---|
| Australia | A$1 | CDF775 |
| Canada | C$1 | CDF776 |
| Euro | €1 | CDF1116 |
| Japan | ¥100 | CDF964 |
| NZ | NZ$1 | CDF731 |
| UK | UK£1 | CDF1295 |
| US | US$1 | CDF1028 |

For current exchange rates, see www.xe.com.

## OPENING HOURS

**Banks & offices** 8.30am–3pm Monday to Friday, 8.30am–noon Saturday
**Shops** 8am–6pm Monday to Saturday
**Restaurants** noon–10pm
**Bars** 6pm–midnight

## PUBLIC HOLIDAYS

Public holidays are as follows:

**New Year's Day** 1 January
**Martyrs of Independence Day** 4 January
**Heroes' Day** 16–17 January
**Easter** March/April
**Labour Day** 1 May
**Liberation Day** 17 May
**Independence Day** 30 June
**Parents' Day** 1 August
**Christmas Day** 25 December

## SAFE TRAVEL

DRC is fraught with potential danger, and almost any government website will warn you against travel here. This is alarmist, however: be sensible, ask for and follow local advice, keep your wits about you and you should be absolutely fine. There are, however, a large number of things to consider and be aware of.

There are still rebel armies and bandits (plus government soldiers, who are often just as dangerous) terrorising people in large swathes of northern and eastern DRC. North Kivu province around the city of Beni was particularly unstable at the time of writing. Political unrest is another danger: late 2016 saw violence that left many people dead in several cities in DRC, including Kinshasa.

Though the situation is improving, police and other officials, particularly those working in customs and immigration, frequently request money, though they rarely demand it. In all cases, calm. friendly and confident is your best play. Do all you can to avoid handing over your passport (present copies instead) since it might cost you to get it back.

Photography in towns and cities across DRC attracts attention and should only be done if you're sure it's safe. The best plan is to ask a local, and if in doubt, don't take the photo. Travellers have been arrested for taking photos in Kinshasa and other towns. In the countryside things are generally easier, but avoid taking photos within sight of police.

## TELEPHONE

SIM cards cost very little in DRC and can be purchased from one of the major mobile-phone providers, including Airtel, Tigo and Vodacom. When going to buy one, be sure to bring your passport and go to an official office of the operator, rather than buying a SIM card from a street hawker. Only official vendors can register your SIM, which is necessary before it can be used.

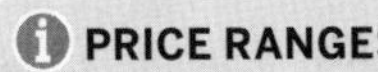

### PRICE RANGES

The following price ranges refer to a double room with bathroom. Unless otherwise stated, breakfast is included in the price.

**$** less than US$50

**$$** US$50–US$100

**$$$** more than US$100

The following price ranges refer to a main course.

**$** less than US$10

**$$** US$10–US$20

**$$$** more than US$20

## TOURIST INFORMATION

There is an **Office National du Tourisme** (☎0998319053; Blvd du 30 Juin; ⊗8am–5pm Mon–Fri) bureau in Kinshasa, though despite having an impressive website, there's very little in the way of practical information to be had from its staff. Your best source of up-to-date tourist information is travel agencies or tour operators.

The **Wildlife Conservation Society** (☎0820459075; https://drcongo.wcs.org; 56 Ave Col Ebeya) in Kinshasa is a good place to get up-to-date information about visiting the various national parks in DRC.

## VISAS

All visitors to DRC need visas, and they're not available on arrival. You must apply at the DRC embassy in your home country or country of residence.

### Obtaining Visas

The exact requirements for visas vary from embassy to embassy, but in general you will need proof of hotel booking, yellow fever vaccination and a legalised letter from a sponsor in DRC. Visa fees tend be between US$100 and US$200, and normally require several weeks to be processed.

The only current alternative to getting a visa at home is the two-week, single-entry tourist visa issued for people visiting Parc National des Virunga. The cost of this visa is US$105, and on top of that you'll need to purchase a mountain-gorilla trek permit, a Nyiragongo trek permit or accommodation at the Mikeno Lodge in order to get the paperwork issued. The visa limits you to visiting North Kivu province, and is issued on arrival, though all the bookings need to have been made several weeks in advance. See http://visitvirunga.org for more information.

## DEPARTURE TAX

DRC's departure tax is US$15/50 for domestic/international flights and needs to paid in cash at the airport. You will also need to purchase something called a 'go pass' for all flights. This is currently US$5 and is paid at the same time as the departure tax.

### Visas for Onward Travel

**Congo** Bring a photo and US$80/120 for a 15-day/three-month visa. They're typically ready in two days, but you can pay an extra US$90/170 for same-day service.

**Tanzania** Single-entry tourist visas cost US$50, though Americans pay twice that. Multiple entry visas cost US$100. Bring two passport photos and expect it to take 48 hours.

**Zambia** Single-entry tourist and transit visas cost US$50. Transit visas are easy to come by, but tourist visas are complicated and involve multiple letters of invitation from a host in Zambia.

### WOMEN TRAVELLERS

Female travellers should exercise extra caution in DRC. Travelling alone is unwise, and even taking taxis or walking on the streets alone during the daytime is not generally advisable unless you know the driver or are familiar with the town.

## Getting There & Away

### AIR

The three main international airports in DRC are in Kinshasa (p516), **Goma** (Ave de l'Aéroport) and Lubumbashi. None of them is particularly pleasant, but Kinshasa is definitely rather a headache, especially if you're flying domestically. Count on lots of hassle, frequent demands for bribes, tough security and long lines.

Since 2015, **Congo Airways** (☎0829781922; www.congoairways.com; Blvd 30 de Juin; ⏲8am–6pm Mon–Sat) has been the DRC's national carrier, taking the place of former national airline Hewa Bora, which ceased operations in 2011.

### LAND

**Republic of Congo** Crossing the Congo River between Kinshasa (the port is called Beach Ngobila, or just 'Beach') and Brazzaville (Le Beach) can be a real headache. It helps to travel in the afternoon and on weekends when the crowds are thinner. The crossing involves taking a *canot rapide* (speedboat), which takes 10 minutes and costs US$25. Boats sail 8.30am to 4pm Monday to Saturday, and until noon on Sunday. In reality you need to allow at least a half day to complete all formalities and cross the river – sometimes even longer.

**Rwanda** Whether you're heading to Goma or Bukavu, normally crossing from Rwanda couldn't be any easier. Transport from Kigali to the border towns of Gisenyi and Cyangugu is frequent, and from there you just walk into DRC and hire a moto-taxi to take you to your destination in town. In the case of Gisenyi, you cross directly into the city of Goma, and can even walk to your hotel.

**Tanzania** There is no land border with Tanzania, so your only option to go directly from DRC to Tanzania is to cross Lake Tanganyika. Head to the port of Kalemie and try to negotiate passage with a cargo boat to Kigoma.

**Uganda** The principal route to Uganda is from Beni to Kasindi, where you walk over the border and get another taxi to Kasese.

**Zambia** The main crossing is just south of Lubumbashi at Kasumbalesa, and it's safe and straightforward to cross here. Take a taxi to Kasumbalesa and walk across the border. Once across, take a shared taxi to Chingola, from where there are buses to Kitwe and Ndola.

## Getting Around

### AIR

**CAA Congo** (☎0995903811; www.caacongo.com; Blvd de 30 Juin; ⏲8am–6pm Mon–Sat), **KIN-AVIA** (☎0816303331; www.kinavia.com; N'dolo Airport; ⏲7am–5pm) and Congo Airways are generally considered to be the best of the domestic airlines. Air travel is not cheap, however; reckon on paying US$300 one way from Kinshasa to Goma.

### TOUR COMPANIES

Getting around the DRC can be a slog. The transport network is virtually nonexistent, there are danger areas to be avoided and even getting a visa can give you a migraine. So no surprise, then, that some travellers find it easier to just let someone else organise everything for them. The following tour companies are highly recommended and can help with everything from obtaining a visa to organising a full expedition down the Congo River.

**Go Congo** (☎0811837010; www.gocongo.com)

**Kivu Travel** (p518)

**Okapi Tours & Travel** (☎0994328077; www.okapitoursandtravel.org)

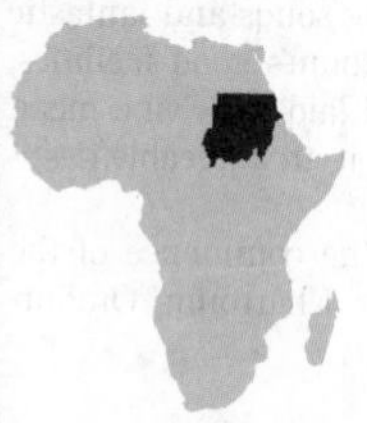

# Sudan

POP 42 MILLION / ☎249

## Includes ➡



## Best Places to Eat

- ➡ Al-Housh (p531)
- ➡ Amwaj (p531)
- ➡ Laziz (p531)
- ➡ Fish Wok (p531)
- ➡ Assaha Village (p531)

## Best Places to Sleep

- ➡ Meroe Lodge (p532)
- ➡ Nubian Rest-House (p536)
- ➡ Acropole Hotel (p530)
- ➡ Bougainvilla Guesthouse (p529)
- ➡ Abdu Rabbo Guesthouse (p534)

## Why Go?

Wake at the break of day under the golden pyramids of god-like kings of old, traverse a searing desert to the place where two Niles become one, and watch a million blood-red fish swarm through gardens of coral. Whichever way you look at it, there's just no denying that among Sudan's sweeping hills of sand lie treasures the rest of the world are only just beginning to discover. For the few travellers who venture here, Sudan comes as a fantastic surprise. Visitors invariably agree that the Sudanese are among the friendliest and most hospitable people on earth. And although various ongoing conflicts mean part of this vast nation remains off limits, the northeast is one of the safest places in the world. Whether you rush through on a Cairo-to-Cape Town trip, or spend a slow month soaking up the history and hospitality, visiting Sudan is a memorable experience.

## When to Go

### Khartoum

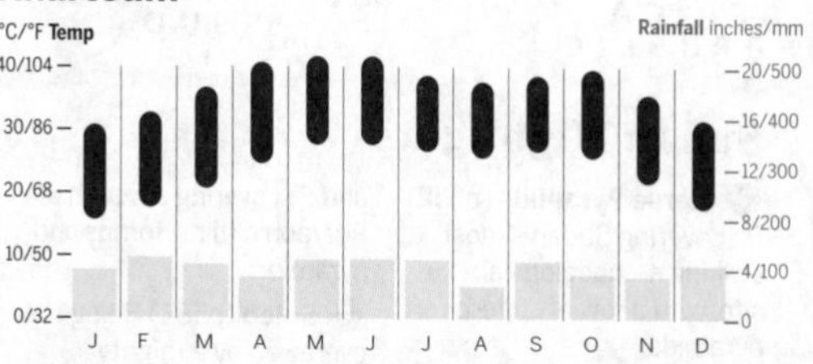


**Mar–May** Best time for a live-aboard dive trip in the Red Sea.

**Sep–Oct** Catch the camel races in Kassala.

**Nov–Feb** Coolest months; perfect temperatures and clear skies.

## KHARTOUM

POP

Built where the Blue and White Niles meet, Khartoum defies expectations. It's a boisterous, modern, flashy city with an ever-increasing number of glass tower blocks altering its skyline. As well as an excellent museum, some fascinating souqs and fantastic Nile-side views, Khartoum's good facilities, hospitable people and laid-back vibe mean that most people find it an agreeable destination in itself.

Three cities sit at the confluence of the White and Blue Niles: Khartoum, Omdur-

## Sudan Highlights

**1 Meroe Pyramids** (p532) Discovering Sudan's most striking archaeological site, with a row of superb pyramids.

**2 Kassala** (p536) Diving into exotic markets and scrambling around the photogenic Taka Mountains.

**3 Karima** (p535) Sweeping away the sandy layers of time and discovering a wealth of Pharaonic ruins, tombs and pyramids.

**4 Soleb** (p534) Being overawed by a mighty Egyptian temple.

**5 Kerma** (p534) Surveying the world from the top of a mudbrick fortress.

**6 Port Sudan** (p537) Diving into a rainbow of colour on the pristine coral reefs of the Sudanese Red Sea.

**7 National Museum** (p527) Taking a lesson in history at Sudan's best museum.

**8 Naqa** (p533) Visiting two spellbinding temples that are some of the finest examples of Kushite architecture.

man and Bahri (Khartoum North), each separated by an arm of the river. You'll find everything you need in central Khartoum; continuing south, the city gets more upscale and international.

## Sights

### Khartoum

**★National Museum** MUSEUM
(Map p528; al-Nil St; S£2; ⏲9.30am-6.30pm Tue-Thu, Sat & Sun, 9am-noon & 3-6.30pm Fri) This museum, the best in Sudan, has some breathtaking exhibits. The ground floor covers the rise and fall of the kingdoms of Kerma, Kush and Meroe. There's some stunning royal statues and perfectly preserved 3500-year-old artefacts from Kerma. Upstairs are numerous medieval Christian frescos removed from the ruined churches of Old Dongola and elsewhere. Outside are some temples rescued, Abu Simbel–style, from the rising waters of Lake Nasser. Allow at least 1½ to two hours for a visit.

**Ethnographical Museum** MUSEUM
(Map p530; al-Jamia St; ⏲8.30am-6pm Tue-Thu & Sat) FREE This museum contains a small but fascinating collection of tribal artefacts from across Sudan. Displays are ordered by geographic region and illustrate how people adapt to each climatic area. It begins with the tropics of (what is now) South Sudan followed by the savannah regions south of Khartoum, finishing up with the deserts of the north.

**White Nile Bridge** VIEWPOINT
(Map p528) The confluence of the Blue and White Niles, best seen from this bridge, is a languid high point of the world's longest river. You can actually see the different colours of each Nile flowing side by side before blending further downstream – although neither are blue or white! Don't attempt to take a photograph of the Nile from this bridge; numerous foreigners have been arrested for doing so.

### Omdurman

**★Hamed el-Nil Tomb** ISLAMIC SITE
(Map p528; Omdurman; ⏲Fri (except Ramadan)) FREE Every Friday afternoon you can see an incredible Sufi ritual, where a colourful local troupe of whirling dervishes belonging to the Sufi community stirs up the dust in worship of Allah, at this imposing mausoleum located in a large Islamic cemetery. Things start around 4.30pm (5pm in winter), but it doesn't really get going until about 5.30pm and they don't dance during Ramadan. If you're used to the dour colours of Arabian Islam, you'll find the circus-like atmosphere here refreshingly colourful and laid-back – don't miss it!

**Omdurman Souq** MARKET
(Map p528; Omdurman; ⏲8am-5pm) This famous souq – the largest in Sudan – is abuzz with noise, activity and colour, and a couple of hours' exploration is bound to turn up all manner of surprises.

**Mahdi's Tomb** MONUMENT
(Map p528; Omdurman; ⏲8am-5pm Fri) FREE This rocket-topped tomb is worth making the effort to see. Respectfully dressed foreigners are generally allowed inside. The original was destroyed on Kitchener's orders by General Gordon's nephew 'Monkey', who, somewhat unsportingly, threw the Mahdi's ashes into the Nile.

**Camel Market** MARKET
(Souq Moowaileh; Omdurman; ⏲8am-2pm) On the far western edge of Khartoum, this market is spectacular, especially on Saturday, but there is no public transport (a taxi will cost at least S£150). The majority of camels come from Darfur.

### Bahri

**Nuba Wrestlers** WRESTLING
(Map p528; Souq Seta; S£2; ⏲from 4pm Fri) In this Khartoum wrestling area, you'll find traditional wrestlers going through their paces at roughly 4pm on Fridays. The tournament attracts hundreds of spectators. Get there by taxi from the centre (about S£15, 15 minutes). Photography is permitted.

## Tours

**Lendi Travel** TOURS
(Map p530; ☎091 287 4080; www.lenditravel.com; Eid Allah bldg, Sayyd Abd al-Rahman St, Khartoum) Friendly and competent, this operator is easily the one of the most professional tour companies in the country. The owner, Waleed Arafat, can supply cars and drivers, book hotels, help organise visas and travel permits, and he can arrange all kinds of customised tours throughout Sudan at competitive prices.

**Italian Tourism Company** TOURS
(Map p528; ☎018 348 7961; www.italtoursudan.com; St 31, Amarat, Khartoum) This Italian-run

## Greater Khartoum

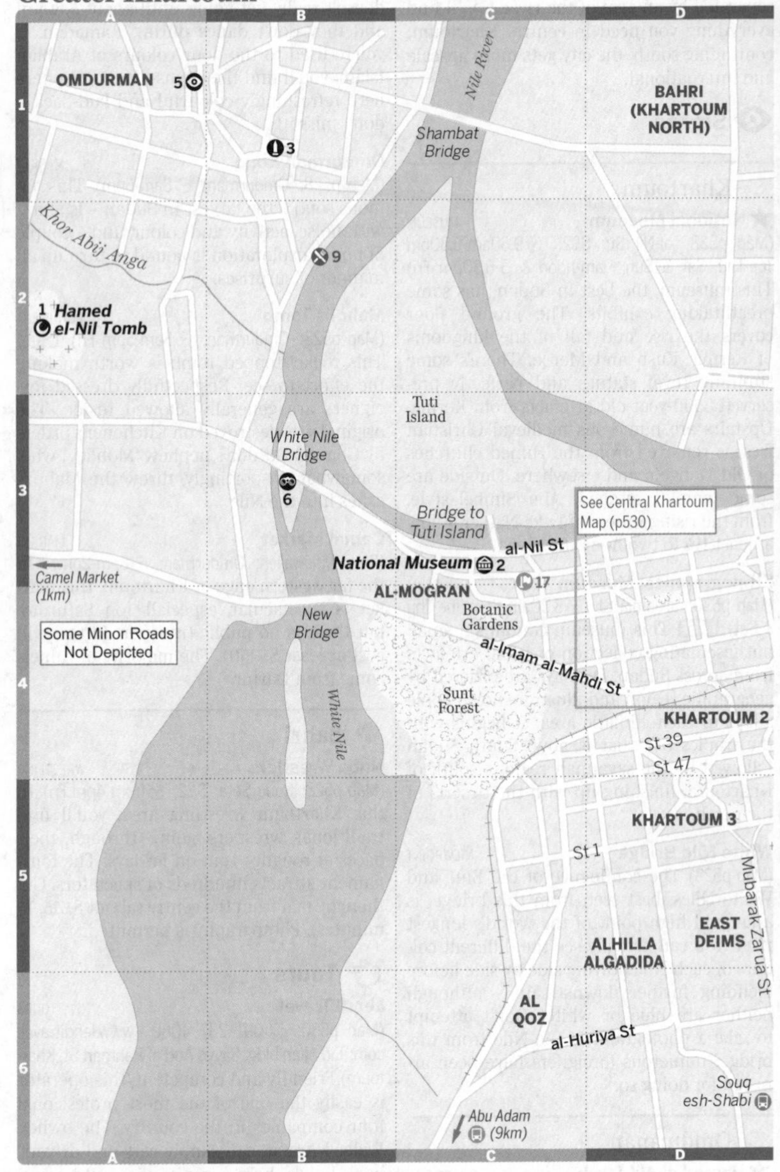


agency is easily the most professional tour company in the country and is the one that virtually every overseas tour company offering trips to Sudan uses for on-ground organisation. It can plan all kinds of trips and tours in Sudan.

## Sleeping

Upmarket hotels quote rates in US dollars and won't accept payment in Sudanese pounds. Cheaper accommodation is conveniently located near **Al-Kabir mosque** (off al-Tayyar Zulfu St), right in the centre. There is high demand

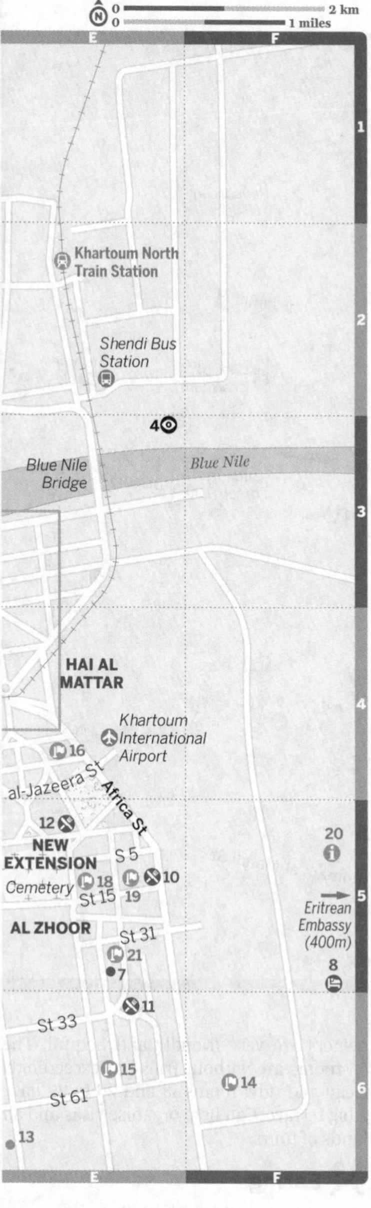


## Greater Khartoum

**Top Sights**
1 Hamed el-Nil Tomb .......... A2
2 National Museum .......... C3

**Sights**
3 Mahdi's Tomb .......... B1
4 Nuba Wrestlers .......... E3
5 Omdurman Souq .......... A1
6 White Nile Bridge .......... B3

**Activities, Courses & Tours**
7 Italian Tourism Company .......... E5

**Sleeping**
8 Bougainvilla Guesthouse .......... F5

**Eating**
9 Al-Housh .......... B2
10 Amwaj .......... E5
11 Fish Wok .......... E6
12 Laziz .......... E5

**Information**
13 Aliens Registration Office .......... E6
14 Central African Republic Embassy .......... F6
15 Chadian Embassy .......... E6
16 Dutch Embassy .......... E4
17 Egyptian Embassy .......... C3
18 Ethiopian Embassy .......... E5
19 French Embassy .......... E5
20 Ministry of Tourism and Wildlife .......... F5
21 Saudi Arabian Embassy .......... E5

between December and March for accommodation, so advance booking is recommended.

**Kabri Hotel** HOTEL **$**
(Map p530; ☎018 374 0133; al-Tayyar Izz al-Din St; s S£300-350, d S£400-450, incl breakfast; ❄📶) The Kabri's main draw is its reasonable rates, something lost to many Khartoum hoteliers. Of course you get what you pay for, but here at least that means secure, well looked-after doubles with salubrious albeit pint-sized bathrooms and a prime location.

**★Bougainvilla Guesthouse** BOUTIQUE HOTEL **$$**
(Map p528; ☎092 261 5445; www.bougainvillaguesthouse.net; Bldg 314, Block 21, Riyadh; s US$65-75, d US$91-105, incl breakfast; ❄📶🏊) This oasis of low-key luxury and tranquillity in the upscale Riyadh neighbourhood is the perfect soft landing into Khartoum. Featuring plush bedding, gleaming bathrooms and tiled floors, the 26 rooms exemplify functional simplicity. Added bonuses include free laundry, an excellent restaurant, a small indoor pool and a gym. Staff can also help organise visas. A fab choice.

**★Khartoum Plaza Hotel** HOTEL **$$**
(Map p530; ☎018 379 2986; www.khartoumplaza-hotel.com; Sayyd Abd al-Rahman St; s/d incl breakfast S£650/800; ❄📶) Deservedly popular

## Central Khartoum

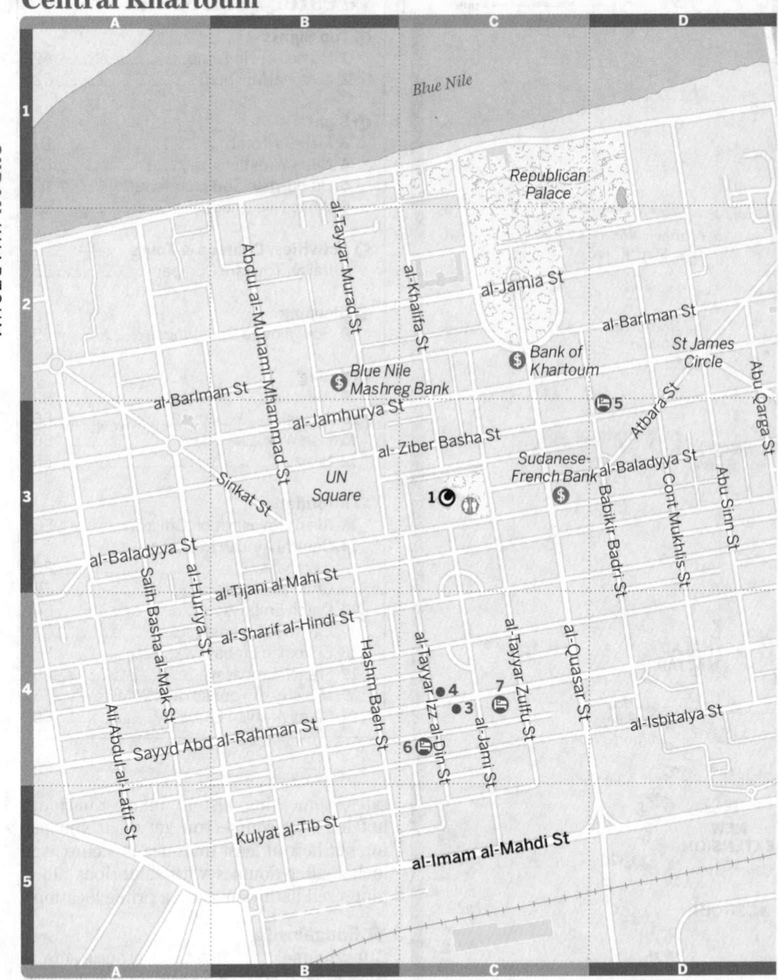


with tour operators, the Plaza has a central location, large rooms with pleasant bathrooms, efficient wi-fi, a decent restaurant and a couple of sinkworthy sofas in the vast lobby. It won't win any style awards but it makes for a cost-effective base from which to explore Khartoum. Excellent breakfast buffet.

**★Acropole Hotel** HISTORIC HOTEL **$$$**
(Map p530; ☎018 377 2860; www.acropolekhartoum.com; al-Ziber Basha St; s/d incl breakfast US$80/100; ❄@📶) This family-run hotel in Khartoum, the first choice of archaeologists, reeks of history and atmosphere. The Greek owners are very friendly and helpful. The 35 rooms are without frills but exceedingly clean and tidy; rooms 18 and 26 to 29 have a big terrace. Can help organise visas and all kinds of tours.

## Eating

Khartoum has the best choices of restaurants in the country, and the food will seem like haute cuisine if you're returning to the city after time spent elsewhere in Sudan. Most upscale hotels also have quality restaurants. No alcohol is served.

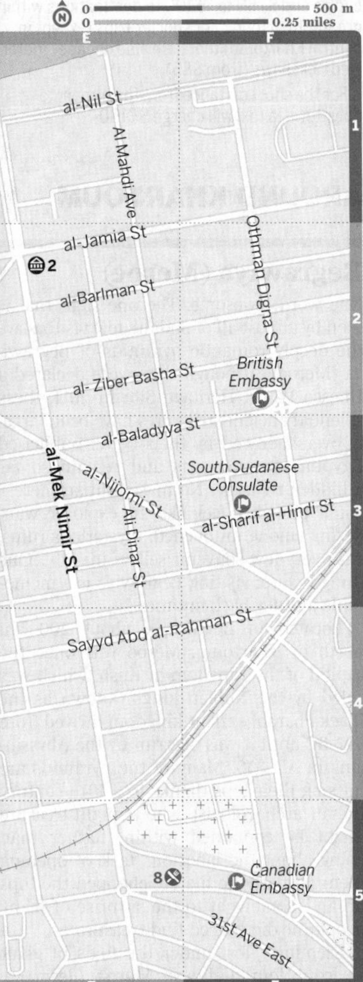


## Central Khartoum

**Sights**
1 Al-Kabir Mosque .......... C3
2 Ethnographical Museum .......... E2

**Activities, Courses & Tours**
3 Lendi Travel .......... C4
4 Mashansharti Travel Agency .......... C4

**Sleeping**
5 Acropole Hotel .......... D3
6 Kabri Hotel .......... C4
7 Khartoum Plaza Hotel .......... C4

**Eating**
8 Assaha Village .......... E5

**★ Laziz** SUDANESE $
(Map p528; al-Mufti St; mains S£15-80; 10am-midnight Sat-Thu, 2pm-midnight Fri) Elbows out – this is indisputably the most popular eatery in the centre of Khartoum and it's always busy, whether it be with takeaway orders, hungry employees helping themselves at the salad bar, or friends sipping a cup of tea on the outdoor terrace in the evening. One thing is sure: its shwarma (kebablike dish) is the best this side of the Nile.

**★ Al-Housh** SUDANESE $$
(Map p528; 099 466 7945; Omdurman; mains S£50-120; 9.30am-11.30pm Sat-Thu, 3-11.30pm Fri) Everyone, from cabbies to well heeled families, flocks to this legendary eatery in Omdurman, where you dine like a prince and pay like pauper. Loosen that belt for succulent *agashi* (fish or meat seared over charcoal), heaping helpings of salads and perky meatballs.

**★ Assaha Village** LEBANESE $$
(Map p530; 018 348 1919; www.assahavillage.com; Africa St; mains S£50-130; 8am-11pm; ) With its vaulted dining room, brick walls and elegantly set tables, Assaha is poised to take you on a culinary magic-carpet ride. Nibble on a platter of olives while perusing the huge menu, perhaps settling on delicious meze (with great hummus) followed by a classic shwarma. The attractive terrace at the back is highly sought after at dinner.

**★ Amwaj** SUDANESE $$
(Map p528; 091 828 8890; Africa St; mains S£40-140; 10am-midnight Sat-Thu, 2pm-midnight Fri) A Khartoum institution. The waiters are snappy, ingredients are fresh, and prices are reasonable for scrumptious dishes such as grilled chicken, roast lamb and shwarma. Those who enjoy a sweet at the end of the meal will be impressed by the delicious baklava and other treats on offer. Some might find the decor a bit too hospital-like but that's the only gripe.

**★ Fish Wok** SEAFOOD $$$
(Map p528; 099 911 1999; off King Abdelaziz St; mains S£70-150; 10am-11pm) Everyone loves an insider's tip, and Fish Wok is that easy-to-miss 'secret spot' that locals like to recommend. Hidden behind a row of dull multistorey buildings, it prepares delectable fish dishes – the *bulti* (Nile perch) served with bread and salad is the best we've had in Sudan. The setting is appealing too, with wooden low tables and chairs under a vast tent.

## Information

### DANGERS & ANNOYANCES

Khartoum has to be one of the safest cities in Africa. Petty crime is rare, although, as a 'rich' foreigner, care should be taken in crowded areas. Violent crime against foreigners is virtually unheard of.

There is a risk of terrorist acts (or, in the case of political demonstrations, attacks by overzealous police and military) and you should keep away from political gatherings and demonstrations. At the other end of the spectrum, rumour has it that plain-clothed intelligence agents are everywhere, so be careful of talking politics with locals in public places.

Aside from when you're visiting museums, taking photos in Khartoum (even with a photo permit) is asking for trouble.

### MONEY

The following all do foreign exchange.

**Bank of Khartoum** (Map p530; al-Barlman St; ⏲8am-4pm Sat-Thu)

**Blue Nile Mashreg Bank** (Map p530; al-Barlman St; ⏲8am-4pm Sat-Thu) Handles Western Union money transfers.

**Sudanese-French Bank** (Map p530; al-Quasar St; ⏲8am-noon & 3-5pm Sat-Thu)

## Getting There & Away

### AIR

**Khartoum International Airport** (Map p528) is virtually in the city centre.

### BUS

Most road transport departs from one of Khartoum's four bus stations.

**Mina al-Barri** (Khartoum South; S£1.50) Gedaref (S£140, five hours), Kassala (S£200, seven hours), Port Sudan (S£265, 10 hours) and El-Obeid (S£140, eight hours). Note this station has a S£1.50 entrance fee even if you're just reserving a ticket.

**Abu Adam Bus Station** For Dongola (S£160, six hours), Wadi Halfa (S£280, 11 hours) and other points north.

**Souq esh-Shabi** (Map p528; off St 61, Omdurman) For other buses to the north (including Dongola and Karima), as well as El-Obeid and Port Sudan.

**Shendi Bus Station** (Map p528; Khartoum North) For Atbara (S£100, five hours) and Port Sudan (S£265, 10 hours).

## Getting Around

Buses (S£1) and minibuses (from S£2) cover most points in Khartoum and run from early to very late.

Taxi prices are negotiable: expect to pay around S£20 to S£50 for journeys within the city centre and S£50 to S£100 to destinations within greater Khartoum. For shorter trips (except in central Khartoum) there are also cheaper motorised rickshaws (from S£5).

For the short distance from the airport to downtown, a taxi will charge S£100.

# AROUND KHARTOUM

## Begrawiya (Meroe)

One word: awesome. The one sight that is seen by almost all of Sudan's few visitors are the deeply romantic pyramids of Begrawiya (Meroe). Although they were declared a Unesco World Heritage Site in 2011, these splendid ancient structures have been largely overshadowed by their better-publicised Egyptian counterparts and remain so far a hidden treasure. No mass tourism here – you'll probably feel like an explorer wandering among untouched, mysterious ruins, with very few souvenir sellers in sight. One thing is sure: visiting Begrawiya is a memorable journey back in time.

Located in Begrawiya, about 200 km north of Khartoum, Meroe was once the capital of the Kingdom of Kush, which was ruled by the Nubian kings (known as the Black Pharaohs). This kingdom thrived from 592 BC until it was overrun by the Abyssinians in AD 350. Many of the pyramids are missing their tops thanks to a 19th-century Italian 'archaeologist' who thought treasure might be contained within. Rather than going about the laborious task of opening them properly he merely chopped the tops off and, somewhat to the surprise of many people, he did indeed find treasure.

Seemingly lost under the folds of giant apricot-coloured dunes, **Meroe** (Begrawiya; US$25; ⏲6am-6pm) with its clusters of narrow pyramids blanketing the sand-swept hills, is one of the most spectacular sights in eastern Africa. The pyramids range from 6m to 30m high and were built in the Nubian style, which is characterised by narrow bases and steep slopes. Like the pyramids of ancient Egypt, Meroe is an ancient royal cemetery, where the structures served as tombs for kings and queens.

There are two sleeping options in Begrawiya, both within easy reach of the pyramids, and both with on-site restaurants. **Meroe Lodge** (☎091 512 4871; www.italtoursudan.com; s/d with half board S£1400/1700; ⏲Oct-Apr; P 📶) is an Italian-run venture set on a sandy ridge about 2km away from the pyramids, where you can enjoy a sundowner on the rooftop terrace. Digs are in comfy walk-in safari-style tents with exterior bathrooms. They were in the process of being replaced by 24 luxurious stone-and-thatch lodges when we visited. **Raidane's Place** (☎018 379 8548; raidantravel@gmail.com; s/d incl breakfast US$100/120; P❄📶) is a new midrange venture that has 20 well equipped rooms in a low-slung building in a secluded place about 3km from the pyramids. You can also camp in the desert near the pyramids, but you'll need to be fully self-sufficient.

The ruins are easily visited as a day trip from Khartoum. If you hire a car and driver (starting at about US$110 plus fuel), you can visit the Sixth Cataract (Sabalooka Falls) too. Begrawiya is just 700m off the highway and easily reached by public transport: take an Atbara bus (S£55, two to three hours) from Bahri and ask to be let out at Al-Ahram (Pyramids). Coming back, flag down vehicles heading south; you'll probably have to change in Shendi. Note that while most tourists refer to the pyramids at Begrawiya as Meroe, if you were to tell a Sudanese person that you want to go to Meroe, you'd probably end up by the dam near Karima.

## Naqa & Musawarat es-Suffra

These two Meroitic sites lie in an area of wild and remote desert 35km off the highway southeast of Shendi. They are about the same distance from each other and are best visited with a tour (p527) combining Meroe pyramids, Naqa and Musawarat out of Khartoum. **Naqa** (US$25; ⏲6am-6pm) consists of a large and well preserved **temple of Amun** dating from the 1st century AD. Notable features include a hypostyle hall with splendid columns and hieroglyphics and a row of statues representing rams. Very close by is the **Lion Temple**. Dating from the same period, this temple is dedicated to the lion-headed god Apedemak and has wonderful exterior carvings depicting the temples creators, King Natakamani and Queen Amanitore. The exact purpose of the site remains unclear as it's located in an area that has never really been inhabited. There is a small kiosk in front of the Lion Temple.

**Musawarat** (US$25; ⏲6am-6pm) is the largest Meroitic temple complex in Sudan. Its purpose remains a little unclear, though it's believed to have served as a pilgrimage site. The enormous Great Enclosure consists of numerous tumbledown columns and walls carved with reliefs of wild animals that once inhabited this region. Check out the former elephant stables and the marriage room with the engravings of newly-weds getting to know one another. A few hundred metres away is another large **Lion Temple** dating to the 3rd century BC.

# NORTHERN SUDAN

## Wadi Halfa

POP 18,000

Wadi Halfa is the gateway to Aswan (Egypt) and a vital pit stop on the long road north. With the recent reopening of Sudan's land border with Egypt, business is thriving again between the two countries, and Wadi Halfa is now a booming town – far from than the backwater it used to be. Good news: it has kept its very relaxed, unhurried pace of life.

If you want an authentic local fish-fry, there is no better place than the handful of restaurants along the main drag.

**Cleopatra Hotel** HOTEL $
(☎012 317 6725; d S£180; ❄) The Cleopatra (pronounced 'Kilopatra') is a commendable haunt located behind the Agricultural Bank of Sudan. A recent coat of orange paint has spruced up the rooms, which are well equipped and serviceable. No meals are served but you're in spitting distance of the market and restaurants.

**Ibrahim Agha Hotel** HOTEL $
(☎011 463 7993; d with shared bathroom S£100; ❄) No frills, flounces or phones here, but this typical cheapie 200m south of Wadi Halfa's main road still does the trick if you're watching the pennies, with 12 unadorned rooms and acceptable shared bathrooms.

**Nasreddin** SEAFOOD $
(☎012 457 6165; mains S£20-25; ⏲10am-11pm) Tuck into a plate of faultlessly grilled (or fried) *bulti* (Nile perch) at this welcoming restaurant. It doesn't have a sign in English; find it 30m off the main drag, virtually opposite the Agricultural Bank of Sudan.

**Debena** FAST FOOD $
(☎012 212 0524; mains S£30-35; ⏲11am-10pm Sat-Thu, 3-10pm Fri) This place on the main drag lacks any pretensions but is all the better for it. It specialises in chicken, served roasted or grilled on charcoal and accompanied with rice. The sign is in Arabic; it's 50m east of the Agricultural Bank of Sudan, across the street.

DON'T MISS

### SAI ISLAND

With a temple from Egypt's Middle Kingdom, an **Ottoman fort** and a medieval **church** among the many ruins, **Sai Island** is something of a synopsis of ancient Sudanese history. The fort is actually built on the foundations of a 1500 BC Egyptian town, and the ground around the ruins is littered with millions of bits of broken pottery. Little but three upright granite columns and a few walls remain of the medieval church, but physically it's probably the most striking site on the island. If you choose to stay overnight, try the lovely **Magzoub Nubian Guesthouse** (☎012 288 6586, 091 122 0984; Abri; d/tw with shared bathroom S£250/300, incl breakfast; P).

Minibuses to Wadi Halfa (S£60, three hours) stop at a junction on the main road, from where you'll need to take a taxi (S£20, five minutes) to the centre of Abri. There's also one morning minibus to Kerma (S£50, three hours) and regular daily minibuses to Dongola (S£60, four hours).

## Information

**Internet Cafe** (Hali Center; Wada Halfa; per hr S£3; 8am-4.30pm; wi-fi) offers both internet computers and wi-fi access.

There's no tourist office in Wadi Halfa, but you can contact **Mazar Mahir** (☎012 238 0740; mazarhalfa@gmail.com; Wadi Halfa) or **Magdi Boshara** (☎012 173 0885; nubatia51@yahoo.com) – both are reliable individuals who can assist with visa and border formalities and provide letters of invitation, as well as bus and ferry tickets once you're in town. For overlanders with a vehicle, the two are also the best sources of information. Both can usually be found at the Egyptian–Sudanese border. Contact them by email a few days before your intended arrival.

## Getting There & Away

With the reopening of the road between Wadi Halfa and Aswan, the weekly passenger ferry on Lake Nasser from Wadi Halfa to the port near Aswan (Egypt) has become much less popular with travellers, who find the bus faster, much more frequent and more reliable. That said, the ferry usually heads south to Wadi Halfa on Sunday, returning to Egypt on Monday afternoon. It costs S£350/210 1st/2nd class. The journey takes about 18 hours plus immigration time.

Buses head from Wadi Halfa to Khartoum (S£210, 11 hours), Abri (S£25, three hours) and Kerma (S£60, six hours). Buses also ply the route to Aswan in Egypt (S£170, 12 hours) via Abu Simbel: they run daily except Friday.

Buses leave from the **new bus station** (Wadi Halfa), about 400m south of the main drag.

# Wawa

POP 2200

One word: Soleb. A modest town on the eastern bank of the Nile, Wawa has little of specific interest to travellers, but it's an excellent base if you plan to visit the ruins of the grandiose Egyptian temple of Soleb, which lies on the Nile's west bank.

**★Soleb** HISTORIC SITE

A little south of Abri, for many travellers the evocative Egyptian temple of Soleb is the highlight of the journey between Dongola and Wadi Halfa. It was built in the 14th century BC by Amenhotep III, the same pharaoh who gave us Luxor in Egypt. It features a sanctuary and a hypostyle hall that consists of massive columns with elaborately carved capitals and splendid relief carvings.

**★Abdu Rabbo Guesthouse** GUESTHOUSE $

(☎012 289 9925; s/d with shared bathroom S£100/200; P) Besides being a charmingly decorated place, this guesthouse has unadorned but clean rooms. It's super traditional, but the welcome is warm and the shared bathrooms are kept in good nick. The owner has a boat and can take you to Soleb. It's about 4km south of Wawa.

## Getting There & Away

Minibuses run fairly frequently from Wawa, north to Abri (S£20, 45 minutes) and south to Kerma (S£25, two hours) and Dongola (S£50, three hours), stopping at various villages. There's no real bus station in Wawa; most minibuses stop on the Dongola–Wadi Halfa road.

# Kerma

Kerma is one of the oldest inhabited towns in Africa and a place of immense historical importance. The area around Kerma has been occupied for at least 8000 to 10,000 years, but the town reached its peak around 1800 BC to 1600 BC, when it was capital of the Kingdom of Kush and an important trade centre during Egypt's Middle Kingdom. It was at this time that Kerma's kings built two monumental mudbrick temples, known as *deffufa*; the oldest, and arguably largest, mudbrick buildings on the continent. North of Kerma, the site of **Tombos** is also well worth a detour.

## Sights

**★Western Deffufa** ARCHAEOLOGICAL SITE

(Kerma; combined ticket with museum US$10; ⌚8.30am-sunset Tue-Sun) A 15-minute walk away from town, this massive mudbrick temple stood about 19m high and stretched 50m long. Nobody is really certain what it was used for but most agree it served a religious purpose. Today it has crumbled into an oddly appealing form and you can still climb to the top and enjoy breathtaking views.

**★Kerma Museum** MUSEUM

(combined ticket with western deffufa US$10; ⌚8.30am-sunset Tue-Sun) Next to Kerma's western *deffufa* is this well organised museum that contains interesting relics from the site, including granite statues and various Nubian artefacts. There's also a section dedicated to the Christian and Islamic heritage of the area. Ask for Mahamad Hassan, the director of the museum, who speaks good English. Although the museum is technically closed on Monday, if you do turn up then someone will be sent to find the keys and open up.

## Sleeping & Eating

You won't find many restaurants in Kerma, just modest cafes serving Sudanese staples and sweets. Some have Nile views. For more options, press on to Dongola.

**Deffufa Resthouse** GUESTHOUSE $

(☎091 805 5243; triso79@yahoo.com; Kerma; per person US$15; ❄) Just next to the museum, this guesthouse that has long been used by foreign archaeologists now welcomes visitors. It has five rooms set around a vast dining room. They're simple but well kept.

**Radwane** GUESTHOUSE $

(☎091 827 9467; Tombos; s/d with shared bathroom S£100/200; ❄) This is a simple yet mellow and neat Nubian house with three rooms at the northern end of Tombos village, a short stroll from the archaeological site. Meals can be arranged on request.

## Getting There & Away

Buses and minibuses run fairly frequently north from Kerma to Abri (S£35, three hours) and south to Dongola (S£20, one hour). They leave from a small bus station near the market.

# Dongola

POP 15,500

One of the most attractive towns along the Nile, Dongola is considered the heart of Nubia. Famous for its lush palm groves, this relaxed little town is full of character and boasts good amenities – bliss for travellers on their way to Wadi Halfa.

## Sleeping & Eating

Most *lokandas* (basic hotels) are clustered together on the main road, near the market.

A not-to-be-missed experience at dinner consists of sampling fried fish with *fuul* (stewed broad beans) at one of the stalls on the main road near Dongola's market.

**Qasr Diyafa** HOTEL $

(☎011 967 9790; Hosbitalia St; S£200; P 📶) A good bang-for-your-buck choice, the Qasr has large rooms that are thoroughly sanitised. It's on a peaceful stretch of Hosbitalia St, a mere five minutes' stroll south of Dongola's market. The property opens onto the Nile; unfortunately, the rooms don't face the river.

**★Charles Bonnet Nubian Village** HOTEL $$

(☎091 213 9730; tudmstour@gmail.com; Es Seleim; s/d incl breakfast S£500/600; P ❄ 📶) This secluded property opens onto the eastern bank of the Nile (it's actually in Es Seleim, across the river from Dongola). It features seven well designed Nubian-style bungalows brimful of local charm, and 10 well organised adjoining rooms with good bedding and large bathrooms. Pity about the impersonal dining room, though.

**Marafi** ARABIC $

(☎091 556 1880; Hosbitalia St; mains S£20-45; ⌚8am-11pm) With its flashy sign (in Arabic only) and dramatic bright-orange facade and walls adorned with tacky posters, this unmissable joint on the main drag has to be Dongola's kookiest spot. It churns out the usual Sudanese staples as well as pizzas, soups and salads. It's about 200m east of the hospital and almost opposite the green mosque, in a curve.

## Getting There & Away

There are regular buses from Dongola to Kerma (S£25, one hour), Karima (S£50, 2½ hours), Khartoum (S£165, six hours) and Wadi Halfa (S£100, five to six hours). The bus station is west of Dongola's centre.

# Karima

This dusty Nile-side Nubian town boasts an extraordinary collection of ancient sites, which together have given the whole area Unesco World Heritage status. The majesty of Karima's past will probably remain with

DON'T MISS

## OLD DONGOLA

If you're travelling in your own car between Dongola and Karima, it's well worth making the short detour to beautiful, sandswept Old Dongola with its faded Christian glories and massive Sufi saints' tombs.

The city of **Old Dongola** (US$10) was capital of the Christian kingdom of Makuria between the 7th and 14th centuries and at its peak it was home to dozens of churches. The church exteriors were generally plain, but the interiors were painted in beautiful frescos. Today little but scattered blocks, tumbledown walls and a few rows of columns remain of Old Dongola, but the sand-swept setting is sublime and you'll have the place to yourself.

you for a long time. Its setting, too, is unforgettable, with the impressive Jebel Barkal lording over the town.

## Sights

**Jebel Barkal** ARCHAEOLOGICAL SITE

Jebel Barkal, the tabletopped mountain hanging on the town's south side, was sacred ground for the Egyptians at the time of the 18th-dynasty pharaohs. At the base of the mountain are some well preserved pyramids and the **Temple of Amun**. Buried into the belly of the mountain is the **Temple of Mut** (US$10), dedicated to the Egyptian sky goddess. Close to the Temple of Amun there's a small **museum** (S£20; 8am-4pm Sat-Thu) with finds from around Jebel Barkal.

**El Kurru** RUINS

(US$10) The royal cemetery of El Kurru, 20km south of Karima, contains the remains of dozens of tombs. Most have either faded away to virtually nothing, or the entrances have been buried under tonnes of sand. However, two tombs containing wonderfully preserved paintings, can still be entered down a flight of stairs cut out of the rock. Dating to the 7th century BC, they were the final resting place of King Tanwetamani and his mother, Queen Qalhata.

**Nuri** MONUMENT

(US$10; 6am-sunset) At Nuri, across the river from Jebel Barkal, there are some delightfully dilapidated pyramids – among the largest in Sudan – lost among a stormy sea of orange sand. Dating from around the 7th century BC, these are both the oldest and largest pyramids in Sudan. Take a minibus (S£5, 15 minutes) from Karima. You must buy an entry ticket from the museum in Karima in advance.

## Sleeping & Eating

Plenty of cheap eateries can be found in Karima's centre and near the market, but if you want a memorable dining experience, make a beeline for Nubian Rest-House.

**Ahmed Mousa Homestay** GUESTHOUSE $

(091 258 5462; s/d with shared bathroom S£75/150) Ahmed has a couple of spartan but clean rooms with fans set around a sandy courtyard, not far from the museum and the temple. The communal bathrooms are spotless. You can normally find Ahmed at the ticket office for the museum, where he works, otherwise call ahead for directions.

★ **Nubian Rest-House** LODGE $$$

(091 282 3247, 011 554 5201; www.italtoursudan.com; s/d with half board S£1600/2000; P) Privacy, luxury and service are hallmarks of this lovely mudbrick Nubian-style structure built around flowering gardens with Jebel Barkal as a backdrop. It shelters 22 rooms that are elegantly furnished and decorated. Another draw is the superb restaurant (open to nonguests by reservation; set meals S£300), with refined Italian and Sudanese specialities.

## Getting There & Away

There are frequent buses from Karima to Dongola (S£50, 2½ hours) and Atbara (S£110, four hours), as well as less regular ones to Khartoum (S£120, six hours). For Wadi Halfa, change in Dongola. The bus station is east of the centre, near the railway station.

# EASTERN SUDAN

## Kassala

POP 419,000

Kassala, with its wonderful setting at the foot of the melting granite peaks of the Taka Mountains, is easily the most exotic corner of northeastern Sudan and a fitting reward for the long journey here. Its huge souq is where half the tribes of northern Sudan, including the Beja and the Rashaida, seem to meet – expect an ethnic mosaic of colours, smells, noises and experiences. It's also a popular destination for honeymooners, whom you can usually see enjoying a cup of tea in the nearby village of Toteil. If you happen to be here in September or October, don't miss the famous camel races.

## Sights

### ★Khatmiyah Mosque MOSQUE

At the base of the Taka Mountains is this spectacular mosque, centre of the Khatmiyah Sufi sect. It's a lovely mudbrick building with a pointed octagonal minaret and a photogenic arcade of columns in the main prayer hall. Non-Muslims are quite welcome to take a peek about. Afterwards have a little scramble around the bizarre peaks of the mountains. It's about 4km southeast of Kassala's centre; get there by taxi (S£20) or minibus (S£2).

### Kassala Souq MARKET

Kassala has one of Sudan's best markets, and a visit is a must. It's a maze of alleys and side streets lined with shops and stalls where myriad items are sold, from traditional products like cloth, jewels, henna or spice, to plastic buckets and electronic goods. One section of the souq caters mainly to Rashaida nomads. The magnificent Rashaida women are famous for their black-and-red geometrically patterned dresses, and their long, heavy veils.

### Toteil VILLAGE

Don't miss this village at the southern edge of the Taka Mountains. It's noted for its atmospheric cafes serving delicious coffee and popcorn in lovely surrounds .

## Sleeping

### Almak Nimir Tower HOTEL $

(091 449 9966; d S£200-300; P ) The rooms at this newish place are among Kassala's best, with tiled floors, decent bathrooms, city views from the top floors, a convenient location near the market and pretty good service.

### Saray Timintay Resort Tourist HOTEL $$

(015 488 2727; strtourist@gmail.com; d S£450-675) Saray Timintay's top selling points are its attractive gardens and relaxing setting. It features 16 sparse yet cleanish chalet-like rooms that are tightly packed together. Maintenance may not be the hotel's strong point, and there's no hot water, but what you want is the location and friendly service. There's an on-site restaurant.

## Eating

Cheap eats abound near Kassala's market. You'll also find a smattering of stand-alone eateries in the centre.

### ★Rawabi Pizza Ice Cream PIZZA $

(Turaa St; mains S£30-60; 10am-10pm Sat-Thu, 2-10pm Fri) The sign is in Arabic only, but you can't miss this lively, bright and sleek place south of the souq – look for the flashy pink-and-yellow facade on Turaa St. Locals love it to bits and once you've tasted the pizza, you'll know why. Oh, and the ice creams are irresistible too.

### Al Moringa Garden Restaurant SUDANESE $

(0911 078 505; mains S£15-40; 10am-midnight Sat-Thu, 3pm-midnight Fri) Sure, Al Moringa is a bit out of the way, but this enticing garden restaurant is well worth the short taxi ride (about £10) from the centre. Clued-up locals claim it serves the best meat dishes in town, and after tasting its delicious shish kebab we'd be silly to argue.

## Getting There & Away

Minibuses (S£2) and taxis (S£20) shuttle from Kassala to Souq esh-Shabi (about 6km), where the buses to Port Sudan (S£185, eight hours), Gedaref (S£70, three hours) and Khartoum (SD£210, nine hours) arrive and depart.

# Port Sudan

POP 530,000

Sudan's only major industrial port is the base for some of the world's most spectacular and undeveloped diving. Above the waves, sights are scarce – don't expect masses of historical buildings or sweeping beaches and translucent waters lapping your toes – but there's a laid-back atmosphere that's supremely enjoyable. Port Sudan is also an ideal base to visit the nearby historical town of Suakin.

## Sights & Activities

Port Sudan has a vibrant fishing industry, and the lively **fish market** (8am-4pm) near the beach is a sight to behold. The men are amazingly deft at gutting, scaling and skinning their catches. The fish restaurants near the market run glass-bottom **boat trips**. During the 30-minute outing, the boat chugs around the lagoon and you're bound to see plenty of rainbow-coloured fish species.

## Sleeping

Accommodation-wise, there's a bit of everything in Port Sudan, including a few guesthouses and a smattering of modern hotels with all mod cons.

★**Baasher Palace Hotel** HOTEL $$
(☎031 182 3343; ageeg@yahoo.com; Cornish St; s S£450-680, d S£520-750; P ❄ ☎) Even if you're on a tight budget, consider spending a little more to enjoy the comforts of this well organised midrange venture. By far Port Sudan's sweetest deal, there are spotless, quiet rooms complete with fresh linen and functional bathrooms. Pluses include a neatly manicured garden, a coffee shop, a sleek restaurant and a tough-to-beat location.

**Sudan Red Sea Resort** RESORT $$
(☎012 933 3453; d with half board S£750-1500; P ❄) Friendly, low-key and peaceful are good descriptions of the atmosphere that prevails in this compact resort perched only a metre or so from the sea. Don't get too excited, though: swimming is not *that* tempting here due to shallow (and sometimes murky) waters. The attached restaurant is a winner. The resort is about 20km north of Port Sudan.

**Basiri Plaza** HOTEL $$
(☎031 182 1999; basiriplaza@hotmail.com; s/d incl breakfast S£750/950; ❄ ☎) Sure, the exterior of the Basiri looks like a common apartment block, but once you enter the lobby things get much better, with nicely laid-out rooms (some with sweeping city–sea views), enticing bathrooms and a restaurant. It's right in the thick of things, a shwarma's throw from the market and restaurants.

## Eating

Both Baasher Palace Hotel and **Coral Port Sudan** (☎031 183 9800; Cornish St) have an excellent on-site restaurant. There's a clutch of restaurants and fast-food outlets along Port Sudan's waterfront, which spring to life in the evening and do a good range of local dishes for a few bucks. Fans of fresh fish may want to sample a simple fish stew at one of the restaurants located just north of the fish market.

**Ice Cream Dream** FAST FOOD $
(Cornish St; mains S£30-80; ⌚9am-11pm) With an selection of burgers, wraps and pizzas,

DON'T MISS

### DIVING PORT SUDAN

The reefs off Port Sudan offer some of the best diving in the Red Sea. Outstanding marine life, dramatic seascapes, atmospheric wrecks and a true sense of wilderness – it's impossible to be bored. For lack of a reliable land-based dive centre, the only way to explore the area is by live-aboard boat. All live-aboard boats depart from Port Sudan and make either one-week or 10- to 12-day trips along the coast, offering a variety of itineraries.

**Dahrat Abid** One of Sudan's iconic dives, Dahrat Abid is part of the southern Suakin archipelago. What to expect? Pure blue water, dizzying drop-offs, as well as prolific fish life, including loads of whitetips, silvertips and hammerheads. The reef is ablaze with black coral bushes and sensational hard and soft corals.

**Sha'ab Rumi** One of Sudan's most magical dives, Sha'ab Rumi is known for its sheer abundance of underwater life and superb topography. This is where Jacques Cousteau established his underwater village Conshelf II in 1963, the remnants of which can still be seen. Divers are bedazzled by the incredible variety of fish, including barracudas, grey reef sharks and Napoleon wrasses.

**Umbria** One of the Red Sea's best wreck dives, this massive freighter, which was sunk during WWII, is a treasure trove of war matériel and ship artefacts, including Fiat 1100 Lunga cars. It's 155m long and lies between 18m and 40m. It supports all sorts of fish life and is overgrown with soft and hard species of coral.

**Sanganeb Reef** Sanganeb is a long ellipse of reef with a shallow lagoon at its centre and a lighthouse on its southern tip. It offers two main dive sites: a long ridge at the north end and a stunning plateau to the southwest. The north ridge tumbles down to about 55m. Hammerheads are regularly seen in the blue. The south plateau is a mixture of sand and soft-coral-covered pinnacles at about 25m, patrolled by grey reef sharks. Groupers, jacks, barracudas and sharks dominate this zone.

**Angarosh** Sharks galore! The northeast point of Angarosh reef is where hammerheads hang out. Silvertip sharks, grey sharks as well as large schools of barracuda and trevally can also be spotted along the reef. Because of almost-constant currents, this dive is suitable for experienced divers only.

this colourful outlet is a good place to fill your belly. As the name suggests, it also serves dangerously good ice creams (from S£10), although the choice of flavours is fairly limited.

**Sea Side Restaurant & Coffee Shop** SEAFOOD **$$**
(mains S£65-130; ⏲9am-11pm) One of many fish restaurants near the fish market, the Sea Side's distinctive asset is its sign in English. It's a popular place serving fish dishes in a pleasant convivial space that combines atmosphere with great sea views. *Nagil* (grouper) served with rice is the pick of the menu. Excellent fruit juices too.

## Getting There & Away

### AIR

**Badr/Tarco Airlines** (☎096 204 0871; www.badrairlines.com; ⏲9am-4pm Sat-Thu) and **Nova Airways** (☎031 182 6679; www.novaairways.com; 8am-4pm Sat-Thu) have daily flights to Khartoum (S£965, one hour). **Nile Air** (☎090 000 8913; www.nileair.com; ⏲8am-4pm Sat-Thu) has a once-weekly flight to Cairo (Egypt; US$105, two hours).

### BUS

Minibuses (S£15, one hour) for Suakin leave from the centre of Port Sudan. The major bus companies serve Kassala (S£155, seven hours), Atbara (S£135, seven hours) and Khartoum (S£220, 10 hours). The bus station is northwest of the centre; get there by rickshaw (S£20, five minutes).

## Suakin

POP 47,000

Suakin exudes a kind of tranquil charm, light years away from the hullabaloo of Port Sudan. Its main attraction is Suakin Island, which has a palpable historical aura. Amenities are limited, but it's easily visited as a day trip if you're based in Port Sudan.

**Suakin Island** (S£10; ⏲6am-6pm) was Sudan's only port before the construction of Port Sudan. Abandoned in the 1930s, it's now a melancholy ghost town, full of crumbling coral buildings, demonic cats said to be cursed, and circling kites and hawks with a devil's shrill call. A few buildings have been recently renovated by Turkish investors. The ruins, connected to the mainland by a short causeway, are fascinating to explore.

With **Captain Jack Croisière** (☎090 402 3935; www.facebook.com/captainjackcroisiere; per person per day US$75; ⏲mid-Dec–mid-April) French sailor Jacques runs good-value cruises on a monohull that takes you to various scenic spots on Suakin's lagoon for swimming, snorkelling and trying your hand at fishing. The itinerary is flexible. Minimum of two days and two people.

Lap up a reviving soft drink and scoff a grilled fish at ramshackle **Garmushi** (mains from S£35; ⏲8am-6pm) overlooking the fishing harbour, and you'll leave with a smile on your face. Everything's super fresh – it helps that the owner is a fisherman. The sign is in Arabic: just look for the shack painted in blue.

There's nowhere we recommend to stay in Suakin. Your best bet is to base yourself in Port Sudan, which is less than an hour away by minibus.

Suakin is best visited as a day trip from Port Sudan. Get there by minibus (S£15, about one hour) or by taxi (S£140, 45 minutes).

# SOUTH OF KHARTOUM

## Gedaref

POP 375,000

The busy market- and farming-town of Gedaref lies just a couple of hours from the main border crossing into Ethiopia. If you're heading to or from Ethiopia, you stand a good chance of spending a night here.

There are several cheap and grotty places to stay around Gedaref's central market area. The **Almotwakil Hotel** (☎044 184 3232; s/d S£400/600; ❄) is probably the best of the town's hotels, with basic unadorned rooms and passable bathrooms.

Gedaref has a handful of good places to eat. The downstairs restaurant (mains S£20 to S£60) at Almotwakil Hotel churns out well priced Sudanese specialities as well as sandwiches. **Bet Urduni Siyahi** (☎012 597 5555; mains S£20-80; ⏲9am-10pm) is a good place to break up the Khartoum–Kassala journey with an eclectic menu that features well prepared salads, fish and meat dishes. It occupies a peaceful compound, complete with a cluster of snug, traditional-style huts. The sign is in Arabic and the restaurant is just north off the disused railway station.

From Souq al-Koda, buses run along the smooth road to Gallabat (the Sudanese border town with Ethiopia) for S£36; the journey takes two hours. From the main bus station, which is on the Wadi Medani–Kassala road, a short taxi ride north of the centre, buses head to Khartoum (S£135, seven hours), Kassala (S£30, 2½ hours) and Wadi Medani (S£75, 3½ hours).

# UNDERSTAND SUDAN



## Sudan Today

Sudan is entering new territory and its future has never been so unpredictable. Most Sudanese consider South Sudan's independence something of a disaster for the future of this now-shrunken nation. The loss of the oil revenue since the south obtained independence has sent the Sudanese economy on a sharp downward spiral and the cost of basic daily goods has skyrocketed.

While the conflict in Darfur has reduced in intensity (though it is still not over), the security situation elsewhere has taken a serious turn for the worse. There are near-constant fears of renewed war with South Sudan over the oil-rich flashpoint region of Abyei, which is claimed by both countries. Also, since 2011, there has been serious conflict in the Nuba Mountains and other parts of South Kordofan as well as Blue Nile state. Many accounts speak of widespread aerial bombardment by Sudanese air-force planes and the specific targeting of civilians.

Dissatisfaction with the al-Bashir government is growing by the day and street protests have taken place in Khartoum and a number of other major urban centres. High youth unemployment is another major concern. Many young Sudanese, including university students, have little perspective and seek to emigrate to Europe.

Many outside observers agree that the al-Bashir government is starting to lose control. But what will come next nobody knows.

## History

Modern Sudan is situated on the site of the ancient civilisation of Nubia, which predates Pharaonic Egypt. For centuries sovereignty was shuttled back and forth between the Egyptians, indigenous empires such as Kush and a succession of independent Christian kingdoms. After the 14th century AD the Mamelukes (Turkish rulers in Egypt) breached the formidable Nubian defences and established the dominance of Islam. By the 16th century the kingdom of Funj had become a powerful Muslim state.

### Colonialism & Revolt

In 1821 the viceroy of Egypt, Mohammed Ali, conquered northern Sudan and opened the south to trade. Within a few decades British interests were also directed towards Sudan, aiming to control the Nile, contain French expansion from the west and draw the south into a British–East African federation. The European intrusion, and in particular the Christian missionary zeal that accompanied it, was resented by many Muslim Sudanese.

The revolution came in 1881, when one Mohammed Ahmed proclaimed himself to be the Mahdi – the person who, according to Muslim tradition, would rid the world of evil. Four years later he rid Khartoum of General Gordon, the British-appointed governor, and the Mahdists ruled Sudan until 1898, when they were defeated outside Omdurman by Lord Kitchener and his Anglo-Egyptian army. Sudan then effectively became a British colony.

### Independence & Revolt

Sudan achieved independence in 1956, but General Ibrahim Abboud, the deputy commander-in-chief of the Sudanese army, summarily dismissed the winners of the first postindependence elections and made himself president.

In 1969 Colonel Jaafar Nimeiri assumed power and held it for 16 years. Most importantly, by signing the 1972 Addis Ababa Agreement to grant the southern provinces a measure of autonomy, he quelled the civil war for more than a decade. But in 1983 Nimeiri scrapped the autonomy accord and imposed Sharia (Islamic law) over the whole country. Hostilities between north and south recommenced almost immediately. Army commander John Garang deserted to form the Sudanese People's Liberation Army (SPLA), which quickly took control of much of the south.

Nimeiri was deposed in 1985 and replaced first by a Transitional Military Council, then, after elections the next year, Sadiq al-Mahdi became prime minister. In July 1989 power was seized by the current president, Lieutenant General Omar Hassan Ahmad al-Bashir; however, Hassan al-Turabi, fundamentalist leader of the National Islamic Front (NIF), was widely seen as the man with real power.

### Infighting (& Revolt)

The year 1999 was something of a watershed in Sudanese politics: in December, President al-Bashir dissolved parliament, suspended the constitution and imposed a three-month state of emergency, all as part of an internal power struggle with al-Turabi. The subsequent elections in December 2000 were boycotted by opposition parties, giving al-Bashir an easy win.

By 2002 things were looking up again – the economy had stabilised and a ceasefire was called after President al-Bashir and SPLA leader John Garang met in Nairobi – but it seems good news in Sudan is always followed by bad. In February 2003 rebels in the western Darfur region rose up against the government, which they accused of oppression and neglect. The army's heavy-handed response, assisted by progovernment Arab militias (the Janjaweed), escalated to what many have called genocide. The government's scorched-earth campaign is thought to have killed between 200,000 and 400,000 Sudanese and uprooted millions more. The Sudanese government say the real death toll is 10,000.

### A New Sudan (& More War)

While Darfur spun out of control, peace crept forward in the south, and in January 2005 a deal was signed ending Africa's longest civil war. It included accords on sharing power and wealth (including equal distribution of oil-export revenue), and six years of southern autonomy followed by a referendum on independence.

In March 2009 an international arrest warrant was issued for al-Bashir after the International Criminal Court accused him of war crimes and crimes against humanity in Darfur. However, both the African Union and the Arab League condemned the arrest warrant. In January 2011, the South Sudanese went to the polls and voted overwhelmingly for independence. Almost before the new flag was raised in Juba, capital of South Sudan, the new neighbours were at each other's throats over the oil-rich territory of Abyei, which both nations claimed as theirs. In 2013, Sudan and South Sudan managed to strike a deal about oil and agreed upon the principle of a demilitarised zone along their borders.

## Culture

Sudan's 41 million people are divided into many ethnic groups. Some 70% of Sudan's population is of Arab descent; much of the remainder of the population consists of Arabized ethnic groups such as the Nubians of the northern Nile valley and the sword-wielding Beja of the east. There is a significant nomadic population concentrated largely in the west and east. About 97% of the population is Muslim (Sunnis, mostly), but there are populations of Coptic Christians throughout the country. The people of the Nuba Mountains practise a mixture of Islam, Christianity and shamanistic beliefs.

# SURVIVAL GUIDE

## Directory A–Z

### ACCOMMODATION

Most high-standard hotels are in Khartoum and Port Sudan, with limited options outside. Many upmarket hotels quote rates in US dollars and won't accept payment in Sudanese pounds; all other hotels quote in Sudanese pounds. Cheaper options include *lokandas* (basic hotels) and family-run guesthouses. All hotels will request a copy of each of your travel permit, passport and visa. Bring plenty of copies as hotels will keep them.

### ACTIVITIES

Though largely overshadowed by the iconic Egypt, Sudan's Red Sea dive sites are as good as Egypt's, but without the crowds. Expect rainbow-coloured fish and pelagic species (including plenty of sharks), a splendid seascape, a few iconic wrecks and a host of dizzying drop-offs and healthy reefs. The best season for diving is from December to May. During July and August, the seas may be too rough.

Most people use European-run, all-inclusive live-aboard operations that operate from Port Sudan. They must generally be booked in advance. One recommended operator is UK-based **Regal Dive** (☎ 0044 1353 659999 in the UK; www.regal-diving.co.uk). Other reputable companies include the French-run **Diving Attitude** (☎ +33 7 81 08 03 38 in France; www.divingattitude.com) and **Dune World** (☎ +33 4 88 66 48 13 in France; www.dune-world.com).

All operators will arrange your visa, which is collected on arrival in Port Sudan.

### ELECTRICITY

Sudan uses 230V, 50Hz AC; plugs in general have two-round-pin plugs.

### EMBASSIES & CONSULATES

Countries with diplomatic representation in Sudan include the following, all of which are in Khartoum:

**British Embassy** (Map p530; ☎ 015 677 5500; www.facebook.com/ukinsudan; al-Baladyya St; ⏰ 8-11am Sat-Thu)

**Canadian Embassy** (Map p530; ☎ 015 655 0500; www.canadainternational.gc.ca/sudan-soudan; Block 56, Africa St; ⏰ 8am-noon Sat-Thu)

**Central African Republic Embassy** (CAR; Map p528; ☎ 015 522 9562; Block 344, El-Maamura; 9am-noon Sat-Thu)

### PRICE RANGES

The following price ranges refer to a double room with bathroom:

**$** less than S£500

**$$** S£500–1000

**$$$** more than S£1000

These price ranges refer to a main course:

**$** less than S£50

**$$** S£50–100

**$$$** more than S£100

**Chadian Embassy** (Map p528; ☎018 347 1084; St 57, Amarat; ⏲8-11am Sat-Thu)

**Dutch Embassy** (Map p528; ☎018 347 1020; www.dutch-embassy/sudan-khartoum.html; St 47; ⏲8am-noon Sat-Thu)

**Egyptian Embassy** (Map p528; ☎018 377 7646; al-Jamia St; ⏲8-11.30am Sat-Thu)

**Eritrean Embassy** (☎018 352 1000; al-Jazar St, Riyadh; ⏲8am-noon Sat-Thu)

**Ethiopian Embassy** (Map p528; ☎018 347 1379; www.facebook.com/ethioembassysudan; St 11; ⏲8.30am-noon & 2-4pm Sat-Thu)

**French Embassy** (Map p528; ☎018 347 1082; www.ambafrance-sd.org; St 13; ⏲8am-noon Sat-Thu)

**German Embassy** (☎018 534 9622; www.khartum.diplo.de) Phone and email only.

**Saudi Arabian Embassy** (Map p528; ☎018 346 4646; St 29; ⏲8.30am-noon Sat-Thu)

**South Sudanese Consulate** (Map p530; ☎092 628 9590; Sheikh Mustafa al-Amin St; ⏲8-11am Sat-Thu)

**Ugandan Embassy** (☎091 215 8571; khartoum@mofa.go.ug; ⏲8am-noon Sat-Thu)

**US Embassy** (☎018 702 2000; https://sudan.usembassy.gov; Kilo 10, Soba; ⏲8-11am Sat-Thu)

## FOOD

Sudanese food isn't particularly varied – the staples are *fuul* (stewed broad beans) and *ta'amiya*, known elsewhere as felafel. Outside the larger towns you'll find little else. That said, the food is generally fresh, tasty and healthy.

Meat dishes include *kibda* (liver), shish kebabs and shwarma (hunks of chicken or lamb sliced fresh from the classic roasting spit). Along the Nile you can find excellent fresh perch and tilapia.

## INTERNET ACCESS

Internet access is generally very good in Sudan – even in small towns connection speeds are decent and prices low. Most towns have an internet cafe (or perhaps internet cabin is a better description) or two – although they're slowly disappearing in favour of 3G – and most midrange and top-end hotels have wi-fi. It's also possible to access the internet on your phone using a Zain (www.sd.zain.com) or MTN (www.mtn.sd) SIM with mobile-phone data.

## LGBTIQ TRAVELLERS

Homosexual practices are illegal in Sudan, which is under Sharia (Islamic) law, and homosexuality remains a topic of absolute taboo. That said, Western travellers are unlikely to encounter outright prejudice or harassment so long as they remain discreet. However, this may well change if you become involved with a local. Room sharing is generally not a problem (it will be assumed that you're economising).

## MONEY

- The official currency is the Sudanese pound (S£/SDG), which is divided into 100 piastres.
- In the last couple of years the Sudanese pound has started to lose value against the US dollar at a steady rate, and with inflation increasing an exchange black market has sprung up. Official rates massively overvalue the Sudanese pound (up to triple!). If you use the black market be very discreet. Hotels and shops are good places to enquire. You can also ask your driver if you're on a tour.
- To curb the black market, the government has allowed a few private exchange offices that offer much better rates than the banks, and longer working hours. The rates offered by these offices is generally only a little lower than the black-market rate. The exchange office in the arrival hall at the airport in Khartoum is the best one.
- You can't pay with a foreign credit card in Sudan and ATMs don't accept foreign cards.
- Cash is king. Euros and US dollars are the easiest to change (outside Khartoum you'll be hard-pressed to change anything else). Bring clean, uncreased notes, preferably in denominations of US$50 or US$100 printed since 2006. The only way to change Egyptian pounds and Ethiopian birr is on the black market, which is easy at the borders.
- Money can be wired to Khartoum and Port Sudan (even from the US and UK, though this could always change because of sanctions) with Western Union and Travelex.

### Exchange Rates

| | | |
|---|---|---|
| Australia | A$1 | S£4.80 |
| Canada | C$1 | S£4.77 |
| Euro zone | €1 | S£6.80 |
| Japan | ¥100 | S£5.55 |
| New Zealand | NZ$1 | S£4.54 |
| UK | UK£1 | S£8.62 |
| USA | US$1 | S£6.35 |

For current exchange rates, see www.xe.com. Note that these rates are the official rates.

## OPENING HOURS

The following are common business hours in Sudan. Friday is the weekly holiday for offices and most shops.

**Government offices** 8am–12.30pm and 4–6pm Saturday to Thursday

**Restaurants** Breakfast 8–10am, lunch noon–3pm, dinner 6.30–10pm

**Shopping centres** 10am-10pm

**Shops and businesses** Typically 7.30am–1.30pm and 4pm–7pm Saturday to Thursday

## PHOTOGRAPHY

Photo permits are obligatory for foreigners and they form part of your travel permit. On the permit you must write down everything you want to photograph. Put 'historical sites, landscapes and tourist sites'. Permits are issued by Khartoum's Ministry of Tourism and Wildlife. Photography along the northern Nile route is generally a breeze and people will be keen to pose. Anywhere else it can be a pain thanks to overzealous officials. Photography in Khartoum (away from recognised tourist attractions) is asking for trouble.

## PUBLIC HOLIDAYS

In addition to the main Islamic holidays, the following are the principal public holidays in Sudan:

**Independence Day** 1 January

**Christmas Day** 25 December

## SAFE TRAVEL

While there are still many no-go areas, the rest of Sudan is a very safe place – one of the safest in Africa, in fact. Crime is almost unheard of, but watch your wallet among crowds and lock your luggage in hotels. The Nuba Mountains, Darfur and the borderlands with South Sudan are generally dangerous and out of bounds to foreign travellers.

## TELEPHONE

- Mobile-phone reception is excellent throughout the country.
- Depending on which mobile network you use at home, your phone may or may not work while in Sudan – ask your network provider.
- If you have a GSM phone and it has been 'unlocked', you can use a local SIM card purchased from one of the three providers (Sudani, Zain or MTN). It's an easy process involving only a few photocopies of your passport.
- You can buy credit at many shops in the form of scratch cards.

## TIME

Sudan is three hours ahead of GMT/UTC. Sudan does not operate a system of daylight saving.

## TOURIST INFORMATION

There's no tourist office in Sudan. Local tour operators and some hotels in Khartoum are the most reliable sources of travel information. Info for travellers is hard to come by outside the country.

## VISAS

Everyone, except Egyptians, needs a visa, and getting one could be the worst part of your trip.

### Obtaining a Visa

A transit visa (which gives you up to a fortnight to transit the country) is easier to get than a month-long tourist visa. Note that if there is evidence of travel to Israel in your passport you will be denied a visa. Currently Aswan (Egypt) remains the easiest place to get a visa; they are normally issued in a couple of days or even less there. A tourist visa is very hard to get in Addis Ababa (Ethiopia), but transit visas are possible.

For a tourist visa, it helps a lot to let a Sudanese tour operator arrange it. Most of the time they will get you a counter visa: you email them a copy of the first page of your passport and they arrange everything at the Ministry of Interior in Khartoum; after this they email you an entry permit, which you'll need to board the plane to Sudan; on arrival you show your entry permit at immigration, pay US$100 (US$150 for American citizens) and collect the visa. Sudanese tour operators typically charge US$150 per person for the visa service.

If the tour companies give you the runaround (some may be reluctant to offer this service if you don't book a tour with them), some hotels in Khartoum can also arrange an entry permit. The Bougainvilla Guesthouse (p529) and Acropole Hotel (p530) are very helpful in this regard. They may ask you to book a few nights on top of the service fees.

### Registration

You have to register within three days of arrival in Khartoum, Port Sudan, Gallabat or Wadi Halfa. In Khartoum, go to the **Aliens Registration Office** (Map p528; Souq esh-Shabi, Al-Diyum East; ⏲8am-2.15pm); the process costs S£250. You need one photo and photocopies of your passport and visa (there's a photocopier in the building) and a letter from a sponsor in Sudan; your hotel will normally act as your sponsor and provide you with the required letter. If you're travelling with a tour company they will take care of this for you. If doing it all independently allow several hours and a headache.

In all towns where you overnight you will need to register with the police – this is free, and it's a straightforward process; most hotels or guesthouses can do it on your behalf.

### Travel Permits

All travel outside Khartoum requires a travel permit. Take one photo and a copy of your passport and visa to the **Ministry of Tourism and Wildlife** (Map p528; ☎091 112 1856; al-Mashtal St, Riyadh; ⏲8.30am-3.30pm Sun-Thu) in the Riyadh area south of the city centre. A permit covering everywhere you intend to visit (except the no-go zones) can be issued on the spot. This permit is a combined travel and photograph permit. Carry dozens of photocopies of this permit along with copies of your passport and visa to give to police at checkpoints and when checking in at hotels.

### Visas for Onward Travel

Visas for the following neighbouring countries are available from embassies in Khartoum.

**Egypt** This embassy is not the most organised place – it's easier to get a tourist visa on arrival (which most, but not all, nationalities can do), especially if you're flying, or at the border (US$20) if you're travelling from Wadi Halfa.

**Ethiopia** One-month visas cost S£250 and require two photos. You can pick your visa up the same day.

**South Sudan** You will need a hotel reservation/ letter of invitation, a letter or invitation from your embassy, US$100 and two passport photos. Visas take one or two days to issue.

### WOMEN TRAVELLERS

Contrary to expectations, women travelling alone or in groups in Sudan are unlikely to face any major problems bar the odd cheap hotel refusing to rent you a room. What you will encounter though is general astonishment that you are here alone. People (particularly families and Sudanese women) will constantly try and take you under their wing and there will be lots of invites to people's houses. You should dress conservatively – a headscarf will likely make you feel more comfortable.

## Getting There & Away

### AIR

Sudan has two international gateways for arrival by air, **Khartoum International Airport** (p532) and **Port Sudan New International Airport** (Port Sudan). Khartoum is the main international airport. Sudan's international carrier is **Sudan Airways** (www.sudanair.com).

### LAKE

You can take the weekly passenger (and car) ferry on Lake Nasser from Wadi Halfa, Sudan, to the port near Aswan in Egypt. The journey takes around 17 hours plus immigration time. You can buy tickets in Wadi Halfa at the port.

### LAND

Sudan shares borders with many countries, but there are few crossing options. The security situation along the border with South Sudan is highly volatile, and though locals are taking boats down the White Nile between the two countries we've not heard of any travellers doing it. Most people consider an overland crossing between Sudan and South Sudan too dangerous to attempt. Libya is also risky, and while the Chadian border is technically open (but dangerous), there's no way a foreign traveller will be granted travel permits for Darfur, which borders Chad.

#### Border Crossings

**Egypt** The border between Wadi Halfa and Aswan is at Eshket and is open for all.

**Eritrea** The crossing between Kassala and Teseney is open, but the Eritrean side of the border area is closed to foreigners.

**Ethiopia** The border crossing is at Gallabat.

#### Bus

There are several daily (except Friday) bus services between Aswan (Egypt) and Wadi Halfa (Sudan). The whole trip takes about 12 hours. Border formalities are fairly straightforward. Sudanese visas are *not* issued at the border.

For Ethiopia, head to Gedaref, from where you'll find minibuses to the border town of Gallabat. Walk over the bridge to Metema (Ethiopia), where buses go direct to Gonder or, if you miss the bus, you can reach Gonder by changing vehicles in Shihedi. Note that you cannot get Ethiopian visas on the border.

#### Car & Motorcycle

The roads between Sudan and Egypt have been recently reopened. The road between Wadi Halfa and Aswan is the most convenient for overlanders.

Mazar Mahir (p534) and Magdi Boshara (p534) have a good reputation for speeding people through the paperwork at the border: contact them by email before your arrival.

## Getting Around

### AIR

A couple of airlines connect Khartoum to all large Sudanese cities. The most reliable ones include **Badr/Tarco Airlines** (www.badrairlines.com) and **Nova Airways** (www.novaairways.com), which both fly from Khartoum to Port Sudan. There's also Sudan Airways, but it's notorious for its last-minute cancellations.

### BUS & MINIBUS

Sudan is undergoing a road-building frenzy and all significant towns northeast of El-Obeid are now linked by excellent paved roads. Fast, comfortable buses have almost totally replaced most of the *bokasi* (pick-up trucks) that formerly bounced over the desert between big northern towns. There are also plenty of minibuses between the smaller towns; they usually leave when they're full. It's best to buy bus tickets a day in advance.

### CAR & MOTORCYCLE

Sudan has an excellent road network that links most cities and towns of interest to travellers. Most tour operators in Khartoum can arrange car hire, and all make hiring a driver compulsory with their vehicles. For a 4WD with driver expect to pay around US$110 a day. Fuel is generally extra, but it's very cheap.

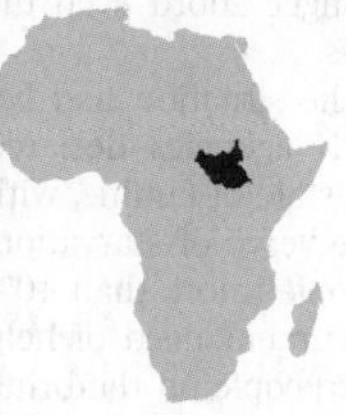

# South Sudan

POP 12.39 MILLION / ☎ 211



## Fast Facts

**Capital** Juba

**Population** 12.53 million

**Languages** English, Arabic, numerous tribal languages

**Area** 644,329 sq km

**Currency** South Sudanese pound (SSP)

## Introduction

In July 2011 Africa's largest country, Sudan, split into two and with that South Sudan, the world's newest country, was born.

The birthing process was a violent and bloody one. For decades the people of South Sudan have known little but war as they fought for independence from the north – and sadly it didn't take long for the infant nation to turn on itself, with a civil war erupting between the new government and various rebel groups.

South Sudan is one of the poorest and least developed nations on the planet, but the very fact that South Sudan remains such an unknown is the thing that will likely attract the first visitors back here. Until stability is established, however, even the most intrepid travellers will have to wait to be amazed by its wealth of tribal groups and excited by its national parks packed with vast numbers of large mammals.

## South Sudan at a Glance

**Boma National Park** This vast wilderness is home to huge quantities of wildlife, including migrating herds of over a million antelope.

**Nimule National Park** Home to hippos, Ugandan kobs, elephants, buffaloes and beautiful scenery.

**Bandingalo National Park** A paradise for giraffes, hippos and wild dogs, this park also welcomes hundreds of thousands of migrating antelope.

**Juba** The capital is a bustling boom town with busy markets and the grave of John Garang, the former leader of the South Sudan independence movement.

**Tribal people** Possibly no other corner of Africa has such a wide diversity of tribal peoples, many of whom continue to live a largely traditional lifestyle.

# UNDERSTAND SOUTH SUDAN

## South Sudan Today

With the resumption of civil war, South Sudan's fledgling economy has stuttered to a halt, development has foundered and, by almost all measures, South Sudan remains one of the world's most unfortunate nations. There are almost no surfaced roads, and outside the main towns virtually no hospitals or medical centres, few schools and little industry. Almost all South Sudanese survive by subsistence agriculture. According to the World Bank, 65.9% of the population live in extreme poverty.

South Sudan is the most oil-dependent country on earth, with oil accounting for almost all its exports and around 60% of its GDP, and yet with the current fighting oil exports are down (and even at normal rates of use, oil reserves are expected to have almost dried up by 2035). This decline in oil revenue has led to a financial crisis and an inflation rate of 730% (up to August 2016). This, combined with the civil war and a catastrophic drought in 2016, has meant that the cost of basic food items has spiralled upwards to the point where a majority of households can no longer afford even th most basic of foodstuffs.

By February 2017 the situation had be come so bad that UN agencies declare South Sudan was in a state of famine, wit 100,000 people on the verge of starvation nearly five million people (more than 40% of the population) in urgent need of hel and a million of those people on the brin of famine. Aid agencies say that the famin is almost entirely caused by humans an that a million children under five years o age are already acutely malnourished an that 1.5 million people have fled the countr

Whatever way you look at it, the futur for the world's newest nation is looking pre cariously grim.

## History

The history of South Sudan is very muc tied up with that of its northern neighbou Sudan.

### Early History & the British

We know little of the history of early Sout Sudan, although there is evidence that tran shumant cattle-raisers have inhabited th region for around 5000 years. Around th 1500s Nilotic-speakers such as the Dink

## South Sudan

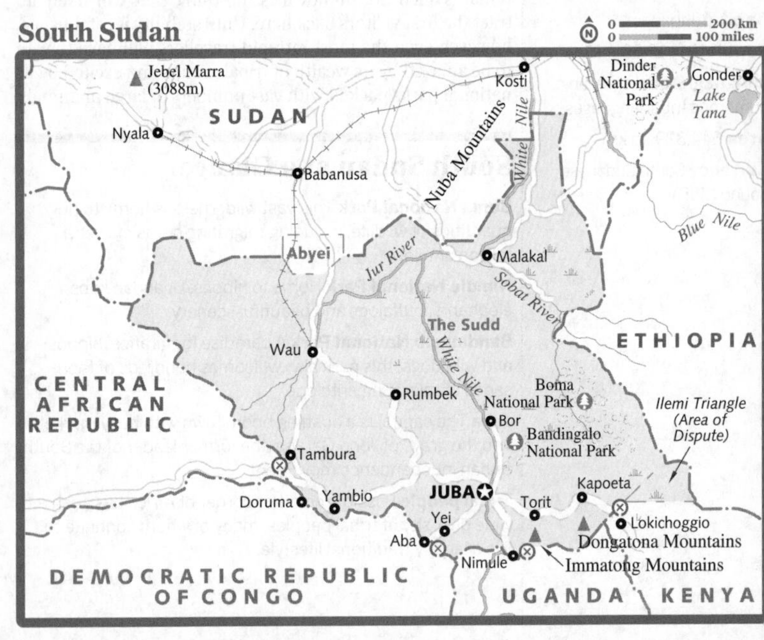

and Luo are thought to have moved down into what is now South Sudan from further north.

In 1899 South Sudan became a part of Anglo-Egyptian Sudan under the control of Britain and Egypt. Almost no development at all took place in the area that is today South Sudan, although the British encouraged Christian missionaries to work in the area in order to counter the spread of Islam southwards.

## Independence & Rebellion

In 1956 Sudan as a whole became independent and the people of South Sudan found themselves being ruled by Khartoum. Almost straight away southerners complained of discrimination and an unfair division of wealth, opportunities and political power between northerners and southerners. In addition, southern leaders accused Khartoum of trying to impose an Islamic and Arabic identity on the south and of reneging on promises to create a federal system.

In 1962 a rebellion originally launched by southern army officers seven years earlier turned into a full-scale civil war against Khartoum led by the Anya Nya guerrilla movement. In 1969 a group of socialist and communist Sudanese military officers led by Colonel Jaafar Muhammad Numeiri seized power in Khartoum. For the people of South Sudan the defining moment of Numeiri's 16 years in power came in 1972 when he signed the Addis Ababa Agreement which granted the southern provinces a degree of autonomy.

## War

The future looked bright in 1978 when the first oil was discovered in South Sudan: however, civil war broke out again in 1983 after Khartoum cancelled the autonomy arrangements. This time the southerners were led by John Garang's Sudan People's Liberation Movement (SPLM) and its armed wing, the Sudan People's Liberation Army (SPLA).

In the ensuing 22 years of fighting around 1.5 million people are thought to have lost their lives and more than four million were displaced.

The conflict finally ended with the 2005 Comprehensive Peace Agreement, under which the south was granted regional autonomy along with guaranteed representation in a national power-sharing government, as well as a referendum for the south on independence. In July of that year John Garang was sworn in as first vice president of Sudan, but then, just one month later, he was killed in a plane crash. Many southerners suspected foul play and demonstrations and fighting broke out again. John Garang was replaced by Salva Kiir Mayardit.

Despite the establishment in Khartoum of a power-sharing government between Omar al-Bashir and Salva Kiir, numerous deadly skirmishes occurred. The oil-rich state of Abyei, which sits on the frontier of Sudan and South Sudan, is, and continues to be, a particular flashpoint.

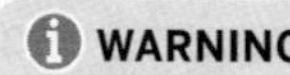

**WARNING**

Armed conflict in South Sudan is ongoing across the country. Most Western governments advise against all travel to anywhere in the country.

## The Second Independence & Civil War

After many long years of war, in January 2011 99% of southern Sudanese voted in the long-promised referendum to split from the rest of Sudan. In July of that year South Sudan became an independent country.

The independence honeymoon was shortlived: even before the new nation's first birthday South Sudan was back at war with itself after fighting broke out between Nuer and Murle tribal groups in the northeast of the country.

In December 2013, with intertribal conflict erupting in many parts of the country, things went from bad to worse after President Kiir accused his deputy, Riek Machar, of attempting to overthrow him in a coup. Machar fled into the bush and a full-scale civil war erupted between supporters of Kiir and supporters of Machar. Trapped in the middle were the ordinary citizens, and atrocities were committed against them by both sides.

After numerous international attempts at ceasefires – all of which failed – a peace agreement was finally signed in 2015 and Machar returned to Juba as vice president. No sooner had the ink dried on the peace agreement than fighting once again broke out between supporters of the two men, and by 2016 the country had plunged back into civil war.

### THE GREATEST (WILDLIFE) SHOW ON EARTH

So you've heard all about the wildebeest migration in Kenya and Tanzania and how it's been described as the greatest wildlife show on earth. Well, have you heard about South Sudan's own wildlife migration involving possibly even larger numbers of animals? When the Wildlife Conservation Society (www.wcs.org) conducted aerial surveys of what is now South Sudan in 2007, the last thing they expected to see was migrating herds of over a million white-eared kob, tiang antelope and Mongalla gazelle, but that's exactly what they found. In addition there are thought to be over 8000 elephants, 8900 buffaloes and 2800 ostriches, as well as lions, leopards, giraffes, hippos and numerous other species.

Looking at how big-buck-spending tourists flock to the national parks of neighbouring Kenya, the new government of South Sudan wasn't slow to recognise the tourist goldmine these animals might represent, and started trying to promote wildlife-watching tourism. The focus of these efforts was Boma National Park. This huge park, abutting the Ethiopian border, is crawling in megafauna.

Sadly, Boma is in a particularly volatile part of the country and it hasn't been safe to visit for the last few years. There is not yet any information on how the wildlife is faring during the current round of violence.

## Culture

South Sudan boasts numerous ethnic groups, with around 60 different languages spoken. The main ethnic groups are the Dinka, who make up around 15% of the population, the Nuer (around 10%), the Bari and the Azande. Indigenous traditional beliefs are widespread and even though Christianity has made inroads, it's still very much a minority religion that's often overlaid with traditional beliefs and customs.

Despite the potential oil wealth the vast majority of South Sudanese live a life of subsistence farming and cattle herding. For many tribes cattle are of huge cultural importance. They are the source of wealth and the key to marriage. A young boy is traditionally given an ox to care for by his father and he is even given a 'bull name', which often relates to the colour of his ox. Many tribes have a large vocabulary for cattle and their different colours. Cattle rustling is very common and clashes between tribal groups occur frequently.

## Environment

South Sudan is made up of vast areas of savannah (including the biggest savannah ecosystem in Africa), swamps (the Sudd, a swamp the size of England, is the largest such habitat in Africa), and flood plains interspersed with areas of woodland.

The wildlife of South Sudan has fared the years of the independence wars remarkably well. For the moment nobody really knows how the current rounds of fighting are impacting the great herds of large mammals that wade through the swamps and stride across the grasslands of South Sudan. Before these current outbreaks of violence environmental threats were coming in other forms: oil companies were looking for oil in a number of wildlife-rich areas, and illegal hunting, farming and construction work was taking place in and around protected zones. A big potential threat is water-diversion projects, which could have a dramatic impact on the annual flooding of the White Nile.

# East Africa

EVGENII ZOTOV/GETTY IMAGES ©

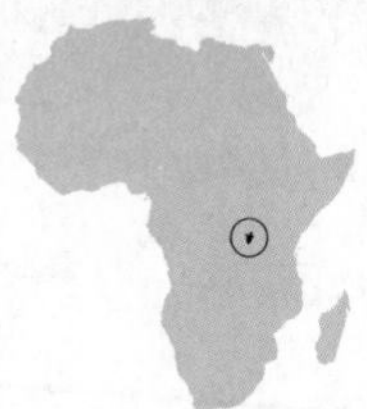

# Burundi

POP 10.16 MILLION / ☎257

**Includes ➡**



## Fast Facts

**Capital** Bujumbura

**Population** 11.1 million

**Languages** Kirundi, French

**Area** 27,830 sq km

**Currency** Burundian franc (BIF)

## Introduction

Tiny Burundi is an incongruous mix of soaring mountains, languid lakeside communities and a tragic past blighted by ethnic conflict. Despite their troubles, Burundians have an irrepressible joie de vivre, and their smiles are as infectious as a rhythm laid down by a drummer from Les Tambourinaires (a Burundian dance group).

When civil war broke out in 1993, the economy was destroyed and the tourist industry succumbed to a quick death. When the war finally ended in 2005, a trickle of travellers returned to rediscover the steamy capital, Bujumbura, with its lovely Lake Tanganyika setting and some of the finest inland beaches on the continent.

The new peace, however, came to a shattering end in 2015 when President Nkurunziza decided to run for what many Burundians believed to be a constitution-breaking third term in office. Violence broke out before the election, and has escalated since. The entire country is now considered unsafe to visit.

## Burundi at a Glance

**Bujumbura** The sultry capital has great nightlife and delicious food.

**Saga Beach** Soft white sands, warm waters and a stash of cool beach bars make this one of the most enticing inland beaches in Africa.

**Chutes de la Karera** Four different waterfalls make up this gorgeous cascade.

**Source du Nil** Burundi's very own pyramid, a memorial marking a small stream in Kasumo, at the southernmost source of the Nile.

**Parc National de la Rusizi** Antelopes and hippos splash and stomp through this national park just outside Bujumbura.

# UNDERSTAND BURUNDI

## Burundi Today

The political situation in Burundi is highly unstable, with frequent acts of violence throughout the country. This instability is having a very negative impact on a country that has long been one of the poorest and least developed in East Africa.

According to both the International Monetary Fund (IMF) and World Bank, Burundi is one of the five poorest countries in the world. Civil wars, corruption, landlocked geography, poor education, AIDS and a lack of economic freedom have all but economically crippled the country, and today it is largely dependent on foreign aid.

The country sits at just 180 out of 186 countries on the Human Development Index and 64.9% of the population are thought to live below the poverty line. Although Burundi's largest industry is agriculture (employing around 90% of the workforce), the sheer number of people living in such a small country (Burundi is the second most densely populated country in Africa) means that not enough food is produced to keep everyone fed. According to the Global Hunger Index almost half of all households are food insecure and slightly over half of the children of Burundi have stunted growth due to a lack of food.

Economically things are grim as well, with the country recording a negative economic growth rate in 2016, which can primarily be put down to the unstable political situation and a recent contraction in food production.

## History

### Independence & Coups

Burundi, like Rwanda, was colonised first by Germany and then later by Belgium, and like its northern neighbour, the Europeans



## Burundi

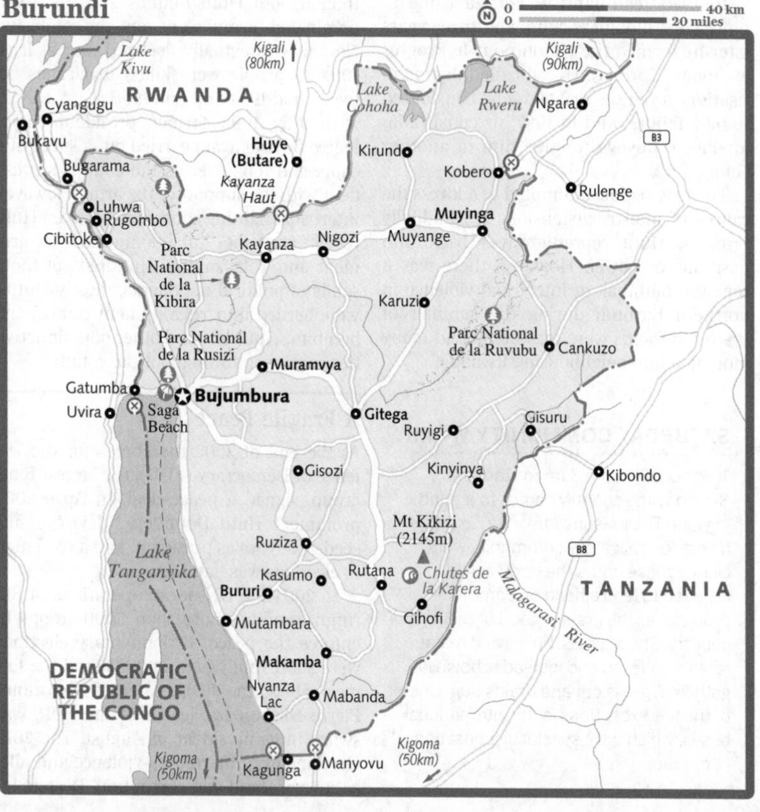

played on ethnic differences to divide and conquer the population. Power was traditionally concentrated in the hands of the minority Tutsi, though Hutus began to challenge the concentration of power following independence in 1962.

In the 1964 elections, Tutsi leader Mwami Mwambutsa refused to appoint a Hutu prime minister, even though Hutu candidates attracted the majority of votes. Hutu frustration soon boiled over, and Hutu military officers and political figures staged an attempted coup. Although it failed, Mwambutsa was exiled to Switzerland, and replaced by a Tutsi military junta.

A wholesale purge of Hutu from the army and bureaucracy followed, and in 1972 another large-scale Hutu revolt resulted in more than 1000 Tutsi being killed. The Tutsi military junta responded with the selective genocide of elite Hutu; after just three months, an estimated 200,000 Hutu had been killed and another 100,000 had fled into neighbouring countries.

In 1976 Jean-Baptiste Bagaza came to power in a bloodless coup, and three years later he formed the Union pour le Progrès National (Uprona). His so-called democratisation program was largely considered to be a failure, and in 1987 his cousin Major Pierre Buyoya toppled him in another coup.

The new regime attempted to address the causes of intertribal tensions by gradually bringing Hutu representatives back into positions of power. However, there was a renewed outbreak of intertribal violence in northern Burundi during the summer of 1988; thousands were massacred and many more fled into neighbouring Rwanda.

### SATURDAY COMMUNITY WORK

Traditionally, from 8am to 11am every Saturday the country comes to a grinding halt. The reason? *Ibikorwa rusangi* – a time for obligatory community work. During these hours the populace is required to lend a hand on community projects for the greater good of their country. Shops, taxis, buses and restaurants are closed and instead rubbish is gathered, grass cut and drains dug. One of the few exceptions is the international buses, which have special dispensation to operate.

## A Bloody Civil War

Buyoya finally bowed to international pressure, and multiparty elections were held in June 1993. These brought a Hutu-dominated government to power, led by Melchior Ndadaye, himself a Hutu. However, Ndadaye's rule was to be short-lived, as by October of that year he had been assassinated by unknown military assailants in an attempted coup (a 1996 UN investigation accused the army command of being responsible for Ndadaye's death, but the report did not name names). The coup eventually failed, though thousands were massacred in intertribal fighting, and almost half a million refugees fled across the border into Rwanda.

In April 1994 Cyprien Ntaryamira, the new Hutu president, was killed in the same plane crash that killed Rwanda's President Juvénal Habyarimana – an event that ignited the subsequent genocide in Rwanda. In Burundi, Sylvestre Ntibantunganya was immediately appointed interim president, though both Hutu militias and the Tutsi-dominated army went on the offensive. No war was actually declared, but at least 100,000 people were killed in clashes between mid-1994 and mid-1996.

In July 1996 former president Major Pierre Buyoya again carried out a successful coup, and took over as the country's president with the support of the army. However, intertribal fighting continued between Hutu rebels and the Tutsi-dominated government and Tutsi militia. Hundreds of thousands of political opponents, mostly Hutus, were herded into 'regroupment camps', and bombings, murders and other horrific activities continued throughout the country.

## A Fragile Peace

At the end of 2002 the Forces for the Defence of Democracy (FDD), the largest rebel group, signed a peace deal. In April 2003 prominent Hutu Domitien Ndayizeye succeeded Buyoya as president, and a road map to elections was hammered out.

In 2004 the UN began operations in Burundi, sending more than 5000 troops to enforce the peace. Parliamentary elections were successfully held in 2005, and the former rebels, the FDD, emerged victorious. Pierre Nkurunziza, leader of the FDD, was sworn in as president in August. The 2010 elections were marred by violence and allegations of fraud and corruption. Despite in ternational observers recognising the local elections as mainly free and fair, a growing mistrust of the incumbent's commitments to democracy saw all opposition withdraw their candidacy and Nkurunziza was re-elected unopposed.

Between 2010 and early 2015 the peace largely held and Burundi continued on its (very shaky) road to recovery: foreign investment started to arrive; the infrastructure of the country started to be over-hauled; the economy climbed slowly upward, with tourism increasing; and for a few short years things looked more positive than they had in many a year.

But then in April 2015 Domitien Ndayizeye announced that he intended to run for a third term as president. Opposition parties said that this would be against the constitution, which limits a president to two terms. Ndayizeye, though, claimed that his first term didn't count as he was appointed by parliament and not voted for by the people. But the people weren't happy and by the end of April angry protests had broken out on the streets of Bujumbura. On 26 April six demonstrators were killed in clashes with police during a protest. This led to more protests, much more violence, a government shutdown of independent radio stations and media outlets, an attempted coup, and tens of thousands of people fleeing the worsening situation for Rwanda and Tanzania.

Despite the rapid breakdown in law and order, elections were held in late July 2015. These were boycotted by the opposition and Ndayizeye was duly re-elected.

### WARNING

The security situation in Burundi is very unstable and violence has, and could again, flare up with little notice. Most Western governments advise against all but essential travel to most of the country, including Bujumbura, and all travel to certain parts of the northwest and northeast.

If you do visit the country, the following precautions should apply:

- Do not walk around Bujumbura at night.
- The road north of Bujumbura towards Cibitoke should be avoided.
- Do not attempt to visit the Parc National de la Kibira or Parc National de la Ruvubu.
- Do not travel anywhere by road at night.
- Avoid the Democratic Republic of the Congo (DRC) border areas.
- Carry your passport at all times.

## Culture

Burundi's population comprises 84% Hutu,15% Tutsi and 1% Twa. Like Rwanda in 1994, Burundi has been torn apart by tribal animosities, and the conflict between Hutus and Tutsis has claimed hundreds of thousands of lives since independence. The Belgians masterminded the art of divide and rule, using the minority Tutsis to control the majority Hutus. Generations of intermarriage and cooperation went out the window, as the population was forced into choosing sides, Hutu or Tutsi. The pattern continued into independence as the minority Tutsis clung to power to protect their privileges, and marginalised the Hutu majority.

The one (very slight) silver lining to the most recent violence is that it hasn't taken as much of a Tutsi-against-Hutu angle as in the past.

## Environment

Taking up a mere 27,830 sq km, most of the country is made up of mountains that vanish into the horizon. Like its neighbour Rwanda, this is a very densely populated country and most areas that can be farmed are being utilised as such. There are three national parks worthy of the name and, at least prior to the latest round of violence, there were surprisingly healthy animal populations within them.

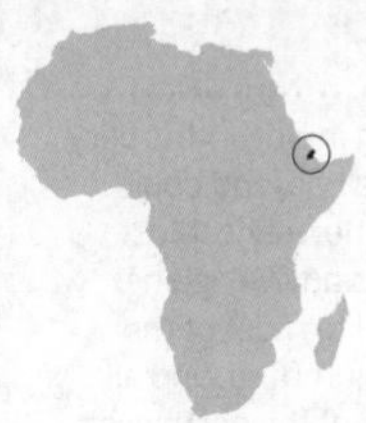

# Djibouti

POP 920,000 / ☎253

**Includes ➡**



## Best Places to Eat

- Mukbassa Central – Chez Youssouf (p559)
- Café de la Gare (p559)
- La Terrasse (p559)
- Hôtel-Restaurant Le Golfe (p561)

## Best Places to Sleep

- Le Héron Auberge (p558)
- Atlantic Hotel (p558)
- Hôtel Village Vacances Les Sables Blancs (p561)
- Campement Touristique de la Forêt du Day (p562)
- Campement Touristique d'Asboley (p561)

## Why Go?

This tiny speck of a country packs a big punch. What it lacks in size, it more than makes up for in beauty. Few countries in the world, with the possible exception of Iceland, offer such weird landscapes – think salt lakes, extinct volcanoes, sunken plains, limestone chimneys belching out puffs of steam, basaltic plateaus and majestic canyons. Outdoorsy types will enjoy a good mix of land and water activities, including hiking, diving and whale-shark spotting in the Gulf of Tadjoura.

Barring Djibouti City, the country is refreshingly devoid of large-scale development. It's all about ecotravel, with some sustainable stays in the hinterland that provide a fascinating glimpse into the life of nomadic tribes.

Travelling independently around Djibouti may not come cheap, but despite the high cost of living, you'll surely leave this little corner of Africa with new experiences and wonderful memories.

## When to Go

### Djibouti City

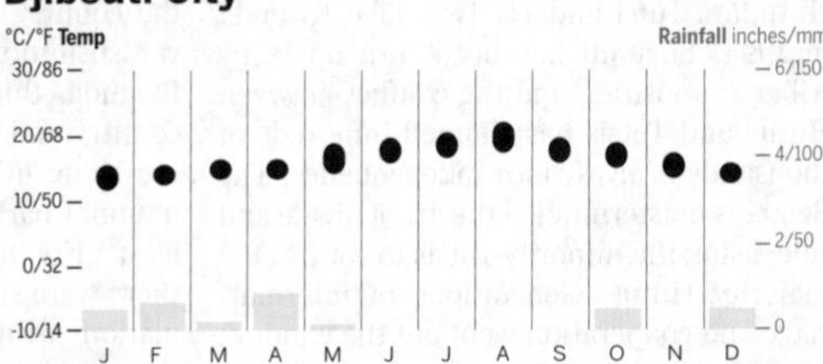


**May–Sep** Some like it hot…some like it *hot*.

**Oct & Feb–Apr** Shoulder seasons are not a bad time to visit. Calm waters for diving.

**Nov–Jan** Coolest months; perfect for outdoor activities. Whale sharks make their annual visit.

# DJIBOUTI CITY

POP 610,000

Djibouti's capital is evolving at a fast pace, and there's a palpable sense of change in the air. Thanks to its geostrategic importance and its busy port, Djibouti City has been transformed from a sleepy capital to a thriving place. Yet under its veneer of urban bustle, the city remains a down-to-earth place. Traditionally robed Afar tribesmen, stalwart GIs, colourfully dressed Somali ladies and frazzled businessmen with the latest mobile phones stuck to their ear all jostle side by side.

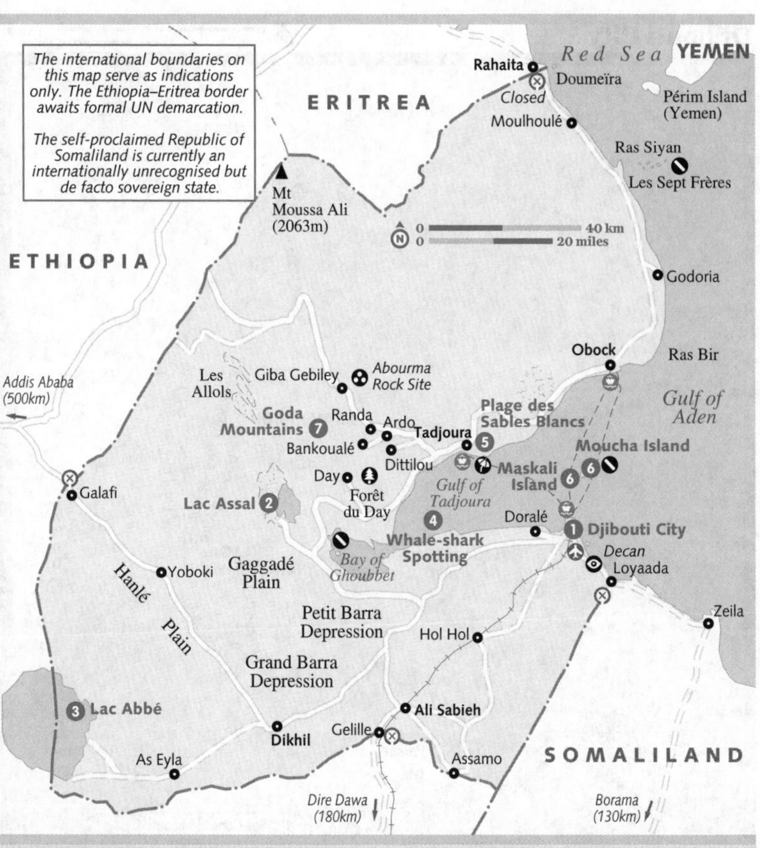


## Djibouti Highlights

1 **Djibouti City** (p555) Catching local vibes while wandering through the animated streets of the capital and enjoying its culinary delights.

2 **Lac Assal** (p560) Descending to the lowest point on the African continent at 155m below sea level.

3 **Lac Abbé** (p560) Wandering flabbergasted in a Martian landscape, with hundreds of spikelike limestone chimneys.

4 **Whale-shark spotting** (p557) Sighting and swimming with whale sharks from November to January in the Gulf of Tadjoura.

5 **Plage des Sables Blancs** (p561) Unwinding on Djibouti's most scenic beach.

6 **Diving** (p557) Exploring some superb shipwrecks in the Gulf of Tadjoura.

7 **Goda Mountains** (p561) Taking a guided walk amid spectacular mountain scenery and spending a night in a traditional *campement touristique* (tourist camp).

## Sights

**L'Escale** HARBOUR

(Map p556) In the early evening, the walk along the causeway northwest of the centre makes a very pleasant stroll. The Moorish-inspired **presidential palace** (not open to the public) marks one end, the harbour of L'Escale, the other. The little marina is home to a variety of boats, from the traditional and picturesque Arab dhows to the simple local fishing skiffs and ferries to Tadjoura and Obock.

## Djibouti City

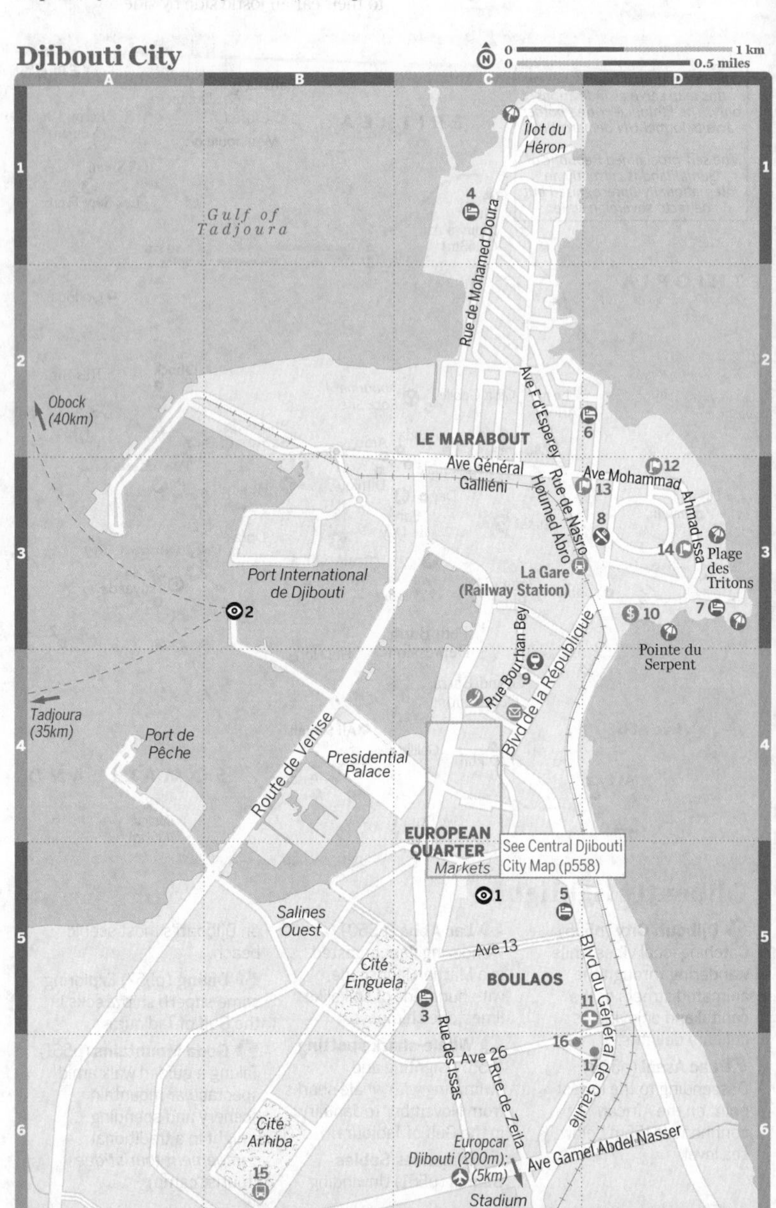

**African Quarter** AREA
(Map p556) The vast **Place Mahmoud Harbi** (aka Pl Rimbaud), which is dominated by the minaret of the great **Hamoudi Mosque** (Map p558), Djibouti City's most iconic building, is considered the real soul of the city. Eastward, the chaotic **Quartier 1** is a crisscross of alleyways where stalls and shops are lined cheek by jowl. Spreading along Blvd de Bender are the stalls of **Les Caisses Market** (Map p558; Blvd de Bender; ⌚8am-10pm Sat-Thu). Crammed with every type of souvenir from woodcarvings to clothing, it's a colourful place for soaking up the atmosphere.

## Activities

For a capital that's surrounded by water, Djibouti City is not well endowed with beaches. The only decent stretch of sand is at the **Djibouti Palace Kempinski** (Map p556; Îlot du Héron), but there's an entrance fee of DFr4000, and the swimming is not *that* tempting, with shallow waters and a profusion of algae. South of the Djibouti Palace Kempinski, the **Plage du Héron** is much wider but is average. There's also a postage-stamp-sized beach at the **Sheraton Djibouti Hotel** (Map p556; Plateau du Serpent). For a dip, your best bet is to use the pools at both hotels.

For diving and whale-shark spotting, try **Dolphin** (☎21347807, 77103395; www.dolphin-services.com; Haramous; ⌚7am-5pm), **Siyyan Travel & Leisure** (☎77103674; www.dive-lucy.com) or **Youssouf Travel** (☎77828166; ⌚by reservation).

### Diving

Most diving takes place off the islands of Maskali and Moucha in the **Gulf of Tadjoura**, where you'll find a variety of dive sites for all levels. Wreck enthusiasts will make a beeline for monster-sized **Le Faon**, a 120m-long cargo ship that lies in 27m of water on a sandy floor. Other shipwrecks worthy of exploration include **L'Arthur Rimbaud**, a tugboat that was scuttled in 2005, and the nearby **Nagfa**, a small Ethiopian boat that lies in about 32m of water. If you need a break from wreck dives, some excellent reef dives beckon, including **Tombant Point**, where you'll see a smorgasbord of reef fish; and the **Canyon**, a relaxing site suitable for novices.

There's also an array of spectacular sites scattered along the southern shoreline of the Gulf of Tadjoura and the **Bay of Ghoubbet**, furthest west.

Most sites around the Gulf of Tadjoura can be accessed with organised boat trips from the capital, particularly at the weekend (Friday).

### Whale-Shark Spotting

The Bay of Ghoubbet, at the western end of the Gulf of Tadjoura, is one of the most dependable locations in the world to swim alongside a massive whale shark *(Rhincodon typus)*, the world's largest fish. The peak season runs from November to January. There are between two and 10 individuals, close to the shore, and it's very easy to snorkel with these graceful creatures.

This activity has exploded in recent years, and plenty of unprofessional operators can arrange trips. It's better to stick to well established outfits that are ecologically sensitive and follow protocols. Give the sharks a berth of at least 4m. Touching is an absolute no-no.

## Sleeping

**Dar Es Salam** HOTEL $
(Map p556; ☎21353334; off Rue des Issas; s DFr6000, d DFr7000-8400; ❄📶) Right in the

## Djibouti City

**Sights**
1 African Quarter ... C5
2 L'Escale ... B3

**Sleeping**
3 Dar Es Salam ... C5
4 Djibouti Palace Kempinski ... C1
5 Hôtel Horseed ... C5
6 Le Héron Auberge ... D2
7 Sheraton Djibouti Hotel ... D3

**Eating**
8 Café de la Gare ... D3

**Drinking & Nightlife**
9 Association de la Communauté Ethiopienne de Djibouti ... C4

**Information**
10 BCIMR ... D3
11 CHA Bouffard ... D5
12 Ethiopian Embassy ... D3
13 French Embassy ... D3
14 Somaliland Bureau de Liaison ... D3

**Transport**
15 Cité Arhiba minibus station ... B6
Ferries to Obock & Tadjoura ... (see 2)
16 Garage Roberto ... C6
17 Pyramid ... D6

African Quarter, the Dar Es Salam is a dependable budget choice if you're strapped for cash. Rooms are presentable but vary in size, light and noisiness so ask to see a couple before you settle on one. Facilities include a small restaurant and an internet café. Overall, not a bad deal provided you keep your expectations in check.

**Hôtel Horseed** HOTEL $
(Map p556; ☎77017804, 21352316; horseedhotel@gmail.com; Blvd du Général de Gaulle; s with shared bathroom Dfr5000-6500, d DFr7500-9000, with shared bathroom Dfr6500-8000; ❄📶) The Horseed is a reliable choice for unfussy budgeteers, with bare but serviceable rooms and a couple of dorms with mattresses (and air-con) at the back. It all feels very compact, but it's well managed and the shared bathrooms are well scrubbed. The owner, Kadar Ismael, lived in Canada for 10 years and speaks excellent English; he's a mine of local information.

★**Le Héron Auberge** HOTEL $$
(Map p556; ☎21324343; www.aubergeleheron.net; Rue de l'Imam Hassan Abdallah Mohamed; s/d incl breakfast DFr13,000/15,800; ❄📶) An attractive, secure compound in a residential area, Le Héron is one of Djibouti City's best-value hotels, with 29 rooms that are well appointed and clean as a whistle. The slightly off-the-beaten-path location on a peaceful street means you can actually get a good night's sleep here. Credit cards (Visa) are accepted but there's a 3% commission. Book ahead.

**Menelik Hotel** HOTEL $$
(Map p558; ☎21351177; Pl du 27 Juin 1977; s DFr16,000-18,000, d DFr20,500, all incl breakfast; ❄📶) It's hard to top the Menelik's location, smack-dab in the centre. The rooms, some with good views of the main square, have started to show their age but provide good levels of comfort and hygiene, and there's an on-site restaurant. Cash only.



## Central Djibouti City

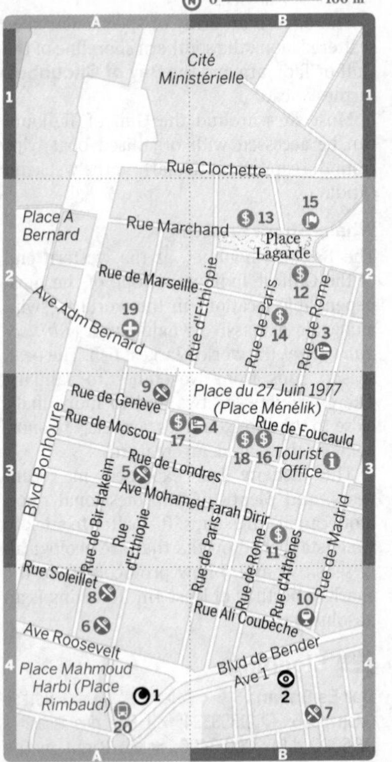


### Central Djibouti City

**Sights**
1 Hamoudi Mosque ........ A4
2 Les Caisses Market ........ B4

**Sleeping**
3 Atlantic Hotel ........ B2
4 Menelik Hotel ........ B3

**Eating**
5 Bunna House ........ A3
6 La Terrasse ........ A4
7 Mukbassa Central – Chez Youssouf ........ B4
8 Nil Bleu ........ A4
9 Time Out ........ A3

**Drinking & Nightlife**
10 Jus de Fruits Chez Mahad ........ B4

**Information**
11 Amal Express ........ B3
12 Bank of Africa ........ B2
13 BCIMR ........ B2
14 CAC International Bank ........ B2
15 Canadian Consulate ........ B2
16 Dilip Corporation ........ B3
17 East Africa Bank ........ A3
18 Mehta ........ B3
19 Pôle Médical ........ A2

**Transport**
20 City Minibuses Central Hub ........ A4

### ★ Atlantic Hotel HOTEL $$$

(Map p558; ☎21331100; www.atlantichoteldjibouti.com; Rue de Rome; s/d incl breakfast DFr26,000/30,000; P ❄ ☎) Opened in 2016, the professionally run Atlantic is a great place to drop anchor in the centre. Expect efficient service, spacious rooms with balcony, excellent bedding, sparkling bathrooms and a good Italian restaurant beside the reception. Its central location is ideal if you want to immerse yourself in Djibouti City.

Rooms 401, 403, 405, 407, 409 and 411 are blessed with sea views.

## Eating

For sheer choice and quality of food, Djibouti City ranks among the best places in Africa, with a wide array of eating options. This is your chance to relish French specialities, scoff absolutely fresh local seafood, savour tasty meat dishes, devour delicious pizzas and treat yourself to exquisite fruit juices or pastries.

No alcohol is served in the cheaper places.

### ★ La Terrasse ETHIOPIAN $

(Map p558; ☎21350227; Rue d'Ethiopie; mains DFr900-1600; ⊙6.30-10.30pm Sat-Thu) This place has plenty of character and serves up good Ethiopian food as well as pasta and sandwiches at puny prices. It occupies a rooftop, with a moodily lit dining area and an open kitchen – not to mention the heady scents of incense. If only it was licensed!

### Bunna House CAFETERIA $

(Map p558; Rue d'Ethiopie; mains DFr400-800; ⊙7am-10.30pm Sat-Thu, 8am-2pm & 4-9pm Fri) Located right in the centre, this trendy cafeteria-cum-fast-food outlet is a handy spot for a cheap, uncomplicated, walk-in bite. Tuck into well made sandwiches, panini or burgers. The concise menu also includes pastries and pancakes.

### Nil Bleu FAST FOOD $

(Map p558; Rue d'Ethiopie; mains DFr500-1200; ⊙11am-2pm & 6-10pm Sat-Thu) A great place to quieten a growling stomach without breaking the bank, this busy Djiboutian place serves simple fish dishes, salads, rice and spags. It serves great *shwarmas* (kebablike dishes) in the evening too.

### ★ Mukbassa Central – Chez Youssouf YEMENI $$

(Map p558; ☎21351899; off Ave 1; fish menu DFr3000; ⊙11am-2pm Sat-Thu, 6-10pm daily) In business for ages, this Djibouti City icon is famous for one thing and one thing only: *poisson yemenite* (oven-baked fish). It's served with a chapati-like bread and a devilish *mokbasa* (purée of honey and either dates or banana). The colourful, wooden building feels a bit ramshackle, but that's part of the experience. Dessert (pancakes) is extra (DFr400). No alcohol is served.

### ★ Café de la Gare FRENCH $$$

(Map p556; ☎21351530; Rue de Nasro Houmed Abro; mains DFr3200-6000; ⊙noon-2.30pm & 6.30-10pm Sat-Thu) Dining at this upscale gourmet restaurant is a treat. The elegant dining room is decorated with earthy tones and classy furniture, and Café de la Gare is justly revered for its refined French-inspired cuisine with a bow to local ingredients. Highlights include *magret aux girolles* (duck with mushrooms), beefsteak and king prawns. Another draw is the cosy cocktail bar upstairs.

## Drinking & Nightlife

There's no shortage of watering holes in Djibouti City, especially around Pl du 27 Juin 1977. Plenty of tea houses are also scattered around the centre.

Most clubs are on or around Rue d'Ethiopie, in the European Quarter. They are at their liveliest on Thursday and Friday nights. Entrance is free, but a beer costs upwards of DFr1000.

### ★ Jus de Fruits Chez Mahad JUICE BAR

(Map p558; ☎77866305; Rue Ali Coubèche; juices DFr400-800; ⊙7am-noon & 4-8pm Sat-Thu, 4-8pm Fri) Ah, Mahad and its oh-so-smooth, oh-so-thick fruity concoctions (over 45 varieties)! Grab a seat outside and watch the world go by. Also serves tea, coffee and pastries.

### Association de la Communauté Ethiopienne de Djibouti BAR

(Club Éthiopien; Map p556; off Rue Bourhan Bey; ⊙5-10pm) This down-to-earth bar, with its large outdoor courtyard, is a pleasant place to enjoy a very cheap beer – a bottle of St George costs only DFr350. Also known as 'Club Éthiopien', this simple establishment also serves good Ethiopian fare at economical prices.

## Information

### MEDICAL SERVICES

You'll find several well stocked pharmacies in the centre.

**CHA Bouffard** (Map p556; 21351351; Blvd du Général de Gaulle) The best equipped hospital, south of the city.

**Pôle Médical** (Map p558; 21352724; off Pl du 27 Juin 1977; 8am-noon & 4-7pm Sat-Thu) A small clinic.

### MONEY

**Amal Express** (Map p558; Ave Mohamed Farah Dirir; 7am-noon & 4-9pm Sat-Thu) Bureau de change.

**Bank of Africa** (Map p558; Pl Lagarde; 7.30am-noon & 4.15-6pm Sun & Wed, 7.30am-noon Mon, Tue & Fri) Changes cash and has two ATMs.

**BCIMR** (Map p558; Pl Lagarde; 7.30-11.45am Sun-Thu) Changes cash and has ATMs. The branch at **Plateau du Serpent** (Map p556; Rue Mohamed Dileita Chehem) has an ATM (Visa only).

**CAC International Bank** (Map p558; Rue de Marseille; 7.30-11.45am & 4-6pm Sun-Thu) Changes cash and has two ATMs (Visa and MasterCard).

**Dilip Corporation** (Map p558; Pl du 27 Juin 1977; 8am-noon & 4-7.30pm Sat-Thu) Bureau de change.

**East Africa Bank** (Map p558; Pl du 27 Juin 1977; 7.30am-12.30pm & 4.30-6pm Sun-Wed, 7.30am-noon Thu & Sat) Changes cash and has an ATM (Visa and MasterCard).

**Mehta** (Map p558; 21353719; Pl du 27 Juin 1977; 7.30am-noon & 4-7.30pm Sun-Thu) Bureau de change.

### POST

**Main post office** (Map p556; Blvd de la République; 7am-1pm & 4-9pm Sat-Thu) North of the centre.

### TOURIST INFORMATION

**Tourist Office** (Map p558; 21352800; www.visitdjibouti.dj; Rue de Foucauld; 7am-1.30pm Sat-Thu, plus 4-6pm Sat, Mon & Wed) Mildly helpful. Sells a map of the city (DFr1000 to DFr1500). For details on tours, you're better off at a travel agency. On the southeastern side of Pl du 27 Juin 1977.

## Getting There & Away

### AIR

**Djibouti-Ambouli airport** (21341646; www.aeroport-jib.com) is 5km south of town.

### BOAT

A **ferry** (Map p556; L'Escale) plies the Djibouti–Tadjoura and Djibouti–Obock routes two to three times a week (DFr700 one way, about three hours for either journey). It doesn't operate from mid-June to mid-September. Boats leave from L'Escale.

### BUS

Minibuses leave from various departure points south of town, including **Cité Arhiba** (Map p556). They connect Djibouti City to Tadjoura (DFr 1500, three hours), Galafi (at the Ethiopian border) and Obock (DFr2000, about 4½ hours).

### CAR & MOTORCYCLE

For 4WD rental (from DFr25,000 per day, with driver), contact the following outfits.

**Europcar Djibouti** (Marill; 21329425; www.europcar-djibouti.com; Route de l'Aéroport)

**Garage Roberto** (Map p556; 21352029; robertosanges@yahoo.fr; Route de Boulaos)

**Pyramid** (Map p556; 21358203; www.pyramidrental.com; Route de Boulaos)

## Getting Around

The central hub for **city minibuses** (Map p558; all tickets DFr50) is on Pl Mahmoud Harbi. A taxi ride within the centre costs about DFr600 (DFr1200 to or from the airport).

# AROUND DJIBOUTI

## Lac Assal

Just over 100km west of the capital lies one of the most spectacular natural phenomena in Africa: Lac Assal. Situated 155m below sea level, this crater lake is encircled by dark, dormant volcanoes. The vast depression, which represents the lowest point on the continent, is an impressive sight. The aquamarine water is ringed by a huge salt field, 60m in depth. The banks of salt and gypsum surround the lake for more than 10km, and the blinding white contrasts starkly with the black lava fields around it. The water is totally saturated with salt, so there's not much chance of a swim.

Lying 107km west of the capital and connected by a decent sealed road, Lac Assal is within easy reach of Djibouti City. That said, there's no public transport – most visitors come with tours out of the capital.

## Lac Abbé

You'll never forget your first glimpse of Lac Abbé. The scenery is sensational: the plain is dotted with hundreds of limestone chimneys, some standing as high as 50m, belching out puffs of steam. Located 140km southwest of Djibouti City, it is often described as 'a slice of moon on the crust of earth'.

The best time to visit the lake is in the early morning, when the chimneys appear to belch smoke in the cool morning air. An even better plan is to arrive in the late afternoon, stay the night, and leave after sunrise the following morning. In the evening, when the sun sets behind the chimneys, the landscape can look almost magical.

Friendly **Houmed Loita** (☎77822291, 21357244; houmed_asboley@hotmail.fr) runs the Campement Touristique d'Asboley and can organise all kinds of cultural trips and excursions in the area.

Set in the most surreal landscape you've ever imagined, **Campement Touristique d'Asboley** (huts with full board & transfers per person DFr21,500; P) lies on a plateau that proffers stupendous views of the big chimneys – whatever the time of the day, you're guaranteed to be hypnotised by the scenery. It offers traditional Afar huts with shared showers and toilets – the ablution block is rudimentary but OK. Prices include a guided walk to the chimneys.

The only way of getting here is by hiring a 4WD with driver or by taking a tour. If you are (or can find) a party of four, the *campement touristique* can arrange all-inclusive packages for about DFr24,000 per person per day: prices include transfers from Djibouti City, accommodation, meals and guided walks.

## Tadjoura

POP 26,000

Nestled in the shadow of the green Goda Mountains with the bright-blue sea lapping at its doorstep, Tadjoura is a picturesque little place. With its palm trees, whitewashed houses and numerous mosques, it has an Arabian feel to it. There's little to do here besides stroll around and soak up the atmosphere, but it's a great place to spend a few hours before heading to Plage des Sables Blancs or Obock.

WORTH A TRIP

### PLAGE DES SABLES BLANCS

Plage des Sables Blancs, 7km east of Tadjoura, is tranquillity incarnate and a lovely place to sun yourself, with a good string of white sand and excellent facilities. Small wonder that it's hugely popular with weekending expats. Your biggest quandary here: a bout of snorkelling, kayaking, or a snooze on the beach? **Hôtel Village Vacances Les Sables Blancs** (☎77073377, 77182822; www.sablesblancs.com; beds with full board DFr12,000, d/q incl breakfast DFr 25,000/35,000; P❄📶), right on the beach, is a lovely place to chill for a few days.

### Sleeping & Eating

**Hôtel-Restaurant Le Golfe** HOTEL **$$**

(☎77839533, 77846598; http://hotel-restaurant-le-golfe-djibouti-tadjourah.e-monsite.comite.com; bungalow d/q incl breakfast DFr11,000/15,000; P❄📶) Under French-Ethiopian management, this low-key but well kept resort with a family atmosphere is situated in a relaxing waterfront setting, about 1.5km from the town centre. The 28 units, 10 of which come with sea views, are not fancy but are functional, and there's an excellent on-site restaurant (mains DFr1500 to DFr2600) with a terrace facing the Gulf of Tadjoura.

**Le Corto Maltese** HOTEL **$$**

(☎77859574; d incl breakfast DFr12,000; P❄📶) Le Corto Maltese is right on the seashore, about 1.5km west of the town centre, but there's no real beach. The adjoining 18 rooms are well organised, with good bedding and large bathrooms, and we hear good things about the on-site restaurant (mains DFr1200 to DFr2600). It feels a tad impersonal, though. Transfers to Plage des Sables Blancs can be arranged.

### Getting There & Away

Regular morning buses ply the route between Cité Arhiba in Djibouti City and Tadjoura (DFr1500, three hours). A passenger ferry runs two to three times weekly between L'Escale in Djibouti City and Tadjoura (DFr700 one way, about three hours).

# GODA MOUNTAINS

Northwest of the Gulf of Tadjoura, the Goda Mountains rise to a height of 1750m and are a spectacular natural oddity. This area shelters one of the rare speckles of green on Djibouti's parched map, like a giant oasis – a real relief after the scorched desert landscapes. A few Afar villages are scattered around and merit at least a couple of days of your time to soak up their charm. It won't be long before you're smitten by the region's mellow tranquillity and laid-back lifestyle. For outdoorsy types, this area offers ample hiking opportunities.

## Sleeping & Eating

There aren't any independent eateries in the region. The three *campements touristiques* – Forêt du Day, Bankoualé and Dittilou – provide full-board accommodation.

**★Campement Touristique de la Forêt du Day** HUT $
(☎77728544, 77829774; Day; per person full board DFr8000) If you like peace, quiet and sigh-inducing views, you'll have few quibbles with this atmospheric *campement* in the village of Day, at an altitude of 1500m, close to the Forêt du Day. The traditional huts are welcoming and the toilet blocks are kept clean. Other draws include the host of walking options available and the healthy food, including delicious *kemir* (pancakes) for breakfast.

**Campement Touristique de Bankoualé** HUT $
(☎77814115; Bankoualé; per person full board DFr8000; P) This ecofriendly camp (electricity is solar powered) in a scenic location – it's perched on a hillside and overlooks a deep valley – is a lovely place to spend a couple of days, particularly if you're keen on hiking. Huts are equipped with traditional Afar beds made of wood, and the views of the valley are sensational.

**Campement Touristique de Dittilou** HUT $
(☎77810488, 21354520; Dittilou; per person full board DFr8000; P) This *campement* has helpful and friendly management offering a series of well designed *daboytas* (traditional huts) brimful of rustic charm. They are set against a spectacular and peaceful landscape. The laid-back restaurant is chilled and the food is great. The gang of green monkeys that roam around the place is either a nuisance or an attraction, depending on your perspective.

## Getting There & Away

Public transport is virtually nonexistent. The most convenient way to visit the area is on a tour or with a rental 4WD. Transport can also be organised by the *campements touristiques* if there's a group (usually a minimum of four people). Count on DFr21,500 per person, including transfers and one night's accommodation with full board.

# UNDERSTAND DJIBOUTI

## Djibouti Today

Djibouti's stability and neutrality, combined with its strategic position, have brought lots of benefits, especially in terms of foreign assistance, economic growth and employment – Djibouti is not dubbed 'the Dubai of the Horn' for nothing. The total number of foreign soldiers on the Djiboutian territory is estimated at 7000, which contributes directly or indirectly to the country's income.

Djibouti City's strategic value as a port is today as important as ever. As a key trade hub to Asia, Europe and the rest of Africa, it provides the biggest source of income in a country devoid of natural resources. The port handles most of Ethiopia's imports and exports, which brings lots of fees and transit taxes. Foreign investors from Asia and the Gulf are increasingly active in Djibouti, and there are building projects springing up all over the capital.

## History

### From Aksum to Islam

Around the 1st century AD, Djibouti made up part of the powerful Ethiopian kingdom of Aksum, which included modern-day Eritrea and even stretched across the Red Sea to parts of southern Arabia. It was during the Aksumite era, in the 4th century AD, that Christianity first appeared in the region.

As the empire of Aksum gradually fell into decline, a new influence arose that would forever supersede the Christian religion in Djibouti: Islam. It was introduced to the region around AD 825 by Arab traders from Southern Arabia.

## European Ambitions

In the second half of the 19th century, European powers competed to grab new colonies in Africa. The French, seeking to counter the British presence in Yemen on the other side of the Bab al-Mandab Strait, made agreements with the Afar sultans of Obock and Tadjoura that gave them the right to settle. In 1888 construction of Djibouti City began on the southern shore of the Gulf of Tadjoura. French Somaliland (present-day Djibouti) began to take shape.

France and the emperor of Ethiopia then signed a pact designating Djibouti as the 'official outlet of Ethiopian commerce'. This led to the construction of the Addis Ababa–Djibouti City railway, which was of vital commercial importance until recently.

## Throwing Off the French Yoke

As early as 1949 there were a number of anticolonial demonstrations that were led by the Issa Somalis, who were in favour of the reunification of the territories of Italian, British and French Somaliland. Meanwhile, the Afars were in favour of continued French rule.

Major riots ensued, especially after the 1967 referendum, which produced a vote in favour of continued French rule – a vote achieved partly as a result of the arrest of opposition leaders and the massive expulsion of ethnic Somalis. After the referendum, the colony's name was changed from French Somaliland to the French Territory of the Afars and Issas.

In June 1977 the colony finally won its sovereignty from France. The country became the Republic of Djibouti.

Despite continuous clan rivalries between the two main ethnic groups, Afars and Issas, who have been jostling for power since the 1970s, Djibouti has learned to exploit its strategic position, keeping both sides happy during the two Gulf Wars.

# Culture

Of Djibouti's estimated 920,000 inhabitants, about 35% are Afars and 60% are Issas. Both groups are Muslim. The rest of the population is divided between Arabs and Europeans. The south is predominantly Issa, while the north is mostly Afar. Ethnic tensions between Afars and Issas have always dogged Djibouti. These tensions came to a head in 1991, when Afar rebels launched a civil war in the north. A peace accord was brokered in 1994, but ethnic hostility has not completely waned.

# SURVIVAL GUIDE

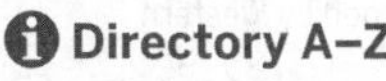

## Directory A–Z

### ACCOMMODATION

Most hotels are in the capital, with few options outside. Hotel categories are limited in range; most of them fit into the upper echelon and are expensive. At the lower end, the few budget hotels that exist tend to be pretty basic. There's a limited choice in between.

### ACTIVITIES

Djibouti is a great place for anyone in search of an active holiday. Out on the water there's everything from diving and snorkelling to whale-shark spotting. Away from the water's edge there's great hiking amid superb scenery.

### EMBASSIES & CONSULATES

The following is a list of nations with diplomatic representation in Djibouti City.

**Canadian Consulate** (Map p558; ☎21355950; Pl Lagarde; ⊙8am-noon Sun-Thu)

**Ethiopian Embassy** (Map p556; ☎21350718; Blvd Idriss Omar Guelleh; ⊙8am-2pm Sun-Thu, to noon Sat)

**French Embassy** (Map p556; ☎21350963; www.ambafrance-dj.org; Ave Mohammad Ahmad Issa; ⊙7am-1.30pm & 3-6pm Mon & Wed, 7am-1.30pm Sun, Tue & Thu)

**Somaliland Bureau de Liaison** (Somaliland Liaison Office; Map p556; ☎21358758; Ave Mohammad Ahmad Issa; ⊙8am-2pm Sat-Thu)

### PRACTICALITIES

**Electricity** Djibouti uses 220V, 60Hz AC; plugs in general have two-round-pin plugs.

**Newspapers** The most widely read newspaper is *La Nation* (www.lanation.dj), published weekly in French.

**TV** Radiodiffusion Television Djibouti (RTD) broadcasts news and sports. Programs are in Somali, Afar, Arab and French. Most top-end hotels also offer satellite TV.

**US Embassy** (☎21453000; https://dj.usembassy.gov; Lotissement Haramous; ⏰by appointment)

## INTERNET ACCESS

➡ There are a couple of internet cafes in Djibouti City. Outside the capital, internet cafés are virtually nonexistent.

➡ Wireless is widespread and free in most hotels in Djibouti City.

➡ Connection is fairly good by Western standards.

## LGBTIQ TRAVELLERS

Although homosexuality is not illegal per se in Djibouti, it's severely condemned by both traditional and religious cultures, and remains a topic of absolute taboo. Although gay locals obviously exist, they behave with extreme discretion and caution. Gay and lesbian travellers are advised to do likewise.

## MONEY

➡ The unit of currency is the Djibouti franc (DFr). Coins are in denominations of DFr1, 2, 5, 10, 20, 50, 100 and 500. Notes are available in DFr1000, 2000, 5000 and 10,000.

➡ All the ATMs in Djibouti City accept Visa. ATMs accepting MasterCard are harder to find.

➡ Visa credit cards are accepted at some upmarket hotels and shops, and at some larger travel agencies and airline offices. Some places levy a commission of about 5% for credit-card payment.

➡ There are many banks and a couple of authorised foreign exchange bureaux in the capital. Outside the capital, banking facilities are almost nonexistent.

➡ The euro and the US dollar are the favoured hard currencies; euros and dollars in cash and an ATM card – preferably Visa – are the way to go.

### Exchange Rates

| | | |
|---|---|---|
| Australia | A$1 | DFr134 |
| Canada | C$1 | DFr132 |
| Euro zone | €1 | DFr192 |
| Japan | ¥100 | DFr194 |
| New Zealand | NZ$1 | DFr126 |
| UK | UK£1 | DFr215 |
| USA | US$1 | DFr176 |

For current exchange rates, see www.xe.com.

### ℹ PRICE RANGES

The following price ranges refer to a double room with bathroom.

**$** less than DFr10,000

**$$** DFr10,000 to DFr25,000

**$$$** more than DFr25,000

The following price ranges refer to a main course.

**$** less than DFr1000

**$$** DFr1000-2500

**$$$** more than DFr2500

## OPENING HOURS

The following are common business hours in Djibouti. Friday is the weekly holiday for offices and most shops.

**Banks** 7.30am–12.30pm and 4-6pm Sun–Thu

**Government offices** 8am–12.30pm and 4–6pm Sat–Thu

**Restaurants** Breakfast 6.30am–8am, lunch 11.30am–2.30pm, dinner 6.30–10pm

**Shops and businesses** Typically 7.30am–1.30pm and 4–6.30pm Sat–Thu

## PUBLIC HOLIDAYS

As well as Islamic holidays, which change dates every year, the following are the principal public holidays in Djibouti:

**New Year's Day** 1 January

**Labour Day** 1 May

**Independence Day** 27 June

**Christmas Day** 25 December

## SAFE TRAVEL

Djibouti is one of the safest destinations in Africa, partly because of the large Western military presence.

➡ Serious crime or hostility aimed specifically at travellers is very rare, and there's no more to worry about here than in most other countries.

➡ In Djibouti City, take care in crowded areas and markets, as pickpockets may operate, and avoid walking on your own in the Quartier 1, immediately south of Les Caisses market.

➡ The risk of theft and pickpocketing diminishes considerably outside the capital.

➡ Note that Djibouti's security services are sensitive and active. Remain polite and calm if questioned by police officers.

## TELEPHONE

➡ Mobile-phone coverage is pretty good across Djibouti.

➡ Depending on which mobile network you use at home, your phone may or may not work while in Djibouti: ask your mobile network provider.

➡ If you have a GSM phone and it has been 'unlocked', you can use a local SIM card (DFr1000) purchased from **Djibouti Telecom** (Map p556; www.adjib.dj; Rue Bourhan Bey; ⏰7.30am-noon & 5-7pm Sat-Thu).

- You can buy credit at some shops in the form of scratch cards (DFr500 to DFr5000).

### Emergency & Important Numbers

Djibouti does not use area codes.

| | |
|---|---|
| Djibouti's country code | ☎253 |
| International access code | ☎00 |
| Emergency | ☎119 |
| Police | ☎17 |

### TOURIST INFORMATION

The Office National du Tourisme de Djibouti (ONTD; www.visitdjibouti.dj) is the only tourist-information body in Djibouti. It has one tourist office (p560) in the capital. Tour agencies are also reliable sources of travel information.

Information for travellers is hard to come by outside the country. In Europe, contact **Association Djibouti Environnement Nomade** (ADEN; ☎France 01 48 51 71 56; domglobetrotter@gmail.com; 64 rue des Meuniers, 93100 Montreuil-sous-Bois, France), which functions as a kind of tourist office abroad. Run by Dominique Lommatzsch, a French national, it promotes sustainable tourism and can help with bookings in the *campements touristiques*.

### VISAS

All visitors, including French nationals, must have a visa to enter Djibouti.

### Obtaining a Visa

Tourist visas cost from US$50 to US$80 depending on where you apply, and are valid for one month. Visas can be obtained at the nearest Djibouti embassy (including Addis Ababa, Ethiopia, if you're in the Horn). Some embassies are easier to deal with than others.

Travellers from most Western countries can also obtain a single-entry tourist visa on arrival at the airport, but you'll need a letter of invitation from a sponsor – a local tour operator or a hotel. Be sure to arrange it a few days prior to arrival. If you're travelling with a tour company it will take care of this for you. The visa costs €55 for three days and €80 for one month. Payment can also be made in US dollars.

You must have a valid visa to enter overland as none are available at borders. That said, travellers coming from Somaliland have reported having been allowed to purchase their visa at the Loyaada border for €80 or the equivalent in US dollars.

### Visas for Onward Travel

Visas for the following neighbouring countries are available from embassies in Djibouti City.

**Ethiopia** A one-month, single-entry visa costs DFr7200 (DFr12,600 for US nationals). You need to supply two photos. It takes 24 hours to process. Visas are also easily obtained at Bole International Airport in Addis Ababa.

**Somaliland** A one-month, single-entry visa costs DFr5600. You need to supply one photo and it's issued within 24 hours.

## Getting There & Away

### AIR

For most travellers, your best bet is to fly to Dubai, Doha, Addis Ababa, Istanbul or Nairobi and find an onward connection to Djibouti. You can also fly direct from Paris.

Djibouti has one international gateway for arrival by air, Djibouti-Ambouli Airport (p560), about 5km south of Djibouti City. Djibouti does not have a national airline.

### LAND

### Border Crossings

**Eritrea** The border with Eritrea is closed.

**Ethiopia** The two crossings from Ethiopia are Gelille and Galafi.

**Somaliland** The border crossing is at Loyaada.

All borders are open daily. Border posts are generally open at least between 8am and 5pm.

### Bus

There is a daily bus service between Djibouti City and Dire Dawa (Ethiopia) – a strenuous 10- to 12-hour ride on a gravel road (which is being upgraded and asphalted). Take your first bus to the border town of Gelille (DFr1500), then another bus to Dire Dawa (Birr185). Bring plenty of water.

### Train

Launched in 2017, a Chinese-built railway line links Djibouti City to Addis Ababa in Ethiopia. It should carry passengers.

## Getting Around

### BOAT

A reliable passenger boat operates twice weekly between Djibouti City and Tadjoura and between Djibouti City and Obock, north of the Gulf of Tadjoura.

### BUS

Public transport is available between Djibouti City and major towns, including Dikhil, Tadjoura, Obock and Galafi. It's a cheap way to get around but services are infrequent in remote areas.

### CAR & MOTORCYCLE

The Rte de l'Unité, a good sealed road, covers the 240km from the capital around the Gulf de Tadjoura, as far as Obock.

Most rental agencies make hiring a driver compulsory with their vehicles.

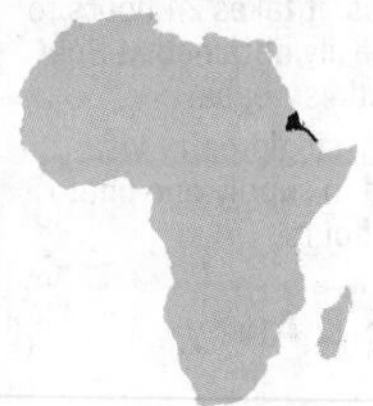

# Eritrea

POP 5.87 MILLION / ☎291

## Includes ➡



## Best Places to Eat

- ➡ Sallam Restaurant (p573)
- ➡ Napoli Pizzeria (p571)
- ➡ Hamasien Restaurant (p571)
- ➡ American Bar (p571)

## Best Places to Sleep

- ➡ Albergo Italia (p570)
- ➡ Grand Hotel Dahlak (p573)
- ➡ Africa Pension Hotel (p570)

## Why Go?

Historically intriguing, culturally compelling and scenically inspiring, Eritrea is one of the most secretive countries in Africa. For those with a hankering for off-the-beaten-track places, it offers challenges and excitement alike, with a unique blend of natural and cultural highlights.

Eritrea wows visitors with its scenery, from the quintessentially Abyssinian landscapes – escarpments, plateaus and soaring peaks – to the deserted and desertified beaches of the Red Sea coast. Culturally, Eritrea is a melting pot. It might be a tiny country by Africa's standards, but it hosts a kaleidoscopic range of ethnic groups. It also features a superb array of archaeological sites that tell volumes of history. The cherry on top is Asmara, Eritrea's delightful capital and a whimsical art deco city. Despite the tough political and economic situation, and the odd travel restrictions, this country remains one of the most inspiring destinations in Africa, particularly for travellers that want something a little different.

## When to Go

### Asmara

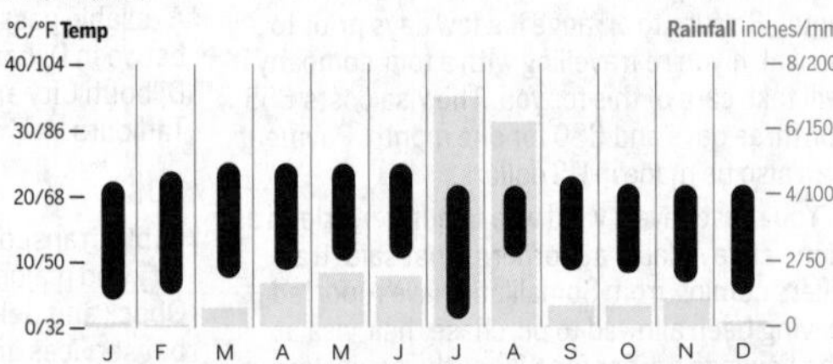


**Jan** Followers of the Orthodox church celebrate Christmas (7th) and Epiphany (19th) in the highlands.

**May** Eritreans take to the streets in celebration of Independence Day on the 24th.

**Sep** Sombre celebrations mark the anniversary of the beginning of the War for Independence on the 1st.

## ASMARA

POP 805,000 / ☎01 / ELEV 2347M

An unexpectedly delightful capital city, Asmara is dotted with art deco and modernist architecture, authentic street-front coffee shops that make for prime people-watching, and sobering testaments to the many difficult years of fighting in the lead up to, and ensuing years since, independence. Also, as long as travel restrictions remain in place for the rest of the country, Asmara offers the most freedom to travellers, with anywhere within 25km of the city fair game for exploration without needing to apply for travel permits.

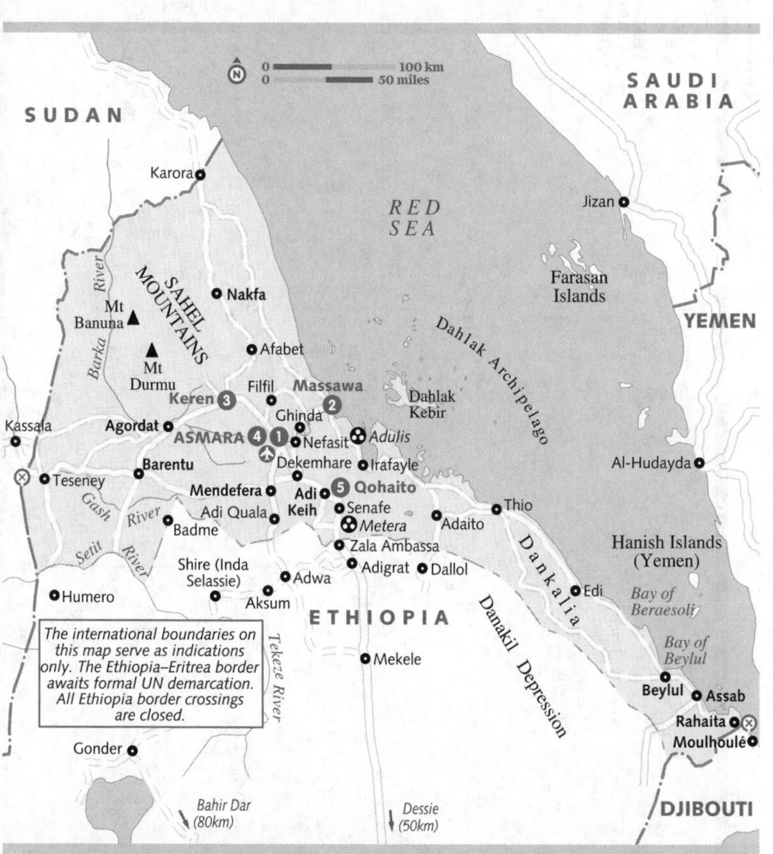


## Eritrea Highlights

1 **Art Deco Architecture** (p572) Discovering Asmara's dazzling collection of colonial-era architectural wonders.

2 **Massawa Old Town** (p573) Exploring the ruined alleyways and faded-glory buildings of this historic coastal town, which suffered heavy bombing at the tail end of the War for Independence.

3 **Keren Camel Market** (p572) Soaking up the languid atmosphere of Eritrea's beguiling and multicultural second city, and joining the weekly walk out to haggle for camels and other livestock on the edge of town.

4 **Tank Graveyard** (p569) Getting a first-hand look at the devastation wrought by decades of war at this military-hardware dumping ground on the outskirts of the capital.

5 **Qohaito** (p573) Speculating on Eritrea's mysterious past at these enigmatic ruins on an old Aksumite trade route.

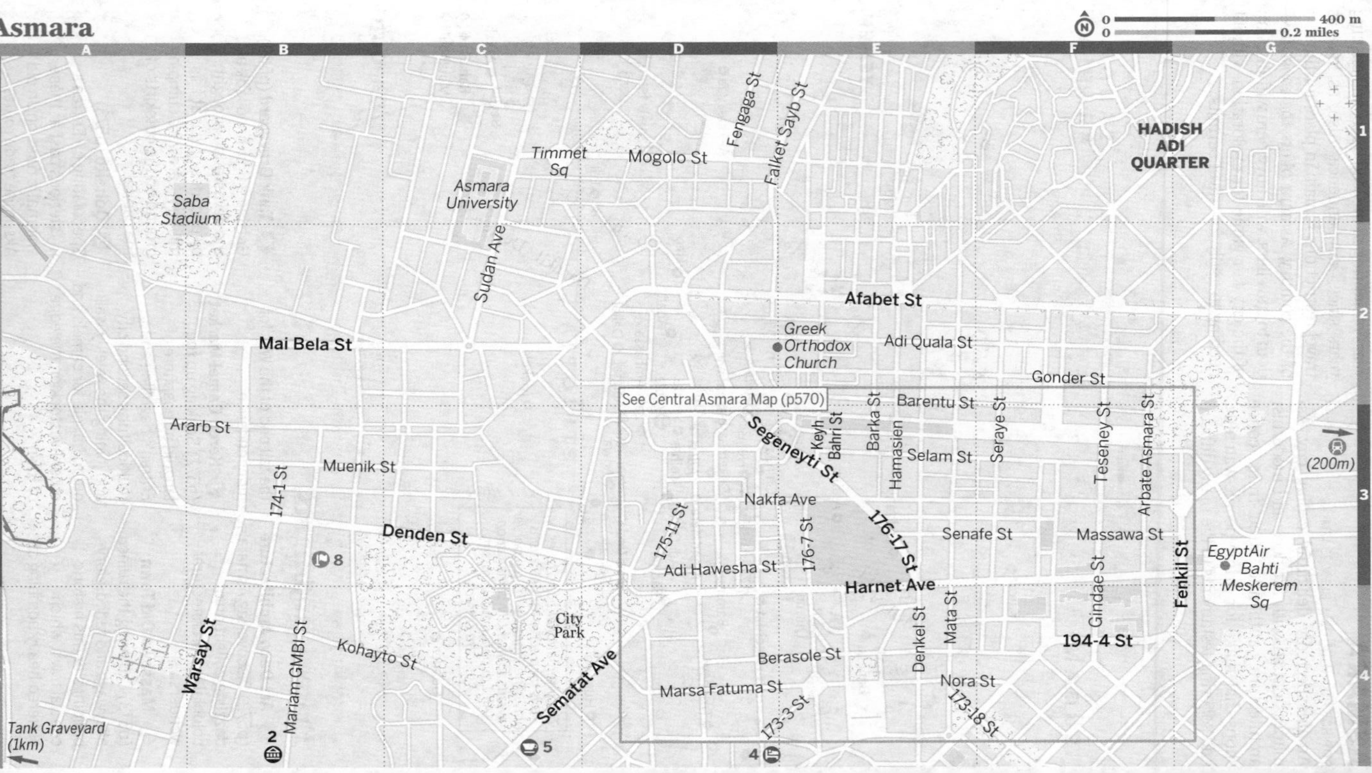
Asmara
400 m
0.2 miles
HADISH ADI QUARTER
Fengaga St
Falket Sayb St
Timmet Sq
Mogolo St
Asmara University
Saba Stadium
Sudan Ave
Afabet St
Mai Bela St
Greek Orthodox Church
Adi Quala St
Gonder St
See Central Asmara Map (p570)
Barentu St
Keyh Bahri St
Barka St
Hamasien
Selam St
Seraye St
Teseney St
Arbate Asmara St
Segeneyti St
Ararb St
Muenik St
174-1 St
Nakfa Ave
175-11 St
176-7 St
176-17 St
Senafe St
Massawa St
Fenkil St
(200m)
EgyptAir
Bahti Meskerem Sq
Denden St
8
Adi Hawesha St
Harnet Ave
Gindae St
Mata St
Denkel St
194-4 St
City Park
Warsay St
Mariam GMBI St
Kohayto St
Sematat Ave
Berasole St
Nora St
Marsa Fatuma St
173-3 St
173-18 St
Tank Graveyard (1km)
2
5
4

## Asmara

**Sights**
1 Fiat Tagliero Building ........ B6
2 National Museum ........ B4

**Activities, Courses & Tours**
3 Asmara Grande ........ A5

**Sleeping**
4 Africa Pension Hotel ........ D4

**Drinking & Nightlife**
5 Cinema Roma ........ C4

**Information**
6 Dutch Honorary Consulate ........ D5
7 Italian Embassy ........ C5
8 UK Embassy ........ B3
9 US Embassy ........ D6

# Sights

**★Bowling Alley** ARCHITECTURE
(Map p570; 22 194-4 St; ⏲7am-1am) A block south of the Municipality Building, the Bowling Alley is one of the few genuine 1950s alleys left in the world. It was probably built for US servicemen when they were manning military bases in the region.

**Fiat Tagliero Building** HISTORIC BUILDING
(Map p568; Sematat Ave) A futurist departure from the art deco standard that defines most of the notable Italian-era buildings in Asmara, this former petrol station was constructed in the late 1930s to resemble an airplane and may be the single most-photographed structure in the city. It's on the northwestern side of the large intersection at Sematat Ave and Mereb St.

**★Opera House** HISTORIC BUILDING
(Map p570; 14 Harnet Ave; ⏲7am to 9pm) FREE The Opera House, completed around 1920, is one of Asmara's most elegant early–20th-century buildings. It's free to have a look around during the resident cafe's opening hours. Or hang around and soak up the atmosphere over a coffee (nfa8; shockingly low quality by Asmara standards) or to use the on-site wi-fi (from nfa20 per hour).

**★Tank Graveyard** MEMORIAL
Part junkyard, part memorial, the ruins of military vehicles from around the country have been dragged to this open field in the years since heavy fighting ended, and make for poignant reflection on the damage done during decades of fighting. Local families have made their homes in a number of

shipping containers in the centre of the area, which you'll need a permit from the Tourist Information Centre to enter, but wander (and photograph) at will apart from this area.

## Tours

**Asmara Grande** TOURS
(Map p568; ☎01 110672, 07 116317; www.asmara-grande.com; 2nd fl, 76 Harbinyatat St; ⊙8am-noon & 3-6pm) Owner Tekeste organises trips to anywhere travel permits can be issued for, including the sometimes-tricky Dahlak Islands, for around $150 per day for transport. The sign is hard to spot, but it's the building on the corner with Warsay St.

## Sleeping

**Africa Pension Hotel** GUESTHOUSE $$
(Map p568; ☎01 121436; 21 Keskese St; d nfa500, with shared bathroom nfa400) A good place to bunk down if you're after style without breaking the bank. This mellow pension from the early 1900s is set in a converted villa and features generous-sized rooms overlooking a pleasantly manicured garden. It's in a residential neighbourhood, a jaunt from Harnet Ave. A tad overpriced, but the historic aura that shrouds the place sweetens the deal.

**Khartoum Hotel** HOTEL $$
(Map p570; ☎01 128008; 35 176-13 St; d from nfa500, with shared bathroom nfa300) One block south of Harnet Ave, the Khartoum offers super-clean rooms, and the shared bathrooms are probably the cleanest-smelling bathrooms this side of the Rift Valley. Friendly owner Yamani can arrange drivers for trips to explore outside of Asmara, and the on-site restaurant whips up tasty local dishes.

★**Albergo Italia** BOUTIQUE HOTEL $$$
(Map p570; ☎01 120740; www.albergoitaliaasmara.com; 1 Nakfa Ave; r/ste nfa1500/1750; 📶) A lovely boutique-ish hotel housed in an Italian villa constructed in 1899, with cushy rooms decorated with period furniture and communal

## Central Asmara

areas awash with heritage aesthetics. You won't have to go far for nosh, either, as the in-house restaurant serves up a decent pizza and coffee.

## Eating

If you're craving generously portioned curries ladled over spongy *injera* bread or Italian classics straight from the old country, Asmara is a culinary heaven. What the local menu lacks in diversity of choice, it makes up for in quality and taste; you're not going hungry while you're here.

**American Bar** FAST FOOD $
(Map p570; ☎01 120564; 47 Harnet Ave; coffee nfa10, mains nfa50; ⏰6am-9pm) This snazzy fast-food joint serves up decent burgers and explosively fruity cocktails. The streetside terrace allows for a dash of people-watching panache with the historic Opera House in the background.

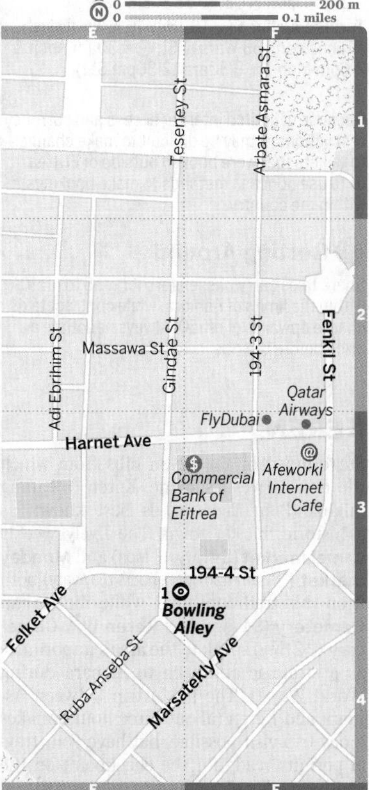


**Cathedral Snack Bar** CAFE $$
(Map p570; 82 Harnet Ave; mains nfa78; ⏰8am-10pm) An inviting spot almost opposite the Catholic cathedral, serving a small food selection and a range of drinks (nfa8).

**Napoli Pizzeria** PIZZA $$$
(Map p570; ☎01 123784; 36 Adi Hawesha St; mains nfa130-240; ⏰10am-11pm) Italian-style pizza in a cosy parlour, with warm staff and cold beer. This is comfort food in a comfortable setting, with no pretensions to being otherwise.

**Hamasien Restaurant** ERITREAN $$$
(Map p570; ☎01 122981; 19 Seraye St; mains nfa150-300; ⏰7am-10pm) The huge platters of *injera* and Eritrean curries are the stars of the show here, but there's also a wide selection of Italian and fast-food options.

## Drinking & Nightlife

Lingering long over a drink is something of a way of life in Asmara. During the early-evening *passeggiata* there's nowhere better than the streetside seating on Harnet Ave, but after dark it's worth heading out to some of the cool retro bars outside the city centre.

★**Cinema Roma** CAFE
(Map p568; ☎01 116689; 97 Sematat Ave; ⏰7.30am-10.30pm) An inspiring place from the late 1930s, with one of Asmara's finest historic interiors and playbills for films by Frederico Fellini still posted out front. Enjoy a beer or a coffee in the cinema-themed lobby, or on weekends pack into the old theatre with cheering local crowds for irregular live screenings of international football matches.

## Information

### INTERNET ACCESS

While it *is* the fastest in the country, internet access in Asmara is still painfully slow.

### Central Asmara

**Top Sights**
1 Bowling Alley ... E3
2 Opera House ... B3

**Sleeping**
3 Albergo Italia ... A2
4 Khartoum Hotel ... D3

**Eating**
5 American Bar ... B3
6 Cathedral Snack Bar ... C3
7 Hamasien Restaurant ... D2
8 Napoli Pizzeria ... A3

DON'T MISS

## ART (DECO) ATTACK IN ASMARA

Asmara is one of the most entrancing cities in Africa. It usually comes as a surprise to travellers to discover a slick city crammed with architectural gems harking back to the city's heyday as the 'Piccolo Roma' (small Rome). Isolated for nearly 30 years during its war with Ethiopia, Asmara escaped both the trend to build post-colonial piles and the push towards developing-world urbanisation. Thus, it has kept its heritage buildings almost intact. Wander the streets in the centre and you'll gaze upon a showcase of art deco, international, cubist, expressionist, functionalist, futurist, rationalist and neoclassical architectural styles. Among the most outstanding buildings are the Opera House, the Ministry of Education, the Cinema Impero, the Municipality Building and the Cinema Roma. But nothing can compare with the Fiat Tagliero Building, a superb example of a futuristic architecture. Built in 1938, it is designed to look like an aeroplane (or a spaceship, or a bat). The best way to see Asmara's architectural heritage is to simply walk around town.

**Afeworki Internet Cafe** (Map p570; ☎01 111820; 222 Harnet Ave; per hour from nfa20; ⏲8am-11pm; 📶) Wi-fi plus comfy couches to sink into while you wait for pages to load. If you really need a fast connection, buy a timed ticket and then come back early the next morning before the rest of the city starts hitting the bandwidth.

**Erena Internet Cafe** (Map p570; 129 Harnet Ave; per hour from nfa20; ⏲9am-11pm; 📶) There's wi-fi (always) and computers (when the city's power is working) in this 2nd-floor internet cafe.

### MEDICAL SERVICES

**Sembel Hospital** (☎01 150175; Warsay St) The most reputable hospital in town, on the road to the airport.

### MONEY

Any of the many *himbol* (exchange) shops around town can change foreign currencies.

**Commercial Bank of Eritrea** (Map p570; ☎01 122425; 208 Harnet Ave; ⏲8-11am & 2-4pm Mon-Sat) Changes cash and travellers cheques at the official rate, but you'll need your passport; if there's no line, this will often be the quickest currency-exchange option. Also acts as an agent for Western Union.

### TOURIST INFORMATION

**Tourist Information Centre** (Map p570; ☎01 124871; 108 Harnet Ave; ⏲8.30am-noon & 2.30-6pm Mon-Fri) Has some brochures and issues the compulsory travel permit (p577).

## ℹ Getting There & Away

The small **airport** (p577) is around 7km from Harnet Ave and is the country's only international air connection to the rest of the world. While services at the airport itself are limited, there are offices in town for the following major international airlines:

**EgyptAir** (Map p568; ☎01 127510; www.egyptair.com; Harnet Ave; ⏲9am-noon & 2-6pm Mon-Fri, 10am-noon Sat)

**FlyDubai** (Map p570; ☎01 112860; www.flydubai.com; 25 194-3 St; ⏲8-11.30am & 2.30-5.30pm Mon-Sat)

**Qatar Airways** (Map p570; ☎01 112690; www.qatarairways.com; 263 Harnet Ave; ⏲8.30am-4.30pm Mon-Fri, 8.30-11.30am Sat)

**Turkish Airlines** (☎01 184949; www.turkishairlines.com; 53 Warsay St; ⏲8.30am-noon & 2-6pm Mon-Fri, 9.30am-12.30pm Sat).

Because of limited internet access and currency restrictions, it may be difficult to make changes to tickets that were booked outside of Eritrea or to use noncash methods to make bookings within the country.

## ℹ Getting Around

Share taxis carry passengers for nfa5 to nfa10 within the limits of Asmara, while contract taxis charge upwards of nfa50. Always negotiate a price before the ride.

# KEREN

Surrounded by the seven hills from which the city derives its name, Keren (meaning 'highland' in Tigrinya) is best known as a historic market town. The lively weekly **camel market** (S-1 Hwy; ⏲Mon) and **Monday market** (⏲8am-4pm Mon, hours may vary) both keep this tradition alive, while the **Italian Cemetery** (S-1 Hwy) and **Keren War Cemetery** (P-2 Hwy) speak to the area's importance as a strategic approach to Asmara during World War II. The 95km trip between Asmara and Keren (about three hours) makes a day-trip visit possible, but have your travel permits ready for the checkpoint on the southern edge of town.

# MASSAWA

POP 53,090 / ☎01

Once called the 'Pearl of the Red Sea', Massawa is now a more faded-glory beauty, as the historic Ottoman, Egyptian and Italian architecture continues to fall further into the disrepair originally inflicted by the final days of fighting of the War for Independence in 1991. Budding historians and photographers continue to explore the **Old Town** in small numbers, while nearby beaches (both on the mainland and in the Dahlak Islands) and the archaeological excavations at Adulis also draw their share of visitors.

The road from Asmara to Massawa winds down from the highlands through several large canyons before finally reaching sea level and the empty desert on the final approach to the coast. En route you'll pass though the highland market town of **Ghinda**; it's worth a wander if you have time to spare, particularly on Wednesdays when residents of surrounding villages come in for the weekly market.

## Sights

**Imperial Palace** PALACE

(Taulud Island) Overlooking the harbour just north of the gates of the Dahlak Hotel is the Imperial Palace, the original iteration of which was built by the Turkish Osdemir Pasha in the 16th century. The present building dates from 1872, when it was built for the Swiss adventurer Werner Munzinger. During the federation with Ethiopia, it was used as a winter palace by Emperor Haile Selassie, whose heraldic lions still decorate the gates and by whose name the building is still commonly referred to.

**House of Mammub Mohammed Nahari** HISTORIC BUILDING

(Old Town) The ancient House of Mammub Mohammed Nahari was built with magnificent soaring Ottoman-style windows on every side. Unfortunately they are particularly decrepit and, like the rest of the house, seem ready to crumble at any moment, so take particular care about wandering inside. Nearby are several large and ornate 18th-century Armenian and Jewish merchant houses.

## Sleeping

**Red Sea Hotel** HOTEL $$

(☎01 552839; Taulud Island; s/d nfa660/780; ❄) This Italian-designed hotel is well arranged and has 50 tidy rooms with big bathrooms, air-con, satellite TV, balcony and sea views. Facilities include a restaurant, and gardens in which to curl up with a book.

**Grand Hotel Dahlak** BOUTIQUE HOTEL $$$

(Dahlak Hotel; ☎01 552782; Taulud Island; s/d nfa725/1450; ❄ 📶 🏊) This faded-beauty anchor of Taulud Island's waterfront is the top choice in town, with a colonial-era vibe, but at Western prices. Usually referred to locally as the 'Dahlak Hotel', it's also the site of the only wi-fi on the islands.

## Eating

★ **Sallam Restaurant** SEAFOOD $$$

(☎01 552187; Old Town; mains nfa160-300; ⏲7-11pm) It doesn't look like much from the outside and even worse inside, but this place is *the* culinary gem of Massawa. Here you can relish the Yemeni-style fresh fish sprinkled with hot pepper and baked in a tandoori oven. The fish, served with a chapatti flat bread, is absolutely superb.

**Seghen Restaurant** SEAFOOD $$$

(☎01 180250; Old Town; mains nfa180-250; ⏲6am-11pm) In the same colonnaded arcades that house the Hotel Savoiya, the outdoor seating here is popular for breakfast and dinner when the mercury is manageable. There's a range of cuisines on the menu, but you'll do best to stick with the seafood – especially the 'finger fish'.

## Information

Change cash or travellers cheques at the **Commercial Bank of Eritrea** (Old Town; ⏲7.30-11.30am & 4-5.30pm Mon-Fri, 7-10.30am Sat) or the front desk of the Dahlak Hotel, both of which offer the official rate.

WORTH A TRIP

### QOHAITO

Historians debate whether or not the ruins of **Qohaito** were once the inhabited walls of the ancient town of Koloe, a settlement that predated, but grew to commercial importance during, the Aksumite kingdom. Even if it wasn't, the city's impressively large remains are testament to its once-great stature.

Though there's no admission fee, a permit from the **National Museum** (Map p568; 43 Mariam GMBI St; ⏲9-11am & 3-5pm Thu-Tue) FREE is mandatory – as is on-site guide Ibrahim who lives in the upper village of Qohaito and expects a gratuity for his time. Nfa200 or so is suggested. The village of Adi Keih is approximately 110km from Asmara, and from here it's a further 25km to Qohaito.

# Massawa

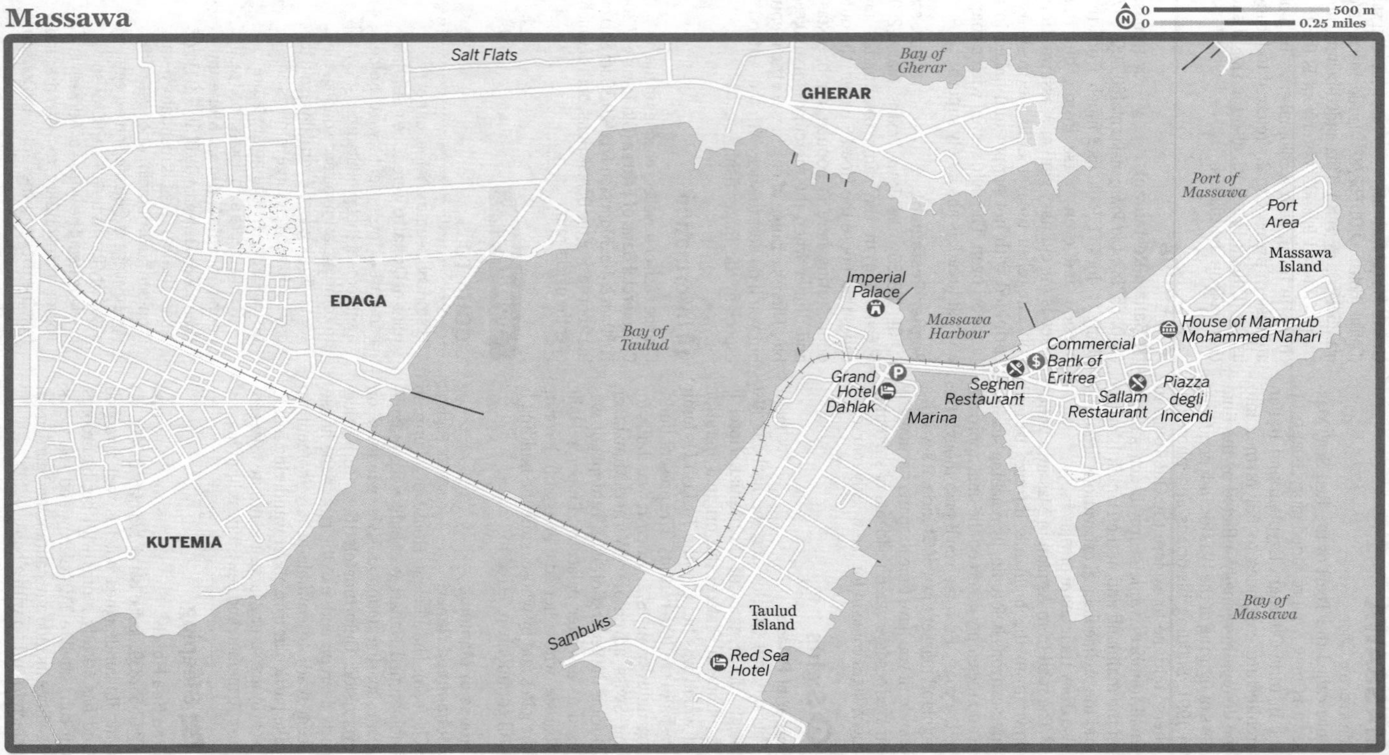

0 500 m
0 0.25 miles

Salt Flats
Bay of Gherar
GHERAR
Port of Massawa
Port Area
Massawa Island
EDAGA
Imperial Palace
Bay of Taulud
Massawa Harbour
House of Mammub Mohammed Nahari
Commercial Bank of Eritrea
Grand Hotel Dahlak
Seghen Restaurant
Sallam Restaurant
Piazza degli Incendi
Marina
KUTEMIA
Taulud Island
Bay of Massawa
Sambuks
Red Sea Hotel

### Getting There & Away

The town of Massawa is approximately 120km (around three hours) from Asmara; from here it's a further 56km (around 1½ hours) to Adulis.

# UNDERSTAND ERITREA

## Eritrea Today

Today Eritrea is not exactly a wonderland. Freedom of press and speech is nonexistent, the state has taken control of all private companies, and the country has one of the most restrictive economies on the planet. Mass conscription has deprived many industries of manpower. The end result? Eritrea has won the less-than-enviable sobriquet of 'the North Korea of Africa', while the slightly more generous might realistically compare it to Cuba. Despite these harsh realities and the clampdown on civil liberties, Eritreans show an exceptional resilience and have not entirely lost hope in the future of their country.

## History

### Aksum, Islam & the Ottomans

Around the 4th century BC the powerful kingdom of Aksum, situated in Tigray in the north of modern Ethiopia, began to develop. Much foreign trade – on which Aksum's prosperity depended – was seaborne, and came to be handled by the ancient port of Adulis in what is now Eritrea. Islam, the arrival of which coincided with the beginning of Christian Aksum's decline in the 7th century, was the other great influence on the region. Islam made the greatest inroads in the Dahlak Islands, while Muslim traders also settled in nearby Massawa on the mainland.

The Turks first arrived in the Red Sea at the beginning of the 16th century. For the next 300 years (with a few short-lived intervals) the coast, including the port of Massawa, belonged to the Ottomans.

### European Aspirations & WWII

Following the Battle of Adwa in 1896, when the Ethiopians resoundingly defeated the Italian armies, new international boundaries were drawn up: Ethiopia remained independent and Eritrea became, for the first time, a separate territory – and an Italian colony. Of all Italy's colonies (Eritrea, Libya and Italian Somaliland), Eritrea was considered the jewel in the crown, and much effort was put into industrialising the little territory. The year 1941 marked a turning point: the British took the strategically important town of Keren and forced the Italians to flee from Asmara.

### Fight for Independence

In 1950 the contentious Resolution 390 A (V) was passed. Eritrea became Ethiopia's 14th province and disappeared from the map of Africa. When in the early 1960s Ethiopia formally annexed Eritrea in violation of international law, Cold War politics ensured that both the US and the UN kept silent.

In 1961 the fight for independence began. In 1990, amid some of the fiercest fighting of the war, the Eritrean People's Liberation Front (EPLF) took the strategically important port of Massawa. By a fortunate turn of events, the Ethiopian dictator Mengistu was overthrown in 1991, his 140,000 troops fled Eritrea and a final confrontation in the capital was avoided. The EPLF walked into Asmara without having to fire a single bullet.

In April 1993 the provisional government of Eritrea held a referendum on Eritrean independence. More than 99% of voters opted for full Eritrean sovereignty, and on 24 May 1993 independence was declared.

### Postindependence

After the war, the little nation worked hard to rebuild its infrastructure, repair the economy and improve conditions for its people. Eritrea was also at pains to establish good international relations with, among others, Ethiopia, the Gulf States, Asia, the USA and Europe. However, this progress was seriously undermined in 1998, when war broke out with Ethiopia. In February 1999 a full-scale military conflict broke out that left tens of thousands dead on both sides before it finally ceased for good in mid-2000. UN forces remained in the country until 2008.

For the moment a wary calm prevails, but everyone knows that the merest spark could reignite a war that neither country can afford, as seemed likely as recently as June 2016 when hundreds died in clashes between the two countries.

## Religion

The population of Eritrea is almost equally divided between Christians and Muslims. Christians are primarily Orthodox; the

Eritrean Orthodox Church has its roots in the Ethiopian one but separated after liberation. There are also small numbers of Roman Catholics and Lutheran Protestants.

# SURVIVAL GUIDE

## Directory A–Z

### ACCOMMODATION

There is a solid range of accommodation in Asmara and Massawa. Outside of these cities, , expect only the basics.

### DANGERS & ANNOYANCES

Eritrea is a safe country for travellers, certainly one of the safest in Africa, but you should take the usual precautions.

➜ Be careful of discussing sensitive topics with locals you don't know well; being overheard by the wrong ears can land both of you in trouble.

➜ When travelling throughout the country be aware of conditions on winding rural roads, and try to avoid driving at night.

### EMBASSIES & CONSULATES

Australia, New Zealand and Ireland do not have diplomatic representation in Eritrea. The following offices are all in Asmara.

**Canadian Honorary Consulate** (☎01 186490; mkcca1@yahoo.com)

**Dutch Honorary Consulate** (Map p568; ☎01 125039, emergency 07 128351; http://sudan.nlembassy.org/organization/honorary-consulates/honorary-consulate-in-asmara-eritrea; 187 171-3 St)

**French Embassy** (☎01 182875, emergency 07 116392; 8th fl, 53 Warsay St; ⏲8am-5pm Mon-Fri)

**German Embassy** (☎01 186670, emergency 07 115571; www.asmara.diplo.de; 8th fl, 53 Warsay St; ⏲9am-noon Mon-Fri or by appointment)

**Italian Embassy** (Map p568; ☎01 121852; BDHO Ave; ⏲10am-noon Mon-Fri) Look for Villa Milloni on BDHO Ave, from which the consular entrance is up the small side street to the left.

**UK Embassy** (Map p568; ☎01 120145, emergency 07 165316; 68 Mariam GMBI St; ⏲8am-12.30pm & 1.30-4.30pm Mon-Thu, 8am-12.30pm Fri)

**US Embassy** (Map p568; ☎01 120004; http://eritrea.usembassy.gov; 179 Alaa St; ⏲by appointment only)

### EMERGENCY & IMPORTANT NUMBERS

| | |
|---|---|
| Eritrea's country code | ☎291 |
| Police | ☎01 127799 |
| Ambulance | ☎01 202914 |

### INTERNET ACCESS

Accessing the internet has grown much easier in the past few years, and every small town seems to have at least one or two internet cafes. These will generally sell login details for set blocks of time (anywhere from 30 minutes to four or more hours) that are valid for a certain period, usually a few days. However, speeds are stiflingly slow at best and downright unusable at worst.

### MONEY

There are no international ATMs in Eritrea and credit cards aren't much use. Bring all the cash (US dollars get the best rates) you expect to need.

#### Exchange Rates

| | | |
|---|---|---|
| Australia | $1 | nfa11.7 |
| Canada | $1 | nfa11.7 |
| Euro zone | €1 | nfa16.2 |
| Japan | ¥100 | nfa13.5 |
| New Zealand | $1 | nfa11 |
| UK | £1 | nfa19 |
| US | $1 | nfa15.3 |

For current exchange rates, see www.xe.com.

### OPENING HOURS

Most businesses and offices are open from 8am to 6pm, with a midday break between noon and 2pm for lunch at government offices and smaller businesses.

**Banks** 8am–noon and 2pm–6pm Monday to Friday

**Bars and clubs** 6pm–midnight Monday to Saturday

**Government offices** 8am–noon and 2pm–6pm Monday to Friday

**Restaurants and cafes** 7am–10pm

**Shops** 9am–noon and 2pm–7pm Monday to Saturday

#### PRICE RANGES

The following price ranges refer to a double room with bathroom in high season.

**$** less than nfa375

**$$** nfa375–nfa1125

**$$$** more than nfa1125

Average prices for a main course:

**$** less than US$5 (nfa75)

**$$** US$5–US$10 (nfa75–nfa150)

**$$$** more than US$10 (nfa150)

## TRAVEL PERMITS

- Travel permits are necessary for all travel outside of the Greater Asmara region, defined as roughly 25km from the city. At the time of writing, permits were being issued for (and so tourists were allowed to visit) the areas of Massawa, Keren, Ghinda, Adulis, Senefe and Adi Keih. Any number of sites may be added to a single permit, but the schedule submitted with the permit must be adhered to and cannot be amended once the permit is issued.
- To visit archaeological sites such as Adulis and Qohaito, an additional cultural permit from the directorate of the National Museum (p573) in Asmara is required. In practice it is often impossible to do this without either a tour agency or local contacts.
- The Dahlak Islands, Semenawi Bahri National Park, Nakfa and Teseney were all closed to foreigners at the time of writing; international residents of Asmara, however, report that the Dahlak Archipelago is generally accessible.
- Asmara's Tourist Information Centre (p572) issues travel permits. To obtain one, you'll need to present a photocopy of your passport details and visa pages. If you're renting a car you'll need to record the licence-plate number of the car, and if you're hiring a driver you'll also need a photocopy of their national ID. If documents are dropped off in the morning, it's generally possible to process a permit same-day.

### PUBLIC HOLIDAYS

Eritrea observes the following national holidays:

**Lidet (Orthodox Christian Christmas)** 7 January

**Timket (Orthodox Christian Epiphany)** 19 January

**Fenkil Day** 10 February

**Women's Day** 8 March

**Easter** March/April

**Fasika (Orthodox Christian Easter)** April/May

**International Day of Workers** 1 May

**Independence Day** 24 May

**Martyr's Day** 20 June

**Eid-Al-Fitr** June/July

**Eid-Al-Adha** August/September

**Revolution Day** 1 September

**Geez New Year** 11 September

**Discovery of the True Cross (Meskel)** 27 September

**Birth of the Prophet** November/December

**Christmas Day** 25 December

### TELEPHONE

Procuring a local SIM card is nearly impossible for international visitors, and SIM cards from international providers will not connect to Eritrean networks.

### TOURIST INFORMATION

Guidance and travel tips are available at the Tourist Information Centre (p572) in Asmara.

### VISAS

While citizens of Uganda and Kenya may visit visa-free and citizens of Sudan can obtain visas on arrival, all other foreign nationals require a valid visa to enter Eritrea. In the majority of cases visitors are required to apply at the embassy or consulate that is accredited to their place of residence, a process than can often take months between application and approval, but increasingly travellers report that tour agencies in Asmara are able to provide visa-on-arrival invitations with minimal fuss. Whichever route you decide to pursue, begin the process before your travels begin.

## Getting There & Away

### AIR

There is currently no functioning national airline, but even when there was, it never got off the European Commission blacklist. Stick with international operators. The only airport currently accepting commercial flights in the country is Asmara International Airport, though in theory Massawa is another possible option.

### LAND

For a number of years the only open land border crossings have been those between Eritrea and Sudan, and these are officially open only to citizens of these two countries.

## Getting Around

### BUS

There is an extensive bus network through Eritrea, though departures to outlying areas are infrequent and conditions are quite basic. That said, public buses are generally faster, cheaper and more comfortable than private buses. Until mid-2017 international tourists weren't permitted to use public transport at all, but it should now be possible to get permits to travel on buses to Keren and Massawa.

### CAR & MOTORCYCLE

Travel by private vehicle is the only officially allowed method of transportation for international visitors, and will almost certainly be your single largest expense if you go beyond Asmara.

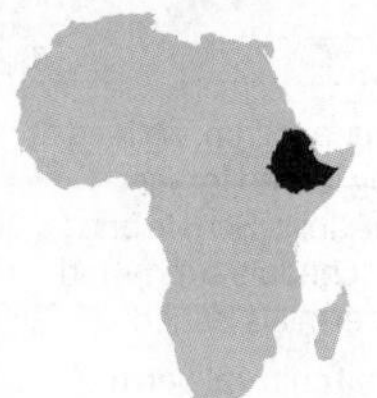

# Ethiopia

POP 102 MILLION / ☎251

### Includes ➡



## Best Places to Eat

- Four Sisters (p588)
- Yod Abyssinia (p583)
- Kategna (p582)
- Itegue Taitu Hotel (p583)
- Hirut Restaurant (p596)
- Fresh Touch Restaurant (p596)

## Best Places to Sleep

- Addissinia Hotel (p582)
- Sheraton Hotel (p582)
- Grand Gato (p596)
- Hotel Maribela (p595)

## Why Go?

Ethiopia is truly a world apart. Here there are over two millenniums' worth of ancient treasures scattered about, from the hidden tombs of the legendary Queen of Sheba to castles that would make Camelot jealous and the breathtaking rock-carved churches of Lalibela, the New Jerusalem.

Not to be outdone by human craftspeople, Mother Nature also let her creative juices flow here. East Africa's great Rift Valley has left some of its most memorable signatures in Ethiopia: milky-brown lakes scar the south and deep canyons and steep peaks wrinkle the land...well, just about everywhere.

Though you can hit the highlights in a couple of weeks it takes three or four for proper exploration. But no matter how long you stay, you'll probably wish for just a few more days.

## When to Go

### Addis Ababa

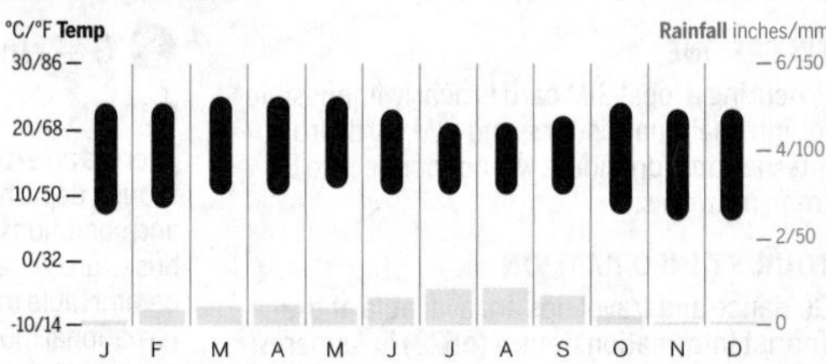


**Jan–Mar** Good for wildlife watching and Ethiopia's most colourful festivals, including Timkat and Leddet.

**Oct–Dec** The country is green, trekking is great and there are fewer visitors.

**Apr–Sep** The rainy season in southern Ethiopia with scorching hot temperatures in the lowlands.

# ADDIS ABABA

POP 4.5 MILLION

Addis – Africa's fourth-largest city and its diplomatic capital – is a traffic-choked, sprawling city of no discernible beauty that many foreign visitors try to transit as quickly as possible. But take note: by skipping out on the contradictions of this complex city you run the risk of failing to understand Ethiopia altogether. And apart from anything else, Addis is the best place in the country to sample Ethiopian food, and has some wonderful museums and places to stay.

## Sights

Most sights are scattered throughout the city centre and Piazza, though there is a concentration of major museums and other sights in the vicinity of Arat Kilo and Siddist Kilo, which sit east of Piazza and north of the city centre.

**★'Red Terror' Martyrs Memorial Museum** MUSEUM

(የቀይ ሽብር ተጠቂዎች ማስታወሻ ሙዚየም; Meskal Sq; by donation; 8.30am-6.30pm) 'As if I bore them all in one night, they slew them in a single night.' These were the words spoken by the mother of four teenage children all killed on the same day by the Derg, as she officially opened the small but powerful 'Red Terror' Martyrs Memorial Museum in 2010. Over a couple of rooms the museum reveals the fall of Emperor Haile Selassie and the horrors of life under Mengistu's Derg regime.

**★Ethnological Museum** MUSEUM

(ብሄራዊ ሙዚየም; 011 123 1068; Addis Ababa University, Algeria St; adult/student Birr100/50; 8am-5pm Mon-Fri, 9am-5pm Sat & Sun) Set within Haile Selassie's former palace, and surrounded by the beautiful gardens and fountains of the university's main campus, is the enthralling Ethnological Museum. Even if you're not a museum fan, this one is worth a bit of your time – it's easily one of the finest museums in Africa, showing the full sweep of Ethiopia's cultural and social history across two floors.

**★National Museum** MUSEUM

(ብሔራዊ ሙዚየም; 011 111 7150; King George VI St; Birr10; 8.30am-5.30pm) The collection on show at the National Museum is ranked among the most important in sub-Saharan Africa, but sadly many of its exhibits are poorly labelled, lit and displayed. Far and away the highlight is the palaeontological exhibition in the basement, the home of world-famous **Lucy**. Her 1974 discovery in the Afar region of northwestern Ethiopia changed our understanding of human origins forever. This section is well labelled in English, so if your time is limited spend most of it here.

**★St George Cathedral & Museum** CHURCH

(ቅዱስጊዮርጊስ ቤተክርስቲያን; Fitawrari Gebeyehu St; museum Birr100; museum 9am-noon & 2-5pm Tue-Sun) Commissioned by Emperor Menelik II to commemorate his stunning 1896 defeat of the Italians in Adwa, and dedicated to St George (Ethiopia's patron saint), whose icon was carried into the battle, this Piazza cathedral is one of Addis' most beautiful churches. The grey stone exterior is easily outdone by the interior's flashes of colour and art. Sections of ceiling glow sky-blue and boast gilded stars, while the outer walls of the innermost shrine are covered in paintings and mosaics by the renowned Afewerk Tekle.

## Tours

There are no scheduled tours of the city itself; however, if you contact one of Addis Ababa's many travel agencies, most can usually arrange something.

**★Go Addis Tours** TOURS

(094 307 6240; www.goaddistours.com; per person US$60-135) This fantastic new kid on the block is your window into the best Addis has to offer. Eliza and Xavier offer a range of city tours, with a particular focus on the capital's best Ethiopian food. Their five-hour Highlights tour is probably our pick with a good mix of sightseeing, a fine lunch stop and good coffee.

**Mandril Wenni Tour & Travel** TOURS

(091 139 3944, 092 794 9257; www.ethiomandriltour.com; Cameroon St) An excellent and relatively new company offering professionally run tours around Ethiopia.

**GETTS Ethiopia** TOURS

(091 123 3289; www.getts.com.et; off Bole Rd/Africa Ave) Well-regarded and professional operator, with countrywide tours with good drivers, guides and vehicles.

**Abeba Tours Ethiopia** TOURS

(011 557 0881, mobile 092 781 9331; www.abebatoursethiopia.com; off Democratic Republic Congo St) Friendly and very professional, this operator seems to go the extra mile for its customers. It organises general tours throughout the country and the drivers it uses are

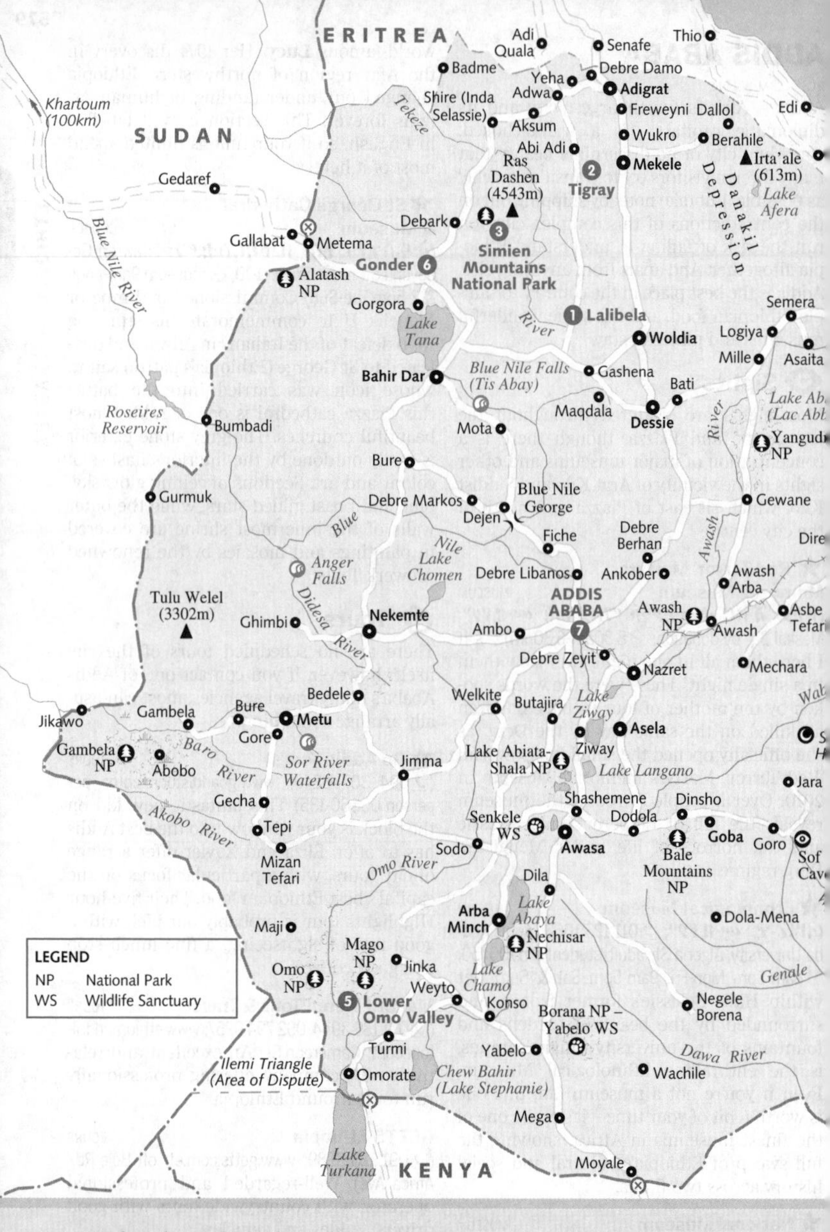


# Ethiopia Highlights

**1 Lalibela** (p593) Immersing yourself in Christianity's most raw and powerful form at these rock churches.

**2 Rock-Hewn Churches of Tigray** (p591) Staring from Abuna Yemata Guh then climbing to the monastery at Maryam Korkor.

**3 Simien Mountains National Park** (p589) Lacing up your boots to hike through the home of magnificent wildlife and unparalleled panoramas.

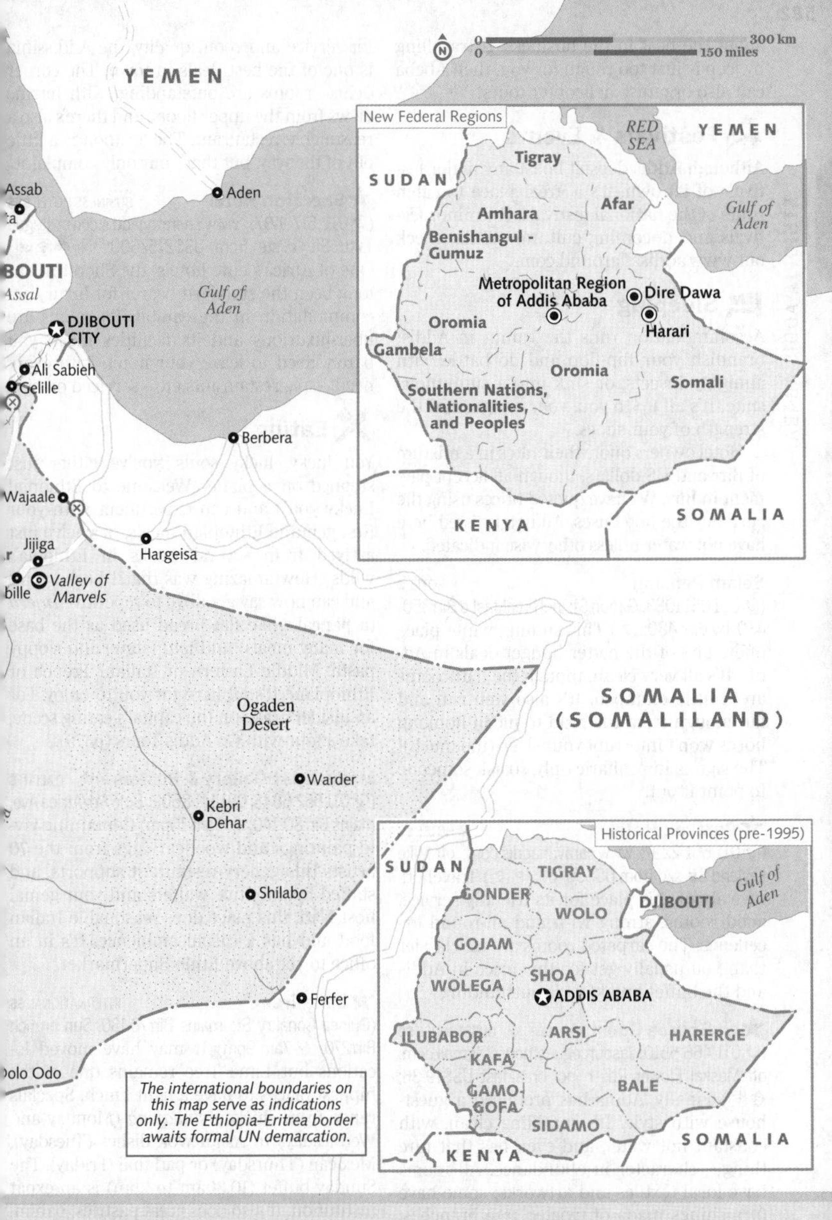


*The international boundaries on this map serve as indications only. The Ethiopia–Eritrea border awaits formal UN demarcation.*

4 **Harar** (p595) Exploring the labyrinth of alleyways and shrines in this old walled city.

5 **Lower Omo Valley** (p596) Visiting 'Africa's last great wilderness' and possibly the continent's most diverse and fascinating peoples.

6 **Gonder** (p587) Feeling the thrill of Africa's 'Camelot' wreathed in legends and full of fascinating historical sites.

7 **Addis Ababa** (p579) Getting to know the capital's superb museums, diverse restaurants and happening nightlife.

about the best in the business. If travelling by jeep is just too rough for you, then Abeba can also organise helicopter tours!

## Festivals & Events

Although Addis doesn't boast any major festivals of its own, it's a great place to catch some of the national festivals. For minor festivals and upcoming cultural events, check out www.addisallaround.com.

## Sleeping

Accommodation runs the gamut in Addis: brandish your flip-flop and do battle with almighty insects, or sink into a sumptuous suite. It's all up to you, your budget and the strength of your shoes.

Hotel owners quote their rates in a mixture of Birr and US dollars, though all accept payment in Birr. We have quoted prices using the currency the hotel uses. All hotels listed here have hot water unless otherwise indicated.

**Selam Pension** HOTEL **$**
(☎091 051 1083; Gabon St; incl breakfast d Birr350-430, tw Birr 480; 📶) This shining white place offers one of the better budget deals in Addis. It's all very clean, though the bathrooms are a little cramped. It's also well run and far enough from the road to mean honking horns won't interrupt your sleep (too much)! The sign is in Amharic only, so ask someone to point it out.

★**Caravan Hotel** HOTEL **$$**
(☎011 661 2297; www.caravanaddis.com; off Mike Leyland St; s/d from US$56/66; P📶) Travellers rave about this place for its friendly service, good rooms, strong wi-fi and all-round excellence. The carpeted rooms are far classier than you usually get for this price in Addis and the buffet breakfast is outstanding.

★**La Source Guest House** GUESTHOUSE **$$**
(☎011 466 5510; lasourceguesthouse@gmail.com; off Meskal Flower Rd; r incl breakfast US$19-36; @📶) Finally, Addis has produced a guesthouse with style. It's sparkling clean, with constant hot water, and even has that rare thing – character in abundance. All rooms have local textiles and artworks; some have furnishings made of twisted tree branches. Service is friendly and, very unusually in this price bracket, it offers a free airport shuttle. The front-facing rooms can be very noisy.

★**Addissinia Hotel** HOTEL **$$$**
(☎011 662 3634; www.addissiniahotel.com; Djibouti St; s/d/tw from US$89/99/129) Getting consistently good reviews from travellers both for service and room quality, the Addissinia is one of the best deals in town. The corner deluxe rooms are outstanding, with terrific views from the upper floors, and there's also a reasonable restaurant. The location is a little out of the way, but that's our only complaint.

★**Sheraton Hotel** BUSINESS HOTEL **$$$**
(☎011 517 1717; www.sheratonaddis.com; Itegue Taitu St; d/ste from US$275/600; ❄@📶🏊) One of Africa's elite hotels, the Sheraton has long been the standard bearer for luxury accommodation in the capital. Its rooms are uber-luxurious and its facilities mean you barely need to leave your hotel, with every need – spa, restaurants etc – serviced on-site.

## Eating

You lucky, lucky souls…you've either just stepped off a plane (Welcome to Ethiopia! Lucky you!) and can experiment with your first genuine Ethiopian meals, or you've just arrived from several weeks in Ethiopia's wilds (How amazing was that?! Lucky you!) and can now say goodbye to repetitive *injera* (a pancake-like flat bread used as the base for many meals) and *wat* (stew) and sloppy pasta. Middle Eastern or Italian? French or Ethiopian? It's all here for you to enjoy. For an insider's take on the capital's eating scene, take a tour with Go Addis Tours (p579).

**Makush Art Gallery & Restaurant** ITALIAN **$**
(☎011 552 6848, 091 141 8602; Bole Rd/Africa Ave; mains Birr80-140; ⊙9am-10pm) Containing vivid paintings and woodcarvings from the 70 artists this gallery-restaurant supports, and staffed by attentive waiters and your genial host Nati, this place does reasonable Italian food and has a casual ambience. It's in an office tower above Ethio Supermarket.

★**Lime Tree** INTERNATIONAL **$$**
(Guinea Conakry St; mains Birr78-130, Sun brunch Birr270; ⊙7am-9pm) It may have moved locations but Lime Tree remains one of the hippest places to have a light lunch. Specials range from chicken *shwarma* (Monday and Wednesday) to Asian wok dishes (Tuesday), Mexican (Thursday) or pad thai (Friday). The Sunday buffet (10.30am to 2pm) is an expat institution. It also does great pastries, panini, felafel, juices and pizzas all day Saturday.

★**Kategna** ETHIOPIAN **$$**
(☎091 152 0183; off Bole Rd/Africa Ave; mains Birr60-160; ⊙8am-10pm) A pleasingly modern take on the traditional Ethiopian restaurant, Kategna feels like a classy urban cafe with its soothing colour scheme, low wood-

en stools and well-to-do young crowd. The menu covers all corners of the Ethiopian culinary scene and does so exceptionally well – its special *kitfo* (like an Ethiopian version of steak tartare) is one highlight among many.

**★Itegue Taitu Hotel** ETHIOPIAN $$
(☎011 156 0787; www.taituhotel.com; mains Birr44-120, lunch buffet Birr70; ⏲7am-10pm, buffet noon-3pm; ✎) If you've travelled overland to Addis Ababa, and eaten in a succession of cheap local restaurants serving less-than-inspiring *injera,* then reward yourself with high-quality, delicious Ethiopian fare served up in the refined and stately atmosphere of this hotel's renovated dining room. Its bargain-priced vegan lunchtime buffet is immensely popular with both foreigners and well-to-do locals.

**★Yod Abyssinia** ETHIOPIAN $$$
(☎011 661 2985, 091 121 6127; www.yodethiopia.com; off Cameroon St; mains Birr160-385; ⏲10am-midnight) Yes, it's touristy, but they sure put on a show at Yod Abyssinia. The large dining area is crammed with low wooden stools that all face a stage; at around 7.30pm, musicians, dancers and singers perform traditional acts from around Ethiopia. The food, too, is some of the best traditional food and it's a good place to try *tej* (honey wine).

## Drinking & Nightlife

You won't go thirsty in Addis Ababa. Sip some of the world's best (and cheapest) coffee, down a healthy juice or simply sway home after swallowing your share of *tej*.

**★Galani Cafe** COFFEE
(☎091 144 6265; www.galanicafe.com; Salite Mehret Rd; coffee Birr27-40; ⏲8.30am-7pm Thu-Sun) This one's worth taking a taxi across Addis for. A cool and contemporary space, Galani serves up Ethiopia's finest barista-poured coffees, from espresso to *piccolo* and from drip-filter coffee to cold coffees. It's also a fine restaurant and dynamic cultural space with art exhibitions, a shop selling coffee, honey and the like, and coffee tastings or 'cuppings'.

**★Tomoca** CAFE
(Wavel St; coffee from Birr10; ⏲6.30am-8.30pm Mon-Sat, to 6pm Sun) Ahh, if only all cafes were like this! Coffee is serious business at this great high-stooled Italian cafe (around since 1953) in Piazza. The beans are roasted on-site (you can literally smell them from a block away) and Tomoca serves some of the capital's best coffee. Beans are also sold by the half-kilo and there's an Ethiopian coffee map on the wall.

### SOLEREBELS FOOTWEAR

Designer Bethlehem Tilahun Alemu set up **soleRebels Footwear** (☎091 059 1180; www.solerebels.com; 2nd fl, Adams Pavilion, Sar Bet; ⏲9.30am-7pm Mon-Sat) as a way of helping the unemployed but tremendously talented artisans in her Addis neighbourhood. Just eight years later, soleRebels is one of Ethiopia's best-known companies internationally and the world's first shoe company to have been certified by the World Fair Trade Organization (WFTO). All its shoes are made using locally sourced natural fibres, handmade fabric and, for soles, old car and truck tyres, and staff are paid up to four times the average wage in Ethiopia.

SoleRebels shoes are available in around 55 countries, including a flagship shop in Addis Ababa.

**★Topia Tej Bet** BAR
(off Haile Gebreselassie Rd; 500ml/1L tej Birr60/120; ⏲10am-9.30pm) Tucked up an alley behind the Axum Hotel, this is Addis' top *tej bet* (honey wine) and the only one to serve pure-honey *tej*. Signposted only in Amharic but with menus in English, it's a congenial place with tables surrounding a tiny garden. The smallest serve is 500ml...

**Black Rose** BAR
(☎011 663 9884; Bole Rd/Africa Ave; ⏲5.30pm-2.30am Mon-Sat, to 12.30am Sun) Hiding in a modern building above the Boston Day Spa, this plush bar possesses a cool vibe and a refined clientele. Music ranges from Ethiopian to Western and Indian, and it's a classy place to spend an evening.

## Shopping

The spectrum of prices and quality of goods for sale in the Ethiopian capital is vast. You'll find most of the cheap souvenir stalls along or around Churchill Ave and in Piazza – haggling is always recommended.

**★St George Interior Decoration & Art Gallery** ARTS & CRAFTS
(☎011 551 0983; www.stgeorgeofethiopia.com; Itegue Taitu St; ⏲9am-1pm & 2.30-6.30pm Mon-Sat) One of Addis Ababa's classiest places to shop, St George has everything from antique silver crosses and contemporary textiles to books about Ethiopia and designer jewellery. Everything here, both modern and traditional, is exquisite and it's worth a wander.

# Addis Ababa

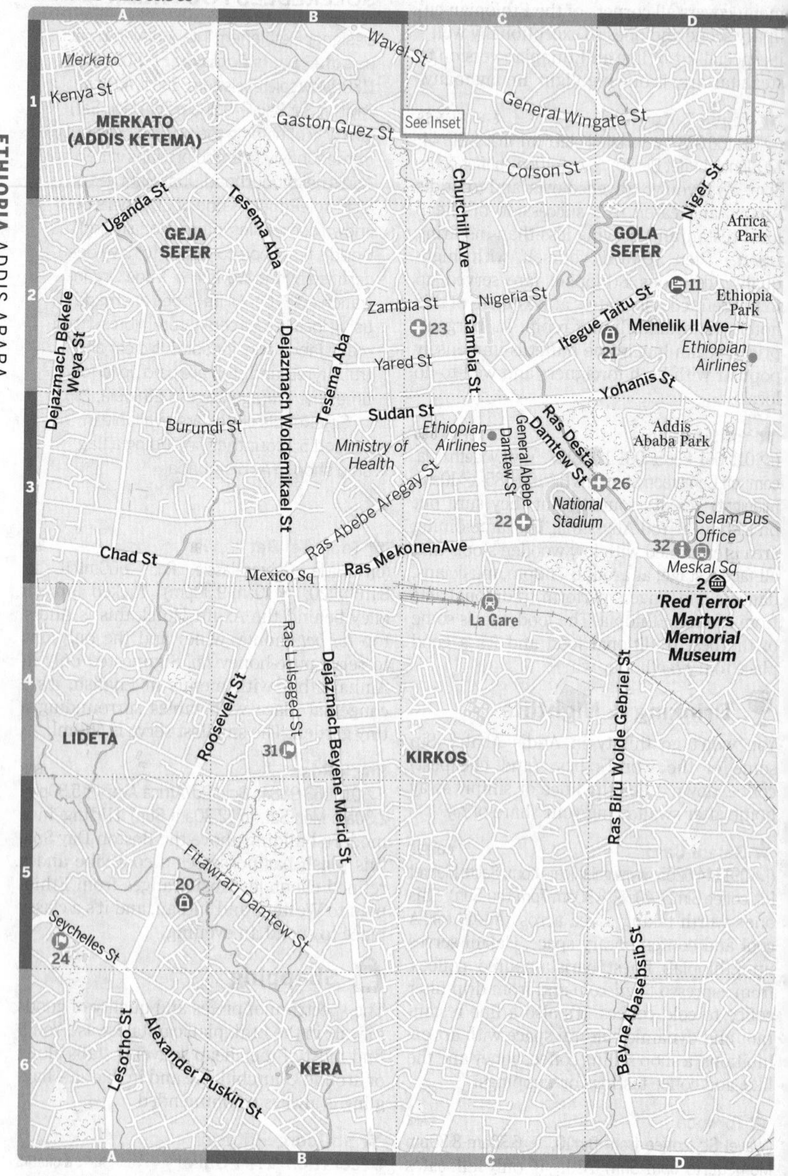


# Information

## DANGERS & ANNOYANCES

Violent crime in Addis Ababa is fortunately rare, particularly where visitors are concerned. However, petty theft and confidence tricks are problematic. The Merkato has the worst reputation for pickpockets. Other spots where you should be vigilant include Piazza, where many foreigners get pickpocketed or mugged; Meskal Sq; minibus stands; outside larger hotels; and Churchill Ave, where adult gangs have been known to hang around the National Theatre. Don't let any of this scare you, though – Addis

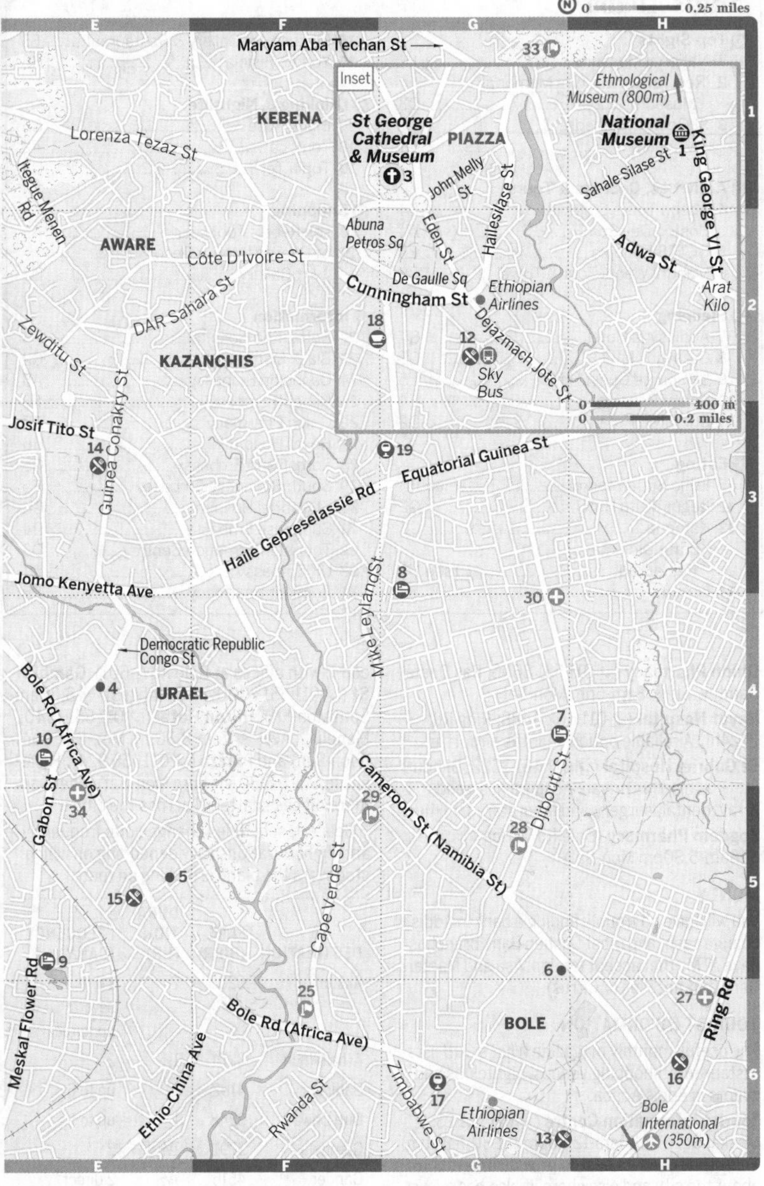


is very safe compared with many other African capitals.

## EMERGENCY

**Police** ☎ 991

**Red Cross Ambulance Service** ☎ 917

## MEDICAL SERVICES

**Bethzatha Hospital** (☎ 011 551 4470; ⏰ 24hr) This quality private hospital, off Ras Mekonen Ave, is recommended by most embassies.

**Black Lion Hospital** (☎ 011 111 1111; ⏰ 24hr) Public hospital

## Addis Ababa

**Top Sights**
1 National Museum .......... H1
2 'Red Terror' Martyrs Memorial Museum .......... D3
3 St George Cathedral & Museum .......... G1

**Activities, Courses & Tours**
4 Abeba Tours Ethiopia .......... E4
Boston Day Spa .......... (see 17)
5 GETTS Ethiopia .......... E5
6 Mandril Wenni Tour & Travel .......... G5

**Sleeping**
7 Addissinia Hotel .......... G4
8 Caravan Hotel .......... G3
9 La Source Guest House .......... E5
10 Selam Pension .......... E4
11 Sheraton Hotel .......... D2

**Eating**
Ethio Supermarket .......... (see 15)
12 Itegue Taitu Hotel .......... G2
13 Kategna .......... G6
Kuriftu Diplomat Restaurant .......... (see 17)
14 Lime Tree .......... E3
15 Makush Art Gallery & Restaurant .......... E5
16 Yod Abyssinia .......... H6

**Drinking & Nightlife**
17 Black Rose .......... G6
18 Tomoca .......... F2
19 Topia Tej Bet .......... G3

**Shopping**
20 soleRebels Footwear .......... A5
21 St George Interior Decoration & Art Gallery .......... D2

**Information**
22 Bethzatha Hospital .......... C3
23 Black Lion Hospital .......... C2
24 Canadian Embassy .......... A5
25 Djibouti Embassy .......... F6
26 Ghion Pharmacy .......... D3
27 Hayat Hospital .......... H6
28 Somaliland Embassy .......... G5
29 South Sudanese Embassy .......... F5
30 St Gabriel Hospital .......... G4
31 Sudanese Embassy .......... B4
32 Tourist Information Centre .......... D3
33 UK Embassy .......... G1
34 Zogdom Pharmacy .......... E5

**Ghion Pharmacy** (☎011 551 8606; Ras Desta Damtew St; ⊙8am-6pm Mon-Sat)

**Hayat Hospital** (☎011 662 4488; Ring Rd; ⊙24hr) A reliable option near the airport.

**St Gabriel Hospital** (☎011 661 3622; Djibouti St; ⊙24hr) This private hospital has good X-ray, dental, surgery and laboratory facilities.

**Zogdom Pharmacy** (Bole Rd/Africa Ave; ⊙8am-5.30pm Mon-Sat)

### MONEY

You will have no trouble finding a bank in Addis to change cash, and most Dashen Bank branches have ATMs that accept foreign Visa and MasterCard (but not Plus or Cirrus).

### TOURIST INFORMATION

The useful, monthly magazine *What's Out!* lists restaurants, shopping venues, nightclubs and events in Addis Ababa.

**Tourist Information Centre** (☎011 551 2310; Meskal Sq; ⊙8.30am-12.30pm & 1.30-5.30pm) This office does its best to provide information about the city and elsewhere. It also has a few informative brochures about the rest of Ethiopia.

## Getting There & Away

### AIR

All domestic flights to/from Addis are operated by Ethiopian Airlines (www.ethiopianairlines.com), with offices at Bole Rd (p601), **Gambia St** (☎011 551 7000; off Gambia St; ⊙8.30am-5pm Mon-Fri), **Hilton Hotel** (☎011 551 1540; Menelik II Ave; ⊙7am-8.30pm Mon-Sat, 8am-noon Sun) and **Piazza** (☎011 156 9247; Hailesilase St; ⊙8.30am-5pm Mon-Sat). There are more offices scattered across the city.

Be alert: schedules change quite frequently and flight durations vary depending on which stopovers the plane is making en route.

| DESTINATION | FARE (BIRR) | DURATION (HR) | FREQUENCY (DAILY) |
|---|---|---|---|
| Aksum | 5200 | 2 | 1 direct, several nondirect |
| Arba Minch | 3274 | 1½ | 2 |
| Bahir Dar | 4192 | 1 | up to 6 |
| Dire Dawa | 3248 | 1 | up to 5 |
| Gambela | 3791 | 1½ | 2 |
| Gonder | 4515 | 1½ | 2 direct, several nondirect |
| Jimma | 2621 | 1 | 2 |
| Lalibela | 4295 | 2-2½ | 1 direct, several nondirect |
| Mekele | 4026 | 1 | 3-5 |

### BUS

The best-established company is **Selam Bus** (☎011 554 4831, 011 554 8800; Meskal Sq; ⏲5am-5pm); its ticket office is on Meskal Sq. It has daily services (all departing at 4.30am or 5am) to Bahir Dar (Birr340, 10 hours), Gonder (Birr420, 13 hours) and Harar (Birr330, 8½ hours). Possibly even slicker is **Sky Bus** (☎011 156 8080, 011 467 3331; http://skybusethiopia.com; Itegue Taitu Hotel; ⏲4.30am-5pm), which also leaves from Meskal Sq, but the ticket office is inside the Itegue Taitu Hotel. These buses have air-con and toilets, and breakfast is included in the ticket price. Book tickets up to a week beforehand if possible.

## Getting Around

### MINIBUS

Minibus stops can be found near almost every major intersection. Major ones include Arat Kilo, De Gaulle Sq in Piazza, Meskal Sq, Ras Mekonen Ave near La Gare and in front of the main post office on Churchill Ave. Journeys cost roughly Birr2 (though exact prices depend on the distance).

### TAXI

Most taxis in Addis operate from 6am to 11pm. Short journeys (up to 3km) usually cost foreigners Birr60 to Birr80 (more at night). Medium/long journeys cost Birr100/140. If you share a taxi with strangers, the normal fare is split between the group.

# NORTHERN ETHIOPIA

For most visitors to Ethiopia, it's all about the north. More than anywhere else on earth, northern Ethiopia has the ability to wow you day after day after day.

Known as the historical circuit, there are over two millenniums' worth of ancient treasures scattered about, from giant obelisks and hidden tombs at Aksum to a collection of castles in and around Gonder, and unique churches in Lalibela, Tigray, Lake Tana and many other places. The Danakil Depression, an esteemed destination among adventure travellers, features a permanent lava lake and a bright-yellow sulphuric plain, while the Simien Mountains wrinkle the land with canyons and peaks with a beauty you'll struggle to find anywhere else in Africa.

# Gonder

POP 323,900 / ELEV 2300M

It's not what Gonder (ጎንደር) is, but what Gonder was that's so enthralling. The city lies in a bowl of hills where tall trees shelter tin-roofed stone houses, but rising above these, and standing proud through the centuries, are the walls of castles bathed in blood and painted in the pomp of royalty. It's often called the 'Camelot of Africa', a description that does the royal city a disservice: Camelot is legend, whereas Gonder is reality.

## Sights

**★Debre Berhan Selassie** CHURCH

(Birr100, video camera Birr75; ⏲7.30am-12.30pm & 1.30-5.30pm) Welcome to one of Ethiopia's most beautiful churches. Appealing as it is on the outside with its stone walls, arched doors and two-tiered thatch roof, it's the inner sanctuary of Debre Berhan Selassie, with its glorious frescos, that really shines. But it was very nearly destroyed like most of Gonder's other churches. When the marauding Sudanese dervishes showed up outside the church gates in the 1880s, a giant swarm of bees surged out of the compound, chasing the invaders away.

**Royal Enclosure** CASTLE

(adult/student Birr200/100, video camera Birr75; ⏲8.30am-12.30pm & 1.30-6pm) The Gonder of yesteryear was a city of extreme brutality and immense wealth. Today the wealth and brutality are gone, but the memories linger in this amazing World Heritage site. The entire 70,000-sq-metre compound containing numerous castles and palaces has been restored with the aid of Unesco. Knowledgable, well-trained guides cost Birr200 and are well worth it.

## Festivals & Events

**Timkat** RELIGIOUS

(⏲Jan) This three-day celebration of the Epiphany (Christ's baptism), is marked with special fervour in Gonder. White-robed faithful throng the streets and churches in solemn processions, with a less solemn event at **Fasiladas' Bath** (included in Royal Enclosure ticket; ⏲8.30am-6pm).

**Meskel** RELIGIOUS

(⏲Sep) Gonder is a fine place to be for this important national festival that marks the 'finding of the True Cross' by the Empress Helena in the 4th century. Expect bonfires, priests in full regalia and much pageantry.

## Sleeping

**Zozamba Hotel** HOTEL $

(☎0582-110131; s/d Birr300/400; P) Between the piazza and Debre Berhan Selassie, this quiet, newish hotel is excellent value – the

WORTH A TRIP

## DANAKIL DEPRESSION

Bubbling volcanoes light up the night sky, sulphurous mounds of yellow contort into other-worldly shapes, and mirages of camels cross lakes of salt. Lying 100m and more below sea level, the Danakil Depression (የዳንኪል በረሃ) is about the hottest and most inhospitable place on earth. In fact it's so surreal that it doesn't feel like part of earth at all. If you want genuine, raw adventure, few corners of the globe can match this overwhelming wilderness. But come prepared because with temperatures frequently saying hello to 50°C and appalling 'roads', visiting this region is more an expedition than a tour.

Private travel is no longer allowed but trips to the Danakil Depression can be organised through tour operators in Addis Ababa, Mekele and elsewhere. The going rate in Mekele is US$600 per day with a big-enough group, but all prices are negotiable – remember, however, that obtaining a discount may be a false economy as the operators may then be forced to cut back on essentials such as food and water.

Two days is a minimum for visiting the Danakil, including a visit to Irta'ale Volcano, but three- and four-day excursions are also possible; the latter will enable you to visit Irta'ale, Dallol and Lake Asale.

rooms are tidy and large enough to put your backpack down without tripping over it. It has a surprisingly decent kitchen where it can rustle up simple but hearty Ethiopian meals.

**★Lodge du Chateau** HOTEL **$$**
(☎0918-152001; www.lodgeduchateau.com; dm/s/d & tw incl breakfast US$20/45/55; @🛜) Doing things its own way, this owner-managed spot next to the Royal Enclosure has the friendliest service in town, attention to detail and a real commitment to community involvement. The rooms are nicely decorated and have good mattresses, renovated bathrooms and Gonder's best breakfast served in a dining room–lounge perched high to make the best of the valley views.

**Gonder Landmark Hotel** HOTEL **$$**
(☎0581-122929; www.gonderlandmark.com; s/d/tw/ste US$60/68/72/85) Lording it over the town's northern end and with terrific city views from most rooms (avoid the 'Mountain View' rooms), the Landmark is an excellent choice if you like modern, light-filled rooms. The suites may look like they didn't quite know what to do with all that space, but even the standard rooms are some of the nicest in town.

## Eating & Drinking

There's not a lot to choose from in Gonder, but you won't go hungry. Four Sisters is one of northern Ethiopia's best places to eat, with a handful of other places for decent Ethiopian food. Gonder has plenty of fine coffee houses dotted around the town centre, while nightlife is a mix of bars, nightclubs and garden restaurants where people like to linger after the business of eating is done.

**★Four Sisters** EUROPEAN, ETHIOPIAN **$**
(☎0581-122031; www.thefoursistersrestaurant.com; mains Birr70-100; ⏱noon-10pm) Now here's something special. One of the best places in northern Ethiopia for both food and atmosphere, Four Sisters has brilliant traditional food (order 'national food' for an overview of what it's capable of), a lovely, leafy setting with stone walls and Debre Berhan Selassie–inspired paintings and nightly traditional music and dance.

**Lodge Fasil** ETHIOPIAN, INTERNATIONAL **$$**
(☎0581-110637; mains Birr55-120; ⏱7am-10pm) With an agreeable garden setting (there's a more formal dining area inside), Lodge Fasil in the hotel of the same name does a good mix of Ethiopian dishes with European comfort food such as steak sandwiches and pizzas. Nothing special, but a reliable central choice.

**★Senait Coffee Shop** COFFEE
(⏱9am-5pm) Serving up Gonder's best coffee, Senait is brought to you by the same people who run Four Sisters and it shows. With a small but lovely, character-filled outdoor setting opposite the exit to the Royal Enclosure, it's a nice place to rest during your exploration of the city. The coffee is strong and traditional and of the highest quality.

## Information

**Dashen Bank** (⏱8.30am-11am & 1.30-3.30pm Mon-Fri, 8.30-11am Sat) The branch north of the piazza has an ATM, as do some others further out of town.

**Wegagen Bank** (8.30-11am & 1.30-3.30pm Mon-Fri, 8.30-11am Sat) Also has an **ATM** (24hr) inside Taye Hotel.

## Getting There & Away

### AIR

**Ethiopian Airlines** (0581-117688; 8am-1pm & 2-6pm Mon-Sat) flies twice daily to Addis Ababa (Birr4516, one hour) and once to Aksum (Birr2113, two hours) via Lalibela (Birr1781, one hour).

### BUS

Ordinary buses leave from the bus station.

**Addis Ababa** Few travellers go direct to/from Addis, but it can be done in 15 hours with the luxury buses. Options include Sky Bus (Birr422, 5am), which departs from the Royal Enclosure entrance gate, and Selam (Birr420, 5.30am), which, just to be different, departs from the Royal Enclosure exit gate.

**Aksum** For Aksum, you'll need to change in Shire (Birr160, 10 to 11 hours, 5.30am).

**Bahir Dar** Two daily buses make the trip between Gonder and Bahir Dar (Birr75, three hours).

**Debark (Simien Mountains)** Minibuses and an early morning bus connect Gonder with Debark (Birr65, 2½ hours).

**Lalibela** There are no direct buses to Lalibela so take the 5.30am bus (Birr115, four to five hours) or one of the minibuses (Birr210, four hours) headed to Woldia and get off in Gashena, where you can catch a connection as long as you don't arrive too late in the day.

# Simien Mountains National Park

No matter how you look at it, the Unesco World Heritage–listed Simien Mountains National Park (የሰሜን ተራሮች ብሔራዊ ፓርክ) is one of Africa's most beautiful ranges. This massive plateau, riven with gullies and pinnacles, offers tough but immensely rewarding trekking along the ridge that falls sheer to the plains far below. It's not just the scenery (and altitude) that will leave you speechless, but also the excitement of sitting among a group of gelada monkeys, or watching magnificent walia ibex joust on rock ledges. Whether you come for a stroll or a two-week trek, the Simiens make a great companion to the historical circuit's monument-viewing.

Organising trekking yourself at **park headquarters** (0581-170016; Debark; 8.30am-12.30pm & 1.30-5.30pm) in Debark is straightforward, but it can take up to two hours so it's best to arrive the afternoon before you plan to trek, or to book through a reputable agency in advance of your visit. Park fees are payable at the park headquarters in Debark.

Our pick of the budget options in Debark, **Pension Everlasting** (0918-724558, 0581-171173; simienpensioneverlasting@gmail.com; Debark; s/d/tw/tr Birr300/400/500/600; ) has a friendly English-speaking owner and a fine little restaurant where mostly local, organic ingredients are used. The rooms are fairly similar to those elsewhere, but the quiet location and friendly service are what stand out.

**Limalimo Lodge** (0918-776499, 0931-688062; www.limalimolodge.com; s/d/tr full board Oct-Apr US$220/320/410, May & Jun US$185/270/360, Sep US$150/220/310; closed Jul & Aug) is something special – one of the best places to stay in Ethiopia. The location is the best in the Simiens, with incredible views from the terrace; the architect-designed look is clean-lined and contemporary, and the lodge supports local development projects and was built by members of the local community. Rooms are supremely comfortable with massive windows and lovely day beds.

Two morning buses and lots of minibuses run from Debark to Gonder (Birr40, 2½ hours). The only bus to Shire (for Aksum) is the Gonder service that passes through Debark around 8am, but it's often full. If you want to guarantee a seat, the national-park office, your guide or hotel will reserve you a place by getting somebody in Gonder to ride in your seat between Gonder and Debark. They charge Birr300 to Birr350 for this service; arrange it a day in advance. Hitching is possible, but you may need more than one day to reach Shire.

# Aksum

POP 56,500 / ELEV 2130M

Aksum (አክሱም) is a riddle waiting to be solved. Did the Queen of Sheba really call the town's dusty streets home? Does the Ark of the Covenant that holds Moses' 10 Commandments reside in a small Aksum chapel? Is one of the Three Wise Men really buried here? And what exactly do those famous stelae signify? This Unesco World Heritage site has revealed only a tiny fraction of its secrets, and an exploration of its ruined tombs and palaces is sure to light a spark of excitement.

## Sights

Ancient Aksum obelisks pepper the area, and whether you're looking down on a small specimen or staring up at a grand tower, you'll be duly bowled over. The closer you get, the more amazing they are. A full day is a minimum for seeing everything worth seeing. And carry a torch for the tombs.

**★Ark of the Covenant Chapel** LANDMARK
In between the old and new St Mary of Zion churches is the real reason for most people's devotion: a tiny, carefully guarded chapel that houses what most Ethiopians believe is the legendary Ark of the Covenant. Don't think you can take a peek: just one specially chosen guardian has access to the Ark, and even he is not allowed to look at it.

**★Northern Stelae Field** ARCHAEOLOGICAL SITE
(archaeological sites combined ticket Birr50; 8am-5.30pm) Despite the dizzying grandeur of the numerous rock needles reaching for the stars, it's what's under your feet here that's most important. Amazingly, about 90% of the field hasn't yet been dug, so no matter where you walk, there's a good chance there's an undiscovered tomb with untold treasures beneath. This is part of Aksum's appeal: the thought that fascinating finds and secrets lurk in the depths. That said, these are some of the ancient world's most striking monuments.

**★St Mary of Zion Churches Complex** CHURCH
(Birr200, video camera Birr100; 8am-12.30pm & 2.30-5.30pm Mon-Fri, 9am-noon & 2.30-5.30pm Sat & Sun) Though religions have come and gone, Aksum has always remained a holy city – welcome to the centre of the universe for Christian Ethiopians. A church of some form has stood here since the earliest days of Ethiopian Christianity and it was God himself who, descending from heaven, indicated that a church should be built here, though the original church is long gone. The complex includes the new church, old church, museum and the chapel said to house the Ark of the Covenant.

**Dungur (Queen of Sheba's) Palace** RUINS
(ደንጉር (የንግስት ሳባ) ቤተ-መንግስት; archaeological sites combined ticket Birr50; 8am-5.30pm) The structure at Dungur is popularly known as Queen of Sheba's Palace, though archaeologists are divided over whether it was the great woman's palace or the 6th-century-AD mansion of a nobleman. Most leaned towards the latter, but the find during recent excavations of a relief carving depicting a beautiful woman (in the museum at St Mary of Zion Church) has caused some to wonder whether her palace may lie beneath the current ruins.

## Tours

**Tedros Girmay** TOURS
(0910-081534; tedrosaxum21@gmail.com) An outstanding Aksum guide.

**Rufael Fitsum** TOURS
(0913-125540; rufael12@yahoo.com) One of Aksum's best guides.

## Festivals & Events

Aksum's calendar is filled with Christian celebrations – if you're in Ethiopia for any of the most important dates in the Orthodox calendar, make your way to Aksum (but make sure you've booked your hotel well in advance).

**Timkat** RELIGIOUS
(Jan) Though smaller than those in Gonder, Aksum's Timkat celebrations are held at the Queen of Sheba's Bath, and are just as interesting.

**Festival of Maryam Zion** RELIGIOUS
(Nov) This is one of Ethiopia's largest festivals. In the days leading up to the event on 30 November, thousands of pilgrims arrive and sleepy Aksum truly awakens. Celebrations start in front of the Northern Stelae Field, where the monarchs of the Orthodox church line the steps and watch performers in the street below.

## Sleeping

Aksum has excellent budget and midrange choices, but there's nothing at the top end. Rooms become scarce and prices rise during major festivals, when reservations are essential. When things are quiet, it's always worth asking for a discount.

**Kaleb Hotel** HOTEL $
(0911-546823, 0347-752222; s/tw Birr300/600; P ) With quiet rooms set around possibly Aksum's loveliest garden courtyard and with a popular pizza restaurant, Kaleb has the nicest budget setting. The rooms are large and uninspiring, but the setting makes up for it. Its twin rates are just silly – ask for a discount. Although it's signposted off the main road, it's only in Amharic at the property itself.

**Yared Zema Hotel** HOTEL $$
(0347-754817; www.yaredzemainternationalhotel.com; incl breakfast s US$40-55, d or tw

US$50-65, ste US$65-80; ) One of a clutch of new hotels along the main road through town, the Yared Zema has some of Aksum's best beds. Attractive wood-floored rooms are easy on the eye with comfy beds and some of the bathrooms have bath-tubs. There's a reasonable on-site bar and restaurant.

**Sabean International Hotel** HOTEL $$
(0347-751224; www.sabeanhotel.com; s/d incl breakfast US$50/60) The rooms at this new place are among Aksum's best: wooden floors, decent bathrooms and pretty good service. The walls are a tad thin and you've a right to expect a better breakfast for this price, but otherwise it's a good choice.

## Eating & Drinking

Aksum has plenty of good restaurants, including a number that are approximations of traditional Ethiopian eating dens.

For something entirely different, seek out a *tella bet* (local bar serving home-brewed barley and millet beer; *suwa* in Tigrinya) in the tiny streets around town. They're marked by cups on top of small poles, but you'll need a local to decode the various colours.

**Lucy Traditional Restaurant** ETHIOPIAN $
(0914-768399; mains Birr35-80; 7am-11pm) Slightly cheaper than some of the other traditional restaurants around town, Lucy has low wooden stools and attracts a predominantly local crowd who come for the soups, grilled fish or *tibs* (lamb stew). There's occasional live music in the evenings.

**AB Traditional Restaurant** ETHIOPIAN $
(0920-877382; mains Birr50-120; 7am-11pm) Decorated with bamboo and crafts and with traditional low-stool seating, this restaurant is peaceful and a great spot to dig into *shekla tibs*, with goat fresh from the butchery inside the dining room (don't look too closely at the flies...), or *doro wat* (chicken stew). Give the pasta and rice dishes a pass: they can take forever to prepare and can be disappointing.

## Shopping

Aksum has more souvenir shops than any other town in Ethiopia and the road between the piazza and Northern Stelae Field is lined with them; the main road through town also has its fair share. Most feature basketry and weavings, but you can also buy silver crosses and old triptych paintings.

★ **St George Gallery Axum** ARTS & CRAFTS
(0914-744109; 7.30am-8.30pm) One of the best shops in northern Ethiopia, St George has that rare combination of simple tourist items and fine pieces of art and antiques, although the quality tends towards the latter. Religious paintings (including triptych and on goat skin), silver crosses and jewellery make up the bulk of the collection.

## Information

**Aksum Visitor Centre** (0347-753924; aksumtourismoffice@ethionet.net; 8am-5.30pm) One of the country's most helpful offices.

## Getting There & Away

**Ethiopian Airlines** (0347-752300; www.ethiopianairlines.com) flies twice daily to Addis Ababa (US$240, one to three hours), sometimes direct and sometimes via Lalibela (US$130, 45 minutes) and Gonder (US$130, 40 minutes).

For buses to Gonder and Debark (for the Simien Mountains), go to Shire (Birr45, 1½ hours) first. There's only one bus (6am) and a few minibuses to Adigrat (Birr58, 3½ hours), but services are more frequent from Adwa (Birr10, 30 minutes). There are two morning buses to Mekele (Birr85, seven hours, 6am), as well as minibuses (Birr120), any of which can drop you in Wukro (Birr70, six hours). All buses leave from the bus station.

Aksum's travel agencies and numerous freelance agents rent vehicles (including driver and guide) for trips to Yeha, Debre Damo and the rock churches of Tigray.

# Rock-Hewn Churches of Tigray

The landscapes of northern Tigray seem to spring from some hard-bitten African fairy tale. The luminous light bathes scattered sharp peaks that rise into the sky out of a sandy, rolling semidesert. The stratified plateaus, particularly between Dugem and Megab in the Gheralta region, lead to inevitable comparisons with the USA's desert southwest.

The 120-odd churches are as intriguing as the landscape is beautiful. Very different from the more famous monolithic (carved out of the ground and only left attached to the earth at the base) churches of Lalibela, the Tigrayan churches are carved from cliff faces, built into pre-existing caves or constructed high atop some improbable perch – getting to some of them may not be for the faint-hearted, but getting there is almost always half the fun. And beyond a few famous churches, you'll likely get to explore on your own, even in the high season.

## Sights

Most churches are spread out across the eastern Tigray region and it helps when planning to group them together in clusters. Hawzien and the surrounding area is generally the base/starting point of choice for most travellers. Guides can be arranged through the Gheralta Local Guide Association. One guide we recommend is **Tewelde Hileselassie** (☎0914-616851).

**★Abuna Yemata Guh** CHURCH

(Gheralta Cluster; Birr150; ⊙8am-5.30pm) There's nowhere on earth quite like Abuna Yemata Guh. Although less impressive architecturally than most, the church is spectacularly sited within a cliff face, halfway up a sheer rock pinnacle 4km west of Megab. The first 45 minutes of the climb is mildly challenging, with a couple of tricky sheer sections requiring toehold action; guides carry ropes (Birr150) for the final push. The last two minutes require nerves of steel to make the final scramble and precarious ledge walk over a 200m drop.

**★Mikael Debre Selam** CHURCH

(ሚካኤል ደብረ ሰላም; Atsbi Cluster; Birr150; ⊙8am-5.30pm) This church or 'church within a church' has an exceptional brown-and-white, Aksumite-style facade fronting its inner rock-hewn section. The bright, modern paintings at the front and its beautiful carved arch add an odd but interesting contrast. The setting is lovely and it's one of our favourites. The 45-minute, one-way climb is strenuous but otherwise not difficult.

**★Abuna Abraham** CHURCH

(አቡነ አብርሀም; Gheralta Cluster; Birr150; ⊙8am-5.30pm) Rectangular in shape, with six massive free-standing pillars, this large and impressive 14th-century church (also known as Debre Tsion) is known for its diverse architectural features, including decorated cupolas, bas-reliefs and carved crosses on the walls and ceiling. It also has beautiful, though faded and damaged, 16th-century murals and an unusual, large 15th-century ceremonial fan. It sits like a fortress on a hill about 500m south of Dugem.

**★Abraha We Atsbeha** CHURCH

(አብርሃ ወ አጽበሃ; Wukro Cluster; Birr250; ⊙8am-5.30pm) Architecturally speaking, this 10th-century church is one of Tigray's finest. It's large and cruciform in shape, with cruciform pillars and well-preserved 17th- and 18th-century murals and a wonderful wooden door. Some of the church treasures, including what's believed to be King Atsbeha's golden shoes, are properly displayed in glass cases in the adjacent **museum**. It's by the road 15km west of Wukro or 23km from Megab.

**★Maryam Korkor** CHURCH

(ማርያም ቆርቆር; Gheralta Cluster; Birr150; ⊙8am-5.30pm) Although an unsightly green from the outside, this impressive, cross-shaped church is known for its architectural features (cruciform pillars, arches and cupolas), fine 17th-century frescos and church treasures. It's also one of the largest churches in the area. The path begins around 1km from the road just southeast of Megab and involves a fairly steep one-hour ascent. Maryam Korkor is easily combined with nearby Abuna Yemata Guh into an all-day trek from Megab.

## Sleeping

There's accommodation in many towns around the churches, but only Wukro, Abi Adi and Hawzien provide a level of comfort and cleanliness that most people expect.

**★Vision Hotel** HOTEL $

(☎0924-293314; Main Rd, Hawzien; s/d/tw/tr incl breakfast Birr329/429/459/699; ) If only all Ethiopian budget hotels were this good. Overseen by the professional Geshu, and with one of the faster wi-fi connections we came across in Ethiopia, it's an excellent place. The rooms are clean, well-sized and reached via a courtyard with more greenery than most places at this price. All in all, it's excellent value for money.

**★Wukro Lodge** LODGE $$

(☎0115-150698, 0921-117028; www.wukrolodge.com; Wukro; s/d/tw incl breakfast Birr880/1020/1150; P) Finally nearing completion during our recent visit, Wukro Lodge has been worth the wait. The rooms feature traditional designs – split levels like many local homes, walls carved from the rock like the region's churches, traditional building materials and even 'soil' ceilings – and all have fabulous views over the surrounding valleys. Add in eminently reasonable prices and we're already hooked.

**★Gheralta Lodge** LODGE $$$

(☎0346-670344, Addis Ababa office 011 663 2893; www.gheraltalodgetigrai.com; Hawzien; per person incl breakfast Birr950; P) In a word: fantastic. This lovely Italian-owned, African-themed lodge has great facilities and service and many guests declare it their best night in Ethiopia. Rooms in the stone buildings are large and lovely. Don't miss eating at the restaurant, which provides a set Italian-inspired menu (lunch/dinner Birr210/250) that may be some of the finest food you eat in Ethiopia. Book as far ahead as possible.

## Eating

Hawzien has the best selection of restaurants. Gheralta Lodge is the best place to eat in town. Wukro also has a few good choices.

**Tesfay Restaurant** ETHIOPIAN $
(0914-784425; Hawzien; mains Birr50-100; 7am-9pm) Opened in 2016, this friendly place is a good, simple choice. It does all the usual Ethiopian staples, as well as sandwiches. It's not signposted: take the road heading south down the hill off the main road through Hawzien, around 100m east of the local guide association office; once on this road, it's 200m down the hill on your right.

**Fisseha Hotel** ETHIOPIAN $
(0914-730898; Wukro; mains Birr55-150; 7am-10pm; ) The main reason to come here is not the large and loud TV screen in the dining room, but the roast goat served with rice – it's a great meal and easily our favourite dish in town. Get your hands all greasy, pick it up and tuck in. The rooms here are rather nondescript, and if you can work out the pricing system (rooms from Birr400), let us know.

## Information

**Gheralta Local Guide Association** (0914-616851; 1-3 people per day Birr250, 4-6 350) Official guides are mandatory for Abuna Yemata Guh and Maryam Korkor (where going alone is potentially dangerous), but they can be hired for other places too, which we recommend. This office is at the main junction in Megab. You can also hire local scouts (Birr100) to carry bags and chase away children.

**Tigray Tourism Commission** (0344-430340; 8am-noon & 1.30-5pm Mon-Sat) The helpful staff at the tourist offices in Wukro, Aksum and Mekele (0914-721280; Axum Hotel; 8.30am-noon & 2-6pm) advise (sometimes) on itineraries and provide brochures.

## Getting There & Around

Quite good gravel roads now connect the villages with the trailheads to most churches. Contract minibuses (per group per day Birr1300) are available in Hawzien, Wukro and Abi Adi, or ask at the Gheralta Local Guide Association office in Megab.

If you're patient, exploration by public transport is possible. There are many minibuses from Adigrat (Birr35, 1½ hours) to Wukro and also from Mekele to Wukro (Birr26, one hour) and Hawzien (Birr48, 2½ hours) via Freweyni. There's always much more traffic on market days.

# Lalibela

POP 25,000 / ELEV 2630M

Lalibela (ላሊበላ) is history and mystery frozen in stone, its soul alive with the rites and awe of Christianity at its most ancient and unbending. No matter what you've heard about Lalibela, no matter how many pictures you've seen of its breathtaking rock-hewn churches, nothing can prepare you for the reality of seeing it for yourself. It's not only a World Heritage site, but truly a world wonder. Spending a night vigil here during one of the big religious festivals, when white-robed pilgrims in their hundreds crowd the courtyards of the churches, is to witness Christianity in its most raw and powerful form.

## Sights

Lalibela's rock-hewn churches, all built below ground level, aren't just carved into the rock but freed from it. And the carving, both inside and out, is exceptionally refined. Although time has treated most with gentle gloves, Unesco has built protective roofing. Fortunately, despite the intrusive design, this won't detract much from your enjoyment.

There are two main church clusters around the town, and it will take you the best part of a day to visit them all. There are also some wonderful churches and monasteries outside of town that can be explored on day trips.

★**Bet Giyorgis** CHURCH
(ቤተ ጊዮርጊስ, St George's Church; adult/child 9-13yr with combined Lalibela church ticket US$50/25; 8am-noon & 2-5.30pm) When you think of Lalibela, you're thinking of Bet Giyorgis. Resting off on its own, St George's Church is Lalibela's masterpiece. Representing the apogee of the rock-hewn tradition, it's the most visually perfect church of all, a 15m-high three-tiered plinth in the shape of a Greek cross – a perfectly proportioned shape that required no internal pillars. Due to its exceptional preservation, it also lacks the obtrusive roofing seen over the other churches.

★**Yemrehanna Kristos** CHURCH
(ይምርሃነ ክርስቶስ; Birr300, personal video cameras Birr50; 8am-5.30pm) Despite Yemrehanna Kristos being one of Ethiopia's best-preserved late-Aksumite buildings, few people reward themselves with a visit. And a reward it is. The church is different because it's built rather than excavated. Seeing the stepped exterior facade, created from alternating wood and stone layers,

you'll understand why so many of Lalibela's rock-hewn churches look like they do. And knowing that Yemrehanna Kristos may predate Lalibela's churches by up to 80 years, you have before you a virtual blueprint of greatness.

★**Bet Medhane Alem** CHURCH
(ቤተ መድኃኔዓለም, House of the Saviour of the World; Northwestern Group of Churches; adult/child 9-13yr with combined Lalibela church ticket US$50/25; ⊙8am-noon & 2-5.30pm) Resembling a massive Greek temple more than a traditional Ethiopian church, Bet Medhane Alem is impressive for its size and majesty. Said to be the largest rock-hewn church in the world, it measures 33.5m by 23.5m and is more than 11.5m high. Some scholars have suggested it may have been a copy in rock of the original St Mary of Zion church (p590) in Aksum.

★**Bet Maryam** CHURCH
(ቤተ ማርያም; Northwestern Group of Churches; adult/child 9-13yr with combined Lalibela church ticket US$50/25; ⊙8am-noon & 2-5.30pm) Connected to Bet Medhane Alem by a tunnel is a large courtyard containing three churches. The first, Bet Maryam, is small, yet designed and decorated to an exceptionally high standard. It's also the only church with porches extending off it. Dedicated to the Virgin (who's particularly venerated in Ethiopia), this is the most popular church among pilgrims. Some believe it may have been the first built in Lalibela.

★**Bet Amanuel** CHURCH
(ቤተ አማኑኤል; Southeastern Group of Churches; adult/child 9-13yr with combined Lalibela church ticket US$50/25; ⊙8am-noon & 2-5.30pm) Free-standing and monolithic, Bet Amanuel is Lalibela's most finely carved church. Some have suggested it was the royal family's private chapel. It perfectly replicates the style of Aksumite buildings, with its projecting and recessed walls mimicking alternating layers of wood and stone seen at places such as Yemrehanna Kristos and Debre Damo. The most striking feature of the interior is the double Aksumite frieze atop the nave.

## Festivals & Events

The most exciting time to visit is during a major festival, when thousands of pilgrims crowd in. **Timkat** and **Leddet** are the biggest, but Lalibela draws masses for all the major ones. Outside these periods, try to attend at least one church's monthly saint day.

## Tours

**Zenebe Minale** TOURS
(☎0913-420383; zenebeminale2017@yahoo.com) An excellent and enthusiastic guide to the churches of Lalibela.

**Girma Derbie** TOURS
(☎0913-513763; girmaderbie123@yahoo.com) Lalibela guide who can also lead community treks in the mountains around Lalibela.

## Sleeping

Lalibela's sleeping choices are improving all the time, especially in the midrange.

Discounts, often very large ones, are negotiable in most hotels from April through August. Vacancies are almost nonexistent during the festival period and European Christmas, so reservations are essential. However, prices for reserved rooms during these times can quintuple or more. If you arrive during a festival without reservations, look for brokers who work the centre of town hiring out rooms in people's homes.

**Asheton Hotel** HOTEL $
(☎0333-360030; hailu_mher@yahoo.com; s/d/tw Birr300/400/500; P 📶) This classic budget-traveller haunt offers older whitewashed rooms – don't be fooled by the intricately carved doorways as what lies within is far simpler. The whole place is running down slowly, so the doubling of prices since we were last here is most unwelcome. One big plus: it's across the road from Unique Restaurant.

★**Old Abyssinia Lodge** BUNGALOW $$
(☎0338-362758; www.oldabyssinia.com; incl breakfast s US$55-75, tw US$65-85; P 📶) There were just three *tukul*-style rooms here when we visited, but they certainly caught our eye. Stunning wood furnishings, many with intricately carved traditional local designs, inhabit stone-walled rooms that are lovely and large and come with good-sized bathrooms. The balconies have wonderful views. It's *very* quiet.

**Sora Lodge Lalibela** HOTEL $$
(☎0911-637211; www.soralodgelalibela.com; s/d/tw incl breakfast main bldg US$45/55/60, d/f tukul cottages US$65/99; P 📶) A friendly place out on the tip of one of Lalibela's many ridges, Sora Lodge has a modern main building with tidy rooms and sweeping views from the upper floors, as well as nicely decorated *tukul*-style rooms, also with terrific views. It grows many of its own vegetables for the onsite restaurant.

**★Hotel Maribela** HOTEL **$$$**
(☎0333-360345; www.hotelmaribela.com; s/d & tw/ste US$65/99/110) Of all the hotels lined up along the ridges that face out over the valleys and mountains, this is the one we like best. With just 15 rooms, it has a more intimate feel than most and the rooms are filled with light and a light touch that gets the mix of modern and traditional just right.

## Eating & Drinking

Lalibela has some fine places for a coffee or something a little stronger – try the restaurants or hotel terraces. It also has one of northern Ethiopia's better places for trying honey wine.

**Old Abyssinia Restaurant** ETHIOPIAN **$**
(☎0338-362758; www.oldabyssinia.com; mains Birr40-95; ⏲6am-10pm) The combination of excellent food (mostly Ethiopian with a few European dishes), fine views and an on-site **cooking school** (per person US$25) means you can take care of all of your culinary needs in one go here. It's lovely and quiet, not least because it's a fair hike out of town (downhill on the way here, uphill the way back...).

**Unique Restaurant** EUROPEAN, ETHIOPIAN **$**
(☎0333-360125; breakfast Birr30-40, mains Birr40-70; ⏲6am-10pm) This basic but cosy little restaurant ('bad house, good food' is what the charming and irrepressible owner Sisaynesh tells people who hesitate outside her door) serves the usual mix of national and *faranji* (foreigner) dishes. It's the kind of place you'll wonder about as you enter, then find yourself staying to take **cooking classes** (per person US$20).

**★Ben Abeba** EUROPEAN, ETHIOPIAN **$$**
(☎0922-345144, 0333-360215; www.benabeba.com; mains Birr45-110; ⏲6am-10pm) Easily one of Ethiopia's coolest restaurants, this Ethio-Scottish-owned, Dalí-esque jumble of walkways, platforms and fire pits is perched on the edge of the ridge for 360-degree views. The food is tasty – we especially like that the restaurant makes its own traditional bread and uses it to make an excellent goat burger. Stop by at 11am to see *injera* being made.

**Torpido Tej House** BAR
(⏲7am-midnight) Also known as Askalech, Torpido serves *tej* along with traditional *azmari* song and dance after 8pm. It gets a lot of tourists, but locals usually outnumber them. And unlike the more earthy *tej* houses, you are ensured good-quality wine – it comes in three strengths. Everyone is expected to dance – it's all in the shoulders...

## Information

The **Tourism Information Centre** (⏲8.30am-12.30pm & 1.30-5.30pm Mon-Fri) is unsigned and located behind the church ticket office.

## Getting There & Away

**Ethiopian Airlines** (☎0333-360046; ⏲8am-5pm Mon-Sat) flies between Lalibela and Addis Ababa (Birr3224, 45 minutes, twice daily), Aksum (Birr2190, 45 minutes), Bahir Dar (Birr1781, 30 minutes, weekly) and Gonder (Birr4298, two hours, daily).

There are two morning buses (Birr75, four hours) and usually four minibuses (Birr95) to/from Woldia, the last leaving about 2pm. If you're travelling to/from Bahir Dar or Gonder, you'll need to change in Gashena.

A bus departs daily for Addis Ababa (Birr295, two days, 6am), overnighting in Dessie (Birr125, eight to nine hours).

# EASTERN ETHIOPIA

Most of eastern Ethiopia is a stark landscape of dust-stained acacia scrub and forgettable towns. But scattered around this cloak of the commonplace are gems of genuine adventure, with the east's pièce de résistance being the walled city of Harar.

## Harar

POP 196,000 / ELEV 1850M

World Heritage–listed Harar (ሐረር) is a place apart. With its 368 alleyways squeezed into just 1 sq km, it's more reminiscent of Fez in Morocco than any other city in the Horn. Its countless mosques and shrines, animated markets, crumbling walls and charming people will make you feel as if you've floated right out of the 21st century. It's the east's most memorable sight and shouldn't be missed. As if that wasn't enough, there are many chances to get up close and personal with wild hyenas. It's a rare traveller who doesn't enjoy it here.

### Sights

No visit to Harar would be complete without wading through its shambolic markets. They're packed with Oromo people from the surrounding countryside coming to town to sell their goods (mostly firewood) and then spend their earnings on food and household goods. All the fresh markets are busiest after 3pm and are pretty quiet on Sundays.

WORTH A TRIP

## THE LOWER OMO VALLEY

If there's anything in southern Ethiopia that can rival the majesty of the north's historical circuit, it's the people of the Lower Omo Valley. The villages are home to some of Africa's most fascinating ethnic groups and a trip here represents a unique chance for travellers to encounter a culture markedly different from their own. Whether it's wandering through traditional Daasanach villages, watching Hamer people performing a Jumping of the Bulls ceremony or seeing the Mursi's mind-blowing lip plates, your visit here will stick with you for a lifetime. This is quite a beautiful region too. The landscape is diverse, ranging from dry, open savannah plains to forests in the high hills and along the Omo and Mago Rivers. The former meanders for nearly 800km, from southwest of Addis Ababa all the way to Lake Turkana on the Kenyan border.

**Northern Hyena Feeding Site** WILDLIFE
(ጅብ መመገቢያ ስፍራ; Birr100; ⏲from 6.30pm) Located north of Fallana Gate, this is one of Harar's two hyena feeding stations. A highlight of any visit to Harar, this impressive spectacle begins around 6.30pm. There are generally two to four hyenas that make an appearance after the 'hyena man' calls them. If none turn up, you'll be taken to a nearby hyena den where hyenas can be seen with their pups.

**Old Town** AREA
(በግንብ የታጠረ ከተማ) Harar's old walled town (known as Jugal) is a fascinating place that begs exploration. The thick, 5m-high walls running 3.5km around town were erected in the 16th century in defensive response to the migrations northward of the Oromo, and little development occurred outside them until the early 20th century. There are six gates: five 16th-century originals and the car-friendly **Harar Gate**, also known as Duke's Gate after Ras Makonnen, the first duke of Harar, who added it in 1889.

## Sleeping

**Belayneh Hotel** HOTEL $
(☎025 666 2030; New Town; d/tw Birr300/350; Wi-Fi) The big drawcards here are the balcony views over the Shoa Gate Market and the hotel's proximity to the bus station and old town. The rooms themselves are noisy and tired, but will do for a night's kip. Give the bathrooms a smell test before choosing a room; some won't pass.

**★Rawda Waber Harari Cultural Guesthouse** GUESTHOUSE $$
(☎091 575 6439; Old Town; d/tw with shared bathroom incl breakfast Birr400/700) This genuine Adare house percolates tradition and history into a comfy brew of warm welcome amid exotic decorations. Set in the heart of the old town, down a nondescript side street, the four snug bedrooms share two bathrooms (hot water). The place feels a tad cramped, but that shouldn't mar the experience. Breakfast is in a wonderfully atmospheric living room.

**★Grand Gato** BOUTIQUE HOTEL $$$
(☎025 466 0036; New Town; d/tw incl breakfast Birr1500/2000; P Wi-Fi) This great collection of 14 stylish suites – at what is possibly the first hotel with an ounce of character in Harar – is perfect for well-heeled travellers who are after some sophistication. Spacious rooms with pristine bathroom and balcony are awash with calming tones, boldly accented by carpet or laminate floors and lavish furniture.

## Eating

Harar has a handful of quality eateries and cafeterias. Most hotels have their own restaurants and serve average to excellent local and international food. The restaurant inside **Ras Hotel** (☎025 666 0027; New Town; P @ Wi-Fi) is the best of the lot.

**★Hirut Restaurant** ETHIOPIAN $
(☎096 217 4799; New Town; mains Birr75-100; ⏲11am-11pm) Decorated with traditional woven baskets and specialising in authentic local cuisine, this is the most atmospheric place in Harar to sink your teeth into a filling *kwanta firfir* (dried strips of beef rubbed in chilli, butter, salt and *berbere*) or swill a glass of Gouder wine. It also serves a selection of pizzas, salads and sandwiches.

**Kim Café & Restaurant** CAFETERIA $
(New Town; mains Birr50-100) This unmissable spot on the main avenue in the new town has a wide variety of cavity-inducing pastries, as well as excellent fruit juices and acceptable pizzas, burgers, pasta and Ethiopian dishes. It's also a great place to grab a coffee and watch the world go by.

**★Fresh Touch Restaurant** EUROPEAN $$
(☎091 574 0109; New Town; mains Birr80-190; ⏲7.30am-11pm; Wi-Fi) The king of restaurants in Harar, snazzy Fresh Touch is a hot favour-

ite among well-heeled locals and visitors. That's all thanks to four winning details: its convenient location near the old town; the uplifting ambience; the attractive open-air terrace; and the excellent something-for-everyone menu. Try the burgers.

## Information

### MONEY

Banks with foreign-exchange facilities and ATMs can be found in the new town alongside the avenue heading west from Harar Gate.

**Awash International Bank** (New Town; ⌚8am-6pm Mon-Fri, to 2pm Sat)

**Commercial Bank** (New Town; ⌚8-11.30am & 1.30-4.30pm Mon-Fri, 8-11am Sat)

### TOURIST INFORMATION

**Tourist Office** (☎025 666 9300; Ras Makonnen's Palace, Old Town; ⌚8am-noon & 2-5pm Mon-Fri) Can help with finding a guide.

## Getting There & Away

There are no direct flights to Harar. The nearest airport is in Dire Dawa, from where you can catch a minibus to Harar.

The **bus station** (New Town) is near Harar Gate. Minibuses run frequently to Dire Dawa (Birr20, one hour) and Babille (Birr12, 45 minutes). There are also frequent buses to Jijiga (Birr42, 1½ hours).

For Addis Ababa (Birr300, nine to 10 hours), **Sky Bus** (New Town) and **Selam Bus** (New Town) depart around 5am from their ticket offices on the north side of the main road to Addis Ababa, between Harar Gate and Ras Makonnen Circle. The minibuses that do the capital run are less comfortable and more dangerous than the buses, but they do travel faster and they'll pick you up at your hotel. You can book minibus tickets departing for Addis with **Adil Transport** (☎091 195 5521; New Town). You can also buy tickets from your hotel, but you'll pay a commission. Most minibuses leave between 4am and 2pm.

# UNDERSTAND ETHIOPIA

## Ethiopia Today

Ethiopia prides itself on having attained political stability and has an enviable rate of economic growth thanks to huge foreign investment and the development of a manufacturing industry. Despite the apparent economic boom, the country faces numerous challenges as it grapples with finding job opportunities for an expanding population – not to mention the growing political dissent from the Oromo people, who feel marginalised by the ruling elites. To achieve long-term stability, Ethiopia is in need of better governance and democratic reforms.

## History

Ethiopia's human history dates back at least 4.4 million years, landing it squarely in East Africa's heralded cradle of humanity. Recorded history dates to 1500 BC, when a civilisation with Sabaean influences briefly blossomed at Yeha.

### Kingdom of Aksum

This kingdom, ranking among the ancient world's most powerful, rose shortly after 400BC. Its capital, Aksum, sat in a fertile area lying at an important commercial crossroads between Egypt, Sudan's goldfields and the Red Sea. At its height the kingdom extended well into Arabia. Aksum grew on trade, exporting frankincense, grain, skins, apes and, particularly, ivory. In turn, exotic imports returned from Egypt, Arabia and India. Aksumite architecture was incredible, and impressive monuments still stand today.

The 4th century AD brought Christianity, which enveloped Aksum and shaped Ethiopia's future spiritual, cultural and intellectual life. Aksum itself flourished until the 7th century, when its trading empire was fatally isolated by the rise of Arabs and Islam in Arabia. Ethiopia soon sank into its 'dark ages', a period that has left few traces.

### Early Dynasties

The Zagwe dynasty rose in Lalibela around 1137. Although only lasting until 1270, it produced arguably Ethiopia's greatest treasures: the rock-hewn churches of Lalibela. Yet, the period remains shrouded in mystery as there is no written evidence of it. The dynasty was overthrown by Yekuno Amlak, self-professed descendant of King Solomon and the Queen of Sheba. His 'Solomonic dynasty' would reign for 500 years.

Although Islam expanded into eastern Ethiopia during the 12th and 14th centuries, it wasn't until the late 15th century, when Ottoman Turks intervened, that hostilities erupted. After jihad was declared on the Christian highlands, Ethiopia experienced some of the worst bloodshed in its history. Only Portuguese intervention helped save the Christian empire.

## Towards a United Empire

Filling the power vacuum that was created by the weakened Muslims, Oromo pastoralists and warriors migrated from what is now Kenya. For 200 years intermittent conflict raged. Two 17th-century emperors, Za-Dengel and Susenyos, converted to Catholicism to gain the military support of Portuguese Jesuits.

In 1636 Emperor Fasiladas founded Ethiopia's first permanent capital since Lalibela. By the close of the 17th century, Gonder boasted magnificent palaces, beautiful gardens and extensive plantations. Gonder collapsed in the mid-19th century and Ethiopia disintegrated into a cluster of feuding fiefdoms. The empire was eventually reunified by Kassa Haylu, who crowned himself Emperor Tewodros. His successor, Yohannes IV, fought to the throne with weapons gained by aiding the British.

Later, Menelik II continued acquiring weaponry, using it to thrash the advancing Italians in 1896 and thus stave off colonisation. In 1936 Mussolini's troops overran Ethiopia. They occupied it until capitulating to British forces in 1941.

With the arrival of the British, Haile Selassie, the Ethiopian emperor at the time of Mussolini's invasion, reclaimed his throne and Ethiopia its independence, and the country started to modernise.

## The Derg to Democracy

By 1973 a radical military group, known as the Derg, had emerged. They used the media with consummate skill to undermine and eventually depose Emperor Haile Selassie, before their leader, Colonel Mengistu Haile Mariam, declared Ethiopia a socialist state in 1974, called the People's Democratic Republic of Ethiopia.

Despite internal tensions, external threats initially posed the Derg's biggest problem. Only state-of-the-art weaponry, gifted by the Soviet Union, allowed them to beat back an attempted invasion by Somalia in 1977. In Eritrea (which had been annexed by Ethiopia in 1962), however, the secessionists continued to thwart Ethiopian offensives.

## The Ethiopian-Eritrean War

During the 1980s, numerous Ethiopian armed liberation movements arose. For years, with limited weaponry, they fought the Soviet-backed Derg's military might. Mengistu lost Soviet backing after the Cold War, and the rebel Ethiopian and Eritrean coalition forces finally claimed victory in 1991. Eritrea was immediately granted independence, Mengistu's failed socialist policies were abandoned, and in 1995 the Federal Democratic Republic of Ethiopia was proclaimed.

Elections followed, and the second republic's constitution was inaugurated. Meles Zenawi, as prime minister, formed a new government. Despite having fought together against the Derg for over a decade, Meles Zenawi and Eritrea's President Isaias soon clashed. Bickering over Eritrea's exchange-rate system for its new currency led to Eritrea occupying the border town of Badme in 1998. Soon full-scale military conflict broke out, leaving tens of thousands dead on both sides before ceasing in mid-2000.

## The New Century

In 2005 controversial elections were held, followed by heavy-handed government reprisals.Tensions with Eritrea continued and the two neighbours almost came to blows again in 2005. Ethiopian troops entered Somalia in 2006 in support of the Somali government's fight against the Islamic milita who controlled Mogadishu. Officially Ethiopia withdrew its troops in early 2009, but by the middle of that year Ethiopia admitted that some of its forces had returned to Somalia.

In late 2011 the Ethiopian military, working with the transitional government of Somalia, African Union forces and the Kenyan military, officially reentered Somalia as part of a concerted drive to destroy al-Shabaab, an al-Qaeda-affiliated Somali group. The elections of 2010 saw Zenawi and the Ethiopian People's Revolutionary Democratic Front (EPRDF) returned to power. There was none of the violence that had marked the 2005 election, but international observers criticised the elections for falling short of international standards.

# People of Ethiopia

Ethiopia's population has squeezed past the 100-million mark, an astounding figure considering the population was just 15 million in 1935. Ethiopia has one of the fastest-growing populations in the world. This population explosion is arguably the biggest problem facing Ethiopia today. In 2015 its population-growth rate was estimated at a worryingly high 2.5%; which, if growth rates continue at around that level, will leave Ethiopia bursting at the seams with almost 120 million people in 2025. Eighty-four languages and 200 dialects are spoken in Ethiopia.

## Food & Drink

Eating Ethiopian-style means rethinking many things you might assume about eating. That's because the foundation of almost every meal in Ethiopia is *injera*, a one-of-a-kind pancake of near-universal proportions. At seemingly every turn, plates, bowls and even utensils are replaced by *injera*. Atop its rubbery surface sit delicious multicoloured mounds of spicy meat stews, tasty vegetable curries and even cubes of raw beef.

Other staples that are ever-present on most menus are the much-heralded *wat* (stew), *kitfo* (mince meat) and *tere sega* (raw meat).

### PRICE RANGES

The following price ranges refer to a double room with bathroom in high season.

**$** less than US$25

**$$** US$25 to US$75

**$$$** more than US$75

The following price ranges refer to a standard main course.

**$** less than US$5

**$$** US$5 to US$10

**$$$** more than US$10

# SURVIVAL GUIDE

## Directory A–Z

### ACCOMMODATION

Anyone who visited Ethiopia 15 to 20 years ago will recall joyous nights sleeping in rural hotels that may as well have been stables for animals, and urban hotels that were essentially brothels. No matter where you stayed, fleas were a constant companion. Fortunately, Ethiopian accommodation has come on in leaps and bounds, and it continues to get better, especially in the midrange category. Fleas and sheep mostly stay elsewhere now and hotels functioning as brothels are the exception rather than the rule.

### ACTIVITIES

There aren't many organised activities to get involved in while in Ethiopia – wildlife watching is a notable exception, while horse riding is possible in some areas. But one widely available activity more than compensates – the country offers some of Africa's most rewarding trekking opportunities.

### EMBASSIES & CONSULATES

The following list isn't exhaustive (almost every African nation has representation in Addis Ababa), but it covers the embassies that are most likely to be needed.

**Canadian Embassy** (☎ 011 317 0000; www.canadainternational.gc.ca/ethiopia-ethiopie/index.aspx?lang=eng; Seychelles St; ⏲ 8.30am-noon Mon-Wed & Fri) Also represents Australia.

**Djibouti Embassy** (☎ 011 661 3200; off Bole Rd/Africa Ave; ⏲ 9am-noon Mon-Thu)

**French Embassy** (☎ 011 140 0000; www.ambafrance-et.org; Angola St; ⏲ 8.30am-12.30pm & 2-6.30pm Mon-Thu, 8.30am-12.30pm Fri)

**German Embassy** (☎ 011 123 5139; www.addis-abeba.diplo.de; off Comoros St; ⏲ 7.45am-1pm & 1.30-5pm Mon-Thu, 7.45am-1.45pm Fri)

**Italian Embassy** (☎ 011 123 5684; www.ambaddisabeba.esteri.it; Villa Italia Kebenà; ⏲ 9am-noon Mon-Fri)

**Kenyan Embassy** (☎ 011 661 0033; www.kenyaembassyaddis.org; Comoros St; ⏲ 9am-5pm Mon-Thu)

**Netherlands Embassy** (☎ 011 317 0360; http://ethiopia.nlembassy.org; Ring Rd; ⏲ 8am-5pm Mon-Thu, to 2pm Fri)

**Somaliland Embassy** (☎ 011 663 5921; off Djibouti St; ⏲ 9am-noon Mon-Thu)

**South Sudanese Embassy** (☎ 011 662 0245; off Cameroon St; ⏲ 9am-noon Mon-Fri)

**Sudanese Embassy** (☎ 011 551 6477; sudan.embassy@ethionet.et; Ras Lulseged St; ⏲ 9am-12.30pm Mon-Thu)

**UK Embassy** (☎ 011 617 0100; www.gov.uk/government/world/ethiopia; Comoros St; ⏲ 8am-4.45pm Mon-Thu)

**US Embassy** (☎ 011 130 6000; http://ethiopia.usembassy.gov; Entoto Ave; ⏲ 7.30am-5pm Mon-Thu, to 12.30pm Fri)

### INTERNET ACCESS

Internet cafes are everywhere in Addis Ababa and other major towns and fairly easy to come by in smaller places that see few tourists.

In-room wi-fi is increasingly common in most hotels, including most budget hotels. Before you get too excited, remember that internet connections in Ethiopia can be among the worst on the continent. The Ethiopian government is highly suspicious of the internet. Opposition websites and all social media (Twitter, Facebook, Skype etc) are frequently blocked.

## LGBTIQ TRAVELLERS

In Ethiopia and the rest of the Horn, homosexuality is severely condemned – traditionally, religiously and legally – and remains a topic of absolute taboo. Don't underestimate the strength of feeling. Reports of gays being beaten up or worse aren't uncommon.

In Amharic, the word *bushti* (homosexual) is a very offensive insult, implying immorality and depravity. One traveller wrote to us to report expulsion from a hotel and serious threats just for coming under suspicion. If a hotel only offers double beds, rather than twins, you and your companion will pay more or may even be refused occupancy.

Women may have an easier time: even the idea of a lesbian relationship is beyond the permitted imaginings of many Ethiopians! Behave discreetly, and you will be assumed to be just friends.

Note that the Ethiopian penal code officially prohibits homosexual acts, with penalties of between 10 days' and 10 years' imprisonment for various 'crimes'. Although gay locals obviously exist, they behave with extreme discretion and caution. Gay travellers are advised to do likewise.

## MONEY

ATMs in major towns. Credit cards accepted in some top-end hotels (especially in Addis), but in very few restaurants or even midrange hotels. Bring US dollars in cash.

### Exchange Rates

| | | |
|---|---|---|
| Australia | A$1 | Birr16.82 |
| Canada | C$1 | Birr16.82 |
| Eurozone | €1 | Birr23.99 |
| Japan | ¥100 | Birr19.95 |
| New Zealand | NZ$1 | Birr16.08 |
| UK | UK£1 | Birr28.16 |
| USA | US$1 | Birr22.56 |

For current exchange rates, see www.xe.com.

## OPENING HOURS

**Banks** 8.30am–11am and 1.30pm–3.30pm Monday to Friday, 8.30am–11am Saturday
**Cafes** 6am–9pm or 10pm
**Government offices** 8.30am–11am and 1.30pm–3.30pm Monday to Friday, 8.30am–11am Saturday
**Internet cafes** 8am–8pm Monday to Saturday, limited hours Sunday
**Post offices** 8.30am–11am and 1.30pm–3.30pm Monday to Friday, 8.30am–11am Saturday
**Restaurants** 7am–10pm; upmarket restaurants in Addis and other big towns generally open noon–3pm and 6pm–10pm daily
**Shops** 8am–1pm and 2pm–5.30pm Monday to Saturday
**Telecommunications offices** 8.30am–11am and 1.30pm–3.30pm Monday to Friday, 8.30am–11am Saturday

## PUBLIC HOLIDAYS

Ethiopia observes the following national holidays:
**Leddet (Christmas)** 6 or 7 January
**Timkat (Epiphany)** 19 or 20 January
**Victory of Adwa Commemoration Day** 2 March
**Good Friday** March or April
**Easter Saturday** March or April
**International Labour Day** 1 May
**Ethiopian Patriots' Victory Day** (also known as Liberation Day) 5 May
**Downfall of the Derg** 28 May
**Kiddus Yohannes (New Year's Day)** 11 September
**Meskel (Finding of the True Cross)** 27 September

## SAFE TRAVEL

Compared with many African countries, Ethiopia is remarkably safe – most of the time. Serious or violent crime is rare; against travellers it's extremely rare. Outside the capital, the risk of petty crime drops still further.

A simple tip for travellers: always look as if you know where you're going. Thieves and con artists get wind of an uncertain newcomer in a minute.

It's very unlikely you'll encounter any serious difficulties – and even less likely if you're prepared for them.

## TELEPHONE

All mobile phones are operated by Ethio Telecom (www.ethionet.et). Whether you're using your home phone on a roaming plan or a locally bought phone and SIM card, expect connection problems, although the situation is improving.

## TIME

Ethiopia is three hours ahead of GMT/UTC.

The Ethiopian daily clock sits six hours behind European time – beginning each day with sunrise, which is 12 o'clock. After one hour of sunshine it's 1 o'clock. After two hours of sunshine? Yes, 2 o'clock. Also, the 24-hour clock is used occasionally in business. In short, be careful to ask if a time quoted is according to the Ethiopian or 'European' clock (*Be habesha/faranji akotater no*? – Is that Ethiopian/foreigners' time?). Additionally, note that instead of using 'am' or 'pm', Ethiopians use 'in the morning', 'in the evening' and 'at night' to indicate the period of day.

### VISAS

- Currently, all visitors except Kenyan and Djiboutian nationals need visas to visit Ethiopia.
- Nationals of most Western countries (including the US, UK, Australia, New Zealand, South Africa and most Western European countries) can obtain tourist visas on arrival at Bole International Airport. Aside from some (usually minor) queuing, the process upon arrival is painless and a tourist visa costs US$50.
- Normally immigration staff automatically grant a one-month visa, but if you request it, three months doesn't seem to be an issue.
- Visas are *not* available at any land border.

## Getting There & Away

### AIR

Addis Ababa's **Bole International Airport** (☎ 011 551 7000; www.addisairport.com) is Ethiopia's only international airport.

Ethiopia's only international and national carrier, **Ethiopian Airlines** (☎ 011 663 3163; www.ethiopianairlines.com; Bole Rd/Africa Ave; ⊙ 8.30am-5pm Mon-Sat) is rated as one of the best (and largest) airlines in Africa, with a modern fleet and a good safety record.

### LAND

#### Djibouti

Border formalities are usually pretty painless crossing between Djibouti and Ethiopia, but you *must* have your visa prior to arriving as none are issued at the land border.

#### Eritrea

All border crossings between Ethiopia and Eritrea have been closed for many years.

#### Kenya

- There are usually few problems crossing between Ethiopia and Kenya. The only feasible crossing is at Moyale, 772km south of Addis Ababa by road. Moyale has two incarnations, one on either side of the border.
- The northern, Ethiopian, version of Moyale is well connected to the north and Addis Ababa by bus, along a pretty good, but often potholed, section of sealed road. The southern, Kenyan, side of Moyale is truly in the middle of nowhere: around 800km north of Nairobi. A daily bus connects Moyale with Marsabit, from where transport is available onto Isiolo and then onward to Nairobi.
- If driving, make sure you fill up before leaving Ethiopia as petrol is half the price on the Ethiopian side of the border.The Ethiopian and Kenyan borders at Moyale are open daily. Kenyan three-month visas are painlessly produced at Kenyan immigration for the grand sum of US$50.
- Ethiopian immigration cannot issue Ethiopian visas; these must be obtained at an Ethiopian embassy prior to arrival at the border.

#### Sudan

The main border-crossing point with Sudan is the Metema crossing, 180km west of Gonder. The road between Gonder and Khartoum is now paved all the way. It's imperative that you've obtained your Sudan visa in Addis Ababa (not an easy task) or elsewhere before heading this way.

In Gonder minibuses leave daily for Metema (Birr105, three hours). There is also a direct bus from Addis (Birr375, two days). After reaching Metema walk across the border into the Sudanese town of Gallabat. From Gallabat, transport can be found to Gedaref (three hours) and onward to Khartoum.

## Getting Around

### AIR

Ethiopian Airlines (www.ethiopianairlines.com) is the only domestic carrier, with a comprehensive domestic route service and a solid safety record. It's well worth considering a domestic flight or two, even if you're travelling on a budget. Most flights leave from Addis Ababa, but not all are nonstop, which means you can also jump from one town to another.

Buying domestic tickets from an agency on arrival in Ethiopia is almost always cheaper than buying them online from outside the country.

### BUS

Recently a new breed of bus has taken to the roads of Ethiopia and these ones actually are pretty plush (air-con, reclining seats, on-board toilets, TVs and even free snacks). The biggest and best companies are **Selam Bus** (☎ 011 554 8800) and **Sky Bus** (☎ 011 156 8080; www.skybusethiopia.com). We strongly recommend that you pay extra to travel on one of these newer private bus operators. Apart from being much more comfortable, they rarely travel at night and are generally safer. Otherwise, you'll find yourself at the mercy of the government buses and similar private services.

The major drawback with bus travel is the size of the country. For the historical circuit alone, you'll spend a total of at least 10 days sitting on a bus to cover the 2500km.

### CAR & MOTORCYCLE

- Most people hire a 4WD with a driver.
- Despite competition between the numerous tour agents in Addis Ababa that hire 4WDs, prices are steep and start from US$180 per day. Most companies include unlimited kilometres, a driver, driver allowance (for their food and accommodation), fuel, third-party insurance, a collision-damage waiver and government taxes in their rates; check all these details, and ask if service charges will be added afterwards and if there are set driver's hours. Some companies allow you to pay for fuel separately. This is almost always cheaper than paying an all-inclusive rate.

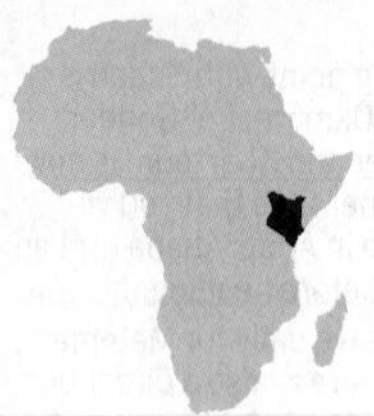

# Kenya

POP 47.7 MILLION / ☎254

**Includes ➡**



## Best Places to Eat

- ➡ Pili Pan (p628)
- ➡ Baby Marrow (p627)
- ➡ Shehnai Restaurant (p624)
- ➡ The Fort (p625)
- ➡ Tin Roof Cafe (p606)

## Best Places to Sleep

- ➡ Kobe Suite Resort (p628)
- ➡ Dea's Gardens (p611)
- ➡ Basecamp Masai Mara (p621)
- ➡ Camp Carnelley's (p611)
- ➡ Wildebeest Eco Camp (p603)

## Why Go?

Kenya is the Africa you always dreamed of: a land of vast savannah, immense herds of wildlife, and peoples with proud traditions rooted in the soil where human beings emerged. The Maasai, the Samburu, the Turkana, the Swahili, the Kikuyu: these are the peoples whose histories and daily struggles tell the story of a country and of a continent – the struggle to maintain traditions as the modern world crowds in, the daily fight for survival, the ancient tension between those who farm and those who roam.

Then, of course, there's the wildlife. From the Masai Mara to Tsavo, this is a country of vivid experiences – elephant families wallowing in swamps in the shadow of Mt Kilimanjaro, the massed millions of pink flamingos bathing in lake shallows, the landscape suddenly fallen silent and brought to attention by the arrival of an as-yet-unseen predator. There's nowhere better than Kenya to answer the call of the wild.

## When to Go

### Nairobi

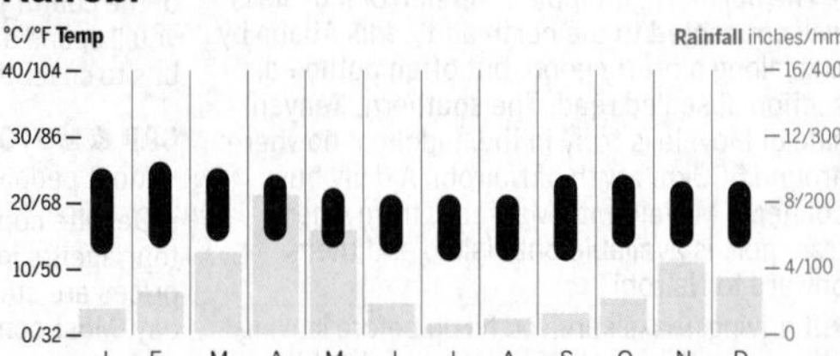


**Jul–Oct** The annual wildebeest migration arrives in the Masai Mara in all its epic glory.

**Jan–Feb** Hot, dry weather with high concentrations of wildlife in the major parks.

**Nov–Mar** Migratory birds present in their millions throughout the country.

# NAIROBI

POP 3.5 MILLION / ELEV 1661M

East Africa's most cosmopolitan city, Nairobi is Kenya's beating heart, an exciting, maddening concrete jungle that perfectly counterpoints the untrammelled natural beauty to be found elsewhere in the country.

Nairobi's polarising character ensures that the city is reviled and loved in equal measure, and even those who love it might well admit that it's the kind of place many rave about only once they're away from it. For those who call it home, the city's charms include a vibrant cultural life, fabulous places to eat and exciting nightlife. Its detractors point to its horrendous traffic, poor safety levels ('Nairobbery' is a common expat nickname) and its less-than-gorgeous appearance.

However, with a fantastic national park on its doorstep, the excellent National Museum and a series of quirky sights, Nairobi's reality – like that of so many places with a bad reputation – will often come as a pleasant surprise.

## Sights

**★Nairobi National Park** NATIONAL PARK
(☎020-2423423; www.kws.go.ke/parks/nairobi-national-park; adult/child US$43/22) Welcome to Kenya's most accessible yet incongruous safari experience. Set on the city's southern outskirts, Nairobi National Park (at 117 sq km, it's one of Africa's smallest) has abundant wildlife that can, in places, be viewed against a backdrop of city skyscrapers and planes coming in to land – it's one of the only national parks on earth bordering a capital city. Remarkably, the animals seem utterly unperturbed by it all.

**★Giraffe Centre** WILDLIFE RESERVE
(☎020-8070804; www.giraffecenter.org; Koitobos Rd; adult/child KSh1000/500; ⏲9am-5pm) This centre, which protects the highly endangered Rothschild's giraffe, combines serious conservation with enjoyable activities. You can observe, hand-feed or even kiss one of the giraffes from a raised structure, which is quite an experience. You may also spot warthogs snuffling about in the mud, and there's an interesting self-guided forest walk through the adjacent Gogo River Bird Sanctuary.

**★David Sheldrick Wildlife Trust** WILDLIFE RESERVE
(☎020-2301396; www.sheldrickwildlifetrust.org) Occupying a plot within Nairobi National Park, this non-profit trust was established in 1977, shortly after the death of David Sheldrick, who served as the anti-poaching warden of Tsavo National Park. Together with his wife Daphne, David pioneered techniques for raising orphaned black rhinos and elephants and reintroducing them into the wild, and the trust retains close links with Tsavo for these and other projects. The centre is one of Nairobi's most popular attractions, and deservedly so.

**★National Museum** MUSEUM
(☎020-8164134; www.museums.or.ke; Museum Hill Rd; adult/child KSh1200/600, combined ticket with Snake Park KSh1500/1000; ⏲8.30am-5.30pm) Kenya's wonderful National Museum, housed in an imposing building amid lush, leafy grounds just outside the centre, has a good range of cultural and natural-history exhibits. Aside from the exhibits, check out the life-sized fibreglass model of pachyderm celebrity Ahmed, the massive elephant that became a symbol of Kenya at the height of the 1980s poaching crisis, and who was placed under 24-hour guard by Jomo Kenyatta; he's in the inner courtyard next to the shop.

**★Karen Blixen's House & Museum** HISTORIC BUILDING
(www.museums.or.ke; Karen Rd; adult/child KSh1200/600; ⏲8.30am-6pm) If you loved *Out of Africa,* you'll love this museum in the farmhouse where author Karen Blixen lived between 1914 and 1931. She left after a series of personal tragedies, but the lovely colonial house has been preserved as a museum. The museum is set in expansive gardens, and is an interesting place to wander around. That said, the movie was actually shot at a nearby location, so don't be surprised if things don't look entirely right!

## Sleeping

You can expect to pay a bit more in Nairobi than you would for the same facilities elsewhere in Kenya. However, in a city where personal safety is something of an issue, it's worth shelling out more for secure surroundings. The majority of midrange and top-end places also tend to throw in a hearty buffet breakfast.

**★Wildebeest Eco Camp** TENTED CAMP $
(☎0734770733; http://wildebeestecocamp.com; 151 Mokoyeti Rd West, Langata; dm tents KSh1500, garden tent s/d from KSh4000/6000, luxury safari tents s/d/tr KSh10,000/12,500/15,000; ) This fabulous place in Langata is arguably Nairobi's outstanding budget option. The atmosphere is relaxed yet switched on, and the accommodation is spotless and great

# Kenya Highlights

**1 Masai Mara National Reserve** (p620) Experiencing the savannah, unmatched wildlife and the world's most fascinating traffic jam in the annual wildebeest migration.

**2 Amboseli National Park** (p629) Checking out the elephants and Kilimanjaro, two of Kenya's most famous picture-postcard views.

**3 Mt Kenya** (p613) Enjoying the tremendous hikes and jagged peaks that await on Kenya's highest mountain.

**4 Samburu National Reserve** (p617) Watching wildlife, hoping to spot the blue-legged Somali ostrich and the endangered Grevy's zebra.

**5 Lake Nakuru** (p613) Spotting rhinos, tree-climbing lions and Rothschild's giraffes by one of the Rift Valley's most beautiful lakes.

value, however much you're paying. The deluxe garden tents are as good as many exclusive such places out on safari – for a fraction of the price. A great Nairobi base.

**Milimani Backpackers & Safari Centre** HOSTEL $
(☎0718919020, 0722347616; www.milimanibackpackers.com; Karen St, St Helens Lane, off Langata Rd, Milimani; camping KSh800, dm KSh1500, cabins s/d KSh2700/3000; @📶) This terrific place within a very secure gated community is one of the friendliest accommodation options in town, and whether you camp out back, cosy up in the dorms or splurge on your own cabin, you'll end up huddled around the fire at night, swapping travel stories and dining on home-cooked meals (from KSh500) with fellow travellers.

**★Lotos Inn & Suites** HOTEL, SUITES $$
(☎0727 168169; http://lotos.co.ke/; 19 Mpaka Road, Westlands; d from KSh13,000; 📶) Despite the bizarre spelling, this fantastic new addition to the city's hotel scene offers spacious, great-value and super-comfortable rooms within easy walking distance of Westland's eating and nightlife attractions. There's a great breakfast buffet in the top-floor restaurant and very friendly staff. The only negative is a lack of mosquito nets or suitable prophylaxis – bring your own.

**★Kahama Hotel** HOTEL $$
(☎0704857475; www.kahamahotels.co.ke; Murang'a Rd; s/d from US$45/55; P📶) Almost equidistant between the city centre and the National Museum, this place is a terrific budget choice. Billing itself 'economy with style', it provides just that with pleasant rooms and comfy beds. The only downside? The new highway passes by the front door – ask for a room at the back.

**Bush House & Camp** GUESTHOUSE $$
(www.bush-house.com; Karen Triangle, Karen Rd, Karen; s/d US$60/80; 📶) Tucked away inside a gated community, this friendly and quiet place offers good-value midrange accommodation in a large house set in a well-tended garden. The various rooms differ quite a bit in size and decor, but they enjoy a cosy atmosphere and breakfast is good. Check-in is done at the next-door Karen Inn, run by the same management.

**★Sarova Stanley Hotel** HOTEL $$$
(☎0719048000; www.sarovahotels.com/stanley-nairobi; cnr Kimathi St & Kenyatta Ave; s/d from US$455/505; P❄📶🏊) A Nairobi classic. The original Stanley Hotel was established in 1902 – past guests include Ernest Hemingway, Clark Gable, Ava Gardner and Gregory Peck. The latest version comes with an eye-watering price tag, but boasts large and luxurious rooms and a timeless lobby characterised by plush green leather banquettes, opulent chandeliers and lots of dark-wood trimmings.

## Eating

If you're planning on having dinner anywhere in the city centre, be sure to take a taxi back to your accommodation as the streets empty out once the sun goes down. For dinner it's worth heading out to the suburbs, where there are dozens of choices of cuisine from all over the world. Karen has the best range.

**Pasara Café** INTERNATIONAL $
(ground fl, Lonrho Bldg, Standard St; mains KSh300-600; ⌚6am-11pm Mon-Sat; 📶) This curiously charming city-centre cafe is a sort of Kenyan greasy spoon where time has rather stood still; think Formica tables and cloth booths. But it's a good spot for a quick lunch in the CBD, with a wide selection of sandwiches, grills and breakfasts.

**Nyama Choma Stalls** KENYAN $
(Haile Selassie Ave; mains around KSh500) At these backstreet stalls near the Railway Museum, behind the Shell petrol station, foreigners are a rare sight, but you'll be warmly welcomed and encouraged to sample Kenyan dishes such as *matoke* (cooked mashed plantains) and wonderful barbecued meat.

**★Tin Roof Cafe** INTERNATIONAL $$
(☎0706348215; www.facebook.com/TinRoofCafe; Dagoretti Rd, Karen; mains KSh950-1100 ⌚8.30am-5.30pm; 📶) This place has all the necessary ingredients to be a Nairobi favourite – a quiet garden setting in Karen, great coffee, amazing juices, an Ottolenghi salad bar and a commitment to healthy eating. Despite having a cafe vibe, full meals are possible and there's a set lunch for KSh750. Our only complaint? It doesn't open for dinner.

**★Talisman** INTERNATIONAL $$
(☎0705999997; www.thetalismanrestaurant.com; 320 Ngong Rd, Karen; mains KSh1200-2500 ⌚8am-midnight Tue-Sun; 📶) This classy cafe bar-restaurant remains fashionable with the Karen in-crowd, and rivals any of Kenya's top eateries for imaginative international food. The comfortable lounge-like rooms mix modern African and European styles; the courtyard provides some welcome air and specials such as pan-seared ostrich fillet and twice-cooked pork belly perk up the palate no end.

**Thorn Tree Café** INTERNATIONAL $$
(☎0719048000; Sarova Stanley Hotel, cnr Kimathi St & Kenyatta Ave; mains KSh1200-2400; ⊙6am-9.30pm) The Stanley Hotel's legendary pavement cafe still serves as a traveller favourite, and caters to most tastes with a good mix of food. The original thorn-tree noticeboard in the courtyard gave rise to the general expression, and inspired Lonely Planet's own online Thorn Tree Travel Forum. The menu ranges from grilled giant prawns to Kenyan-style chicken stew.

**Amaica** KENYAN $$
(☎020-5202200; www.amaica.co.ke; Getathuru Garden, off Peponi Rd, Westlands; mains KSh1000-2500; 📶) Dining at this wonderful place magically takes you out of the city for an hour or two, with views into the lush Karura Forest from the open terrace. The cooking also takes you on a journey through Kenya with its stellar menu of indigenous Kenyan cooking from all parts of the country. Don't miss the peanut soup!

**Carnivore** GRILL $$$
(☎0733611608, 020-5141300; www.tamarind.co.ke/carnivore; off Langata Rd, Karen; buffet from KSh3000; ⊙noon-3pm & 6.30-11pm; P) Love it or hate it, Carnivore is hands down the most famous *nyama choma* (barbecued meat) in Kenya – an icon among tourists, expats and wealthier locals for over 25 years. At the entrance is a huge barbecue pit laden with real swords of beef, pork, lamb, chicken and farmed game meats. Prices are high, but it's a memorable night out.

## Drinking & Nightlife

Nairobi has an enormous, exuberant and sometimes rather intimidating nightlife. Such a massive city naturally has almost endless opportunities for hedonistic nights out, but the real trick for visitors is finding places where foreigners won't be harrassed. Westlands is generally the neighbourhood best for this – foreigners will still get attention, of course, but it's not as relentless as elsewhere.

**★Gipsy's Bar** BAR
(Woodvale Grove; ⊙11am-4am) This is one of the most popular bars in Westlands, pulling in a large, mixed crowd of Kenyans, expats and prostitutes. Snacks are available and there's decent Western and African music, with parties frequently spilling out onto the pavement.

**Black Diamond** CLUB
(1st fl, Bishan Plaza, Mpaka Rd, Westlands; ⊙6pm-6am) If you want to explore real Nairobi nightlife, Black Diamond would be an obvious place to start. The crowd is as lively as the music, which is mainly Kenyan and other African pop. While it's all a lot of fun, do watch your belongings and never leave your drink unattended. Things get going around midnight.

### COFFEE CULTURE

Western cafe culture has hit Nairobi and been seized upon enthusiastically by expats and residents pining for a decent cup of Kenyan coffee, most obviously at the now-ubiquitous Java House outlets (a kind of Kenyan Starbucks surrogate). Most cafes offer at least some form of food, whether it's a few cakes or a full menu, but don't serve alcohol.

## Shopping

Nairobi is a good place to pick up souvenirs before heading home. There are loads of souvenir shops in the city centre and in the area northwest of Kenyatta Ave, so you're spoiled for choice. Be warned, though, that prices are usually higher than elsewhere in the country.

**★Souk** ARTS & CRAFTS
(☎0706348215; www.souk-kenya.com; Dagoretti Rd; ⊙9.30am-5.30pm Mon-Sat) Some of Kenya's more creative artists, photographers, leatherworkers and other high-quality artisans and artists have come together under one roof – the result is one of Kenya's most discerning shopping experiences. It shares premises with the equally excellent Tin Roof Cafe.

**★Utamaduni** ARTS & CRAFTS
(www.utamadunicraftshop.com; Bogani East Rd, Karen; ⊙9am-6pm) Utamaduni is a large crafts emporium and easily one of the best places to souvenir shop in Nairobi, with more than a dozen separate shops selling all kinds of excellent African artworks and souvenirs. Prices start relatively high, but there's *none* of the hard sell you'd get in town. A portion of all proceeds goes to the Kenya Wildlife Foundation.

## Information

### DANGERS & ANNOYANCES

First-time visitors to Nairobi are understandably daunted by the city's unenviable reputation. 'Nairobbery', as it has been nicknamed by jaded residents and expats, is often regarded as the most dangerous city in Africa, beating stiff competition from Johannesburg, Abidjan and Lagos.

# Nairobi



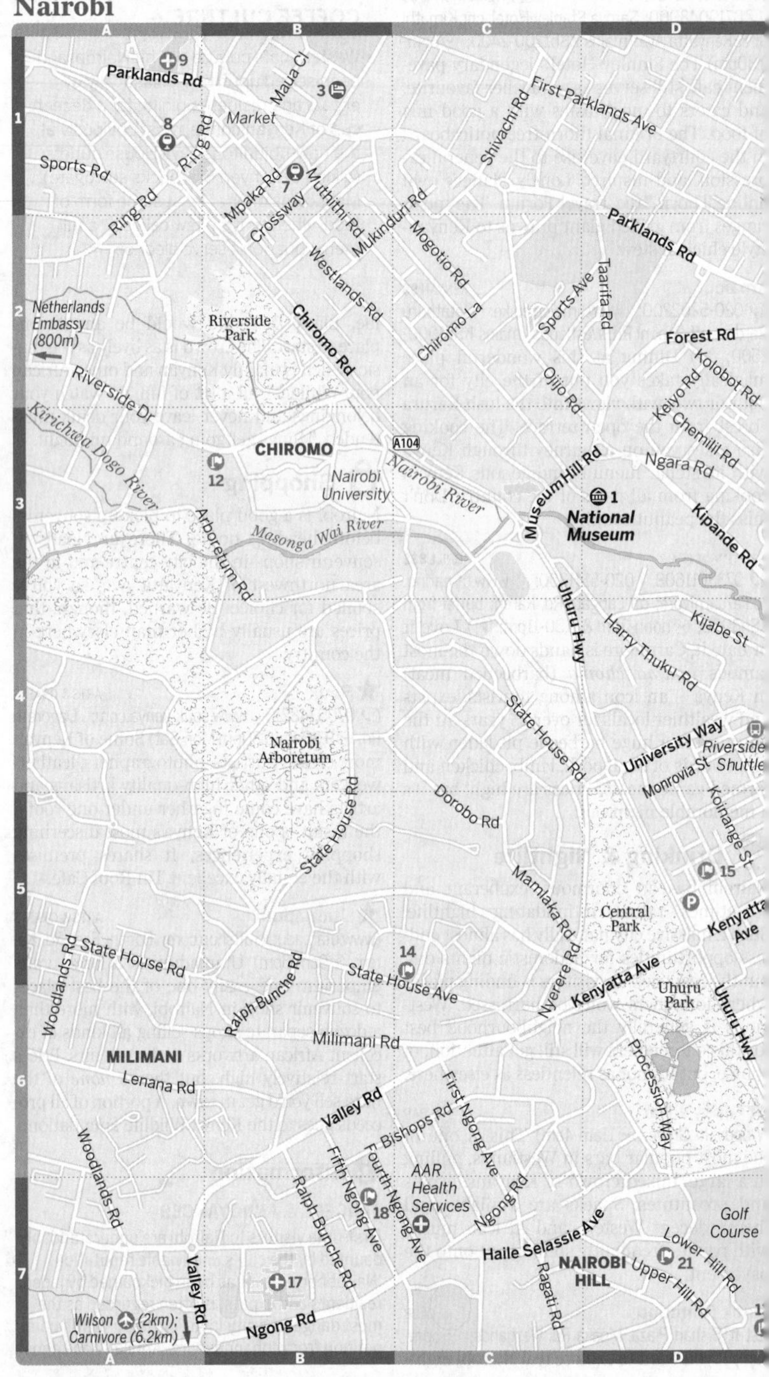
A
B
C
D
1
2
3
4
5
6
7
Parklands Rd
Maua Cl
Market
Ring Rd
Sports Rd
Mpaka Rd
Muthithi Rd
Crossway
Mukinduri Rd
Mogotio Rd
Westlands Rd
Shivachi Rd
First Parklands Ave
Parklands Rd
Sports Ave
Taarifa Rd
Chiromo La
Chiromo Rd
Riverside Park
Netherlands Embassy (800m)
Riverside Dr
Kirichwa Dogo River
Forest Rd
Kolobot Rd
Keiyo Rd
Chemilil Rd
Ojijo Rd
Ngara Rd
CHIROMO
Nairobi University
A104
Nairobi River
Museum Hill Rd
National Museum
Kipande Rd
Masonga Wai River
Arboretum Rd
Uhuru Hwy
Harry Thuku Rd
Kijabe St
State House Rd
University Way
Riverside Shuttle
Monrovia St
Koinange St
Nairobi Arboretum
State House Rd
Dorobo Rd
Mamlaka Rd
Central Park
Kenyatta Ave
State House Rd
Woodlands Rd
Ralph Bunche Rd
State House Ave
Nyerere Rd
Kenyatta Ave
Uhuru Park
Uhuru Hwy
Milimani Rd
MILIMANI
Lenana Rd
Valley Rd
Procession Way
First Ngong Ave
Bishops Rd
Woodlands Rd
Fifth Ngong Ave
Fourth Ngong Ave
Ralph Bunche Rd
AAR Health Services
Ngong Rd
Golf Course
Lower Hill Rd
Haile Selassie Ave
NAIROBI HILL
Ragati Rd
Upper Hill Rd
Valley Rd
Ngong Rd
Wilson (2km); Carnivore (6.2km)
1
3
7
8
9
12
14
15
17
18
21

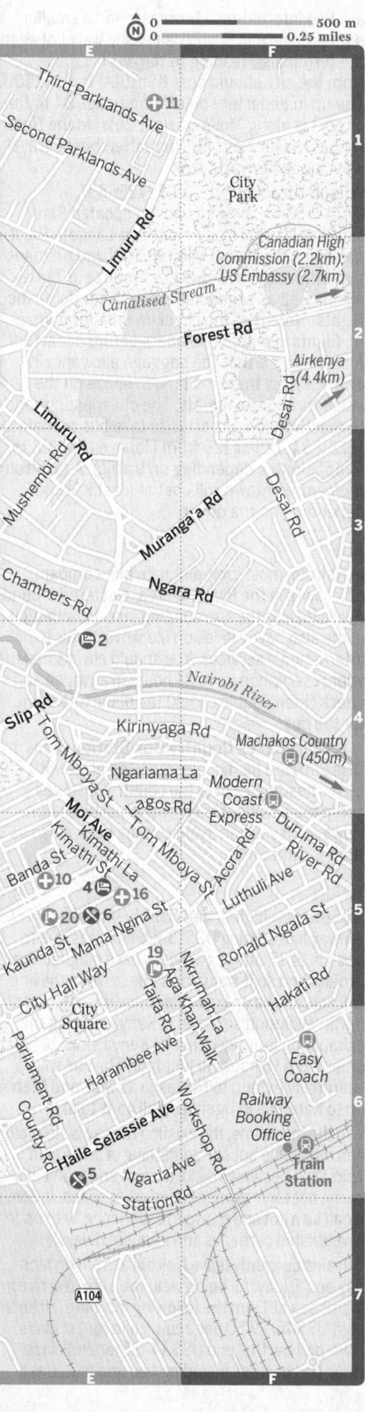


## Nairobi

**Top Sights**

1 National Museum ... D3

**Sleeping**

2 Kahama Hotel ... E4
3 Lotos Inn & Suites ... B1
4 Sarova Stanley Hotel ... E5

**Eating**

5 Nyama Choma Stalls ... E6
6 Pasara Café ... E5
Thorn Tree Café ... (see 4)

**Drinking & Nightlife**

7 Black Diamond ... B1
8 Gipsy's Bar ... A1

**Information**

9 AAR Health Services Clinic ... A1
10 Acacia Medical Centre ... E5
11 Aga Khan Hospital ... E1
12 Australian High Commission ... B3
13 British Embassy ... D7
14 Ethiopian Embassy ... C5
15 French Embassy ... D5
16 KAM Pharmacy ... E5
17 Nairobi Hospital ... B7
18 South Sudan Embassy ... B7
19 Tanzanian Embassy ... E5
20 Uganda High Commission (Consular Section) ... E5
21 UK High Commission ... D7

Read the local newspapers and you'll quickly discover that carjacking, robbery and violence are daily occurrences, and the social ills behind them are unlikely to disappear in the near future.

The most likely annoyance for travellers is petty theft, which is most likely to occur at budget hotels and campsites. As a general rule, you should take advantage of your hotel's safe and never leave your valuables out in the open. While you're walking around town, don't carry anything that you wouldn't want to lose. As an extra safety precaution, it's best to only carry money in your wallet, hiding your credit cards and bank cards elsewhere.

In the event that you are mugged, never, ever resist – simply give up your valuables and, more often than not, your assailant will flee the scene rapidly. Remember that a petty thief and a violent aggressor are very different kinds of people, so don't give your assailant any reason to do something rash.

While it's important to understand the potential dangers and annoyances that are present, you shouldn't let fear exile you to your hotel room – remember that the majority of foreign visitors in Nairobi never experience any kind of problem. Exude confidence, practise street smarts and don't wear anything too flashy and you should encounter nothing worse than a few persistent safari touts and the odd con artist.

### MEDICAL SERVICES

Nairobi has plenty of health-care facilities that are used to dealing with travellers and expats, which is a good thing as you're going to want to avoid the Kenyatta National Hospital – although it's free, stretched resources mean you may come out with something worse than you had when you went in.

**AAR Health Services** (☎0731191070, 0709701000; http://aar-healthcare.com; Williamson House, Fourth Ngong Ave; ⏰24hr) Probably the best of a number of private ambulance and emergency air-evacuation companies. It also runs private clinics at various locations around Nairobi, including in **Westlands** (☎0731191064; http://aar-healthcare.com; 4th fl, Sarit Centre Mall, Westlands; ⏰8am-7pm Mon-Fri, 8am-4pm Sat, 10am-2pm Sun).

**Acacia Medical Centre** (☎020-2212200; http://acaciamedcentre.com; ICEA Bldg, Kenyatta Ave; ⏰7am-7pm Mon-Fri, 7am-5pm Sat, 8am-5pm Sun) Privately run clinic in the city centre.

**Aga Khan Hospital** (☎020-3662020; Third Parklands Ave; ⏰24hr) A reliable hospital with 24-hour emergency services.

**KAM Pharmacy** (☎020-2227195; www.kampharmacy.com; Executive Tower, IPS Bldg, Kimathi St; ⏰8.30am-6pm Mon-Fri, 9am-2pm Sat) A one-stop shop for medical treatment, with a pharmacy, doctor's surgery and laboratory.

**Nairobi Hospital** (☎020-2846000; www.nairobihospital.org; off Argwings Kodhek Rd; ⏰24hr) One of the city's largest hospitals.

### TOURIST INFORMATION

Despite the many safari companies with signs saying 'Tourist Information', there is still no official tourist office in Nairobi. For events and other listings you'll have to check the local newspapers, search online or ask at your hotel.

The vast noticeboards at the Sarit Centre and Yaya Centre are good places to look for local information. All sorts of things are advertised here, including language courses, vehicles for sale and houses for rent.

## ℹ Getting There & Away

### AIR

Nairobi is the main arrival and departure point for international flights, although some touch down in Mombasa as well.

Nairobi has two airports:

**Jomo Kenyatta International Airport** (NBO; ☎0722205061, 020-6822111; www.kaa.go.ke) Most international flights to Nairobi arrive at this airport, 15km southeast of the city. There are two international terminals and a smaller domestic terminal; you can easily walk between the terminals. Heading to the airport, taxis from the city should cost KSh1500 to KSh2500. The main departure point for city bus 34 to the airport is along Moi Ave, right outside the Hotel Ambassadeur Nairobi. Thereafter, buses travel west along Kenyatta Ave.

**Wilson Airport** (WIL; ☎0724256837, 0724255343; www.kaa.go.ke) Located 6km south of Nairobi's city centre on Langata Rd; it has some flights between Nairobi and Kilimanjaro International Airport or Mwanza in Tanzania, as well as scheduled and charter domestic flights. Note that the check-in time for domestic flights is one to two hours before departure. Also be aware that the baggage allowance is only 15kg, as there isn't much space on the small turboprop aircraft. The cheapest option to reach Wilson Airport is to take bus or matatu 15, 31, 34, 125 or 126 from Moi Ave (KSh35, 15 to 45 minutes depending on traffic). A taxi from the centre of town will cost at least KSh1000, depending on the driver.

### BUS

In Nairobi, most long-distance bus-company offices are in the River Rd area, clustered around Accra Rd and the surrounding streets, although some also have offices on Monrovia St for their international services. You should always make your reservation up to 24 hours in advance and check (then double check) the departure point for the bus.

The **Machakos Country Bus Station** (Landhies Rd) is a hectic, disorganised place with buses heading all over the country; it serves companies without their own departure point. However, if you can avoid coming here, do so as theft is rampant.

### TRAIN

A brand new high-speed Nairobi–Mombasa railway line costing US$13.8 billion was due to open in 2017, although delays have plagued the project and so it's anyone's guess when the line will actually be operational. Once it is, however, it will revolutionise travel in Kenya, cutting the exhausting journey between Kenya's two biggest cities from 18 hours to just four. The line will eventually extend to Naivasha as well, and then on to Kampala in Uganda, if all goes to plan.

In the meantime, the existing railway is slow, old and unreliable but still something of an African epic. Do it because you love trains and aren't in a hurry, not for reasons of comfort or speed. Indeed, it can be a hot and crowded experience, with poorly ventilated carriages and frequent delays.

Trains currently leave Nairobi at 5pm on Monday and Friday. All being well, you should arrive in Mombasa at 11am the following morning. Tickets cost US$45/27.50 per adult/child for 1st class (two-bed berths) and US$34/22 for 2nd class (four-bed berths), including bed and breakfast (you also get dinner with 1st class). Book as far in advance as possible. Trains return to Nairobi from Mombasa on Wednesday and Sunday.

Nairobi train station has a small **booking office** (Station Rd; ⏲9am-noon & 2-6.30pm). You can book via one of many travel agencies online, or come in person to book tickets a few days in advance of your intended departure. On the day of departure, arrive early.

# SOUTHERN RIFT VALLEY

It's hard to believe that the geological force that almost broke Africa in two instead created such serene landscapes. But this southern slice of Africa's Great Rift Valley is cool and calm, swathed in forest and watered by moody mineral lakes that blanch and blush with the movements of pelicans and flamingos. The altitude peaks and dips all the way from Nairobi to Nakuru, ensuring pleasant weather almost year-round.

## Lake Naivasha

POP 182,000 / ☎050

A short drive from Nairobi and a world away from the capital's choked arteries is Lake Naivasha, the highest of the Rift Valley lakes (at 1884m above sea level). Hugged by grassy banks and shingled with cacti and sand olive trees, the lake extends like a vast, sunlit sea. But there's more to this spot than the lovely blue lake. You can ride among giraffes and zebras, sip on a glass of Rift Valley red, and relax in the garden at Elsamere, the former home of late *Born Free* personality Joy Adamson. Most of the lake is ringed by an electric fence, so hippo attacks are rare. A greater threat is the traffic, which loops around the road at speed: take care when out walking.

### Sights

**★Elsamere** MUSEUM
(☎050-2021247, 0726443151; www.elsamere.com; KSh1050; ⏲9am-6pm; P) Stippled with sisal, yellow fever trees and candelabra euphorbia, this is the former home of the late Joy Adamson of *Born Free* fame. She bought the house in 1967 with her husband George, and did much of her painting, writing and conservation work here until her murder in 1980. Guests can attend regular screenings of a flickering 1970s film about Joy's life and her myriad love affairs, notably with Elsa the lioness.

**★Crescent Island** WILDLIFE RESERVE
(www.crescentisland.co; adult/student US$30/20; ⏲8am-6pm) This private island sanctuary can be reached by boat, or by driving across the narrow, swampy causeway from Sanctuary Farm. It's one of the few places in the Rift Valley where you can walk among giraffes, zebras, waterbucks, impalas and countless bird species. Lucky visitors might even spot a leopard. Island walks, led by a guide, last between 90 minutes and three hours. It's also a good spot for a picnic lunch.

### Sleeping

Lake Naivasha has some wonderful accommodation options and because much of the lake's shoreline is taken up by camps, hotels and guesthouses of various sorts, it's never likely to be a struggle to find somewhere to stay.

**★Camp Carnelley's** CAMPGROUND, BANDAS $
(☎050-50004, 0722260749; www.campcarnelleys.com; Moi South Lake Rd; camping KSh800-1000, dm KSh1000, r from KSh3000, bandas KSh8000-16,000; P) Right on the shoreline, this gorgeous budget spot has comfortable *bandas* (thatched huts), simple twin rooms with woolly blankets and one of the cleanest and most attractive campsites in Kenya. Come evening, head to the fantastic wooden-beamed bar and restaurant with its hip couches, roaring fireplace and creative menu – another highlight.

**★Dea's Gardens** GUESTHOUSE $$
(☎0733747433, 0734453761; www.deasgardens.com; Off Moi South Lake Rd; half-board per person KSh9500; ) This charming guesthouse is run by the charismatic and elegant Dea. The main house has three guest rooms and is a gorgeous chalet of Swiss inspiration, while the cottages in the lush grounds are large and comfortable. Meals are served family style with Dea as your host, and it's hard to imagine a warmer welcome.

**Elsamere Lodge** HOTEL $$$
(☎050-2021055; www.elsamere.com; s/d full board US$150/245; P) The conservation centre at the very lovely former home of Joy Adamson (p611) also doubles as a lodge with high novelty value. You can stay here in one of the 10 pleasant rooms dotted through the pretty garden where wild colobus monkeys roam, and enjoy high tea in the Adamsons' dining room.

WORTH A TRIP

### HELL'S GATE NATIONAL PARK

Dry and dusty but infinitely peaceful, **Hell's Gate** (☎0726610508, 020-2379467; www.kws.org; adult/child US$26/17, bike hire KSh500, car entry KSh300; ⏰6am-6pm; P) is that rare Kenyan park made for bicycles and exploring on foot. Large carnivores are very rare indeed, so you can cycle past grazing zebras and bison, spot rock hyraxes as they clamber up inclines and watch dust clouds swirl in the wind. In the early morning the park is all aglow with its rich ochre soils and savannah grasses squeezed between looming cliffs of rusty columnar basalt.

## Eating & Drinking

Almost all of the campsites and guesthouses have their own restaurants, so there's little in the way of independent dining, though most accommodation places happily welcome non-guests to their restaurants.

There's not much nightlife along the lakeshore, though most hotels have a bar where you can enjoy a drink after dark.

## Getting There & Away

Frequent matatus (KSh100, one hour) run along Moi South Lake Rd between Naivasha town and Kongoni on the lake's western side, passing the turn-offs to Hell's Gate National Park and Fisherman's Camp (KSh70). Taxis charge upwards of KSh2000 for the hop from Naivasha. Contact **Nickson Gatimu** (☎0726797750) if you'd like to arrange a pick up.

# Nakuru

POP 308,000 / ☎051

Speed through Nakuru on your way to the lakes and you might wonder why anyone would choose to stay here. At first glance, Kenya's fourth-largest city is grim and provincial, without much to offer besides a convenient refuel. But stick around longer and we bet you'll start to like it: Nakuru is changing fast, gentrifying around the edges and adopting some of the better aspects of Nairobi – minus the stress and the crime.

If you don't want to fork out to overnight at Lake Nakuru, the city makes a good base for exploring the park and surrounds.

## Sleeping & Eating

Nakuru has plenty of hotels and they're generally cheaper than staying by the lake itself. The smarter places tend to be some way up the hillside, out of the traffic-clogged city centre and with views towards the lake.

There's a good range of restaurants in Nakuru, and finding a decent bite to eat in the city centre should never be a problem.

**★Milimani Guest House** GUESTHOUSE **$$**
(☎0753616263; www.nakurumilimaniguesthouse.co.ke; Maragoli Ave; s/d KSh5500/6600; P 📶) Perched above the town with soaring views towards the lake, this well-run, stylish place is a tranquil escape from the traffic below. Rooms wrap around a living room furnished with sofas and a fireplace, and breakfast is served in the pretty garden. The rooms are bright and clean with hip touches, and the welcome is warm.

**Midland Hotel** HOTEL **$$**
(☎051-2212125, 0738900380; www.midlandhotel.co.ke; Geoffrey Kamau Way; s/d from US$69/99; P 📶) A Nakuru institution, the Midland first opened in 1906 as a hotel for first-class rail travellers. More than a century later, it's still going strong. The architecture won't excite you, but the renovated rooms are modern, clean and stylish and there's a new block being constructed, which is likely to raise standards further.

**Hygienic Butchery** KENYAN **$**
(Tom Mboya Rd; mains KSh180-270; ⏰8am-10pm) Great name, great place. The Kenyan tradition of *nyama choma* (barbecued meats) is alive and well here. Sidle up to the counter, try a piece of tender mutton or beef and order half a kilo (per person) of whichever takes your fancy, along with chapatis or ugali (no sauce!).

The meat will then be brought to your table, carved up and you dig in with your hands. Bliss! It also serves stews, barbecued chicken and other dishes.

## Drinking & Nightlife

Nakuru is a lively town, with plenty going on after dark. There are several bars and clubs in the city centre, particularly around Kenyatta Ave and West Rd. Nakuru is generally a safe place, but it's still a good idea to take a taxi after dark.

## Getting There & Away

**Easy Coach** (www.easycoach.co.ke; Kenyatta Ave) is one of several bus companies offering services to Nairobi (KSh500, three hours), Eldoret (KSh650, 2¾ hours) and Kisumu (KSh750, 3½ hours).

## Lake Nakuru National Park

Just two hours' drive from Nairobi, **Lake Nakuru** (☎0728355207, 0728355267; www.kws.go.ke; adult/child US$60/30; ⏲6.30am-6.30pm) is among Kenya's finest national parks. Flanked by rocky escarpments, pockets of forest and at least one waterfall, the park is gorgeous year-round and is home to both black and white rhinos, lions, leopards, hippos and giraffes. Rising water levels in 2014 forced the park's famous flamingos to flee, as well as the park authorities to move the entrance gate – the old one now stands submerged by the lake along with hundreds of now-dead trees, creating a fairly haunting first impression.

The southern end of the lake is the best place to see wildlife, away from the busy city of Nakuru, which borders the park's northern extent. The forested area below Flamingo Hill is a favourite lion-spotting point – lionesses love to sleep in the trees – while leopards frequent the same area, and are also seen around Makolia camp.

### Sleeping & Eating

There are plenty of sleeping options inside the national park itself, including a number of fancy safari lodges, some simple guesthouses and four excellent bush campsites. Alternatively you can sleep in a hotel in Nakuru town. If you're camping you'll have to bring your own food or eat in the pricey lodges, most of which welcome non-guests for meals. Campers should always make sure that tents are securely zipped or the vervet monkeys and baboons will make a right mess while cleaning you out. Most lodges include full board in their packages, though some guesthouses are self-catering.

**Wildlife Club of Kenya Guesthouse** HOSTEL $
(☎0720456546, 0723760970; per person without bathroom KSh1250) Hands down Nakuru's best budget choice, this rather charming cottage inside the park looks out towards the lake and often finds its own gardens frequented by zebra and buffalo. Inside it's nothing special, but there are six simple rooms with shared bathrooms, as well as a moderately well-equipped kitchen and a comfortable dining room. Self-catering only.

**Sarova Lion Hill Lodge** LODGE $$$
(☎020-2315139, 0709111000; www.sarovahotels.com/lionhill-nakuru; s/d full board from US$200/269; P🛜🏊) Sitting up the lake's eastern slopes, this lodge offers first-class service and comfort. The views from the open-air restaurant-bar and from most rooms are great. Rooms are understated but pretty, while the flashy suites are large and impressive. On quiet days you may even get the residents' rate, which is half that quoted here.

**Flamingo Hill Tented Camp** TENTED CAMP $$$
(☎0727525279; www.flamingohillcamp.com; full board per person from US$110; P🛜🏊) 🍃 Flamingo Hill strikes a nice balance between chic and wild, and by the standards of national-park lodges it offers a good deal. There's a smart wooden communal area, 30 luxury tents, a spa and pool. The camp is just a short drive from the main gate, and it's also possible for non-guests to have lunch here.

### ℹ Getting There & Away

The park begins on the outskirts of Nakuru town, so simply head there to access the park.

# CENTRAL HIGHLANDS & LAIKIPIA

The Central Highlands are the spiritual heartland of Kenya's largest tribe, the Kikuyu. This is the land the Mau Mau fought for, that the colonists coveted and whose natural, cyclical patterns define the lives of the country's largest rural population. These highlands form one of the most evocative sections of Africa's Great Rift Valley. It is here that Mt Kenya, Africa's second-highest mountain, rises into the clouds – climbing it is one of the great rites of passage of African travel. In its shadow lies one of Kenya's most intriguing national parks: Aberdare National Park, home to some of the oldest mountains on the continent.

## Mt Kenya National Park

Africa's second-highest mountain is also one of its most beautiful. Here, mere minutes from the equator, glaciers carve out the throne of Ngai, the old high god of the Kikuyu. To this day the tribe keeps its doors open to the face of the sacred mountain, and some still come to its lower slopes to offer prayers. Besides being venerated by the

Kikuyu, Mt Kenya and **Mt Kenya National Park** (☎0712294084, Nairobi 020-3568763; www.kws.go.ke; adult/child day entry US$52/26, 4-/5-/6-day package adult US$208/260/312, child US$104/130/156) have the rare honour of being both a Unesco World Heritage Site and a Unesco Biosphere Reserve.

The highest peaks of Batian (5199m) and Nelion (5188m) can only be reached by mountaineers with technical skills, but Point Lenana (4985m), the third-highest peak, can be reached by trekkers and is the usual goal for most mortals. When the clouds part, the views are simply magnificent.

## Activities

There are at least seven different routes up Mt Kenya. Of those, we cover Naro Moru, the easiest and most popular, as well as Sirimon and Chogoria, which are excellent alternatives, and the exciting but demanding Summit Circuit, which circles Batian and Nelion, thus enabling you to mix and match ascending and descending routes. Other routes include the Timau Route and Burguret Route.

### Naro Moru Route

Although the least scenic, this is the most straightforward, popular route, and still a spectacular and very enjoyable trail. Allow a minimum of four days for the hike; it's possible in three if you arrange transport between Naro Moru and the Met Station Hut, but doing it this quickly risks serious altitude sickness.

### GUIDES, COOKS & PORTERS

Having a porter for your gear is like travelling in a chauffeured Mercedes instead of a matatu. With both on your team, your appreciation of this mountain will be enhanced a hundredfold. If you hire a guide or porter who can also cook, you won't regret it.

The KWS issues vouchers to all registered guides and porters, who should also hold identity cards; they won't be allowed into the park without them.

The cost of guides varies depending on the qualifications of the guide, whatever the last party paid and your own negotiating skills. You should expect to pay a minimum of US$30/25/20 per day for a guide/cook/porter.

### Sirimon Route

A popular alternative to Naro Moru, this route has more spectacular scenery, greater flexibility and a gentler rate of ascent, although it is still easy to climb too fast, so allow at least five days for the hike. It's well worth considering combining it with the Chogoria route for a six- to seven-day traverse that will really bring out the best of Mt Kenya.

### Chogoria Route

This route is justly famous for crossing some of the most spectacular and varied scenery on Mt Kenya, and is often combined with the Sirimon route (usually as the descent). The only disadvantage is the long distance between Chogoria village and the park gate. Allow at least five days for a hike here.

## Tours

**IntoAfrica** TREKKING
(☎Nairobi 0722511752, UK 0797-4975723; www.intoafrica.co.uk) An environmentally and culturally sensitive company offering both scheduled and exclusive seven-day trips ascending Sirimon route and descending Chogoria. All trips are calculated to ensure that local contractors earn a fair living wage from their work.

**KG Mountain Expeditions** TREKKING
(☎0733606338, Nairobi 020-2033874; www.kenyaexpeditions.com) Run by a highly experienced mountaineer and a team of knowledgeable trekkers, KG offers all-inclusive scheduled treks. It also runs an outdoor-gear rental shop from its office in Naromoru, at the base of Mt Kenya.

## Sleeping & Eating

As well as the official sleeping options on each route, it is possible to camp anywhere on the mountain; the cost of camping is included in the four- to six-day park-fee packages payable at any gate. Most people camp near the huts or bunk-houses, as there are often toilets and water nearby.

You'll need to be totally self-sufficient if you're climbing Mt Kenya, as none of the lodges or camps on the route offer meals. However, most packages include cooks who both carry and prepare all meals for you on the way. Even if that is the case, take citrus fruits and/or citrus drinks as well as chocolate, sweets or dried fruit to keep your blood-sugar level up.

## Mt Kenya National Park

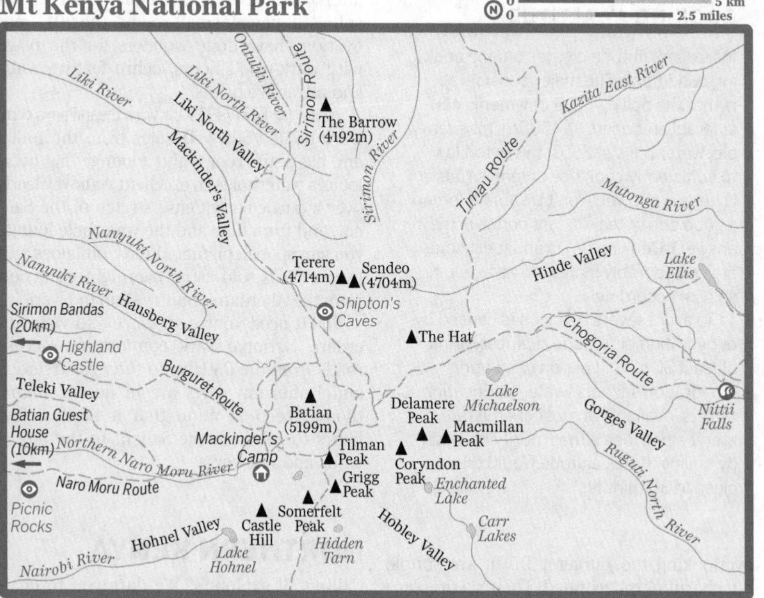


**Batian Guest House** GUESTHOUSE $
(www.kws.go.ke/content/batian-guest-house; 8-bed banda US$180) Those needing a bit of luxury can sleep in lovely, KWS-run Batian Guest House, which sleeps eight people in several different bedrooms. You are required to book the entire house, however; it's not possible simply to book a room. It's around 1km from the Naro Moru gate.

**Mackinder's Camp** HUT $
(☎0724082754; dm US$30) At 4200m on the Naro Moru route. Book through Naro Moru River Lodge (p615).

**Sirimon Bandas** BANDA $$
(www.kws.go.ke/content/sirimon-cottage; banda US$80) The excellent KWS-run Sirimon Bandas are located 9km from the Sirimon gate and make for a comfortable place to acclimatise to the altitude before a climb. Each *banda* sleeps four.

# Naro Moru

POP 9000 / ☎062

Naro Moru may be little more than a string of shops and houses, with a couple of very basic hotels and a market, but it's the most popular starting point for treks up Mt Kenya. There's a post office and internet access but no banks, so be sure to bring all the cash you'll need for your trek.

## Sleeping & Eating

As a general rule, the basic hotels are in town, while the more tourist-oriented options are in the surrounding countryside, particularly on the bumpy road between Naro Moru and the park gates. Eating options in town are slim, but you won't starve if you like greasy chips and dining on goats that have lived long and eventful lives. Bring all the supplies you'll need for climbing Mt Kenya with you from elsewhere.

★ **Naro Moru River Lodge** LODGE $$
(☎0724082754; www.naromoruriverlodge.com; campsites/dm US$18/34, s full board US$126-177, d & tw full board US$176-227; P 📶 🏊) A bit like a Swiss chalet, the River Lodge is a lovely collection of dark, cosy cottages and rooms embedded into a sloping hillside that overlooks the rushing Naro Moru River, 3km from town. All three classes of room are nice, but the middle-of-the-road 'superior' option seems the best value of the lot.

**Colobus Cottages** COTTAGE $$
(☎0722840195, 0753951720; www.colobuscottages.wordpress.com; per person without breakfast KSh3500) These wooden cottages, some almost completely enveloped by the forest

### COOKING AT ALTITUDE

Increased altitude creates unique cooking conditions. The major consideration is that the boiling point of water is considerably reduced. At 4500m, for example, water boils at 85°C; this is too low to sufficiently cook rice or lentils (pasta is better) and you won't be able to brew a good cup of tea (instant coffee is the answer). Cooking times and fuel usage are considerably increased as a result, so plan accordingly.

To avoid severe headaches caused by dehydration or altitude sickness, drink at least 3L of fluid per day and bring rehydration sachets. Water-purification tablets, available at most chemists, aren't a bad idea either (purifying water by boiling at this altitude would take close to 30 minutes).

overlooking the Burgeret River, are simple but charmingly decorated. There's a fireplace in each, a barbecue area and a communal treetop bar. Note that the minimum booking is for two people. It's 2km off the main highway; the turn-off is 6km north of Naro Moru.

### Getting There & Away

There are plenty of buses and matatus heading to Nanyuki (KSh80, 30 minutes), Nyeri (KSh180, 45 minutes) and Nairobi (KSh600, three hours) from either the northbound or southbound bus parks.

## Aberdare National Park

Herds of wildlife thunder over an open African horizon, elephants emerge from a thicket of plants and the mysterious black rhino munches tranquilly on leaves. This is Aberdare National Park, packed with 300m-high waterfalls, dense forests and serious trekking potential. Also commonly seen here are buffaloes, black rhinos, spotted hyenas, bongo antelope, bush pigs, black servals and rare black leopards.

**Treetops** (0722207761; www.treetops.co.ke; s/d US$141/256, s/d ste US$166/282; P @ wi-fi) is one of the most famous hotels in Kenya. It is booked through the **Outspan Hotel** (061-2032424, Nairobi 020-4452095; www.aberdaresafarihotels.com; s/d from US$179/276; P wi-fi pool) in Nyeri, where check-in happens. From here guests must drive themselves to Treetops, where they dine, sleep and have breakfast, after which they leave at their leisure. Despite still having small rooms, the 2012 renovations have done wonders for the place with dark-wood floors, ochre feature walls and attractive prints.

**Ark** (0737799990; www.thearkkenya.com; s/d/tr US$180/305/434) dates from the 1960s and has petite rooms and a lounge that overlooks a waterhole. An excellent walkway leads over a particularly dense stretch of the Salient, and from here and the waterhole lounge you can spot elephants, rhinos, buffaloes and hyenas. It is sold as an overnight excursion from the Aberdare Country Club in Nyeri.

You'll need your own wheels to visit Aberdare National Park comfortably. Access roads from the B5 Hwy to the Ark, Treetops and Ruhuruini gates are in decent shape, though keep in mind that it takes a few hours to get from the Salient to the moorlands and vice versa.

# NORTHERN KENYA

Calling all explorers! We dare you to challenge yourself against some of the most exciting wilderness in Africa. Step forward only if you're able to withstand appalling roads, searing heat, clouds of dust torn by relentless winds, primitive food and accommodation, vast distances and more than a hint of danger. The rewards include memories of vast, shattered lava deserts, camel herders walking their animals to lost oases, elephant encounters in scrubby acacia woodlands and the chance to walk barefoot along the fabled shores of a sea of jade.

## Isiolo

Isiolo is where anticipation and excitement first start to send your heart aflutter. This vital pit stop on the long road north is a true frontier town, a place on the edge, torn between the cool, verdant highlands just to the south and the scorching badlands – home of nomads and bandits – to the north. On a more practical note, it's also the last place with decent facilities until Maralal or Marsabit.

Among the first things you'll undoubtedly notice is the large Somali population (descendants of WWI veterans who settled here) and the striking faces of Boran, Samburu and Turkana people walking the streets. It's this mix of people, cultures and religions that's the most interesting thing about Isiolo. Nowhere is this mixture better illustrated than in the hectic market.

**Rangeland Hotel** COTTAGE $
(☎0710114030; A2 Hwy; campsite per person KSh1000, s/d cottages KSh3500/4500; P 📶) About 4km south of town, this is a nice option for those with their own set of wheels. The sunny campsite has bickering weaver birds and busy rock hyraxes in abundance, as well as neat-and-tidy stone bungalows with hot showers. Many people come to laze around in the gardens at the weekend, but during the week it's quiet.

**Bomen Hotel** HOTEL $
(☎064-52389; Great North Rd; s/tw KSh2500/3500; P 📶) The NGOs' favourite home, the Bomen Hotel has the town's most toe-curlingly frilly pink bed sheets! It also has TVs, shared terraces with views and unfailingly polite staff.

# Samburu, Buffalo Springs & Shaba National Reserves

Studded with termite skyscrapers, cleaved by the muddy Ewaso Ngiro River and heaving with heavyweight animals, this triumvirate of national reserves has a beauty that is unsurpassed, as well as a population of creatures that occur in no other major Kenyan park. These species include blue-legged Somali ostrich, endangered Grevy's zebra, beisa oryx, reticulated giraffe and gerenuk – gazelles that dearly wish to be giraffes. Despite covering just 300 sq km, the reserves' variety of landscapes and vegetation is amazing.

## Sights

**Samburu National Reserve** NATIONAL PARK
(adult/child US$70/40, vehicle KSh1000) The most popular park in northern Kenya, Samburu's dominant feature is the Ewaso Ngiro River, which slices through the otherwise bone-dry country. The river acts as a magnet for thirsty animals and large numbers of elephants, Grevy's zebras, giraffes and lions gather along the riverbanks.

**Shaba National Reserve** NATIONAL PARK
(adult/child US$70/40, vehicle KSh1000) Shaba, with its great rocky kopjes (isolated hills), natural springs and doum palms, is more physically beautiful than the nearby national reserves of Samburu and Buffalo Springs. It is also much less visited, so you'll almost have it to yourself. But it also often has less visible wildlife.

**Buffalo Springs National Reserve** NATIONAL PARK
(adult/child US$70/40, vehicle KSh1000) The twin sister of Samburu National Reserve, which sits on the opposite, northern side of the river, Buffalo Springs has a wide variety of animals, including lots of elephants, but surprisingly few safari goers, which helps make it a joy to explore.

## Getting There & Away

The vehicle-less can wangle a 4WD and driver in Archer's Post for about US$100 per half-day. **Airkenya** (☎Nairobi 020-3916000; www.airkenya.com) and **Safarilink** (www.flysafarilink.com) have frequent flights from Nairobi's Wilson Airport to Samburu and Kalama. The bridge between Samburu and Buffalo Springs has been collapsed for years, despite promises to rebuild it. At present, if you want to visit both Samburu and Buffalo Springs, you'll need to make a long detour back to Archer's Post and the main A2 road, which can take up to three hours.

# Marsabit

☎069

The small town of Marsabit sits on the side of a 6300-sq-km shield volcano, the surface of which is peppered with 180 cinder cones and 22 volcanic craters, many of which house lakes – or at least they do when the rains have been kind. While the town is less attractive than its surrounds, which also comprise the enormous 1500-sq-km Marsabit National Reserve and the smaller Marsabit National Park, it's an interesting and lively place, thanks to colourful nomads passing through and a busy market.

In 2013 the **Shurr Community Conservancy** (www.nrt-kenya.org/shurr) was established immediately to the east of Marsabit. The conservancy has a lot of potential and there's more wildlife around here than many people realise. However, there are currently no visitor facilities.

**Chicho** GUESTHOUSE $
(☎0706153827, 069-2102846; www.chichohotel.com; Post Office Rd; s/d KSh2500/3000; P 📶) Located very close to the post office, but up a quiet side road, this family-run place has colourful rooms with some character, small bathrooms with hot water and bed sheets that will shock you with their absence of dubious stains! All up it's the best bet in the town centre. Book ahead.

### Getting There & Away

Although improved security means convoys and armed guards are no longer being used to Moyale or Isiolo, it's still wise to get the latest security and Ethiopian border information from locals and the police station before leaving town. As a rule, if buses and trucks travel in a convoy, or take armed soldiers on board, you should too!

## Loyangalani

Standing in utter contrast to the dour desert shades surrounding it, tiny Loyangalani assaults all your senses in one crazy explosion of clashing colours, feather headdresses and blood-red robes. Overlooking Lake Turkana and surrounded by small ridges of pillow lava (evidence that this area used to be underwater), the sandy streets of this one-camel town are a meeting point of the great northern tribes: Turkana and Samburu, Gabbra and El Molo. It's one of the most exotic corners of Kenya and a fitting reward after the hard journey here.

**★Malabo Resort** BANDA $

(☎0724705800; www.malaboresort.co.ke; camping KSh2000, huts from KSh2000, bandas KSh3000-4000; P ≋) The newest, and best, place to stay in Loyangalani is a few hundred metres north of the village and has slight lake views. There's a range of decent *bandas* with arty wooden beds and attached bathrooms, or there are thatched huts based on a traditional Turkana design. The bar-restaurant area is a good place to hang out.

### Getting There & Away

Trucks loaded with fish (and soon-to-be-smelly passengers) leave Loyangalani for Maralal (around KSh1000, nine to 12 hours) once or twice a week at best. Trucks heading in any other direction are even rarer and locals talk of waits of between a week and a month for transport to North Horr (around KSh1000) or Marsabit. When trucks do travel to Marsabit, they tend to take the slightly easier southern route via Kargi and charge a flexible KSh1000. It's better to travel from Loyagalani to North Horr rather than the other way around because with buses every other day from North Horr to Marsabit you won't get stuck for more than a night – going from North Horr to Loyagalani could mean waiting in North Horr for a week or more. This would be bad.

If you're travelling in your own vehicle, you have two options to reach Marsabit: continue northeast from Loyangalani across the dark stones of the Chalbi Desert towards North Horr, or head 67km south towards South Horr and take the eastern turn-off via Kargi. The 270km Chalbi route (10 to 12 hours) is hard in the dry season and impossible after rain. It's also wise to ask for directions every chance you get, otherwise it's easy to take the wrong track and not realise until hours later. This also would be bad. The 241km southern route (six to seven hours) via the Karoli Desert and Kargi is composed of compacted sands and is marginally less difficult in the rainy season.

## Lake Turkana

If you go to Loyangalani you can't help but visit Lake Turkana. Formerly known as Lake Rudolf, and nowadays often evocatively called the 'Jade Sea', vast Lake Turkana stretches all the way to Ethiopia. High salt levels render the sandy, volcanic area around the lake almost entirely barren, but its desolation and stark, surreal beauty contrast with the colourful tribespeople who inhabit the lake's shore.

# WESTERN KENYA

For most people the magic of western Kenya is summed up in two poetic words: Masai Mara. Few places on earth support such high concentrations of animals, and the Mara's wildebeest-spotted savannahs are undeniably the region's star attraction. Drama unfolds here on a daily basis, be it a stealthy trap coordinated by a pride of lions, the infectious panic of 1000 wildebeest crossing a river, or the defensive march of a herd of elephants protecting their young from predators.

But there's much more to western Kenya than these plains of herbivores and carnivores. The dense forests of Kakamega are buzzing with weird and wonderful creatures, Kisumu is a laid-back port city with lively nightlife, and amid the boat-speckled waters of Lake Victoria lies a smattering of seldom-visited islands crying out for exploration.

## Lake Victoria

Spread over 68,000 sq km, yet never more than 80m deep, Lake Victoria, one of the key water sources of the White Nile, might well be East Africa's most important geographical feature, but is seen by surprisingly few visitors. This is a shame, as its humid shores hide some of the most beautiful and rewarding parts of western Kenya – from untouched national parks to lively cities and tranquil islands.

## Kisumu

POP 410,000 / ☎057

Set on the sloping shore of Lake Victoria's Winam Gulf, Kisumu might be the third-largest city in Kenya, but its relaxed atmosphere is a world away from that of Nairobi and Mombasa. Until 1977 the port was one of the busiest in Kenya, but decline set in with the collapse of the East African Community (EAC; the common market between Kenya, Tanzania and Uganda) and the port sat virtually idle for two decades. Since the revival of the EAC in 2000, Kisumu has begun to thrive again, and though it was declared a city during its centenary celebrations in 2001, it still doesn't feel like one and remains a pleasant and laid-back place with a number of interesting sights and activities nearby.

### Sights

**Kisumu Main Market** MARKET

(off Jomo Kenyatta Hwy; ⏲7am-6pm) Kisumu's Main Market is one of Kenya's most animated, and certainly one of its largest, now spilling out onto the surrounding roads. If you're curious, or just looking for essentials such as suits or wigs, it's worth a stroll around.

**Ndere Island National Park** NATIONAL PARK

(http://www.kws.go.ke/content/ndere-island-national-park; adult/child US$25/15; ⏲6am-6pm) Gazetted as a national park in 1986, this 4.2-sq-km island has never seen tourism take off. It is forested and very beautiful, housing a variety of bird species, plus occasionally sighted hippos, impalas (introduced) and spotted crocodiles, a lesser-known cousin of the larger Nile crocodiles.

### Sleeping

There's plenty of hotel choice in Kisumu. If you're finding the humidity hard to deal with, you'll be pleased to know that most rooms in Kisumu are equipped with fans. Be careful in the budget hotels here – many have a reputation for petty theft.

★**New East View Hotel** HOTEL $

(☎0711183017; Omolo Agar Rd; s KSh1800-2500, d KSh2500-3000; P 📶) The town's standout budget option is one of many family homes in the area that have been converted into small hotels. Splashed in bright colours, the rooms have a homely, preloved feel and the welcome is, even for Kenya, unusually warm. Good hot showers with decent water pressure are another plus. Security is also tight.

**Scottish Tartan Hotel** HOTEL $$

(☎0722202865; www.scottishtartanhotel.co.ke; Ogada St; s/d from US$55/70; ❄📶) The oddly named Scottish Tartan is generally held to be the best hotel in town, and while it's true that its large rooms and furnishings carved from tree trunks are a great deal, do be aware that some rooms get noise from the next-door nightclub.

### Eating & Drinking

As you'd expect from a town on Lake Victoria, fish is abundant on the menus of Kisumu. If you want an authentic local fish fry, there are no better places than the dozens of smoky tin-shack restaurants sitting on the lake's shore at Railway Beach at the end of Oginga Odinga Rd.

Kisumu's nightlife has a reputation for being even livelier than Nairobi's. Check flyers and ask locals who are plugged into the scene. Be careful when leaving venues as muggings and worse have occurred, and don't go out alone. Clubs are busiest on Friday and Saturday night.

### Getting There & Away

Buses, matatus and Peugeots (shared taxis) to numerous destinations within Kenya battle it out at the large bus and matatu station just north of the main market. Peugeots cost about 25% more than matatus.

**Easy Coach** (www.easycoach.co.ke; Jomo Kenyatta Hwy) offers the smartest buses out of town. Its booking office and departure point are in the car park just behind (and accessed through) Tusky's Shopping Centre. It has daily buses to Nairobi (KSh1400, seven hours, every couple of hours), Nakuru (KSh800, 4½ hours, every couple of hours) and Kampala (KSh1500, seven hours, 1.30pm and 10pm).

## Kakamega Forest

Not so long ago, much of western Kenya was hidden under a dark veil of jungle and formed a part of the mighty Guineo–Congolian forest ecosystem. However, the British turned much of that virgin forest into tea estates. Now all that's left is Kakamega Forest National Reserve, a slab of tropical rainforest surrounding the town of Kakamega.

## Sights & Activities

**Kakamega Forest National Reserve** PARK
(www.kws.go.ke; adult/child US$25/15, vehicles KSh300) All that's now left in Kenya of the massive Guineo-Congolian rainforest, the Kakamega Forest National Reserve, though seriously degraded, is unique in Kenya and contains plants, animals and birds that occur nowhere else in the country. Kakamega is especially good for birders, with turacos, flocks of African grey parrots and noisy hornbills that sound like helicopters when they fly overhead. If you prefer your animals furrier, Kakamega is home to several primates, including graceful colobus monkeys, black-cheeked-white-nosed monkeys and Sykes monkeys.

**Kakamega Rainforest Tour Guides** WALKING
(☎0726951764; short/long walk per person KSh500/1000) Next to the forest reserve office, KRTG supplies knowledgeable guides to the forest for a variety of walks, including recommended night walks (KSh1500 per person) and sunrise/sunset walks (KSh1000 per person). These are some of the best-value nature walks you'll find in Kenya, with lots of wildlife to spot.

## Sleeping & Eating

As with almost any reserve in Kenya, if you stay within the Kakamega Forest National Reserve you'll have to pay park entry fees for each night. All lodges and guesthouses within the Kakamega Forest have their own restaurants where guests eat. Campsites generally have basic cooking facilities and you'll need to bring your own food.

**KEEP Bandas** BANDA $
(☎0704851701; safari tent per person KSh700, banda per person with shared bathroom KSh1000) If you want a jungle adventure, look no further than this rustic place for a night or two's stay. All you get is a small hut with no electricity and communal cold-water showers, but surrounded by rainforest it's very atmospheric. Meals can be arranged at the small canteen if you don't wish to self-cater in the basic kitchen.

★ **Rondo Retreat** GUESTHOUSE $$$
(☎0733299149, 056-2030268; www.rondoretreat.com; s/d half-board US$180/240; P) To arrive at Rondo Retreat is to be whisked back to 1922 and the height of British rule. Consisting of a series of wooden bungalows filled with a family's clutter, this gorgeous and eccentric place is a wonderful retreat from modern Kenya. The gardens are absolutely stunning and worth visiting even if you're not staying.

## Getting There & Away

**BUYANGO AREA**

Matatus heading north towards Kitale can drop you at the access road, about 18km north of Kakamega town (KSh100). It's a well-signposted 2km walk from there to the park office.

**ISECHANO AREA**

Regular matatus link Kakamega with Shinyalu (KSh80), but few go on to Isecheno. Shinyalu is also accessed by a rare matatu service from Khayega. From Shinyalu you will probably need to take a *boda-boda* (motorcycle taxi) to Isecheno (KSh100).

The improved roads are still treacherous after rain and you may prefer to walk once you've seen the trouble vehicles can have. Shinyalu is about 7km from Khayega and 10km from Kakamega. From Shinyalu it's 5km to Isecheno.

The dirt road from Isecheno continues east to Kapsabet, but transport is rare.

# Masai Mara National Reserve

The world-renowned **Masai Mara National Reserve** (www.maratriangle.org; adult/child US$80/45, subsequent days if staying inside the reserve US$70/40; ⏰6.30am-6.30pm) is a huge expanse of tawny, sunburnt grasslands pocked with acacia trees and heaving with animals big and small. Impressive at any time of year, it's at its best between July and October when around a million migrating wildebeest and thousands of topis, zebras and other animals pour into the reserve from Tanzania in search of the fresh grass generated by the rains. It is, arguably, the most spectacular wildlife show on the planet and the one thing that no visitor to Kenya should even consider missing.

Reliable rains and plentiful vegetation underpin this extraordinary ecosystem and the millions of herbivores it supports. Wildebeest, zebras, impalas, elands, reedbucks, waterbucks, black rhinos, elephants, Masai giraffes and several species of gazelle all call the Mara home. Predators here include cheetahs, leopards, spotted hyenas, black-backed jackals, bat-eared foxes and caracals, plus it has the highest lion density in the world.

## Activities

Virtually all lodges organise wildlife drives through the park. At some cheaper places it will be in a battered old Land Rover or similar, while in the more expensive places safaris will be conducted in 'pop-top' minivans with other guests. The super-exclusive lodges will use state-of-the-art customised vehicles with open sides. Self-drive safaris in your own vehicle are also perfectly possible.

One of the best ways to experience the African bush is on foot. You'll learn all about the medicinal properties of various plants, see the telltale signs of passing animals and have some thrilling encounters with wildlife. As it's forbidden to walk within the reserve due to predators, guided walks generally take place in the company of a Maasai *moran* (warrior) outside the park itself.

## Sleeping & Eating

Make no mistake about it, accommodation in the Masai Mara can be very expensive. Remember, though, that in most cases all meals are included, and in many of the top-end places drinks and safari activities are also part of the deal. It's possible to keep prices right down by camping and self-catering. This also adds to the excitement, with just a thin sheet of canvas between you and the great outdoors – and all its toothy creatures.

All lodges and camps provide food to their guests, with only very simple campsites requiring self-catering. In lodges meals tend to be hefty and elaborate to ensure that guests are full all day, and cooking tends to be generic European dishes with little Kenyan influence. Standards are generally high, though you're unlikely to come home raving about the food. Packed lunches are provided by lodges if you're going to be out on safari all day.

**Acacia Camp** TENTED CAMP **$**
(☎0733601441; mara@acaciacamp.com; Ololaimutiek Gate; camping US$6, tent without breakfast s/d US$22/36) A little tricky to find, Acacia is 2.5km over sand roads from Ololaimutiek Gate, just outside the park. Here you'll find thatched roofs sheltering simple tents in a pleasant garden against a beautiful backdrop of bougainvillea. There's a kitchen, bar and a campfire, as well as a canteen providing meals at US$7 a pop. The bathrooms have evening hot water.

★**Ewangan** HOMESTAY **$$**
(☎0721817757; www.maasaimaravillage.com; Sekenani Gate; full board per person US$70, children free) A traditional Maasai *manyatta* 2km north of Sekenani Gate, offering a homestay with the Maasai. During your stay you'll help with daily chores such as milking the cows and goats, learn skills such as jewellery making and enjoy nature walks with a Maasai guide. At least 25% of your money goes to help support local community projects.

★**Aruba Mara Camp** TENTED CAMP **$$**
(☎0723997524; www.aruba-safaris.com; Talek Gate; camping KSh820, bush tent without bathroom per person KSh2700, safari tent full board per person KSh9200; ) Set alongside a narrow river where animals often come to drink, this is arguably the Mara's best-value camp. There are three categories of wonderfully plush tents with good self-contained bathrooms as well as several small, but comfortable, tents (meals not included) that share bathrooms. The nearby campsite is decent, with a kitchen area and reliable hot water in the showers.

**Manyatta Camp** TENTED CAMP **$$**
(☎072059252547; Ololaimutiek Gate; full board per person KSh4000) This is an excellent-value choice just moments from the park gates. The large camp has 40 tents spread out in its rather chaotically tended gardens, all of which have their own bathrooms with hot water and thatch shelter. There is none of the sheen of the pricier camps, but it's cheap and cheerful.

★**Basecamp Masai Mara** LODGE **$$$**
(☎0733333909; www.basecampexplorer.com; tent s/d full board from US$300/600; ) This upmarket lodge has 16 luxuriously appointed tents with large wooden verandas and smart bathrooms. The camp is very serious about sustainabilty and recycling, and enjoys a gold eco rating from Ecotourism Kenya. It also enjoys huge grounds and overlooks the river and the Mara beyond. Don't miss the trees planted by the Obama family on their stay here.

**Keekorok Lodge** LODGE **$$$**
(☎0703048100; www.sunafricahotels.com; s/d full board US$280/400; ) This may be the oldest lodge in the Mara, but thanks to a recent makeover the 101 rooms are modern, bright and tastefully decorated with tribal arts and crafts. As well as being in the middle of the Mara, you also have manicured gardens and a wooden boardwalk that leads to a gazebo overlooking a hippo pool.

## Getting There & Away

### AIR

**Airkenya** (☎Nairobi 020-3916000; www.airkenya.com); **Mombasa Air Safari** (☎0734400400; www.mombasaairsafari.com);

**Safarilink** (☎020-6690000; www.flysafarilink.com) and **Fly540** (☎0710540540; www.fly540.com), flying under the name of SAX, each have daily flights to any of the eight airstrips in and around the Masai Mara. Flights from Nairobi's Wilson Airport start at US$300 return.

### CAR

If you're driving to the Mara, be sure to get petrol in Narok, the last chance to fill your vehicle at normal prices on the road from Nairobi. Expensive petrol is available at Mara Sarova, Mara Serena and Keekorok Lodges, as well as in Talek village.

The first 52km west of Narok on the B3 and C12 are smooth enough, but after the bitumen runs out you'll find yourself on Kenya's most notorious road – a bone-shaking dirt road that many drivers simply dread. Most people drive in the sandy verges of the road, which makes for a far smoother experience, but either way the road is a pain and you might well wonder why you didn't fly.

That said, having your own wheels in the Mara is a wonderful thing. Even if most safari drives will be done with a guide in their own vehicle, it still means you're free to self-drive through the reserve, which is a huge pleasure in itself, although getting lost is always a slight risk. It's possible to access Talek and Sekenani gates from Narok by matatu (KSh600), after which you'll need to arrange pick-ups from a lodge.

# THE COAST

From the hypnotic port city of Mombasa south to the border with Tanzania, Kenya's South Coast is anything but ordinary. Where else can you see snow-white beaches framed by *kayas* (sacred forests), soft-sailed dhows and elephant watering holes, all in one day?

Governed by Swahili rhythms and the rise and fall of the tides, life here moves to its own beat. Thanks to the long interplay of Africa, India and Arabia, this coast feels wildly different from the rest of Kenya. Its people, the Swahili, have created a distinctive Indian Ocean society – built on trade with distant shores – that lends real romance to the coast's beaches and to Mombasa, a city poets have embraced for as long as ivory has been traded for iron.

Kenya's Indian Ocean coastline is where the exotic permeates everything, blending spice, soul and sand. The attractions of this slice of paradise have historically not been lost on anyone lucky enough to visit, whether it be Portuguese explorers, Cushitic Somalis, Bantu-speaking Mijikenda, cattle-herding Orma, Italian holidaymakers or, of course, the Swahili. Many of these people stayed on and have left their own mark on the coast, from the ancient ruins at Gede to the holiday resorts built by Italians in more recent times.

Watamu and Malindi remain popular beach destinations for Europeans, though sadly the jewel of the north coast, Lamu, is little visited these days, as the road to the island city is not currently considered safe due to Al-Shabaab terrorist activity in the area. If you do decide to visit, fly rather than drive.

## Mombasa

POP 1.2 MILLION / ☎041

Mombasa, a melting pot of languages and cultures from all sides of the Indian Ocean, awaits travellers like an exotic desert. Having more in common with Dakar or Dar es Salaam than Nairobi, Mombasa's blend of India, Arabia and Africa can be intoxicating, and many visitors find themselves seduced by East Africa's biggest and most cosmopolitan port despite its grime and sleaze, which somehow only adds to the place's considerable charm.

Indeed, the city dubbed in Swahili *Kisiwa Cha Mvita* – the Island of War – has many faces, from the ecstatic passion of the call to prayer over the old town to the waves crashing against the coral beaches below Fort Jesus and the sight of a Zanzibar-bound dhow slipping over the horizon. As the Swahili people themselves say in an old proverb: 'Mombasa is famous, but its waters are dangerously deep. Beware!'

### Sights

**★Fort Jesus** MUSEUM

(Map p624; adult/child KSh1200/600; ⏲8am-6pm) This Unesco World Heritage treasure is Mombasa's most visited site. The metre-thick walls, frescoed interiors, traces of European graffiti, Arabic inscriptions and Swahili embellishment aren't just evocative – they're a record of the history of Mombasa and the coast writ in stone. These days the fort houses a museum, which would ideally give a good insight into Swahili life and culture but, like the rest of the complex, is poorly labelled and woefully displayed. Despite this, the fort is unmissable.

**Old Town** HISTORIC BUILDINGS

(Map p624) This doesn't have the medieval charm of Lamu or Zanzibar, but it's still an

## Mombasa

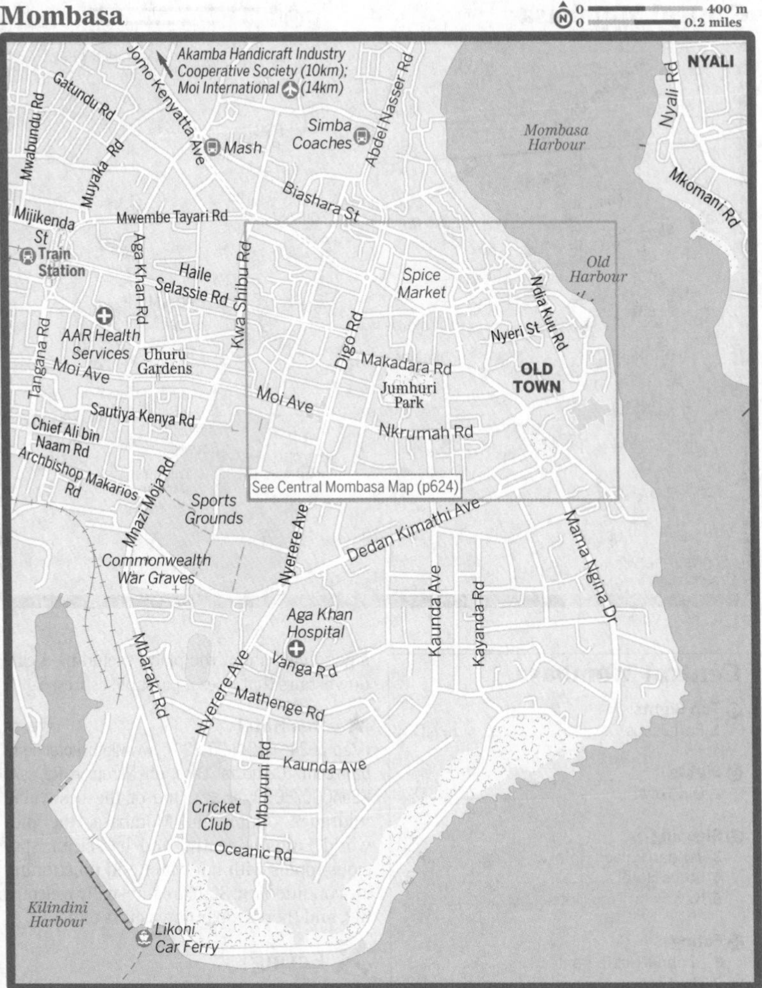


interesting area to wander around. The houses are characteristic of coastal East African architecture, with ornately carved doors and window frames and fretwork balconies. Don't wander too deep into the narrow side streets alone, however, as they can be a little sketchy even during the day. Be aware that numerous touts and scammers work the area: be suspicious of anyone who approaches you.

### Sleeping

**Jundan Palace Hotel** HOTEL $
(Map p624; ☎0725376784, 0722200442; Taita St; s/d/tr incl breakfast KSh2500/3000/3500; ❄📶) The palace in the name may be entirely fanciful, but don't dismiss this city-centre cheapie immediately, as its rooms are far better than you'd expect from its market exterior and cramped lobby. Awaiting you upstairs are spotless tile-floored rooms with TVs and fridges. There's also the room number embroidered on each pillow case in case you forget it.

**New Palm Tree Hotel** HOTEL $
(Map p624; ☎0715442017; www.newpalmtreehotel.com; Nkrumah Rd; s/d/tr KSh2500/3500/4500; 📶) If you're looking for central, budget-friendly but reasonably comfortable digs, this

## Central Mombasa

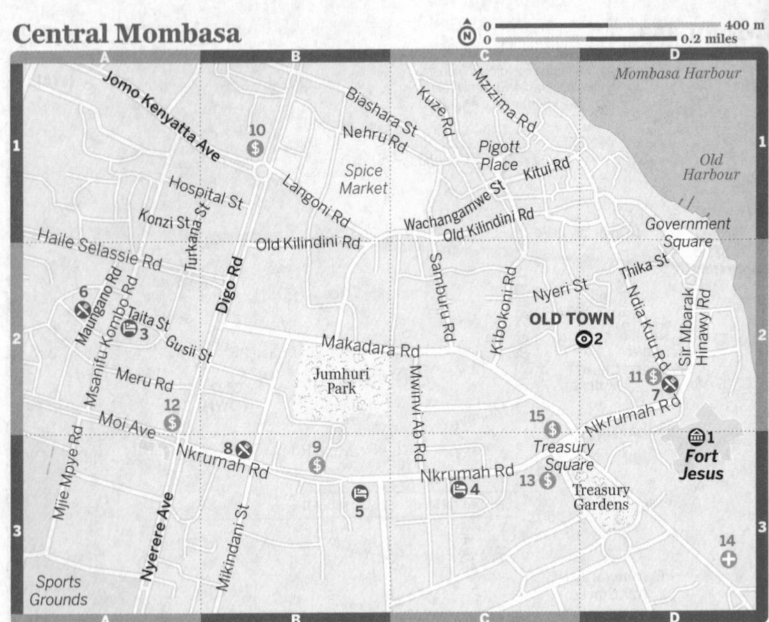


### Central Mombasa

**Top Sights**
1 Fort Jesus ... D3

**Sights**
2 Old Town ... D2

**Sleeping**
3 Jundan Palace Hotel ... A2
4 Lotus Hotel ... C3
5 New Palm Tree Hotel ... B3

**Eating**
6 Shehnai Restaurant ... A2
7 The Fort ... D2
8 Urban Street Food ... B3

**Information**
9 Barclays Bank ... B3
10 Barclays Bank ... B1
11 Fort Jesus Forex Bureau ... D2
12 Kenya Commercial Bank ... A2
13 Kenya Commercial Bank ... C3
14 Mombasa Hospital ... D3
15 Standard Chartered Bank ... C2

place delivers. Rooms are arranged around a courtyard and while the amenities (such as hot water) aren't always reliable, the service is fine, it's generally well cared for and there's a good vibe about the place, including a cafe downstairs that does a passable espresso.

**★Lotus Hotel** HOTEL $$
(Map p624; ☎041-2313207; www.lotushotelmombasa.com; Cathedral Lane, off Nkrumah Rd; s/d KSh4000/6000; ❄📶) One of the best-value midrange options in Mombasa, the old-world Lotus is central and has clean, spacious rooms with hot water and functioning air-conditioning. Staff are unusually welcoming, and there's a bar downstairs to boot.

## Eating

Mombasa has a variety of cuisines on offer to match the breadth of its cultural influences. Explore the Old Town for cheap, authentic Swahili cuisine; if in doubt, follow the locals to find the best places. Be aware that most places are Muslim-run, so alcoholic drinks are rarely on the menu and most places are closed until after sunset during Ramadan.

**★Shehnai Restaurant** INDIAN $
(Map p624; ☎041-2224801; Fatemi House, Maungano Rd; mains KSh400-800; ⏰noon-2pm & 7.30-10.30pm Tue-Sun) This reputable *mughlai* (North Indian) curry house does delicious dishes such as *gosht palakwalla* (lamb with masala and spinach) and a superb chicken

biryani. The staff are friendly and fast, while the entire place has an air of gentility absent elsewhere in Mombasa. There's no alcohol.

**Urban Street Food** INTERNATIONAL $
(Map p624; ☎0700907363; www.urbanstreetfood.co.ke; Nkrumah Rd; mains KSh500-750; ⏰7am-11pm Mon-Sat; 📶) This textbook hip, yellow-walled place with an industrial vibe in central Mombasa does several things few other local establishments do, including great coffee, small plates of hummus, juicy burgers and gorgeous fresh juices. There's a distinct Middle Eastern slant to the otherwise international menu, with shawarma jostling with pizza and a selection of good breakfasts. Delivery is available.

**★The Fort** SEAFOOD $$
(Map p624; ☎0722776399; www.thefort.co.ke; Nkrumah Rd; mains KSh1000-2000; ⏰noon-11pm Tue-Sun; 📶) Right opposite the entrance to Fort Jesus, Mombasa's main sight, this excellent new restaurant is an obvious place for a meal after your visit. The speciality here is local seafood cooked in a variety of Swahili sauces, but there's lots of other choice, including seafood risotto and pizzas.

## Information

### DANGERS & ANNOYANCES

High crime levels and security issues make it unwise to walk around alone after dark. During the day you shouldn't have a problem, although women in particular can expect to be hassled when walking alone through the Old Town. When in doubt, hailing a tuk-tuk is an easy (and cheap) answer. Wrapping a headscarf around your hair is also a quick solution to unwanted male attention.

### MEDICAL SERVICES

The following are the best medical services in Mombasa.

**AAR Health Services** (Map p623; ☎0731191067; www.aar-healthcare.com; Pereira Bldg, Machakos St, off Moi Ave; ⏰24hr) Medical clinic.

**Aga Khan Hospital** (Map p623; ☎041-2227710; www.agakhanhospitals.org; Vanga Rd)

**Mombasa Hospital** (Map p624; ☎041-2312191; www.mombasahospital.com; off Mama Ngina Dr)

### MONEY

Outside business hours you can change money at most major hotels, although rates are usually poor. Exchange rates are generally slightly lower here than in Nairobi, especially if you're changing travellers cheques. ATMs can be found everywhere and nearly all accept international credit and debit cards.

**Barclays Bank** (Map p624; Digo Rd) Has an ATM, as does another branch on Nkrumah Rd (Map p624).

**Fort Jesus Forex Bureau** (Map p624; ☎041-316717; Ndia Kuu Rd) Currency exchange.

**Kenya Commercial Bank** (Map p624; Nkrumah Rd) With ATM. Another on Moi Ave (Map p624).

**Standard Chartered Bank** (Map p624; Treasury Sq, Nkrumah Rd) With ATM.

> DON'T MISS
>
> **STREET FOOD**
>
> Mombasa is good for street food: stalls sell cassava, samosas, bhajis, kebabs and the local take on pizza (meat and onions wrapped in soft dough and fried). A few dish out stew and ugali. For dessert, seek out *haluwa* (an Omani version of Turkish delight), fried taro root, sweet baobab seeds and sugared doughnuts.

## Getting There & Away

### AIR

Both **Kenya Airways** (☎041-2125251, booking 020-3274747; www.kenya-airways.com; Nyali City Mall) and **Fly540** (☎041-2319078, booking 0710540540; www.fly540.com; Moi International Airport) have multiple daily flights between Mombasa and Nairobi. Prices start at around KSh9500.

### BUS & MATATU

Most bus offices are on either Jomo Kenyatta Ave or Abdel Nasser Rd. Services to Malindi and Lamu leave from Abdel Nasser Rd, while buses to destinations in Tanzania leave from the junction of Jomo Kenyatta Ave and Mwembe Tayari Rd.

For buses and matatus to the beaches and towns south of Mombasa, you first need to get off the island on the **Likoni ferry** (Map p623; www.kenyaferry.co.ke). Frequent matatus run from Nyerere Ave to the transport stand by the ferry terminal.

For Nairobi, there are dozens of daily departures in both directions (mostly in the early morning and late evening). Daytime services take at least eight hours, and overnight trips take 10 to 12 hours, and include a meal break about halfway. Fares range from KSh500 to KSh3000.

There are numerous daily buses and matatus up the coast to Malindi, leaving from in front of the Noor Mosque on Abdel Nasser Rd. Buses

DON'T MISS

### BOMBOLULU WORKSHOPS & CULTURAL CENTRE

A non-profit organisation, **Bombolulu Workshops & Cultural Centre** (www.apdkbombolulu.org; adult/child KSh750/350, workshops & showroom free; ⏲8am-6pm Mon-Sat, 10am-3pm Sun) produces crafts of a high standard and gives vocational training to physically disabled people. Visit the workshops and showroom to buy jewellery, clothes, carvings and other crafts. The turn-off for the centre is on the left, about 3km north of Nyali Bridge. Bombolulu matatus run here from Msanifu Kombo Rd, and Bamburi services also pass the centre.

take up to three hours (around KSh600) and matatus take about two hours (KSh400 rising to KSh600 during holidays and very busy periods).

**Simba Coaches** (Map p623; Abdel Nasser Rd), **Mash** (Map p623; ☎0733623260; www.masheastafrica.com) and **Coast** (☎0722206446; www.coastbus.com) have daily departures from their offices on Jomo Kenyatta Ave to Dar es Salaam (KSh1200 to KSh1600, 10 to 12 hours) via Tanga.

#### TRAIN

The **Mombasa–Nairobi train** (☎0722106395, 0733681061, Nairobi 020-3596750; www.kenyatrainbooking.com; Mombasa Railway Station) leaves Mombasa for Nairobi at 5pm Wednesday and Sunday, arriving the next day (if you're lucky) at 11am. You can reserve online, by phone or in person at the station from Monday to Friday (9am to 5pm). This ancient and extremely slow service will soon be replaced with a modern high-speed service that will take just four hours.

## Malindi

POP 207,000 / ☎042

Malindi is one of the most charming and sophisticated towns on Kenya's coast and boasts several worthwhile sights, its own marine national park and some fantastic stretches of beach. Despite being beloved by Italians – many of whom have settled here – Malindi is far more than just another European holiday resort and is in fact a melting pot of local cultures with a rich and fascinating history. Wander through the alleys of the atmospheric old town, stop for fresh oysters beside the Indian Ocean, or take a plunge into the crystal-clear waters of the national park and you'll discover for yourself that Malindi is quite the charmer.

### Sights

**Malindi Historic Circuit** HISTORIC SITE
(adult/child KSh500/250; ⏲8am-6pm) National Museums of Kenya has cleverly grouped the major cultural sites of Malindi under the one general ticket. The most compelling attraction covered in the Historic Circuit is the **House of Columns** (Mama Ngina Rd), a good example of traditional Swahili architecture, containing exhibits of all sorts of archaeological finds dug up around the coast.

**Malindi Marine National Park** NATIONAL PARK
(www.kws.go.ke; adult/child US$17/13, boats KSh3000; ⏲6am-6pm) The oldest marine park in Kenya covers 213 sq km and boasts powder-blue fish, organ-pipe coral, green sea turtles and beds of Thalassia seagrass. If you're extremely lucky, you may spot mako and whale sharks. Unfortunately these reefs have suffered (and continue to suffer) extensive damage, evidenced by the piles of seashells on sale in Malindi. Monsoon-generated waves can reduce visibility from June to September.

### Activities

**Blue Fin** DIVING
(☎0722261242; www.bluefindiving.com) With the marine park just offshore from Malindi, scuba diving is a popular activity, although the visibility is greatly reduced by silt between March and June. Blue Fin operates out of several resorts in town.

**Aqua Ventures** DIVING
(☎0703628102; www.diveinkenya.com; Driftwood Beach Club) Based at the Driftwood Beach Club, Aqua Ventures is one of the best diving outfits in town. Dives start at US$45, but buying a package reduces the cost considerably.

### Sleeping

Tourism is the lifeblood of Malindi, and there's an almost-unbroken stretch of hotels and resorts along the town's coastline. As visitor numbers have fallen in recent years, prices have also fallen, meaning some excellent deals are available, and you can often snag a room at well below the normal rack rate. Do note that some places close or scale down operations in October and between April and June.

**Marine Park Bandas & Camping** CAMPGROUND $
(Nairobi 020-6000800; www.kws.go.ke; Marine National Park; camping KSh1500, bandas KSh1500-3000; P) Malindi Marine National Park has set aside a small area for pitching tents on the rather sandy ground. There's some – but not much – shade, and a shower and toilet block to use. Better value is the handful of *bandas* – one has been modernised and is very comfortable; the cheaper ones are far simpler but clean and cosy.

★**Scorpio Villas** RESORT $$
(042-2120194, 0700437680; www.scorpio-villas.com; Mnarani Rd; s/d from KSh4000/7000; P) Right by the ocean and within walking distance of some good restaurants, Scorpio Villas offers excellent value for money. The 40-or-so rooms follow the hotel theme – gorgeous dark wood, white linen sofas and Swahili carvings – while the bathrooms have huge monsoon showers.

★**Driftwood Beach Club** RESORT $$$
(042-2120155, 0721724489; www.driftwoodclub.com; Mama Ngina Rd; s/d from KSh10,000/14,600; ) This charming place gets it all just about right – it has a beachfront location, a decent-sized pool, large and spotless rooms and a very chilled out bar-restaurant area where guests and local club members mingle as the waves crash on the beach out front.

## Eating & Drinking

With great seafood and strong Italian influences, Malindi is one of the best places to eat on the coast and there's no reason to stay holed up in your resort. Street-food heaven is Jamhuri St, where stalls line both sides of the road selling deep-fried goodies, bhajis, dates and chapattis.

There's plenty going on after dark in Malindi. There are several nightclubs that are rammed at weekends, while beach bars attract a steady crowd of tourists and locals throughout the week. Expect lots of working-girl and beach-boy attention.

★**Baby Marrow** ITALIAN, SEAFOOD $$
(0700766704; Mama Ngina Rd; mains KSh800-2000; noon-3pm & 6-11pm) This standout restaurant is not only one of the best on the coast, but also in the entire country. The gorgeous, leafy setting is absolutely charming, as are the staff who will bring you house specialities such as smoked sailfish, pizza bianca, vodka sorbet or Sicilian ice cream. The jungle bar is a good spot for a digestif.

★**I Love Pizza** ITALIAN $$
(042-20672; nwright@africaonline.co.ke; Mama Ngina Rd; pizzas around KSh900, pastas KSh400-700; 11am-3pm & 6-11pm) We do too, and the pizza is done really well here – way better than you might expect this far from Naples. No matter how good the pizza, many people come instead for the seafood and pasta. The hip, renovated colonial building has a lovely terrace that is gorgeously lit at night and perfect for a romantic meal.

## Information

### DANGERS & ANNOYANCES

Being on the beach alone at night is asking for trouble, as is walking along any quiet beach back road at night. Avoid the far northern end of the beach, or any deserted patches of sand, as muggings are common. There are lots of guys selling drugs, so remember: everything is illegal. Drug sales often turn into stings, with the collusive druggie getting a cut of whatever fee police demand from you (if they don't throw you in jail).

### MONEY

**Barclays Bank** (Lamu Rd) With ATM.

**Dollar Forex Bureau** (042-30602; Lamu Rd) Rates may be slightly better here than at the banks.

**Standard Chartered Bank** (042-20130; Stanchart Arcade, Lamu Rd) With ATM.

### TOURIST INFORMATION

**Malindi Tourist Office** (042-20689; Malindi Complex, Lamu Rd; 8am-12.30pm & 2-4.30pm Mon-Fri)

## Getting There & Away

### AIR

**Airkenya** (042-2120411; www.airkenya.com; Malindi Airport), **Fly540** (0710540540; www.fly540.com; Wilson Airport) and **Kenya Airways** (0734102851; www.kenya-airways.com; Lamu Rd) all have daily flights from Malindi to Nairobi. Prices start around US$120 one way.

### BUS & MATATU

**Lamu** There are usually at least six buses a day to Lamu (KSh800 but can rise in periods of high demand, four to five hours). Most leave around 9am. TSS Buses and Tawakal are the biggest operators.

**Mombasa** There are numerous daily buses and matatus to Mombasa (bus/matatu KSh400/450, two hours). During periods of high demand, fares can rise to KSh600.

**Nairobi** All the main bus companies have daily departures to Nairobi, via Mombasa, at around 7am and/or 7pm (KSh700 to KSh3000, 12 to 14 hours).

**Watamu** Matatus to Watamu (KSh100, one hour) leave from the not-very-new New Malindi Bus Station on the edge of town.



# Watamu

POP 1900 / ☎042

Laid-back little Watamu looks out over the Indian Ocean and enjoys a blinding white-sand beach and a soft breeze coming off the water. It's a gorgeous slice of coastline and one that includes its own marine national park. As well as its natural endowments, Watamu also has a number of excellent hotels and restaurants spread along its beach road, so it's hardly a surprise that it's the kind of place visitors return to again and again. Far more sleepy than nearby Malindi, village-like Watamu is a perfect counterpoint to its larger northern neighbour.

## Sights

**★Watamu Turtle Watch** WILDLIFE RESERVE
(☎0713759627; www.watamuturtles.com; suggested donation KSh300; ⏲9.30am-noon & 2.30-4pm Mon-Fri, 9.30am-noon Sat) This excellent organisation protects the approximately 50 hawksbill and green turtles that lay their eggs on Watamu beach. The centre provides much-needed education in the local community about the fragility of sea turtles and actively patrols for people selling turtle shell. At the trust's rehabilitation centre you can normally see turtles being treated for injury or illness and learn about these magnificent creatures. It's a very worthwhile visit.

**Watamu Marine National Park** NATIONAL PARK
(adult/child US$17/13) The southern part of Malindi Marine National Reserve, this park includes some magnificent coral reefs, abundant fish life and sea turtles. To get here to snorkel and dive, you'll need a boat, which is easy enough to hire at the KWS office, where you pay the park fees, at the end of the coast road. Boat operators ask anywhere from KSh2500 to KSh5000 for two people for two hours; it's all negotiable.

## Sleeping

There are some truly lovely accommodation options in Watamu, nearly all of which are spread along the beach road. Do note that most of Watamu's major hotels close from May to mid-July for the low (and rainy) season.

**★Mwamba Field Study Centre** GUESTHOUSE $
(☎042-2332023, Nairobi 020-2335865; www.arocha.org; plot 28, Watamu Beach; per person with breakfast/full board US$25/45; ) This lovely guesthouse, set amid a pleasant garden and thick woods, is just a short wander from the beach. Run by a Christian conservation society, it's a fantastic deal with simple, clean and charming rooms with bright colour schemes and the noise of waves crashing onto the beach as you drift off to sleep.

**★Kobe Suite Resort** BOUTIQUE HOTEL $$$
(☎Nairobi 0722658951; www.kobesuiteresort.com; s/d US$90/175; ) With five rooms facing the ocean and a further 18 set back around a saltwater pool, this boutique hotel works a sleek, dreamy vibe. Expect Swahili archways, bougainvillea window frames, brushed concrete surfaces and a minimalist feel. The garden hides intimate coves and a firepit, there's a beautiful rooftop terrace and the restaurant serves fine food.

## Eating

There are some excellent eating options in well-heeled Watamu. One dining experience you shouldn't miss is chic **Pili Pan** (☎0713993776; Turtle Bay Rd; mains KSh1000-1600; ⏲noon-2.30pm & 6-10pm Tue-Sun; ), set on a breezy Swahili-style outdoor terrace facing mangrove-strewn Prawn Lake. The menu includes things such as salt-and-pepper squid, tikka skewers with tamarind and tuna carpaccio. Service is good and there's a stylish bar area for aperitifs.

For local cuisine, try the tiny stalls lining Beach Way Rd, selling kebabs, chicken, chips, samosas, chapattis and the like.

## Information

There's a KCB with an ATM on Beach Way Rd.

**Barclays Bank** (Watamu Supermarket, Jacaranda Rd)

**Kenya Commercial Bank** (Beach Way Rd)

## Getting There & Away

Watamu is about a two-hour drive north of Mombasa and about a 40-minute drive south of

Malindi. Matatus run regularly between the three destinations. Heading north, they depart from Watamu village; southbound vans leave from Gede ruins. Matatus to Malindi charge KSh100; to Mombasa they charge KSh400 to KSh600.

# SOUTHEASTERN KENYA

Southeastern Kenya is one of the great wildlife-watching destinations in Africa. Here you'll find a triumvirate of epic Kenyan parks – Amboseli, Tsavo West and Tsavo East – that are home to the Big Five and so much more.

## Amboseli National Park

**Amboseli** (☎0716493335, Nairobi 020-8029705; www.kws.go.ke; adult/child US$60/35; ⏰6am-6pm) belongs in the elite of Kenya's national parks, and it's easy to see why. Its signature attraction is the sight of hundreds of big-tusked elephants set against the backdrop of Africa's best views of Mt Kilimanjaro (5895m). Africa's highest peak broods over the southern boundary of the park, and while cloud cover can render the mountain's massive bulk invisible for much of the day, you'll be rewarded with stunning vistas when the weather clears, usually at dawn and/or dusk.

Apart from guaranteed elephant sightings, you'll also see wildebeest and zebras, and you've a reasonable chance of spotting lions and hyenas. The park is also home to over 370 bird species, and it has an excellent array of lodges and a gorgeous climate.

### Sights

The park's permanent swamps of **Enkongo Narok**, **Olokenya** and **Longinye** create a marshy belt across the middle of the park and this is where you'll encounter the most wildlife. Elephants love to wallow around in the muddy waters and you've a good chance of seeing hippos around the edge. For really close-up elephant encounters, **Sinet Causeway**, which crosses Enkongo Narok near Observation Hill, is often good. The surrounding grasslands are home to grazing antelope, zebras and wildebeest, with spotted hyenas, cheetahs and lions sometimes lurking nearby. Birdlife is especially rich in these swamps when the migrants arrive in November.

**Normatior (Observation Hill)** VIEWPOINT

This pyramid-shaped hill is one of the only places in the park where you can get out and walk. The summit provides an ideal lookout from which to orient yourself to the plains, swamps and roads below. The views from here are also pretty special, whether south to Kilimanjaro or east across the swamps. Wildlife is generally a fair way off, but the views here put them in their context.

**Sinet Delta** LAKE

From Observation Hill, the northern route runs across the Sinet Delta, which is an excellent place for birdwatching. The vegetation is thicker the further south you go, providing fodder for giraffes and also framing some of the park's best Kilimanjaro views.

### Sleeping & Eating

Despite being on almost every Kenyan itinerary, there's a real lack of midrange accommodation in Amboseli, and almost everything here is either top-end luxury or budget simplicity. That said, there are excellent examples in both categories, so whether you plan to camp and cook for yourself or enjoy pampering in a fancy lodge, you'll find something suitable here. Most accommodation is outside the park, but there are three lodges inside.

All but the most basic camps provide meals, normally on a full-board basis included in the price, and these are nearly always served as buffets. Campsites are aimed at self-caterers and usually have basic cooking facilities on site, though some require you to bring your own gas cooker. Some campsites also sell meals.

**Kimana Camp** TENTED CAMP $

(☎0715059635; per person from US$31, camping per person US$10) A good deal within easy reach of Amboseli's main Kimana Gate, this dusty but great-value tented camp has 20 permanent tents and six cottages, all of which enjoy electricity and 24-hour hot water, although the bathrooms are extremely simple in both cases. There's a restaurant, a kitchen that guests can use and staggering views of Kilimanjaro.

**KWS Campsite** CAMPGROUND $

(www.kws.go.ke; camping per adult/child US$30/25) Just inside the park's southern boundary, the KWS campsite has toilets, an unreliable water supply (bring your own) and a small bar selling warm beer and soft drinks. It's fenced off from the wildlife, so you can walk around safely at night, though *don't* keep food in your tent, as baboons visit during the day looking for an uninvited feed.

★**Ol Tukai Lodge** LODGE $$$
(☎0726249697, Nairobi 020-4445514; www.oltukailodge.com; s/dtr full board Jul-Oct US$410/520/730, Nov-Mar US$350/450/630, Apr-Jun US$170/315/435; P @ ☎ ≋) Lying at Amboseli's heart, on the edge of a dense acacia forest, Ol Tukai is a splendidly refined lodge with soaring *makuti* (thatched roofs of palm leaves) and tranquil gardens defined by towering trees. Accommodation is in wooden chalets, which are brought to life with vibrant zebra prints. The split-level bar has a sweeping Kili view and a pervading atmosphere of peace and luxury.

**Kibo Safari Camp** TENTED CAMP $$$
(☎0721380539; www.kibosafaricamp.com; per person from US$160; P ☎ ≋) Around 2km from Kimana Gate, Kibo Safari Camp gives you the experience of a tented camp without asking the prohibitive fees of the lodges inside the park proper. The 72 tents and expansive grounds are beautifully kept and there are astonishing views of Kilimanjaro to be had, as well as a good restaurant serving high-quality buffet meals.

## ℹ Getting There & Away

### AIR

**Airkenya** (www.airkenya.com; adult/child one way US$187/138) has daily flights between Nairobi's Wilson Airport and Amboseli. You'll need to arrange with one of the lodges or a safari company for a vehicle to meet you at the airstrip, which is inside the park proper, near Ol Tukai Lodge.

### CAR & 4WD

There are four gates. Approaches to the park from the west (Kitirua and Meshanani gates) are in poor condition; the Iremito (northeast) and Kimana (southeast) gates are in better condition. The park is accessible in 2WD, but 4WD is always the best option, particularly after rain.

# Tsavo West National Park

Welcome to the wilderness. **Tsavo West** (☎0720968527, Nairobi 0800597000, Nairobi 020-2384417; www.kws.go.ke/tsavo-west-national-park; adult/child per day US$52/35; ⊙6am-6pm) is one of Kenya's larger national parks (9065 sq km), covering a huge variety of landscapes from swamps, natural springs and rocky peaks to extinct volcanic cones, rolling plains and sharp outcrops dusted with greenery.

This is a park with a whiff of legend about it, first for its famous man-eating lions in the late 19th century and then for its devastating levels of poaching in the 1980s. Despite the latter, there's still plenty of wildlife here, although you'll have to work harder and be much more patient than in Amboseli or the Masai Mara; the foliage is generally denser and higher here. Put all of these things together, along with its dramatic scenery, fine lodges and sense of space, and this is one of Kenya's most rewarding parks.

**Kitani Bandas** BANDAS $$
(☎0716833222, 041-2004154; www.severinsafaricamp.com; bandas Jul-Mar US$125, Apr-Jun US$100; P ☎ ≋) Run by the same people as Severin Safari Camp, Kitani is located 2km past its sister site, but is far better value. These thatched concrete *bandas* (which have their own simple kitchens) have far more style than your average budget camp and you can use Severin's facilities (including the pool and free wi-fi). Great value, though do call ahead.

★**Rhino Valley Lodge** TENTED CAMP $$$
(Ngulia Bandas; ☎043-30050; www.tsavolodgesandcamps.com; bandas full board s/d/tr US$150/200/280; P) This hillside camp is Tsavo's best bargain and one of the most reasonably priced choices in the parks of southern Kenya. The thatched stone cottages and tents perch on the lower slopes of the Ngulia Hills with sweeping views of Rhino Valley, overlooking a stream. The decor is designer rustic with plenty of space and private terraces.

**Finch Hatton's Safari Camp** TENTED CAMP $$$
(☎0716021818, Nairobi 020-8030936; www.finchhattons.com; s/d full board Jul-mid-Oct US$1225/1960, family tent full board Jul-mid-Oct US$3240, rates vary rest of year; P ☎ ≋) This luxurious tented camp, arranged around a stream full of crocs and hippos, is now looking fancier than ever after a 2014 renovation. The 17 massive, glamorous tents have vast beds, huge verandas and incredible outdoor bathrooms complete with copper bathtubs. There's a spa, gym and pool, courteous staff and a wonderfully stylish air to the place.

## ℹ Getting There & Away

There are six gates into Tsavo West, but the main access is just off the Nairobi–Mombasa

Hwy at Mtito Andei and Tsavo gates. Do be aware that unless you have a charged safari card, you'll need to enter at the main Mtito Andei gate, where they are able to process payments. Other gates may let you enter, but you'll have to leave from Mtito Andei in order to pay for your entry.

**Safarilink** (☎ Nairobi 020-6690000; www.flysafarilink.com; adult/child one-way US$224/170) has daily flights between Nairobi's Wilson Airport and Tsavo West, with airstrips near Finch Hatton's Camp and Kilaguni Serena Lodge. You'll need to arrange with one of the lodges or a safari company for a vehicle to meet you at the airstrip.

## Tsavo East National Park

Kenya's largest national park, **Tsavo East** (http://www.kws.go.ke/content/tsavo-east-national-park; adult/child per day US$52/35) has an undeniable wild and primordial charm and is a terrific wildlife-watching destination. Although one of Kenya's largest rivers flows through the middle of the park, the landscape here is markedly flatter and drier and lacks the drama of Tsavo West. The flip side is that spotting wildlife is generally easier thanks to the thinly spread foliage.

Despite the size of the park, the area of most wildlife activity is actually quite compact – the northern section of the park is largely closed and can only be visited with advance permission due to the threat of banditry and ongoing campaigns against poachers. The demarcation point is the Galana River.

**KWS Campsite** CAMPGROUND $
(camping per adult/child US$20/15) Decent site with toilets, showers and a communal kitchen.

**Lion Hill Lodge** LODGE $$
(☎ 0735877431, Nairobi 020-8030828; www.lionhilllodge.com; s/d US$80/120) Just before the park entrance, this quiet place sits atop an impossibly steep hill and the views that result from this location are extraordinary. The best views are from rooms 5 and 6, which are large rooms with balconies, or, failing that, rooms 7 to 10 also boast fine panoramas. Tents are also available.

**Satao Camp** TENTED CAMP $$$
(☎ Nairobi 020-2434610; www.sataocamp.com; s/d full board Jul-Oct US$337/436, rates vary rest of year; P 📶) Located on the banks of the Voi River, this luxury camp was recently renovated and now looks better than ever. There are 20 canopied tents, all of which are perfectly spaced within sight of a waterhole that's known to draw lions, cheetahs and elephants on occasion.

### ℹ Getting There & Away

You'll need your own wheels to explore Tsavo East, and even though it's perfectly easy to access the park on public transport from the town of Mtito Andei on the main road between Nairobi and Mombasa, it's not very useful unless you've got onward transport into the park booked.

A track through the park follows the Galana River from the Tsavo Gate to the Sala Gate; others fan out from Voi Gate. To access the park with your own vehicle use the following park gates.

**To/from Nairobi or Tsavo West** Voi, Tsavo or Manyani gates.

**To/from Mombasa** Sala or Buchuma gates.

# UNDERSTAND KENYA

## Kenya Today

Despite the horrific attacks carried out by the radical Islamic terrorist group Al-Shabaab in recent years, Kenya has found itself growing in confidence as a nation, unified rather than divided by the threat of terrorism and increasingly confident of its status as an East African powerhouse. Nevertheless, as the presidency of Uhuru Kenyatta nears the end of its first term, Kenyans are looking nervously towards the elections in August 2017, a time when tribal tensions have typically overflown into violence.

## History

The patchwork of ethnic groups, each with its own culture and language, that today exist side by side in modern Kenya are the result of waves of migration. These waves – some occurring as early as 2000 BC – came from every corner of Africa: Turkanas from Ethiopia; Kikuyu, Akamba and Meru from West Africa; and the Maasai, Luo and Samburu from the southern part of Sudan.

Kenya, however, was occupied long before this: archaeological excavations around Lake Turkana in the 1970s revealed skulls thought to be around two million years old and those of the earliest human beings ever discovered. By around the 8th century, Arabic, Indian, Persian and even Chinese merchants were arriving on the Kenyan coast, intent on trading skins, ivory, gold and spices. These new arrivals helped set up a string of commercial cities along the whole of the East African coast, intermarrying with local dynasties to found a prosperous new civilisation, part African, part Arabic, known as the Swahili.

By the 16th century, Europeans too had cottoned on to the potential of the East African coast, and most of the Swahili trading towns, including Mombasa and Lamu, were either sacked or occupied by the Portuguese. Two centuries of harsh military rule followed, punctuated by regular battles for control of the former Swahili empire. The Omani Arabs finally ousted the Portuguese in 1720, but it wasn't long before the coast came into the control of more European colonisers – the British, who used their battleships to protect their lucrative route to India and to suppress the hated slave trade.

## Mau Mau Rebellion & Independence

Despite plenty of overt pressure on Kenya's colonial authorities, the real independence movement was underground. Groups from the Kikuyu, Maasai and Luo tribes vowed to kill Europeans and their African collaborators. The most famous of these movements was Mau Mau, formed in 1952 by the Kikuyu people, which aimed to drive the white settlers from Kenya forever. The Mau Mau rebellion was a brutal war of attrition on white people, property and 'collaborators'. The various Mau Mau sects came together under the umbrella of the Kenya Land Freedom Army, led by Dedan Kimathi, and staged frequent attacks against white farms and government outposts.

By the time the rebels were defeated in 1956, the death toll stood at over 13,500 Africans (guerrillas, civilians and troops) and just over 100 Europeans. In 1960 the British government officially announced its plan to transfer power to a democratically elected African government. Independence was scheduled for December 1963, accompanied by grants and loans of US$100 million to enable the Kenyan assembly to buy out European farmers in the highlands and restore the land to the tribes.

The run-up to independence was surprisingly smooth, although the redistribution of land wasn't a great success. The immediate effect was to cause a significant decline in agricultural production, from which Kenya has never quite recovered.

Jomo Kenyatta became Kenya's first president on 12 December, ruling until his death in 1978. Under Kenyatta's presidency, Kenya developed into one of Africa's most stable and prosperous nations. But while Kenyatta is still seen as a success story, he was excessively biased in favour of his own tribe and became paranoid about dissent. Opponents of his regime who became too vocal for comfort frequently 'disappeared', and corruption soon became endemic at all levels of the power structure.

## The 1980s & '90s

Kenyatta was succeeded in 1978 by his vice president, Daniel arap Moi, a member of the Kalenjin people. He became one of the most enduring 'Big Men' in Africa, ruling in virtual autocracy for nearly 25 years. In the process, he accrued an incredible personal fortune; today many believe him to be the richest man in Africa.

Moi's regime was also characterised by nepotism, corruption, arrests of dissidents, censorship, the disbanding of tribal societies and the closure of universities. Faced with a foreign debt of nearly US$9 billion and blanket suspension of foreign aid, Moi was pressured into holding multiparty elections in early 1992. Independent observers reported a litany of electoral inconsistencies, and about 2000 people were killed during ethnic clashes widely believed to have been triggered by Kenya African National Union (KANU) agitation. Nonetheless, Moi was overwhelmingly re-elected.

Preoccupied with internal problems, Kenya was quite unprepared for the events of 7 August 1998. Early in the morning massive blasts simultaneously ripped apart the American embassies in Nairobi and Dar es Salaam in Tanzania, killing more than 200 people. The effect on Kenyan tourism, and the economy as a whole, was devastating. Further terrorist activity shook the country on 28 November 2002, when suicide bombers slammed an explosives-laden car into the lobby of the Paradise Hotel at Kikambala, near Mombasa. Moments before, missiles were fired at an Israeli passenger plane taking off from Mombasa's airport. Al-Qaeda subsequently claimed responsibility for both the 1998 and 2002 acts.

# Culture

Many residents of Kenya are more aware of their tribal affiliation than of being 'Kenyan'; this lack of national cohesion undoubtedly presents the nation with some challenges, but is generally accompanied by an admirable live-and-let-live attitude.

Education is of primary concern to Kenyans. Literacy rates are around 85% and are considerably higher than in neighbouring countries. Although education isn't compulsory, the motivation to learn is huge, particularly now that it's free, and you'll see children in school uniform everywhere in Kenya, even in the most impoverished rural communities. For all this, as Kenya gains a foothold in the 21st century it is grappling with ever-increasing poverty. Once categorised as a middle-income country, Kenya has become a low-income country, with the standard of living dropping drastically since the start of the new millennium.

# People

Most Kenyans outside the coastal and eastern provinces are Christians of one sort or another, while most of those on the coast and in the eastern part of the country are Muslim. Muslims make up some 30% of the population. In the more remote tribal areas you'll find a mixture of Muslims, Christians and those who follow their ancestral tribal beliefs, such as animism, though this last group is in the minority.

# Kenyan Cuisine

The Kenyan culinary tradition has generally emphasised feeding the masses as efficiently as possible, with little room for flair or innovation. Most meals are centred on ugali, a thick, doughlike mass made from maize and/or cassava flour. While traditional fare may be bland but filling, there are some treats to be found. Many memorable eating experiences in Kenya are likely to revolve around dining alfresco in a safari camp, surrounded by the sights and sounds of the African bush.

## Counting Carbs

Kenyan cuisine has few culinary masterpieces and is mainly survival food, offering the maximum opportunity to fill up at minimum cost. Most meals in Kenya consist largely of heavy starches.

In addition to ugali, Kenyans rely on potatoes, rice, chapati and *matoke*. The rice-based dishes, biryani and pilau, are clearly derived from Persia – they should be delicately spiced with saffron and star anise and liberally sprinkled with carrot and raisins. The chapati is identical to its Indian predecessor, while *matoke* is mashed green plantains that, when well prepared, can taste like buttery, lightly whipped mashed potato. Also look out for *irio* (or *kienyeji*), made from mashed greens, potato and boiled corn or beans; *mukimo,* a kind of hash made from sweet potatoes, corn, beans and plantains; and *githeri,* a mix of beans and corn.

## Flesh & Bone

Kenyans are enthusiastic carnivores and their unofficial national dish, *nyama choma* (barbecued meat), is a red-blooded, hands-on affair. Most places have their own on-site butchery, and *nyama choma* is usually purchased by weight, often as a single hunk of meat. Half a kilogram is usually enough for one person (taking into account bone and gristle). It'll be brought out to you chopped into small bite-sized bits, often with a salad or vegetable mash and greens.

Goat is the most common meat, but you'll see chicken, beef and some game animals (ostrich and crocodile) in upmarket places. Don't expect *nyama choma* to melt in the mouth – its chewiness is probably indicative of the long and eventful life of the animal you're consuming and you'll need a good half-hour at the end of the meal to work over your gums with a toothpick. We find that copious quantities of Tusker beer also tend to help it go down.

In addition to *nyama choma,* Kenyans are fond of meat-based stews, which help make their carb-rich diet more palatable. Again, goat, chicken and beef, as well as mutton, are the most common cuts on the menu, though they tend to be pretty tough, despite being cooked for hours on end.

# SURVIVAL GUIDE

## Directory A–Z

### ACCOMMODATION

Kenya has a wide range of accommodation options, from basic hotels with cells overlooking city bus stands to luxury tented camps hidden away in remote corners of the country. There

**PRICE RANGES**

The following price ranges refer to a double room with bathroom in high season.

**$** less than US$75

**$$** US$75 to US$200

**$$$** more than US$200

The following price ranges refer to a standard main course.

**$** less than US$5

**$$** US$5 to US$10

**$$$** more than US$10

are also all kinds of campsites, budget tented camps, *bandas* (thatched-roof wood or stone huts) and cottages scattered around the parks and rural areas.

## ACTIVITIES

Kenya is not just about seeing – there's also so much to do here, from walking up some of Africa's highest peaks to drifting out over the Masai Mara in a balloon, and from snorkelling the Indian Ocean to cycling within sight of wild rhinos. So get down from your vehicle and explore.

## DANGERS & ANNOYANCES

While Kenya can be quite a safe destination, there are still plenty of pitfalls for the unwary or inexperienced traveller, from everyday irritations to more serious threats. A little street sense goes a long way here, and getting the latest local information is essential wherever you intend to travel.

### Hotel Security

Although hotels give you room keys, it is recommended that you carry a padlock for your backpack or suitcase as an extra deterrent. Furthermore, don't invite trouble by leaving valuables, cash or important documents lying around your room or in an unlocked bag.

Upmarket hotels will have safes (either in the room or at reception) where you can keep your money and passport (and sometimes even your laptop), so it's advised that you take advantage of them. It's usually best not to carry any valuables on the street, but if your budget accommodation is a bit rough around the edges, you may want to consider hiding your valuables on your person and carrying them at all times. Of course, use discretion, as muggings do happen in large towns and cities. Sadly, theft is perhaps the number-one complaint of travellers in Kenya, so it can't hurt to take a few extra precautions.

### Crime

Even the staunchest Kenyan patriot will readily admit that one of the country's biggest problems is crime. It ranges from petty snatch theft and mugging to violent armed robbery, carjacking and, of course, white-collar crime and corruption. As a visitor you needn't feel paranoid, but you should always keep your wits about you, particularly at night.

Although crime is a fact of life in Kenya, it needn't spoil your trip. Above all, don't make the mistake of distrusting everyone you meet – the honest souls you encounter will far outnumber any crooks who cross your path.

**Precautions** Perhaps the best advice for when you're walking around cities and towns is not to carry anything valuable with you – that includes jewellery, watches, cameras, bumbags, daypacks and money. Most hotels provide a safe or secure place for valuables, although you should also be cautious of the security at some budget places.

**Mugging** While pickpocketing and bag snatching are the most common crimes, armed muggings do occur in Nairobi and on the coast. Always take taxis after dark.

**Snatch and run** Snatch-and-run crimes happen more in crowds. If you suddenly feel there are too many people around you, or think you are being followed, dive straight into a shop and ask for help.

**Luggage** This is an obvious signal to criminals that you've just arrived. When arriving anywhere by bus, it's sensible to take a 'ship-to-shore' approach, getting a taxi directly from the bus station to your hotel. You'll have plenty of time to explore once you've safely stowed your belongings. Also, don't read a guidebook or look at maps on the street – it attracts unwanted attention.

**Reporting crime** In the event of a crime, you should report it to the police, but this can be a real procedure. You'll need to get a police report if you intend to make an insurance claim. In the event of a snatch theft, think twice before yelling 'Thief!' It's not unknown for people to administer summary justice on the spot, often with fatal results for the criminal.

## EMBASSIES & CONSULATES

**Australian High Commission** (☎020-4277100; www.kenya.embassy.gov.au; ICIPE House, Riverside Dr, Nairobi)

**British Embassy** (☎020-2844000; http://ukinkenya.fco.gov.uk/en; Upper Hill Rd, Nairobi)

**Canadian High Commission** (☎020-3663000; www.canadainternational.gc.ca/kenya/index.aspx; Limuru Rd, Gigiri, Nairobi)

**Ethiopian Embassy** (☎020-2732050; State House Ave, Nairobi)

**French Embassy** (☎020-2778000; www.ambafrance-ke.org; 15th fl, Barclays Plaza, Loita St, Nairobi)

**German Embassy** (☎020-4262100; www.nairobi.diplo.de; 113 Riverside Dr, Nairobi)

**Netherlands Embassy** (☎020-4288000; http://kenia.nlembassy.org; Riverside Lane)

**South Sudan Embassy** (☎020-2711384; 6th fl, Bishops Gate House, 5th Ngong Ave, Nairobi)

**Tanzanian Embassy** (☎020-331057, 020-2311948; Reinsurance Plaza, Aga Khan Walk, Nairobi)

**Uganda High Commission (Consular Section)** (☎020-311814; 1st fl, Uganda House, Kenyatta Ave) The consular section is in the city centre. There's also a High Commission office further out.

**UK High Commission** (☎020-2873000; www.gov.uk/government/world/kenya; Upper Hill Rd, Nairobi)

**US Embassy** (☎020-3636000; http://nairobi.usembassy.gov; United Nations Ave, Nairobi)

## INTERNET ACCESS

**Wi-fi** You'll find wi-fi in all but the cheapest or most remote hotels, though speeds vary enormously. Many wildlife lodges have wi-fi access, but it tends to be unreliable. Budget and midrange lodges rarely have internet access at all.

**Mobile Networks** Safari.com, Orange and Airtel are your best bets for internet access on your phone. Data is cheap and speeds are generally decent, especially compared to other countries in East Africa.

## LBGTIQ TRAVELLERS

Negativity towards homosexuality is widespread in Kenya and recent events ensure that it's a brave gay or lesbian Kenyan who comes out of the closet. Frequent denunciations by those in power have created a toxic atmosphere of homophobia, which sometimes spills over into violence and, more often, into government harassment.

While there are very few prosecutions under the law, it is certainly better to be discreet as a gay foreigner in Kenya. Some local con artists do a good line in blackmail, picking up foreigners then threatening to expose them to the police.

## MONEY

All banks change US dollars, euros and UK pounds into Kenyan shillings. ATMs are found in medium-sized towns, so bring cash and a debit or credit card.

### Exchange Rates

| | | |
|---|---|---|
| Australia | A$1 | KSh79 |
| Canada | C$1 | KSh79 |
| Europe | €1 | KSh118 |
| Japan | ¥100 | KSh92 |
| New Zealand | NZ$1 | KSh75 |
| UK | UK£1 | KSh133 |
| USA | US$1 | KSh104 |

For current exchange rates, see www.xe.com.

## OPENING HOURS

**Banks** 9am to 3pm Monday to Friday; 9am to 11am Saturday

**Post Offices** 8.30am to 5pm Monday to Friday; 9am to noon Saturday

**Restaurants** 11am to 2pm and 5pm to 9pm; some remain open between lunch and dinner

**Shops** 9am to 3pm Monday to Friday; 9am to 11am Saturday

**Supermarkets** 8.30am to 8.30pm Monday to Saturday; 10am to 8pm Saturday

## PUBLIC HOLIDAYS

**New Year's Day** 1 January

**Good Friday and Easter Monday** March/April

**Labour Day** 1 May

**Madaraka Day** 1 June

**Moi Day** 10 October

**Kenyatta Day** 20 October

**Independence Day** 12 December

**Christmas Day** 25 December

**Boxing Day** 26 December

## TELEPHONE

Landlines continue to be used by most businesses in Kenya, but otherwise the mobile phone is king. Prices are low, data is fast and coverage is excellent in most towns and cities.

### Mobile Phones

**Coverage** While coverage is excellent in Kenya, you'll often not be able to use your phone or data in more remote areas, including many national parks.

**SIM cards** Pick up a SIM card from one of the Kenyan mobile-phone companies: **Safaricom** (www.safaricom.co.ke), **Airtel** (www.africa.airtel.com/kenya/) or **Orange** (orange.co.ke). A SIM card costs about KSh100, and you can then buy top-up scratch cards and use them either for data or calling credit.

## TIME

Kenya is three hours ahead of Greenwich Mean Time (GMT) all year round.

## VISAS

**Visa on arrival** Tourist visas can be obtained on arrival at all three international airports and at the country's land borders with Uganda and Tanzania. This applies to Europeans, Australians, New Zealanders, Americans and Canadians, although citizens from a few smaller Commonwealth countries are exempt. Visas cost US$50/€40/£30 and are valid for three months from the date of entry. Tourist visas can be extended for a further three-month period.

**E-visa** The Kenyan government's online visa portal (http://evisa.go.ke) issues single-entry tourist visas (US$51) valid for up to 90 days from the date of entry, as well as transit visas (US$21). Simply register, apply and pay online and once it's approved (within two business days) you'll be sent a PDF visa document to print out, which you then present on entry to Kenya.

### WOMEN TRAVELLERS

In their day-to-day lives, Kenyans are generally respectful towards women, although solo women in bars will attract a lot of interest from would-be suitors.

**Trouble spots** In most areas of Kenya, and certainly on safari, women are unlikely to experience any difficulties. The only place you are likely to have problems is at the beach resorts on the coast, where women may be approached by male prostitutes as well as local aspiring Romeos. It's always best to cover your legs and shoulders when away from the beach so as not to offend local sensibilities.

**Safety** Women should avoid walking around at night. The ugly fact is that while men are likely just to be robbed without violence, rape is a real risk for women. Lone night walks along the beach or through quiet city streets are a bad idea and criminals usually work in gangs, so take a taxi, even if you're in a group.

**Discrimination** Regrettably, black women in the company of white men are often assumed to be prostitutes, and can face all kinds of discrimination from hotels and security guards as well as approaches from Kenyan hustlers offering to help rip off the white 'customer'. Again, the worst of this can be avoided by taking taxis between hotels and restaurants etc.

## ℹ Getting There & Away

### AIR

#### Airports

Kenya has three international airports; check out the website www.kaa.go.ke for further information.

**Jomo Kenyatta International Airport** (p610) Most international flights to and from Nairobi arrive at this airport, 15km southeast of the city. There are two international terminals and a smaller domestic terminal; you can easily walk between the terminals.

**Moi International Airport** (MBA; ☎020-3577058, 041-3433211) In Mombasa, 9km west of the centre, and Kenya's second-busiest international airport. Apart from flights to Zanzibar, this is mainly used by charter airlines and domestic flights.

**Wilson Airport** (p610) Located 6km south of Nairobi's city centre on Langata Rd. Has some flights between Nairobi and Kilimanjaro International Airport or Mwanza in Tanzania, as well as scheduled and charter domestic flights.

#### Airlines

**Kenya Airways** (www.kenya-airways.com) is the main national carrier, and has a generally good safety record, with just one fatal incident since 1977.

### LAND

#### Ethiopia

**Security** With ongoing problems in Sudan and Somalia, Ethiopia offers the only viable overland route into Kenya from the north. The security situation around the main entry point at Moyale is changeable – the border is usually open, but security problems often force its closure. Most foreign governments warn against travel to areas of Kenya bordering Ethiopia and even along the highway between Isiolo and Moyale. Even so, cattle- and goat-rustling are rife, triggering frequent cross-border tribal wars, so check the security situation carefully before attempting this crossing.

**Visas** Theoretically Ethiopian visas can be issued at the Ethiopian embassy in Nairobi, but expect a number of hurdles, including having to provide a letter of introduction from your own embassy in Nairobi, which is likely to be hard to get. Persistence generally pays off, however, so if you have plenty of time, it should be possible to get an Ethiopian visa eventually.

There were no cross-border bus services at the time of writing. If you don't have your own transport from Moyale, there's a daily bus between Moyale and Marsabit (KSh800), while lifts can be arranged with the trucks (KSh500).

From immigration on the Ethiopian side of town it's a 2km walk to the Ethiopian and Kenyan customs posts. A yellow-fever vaccination is required to cross either border at Moyale. Unless you fancy being vaccinated at the border, get your jabs in advance and keep the certificate with your passport. A cholera vaccination may also be required.

#### Tanzania

The main land borders between Kenya and Tanzania are at Namanga, Loitokitok, Taveta, Isebania and Lunga Lunga, and can be reached by public transport. There are no train services between the two countries.

Although all of the routes may be done in stages using a combination of buses and local matatus, there are six main routes to/from Tanzania:

- Mombasa–Tanga/Dar es Salaam
- Mombasa–Arusha/Moshi
- Nairobi–Arusha/Moshi (via Namanga)
- Nairobi-Moshi (via Loitokitok)
- Nairobi–Dar es Salaam
- Nairobi–Mwanza

The main bus companies serving Tanzania are as follows:

**Riverside Shuttle** (☎ 0722328595; www.riverside-shuttle.com; Lagos House, Monrovia St)

**Modern Coast Express** (Oxygen; ☎ 0705700888, 0737940000; www.modern.co.ke; cnr Cross Lane & Accra Rd)

### Uganda

The main border post for overland travellers is Malaba, with Busia an alternative if you're travelling via Kisumu.

Numerous bus companies run between Nairobi, Nakuru or Kisumu and Kampala. From the Kenyan side, we recommend **Easy Coach** (☎ 0738200301, 0726354301; www.easycoach.co.ke; Haile Selassie Ave, Nairobi) and Modern Coast Express.

### TOURS

Most people come to Kenya on safari but it's also possible to reach the country as part of an overland truck tour originating in Europe or other parts of Africa – many also start in Nairobi bound for other places in Africa. Most companies are based in the UK or South Africa.

**Acacia Expeditions** (www.acacia-africa.com) Covers East and southern Africa with some small-group options.

**Africa Travel Co** (www.africatravelco.com) Focuses on East and southern Africa.

**Dragoman** (www.dragoman.co.uk) There are few places in Africa it doesn't go, with good links to trips across the continent.

**Oasis Overland** (www.oasisoverland.co.uk) A range of East and southern African overland trips, as well as some more conventional tours.

## Getting Around

### AIR

**Airkenya** (☎ 020-3916000; www.airkenya.com) Amboseli, Diani, Lamu, Masai Mara, Malindi, Meru, Mombasa, Nakuru, Nanyuki, Lewa and Samburu.

**Fly540** (p627) Eldoret, Kisumu, Lamu, Lodwar, Malindi, Masai Mara and Mombasa.

**Jambo Jet** (☎ 020-3274545; www.jambojet.com) Subsidiary of Kenya Airways that flies to Diani Beach, Eldoret, Kisumu, Lamu, Malindi and Mombasa.

**Kenya Airways** (www.kenya-airways.com) Kisumu, Malindi and Mombasa.

**Mombasa Air Safari** (p621) Amboseli, Diani Beach, Kisumu, Lamu, Malindi, Masai Mara, Meru, Mombasa, Samburu and Tsavo West.

**Safarilink** (☎ 020-6690000; www.flysafarilink.com) Amboseli, Diani Beach, Kiwayu, Lamu, Lewa Downs, Loisaba, Masai Mara, Naivasha, Nanyuki, Samburu, Shaba and Tsavo West.

### BUS

**Services** Kenya has an extensive network of long- and short-haul bus routes, with particularly good coverage of the areas around Nairobi, the coast and the western regions. Services thin out the further from the capital you get, particularly in the north, and there are still plenty of places where you'll be reliant on matatus.

**Operators** Buses are operated by a variety of private companies that offer varying levels of comfort, convenience and roadworthiness. They're considerably cheaper than taking the train or flying and, as a rule, services are frequent, fast and can be quite comfortable.

**Facilities** In general, if you travel during daylight hours, buses are a fairly safe way to get around – you'll certainly be safer in a bus than in a matatu. The best coaches are saved for long-haul and international routes and offer movies, drinks, toilets and reclining airline-style seats; some of the newer ones even have wi-fi. On shorter local routes, however, you may find yourself on something resembling a battered school bus.

**Seating tips** Whatever kind of conveyance you find yourself in, don't sit at the back (you'll be thrown around like a rag doll on Kenyan roads) or right at the front (you'll be the first to die in a head-on collision, plus you'll be able to see the oncoming traffic, which is usually best left to the driver or those with nerves of steel).

**Safety** There are a few security considerations to think about when taking a bus in Kenya. Some routes, most notably the roads from Malindi to Lamu and Isiolo to Marsabit, have been prone to attacks by *shiftas* (bandits) in the past; check things out locally before you travel. Another possible risk is drugged food and drink: it is best to politely refuse any offers of drinks or snacks from strangers.

The following are the main national bus operators in Kenya:

**Busways** (☎ 020-2227650) Western Kenya and the coast.

**Coastline Safaris** (Coast Bus; ☎ 0722206446; www.coastbus.com) Western and Southern Kenya and Mombasa.

**Dreamline Executive** (☎ 0731777799) Nairobi, Mombasa and Malindi.

**Easy Coach** Rift Valley and Western Kenya.

**Modern Coast Express** Nairobi, Mombasa, Malindi and Western Kenya.

### CAR & MOTORCYCLE

Many travellers bring their own vehicles into Kenya as part of overland trips and, expense notwithstanding, it's a great way to see the country at your own pace. Otherwise, there are numerous car-hire companies that can rent you anything from a small hatchback to a 4WD, although hire rates are very high.

### Hire

Hiring a vehicle to tour Kenya (or at least the national parks) is an expensive way of seeing the country, but it does give you freedom of movement and is sometimes the only way of getting to more remote parts of the country. However, unless you're sharing with a sufficient number of people, it's likely to cost more than you'd pay for an organised camping safari with all meals.

**Four-wheel drive** Unless you're just planning on travelling on the main routes between towns, you'll need a 4WD vehicle. Few of the car-hire companies will let you drive 2WD vehicles on dirt roads, including those in the national parks, and if you ignore this proscription and have an accident you'll be personally liable for any damage to the vehicle.

**Driver requirements** A minimum age of between 23 and 25 years usually applies for hirers. Some companies require you to have been driving for at least two years. An international driving licence is not required, but you will need to show your passport.

**Vehicle condition** It's generally true to say that the more you pay for a vehicle, the better its condition will be. The larger companies are usually in a better financial position to keep their fleet in good order. Always be sure to check the brakes, the tyres (including the spare), the windscreen wipers and the lights before you set off.

**Breakdowns** The other factor to consider is what the company will do for you (if anything) if you have a serious breakdown. The major hire companies *may* deliver a replacement vehicle and make arrangements for recovery of the other vehicle at their expense, but with most companies you'll have to get the vehicle fixed and back on the road yourself, and then try to claim a refund.

**Crossing borders** If you plan to take the car across international borders, check whether the company allows this – many don't, and those that do charge for the privilege.

## MATATU

Local matatus are the main means of getting around for local people, and any reasonably sized city or town will have plenty of services covering every major road and suburb.

**Fares** These start at around KSh40 and may reach KSh100 for longer routes in Nairobi.

**Vehicles** The vehicles themselves can be anything from dilapidated Peugeot 504 pick-ups with a cab on the back to big 20-seater minibuses. The most common are white Nissan minibuses (many local people prefer the name 'Nissans' to matatus).

**Safety** Despite a periodic government drives to regulate the matatu industry, matatus remain notorious for dangerous driving, overcrowding and general shady business. A passenger backlash has seen a small but growing trend in more responsible matatu companies offering less crowding, safer driving and generally better security on intercity services. Mololine Prestige Shuttle is one of these plying the route from Nairobi to Kisumu.

**Services** Apart from in the remote northern areas, where you'll rely on occasional buses or paid lifts on trucks, you can almost always find a matatu going to the next town or further afield, so long as it's not too late in the day. Simply ask around among the drivers at the local matatu stand or 'stage'. Matatus leave when full and the fares are fixed. It's unlikely you will be charged more than other passengers.

**Accidents** As with buses, roads are usually busy enough for a slight shunt to be the most likely accident, though of course congestion never stops drivers jockeying for position like it's the Kenya Derby. Wherever you go, remember that most matatu crashes are head-on collisions – under no circumstances should you sit in the 'death seat' next to the matatu driver. Play it safe and sit in the middle seats away from the window.

## TRAIN

The Uganda Railway was once the main trade artery in East Africa, but these days the network has dwindled to one functioning route between Nairobi and Mombasa; the Nairobi–Kisumu service was not operating at the time of research. However, the brand-new Chinese-built Nairobi–Mombasa high-speed railway is due to open in 2017, and when it does, it will be little short of a revolution in Kenya transport, cutting travel time between the capital and the coast from 18 hours to four.

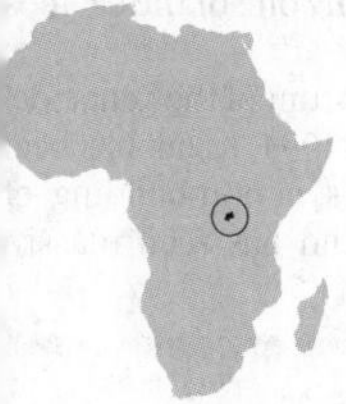

# Rwanda

OP 11.53 MILLION / ☎250

### Includes ➡



### Best Places to Eat

- Heaven Restaurant (p644)
- Shokola Cafe (p643)
- Nehemiah's Best Coffee p648)
- Khana Khazana (p644)

### Best Places to Sleep

- Discover Rwanda Youth Hostel (p641)
- Garden House (p645)
- Cormoran Lodge (p646)
- Ruzizi Tented Lodge p649)
- Iby'Iwacu Cultural Village p647)

## Why Go?

Tiny Rwanda's name may evoke memories of the horrific genocide that brutalised this country in 1994, but the country is better known today as one of Africa's most stable nations, a plucky survivor that has come together in the decades since the dark times to create a promising and dynamic future.

Tourism is once again a key contributor to the economy and the industry's brightest star is the chance to track mountain gorillas through bamboo forests in the shadow of the Virunga volcanoes. These conical mountains are shrouded in equatorial jungles and helped earn Rwanda the moniker of 'Le Pays des Mille Collines' (Land of a Thousand Hills).

So, while Rwanda's scars may run deep, now is the time to help the country look to its future and embrace its newfound optimism.

## When to Go

### Kigali

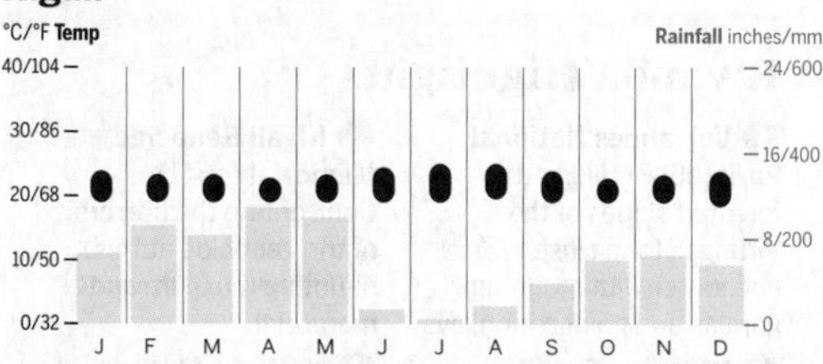


**Dry seasons** Rains ease from mid-May to September and from mid-December to mid-March.

**Jun–Jul** Baby gorillas are named during the Kwita Izina ceremony.

**The long rains** Although often wet from mid-March to mid-May, travel is still possible.

## KIGALI

POP 1.2 MILLION

Spanning several ridges and valleys, Kigali, with its lush hillsides, flowering trees, winding boulevards and bustling streets, is arguably one of the most attractive capital cities in Africa, as well as easily one of the cleanes[t] and safest.

Despite bearing the brunt of the genocide'[s] unspeakable horrors in 1994, Kigali has bee[n] the centre of Rwanda's nation-building ef[-]forts since that time and has seen massiv[e]

## Rwanda Highlights

1. **Volcanoes National Park** (p647) Hiking the forested slopes of the Virungas for a close encounter with mountain gorillas and golden monkeys.
2. **Nyungwe Forest National Park** (p650) Hacking through steamy rainforests in search of colobus monkeys and chimpanzees.
3. **Kigali Genocide Memorial** (p641) Confronting the horrors of the genocide at this haunting museum and memorial.
4. **National Museum of Rwanda** (p648) Watching an Intore dance performance at the finest museum in the country, in Huye (Butare).
5. **Kibuye** (p646) Kicking back on the sandy shores of Lake Kivu with views of the islands out in the bay at this much-overlooked resort town.
6. **Akagera National Park** (p649) Going on safari in this quickly replenishing national park, a victim of the genocide but still one of Rwanda's best.
7. **Kigali** (p640) Getting to know Rwanda's charming and hilly capital, full of great eating opportunities.

amounts of state and foreign investment pouring in over the past two decades. Indeed, the rebirth of the capital has seen a cosmopolitanism arrive in the city and Kigali now boasts a slew of new skyscrapers, several international hotels and a host of excellent eating options. Few people leave Kigali without being impressed by this plucky and charismatic survivor.

## Sights

**★Kigali Genocide Memorial** MEMORIAL
(www.kgm.rw; 8am-5pm, last entry 4pm; closed public holidays) FREE In the span of 100 days, an estimated one million Tutsis and moderate Hutus were systematically butchered by the Interahamwe army. This memorial honours the estimated 250,000 people buried here in mass graves and also has an excellent exhibition that tries to explain how it was that the world watched as the genocide unfolded. This is an intensely powerful and moving memorial to which you should dedicate at least half a day.

**Inema Art Center** GALLERY
(0783187646; www.inemaartcenter.com; KG 563 St, Kacyiru; 9am-7pm) FREE Opened in 2012, the privately run Inema Art Center is a collective of 10 resident artists and guests. It's quickly established itself as the foremost modern art gallery in Kigali. As well as paintings, sculptures and contemporary takes on traditional crafts, there are dance and music performances and courses. Much of the art is for sale (and can be shipped internationally), but if you're not buying you're welcome just to admire.

**Hotel des Mille Collines** HISTORIC SITE
(Hotel Rwanda; 0788192530; www.millecollines.rw; KN 6 Ave) The inspiration for the film *Hotel Rwanda,* this still-functioning luxury hotel was owned by the Belgian airline Sabena in 1994. At the time of the genocide, the hotel's European managers were evacuated and control was given to local employee Paul Rusesabagina, who used his position to hide fleeing Tutsis and moderate Hutus, thus saving hundreds of lives.

**Camp Kigali Memorial** MEMORIAL
(KN 3 Ave; 8am-5pm) FREE The 10 stone columns you find here mark the spot where 10 Belgian UN peacekeepers were murdered on the first day of the genocide. Originally deployed to protect the home of moderate prime minister Agatha Uwilingimana, the soldiers were captured, disarmed and brought here by the Presidential Guard before being killed. Each stone column represents one of the soldiers and the horizontal cuts in it represent the soldier's age.

## Festivals & Events

**Kigali Up** MUSIC
(www.kigaliup.rw; RFr5000; Jul) Kigali's annual music festival features world music, blues, funk and roots artists from around the globe.

**Rwanda Film Festival** FILM
(www.rwandafilmfestival.net; Jul) The Rwanda Film Festival, otherwise known as Hillywood to locals, runs in cinemas around the city in July, showcasing new Rwandan film.

## Sleeping

**★Discover Rwanda Youth Hostel** HOSTEL $
(0782265679; www.discoverrwanda.hostel.com; Bldg 14, KN 14 Ave, Kimihurura; 4-/6-/8-bed dm US$20/18/17, tw without bathroom US$25, d US$50; P@) Now in a new location, this long-running backpackers' hostel offers a very sociable atmosphere, lots of fun events and plenty of tours and excursions. Accommodation is either in dorms with four to eight beds and shared bathrooms or in private en suite rooms.

**Centre Saint Paul** GUESTHOUSE $
(0252576371; cnpsaintpaul@yahoo.fr; KN 32 St; s/tw incl breakfast US$21/30 apt US$28-42; ) This central and spotless Catholic church-run complex has four blocks of spartan but spacious rooms and apartments set around a well-manicured garden. Each room has its own bathroom, mosquito net and a small desk (presumably for reading your Bible at).

**★Gloria Hotel** HOTEL $$
(0788930233; www.gloriahotelrwanda.com; KN 76 St; s/d incl breakfast from US$70/90) This excellent, central midrange place appears sometimes to spill over into top end with its lavish buffet breakfast served in the gorgeous open-sided restaurant and charming staff that seems genuinely happy to see you. The rooms are modern with comfortable mattresses, even if the spacious bathrooms can flood and the desks are too high – these are small quibbles overall.

**Garr Hotel** GUESTHOUSE $$
(0783831292; www.garrhotel.com; 52 KG 9 Ave, Nyarutarama; s/d/tw/ste US$95/110/130/160; P) Head and shoulders above much of the competition, this homely guesthouse has

# Kigali

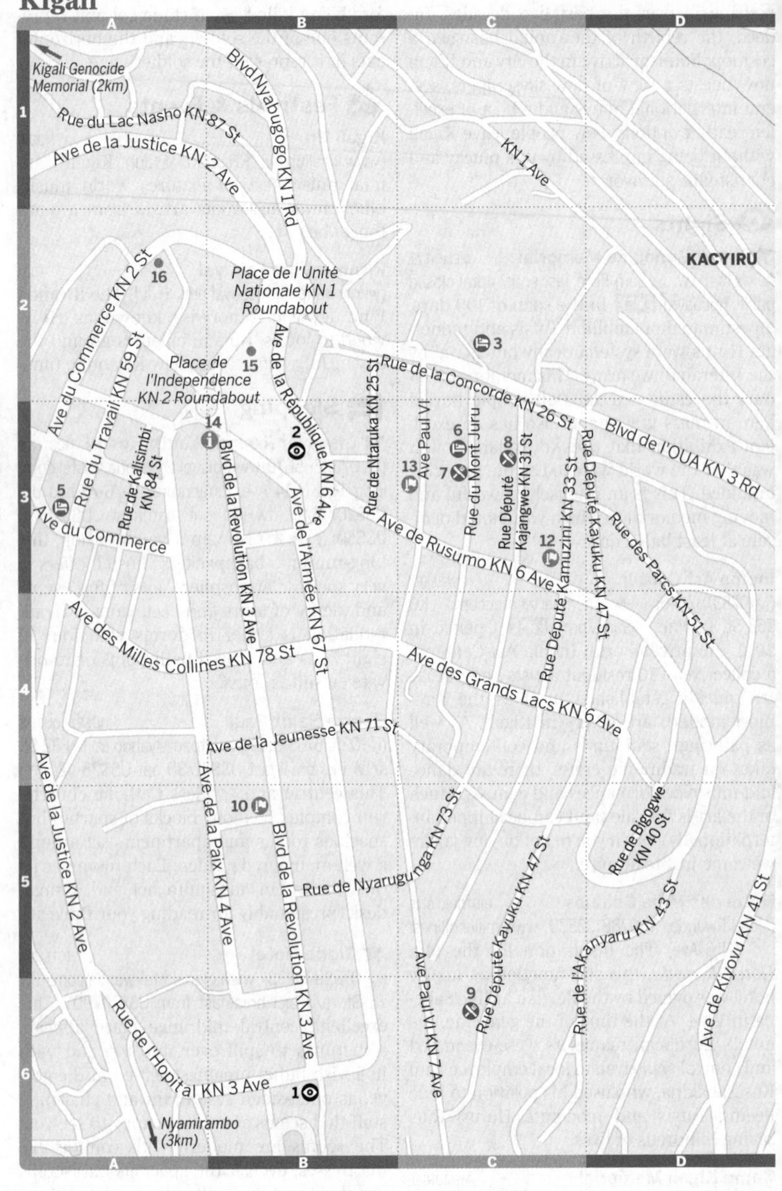




large and rather classically styled rooms with wood furnishings and quality beds. It's in a smart part of town (but it's a long way from the city centre) and there are a number of excellent places to eat within walking distance. The swimming pool is another nice touch.

**Heaven Boutique Hotel** BOUTIQUE HOTEL **$$$**
(☎0737886307; www.heavenrwanda.com; KN 29 St, Kiyovu; r US$135-165; ❄📶) This American-run boutique hotel is a breath of fresh air in Kigali, where charming accommodation is hard to come by. There are three rooms in

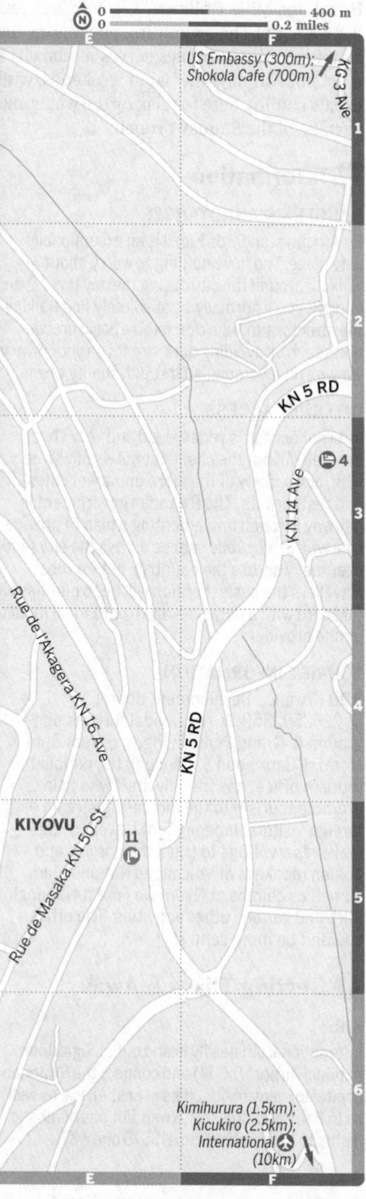


the same building as the Heaven restaurant and 15 newer rooms in a purpose-built villa just a little down the road. Rooms are stylish and colourfully decorated and the welcome is warm.

## Kigali

**Sights**

| | | |
|---|---|---|
| 1 | Camp Kigali Memorial | B6 |
| 2 | Hotel des Mille Collines | B3 |

**Sleeping**

| | | |
|---|---|---|
| 3 | Centre Saint Paul | C2 |
| 4 | Discover Rwanda Youth Hostel | F3 |
| 5 | Gloria Hotel | A3 |
| 6 | Heaven Boutique Hotel | C3 |

**Eating**

| | | |
|---|---|---|
| 7 | Heaven Restaurant | C3 |
| 8 | Khana Khazana | C3 |
| 9 | New Cactus | C6 |

**Drinking & Nightlife**

| | | |
|---|---|---|
| | Hotel des Mille Collines | (see 2) |

**Information**

| | | |
|---|---|---|
| 10 | Belgian Embassy | B5 |
| 11 | Canadian Embassy | E5 |
| 12 | French Embassy | C3 |
| 13 | German Embassy | C3 |
| 14 | RDB | B3 |

**Transport**

| | | |
|---|---|---|
| | Brussels Airlines | (see 2) |
| 15 | Ethiopian Airlines | B2 |
| | Kenya Airways | (see 15) |
| | KLM | (see 15) |
| 16 | Qatar Airways | A2 |
| | RwandAir | (see 15) |
| | South African Airways | (see 2) |
| | Turkish Airlines | (see 14) |

## Eating

**Shokola Cafe** INTERNATIONAL $

(0788350530; Kigali Public Library, KN 8 Ave, Kimihurura; mains RFr4000-7000; 7am-9pm; ) This gorgeous, bright and breezy space on the top floor of the Kigali Public Library (go round the back and take the stairs) is emblematic of just how progressive and sophisticated Kigali has become in a short time. Read a book on one of the comfy sofas, order food from the interesting international menu or just have a great coffee.

**New Cactus** FRENCH $

(0788678798; KN 47 St; mains RFr5000-7500; noon-2pm & 6-10.30pm; ) This attractive hacienda is set on a ridge where you can soak up the sparkling lights of Kigali by night or get a bird's-eye appreciation of the city during the day. It boasts a broad menu of French favourites and, for something a little different, some delicious Congolese dishes full of spices and flavours.

WORTH A TRIP

### NTARAMA & NYAMATA

**Ntarama Church** (Ntarama; ⏲8am-4.30pm Mon-Thu, 9am-4pm Fri-Sun), about 25km south of Kigali, has not been touched since the genocide ended and the bodies were removed. Today, there are many bits of clothing scraps still on the floor.

**Nyamata Church** (Nyamata; ⏲8am-4.30pm Mon-Thu, 9am-4pm Fri-Sun), about 30km south of Kigali, is a deeply disturbing genocide memorial where some 50,000 people died. Today the skulls and bones of the many victims are on display. While the visual remains of the deceased are a visceral sight, their inclusion here is to provide firm evidence to would-be genocide deniers.

★**Heaven Restaurant** INTERNATIONAL **$$**
(☎0788486581; 7 KN 29 St; mains RFr11,000-15,000; ⏲noon-10.30pm Mon-Fri, 10am-10.30pm Sat & Sun) A highlight of the Kigali restaurant scene, Heaven has a relaxed, open-air deck bistro with a wide-ranging menu drawing from a variety of international influences. It's hugely popular with expats and travellers, so look elsewhere for local atmosphere, but do come here for an excellent and innovative menu that combines local flavours with international dishes.

**Khana Khazana** INDIAN **$$**
(☎0788499600; www.khanakhazana.rw; KN 31 St, Kiyovu; mains RFr5000-12,000; ⏲noon-3.30pm & 6-10.30pm) Statues of a rotund Ganesh and a blissed-out Shiva dot what locals generally agree is the best Indian restaurant in Kigali. The menu has a long list of all the Indian classics (which are prepared with panache) and waitstaff are dressed in imitation traditional Indian dress.

## Drinking & Nightlife

**K-Club** CLUB
(KG 9 Ave, Nyarutarama; Sat & Sun RFr5000; ⏲10pm-3am Mon-Thu, 10pm-5am Fri-Sun) The general consensus is that K-Club is currently the best spot in town for a night out and come the weekends (the only time admission is charged) it's packed with a young and well-off crowd enjoying the cheap drinks, flashy atmosphere and air-conditioned dance floor. Dress up if you plan to join them.

**Hotel des Mille Collines** BAR
(KN 6 Ave; 📶) The swimming pool bar at the Hotel des Mille Collines serves as the city's most popular daytime bar at weekends, with expats coming here to relax by the water and partake of the Sunday brunch.

## Information

### DANGERS & ANNOYANCES

By African standards Kigali is an exceptionally safe place. You have nothing to worry about walking around the city during the day time. Even at night you'll normally be absolutely fine walking the streets, although do exercise basic precautions such as avoiding dark streets on your own or walking unaccompanied through shanty towns.

### INTERNET ACCESS

Internet access is widespread and very cheap in Kigali. All but the cheapest hotels offer free wi-fi, as do many of the more upmarket cafes and restaurants. The Rwandan government is halfway through implementing a plan to provide free wi-fi in all public spaces across the city (and eventually across the country), but for most travellers the easiest option will be to purchase a SIM card with a data package from a local mobile phone provider.

### TOURIST INFORMATION

**RDB** (Rwanda Development Board; ☎0252502350; www.rwandatourism.com; ground fl, Grand Pension Plaza; ⏲7am-5pm Mon-Fri, 8am-noon Sat & Sun), the national tourism office, has friendly staff who help promote tourism to the increasing stream of foreign visitors. Independent travellers can make reservations to track the gorillas and golden monkeys at Volcanoes National Park as well as chimps at Nyungwe Forest National Park and various other activities. The office couldn't be more central.

## Getting There & Away

### AIR

International airlines fly in and out of Kigali International Airport (p654) and connect the Rwandan capital to many major cities in East Africa, as well as to Paris and Brussels. RwandAir has domestic flights to Kamembe (from US$75 one way).

### BUS

Several bus companies operate services to major towns and these are safer and less crowded than local minibuses. The **Nyabugogo bus terminal** (KN1 Rd), about 2km north of the city centre, is a bustling place where each bus company has a separate office. Buses usually depart from outside the office you bought your ticket at, but double check. Most bus services dry up around mid-afternoon.

**Capital** Half-hourly departures for Kibuye (RFr2600, 2½ hours) via Gitarama (RFr1000, one hour).

**Horizon Express** To Nyanza (RFr1700, 1¾ hours) and Huye (Butare; RFr2500, 2½ hours) every half hour. Horizon operates some of the better buses.

**International** Heads to the town of Gatuna, on the border with Uganda, every half hour (RFr3500, 2½ hours).

**Select Express** Buses to the Rwanda–Tanzania border crossing of Rusumo (RFr3000, three hours) every half hour.

**Volcano Express** Reliable operator for Huye (Butare; RFr2510, 2½ hours) and Nyanza (RFr1670, 1¾ hours) every half hour.

#### MINIBUS

Local minibuses depart from the Nyabugogo bus terminal for towns all around Rwanda, including Huye (Butare; RFr2500, two hours), Katuna (RFr1500, 1½ hours), Kibuye (RFr3000, two hours), Musanze (Ruhengeri, RFr1700, two hours) and Gisenyi (RFr3000, four hours). These minibuses leave when full throughout the day, except at weekends when they tend to dry up after 3pm.

### Getting Around

#### MINIBUS

Minibuses cruise the streets looking for passengers. All advertise their destination in the front window and run to districts throughout the city. They charge a flat price of RFr200.

#### MOTO TAXI

These small Japanese trail bikes can be a swift way to get around Kigali and, unlike in many other parts of Africa, helmets are provided. Short hops are just RFr300 to RFr500, while trips out to the suburbs cost RFr700 to RFr1000.

#### TAXI

Taxis are not metered but a fare within the city centre costs, on average, RFr3000 to RFr4000, and double that out to the suburbs or later at night. A trip to the airport costs RFr10,000.

# NORTHWESTERN RWANDA

## Musanze (Ruhengeri)

POP 86,700

For most travellers, Musanze (Ruhengeri) is the preferred staging post for the magnificent Volcanoes National Park, one of the best places in East Africa to track mountain gorillas. Since permit holders are required to check in at the park headquarters in nearby Kinigi at 7am on the day of tracking, staying in Musanze is a much safer and easier option than leaving from Kigali at the crack of dawn.

Musanze is a pleasant enough town to explore on foot, and it's situated near a number of interesting natural sights, with the massive Virunga volcanoes looming to the north and west.

### Tours

**Amahoro Tours** WILDLIFE, CULTURE
(0788655223; www.amahoro-tours.com) A small, locally run operator that can help arrange gorilla-tracking permits, cultural activities and homestays in the surrounding area at reasonable prices. The office is unsigned and down a small dirt alleyway next to the brick 'COODAF' building, behind the bus station.

### Sleeping

★ **Amahoro Guesthouse** GUESTHOUSE $
(0788594521, 0784424866; www.amahoro-guesthouse.com; dm/s/d/tr US$15/35/50/60; P) The best budget place in town, Amahoro Guesthouse is run by the excellent Amahoro Tours, who take good care of gorilla tour groups at this spotless, fun and friendly spot. The rooms are painted in bright, primary colours and there's a fresh, young feel to the place. Most rooms have several beds in them and share a common bathroom.

★ **Garden House** GUESTHOUSE $$
(0788427200, 0781626504; emgardner1@yahoo.co.uk; NM 202 St 3; s/d/tr US$60/80/90; P) This English-Rwandan-run guesthouse in a beautifully converted villa has five cute, artistically decorated, whitewashed rooms with double glass doors giving views of the large, leafy gardens. The hosts are extremely kind and welcoming, the dogs friendly and the breakfast, which consists of homemade breads, jams and local honey, is as good as you'll get anywhere in Rwanda.

**Five Volcanoes Boutique Hotel** BOUTIQUE HOTEL $$$
(0789924969; www.fivevolcanoesrwanda.com; r from US$400; ) This is the best top-end option in Musanze and, while it's certainly very pricey, you do get tuned in and efficient staff, a great location between the town and the national park, very attractive

WORTH A TRIP

## LAKE KIVU

One of the Great Lakes in the Albertine Rift Valley, Lake Kivu has a maximum depth of nearly 500m and is one of the 20 deepest and most voluminous lakes in the world.

### Gisenyi

Gisenyi, right on the border with the DRC, is one of Rwanda's loveliest spots and the closest this landlocked country has to a beach resort. With some attractive stretches of sand fringed with all manner of tropical vegetation along Lake Kivu's long shore, Gisenyi is unsurprisingly a popular destination for wealthy Rwandans, expats and independent travellers alike.

**Centre d'Accueil de l'Église Presbytérienne** (0783029600, 0784957945; Ave du Marché; dm/s/d/tr RFr3000/5000/10,000/15,000; P) This church-run hotel has the cheapest beds in town – dorms come with varying numbers of beds, while the double rooms are spick and span with en suite facilities. Basic meals are served in a small restaurant and there's a craft shop selling banana-leaf cards and stuffed toys to raise money for local women's groups.

**Gorillas Lake Kivu Hotel** (0788200522; www.gorillashotels.com; Ave de l'Indépendance; s/d from US$80/90; P) Part of the successful Gorilla chain, this hotel has more of a resort feel than its sisters elsewhere in Rwanda, largely thanks to the big, phallic-shaped swimming pool. The rooms themselves are plain, sturdy and good value for those after something approaching luxury.

### Kibuye

Although it has a stunning location, spread across a series of tongues jutting into Lake Kivu, Kibuye has not caught on as a tourist destination for sun and sand in the same way that Gisenyi has, but for our money – and there are plenty who will disagree – this is the better of the two. True, on this part of the lake good beaches are a lot less common, but the steep hills that fall into the deep green waters and the indented shoreline with a smattering of islands nearby make it extremely picturesque. It's also, even by Rwandan standards, a very clean and green little town where nothing much seems to happen in a hurry.

**Hotel Centre Béthanie** (0784957945; s RFr25,000-40,000, d RFr30,000-48,000; P) This sprawling guesthouse occupies a charming location on a wooded peninsula jutting into the lake. The older rooms are in red-brick blocks and are small but cosy. There are also some bright, modern, tiled rooms in a new block. Whichever you choose, all are kept spick and span and many have amazing views to the islands. There's a decent restaurant (mains RFr5500 to RFr8000).

**Cormoran Lodge** (0728601515; www.cormoranlodge.com; s/d from US$135/180; P) Outside of town along a very rough road, this stunner of a lodge melds rock, lake and wood into a truly memorable place to stay. The rooms, which are all freestanding and spaced throughout landscaped grounds tumbling to the lake shore, are like luxurious treehouses on stilts and are built entirely out of logs and beach pebbles.



accommodation and an excellent restaurant. Extras such as a spa, a good pool and even a complimentary shoe cleaning service make all the difference.

## Eating

**La Paillotte** PIZZA $
(Ave de la Nutrition; pizza RFr2500-6000; ) This popular local haunt is streets ahead of the hotel restaurants in town, at least in terms of atmosphere. There's a funky interior and seating on a breezy roadside terrace. Pizzas are the most popular item on the menu, but there's also a selection of other dishes, as well as an in-house bakery.

★**Volcana Lounge** ITALIAN $
(Ave du 5 Juillet; mains RFr6500; 11am-until last customer leaves) With a roaring wood fire in the corner, a sort of rainforest lodge atmosphere (despite being on Musanze's main street) and a laid-back feel, this is one of the better places to eat and hang out in town. The menu consists primarily of Rwandan versions of pizzas and pasta.

## Information

**RDB** (Rwanda Development Board; ☎0788519727; www.rdb.rw; Ave du 5 Juillet; ⏰8am-5pm) Located in the prefecture headquarters, this RDB office is a small administrative branch. If you already have a gorilla permit, there's no reason to stop here. Although the staff is happy to offer advice about any RDB-organised activity, it couldn't issue permits or tickets at the time of research. It will, however, phone the Kigali or Kinigi office to see if gorilla permits or others are available.

## Getting There & Away

Numerous bus companies offer scheduled hourly services between Musanze and Kigali (RFr1700, two hours) and between Musanze and Gisenyi (RFr1100, 1½ hours). The three most reliable are **Kigali Safaris** (Nyabugogo bus terminal), **Horizon** (Rue Muhabura) and **Virunga Express** (Rue du Commerce). Virunga Express (and an armada of minibuses) also travels to Cyanika (RFr400, 45 minutes) on the Rwanda–Uganda border.

# Volcanoes National Park

Running along the border with the Democratic Republic of Congo (DRC) and Uganda, **Volcanoes National Park** (www.volcanoesrwanda.org; gorilla permit US$1500) is home to the Rwandan section of the Virungas. Comprising five volcanoes, the Virungas are utterly spellbinding and few would argue that this is not one of the most exciting national parks in Africa. Of all the extraordinary sights and attractions around the Virungas, it is the mountain gorillas that really draw people here.

While most travellers are driven by the desire to have a face-to-face encounter with real gorillas in the mist, rare golden monkeys, a troop of which have been habituated to human contact, can also be visited.

## Activities

### Gorilla Tracking

An up-close encounter with the mountain gorillas while gorilla tracking (US$750 per person) is the highlight of a trip to Africa for many visitors. A close-quarters encounter with a silverback male gorilla can be a hair-raising experience, especially if you've only ever seen large wild animals behind the bars of a cage or from the safety of a car. Yet despite their intimidating size, gorillas are remarkably nonaggressive animals, entirely vegetarian and quite safe to be around. You'll be given a safety briefing by park rangers before leaving to track the habituated gorilla groups.

### Golden Monkey Tracking

Golden monkey tracking (US$100 per person) is a relative newcomer on the wildlife scene of East Africa, but is rapidly rising in popularity. More like chimp-viewing than a gorilla encounter, these beautiful and active monkeys bound about the branches of bigger trees. If you're looking for a reason to spend an extra day in the park, don't miss the chance to track these rare animals.

Permits to track the golden monkeys are easy to get hold of – simply enquire at the RDB office in Kigali or Musanze, or at the park headquarters. As with the gorillas, your time with the monkeys is limited to one hour. But unlike the gorillas, children are allowed to take part (permit price is the same as for adults).

## Sleeping

**La Paillotte Gorilla Place** HOTEL **$**
(☎0785523561; www.lapaillottegorillaplace.com; s & d RFr10,000-15,000; 🅿📶) Right in Kinigi village, not far from the market and bus stand, this small hotel offers exceptional value for money. Rooms come in two categories, with the pricier ones having stone floors with bamboo matting, cool ceilings and other local decorative touches. Cheaper rooms lack these but are polished white and very comfortable.

★ **Iby'Iwacu Cultural Village** HUT **$$**
(☎0788352009, 0788374545; www.cbtrwanda.org; per adult/child half board US$75/60) This re-creation of a traditional village is one of the most novel places to stay in Rwanda. Although it is mainly used to provide day trippers with a 'cultural experience', you can also stay the night, and that's when things get interesting. Guests sleep in one of the cosy huts and are entertained long into the evening by local villagers.

★ **Sabyinyo Silverback Lodge** LODGE **$$$**
(www.governorscamp.com; s/d full board US$1090/1630; 🅿📶) This incredible travel experience will be beyond most travellers' means, but if you want to splurge on your visit to the gorillas, then this is without a doubt the place to do it. Intimate and immaculate accommodation is in Venetian plaster cottages with Rwandese-style terracotta-tile roofs, spacious sitting areas, individual fireplaces, stylish en suite bathrooms and sheltered verandas.

## Information

**Volcanoes National Park Headquarters** (RDB; ☎0788771633; ⏲6am-4pm) You are required to register at this office, 3km east of the village of Kinigi, at 7am on the day of your scheduled gorilla tracking. If you are late, your designated slot will be forfeited. This is also the place to arrange permits for golden monkey tracking, as well as climbs and treks in the Virunga volcanoes.

## Getting There & Away

The main access point for Volcanoes National Park is the nearby town of Musanze (Ruhengeri). The park headquarters is located near the village of Kinigi, approximately 12km north of Musanze. Virunga District Service runs buses every 30 minutes between Musanze and Kinigi (RFr400, 35 minutes, first departure 6am). From Kinigi it's a further 3km to the park headquarters (reckon on paying around RFr1000 by moto-taxi).

It's also necessary to arrange transport from the park headquarters to the point where you start climbing up to where the gorillas are situated. It's best to arrange for a taxi. If you want the assurance of your own wheels and the peace of mind of knowing that you'll meet the critical 7am meeting time, the best option is to join a group in Musanze. Ask around at Amahoro Tours (p645) or **Hotel Muhabura** (☎0788364774; www.muhaburahotel.com; Ave du 5 Juillet; s/d from US$45/55; P 📶).

# SOUTHWESTERN RWANDA

## Huye (Butare)

POP 89,600

Huye is one of the most distinguished towns in Rwanda, having served as the country's most prominent intellectual centre since the colonial era, when it was known as Butare, a name most Rwandans still use for it. Home to the National University of Rwanda, the National Institute of Scientific Research and the excellent National Museum, Huye isn't a tourist destination in the traditional sense. But it's nevertheless an interesting stopover and the concentration of liberal college students roaming the streets makes for an interesting contrast to the chaotic whirl of Kigali.

### Sights

**★National Museum of Rwanda** MUSEUM

(Ethnographic Museum; www.museum.gov.rw; Rue de Kigali; adult/child RFr6000/3000; ⏲8am-6pm, last Sat of month from 11am) This outstanding museum was given to the city as a gift from Belgium in 1989 to commemorate 25 years of independence. While the building itself is certainly one of the most beautiful structures in the city, the museum wins top marks for having one of the best ethnological and archaeological collections in the entire region. The seven exhibition halls contain some very interesting items and everything is unusually well lit and presented.

### Sleeping

**Hotel Ibis** HOTEL $

(☎0738323000; campionibis@hotmail.com; Rue de Kigali; s RFr15,000-30,000, d RFr21,000-35,000, apt RFr33,000-41,000; P 📶) The stock choice for travellers passing through Huye, the Ibis is an upmarket, motel-style place with spacious but decidedly aged rooms that enjoy quiet and have a certain old-fashioned charm. The price system is a little bewildering – ask to see a few rooms before committing.

**★Centre d'Accueil Matar Boni Consilii** HOTEL $$

(☎0783777626, 0788283903; http://mbcrwanda.com; s/d/tw/ste RFr30,000/60,000/70,000/120,000; P 📶) It's definitely unusual to find a church-run place offering such a comfortable hotel experience, but that's just what you get here. In a quiet residential area 500m from the main road, the hotel provides plenty of peace and quiet, whiles its spotless rooms have rain showers and are an excellent deal.

### Eating

**★Nehemiah's Best Coffee** CAFE $

(Rue de Kigali; ⏲6.30am-10pm Mon-Sat, 10am-10pm Sun; 📶) On the main drag running from the upper town to the university, this wonderful surprise serves up pastries, omelettes, freshly made smoothies and – most importantly of all – great coffee, making it by far the best breakfast spot in town. It's right next to Ecobank.

**Hotel Ibis Restaurant** INTERNATIONAL $$

(Rue de Kigali; meals RFr4000-8000; ⏲6am-11pm; 📶) This hotel restaurant, with its open-air terrace and pleasantly faded dining room, is the most popular place in town for locals and tourists alike. The menu is something of a culinary tour of the world and includes a selection of meats, fish, pizzas, pastas and a wholesome range of salads.

### Information

**Ecobank** (Rue de Kigali) has an ATM accepting international credit and debit cards.

WORTH A TRIP

## AKAGERA NATIONAL PARK

Created in 1934 to protect the lands surrounding the Kagera River, **Akagera National Park** (www.african-parks.org/the-parks/akagera; adult/child 1 day US$35/25, vehicle from US$6; ⏲6am-6pm) once protected nearly 10% of Rwanda and was considered to be one of the finest wildlife reserves in the whole of Africa. Sadly, due to the massive numbers of refugees who returned to Rwanda in the late 1990s, over half of the park was de-gazetted and resettled with new villages. The increased human presence took an incredible toll on what had until recently been semiwilderness. Human encroachment facilitated poaching and environmental degradation and Akagera's wildlife was very nearly decimated. However, strict conservation laws, the reintroduction of lions and black rhinos, the revamping of old camps and the building of new ones has meant that all is not lost and Akagera is quickly recovering. While it's a long road ahead, visiting Akagera is a great way to support Eastern Rwanda's efforts to preserve its fabulous natural heritage.

### Activities

**Lake Ihema Boat Trips** (1hr tour per person US$30, sunset tour per person US$40; ⏲departures 7.30am, 9am, 3pm & 4.30pm) Park authorities can arrange trips on Lake Ihema to see the hippo pods and some of the huge Nile crocodiles that are otherwise difficult to observe. This is also the best way to view the park's abundant waterbirds, including breeding colonies of noisy and smelly cormorants and open-bill storks.

### Tours

**Behind the Scenes Tour** (☎0786182871, 0782166015; per person US$20) Requiring a minimum of four people, this fascinating and innovative tour takes you into the daily reality of rangers, antipoaching patrols and community projects managers. It's a fascinating insight into the often very political world of modern wildlife conservation in East Africa and the day-to-day running of a protected zone.

### Sleeping

**Akagera Game Lodge** (☎0782535717, 0785201206; www.akageralodge.com; s/d/ste US$100/120/170; P 🛜 🏊) Recently revamped, this motel-like place has large and comfortable rooms with views over the hills to the hippo-filled lake below for a very good price. The restaurant is kind of soulless. The lodge does at least have a decent pool and a kids' play area.

**Ruzizi Tented Lodge** (☎0787113300; www.ruzizilodge.com; half board s/d US$230/330; P 🛜) Hidden under a tangle of dense riverine trees on the shore of Lake Ihema, this gorgeously refined tented camp is managed by African Parks, with all profits going back into conservation projects. While it's not as ornate as some top-end camps elsewhere in East Africa, you can't fault the price – a steal for such comfort inside a national park.

### Information

The very helpful **Park Office** (☎0782166015, 0786182871; Kiyonza; ⏲6am-6pm) is where you need to book most activities. It also houses an interesting display on the park.

### Getting There & Away

Akagera is really only accessible for those with their own transport. Safari and tour companies in Kigali can arrange a vehicle with a driver or you can simply hire your own and self drive – a far cheaper option.

## ℹ Getting There & Away

There are several bus companies found on Rue de Kigali that operate between Huye and Kigali (RFr2500, 2½ hours); some of these also have services to Nyamagabe (RFr500, 30 minutes), Nyanza (RFr600, 45 minutes) and Cyangugu (RFr4000, four hours).

The local minibus stand is just a patch of dirt about 1km north of the town centre, by the stadium. Arriving buses often drop passengers here first before continuing to the centre of town.

## Nyungwe Forest National Park

Quite simply, **Nyungwe Forest National Park** (☎0788558880; www.nyungwepark.com; US$40; ⏰6am-6pm) is Rwanda's most important area of biodiversity. It has been rated the highest priority for forest conservation in Africa and its protected area covers one of the oldest rainforests in Africa. Despite its huge biodiversity, Nyungwe is little known outside of East Africa and remains overlooked by many tourists. This is a shame as the park offers some superb hiking and the chance to track chimpanzees that have been habituated to human visits.

### Activities

**Canopy Walkway** HIKING

(per person US$60) The construction of a 160m-long and at times 60m-high canopy walkway is a big draw for birders. You won't encounter much wildlife while on the suspension bridge, but you'll certainly appreciate the jungle anew from this unique monkey's-eye perspective, and have the chance to see some unique birds. The walkway is on the **Igishigishigi Trail**, which begins 1km from Uwinka.

### Sleeping

**Uwinka Campsite** CAMPGROUND $

(Uwinka; camping per person from US$30) The campsite at RDB's reception centre is currently the only option at Uwinka. There are several choice spots, many with impressive views overlooking the forest and one under a shelter with a tin roof that's a godsend in the likely event of rain.

★**Nyungwe Forest Lodge** LODGE $$$

(☎0252589106; www.nyungweforestlodge.com; Gisakura; d full board US$315-680; P wi-fi pool) Located in the heart of a tea plantation with a stunning jungle backdrop, it is very easy to while away days here as you lounge in the heated infinity pool or sip cocktails on the terrace. The rooms are as impressive as the views: all have wood burners, flat-screen satellite TVs, lounging areas and classy decor.

### Information

**Uwinka Reception Centre** (☎tourist warden for bookings 0788436763; kambogoi@yahoo.fr) The park headquarters is a little over halfway to Cyangugu from Huye (Butare). It got a revamp in 2010 and there is now a small but informative display on the ecology of the park, a new toilet block and an outdoor terrace area. From here you can get a good overview of the trails, arrange guides, book activities and pay fees.

**Gisakura Booking Office** (☎0788841079) This booking office can be found in Gisakura (near the Gisakura Guest House) and you can pay fees and organise chimpanzee tracking here. This is the one most frequently used by park visitors.

# UNDERSTAND RWANDA

## Rwanda Today

Rwanda is easily one of Africa's most progressive and better-run nations, and has done an impressive job in the past two decades of coming to terms with and moving on from its dark past. That said, the news is not all positive, with the increasingly autocratic rule of President Paul Kagame worrying many observers who see definite signs of the now veteran leader making moves to ensure he can remain in power long term.

### Building National Unity

Despite all the efforts at nation building since the genocide, Rwanda remains the home of two tribes, the Hutu and the Tutsi. The Hutu presently outnumber the Tutsi by more than four to one and, while the RPF government is one of national unity with a number of Hutu representatives, it's viewed in some quarters as a Tutsi government ruling over a predominantly Hutu population.

However, the RPF government has done an impressive job of promoting reconciliation and restoring trust between the two communities. This is no small achievement after the horrors that were inflicted on the Tutsi community during the genocide of 1994, especially since it would have been all too easy for the RPF to embark on a campaign of revenge and reprisal.

Officially there are no more Tutsis and no more Hutus – only Rwandans. Rightly or wrongly, Paul Kagame has plenty of detractors, but on the surface, at least, it's hard not to see Rwanda today as anything other than buzzing with potential for the future.

### Signs of Authoritarianism

Despite being a genuinely popular leader who many credit with single-handedly leading Rwanda's impressive transformation since 2000, Paul Kagame has in recent years displayed a worrying strain of authoritarianism and has undertaken various measures that suggest he plans to remain in power indefinitely.

In 2015 an incredible 3.7 million Rwandans – over half the total number of people in the country registered to vote – signed a petition seeking a constitutional amendment to allow Kagame to stand again for re-election in 2017, and effectively clearing the way for him to run for office until 2034. When the matter was put to a referendum later the same year, an amazing 98% of the electorate supported the move, though there were reports of voter intimidation and coercion.

Amnesty International has repeatedly reported declining press freedom, human rights abuses and repression of opposition parties. While it is certain that Kagame will win the 2017 presidential election, what his plans entail beyond that is currently anyone's guess.

# History

## Early Days

The original Rwandans, the Twa, were gradually displaced by bigger groups of migrating Hutu tribespeople from AD 1000. Later came the Tutsi from the north, arriving from the 16th century onwards. The authority of the Rwandan *mwami* (king) was far greater than that of his opposite number in Burundi, and the system of feudalism that developed here was unsurpassed in Africa outside Ethiopia. Tutsi overlordship was reinforced by ceremonial and religious observance.

## European Meddling

The Germans took the country in 1890 and held it until 1916, when their garrisons surrendered to Belgian forces during WWI. During Belgian rule, the power and privileges of the Tutsi increased, as the new masters found it convenient to rule indirectly through the *mwami* and his princes.

However, in 1956 Mwami Rudahigwa called for independence from Belgium and the Belgians began to switch allegiance to the Hutu majority. The Tutsi favoured fast-track independence, while the Hutus wanted the introduction of democracy first. Following the death of the *mwami* in 1959, armed clashes began between the two tribes, marking the start of an ethnic conflict that was to culminate in the 1994 genocide.

Following independence in 1962, the Hutu majority came to power under Prime Minister Grégoire Kayibanda. The new government introduced quotas for Tutsis, limiting opportunities for education and work, and small groups of Tutsi exiles began to launch guerrilla raids from neighbouring Uganda. In the round of bloodshed that followed, thousands more Tutsis were killed by Hutus and Hutu sympathisers, and tens of thousands fled to neighbouring countries.

## A Simmering Conflict

The massacre of Hutus in Burundi in 1972 reignited the old hatreds in Rwanda and prompted the army commander, Major General Juvenal Habyarimana, to oust Kayibanda in 1973. Habyarimana made some progress towards healing the ethnic divisions during the early years of his regime, but before long it was business as usual.

In October 1990 the entire intertribal issue was savagely reopened when 5000 well-armed rebels of the RPF, a Tutsi military front, invaded Rwanda from their bases in western Uganda. Two days later, at Habyarimana's request, France, Belgium and Zaïre (as DRC was then known) flew in troops to assist the Rwandan army to repulse the rebels. The RPF invaded again in 1991, this time better armed and prepared. By early 1992 the RPF was within 25km of Kigali. A ceasefire was cobbled together and the warring parties brought to the negotiating table. A peace accord between the government and the RPF was finally signed in August 1993.

## The Genocide

In 1994 the conflict erupted again on an incomprehensible scale. An estimated one million Rwandans were killed in just three months, mostly by Interahamwe militias – gangs of youths armed with machetes, guns and other weapons supplied by officials close to Habyarimana. Three million people fled to refugee camps in Tanzania, DRC and Uganda,and an estimated seven million of the country's nine million people were displaced.

The spark for the carnage was the death of Habyarimana and his Burundian counterpart, Cyprien Ntaryamira, on 6 April as their plane was shot down attempting to land in Kigali on their return from peace talks in Tanzania. Whoever was responsible, the event unleashed one of the 20th century's worst explosions of bloodletting.

The massacres that followed were, according to political analysts, no spontaneous outburst of violence but a calculated 'final solution' by extremist elements of Habyarimana's government to rid the country of all Tutsi and the Hutu reformists. Rwandan army and Interahamwe death squads ranged over the countryside killing, looting and burning, and roadblocks were set up in every town and city.

The UN Assistance Mission for Rwanda (UNAMIR) was in Rwanda throughout the genocide, but was powerless to prevent the killing due to an ineffective mandate. By the time UNAMIR was finally reinforced in July, it was too late. By the time the Tutsi-backed Rwandan Patriotic Front (RPF), backed by Paul Kagame, retook control of the country, the genocide was already over.

## The Aftermath

Hutu extremists and their allies fled into eastern DRC to regroup and launched cross-border raids into both Rwanda and Burundi from the refugee camps in the Goma and Uvira regions. Rwanda responded with raids into eastern DRC and support for Tutsi rebels north of Goma. The Hutu fought alongside the Congolese army, and the entire situation turned ugly, as one million or so refugees were caught in the middle.

But the RPF and their allies soon swept across DRC, installing Laurent Kabila in power and breaking the grip of the extremists on the camps. However, they soon decided Kabila was not such a reliable ally and became embroiled in Africa's biggest war to date, fighting over DRC's mineral wealth with nine other African states.

The International Criminal Tribunal for Rwanda (www.ictr.org) was established in Arusha (Tanzania) in November 1994 to bring to justice former government and military officials for acts of genocide. Several big fish have been sentenced in the past decade and in Rwanda the prisons are still overflowing with smaller players.

# SURVIVAL GUIDE

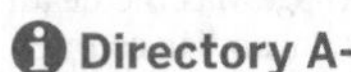

## Directory A–Z

### ACCOMMODATION

Generally, the price and quality of Rwandan budget accommodation is on a par with Kenya and Uganda and better value than Tanzania. Cheap hotels are often noisy, though mission- and church-run hostels are quieter and cleaner than most. Top-end hotels and ecolodges are found mostly in Kigali, Gisenyi and inside the national parks.

### DANGERS & ANNOYANCES

Mention Rwanda to most people and they think of it as a highly dangerous place. However, this is actually one of the safest countries in East Africa to travel in today. Kigali is a genuine contender for the safest capital in Africa, though, as in any big city the world over, take care at night and don't take unnecessary risks, such as walking alone down a dark street after dark.

Never take photographs of anything connected with the government or the military (post offices, banks, bridges, border crossings, barracks, prisons and dams) – cameras can and will be confiscated by the rather overzealous police or security services.

### ELECTRICITY

Electricity in Rwanda is 240V, 50 cycles, and plugs are mainly two-pin.

### EMBASSIES & CONSULATES

Australia's embassy in Nairobi, Kenya, handles Rwanda, while New Zealand's embassy in Addis Ababa, Ethiopia is responsible for Rwanda. Ireland handles its affairs from its embassy in Kampala, Uganda.

**Belgian Embassy** (☎252575553; www.diplomatie.be/kigali; KN 3 Ave)

**British High Commission** (☎252556000; http://ukinrwanda.fco.gov.uk; KG 7 Ave, Kacyiru)

**Burundi Embassy** (☎252517529; KG 7 Ave, Kacyiru)

**Canadian Embassy** (☎252573210; KN 16 Ave)

**French Embassy** (☎252551800; http://ambafrance-rw.org; KN 33 St)

**German Embassy** (☎280575141; www.kigali.diplo.de; KN 27 St; ⏰9am-11am Mon-Thu)

**Kenyan Embassy** (☎252-583332; KG 7 Ave, Kacyiru)

**Netherlands Embassy** (☎280280281; www.rwanda.nlembassy.org; KG 7 Ave; ⏰8am-12.30pm & 1.15-5.30pm Mon-Fri)

**Tanzanian High Commission** (☎252505400; KG 9 Ave, Kacyiru)

**Ugandan High Commission** (☎252503537; kigali.mofa.go.ug; KG 569 St, Kacyiru)

**US Embassy** (☎252596400; http://rwanda.usembassy.gov; KG 3 Ave, Kacyiru)

### INTERNET ACCESS

Internet access is widely available in all towns and cities. All midrange and top-end hotels, bar a few remote ecolodges, have wi-fi available (often in rooms but sometimes just around the reception area) and an increasing number of budget hotels and restaurants offer wireless. However, speeds are slow and service is often cut off for no reason.

## MONEY

The unit of currency is the Rwandan franc (RFr).

Most banks in larger towns have international ATMs. Credit cards are not often taken outside cities and higher-end tourist hotels.

### Exchange Rates

| | | |
|---|---|---|
| Australia | A$1 | RFr585 |
| Canada | C$1 | RFr604 |
| Europe | €1 | RFr854 |
| Japan | ¥100 | RFr694 |
| New Zealand | NZ$1 | RFr562 |
| UK | UK£1 | RFr1002 |
| USA | US$1 | RFr812 |

For current exchange rates, see www.xe.com.

## OPENING HOURS

The following are standard opening hours for various kinds of establishments.

**Banks** 8am–1pm and 2pm–4pm Monday to Friday

**Bars and clubs** 9pm–3am

**Cafes** 7am–7pm

**Restaurants** noon–3pm and 7pm–11pm

**Shops** 9am–1pm and 2pm–5pm Monday to Saturday

## PUBLIC HOLIDAYS

**New Year's Day** 1 & 2 January

**National Heroes Day** 1 February

**Easter** (Good Friday, Holy Saturday and Easter Monday) March/April

**Genocide against the Tutsi Memorial Day** 7 April

**Labour Day** 1 May

**Independence Day** 1 July

**Liberation Day** 4 July

**Umuganura Day** First Friday in August

**Assumption** 15 August

**Christmas Day** 25 December

**Boxing Day** 26 December

## TELEPHONE

Most businesses use mobile phones rather than landlines. It's cheap, fast and painless to get a Rwandan SIM card for your phone; just go to any operator with your passport. The main operators in Rwanda are MTN, Tigo and Airtel.

Top-up cards start from as little as RFr100. Mobile phone calls cost about RFr1 per second, although rates vary depending on when you call. Mobile numbers begin with either ☎078 or ☎072.

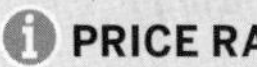

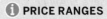

### PRICE RANGES

The following price ranges refer to a double room with bathroom in high season.

**$** US$15 to US$40

**$$** US$40 to US$70

**$$$** more than US$100

Average prices for a main course:

**$** US$3to US$6

**$$** US$10 to US$15

**$$$** more than US$25

## TIME

Rwanda is two hours ahead of GMT/UTC. If you're coming from Uganda or Tanzania, be advised that Rwanda is one hour behind the rest of East Africa.

## TOURIST INFORMATION

The Rwanda Development Board (RDB; www.rwandatourism.com) runs the state tourist board. Currently it has several tourist offices: two in Kigali, one in Musanze (Ruhengeri) and another in Gisenyi. While they have only limited amounts of promotional information, the staff is – for East Africa – unusually well trained, knowledgeable and helpful.

## VISAS

Almost everyone now requires a visa to enter Rwanda. Citizens of Australia, Germany, Israel, New Zealand, South Africa, Sweden, the UK and the US can automatically receive visas on arrival at Kigali International airport and all land borders (US$30). All other passport holders must obtain a visa before entering the country at the Rwandan embassy in their country of residence. These visas (called class T2) cost US$50, are valid for 90 days and are good for multiple entries within that time.

If Rwanda isn't represented in your country then you need to register online at Rwanda Immigration (www.migration.gov.rw) before you travel. The website is a little confusing, but once you've submitted the online form you'll receive your letter of entitlement within three days. Present this letter at the border along with the US$30 fee to obtain a single-entry, 30-day visa (called a V1 visa).

Rwanda is one of the countries covered by the East Africa Tourist Visa and for those also visiting Kenya and Uganda on the same trip it is a cheaper alternative. The visa costs US$100, is valid for 90 days and is multiple entry – it is available upon arrival or from embassies abroad.

## Getting There & Away

### AIR

Kigali International Airport is located at Kanombe, 10km east of Kigali's city centre. The most useful international airlines include the following:

**Brussels Airlines** (SN; ☎252575290; www.brusselsairlines.com; Hotel des Mille Collines, KN 6 Ave)

**Ethiopian Airlines** (ET; ☎0252570440; www.ethiopianairlines.com; Union Trade Centre, KN Ave 4)

**Kenya Airways** (☎280306850; www.kenya-airways.com; Union Trade Centre, KN Ave 4)

**KLM** (☎280306850; www.klm.com; Union Trade Centre, KN 4 Ave)

**Qatar Airways** (☎0786387233; www.qatarairways.com; Kigali City Towers, 11th fl, KN 2 St)

**RwandAir** (☎0788177000; www.rwandair.com; Union Trade Centre, KN Ave 4)

**South African Airways** (☎252577777; www.flysaa.com; Easy Travel, Hotel des Mille Collines, KN 6 Ave)

**Turkish Airlines** (☎786730231; www.turkishairlines.com; 4th fl, Grand Pension Plaza)

### LAND

Rwanda shares land borders with Burundi, the DRC, Tanzania and Uganda.

#### Tanzania

Only one bus company, **Taqwa** (Nyabugogo bus terminal, Kigali), operates cross-border buses to Tanzania and this goes all the way to Dar es Salaam. But doing it, as most people do, in stages is no great hassle.

#### The DRC

There are two crossings between Rwanda and the DRC, both are on the shores of Lake Kivu. To the north is the crossing between Gisenyi and Goma. The southern border is between Cyangugu and Bukavu. Providing the DRC remains politically stable and you have prearranged visas, the crossings are surprisingly straightforward, and you can walk across the borders directly from town to town.

#### Uganda

There are two main crossing points for foreigners: between Kigali and Kabale via Gatuna/Katuna (called Gatuna on the Rwandan side, Katuna on the Ugandan side); and between Musanze (Ruhengeri) and Kisoro via Cyanika.

There are direct buses between Kigali/Musanze and Gisenyi and Kampala. Buses also run between Kigali and the border at Gatuna (RFr3500, 1½ hours) throughout the day. Plenty of shared taxis (USh4000) and special-hire taxis (USh20,000 for the whole car) travel back and forth between Katuna and Kabale.

From Musanze (Ruhengeri) to Kisoro via Cyanika, the road is in excellent shape on the Rwandan side and in rather poor condition on the Ugandan side. Minibuses link either side of the border with Musanze (RFr500, 25km).

## Getting Around

### AIR

RwandAir operates domestic flights between Kigali and Kamembe (Cyangugu). There are no other services within the country.

### BUS & MINIBUS

Rwanda has efficient and reliable public transport. Privately run buses cover the entire country and, with scheduled departure times, you won't find yourself waiting for hours while the driver scouts for more passengers. Tickets are bought in advance from a ticket office, which is usually at the point of departure.

You will also find plenty of well-maintained, modern minibuses serving all the main routes. Head to the bus stand in any town between dawn and about 3pm and it is quite easy to find one heading to Kigali and nearby towns. Destinations are displayed in the front window and the fares are fixed. Neither buses nor minibuses are supposed to charge extra for baggage.

### CAR & MOTORCYCLE

Cars are suitable for most of the country's main roads, but those planning to explore Akagera National Park or to drive the road between Kibuye and Gisenyi will be better off with a 4WD.

Car hire isn't well established in Rwanda, but there are plenty of small local agencies in Kigali that can organise something. Prices are low by African standards and start at around US$50 per day. If you prefer to have a car and driver, Kigali-based **Jean-Paul Birasa** (☎0788517440; birasajeanpaul@yahoo.fr) can organise no-frills car and jeep rental (the jeeps are small 4WDs, such as a RAV4, which is fine for anywhere in Rwanda) with drivers for considerably lower prices than any of the big travel agencies.

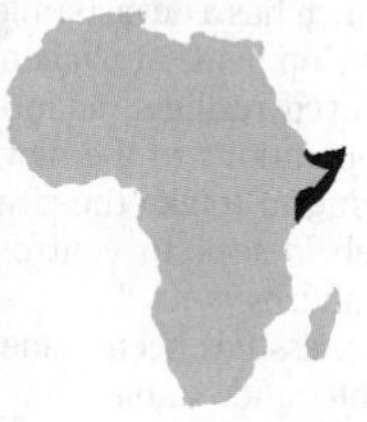

# Somalia

POP 11 MILLION / ☎ 252

**Includes ➡**



## Fast Facts

**Capital** Mogadishu

**Population** 10.82 million

**Languages** Somali, Arabic, Italian, English

**Area** 637,657 sq km

**Currency** Somali shilling (SOS), Somaliland shilling (Ssh)

## Introduction

A few decades ago Somalia was a magnet for travellers and, with a bit of luck and a following wind, it could be again. But right now the country is still unsafe for foreigners, with its people, places and infrastructure still recovering from over 25 years of brutal civil war. The situation is not insurmountable. There are increasing signs of hope and Mogadishu, the capital, is experiencing an urban boom thanks to massive investments from returning Somalis. And amid chaos, there is a success story: the self-proclaimed nation of Somaliland, north of the country, which has managed to retain something close to peace and stability. If Somalia does open up for travel, visitors will again be able to experience its fascinating culture and enjoy its natural attractions, bask on pristine beaches and trek across arid mountains.

## Somalia at a Glance

**Mogadishu** The fascinating streets of the former 'Pearl of the Indian Ocean'.

**Hargeisa** A lively gold market where haggling erupts over jewellery.

**Berbera** The pleasure of a soft drink and fresh fish while relaxing on white-sand beaches.

**Las Geel** This astounding archaeological site, festooned in ancient rock art, tells of Somalia's mysterious past.

**Raas Xaafun** A remarkable vista at the tip of the Horn of Africa.

**Merca** Myriad alleyways in this wonderful old Arab coastal town.

**Bajuni Islands** A fantastic archipelago blessed with glistening white-sand beaches.

# UNDERSTAND SOMALIA



## Somalia Today

In terms of security and stability, there has been some improvement over the last few years in Somalia but gains are fragile. Life has not returned to normal yet and, bar a few pockets of economic activity, deep poverty is widespread. The national army, backed by peacekeepers from the African Union Mission in Somalia (Amisom) force, has managed to dislodge many Islamic fundamentalists of the Al Shabab movement from many towns and cities, including Mogadishu and the strategic port town of Kismayo. The situation remains highly unpredictable, however: Al Shabab groups still control swaths of the country and remain very active. They regularly launch guerilla-style attacks and assassinations in the capital in order to destabilise the fragile Somali government, which has a devastating effect on economic development. Al Shabab militants have also proved resilient, adapting their destructive operations to the new context; instead of trying to retake the city centres, Al Shabab rebels seek to control neighbourhoods and suburbs.

Politically, some progress has been made in reestablishing viable and stable state structures and a central government – no mean feat after three decades of conflict and lawlessness. The African Union and UN have played a key part in revitalising institutions. Somalia turned a corner in 2012 when the first presidential elections were held, but voting took place only in Mogadishu. Another breakthrough took place in February 2017, when Somalia's MPs elected Mohamed Abdullahi Farmajo, a Somali-US national, as the country's new president; the vote was held at the heavily guarded Mogadishu airport. This vote is seen by the UN and the African Union as a milestone towards a stable democracy, in the hope that the next president will be chosen in a one-person one-vote election. Farmajo's challenges are enormous, and he has pledged to tackle corruption during his term in office.

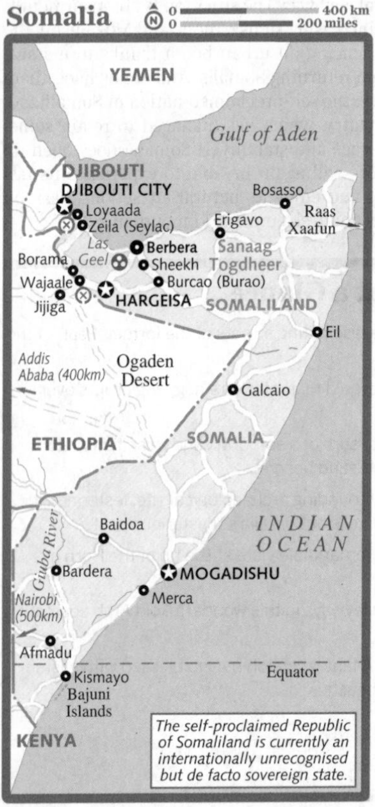

**Somalia**

*The self-proclaimed Republic of Somaliland is currently an internationally unrecognised but de facto sovereign state.*

## History

### Somalia's Roots

Originally, Somalis probably hail from the southern Ethiopian highlands. As a people, they have been subject to a strong Arabic influence ever since the 7th century, when the Somali coast formed part of the extensive Arab-controlled trans–Indian Ocean trading network.

### Foreign Interventions

In the 19th century much of the Ogaden Desert – whose people are ethnically a part of Somalia – was annexed by Ethiopia (an invasion that has been a source of bad blood ever since), then in 1888 the country was divided by European powers. The French got the area around Djibouti, Britain much of the north, while Italy got Puntland and the south. Sayid Maxamed Cabdulle Xasan (known affectionately as 'the Mad Mullah') fought the British for two decades, but it wasn't until 1960 that Somaliland, Puntland and southern Somalia were united, which wasn't altogether a good idea.

**WARNING**

Travelling in Somalia remains unsafe, and most Western governments warn against *all* travel to the country (and note that by ignoring these warnings you may well be making your travel insurance invalid). There is a dangerous level of criminal activity by armed militia and terrorist groups throughout the country as well as regular outbreaks of interclan violence. Despite some signs of improvement in some big cities, including Mogadishu, at the time of writing Somalia was still considered highly dangerous and we do not recommend travelling there given the unstable security situation.

What about Somaliland? While it's definitely much safer than the rest of Somalia, there is still a large element of uncertainty regarding the security situation, with the threat of kidnap and terrorism being highlighted by Western governments – after all, borders with Puntland and southern Somalia are not terrorist-proof.

Sadly, between 1960 and 1991, interclan tensions, radical socialism, rearmament by the USSR and the occasional (often disastrous) war with Ethiopia helped tear the country apart. Mohamed Siad Barre, Somalia's last recognised leader, fled to Nigeria in 1991 after the forces of General Aideed took Mogadishu. At the same time the Somali National Movement (SNM) moved quickly and declared independence for Somaliland. Puntland also broke away.

## Civil Wars

Fierce battles between warring factions throughout southern Somalia took place throughout the 1990s, but in 1992 the US led a UN mission (Operation Restore Hope) to distribute food aid to the southern population. Without much ado, a nasty little conflict between the US-UN and warlord General Aideed began, during which it's estimated that thousands of Somalis died. The last UN troops pulled out in 1995, having alleviated the famine to some extent, but the nation was still a disaster area.

Designed to establish control across the whole of the country, Somalia's lame-duck Transitional National Government (TNG) was set up in 2000. Alas, it still only controls only parts of Mogadishu. In 2002 the Somali Reconciliation and Restoration Council (SRRC) created a government for southwest Somalia; later that year 21 warring factions in the south and the TNG agreed to a cessation of hostilities for Kenyan-sponsored peace talks, although most of the delegates seemed more concerned with their private fiefdoms and the quality of their Kenyan hotel accommodation than creating a viable state. In 2004 a transitional federal president was elected, but with limited influence and power.

## Islamist Conflicts

In 2007 President Abdullahi Yusuf Ahmed entered Mogadishu for the first time since taking office. That year, African Union troops landed in Mogadishu to help the government forces, backed by Ethiopian troops, fight Al Shabab (an Islamist insurgency group). After the withdrawal of the Ethiopian army in 2009, the Islamist fundamentalists managed to recapture Mogadishu and the southern port of Kismayo. In 2011, Kenyan troops entered the scene; they set up military bases in various areas in the country to help the weak Somali government forces oust the Al Shabab groups. Over the next few years, the Islamist insurgents retaliated by carrying out a number of terrorist attacks and mass killings both in Somalia and in Kenya.

To complicate matters further, a crippling drought caused by rainfall failure has threatened the lives of hundreds of thousands of people in southern Somalia since 2010. In 2011, three regions were formally declared famine zones by the UN.

# Culture

Somalis all hail from the same tribe, which is divided into four main clans and loads of subclans. The clan in particular, and genealogy in general, is hugely important to Somalis, who are more likely to ask a stranger 'Whom are you from?' than 'Where are you from?' This interclan rivalry has fuelled two decades of conflict.

Saving face is important to Somalis, so indirectness and humour are common in conversation, along with enthusiastic hand and arm gestures. Somalis can be quiet and dignified, with a tendency to ignore strangers,

### SOMALILAND: THE COUNTRY NOBODY KNOWS

It has a parliament. It has a broadly representative government. It has a capital. It has a flag. It has a currency. It has a university. It has an army. It has multiparty elections. But nobody recognises it. Welcome to Somaliland, the country that does not exist.

The self-proclaimed Republic of Somaliland was formed in 1991 after the collapse of unitary Somalia. Although its leaders desperately struggle to gain formal international recognition, Somaliland is still treated as a pariah by the international community. It does have political contacts with a few states, including Ethiopia, Djibouti, France, the UK, the US and South Africa, but it is not recognised as a separate state. The main reason why the world is reluctant to accept Somaliland's independence is that the rest of Somalia does not want it, and other nations prefer a unitary Somalia instead of a split country. Somaliland Somalis from the diaspora keep doing their best to influence diplomatic corps in Europe, in East Africa and in North America – in vain, so far.

As recently as 2013 Somaliland was a Shangri La for the savvy travellers who wanted to break the rules of conventional travel. While the rest of Somalia had been a travellers' no-go zone for three decades, Somaliland had managed to restore law and order within its boundaries and the safety of Westerners was taken very seriously. The local authorities were so protective of foreigners outside the capital, all travellers were assigned an armed bodyguard (US$20 per day), the price to pay for being a special guest. However, the threat of terrorism and kidnap has risen to such a level that travel to Somaliland can no longer be recommended.

but have a tremendous oral (often poetic) tradition. Poetry recitation is the premier art form. It's often accompanied by an oud (a lute-type instrument). Visual arts are quite developed, especially in the form of brightly painted murals.

Written Somali is a very young language – spelling variation, especially for place names, is very common. English is widely used in the north, while Italian remains the foreign language of choice in the south.

Well over a million Somalis are scattered across Europe, North America and the Middle East; together they send hundreds of millions of dollars back to Somalia each year. In addition, there are Somalis in Djibouti, Ethiopia (in the Ogaden region) and Kenya.

## Environment

Africa's easternmost country, Somalia is bordered by Djibouti to the north, Ethiopia to the west and Kenya to the south. It is characterised by desert or semidesert terrain and is distinguished by three main topographical features: the Oogo, a mountainous highland region in the north dominated by the Gollis Mountains; the Guban, a relatively barren, hot and humid coastal region (dominating southern Somalia); and the Hawd, a sweeping area of rich, rainy-season pasture prone to overgrazing and desertification. Serious drought continues to plague Somalia's south. Such a harsh environment is only suitable for nomadic pastoralism; agricultural production is limited to the southwest, where there's moderate rainfall. Livestock (especially camel) rearing is the most important type of farming.

Unfortunately, the civil war that's been raging for more than 25 years has overshadowed Somalia's great natural wonders. There are thousands of kilometres of pristine beaches along the Gulf of Aden and the Indian Ocean. The islands off Zeila, close to the Djibouti border, are also completely unspoilt and ablaze with technicolour tropical fish. The wild expanses of the Sheekh Mountains (Somaliland) have a rugged beauty and afford stunning views over the coast, as far as Berbera.

Before civil war, Somalia boasted national parks with cheetahs, leopards, lions and antelope. Today you'd be lucky to see any predator bigger than a mongoose.

# Tanzania

POP 52.5 MILLION / ☎255

### Includes ➡



### Best Places to Eat

- ➡ Chapan Bhog (p663)
- ➡ Lukmaan Restaurant (p671)
- ➡ Hot Plate (p689)
- ➡ Khan's Barbecue (p690)

### Best Places to Sleep

- ➡ Old Boma at Mikindani (p702)
- ➡ Tarangire Safari Lodge (p692)
- ➡ Kisiwa House (p671)
- ➡ Wayo Green Camp (p694)

## Why Go?

Tanzania is the land of safaris, with wildebeest stampeding across the plains, hippos jostling for space in rivers, elephants kicking up the dust and chimpanzees swinging through the treetops.

Tanzania's magical Indian Ocean coastline also entrances, with its tranquil islands, long beaches and sleepy villages steeped in centuries of Swahili culture. Coconut palms sway in the breeze, dhows glide by on the horizon and colourful fish flit past spectacular corals in the turquoise waters.

More than anything, though, it is Tanzania's people that make a visit so memorable, with their characteristic warmth and politeness, and the dignity and beauty of their cultures. The chances are you will want to come back for more, to which most Tanzanians would say 'karibu tena' (welcome again).

## When to Go

### Dodoma

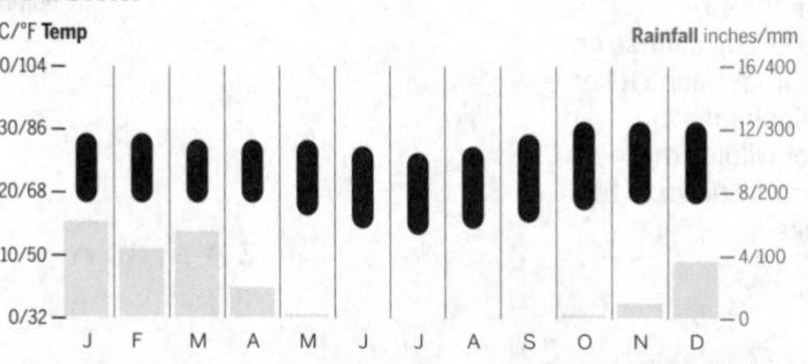


**Mar–May** Heavy rains bring green landscapes, lower prices, top-notch birding and muddy roads.

**Jun–Aug** The weather is cool and dry throughout, and wildlife watching is at its prime.

**Sep–Oct** The weather continues dry, and wildlife watching remains good, without the crowds.

# Tanzania Highlights

1. **Serengeti National Park** (p694) Marvelling at nature's rhythms.
2. **Zanzibar Town** (p668) Taking in the skyline and wandering through narrow alleys.
3. **Ngorongoro Crater** (p693) Enjoying sublime views over the enormous crater.
4. **Mt Kilimanjaro National Park** (p685) Scaling the mountain's heights or hiking on its lower slopes.
5. **Usambara Mountains** (p682) Enjoying the rolling hill panoramas, hiking and local culture.
6. **Mahale Mountains National Park** (p698) Tracking chimpanzees through dense vegetation.
7. **Selous Game Reserve** (p700) Taking a boat safari to glide past borassus palms, slumbering hippos and motionless crocodiles.
8. **Ruaha National Park** (p699) Witnessing sunrise on the Great Ruaha River as elephants and other wildlife make their way down to the banks.

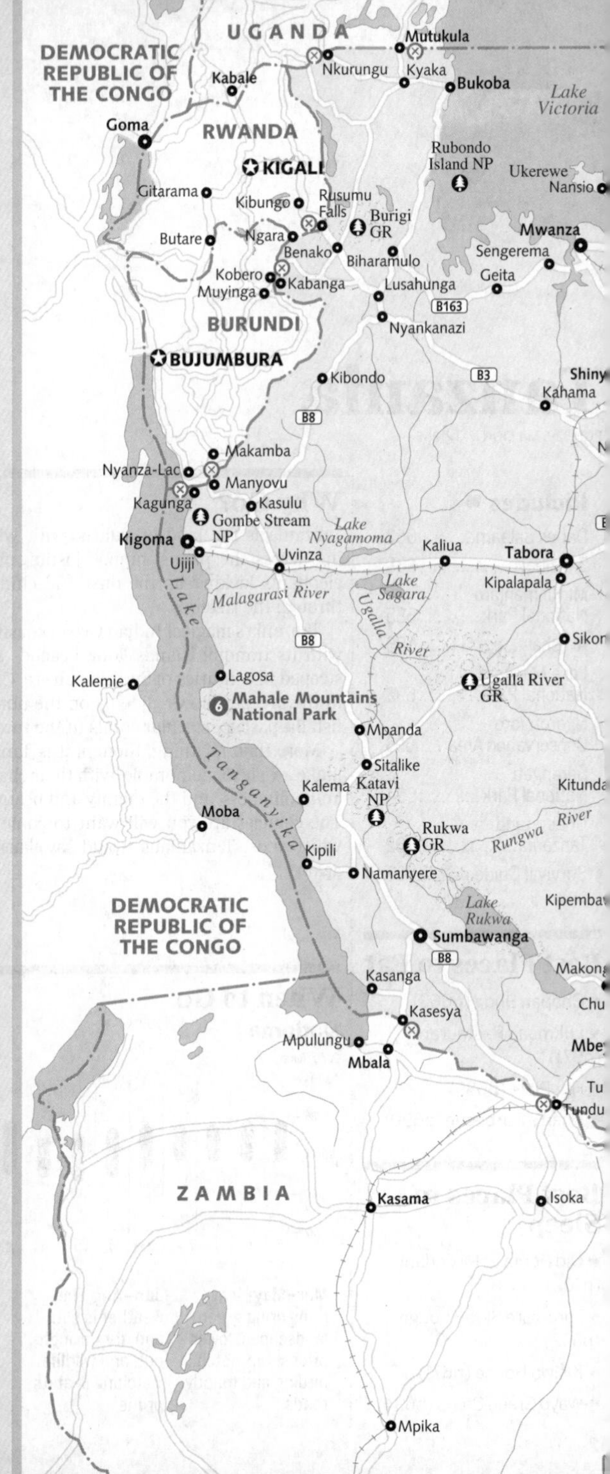

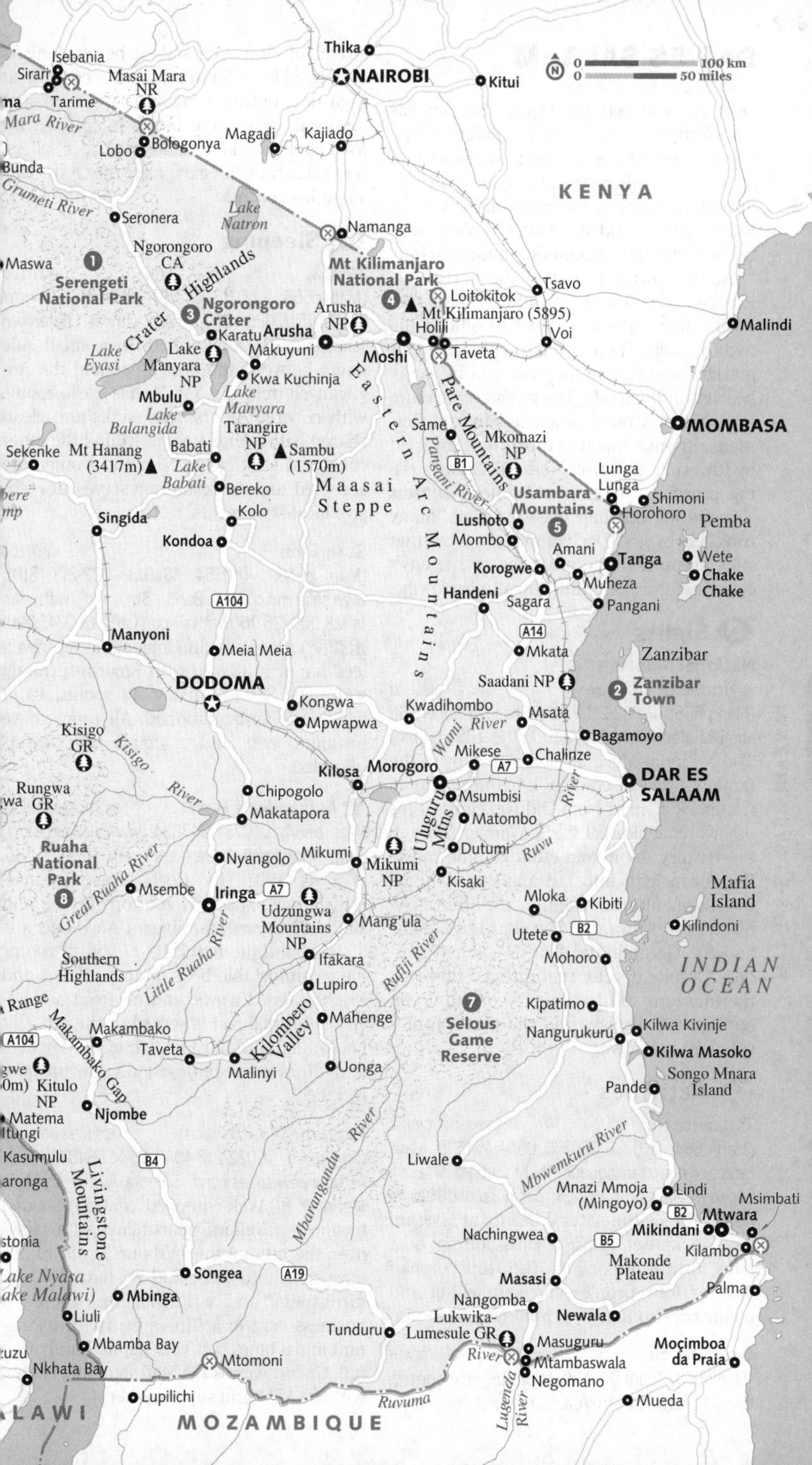

0 100 km
0 50 miles
KENYA
Thika
NAIROBI
Kitui
Isebania
Sirari
Tarime
Masai Mara NR
Mara River
Magadi
Kajiado
Bologonya
Lobo
Bunda
Grumeti River
Seronera
Lake Natron
Namanga
Maswa
1 Serengeti National Park
Ngorongoro CA
Highlands
Crater
3 Ngorongoro Crater
Mt Kilimanjaro National Park
4
Loitokitok
Mt Kilimanjaro (5895)
Tsavo
Arusha NP
Arusha
Holili
Moshi
Taveta
Voi
Malindi
Karatu
Lake Eyasi
Lake Manyara NP
Makuyuni
Kwa Kuchinja
Lake Manyara
Mbulu
Lake Balangida
Eastern Arc Mountains
Pare Mountains
Same
Mkomazi NP
MOMBASA
Sekenke
Mt Hanang (3417m)
Babati
Lake Babati
Tarangire NP
Sambu (1570m)
Bereko
Maasai Steppe
B1
Pangani River
Lunga Lunga
Shimoni
Horohoro
Usambara Mountains
5
Singida
Kolo
Kondoa
Lushoto
Mombo
Pemba
Wete
Chake Chake
Amani
Korogwe
Tanga
Muheza
Handeni
Sagara
Pangani
A104
A14
Manyoni
Meia Meia
Mkata
Zanzibar
DODOMA
Saadani NP
2 Zanzibar Town
Kongwa
Mpwapwa
Kwadihombo
Msata
Wami River
Bagamoyo
Kisigo GR
Kisigo River
Mikese
A7
Chalinze
Kilosa
Morogoro
DAR ES SALAAM
Rungwa GR
Chipogolo
Msumbisi
Makatapora
Uluguru Mtns
Matombo
Ruvu River
Ruaha National Park
8
Great Ruaha River
Nyangolo
Mikumi
Dutumi
Mikumi NP
Kisaki
Msembe
Iringa
Udzungwa Mountains NP
Mloka
Kibiti
Mafia Island
Mang'ula
Kilindoni
Utete
B2
Little Ruaha River
Southern Highlands
Ifakara
Rufiji River
Mohoro
INDIAN OCEAN
Lupiro
7
Kipatimo
Range
Mahenge
Selous Game Reserve
Kilombero Valley
Makambako Gap
Makambako
Nangurukuru
Kilwa Kivinje
Kilwa Masoko
Taveta
Malinyi
Uonga
Songo Mnara Island
Kitulo NP
Pande
Njombe
Matema
Kasumulu
Livingstone Mountains
B4
Liwale
Mbwemkuru River
Mbarangandu River
Lindi
Mnazi Mmoja (Mingoyo)
B2
Mtwara
Msimbati
Mikindani
Nachingwea
B5
Kilambo
Makonde Plateau
Songea
A19
Masasi
Lake Nyasa (Lake Malawi)
Mbinga
Palma
Liuli
Nangomba
Newala
Lukwika-Lumesule GR
Tunduru
Masuguru
Mbamba Bay
Moçimboa da Praia
Mtomoni
Mtambaswala
Nkhata Bay
Negomano
Lupilichi
Ruvuma
Lugenda River
Mueda
MOZAMBIQUE

# DAR ES SALAAM

POP 4.36 MILLION / ☎022

Over the last century, Dar es Salaam has transformed from a sleepy Zaramo fishing village into a thriving metropolis of over four million people (and growing). Straddling some of the most important sea routes in the world, it is East Africa's second-busiest port and Tanzania's commercial hub.

At the northern end of the harbour is Kivukoni Front, with a bustling fish market where dhows dock at dawn to offload the night's catch. There are also excellent craft markets and restaurants, and nearby sandy beaches and islands. The city's architecture is a mix of African, Arab, Indian and German, although much of this is now dwarfed by towering high-rises that reflect Dar's rising prosperity in the golden-hued sunsets shimmering off their glass exteriors. Many travellers bypass 'Dar' completely; those that stick around will be rewarded by the city's eclectic cultural mix and down-to-earth vibe.

## Sights

**National Museum & House of Culture** MUSEUM

(Map p666; ☎022-211 7508; Shaaban Robert St; adult/student Tsh6500/2600; ⏲9.30am-6pm) The National Museum houses a copy of the famous fossil discoveries of *zinjanthropus* (nutcracker man) from Olduvai Gorge, plus other archaeological finds. Wander through the History Room and ethnographic collection for insights into Tanzania's past and its mosaic of cultures, including the Shirazi civilisation of Kilwa, the Zanzibar slave trade, and the German and British colonial periods. Despite recent renovations, however, the museum still has much work to do on appropriate displays and the curation of a coherent narrative.

## Activities

**Tanzaquatic** FISHING, CRUISE

(Map p664; ☎0786 058370, 0654 454535; www.facebook.com/tanzaquatic; Yacht Club Rd, Msasani Slipway; glass-bottom boat per person US$10 to US$20) Enjoy the natural beauty of Msasani Bay on sunset cruises, glass-bottom boat trips, fishing excursions (US$450 per half day for four people) and snorkelling and picnic trips to Bongoyo, Mbudya and Sinda.

**Coco Beach** BEACH

(Map p664; Toure Dr) North of the city centre, the Msasani Peninsula is fringed by a long stretch of sand and coral rag beach along its eastern side. Swimming is only possible at high tide, but it's a favourite weekend spot for locals, when the beach is dotted with food stalls, coconut stands and beer sellers, particularly the area opposite the Oyster Bay shopping centre.

## Sleeping

**YWCA** HOSTEL $

(Map p666; ☎0713 622707; Maktaba St; dm/tr Tsh15,000/50,000, s/d without bathroom Tsh20,000/30,000) Located on a small side street between the post office and the Anglican church, the YWCA has basic rooms with concrete floors, fans, sinks and clean shared bathrooms. Rooms around the inner courtyard are quieter. Men and women are accepted, and the restaurant serves inexpensive local-style meals.

**Safari Inn** HOTEL $

(Map p666; ☎0754 485013, 022-213 8101; www.safariinn.co.tz; Band St; s/d with fan Tsh28,000/35,000, with air-con Tsh35,000/45,000; ❄@📶) A popular and long-standing travellers' haunt in Kisutu with English-speaking staff. The Safari Inn has 42 rooms, 10 of which are air-conditioned. All rooms have mosquito nets and a simple breakfast is provided.

★**Alexander's Hotel** BOUTIQUE HOTEL $$

(Map p664; ☎0754 343834; www.alexanders-tz.com; Maryknoll Lane; s/d from US$150/185; ❄📶🏊) With its Corbusier-style modernist lines, spacious rooftop terrace and shady courtyard, family-run Alexander's is a true boutique hotel. Its 17 stylish rooms have comfortable beds, plump pillows and bright *kikoi* throws, and all front a shaded pool. Breakfast is served in the art- and book-filled dining room, while sundowners and dinners are enjoyed on the upstairs terrace.

**Harbour View Suites** BUSINESS HOTEL $$

(Map p666; ☎022-212 4040, 0784 564848; www.harbourview-suites.com; Samora Ave; r US$125-175; ❄📶🏊) Well-equipped, centrally located business travellers' apartments with views over the city or the harbour. Some rooms have mosquito nets, and all have modern furnishings and a kitchenette. There's a business centre, a fitness centre, a restaurant and a blues bar. Very popular and often full. Underneath is JM Mall shopping centre, with an ATM and supermarket.

**Dar es Salaam Serena Hotel** HOTEL $$$
(Map p666; 022-211 2416, 022-221 2500; www.serenahotels.com/serenadaressalaam; Ohio St; s/d from US$242/268; ) Serena has an unbeatable location in enormous gardens overlooking the golf course of the Gymkhana Club, and a lovely, large swimming pool. Rooms offer all the bells and whistles you'd expect from a five-star hotel.

## Eating

★**Chapan Bhog** INDIAN $
(56 Bhog; Map p666; 0685 401417; www.facebook.com/56Bhog; Kisutu St; meals Tsh6000-15,000; 7am-10pm; ) Chapan's Gujurati *dhoklas* (savoury steamed chickpea cakes), south Indian dosas (fermented crepes) and thalis are a vegetarian nirvana in a sea of *nyama choma* (roasted meat). The all-vegetarian menu is extensive, and the restaurant has a prime position on temple-lined Kisutu St.

**Épi d'Or** CAFE $
(Map p664; 0786 669889, 022-260 1663; www.epidor.co.tz; cnr Chole & Haile Selassie Rds; meals Tsh10,000-30,000; 8am-7pm Mon-Sat) This French-run bakery-cafe has a good selection of freshly baked breads, pastries, light lunches, paninis, banana crêpes and Middle Eastern dishes, plus good coffee.

**Chef's Pride** TANZANIAN $
(Map p666; Chagga St; meals Tsh6000-12,000; 6am-11pm, closed during Ramadan) This long-standing and popular local eatery serves roasted chicken, biryani and coconut-crusted fish. In addition, the large menu features fast-food favourites such as pizza and Indian and vegetarian dishes, popular with hungry office workers.

**Al Basha** LEBANESE $$
(Map p666; 022-212 6888; Bridge St; mains Tsh20,000-35,000; 7am-10am & noon-11pm) Dar's best Lebanese restaurant serves a good selection of hot and cold mezze dishes, shish kebabs and salads. No alcohol is served but there's a wide selection of fresh juices. They also have a branch at Sea Cliff Village on the Msasani Peninsula.

**Ristorante Bella Napoli** ITALIAN $$
(Map p664; 022-260 0326, 0778 497776; www.bellanapolitz.com; 530 Haile Selassie Rd; mains Tsh12,000-25,000; 6pm-10pm Tue-Fri, noon-10pm Sat & Sun; ) Delicious Italian food served in a pleasant garden setting or in the air-con indoor dining room, plus a children's playground.

## Drinking & Nightlife

**Waterfront** BAR
(Map p664; 022-260 0893; Slipway, Yacht Club Rd, Msasani; 11.30am-midnight; ) This is a popular place for sundowners with prime sunset views. Meals are also available.

**Level 8 Bar** BAR
(Map p666; 0764 701234; 8th fl, Hyatt Regency, Kivukoni Front; 5pm-1am) The Hyatt's chic rooftop bar has wonderful views over the harbour, lounge seating and live music some evenings.

## Shopping

★**Wonder Workshop** ARTS & CRAFTS
(Map p664; 0754 051417; http://wonderworkshop.squarespace.com/; 1372 Karume Rd, Msasani; 8.30am-6pm Mon-Fri, 10am-6pm Sat) At this excellent workshop, disabled artists create world-class jewellery, sculptures, candles, stationery and other crafts from old glass, metal, car parts and other recycled materials. There's a small shop on the grounds. Crafts can also be commissioned (and sent abroad) and, Monday through Friday, you can watch the artists at work.

**Tingatinga Centre** ARTS & CRAFTS
(Map p664; www.tingatinga.org; Morogoro Stores, off Haile Selassie Rd; 9am-6pm) This excellent centre is at the spot where Edward Saidi Tingatinga originally marketed his designs, and it's still one of the best places to buy Tingatinga paintings and to watch the artists at work.

## Information

### DANGERS & ANNOYANCES

Take the usual precautions:

- Watch out for pickpocketing in crowded areas, and for bag snatching through vehicle windows.
- Stay aware of your surroundings and leave your valuables in a reliable hotel safe.
- At night, always take a taxi rather than taking a dalla-dalla or walking.
- Avoid walking alone along the path paralleling Barack Obama Drive, on Coco Beach, and at night along Chole Rd.
- Only use taxis from reliable hotels or established taxi stands. Avoid taxis cruising the streets, and never get in a taxi that has a 'friend' of the driver or anyone else already in it.

### INTERNET ACCESS

Most hotels, even budget ones, now have either a fixed internet point or wi-fi. Internet cafes abound in the city centre; the more professional

# Greater Dar es Salaam

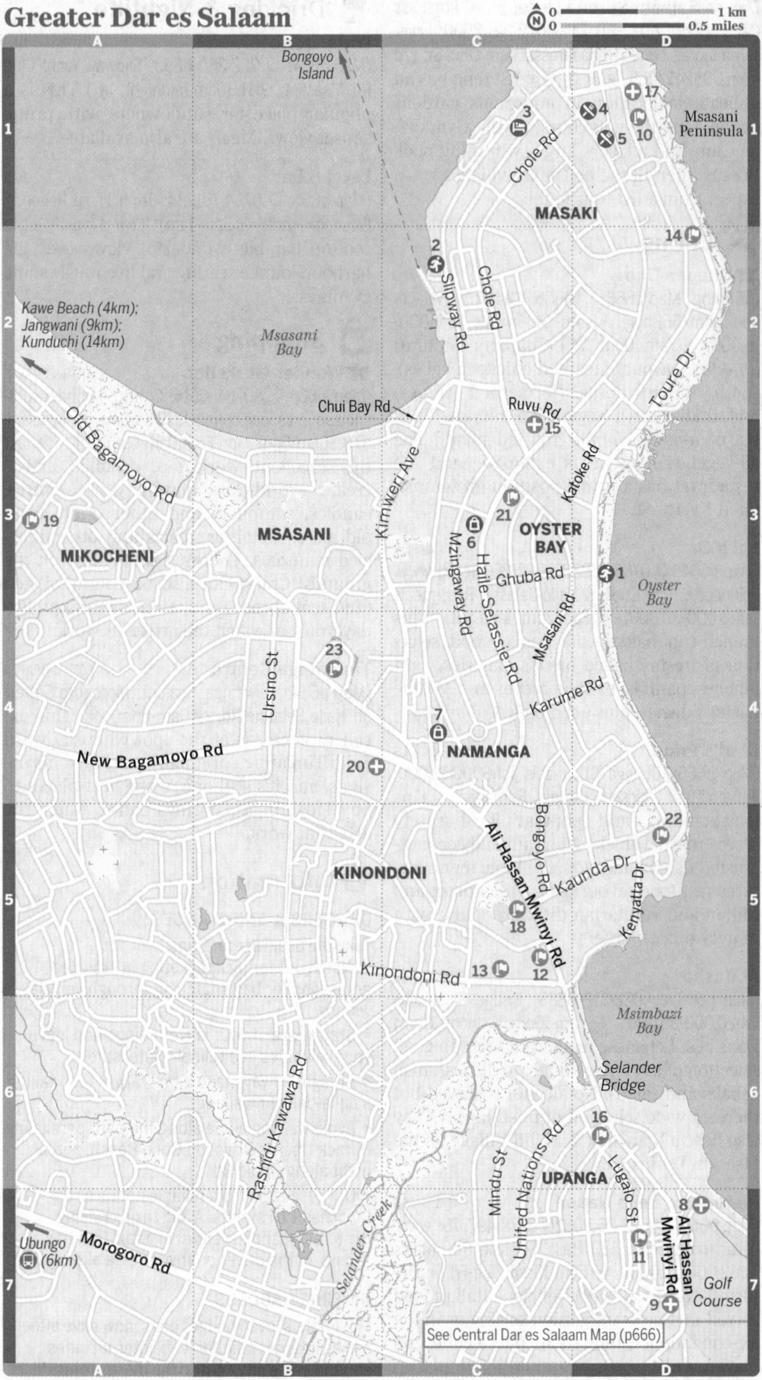

0 — 1 km
0 — 0.5 miles

Bongoyo Island
Msasani Peninsula
MASAKI
Chole Rd
Slipway Rd
Kawe Beach (4km); Jangwani (9km); Kunduchi (14km)
Msasani Bay
Toure Dr
Chui Bay Rd
Ruvu Rd
Old Bagamoyo Rd
Kimweri Ave
Katoke Rd
MSASANI
MIKOCHENI
OYSTER BAY
Mzingaway Rd
Haile Selassie Rd
Ghuba Rd
Oyster Bay
Msasani Rd
Ursino St
Karume Rd
New Bagamoyo Rd
NAMANGA
Ali Hassan Mwinyi Rd
Bongoyo Rd
KINONDONI
Kaunda Dr
Kenyatta Dr
Kinondoni Rd
Msimbazi Bay
Selander Bridge
Rashidi Kawawa Rd
Mindu St
United Nations Rd
UPANGA
Lugalo St
Selander Creek
Ubungo (6km)
Morogoro Rd
Golf Course

See Central Dar es Salaam Map (p666)

## Greater Dar es Salaam

**Activities, Courses & Tours**
1 Coco Beach .......... D3
2 Tanzaquatic .......... C2

**Sleeping**
3 Alexander's Hotel .......... C1

**Eating**
4 Épi d'Or .......... D1
5 Ristorante Bella Napoli .......... D1

**Drinking & Nightlife**
Waterfront .......... (see 2)

**Shopping**
6 Tingatinga Centre .......... C3
7 Wonder Workshop .......... C4

**Information**
8 Aga Khan Hospital .......... D7
9 Amref Flying Doctors .......... D7
10 Australian Honorary Consulate .......... D1
Burundian Embassy .......... (see 16)
Coastal Travels .......... (see 2)
11 Democratic Republic of the Congo Embassy (Formerly Zaïre) .......... D7
12 French Embassy .......... C5
13 Indian High Commission .......... C5
14 Irish Embassy .......... D2
15 IST Clinic .......... C3
16 Italian Embassy .......... D6
17 JD Pharmacy .......... D1
18 Kenyan High Commission .......... C5
19 Malawian High Commission .......... A3
20 Premier Care Clinic .......... B4
21 Rwandan Embassy .......... C3
22 Ugandan Embassy .......... D5
23 US Embassy .......... B4

ones are tucked away in commercial centres such as Harbour View Towers and Osman Towers. Most charge between Tsh1000 and Tsh2000 per hour.

**Main post office** (Map p666; Azikiwe St; Tsh1500 per hr; ⏲8am-4.30pm Mon-Fri, 9am-noon Sat) Has terminals.

**YMCA Internet Café** (Map p666; Upanga Rd; per hour Tsh1000; ⏲8am-7.30pm Mon-Fri, to 2pm Sat)

### MEDICAL SERVICES

There are good pharmacies at all the main shopping centres including the Slipway, Oyster Bay and Sea Cliff Village.

**Aga Khan Hospital** (Map p664; ☎022-211 5153, 022-211 5151; www.agakhanhospitals.org/DarEsSalaam; Barack Obama Dr) A multi-speciality hospital with internationally qualified doctors offering general medical services, specialist clinics and accident and emergency services.

**Amref Flying Doctors** (Map p664; ☎0719 881887, 0784 240500, in Kenya 020-699 2299; www.flydoc.org; Ali Hassan Mwinyi Rd) For emergency air evacuations.

**IST Clinic** (Map p664; ☎022-260 1307, 24hr emergency 0754 783393; www.istclinic.com; Ruvu Rd, Msasani; ⏲8am-6pm Mon-Thu, 8am-5pm Fri, 9am-noon Sat) A fully equipped Western-run clinic, with a doctor on call 24 hours.

**JD Pharmacy** (Map p664; ☎022-286 3663, 022-211 1049; www.jdpharmacy.co.tz; opposite Seacliff Village, Toure Dr & Mhando St; ⏲9am-8pm Mon-Sat, 9am-2pm Sun) Well-stocked pharmacy; also has a number of other branches around town.

**Premier Care Clinic** (Map p664; ☎0715 254642, 0752 254642; www.premiercareclinic.com; 259 Ali Hassan Mwinyi Rd, Namanga; ⏲8am-5pm Mon-Fri, to noon Sat) Western standards and facilities, next to the Big Bite restaurant; also has a branch in Masaki.

### TOURIST INFORMATION

**Tanzania Tourist Board Information Centre** (Map p666; ☎022-212 8472; www.tanzaniatouristboard.com; Samora Ave; ⏲8.30am-4pm Mon-Fri, to noon Sat) Free tourist maps and brochures, and limited city information.

## Getting There & Away

### AIR

**Julius Nyerere International Airport** (p706) is Tanzania's hub airport. Verify the departure terminal when purchasing your ticket.

### BOAT

Four fast **Azam Marine** (Map p666; ☎022-212 3324; www.azammarine.com; Kivukoni Front) catamarans operate daily between Dar and Zanzibar (economy/VIP US$35/50, economy child US$25). All take about two hours, with a luggage allowance of 25kg per person.

The only place at the port to buy legitimate ferry tickets is the tall, blue-glass building at the southern end of the ferry terminal on Kivukoni Front.

The large Azam Sealink I ferry to Pemba (adult/child US$70/50) departs Dar on Tuesday and Friday evening at 7.45pm, arriving in Pemba about 2pm the next day, following a stop in Zanzibar. Tickets are purchased at the same blue Azam Marine building selling Zanzibar tickets.

# Central Dar es Salaam

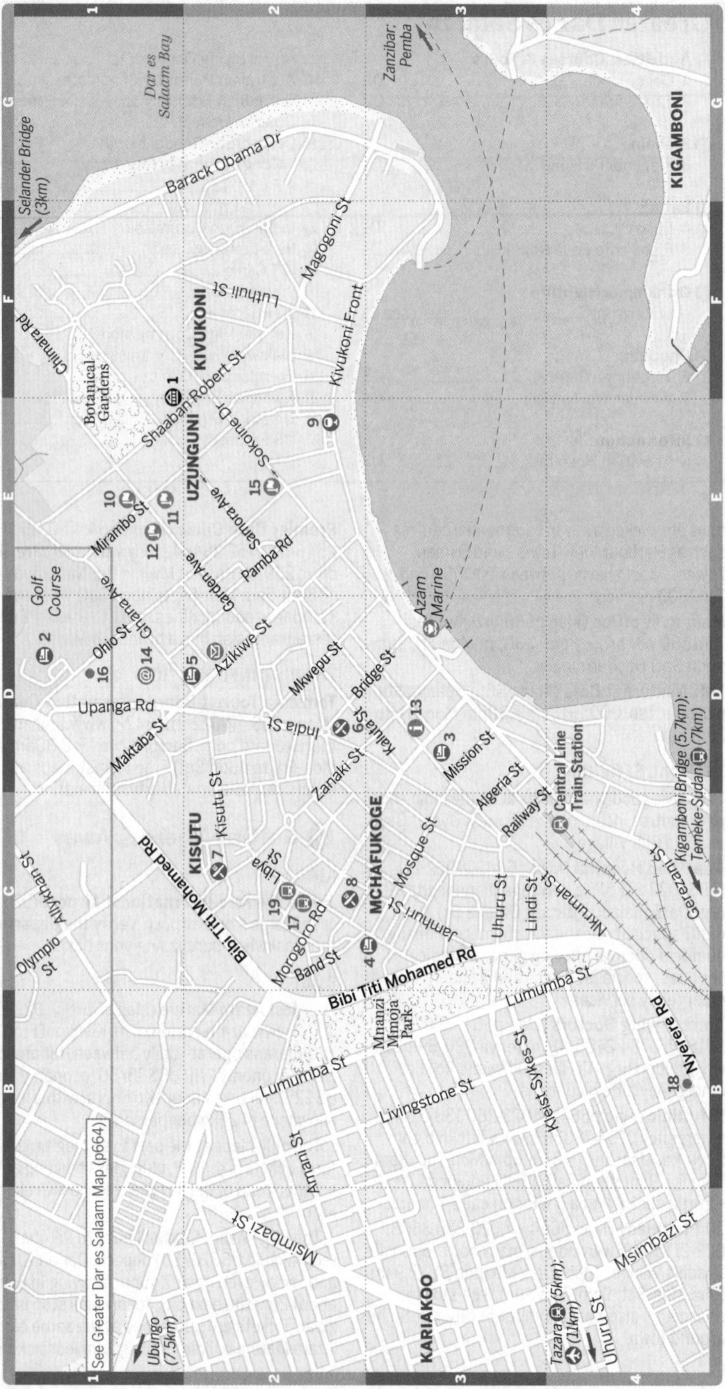

0 500 m
0 0.25 miles

See Greater Dar es Salaam Map (p664)

Ubungo (7.5km)
Selander Bridge (3km)
Zanzibar; Pemba
Tazara (5km); (11km)
Kigamboni Bridge (5.7km); Temeke-Sudan (7km)

Dar es Salaam Bay
Golf Course
Botanical Gardens
Mnanzi Mmoja Park
Azam Marine
Central Line Train Station

KISUTU
UZUNGUNI
KIVUKONI
MCHAFUKOGE
KARIAKOO
KIGAMBONI

Olympio St
Allykhan St
Chimara Rd
Upanga Rd
Ohio St
Ghana Ave
Mirambo St
Maktaba St
Bibi Titi Mohamed Rd
Kisutu St
Azikiwe St
Garden Ave
Samora Ave
Shaaban Robert St
Sokoine Dr
Pamba Rd
Luthuli St
Barack Obama Dr
Magogoni St
Kivukoni Front
Msimbazi St
Amani St
Lumumba St
Libya St
Morogoro Rd
Band St
India St
Mkwepu St
Zanaki St
Kaluta St
Bridge St
Jamhuri St
Mosque St
Mission St
Algeria St
Railway St
Uhuru St
Lindi St
Livingstone St
Kleist Sykes St
Nkrumah St
Gerezani St
Nyerere Rd

1 2 3 4 5 6 7 8 9 10 11 12 13 14 15 16 17 18 19

## Central Dar es Salaam

**Sights**
1 National Museum & House of Culture ... F1

**Sleeping**
2 Dar es Salaam Serena Hotel ... D1
3 Harbour View Suites ... D3
4 Safari Inn ... C3
5 YWCA ... D2

**Eating**
6 Al Basha ... D2
7 Chapan Bhog ... C2
8 Chef's Pride ... C2

**Drinking & Nightlife**
9 Level 8 Bar ... E2

**Information**
10 British High Commission ... E1
11 Canadian High Commission ... E1
German Embassy ... (see 10)
12 Mozambique High Commission ... E1
Netherlands Embassy ... (see 10)
13 Tanzania Tourist Board Information Centre ... D3
14 YMCA Internet Café ... D1
15 Zambian High Commission ... E2

**Transport**
16 Avis ... D1
17 Dar Express ... C2
18 Green Car Rentals ... B4
Jumanne Mastoka ... (see 16)
19 Kilimanjaro Express ... C2

### BUS

Except as noted, all buses currently depart from and arrive at the main bus station at Ubungo, 8km west of the city centre on Morogoro Rd, from where you can take a taxi (from Tsh30,000, about one hour, more with heavy traffic).

**Dar Express** (Map p666; Libya St, Kisutu; ⏲6am-6pm) Daily buses to Moshi (Tsh30,000 to Tsh33,000, 8½ hours) and Arusha (Tsh30,000 to 36,000, 10 hours) depart hourly between 6am and 8am from Ubungo bus station. There's also a daily bus to Nairobi (Tsh65,000, 15 hours) at 6am.

**Kilimanjaro Express** (Map p666; Libya St, Kisutu; ⏲4.30am-7pm) Two daily buses to Moshi (Tsh33,000 to Tsh36,000, 8½ hours) and Arusha (Tsh33,000 to Tsh36,000, 10 hours) depart at 6am and 7am from outside the Kilimanjaro Express office on Libya St, and then about 45 minutes later from Ubungo.

### TRAIN

**Tazara** (Tanzanian Zambia Railway Authority; ☎0713 354648, 0732 998855, 022-286 5187; www.tazarasite.com; cnr Nyerere & Nelson Mandela Rds; ⏲ticket office 7.30am-noon & 2-4.30pm Mon-Fri, 9am-noon Sat) The train station is 6km southwest of the city centre (Tsh15,000 to Tsh20,000 in a taxi). Dalla-dallas to the station leave from the New Posta transport stand, and are marked Vigunguti, U/Ndege or Buguruni. Train services run between Dar es Salaam, Mbeya and Kapiri Mposhi (Zambia).

**Tanzanian Railways Limited** (☎022-211 7833; www.trl.co.tz; cnr Railway St & Sokoine Dr) The train station is just southwest of the ferry terminal in the city centre. 'Central Line' services connect Dar es Salaam with Kigoma and Mwanza via Tabora.

## Getting Around

### CAR & MOTORCYCLE

Most rental agencies offer self-drive options in town; none offers unlimited kilometres. Another option is to negotiate a daily or half-day rate with a reliable taxi driver such as **Jumanne Mastoka** (☎0659 339735, 0784 339735; mjumanne@yahoo.com).

**Avis** (Map p666; ☎022-211 5381, 0754 451111; www.firstcarrental.co.tz; Amani Place, Ohio St) Not the cheapest prices, but offers a professional service. Has desks at the Hyatt Regency and the airport, as well as branch offices in Arusha and Stone Town.

**Green Car Rentals** (Map p666; ☎0713 227788, 022-218 3718; www.greencarstz.com; Nyerere Rd) A reputable company with over 20 years of experience. It also has branch offices in Arusha and Zanzibar. You'll find it next to Dar es Salaam Glassworks.

### PUBLIC TRANSPORT

Dalla-dallas (minibuses and 30-seater buses) – long the mainstay of Dar's public transport system – service many city destinations for an average price of Tsh400.

The Dar Rapid Transit project in Dar es Salaam is gradually taking over old dalla-dalla routes. The Kimara–Kivukoni line of the new system runs express buses between the city centre and Ubungo (Tsh650, about 20 minutes). Purchase your ticket from any station in advance of boarding.

### TAXI

Taxis don't have meters. Short rides within the city centre cost from Tsh5000.

For a reliable taxi driver, highly recommended also for airport pick-ups and for travel elsewhere in Tanzania, contact **Jumanne Mastoka** (☎0659 339735, 0784 339735; mjumanne@yahoo.com).

WORTH A TRIP

### JOZANI-CHWAKA NATIONAL PARK

A cool and shady patch of green, **Jozani-Chwaka National Park** (Map p670; ☎024-223 8628, 0777 469911; adult/child with guide Tsh23,600/11,800; ⏲7.30am-5pm) is the largest area of mature, indigenous forest left on Zanzibar. Situated inland from Chwaka Bay on low-lying land, the area is prone to flooding, which nurtures a unique swamp forest of moisture-loving trees and lush, feathery ferns. Living among Jozani Forest's tangle of vines and branches are populations of the endangered red colobus monkey, as well as Sykes monkeys, bushbabies, Ader's duikers and more than 40 species of birds.

# ZANZIBAR ARCHIPELAGO

Step off the boat or plane onto the Zanzibar Archipelago, and you'll be transported through the centuries – to ancient Persia and tales of Shirazi merchants, to the courts of Swahili princes and Omani sultans, and to the west coast of India, with its heavily laden scents.

## Zanzibar

Zanzibar is the archipelago's focal point, and with good reason. Its old Stone Town is one of Africa's most evocative locations, with a mesmerising mix of influences from the Indian subcontinent, the Arabian peninsula, the African mainland and Europe.

An easy drive away are Zanzibar's beaches, which are among the finest stretches of sand to be found anywhere. Along the east coast, rural villages dot the coastline, from community-minded Jambiani through the surf-and-party hub of Paje to traditional Matemwe with its seaweed harvesting, and its snorkelling around lovely Mnemba Atoll.

At Zanzibar's northern tip, tourist activity centres on Nungwi and Kendwa, with their beaches, bars and dance-till-dawn full-moon parties. Choose your spot carefully here, as increasing development threatens the area's ineluctable magic and fragile community resources.



### Zanzibar Town

POP 495,000 / ☎024

Zanzibar Town, on the western side of Zanzibar (Unguja) island, is the Zanzibar Archipelago's heart and the first stop for most travellers. It is divided in two by Creek Rd, which separates the old Stone Town (Mji Mkongwe – the main destination for visitors) from the 'Other Side' or Ng'ambo, with its offices, apartment blocks and crowded neighbourhoods.

Wander through Stone Town's winding alleyways, with their carved doors and latticework balconies, and you'll easily lose yourself in centuries of history. Each twist and turn brings something new, be it a school full of children chanting verses from the Quran, an abandoned Persian bathhouse, or a coffee vendor with his long-spouted pot fastened over coals.

#### Sights

Shaped like a triangle, **Stone Town** sits on a cape, Ras Shangani. It is bounded on two sides by the sea, and along the third by Creek Rd (Benjamin Mkapa Rd), which is also the site of the chaotic and colourful Darajani Market. The harbour and port are located to the north and most of the major sights sit along the seafront opposite. The modern city expands to the east of Creek Rd.

South and north of Zanzibar Town, beyond the heat and bustle, are the wealthy residential area of Mbweni and the northern beaches of Mtoni and Bububu, where Omani royalty once retired for the weekend.

Within these boundaries are grand sultan's palaces, old Persian baths, graceful mosques, lively markets and much more to explore.

**Forodhani Gardens** GARDENS

(Jamituri Gardens; Map p672) One of the best ways to ease into life on the island is to stop by these formal gardens, laid out in 1936 to commemorate the Silver Jubilee of Sultan Khalifa (r 1911–60). In the centre of the grassy plaza is a domed podium where a brass band would play; the marooned ceremonial arch near the waterfront was built to welcome Princess Margaret on a state visit in 1956. Renovated in 2010 by the Aga Khan Trust for Culture, the gardens are a social hub, with several waterfront cafes, shady benches and an evening food market.

**Slave Chambers** HISTORIC SITE

(Map p672; off New Mkunazini Rd; incl slave chambers & slavery exhibit Tsh10,000; ⏲8.30am-6pm

Mon-Sat, noon-6pm Sun) Although nothing of the old slave market remains, some 15 holding cells are located beneath the Anglican Cathedral and St Monica's Hostel. Two of them, beneath St Monica's, are open to the public and offer a sobering glimpse of the appalling realities of the trade. Dank, dark and cramped, each chamber housed up to 65 slaves awaiting sale. Tiny windows cast weak shafts of sunlight into the gloom and it's hard to breathe even when they're empty.

**Beit el-Ajaib** HISTORIC BUILDING

(House of Wonders; Map p672; Mizingani Rd) Built for ceremonial purposes by Sultan Barghash in 1883, the 'House of Wonders' rises in impressive tiers of slender steel pillars and balconies overlooking the Forodhani Gardens. It is the grandest structure in Zanzibar and in its heyday sported fine marble floors, panelled walls and never-before-seen electricity and running water. Now it houses the Zanzibar National Museum of History & Culture with exhibits on the dhow culture of the Indian Ocean and Swahili civilisation.

**Beit el-Amani** HISTORIC BUILDING

(Map p672; cnr Kaunda & Creek Rds) This domed building, formerly the Peace Memorial Museum and now an archive, dates from 1925, when it was inaugurated as a memorial to the accords ending WWI. It was designed by British architect JH Sinclair, who also designed the High Court, further up on Kaunda Rd.

**Zanzibar National Museum of History & Culture** MUSEUM

(Map p672; Mizingani Rd; adult/child US$4/1; ⌚9am-6pm) Housed in the imposing Beit el-Ajaib (House of Wonders), this museum has exhibits on Swahili civilisation, the history of Stone Town and a *mtepe* (a traditional Swahili sailing vessel made without nails). It is currently closed, awaiting renovations.

**Beit el-Sahel** MUSEUM

(Palace Museum; Map p672; Mizingani Rd; adult/child US$4/1; ⌚9am-6pm) Occupying several blocks along the waterfront, the imposing Palace Museum is a reconstruction of the Sultan Seyyid Said's 19th-century palace home, which was destroyed by the British bombardment of 1896. It was renamed the People's Palace in 1964 when the last sultan, Jamshid, was overthrown.

**Old Fort** HISTORIC BUILDING

(Map p672; ⌚9am-10pm) FREE Among the defining features of Stone Town's waterfront are the ragstone ramparts of Ngome Kongwe, the Old Fort. It was the first defensive structure built by the Busaidi Omani Arabs when they seized the island from the Portuguese in 1698, and did duty as a prison and place of execution until the British transformed it into a women's tennis club in 1949.

**Darajani Market** MARKET

(Map p672; Creek Rd; ⌚6am-4pm) Zanzibar's main market is well worth a visit and best undertaken in the morning, when things are still fresh. You'll find everything here – from colourful piles of spices, slabs of meat, fresh fish and huge baskets full of live chickens to sandals and mobile phones – all set out in a series of covered halls and twisting alleys.

## Activities & Tours

**One Ocean** DIVING

(Map p672; ☎024-223 8374, 0773 048828; www.zanzibaroneocean.com; off Shangani St; ⌚8am-6pm) This five-star PADI centre has more than a decade of experience on Zanzibar. In addition to its main office in Stone Town, it has branches at a number of locations along the east coast. It organises dives all around the island, for divers of all levels.

**Grassroots Traveller** CULTURAL

(☎0772 821725; www.grassroots-traveller.com) Working closely with community-based projects, NGOs and organisations striving for sustainable development, this forward-thinking company helps travellers craft interesting itineraries blending adventure with community engagement to discover that there's more to Zanzibar than sun, sand and sea. It also helps volunteers hook up with successful short- and long-term projects.

### ZANZIBAR FESTIVALS

**Zanzibar International Film Festival** (Festival of the Dhow Countries; www.ziff.or.tz; ⌚Jul) celebrates and nurtures arts from Indian Ocean countries as diverse as India, Iran, Madagascar and the Horn of Africa. For 16 days in July, venues around Stone Town host screenings, performing-arts groups, media-related workshops and musical masterclasses.

**Sauti za Busara** (Voices of Wisdom; www.busaramusic.com; festival pass nonresident US$80-120; ⌚Feb) showcases some of the hottest musical talent in Africa. This three-day festival fills the Old Fort and venues across the island with the best *taarab*, jazz, Afro-pop and bongo flava (Tanzanian hip-hop).

# Zanzibar

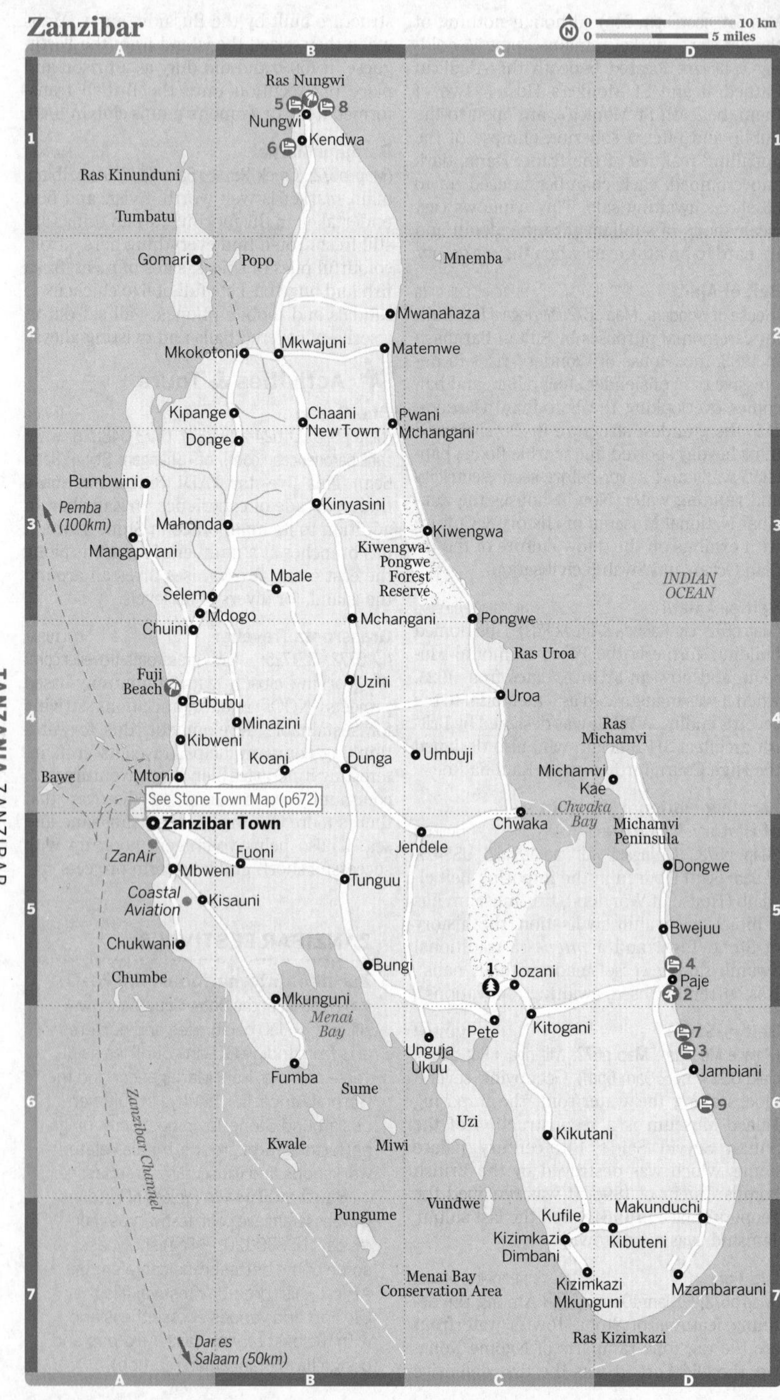
0 10 km
0 5 miles
A
B
C
D
1
2
3
4
5
6
7
Ras Nungwi
5
8
Nungwi
6
Kendwa
Ras Kinunduni
Tumbatu
Gomari
Popo
Mnemba
Mwanahaza
Mkokotoni
Mkwajuni
Matemwe
Kipange
Chaani
New Town
Pwani
Mchangani
Donge
Bumbwini
Pemba
(100km)
Kinyasini
Mahonda
Kiwengwa
Mangapwani
Kiwengwa-
Pongwe
Forest
Reserve
Mbale
INDIAN
OCEAN
Selem
Mdogo
Mchangani
Pongwe
Chuini
Ras Uroa
Fuji
Beach
Uzini
Uroa
Bububu
Minazini
Ras
Michamvi
Kibweni
Koani
Dunga
Umbuji
Bawe
Mtoni
Michamvi
Kae
See Stone Town Map (p672)
Chwaka
Bay
Zanzibar Town
Chwaka
Michamvi
Peninsula
ZanAir
Jendele
Fuoni
Mbweni
Dongwe
Tunguu
Coastal
Aviation
Kisauni
Bwejuu
Chukwani
Bungi
4
Chumbe
1
Jozani
Paje
2
Mkunguni
Menai
Bay
Pete
Kitogani
7
3
Unguja
Ukuu
Jambiani
Fumba
Sume
9
Zanzibar Channel
Uzi
Kikutani
Kwale
Miwi
Vundwe
Makunduchi
Pungume
Kufile
Kizimkazi
Dimbani
Kibuteni
Menai Bay
Conservation Area
Kizimkazi
Mkunguni
Mzambarauni
Ras Kizimkazi
Dar es
Salaam (50km)

## Zanzibar

**Sights**

1 Jozani-Chwaka National Park .............. C5

**Activities, Courses & Tours**

2 Paje by Kite .............. D5
Scuba Do .............. (see 6)

**Sleeping**

3 Blue Oyster Hotel .............. D6
Casa del Mar Hotel .............. (see 3)
4 Dhow Inn .............. D5
5 Flame Tree Cottages .............. B1
Garden Bungalows .............. (see 3)
Jambo Beach Bungalows .............. (see 4)
6 Kendwa Rocks .............. B1
7 Mango Beach House .............. D6
8 Mnarani Beach Cottages .............. B1
Nungwi Guest House .............. (see 5)
Paradise Beach Bungalows .............. (see 4)
Ras Nungwi Beach Hotel .............. (see 8)
9 Red Monkey Lodge .............. D6
Safina Bungalows .............. (see 5)
Sunset Kendwa .............. (see 6)

**Eating**

Kiddo's Cafe .............. (see 7)
Kim's Restaurant .............. (see 3)

## Sleeping

**★Jambo Guest House** GUESTHOUSE $
(Map p672; ☎024-223 3779, 0653 943548; www.jamboguest.com; off Mkunazini St; s/d/tr with shared bathroom US$30/45/65; ❄@) Probably the best budget accommodation in town and extremely popular with backpackers, Jambo runs smooth as clockwork. Nine spick-and-span rooms with Zanzibari beds share four bathrooms, there's complimentary tea and coffee, and the Green Garden Restaurant, opposite, provides an easy dinner.

**Garden Lodge** GUESTHOUSE $
(Map p672; ☎024-223 3298; gardenlodge@zanlink.com; Kaunda Rd, Vuga; s/d/tr US$40/60/70; ❄) This efficient, friendly, family-run place offers 18 rooms (two with air-con; US$10 extra per room) in a characterful Swahili house fringed with balconies and decorated with stained-glass windows. Rooms are good value, especially the upstairs ones, which are bright and spacious, and all have hot water, ceiling fans and Zanzibari beds. There's a rooftop breakfast terrace, and lunch can be arranged with advance order.

**Stone Town Café B&B** B&B $$
(Map p672; ☎0773 861313, 0778 373737; www.stonetowncafe.com; Kenyatta Rd; s/d from US$65/80; ❄@) Simple, unpretentious and uncluttered, the Stone Town Café has five rooms with Zanzibari beds dressed in pristine white linens. Black-and-white photos, decorative chests and rugs lend atmosphere, while breakfast smoothies, coffee and avocado toast are served downstairs on the palm-shaded patio.

**Seyyida Hotel & Spa** BOUTIQUE HOTEL $$
(Map p672; ☎024-223 8352; www.theseyyida-zanzibar.com; off Nyumba Ya Moto St; s/d from US$100/140; ❄@令) Lighter, brighter and different in style to many Stone Town hotels, the Seyyida is arranged around a verdant courtyard hung with island art. Rooms are modern and styled in neutral tones; all have satellite TV, and some have sea views and balconies. There's also a rooftop terrace restaurant and a spa.

**Warere Town House** HOTEL $$
(Map p672; ☎0782 234564; www.warere.com; off Funguni Rd; s/tr/f US$35/85/100, d US$55-70; ❄令) A well-run budget hotel with front-room balconies overlooking a flowering garden. Ten rooms come with Zanzibari beds dressed with kanga-lined mosquito nets, blue stucco trim and palm-woven furniture. Laundry and good wi-fi are available and the reception will organise taxis to the beach and local excursions. It's just a few minutes' walk from the port (staff will meet you).

**★Kisiwa House** BOUTIQUE HOTEL $$$
(Map p672; ☎024-223 5654; www.kisiwahouse.com; off Kenyatta Rd; r US$185-240; ❄令) The lovely Kisiwa House has nine spacious rooms and an excellent rooftop restaurant with sea views. Reached via a grand, steep staircase, all rooms have king-size Zanzibari beds, Persian rugs and dark-beamed ceilings. A mix of minimalist ethnic and European decor and grand proportions gives the house an understated glamour, making it popular as a honeymoon destination.

## Eating

**★Lukmaan Restaurant** ZANZIBARI $
(Map p672; New Mkunazini Rd; meals Tsh4500-7000; ⏰7am-9pm) Probably the best local restaurant for quality Zanzibari food. There's no menu – just make your way inside to the 1950s counter and see what's on offer. Servings are enormous and include various biryanis, fried fish, coconut curries and freshly

# Stone Town

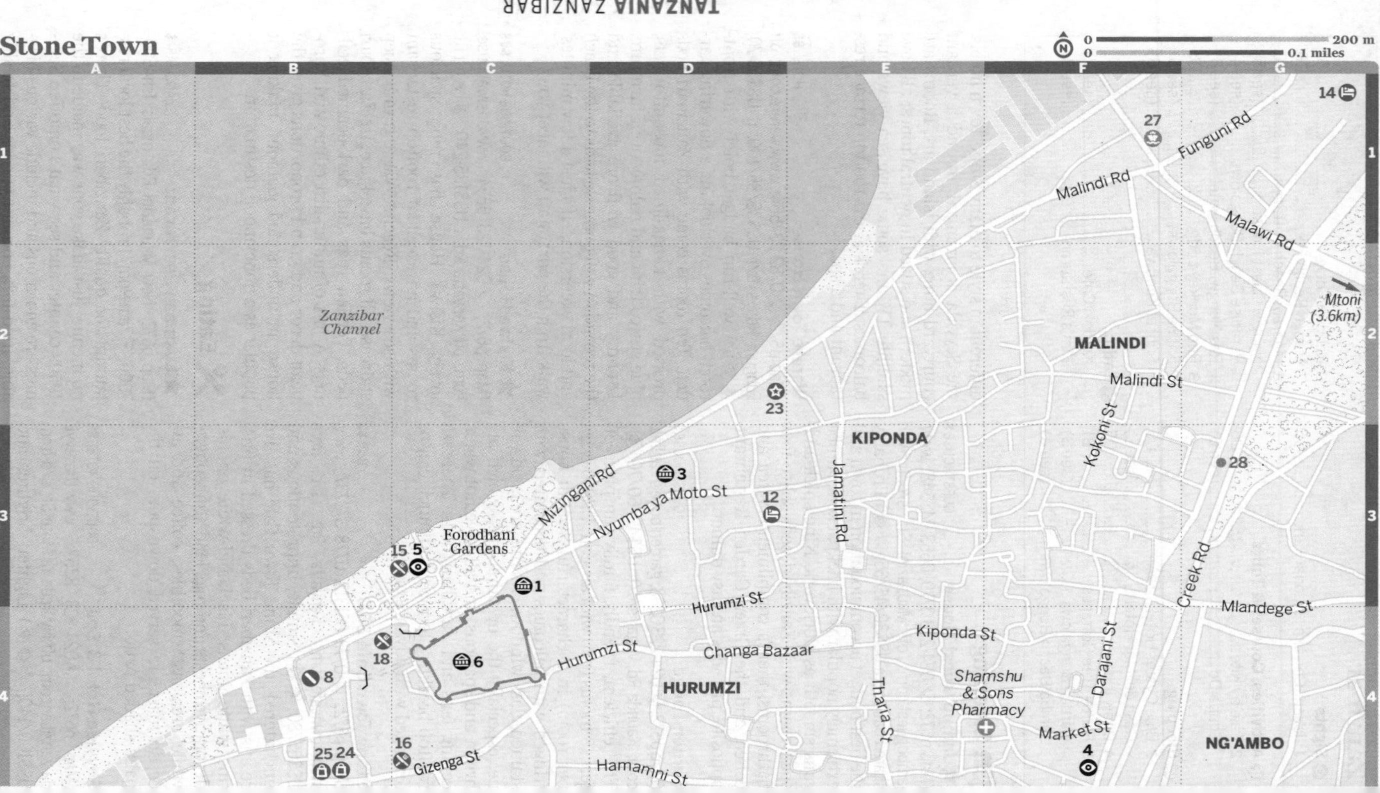

200 m
0.1 miles
A
B
C
D
E
F
G
1
2
3
4
Zanzibar Channel
Mtoni (3.6km)
MALINDI
KIPONDA
HURUMZI
NG'AMBO
Forodhani Gardens
Funguni Rd
Malindi Rd
Malawi Rd
Malindi St
Kokoni St
Creek Rd
Mlandege St
Mizingani Rd
Nyumba ya Moto St
Jamatini Rd
Hurumzi St
Kiponda St
Changa Bazaar
Darajani St
Tharia St
Shamshu & Sons Pharmacy
Market St
Gizenga St
Hamamni St
1
3
4
5
6
8
12
14
15
16
18
23
24
25
27
28

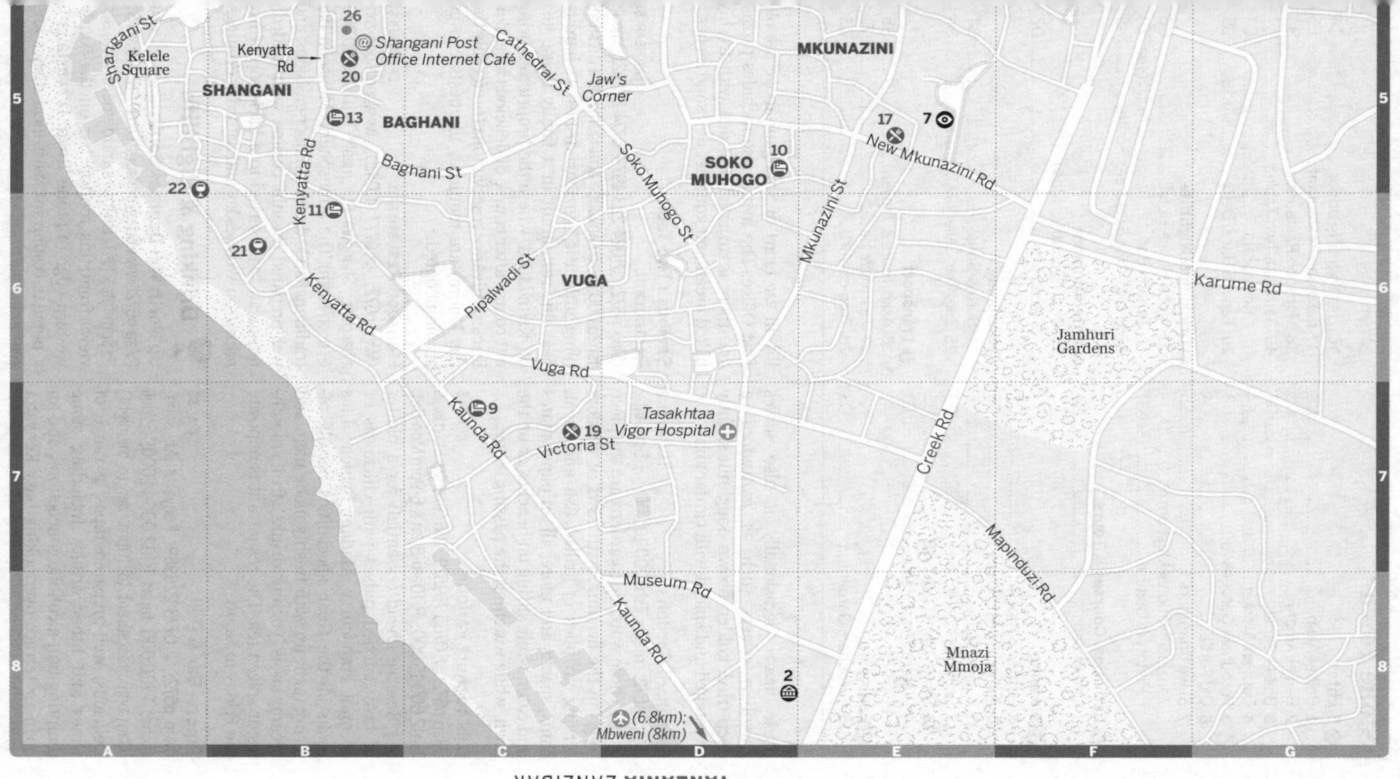

5
6
7
8
A
B
C
D
E
F
G
Shangani St
Kelele Square
Kenyatta Rd
26
@ Shangani Post Office Internet Café
20
SHANGANI
13
BAGHANI
Cathedral St
Jaw's Corner
MKUNAZINI
17
7
New Mkunazini Rd
SOKO MUHOGO
10
Baghani St
Kenyatta Rd
22
11
21
Soko Muhogo St
Mkunazini St
Pipalwadi St
VUGA
Kenyatta Rd
Karume Rd
Jamhuri Gardens
Vuga Rd
9
Kaunda Rd
Tasakhtaa
19
Vigor Hospital
Victoria St
Creek Rd
Museum Rd
Mapinduzi Rd
Kaunda Rd
Mnazi Mmoja
2
(6.8km); Mbweni (8km)

## Stone Town

**Sights**
1 Beit el-Ajaib ........ C3
2 Beit el-Amani ........ D8
3 Beit el-Sahel ........ D3
4 Darajani Market ........ F4
5 Forodhani Gardens ........ C3
6 Old Fort ........ C4
7 Slave Chambers ........ E5
Zanzibar National Museum of History & Culture ........ (see 1)

**Activities, Courses & Tours**
8 One Ocean ........ B4

**Sleeping**
9 Garden Lodge ........ C7
10 Jambo Guest House ........ D5
11 Kisiwa House ........ B6
12 Seyyida Hotel & Spa ........ D3
13 Stone Town Café B&B ........ B5
14 Warere Town House ........ G1

**Eating**
15 Forodhani Gardens ........ C3
16 Luis Yoghurt Parlour ........ C4
17 Lukmaan Restaurant ........ E5
18 Monsoon Restaurant ........ B4
19 Sambusa Two Tables Restaurant ........ C7
20 Tapería Bar & Deli ........ B5

**Drinking & Nightlife**
21 Africa House Hotel ........ B6
Tapería Bar ........ (see 20)
22 Up North @ 6 Degrees South ........ A5

**Entertainment**
23 Dhow Countries Music Academy ........ D2

**Shopping**
24 Surti & Sons ........ B4
25 Zanzibar Gallery ........ B4

**Transport**
26 Asko Tours & Travel ........ B5
27 Azam Marine ........ F1
28 Tropical Air ........ G3



made naan. Occasionally it also serves Zanzibari sweets such as *maandazi* (a deep fried, golden brown doughnut slightly sweetened and spiced with cardamom).

**Forodhani Gardens** TANZANIAN $
(Map p672; meals Tsh3000-10,000; 5pm-late; ) These waterside gardens are the place to go in the evening, with rows of vendors serving up piles of grilled fish and meat, chips, snacks and more, all on paper plates and eaten while sitting on benches or on the lawn, while watching the passing scene.

**Luis Yoghurt Parlour** INDIAN $
(Map p672; 0765 759579; 156 Gizenga St; meals Tsh12,000-15,000; 10am-3pm & 6-9pm Mon-Sat; ) Reserve ahead (essential) for a platter of tasty curried pulses with chickpeas or coconut crab curry. Madam Blanche Luis cooks all the Goan specialities herself, offering them up with freshly made naan and creamy lassis (yoghurt drinks), fruit smoothies or spiced tea. The restaurant is opposite the Friday mosque.

**Tapería Bar & Deli** TAPAS $$
(Map p672; 0773 226989; Kenyatta Rd; sandwiches Tsh10,000, tapas Tsh12,000-14,000; deli 10am-6pm, restaurant to 10pm, bar to midnight) Delicious, well-prepared tapas, a range of wines and other drinks, including some tempting non-alcoholic concoctions, and an open-air terrace overlooking busy Kenyatta Rd, in the heart of Shangani above the old Post Office. The menu also includes pizzas and there is an adjoining deli with freshly baked bread and gourmet deli sandwiches.

**Sambusa Two Tables Restaurant** ZANZIBARI $$
(Map p672; 024-223 1979, 0774 881921; meals Tsh25,000; by advance arrangement) For sampling authentic Zanzibari dishes, it's hard to beat this restaurant in a family house just off Kaunda Rd, where the proprietors bring out course after course of delicious local delicacies. Advance reservations (preferably the day before) are required; 15 guests can be accommodated.

**Monsoon Restaurant** ZANZIBARI $$
(Map p672; 0777 410410; www.monsoon-zanzibar.com; Shangani St; meals Tsh17,000-30,000; noon-10pm) The atmospheric Monsoon has traditional-style dining on floor cushions, and well-prepared Swahili cuisine with a Mediterranean twist served to a backdrop of live *taarab* on Wednesday and Saturday evenings.

## Drinking & Nightlife

**Up North @ 6 Degrees South** BAR
(Map p672; www.6degreessouth.co.tz; Shangani St; 5pm-late; ) Enjoy sundowners and sea views from this rooftop bar on the southwestern edge of Stone Town. Downstairs is a popular restaurant with local dishes and seafood.

**Tapería Bar** BAR
(Map p672; ☎0773 226989; Kenyatta Rd; ⏰10am-midnight; 📶) Located above the historic Post Office, this contemporary wine and tapas bar serves a long list of wine and beer accompanied by tapas, plates of prawns, *patatas bravas* (spicy potatoes) and cheesy croquettes. The friendly staff, indoor-outdoor seating and rowdy scene, especially on big football nights, have made it a popular local hangout.

**Africa House Hotel** BAR
(Map p672; www.africahousehotel.co.tz; Shangani St; ⏰5pm-midnight) With a front-row view of the sunset, the terrace bar of the Africa House Hotel – once the British Club – is a perennially popular place for sundowners.

## ☆ Entertainment

**Dhow Countries Music Academy** LIVE MUSIC
(Map p672; ☎0777 416529; www.zanzibarmusic.org; Old Customs House, Mizingani Rd; concerts Tsh10,000; ⏰9am-6pm) Zanzibar's celebrated music genre, called *taarab,* is a form of mellifluously sung poetry. The tradition is kept alive by this dynamic academy, which trains next-generation masters and hosts weekly *taarab* concerts as well as a lively program of Afro-jazz and fusion bands. If you like what you hear you can always take a lesson. Concerts start at 8pm and CDs are on sale.

## Shopping

**Surti & Sons** SHOES
(Map p672; ☎0777 472742; www.surtiandsons.wordpress.com; Gizenga St; ⏰10am-2pm & 3-7pm) For over 30 years, Parvin Surti and his family have been shoeing Zanzibaris in beautiful, durable leather sandals (US$25 to US$35) in a range of understated styles in soft, natural colours. All the sandals are handstitched and made from good-quality leather, and great attention is paid to comfort and customer satisfaction. Belts and bags are also available.

**Zanzibar Gallery** GIFTS & SOUVENIRS
(Map p672; ☎024-223 2721; www.zanzibargallery.net; cnr Kenyatta Rd & Gizenga St; ⏰9am-6.30pm Mon-Sat, to 1pm Sun) This long-standing gallery has a collection of souvenirs, textiles, woodcarvings, antiques and more.

## ℹ Information

### DANGERS & ANNOYANCES

While Zanzibar remains a relatively safe place, robberies and muggings do occur, notably in Zanzibar Town.

- Avoid isolated areas, especially isolated stretches of beach, and leave your valuables in a hotel safe.
- At night in Zanzibar Town, take a taxi or walk in a group. Should your passport be stolen, get a written report from the police. With this, Immigration will issue you a travel document that will get you back to the mainland.
- If you've rented a bicycle or motorcycle, be prepared for stops at checkpoints. Assuming your papers are in order, the best tactic is respectful friendliness.

### INTERNET ACCESS

Most hotels, and many cafes and restaurants, offer wi-fi. It doesn't always work well in historic buildings due to the thick walls and weak signal, but it is generally not difficult to get connected.

**Shangani Post Office Internet Café** (Map p672; Kenyatta Rd; per hour Tsh1000; ⏰8am-4.30pm Mon-Fri, to 12.30pm Sat) At the main post office in Shangani.

### MEDICAL SERVICES

There are several private medical centres in Zanzibar Town (consultations US$30 to US$50), and top-end hotels usually have an internationally trained doctor on call for a fee, but anything serious should be treated in Dar es Salaam.

**Shamshu & Sons Pharmacy** (Map p672; ☎024-223 2199, 0715 411480; Market St; ⏰9am-8.30pm Mon-Thu & Sat, 9am-noon & 4-8.30pm Fri, 9am-1.30pm Sun) Convenient, reasonably well stocked pharmacy behind the Darajani Market.

**Tasakhtaa Vigor Hospital** (Map p672; ☎024-223 2341, 024-223 2222; info@tasakhtaahospital.co.tz; Victoria St, Vuga) Modern medical facilities.

### TOURIST INFORMATION

There is a small tourist information kiosk at the Old Fort, with information on upcoming events in Zanzibar Town. Staff can also help arrange town tours. The official Zanzibar Commission for Tourism website is www.zanzibartourism.net.

## ℹ Getting There & Away

### AIR

**Zanzibar International Airport** (p706) is about 7km southeast of Zanzibar Town. A taxi to/from the airport costs Tsh15,000. Dalla-dalla 505 also does this route (Tsh500, 30 minutes), departing from the corner opposite Mnazi Mmoja hospital.

**Coastal Aviation** (Map p670; ☎024-223 3489, airport 024-223 3112; www.coastal.co.tz) and **ZanAir** (Map p670; ☎024-223 3670, 024-223 3678; www.zanair.com; Nyerere Rd) have daily flights connecting Zanzibar with Dar es Salaam (US$75), Arusha (US$250), Pemba (US$95), Selous Game Reserve and the northern parks.

Coastal Aviation goes daily to/from Tanga via Pemba (US$130), and has good-value day-excursion packages from Dar es Salaam to Stone Town. **Tropical Air** (Map p672; ☎0777 431431, 0687 522912; www.tropicalair.co.tz; Creek Rd) flies daily between Zanzibar and Dar es Salaam (US$70), and **Precision Air** (www.precisionairtz.com) has connections to Nairobi (Kenya).

#### BOAT

**Azam Marine** (Map p672; ☎Dar es Salaam 022-212 3324, Zanzibar 024-223 1655, Zanzibar 0774 707172; www.azammarine.com) operates the most reliable scheduled service between Dar es Salaam, Zanzibar and Pemba aboard a fleet of fast, modern catamarans. There are four daily services from Dar to Zanzibar (VIP/adult/child US$40/35/25, two hours) on smaller, fairly fast catamarans and three weekly services from Zanzibar to Pemba (VIP/adult/child US$40/35/25, six to seven hours).

## Getting Around

#### CAR & MOTORCYCLE

Daily rental rates average from about US$30 for a moped or motorcycle, and US$40 to US$65 for a Suzuki 4WD, excluding petrol.

**Asko Tours & Travel** (Map p672; ☎024-223 4715, 0777 411854, 0777 412848; askotour@hotmail.com; Kenyatta Rd) Offers reasonable rates for car hire.

#### DALLA-DALLAS

Open-sided dalla-dallas piled with people link all major towns on the island. None of the routes cost more than Tsh2500, and all take plenty of time (eg between one and 1½ hours from Zanzibar Town to Jambiani).

#### PRIVATE MINIBUS

Private tourist minibuses run daily to the north- and east-coast beaches and are cheaper than hotel transfers and taxis, which routinely cost US$50. Travel takes from one to 1½ hours to most destinations, and costs Tsh10,000 to Tsh15,000 per person.

#### TAXI

Taxis don't have meters, so you'll need to agree on a price with the driver before getting into the car. Town trips cost from Tsh4000, and more at night.



## Nungwi

POP 8000 / ☎024

This large village at Zanzibar's northernmost tip is a dhow-building centre and one of the island's major tourist destinations. Nungwi is also where the traditional and modern knock against each other with full force. Fishing and dhow-building are the centuries-old trades here, yet you only need to take a few steps back from the waterfront to enter another world, with party music and a collection of slightly scruffy guesthouses interspersed with five-star hotels. For some travellers it's the only place to be on the island (it's one of the few places you can swim throughout the day, and the beach is lovely) others will probably want to give it a miss.

## Sleeping

**Safina Bungalows** GUESTHOUSE $
(Map p670; ☎0777 415726, 0777 415856; www.newsafina.com; s/d/tr from US$30/50/70) Safina is a decent budget choice, with no-frills bungalows around a small garden, just in from the beach in the centre of Nungwi and meals in a double-storey pavilion. A few rooms have air-con.

**Nungwi Guest House** GUESTHOUSE $
(Map p670; ☎0772 263322; http://nungwiguesthouse.tripod.com; Nungwi village; s/d excl breakfast Tsh45,000/68,000) A good, brightly painted budget option in the village centre, with simple, clean en suite rooms around a small garden courtyard, all with fans. There's no food.

**Mnarani Beach Cottages** LODGE $$
(Map p670; ☎0777 415551, 024-224 0494; www.lighthousezanzibar.com; East Nungwi; half board s US$80-95, d US$140-250; ) Mnarani is set on a small escarpment with a lovely waterside terrace and easy access to the beach just below. There's a mix of rooms including pleasant garden cottages, family rooms, the two-storey Zanzibar House, and a honeymoon suite. It is well suited to couples and families, and has a surprising feeling of space despite often being fully booked.

**Flame Tree Cottages** B&B $$
(Map p670; ☎024-224 0100, 0777 479429; www.flametreecottages.com; s/d US$130/170; ) The cosy Flame Tree offers simply but thoughtfully furnished cottages in a flowering garden with a small pool. It's a perfect spot for families or romancing couples in a quieter location on the northeastern edge of Nungwi. Breakfast is served on your veranda dinner can be arranged with advance order.

★**Ras Nungwi Beach Hotel** HOTEL $$$
(Map p670; ☎024-294 1025, 0777 417316 www.rasnungwi.com; East Nungwi; s/d from US$190/250; ⏲Jun-Mar; ) This beautifully situated, upmarket place has long been a standout in Nungwi, with a low-key ambience, luxurious sea-view chalets in mature tropical gardens, and less-expensive room

in the main lodge. The hotel can organise fishing and watersports, and there's a dive centre and a spa.

## Kendwa

Kendwa lies about 3km southwest of the tip of Zanzibar Island. It's a long, wonderfully wide stretch of sand with a string of resorts interspersed with some smaller places, and a lively party vibe. Its attractions include lots of space on the beach, and favourable tidal patterns that ensure swimming at all hours.

### Activities

The scene in Kendwa is all about the beach, with volleyball nets, snorkelling and dive outlets dotted along the sand. Dhow cruises, boat trips to nearby Tumbatu island and to Nungwi – several kilometres north on the tip of Zanzibar Island – and diving can be arranged through most hotels.

★**Scuba Do** DIVING
(Map p670; ☎0777 417157; www.scuba-do-zanzibar.com; 2/6 dives US$150/330) Tammy and Christian's five-star Gold Palm dive centre has been operating for over a decade and is one of the most forward-thinking and ecofriendly outfits on the island. Committed to the local community, they have a well-trained, professional crew of 10 dive masters and offer excellent courses and excursions.

### Sleeping

**Sunset Kendwa** BUNGALOW $$
(Map p670; ☎0777 414647; www.sunsetkendwa.com; s US$45-85, d US$60-98; ❄) This long-standing place has a mix of rooms on the beach and on the cliff top, some with air-con and all with bathrooms with hot water, plus some cliff-top rooms in two-storey blocks. There's a good resident dive operator (p677), and a popular beachside restaurant-bar with evening bonfires on the beach.

**Kendwa Rocks** BUNGALOW $$
(Map p670; ☎0777 415475, 024-294 1113; www.kendwarocks.com; s/d/tr bandas with shared bathroom US$40/50/70, s/d bungalows from US$60/90; ❄) This is a Kendwa classic, although it has considerably expanded from its humble beginnings. Accommodation is in no-frills beach *bandas* sharing toilets, nicer self-contained bungalows on the sand, cool stone garden cottages, and suites and rooms up on the cliff top. Full-moon parties are an institution.

### Getting There & Away

From Stone Town, dalla-dalla 116 (Nungwi) can drop you at the Kendwa turn-off, from where it's about a 2km walk to the beach along an unpaved track. If you're driving, this access road is passable in 2WD, with some care needed over the rocky patches.

From Nungwi, it's possible to walk to Kendwa at low tide along the beach in about 30 minutes, but take care as there have been some muggings. Alternatively, you can arrange boat transfers with hotels in both Nungwi and Kendwa.

## Paje

☎024

Paje has a wide, white beach at the junction where the coastal road north to Bwejuu and south to Jambiani joins with the road from Zanzibar Town. It's quite built up, with a cluster of small-scale places on the beach and a party atmosphere. Paje is also Zanzibar's main kite-surfing centre; during the season, between December and June, the sea is filled with surfers, often so much so that it can be difficult to find a quiet spot to swim.

### Activities

**Paje by Kite** KITESURFING
(Map p670; www.pajebykite.net; board & kite rental per half-day from US$20) Affiliated with Paje by Night hotel, this IKO centre offers kite rental and courses, as well as wake-boarding, speed-boating and other thrill-seeking water sports.

### Sleeping & Eating

**Jambo Beach Bungalows** BUNGALOW $
(Map p670; ☎0774 529960; jambo.booking@hotmail.com; dm/d/tr US$23/55/75) The frayed and laid-back Jambo is on the beach just north of Paje village. Its rather tatty thatched bungalows have a mix of sand and concrete floors, rustic wooden furniture, fans and mosquito nets. There's a beach bar, a simple restaurant and Friday night parties.

**Paradise Beach Bungalows** BUNGALOW $$
(Map p670; ☎0777 414129, 0785 340516; http://nakama.main.jp/paradisebeachbungalows; s/d US$60/70) This long-standing Japanese-run place is hidden among the palm trees in a quiet beachside compound at the northern edge of Paje and slightly removed from the main cluster of hotels. Each room has two large beds, and there's a restaurant serving tasty food, including sushi and other Japanese cuisine with advance order, plus local fare.

**Dhow Inn** BOUTIQUE HOTEL **$$$**
(Map p670; ☎0777 525828; www.dhowinn.com; d US$150-250; P❄📶🏊) With its 28 architect-designed bungalows clustered around three pools and set amid sculptural gardens of bright-red canna flowers and palms, Dhow Inn is a vision of style amid Paje's rough-and-ready hotel scene. Beige-on-white interiors soothe heat-weary travellers, while the main clubhouse offer a games room, a laundry (Tsh10,000 per load) and a spa.

## ℹ Getting There & Away

Dalla-dalla 324 runs several times daily between Paje and Stone Town (Tsh1500) en route to/from Bwejuu. The Makunduchi–Michamvi dalla-dalla also stops at Paje.

# Jambiani

POP 8000 / ☎024

Jambiani is a long village on a stunning stretch of coastline. The village itself, a sun-baked and somnolent collection of thatch and coral-rag houses, is stretched out over more than a kilometre starting just south of Paje. The sea is an ethereal shade of turquoise and is usually dotted with *ngalawa* (outrigger canoes), while on the beach women tend seaweed farms. It's one of the best places on the island to gain an insight into village life.

## Sleeping

**Garden Bungalows** BUNGALOW **$**
(Map p670; ☎0779 121002, 0777 497718; info@garden-bungalows.com; dm US$25, s/d/tr from US$35/60/75) These beautifully constructed bungalows with terraces and *makuti*-thatch roofs are located right on the beach and presided over by the creative owner, Dulla. The popular bar serves pina coladas as well as *dafu* (young coconuts), fresh juices and shakes, and there's some tasty Swahili cuisine on offer, from coconut-crusted fish to *pili pili* (spicy) prawns.

★ **Red Monkey Lodge** BUNGALOW **$$**
(Map p670; ☎0777 713366; www.redmonkeylodge.com; r US$65-110; 📶) 🍃 Red Monkey has nine minimal-chic rooms overlooking the beach at the southern end of Jambiani village. It has an ethical, environmentally friendly outlook with furniture made from recycled dhows, soaps supplied by the Seaweed Centre in Paje and a free water dispenser in the restaurant.

**Casa del Mar Hotel** HOTEL **$$**
(Map p670; ☎0778 067510, 0777 455446; www.casa-delmar-zanzibar.com; r downstairs/upstairs from US$90/110; 🏊) Colourful Casa del Mar brings a dash of design to Jambiani with 14 rooms in two double-storey houses set amid tropical gardens full of papaya, guava and fragrant frangipani. All the furniture and artworks were made in Jambiani and many of the staff come from the village.

**Blue Oyster Hotel** HOTEL **$$**
(Map p670; ☎0783 045796, 0779 883554; www.blueoysterhotel.com; s US$65-135, d US$75-150; P📶) Personable and professional, Blue Oyster offers good-value accommodation in Jambiani with locally furnished rooms in two-storey villas overlooking the sea on a lovely stretch of beach. Loungers dot the beach in front and there's an open-air terrace restaurant serving plates of coconut curry and mango kingfish.

## Eating

**Kiddo's Cafe** ZANZIBARI **$**
(Map p670; ☎0773 498949; meals Tsh8000-18,000; ⏲10am-6pm; 🍸👪) Sit beneath suspended dhow sails downstairs or climb to the treehouse-style upper bar decorated with interesting flotsam and bright soft furnishings. Gourmet juices are similarly colourful, combining pineapple, mango, passionfruit and coconut milk, and are accompanied by light snacks of pancakes, omelettes, salads and grilled fish. Affiliated with **Mango Beach House** (Map p670; ☎0784 405391, 0773 498949; www.mango-beachhouse.com); you'll need to book ahead for dinner.

**Kim's Restaurant** ZANZIBARI **$**
(Map p670; ☎0777 457733; meals Tsh5000-15,000; ⏲11am-9pm) Dig your toes into the sandy floor of this palm-thatched restaurant and tuck into spicy fish samosas, whole grilled fish and octopus curry. It's best to order in advance and with time to spare. Eating here is a leisurely experience. It's signposted from the easily located Blue Oyster Hotel.

## ℹ Getting There & Away

Dalla-dalla 309 runs several times daily from Darajani Market in Stone Town to Jambiani (Tsh1200). The Makunduchi–Michamvi dalla-dalla also stops at Jambiani. South of Jambiani the coastal road deteriorates to become a sandy, rocky track. All public transport uses the new tarmac road.

## Pemba

For much of its history, Pemba has been overshadowed by Zanzibar, its larger neighbour to the south. Although the islands are separated by only 50km of water, relatively few tourists cross the channel. Those who do, however, are seldom disappointed.

Unlike flat, sandy Zanzibar, Pemba's terrain is hilly, fertile and lushly vegetated. In the days of the Arab traders, it was even referred to as Jazirat al Khuthera (the Green Island). Much of Pemba's coast is lined with mangroves and lagoons, interspersed with a few good stretches of sand and some idyllic islets. Offshore, coral reefs, the steeply dropping walls of the Pemba Channel and an abundance of fish offer some of East Africa's best diving.

Throughout, Pemba remains largely 'undiscovered', and you'll still have most things to yourself, which is a big part of the island's appeal.

### Sleeping

**Pemba Island Hotel** HOTEL **$$**
(☎0777 490041; pembaisland@gmail.com; Wesha Rd, Chake Chake; s/d/tr US$50/70/100; ❄📶) Clean rooms with cable TV, air-conditioning, nets and hot water, plus a rooftop restaurant serving good home-cooked meals such as *samaki na wali* (fish and rice) with spicy *kachumbari* salad. Nothing special, nothing wrong, and the location is conveniently central.

**Hotel Archipelago** HOTEL **$$**
(Hifadhi Hotel; ☎024-245 2775; baraka@zanlink.com; Tibirinzi St, Chake Chake; s/d US$60/80; ❄📶🏊) This glass-fronted hotel brings a shock of modernity to Chake Chake with 14 turquoise rooms with swagged curtains, Zanzibari beds, mini-fridges and bathroom toiletries. It also has the only pool in town, and two Swahili restaurants.

**Manta Resort** RESORT **$$$**
(☎0776 718853, 0776 718852; www.themantaresort.com; Verani Beach, Kigomasha Peninsula; s/d from US$340/570, underwater r US$1500, all with full board; ❄@📶🏊) Superbly situated on Verani Beach, the Manta Resort rests on a breezy escarpment with perfect ocean views. Accommodation is in a mix of seafront and garden cottages with private terraces, polished concrete floors and comfy king-sized beds. There's also an 'underwater room' with amazing views of manta rays, octopus and tropical fish.

### Getting There & Away

**AIR**

**Pemba-Karume Airport** (PMA; Chake Chake) is 6km east of Chake Chake. ZanAir (www.zanair.com), Coastal Aviation (www.coastal.co.tz) and Auric Air (www.auricair.com) offer daily flights from Dar es Salaam to Pemba via Zanzibar (from US$125/100 from Dar/Zanzibar to Pemba). Connections to Tanga are also possible with Coastal (US$100) and Auric (US$65).

**BOAT**

Ferries to/from Zanzibar and Dar es Salaam dock in Mkoani.

**Azam Marine** (p676) Offers the most reliable service twice weekly from Dar es Salaam (VIP/adult/child US$80/70/50). Zanzibar to Pemba tickets cost US$40/35/25.

An immigration officer usually checks passports on arrival. If you don't see them at the port and you aren't coming from Zanzibar, you're required to go the immigration office and sign in.

# NORTHEASTERN TANZANIA

Northeastern Tanzania's highlights are its coastline, its mountains and its cultures. These, combined with the area's long history, easy access and lack of crowds, make it an appealing focal point for a Tanzania sojourn.

## Bagamoyo

POP 15,000 / ☎023

Strolling through Bagamoyo's narrow, unpaved streets takes you back to the mid-19th century, when the town was one of the most important settlements along the East African coast and the terminus of the trade caravan route linking Lake Tanganyika with the sea. Slaves, ivory, salt and copra were unloaded before being shipped to Zanzibar and elsewhere, and many European explorers, including Richard Burton, Henry Morton Stanley and David Livingstone, began and ended their trips here. In 1868 French missionaries established Freedom Village at Bagamoyo as a shelter for ransomed slaves, and for the remainder of the century the town served as a way station for missionaries travelling from Zanzibar to the interior.

Bagamoyo's unhurried pace and long history make it an agreeable day or weekend excursion from Dar es Salaam. But visit soon: once disputed plans for a new port go through, the ambience is likely to rapidly change.

## Sights

**Bagamoyo Town** HISTORIC SITE
(adult/child Tsh20,000/10,000) With its cobwebbed portals and crumbling German-era colonial buildings, central Bagamoyo, or *Mji Mkongwe* (Stone Town) as it's known locally, is well worth exploration. The most interesting area is along Ocean Rd. Here you'll find the old German **boma**, built in 1897, and **Liku House**, which served as the German administrative headquarters.

**Kaole Ruins** RUINS
(adult/child Tsh20,000/10,000; 8am-4pm Mon-Fri, 9am-5pm Sat & Sun) Just southeast of Bagamoyo are these atmospheric ruins. At their centre are the remains of a 13th-century mosque, which is one of the oldest in mainland Tanzania and also one of the oldest in East Africa. It was built in the days when the Sultan of Kilwa held sway over coastal trade, and long before Bagamoyo had assumed any significance.

## Sleeping

**Funky Squids B&B** B&B $
(0755 047802; the.funky.squids@gmail.com; s/d US$37/47; P) This beachside place has a handful of modest rooms in a small house just back from the beach, and a large beachfront bar-restaurant. It's at the southern end of town, next door to (and immediately south of) the Bagamoyo College of Arts (Chuo cha Sanaa).

**Firefly** HISTORIC HOTEL $$
(0759 177393; www.fireflybagamoyo.com; India St; camping US$10, dm/r US$15/60; ) This is a fine choice, with camping on a large lawn sloping down towards the sea (although there is no beach access) and mostly very spacious and atmospheric rooms (including a large family room) in an old Arab merchant's house. There's a small restaurant and an outdoor poolside lounge. The location on the edge of the old town is excellent.

**Travellers Lodge** LODGE $$
(023-244 0077, 0754 855485; www.travellers-lodge.com; camping US$8, cottages s US$60-70, d US$80-90; ) With its relaxed atmosphere and reasonable prices, this is among the best-value beach places. Accommodation is in clean, pleasant cottages scattered around expansive grounds, some with two large beds. There's a restaurant and a good children's play area. It's just south of the entrance to the Catholic mission.

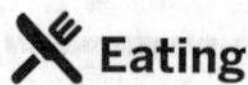

## Eating

**Nashe's Cafe** CAFE $
(0676 506705, 023-244 0171; Mji Mkongwe; mains Tsh6000-15,000; 9am-10pm Mon-Sat, 10am-10pm Su; ) Tasty seafood and meat grills served on a nice rooftop terrace in the centre of the old town. It also does good coffee.

**Funky Squids Beach Bar & Grill** TANZANIAN, EUROPEAN $
(0755 047802; funky.squids@gmail.com; meals Tsh10,000-20,000; 11am-10pm; P) This large, beachfront bar-restaurant serves a good selection of tasty meat and seafood grills, which can be enjoyed on a large terrace looking out over the sea.

## Information

**Tourist Information Office** (8.30am-4.30pm) The tourist information office at the town entrance can set you up with guides for walking tours of the old town, as well as for excursions to the Kaole Ruins and further afield.

## Getting There & Away

**BUS**

Dalla-dallas from 'Makumbusho' (north of Dar es Salaam along the New Bagamoyo road, and accessed via dalla-dalla from New Posta, Tsh500) head to Bagamoyo (Tsh2200, two hours) throughout the day. The transport stand in Bagamoyo is about 700m from the town centre just off the road heading to Dar es Salaam. Taxis to the town centre charge from Tsh2000, and *bajajis* (tuk-tuks) slightly less. There is also a daily dalla-dalla to Saadani village via Msata on the main Arusha highway, departing Bagamoyo at about 10am (Tsh10,000, three hours).

**BOAT**

Nonmotorised dhows to Zanzibar cost around Tsh5000 (around Tsh10,000 to Tsh15,000 for motorised boats) and take around four hours with a good wind. You'll need to register first with the immigration officer in the old customs building, which is also the departure point. Departure times vary, and are often around 1am, arriving in Zanzibar sometime the next morning if all goes well. There is no regular dhow traffic direct to Saadani or Pangani.

# Tanga

POP 273,300 / 027

Tanga, a major industrial centre until the collapse of the sisal market, is Tanzania's second-largest seaport and its fourth-largest town behind Dar es Salaam, Mwanza and Arusha. Despite its size, it's an agreeable place with a sleepy, semicolonial atmosphere, wide streets filled with cyclists and motorcycles, intriguing architecture and faded charm. It makes a pleasant stop en route to or from Mombasa, and is a springboard to the beaches around Pangani, about 50km south.

## Sights

**Urithi Tanga Museum** MUSEUM
(0784 440068; Independence Ave; Tsh5000; 9am-5pm) Tanga's old *boma* has been rehabilitated, and now houses this small but worthwhile museum, with historical photos and artefacts from the area.

**Toten Island** HISTORIC SITE
Directly offshore from Tanga is this small, mangrove-ringed island ('Island of the Dead') with the overgrown ruins of a mosque dating at least from the 17th century and some 18th- and 19th-century gravestones. Pottery fragments from the 15th century have also been found, indicating that the island may have been settled during the Shirazi era. Toten Island's apparently long history ended in the late 19th century, when its inhabitants moved to the mainland.

## Sleeping

**ELCT Mbuyukenda Tumaini Hostel** GUESTHOUSE $
(0658131557, 0763410059; mbuyukendahostel@elct-ned.org; Hospital Rd; s/d Tsh25,000/30,000; P ❄) Rather faded overall, but the newer rooms (all doubles) are decent value for the price, and the compound is quiet, spacious and green, making this a good budget choice. It's just southwest of Bombo Hospital, and diagonally opposite Katani House. Meals (Tsh7000) can be arranged with advance notice. Taxis charge Tsh5000 from the bus stand.

**Majuba's B&B** B&B $$
(0784 395391, 0715 395391; graberh1@gmail.com; Hospital Rd; r US$100; P ❄ 📶 🏊) This B&B offers two quiet, spacious and beautifully decorated luxury rooms, each with a minifridge and satellite TV.

**Mkonge Hotel** HOTEL $$
(027-264 3440, 027-264 4444; www.mkongehotel.com; Hospital Rd; s/d US$82/92, with sea view US$92/102; P ❄ 📶 🏊) The imposing Mkonge Hotel, in a lovely setting on a vast, grassy lawn overlooking the sea, has reasonably comfortable rooms (worth the extra money for a sea view), a restaurant and wonderful views.

## Eating

**Pizzeria d'Amore** ITALIAN $
(0715 395391, 0784 395391; Hospital Rd; meals Tsh15,000-20,000; 11.30am-2pm & 6.30-10pm Tue-Sun) A small garden restaurant with tasty pizzas, pasta, seafood and continental fare. It has an upstairs, breezy terrace for dining, and a bar.

**Food Palace** INDIAN $
(027-264 6816; Market St; meals Tsh6000-10,000; 7.30am-3.30pm Mon-Thu, 7.30am-3.30pm & 7-10pm Fri-Sun; ✍) Tasty Indian snacks and meals, including some vegetarian selections, and good local ambience. Overall good value.

**Tanga Yacht Club** EUROPEAN $$
(027-264 4246; Hospital Rd, Ras Kazone; admission Tsh6000, meals Tsh12,000-20,000; 10am-2.30pm & 5.30pm-10pm Mon-Thurs, 10am-11pm Fri-Sun; 📶) Seafood and mixed grill dishes, overlooking the water.

## Information

### DANGERS & ANNOYANCES

The harbour area is seedy and best avoided. In the evenings, take care around Port Rd and Independence Ave near Jamhuri Park.

### MONEY

**Barclays** (Independence Ave)
**CRDB** (Tower St)
**Exim** (Independence Ave) Next to Barclays.
**NBC** (cnr Bank & Market Sts) Just west of the market; changes cash.

### TOURIST INFORMATION

**Tanga Cultural Tourism Enterprise** (027-264 5254, 0765 162875, 0713 375367; www.tangatourismcoalition.com; 8.30am-4pm Mon-Fri, to 1pm Sat) The helpful staff here can provide information on nearby attractions, and advice for accommodation and transport options. They also arrange excursions and guides for tours in town and nearby.

## Getting There & Away

### BOAT

Ferry service between Tanga and Wete on Pemba is currently suspended, and dhows are not recommended on this route.

### BUS

Ratco and other buses for Dar es Salaam depart daily every few hours from 6am to 2pm in each direction (Tsh15,000 to Tsh17,000, six hours).

To Arusha there are at least three departures daily between about 6am and 11am (Tsh17,000 to Tsh19,000, seven to eight hours). To Lushoto there are several direct buses daily departing from 7am (Tsh7000 to Tsh8000, four hours)

To Pangani (Tsh3000, 1½ hours) there are several larger buses and many dalla-dallas throughout the day along the coastal road.

All transport leaves from the main bus stand on Taifa Rd ('Double Rd'), at the corner of Street No 12. It's about 1.5km south of the town centre (Tsh5000 in a taxi), and south of the railway tracks in the Ngamiani section.

# Usambara Mountains

With their wide vistas, cool climate, winding paths and picturesque villages, the Usambaras are one of northeastern Tanzania's delights. Rural life revolves around a cycle of colourful, bustling market days that rotate from one village to the next, and is largely untouched by the booming safari scene and influx of 4WDs in nearby Arusha. It's easily possible to spend at least a week trekking from village to village or exploring with day walks.

The Usambaras, which are part of the ancient Eastern Arc chain, are divided into two ranges separated by a 4km-wide valley. The western Usambaras, around Lushoto, are the more accessible. The eastern Usambaras, around Amani, are less developed. Both ranges are densely populated, with an average of more than 300 people per sq km. The main tribes are the Sambaa, Kilindi, Zigua and Mbugu.

## Lushoto

POP 500,000 / ☎027

This leafy highland town is nestled in a fertile valley at about 1200m, surrounded by pines and eucalyptus mixed with banana plants and other tropical foliage. It's the centre of the western Usambaras and makes an ideal base for hikes into the surrounding hills. Lushoto is also the heartland of the Wasambaa people (the name 'Usambara' is a corruption of Wasambaa or Washambala, meaning 'scattered'). Local culture is strong. In Muheza and parts of the Tanga region closer to the coast, Swahili is used almost exclusively. Here however, Sambaa is the language of choice for most residents.

### Sleeping & Eating

**St Eugene's Lodge** GUESTHOUSE $

(☎027-264 0055, 0784 523710; www.s243760778.onlinehome.us/lushoto; s/tw/tr/ste US$25/45/54/60) Run by an order of sisters, the unpretentious St Eugene's has pleasant rooms with balconies and views over the surrounding gardens. Tasty meals are served, and homemade cheese and jam are for sale. St Eugene's is along the main road, about 3.5km before Lushoto, on the left coming from Soni. Ask to get dropped at the Montessori Centre.

**Lawns Hotel** LODGE $$

(☎0652 315914, 0759 914144; www.lawnshotel.com; camping Tsh15,000, s Tsh30,000, d Tsh50,000-130,000, f from Tsh185,000; P 📶) This Lushoto institution is now under new ownership, and is getting a facelift. It's full of charm, with vine-covered buildings, extensive gardens and fireplaces in some rooms. There's also good camping, a sauna, a restaurant, a lovely terrace and plenty to do for children. It's signposted at the entrance to town.

**Mamma Mia Pizza** PIZZA $

(Main Rd; mains Tsh14,000-17,000; ⏰11am-9pm Tue-Sat, 2.30-9pm Sun & Mon) Very good pizzas, pastas, brownies, shakes, smoothies and more in this slick eatery on the main road.

**Tumaini Cafe & Makuti African Restaurant** TANZANIAN, EUROPEAN $

(☎027-266 0094; Main Rd; meals Tsh6000-12,000; ⏰7am-9.30pm) Tumaini Cafe – on the main road next to the Telecom building – offers cheap snacks, breakfasts and meals, including banana milkshakes, freshly baked rolls and well-prepared continental fare. In the same compound and under the same management is Makuti African Restaurant, which is open for lunch and dinner only and serves tasty local food.

### Information

There are several ATMs in the town centre.

**CRDB** (Main Rd) ATM (MasterCard only); at the Western Union building, diagonally opposite the prison, at the northern (uphill) end of the main road.

**National Microfinance Bank** (Main Rd; ⏰8.30am-3.30pm Mon-Fri) Exchanges dollars to Tanzanian shillings.

### Getting There & Away

Dalla-dallas go throughout the day between Lushoto and Mombo (Tsh4000, one hour), the junction town on the main highway.

Daily direct buses travel from Lushoto to Tanga (Tsh7000, four hours), Dar es Salaam (Tsh15,000 to Tsh17,000, six to seven hours) and Arusha (Tsh15,000, six hours), with most departures from 7am. To get to the lodges near Migambo, take the road heading uphill and northeast of town to Magamba, turn right at the signposted junction and continue for 7km to Migambo junction, from where the lodges are signposted.

# NORTHERN TANZANIA

## Moshi

POP 184,290 / ☎027

The noticeably clean capital of the densely populated Kilimanjaro region sits at the foot of Mt Kilimanjaro and makes a good introduction to the splendours of the north. It's a low-key place with an appealing blend of African and Asian influences and a self-sufficient, prosperous feel, due in large part to it being the centre of one of Tanzania's major coffee-growing regions. Virtually all visitors are here to climb Mt Kilimanjaro or to recover after having done so. Yet, there is much more to do, including cultural tours and hikes on the mountain's lower slopes.

### Tours

**TinTin Tours** SAFARI, TREKKING
(☎0657 123766; www.tintintours.org) This low-key, friendly but very professional outfit offers reliable Kilimanjaro treks and northern circuit safaris.

**African Scenic Safaris** SAFARI, TREKKING
(☎0783 080239; www.africanscenicsafaris.com) Well-organised cultural tours, northern circuit safaris and Kilimanjaro treks.

**Summit Expeditions & Nomadic Experience** CYCLING, TREKKING
(☎0787 740282; www.nomadicexperience.com) Expertly guided Kilimanjaro treks, plus cycling, walks and cultural excursions on the mountain's lower slopes, and customised northern circuit wildlife safaris.

**Just Kilimanjaro** TREKKING
(☎0789 743272; www.just-kilimanjaro.com) A small, highly regarded operator offering expertly guided Kilimanjaro treks.

**Tanzania Journeys** SAFARI, TREKKING
(☎0787 834152, 027-275 4295; www.tanzaniajourneys.com) High-quality northern circuit, community-focused vehicle, active and cultural safaris, including Kilimanjaro treks, day hikes and cultural tours in the Moshi area.

### Sleeping

**Nyota Bed & Breakfast** B&B $
(www.nyotabedandbreakfast.com; Rengua Rd; tw/tr with shared bathroom US$40/60) This small place has spacious, spotless rooms with fans and some with verandas, plus carefully prepared breakfasts and a convenient central location. Overall, a recommended budget choice.

**Hibiscus** B&B $
(☎0766-312516; www.thehibiscusmoshi.com; Paris St; s/tw US$30/40; ) This cosy B&B has spotless, nicely decorated rooms, all with fan and most with private bathroom, plus a pleasant garden and meals on request. It's in a quiet residential area just northwest of the town centre off the Arusha road.

★ **AMEG Lodge** LODGE $$
(☎0754 058268, 027-275 0175; www.ameglodge.com; off Lema Rd; s/d from US$82/106, s/d ste US$135/159; P) This friendly place wins plaudits from travellers for its lovely setting in 4.5 acres of manicured gardens with palm trees and frangipanis, 4km northwest of the town centre. Attractive rooms with broad verandas and plenty of space lie dotted around the compound, service is friendly, and the overall feel is that of a rural oasis on the fringe of the city.

**Bristol Cottages** HOTEL $$
(☎027-275 5083; www.bristolcottages.com; 98 Rindi Lane; s/d US$60/90, s/d/tr cottage US$70/100/130, s/d/tr ste US$80/110/140; P) This place exudes a sense of peace upon entering – the leafy compound is an attractive counterpoint to the busy Moshi streets – and the rooms are well presented; the suites are particularly spacious. For all this talk of peace, however, early morning noise can be a problem. Even so, it's our midrange pick in the downtown.

### Eating

**Jay's Kitchen** KOREAN $
(☎0768 607456, 0765 311618; www.facebook.com/JaysAdventureTanzania; Boma Rd; meals Tsh8000-20,000; 11am-9pm Wed-Mon) Jay's boasts tasty Korean food and sushi, a central location, and good garden seating. Also offers takeaway service.

**Mr Feng Chinese Restaurant** CHINESE $
(☎0768 565656; meals Tsh8000-17,000; noon-3pm & 6.30-10pm Mon-Fri, 11am-10pm Sat & Sun; ) Delicious Chinese food, including many veg options, plus tranquil garden seating and a friendly, helpful proprietor make this a recommended spot for a meal in Moshi.

**Milan's** INDIAN $
(Makinga St; meals Tsh6000-10,000; 11am-9.30pm; ) This colourful all-vegetarian spot is our favourite Indian restaurant, and not only because the prices are so low: it's also really delicious.

# Moshi

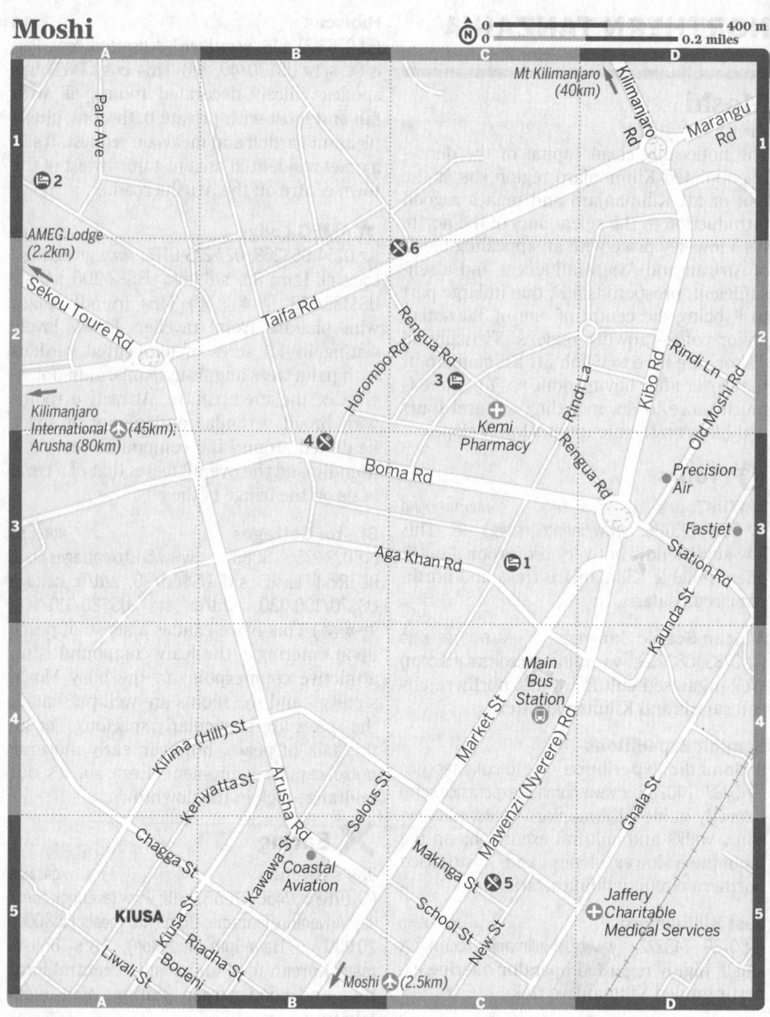


## Moshi

**Sleeping**

1 Bristol Cottages ........ C3
2 Hibiscus ........ A1
3 Nyota Bed & Breakfast ........ C2

**Eating**

4 Jay's Kitchen ........ B3
5 Milan's ........ C5
6 Mr Feng Chinese Restaurant ........ C2

## Information

**Jaffery Charitable Medical Services** (027-275 1843; Ghala St; 8.30am-5pm Mon-Fri, to 1pm Sat) Medical clinic with Moshi's most reliable laboratory.

**Kemi Pharmacy** (027-275 1560; Rengua Rd; 7am-7pm Mon-Sat) One of numerous pharmacies dotted around the city centre.

**Kilimanjaro Christian Medical Centre** (027-275 4377/80; www.kcmc.ac.tz; off Sokoine Rd; 24hr) Around 4.5km north of the centre.

## Getting There & Away

### AIR

Kilimanjaro International Airport (KIA) is 50km west of town, halfway to Arusha.The standard taxi fare to/from Moshi is Tsh50,000, although drivers will often request more. There's also the small Moshi airport just southwest of town along the extension of Market St (Tsh5000 to central hotels), which handles Coastal Aviation flights and occasional charters.

**Coastal Aviation** (0785 500445, 0785 500729; www.coastal.co.tz; Arusha Rd; 8.30am-5pm Mon-Fri, to noon Sat) Flies daily to and from Moshi airport (if there are enough passengers) on the Arusha–Tanga–Pangani–Pemba–Zanzibar–Dar es Salaam circuit, with links also possible to the northern national parks.

**Fastjet** (0784 108900; www.fastjet.com; Kaunda St) Daily flights between KIA and Dar es Salaam with onward connections across Tanzania and East Africa.

**Precision Air** (0787 800820, 027-275 3495; www.precisionairtz.com; Old Moshi Rd; 8am-5pm Mon-Fri, 9am-1pm Sat & Sun) Flies from KIA to Dar es Salaam, Zanzibar and Mwanza.

### BUS

Buses and minibuses run throughout the day to Arusha (Tsh3000, two hours) and Marangu (Tsh1500 to Tsh2000, 1½ hours).

The **bus station** (Market St) is conveniently located in the middle of the city.

# Marangu

POP 23,000 / 027

Nestled on the lower slopes of Mt Kilimanjaro, 40km northeast of Moshi amid dense stands of banana and coffee plants, is the lively, leafy market town of Marangu. It has an agreeable highland ambience, a cool climate and a good selection of hotels, all of which organise treks. While you'll sometimes get slightly better budget deals in Moshi, Marangu makes a convenient base for Kili climbs using the Marangu or Rongai routes, and it's an enjoyable stop in its own right.

Marangu is also the heartland of the Chagga people, and there are many possibilities for walks and cultural activities. *Marangu* means 'place of water' and the surrounding area is laced with small streams and waterfalls (most with a small entry charge to visit).

## Sleeping

**Coffee Tree Campsite** CAMPGROUND $

(027-275 6604, 0754 691433; kilimanjaro@iwayafrica.com; camping/chalet per person US$8/15; @) This place has expansive, trim grounds, hot-water showers, tents for hire and chalets of varying sizes. It's about 5km north of Marangu and 700m east of the main road and signposted. There's no food, but there are several eateries nearby. The owner is committed to slowing the environmental destruction of Kilimanjaro, and is a good source of information on local conservation efforts.

**Babylon Lodge** LODGE $$

(027-275 6355, 0762 016016; www.babylonlodge.com; s/d/tr US$50/70/80; P @ ) Friendly Babylon has straightforward, clean twin- and double-bedded rooms clustered around small, attractive gardens. It's often somewhat more flexible than other properties on negotiating Kili trek packages, and staff are very helpful with helping you sort out arrivals and departures via public transport. It's 700m east of the main junction.

**Marangu Hotel** LODGE $$

(027-275 6594, 0754 886092; www.marangu-hotel.com; camping US$10, s/d/tr with half board US$120/200/275; ) This long-standing hotel is the first place you reach coming from Moshi. It has a cosy and appealing Old World ambience, pleasant rooms in expansive, flowering grounds, lovely gardens, and a campsite with hot-water showers. Room prices are discounted if you join one of the hotel's fully equipped climbs.

## Getting There & Away

Minibuses run throughout the day between Moshi and Marangu's main junction (Marangu Mtoni; Tsh1500 to Tsh2000, 1½ hours). Once in Marangu, there are sporadic pick-ups from the main junction to the park gate (Tsh1500), 5km further on. For the Holili border crossing, change at Himo junction.

If you're travelling to Marangu via public bus from Arusha or Dar es Salaam, ask the driver to drop you at Himo Junction, from where frequent dalla-dallas go up to Marangu junction (Tsh1000).

# Mt Kilimanjaro National Park

**Mt Kilimanjaro National Park** (027-275 6602; www.tanzaniaparks.go.tz; adult/child US$83/24; park gates 6.30am-6.30pm, park headquarters 8am-5pm) is one of Tanzania's most visited parks. Unlike the other northern parks, this isn't for the wildlife, although wildlife is there. Rather, it is to gaze in awe at a snow-capped equatorial mountain, and to climb to the top of Africa.

At the heart of the park is the 5896m Mt Kilimanjaro, Africa's highest mountain and one of the continent's most magnificent

## CLIMBING MT KILIMANJARO

Mt Kilimanjaro can be climbed at any time of year, though weather patterns are notoriously erratic and difficult to predict. Overall, the best time for climbing the mountain is in the dry season, from late June to October, and from late December to February or early March, just after the short rains and before the long rains. During November and March/April, it's more likely that paths through the forest will be slippery, and that routes up to the summit, especially the Western Breach, will be covered by snow. That said, you can also have a streak of beautiful, sunny days during these times.

### Costs

Kilimanjaro can only be climbed with a licensed guide, and we recommend organising your climb through a tour company. No-frills four-night/five-day treks up the Marangu Route start at about US$1500, including park fees and taxes, and no-frills six-day budget treks on the Machame Route start at around US$1900. Prices start at about US$1500 on the Rongai Route, and about US$2000 for a seven-day trek on the Shira Plateau Route. For other routes, the starting points are further from Moshi and transport costs can be significant, so clarify whether they're included in the price.

Most of the better companies provide dining tents, decent-to-good cuisine and various other extras to both make the experience more enjoyable and to maximise your chances of getting to the top. If you choose a really cheap trip you risk having inadequate meals, mediocre guides, few comforts, and problems with hut bookings and park fees. Also remember that an environmentally responsible trek usually costs more.

Whatever you pay for your trek, remember that the following park fees are not negotiable and should be part of any quote from your trekking operator:

**National park entry fees** US$83 per adult per day

**Hut/camping fees** US$71/59 per person per night

**Rescue fee** US$24 per person per trip

Other costs will vary depending on the company, which should handle food, tents (if required), guides and porters, and transport to/from the trailhead, but not tips.

### Guides & Porters

Guides, and at least one porter (for the guide), are obligatory and are provided by your trekking company. You can carry your own gear on the Marangu Route, although porters are generally used, but one or two porters per trekker are essential on all other routes.

All guides must be registered with the national park authorities. If in doubt, check that your guide's permit is up to date. On Kili, the guide's job is to show you the way and that's it.

sights. It's also one of the world's highest volcanoes, and the highest free-standing mountain in the world, rising from cultivated farmlands on the lower slopes, through lush rainforest to alpine meadows, and finally across a barren lunar landscape to the twin summits of Kibo and Mawenzi. Kilimanjaro's third volcanic cone, Shira, is on the mountain's western side. The lower rainforest is home to many animals, including buffaloes, elephants, leopards and monkeys, and elands are occasionally seen in the saddle area between Kibo and Mawenzi.

# Arusha

POP 416,440 / ☎027

Arusha is a large, sprawling city with all of the contradictions that brings.

On the one hand, Arusha offers a nice break from the rigours of life on the African road – it has excellent places to stay and eat and, for the most part, it is lush, green and enjoys a temperate climate throughout the year, thanks to its altitude (about 1300m) and location near the foot of Mt Meru. It's also the starting point for many safaris and cultural tours.

Only the best guides, working for reputable companies, will be able to tell you about wildlife, flowers or other features on the mountain.

Porters will carry bags weighing up to 15kg (not including their own food and clothing, which they strap to the outside of your bag), and your bags will be weighed before you set off.

### Trekking Routes

There are seven main trekking routes to the summit. Trekkers on all but the Marangu Route must use tents.

Officially a limit of 60 climbers per route per day is in effect on Kilimanjaro. It's not always enforced, except on the Marangu Route, which is self-limiting because of maximum hut capacities.

**Marangu Route** A trek on this route is typically sold as a four-night, five-day return package, although at least one extra night is highly recommended to help acclimatisation, especially if you've just flown in to Tanzania or arrived from the lowlands.

**Machame Route** This increasingly popular route has a gradual ascent, including a spectacular day contouring the southern slopes before approaching the summit via the top section of the Mweka Route.

**Umbwe Route** Steeper and with a more direct way to the summit than the other routes; it's very enjoyable if you can resist the temptation to gain altitude too quickly. Although this route is direct, the top, very steep section up the Western Breach is often covered in ice or snow, which makes it impassable or extremely dangerous. Many trekkers who attempt it without proper acclimatisation are forced to turn back. An indication of its seriousness is that until fairly recently, the Western Breach was considered a technical mountaineering route. Only consider this route if you're experienced, properly equipped and travelling with a reputable operator.

**Rongai Route** This popular route starts near the Kenyan border and goes up the northern side of the mountain.

**Shira Plateau Route** Also called the Londorosi Route, this attractive route is somewhat longer than the others, but good for acclimatisation if you start trekking from Londorosi gate (rather than driving all the way to the Shira Track trailhead), or if you take an extra day at Shira Hut.

**Mweka Route** For descent only, and often used as part of the Machame, Umbwe and (sometimes) Marangu routes.

**Northern Circuit Route** This route – the longest – initially follows the same path as Shira Plateau Route before turning northwards near Lava Tower and then continuing around the northern ('back') side of Kilimanjaro before tackling the summit via Gilman's Point.

Which brings us to Arusha's alter ego. As the safari capital of northern Tanzania, Arusha is where you're most likely to encounter touts offering safaris, souvenirs and all manner of deals - some genuine, many of them not. Their main haunts are the bus stations and along Boma Rd. The city's downtown area and the main road towards Dodoma are also noisy and packed with people and traffic.

## Tours

**Peace Matunda Tours** CULTURAL
(☎0787 482966, 0757 198076; www.peacematunda.org) Cultural walks and tours around Arusha, plus northern circuit wildlife safaris. Profits go to support the organisation's school and other community projects.

**Wayo Africa** CYCLING, SAFARI
(www.wayoafrica.com) Northern circuit active safaris, including Serengeti walking safaris, cycling around Lake Manyara, canoeing in Arusha National Park and much more.

**IntoAfrica** SAFARI, TREKKING
(www.intoafrica.co.uk) This reliable, long-standing company offers fair-traded cultural safaris and treks in northern Tanzania, including a fascinating seven-day wildlife-cultural safari in Maasai areas.

# Arusha

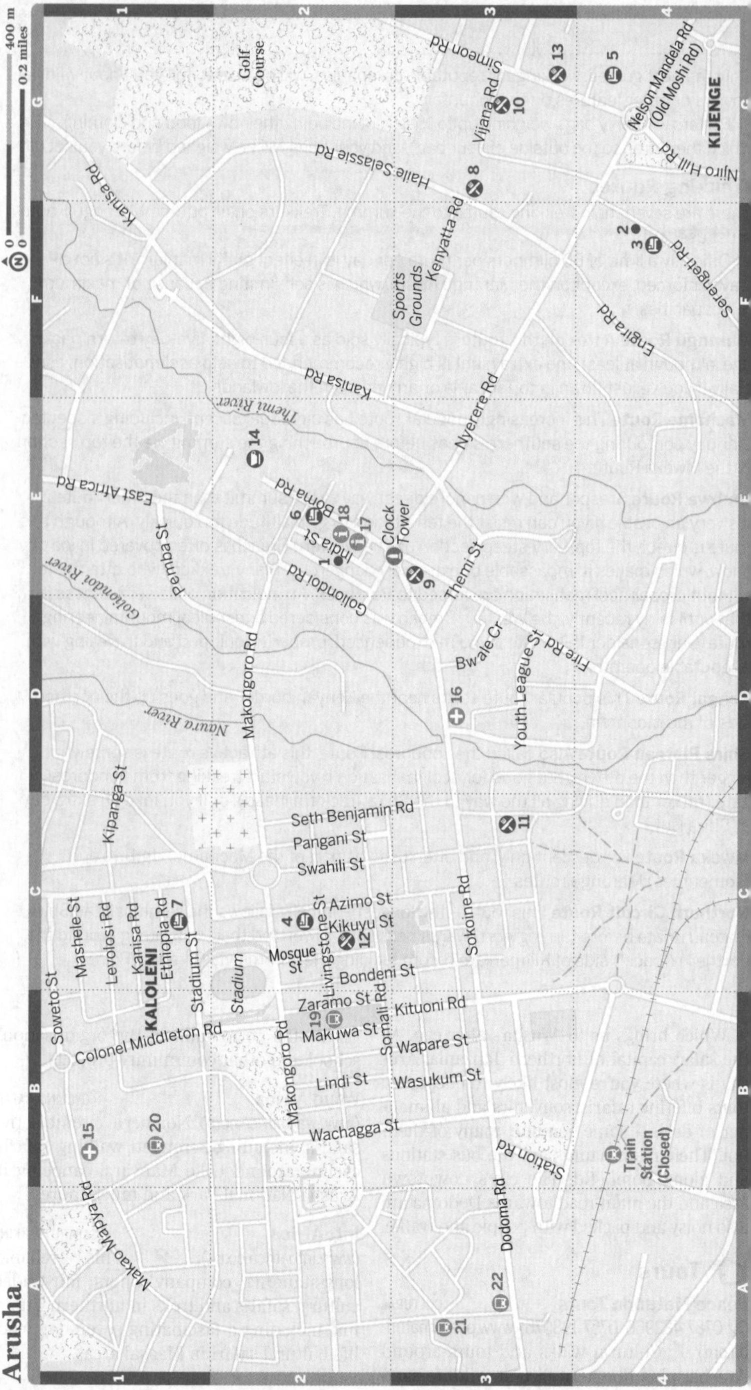

0 400 m
0 0.2 miles

Soweto St
Mashele St
Levolosi Rd
Kanisa Rd
KALOLENI
Ethiopia Rd
7
Stadium St
Colonel Middleton Rd
Makao Mapya Rd
15
20
Kipanga St
Naura River
Goliondoi River
East Africa Rd
Pemba St
Kanisa Rd
Stadium
Makongoro Rd
Makongoro Rd
14
Themi River
Golf Course
Mosque St
4
Livingstone St
19
Zaramo St
Makuwa St
Lindi St
Wachagga St
12
Kikuyu St
Azimo St
Swahili St
Pangani St
Seth Benjamin Rd
Somali Rd
Bondeni St
Kituoni Rd
Wapare St
Wasukum St
Goliondoi Rd
India St
Boma Rd
6
1
18
17
Clock Tower
9
Kanisa Rd
Haile Selassie Rd
Sports Grounds
Kenyatta Rd
8
Vijana Rd
Simeon Rd
10
13
5
21
22
Dodoma Rd
Sokoine Rd
16
Bwale Cr
Themi St
Nyerere Rd
Station Rd
11
Youth League St
Fire Rd
Train Station (Closed)
Engira Rd
2
3
Serengeti Rd
Njiro Hill Rd
Nelson Mandela Rd (Old Moshi Rd)
KIJENGE

## Arusha

**Activities, Courses & Tours**
1 Hoopoe Safaris .......... E2
2 Roy Safaris .......... F4

**Sleeping**
3 African Tulip .......... F4
4 Flamingo Inn .......... C2
5 Impala Hotel .......... G4
6 New Safari Hotel .......... E2
7 Raha Leo .......... C1

**Eating**
8 Blue Heron .......... G3
9 Cafe Barrista .......... E3
10 Eight .......... G3
11 Hot Plate .......... C3
12 Khan's Barbecue .......... C2
13 Spices & Herbs .......... G3

**Drinking & Nightlife**
14 Via Via .......... E2

**Information**
15 Arusha Lutheran Medical Centre .......... B1
16 Moona's Pharmacy .......... D3
17 Ngorongoro Conservation Area Authority Information Office .......... E2
18 Tanzania Tourist Board Tourist Information Centre .......... E2

**Transport**
19 Central Bus Station .......... B2
20 Dar Express .......... B1
21 Kilombero Station .......... A3
22 Mtei Express .......... A3

**Hoopoe Safaris** SAFARI, TREKKING
(027-250 7011; www.hoopoe.com; India St; 8.30am-5.30pm Mon-Fri, to 2pm Sat) A highly regarded company offering community-integrated luxury camping and lodge safaris in the northern circuit; also has its own tented camps at Lake Manyara and mobile camps in the Serengeti.

**Roy Safaris** SAFARI, TREKKING
(027-250 2115; www.roysafaris.com; Serengeti Rd; 8am-5.30pm) A long-standing, reliable operator offering budget and semiluxury camping safaris in the northern circuit, as well as luxury lodge safaris, and Kilimanjaro and Meru treks.

### Sleeping

**★Flamingo Inn** GUESTHOUSE $
(0754-260309; flamingoarusha@yahoo.com; Kikuyu St; s/tw US$20/25; ) This low-key place has sparse but spotlessly clean rooms with fans and nets, a convenient central location, decent breakfasts and friendly staff. Wi-fi costs Tsh1000 per hour, although prices drop the longer you use it.

**Raha Leo** GUESTHOUSE $
(0753 600002; Stadium St; s/d Tsh30,000/40,000; ) This welcoming place has simple but adequate double and twin rooms, some along the corridor, others around an open-air lounge. With hot water and cable TV it's one of the best-value budget options in town. The location is central, but quieter than most.

**Impala Hotel** HOTEL $$
(027-254 3082; www.impalahotel.com; Simeon Rd; s/d/tr US$100/130/160; ) Filling a gap between the small family-run guesthouses and the big luxury hotels, the Impala offers a convenient location, reasonable rooms (ask for a newer one with parquetry floors and safari-themed furnishings) and abundant services such as a foreign-exchange bureau and a restaurant. It's always worth asking for discounts.

**New Safari Hotel** HOTEL $$
(0787 326122, 027-254 5940; www.newsafarihotel.com; Boma Rd; s/d/tr US$100/125/180; ) Once the favourite of white hunters and their tall tales from the African bush, the New Safari was reborn in 2004 and is the pick of the city-centre midrange options. Rooms are generally large, have tiled floors, and boast a touch of class in the decor.

**★African Tulip** BOUTIQUE HOTEL $$$
(027-254 3004, 0783 714104; www.theafricantulip.com; Serengeti Rd; s/d/tr US$190/250/330, ste US$350-550; ) Marketing itself as a luxury boutique hotel, the deservedly popular African Tulip inhabits a quiet green side street and successfully combines an African safari theme with a genteel ambience. The large rooms are supremely comfortable havens from Arusha's noise. There's a whimsical baobab tree in the restaurant, carved wood around the common areas and a small garden around the swimming pool at the back.

### Eating

**★Hot Plate** INDIAN $
(0715 030730, 0783 030730; Navrat St, off Sokoine Rd; mains Tsh6000-12,000; 7.30am-10pm Tue-Sun; ) Delicious Indian food – including southern Indian dishes plus some Punjabi and other dishes, both veg and

non-veg – in a shady, street-side setting. It's down the small side street just next to Manji's petrol station, tucked away behind a leafy green stand of bamboo.

★**Khan's Barbecue** BARBECUE $
(Mosque St; meals Tsh9000-10,000, mixed grill Tsh13,000; 6.30-11pm Mon-Fri, 5-11pm Sat & Sun) This Arusha institution is an auto-spares shop by day (look for the Zubeda Auto Spares sign) and the best known of many earthy roadside barbecues around the market area by night. It lays out a heaping spread of grilled, skewered meat and salad. If you want to experience Arusha like a local, this is a fine place to begin.

**Spices & Herbs** ETHIOPIAN, EUROPEAN $
(0754 313162, 0685 313162; Simeon Rd; mains Tsh14,000-19,000; 11am-10.30pm; ) Unpretentious al fresco spot serving two menus: Ethiopian and continental – ignore the latter and order *injera* (Ethiopian bread) soaked in beef, chicken or lamb sauce, or *yegbeg tibs* (fried lamb with Ethiopian butter, onion, green peppers and rosemary). The service is good and there's plenty of art on the walls.

**Eight** EUROPEAN $$$
(Bay Leaf; 027-254 3055; www.bayleaftz.com; Vijana Rd; mains Tsh16,000-40,000; 8am-11pm; ) Arusha's poshest menu features fresh ingredients and creative dishes such as slow-cooked West Kili lamb shanks. Seating is in a quiet indoor dining room or in the shaded, walled garden. It also offers a great wine list (by the glass and bottle), as well as separate lunch and dinner menus.

## Drinking & Nightlife

**Via Via** CAFE
(Boma Rd; 9am-10pm Fri-Wed, to midnight Thu) This cafe is a good spot for a drink, and one of the best places to find out about upcoming cultural events, many of which are held here. On Thursday nights there's karaoke and a live band (admission Tsh10,000). Things get started at 9pm.

## Information

### DANGERS & ANNOYANCES

At night, take a taxi if you go out. It's not safe to walk after dusk except around the market where the streets remain crowded for a few hours after dark. But even here, be wary and don't carry anything valuable.

### INTERNET ACCESS

There are numerous internet cafes around the market and Clock Tower areas. The normal rate is Tsh2000 per hour. New Safari Hotel has internet in the hotel lobby.

**Cafe Barrista** (0754 288771, 027-254 5677; www.cafebarrista.com; Sokoine Rd; meals Tsh9000-14,000; 7am-6.30pm Mon-Sat, to 2.30pm Sun; ) Has computers and wi-fi (the latter is free if you buy a meal).

### MEDICAL SERVICES

**Akaal Pharmacy** (0715 821700, 0718 444222; Sable Square Shopping Village, Dodoma Rd; 9am-5.30pm Mon-Sat, 11am-4pm Sun) Well-stocked pharmacy en route to the northern parks.

**Arusha Lutheran Medical Centre** (027-254 8030; www.selianlh.habari.co.tz; Makao Mapya Rd; 24hr) This is one of the better medical facilities in the region, but for anything truly serious, go to Nairobi.

**Moona's Pharmacy** (0754 309052, 027-254 5909; Sokoine Rd; 8.45am-5.30pm Mon-Fri, to 2pm Sat) Well-stocked pharmacy, west of NBC bank.

### MONEY

Foreign-exchange bureaus are clustered along Joel Maeda St, India St, and Sokoine Rd between the Nakumatt supermarket and the Clock Tower. Most are open from 8am to 6pm daily, including public holidays. ATMs are scattered around the city centre, and easy to find, although be prepared for long waits, especially on Friday afternoons.

### TOURIST INFORMATION

The bulletin boards at the tourist board tourist info centre and at Cafe Barrista are good spots to find safari mates.

**Ngorongoro Conservation Area Authority (NCAA) Information Office** (027-254 4625; www.ngorongorocrater.go.tz; Boma Rd; 8am-4pm Mon-Fri, 9am-1pm Sat, 10am-1pm Sun) Has free Ngorongoro booklets and a relief map of the conservation area. You'll also need to stop here to arrange payment of your entry fees prior to heading out to the crater.

**Tanzania National Parks Authority** (Tanapa; 027-250 3471; www.tanzaniaparks.go.tz; Dodoma Rd; 8am-4pm Mon-Fri) Just west of town, this office has info on Tanzania's national parks and can help with general information and bookings of park accommodation.

**Tanzania Tourist Board Tourist Information Centre** (TTB; 027-250 3842, 027-250 3843; www.tanzaniatouristboard.com; Boma Rd; 8am-4pm Mon-Fri, 8.30am-1pm Sat) Knowledgeable and helpful staff have information on Arusha, northern circuit parks and other area attractions. They can book Cultural Tourism

Program tours and provide a good free map of Arusha and Moshi. The office also keeps a 'blacklist' of tour operators and a list of registered tour companies.

## Getting There & Away

Arusha has several bus stations. If you want to avoid the bus stations altogether, most buses make a stop on the edge of town before going to the stations. Taxis will be waiting at that location.

When leaving Arusha, the best thing to do is book your ticket the day before, so that in the morning when you arrive with your luggage you can get straight on your bus. For pre-dawn buses, take a taxi to the station and ask the driver to drop you directly at your bus.

Despite what you may hear, there are no luggage fees (unless you have an extraordinarily large pack).

**Central Bus Station** (cnr Somali Rd & Zaramo St) Arusha's biggest bus station is intimidatingly chaotic in the morning and is popular with touts. If you get overwhelmed head straight for a taxi, or duck into the lobby of one of the hotels across the street to get your bearings.

**Dar Express Bus Station** (Makao Mapya Bus Station; Wachagga St) Most of the luxury buses to Dar es Salaam depart from here, including Dar Express and Kilimanjaro Express.

**Kilombero Station** (Makao Mapya Rd) Several companies serving Babati, Singida, Mwanza and other points generally west, including Mtei Express, have their offices and departure points here, about 300m north of Nakumatt supermarket, near Kilombero market.

# Arusha National Park

At 552 sq km, **Arusha National Park** (www.tanzaniaparks.go.tz; adult/child US$54/18; 6.30am-6.30pm) is one Tanzania's smallest, but most beautiful and topographically varied, northern circuit parks. It's dominated by **Mt Meru**, an almost perfect volcanic cone with a spectacular crater. Also notable is **Ngurdoto Crater** (often dubbed Little Ngorongoro) with its swamp-filled floor. Wildlife is present, but for the most part it's a sideshow to the scenery and the trekking and climbing possibilities.

## Sleeping

**Momella Gate Public Campsite** CAMPGROUND **$**
(camping US$36) Arusha National Park has three public campsites in the vicinity of Momella gate, including one with a shower.

**African View Lodge** LODGE **$$**
(0784 419232; www.african-view.com; s/d US$100/140; ) This good-value place features prime views of Mt Meru, an infinity pool, a good restaurant and accommodation in stylishly furnished bungalows dotted around lovely gardens. The in-house tour operator also organises northern circuit safaris, Meru and Kilimanjaro climbs, and add-on excursions to Zanzibar and other coastal destinations.

**Kiboko Lodge** LODGE **$$**
(0765 688550; www.kibokolodge.nl; s/d with half board from US$83/120) Most employees at this non-profit, charity-run lodge are former street kids who received training at the Watoto Foundation's vocational training school, and a stay here supports the project. The slightly frayed but spacious stone cottages have fireplaces, hot water and safes, and the thatched-roof lounge is almost homey. It's 5km down a 4WD-only road east of Ngongongare gate.

## Getting There & Away

The entrance to Arusha National Park is about 35km northeast of Arusha. Take the main road between Arusha and Moshi to the signposted turn-off, from where it's about 10km north to **Ngongongare gate** (6.30am-6.30pm), where you pay your entry fees. **Momella gate** (6.30am-6.30pm) – where **park headquarters** (arusha@tanzaniaparks.go.tz) are located – is about 14km further on. From Momella gate, it's possible to continue along a rough track to Lariboro, on the main Nairobi highway, passing Ngare Nanyuki village (6km north of Momella gate) en route.

There are several buses daily between Arusha and Ngare Nanyuki village, departing Arusha between 1.30pm and 4pm and Ngare Nanyuki between 7am and 8am. Buses stop at Ngongongare gate (Tsh5000, 1½ hours). A taxi from Arusha should cost about Tsh50,000.

# Tarangire National Park

Welcome to one of Africa's most underrated parks. Thanks to its proximity to Serengeti National Park and Ngorongoro Crater, **Tarangire National Park** (www.tanzaniaparks.go.tz; adult/child US$54/18; 6am-6pm) is usually assigned only a day visit as part of a larger northern circuit itinerary. Yet it deserves much more, at least in the dry season (August through October). It's a place where elephants dot the plains like cattle, and where lion roars and zebra barks fill the night.

But this is one place where the wildlife tells only half the story. Dominating the park's 2850 sq km, Tarangire's great stands of epic baobabs should be reason enough to come here. There are also sun-blistered termite mounds in abundance, as well as grassy savannah plains and vast swamps. And cleaving the park in two is the Tarangire River, its meandering course and (in some places) steep riverbanks providing a dry-season lure for so many stirring wildlife encounters.

## Sleeping

**Public Campsite** CAMPGROUND **$**
(tarangire@tanzaniaparks.go.tz; camping US$36) Tarangire's public campsite is just a short drive into the park near the northwestern tip. It has a good bush location and simple cold-water facilities. Bring supplies from Arusha. Bookings can be made in advance via email, or on arrival at the park gate.

**★Tarangire Safari Lodge** LODGE, TENTED CAMP **$$$**
(0756 914663, 027-254 4752; www.tarangire-safarilodge.com; s/d with full board US$270/440; P) A fabulous location overlooking the Tarangire River, good food and service, and well-priced accommodation make this lodge our pick of the in-park options. The sweeping vistas are such that there's no need to go elsewhere for a sundowner. Accommodation includes stone bungalows or standard en suite safari tents; the latter have good views from their doorsteps. It's 10km inside the park gate.

**★Sanctuary Swala** TENTED CAMP **$$$**
(027-250 9817; www.sanctuaryretreats.com; s/d with full board US$1106/1622; Jun-Mar; P@) Arguably the most refined safari experience inside Tarangire, this premier-class camp nestles in a grove of acacia trees and overlooks a busy waterhole in the south-western part of the park by Gurusi Swamp. Each of the 12 lovely tents has a big deck and its own butler. It's in a great wildlife-watching location with lots of lions.

## Getting There & Away

Tarangire is 130km from Arusha via Makuyuni (which is the last place for petrol and basic supplies). At Kigongoni village, there's a sign-posted turn-off to the main park gate, which is 7km further down a good dirt access road. The only other entrance is Boundary Hill gate along the northeast border, which provides access to some lodges located in the area. The park doesn't rent vehicles.

**Coastal Aviation** (027-250 0343; www.coastal.co.tz; Arusha Airport; 7am-6pm) and **Air Excel** (027-297 0249, 027-297 0248; www.airexcelonline.com; Arusha Airport) sometimes stop at Tarangire's Kuro airstrip on request on their flights between Arusha and Lake Manyara.

# Lake Manyara National Park

One of Tanzania's smaller parks, **Lake Manyara National Park** (www.tanzaniaparks.go.tz; adult/child US$54/18; 6am-6pm) is skipped by many safari itineraries, but we highly recommend you make the detour. The dramatic western escarpment of the Rift Valley forms the park's western border. To the east is the alkaline Lake Manyara, which covers one-third of the park, but shrinks considerably in the dry season. During the rains, the lake hosts millions of flamingos and other birdlife.

While Manyara lacks the raw drama of other northern circuit destinations, its vegetation is diverse, ranging from savannah to marshes to evergreen forest (11 different ecosystems in all) and it supports one of the highest biomass densities of large mammals in the world. Elephants, hippos, zebras, giraffes, buffaloes and wildebeest are often spotted. Leopards and hyenas are also here. Lake Manyara is also home to a famous population of tree-climbing lions.

## Sights

**Lake Manyara Treetop Walkway** VIEWPOINT
(0756 977384; www.wayoafrica.com/tree-top-walkway; US$30) Enjoy a bird's-eye view of Manyara on Tanzania's first treetop walkway (370m). Highly recommended.

## Sleeping

**Panorama Safari Campsite** CAMPGROUND **$**
(0763 075130; www.panoramasafaricamp.com; camping per tent US$10, permanent tent/igloo per person US$12/25) Located near the top of the escarpment is this hot, sometimes dusty place with camping and faded warm-water ablutions. The price is great, however, and the views are as wonderful as those at any of the nearby luxury lodges. There's also a restaurant. Dalla-dallas running between Mto wa Mbu and Karatu will drop you at the entrance.

**Public Campsite No 2** CAMPGROUND **$**
(www.tanzaniaparks.go.tz; camping US$36) Shaded Campsite 2 ('Riverside' or 'Endabash' campsite), set amid sausage trees and other

vegetation near the Endabash River about an hour's drive from the gate, has relatively new toilet and shower facilities, and tank water for cooking (and, if treated, for drinking).

## Getting There & Away

Buses and dalla-dallas run frequently from Arusha (Tsh6000, two hours) and Karatu (Tsh3000, one hour) to Mto wa Mbu, the gateway village for Lake Manyara park. Once at Mto wa Mbu, it is straightforward to get onward transport to Lake Manyara park lodges and camps, or to hire a vehicle (from US$150 including fuel and driver) to explore the park.

# Ngorongoro Conservation Area

Lying within the boundaries of the 8292-sq-km **Ngorongoro Conservation Area** (NCA; 027-253 7019, 027-253 7046; www.ngorongoro-crater.go.tz; adult/child US$71/24, crater services fee per vehicle per 24hr US$295; 6am-6pm) are some of northern Tanzania's greatest sights: Ngorongoro Crater, Oldupai Gorge and much of the Crater Highlands (although not Ol Doinyo Lengai and Lake Natron).

## Sights

**Ngorongoro Crater** PARK

(027-253 7019, 027-253 7046; www.ngorongoro-crater.go.tz; adult/child US$71/24, crater service fee per vehicle US$295) At 19km wide and with a surface of 264 sq km, Ngorongoro is one of the largest unbroken calderas in the world that isn't a lake. Its steep walls soar 400m to 610m and provide the setting for an incredible natural drama as prey and predators graze and stalk their way around the open grasslands, swamps and acacia woodland on the crater floor. It's such an impressive sight that, other vehicles aside, you'll wonder whether you've descended into a wildlife paradise.

## Sleeping

**Simba A Public Campsite** CAMPGROUND $

(027-253 7019; www.ngorongoro.go.tz; camping US$48) Ngorongoro's only public campsite is Simba A, up on the crater rim not far from headquarters. It has basic facilities and can get very crowded, so hot water sometimes runs out. Even so, it's a fine location and by far the cheapest place to stay up on the rim.

**Rhino Lodge** LODGE $$$

(0785 500005; www.ngorongoro.cc; s/d with half board US$145/260; ) This small, friendly lodge, run by Italians in conjunction with the Maasai community, is one of the cheapest places in the NCA. The rooms are simple and tidy, and the balconies have fine forest views, often with bushbucks or elephants wandering past. It's arguably the best-value place up here, as long as you don't need a crater view.

## Information

The crater falls within the Ngorongoro Conservation Area Authority (NCAA), which has its **headquarters** (027-253 7019, 027-253 7006; www.ngorongorocrater.go.tz; 8am-4pm) at Park Village at Ngorongoro Crater and information centres in both Arusha (p690) and **Karatu** (www.ngorongorocrater.go.tz; Main road; 7.30am-4.30pm Mon-Fri, to 12.30pm Sat & Sun).

The two entry points for the NCAA are Lodoare gate, just south of Ngorongoro Crater on the road from Arusha and about 14km west of Karatu, and Naabi Hill gate on the border with Serengeti National Park.

Payment of all fees for visiting the crater and the NCAA *must* be made in advance at a local Tanzanian bank. First contact the NCAA information centre in Arusha or Karatu, where you will be given an invoice, based on the amount of time you are planning to spend in the NCAA. Take this to a local Tanzanian bank (currently NCAA has designated both NBC and CRDB banks), following which you will be given a receipt slip. This slip can be presented at either one of the NCAA information centres, or at the park gate itself, in order to get an actual entry permit. In practice, both Lodoare Gate and Naabi Hill Gate seem ready to also sometimes accept cash payments (no credit cards). Should you wish to add days or activities to your visit, you can pay fees (cash only) at NCAA headquarters. A credit card payment system is planned for the future (but at the time of writing no date had been set for implementation).

## Getting There & Away

There's no public transport to the crater. If you aren't travelling on an organised safari and don't have your own vehicle, the easiest thing to do is hire one in Karatu, where most lodges charge from US$160 per day for a 4WD with a pop-up top including fuel and driver but excluding entry and vehicle fees. Vehicle rental from Mto wa Mbu costs from US$220 per day including fuel and driver. Note that any vehicle with a pop-up top or any vehicle operated by a safari company will not be permitted to enter the NCAA without an up-to-date TALA licence. Be sure to verify this before making any payments.

## Serengeti National Park

Few people forget their first encounter with **Serengeti National Park** (☎0689 062243, 0767 536125, 028-262 1515; www.tanzaniaparks.go.tz; adult/child US$71/24; ⊙6am-6pm). Perhaps it's the view from Naabi Hill at the park's entrance, from where the Serengeti's grasslands appear to stretch to the ends of the earth. Or maybe it's a coalition of lions stalking across open plains, their manes catching the breeze. Or it could be the migration of wildebeest and zebra in their millions, following the ancient rhythm of Africa's seasons. Whatever it is, welcome to one of the greatest wildlife-watching destinations on earth.

The 14,763-sq-km Serengeti is also renowned for its predators, especially its lions. Cheetahs, leopards, hyenas and jackals are on the hunt here, too, feasting on zebras, giraffes, buffaloes, gazelles, topis, elands, hartebeests, impalas and more. It's also an incredible birdwatching destination, with over 500 species to spot. A few black rhinos around Moru Kopjes offer a chance for the Big Five, although they're rarely seen.

### Sleeping

**Serengeti Stop-Over** CAMPGROUND $
(☎028-262 2273, 0757 327294; www.serengetistopover.com; camping US$10, s/d US$45/70; P) Just 1km from Ndabaka gate along the Mwanza–Musoma road, this sociable place has camping with hot showers and a cooking area, plus 14 simple rondavels, and a restaurant-bar. Safari vehicle rental is available with advance notice and Serengeti day trips are feasible. It also offers trips on Lake Victoria with local fishermen, visits to a traditional healer and other Sukuma cultural excursions.

**Twiga Resthouse** GUESTHOUSE $$
(☎028-262 1510; www.tanzaniaparks.go.tz; r per person US$36; P) Simple but decent rooms with electricity and hot showers, and satellite TV in the lounge. Guests can use the kitchen or meals can be cooked for you if you order way in advance. There's a well-stocked little bar and a bonfire at night. If Twiga is full, there might be room at the similar Taj Resthouse, used mostly by visiting park officials.

★ **Wayo Green Camp** TENTED CAMP $$$
(☎0784 203000; www.wayoafrica.com; per person with full board from US$270) These 'private mobile camps' combine the best aspects of both tented camps and budget camping safaris and are the best way possible to get a deep bush experience in the Serengeti. They use 3m x 3m dome tents and actual mattresses (off the ground) and move from site to site every couple of days. Wayo also runs excellent walking safaris.

**Serengeti Serena Safari Lodge** LODGE $$$
(☎027-254 5555; www.serenahotels.com; s/d with full board US$426/711; P @ 🛜 ≋) Serena's Maasai-style bungalows boast well-appointed rooms with lovely furnishings and views. The top-floor rooms are best. Guides lead short nature walks and the Maasai do an evening dance show. A good location for those who want to explore several parts of the park but not switch accommodation, and the hilltop site offers fine views when the migration's in town.

### Information

**Serengeti Visitor Centre** (serengeti@tanzaniaparks.go.tz; ⊙8am-5pm) This office at Seronera has an excellent self-guided walk through the Serengeti's history and ecosystems, and it's well worth spending time here before exploring the park. The gift shop sells various booklets and maps, and there's a coffee shop with snacks and cold drinks.

### Getting There & Away

The park has four main entry and exit points, plus two lesser-used gates at Handajega and Fort Ikoma.

**Naabi Hill Gate** (⊙6am-6pm) The main (and most heavily trafficked) access gate if coming from Arusha; 45km from Seronera, in central Serengeti.

**Ndabaka Gate** (⊙6am-6pm, last entry 4pm) Main gate for the Western Corridor; a 1½-hour drive from Mwanza and 145km from Seronera.

**Klein's Gate** (⊙6am-6pm, last entry 4pm) In the far northeast, it allows a loop trip combining Serengeti, Ngorongoro and Lake Natron, the latter just two to three hours from the park.

**Bologonya Gate** (⊙6am-6pm) This gate would be on the route to/from Kenya's Masai Mara National Reserve, but the border is closed and unlikely to open any time soon.

# LAKE VICTORIA

Tanzania's half of Africa's largest lake sees few visitors, but the region holds many attractions for those with a bent for the offbeat and a desire to immerse themselves in the rhythms of local life beyond the tourist trail. The cities of Musoma and Bukoba have a quiet waterside charm, while most villagers on Ukerewe Island follow a subsistence lifestyle with little connection to the world beyond the shore.

Mwanza is appealing in its own way and it's the perfect launching pad for a Serengeti–Lake Natron–Ngorongoro loop. Add the forests of idyllic Rubondo Island National Park, deep in the lake's southwest reaches, for a well-rounded safari experience.

# Mwanza

Tanzania's second-largest city, and the lake region's economic heart, Mwanza is set on Lake Victoria's shore, surrounded by hills strewn with enormous boulders. It is notable for its strong Indian influences, as well as for being a major industrial centre and a busy port. Yet, despite its rapidly rising skyline, Mwanza manages to retain a casual feel. In addition to being a stop on the way to Rubondo Island National Park, Mwanza is a great starting or finishing point for safaris through Ngorongoro and the Serengeti, ideally as a loop by adding in Lake Natron.

## Tours

Several travel agencies in town hire 4WDs and can organise complete safaris to Serengeti and Rubondo Island National Parks. While Mwanza's operators may not be as good as the best agencies in Arusha, they provide solid service and we're unaware of any in town that will blatantly rip you off. It's not easy to meet other travellers in Mwanza, but you can ask the agencies whether they have other clients interested in combining groups to save money, or try posting a notice at Kuleana Pizzeria.

## Sleeping

**St Dominic's Pastoral Centre** HOSTEL $
(Nyakahoja Hostel; 0788 556532, 0689 413159, 028-250 0830; off Balewa Rd; s/d Tsh30,000/40,000, r with air-con Tsh50,000-60,000) This centrally located church-run hostel offers simple rooms plus meals on order (Tsh7000). It's about five minutes' walk north of the Clock Tower roundabout, and good value.

**Hotel Tilapia** HOTEL $$
(0784 700500, 028-250 0617; www.hoteltilapia.com; Capri Point Rd; s/d/ste US$100/120/150; ) The ever-popular Tilapia, on the city side of Capri Point, has a variety of rooms, most of which are dated but decent and look out at the lake. It also has rooms on a historic boat; though these are smaller and a little off-kilter, their special character makes them fun, and the two end ones have prime lake views.

**Ryan's Bay** RESORT $$
(028-254 1702, 0784 699393; www.ryansbay.com; Station Rd, Capri Point; s/d from US$110/140; P) The flashest place in Mwanza has lake views and large, well-appointed rooms with acacia-tree murals on the walls. There's a good pool, and one of the best Indian restaurants in town (mains Tsh12,000 to Tsh20,000).

## Eating

**Salma Cone** STREET FOOD $
(Bantu St; snacks Tsh500-5000; 9am-10pm) *Sambusas* (Indian pastry snacks stuffed with curried meat or vegetable), soft ice cream and juice are all pleasers here, but it's the smell of barbecuing meat that will draw you in for a kebab. With plastic outdoor tables, this a fun corner to lounge in the evening.

**DVN Restaurant** TANZANIAN $
(Nyamagana Rd; meals around Tsh5000; 7am-5pm Mon-Sat) Excellent local fare served fast and cheap in this church-run place with an old-fashioned cafe look and feel. It's behind the post office and behind St Nicholas Anglican Church – quite hidden with just a small sign above a tucked-away door. You might need to ask for someone to point it out.

**Kuleana Pizzeria** INTERNATIONAL $
(028-256 0566; Post St; snacks Tsh2000-6000, pizzas Tsh15,000-17,000; 7am-9pm; ) Don't expect Italian-class food, but this is a relaxed and popular place for pizzas and snack-style food (omelettes, sandwiches and breads) with a good mix of locals and expats. The friendly owner feeds many street children.

## Information

**Tourist Office** (028-250 0818; www.tanzaniatouristboard.com; New Mwanza Hotel, Post St; 8am-5pm Mon-Fri, to 1pm Sat) There's a small tourist-office branch inside the lobby of the New Mwanza Hotel.

The Mwanza Guide website (www.mwanza-guide.com) has dated but useful tourist information.

## Getting There & Away

### AIR

The **airport** (MWZ) is 10km north of the centre; taxis should cost between Tsh15,000 and Tsh20,000

**Precision Air** (☎ 028-250 0819; www.precisionairtz.com; Kenyatta Rd) flies daily to Dar es Salaam, Zanzibar and Kilimanjaro. **Auric Air** (☎ 0783 233334; www.auricair.com; Mwanza Airport) and **Air Tanzania** (☎ 0756 067783; www.airtanzania.co.tz; Kenyatta Rd) fly daily to Bukoba. Air Tanzania also has at least five flights weekly to Dar es Salaam and Zanzibar. **Fastjet** (☎ 0784 108900; www.fastjet.com; Kenyatta Rd) flies daily to Dar. One-way fares to Bukoba/Dar average Tsh180,000/Tsh200,000. **Coastal Aviation** (☎ 0736 200840; www.coastal.cc; Mwanza Airport) has a daily flight to Arusha airport stopping at various Serengeti National Park airfields. It also flies to Dar es Salaam and Zanzibar.

Flight schedules and destinations constantly change so it pays to check each airline's website for the latest.

### BUS

About 10km south of town, **Nyegezi Bus Station** (Shinyanga Rd) handles buses to all points east, south and west including to Dar es Salaam (Tsh45,000, 15 to 17 hours), Arusha (Tsh35,000, 12 to 13 hours) and Moshi (Tsh38,000, 14 to 15 hours). The Arusha and Moshi buses go via Singida (Tsh25,000, six hours). There are no buses between Mwanza and Arusha via the Serengeti – you will need to catch these in Musoma. Buses also go to Babati (Tsh30,000, nine to 10 hours), Dodoma (Tsh32,000, 10 hours) and Iringa (Tsh38,000, 14 hours).

Buses to Bukoba (Tsh20,000, six to seven hours) via Chato depart between 6am and 1pm and mostly use the Busisi ferry, but if they're redirected to the Kamanga ferry in central Mwanza, you can meet them there.

Adventure is probably the best of several companies departing daily at 5.30am to Kigoma (Tsh35,000, 12 hours) via Tabora (Tsh16,000, six hours). You can also find buses to Kigoma taking the route via Kasulu. Both take about the same amount of time, but as of late 2016, there was more tarmac going via Tabora than via Kasulu.

Buses for Musoma (Tsh8000, three to four hours, last bus 4pm) and other destinations en route to the Kenyan border depart from **Buzuruga Bus Station** (Nyakato), 4km east of the centre.

### TRAIN

Mwanza is the terminus of a branch of the **Central Line** (p707) and trains run to Tabora (1st-class sleeping/2nd-class sleeping/economy Tsh29,600/22,700/11,800, 11 hours) on Sunday, Tuesday and Thursday at 5pm. From Tabora you can connect to Kigoma (Tsh51,800/38,400/19,300 from Mwanza) or continue to Dar es Salaam (Tsh75,000/54,800/27,300 from Mwanza). If travelling to Kigoma, you'll need to disembark in Tabora (arrivals are in the morning) and spend the day there before boarding the train to Kigoma in the evening. For Dar es Salaam, just stay on the same train.

## Getting Around

Dalla-dallas (labelled Buhongwa) to Nyegezi bus station (Tsh400) run south down Kenyatta and Pamba roads. The most convenient place to find a dalla-dalla (labelled Igoma) to Buzuruga bus station (Tsh400) is just northeast of the clock tower, where they park before running down Uhuru St. Dalla-dallas to the airport (Tsh400) follow Kenyatta and Makongoro roads.

There are taxi stands all around the city centre, with prices averaging Tsh3000 to Tsh5000 within the centre. Taxis to Buzuruga cost from Tsh7000, and to Nyegezi about Tsh15,000. Taxis to the airport cost between Tsh15,000 and Tsh20,000. Motorcycle taxis are everywhere and charge Tsh1000 within the centre.

# Bukoba

Bustling, green-leafed Bukoba has an attractive waterside setting and a pleasing small-town feel. Everyone who comes to visit here seems to like it, even though it's a little hard to put your finger on exactly why.

**Kiroyera Tours** (☎ 0759 424933, 0713 526649; www.kiroyeratours.com; Shore Rd), a well-informed agency leading cultural tours in Bukoba and the Kagera region, is an essential stop for travellers in Bukoba. Its half- and full-day tours include visiting ancient rock paintings and walking in Rubale Forest. If you liked your Zanzibar spice tour, consider a Kagera vanilla and coffee tour. It also sells bus, boat and plane tickets; supplies boats to go to Musira Island; and organises visits to national parks in Tanzania and gorilla tracking in Uganda.

**ELCT Bukoba Hotel** (☎ 0754 415404, 028-222 3121; www.elctbukobahotel.com; Aerodrome Rd; s/tw/ste US$40/45/60; P @) has comfortable rooms and pleasant grounds. **Kiroyera Campsite** (☎ 0757 868974; www.kiroyeratours.com; Shore Rd; camping/banda US$5/20; P) is a great backpackers' spot on the beach with meals and three Haya *msonge* (grass huts) with beds and electricity. Even if you don't sleep here, at least stop for a drink and some fried fish and rice in the chilled beach-shack restaurant.

There are daily flights to and from Mwanza (US$75 one way) on **Auric Air** (www.auricair.com), and to and from Dar es Salaam (from US$225) via Mwanza with **Precision Air** (☎0782 351136, 028-222 0204; www.precisionairtz.com; Kawawa Rd).

All bus companies have ticket offices at or near the bus stand, with buses to Kigoma (Tsh30,000, 13 to 15 hours, every other day at 6am) and Mwanza (Tsh20,000, six to seven hours, frequent between 6am and 1pm).

# LAKE TANGANYIKA

## Kigoma

POP 144,260 / ☎028

This agreeable little town is the regional capital and only large Tanzanian port on Lake Tanganyika. It's also the end of the line for the Central Line train and a starting point for the MV *Liemba* and visits to Gombe National Park. It's hardly a bustling metropolis, but it feels that way if you've slogged across Western Tanzania by road to get here.

### Sights

**Jakobsen's (Mwamahunga) Beach** BEACH
(adult/child Tsh7000/2500) Jakobsen's is actually two tiny, beautiful sandy coves below a wooded hillside. The overall setting is idyllic, especially if you visit during the week when few people are around. There are some *bandas* for shade, and soft drinks and water are sold at the guesthouse.

**Katonga** VILLAGE
This large and colourful fishing village is quite a spectacle when the 200-plus wooden boats pull in with their catch. During the darkest half of the moon's cycle they come back around 8am after they've spent the night on the lake fishing by the light of lanterns. Dalla-dallas (Tsh400) come here frequently.

**Kibirizi** VILLAGE
There are many fishermen at Kibirizi, 2km north of town by the oil depots. The early afternoon loading of the lake taxis is impressive in a noisy, colourful and rather chaotic kind of way. You can walk here by following the railway tracks or the road around the bay.

### Sleeping & Eating

★ **Jakobsen's Guesthouse** GUESTHOUSE $
(☎0753 768434; www.newsite.kigomabeach.com; camping Tsh20,000, tent or r per person without breakfast Tsh30,000-75,000; P) This comfortable place has a guesthouse with a lovely clifftop perch above Jakobsen's Beach, two cottages and some standing tents, plus two shady campsites with bathrooms, lanterns and grills closer down near the lake. It's good value and a wonderful spot for a respite, but there is no food available so you'll need to self-cater.

**Coast View Resort** HOTEL $
(☎0713 491570, 028-280 3434; r Tsh50,000-60,000; P❄📶) The highest hotel in town doesn't have rooms with views, but you can see everything from the restaurant's gazebo tower. The limited sightlines are the only shortcoming here; rooms and service are solid.

**Sun City** TANZANIAN $
(Lumumba St; meals Tsh6000-8000; ⊙7am-8pm) This long-standing establishment is a clean and almost artistic spot for *wali maharagwe* (rice and beans) and other local meals. There's also chicken biryani on Sunday.

### Information

**Gombe/Mahale visitors information centre** (☎028-280 4009, 0689 062303; gonapachimps@yahoo.com; ⊙9am-4pm) This helpful office for general information and for booking park-run accommodation is signposted off Ujiji Rd near the top of the hill; turn left at the T-junction. Although it is officially for both Gombe and Mahale Mountains parks, staff are primarily informed about Gombe.

### Getting There & Away

#### AIR

**Air Tanzania** (☎0787 737251; www.airtanzania.co.tz; CRDB Building, Lumumba St; ⊙8am-5pm Mon-Fri, 9am-2pm Sat & Sun) flies four times weekly between Kigoma and Dar es Salaam (US$200). **Precision Air** (☎0784 298929; www.precisionairtz.com; Kibirizi road; ⊙9am-4pm Mon-Fri, to noon Sat) flies five times weekly between Kigoma and Dar es Salaam via Tabora (US$226). Both airlines accept cash only. Air travel to Kigoma is in a constant state of flux, so expect this information to change.

The airport (TKQ) is about 5km east of the town centre (about Tsh5000 in a taxi).

#### BUS

All buses depart from the dusty streets behind Bero petrol station (coming from Kigoma, look for the large, white petrol station with an NBC

ATM). The bus station is surprisingly well organised with all the bus companies having little ticket offices with destinations clearly signed in a long row. Other bus ticket offices are scattered around the Mwanga area, just to the west.

Buses go to the following:

**Arusha** (Tsh60,000, 20 hours)

**Bukoba** (Tsh30,000, 6am, 12 hours), via Biharamulo (Tsh27,000, eight hours).

**Mpanda** (Tsh23,000, 6am, eight hours)

**Mwanza** (Tsh35,000, 6am, 10 to 12 hours), via Nyankanazi (Tsh22,000, seven hours).

**Tabora** (Tsh25,000, 6am, eight hours)

**Uvinza** (Tsh5000, four hours) All buses to Tabora or Mpanda pass through Uvinza.

# Gombe National Park

With an area of only 56 sq km, **Gombe National Park** (☎0689 062303, 028-280 4009; www.tanzaniaparks.go.tz; adult/child US$118/24, trekking fee US$24; ⏲6.30am-6.30pm) is Tanzania's smallest national park, but its famous primate inhabitants and its connection to Jane Goodall has given it worldwide renown. Many of Gombe's 100-plus chimps are well habituated, and though it can be difficult, sweaty work traversing steep hills and valleys, if you head out early in the morning sightings are nearly guaranteed.

As well as chimp tracking, you can take walks along the lake shore, and go and see Jane's old chimp-feeding station, the viewpoint on Jane's Peak and Kakombe Waterfall.

## Sleeping

**Tanapa Resthouse** GUESTHOUSE $

(☎028-280 4009; r per person US$24) Next to the visitor centre at Kasekela, this amenable place has six simple rooms with electricity mornings and evenings. Two overflow facilities have rooms of lesser quality, and toilets at the back. The restaurant's prices are high (breakfast US$10, lunch US$15, dinner US$15) but you can bring your own food and use the kitchen for free.

**Gombe Forest Lodge** TENTED CAMP $$$

(☎0732 978879; www.mbalimbali.com; s/d all-inclusive except drinks US$800/1250; ⏲May-Feb) Gombe's only private lodge has a shady, waterside location with just seven tents that offer a certain class and sophistication in the jungle. The tents are luxurious without being ostentatious.

## Getting There & Away

Gombe is 26km north of Kigoma and the only way there is by boat.

At least one lake taxi to the park (Tsh5000, three to four hours) departs from Kibirizi village, just north of Kigoma, around noon. Returning, it passes Kasekela as early as 7am.

It's safer and more comfortable (in part because there will be sun shade) to arrange a charter with an established company. Chartering the Tanapa boat costs US$354 return, plus US$24 for each night you spend at Gombe. Organise it through the visitors information centre in Kigoma. Boats take 1½ to two hours.

# Mahale Mountains National Park

It's difficult to imagine a more idyllic combination: clear, blue waters and white-sand beaches backed by lushly forested mountains soaring straight out of Lake Tanganyika, as well as some of the continent's most intriguing wildlife. And, because of the unrivalled remoteness, visitor numbers to **Mahale Mountains National Park** (www.mahalepark.org; adult/child US$95/24; ⏲6am-6pm) are low, adding to the allure.

The rainforest blanketing Mahale's western half is, in essence, a small strip of the Congo. It's most notable as a chimpanzee sanctuary, and there are around 900 of our primate relatives split into 14 groups residing in and around the park, along with leopards, blue duikers, red-tailed monkeys, red colobus monkeys, giant pangolins and many Rift Valley bird species not found elsewhere in Tanzania. There are also hippos, crocodiles and otters in the lake, and lions, elephants, buffaloes and giraffes roaming the savannah of the difficult-to-reach eastern side of the mountains.

## Sleeping

**Mango Tree Bandas** BUNGALOW $$

(sokwe@tanzaniaparks.go.tz; Kasiha; bandas per person US$48) The cosy Mango Tree *bandas* are set in the forest about 100m from the shore in Kasiha (about 10km south of park headquarters). While they lack lake views, the night sounds are wonderful. You will need to be completely self-sufficient with food and drink, and bring everything you might need with you. The kitchen is well equipped.

**Kungwe Beach Lodge** TENTED CAMP $$$

(☎0737 206420; www.mbalimbali.com; s/d with full board & chimpanzee trekking US$962/1573; ⏲mid-May–mid-Feb; 📶) This is a low-key and enjoyable luxury camp with well-appointed safari tents that boast big four-poster beds, weathered storage chests and piping-hot showers, all hidden under the trees fringing a lovely beach. The centrepiece of the camp is the dhow-shaped dining area. The price includes daily chimp tracking and a boat safari.

## Information

**Park Headquarters** (sokwe@tanzaniaparks.go.tz; ⏲7am-6pm) Located at Bilenge, in the park's northwestern corner, and about 10km north of Kasiha, where the park-run *bandas* and several top-end camps are located. Unless you have made other arrangements with one of the lodges, you will need to stop here to pay your park fees.

## Getting There & Away

### AIR

**Safari Airlink** (☎0777 723274; www.flysal.com) and **Zantas Air** (☎0688 434343; www.zantasair.com) fly to Mahale twice weekly (assuming there are enough passengers to cover costs: usually four). The former starts in Ruaha National Park or Arusha and the latter in Arusha. Zantas flights sometimes also stop in Kigoma. All flights stop at Katavi National Park en route, and thus the parks are frequently visited as a combination package. Expect to pay approximately US$960 one way from Arusha, US$675 one way from Ruaha and US$400 to US$520 one way between Mahale and Katavi National Parks.

If you've booked with one of the lodges, a boat will meet your flight. Otherwise, arrange a boat in advance with park headquarters.

### FERRY

It's hard to beat the satisfyingly relaxing journey to Mahale via ferry. The MV *Liemba* (p707) stops at Lagosa (also called Mugambo) to the north of the park (1st/2nd/economy class US$40/35/30), about 10 hours from Kigoma. Under normal scheduling, it reaches Lagosa around 3am whether coming from the north (Thursday) or south (Sunday), but with the frequent delays, southern arrivals present a good chance of passing the park during daylight, which makes for a very beautiful trip. Services are on alternate weeks.

You can arrange in advance at the Gombe/Mahale visitors information centre (p697) in Kigoma or through Mahale park headquarters for a park boat (holding eight people with luggage) to meet the *Liemba*. It's one hour from the *Liemba* to the *bandas*, including a stop to register and pay at park headquarters, and costs US$192 return. Lagosa has a basic guesthouse where you can wait for the *Liemba* after leaving the park.

# SOUTHERN HIGHLANDS

## Ruaha National Park

**Ruaha National Park** (www.tanzaniaparks.go.tz; adult/child US$36/12) forms the core of a wild and extended ecosystem covering about 40,000 sq km and provides home to Tanzania's largest elephant population. In addition to the elephants, which are estimated to number about 12,000, Tanzania's largest national park hosts large herds of buffaloes, greater and lesser kudus, Grant's gazelles, wild dogs, ostriches, cheetahs, roan and sable antelopes, and more than 400 different types of birds.

Ruaha is notable for its wild and striking topography, especially around the Great Ruaha River, which is its heart. Much of this topography is undulating plateau averaging about 900m in height with occasional rocky outcrops and stands of baobabs. Mountains in the south and west reach to about 1600m and 1900m, respectively. Running through the park are several 'sand' rivers, most of which dry up during the dry season, when they are used by wildlife as corridors to reach areas where water remains.

### Activities

Besides wildlife drives, it's possible to organise two- to three-hour walking safaris (park walking fee US$20 per group) from June to January.

**Ruaha Cultural Tourism Program** CULTURAL
(☎0752 142195, 0788 354286; www.ruahaculturaltours.com; half-/full-day tour US$20/40, per person with full board in Maasai village US$27) Cultural tours of a Maasai *boma* (including the chance to spend the night), traditional cooking lessons, nature walks and more. Recommended stop en route to or from Ruaha.

### Sleeping

**Chogela Campsite** CAMPGROUND $
(☎0782 032025, 0757 151349; www.chogelasafaricamp.wix.com/chogelasafaricamp; camping US$10, s/d safari tents US$30/50; P) Shaded grounds, a large cooking-dining area and hot-water showers make this a popular budget choice. There are also twin-bedded safari-style tents. Vehicle rental can be arranged (US$250 for a full-day safari, advance notice required; US$350 including pick-up and drop-off in Iringa), as can meals. The camp is about

34km from the park gate along the Tungamalenga road.

**Ruaha Park Bandas & Cottages** COTTAGE $$ (0756 144400; ruaha@tanzaniaparks.go.tz; s/d bandas with shared bathroom US$36/71, s/d/f cottages US$59/118/118) Ruaha's 'old' park *bandas,* in a fine setting directly on the river near park headquarters, have been partially upgraded. Several have private bathroom, and meals can be arranged or cooked yourself. About 3km beyond here, on a rise overlooking the river in the distance, are the 'new' tidy concrete cottages (all with private bathroom). There's a dining hall next door with inexpensive meals.

## Getting There & Away

### AIR

There is an airstrip at Msembe.

**Coastal Aviation** (0752 627825; www.coastal.co.tz) flies from Dar es Salaam and Zanzibar to Ruaha via Selous Game Reserve (one way US$365 from Dar es Salaam, US$425 from Zanzibar) and between Ruaha and Arusha (US$365). Safari Airlink has similarly priced flights connecting Ruaha with Dar es Salaam, Selous and Arusha, and also with Katavi and Mikumi.

### BUS

There's a daily bus between Iringa and Tungamalenga village (Tsh6500, five hours), departing Iringa's Mwangata bus stand (on the southwestern edge of town at the start of the Ruaha road) at 1pm. Look for the vehicle marked 'Idodi-Tungamalenga'. Departures from Tungamalenga's village bus stand (along the Tungamalenga road, just before Tungamalenga Camp) are at 6am. From Tungamalenga, there's no onward transport to the park, other than rental vehicles arranged in advance through the Tungamalenga road camps (prices start at US$250 per day). There's no vehicle rental once at Ruaha, except what you've arranged in advance with the lodges.

# SOUTHEASTERN TANZANIA

## Selous Game Reserve

**Selous Game Reserve** (mtbutalii@gmail.com; adult/child US$59/36 plus daily conservation fee US$17.70) is a vast, 48,000-sq-km wilderness area lying at the heart of southern Tanzania. It is Africa's largest wildlife reserve, and home to large herds of elephants, plus buffaloes, crocodiles, hippos, wild dogs, many bird species and some of Tanzania's last remaining black rhinos. Bisecting it is the Rufiji River, which cuts a path past woodlands, grasslands and stands of borassus palm, and provides unparalleled water-based wildlife-watching.

Only the section of the reserve north from the Rufiji River is open for tourism; large areas of the south are zoned as hunting concessions. Yet the wealth of Selous' wildlife and its stunning riverine scenery rarely fail to impress.

Another draw is the Selous' relative lack of congestion in comparison with Tanzania's northern parks.

### Sleeping

**Lake Tagalala Public Campsite** CAMPGROUND $ (mtbutalii@gmail.com; per adult/child US$35.40/23.60) Lake Tagalala campsite has basic but good facilities. There is usually water, but it is worth also filling up a container when entering the reserve. The campsite is located roughly midway between Mtemere and Matambwe on a low rise near Lake Tagalala. Booking and payment should be made when entering the reserve.

**Selous River Camp** TENTED CAMP $$ (0784 237525; www.selousrivercamp.com; camping US$10, s/d tent with full board US$100/155, s/d/tr mud hut with full board US$230/300/348; Jun-Feb) This friendly place is the closest camp to Mtemere gate. It has cosy, river-facing 'mud huts' with bathrooms, plus small standing tents surrounded by forest with cots and shared facilities. The bar-restaurant area is lovely, directly overlooking the river at a scenic spot. Overall, it's a good choice for budget travellers.

**Selous Mbega Camp** TENTED CAMP $$ (0784 748888, 0784 624664; www.selous-mbega-camp.com; s/d with full board from US$140/200, s/d backpackers' special with full board from US$95/140) This laid-back camp is about 1km outside the eastern boundary of the Selous near Mtemere gate and just west of Mloka village. It has raised, no-frills tents set in the foliage overlooking the river, and reasonably priced boat and vehicle safaris. Pick-ups and drop-offs to and from Mloka are free. It is good budget value.

★ **Selous Impala Camp** TENTED CAMP $$$ (0753 115908, 0787 817591; www.selousimpalacamp.com; s/d with full board & excursions US$690/1200; Jun-Mar; P) Impala

Camp has eight well-spaced, nicely appointed tents in a prime setting on the river near Lake Mzizimia. Its restaurant overlooks the river and has an adjoining bar area on a deck jutting out towards the water, and the surrounding area is rich in wildlife.

## Getting There & Away

Tokyo Bus Line runs a daily bus between Temeke's Sudan Market (Majaribiwa area) and Mloka village (Tsh15,000, eight to 10 hours), which is about 10km east of Mtemere gate. Departures in both directions are at 5am. From Mloka you'll need to arrange a pick-up in advance with one of the camps. Hitching within the Selous isn't permitted, and there are no vehicles to rent in Mloka.

# Mtwara

POP 108,300 / ☎023

Once an obscure fishing village and then an empty shell of a city after the failed East African Groundnut Scheme, sprawling Mtwara is now southeastern Tanzania's major town. The discovery of offshore natural gas reserves has shattered the somnolent, sunbaked atmosphere that characterised the city for so long. Whether recent developments will ultimately be to the benefit of local residents remains to be seen, but for now, Mtwara is hopping. The city lacks the historical appeal of nearby Mikindani and other places along the coast, and has little to recommend it as a tourist destination. However, with its decent infrastructure and easy access, it makes a convenient entry or exit point for those travelling between Tanzania and Mozambique.

## Sleeping & Eating

**VETA** HOSTEL $

(☎023-233 4094; Shangani; s/ste Tsh35,000/60,000; P ❄ ≋) This large compound has clean rooms, all with one large twin bed, fan, TV and views towards the water, plus a restaurant. It's in Shangani, about 200m back from the water (though there's no swimming beach here). From the T-junction in Shangani, go left and continue for about 2km. There's no public transport; *bajaji* charge around Tsh3000 from town.

**Drive-In Garden & Cliff Bar** GUESTHOUSE $

(☎0784 503007; Shangani Rd; camping per tent Tsh5000, r without breakfast Tsh20,000-25,000; ⏲restaurant 11am-2pm & 5.30-9pm) This friendly place allows campers to pitch their tent in the garden. There are also several simple, good-value rooms. The restaurant offers simple, delicious and generously portioned meals (Tsh12,000) of grilled fish or chicken and chips, plus cold drinks, in a peaceful garden setting just back from the water. Call in advance to place your order to minimise waiting time.

The guesthouse is just across the road from the beach, although for swimming you'll need to walk up to the main Shangani beach area near Shangani junction.

**Fish Market** MARKET $

(off Shangani Rd, at Msangamkuu ferry dock; ⏲6am-4pm) The fish market at the Msangamkuu boat dock is good for street food, selling grilled *pweza* (octopus), *vitambua* (rice cakes) and other delicacies.

## Getting There & Away

All long-distance buses depart between about 5am and noon from the main bus stand just off Sokoine Rd near the market.

To Dar es Salaam (Tsh26,000, eight hours), JM Luxury Coach and several other lines depart daily in each direction between 6am and 7.30am, starting and terminating at Temeke's Sudan Market area, where all the southbound bus lines also have booking offices. Book in advance.

To Mozambique there are several pick-ups and at least one minivan daily to Mahurunga and the Tanzanian immigration post at Kilambo (Tsh5000), departing Mtwara between about 5am and 10am.

# Mikindani

☎023

Mikindani – set on a picturesque bay surrounded by coconut groves – is a quiet, charming Swahili town with a long history. Although easily visited as a day trip from the nearby regional travel hub of Mtwara, many travellers prefer Mikindani to its larger neighbour as a base for exploring the surrounding area.

## Sleeping

**Ten Degrees South Lodge** LODGE $

(ECO2; ☎0684 059381, 0766 059380; www.tendegreessouth.com; s/d US$60/70, with shared bathroom US$20/30; @) This good budget travellers' base has four refurbished rooms, all with large double beds and shared bathrooms, plus bay views and deck chairs up on the roof. Next door are a handful of newer, self-contained double-bedded rooms with hot-water showers. There's also an outdoor restaurant-bar with tasty wraps, pancakes, curries and other meals from about Tsh15,000.

★ **Old Boma at Mikindani** HISTORIC HOTEL $$
(☎023-233 3875, 0757 622000; www.mikindani.com; s US$60-110, d US$110-140; P@🛜🏊) This beautifully restored building is on a breezy hilltop overlooking the town and Mikindani Bay. It offers spacious, atmospheric, high-ceilinged doubles and the closest to top-end standards that you'll find in these parts. There's a sunset terrace overlooking the bay, a pool surrounded by bougainvillea bushes and lush gardens, and a good restaurant.

### ℹ Getting There & Away

Mikindani is 10km from Mtwara along a sealed road. Minibuses (Tsh500) run between the two towns throughout the day. *Bajajis* (tuk-tuks) from Mtwara charge about Tsh10,000 (or it's about Tsh30,000 for a taxi).

# UNDERSTAND TANZANIA

## Tanzania Today

Tanzania today is moving fast and looking forward. Its urban areas are growing exponentially, and it is one of Africa's top tourist destinations thanks to its magnificent national parks. It is also sitting on a potential goldmine in the form of recently discovered natural gas reserves. Politically, the country's focus is on the new president, Dr John Magufuli, who is moving full steam ahead to eradicate corruption and yank up the country by the bootstraps.

A major impediment to real progress is corruption. In the most sweeping effort to date to combat it, President Magufuli has eliminated thousands of 'ghost workers' from government payrolls, fired anyone with even a suspicion of involvement in shady dealings, and in general succeeded in creating the seeds of a new mentality.

An ongoing challenge for the Tanzanian government is keeping ties happy between the mainland and proudly independent Zanzibar. While dialogue is generally amicable, the relationship requires ongoing attention.



## History

### Dr Livingstone, I Presume?

The first Europeans to arrive in East Africa were the Portuguese, who clashed with the Omanis for control of the lucrative trade routes to India. Later came British, Dutch and American merchant adventurers. By the 19th century, European explorers were setting out from Zanzibar into the unknown African interior. While searching for the source of the Nile, Dr David Livingstone became so famously lost that a special expedition headed by Henry Stanley was sent out to find him. Stanley caught up with Livingstone near modern-day Kigoma after a journey of more than a year, whereupon he allegedly uttered the famous words: 'Dr Livingstone, I presume?'

British efforts to suppress the slave trade ultimately led to the downfall of the Omani Empire. But it was Germany that first colonised what was then known as Tanganyika. Following WWI, the League of Nations mandated Tanganyika to Britain.

### Independence

In 1959 Britain agreed to growing demands for the establishment of internal self-government. On 9 December 1961, Tanganyika became independent and on 9 December 1962 it was established as a republic, with Julius Nyerere as president.

On the Zanzibar Archipelago, which had been a British protectorate since 1890, the main push for independence came from the radical Afro-Shirazi Party (ASP), but when independence was granted in December 1963, two British-favoured minority parties formed the first government. Within a month, a Ugandan immigrant named John Okello initiated a violent revolution that toppled the government and the sultan, and led to the massacre or expulsion of most of the islands' Arab population. The sultan was replaced by the Zanzibar Revolutionary Council headed by Abeid Karume.

On 26 April 1964, Nyerere signed an act of union with Karume, creating the United Republic of Tanganyika (renamed the United Republic of Tanzania the following October). The union was resented by many Zanzibaris from the outset. In 1972 Karume was assassinated. Shortly thereafter, in an effort to subdue the ongoing unrest, Nyerere authorised the formation of a one-party state and combined his ruling Tanganyika African National Union (TANU) party and the ASP into Chama ChaMapinduzi (CCM; Party of the Revolution). CCM's dominance of Tanzanian politics endures to this day.

## The Socialist Experiment

The Arusha Declaration of 1967 committed Tanzania to a policy of socialism and self-reliance. The policy's cornerstone was the *ujamaa* (familyhood) village: an agricultural collective run along traditional African lines, whereby basic goods and tools were held in common and shared among members, while each individual was obliged to work on the land. After an initial period of euphoric idealism, resentment at forced resettlement programs and other harsh measures grew, and the economy rapidly declined – precipitated in part by steeply rising oil prices and sharp drops in the value of coffee and sisal exports.

## Democracy At Last

In 1985 Nyerere resigned, handing overpower to Ali Hassan Mwinyi. Mwinyi tried to distance himself from Nyerere and his policies, and instituted an economic recovery program. The fall of European communism in the early 1990s and pressure from Western donor nations accelerated the move towards multiparty politics, and in 1992 the constitution was amended to legalise opposition parties.

The first elections were held in 1995 in an atmosphere of chaos, and the voting for the Zanzibari presidency was denounced for its dishonesty. In the ensuing uproar, foreign development assistance was suspended and most expatriates working on the islands left. Similar problems have plagued successive elections, and tensions continue to simmer.

# People

Tanzania is home to about 120 tribal groups, plus relatively small but economically significant numbers of Asians and Arabs, and a tiny European community. Most tribes are very small; almost 100 of them combined account for only one-third of the total population. As a result, none has succeeded in dominating politically or culturally, although groups such as the Chagga and the Haya, who have a long tradition of education, are disproportionately well represented in government and business circles.

About 95% of Tanzanians are of Bantu origin. Tribal structures range from weak to non-existent – a legacy of Julius Nyerere's abolishment of local chieftaincies following independence. About 3% of Tanzania's population lives on the Zanzibar Archipelago.

# SURVIVAL GUIDE

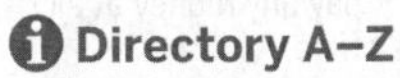

## Directory A–Z

### ACCOMMODATION

Tanzania has a wide range of accommodation, from dingy rooms with communal bucket baths to luxurious safari and island lodges. It's generally not necessary to book in advance, except at holiday times and in popular beach and safari areas, where accommodation fills quickly.

- **Camping** Campsites range from completely wild to reasonably well-outfitted places with running water and cooking facilities.
- **Hotels** Vary from modest mid-range properties with en suite rooms, often with air-con, right up to top-notch establishments.
- **Guesthouses** Range from poorly ventilated concrete-block rooms with shared bathroom to homey, simple but pleasant places with fan and private bathroom.

### DANGERS & ANNOYANCES

- Avoid isolated areas, especially isolated stretches of beach.
- In cities and tourist areas take a taxi at night. Only take taxis from established taxi ranks or hotels. Never enter a taxi that already has someone else in it other than the driver.

### PRICE RANGES

The following price ranges refer to a standard double room with bathroom in high season. Unless otherwise stated, VAT of 18%, and continental breakfast, is included in the price. For midrange and top-end hotels, full breakfast is usually included.

**$** less than US$50

**$$** US50 to US$200

**$$$** more than US$200

The following price ranges refer to a standard main course.

**$** less than US$10

**$$** US$10 to US$20

**$$$** more than US$20

- When using public transport, don't accept drinks or food from someone you don't know. Be sceptical of anyone who comes up to you on the street asking whether you remember them from the airport, your hotel or wherever. Take requests for donations from 'refugees', 'students' or others with a grain of salt. Contributions to humanitarian causes are best done through an established agency or project.
- Never pay any money for a safari or trek in advance until you've thoroughly checked out the company, and never pay any money at all outside the company's office.
- In western Tanzania, especially along the Burundi border, there are sporadic outbursts of banditry and political unrest. At the time of writing, things were quiet, but it's worth getting an update locally.
- In tourist areas, especially Arusha, Moshi and Zanzibar, touts can be quite pushy, particularly around bus stations and budget tourist hotels. Do everything you can to minimise the impression that you're a newly arrived tourist: walk with purpose. Duck into a shop if you need to get your bearings or look at a map.
- Arriving for the first time at major bus stations, have your luggage as consolidated as possible, with your valuables well hidden under your clothes. Try to spot the taxi area before disembarking and make a beeline for it. It's well worth a few extra dollars for the fare. While looking for a room, leave your bag with a friend or reliable hotel rather than walking around town with it. Buy your bus tickets a day or two in advance (without your luggage).
- Carry your passport, money and other documents in a pouch against your skin, hidden under loose-fitting clothing. Or, store valuables in a hotel safe, if there's a reliable one, ideally inside a pouch with a lockable zip to prevent tampering.
- Keep the side windows up in vehicles when stopped in traffic and keep your bags out of sight (eg on the floor behind your legs).
- When bargaining or discussing prices, don't do so with your money or wallet in your hand.

## EMBASSIES & CONSULATES

Most embassies and consulates in Dar es Salaam are open from 8.30am to 3pm Monday to Friday, often with a midday break. Visa applications for all countries neighbouring Tanzania should be made in the morning.

**British High Commission** (Map p666; ☎022-229 0000; www.gov.uk/government/world/tanzania; Umoja House, cnr Mirambo St & Garden Ave)

**Burundian Embassy** (Map p664; ☎022-212 7007/8; burundiembassydar@yahoo.com; 1007 Lugalo St, Upanga)

**Canadian High Commission** (Map p666; ☎022-216 3300; www.canadainternational.gc.ca/tanzania-tanzanie/; 38 Mirambo St)

**Democratic Republic of the Congo Embassy (Formerly Zaïre)** (Map p664; ☎022-215 2388; www.ambardc-tz.org; 20 Malik Rd, Upanga)

**French Embassy** (Map p664; ☎022-219 8800; www.ambafrance-tz.org; 7 Ali Hassan Mwinyi Rd)

**German Embassy** (Map p666; ☎022-211 7409/15; www.daressalam.diplo.de; Umoja House, cnr Mirambo St & Garden Ave)

**Indian High Commission** (Map p664; ☎022-211 3094, 022-211 3079; www.hcindiatz.org; Shaaban Robert St)

**Irish Embassy** (Map p664; ☎022-260 0629, 022-260 2355; www.dfa.ie/irish-embassy/tanzania/; 353 Toure Dr)

**Italian Embassy** (Map p664; ☎022-211 5935; www.ambdaressalaam.esteri.it; 316 Lugalo St, Upanga)

**Kenyan High Commission** (Map p664; ☎022-266 8285/6; www.kenyahighcomtz.org; cnr Ali Hassan Mwinyi Rd & Kaunda Dr, Oyster Bay)

**Malawian High Commission** (Map p664; ☎022-277 4220; www.malawihctz.org; Rose Garden Rd, Mikocheni A)

**Mozambique High Commission** (Map p666; 25 Garden Ave; ⏰9am-3pm Mon-Thurs, 9am-noon Fri)

**Netherlands Embassy** (Map p666; ☎022-219 4000; www.netherlandsworldwide.nl/countries/tanzania; Umoja House, cnr Mirambo St & Garden Ave)

**Rwandan Embassy** (Map p664; ☎0754 787835, 022-260 0500; www.tanzania.embassy.gov.rw; 452 Haile Selassie Rd)

**Ugandan Embassy** (Map p664; ☎022-266 7391; www.daressalaam.mofa.go.ug; 24 Mkwawa Rd)

**US Embassy** (Map p664; ☎022-229 4000; http://tanzania.usembassy.gov; 686 Old Bagamoyo Rd)

**Zambian High Commission** (Map p666; ☎022-212 5529; ground fl, Zambia House, cnr Ohio St & Sokoine Dr)

## INTERNET ACCESS

There are internet cafes in all major towns, and wi-fi hotspots are widespread, except in rural areas. Prices at internet cafes average Tsh1000 to Tsh2000 per hour. Speed varies greatly; truly fast connections are rare. Almost all midrange and top-end hotels, including on the safari circuits, and some budget places have wireless access points; some are free, others charge a modest fee. The best way to connect is either with your smart phone or by purchasing a wi-fi hotspot from one of the mobile providers (about Tsh70,000, including 10GB of initial credit).

For topping up, various packages are available, averaging about Tsh35,000 for 10GB, valid for one month. Top-up credit vouchers are sold at roadside shops countrywide.

## MONEY

- Tanzania's currency is the Tanzanian shilling (Tsh).
- A Visa or MasterCard is essential for accessing money from ATMs and for paying entry fees at most national parks.
- Credit cards are not widely accepted for hotel payment.
- US dollar bills dated prior to 2006 are not accepted anywhere.

### Exchange Rates

| | | |
|---|---|---|
| Australia | A$1 | Tsh1701 |
| Canada | C$1 | Tsh1701 |
| Europe | €1 | Tsh2554 |
| Japan | ¥100 | Tsh1995 |
| New Zealand | NZ$1 | Tsh1627 |
| UK | UK£1 | Tsh2890 |
| USA | US$1 | Tsh2237 |

## OPENING HOURS

Opening hours are generally as follows.

**Banks and government offices** 8am–3.30pm Monday to Friday

**Restaurants** 7am–9.30am, noon–3pm and 6.30pm–9.30pm; reduced hours low season

**Shops** 8.30am–5pm or 6pm Monday to Friday, 9am–1pm Saturday; often closed Friday afternoon for mosque services

**Supermarkets** 8.30am–6pm Monday to Friday, 9am–4pm Saturday, 10am–2pm Sunday

## PUBLIC HOLIDAYS

The dates of Islamic holidays depend on the moon and are known for certain only a few days in advance. They fall about 11 days earlier each year and include Eid al-Kebir (Eid al-Haji), Eid al-Fitr and Eid al-Moulid (Maulidi).

**New Year's Day** 1 January

**Zanzibar Revolution Day** 12 January

**Easter** March/April – Good Friday and Easter Monday

**Karume Day** 7 April

**Union Day** 26 April

**Labour Day** 1 May

**Saba Saba (Peasants' Day)** 7 July

**Nane Nane (Farmers' Day)** 8 August

**Nyerere Day** 14 October

**Independence Day** 9 December

**Christmas Day** 25 December

**Boxing Day** 26 December

## TELEPHONE

- The mobile network covers major towns throughout the country, plus most rural areas, though signal availability can be erratic.
- The major companies are currently Vodacom, Airtel, Tigo, Halotel and (on Zanzibar) Zantel.
- All the companies sell pre-paid starter packages for about US$2, and top-up cards are widely available at shops and roadside vendors throughout the country.
- Local SIM cards can be used in European and Australian phones. Other phones must be set to roaming.

## VISAS

Almost everyone needs a visa, which costs US$50 for most nationalities (US$100 for citizens of the USA) for a single-entry visa valid for up to three months. Officially, visas must be obtained in advance by all travellers who come from a country with Tanzania diplomatic representation. One-month single-entry visas (but not multiple-entry visas) are also currently issued on arrival (no matter your provenance) at both Dar es Salaam and Kilimanjaro International Airports, at the Namanga border post between Tanzania and Kenya, and at Tunduma border (between Tanzania and Zambia).

### East Africa Tourist Visa

Tanzania is not currently a party to the East Africa Tourist Visa (EATV), and the EATV does not apply to travel in the country.

### Visas for Onward Travel

#### DRC

Visas are only issued to Tanzania residents. Any Congolese visa issued in Tanzania will not be honoured on entry in the DRC unless you have a Tanzania resident's permit.

#### Kenya

Kenyan visas should be applied for online in advance of travel at www.evisa.go.ke. If this is not possible, they are issued at Kenya's borders with Tanzania for US$50 plus one photo. The Kenyan High Commission in Dar es Salaam does not issue visas.

#### Malawi

Malawi visas issued in Dar es Salaam cost US$100 plus two photos. If application is made in the morning, they are often issued on the same day.

#### Mozambique

One-month single-entry visas cost US$60 plus two photos, and are issued within five days (US$100 for 24-hour service). In addition, you will require an application letter, a bank statement for the past six months, a return ticket, a hotel booking, a photocopy of your passport and a valid yellow fever certificate.

### Rwanda

Three-month single-entry visas cost US$50 plus one photo, and are issued within four days.

### Uganda

One-month single-entry visas cost US$50 plus two photos and are issued within 48 hours. Located near Yasser Arafat Rd and Uwanjwa wa Farasi.

### Zambia

One-month single-entry visas cost US$50 plus two photos, and are issued within two days or less. Visa applications are only accepted on Monday, Wednesday and Friday mornings between 10am and noon.

##  Getting There & Away

### AIR

**Julius Nyerere International Airport** (DAR; ☎022-284 2402; www.taa.go.tz) Dar es Salaam; Tanzania's air hub.

**Kilimanjaro International Airport** (JRO; ☎027-255 4252, 027-255 4707; www.kilimanjaroairport.co.tz) Between Arusha and Moshi, and the best option for itineraries in Arusha and the northern safari circuit. Note: not to be confused with the smaller Arusha Airport (ARK), 8km west of Arusha, which handles domestic flights only.

**Zanzibar International Airport** (ZNZ, Abeid Amani Karume International Airport; Map p670) On Zanzibar Island, at the southern edge of Zanzibar Town; handles frequent charter flights from Europe, as well as several international carriers.

A useful website for researching and booking East African regional flights is www.flyezee.com.

Tanzania's flagship carrier is **Air Tanzania** (☎0782 737730, 0782 782732; www.airtanzania.co.tz), with domestic destinations, plus a small but growing network of regional and (soon) international destinations.

### LAND

### Kenya

The main route to/from Kenya is the good sealed road connecting Arusha (Tanzania) and Nairobi (Kenya) via Namanga border post (open 24 hours). There are also border crossings at Horohoro (Tanzania), north of Tanga; at Holili (Tanzania), east of Moshi; at Loitokitok (Kenya), northeast of Moshi; and at Sirari (Tanzania), northeast of Musoma. With the exception of the Serengeti–Masai Mara crossing (which is currently closed), there is public transport across all Tanzania–Kenya border posts.

### Malawi

From Mbeya's Nane Nane bus stand, there are daily minibuses and 30-seater buses (known as 'coastals' or thelathini) to the border (Tsh5000, two hours). Once through the Tanzanian border post, there's a 300m walk to the Malawian side, and minibuses to Karonga. There's also one Malawian bus daily from the Malawi side of the border and Mzuzu (Malawi), departing the border by mid-afternoon and arriving in Mzuzu by evening.

### Mozambique

Vehicles depart daily from Mtwara from 6am to the Kilambo border post (Tsh6000, one hour) and on to the Ruvuma River, which in theory is crossed daily by the MV *Kilambo* ferry. The ferry, again in theory, takes half a dozen cars plus passengers (Tsh500 per person). However, its passage depends on tides, rains and mechanical issues. If it is not operating, you'll need to negotiate a ride in a smaller boat or a dugout canoe (about Tsh5000, 10 minutes to over an hour, depending on water levels, and dangerous during heavy rains).

Once in Mozambique, several pick-ups go daily to the Mozambique border crossing at Namiranga, 4km further on, and from there to Palma and Moçimboa da Praia (US$13, three hours). The road on the Mozambican side is poor at the border, but improves closer to Palma.

Further west, one or two vehicles daily depart from Songea's Majengo C area by around 11am (Tsh12,000, three to four hours) to Mtomoni village and the Unity 2 bridge. Once across, you can get Mozambique transport on to Lichinga (Tsh30,000, five hours).

### Rwanda

There are no direct buses to Kigali. From Mwanza, you will need to go via Kahama and Benaco (Nyakasanza) to the border, which you can cross on foot and then get Rwandan transport on the other side to Kigali; reckon on about 12 to 14 hours and Tsh32,000 for the entire journey.

### Uganda

Kampala Coach has a daily bus from Arusha to Kampala via Nairobi (Tsh70,000, 20 hours). The cost to Jinja is the same as Kampala.

Several companies leave Bukoba at 6am for Kampala (Tsh15,000, six hours). Departures from Kampala are at 7am and usually again at 11am.

From Mwanza, there are currently no direct buses. You will need to travel in stages; allow about 16 to 18 hours for the journey.

### Zambia

Minibuses go several times daily between Mbeya and Tunduma (Tsh4000, two to three hours), where you walk across the border for Zambian transport to Lusaka (about US$20, 18 hours).

### LAKE

The venerable **MV Liemba** (☎ 028-280 2811) has been plying the waters of Lake Tanganyika for more than a century on one of Africa's classic adventure journeys. It connects Kigoma with Mpulungu in Zambia every other week (in theory), with prices for 1st/2nd/economy class costing US$105/95/75 (payment must be in US dollars cash). The trip takes at least 40 hours and stops en route at various lakeshore villages, including Lagosa (for Mahale Mountains National Park; US$40 for 1st class from Kigoma). Delays are common.

Food, soft drinks, beer and bottled water are sold on board, but it's a good idea to bring supplements.

## Getting Around

### AIR

Always reconfirm your bookings at least once, and expect delays. Sample one-way fares: Dar es Salaam to Mbeya from Tsh225,000; Dar to Mwanza from Tsh140,000; Dar to Kigoma from Tsh400,000; and Dar to Arusha or Kilimanjaro International Airport (KIA) Tsh200,000 to Tsh400,000

**Air Excel** (☎ 027-297 0248; www.airexcelonline.com)

**Air Tanzania** (p706)

**Coastal Aviation** (p700)

**Fastjet** (☎ 0784 108900; www.fastjet.com)

**Tropical Air** (☎ 0777 431431, 024-223 2511; www.tropicalair.co.tz)

### BOAT

Ferries operate on Lake Victoria, Lake Tanganyika and Lake Nyasa, and between Dar es Salaam, Zanzibar and Pemba. There is a US$5 port tax per trip.

### BUS

Bus travel is an inevitable part of the Tanzania experience for many travellers. Prices are reasonable for the distances covered, and there's often no other way to reach many destinations.

➡ On major long-distance routes, there's a choice of express and ordinary buses. Express buses make fewer stops, are less crowded and depart on schedule. Some have toilets and air-conditioning, and the nicest ones are called 'luxury' buses.

➡ For popular routes, book in advance. Buy your tickets at the office and not from the touts, and don't believe anyone who tries to tell you there's a luggage fee, unless you are carrying an excessively large pack.

### CAR & MOTORCYCLE

Unless you have your own vehicle and/or are familiar with driving in East Africa, it's relatively unusual for fly-in travellers to tour mainland Tanzania by car. More common is to focus on a region and arrange local transport through a tour or safari operator. On Zanzibar, however, it's easy, though not so common these days, to hire a car or motorcycle for touring, and self-drive is permitted.

#### Hire

In Dar es Salaam, daily rates for a 2WD vehicle start at about US$80, excluding fuel, plus from US$30 for insurance and tax. Prices for 4WDs are US$100 to US$250 per day plus insurance (US$30 to US$45 per day), fuel and driver (US$20 to US$50 per day). There's also an 18% value-added tax.

You can hire 4WD vehicles in Arusha, Karatu, Mwanza, Mbeya, Zanzibar Town and other centres through travel agencies, tour operators and hotels. Except on Zanzibar, most come with driver. Rates average US$100 to US$250 per day plus fuel; less on Zanzibar.

For vehicle hire with driver, contact the Dar es Salaam-based **Jumanne Mastoka** (Map p666; ☎ 0659 339735, 0784 339735; mjumanne@yahoo.com).

### LOCAL TRANSPORT

Local routes are serviced by dalla-dallas (minivans) and, in rural areas, by pick-up trucks or old 4WDs. Prices are fixed and inexpensive. The vehicles make many stops and are extremely crowded. Accidents are frequent, particularly in minibuses.

### TRAIN

For those with plenty of time, train travel offers a fine view of the countryside and local life. There are two lines: **Tazara** (Tanzania-Zambia Railway; www.tazarasite.com), linking Dar es Salaam with New Kapiri Mposhi in Zambia via Mbeya and Tunduma; and the Tanzania Railways Limited **Central Line** (☎ 0754 460907, 022-211 6213; www.trl.co.tz), linking Dar es Salaam with Kigoma and Mwanza via Tabora. A Central Line branch also links Tabora with Mpanda.

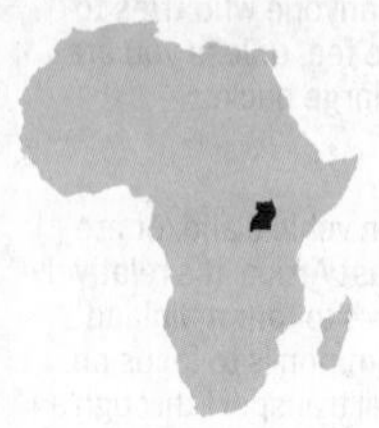

# Uganda

POP 40.9 MILLION / ☎256

**Includes ➡**



## Best Places to Eat


➡ Prunes (p712)
➡ Anna's Corner (p718)
➡ Dutchess (p723)
➡ EcoBurrito (p724)
➡ Mediterraneo (p712)


## Best Places to Sleep


➡ Byoona Amagara (p729)
➡ Emin Pasha Hotel (p712)
➡ Red Chilli Hideaway (p712)
➡ Chimpanzee Forest Guest House (p723)
➡ Katara Lodge (p727)


## Why Go?

Emerging from the shadows of its dark history, a new dawn of tourism has risen in Uganda, polishing a glint back into the 'pearl of Africa'. Travellers are streaming in to explore what is basically the best of everything the continent has to offer.

For a relatively small country, there's a lot that's big about the place. It's home to the tallest mountain range in Africa (Rwenzori Mountains), the source that feeds the world's longest river and the continent's largest lake. And with half the planet's remaining mountain gorillas residing here, as well as the Big Five to be ticked off, wildlife watching is huge.

While anti-gay sentiments have cast a shadow over an otherwise positive tourism picture, Uganda remains one of the safest destinations in Africa. Other than watching out for the odd hippo at your campsite, there's no more to worry about here than in most other countries.

## When to Go

### Kampala

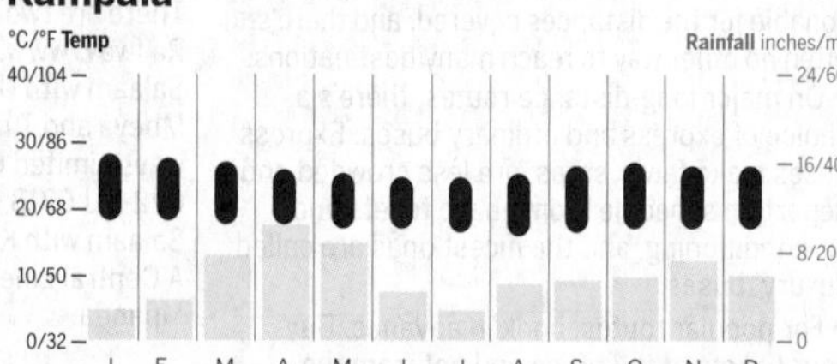


**Jun–Sep** The best bet weatherwise: not too hot with minimal rainfall.

**Jan–Feb** Perfect climate to head for the hills to climb the Rwenzoris or Mt Elgon.

**Oct–Nov** Can be rainy, but fewer travellers means gorilla permits are much easier to obtain.

# KAMPALA

POP 1.6 MILLION / 0414

Bustling Kampala makes a good introduction to Uganda. It's a dynamic and engaging city, with few of the hassles of other East African capitals and several worthy attractions to keep you occupied for a couple of days. As the heartland of the Buganda kingdom, Kampala has a rich and colourful history, visible in several fascinating palaces and compounds from where the nation was run until the arrival of colonialism.

## Sights

**★Mengo Palace** HISTORIC SITE

(Lubiri Palace; Map p713; Lubiri Ring Rd, Twekobe; admission incl guide USh15,000; 8am-5pm) Built in 1922, this small palace is the former home of the king of Buganda, though it has remained empty since 1966 when Prime Minister Milton Obote ordered a dramatic attack to oust Kabaka Mutesa II, then president of Uganda. Led by the forces of Idi Amin, soldiers stormed the palace and, after several days of fighting, Mutesa was forced into exile. The building's interior cannot be visited, but the notorious underground prison here is open to tours.

**Kasubi Tombs** MAUSOLEUM

(Map p713; www.kasubitombs.org; Kasubi Hill; USh10,000; 8am-5pm) The Unesco World Heritage-listed Kasubi Tombs are of great significance to the Buganda kingdom as the burial place of its kings and royal family. The huge thatched-roof palace was originally built in 1882 as the palace of Kabaka Mutesa I, before being converted into his tomb following his death two years later. The tombs were destroyed in an arson attack in March 2010, however, and are still being rebuilt, with no end to the work in sight.

**National Mosque** MOSQUE

(Map p714; Old Kampala Rd; entry incl tour USh10,000) One of Kampala's premier sights, the prominent National Mosque (widely known as the Gadaffi Mosque) was begun by Idi Amin in 1972 but only completed in 2007 following a donation from Libya's Colonel Gadaffi. The hour-long tour allows you to scale its soaring minaret for the best views of Kampala, and takes you within its gleaming interior. Free entry for Muslims.

**Uganda Museum** MUSEUM

(Map p714; Kira Rd; adult/child USh5000/2500; 10am-5.30pm) There's plenty to interest you here with a varied and well-captioned ethnographic collection covering clothing, hunting, agriculture, medicine, religion and recreation, as well as archaeological and natural-history displays. Highlights include traditional musical instruments, some of which you can play, and the fossil remains of a Napak rhino, a species that became extinct eight million years ago. Head outside to wander through the traditional thatched homes of the various tribes of Uganda; plus get a look at Idi Amin's Mercedes.

## Tours

**Red Chilli Hideaway** SAFARI

(Map p713; 0772-509150; www.redchillihideaway.com; 3-day safaris from US$320) An excellent choice for budget safaris to Murchison Falls and Queen Elizabeth National Parks. Also very affordable car-hire rates.

**Coffee Safari** TOURS

(Map p714; 0772-505619; www.1000cupscoffee.com; 18 Buganda Rd; US$100; 7.30am Fri) You can trace your coffee from the cup to the farm on day tours run by 1000 Cups Coffee House (p713). Book before noon on Thursday.

## Festivals & Events

**Kampala City Festival** CULTURAL

(www.kcca.go.ug; 1st week Oct) One of East Africa's biggest street parties is held early each October with floats and performers celebrating Ugandan culture. Traditional and contemporary art, fashion and music are all showcased over multiple stages.

**Amakula International Film Festival** FILM

(www.amakula.org) Hosted at the Uganda Museum, the Amakula International Film Festival is one of Africa's oldest independent film festivals, and shows Ugandan and international features and shorts.

## Sleeping

**★Bushpig** HOSTEL $

(Map p714; 0772-285234; www.bushpigkampala.com; 31 Acacia Ave, Kololo; d US$45, dm/s/d/tr without bathroom US$15/25/35/53; ) A slice of luxury by the standards of African hostels, Bushpig is housed in a smart complex that also functions as a posh hotel and restaurant. The staff are exceptionally friendly and the cool vibe in the dorms and spacious doubles makes up for the street noise outside. Best of all is the excellent hostel restaurant and great water pressure.

# Uganda Highlights

1 **Bwindi Impenetrable National Park** (p727) Trekking through the jungle to marvel at critically endangered mountain gorillas.

2 **Nile River** (p719) Taking on the wild waters at the source of the Nile, some of the best white-water rafting in East Africa.

3 **Murchison Falls** (p731) Witnessing the world's most powerful waterfall during a boat ride up the Victoria Nile.

4 **Lake Bunyonyi** (p729) Chilling out on a remote island on the most beautiful lake in Uganda.

5 **Kidepo Valley National Park** (p733) Exploring unvarnished Africa at its wild and colourful best.

6 **Rwenzori Mountains** (p725) Tackling the ice-capped peaks of Africa's highest range, evocatively known as the 'Mountains of the Moon'.

7 **Ssese Islands** (p731) Lazing in a hammock on a powdery white-sand beach in the middle of Lake Victoria.

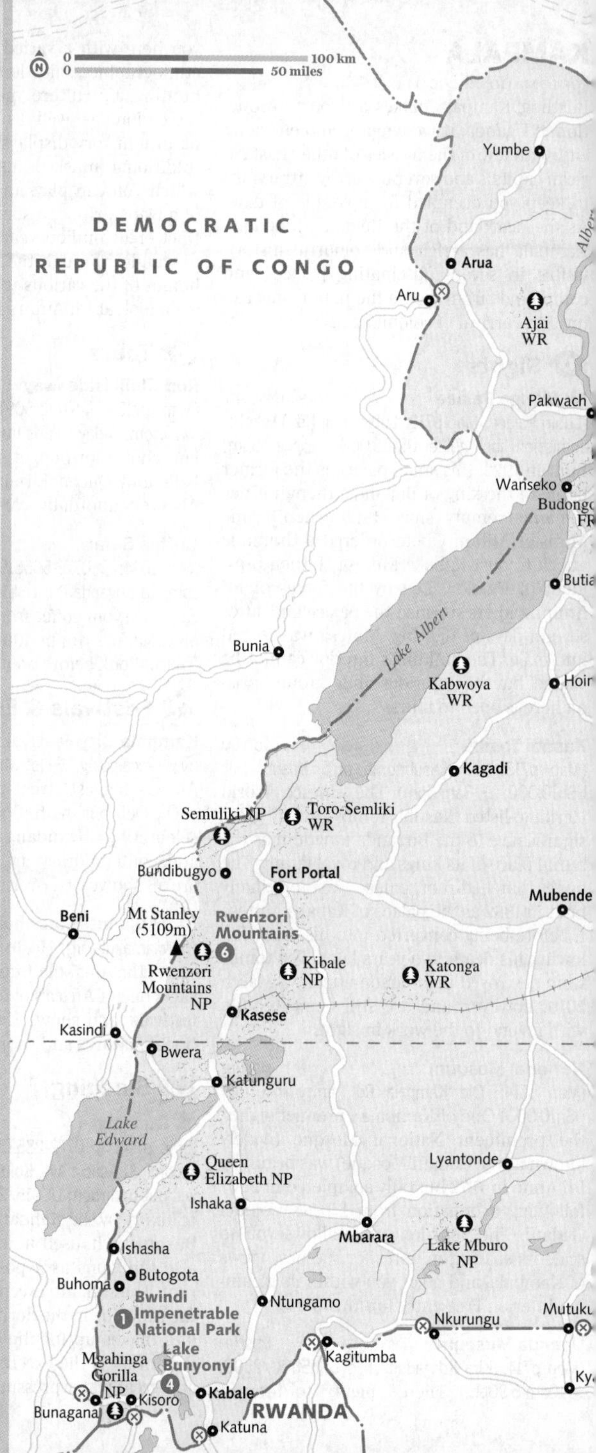

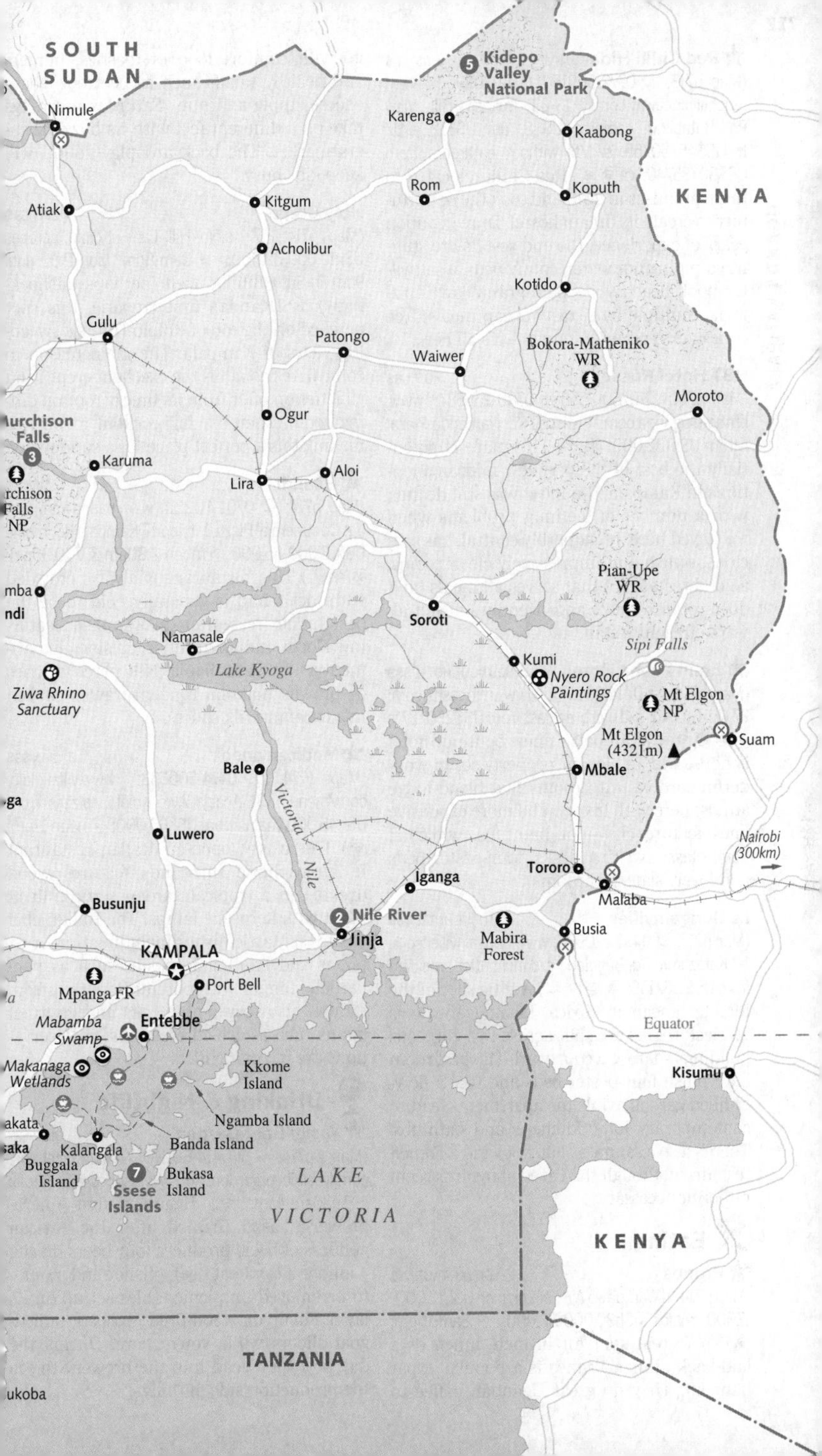

SOUTH SUDAN
Kidepo Valley National Park
Nimule
Karenga
Kaabong
Rom
Koputh
KENYA
Atiak
Kitgum
Acholibur
Kotido
Gulu
Patongo
Bokora-Matheniko WR
Waiwer
Moroto
Ogur
Karuma
Aloi
Lira
Pian-Upe WR
Soroti
Sipi Falls
Namasale
Kumi
Lake Kyoga
Nyero Rock Paintings
Mt Elgon NP
Ziwa Rhino Sanctuary
Mt Elgon (4321m)
Suam
Bale
Mbale
Victoria Nile
Luwero
Nairobi (300km)
Tororo
Iganga
Malaba
Busunju
Nile River
Jinja
Busia
Mabira Forest
KAMPALA
Port Bell
Mpanga FR
Mabamba Swamp
Entebbe
Equator
Makanaga Wetlands
Kkome Island
Kisumu
Ngamba Island
Banda Island
Kalangala
Buggala Island
Bukasa Island
Ssese Islands
LAKE VICTORIA
KENYA
TANZANIA

**★Red Chilli Hideaway** HOSTEL $

(Map p713; ☎0772-509150, 0312-202903; www.redchillihideaway.com; 13-23 Bukasa Hill View Rd, Butabika; camping US$8, dm US$12, s/d/tr US$45/50/55, s/d/tr without bathroom from US$30/35/40; ) Red Chilli relocated to these premises in 2013 and took the opportunity to create its dream hostel. Drawing upon years of experience, the end results are stunning: piping hot water, comfy beds, a saltwater pool, beach volleyball, grassy lawn, pizzeria, multiple bars, tasty/cheap meals, free computers and a TV lounge – it's all here.

**HBT Hotel Russell** HOTEL $$

(Map p714; ☎0780-255581, 0780-255584; www.hbthoteluganda.com; 1 Russell Rd, Namanda Plaza; r from USh182,000; ) This place is potentially the best of the very few midrange options in Kampala, though it was still dealing with a number of teething problems when we stayed here. It's superbly central, has spacious, stylish and impressively clean rooms, a good restaurant that serves all meals (and does room service) and friendly – if not always efficient – staff.

**★Emin Pasha Hotel** BOUTIQUE HOTEL $$$

(Map p714; ☎0414-236977; www.eminpasha.com; 27 Akii Bua Rd; s/d incl breakfast from US$250/270; ) Kampala's finest boutique hotel is housed in an elegant property set in wonderful gardens with rooms that blend lodge atmosphere with luxury. The more expensive ones feature claw-foot bathtubs, while all have classic writing desks, four-poster beds and lovely slate bathrooms.

**Le Bougainviller** BOUTIQUE HOTEL $$$

(Map p713; ☎0414-220966; www.bougainviller.com; 1-7 Katazamiti Rd, Bugolobi; s/d incl buffet breakfast from US$116/136; ) A little slice of the Mediterranean in Africa, Le Bougainviller's 20 sleek rooms are split across two gorgeous buildings sharing a courtyard. The best room have plush four-poster beds and face a flower-filled garden, while the apartments feature contemporary lofts, kitchens and bathtubs. There's also a sauna, a slate pool and a French restaurant, though the caged songbirds seem rather unnecessary.

## Eating

**★Prunes** INTERNATIONAL $

(Map p714; 8 Wampewo Ave; set brunch USh12,000-17,000, mains USh20,000-32,000; 8am-10pm; ) A great spot for brunch, lunch or a laid-back dinner, Prunes is a popular expat hangout. They do great Ugandan coffee to go with comfort food of toasties, burgers and healthy salads such as beetroot, goat's cheese, apple and nuts. Saturday mornings take on a different feel with its buzzy farmers market. The backyard playground will keep kids busy.

**Holy Crêpe** CRÊPES $

(Map p714; 17 Kololo Hill Lane, Kololo; crepes USh12,000-32,000; 8am-8pm Mon-Thu, until 9pm Fri-Sun) Billing itself (perhaps unshockingly) as Uganda's first creperie, this spot perched on the top of Kololo Hill has sweeping views of Kampala. The main reason to come here though is the excellent crepes and gallettes on offer from its breezy rooftop dining room. There's a full cocktail menu too, making this a perfect place for a sundowner.

**★Haandi** INDIAN $$

(Map p714; ☎0701-411221; www.haandikampala.ug; Commercial Plaza, 1st floor, 7 Kampala Rd; mains USh18,000-65,000; noon-2.30pm & 7-10.30pm; ) This restaurant is always crowded with locals and is generally held to be the best Indian restaurant in Kampala, featuring North Indian frontier cuisine. Experiment a little with tilapia (Nile perch) curries or prawns makhini (queen prawns cooked in a coconut milk sauce).

**★Mediterraneo** ITALIAN $$$

(Map p714; ☎0414-500533; www.villakololo.com/menu/; 31 Acacia Ave, Kololo; pizzas from USh45,000, mains from USh60,000; noon-11pm; ) This classy, open-air Italian restaurant in atmospheric surrounds features wood decking in a tropical garden setting, lit at night with kerosene lamps. The Italian chef creates fantastic dishes including thin-crust pizzas and handmade pastas such as pappardelle funghi with porcini imported from Italy. It also serves up steaks and gourmet mains such as grilled rock lobster. Reservations are recommended.

## Drinking & Nightlife

**★Yasigi Beer Garden** BREWERY

(Map p714; ☎0414-661110; www.facebook.com/yasigibeergarden; 40 Windsor Cres, Kololo; 11.30am-4am; ) Uganda's first microbrewery, Yasigi (named after the African goddess of beer) produces four beers on site – amber ale, wheat beer, pilsner and stout – to be enjoyed on picnic tables set up on its lawn. Fill up on wood-fired pizzas or pulled-goat sliders while you're here. During the day pop your head into the brewery to see the production side of things.

## Kampala

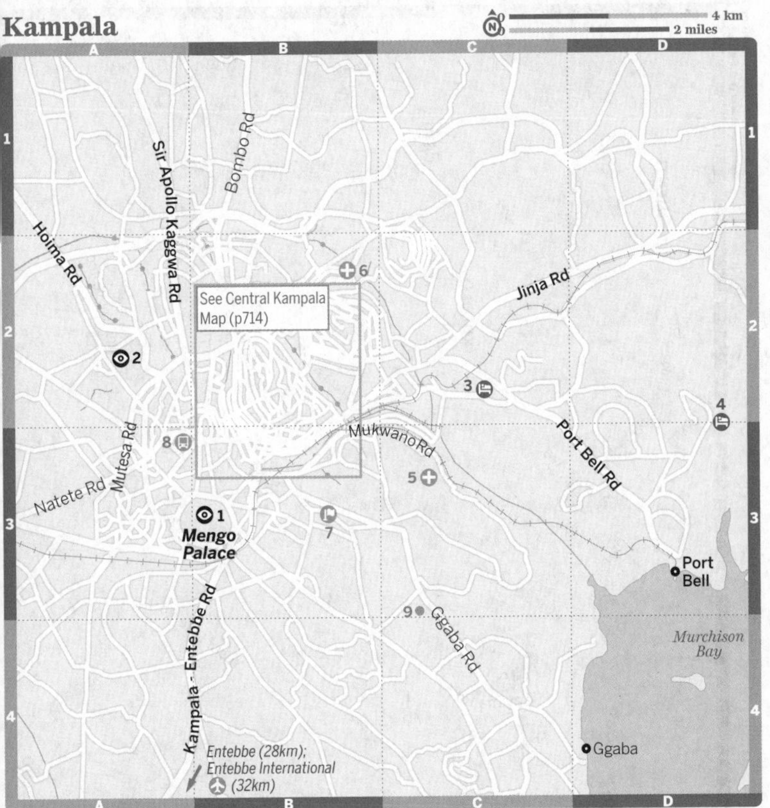




**1000 Cups Coffee House** CAFE
(Map p714; ☎0772-505619; www.1000cupscoffee.com; 18 Buganda Rd; coffee from USh7000; ⊙8am-9pm Mon-Sat, 8am-7pm Sun) For espresso, aeropress or cold drip, caffeine aficionados will want to head here. There's a good range of single-origin beans from across East Africa – expect to pay a premium – and a menu of light bites, along with a selection of international newspapers and magazines.

### ☆ Entertainment

**Musicians Club** CONCERT VENUE
(Map p714; Siad Barre Ave; admission free; ⊙8pm-midnight) Kampala musicians get together every Monday at the National Theatre (www.uncc.co.ug) for informal jam sessions and live performances. This is a must if you are in the city, as the place fills up with Ugandans letting off steam after a Monday back at work and the drinks flow. On the second and last Monday of the month, the

# Central Kampala

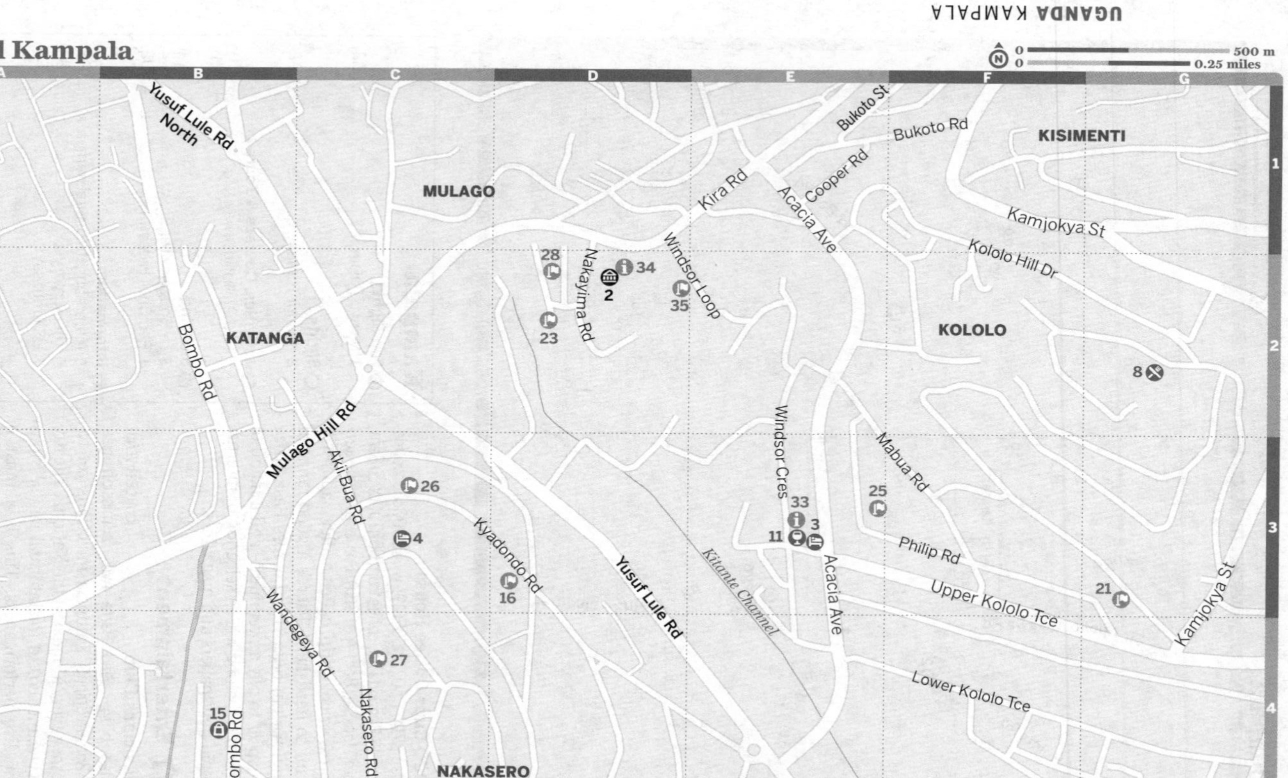

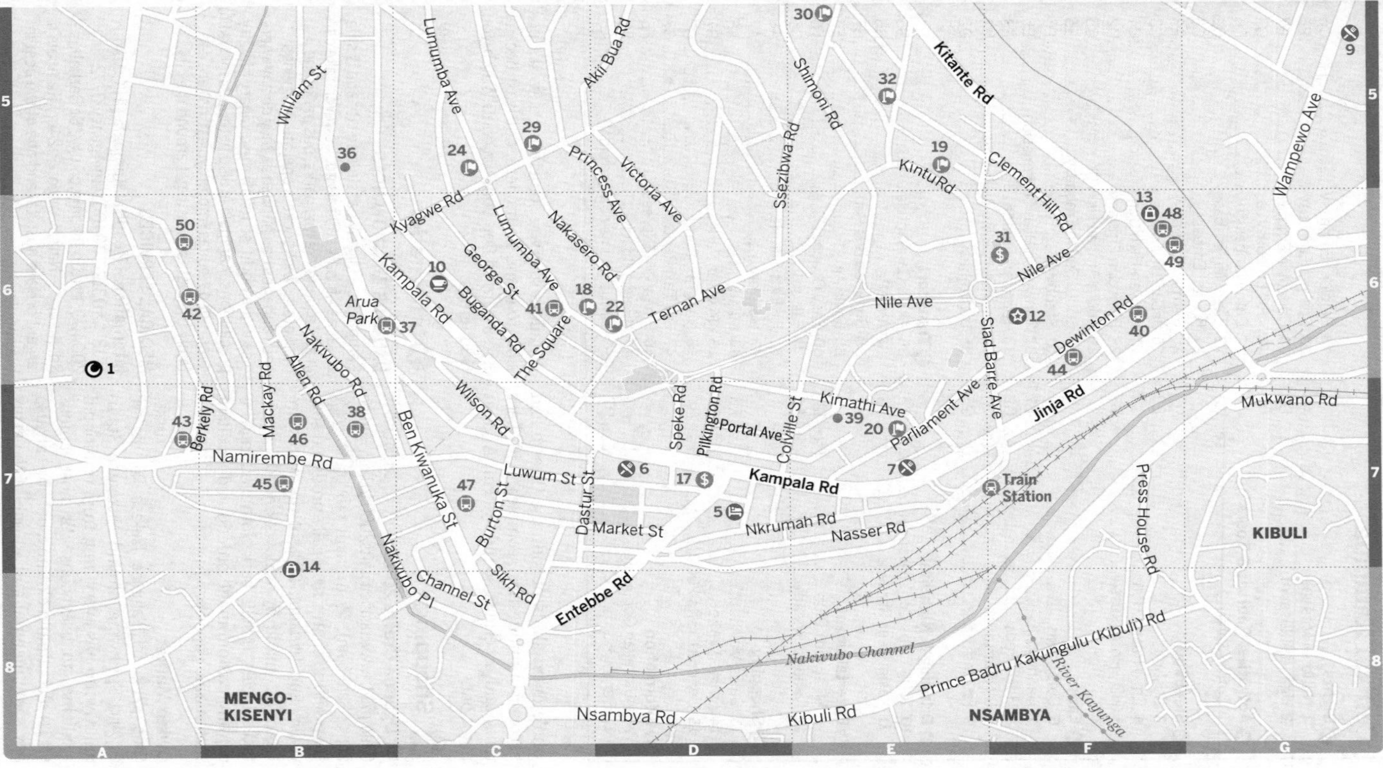
Wampewo Ave
Mukwano Rd
KIBULI
Press House Rd
Kitante Rd
Clement Hill Rd
Nile Ave
Dewinton Rd
Jinja Rd
Siad Barre Ave
Train Station
Parliament Ave
Kintu Rd
Kimathi Ave
Kampala Rd
Nasser Rd
Nkrumah Rd
Shimoni Rd
Ssezibwa Rd
Colville St
Portal Ave
Pilkington Rd
Speke Rd
Ternan Ave
Victoria Ave
Princess Ave
Akii Bua Rd
Nakasero Rd
Lumumba Ave
The Square
George St
Buganda Rd
Wilson Rd
Luwum St
Dastur St
Market St
Entebbe Rd
Burton St
Sikh Rd
Channel St
Ben Kiwanuka St
Nakivubo Pl
Kyagwe Rd
Arua Park
Nakivubo Rd
Allen Rd
Mackay Rd
Namirembe Rd
Berkely Rd
William St
MENGO-KISENYI
NSAMBYA
Nsambya Rd
Kibuli Rd
Nakivubo Channel
Prince Badru Kakungulu (Kibuli) Rd
River Kayunga

## Central Kampala

**Sights**
1 National Mosque ... A6
2 Uganda Museum ... D2

**Activities, Courses & Tours**
Coffee Safari ... (see 10)

**Sleeping**
3 Bushpig ... E3
4 Emin Pasha Hotel ... C3
5 HBT Hotel Russell ... D7

**Eating**
6 Cafe Javas ... D7
7 Haandi ... E7
8 Holy Crêpe ... G2
Mediterraneo ... (see 3)
9 Prunes ... G5

**Drinking & Nightlife**
10 1000 Cups Coffee House ... C6
11 Yasigi Beer Garden ... E3

**Entertainment**
Musicians Club ... (see 12)
12 National Theatre ... F6

**Shopping**
13 Oasis Mall ... F6
14 Owino Market ... B7
15 Uganda Crafts 2000 ... B4

**Information**
16 Australian Consulate ... D3
17 Barclays ... D7
18 Belgium Embassy ... C6
19 Burundi Embassy ... E5
20 Canadian Embassy ... E7
21 DRC Embassy ... G3
22 Dutch Embassy ... D6
23 Ethiopian Embassy ... D2
24 French Embassy ... C5
25 German Embassy ... E3
26 Japanese Embassy ... C3
27 Kenyan High Commission ... C4
28 Rwandan Embassy ... D2
29 South African High Commission ... C5
30 South Sudan Embassy ... E5
31 Stanbic ... F6
32 Tanzanian High Commission ... E5
33 Tourism Uganda ... E3
34 Uganda Wildlife Authority ... D2
35 UK Embassy ... D2

**Transport**
36 Alpha Car Rentals ... B5
37 Arua Park ... B6
38 Buganda Bus Park ... B7
39 Eagle Air ... E7
40 Easy Coach ... F6
41 Falcon ... C6
42 Friends Safari ... A6
43 Horizon ... A7
44 Mash ... F6
45 New Bus Park ... B7
46 New Taxi Park ... B7
47 Old Taxi Park ... C7
48 Pineapple Express ... F6
49 Queens Coach ... F6
50 Simba (Namayiba Terminal) ... A6

whole event shifts outside the theatre and becomes a minifestival, complete with beer tents and a serious sound system. A great night out.

## Shopping

**★Uganda Crafts 2000** ARTS & CRAFTS
(Map p714; www.ugandacrafts2000ltd.org; Bombo Rd; ⏲8am-6pm) A small fair-trade craft shop selling charming locally produced souvenirs and trinkets; 90% of the wares are Ugandan, made by widows and disadvantaged locals. It sells bark-cloth clothing (including custom-made orders) and excellent sustainable paper products.

**Owino Market** MARKET
(Map p714; off Kafumbe Mukasa Rd, Kisenyi; ⏲24hr) Sprawling around Nakivubo Stadium, Owino has everything from traditional medicines to televisions. It's most famous for its secondhand clothing, but you can also buy some material and let one of the army of tailors sew you something new. It's possible to spend hours here, not least because it's so hard to find your way out. Watch your belongings.

## Information

### DANGERS & ANNOYANCES

Kampala is a largely hassle-free city and is safe as far as Africa's capitals go. However, take care in and around the taxi parks, bus parks and markets, as pickpockets operate. Muggings and robberies can happen as they do anywhere else in the world, so follow the ordinary big-city precautions. Kampala is also notorious for traffic jams – *boda-bodas* (motorcycle taxis) are certainly the fastest way to get around the city.

### MEDICAL SERVICES

**International Hospital Kampala** (IHK; Map p713; ☎0312-200400, emergency 0772-200400; http://ihk.img.co.ug/; St Barnabus Rd, Kisugu – Namuwongo; ⏲24hr) Kampala's largest private hospital and one of the best in the country.

**The Surgery** (Map p713; ☎emergency 0752-756003, 0312-256001; www.thesurgeryuganda.org; 42 Naggulu Dr, Naguru; ⊙8am-6pm Mon-Sat, emergency 24hr) A highly respected clinic run by Dr Dick Stockley, an expat British GP. Stocks self-test malaria kits.

### MONEY

**Stanbic** (Map p714; 17 Hannington Rd, Crested Towers Bldg) and **Barclays** (Map p714; Kampala Rd) are the most useful banks in Kampala.

### TOURIST INFORMATION

Kampala has no official tourist office, but it does have a number of useful online resources and magazines.

**Uganda Wildlife Authority** (UWA; Map p714; ☎0414-355000; www.ugandawildlife.org; 7 Kira Rd; ⊙8am-5pm Mon-Fri, 9am-1pm Sat) Administers all of Uganda's protected areas. It's the place to make bookings to see the gorillas in Bwindi Impenetrable National Park, and should be the first port of call for those needing to book permits and accommodation for elsewhere.

**The Eye** (www.theeye.co.ug) Free, bi-monthly magazine and website with listings and reviews for Kampala and other tourist towns.

**Pearl Guide** (www.thepearlguide.co.ug) Online and hard-copy upmarket magazine with good info on upcoming events, food reviews and features on Uganda.

**Tourism Uganda** (Map p714; ☎0414-342196; www.visituganda.com; 42 Windsor Cres; ⊙8.30am-5pm Mon-Fri, 9am-1pm Sat) Has a good website.

**Visit Kampala** (www.visitkampala.net) Handy website with good overview of things to see and do in Kampala, upcoming events and general tourist info.

## Getting There & Away

### BUS

Buses leave early if they're full. Fares vary enormously, but sample destinations and fares include Fort Portal (USh20,000, five hours), Gulu (USh20,000, five hours), Jinja (USh10,000, two hours), Kabale USh30,000, eight hours) and Mbale (USh15,000, five hours).

**Arua Park** (Map p714; Johnston St) Buses to Murchison Falls National Park.

**Buganda Bus Park** (Main Bus Park; Map p714; off Namirembe Rd) Kampala's main bus terminal has the most departures.

**New Bus Park** (Map p714; off Namirembe Rd) Buses to Kisoro, Kabale, Gulu and Kihihi.

### MINIBUS TAXIS

**New Taxi Park** (Map p714) Services western and northern destinations.

**Old Taxi Park** (Map p714) The busier of the two taxi parks serves towns in eastern Uganda.

## Getting Around

### BODA-BODAS

Motorbike taxis are the fastest way to get around Kampala since they can weave in and out of the traffic jams – though they come with the catch of a horrendous safety record. The fare from the centre out to the UWA office or museum is likely to be USh3000.

### MINIBUS TAXIS

The ubiquitous white and blue minibus taxis fan out from the city centre to virtually every point in Kampala. Many start in the taxi parks (for most destinations you can use either park), but it's quicker to flag one down on Kampala Rd as they don't need to navigate the nightmare tailbacks around the taxi parks.

### SPECIAL-HIRE TAXIS

If you see a car with its door open or with the driver sitting behind the wheel while parked, it's probably a special-hire. It's best to grab the number of a recommended driver through your hotel or a trusted local contact. Prices will be higher at night and during rush hour.

# AROUND KAMPALA

## Entebbe

POP 79,700 / ☎0414

On the shores of gorgeous Lake Victoria, Entebbe is an attractive, verdant town that served as the capital city during the early years of the British protectorate. Today it's the relaxed pace of life and nearby natural attractions that give the city its charm rather than any notable colonial relics.

## Sights

**★Ngamba Island Chimpanzee Sanctuary** WILDLIFE RESERVE

(☎0758-221880; www.ngambaisland.org; 24 Lugard Ave; half-/full-day trip US$50/90, s/d incl full board US$309/420) This sanctuary in Lake Victoria is home to around 50 orphaned chimps that have been rescued from elsewhere in Uganda and are being rehabilitated as much as possible on this thickly forested island. Day trips to see the residents are superb. Plan ahead and you can join the overnight experience and a forest-walk with the chimps, who'll climb all over you. It's a 50-/90-minute speedboat/motorised canoe ride from Entebbe to get here.

**Uganda Wildlife Education Centre** ZOO
(UWEC; 0414-320520; www.uwec.ug; 56/57 Lugard Ave; adult/child USh30,000/15,000; 8am-6pm) While it functions primarily as a zoo, this centre is actually a world-class animal refuge that has benefited from international assistance in recent years. Most of the animals on display were once injured or were recovered from poachers and traffickers. Star attractions include chimpanzees (a good alternative to pricier Ngamba Island), southern white rhinos, lions, leopards and shoebill storks. Keep an eye out for the baby elephant wandering about too.

## Sleeping

**Entebbe Backpackers Hostel & Campsite** HOSTEL $
(0414-320432; www.entebbebackpackers.com; 33/35 Church Rd; camping with/without tent US$4/5, dm US$7, r from US$15, s/d without bathroom US$9/10; ) A popular, colourful and straight-down-the-line backpackers without the whole party scene. The pricier rooms are spacious, while all are spotless. The helpful owners can suggest things to do around town and beyond. It's often full, so book ahead. All rooms come with mosquito nets, and much of the place runs on solar electricity.

★ **Airport Guesthouse** GUESTHOUSE $$
(0414-370932; www.gorillatours.com; 17 Mugula Rd; s/d/tr US$70/82/115; ) One of the best-value options in town, this guesthouse's recently renovated rooms maintain a great balance between style and homeliness. Rooms feature verandas looking out to the peaceful garden full of birdlife and huge beds laden with pillows. The delicious three-course dinners (USh25,000) served on the lawn are some of the best in town.

★ **Karibu Guesthouse** GUESTHOUSE $$$
(0777-044984; www.karibuguesthouse.com; 84 Nsamizi Rd; s/d from US$125/145; ) Entebbe does boutique guesthouses superbly, and Karibu is no exception. It has peaceful gardens full of fruit trees and a boules pit, while its stylish rooms are decked in colourful African motifs. There's a saltwater pool, a fantastic restaurant and extremely friendly and helpful staff.

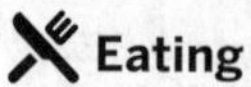

## Eating

**Goretti's Beachside Pizzeria and Grill** PIZZA $
(Nambi Rd; pizzas USh 20,000-35,000; 8.30am-10pm; ) What could be better than eating a wood-fired pizza on the beach with Lake Victoria lapping at your feet? Not much, actually, and it's the reason why Goretti's is such a consistent favourite with locals and visitors alike.

★ **Anna's Corner** CAFE $$
(0789-593196; 12 Queens Rd; coffee USh5000, pizzas USh14,000-20,000; 8am-9pm; ) This wonderful expat institution has recently moved location, but is going from strength to strength. Its woodfired pizzas and coffee are the best in town, while proceeds from its home-baked cakes go to a local orphanage. There's also a Congolese craft store, Friday movie nights, Tuesday salsa lessons, regular coffee tasting and a farmers market one Sunday a month.

## Information

Exchange rates at the banks in town are better than those at the airport, but lower than in Kampala.

**Barclays ATM** (off Airport Rd)

**Stanbic Bank** (Kampala Rd) ATM.

## Getting There & Away

The brand new four-lane Entebbe Express Hwy was nearing completion in early 2017 and will slash journey times between Entebbe International Airport and Kampala when it opens. At present the journey takes around an hour and a half, though in traffic it can be two hours or more.

### BUS

**Pineapple Express** (Map p714; 0787-992277; www.entebbejinjashuttle.com; Oasis Mall, Yusuf Lule Rd) shuttle runs daily from the airport and guesthouses to Kampala (US$12, two hours) at 5am, 2.30pm and 11pm. The first two buses also serve Jinja (US$24, four hours).

Minibus taxis run between Entebbe and either taxi park in Kampala (USh2500, 1½ hours) throughout the day. A special-hire from the airport to Kampala will cost you anywhere from USh70,000 to USh100,000.

# EASTERN UGANDA

Eastern Uganda, where the mighty Nile begins its epic journey north, is a must on any East African journey thanks to an intoxicating blend of adrenaline adventures and superb scenery. White-water rafting on the Nile River undoubtedly leads the way as the biggest draw card, but trekking through Mt Elgon National Park and visiting stunning Sipi Falls are two other big reasons not to miss Uganda's eastern flank. The region's capital, Jinja, is a charming and friendly place on the shore of Lake Victoria where many backpackers find themselves spending a week or more enjoying the chilled atmosphere and top-notch activities.

## Jinja

POP 72,900 / ☎0434

Famous as the historic source of the Nile River, Jinja is these days the adrenaline capital of East Africa. Here you can get your fix of white-water rafting, kayaking, quad biking, mountain biking and horseback riding in a town with a gorgeous natural setting and some wonderful, crumbling colonial architecture.

### Activities

The source of the Nile is one of the most spectacular white-water rafting destinations in the world and for many visitors to Uganda a rafting trip is the highlight of their visit. Here you can expect long, rollicking strings of Grade IV and V rapids, with plenty of thrills and spills. Despite the intensity of some of the rapids, most people who venture here are first-time rafters; it's the perfect opportunity to get out of your comfort zone and try something different.

The three most reputable rafting companies are **Nile River Explorers** (NRE; ☎0772-422373; http://raftafrica.com), **Nalubale Rafting** (☎0782-638938; www.nalubalerafting.com; half-/1-/2-day trips US$125/140/255) and **Adrift** (☎0772-286433, 0312-237438; www.adrift.ug; half-/full-day trips US$125/140), all equal in terms of professionalism and pricing, and each places an outstanding emphasis on safety (all rafting trips are accompanied by a fleet of rescue kayaks and a safety boat you can retreat to if you find things a bit too hairy for your liking).

### Sleeping & Eating

Jinja has some wonderful guesthouses in its leafy suburbs away from the dusty city centre, as well as along its gorgeous shoreline on Lake Victoria. There are also some fantastic options further downriver, near Bujagali, around 8km from Jinja. This is where most of the backpacker and activities bases are. Due to its sizeable expat and NGO community, Jinja has some good eating options, while the steady stream of travellers in the town has contributed to the eating scene too, and has led to a string of rather hip cafes and coffee shops lining Main St. Various international cuisines dominate the selection, but Ugandan food is also available.

**Nile River Explorers Campsite** HOSTEL $
(☎0772-422373; http://aftafrica.com/site/accommodation/explorers-river-camp.html; Bujagali; camping US$7, dm US$12, r from US$50, r without bathroom from US$30; @ 📶) The most popular place to stay at Bujagali, this attractive camp is set on a grassy site with sensational river views. There's a good mix of budget rooms, often full with overland truckers and backpackers, but the pick of accommodation are the tented camps sloped along the terraced hill, which have superb outlooks – as do the showers!

★**Hairy Lemon** BANDAS $$
(☎0434-130349, 0772-828338; www.hairylemonuganda.com; incl full board camping US$35, dm from US$38, bandas US$42-70) Situated 15km downstream from the starting point for rafting, Hairy Lemon's isolated location on a small island makes it the perfect getaway retreat. More rustic than luxurious, dorms and *bandas* (thatched-roofed huts) are basic and mostly share bathrooms. A short paddle away is Nile Special, a world-class wave for kayakers. It's essential to book ahead.

★**Gately on Nile** BOUTIQUE HOTEL $$
(☎0434-122400, 0772-469638; www.gatelyonnile.com; 47 Nile Cres; s US$59-80, d US$89-105, house s/d US$130/175; @ 📶) The classiest guesthouse in Jinja, Gately's stylish rooms are split between a lovely garden premises with a selection of thoughtfully decorated rooms, and loft apartments and a gigantic villa across the road, all of which have views of Lake Victoria. The Mediterranean-style house is a great choice for honeymooners and families. The **restaurant** (mains USh19,000-27,000; ⏰7am-9.30pm; 📶) is one of the best in town.

**Source of the Smile Guesthouse** GUESTHOUSE $$
(☎0783-842021; www.sourceofthesmile.com; 39 Kiira Rd; s/d/tr from US$80/88/125; 📶 🏊) Mixing a relaxed vibe with a bohemian design

## Jinja

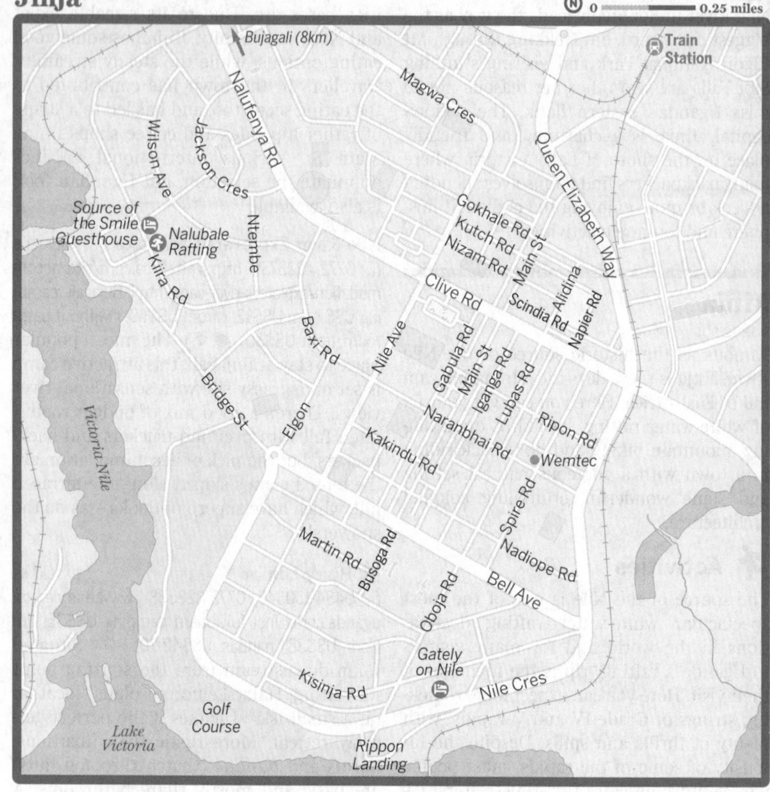


scheme, a gorgeous garden and a pleasant pool, this guesthouse is indeed likely to bring a smile to one's face, even if the name makes you cringe. For a bit of character, opt for the poolside rooms; otherwise there are cheaper, more conventional rooms out the back.

### Getting There & Around

Coming from Kampala, be prepared for a slow and frustrating ride on the two-lane road to Jinja. The Nalubaale Power Station (formerly known as the Owen Falls Dam) provides a spectacular gateway into the town, but don't take pictures – people have been arrested for doing so, even though there are no signs informing people of this law.

The centre of Jinja is compact enough to wander about on foot. For getting elsewhere you'll want a *boda-boda;* a ride to Bujagali will cost about USh5000.

## Mbale

POP 96,200 / ☎0454

You'll pass through Mbale, a bustling provincial city, if you're planning an assault on Mt Elgon or en route to Sipi Falls. Away from the dusty centre there are pockets of charm and it does have a scenic mountain backdrop, but there's no real reason to hang around here.

### Sleeping & Eating

**Casa Del Turista** HOSTEL $

(☎0772-328085; https://casadelturistablog.wordpress.com/; 18 Nkokonjeru Tce; dm/s/d US$12/18/26; 📶) This friendly guesthouse is a relaxed place to hang out, with high-speed internet, spotless dorms and private beds. Its Eco Shamba cafe has quality food and top organic Mt Elgon coffee, and with proceeds going to a local school, why would you want to stay anywhere else?

**Nurali's Café** INDIAN $

(☎0772-445562; 5 Cathedral Ave; mains USh10,000-20,000; ⊙8.30am-10.30pm) Nurali's is a popular Indian restaurant delivering delicious flavours from the tandoor. It has a great biriyani selection, plus some less reliable Chinese, a few Ugandan greatest hits and creative pizzas, including topping such as steak and kidney, or sausage and apple. Its bar is the closest thing to a proper pub in Mbale and it's a friendly and fun place.

### Information

**National Park Headquarters** (☎0454-433170; www.ugandawildlife.org; 19 Masaba Rd; ⊙8am-5pm Mon-Fri, 8am-3pm Sat & Sun) Organise your Mt Elgon visit here, about 1km from the city centre.

### Getting There & Away

There are frequent buses or minibuses to Kampala (USh15,000, four hours) and Jinja (USh10,000, three hours) from the main taxi park off Manafa Rd. Behind it is the bus stand, with less frequent transport to Jinja, Kampala, and Soroti. Prices are similar to minibus prices.

For Sipi Falls (USh7000, one hour), head to the Kumi Rd taxi park northeast of town. Services are infrequent so it's best to travel in the morning.

## Mount Elgon National Park

Trekking in **Mt Elgon National Park** (www.ugandawildlife.org; adult/child US$35/5, trekking per day incl fees & guide US$90) offers some of East Africa's most memorable climbing experiences, and boasts a milder climate, lower elevation and much more reasonable prices than climbs available in neighbouring Kenya or Tanzania. Mt Elgon has five major peaks and the highest, Wagagai (4321m), is on the Ugandan side. It's the second tallest mountain in Uganda and the eighth tallest in Africa.

### Activities

There are four routes up the mountain. Many people combine different routes going up and down for maximum variety. If summiting at Wagagai, it only takes an extra hour to hit Jackson's Summit (4165m) via Jackson's Pool, a little crater lake. You must use designated campsites, all of which have tent pads, latrines, rubbish pits and nearby water sources.

There are also many options for day hikes, with the most popular being a trio of short loops around the Forest Exploration Centre at the start of the Sipi Trail. Rose's Last Chance offers day walks for USh30,000 (including lunch) or a two-day Budadari to Sipi Falls walk along the slopes of Mt Elgon, visiting villages and coffee plantations en route (USh300,000 per person inclusive of food, tents, guide and porter); no park permit required.

Trekking on Mt Elgon costs US$90 per person per day, which covers park entry fees and a ranger-guide. Permits are issued at UWA offices at each trailhead. Guides are mandatory whether heading to the summit or just doing a day trip. Camping fees are USh15,000 more per night and porters, who are highly recommended, charge USh15,000 per day for carrying 18kg. Also factor in tips, which are highly appreciated.

### Sleeping

★**Rose's Last Chance** GUESTHOUSE $

(☎0772-623206, 0752-203292; www.roseslastchance.yolasite.com; Budadiri; incl half board camping USh12,000, dm USh15,000, s/d USh20,000/30,000) Located near the trailhead in Budadari, Rose's is a laid-back, comfortable, fun and friendly place that brings guests closer to the local scene. Testing local brews is a favourite activity and Rose sometimes brings in musicians and dancers at night. The dining room has good vibes and bedrooms are cosy and clean. It's located a few doors down from the UWA office.

**Forest Exploration Centre** GUESTHOUSE $

(☎0772-674063; Kapkwai; camping USh15,000, dm USh10,000, s/d USh40,000/55,000) This lovely spot run by Uganda Wildlife Authority (UWA) is right at the Sipi trailhead and has a little restaurant. Book via the National Park Headquarters office in Mbale.

### Getting There & Away

There are regular minibuses from Mbale to Budadari (USh5000, one hour).

## Sipi Falls

Sipi Falls, in the foothills of Mt Elgon, is a stunner – arguably the most beautiful waterfall in all of Uganda. There are three levels, and though the upper two are beautiful, it's the 95m main drop that attracts the crowds, and most of Sipi's lodging looks out over it. It's well worth spending a night or two in this peacefully magnificent place, which also allows you time to enjoy some of the excellent walks in the area, including the show-stopping descent to the bottom of the falls.

## Activities

Aside from gawking at the views, the main activity here is hiking. Guides for activities are best organised through your hotel or the grassroots **Sipi Falls Tourism Guide Association** (☎0772-646364, 0773-068977) based outside **Sipi Falls Resort** (☎0753-153000; sipiresort@gmail.com; camping USh30,000, s/d/tr USh160,000/190,000/230,000).

## Sleeping

**Lacam Lodge** LODGE $$
(☎0752-292554; www.lacamlodge.co.uk; incl full board camping from USh65,000, dm from USh85,000, r without bathroom from s/d USh95,000/125,000, bandas s/d/tr from USh140,000/230,000/300,000) This attractive lodge is the closest to the big waterfall, and from the viewing area you can see the water crash on land. Accommodation here, from the three-bed dorms to the large *bandas* (thatched-roofed huts), is very stylish and comfortable, and the service is good. Rates include full board and fluctuate seasonally.

**Sipi River Lodge** LODGE $$
(☎0751-796109; www.sipiriverlodge.com; incl full board dm US$67, banda s/d US$112/138, cottage d/q US$219/374) This attractive lodge has a tranquil setting among a garden full of flowers, with a flowing creek and Sipi's second waterfall as a memorable backdrop. Rooms range from charming country-style cottages to *bandas* and 'dorms' (which you're unlikely to have to share) with wide, comfy beds.

## Getting There & Away

Minibus taxis run between Mbale and Sipi Falls (USh10,000, one hour), but can take a long time to fill up. For the return trip, most minibuses start at Kapchorwa and are often full when they pass through Sipi, so you may end up waiting a while. Ask at your lodge if they know when any minibuses will start the trip in Sipi.

# SOUTHWESTERN UGANDA

## Fort Portal

POP 54,300 / ☎0483

The fort may be gone, but this dynamic and friendly town is definitely still a great portal to numerous places offering sublime scenery, amazing nature and genuine adventure. Here you can explore the beautiful Crater Lakes, track the chimps in Kibale Forest National Park or drop into Semuliki National Park with its hot springs and central African wildlife, while all the time having the pleasant hotels of Fort Portal to return to afterwards.

### Sights & Activities

**Tooro Palace** PALACE
(guide USh5000, camera USh20,000) Looking down over the town from its highest hill, the palace is worth a visit purely for its 360-degree panoramic views. It's the residence of King Oyo, who ascended the throne in 1995 at the age of three! A guide will give you a quick history of the kingdom and explain the ceremonies that take place on the hill, but you can't go inside.

**Kabarole Tours & Safari** TOURS
(☎0774-057390, 0483-422183; https://kabarole-tours.com; 1 Moledina St; ⏲8am-6pm Mon-Sat, 10am-4pm Sun) A local leader in community tourism and an impressive advocate for sustainable travel, Kabarole Tours can take you anywhere in Uganda, but focuses on this little corner of the country. Popular day trips include those to the Crater Lakes, mountain bike tours, birdwatching, village walks and treks in the foothills of the Rwenzoris. It can arrange gorilla permits for both Uganda (US$30) and Rwanda (US$50).

### Sleeping & Eating

★**Ruwenzori View Guesthouse** GUESTHOUSE $
(☎0483-422102, 0772-722102; www.ruwenzoriview.com; Lower Kakiiza Rd, Boma; s/d USh135,000/195,000, without bathroom USh70,000/115,000; P wi-fi) A blissful little guesthouse run by a Dutch–Anglo couple, with a refreshingly rural and lovely homely atmosphere. The rooms with attached bathrooms have their own patios overlooking the superb garden and Rwenzori mountain backdrop. Rates include a hearty breakfast, while its social dinners (USh35,000) served around the family table are an institution (nonguests also welcome).

★**Y.E.S. Hostel** HOSTEL $
(Youth Encouragement Services; ☎0772-780350, 0787-291183; www.yesugandahostel.weebly.com; Lower Kakiiza Rd; camping USh10,000, dm USh20,000, d with shared bathroom USh30,000; wi-fi) This wonderful project is the work of Carol, a Hawaiian who moved to Uganda to make a difference over two decades ago, and boy,

has she! Y.E.S. supports the Mama Rescue Home, where 30 HIV+ children live, through its exceptional-value hostel with a peaceful pastoral setting. Rooms are configured as dorms, but usually you'll get one to yourself.

**Dutchess Guesthouse** GUESTHOUSE **$$**
(☎0704-879474, 0718-746211; www.dutchessuganda.com; 11 Mugusrusi Rd; s/d/tr US$65/80/105, s without bathroom US$30; P@☎) Dutchess offers excellent-value boutique rooms with plenty of flair, big beds, couches, powerboard adaptors and safes for laptops. Sadly there are just a few rooms, so it's a good idea to book ahead. The excellent downstairs restaurant is another reason to stay here, as is its central location and kindly staff.

★**Dutchess** INTERNATIONAL **$**
(www.dutchessuganda.com; 11 Mugusrusi Rd; mains USh10,000-30,000; ⏲7am-11pm; ☎) Easily Fort Portal's best place to eat (if not the entire country's), Dutchess has a creative menu featuring crocodile burgers, Flemish beef stew with Guinness and mash, and a selection of 46 excellent woodfired pizzas, including a superb calzone to keep visiting *mzungus* happy. The only lacklustre offering on our last visit was the dessert menu.

### Getting There & Away

**Kalita** (☎0483-422959; www.kalita.co.ug; Lugard Rd) and **Link** (☎0312-108830; www.link.co.ug) have regular buses to Kampala (USh20,000, five hours). Both also head to Kasese (USh5000, two hours), but only Kalita makes the journey to Kabale (USh35,000, eight hours), via Katunguru (USh9000, 1½ hours) in Queen Elizabeth National Park.

## Crater Lakes

The landscape south of Fort Portal is dotted with picturesque crater lakes, all of which are ringed with improbably steep hills. It's a great spot to settle in for a few days to explore the footpaths or cycle the seldom-used roads. Much of the land is cultivated, but there are still plenty of primates and birds at the lakeshores.

### Lake Kasenda

Little Lake Kasenda isn't at the end of the road, but it sure feels like it. **Afritastic Planet Ruigo** (☎0701-370674; incl breakfast camping USh10,000, s/d USh50,000/60,000, r without bathroom USh30,000) is a tiny refuge from the world, sitting right on the shore of Lake Kasenda looking up at the steep hills on the other side. Considering how few people come here, the three self-contained *bandas* are well maintained. The 'treehouse' is secluded on the other side of the lake, and is great for those who want solitude.

### Lake Nkuruba

Probably the winner among the contenders for the title of most beautiful crater lake, Nkuruba is one of the few still surrounded by forest. Many monkeys, including black-and-white and red colobus, frolic here, giving it the feel of wild paradise.

**Lake Nkuruba Nature Reserve Community Campsite** (☎0782-141880, 07732-66067; www.nkuruba.com; Lake Nkuruba; camping USh10,000, s/d without bathroom USh36,000/52,000, cottage USh75,000) is the best place to stay on the lake (not to be confused with the imitating lodge next door) with funds going towards community projects. The camp is set on a hill with nice views and easy access to the lake. The *bandas* are basic, but clean and comfortable. The cottage is down on the lakeshore for more privacy.

### Lake Nyabikere

The 'Lake of Frogs' (you'll hear how it got its name at night!) lies just off the road to Kibale Forest National Park, 12km northwest of Kanyanchu visitor centre or 21km from Fort Portal. An enjoyable footpath circles the lake.

Not actually on Lake Nyabikere, but near enough to snatch some views of it, is the wonderful **Chimpanzee Forest Guesthouse** (☎0772-486415; www.chimpanzeeforestguesthouse.com; camping US$10, incl breakfast s/d guesthouse US$65/95, cottage US$70/110; ☎). Set in manicured gardens overlooking tea plantations, there's a choice of *banda* cottages or rooms in the atmospheric 1950s colonial building with a fireplace and a superb collection of antique books on Africa.

### Lake Nyinabulitwa

A beautiful and tranquil spot, the mid-sized 'Mother of Lakes' is set back a bit off the road to Kibale Forest National Park.

**Nyinabulitwa Country Resort & Safari Camp** (☎0712-984929; www.nyinabulitwaresort.com; Lake Nyinabulitwa; incl breakfast camping US$15, s/d/tr from US$70/120/180) is an intimate little place on the lake's south shore with five *bandas* and an excellent campsite. With a beautiful garden setting, it's the perfect place to catch up on your journal. It runs boat trips (US$10 per person) around the lake and can deliver you to a treehouse for bird- and primate-watching. Alternatively, you can paddle around yourself for free.



### Lake Nyinambuga

Emblazoned on Uganda's USh20,000 note, picturesque Lake Nyinambuga is a worthwhile stop with some excellent photo ops.

Luxurious, colonial-style **Ndali Lodge** (☎0772-221309; www.ndalilodge.com; Lake Nyinambuga; s/d incl full board US$545/738; @📶🏊) has a stunning location on a ridge above the lake. Its elegant (but well overpriced) cottages face west towards Mwamba and Rukwanzi lakes with the Rwenzori Mountains looming on the horizon. Day-trippers should aim for a lunch stop here with homely toasted sandwiches served on a tranquil porch overlooking the lake.

## Kibale Forest National Park

☎0483

This 795-sq-km **national park** (☎0483-425335; www.ugandawildlife.org; adult/child US$40/20) just outside Fort Portal is made up of dense tropical rainforest, within which dwell enormous numbers of primates. If you can't afford the lavish cost of mountain gorilla tracking, then visiting one of the five habituated groups of chimpanzees here is a very worthy substitute, not to mention a far less financially draining one. Also regularly seen here are the rare red colobus and L'Hoest's monkeys.

Larger but rarely seen residents include bushbucks, sitatungas, buffaloes, leopards and quite a few forest elephants. There are also an incredible 250 species of butterfly and 372 species of bird here. The park visitor centre is at Kanyanchu, 35km southeast of Fort Portal.

### Activities

With around a 90% chance of finding chimpanzees on any particular day, Kibale National Park is undoubtedly the most popular place to track them in Uganda. There's a morning (8am) and afternoon (2pm) departure. Children aged 12 and under aren't permitted.

While you've a good chance of being issued a chimp permit (US$150) at the park, it occasionally gets booked out during the holiday season, so reservations at the UWA office (p717) in Kampala are a good idea. Regular trackers get just one hour with the playful primates, but those on the **Chimpanzee Habituation Experience** (1/2/3 days US$220/440/660; ⏲Mar, Apr, May & Nov) can spend the whole day with them.

### Sleeping

**UWA Campsite** CAMPGROUND $
(☎0486-424121; camping per person US$12) This pleasant campsite is enclosed by the rainforest, but offers some attractive grass on which to pitch your tent. There are showers and toilets on site and you can take meals at the nearby **Primate Lodge** (☎0414-267153; www.ugandalodges.com/primate; Kanyanchu; camping without breakfast US$14, incl full board s/d safari tent US$178/254, cottage US$340/480; 📶) if you don't want to cook for yourself.

★**Kibale Forest Camp** LODGE $$
(☎0312-294894; www.naturelodges.biz/kibale-forest-camp; Bigodi; camping US$10, s/d lazy camping US$35/60, tented camping US$90/115) This atmospheric camp is hidden away deep in the forest, offering tented camping with stone floors and porches, fire-heated hot water, and even ready-made 'lazy camping' for the budget minded. There's also a safari-style restaurant in an attractive *banda*. It's on the outskirts of Bigodi, 1km down a side road off the Kamwenge Rd.

★**EcoBurrito** TEX-MEX $
(☎0780-142926; www.ecoburrito.com; Bigodi; burritos USh9000-10,000; ⏲8am-5pm Mon-Fri) This brilliant and highly unexpected roadside find is likely to elicit squeals of glee from even the most seasoned Africa hands. An American doctoral student studying the chimps in the park trained locals in the ways of Tex-Mex, and EcoBurrito is the result. Enjoy succulent and delicious chapattis and tortillas stuffed full of tasty fillings and washed down with beer.

### Getting There & Away

Minibuses to Kamwenge from Fort Portal pass the park visitor centre (USh8000, one hour). For Sebitoli, take any minibus (USh2000, 30 minutes) heading east from Fort Portal.

## Semuliki National Park

Covering 220 sq km of the valley floor connecting Uganda to the steamy jungles of central Africa, **Semuliki National Park** (☎0382-276424; www.ugandawildlife.org; adult/child US$35/5) harbours some intriguing wildlife, although sightings are not always easy due to the thick vegetation. It's most famous for its primordial hot springs, sites for traditional rituals for the local Bamaga people. Birdwatchers come to look for over 440 birds; at least 133 of the 144 Guinea-Congo forest species have been recorded here and nearly 50 species are found nowhere else in East Africa. There are nine primate species, including De Brazza's monkey, and many mammals not found elsewhere in Uganda, such as Zenker's flying mice.

**Bumaga Campsite** (☎0772-367215; camping USh20,000, banda USh90,000-135,000) is a pleasant, grassy spot on the edge of the forest with several *bandas* and a campsite with showers and latrines. There's a lovely elevated dining area, but you will need to bring your own food. You'll need to arrange accommodation at the UWA office at the Sempaya Gate. The campsite is located 2km past the gate.

There are regular minibuses and pick-ups between Fort Portal and Bundibugyo that pass the park (USh12,000, three hours). The last one heads to Fort Portal around 4pm, so if you leave early you can do the park as a day trip.

## Toro-Semliki Wildlife Reserve

Once one of the best-stocked and most popular wildlife parks in East Africa, the **Toro-Semliki Wildlife Reserve** (☎0772-649880; adult/child US$35/5) suffered significant poaching during the civil-war years and after the war with Tanzania. However, wildlife is recovering well and you may encounter waterbucks, reedbucks, bushbucks, chimpanzees, pygmy hippos, buffaloes, leopards, elephants and hyenas here. A number of lions have also recently returned to the reserve, which is also the oldest protected natural area in Uganda, having first been set aside in 1926.

The small **Uganda Wildlife Authority (UWA) campsite** (☎0772-911499; www.ugandawildlife.org; camping USh15,000, banda with shared bathroom USh50,000) at Ntoroko is on the shores of Lake Albert, meaning you often have hippos joining you in the evening. There are three *bandas* with shared bathrooms and a small canteen where staff prepare your meals.

One of the first luxury lodges in Uganda, **Semliki Safari Lodge** (☎0414-251182; www.wildplacesafrica.com; s/d incl full board & activities US$180/300; 📶🚭) has eight luxury tents set under *bandas,* all with sumptuous Persian carpets and four-poster beds. It's extremely good value for what you get, as the prices include all food, one game drive or boat trip per day, transfers from the airport and local taxes.

Toro-Semliki can be reached very easily by public transport or your own wheels from Fort Portal, and even from Kampala if you fly.

## Kasese

POP 101,700 / ☎0483

The only reason to visit Kasese is to organise a trip to the Rwenzori Mountains.

A mix of cleanliness and good prices makes **White House Hotel** (☎0782-536263; whitehse_hotel@yahoo.co.uk; 46 Henry Bwambale Rd; r USh40,000, s/d without bathroom USh21,000/35,000; @📶) one of Kasese's most popular budget options. The garden restaurant next door is the best in town for a feed and cold beer (mains from USh15,000).

The quickest connection to Kampala (USh20,000, five hours) is the Link or Kalita bus via Fort Portal (USh4000, one hour).

Getting to Queen Elizabeth National Park is straightforward. Catch any Mbarara-bound vehicle to Katunguru (USh4000, one hour).

## Rwenzori National Park

The Unesco World Heritage–listed **Rwenzori Mountains National Park** (www.ugandawildlife.org; adult/child US$35/5) contains the tallest mountain range in Africa, including several peaks that are permanently covered by ice. The three highest peaks in the range are Margherita (5109m), Alexandria (5083m) and Albert (5087m), all on Mt Stanley, the third highest mountain in Africa. Two mammals are endemic to the range, the Rwenzori climbing mouse and the Rwenzori red duiker, as are 19 of the 241 known bird species. This is one of Uganda's less visited national parks, and so nature lovers wanting to escape the safari crowds should definitely put it on their list.

### Activities

Back in Uganda's heyday, the Rwenzoris were as popular with travellers as Mt Kilimanjaro and Mt Kenya, but this is definitely a more demanding expedition. The Rwenzoris (known locally as the 'Rain Maker') have a well-deserved reputation for being very wet and muddy, with trails that are often slippery and steep. There are treks available to suit all levels and needs, from one-day jaunts in the forest to 10-day treks with technical climbs. The six-day treks are the most popular. The popular **Rwenzori Trekking Services** (RTS; ☎Kampala 0774-114499, Kilembe 0774-199022; www.rwenzoritrekking.com) looks after the Kilembe Trail. The Muhoma Nature Trail is open to all, but Ruboni Community Campsite can assist with arranging guides, as can Uganda Wildlife Authority (UWA).

The best times to trek are from late December to mid-March and from mid-June to mid-August, when there's less rain. Guides, who are compulsory even if you've conquered the seven summits, are on perpetual standby so you can book in the morning and leave the same day.

### Sleeping

**Ruboni Community Campsite** HUT $
(☎0752-503445; www.rubonicamp.com; camping with/without tent US$5/15, banda per person US$25, r without bathroom per person US$20) This community-run place down the road from Nyakalengija is at the base of the hill just outside the park boundary, with an attractive setting and comfortable lodging. All profits go towards a health centre, tree planting projects and more. It also offers guided walks into the hills outside the park, drumming lessons and traditional dance performances.

★**Equator Snow Lodge** LODGE $$
(☎0414-258273; http://geolodgesafrica.com/index.php/equator-snow-lodges/; s/d/tr incl full board US$132/242/342; ) Conveniently located for the Central (and Mahoma) Trail, this luxury mountain lodge at the foot of the Rwenzoris has large cottages surrounded by forest and views from its porch. There are plenty of superb trekking opportunities in the immediate area, even if you're not keen on a hardcore mountaineering expedition. All up, it's excellent value.

### Getting There & Away

Nyakalengija is 25km from Kasese, though minibuses only run as far as Ibanda (USh5000, one hour). From here you can take a *boda-boda* to Nyakalengija (USh4000) or Ruboni Community Camp (USh3500). For Kilembe (USh4000, 30 minutes), take one of the frequent shared-car taxis from near the Shell petrol station on Kilembe Rd.

## Queen Elizabeth National Park

Covering 1978 sq km, scenic **Queen Elizabeth National Park** (☎0782-387805; www.ugandawildlife.org; adult/child US$40/20; ⏰6.30am-7pm, park gates 7am-7pm) is one of the most popular parks in Uganda. Few reserves in the world can boast such a high biodiversity rating, and with landscapes including savannah, bushland, wetlands and lush forests, the park is inhabited by 96 species of mammals, including healthy numbers of hippos, elephants, lions and leopards as well as chimps and hyenas. The remote Ishasha sector, in the far south of the park, is famous for its tree-climbing lions. Don't miss the superb birdlife or the wonderful boat trip on the Kazinga Channel either.

### Activities

#### Boat Trips

Almost every visitor takes the two-hour launch trip (US$30) up the Kazinga Channel to see the thousands of hippos and pink-backed pelicans, plus plenty of crocodiles, buffaloes and fish eagles. The boat docks below Mweya Safari Lodge, but you buy tickets at the UWA visitor centre up on the top of the hill. Trips depart at 9am, 11am, 3pm and 5pm.

#### Wildlife Drives

Most of the wildlife-viewing traffic is in the northeast of the park in Kasenyi, which offers the best chance to see lions, as well as elephants, waterbucks and kobs. Night game drives (US$30 per person, including guide) are also available. Pay for drives or book guides at any of the park gates or at the Mweya Visitor Information Centre.

As well as being famous for its tree-climbing lions, Ishasha, in the south of the Queen Elizabeth National Park, is the only place to see topis and sitatungas.

## Sleeping

**Bush Lodge** LODGE $

(☎0312-294894; www.naturelodges.biz/the-bush-lodge; Kazinga Channel; lazy camping s/d US$35/60, s/d US$105/140) One of the park's most popular budget choices, this bush camp sits on the banks of Kazinga Channel where elephants and hippos often hang out. There's a choice between basic tents with beds (and power points), and pricier safari-tent rooms with outdoor stone bathrooms. At dinner, tables are brought around the campfire to provide some atmosphere.

★ **@The River** LODGE $$

(☎0772-722688; www.attheriverishasha.com; Ishasha; camping incl full board US$35, tented camp without bathroom per person US$60, s/d US$95/190, bush camping per person US$180; ) Word of this fantastic lodge has spread all over Uganda, and it's definitely one of Queen Elizabeth's best offerings. While its vibe and standards are very similar to that of the luxury camps, @The River boasts far more affordable rates. It has a laid-back camp atmosphere, with tasteful cottages, a plunge pool, a riverside beach and open-air showers.

★ **Katara Lodge** LODGE $$$

(☎0773-011648; www.kataralodge.com; Kichwamba; s/d incl full board US$250/400; @) It's hard not to be seduced by this exceptionally gorgeous place. With just five wood, thatch and canvas cottages made for taking in the stunning savannah views, it's quite simply a sublime choice, even if the rooms do feel rather dark sometimes. The best bit: the sides roll up and even the bed rolls out for sleeping under the stars.

**Mweya Safari Lodge** LODGE $$$

(☎0312-260260; www.mweyalodge.com; Mweya; s/d incl full board from US$227/402; @) Queen Elizabeth's iconic, classic safari lodge has a commanding location with excellent views over Lake Edward and the Kazinga Channel – full of hippos and buffaloes. Set in a resort-like complex, it offers everything from hotel-style rooms to luxury tents and plush cottages, most with views of the water. Come sunset, the terrace overlooking the water is the place to be.

## Eating

**Tembo Canteen** INTERNATIONAL $

(Mweya Peninsula; meals USh10,000-20,000; ⌚6.30am-11pm) A wonderful safari-style canteen, Tembo buzzes with campers, UWA staff, guides and drivers, all here for cheap, tasty food and cold beer. Head outdoors to its tables with epic lake views.

## Information

**Mweya Visitor Information Centre** (☎0392-700694; Mweya Peninsula; ⌚6.30am-6.30pm) Helpful and busy visitor information centre on the Mweya Peninsula with info on activities and UWA's accommodation and campgrounds.

## Getting There & Away

Park gates are open from 7am to 7pm. Katunguru is the main village in the park's centre, which is linked by buses from Kampala and Kasese.

# Bwindi Impenetrable National Park

As names go alone, there can hardly be a more evocative African destination than the so-called Impenetrable Forest of Bwindi. But unlike many other alluringly named places, this one is just as magnificent as it sounds. A swath of steep mountains covered in thick, steamy jungle, the 331-sq-km World Heritage–listed **Bwindi Impenetrable National Park** (☎0414-355409, 0486-424121; www.ugandawildlife.org; adult/child US$40/20; ⌚park office 7.45am-5pm) is one of Africa's most ancient habitats, even surviving the last Ice Age as most of the continent's other forests disappeared.

The combination of its broad altitude span (1160m to 2607m) and its antiquity has produced an incredible diversity of flora and fauna, resulting in some 120 species of mammal and over 350 species of bird calling Bwindi home. The stars of the show, however, are the approximately 340 mountain gorillas living here, which is why most people come. Seeing these critically endangered creatures up close is an unforgettable experience.

## Activities

A genuine once-in-a-lifetime experience, hanging out with mountain gorillas is one of the most thrilling wildlife encounters in the world, and Bwindi Impenetrable National Park is one of the best places to see them. There are theoretically 96 daily permits available to track gorillas in Bwindi. Permits cost US$600 (including park entry) and are booked through the UWA office (p717) in

Kampala. Note you must be over 15 years of age to track the gorillas.

Trips leave from the park office nearest the group you'll be tracking at 8.30am daily, but you should report to park headquarters by 7.45am.

Once you join a tracking group, your chances of finding the gorillas are almost guaranteed. But, as the terrain in Bwindi Impenetrable National Park is mountainous and heavily forested, if the gorillas are a fair distance away it can be quite a challenge to get close. The path is often steep and slippery, and it can take anywhere from 30 minutes to five hours to reach them, so you'll need to be in reasonable shape.

## Tours

**Ride 4 A Woman** CYCLING

(☎0785-999112; www.ride4awoman.org; Buhoma; bike rental from US$25, tours from US$25) This NGO runs guided mountain-bike tours through the forest or village and rents out bikes if you want to go exploring yourself. They also have a clothing and craft shop near Buhoma Hospital, where they offer sewing classes from USh30,000. All proceeds go to helping women in the community.

**Batwa Experience** CULTURAL

(☎0772-901628; www.batwaexperience.com; per person US$60-85) The Twa (Batwa) people were displaced from their forest habitat when Bwindi became a national park, but this community-owned company allows you to both meet them and see how they lived in the forest. The five-hour tours include witnessing a mock hunting party with bow and arrows and watching stories from Twa legend being told alongside traditional song and dance. Price depends on the number of participants.

## Sleeping

**★Buhoma Community Rest Camp** LODGE $

(☎0772-384965; www.buhomacommunity.com; Buhoma; camping US$12, dm without breakfast US$30, s/d US$85/126) Next door to the park headquarters, this camp is Bwindi's most popular budget option with a stunning location looking directly out to the forest. *Bandas* (thatched-roofed huts) and safari tents are spaced out on a hill heading down the valley, and the best are at the bottom, which puts you right at the jungle; gorillas sometimes even pass by the clearing here.

**Bwindi Backpackers** LODGE $

(☎0772-661854; www.bwindibackpackerslodge.com; Nkuringo; camping US$15, dm US$20-25, s/d US$45/90, s/d without bathroom US$30/60; 📶) Colourful if somewhat dilapidated, Bwindi Backpackers offers the best budget digs on the south side of the park. Rooms are basic but have mosquito nets and many boast incredible full-frontal forest views. The cottages are a little bigger and have simple en suite bathrooms, while the restaurant boasts the best views of all over the jungle canopy.

**★Nkuringo Bwindi Gorilla Lodge** LODGE $$$

(☎0754-805580; www.mountaingorillalodge.com; Nkuringo; incl full board lazy camping s/d US$82/143, s/d US$200/250, cottages with bathroom s/d US$300/418; 📶) A wonderful set-up with views looking out to the misty Virungas, the Nkuringo Gorilla Camp is one of the best places to stay in Bwindi. Comfortable rooms and cottages mix safari-chic with boutique touches, while lazy camping (sleeping in pre-erected tents) provides a more cost-effective option. Little touches such as turn-over service, fabulous bathrobes and hot-water bottles go a long way.

**Bwindi Lodge** LODGE $$$

(☎0414-346464; www.volcanoessafaris.com/lodges/bwindi-lodge; Buhoma; s/d incl full board & activities US$250/500; 📶) An ultra-luxurious offering by Volcanos hotel group, Bwindi Lodge has superb thatched, farm-style cottages that open up to thick jungle. Activities include game drives, coffee plantation visits, forest walks and trips to nearby Batwa villages.

# Kabale

POP 49,700 / ☎0486

A dusty provincial town, Kabale is the kind of place most people get through as fast as possible. It is of most interest to travellers as a transport hub and gateway to both Lake Bunyonyi and Bwindi Impenetrable National Park, though given its proximity to both, most travellers try to avoid overnighting here and carry straight on to Bunyoni and Bwindi's far more obvious charms.

## Sleeping & Eating

**Kabale Backpackers** HOSTEL $

(☎0782-421519; Muhumuza Rd; dm USh15,000, r per person without breakfast USh20,000-35,000; 📶) Despite its name, this budget place isn't particularly attuned to the needs of backpackers (paid wi-fi, very basic toilets), but it's a good overnight choice for those on a budget, and there's a pool table and cafe downstairs. Rooms are very simple, but beds have mosquito nets and there's a friendly vibe.

**★White Horse Inn** HOTEL **$$**
(☎0772-459859, 0486-423336; www.whitehorseinnkabale.com; Rwamafa Rd; s/tw/d US$40/40/60; ) Set on five grassy acres on the outskirts of town, this faded colonial hotel (built in 1937) has hosted many a visiting dignitary, including Jimmy Carter and Bill Gates. These days its still living in the shadow of its glory days; but remains a good midrange option for those who like their accommodation to have some character.

**Cafe Barista** CAFE **$**
(Kabale-Kisoro Rd; mains USh8000-20,000; ⏲8am-11pm) This friendly cafe on Kabale's main drag serves up pizzas, burgers and curries to hungry travellers. It also has decent coffee and pastries.

## Getting There & Away

The **Post Bus** heads to Kabale to/from Kampala (USh25,000, eight hours) en route from/to Kisoro (USh14,000, two hours) at around 3pm from the post office. There are buses to Fort Portal (USh30,000, eight hours) via Queen Elizabeth National Park and Kasese (USh25,000, seven hours). Minibus taxis to the Rwandan border at Katuna (USh5000, 30 minutes) and on to Kigali are frequent.

# Lake Bunyonyi

Lake Bunyonyi ('place of many little birds') is undoubtedly the loveliest lake in Uganda. Its contorted shore encircles 29 islands, and the steep surrounding hillsides are intensively terraced, reminiscent of parts of Nepal. A magical place, especially with a morning mist rising off the placid waters, it has supplanted the Ssese Islands as the place for travellers to chill out on their way through Uganda, and has a selection of gorgeously remote and bucolic places to stay on distant islands, where you've only the birds for company. Best of all – unlike many lakes in East Africa – Bunyoni is bilharzia, croc and hippo free, and so its crystal clear waters are all yours to swim in. Bliss.

## Activities

All guesthouses on the lake can arrange boat trips, either in motorboats or dugout canoes, which is still how most locals get about. This is one of the few places in Uganda where you can swim, so go ahead and jump in.

## Sleeping & Eating

**★Byoona Amagara** LODGE **$**
(☎0752-652788; www.lakebunyonyi.net; Itambira Island; camping USh12,000, dm USh20,000-26,000, geodome per person USh46,000-60,000, cabin per person USh50,000, cottage USh225,000; @) Marooned perfectly on an idyllic island, Byoona Amagara bills itself as a backpacker's paradise, and it's hard to disagree. The rooms are built with all-natural materials and are very reasonably priced, though the open-faced geodome huts are the pick of the litter and have some of the most extraordinary views you'll see anywhere in Uganda.

**Birdnest@Bunyoni Resort** RESORT **$$**
(☎0754-252560; www.birdnestatbunyonyi.com; s/d US$160/190, cottage US$210; ) Belgian-owned Birdnest is an impressive sight. It's the most upmarket choice in Bunyonyi, but remains excellent value. Open-plan rooms have vibrant decor, with lovely, private balconies looking out to the lake, while the outside terrace decking has a swimming pool with huge hammocks and free canoe hire. The secluded cottages (which sleep four) can only be reached by canoe.

**Lake View Coffee House** CAFE **$**
(Kachwekano; mains USh8000-20,000; ⏲7am-9pm; ) This open-air cafe has a fantastic wooden deck with sweeping views over the lake. There's a full menu of delicious Indian and Western food (including pizza), though portions tend to be on the small side.

**Yared's Island Cafe** SEAFOOD **$**
(Itambira Island; meal USh13,000; ⏲dawn-dusk) If you're staying on Itambira Island, then search out this small hut on the path between Cities of Hope and Green Lodge. Here John will serve you a meal of delicious crayfish chapattis and welcome you into his simple home and introduce you to his young family. Experiences don't come much more local than this.

# Kisoro

POP 17,500 / ☎0486

While Kisoro – a gritty town with a frontier atmosphere – may not be much to look at, its verdant surrounds are undeniably beautiful. On a clear day the backdrop of the Virunga chain of volcanoes is stunning. Kisoro serves as a popular base for tourists, here primarily to access nearby Mgahinga Gorilla National Park to see mountain gorillas, track golden monkeys or climb volcanoes. It's also a convenient base for those with gorilla permits in the southern sector of Bwindi Impenetrable National Park or even Parc National des Virunga at Djomba, just over the border in the DRC. If you're en route to/from Rwanda it makes a pleasant place to spend the night.

## Sleeping & Eating

**Golden Monkey Guesthouse** HOSTEL $
(☎0772-435148; www.goldenmonkeyguesthouse.com; dm/s/d US$10/30/40, r with shared bathroom US$15; 📶) Friendly and welcoming, Golden Monkey is popular with NGOs and return visitors. Well-maintained rooms are basic but good value, and it has the best menu in town in its popular restaurant. It also runs Virunga Adventure Tours, and can arrange trips across Uganda as well as decent-value transfers to the nearby parks.

★**Travellers Rest Hotel** HOTEL $$
(☎0772-533029; www.gorillatours.com/accommodations/travellers-rest/; Mahuabura Rd; s/d/tr US$85/100/130; @📶) This is a hotel with a history. It was once run by the so-called father of gorilla tourism, Walter Baumgärtel, and Dian Fossey regularly stayed here. Through various thoughtful touches such as Congolese crafts, this otherwise simple place has become a lovely little oasis. The garden has lots of shade, and an atmospheric bar with fireplace.

**Coffee Pot Café** CAFE $
(www.coffee-pot-cafe.com; Bunagana Rd; mains USh5,000-10,000; ⏲8.30am-9.30pm; 📶) A smart German-owned cafe with decent coffee, burgers, BLTs and meatball dishes. It sells secondhand books and quality crafts next door.

## Information

**Mgahinga Gorilla National Park Office**
(☎0414-680793; www.ugandawildlife.org; Main St; ⏲8am-5pm) The place to book your gorilla permits, they have information about everything in and around Kisoro.

## Getting There & Away

**Post Bus** (Main St) heads to Kampala (USh30,000, nine hours) via Kabale (USh10,000, 1½ hours) daily at 6am. Several bus companies also have departures during the morning, as do minibus taxis.

The Rwandan border south of Kisoro at Cyanika is open 24 hours and it's a pretty simple, quick trip to Musanze (Ruhengeri). To the border a *boda-boda* is around USh5000; special-hire taxi is USh25,000.

# Mgahinga Gorilla National Park

The tiny 34-sq-km **Mgahinga Gorilla National Park** (☎0486-430098; www.ugandawildlife.org; adult/child US$40/20) in the far southwest corner of the country is Uganda's slice of volcanic Virunga range, most of which can be found in the dense tropical rainforest of Eastern DRC and northern Rwanda. While the 434-sq-km Virunga Conservation Area that is shared between the three countries is home to half the world's mountain gorilla population, Uganda's small share of the park means that its one habituated gorilla family regularly ducks across the mountains into Rwanda or the DRC. Mgahinga also serves up some challenging but rewarding treks, plus golden monkeys, elephants, buffaloes and many rare bird species.

**Batwa Trail** (tour incl guide US$80) forest tours are led by the local Twa (Batwa), who explain how they used to live in the forest before they were forcibly removed from Mgahinga when it was turned into a national park. The 3½-hour tours include tales from Twa legend, demonstrations of day-to-day practices such as hunting and fire lighting, and a visit to the 342m-long Garama Cave, a historic residing spot of the Twa, where you'll get a song-and-dance performance.

Right at the park's gate, **Amajambere Iwacu Community Campground** (☎0774-954956, 0782-306973; www.amajamberecamp.com; camping with/without tent US$5/10, dm US$10, banda s/d/tr US$30/40/50) 🍃 is friendly and extremely peaceful. Set up and run by the local community, it has a variety of rooms with nice verandas for relaxing. It's a good choice for those seeking a local experience, and has volunteer opportunities. Proceeds fund school projects in the area.

There's no scheduled transport along the rough 14km track between Kisoro and the park headquarters. A special-hire taxi (around USh60,000) or *boda-boda* (motorcycle taxi; USh10,000) are the most straightforward way of getting to the park, but be prepared for a long, rough, slippery ride if it's wet.

## Ssese Islands

If you're looking for a place to slow it right down, Ssese's lush archipelago of 84 islands along Lake Victoria's northwestern shore boasts some stunning white-sand beaches. There's not much to do other than grab a good book and relax. There are canoes for hire, but swimming is not advised due to the risks of bilharzia, and some outlying islands have the occasional hippo and crocodile.

**Banda Island Resort** (☎0772-222777, 0774-728747; www.bandaisland.biz; Banda Island; incl full board camping USh110,000, dm & tented camping USh150,000, cottage USh195,000) is exactly what an island escape should be: it has a picturesque beach and laid-back vibe, and days here feel like weeks. This decidedly rustic place nonetheless has running water, cold beer and hot showers. Accommodation is in comfortable cottages, decent dorms or tented camps. Food is a highlight. Hippos are common visitors come full moon.

**Brovad Sands Lodge** (☎0758-660020; www.sseseislandsresorthotel.com; Bugala Island; s/d USh135,000/200,000; ) is a stunning property comprising large, plush thatched cottages in a tropical garden with a soaring *banda* restaurant and direct beach access. Though it has its imperfections (eg some shoddy materials), all is forgiven when lazing in its pool or hanging out on the beach by the bonfire. Discounts available.

Departure times from Buggala are at 1.30pm, arriving at Port Bell by 6pm. Fares are USh30,000/70,000 for economy/first class; you'll need to arrive 30 minutes before departure.

# NORTHERN UGANDA

## Murchison Falls National Park

**Murchison Falls National Park** (☎0392-881348; www.ugandawildlife.org; adult/child US$40/20; 7am-7pm) is Uganda's best-known and biggest nature reserve, and its impressive animal populations and superb activities are further augmented by its location, which straddles the Victoria Nile as it makes its way through multiple rapids and waterfalls (including the enormously impressive Murchison Falls) to Lake Albert. This is an exceptional place to see wildlife and a trip along the Nile should not be missed.

### Sights & Activities

Wild Frontiers (www.wildfrontiers.co.ug) offers the most comfortable boat trips up the Nile to the falls (US$32 per person; 2.30pm daily, 8.30am Monday, Wednesday and Friday). Cheese-and-wine sunset cruises (US$75 per person) are also available, as are longer boat trips downstream to the papyrus-filled delta where the Nile empties into Lake Albert (US$55 per person). Full-day fishing trips start at US$115 per person (excluding permits).

**★Top of the Falls** WATERFALL

Once described as the most spectacular thing to happen to the Nile along its 6700km length, the 50m wide Victoria Nile is squeezed here through a 6m gap in the rock and crashes through this narrow gorge with unbelievable power. The 45m waterfall was featured in the Katharine Hepburn and Humphrey Bogart film *The African Queen*. Murchison was even stronger back then, but in 1962 massive floods cut a second channel creating the smaller Uhuru Falls 200m to the north.

**Budongo Forest Reserve** PARK

(www.budongo.org) The Budongo Forest Reserve is a large (825 sq km) tract of virgin tropical forest on the southern fringes of Murchison Falls National Park. Its main attractions are chimpanzees and birds (366 species), but the huge mahogany trees are also worth a look. It's a great add-on to your Murchison Falls National Park visit, with your park permit allowing you entry to Budongo too.

### Sleeping

**★Red Chilli Rest Camp** HOSTEL $

(☎0772-509150; www.redchillihideaway.com; Paraa; camping US$7, d safari tents US$30, d/f banda US$50/85, d banda without bathroom US$35; ) The excellent Red Chilli team offers the best budget option in Murchison. The *bandas* (thatched-roofed huts) are great value, while well-priced safari tents get the job done. The restaurant-bar is set under a thatched roof with good river views and a roaring evening fire. Meals are good value, as are the hearty breakfasts before each day's safari drive. Book well in advance.

**Pakuba Safari Lodge** LODGE $$$

(☎0414-253597, 0786-657070; www.pakubasafarilodge.com; s/d US$163/189; ) Overlooking the Albert Nile, this lodge deep inside the park

## Murchison Falls National Park

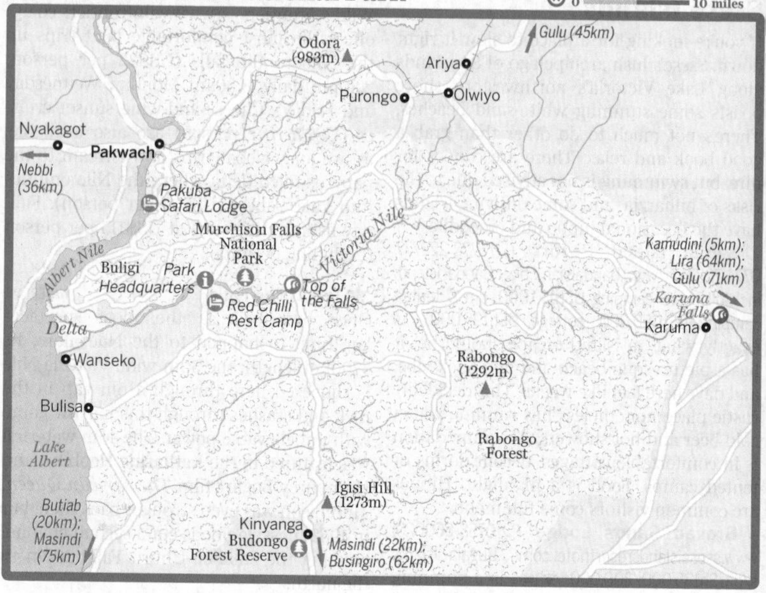

was built on a site just up from the ruins of an old safari lodge formerly used by Idi Amin, now a picturesque ruin favoured as a hangout by giraffes. Rooms are huge, stylish and rather minimalist, even if they're rather tightly packed in together in terraced rows.

### Information

**Park Headquarters** (www.ugandawildlife.org; Paraa; ⊙6.30am-6.30pm) Buy permits, book tours and pay for ferry crossings across the Nile here.

### Getting There & Away

Public transport can be used to get to the fringes of the park, but you'll need a vehicle to get within; numerous hostels offer budget tours, which are the best option for backpackers without wheels.

## Ziwa Rhino Sanctuary

The Big Five are back. Twenty years after poachers shot the nation's last wild rhino in Uganda, Rhino Fund Uganda opened this private 70-sq-km reserve, 170km northwest of Kampala. There are now 19 southern white rhinos roaming the savannah and wetland, many of which were born in the wild in Uganda.

**Ziwa Rhino Lodge** (☎0775-521035; www.ziwarhino.com; camping per tent US$10, r with shared bathroom US$15, cottage US$40) is set around the park headquarters, and you can choose between the cottages or rows of basic rooms with small porches. There's also a restaurant serving simple food and cold drinks, plus camping for overlanders with cooking facilities and ablutions. There's plenty of wildlife about, including the occasional rhino.

Deep in the sanctuary (a 20-minute drive from park headquarters), tasteful **Amuka Safari Lodge** (☎0771-600812; www.amukalodgeuganda.com; banda incl half board per person US$153; ) has secluded cottages and a common area with lovely decking, a swimming pool, a bar and an open-air restaurant.

All buses from Kampala heading to Gulu or Masindi pass nearby. Get off at little Nakitoma (USh15,000, three hours) and take a *boda-boda* (motorcycle taxi) 7km to the sanctuary gate for USh6000.

## Gulu

POP 152,000 / ☎0471

Unless you're here volunteering or en route to Kidepo Valley National Park, there's no real reason to visit Gulu. It's the largest town in northern Uganda and one of the hardest hit during the Lord's Resistance Army (LRA) conflict. It's a town in transition and, in a sure sign of optimism, shop shelves are full and people are arriving from elsewhere in the country hoping to cash in on the coming boom.

## Sleeping & Eating

**Hotel Pearl Afrique** HOTEL $

(☎0774-072277; www.hotelpearlafrique.co; Paul Odong Rd; s/d from USh75,000/90,000) A comfortable, good-value choice with spotless rooms, some with bathtubs. Pricier rooms are worth it, with tonnes more space. There's a restaurant and bar with live music on weekends.

**Bomah Hotel** HOTEL $$

(☎0779-945063; http://bomahhotels.com; 8 Eden Rd; s/d/ste US$47/70/195; ❄@☜≋) In a leafy part of town, the colonial-style Bomah is Gulu's smartest option with sparkling rooms in a hotel block set over many levels. There's also an excellent gym overlooking the pool and a popular thatched-roof restaurant (mains USh18,000 to USh22,000).

**Coffee Hut** CAFE $

(Awich Rd; coffee USh4000, wraps USh8000; ☜) Across from the bus park, this modern cafe is the place to go for excellent coffee, w-fi, breakfast and tasty wraps.

## Getting There & Away

To get here your best option is the Kampala–Gulu Post Bus, which continues through to Kitgum. Otherwise buses and minivans run between Kampala and Gulu (USh25,000, five hours) all day long departing from and arriving at Gulu's bus park. Those heading to Kidepo can get a bus to Kitgum (USh12,000, three hours).

# Kidepo Valley National Park

This **national park** (www.ugandawildlife.org; adult/child US$40/20) is most notable for harbouring a number of animals found nowhere else in Uganda, including cheetahs, bat-eared foxes, aardwolves, caracal, and greater and lesser kudus. There are also large concentrations of elephants, zebras, buffaloes, bushbuck, giraffes, lions, jackals, leopard, hyenas and Nile crocodiles. The park also offers some of the most stunning scenery of any protected area in Uganda; the rolling, short-grass savannah of the 1442-sq-km park is ringed by mountains and cut by rocky ridges.

**Apoka Hostel** BANDAS $

(☎0392-899500; camping USh15,000, s/d USh60,000/70,000, s/d without bathroom USh40,000/50,000) The best of Uganda Wildlife Authority (UWA)'s park lodges, laid-back Apoka has basic *bandas* (thatched-roofed huts) spread over its grassy site. There's plenty of wildlife about, so be sure to keep your distance and always carry a torch. You've got a good chance of hearing lions roaring at night. There's a small restaurant with a limited menu (meals USh8000) and cold beers to enjoy around the nightly campfire.

★**Apoka Safari Lodge** LODGE $$$

(☎0414-251182; www.wildplacesafrica.com; s/d incl full board & 2 activities US$550/755; ☜≋) If you want something really special, you want Apoka Safari Lodge. Its large, private cottages with thatched roofs and canvas walls all look out to wildlife grazing right on your doorstep. Each features an outdoor tub (watch animals graze while you have a bath), stone showers, perfect views and a writing desk that would suit Hemingway to a tee.

## Getting There & Away

The vast majority of visitors take the route through to Kitgum via Gulu, which is the shortest, easiest and safest route. Undoubtedly your best bet is to rent a car, in which case you can make it in one day from Kampala to Kidepo if you get a very early start. Alternatively you could take a bus to Kitgum and negotiate a special-hire from there.

# UNDERSTAND UGANDA

## Uganda Today

Surprising almost nobody, President Museveni won a thumping victory in the 2016 presidential elections, earning an impressive 61% of the vote. As he began his fifth term as president, Museveni looked more and more like one of the African big men he himself used to rage against, and though his popularity is waning, no credible opposition has arisen that can make an impact at the polls.

Though there's been no further incident since the horrific bombings in Kampala in 2010 that left 74 dead, threats of terrorism remain a concern. The ongoing involvement of Ugandan troops in peace-keeping missions in Somalia have put the nation firmly in the targets of the Al-Shadab militia group. In light of the Nairobi attacks in 2013, Kampala remains on high alert with thorough security checks at malls, bars and restaurants now an everyday part of life.

# History

Uganda experienced two great waves of migration. The first brought the Bantu-speaking peoples from further west in Africa, and the second, the Nilotic people from Sudan and Ethiopia. These broad families are still geographically split today: the Bantu in the centre and south of the country and the Nilotic peoples in the north.

## The British Arrive

After the Treaty of Berlin in 1890, when Europeans carved up Africa, Uganda, Kenya and Zanzibar were declared British Protectorates. The Brits ruled indirectly, giving the traditional kingdoms a considerable degree of autonomy, but favoured the Baganda (the name of the people of the Buganda Kingdom) people for their civil service. The Acholi and Lango people from the north soon became dominant in the military. Thus were planted the seeds for the intertribal conflicts that were to tear Uganda apart following independence.

## Independence Time

By the mid-1950s a Lango schoolteacher, Dr Milton Obote, had cobbled together a loose coalition that led Uganda to independence in 1962, on the promise that the Baganda would have autonomy. The *kabaka* (king), Edward Mutesa II, became the new nation's president, and Milton Obote became prime minister. It soon became obvious that Obote had no intention of sharing power. In 1966 he arrested several cabinet ministers and ordered his army chief of staff, Idi Amin, to storm the *kabaka's* palace. Obote became president, and the Bugandan monarchy (and all others) was abolished.

## Enter Idi Amin

Idi Amin staged a coup in January 1971, and so began Uganda's first reign of terror. All political activities were suspended and the army was empowered to shoot on sight anyone suspected of opposition to the regime. Over the next eight years an estimated 300,000 Ugandans lost their lives, often in horrifying ways. Amin's main targets were the educated classes; the Acholi and Lango people of Obote; and the 70,000-strong Asian community, which in 1972 was given 90 days to leave the country.

Meanwhile, the economy collapsed, infrastructure crumbled, prolific wildlife was slaughtered by soldiers and the tourism industry evaporated. The stream of refugees fleeing the country became a flood, inflation hit 1000% and the treasury ran out of money to pay the soldiers. By the end of 1978 Amin had invaded Tanzania – ostensibly to teach that country a lesson for supporting anti-Amin dissidents – as a diversion from problems at home. However, the Tanzanians, with the help of exiled Ugandans, soundly defeated Amin and pushed on into the heart of Uganda in early 1979.

## Obote Rides Again

The rejoicing in Uganda after Amin's downfall was short-lived. The 12,000 Tanzanian soldiers who remained in Uganda turned on the Ugandans as soon as their pay dried up. Once again the country slid into chaos and gangs of armed bandits roamed the cities, killing and looting. Yusufu Lule and Godfrey Binaisa came and went as leaders before Obote returned from exile in Tanzania. He swept to victory in an election that was widely reported to be rigged.

Obote continued a policy of tribal favouritism, replacing many southerners in military and civil-service positions with his northern Lango and Acholi supporters, and the prisons began to fill again. Reports of atrocities leaked out of the country and several mass graves were discovered. In mid-1985 Obote was overthrown in a coup staged by the army under the leadership of Tito Okello.

## A New Beginning

Okello, who turned out not to be much different from his predecessors, had many enemies, including Yoweri Museveni, who built a guerrilla army in western Uganda. Museveni's National Resistance Army (NRA) was different from the armies of Amin and Obote – new recruits, many of them orphans, were taught to be servants of the people, not oppressors, and discipline was tough.

By January 1986 it was clear that Okello's days were numbered. The NRA launched an all-out offensive and easily took Kampala since most of Okello's troops chose to loot the capital rather than fight. Museveni was a pragmatic leader. He appointed a number of arch-conservatives to his cabinet, and made an effort to avoid the tribal nepotism that had divided the country. The economy improved, and aid and investment returned. Political parties were banned to avoid a polarisation along tribal lines. Prosperity followed stability, and this was helped by Museveni's bold decision to invite Asians back. He also restored the monarchies. In 1996 he agreed to elections,which he won overwhelmingly. He was easily re-elected in 2001.

The darkness didn't end for northern Uganda, however, due to the Lord's Resistance Army (LRA). Its leader, Joseph Kony, grew increasingly delusional and paranoid during the 1990s and shifted his focus from attacking soldiers to attacking civilians in his attempt to found a government based on the biblical Ten Commandments. Eventually more than one million northerners fled their homes to refugee camps and tens of thousands of children became 'night commuters', walking from their villages each evening to sleep in schools and churches or on the streets of large towns.

## Daily Life

Life in Uganda has been one long series of upheavals for the older generations, while younger generations have benefited from the newfound stability. Society has changed completely in urban areas in the past couple of decades, but in the countryside it's often business as usual.

Uganda has been heavily affected by HIV/AIDS. One of the first countries to be struck by an outbreak of epidemic proportions, Uganda acted swiftly in promoting AIDS awareness and safe sex; Uganda went from experiencing an infection rate of around 25% in the late 1980s to one that dropped as low as 4% in 2003.

But things have changed. Due in large part to pressure from the country's growing evangelical Christian population, led on this issue by President Museveni's outspoken wife (though the president himself has taken her lead), Uganda has reversed its policy on promoting condoms and made abstinence the focus of fighting the disease. The result is no surprise: the infection rate has since risen to 7.1%.



# SURVIVAL GUIDE

## Directory A–Z

### DANGERS & ANNOYANCES

Uganda is generally a very safe destination today. As a traveller your main dangers are those of mosquito-borne disease and dangerous driving. Gay travellers should be aware that recent evangelical-led campaigns against homosexuality have resulted in a high level of homophobia.

Despite a disarmament program, banditry remains rife in the Karamojong area of the far northeast (though not within Kidepo Valley National Park). Various rebel groups hang out in the far eastern DRC and they occasionally slip across the porous border to wreak havoc.

### ELECTRICITY

**Electricity** 240V, 50 cycles; British three-pin plugs are used.

### EMBASSIES & CONSULATES

Embassies and consulates are located in Kampala.

**Australian Consulate** (Map p714; ☎0312-515865; 40 Kyadondo Rd, Nakasero; ⏰9am-12.30pm & 2-5pm Mon-Fri)

**Belgium Embassy** (Map p714; ☎0414-349559; www.diplomatie.be/kampala; Lumumba Ave, Rwenzori House; ⏰8.30am-1pm & 2-4pm Mon-Thu, 8.30am-1pm Fri)

**Burundi Embassy** (Map p714; ☎0414-235850; 12a York Tce; ⏰visas 10am-1pm Mon-Thu)

**Canadian Embassy** (Map p714; ☎0414-258141; canada.consulate@utlonline.co.ug; 14 Parliament Ave; ⏰9.30am-noon &1-4.30pm Mon-Thu)

**DRC Embassy** (Map p714; ☎0414-250099; 20 Philip Rd, Kololo; ⏰9am-4pm Mon-Fri)

**Dutch Embassy** (Map p714; ☎0414-346000; http://uganda.nlembassy.org; Nakasero Rd, Rwenzori Courts; ⏰10am-noon Mon-Thu, by appointment)

**Ethiopian Embassy** (Map p714; ☎0414-348340; ethiokam@utlonline.co.org; 3 Kira Rd,

### PRICE RANGES

The following price ranges refer to a double room with bathroom in high season.

**$** less than Ush170,000 (US$50)

**$$** Ush170,000–340,000 (US$50–100)

**$$$** more than Ush340,000 (US$100)

The following price ranges refer to a standard main course.

**$** less than USh35,000

**$$** USh35,000–70,000

**$$$** more than USh70,000

Kitante Close; 8.30am-12.30pm & 2-5.30pm Mon-Fri)

**French Embassy** (Map p714; 0414-304500; www.ambafrance-ug.org; 16 Lumumba Ave; 9am-5pm Mon-Thu, to 1pm Fri)

**German Embassy** (Map p714; 0414-501111; www.kampala.diplo.de; 15 Philip Rd, Kololo; 8am-11am Mon-Fri by appointment only)

**Japanese Embassy** (Map p714; 0414-349542; www.ug.emb-japan.go.jp; 8 Kyadondo Rd; 8.30-12.30pm & 1.30-5.15pm Mon-Fri)

**Kenyan High Commission** (Map p714; 0414-258235; kampala@mfa.go.ke; 41 Nakasero Rd; 9am-12.30pm & 2-4pm Mon-Fri)

**Rwandan Embassy** (Map p714; 0414-344045; www.uganda.embassy.gov.rw; 2 Nakayima Rd, Kitante; 9am-12.30pm Mon-Fri)

**South African High Commission** (Map p714; 0417-702100; www.dirco.gov.za/uganda; 15A Nakasero Rd; 8.30am-noon Mon-Fri)

**South Sudan Embassy** (Map p714; 0414-271625; 2 Ssezibwa Rd; 9am-12pm Thu)

**Tanzanian High Commission** (Map p714; 0414-256272; 9am-12.30pm & 2-5pm Mon-Thu, to 1pm Fri)

**UK Embassy** (Map p714; 0312-312000; http://ukinuganda.fco.gov.uk; Windsor Loop, Kamwokya; 8.30am-1pm & 2-5pm Mon-Thu, 8.30am-1pm Fri)

**US Embassy** (Map p713; 0414-259791; https://ug.usembassy.gov; Ggaba Rd, Nsambya; 8-11.45am Mon-Wed, 8-10.45am Fri)

## INTERNET ACCESS

Free wireless is available at all but the simplest hotels, as well as some better restaurants and cafes. However, it's much less likely (or very slow) in national parks and remote regions.

Smart-phone users can easily purchase a local SIM card with data, and this remains the most reliable way to connect. Laptop users can easily get a wireless USB internet/dongle for around US$30. The best networks are MTN and Orange, which have reliable access for most parts of the country (but not in the remote parks).

Internet cafes can be found in cities and most medium-sized towns.

## LGBTIQ TRAVELLERS

Homosexuality has been illegal in Uganda since the time of British colonial rule, and in theory can result in a sentence of up to 14 years in prison. Not satisfied with this relative lenience, in 2014 the Ugandan government passed legislation that punished homosexuality with life imprisonment (watered down from the death sentence proposed by the original law), but this draconian measure was thrown out by the Constitutional Court. As you might expect, the gay community here remains very much underground. LBGTQ tourists are advised to likewise keep things discrete, although there's no need to be overly worried as foreigners are rarely the subject of investigation.

## MONEY

The local currency is the Ugandan shilling (USh), though most tour operators and upscale hotels quote in US dollars. ATMs are abundant and US dollars are widely accepted.

### Exchange Rates

| | | |
|---|---|---|
| Australia | A$1 | USh2315 |
| Canada | C$1 | USh2370 |
| Europe | €1 | USh3360 |
| Japan | ¥100 | USh2465 |
| New Zealand | NZ$1 | USh2080 |
| UK | UK£1 | USh4265 |
| USA | US$1 | USh2650 |

## OPENING HOURS

**Government offices** 8.30am–5pm Mon–Fri

**Shops** 8am–5pm Mon–Sat

**Banks** 9am–3pm Mon–Fri

**Restaurants** 8am–10pm

## PUBLIC HOLIDAYS

**New Year's Day** 1 January

**Liberation Day** 26 January

**International Women's Day** 8 March

**Easter** (Good Friday, Holy Saturday and Easter Monday) March/April

**Labour Day** 1 May

**Martyrs' Day** 3 June

**Heroes' Day** 9 June

**Independence Day** 9 October

**Christmas Day** 25 December

**Boxing Day** 26 December

Banks and government offices also close on the major Muslim holidays.

### TELEPHONE

Mobile (cell) phones are very popular as the service is better than landlines, although there are still large areas of rural Uganda with little or no coverage. MTN and Orange currently have the best coverage across the country. All mobile numbers start with 07. Mobile phone companies sell SIM cards for USh2000 and then you buy airtime vouchers for topping up calling credit or data packs from street vendors.

### TIME

Uganda is three hours ahead of GMT/UTC. There is no daylight saving.

### VISAS

Most passport holders visiting Uganda require visas, including citizens of the US, Canada, EU, Australia and New Zealand. The process for obtaining visas was moved almost entirely online in July 2016, and it's important to note that visas on arrival are no longer available without online approval first, and this can take up to five days.

To apply for your visa, go to the immigration website (http://visas.immigration.go.ug) and follow the instructions. Here, you will have to upload a scan of both your passport's photograph page and your yellow fever certificate, as well as fill in an application form. Once submitted, you should have your approval notification within three working days. You should print this out and present it at immigration when you arrive in Uganda to then get your visa on arrival.

When you receive your visa, you'll need to pay in cash at the immigration desk. Single-entry tourist visas valid for up to 90 days cost US$50; however, do be sure to ask for a 90-day visa, or you'll probably be given 30 or 60 days. Your yellow-fever certificate may be required again, so do bring it with you. Multiple-entry visas aren't available on arrival, but it is possible for embassies abroad to issue them (US$100 for six months).

Uganda is one of the countries covered by the East Africa Tourist (EAT) visa, and for those also visiting Kenya and Rwanda on the same trip it is a cheaper alternative. The visa costs US$100, is valid for 90 days and is multiple entry – it is available upon arrival or from embassies abroad. If acquiring the visa before travel, your first port of call must be the country through which you applied for the visa. If Uganda is your first destination, then you have to apply for the EAT visa in a Ugandan embassy abroad – it is not available by applying online and then obtaining it on arrival.

## Getting There & Away

### AIR

Uganda is well linked to its East African neighbours with daily flights to Kenya, Tanzania, Rwanda, Democratic Republic of Congo and Sudan, even if it doesn't currently have a national airline.

Entebbe International Airport (EBB), located about 40km south of the capital, is the only international airport in Uganda.

### LAND

#### Kenya

The busiest border crossing is at Busia on the direct route to Nairobi through Kisumu. Frequent minibuses link Jinja to Busia (USh10,000, 2½ hours), and then again between Busia and Kisumu or Nairobi.

The other busy border crossing to Kenya is through Malaba, a bit north of Busia and just east of Tororo. Onward transport from here to Nairobi is less frequent than at Busia.

Trekkers in either the Ugandan or Kenyan national parks on Mt Elgon also have the option of walking over the border.

Buses run between Kampala and Nairobi. The journey takes about 12 to 13 hours.

**Easy Coach** (Map p714; ☎0757-727273, 0776-727270; www.easycoach.co.ke; Dewinton Rd) Daily departures to Nairobi (USh80,000) at 6.30am, 2pm and 7pm.

**Mash** (Map p714; ☎0793-234312; www.masheastafrica.com; 7 Dewinton Rd, Kampala) Twice daily departures to Nairobi (USh70,000) at 5pm and 10pm.

**Queens Coach** (Map p714; ☎0773-002010; Oasis Mall, Yusuf Lule Rd) Comfortable bus servicing Nairobi (USh75,000) departing 8pm.

#### Rwanda

There are two main border crossing points between Uganda and Rwanda: between Kabale and Kigali via Katuna (Gatuna on the Rwandan side), and between Kisoro and Musanze (Ruhengeri) via Cyanika. The Kagitumba border isn't very practical for most people, but there is public transport on both sides.

There's also the option of taking a direct bus between Kampala and Kigali (USh35,000 to USh40,000), a seven- to nine-hour journey including a slow border crossing.

**Horizon** (Map p714; ☎0772-504565; 2 Berkely Rd, Kampala) Daily 8pm bus to Kigali from Monday to Saturday.

**Jaguar Executive Coaches** (Map p713; ☎0782-417512; Namirembe Rd, Kampala) Reliable company with daily services to Kigali at 7am, 9am, 8pm and 9pm. Also has a 'VIP' option with more comfortable seats.

**Simba** (Namayiba Terminal; Map p714; Rashid Khamis Rd, Kampala) Daily buses to Kigali (USh40,000, 11 hours) at 2am.

#### Tanzania

The most commonly used direct route between Uganda and Tanzania is on the west side of

Lake Victoria between Bukoba and Kampala, via Masaka; the border crossing is at Mutukula. Road conditions are good and the journey takes about six hours by bus from Kampala (you can also catch these buses in Masaka).

**Falcon** (Map p714; ☎0781-338066; 4 Lumumba Ave, Kampala) Departs for Dar-es-Salaam (USh140,000, 28 hours) on Wednesday, Friday and Sunday at 6am.

**Friends Safari** (Map p714; ☎0788-425952; Rashid Khamis Rd, Kampala) Recommended bus departs at 11am for Bukoba (USh35,000, seven hours) and Mwanza (USh65,000, 12 hours) at 6am.

### The Democratic Republic of Congo

The main border crossings into the DRC are at Bunagana (8km from Kisoro) and Arua, and visitor numbers to DRC are thriving, though do check the current security situation before heading across the border here. There are no direct buses; you'll need to get to Kisoro and continue by special-hire taxi to the border.

#### LAKE

The 'passenger' service on Lake Victoria to Mwanza (Tanzania) is more one for adventure travellers, via the MV *Umoja* cargo ferry that departs from Kampala's Port Bell. Typically these sail two or three days a week. Check the schedule at the Marine Services offices on the 2nd floor of the train station in downtown Kampala. Enter through the eastern gate. Pay your USh5000 port fee in the office in the green shipping container and then USh40,000 directly to the captain. The trip takes 16 to 17 hours and it's usually possible to make a deal with one of the crew for their bunk.

## Getting Around

#### AIR

Several airlines operate charter flights, which get you to the national parks in comfort, but cost a fortune.

**Aerolink** (☎0317-333000; www.aerolinkuganda.com; Entebbe International Airport)

**Eagle Air** (Map p714; ☎0414-344292; www.eagleair-ug.com; 11 Portal Ave, Kampala)

**Fly Uganda** (☎0772-706107; www.flyuganda.com; Kajjansi Airfield)

#### BUS

Standard buses and sometimes half-sized 'coasters' connect major towns on a daily basis. The longer your journey is, the more likely it will be on a bus rather than a minibus. Bus fares are usually a little less than minibus fares and buses stop far less frequently, which saves time. Buses generally leave Kampala at fixed departure times; however, returning from provincial destinations, they usually leave when full. There are many reckless drivers, but buses are safer than minibuses. Night travel is best avoided.

The safest bus company to travel with are the post buses run by the Ugandan Postal Service (UPS). Post buses run daily (except Sunday) from Kampala to Kasese (via Mbarara), Kabale (via Masaka and Mbarara), Soroti (via Mbale) and Hoima (via Masindi).

#### CAR & MOTORCYCLE

There's a pretty good system of sealed roads between most towns in Uganda. Keep your wits about you when driving: cyclists, cows and large potholes often appear from nowhere.

As with other transport, avoid travelling at night due to higher risks of accidents and banditry. Take care in the national parks where there's a US$500 fine for hitting animals and US$150 fine for off-track driving.

### Hire

Due to high taxes and bad roads, car-hire prices tend to be expensive compared to other parts of the world. Add fuel costs and there will be some real shock at the total price if you're considering driving around the country.

**Alpha Car Rentals** (Map p714; ☎0772-411232; www.alpharentals.co.ug; 3/5 Bombo Rd, EMKA House) A car with driver costs USh80,000 for the day around Kampala, while a 4WD with driver is US$100 (his food and lodging inclusive) if you head upcountry, or US$70 for self-drive.

**Road Trip Uganda** (Map p713; ☎0773-363012; www.roadtripuganda.com; off Ggaba Rd) Popular company hiring self-drive fully equipped RAV4s from US$50 per day. Also offers a car with driver.

**Wemtec** (☎0772-221113; wemtec@source.co.ug; 14 Spire Rd, Jinja) Well-known company based in Jinja but delivers country-wide. Hires out a variety of Land Rovers with driver from around USh200,000. Prices all-inclusive (minus fuel), with no limits on mileage.

#### LOCAL TRANSPORT

Kampala has a local minibus network, as well as special-hire taxis for private trips. Elsewhere you'll have to rely solely on two-wheel taxis, known as *boda-bodas* as they originally shuttled people between border posts: from '*boda* to *boda*'. Never hesitate to tell a driver to slow down if you feel uncomfortable with his driving skills, or lack thereof. Outside Kampala, there are few trips within any town that should cost more than USh3000.

# Southern Africa

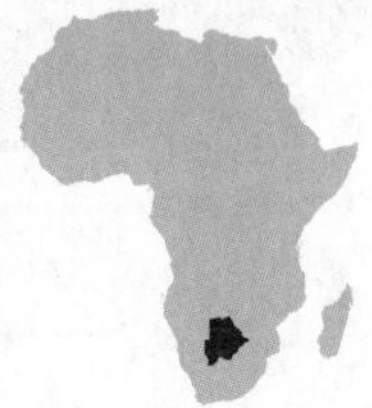

# Botswana

POP 2.183 MILLION / ☎27

### Includes ➡



## Best Places to Eat

➡ Courtyard Restaurant (p744)

➡ Cafe Dijo (p741)

➡ Hilary's (p756)

➡ French Connection (p755)

## Best Places to Sleep

➡ Mombo Camp (p759)

➡ Vumbura Plains Camp (p758)

➡ Sandibe Safari Lodge (p757)

➡ Jao Camp (p758)

➡ Kalahari Plains Camp (p760)

## Why Go?

Blessed with some of the greatest wildlife spectacles on earth, Botswana is one of the great safari destinations in Africa. There are more elephants in Botswana than any other country on earth, the big cats roam free and there's everything from endangered African wild dogs to aquatic antelopes, and from rhinos making a comeback to abundant birdlife at every turn.

This is also the land of the Okavango Delta and the Kalahari Desert, at once iconic African landscapes and vast stretches of wilderness. Put these landscapes together with the wildlife that inhabits them, and it's difficult to escape the conclusion that this is wild Africa at its best.

Botswana may rank among Africa's most exclusive destinations – accommodation prices at most lodges are once-in-a-lifetime propositions – but self-drive expeditions are also possible. And whichever way you visit, Botswana is a truly extraordinary place.

## When to Go

### Gaborone

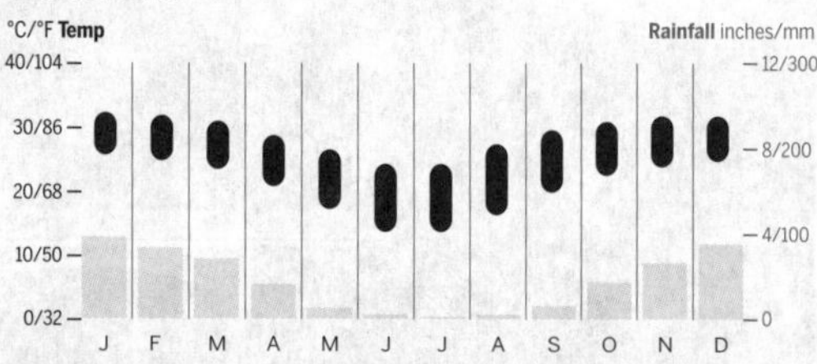


**Jun or Jul–Oct** Warm days and mild nights, but October can be oppressively hot.

**Apr, May & Nov** May nights can be cold, but otherwise a lovely, cheaper time to visit.

**Dec–Mar** Cheaper rates and high availability, except over Christmas/New Year.

# GABORONE

POP 234,500

Depending on your perspective, low-key Gaborone (or Gabs to its friends) is either terribly unexciting or one of Africa's more tranquil capital cities. There aren't that many concrete reasons to come here – it's a world of government ministries, shopping malls and a seemingly endless urban sprawl – and most travellers can fly to Maun or cross overland elsewhere. Yet, it can be an interesting place to take the pulse of the nation.

## Sights

**Gaborone Game Reserve** WILDLIFE RESERVE

(☎318 4492; adult/child/vehicle P10/5/10; ⏲6.30am-6.30pm) This reserve was established in 1988 by the Kalahari Conservation Society to give the Gaborone public an opportunity to view Botswana's wildlife in a natural and accessible location. It seems to be working: although the reserve is only 5 sq km, it's the third busiest in the country and boasts wildebeest, elands, gemsboks, kudus, ostriches and warthogs. The birdlife, which includes kingfishers and hornbills, is particularly plentiful and easy to spot from observation areas.

## Tours

**Africa Insight** TOURS

(☎316 0180, 72 654 323; www.africainsight.com; half-/full-day tours P545/1198) This outfit offers half- and full-day *No. 1 Ladies' Detective Agency* tours endorsed by author Alexander McCall-Smith himself, with more wide-ranging excursions around Gaborone and beyond also possible. Among the latter are 'Predator Weekends' – weekend safaris to Khutse Game Reserve.

**Garcin Safaris** TOURS

(☎71 668 193, 393 6773; garcinsafaris@info.bw; half-/full-day tours from US$140/220) Resident and Gaborone expert Marilyn Garcin does great tours of the city, including a *No. 1 Ladies' Detective Agency*–focused jaunt. She also offers recommended safaris around Botswana.

## Festivals & Events

**Maitisong Festival** PERFORMING ARTS

(☎397 1809; www.maitisong.org; ⏲Mar-Apr) Botswana's largest performing-arts festival has been running since 1987 and is held over seven days in late March or early April. It features an outdoor program of music, theatre, film and dance, as well as an indoor program at the Maitisong Cultural Centre and the Memorable Order of Tin Hats (MOTH) Hall. Highlights include top performing artists from around Africa.

## Sleeping

★**Mokolodi Backpackers** HOSTEL $

(☎74 111 164; www.backpackers.co.bw; camping/dm/s P135/235/325, 2-person units/chalets P550/645, 3-person rondavels P750; @ ≋) This great place, around 14km south of the city centre, is the only accommodation with a real backpacker vibe around Gaborone. It has everything from comfortable rondavels (round huts with conical roofs) and attractive chalets to good campsites (you can use your own tent or rent one) and four-bed dorms.

★**Metcourt Inn** HOTEL $$

(☎363 7907; www.peermont.com; r P620-1060; ❄ 📶) Located within the Grand Palm Resort complex, this affordable business hotel has classy if smallish rooms with a hint of Afro-chic in the decor. If this is your first stop in Africa, you'll wonder what all the fuss is about, but if you've been out in the bush, it's heaven on a midrange budget.

**Capital Guesthouse** GUESTHOUSE $$

(☎391 5905; www.thecapitalguesthouse.co.bw; 28492 Batsadi Rd, Block 3; r P950-1500; P ❄ 📶 ≋) One of a number of newer, more personal guesthouses and B&Bs opening up around Gabs, the Capital is quietly elegant and reasonably central. It's on a quiet street and already has something of a following among business people, expats and travellers.

## Eating

Gabs has numerous good restaurants aimed at an expat market. The upmarket hotels are another good place to try. For cheap African food, stalls near the bus station (and on the Mall during lunchtime) sell plates of traditional food, such as *mealie pap* (maize-meal porridge) and stew. For self-caterers, there are well-stocked supermarkets across the city.

★**Cafe Dijo** CAFE $$

(☎318 0575; Kgale Hill Shopping Mall, Lobatse Rd; mains from P79; ⏲7am-4pm Mon-Fri, 8am-1pm Sat; 📶) This classy but casual place is one of our favourite haunts in Gabs. The lunch specials

## Botswana Highlights

1. **Safaris** (p758) Going on the perfect safari with a luxury camp such as Vumbura Plains.
2. **Mokoro Trips** (p757) Gliding through the vast unspoiled wilderness of the Okavango Delta.
3. **Chobe National Park** (p749) Getting up close and personal with Africa's largest elephant herds.
4. **Central Kalahari Game Reserve** (p759) Looking for black-maned lions in the heart of the Kalahari Desert.
5. **Makgadikgadi Pans National Park** (p748) Watching the wildlife gather by the banks of the Boteti River.
6. **Rock Art** (p750) Leaving behind the crowds and searching for ancient rock art in the soulful and beautiful Tsodilo Hills.

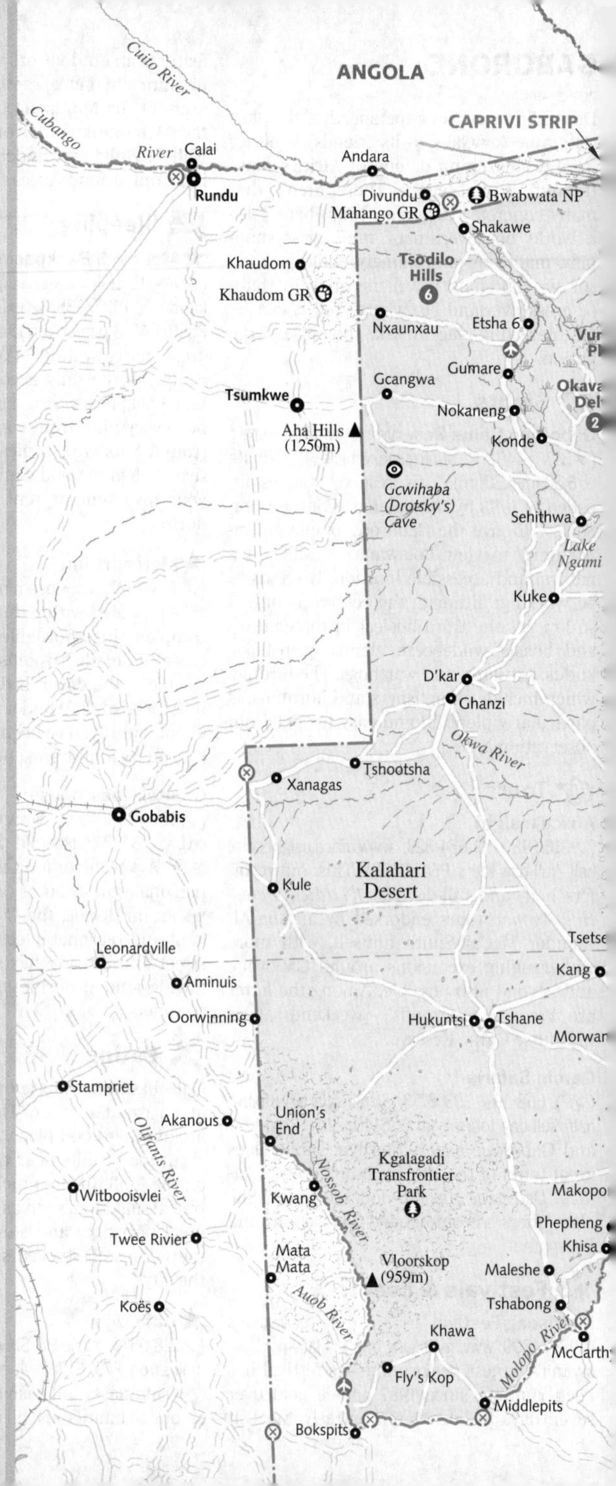

ZAMBIA
Lake Kariba
0 100 km
0 60 miles
FR Forest Reserve
GR Game Reserve
NP National Park
NR Nature Reserve
Sesheke
Mpalila Island
Mosi-oa-Tunya NP
Katima
Chobe River
Kasane
Livingstone
Kazungula
Victoria Falls
Zambezi NP
Zambezi River
Linyanti
Chobe FR
Hwange
Savuti
Pandamatenga
Chobe NP
Sibuyu FR
ZIMBABWE
Nxai Pan
Shorobe
Nxai Pan NP
Gweta
Nata
Nata Sanctuary
Bulawayo
Makgadikgadi Pans NP
Sowa
Plumtree
Ntwetwe Pan
Sowa (Sua) Pan
Gulubane
Gwanda
Mmatshumo
Francistown
Orapa
Letlhakane
Matsiloje
BOTSWANA
Mmashoro
Serule
Selebi-Phikwe
North-East Tuli GR
Khama Rhino Sanctuary
Pont Drift
Serowe
Tuli Block
Mawana NR
Palapye
Zanzibar
Quoxo River
Sherwood
Swartwater
Martin's Drift
Tom Burke
Mahalapye
Parr's Halt
Tropic of Capricorn
Khutse GR
Salajwe
Buffel's Drift
Takatokwane
Letlhakeng
Spanwerk
Ditshegwane
Molepolole
Mochudi
Jwaneng
GABORONE
SOUTH AFRICA
Khakea
Mokolodi NR
Kanye
Mannyelanong GR
Otse Hill (1489m)
Lobatse
Pioneer Gate
Phitshane
Ramatlabama
PRETORIA
Mabule
Tshidilamolomo
Mafikeng
JOHANNESBURG
Soweto
Vryburg

change regularly, but usually include Thai chicken curry, chicken tandoori wraps and excellent salads, alongside toasted ciabatta, wraps and Botswana's best carrot cake. With free wi-fi and great coffee (from filter coffee to Australian iced coffee), you could easily spend hours here.

**★Courtyard Restaurant** AFRICAN, INTERNATIONAL **$$**
(392 2487; www.botswanacraft.bw; Western Bypass, off Airport Rd; mains P65-110; 8am-5pm Mon-Sat) In the garden area out the back of Botswanacraft, this tranquil spot serves up imaginative African cooking (including guinea fowl pot), with other local staples making a rare appearance. It also serves salads and sandwiches and there's even occasional live music.

**Bull & Bush Pub** INTERNATIONAL **$$**
(Map p744; 397 5070, 71 212 233; off Sebone Rd; mains P55-126; noon-10.30pm Mon-Fri, to 11.30pm Sat & Sun) This long-standing South African–run Gabs institution is deservedly popular with expats, tourists and locals alike. Though there's something on the menu for everyone, it's renowned for its thick steaks, pizzas and cold beers. It has some themed nights – Monday is ribs night, Thursday is pizzas – while on any given night, the outdoor beer garden is buzzing with activity.

## Information

### DANGERS & ANNOYANCES

➡ Always take cabs at night, especially if you're a woman or on your own.

➡ Use drivers recommended by hotels and try to keep their phone numbers, as some people have been robbed in unmarked cabs.

➡ The Main Mall is fine to walk around in during the day but is best avoided after dark.



## Gaborone

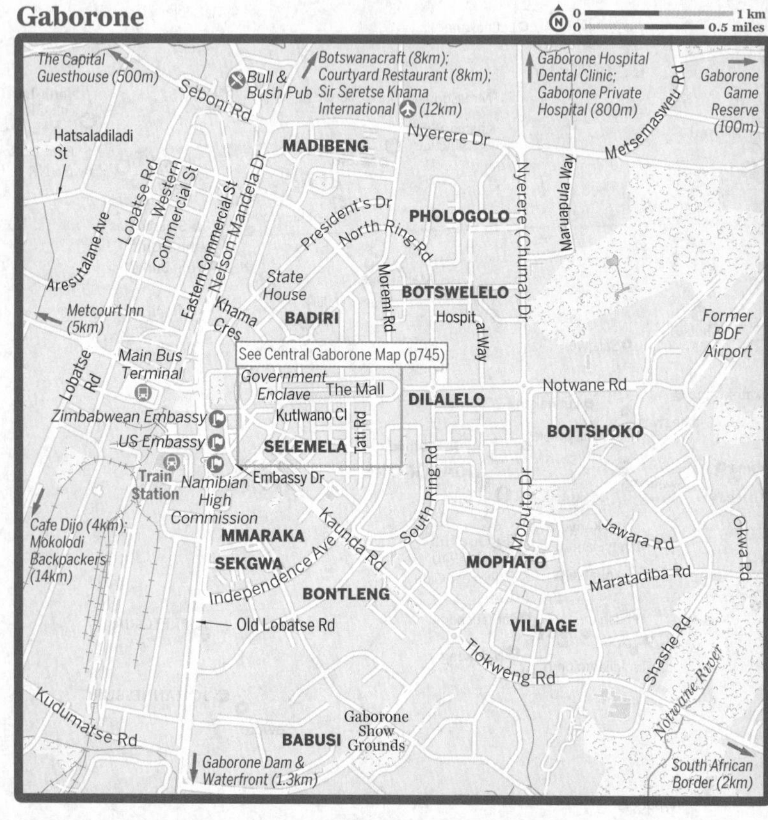

## Central Gaborone

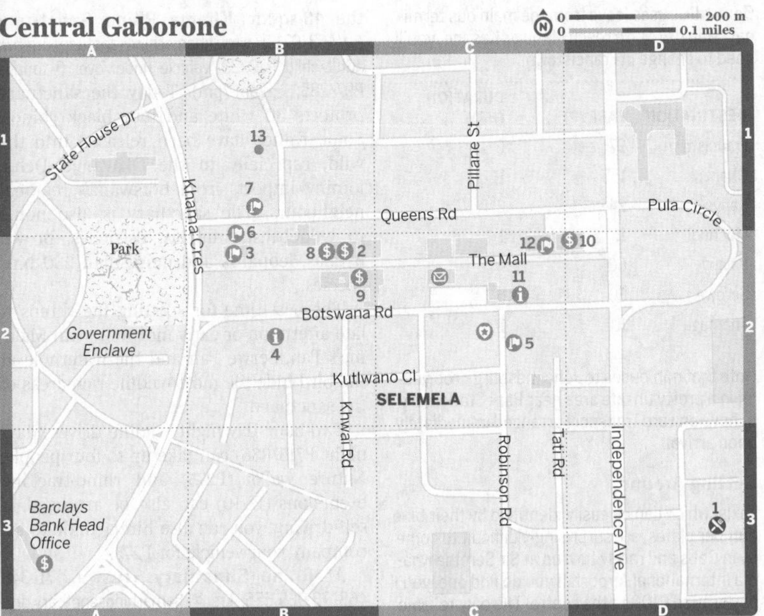


### Central Gaborone

**Eating**

1 Caravela Portuguese Restaurant.......D3

**Information**

2 Barclays Bank .......B2
3 British Embassy .......B2
4 Department of Wildlife & National Parks.......B2
5 French Embassy .......C2
6 German Embassy .......B1
7 South African Embassy .......B1
8 Standard Chartered ATM .......B2
9 Standard Chartered Bank .......B2
10 Standard Chartered Bank .......D2
11 Tourist Office.......C2
12 Zambian Embassy .......C2

**Transport**

13 Air Botswana .......B1

### MEDICAL SERVICES

**Gaborone Private Hospital** (☎300 1999; Segoditshane Way) The best facility in town.

### MONEY

**American Express** (Shop 113, 1st fl, Riverside Mall; ⊙9am-5pm Mon-Fri, to 1.30pm Sat)

**Barclays Bank** (Map p745; The Mall; ⊙8.30am-3.30pm Mon-Fri, 8.15-10.45am Sat)

**Standard Chartered Bank** (Map p745; The Mall; ⊙8.30am-3.30pm Mon-Fri, 8.15-11am Sat)

**UAE Foreign Exchange** (1st fl, Riverwalk Mall; ⊙9am-5pm Mon-Fri, to 1.30pm Sat)

### TOURIST INFORMATION

**Tourist Office** (Botswana Tourism; Map p745; ☎395 9455; www.botswanatourism.co.bw; Botswana Rd; ⊙7.30am-6pm Mon-Fri, 8am-1pm Sat) Next to the Cresta President Hotel, this office has a moderately useful collection of brochures.

### TRANSPORT

#### Getting There & Away

From **Sir Seretse Khama International Airport** (GBE; ☎391 4401; www.caab.co.bw), 14km northeast of the centre, **Air Botswana** (Map p745; ☎368 0900; www.airbotswana.co.bw; Matstitam Rd; ⊙9.30am-5pm Mon-Fri, 8.30-11.30am Sat) operates international services to Harare (Zimbabwe), Johannesburg (South Africa) and Lusaka (Zambia), as well as domestic services.

| DESTINATION | ONE-WAY FARE (P) |
|---|---|
| Francistown | 1406 |
| Kasane | 2060 |
| Maun | 1791 |

Domestic buses leave from the main bus terminal (Map p744). To reach Maun or Kasane, you'll need to change in Francistown.

| DESTINATION | FARE (P) | DURATION (HR) |
|---|---|---|
| Francistown | 97 | 6 |
| Ghanzi | 155 | 11 |
| Kanye | 24 | 2 |
| Mochudi | 15 | 1 |
| Palapye | 60 | 4 |
| Serowe | 60 | 5 |
| Thamaga | 10 | 1 |

Note that minibuses to Johannesburg drop you off in a pretty unsafe area near Park Station; try to have onward transport arranged immediately upon arrival.

### Getting Around

Taxis, which can be easily identified by their blue number plates, are surprisingly difficult to come by in Gabs and rarely turn up at Sir Seretse Khama International Airport. If you do find one, you'll pay around P100 to the centre. The only reliable transport between the airport and town are the courtesy minibuses operated by top-end hotels for their guests. If there's space, non-guests may talk the driver into a lift.

Around Gabs, you're better off arranging a taxi through your hotel.

**Final Bravo Cabs** (☎312 1785)

**Speedy Cabs** (☎390 0070)

# EASTERN BOTSWANA

Eastern Botswana is the most densely populated corner of the country and it's rich in historical resonance as the heartland of the Batswana (people of Botswana). Most travellers visit here on their way between South Africa and Botswana's north, and if you're in Botswana for a two-week safari, you're unlikely to do more than pass through.

But if you've a little more time and are keen to see a different side to the country, Botswana's east does have considerable appeal and is home to the country's most important rhino sanctuary and the Tuli Block, one of Botswana's most underrated wildlife destinations.

## Khama Rhino Sanctuary

With the rhinos all but disappeared from Botswana, the residents of Serowe banded together in the early 1990s to establish the 43-sq-km **Khama Rhino Sanctuary** (☎463 0713; www.khamarhinosanctuary.org.bw; adult/child P79/39, vehicle under/over 5 tonnes P97/285; ⏲7am-7pm). Today the sanctuary protects 30 white and four black rhinos. Some rhinos have been released into the wild, especially in the Okavango Delta, joining imports from Botswana's regional neighbours. The sanctuary is also home to wildebeest, impalas, ostriches, brown hyenas, leopards and more than 230 bird species.

The best time for spotting the rhinos is late afternoon or early morning, with Malema's Pan, Serwe Pan and the waterhole at the bird hide the most wildlife-rich areas of the sanctuary.

Two-hour day/night wildlife drives (day/night P715/836) can take up to four people. Nature walks (P275) and rhino-tracking excursions (P440) can also be arranged. If self-driving, you can also hire a guide to accompany your vehicle for P275.

At **Rhino Sanctuary Trust** (☎71 348 468, 73 965 655; krst@khamarhinosanctuary.org.bw; Khama Rhino Sanctuary; camping per adult/child 103/51, dm P440, chalets P660-880; P 🏊), shady campsites with braai pits (barbecue) are adjacent to clean toilets and (steaming-hot) showers, while there are also some pricey six-person dorms. For a little more comfort, there are rustic four-person chalets and six-person A-frames; both have basic kitchen facilities and private bathrooms. There's also a restaurant, bar and a swimming pool.

The entrance gate to the sanctuary is 26km northwest of Serowe along the Serowe–Orapa road (turn left at the poorly signed T-junction about 5km northwest of Serowe). Khama is accessible by any bus or combi (minibus) heading towards Orapa, with the entrance right next to the road.

## Francistown

POP 98,961

Francistown is Botswana's second-largest city and an important regional centre – there's a fair chance you'll overnight here if you're on the way north from South Africa, or driving without haste between Gaborone and Maun. There's not much to catch the eye, but there are places to stay and eat, as well as excellent supermarkets for those heading out into the wilds.

## Sleeping & Eating

**★A New Earth Guest Lodge** GUESTHOUSE $
(71 846 622; anewearthguestlodge@gmail.com; Bonatla St; r from P520; ) Out in the quiet southeastern suburbs of Francistown, this lovely little guesthouse has a family-run feel and rooms decorated in earth tones or with exposed-stone walls and down-home furnishings. Patricia, your host, is a delight and reason alone to stay here. It can be a little tricky to find, so ring ahead for directions.

**★Woodlands Stop Over** CAMPGROUND, BUNGALOW $$
(244 0131, 73 325 911; www.woodlandscampingbots.com; off A3, S 21°04.532', E 27°27.507'; camping per adult/child P115/95, s/d P725/865, with shared bathroom P415/610, q P1740; ) A wonderfully tranquil place, 15km north of town off the road to Maun, Woodlands is easily the pick of places to stay around Francistown if you have your own wheels. The budget chalets are tidy, the bungalows are nicely appointed and come with loads of space, while the immaculate campsites are Botswana's cleanest and a wonderful respite from dusty trails.

**★Barbara's Bistro** INTERNATIONAL $$
(241 3737; Francistown Sports Club; mains from P75; noon-2pm & 7-10pm Mon-Sat) Located in the town's eastern outskirts in the sports club, this leafy spot is a fabulous choice. Barbara, the German owner, is a charismatic host and loves nothing better than to sit down and run through the specials. The food – German pork dishes like *eisbein* are recurring themes, while the Karoo lamb is outstanding – is easily Francistown's best.

**★Thorn Tree** CAFE $$
(St Patrick St, Village Mall; breakfast P30-70, mains P55-100; 6am-3pm Mon-Sat; ) An oasis of sophistication at the northern end of Francistown, Thorn Tree (no relation to Lonely Planet's famous online bulletin board) does burgers, salads, pizza, pasta, jacket potatoes, fresh fish and great coffee. The outdoor terrace is lovely. This place is highly recommended.

## Information

The **Tourist Office** (244 0113; www.botswanatourism.co.bw; St Patrick St, Village Mall; 7.30am-6pm Mon-Fri, 9am-2pm Sat) is moderately useful for brochures and basic local information, but little else.

## Getting There & Away

From the **main bus terminal** (Haskins St), located between the train line and Blue Jacket Plaza, buses and combis connect Francistown with the following places.

| DESTINATION | FARE (P) | DURATION (HR) |
|---|---|---|
| Gaborone | 97 | 6 |
| Kasane | 110 | 7 |
| Maun | 105 | 5 |
| Nata | 40 | 2 |

# Tuli Block

Tucked into the nation's right-side pocket, the Tuli Block is one of Botswana's best-kept secrets. This 10km- to 20km-wide swath of freehold farmland extends over 300km along the Limpopo River's northern banks and is made up of a series of private properties, many with a conservation bent.

Wildlife is a big attraction, but so too is the landscape, which is unlike anywhere else in Botswana. With its moonscapes of muddy oranges and browns, its kopjes overlooked by deep-blue sky, it's the sort of Dalí-esque desert environment reminiscent of Arizona or Australia. Yet the barren beauty belies a land rich in life. Elephants, hippos, kudus, wildebeest and impalas, as well as small numbers of lions, cheetahs, leopards and hyenas, circle each other among rocks and kopjes (hills) scattered with artefacts from the Stone Age onwards. More than 350 species of bird have been recorded.

**Wild at Tuli** (72 113 688; www.wildattuli.com; Kwa-Tuli Game Reserve; s/d with full board US$250/400) is a fabulous camp on an island in a branch of the Limpopo River, run by respected conservationists Judi Gounaris and Dr Helena Fitchat, who bring a winning combination of warmth and conservation knowledge to the experience. Meals are home-cooked and eaten around the communal table and the tents are extremely comfortable.

**Mashatu Game Reserve** (in South Africa +27 11-442 2267; www.mashatu.com; luxury tents s/d US$562/750, chalet s/d US$765/1020;

WORTH A TRIP

### KUBU ISLAND

Along the southwestern edge of Sowa Pan is a ghostly, baobab-laden rock, entirely surrounded by a sea of salt. In Setswana, *kubu* means 'hippopotamus' (in ancient times this was a real island on a real lake inhabited by hippos).

The sprawling **Kubu Island Campsite** (☎75 494 669; www.kubuisland.com; Lekhubu, S 20°53.460', E 25°49.318'; camping per adult/child P100/50) has 14 sites and is one of Botswana's loveliest, with baobabs as a backdrop to most campsites, many of which also have sweeping views of the pan. There are bucket showers and pit toilets.

) and **Tuli Safari Lodge** (☎264 5303; www.tulilodge.com; s/d with full board & wildlife drives US$630/840; ) are also good accommodation options.

Unless you're flying in, you'll need your own vehicle to reach (and explore) the Tuli Block. Once there, most roads in the Tuli Block are negotiable by 2WD, though it can get rough in places over creek beds, which occasionally flood during the rainy season.

Until it has been upgraded, avoid the deeply corrugated gravel road that runs north and roughly parallel to the South African border from Sherwood and Martin's Drift. Far better if you're coming from South Africa is to approach via the border crossings of Platjan or Pont Drift. From elsewhere in Botswana, the lodges can be accessed from the west on the paved road from Bobonong.

# MAKGADIKGADI & NXAI PANS

Within striking distance of the water-drowned terrain of the Okavango Delta, Chobe River and Linyanti Marshes lies **Makgadikgadi** (per day per nonresident/vehicle P120/50; ⏲6am-6.30pm Apr-Sep, 5.30am-7pm Oct-Mar), the largest network of salt pans in the world. Here the country takes on a different hue, forsaking the blues and greens of the delta for the burnished oranges, shimmering whites and golden grasslands of this northern manifestation of the Kalahari Desert. It's as much an emptiness as a place, a land larger than Switzerland, mesmerising in scope and in beauty.

Two protected areas – Makgadikgadi and Nxai Pans – preserve large tracts of salt pans, palm islands, grasslands and savannah. Although enclosing a fraction of the pan networks, they provide a focal point for visitors: Nxai Pan has a reputation for cheetah sightings, and Makgadikgadi's west is a wildlife bonanza of wildebeest, zebras and antelope species pursued by lions. Fabulous areas exist outside park boundaries too, with iconic stands of baobab trees and beguiling landscapes.

## Sights

**Nata Bird Sanctuary** WILDLIFE RESERVE
(☎71 544 342; P55; ⏲7am-7pm) This 230-sq-km community-run wildlife sanctuary was formed when local people voluntarily relocated 3500 cattle and established a network of tracks throughout the northeastern end of Sowa Pan. Although the sanctuary protects antelope, zebras, jackals, foxes, monkeys and squirrels, the principal draw is the birdlife – more than 165 species have been recorded here. It's at its best in the wet season when the sanctuary becomes a haven for Cape and Hottentot teals, white and pink-backed pelicans and greater and lesser flamingos.

## Sleeping

**Khumaga Campsite** CAMPGROUND $
(☎686 5365; www.sklcamps.com; S 20°27.311', E 24°30.968'; camping per adult/child US$50/25) The Khumaga Campsite sits high above the Boteti River and is an attractive site with good shade, braai pits and an excellent ablutions block with flush toilets and (usually) hot showers. Some readers have complained of night-time noise from the village across the river, but the last time we slept here all we could hear was a frog symphony.

★**Baines' Baobabs** CAMPGROUND $
(☎reservations 686 2221; www.xomaesites.com; S 20°08.362', E 24°46.213'; camping per adult/child P400/200) Just three sites sit close to the famed baobabs, and it's a wonderfully evocative site once the day trippers go home – this is the best place to camp in the park, though wildlife is scarce. There are bucket showers and pit toilets.

★**Elephant Sands** LODGE $
(☎7353 6473; www.elephantsands.com; camping P60, s/d/f safari tents & chalets from P600/810/910; ) Some 52km north of Nata, Elephant

Sands, run by Mike and Saskia, is a fabulous place to stay. Excellent and spacious safari tents, some chalets and a few campsites encircle a natural waterhole that is always filled with elephants; in the bar, restaurant and pool area, you'll be as close to wild elephants as it's possible to be.

**Gweta Lodge** LODGE **$$**
(☎76 212 220; www.gwetalodge.com; camping P80, standard/premium r P700/1100, f P1000; ❄📶🏊) In the centre of town, Gweta Lodge is a friendly place that combines a lovely bar and pool area with a range of accommodation options spread around the leafy grounds. The rooms are large and comfortable, the campsites are excellent, and activities include half-day/overnight tours of Ntwetwe Pan and its human-habituated meerkats (P650/1150) and walking tours of the village (P150).

**Planet Baobab** LODGE **$$**
(☎in South Africa +27 11-447 1605; www.unchartedafrica.com; camping per adult/child US$15/8, s/d/q huts from US$165/190/600; 📶🏊) About 4km east of Gweta, a huge concrete aardvark marks the turn-off for Planet Baobab. This inventive lodge forsakes masks and wildlife photos, replaced by a great open-air bar-restaurant (meals P45 to P90) filled with vintage travel posters, metal seats covered in cowhide, beer-bottle chandeliers and the like. Outside, colourfully painted rondavels lie scattered over the gravel.

# NOTHERN BOTSWANA

## Chobe National Park

Famed for its massive elephants, and some of the world's largest herds of them, **Chobe National Park** (per day per nonresident/vehicle P120/50; ⏲6am-6.30pm Apr-Sep, 5.30am-7pm Oct-Mar) in Botswana's far northeastern corner is one of the great wildlife destinations of Africa. In addition to the mighty pachyderms, a full suite of predators and more than 440 recorded bird species are present – watch for roan antelope and the rare oribi antelope.

Chobe was first set aside as a wildlife reserve in the 1930s and became Botswana's first national park in 1968. It encompasses three iconic wildlife areas that all carry a whiff of safari legend: Chobe Riverfront, which supports the park's largest wildlife concentration; the newly accessible and Okavango-like Linyanti Marshes; and the remote and soulful Savuti, with wildlife to rival anywhere.

Whether you're self-driving and camping under the stars, or flying into your luxury lodge, Chobe can be enjoyed by everyone.

### Chobe Riverfront

The Chobe Riverfront rarely disappoints, with arguably Botswana's densest concentration of wildlife. Although animals are present along the riverfront year-round, the density of wildlife can be overwhelming during the dry season, especially in September and October. Whether you cruise along the river in a motorboat, or drive along the banks in a 4WD, you're almost guaranteed an up-close encounter with some of the largest elephants on the continent.

If you don't have your own wheels, any of the hotels and lodges in Kasane can help you organise a wildlife drive or boat cruise along the river. Two- to three-hour cruises and wildlife drives typically cost around P200, though you will also have to pay separate park fees. As always, shop around, compare prices and choose a trip that suits your needs.

#### Sleeping

**Ihaha Campsite** CAMPGROUND **$**
(kwalatesafari@gmail.com; S 17°50.487', E 24°52.754'; camping per adult/child P260/130) Ihaha is the only campsite for self-drivers inside the park along the Chobe Riverfront and it's a wonderful base for watching wildlife. The trees need time to mature and shade can be in short supply at some sites, but the location is excellent – it's by the water's edge 27km from the Northern Gate. There's an ablutions block and braai areas.

**Chobe Chilwero Lodge** LODGE **$$$**
(☎in South Africa +27 11-438 4650; www.sanctuarylodges.com; Airport Rd; per person low/high season from US$590/990; ❄📶🏊) Chilwero means 'place of high view' in Setswana, and indeed this exclusive lodge boasts panoramic views. Accommodation is in one of 15 elegant bungalows featuring romantic indoor and outdoor showers, private terraced gardens and colonial fixtures adorned with plush linens. The lodge is on expansive grounds that contain a pool, a spa, an outdoor bar and a well-reviewed gourmet restaurant.

WORTH A TRIP

## TSODILO HILLS

The Unesco World Heritage–listed Tsodilo Hills rise abruptly from a rippled, ocean-like expanse of desert northwest of Maun and west of the Okavango Panhandle. They are threaded with myth, legend and spiritual significance for the San people, who believe this was the site of Creation. More than 4000 instances of ancient rock art and carvings have been discovered at well over 200 sites. The majority of these are attributed to ancestors of today's San people. The hills can be explored along any of five walking trails.

Although there are some signposts, most trails require a guide (expect to pay around P50 to P60 for a two- to three-hour hike, or P100 per day), which can be arranged at the Main (Rhino) Camp. The hills are well signposted off the Sehitwa–Shakawe road, along a good gravel track. The turn-off is just south of Nxamasere village. It's around 35km from the main road to the entrance to the site.

**Chobe Game Lodge** LODGE $$$
(☎625 0340, 625 1761; www.chobegamelodge.com; River Rd; s/d Jul-Oct US$1470/2370, per person Apr-Jun & Nov US$995, Jan-Mar & Dec US$795; ❄📶🏊) This highly praised safari lodge is one of the best in the Chobe area. The lodge is constructed in the Moorish style and flaunts high arches, barrel-vaulted ceilings and tiled floors. The individually decorated rooms are elegant yet soothing, and some have views of the Chobe River and Namibian floodplains – the views from the public areas are sublime.

### ℹ Getting There & Away

From central Kasane, the Northern Gate is about 6km to the southwest. Unlike all other national parks operated by the Department of Wildlife & National Parks (DWNP), you do not need a campsite reservation to enter, though you will be expected to leave the park prior to closing if you do not have one. All tracks along the riverfront require a 4WD vehicle, and you will not be admitted into the park without one.

You can either exit the park through the Northern Gate by backtracking along the river or via the Ngoma Bridge Gate near the Namibian border. If you exit via Ngoma, you can return to Kasane via the Chobe transit route. (If you're simply bypassing Chobe en route to/from Namibia, you do not have to pay park fees to travel on this road.) Be advised that elephants frequently cross this road, so keep your speed down and do not drive at night.

## Savuti

Savuti's flat, wildlife-packed expanses and rocky outcrops, awash with distinctly African colours and vistas, make it one of the most rewarding safari destinations on the continent. With the exception of rhinos, you'll find all of Africa's most charismatic megafauna in residence here or passing through – on one afternoon wildlife drive, we encountered 15 lions and two leopards.

The area, found in the southwestern corner of Chobe National Park, contains the remnants of the 'superlake' that once stretched across northern Botswana – the modern landscape has a distinctive harsh and empty feel to it. Because of the roughness of the terrain, the difficulty in reaching the area and the beauty you'll find when you get here, Savuti is an obligatory stop for all 4WD enthusiasts en route between Kasane and Maun.

### Sleeping

**Savuti Campsite** CAMPGROUND $$
(www.sklcamps.com; S 18°34.014', E 24°03.905'; camping per adult/child US$50/20) One of the best campgrounds in Chobe, with five of the seven sites (all with braai pits) overlooking the (usually dry) river: sites one to four could do with a little more shade, while Paradise camp is our pick. The ablutions block has sit-down flush toilets and showers (usually hot).

★**Savute Elephant Camp** LODGE $$$
(☎686 0302; www.belmondsafaris.com; s/d Jun-Oct US$4058/5680; ❄📶🏊) The premier camp in Savuti is made up of 12 lavishly appointed East African–style linen tents on raised wooden platforms, complete with antique-replica furniture that will appeal to colonial safari nostalgics. The main tent houses a dining room, lounge and bar, and is next to a swimming pool that overlooks a pumped waterhole.

★**Savute Under Canvas** TENTED CAMP $$$
(☎in South Africa +27 11-809 4300; www.andbeyond.com/savute-under-canvas/; per person

Jul-Oct US$725, Apr-Jun & Nov US$590, Feb & Mar US$480) This cross between a tented camp and luxury mobile safari enables you to experience the freedom of camping (sites are moved every few days) with the exclusivity that comes with having a beautifully appointed tent, butler and excellent meals served in between your game drives. Tents have bathroom facilities, including hot bucket showers. No children under 12.

### Getting There & Away

Tracks in the Savuti area can be hard slogs – deep sand, hidden troughs to jolt the unwary and deep corrugations.

# OKAVANGO DELTA

Welcome to one of Africa's most extraordinary places. There is something elemental about the Unesco World Heritage–listed Okavango Delta: the rising and falling of its waters; the daily drama of its wildlife encounters; its soundtrack of roaring lions, saw-throated leopard barks and the crazy whoop of a running hyena; and the mysteries concealed by its papyrus reeds swaying gently in the evening breeze. Viewed from above on a flight from Maun, the Okavango is a watery paradise of islands and oxbow waterways. At ground level, the silhouettes of dead trees in the dry season give the delta a hint of the apocalypse.

The stirring counterpoint to Botswana's Kalahari Desert, the Okavango Delta, the up-to-18,000-sq-km expansion and expiration of the Okavango River, is one of the world's largest inland deltas. Best of all, the waters sustain vast quantities of wildlife that shift with the seasons.

Generally, the best time to visit the delta is from July to September or October, when the water levels are high and the weather is dry. Tracks can get extremely muddy and trails are often washed out during and after the rains (November to March). From January to March, the Moremi Game Reserve can be inaccessible, even with a state-of-the-art 4WD. Bear in mind that several lodges close down for part or all of the rainy season, but others revel in the abundant birdlife. Mosquitoes are prevalent, especially in the wet season.

Although a few visitors arrive from Chobe National Park and Kasane, Maun is where you'll have the most choice when it comes to organising safaris. Charter flights into the lodges and camps of the delta from Maun are considerably cheaper than those from Kasane.

## Maun

POP 60,263

As the main gateway to the Okavango Delta, Maun (pronounced 'mau-*uu*nn') is Botswana's primary tourism hub. With good accommodation and a reliably mad mix of bush pilots, tourists, campers, volunteers and luxury safariphiles, it's a decent-enough base for a day or two. That said, if your only business in Botswana involves staying in the lodges and tented camps of the delta, you may do little more than hang around the airport. No great loss: the town itself has little going for it – it's strung out over kilometres with not much of a discernible centre – but some of the hotels and camps have riverside vantage points.

### Activities

**Helicopter Horizons** SCENIC FLIGHTS
(☎680 1186; www.helicopterhorizons.com; per person from US$150, min 3 people) A range of helicopter options, all with the passenger doors removed to aid photography. If you're willing to drive out to the buffalo fence and take your flight from there, the 22-minute flight will be almost entirely over the delta, rather than wasting time and money flying there. You may need to combine this option with a *mokoro* (dugout canoe) excursion.

**Wilderness Air** SCENIC FLIGHTS
(☎686 0778; www.sefofane.com) Part of Wilderness Safaris (p755). Offers scenic flights and flies in guests to Wilderness Safaris' lodges and camps.

**Mack Air** SCENIC FLIGHTS
(☎686 0675; www.mackair.co.bw; Mathiba I St) Offers scenic flights; located around the corner from Wilderness Safaris. It costs P2900/3600 for the whole plane for 45/60 minutes; how much you pay depends on how many people are on the flight.

### Tours

**Audi Camp Safaris** SAFARI
(☎686 0599; www.audisafaris.com; Shorobe Rd, Matlapaneng) Well-run safaris into the delta and further afield out of the popular Audi Camp (p755).

# Okavango Delta

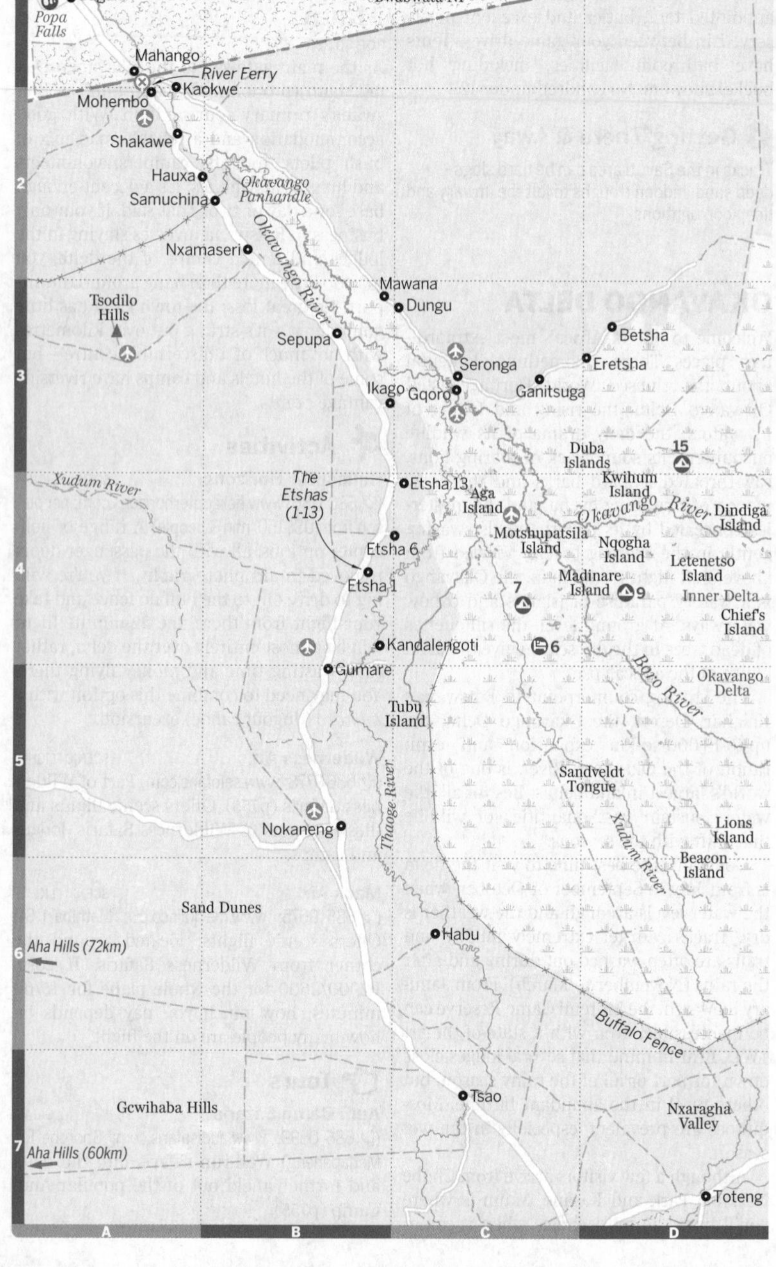

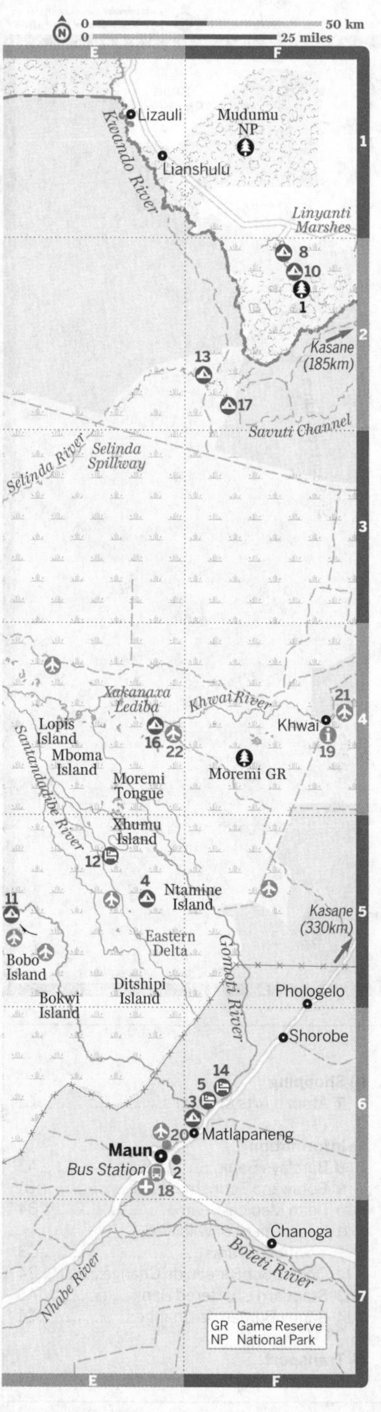


## Okavango Delta

**Sights**

1 Nkasa Rupara National Park .............. F2

**Activities, Courses & Tours**

Audi Camp Safaris ...................... (see 3)
2 Lelobu Safaris ............................ E6
Old Bridge Backpackers ............. (see 3)

**Sleeping**

3 Audi Camp ................................ F6
4 Chitabe Lediba ........................... E5
5 Discovery Bed & Breakfast ............. F6
6 Jao Camp ................................. C4
Kraal Lodging ........................... (see 3)
7 Kwetsani Camp ........................... C4
8 Livingstone's Camp ..................... F2
9 Mombo Camp .............................. D4
10 Nkasa Lupala Lodge ..................... F2
11 Nxabega Okavango Camp ............... E5
Old Bridge Backpackers ............. (see 3)
12 Sandibe Safari Lodge .................. E5
13 Selinda Camp ............................ F2
14 Thamalakane Lodge ..................... F6
15 Vumbura Plains Camp .................. D3
16 Xakanaxa Campsite ..................... E4
Xaranna Camp ......................... (see 11)
17 Zarafa Camp .............................. F2

**Information**

18 Maun General Hospital .................. E6
19 North (Khwai) Gate & Park Headquarters ................................ F4

**Transport**

20 Air Botswana ............................. E6
21 Khwai River Airstrip ..................... F4
22 Xakanaxa Airstrip ........................ E4

**Ker & Downey** SAFARI

(☎686 0570; www.kerdowney.com; Mathiba I St) One of Africa's most exclusive tour operators, Ker & Downey is all about pampering and luxury lodges.

**Lelobu Safaris** SAFARI

(☎74 511 600; www.botswanabudgetsafaris.com) A flexible and professional operator (the name means 'chameleon' in Setswana) run by Rebecca and Anton, Lelobu organises excellent custom-designed itineraries with a focus on getting you out into the delta, especially around Chief's Island, with reasonable price tags attached.

**Old Bridge Backpackers** SAFARI

(☎686 2406; www.maun-backpackers.com; Shorobe Rd, Matlapaneng) This experienced budget operation is run from the Old Bridge Backpackers and we're yet to hear a bad word about its expeditions.

## Maun

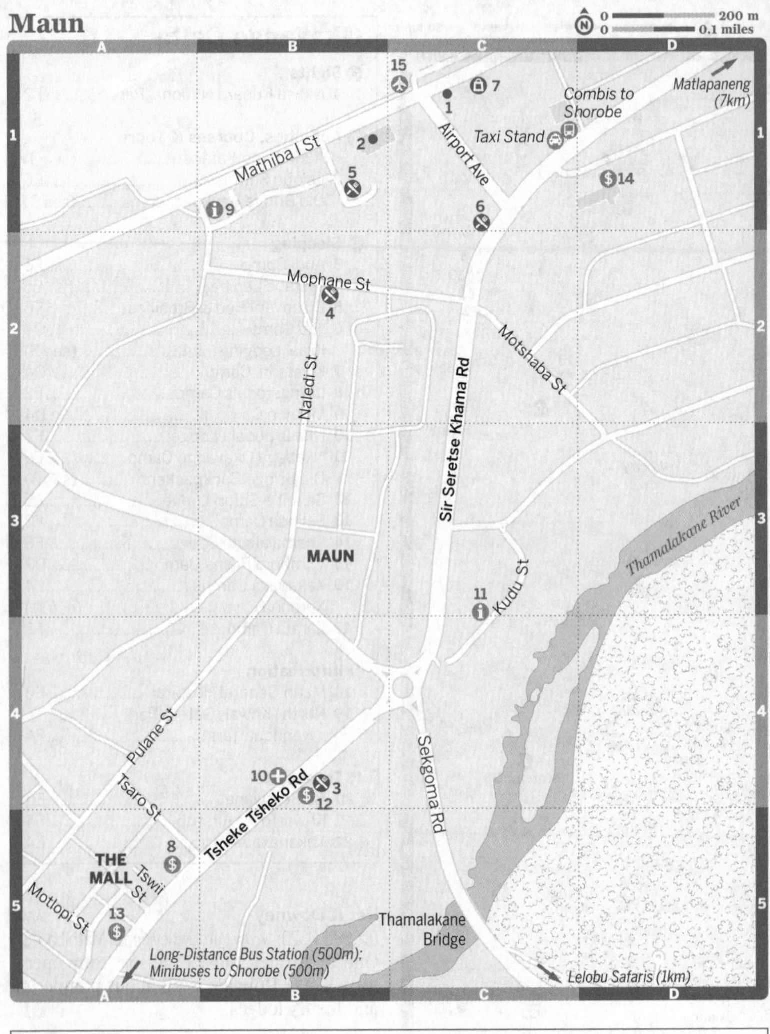


## Maun

**Activities, Courses & Tours**

- Helicopter Horizons ........................ (see 9)
- 1 Ker & Downey ........................ C1
- Mack Air ........................ (see 2)
- Okavango Kopano Mokoro Community Trust ........................ (see 9)
- Wilderness Air ........................ (see 2)
- 2 Wilderness Safaris ........................ B1

**Eating**

- 3 Delta Deli ........................ B4
- 4 French Connection ........................ B2
- 5 Hilary's ........................ B1
- 6 Wax Apple Cafe ........................ C1

**Shopping**

- 7 African Arts & Images ........................ C1

**Information**

- 8 Barclays Bank ........................ A5
- 9 Botswana Tourism ........................ B1
- 10 Delta Medical Centre ........................ B4
- 11 Department of Wildlife & National Parks ........................ C3
- 12 Open Door Bureau de Change ........................ B4
- 13 Standard Chartered Bank ........................ A5
- 14 Sunny Bureau de Change ........................ D1

**Transport**

- 15 Maun Airport ........................ C1

**Wilderness Safaris** SAFARI
(☎686 0086; www.wilderness-safaris.com; Mathiba I St) Near the airport, this operator specialises in upmarket safaris and owns many of Botswana's best camps.

## Sleeping

The Okavango Delta has some of the finest and most exclusive accommodation anywhere in Africa. Remote, fly-in, utterly luxurious lodges and tented camps may be expensive, but they could just be the safari you've always dreamed about. Everything is included in their all-inclusive packages: meals, safari activities, great wildlife...

It's also possible to gain a delta foothold on a lesser budget on a mobile safari from Maun, or by self-drive camping in Moremi Game Reserve.

**★Old Bridge Backpackers** CAMPGROUND $
(☎686 2406; www.maun-backpackers.com; Hippo Pools, Old Matlapaneng Bridge; camping P80, dm P150, s/d tents without bathroom P330/400, s/d tents with bathroom P480/580; @ ) One of the great boltholes on Southern African overland trails, 'the Bridge' has a great bar-at-the-end-of-the-world kind of vibe. Accommodation ranges from dome tents by the riverbank to well-appointed campsites and some tents that extra private.

**Audi Camp** CAMPGROUND $
(☎686 0599; www.audisafaris.com/audi-camps; Matlapaneng; camping from P70, s/d tents without bathroom from P160/190, s/d tents with bathroom P630/760; @ ) Off Shorobe Rd, Audi Camp is a fantastic campsite that's become increasingly popular with families, although independent overlanders will also feel welcome. Management is friendly and helpful, and there's a wide range of safari activities. The restaurant does a mean steak. If you don't have your own tent, the pre-erected tents complete with fan are a rustically luxurious option.

**★Kraal Lodging** GUESTHOUSE $$
(☎72 320 090; http://thekraallodgingbotswana.com; exit 6, Disaneng Rd; r P1200-2000; P ) Run by respected film-makers June and Tim Liversedge, the Kraal is a terrific place to stay. The attractive thatched rondavels are beautifully appointed with just the right blend of safari prints, earth tones and African handicrafts and artwork. There's a pool, free wi-fi and a barbecue area, and the owners are a mine of information on the region.

**Discovery Bed & Breakfast** B&B $$
(☎72 448 298; www.discoverybedandbreakfast.com; Matlapaneng; s/d from US$60/80; ) Dutch-run Discovery does a cool job of creating an African-village vibe in the midst of Maun – the owners strive for and achieve 'affordable accommodation with a traditional touch'. The thatched, rondavel-style housing looks pretty bush from the outside and feels as posh as a nice hotel on the inside.

**Thamalakane Lodge** LODGE $$$
(☎72 506 184; www.thamalakane-lodge.com; Shorobe Rd; d/f chalets US$238/345; @ ) With a beautiful setting on a sun-drenched curve of the Thamalakane River, overlooking wading hippos and waving reeds (when there's enough water), Thamalakane wins in the location stakes, at least for Maun. It has beautiful little stone chalets stuffed with modern amenities and dressed up in safari-chic tones. The lodge is 19km northeast of Maun, off the road to Shorobe.

## Eating

**French Connection** FRENCH $
(Mophane St; breakfast P40-75, mains P40-95; 8.30am-5pm Mon-Fri, to 2pm Sat) Close to the airport, but on a quiet backstreet, this fine place serves up fresh tastes that might include Turkish pide, Moroccan lamb or Creole fish cakes; the meze platter is especially good. Run by a delightful French owner and driven by a far-ranging passion for new tastes, it's a lovely spot to eat with a shady garden setting.

**Delta Deli** DELI $
(☎686 1413; Tsheke Tsheko Rd; 8am-5.30pm Mon-Fri, to 1.30pm Sat) Ask anyone in Maun the best place to buy meat in town for your next barbecue or camping expedition and they're likely to send you here. Part of the Riley's Garage service station set-up, it has easily the most appealing meat selection we found in Botswana – terrific steaks, marinated cuts and excellent sausages.

**Wax Apple Cafe** CAFE $
(☎72 703 663; Airport Ave; breakfast P20-45, light meals P30-45; 7.30am-5pm Mon-Fri, to 2pm Sat; ) Handy for the airport (a 100m walk away) and with a lovely casual atmosphere, Wax Apple is a wonderful addition to Maun's eating scene. Apart from great teas and coffees, it serves tasty baguettes and wraps, with the odd local dish on the short-but-sweet menu. There's also a gift shop with some nice jewellery and paintings and free wi-fi.

★ **Hilary's** INTERNATIONAL $$
(breakfast P16-92, light meals P46-56, mains P82; ⏲8am-4pm Mon-Fri, 8.30am-noon Sat; ) This homey place offers a choice of wonderfully earthy meals, including homemade bread, homemade lemonade, filter coffee, baked potatoes, soups and sandwiches. It's ideal for vegetarians and anyone sick of greasy sausages and soggy chips. We're just sorry it doesn't open in the evenings.

## Information

### MEDICAL SERVICES

**Delta Medical Centre** (☎686 1411; Tsheke Tsheko Rd) Along the main road; this is the best medical facility in Maun. It offers a 24-hour emergency service.

**Maun General Hospital** (☎686 0661; Shorobe Rd) About 1km southwest of the town centre.

**MedRescue** (☎390 1601, 680 0598, 992; www.mri.co.bw) For evacuations in the bush.

### MONEY

**Barclays Bank** (Tsheke Tsheko Rd; ⏲8.30am-3.30pm Mon-Fri, 8.15-10.45am Sat) Has foreign-exchange facilities and offers better rates than the bureau de change.

**Open Door Bureau de Change** (Tsheke Tsheko Rd; ⏲7.30am-6pm Mon-Fri, 8am-4pm Sat, 9am-4pm Sun)

**Standard Chartered Bank** (Tsheke Tsheko Rd; ⏲8.30am-3.30pm Mon-Fri, 8.15-11am Sat) Has foreign-exchange facilities and offers better rates than the bureaux de change. Standard Chartered charges 3% commission for cash and travellers cheques, but isn't as well set up as Barclays Bank.

**Sunny Bureau de Change** (Sir Seretse Khama Rd, Ngami Centre; ⏲8am-6pm) Although you will get less favourable exchange rates than at the banks, this is a convenient option if the lines at the banks are particularly long.

### TOURIST INFORMATION

**Department of Wildlife & National Parks** (DWNP; ☎686 1265; Kudu St; ⏲7.30am-4.30pm Mon-Fri, 7.30am-12.45pm & 1.45-4.30pm Sat, 7.30am-12.45pm Sun) To pay national park entry fees and book park campsites not in private hands.

**Tourist office** (☎686 1056; off Mathiba I St; ⏲7.30am-6pm Mon-Fri, 9am-2pm Sat) Provides information on Maun's many tour companies and lodges.

## Getting There & Away

**Air Botswana** (☎686 0391; www.airbotswana.co.bw) has flights from **Maun Airport** (MUB; 686 1559) to Gaborone (from P1791) and Kasane (from P715). There are also international flights between Maun and Johannesburg (South Africa), Victoria Falls (Zimbabwe) and Livingstone (Zambia).

The **bus station** (Tsheke Tsheko Rd) for long-distance buses and combis is southwest of the centre. For Gaborone, you'll need to change in Ghanzi or Francistown. Combis to Shorobe leave from Sir Seretse Khama Rd near the taxi stand. Destinations by bus or combi include Francistown (P105, five hours), Ghanzi (P75, five hours), Nata (P92, five hours) and Kasane (P120, six hours).

### OKAVANGO DELTA SEASONS

**November–December** Rains begin to fall in the highlands of Angola, in the catchment areas of the Cubango and Cuito Rivers. Down in the delta, waters are receding, despite rains falling in the delta itself and surrounding area. By December, the waters have begun to flow down these two rivers towards Botswana.

**January–February** The waters of the Cubango flow more quickly and near the Okavango River, arriving before the waters of the Cuito. Water levels in the delta remain low.

**March–April** Continuing rainfall (in good years) adds to the growing volume of water that flows southeast through the Okavango Panhandle and begins to enter the delta proper.

**May–June** The flooding of the Okavango Delta begins in earnest, and water levels rise across the delta. Depending on the year and its rains, waters may reach further into the southeast via the Boteti River and Selinda Spillway.

**July–September** The flooding of the delta peaks and the waters reach their southeasternmost limits, a point that can vary considerably from one year to the next.

**October** Having reached their limits some time in September, the waters begin to evaporate and disappear, and water levels recede towards the northwest.

### THE MOKORO EXPERIENCE

One of the best (and also cheapest) ways to experience the Okavango Delta is to glide across the waters in a *mokoro* (plural *mekoro*), a shallow-draft dugout canoe traditionally hewn from an ebony or sausage-tree log. With encouragement from several international conservation groups, however, the Batswana have now begun to construct more *mekoro* from fibreglass. The rationale behind this is that ebony and sausage trees take over 100 years to grow while a *mokoro* only lasts for about five years.

A *mokoro* may appear precarious at first, but it is amazingly stable and ideally suited to the shallow delta waters. It can accommodate two passengers and limited luggage, and is propelled by a poler who stands at the back of the canoe with a *ngashi,* a long pole made from the mogonono tree.

The quality of a *mokoro* trip often depends on the passengers' enthusiasm, the meshing of personalities and the skill of the poler. Most polers (but not all) speak at least some English and can identify plants, birds and animals, and explain the cultures and myths of the delta inhabitants. Unfortunately, polers are often shy and lack confidence, so you may have to ask a lot of questions to get the information.

How much you enjoy your trip will depend partly on your expectations. If you come in the spirit of immersing yourself in nature and slowing down to the pace of life here on the delta, you won't leave disappointed. It's important to stress, however, that you should not expect to see too much wildlife. From the *mokoro,* you'll certainly spot plenty of hippos and crocs, and antelope and elephants are frequently sighted during hikes. However, the main attraction of a *mokoro* trip is the peace and serenity you'll feel as you glide along the shallow waters of the delta. If, however, your main interest is viewing wildlife, consider spending a night or two in the Moremi Game Reserve.

## Eastern Delta

The Eastern Delta includes the wetlands between the southern boundary of Moremi Game Reserve and the buffalo fence that crosses the Boro and Santandadibe Rivers, north of Matlapaneng. If you're short of time and/or money, this part of the Okavango Delta remains an affordable and accessible option. From Maun it's easy to arrange a day trip on a *mokoro* (see p758), or a two- or three-night *mokoro* trip combined with bush camping.

Then again, the Chitabe concession and surrounding area has been quietly building a reputation as one of the wildlife hot spots of recent times, and a luxury experience is very much a possibility here as well.

As with elsewhere in the delta, Wilderness Safaris' camps are serviced by Wilderness Air (p751), with Mack Air (p751) the other most popular charter company. Enquire with your lodge.

**★Chitabe Lediba** TENTED CAMP **$$$**

(☎686 0086; www.wilderness-safaris.com; s/d Jun-Oct US$1950/3280, rates vary rest of year; ❄ ≋) One of the more intimate camps run by Wilderness Safaris, Chitabe Lediba has just five tents (including two family ones) and a warm and intimate atmosphere. The larger-than-usual tents here are supremely comfortable, and the whole place is also distinguished by the warm service and brilliant game drives.

**★Sandibe Safari Lodge** LODGE **$$$**

(☎in South Africa +27 11-809 4300; www.andbeyondafrica.com; per person Jun-Oct US$2350, rates vary rest of year; ᯤ ≋) This riverine forest retreat is the architectural jewel of the Okavango Delta, as well as one of the premier safari camps anywhere in Southern Africa. Service is warm and welcoming, the accommodation is exceptional in its style and comfort, and the location (next to the famed Chitabe concession) is one of the best anywhere in the delta.

## Inner Delta

Welcome to the heart of the Okavango, a world inaccessible by roads and inhabited by some of the richest wildlife concentrations on earth. Not surprisingly, these are some of the most exclusive patches of real estate in Botswana, with luxury lodges and tented camps inhabiting some of the delta's prettiest corners.

## BOOKING A MOKORO TRIP

A day trip from Maun into the Eastern Delta usually includes a two- to three-hour return drive in a 4WD to the departure point, two to three hours in a *mokoro* (perhaps longer each day on a two- or three-day trip), and two to three hours' hiking. At the start of a *mokoro* trip, ask the poler what he has in mind, and agree to the length of time spent per day in the *mokoro*, out hiking and relaxing at the campsite – bear in mind that travelling by *mokoro* is tiring for the poler.

One of the most refreshing things about booking *mokoro* trips is the absence of touts wandering the streets of Maun. That's because all polers operating *mokoro* trips out of Maun are represented by the **Okavango Kopano Mokoro Community Trust** (☎686 4806; www.okmct.org.bw; off Mathiba 1 St; ⏰8am-5pm Mon-Fri, to noon Sat). This trust sets daily rates for the polers (P180 per poler per day, plus a P68 daily membership fee for the trust) by which all safari operators have to abide. Other costs include a guide (P200 per day) and a camping fee (P50 per person per night) if your expedition involves an overnight component.

In terms of pricing, catering is an important distinction. 'Self-catering' means you must bring your own food as well as cooking, sleeping and camping equipment. This option is a good way to shave a bit off the price, though most travellers prefer catered trips. It's also easier to get a lower price if you're booking as part of a group or are planning a multi-day tour.

A few other things to remember:

- Ask the booking agency if you're expected to provide food for the poler (usually you're not, but polers appreciate any leftover cooked or uncooked food).
- Bring good walking shoes and long trousers for hiking, a hat and plenty of sunscreen and water.
- Water from the delta (despite its unpleasant colour) can be drunk if boiled or purified.
- Most campsites are natural, so take out all litter and burn toilet paper.
- Bring warm clothes for the evening between about May and September.
- Wildlife can be dangerous, so make sure to never swim anywhere without checking with the poler first.

## Sleeping

**★Jao Camp** LODGE $$$
(☎686 0086; www.wilderness-safaris.com; s/d Jun-Oct US$2700/4700, rates vary rest of year; 📶❄) Part of Wilderness Safaris' portfolio of premier camps, Jao is a special place that combines Asian style (the public areas and the rooms were inspired by a Balinese longhouse) with a very African feel (jackalberry and mangosteen trees, liberal use of thatch). Rooms are uberluxurious and the staff are extremely professional and attentive to your every need.

**★Kwetsani Camp** TENTED CAMP $$$
(☎686 0086; www.wilderness-safaris.com; s/d Jun-Oct US$1820/3000, rates vary rest of year; ❄) This highly recommended camp has the usual high levels of comfort, but there are some very special selling points. First, the recently overhauled rooms, elevated high above the water, are simply stunning, while the camp manager, Dan Myburg, is a top-class photographer who can help elevate your photography above the usual even in just a few days.

**★Vumbura Plains Camp** TENTED CAMP $$$
(☎686 0086; www.wilderness-safaris.com; s/d Jun-Oct US$2810/4890, rates vary rest of year; ❄) One of Wilderness Safaris' flagship properties, this regally luxurious twin camp is on the Duba Plains in the transition zone between the savannahs and swamps north of the delta. Although divided into north and south sections, with separate eating and other common areas, this is essentially a single lodge. It inhabits the Kwedi Concession and the wildlife viewing is superlative.

**★Nxabega Okavango Camp** TENTED CAMP $$$
(☎in South Africa +27 11-809 4300; www.andbeyond.com; per person Jun-Oct US$1665, rest of year US$755-1035; 📶❄) In a grove of ebony trees

on the flats near the Boro River, this exquisitely designed tented camp has sweeping views of the delta floodplains. The rooms are magnificent – the private terraces in each are large with lovely swing chairs, each built around water's-edge termite mounds or trees, lending a real sense of intimacy with the landscape.

## Getting There & Away

The only way into and out of the Inner Delta for most visitors is by air. This is an expensive extra, but the pain is alleviated if you look at it as two scenic flights. Chartered flights to the lodges typically cost about US$200 per leg. A *mokoro* or 4WD vehicle will meet your plane and take you to the lodge.

# Moremi Game Reserve

Moremi Game Reserve, which covers one-third of the Okavango Delta, is home to some of Africa's densest concentrations of wildlife. It's also one of the most accessible corners of the Okavango, with well-maintained trails and accommodation that ranges from luxury lodges to public campsites for self-drivers.

With the recent reintroduction of rhinos, Moremi is now home to the Big Five (lions, leopards, buffaloes, elephants and rhinos), and notably Africa's largest population of red lechwe (a type of antelope). The reserve also protects one of the largest remaining populations of endangered African wild dogs.

## Sleeping

**★Xakanaxa Campsite** CAMPGROUND **$**
(Xakanaxa Lediba; kwalatesafari@gmail.com; S 19°10.991', E 23°24.937'; camping per adult/child P260/130) A favourite Moremi campground, Xakanaxa occupies a narrow strip of land surrounded by marshes and lagoons. It's no coincidence that many upmarket lodges are located nearby – the wildlife in the area can be prolific and campers are frequently woken by elephants or serenaded by hippo grunts. Be warned: a young boy was tragically killed by hyenas here in 2000.

**★Mombo Camp** TENTED CAMP **$$$**
(☎686 0086; www.wilderness-safaris.com; s/d Jun-Oct US$3564/5736, rates vary rest of year; ) Ask anyone in Botswana for the country's most exclusive camp and they're likely to nominate Mombo. The surrounding delta scenery is some of the finest in the Okavango and the wildlife watching is almost unrivalled. The rooms are enormous and the entire package – from the service to the comfort levels and attention to detail – never misses a beat.

**★Xaranna Camp** TENTED CAMP **$$$**
(☎in South Africa +27 11-809 4300; www.andbeyond.com; per person Jun-Oct US$1770, rates vary rest of year; ) Xaranna is a worthy member of the elite group pf camps run by &Beyond, which mixes daringly designed luxury accommodation with serious conservation work. Xaranna's large rooms have expansive terraces, private pools and as little to separate you from the delta surrounds as is possible. The food is excellent and the service first-rate.

## Information

**North (Khwai) Gate & Park Headquarters**
(6am-6:30pm 1 April to 30 September; 5.30am-7pm 1 October to 31 March) Pick up your photocopied map of the reserve (they sometimes run out) and pay your park fees here.

## Getting There & Away

Chartered flights (and/or 4WD) are usually the only way to reach the luxury lodges of Moremi, with the Khwai River and Xakanaxa strips being regularly used.

If you're driving from Maun, the reserve entrance is at South (Maqwee) Gate, about 99km north of Maun via Shorobe. From Kasane and the east, a track links Chobe National Park with the other gate at North (Khwai) Gate.

# KALAHARI

The parched alter ego of the Okavango Delta, the Kalahari is a primeval landscape, recalling in stone, thorns and brush the earliest memories of the human experience. It's no surprise that the Tswana call this the Kgalagadi: Land of Thirst.

# Central Kalahari Game Reserve

The dry heart of the dry south of a dry continent, the **Central Kalahari Game Reserve** (CKGR; per day per non-resident/vehicle P120/50; 6am-6.30pm Apr-Sep, 5.30am-7pm Oct-Mar) is an awesome place. If remoteness, desert silences and the sound of lions roaring in the night are your thing, this could become one of your favourite places in Africa. Covering 52,800 sq km (about the size of Denmark), it's also one of Africa's largest protected areas. This is big-sky country, home to black-maned Kalahari lions, a full suite of predators and an utterly wonderful sense of the remote.

The park is most easily accessible during the dry season (May to September) when tracks are sandy but easily negotiated by 4WD vehicles. Nights can be bitterly cold at this time and daytime temperatures are relatively mild. During the rainy season (November to March or April), tracks can be muddy and nearly impassable for inexperienced drivers. Watch for grass seeds clogging engines and searing temperatures in October.

## Sleeping

You will not be permitted into the park without a campsite reservation. Collecting firewood is banned in the CKGR, so bring your own.

**★Passarge Valley Campsites** CAMPGROUND $
(☎395 3360; www.bigfoottours.co.bw; camping per adult/child P200/100) These three campsites have no facilities, but their location on the valley floor (some kilometres apart) is among the best in the Kalahari. Site No 2 (S 21°26.847', E 23°47.694'), under a shady stand of trees in the centre of the valley floor, is simply wonderful and the world is yours and yours alone.

**★Piper Pan Campsites** CAMPGROUND $
(☎395 3360; www.bigfoottours.co.bw; camping per adult/child P200/100) Slightly removed from the main circuit, the two Piper Pan sites have a wonderfully remote feel and wildlife watching is good thanks to a waterhole. The pans are 26km southwest off the main Letiahau track. Site No 1 (S 21°76.827', E 23°19.843'), overlooking the main pan, is probably our favourite, but No 2 (S 21°76.827', E 23°19.843') is also excellent.

**Kori Campsites** CAMPGROUND $
(☎381 0774; dwnp@gov.bw; camping P30) The four campsites known as Kori sit on the hill that rises gently from the western edge of Deception Valley. There's plenty of shade and some have partial views of the valley, making any of them a wonderful base. There are braai pits and pit latrines.

**★Kalahari Plains Camp** TENTED CAMP $$$
(☎in South Africa +27 11-807 1800; www.wilderness-safaris.com; per person mid-Jan–May US$965, Nov–mid-Jan US$935, Jun-Oct US$650; ) If we could choose one place to stay in the CKGR, this would be it. These lovely solar-powered tents inhabit a gorgeous location southeast of Deception Valley and face the setting sun with stunning views. The spacious tents have wooden floors, extremely comfortable beds, 24-hour electricity, yoga mats and a roof terrace (for those wishing to sleep under the stars).

## Getting There & Around

Gateway towns for the reserve are Ghanzi, Rakops and (at a stretch) Maun.

A 4WD is essential to get around the reserve, and a compass (or GPS equipment) and petrol reserves are also recommended.

# UNDERSTAND BOTSWANA

## Botswana Today

By any standards, Botswana's recent history is a lesson to other African countries. Instead of suffering from Africa's oft-seen resource curse, Botswana has used the ongoing windfall from its diamond mines to build a stable and, for the most part, egalitarian country, one whose economic growth rates have, for decades, been among the highest on earth. When the country celebrated 50 years of independence in 2016, there was much to celebrate.

This is a place where things work, where education, health and environmental protection are government priorities; even when faced with one of the most serious challenges faced by Africa in the 20th century, HIV/AIDS, the government broke new ground in making antiretroviral treatment available to all. For all such promising news, Botswana is far from perfect. The country's dependence on diamonds is, however, also a major concern when looking into Botswana's future; diamonds make up 85% of the country's export earnings and one-third of government revenues. As such, the economy remains vulnerable to a fluctuating world economy – in 2015, the economy grew by just 1% (which is very low by the country's recent, albeit lofty, standards) and unemployment sits at

**BOTSWANA LITERATURE**

Botswana's most famous modern literary figure was South African–born Bessie Head (1937–86), who fled apartheid in South Africa and settled in Sir Seretse Khama's village of Serowe. Her writings, many of which are set in Serowe, reflect the harshness and beauty of African village life and the physical attributes of Botswana itself. Her most widely read works include *Serowe – Village of the Rain Wind* (1981), *When Rain Clouds Gather* (1968), *Maru* (1971), *A Question of Power* (1973), *The Cardinals* (1993), *A Bewitched Crossroad* (1984), and *The Collector of Treasures* (1977), which is an anthology of short stories.

Since the 1980s Setswana novel writing has had something of a revival with the publication in English of novels like Andrew Sesinyi's *Love on the Rocks* (1983) and Gaele Sobott-Mogwe's haunting collection of short stories, *Colour Me Blue* (1995), which blends fantasy and reality with the everyday grit of African life.

Unity Dow, Botswana's first female high-court judge, also writes novels dealing with contemporary social issues in the country; we recommend *Far and Beyon'* (2002).

a worrying 20%, prompting the government to announce an economic stimulus package in 2016.

# History

## Precolonial History

Archaeological evidence and rock art found in the Tsodilo Hills suggests the San took shelter in caves throughout the region from around 17,000 BC. Perhaps the most significant development in Botswana's history was the evolution of the three main branches of the Tswana tribe during the 14th century. It's a King Lear–ish tale of family discord, where three brothers – Kwena, Ngwaketse and Ngwato – broke away from their father, Chief Malope, to establish their own followings in Molepolole, Kanye and Serowe respectively. These fractures probably occurred in response to drought and expanding populations eager to strike out in search of new pastures and arable land.

## Colonial History

From the 1820s the Boers began their Great Trek across the Vaal River; 20,000 Boers crossed into Tswana and Zulu territory and established themselves as though the lands were unclaimed and uninhabited. At the Sand River Convention of 1852, Britain recognised the Transvaal's independence. The Boers informed the undoubtedly surprised Batswana (people of Botswana) that they were now subjects of the South African Republic.

Prominent Tswana leaders Sechele I and Mosielele refused to accept white rule and incurred the wrath of the Boers. By 1877 the British had annexed the Transvaal and launched the first Boer War. In 1882, Boers again moved into Tswana lands and subdued the town of Mafikeng, threatening the British route between the Cape and suspected mineral wealth in Zimbabwe. In 1885, thanks to petitions from John Mackenzie (a friend of the Christian Chief Khama III of Shoshong), lands north of the Molopo River became the British Crown Colony of Bechuanaland, attached to the Cape Colony. The area north became the British Protectorate of Bechuanaland.

A new threat to the Tswana chiefs' power base came from Cecil Rhodes and his British South Africa Company (BSAC). By 1894 the British had all but agreed to allow him to control the country. An unhappy delegation of Tswana chiefs – Bathoen, Khama III and Sebele – accompanied by a sympathetic missionary, WC Willoughby, sailed to England to appeal for continued government control (far less intrusive than Rhodes' proposed rule). Public pressure mounted and the British government was forced to concede.

In 1923 Chief Khama III died and was succeeded by his son Sekgoma, who died only two years later. The heir to the throne, four-year-old Seretse Khama, wasn't ready for the job of ruling the largest Tswana chiefdom, so his 21-year-old uncle, Tshekedi Khama, became clan regent.

After WWII, Seretse Khama went to study in England where he met and married an Englishwoman. Tshekedi Khama was furious at this breach of tribal custom, and apartheid-era South African authorities were none too happy either. The British government blocked Seretse's chieftaincy and he was exiled to England. Bitterness continued until 1956 when Seretse Khama renounced his right to power and returned with his wife to Botswana to serve as a minor official.

## Nationalism & Independence

The first signs of nationalist thinking among the Tswana occurred in the late 1940s, and over time it became apparent that Britain was preparing to release its grip on Bechuanaland. In 1962 Seretse Khama and Kanye farmer Quett Masire formed the moderate Bechuanaland Democratic Party (BDP).

The BDP formulated a schedule for independence, drawing on support from local chiefs and traditional Batswana. They promoted the transfer of the capital into the country (from Mafikeng to Gaborone), drafted a new nonracial constitution and set up a countdown to independence to allow a peaceful transfer of power. General elections were held in 1965 and Seretse Khama was elected president. On 30 September 1966, the Republic of Botswana gained independence.

Sir Seretse Khama – he was knighted shortly after independence – adopted a neutral stance (until near the end of his presidency) towards South Africa and Rhodesia (on each of which Botswana was economically dependent). Nevertheless, Khama refused to exchange ambassadors with South Africa and, in international circles, officially disapproved of apartheid.

Botswana was transformed by the discovery of diamonds near Orapa in 1967. The mining concession was given to De Beers, with Botswana taking 75% of the profits. For 40 years the BDP managed the country's diamond windfall relatively wisely. Diamond dollars were ploughed into infrastructure, education and health. Private businesses were allowed to grow and foreign investment was welcomed. From 1966 to 2005, Botswana's economy grew faster than any other in the world.

After the death of Khama in 1980, Dr Ketumile Masire took the helm. His popular presidency ended in March 1998, when President Festus Mogae assumed control of Botswana. He was succeeded in April 2008 by Ian Khama, son of Sir Seretse Khama.

# People of Botswana

All citizens of Botswana – regardless of colour, ancestry or tribal affiliation – are known as Batswana (plural) or Motswana (singular). Almost everyone, including members of non-Tswana tribes, communicates via the lingua franca of Tswana, a native language, rather than the official language of English. Alongside language, education has played an important role in building a unified country, and the government proudly claims that its commitment of over 30% of its budget to education is the highest per capita in the world.

The three major tribal groupings are the ethnic Tswana (80% of Botswana's population claims Tswana heritage), the Bakalanga (11%) and the indigenous San (3%).

# Environment

Botswana is the geographic heart of sub-Saharan Africa, extending over 1100km from north to south and 960km from east to west, an area of 582,000 sq km that's equivalent in size to France. The country is entirely landlocked, and is bordered to the south and southeast by South Africa, across the Limpopo and Molopo Rivers; to the northeast by Zimbabwe; and to the north and west by Namibia.

Botswana is home to anywhere between 160 and 500 different mammal species, 593 recorded bird species, 150 different reptiles, over 8000 insect and spider species, and more than 3100 types of plants and trees.

# National Parks & Reserves

All public national parks and reserves in Botswana are run by the **Department of Wildlife & National Parks** (DWNP; Map p745; ☎381 0774; dwnp@gov.bw; Millennium Office Park, New Lobatse Rd, Gaborone; ⏰7.30am-4.30pm Mon-Fri, 7.30am-12.45pm & 1.45-4.30pm Sat, 7.30am-12.45pm Sun). There are other park offices in Maun (p756) and **Kasane** (☎625 0235; Sedudu Gate), as well as a rarely visited outpost in **Kang** (☎651 7036; off Trans Kalahari Hwy/A2; ⏰7.30am-12.45pm & 1.45-4.30pm).

There are a few things worth remembering about visiting Botswana's national parks and reserves:

➡ Park fees have long been slated for a significant rise – we thought it would have happened by now, but don't be surprised if they're significantly above those we've provided by the time you arrive.

- Although there are exceptions (such as the Chobe Riverfront section of Chobe National Park) and it may be possible on rare occasions to get park rangers to bend the rules, no one is allowed into a national park or reserve without an accommodation booking for that park.
- It is possible to pay park entrance fees at park entrance gates, after a spell in which places had to be reserved and fees paid in advance at DWNP offices in Gaborone, Maun or Kasane (you'll still see some signs around Botswana to that effect). Even so, you should always try to book and pay in advance.
- The gates for each DWNP park are open from 6am to 6.30pm 1 April to 30 September and from 5.30am to 7pm 1 October to 31 March. It is vital that all visitors be out of the park, or settled into their campsite, outside of these hours. Driving after dark is strictly forbidden (although it is permitted in private concessions).

# SURVIVAL GUIDE

##  Directory A–Z

### ACCOMMODATION

The story of Botswana's accommodation is a story of extremes. At one end, there are fabulously located campsites for self-drivers (the closest the country comes to budget accommodation outside the main towns). At the other extreme, there are top-end lodges where prices can be eye-wateringly high. In between, you will find some midrange options in the major towns and places such as the Okavango Panhandle, but elsewhere there's very little for the midrange (and nothing for the noncamping budget) traveller.

#### Seasons

While most budget and midrange options tend to have a standard room price, many top-end places change their prices according to season. High season is usually from June to November (and may also apply to Christmas, New Year and Easter, depending on the lodge), low season corresponds to the rains (December to March or April) and the shoulder is a short April and May window. The only exception is the Kalahari, where June to November is generally considered to be low season.

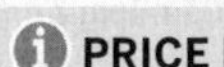

#### PRICE RANGES

The following price ranges refer to a double room with bathroom. Unless otherwise stated, breakfast is included in the price. Upmarket places tend to price in US dollars rather than pula.

**$** less than P800 (US$75)

**$$** P800 to P1600 (US$75–150)

**$$$** more than P1600 (US$150)

The following price ranges refer to a main course.

**$** less than US$10

**$$** US$10 to US$20

**$$$** more than US$20

#### Camping

Just about everywhere of interest, including all major national parks, has a campsite. Once the domain of the Department of Wildlife and National Parks (DWNP), many of the campsites are now privately run.

All campsites *must* be booked in advance and they fill up fast in busy periods, such as during South African school holidays. It is very important to remember that you will not be allowed into almost every park run by the DWNP without a reservation for a campsite.

Camping prices in reviews are per person and per night (eg camping P80), unless otherwise noted.

### ACTIVITIES

Such is the nature of travelling in Botswana that even the most tranquil holidays will involve some form of activity, such as a rugged 4WD excursion or poling gently along the Okavango Delta's waterways in a traditional *mokoro* (dugout canoe). Beyond these activities there are few options, and most activities that are possible are organised as part of lodge packages rather than designed for individual travellers.

### EMBASSIES & HIGH COMMISIONS

Most diplomatic missions are in Gaborone. Many more countries (such as Australia and New Zealand) have embassies or consulates in South Africa.

**French Embassy** (Map p745; ☎368 0800; www.ambafrance-bw.org; 761 Robinson Rd, Gaborone; ⏲8am-4pm Mon-Fri)

**German Embassy** (Map p745; ☎395 3143; www.gaborone.diplo.de; Queens Rd, Gaborone; ⏲9am-noon Mon-Fri)

**Namibian High Commission** (Map p744; ☎390 2181; namibhc@info.bw; Plot 186,

Morara Close, Gaborone; ⏲7.30am-1pm & 2-4.30pm Mon-Fri)

**South African High Commission** (Map p745; ☎390 4800; sahcgabs@botsnet.bw; 29 Queens Rd, Gaborone; ⏲8am-noon & 1.30-4.30pm Mon-Fri)

**UK High Commission** (Map p745; ☎395 2841; www.gov.uk/government/world/botswana; Queens Rd, Gaborone; ⏲8am-4.30pm Mon-Thu, to 1pm Fri)

**US Embassy** (Map p744; ☎395 3982; http://botswana.usembassy.gov; Embassy Dr, Government Enclave, Gaborone; ⏲7.30am-5pm Mon-Thu, to 1.30pm Fri)

**Zambian High Commission** (Map p745; ☎395 1951; zamhico@work.co.bw; Plot No 1118, Queens Rd, The Mall, Gaborone; ⏲8.30am-12.30pm & 2-4.30pm Mon-Fri)

**Zimbabwean Embassy** (Map p744; ☎391 4495; www.zimgaborone.gov.zw; Plot 8850, Orapa Close, Government Enclave, Gaborone; ⏲8am-1pm & 2-4.30pm Mon-Fri)

## EMERGENCY

| | |
|---|---|
| Emergency | ☎999 |
| Ambulance | ☎997 |
| Fire | ☎998 |
| Police | ☎999 |

## INTERNET ACCESS

**Cyber cafes** Common in large and medium-sized towns; connection speeds fluctuate wildly.

**Post offices** Some post offices, including in Kasane, have a few internet-enabled PCs.

**Wi-fi** Reasonably common in midrange and top-end hotels in towns, but very rarely available in safari lodges.

## LGBTIQ TRAVELLERS

Homosexuality, both gay and lesbian, is illegal in Botswana. Intolerance has increased in the region over the last few years due to the homophobic statements of leaders in neighbouring Namibia and Zimbabwe. Gay and lesbian people with whom we spoke in Botswana suggested that the situation, at least in Gaborone, is relatively relaxed but it is advisable to refrain from any overt displays of affection in public.

## MAPS

The best paper map of Botswana is the *Botswana* (1:1,000,000) map published by Tracks4Africa (www.tracks4africa.co.za). Updated every couple of years using detailed traveller feedback, the map is printed on tearproof, waterproof paper and includes distances *and* estimated travel times. Used in conjunction with Tracks4Africa's unrivalled GPS maps, it's far and away the best mapping product on the market.

## MONEY

Botswana's unit of currency is the pula (P), which is divided into 100 thebe. *Pula* means 'rain' – a valuable commodity in this desert land.

Full banking services are available only in major towns, although ATMs are sprouting up all over the country. Most credit cards are accepted at hotels and restaurants, and cash advances are available at major banks (but not through ATMs).

## OPENING HOURS

**Banks** 8.30am–3.30pm Monday to Friday, 8.15am–10.45am Saturday

**National Parks** 6am–6.30pm April to September, 5.30am–7pm October to March

**Post Offices** 9am–5pm Monday to Friday, 9am–noon Saturday, or 7.30am–noon and 2pm–4.30pm Monday to Friday, 7.30am–12.30pm Saturday

**Restaurants** 11am–11pm Monday to Saturday; some also open the same hours on Sunday

## PUBLIC HOLIDAYS

During official public holidays, all banks, government offices and major businesses are closed. However, hotels, restaurants, bars, smaller shops, petrol stations, museums and national parks and reserves stay open, while border crossings and public transport continue operating as normal. Government offices, banks and some businesses also take the day off after New Year's Day, President's Day, Botswana/Independence Day and Boxing Day.

**New Year's Day** 1 January

**Easter** Good Friday, Easter Saturday and Easter Monday March/April

**Labour Day** 1 May

**Ascension Day** May/June, 40 days after Easter Sunday

**Sir Seretse Khama Day** 1 July

**President's Day** Third Friday in July

**Botswana/Independence Day** 30 September

**Christmas Day** 25 December

**Boxing Day** 26 December

## SAFE TRAVEL

Crime is rarely a problem in Botswana, and doesn't usually extend beyond occasional pick-pocketing and theft from parked cars. Gaborone is one of Africa's safer cities, but it still pays to take a taxi after dark.

## TELEPHONE

Botswana's country code is ☎267, and the international access code is ☎00. Botswana has two main mobile-phone networks, Mascom Wireless (www.mascom.bw) and Orange Botswana (www.orange.co.bw), of which Mascom is the largest provider. All providers have dealers in most large and medium-sized towns where you can buy phones, SIM cards and top up your credit. Government-run Botswana Telecommunications Corporation (www.btc.bw) runs the beMobile network, but its future was uncertain at the time of writing.

The coverage map for the two main providers is improving with each passing year, but when deciding whether to get a local SIM card, remember that there's simply no mobile coverage across large parts of the country (including much of the Kalahari and Okavango Delta). That said, the main highway system is generally covered.

Mobile-phone numbers are eight-digit numbers starting with a 7.

### TIME

Botswana is two hours ahead of GMT/UTC.

### TOURIST INFORMATION

There are tourist offices in the following places:

- **Francistown** (p747)
- **Gaborone** (p745)
- **Kang** (☎651 7070; www.botswanatourism.co.bw; Trans Kalahari Hwy/A2; ⊙7.30am-4.30pm Mon-Fri, 9am-2pm Sat)
- **Kasane** (☎625 0555; www.botswanatourism.co.bw; Hunters' Africa Mall, off President Ave; ⊙7.30am-6pm Mon-Fri, 9am-2pm Sat)
- **Maun** (p756)

### VISAS

Most visitors can obtain tourist visas at the international airports and borders (and the nearest police stations in lieu of an immigration official at remote border crossings). Visas on arrival are valid for 30 days – and possibly up to 90 days if requested at the time of entry – and are available for free to passport holders from most Commonwealth countries (but not Ghana, India, Nigeria, Pakistan and Sri Lanka), all EU countries, the USA and countries in the Southern African Customs Union (SACU), ie South Africa, Namibia, Lesotho and Swaziland.

## RENTING A FOUR-WHEEL DRIVE

If you're looking to rent a car to explore Botswana, we recommend booking through companies that offer specialist rental of fully equipped 4WDs with all camping equipment. Most can also arrange for pick ups/drop offs in Maun, Kasane, Gaborone, Windhoek (Namibia), Victoria Falls (Zimbabwe/Zambia), Harare (Zimbabwe) or Livingstone (Zambia), but remember that you'll usually pay a fee if you decide to pick up your vehicle in a place away from the company's main office, or if you drop off your vehicle in a place that's different from where you picked it up: fees range between £200 and £500 for either service.

Among the better 4WD-rental agencies are the following:

**Avis Safari Rentals** (☎in South Africa +27 11-387 8431; www.avisvanrental.co.za/avis-safari-rental.aspx)

**Bushlore** (☎in South Africa +27 11-312 8084; www.bushlore.com)

**Travel Adventures Botswana** (☎74 814 658, 686 1211; www.traveladventuresbotswana.com)

If you hire directly through the rental company, you'll get just the vehicle and you'll need to make all of the other travel arrangements on your own. For most travellers, it works out more convenient to book through an operator who can also make campsite and other accommodation bookings, arrange a satellite phone and make any other necessary arrangements. For this, try the following:

**Drive Botswana** (☎in Palapye 492 3416; www.drivebotswana.com) This excellent operator arranges 4WDs and also organises a complete package itinerary, including maps, trip notes and bookings for campsites. Although Botswana is where it all began, Drive Botswana arranges trips and can also make bookings for Namibia, Zambia and Zimbabwe. We found the owner, Andy Raggett, to be outstanding and unfailingly professional.

**Safari Drive** (☎in the UK 01488 71140; www.safaridrive.com) Expensive but professional and upmarket company with its own fleet of recent-model vehicles. Prices include all equipment, emergency backup, detailed route preparation and bookings, sat phone and free tank of fuel.

**Self Drive Adventures** (☎686 3755; www.selfdriveadventures.com) 4WD rentals and all bookings made on your behalf. Although you do the driving, you'll be accompanied by a support vehicle and a local guide.

If you hold a passport from any other country, apply for a 30-day tourist visa at an overseas Botswanan embassy or consulate.

## Getting There & Away

### ENTERING BOTSWANA

Entering Botswana is usually straightforward provided you are carrying a valid passport. Visas are available on arrival for most nationalities and are issued in no time. If you're crossing into the country overland and in your own (or rented) vehicle, expect to endure (sometimes quite cursory, sometimes strict) searches for fresh meat, fresh fruit and dairy products, most of which will be confiscated if found. For vehicles rented in South Africa, Namibia or other regional countries, you will need to show a letter from the owner that you have permission to drive the car into Botswana, in addition to all other registration documents.

At all border crossings you must pay P120 (a combination of road levy and third-party insurance) if you're driving your own vehicle. Hassles from officialdom are rare.

#### Passport

All visitors entering Botswana must hold a passport that is valid for at least six months. Also, allow a few empty pages for stamp-happy immigration officials, especially if you plan on crossing over to Zimbabwe and/or Zambia to Victoria Falls.

### AIR

Botswana's main airport, **Sir Seretse Khama International Airport** (GBE; ☎391 4401; www.caab.co.bw), is located 11km north of Gaborone. Although it's well served with flights from Jo'burg (South Africa) and Harare (Zimbabwe), it's seldom used by tourists as an entry point into the country.

Other, more popular entry points are **Kasane Airport** (BBK; ☎625 0133, 368 8200) and **Maun Airport** (p756).

The national carrier is **Air Botswana** (BP; ☎390 5500; www.airbotswana.co.bw), which flies routes within Southern Africa. Air Botswana has offices in Gaborone, Francistown, Maun, Kasane and Victoria Falls (Zimbabwe). It's generally cheaper to book Air Botswana tickets online than through one of its offices.

In addition to **Air Namibia** (☎in Maun 686 0391; www.airnamibia.com) and **South African Airways** (☎in Gaborone 397 2397; www.flysaa.com), which do fly into Botswana, the country is served by a number of special charter flights.

### LAND

Overland travel to or from Botswana is usually straightforward as most travellers either arrive by private vehicle or by Intercape Mainliner (www.intercape.co.za) from South Africa. The main border crossings into Botswana are as follows:

**From Namibia** (five) Mamuno, Mohembo and Ngoma Bridge.

**From South Africa** (14 crossings) Martin's Drift (from Northern Transvaal), Tlokweng, Pioneer Gate and Ramatlabama (from Mafikeng).

**From Zimbabwe** (three) Kazungula and Ramokgweban/Plumtree.

**From Zambia** (one) Kazungula River Ferry.

## Getting Around

### AIR

Air Botswana operates a limited number of domestic routes. Sample one-way fares at the time of writing:

**Gaborone–Francistown** P1406

**Gaborone–Kasane** P2060

**Gaborone–Maun** P1791

**Kasane–Maun** P715

### BUS & COMBI

Buses and combis (minibuses) regularly travel to all major towns and villages throughout Botswana, but are less frequent in sparsely populated areas such as western Botswana and the Kalahari. Public transport to smaller villages is often nonexistent, unless the village is along a major route.

Buses are usually comfortable and normally leave at a set time, regardless of whether they're full. Finding out the departure times for buses is a matter of asking around the bus station, because schedules are not posted anywhere. Combis leave when full, usually from the same station as buses. Tickets for all public buses and combis cannot be bought in advance; they can only be purchased on board.

### CAR & MOTORCYCLE

The best way to travel around Botswana is to hire a vehicle. With your own car you can avoid public transport and organised tours. Remember, however, that distances are long.

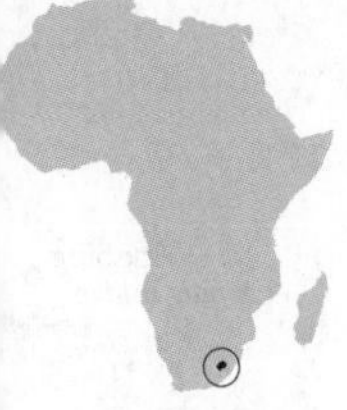

# Lesotho

POP 2.1 MILLION / ☎266

## Includes ➡



## Best Places to Eat

- Maliba Lodge (p774)
- No.7 Restaurant (p771)
- Semonkong Lodge (p775)
- Piri Piri (p771)

## Best Places to Sleep

- Malealea Lodge (p776)
- Maliba Lodge (p774)
- Semonkong Lodge (p775)
- Sani Mountain Lodge (p774)
- Kick4Life Hotel (p770)

## Why Go?

Beautiful, culturally rich, safe, affordable and easily accessible from Durban and Johannesburg, mountainous Lesotho (le-*soo*-too) is a vastly underrated travel destination. The contrast with South Africa could not be more striking, with the Basotho people's distinct personality and the altitudinous terrain's topographical extremes. Even a few days in Lesotho's hospitable mountain lodges and trading posts will give you a fresh perspective on Southern Africa.

This is essentially an alpine country, where villagers on horseback in multicoloured balaclavas and blankets greet you round precipitous bends. The hiking and trekking – often on a famed Basotho pony – is world class and the infrastructure of the three stunning national parks continues to improve.

The 1000m-high 'lowlands' offer craft shopping and sights, but don't miss a trip to the southern, central or northeastern highlands, where streams traverse an ancient dinosaur playground. This is genuine adventure travel.

## When to Go

### Maseru

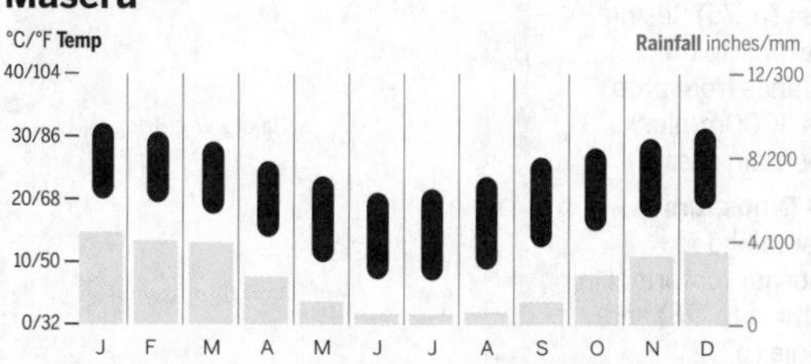


**Mar–Apr** Purple cosmos flowers in the green meadows and cool autumn temperatures.

**Jun–Aug** See snow frosting the mountaintops and do some short hikes.

**Sep** Morija Festival celebrates Sotho culture; peach blossoms colour the landscape.

# Lesotho Highlights

❶ **Trading Posts** (p776) Staying in a former trading post for mountain views and authentic village life.

❷ **Pony trekking or hiking** (p775) Making your way through the highlands, staying in traditional Basotho huts.

❸ **Southern Africa's Highest Pub** (p774) Raising a glass at Sani Mountain Lodge, perched atop the Sani Pass in Sani Top.

❹ **Sehlabathebe National Park** (p774) Finding rugged isolation in this remote and beautiful park.

❺ **Maletsunyane Falls** (p775) Abseiling 200m down these awesome falls in Semonkong.

❻ **Katse Dam** (p775) Admiring feats of aquatic engineering.

❼ **Ts'ehlanyane National Park** (p774) Experiencing the park's raw beauty.

❽ **Mafika-Lisiu Pass** (p775) Seeing forever into the distance from atop this 3000m-plus mountain pass.

❾ **Dinosaurs** Searching for dinosaur footprints in Quthing (p776) and Morija (p772).

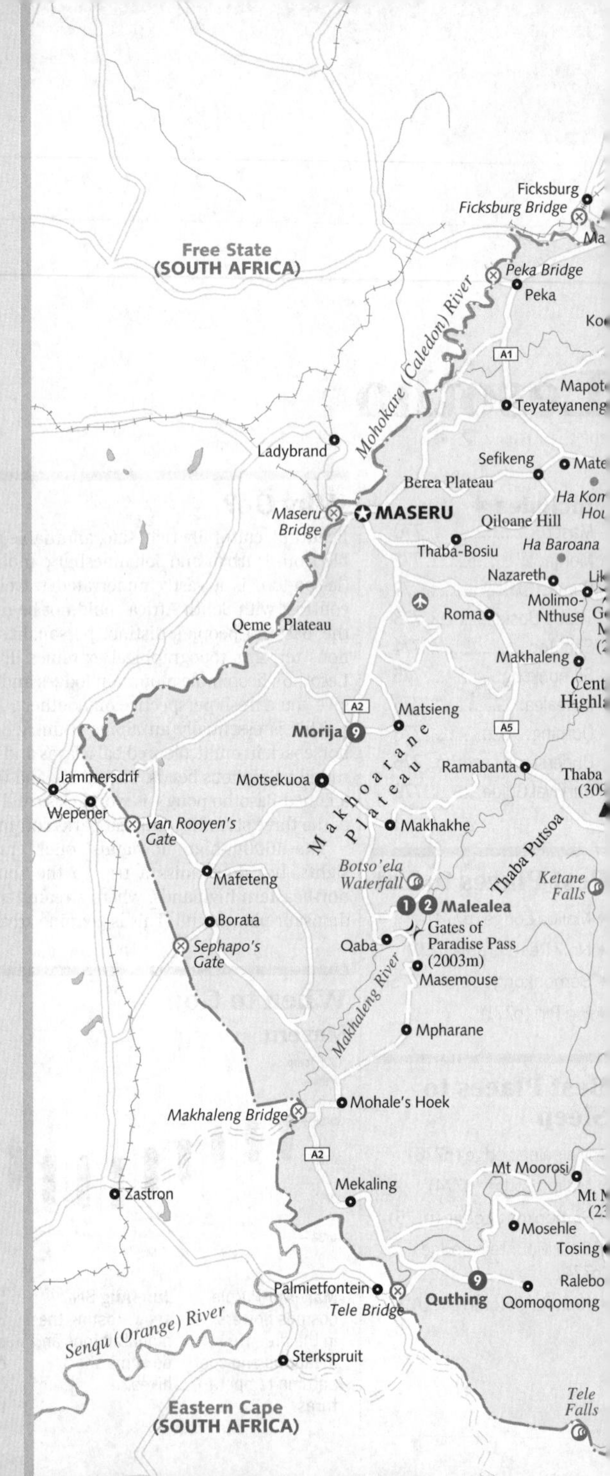

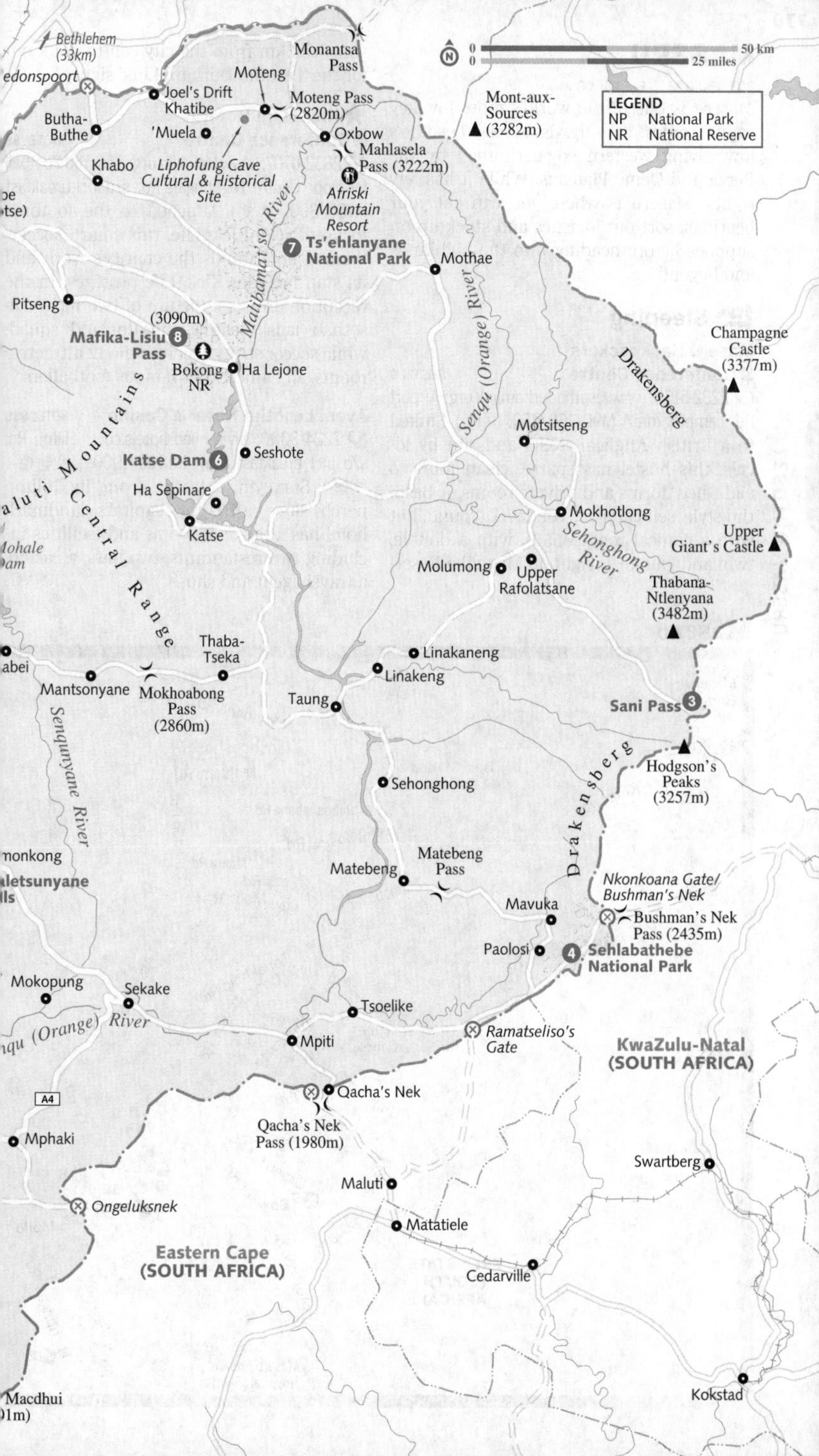

Bethlehem (33km)
Monantsa Pass
Moteng
Joel's Drift
Khatibe
Moteng Pass (2820m)
Butha-Buthe
'Muela
Oxbow
Mahlasela Pass (3222m)
Khabo
Liphofung Cave Cultural & Historical Site
Afriski Mountain Resort
Malibamat'so River
Ts'ehlanyane National Park
Mothae
Mont-aux-Sources (3282m)
LEGEND
NP National Park
NR National Reserve
50 km
25 miles
Pitseng
(3090m)
Mafika-Lisiu Pass
Bokong NR
Ha Lejone
Senqu (Orange) River
Drakensberg
Champagne Castle (3377m)
Motsitseng
Maluti Mountains
Central Range
Katse Dam
Seshote
Ha Sepinare
Katse
Mokhotlong
Sehonghong River
Upper Giant's Castle
Molumong
Upper Rafolatsane
Thabana-Ntlenyana (3482m)
Thaba-Tseka
Linakaneng
Linakeng
Mantsonyane
Mokhoabong Pass (2860m)
Taung
Sani Pass
Hodgson's Peaks (3257m)
Senqunyane River
Sehonghong
Drakensberg
Matebeng Pass
Matebeng
Nkonkoana Gate/ Bushman's Nek
Bushman's Nek Pass (2435m)
Mavuka
Paolosi
Sehlabathebe National Park
Mokopung
Sekake
Tsoelike
Ramatseliso's Gate
Senqu (Orange) River
Mpiti
KwaZulu-Natal (SOUTH AFRICA)
A4
Qacha's Nek
Qacha's Nek Pass (1980m)
Mphaki
Swartberg
Maluti
Ongeluksnek
Matatiele
Eastern Cape (SOUTH AFRICA)
Cedarville
Kokstad
Macdhui

# MASERU

POP 430,000 / ELEV 1600M

Maseru is one of the world's more low-key capital cities. It sprawls across Lesotho's lower-lying western edge, rimmed by the Berea and Qeme Plateaus. While it has few sights, Maseru is where you can get your bearings, sort out logistics and stock up on supplies before heading into the highlands and beyond.

## Sleeping

**Maseru Backpackers & Conference Centre** HOSTEL $
(2232 5166; www.lesothodurhamlink.org; Airport Rd; camping/dm/r M90/160/450; P 📶) Linked to a British Anglican NGO and run by locals, this hostel has sparse, clean four- to eight-bed dorms and private rooms. A Basotho-style self-catering rondavel (round hut with a conical roof; M550), with a double, twin and lounge, is right on Maqalika Reservoir. It's 3km from the city centre; look out for the 'Lesotho Durham Link' sign.

**★Kick4Life Hotel & Conference Centre** HOTEL $$
(2832 0707; www.kick4life.org; Lesotho Football for Hope Centre, Nightingale Rd; s/d incl breakfast M750/800; P 📶) Attached to the football-focused NGO Kick4Life, this smart, soccer-themed hotel funds the charity's work and its staff includes Kick4Life protégés. In the reception area is a picture of two lucky Lesothan lads meeting the England squad, while soccer strips decorate the 12 attractive rooms, all named after famous footballers.

**Avani Lesotho Hotel & Casino** HOTEL $$$
(2224 3000; www.minorhotels.com; Hilton Rd; s/d incl breakfast from M1800/1900; P ❄ @ 📶 🏊) Surveying Maseru from its hilltop perch since 1979, the capital's landmark hotel has a range of rooms and facilities including two restaurants, two bars, a casino, a travel agent and shops.

## Maseru

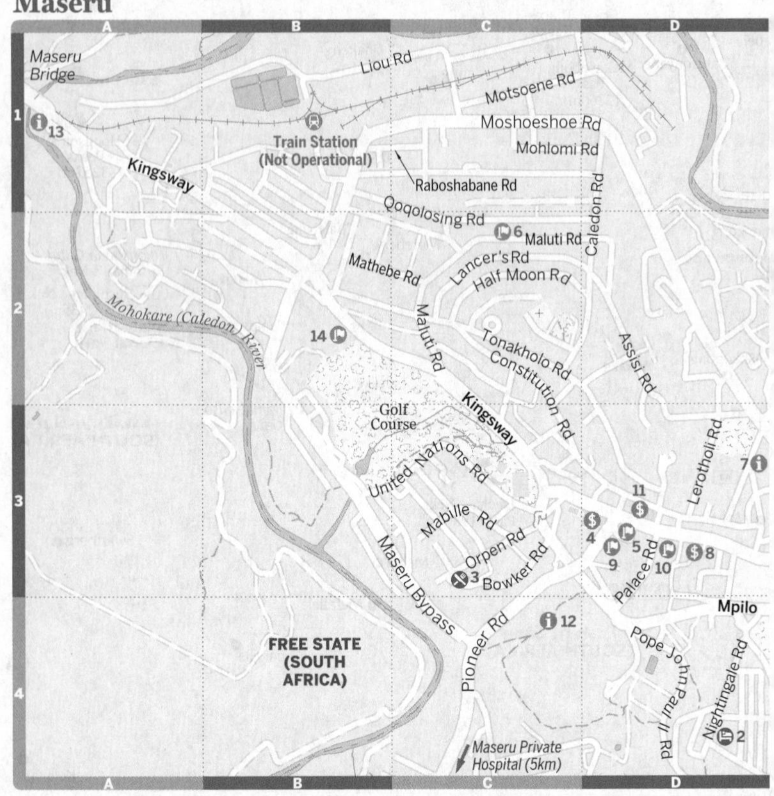

## Eating

**★No.7 Restaurant** INTERNATIONAL $$

(☎2832 0707; www.kick4life.org; Lesotho Football for Hope Centre, Nightingale Rd; mains lunch M60-95, dinner M75-130; ⏰7am-10pm Mon-Sat, to noon Sun; ) Attached to football-focused NGO Kick4Life and its hotel, No.7 pumps its profits back into Kick4Life's charitable work and the team includes young locals training for a career in hospitality. The restaurant is a stylish spot with city views and a menu fusing European sophistication with Basotho touches, offering dishes such as fillet steak and bouillabaisse. The halloumi salad is superb.

**Piri Piri** INTERNATIONAL $$

(Orpen Rd; mains M85-130; ⏰11am-10pm Mon-Sat) This restaurant near the Maseru Sun does Portuguese, Mozambican and South African dishes, including steaks, seafood, *feijoada* (a traditional Portuguese stew) and piri-piri chicken. Choose between romantic, low-lit rooms and a gazebo in the garden.

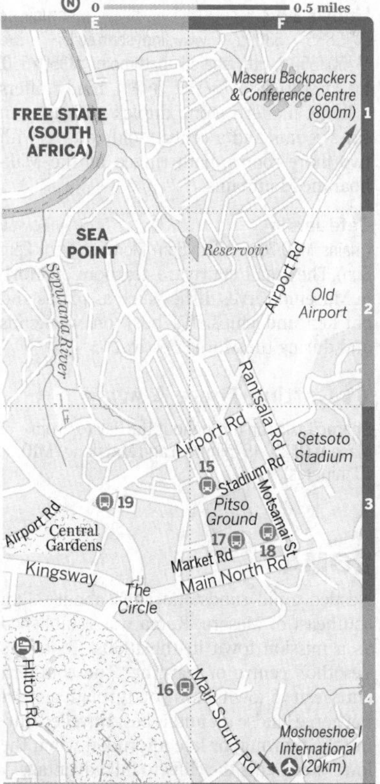


## Information

### MEDICAL SERVICES

**Maseru Private Hospital** (☎2231 3260; off Pioneer Rd, Ha Thetsane) In the suburb of Ha Thetsane, about 7km south of central Maseru.

### MONEY

There are several banks with ATMs on Kingsway. The top-end hotels will do foreign-exchange transactions (at poor rates).

**FNB** (Kingsway)

**Nedbank** (Kingsway) Does foreign-exchange transactions Monday to Friday.

**Standard Lesotho Bank** (Kingsway)

### TOURIST INFORMATION

**Tourist information office** (☎2833 2238; http://visitlesotho.travel; Pioneer Mall, cnr Pioneer & Mpilo Rds; ⏰9am-6pm Mon-Fri, to 3pm Sat, to 1pm Sun) Has lists of tour guides, information on public transport and, when in stock, free Maseru city maps. Tourist offices can also be found at Maseru Bridge Border Post (☎2231 2427; ⏰8am-5pm Mon-Fri, 9am-1pm Sat & Sun), Moshoeshoe I International

### Maseru

**Sleeping**

1 Avani Lesotho Hotel & Casino ........... E4
2 Kick4Life Hotel & Conference Centre ........... D4

**Eating**

No.7 Restaurant ........... (see 2)
3 Piri Piri ........... C3

**Drinking & Nightlife**

Lesotho Sun ........... (see 1)

**Information**

4 FNB ........... D3
5 French Honorary Consul ........... D3
6 German Honorary Consul ........... C2
7 Lesotho Tourism Development Corporation ........... D3
8 Nedbank ........... D3
9 Netherlands Honorary Consul ........... D3
10 South African High Commission ........... D3
Standard Lesotho Bank ........... (see 10)
11 Standard Lesotho Bank ........... D3
12 Tourist Information ........... C4
13 Tourist Information Office ........... A1
14 US Embassy ........... B2

**Transport**

15 Buses to Mokhotlong ........... F3
16 Buses to Qacha's Nek ........... E4
17 Manonyane Bus Stop ........... F3
18 Motsamai Street Taxi Rank ........... F3
19 Sefika Taxi Rank ........... E3

Airport (☎2835 0479; ⏰9am-4.30pm Mon-Fri, 10am-4pm Sat & Sun) and the headquarters of the Lesotho Tourism Development Corporation (LTDC; ☎2231 2231; cnr Linare Rd & Parliament St; ⏰8am-5pm Mon-Fri).

## Getting There & Away

**Buses to Mokhotlong** Depart from Stadium Rd behind Pitso Ground, while those to Qacha's Nek depart from next to St James Primary and High Schools on Main Rd South.

**Manonyane bus stop** (Market Rd) Shared taxis to Thaba-Bosiu and Semonkong, Leribe and points north. Also Lesotho Freight Service buses to destinations including Leribe and Thaba-Tseka. The stop is located near Pitso Ground.

**Motsamai Street taxi rank** (cnr Motsamai St & Market Rd) Services to local destinations (including Motsekuoa) and points north such as Maputsoe and Leribe (Hlotse). The rank is behind KFC located on Main North Rd, between Pitso Ground and Setsoto Stadium.

**Sefika taxi rank** (Airport Rd) A major stand located behind Sefika Mall with services to nationwide destinations, including Roma, Motsekuoa (for Malealea) and points south.

## Getting Around

**Moshoeshoe I International Airport** (MSU; ☎2235 0777) is 21km south of town, off Main South Rd en route to Morija. Shared taxis to the airport depart from Sefika taxi rank. Maseru accommodation, tourist offices and travel agencies can organise private transfers, which cost around M100.

The standard fare for a seat in a shared 'four-plus-one' taxi travelling around town is M6.50. For a private taxi try **Superb Taxis** (☎2831 9647): the standard fee for a trip around town is M40. **Luxury** (☎2232 6211) taxis is another option.

# MORIJA

Tiny Morija is the site of the first European mission in Lesotho. It's an important and attractive town with a rich cultural heritage that makes a pleasant stopover or day trip from Maseru.

## Sights & Activities

The **Morija Museum** (☎2236 0308; www.morija.co.ls; M20; ⏰8am-5pm Mon-Sat, from 2pm Sun; P) is the unofficial national one. If you're here in late September or early October, don't miss the **Morija Festival** (www.morija.co.ls/festival).

**Pony trekking** (one person per hour/half-day/day M220/600/880), guided hikes to dinosaur footprints (per person M50) and village sleepovers (per hiker/rider M440/1060 including full board) can be organised through Morija Guest Houses. Reserve a day in advance. An optional pack-horse for luggage is M480 extra.

## Sleeping & Eating

★**Morija Guest Houses** GUESTHOUSE $
(☎6306 5093; www.morijaguesthouses.com; camping M110, r per person with shared bathroom M260-340, breakfast/lunch/dinner M70/130/150; P 📶) At this sterling stone-and-thatch house perched high above the village, guests can choose between cosy rooms in the main building and cottages below. Activities such as mountain biking, and entertainment such as traditional choir and dance performances are offered, making this a top spot to experience the area. Backpackers who arrive by public transport pay R200 per person, regardless of the room.

**Lindy's B&B** GUESTHOUSE $
(☎5885 5309; www.lindysbnb.co.ls; s/d M450/650, with shared bathroom M350/560, breakfast/dinner M75/130; P 📶) Lindy offers a large, modern stone duplex with two en suite rooms and a century-old cottage with two more rooms, both ringed by the Makhoarane Mountains.

**Cafe Jardin** CAFE $
(mains M40-70; ⏰8am-5pm Mon-Sat, from 2pm Sun) The small courtyard tearoom at Morija Museum serves dishes such as pizzas and chicken and chips. It's busy on weekends and during the Morija Festival.

## Getting There & Away

Shared taxis run throughout the day to/from Maseru (M25, 45 minutes) and Matsieng (M10, 10 minutes).

# ROMA

Nestled amid sandstone cliffs about 35km southeast of Maseru, Roma was established as a mission town in the 1860s. Today it's Lesotho's centre of learning. The southern entry/exit to town takes you through a striking gorge landscape and is best travelled during the morning or late afternoon when the lower sun lights the cliffs to full advantage.

WORTH A TRIP

## LIPHOFUNG CAVE CULTURAL & HISTORICAL SITE

Just beyond the village of Muela is the signposted turn-off for this small Lesotho Northern Parks–administered **site** (☎6718 5155, 2246 0723; adult/child M30/15; ⊙8.30am-4.30pm Mon-Fri, from 9am Sat & Sun; P), which includes a cave with some San paintings and Stone Age artefacts. King Moshoeshoe the Great is rumoured to have stopped here on his travels around Lesotho.

There is a cultural centre and a small shop selling local crafts. Day walks are possible and, with notice, you can arrange guided hikes and pony treks.

Accommodation is available in simple, but comfortable, stone, four-person rondavels with kitchen facilities and sweeping views. It is also possible to camp in the cave – a novel and atmospheric experience. Either way, you'll need to bring your own food.

**Roma Trading Post** (☎2234 0203, 2234 0267; www.tradingpost.co.za; camping M85, r per person M350, per person with shared bathroom M200, breakfast/dinner M55/100; P) is a charming fourth-generation trading post operated since 1903 by the Thorn family. The attached guesthouse includes garden rooms, rondavels and the original sandstone homestead, with shared kitchen, set in a lush garden. The accommodating and personable staff can organise adventures including pony trekking, hiking, visits to nearby *minwane* (dinosaur footprints) and local attractions.

Sister property **Ramabanta Trading Post** (☎5844 2309; s/d M300/600; P) is about 40km southeast of Roma, off the tar road to Semonkong and the south. Set in neat grounds with mountain views, its smart and spacious rondavels have a lounge and dining room, three have a kitchenette and the main building features a lounge, bar and restaurant.

There are a couple of lively fast-food joints on the main road and Kaycees is a popular student hang-out off the main drag.

Shared taxis run throughout the day to/from Maseru (M30, 45 minutes).

# THABA-BOSIU

About 25km east of Maseru is the famed and flat-topped Thaba-Bosiu (Mountain at Night), where King Moshoeshoe the Great established his mountain stronghold in 1824. It's regarded as the birthplace of the Basotho nation and, although an unassuming spot, is Lesotho's most important historical site.

## Sights & Activities

At the mountain's base is a **visitor information centre** (☎2835 7207; ⊙8am-5pm Mon-Fri, from 9am Sat, 9am-1pm Sun) where you can organise a guide to walk with you to the top (M40, two hours). Horse riding is also available (M100 per hour; book ahead), as are two-hour walks to see rock art (M50).

From the summit, there are good views over the surrounding area, including Qiloane Hill, which allegedly provided the inspiration for the Basotho hat.

★ **Cultural Village** MUSEUM
(☎5884 0018; www.thababosiu.com; M20; ⊙8am-sunset; P) Revamped in 2016, the well-maintained cultural village is a highly worthwhile stop. Excellent guided tours of the complex explain traditional Basotho culture and history and end with a visit to a statue of the much-revered Moshoeshoe I. There's a restaurant (mains M60 to M160) with a wraparound verandah – a great place for an afternoon drink.

## Sleeping

Thaba-Bosiu's accommodation options are within walking distance of each other on the main road. It's a fine alternative to staying in Maseru.

**Mmelesi Lodge** LODGE $
(☎5250 0006; www.mmelesilodge.co.ls; s/d incl breakfast M520/700; P) Mmelesi Lodge has sandstone chalets in the style of thatched *mokhoro* (traditional Basotho huts), reached along flower-lined paths. The bar often fills with government workers, while the restaurant serves surprisingly good food (mains M50 to M75).

## Getting There & Away

If you're driving, take the Mafeteng Rd for about 13km and turn left at the Roma turn-off; after about 6km take the signposted road left. Thaba-Bosiu is 10km further along. Shared taxis to Thaba-Bosiu (M20, 30 minutes) depart from the Manonyane transport stand in Maseru.

## NORTHEASTERN HIGHLANDS

East of Butha-Buthe, the road weaves up dramatically through spectacular mountains – part of the Drakensberg range – with rocky cliffs and rolling hills. South Africa does a good job of marketing its portion of the Drakensberg escarpment, but the raw beauty of the Lesotho section is hard to beat, with stunning highland panoramas, low population density and plenty of winter snow.

This area has many of the country's worst stretches of main road. In places the asphalt has actually made the road more potholey, making for a wild and slow ride in a regular vehicle. Lesotho's mass, Chinese-run roadwork program is another complication, as the work can further slow traffic.

### Sani Top

Sani Top sits atop the steep Sani Pass, the famous road into Lesotho through the Drakensberg range in KwaZulu-Natal. South Africa's highest mountain pass, it offers stupendous views on clear days and unlimited hiking possibilities.

Besides local hikes, a rugged three- to four-day trek south to Sehlabathebe National Park is possible. The route follows a remote Drakensberg escarpment edge and should only be attempted if you're well prepared, experienced and in a group of at least four people.

Africa's highest peak south of Mt Kilimanjaro, **Thabana-Ntlenyana** (3482m) is a popular but long and arduous hike (12km, nine hours). There's a path, but a guide (from M350) would be handy; arrange the night before through **Sani Mountain Lodge** (☎in South Africa 073 541 8620, in South Africa 078 634 7496; www.sanimountain.co.za; dm/camping M250/95, s/d/tr with half board M1520/2290/3165; P). It's also possible to do the ascent on horseback.

**Hodgson's Peaks** (3256m) is a 6km, five-hour hike up a valley. There are views of KwaZulu-Natal from the summit.

About 8km from Sani Top, Basotho-run **Sani Stone Lodge** (☎5631 0331, 2892 4000; www.sanistonelodge.co.za; camping M90, dm/d M170/500; P) offers simple rooms, an en suite dorm and three cosy rondavels (d M800) with all-important fireplaces. Guided hikes, village visits and pony treks are available and the bar-restaurant is a welcome sight after a trek in the highlands.

At 2874m, atop the Sani Pass, **Sani Mountain Lodge** (☎in South Africa 073 541 8620, in South Africa 078 634 7496; www.sanimountain.co.za; dm/camping M250/95, s/d/tr with half board M1520/2290/3165; P) stakes a claim to 'highest drinking hole in Southern Africa'. Pub trivia aside, cosy rondavels and excellent meals reward those who make the steep ascent from KwaZulu-Natal. Backpackers doss

WORTH A TRIP

#### HIGHLANDS PARKS & RESERVES

**Bokong Nature Reserve** (☎2246 0723, 5950 2291; adult/child M10/5, chalets M500; ⏲8am-5pm) Bokong has perhaps the most dramatic setting of the northern parks, with stunning vistas over the Lepaqoa Valley from the **visitors centre** (☎5950 2291; adult/child M10/5; ⏲8am-4pm), various short walks and a good, rugged two- to three-day hike to Ts'ehlanyane National Park. Bearded vultures, rock shelters and valleyhead fens (wetland areas) are features here.

**Ts'ehlanyane National Park** (☎in Leribe 2246 0723; adult/vehicle M40/10; ⏲gate 8am-4.30pm; P) This Lesotho Northern Parks–administered national park protects a beautiful, 56-km-sq patch of rugged wilderness, including one of Lesotho's only stands of indigenous forest, at a high altitude of 2000m to 3000m. This underrated and underused place is about as far away from it all as you can get and is perfect for hiking.

**Maliba Lodge** (☎in South Africa +27 31-702 8791; www.maliba-lodge.com; chalet s/d with full board M2570/3440; P 📶) Maliba ('Madiba') offers a range of accommodation in Ts'ehlanyane National Park, but its signature offering is six lavish chalets – Lesotho's plushest accommodation. Each features a four-poster bed, antique furniture, terrace and hot tub facing the mountain range, heated towel racks and sherry by the door. Go for the secluded number 6, the honeymooners' choice. There's also an excellent restaurant.

down the road in modern rooms that hold between two and six people.

The road to Sani Top is tarred all the way from Butha Buthe. There is a daily shared taxi from Mokhotlong (M90, two hours), departing early in the morning.

## CENTRAL HIGHLANDS

Lesotho's rugged interior boasts the country's two trademark sights: the breathtaking Maletsunyane Falls (204m), which are almost twice the height of the Victoria Falls and has a word-record-holding abseil drop (operated by **Semonkong Lodge** (☎2700 6037; www.semonkonglodge.com; camping M100, dm/s/d from M175/560/860; P) ); and the human-made spectacle of **Katse Dam**, an engineering feat holding a shimmering lake surrounded by rippling mountain slopes. The area offers an incredible mix of scenery, activities and engineering marvels, accessed from the lowlands up tortuous but stunning passes such as the excellently named God Help Me Pass (2281m) and the **Mafika-Lisiu Pass** (3090m), one of Lesotho's most beautiful roads.

### Semonkong

Semonkong (Place of Smoke), a one-pony town in the rugged Thaba Putsoa range, gets its name from the nearby **Maletsunyane Falls** (204m), which are at their loudest in summer. The town is the starting point for many fine hiking and pony-trekking trails, including the two-day ride via the peaks of the Thaba Putsoa to **Ketane Falls** (122m).

Near the Maletsunyane River, Semonkong Lodge is a model of community tourism and a great place for everyone from families to adventure seekers. If the inviting accommodation, including cosy rondavels with fireplaces, doesn't make you extend your stay in the mountains, fireside feasts in the lodge's **Duck & Donkey Tavern** (lunch/dinner mains M75/120) surely will.

Staff can arrange all kinds of tours and hikes, employing locals to navigate the villages and steep trails, including extreme fishing expeditions, pony trekking and even pub crawls by donkey. Then there's the world's longest commercially operated, single-drop abseil (204m) down the Maletsunyane Falls.

DON'T MISS

**SEHLABATHEBE NATIONAL PARK**

Lesotho's most undervisited **national park** (☎2232 6075; per person/vehicle M60/15; ⏲gate 8am-4.30pm) is remote, rugged and beautiful. The rolling grasslands, wildflowers and silence provide complete isolation, with only the prolific birdlife (including the bearded vulture) and the odd rhebok for company. Hiking (and horse riding from Sani Top or the Drakensbergs) is the main way to explore and angling is possible in the dams and rivers.

Semonkong is about 110km southeast of Maseru on the tar road to Qacha's Nek; both are a three-hour drive. Shared taxis run all day to/from Maseru (M70) and leave throughout the morning to/from Qacha's Nek (M120). A private taxi to/from Qacha's Nek costs around M250.

## SOUTHERN LESOTHO

The region south of Morija, across to Sehlabathebe National Park in the southeast, is less developed than the northwest but lingers in the memory banks of all who pass through. The mountain ranges eat up the sky out here, where a velvety orange-pink light pours over rocky peaks and yawning valleys. If you like hiking and pony trekking in rugged isolation, head south.

The road from Quthing to Qacha's Nek is one of Lesotho's most impressive drives, taking you along the winding Senqu (Orange) River gorge and through some striking canyon scenery before climbing up onto the escarpment. Another stunner is the road through the interior from Semonkong down to Qacha's Nek. Despite what some maps show, both are tarred all the way to Qacha's Nek.

### Malealea

This remote village has three travel trump cards: its breathtaking mountain scenery, its trading-post lodge and its successful community-based tourism. Many visitors to Lesotho head straight here to sample traditional Basotho life or, as the sign outside town says, to just 'pause and look upon a gateway of paradise'. The area has been inhabited for centuries, as shown by the many instances of **San rock art** in the vicinity.

## Activities

Malealea is one of the best places in Lesotho to organise a village visit, hike or pony trek in the mountains – you can even rent a mountain bike if you prefer to explore on wheels. Organise activities through Malealea Lodge.

## Festivals & Events

**Malealea Monster Weekend** SPORTS
(www.malealea.com; late May) The 'weekend of adventure' hosted by Malealea Lodge features 8km to 80km mountain-bike races, 7km and 15km trail runs and a 2km night run. All take advantage of the mountainous terrain and gorges around Malealea.

**Lesotho Sky** SPORTS
(http://lesothosky.com; late Sep) This six-day, 350km, team mountain-bike race begins in Maseru and climbs through the highlands to Malealea and on to Semonkong.

## Sleeping

★ **Malealea Lodge** LODGE $
(5018 1341, in South Africa 082 552 4215; www.malealea.com; camping M110, s/d from M450/600, with shared bathroom from M277.50/370; P) Offering 'Lesotho in a nutshell', Malealea is a deserving poster child for the mountain kingdom. Every sunset, village choirs and bands perform at the mountaintop lodge. Activities are community run and a proportion of tourist revenues and donations goes directly to supporting local projects. The views, meanwhile, are stupendous.

## Getting There & Away

Early-morning shared taxis connect Maseru and Malealea (M100, 2½ hours). Later in the day, catch a shared taxi to the junction town of Motsekuoa (M50, 1½ hours), from where there are connections to Malealea (M40, one hour). Services from Mafeteng and the south also stop in Motsekuoa.

# Quthing

POP 20,000

Quthing, the southernmost major town in Lesotho, is also known as Moyeni (Place of the Wind). It was established in 1877, abandoned during the Gun War of 1880 and then rebuilt at the present site. Activity centres on the new part of town, Lower Quthing, with its bustling main road.

## Sights

**Dinosaur Footprints** ARCHAEOLOGICAL SITE
(M15; 8am-5pm; P) One of Quthing's main claims to fame is the proliferation of dinosaur footprints in the surrounding area. The most easily accessible are signposted on the left as you leave town heading northeast towards Qacha's Nek. In this building are 230-million-year-old footprints and a craft shop. Children will offer to guide you to more footprints for a small tip.

**Masitise Cave House Museum** MUSEUM
(2700 3259; http://masitisecavehouse.blogspot.co.za; adult/child M10/3; 8.30am-5pm Mon-Fri, to 2pm Sat & Sun; P) Five kilometres west of Quthing is this intriguing section of an old mission, built directly into a San rock shelter in 1866 by Reverend David-Frédéric Ellenberger, a Swiss missionary who was among the first to Lesotho. There's a cast of a dinosaur footprint in the ceiling, a museum with displays on local culture and history, and San rock art nearby.

## Sleeping & Eating

There are a few basic fast-food stands, but you're better off eating at your guesthouse.

**Fuleng Guest House** GUESTHOUSE $
(2275 0260; info.fulengguesthouse@gmail.com; s/d from M450/570; P) This hillside guesthouse offers rondavels with a view, a restaurant, cheeky garden gnomes, a rock feature and a friendly local experience. Find it by the main road on the way up to Upper Quthing. Rates are higher if you pay by card.

## Getting There & Away

The transport stand is in Lower Quthing. Shared taxis serve Maseru (M80, 2½ hours) and Qacha's Nek (M90, 2½ hours), as do faster, more expensive sprinters and slower, cheaper buses.

# UNDERSTAND LESOTHO

## Lesotho Today

A bloodless coup attempt rocked Lesotho in August 2014, harking worryingly back to 1998, when South African Development

Community (SADC) forces had to restore order. Prime Minister Thomas Thabane fled the country and accused the military of trying to overthrow him; following SADC mediation, peaceful general elections took place in February 2015. Thabane's All Basotho Convention lost narrowly and a coalition government was formed by seven other parties. The Basotho-dominated country did not experience apartheid and, with life revolving around subsistence farming, levels of social inequality and crime are lower than in South Africa. The mountain kingdom does face serious issues, though, including unemployment, food shortages, a 23% HIV/AIDS rate and an average life expectancy of 49 years.

# History

## The Early Days

Neighbouring South Africa has always cast a long shadow over Lesotho, fuelling a perpetual struggle for a separate identity on an ever-diminishing patch of territory.

The first inhabitants of the mountainous region that makes up present-day Lesotho were the hunter-gatherer people known as the Khoe-san. They have left many examples of their rock art in the river valleys. Lesotho was settled by the Sotho peoples in the 16th century.

## Moshoeshoe the Great

King Moshoeshoe ('mo-shweshwe' or 'mo-shesh') is the father figure of Lesotho's history. In about 1820, while a local chief of a small village, he led his villagers to Butha-Buthe, a mountain stronghold, where they survived the first battles of the *difaqane* (forced migration in Southern Africa), caused by the violent expansion of the nearby Zulu state. The loosely organised southern Sotho society managed to survive due largely to the adept political and diplomatic abilities of the king. In 1824 Moshoeshoe moved his people to Thaba-Bosiu, a mountaintop that was even easier to defend.

From Thaba-Bosiu, Moshoeshoe played a patient game of placating the stronger local rulers and granting protection, as well as land and cattle, to refugees. These people were to form Basutholand; at the time of Moshoeshoe's death in 1870, Basutoland had a population of more than 150,000.

As the *difaqane* receded a new threat arose. The Voortrekkers had crossed the Senqu (Orange) River in the 1830s and established the Orange Free State. By 1843 Moshoeshoe was sufficiently concerned by their numbers to ally himself with the British Cape Colony government. The British Resident in Basutoland decided that Moshoeshoe was becoming too powerful and engineered an unsuccessful attack on his kingdom.

Treaties with the British helped define the borders of Basutoland but the Boers pressed their claims on the land, leading to wars between the Orange Free State and the Basotho people in 1858 and 1865; Moshoeshoe was forced to sign away much of his western lowlands.

## The Road to Independence

In 1868 the British government annexed Basutoland and handed it to the Cape Colony to run in 1871. After a period of instability, the British government again took direct control of Basutoland in 1884, although it gave authority to local leaders.

Lesotho's existence is attributable to a quirk of history and fortuitous timing. In the 1880s locals resented direct British rule as it was seen as an infringement on Basutoland's freedom and sovereignty. Ironically, British occupation secured the future independence of Lesotho: at the precise moment when the Union of South Africa was created, Basutoland was a British Protectorate and was not included in the Union.

In 1910 the advisory Basutoland National Council was formed from members nominated by the chiefs. In the mid-1950s the council requested internal self-government from the British; by 1960 a new constitution was in place and elections were held for a legislative council. The main contenders were the Basutoland Congress Party (BCP; similar to South Africa's African National Congress) and the conservative Basutoland National Party (BNP) headed by Chief Leabua Jonathan. The BCP won the 1960 elections, then paved the way for full independence from Britain (achieved in 1966). However, at the elections in 1965 the BCP lost to the BNP and Chief Jonathan became the first prime minister of the new Kingdom of Lesotho, which allied itself with the apartheid regime across the border.

**MALOTI OR RAND?**

The South African rand is universally accepted in Lesotho, but even though it's tied to its neighbour's currency, the maloti is not accepted in South Africa. Most ATMs dispense maloti, so don't get caught with a pocketful. If you are spending a short time here before returning to South Africa, stocking up on rand will eliminate the worry of having to spend all your maloti before leaving Lesotho.

### Big Brother

Stripping King Moshoeshoe II of the few powers that the new constitution had left him did not endear Jonathan's government to the people and the BCP won the 1970 election. After his defeat, Jonathan suspended the constitution, expelled the king and banned all opposition political parties.

Jonathan changed tack, distancing himself from South Africa and calling for the return of land in the Orange Free State that had been stolen from the original Basutholand. He also offered refuge to ANC guerrillas and flirted with Cuba. South Africa closed Lesotho's borders, strangling the country. Jonathan was deposed in 1986 and the king was restored as head of state. Eventually agitation for democratic reform rose again.

In 1990 King Moshoeshoe II was deposed by the army in favour of his son, Prince Mohato Bereng Seeisa (Letsie III). Elections in 1993 resulted in the return of the BCP. In 1995 Letsie III abdicated in favour of his father, Moshoeshoe II was reinstated and calm was restored after a year of unrest. Less than a year later Moshoeshoe II was killed when his 4WD plunged over a cliff in the Maluti Mountains. Letsie III became king for the second time.

A split in the BCP resulted in the breakaway Lesotho Congress for Democracy (LCD) taking power. The 1998 elections saw accusations of widespread cheating by the LCD, which won by a landslide, with Pakalitha Mosisli becoming prime minister. Major tensions arose between the public service and the government; the military was also split over the result.

Following months of protests, the government appeared to be losing control. In late September 1998 it called on the Southern African Development Community (SADC) treaty partners – Botswana, South Africa and Zimbabwe – to help restore order. Troops, mainly South African, invaded the kingdom. Rebel elements of the Lesotho army put up strong resistance and there was heavy fighting in Maseru. The government agreed to call new elections, but the political situation remained tense with the spectre of South African intervention never far away. Political wrangling delayed the elections until May 2002.

The LCD won again and Prime Minister Mosisili began a second – and peaceful – five-year term. The 2007 elections were highly controversial. A newly formed All Basotho Convention (ABC) party accused the LCD party of manipulating the allocation of seats. National strikes followed and several ministers were allegedly attacked by gunmen. There was an assassination attempt on ABC's leader, Thomas Thabane, and many people were detained and tortured. In May 2012 Thabane's coalition government ousted Pakalitha Mosisili, who had ruled for 14 years.

## The Culture

Traditional Basotho culture is flourishing, and colourful celebrations marking milestones, such as birth, puberty, marriage and death, are a central part of village life. Cattle hold an important position in daily life, both as sacrificial animals and as symbols of wealth.

The Basotho believe in a Supreme Being and place a great deal of emphasis on *balimo* (ancestors), who act as intermediaries between people and the capricious forces of nature and the spirit world. Evil is a constant danger, caused by *boloi* (witchcraft; witches can be either male or female) and *thkolosi* (small, mischievous beings, similar to the Xhosa's *tokoloshe*). If these forces are bothering the Basotho, they visit the nearest *ngaka* (a learned man, part sorcerer and part doctor) who can combat them. Basotho are traditionally buried in a sitting position, facing the rising sun and ready to leap up when called.

## Environment

The Drakensberg range is at its most rugged in tiny Lesotho – a 30,355-sq-km patch of mountain peaks and highland plateau that is completely surrounded by South Africa. It has the highest lowest point of any country in the world – 1400m, in southern Lesotho's Senqu (Orange) River valley.

Due primarily to its altitude, Lesotho is home to fewer animals than much of the rest of the region. Those you may encounter include rheboks, jackals, mongooses, meerkats, elands and rock hyraxes.

The country's almost 300 recorded bird species include the lammergeier (bearded vulture) and the southern bald ibis.

# SURVIVAL GUIDE

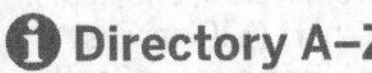

## Directory A–Z

### ACCOMMODATION

The best accommodation options, and a highlight of travelling in Lesotho, are the various tourist lodges, which offer excellent digs, good food and a range of activities. Family-run guesthouses of varying quality can be found across the country. Top-end accommodation is scarce – exceptions are a few hotels in Maseru and one superb lodge in Ts'ehlanyane National Park. Camping opportunities abound away from major towns but always ask locally for permission.

### ACTIVITIES

Lesotho is a supreme destination for lovers of rugged outdoor adventure. The mountains offer endless opportunities to explore on foot or on a Basotho pony. You'll find guides and maps available at the main lodges. Lesotho is also excellent 4WD country, though you need to be experienced and come well-equipped.

### EMBASSIES & CONSULATES

Embassies and consulates are in Maseru.

**French Honorary Consul** (☎2232 5722; www.ambafrance-rsa.org/-Lesotho-320; Alliance Française, cnr Kingsway & Pioneer Rd)

**German Honorary Consul** (☎2233 2292, 2233 2983; www.southafrica.diplo.de; 70c Maluti Rd)

**Netherlands Honorary Consul** (☎2231 2114; www.dutchembassy.co.za; Lancer's Inn, cnr Kingsway & Pioneer Rd)

**South African High Commission** (☎2222 5800; www.dirco.gov.za; cnr Kingsway & Old School Rd)

**US Embassy** (☎2231 2666; https://maseru.usembassy.gov; 254 Kingsway)

### EMERGENCY

**Ambulance** ☎2231 3260, 112
**Fire** ☎112
**Police** ☎5888 1010, 5888 1024, 112

### TAP WATER

It's best to purify it or use bottled water in Lesotho.

### INTERNET ACCESS

Web access is available in Maseru and a few accommodation options elsewhere have wi-fi.

### LGBTIQ TRAVELLERS

The country's law does not protect against discrimination based on sexual orientation or gender identity. Gay sexual relationships are taboo, with open displays of affection frowned upon.

### MONEY

The unit of currency is the loti (plural maloti; symbol: M), made up of 100 lisente. The loti is fixed at the value of the South African rand; rands are accepted everywhere in Lesotho, but maloti are not accepted back in South Africa. The only currency-exchange banks (including Nedbank and Standard Bank) are in Maseru and Maseru has the only ATMs.

### OPENING HOURS

**Banks** 9am–3.30pm Monday–Friday, 8.30am–noon Saturday
**Post Offices** 8am–4.30pm Monday–Friday, 8am–noon Saturday
**Government Offices** 8am–12.45pm & 2pm–4.30pm Monday–Friday
**Cafes** 8am–5pm
**Restaurants** 11.30am–3pm & 6–10pm (last orders); many open 3–6pm
**Bars** Noon–midnight
**Businesses and Shopping** 8.30am–6pm Monday–Friday, 8.30am–1pm Saturday; many supermarkets also 9am–noon Sunday; major shopping centres until 9pm daily

### PRICE RANGES

The following price ranges refer to a double room with bathroom.

**$** less than M700 (US$50)

**$$** M700 to M1400 (US$50 to US$100)

**$$$** more than M1400 (US$100)

The following price ranges refer to a main course.

**$** less than M75 (US$5)

**$$** M75 to M150 (US$5 to US$10)

**$$$** more than M150 (US$10)

### PRACTICALITIES

**Media** The *Sunday Express* (sundayexpress.co.ls) and *Lesotho Times* (www.lestimes.com) carry Lesothan news.

**Electricity** Lesotho's electricity is generated at 220V. Plugs have three round prongs as used in South Africa.

**Weights & measures** Lesotho uses the metric system.

### PUBLIC HOLIDAYS

**New Year's Day** 1 January
**Moshoeshoe's Day** 11 March
**Good Friday** March/April
**Easter Monday** March/April
**Workers' Day** 1 May
**Africa or Heroes' Day** 25 May
**Ascension Day** May/June
**King's Birthday** 17 July
**Independence Day** 4 October
**Christmas Day** 25 December
**Boxing Day** 26 December

### TELEPHONE

- Lesotho's telephone system works reasonably well in the lowlands, but even landlines are temperamental in the highlands.
- There are no area codes.
- Mobile-phone signals are rare in the highlands and can only be picked up on a few mountain passes.
- The main mobile-phone service providers are Vodacom Lesotho (www.vodacom.co.ls) and Econet Telecom (www.etl.co.ls).
- Most villages have a Vodacom or Econet booth, selling credit and SIM cards (about M20; bring your passport).
- South African SIMs work on roaming.

### TIME

Lesotho is on SAST (South Africa Standard Time), which is two hours ahead of GMT/UTC.

### TOURIST INFORMATION

There is a tourist office in Maseru; elsewhere they are thin on the ground.

**Lesotho Tourism Development Corporation** (visitlesotho.travel)
**See Lesotho** (www.seelesotho.com)

### VISAS

Citizens of most Western European countries, the USA and most Commonwealth countries are granted a free entry permit at the border or airport.

## Getting There & Away

### AIR

**Airlink** (☎2235 0418; www.flyairlink.com) has daily flights between Johannesburg (South Africa) and Moshoeshoe I International Airport, 21km south of Maseru (from R1100, one hour). Flying to Bloemfontein airport (130km west of Maseru) is cheaper, as is hiring a car in South Africa.

New local airline **Maluti Sky** (☎2231 7733; www.flymalutisky.com) also offers flights between Maseru and Johannesburg.

### LAND

All Lesotho's borders are with South Africa. Most people enter via Maseru Bridge (open 24 hours). Other main border crossings include Ficksburg Bridge (open 24 hours), Makhaleng Bridge (open 8am to 4pm) and Sani Pass (open 6am to 6pm, but ask around, as times change); however, these often have long queues.

Intercape (www.intercape.co.za) offers bus services to a changing timetable between Bloemfontein and Maseru (from M550,1¾ hours). After your passport is stamped you need to catch a car taxi (called a four-plus-one) from the Lesotho border to the Maseru taxi rank. Via minibus taxi, daily minibuses run between Bloemfontein and Maseru (two hours).

## Getting Around

You can now access most of Lesotho in a 2WD car, but it is still not possible to do a complete circuit without a 4WD, due to rough gravel roads in the east between Mokhotlong and Qacha's Nek. Bus and shared-taxi networks cover the country; taxis do not normally operate to a schedule but leave only when full.

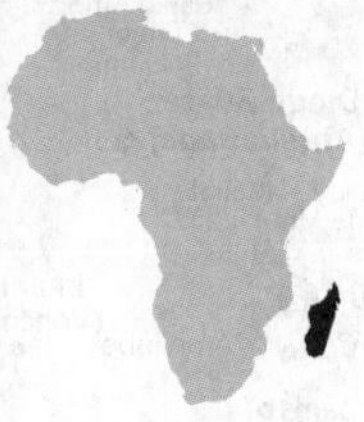

# Madagascar

POP 24.2 MILLION / ☎261

**Includes ➡**



## Best Places to Eat

- L'Estérel (p794)
- Chez Maman (p796)
- La Bodega (p797)
- Saka Express (p784)
- Café Mirana (p789)

## Best Places to Sleep

- Bakuba (p793)
- Auberge Peter Pan (p794)
- Chez Billy (p788)
- Hôtel Niaouly (p783)
- Auberge de la Table (p793)

## Why Go?

Lemurs, baobabs, rainforest, beaches, desert, trekking and diving: Madagascar is a dream destination for lovers of nature and the outdoors. The world's fourth-largest island is also a relatively easy destination: hassle-free, with good tourism infrastructure (but poor roads), sensational national parks, a plethora of activities and divine food. The drawcard for many travellers is the country's incredible natural diversity – you can go from rainforest to desert or high altitude in just 300km – and unique wildlife: 5% of all known animal and plant species are endemic to Madagascar. Less well known but just as fascinating is Malagasy culture, in which ancestors and their spirits play a central role, and death is only the beginning of the (permanent) afterlife. The hardest thing will be to choose what to do: Madagascar is vast and unless you have unlimited time and/or money, you'll have to spend them wisely.

## When to Go

### Antananarivo

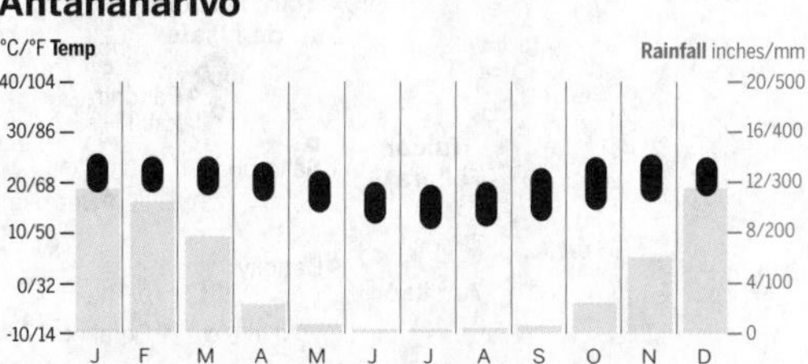


**Jul & Aug** It's winter – balmy temperatures by day and cool nights (cold in the highlands).

**Apr–Jun, Sep–Dec** The best time to go: warm temperatures and fewer visitors.

**Jan–Mar** Cyclone season on the east coast; rainy season everywhere.

# Madagascar Highlights

**1 Parc National de l'Isalo** (p792) Taking a dip in natural swimming pools after a day's trek.

**2 Nosy Be** (p794) Snorkelling and diving to your heart's content.

**3 Anakao** (p794) Snorkelling, diving and paddling at Madagascar's Great Reef.

**4 Tropical Haute Cuisine** (p783) Sampling a divine strand of fusion cuisine in Antananarivo.

# ANTANANARIVO

POP 1.39 MILLION

Tana, as the capital is universally known, is all about eating, shopping, history and day trips. The town centre itself, with its pollution and dreadful traffic, puts off many travellers from staying, but bypassing the capital altogether would be a mistake: Tana has been the home of Malagasy power for three centuries and there is a huge amount of history and culture to discover, as well as some unexpected wildlife options.

## Sights

Central Tana is relatively compact, which means that it is easily explored on foot. The catch is that it's hilly, with plenty of stairs. The Haute-Ville, with its numerous old buildings, is a great place to explore. Don't linger on Ave de l'Indépendance in the Basse-Ville, however; pickpockets are rife.

**★Rova** HISTORIC BUILDING

(Palais de la Reine; Rue Ramboatiana; Ar10,000; 9am-5pm) Tana's *rova* (fortified palace), known as Manjakamiadana (A Fine Place to Rule), is the imposing structure that crowns the city's highest hill. Gutted in a fire in 1995, it is still under restoration but the compound can be visited. The palace was designed for Queen Ranavalona I by Scottish missionary James Cameron. The outer stone structure was added in 1867 for Queen Ranavalona II, although the roof and interior remained wooden, much to everyone's regret in 1995...

**Musée Andafivaratra** MUSEUM

(Ar10,000; 9am-5pm) Housed in a pink baroque palace, this museum is the former home of Prime Minister Rainilaiarivony, the power behind the throne of the three queens he married in succession (Rasoherina, Ranavalona II and Ranavalona III) between 1864 and 1895. The museum's collection is a dusty assortment of memorabilia from Merina (a tribal group) kings and queens, but it illuminates some colourful characters of that era. The museum has been closed since 2012 due to works; it's unclear when it will reopen.

## Sleeping

Accommodation in Tana is pricier than in the rest of the country. A number of hotels offer 'day rates', which allow guests to keep their room until early evening, as many flights out of the country leave late at night.

**Hôtel Moonlight** HOTEL $

(020 22 268 70, 034 06 265 15; hasinaherizo@yahoo.fr; Rue Rainandriamapandry; s/d/tr Ar27,000/32,000/43,000; ) This budget stalwart is an excellent option in a lively part of town. Rooms have brightly coloured walls, parquet floors and brand-new bathrooms (most rooms now have showers but share toilets). The staff is friendly and there are two large communal terraces from where you can watch the world go by.

**★Hôtel Niaouly** HOTEL $$

(020 22 627 65; www.niaouly.com; Rue Tsiombikibo; r Ar35,000-50,000; ) Located between the beautiful Haute-Ville and the trendy bars and restaurants of Isoraka, the Niaouly punches well above its weight for the price. The rooms are pretty with polished wooden floors, Madagascan crafts and modern bathrooms (the cheaper rooms are very dark, however). And as if this were not enough, there is also a panoramic terrace and a good restaurant.

**Hôtel Tana-Jacaranda** GUESTHOUSE $$

(020 22 694 63, 034 22 562 39; www.tana-jacaranda.com; 24 Rue Rainitsarovy; s without bathroom Ar35,000, d Ar55,000-80,000; @) Rooms at this superfriendly, family-run hotel are simple, quiet and clean. There is also a tip-top dining room with fabulous views of the Rova and the Haute-Ville, piping-hot water in the showers, good wi-fi, a guest computer and multilingual, wonderfully helpful staff.

**Chez Francis** HOTEL $$

(020 22 613 65; hotelchezfrancis@yahoo.fr; Rue Rainandriamapandry; d Ar35,000-55,000; ) Owners Sébastien and Gina took over this great-value establishment in 2015. One thing that hasn't changed, however, is the superb panorama, so ask for a room with a view.

**★Résidence Lapasoa** BOUTIQUE HOTEL $$$

(020 22 611 40; www.lapasoa.com; 15 Rue Réunion; d/ste Ar157,500/245,000; @) The exquisite Lapasoa is a modern twist on colonial decor: there are polished wood floors, beautiful wooden furniture (including stunning four-poster beds), colourful fabrics and light flooding in from skylights and big windows. The top-floor rooms, with their high, sloped ceilings, are the loveliest. The same owners run the superb **Kudéta** (020 22 611 40; www.kudeta.mg; 16 Rue Réunion; mains Ar15,000-25,000, 2-course lunch menu Ar20,000; ) restaurant next door.

## Eating

Tana excels at cooking: you'll find some of the country's best restaurants in the capital, and although they're slightly more expensive than in the rest of the country, they're often great value for the quality.

## Central Antananarivo

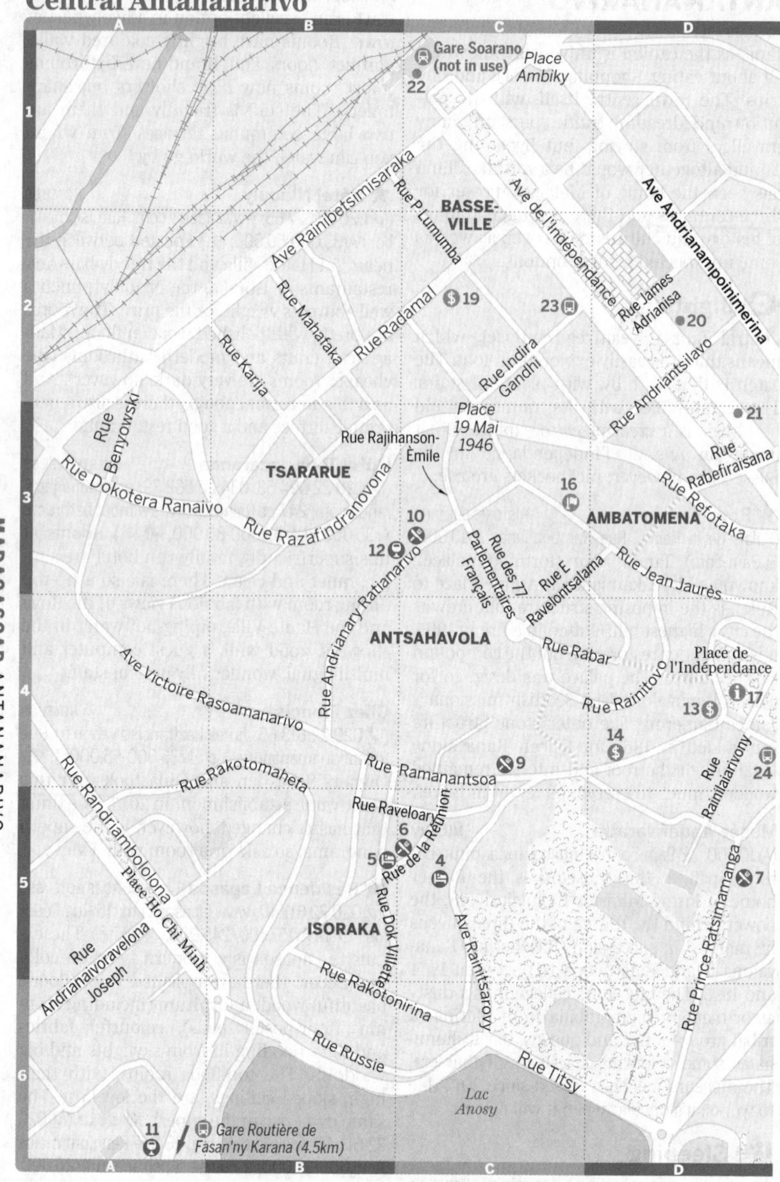




★ **Saka Express** CAFE $

(www.sakamanga.com; Rue Andrianary Ratianarivo; mains Ar7000-12,000; ⏰11am-9pm; 📶📝) The Hôtel Sakamanga's snack cafeteria and takeaway outlet is the best place in town for lunch on the go. There are pizzas, kebabs and sandwiches, all bursting at the seams with fillings. There are a few tables inside, which fill quickly at lunchtime. Delivery to neighbouring hotels (including in Isoraka) is possible.

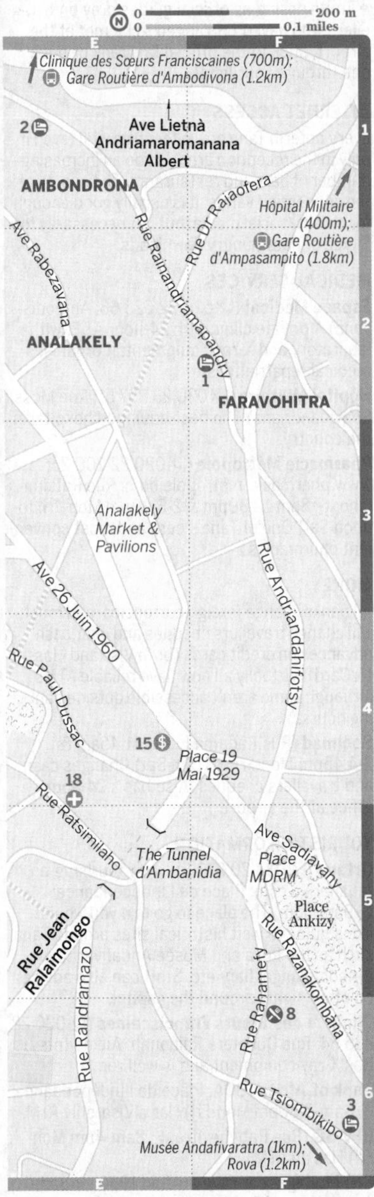


## Central Antananarivo

**Sleeping**

| | | |
|---|---|---|
| 1 | Chez Francis | F2 |
| 2 | Hôtel Moonlight | E1 |
| 3 | Hôtel Niaouly | F6 |
| 4 | Hôtel Tana-Jacaranda | C5 |
| 5 | Résidence Lapasoa | B5 |

**Eating**

| | | |
|---|---|---|
| 6 | Kudéta | C5 |
| 7 | La Varangue | D5 |
| 8 | Le Petit Verdot | F6 |
| 9 | Mad'Délices | C4 |
| 10 | Saka Express | C3 |

**Drinking & Nightlife**

| | | |
|---|---|---|
| 11 | Kudéta Urban Club | A6 |
| 12 | Outcool Web Bar | B3 |

**Information**

| | | |
|---|---|---|
| 13 | Bank of Africa | D4 |
| 14 | BFV-SG | D4 |
| 15 | BNI Madagascar | E4 |
| 16 | French Embassy | C3 |
| 17 | Ortana | D4 |
| 18 | Pharmacie Métropole | E4 |
| 19 | Socimad | C2 |

**Transport**

| | | |
|---|---|---|
| 20 | Air Austral | D2 |
| 21 | Air Madagascar | D3 |
| 22 | Corsair | C1 |
| 23 | Transport Première Class | C2 |
| 24 | Transpost | D4 |

**Mad'Délices** MADAGASCAN $
(Rue Ramanantsoa; mains Ar5000-7000; 6.30am-9.30pm Mon-Sat; ) This cheerful little restaurant in the heart of Isoraka serves hearty Madagascan meals such as pork with greens, zebu stew and omelettes. It's also a good place for breakfast: the pastries are excellent and there is an espresso machine.

**Le Petit Verdot** FRENCH $$
(034 97 963 85; www.lepetitverdot-tana.com; 27 Rue Rahamefy; mains Ar12,000-20,000; noon-2pm & 6.30-10pm Mon-Fri, 6.30-10pm Sat) This tiny red-brick bistro, spread over three floors from cellar to mezzanine, scores high on homey atmosphere and hearty French food. There is a fantastic selection of meat and fish dishes and the wine selection is the best in Madagascar (261 references from around the world, including some local vintages).

## Drinking & Nightlife

Tana has a lively nightlife, with a number of good bars and busy nightclubs. Beer and rum are the tipples of choice and live music is a popular fixture in many establishments.

**Kudéta Urban Club** LOUNGE
(www.kudeta.mg; Hôtel Carlton, Anosy; 10am-late Mon-Sat) Tana's most exclusive (and expensive) bar turns from bar/lounge during

the day to nightclub/DJ platform as the night draws in; there are regular parties and events.

**Outcool Web Bar** BAR
(Rue Andrianary Ratianarivo; 10am-12.30am; ) This sociable bar is one of the nicest hang-outs in Tana: it's laid-back, cheerful and very popular with young and cool Malagasies, many of whom come here partly for the free wi-fi. Draft beer (Ar2500) is the most popular tipple; light meals are available.

## Shopping

The shopping in Tana is top-notch, with an excellent range of souvenirs from across the country as well as original boutiques. The city has a couple of shopping malls, including **Tana Water Front** (www.centre-commercial-tanawaterfront.com; Ambodivona; 9am-6.30pm Mon-Sat, to 1pm Sun), 2km north of the centre, with a food court, a supermarket and the usual amenities. English books are hard to come by: your best bet are hotel libraries/swap shelves.

**Lisy Art Gallery** GIFTS & SOUVENIRS
(Route du Mausolée; 8.30am-6pm Mon-Sat) This huge shop stocks anything and everything you could possibly want to bring back from Madagascar, from bottles of *rhum arrangé* (rum with macerated fruit) to leather goods, raffia baskets, hats and spices. The only thing you won't find are gemstones. Prices are fixed but reasonable. It's a short taxi ride from the centre (Ar5000 one way). Card payments accepted.

**Marché Artisanal de La Digue** GIFTS & SOUVENIRS
(La Digue; 9am-5.30pm) A popular place to pick up souvenirs is this market located about 12km out of town on a bend in the Ivato airport road. There are products from all over the country, including embroidered tablecloths, raffia products, woodcarvings, spices, vanilla, gemstones etc. Bargaining is essential – divide the initial price by three or four and work from there.

## Information

### DANGERS & ANNOYANCES

- Insecurity has increased in Tana since the political events of 2009. It is not safe to walk after dark; you should always travel by taxi at night.
- Pickpocketing is rife around Ave de l'Indépendance and Analakely, so be very careful with your belongings.
- Touts posing as official guides prey on travellers who haven't arranged to be met at the airport; stick to the official taxi rank or book one through your hotel.

### INTERNET ACCESS

Every hotel in Tana now offers free wi-fi (even if only in the reception area), as do an increasing number of bars and restaurants. The quality of the connection varies; it is usually good enough for emails/social media, but not necessarily for Skype or data-hungry downloads.

### MEDICAL SERVICES

**Espace Médical** (020 22 625 66; Ambodivona) A private clinic with 24-hour A&E, with laboratory and X-ray equipment; it organises medical repatriations.

**Hôpital Militaire** (020 23 397 51; Rue Moss, Soavinandriana) The best-equipped hospital in the country.

**Pharmacie Métropole** (020 22 200 25; www.pharmacie-metropole.com; Rue Ratsimilaho; 8am-12.30pm & 2-6.30pm Mon-Fri, to noon Sat) One of Tana's best and most convenient pharmacies.

### MONEY

All banks change foreign currencies, and most will change travellers cheques and offer cash advances on credit cards (both Visa and MasterCard). Virtually all now have reliable ATMs although some aren't accessible outside banking hours.

**Socimad** (Rue Radama I; 8-11.45am & 2-4.45pm Mon-Fri, 8-11am Sat) Changes cash and travellers cheques. Also has a 24-hour office at the airport.

### TOURIST INFORMATION

**Ortana** (034 20 270 51; www.tourisme-antananarivo.com; Place de l'Indépendance; 9am-5pm) The place to go to if you would like a guide to visit historical sites around Tana such as the Rova and Musée Andafivaratra, Ambohimanga, Ilafy etc. Staff can also advise on other sights around the capital.

**Clinique des Sœurs Franciscaines** (020 22 235 54; Rue Dokotera Rajaonah, Ankadifotsy) Has X-ray equipment and is well run.

**Bank of Africa** (BOA; Place de l'Indépendance; 8am-3.30pm Mon-Fri) Has a Visa-only ATM.

**BFV-SG** (Rue Rabehevitra; 8am-4pm Mon-Fri) Has an ATM.

**BNI Madagascar** (Ave 26 Juin 1960; 8am-4pm) Has an ATM (Visa and MasterCard).

## Getting There & Away

### AIR

You can get domestic and international flights to and from Ivato airport. The following airlines have offices in Tana:

**Air Austral** (☎020 22 303 31; www.air-austral.com; 23 Ave de l'Indépendance – Analakely)

**Air France** (☎020 23 230 23; www.airfrance.com; Tour Zital, Rte des Hydrocarbures, Ankorondrano)

**Air Madagascar** (☎020 22 510 00; www.airmadagascar.com; 31 Ave de l'Indépendance)

**Corsair** (☎020 22 633 36; www.corsair.fr; Gare Soarano, 1 Ave de l'Indépendance – Analakely)

**Madagasikara Airways** (☎032 05 970 07; www.madagasikaraairways.com; La City, Ivandry)

#### BUS & MINIBUS

**Cotisse** (☎032 11 027 33; www.facebook.com/cotisse.transport; Ambodivona) Nice 16- or 19-seater Mercedes minibuses that link Tana with Tamatave (Ar20,000, seven hours)

**Transport Première Class** (☎033 15 488 88, 034 22 588 88; www.malagasycar.com; Hôtel Le Grand Mellis, 3 Rue Indira Gandhi) Runs comfortable, air-con vehicles only between Tana and Majunga (Ar78,000, 10 hours, daily). It sometimes runs services to Nosy Be too.

**Transpost** (Post Office, Rue Ratsimilaho; ⏲7.30am-5pm Mon-Fri, to noon Sat) More punctual than normal *taxis-brousses* (bush taxis), but similar in comfort and price. It has minibuses between Majunga and Tana only (Ar25,000, 12 hours).

#### TAXI-BROUSSE

For morning departures, turn up early (6am); for afternoon departures, come around 2pm. It may take up to four hours for some vehicles to fill.

**Gare Routière d'Ambodivona** (Northern Taxi-brousse Station; Ambodivona) About 2km northeast of the city centre. A taxi to/from the centre costs Ar4000.

**Gare Routière d'Ampasampito** (Eastern Taxi-brousse Station; Ampasampito) About 3.5km northeast of the centre. A taxi to/from the centre will cost Ar6000.

**Gare Routière de Fasan'ny Karana** (Southern Taxi-brousse Station; Anosibe) About 4km southwest of Lac Anosy. A taxi to/from the centre costs Ar10,000.

# CENTRAL MADAGASCAR

The classic tourist route from Tana takes you south along the RN7 through central Madagascar, a high plateau stretching all the way to Fianarantsoa. You'll twist and turn through these highlands, a region of scenic hills and rice paddies that resists generalisation.

Here you'll find a potpourri of travellers' delights: bustling market towns clogged with colourful pousse-pousse (rickshaws); a distinctive architecture of two-storey mudbrick homes; a mountain stronghold of lemurs, the legacy of French colonialism; national parks with landscapes ranging from thick jungle to wide-open grandeur; and some of the best hiking Madagascar has to offer.

## Antsirabe

POP 186,253

Antsirabe is best-known for its thermal springs. The city emerged as a spa town in the late 1800s when Norwegian missionaries built a health retreat here (still in use to this day). French colonists then turned it into a chic getaway from nearby Tana, hence the numerous turn-of-the-century villas and the broad tree-lined avenues so typical of French cities. Much of this colonial heritage is fading now, nut the city itself is full of life.

### Sights

Antsirabe is famed for its skilled artisans and a popular activity is to visit a few workshops over the course of a morning or afternoon. Some people charter a pousse-pousse for the occasion and let the driver take charge of the itinerary (make sure you discuss the number of stops, length and price beforehand; allow Ar20,000 to Ar40,000 for a circuit) but you could simply take a different pousse-pousse between each stop, if you know where you want to go.

**Atelier Corne de Zébu** WORKSHOP

(Parc de l'Est; ⏲9am-5pm) Zebu horn is a versatile – and beautiful – material, which artisans at this workshop turn into numerous objects, from jewellery to salad spoons, sculpted animals and accessories. You'll see the whole production process: from how to separate the bone from its keratin shell to polishing the final products with old denims.

**Chez Mamy Miniatures** WORKSHOP

(Parc de l'Est; ⏲9am-5pm) This family workshop specialises in the creation of miniature objects (cars, rickshaws, bicycles etc) made from recycled materials – anything from aluminium cans to (unused) intravenous tubes, textiles and old cables. They'll demonstrate how to make parts of their models; it's an incredibly fiddly and inventive process.

### Tours

**★Rando Raid Madagascar** MOUNTAIN BIKING

(☎032 04 900 21; Rue Stavanger; half-/full-day mountain-biking excursion Ar50,000/90,000; ⏲8.30am-noon & 3-6pm Mon-Sat) The area around Antsirabe is a paradise for outdoor sports and Bazoly and Jean-Marc have devised a plethora of activities (mountain

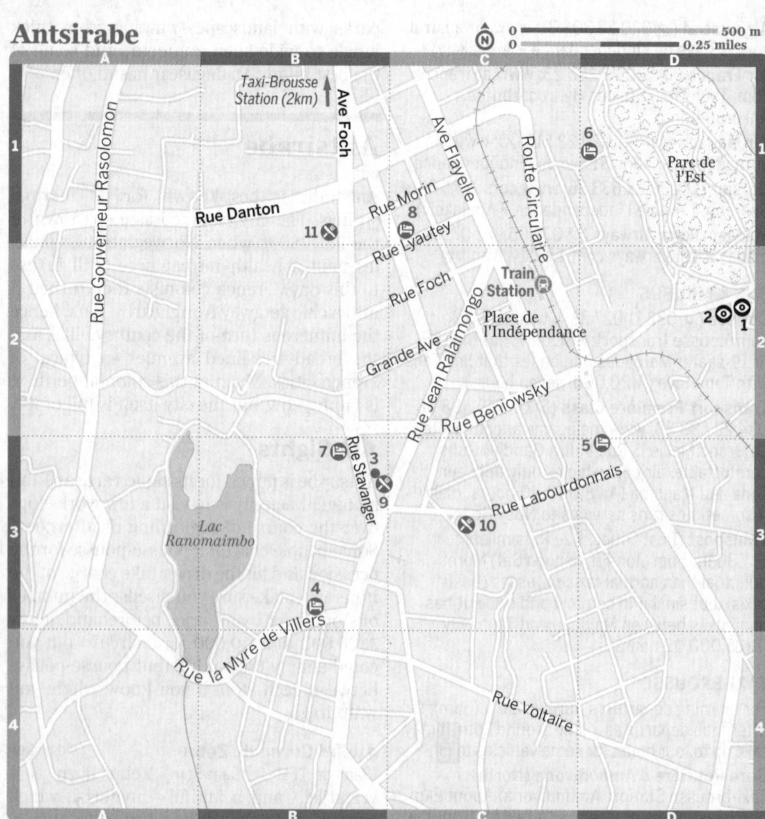


## Antsirabe

**Sights**
1 Atelier Corne de Zébu ........ D2
2 Chez Mamy Miniatures ........ D2

**Activities, Courses & Tours**
3 Rando Raid Madagascar ........ B3

**Sleeping**
4 Chez Billy ........ B3
5 Couleur Café ........ D3
6 Les Chambres du Voyageurs ........ D1
7 Lovasoa ........ B3
8 Résidence Camélia ........ C1

**Eating**
9 Café Mirana ........ B3
10 Chez Jenny ........ C3
11 Zandina ........ B1

biking, hiking, horse riding, canoeing, quad bikes and motorbikes, often in combination) and excursions (lakes, mountains, Betafo, anything from half a day to several days) to make the best of this amazing playground.

## Sleeping

Antsirabe offers a fascinating array of sleeping options and caters particularly well to budget travellers. Do ask for extra blankets on winter nights.

**★Chez Billy** GUESTHOUSE $
(☎020 44 484 88; www.chez-billy.com; Antsenakely; d/tr/q without bathroom Ar28,000/38,000/48,000; ) This eclectic melange of guesthouse, bar and restaurant, awash in loud art, inspires a hostel-like conviviality among the staff, backpackers, guides and in-the-know *vazaha* (foreigners) who form its crossroads clientele. The rooms are simple but well kept, the showers hot and powerful and the jovial owner Billy, a former guide,

is a mine of information. It's always full so book ahead.

★ **Les Chambres du Voyageurs** GUESTHOUSE $$$
(☎032 83 083 61; androdenis@yahoo.fr; d/tr/f bungalows Ar110,00/130,000/220,000; ) This ecolodge is a rarity in Antsirabe, an island of nature on the edge of the city. The owner's passion is gardening and you'll find some 800 species of plant in the themed gardens (Majorelle, Alhambra, Japanese etc) as well as 14 species of bird, tortoises and chameleons. The brick bungalows are pretty, spacious and very comfortable.

**Lovasoa** GUESTHOUSE $$$
(☎020 44 486 85; www.lovasoa.mg; Rue Stavanger; dm Ar15,000, d with/without bathroom Ar89,000/40,000; ) Run by the Lutheran Church and a Norwegian aid agency, this guesthouse in the centre of town is a little gem. The grounds are large and feel like an oasis. Inside, the dorms (sleeping eight) are immaculate and cheerful, with separate bathrooms for men and women. There are gorgeous double rooms too, which are surprisingly high-end and therefore more expensive.

## Eating

Food is excellent and inexpensive in Antsirabe, even at top-end hotels. Among the latter, **Résidence Camélia** (☎020 44 488 44; laresidencecamelia@gmail.com; Ave de l'Indépendance; d Ar72,000-128,000) and **Couleur Café** (☎020 44 485 26; www.couleurcafeantsirabe.com; Route d'Ambositra; d/f Ar125,000/175,000; ) are the best. Chez Billy also serves delicious and cheap meals.

★ **Café Mirana** MADAGASCAN, BAKERY $
(Rue Ralaimongo; mains Ar4000-7000; ⏲7am-6.30pm) This cafeteria is one of the busiest in town, with reason: its bakery is the best for kilometres (the croissants get top marks, as does the bread), and the restaurant out back churns out tasty, great-value Madagascan staples such as *vary' aminana* (rice soup served for breakfast), *mi sao* (noodle stir-fry), zebu stews etc. The terraces at the front are perfect for people watching.

★ **Chez Jenny** INTERNATIONAL $$
(Rue Labourdonnais; mains Ar10,000-15,000; ⏲11am-2.30pm & 6-9.30pm Tue-Sun; ) Hands down the best restaurant in town, Chez Jenny is a winning combination of colourful decor, delicious food, warm service and atmosphere, complete with a well-stocked bar and a cosy fireplace for cold winter nights. Try the duck in three pepper sauce or opt for one of the lovely pizzas.

**Zandina** PIZZA $$
(5 Ave Foch; mains Ar10,000-15,000; ⏲11.30am-10pm; ) Zandina has become something of an institution thanks to its all-day service, good wi-fi connection, satellite TV, and generally warm and relaxed atmosphere. The food is good too, a mixture of salads, grills and pizzas. Portions are huge.

## Getting There & Away

Antsirabe is 170km south of Tana. The *gare routière* (*taxis-brousse* station) is located about 2.5km north of town, behind the Jovenna petrol station. *Taxi-brousse* services include Ambositra (Ar7000, three hours), Tana (Ar10,000, four hours), Fianarantsoa (Ar15,000, six hours) and Tamatave (Toamasina, Ar 32,000, ten hours).

# Fianarantsoa

POP 167,227

Fianarantsoa (fi-a-nar-ant-soo), or Fianar for short, is like a mild version of Tana. Surrounded by hills, it is both a regional commercial, administrative and religious centre as well as a major transit point. Tourists typically come here to spend the night on their way to Ranomafana or Isalo, or to take the train to Manakara. But visitors can enjoy a historic old town, a great local market, some interesting places to stay and a more laid-back ambience than that of the capital.

**Mad Trekking** (☎034 14 221 73; mad.trekking@moov.mg; Rue Philibert Tsiranana; ⏲8.30am-noon & 2-5.30pm Mon-Fri) is a reliable operator specialising in multiday excursions around Fianarantsoa and hiking packages in hard-to-reach places such as Andringitra or the Makay (north of Isalo National Park). For two people, allow around €30 per person per day for local excursions, €60 to €70 for more adventurous hikes (prices include transport).

Don't be fooled by the facade of **Chez Ninie** (Rue Rondriantsilanizaka; mains Ar4500-7000; ⏲8am-8.30pm): lurking out back is a rather chic open-porch dining area with an extensive, inexpensive and very tasty Madagascan menu that keeps this place very popular. Dirt cheap beer (Ar2000) too.

Minibuses go daily to Ambalavao (Ar3000, two hours), Ranohira (Ar25,000, seven hours) and on to Tuléar (Ar30,000, 12 hours). Heading east there are multiple vehicles daily between Fianarantsoa and Ranomafana (Ar7000, two hours) and Manakara (Ar13,000, eight hours).

Frequent *taxis-brousses* connect Fianarantsoa with Ambositra (Ar10,000, five hours), Antsirabe (Ar15,000, seven hours) and Tana (Ar26,000, 10 hours).

## Parc National de Ranomafana

Ranomafana appears after a fantastic entrance through a dry rocky valley spotted with two-storey highlands houses. After a long day's travel, it feels like you have reached a mysterious island. The air is fresh and cool, and the nearby presence of the forest, with all of its strange sounds, is alluring.

Created in 1991 largely to protect two rare species of lemur (the golden bamboo lemur and the greater bamboo lemur, the former discovered only in 1986), **Parc National de Ranomafana** (http://parcs-madagascar.com/aire-protegee/parc-national-ranomafana; entry permits per day Ar55,000) contains 400 sq km of oddly shaped rolling hills carpeted in jungle and fed by rushing streams.

The park is known for its diverse wildlife, although some of it is quite elusive. There are 29 mammal species, including 12 species of lemur. The forest abounds with reptiles and amphibians, and the birdlife is exceptional. Although famous for its animals, the park's plant life is just as impressive, with orchids, tree ferns, palms, mosses and stands of giant bamboo.

### Sleeping

**Rianala Gîte** HOSTEL $

(034 14 360 36; rianalagite@gmail.com; Ranomafana National Park entrance; dm/camping per site Ar14,000/5000) This is a great budget option right by the park entrance, which will save you toing and froing between the village and the park. The rooms are clean and come with blankets and hot water and there is a nice porch to sit on. A short walk away there are also some great campsites, with pitched thatched roofs.

**Chez Gaspard** BUNGALOW $$

(032 87 115 15, 033 01 155 05; chezgaspard.ranomafana@gmail.com; Ranomafana; bungalow Ar55,000-100,000) These pretty bungalows, in a scenic tropical setting stretching along the river, are great value. Those furthest upstream are best; room 14 is a great family room that holds five. No on-site restaurant.

**Cristo** LODGE $$$

(034 12 353 97; http://cristohotel.cabanova.fr; RN25; r Ar100,000; wi-fi) This lodge on the outskirts of town, perched on a gorgeous bend in the Namorona River, has idyllic views of the rainforest and hills. The upper-floor rooms in the main building bask in the glorious panorama, while the riverside bungalows are more secluded.

### Information

The **Madagascar National Parks office** (MNP; 7am-4.30pm) is located right at the entrance of the park. Park visitors pay the entry fee here, part of which goes to the community, and a guide fee (full day Ar75,000). Several guides speak good English.

### Getting There & Away

The gateway town for the park is Ranomafana, which is 6km east of the park entrance on the RN25. If you don't have a private car, travelling between Ranomafana and the park will be tricky. *Taxis-brousses* heading in/out of the village may be happy to take you (Ar2000); some hotels arrange transfer for about Ar10,000. Alternatively, hitch a ride with other travellers.

## Ambalavao

POP 28,027

Set amid beautiful mountainous countryside with numerous boulder-like peaks, Ambalavao is like a charming French village reduced through years of neglect to a Wild West outpost. The Gothic cathedral looks as if it's been parachuted in from the Loire Valley, although the surrounding landscape is signature Madagascan highlands. There are no banks in Ambalavao.

### Sights

**Soalandy** WORKSHOP

(033 14 987 45; RN7; 7.30am-5pm) Madagascar is home to an endemic species of silkworm, which feeds on tapia trees in the wild and whose cocoons are threaded and woven like 'conventional' silk. The fascinating production process of this 'wild silk' is laid out in this workshop. You can buy beautiful scarves (Ar50,000 to Ar70,000) in the adjoining shop.

**Zebu Market** MARKET

(RN7; Wed) Ambalavao hosts the largest zebu market in the country. Tough, wizened herders walk from as far away as Tuléar and Fort-Dauphin to sell their cattle. It is quite a spectacle, especially as the animals make their way up the bluff where the huge enclosure is located. The market reaches fever pitch around 10am or 11am. It's located about 1km south of Ambalavao.

**Réserve d'Anja** WILDLIFE RESERVE
(Ar10,000) This 370,000-sq-metre reserve encompasses three mountain-size boulders (the three sisters) ringed at the base by a narrow forest full of ring-tailed lemurs. Anja's lemurs are famous for sunning themselves on the boulders (generally early in the morning); there are around 400 individuals in the reserve and they have grown accustomed to visitors so you'll get the chance to get relatively close. The reserve is a completely community-run initiative and has been extremely successful, generating revenues and jobs for the village.

**Fabrique de Papier Antaimoro** WORKSHOP
(020 75 340 01; 7.30-11.30am & 1-5pm Sat, 8.30am-noon Sun) This workshop showcases the production of a unique kind of paper, made from the bark of a local bush, which has flowers pressed into it. Antaimoro cards, envelopes and picture frames are all for sale.

## Sleeping & Eating

**Résidence du Betsileo** HOTEL $$
(032 28 259 80, 034 10 665 45; residencedubetsileo@gmail.com; s/d Ar35,000/45,000; ) This charming bargain is the best place to stay – and eat – in town. New owners Holly and Jean-Marie are slowly renovating the building (the rooms do need updating), but the atmosphere is already great and Jean-Marie is a mean cook. Choose the off-street rooms.

**La Varangue du Betsileo** GUESTHOUSE $$$
(032 63 376 48; www.varangue-betsileo.com; RN7; d//f Ar80,000/150,000, s bungalows Ar140,000; ) Located 8km south of Ambalavao on the RN7, the Varangue basks among glorious landscapes and enormous skies. The pretty rooms and bungalows (all newly built) are incredibly homely and the friendly owners will bend over backwards to help their guests. The pool is a lovely bonus. Dinner is a set menu (Ar30,000).

## Getting There & Away

Ambalavao lies 56km south of Fianarantsoa. The town has direct *taxi-brousse* connections with Fianarantsoa (Ar3000, 1½ hours), Ihosy (Ar8000, three hours) and Ranohira (Ar14,000, six hours). For destinations further north, you'll have to go to Fianarantsoa first.

# SOUTHERN MADAGASCAR

Southern Madagascar is a wide-open adventure among some of nature's most dramatic forms. The stark desert canyons of Parc National de l'Isalo rival those of Arizona. The west coast offers gorgeous coastal settlements that serve as gateways to the fifth-largest coral reef in the world. And

WORTH A TRIP

### PARC NATIONAL D'ANDRINGITRA

Parc National d'Andringitra is the pièce de résistance of the wider Massif de l'Andringitra. It encompasses high-altitude plateaux of epic beauty, small tracts of primary rainforest, scenic trails along mountain streams and waterfalls, and Pic Boby, the highest accessible mountain in Madagascar. The best time to visit the **national park** (http://parcs-madagascar.com/aire-protegee/parc-national-andringitra; entry permits per day Ar45,000) is from June to November, when the rains aren't relentless (the park is officially closed from January to March, when heavy rains make access difficult). Afternoon mists are common at these high altitudes, and you should be prepared for bad weather at any time of year. If you are climbing Pic Boby, you will need a flashlight with several hours of battery life.

The **Madagascar National Parks office** (MNP; 020 75 340 81; www.parcs-madagascar.com; 6.30am-4pm) in Namoly has all you need to hike into the park, including entry permits. Here you can hire guides, porters and cooking utensils (but not camping equipment: you'll need to organise this in Ambalavao).

Guide fees are Ar20,000/35,000/50,000/70,000 for one/two/three/four days; porters (who will also cook for you) cost Ar20,000 per day and can carry up to 20kg. Note that only a couple of guides speak basic English.

The Namoly Valley is a nearly three-hour drive from Ambalavao, with some iffy bridges, but it is also a scenic trip through rocky hill country full of small villages, rice paddies and smiling children. The track is very rough and requires a 4WD.

vast kilometres of spiny forest contain the strangest and most formidable plants on earth. The cape is also the last stop before Antarctica.

## Parc National de l'Isalo

**Parc National de l'Isalo** (www.parcs-madagascar.com; adult/child per day Ar65,000/25,000) is like a museum dedicated to the art of the desert canyon. Gorges here are filled with yellow savannah grasses, sculpted buttes, vertical rock walls and, best of all, deep canyon floors shot through with streams, lush vegetation and pools for swimming. All of this changes with the light, culminating in extraordinary sunsets beneath a big sky. Add all this to easy access off the RN7 and you understand why this is Madagascar's most visited park.

### Sleeping

**★Chez Alice** BUNGALOW $$
(032 02 055 68, 033 07 134 44; chezalice@yahoo.fr; off RN7; camping for 2 people Ar20,000, paillote Ar33,00, d/tr/f bungalows Ar39,000/53,000/65,000) It's a rough drive in, and somewhat-bare surrounds hide this convivial backpacker's hang-out and budget gem not far from the centre of Ranohira. Run by the irrepressible Alice, who would otherwise be running an Old West saloon, this place has bungalows of various types and prices, all of which are colourfully painted and excellent value.

**L'Orchidée de l'Isalo** HOTEL $$
(032 44 676 89; www.orchidee-isalo.com; RN7; d Ar41,000-71,000, f Ar97,000; ) In the centre of town, just before the RN7 doglegs south if you're coming from the north, Le Orchidée d'Isalo has simple but tidy rooms with tiled floors, mosquito nets and hot water. Its top-of-the-range newer rooms, built in 2014, are the best in Ranohira itself. Management is friendly.

**★Isalo Rock Lodge** LODGE $$$
(020 22 328 60; www.isalorocklodge.com; off RN7; r €120; ) This stylish hotel has a beautiful terrace overlooking sandstone formations as well as a spa and fitness room and a fluorescent pool with ever-changing colours. The restaurant (set menu €20) serves works of art, while the rooms, bathed in soothing earth tones, are triumphs of contemporary design. A sharp manager ensures perfection.

### Getting There & Away

For points north, you may be lucky enough to find a *taxi-brousse* travelling between Tuléar and Tana with an empty seat. Each morning one or two *taxis-brousses* connect Ranohira directly with Ihosy (Ar25,000, two hours, 91km), from where there are more options.

Public transport from Tuléar generally arrives in Ranohira between 10am and 1pm, while vehicles from the north usually arrive before 10am.

## The Great Reef

A reef stretches over 450km along the southwestern coast of Madagascar, making it the fifth-largest coral reef in the world. Running from Andavadoaka in the north to Itampolo in the south, it's the main attraction in the region, with its own changing personality.

The Great Reef comes in three forms: a fringing reef close in, a patch reef of coral heads and an outer barrier reef. The last creates very broad and shallow inshore lagoons and makes for dramatic scenery, with large waves crashing in the distance, forming a vibrant line of white. The beaches range from broken coral to spectacular white powder. There are many activities to pursue here: sunbathing, snorkelling, diving, fishing, whale watching (mid-June or early July to September), surfing and sailing among them.

### Tuléar (Toliara)

POP 115,319

Tuléar is where the sealed road (the RN7) ends and many adventures begin – its main appeal is as most travellers' gateway to The Great Reef (found both north and south of the city). Your most enduring memory here is likely to be a sea of pousse-pousse bouncing down dusty lanes – the city itself has little to detain you beyond an outstanding out-of-town arboretum and some fine hotels and restaurants. Add a somewhat-raffish tropical ambience fuelled by local French and Italian expats and you have the setting for your first novel. Do take taxis after dark.

### Sights

**★Arboretum d'Antsokay** GARDENS
(034 07 600 15; www.antsokayarboretum.org; off RN7; adult/child Ar15,000/5000; 7.30am-5.30pm, closed Feb) This is the one must-see attraction in Tuléar. Essentially a 400,000-sq-metre distillation of the entire

spiny forest in one place, it's a fantastic collection of 900 plant species. Established by a Swiss botanist and conservationist in 1980, it's also a model for how much-larger parks should be run. There's a classy interpretation centre, a small museum, shop, self-guided tours in English, a stylish restaurant and some excellent, inexpensive bungalows, Auberge de la Table, with pool. MNP take note: clone this place.

## Sleeping & Eating

**Chez Lala** HOTEL $

(☎020 94 434 17; Ave de France; d Ar22,000-40,000, without bathroom Ar18,000; ) This laid-back and genial guesthouse is your best budget option; most nights there are more Malagasy guests than foreigners. The simple rooms in the tropical courtyard are smaller than those in the parquet-tiled main block, but they're all decent value. A TV lounge, great espresso, loads of info and free wi-fi help clinch the deal.

**★Auberge de la Table** BUNGALOW $$$

(☎034 07 600 15; www.aubergedelatable.com; off RN7; d bungalows Ar100,000-140,000, tr Ar135,000-175,000; ) The bungalows at the Arboretum d'Antsokay, 12km east of the city, represent fabulous value as long you don't need to be in town. They're beautifully appointed with some original stone furnishings and they're lovely and quiet. The on-site restaurant is similarly excellent.

**★Bakuba** GUESTHOUSE $$$

(☎032 51 528 97; www.bakuba-lodge.com; r/ste €105/140) It would be more accurate to describe this place as a work of art that you stay in rather than an arty guesthouse. The work of Bruno Decorte (a Frenchman who has spent much of his life in Africa), Bakuba has five unique rooms, with features such as a water wall, a dugout-canoe-turned-bath-tub and lamps made of gourds.

## Tuléar (Toliara)

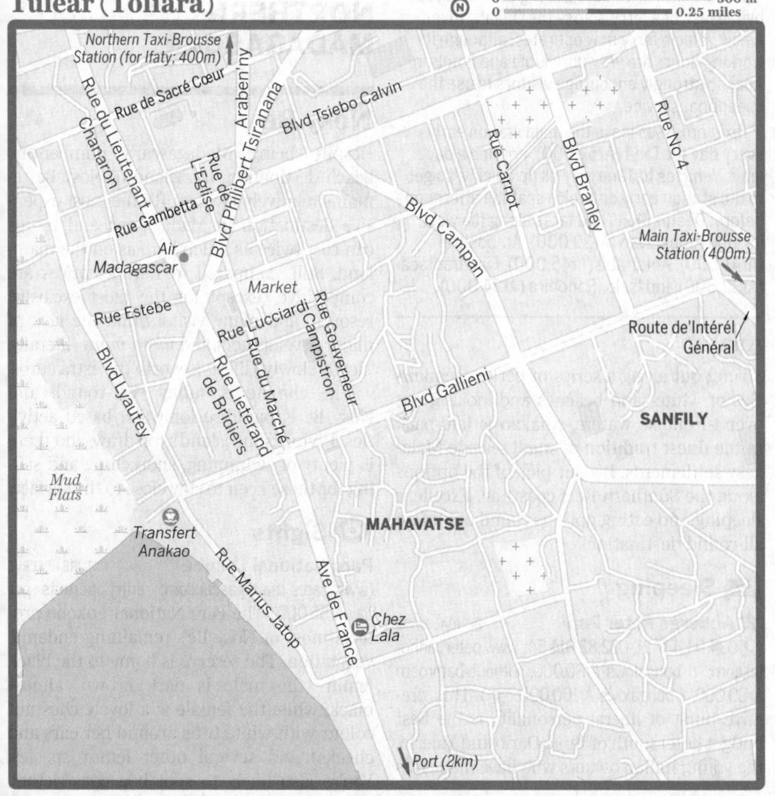

★ **L'Estérel** ITALIAN $$

(☎ 032 40 618 66; Rue de la Voirie; pizzas Ar9000-12,000, mains Ar11,000-14,000; ⊙ noon-2pm & 7-10pm Mon-Sat) Our pick of the restaurants in Tuléar, Italian-run L'Estérel has a tranquil garden setting and a menu that includes some of the best Italian cooking in southern Madagascar – pasta, pizzas, salads you can trust – as well as the occasional French dish. Service is attentive without being in your face.

### Getting There & Away

**Air Madagascar** (☎ 034 11 222 15, 020 94 415 85; Rue Henri Martin) has an office in town, but not at the airport. It flies from Tuléar to Tana (€247), Fort Dauphin (€202) and Morondava (€247). The schedule is a moving target.

**Transfert Anakao** (☎ 034 91 468 36; www.transfert-anakao.com; Restaurant Le Blu; per person one way/return Ar50,000/100,000), an enjoyable speedboat, departs from the tourist port for Anakao every day at 9.30am. This is the best and safest option.

Travel south of Tuléar has long been delayed by the lack of a ferry across the Onilahy River. A new vehicle ferry now operates, although its working hours are very unreliable and hotels in Anakao strongly encourage visitors to use the speedboat service.

*Taxis-brousses* leave the main station early every day for Tana (Ar52,000), arriving a day later. Vehicles to Tana may fill up quickly, so get to the station early or book a seat the afternoon before. Destinations and fares along the way include Ambalavao (Ar29,000), Ambositra (Ar41,000), Antsirabe (Ar45,000), Fianarantsoa (Ar32,000) and Isalo/Ranohira (Ar24,000).

## Anakao

Strung out along a series of perfect semicircles of white-sand beaches and looking out over turquoise waters, Anakao is laid-back in the finest tradition of small seaside Malagasy settlements. It's our pick of the options along the Southern Reef coastline. Excellent sleeping and eating options round out a fine all-round destination.

### Sleeping

★ **Auberge Peter Pan** BUNGALOW $$

(☎ 034 94 437 21, 032 82 614 54; www.peterpanhotel.com; d bungalows Ar80,000, without bathroom Ar30,000, f bungalows Ar100,000; 📶) This creative burst of liberal personality is the best budget hotel south of Tana. Dario and Valerio, the young Italian owners who have made this place their life's work, have crafted a funky selection of eight warmly eclectic bungalows, set in a playful yard of political art contained by a fence of enormous crayons.

★ **Anakao Ocean Lodge** LODGE $$$

(☎ 020 94 919 57, 020 94 921 76; www.anakao-oceanlodge.com; s/d/f bungalows €120/155/180, ste €190; 📶) This is the premier resort on The Great Reef. It's not that any of the elements are unique, but each one is carried off to perfection. The bungalows, with enormous baths, are beautiful, the smiling uniformed staff members are always there when you need them and the food (set menu €20) is a work of art.

### Getting There & Away

Almost everyone coming to Anakao arrives by speedboat. By 'road' (a relative term), it's a rough, bone-shaking seven- to eight-hour drive from Tuléar.

# NORTHERN MADAGASCAR

## Nosy Be

Despite being Madagascar's number-one beach destination, the island of Nosy Be remains relatively low-key. It's the most expensive destination in Madagascar, and rooms can cost twice as much here as on the mainland. Still, compared to Europe, prices are competitive (except for the most exclusive resorts), and many visitors find the lack of major development and *mora mora* (literally, 'slowly slowly') lifestyle worth the extra euros.

The climate is sunny year-round, and Nosy Be is paradise for water-based activities. Diving is the island's top draw, and there is plenty of swimming, snorkelling and sailing for those keen to stay close to the surface.

### Sights

**Parc National Lokobe** NATURE RESERVE

(www.parcs-madagascar.com; entry permits per day Ar55,000) The Parc National Lokobe protects most of Nosy Be's remaining endemic vegetation. The reserve is home to the black lemur (the male is dark brown, almost black, while the female is a lovely chestnut colour with white tufts around her ears and cheeks) and several other lemur species. You're also likely to spot boa constrictors,

# Nosy Be Island

0 5 km
0 2.5 miles

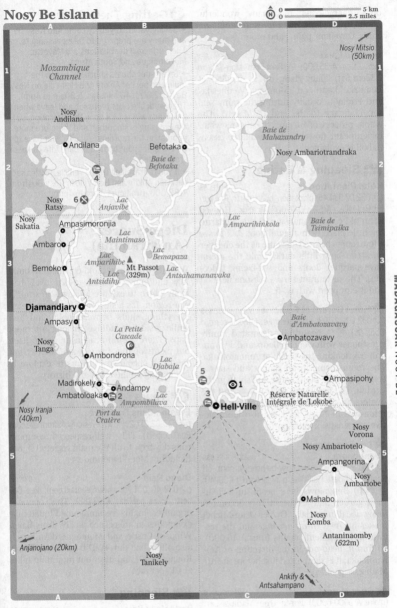

Nosy Mitsio (50km)
Mozambique Channel
Nosy Andilana
Andilana
Befotaka
Baie de Befotaka
Baie de Mahazandry
Nosy Ambariotrandraka
Nosy Ratsy
Lac Anjavibe
Nosy Sakatia
Ampasimoronjia
Lac Amparihinkola
Baie de Tsimipaika
Lac Maintimaso
Ambaro
Lac Bemapaza
Lac Amparihibe
Mt Passot (329m)
Lac Antsahamanavaka
Bemoko
Lac Antsidihy
Djamandjary
Baie d'Ambatozavavy
Ampasy
La Petite Cascade
Ambatozavavy
Nosy Tanga
Ambondrona
Lac Djabala
Ampasipohy
Madirokely
Andampy
Ambatoloaka
Lac Ampombilava
Réserve Naturelle Intégrale de Lokobe
Hell-Ville
Nosy Iranja (40km)
Port du Cratère
Nosy Vorona
Nosy Ambariotelo
Ampangorina
Nosy Ambariobe
Mahabo
Nosy Komba
Antaninaomby (622m)
Anjanojano (20km)
Nosy Tanikely
Ankify & Antsahampano

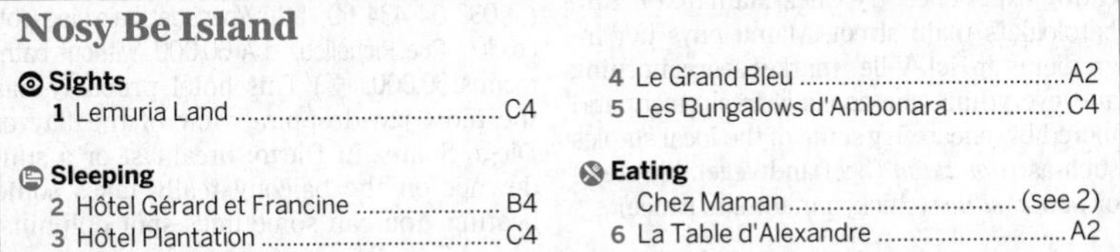

## Nosy Be Island

**Sights**
1 Lemuria Land ........ C4

**Sleeping**
2 Hôtel Gérard et Francine ........ B4
3 Hôtel Plantation ........ C4
4 Le Grand Bleu ........ A2
5 Les Bungalows d'Ambonara ........ C4

**Eating**
Chez Maman ........ (see 2)
6 La Table d'Alexandre ........ A2

owls, chameleons and many wonderful plants, from ylang-ylang trees to vanilla orchids, travellers' palms and more.

**Lemuria Land** DISTILLERY

(admission Ar35,000; ⊙8am-5pm Mon-Sat, to 2.30pm Sat) Ylang-ylang oil is distilled at Lemuria Land on Monday, Wednesday and Friday and daily during the rainy season (January to the end of March). The whole process of turning these somewhat-insignificant flowers into a valuable essential oil is explained.

## Sleeping & Eating

**Hôtel Plantation** HOTEL $$

(032 07 934 45; plantation_b@yahoo.fr; Rue Fortin, Hell-Ville; r Ar57,000-76,000; ) Housed in an old colonial mansion, this is a charming little place with a small pool. Ask to see a few rooms before you settle as the cheaper ones can be a little dark, while the nicest have parquet floors and sea-facing balconies. The restaurant serves reasonable food and is equipped with wi-fi.

★**Hôtel Gérard et Francine** GUESTHOUSE $$$

(032 07 127 93; www.gerard-et-francine.com; d €55; ) A beautifully decorated family guesthouse with wooden floors and a verandah overlooking the beach at Ambatoloaka. The rooms come in all shapes and sizes – some are in the main house and some in the garden. The hotel uses solar power and the owners are very involved in environmental initiatives in Nosy Be. They also lobby actively against sex tourism.

★**Les Bungalows d'Ambonara** GUESTHOUSE $$$

(020 86 613 67; www.nosy-be-holidays.com; off Route de l'Ouest, Hell-Ville; bungalows d/f €30/40; ) Bungalows here nestle in a luxuriant garden and are beautifully decorated using local materials. Owner Jean-Michel makes his own *rhum arrangé* and the restaurant is excellent (mains from Ar16,000). To find it, head out in the direction of Ambatoloaka; it is signposted just before the Air Madagascar office.

★**Chez Maman** MADAGASCAN $

(mains Ar5000-6000) For a true Madagascan eating experience, try Chez Maman, on Ambatoloaka's main street. Mama buys her ingredients at Hell-Ville's market every morning and everything she cooks is fresh, tasty and incredibly cheap. Try some of the local staples such as *romazava* (beef and vegetable stew) or *poulet sauce* (chicken in tomato sauce).

## Getting There & Away

- Sailing yachts regularly come into Nosy Be and many are prepared to take passengers. Their principal destinations are Mayotte, Mozambique and South Africa.
- Small speedboats shuttle between the mainland port of Ankify and Hell-Ville on Nosy Be (Ar12,000, 40 minutes, 5.30am to 4pm). They work like *taxis-brousses* and leave when full. Trade winds pick up in the afternoon, so the crossing is smoother, and therefore more popular, in the morning – you'll never have to wait long for your boat to depart. Life jackets are provided.
- If you're travelling with a vehicle, ferries sail between Ankify and Hell-Ville in Nosy Be (from Ar80,000, two hours, 6am to 4pm).

# Diego Suarez (Antsiranana)

POP 82,937

With its wide streets, old colonial-era buildings and genteel air, Diego is a lovely base from which to explore Madagascar's northern region. It's a slow-moving place; nearly everything shuts between noon and 3pm while residents indulge in long afternoon naps. There are no beaches in Diego itself, but plenty of amazing views of the bay, and the town encourages visitors to explore its fascinating architecture and history.

## Tours

**Evasion Sans Frontière** TOURS

(020 82 217 23; www.evasionsansfrontiere.com; Rue Colbert) This well-respected company runs day trips to all the main regional sights, including Mer d'Emeraude.

**Diego Raid** DRIVING

(032 40 001 75; www.diegoraid.com; Rue Colbert; tours per day €107-182) This operator organises highly recommended quad-bike excursions to areas such as Les Trois Baies, Windsor Castle and Montagne d'Ambre. It also offers half-day 4WD trips to the Tsingy Rouges (€90) and hires out mountain bikes at €15 per day.

## Sleeping

**Perle de la Baie** GUESTHOUSE $$

(032 04 434 50; http://perledelabaie.blogspot.co.uk/; Rue Richelieu; d Ar60,000, without bathroom Ar50,000; ) This hotel probably has the most jaw-dropping view of the Bay of Diego Suarez in Diego: breakfast or a sundowner on the balcony really takes some beating. You can sometimes spot dolphins,

and watching container or cruise ships come in is majestic. The rooms are sparsely furnished but spacious and light (opt for one upstairs). Some share bathrooms.

**La Belle Aventure** GUESTHOUSE **$$**
(☎032 44 153 83; www.labellaventure-diego.com; 13 Rue Freppel; d €17-28; ❄📶) Gilles and Elisabeth built their Beautiful Adventure in a great neighbourhood of Diego: quiet, yet close to the centre and with good views of the bay. Everything is bright, fresh and impeccable, with colourful sheets and lemur and baobab friezes on the walls. Rooms upstairs have a balcony and sea view. There's a friendly bar and restaurant at street level.

★**Le Jardin Exotique** BOUTIQUE HOTEL **$$$**
(☎020 82 219 33; www.jardinexotique-diegosuarez.com; Rue Louis Brunet; r Ar77,000-102,000; ❄📶) Rooms at this quirky boutique place all come with parquet floors, four-poster beds, mosquito nets, bold and creative paint jobs and Italian showers in the bathrooms. The rooftop terrace has picnic tables and the views over the bay of Diego Suarez are awesome. The garden, with its indigenous plants and tumbling bougainvilleas, is wonderful. Massage is available.

## Eating

**Pâtisserie Le Grand Hôtel** BAKERY **$**
(Rue Colbert; cakes & sandwiches Ar3000-9000; ⏲5am-9.30pm) This excellent bakery doubles up as a cafe that's popular with tourists. It's a great choice for an economical and light breakfast, or a cheap lunch of salad or a sandwich. There are some lovely pastries too, which you can devour with real espresso.

★**La Bodega** MADAGASCAN **$$$**
(cnr Rue Colbert & Rue Flacourt; mains Ar16,000-35,000; ⏲9am-2pm Tue-Sat, 5-11pm daily) The name suggests Spanish influence, but owner Cyrille is from France and the colourful restaurant is in Madagascar, so it's hardly surprising the menu is a mix of all three nationalities. We loved the tapas à la Malagasy, the fish carpaccio with avocado and lime mousse and the amazing rum cocktails. It's always busy and has a great atmosphere.

**La Terrasse du Voyageur** MADAGASCAN **$$$**
(☎020 82 240 63; www.terrasseduvoyageur-hotel.com; Rue du Mozambique; set menu Ar25,000; ⏲dinner) 🍃 The 4th-floor restaurant at hotel La Terrasse du Voyageur has sweeping views of Diego. It's a cosy and convivial space, with a TV lounge, library and bar. The set taster menu of Madagascan dishes is good value: portions are gargantuan and the food delicious. The restaurant is only open for dinner and you must book.

## Getting There & Away

There are *taxi-brousse* services to Tana (Ar74,000, 24 hours, departs morning and afternoon), Ankify (Ar4000, nine hours, departs 1am) and Ramena (Ar3000, one hour, frequent).

# EASTERN MADAGASCAR

Eastern Madagascar is travel the way it used to be. Travelling here requires a combination of plane, car, 4WD, dirt bike, scooter, pirogue (dugout canoe), ferry, cargo boat, *taxi-brousse* and motorboat. This inaccessibility results in isolated communities and, for the traveller, a constant sense of coming upon undiscovered locales, including entire national parks. There's no doubt it can be frustrating at times, but eastern Madagascar produces more travellers' tales than anywhere else. If you value that, come here first.

## Parc National Andasibe Mantadia

The Parc National Andasibe Mantadia comprises two distinct parks. More accessible and fairly flat for easy walking is the 8-sq-km **Parc National Analamazaotra** (Périnet; www.parcs-madagascar.com; entry permits per day Ar45,000), with its entrance and large information centre on the main road to Andasibe. Some 17km to the north lies the wilder, primary forest of 155-s-km **Parc National de Mantadia** (www.parcs-madagascar.com; entry permits per day Ar45,000). This is harder terrain but worth the effort.

Analamazaotra gets the most visitors and tends to fill up from July to October, Madagascar's tourist high season. Because the park is small, most of it can be covered in short walks, including to two small lakes, **Lac Vert** (Green Lake) and **Lac Rouge** (Red Lake). The best time for seeing (and hearing) *indris* (lemurs) is early in the morning, from 7am to 11am.

Accommodation is available in the nearby town of Andasibe.

The **MNP office** (⏲6am-4pm) for Parc National Andasibe Mantadia is located at the entrance of the Parc National Analamazaotra and contains a helpful interpretation centre. Entrance permits and guides are available here. The office also sells an informative booklet (Ar5000).

## Andasibe

The small town of Andasibe is surrounded by several parks and reserves whose unique wildlife and close proximity to the capital have made this area extremely popular with travellers. The largest is the Parc National Andasibe Mantadia. This is actually the organisational union of two separate parks, the northern Parc National de Mantadia and the much smaller Parc National Analamazaotra. To these are added Parc Mitsinjo, Réserve de Torotorofotsy and Mahay Mitia Ala (MMA).

Bring warm clothing in winter, and enough cash to see you through, as the nearest banks/ATMs are in Moramanga.

### Sleeping

**Vohitsara Guest House** GUESTHOUSE $
(034 15 854 24; vohitsara@hotmail.com; d/tr Ar30,000/50,000) This family-run operation, on the edge of the village near the station, offers a varied selection of spick-and-span budget rooms with external showers and Madagascan food on request. Reception is in the Mitsinjo building.

★**Hôtel Feon'ny Ala** BUNGALOW $$
(033 05 832 02, 020 56 832 02; d/tr bungalows Ar74,000/78,500) Whoever named this garden hotel 'Song of the Forest' was absolutely right: the site is virtually part of the forest in Parc National Analamazaotra, so close that you can hear the *indris*. The thatched bungalows are close together but comfortable enough and they have hot showers.

★**Andasibe Hotel** LODGE $$$
(034 14 326 27; www.andasibehotel-resto.com; d/f Ar220,000/370,000; ) This hotel on the west side of the village shines: it has the best double rooms around, with split levels, bold Asian styling and knockout views across a verdant rice paddy. The restaurant (menu Ar45,000) has creative French cuisine and there's a nice pool deck. Located on a forest lake, the hotel also offers kayaking.

### Getting There & Away

From Tana, the best way to reach Andasibe is to take a *taxi-brousse* to Moramanga first, then another to Andasibe. Ask the driver to drop you at your hotel. Otherwise, you can take any *taxi-brousse* along the RN2 for 26km to the Andasibe junction at Antsapanana, then walk or hitch the 3km to the village itself.

## Tamatave (Toamasina)

POP 206,373

Tamatave is very much like its cousin Tuléar (Toliara) on the western coast. It is a hot, dusty and chaotic port town full of decaying colonial buildings, roadside markets and throngs of pousse-pousse carts. The emphasis is on commerce, not tourism, apart from being an important transit point.

### Sleeping & Eating

**Hôtel Eden** HOTEL $
(020 53 312 90; calypsotour@netcourrier.com; Blvd Joffre; r Ar30,000, without bathroom Ar20,000) This popular backpackers' hotel is a good budget choice, with a mix of shared and private bathrooms and helpful staff. Expect slightly higher rates as it was being upgraded at the time of writing. **Calypso Tours** (032 04 628 82, 032 40 247 78; www.chrismiatoursmada.com; tours incl lunch Ar80,000) is based here, so it's a good place to organise a tour of the Canal des Pangalanes.

**Génération Hôtel** HOTEL $$
(020 53 321 05; www.generationhotel-tamatave.com; Blvd Joffre; d Ar52,000-75,000; ) At this slightly cluttered but genial hotel all rooms have balconies and fridges; the good-value suites are larger. Furnishings are old-style, but it all works and the staff are friendly. The restaurant serves reasonable food (mains from Ar11,000) and has a pleasant terrace.

**La Véranda** INTERNATIONAL $
(020 53 340 86; http://veranda-hotel-restaurant-tamatave.com; Rue Lieutenant Bérard; mains from Ar9000; breakfast, lunch & dinner Mon-Sat; ) A popular choice for French expats and visitors thanks to its wide-ranging menu of European, Chinese and Madagascan dishes and very reasonable prices. The three-course set menu (Ar15,000) changes daily and is far

**Tamatave (Toamasina)**

**Activities, Courses & Tours**
1 Calypso Tours ........ C6

**Sleeping**
2 Génération Hôtel ........ C2
3 Hôtel Eden ........ C6

**Eating**
4 La Terrasse ........ C4
5 La Véranda ........ C4

too tempting to settle for less. Eat inside or on the lovely colonial-style terrace.

**La Terrasse** PIZZA **$$**
(Blvd Joffre; mains/menus Ar14,000/12,000; ⏰7am-1am; 📶) This hopping streetside bistro with tasty pizza and grills is the go-to lunch spot for people on the move.

## ℹ Information

There are many banks in the centre with ATMs; **BNI** (Blvd Joffre) takes MasterCard. There are also plenty of exchange bureaus.

## Tamatave (Toamasina)

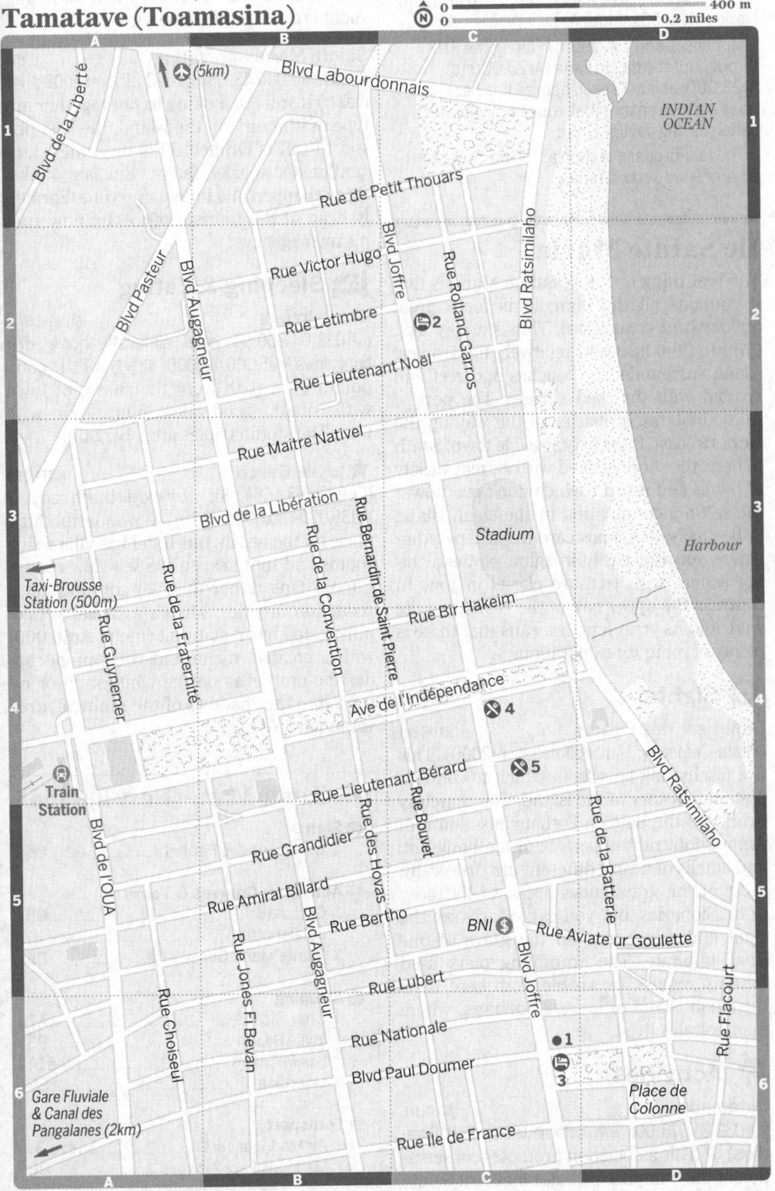

### Getting There & Away

Air Madagascar flies daily between Tamatave and Tana (€227, one hour) and three times weekly to Île Sainte Marie (€227, 30 minutes).

**Madagasikara Airways** (032 05 970 09, 034 05 970 09; www.madagasikaraairways.com; Airport Ambalamanasy) has between one and three flights a week to Tana (€104, one hour). There is also a weekly service to Île Sainte Marie (€101, 30 minutes).

Minibuses and coaches run along the RN2 throughout the day to Tana (Ar20,000 to Ar23,000, at least seven hours). It is best to leave early to ensure that you reach your destination during daylight hours.

The taxi-brousse station at the northwestern edge of town serves Tana.

## Île Sainte Marie

The best thing about Île Sainte Marie is that it contains all the ingredients for a great holiday *and* great travel. This is a very long (57km), thin, lush and relatively flat tropical island surrounded by beaches and reef and spotted with thatched villages. The port of Ambodifotatra, a quarter of the way up the western coast, is the only sizeable town. South of here, the shore is lined with a great variety of hotels and resorts, which don't overpower the setting, culminating in the small island of Île aux Nattes, a postcard tropical paradise where you can easily imagine pirates coming ashore with treasure chests in tow. In contrast, the upper half of the island is quite wild, and its great length means that there is plenty of room for exploration.

### Sights

**Cimetière des Pirates** CEMETERY
(Pirate Cemetery; Ambodifotatra; Ar2000) This is a fascinating spot from which to contemplate the history of the island. The cemetery overlooks the Baie de Forbans just south of Ambodifotatra, the perfect pirate hang-out, and smells of a very different era. Ironically, most of the gravestones are actually those of missionaries, but you can clearly see the skull and crossbones on the grave of one English pirate. The crumbling piers used for ship repairs are visible from here, as is the small island of **Île aux Forbans**, where many pirates lived.

### Activities

**Cétamada** WILDLIFE
(032 81 973 00; www.cetamada.org; Port Barachois) This association promotes conservation of the humpback whales that visit Sainte Marie between July and October. Some members offer whale-watching expeditions. Artisanal products are sold at the office here to raise money for educational projects.

**Il Balenottero** DIVING
(020 57 400 36; www.il-balenottero.com; Ambodifotatra) A large operation with five boats. It also offers PADI courses, whale watching, yacht cruises and fishing trips.

**Sainte Marie Consulting** TOURS
(032 40 084 43, 034 01 793 81; orpheu09@hotmail.fr) If you are looking to put together any type of itinerary on the island, the best person to call is Orpheu. This dynamic young gentleman speaks fluent English, makes things happen and knows everyone. Formerly head of the tourism office, he now runs his own agency.

### Sleeping & Eating

**Les Palmiers** BUNGALOW $
(032 04 960 94; hotel.palmiers@yahoo.fr; d/tr bungalows Ar35,000/45,000; @ wifi) A little compound up a path from the centre of town with smart, good-value bungalows with fans. The studio triples are a bargain.

★ **Idylle Beach** HOTEL $$$
(032 48 684 81; www.idyllebeach.com; r Ar135,000-150,000; air-con wifi) A wonderful little place on the beach, this hotel has villageside rooms and more expensive sea-view rooms. Choose fans rather than air-con and get a reduction in price. There's a casual yet sophisticated bar-restaurant (menu Ar60,000) with a creative menu and you can eat under the umbrellas on the white sand or retreat into the shadows of the multicoloured verandah.

**Île Sainte Marie (Nosy Boraha)**

**Sights**
1 Cimetière des Pirates .......... B5

**Activities, Courses & Tours**
2 Cétamada .......... B5
Il Balenottero .......... (see 2)
3 Sainte Marie Consulting .......... B5

**Sleeping**
4 Chez Sica .......... A7
5 Idylle Beach .......... B5
Les Palmiers .......... (see 5)
6 Libertalia .......... B5

**Transport**
Air Madagascar .......... (see 3)
7 Madagasikara Airways .......... B6

# Île Sainte Marie (Nosy Boraha)

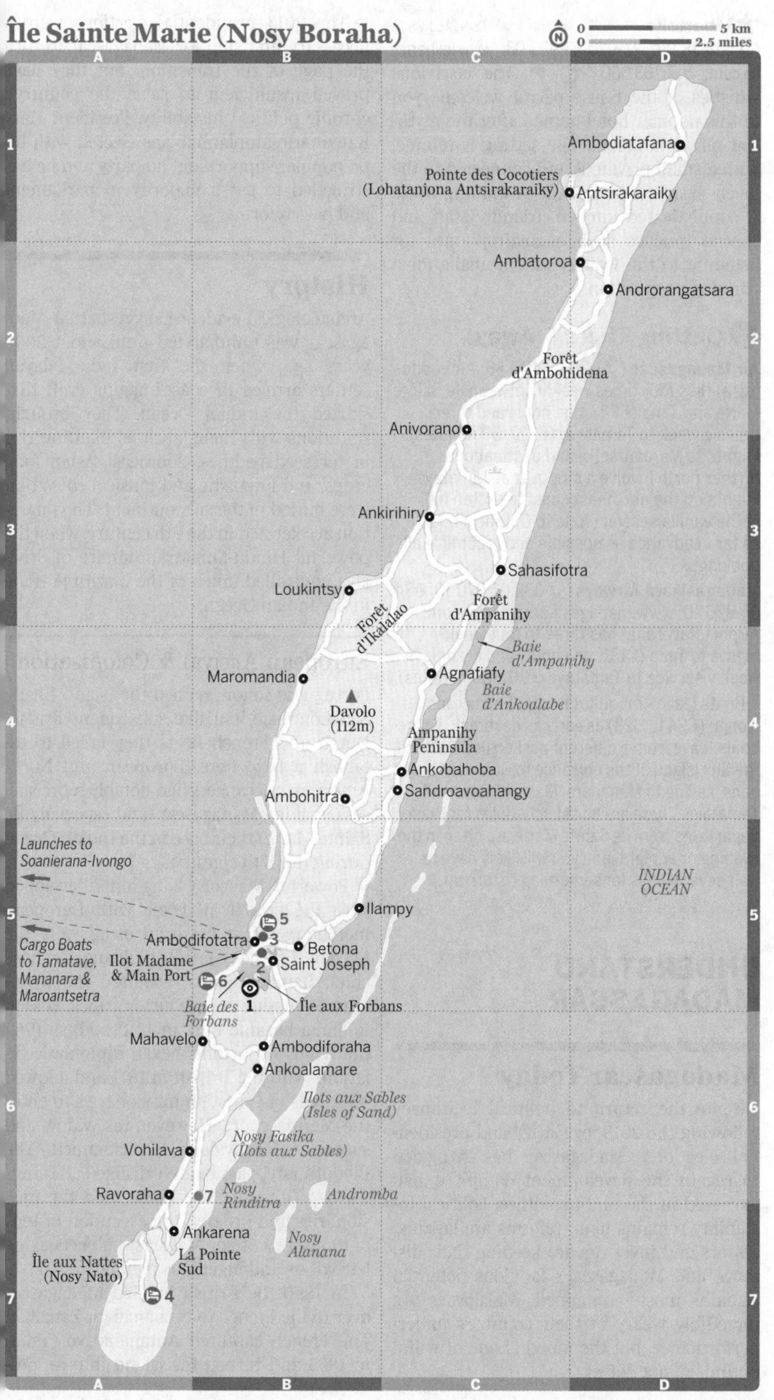

**★Libertalia** BUNGALOW **$$$**
(☎034 18 997 27, 020 57 923 03; www.leliberta-lia.com; d Ar163,000; 📶) 🍃 The lascivious whistles of the house parrot welcome you to this popular hotel named after the mythical pirate kingdom. The setting is unique, with a small private island connected to the lovely beach, and a great swimming dock. A sophisticated kitchen, friendly staff and special touches such as hydrophones for listening to the whales singing make for a winning proposition.

## ℹ Getting There & Away

**Air Madagascar** (☎020 57 400 46; Ambodifotatra) flies four times weekly between Île Sainte Marie and Tana (€227, one hour) and three times a week to Tamatave (€227, 30 minutes). Flights to Maroantsetra and destinations further north involve a stopover at Tamatave. Flights up the northeast coast are often full; in the vanilla season (June to October) book as far in advance as possible and reconfirm all bookings.

**Madagasikara Airways** (☎032 05 970 10, 034 05 970 10; www.madagasikaraairways.com; Airport Ravoraha) has three to four weekly flights to Tana (€131, one hour) and a single weekly service to Tamatave (€101, 30 minutes).

Boats leave Ambodifotatra for Soanierana-Ivongo (€24 to €28) as early as daybreak. Cargo boats leave from a different port on Ilot Madame, the tiny island at the entrance to Baie des Forbans, sailing to Mananara, Maroantsetra and Tamatave. There are no set schedules for these; departures from Île Sainte Marie are often in the evening or at night, and you will likely have to wait several days for something to turn up.

# UNDERSTAND MADAGASCAR

## Madagascar Today

Despite the return to political legitimacy following the 2013 legislative and presidential elections, Madagascar has struggled to regain the development oomph it had garnered in the mid-naughties. Political instability remains high, reforms are lagging, donors and investors are keeping their distance and Madagascar's fabulous potential remains mostly untapped. Malagasies are incredibly weary of their country's underperformance, but the mood is one of wilful optimism, not defeat.

The 2013 presidential elections were a necessary first step for Madagascar to turn the page of the transition, but they have proved insufficient to solve the country's chronic political instability. President Hery Rajaonarimampianina was elected with little popular support and no party and he has struggled to get a majority in parliament and pass reforms.

## History

Archaeological evidence suggests that Madagascar was uninhabited until about 2000 years ago, when the first Indo-Malayan settlers arrived in coast-hugging craft that skirted the Indian Ocean. They brought traditions with them, such as planting rice in terraced paddies, Southeast Asian food crops, and linguistic and musical roots that were buried in the subcontinent. The migration accelerated in the 9th century, when the powerful Hindu-Sumatran empire of Srivijaya controlled much of the maritime trade in the Indian Ocean.

### European Arrival & Colonisation

Portuguese sailors named the island Ilhade São Lourenço, but like subsequent British, Dutch and French fleets they failed to establish a base here. European and North American buccaneers had notably more success, making Madagascar (and especially Île Sainte Marie) their base in the Indian Ocean during the 17th century.

Powerful Malagasy kingdoms developed with the growth of trade with European merchants. Most powerful of all were the Merina of the central highlands, whose chief, Ramboasalama, acquired the weaponry to subdue neighbouring tribes. Hisson Radama became king in 1810 and, sniffing the winds of fortune, began diplomatic relations with the British in 1817 and allowed hundreds of Christian missionaries to enter the Merina court. However, his widow and successor, Ranavalona I, nicknamed 'The Bloodthirsty', passionately disliked all things *vahaza* (foreign); she persecuted the missionaries and ordered the execution of tens of thousands of her Malagasy subjects using barbarous and ingenious methods.

In 1890 the British handed Madagascar over to the French in exchange for Zanzibar. The French captured Antananarivo (Tana) in 1895 and turned the island into an official colony in 1897. The French suppressed the Malagasy language; however, they constructed roads, expanded the education network and abolished slavery. Resentment of the French colonial presence grew in all levels of society, and nationalist movements had developed by the 1920s. Strikes and demonstrations culminated in a revolt in 1947, which the French suppressed after killing an estimated 80,000 people and sending the rebel leaders into exile.

## Nationalism & Independence

By 1958 the Malagasy had voted in a referendum to become an autonomous republic within the French community of overseas nations. Philibert Tsiranana became Madagascar's first president, and allowed the French to keep control of most of Madagascar's trade and industry. Tsiranana was forced to resign in 1972 and was succeeded by army general Gabriel Ramantsoa.

The socialist Ramantsoa made friends with China and the USSR, closed down the French military bases and collectivised the farming system, which led to an exodus of French farmers. The economy took a nosedive and Ramantsoa was forced to resign. His successor, Richard Ratsimandrava, lasted just one week before being assassinated by rebel army officers. They were almost immediately routed by Ramantsoa loyalists, and a new government headed by Admiral Didier Ratsiraka came to power.

The Ratsiraka years were characterisedby more socialist reforms, but a debt crisis in the early 1980s forced him to abandon the reforms and obey the International Monetary Fund. In 1989 Ratsiraka was dubiously 'elected' to his third seven-year term, sparking riots that left six people dead. People were still demanding his resignation by 1991, and the ensuing demonstrations brought the economy to a standstill. In 1992 the Malagasy voted in a referendum to limit the presidential powers. General elections were held that year, and Professor Albert Zafy thrashed Ratsiraka, ending his 17 years in power.

Years of communist-style dictatorship and economic mismanagement made it hard for Zafy to ignite the economy and gain the trust of the people. He was eventually impeached for abuse of constitutional powers. Elections were called in 1996 and Ratsiraka surprised everyone by scraping by with a victory.

## Ravolomanana

In the first round of the 2001 general election, Marc Ravalomanana, a dairy businessman, claimed victory, but Ratsiraka refused to accept the vote. Ravalomanana and his supporters mounted mass protests and a general strike at the beginning of 2002. A month later Ravalomanana went ahead and declared himself president anyway, sparking off clashes between rival supporters that nearly brought Madagascar to civil war. Bridges were bombed, and Ratsiraka's supporters blockaded Tana, cutting off its fuel and food supply for weeks. The Supreme Court held a recount of the votes and declared Ravalomanana the winner. When the US recognised Ravalomanana as the rightful president, Ratsiraka fled in exile to Paris.

Ravalomanana's 'I Love Madagascar' party sealed its popularity at parliamentary elections in December 2002. The new president set about reforming the country's ruined economy, and announced salary increases for politicians in an effort to stamp out corruption. His government generally made the right noises to the World Bank, which, along with France and the US, pledged a total of US$2.3 billion in aid. Under his leadership, main roads were repaired and maintained, and tourism was promoted by the declaration of new national parks.

But it was Ravalomanana's business drive that eventually brought about his demise: in July 2008 he signed a 99-year lease with Korean company Daewoo Logistics for 13,000 sq km of land for maize cultivation, half of all arable land on the island. The deal caused consternation (and was later rescinded) in a country where land customarily belongs to ancestors. What had been simmering discontent grew to a boil and led to the 2009 coup.

# Madagascar's People

Malagasy people are divided into 19 tribes, whose boundaries are roughly based on old kingdoms. Tribal divisions are still evident between ancient enemies such as the Merina and the Antakàrana. Also important is the distinction between Merina highlanders, who have more prominent Asian origins and are associated with the country's aristocracy, and so-called *côtiers* (literally, 'those from the coast'), whose African influences are more pronounced and who are often looked down on by the Merina. In Tana, well-off *côtières* (women from the coast) often straighten their hair to avoid discrimination against their coastal origins.

The main tribal groups are Merina, who make up 27% of the population, Betsimisaraka (15%), Betsileo (12%), Tsimihety (7%), Sakalava (6%), Antaisaka (5%) and Antandroy (5%). There are also small groups of Indian, Chinese, Comorian and French people living on the island.

## Religion

About half of Madagascar's population adheres to traditional beliefs, while the efforts of proselytising Europeans during the 19th century have resulted in the other half worshipping at Catholic and Protestant churches. A small proportion is Muslim. In recent years evangelical churches have become popular too, with charismatic preachers, inspirational singing and dancing, and unusual venues (from stadiums to town halls).

Christian Malagasies often retain great respect for traditional beliefs, which are rooted in reverence for one's ancestors and their spirits. Among most tribes, this is manifested in a complex system of *fady* (taboos) and burial rites, the best known of which is the ceremonial exhumation and reburial known as *famadihana* (literally, 'the turning of the bones').



## Environment

Madagascar is the world's fourth-largest island, after Greenland, Papua New Guinea and Borneo. Its incredibly diverse landscapes and unique wildlife are a product of history: cast adrift from Africa about 165 million years ago, Madagascar took with it a cargo of animals and plants that have been evolving in isolation ever since.

Madagascar's 80-million-year isolation has allowed its wildlife to take a remarkable evolutionary turn. Undisturbed by outside influences and human beings (who 'only' arrived 2000 years ago), the various fauna and flora followed their own interpretation of the evolution manual. The result is that 70% of animals and 90% of plants found in Madagascar are endemic.

As well as being completely unique, their sheer variety is staggering: Madagascar hosts 5% of all known animal and plant species. Habitat degradation threatens much of this incredible natural wealth, though, and habitat conservation is now a priority.

# SURVIVAL GUIDE

## Directory A–Z

### ACCOMMODATION

Accommodation in Madagascar is cheap compared to Europe or North America, but not as cheap as you might perhaps expect.

Madagascar's winter months (July to September) are the busiest. It's a good idea to book ahead at this time of year, particularly in popular destinations such as Nosy Be, Île Sainte Marie or Parc National des Tsingy de Bemaraha.

Few hotels have official low-/high-season prices, although many offer discounts in quiet periods, notably during the rainy season (January to the end of March).

Top-end places are the most heterogeneous, with some luxury resorts costing as much as €500 (Ar1.5 million) per night for a double room with full board.

Because of the depreciation of the ariary, an increasing number of hotels (even midrange ones) are quoting their prices in euros. You then settle in ariarys, at the day's exchange rate (some places will accept euros).

In 2016 the *vignette* (tourist tax) of Ar600 to Ar3000 per night, which was included in prices, was abolished and replaced with a one-off €10 charge at the airport upon arrival in Madagascar.

### ACTIVITIES

Madagascar is an excellent destination for sporting activities. Climbing, diving, hiking and canoeing/kayaking are all in plentiful supply.

Whatever activity you embark on, pick a reliable operator, especially with high-risk activities such as diving, kitesurfing and rock climbing. Check the operator's affiliations, the instructors' qualifications and inspect your gear.

Divers, note that there is no hyperbaric chamber in Madagascar, so should you have a mishap underwater, you will have to go to Réunion to be depressurised.

### EMBASSIES & CONSULATES

**Australian High Commission** (in Mauritius +230 202 0160; www.mauritius.embassy.gov.au; Mauritius) The Australian High Commission in Mauritius has consular responsibility for Madagascar.

**Canadian Consulate** (☎ in South Africa +27 12-422 3000; Pretoria, South Africa) Consulate under the responsibility of the High Commission of Canada in Pretoria, South Africa.

**French Embassy** (☎ 020 22 398 98; www.ambafrance-mada.org; 3 Rue Jean Jaurès, Ambatomena) There are also representatives in Diego Suarez (Antsiranana), Majunga (Mahajanga) and Tamatave (Toamasina).

**German Embassy** (☎ 020 22 238 02; www.antananarivo.diplo.de; 101 Rue Pasteur Rabeony, Ambodiroatra)

**Netherlands Consulate** (☎ 020 23 682 31; nl.mg@moov.mg; Villa Christina No 88, Lotissement Bonnet, Ivandry) Consulate under the responsibility of the Dutch Embassy in Dar Es Salaam, Tanzania.

**South African Embassy** (☎ 020 22 433 50; antananarivo.consular@dirco.gov.za; Rue Ravoninahitriniarivo, Ankorondrano)

**UK Embassy** (☎ 020 22 330 53; http://ukinmadagascar.fco.gov.uk; 9th fl, Tour Zital, rue Ravoninahitriniarivo, Ankorondrano) The embassy reopened in 2013 after an eight-year hiatus.

**US Embassy** (☎ 020 23 480 00; www.antananarivo.usembassy.gov; Point Liberty, Andranoro, Antehiroka) Located about 15km north of Tana, on the road to Ivato airport.

## INTERNET ACCESS

Virtually every hotel (even budget ones) now offers complimentary wi-fi, even if only in the reception area. The same is true for midrange and top-end restaurants. The connection is generally good enough for emails, but can struggle with more demanding applications such as Skype/FaceTime or downloads.

Internet cafes can be found in all major towns and cities. Connection speeds vary from pretty good to woefully slow. Prices range from Ar30 to Ar50 per minute.

If you have a smartphone, an excellent alternative is to buy a local SIM card and a 3G package: Ar25,000 will buy you 1GB of data. The mobile coverage is excellent, so you should be connected reliably, except in very remote areas.

## LGBTIQ TRAVELLERS

Homosexuality is legal in Madagascar, but not openly practised. The age of consent is 21.

Overt displays of affection – whether the couple is of the same or opposite sex – are considered to be culturally inappropriate.

## MONEY

ATMs (Visa and MasterCard) are widely available in large towns and cities. In rural areas, cash rules. Euros are the easiest foreign currency to exchange.

### Exchange Rates

| | | |
|---|---|---|
| Australia | A$1 | Ar2500 |
| Canada | C$1 | Ar2400 |
| Euro zone | €1 | Ar3500 |
| Japan | ¥100 | Ar3000 |
| New Zealand | NZ$1 | Ar2300 |
| South Africa | R10 | Ar2300 |
| UK | £1 | Ar4100 |
| US | US$1 | Ar3300 |

For current exchange rates, see www.xe.com.

## OPENING HOURS

Shops geared towards tourists tend to open longer at the weekend.

**Banks** (Tana) 8am to 4pm Monday to Friday

**Banks** (rest of the country) 7.30am to 11.30am and 2pm to 4.30pm Monday to Friday

**Bars** 5pm to 11pm

**Restaurants** 11.30am to 2.30pm and 6.30pm to 9.30pm

**Shops** 9am to noon and 2.30pm to 6pm Monday to Friday, 9am to noon Saturday

## PUBLIC HOLIDAYS

Accommodation and flights can be harder to find during French school holidays, when residents from neighbouring French territories Mayotte and Réunion travel in the region. To find out when these holidays are, visit www.ac-reunion.fr/calendrier-scolaire.html.

Government offices and private companies close on the following public holidays. Banks are generally also closed the afternoon before a public holiday.

**New Year's Day** 1 January

**Insurrection Day** 29 March; celebrates the rebellion against the French in 1947

**Easter Monday** March/April

**Labour Day** 1 May

**Ascension Thursday** May/June; occurs 40 days after Easter

**Pentecost Monday** May/June; occurs 51 days after Easter

**National Day** 26 June; Independence Day

**Assumption** 15 August

**All Saints' Day** 1 November

**Christmas Day** 25 December

## SAFE TRAVEL

Insecurity has increased in Tana since the 2009 coup, so always travel by taxi at night and watch out for pickpockets, especially around Ave de l'Indépendance.

Batterie Beach near Tuléar is also to be avoided following a series of attacks on foreigners.

### PRICE RANGES

The following price ranges refer to a double room with bathroom in high season.

**€** less than Ar35,000

**€€** Ar35,000 to Ar80,000

**€€€** more than Ar80,000

The following price ranges refer to a standard main course.

**€** less than Ar10,000

**€€** Ar10,000 to Ar17,000

**€€** more than Ar17,000

Cyclone season runs from December to March. The east coast is the most affected but cyclones can also hit the west coast. Heed local warnings and seek advice at the time for transport and activities.

Vehicles travelling at night have been subject to attacks over the past few years. *Taxis-brousses* are now therefore required to travel in convoy at night, but private vehicles should avoid being on the road after dark (many drivers will, in fact, refuse to drive at night).

The area between Ihosy and Ambovombe should also be avoided because of banditry.

### TELEPHONE

Phone numbers are generally 10 digits. Landlines start with ☎020, mobiles with ☎03. Mobile phone coverage is excellent in Madagascar. The main networks are Telma (www.telma.mg), which is government owned, Airtel (www.africa.airtel.com/madagascar) and Orange (www.orange.mg). Some remote areas only have coverage from one network.

SIM cards are very cheap (Ar500 to Ar2000) and can be bought from the mobile networks' offices.

You can buy credit at literally every street corner in towns and cities and in grocery shops in the form of electronic credit or scratch cards (Ar1000 to Ar100,000).

A national/international SMS costs around Ar120/340. National calls cost around Ar720 per minute. International calls from mobile phones cost Ar870 to Ar4500 per minute.

### TIME

Madagascar is three hours ahead of GMT; there is no daylight saving.

### TOURIST INFORMATION

Madagascar's tourist offices (www.madagascar-tourisme.com) range from useless to incredibly helpful. They will generally be able to provide listings of hotels and restaurants in the area and, in the best cases, help you organise excursions or find a guide.

MNP (www.parcs-madagascar.com) offices are generally excellent (with a couple of exceptions) when it comes to logistics and practical advice, but they often have little in the way of maps or literature.

### VISAS

All visitors must have a visa to enter Madagascar. Travellers will need to provide a return plane ticket, have a passport valid for at least six months after the intended date of return and one free page in the passport for the visa stamps.

Visas of up to 90 days can be purchased at the airport upon arrival.

- 30-day visas cost €31
- 60-day visas cost €39
- 90-day visas cost €54

Longer or different types of visas must be arranged before travel – note that application times can be long.

Always check with your country's embassy on the latest conditions and fees.

## Getting There & Away

### AIR

International flights come into **Ivato airport** (www.antananarivoairport.com), 20km north of Antananarivo (Tana). The airports in Majunga (Mahajanga), Diego Suarez (Antsiranana) and Tamatave (Toamasina) also handle flights from Réunion, Mauritius and the Comoros.

### TOURS

The following European, American and Australian tour operators offer all-inclusive trips to Madagascar, whether tailor-made or as part of a group.

**Adventure Associates** (www.adventureassociates.com; Australia) Runs two trips a year to Madagascar, some of them led by famous wildlife TV presenter Richard Morecroft.

**Baobab Travel** (www.baobab.nl; Netherlands) Offers a south and east circuit.

**Comptoir de Madagascar** (www.comptoirde-madagascar.com; France) Numerous circuits offered, from general discovery to activity-led (mountain biking) and beach-based (Nosy Be, Île Sainte Marie etc).

**Cortez Travel & Expeditions** (www.air-mad.com; USA) Well-established operator with an agency in the USA and one in Madagascar. Offers organised tours as well as customised trips.

**Madagaskar Travel** (www.madagaskar-travel.de; Germany) General and specialist fauna-and-flora itineraries.

**Priori** (www.priori.ch; Madagascar) Cultural and wildlife tours, run by a Swiss national who is a long-time Madagascar resident.

**Rainbow Tours** (www.rainbowtours.co.uk; UK) Specialist and general-interest guided trips to Madagascar; highly recommended by travellers.

**Reef & Rainforest Tours** (www.reefandrainforest.co.uk; UK) Focuses on top-end wildlife holidays.

**Terre Voyages** (www.terre-voyages.com; France) A wide range of tours to Madagascar.

**Wildlife Worldwide** (www.wildlifeworldwide.com; UK) Wildlife-viewing tours.

**Zingg Event Travel** (www.zinggsafaris.com; Switzerland) Individual and group circuits.

## Getting Around

Madagascar is a huge place, the roads are bad and travel times long (it takes 24 hours to drive from Tana to Diego Suarez, 18 hours to Tuléar etc), so be realistic about how much ground you want to cover or you'll spend every other day in the confines of a vehicle.

**Private vehicle** If you can afford it, this is the best way to explore Madagascar. You'll be able to go anywhere, whenever suits you. The off-road driving can be great fun too.

**Taxi-brousse (bush taxi)** They are slow, uncomfortable and not always safe, but they are cheap, go (almost) everywhere and you can't get more local than that.

**Plane** Can be huge time savers, but they can be expensive and subject to frequent delays and cancellations.

### AIR

Air Madagascar (www.airmadagascar.com;) is the main airline to provide domestic flights. Cancellations and delays are unamusingly frequent.

Tickets are expensive (upwards of €200 for a one-way ticket), but generally exchangeable.

You can pay for tickets by credit card or in ariary, euros or US dollars at the head office in Antananarivo and Air Madagascar offices in larger towns. Smaller offices may only accept ariary or euros, however.

Certain routes, such as Morondava–Tuléar (Toliara) during the high season (May to September) and all flights to/from Sambava during the vanilla season (June to October), are often fully booked months in advance.

A new airline, Madagasikara Airways (www.madagasikaraairways.com), started flights in late 2015 between Tana and all major cities as well as Nosy Be and Île Sainte Marie.

### CAR & MOTORCYCLE

Due to the often-difficult driving conditions, most rental agencies make hiring a driver compulsory with their vehicles.

Of Madagascar's approximately 50,000km of roads, less than 20% are sealed, and many of those are riddled with potholes the size of an elephant. Routes in many areas are impassable or very difficult during the rainy season.

The designation *route nationale* (RN) is sadly no guarantee of quality.

- Driving in Madagascar is on the right-hand side.
- Police checkpoints are frequent (mind the traffic spikes on the ground) – always slow down and make sure you have your passport and the vehicle's documents handy.
- If you see a zebu on the road, slow right down as it can panic; also, there may be another 20 in the bushes that haven't yet crossed.

### TAXI-BROUSSE

The good news is that *taxis-brousses* are cheap and go everywhere. The bad news is that they are slow, uncomfortable, erratic and sometimes unsafe.

Despite the general appearance of anarchy, the *taxi-brousse* system is actually relatively well organised. Drivers and vehicles belong to transport companies called *coopératives* (cooperatives). *Coopératives* generally have a booth or an agent at the *taxi-brousse* station (called *gare routière* or *parcage*), where you can book your ticket.

Although the going can be slow, *taxis-brousses* stop regularly for toilet breaks, leg stretching and meals (at *hotelys* along the road).

There are national and regional services (called *ligne nationale* and *ligne régionale*). They can cover the same route, the difference being that on national services the *taxis-brousses* go from A to B without stopping and only squeeze three people to a row. On regional services, people hop on and off along the way, and there are four people per row, so tickets are cheaper. Make sure you stipulate which service you'd like when booking your ticket.

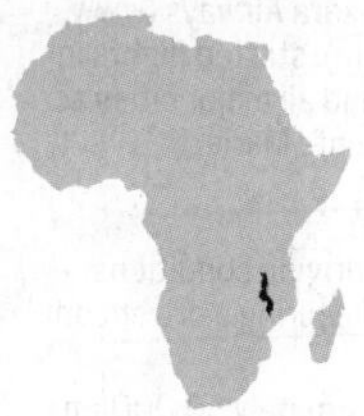

# Malawi

POP 18.6 MILLION

**Includes ➡**



## Best Places to Eat

➡ Casa Rossa (p824)

➡ L'Hostaria (p825)

➡ Macondo Camp (p817)

## Best Places to Sleep

➡ Kaya Mawa (p819)

➡ Mkulumadzi Lodge (p828)

➡ Mvuu Camp (p823)

➡ Chelinda Lodge (p816)

➡ Mumbo Island Camp (p821)

## Why Go?

Apart from the legendary Malawian friendliness, what captures you first about this vivid country is its geographical diversity. Slicing through the landscape in a trough formed by the Great Rift Valley is Africa's third-largest lake: Lake Malawi, a shimmering mass of clear water, its depths swarming with colourful cichlid fish. A visit to the lake is a must, whether for diving, snorkelling, kayaking or chilling out on beaches and desert islands.

Suspended in the clouds in Malawi's deep south are the dramatic peaks of Mt Mulanje and the mysterious Zomba Plateau, both a hiker's dream, with mist-cowled forests and exotic wildlife. Further north is the other-worldly beauty of the Nyika Plateau, its rolling grasslands resembling the Scottish Highlands. Malawi was once dismissed as a safari destination, but all that changed with a lion-reintroduction program at Majete Wildlife Reserve, which is now one of a few worthwhile wildlife-watching destinations nationwide.

## When to Go

### Lilongwe

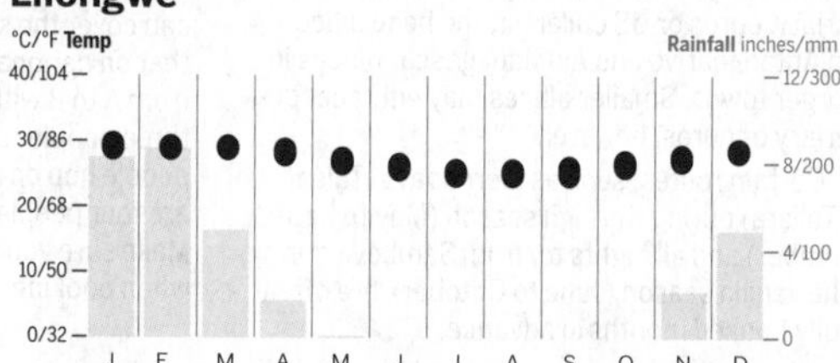


**May–Jul** Dry season, with cooler temperatures and lush vegetation.

**Aug** Interesting cultural festivals and good beach weather; the higher areas are chilly.

**Sep & Oct** The end of the dry season brings great wildlife-watching conditions, but temperatures are high.

# Malawi Highlights

**1 Lake Malawi** (p820) Kayaking across the bottle-green lake from ultra-chilled Cape Maclear to Mumbo Island.

**2 Majete Wildlife Reserve** (p828) Searching for reintroduced lions in Malawi's only Big Five park.

**3 Mt Mulanje** (p827) Scrambling up the twisted peaks and admiring the astounding views.

**4 Liwonde National Park** (p822) Spotting hippos and crocs on the Shire River and getting up close to elephants.

**5 Kaya Mawa** (p819) Escaping to this dreamy boutique hotel on Likoma Island.

**6 Nkhotakota Wildlife Reserve** (p821) Kayaking past crocs in the Bua River.

**7 Nyika National Park** (p816) Cycling the rugged grasslands, home to zebras and antelope.

**8 Nkhata Bay** (p817) Diving among cichlids and feeding fish eagles in northern Malawi's up-and-coming beach town.

**9 Livingstonia** (p815) Heading to the hills to find this atmospheric mission, home to fantastic ecolodges.

# LILONGWE

POP 1,077,116 / ELEV 1050M

Sprawling, chaotic and bustling with commerce, Lilongwe feels fit to burst. The nation's capital is initially a little underwhelming and it takes some time to get your bearings – you may wonder where the centre is – but once you've decided on your favourite restaurants, ferreted out the best malls and discovered those hidden leafy oases, the place grows on you.

## Sights & Activities

**Lilongwe Wildlife Centre** WILDLIFE RESERVE
(0881 788999; www.lilongwewildlife.org; Kenyatta Rd; MK3500; 8am-5pm) This 1.1-sq-km wilderness area is Malawi's only sanctuary for orphaned, injured and rescued wild animals, and plays an active role in conservation. Local residents include a one-eyed lion rescued from Romania, a python, two cobras, baboons, duikers, servals, and blue and vervet monkeys. The entry fee includes a one-hour tour of the enclosures. Tours run on the hour from 9am to 4pm.

**Kamuzu Mausoleum** SHRINE
(Capital Hill, Presidential Way; 24hr) This marble and granite mausoleum is the final resting place of Malawi's 'president for life', Dr Hastings Kamuzu Banda. Between four pillars bearing the initials of his most prized principles – unity, loyalty, obedience and discipline – is a wrinkled portrait of the 'lion of Malawi'. Guides at the entrance will show you around in exchange for a small tip.

## Tours

**Ultimate Travel** (01-776000; www.ultimatetravel.mw; President Walmont Hotel, Umodzi Park) offers city tours and nocturnal experiences of Lilongwe nightlife. For a day trip into the surrounding countryside, contact the **Adventure Office** (0996 347627; www.theadventureoffice.com; Mabuya Camp, Livingstone Rd) or **Land & Lake Safaris** (01-757120; www.landlake.net; Area 3).

## Sleeping

Most budget and midrange digs are located in Old Town, which is handy for restaurants and transport links, while City Centre and Area 10 have more high-end hotels and guesthouses. There are also some stunning lodges fringing the bush on the city's outskirts.

**Mabuya Camp** HOSTEL $
(01-754978; www.mabuyacamp.com; Livingstone Rd; camping/tent hire/dm US$7/9/12, r US$45, with shared bathroom US$30; P) Lilongwe's liveliest backpacker spot buzzes with a mix of travellers, overlanders and volunteers relaxing by the pool and in the large, shady gardens. There are dorms in the main house, as well as chalets, A-frame huts, en suite rooms and camping pitches in the garden, with shared ablutions in thatched rondavels (round, traditional-style huts).

**St Peter's Guesthouse** GUESTHOUSE $
(0995 299364; Glyn Jones Rd; incl breakfast dm MK4000, r MK8000-10,000; P) Anglican-owned St Peter's has four pleasant rooms next to a red-brick church. All rooms and the four-bed dorm are en suite. It's very peaceful, with a tranquil, leafy garden.

**Korea Garden Lodge** HOTEL $$
(01-759774, 01-757854, 01-753467; www.kglodge.net; Tsiranana Rd; s/d from MK25,000/35,000, with shared bathroom MK18,000/22,000; P@) This good-value hotel has numerous rooms of varying standards; the more you pay, the larger and better equipped they get, and you can choose if you want an en suite bathroom, TV, air-con and self-catering facilities. There's a tempting pool, flanked by a **restaurant** (01-753467; mains MK5000; 6.30am-9pm; P) serving Asian food, and the grounds are replete with plants.

**★Latitude 13°** BOUTIQUE HOTEL $$$
(0996 403159; www.latitudehotels.com; Mphonongo Rd, Area 43; r US$220; P@) Lilongwe's first world-class boutique hotel, this gated, nine-suite retreat raises the bar for Malawian accommodation. From the moment you step into its rarefied atmosphere of shadowy chic pulsing with glowing pod lights you're transported right off the African continent.

**★Kumbali Country Lodge** LODGE $$$
(0999 963402; www.kumbalilodge.com; Capital Hill Dairy Farm, Plot 9 & 11, Area 44; s/d incl breakfast from US$200/240; P) A short drive from the city centre, on a 650-hectare forest reserve, is a choice of swanky individual thatched chalets (Madonna has stayed here on her controversial visits to Malawi) with beautiful views of nearby Nkhoma Mountain.

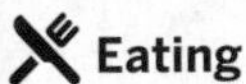

## Eating

**Land & Lake Cafe** CAFE $

(☎01-757120; Land & Lake Safaris, Area 3; mains MK3000; ⌚8am-4.30pm Mon-Fri, to 2pm Sat; P📶✎) This garden cafe at Land & Lake Safaris' headquarters, off Laws Ave, serves croissants, bagels and English breakfasts, light lunches from quesadillas to spuds, and tempting desserts.

★**Ad Lib** INTERNATIONAL $$

(☎0994 350630; www.adlibglasgow.com; Mandala Rd; mains MK6000; ⌚9am-late) An adventurous extension of a hip Glaswegian diner chain, this popular local gathering spot has a covered street-front terrace and a jolly red-walled interior with a long bar. The menu gallops enthusiastically across a broad spectrum, including steaks, jerk chicken, fish and chips, wood-smoked meats, nachos, quesadillas, Angus-beef burger (recommended) and southern fried chicken popcorn.

★**Koko Bean** CAFE $$

(☎0994 263363; Lilongwe Wildlife Centre, Kenyatta Rd; mains MK5000; ⌚8am-5pm) Soundtracked by world music, this breezy urban sanctuary is surrounded by lawns, thatched shelters and a bar overlooking a sprawling jungle gym – perfect for a family visit. Come for breakfasts from French toast to hearty 'hangover' omelettes, with a pot of tea or coffee; sandwiches, wraps and burgers; and pizzas with zingy toppings.

★**Ama Khofi** CAFE $$

(☎0998 196475; Four Seasons Centre, Presidential Way; mains MK5000; ⌚7.30am-5pm Mon-Sat, 9am-5pm Sun; P📶✎) Follow your nose to this delightful Parisian-style garden-centre cafe with wrought-iron chairs, a bubbling fountain and leafy surrounds. The menu has salads, main courses such as beef burgers and roast-beef sandwiches, and homemade sweet treats that include cakes and ice cream.

## Drinking & Nightlife

In addition to Lilongwe's dedicated watering holes, the garden cafes Ama Khofi, **Kiboko Town Hotel** (www.kibokohotel.com; Mandala Rd; ⌚7am-5pm; P📶✎👪), Koko Bean, Land & Lake Cafe and Mimosa Food Court at the **Sunbird Capital Hotel** (☎01-773388; www.sunbirdmalawi.com; Chilembwe Rd) are delightful spots for a coffee. Ad Lib is hugely popular for beers and live music, while the air-conditioned bars at swish hotels such as the **President Walmont** (www.umodzipark.co.mw; Umodzi Park) are appealing on a hot sub-Saharan day.

**Living Room** CAFE, BAR

(☎0881 615460; www.facebook.com/thelivingroomlilongwe; cocktails MK2000; ⌚8am-late) With woodcarvings on its shaded veranda, this tucked-away chill-out den (find it off Mzimba St) offers coffee, cocktails, board games and dishes from steaks to *chambo* (a bream-like fish) and chips (mains MK4000). Check Facebook for details of events, which include live music on Tuesdays and poetry on Wednesdays. The adjoining sports bar, Champions, opens at 11am; Amazon nightclub opens at 7pm on Friday and Saturday.

**Chameleon Bar** BAR

(☎0888 833114; Four Seasons Centre, Presidential Way; ⌚4-11pm Mon-Wed, to midnight Thu, to 1am Fri & Sat, 2-11pm Sun; 📶) This Scottish-owned watering hole faces Buchanan's Grill in a leafy compound, with tables outside and a glass bar and purple walls within. It's popular with Malawians and expats both, and Sundays are big here, with live music from 2pm to 9.30pm. Karaoke is offered on the last Thursday of the month and soccer matches are screened.

## Shopping

**African Habitat** ARTS & CRAFTS

(☎01-752363; grabifem@hotmail.com; Old Town Mall; ⌚8.30am-5pm Mon-Fri, to 1pm Sat) Excellent for sculpture, woodcarvings, sarongs, cards and jewellery, as well as T-shirts and bags.

**Craft Market** MARKET

(cnr Mandala & Kamuzu Procession Rds; ⌚8am-4pm Mon-Sat) At these stalls outside the Old Town post office, vendors sell everything from trinket woodcarvings, basketware and jewellery to traditional Malawian chairs.

## Information

### DANGERS & ANNOYANCES

During the day it's fine to walk around most of Old Town and City Centre, although City Centre is quieter at the weekend, so you should be on your guard then. Malangalanga Rd and the area around the main bus station and market can be dangerous, and walking to Old Town from there is not recommended. Muggers' haunts en route include the Kamuzu Procession Rd bridge between Area 2 and Area 3.

# Lilongwe

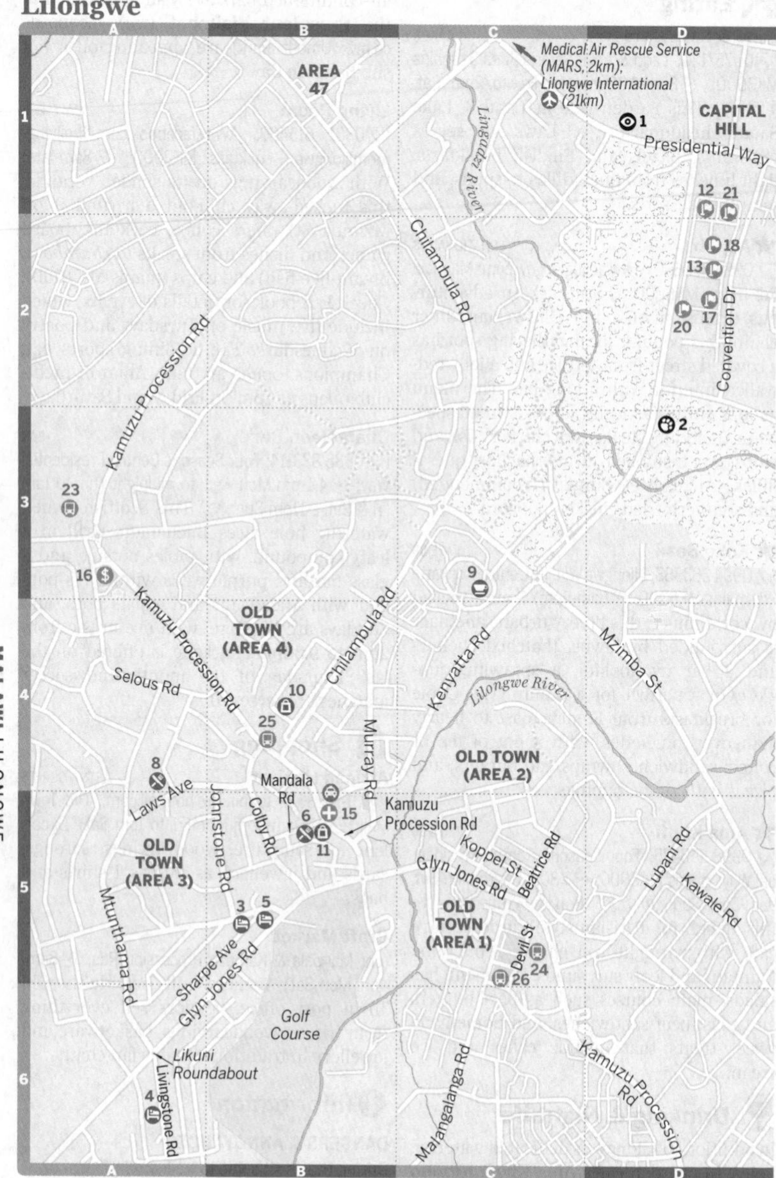


Always watch out for your things while at the bus station, and if you arrive after dark take a taxi or minibus to your accommodation. As a general rule, it isn't safe to walk around anywhere in the city after dark. Following a spate of carjackings, many local motorists run red lights after dark. Bus tickets should only be bought at the bus station; travellers have been conned out of money by buying tickets for nonexistent services on the street.

You definitely don't want to be around Lilongwe Wildlife Centre after dark due to late-night hyena appearances – hyenas have taken a few locals over the years.

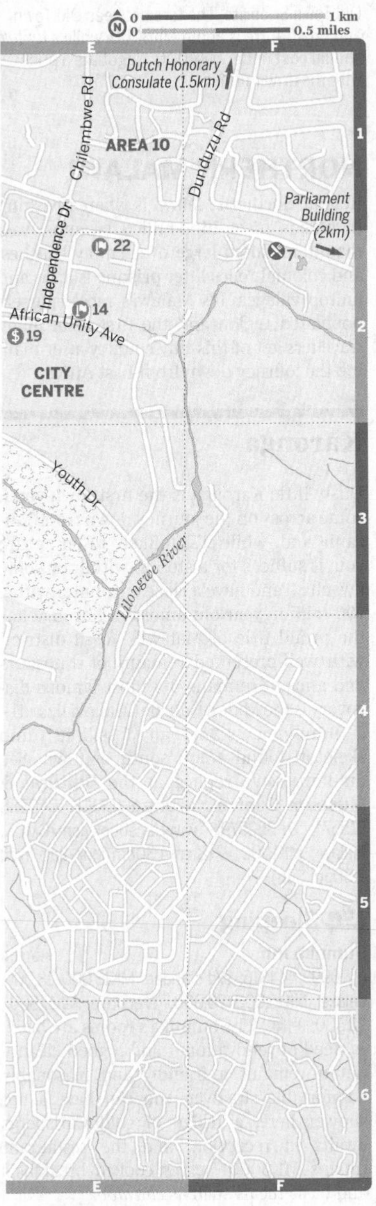


## Lilongwe

**Sights**

1 Kamuzu Mausoleum ........ D1
2 Lilongwe Wildlife Centre ........ D3

**Sleeping**

3 Korea Garden Lodge ........ B5
4 Mabuya Camp ........ A6
5 St Peter's Guesthouse ........ B5

**Eating**

6 Ad Lib ........ B5
7 Ama Khofi ........ F2
Buchanan's Grill ........ (see 7)
Koko Bean ........ (see 2)
Korea Garden Restaurant ........ (see 3)
8 Land & Lake Cafe ........ A4

**Drinking & Nightlife**

Chameleon Bar ........ (see 7)
9 Living Room ........ C3

**Shopping**

10 African Habitat ........ B4
11 Craft Market ........ B5

**Information**

12 British High Commission ........ D1
13 German Embassy ........ D2
14 Irish Embassy ........ E2
15 Michiru Pharmacy ........ B5
16 Money Bureau ........ A3
17 Mozambican High Commission ........ D2
18 South African High Commission ........ D2
19 Standard Bank ........ E2
20 US Embassy ........ D2
21 Zambian High Commission ........ D1
22 Zimbabwean Embassy ........ E2

**Transport**

23 AXA Coach Terminal ........ A3
24 Buses to Dar es Salaam & Lusaka ........ C5
25 Intercape ........ B4
Local Minibus Rank ........ (see 26)
Long Distance Minibuses ........ (see 26)
26 Main Bus Station ........ C5

### MEDICAL SERVICES

**Daeyang Luke Hospital** (☎01-711395; www.hospital.daeyangmission.org; Area 27; ⌚casualty 24hr, inpatients 8am-4.30pm Mon-Fri) Recommended private hospital. Off the M1 en route to the airport.

**Likuni Mission Hospital** (☎01-766574, 01-766602; Likuni) This hospital, 7km southwest of Old Town, has public wards, private rooms and some expat European doctors on staff.

**Michiru Pharmacy** (☎01-754294; Nico Shopping Centre, Kamuzu Procession Rd; ⌚8am-5pm Mon-Fri, to 1pm Sat & Sun) Sells antibiotics and malaria pills as well as the usual offerings.

### MONEY

**Money Bureau** (☎01-750875; www.fdh.co.mw; Crossroads Complex, Kamuzu Procession Rd; ⌚8am-4pm Mon-Fri, to noon Sat) Has good rates.

**Standard Bank** (African Unity Ave, City Centre; ⏲8am-3pm Mon-Fri, 9-11am Sat) You can change money here and get a cash advance on your Visa card. There's a 24-hour ATM that accepts Visa, MasterCard, Cirrus and Maestro.

## Getting There & Away

**AXA** (☎01-820100; www.axacoach.com; City Mall) buses run daily from outside its office to Blantyre (MK11,300, four hours), leaving at 7am, noon and 4.30pm. Buses leave around noon for Mzuzu (MK7000, four hours).

Destinations from the **main bus station** (Malangalanga Rd, Area 2) include Mzuzu (MK4000, five hours), Blantyre (MK3500, four hours), Kasungu (MK2500, two hours), Nkhata Bay (MK4000, five hours) and Dedza (MK2000, one hour).

Long-distance minibuses depart from the main bus station area to nearby destinations such as Zomba (MK5000, four to five hours), Dedza (MK2000, 45 minutes to one hour), the Zambian border at Mchinji (MK2500, two hours), Mangochi (MK5000, 4½ hours), Limbe (for Blantyre; MK4000, three to four hours) and Nkhotakota (MK4000, three hours).

**Intercape** (☎0999 403398; www.intercape.co.za; Kamuzu Procession Rd; ⏲ticket office 5am-5pm Mon-Fri, to 2pm Sat, to 11am Sun) has modern buses to Johannesburg (South Africa; MK36,000 to MK43,000, 36 hours), leaving daily from outside its office at 6am and departing Jo'burg daily at 8.30am. Intercape also operates a bus to Mzuzu (MK15,000 to MK23,000, five hours, daily except Friday and Sunday), which waits for the service from Jo'burg to arrive and leaves between 9pm and 11pm.

**Kob's Coach Services** (☎in Zambia +260 977 794073) leaves for Lusaka (Zambia) on Wednesday and Saturday at 5.30am, arriving at 5pm (MK20,000). **Taqwa Coach Company** (☎in Zambia +260 977 114825) departs five evenings a week to Dar es Salaam (Tanzania; US$60, 30 hours) via Mzuzu, with onward connections to Nairobi (Kenya). In both cases, get there a good hour early for a decent seat. Both the Lusaka and the Dar es Salaam services (Devil St) leave from Devil St, adjacent to the main bus station.

## Getting Around

The most useful local minibus route for visitors is between Old Town and City Centre. The journey should cost around MK200; you can cross the whole city for MK300.

You can also catch minibuses to Old Town and City Centre from the main bus-station area.

The best places to find taxis are at the big hotels and major shopping malls, including outside Old Town Shoprite. The fare between Old Town and City Centre is about MK6000, while a *tuktuk* should cost under MK4000. Negotiate a price with the driver first.

# NORTHERN MALAWI

Remote northern Malawi is where ravishing highlands meet hippo-filled swamps, vast mountains loom large over empty beaches, and colonial relics litter pristine islands and hilltop villages. It's Malawi's most sparsely populated region and the first taste many travellers get of this tiny country after making the journey down from East Africa.

## Karonga

POP 43,000

Dusty little Karonga is the first town you'll come across on the journey down from Tanzania and, while it's unlikely to enrapture you, it suffices for a stop to withdraw some kwacha – and have a close encounter with a 100-million-year-old dinosaur. Karonga has the proud title of Malawi's 'fossil district', with well-preserved remains of dinosaurs and ancient humans. Its most famous discovery is the Malawisaurus (Malawi lizard) – a 9.1m-long, 4.3m-high fossilised dino skeleton found 45km south of town. See an impressive replica at the **Cultural & Museum Centre Karonga** (CMCK; ☎0888 515574, 01-362579; www.facebook.com/CMCK.Malawi; MK1000; ⏲8am-4.30pm Mon-Sat, from 2.30pm Sun).

### Sleeping

**Sumuka Inn** HOTEL $

(☎0999 444816; s/d standard MK13,000/18,000, deluxe MK15,000/20,000, executive MK17,500/22,500; P ❄) The Sumuka's rooms are badly in need of renovation – and a good clean – but it remains a friendly and reasonably comfortable stopover. You can have a hot shower here, a fridge of cold Carlsbergs awaits in reception, and the restaurant (mains MK3000) serves cooked breakfasts and basic meals such as *chambo*.

**Safari Lodge** HOTEL $

(☎01-362340; incl breakfast s/d standard MK5500/6500, executive MK9000/11,500) This fallback option has spacious but basic rooms with tiled floors and a bar where drinkers watch the football or sit outside amid the chirping crickets.

## Getting There & Away

AXA deluxe buses leave Karonga at noon daily for Blantyre (MK12,000, 18 hours), stopping in Mzuzu (MK4000, four hours) and heading down the lakeshore via Salima (MK11,150, 11 hours). Change in Mzuzu for Lilongwe. In the opposite direction, buses leave Blantyre around 5pm and reach Karonga around 11am the following day.

# Livingstonia

POP 7000 / ☎01

Built by Scottish missionaries, Livingstonia feels sanctified, special and other-worldly, with its tree-lined main street graced by crumbling colonial relics. But for the stunning mountain views, there's not much to do in town other than visit the museum, church and sundry historical curios. Experiencing this piece of mountaintop history, and staying at one of the nearby permaculture farms, will be a magical, peaceful chapter in your Malawian journey.

## Sights

**Stone House Museum** MUSEUM
(☎01-368223; MK700; ⏲7.30am-4.30pm) The fascinating museum in Stone House (once the home of Livingstonia founder Dr Robert Laws, and now a national monument) tells the story of the European arrival in Malawi and the first missionaries. Here you can read Dr Laws' letters and books, including the old laws of Nyasaland, and peruse black-and-white photos of early missionary life in Livingstonia.

**Manchewe Falls** WATERFALL
This impressive waterfall thunders 125m into the valley below, about 4km from Livingstonia (towards the lake). Follow a small path behind the falls and there's a cave where, so the story goes, local people once hid from slave traders.

**Livingstonia Church** CHURCH
(☎01-311344; admission by donation) Dating from 1894, this mission church has a beautiful stained-glass window featuring David Livingstone with his sextant, his medicine chest and his two companions, with Lake Malawi in the background. You can climb the tower for a bird's-eye view of Livingstonia.

## Sleeping

★ **Lukwe EcoCamp** LODGE, CAMPGROUND $
(☎0999 434985; www.lukwe.com; camping US$6, s/d with shared bathroom US$15/25; Ⓟ📶) This serene, tasteful permaculture camp is about being part of the environment and the community: helping local farmers and being completely self-sufficient. Comfortable glass-fronted chalets and thatch-covered tents are set in leafy terraced gardens, with private balconies and shared solar- and donkey-boiler-heated showers, composting loos and self-catering kitchen. See the mountain drop into infinity and spy Manchewe Falls from the swing chair.

★ **Mushroom Farm** LODGE, CAMPGROUND $
(☎0999 652485; www.themushroomfarmmalawi.com; camping US$5, dm US$8-10, s/d US$30/40, with shared bathroom from US$15/25; Ⓟ📶) Perched on the edge of the Livingstonia escarpment (aka an abyss!), this permaculture ecolodge and campsite is worth the arduous journey for the warm welcome and views that will have you manually closing your jaw. The safari tents, hardwood A-frames and dorms provide charmingly rustic accommodation; better still is the en suite cob house with cliffside shower.

**Hakuna Matata** HOSTEL, CAMPGROUND $
(☎0991 092027, 0882 297779; www.facebook.com/chitimbahakunamatata; camping/dm MK3500/4900, s/d with shared bathroom MK7000/11,000; Ⓟ📶) At the foot of the mountain in lakeside Chitimba, this beach camp is an excellent launch pad for tackling the ascent to Livingstonia. The whitewashed rooms have mozzie nets and fans, and one room has a private bathroom. Chat to the personable South African host, Willie, in the refreshingly shaded cafe (mains MK2000, pre-ordered dinner MK4000).

## Getting There & Away

From the main north–south road between Karonga and Mzuzu, the road to Livingstonia (known as the Gorode) turns off at Chitimba, forcing its way up the escarpment. This twisting, ulcerated road is a test for the most steely drivers: a white-knuckle experience of 20 switchbacks and hairpins, with a boulder-strewn, mainly unpaved surface – at times single track – with the mountain abysmally close to you. Don't attempt this in anything but a 4WD and *never* in rain.

# Nyika National Park

It's a rough drive to these beguiling highlands, but Malawi's oldest reserve is worth every bump. Towering over 2000m above sea level, the 3200-sq-km **Nyika National Park** (person/car US$10/3; ⏰6am-6pm) is easily one of the country's most magical experiences. Turning burnt amber in the afternoon sun, the highland grass flickers with the stripes of zebras and is punctuated by glittering boulders that look like set dressing from a *Star Trek* movie.

## Activities

Thanks to the top guides of **Central African Wilderness Safaris** (☎01-771393, 0881 085177; www.cawsmw.com), your chances of seeing animals on a morning wildlife drive (US$35 per person) or walk (US$20 per person) are extremely high.

The most exciting wildlife drives, however, are by night, with decent chances of your guide scoping out leopards. The current population of around 100 is one of the region's densest. Wildlife viewing is good year-round, although in July and August the cold weather means the animals move off the plateau to lower areas. Birdwatching is particularly good between October and April, when migratory birds are on the move.

## Sleeping

Self-caterers should stock up in either Mzuzu or Rumphi.

**Chelinda Campground** CAMPGROUND $
(☎01-771393, 0881 085177; www.cawsmw.com; camping US$15; P) Set in a secluded site with vistas of the plateau's rolling hills, this camp has permanent security, clean toilets, hot showers, endless firewood and shelters for cooking and eating. There's a small shop at Chelinda for national-park staff, but provisions are often basic and supplies sporadic.

★**Chelinda Lodge** LODGE $$$
(☎0881 085177, 01-771393; www.cawsmw.com; s/d all-inclusive US$450/700; P@) Sitting on a hillside in a clearing of pine trees, upmarket Chelinda is a traveller's dream. The main building crackles with fires at every turn, complemented by inviting couches, walls adorned with lush wildlife photography, pillars hung with woodcarvings, glittering chandeliers and high beams. Rates include park entrance fees and wildlife-watching activities.

★**Chelinda Camp** CHALET $$$
(☎01-771393, 0881 085177; www.cawsmw.com; s/d all-inclusive US$355/530; P) Nestled into the lee of a valley beside a small lake, this Central African Wilderness Safaris lodge is insanely picturesque. Its bungalows have an unfussy '70s aspect to them and are ideal for families, with small kitchen, cosy sitting room and stone fireplace. Rates include park entrance fees and wildlife-watching activities.

## Getting There & Around

The main Thazima Gate (pronounced and sometimes spelled Tazima) is 55km northwest of Rumphi – about two hours' drive. Once inside the park, it's another 60km, two-hour drive to Chelinda. Especially from Rumphi to Thazima Gate, the corrugated road is appallingly bumpy; call one of the accommodation options to check on its condition in the wet season. Petrol is available at Chelinda but in limited supply, so fill up before you enter the park.

# Vwaza Marsh Wildlife Reserve

This compact, 1000-sq-km **reserve** (☎0884 203964, 0991 912775; moyoleonard52@gmail.com; person/vehicle US$10/3; ⏰6am-6pm) is home to plentiful wildlife (although it currently suffers from poor management), and ranges from large, flat areas of mopane (woodland) to open swamp and wetlands. The Luwewe River runs through the park, draining the marshland, and joins the South Rukuru River (the reserve's southern border), which flows into Lake Kazuni.

**Lake Kazuni Safari Camp** (☎0991 912775, 0884 203964; moyoleonard52@gmail.com; camping per site MK7500, r MK10,000; P) offers basic accommodation, and *matolas* (pick-ups) run here from Rumphi, but visiting on a tour with the likes of Nkhata Bay Safaris (p818) is the easiest option.

The best time to visit is the dry season; just after the rainy season, the grass is high and you might go away without seeing anything.

If you're travelling by public transport, first get to Rumphi (reached from Mzuzu by minibus for MK2000). From Rumphi, *matolas* travel to/from the Kazuni area and you should be able to get a lift to the main gate for around MK1500. Minibuses also ply this route to/from Kazuni village, and can drop you by the bridge, 1km east of the park gate and camp.

By car, head west from Rumphi. Turn left after 10km (Vwaza Marsh Wildlife Reserve is signposted) and continue for about 20km. Where the road swings left over the bridge, go straight on to reach the park gate and camp after 1km.

# Mzuzu

POP 239,000

Dusty, sprawling Mzuzu is Malawi's third-largest city, northern Malawi's principal town and the region's transport hub. Travellers heading along the M1 – across to Nkhata Bay, Nyika or Viphya, or up to Tanzania – are likely to spend a night or two here. With some good accommodation options, Mzuzu is an appealingly authentic and laid-back spot to experience everyday Malawian life.

Mzuzu has banks, shops, a post office, supermarkets, pharmacies, petrol stations and other facilities, which are especially useful if you've entered Malawi from the north.

## Sleeping

**★Macondo Camp** GUESTHOUSE $

(☎0991 792311; www.macondocamp.com; Chimaliro 4; camping MK3000, dm MK5000, s/d with shared bathroom MK14,000/17,000, apt MK35,000; P 📶) Run by Italian couple and serial overlanders Luca and Cecilia, Macondo has cute rooms in the main house, tented chalets with wooden decks overlooking the lawn and banana trees, and an annexe with dorm beds.

**Umunthu Camp** LODGE $

(☎0992 417916, 0881 980019; umunthucamp@gmail.com; dm/r MK5000/12,000; P 📶) The brainchild of South African couple Andries and Farzana, Umunthu has coolly decorated, sparsely furnished rooms and a four-bed dorm with adjoining bathroom. The bar-restaurant (mains MK5000; restaurant open 7am to 9pm Tuesday to Sunday) draws on the resident kitchen garden, serving dishes including pizza, pasta, burgers and steaks. It's behind Shoprite supermarket, signposted from the main drag.

**Sunbird Mzuzu** HOTEL $$$

(☎01-332622; www.sunbirdmalawi.com; Kabunduli Viphya Dr; s/d/ste incl breakfast from US$120/150/240; P ❄ @ 📶) Easily the city's plushest digs, this large hotel in imposing grounds has huge rooms with deep-pile carpet, flat-screen DSTV (a digital satellite TV service in sub-Saharan Africa), fridge and views of Mzuzu's golf course. As you'd expect from Sunbird, the service is friendly and efficient and the place is of an international standard.

## Eating

**Soul Kitchen** MALAWIAN $

(☎0884 957150; St Denis Rd; mains MK2000; ⏲7am-10pm Mon-Sat) Watch Mzuzu go by on Soul Kitchen's shaded stoep with a barbecue smoking away at one end and a view of the city's only traffic light. Barbecued chicken, *chambo*, omelette and T-bone steak are on the menu.

**★Macondo Camp** ITALIAN $$

(☎0991 792311; mains MK4500; ⏲7am-9pm; P 📶) This Italian restaurant offers treats such as homemade pasta made daily, Parmesan flown from Italy and monthly live music on the stoep. Dishes include pizza, steaks, spring rolls and the ever-popular ravioli with blue cheese, which can be accompanied by a good selection of Italian and South African wines. It's at the namesake guesthouse northeast of central Mzuzu.

## Getting There & Away

AXA buses leave at 5pm for Blantyre (MK8000, 13 hours) via the lakeshore, and at 7am for Karonga (MK4000, four hours). AXA departs at 7pm for Lilongwe (MK7000, four hours).

Minibuses and shared taxis go to Nkhata Bay (MK1500, one to two hours), Karonga (MK4000, four hours), Chitimba (MK2000, 2½ hours), Rumphi (MK2000, one hour) and the Tanzanian border (MK5200, five hours).

# Nkhata Bay

POP 15,000

Nkhata Bay has an almost Caribbean feel, with its fishing boats buzzing across the green bay, market stalls hawking barbecued fish, and reggae filling the languorous afternoons. There are also loads of activities to enjoy before you hammock flop, be it snorkelling, diving, fish-eagle feeding, kayaking or forest walks.

## Sights & Activities

Accommodation and **Monkey Business** (☎0999 437247; http://monkeybusinesskayaking.blogspot.co.za; Butterfly Space) offer enjoyable boat or kayak trips to feed fish eagles out on the lake. Cliff jumping and snorkelling trips are also popular.

**Chikale Beach** BEACH

On the southern side of Nkhata Bay, Chikale Beach is a popular spot for swimming and lazing on the sand, especially at weekends. After church on Sunday, the locals set up a speaker stack and enjoy a few beers.

**Aqua Africa** DIVING

(☎0999 921418; www.aquaafrica.co.uk) This dependable British-run outfit offers dives for certified divers (from US$50) and numerous courses, including the three- to four-day PADI Open Water course (US$380 including all materials). Colourful cichlid fish, the kind you've probably seen in a dentist's aquarium, swim throughout the lake, but more spectacular are the schools of dolphinfish that are drawn to your torch (flashlight) on night dives.

## Tours

**Nkhata Bay Safaris** TOURS

(☎0999 265064; www.nkhatabaysafaris.com; 4-day tour for 2 people camping/chalets US$655/755) Run by a Malawian team headed by Davie, this tour operator offers four- to 10-day trips to Vwaza Marsh Wildlife Reserve, Nyika National Park, Livingstonia and further afield. It can help with local activities, transport and accommodation bookings, and has recently introduced day and overnight wildlife-watching tours to Vwaza and overnight safaris to Nkhotakota Wildlife Reserve (US$275 per person).

## Sleeping

★**Mayoka Village** LODGE $

(☎0999 268595, 01-994025; www.mayokavillagebeachlodge.com; camping/dm US$5/12, chalet s/d US$30/45, f US$50-70, s/d/tr/q with shared bathroom US$20/35/45/60; P 📶) Cleverly shaped around the rocky topography of a cliff, boutique-style Mayoka cascades down in a series of beautiful bamboo-and-stone chalets. There are myriad romantic nooks for taking in the lake below or grabbing some rays on sun loungers. The waterfront bar-restaurant (mains MK2500) is a beach hideaway serving cocktails and dishes from wraps and burgers to Malawian red-bean stew.

**Butterfly Space** HOSTEL $

(☎0999 265065, 0999 156335; www.butterfly-space.com; camping/dm MK1500/3000, chalets per person MK8000, with shared bathroom MK7000; P @ 📶) Run by Alice and Josie, inspiring, colourful and socially committed Butterfly is a rare backpackers oasis. There's a *palapa*-style lounge or spacious beachfront bar to chill in, a private beach, an internet cafe, a media centre, a self-catering block and a restaurant serving authentic Tongan cuisine (The Tonga are one of Malawi's ethnic groups), as well as sandwiches, chapattis, pasta and burgers (mains MK2000, pre-ordered dinner MK3000).

**Aqua Africa** GUESTHOUSE $$

(☎0999 921418; www.aquaafrica.co.uk; standard s/tw US$30/40, deluxe s/d incl breakfast US$60/80; ⏰restaurant 7am-6pm; P ❄ 📶) With whitewashed rooms featuring polished-stone floors, step-in mozzie nets and blue curtains opening onto balconies overlooking the bay, this dive school's four rooms often host its students. The **Dive Deck Cafe** (mains MK2500; ⏰7am-6pm), complete with wicker loungers and viewing deck, has an excellent menu ranging from full breakfasts to nachos, Cajun chicken, fish burgers and peanut-coated chicken strips.

## Eating & Drinking

**Crest View** MALAWIAN $

(☎0881174804; mains MK2000; ⏰6am-9pm; 🖉) Thrifty travellers appreciate this local hangout with football on the TV and a good view of the action happening on the main street. *Nsima* (a filling porridge-like dish made from white maize flour and water) with beans, omelettes and other local favourites are on the menu.

**One Love** CAFE $

(☎0996 955164; www.facebook.com/onelovehandmadeart) At One Love, with an unbeatable view of the bay, Kelvin the Rasta serves cold beers and simple dishes such as chapattis, *nsima* and beans (mains MK1300). He also sells his woodcarvings and drums. Hours are variable, so call ahead before making a special trip.

★**Kaya Papaya** THAI $$

(☎0993 688884, 0888 576489; mains MK4000; ⏰11am-10pm, last food orders 8.45pm; 📶 🖉) Close to the harbour, with a big upstairs balcony overlooking the main street, Kaya Papaya has an appealing Afro-Asian-fusion chic that's matched by a menu of zesty salads, pizza and Thai fare such as green curry, chicken satay and stir-fries. If you're still hungry, try a banana pancake.

## Information

Travellers have been mugged when walking outside the town centre (in particular to and from Chikale Beach and the surrounding lodges at night), so take extra care when walking this route as it's unlit and can be quite deserted.

## Getting There & Away

Most transport leaves from the bus stop in the market area. AXA (p833) runs to Karonga via Mzuzu, leaving around 5.30am, and down the lake to Blantyre via Salima, departing around 6.30pm. Minibuses run to Nkhotakota (MK1500, five hours), Chintheche (MK950, one hour) and Mzuzu (MK1000, 1½ hours). There are also regularly departing and less cramped shared taxis (MK1500 to Mzuzu) and a daily bus to Salima (MK8000, nine hours, 5am), which respectively leave from the main bus stop and from outside the Admarc maize store.

To reach Lilongwe the quickest option is to head down the lake to Salima and change; alternatively, travel inland to Mzuzu and pick up a service going south.

# Likoma Island

Blissful Likoma Island – situated on the Mozambican side of Lake Malawi but part of Malawi – measures 17 sq km and is home to around 9000 people.

Likoma's flat and sandy south is littered with baobabs and offers an uninterrupted panoramic view of Mozambique's wild coast. The island's main drawcards are its abundance of pristine beaches and the attendant snorkelling, diving and water sports, but there's a healthy dose of other activities, both cultural and physical, to fill several days here.

## Sights & Activities

Swimming is a must on Likoma and is best on the long stretches of beach in the south. The tropical-fish population has been unaffected by the mainland's overfishing, and the snorkelling is excellent. Snorkels are on hand at the island's accommodation options, which can arrange scuba diving and PADI courses too.

**Cathedral of St Peter** CHURCH

(Chipyela; dawn-dusk) Likoma's huge Anglican cathedral (1911), said to be the same size as Winchester Cathedral, should not be missed. Its stained-glass windows, crumbling masonry and sheer scale are testament to the zeal of its missionary creators' religious conviction.

## Sleeping

**★Mango Drift** HOSTEL $$

(0999 746122; www.mangodrift.com; camping US$6, tent rental US$1, dm US$8, s/d US$60/70, with shared bathroom US$25/30; @ ) Far from backpacker hardship, this affordable island idyll is one of Malawi's most luxurious hostels. Its stone chalets are the closest you'll come to boutique this side of US$100, with hibiscus petals scattered on snow-white linen, wicker furniture, sundown verandas and loungers on the sand. The shared toilets and shower block are no less immaculate.

**★Kaya Mawa** BOUTIQUE HOTEL $$$

(0999 318360; www.kayamawa.com; full board per person from US$415; @ ) Remember Scaramanga's pad in *The Man with the Golden Gun*? Kaya Mawa, set on an amber-coloured beach lapped by turquoise water, is the ultimate location to live out your inner Bond. Its cliffside chalets, cleverly moulded around the landscape, are so beautiful you'll never want to leave.

## Getting There & Away

Ulendo Airlink (www.flyulendo.com) flies daily to Likoma from Lilongwe (adult/child one way US$295/211), with further scheduled departures from several other locations. The *Ilala* ferry stops at Likoma Island twice a week, usually for three to four hours, so even if you're heading elsewhere, you might be able to nip ashore to have a quick look at the cathedral. Check with the captain before you leave the boat.

# CENTRAL MALAWI

This small corner of Malawi is chiefly famed for its dazzling white beaches, like the backpacker magnet Cape Maclear, and for its desert islands like Mumbo and Domwe – both reached by sea kayak or boat. Nkhotakota Wildlife Reserve, its wildlife stocks increased by a major elephant translocation, has fine lodges and good access from the coast. North of here is the Viphya Plateau, a haunting wilderness of mountains, grasslands and mist-shrouded pines. For cultural appeal, meanwhile, you can't beat the Kungoni complex and mission buildings in Mua.

WORTH A TRIP

### MUA

Sitting on a hill aglow with flame trees, Mua is a rare treat; its red-brick terracotta-tiled mission seems transplanted from Tuscany, its **church** strangely beautiful. The Roman Catholic mission was established in 1902, and a visit to its sepia-tinted structures is complemented by the excellent **Kungoni Centre of Culture & Art** (☎0999 035870, 01-262706; www.kungoni.org; ⏰7.30am-4pm Mon-Sat). With the **Chamare Museum** offering gripping insights into the culture of Malawi's various ethnic groups, plus the nearby **Kungoni Art Gallery**, Mua could be an unexpected highlight of your trip. For accommodation, try **Namalikhate Lodge** (☎01-262706; www.kungoni.org; camping MK5000, s/d MK17,000/22,000; ⏰restaurant 7.30am-6.30pm; P).

Mua is about 50km south of Salima on the road to Balaka. The Mua Mission is about 2km from the main road and is signposted (the Mua Mission Hospital sign is clearest). The road uphill is quite rough, so call ahead to check on its current condition if you're driving a 2WD.

## Monkey Bay

Hidden behind the Cape Maclear headland, sultry Monkey Bay is enchantingly slow: languid locals, a petrol station and a few shops are all that you'll find here. It's backpacker country, with two beachfront traveller joints, and the harbour is the launch pad for the *Ilala* ferry's long journey up the lake. Fish, snorkel or hammock flop – whatever you do, you may need to recalibrate your calendar.

The main reason to hang around in Monkey Bay is **Mufasa Ecolodge** (☎0993 080057; www.facebook.com/MufasaRusticLodgeBackpackers; camping/tent hire/dm MK3000/3500/5000, s/d with shared bathroom MK8000/12,000; P ), a traveller's magnet with a sheltered beach bookended by smooth boulders and campsites on the sand or mountainside. Rooms are basic bamboo affairs, but the beach bar is appealing, with lounging cushions, wicker swing chairs and a relaxed vibe. Come dusk expect communal fires, drum circles and backpacker bonhomie.

Another option, **Norman Carr Cottage** (☎0999 207506, 0888 355357; www.normancarrcottage.com; s/d all-inclusive from US$145/240; P ) is a good balance of simplicity, character and luxury. The beach retreat's six suites and two-bedroom family cottage have massive handmade king-size beds, small living areas and open-air garden showers. The beach and gardens are full of hanging chairs and sunbeds and there's a beachside pool and whirlpool – perfect for a Malawian gin and tonic.

From Lilongwe, buses run to Monkey Bay, usually via Salima and the southern lakeshore (MK3000, four hours). It's probably quicker to catch a minibus to Salima (MK1700, two hours), where you should find a minibus or *matola* going direct to Monkey Bay. From Blantyre, it's easiest to reach Monkey Bay by minibus with a change in Mangochi (total MK6000, five to six hours).

## Cape Maclear

A long stretch of powder-fine sand bookended by mountains and lapped by dazzling water, Cape Maclear deserves all the hype thrown at it. By day the bay glitters a royal blue, studded with nearby islands and puttering, crayon-coloured fishing boats. Especially in the early morning, the tideline is a hub of local life, with women washing clothes and their children, while fisherfolk spread out vermilion nets to dry and tourists emerge onto the verandas of nearby beach cabanas. Come afternoon the sleepy lanes ring with music from backstreet gospel choirs, while the evenings fill with reggae from the tinny sound system of that bar under the baobab. Much of the surrounding area is part of **Lake Malawi National Park** (person/car US$10/3), a Unesco World Heritage Site.

### Activities

There's a range of hikes and walks in the hills. Entry into the national park is US$10, which you can pay at the **Lake Malawi National Park Headquarters** (Otter Point Rd; ⏰7.30am-noon & 1-5pm Mon-Sat, 10am-noon & 1-4pm Sun) or the nearby gate, and the rate for a Cape Maclear Tour Guides Association guide is US$15 per person. It's better to hire a guide.

Diving is possible with **Cape Maclear Scuba** (☎0999 952488; www.capemaclearscuba.com; Thumbi View Lodge; casual dive US$50, PADI Open Water course US$400) and kayaking with **Kayak Africa** (☎0999 942661, in South Africa +27 21-783 1955; www.kayakafrica.co.za).

## Sleeping

**★Funky Cichlid** HOSTEL $
(☎0999 969076; www.thefunkycichlid.com; camping/dm US$5/10, s/d with shared bathroom from US$20/30; P 📶) With its cheeky logo of a cichlid clad in sunglasses, this backpacker beach resort is Cape Mac's top spot to chill by day and party by night. Cool whitewashed rooms and six- to eight-bed dorms are decorated with funky murals, with well-maintained shared ablutions and packages available including breakfast, full or half board, drinks and water sports.

**Gecko Lounge** LODGE $$
(☎0999 787322; www.geckolounge.net; dm/r/chalet q US$15/75/90; P 📶) A firm family favourite and with good reason, Gecko's self-catering chalets are right on the manicured beach. Each has a double and a bunk bed, fridge, fan, tile floor, mozzie nets and private veranda, as well as plenty of hammocks and swing chairs outside. Equally pleasant are the subdivided eight-bed dorm and the double and family rooms, replete with African decor.

**★Pumulani** LODGE $$$
(☎01-794491; www.robinpopesafaris.net; per person all-inclusive US$355-470; ⏰Apr-Jan; P 🚭 ❄ @ 📶 🏊) Pumulani is a stylish lakeside lodge with nature-inspired rooms – think grass roofs and huge windows to let in the light, views of the surrounding forest and lake, and massive wooden terraces from which to gaze at the clear waters and sweep of golden sand below. The food, served in the open bar-restaurant, is equally amazing.

**★Mumbo Island Camp** CAMPGROUND $$$
(☎0999 942661, in South Africa +27 21-783 1955; www.kayakafrica.co.za; per person all-inclusive US$260) Situated exclusively on Mumbo Island, this eco-boutique camp has chalets and a walk-in tent on wooden platforms (with en suite bucket showers and eco-loos), tucked beneath trees and above rocks, with spacious decks and astounding views. Accommodation rates include boat transfers, full board, kayaking, snorkelling and guided hikes.

**★Domwe Island Adventure Camp** CAMPGROUND $$$
(☎0999 942661, in South Africa +27 21-783 1955; www.kayakafrica.co.za; camping US$30, safari tents per person US$60) 🌿 Domwe is the smaller and more rustic of Kayak Africa's two neighbouring island lodges, run on solar power and romantically lit by paraffin lamps. It's self-catering, with furnished safari tents, kitchen, shared eco-showers and composting toilets. It has a bar and a beautiful staggered dining area, open to the elements and set among boulders. Food can be provided on request.

## Eating

**Thumbi View Lodge** CAFE $
(☎0997 463054, 0998 599005; www.thumbiviewlodge.com; mains MK3000; ⏰7am-8pm) On the lane opposite Thumbi View's gate, this cafe



WORTH A TRIP

### NKHOTAKOTA WILDLIFE RESERVE

West of the main lakeshore road lies **Nkhotakota Wildlife Reserve** (☎0999 521741; www.african-parks.org; person/car US$10/3; ⏰6am-6pm), comprising 1800 sq km of rough, inhospitable terrain inhabited by animals from elephants to buffaloes.

The best way to experience the bush is by staying at one of the reserve's two excellent lodges and walking with a guide, or by kayaking down the Bua River from Tongole, your heart in your mouth as crocs upstream slip soundlessly into the murk to come and take a closer look.

**Tongole Wilderness Lodge** (☎01-209194, 0999 055778; www.tongole.com; per person with full board US$435; P 📶 🏊) 🌿 and **Bua River Lodge** (☎0995 476887, 0885 181834; www.buariverlodge.com; camping US$10, with full board island/riverside tents US$150/120, hillside r US$95; P) 🌿 are excellent places to stay.

The turn-off to the reserve's main gate is 10km north of Nkhotakota town. Public transport along the coast road north of Nkhotakota can you drop you at this turn-off, from where the gate is 10km away along a dirt track.

serves light meals and snacks such as vegetable curry, spaghetti bolognese, lasagne, fish, burgers and toasted sandwiches. Book by 1pm to join the set dinner, which typically consists of Indian or South African dishes such as slow-cooked oxtail from the owners' homeland, in the main lodge.

**Mphipe Lodge** ITALIAN $
(☎0884 997481; www.andiamotrust.org; mains MK2500; ⏲7am-9pm; P) For a different take on lake fish, Mphipe serves it in pasta dishes. Malawian staples such as *kampango* (catfish) and *nsima* are also on the menu. The lodge funds a children's hospital in Balaka.

### Getting There & Away

By public transport, first get to Monkey Bay, from where a *matola* to Cape Maclear costs MK1000 and a motorbike costs MK1500. The journey takes about an hour and they drop off at the lodges.

# SOUTHERN MALAWI

Southern Malawi is home to the country's commercial capital, Blantyre, and incredibly diverse landscapes. These include mist-shrouded Mt Mulanje, Malawi's highest peak, and the Zomba Plateau, a stunning highland area. Safari lovers can experience luxury and adventure combined in two of the country's best wildlife reserves: Liwonde and Majete, the country's only park with the Big Five (lions, leopards, buffaloes, elephants and rhinos).

## Liwonde

Straddling the Shire River, Liwonde is the main gateway to Liwonde National Park. The river divides the town in two, with the market and most services found on the eastern side, along with the turn-off to the park. If you're unable to stay in the park, it's possible to use Liwonde as a base for a short safari by road or river.

**Hippo View Lodge** (☎01-542116/8; www.hippoviewlodge.com; incl breakfast s/d superior MK35,000/55,500, deluxe MK48,000/65,500; P❄📶🏊), a 111-room behemoth, does its best to banish a lingering feeling of faded grandeur, with rooms in blocks overlooking riverside gardens shaded by palms and a huge baobab. Superior rooms have tiled floor, fridge, phone and plasma-screen TV; it's worth upgrading to the more attractive and modern deluxe rooms, with larger bathrooms and tea and coffee.

Regular minibuses run along the main road through town to/from Zomba (MK1000, 45 minutes), Limbe (for Blantyre; MK2500, three hours), Mangochi (MK2500, two hours) and the Mozambique border at Nayuchi (MK3000, 2½ to three hours).

There are two petrol stations east of the river en route to the Liwonde National Park turn-off.

## Liwonde National Park

Set in 584 sq km of dry savannah and forest alongside the serene Shire River, the relatively small **Liwonde National Park** (www.african-parks.org; person/car US$20/4; ⏲6am-6pm) is one of Africa's best spots for river-based wildlife watching, with around 550 elephants, 2000 hippos and innumerable crocs. Animals including black rhinos, buffaloes and sable antelopes are found on dry land, where the terrain rolls from palm-studded flood plains and riverine forests to mopane and acacia woodlands interspersed with candelabra succulents.

The park's excellent lodges offer a fantastic range of wildlife-spotting drives, walks and boat trips.

### Activities

**Njobvu Cultural Village** CULTURAL
(☎0888 623530; www.njobvuvillage.org; r incl breakfast per person US$16, all-inclusive US$50) Near Liwonde National Park's Makanga Gate, Njobvu offers visitors a rare opportunity to stay in a traditional Malawian village, sleeping in mudbrick huts (with or without a mattress – your choice!). During the day you are invited to take part in the villagers' daily lives, visiting traditional doctors and the village school, and eating local food such as the porridge-like *nsima*.

### Sleeping

The park has excellent midrange and top-end lodges. They remain open all year – you can reach them by boat even if rain closes some of the park tracks. (Be warned, though: the rains send the elephants further inland, making them harder to spot.) You can also stay at Njobvu Cultural Village.

★ **Bushman's Baobabs** LODGE, CAMPGROUND $$
(☎0995 453324, 0884 659901; www.bushmans-baobabs.com; camping US$7.50, dm US$15, s US$65-85, d US$90-120, tr/f US$180/240, s/d with shared bathroom US$25/50; P) The former Chinguni Hills Lodge is a fun place to experience a night in the bush and a safari. In an accessible location in the south of the park, Bushman's offers 14-bed dorms, thatched A-frame tents, luxurious en suite tents, en-suite chalets, and campsites with barbecue spots and a self-catering kitchen. Wildlife drives, walks, and boat and canoe trips are offered.

**Liwonde Safari Camp** LODGE, CAMPGROUND $$
(☎0881 813240; www.liwondesafaricamp.com; camping/dm US$10/15, safari tents s/d US$40/60; P) This rustic camp is immersed in the park, with stilted safari tents, dorm and campsite sharing ablutions and a self-catering kitchen. There's a plunge pool, a thatched bar, meals (buffet dinner US$15), and – if you don't spot animals from the viewing decks – wildlife walks (US$5 per person), drives and boat trips (US$25 per person).

★ **Mvuu Camp** LODGE $$$
(☎01-771393, 01-821219; www.cawsmw.com; camping US$15, chalets all-inclusive s/d US$360/520; P@) Run by the excellent Central African Wilderness Safaris, Malawi's premier safari operator, Mvuu sits on the river in the realm of myriad hippos and crocs. The camp comprises a main restaurant building and, nearby, scattered chalets with cosy interiors, step-in mozzie nets, comfy beds, immaculate linen and stone-walled bathrooms.

## Getting There & Around

The main park gate is 6km east of Liwonde town. From the gate to Mvuu Camp is 28km along the park track (closed in the wet season); a 4WD vehicle is recommended for this route. The park lodges offer transfers from Liwonde.

> **LIWONDE RHINO SANCTUARY**
>
> The **rhino sanctuary** (☎01-771393, 01-821219; www.cawsmw.com; US$80) is a fenced-off area within Liwonde National Park, developed for breeding rare black rhinos, and expanded to protect other mammal species from poaching. With a scout from Mvuu Camp or Mvuu Lodge in the park, you can go on a three-hour hike, searching for the rhinos in the 48-sq-km reserve.
>
> In late 2016, 10 black rhinos were living in the enclosure, along with populations of Lichtenstein's hartebeest, Cape buffalo, Burchell's zebra, eland and roan antelope.

# Zomba

POP 147,100

With its chilly elevation and atmospheric old colonial and missionary buildings nestled in the wooded foothills, Zomba is hauntingly special – like a chapter of the British Empire hanging by a tenuous thread. It has the typical chaos of a dusty market town, but the higher you climb towards the Zomba Plateau, the more stunning and pristine the scenery becomes. The capital from 1891 to 1974 of British Central Africa, Nyasaland and, finally, Malawi, it's home to wide, tree-lined streets and an easy charm. This is perhaps Malawi's most appealing city, and a great base for exploring the plateau to the north.

## Tours

**African Heritage** ADVENTURE, CULTURAL
(Luso Lathu Art & Coffee Shop; ☎0999 235823; www.africanheritage.mw; Zomba Gymkhana Club) This craft shop doubles as a tourism hub, offering guided tours, shuttles to the Zomba Plateau (US$10), mountain-bike rental (MK1000 per hour) and a detailed plateau map (MK1000). Half-day tours cover the plateau and historical Zomba, while longer itineraries go further afield to Mt Mulanje, Mua, Lake Chilwa and beyond.

## Sleeping

**Pakachere Backpackers & Creative Centre** HOSTEL $
(☎0994 685934, 0882 858089; www.pakachere.com; camping/tent hire/dm US$5/7/10, r/tr US$40/45, r with shared bathroom US$35; P) This locally run hostel is nicely decorated, and has craftwork for sale and a bar-restaurant opening onto a garden with thatched seating areas. The spacious rooms are worn but clean, with tiled floors and mozzie nets, and there's six-bed dorm and an en-suite 10-bed dorm with secure storage space.

★ **Casa Rossa** GUESTHOUSE, CAMPGROUND $$
(☎0881 366126, 0991 184211; www.casarossamw.com; Mountain Rd 5; incl breakfast camping US$5, r US$50-60, without bathroom US$40; P)

WORTH A TRIP

### ZOMBA PLATEAU

Rising nearly 1800m behind Zomba town, and carpeted in thick stands of pine, the Zomba Plateau is beguilingly pretty. As you ascend the snaking road past wildflowers, stoic locals heaving huge burdens of timber, and roadside strawberry vendors, the place almost feels like alpine France; then a vervet monkey jumps out, a pocket of blue mist envelops your car, and you remember you're in Africa. This gorgeous highland paradise, replete with streams, lakes and tumbling waterfalls, is home to monkeys, bushbucks, and birds including mountain wagtails and Bertram's weavers.

Named after its ox-blood-coloured overlooking town, this Italian-owned guesthouse offers hillside tranquillity and the best **restaurant** (mains MK3100-8100; 9am-9pm Tue-Sun, residents only Mon; P) around. Rooms in the old colonial house are simple but comfortable and the campsites in the leafy garden have electricity, fireplace and two barbecues.

**★Annie's Lodge** LODGE **$$**
(01-951636, 01-527002; www.annieslodge.com; Livingstone Rd; incl breakfast s US$40-70, d US$50-80; P) Set in the foothills of the Zomba Plateau, Annie's has a bar-restaurant with an appealing terrace for a sundowner, and black-and-white-brick chalets with green tin roofs, engulfed in palm trees and flowers. The 40-plus rooms are carpeted, clean and welcoming, with DSTV, bathroom and fan or air-con.

### Getting There & Away

Zomba is on a main route between Lilongwe and Blantyre. The bus station is in the town centre, off Namiwawa Rd. Minibuses depart every hour or so to Limbe (for Blantyre; MK1500, one hour) and Lilongwe (MK6000, five hours), and head to Liwonde (MK1000, 45 minutes). There are more services in the morning.

## Blantyre & Limbe

Founded by Scottish missionaries in 1876, and named after the town in South Lanarkshire, Scotland, where explorer David Livingstone was born, Blantyre is Malawi's second-largest city. It's more appealing and cohesive than Lilongwe thanks to its compact size and hilly topography, and though there's not much to do here, it makes a good springboard for exploring Majete Wildlife Reserve and Mt Mulanje. Malawi's commercial and industrial hub, Blantyre has the country's best and most diverse choice of restaurants and a small selection of lively watering holes. Add to that tour operators, banks, internet cafes and other practicalities, and Blantyre makes a pleasant stopover.

Attached to the Blantyre's eastern side, Limbe is home to a grand old mission church, a minibus station and a golf club. Unlike Blantyre, however, which has seen a finessing of its restaurants and hotels, Limbe has fallen into disrepair over the last couple of decades. You may have to change minibuses here, but it's best to head straight on.

### Sights & Activities

**Mandala House** HISTORIC BUILDING
(01-871932; Kaoshiung Rd; 8.30am-4.30pm Mon-Fri, to 12.30pm Sat) This is the oldest building in Malawi, built in 1882 as a home for the managers of the African Lakes Corporation. It's a quietly grand colonial house, encased in wraparound verandas and set in lovely gardens. Inside are the inviting Mandala Cafe, an eclectic art gallery and the **Society of Malawi Library & Archive** (01-872617; www.societyofmalawi.org; 1st fl, Mandala House, Kaoshiung Rd; 9am-4pm Mon-Fri) FREE.

**Museum of Malawi** MUSEUM
(Chichiri Museum; 01-873258; Kasungu Cres; adult/child under 13yr MK500/100; 7.30am-4.30pm) Malawi's interesting national museum has a few gems, including a royal ceremonial stool dating from the 16th century and a display on Gule Wamkulu dances. The museum is between central Blantyre and Limbe, accessed from Moi Rd opposite Chichiri Shopping Mall. Take a minibus headed for Limbe and ask to be let off at the museum.

**St Michael and All Angels Church** CHURCH
(CCAP Church; www.stmichaelchurchmw.com; services 6am, 7am, 8.30am, 10.30am & 5pm Sun) This magnificent red-brick Church of Central Africa Presbyterian building was preceded by a simpler structure, built by Scottish missionary Reverend DC Scott in 1882. In 1888 the missionaries started work on a new, more impressive church with elab-

orate brickwork moulded into arches, buttresses, columns and towers, topped with a grand basilica dome. The church is off Old Chileka Rd.

## Sleeping

**★Doogles** HOSTEL $

(☎0999 186512; www.dooglesmalawi.com; Mulomba Pl; dm US$15, r US$30-45; P@🛜≋) Doogles is popular with discerning travellers of all stripes, its inviting pool and bar ringed by walls with a cool sunset-safari design. From there, the complex leads to a big TV lounge, lush gardens, superfresh en suite rooms with shower, clean six-bed dorms, and thatched en suite chalets with mozzie nets and fans.

**Hotel Victoria** HOTEL $$

(☎01-823500; www.hotelvictoriamw.com; Lower Sclater Rd; s/d incl breakfast from MK45,000/50,000; P❄@🛜≋) Upmarket Victoria attracts corporate types and aid workers with its pool, marble lobby and air-conditioned restaurant. Eighty rooms enjoy plump pillows, thick carpet, DSTV, writing desk, fridge and less impressive bathroom. Deluxe and larger executive rooms are a big step up, with flat-screen TV, office chair, and bathroom with oval tub and shower. Ask for one away from Victoria Ave.

**Malawi Sun Hotel** HOTEL $$$

(☎01-824808; www.malawisunhotel.com; Robins Rd; incl breakfast s/d standard US$100/125, executive US$145/170; P⊖❄@🛜≋) This comfortable hotel has a small African-style lounge with mountain views, a tempting swimming pool and a **food court** (☎0997 915519; Blue Savannah mains MK2000; ⊙8am-9pm; ✎). The 73 rooms are decent, with DSTV, comfy beds, fridge, tea and coffee. It's worth upgrading to executive from standard (also called 'ethnic' for their Malawian decorative touches); shoot for a balcony overlooking the hills.

## Eating & Drinking

**★L'Hostaria** ITALIAN $$

(☎0888 282828; www.facebook.com/hostariaMW; Sharpe Rd; mains MK5500; ⊙noon-2pm & 6.30-9pm Tue-Sun; P🛜👪) In an atmospheric old house with black-and-white floors and a large veranda overlooking a lawn, L'Hostaria offers Italian recipes and fresh produce that attract local expats in the know. Come for a relaxing evening and wood-fired pizzas, homemade pastas and steaks.

**★Mandala Cafe** CAFE $$

(☎01-871932; Mandala House, Kaoshiung Rd; mains MK5000-6000; ⊙8.30am-4.30pm Mon-Fri, to 12.30pm Sat; P🛜✎) Sit on a breezy stone terrace in the grounds of Mandala House (p824), or inside at this chilled cafe adorned with artworks and guidebooks. Regulars love the Italian cuisine, fillet steak, Thai chicken, freshly brewed coffee, iced tea and gelato. A real oasis.

**★Casa Mia** INTERNATIONAL $$$

(☎01-827871; www.blantyreaccommodation.com; Kabula Hill Rd; mains MK5000-11,000; ⊙6.30am-9.30pm; P❄🛜✎) Don your smarts for dinner at this classy guesthouse restaurant. The wine-stacked interior, with its antique Cinzano prints, white tablecloths and expat clientele, is a pleasant environment for dishes ranging from steaks and carbonara to red wine–marinaded Karoo lamb and *chambo* thermidor. Lunch on the breezy terrace is more casual.

**Kwa Haraba** CAFE

(☎0993 801564, 0994 764701; www.facebook.com/KwaHaraba-138690532886703/; Phekani House; ⊙7.30am-5pm Sun-Tue & Thu, to 8pm Wed, to 10pm Fri & Sat) This craft shop and cafe serves fresh juices bursting with goodness and light meals such as feta pizza, ham and cheese pita sandwiches, salads and toasted sandwiches. The wonderful masks, paintings, secondhand paperbacks and fabric make a creative environment. Cocktails and music from 6pm Friday and Saturday, and poetry between 6pm and 7pm Wednesday. Phekani House is off Glyn Jones Ave.

## Information

### MEDICAL SERVICES

**Blantyre Adventist Hospital** (☎hospital 01-820006, medical appointments 01-820399; Kabula Hill Rd; ⊙casualty 24hr) This private hospital and medical and dental clinic charges MK5400 for a doctor's consultation and MK2000 for a malaria test. Cash only.

**One Stop Pharmacy** (☎01-824148, 0888 860230; Chilembwe Rd; ⊙8am-5.30pm Mon-Fri, 9am-2pm Sat) This well-stocked pharmacy sells bilharzia tablets (if you've been swimming in the lake), as well as malaria prophylaxis.

### TOURIST INFORMATION

**Jambo Africa** (☎0111 572709, 0882 904166; www.jambo-africa.com; Uta Waleza Centre, Kidney Cres; ⊙8am-5pm Mon-Fri, 9am-noon Sat) A great one-stop shop for travel tickets, car hire, excursions and accommodation. Jambo owns

# Blantyre City Centre

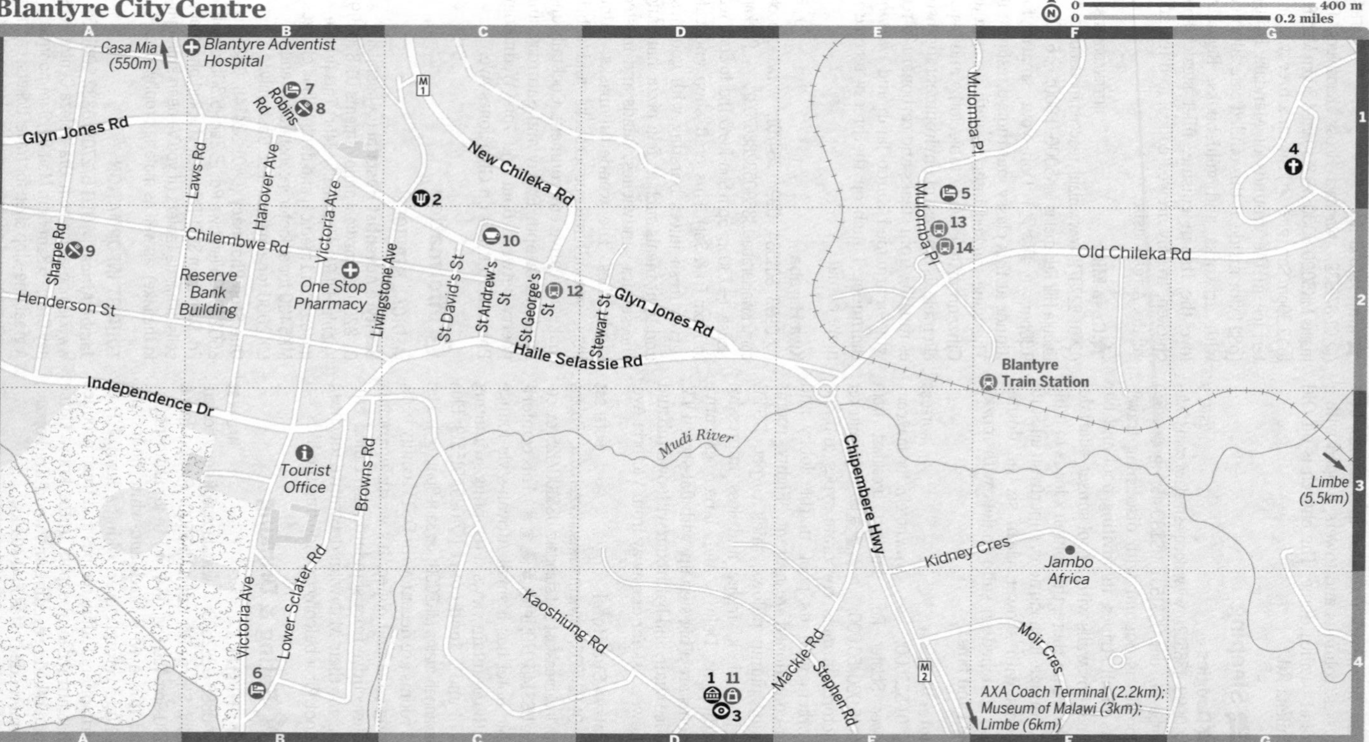

## Blantyre City Centre

**Sights**
1 Mandala House ........ D4
2 Shree Hindu Temple ........ C1
3 Society of Malawi Library & Archive ........ D4
4 St Michael and All Angels Church ........ G1

**Sleeping**
5 Doogles ........ E1
6 Hotel Victoria ........ B4
7 Malawi Sun Hotel ........ B1

**Eating**
8 Food Court ........ B1
9 L'Hostaria ........ A2
Mandala Cafe ........ (see 3)

**Drinking & Nightlife**
10 Kwa Haraba ........ C2

**Shopping**
11 Mandala House ........ D4

**Transport**
12 AXA House Coach Terminal ........ C2
13 National Bus Company ........ E2
14 Wenela Bus Station ........ E2

a park lodge and two self-catering cottages on the lake. It has a second office next to the Shree Hindu Temple (01-820761; Glyn Jones Rd).

**Tourist office** (01-827066; Government Complex, Victoria Ave; 7.30am-4.30pm Mon-Fri) In a cottage-like tax building dating to 1939, this small office covers the whole country. It stocks a few leaflets and maps, sells wall maps of Malawi (MK5000), and can offer enthusiastic, though not always particularly helpful, advice.

### Getting There & Around

Blantyre's **Chileka International Airport** (01-827900) is about 15km north of the city centre. A taxi to the city costs around MK15,000, but agree on a price with the driver first.

Blantyre's main bus station for long-distance buses is **Wenela Bus Station** (Mulomba Pl), east of the centre. Companies including **National Bus Company** (0888 561365; Wenela Bus Station, Mulomba Pl) have daily services to Lilongwe (MK3500, four hours), Mzuzu (MK7500, nine to 10 hours), Zomba (MK1500, 1½ to two hours), Mulanje (MK1500, 1½ hours) and Karonga (MK10,500, 14 hours).

AXA buses depart from the **terminal** (Chipembere Hwy) next to the Chichiri Shopping Mall, then pick up at the central **office** (01-820100, 01-820411; www.axacoach.com; St George's St; ticket office 6am-5pm) en route to Lilongwe (MK11,300).

# Mt Mulanje

A huge hulk of twisted granite rising majestically from the surrounding plains, Mt Mulanje towers over 3000m high. All over the mountain are dense green valleys and rivers that drop from sheer cliffs to form dazzling waterfalls. The locals call it the 'Island in the Sky', and on misty days (and there are many) it's easy to see why: the massif is shrouded in a cotton-wool haze, its highest peaks bursting through the cloud to touch the heavens.

## Festivals

**Mt Mulanje Porters Race** SPORTS

(Jul) Taking place on the second Saturday in July, this 20-year-old competition follows a gruelling, rocky route over the country's highest peak. It was originally only for porters and guides, but these days anyone can take the 22km challenge. Contact Mulanje Infocentre (p828) for details.

## Sleeping

There are eight forestry huts on Mulanje: Chambe, Chisepo, Lichenya, Thuchila, Chinzama, Minunu, Madzeka and Sombani. Each is equipped with benches, tables and open fires with plenty of wood. Some have sleeping platforms (no mattresses); in others you just sleep on the floor. You provide your own food, cooking gear, candles, sleeping bag and stove (although you can cook on the fire). A caretaker chops wood, lights fires and brings water, for which a small tip should be paid. Payments must be made at Likhubula Forestry Office; show your receipt to the hut caretaker.

**Likhubula Forest Lodge** LODGE $

(0111 904005, 0888 773792; Likhubula; camping MK3500, s/d from MK12,100/14,100; P) This faded but lovely old colonial house has lots of character: a homey kitchen, five clean rooms (two with their own bathroom), a veranda, a communal lounge with rocking chairs, and a nightly fire crackling. The easy charm of the staff and the recommended food make it a memorable place to overnight, with breakfast, half board and full board available.

**CCAP Guesthouse** GUESTHOUSE $

(0888 863632, 0881 188887; www.ccapblantyresynod.org/ccap-likhubula-mulanje.html; Likhubula; camping US$5, dm US$11, s/d/q from US$47/55/93, r with shared bathroom per person US$16) The CCAP Mission, after the Likhubula gate, has

### HIKING ON MT MULANJE

There are about six main routes up and down Mulanje. The three main ascent routes go from Likhubula: the **Chambe Plateau Path** (also called the Skyline Path), the **Chapaluka Path** and the relatively easy **Lichenya Path** (aka the Milk Run). Other routes, more often used for the descent, are Thuchila Hut to Lukulezi Mission, Sombani Hut to Fort Lister Gap, and Minunu Hut to the Lujeri Tea Estate.

Once you're on the massif, a network of paths links the huts and peaks, and many permutations are possible. It takes anything from two to six hours to hike between one hut and the next.

Hiking on Mt Mulanje is controlled by the **Likhubula Forestry Office** (☎0888 773792, 0111 904005; ⏲7.30am-4.30pm), at the small village of Likhubula, about 15km north of Mulanje town centre. Entry fees payable at the gate are MK1000 per person, MK500 per vehicle, and MK1000 per day for parking.

cosy rooms, four- and 12-bed dorms, and one- and two-bedroom self-catering chalets (number one is homey). The friendly guesthouse among jacaranda trees is a pleasant place to rest after a long hike. Breakfast (US$4), and lunch and dinner (US$6), are available to both guests and nonguests.

## Information

**Mulanje Infocentre** (☎01-466466, 0888 122645; infomulanje@sdnp.org.mw; Phalombe Rd, Chitakale Trading Centre; ⏲8am-5pm Mon-Fri, by appointment Sat & Sun) Excellent for information and bookings.

## Getting There & Away

The dirt road to Likhubula turns off the main sealed Blantyre–Mulanje road at Chitakale Trading Centre, about 2km northwest of the centre of Mulanje town; follow the signpost to Phalombe.

If you're coming from Blantyre on the bus, ask to be dropped at Chitakale. From there, you can pick up a *matola*, minibus (MK1000) or bicycle taxi (MK700) to Likhubula. Alternatively you can walk (11km, two to three hours); it's a pleasant hike with good views of the southwestern face of Mulanje on your right.

# Majete Wildlife Reserve

Malawi's only Big Five park, this rugged wilderness of hilly miombo (woodland) and savannah hugs the west bank of the Shire River. Since African Parks took over its management in 2003, things have really been looking up for the once heavily poached reserve. A perimeter fence has been erected, and accommodation and roads have been massively upgraded. With Majete's lion-reintroduction program, the **park** (☎0999 521741; www.african-parks.org; person/vehicle US$20/4; ⏲6am-6pm) is now a conservation case study and an exciting destination.

## Sleeping

**Community Campsite** CAMPGROUND **$**
(☎0999 521741; www.african-parks.org; camping/tent hire US$10/25, gazebos s/d US$12/15; P) Enabling visitors on a budget to stay in the reserve and fully immerse themselves in the wildlife-viewing activities, this campingground has shady places to pitch up, park or sleep on a stilted gazebo under the stars. There's drinkable borehole water, a thatched bar, clean ablution blocks and hot showers, as well as barbecues, cooking utensils and free firewood.

★**Mkulumadzi Lodge** LODGE **$$$**
(☎01-794491; www.mkulumadzi.com; per person all-inclusive US$445; P ❄ @ 📶 ≋) Romantically reached by a suspension bridge over a croc-infested river, this extraordinary lodge is a fusion of African tradition and boutique chic. The eight chalets are artfully blended with the bush, with grass roofs, step-in rain showers and windows offering widescreen views of the Shire River as you flop in a sunken, candlelit bath.

★**Thawale Camp** LODGE **$$$**
(☎0999 521741; www.african-parks.org; chalets per person with half board/full board/full board plus activities from US$138/150/180; P) 🍃 Situated around a watering hole frequented by antelopes and warthogs, this upmarket bush camp is about 3km inside the reserve from the main entrance. The standard, luxury and family tented chalets on raised wooden platforms feel safari-ready with their khaki sheets, outside barbecues and private verandas overlooking the floodlit watering hole.

### Getting There & Away

Majete lies west of the Shire River, some 70km southwest of Blantyre. Take the M1 to Chikwawa, from where signs will direct you 20km to the reserve along 2WD-accessible roads. By public transport, the nearest you can get is Chikwawa.

# UNDERSTAND MALAWI

## Malawi Today

The smiles travellers encounter in 'the warm heart of Africa' belie a country grappling with the disasters of drought, flooding and food shortages. These environmental challenges are set against a background of political corruption, unsustainable population growth and deforestation, and one of the world's highest HIV/AIDS infection rates at about 10%. At the time of writing, leadership difficulties continue to dominate headlines. However, there is good news in the conservation sector, with animal translocations proceeding apace. Among the highlights: 250 elephants were translocated from Majete to Nkhotakota in 2017 and Liwonde's rhino sanctuary continues to conserve endangered black rhinos.

## History

Since the first millennium, the Bantu people had been migrating from central Africa into the area now called Malawi, but migration to the area stepped up with the arrival of the Tumbuka and Phoka, who settled around the highlands of Nyika and Viphya during the17th century, and the Maravi, who established a large and powerful kingdom in the south.

The early 19th century brought with it two significant migrations. The Yao invaded southern Malawi from western Mozambique, displacing the Maravi, while groups of Zulu migrated northward to settle in central and northern Malawi. This century also saw the escalation of the East African slave trade.

### Enter the British

The most famous explorer to reach this area was Dr David Livingstone. He reached Lake Malawi in September 1859, naming it Lake Nyasa. His death in 1873 inspired a legion of missionaries to come to Africa, bringing the more 'civilised' principles of commerce and Christianity.

The early missionaries blazed the way for various adventurers and pioneer traders and it wasn't long before European settlers began to arrive in their droves. In 1889 Britain allowed Cecil Rhodes' British South Africa Company to administer the Shire Highlands, and in 1891 the British Central Africa (BCA) Protectorate was extended to include land along the western side of the lake. In 1907 the BCA Protectorate became the colony of Nyasaland.

Colonial rule brought with it an end to slave traders and intertribal conflicts, but it also brought a whole new set of problems. As more European settlers arrived, land was increasingly taken away from the locals and Africans were forced to pay taxes to the administration.

### Transition & Independence

Not surprisingly, this created opposition to colonial rule and in the 1950s the Nyasaland African Congress (NAC) party, led by Dr Hastings Kamuzu Banda, pushed for independence. This came, after considerable struggle, in 1964, and Nyasaland became the independent country of Malawi. Two years later Malawi became a republic and Banda was made president, eventually declaring himself 'president for life' in 1971. He ruled for over 20 years before his downfall and died three years later. Many achievements were made during his presidency but these were overshadowed by his stringent rule: banning of foreign press, imposition of dress codes and vendettas waged against any group regarded as a threat.

In June 1993 Banda agreed to a referendum that resulted in the introduction of a multiparty political system; at Malawi's first full multiparty election in May 1994, the victor was the United Democratic Front (UDF), led by Bakili Muluzi. On becoming president, Muluzi closed political prisons, permitted freedom of speech and print, and instituted several economic reforms. Muluzi was reelected in May 1999. Muluzi was followed by Bingu wa Mutharika in 2004; Mutharika quit the UDF, established his own party and began eight years of rule that delivered the country to its knees by the time he died in 2012.

DON'T MISS

**LAKE OF STARS MUSIC FESTIVAL**

One of the region's largest spectacles, this three-day **music festival** (www.lakeofstars.org; ⌚ late Sep-early Oct) features live acts from around Africa and Europe. It takes place in a different lakeshore venue each year, with proceeds benefiting charity. Booking accommodation well in advance is essential, but there are normally camping spots available until the last minute.

## The Culture

Malawi's main ethnic groups are Chewa, dominant in the centre and south; Yao in the south; and Tumbuka in the north. Other groups include the Ngoni (also spelt Angoni), inhabiting parts of the central and northern provinces; the Chipoka (or Phoka) in the central area; the Lambya; the Ngonde (also called the Nyakyusa) in the northern region; and the Tonga, mostly along the lakeshore.

Around 83% of Malawians are Christians. Some are Catholic, while many follow indigenous Christian faiths that have been established locally. Malawi has a significant Muslim population of around 13%, mostly living in the south. Alongside the established churches, many Malawians also follow traditional animist religions.

## The Arts

Malawi's most acclaimed novelist is the late Legson Kayira, whose semiautobiographical *The Looming Shadow* and *I Will Try* earned him acclaim in the 1970s. A later work to look out for is *The Detainee*. Another novelist is Sam Mpasu; his *Nobody's Friend* was a comment on the secrecy of Malawian politics – it earned him a two-year prison stint in 1975. After his release he wrote *Political Prisoner 3/75* and later became minister for education in the new UDF government. He served a two-year jail sentence following a corruption scandal in the 2000s.

## Environment

Pint-sized, landlocked Malawi is no larger than the US state of Pennsylvania. It's wedged between Zambia, Tanzania and Mozambique, measuring roughly 900km long and between 80km and 150km wide, with a total area of 118,484 sq km.

### Wildlife

In 2012 Malawi began reintroducing lions at Majete Wildlife Reserve, finally giving the country its 'Big Five' stamp. Many people head for Liwonde National Park, noted for its herds of elephants and myriad hippos. Along with Majete, it's the only park in the country where you might see rhinos.

Elephants are also regularly seen in Nkhotakota Wildlife Reserve, Majete and Nyika National Park. Nyika has the country's largest population of leopards and Nkhotakota has been bolstered by a historic elephant translocation from Liwonde and Majete. Vwaza Marsh Wildlife Reserve is known for its hippos, as well as elephants, buffaloes and antelope, but is currently in poor shape due to unsatisfactory management.

Lake Malawi has more fish species than any other inland body of water in the world, with a total of over 1000, of which more than 350 are endemic. The largest family of fish in the lake is the Cichlidae (cichlids).

For birdwatchers, Malawi is rewarding: over 600 species have been recorded in the country.

# SURVIVAL GUIDE

## ℹ Directory A–Z

### ACCOMMODATION

There are generally good selections of backpacker hostels and top-end accommodation but fewer midrange guesthouses and hotels. One tip: consider sharing a bathroom; many budget and midrange options have lovely rooms with a bathroom for every two rooms. Camping offers affordable access to high-end lodges, as many have campsites. Camping prices in reviews are per person and per night (eg camping US$10), unless otherwise noted.

### ACTIVITIES

Malawi provides a hugely exciting range of activities for travellers. Lake Malawi is the main destination, so diving and snorkelling are particularly popular.

### EMBASSIES & CONSULATES

**Australia** Contact the Australian Embassy in Harare, Zimbabwe.

**Canada** Contact the Canadian High Commission in Maputo, Mozambique.

**France** Contact the French Embassy in Harare, Zimbabwe.

**New Zealand** Contact the New Zealand High Commission in Pretoria, South Africa.

The following are in Lilongwe:

**British High Commission** (01-772400; www.gov.uk; City Centre)

**German Embassy** (01-772555; www.lilongwe.diplo.de; Convention Dr, City Centre)

**Irish Embassy** (0888 207543; www.dfa.ie/irish-embassy/malawi; 3rd fl, Arwa House, African Unity Ave, City Centre)

**Mozambican High Commission** (01-774100; www.minec.gov.mz; Convention Dr, City Centre)

**Netherlands Honorary Consulate** (0999 960481; https://zimbabwe.nlembassy.org; Heavenly Close, Area 10)

**South African High Commission** (01-773722; www.dirco.gov.za; Plot 19)

**US Embassy** (01-773166; lilongwe.usembassy.gov; 16 Kenyatta Rd, City Centre)

**Zambian High Commission** (01-772590; www.facebook.com/zambiahighcommissionlilongwe; City Centre)

**Zimbabwean Embassy** (01-774413, 01-774988; www.zimfa.gov.zw; Area 13)

## EMERGENCY

| | |
|---|---|
| Ambulance | 998 |
| Police | 997 |
| Fire | 999 |

## INTERNET ACCESS

Across the country, most accommodation and restaurants catering to foreigners offer wi-fi, generally operated by Skyband (www.skyband.mw). The advantage of this system is that you can buy a voucher (typically MK2000 for 500MB) and use it at multiple locations.

Wi-fi is rarely free in budget accommodation but may be in midrange and top-end places. You'll find internet cafes in Lilongwe, Blantyre and most towns.

## LGBTIQ TRAVELLERS

Male and female homosexuality is illegal in Malawi. On top of this, the people of Malawi are conservative in their attitudes towards gays and lesbians, and gay sexual relationships are culturally taboo.

## MONEY

Malawi's unit of currency is the Malawi kwacha (MK). This is divided into 100 tambala (t).

At big hotels that quote in US dollars you can pay in hard currency or kwacha at the prevailing exchange rate.

Standard Bank and National Bank ATMs are the best bet for foreigners wishing to draw money from their home account. Standard Bank accepts foreign Visa, MasterCard, Cirrus and Maestro cards. National Bank ATMs only take Visa cards. You can use Visa cards at many large hotels and top-end restaurants, though there may be a surcharge of around 5%.

### Exchange Rates

| | | |
|---|---|---|
| Australia | A$1 | MK541 |
| Canada | C$1 | MK532 |
| Euro zone | €1 | MK783 |
| Japan | ¥100 | MK680 |
| New Zealand | NZ$1 | MK511 |
| South Africa | ZAR10 | MK515 |
| UK | UK£1 | MK869 |
| USA | US$1 | MK713 |

For current exchange rates, see www.xe.com.

## OPENING HOURS

**Banks** Usually 8am to 3.30pm weekdays

**Bars** Noon to 11pm

**Post Offices** Generally 7.30am to 5pm weekdays, sometimes with a break for lunch; in Blantyre and Lilongwe, they're open Saturday morning too

**Restaurants** If they don't serve breakfast, 11am to 10pm

**Shops and Offices** 8am to noon and 1pm to 5pm weekdays; many shops also open Saturday morning

## PUBLIC HOLIDAYS

**New Year's Day** 1 January

**John Chilembwe Day** 15 January

**Martyrs' Day** 3 March

**Easter** (Good Friday, Holy Saturday and Easter Monday) March/April

**Labour Day** 1 May

**Kamuzu Day** 14 May

**Independence Day** 6 July

**Mother's Day** October, second Monday

**Christmas Day** 25 December

**Boxing Day** 26 December

## TELEPHONE

Malawi's country code is 265 and it's international access code is 00.

Mobile phones are in use everywhere, and coverage is extensive. The major networks are Airtel and TNM, with 099 and 088 prefixes respectively. TNM has better coverage in rural areas and is popular with locals. Airtel is popular among expats and travellers; it also has good coverage, and works better in the cities, especially for using the internet and social-media apps.

SIM cards are readily available from street vendors for around MK1000.

### TIME

Malawi follows Central Africa Time, which is two hours ahead of Greenwich Mean Time (GMT/UTC). There is no daylight saving time.

### TOURIST INFORMATION

There are tourist-information offices in Blantyre and Lilongwe, but you're much better off asking for advice from your accommodation or a travel agency. Outside Malawi, tourism promotion is handled by UK-based **Malawi Tourism** (☎ in the UK 0115-972 7250; www.malawitourism.com), which responds to enquiries from all over the world.

### VISAS

Most nationalities require a visa, which is issued (in most cases) upon arrival at the airport or major land border.

A one-month single-entry visa costs US$75, six- and 12-month multiple-entry visas cost US$150 and US$250 respectively; a seven-day transit visa costs US$50. Card payments should be possible at the airports, but it would be wise to have the fee handy in cash US dollars.

Check the Malawian Department of Immigration website, www.immigration.gov.mw/visa.html, for more info.



## Getting There & Away

### AIR

**Lilongwe International Airport** (Kamuzu International Airport, LLW; ☎ 0992 991097), 25km north of Lilongwe City Centre, handles the majority of international flights, while **Chileka International Airport** (☎ 01-827900), 15km north of central Blantyre, also receives numerous flights.

**PRICE RANGES**

The following price ranges refer to a double room with bathroom in high season.

**$** less than MK35,000 (US$50)

**$$** MK35,000 to MK70,000 (US$50 to US$100)

**$$$** more than MK70,000 (US$100)

The following price ranges refer to a standard main course.

**$** less than MK3500 (US$5)

**$$** MK3500 to MK7000 (US$5 to US$10)

**$$$** more than MK7000 (US$10)

### LAND

Overland, travellers can enter the country from Zambia, Mozambique or Tanzania. Indeed, Malawi is a popular staging post for overland trucks heading between Nairobi and Cape Town. Most border crossings close from 6pm to 7am.

#### Mozambique

**South** Take a minibus to the Mozambican border crossing at Zóbuè and then a minibus to Tete, from where buses go to Beira and Maputo. You could also get a Blantyre–Harare bus to drop you at Tete.

**Central** There are daily buses from Blantyre to the Mozambican border at Marka; failing that, take a bus to Nsanje and continue by minibus or *matola* (pick-up). It's a few kilometres between the border crossings – you can walk or take a bicycle taxi – and you can change money on the Mozambique side. From here pick-ups go to Mutarara and over the bridge to Vila de Sena.

**North** There are three border crossings from Malawi into northern Mozambique: Muloza, from where you can reach Mocuba in Mozambique, and Nayuchi and Chiponde, both of which lead to Cuamba in Mozambique.

#### South Africa

A number of bus companies run services from Lilongwe and Blantyre to Johannesburg. The best option is Intercape (p814), which operates daily services between Jo'burg and both Blantyre and Lilongwe, with a service continuing north five days a week from the latter to Mzuzu.

#### Tanzania

If you're going in stages, Mbeya in southern Tanzania is handy for crossing to/from northern Malawi. Buses and minibuses ply the M1 between Mzuzu and Karonga, from where you can get a minibus or taxi to the Songwe border crossing.

Once on the Tanzanian side of the border, minibuses travel 115km north to Mbeya. You can change money with the bicycle-taxi boys, but beware of scams.

#### Zambia

Four direct **Kob's Coach Services** (☎ in Zambia +260 977 794073) buses per week link Lilongwe and Lusaka (MK20,000, 12 hours). Regular minibuses run between Lilongwe and Mchinji. From here, it's 12km to the border. Local shared taxis shuttle between Mchinji and the border crossing.

### BOAT

Dhows sail in the morning from Mdamba on Likoma Island (Malawi) to Cóbuè (Mozambique). If you're planning to visit Mozambique you must get a visa in advance and be sure to get your passport stamped at Malawian immigration in Mdimba. Operated by the **Malawi Shipping Company** (☎ 01-587411), the *Chambo* connects Metangula

## SAMPLE ROUTES & FARES

The following are sample boat fares from Nkhata Bay.

| DESTINATION | OWNER'S CABIN (MK) | STANDARD CABIN (MK) | UPPER DECK (MK) | 2ND (MK) | ECONOMY (MK) |
|---|---|---|---|---|---|
| Nkhotakota | 25,770 | 19,850 | 12,490 | 7160 | 5120 |
| Monkey Bay | 44,800 | 34,440 | 20,450 | 11,860 | 8120 |

(Mozambique) with Likoma Island, Chizumulu and Nkhata Bay. It leaves Metangula at 5am on Wednesday, and reaches Likoma around 11.30am, Chizumulu around 12.30pm and Nkhata Bay around 2pm.

The Tanzanian *Songea* (www.mscl.go.tz) sails south, at 1pm on Thursday, from Itungi via Liuli and Mdamba Bay (all in Tanzania) to Nkhata Bay. A 1st-class ticket from Mdamba Bay to Nkhata Bay costs around US$5.

## Getting Around

### AIR

**Malawian Airlines** (☎01-774605, 01-827900; www.malawian-airlines.com) The national carrier operates daily flights between Lilongwe and Blantyre (US$50, one hour), a good alternative to the bus. Its booking system isn't always reliable, so it's worth confirming your flight by phone or at an office.

**Ulendo Airlink** (☎01-794638; www.flyulendo.com) The aviation wing of Ulendo Travel Group operates scheduled and charter flights on safe twin-prop planes to locations including Likoma Island and all the major wildlife parks. Check the 'bid to fly' section of Ulendo Airlink's website for discounted seats on upcoming flights.

### BOAT

The *Ilala* ferry chugs passengers and cargo up and down Lake Malawi once a week in each direction. You can normally download the latest schedules from Malawi Tourism.

### BUS

Malawi's best bus company is **AXA Coach Service** (☎01-820100; www.axacoach.com), with three classes of vehicle: Super Executive, Executive and Special.

Other smaller bus companies, including the National Bus Company, have daily services up and down the lake and between the country's main centres. These are marginally more comfortable than minibuses, but no more efficient, and they generally cost the same.

Minibuses are the most popular option because they leave regularly throughout the day.

### TAXI

You can often share a taxi instead of waiting for the minibus to depart – a safer, more comfortable and faster option.

Privately hiring a taxi will likely work out cheaper than renting a car with a driver, plus it will remove driving stress and give you an unofficial guide and interpreter. **High Class Taxi Services** (☎0999 356920, 0888 100223; justinchimenya@yahoo.com) in Blantyre and **Mawaso Taxi Service** (☎0995 769772, 0999 161111; plizimba@gmail.com) in Lilongwe both offer multiday services.

# Mozambique

POP 25.3 MILLION

### Includes ➡



## Best Places to Eat

➡ Cinco Portas (p852)

➡ Rickshaws Cafe (p849)

➡ Restaurante Maúa (p847)

➡ Restaurante Costa do Sol (p840)

➡ Karibu (p850)

## Best Places to Sleep

➡ Ibo Island Lodge (p852)

➡ &Beyond Benguerra (p845)

➡ Montebelo Gorongosa Lodge & Safari (p846)

➡ Jardim dos Aloés (p849)

## Why Go?

Mozambique beckons with its coastline and swaying palms, its traditions, its cultures, its vibe and its opportunities for adventure. This enigmatic southeast African country is well off most travellers' maps, but it has much to offer those who venture here: long, dune-fringed beaches, turquoise waters abounding in shoals of colourful fish, well-preserved corals, remote archipelagos in the north, pounding surf in the south and graceful dhows with billowing sails. Add to this colonial-style architecture, pulsating nightlife, a fascinating cultural mix and vast tracts of bush. Discovering these attractions is not always easy, but it is unfailingly rewarding. Bring along patience, a tolerance for long bus rides, some travel savvy and a sense of adventure, and jump in for the journey of a lifetime.

## When to Go

### Maputo

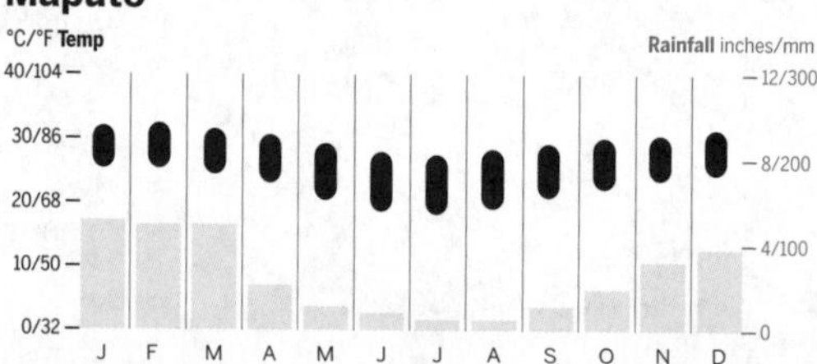


**May–Nov** Cooler, dry weather makes this the ideal time to visit.

**Dec–Apr** Rainy season can bring washed-out roads and occasional flooding in the south and centre.

**Holidays** During Christmas, Easter and August holidays southern resorts fill up; advance booking suggested.

# MAPUTO

With its Mediterranean-style architecture, waterside setting and wide avenues lined with jacaranda and flame trees, Maputo is easily one of Africa's most attractive capitals. It's also the most developed place in Mozambique, with a wide selection of hotels and restaurants, well-stocked supermarkets, shady sidewalk cafes and a lively cultural scene. Getting to know the city is a highlight of visiting Mozambique and essential to understanding the country. Don't miss spending time here before heading north.

## Sights

**National Art Museum** MUSEUM
(Museu Nacional de Arte; 21-320264; artemus@tvcabo.co.mz; 1233 Avenida Ho Chi Minh; Mtc20, Sun free; 11am-6pm Tue-Fri, 2-6pm Sat & Sun) Half a block west of Avenida Karl Marx, the National Art Museum has an excellent collection of paintings and sculptures by Mozambique's finest contemporary artists, including Malangatana and Alberto Chissano.

**Fort** FORTRESS
(Fortaleza; Praça 25 de Junho; Mtc20; 9.30am-4pm) The old fort was built by the Portuguese in the mid-19th century near the site of an earlier fort. Inside is a garden and a small museum with remnants from the era of early Portuguese forays to the area. The sealed, carved wooden coffin of Ngungunhane – final ruler of the famed kingdom of Gaza – is on display in one of the side rooms.

**Praça da Independência** PLAZA
This wide and imposing plaza is the gateway from the upper part of town to the *baixa* (downtown area). It's rimmed by several notable buildings and well worth a stroll.

## Tours

**★Bairro Mafalala Walking Tour** CULTURAL
(82 415 1580, 82 418 0314; www.iverca.org; 3hr tour per person Mtc1000-1500) This excellent walking tour through Mafalala *bairro* (region) focuses on exploring the area's rich historical and cultural roots. It includes a stop at a local *curandeiro* (healer) and a traditional dance performance. The per-person price varies depending on group size; tours depart off Avenida Marien N'gouabi. Highly recommended.

## Festivals & Events

**Marrabenta Festival** CULTURAL
(http://ccfmoz.com; Feb) To hear *marrabenta* – Mozambique's national music – at its best, don't miss the annual Marrabenta Festival. It's held mostly in Maputo but also takes place in Beira, Inhambane and several other locations. The timing is set to coincide with Marracuene's **Gwaza Muthini** (Commemoration of the Battle of Marracuene; Feb) commemorations.

**Festival Azgo** CULTURAL
(www.azgofestival.com; May) This Maputo-based extravaganza has become Mozambique's largest arts and culture festival, featuring artists from Mozambique as well as elsewhere in the region.

## Sleeping

**Maputo Backpackers** HOSTEL $
(21-451213, 82 467 2230; maputobp@gmail.com; 95 Quarta Avenida (Rua das Palmeiras), Bairro Triunfo; dm/d Mtc750/3200, s/d without bathroom Mtc2100/2500) A small, quiet place well away from the centre and near Costa do Sol, with a handful of rooms (including eight- and 10-bed dorms) with fans but no nets. *Chapas* to/from town (Mtc7) stop nearby: ask the driver to let you off at 'Escola', which is on Quinta Avenida; walk back one block to Maputo Backpackers. Taxis charge from Mtc300.

**Base Backpackers** HOSTEL $
(21-302723, 82 452 6860; thebasebackpackers@gmail.com; 545 Avenida Patrice Lumumba; dm/d Mtc500/1500; @) This scruffy but friendly backpackers is small, but justifiably popular and often full, with a convenient, quiet location on the edge of the *baixa*. It has a kitchen, backyard bar, terrace and braai (barbecue) area with views to the port. Via public transport from Junta, take a 'Museu' *chapa* (minivan) to the final Museu stop, from where it's a short walk.

**Residencial Palmeiras** BOUTIQUE HOTEL $$
(21-300199, 82 306 9200; www.palmeiras-guesthouse.com; 948 Avenida Patrice Lumumba; s/tw/d Mtc3950/4850/4850; ) This popular place has bright decor, comfortable and good-value rooms (all but one with private bathroom) and a tiny garden. It's near the British High Commission on a quiet but central street, and just a short walk from the *baixa*.

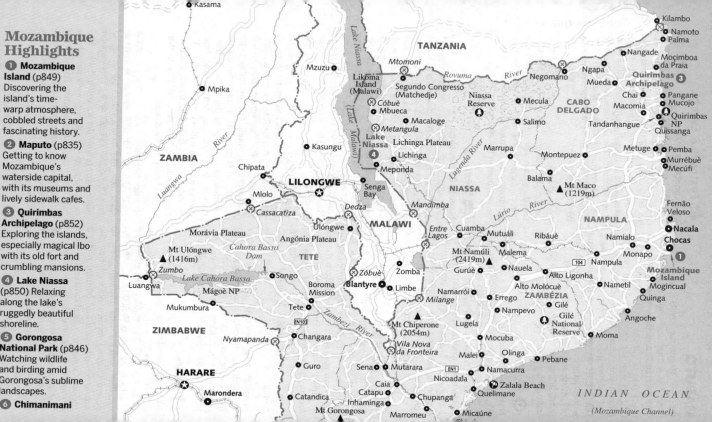

## Mozambique Highlights

1. **Mozambique Island** (p849) Discovering the island's time-warp atmosphere, cobbled streets and fascinating history.
2. **Maputo** (p835) Getting to know Mozambique's waterside capital, with its museums and lively sidewalk cafes.
3. **Quirimbas Archipelago** (p852) Exploring the islands, especially magical Ibo with its old fort and crumbling mansions.
4. **Lake Niassa** (p850) Relaxing along the lake's ruggedly beautiful shoreline.
5. **Gorongosa National Park** (p846) Watching wildlife and birding amid Gorongosa's sublime landscapes.
6. **Chimanimani**

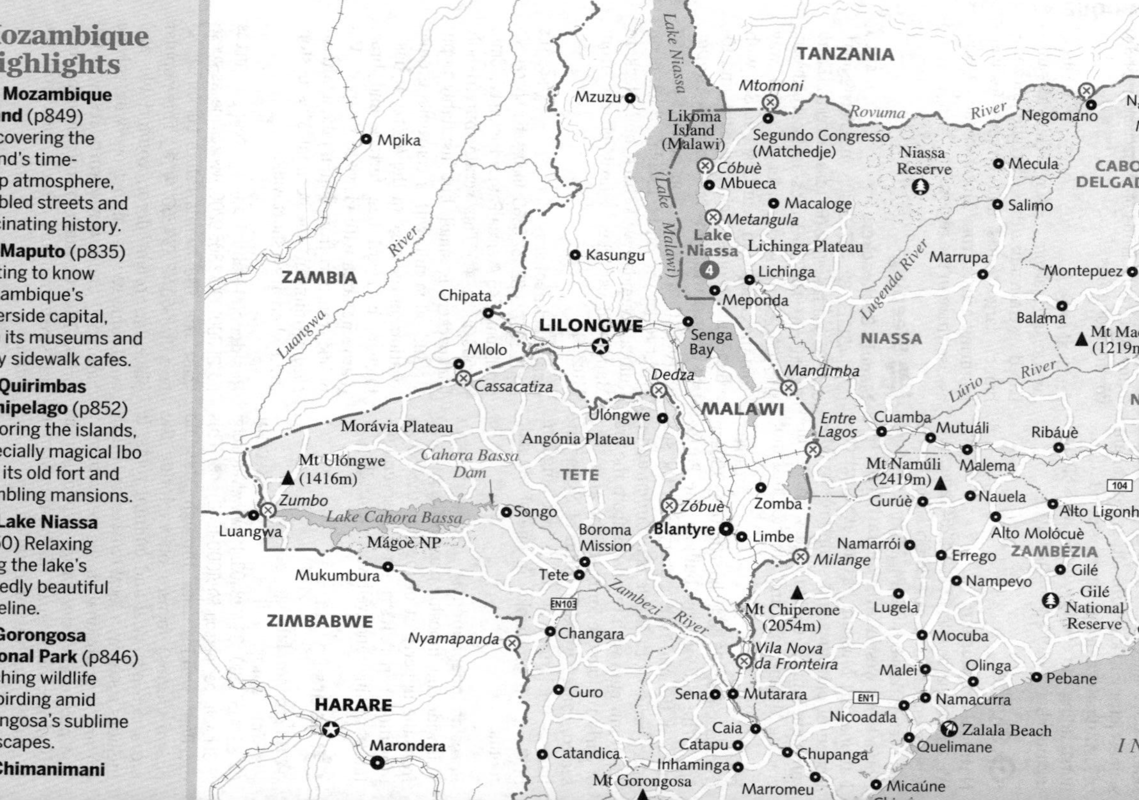

**Mountains** (p847) Hiking and learning about local culture.

7 **Inhambane** (p842) Wandering the town's quiet streets before relaxing on nearby beaches.

8 **Bazaruto Archipelago** (p845) Snorkelling around the islands and enjoying Bazaruto's lodges.

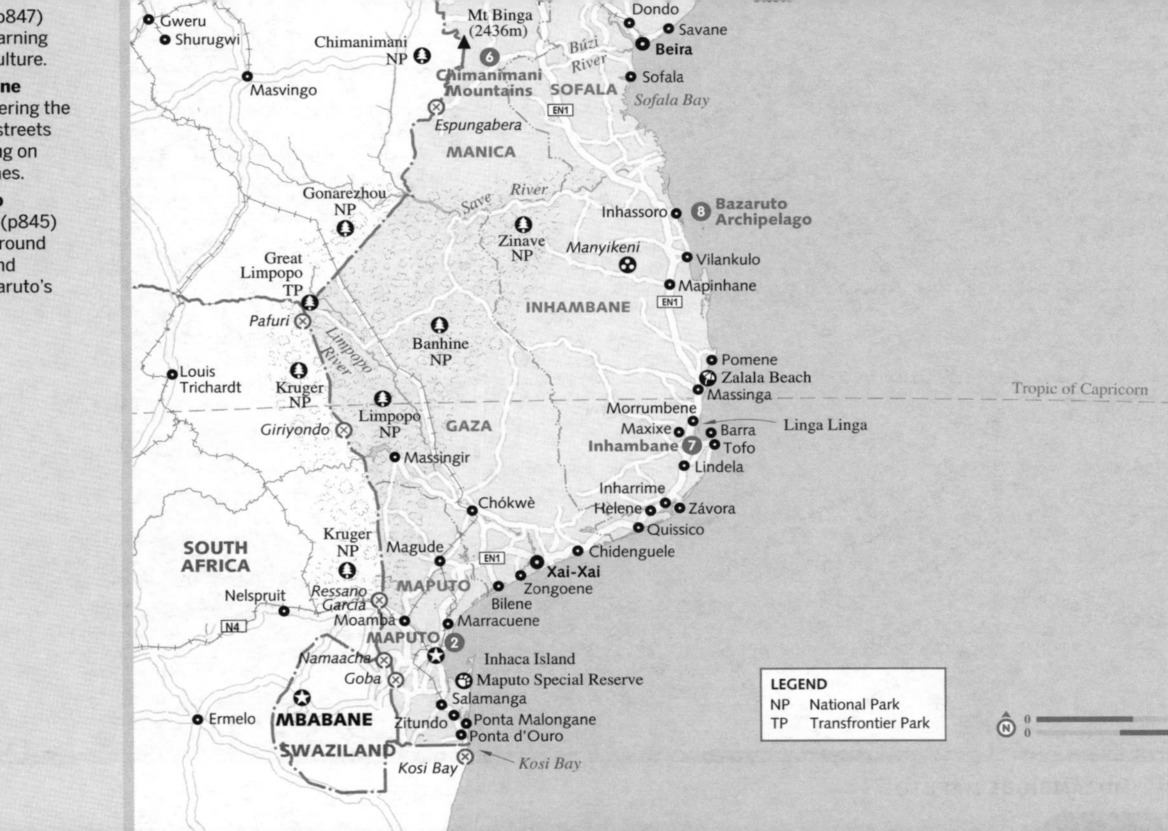

# Central Maputo

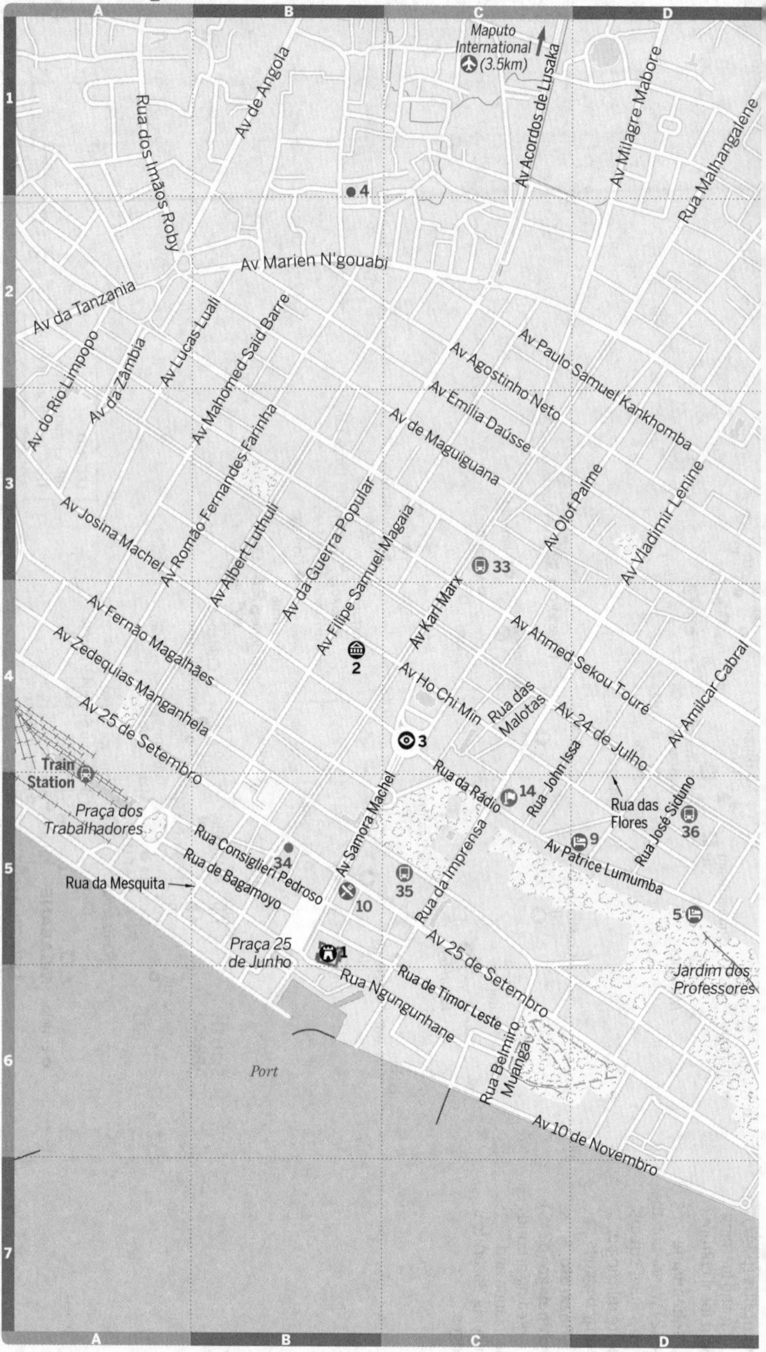

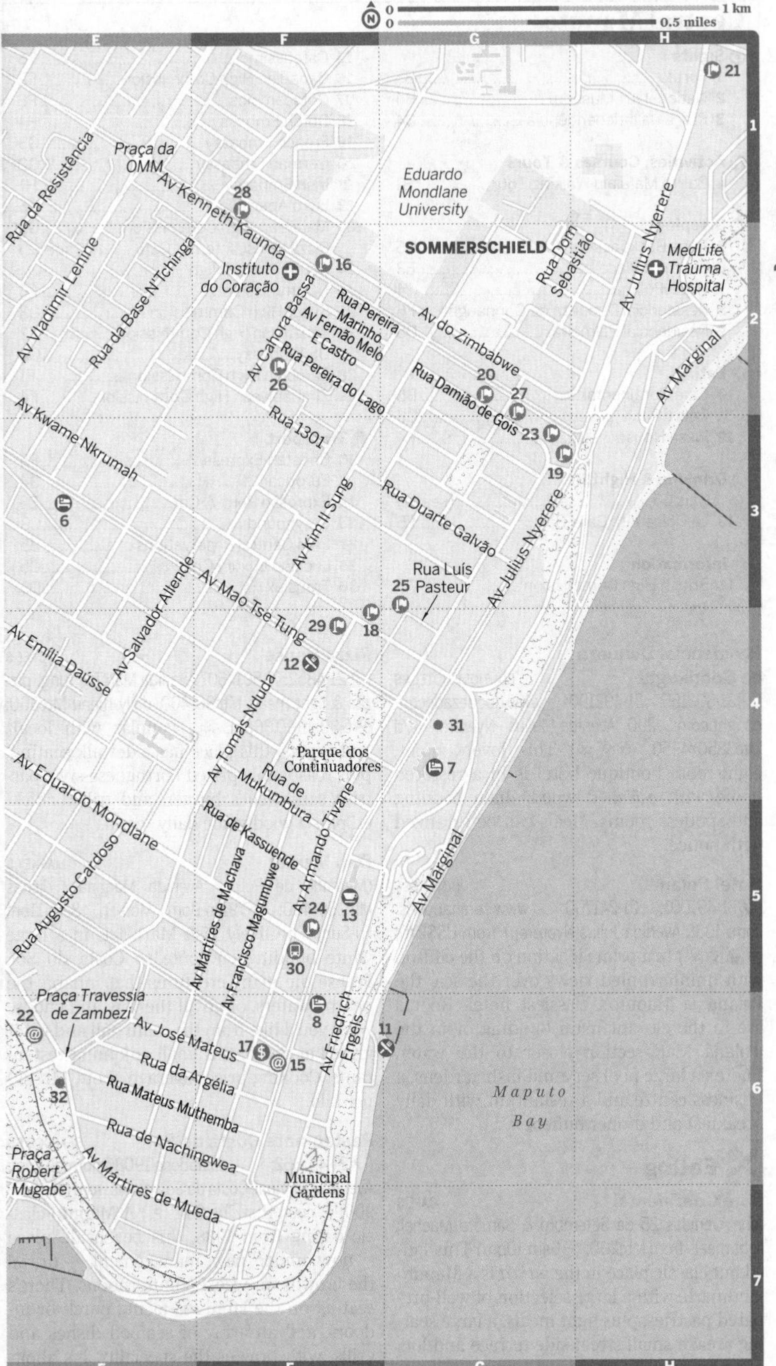

0 1 km
0 0.5 miles
E
F
G
H
1
2
3
4
5
6
7
Praça da OMM
Rua da Resistência
Av Kenneth Kaunda
28
Eduardo Mondlane University
SOMMERSCHIELD
Rua Dom Sebastião
Av Julius Nyerere
MedLife Trauma Hospital
21
Av Vladimir Lenine
Rua da Base N'Tchinga
Instituto do Coração
16
Av Cahora Bassa
Rua Pereira Marinho
Av Fernão Melo E Castro
Rua Pereira do Lago
26
Av do Zimbabwe
20
27
Rua Damião de Gois
23
19
Av Marginal
Av Kwame Nkrumah
Rua 1301
6
Av Kim Il Sung
Rua Duarte Galvão
Av Julius Nyerere
Rua Luís Pasteur
25
Av Salvador Allende
Av Mao Tse Tung
29
18
Av Emília Daússe
12
31
Av Tomás Nduda
Parque dos Continuadores
7
Rua de Mukumbura
Av Armando Tivane
Av Eduardo Mondlane
Rua de Kassuende
Rua Augusto Cardoso
Av Mártires de Machava
Av Francisco Magumbwe
Av Marginal
24
13
30
Praça Travessia de Zambezi
22
8
Av Friedrich Engels
11
Av José Mateus
17
15
Rua da Argélia
32
Rua Mateus Muthemba
Maputo Bay
Rua de Nachingwea
Praça Robert Mugabe
Av Mártires de Mueda
Municipal Gardens

## Central Maputo

**Sights**
1 Fort ........ B5
2 National Art Museum ........ B4
3 Praça da Independência ........ C4

**Activities, Courses & Tours**
4 Bairro Mafalala Walking Tour ........ B1

**Sleeping**
5 Base Backpackers ........ D5
6 Fatima's Place ........ E3
7 Hotel Polana ........ G4
8 Residencial Duqueza de Connaught ........ F6
9 Residencial Palmeiras ........ D5

**Eating**
10 Café Continental ........ B5
11 Cais 66 ........ G6
12 Pizza House ........ F4

**Drinking & Nightlife**
Cais 66 ........ (see 11)
13 La Dolce Vita Café-Bar ........ F5

**Information**
14 British High Commission ........ C5
15 Cafetíssimo ........ F6
16 Canadian High Commission ........ F2
17 Cotacambios ........ F6
18 Dutch Embassy ........ F4
19 French Embassy ........ G3
20 German Embassy ........ G2
21 Irish Embassy ........ H1
22 Livro Aberto ........ E6
23 Malawian High Commission ........ G3
Pizza House Internet Café ........ (see 12)
24 South African High Commission ........ F5
25 Swazi High Commission ........ G3
26 Tanzanian High Commission ........ F2
27 US Embassy ........ G2
28 Zambian High Commission ........ F1
29 Zimbabwean High Commission ........ F4

**Transport**
30 Cheetah Express ........ F5
31 Europcar ........ G4
32 Expresso Rent-A-Car ........ E6
33 Greyhound ........ C3
34 LAM Central Reservations ........ B5
35 Luciano Luxury Coach ........ C5
36 Translux ........ D5

**Residencial Duqueza de Connaught** BOUTIQUE HOTEL $$
(21-302155, 21-492190; www.duquezadeconnaught.com; 290 Avenida Julius Nyerere; s/d Mtc3850/4950; ) This lovely, quiet, eight-room boutique hotel is in a restored home with polished wood, linen bedding and spotless rooms. Meals can be arranged with notice.

**Hotel Polana** HOTEL $$$
(21-491001, 21-241700; www.serenahotels.com; 1380 Avenida Julius Nyerere; r from US$270; @) In a prime location on the clifftop with uninterrupted views over the sea, the Polana is Maputo's classiest hotel. Rooms are in the elegant main building or in the 'Polana Mar' section closer to the water. There's a large pool set amid lush gardens, a business centre and a restaurant with daily breakfast and dinner buffets.

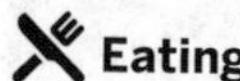

## Eating

**Café Continental** CAFE $
(cnr Avenidas 25 de Setembro & Samora Machel; light meals from Mtc200; 6am-10pm) This faded but classic place in the *baixa* is a Maputo landmark, with a large selection of well-prepared pastries, plus light meals, a large seating area, a small street-side terrace and lots of ambience.

**Pizza House** CAFE $
(21-485257; 601/607 Avenida Mao Tse Tung; pizzas & light meals Mtc80-400, daily menu Mtc300; 6.30am-10.30pm; ) Popular with locals and expats, this place has sidewalk seating, plus reasonably priced Portuguese-style pastries, sandwiches, burgers and grilled chicken plus a good-value daily menu.

**Fish Market** MARKET $
(Mercado de Peixe; Avenida Marginal; dishes Mtc250-400; 9am-9pm Mon-Fri, 8am-11pm Fri-Sun) The lively Fish Market is in a large white building en route to Costa do Sol. Peruse the many creatures that inhabit the nearby waters, or go all the way and choose what you'd like from the main hall and get it grilled at one of the small adjoining restaurants. Cooking prices average about Mtc160 per kilo.

**Restaurante Costa do Sol** SEAFOOD $$
(21-451662; costadosol1908@hotmail.com; Avenida Marginal, Costa do Sol; mains from Mtc400-900; noon-11pm Tue-Sun; P) A Maputo classic dating from 1938, this beachside place – now under new management – draws the crowds on weekend afternoons. There's seating on the large sea-facing porch or indoors, and an array of seafood dishes and grills, with prawns the speciality. It's about

5km from the centre at the northern end of Avenida Marginal.

**Cais 66** SEAFOOD $$
(☎84 547 5906; Avenida Marginal, at Clube Naval; mains from Mtc400; ⊙10am-midnight) Enjoy sushi and snacks on the upstairs deck or seafood grills in the breezy waterside dining area downstairs. It's located at Clube Naval, Maputo's long-standing yacht club.

## Drinking & Nightlife

**Cais 66** BAR
(☎21-493204; Clube Naval, Avenida Marginal; ⊙10am-2am) The late-night waterside bar at the yacht club is especially popular with old-timers on Thursday and Friday.

**La Dolce Vita Café-Bar** CAFE
(822 Avenida Julius Nyerere; ⊙10am-late Tue-Sun; 📶) This sleek tapas and late-night place has live music on Thursday evening. By day, try the juices and smoothies.

## Information

### INTERNET ACCESS

Internet cafes:

**Cafetíssimo** (3rd fl, Polana Shopping Centre, cnr Avenidas Julius Nyerere & 24 de Julho; ⊙8.30am-9pm Mon-Sat; 📶) Wi-fi free with food/drink purchase.

**La Dolcé Vita Café-Bar** (822 Avenida Julius Nyerere; ⊙10am-late Tue-Sun; 📶)

**Livro Aberto** (Maputo Community Library; www.livroaberto.org; Avenida Patrice Lumumba; ⊙8am-4pm Mon-Fri, 9am-4pm Sat; 📶)

**Pizza House Internet Café** (Avenida Mao Tse Tung; per hr Mtc60; ⊙7.30am-10pm Mon-Fri, 9am-5pm Sat; 📶) Upstairs at Pizza House.

### MEDICAL SERVICES

**Instituto do Coração** (☎21-416347, 82 327 4800, 82 305 3097; 1111 Avenida Kenneth Kaunda; ⊙24hr) Western standards and facilities for all ailments (not just cardiac issues); meticals, US dollars and Visa cards accepted.

**MedLife Trauma Hospital** (☎84 302 0999; 2986 Avenida Julius Nyerere; ⊙24hr) Western standards and facilities; meticals, US dollars and Visa cards accepted.

### MONEY

There are 24-hour ATMs all over town, including at the airport. Changing cash is easy. Travellers cheques are not accepted anywhere.

**Cotacambios** (ground fl, Polana Shopping Centre, cnr Avenida Julius Nyerere & Mao Tse Tung; ⊙9am-9pm Mon-Sat, 10am-8pm Sun) Useful for changing cash out of hours.

### SAFE TRAVEL

Although most tourists visit Maputo without mishap, be vigilant and take precautions.

- Avoid carrying a bag (thieves may think you have something valuable).
- Avoid situations in which you are isolated.
- At night, always take a taxi.
- Avoid the stretches of Avenida Marginal between Praça Robert Mugabe and the Southern Sun hotel; the access roads leading down to the Marginal from Avenida Friedrich Engels; and the area below the escarpment south of Avenida Patrice Lumumba.
- Areas off-limits to pedestrians (no photos) include the eastern footpath on Avenida Julius Nyerere in front of the president's residence and the Ponta Vermelha zone in Maputo's southeastern corner.

## Getting There & Away

### AIR

Kenya Airways, LAM, South African Airways and TAP Air Portugal have regular flights to Maputo.

### BUS

Maputo's main long-distance bus depot for up-country arrivals and departures is **'Junta'** (Terminal Rodovia'ria Interprovincial da Junta; cnr Avenida de Moçambique & Rua Gago Coutinho), about 7km (Mtc300 in a taxi) from the city centre. Time your travels to avoid arriving at night.

Sample prices and travel times for daily routes from Maputo include Inhambane (Mtc600, seven hours), Tofo (Mtc750, 7½ hours), Vilankulo (Mtc900, nine hours) and Beira (Mtc1700, 17 hours). There is twice-weekly service from Junta to Nampula (Mtc3100, 36 hours) and Pemba (Mtc3600), with overnight stops en route, although it's better to do these journeys in stages.

### South Africa

Departure and ticketing points for express buses to Johannesburg:

**Greyhound** (☎21-302771, in South Africa 011-611 8000; www.greyhound.co.za; Avenida Karl Marx; ⊙6.30am-7pm Mon-Fri, 6.30am-noon & 6-7pm Sat, 6.30am-7am & 6-7pm Sun) Avenida Karl Marx, just south of Avenida Eduardo Mondlane.

**Luciano Luxury Coach** (☎84 661 5713, in South Africa 083 993 4897, in South Africa 072-278 1921; Avenida Zedequías Manganhela) Behind the main post office.

**Translux** (☎21-303825, 21-303829, in South Africa 086 158 9282; www.translux.co.za; Simara Travel & Tours, 1249 Avenida 24 de Julho;

⌚ticket sales only 7am-5pm Mon-Fri, to 10am Sat & Sun) At Simara Travel & Tours.

**Cheetah Express** (☎84-244 2103, in South Africa 013-755 1988; cheetahexpressmaputo@gmail.com; cnr Avenidas Eduardo Mondlane & Julius Nyerere) Daily between Maputo and Nelspruit (Mtc1300 return, no one-way option), departing Maputo at 6am from Avenida Eduardo Mondlane next to Mundo's.

**Fatima's Place** (☎82 185 1577, 21-302994) Has a daily shuttle between Maputo and Tofo (Mtc800). With notice, it does pick-ups from other Maputo hotels. If seats are still remaining, it will also stop at Junta to take on additional passengers.

## Getting Around

### TO/FROM THE AIRPORT

**Maputo International Airport** (☎21-465827/8; www.aeroportos.co.mz) is 6km northwest of the city centre (Mtc400 to Mtc600 in a taxi).

### BUS & CHAPA

Buses have name boards with their destination. City rides cost about Mtc5.

*Chapas* go everywhere, with the average price for town trips Mtc5 to Mtc7. Most are marked with route start and end points, but you should also listen for the destination called out by the conductor.

### CAR

**Avis** (☎21-321243; www.avis.co.za; Maputo International Airport) At the airport, with offices also in Beira, Nampula and Tete; good deals often available.

**Europcar** (☎21-497338, 84 302 8330; www.europcar.co.mz; 1418 Avenida Julius Nyerere) Next to Hotel Polana and at the airport. Offices also in Beira, Nampula and Tete.

**Expresso Rent-A-Car** (☎21-493619; timisay@tropical.co.mz; Avenida Mártires de Mueda) At Hotel Cardoso; 2WD vehicles only.

**Sixt** (☎21-465250, 82 302 3555; www.sixt.co.mz; Maputo International Airport) Offices also in Beira, Tete, Nampula and Pemba.

# SOUTHERN MOZAMBIQUE

## Inhambane

POP 65,150

With its serene waterside setting, tree-lined avenues, faded colonial-style architecture and mixture of Arabic, Indian and African influences, Inhambane is one of Mozambique's most charming towns and well worth a visit on the way to Tofo. It has a history that reaches back at least a millennium, making it one of the oldest settlements along the coast.

### Sleeping & Eating

**Hotel África Tropical** PENSION $

(Sensasol; ☎84 641 7312; Rua da Liberdade; r Mtc1500; ❄) África Tropical has a row of small, tidy rooms facing a tiny garden. Some rooms have a double bed, others a double plus a single; all have fan, net and hot water. Breakfast is extra, and there's a small restaurant. The hotel's just off Avenida da Independência.

**Casa do Capitão** HOTEL $$$

(☎293-21408/9, 84 026 2302; www.hotelcasadocapitao.com; Avenida Maguiguana; r from Mtc9750; ❄📶🏊) This low-key hotel is in a fantastic location overlooking Inhambane Bay on two sides. Views are wonderful and rooms are well appointed. It's the most upmarket choice in town – a nice treat if you're in Inhambane on a honeymoon or if you just want pampering.

**TakeAway Sazaria** CAFE $

(Avenida da Independência; mains from Mtc100; ⌚8am-5pm Mon-Fri) Tasty, inexpensive soups, *pregos* (steak rolls) and sandwiches to eat there or take away.

**Verdinho's** EUROPEAN $$

(☎84 563 1260; 70 Avenida Acordos de Lusaka; mains Mtc250-450; ⌚8am-10pm Mon-Sat; 📶) The popular Verdinho's features a large menu including tasty salads, burgers, pizzas, pasta and continental dishes. It has seating indoors or at shaded tables outside on the patio where you can watch the passing scene.

### Getting There & Away

#### AIR

**LAM** (☎21-326001, 21-468800, 84 147, 82 147; www.lam.co.mz; cnr Avenidas 25 de Setembro & Karl Marx) has five flights weekly connecting Inhambane with Maputo, Vilankulo and Johannesburg (from about US$100 one way).

#### BOAT

Small motorised passenger boats operate from sunrise to sundown between Inhambane and Maxixe (Mtc10, 25 minutes).

### BUS & CAR

The bus station is behind the market. *Chapas* to Tofo run throughout the day (Mtc15 to Mtc18, one hour). There is a daily direct bus to Maputo, departing at 5.30am (Mtc600, seven hours, 450km). Fatima's Nest in Tofo has a daily shuttle to Maputo (Mtc800) that stops at Inhambane. There's also at least one bus daily in the morning from Inhambane to Vilankulo (Mtc300). For all other southbound and northbound transport, you'll need to head to Maxixe.

# Tofo

Thanks to its sheltered azure waters, white sands, easy access and fine diving, the beach at Tofo has long been legendary on the Southern Africa holiday circuit. The magnificent beach runs in a long arc, at the centre of which is a small town with a perpetual party atmosphere. Many people come to Tofo expecting to spend a few days and instead stay several weeks or more. For something quieter, head around the point to Barra or further north or south.

## Activities

**Tofo Scuba** DIVING

(82 826 0140; www.tofoscuba.com) This PADI five-star Gold Palm resort offers a full range of instruction, dives and equipment, and also has nitrox and a heated training pool. It's at the northern end of the beach, with a surf shop and a good cafe adjoining.

**Liquid Dive Adventures** DIVING

(0846 130 316, 0846 512 737; www.liquiddiveadventures.com) This PADI Green Star outfit offers Open Water courses and other instruction plus a full range of diving. It's at the entrance to town: go left at the first Y-intersection and Liquid Dive Adventures is about 150m up on the left.

## Sleeping

**Wuyani Pariango** HOSTEL $

(84 712 8963; www.pariangobeach.com; camping Mtc300, dm Mtc500, r Mtc2500, with shared bathroom Mtc1500-1800; ) This good budget place is in the centre of Tofo, just north of the market and just back from the beach. It has various simple reed-and-thatch rooms in the backyard walled garden plus space to pitch a tent.

**Fatima's Nest** HOSTEL $

(82 185 1575; www.mozambiquebackpackers.com; camping Mtc400, dm Mtc500, s/d/tr Mtc1600/2200/3200, without bathroom Mtc1000/2000/2600) The long-standing Fatima's, ever popular and now considerably expanded, has camping, dorm beds and a mix of very basic bungalows and rooms, all on low dunes overlooking the beach just north of the town centre. There's also kitchen, bar, pool table and evening beach bonfires.

**Casa Na Praia** GUESTHOUSE $$

(82 821 5921; www.casanapraiatofo.com; d Mtc5500-8800, tr Mtc4500-10,000) This place in the centre of Tofo beach has accommodation in three buildings: the more luxurious Casa Amarela, with lovely, attached beach-facing rooms with verandas; the cosy Bungalow Africa; and Casa Azul, a cheery white-with-blue trim, colonial-era house. There are semi-open-air bathrooms, each one different, and a very nice, beachside cafe–breakfast area.

## Eating

**Café Happi** CAFE $

(snacks & light meals from Mtc100; 7am-5pm; ) This good veg-only cafe at Liquid Dive Adventures (p843) has tasty breakfasts, salads, sandwiches, smoothies and more. It's near the entrance to town: go left at the Y-junction and it's about 100m further on the left.

**What U Want** ITALIAN $$

(mains Mtc300-500) Tasty Italian and Mozambican cuisine, good pizzas and starters like focaccia and bruschetta. It's in the centre of town, just northwest of the market area.

## Getting There & Away

*Chapas* run throughout the day along the 22km sealed road between Tofo and Inhambane, departing Tofo from about 5am (Mtc15 to Mtc18 for a large bus, one hour). To Maputo's Junta, there's usually one direct bus daily, departing Tofo by about 5am (Mtc750, 7½ hours). Fatima's Nest also has a daily shuttle to Maputo (Mtc800).

# Vilankulo

Vilankulo is the finishing (or starting) point of Mozambique's southern tourism circuit. It's also the gateway for visiting the nearby Bazaruto Archipelago, separated from the mainland by a narrow channel of turquoise sea. During South African holidays, Vilankulo is overrun with pickups and 4WDs, but otherwise it's a quiet, slow-paced town with some lovely nearby beaches.

## Activities

### Diving

Diving here is rewarding, and it's possible year-round. The best months are April to September and the worst are December and January, although conditions can vary markedly within these periods. The main sites are well offshore around the Bazaruto Archipelago (about a 45-minute boat ride away).

**Odyssea Dive** DIVING
(☎82 781 7130; www.odysseadive.com) This reliable outfit is the main dive outfitter in Vilankulo, offering a range of dives and PADI instruction. It's at the southern end of town, about 500m south of the Old Market on the beach.

### Dhow Safaris

Several outfits offer day or overnight dhow safaris around the Bazaruto Archipelago. Besides the recommended **Sailaway** (☎82 387 6350, 293-82385; www.sailaway.co.za; per person snorkelling excursion/overnight safari from US$75/260), **Marimba Secret Gardens** (☎84 048 9098, 82 005 3015; www.marimba.ch; dm/d/tw US$18/104/110; @) also organises good day trips to Bazaruto (from US$60 per person) as well as to lovely Santa Carolina Island (from US$70 per person) – all including park fees, lunch and snorkelling equipment. There is officially no camping on the islands in the park; operators running overnight tours camp along the mainland coast.

### Kite Surfing

**Kite Surfing Centre** KITESURFING
(www.kitesurfingcentre.com) Lessons, rentals and – best of all – kitesurfing safaris to the islands. It's north of town, next to the signposted Casbah Beach Bar.

## Sleeping

**Baobab Beach Backpackers** HOSTEL, CAMPGROUND $
(☎84 413 3057, 82 731 5420; www.baobabbeach.net; Rua do Palacio, Bairro Desse; camping US$7, dm US$10, bungalow d from US$34, with shared bathroom from US$26) With its waterside setting, chilled vibe and straightforward, good-value bungalows, Baobab Beach is a favourite with the party set. It has a popular, reasonably priced restaurant and an area for self-catering. It's about 500m south of the Old Market. Walking here from town is fine by day; at night, it's best to take a taxi.

**Casa Jules & Zombie Cucumber Backpackers** HOSTEL $
(☎84 686 9870, 84 421 2565; www.casajules.com; dm Mtc500, s/d from Mtc2500/3000; ) This place, just back from the beach road, offers a quiet vibe, hammocks, a bar, restaurant, tranquil gardens and helpful staff. Accommodation is in dorms or simple, tidy, thatched garden huts (as part of the original Zombie Cucumber Backpackers) or more spacious double and triple rooms up on the hillside at the newer 'Casa Jules'.

**Archipelago Resort** RESORT $$
(☎293-84022, 84 775 8433; www.archipelago-resort.com; 6-person garden/sea-view bungalows from US$170/190; ) This wonderful resort has 18 spacious, well appointed, Indonesian-style self-catering bungalows set in expansive green grounds overlooking the sea. All have large verandas, two bedrooms and two bathrooms downstairs as well as a two-bed loft.

## Eating

**Café Zambeziana** CAFE $
(light meals from Mtc250) Immediately to your right when exiting the old market, this local place has tasty but inexpensive grilled chicken and barbecue sandwiches.

**Kilimanjaro Café** CAFE $
(breakfast Mtc150-200, sandwiches & light meals Mtc250-300; ⊙8am-5pm Mon-Sat; ) Salads, sandwiches, pizza, pasta and a changing daily menu, plus smoothies and gourmet coffees. It's in the Lexus shopping mall.

## Getting There & Away

### AIR

**LAM** (p842) has daily flights to/from Maputo (from about US$150 one way) and **SAAirlink** (☎in South Africa 011-451 7300; www.flyairlink.com) has daily flights from Johannesburg (about US$150 one way).

### BUS

**Beira** (Mtc550 to Mtc600, 10 hours) Buses depart Vilankulo between 4.30am and 6am at least every second day; book the afternoon before.

**Maputo** (Mtc950, nine to 10 hours, usually two daily, departing from 3.30am) Book your ticket with the drivers the afternoon before and verify the time. Coming from Maputo, departures from Junta are at about 5am.

**Maxixe** (Mtc200, three to four hours) Several minibuses depart each morning to Maxixe (for Inhambane and Tofo). Allow six to seven hours for the entire journey from Vilankulo to Tofo.

## Bazaruto Archipelago

The Bazaruto Archipelago has clear, turquoise waters filled with colourful fish and offers diving, snorkelling and birding. It makes a fine upmarket holiday if you're looking for the quintessential Indian Ocean getaway.

Since 1971 much of the archipelago has been protected as **Bazaruto National Park** (Parque Nacional de Bazaruto; adult Mtc400). You'll see dozens of bird species, including fish eagles and pink flamingos. There are also red duikers, bushbucks and, especially on Benguera, Nile crocodiles. Dolphins swim through the clear waters, along with 2000 types of fish, plus loggerhead, leatherback and green turtles. Most intriguing are the elusive dugongs.

### Activities

Diving is generally best from about May to September, although it's possible year-round, and visibility can vary greatly even from day to day. Dives, equipment rental and dive-certification courses can be organised at any of the island lodges or in Vilankulo.

### Sleeping & Eating

**★&Beyond Benguerra** LODGE **$$$**

(in South Africa 011-809 4300; www.andbeyond.com/benguerra-island/; r per person all-inclusive from US$765; ) This is perhaps the most intimate of the archipelago lodges, with lovely, well-spaced beach chalets (cabanas) and villas (*casinhas*), fine beachside dining under the stars and a good selection of activities. The entire lodge is open design, with open-air showers, luxury bathtubs with views and private infinity plunge pools. It's well worth the splurge, if your budget allows.

**Azura Benguerra** RESORT **$$$**

(84 731 0871, in South Africa 011-467 0907; www.azura-retreats.com; r per person all-inclusive from US$655; ) This lovely place is one of the archipelago's most luxurious retreats. Accommodation is in secluded beach villas nestled amid tropical vegetation, with private plunge pools, wonderful cuisine, outdoor showers under the stars, fine views and a selection of activities.

### Getting There & Away

All the top-end lodges arrange speedboat transfers for their guests. Most day visitors reach the islands by dhow from Vilankulo, where there are a number of dhow safari operators.

# CENTRAL MOZAMBIQUE

## Beira

POP 546,000

Faded, withered and decidedly rough around the edges, Mozambique's second-largest city seems like a place that's been left behind. Yet even seedy Beira has its highlights. There's **Macuti Beach** (Praia de Macuti; Avenida das FPLM), an unkempt but broad swath of sand commandeered by weekend footballers and haunted by shipwrecks, some glorious if grimy examples of colonial architecture and a few eating surprises if you know where to look.

### Sleeping

**Royal Guest House** GUESTHOUSE **$**

(23-324030; 1311 Avenida Eduardo Mondlane; r incl breakfast Mtc3000; ) This intimate, residential-style B&B in the shady Ponta Gêa area has large, characterful rooms with mini fridge, TV and laundry service. No meals (apart from breakfast) are available. There's a pleasant garden and small pool out the back.

#### TRAVEL & SECURITY IN CENTRAL MOZAMBIQUE

Following attacks by Renamo opposition forces on buses in the provinces of Sofala, Manica, Tete and Zambézia in 2016, the public-transport system has been in a state of flux. Some services are suspended, several routes are subject to military convoys and a couple of bus companies are not operating at all. As a result, transport information for the region is particularly liable to change. Check ahead before travelling in central Mozambique and always review the current security situation before setting out.

## GORONGOSA NATIONAL PARK

About 170km northwest of Beira is **Gorongosa National Park** (Parque Nacional de Gorongosa; ☎82 308 2252; www.gorongosa.org; adult/child per day US$20/10; ⏰6am-6pm Apr-Dec), which was gazetted in 1960 and soon made headlines as one of Southern Africa's premier wildlife parks. It was once renowned for its large prides of lions, as well as for its elephants, hippos, buffaloes and rhinos, but the civil war during the 1980s and early 1990s destroyed its infrastructure. Rehabilitation work began in 1995, and in 1998 Gorongosa reopened to visitors.

In recent years the park has received a major boost thanks to assistance from the US-based Carr Foundation, which has joined with the government of Mozambique to fund Gorongosa's long-term restoration and ecotourism development.

**Montebelo Gorongosa Lodge & Safari** (☎82 308 2252; www.gorongosa.org; s/d Mtc3300/4300, bungalow s/d Mtc4125/5125; P ❄ 📶 ≋) Located at Chitengo park headquarters, Montebelo has lovely comfortable rooms in rondavels or standard blocks. Count on hot water, soap, mosquito nets and night-time coffee. It also offers the opportunity to organise 'fly camps', depositing you deep in the bush with your own tent and guide (US$500 per person for two nights including flight, meals and guide).

### Getting There & Away

The park turnoff is at Inchope, about 130km west of Beira, from where it's 43km north along reasonable tarmac to Nota village and then 11km east along an all-weather gravel road to the park gate. From the gate it's another 18km to Montebelo Gorongosa Lodge and park HQ.

**VIP Inn Beira** HOTEL $$
(☎23-340100; www.viphotels.com; 172 Rua Luís Inácio; s/d incl breakfast from Mtc4100/4400; ❄ 📶) All things considered, the VIP is probably your best accommodation bet in Beira's *baixa,* a little oasis of light in an otherwise dark and dingy quarter. The clean, spacious entrance opens a theme that continues upstairs in rooms that are comfortable, if lacking in wow factor. Bank on a substantial buffet breakfast, a relaxing bar and very helpful staff.

★**Jardim das Velas** HOTEL $$$
(☎23-312209; www.jardimdasvelas.wixsite.com; 282 Avenida das FPLM, Makuti Beach; d/q US$105/120; P ❄ 📶) For a fantastic alternative to the business hotels of Macuti, check into this quiet Mediterranean-style place near the lighthouse. Upstairs are six spotless, modern doubles with views of the sea, and there are six equally well equipped, four-person family rooms with bunks downstairs. A lush walled garden hosts breakfast and an all-day cafe and snack bar that makes excellent waffles.

## Eating

**Café Riviera** CAFE $
(Praça do Município; mains from Mtc150; ⏰7.30am-9pm Mon-Sat, to 7pm Sun) Head to this old-world street-side cafe for caffeine Portuguese style and a *bolo* (cake) as you watch the passing Beira scene – both the pretty and the gritty. It offers all the usual snacks, including chicken and samosas, in an African colonial atmosphere that'll make you feel as though you've slipped into a Graham Greene novel.

★**Biques** INTERNATIONAL $$
(☎84 597 7130, 23-313051; Macuti Beach; mains from Mtc400; ⏰10am-10pm) Biques (pronounced '*beaks*') is a sight for sore eyes if you've just emerged bleary-eyed from the bush. Perched on a rise overlooking a windswept scoop of Macuti Beach, it's long been revered by overlanders for its pizza oven, triple-decker club sandwiches and sweet chocolate brownies. Wash your meal down with a frosty beer (served in a *real* beer glass).

★**Tutto D'Italy** ITALIAN $$$
(☎87 427 4569; Rua Vasco Fernando Homen; pasta Mtc400-600, mains Mtc650-850; ⏰11am-10pm; 👪) Top of the list of 'weird epiphanies in Beira' is this fabulous Italian restaurant hidden (there's no sign) in a children's park on the cusp of the Ponta Gêa neighbourhood. All the Italian favourites – antipasti, veal, octopus and pasta dishes – are served here, and all taste as though they've been teleported from Rome or Naples.

## Getting There & Away

**AIR**

**Beira Airport** is 7km northwest of town. There are flights on **LAM** (☎23-303112, 23-324142; www.lam.co.mz; 85 Rua Major Serpa Pinto) twice weekly to/from Johannesburg, daily to/from Maputo and several times weekly to/from Tete, Nampula, Pemba and Lichinga.

**BUS & CHAPA**

**Chimoio**

To Chimoio (Mtc200, three hours), *chapas* go throughout the day from the **main transport stand** in the city centre. For Gorongosa National Park you'll need to change at Inchope.

**Maputo**

Numerous companies serve Maputo (Mtc1700, 17 hours), including **Etrago** (☎82 320 3600; www.etrago.co.mz), departing Tuesday and Thursday at 3pm and Saturday at 3am from Praça do Maquinino in the city centre.

**Vilankulo**

To Vilankulo (Mtc550 to Mtc600, 10 hours, daily), there's a direct bus departing by about 4.30am.

# Chimoio

Chimoio is a gateway city, not just for travellers heading into and out of Zimbabwe (located 100km west), but also for the lure of the **Chimanimani Mountains** (Reserva Nacional de Chimanimani; adult/vehicle/camping Mtc400/400/200), the rugged mountainous frontier that is loaded with DIY, back-to-nature experiences.

## Sleeping

**Pink Papaya** HOSTEL $

(☎82 555 7310; http://pinkpapaya.atspace.com; cnr Ruas Pigivide & 3 de Fevereiro; dm/s/d/q Mtc500/1000/1300/2000) Pink Papaya is one of the few genuine backpacker hostels in central Mozambique and an excellent orientation point if you've just arrived from Zimbabwe. Located in a salubrious part of town near the governor's mansion, it has helpful management, clean dorm beds and doubles, and a well-equipped kitchen and braai area. Breakfast is available on request.

★**Residencial Chinfura** B&B $$

(☎251-22640; Avenida Liberdade; r Mtc2200-3300; P ❄ 📶) In terms of value for money, this is probably the best accommodation option in Chimoio. Located on the edge of the main town behind a guarded entrance, the large rooms are separated from the main house and have their own pleasant terrace and breakfast room. Beds are large, towels are thick, there are coffee-making facilities and the wi-fi is strong.

## Eating

**Banana Split** BURGERS, SNACKS $

(cnr Ruas Pigivide & Dr Araujo de la Cerda; snacks Mtc150-400; ⏲7am-9pm) This new, locally run place offers a Mozambican take on fast food, with burgers, wraps, samosas and desserts served in a small, bright four-table cafe or available for takeaway. The daily cakes are delightful.

★**Restaurante Maúa** AFRICAN $$$

(Feria Popular, EN6; mains Mtc500-800; ⏲11am-10pm Tue-Sun) Tap any local with taste buds and they'll probably tell you that this place – one of several restaurants in the Feria Popular complex – serves the best food in Chimoio, possibly even central Mozambique. The menu leans heavily towards Mozambican flavours, with excellent tiger prawns, piri-piri chicken, steak and *matapa* (cassava leaves sauteed with cashews and coconut milk).

## Information

**Eco-Micaia Office** (☎82 303 4285; www.micaia.org) The office of local foundation Eco-Micaia can offer info on Ndzou Camp and the Chimanimani Reserve in general. It's behind the Shoprite (EN6; ⏲9am-8pm Mon-Sat, to 3pm Sun) supermarket just off the main EN1 highway.

## Getting There & Away

Most transport leaves from the main bus station, near the train station. Several bus companies operate out of Chimoio, including national stalwarts Maning Nice and Nagi Investimentos. The Nagi office is next to Shoprite supermarket.

# Quelimane

POP 245,000

Quelimane is a small city with a scruffy sensibility that acts as a convenient waystation for travellers jockeying between northern and southern Mozambique, or overlanders heading for the border with Malawi. The mainstay of the local economy is the coconut, best enjoyed in a sauce atop chicken known as *frango à zambeziana*.

## Sleeping & Eating

**Hotel Chuabo** HOTEL $

(☎24-213181, 24-213182; 232 Avenida Samora Machel; s/d Mtc2975/3150; ) The Chuabo is a Quelimane institution, one of the few hotels anywhere in Mozambique that managed to stay running throughout the war years. These days the whole place reeks of another era – if you like (unintentional) retro, this is your bag. Drink in the furry carpets, oversized bedrooms, wood-strip walls and – best of all – the curvaceous staircase that spirals down six levels.

**Hotel Elite** HOTEL $$

(☎24-219900; www.elitehotels.com; cnr Avenidas 7 de Setembro & Eduardo Mondlane; r/ste Mtc3900/5600; ) Look out, Quelimane, the accommodation bar has been raised! Seeming small and relatively modest, the new Hotel Elite is something of a palace behind its outer skin and not as small as the exterior suggests. The 23 deluxe rooms come with all mod-cons and a number are equipped with king-sized beds and sofas.

## Getting There & Away

The transport stand (known locally as 'Romoza') is at the northern end of Avenida Eduardo Mondlane. *Chapas* run frequently to/from Nicoadala from the junction with the main road (Mtc50, 45 minutes). Routes south towards Beira were in flux in late 2016 due to political unrest.

# NORTHERN MOZAMBIQUE

## Nampula

POP 477,000

Anchored by its white cathedral and embellished with a museum, Nampula is worth a brief stopover if you're in the area. Indeed, many travellers find themselves resting up here before pitching north to Pemba or east to Mozambique Island.

### Sleeping

**Complexo Bamboo** CHALET $

(☎26-217838, 26-216595; bamboo@teledata.mz; Ribáuè Rd; s/d/ste Mtc2350/2750/3750; ) Well-maintained rooms (the twins are nicer than the doubles) in expansive grounds with a playground make this a good choice for families. All rooms have TV and minifridge, and there's a popular restaurant. It's about 7km out of town; follow Avenida de Trabalho west from the train station, then right onto Ribáuè Rd; Bamboo is 1.5km down on the left.

★**Hotel Milénio** HOTEL $$

(☎26-218877; 842 Avenida 25 de Setembro; d/ste Mtc3900/4500; ) What might look like a standard business hotel has raised the game in Nampula with some useful bonuses, most notably a gym (with proper working machines); a sizeable outdoor pool; well-equipped, surgically clean rooms; and, arguably, the best restaurant in town. For what you get, the price is a veritable bargain.

### Eating

★**Hotel Milénio Restaurant** INDIAN $$

(842 Avenida 25 de Setembro; mains Mtc450-700; ⏲12.30-3pm & 6.30-10pm) Equipped with a chef from Mumbai, this sleek restaurant at Hotel Milénio (p848) knocks out the best Indian food in northern Mozambique, with excellent meat and vegetarian dishes. Recommended is the lamb biriyani, the *bhuna* (curry) and the chicken tikka. All come with lashings of rice and/or naan. Equally spicy are some finely seasoned Mozambican standards. No alcohol served.

**VIP Cafe** INTERNATIONAL $$

(cnr Avenidas Eduardo Mondlane & Josina Machel; snacks from Mtc100, mains Mtc400-600; ⏲7am-10pm) This clean, new, impossibly inviting nook in a glassy shopping centre draws you in with its shiny espresso machine and display case replete with fresh pastries. Cakes aside, there's a full laminated menu of sandwiches, burgers and fuller dishes, some with Lebanese inflections.

### Getting There & Away

#### AIR

**Nampula Airport** is very handily positioned just 4km northeast of the city centre (Mtc200 in a taxi). There are flights on **LAM** (☎26-212801, 26-213322; Avenida Francisco Manyanga; ⏲8am-4pm Mon-Fri, 9.30am-11.30am Sat) to Maputo daily, and to Beira, Lichinga, Quelimane, Tete and Pemba several times weekly. There are also flights to Johannesburg (South Africa), Nairobi (Kenya) and Lilongwe (Malawi).

#### BUS & CHAPA

Most long-distance buses depart from next to the Petromac petrol station in the Antiga Gorongosa area (from the train station, follow Avenida de Trabalho west for around 2km).

**TRAIN**

A twice-weekly passenger train connects Nampula and Cuamba. The spectacular but typically African journey takes 10 to 12 hours. There are theoretically three classes of carriage (executive/1st/2nd Mtc600/400/170), although they might not function on all trips. It's well worth investing in executive if you can.

# Mozambique Island

Dhows shifting silently through shallow seas, bruised colonial buildings withering elegantly in the tropical heat and the voices of a church choir competing with the muezzin's call to prayer. You'll encounter all this and more within the crowded confines of Mozambique Island, one of the historical highlights of Africa, a fragrant melange of African, Portuguese, Swahili, French and Goan flavours left to mellow in the iridescent waters of the Indian Ocean for centuries.

## Sights

**Fort of São Sebastião** FORTRESS
(adult/child Mtc100/50; 8am-4.30pm) The island's northern end is dominated by the massive Fort of São Sebastião – the oldest complete fort still standing in sub-Saharan Africa and, arguably, the finest military building on the continent. Construction began in 1558 and took 62 years. The fort has withstood numerous Dutch, British and Omani bids to diminish it. While the structure remains in a pretty unkempt state, with little explanatory information, it size and aura, along with the views from its battlements, are awe-inspiring.

## Activities

Strong tidal flows make it dangerous to swim around Mozambique Island's northern and southern ends. The cleanest of the island's patches of sand is Nancaramo Beach, next to the fort. For beautiful, clean sand, head across Mossuril Bay to Chocas and Cabaceira Pequena or to the beach on Goa Island.

**Ilha Blue** TOURS
(84 396 9438; www.ilhablue.com; Avenida dos Heróis) Run by an expat British-Australian couple, this professional, community-involved tour company offers cycling, snorkelling, kayaking and dhow safaris, all led by local guides. It shares digs with a clothes shop called Orera Orera in Stone Town.

## Sleeping

**Ruby Backpacker** HOSTEL $
(84 866 0200; ruby.backpackers@gmail.com; Travessa da Sé; dm/d Mtc650/1550; ) Located in a renovated 400-year-old house, the island's only backpackers is a good one. It has dorm beds upstairs and downstairs, twin and double rooms, a self-catering kitchen, hot showers, a bar, a fantastic rooftop terrace, bicycle rental, laundry service, a travellers' noticeboard and lots of information about onward travel.

★ **O Escondidinho** HOTEL $$
(26-610078; www.oescondidinho.net; Avenida dos Heróis; s/d Mtc3900/4400, with outside bathroom Mtc2500/3300; ) In a sturdy but genteel old trading house in Stone Town, you can recline like a colonial lord in atmospheric, high-ceilinged rooms furnished with four-poster beds draped with mosquito nets. Seven of the 10 rooms have large bathrooms and there are more refinements downstairs, with a flower-embellished garden and small pool overlooked by one of the town's best restaurants.

★ **Jardim dos Aloés** B&B $$$
(87 827 4645; www.jardim-dos-aloes.com; Rua Presidente Kaunda; r incl breakfast Mtc10,500-11,200; ) These three exquisite suites are relatively new on the island scene and have upped the ante, mixing retro decor (record players, antique phones) and interesting books with elements of the island's past and present. It's a beautiful melange of hammocks, terraces and alcoves hidden behind high walls in the heart of Stone Town.

## Eating

**Sara's Place** AFRICAN $
(Avenida 25 de Junho; mains Mtc150-300; 8am-10pm) Inhabiting a reed house in the square opposite the hospital, Sara's is a confirmed local favourite – small and scruffy, but salt-of-the-earth – where you can taste chicken and fish served with the unique island speciality *matapa de siri siri* (seaweed with coconut milk).

★ **Rickshaws Cafe** INTERNATIONAL $$
(82 678 0098; Rua dos Trabalhadores; mains Mtc495-610; 7am-11pm) The new kids on the block have nabbed a beautiful sunset

location on the island's western side where you can sit alfresco and relish food from a menu that mixes Mozambican favourites with fish tacos, pizza, brownies and burgers. It's American run, and the name harks back to a method of transport once popular on the island.

**★Karibu** SEAFOOD **$$**
(☎84 380 2518; Barrio do Museu; mains Mtc400-800; ⏲11am-3pm & 6-9.15pm Tue-Sun) This excellent new restaurant in Stone Town specialises in the island's seafood bounty. Tuna, prawns, marlin and lobster are all done to perfection here, overseen by the hands-on Portuguese owner. Choose from the chalkboard menu and sit alfresco in front of artfully arranged antiques in the window.

## ℹ Getting There & Away

### BOAT

There's at least one dhow daily connecting Mozambique Island with Cabaceira Grande and Mossuril. For **Pensão-Restaurant Sunset Boulevard** (☎82 401 5416; www.hotelsunsetboulevard.com; dm/d US$8/20), ask to be dropped off at 'São João', from where the *pensão* is just a five- to 10-minute walk up from the beach. From Mossuril village, it's about 1½ hours on foot to Cabaceira Grande.

However, most travellers charter a motorised dhow (about Mtc1500 if you haggle) to the Cabaceiras so they can come back the same day.

### BUS & CHAPA

Mozambique Island is joined by a one-lane, 3.5km bridge (built in 1967) to the mainland (there are half-a-dozen passing places). Most *chapas* stop about 1km before the bridge in Lumbo, where you'll need to get into a smaller pickup to cross over Mossuril Bay, due to vehicle weight restrictions on the bridge. (Thanks to lack of traffic, it's perfectly pleasant to walk the 3.5km across the bridge.)

# Cuamba

This lively if unexciting rail and road junction was formerly known as Novo Freixo. With its dusty streets, flowering trees and large student population, it's the economic centre of Niassa province and a convenient stop-off if you're travelling to/from Malawi, especially if you're catching the train. The area is known for its garnet gemstones and for its scenic panoramas, especially to the east around Mt Mitucué (Serra Mitucué).

**Quinta Timbwa** CHALET **$**
(☎82 692 0250, 82 300 0752; quintatimbwa@yahoo.com.br; Cruze dos Chiapas; rondavels Mtc2500; ❄) This place is set on a large estate about 2.5km from town, and signposted. It's tranquil and good value, with spotless, pleasant rooms – some in attached rows, some in small rondavels – surrounded by expansive grounds featuring a small lake. It's ideal for families or for anyone with their own transport. There's also a restaurant (mains Mtc350 to Mtc600).

**Pensão São Miguel** PENSION **$**
(☎271-62701; Avenida 3 de Fevereiro; r with fan/air-con incl breakfast Mtc1000/1200; ❄) This long-standing, local-style guesthouse has small, clean rooms crowded behind the restaurant-bar area. Each room has one small double bed. While it's not the most luxurious of establishments, it's the best value-for-price option in the town centre, and located an easy 10-minute walk from the train station and bus stand.

## ℹ Getting There & Away

A passenger train connects Cuamba and Nampula, leaving Cuamba on Sunday and Thursday at 5am. The journey takes 10 to 12 hours. There are theoretically three classes of carriage (executive/1st/2nd Mtc600/400/170), although they might not function on all trips. It's well worth investing in executive if you can.

# Lake Niassa

Most people think of Lake Malawi as – well – Malawian, but 25% of its waters lie within Mozambique. Guarding the quieter, less developed side of the lake (which is called Lago Niassa in these parts), the Mozambican shoreline sees a small but steady stream of adventure travellers who quickly realise they've stumbled upon a wild and wonderful African paradise that few others know about.

**Mbuna Bay** CHALET **$$$**
(☎82 536 7781; www.mbunabay.ch; s/d with full board in bush bungalow US$150/240, in beach chalet US$210/340) 🍃 About 15km south of Metangula, ecofriendly Mbuna Bay has four wooden beachfront cottages, four brick cottages set back in the bush and one wattle-and-daub cottage. All have creatively designed bathrooms (some open-air), and all are comfortable in a rustic way. Snorkelling, dhow sails, kayaking

and yoga can be arranged, as can transfers from Lichinga. Food (included) is entirely vegetarian.

## Getting There & Away

**BUS**

The lakeshore is best accessed from the provincial capital, Lichinga, from where *chapas* head out to Metangula (two hours) and Cóbuè (four hours).

**FERRY**

The MV *Chambo* connects Likoma Island and other Malawian ports with the villages on the Mozambican side of the lake. There are departures from Metangula three times a week. Services on the route north from Metangula to Likoma Island also call in at Cóbuè.

# Pemba

POP 208,000

The gateway to the north, Pemba sprawls across a small peninsula that juts into the enormous and magnificent Pemba Bay, one of the world's largest natural harbours. The mildewed *baixa* area is home to the low-lying port, the old town and the lively township of **Paquitequete**. Steeply uphill from here, the busier and less atmospheric town centre is the place to get things done, with banks and offices, a few restaurants and the main bus stand. About 5km east of the town centre is **Wimbi Beach** (also spelled Wimbe), the hub of tourist activity and the favoured destination of most visitors.

## Activities

**CI Divers** DIVING

(☎272-20102; www.cidivers.co.za; Pieter's Place, Avenida Marginal, Wimbi Beach) The only independent dive operator in Pemba, CI Divers is based at South African–run Pieter's Place. It offers PADI open-water certification (US$560 for a four-day course) and guided dive immersions (US$70). Boats launch from the Náutilus Hotel and sail roughly 1km out to sea to a 12m to 30m wall replete with coral and marine life.

## Sleeping

**Pemba Magic Lodge** CAMPGROUND, BUNGALOW $

('Russel's Place'; ☎272-21429; www.pembamagiclodge.com; Avenida Marginal; camping per site Mtc700, tent hire Mtc1000, dm/s/d Mtc1000/3500/5200; ) In business since 1998, Russel's Place is Pemba's nominal backpackers, located on the eastern extension of Wimbi Beach (called Nanhimbe) about 3.5km beyond Complexo Náutilus. It offers the full gamut of budget accommodation: campsites, rent-a-tents, a five-bed dorm and private bungalows made out of local materials (one of which sleeps six).

**Pieter's Place** GUESTHOUSE $$

(☎82 682 2700; www.pietersdiversplace.co.za; Avenida Marginal; r US$60-100; ) Built around a huge, ancient baobab tree (into which you can climb and have breakfast in an improvised treehouse), Pieter's Place has an amiable African-backpackers feel to it. It's also diving central, thanks to the on-site CI Divers. Building work was being completed on some new rooms in late 2016; all will have private bathroom, mosquito nets and coffee-making tray.

★**Avani Pemba Beach Hotel** HOTEL $$$

(☎272-21770; www.pembabeachresort.com; 5470 Avenida Marginal; s US$264-366, d US$310-430; P@) If you're a romantic with a penchant for luxurious beachside hotels that have an Arabian bent, then this five-star establishment is the business. Sitting like a mini-Alhambra in expansive grounds north of Wimbi Beach, it has well-equipped rooms, a dreamy restaurant, gym, spa and infinity pool, a handy travel agent and staff who touch their heart when they say 'good morning'.

## Eating

**Pastelaria Flor d'Avenida** CAFE $

(☎272-20514; Avenida Eduardo Mondlane; mains Mtc300-350; 6am-10pm Mon-Sat) It doesn't look much from the outside, but this long-standing, informal eatery with mainly outdoor tables delivers the goods when it comes to coffee and pastries.

★**Locanda Italiana** ITALIAN $$

(☎272-20672, 82 688 9050; 487 Rua Jerónimo Romero; pizza & pasta Mtc300-400, mains Mtc500-600; 10am-10pm) Something of a vision in the quiet, well-worn streets of the *baixa*, this Italian-run restaurant serves up al dente pasta (the *ragú* is excellent) and wood-fired-oven pizzas in the flower-embellished courtyard of a restored building. If you're looking for a day off root vegetables and chicken piri-piri, this is the place to go.

### Information

**Kaskazini** (☎82 309 6990, 272-20371; www.kaskazini.com; Pemba Beach Hotel, Avenida Marginal; ⏲8am-3pm Mon-Fri, 9am-noon Sat) Efficient, knowledgeable and a good first stop. It gives free information on Pemba and elsewhere in northern Mozambique, helps with accommodation and flight bookings, and can organise everything from dhow safaris to sunset cruises.

### Getting There & Away

**AIR**

**Pemba Airport** is 4km southwest of the city centre. **LAM** (☎272-21251; Avenida Eduardo Mondlane; ⏲7am-4.30pm Mon-Fri, 9.30-11.30am Sat) flies daily to/from Maputo (via Nampula and/or Beira) and twice weekly to/from Dar es Salaam (Tanzania) and Nairobi (Kenya). **SAAirlink** (☎272-21700; www.flyairlink.com; Airport) flies twice weekly to Johannesburg. Expect to pay from Mtc400 to Mtc500 for a taxi from the airport to town.

**BUS & CHAPA**

**Ibo & Quirimbas Islands**

For the Quirimbas get a *chapa* (minibus) from the **Mcel Transport Stand** to the boat dock at Tandanhangue (Mtc300 to Mtc400, four to eight hours) via Quissanga. *Chapas* leave daily between 4am and 5am.

**Mozambique Island**

For Mozambique Island the best bet is to go to Nampula and then get onward transport from there the next day. You can also try your luck getting out at Namialo junction and looking for onward transport from there, but the timing often doesn't work out and Namialo is unappealing as an overnight spot.

## Quirimbas Archipelago

Hidden like pirate treasure off Mozambique's north coast, the islands of the Quirimbas archipelago conceal a multitude of secrets, from the brilliant coral reefs of Medjumbe to the ancient baobab trees of Quilaluia. But none of the 31 islands can equal mysterious Ibo, the archipelago's de facto capital. Haunted by a tumultuous history, and now a bubbling blend of Portuguese, Swahili, Indian and African cultures, Ibo feels as though it fell into a stupor in the 1850s and has yet to awaken.

### Sleeping

**Karibuni** CABIN, CAMPGROUND $

(☎82 703 2200; camping Mtc120, r Mtc400-700) Karibuni is Ibo on a budget, with very basic rooms in local-style thatched huts and space in a small garden to pitch your tent. Meals can be prepared, but you'll need to bring your own food.

★ **Cinco Portas** GUESTHOUSE $$

(☎86 926 2399; www.cincoportas.com; Avenida República; s US$50-80, d US$85-140, apt US$160-195; ) Ibo is an idyll wherever you stay, but Cinco Portas could well offer the best deal when you factor in price, friendly ambience and flawless, nothing-is-too-much-trouble service. Housed in a spruced-up old warehouse with a brilliant waterside setting, its small but comfortable rooms are complemented by lovely communal areas embellished with mahogany carvings and the best restaurant on the island.

★ **Ibo Island Lodge** LODGE $$$

(www.iboisland.com; s/d with full board US$460/720; ) This nine-room luxury boutique hotel – the most upmarket accommodation on Ibo – is housed in three restored 19th-century mansions in a prime setting overlooking the water near the dhow port. Furnishings throughout reflect the nuances of Ibo's past (Swahili, Indian, Portuguese and African), with mahogany chests, four-poster beds, and indoor and open-to-the-stars showers.

### Eating

**Kumawe** SEAFOOD $

(☎82 741 4616; Rituto; mains Mtc300) A couple of homes in the *bairro* known as Rituto offer meals if organised in advance (enquire at Cinco Portas). A local will pick you up and take you to their small house, where you'll likely dine on the catch of the day, along with *matapa* and rice.

# UNDERSTAND MOZAMBIQUE

## Mozambique Today

In Mozambique's hotly contested 2014 national elections, Frelimo insider Filipe Nyusi won at the national level. However, Renamo, which won at the parliamentary level in five central and northern provinces, alleged widespread irregularities and rejected the results.

Since then, ongoing low-level conflict between Frelimo and Renamo – fuelled also by the discovery of major coal and natural-gas deposits in the country's north – has marred Mozambique's once glowing image as a postwar success story. While economic forecasts remain positive overall, other challenges include corruption and lack of free political debate in the public arena.

# History

From Bantu-speaking farmers and fishers to Arabic traders, Goan merchants and adventuring Europeans, Mozambique has long been a crossroads of cultures.

## Resistance

Resistance was kindled, and the independence movement brought to life after the'Mueda Massacre' in 1960, in which peacefully protesting villagers were gunned down by Portuguese troops.

In 1962 the Front for the Liberation of Mozambique (Frelimo) was formed, led by the charismatic Eduardo Mondlane. Mondlane was assassinated in 1969 and succeeded by Frelimo's military commander, Samora Machel. Frelimo decided early on a policy of violent resistance. Finally, after bitter struggle, the independent People's Republic of Mozambique was proclaimed on 25 June1975, with Frelimo as the ruling party and Samora Machel as president.

The Portuguese pulled out virtually overnight – after sabotaging vehicles and pouring concrete down wells – and left Mozambique in chaos with few skilled professionals and virtually no infrastructure. Mozambique's new government threw itself into a policy of radical social change. Ties were established with European communist powers, cooperative farms replaced private land, and companies were nationalised. Mass literacy programs and health initiatives were launched. For a while, the future looked rosy and Mozambique was feted in left-wing Western circles as a successful communist state.

## Civil War

By 1983 the country was almost bankrupt. The roots of the crisis were both economic and political. Concerned by the government's support for resistance movements such as the African National Congress (ANC), the white-minority-ruled countries of Rhodesia and South Africa deliberately 'destabilised' their neighbour with the creation of a manufactured guerrilla movement known as the Mozambique National Resistance (Renamo).

Renamo was made up of mercenaries, co-opted soldiers and disaffected Mozambicans, and funded by the South African military and a motley collection of Western interests. Renamo had no desire to govern – its only ideology was to paralyse the country. Roads, bridges, railways, schools and clinics were destroyed. Villagers were rounded up, anyone with skills was shot, and atrocities were committed on a massive scale.

By the late 1980s, change was sweeping through the region. The USSR's collapse altered the political balance in the West, and new, more liberal policies in South Africa restricted Renamo support. Samora Machel died under questionable circumstances in 1986 and was succeeded by the more moderate Joaquim Chissano. Frelimo switched from a Marxist ideology to a market economy and Renamo began a slow evolution into a genuine opposition party. A formal peace agreement was signed in October 1992.

## Peace

In October 1994 Mozambique held its first democratic elections. Frelimo won, but narrowly, with Renamo netting almost half the votes. The 1999 election produced similar results, this time followed by rioting and discord.

Since then, things have settled down. In December 2004 prominent businessman and long-time Frelimo insider Armando Guebuza was elected with a solid majority to succeed Chissano, who had earlier announced his intent to step down. Since taking the reins, Guebuza has pursued a more hard-line approach than Chissano and tensions between Frelimo and Renamo have sharpened. Frelimo has also increased its dominance of political life, and an easy re-election for Guebuza followed in 2009.

There were some isolated incidences of political unrest in the early lead-up to the 2014 elections. Yet, throughout its long history, Mozambique has shown a remarkable ability to rebound in the face of adversity, and most observers count the country among the continent's bright spots.

## People

There are 16 main tribes in Mozambique, including the Makua and Makonde in the north and the Shangaan in the south. Although Mozambique is relatively free of tribal rivalries, there has long been an undercurrent of north–south difference, with geographically remote and independent-minded northerners often feeling neglected by the upwardly mobile denizens of powerhouse Maputo.

Once suppressed under the Marxist regime, religion now flourishes and most villages have a church, a mosque or both. About 60% of Mozambicans are Christians, about 20% are Muslims (mostly in the north and along old trading routes), with the remainder following traditional animist beliefs.

## Food

Mozambique's cuisine blends African, Indian and Portuguese influences, and is especially noted for its seafood as well as its use of coconut milk and piri-piri (chilli pepper).

Roadside or market *barracas* (food stalls) serve plates of local food such as *xima* (a maize- or cassava-based staple) and sauce for about Mtc400 or less.

Most towns have a cafe, *pastelaria* or *salão de chá* serving coffee, pastries and inexpensive snacks and light meals such as omelettes, *pregos* (thin steak sandwiches) and burgers.

Restaurant prices and menu offerings are remarkably uniform throughout the country, ranging from about Mtc300 to Mtc500 for meals such as grilled fish or chicken served with rice or potatoes. Most restaurants also offer hearty Portuguese-style soups.

Markets in all larger towns sell an abundance of fresh tropical fruit along with a reasonably good selection of vegetables. High-quality meats from nearby South Africa are sold in delis and supermarkets.

## Wildlife

While more than 200 types of mammal wander the interior, challenging access, dense vegetation and skittishness on the part of the animals can make spotting them difficult. Mozambique shouldn't be viewed as a 'Big Five' destination. Work is proceeding in reviving several parks and reserves, especially Gorongosa National Park, which offers Mozambique's most accessible wildlife watching. However, poaching is taking a heavy toll, especially on the country's elephant population.

Of the approximately 900 bird species that have been identified in the Southern Africa region, close to 600 have been recorded in Mozambique.

## National Parks & Reserves

Mozambique has seven national parks: Gorongosa, Zinave, Banhine, Limpopo and Mágoè in the interior; Bazaruto National Park offshore; and Quirimbas National Park, encompassing both coastal and inland areas in Cabo Delgado province.

# SURVIVAL GUIDE

## Directory A–Z

### ACCOMMODATION

Accommodation in coastal areas fills during Christmas and New Year, Easter and other South African school holidays; advance bookings are recommended. Ask about rainy-season and children's discounts.

When quoting prices, many establishments distinguish between a *duplo* (room with two twin beds) and a *casal* (room with double bed). Rates are often quoted in US dollars or South African rand. Payment can almost always be made in meticals, dollars or rand.

### ACTIVITIES

There are numerous opportunities to get active in Mozambique, with highlights being birdwatching, wildlife-watching, diving and snorkelling, hiking, surfing and kitesurfing.

### DANGERS & ANNOYANCES

Mozambique is a relatively safe place and most travellers shouldn't have any difficulties. Petty theft and robbery are the main risks: watch your pockets or bag in markets; don't leave personal belongings unguarded on the beach or elsewhere; and minimise trappings such as jewellery, watches and external money pouches.

If you leave your vehicle unguarded, don't be surprised if windscreen wipers and other accessories are gone when you return. Don't leave anything inside a parked vehicle.

In Maputo and southern Mozambique, carjackings and more violent robberies do occur, although most incidents can be avoided by taking the usual precautions: avoid driving at night; keep the passenger windows up and the doors locked if you are in a vehicle (including a taxi) at any time during the day or night; avoid walking alone or in a group at dusk or at night, particularly in isolated areas; and avoid isolating situations in general. Don't walk alone along the beach away from hotel areas. If you're driving and your car is hijacked, hand over the keys immediately.

All this said, don't let these warnings deter you; simply be a savvy traveller. The vast majority of visitors enjoy this beautiful country without incident.

## ELECTRICITY

Electricity is 220V to 240V AC, 50Hz, usually accessed with South African-style three-round-pin plugs or two-round-pin plugs.

## EMBASSIES & CONSULATES

All of the following embassies are located in Maputo. The closest Australian representation is in South Africa.

**British High Commission** (☎82 313 8580; www.gov.uk/government/world/mozambique; 310 Avenida Vladimir Lenine)

**Canadian High Commission** (☎21-492623; www.canadainternational.gc.ca/mozambique; 1138 Avenida Kenneth Kaunda)

**Dutch Embassy** (☎21-484200; http://mozambique.nlembassy.org; 324 Avenida Kwame Nkrumah)

**French Embassy** (☎21-484600; www.ambafrance-mz.org; 2361 Avenida Julius Nyerere)

**German Embassy** (☎21-482700; www.maputo.diplo.de; 506 Rua Damião de Gois)

**Irish Embassy** (☎21-491440; www.dfa.ie/mozambique; 3630 Avenida Julius Nyerere)

**Malawian High Commission** (☎21-492676; 75 Avenida Kenneth Kaunda)

**South African High Commission** (☎21-243000; www.dfa.gov.za/foreign/sa_abroad/sam.htm; 41 Avenida Eduardo Mondlane)

**Swazi High Commission** (☎21-492117, 21-491601; 1271 Rua Luís Pasteur)

**Tanzanian High Commission** (☎21-490110, 21-490112; ujamaa@zebra.uem.mz; 115 Rua 301)

**US Embassy** (☎21-492797; http://maputo.usembassy.gov; 193 Avenida Kenneth Kaunda)

**Zambian High Commission** (☎21-492452; 1286 Avenida Kenneth Kaunda)

**Zimbabwean High Commission** (☎21-488877, 21-490404; zimmaputo@zimfa.gov.zw; 1657 Avenida Mártires de Machava)

## INTERNET ACCESS

Internet access is easy and fast in Maputo and other major centres, where there are numerous wi-fi spots and internet cafes. Most midrange and top-end hotels also offer wi-fi.

### PRICE RANGES

The following price ranges refer to a double room in high season.

**$** less than Mtc3500 (US$50)

**$$** Mtc3500 to Mtc7000 (US$50 to US$100)

**$$$** more than Mtc7000 (US$100)

The following price ranges refer to a standard main course.

**$** less than Mtc325 (US$5)

**$$** Mtc325 to Mtc650 (US$5 to US$10)

**$$$** more than Mtc650 (US$10)

## LGBTIQ TRAVELLERS

Mozambique tends to be more tolerant than some of its neighbours, and in 2015 it officially decriminalised homosexuality. However, gay sexual relationships remain for the most part culturally taboo. The country's small gay scene, centred on Maputo, has traditionally been quite discreet, but things are starting to open up.

## MONEY

Mozambique's currency is the metical (plural meticais, pronounced 'meticaish'), abbreviated here as Mtc.

Visa card withdrawal from ATMs is the best way of accessing money. All larger and many smaller towns have ATMs for accessing cash meticais. Most (including Barclays, BCI and Standard Bank) accept Visa card only; Millennium BIM machines also accept MasterCard.

Carry a standby mixture of US dollars (or South African rand, especially in the south) and meticais (including a good supply of small denomination notes, as nobody ever has change) for times when an ATM is not available or not working.

Except for Millennium BIM, most banks don't charge commission for changing cash.Travellers cheques can only be exchanged with difficulty (try BCI) and with a high commission; you'll need original purchase receipts.

### Exchange Rates

| | | |
|---|---|---|
| Australia | A$1 | Mtc60 |
| Canada | C$1 | Mtc60 |
| Japan | ¥100 | Mtc77 |
| New Zealand | NZ$1 | Mtc57 |
| UK | UK£1 | Mtc102 |
| US | US$1 | Mtc78 |

For current exchange rates, see www.xe.com.

### OPENING HOURS

**Banks** 8am to 3pm Monday to Friday
**Bars** 5pm to late
**Cafes** 7.30am to 9pm
**Exchange bureaus (casas de câmbio)** 8.30am to 5pm Monday to Friday, to noon Saturday
**Government offices** 7.30am to 3.30pm Monday to Friday
**Restaurants** Breakfast 7am to 11am, lunch noon to 3pm, dinner 6.30pm to 10.30pm
**Shops** 8am to noon and 2pm to 6pm Monday to Friday, 8am to 1pm Saturday

### PUBLIC HOLIDAYS

**New Year's Day** 1 January
**Mozambican Heroes' Day** 3 February
**Women's Day** 7 April
**International Workers' Day** 1 May
**Independence Day** 25 June
**Lusaka Agreement/Victory Day** 7 September
**Revolution Day** 25 September
**Peace & Reconciliation Day** 4 October
**Christmas/Family Day** 25 December

For South African school-holiday dates, see the calendar link at www.saschools.co.za.

### TELEPHONE

Mobile phone numbers are seven digits long, preceded by ☎82 for Mcel, ☎84 for Vodafone and ☎86 for Movitel.

All companies have outlets in major towns at which you can buy Sim-card starter packs (from Mtc50), fill out the necessary registration form and buy top-up cards.

### TIME

Mozambique time is GMT/UTC plus two hours. There is no daylight-saving time.

### VISAS

Travellers residing in a country with Mozambique diplomatic representation are required to obtain visas in advance of arrival in Mozambique or they must pay an additional 25% for visas obtained at the border. However, in an effort to encourage tourism, the government announced in early 2017 that one-month, single-entry tourist visas could now be obtained on arrival at 44 land borders (including all major aiports and many major borders, but not the border with Tanzania) for Mtc2000. It is too early to tell how this new announcement will be implemented. Our advice is to try to get your visa in advance, especially if you will be arriving in Maputo via bus from Johannesburg. But failing that, it is well worth trying your luck at the border.

## Getting There & Away

### AIR

#### Airports & Airlines

Airports in Mozambique:
**Maputo International Airport** (p842) Mozambique's main airport.
**Vilankulo** Regional flights.
**Beira** (p847) Regional flights.
**Nampula Airport** (p848) Regional flights.
**Moçimboa da Praia** Regional charter flights.
**Pemba Airport** (p852) Regional flights.

Airlines servicing Mozambique:
**Coastal Aviation** (safari@coastal.co.tz) Charter flights between Dar es Salaam (Tanzania) and Moçimboa da Praia, with connections to Pemba and the Quirimbas Archipelago.
**Linhas Aéreas de Moçambique** (LAM; ☎21-468800, 21-326001, 84 147, 82 147; www.lam.co.mz) The national airline. Offers flights connecting Johannesburg (South Africa) with Maputo, Vilankulo and Beira; and Dar es Salaam (Tanzania) with Pemba, Nampula and Maputo.
**Kenya Airways** (www.kenya-airways.com) Nairobi (Kenya) to Pemba and Maputo.
**SAAirlink** (p844) Johannesburg (South Africa) to Vilankulo, Beira, Nampula, Tete and Pemba; and Durban (South Africa) to Maputo.
**South African Airways** (www.flysaa.com) Johannesburg (South Africa) to Maputo and Vilankulo.
**TAP Air Portugal** (www.flytap.com) Lisbon (Portugal) to Maputo.

### LAKE

#### Malawi

The MV *Chambo* ferry (Mtc300, 6½ hours between Metangula and Likoma Island; Mtc40, 1½ hours between Cóbuè and Likoma Island; and Mtc500, 12 to 13 hours between Metangula and Nkhata Bay) connects Metangula and Cóbuè twice weekly with Likoma Island (Malawi) and weekly with Nkhata Bay (Malawi). A southern route connecting Metangula with Chipoka (Malawi, Mtc550, 11 to 12 hours) via Meponda is also running. Contact the Malawi Shipping Company (p833) for confirmation of prices and schedules.

### BORDER CROSSINGS

#### Malawi

**Cóbuè** On Lake Niassa.
**Dedza** 85km southwest of Lilongwe.
**Entre Lagos** Southwest of Cuamba.
**Mandimba** Northwest of Cuamba.
**Metangula** On Lake Niassa.
**Milange** 120km southeast of Blantyre.

**Vila Nova da Fronteira** At Malawi's southern tip.

**Zóbuè** On the Tete Corridor route linking Blantyre (Malawi) and Harare (Zimbabwe); this is the busiest crossing.

### South Africa

**Giriyondo** (8am to 4pm October to March, to 3pm April to September) 75km west of Massingir town, 95km from Kruger National Park's Phalaborwa Gate.

**Kosi Bay** (8am to 5pm) 11km south of Ponta d'Ouro.

**Pafuri** (8am to 4pm) 11km east of Pafuri Camp in Kruger National Park.

**Ressano Garcia–Lebombo** (6am to midnight) Northwest of Maputo; very busy.

### Swaziland

**Goba–Mhlumeni** (open 24 hours) Southwest of Maputo.

**Lomahasha–Namaacha** (7am-8pm) In Swaziland's extreme northeastern corner.

### Tanzania

For all Mozambique–Tanzania crossings it is essential to arrange your Mozambique (or Tanzania) visa in advance.

**Kilambo** 130km north of Moçimboa da Praia, and called Namiranga or Namoto on the Mozambique side.

**Moçimboa da Praia (Mozambique)** Immigration and customs for those arriving by plane or dhow.

**Mtomoni** Unity Bridge 2; 120km south of Songea (Tanzania).

**Negomano** Unity Bridge.

**Palma (Mozambique)** Immigration and customs for those arriving by dhow or charter flight.

### Zambia

**Cassacatiza** (7am to 5pm) 290km northwest of Tete; main crossing.

**Zumbo** (7am to 5pm) At the western end of Lake Cahora Bassa.

### Zimbabwe

**Espungabera** In the Chimanimani Mountains.

**Machipanda** On the Beira Corridor linking Harare with the sea.

**Mukumbura** (7am to 5pm) West of Tete.

**Nyamapanda** On the Tete Corridor, linking Harare with Tete and Lilongwe (Malawi).

## Getting Around

### AIR

#### Airlines in Mozambique

**Linhas Aéreas de Moçambique** The national airline, with flights linking Maputo with Inhambane, Vilankulo, Beira, Chimoio, Quelimane, Tete, Nampula, Lichinga and Pemba. Sample one-way fares and flight frequencies include Maputo to Pemba (US$200, daily), Maputo to Vilankulo (US$150, daily) and Maputo to Lichinga (US$200, five weekly).

**CR Aviation** (www.craviation.co.mz) Scheduled and charter flights to the Bazaruto Archipelago, Quirimbas Archipelago, Inhaca and Gorongosa National Park.

### BOAT

On Lake Niassa there is a twice-weekly passenger service on the MV *Chambo* between Metangula, Cóbuè, Mbueca and several other villages along the Mozambican lakeshore.

### BUS

Sample journey fares, times and frequencies:

| ROUTE | FARE (MTC) | DURATION (HR) | FREQUENCY |
|---|---|---|---|
| Maputo–Vilanculos | 950 | 10 | daily |
| Nampula–Pemba | 500 | 7 | daily |
| Maputo–Beira | 1700 | 17-18 | daily |
| Lichinga–Maputo | 4200 | 2-3 days | weekly |

### CAR & MOTORCYCLE

- A South African or international driving licence is required to drive in Mozambique.
- *Gasolina* (petrol) is scarce off main roads, especially in the north. *Gasóleo* (diesel) supplies are more reliable.
- In late 2016 Mozambique introduced *livre-trânsito* (free pass) cards. The cards – given to drivers following inspection at the border to minimise traffic-police stops – should be displayed in the front windscreen to show that the car has already been inspected.

#### Car Hire

- There are rental agencies in Maputo, Vilankulo, Beira, Nampula, Tete and Pemba, most of which take credit cards. Elsewhere, you can usually arrange something with upmarket hotels.
- Rates start at about US$100 per day for 4WD (US$80 for 2WD), excluding fuel.
- With the appropriate paperwork, rental cars from Mozambique can be taken into South Africa and Swaziland but not into other neighbouring countries. Most South African rental agencies don't permit their vehicles to enter Mozambique.

## LOCAL TRANSPORT

### Chapa

- The main form of local transport is the *chapa*, the name given to any public transport that runs within a town or between towns and isn't a bus or truck. On longer routes, your only option may be a *camião* (truck).
- *Chapas* can be hailed anywhere and prices are fixed.
- *Chapa* drivers are notorious for their unsafe driving and there are many accidents. Bus is always a better option.

## TRAIN

The only passenger train regularly used by tourists is the twice-weekly slow line between Nampula and Cuamba. Vendors are at all stations, but bring extra food and drink. Second class is reasonably comfortable and most cabins have windows that open. Third class is hot and crowded. Book the afternoon before travel.

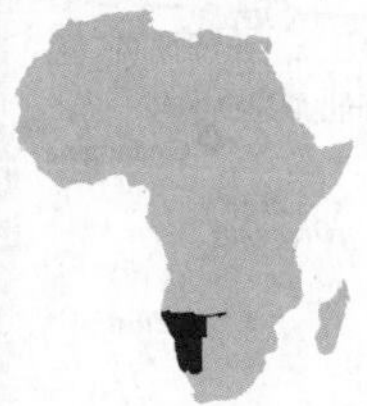

# Namibia

POP 2.4 MILLION / ☎264

**Includes ➡**



## Best Places to Eat

- ➡ Leo's (p865)
- ➡ Sam's Giardino Hotel (p881)
- ➡ 22° South (p882)
- ➡ Restaurant Gathemann (p865)

## Best Places to Sleep

- ➡ Serra Cafema Camp (p878)
- ➡ Sossusvlei Desert Lodge (p884)
- ➡ Little Kulala (p884)
- ➡ Hoanib Skeleton Coast Camp (p878)

## Why Go?

Namibia possesses some of the most stunning landscapes in Africa, and a trip through the country is one of the great road adventures. Natural wonders such as that mighty gash in the earth at Fish River Canyon and the wildlife utopia of Etosha National Park enthral, but it's the lonely desert roads, where mighty slabs of granite rise out of swirling desert sands, that will sear themselves in your mind. It's like a coffee-table book come to life as sand dunes in the world's oldest desert meet the crashing rollers along the wild Atlantic coast.

Among all this is a German legacy, evident in the cuisine and art nouveau architecture and in festivals such as Windhoek's legendary Oktoberfest. Namibia is also the headquarters of adventure activities in the region, so whether you're a dreamer or love hearing the crunch of earth under your boots, travel in Namibia will stay with you long after the desert vistas fade.

## When to Go

### Windhoek

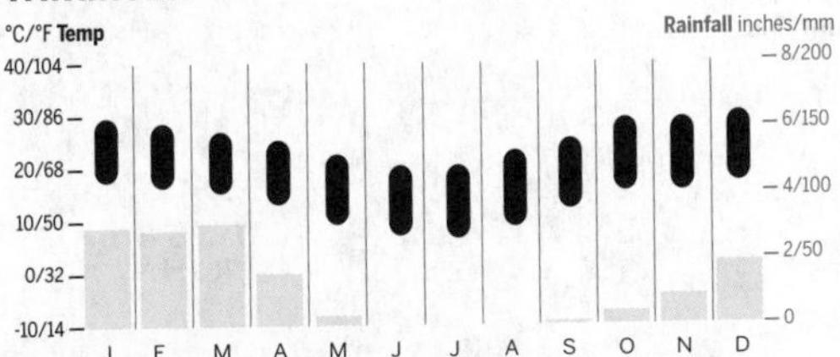


**Jun–Oct** Accommodation at a premium. Temperatures soar by September.

**May & Nov** Cheaper accommodation. Heavy rains sometimes occur in November; May is mild.

**Dec–Apr** Rains begin in December. Humidity and high temperatures can make days unpleasant.

# Namibia Highlights

**1 Etosha National Park** (p870) Crouching by a water hole in one of the world's premier wildlife venues.

**2 Sossusvlei** (p883) Watching the sun rise from the top of the fiery coloured dunes.

**3 Fish River Canyon** (p885) Hiking through one of Africa's greatest natural wonders.

**4 Skeleton Coast** (p878) Getting off the beaten track (and the tarred road) in the true African wilderness.

**5 Waterberg Plateau** (p869) Hiking to the top for breathtaking views, while keeping an eye out for rare sable and roan antelope.

**6 Swakopmund** (p878) Getting your adrenaline fix at Namibia's extreme-sport capital.

**7 Damaraland** (p874) Tracking rhinos and desert elephants in a stunning landscape of red-bouldered mountains.

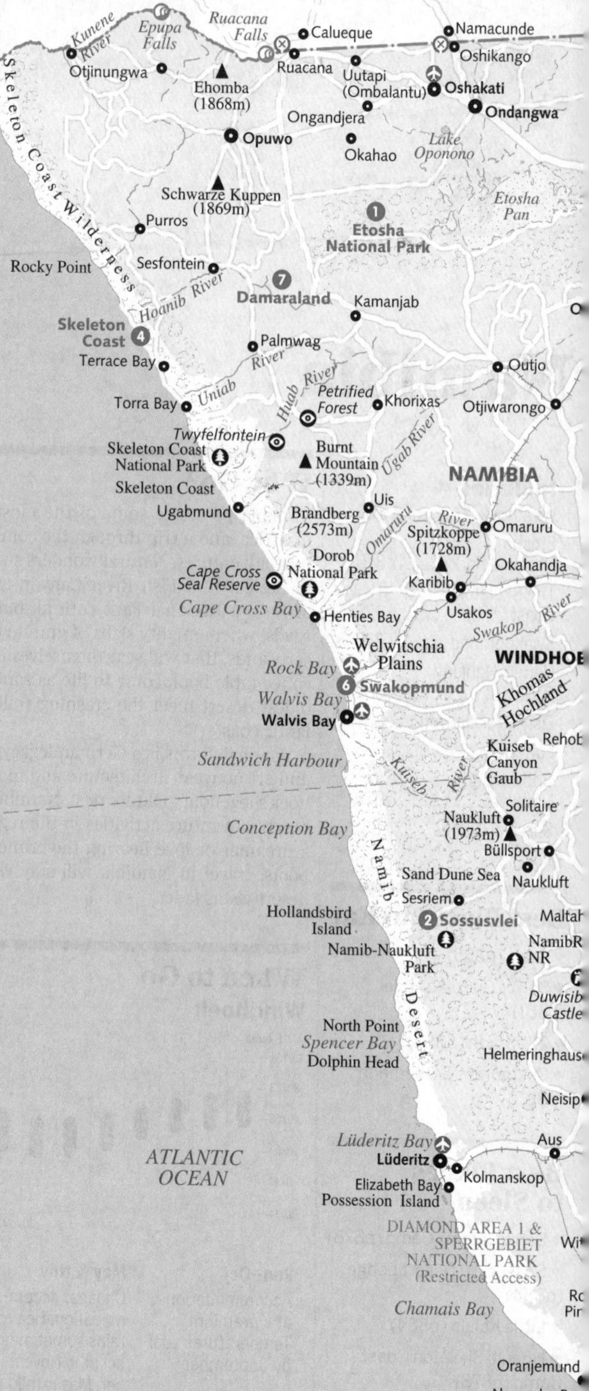

ANGOLA
NAMIBIA
BOTSWANA
SOUTH AFRICA
Cubango River
Calai
Rundu
Andara
Divundu
Mahango GR
Bwabwata NP
Shakawe
Katima
Kasane
Kongola
Mudumu NP
Linyanti
Nkasa Rupara NP
Chobe FR
Savuti
Mangetti
Khaudum NP
Tsumeb
Grootfontein
Tsumkwe
Aha Hills (1250m)
Nxai Pan
Nxai Pan NP
Konde
Maun
Sehithwa
Lake Ngami
Kuke
Deception Pan
Eiseb River
Okanuwa
Otjosondu
Labora
Epukiro River
Rietfontein
Ghanzi
Okwa River
Quoxo River
Xanagas
Omitara
Gobabis
Seeis
Dorbabis
Kalahari Desert
Khutse GR
Leonardville
Aminuis
Kang
Salajwe
Oorwinning
Hukuntsi
Tshane
Takatokwane
Kalkrand
Stampriet
Sekoma
Akanou
Union's End
Gochas
Olifants River
Kwang
Nossob River
Witbooisvlei
Twee Rivier
Mata Mata
Vloorskop (959m)
Katzies
Koës
Aoub River
Garinais
Khawa
Molopo River
McCarthysrus
Fly's Kop
Middlepits
Rietfontein
Bokspits
Seeheim
Tsaraxaibis
Fish River Canyon
Upington
Richtersveld NP
Warmbad
Noordoewer
Onseepkans
Orange River
Vioolsdrif
Goodhouse
Vaal River
Kimberley
FR Forest Reserve
GR Game Reserve
NP National Park
NR Nature Reserve
0 100 km
0 50 miles

# WINDHOEK

POP 325,860

If Namibia is Africa for beginners, then Windhoek is very much its capital in more than name only. It's the sort of place that divides travellers, with those who love it for the respite it offers from the rigours of life on the African road facing off against those who find it a little too 'Western' for their African tastes. And they're both right: Windhoek is a modern, well-groomed city where office workers lounge around **Zoo Park** (dawn-dusk) FREE at lunchtime, tourists funnel through Post St Mall admiring African curios, and taxis whizz around honking at potential customers. Neo-baroque cathedral spires, as well as a few seemingly misplaced German castles, punctuate the skyline, and complement the steel-and-glass high-rises.

## Sights

**Christuskirche** CHURCH

(Fidel Castro St) FREE Windhoek's best-recognised landmark, and something of an unofficial symbol of the city, this German Lutheran church stands on a traffic island and lords it over the city centre. An unusual building, it was designed by architect Gottlieb Redecker in conflicting neo-Gothic and art nouveau styles, and constructed from local sandstone in 1907. The resulting design looks strangely edible, and is somewhat reminiscent of a whimsical gingerbread house. The altarpiece, the *Resurrection of Lazarus,* is a copy of the renowned work by Rubens.

**Daan Viljoen Game Park** WILDLIFE RESERVE

(061-232393; per person/vehicle N$40/10; sunrise-sunset) This beautiful wildlife park sits in the Khomas Hochland about 18km west of Windhoek. You can walk to your heart's content through lovely wildlife-rich desert hills, and spot gemsbok, kudu, mountain zebras, springbok, hartebeests, warthogs and elands. Daan Viljoen is also known for its birdlife, and over 200 species have been recorded, including the rare green-backed heron and pin-tailed whydah. Daan Viljoen's hills are covered with open thorn-scrub vegetation that allows excellent wildlife viewing, and three walking tracks have been laid out. There's also an on-site luxury **lodge** (061-232393; www.sunkarros.com; camping N$260, s/d chalets from N$1774/2818; @).

**Independence Memorial Museum** MUSEUM

(061-302236; www.museums.com.na; Robert Mugabe Ave; 9am-5pm Mon-Fri, 10am-5pm Sat & Sun) FREE Opened in 2014, this good museum is dedicated to the country's anti-colonial and independence struggle. The first floor tells the story of Namibia under colonial rule, with the next floor up shifting gears to the resistance movement, and the top floor dominated by the road to independence. Don't miss taking the glass elevator up the outside of the building for great views out over Windhoek. There's a statue of founding president Sam Nujoma outside.

**National Museum of Namibia** MUSEUM

(061-302230; www.museums.com.na; Robert Mugabe Ave; 9am-6pm Mon-Fri, 3-6pm Sat & Sun) FREE Namibia's National Museum hosts an excellent display on Namibia's independence at the country's historical museum, which provides some enlightening context to the struggles of this young country. But probably the most interesting part of the museum is the rock-art display, with some great reproductions; it would definitely be worth a nose around before heading to the Brandberg or Twyfelfontein. It's housed in Windhoek's oldest surviving building, dating from the early 1890s; it originally served as the headquarters of the German Schutztruppe.

## Festivals & Events

**Mbapira/Enjando Street Festival** CARNIVAL

(Mar) Windhoek's big annual bash is held in March around the city centre. It features colourful gatherings of dancers, musicians and people in ethnic dress.

**Windhoek Karneval (WIKA)** CARNIVAL

(http://windhoek-karneval.org/en/; Apr) This German-style carnival takes place in late April and features music performances, a masked ball and a parade down Independence Ave.

**Oktoberfest** BEER

(www.windhoekoktoberfest.com; Oct) True to its partially Teutonic background, Windhoek stages this festival towards the end of October – beer lovers should not miss it.

## Tours

★ **Cardboard Box Travel Shop** TOURS

(061-256580; www.namibian.org; 15 Bismark St) Attached to the backpacker hostel of the same name, this recommended travel agency can arrange both budget and upmarket bookings all over the country. Great website, too.

## Sleeping

Whether you bed down in a bunkhouse or a historic castle, Windhoek has no shortage of appealing accommodation options. Compared to the rest of the country, prices in the capital are relatively high, though you can usually be assured of a corresponding level of quality. Note that in a city this small, space is limited, so consider booking your bed well in advance, especially in high season, during holidays or even on busy weekends.

**★Cardboard Box Backpackers** HOSTEL $
(061-228994; www.cardboardbox.com.na; 15 Johann Albrecht St; camping/dm N$90/150, r/tr/q N$450/550/660; ) Hostels are hard to come by in this country but 'The Box' has been doing it for years, with a rep as one of Windhoek's better backpackers. It has a fully stocked bar and a swimming pool to cool off in, and travellers have a tough time leaving. Rates include free coffee and pancakes in the morning and there are free pick-ups from the Intercape bus stop.

**Chameleon Backpackers Lodge & Guesthouse** HOSTEL $
(061-244347; www.chameleonbackpackers.com; 5-7 Voight St; dm/s/d incl breakfast from N$170/280/350; ) With a chilled vibe emanating from its considerable range of accommodation options, this well-matched rival to the Cardboard Box caters to a slightly more subdued crowd. It offers decent-sized, luxurious African-chic rooms and spick-and-span dorms at shoestring prices. There are also three self-catering flats if you're in town for an extended period. The on-site safari centre offers some of the most affordable trips in Namibia.

**★Guesthouse Tamboti** GUESTHOUSE $
(061-235515; www.guesthouse-tamboti.com; 9 Kerby St; s/d from N$560/820; ) Hands-down our favourite place in Windhoek to stay, Tamboti is very well priced, has a great vibe and terrific hosts who will go out of their way to ensure you are comfortable (such as driving you to the airport if you have a flight to catch). The rooms here are spacious and well set up – it's situated on a small hill just above the city centre. Book ahead as it's popular.

**★Hotel Heinitzburg** HOTEL $$$
(061-249597; www.heinitzburg.com; 22 Heinitzburg St; s/d from N$2137/3154; ) Inside Heinitzburg Castle, which was commissioned in 1914 by Count von Schwerin for his fiancée, Margarethe von Heinitz, Hotel Heinitzburg is a member of the prestigious Relais & Chateaux hotel group, and far and beyond the most personable upmarket accommodation in Windhoek. Rooms have been updated for the 21st century with satellite TV and air-con.

**★Olive Grove** BOUTIQUE HOTEL $$$
(061-302640; www.olivegrove-namibia.com; 20 Promenaden St; s/d standard N$995/1610, luxury N$1319/2370; ) Refined elegance is the order of the day at this boutique hotel in Klein Windhoek, which features 10 individually decorated rooms and two suites awash in fine linens, hand-crafted furniture and all-around good taste. Guests in need of some pampering can indulge in a massage, or warm their toes on a cold Windhoek night in front of the crackling fire.

## Eating

Namibia's multicultural capital provides a range of restaurants. It's worth stretching your budget and indulging in the gourmand lifestyle while you're in town. Be advised that reservations are a very good idea on Friday and Saturday nights.

Windhoek is a grocery paradise for self-caterers. The big names are **Pick & Pay** (Wernhill Park Centre; 9am-6pm Mon-Fri, to 2pm Sat, to 1pm Sun) and **Checkers** (Gustav Voigts Centre; 8am-7pm Mon-Fri, to 6pm Sat, to 3pm Sun).

**Namibia Crafts Cafe** CAFE $
(Old Breweries Complex, cnr Garten & Tal Sts; mains N$35-90; 9am-6pm Mon-Fri, to 3.30pm Sat & Sun) This cafe-restaurant-bar is a great spot to perch yourself above Tal St, checking out the local action and taking in the breeze from the outside deck. The extensive drinks menu includes health shakes and freshly squeezed juices. Meals in the way of salads, large pitas, cold meat platters, open sandwiches and healthy (or just filling) breakfasts hit the spot.

**★Joe's Beerhouse** PUB FOOD $$
(061-232457; www.joesbeerhouse.com; 160 Nelson Mandela Ave; mains N$74-179; 4.30-11pm Mon-Thu, 11am-11pm Fri-Sun) A legendary Windhoek institution, this is where you can indulge (albeit with a little guilt...) in

## Central Windhoek

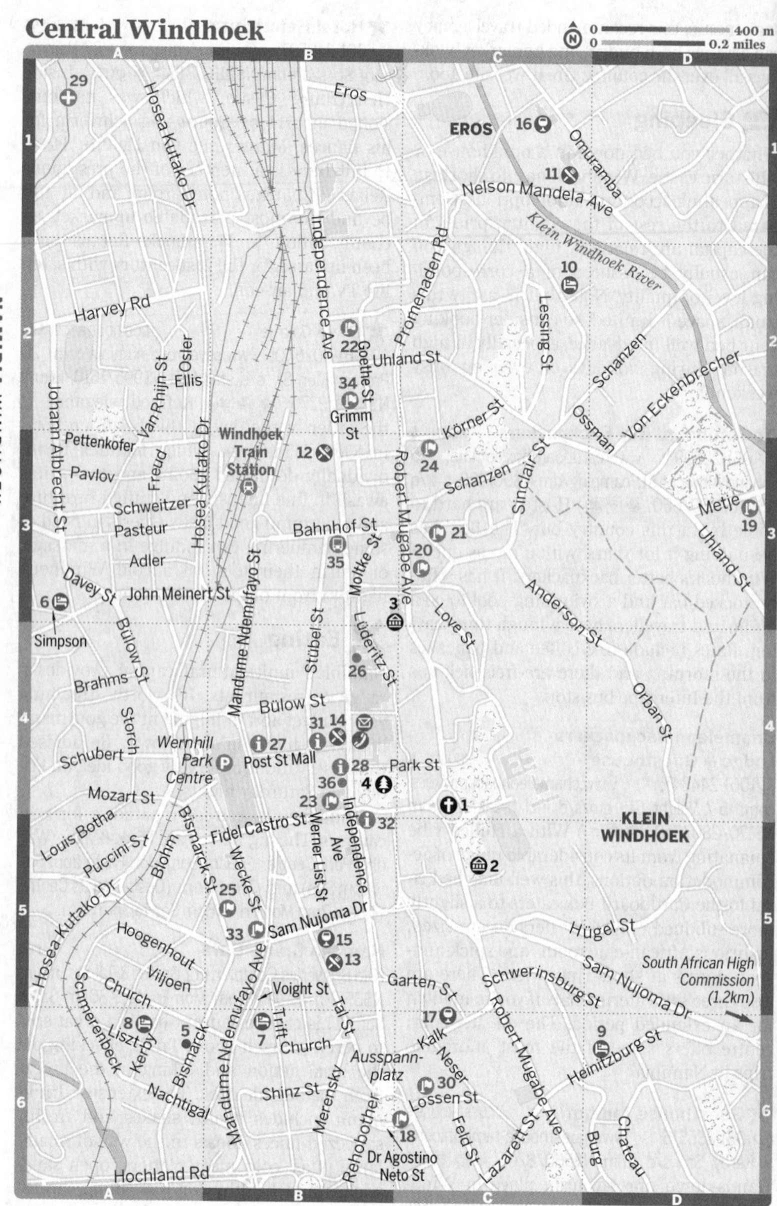


flame-broiled fillets of all those amazing animals you've seen on safari! Seriously. We're talking huge cuts of zebra tenderloin served with garlic butter, ostrich skewers, peppered springbok steak, oryx sirloin, crocodile on a hotplate and marinated kudu steak.

**★Stellenbosch Wine Bar & Bistro** BISTRO **$$**

(☎061-309141; www.thestellenboschwinebar.com; 320 Sam Nujoma Dr; mains N$81-169; ⏰noon-10pm) When well-to-do locals want an enjoyable night out with the guarantee of good

## Central Windhoek

**Sights**
1 Christuskirche .......... C4
2 Independence Memorial Museum .......... C5
3 National Museum of Namibia .......... B3
4 Zoo Park .......... B4

**Activities, Courses & Tours**
5 Cardboard Box Travel Shop .......... A6

**Sleeping**
6 Cardboard Box Backpackers .......... A3
7 Chameleon Backpackers Lodge & Guesthouse .......... B6
8 Guesthouse Tamboti .......... A6
9 Hotel Heinitzburg .......... D6
10 Olive Grove .......... C2

**Eating**
11 Joe's Beerhouse .......... C1
12 La Marmite .......... B3
Leo's .......... (see 9)
13 Namibia Crafts Cafe .......... B5
14 Restaurant Gathemann .......... B4

**Drinking & Nightlife**
15 Boiler Room @ The Warehouse Theatre .......... B5
16 Joe's Beer House .......... C1
17 Wine Bar .......... C6

**Information**
18 Angolan Embassy .......... C6
19 Botswanan Embassy .......... D3
20 British High Commission .......... C3
21 Finnish Embassy .......... C3
22 French Embassy .......... B2
23 German Embassy .......... B4
24 Kenyan High Commission .......... C3
25 Malawian Embassy .......... B5
26 Ministry of Home Affairs .......... B4
27 Namibia Tourism Board .......... B4
28 Namibia Wildlife Resorts .......... B4
29 Rhino Park Private Hospital .......... A1
30 US Embassy .......... C6
31 Windhoek Information & Publicity Office (Branch Office) .......... B4
32 Windhoek Information & Publicity Office (Main Office) .......... B5
33 Zambian High Commission .......... B5
34 Zimbabwean Embassy .......... B2

**Transport**
35 Long-Distance Bus Terminal .......... B3
36 South African Airways .......... B4

food, this is their number-one pick. With a classy outdoor-indoor setting and thoughtfully conceived international food – beef burger with camembert, Bangladeshi lamb curry, crispy pork belly, baked vanilla cheesecake – and excellent service, we can't think of a single good reason not to join them.

**La Marmite** AFRICAN **$$**
(☎061-240306; 383 Independence Ave; mains N$100; ⊙noon-2pm & 6-10pm) Commanding a veritable legion of devoted followers, this humble West African eatery deserves its long-garnered popularity. Here you can sample wonderful North and West African cuisine, including Algerian, Senegalese, Ivorian, Cameroonian (try the curry) and Nigerian dishes, all of which are prepared with the finesse of the finest French haute cuisine. The *jolof* rice is particularly good.

★**Leo's** INTERNATIONAL **$$$**
(☎061-249597; www.heinitzburg.com; 22 Heinitzburg St; mains N$250; ⊙noon-3pm & 6.30-9pm) Leo's takes its regal setting in Heinitzburg Castle to heart by welcoming diners into a banquet hall that previously served the likes of royalty. The formal settings of bone china and polished crystal glassware are almost as extravagant as the food itself, which spans cuisines and continents and land and sea.

★**Restaurant Gathemann** NAMIBIAN **$$$**
(☎061-223853; 179 Independence Ave; mains N$90-250; ⊙noon-10pm) Located in a prominent colonial building overlooking Independence Ave, this splash-out spot serves gourmet Namibian cuisine that fully utilises this country's unique list of ingredients. From Kalahari truffles and Owamboland legumes to tender cuts of game meat and Walvis Bay oysters, Restaurant Gathemann satisfies the pickiest of appetites.

## Drinking & Nightlife

There are a few perennially popular spots where you can enjoy a few drinks and maybe even a bit of dancing. Many restaurants also double as late-night watering holes, particularly tourist-friendly establishments such as **Nice** (☎061-300710; cnr Mozart St & Hosea Kutako Dr; mains N$65-130; ⊙noon-2.30pm Mon-Fri, 6-9pm daily). While the nightlife scene in Windhoek is relaxed and generally trouble-free, you should always travel by taxi when heading to and from establishments.

**★Boiler Room @ The Warehouse Theatre** BAR
(☎061-402253; www.warehousetheatre.com.na; 48 Tal St; ⏰9pm-late) From after-work drinks to live music and a crowd that likes to dance, the Boiler Room at the Warehouse is one of the coolest and most versatile places in town – the latter quality makes us think it might just last the distance.

**★Joe's Beer House** PUB
(☎061-232457; www.joesbeerhouse.com; 160 Nelson Mandela Ave; ⏰noon-late) True to its moniker, Joe's stocks a wide assortment of Namibian and German beers, and you can count on prolonged drinking here until early in the morning. It's the favoured drinking hole of Afrikaners and something of a Windhoek institution.

**Wine Bar** WINE BAR
(☎061-226514; www.thewinebarshop.com; 3 Garten St; ⏰4-10.30pm Mon-Thu, 4-11.30pm Fri, 5-10.30pm Sat) In a lovely historic mansion that actually used to store the town's water supply, but now houses the city's premium wine selection, staff here have an excellent knowledge of their products, pairing an admirable South African wine selection with Mediterranean-style tapas and small snacks. It's a beautiful spot for a glass of wine and a fiery African sunset. There's a wine shop here too.

## ℹ Information

### DANGERS & ANNOYANCES

Central Windhoek is actually quite relaxed and hassle-free. As long as you stay alert, walk with confidence, keep a hand on your wallet and avoid wearing anything too flashy, you should encounter nothing worse than a few persistent touts and the odd con artist. However, you do need to be especially wary when walking with any kind of bag, especially on backstreets.

One popular con is for would-be-thieves to play on the conscience of tourists and get their attention by posing the question 'Why won't you talk to a black man?'. Ignore this and keep walking. As an extra precaution, always travel by taxi at night, even in the wealthy suburbs.

The most likely annoyance for travellers is petty theft, which more often than not occurs at budget hotels and hostels around the city. As a general rule, you should take advantage of the hotel safe, and never leave your valuables out in the open.

If you're driving, avoid parking on the street, and never leave anything of value visible in your vehicle. Also, never leave your car doors unlocked, even if you're still in the car.

### MEDICAL SERVICES

**Mediclinic Windhoek** (☎061-4331000; Heliodoor St, Eros; ⏰24hr) Emergency centre and a range of medical services.

**Rhino Park Private Hospital** (☎061-225434, 061-375000; www.hospital.com.na; Sauer St) Provides excellent care and service, but patients must pay up front.

### POST

**Main post office** (Independence Ave; ⏰8am-4.30pm Mon-Fri, to 11.30am Sat) Modern and can readily handle overseas post. It also has telephone boxes in the lobby, and next door is the **Telecommunications Office** (Independence Ave; ⏰8am-4.30pm Mon-Fri, to 11.30am Sat), where you can make international calls and send or receive faxes.

### TOURIST INFORMATION

**Namibia Tourism Board** (☎061-2906000; www.namibiatourism.com.na; 1st fl, Channel Life Towers, 39 Post St Mall; ⏰8am-1pm & 2-5pm Mon-Fri, to 1pm Sat & Sun) The national tourist office can provide information from all over the country.

**Namibia Wildlife Resorts** (NWR; ☎061-2857200; www.nwr.com.na; Independence Ave) Books national-park accommodation and hikes.

**Windhoek Information & Publicity Office** (☎061-2902596, 061-2902092; www.cityofwindhoek.org.na; Independence Ave; ⏰7.30am-4.30pm) The friendly staff at this main office answer questions and distribute local publications and leaflets, including *What's On in Windhoek* and useful city maps. There's another branch (Post St Mall; ⏰7.30am-noon & 1-4.30pm) in the Post St Mall that is open the same hours but closes from noon to 1pm.

## ℹ Getting There & Away

### AIR

**Chief Hosea Kutako International Airport** (WDH; ☎061-2996602; www.airports.com.na), which is about 40km east of the city centre, serves most international flights into and out of Windhoek.

**Eros Airport** (ERS; ☎061-2955500; www.airports.com.na), immediately south of the city centre, serves most domestic flights into and out of Windhoek. Air Namibia offers around three weekly flights to and from Katima Mulilo, Ondangwa, Rundu and Swakopmund/Walvis Bay.

### BUS

From the main long-distance **bus terminal** (cnr Independence Ave & Bahnhof Sts), the Intercape Mainliner (p894) runs to and from Cape Town, Johannesburg, Victoria Falls and Swakopmund, serving a variety of local destinations along the way. Tickets can be purchased either though your accommodation, from the Intercape Mainliner office at the bus terminal or online; given the popularity of these routes, advance reservations are recommended.

There are some useful shuttle services out to Swakopmund and Walvis Bay such as the **Town Hoppers** (☎ 081 210 3062, 064-407223; www.namibiashuttle.com), departing daily at 2pm (N$270, 4½ hours), and returning in the morning to Windhoek.

### Getting Around

If you're arriving at Chief Hosea Kutako International Airport, taxis typically wait outside the arrivals area. It's a long drive into the city, so you can expect to pay anywhere from N$350 to N$400 depending on your destination. For Eros Airport, fares are much more modest at around N$70. Collective taxis from the main ranks at Wernhill Park Centre follow set routes.

# NORTH-CENTRAL NAMIBIA

## Erongo Mountains (Erongoberg)

The volcanic Erongo Mountains, often referred to as the Erongoberg, rise as a 2216m massif north of Karibib and Usakos and they're among the most beautiful and accessible of Namibia's mountain areas. The Erongo range is best known for its caves and rock art, particularly the 50m-deep Phillips Cave.

### Sights

**Phillips Cave** CAVE

(day permit N$50) This cave, 3km off the road, contains the famous humpbacked white elephant painting. Superimposed on the elephant is a large humpbacked antelope (perhaps an eland), and around it frolic ostriches and giraffes. The Ameib paintings were brought to wider attention in the book *Phillips Cave* by prehistorian Abbè Breuil, but his speculations about their Mediterranean origins have now been discounted. The site is open to day hikers via Ameib Gästehaus.

### Sleeping & Eating

**Camp Mara** CAMPGROUND, GUESTHOUSE $$

(☎ 064-571190; www.campmara.com; camping N$150, s/d with half board N$1025/1750) This lovely spot by a (usually dry) riverbed has shady, well-tended campsites, as well as eclectic but extremely comfortable rooms with whitewashed walls and creative use of wood in the decor. Activities include day tours into the mountains and Bushman activities.

★ **Erongo Wilderness Lodge** LODGE $$$

(☎ 064-570537, 061-239199; www.erongowilderness-namibia.com; tented bungalows with full board s/d from N$2975/5000; ❄@☒) This highly acclaimed wilderness retreat combines spectacular mountain scenery, wildlife viewing, bird-watching and environmentally sensitive architecture to create one of Namibia's most memorable lodges. Accommodation is in one of 10 tented bungalows, which are built on wooden stilts among towering granite pillars crawling with rock hyraxes. The restaurant overlooks a water hole where you might see kudus or genets.

### Getting There & Away

North of Ameib, the D1935 skirts the Erongo Mountains before heading north into Damaraland. Alternatively, you can head east towards Omaruru on the D1937. This route virtually encircles the Erongo massif and provides access to minor 4WD roads into the heart of the mountains.

> WORTH A TRIP
>
> **HARNAS**
>
> The **Harnas Wildlife Foundation & Guest Farm** (☎ 081 140 3322, 061-228545; www.harnas.org; camping N$270, s/d igloos N$1520/2500, s/d cottages N$1900/3100, self-catering units from N$1800; ⏲ 6am-6pm) is a rural development project that likens itself to Noah's Ark. Here you can see wildlife close up, including rescued cheetahs, leopards and lions. A wide range of accommodation is available, including options for full board, and there are plenty of activities here to keep you amused for a couple of days – kids will love it.

## Erindi Private Game Reserve

It may lack the scale of Etosha National Park, but many travellers rank **Erindi** (☎ 081 145 0000, 064-570800; www.erindi.com) as their most memorable wildlife-watching

WORTH A TRIP

### KRISTALL KELLEREI WINERY

One of very few wineries in Namibia, **Kristall Kellerei Winery** (064-570083; www.kristallkellerei.com; 8am-4.30pm Mon-Fri, to 12.30pm Sat) is a lovely spot to come for lunch. In the afternoon you can enjoy light meals – cheese and cold-meat platters – while tasting their wines and other products, and take a tour of the gardens. Apart from schnapps, the winery produces Colombard, a white wine, and Paradise Flycatcher, a red blend of ruby cabernet, cabernet sauvignon and Tinta Barocca. The winery is 4km east of Omaruru on the D2328.

experience in Namibia. With over 700 sq km of savannah grasslands and rocky mountains, Erindi lacks the zoo-like feel of many smaller private reserves in the country and you can reliably expect to see elephants and giraffes, with lions, leopards, cheetahs, African wild dogs and black rhinos all reasonable possibilities. Night drives, too, open up a whole new world of nocturnal species.

## Sleeping

**★Camp Elephant** CAMPGROUND, CHALET $$$
(083 333 1111; www.erindi.com; camping per site N$712, s/d chalets N$1095/2190) In the heart of Erindi, Camp Elephant has 15 excellent self-catering chalets that overlook a water hole that's floodlit at night, while the 30 campsites have some lovely greenery and plenty of shade, not to mention good facilities.

**★Old Traders Lodge** LODGE $$$
(083 330 1111; www.erindi.com; s with half board N$3090-4090, d with half board N$5380-7180; ) Erindi's main lodge has 48 luxury rooms that combine the safari feel (thatched roofs and earth tones) with classic wood-and-four-poster-bed interiors. It's never pretentious, and although it can get a little frenetic when the lodge is full, it's a terrific place to stay on a terrific reserve.

## Getting There & Away

Erindi lies west of Omaruru, northwest of Okahandja and southwest of Otjiwarongo. There are four entrance gates. To reach the main gate, travel 48km north of Okahandja or 124km south of Otjiwarongo along the B1, then turn west onto the D2414, a decent gravel road, for 40km.

# Okonjima Nature Reserve

The 200-sq-km Okonjima Nature Reserve (www.okonjima.com) is the epicentre of one of Namibia's most impressive conservation programs. Home of the AfriCat Foundation, it protects cheetahs and other carnivores rescued from human-wildlife conflict situations across the country, and gives them room to move. Aside from excellent accommodation and fascinating education programs, Okonjima offers the chance to track wild leopards, as well as cheetahs, African wild dogs and (coming soon) lions within the reserve.

## Activities

Activities are not included in the room rates, and cost N$670/340 per adult/child for leopard or cheetah tracking, or N$450/225 per adult/child for guided Bushman nature trails.

**AfriCat Foundation** WILDLIFE
(067-687032; www.africat.org; 10am-4pm) This foundation runs education programs and activities within Okonjima Nature Reserve.

## Sleeping

**★Omboroko Campsite** CAMPGROUND $
(www.okonjima.com; Okonjima Nature Reserve; per adult/child N$330/165; ) These are some of the best campsites in Namibia. There's plenty of shade, firewood is provided, there's a (freezing!) swimming pool, hot showers and flush toilets and the five sites are beautifully maintained in the shadow of one of the large rocky outcrops that dominates the reserve's core. You're also within the 20-sq-km fenced zone and, hence, unlikely to be surprised by wandering predators.

**★Okonjima Plains Camp** LODGE $$$
(067-687032; www.okonjima.com; s/d standard rooms with half board N$2830/4050, view rooms with half board N$3955/6300; ) With 10 'view' and 14 'standard' rooms, these newly built lodgings open out onto the Okonjima grasslands, with the ample terraces and abundant glass taking full advantage of the wildlife-rich views. The view rooms in particular are supremely comfortable, spacious and stylish, decorated with a pleasing mix of soothing earth tones and bold colours, as well as plenty of stunning photographs of Okonjima's wildlife.

### Getting There & Away

Unless you visit Okonjima as part of an organised tour, you'll need your own vehicle to visit. The signpost is impossible to miss, 49km south of Otjiwarongo and 130km north of Okahandja along the B1. After taking the turn-off, you pass through a series of gates and the main lodge is 10km off the main road, along a well-graded gravel track.

## Waterberg Plateau Park

The wild Waterberg is highly recommended – there is nothing quite like it in Namibia. It takes in a 50km-long, 16km-wide sandstone plateau, looming 150m above the desert plains. It doesn't have the traditional big wildlife attractions (such as lions or elephants). What it does have are some rare and threatened species, which include sable and roan antelope, and little-known populations of white and black rhino.

### Activities

**Waterberg Unguided Hiking Trail** HIKING
(per person N$100; 9am Wed) A four-day, 42km unguided hike around a figure-eight track begins at 9am every Wednesday from April to November. It costs N$100 per person, and groups are limited to between three and 10 people. Book through Namibia Wildlife Resorts (p866) in Windhoek. Hikers stay in basic shelters and don't need to carry a tent but must otherwise be self-sufficient. Shelters have drinking water, but you'll need to carry enough to last you between times – plan on drinking at least 3L to 4L per day.

**Waterberg Wilderness Trail** HIKING
(per person N$220; 2pm Thu) From April to November the four-day, guided Waterberg Wilderness Trail operates every Thursday. The walks, which are led by armed guides, need a minimum of two people. They begin at 2pm on Thursday from the visitor centre and end early on Sunday afternoon. They cost N$220 per person and also must be prebooked through NWR (p866) in Windhoek. There's no set route, and the itinerary is left to the whims of the guide. Accommodation is in simple huts, but participants must carry their own food and sleeping bags.

### Sleeping

**Waterberg Camp** CAMPGROUND, LODGE $$
(067-305001; www.nwr.com.na; camping N$160, s/d bush chalets N$810/1320) Together with its sibling properties in Etosha, the Waterberg Camp is part of NWR's Classic Collection. At Waterberg, campers can pitch a tent in any number of scattered sites around braai (barbecue) pits and picnic tables. Campsites benefit from space, views of the plateau and the plains beyond, and well-kept amenities. The lodge rooms and bush chalets are unexciting but nicely kept and well-priced for what you get.

★**Waterberg Wilderness Lodge** LODGE, CAMPGROUND $$
(067-687018; www.waterberg-wilderness.com; off D2512; camping N$170, tented room N$690, r with half board N$1150-1480; ) Waterberg Wilderness occupies a vast private concession within the park and is a wonderful upmarket choice. The Rust family has painstakingly transformed the property (formerly a cattle farm) by repopulating game animals and allowing nature to return to its pregrazed state. The main lodge rests in a sun-drenched, jacaranda-strewn meadow at the end of a valley, where you'll find red-sandstone chalets adorned with rich hardwood furniture.

### Getting There & Away

Waterberg Plateau Park is only accessible by private car – motorcycles are not permitted anywhere within the park boundaries. From Otjiwarongo it's about 90km to the park gate via the B1, C22 and the gravel D512.

## Tsumeb

POP 19,280

Tsumeb is one Namibian town worth a poke around, especially if you are trying to get a feel for the country's urban side. The streets are very pleasant to wander, made more so by the plentiful shady trees; it's reasonably compact, and there's usually a smile or two drifting your way on the busy streets. There are a few attractions to guide your visit, but it's more about getting a window on the world of an appealing northern Namibian town.

### Sleeping

**Mousebird Backpackers & Safaris** HOSTEL $
(067-221777; cnr 533 Pendukeni Iivula-Ithana & 4th Sts; camping N$120, dm/tw N$160/460; ) Tsumeb's long-standing backpacker spot continues to stay true to its roots, offering

economical accommodation without sacrificing personality or character – there's a really good feel to this place. It's a small house-style set-up with decent communal areas, including a kitchen. The best twin rooms share a bathroom inside the house although the twin outside does have its own bathroom. The four-bed dorm is also very good.

**Kupferquelle Resort** RESORT **$$**
(☎067-220139; www.kupferquelle.com; Kupfer St; camping N$115, s/d N$1110/1530; ) This modern, resort-style place has lovely, contemporary rooms with high ceilings, quiet terraces and a real sense of space, style and light. Some are self-catering, with kitchens, and all have modern art on the walls. There's an on-site swimming pool and ample grounds. An excellent choice.

## Information

**Travel North Namibia Tourist Office**
(☎067-220728; 1551 Sam Nujoma Dr; ) Inside the guesthouse of the same name. Provides nationwide information, arranges accommodation, transport, car hire and Etosha bookings, and has internet access. No maps available.

## Getting There & Away

**BUS**

Intercape Mainliner (p894) buses make the trip between Windhoek and Tsumeb (from N$340, 5½ hours, twice weekly).

**CAR & MOTORCYCLE**

Tsumeb is an easy day's drive from Windhoek along paved roads and serves as the jumping-off point for Namutoni and the Von Lindequist Gate of Etosha National Park.

# Etosha National Park

Covering more than 20,000 sq km, **Etosha National Park** (per person per day N$80, per vehicle N$10; ⏲sunrise-sunset) is one of the world's great wildlife-viewing venues. Unlike other parks in Africa, where you can spend days looking for animals, Etosha's charm lies in its ability to bring the animals to you. Just park your car next to one of the many water holes, then wait and watch while a host of animals – lions, elephants, springboks, gemsboks etc – come not two by two, but by the hundreds.

Etosha is also one of the best places to spot the highly endangered black rhino in Southern Africa.

## Sleeping

### In the Park

**Olifantsrus Rest Camp** CAMPGROUND **$**
(☎061-2857200; www.nwr.com.na; camping N$280) The newest of Etosha's rest camps, out in the recently opened-to-the-public western reaches of the park, fenced Olifantsrus occupies an old elephant culling site with some of the gruesome paraphernalia still on show. There's a small kiosk, decent sites and a marvellous elevated hide overlooking a water hole.

**Halali Rest Camp** LODGE, CAMPGROUND **$**
(☎067-229400, 061-2857200; www.nwr.com.na; campsites N$250, plus per person N$150, s/d from N$1150/2040, s/d chalets from N$1530/2800; ) Etosha's middle camp, Halali, nestles between several incongruous dolomite outcrops. The best feature at Halali is its floodlit water hole, which is a 10-minute walk from the rest camp and is sheltered by a glen of trees with huge boulders strewn about. There is a very well-serviced campsite here, in addition to a fine collection of semiluxurious chalets.

**Okaukuejo Rest Camp** LODGE, CAMPGROUND **$$$**
(☎061-2857200, 067-229800; www.nwr.com.na; campsites N$250, plus per person N$150, s/d N$1400/2540, s/d chalets from N$1470/2680; P) Okaukuejo (o-ka-kui-yo) is the site of the Etosha Research Station, and it functions as the official park headquarters and main visitor centre. The Okaukuejo water hole is probably Etosha's best rhino-viewing venue, particularly between 8pm and 10pm. Okaukuejo's campsite can get very crowded, but the shared facilities (washing stations, braai pits and bathrooms with hot water) are excellent.

**Dolomite Camp** LODGE **$$$**
(☎061-2857200, 065-685119; www.nwr.com.na; s/d with half board from N$2040/3580; ) Recently opened in a previously restricted area in western Etosha, Dolomite Camp is beautifully carved into its rocky surrounds. Accommodation is in thatched chalets (actually luxury tents), including a couple with their own plunge pool. The views of surrounding plains are wonderful and

# Etosha National Park

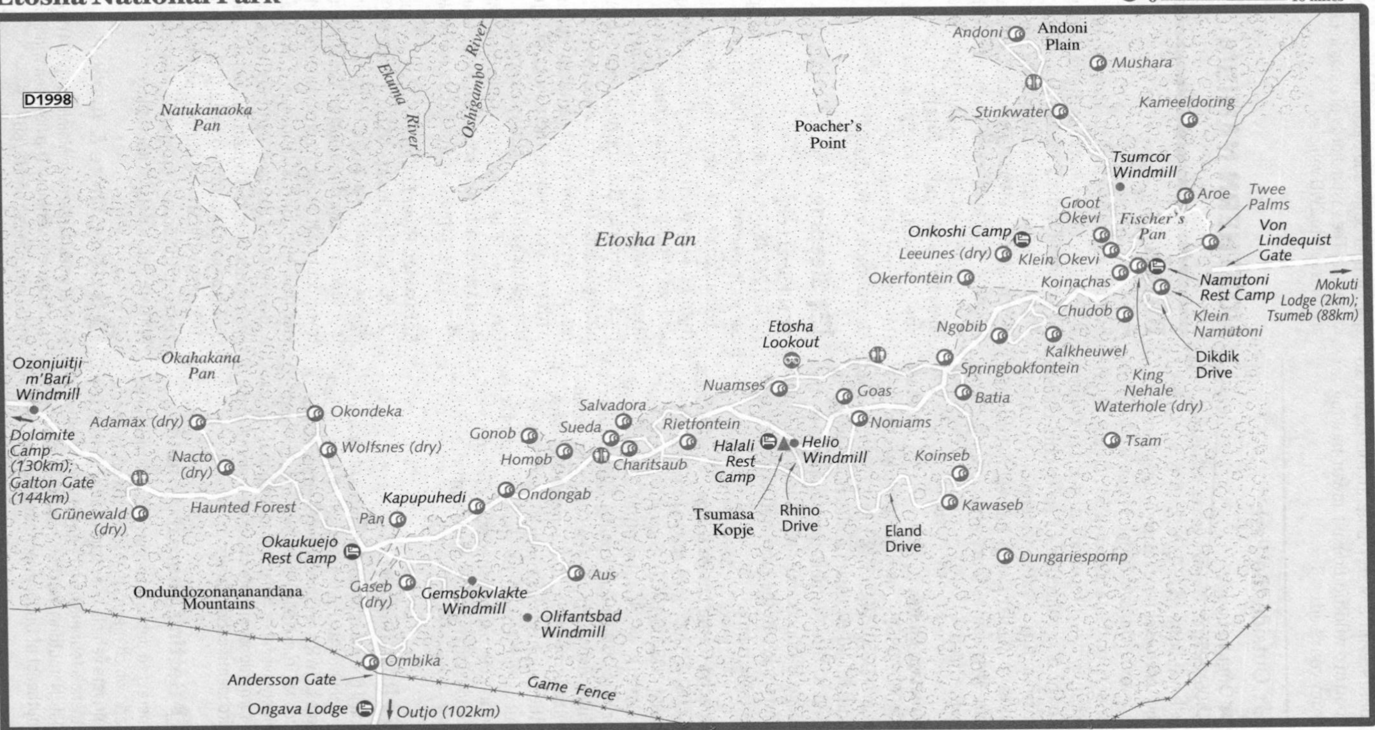

there's even a water hole at the camp, so spotting wildlife doesn't mean moving far from your bed.

## Outside the Park

**★Ongava Lodge** LODGE $$$
(☎061-225178; www.wilderness-safaris.com; s/d with half board N$4771/7632; ) One of the more exclusive luxury lodges in the Etosha area, Ongava Lodge is not far south of Andersson Gate. Ongava is actually divided into two properties: the main Ongava Lodge is a collection of safari-chic chalets surrounding a small water hole, while the Ongava Tented Camp has eight East African–style canvas tents situated a bit deeper in the bush.

**Mushara Lodge** LODGE $$$
(☎061-241880; www.mushara-lodge.com; s/d from N$1850/3700; ) Part of the elegant and varied Mushara Collection (which includes three other fine properties), this lodge is impeccably attired in wood, thatch and wicker in the large and extremely comfortable rooms.

**Epacha Game Lodge & Spa** LODGE $$$
(☎061-375300; www.epacha.com; s/d with full board N$3500/5800) Superb rooms are a hallmark of this beautiful lodge on the private 210-sq-km Epacha Game Reserve. Night drives, great views from its elevated hillside position and a pervasive sense of quiet sophistication are all well and good, but where else in Etosha can you practise your clay-pigeon shooting? There's also a tented lodge and exclusive private villa on the reserve.

## Information

You'll find maps of Etosha National Park across the country and at the shops at most of the park gates. NWR's reliable English-German *Map of Etosha* (from N$40) is the pick and also most widely available. It has the added bonus of park information and quite extensive mammal and bird identification sheets.

## Getting There & Around

There's no public transport into and around the park, which means that you must visit either in a private vehicle or as part of an organised tour. Etosha's four main entry gates are Von Lindequist (Namutoni), west of Tsumeb; King Nehale, southeast of Ondangwa; Andersson (Okaukuejo), north of Outjo; and Galton, northwest of Kamanjab. The vast majority of roads in Etosha are passable to 2WD vehicles.

# NORTHERN NAMIBIA

## Rundu

POP 63,430

Rundu, a sultry tropical outpost on the bluffs above the Okavango River, is a major centre of activity for Namibia's growing Angolan community. Although the town has little of specific interest for tourists, the area is home to a number of wonderful lodges where you can laze along the riverside, and spot crocs and hippos doing pretty much the same. As such, it's a fine place to break up the journey between the Caprivi Strip and Grootfontein or Etosha.

### Sleeping

**★N'Kwazi Lodge** LODGE $
(☎081 242 4897; www.nkwazilodge.com; camping per adult/child N$100/50, s/d N$600/1000) On the banks of the Okavango, about 20km from Rundu's town centre, this is a tranquil and good-value riverside retreat where relaxation is a by-product of the owners' laid-back approach. The entire property blends naturally into the surrounding riverine forest, while the rooms are beautifully laid out, with personal touches; there's a great campsite, although it's sometimes overrun by safari trucks. The lodge represents incredibly good value with no surcharge for singles and a justifiably famous buffet dinner for N$260.

**Sarasungu River Lodge** LODGE $
(☎066-255161; camping N$170, r from N$996; ) Sarasunga River Lodge is situated in a secluded riverine clearing 4km from the town centre. It has attractive thatched chalets that surround a landscaped pool, and a decent-sized grassed camping area with basic amenities and beautiful sunsets. There is also a bar-restaurant on-site. The river excursions don't always happen and they aim more at the local conference market than tourists, but it's still a good place.

### Getting There & Away

Several weekly Intercape Mainliner (p894) buses make the seven-hour trip between Windhoek and Rundu (fares from N$780).

# Khaudum National Park

Exploring the largely undeveloped 3840-sq-km **Khaudum National Park** (adult/child/vehicle N$80/free/10; ⏲sunrise-sunset) is an intense wilderness challenge. Meandering sand tracks lure you through pristine bush and across *omiramba* (fossil river valleys), which run parallel to the east–west-oriented Kalahari dunes. As there is virtually no signage, and navigation is largely based on GPS coordinates and topographic maps, visitors are few, which is precisely why Khaudum is worth exploring – it's home to one of Namibia's most important populations of lions and African wild dogs, although both can be difficult to see.

In addition to African wild dogs and lions, the park protects large populations of elephants, zebras, giraffes, wildebeest, kudus, oryxes and tsessebes, and there's a good chance you'll be able to spot large herds of roan antelopes here. If you're an avid birder, Khaudum supports 320 different species, including summer migratory birds such as storks, crakes, bitterns, orioles, eagles and falcons.

## Sleeping

**Khaudum Camp** CAMPGROUND
(S 18°30.234', E 20°45.180') FREE Khaudum Camp is somewhat akin to the Kalahari in miniature, but this is true wilderness camping – shade can be meagre and facilities are nonexistent. The sunsets here are the stuff of legend.

**Sikereti Camp** CAMPGROUND
(S 19°06.267', E 20°42.300') FREE 'Cigarette' camp, in the south of the park, inhabits a shady grove of terminalia trees, though full appreciation of this place requires sensitivity to its subtle charms, namely isolation and silence. This is true wilderness camping with no facilities whatsoever.

## Getting There & Away

From the north, take the sandy track from Katere on the B8 (signposted 'Khaudum'), 120km east of Rundu. After 45km you'll reach the Cwibadom Omuramba, where you should turn east into the park.

From the south, you can reach Sikereti Camp via Tsumkwe. From Tsumkwe, it's 20km to Groote Döbe and another 15km from there to the Dorslandboom turning. It's then 25km north to Sikereti Camp.

# The Caprivi Strip

Namibia's spindly northeastern appendage, the Caprivi Strip (now officially known as Namibia's Zambezi region, although the name is taking time to catch on...) is typified by expanses of mopane and terminalia broadleaf forest, and punctuated by *shonas* (fossilised parallel dunes that are the remnants of a drier climate). For most travellers, the Caprivi serves as the easiest access route connecting the main body of Namibia with Victoria Falls and Botswana's Chobe National Park.

But Caprivi is also one of Southern Africa's wildlife destinations to watch. After decades of poaching, the region's wildlife is returning and visitors with time and patience can get off the beaten path here, exploring such emerging wildlife gems as Nkasa Rupara and Bwabwata national parks.

## Bwabwata National Park

Only recently recognised as a national park, **Bwabwata** (per person per day N$10, per vehicle N$10; ⏲sunrise-sunset) was established to rehabilitate local wildlife populations. Prior to the 2002 Angolan ceasefire, this area saw almost no visitors, and wildlife populations had been virtually wiped out by rampant poaching instigated by ongoing conflict. But the guns have been silent now for well over a decade and the wildlife is making a slow but spectacular comeback. If you come here expecting Etosha, you'll be disappointed. But you might very well see lions, elephants, African wild dogs, perhaps even the sable antelope and some fabulous birdlife, and you might just have them all to yourself.

### Sleeping

**Ngepi Camp** LODGE $
(☎066-259903; www.ngepicamp.com; camping N$140, bush or tree huts per person from N$770) One of Namibia's top backpacker lodges that appeals beyond the budget market, Ngepi makes a great base for the area. Crash for the night in a bush hut or tree hut, or pitch a tent on grass right by the river's edge and let the sounds of hippos splashing about ease you into a restful sleep; we love the outdoor bath tubs.

★**Nambwa Tented Lodge** LODGE, CAMPGROUND $$$
(www.africanmonarchlodges.com/nambwa-luxury-tented-lodge; camping N$195, s/d Jul-Oct N$6415/9930, Apr-Jun & Nov N$5045/7790,

Dec-Mar N$3195/6390; ) Nambwa, 14km south of Kongola, is one of very few places in the park itself, and it combines an excellent campsite with a luxury lodge, replete with elevated walkways, stunning interiors (tree trunks and antique chandeliers anyone?) and glorious views out over the flood plains. Some of Bwabwata's best wildlife areas are close by, and the lodge overlooks a water hole that's especially popular with animals late in the dry season.

### Getting There & Away

The paved Trans-Caprivi Highway between Rundu and Katima Mulilo is perfectly suited to 2WD vehicles, as is the gravel road between Divundu and Mohembo (on the Botswana border). Drivers may transit the park without charge, but you will incur national-park entry fees if you use the loop drive through the park.

## Nkasa Rupara National Park

Watch this space – this is one of Namibia's, perhaps Southern Africa's, most exciting **national parks** (Map p752; per person/vehicle N$40/10). In years of good rains, this wild and seldom-visited national park (formerly called Mamili National Park) becomes Namibia's equivalent of Botswana's Okavango Delta. Forested islands fringed by reed and papyrus marshes foster some of the country's richest birdwatching, with more than 430 recorded species to count. Poaching has taken a toll on Nkasa Rupara's wildlife, but lions are returning to the area; sightings of wild dogs across the water on the Botswana side are also possible while semiaquatic species, such as hippos, crocodiles, pukus, red lechwes, sitatungas and otters, will still impress.

### Sleeping

**★Livingstone's Camp** CAMPGROUND $
(Map p752; 081 033 2853, 066-686208; www.livingstonescamp.com; camping Nov-Mar/Apr-Oct N$200/250) Overlooking the wetlands and marketing itself as an exclusive campsite, Livingstone's has just five sites, each with their own shower and toilets and all with front-row seats to the water. It can also organise wildlife drives into Nkasa Rupara National Park and *mokoro* (dugout canoe) trips on the Kwando river network.

**★Nkasa Lupala Lodge** TENTED CAMP, LODGE $$
(Map p752; 081 147 7798; www.nkasalupalalodge.com; r per person N$1930) Located 30km from Mudumu, and just outside the entrance to Nkasa Rupara National Park, this remote luxury, Italian-run lodge sits on the banks of the Kwando–Linyanti River system (Nkasa Lupala National Park). The lodge gets rave reviews from travellers and offers activities such as game drives in both national parks, including night drives. Accommodation is in tents on stilts, from where you may just spot elephants trooping past your deck.

### Getting There & Away

Nkasa Lupala Lodge is about 75km from Kongola and 130km from Katima Mulilo. Take the C49 (a maintained gravel road from Kongola and tarred from Katima Mulilo) to Sangwali. From Sangwali, head to the Nkasa Rupara National Park – you'll need a high-clearance 4WD.

# NORTHWESTERN NAMIBIA

## Damaraland

From the glorious rock formations of Spitzkoppe, Erongo and the Brandberg in the south to the equally glorious red-rock, wild-desert mountains around Palmwag in the north, Damaraland is one of Namibia's most dramatic collections of landscapes. Hidden in the rocky clefts is Twyfelfontein, which along with the Brandberg contains some of Southern Africa's finest prehistoric rock art and engravings, and there's even a petrified forest nearby, as well as palm-fringed, oasis-like valleys. Damaraland is also one of Southern Africa's most underrated wildlife-watching areas, one of Namibia's last 'unofficial' wildlife areas with critically endangered black rhinos, desert-adapted lions and elephants, as well as the full range of Namibia specialities such as gemsbok, zebra, giraffe and spotted hyena.

### The Spitzkoppe

One of Namibia's most recognisable landmarks, the 1728m-high **Spitzkoppe** (Groot Spitzkoppe village; per person/car N$50/20; sunrise-sunset) rises mirage-like above the dusty pro-Namib plains of southern Damaraland. Its dramatic shape has inspired its nickname, the Matterhorn of Africa, but similarities between this ancient volcanic remnant and the glaciated Swiss alp begin and end with its sharp peak. First summited in 1946, the Spitzkoppe continues to attract hard-core rock climbers bent on tackling Namibia's most challenging peak.

## Sleeping

**Sptitzkoppe Campsites** CAMPGROUND $
(064-464144; www.spitzkoppe.com; camping N$135) These wonderful campsites in the nooks and crannies that surround the Spitzkoppe massif perfectly capture the area's other-worldly landscapes. Run by the same people that run Spitzkoppen Lodge, it's a professionally operated place with carefully chosen sites and good facilities.

★ **Spitzkoppen Lodge** LODGE $$$
(www.spitzkoppenlodge.com; s/d N$2900/5000; ) Due to open not long after our visit, this place promises to be the pick of the Spitzkoppe choices. Run by the same people that brought you **Kalahari Bush Breaks** (www.kalaharibushbreaks.com), the lodge consists of 15 wonderfully secluded chalets with gorgeous views, all connected by an elevated walkway. The design in places evokes the Spitzkoppe mountain and there is an enduring sense of isolation and luxury.

## Getting There & Away

Under normal dry conditions, a 2WD is sufficient to reach the mountain. Turn northwest off the B2 onto the D1918 towards Henties Bay. After 18km, turn north onto the D3716.

# The Brandberg

Driving around this massive pink granite bulge, and marvelling at the ethereal light during sunset which appears to bounce off it, is a highlight of the region. But inside lies the real treasure – one of the finest remnants of prehistoric art on the African continent.

## Sights

**Tsisab Ravine** ROCK ART
Tsisab Ravine is the epicentre of the Brandberg's rock-art magic. The most famous figure in the ravine is the White Lady of the Brandberg, in Maack's Shelter. The figure, which isn't necessarily a lady (it's still open to interpretation), stands about 40cm high, and is part of a larger painting that depicts a bizarre hunting procession. In one hand, the figure is carrying what appears to be a flower or possibly a feather. In the other, the figure is carrying a bow and arrows.

**Numas Ravine** ROCK ART
Numas Ravine, slicing through the western face of the Brandberg, is a little-known treasure house of ancient paintings. Most people ask their guide to take them to the rock facing the southern bank of the riverbed, which bears paintings of a snake, a giraffe and an antelope. It lies about 30 minutes' walk up the ravine. After another half-hour you'll reach an oasis-like freshwater spring and several more paintings in the immediate surroundings.

## Sleeping

**Brandberg White Lady Lodge** LODGE $$
(064-684004, 081 791 3117; www.brandbergwllodge.com; D2359; camping N$110, s/d luxury tents N$550/770, s/tw with half board N$1075/1846) The Brandberg White Lady has something for just about every kind of traveller. Campers can pitch a tent along the riverine valley, all the while taking advantage of the lodge's upmarket facilities, while lovers of their creature comforts can choose from rustic bungalows and chalets that are highlighted by their stone interiors and wraparound patios. There are also luxury tents.

## Getting There & Away

To reach Tsisab Ravine from Uis, head 15km north and turn west on the D2359, which leads 26km to the Tsisab car park. To reach Numas Ravine, head 14km south of Uis and follow the D2342 for 55km, where you'll see a rough track turning eastward. After about 10km, you'll reach a fork; the 4WD track on the right leads to the Numas Ravine car park.

# Twyfelfontein Area

Unesco World Heritage–listed Twyfelfontein (Doubtful Spring), at the head of the grassy Aba Huab Valley, is one of the most extensive rock-art galleries on the continent. To date over 2500 engravings have been discovered. Guides are compulsory; note that tips are their only source of income.

## Sleeping

**Abu Huab Rest Camp** CAMPGROUND $
(camping N$120) Well-shaded, close to the Twyfelfontein rock art and often visited by desert elephants, Abu Huab is an appealing

## TWYFELFONTEIN'S ROCK ENGRAVINGS

Mostly dating back at least 6000 years to the early Stone Age, Twyfelfontein's **rock engravings** (adult/child/car N$80/free/10; ⏲ sunrise-sunset) were probably the work of ancient San hunters, and were made by cutting through the hard patina covering the local sandstone. In time, this skin reformed over the engravings, protecting them from erosion. From colour differentiation and weathering, researchers have identified at least six distinct phases, but some are clearly the work of copycat artists and are thought to date from the 19th century.

In the ancient past, this perennial spring most likely attracted wildlife, creating a paradise for the hunters who eventually left their marks on the surrounding rocks. Animals, animal tracks and geometric designs are well represented here, though there are surprisingly few human figures. Many of the engravings depict animals that are no longer found in the area – elephants, rhinos, giraffes and lions – and an engraving of a sea lion indicates contact with the coast more than 100km away.

choice for self-drivers, at least at first glance. There's also a small bar, but service at the whole place definitely needs a rethink and facilities (such as the nonexistent electricity) need an overhaul.

**★Doro Nawas Camp** LODGE **$$$**
(☎061-225178; www.wilderness-safaris.com; s/d Jun-Oct N$6510/11,270, rates vary rest of year; 📶🏊) Part of the elite Wilderness Safari portfolio, Doro Nawas is a magnificent place. The thatched rooms are massive and luxurious, the terraces open on to vast views and there's a great mix of excursions, from Twyfelfontein rock art to wildlife drives in search of desert-adapted elephants and lions. Prices are high by Namibian standards, but the quality and service are unimpeachable.

### ℹ Getting There & Away

There's no public transport in the area and little traffic. Turn off the C39, 73km west of Khorixas, then turn south on the D3254 and continue 15km to a right turning signposted Twyfelfontein. It's 5km to the petroglyph site.

## Palmwag

The 5000-sq-km Palmwag Concession and the surrounding areas together make up a rich wildlife area amid stark red hills and plains, surrounded by a bizarre landscape of uniformly sized red stones. It serves as something of a buffer zone between Etosha in the north and the Skeleton Coast, with a reasonable chance that you'll see black rhinos (most of the camps offer rhino tracking), desert elephants and lions, as well as spotted hyenas, giraffes, gemsboks and other antelopes. The area is home to a handful of luxury lodges, and also serves as a study centre for the Save the Rhino Trust (SRT), making it a good mix of great wildlife watching and serious conservation, quite apart from being stunningly beautiful country.

### 🛏 Sleeping

**Hoada Campsite** CAMPGROUND **$**
(☎081 289 0982, 061-228104; www.grootberg.com/hoada-campsite; camping N$185; 🏊) Run by Grootberg Lodge, this superb campsite sits among towering boulders with excellent facilities (including a fine swimming pool, flush toilets and outdoor showers).

**★Desert Rhino Camp** TENTED CAMP **$$$**
(☎061-225178; www.wilderness-safaris.com; s/d with full board high season N$11,600/17,010; 🏊) These safari-style tents in a remote corner of Damaraland are certainly luxurious and a worthy member of the elite Wilderness Safaris classic collection. But even more than the rooms, it's the ethos of this place – the camp has been at the centre of efforts to save Namibia's black rhino population – that impresses. Rhino-tracking, and the chance to see desert lions and elephants, are other highlights.

**Damaraland Camp** LODGE **$$$**
(☎061-225178; www.wilderness-safaris.com; s/d with full board high season N$9030/13,120; 🏊) This solar-powered desert outpost 60km south of Palmwag has all-encompassing views of stark, truncated hills and is an oasis of luxury amid a truly feral and outlandish setting. When you're not living out your end-of-the-world fantasies in your luxury tent with wood floors, adobe walls and outdoor

showers, you can do a few laps in the novel pool that occupies a rocky gorge formed by past lava flows.

### Getting There & Away

Palmwag is on the D3706, 157km from Khorixas and 105km from Sesfontein. Coming from the south, you'll cross the Red Line, 1km south of Palmwag Lodge – you can carry meat heading north, but not south.

## The Kaokoveld

The Kaokoveld is a photographer's dreamscape of wide-open vistas, lonely desert roads and hardly another person around to ruin your shot. A vast repository of desert mountains, this is one of the least developed regions of the country, and arguably Namibia at its most primeval. The Kaokoveld is also the ancestral home of the Himba people, a culturally rich tribal group who have retained their striking appearance and dress.

### Opuwo

POP 7660

In the Herero language, Opuwo means 'The End', which is certainly a fitting name for this dusty collection of concrete commercial buildings ringed by traditional rondavels (round huts with conical roofs) and huts. While first impressions are unlikely to be very positive, a visit to Opuwo is one of the cultural highlights of Namibia, particularly for anyone interested in interacting with the Himba people. As the unofficial capital of Himbaland, Opuwo serves as a convenient jumping-off point for excursions into the nearby villages, and there is a good assortment of lodges and campsites in the area to choose from.

### Sleeping

**Ohakane Lodge** LODGE $

(065-273031, 081 295 9024; ohakane@iway.na; s/d N$620/1030; ) This well-established and centrally located lodge sits along the main drag in Opuwo and does good business with tour groups. Fairly standard but fully modern rooms are comfortable enough, but if it's in your budget, it's worth shelling out a bit more for a bungalow at the Opuwo Country Lodge.

★ **Opuwo Country Lodge** HOTEL $$$

(064-418661, 065-273461; www.opuwolodge.com; camping N$160, s/d standard incl breakfast N$1260/1800, s/d luxury incl breakfast N$1820/2560; @) Far and away the area's swankiest accommodation option with lovely rooms, the hilltop Opuwo Country Lodge is an enormous thatched building (reportedly the largest in Namibia) that elegantly lords it over the town below. The hotel faces across a valley towards the Angolan foothills, and most of your time here will be spent soaking your cares away in the infinity-edge pool.

### Information

**Kaoko Information Centre** (065-273420, 081 284 3681; 8am-6pm) KK and Kemuu, the friendly guys at this information centre (look for the tiny, tiny yellow shack), can arrange visits to local Himba villages in addition to providing useful information for your trip through the Kaokoveld region.

### Getting There & Away

The paved C41 runs from Outjo to Opuwo, which makes Himbaland accessible even to 2WD vehicles. Although there is a temptation to speed along this long and lonely highway, keep your

WORTH A TRIP

**EPUPA FALLS**

At Epupa, which means 'Falling Waters' in Herero, the Kunene River fans out into a vast flood plain and is ushered through a 500m-wide series of parallel channels, dropping a total of 60m over 1.5km. The greatest single drop, an estimated 37m, is commonly identified as the Epupa Falls. Here the river tumbles into a dark, narrow, rainbow-wrapped cleft, a stunning sight to behold, particularly when the Kunene is in peak flow from April to May.

Although you'd think this remote corner of the Kaokoveld would be off the tourist trail, Epupa Falls is a popular detour for overland trucks and organised safaris, and can get swamped with tourists. But if you're passing through the area, the falls are certainly worth the detour – the sight of so much water in the middle of the dry Kaokoveld is miraculous to say the least, and if the pools are free from crocs, a dip is a possibility.

**HOANIB SKELETON COAST CAMP**

Now here's something special. So far from the nearest publicly accessible road, and built in a splendid amalgam of canopied canvas and light woods, this uberluxurious tented **camp** (☎061-225178; www.wilderness-safaris.com; s/d all-inclusive high season N$16,350/26,100, rates vary rest of year; 🅧) is one of the most beautiful places to stay in Namibia. With a more contemporary look than many safari camps in the region, and all the better for it, Hoanib exudes light and space and end-of-the-earth romance.

lead foot off the pedal north of the veterinary control fence, as herds of cattle commonly stray across the road. If you're heading deeper into the Kaokoveld, be advised that Opuwo is the last opportunity to buy petrol before Kamanjab, Ruacana or Sesfontein.

### The Northwest Corner

West of Epupa Falls is the Kaokoveld of travellers' dreams: stark, rugged desert peaks, vast landscapes, sparse, scrubby vegetation, drought-resistant wildlife, and nomadic bands of Himba people and their tiny settlements of beehive huts. This region, which is contiguous with the Skeleton Coast Wilderness, has been designated the Kaokoveld Conservation Area and it's one of Namibia's true gems. It's also a pretty rough ride on bad tracks – getting here and around is part of the adventure.

Allow plenty of time to explore the wild and magical **Otjinjange** (better known as Marienflüss) and **Hartmann's Valleys** – broad sandy and grassy expanses descending gently to the Kunene River. Note that camping outside campsites is prohibited at both valleys.

**Serra Cafema Camp** (www.wilderness-safaris.com; s/d high season N$16,320/25,140; 🅧) is one of Namibia's most opulent and remote safari experiences. Stunning desert scenery, combined with a special riverside location and excellent cultural-immersion opportunities with the local Himba are big selling points here. The public areas open onto some gorgeous views, while the rooms, each with a private terrace overlooking the river, are large and lovely.

## The Skeleton Coast

This treacherous coast – a foggy region with rocky and sandy coastal shallows, and soaring dunes – has long been a graveyard for unwary ships and their crews, hence its forbidding name. Early Portuguese sailors called it As Areias do Inferno (The Sands of Hell), as once a ship washed ashore, the fate of the crew was sealed. This protected area stretches from Sandwich Harbour, south of Swakopmund, to the Kunene River, taking in around 20,000 sq km of dunes and gravel plains to form one of the world's most inhospitable waterless areas in the world's oldest desert.

### Cape Cross Seal Reserve

The best-known breeding colony of Cape fur seals along the Namib coast is at this **reserve** (per person/car N$80/10; ⏲10am-5pm), where the population has grown large and fat by taking advantage of the rich concentrations of fish in the cold Benguela Current. The sight of more than 100,000 seals basking on the beach and frolicking in the surf is impressive to behold. There are **campsites** (camping N$100) on the water's edge 1.7km back along the coast from the seal colony. They're far enough away from the stink and have uninterrupted sea views, but facilities are basic and they only open from November to July. They operate on a first-come, first-served basis; ask at the entry to the reserve.

**Cape Cross Lodge** (☎064-694012, 064-461677; www.capecross.org; camping per adult/child N$100/50, s/d N$1600/2450; ❄📶) has an odd but strangely appealing architecture, which is self-described as a cross between Cape Dutch and fishing-village style. The nicer rooms have outdoor patios that overlook the coastline, though you really can't choose a bad room at this stunner of a lodge, conveniently located just before the official reserve entrance.

Cape Cross lies 46km north of Henties Bay along the coastal salt road. There's no public transport here, but a 2WD is all you'll need to get here from the south.

# CENTRAL NAMIBIA

## Swakopmund

POP 44,730

Sandwiched between Atlantic rollers and the Namib Desert, Swakopmund is one of those great traveller waystations along the

African road. At once Namibia's adventure capital and surreal colonial remnant, part destination in its own right and part launch pad for an exploration of the Skeleton Coast and Namib Desert, this is a city with as much personality as it has sea frontage.

## Sights

Swakopmund brims with numerous historic examples of traditional German architecture. For further information on the town's colonial sites, pick up *Swakopmund – A Chronicle of the Town's People, Places and Progress*, which is sold at Swakopmund Museum and in local bookshops.

**★Jetty** LANDMARK

In 1905 the need for a good cargo- and passenger-landing site led Swakopmund's founders to construct the original wooden pier. In the years that followed, it was battered by the high seas and damaged by woodworm, and in 1911 construction began on a 500m iron jetty. When the South African forces occupied Swakopmund, the port became redundant (they already controlled Walvis Bay), so the old wooden pier was removed in 1916, and the unfinished iron pier – a starkly beautiful thing – was left to the elements.

**★National Marine Aquarium** AQUARIUM

(☎064-4101214; Strand St; adult/child N$40/20; ⊙10am-4pm Tue-Sun) This recently overhauled waterfront aquarium provides an excellent introduction to the cold offshore world in the South Atlantic Ocean. Most impressive is the tunnel through the largest aquarium, which allows close-up views of graceful rays, toothy sharks (you can literally count the teeth!) and other little marine beasties.

**Alte Gefängnis (Old Prison)** HISTORIC BUILDING

(Nordring St) This impressive 1909 structure, on Nordring St, was built as a prison, but if you didn't know this, you'd swear it was either an early train station or a health-spa hotel. The main building was used only for staff housing, while the prisoners were relegated to much less opulent quarters on one side.

**Swakopmund Museum** MUSEUM

(☎064-402046; Strand St; adult/student N$30/15; ⊙8am-1pm & 3-5pm Mon-Fri, 10am-noon Sat) When ill winds blow, head for this museum at the foot of the lighthouse, where you can hole up and learn about the town's history. The museum occupies the site of the old harbour warehouse, which was destroyed in 1914 by a 'lucky' shot from a British warship. Displays include exhibits on Namibia's history and ethnology, including information on local flora and fauna. Especially good is the display on the !nara melon, a fruit which was vital to the early Khoekhoen people of the Namib region.

## Activities

Adventure sports and Swakopmund go hand in hand. From quad biking up the crest of a soaring seaside dune to jumping out of a plane at 3000m, Swakop is one of the top destinations in Southern Africa for extreme-sports enthusiasts. Although filling your days with adrenaline-soaked activities is certainly not cheap, there are few places in the world where you can climb up, sandboard down and soar over towering sand dunes.

Most activity operators don't have offices in town, which means that you need to arrange all of your activities through either your accommodation or the Namib-i (p882) tourist information centre.

## Tours

If you've arrived in Swakopmund by public transport, and don't have access to a private vehicle, then consider booking a tour through a recommended operator. Central Swakop is compact and easily walkable, but you need to escape the city confines if you really want to explore the area.

Prices are variable depending on the size of your party and the length of tour. As with

WORTH A TRIP

### SANDWICH HARBOUR

Situated 56km south of Walvis Bay in Dorob National Park, Sandwich Harbour is one of the most dramatic sights in Namibia – dunes up to 100m-high plunge into the Atlantic, which washes into the picturesque lagoon. The harbour is now deserted and a stirring wilderness devoid of any human settlement. Birdwatchers will have a field day and **Sandwich Harbour 4x4** (☎064-207663; www.sandwich-harbour.com; Waterfront; adult/child half-day N$1100/850, full day N$1300/1050) facilitate half- and full-day trips down here.

# Swakopmund

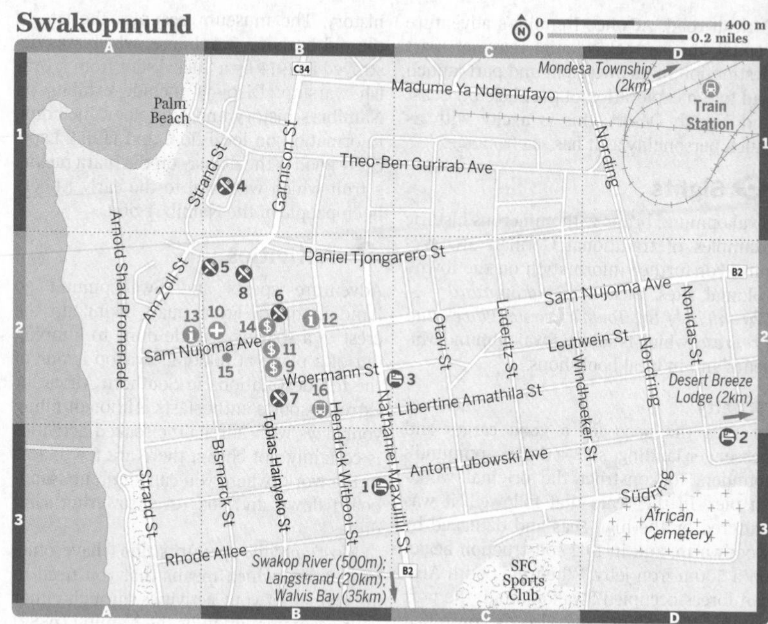


## Swakopmund

**Sleeping**
1 Desert Sky Backpackers ... B3
2 Sam's Giardino Hotel ... D3
3 Swakop Lodge ... C2

**Eating**
4 22° South ... B1
5 Cafe Anton ... B2
6 Die Muschel Art Cafe ... B2
7 Kücki's Pub ... B2
8 Raith's Gourmet ... B2

**Information**
9 Bank of Windhoek ... B2
10 Bismarck Medical Centre ... B2
11 First National Bank ... B2
12 Namib-i ... B2
13 Namibia Wildlife Resorts ... A2
14 Swakopmunder Buchhandlung Commercial Bank ... B2

**Transport**
15 Air Namibia ... B2
16 Intercape Mainliner Bus Stop ... B2

activities in Swakop, money stretches further if you get together with a few friends and combine a few destinations to make a longer outing.

Possible tours include the Cape Cross seal colony, Rössing Mine gem tours, Welwitschia Drive, Walvis Bay Lagoon, and various destinations in the Namib Desert and Naukluft Mountains.

The most popular operators are **Charly's Desert Tours** (☎064-404341; www.charlysdeserttours.com; Sam Nujoma Ave), **Namib Tours and Safaris** (☎064-406038; www.namibia-tours-safaris.com; cnr Sam Nujoma Ave & Nathaniel Maxuilili St) and **Turnstone Tours** (☎064-403123; www.turnstone-tours.com; day tours from N$1550). With the exception of Charly's, most operators do not have central offices, so it's best to make arrangements through your accommodation.

**Hafeni Cultural Tours** CULTURAL
(☎081 146 6222, 064-400731; hafenictours@gmail.com; 4hr tour N$450) If you're interested in arranging a visit to the Mondesa township, Hafeni Cultural Tours runs a variety of different excursions that provide insight into how the other half of Swakopmunders live.

**Hata Angu Cultural Tours** CULTURAL
(☎081 124 6111; www.culturalactivities.in.na; tours from N$400; ⏲10am & 3pm) These four-hour tours are a refreshing change from your

typical Swakop adventure. Here you'll meet an African herbalist, try homemade local dishes, drink at a local shebeen in a Swakop township and even shake hands with a chief. It can also organise sandboarding.

## Sleeping

Given Swakopmund's chilly climate, air-conditioning is absent at most hotels, though you won't miss it once the sea air starts blowing through your room. On the contrary, a heater is something of a requirement in the winter months when the mercury drops along the coast.

During the school holidays in December and January, accommodation books up well in advance – make reservations as early as possible.

**Desert Sky Backpackers** HOSTEL $
(064-402339; www.desertskylodging.com; Anton Lubowski Ave; camping/dm N$160/200, d N$650, with shared bathroom N$600; @) This centrally located backpackers haunt is an excellent place to drop anchor in Swakopmund. The indoor lounge is simple and homey, while the outdoor picnic tables are a nice spot for a cold beer and warm conversation. Free coffee is available all day, and you're within stumbling distance of the pubs if you want something stronger.

**Swakop Lodge** HOSTEL $
(064-402030; 42 Nathaniel Maxuilili St; dm/s/d N$150/450/650; ) This backpacker-oriented hotel is the epicentre of the action in Swakopmund, especially since this is where many of the adrenaline activities depart from and return to, and where many of the videos are screened each night. The hotel is extremely popular with overland trucks, so it's a safe bet that the attached bar is probably bumping and grinding most nights of the week.

**★Sam's Giardino Hotel** HOTEL $$
(064-403210; www.giardinonamibia.com; 89 Anton Lubowski Ave; s/d from N$1000/1500; ) Sam's Giardino Hotel is a wonderfully personal place in the backstreets emphasising superb wines, fine cigars and relaxing in the rose garden with a friendly dog named Beethoven. There's a lovely front garden and a lot of common areas with books, and a grotto with stacks of wine bottles. The rooms are simple but very comfortable. Book ahead for the five-course dinner (N$280), and preview with some wine tasting (N$190).

**★Atlantic Villa** BOUTIQUE HOTEL $$
(064-463511; www.atlantic-villa.com; Plover St; s/d N$980/1380, with sea view N$1200/1720, ste N$2100/2940) Styling itself as a boutique guesthouse, Atlantic Villa is a stylish place. Expect clean-lined rooms decked all in white and Nespresso coffee machines; many rooms have ocean views. In the northern part of town, it's also blissfully quiet.

**★Desert Breeze Lodge** LODGE $$$
(064-406236, 064-400771; www.desertbreezeswakopmund.com; off B2; s/d from N$1570/2140) The 12 luxury bungalows here are lovely, modern and comfortable but it's the views you come here for: set on Swakopmund's southern outskirts but still close to the centre, Desert Breeze has sweeping views of the sand dunes from its perch above the Swakop riverbed. The views are, quite simply, sublime.

## Eating

True to its Teutonic roots, Swakopmund's restaurants have a heavy German influence, though there's certainly no shortage of local seafood and traditional Namibian favourites, as well as a surprising offering of truly cosmopolitan fare. While Windhoekers might disagree, Swakopmund can easily contend for the title of Namibia's culinary capital.

Self-caterers can head for the well-stocked supermarket on Sam Nujoma Ave near the corner with Hendrick Witbooi St. Most backpacker spots have kitchens on the premises.

**Die Muschel Art Cafe** CAFE $
(081 849 5984; Brauhaus Arcade, off Tobias Hainyeko St; snacks & light meals N$26-50; 9am-6pm Mon-Fri, 8.30am-5pm Sat, 10am-5pm Sun) The size of a postage stamp and cute as a button, this fine little cafe next to the bookshop of the same name does great coffee to go with its oven-baked rolls and cupcakes. Enjoy it all at one of the tables on the pedestrianised street outside.

**Raith's Gourmet** CAFE $
(Tobias Hainyeko St; snacks & mains N$20-50; 7am-5pm Mon-Fri, to 2pm Sat & Sun) Very central and convenient and open all weekend, this is a self-proclaimed bakery-deli-bistro-gelateria (though 'bistro' might be stretching it...). It's mainly a bakery with fresh-made rolls and sandwiches for lunch, and pies and pasties. Indulge in a croissant

and scrambled eggs for breakfast. There's a good selection of meats and cheeses too if you're self-catering or just planning a picnic.

**Cafe Anton** CAFE $
(☎064-400331; 1 Bismarck St; light meals N$40-70; ⏲7am-7pm) This much-loved local institution, located in Schweizerhaus Hotel, serves superb coffee, *Apfelstrudel, Kugelhopf* (cake with nuts and raisins), *Mohnkuchen* (poppy seed cake), *Linzertorte* (cake flavoured with almond meal, lemon and spices, and spread with jam) and other European delights. The outdoor seating is inviting for afternoon snacks in the sun.

**★22° South** ITALIAN $$
(☎064-400380; Strand St; mains N$80-190; ⏲noon-2.30pm & 6-9.30pm Tue-Sun) Inside the ground floor of the lighthouse, this atmospheric place is run by an Italian-Namibian couple who prepare Swakopmund's best (and homemade) Italian food. It's a slightly more formal option than the many pizzerias around town, and the quality of the food is similarly elevated.

**★Kücki's Pub** PUB FOOD $$
(☎064-402407; www.kuckispub.com; Tobias Hainyeko St; mains N$95-160) A Swakopmund institution, Kücki's has been in the bar and restaurant biz for a couple of decades. The menu is full of seafood and meat dishes alongside comfort food, and everything is well prepared. The warm and congenial atmosphere is a welcome complement to the food.

## ℹ Information

### DANGERS & ANNOYANCES

Although the palm-fringed streets and cool sea breezes in Swakopmund are unlikely to make you tense, you should always keep your guard up in town. Regardless of how relaxed the ambience might be, petty crime unfortunately occurs.

If you have a private vehicle, be sure that you leave it all locked up with no possessions inside visible during the day. At night, you need to make sure you're parked in a gated parking lot and not on the street. When possible, take a taxi to and from your accommodation.

### MEDICAL SERVICES

**Bismarck Medical Centre** (☎064-405000; cnr Bismarck St & Sam Nujoma Ave) To visit a doctor, go to this recommended centre.

### MONEY

There are plenty of banks in the centre of town with ATMs. Find branches of **Bank of Windhoek**, **First National Bank** and **Swakopmunder Buchhandlung Commercial Bank** around the corner of Tobias Hainyeko St and Sam Nujoma Ave.

### TOURIST INFORMATION

**Namib-i** (☎064-404827; Sam Nujoma Ave; ⏲8am-1pm & 2-5pm Mon-Fri, 9am-1pm & 3-5pm Sat, 9am-1pm Sun) This tourist information centre is a very helpful resource. In addition to helping you get your bearings, it can also act as a booking agent for any activities and tours that happen to take your fancy.

**Namibia Wildlife Resorts** (NWR; ☎064-402172; www.nwr.com.na; Woermannhaus, Bismarck St; ⏲8am-1pm & 2-5pm Mon-Fri, park permits only 8am-1pm Sat & Sun) Like its big brother in Windhoek, this office sells Namib-Naukluft Park and Skeleton Coast permits, and can also make reservations for other NWR-administered properties around the country.

## ℹ Getting There & Away

### AIR

**Air Namibia** (☎064-405123; www.airnamibia.com.na) has several flights a week between Windhoek's Eros Airport and Walvis Bay, from where you can easily catch a bus or taxi to Swakopmund.

### BUS

There are twice-weekly buses between Windhoek and Swakopmund (from N$200, five hours) on the Intercape Mainliner (p894) from the company's bus stop. You can easily book your tickets in advance online.

Also consider **Town Hopper** (☎064-407223; www.namibiashuttle.com), which runs private shuttle buses between Windhoek and Swakopmund (N$270), and also offers door-to-door pick-up and drop-off service.

# Namib-Naukluft Park

Welcome to the Namib, the oldest desert on earth and certainly one of the most beautiful and accessible desert regions on the planet. This is sand-dune country par excellance, silent, constantly shifting and ageless, and an undoubted highlight of any visit to Namibia. The epicentre of its appeal is at Sossusvlei, Namibia's most famous strip of sand, where gargantuan dunes tower more than 300m above the underlying strata. Elsewhere, the land lives up to its name: the Nama word *namib* inspired the name of the entire country and rather prosaically means 'vast dry plain'. And then there are the Naukluft Mountains – barren and beautiful and filled with an appeal all of their own.

## Naukluft Mountains

ELEV 1973M

The Naukluft Mountains, which rise steeply from the gravel plains of the central Namib, are characterised by a high plateau bounded by gorges, caves and springs cut deeply from dolomite formations. The Tsondab, Tsams and Tsauchab Rivers all rise in the massif, and the relative abundance of water creates an ideal habitat for mountain zebras, kudus, leopards, springboks and klipspringers. In addition to wildlife watching, the Naukluft is home to a couple of challenging treks that open up this largely inaccessible terrain.

If you're an avid hiker (or just love excellent settings!), **Tsauchab River Camp** (☎063-293416; www.tsauchab.com; campsites N$150, plus per adult/child N$110/65, s/d chalets N$760/1400; ) will be a treat. The scattered campsites here sit beside the Tsauchab riverbed – one occupies a huge hollow tree – and each has a private shower block, a sink and braai area. The stone-built chalets grow in number with each passing year; also down in the riverbed, they're lovely and quiet.

Occupying a magical setting in the Tsaris Mountains, **Zebra River Lodge** (☎061-301934; www.zebra-river-lodge.com; s/d with full board from N$1275/1610; ) is Rob and Marianne Field's private Grand Canyon. Go for one of the more expansive rock chalets – you'll feel like you're sleeping inside the mountain and they're some of Namibia's more original rooms.

The Naukluft is best reached via the C24 from Rehoboth and the D1206 from Rietoog; petrol is available at Büllsport and Rietoog. From Sesriem, 103km away, the nearest access is via the dip-ridden D854.

## Sesriem & Sossusvlei

Appropriate for this vast country with its epic landscapes (its number-one tourist attraction) Sossusvlei still manages to feel isolated. The dunes, appearing otherworldly at times, especially when the light hits them just so near sunrise, are part of the 32,000-sq-km sand sea that covers much of the region. The dunes reach as high as 325m, and are part of one of the oldest and driest ecosystems on earth. However, the landscape here is constantly changing – wind forever alters the shape of the dunes, while colours shift with the changing light, reaching the peak of their brilliance just after sunrise.

### Sights

**★Sossusvlei** PAN

(round trip N$100) Sossusvlei, a large ephemeral pan, is set amid red sand dunes that tower up to 325m above the valley floor. It rarely contains any water, but when the Tsauchab River has gathered enough volume and momentum to push beyond the thirsty plains to the sand sea, it's completely transformed. The normally cracked dry mud gives way to an ethereal blue-green lake, surrounded by greenery and attended by aquatic birdlife, as well as the usual sand-loving gemsboks and ostriches.

**★Deadvlei** NATURAL FEATURE

Although it's much less famous than its neighbour Sossusvlei, Deadvlei is actually the most alluring pan in the Namib-Naukluft National Park – it's arguably one of Southern Africa's greatest sights. Sprouting from the pan are seemingly petrified trees, with their parched limbs casting stark shadows across the baked, bleached-white canvas. The juxtaposition of this scene with the cobalt-blue skies and the towering orange sands of Big Daddy, the area's tallest dune (325m), is simply spellbinding.

**★Hidden Vlei** NATURAL FEATURE

This unearthly dry vlei (pan) amid lonely dunes, makes a rewarding excursion. It's a 4km return hike from the 2WD car park. The route is marked by white-painted posts. It's most intriguing in the afternoon, when you're unlikely to see another person.

**★Sesriem Canyon** CANYON

The 3km-long, 30m-deep Sesriem Canyon, 4km south of the Sesriem headquarters, was carved by the Tsauchab River through the 15-million-year-old deposits of sand and gravel conglomerate. There are two pleasant walks: you can hike upstream to the brackish pool at its head or 2.5km downstream to its lower end. Check out the natural sphinxlike formation on the northern flank near the canyon mouth.

## Sleeping

Advance reservations are essential, especially during the high season, school holidays and busy weekends. For an overview of accommodation options in the area, visit Sossusvlei Accommodation (www.sossusvlei.org/accommodation).

**Sossus Oasis Campsite** CAMPGROUND $
(☎063-293632; www.sossus-oasis.com; camping N$180) Nicer than the main Sesriem Camp Site but outside the main gate, Sossus Oasis has an on-site petrol station, kiosk, restaurant and decent if dusty sights with good shade and a private ablutions block for each site.

**Sesriem Camp Site** CAMPGROUND $
(☎061-2857200; www.nwr.com.na/resorts/sesriem-camp; camping N$200) With the exception of the upmarket **Sossus Dune Lodge** (☎061-2857200; www.nwr.com.na/resorts/sossus-dune-lodge; s/d chalets with half board N$3190/5940; ), this is the only accommodation inside the park gates – staying here guarantees that you will be able to arrive at Sossusvlei in time for sunrise. The campsite is rudimentary – sandy sites with bins, taps, and trees for shade – and expensive for what you get. It can also get really noisy, which defeats the purpose of why you came out here.

**Desert Quiver Camp** LODGE $$
(☎081 330 6655; www.desertquivercamp.com; s with half board N$1419-1587, d with half board N$2142-2364) Lined up across the desert 5km from the park entrance off the road in from Solitaire, Desert Quiver Camp has striking A-frame chalets that are nicely turned out, but they could benefit from a few more windows to really make you feel a part of the desert. Meals are at the nearby **Sossusvlei Lodge** (☎063-293636; www.sossusvleilodge.com), but self-catering rates are also available.

★**Little Kulala** LODGE $$$
(☎061-225178; www.wilderness-safaris.com; s/d all-inclusive Jun-Oct N$13,480/20,750, rates vary rest of year) Part of Wilderness Safaris' Classic portfolio, Little Kulala is simply stunning. Expansive rooms, each with their own plunge pools, watch over rippling sands and silhouetted desert trees with the sand sea dominating the view not far away. Meals are outstanding, there's a well-stocked wine cellar, the public areas are gorgeous and the whole effect is of a near-perfect sophisticated oasis.

## Getting There & Away

Sesriem is reached via a signposted turn-off from the C14, and petrol is available in town. There is no public transport leading into the park, though hotels can arrange tours if you don't have your own vehicle.

## NamibRand Nature Reserve

Bordering the Namib-Naukluft Park, this reserve (www.namibrand.org) is essentially a collection of private farms that together protect over 20,000 sq km of dunes, desert grasslands and wild, isolated mountain ranges. Currently, several concessionaires operate on the reserve, offering a range of experiences amid one of Namibia's most stunning and colourful landscapes. A surprising amount of wildlife can be seen here, including large herds of gemsboks, springboks and zebras, as well as kudus, klipspringers, spotted hyenas, jackals, and Cape and bat-eared foxes.

**NamibRand Family Hideout** FARMSTAY $
(☎061-226803; www.nrfhideout.com; camping N$150) Run on solar energy and making a virtue of its remoteness, NamibRand's hosts Andreas and Mandy offer a warm welcome, two wonderfully isolated campsites and accommodation in the farmhouse (sleeps 10); much of the old farm infrastructure, now defunct, has been left in situ to evoke the property's sheep-farming days

★**Sossusvlei Desert Lodge** LODGE $$$
(☎in South Africa 27-11-809 4300; www.andbeyond.com; per person all-inclusive high/low season N$10,185/6345; ) This stunning place frequently appears in *Condé Nast* as one of the top lodges in the world, and we're inclined to agree. The property contains 10 chalets, which are constructed from locally quarried stone, and appear to blend effortlessly into the surrounding landscape. The interiors showcase contemporary flair with lovely earth tones, and feature personal fireplaces, marble baths and linen-covered patios.

## Getting There & Away

Access by private vehicle is restricted in order to maintain the delicate balance of the reserve. Accommodation prices are also extremely high, which seeks to limit the tourist footprint. As a result, you must book in advance through a lodge, and then arrange either a 4WD transfer or a chartered fly-in.

# SOUTHERN NAMIBIA

## Fish River Canyon

Nowhere else in Africa will you find anything quite like **Fish River Canyon** (per person per day N$80, per vehicle N$10). Whether you're getting a taste of the sheer scale and beauty of the place from one of the lookouts, or hiking for five days to immerse yourself in its multifaceted charm, Fish River Canyon is a special place.

### Activities

Hiking is obviously the main event here, but following the death of an ill-prepared hiker in 2001, the NWR decided to prohibit day hikes and leisure walks into Fish River Canyon.

**Fish River Hiking Trail** HIKING
(per person N$250; ⏲15 Apr-15 Sep) The five-day hike from Hobas to Ai-Ais is Namibia's most popular long-distance walk – and with good reason. The magical 85km route, which follows the sandy riverbed past a series of ephemeral pools, begins at Hikers' Viewpoint, and ends at the hot-spring resort of Ai-Ais.

### Sleeping

Accommodation inside the park must be prebooked through the NWR office (p866) in Windhoek. In addition to the accommodation inside and close to the park, other excellent possibilities can be found at Gondwana Cañon Park.

**Hobas Camp Site** CAMPGROUND $
(camping N$170, s/d N$1080/1760; 🏊) Administered by NWR, this pleasant and well-shaded camping ground near the park's northern end is about 10km from the main viewpoints. Facilities are clean and there's a kiosk and swimming pool, but no restaurant or petrol station. Rooms in bush chalets were under construction when we last passed through.

**Ai-Ais Hot Springs Spa** RESORT $$
(www.nwrnamibia.com/ai-ais.htm; camping N$190, mountain-/river-view d N$1330/1620; 🏊) Administered by NWR, amenities here include washing blocks, braai pits and use of the resort facilities, including the hot springs. The rooms are tidy, if a touch overpriced, and there are also slightly more expensive river-view rooms. There are family chalets available and an on-site restaurant and small grocery store.

★ **Fish River Lodge** LODGE $$$
(☎061-228104, 063-683005; www.fishriver-lodge-namibia.com; s/d N$1995/3056) With 20 chalets located on the western rim of the canyon, Fish River Lodge is a magical spot to enjoy the landscape. Rooms are gorgeous, modern and come with superlative views. Activities include a five-night canyon hike (85km, April to September), or a day hike for the less ambitious.

### Information

The main access points for Fish River Canyon are at Hobas, near the northern end of the park, and Ai-Ais, near the southern end. Both are administered by the NWR.

Accommodation must be booked in advance through the Windhoek office (p866). Daily park permits (N$80 per person and N$10 per vehicle) are valid for both Hobas and Ai-Ais.

The **Hobas Information Centre** (⏲7.30am-noon & 2-5pm), at the northern end of the park, is also the check-in point for the five-day canyon hike. Packaged snacks and cool drinks are available here, but little else. If you're on your way to view the canyon, use the toilets here – there are none further on.

The Fish River typically flows between March and April. Early in the tourist season, from April to June, it may diminish to a trickle, and by midwinter, to just a chain of remnant pools along the canyon floor.

### Getting There & Around

There's no public transport to Hobas or Ai-Ais, and you'll really need a private vehicle to get around. The drive in from Grünau to Hobas is on a decent gravel road, accessible most of the year in a 2WD, although it can be problematic immediately after heavy rain.

# Lüderitz

Before travelling to Lüderitz, pause for a moment to study the country map and how the town is sandwiched between the barren Namib Desert and the windswept South Atlantic coast. As if Lüderitz' unique geographical setting wasn't impressive enough, its surreal German art nouveau architecture will seal the deal. A colonial relic scarcely touched by the 21st century, Lüderitz recalls a Bavarian *dorfchen* (small village), with churches, bakeries and cafes. Unlike its more well-heeled Teutonic rival Swakopmund, Lüderitz feels stuck in a time warp, a perception that delivers both gloom and a certain charm (at least for visitors). In short, it's one of the most incongruous places in Africa.

## Sights

Lüderitz is chock-a-block with colonial buildings, and every view reveals something interesting. The curiously intriguing architecture, which mixes German imperial and art nouveau styles, makes this bizarre little town appear even more other-worldly. Check out the prominent Evangelical Lu-

## Lüderitz

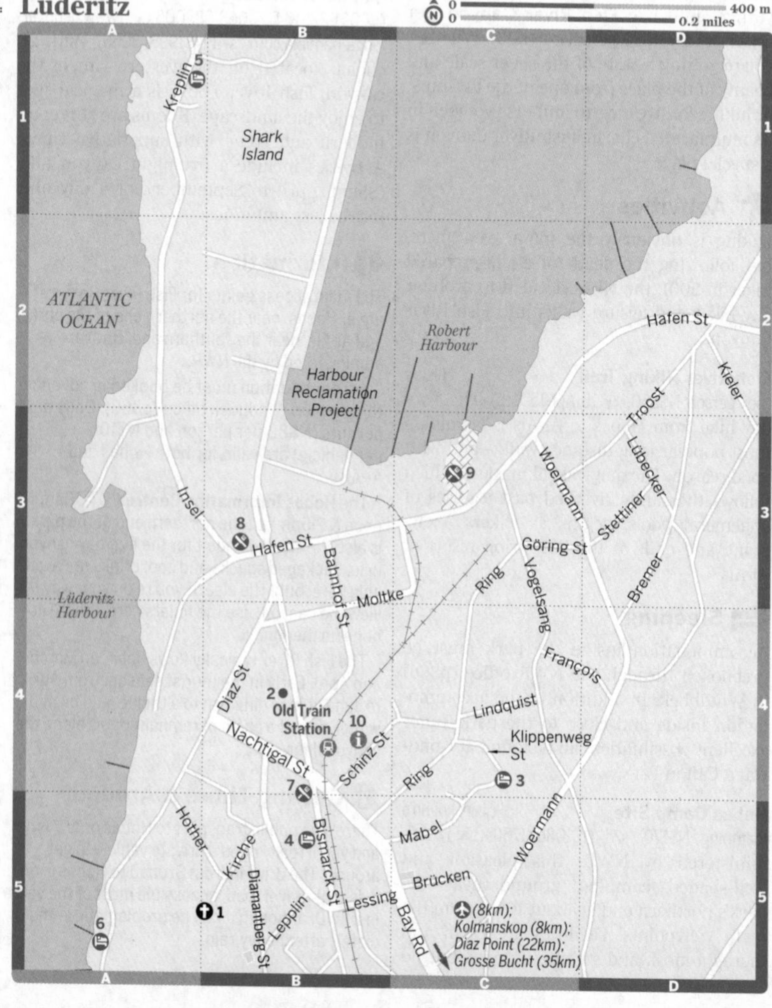

theran church, **Felsenkirche** (Kirche St; ⏲4-5pm Mon-Sat) FREE, for views over the water and the town.

The Lüderitz Peninsula, much of which lies outside the Sperrgebiet, makes an interesting half-day excursion from town.

## Sleeping

**★Hansa Haus Guesthouse** GUESTHOUSE $
(☎063-203699; www.hansahausluderitz.co.za; 85 Mabel St; s/d from N$552/650; 📶) This family-run guesthouse in an early-20th-century German-style house is one of the better places in town. The wood floors, white-linen look and the sea breezes (especially on the upstairs terrace) round out a lovely package.

**★Haus Sandrose** APARTMENT $
(☎063-202630; www.haussandrose.com; 15 Bismarck St; s/d from N$530/760) Haus Sandrose is comprised of uniquely decorated self-catering rooms surrounding a sheltered garden. The bright rooms are good value and exude a cheerful and roomy feel; note some rooms are bigger than others. It's a great location and very friendly.

**★Kairos B&B** B&B $
(☎063-203080, 081 650 5598; http://kairoscottage.com/; Shark Island; s/d N$480/680) This brand-spanking-new, cheerful, whitewashed building houses a promising new guesthouse and overlooks the water just before Shark Island. It's in a lovely location and is just a few minutes' drive from the town centre. Also here is a coffee shop serving breakfast and lunch.

### Lüderitz

**Sights**
1 Felsenkirche .......... B5

**Activities, Courses & Tours**
2 Lüderitz Safaris & Tours .......... B4

**Sleeping**
3 Hansa Haus Guesthouse .......... C4
4 Haus Sandrose .......... B5
5 Kairos B&B .......... A1
6 Lüderitz Nest Hotel .......... A5

**Eating**
7 Diaz Coffee Shop .......... B4
8 Garden Cafe .......... B3
9 Ritzi's Seafood Restaurant .......... C3

**Information**
10 Namibia Wildlife Resorts .......... B4

**Lüderitz Nest Hotel** HOTEL $$$
(☎063-204000; www.nesthotel.com; 820 Diaz St; s/d from N$1320/2100; ❄🏊) Lüderitz' oldest upmarket hotel occupies a jutting peninsula in the southwest corner of town, complete with its own private beach. Each room is stylishly appointed with modern furnishings and faces out towards the sea. Amenities include a pool, sauna, kids playground, car hire, terraced bar and a collection of gourmet restaurants. It's overpriced but this hotel's drawcard is the magnificent water views from the rooms.

## Eating

**★Diaz Coffee Shop** CAFE $
(☎081-700 0475; cnr Bismarck & Nachtigal Sts; mains from N$45; ⏲8am-9pm) The cappuccinos are strong, the pastries are sweet, and the ambience wouldn't at all seem out of place in Munich. The coffee shop has recently broadened its horizons to become an evening oyster and wine bar – very cool. Try the speciality coffee...if you dare.

**★Garden Cafe** CAFE $
(☎081-124 8317; 17 Hafen St; light meals from N$25) The garden setting, white-wood furnishings, great coffee and filled rolls add up to one of our favourite little haunts in town. The baked treats, Black Forest gateau among them, are also highlights.

**Ritzi's Seafood Restaurant** SEAFOOD $$
(☎063-202818; Waterfront Complex; mains from N$75; ⏲8am-9pm Tue-Sat, noon-9pm Mon) Occupying a choice location in the waterfront complex, Ritzi's is the town's top spot for seafood matched with fine sunset views. The food can be a little hit-or-miss, but the location is difficult to beat and outside dining catches the breeze and the views.

## Getting There & Away

Air Namibia (www.airnamibia.com.na) travels about three times a week between Windhoek and Lüderitz. The airport is 8km southeast of town.

Somewhat-irregular combis (minibuses) connect Lüderitz to Keetmanshoop, with fares averaging around N$250. Buses depart from the southern edge of town at informal bus stops along Bismarck St.

Lüderitz and the scenery en route are worth the 334km trip from Keetmanshoop via the tarred B4.

DON'T MISS

**KOLMANSKOP GHOST TOWN**

Named after early Afrikaner trekker Jani Kolman, whose ox wagon became bogged in the sand here, **Kolmanskop** (N$75; ⏲9.30am & 11am Mon-Sat, 10am Sun) was originally constructed as the Consolidated Diamond Mines (CDM) headquarters. Although Kolmanskop once boasted a casino, bowling alley and a theatre with fine acoustics, the slump in diamond sales after WWI and the discovery of richer pickings at Oranjemund ended its heyday. By 1956, the town was totally deserted, and left to the mercy of the shifting desert sands.

Today, Kolmanskop has been partially restored as a tourist attraction, and the sight of decrepit buildings being invaded by dunes is simply too surreal to describe. You can turn up at any time, and you're not required to arrive as part of an organised tour, though you do need to purchase a permit in advance through either the Lüderitz office of **Namibia Wildlife Resorts** (NWR; ☎063-202752; www.nwr.com.na; Schinz St; ⏲7.30am-1pm & 2-4pm Mon-Fri) or a local tour operator. Guided tours (in English and German), which are included in the price of the permit, depart from the museum in Kolmanskop. After the tour, you can return to the museum, which contains relics and information on the history of Namibian diamond mining.

Unfortunately the coffee shop and gift shop and often-large tourist numbers dampen the potentially eerie effect of this old town. If there are a lot of tourists around (likely) then you're better off skipping the organised part of the trip here and focusing instead on wandering around the decrepit buildings and piles of sand, getting a bit of a taste for this old deserted town.

Kolmanskop is only a 15-minute drive from Lüderitz, just off the main B4 highway. Tour agencies sell tours to Kolmanskop, or you can drive yourself so long as you have arranged the permit beforehand.

# UNDERSTAND NAMIBIA

## Namibia Today

As a relative newcomer to the world of nations, Namibia has mastered political stability and economic prosperity better than most African veterans. This is a country that works. Yes, many of its people live in grinding poverty and wealth disparity is a major issue, but Namibia's economy continues to roll along nicely. Although it was affected by the global recession in 2008–09, its mineral deposits ensured its economy rebounded as uranium and diamond prices recovered. By 2015 the country was again reporting a growth rate in excess of 5%.

There is much to be excited about when it comes to the country's economic future. Offshore oil and natural-gas exploration has thrown up some promising signals; the country is one of the world's largest producers of diamonds and uranium, with large deposits of gold, copper and zinc; while its tourism industry goes from strength to strength.

Like many countries in Southern Africa, Namibia is struggling to balance the needs of a growing population with the demands of a fragile environment.

## History

### In the Beginning

Namibia's history extends back into the mists of time, a piece in the jigsaw that saw the evolution of the earliest human beings. The camps and stone tools of *Homo erectus* (literally 'man who stands upright') have been found scattered throughout the region. By the middle Stone Age, the Boskop, the presumed ancestors of the San, had developed into an organised hunting-and-gathering society. Use of fire was universal, tools had become more sophisticated and natural pigments were being used for personal adornment. From around 8000 BC they began producing pottery, and started to occupy rock shelters and caves such as those at Twyfelfontein and Brandberg.

### Early Settlement

The archaeological connection between the late Stone Age people and the first Khoe-San arrivals isn't clear, but it is generally accepted that the earliest documented inhabitants of Southern Africa were the San, a nomadic people organised into extended family groups who were able to adapt to the severe terrain.

During the early Iron Age, between 2300 and 2400 years ago, rudimentary farming techniques appeared on the plateaus of south-central Africa. As the centuries came and went, Bantu-speaking groups began to arrive in sporadic southward waves. The first agriculturists and iron workers of definite Bantu origin belonged to the Gokomere culture. Cattle ranching became the mainstay of the community, and earlier hunting and gathering San groups retreated to the west, or were enslaved and/or absorbed.

At the same time, the San communities were also coming under pressure from the Khoekhoen (the ancestors of the Nama), who probably entered the region from the south. The Khoekhoen were organised loosely into tribal groups and were distinguished by their reliance on raising livestock. They gradually displaced the San, becoming the dominant group in the region until around AD 1500.

## European Exploration & Incursion

In 1486 the Portuguese captain Diego Cão sailed as far south as Cape Cross, where he erected a stone cross in tribute to his royal patron, João II. It wasn't really until the early 17th century that Dutch sailors from the Cape colonies began to explore the desert coastline, although they refrained from setting up any permanent stations.

In 1750 the Dutch elephant hunter Jacobus Coetsee became the first European to cross the Orange River. In his wake came a series of traders, hunters and missionaries, and by the early 19th century there were mission stations at Bethanie, Windhoek, Rehoboth, Keetmanshoop and various other sites. In 1844 the German Rhenish Missionary Society, under Dr Hugo Hahn, began working among the Herero.

By 1843 the rich coastal guano deposits of the southern Namib Desert were attracting commercial attention. In 1867 the guano islands were annexed by the British, who then proceeded to take over Walvis Bay in 1878.

## Colonial Period

Because Namibia has one of the world's most barren and inhospitable coastlines, it was largely ignored by European nations until relatively recently. The first European visitors were Portuguese mariners seeking a route to the Indies in the late 15th century, but they confined their activities to erecting stone crosses at certain points as navigational aids. It wasn't until the last-minute scramble for colonies towards the end of the 19th century that Namibia was annexed by Germany (except for the enclave of Walvis Bay, which was taken in 1878 by the British for the Cape Colony).

In 1904 the Herero launched a rebellion and, later that year, were joined by the Nama, but the rebellions were brutally suppressed. The Owambo in the north were luckier and managed to avoid conquest until after the start of WWI, when they were overrun by Portuguese forces fighting on the side of the Allies. Soon after, the German colony abruptly came to an end when its forces surrendered to a South African expeditionary army also fighting on behalf of the Allies. At the end of WWI, South Africa was given a mandate to rule the territory (then known as South West Africa) by the League of Nations.

Following WWII, the mandate was renewed by the UN, who refused to sanction the annexation of the country by South Africa. Undeterred, the South African government tightened its grip on the territory, and in 1949 it granted parliamentary representation to the white population. The bulk of southern Namibia's viable farmland was parcelled into some 6000 farms owned by white settlers, while indigenous families were confined by law to their 'reserves' (mainly in the east and the far north) and urban workplaces.

## Nationalism & the Struggle for Independence

Forced labour had been the lot of most Namibians since the German annexation. This was one of the main factors that led to mass demonstrations and the development of nationalism in the late 1950s. Around this time, a number of political parties were formed and strikes organised. By 1960 most of these parties had merged to form the South-West African People's Organization (Swapo), which took the issue of South African occupation to the International Court of Justice. The outcome was inconclusive, but in 1966 the UN General Assembly voted to terminate South Africa's mandate and set up a Council for South West Africa (in 1973

## WHERE TO WATCH WILDLIFE

Undoubtedly Namibia's most prolific wildlife populations are in Etosha National Park (p870), one of Africa's premier wildlife reserves. Its name means 'Place of Mirages', for the dusty salt pan that sits at its centre. During the dry season, huge herds of elephants, zebras, antelope and giraffes, as well as rare black rhinos, congregate here against an eerie, bleached-white backdrop. Predators, too, are commonly sighted here.

Namibia's other major parks for good wildlife viewing are Bwabwata National Park (p873) and Nkasa Rupara National Park (p874) in the Caprivi Strip.

Along the coast, penguins and seals thrive in the chilly Atlantic currents; the colony of Cape fur seals at Cape Cross Seal Reserve (p878) is one of the country's premier wildlife-watching attractions.

Not all of Namibia's wildlife is confined to national parks. Unprotected Damaraland (p874), in the northwest, is home to numerous antelope species and other ungulates, and is also a haven for desert rhinos, elephants, lions, spotted hyenas and other specially adapted subspecies.

renamed the Commission for Namibia) to administer the territory.

At the same time, Swapo launched its campaign of guerrilla warfare. The South African government reacted by firing on demonstrators and arresting thousands of activists. In 1975 the Democratic Turnhalle Alliance (DTA) was officially established. Formed from a combination of white political interests and ethnic parties, it turned out to be a toothless debating chamber, spending much of its time in litigation with the South African government over the scope of its responsibility. The DTA was dissolved in 1983 after it had indicated it would accommodate members of Swapo. It was replaced by the Multiparty Conference, which had even less success and quickly disappeared. And so control of Namibia passed back to the South African–appointed administrator-general.

These attempts to set up an internal government did not deter South Africa from maintaining its grip on Namibia. It refused to negotiate on a UN-supervised program for Namibian independence until the estimated 19,000 Cuban troops were removed from neighbouring Angola. In response, Swapo intensified its guerrilla campaign.

In the end, however, it was neither the activities of Swapo alone nor the international sanctions that forced the South Africans to the negotiating table. The white Namibian population itself was growing tired of the war and the South African economy was suffering, making sustaining the war financially difficult.

The stage was finally set for negotiations on the country's future. Under the watch of the UN, the USA and the USSR, a deal was struck between Cuba, Angola, South Africa and Swapo, in which Cuban troops would be removed from Angola and South African troops from Namibia. This would be followed by UN-monitored elections held in November 1989 on the basis of universal suffrage. Swapo collected a clear majority of the votes but an insufficient number to give it the sole mandate to write the new constitution.

## Independence

Following negotiations between the various parties, a constitution was adopted in February 1990. Independence was granted the following month under the presidency of the Swapo leader, Sam Nujoma. Initially, his policies focused on programs of reconstruction and national reconciliation to heal the wounds left by 25 years of armed struggle.

In 1999, however, Nujoma had nearly served out his second (and constitutionally, his last) five-year term, and alarm bells sounded among watchdog groups when he changed the constitution to allow himself a third five-year term, which he won with nearly 77% of the vote. In 2004 he announced that he would finally be stepping down in favour of his chosen successor, Hifikepunye Pohamba. After Pohamba took power, Namibia profited considerably from the extraction and processing of minerals for export. Rich alluvial diamond deposits alongside uranium and other metal reserves put the country's budget into surplus in 2007 for the first time since independence.

In line with the constitution, and in keeping with Namibia's impressive postindependence record of largely peaceful transitions, President Pohamba honoured his pledge to stand aside in 2014. His successor, Hage Geingob, easily won elections in November of that year.

## The Namibian People

The population of Namibia comprises 12 major ethnic groups. Half the people come from the Owambo tribe (50%), with other ethnic groups making up a relatively small percentage of the population: Kavango (9%), Herero/Himba (7%), Damara (7%), Afrikaner and German (6%), Nama (5%), Caprivian (4%), San (3%), Baster (2%) and Tswana (0.5%).

## Environment

The Namib, the desert of southwestern Africa that so appropriately gives its name to the driest country south of the Sahara, is the oldest desert on the planet. It is a scorched earth of burned and blackened-red basalt that spilled from beneath the earth 130 million years ago, hardening to form what we now know as Namibia. Precious little can grow or thrive in this merciless environment. That anything survives out here owes everything to the sheer ingenuity of the natural world and the resilience of its human population.

# SURVIVAL GUIDE

## Directory A–Z

### ACCOMMODATION

Accommodation in Namibia is some of the best priced and most well kept in Southern Africa, and covers a huge range of options.

Backpacker hostels inhabit Windhoek, Swakopmund and elsewhere. Hotels are everywhere, with a vast range in quality.

Most rest camps, campsites and caravan parks are fenced, and may have a small kiosk and even a swimming pool. Camping prices quoted in this chapter are indicative of the per person, per night rates, unless otherwise noted.

Guest farms are often in remote areas with rustic accommodation and activities. B&Bs and guesthouses are found all across Namibia and are often simple but welcoming and well priced.

Accommodation in safari lodges ranges from well priced and relatively simple to opulent with sky's-the-limit prices.

### ACTIVITIES

Given its stunning landscapes, Namibia provides a photogenic arena for the multitude of outdoor activities that are on offer. These range from the more conventional hiking and 4WD trails to sandboarding down mountainous dunes, quad biking, paragliding, ballooning and camel riding. Most of these activities can be arranged very easily locally, and are relatively well priced.

### ELECTRICITY

Electrical plugs have three round pins (like South Africa).

### EMBASSIES & CONSULATES

The embassies and high commissions listed here are all in Windhoek.

**Angolan Embassy** (☎061-227535; 3 Dr Agostino Neto St; ⏲9am-4pm)

**Botswanan Embassy** (☎061-221941; 101 Nelson Mandela Ave; ⏲8am-1pm & 2-5pm)

**British High Commission** (☎061-274800; www.gov.uk/government/world/organisations/british-high-commission-windhoek; 116 Robert Mugabe Ave; ⏲8am-noon Mon-Thu)

**Finnish Embassy** (☎061-221355; www.finland.org.na; 2 Crohn St, cnr Bahnhof St; ⏲9am-noon Mon, Wed & Thu)

**French Embassy** (☎061-276700; www.ambafrance-na.org; 1 Goethe St; ⏲8am-12.30pm & 2-5.45pm Mon-Thu, to 1pm Fri)

**German Embassy** (☎061-273100; www.windhuk.diplo.de; 6th fl, Sanlam Centre, 154 Independence Ave; ⏲9am-noon Mon-Fri, plus 2-4pm Wed)

**Kenyan High Commission** (☎061-226836; www.khcwindhoek.com; 5th fl, Kenya House, 134 Robert Mugabe Ave; ⏲8.30am-1pm & 2-4.30pm Mon-Thu, to 3pm Fri)

### PRICE RANGES

Price ranges refer to a high-season double room with bathroom:

**$** less than N$1050 (US$75)

**$$** N$1050–N$2100 (US$75–US$150)

**$$$** more than N$2100 (US$150)

The following price ranges refer to a main course.

**$** less than N$75 (US$5)

**$$** N$75–N$150 (US$5–US$10)

**$$$** more than N$150 (US$10)

**Malawian Embassy** (☎061-221391; 56 Bismarck St, Windhoek West; ⏰8am-noon & 2-5pm Mon-Fri)

**South African High Commission** (☎061-2057111; www.dirco.gov.za/windhoek; cnr Jan Jonker St & Nelson Mandela Dr, Klein Windhoek; ⏰8.15am-12.15pm)

**US Embassy** (☎061-2958500; https://na.usembassy.gov; 14 Lossen St; ⏰8.30am-noon Mon-Thu)

**Zambian High Commission** (☎061-237610; www.zahico.iway.na; 22 Sam Nujoma Dr, cnr Mandume Ndemufeyo Ave; ⏰9am-1pm & 2-4pm)

**Zimbabwean Embassy** (☎061-228134; www.zimwhk.com; Gamsberg Bldg, cnr Independence Ave & Grimm St; ⏰8.30am-1pm & 2-4.45pm Mon-Thu, to 2pm Fri)

### INTERNET ACCESS

Internet access is firmly established and widespread in Namibia, and connection speeds are fairly stable. Most larger or tourist-oriented towns have at least one internet cafe. Plan on spending around N$50 per hour online. An increasing number of backpacker hostels, hotels in larger towns and some lodges and guesthouses also offer wi-fi internet access, although this rarely extends beyond the hotel reception area.

### LGBTIQ TRAVELLERS

As in many African countries, homosexuality is illegal in Namibia, based on the common-law offence of sodomy or committing 'an unnatural sex crime'. Namibia is also very conservative in its attitudes, given the strongly held Christian beliefs of the majority. In view of this, discretion is certainly the better part of valour, as treatment of gay men and lesbians can range from simple social ostracism to physical attack.

The climate for gays and lesbians in Namibia has, however, eased somewhat in recent years. With no prosecutions recorded under the sodomy law since independence, the UN Human Rights Committee called in 2016 for the law against sodomy to be abolished and for laws to be introduced prohibiting discrimination on the grounds of sexual orientation. The call received the public support of Namibia's ombudsman and stirred little public debate. In the same year, an Afrobarometer opinion poll found that 55% of Namibians would welcome, or would not be bothered by, having a gay neighbour. Namibia was one of only four African countries polled to have a majority in favour of the proposition.

### MONEY

Credit cards can be used in ATMs displaying the appropriate sign or to obtain cash advances over the counter in many banks; Visa and MasterCard are among the most widely recognised. You'll find ATMs at all the main bank branches throughout Namibia, and this is undoubtedly the simplest (and safest) way to handle your money while travelling.

While most major currencies are accepted in Windhoek and Swakopmund, once away from these two centres you'll run into problems with currencies other than US dollars, euros, UK pounds and South African rand (you may even struggle with pounds). Play it safe and carry US dollars – it makes life much simpler.

Credit cards and debit cards are accepted in most shops, restaurants and hotels, and credit- and debit-card cash advances are available from ATMs. Check charges with your bank.

### OPENING HOURS

**Banks** 8am or 9am–3pm Monday–Friday, 8am–12.30pm Saturday

**Information Centres** 8am or 9am–5pm or 6pm Monday–Friday

**Petrol Stations** Only a few open 24 hours; in outlying areas fuel hard to find after hours or Sunday

**Post Offices** 8am–4.30 Monday–Friday, 8.30–11am Saturday

**Pubs & Clubs** 5pm to close (midnight–3am) Monday–Saturday

**Restaurants** breakfast 8am–10am, lunch 11am–3pm, dinner 6pm–10pm; some places open 8am–10pm Monday–Saturday

**Shopping** 8am or 9am–5pm or 6pm Monday–Friday, 9am–1pm or 5pm Saturday; late-night shopping to 9pm Thuday or Friday

### PUBLIC HOLIDAYS

Banks, government offices and most shops are closed on public holidays; when a public holiday falls on a Sunday, the following day also becomes a holiday.

**New Year's Day** 1 January

**Good Friday** March or April

**Easter Sunday** March or April

**Easter Monday** March or April

**Independence Day** 21 March

**Ascension Day** April or May

**Workers' Day** 1 May

**Cassinga Day** 4 May

**Africa Day** 25 May

**Heroes' Day** 26 August

**Human Rights Day** 10 December

**Christmas Day** 25 December

**Family/Boxing Day** 26 December

### SAFE TRAVEL

Namibia is one of the safest countries in Africa. It's also a huge country with a very sparse population, and even the capital, Windhoek, is more like a provincial town than an urban jungle.

Unfortunately, however, crime is on the rise in the larger cities, in particular Windhoek, but a little street sense will go a long way here.

### Theft

Theft isn't rife in Namibia, but Windhoek, Swakopmund, Walvis Bay, Tsumeb and Grootfontein have problems with petty theft and muggings, so it's sensible to conceal your valuables, not leave anything in your car and avoid walking alone at night. It's also prudent to avoid walking around cities and towns bedecked in expensive jewellery, watches and cameras. Most hotels provide a safe or secure place for valuables, although you should be cautious of the security at some budget places.

### TELEPHONE

MTC (www.mtc.com.na) is the largest mobile service provider in Namibia, operating on the GSM 900/1800 frequency, which is compatible with Europe and Australia but not with North America (GSM 1900) or Japan. The other provider is Telecom Namibia (www.telecom.na).

Both providers offers prepaid services. For visitors to the country, you're better off paying a one-off SIM-card fee then buying prepaid vouchers at the ubiquitous stores across Namibia.

Namibian mobile-phone numbers start with ☎08, landlines with ☎06.

### TOURIST INFORMATION

Namibia's national tourist office, Namibia Tourism (p866), is in Windhoek, where you'll also find the local Windhoek Information & Publicity Office (p866).

Also in Windhoek is the office of Namibia Wildlife Resorts (p866), where you can pick up information on national parks and make reservations for any NWR campsite.

Other useful tourist offices include **Lüderitz Safaris & Tours** (☎063-202719; ludsaf@africaonline.com.na; Bismarck St) in Lüderitz and Namib-i (p882) in Swakopmund.

### VISAS

Nationals of many countries, including Australia, the EU, USA and most Commonwealth countries do not need a visa to visit Namibia. Citizens of most Eastern European countries do require visas.

Tourists are granted an initial 90 days, although most immigration officials will ask how long you plan to stay in the country and tailor your visa duration accordingly.

Visas may be extended at the **Ministry of Home Affairs** (☎061-2922111; www.mha.gov.na; cnr Kasino St & Independence Ave; ⊙8am-1pm Mon-Fri) in Windhoek. For the best results, be there when the office opens at 8am and submit your application at the 3rd-floor offices (as opposed to the desk on the ground floor).

## ℹ Getting There & Away

### ENTERING THE COUNTRY

All visitors entering Namibia must hold a passport that is valid for at least six months after their intended departure date from Namibia.

### AIR

Most international airlines stop at Johannesburg or Cape Town in South Africa, where you'll typically switch to a **South African Airways** (☎061-273340; www.flysaa.com; Independence Ave, Windhoek) flight for your final leg to Windhoek. South African Airways has daily flights connecting Cape Town and Johannesburg to Windhoek. Johannesburg is also the main hub for connecting flights to other African cities.

Most international flights into Namibia arrive at Windhoek's Chief Hosea Kutako International Airport (p866), 42km east of the capital.

The main domestic carrier is Air Namibia (www.airnamibia.com.na), which flies routes to other parts of Southern Africa as well as long-haul flights to Frankfurt.

### LAND

Thanks to the Southern African Customs Union, you can drive through Namibia, Botswana, South Africa and Swaziland with a minimum of ado. To travel further north requires a *carnet de passage*, which can amount to heavy expenditure.

If you're driving a hire car to/from Namibia you will need to present a letter of permission from the rental company saying the car is allowed to cross the border.

### Border Crossings

Namibia has a well-developed road network with easy access from neighbouring countries. The main border crossings into Namibia are as follows:

**Angola** Oshikango, Ruacana, Rundu

**Botswana** Buitepos, Mahango and Ngoma

**South Africa** Noordoewer, Ariamsvlei

**Zambia** Katima Mulilo

All borders are open daily, and the main crossings from South Africa are open 24 hours. Otherwise, border crossings are generally open at least between 8am and 5pm, although most open from 6am to 6pm. Immigration posts at some smaller border crossings close for lunch between 12.30pm and 1.45pm. It is always advisable to reach the crossings as early in the day as possible to allow time for any potential delays. For more information on opening hours, check out the website www.namibweb.com/border.htm.

### Bus

There's only really one main interregional bus service connecting cities in Namibia with Botswana and South Africa. **Intercape Mainliner** (☎ 061-227847; www.intercape.co.za) has services between Windhoek and Johannesburg and Cape Town (South Africa). It also travels northeast to Victoria Falls, and between larger towns within Namibia. There are also long-distance Intercape Mainliner services running between Windhoek and Livingstone (Zambia).

Making the 12-hour Windhoek–Gaborone (Botswana) run, **Tok Tokkie Shuttle** (☎ 061-300743; www.shuttlesnamibia.com) departs Windhoek at 6pm on Wednesday and Friday, and leaves Gaborone at 1pm on Thursday and Saturday. One-way fares are N$500 and there's free wi-fi and air-con on board.

### Car & Motorcycle

Crossing borders with your own vehicle or a hire car is generally straightforward, as long as you have the necessary paperwork: the vehicle registration documents if you own the car, or a letter from the hire company stating that you have permission to take the car over the border, and proof of insurance. The hire company should provide you with a letter that includes the engine and chassis numbers, as you may be asked for these.

## Getting Around

### AIR

Air Namibia (www.airnamibia.com.na) has an extensive network of local flights operating out of Windhoek's Eros Airport (p866). There are six flights per week to Rundu, Katima Mulilo and Ondangwa.

From Windhoek's **Hosea Kutako International Airport** (p866), domestic destinations include Lüderitz and Oranjemund (three times per week) and Walvis Bay (daily).

### BUS & MINIBUS

Namibia's bus services aren't extensive. Luxury services are limited to the Intercape Mainliner, which has scheduled services from Windhoek to Swakopmund, Walvis Bay, Grootfontein, Rundu, Katima Mulilo, Keetmanshoop and Oshikango. Fares include meals on the bus.

There are also local combis (minibuses), which depart when full and follow main routes around the country. From Windhoek's Rhino Park petrol station they depart for dozens of destinations.

### CAR & MOTORCYCLE

The easiest way to get around Namibia is in your own car. Motorcycle holidays in Namibia are also popular due to the exciting off-road riding on offer. Unfortunately, however, it's difficult to rent a bike in Namibia, though the bigger car companies generally have a couple in their fleet. Note that motorcycles aren't permitted in the national parks, with the exception of the main highway routes through Namib-Naukluft Park.

### TRAIN

**Trans-Namib Railways** (☎ 061-2982032; www.transnamib.com.na) connects some major towns, but trains are extremely slow – as one reader remarked, they move 'at the pace of an energetic donkey cart'. Windhoek is Namibia's rail hub, with services south to Keetmanshoop, west to Swakopmund and east to Gobabis. Trains carry economy and business-class seats, but although most services operate overnight, sleepers are not available.

# South Africa

POP 53 MILLION / ☎27

## Includes ➡



## Best Places to Eat

- Test Kitchen (p907)
- Great Eastern Food Bar (p931)
- Mali's Indian Restaurant (p922)
- Hog House Brewing Co (p906)

## Best Places to Sleep

- Tintswalo Atlantic (p903)
- Motel Mipichi (p931)
- Hog Hollow (p913)

## Why Go?

When Archbishop Desmond Tutu called South Africa the 'Rainbow Nation', his words described the very essence of what makes this country extraordinary. Certainly, the blend of peoples and cultures that his oft-used moniker referred to is instantly evident, but the country's diversity stretches far beyond its people.

Within South Africa's borders you can sleep under the stars in a desert or hike to snowcapped peaks. The hills of Zululand and the Wild Coast provide a bucolic antidote to the bustle of large cities like Johannesburg and Durban. Wildlife watching ranges from remote safari walks to up-close encounters with waddling penguins.

Variety continues in the cuisine, with the delicate (West Coast seafood), the hearty (Karoo meat feasts), the fragrant (Cape Malay stews) and the spicy (Durban curries) all represented. And southwest of it all sits Cape Town, where gourmands, art lovers, thrill seekers and beach babes come together to sip, surf and sunbathe in beautiful surrounds.

## When to Go

### Cape Town

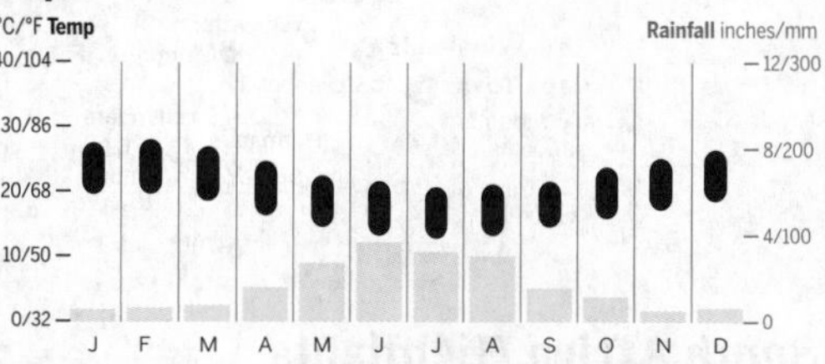


**Apr–Aug** Low season; ideal wildlife-watching conditions; whales on Western Cape coast.

**Sep–Nov** Spring flowers bloom; ideal weather for KwaZulu-Natal beaches and Karoo exploration.

**Dec–Feb** Coastal accommodation fills up; busy, vibrant time to be in the Cape.

## South Africa Highlights

1. **Cape Town** (p898) Tackling Table Mountain, paddling with penguins or just lazing on Atlantic beaches.
2. **Kruger National Park** (p943) Joining rangers on a safari of the most involving kind – on foot.
3. **uKhahlamba-Drakensberg Park** (p927) Hiking past waterfalls and San rock art towards mountain peaks.
4. **Wild Coast** (p918) Choosing between a hammock and the beach at a laid-back hostel.

5 **Winelands** (p910) Sipping on world-class wines and enjoying posh nosh in these magnificent Cape Dutch surrounds.

6 **Kgalagadi Transfrontier Park** (p947) Watching a black-maned lion nap under a thorn tree in this crimson Kalahari wonderland.

7 **iSimangaliso Wetland Park** (p925) Cycling and cruising in nature's playground.

# CAPE TOWN

POP 3.74 MILLION

Prepare to fall in love, as South Africa's 'Mother City' is an old pro at capturing people's hearts. And who wouldn't swoon at the sight of magnificent Table Mountain, its summit draped with cascading clouds, its flanks coated with unique flora and vineyards, its base fringed by golden beaches?

Few cities can boast such a wonderful national park at their heart or provide the range of adventurous activities that take full advantage of it. From the brightly painted facades of the Bo-Kaap and the bathing chalets of Muizenberg to striking street art and the Afro-chic decor of countless guesthouses, this is one good-looking metropolis.

## Sights

### Bo-Kaap

**★Bo-Kaap** AREA

(Map p904; Dorp/Leeuwen) Meaning 'Upper Cape', the Bo-Kaap with its vividly painted low-roofed houses, many of them historic monuments, strung along narrow cobbled streets, is one of the most photographed sections of the city. Initially a garrison for soldiers in the mid-18th century, this area of town was where freed slaves started to settle after emancipation in the 1830s. The most picturesque streets are Chiappini, Rose and Wale.

### Gardens & Around

**★Table Mountain** MOUNTAIN

(Map p900; www.tmnp.co.za) Around 600 million years old, and a canvas painted with the rich diversity of the Cape floral kingdom, Table Mountain is truly iconic. You can admire the showstopper of Table Mountain National Park and one of the 'New Seven Wonders of Nature' (www.new7wonders.com) from multiple angles, but you really can't say you've visited Cape Town until you've stood on top of it.

### Green Point & Waterfront

**★V&A Waterfront** AREA

(Map p900; www.waterfront.co.za; P; Nobel Sq) This historic working harbour has a spectacular setting and many tourist-oriented attractions, including masses of shops, restaurants, bars, cinemas and cruises. The Victoria and Alfred Basins date from 1860 and are named after Queen Victoria and her son Alfred. Too small for modern container vessels and tankers, the Victoria Basin is still used by tugs, fishing boats and various other vessels. In the Alfred Basin you'll see ships under repair.

**★Robben Island** LANDMARK

(021-413 4200; www.robben-island.org.za; adult/child R320/180; ferries depart at 9am, 11am, 1pm & 3pm, weather permitting; Nobel Sq) Used as a prison from the early days of the Vereenigde Oost-Indische Companie (VOC; Dutch East India Company) right up until 1996, this Unesco World Heritage Site is preserved as a memorial to those such as Nelson Mandela who spent many years incarcerated here. You can only go here on a tour, which last around four hours including ferry rides, departing from the **Nelson Mandela Gateway** (Map p900; 9am-8.30pm; Nobel Sq) FREE beside the Clock Tower at the Waterfront. Booking online well in advance is highly recommended as tours can sell out.

### District Six

**★District Six Museum** MUSEUM

(Map p904; 021-466 7200; www.districtsix.co.za; 25A Buitenkant St, East City; adult/child R30/15, walking tours per person R150; 9am-4pm Mon-Sat; Lower Buitenkant) It's impossible not to be emotionally touched by this museum which celebrates the once-lively multiracial area that was destroyed during apartheid in the 1960s and 1970s, its 60,000 inhabitants forcibly removed. Inside the former Methodist Mission Church, home interiors have been re-created, alongside photographs, recordings and testimonials, all of which build an evocative picture of a shattered but not entirely broken community.

Many township tours stop here first to explain the history of the pass laws.

### Southern Suburbs

**★Kirstenbosch Botanical Gardens** GARDENS

(021-799 8782; www.sanbi.org/gardens/kirstenbosch; Rhodes Dr, Newlands; adult/child R60/15; 8am-7pm Sep-Mar, to 6pm Apr-Aug, conservatory 9am-5pm year-round) Location and unique flora combine to make these 52,800-sq-km botanical gardens among the most beautiful in the world. The main entrance at the Newlands end of the gardens is where you'll find the information centre, an excellent souvenir shop and the conservatory.

Added for the garden's centenary in 2013, the Tree Canopy Walkway (informally known as the Boomslang, meaning 'Tree Snake') is a curvaceous steel and timber bridge that rises through the trees and provides amazing views.

## Sea Point to Hout Bay

**Table Mountain National Park** PARK

(Map p900; ☎021-712 2337; www.sanparks.org/parks/table_mountain) Stretching from Signal Hill to Cape Point, this 220-sq-km park is a natural wonder, its range of environments including granite and sandstone mountains, giant boulder-strewn beaches and shady forests. For the vast majority of visitors the main attraction is the 1086m-high mountain itself, the top of which can easily be accessed by the **cableway** (Map p900; ☎021-424 8181; www.tablemountain.net; Tafelberg Rd, Table Mountain; adult one-way/return from R135/255, child R65/125; ⏰8.30am-6pm Feb-Nov, 8am-9.30pm Dec & Jan; 🚌Lower Cable Car), which runs every 10 to 20 minutes.

## Simon's Town & Southern Peninsula

★**Cape of Good Hope** OUTDOORS

(www.tmnp.co.za; adult/child R135/70; ⏰6am-6pm Oct-Mar, 7am-5pm Apr-Sep; P) Commonly called Cape Point, this 77.5-sq-km section of Table Mountain National Park includes awesome scenery, fantastic walks, great birdwatching and often-deserted beaches. Bookings are required for the two-day Cape of Good Hope Trail (p901), a spectacular 33.8km circular route with one night spent at the basic Erica, Protea and Restio huts. Contact the **Buffelsfontein Visitor Centre** (☎021-780 9204; Cape of Good Hope; ⏰9.30am-5.30pm) for further details.

★**Boulders Penguin Colony** BIRD SANCTUARY

(www.tmnp.co.za; Simon's Town; adult/child R70/35; ⏰7am-7.30pm Dec & Jan, 8am-6.30pm Feb, Mar, Oct & Nov, to 5pm Apr-Sep; P; 🚆Simon's Town) Some 3km southeast of Simon's Town, this picturesque area, with enormous boulders dividing small, sandy coves, is home to a colony of 2100 delightful African penguins. A boardwalk runs from the **Boulders Visitor Centre** (☎021-786 2329; 1 Kleintuin Rd, Seaforth, Simon's Town; ⏰8am-4pm) at the Foxy Beach end of the protected area (part of Table Mountain National Park) to Boulders Beach, where you can get down on the sand and mingle with the waddling penguins. Don't, however, be tempted to pet them: they have sharp beaks that can cause serious injuries.

★**Cape Point Vineyards** WINERY

(☎021-789 0900; www.cpv.co.za; 1 Chapmans Peak Dr, Noordhoek; tastings per wine R10; ⏰tastings 11am-6pm, restaurant noon-3pm & 6.30-8.30pm Mon-Wed, Fri & Sat; P 👪) Known for its fine sauvignon blanc, this small vineyard has a spectacular setting overlooking Noordhoek Beach. Enjoy the wines with a picnic (noon-5pm, R395 for two, bookings essential) in the grounds, or at the restaurant. Its Thursday-evening community market (4.30pm-8.30pm), selling mainly food, is a weekly highlight for locals and great for kids, who can play on the lawns.

### CAPE TOWN'S TOP TOURS

If you're short on time, have a specific interest, or want some expert help in seeing Cape Town, there's a small army of tour guides and companies waiting to assist you. The best will provide invaluable insight into Capetonian food and wine, flora and fauna, and history and culture.

**Laura's Township Tours** (☎082 979 5831; www.laurastownshiptours.co.za; from R400) Gugulethu-based Laura Ndukwana gets rave reviews for her tours of her 'hood. She also runs a breakfast club, where she feeds 40 kids daily before they go to school. Itineraries include a Sunday-morning visit to a charismatic evangelist church, and cooking tours (R700).

**Venture Forth** (☎021-555 3864, 086 617 3449; www.ventureforth.co.za; per person from R570) Excellent guided hikes and rock climbs with enthusiastic, savvy guides.

## Clifton Beaches

★**Clifton Beaches** BEACH

(Map p900; Victoria Rd, Clifton; 🚌Clifton, Clifton 2nd, Clifton 3rd, Clifton 4th) Giant granite boulders break up the four beaches at Clifton, all accessible by steps from Victoria Rd. As they're almost always sheltered from the wind, they offer top sunbathing spots. Vendors hawk drinks and ice creams along the beach and sun loungers and shades are available. However, there are no public toilets.

# Cape Town

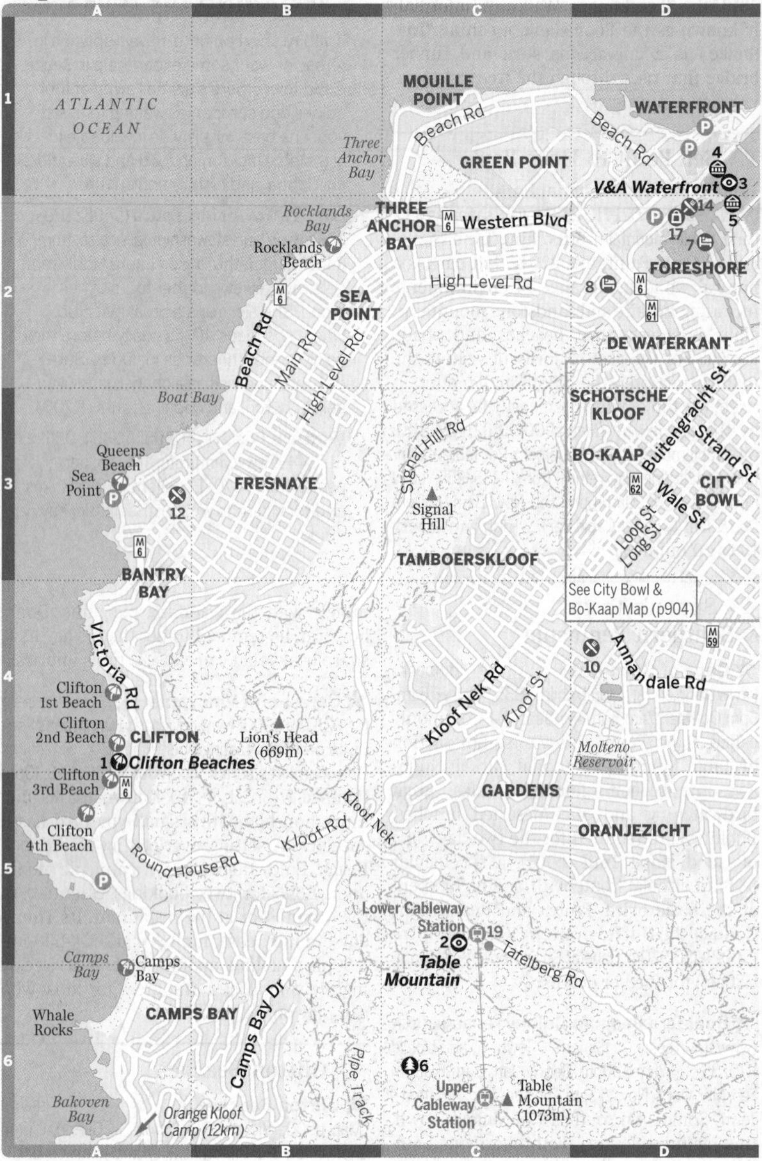

## Activities

**Abseil Africa** ADVENTURE SPORTS

(Map p904; ☎021-424 4760; www.abseilafrica.co.za; 297 Long St; abseiling R995) The 112m drop off the top of Table Mountain with this long-established outfit is a guaranteed adrenaline rush. Don't even think of tackling it unless you've got a head (and a stomach) for heights. You can tag on a guided hike up Platteklip Gorge for R455. It also offers guided hikes without the abseil (R495).

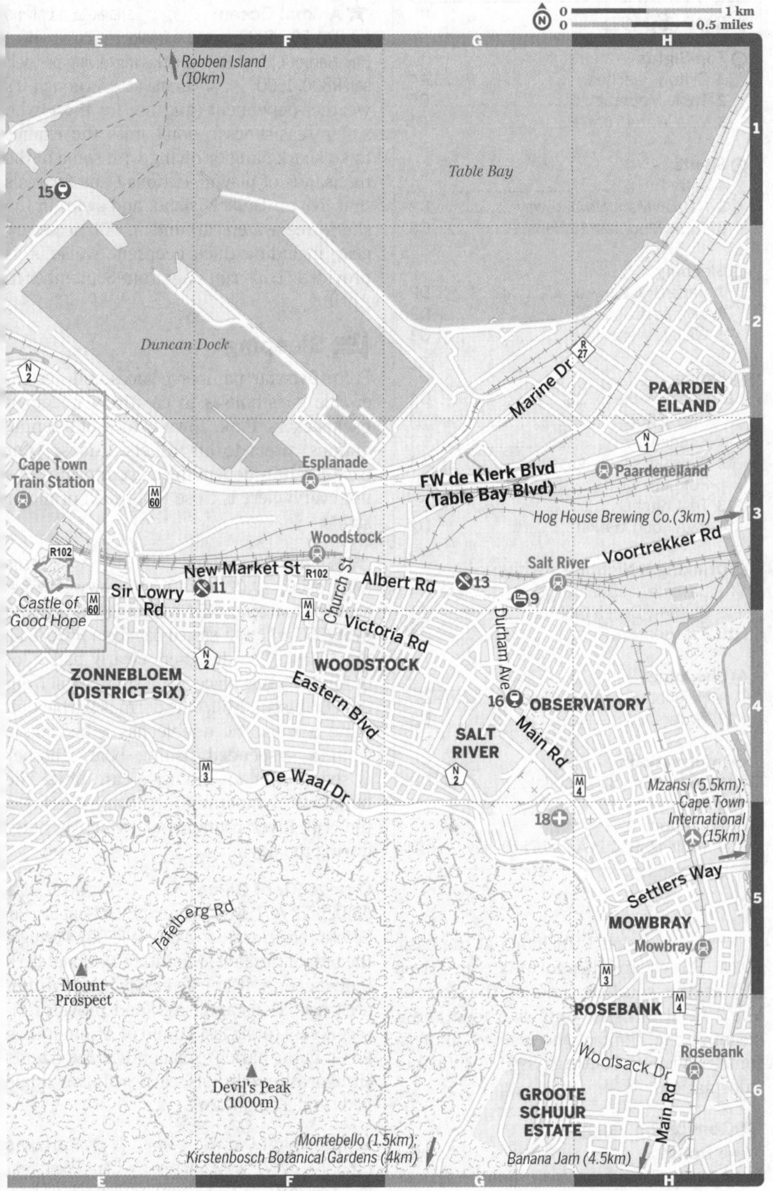


SOUTH AFRICA CAPE TOWN

**★ Sea Kayak Trips** KAYAKING
(☎082 501 8930; www.kayakcapetown.co.za; Simon's Town Jetty, Simon's Town; 🚉Simon's Town) Paddle out to the African penguin colony (p899) at Boulders (R300) with this Simon's Town–based operation.

**Cape of Good Hope Trail** HIKING
(R280, excl reserve entry fee) You'll need to book to walk the two-day/one-night Cape of Good Hope Trail, which traces a spectacular 33.8km circular route through the reserve.

## Cape Town

**Top Sights**
1 Clifton Beaches ... A4
2 Table Mountain ... C5
3 V&A Waterfront ... D1

**Sights**
4 Jetty 1 ... D1
5 Nelson Mandela Gateway ... D2
6 Table Mountain National Park ... C6

**Sleeping**
7 Cape Grace ... D2
8 Villa Zest ... D2
9 Wish U Were Here ... G3

**Eating**
10 Chef's Table ... D4
Dining Room ... (see 11)
11 Kitchen ... F3
12 Kleinsky's Delicatessen ... A3
Pot Luck Club ... (see 13)
13 Test Kitchen ... G3
14 V&A Food Market ... D2

**Drinking & Nightlife**
Bascule ... (see 7)
15 Shimmy Beach Club ... E1
16 Taproom ... G4

**Shopping**
Neighbourgoods Market ... (see 13)
17 Watershed ... D2

**Information**
18 Groote Schuur Hospital ... G5

**Transport**
19 Table Mountain Aerial Cableway ... C5

Accommodation is included at the basic Erica, Protea and Restio huts (each sleep six) at the southern end of the reserve. You'll need to bring your own food and a sleeping bag. Contact the reserve's Buffelsfontein Visitor Centre (p899) for further information.

**★Constantia Valley Wine Route** WINE
(www.constantiawineroute.com) South Africa's wine industry began here back in 1685 when Governor Simon van der Stel chose the area for its wine-growing potential and named his farm Constantia. After Van der Stel's death in 1712 his 7.63-sq-km estate was split up and the area is now the location for this wine route, comprising eight vineyards.

**★Animal Ocean** SNORKELLING, DIVING
(072 296 9132; www.animalocean.co.za; Hout Bay Harbour, Hout Bay; snorkelling/diving per person R800/1600; ; Fishmarket) Although it's weather-dependent (and not for those who suffer seasickness), don't miss the chance to go snorkelling or diving with some of the thousands of playful, curious Cape fur seals that live on Duiker Island, and swim in the shark-free waters around it. All necessary gear, including thick neoprene wetsuits, is provided. Trips run only from September to April.

## Sleeping

From five-star pamper palaces and designer-chic guesthouses to creatively imagined backpackers, Cape Town's stock of sleeping options caters to all wallets. Choose your base carefully depending on your priorities – not everywhere is close to a beach or major sights.

**★Wish U Were Here** HOSTEL $
(Map p900; 021-447 0522; www.wishuwerehere capetown.com; 445 Albert Rd, Salt River; dm/d R255/960, s/d with shared bathroom R530/830; ; Kent) The designers clearly had a lot of fun with this place just a short stroll from the Old Biscuit Mill. One dorm is Barbie-doll pink; a romantic double has a bed made from a suspended fishing boat; another is styled after an intensive care unit! The building's wraparound balcony overlooks the Salt River roundabout (which is noisy during the day).

**Orange Kloof Camp** TENTED CAMP $
(021-712 7471; www.tmbp.co.cz; off Hout Bay Rd, Cecelia Forest; tent for 2 people R590) Perhaps the best of the Table Mountain National Park tented camps. It's tucked away in a beautiful area near Constantia Nek and provides direct access to the last strand of Afromontane forest in the park. Permanently erected tents sit beneath reed roofs, each with two single beds and a small deck.

**Smitswinkel Camp** TENTED CAMP $
(021-712 7471; www.tmnp.co.za; Cape Point; tent for 2 people R725) The bright and spacious permanent tents here are the only ones within the Table Mountain National Park to offer en suite bathrooms. There are also shared kitchen and braai (barbecue) facilities. The camp is steps from the entrance to the Cape of Good Hope section of the park. Note that it does get windy here.

**Simon's Town Boutique Backpackers** HOSTEL $
(☎021-786 1964; www.capepax.co.za; 66 St George's St, Simon's Town; dm R220, s/d 650/760, s/d with shared bathroom R500/640; ; Simon's Town) Best-value place to stay in Simon's Town, with spacious, ship-shape rooms – several overlooking the harbour. Friendly staff can help you arrange a host of activities in the area, and there's bike hire for R200 per day. Rates do not include breakfast.

★**Dutch Manor** HISTORIC HOTEL $$
(Map p904; ☎087 095 1375; www.dutchmanor.co.za; 158 Buitengracht St, Bo-Kaap; s/d incl breakfast R1800/2900; ; Dorp/Leeuwen) Four-poster beds, giant armoires and creaking floorboards lend terrific atmosphere to this six-room property crafted from a 1812 building. Although it overlooks busy Buitengracht, the noise is largely kept at bay thanks to modern renovations. Dinners can be prepared on request by the staff, who can also arrange Bo-Kaap walking tours for R70 (nonguests R100) with a local guide. Parking is R70 per day.

★**Bella Ev** GUESTHOUSE $$
(☎021-788 1293; www.bellaevguesthouse.co.za; 8 Camp Rd, Muizenberg; r incl breakfast from R900; ; Muizenberg) This charming guesthouse, with a delightful courtyard garden, could be the setting for an Agatha Christie mystery, one in which the home's owner has a penchant for all things Turkish – hence the Ottoman slippers for guests' use.

**Villa Zest** BOUTIQUE HOTEL $$
(Map p900; ☎021-433 1246; www.villazest.co.za; 2 Braemar Rd, Green Point; s/d incl breakfast from R1590/1790; ; Upper Portswood) This Bauhaus-style villa has been converted into a quirkily decorated boutique hotel. The lobby is lined with an impressive collection of '60s and '70s groovy electronic goods, including radios, phones, Polaroid cameras and eight-track cassette players. The seven guestrooms have bold, retro-design papered walls and furniture accented with furry pillows and shag rugs.

★**Tintswalo Atlantic** LUXURY HOTEL $$$
(☎021-201 0025; www.tintswalo.com; Chapman's Peak Dr, Hout Bay; s/d with half board from R7020/9370; ; Hout Bay) Destroyed in a disastrous fire in March 2015, this heralded hotel is happily up and running again. Luxurious Tintswalo hugs the edge of a beautiful rocky bay within the Table Mountain National Park, a favourite resting ground for whales. Expect sublime views and rooms rich with natural materials.

**Cape Grace** LUXURY HOTEL $$$
(Map p900; ☎021-410 7100; www.capegrace.com; West Quay Rd, V&A Waterfront; r/ste from R8100/15,000; ; Nobel Sq) One of the Waterfront's most appealing hotels, the Cape Grace sports an arty combination of antiques and crafts decoration – including hand-painted bed covers and curtains – that provide a unique sense of place and Cape Town's history.

## Eating

It's a wonder that Capetonians look so svelte on the beach because this is one damn delicious city to dine in – probably the best in the whole of Africa. There's a wonderful range of cuisines to sample, including local African and Cape Malay concoctions, superb seafood fresh from the boat and chefs working at the top of their game.

★**Kitchen** SANDWICHES, SALADS $
(Map p900; www.lovethekitchen.co.za; 111 Sir Lowry Rd, Woodstock; sandwiches & salads R60-70; 8am-3.30pm Mon-Fri; ; District Six) Of all the swanky restaurants in town, it was this little charmer that Michelle Obama chose for lunch, proving she has excellent taste. Tuck into plates of divine salads, rustic sandwiches made with love, and sweet treats with tea served from china teapots.

**Mzoli's** BRAAI $
(☎021-638 1355; 150 NY111, Gugulethu; meals R50-100; 11am-6pm; Nyanga) Tourists, TV stars and locals gather at this busy butchery serving some of Cape Town's tastiest grilled meat. First buy your meat and make sure you get staff to add Mzoli's special sauce. Take your meat to the kitchen to be braaied (barbecued) and then find a table outside. It gets superhectic here at weekends, so arrive early.

**V&A Food Market** AFRICAN $
(Map p900; www.waterfrontfoodmarket.com; Pump House, Dock Rd, V&A Waterfront; mains from R75; 10am-6pm May-Oct, to 8pm Nov-April; ; Nobel Sq) There's no need to spend big to eat well (and healthily) at the Waterfront, thanks to this colourful, market-style food court in the old Pump House. Grab a coffee or freshly squeezed juice to go with a wrap or muffin, or opt for a larger meal such as Thai, Indian or Cape Malay curry.

# City Bowl & Bo-Kaap

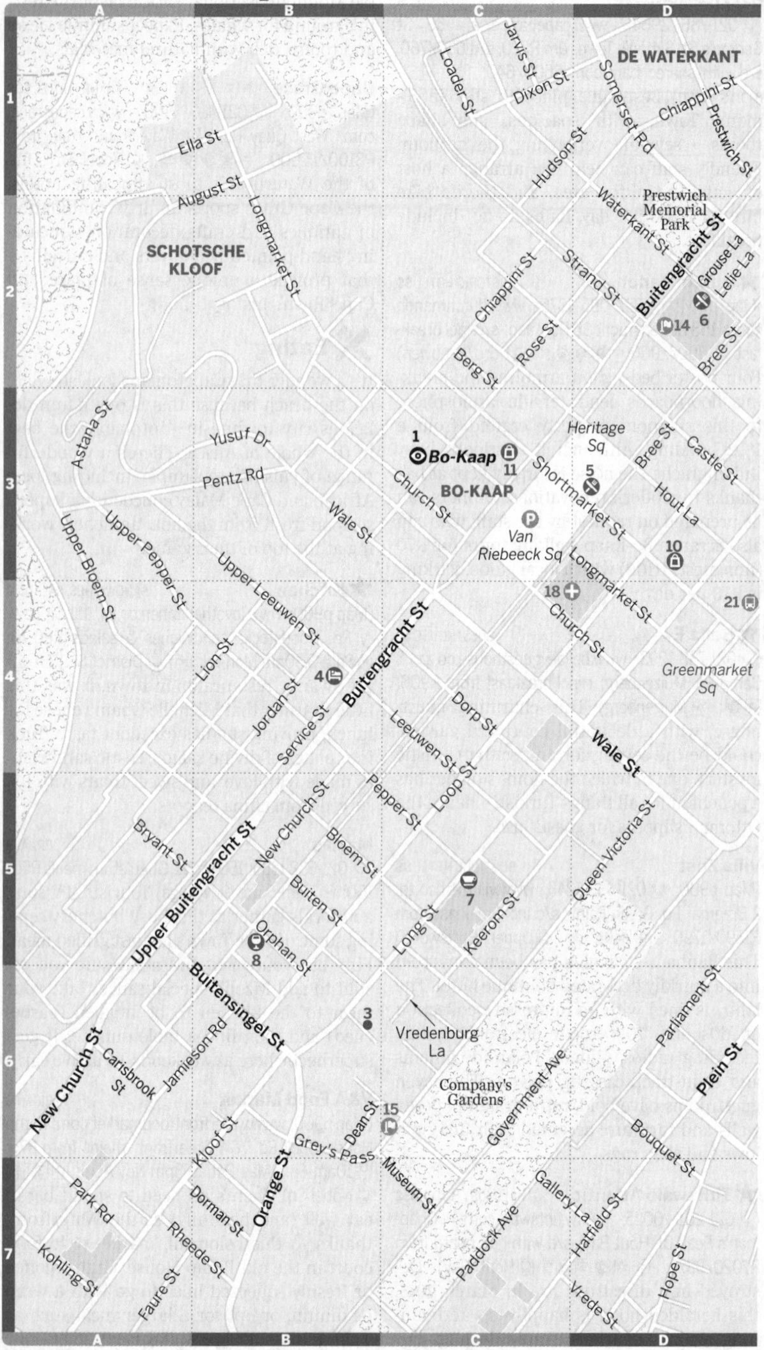

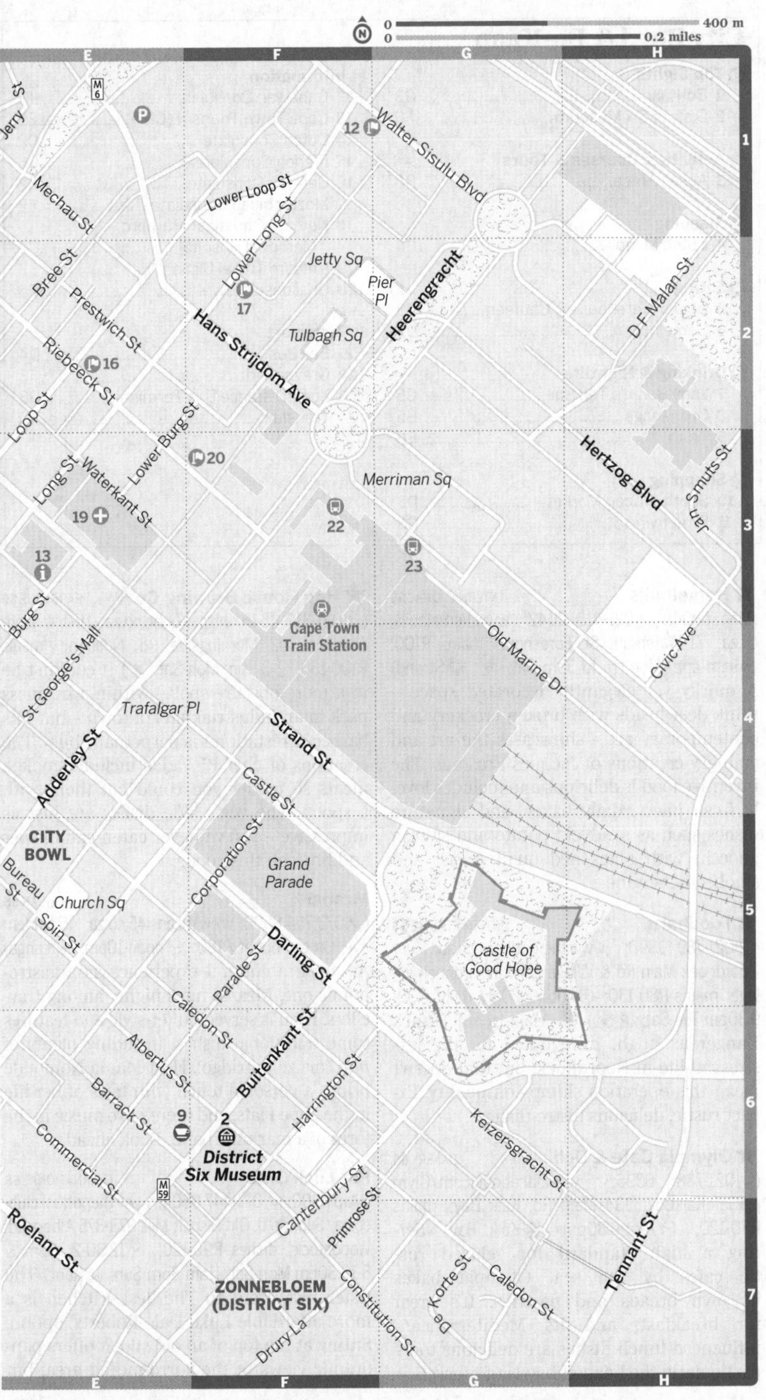

0
400 m
0
0.2 miles
Jerry St
Mechau St
Bree St
Prestwich St
Riebeeck St
Loop St
Long St
Waterkant St
Lower Burg St
Lower Loop St
Lower Long St
Jetty Sq
Pier Pl
Tulbagh Sq
Hans Strijdom Ave
Heerengracht
Walter Sisulu Blvd
D F Malan St
Hertzog Blvd
Jan Smuts St
Merriman Sq
Cape Town Train Station
Old Marine Dr
Civic Ave
Burg St
St George's Mall
Trafalgar Pl
Adderley St
Strand St
Castle St
CITY BOWL
Corporation St
Grand Parade
Bureau St
Church Sq
Spin St
Darling St
Parade St
Castle of Good Hope
Caledon St
Albertus St
Buitenkant St
Harrington St
Barrack St
District Six Museum
Commercial St
Keizersgracht St
Canterbury St
Primrose St
Roeland St
Tennant St
De Korte St
Caledon St
ZONNEBLOEM (DISTRICT SIX)
Constitution St
Drury La

## City Bowl & Bo-Kaap



**★Hemelhuijs** INTERNATIONAL **$$**

(Map p904; 021-418 2042; www.hemelhuijs.co.za; 71 Waterkant St, Foreshore; mains R100; 9am-4pm Mon-Fri, to 3pm Sat; ; Strand) A quirky yet elegantly decorated space – think deer heads with broken crockery and contemporary art – showcases the art and culinary creations of Jacques Erasmus. The inventive food is delicious and includes lovely fresh juices, daily bakes, and signature dishes such as sandveld potato and saffron gnocchi with blackened quail breast and smoked aubergine.

**★Foodbarn** INTERNATIONAL **$$**

(021-789 1390; www.thefoodbarn.co.za; cnr Noordhoek Main Rd & Village Lane, Noordhoek Village; mains R80-130; noon-2.30pm daily, 6.30-9.30pm Tue-Sat; ) Masterchef Franck Dangereux might have opted for the less stressful life in Noordhoek, but that doesn't mean this operation skimps on quality. Expect rustic, delicious bistro dishes.

**★Olympia Café & Deli** BAKERY **$$**

(021-788 6396; www.facebook.com/OlympiaCafeKalkBay; 134 Main Rd, Kalk Bay; mains R80-120; 7am-9.30pm; Kalk Bay) Setting a high standard for relaxed rustic cafes by the sea, Olympia bakes its own breads and pastries. It's great for breakfast, and its Mediterranean-influenced lunch dishes are delicious too – particularly the heaped bowls of mussels.

**★Hog House Brewing Co.** BARBECUE **$$**

(021-810 4545; http://hhbc.co.za; Unit 4 Technosquare, 42 Morningside Rd, Ndabeni; meals R100-150; 5-9pm Mon-Sat; ) It couldn't be in a more obscure spot – within a business park in an industrial part of town – but this barbecue restaurant is perpetually busy. The creations of chef PJ Vadas include smoked meats so tender you could cut them with a spoon. The vegie side dishes are just as impressive – you've never eaten cauliflower and broccoli this good.

**Mzansi** AFRICAN **$$**

(073 754 8502; www.mzansi45.co.za; 45 Harlem Ave, Langa; buffet R180; noon-10pm; Langa) As much a cultural experience as a gastronomic one, Mzansi rates highly among travellers. Food is served buffet-style and features some traditional dishes, including plenty of *pap* (maize porridge). Host Mama Nomonde brings a personal touch with tales of her life in the Cape Flats, and there's live music in the form of a marimba band. Book ahead.

**Pot Luck Club** INTERNATIONAL **$$**

(Map p900; 021-447 0804; www.thepotluckclub.co.za; Silo top fl, Old Biscuit Mill, 373-375 Albert Rd, Woodstock; dishes R90-120; 12.30-2.30pm & 6-10.30pm Mon-Sat, 11am-3pm Sun; Kent) The sister restaurant to The Test Kitchen is a more affordable Luke Dale-Roberts' option. Sitting at the top of an old silo, it offers panoramic views of the surrounding area, but it's what's on the plate that tends to take the breath away. The dishes are designed to be shared; we defy you not to order a second plate of the Chalmar beef with truffle-café-au-lait sauce.

**★Test Kitchen** INTERNATIONAL $$$
(Map p900; ☎021-447 2622; www.thetestkitchen.co.za; Shop 104A, Old Biscuit Mill, 375 Albert Rd, Woodstock; gourmand menu without/with wine R1600/2250; ⏲6.30-9pm Tue-Sat; P; ▣Kent) Luke Dale-Roberts creates inspirational dishes with top-quality local ingredients at his flagship restaurant – generally agreed to be the best in Africa. However, the award-winning UK-born chef is so famous now that bookings several months in advance are essential. Pescatarian and vegetarian menus are available on request.

**★Chef's Warehouse & Canteen** TAPAS $$$
(Map p904; ☎021-422 0128; www.chefswarehouse.co.za; Heritage Sq, 92 Bree St, City Bowl; tapas set for 2 R620; ⏲noon-2.30pm & 4.30-8pm Mon-Fri, noon-2.30pm Sat; ▣Church/Longmarket) Hurry here for a delicious and very generous spread of small plates from chef Liam Tomlin and his talented crew. Flavours zip around the world, from a squid with a tangy Vietnamese salad to comforting coq au vin. If you can't get a seat (there are no bookings) try its takeaway hatch **Street Food** in the space under the stoop (terraced veranda).

**Chef's Table** INTERNATIONAL $$$
(Map p900; ☎021-483 1864; www.belmond.com/mountnelsonhotel; Belmond Mount Nelson Hotel, 76 Orange St, Gardens; lunch R500, dinner without/with wine R745/1285; ⏲noon-3pm Fri, 6.30-9pm Mon-Sat; P🖉; ▣Government Ave) There are several dining options at the Mount Nelson Hotel, but for a real treat book one of the four tables with a front-row view onto the drama and culinary magic unfolding inside the kitchen. The food is superb (vegetarians are catered for) and presented by the chefs, who will take you on a behind-the-scenes tour.

## Drinking & Nightlife

Cape Town didn't become known as the 'Tavern of the Seven Seas' for nothing. There are scores of bars – with stunning views of either beach or mountain – in which to sip cocktails, fine wines or craft beers. If strutting your stuff on the dance floor is more your thing, then there's bound to be a club to suit.

**★Orphanage** COCKTAIL BAR
(Map p904; ☎021-424 2004; www.theorphanage.co.za; cnr Orphange & Bree Sts, City Bowl; ⏲5pm-2am Mon-Thu & Sat, to 3am Fri; ▣Upper Loop/Upper Long) Named after the nearby lane, the mixologists here prepare some tempting artisan libations with curious names including Knicker-Dropper Glory, Dollymop and Daylight Daisy, using ingredients as varied as peanut butter, cumquat compote and 'goldfish'! It's dark, sophisticated and stylish, with outdoor seating beneath the trees on Bree.

**★Bascule** BAR
(Map p900; ☎021-410 7082; www.basculebar.com; Cape Grace Hotel, West Quay Rd, V&A Waterfront; ⏲9am-1am; ▣Nobel Sq) Over 450 varieties of whisky are served at the Grace's sophisticated bar, with a few slugs of the 50-year-old Glenfiddich still available (at just R10,000 a tot). Outdoor tables facing the marina are a superb spot for drinks and tasty tapas. Make a booking for one of Bascule's whisky tastings (from R350), in which you can sample various drams paired with food.

**Tiger's Milk** BAR
(☎021-788 1869; www.tigersmilk.co.za; cnr Beach & Sidmouth Rds, Muizenberg; ⏲11am-2am Mon-Fri, from 8am Sat & Sun; 📶; 🚆Muizenberg) There's a panoramic view of Muizenberg beach through the floor-to-ceiling window of this hangar-like bar and restaurant. Although it's open all day for food (good pizza and steaks), the vibe – with its long bar counter, comfy sofas and quirky decor (a BMW bike and a giant golden cow's head hanging on exposed-brick walls) – is more nightclub.

**★Banana Jam** CRAFT BEER
(www.bananajamcafe.co.za; 157 2nd Ave, Harfield Village, Kenilworth; ⏲11am-11pm Mon-Sat, 5-10pm Sun; 📶; 🚆Kenilworth) Real beer lovers rejoice – this convivial Caribbean restaurant and bar is like manna from heaven, with over 30 beers on tap (including its own brews) and bottled ales from all the top local microbrewers, including Jack Black, Darling Brew and CBC.

**Taproom** MICROBREWERY
(Map p900; ☎021-200 5818; www.devilspeakbrewing.co.za; 95 Durham Ave, Salt River; ⏲11am-2am Mon-Sat, noon-6pm Sun; ▣Upper Salt River) Devil's Peak Brewing Company make some of South Africa's best craft beers. Its taproom and restaurant provide a panoramic view up to Devil's Peak itself. The food is hearty fare (think burgers and fried chicken), designed to balance the stellar

selection of on-tap beers. There are also barrel-aged brews and one-off experiments available on tap.

**★Shimmy Beach Club** CLUB

(Map p900; ☎021-200 7778; www.shimmybeach-club.com; South Arm Rd, V&A Waterfront; cover after 3pm R150; ⊙11am-2am Mon-Fri, 9am-2am Sat, 11am-6pm Sun; 🚌Waterfront Silo) Drive past the smelly fish-processing factories to discover this glitzy megaclub and restaurant, arranged around a small fake beach with a glass-sided pool. Perhaps unsurprisingly, it has pool parties with scantily clad dancers shimmying to grooves by top DJs, including the electro-jazz group Goldfish, who have a summer Sunday residency here (bookings advised).

**Lady Bonin's Tea Bar** TEAHOUSE

(Map p904; ☎021-447 1741; www.ladybonin-stea.com; 213 Long St; ⊙8am-4.30pm Mon-Fri, 9.30am-2.30pm Sat; 🚌Upper Loop/Upper Long) A charmingly decorated, relaxing place in which to sample organic and sustainable artisan teas, fruity and herbal brews, and vegan baked treats.

**Truth** COFFEE

(Map p904; www.truthcoffee.com; 36 Buitenkant St, East City; ⊙7am-6pm Mon-Thu, 8am-midnight Fri & Sat, 8am-2pm Sun; 📶; 🚌Lower Buitenkant) This self-described 'steampunk roastery and coffee bar', with pressed-tin ceilings, naked hanging bulbs and mad-inventor style metalwork, is an awe-inspiring space in which to mingle with city slickers. Apart from coffee, craft beers, baked goods and various sandwiches, burgers and hot dogs are on the menu.

## Shopping

Bring an empty suitcase because the chances are high that you'll be leaving Cape Town laden with booty. There's a practically irresistible range of products on offer, including traditional African crafts, ceramics, fashion, fine wines and contemporary art. You'll also find antiques and curios from all over Africa, but shop carefully as there are many fakes among the originals.

**★South African Market** FASHION, ARTS

(SAM; Map p904; ☎089 690 6476; www.ilovesam.co.za; 67 Shortmarket St, City Bowl; ⊙10am-6pm



DON'T MISS

### CAPE TOWN FESTIVALS

**Cape Town Minstrel Carnival** (www.capetown-minstrels.co.za; ⊙Jan & Feb) Tweede Nuwe Jaar (2 January) is when the satin- and sequin-clad minstrel troupes traditionally march through the city for the Kaapse Klopse (Cape Minstrel Festival). The routes runs from Keizergracht St, along Adderley and Wale Sts to the Bo-Kaap. Throughout January into early February there are Saturday competitions between troupes at Athlone Stadium.

**Cape Town Carnival** (http://capetowncarnival.com; ⊙mid-Mar) Held along the Walk of Remembrance (the former Fan Walk) in Green Point, this is a city-sponsored parade and street party that celebrates the many facets of South African identity.

**Cape Town International Jazz Festival** (www.capetownjazzfest.com; ⊙late Mar/early Apr) Cape Town's biggest jazz event, attracting big names from both South Africa and overseas, is usually held at the Cape Town International Convention Centre at the end of March. It includes a free concert in Greenmarket Sq.

**Cape Town Festival of Beer** (www.capetownfestivalofbeer.co.za; ⊙late Nov) With the stadium as a backdrop, the continent's largest beer festival sees more than 200 beers available for tasting over three days.

**Kirstenbosch Summer Sunset Concerts** (www.sanbi.org/gardens/kirstenbosch/summer-concerts; ⊙late Nov to early Apr) Sunday-afternoon outdoor concerts at Kirstenbosch Botanical Gardens. Bring a blanket and a picnic and join the crowds enjoying anything from arias performed by local divas to a funky jazz combo. There's always a special concert for New Year's Eve too.

**Mother City Queer Project** (www.mcqp.co.za; ⊙Dec) This fabulous fancy-dress dance party is one of the city's main gay events.

Mon-Fri, to 3pm Sat; Church/Longmarket) A showcase for local design talent across fashion, jewellery, homewares, stationery and artworks, with a great selection of menswear, womenswear and clothing for kids here including the cute graphic T-shirts of Mingo Lamberti.

★ **Streetwires** ARTS & CRAFTS
(Map p904; www.streetwires.co.za; Maxton Centre, 354 Albert Rd, Woodstock; 9am-5pm Mon-Fri, to 1pm Sat; Salt River) The motto is 'anything you can dream up in wire we will build'. And if you visit this social project, designed to create sustainable employment, and see the wire sculptors at work, you'll see what that means! It stocks an amazing range, including working radios and chandeliers, life-sized animals and artier products such as the Nguni Cow range.

**Montebello** ARTS & CRAFTS
(www.montebello.co.za; 31 Newlands Ave, Newlands; 9am-5pm Mon-Sat, to 3pm Sun; Newlands) This development project has helped several great craftspeople and designers along the way. In the leafy compound, artists studios are scattered around the central craft shop, where you can buy a great range of gifts, including some made from recycled materials. There's also a plant nursery, the excellent cafe **Gardener's Cottage** and car-washers.

★ **Neighbourgoods Market** MARKET
(Map p900; www.neighbourgoodsmarket.co.za; Old Biscuit Mill, 373-375 Albert Rd, Woodstock; 9am-2pm Sat; Kent) The first and still the best of the artisan-goods markets that are now common across the Cape. Food and drinks are gathered in the main area where you can pick up groceries and gourmet goodies or just graze, while the separate Designergoods area hosts a must-buy selection of local fashions and accessories. Come early unless you enjoy jostling with crowds.

★ **Watershed** SHOPPING CENTRE
(Map p900; www.waterfront.co.za/shop/watershed; Dock Rd, V&A Waterfront; 10am-6pm; Nobel Sq) The best place to shop for souvenirs in Cape Town, this exciting revamped retail market gathers together hundreds of top Capetonian and South African brands in fashion, arts, crafts and design – there's something here for every pocket. On the upper level is an exhibition space, and a wellness centre offering holistic products and massages.

## Information

### MEDICAL SERVICES

**Groote Schuur Hospital** (Map p900; 021-404 9111; www.westerncape.gov.za/your_gov/163; Main Rd, Observatory; Observatory) In an emergency, you can go directly to the casualty (emergency) department.

**Netcare Christiaan Barnard Memorial Hospital** (Map p904; 021-480 6111; www.netcare.co.za/139/netcare-christiaan-barnard-memorial-hospital; 181 Longmarket St, City Bowl; Church/Longmarket) Excellent private hospital. Reception is on the 8th floor.

**Netcare Travel Clinic** (Map p904; 021-419 3172; www.travelclinic.co.za; 11th fl, Picbal Arcade, 58 Strand St, City Bowl; 8am-4pm Mon-Fri; Adderley) For vaccinations and travel health advice.

### TOURIST INFORMATION

**Cape Town Tourism** (Map p904; 021-487 6800; www.capetown.travel; Pinnacle Bldg, cnr Castle & Burg Sts, City Bowl; 8am-5.30pm Mon-Fri, 8.30am-2pm Sat, 9am-1pm Sun; Church/Mid-Long) This head office is centrally located and there are plenty of satellite offices around the city, including one at the airport.

## Getting There & Away

### AIR

**Cape Town International Airport** (CPT; 021-937 1200; www.airports.co.za), 22km east of the city centre, has a tourist information office located in the arrivals hall. There are many direct international flights into Cape Town.

### BUS

Interstate buses arrive at the bus terminus (Map p904) at Cape Town Railway Station, where you'll find the booking offices for the following bus companies, all open from 6am to 6.30pm daily.

**Baz Bus** (Map p904; 0861 229 287; www.bazbus.com; 32 Burg St) Offers hop-on, hop-off fares and door-to-door service between Cape Town and Jo'burg/Pretoria via Northern Drakensberg, Durban and the Garden Route.

**Greyhound** (Map p904; 021-418 4326, reservations 083-915 9000; www.greyhound.co.za; Cape Town Railway Station)

**Intercape** (021-380 4400, 0861 287 287; www.intercape.co.za; Cape Town Railway Station)

**Translux** (Map p904; 0861 589 282, 021-449 6209; www.translux.co.za; Cape Town Railway Station)

### TRAIN

Long distance trains arrive at **Cape Town Railway Station** (Heerengracht, City Bowl). There are services Wednesday, Friday and Sunday to and from Jo'burg via Kimberley on the **Shosholoza Meyl** (☎0860 008 888; www.shosholozameyl.co.za): these sleeper trains offer comfortable accommodation and dining cars. Other services include the luxurious **Blue Train** (☎021-449 2672; www.bluetrain.co.za) and **Rovos Rail** (☎021-421 4020; www.rovos.com).

## Getting Around

### TO/FROM THE AIRPORT

**MyCiTi buses** (☎0800 656 463; www.myciti.org.za) run every 30 minutes between 4.45am and 10.15pm to the city centre and the Waterfront. A single trip fare is R90.

Book **Backpacker Bus** (☎082 809 9185; www.backpackerbus.co.za) in advance for airport transfers (from R220 per person) and pick-ups from hostels and hotels.

Expect to pay around R250 for a nonshared taxi.

### BUS

The MyCiTi network of commuter buses covers the city centre up to Gardens and out to the Waterfront; along the Atlantic seaboard to Camps Bay and Hout Bay; and to the airport.

Fares have to be paid with a stored-value 'myconnect' card (a nonrefundable R30), which can be purchased from MyCiTi station kiosks and participating retailers. It's also possible to buy single-trip tickets.

### TAXI

Consider taking a nonshared taxi at night or if you're in a group. Rates are about R10 per kilometre. Uber (www.uber.com) is very popular and works well.

### TRAIN

**Cape Metro Rail** (☎0800 656 463; http://capetowntrains.freeblog.site) trains are a handy way to get around. Metro trains also run out to Strand on the eastern side of False Bay, and into the Winelands to Stellenbosch and Paarl.

# WINELANDS

Venturing inland and upwards from Cape Town you'll find the Boland, meaning 'Upland'. It's a superb wine-producing area, and indeed the best known in South Africa. The magnificent mountain ranges around Stellenbosch and Franschhoek provide ideal microclimates for the vines.

## Stellenbosch

POP 155,000

Stellenbosch is an elegant, historical town with stately Cape Dutch, Georgian and Victorian architecture along its oak-lined streets – and it is so much more than that. Full of interesting museums, quality hotels and a selection of bars, clubs and restaurants, it is constantly abuzz with locals, students, Capetonians and tourists.

### Sights

**★Villiera** WINERY
(☎021-865 2002; www.villiera.com; ⏲9am-5pm Mon-Fri, to 3pm Sat) FREE Villiera produces several excellent Méthode Cap Classique wines and a highly rated and very well-priced shiraz. Excellent two-hour wildlife drives (adult/child R150/75) with knowledgable guides take in the various antelopes, zebras, giraffes and bird species on the farm.

**Bergkelder** WINERY
(☎021-809 8025; www.bergkelder.co.za; George Blake St; tour & tasting R60; ⏲9am-5pm Mon-Fri, to 2pm Sat; P) For wine lovers without wheels, this cellar a short walk from the town centre is ideal. Hour-long tours are followed by an atmospheric candlelit tasting in the cellar. The tours run at 10am, 11am, 2pm and 3pm Monday to Friday, and at 10am, 11am and noon Saturday. A wine and salt pairing (R95) is also on offer. Bookings are required for all activities.

**Stellenbosch University Botanical Garden** PARK
(☎021-808 3054; cnr Neethling & Van Riebeeck Sts; ⏲8am-5pm) FREE This glorious inner-city garden is an unsung Stellenbosch sight and well worth a wander. There's a pleasant tea garden for coffee, cake or a light lunch (mains R55 to R130).

### Tours

**★Bikes 'n Wines** TOURS
(☎021-823 8790; www.bikesnwines.com; tours from R595) This carbon-negative company comes highly recommended. Cycling routes range from 9km to 21km and take in three or four Stellenbosch wineries. There are also Cape Town city tours and trips to lesser-visited wine regions such as Elgin, Wellington and Hermanus.

**Vine Hopper** TOURS
(☎021-882 8112; www.vinehopper.co.za; cnr Dorp & Market Sts; 1-/2-day pass R300/540) A hop-on, hop-off bus with three routes each covering five or six estates. There are seven departures per day, departing from **Stellenbosch Tourism** (☎021-883 3584; www.stellenbosch.

WORTH A TRIP

## FRANSCHHOEK WINERIES

French Huguenots settled in this spectacular valley over 300 years ago, bringing their vines with them. Ever since, the town has clung to its French roots, and July visitors will find that Bastille Day is celebrated here. Franschhoek bills itself as the country's gastronomic capital, and you'll certainly have a tough time deciding where to eat. Plus, with a clutch of art galleries, wine farms and stylish guesthouses thrown in, it really is one of the loveliest towns in the Cape.

**Boschendal** (021-870 4210; www.boschendal.com; Rte 310, Groot Drakenstein; tastings R75, cellar tours R50, vineyard tours R80; 9am-5.30pm) This is a quintessential Winelands estate, with lovely architecture, food and wine. There are excellent vineyard and cellar tours; booking is essential. Boschendal has three eating options: the huge buffet lunch (adult/child R295/145) in the 1795 homestead, bistro lunches featuring produce grown on the farm at The Werf (mains R200) or a picnic hamper (basket for two R440; bookings essential), served under parasols on the lawn from September to May. Cellar tours run at 10.30am, noon, 1.30pm and 3pm, vineyard tours 11.30am. Mountain-biking trails start from the farm, for those who feel like working up an appetite.

**La Motte** (021-876 8000; www.la-motte.com; Main Rd; tastings R50; 9am-5pm Mon-Sat) There's enough to keep you occupied for a full day at this vast estate just west of Franschhoek. As well as tastings of the superb shiraz range on offer, wine-pairing lunches and dinners are served at the **Pierneef à la Motte** (021-876 8800; www.la-motte.com; Main Rd; mains R160-210; noon-3pm Tue & Wed, noon-3pm & 7-10pm Thu-Sun) restaurant. The restaurant is named for South African artist Jacob Hendrik Pierneef and a collection of his work is on show at the on-site museum. This is also the starting point for historical walks (R50) through the estate, taking in four national monuments and a milling demonstration and ending with a bread tasting (Wednesday 10am; bookings essential). If you've overindulged, walk off a few calories on the 5km circular hike that starts at the farm.

### Getting There & Away

Franschhoek is 32km east of Stellenbosch and 32km south of Paarl. The best way to reach Franschhoek is in your own vehicle. Some visitors choose to cycle from Stellenbosch, but roads are winding and can be treacherous. Alternatively, take a shared taxi from Stellenbosch (R25) or Paarl station (R28).



travel; 36 Market St; 8am-5pm Mon-Fri, 9am-2pm Sat & Sun; ), where you can buy tickets.

## Sleeping & Eating

Stellenbosch is a gourmet's delight, with a plethora of restaurants and bars. The surrounding wineries have some of the most interesting and innovative options in the country.

★**Banghoek Place** HOSTEL $
(021-887 0048; www.banghoek.co.za; 193 Banghoek Rd; dm/r R180/600; ) This stylish suburban hostel provides a quiet budget alternative, away from the town centre. The recreation area has satellite TV and a pool table and there's a nice swimming pool in the garden.

**D'Ouwe Werf** HISTORIC HOTEL $$$
(021-887 4608; www.oudewerfhotel.co.za; 30 Church St; s/d incl breakfast from R2400/2500; ) This appealing, old-style hotel dates back to 1802, though it recently had a dramatic facelift. Deluxe rooms are furnished with antiques and brass beds, while the superior and luxury rooms are bright and modern.

★**Schoon de Companje** DELI $
(www.decompanje.co.za; 7 Church St; mains R55-100; 7am-6pm Tue-Fri, 8am-6pm Sat, 8am-1.30pm Sun; ) A vibrant bakery and deli priding itself on locally sourced ingredients. The menu features salads, sandwiches and meze-style platters, as well as fresh cakes and pastries and local craft beer. There are tables on the pavement, while inside has a market-hall feel, with plenty of seating and some shops to browse.

★**Rust en Vrede** FUSION $$$
(021-881 3757; www.rustenvrede.com; Annandale Rd; 4-course menu R720, 6-course menu without/with wines R850/1450; noon-3pm Mon-Sat, 6.30-11pm Tue-Sat) Chef John Shuttleworth

### PAARL

Surrounded by mountains and vineyards, and set on the banks of the Berg River, Paarl is the Winelands' largest town. It's often overlooked by people heading for Stellenbosch and Franschhoek, but it does have its own charm, including interesting Cape Dutch architecture and gracious homesteads, a good range of places to stay and some decent restaurants. The main road is over 11km long, so not exactly walkable, but there are a couple of wineries within an easy stroll of the train station.

All the major long-distance bus companies offer services going through Paarl, making it easy to build the town into your itinerary. The bus segment between Paarl and Cape Town is disproportionately expensive, so consider taking the cheaper train to Paarl and then linking with the buses.

presides over this stylish winery restaurant. Expect innovative dishes like rabbit-leg wontons or artichoke-and-vanilla mousse. Book ahead.

### Information

The staff at Stellenbosch Tourism are extremely helpful. Pick up the excellent brochure *Historical Stellenbosch on Foot* (R5), with a walking-tour map and information on many of the historic buildings (also available in French and German).

### Getting There & Away

Metro trains run the 46km between Cape Town and Stellenbosch (1st/economy class R22.50/12, about one hour). For inquiries, call Metro Rail (0800 656 463). To be safe, travel in the middle of the day.

# GARDEN ROUTE

High on the must-see lists of most visitors to South Africa is the Garden Route, and with good reason: you can't help but be seduced by the glorious natural beauty. The distance from Mossel Bay in the west to Storms River in the east is just over 200km, yet the range of topography, vegetation, wildlife and outdoor activities is remarkable.

## Knysna

POP 51,000

Embracing an exquisitely beautiful lagoon and surrounded by ancient forests, Knysna (pronounced ny-znah) is probably the most famous town on the Garden Route. With its serene setting, arty and gay-friendly vibe, excellent places to stay, eat and drink, and wide range of activities, Knysna has plenty going for it. But if you're after something quiet and undeveloped, you might like to look elsewhere – particularly in high season (October to March), when the numbers of visitors threaten to overwhelm the town.

### Tours

**★Emzini Tours** CULTURAL
(044-382 1087; www.emzinitours.co.za; adult/child R400/150; 10am & 2pm Mon-Sat) Led by township resident Ella, the three-hour trip visits some of Emzini's community projects. Tours can be tailored to suit your interests, but generally end at Ella's home for tea, drumming and a group giggle as you try to wrap your tongue around the clicks of the Xhosa language.

### Sleeping

**Inyathi Guest Lodge** CHALET $
(044-382 7768; www.inyathiguestlodge.co.za; 38 Trotter St; chalets from R450; ) This lodge has changed address and had a complete overhaul, but the cheery owners and tasteful African decor remain. Accommodation is in self-catering chalets, each with its own private garden. It's an excellent budget option for those who don't fancy a backpackers.

**Brenton Cottages** CHALET $$
(044-381 0082; www.brentononsea.net; 242 CR Swart Drive, Brenton-on-Sea; 2-person cabins R740, 6-person chalets R1480; ) On the seaward side of the lagoon, the hills drop to Brenton-on-Sea, overlooking a magnificent 8km beach. The chalets have a full kitchen while cabins have a kitchenette; many have ocean views. There are plenty of braai areas dotted around the manicured lawns.

### Eating

There are plenty of good snack and coffee places along Main St and some cool spots on Thesen's Island.

**★ Ile de Pain** CAFE, BAKERY $

(044-302 5707; www.iledepain.co.za; Thesen's Island; mains R55-95; 8am-3pm Tue-Sat, 9am-1.30pm Sun; ) Finally back on its feet following a devastating fire, Ile de Pain is a wildly popular bakery and cafe that's as much a hit with locals as it is with tourists. There's an excellent breakfast menu, lots of fresh salads, some inventive lunch specials and quite a bit for vegetarians.

**East Head Café** INTERNATIONAL $$

(044-384 0933; www.eastheadcafe.co.za; 25 George Rex Dr, Eastern Head; mains R75-145; 8am-3.30pm; ) There's an outdoor deck overlooking the lagoon and ocean, lots of fish and seafood, plus a few vegetarian dishes. It's a very popular spot so expect to wait for a table in high season. It doesn't accept reservations.

## Information

**Knysna Tourism** (044-382 5510; www.visitknysna.co.za; 40 Main St; 8am-5pm Mon-Fri, 8.30am-1pm Sat year-round, plus 9am-1pm Sun Dec, Jan & Jul) An excellent office, with very knowledgable staff.

**South African National parks** (SANParks; 044-302 5600; www.sanparks.org; Long St, Thesen's Island; 7.30am-4pm Mon-Fri) For bookings and enquiries.

## Getting There & Away

**Translux** (0861 589 282; www.translux.co.za) and Intercape (p909) stop at the Waterfront; **Greyhound** (customer care 24hr 011-611 8000, reservations 083 915 9000; www.greyhound.co.za) stops at the **Engen petrol station** (Main St); Baz Bus (p909) drops at all the hostels.

Intercape destinations include Port Elizabeth (R350, 4½ hours), Cape Town (R450, eight hours) and Jo'burg (R720, 17½ hours).

# Plettenberg Bay

POP 6500 / 044

Plettenberg Bay, or 'Plett' as it's more commonly known, is a resort town through and through, with mountains, white sand and crystal-blue water making it one of the country's top local tourist spots. As a result, things can get very busy and somewhat overpriced, but the town retains a relaxed, friendly atmosphere and does have very good-value hostels. The scenery to the east in particular is superb, with some of the best coast and indigenous forest in South Africa.

## Sights

**Monkeyland** WILDLIFE RESERVE

(044-534 8906; www.monkeyland.co.za; The Crags; 1hr tour adult/child R230/115; 8am-5pm) This very popular attraction helps rehabilitate wild monkeys that have been in zoos or private homes. The walking safari through a dense forest and across a 128m-long rope bridge is superb. A combo ticket with Birds of Eden costs R280/140 per adult/child.

**Birds of Eden** BIRD SANCTUARY

(044-534 8906; www.birdsofeden.co.za; The Crags; adult/child R230/115; 8am-5pm) This is one of the world's largest free-flight aviaries, with a 200-sq-metre dome over the forest. A combo ticket with Monkeyland costs R360/180 per adult/child.

## Sleeping

**Plett Tourism** (044-533 4065; www.plett-tourism.co.za; Melville's Corner Shopping Centre, Main St; 9am-5pm Mon-Fri, to 1pm Sat) has a full list of accommodation and can tell you about the many camping options, all in nearby Keurboomstrand. In low season there are bargains to be found.

**Abalone Beach House** HOSTEL $

(044-535 9602; www.abalonebeachhouse.co.za; 13 Milkwood Glen, Keurboomstrand; d R700, d with shared bathroom R600; ) This upmarket and extremely friendly backpackers is two minutes' walk from a magnificent beach; surfboards and bodyboards are provided free. To reach the house follow the Keurboomstrand signs from the N2 (about 6km east of Plett), then turn into Milkwood Glen.

**Nothando Backpackers Hostel** HOSTEL $

(044-533 0220; www.nothando.com; 5 Wilder St; dm R160, d R550, with shared bathroom R480; ) This excellent, five-star budget option is owner-run and it shows. There's a great bar area with satellite TV, yet you can still find peace and quiet in the large grounds. Rooms are worthy of a budget guesthouse.

**★ Hog Hollow** LODGE $$$

(044-534 8879; www.hog-hollow.com; Askop Rd, The Crags; s/d incl breakfast R2495/3680; ) Hog Hollow, 18km east of Plett along the N2, provides delightful accommodation in African-art-decorated units overlooking the forest. Each luxurious unit comes with a private wooden deck and hammock. You can walk to Monkeyland from here; staff will collect you if you don't fancy the walk back.

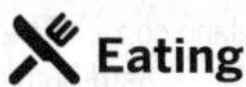

## Eating

**Table** ITALIAN $$
(☎044-533 3024; www.thetable.co.za; 9 Main St; mains R70-130; ⊙noon-11pm Mon-Sat, to 5pm Sun; ) A funky, minimalist venue with pizzas featuring an array of inventive toppings.

★**Nguni** STEAK $$$
(☎044-533 6710; www.nguni-restaurant.co.za; 6 Crescent St; mains R135-200; ⊙11am-10pm Mon-Fri, from 6pm Sat) Tucked away in a quiet courtyard, this is one of Plett's most upscale eateries. The speciality is Chalmar beef, though you'll also find lots of South African favourites including ostrich, Karoo lamb and traditional dishes such as *bobotie* (curry topped with beaten egg baked to a crust). Reservations recommended.

## Information

Plett Tourism (p913) has plenty of useful information on accommodation plus walks in the surrounding hills and reserves.

## Getting There & Away

All the major buses stop at the Shell Ultra City on the N2; the Baz Bus comes into town. Intercape destinations from Plett include George (R330, two hours), Port Elizabeth (R330, 3½ hours), Cape Town (R450, nine hours), Jo'burg (R720, 18 hours) and Graaff-Reinet (R460, 6½ hours).

If you're heading to Knysna you're better off taking a shared taxi (R20, 30 minutes) from Kloof St, near the corner of High St.

# Garden Route National Park (Tsitsikamma Section)

Cut through by dark, coffee-coloured churning rivers, deep ravines and dense forests, the Tsitsikamma section of the **Garden Route National Park** (☎042-281 1607; www.sanparks.org; adult/child R180/90; ⊙gate 6am-9.30pm) encompasses 650 sq km between Plettenberg Bay and Humansdorp, as well a Marine Protected Area covering 80km of coastline and stretching 5km out to sea. Millennium-old sandstone and quartz rock formations line the gorges and rocky shoreline, and southern right whales and dolphins are visible out in the ocean. Birdlife is plentiful, including endangered African black oystercatchers.

## Activities

**Otter Trail** HIKING
(☎in Pretoria 012-426 5111; www.sanparks.org; per person R1075) The 45km Otter Trail is one of South Africa's most acclaimed hikes, hugging the coastline from Storms River Mouth to Nature's Valley. The five-day, four-night walk involves fording a number of rivers and gives access to some superb stretches of coast. A good level of fitness is required for the walk, as it goes uphill and downhill quite steeply in many places.

**Tsitsikamma Mountain Trail** HIKING
(www.mtoecotourism.co.za; per night R155) This 62km trail begins at Nature's Valley and ends at Storms River, taking you inland through the forests and mountains. The full trail takes six days, but you can also opt for two, three, four or five days, because each overnight hut has its own access route. Porterage is also available, as are day hikes (R50) and mountain-bike trails.

## Sleeping

**Storms River Mouth Rest Camp** CAMPGROUND, CHALET $$
(☎042-281 1607; www.sanparks.org; camping per site from R300) This camp offers accommodation ranging from rustic forest huts (from R610) to chalets (from R1155), family cottages with four single beds (R1760), and waterfront 'oceanette' cottages (from R995). Most have single beds with bedding and, apart from the forest huts, kitchens (including utensils) and bathrooms. Rates do not include the park's conservation fee (adult/child R180/90).

## Getting There & Away

There is no public transport to either Nature's Valley or Storms River Mouth. Greyhound, Intercape, Translux and **City to City** (☎0861 589 282; www.citytocity.co.za) stop in Plettenberg Bay and Storms River Bridge. Baz Bus gets you closer to the rest camps, stopping in the Crags (near Nature's Valley), at Bloukrans Bridge and at Storms River en route between Cape Town and Port Elizabeth.

# SUNSHINE COAST

The Sunshine Coast covers a significant chunk of the Eastern Cape coastline, including Port Elizabeth, the seaside town of Jeffrey's Bay, and numerous sandy beaches. In the hinterland are the best wildlife-watching areas within easy reach of the coastline between Cape Town and Durban: Addo Elephant National Park and some nearby private reserves.

## Jeffrey's Bay

POP 27,107

Once just a sleepy seaside town, 'J-Bay' is now one of the world's top surfing destinations. It's certainly South Africa's foremost centre of surfing and surf culture.

### Activities

Dolphin Beach, a beautiful and largely untouched expanse of sand, is perfect for a prebreakfast stroll.

June to September are the best months for experienced surfers, but novices can learn at any time of year.

**Son Surf School** SURFING
(076 501 6191; www.surfschools.co.za; 1½hr lesson R300) Good for intermediate surfers who want a refresher or to improve their technique. Beginner and advanced classes are also on offer.

**Wavecrest Surf School** SURFING
(073 509 0400; www.wavecrestsurfschool.co.za; 6 Drommedaris St; 2hr lesson incl board & wetsuit R300; ) This long-running operation offers daily lessons. Good for children and beginners.

**Supertubes** SURFING
Surfers from all over the planet flock to J-Bay to ride the famous wave at Supertubes, once described as 'the most perfect wave in the world'.

### Sleeping

**Beach Music** GUESTHOUSE $
(042-293 2291; www.beachmusic.co.za; 33 Flame Cres; s R230-430, d R350-700; ) This airy house with a garden leading straight to the beach is great value. The 1st-floor lounge and kitchen have superb ocean views – including a glimpse of Supertubes – and the tastefully decorated rooms have small private patios.

**Island Vibe** HOSTEL $
(042-293 1625; www.jbay.islandvibe.co.za; 10 Dageraad St; dm R160-170, d R550-650; ) Party central in J-Bay, Island Vibe is 500m south of the city centre, and the attendant raft of surfers attests to its prime beachfront location. Accommodation ranges from four- to 12-bed dorms and wooden cabins (numbers one and two have private balconies overlooking the beach), to a beach house and a flashpackers, both with en suite rooms.

**Funky Town** GUESTHOUSE $$
(042-293 3860; www.accommodationjbay.co.za; 12a Oosterland St; r R700-800; ) The eight rooms here are all brightly decorated with original art hanging on the walls. There's also a penthouse apartment (R1700) with kitchen and sitting area. For the rest there's a shared kitchen and TV lounge inside and a braai area, pizza oven, hot tub and pool in the garden. Bikes and boards are available to hire.

### Eating

★**InFood Deli** INTERNATIONAL $
(042-293 1880; www.infood.co.za; cnr Schelde & Jeffrey Sts; mains R50-80; 7am-5pm Mon-Sat; ) The sandwiches, burgers and other fare at this cafe, bakery and deli are far from ordinary. This is not surprising, considering the owner-chef's impressive CV – including once having cooked for Prince William. The mix of organic, locally sourced ingredients (such as Karoo *fynbos* – fine bush – honey) and wide-ranging culinary tastes (quesadillas, handmade pasta and Thai chicken curry) make this a worthy foodie destination.

★**Nina's** INTERNATIONAL $$
(042-296 0281; 126 Da Gama Rd, Wavecrest Centre; mains R65-155; 7am-10pm) Most locals recommend Nina's, with its stylish decor of surfboards and coastal scenes around a paper-disc chandelier. Service can be slow, but the food is worth the wait. Seafood abounds on the wide-ranging menu, which also features burgers, curries, pizza, pasta, Thai food and nachos; the specials menu is a winner, offering dishes such as ostrich fillet and grilled tuna.

### Information

**Jeffrey's Bay Tourism** (042-293 2923; www.jeffreysbaytourism.org; Da Gama Rd; 9am-5pm Mon-Fri, to noon Sat) Friendly and helpful, and can make bookings for accommodation and activities.

### Getting There & Away

Baz Bus stops at several J-Bay backpackers en route between Cape Town and Port Elizabeth.

### ADDO ELEPHANT NATIONAL PARK

Located 70km north of Port Elizabeth, South Africa's third-largest **national park** (☎042-233 8600; www.sanparks.org; adult/child R232/116; ⏰7am-7pm) protects the remnants of the huge elephant herds that once roamed the Eastern Cape. When Addo was proclaimed a national park in 1931, there were only 11 elephants left; today there are more than 600 in the park, and you'd be unlucky not to see some.

A day or two at Addo is a highlight of any visit to this part of the Eastern Cape, not only for the elephants but for the lions, zebras, black rhinos, Cape buffaloes, spotted hyenas and myriad birds. The park is one of few which boasts the 'Big Seven', thanks to sightings of great white sharks and southern right whales (in season) in Algoa Bay (the other 'Big Five' being lions, leopards, buffaloes, elephants and rhinos). Look out, too, for the rare flightless dung beetle, endemic to Addo.

**AdventureNow** (☎076 781 3912; www.adventurenow.co.za; Da Gama Rd) runs shuttles to/from destinations including Storms River (up to three people R640), Bloukrans Bridge (R860) and Port Elizabeth Airport (R550).

Long-distance buses plying the Cape Town–Port Elizabeth–Durban route stop at the Mentors Plaza Caltex garage, at the junction of St Francis St and the N2.

# Port Elizabeth

POP 1.15 MILLION

Port Elizabeth (PE for short) fringes Algoa Bay at the western end of the Sunshine Coast, and offers many good bathing beaches and surf spots. It's also a convenient gateway to worthy destinations in either direction along the coast, as well as to the eastern Karoo.

## Activities

PE is not known as the 'windy city' for nothing; windsurfers and sailors will find what they need at **Hobie Beach**, 5km south of Central.

There are some excellent dive sites around Port Elizabeth, with shipwrecks and reefs all over Algoa Bay.

**Surf Centre** SURFING
(☎041-585 6027; www.surf.co.za; Main Rd, Walmer Park Shopping Centre, Walmer) PE's best surf breaks are found between the harbour wall and Summerstrand, and at Pollok beach. The Surf Centre sells and hires out surfboards and bodyboards. Its surf school will teach you how to use them (1½-hour lesson R250).

**Pro Dive** DIVING
(☎041-581 1144; www.prodive.co.za; 189 Main Rd, Walmer) Pro Dive offers PADI Open Water courses starting at around R3950, with dives from R295 plus equipment rental.

## Sleeping

**★Tree Tops Guest House** GUESTHOUSE $
(☎041-581 0147; www.treetopsguesthouse.co.za; 44 Albert Rd, Walmer; s/d from R450/570; P❄📶🏊) In a suburban area close to the airport, this friendly guesthouse has simple, great-value rooms, each with a fridge, microwave, TV and en suite bathroom. The cheapest rooms are without air-conditioning. Owners offer a free airport shuttle.

**Island Vibe** HOSTEL $
(☎041-583 1256; www.islandvibe.co.za; 4 Jenvey Rd, Summerstrand; dm/d R170/600; P@📶🏊) This 'flashpackers' in a nondescript suburban house is less characterful than its sister in Jeffrey's Bay (p915), but makes a comfortable base with numerous facilities. The bar, pool table, Foosball table and outdoor jacuzzi liven up the 'burbs, while the well-equipped kitchen, secure parking and en suite rooms are welcome. Pollok Beach and the Pipe surf break are within walking distance.

**Forest Hall Guest House** GUESTHOUSE $$
(☎041-581 3356; www.foresthall.co.za; 84 River Rd, btwn 9th & 10th Aves, Walmer; s/d incl breakfast from R700/1000; P📶🏊) At this gracious suburban property, huge rooms with lots of natural light and private patios open onto a beautiful garden with an Italianate swimming pool.

## Eating

On Stanley between Glen and Mackay Sts is a vibey string of more than a dozen restaurants, serving cuisine ranging from Indian to Mediterranean. Most offer outdoor tables and lunch specials.

**★Two Olives** MEDITERRANEAN $$
(☎081 744 2496; www.twoolives.co.za; 3 Stanley St, Richmond Hill; tapas R50-70, mains R75-170;

5.30-10.30pm Mon, noon-3pm & 5.30-10.30pm Tue-Sat, noon-3pm Sun) One of the most upmarket restaurants in Richmond Hill, Two Olives serves a range of Spanish- and Greek-inspired dishes in its busy dining room and on the wraparound balcony (warning: it can get pretty breezy out there). The lamb shank is as delicious as it is enormous. For the not so hungry, try the tapas menu. Reservations recommended.

**Something Good** CAFE $$
(041-583 6986; off Marine Dr, Pollok Beach; mains R60-90; 8am-10.30pm; ) This roadhouse-cum-beach bar is an excellent spot for a sundowner, with a breezy interior, beachfront decks and a children's playground. Dishes include gourmet pizzas, burgers, seafood (try the Cajun calamari) and for the health-conscious, bunless burgers and healthy breakfasts.

## Information

**Nelson Mandela Bay Tourism** (041-585 8884; www.nmbt.co.za; Donkin Reserve; 8am-4.30pm Mon-Fri, 9.30am-3.30pm Sat) has an excellent supply of information and maps, and a cafe with city views. There are also branches at the Boardwalk (041-583 2030; Marine Dr, Summerstrand; 8am-7pm), a good stop for information about the whole province, and the airport (041-581 0456; Port Elizabeth Airport; 7am-9.30pm).

**Wezandla** (041-585 1185; www.wezandla.co.za; 27 Baakens St, Central; 9am-5pm Mon-Fri, to 1pm Sat) This craft shop also dispenses information.

## Getting There & Around

### AIR

**Port Elizabeth Airport** (041-507 7319; www.airports.co.za; Allister Miller Rd, Walmer) is about 5km from the city centre.

**South African Airways** (041-507 7220; www.flysaa.com) and its subsidiaries Airlink, SA Express and Mango, and **FlySafair** (0871 351 351; www.flysafair.co.za) and **Kulula** (0861 585 852; www.kulula.com) all fly daily to/from cities including Cape Town (from R900, 1¼ hours), Durban (from R1500, 1¼ hours) and Jo'burg (from R800, 1¾ hours).

A taxi to the centre costs about R120.

### BUS

Greyhound, **Translux** (041-392 1303; www.translux.co.za; Ring Rd, Ernst & Young Bldg, Greenacres Shopping Centre) and City to City depart from the Greenacres Shopping Centre, about 4km inland from the city centre. Intercape departs from its office behind the old post office.

All have departures to Cape Town (R450, 12 hours). Other destinations include Jo'burg (R500, 16 hours) via Bloemfontein (R480, 9½ hours), and Durban (R520, 14½ hours) via Grahamstown (R290, two hours) and East London (R450, 4½ hours). Baz Bus runs a hop-on, hop-off service four or five days a week in both directions between Port Elizabeth or Durban and Cape Town.

# Hogsback

POP 1029

There's something about Hogsback that inspires people. An Edenic little village 1300m up in the beautiful Amathole Mountains above Alice, the village's name is derived from the 'bristles' (known geologically as a 'hogsback') that cover peaks of the surrounding hills.

## Activities

There are some great walks, bike rides and drives through the area's indigenous forests and pine plantations. A recommended hike (three to five hours) leaves from behind Away with the Fairies backpackers and passes various waterfalls. Purchase a R10 hiking permit at the backpackers.

## Sleeping & Eating

Numerous self-catering cottages are tucked away in the forests surrounding the village; visit www.hogsback.com, www.hogsback.co.za and www.hogsbackinfo.co.za for listings.

**Away with the Fairies** HOSTEL $
(045-962 1031; www.awaywiththefairies.co.za; Ambleside Close; camping/dm/r from R90/160/475; ) Terrific views abound at this magical, mystical clifftop backpackers: take an alfresco bath in the cliffside tub, or climb 15m to the tree house perched in the forest among parrots and monkeys. Activities on offer include Xhosa lessons, picnics in the forest, pancakes at sunrise, fishing, hiking, tree hugging and creative-writing workshops.

★**Edge Mountain Retreat** LODGE $$
(045-962 1159; www.theedge-hogsback.co.za; Perry Bar Lane; s/d incl breakfast R495/900, self-catering cottages R650-1800; ) The tastefully decorated cottages and garden rooms are strung out along a dramatic

WORTH A TRIP

## CEDERBERG WILDERNESS AREA

Some of the Western Cape's finest scenery is found in the desolate **Cederberg Wilderness Area** (027-482 2403; www.capenature.co.za; adult/child R60/35). The 830-sq-km wilderness area boasts San rock art, craggy mountains, clear streams and bumpy dirt roads you can imagine a horse and cart racing along. The peaks and valleys extend roughly north–south for 100km, between Vanrhynsdorp and Citrusdal. The highest peaks are Sneeuberg (2027m) and Tafelberg (1969m).

There are small populations of baboons, rheboks, klipspringers and grysboks; and predators such as caracals, Cape foxes, honey badgers and elusive leopards.

**Sanddrif** (027-482 2825, 044-004 0060; www.sanddrif.com; Dwarsrivier Farm; camping per site R200, 4-person chalets R850) is a great base in the Cederberg, with a winery, brewery, astronomical observatory and a range of top-notch hikes nearby. Accommodation is in simple chalets or campsites, all with wonderful mountain views. Hiking maps and permits are available.

The main camping spot in the area, **Algeria** (027-482 2403; www.capenature.co.za; camping per site R300, chalets/cottages from R580/800) has exceptional grounds in a shaded site alongside the Rondegat River. There is a swimming hole and lovely picnic spots. There are a number of two-person chalets here and six new cottages sleeping four people each. It gets busy at weekends and school holidays. Entrance to the camping ground closes at 4.30pm (9pm on Friday).

The Cederberg range is about 200km from Cape Town, accessible from Citrusdal, Clanwilliam and the N7. You can also drive from Rte 303 via Ceres on the eastern side.

It takes about an hour to get to Algeria from Clanwilliam by car. Algeria is not signposted from Clanwilliam, just follow the gravel road above the dam to the south – it's fairly rough going. Algeria *is* signposted from the N7 and is about 30 minutes from the main road; it's also a gravel road, but in good condition.

Unfortunately, public transport into the mountains is nonexistent.



plateau edge, which once marked the border between the apartheid-era Ciskei homeland and South Africa proper. The cottages vary in size but all have log fires and a small kitchen. The vibe here is peace and relaxation. It's an unbeatable place for a healthy rest or a romantic weekend.

★**Edge Restaurant** INTERNATIONAL **$$**
(Perry Bar Lane; mains R75-130; 7.30am-8.30pm) The Edge's charming garden restaurant serves French toast with local berries and Hogsback's best coffee for breakfast, recommended tapas boards and wood-fired pizzas for lunch, and hearty but refined meat dishes for dinner. Throw in homemade bread, fresh, organic local produce, a cosy dining room, and paths leading to the nearby labyrinth and viewpoint. Dinner bookings essential.

### Information

The helpful **information centre** (045-962 1245; www.hogsbackinfo.co.za; Main Rd; 9am-3pm Mon-Sat, to 1pm Sun) can provide accommodation advice and maps for walks.

### Getting There & Away

The way up to Hogsback on Rte 345 (the turn-off is 4km east of Alice) is sealed, but try to arrive in daylight due to mountain bends and occasional itinerant livestock.

The easiest way to get to Hogsback without a car is in the shuttle run by Away with the Fairies on Tuesday, Wednesday, Friday and Sunday. It picks up at Sugarshack Backpackers in East London (R150, two hours), Buccaneers Lodge in Chintsa (R180, 2½ hours), East London Airport (R180, two hours) and King William's Town (R120, 1½ hours).

City to City stops in Alice daily en route between East London (R140, two hours) and Pretoria via Queenstown, Bloemfontein and Jo'burg.

## THE WILD COAST

This shipwreck-strewn coastline rivals any in the country in terms of beauty, stretching over 350km from just east of East London to Port Edward. Often referred to as the 'Transkei' (the name of the apartheid-era homeland that once covered most of this area), the Wild Coast region also stretches inland, covering pastoral landscapes where clusters of rondavels (round huts with a conical roofs) scatter the rolling hills covered in short grass.

The local Xhosa people are some of the friendliest you'll meet anywhere in South Africa, and you might be invited inside a home or, at the very least, a shebeen (tavern). South of the Mbashe River lives the Gcaleka tribe; the Mpondomise live to the north. In this land of far-flung river estuaries, numerous outdoor activities and cultural tours are on offer. Birdlife is abundant, especially in the parks.

## Port St Johns

POP 6441

Dramatically located at the mouth of the Mzimvubu (or Umzimvubu) River and framed by towering cliffs covered with tropical vegetation, the laid-back town of Port St Johns is the original Wild Coast journey's end. There's a vibrant, if somewhat rundown, quality to the town, which is the largest between East London and Port Edward.

Bull Zambezi sharks calve upriver and there have been several fatal attacks in recent years, all at Second Beach.

### Sleeping & Eating

Outside the large grocery stores on Main St is a small street market where you might be able to buy fresh seafood – mussels, crayfish and fish – to cook your own meal.

**Amapondo Backpackers** HOSTEL **$**
(083 315 3103; www.amapondo.co.za; Second Beach Rd; camping R90, dm from R150, s/d with shared bathroom from R300/390; P ) A mellow place where several low-slung buildings line a hillside with excellent views of Second Beach. A rambling network of verandas, leafy walkways and chill-out spaces leads to the simple rooms, while smarter cottages stand on the hill above. An excellent range of activities is offered, include horse riding, cultural tours, canoeing, hiking to Silaka and sundowners at the airstrip.

**Port St Johns River Lodge** LODGE **$$**
(047-564 0005; www.portstjohnsriverlodge.co.za; Mzimvubu Dr; s/d incl breakfast R640/1000; P ) One of a few riverside lodges north of town, this well-run complex has comfortable rooms, self-catering chalets (R500 per person) and a restaurant (mains R85) gazing across a lawn at the river cliffs. Rates are cheaper on weekends.

**Steve's Pub & Restaurant** SOUTH AFRICAN **$$**
(Main Rd; mains R65-120; 8am-10pm; ) An inviting spot with a covered veranda and cosy bar, Steve's does a mix of pub grub and South African specialities, including bunny chow (hollowed-out bread filled with curry), wood-fired pizzas and steaks.

### Information

Laid-back staff in the **tourist office** (047-564 1187; www.portstjohns.org.za/tourism.htm; Umzimvubu Dr; 8am-4.30pm) have a few pamphlets and will dispense information if asked.

### Getting There & Away

The R61 from Mthatha to Port St Johns is in excellent condition, but it involves switchbacks and sharp curves – beware of speeding minibus taxis. There are regular shared taxis to Port St Johns from Durban (R190, five hours).

# KWAZULU-NATAL (KZN)

KwaZulu-Natal is a region where glassy malls touch shabby suburbs, and action-packed adventurers ooze adrenaline while laid-back beach bods drip with suntan lotion. Mountainscapes contrast with flat, dry savannahs, while the towns' central streets, teeming with African life, markets and noise, are in stark contrast to the sedate tribal settlements in rural areas. Here, too, is traditional Zululand, whose people are fiercely proud of their culture.

Throw in the wildlife – the Big Five (lions, leopards, buffaloes, elephants and rhinos) and rare marine species – as well as the historic intrigue of the Battlefields, fabulous hiking opportunities, and the sand, sea and surf of coastal resort towns, and you get a tantalising taste of local heritage and authentic African highlights that should be on every 'must-do' list.

## Durban

POP 600,000

Cosmopolitan Durban, South Africa's third-largest city (known as eThekweni in Zulu), is sometimes passed over for her 'cooler' Capetonian cousin. But this isn't fair;

## Central Durban

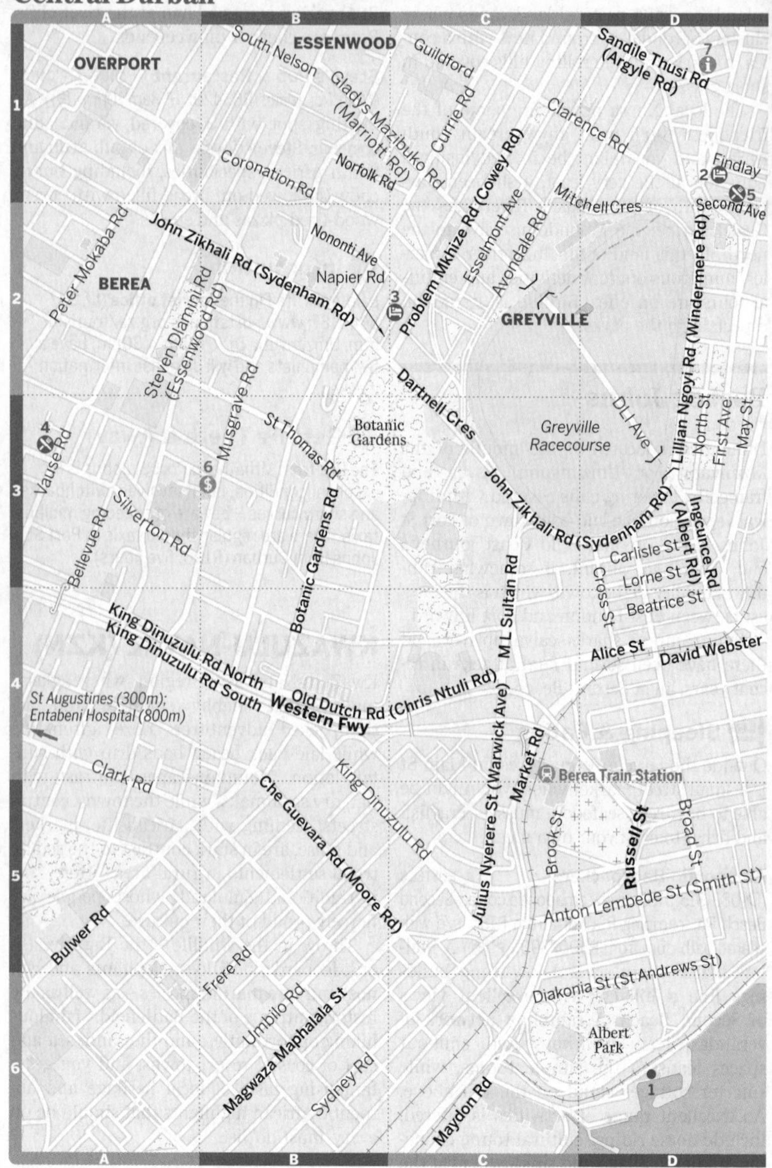


there's a lot more to fun-loving Durbs (as she's affectionately known) than meets the eye.

## Sights & Activities

Both beaches and a promenade extend from the Blue Lagoon (at the mouth of the Umgeni River) to uShaka Marine World on the Point, an area known as the 'Golden Mile', although it's much longer.

At Suncoast Beach, in front of the casino, umbrellas and chairs are available on a first-come, first-served basis. Due to its location

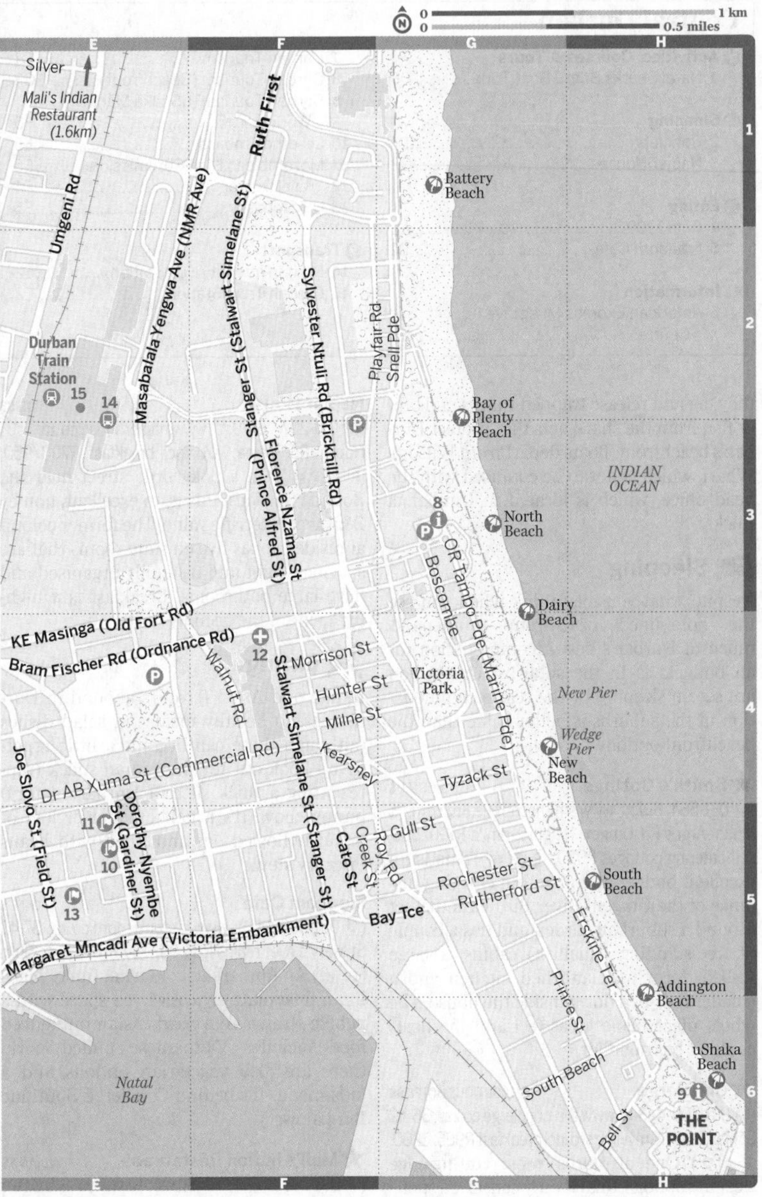




at the strip's southern end, uShaka Beach is often slightly more sheltered and is close to cafes and a small car park. The uShaka Beach has activities including surfing lessons and kayaking.

## Tours

**Natal Sharks Board Boat Tour** BOATING

(☎082 403 9206; www.shark.co.za; Wilson's Wharf; 2hr boat trip R300; ⊙departs 6.30am) A fascinating trip is to accompany Natal Sharks Board personnel in their boat when

## Central Durban

**Activities, Courses & Tours**
1 Natal Sharks Board Boat Tour............. D6

**Sleeping**
2 Concierge.......................................... D1
3 Napier House...................................... C2

**Eating**
4 Cafe 1999............................................ A3
5 Freedom Cafe...................................... D1

**Information**
6 American Express Musgrave Centre............................................ B3
7 Durban Tourism ................................... D1
8 Durban Tourism (Beachfront).............. G3
9 Durban Tourism (uShaka Marine World)................................................ H6
10 Lesotho Embassy................................. E5
11 Mozambican High Commission........... E5
12 Travel Doctor ...................................... F4
13 US Embassy......................................... E5

**Transport**
14 Durban Intercity Bus Station................ E2
15 Durban Train Station ........................... E2



they tag and release trapped sharks and other fish from the shark nets that protect Durban's beachfront. Boats depart from Wilson's Wharf, which is not to be confused with the head office, which is located in Umhlanga Rocks.

## Sleeping

Despite what you may think when you see the hotel-lined beachfront promenade, much of Durban's best accommodation for all budgets is in the suburbs. Unless you are set on sleeping by the sea, accommodation in the suburbs is better value than the beachfront options.

**★Smith's Cottage** HOSTEL $
(☎031-564 6313; www.smithscottage.8m.com; 5 Mount Argus Rd, Umgeni Heights; dm/d R190/500, self-catering cottages R980; P 📶 🏊) This is an excellent budget option within chirping distance of the Umgeni River Bird Park. It's set around a suburban garden and has a couple of free-standing (smallish) cabins, a large 12-bed dorm with attached kitchen and a smaller four-bed dorm inside the house. The whole place has a great feel and the hosts couldn't be friendlier.

**★Concierge** BOUTIQUE HOTEL $$
(☎031-309 4434; www.the-concierge.co.za; 36-42 St Mary's Ave, Greyville; s/d incl breakfast R965/1200; P ❄ 📶) One of Durbs' most cutting-edge sleeping options, this cleverly conceived spot – 12 cosy rooms in four pods – is more about the design (urban, funky, shape-oriented) than the spaces (smallish but adequate). For breakfast, roll out of bed and head to Freedom Cafe, also on the premises.

**Napier House** B&B $$
(☎031-207 6779; www.napierhouse.co.za; 31 Napier Rd, Berea; s/d incl breakfast R700/950; P ❄ 📶 🏊) On a poky little street near the Botanic Gardens, this is an excellent, homey B&B that is terrific value. The former colonial residence has five en suite rooms that are spacious, light and tastefully organised and have large bathrooms. Breakfast is a highlight, as are the friendly hosts.

## Eating

Indian and Asian flavours abound in Durban, as do healthy meat and salad dishes (although these can become a little repetitive). Look out for the Indian snack (representing a thick slice of Durban history) bunny chow. It's a half or quarter loaf of bread hollowed out and filled with beans or curry stew.

**Freedom Cafe** CAFE $
(☎031-309 4453; www.tastefreedom.co.za; 37-43 St Mary's Ave; mains R65-95; ⌚7am-4pm, to 9pm Fri; 👪) An upmarket, colourful, funky place in an imaginatively converted space with a pebble-strewn courtyard. Asian-influenced food includes Vietnamese pulled pork; there are also vegetarian options and a kids menu. It's behind Concierge Boutique Bungalows.

**★Mali's Indian Restaurant** INDIAN $$
(☎031-312 8535; 77 Smiso Nkwanya Rd/Goble Rd, Morningside; mains R90-120; ⌚12.30-3pm & 6-10pm Tue-Thu, to 10.30pm Fri-Sun) In a city that boasts a huge Indian population, this place is about as good as Indian food gets in Durban's restaurant scene. North and South Indian dishes are available at this friendly, family-run spot.

**Cafe 1999** INTERNATIONAL $$
(☎031-202 3406; www.cafe1999.co.za; Silverton Rd, Silvervause Centre, Berea; tapas R60, mains R95-180; ⌚12.30-2.30pm Mon-Fri, 6.30-10.30pm Mon-Sat) This classy restaurant looks unassuming inside, but assume that you will get seriously good modern Mediterranean fusion food here. Tapas including stuffed and deep-fried olives, kudu carpaccio and chilli prawns all hit the spot. There are always lots of daily specials, and friendly wait staff to run you through them.

## ℹ Information

### DANGERS & ANNOYANCES

As with elsewhere in South Africa, crime against tourists and locals can and does occur in Durban. Be aware and careful, but not paranoid. Muggings and pickpocketing, once a problem around the beach esplanade, have declined since that area's upgrade, but be careful here at night. Extra care should also be taken around the Umgeni Rd side of the train station and the Warwick Triangle markets.

Always catch a taxi to and from nightspots, as well as uShaka Marine World (and ride with others, if possible). The best advice is from locals, so ask around when you get here.

### MEDICAL SERVICES

**Entabeni Hospital** (☎031-204 1300, 24hr trauma centre 031-204 1377; 148 Mazisi Kunene Rd/South Ridge Rd, Berea) The trauma centre charges around R700 per consultation.

**St Augustines** (☎031-268 5000; 107 JB Marks Rd, Berea) KwaZulu-Natal's largest private hospital has a good emergency department.

**Travel Doctor** (☎031-360 1122; www.durbantraveldoctor.co.za; 45 Bram Fischer Rd/Old Ordanance Rd, International Convention Centre; ⌚8.30am-4pm Mon-Fri, to 11am Sat) For travel-related advice.

**Umhlanga Hospital** (☎031-560 5500; 323 Umhlanga Rocks Dr, Umhlanga) Handy for the North Coast and north Durban.

### MONEY

There are banks with ATMs and change facilities across the city. These include Standard Bank, FNB, Nedbank and ABSA.

**American Express Musgrave Centre** (☎031-202 8733; FNB House, 151 Musgrave Rd, Musgrave)

**Bidvest Bank** (☎031-202 7833; Shop 311, Level 3, Musgrave Centre, Musgrave Rd, Berea; ⌚9am-5pm Mon-Fri, to 1pm Sat)

### TOURIST INFORMATION

**Durban Tourism** (☎031-322 4164; www.durbanexperience.co.za; 90 Florida Road, Morningside; ⌚8am-4.30pm Mon-Fri) A useful information service on Durban and surrounds. It can help with general accommodation and arranges tours of Durban and beyond. There are also branches at the beachfront (☎031-322 4205; www.durbanexperience.co.za; Old Pavilion Site, OR Tambo Pde/Marine Pde; ⌚8am-5pm) and another at uShaka Marine World (☎031-337 8099; www.durbanexperience.co.za; 1 Bell St, uShaka Marine World; ⌚8am-4.30pm Mon-Fri).

**King Shaka Airport Tourist Information Office** (☎031-322 6046; international arrivals hall; ⌚7am-9pm) Durban Tourism, KwaZulu-Natal Tourism Authority and Ezemvelo KZN Wildlife all share a desk (the last is open 8am to 4.30pm Monday to Friday only) at the airport.

### GETTING THERE & AWAY

#### Air

**King Shaka International Airport** (DUR; ☎032-436 6585; kingshakainternational.co.za) At La Mercy, 40km north of the city.

**Kulula** (p917) A budget airline linking Durban with Jo'burg, Cape Town and Port Elizabeth.

**Mango** (☎0861 001 234; www.flymango.com) A no-frills airline that is a subsidiary of South African Airways, with flights to Jo'burg and Cape Town.

**South African Airlink** (SAAirlink; ☎032-436 2602; www.flyairlink.co.za) Flies daily to Nelspruit, Bloemfontein and George.

**South African Airways** (SAA; ☎032-815 2009; www.flysaa.com) Flies at least once daily to most major regional airports in South Africa.

#### Bus

Long-distance buses leave from the bus station near the Durban train station. Baz Bus (p909) is a hop on and off service to/from Cape Town; you can be picked up and dropped off at selected hostels. The seven-/14-/21-day pass costs R2600/4100/5100.

Greyhound (p913) has daily buses to Jo'burg (R350, eight hours), Cape Town (R750, 22 to 27 hours), Port Elizabeth (R600, 15 hours) and Port Shepstone (R350, 1¾ hours).

Intercape (p909) has several daily buses to Jo'burg (R400, eight hours).

Translux (p913) runs daily buses to nationwide destinations, including Jo'burg (R300, eight hours) and Cape Town (R720, 27 hours).

#### Train

**Durban train station** (Masabalala Yengwa Ave/NMR Ave) is huge. The fully serviced luxury **Premier Classe** (☎086 000 8888, 031-361 7167; www.premierclasse.co.za) has trains between Jo'burg and Durban on Wednesday, Friday and Sunday. Tickets should be booked in advance (R1230, about 14 hours).

# Zululand

Evoking images of wild landscapes and tribal rhythms, this beautiful swath of KwaZulu-Natal offers a different face of South Africa, where fine coastline, mist-clad hills and traditional settlements are in contrast to the ordered suburban developments around Durban. The region is most visited for the spectacular Hluhluwe-iMfolozi Park and its many traditional Zulu villages. Here you can learn about Zulu history and the legendary King Shaka.

## Eshowe

POP 14,800

Situated amid a beautiful indigenous forest and surrounded by green rolling hills, Eshowe has its own particular character. The centre has a rural, rough-and-tumble atmosphere, but the suburbs are leafy and quiet. It is well placed for exploring the wider region and there are decent attractions and accommodation options.

### Tours

**Zululand Eco-Adventures** CULTURAL
(035-474 2298; www.zululandeco-adventures.com; 36 Main St) Zululand Eco-Adventures offers a large range of genuine Zulu activities, from weddings and coming-of-age ceremonies to visits to witch doctors.

### Sleeping & Eating

**Dlinza Forest Accommodation** CABIN $$
(035-474 2377; www.dlinzaforestaccommodation.co.za; 2 Oftebro St; s/d R500/650; ) These four self-catering log cabins are neat, modern, clean and spacious. Follow the signs to the Dlinza Forest Reserve; the guesthouse is just beyond the entrance.

**George Hotel** HOTEL $$
(035-474 4919; www.thegeorge.co.za; 38 Main St; s/d R695/795; ) Dripping with character, this grand old hotel (1902) is a good midrange option. Rooms are a bit old and rickety (and water pressure can be hit-and-miss), but the huge beds are very comfy. The budget wing has been completely renovated and offers good value (s/d R400/600). The restaurant menu is limited, but the food is well prepared.

**Adam's Outpost** INTERNATIONAL $
(035-4741787; 5 Nongqayi St, Fort Nongqayi Museum; mains R50-70; 9am-4pm Mon-Fri & Sun) Find refuge in the garden cafe and cosy, corrugated-iron restaurant, complete with real fireplaces and candles – easily the standout in Eshowe's culinary roll-call. Try a chicken mango salad or beef curry for lunch.

### Getting There & Away

Minibus shared taxis leave from the bus and taxi rank (downhill from KFC near the Osborne and Main Sts roundabout; go across the bridge and to the right) to Empangeni (R60, one hour), which is the best place from which to catch taxis deeper into Zululand, and Durban (R110, 1½ hours).

## Hluhluwe-iMfolozi Park

Rivalling Kruger National Park in its beauty and variety of landscapes, **Hluhluwe-iMfolozi Park** (035-550 8476, central reservations 033-845 1000; www.kznwildlife.com; adult/child R175/90; 5am-7pm Nov-Feb, 6am-6pm Mar-Oct) is one of South Africa's best-known, most evocative parks. Indeed, some say it's better than Kruger for its accessibility – it covers 960 sq km (around a 20th of the size of Kruger) and there's plenty of wildlife, including lions, elephants, rhinos (black and white), leopards, giraffes, buffaloes and African wild dogs.

### Activities

**Wildlife Drives**

Wildlife drives here are very popular. Hilltop Camp offers morning and evening drives, while Mpila Camp does evening drives only. The camp-run drives are open to resort residents only and cost R325 per person. Most visitors to the area self-drive.

**Hiking**

Trail walks are guided and are run by KZN Wildlife (p926). The Base Camp Trail (R3900, three nights) is, as the name suggests, at a base camp. Trailists carry day packs on the daily outings. The Short Wilderness **Trail** (R2350, two nights) is at satellite camps that have no amenities (bucket shower) but are fully catered. Similar is the Extended Wilderness Trail (R3450, three nights), but guests must carry their gear for 7km into camp. Some consider the Primitive Trail (R2900, four nights) to be more fun than the others because you are able to participate more (for example, hikers must sit up in 1½-hour watches during the night).

## Sleeping

**Hilltop Camp** CABIN $$
(☎035-562 0848; s/d rondavels R610/850, 2-person chalets R1600; ❄) The signature resort on the Hluhluwe side: a cold drink followed by dinner on the patio with mountains silhouetted into the distance is a memorable experience.

**Mpila Camp** TENTED CAMP, CHALET $$
(tent for 2 people or chalets R870) The main accommodation centre on the iMfolozi side, spectacular and peaceful Mpila Camp is perched on top of a hill in the centre of the reserve. The safari tents are the most fun, but self-contained chalets are available too. Note: there's an electric fence, but wildlife (lions, hyenas, wild dogs) can still wander through.

## Getting There & Away

You can access the park via three gates. The main entrance, Memorial gate, is about 15km west of the N2, about 50km north of Mtubatuba. The second entrance, Nyalazi gate, is accessed by turning left off the N2 onto R618 just after Mtubatuba on the way to Nongoma. The third, Cengeni gate, on iMfolozi's western side, is accessible by road (tarred for 30km) from Ulundi.

# iSimangaliso Wetland Park

This Unesco World Heritage Site stretches for 200 glorious kilometres from the Mozambican border to Maphelana, at the southern end of Lake St Lucia. With the Indian Ocean on one side, and a series of lakes on the other, the 3280-sq-km park protects five distinct ecosystems, featuring everything from offshore reefs and dolphins to woodlands and zebras.

St Lucia and Sodwana Bay are the main service centres for the park, both offering accommodation, limited eateries and a wealth of ecotour operators.

Activities on offer include birdwatching, boat tours, canoeing, deep-sea fishing, hiking, horse riding, turtle tours, wildlife watching and whale watching (in season)

## Sleeping & Eating

**Mabibi Camp** CAMPGROUND $
(☎035-474-1504; www.mabibicampsite.co.za; camping/chalets R124/680) If you can get here, you'll have heaven to yourself – almost. This rustic community-owned camp is right next to upmarket **Thonga Beach Lodge** (www.thongabeachlodge.co.za), but this is luxury of a different kind – nestled in a swath of forest and only a hop, skip and 137 steps (via a stairway) from the beach. Bring your own tent, food and gear.

**Sodwana Bay Lodge** LODGE $$
(☎035-571 9101; www.sodwanabaylodge.co.za; s/d with half board R925/1700) This resort has neat boardwalks, banana palms and pine-filled, slightly dated rooms. The chalets here are very comfortable, with huge decks. It caters to divers and offers various dive and accommodation packages, which can be great value. It's on the main road on the approach to the park. **Sodwana Bay Lodge Scuba Centre** (☎035-571 0117; www.sodwanadiving.co.za; PADI Open Water course R3750) is on the premises.

**Lodge Afrique** LODGE $$
(☎071 592 0366; www.lodgeafrique.com; 71 Hornbill St; s/d incl breakfast R950/1700; 📶🏊) Smart 'African chic'-style chalets crammed into a suburban block but with lush surrounds. It's a safe bet, if not booked out by groups; reservations required.

**Braza** PORTUGUESE $$
(73 McKenzie St; mains R65-200; ⏲11am-10pm) Cuisine with a touch of Portugal, Brazil, Mozambique and Angola – at least that's what this lively place promotes. It translates as good meaty dishes and grills, although a

DON'T MISS

### UMKHUZE GAME RESERVE

The **uMkhuze Game Reserve** (☎035-573 9004, 031-845 1000; www.kznwildlife.com; adult/child/vehicle R40/30/50; ⏲5am-7pm Nov-Mar, 6am-6pm Apr-Oct) is, in a phrase, a trip highlight. Established in 1912 to protect the nyala antelope, and now part of iSimangaliso Wetland Park, this reserve of dense scrub and open acacia plains covers some spectacular 360 sq km. It successfully reintroduced lions in 2014, and just about every other sought-after animal is represented, as well as more than 400 bird species, including the rare Pel's fishing owl (*Scotopelia peli*). The reserve has fabulous hides, some at water holes; the pans, surrounded by fever trees, offer some of the best wildlife viewing in the country. It's 15km from Mkuze town (18km from Bayla if heading north).

decent vegetarian platter is on offer (but not on the menu). Anything featuring the chorizo is superb.

## Pietermaritzburg

POP 223,500

Billed as the heritage city, and KZN's administrative and legislative capital, Pietermaritzburg and its grand historic buildings hark back to an age of pith helmets and midday martinis. While many buildings have been converted into museums, much of the CBD has, sadly, lost its gloss, especially in the past few years. This is partly due to the dire state of the local-government coffers. Elsewhere, the inner suburbs – plus Hilton, a suburb 9km northwest of the city centre – are green, leafy and pretty.

### Sleeping & Eating

**Tancredi B&B** B&B **$$**
(082 818 1555; www.tancredi.co.za; 41 Woodhouse Rd, Scottsville; s/d incl breakfast R640/890; P ) Just south of the city centre in a quiet suburb, Tancredi has seven rooms in a beautifully restored Victorian house. The top-notch breakfast and personal service from owner Ann make this a popular spot.

**Smith Grove B&B** B&B **$$**
(033-345 3963; www.smithgrove.co.za; 37 Howick Rd; s/d incl breakfast R595/850; ) This beautiful renovated Victorian home offers English-style B&B comforts with spacious, individually styled rooms, each in a different colour. There are free-standIng bath-tubs, and the pick of the rooms is room 5 on the 2nd floor, facing away from the main road with two good-size windows to enjoy the views.

**Tatham Art Gallery Cafe** CAFE **$**
(Chief Albert Luthuli St/Commercial Rd; mains R60-90; 10am-4pm Mon-Sat) Dip into quiche, beef curry or lasagne at the upstairs cafe at Tatham Gallery, or grab a table on the outside balcony. Also on offer are sweet treats like muffins and brownies.

**Traffords** INTERNATIONAL **$$$**
(033-394 4364; http://traffords.co.za; 43 Miller St; mains lunch R65-120, dinner R95-160; noon-3pm Tue-Fri, 6.30-10.30pm Tue-Sat; ) This place serves up quality international cuisine in appealingly quaint surrounds: the rooms of a converted heritage home. Choose from the likes of cherry tobacco duck or smoked, black-pepper-rubbed entrecôte. Lunches include more salad-based offerings. Vegetarians are also catered for. Decor is of the preloved linen-tablecloth variety – it's like having an elegant meal in the home you'd love to have.

### Information

**Ezemvelo KZN Wildlife Headquarters**
(033-845 1000; www.kznwildlife.com; Peter Brown Dr, Queen Elizabeth Park; reception 8am-4.30pm Mon-Fri, reservations 8am-5.30pm Mon-Thu, to 4.30pm Fri, to 12.30pm Sat) Provides information and accommodation bookings for all Ezemvelo KZN Wildlife parks and reserves.

**Msunduzi Pietermaritzburg Tourism** (033-345 1348; www.pmbtourism.co.za; Publicity House, 117 Chief Albert Luthuli St; 8am-5pm Mon-Fri, to 1pm Sat) The tourist office has brand spanking new premises just behind the current office – although when it officially moves is anybody's guess.

### Getting There & Around

The **airport** (033-386 9577) is 7km south of the city. A taxi costs around R90. **Airlink** (033-386 9286; www.flyairlink.com) operates flights to/from Johannesburg (R800, one hour).

The offices of most bus companies, including Greyhound and Intercape, are in Berger St, or directly opposite in McDonalds Plaza. Translux and its no-frills affiliate, City to City, are based at the train station.

Destinations offered from Pietermaritzburg include Jo'burg (R330, seven hours), Pretoria (R330, seven hours) and Durban (R220, 1½ hours). Shosholoza Meyl offers a service to Johannesburg (R320, 12 hours) on Friday and Sunday.

# Drakensberg & uKhahlamba-Drakensberg Park

If any landscape lives up to its airbrushed, publicity-shot alter ego, it is the jagged, green sweep of the Drakensberg's tabletop peaks. This forms the boundary between South Africa and the mountain kingdom of Lesotho, and offers some of the country's most awe-inspiring landscapes.

The Drakensberg range is one of the best hiking destinations in Africa. Valleys, waterfalls, rivers, caves and the escarpment, which rises to an impressive 3000m, provide spectacular wilderness experiences for walkers of all levels. Climbing is popular throughout the Drakensberg; only experienced climbers should attempt peaks in this region.

## Royal Natal National Park

Fanning out from some of the range's loftiest summits, the 80-sq-km **Royal Natal National Park** (☎036-438 6310; www.kznwildlife.com; adult/child/vehicle R40/20/45; ⏰5am-7pm summer, 6am-6pm winter) has a presence that far outstrips its relatively meagre size. With some of the Drakensberg's most dramatic and accessible scenery, the park is crowned by the sublime Amphitheatre, an 8km wall of cliff and canyon that's spectacular from below and even more so from up on high.

### Sights & Activities

**San Rock Art** HISTORIC SITE
(guided walk R40; ⏰9am-4pm) Of several San rock-art sites within the park, this is the only one open to tourists. You can organise a guided walk with community guides. The return trip takes about an hour, including time to rest and chat. Look for the 'San Rock Art' sign near the first bridge after entry.

**Elijah Mbonane** HIKING
(☎073 137 4690; elijahmbonane@yahoo.com) Offers guided hikes ranging from hour-long strolls to overnight treks. Prices vary greatly depending on number of hikers and length of the walk; minimum charge R800.

### Sleeping & Eating

**Amphitheatre Backpackers** HOSTEL $
(☎082 855 9767; www.amphibackpackers.co.za; R74, 21km north of Bergville; camping/dm R95/180, d R360-720; P 📶) This place gets mixed reviews from travellers – some report feeling pressured to do the organised trips (when there are other options around); others enjoy the rolled-out convenience. Amenities, though, are superb, including a bar, Jacuzzi, sauna and restaurant. Facing out over the Amphitheatre, it has a selection of sleeping options from dorms to comfortable four-person en suite rooms and a great campsite.

★**Hlalanathi** RESORT $$
(☎036-438 6308; www.hlalanathi.co.za; camping R195, 2-/4-bed chalets R1100/1800; 🏊) With a location lifted straight from an African chocolate-box lid and next to the local golf course, this pretty, unpretentious resort offers camping and excellent accommodation in thatched chalets on a finger of land overlooking the Tugela River. Go for a site facing the river and mountains. Prices are substantially cheaper outside high season.

**Tower of Pizza** ITALIAN $
(☎036-438 6480; www.towerofpizza.co.za; pizzas R75-100; ⏰noon-8.30pm Tue-Thu, to 9pm Fri & Sat, 10am-9pm Sun) Yep, there really is a tower, where very good wood-fire pizza is prepared. Grab a table on the outside decking and enjoy the clean air and mountain views at this excellent place near the Drakensberg mountains. Be warned: it doesn't accept cash – credit cards only! It also offers quaint rondavels and cottages (s/d R590/1000).

## Central Drakensberg

Crowned with some of the Drakensberg's most formidable peaks, including Giant's Castle peak (3312m), Monk's Cowl (3234m) and Champagne Castle (3377m), the Central Berg is a big hit with hikers and climbers. But with dramatic scenery aplenty, this beautiful region is just as popular with those who prefer to admire their mountains from a safe distance.

In the shadow of the ramparts of Cathedral Peak, **Cathedral Peak Nature Reserve** backs up against a colossal escarpment of peaks between Royal Natal National Park and Giant's Castle, west of Winterton.

### Sleeping

If you arrive late and end up staying in Winterton, **Bridge Lodge** (☎036-488 1554; www.bridgelodge.co.za; 18 Springfield Rd, Winterton; s/d from R330/590) offers excellent-value rooms and cheap pub grub.

**Inkosana Lodge** HOSTEL $
(☎036-468 1202; www.inkosana.co.za; camping/dm R125/225, d 850, with shared bathroom R650; P 📶 🏊) Travellers rave about this lodge. Its indigenous garden, rustic swimming dam, clean rooms and lovely rondavels make it one of the best spots around. Although promoted as a 'backpacker lodge', it's range of rooms would suit any discerning traveller. Centrally located for activities in and around the area, it's on Rte 600, en route to Champagne Castle.

**Didima Camp** CAMPGROUND, CHALET $$
(☎central reservations 033-845 1000; www.kznwildlife.com; camping R200, chalets from R1020; P @ 🏊) One of Ezemvelo KZN Wildlife's swankiest offerings, this upmarket thatched lodge, constructed to resemble San rock shelters, boasts huge views, a restaurant, tennis courts and a range of two- and four-bed self-catering chalets (full-board options

WORTH A TRIP

### GIANT'S CUP TRAIL

If you are planning to stretch your legs anywhere in South Africa, this is the place to do it. Without doubt, the Giant's Cup Trail (60km, five days and five nights), running from Sani Pass to Bushman's Nek, is one of the nation's great walks. Any reasonably fit person can walk it, so it's very popular. Early booking, through Ezemvelo KZN Wildlife (p926), is advisable in local holiday seasons.

Camping is not permitted on this trail, so accommodation is in limited shared **huts** (www.kznwildlife.com; per person R100), hence the need to book ahead. **Sani Lodge** (☎033-702 0330; www.sanilodge.co.za; camping R85, dm/d with shared bathroom R150/430, s/d rondavels R270/540) is almost at the head of the trail; arrange for the lodge to pick you up from Himeville or Underberg.

are also available, on request). The nearby campsites have braai facilities, shared ablutions and kitchen and lovely views. Minimum charges apply.

## Eating

**★Valley Bakery** BAKERY, CAFE $
(☎036-468 1257; Rte 600; mains R35-60; ⏰8am-5pm Mon-Fri, to 2pm Sat; 📶👪) Baguettes, croissants and a range of sticky treats are baked on the premises (the owners even grow and grind their wheat). A quaint wrought-iron veranda is the place for a wonderful selection of breakfasts, including eggs Benedict or muesli with fresh fruit. Wraps, sandwiches and homemade pies feature later in the day.

**Dragon's Rest Pub & Restaurant** PUB FOOD $$
(☎036-468 1218; mains R70-100; ⏰10.30am-2.30pm & 6-8.30pm) Sit outside at this delightful place and drink in the damside and mountain views while enjoying some fine Berg cooking and a cold drink. Inside is a log fire and a cosy bar. Service is painfully slow but the food is tasty and the setting sublime. It's near the auditorium of the boys' choir (www.dbchoir.com).

## Information

Head to the **Park Office** (☎036-488 8000; www.kznwildlife.com) for information on hikes in the area.

## Getting There & Away

Cathedral Peak is 45km southwest of Winterton on a sealed road. There is no public transport unless you hitch a ride on a staff shuttle heading to the hotel.

# Southern Drakensberg

Best accessed from the pleasant towns of Himeville and Underberg, the Southern Berg boasts one of the region's highlights: the journey up to Lesotho over Sani Pass. It is also renowned as a serious hiking area. As well as some great walks (including the fabulous Giant's Cup Trail), the region also offers a smorgasbord of wilderness areas.

## Sleeping

**Ezemvelo KZN Wildlife** CHALET $
(☎033-267 7251; www.kznwildlife.com; chalets from R660) Ezemvelo KZN Wildlife has well-equipped two-bed chalets in the Kamberg section, tastefully decorated with small kitchens and floor-to-ceiling glass overlooking lawns and mountains. Accommodation in the Highmoor section is limited to camping. Bring your own supplies if you're staying in either reserve.

**Cleopatra Mountain Farmhouse** RESORT $$$
(☎033-267 7243; www.cleomountain.com; Balgowan; per person with half board from R2295) If God were to top off the beauty of the Drakensberg with a gourmet treat, Cleopatra Mountain Farmhouse would be it. Guests enjoy a nightly six-course menu of quality produce prepared innovatively and accompanied by rich, creamy sauces. Each of the 11 rooms is decked out in a theme and features quirky touches, such as a picket-fence bedhead and Boer memorabilia.

# FREE STATE

A place of big skies and open pastureland, the Free State is ideal for a road trip. Broad horizons are interrupted only briefly by a smattering of towns and villages and, apart from Bloemfontein, the urban centres are small and manageable.

# Bloemfontein

POP 256,500

With the feel of a small country village, despite its double-capital status (it's the Free State's capital and the judicial capital of the country), Bloemfontein is one of South Africa's most pleasant cities. Although 'Bloem' doesn't possess the type of big-name attractions that make it worth a visit in its own right, you'll likely pass through it at some point on your way across South Africa's heartland.

## Tours

**Manguang Township** CULTURAL

The African National Congress (ANC) was born in the township of Manguang, 5km outside Bloemfontein, in 1912. Today, you can experience township life and learn some important history on a guided tour.

Tours are informal and cost about R500. The operators change, so it's best to ask at the tourist office for an up-to-date list of guides.

## Sleeping

**Reyneke Caravan Park** CARAVAN PARK $

(051-523 3888; www.reynekepark.co.za; Brendar Rd; camping per site up to 4 people R300, s/d/chalets R470/560/980; ) Two kilometres out of town (take the N8 towards Kimberley), this well-organised park has a swimming pool, trampoline and kids play area. It's a good place for families. Basic rooms and modern brick chalets that sleep up to four. Some travellers report that it can be noisy due to its proximity to a busy road.

**★Matanja** GUESTHOUSE $$

(079 494 9740; www.matanja.co.za; 74A Albrecht St, Dan Pienaar; s/d incl breakfast R585/780; ) Small luxuries, such as pure goose-down duvets and a stylish, rustic ambience, set this little B&B apart. There are honesty fridges in the bedrooms, and with only four rooms there's attention to detail. Your comfort seems a priority to the owners, who will even arrange breakfast in bed. Prebooking recommended.

## Eating & Drinking

As a university town, Bloem has a good range of places to drink, party and listen to live music. The corners of 2nd Ave and Kellner St and of Zastron St and Nelson Mandela Ave bustle with revellers in the evening. A slightly older crowd hangs out at the Waterfront.

**Picnic** CAFE $

(051-430 4590; Loch Logan Waterfront; mains R60-90; 8am-5pm Mon-Sat, to 2pm Sun) A cool place with a great outlook over the water, perfect for a long, lazy chill out. The food is excellent, especially the salads and sandwiches. Enjoy the fresh bread, quality ingredients and homemade touches such as tomato chutney (recommended on rye with ham and camembert).

**★Seven on Kellner** INTERNATIONAL $$

(051-447 7928; www.sevenonkellner.co.za; 7 Kellner St, Westdene; mains R80-165; noon-2pm Mon-Fri, from 6.30pm Mon-Sat) Set in an old house with inside and outside dining options, Seven on Kellner offers an informal, intimate atmosphere. Poultry, meat and seafood dishes are delicately prepared with expert hands along a Middle Eastern- and Indian-inspired theme. Excellent wine list.

## Information

**Tourist Information Centre** (051-405 8489; www.bloemfonteintourism.co.za; 60 Park Rd; 8am-4.15pm Mon-Fri, to noon Sat) A mildly useful tourist office.

## Getting There & Away

### AIR

Bloemfontein airport is 10km from the city centre.

**Mango** (086 100 1234; www.flymango.com) connects Bloem with Cape Town (R950, 1½ hours). **Fly Blue Crane** (087 330 2424; www.flybluecrane.com) has flights to Jo'burg (R900, one hour) and Cape Town (R1200, 1½ hours). **CemAir** (in Johannesburg 011-395 4473; www.flycemair.co.za) has flghts to Jo'burg (R1200, one hour), Port Elizabeth (R1600, 1½ hours) and George (R1800, 1½ hours).

### BUS & SHARED TAXI

Long-distance buses leave from the tourist centre on Park Rd. **Translux** (0861 589 282; www.translux.co.za) runs daily buses:

**Cape Town** (R520, 13 hours)

**Durban** (R370, nine hours)

**Jo'burg/Pretoria** (R300, five hours)

**Port Elizabeth** (R500, nine hours)

**Greyhound** (083 915 9000; www.greyhound.co.za; Park Rd) and **Intercape** (in Cape Town 021-380 4400; www.intercape.co.za; Park Rd) also have similar services.

### TRAIN

Shosholoza Meyl operates services three times weekly via Bloemfontein between Jo'burg (tourist/economy R230/130, about seven hours) and Port Elizabeth (R330/210). There's also a service that passes by Bloem on the run between Jo'burg and East London (13 hours, R310/200).

# GAUTENG

If you're in search of urban vibes, Gauteng will enthrall you. This small province is the throbbing heart of the South African nation and the economic engine of Africa. Its epicentre is Johannesburg (Jo'burg), the country's largest city. And what a city! Jo'burg's centre is undergoing an astonishing rebirth and its cultural life has never been so dynamic. Once considered a place to avoid, Jo'burg is now one of the most inspiring and happening metropolises in the world.

## Johannesburg

POP 4.4 MILLION

Johannesburg, more commonly known as Jo'burg or Jozi, is a rapidly changing city and the vibrant heart of South Africa. After almost 20 years of decline and decay, the city is now looking optimistically towards the future. Jo'burg is an incredibly friendly, unstuffy city and there's a lot to see here, from sobering reminders of the country's recent past at the Apartheid Museum to the progressive streets of Melville. So delve in and experience the buzz of a city undergoing an incredible rebirth.

### Sights

**Johannesburg Art Gallery** GALLERY

(JAG; Map p936; ☎011-725 3130; Joubert Park, Inner City; ⏲10am-5pm Tue-Sun) FREE The JAG has the largest art collection in Africa and regularly rotates its incredible collection of 17th- and 18th-century European landscape and figurative paintings with works by leading South African painters and traditional African objects and retrospectives by black artists. It's on the Sophie de Bruyn St (Noord St) side of Joubert Park (the park itself is best avoided).

**Top of Africa** VIEWPOINT

(Map p936; ☎011-308 1331; www.gauteng.net/attractions/carlton_centre; 50th fl, Carlton Centre, 150 Commissioner St, Inner City; adult/child R15/10; ⏲9am-6pm Mon-Fri, to 5pm Sat, to 2pm Sun) The iconic **Carlton Centre** (223m) has been Africa's tallest building for more than 40 years now. The basement shelters a buzzing **shopping mall**. For awesome city vistas, head to the **observation deck** at the top (entrance is via a special lift one floor below street level).

★ **Apartheid Museum** MUSEUM

(Map p932; ☎011-309 4700; www.apartheidmuseum.org; cnr Gold Reef Rd & Northern Parkway, Ormonde; adult/child R80/65; ⏲9am-5pm; P) The Apartheid Museum illustrates the rise and fall of South Africa's era of segregation and oppression, and is an absolute must-see. It uses film, text, audio and live accounts to provide a chilling insight into the architecture and implementation of the apartheid system, as well as inspiring stories of the struggle towards democracy. It's invaluable in understanding the inequalities and tensions that still exist today. Located 8km south of the city centre, just off the M1 freeway.

★ **Joziburg Lane** MARKET

(Map p932; www.joziburglane.co.za; 1 Eloff St, Marshalltown; ⏲10am-5pm Tue-Sat) A gentrified quarter of the city, Joziburg Lane occupies the ground floor of One Eloff, a magnificent art deco building that once stood derelict and is now filled with loft-style apartments. Browse artists' studios, graze on cheese platters, curries and traditional African eats in the hip eateries and sip on good coffee and craft beer. The shops and cafes stay open until 10pm on Fridays.

### Tours

**Dlala Nje** WALKING

(Map p932; ☎011-402 2373; www.dlalanje.org; Shop 1, Ponte City, Hillbrow) Run by Nickolaus Bauer and Mike Luptak, this pioneering company offers unique tours to three of Jo'burg's most impoverished and misunderstood areas: Hillbrow, Berea and the West African immigrant community of Yeoville. This is a great opportunity to change negative perceptions about these districts and learn more about the diverse communities that live there.

### Sleeping

**Curiocity Backpackers** HOSTEL $

(Map p932; ☎011-614 0163; www.curiocitybackpackers.com; 302 Fox St, Maboneng; dm R200, s/d with shared bathroom R330/530; P 📶) This is a superlative place to stay thanks to the dedication of young proprietor Bheki Dube. Occupying a converted printing house in the desirable Maboneng precinct, this quirky, offbeat backpackers features clean dorms, unadorned yet neat rooms and a rooftop suite. It also has a buzzing bar, kitchen facilities and a small restaurant. The congenial atmosphere is hard to beat.

**Joburg Backpackers** HOSTEL $

(Map p932; ☎011-888 4742; www.joburgbackpackers.com; 14 Umgwezi Rd, Emmarentia; dm/d R180/530, s/d with shared bathroom R340/440; P 📶 🏊) This discreet hostel in the leafy streets of Emmarentia is clean, safe and well run, with a range of well-appointed rooms and a relaxed country feel. The en suite rooms are terrific value and open onto big grassy lawns; the eight- and 10-bed dorms are spacious and spotless. No meals are served, but Greenside's eateries are a 10-minute stroll away.

**★12 Decades Art Hotel** BOUTIQUE HOTEL $$

(Map p932; ☎011-026 5601; www.12decadeshotel.co.za; 7th fl, Main Street Life Bldg, 286 Fox St, Maboneng; s/d R950/1260; P ❄ 📶) This terrific concept hotel in the heart of the Maboneng precinct has 12 7th-floor rooms (the rest are residential), each one designed by different international artists and inspired by a particular era in the city's history. The Sir Abe Bailey Suite takes on a late-19th-century Chinese gold rush aesthetic, while Perpetual Liberty is decidedly more contemporary. A special experience.

**★Motel Mipichi** BOUTIQUE HOTEL $$

(Map p932; ☎011-726 8844; www.motelmipichi.co.za; 35 4th Ave, Melville; s/d incl breakfast from R645/895; P 📶) A gem of a place. The design duo behind Motel Mipichi turned two semi-detached 1930s abodes into a genuine alternative to the traditional Melville guesthouse experience. Mipichi is a minimalist delight, with six calming rooms speckled with pastel splotches and walk-through showers. The open-plan kitchen and living area, with original Portuguese tiles, is an ideal place to decompress. Book ahead.

**★Oasis Signature Hotel** HOTEL $$

(Map p932; ☎011-807 4351; www.oasisguesthouse.co.za; 29 Homestead Rd, Rivonia; s/d incl breakfast from R1190/1490; P ❄ 📶 🏊) This is a delightful suburban hideaway, presided over by an astute couple who cater for business people and holidaymakers with equal aplomb. The lush garden surrounds feature a kidney-shaped pool and a spacious *lapa* (South African thatched gazebo). The 14 rooms vary in size and price, but all are stylish and thoughtfully furnished. The breakfast smorgasbord is worthy of special mention.

**★Residence** BOUTIQUE HOTEL $$$

(Map p932; ☎011-853 2480; www.theresidence.co.za; 17 4th Ave, Houghton; d incl breakfast R3165-4975; P ❄ @ 📶 🏊) If you could smell charm, this supersmooth boutique hotel set in a former embassy would reek of it to high heaven. This quiet little paradise is the epitome of a refined cocoon, with 17 opulent, individually designed suites and swish communal areas. After a day of turf pounding, take a dip in the stress-melting pool or relax in the spa.

**★Satyagraha House** GUESTHOUSE $$$

(Map p932; ☎011-485 5928; www.satyagrahahouse.com; 15 Pine Rd, Orchards; d incl breakfast from R2520; P 📶) A wonderful urban sanctuary, Satyagraha is the former home of Mohandas (Mahatma) Gandhi, who lived here between 1907 and 1908. This heritage building has been restored into an innovative guesthouse and museum, with seven rooms built to resemble a traditional African village. The intimate history of Gandhi's time here is on display to reward guests in unexpected ways. Meals are vegetarian.

## Eating

Jo'burg is a fabulous city for foodies, with restaurants to suit all persuasions. Melville, Greenside, Braamfontein, Maboneng and increasingly the Inner City have lots of fun, lively places to feast.

**★Eat Your Heart Out** DELI $

(Map p932; ☎072 586 0600; www.eatyourheartout.co.za; cnr Kruger & Fox Sts, Maboneng; mains R50-80; ⏰7.30am-4pm Tue-Sun; 📶) The best spot in Maboneng to start the day. The Israeli breakfast – omelette, toasted pita, diced salad, pickled cabbage and cottage cheese – is the highlight, while the bagels and cheesecakes will leave your taste buds reeling. Healthy fruit juices, great coffee and sweet treats are also on offer, and there's outdoor seating.

**Post** CAFE $

(Map p936; ☎072 248 2078; 70 Juta St, Braamfontein; mains R45-75; ⏰6.30am-4pm Mon-Fri, 8.30am-2pm Sat; 📶) Fill up at this great little cafe before (or after) delving into Braamfontein. Come for delicious breakfasts, gourmet sandwiches, fresh salads and changing lunch specials. The chalkboard menu adds to the casual atmosphere. Oh, and it serves delectable coffee.

**★Great Eastern Food Bar** ASIAN $$

(Map p932; ☎011-482 2910; Bamboo Centre, cnr 9th St & Rustenburg Rd, Melville; mains R60-140;

# Johannesburg

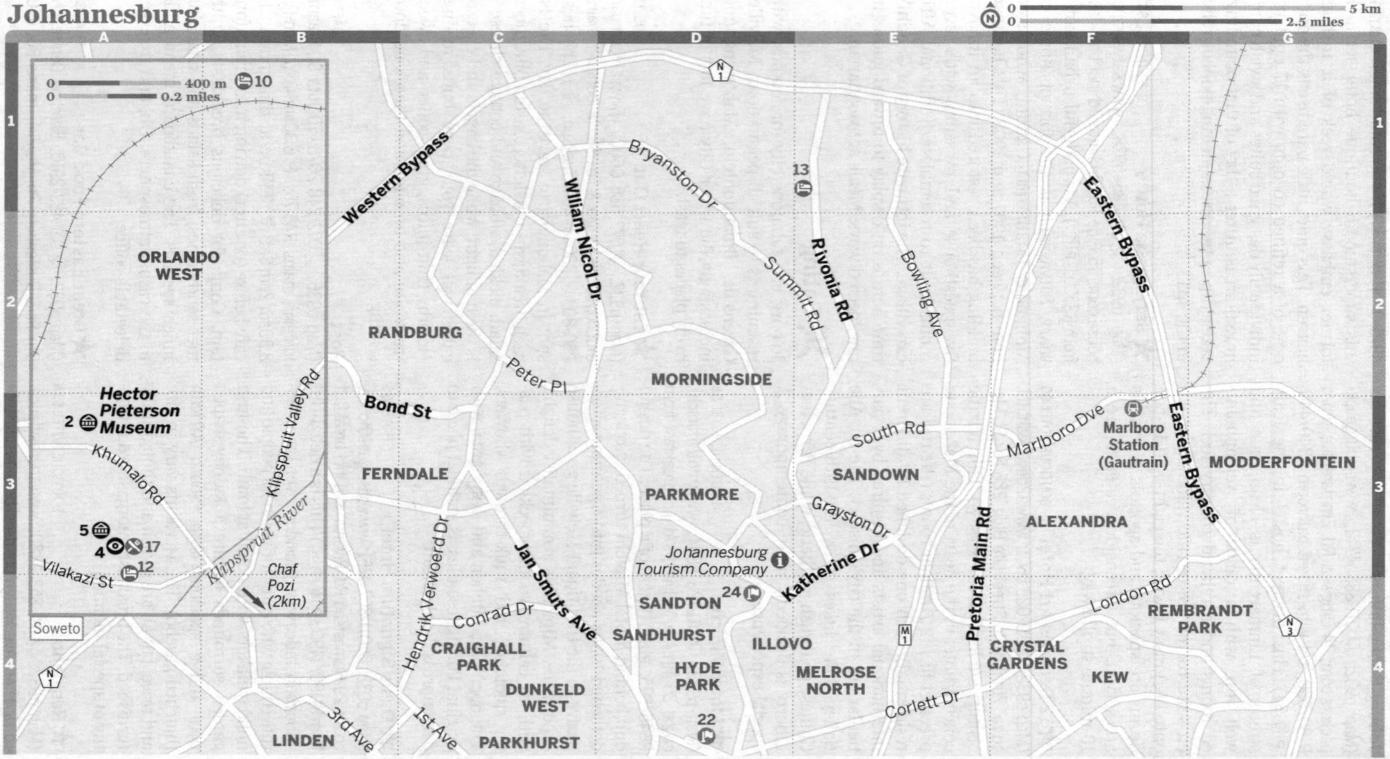

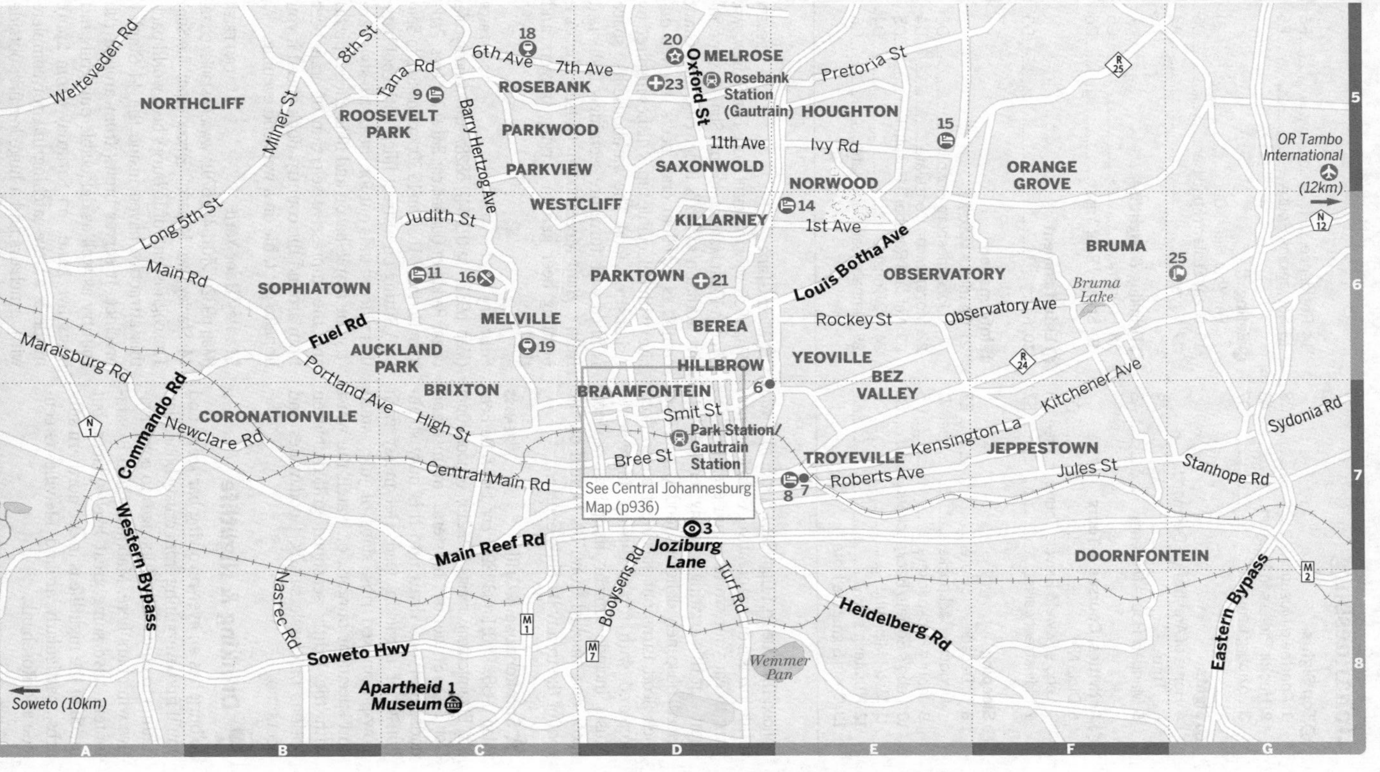

Welteveden Rd
8th St
18
6th Ave
7th Ave
20
MELROSE
Oxford St
Pretoria St
R25
NORTHCLIFF
Milner St
Tana Rd
9
ROSEBANK
23
Rosebank Station (Gautrain)
HOUGHTON
ROOSEVELT PARK
Barry Hertzog Ave
PARKWOOD
11th Ave
Ivy Rd
15
OR Tambo International (12km)
PARKVIEW
SAXONWOLD
NORWOOD
ORANGE GROVE
N12
WESTCLIFF
14
KILLARNEY
1st Ave
Long 5th St
Judith St
BRUMA
25
Main Rd
11
16
SOPHIATOWN
PARKTOWN
21
Louis Botha Ave
OBSERVATORY
Bruma Lake
MELVILLE
BEREA
Rockey St
Observatory Ave
Fuel Rd
19
Maraisburg Rd
AUCKLAND PARK
HILLBROW
YEOVILLE
R24
BEZ VALLEY
Portland Ave
BRIXTON
BRAAMFONTEIN
6
Kitchener Ave
Commando Rd
CORONATIONVILLE
Smit St
N1
Newclare Rd
High St
Park Station/Gautrain Station
Kensington La
JEPPESTOWN
Sydonia Rd
Bree St
TROYEVILLE
Central Main Rd
8
7
Roberts Ave
Jules St
Stanhope Rd
See Central Johannesburg Map (p936)
3
Joziburg Lane
Main Reef Rd
DOORNFONTEIN
Western Bypass
Booysens Rd
Turf Rd
M2
Nasrec Rd
M1
Heidelberg Rd
Eastern Bypass
M7
Soweto Hwy
Wemmer Pan
Apartheid Museum
1
Soweto (10km)

## Johannesburg

**Top Sights**
1 Apartheid Museum ... C8
2 Hector Pieterson Museum ... A3
3 Joziburg Lane ... D7

**Sights**
4 Home of Archbishop Desmond Tutu ... A3
5 Mandela House Museum ... A3

**Activities, Courses & Tours**
6 Dlala Nje ... D7
Lebo's Soweto Bicycle Tours ... (see 10)
7 Mainstreetwalks ... E7

**Sleeping**
8 12 Decades Art Hotel ... E7
Curiocity Backpackers ... (see 7)
9 Joburg Backpackers ... C5
10 Lebo's Soweto Backpackers ... B1
11 Motel Mipichi ... C6
12 Nthateng's B&B ... A3
13 Oasis Signature Hotel ... E1
14 Residence ... E6
15 Satyagraha House ... E5

**Eating**
Eat Your Heart Out ... (see 8)
16 Great Eastern Food Bar ... C6
17 Vuyo's ... A3

**Drinking & Nightlife**
18 Foundry ... C5
19 Stanley Beer Yard ... C6

**Entertainment**
20 Katzy's ... D5

**Information**
21 Charlotte Maxeke Johannesburg Hospital ... D6
22 Mozambican Consulate ... D4
23 Netcare Rosebank Hospital ... D5
24 US Consulate ... D4
25 Zimbabwean Consulate ... G6

noon-11pm Tue-Fri, 1-11pm Sat, 1-8pm Sun) If you think Jozi is a dud at creative Asian food, prepare to eat your words – and everything in sight – at this exciting eatering serving well-priced, obscenely delicious food. Owner-chef Nick Scott turns out succulent concoctions prepared with top-of the-line ingredients. Musts include kimchi dumplings, sashimi tacos and smoked trout. It's located on the roof of the trendy Bamboo Centre.

★ **Smokehouse & Grill** STEAK $$
(Map p936; 011-403 1395; cnr Juta & De Beer Sts, Braamfontein; mains R75-215; noon-10pm Mon-Sat) Students, hipsters, mums and dads: everyone dives into this busy steakhouse for a rockin' feed. Get messy with slow-pit-smoked ribs, slabs of juicy steak and succulent burgers, or watch the waist with the lightly seasoned grilled-chicken options or classic salads. Good wines and beers too.

## Drinking & Nightlife

Jo'burg has an ever-revolving bar scene and you'll find everything from crusty bohemian haunts to chic cocktail lounges to conservative wine bars here. Maboneng and Braamfontein have some great lively places, but much of the nightlife is in the northern suburbs, particularly around Melville, Greenside and Rosebank.

★ **Mad Giant** BREWERY
(Map p936; www.madgiant.co.za; 1 Fox St, Newtown; noon-10pm Mon-Sat, to 6pm Sun) A superlative addition to Jozi's inner city, Mad Giant combines excellent craft beers (brewed on-site) with delectable tapas dishes inspired by Asian street food. The warehouse-like space is filled with furniture seemingly fashioned from a giant Meccano set. Outside there's a bustling beer garden serving burgers and the like.

**Foundry** CRAFT BEER
(Map p932; 011-447 5828; www.foundrycafe.co.za; Parktown Quarter, cnr 3rd & 7th Aves, Parktown North; 11.30am-10.30pm Mon-Sat, to 5pm Sun) Sitting on a street filled with cool bars, this place stands out for the bistro-style fare (try the maple-bacon and blue-cheese pizza) and the impressive selection of craft beer from around the country. Book ahead if you hope to get table on a weekend evening.

**Stanley Beer Yard** CRAFT BEER
(Map p932; 011-481 5791; www.44stanley.co.za; 44 Stanley Ave, Milpark; noon-11pm Tue-Sun) The cognoscenti of Jo'burg's beer world pack this attractive haven inside the 44 Stanley precinct. It serves brews from around the country as well as delectable pub grub and hosts live bands on Saturday (from 2pm). Inside is an eye-catching interior complete with armchairs and a huge log fire; outside are long wooden tables under olive trees.

## Entertainment

**Katzy's** JAZZ

(Map p932; ☎011-880 3945; www.katzys.co.za; The Firs Shopping Centre, cnr Oxford Rd & Bierman Ave, Rosebank; ⊙noon-midnight Mon-Wed, to 2am Thu-Fri, 6.30pm-2am Sat) One of the loveliest hang-outs in the neighbourhood, this swanky den recalls the atmosphere of an old NYC jazz club. You'll find mellow, live jazz five nights a week, as well as the tasty carnivore menu of the restaurant next door, The Grillhouse. A cover charge (R150) applies on Thursday, Friday and Saturday nights.

**Bassline** LIVE MUSIC

(Map p936; ☎011-838 9145; www.bassline.co.za; 10 Henry Nxumalo St, Newtown) This is still the most respected live-music venue in Jo'burg, gaining prominence as a Melville jazz haunt in the late '90s before getting on the world-music trip and relocating to Newtown in 2004. Today it covers the full range of international music, and especially the more-popular reggae, rock and hip-hop styles.

## Shopping

★**Neighbourgoods Market** FOOD

(Map p936; www.neighbourgoodsmarket.co.za; cnr Juta & de Beer Sts, Braamfontein; ⊙9am-3pm Sat) Cape Town's wondrous community market has come to Braamfontein to continually 'reinvent the public market as civic institution'. The two-storey brick warehouse fills with artisan purveyors and their foodie fans, who hoover up healthy brunches, 'slow' beer and stiff coffee. Upstairs you can grab a bench and watch the sun shine off city buildings.

## Information

### DANGERS & ANNOYANCES

Johannesburg has a larger-than-life reputation when it comes to crime, but most visits are trouble-free.

- The city centre, once a no-go area, is fine during the day but best avoided after dark.
- The surrounding neighbourhoods of Braamfontein, Ferreirasdorp, Newtown and Maboneng are generally busy at night and safe to visit – just be vigilant when walking back to your car.
- Avoid Hillbrow and Yeoville unless you're with a guide.
- Carjackings do happen in the city, so keep your wits about you when stopped at traffic lights after dark.

### MEDICAL SERVICES

**Charlotte Maxeke Johannesburg Hospital** (Map p932; ☎011-488 4911; M1/Jubilee Rd, Parktown) Jo'burg's main public hospital.

**Netcare Rosebank Hospital** (Map p932; ☎011-328 0500; www.netcare.co.za; 14 Sturdee Ave, Rosebank; ⊙7am-10pm) A private hospital in the northern suburbs, with casualty (emergency), GP and specialist services.

### TOURIST INFORMATION

**Johannesburg Tourism Company** (Map p932; ☎087 151 2950; www.joburgtourism.com; 4th fl, Nelson Mandela Sq, Sandton; ⊙8am-5pm Mon-Fri) A private endeavour; covers the city of Jo'burg.

## Getting There & Away

### AIR

South Africa's major international and domestic airport is **OR Tambo International Airport** (Ortia; ☎011-921 6262; www.airports.co.za). It's about 25km east of central Johannesburg in Kempton Park.

Smaller budget airlines Kulula, Safair and Mango link Jo'burg with major destinations. For regular flights to national and regional destinations try **South African Airways** (SAA; ☎0861 359 722; www.flysaa.com), **Airlink** (☎0861 606 606; www.flyairlink.com) and **SA Express** (☎0861 729 227; www.flyexpress.aero).

### BUS

There are a number of international bus services that leave Jo'burg from the Park Station (Map p936) complex and head for Mozambique, Lesotho, Botswana, Namibia, Swaziland and Zimbabwe.

**Baz Bus** (p909) Connects Jo'burg with the most popular parts of the region (including Durban, the Garden Route and Cape Town) and picks up at hostels in Jo'burg and Pretoria. A seven-day travel pass costs R2600.

**Citybug** (☎0861 334 433; www.citybug.co.za) Runs a shuttle service between Jo'burg and Nelspruit (R440, 3½ hours).

**City to City** (p914) National and international bus services.

**Greyhound** (☎083 915 9000; www.greyhound.co.za) National and international bus services.

**Intercape** (p909) National and international bus services.

**Lowveld Link** (☎083 918 8075; www.lowveldlink.com) Runs a shuttle between the airport and Nelspruit (R410, four hours), via Pretoria.

**Translux** (p913) National and international bus services.

## Central Johannesburg

A B C D
1 2 3 4 5 6
Hoofd St
Kotze St
Joubert St
Loveday St
South African Institute for Medical Research
Yale Rd
Jan Smuts Ave
Ameshoff St
De Beer St
Melle St
Stiemens St
Hospital St
Jorissen St
BRAAMFONTEIN
Biccard St
Rissik St
De Korte St
Henri St
Station St
Bertha St
Juta St
Smit St
Queen Elizabeth Dr
Wolmarans St
Citysightseeing Joburg
Nelson Mandela Bridge
Leyds St
Long-Distance Buses Booking Offices
Park Station/ Gautrain Station
De Villiers St
Carr St
Gwigwi Mrwebi St
Lilian Ngoyi St (Bree St)
Rahima Moosa St (Jeppe St)
Ntemi Piliso St
Diagonal St
Pixley ka Isaka Seme St (Sauer St)
Simmonds St
Harrison St
Rissik St
Joubert St
Eloff St
Von Brandis St
Henry Nxumalo St
NEWTOWN
Miriam Makeba St
Gerard Sekoto St
Helen Joseph St (President St)
Library Square
Albertina Sisulu Rd
Main Rd
Central Main Rd
Commissioner St
Ferreira St
MARSHALLTOWN
Fox St
Gandhi Square
Metrobus
Main St
Marshall St
Anderson St
Frederick St



**TRAIN**

Trains link Jo'burg with destinations such as Pretoria, Cape Town, Bloemfontein, Kimberley, Port Elizabeth, Durban, Komatipoort and Nelspruit. Get tickets at **Shosholoza Meyl** (Map p936; ☎011-774 4555, 0860 008 888; www.shosholozameyl.co.za) or at Jo'burg's Park Station.

## Getting Around

**BUS**

**Citysightseeing Joburg** (Map p936; ☎0861 733 287; www.citysightseeing.co.za; Park Station) Starting from Park Station, these hop-on, hop-off red buses run to 11 major

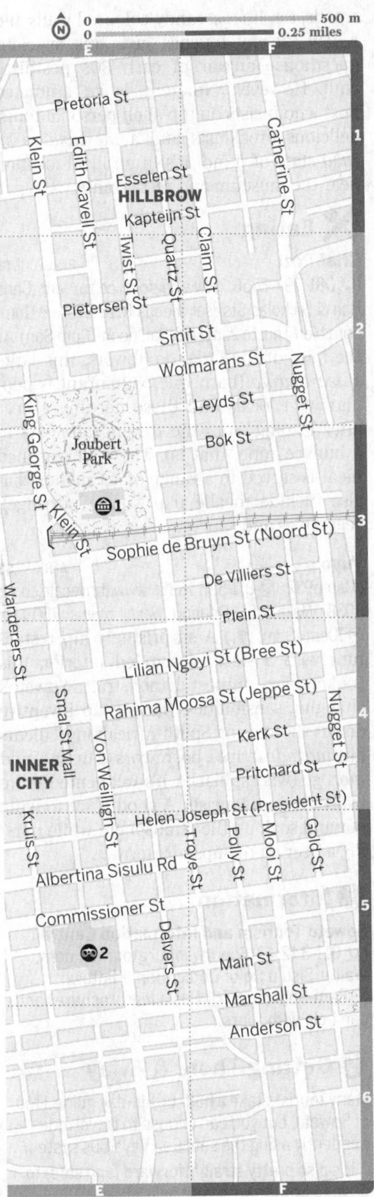


## Central Johannesburg

**Sights**
1 Johannesburg Art Gallery.................E3
2 Top of Africa.................E5

**Eating**
3 Post.................B2
4 Smokehouse & Grill.................B2

**Drinking & Nightlife**
5 Mad Giant.................A6

**Entertainment**
6 Bassline.................A5

**Shopping**
Neighbourgoods Market.................(see 4)

**Information**
7 Botswanan Consulate.................C2
8 Lesotho Embassy.................B2
9 Swazi Consulate.................C1

**Transport**
10 Shosholoza Meyl.................D3

tourist sites around central Johannesburg from roughly 9am to 6pm. A ticket valid for one day costs R190.

**Metrobus** (Map p936; ☎0860 562 874; www.mbus.co.za; Gandhi Sq) A reasonable network of buses across the city.

**Rea Vaya** (☎0860 562 874; www.reavaya.org.za) An inner-city circular route costs R6.20, while a full trip from the feeder routes to the Inner City costs R12.90.

### TAXI

**Rose Taxis** (☎011-403 9625; www.rosetaxis.com) is a reputable firm. These days, most Jo'burgers prefer to use Uber (www.uber.com/cities/johannesburg).

### TRAIN

Jo'burg's pride and joy, the rapid-transit **Gautrain** (☎0800 428 87246; www.gautrain.co.za) offers a direct service between the airport, Sandton, Rosebank, Park Station, Pretoria and Hatfield. A one-way ticket between Pretoria and Park Station costs R72.

## Soweto

POP 1.3 MILLION

The 'South West Townships' have evolved from an area of forced habitation to an address of pride and social prestige and a destination in their own right. Travellers come here to be part of the welcoming township life and to visit places of tremendous historical significance. And while it was considered foolhardy to get there on your own a decade ago, it's now safe to visit the main sights independently.

## Sights

**★Hector Pieterson Museum** MUSEUM
(Map p932; ☎011-536 0611; cnr Pela & Kumalo Sts, Orlando West; adult/child R30/10; ⊙10am-5pm Mon-Sat, to 4pm Sun) This powerful museum illuminates the role of Sowetan life in the history of the independence struggle. On 16 June 1976, a peaceful student protest against the introduction of Afrikaans as a language of instruction in black secondary schools was violently quelled by police. In the resulting chaos police opened fire and a 13-year-old boy, Hector Pieterson, was shot dead.

**Mandela House Museum** MUSEUM
(Map p932; ☎011-936 7754; www.mandelahouse.com; cnr Vilakazi & Ngakane Sts, Orlando West; adult/child R60/20; ⊙9am-5pm) Nelson Mandela lived with his first wife, Evelyn, and later with his second wife, Winnie, in this four-room house, just off Vilakazi St. The museum includes interactive exhibits on the history of the house and some interesting family photos. Just down Vilakazi St, by Sakhumzi Restaurant, is the home of Archbishop Desmond Tutu.

## Tours

**Lebo's Soweto Bicycle Tours** CYCLING
(Map p932; ☎011-936 3444; www.sowetobicycletours.com; 2hr/1-day tour R430/680) Soweto's clay paths and grassy nooks make for fabulous cycling terrain. Walking tours are also offered, and there are *tuk tuk* (auto rickshaw) tours for the less energetic. The tours are organised by Lebo's Soweto Backpackers, with discounts available for guests.

## Sleeping

**Lebo's Soweto Backpackers** HOSTEL $
(Map p932; ☎011-936 3444; www.sowetobackpackers.com; 10823A Pooe St, Orlando West; camping/dm R100/170, s/d with shared bathroom R270/420; P ) For a real township experience, this well-established hostel set by lovely parklands is your answer. It's a healthy walk from the Vilakazi St action, but guests love the shaded beer garden, restaurant (meals from R60) and pool table. Dorms are neat and clean; the double rooms are excellent value. Friendly staff encourage interactivity, and all kinds of tours are available.

**Nthateng's B&B** GUESTHOUSE $$
(Map p932; ☎011-051 9362, 082 335 7956; nthatengmd@gmail.com; 6991 Inhlwathi St, Orlando West; s/d incl breakfast R500/695; P ) Dark woods, tan linens, sandy-coloured walls and a few kitschy touches give this spacious guesthouse an air of early-'80s postdisco chill. However, Nthateng is an animated host who insists on top-shelf personal tours, delicious breakfasts and a *mi casa es su casa* state of mind. It's in an ideal location near the museum and restaurants.

## Eating

**Chaf Pozi** BARBECUE $$
(☎081 797 5756; www.chafpozi.co.za; cnr Chris Han & Nicholas Sts; set menus R110-275; ⊙11am-6pm Mon-Thu, to 2am Fri & Sat, noon-10pm Sun) At the base of the Orlando Towers, this large *shisa nyama* (barbeque) restaurant is popular with locals and those needing a beer after leaping from the towers (attached to a bungee rope, that is). The well-seasoned meat is served in a range of set menus that also include mealie pap (maize porridge), vegetables and sauces.

**Vuyo's** AFRICAN $$
(Map p932; ☎011-536 1838; www.thrivecafe.co.za; 8038 Vilakazi St, Orlando West; mains R50-130; ⊙10am-10pm; ) A surprisingly hip restaurant with a sleek, design-led interior, this cool culinary outpost demonstrates Soweto's changing sensibilities. Serving up inventive dishes showcasing South African ingredients like *mogodo* (tripe), boerewors (sausage) and *morogo* (wild spinach), it's frequented more by locals than tourists. A good place to hang out and soak up the atmosphere while nursing a beer on the upstairs terrace.

## Information

**Soweto Tourism and Information Centre**
(☎011-342 4316; www.joburgtourism.com; Walter Sisulu Sq of Dedication, Kliptown; ⊙8am-5pm Mon-Fri) Has a few brochures and can help with tours.

## Getting There & Away

Many tourists take a half- or full-day guided tour of Soweto, but you can choose to travel independently using the safe Rea Vaya bus system.

It's also pretty straightforward (and safe) to drive to Soweto with your own wheels.

# Pretoria

POP 741,000

South Africa's administrative centre is a handsome city, with a number of gracious old houses in the city centre; large, leafy suburbs; and wide streets that are lined with a purple haze of jacarandas in October and November.

## Sights

**Freedom Park** MEMORIAL

(☎012-336 4000; www.freedompark.co.za; cnr Koch St & 7th Ave; entry incl guided tour R100; ⏰8am-4.30pm, tours 9am, noon & 3pm) This stunning memorial adopts an integrated approach to South Africa's war history and is a place of architectural imagination and collective healing. Located across the kopje (rocky hill) from the austere Voortrekker Monument, Freedom Park honours fallen South Africans in all major conflicts. Highlights include the **Isivivane Garden of Remembrance**; **Sikhimbuto**, the wall of inscribed names of fallen heroes; **//hapo**, a museum and interpretative centre covering Southern African history; and **Mveledzo**, a spiral path that cuts into the natural landscape.

**Voortrekker Monument** MONUMENT, VIEWPOINT

(☎012-326 6770; www.vtm.org.za; Eeufees Rd; adult/child R70/35; ⏰8am-6pm Sep-Apr, to 5pm May-Aug) The imposing Voortrekker Monument was constructed between 1938 and 1949 to honour the journey of the Voortrekkers, who trekked north over the coastal mountains of the Cape into the heart of the African veld. The monument is 3km south of the city and is clearly signposted from the N1 freeway. It is surrounded by a 3.4-sq-km **nature reserve**.

## Sleeping

Most budget options are in Hatfield, near the university and embassies. There are some lovely guesthouses in the southern suburbs.

**Pumbas Backpackers** HOSTEL $

(☎012-362 5343; www.pumbas.co.za; 1232 Arcadia St, Hatfield; camping/dm R100/170, s/d with shared bathroom R300/400; P 📶 🏊) Although this budget-friendly hostel won't knock your socks off, it features an assortment of tidy and serviceable private rooms and dorms and is optimally placed in Hatfield, a short stroll from the Gauteng station. There's a kitchen for guest use and a pocket-sized pool.

**1322 Backpackers International** HOSTEL $

(☎012-362 3905; www.1322backpackers.com; 1322 Arcadia St, Hatfield; dm R170-190, r R550, s/d with shared bathroom from R250/450, all incl breakfast; P @ 📶 🏊) This hostel is a welcoming retreat, where travellers congregate around a backyard pool and a buzzing little bar. You can stay in neat three- to eight-bed dorms, or smallish, converted wood-and-brick sheds at the bottom of the garden (chilly in winter, a bit stifling in summer). Shared bathrooms are clean and all guests have kitchen access. Continental breakfast is included.

★**Foreigners Friend Guesthouse** GUESTHOUSE $$

(☎082 458 4951; www.foreignersfriends.co.za; 409A Om die Berg St, Lynnwood; s/d incl breakfast from R850/1150; P ❄ 📶 🏊) Character and charm – somewhere between a boutique hotel and a B&B, this enchanting abode is an oasis of tranquillity in a wonderfully quiet neighbourhood. It has 10 spacious, well-organised rooms; a well-furnished ground-floor living area; a lush garden; and a spiffing swimming pool. A beautifully presented breakfast is served on a breezy terrace.

## Eating

**Café Riche** BISTRO $

(☎012-328 3173; 2 WF Nkomo St/Church St; mains R45-90; ⏰6am-6pm; 📶) This historic, early 20th-century European bistro in the heart of Church Sq is the ideal place to sip beer and watch the South African capital roll through its day. The street tables are quickly nabbed by local office workers and politicians, while inside the atmospheric bar, unhurried staff serve sandwiches, pastries, salads and very simple bistro meals.

★**Carbon Bistro** STEAK $$

(☎012-340 0029; www.carbonbistro.co.za; 279 Dey St, Brooklyn; mains R80-170; ⏰11am-11pm Mon-Sat, to 3pm Sun) This places oozes hipster chic, with its minimalist decor, craft-beer taps, gin bar and cuts of steak you've never heard of. Knowledgable, friendly staff will explain the meaty menu and pour bespoke cocktails featuring a range of South African gins. And if all that seems too much, grab a draught G&T and watch the world go by from the patio.

**Pacha's** SOUTH AFRICAN $$$

(☎012-460 3220; www.pachas.co.za; 27 Maroelana St, Hazelwood; mains R95-220; ⏰noon-2.30pm & 6-9.30pm Mon-Fri, 6-9.30pm Sat, noon-2.30pm Sun) Fashionable Pacha's is the address of choice for those looking for both style and substance. It's a pleasant modern restaurant

## Pretoria

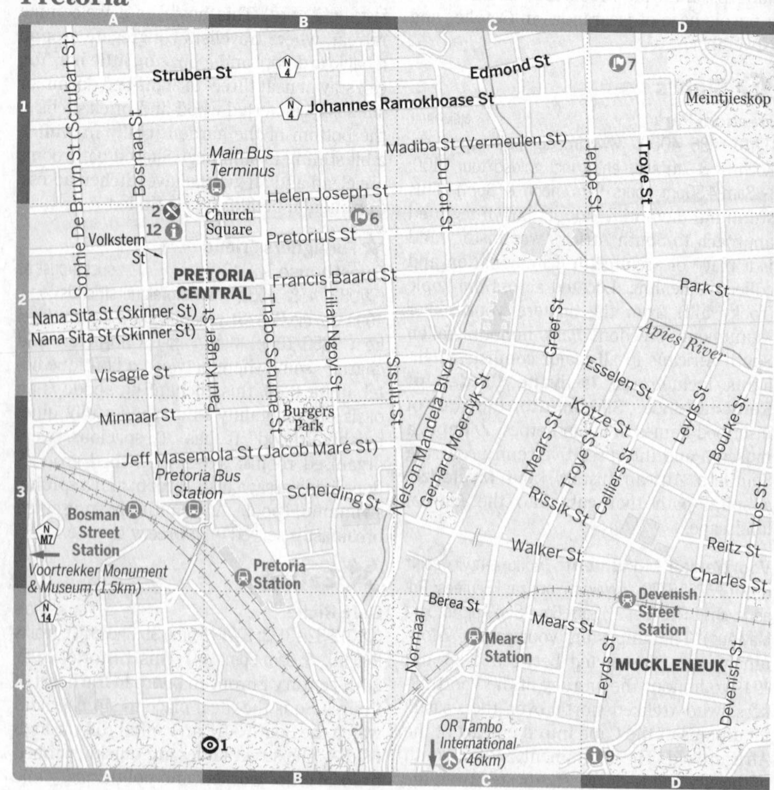


with large picture windows, an aquarium and quality furniture, but high-quality meat dishes, including some traditional fare, are the main attraction here. Feeling more surf than turf? There's also a good selection of seafood dishes.

## Drinking & Nightlife

Hatfield has plenty of bars, restaurants and clubs catering for all types. Hatfield Sq is a university-student stronghold after dark. There are some hip places in Menlo Park and Brooklyn.

**★ Capital Craft** CRAFT BEER

(☎012-424 8601; www.capitalcraft.co.za; Greenlyn Village Centre, cnr Thomas Edison St & 12th St East, Menlo Park; ⏰noon-midnight Tue, 10.30am-midnight Wed-Sat, 10.30am-8pm Sun) Pretoria's premier beer hang-out is a huge place with long tables, both inside the cool bar and out in the garden, that are perpetually packed. The focus here is craft beer from around the country. The selection is impressive – try a few tasters before ordering a pint. Want something to soak up all that ale? The pulled-pork sandwich is superb.

## Information

### MEDICAL SERVICES

**Hatfield Clinic** (☎012-362 7180; www.hatmed.co.za; 454 Hilda St; ⏰8am-7pm Mon-Thu, to 6pm Fri, to 1pm Sat, to noon Sun) A well-known suburban clinic.

**Tshwane District Hospital** (☎012-354 5958; Dr Savage Rd) For medical emergencies.

### TOURIST INFORMATION

**SANParks** (SANParks; ☎012-428 9111; www.sanparks.org; 643 Leyds St, Muckleneuk; ⏰office 7.30am-3.45pm Mon-Fri, call centre 7.30am-5pm Mon-Fri, 8am-1pm Sat) Your best bet for all wildlife-reserve bookings and enquiries.

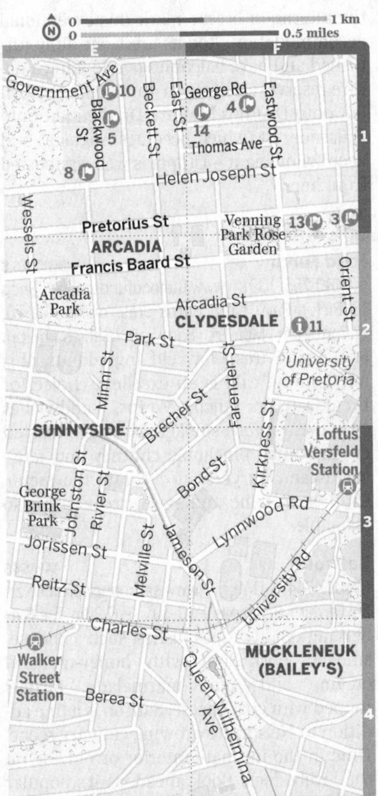


## Pretoria

**Sights**

1 Freedom Park .......... B4

**Eating**

2 Café Riche .......... A2

**Information**

3 Australian High Commission .......... F1
4 French Embassy .......... F1
5 German Embassy .......... E1
6 Lesothan High Commission .......... B2
7 Mozambican High Commission .......... D1
8 Namibian High Commission .......... E1
9 South African National Parks .......... D4
10 Swazi High Commission .......... E1
11 Tourist Information Centre (Hatfield Branch) .......... F2
12 Tourist Information Centre (Main Office) .......... A2
13 US Embassy .......... F1
14 Zimbabwean Embassy .......... F1

**Tourist Information Centre** (☎012-358 1430; www.tshwanetourism.com; Old Nederlandsche Bank Bldg, Church Sq; ⏰7.30am-4pm Mon-Fri) Parking here can be tricky. There's another branch in Hatfield (☎012-358 1675; www.tshwanetourism.com; Kingston House, 311 Eastwood St, Hatfield; ⏰7.30am-4pm Mon-Fri).

## Getting There & Away

### BUS

The **Pretoria Bus Station** (Railway St) is next to Pretoria's train station. Most Translux, City to City, Intercape and Greyhound services running from Jo'burg to Durban, the South Coast and Cape Town originate in Pretoria.

Baz Bus will pick up and drop off at Pretoria hostels.

### TRAIN

The Gautrain service offers regular high-speed connections with Hatfield, Johannesburg (Park Station, Rosebank and Sandton) and onward to the airport. The fare from Pretoria to Sandton is R57. For long distances, Shosholoza Meyl trains running through Pretoria are the *Trans Karoo* (daily from Pretoria to Cape Town) and the *Komati* (daily from Jo'burg to Komatipoort via Nelspruit).

Because of a high incidence of crime, we don't recommend travelling between Pretoria and Jo'burg by Metro.

## Getting Around

### BUS

There's an extensive network of local buses. A booklet of timetables and route maps is available from the enquiry office in the **main bus terminus** (☎012-308 0839; Church Sq) or from pharmacies.

### TAXI

You can get a metered taxi from **Rixi Taxis** (☎086 100 7494; www.rixitaxi.co.za; per km around R10). Locals tend to opt for Uber, which is operational in Pretoria.

# MPUMALANGA

Mpumalanga is one of South Africa's smallest provinces and one of its most exciting. Visually it is a simply beautiful region, with vistas of mountains, lush, green valleys and a collection of cool-climate towns. Its natural assets make it a prime target for outdoor enthusiasts, who head here to abseil down waterfalls, throw themselves off cliffs, negotiate rivers by raft, inner tube or canoe, and hike or bike numerous wilderness trails.

Mpumalanga's major draw, though, is the massive Blyde River Canyon, which carves its way spectacularly through the Drakensberg Escarpment. It is one of South Africa's iconic sights and on a clear day one of the many vantage points can leave you breathless.

And, of course, the province provides access to the southern half of Kruger National Park, with an excellent selection of lodges and wilderness activities right on the mighty park's doorstep.

## Nelspruit (Mbombela)

POP 58,700

Nelspruit (now officially called Mbombela, though locals rarely use the new moniker) is Mpumalanga's largest town and the provincial capital. While not unpleasant, it's more a place to get things done than a worthwhile destination for tourists. There are, however, good accommodation options and a couple of excellent places to eat, so it makes a good-enough stopover on the way elsewhere. It's also a good place to organise a trip to Kruger National Park.

### Sights

**Chimpanzee Eden** ZOO

(☎079 777 1514; www.chimpeden.com; Rte 40; adult/child R190/85) This chimp centre, 12km south of Nelspruit on Rte 40, acts as a sanctuary for rescued chimpanzees. Here you can see chimps in a semiwild environment and learn about the primates' behaviour and plight. The entry fee includes a guided tour (at 10am, noon and 2pm).

### Sleeping

**Nelspruit Backpackers** HOSTEL $

(☎013-741 2237; www.nelback.co.za; Andries Pretorius St; camping/dm R100/160, s/d with shared bathroom R280/450) With a large pool and deck overlooking the adjoining nature reserve, this family home in suburbia is a relaxing budget option. There are rooms in the main house, which has a communal lounge and kitchen, and a couple more in the garden. Tours to Blyde River Canyon and Kruger National Park are available.

**★Utopia in Africa** GUESTHOUSE $$$

(☎013-745 7714; www.utopiainafrica.co.za; 6 Daleen St; s/d incl breakfast from R910/1480; ❄📶🏊) Simplicity, elegance and a masterly design that keeps the premises cool using the afternoon breeze mark this exceptional accommodation. Rooms are beautifully furnished and have balconies overlooking a nature reserve. Head south on Madiba Dr, turn left onto Dr Enos Mabuza Dr, then left onto Halssnoer St (which becomes Augusta) and keep following it – Utopia is well signposted from here.

### Eating

**Food Fundi** SANDWICHES $

(☎013-755 1091; www.thefoodfundi.co.za; Shop 16, Pick n Pay Centre, Sitrus Cres; mains R40-70; ⏰7am-6pm Mon-Fri, 8am-5pm Sat, 8am-2pm Sun) Using fresh lowveld ingredients, this outstanding cafe is an excellent choice for breakfast or lunch. Wraps, sandwiches (try the *rooibos*-smoked chicken, toasted cashew nuts, pineapple chutney and feta), salads and burgers all decorate the menu. Craft beer, wine and sweet treats are also available.

**Saffron** TAPAS $$

(☎013-744 1146; www.saffronnelspruit.co.za; 56 Ferreira St; tapas R30-60; ⏰6-9pm Tue-Sat) Serving quality tapas dishes, such as house-smoked pork loin with honey-mustard cream, and onion-marmalade tartlets topped with goat cheese, Saffron is a fine addition to Nelspruit's growing culinary scene. Dine in the intimate interior or outside on the lovely deck. Book ahead, as it's popular with locals and visitors alike.

### Information

**Lowveld Tourism** (☎013-755 1988; www.krugerlowveld.com; cnr Madiba & Samora Machel Drs; ⏰7am-6pm Mon-Fri, 8am-1.30pm Sat) This helpful office at Nelspruit Crossing Mall (behind News Cafe) takes bookings for all national parks, including Kruger, and can help arrange accommodation and tours.

**Safcol** (South African Forestry Co Ltd; ☎013-754 2724; www.safcol.co.za; 10 Streak St) Provides information and takes bookings for hikes in the area.

### Getting There & Away

**AIR**

**Kruger Mpumalanga International Airport** (KMIA; ☎013-753 7500; www.kmiairport.co.za) is the closest commercial airport to Nelspruit.

**Airlink** (☎013-750 2531, 0861 606 606; www.flyairlink.com) There are daily flights with Airlink to Jo'burg (R1600 to R2200, one hour), Cape Town (R3600 to R4400, 2½ hours) and Durban (R2500 to R3200, 1 hour).

### BUS

The major bus companies, including **Greyhound** (☎083 915 9000; www.greyhound.co.za) and Translux (p913), all stop in Nelspruit as they travel between Jo'burg/Pretoria (R315, five hours) and Maputo (Mozambique; R320, three hours) via Nelspruit. Tickets are sold at the offices in Promenade Mall (Samora Machel Dr).

# Graskop

POP 4000

While it's a popular stop with the tour buses, little Graskop somehow seems to swallow them quite well, leaving plenty of room around town for everyone else. The compact town is one of the most appealing in the area, with a sunny disposition, sleepy backstreets and gently sloping hills in every direction. It's also a useful base for exploring the Blyde River Canyon, and the nearby views over the edge of the Drakensberg Escarpment are magnificent.

## Activities

There's good hiking and mountain biking in the area. **Panorama Info** (☎013-767 1377; www.panoramainfo.co.za; cnr Louis Trichardt & Kerk Sts; ⏲9am-4.30pm Mon-Fri, to 4pm Sat & Sun) can point you in the right direction, or you can hire bikes (per day R200) from Graskop Valley View Backpackers.

**Big Swing** ADVENTURE SPORTS

(☎079 779 8713; www.bigswing.co.za; single/tandem jump R350/R600, zip line only R100; ⏲Tue-Sun 9am-4pm) One of the highest cable gorge swings in the world, Big Swing has a free fall of 68m (that's like falling 19 storeys in less than three seconds) into Graskop Gorge. You then swing like a pendulum across the width of the gorge – which gives you an outstanding view. It's 1km out of town on the Hazyview road.

## Sleeping

**★Graskop Valley View Backpackers** HOSTEL $

(☎013-767 1112; www.valley-view.co.za; 47 De Lange St; camping/dm/r R100/150/390, s/d with shared bathroom R260/320; ❄📶🏊) This friendly backpackers has a variety of rooms in excellent condition, plus rondavels and a self-catering flat. The owners can organise adventure tours and rent out mountain bikes for private use (per day R200). Highly recommended. Take the road to Sabie, turn left at the first four-way stop and take another left on De Lange St.

**★Graskop Hotel** HOTEL $$

(☎013-767 1244; www.graskophotel.co.za; cnr Hoof & Louis Trichardt Sts; s/d incl breakfast R770/1100; ❄📶🏊) This classy hotel is one of our favourites in the province. Rooms here are slick, stylish and individual; several feature art and design by contemporary South African artists. Rooms out the back are little country cottages with dollhouse-like furniture (but are extremely comfortable), an impression exemplified by the glass doors opening onto the lush garden at the rear. Book ahead.

## Eating

**Harrie's Pancakes** CRÊPES $

(cnr Louis Trichardt & Kerk Sts; pancakes R50-80; ⏲8am-7pm) The chic white minimalist interior, full of modern art and quirky touches, is somewhat at odds with the cuisine. You won't find breakfast-style pancakes here but mostly savoury and exotic fillings, as well as some sweet offerings. Its reputation perhaps outdoes what it delivers, but Harrie's is a nice spot for a breakfast croissant and fresh-brewed coffee.

## Information

### MONEY

**First National Bank** (Kerk St) There's an ATM just north of Louis Trichardt St.

### TOURIST INFORMATION

There is no official tourist office and the private enterprises seems to open and close frequently. Panorama Info has some pamphlets and maps.

## Getting There & Away

The **minibus shared taxi stand** (Hoof St) is at the south end of town, with daily morning departures to Pilgrim's Rest (R12, 30 minutes), Sabie (R30, 40 minutes) and Hazyview (R40, one hour).

# KRUGER NATIONAL PARK

In terms of wildlife, **Kruger** (SAN Parks; ☎012-428 9111; www.sanparks.org/parks/kruger) is one of the world's greatest national parks. The diversity, density and sheer numbers of animals is almost unparalleled, and all of Africa's iconic safari species – elephant,

**ENTRY**

Park entry for international visitors costs R304/152 per adult/child per day or for an overnight stay; SANParks' **Wild Card** (pwww.sanparks.org/wild; year pass for 1/couple/family foreigner is R2210/3455/4130) applies. During school holidays park stays are limited to 10 days, and five days at any one rest camp (10 days if you're camping).

Throughout the year authorities restrict the total number of visitors, so in the high season arrive early if you don't have a booking. Bicycles and motorcycles are not permitted.

lion, leopard, cheetah, rhino, buffalo, giraffe, hippo and zebra – live out their dramatic days here, along with a supporting cast of 137 other mammals and over 500 varieties of bird.

## Sights

Kruger encompasses a variety of landscapes and ecosystems, with each favouring particular species. That said, elephants, impalas, buffaloes, Burchell's zebras, wildebeest, kudus, waterbucks, baboons, vervet monkeys, leopards and smaller predators are widespread, and birdlife is incredible, especially along waterways.

## Activities

### Wildlife Walks

Most SANParks rest camps offer three-hour **morning bush walks** (R500) with knowledgeable armed guides, as do all of the lodges in the private concessions. Berg-en-dal, Letaba and Skukuza currently also offer **afternoon walks** (R400), and Olifants offers **river walks** (R275) too. SANParks options can be booked in advance or arranged at the relevant camp upon arrival.

All walking groups limit numbers to eight participants, and no children under 12 are permitted.

### Wildlife Drives

Self-driving is fantastic for so many reasons, but do strongly consider joining some guided drives – they are a great way to maximise your safari experience.

SANParks operates three-hour **sunrise drives** and **sunset drives** at almost all rest camps, bushveld camps and many park gates. Costs vary between R280 and R390, depending on whether a 10- or 20-seat vehicle is used. Two-hour **night drives** (R230 to R320), which are great for nocturnal animals such as bush babies, hippos and big cats, are common too. Book in advance or upon arrival. Children under the age of six are not permitted.

## Courses

**EcoTraining** OUTDOORS
(☎013-752 2532; www.ecotraining.co.za) Various one-week to one-month field-guide training courses for budding professionals and enthusiastic amateurs. Go Bear Grylls wild in the bush for a week on the Wilderness Trails Skills option.

## Sleeping

**★Letaba Rest Camp** BUNGALOW, CAMPGROUND **$$**
(☎013-735 6636, reservations 012-428 9111; www.sanparks.org; camping per site R305, d safari tents/huts with shared bathroom R685/735, bungalows with/without kitchen from R1305/1215; ❄☒) One of Kruger's best rest camps, this leafy Letaba River haven has shady lawns, resident bushbucks, SANParks' most attractive pools and a wide variety of accommodation, with great views from various bungalows (No 32, of BD3U class is best) and six-person cottages (ask for newly refurbished No 101, class FQ6). There's a **Mugg & Bean** (www.themugg.com; mains R55-140), too.

**★Satara Rest Camp** BUNGALOW, CAMPGROUND **$$**
(☎013-735 6306, reservations 012-428 9111; www.sanparks.org; camping per site from R265, d bungalows with/without kitchen R1355/1220; ❄☒) Satara – the second-largest option after Skukuza – may lack the riverside views of other camps, but it's optimally situated in the heart of 'big cat' territory, with open plains making viewing easier. An incongruous **Debonairs Pizza** (www.debonairspizza.co.za; pizzas R35-80) outlet joins Mugg & Bean here.

**★Olifants Rest Camp** BUNGALOW, COTTAGE **$$**
(☎013-735 6606, reservations 012-428 9111; www.sanparks.org; d bungalows with/without kitchenette R1460/1120; ☒) High atop a bluff, this camp offers fantastic views down to the Olifants River, where elephants, hippos and numerous other animals roam.

Bungalow Nos 1 and 9 (of BBD2V class) have the best views, as do the eight-person Nshawu and Lebombo self-catering guesthouses (from R4300). There's also a new camp pool.

**★Lower Sabie Rest Camp** BUNGALOW, CAMPGROUND **$$**
(☎013-735 6056, reservations 012-428 9111; www.sanparks.org; camping per site R305, huts with shared bathroom R595, d safari tents/bungalows with kitchen R955/1310; ❄☒) Kruger's most popular rest camp is set on a gorgeous bend of the Sabie River that attracts elephants, hippos, buffaloes and other animals. LST2U-class safari tents and BD2U/BD3U bungalows have river views. The riverside dining area of the Mugg & Bean is one of Kruger's most scenic, though the pool area is less so.

### ℹ Getting There & Away

There are nine South African entry gates with unified hours of operation, which vary slightly by season (opening times range from 5.30am to 6am; closing times from 5.30pm to 6.30pm). Camp gate times are almost in complete unison with the park gates, and fines are issued for late arrival.

It's also possible to enter Kruger from Mozambique at the Giriyondo and Pafuri border crossings (p952).

# NORTHERN CAPE

With only a million people inhabiting its 373,000 sq km, the Northern Cape is South Africa's last great frontier. Its scattered towns are hundreds of kilometres apart, connected by empty roads across the sublime, surreal wilderness expanses of Namakwa, the Kalahari and Upper Karoo. Under the remorseless sun, vehicles share park roads with lions, dune boards swish down roaring sands, and Kimberley's pubs serve cold beer as they have since the 19th-century diamond rush.

## Kimberley

POP 97,000

Kimberley, the provincial capital, is the centre of the region known as the Diamond Fields. The city that gave birth to De Beers and 'A Diamond is Forever' remains a captivating place, with a Wild West vibe.

The Northern Cape's only real city is also home to fantastic museums, some wonderful accommodation and Galeshewe, a township with plenty of its own history.

### Sights

**★Big Hole** MUSEUM
(☎053-839 4600; www.thebighole.co.za; West Circular Rd; adult/child R100/60; ⏲8am-5pm) Although the R50 million that turned the Big Hole into a world-class tourist destination came from De Beers, touring the world's largest hand-dug hole gives an honest impression of the mining industry's chequered past in Kimberley. Visits start with an entertaining 20-minute film about mining conditions and characters in late 19th-century Kimberley, and a walk along the Big Hole viewing platform. The open-air steel contraption, jutting over the 1.6km-round, 215m-deep chasm, enhances the vertigo-inducing view of the 40m-deep turquoise water. Tours run on the hour.

**Wildebeest Kuil Rock Art Centre** ARCHAEOLOGICAL SITE
(☎053-833 7069; www.wildebeestkuil.itgo.com; Rte 31; adult/child R25/12; ⏲9am-4pm Mon-Fri, by apartment Sat & Sun) On a site owned by the !Xun and Khwe San people, who were relocated from Angola and Namibia in 1990, this small sacred hill has 400-plus rock engravings dating back millenniums. Visits start with a video detailing the troubled history of the !Xun and Khwe, followed by an excellent interpretative **guided tour**.

The centre is 16km northwest of town, en route to Barkly West. A minibus shared taxi costs R35; a private taxi costs R360 return, including waiting time.

### Tours

Local guides **Steve Lunderstedt** (☎083 732 3189; from R200; ⏲6.30pm) and **Jaco Powell** (☎082 572 0065; per person R200) both offer historical and ghost-themed walks around the Kimberley area.

The Kimberley Meander (www.kimberleymeander.co.za) website has information on other local guided tours.

### Sleeping

**★75 on Milner** GUESTHOUSE **$$**
(☎082 686 5994; www.milnerlodge.co.za; 75 Milner St; s/d from R720/890; ❄📶☒) Highly

recommended by travellers, this very friendly guesthouse has spacious, well-equipped rooms with fridge, microwave and cable TV. Rooms are set around a small patio and there's a good-size pool. Little touches set it apart, including a welcome drink, snacks in the room and superb information on local attractions.

★ **Kimberley Club** BOUTIQUE HOTEL **$$$**
(053-832 4224; www.kimberleyclub.co.za; 72 Du Toitspan Rd; s/d from R1010/1450; ) Founded by Rhodes and his diamond cronies as a private club in 1881, and rebuilt following a fire in 1896, this reputedly haunted building became a hotel in 2004. The 21 bedrooms are period-elegant, and offer the chance to pad in the slipper-steps of illustrious visitors such as Queen Elizabeth II. The entrance is on Currey St. Breakfast is R110.

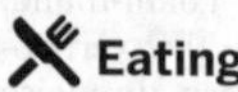

## Eating

**Lemon Tree** CAFE **$**
(053-831 7730; www.nclemontree.co.za; Angel St; mains R50-90; 8am-5pm Mon-Fri, to 1.30pm Sat) A long-established cafe offering light lunches, a range of cakes and a hangover breakfast, in case you've overdone it in Kimberley's historic pubs.

★ **Halfway House** PUB FOOD **$$**
(053-831 6324; www.halfwayhousehotel.co.za; 229 Du Toitspan Rd, cnr Carrington Rd; mains R60-140; 11am-11pm; ) Soak up Kimberley's diamonds-and-drink history – quite literally – in this watering hole dating to 1872. It might be the world's only 'drive-in' bar, stemming from Rhodes' insistence on being served beer without dismounting his horse. The interiors are beautifully historic, with spittoons along the base of the scarred, wood-backed bar, as well as old liquor ads and frosted windows etched with Rhodes quotes.

## Information

**Diamond (Diamantveld) Visitors Centre**
(053-830 6779; www.kimberley.co.za; 121 Bultfontein Rd; 8am-5pm Mon-Fri) Pick up the *Kimberley Meander* brochure, with suggested self-guided walking and driving tours.

## Getting There & Around

### AIR

Taxis connect the city centre with the airport, 6km south.

**SA Express** (053-838 3337; www.flyexpress.aero) Flies to/from Jo'burg (R1000, one hour) and Cape Town (R1000, 1½ hours).

### BUS

**Tickets 4 Africa** (053-832 6040; tickets4africa@hotmail.com; 121 Bultfontein Rd, Diamond Visitors Centre) sells tickets for **Greyhound** (p913), **Intercape** (p909) and **City to City** (p914). There are direct services to Cape Town (R550, 12 hours) and Jo'burg (R400, seven hours). Intercape runs services to Upington (R340, seven hours) on Friday and Sunday via Bloemfontein (R300, two hours).

### TRAIN

Shosholoza Meyl operates trans-Karoo trains that stop in Kimberley en route between Jo'burg (economy/sleeper R160/240, eight hours) and Cape Town (R300/470, 17½ hours).

# Upington

POP 57,000

Home to lush gardens and hundreds of date-palm trees, Upington is a prosperous, orderly town on the banks of the Gariep (Orange) River. The central hub for the Green Kalahari, it's a good place to recoup after a long desert slog – although it gets blazing hot in summer. Wide boulevards, slightly cluttered with supermarkets and chain stores, fill the town centre. Step onto a side street near the river, however, and you'll enter a peaceful world where refreshing, watery views and rows of palms hold quiet court.

## Tours

**Kalahari Safaris** ADVENTURE
(054-332 5653; www.kalaharisafaris.co.za) Runs small-group (two to five people) trips to locations including the Kgalagadi and Augrabies Falls parks, Witsand Nature Reserve and Namakwa. Tours last from one to seven days and cater to all budgets.

## Sleeping

**Island View House** B&B **$$**
(054-331 1328; www.islandviewhouse.co.za; 10 Murray Ave; s/d incl breakfast R700/900; ) The Mocké family offers a friendly welcome and modern rooms with showers and a shared lounge, kitchen and balcony.

★ **Le Must River Residence** GUESTHOUSE **$$$**
(054-332 3971; www.lemustupington.com; 14 Budler St; s/d incl breakfast from 1190/1700; ) This elegant riverside getaway has 11 African-themed rooms with antique fur-

nishings and crisp linen. Sitting rooms and terraces open onto the artful garden with its Italianate pool.

### Eating

**Bi-Lo Bistro** INTERNATIONAL, SUSHI $$
(054-338 0616; 9 Green Point Rd; mains R60-120; 7am-10pm; ) Birds hop between palm trees and kids play on the swings at this popular spot in the suburbs. The vast menu features everything from steak to sushi – the latter is surprisingly decent.

### Information

**Upington Tourist Office** (054-338 7152; www.northerncape.org.za; Mutual St; 7.30am-4.30pm Mon-Fri) This office's location in the municipal building is temporary; there are plans to move it back to the library.

### Getting There & Away

**AIR**

**South African Airways** (0861 606 606; www.flysaa.com) flies to/from Jo'burg (R2200, 1½ hours) and Cape Town (R2500, 1½ hours). The airport is 6km north of town, off the N10.

**BUS**

Intercape buses go to Bloemfontein (R390, nine hours, Thursday and Saturday), Cape Town (R600, 14 hours, Thursday, Friday and Sunday), Jo'burg (R750, 11 hours, daily) and Windhoek, Namibia (R660, 12 hours, Tuesday, Thursday, Friday and Sunday). Buses leave from the Intercape office on Lutz St.

## Kgalagadi Transfrontier Park

A long, hot road leads between crimson dunes from Upington to Africa's first transfrontier **park** (054-561 2000; www.sanparks.org/parks/kgalagadi/; adult/child R304/152), one of the world's last great, unspoilt ecosystems. The Kgalagadi is a wild land of harsh extremes and frequent droughts, where shifting red and white sands meet thorn trees and dry riverbeds. Yet despite the desolate landscape, it's teeming with wildlife. From prides of black-maned lions to packs of howling spotted hyenas, there are some 1775 predators here. It's one of the best places in the world to spot big cats, especially cheetahs. Add in giant, orange-ball sunsets and black-velvet night skies studded with twinkling stars, and you'll feel like you've entered the Africa of story books.

### Activities

The park operates sunrise, sunset, night and full-morning **wildlife drives** (adult/child from R220/110) and three-hour **walking safaris** (adult from R330, no one under 12 years). Both depart from Twee Rivieren, Nossob Rest Camp, Mata-Mata Rest Camp and Kalahari Tented Camp.

### Sleeping

**Twee Rivieren** CHALET $$
(camping from R265, cottages/chalets from R1275/1635; ) The largest camp in the park is also the most convenient, located next to the park entrance and with the most facilities. The cottages have between two and four single beds; the chalet has six. The cheaper campsites don't have power.

★**Kalahari Tented Camp** CAMPGROUND $$$
(d safari tents from R1500; ) Kgalagadi's most luxurious wilderness camp has 14 stilted desert tents with rustic furnishings and views of a water hole in the Auob riverbed – a popular hang-out for herds of wildebeest. It provides a remote, rustic feel while being only 3km from the conveniences of Mata-Mata (and over three hours from Twee Rivieren Gate).

### Information

**Botswana Wildlife** (+267 318 0774; dwnp@gov.bw; Gabarone)

**South African National Parks** (SANParks; 012-428 9111; www.sanparks.org/parks/kgalagadi)

### Getting There & Away

Twee Rivieren Gate is 270km northwest of Upington on the tarred Rte 360.

A 4WD vehicle is useful but not essential – the park's four main routes are gravel/sand roads but they're in decent condition and can be driven in a 2WD if you take care.

# UNDERSTAND SOUTH AFRICA

## South Africa Today

More than two decades after Nelson Mandela came to power (he was president of South Africa from 1994 to 1999 and passed away in 2013), life in South Africa remains dominated by social inequality. Central Cape Town's mountain and beach communities contrast with the townships sprawling across the Cape Flats, lining the N2 with shacks and portaloos. Seeing First-World wealth alongside African poverty is confronting for first-time visitors. Yet every day, millions of South Africans embrace progress by trying to understand and respect the vastly different outlooks of people from other economic and racial groups.

In the 2016 municipal elections, the Democratic Alliance (DA), which already governs the Western Cape, made major gains in African National Congress (ANC) strongholds, particularly in major metropolitan areas such as Tshwane (Pretoria), Johannesburg and Nelson Mandela Bay (Port Elizabeth). Short of the required majority, the DA formed alliances with other parties, including Julius Malema's Economic Freedom Fighters (EFF), best known for their Zimbabwe-style policies of land reform and nationalisation. Almost immediately after taking office, the DA cut lavish spending for city officials, reassigning luxury cars meant for government officials to police officers in the antihijacking unit, and even laid corruption charges against the previous adminstration.

# History

South Africa's history extends back to around 40,000 BC when the San people first settled Southern Africa. By AD 500, Bantu-speaking peoples had arrived from West Africa's Niger Delta.

Widespread colonial settlement of South Africa began in the 19th century. The British annexed the Cape in 1806 and when they abolished slavery in 1833, the Boers (Dutch-Afrikaner farmers) considered it an intolerable interference in their affairs. Dissatisfied with British rule, they trekked off into the interior in search of freedom. This became known as the Great Trek.

The Great Trek coincided with the *difaqane* (forced migration of the Zulu people). This gave rise to the Afrikaner myths that these Voortrekkers (pioneers) moved into unoccupied territory or arrived at much the same time as black Africans. The Boers came into this chaos in search of new lands, and the British were not far behind them. The Zulu were eventually defeated, but relations between the Boers and the British remained tense – particularly after the formation of the Boer republics of the Orange Free State and the Transvaal.

Diamonds were discovered in 1867 at Kimberley, followed by the discovery of gold in 1886 on the Witwatersrand, the area around Jo'burg. The Boer republics were flooded with British business and immigrant labourers, which created resentment among Afrikaner farmers. Wars ensued and while the Boers were victorious in the First Anglo-Boer War (known by Afrikaners as the War of Independence), the Second Anglo-Boer War (1899–1902) ended with the defeat of the Boer republics and the imposition of British rule.

## Independence & Apartheid

In 1910 the Union of South Africa was created, giving political control to the whites. Despite the moderate tone of early black resistance groups, the government reacted by intensifying repression.

The Afrikaner National Party won the election in 1948 and began to brutally enforce laws excluding nonwhites from having any political or economic power. The suppression of black resistance ranged from the Sharpeville massacre of 1960 and the shooting of high-school students in Soweto in 1976, to the forcible evacuation and bulldozing of entire urban areas, and the systematic torture – even murder – of political activists such as Steve Biko.

One of the most important organisations to oppose the racist legislation was the ANC, which took to guerrilla warfare. In the early 1960s, many ANC leaders were arrested, charged with treason and imprisoned, the most famous being Nelson Mandela.

Apartheid was entrenched even further during the early 1970s by the creation of the so-called black homelands. These were, in theory, 'independent' countries. With the creation of the homelands, all black people within white-designated South Africa were deemed foreign guest-workers and were without political rights. Any black person without a residence pass could be 'deported' to a homeland.

The UN imposed economic and political sanctions. The government made some concessions, which included the establishment of a farcical new parliament of whites, 'coloureds' (people of mixed race) and Indians – but no black people.

After the 1989 elections the new president, FW de Klerk, instituted a program that was aimed not only at dismantling the apartheid system, but also at introducing democracy. The release of political prisoners in February 1990 (including Nelson Mandela), the repeal of the Group Areas Act (which set up the homelands), and the signing of a peace accord with the ANC and other opposition groups all opened the way for hard-fought negotiations on the path to majority rule.

## The Post-Apartheid Era

The country's first democratic elections took place in 1994, with the ANC winning 62.7% of the vote; 66.7% would have enabled it to rewrite the interim constitution. The National Party won 20.4% of the vote, enough to guarantee representation in cabinet. Nelson Mandela was made president of the 'new' South Africa.

In 1999 South Africa held its second democratic elections. The National Party lost two-thirds of its seats, losing official opposition status to the Democratic Party. Thabo Mbeki, who had taken over the ANC leadership from Mandela in 1997, became president. While Mbeki was viewed with less affection by the ANC grassroots than the beloved 'Madiba' (Mandela), he was a shrewd politician, leading the ANC to a decisive victory in the 2004 elections. However, Mbeki's effective denial of the AIDS crisis invited global criticism, and his failure to condemn the forced reclamation of white-owned farms in Zimbabwe unnerved both South African landowners and foreign investors.

In 2005 Mbeki dismissed his deputy president Jacob Zuma in the wake of corruption charges against Zuma, setting off a ruthless internal ANC power struggle. In September 2008 Mbeki was asked to step down as president in an unprecedented move by the party.

Corruption charges were dropped and the ANC won the 2009 election, with Jacob Zuma declared president.

# People

The vast majority of South Africans – about 80% – are black Africans. Although subdivided into dozens of smaller groups, all ultimately trace their ancestry to the Bantu-speakers who migrated to Southern Africa in the early part of the 1st millennium AD.

During apartheid, 'coloured' was generally used as a catch-all term for anyone who didn't fit into one of the other racial categories. South Africa's roughly 4.6 million coloured people comprise about 9% of the total population.

Most of South Africa's approximately 4.6 million white people (about 9% of South Africans) are either Afrikaans-speaking descendents of the early European settlers or English-speakers. Afrikaners constitute about 5% of the country's total population.

The majority of South Africa's almost 1.3 million Asians are Indians.

# Religion

Religion plays a central role in the lives of most people in South Africa and church attendance is generally high. Christianity is dominant, with almost 80% of South Africans identifying themselves as Christians. Major South African denominations include the Dutch Reformed Church and the flamboyant Zion Christian Church (ZCC), which has up to six million followers in South Africa.

African traditional believers make up around 1% of South Africa's population, compared with 20% in neighbouring Lesotho.

# SURVIVAL GUIDE

## Directory A–Z

### ACCOMMODATION

**Backpacker hostels** Often have a bar, swimming pool and campsites; ideal for budget or solo travellers.

**Camping** Prices in reviews are per person and per night, unless otherwise noted.

**Guesthouses** Often owner-run, with comfortable rooms, hearty breakfasts and priceless local information.

**Hotels** Everything from stylish boutique hotels to vast and luxurious chains brands.

**Lodges** Can be uber-luxe or fairly rustic but tend to boast some of the best locations.

**Self-catering cottages** Usually spacious and excellent value for money.

### ACTIVITIES

Thanks to South Africa's diverse terrain and pleasant climate, almost any outdoor activity is possible to do here, from abseiling to zip lining. Highlights include hiking, horse riding, mountain biking and surfing, while wildlife possibilities include birdwatching, whale watching

### PRICE RANGES

Accommodation rates quoted are for high season (November to March), with a private bathroom. Price ranges are based on the cost of a double room.

**$** less than R700 (US$50)

**$$** R700–R1400 (US$50–100)

**$$$** more than R1400 (US$100)

In Cape Town, Johannesburg and the Garden Route, accommodation prices are higher:

**$** less than R1050 (US$75)

**$$** R1050–R2100 (US$75–150)

**$$$** more than R2100 (US$150)

The following price ranges refer to a standard main course.

**$** less than R75 (US$5)

**$$** R75–150 (US$5–10)

**$$$** more than R150 (US$10)

and general wildlife safaris. Good facilities and instruction mean that most activities are accessible to all visitors, whatever their experience level.

#### EMBASSIES & CONSULATES

Most countries have their main embassy in Pretoria, with an office or consulate in Cape Town (which may become the embassy during Cape Town's parliamentary sessions).

**Australian High Commission** (☎012-423 6000; www.southafrica.embassy.gov.au; 292 Orient St, Arcadia, Pretoria)

**Botswanan High Commission** (☎012-430 9640; www.mofaic.gov.bw; 24 Amos St, Colbyn, Pretoria) Also has a consulate in Jo'burg (Map p936; ☎011-403 3748; 2nd fl, Future Bank Bldg, 122 De Korte St, Braamfontein).

**Canadian High Commission** (☎012-422 3000; www.canadainternational.gc.ca/southafrica-afriquedusud; 1103 Arcadia St, Pretoria) Also has consulates in Cape Town (Map p904; ☎021-421 1818; 1502 Metlife Centre, Walter Sisulu Ave, Foreshore) and Durban.

**Dutch Embassy** (☎24hr 012-425 4500; http://southafrica.nlembassy.org; 210 Florence Ribeiro/Queen Wilhelmina Ave, cnr Muckleneuk St, New Muckleneuk, Pretoria) Also has missions in Cape Town (Map p904; ☎021-421 5660; http://southafrica.nlembassy.org; 100 Strand St, City Bowl; 🚉Strand) and Durban.

**French Embassy** (☎012-425 1600; www.ambafrance-rsa.org; 250 Melk St, New Muckleneuk, Pretoria) Also has consulates in Cape Town (Map p904; ☎021-423 1575; www.consulfrance-lecap.org; 78 Queen Victoria St, Gardens; 🚉Upper Long/Upper Loop) and Jo'burg (☎011-778 5600; 191 Jan Smuts Ave, Rosebank).

**German Embassy** (☎012-427 8900; www.southafrica.diplo.de; 180 Blackwood St, Arcadia, Pretoria) Also has a consulate in Cape Town (Map p904; ☎021-405 3052; www.southafrica.diplo.de; 19th fl, Triangle House, 22 Riebeeck St, Foreshore; 🚉Lower Long/Lower Loop).

**Irish Embassy** (☎012-452 1000; www.embassyofireland.org.za; 2nd fl, Parkdev Bldg, Brooklyn Bridge Office Park, 570 Fehrsen St, Brooklyn, Pretoria) Also has a liaison office in Cape Town (☎021-419 0637, 021-419 0636; www.embassyofireland.org.za; 19th fl, LG Building, 1 Thibault Sq; ⏰9am-noon Mon-Fri).

**Lesothan High Commission** (☎012-460 7648; www.foreign.gov.ls/home; 391 Anderson St, Menlo Park, Pretoria) Also has embassies in Jo'burg (Map p936; ☎011-339 3653; 76 Juta St, Indent House, Braamfontein) and Durban (☎031-307 2168; 2nd fl, Westguard House, cnr Dr Pixley KaSeme/West St & Dorothy Nyembe/Gardiner St).

**Mozambican High Commission** (☎012-401 0300; www.embamoc.co.za; 529 Edmond St, Arcadia, Pretoria) Also has consulates in Cape Town (Map p904; ☎021-418 2131; 3rd flr, 1 Thibault Square, Long St, City Bowl), Nelspruit (☎013-753 2089; mozconns@mweb.co.za; 32 Bell St; ⏰8am-3pm Mon-Fri), Durban (☎031-304 0200; Room 520, 320 Dr Pixley KaSeme/West St) and Jo'burg (Map p932; ☎011-336 1819; 18 Hurlingham Rd, Illovo).

**Namibian High Commission** (☎012-481 9100; www.namibia.org.za; 197 Blackwood St, Arcadia, Pretoria)

**New Zealand High Commission** (☎012-435 9000; www.nzembassy.com/south-africa; 125 Middle St, New Muckleneuk, Pretoria) Also has an honorary consul in Cape Town (☎021-683 5762; Eastry Rd, Claremont).

**Swazi High Commission** (☎012-344 1910; www.swazihighcom.co.za; 715 Government Ave, Arcadia, Pretoria; ⏰8.30am-4.30pm) Also has a consulate in Jo'burg (Map p936; ☎011-403 2050; www.swazihighcom.co.za; Braampark Forum, 33 Hoofd St, Braamfontein; ⏰8.30am-4.30pm).

**UK High Commission** (☎012-421 7500; http://ukinsouthafrica.fco.gov.uk; 255 Hill St, Arcadia, Pretoria) Also has consulates in Cape Town (Map p904; ☎021-405 2400; www.gov.uk/government/world/organisations/british-consulate-general-cape-town; 15th fl, Norton Rose House, 8 Riebeeck St, Foreshore;

Adderley) and Durban (031-305 7600; http://za.usembassy.gov; 31st fl, Delta Towers, 303 Dr Pixley KaSeme St).

**US Embassy** (012-431 4000; http://za.usembassy.gov; 877 Pretorius St, Arcadia, Pretoria) Also has consulates in Cape Town (021-702 7300; https://za.usembassy.gov; 2 Reddam Ave, Westlake), Durban (031-304 4737; 333 Smith St, 29th fl, Durban Bay House) and Johannesburg (Map p932; 011-290 3000; http://za.usembassy.gov; 1 Sandton Dr, Sandhurst).

**Zimbabwean Embassy** (012-342 5125; www.zimfa.gov.zw; 798 Merton Ave, Arcadia, Pretoria) Also has a consulate (Map p932; 011-615 5879; www.zimbabweconsulate.co.za; 13a Boeing Rd W, Bedfordview; 8.30-noon Mon, Tue, Thu & Fri) in Jo'burg.

## EMERGENCY

| | |
|---|---|
| Ambulance | 10177 |
| Emergencies (from mobiles) | 112 |
| Police | 10111 |

## INTERNET ACCESS

- Internet access is widely available in South Africa, though connections may be slower than you're used to at home.
- Accommodation options usually offer wi-fi or, less commonly, a computer with internet access for guest use.
- Look out for the AlwaysOn (www.alwayson.co.za) network, which generally allows you 30 minutes' of free connection per hot spot if you sign up. It's available at airports and some cafes, malls and banks.

## MONEY

ATMs are found throughout the country and cards are widely accepted. Inform your bank of your travel plans before leaving home to avoid declined transactions.

### Exchange Rates

| | | |
|---|---|---|
| Australia | A$1 | R10.29 |
| Canada | C$1 | R9.98 |
| Euro zone | €1 | R14.74 |
| Japan | ¥100 | R12.78 |
| Lesotho | M1 | R1 |
| New Zealand | NZ$1 | R9.78 |
| Swaziland | E1 | R1 |
| UK | £1 | R16.56 |
| USA | US$1 | R13.35 |

For current exchange rates, see www.xe.com.

## OPENING HOURS

**Banks** 9am–3.30pm Monday–Friday, 9am–11am Saturday

**Bars** 4pm–2am

**Businesses and Shopping** 8.30am–5pm Monday–Friday, 8.30am–1pm Saturday; many supermarkets also 9am–noon Sunday; major shopping centres until 9pm daily

**Cafes** 8am–5pm

**Government Offices** 8am–3pm Monday–Friday, 8am–noon Saturday

**Post Offices** 8.30am–4.30pm Monday–Friday, 8.30am–noon Saturday

**Restaurants** 11.30am–3pm & 6.30pm–10pm (last orders); many open 3pm–7pm

## PUBLIC HOLIDAYS

**New Year's Day** 1 January

**Human Rights Day** 21 March

**Good Friday** March/April

**Family Day** March/April

**Freedom Day** 27 April

**Workers' Day** 1 May

**Youth Day** 16 June

**National Women's Day** 9 August

**Heritage Day** 24 September

**Day of Reconciliation** 16 December

**Christmas Day** 25 December

**Day of Goodwill** 26 December

## SAFETY

Caused by South Africa's poverty and social inequality, crime is the national obsession. Apart from car accidents, it's the major risk that you'll face here. However, try to keep things in perspective: despite the statistics and newspaper headlines, the majority of travellers visit without incident. The risks are highest in Jo'burg, followed by some townships and other urban centres.

## TELEPHONE

South Africa's country code is 027 and the international access code is 00.

South Africa has good telephone facilities, operated by Telkom (www.telkom.co.za).

### Mobile Phones

- The major mobile networks are Cell C (www.cellc.co.za), MTN (www.mtn.co.za), Virgin Mobile (www.virginmobile.co.za) and the Vodafone-owned Vodacom (www.vodacom.co.za).
- You can hire a mobile phone through your car-rental provider.
- A cheaper alternative is to use a local prepaid SIM card in your own phone, provided it's unlocked and on roaming.

### TOURIST INFORMATION

Almost every town in the country has a tourist office. These are often private entities, which will only recommend member organisations and may add commissions to bookings they make on your behalf. South African Tourism (www.southafrica.net) has a helpful website, with practical information and inspirational features.

### VISAS

- Travellers from most Commonwealth countries (including Australia, Canada and the UK), most Western European countries, Japan and the USA are issued with a free, 90-day visitor's permit on arrival. New Zealand citizens require visas.
- Your passport should be valid for at least 30 days after the end of your intended visit, and should have at least two blank pages.
- From June 2015, new immigration regulations require that all children aged under 18 show an unabridged birth certificate, with additional paperwork needed in some cases.
- For more information, visit the websites of the Department of Home Affairs (www.dha.gov.za) and Brand South Africa (www.southafrica.info/travel/advice/disabled.htm).

## Getting There & Away

### AIR

**South African Airways** (www.flysaa.com) is South Africa's national airline, with an excellent route network and safety record. In addition to its long-haul flights, it operates regional and domestic routes together with its partners **Airlink** (0861 606 606; www.flyairlink.com) and **SA Express** (0861 729 227; www.flyexpress.aero).

**OR Tambo International Airport** (Ortia; 011-921 6262; www.airports.co.za), east of Jo'burg, is the major hub for Southern Africa.

The other principal international airports are **Cape Town International Airport** (CPT; 021-937 1200; www.airports.co.za) and **King Shaka International Airport** (DUR; 032-436 6585; kingshakainternational.co.za) in Durban.

### LAND

#### Car & Motorcycle

- If you rent a car in South Africa and plan to take it across an international border, you'll need a permission letter from the rental company.
- Most companies permit entry to most neighbouring counties; some may be reluctant regarding Mozambique.

**Botswana** There are 15 official South Africa–Botswana border crossings, open between at least 8am and 3pm.

**Grobler's Bridge/Martin's Drift** (8am-6pm) Northwest of Polokwane (Pietersburg).

**Kopfontein Gate/Tlokweng Gate** (6am-midnight) Next to Madikwe Game Reserve; a main border crossing.

**Pont Drift** (8am-4pm) Convenient for Mapungubwe National Park (Limpopo) and Tuli Block (Botswana).

**Ramatlabama** (6am-10pm) North of Mahikeng; a main border crossing.

**Twee Rivieren** (7.30am-4pm) At the South African entrance to Kgalagadi Transfrontier Park.

#### Bus

Intercape runs daily between Gaborone (Botswana) and Jo'burg (R290 to R390, seven hours) via Pretoria.

**Lesotho** All of Lesotho's borders are with South Africa and are straightforward to cross.

The main crossing is at Maseru Bridge, east of Bloemfontein. Queues here are sometimes very long upon exiting and, on some weekend evenings, entering Lesotho; use other posts if possible.

Possible shared-taxi routes:

- Butha-Buthe to/from Fouriesburg (Free State).
- Leribe (Hlotse) to/from Ficksburg (Free State).
- Quthing to/from Sterkspruit (Eastern Cape).
- Qacha's Nek to/from Matatiele (Eastern Cape).

**Mozambique** Citizens of Western countries should apply in advance for tourist visas at a Mozambican mission.

**Giriyondo** (8am-4pm Oct-Mar, to 3pm Apr-Sep) Between Kruger National Park's Phalaborwa Gate and Massingir (Mozambique).

**Kosi Bay/Ponta d'Ouro** (8am-4pm) On the coast, well north of Durban.

**Lebombo/Ressano Garcia** The main crossing, east of Nelspruit; also known as Komatipoort.

**Pafuri** (013-735 6888; 6am-6pm with slight seasonal variations) In Kruger National Park's northeastern corner.

Bus companies including Greyhound, Intercape and Translux run daily 'luxury' coaches between Jo'burg/Pretoria and Maputo (Mozambique) via Nelspruit and Ressano Garcia (Komatipoort; R320 to R410, eight hours). Mozambique-based Cheetah Express (p842) runs shuttles between Nelspruit and Maputo.

**Namibia** Border posts include the following:

**Alexander Bay/Oranjemund** (6am-10pm) On the Atlantic coast; access is reliant on the ferry.

**Nakop/Ariamsvlei** (24 hours) West of Upington.

**Rietfontein/Aroab** (8am-4.30pm) Just south of Kgalagadi Transfrontier Park.

**Vioolsdrif/Noordoewer** (24 hours) North of Springbok, en route to/from Cape Town.

Intercape buses run from Windhoek (Namibia) to Cape Town (R780 to R950, 21½ hours) on Monday, Wednesday, Friday and Sunday, returning Tuesday, Thursday, Friday and Sunday.

**Swaziland** There are 11 South Africa–Swaziland border crossings, all of which are hassle-free, including the following. Note that small posts close at 4pm.

**Golela/Lavumisa** (7am-10pm) En route between Durban and Swaziland's Ezulwini Valley.

**Josefdal/Bulembu** (8am-4pm) Between Piggs Peak and Barberton (Mpumalanga); 4WD or a car with high clearance recommended.

**Mahamba** (8am-8pm) The best crossing to use from Piet Retief in Mpumalanga. Casinos nearby attract traffic, especially on weekends – good places to look for lifts into and out of the country.

**Mananga** (8am-6pm) Southwest of Komatipoort.

**Matsamo/Jeppe's Reef** (8am-8pm) Southwest of Malelane and a possible route to Kruger National Park. Casinos nearby attract traffic, especially on weekends – good places to look for lifts into and out of the country.

**Onverwacht/Salitje** (8am-6pm) North of Pongola in KwaZulu-Natal.

**Oshoek/Ngwenya** (7am-10pm) The busiest crossing (and a good place to pick up lifts), about 360km southeast of Pretoria.

Daily shuttles run between Jo'burg and Mbabane. Shared taxi routes:

- Jo'burg to/from Mbabane (four hours); some continue to Manzini.
- Durban to/from Manzini (eight hours).
- Manzini to/from Maputo (3¼ hours).

### Zimbabwe

- Citizens of most Western nations need a visa to enter Zimbabwe, and these should be purchased at the border.
- Beitbridge open 24 hours, on the Limpopo River, is the only border crossing between Zimbabwe and South Africa.

Greyhound and Intercape operate daily buses between Jo'burg and Harare (Zimbabwe; 17 hours, R500), and between Jo'burg and Bulawayo (Zimbabwe; 14 hours, R475), both via Pretoria.

## Getting Around

### AIR

South African Airways has an extensive domestic and regional network. Airlink, South African Airways' partner, has a good network, including smaller destinations such as Upington, Mthatha and Maseru. SA Express, another South African Airways partner, has a good network, including direct flights between Cape Town and Hoedspruit (for Kruger National Park).

#### Budget Airlines

**CemAir** (www.flycemair.co.za) A small airline connecting Port Elizabeth, Bloemfontein, George, Plettenberg Bay and Margate.

**Fly Blue Crane** (www.flybluecrane.com) Connects Jo'burg, Cape Town, Bloemfontein, Kimberley and Mthatha

**FlySafair** (www.flysafair.co.za) A new airline offering cheap fares between Jo'burg, Cape Town, Durban, Port Elizabeth, East London and George.

**Kulula** (www.kulula.com) Budget airline connecting Jo'burg, Cape Town, Durban, George and East London. It also offers discounts on domestic flights with sister airline British Airways.

**Mango** (www.flymango.com) The South African Airways subsidiary flies between Jo'burg, Cape Town, Durban, Port Elizabeth, George and Bloemfontein.

### BUS

A good network of buses, of varying reliability and comfort, links the major cities. Lines are generally safe. Note, however, that many long-distance services run through the night.

For the main lines, purchase tickets at least 24 hours in advance. Tickets can be bought through bus offices, **Computicket** (☎0861 915 4000; www.computickettravel.com) and Shoprite/Checkers supermarkets.

#### Baz Bus

A convenient alternative to standard bus lines, Baz Bus (www.bazbus.com) caters almost exclusively to backpackers and travellers. It offers hop-on, hop-off fares and door-to-door services between Cape Town and Jo'burg via the Garden Route, Port Elizabeth, Mthatha, Durban and the Northern Drakensberg. Baz Bus drops off and picks up at hostels.

One-/two-/three-week travel passes cost R2600/R4100/5100.

### CAR & MOTORCYCLE

- Car rental is inexpensive in South Africa compared with Europe and North America, starting at around R200 per day for longer rentals.
- Many companies stipulate a daily mileage limit, with an extra fee payable for any mileage over this limit. A few local companies offer unlimited mileage.
- South Africa has rental operations in cities, major towns and airports, but it's generally cheapest to hire in a hub such as Jo'burg or Cape Town.

## TRAIN

Shosholoza Meyl (www.shosholozameyl.co.za) offers regular services connecting major cities.

For an overview of services, descriptions of trains and valuable advice, visit The Man in Seat Sixty-One (www.seat61.com).

### Classes

**Tourist class** Recommended: scenic, authentic but safe, and more comfortable than taking the bus, albeit often slower.

**Economy class** Does not have sleeping carriages and is not a comfortable or secure option for overnight travel.

### Routes

**Jo'burg–Cape Town** Via Kimberley and Beaufort West; 26 hours.

**Jo'burg–Durban** Via Ladysmith and Pietermaritzburg; 14 hours.

**Jo'burg–Port Elizabeth** Via Bloemfontein; 20 hours.

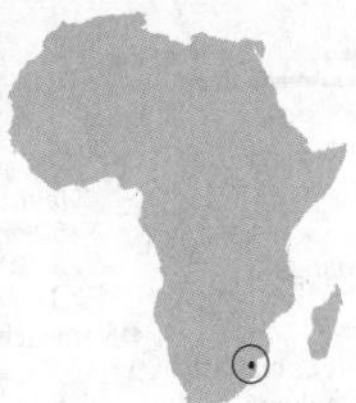

# Swaziland

POP 1.3 MILLION / ☎268

**Includes ➡**



## Best Places to Eat

- ➡ eDladleni (p957)
- ➡ Lihawu Restaurant (p960)
- ➡ Ramblas Restaurant (p957)

## Best Places to Sleep

- ➡ Stone Camp (p965)
- ➡ Sondzela Backpackers (p961)
- ➡ Brackenhill Lodge (p957)
- ➡ Lidwala Backpacker Lodge (p959)
- ➡ Phophonyane Falls Ecolodge & Nature Reserve (p964)

## Why Go?

In short: big things come in small packages. The intriguing kingdom of Swaziland is diminutive but boasts a huge checklist for any visitor. Rewarding wildlife-watching? Tick. Adrenaline-boosting activities such as rafting and mountain biking? Tick. Lively and colourful local culture, with celebrations and ceremonies still common practice? Tick. Plus there are superb walking trails, stunning mountain and flatland scenery, varied accommodation options and excellent, high-quality handicrafts.

Unlike South Africa, Swaziland has managed to hold on to that slow-down-this-is-Africa feeling, and that's why it's gaining in popularity. Everything remains small and personable. Instead of making a flying visit here on your way to Kruger National Park, KwaZulu-Natal or Mozambique, consider staying at least a week to do the country justice. If you plan a visit during the winter months, try to make it coincide with the Umhlanga festival, one of Africa's biggest cultural events.

## When to Go

### Mbabane

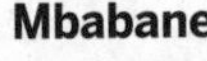

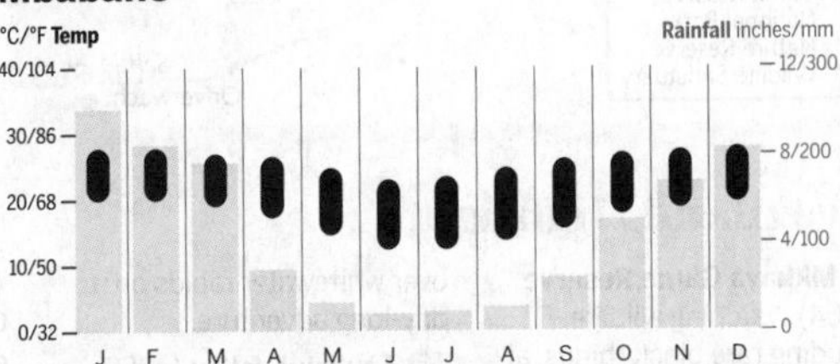


**Dec–Apr** Full rivers and lush vegetation. Incwala festival takes place in Lobamba.

**Feb–Mar** Buganu season – enjoy home-brewed marula beer in rural Swaziland.

**May–Sep** Wonderful wildlife viewing in the lowveld. Don't miss the Umhlanga festival.

## Swaziland Highlights

❶ **Mkhaya Game Reserve** (p964) Watching wildlife, including rare black rhinos, at this excellent reserve.

❷ **Malolotja Nature Reserve** (p962) Walking or hiking in this enchanting wilderness area.

❸ **Great Usutu River** (Lusutfu River; p965) Shooting over whitewater rapids on a day-long adventure.

❹ **Ezulwini Valley** (p959) Browsing the valley's craft shops.

❺ **Mlilwane Wildlife Sanctuary** (p961) Exploring on foot, horseback or by bike and relaxing in the comfortable lodges.

❻ **Sibebe Rock** (p957) Climbing this massive granite dome just outside the capital and soaking up the lovely views.

❼ **Hlane Royal National Park** (p963) Coming face-to-face with a pride of lions or watching white rhinos congregate at at the accessible watering hole.

# MBABANE

POP 38,000 / ELEV 1243M

Mbabane's main draw? Its lovely setting in the craggy Dlangeni Hills. Swaziland's capital and second-largest city, Mbabane is a relaxed and functional place perched in the cool highveld. There's a handful of good restaurants and places to stay, but for the traveller the nearby Ezulwini and Malkerns Valleys have most of the attractions and, on the whole, a better choice of accommodation.

## Sights

**Sibebe Rock** LANDMARK

(Pine Valley; E30; 8am-4pm Mon-Sat) About 8km northeast of Mbabane is Sibebe Rock, a massive granite dome hulking over the surrounding countryside. It's the world's second-largest monolith, after Australia's Uluru, but is considerably less visited. Much of the rock is completely sheer, and dangerous if you should fall, but climbing it is a good adrenaline charge if you're reasonably fit and relish looking down steep rock faces. Community guides operate guided hikes (E50 per person) – ask at the visitor centre.

## Sleeping

**Bombaso's Guesthouse** HOSTEL $

(7681 9191, 7804 0603; www.swazilandhappenings.co.za/photos_bombasos.htm; Lukhalo St, off Pine Valley Rd; dm/s/d E200/550/650, s/d with shared bathroom E450/550; P) Bombaso's offers a buzzy vibe and has a variety of accommodation options, including a self-catering cottage (E850). No meals are served, but there are excellent kitchen facilities. Jason and Lwazi, who run the place, are well clued-up about the country.

★ **Brackenhill Lodge** GUESTHOUSE $$

(2404 2887; www.brackenhillswazi.com; Mountain Dr; s/d incl breakfast E675/950; P) With its wonderfully relaxing atmosphere and bucolic setting, this little cracker located 4.5km northeast of Mbabane is sure to win your heart. It offers eight comfortable, well-equipped and airy rooms, and its 162 hectares have several walking trails, great birdlife and splendid panoramas. Facilities include a gym, sauna, swimming pool and even tennis courts. Lovely owners; evening meals on request.

**Foresters Arms** LODGE $$

(2467 4177; www.forestersarms.co.za; MR19, Mhlambanyatsi; s/d incl breakfast E670/1140; P) Hidden 27km southwest of Mbabane in picturesque hills, Foresters Arms has a haunting but beautiful remoteness. The air is clean, the views suggestive, the peace tangible. It's a superb staging post between KwaZulu-Natal and Kruger National Park, with cosy rooms, attractive gardens and a smorgasbord of activities (horse riding, mountain biking and hiking). Another highlight is the on-site restaurant.

## Eating

**eDish** CAFE $

(2404 5504; Computronics House, Somhlolo St (Gilfillan St); mains E45-75; 8am-5pm Mon-Sat; P) With gourmet sandwiches, comfy couches, good coffee, cold beer and a deck offering fine Mbabane views, eDish is a worthy place to spend an hour. Best of all, there is free wi-fi at decent speeds.

★ **eDladleni** SWAZI $$

(2404 5743; http://edladleni.100webspace.net/index.html; Manzini/Mbabane Hwy, Mvubu Falls; mains E55-80; noon-3pm & 6-10pm Tue-Sun; ) Delicious food, a serene setting and cracking views – if you're after an authentic Swazi experience, eDladleni's hard to beat. Here you can tuck into traditional specialities that are hard to find elsewhere, and it's got excellent vegetarian options. It's about 6km from Mbabane, off the main highway (follow the sign 'Mvubu Falls'); check the website for directions.

**Ramblas Restaurant** INTERNATIONAL $$

(2404 4147; www.ramblasswaziland.webs.com; Mantsholo St; mains E70-160; 8am-10pm Mon-Sat; ) Mbabane's top choice for good cuisine and a buzzing ambience, a stone's throw from the golf course. It's well worth the trip for an eclectic menu including great salads, meat dishes, burgers and appetising desserts. It occupies a small villa with an agreeable terrace, and inside colourful paintings and shades of grey and red create a sophisticated mood.

## Information

### INTERNET ACCESS

Mbabane has internet centres in Swazi Plaza and in the Mall. Access starts from around E30 per hour.

### MEDICAL SERVICES

**Mbabane Clinic** (2404 2423; www.theclinicgroup.com; Mkhonubovu St; 24hr) For emergencies try this well-equipped clinic in the southwestern corner of town, just off the bypass road.

## Mbabane

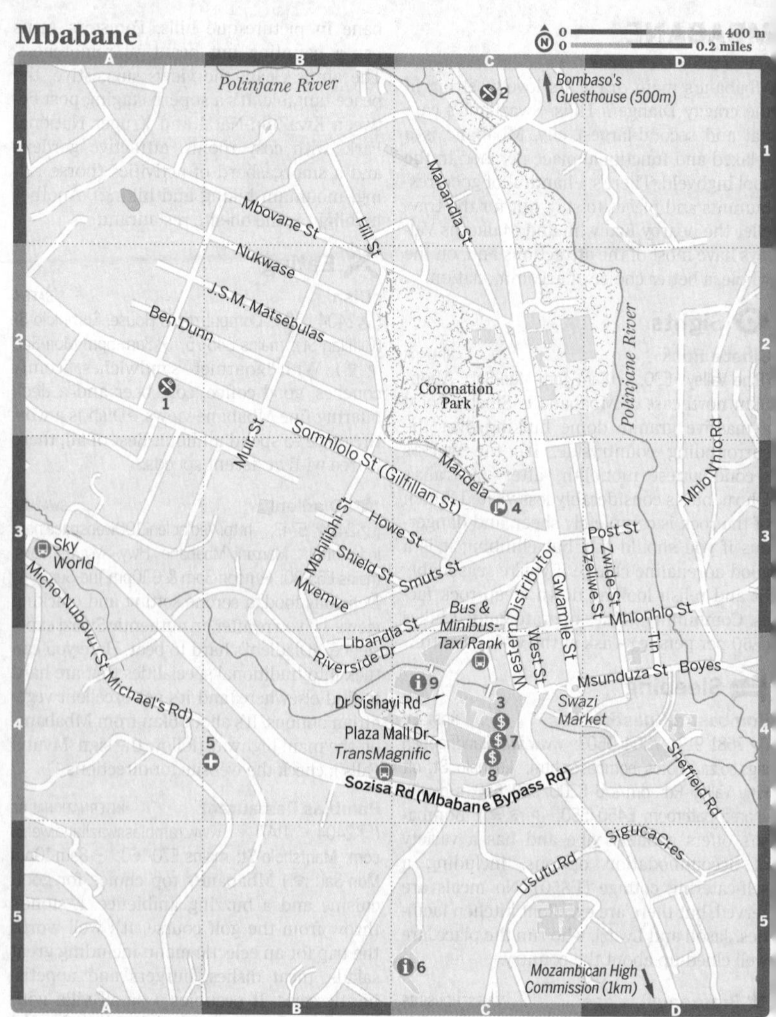


### MONEY

Mbabane's banks with ATMs include **First National Bank** (⏲8.30am-2.30pm Mon-Fri, 9-11am Sat), **Nedbank** (⏲8.30am-2.30pm Mon-Fri, 9-11am Sat) and **Standard Bank** (⏲8.30am-2.30pm Mon-Fri, 9-11am Sat); these are located in Swazi Plaza.

### TOURIST INFORMATION

**Tourism Information Office** (☎2404 2531; www.thekingdomofswaziland.com; Swazi Mall, Dr Sishayi Rd; ⏲8am-5pm Mon-Fri, 9am-1pm Sat) At Mbabane's Swazi Mall. Has maps and brochures.

## ℹ Getting There & Away

Mbabane's main **bus and minibus-taxi rank** (Dr Sishayi Rd) is just behind Swazi Plaza. Minibus shared taxis leave for Jo'burg (E220, four hours) throughout the day.

**TransMagnific** (☎2404 9977; www.goswaziland.co.sz; Cooper Centre, Sozisa Rd) and **Sky World** (☎2404 9921, mobile 7664 0001; www.skyworld.co.sz; Checkers Business Park, Sozisa Rd) offer a daily luxury shuttle service between Johannesburg (stopping at OR Tambo International Airport and Sandton) and Mbabane for E600. Other destinations include Durban (E780) and Nelspruit (from E450).

### Mbabane

**Eating**

1 eDish .......... A2
2 Ramblas Restaurant .......... C1

**Information**

3 First National Bank .......... C4
4 German Liaison Office .......... C3
5 Mbabane Clinic .......... B4
6 Ministry of Home Affairs Immigration Department .......... C5
7 Nedbank .......... C4
South African High Commission .......... (see 9)
8 Standard Bank .......... C4
9 Tourism Information Office .......... C4

# CENTRAL SWAZILAND

The country's tourist hub, central Swaziland is a heady mix of culture, nature and epicurean indulgences, and has plenty to keep you occupied for a few days. There are wildlife reserves to explore, museums to visit, great restaurants to sample and quality handicrafts to bring home.

## Ezulwini Valley

What a difference a few kilometres can make! Swaziland's tourism centre, the Ezulwini Valley, begins just outside Mbabane but feels a world away from the hullabaloo of the capital. With an excellent selection of places to stay and wonderful craft shopping, it's a convenient base for many visitors.

### Sights

**Mantenga Cultural Village & Nature Reserve** NATURE RESERVE
(2416 1151; www.sntc.org.sz/reserves/mantenga.asp; Ezulwini Valley; E100; 8am-6pm) The entrance fee to this tranquil, thickly forested reserve covers a guided tour of the Swazi Cultural Village, a 'living' cultural village with authentic beehive huts and cultural displays, plus a *sibhaca* dance (performed daily at 11.30am and 3.15pm) and a visit to the impressive Mantenga Falls. The reserve is also great for hiking; day hikers pay only E50. Although it's not a big wildlife park, it offers a chance to see vervet monkeys, baboons, warthogs, nyalas and duikers.

### Activities

**Swazi Trails** ADVENTURE SPORTS
(2416 2180, mobile 7602 0261; www.swazitrails.co.sz; Mantenga Craft Centre, Ezulwini Valley; 8am-5pm) Based in the Mantenga Craft Centre in Ezulwini Valley, this is one of the country's major activity companies, and the place to go to for caving, rafting, hikes and general cultural and highlights tours. Also houses the Ezulwini Tourist Office.

**Cuddle Puddle** HOT SPRINGS
(2416 1164; MR103, Ezulwini Valley; adult/child E30/15; 6am-11pm) For personal pampering, head to the Royal Valley's own mineral hot springs. The magnesium-rich waters are a constant 32°C. There's also a spa, complete with sauna, gym and massage services.

### Sleeping

★ **Lidwala Backpacker Lodge** HOSTEL $
(mobile 7690 5865; www.lidwala.co.sz; MR103, Ezulwini Valley; camping per person R100, dm E180, d E440-590; P) What a magical setting. This comfortable, well-run spot is nestled in a splendid garden with a pool, among big boulders and a chuckling stream. Rooms are a typical dorm-style, backpacker set-up, with a laid-back, friendly feel. The separate safari tents are popular (E150 per person), while the private rooms are smallish but neat.

**Legends Backpackers Lodge** HOSTEL $
(2416 1870, mobile 7602 0261; www.legends.co.sz; Mantenga Falls Rd, Ezulwini Valley; camping E80, dm E160, d with shared bathroom E440; P) It's far from flash, but this mellow place is the most obvious choice if funds are short, with an assortment of 10- to 12-bed dorms, a self-catering kitchen, a chill-out lounge with TV and a small pool in the garden. Those needing privacy can opt for the plain but restful private rooms in a separate building. Breakfast costs E50.

**Mantenga Cultural Village & Nature Reserve** BUNGALOW $$
(2416 1178, 2416 1151; www.sntc.org.sz; Ezulwini Valley; s/d incl breakfast E550/850; P) These digs within the Mantenga Nature Reserve offer something different, with a cluster of offbeat bungalows set in lush bushland, many of which overlook a river. Very 'Me Tarzan, you Jane'. With wooden furnishings and modern amenities (but no air-con), they represent a nicely judged balance between comfort, rustic charm and seclusion. Overnight guests don't pay entry to the nature reserve.

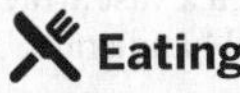

### Eating

**Mantenga Restaurant** INTERNATIONAL $$
(2416 1049; Mantenga Lodge & Restaurant, Mantenga Falls Rd, Ezulwini Valley; mains E70-140; 6.30am-9.30pm) Inside Mantenga Lodge

DON'T MISS

**INCWALA**

Incwala (also known as Ncwala) is the most sacred ceremony of the Swazi people. It is a 'first fruits' ceremony, where the king gives permission for his people to eat the first crops of the new year. It takes place in late December/ early January and lasts one week: dates are announced shortly before the event. It's a fiercely traditional celebration and visitors should take note of strict rules, including restrictions on dress and photography.

(but open to nonguests), this restaurant with a raised wooden deck has a fabulous outlook over the trees. The pasta dishes and grilled meats are good deals, as are the sandwiches.

**Boma Restaurant** INTERNATIONAL **$$**
(2416 2632; Nyonyane Rd, Ezulwini Valley; mains E60-120; 11am-10.30pm; ) This atmospheric, boma-shaped restaurant with thatched roof has a massive menu with all the favourites – grills to pastas – and is within the grounds of Timbali Lodge. You can't really go wrong, everything is pretty good, but if you want a recommendation, go for the wood-fired pizzas.

★ **Lihawu Restaurant** FUSION **$$$**
(2416 7035; www.lihawu.co.sz; Royal Villas, Ezulwini Valley; mains E95-230; noon-2pm & 6-10.30pm; ) Within the swish Royal Villas resort nestles Swaziland's most elegant restaurant, with a tastefully decorated dining room and an outdoor eating area that overlooks a swimming pool. The menu is Afro-fusion, with meaty signature dishes such as oxtail stew and pork belly, but there are a couple of vegetarian options. Needless to say the accompanying wine list is top class.

## Shopping

**Ezulwini Craft Market** ARTS & CRAFTS
(MR103, Ezulwini Valley; 8am-5pm) Don't miss this well-stocked market that's opposite the Zeemans Filling Station on the corner of MR103 and Mpumalanga Loop Rd. Look for the blue tin roofs. The stalls sell a vast array of local carvings, weavings and handicrafts.

**Mantenga Craft Centre** ARTS & CRAFTS
(2416 1136; Mantenga Falls Rd, Ezulwini Valley; 8am-5pm) This colourful, compact craft centre has several shops featuring everything from weaving and tapestries to candles, woodcarvings and T-shirts.

## Information

### MEDICAL SERVICES

**Medi-Sun Clinic** (2416 2800; Mantenga Dr; 24hr) Behind Gables Shopping Centre.

### MONEY

There are ATMs at the **Gables Shopping Centre** (www.thegables.co.sz; MR 103, Ezulwini Valley; 8am-10pm).

### TOURIST INFORMATION

**Big Game Parks** (2528 3943; www.biggameparks.org; Mlilwane Wildlife Sanctuary; 8am-5pm Mon-Fri, 8.30am-12.30pm Sat)

**Ezulwini Tourist Office** (2416 2180, mobile 7602 0261; www.swazitrails.co.sz; Mantenga Craft Centre, Ezulwini Valley; 8am-5pm)

## Getting There & Away

Nonshared taxis from Mbabane to the Ezulwini Valley cost E120 to E200, depending on how far down the valley you go.

During the day you could get on a minibus bound for Manzini, but make sure the driver knows that you want to alight in the valley, as many aren't keen on stopping.

# Lobamba

POP 11,000

Welcome to Swaziland's spiritual, cultural and political heart. Within the Ezulwini Valley lies Lobamba, an area that has played host to Swaziland's monarchy for over two centuries. It's home to some of the most notable buildings in the country. Despite its importance, Lobamba feels surprisingly quiet – except during the spectacular Incwala and Umhlanga ceremonies, when the nation gathers on the surrounding plains for several days of intense revelry.

## Sights

**National Museum** MUSEUM
(2416 1179; Lobamba; adult/child E80/30; 8am-4.30pm Mon-Fri, 10am-4pm Sat & Sun) This museum has some interesting displays of Swazi culture, as well as a traditional beehive village and cattle enclosure, and several of King Sobhuza I's 1940s cars. There's a discounted combo ticket (adult/child E120/40) if you visit both the museum

and the **King Sobhuza II Memorial Park** (☎2416 2131; Lobamba; adult/child E80/30; ⊙8am-4.30pm Mon-Fri, 10am-4pm Sat & Sun).

## Sleeping & Eating

There are no sleeping options in Lobamba itself, but plenty of places to stay in the Ezulwini and Malkerns Valleys.

There are no notable places to eat in Lobamba, but travellers will find cafes, supermarkets and restaurants in the nearby Ezulwini Valley.

## Getting There & Away

Minibus taxis running between Ezulwini and Malkerns stop in Lobamba several times a day. Fares to both destinations are about E10.

# Mlilwane Wildlife Sanctuary

While it doesn't have the drama or vastness of some of the bigger South African parks, the tranquil Mlilwane Wildlife Sanctuary near Lobamba is well worth a visit: it's beautiful, tranquil and easily accessible. The landscape is another highlight; its terrain is dominated by the Nyonyane Mountain, whose exposed granite peak is known as Execution Rock (1110m). Small wonder that the reserve is an outdoors-lover's paradise, with a wide range of activities available.

With easy access from Mbabane and Ezulwini Valley, Mlilwane offers rewarding year-round wildlife-watching and birding, with the chance to see zebras, warthogs, wildebeest, numerous species of antelope (including the rare blue duiker), crocodiles, hippos and rare bird species.

The reserve supports a large diversity of fauna (mostly large herbivores and birds) and flora, and has no dangerous wildlife to worry about (except hippos). The best wildlife and birdwatching areas are the waterhole at the main camp and the main dam to the north. The enclosed area near Reilly's Rock shelters some rare species of antelope and is accessible only on a guided drive.

## Activities

All activities (which include horse riding, mountain biking, walking and wildlife drives) can be booked through reception at Mlilwane Wildlife Sanctuary Main Camp.

## Sleeping

The reserve's beehive huts are cheap and pleasant, and there's also a top-notch backpackers.

**★ Sondzela Backpackers** HOSTEL $
(☎2528 3943; www.biggameparks.org/sondzela; Mlilwane Wildlife Sanctuary; camping per person E100, dm E115, s/d with shared bathroom E275/390, rondavel s/d with shared outside bathroom E295/430; P 🏊) A top choice for budgeteers, in the southern part of the Mlilwane Wildlife Sanctuary, Sondzela boasts fine, breezy dorms, clean private doubles and a clutch of lovely rondavels with wraparound views. And it doesn't end there. The delightful gardens, kitchen, swimming pool and a hilltop perch provide one of the best backpackers' settings in Southern Africa.

**Mlilwane Wildlife Sanctuary Main Camp** CAMPGROUND $$
(☎2528 3943/4; www.biggameparks.org/mlilwane; Mlilwane Wildlife Sanctuary; camping E105, hut s/d E555/790, rondavel s/d E625/890; P 📶 🏊) This homey camp is set in a scenic wooded location about 3.5km from the entry gate, complete with well-appointed rondavels and simple huts – including traditional beehive huts (s/d E580/830) – along with the occasional snuffling warthog. The Hippo Haunt Restaurant serves excellent grilled meat and overlooks a water hole. There are often dance performances in the evening, and the pool is another drawcard.

**Reilly's Rock Hilltop Lodge** LODGE $$$
(☎2528 3943/4; www.biggameparks.org/reilly; Mlilwane Wildlife Sanctuary; s/d with half board

DON'T MISS

### UMHLANGA REED DANCE FESTIVAL

The *umhlanga* (reed) dance is Swaziland's best-known cultural event. Though not as sacred as the Incwala, it serves a similar function in drawing the nation together and reminding the people of their relationship to the king. It is something like a week-long debutante ball for marriageable young Swazi women, who journey from all over the kingdom to help repair the queen mother's home at Lobamba. It takes place in late August or early September.

from E1410/2170; P) Promoted as 'quaintly colonial', this is an oh-so-delightfully tranquil, old-world, nonfussy luxury experience at its best. The main house is in an incredible setting (a Royal Botanic Garden with aloes, cycads and an enormous jacaranda), and shelters four rooms and has striking views of the valley and Mdzimba Mountains. Entry to the reserve is included.

## Getting There & Away

Heading to the sanctuary from Mbabane or Ezulwini Valley, take the MR103 to the south. Drive past Lobamba; the turn-off to the reserve is well signposted on the right. After initial check-in at Sangweni main gate, visitors enjoy 24-hour park access.

# Manzini

Swaziland's largest town, Manzini is a chaotic commercial and industrial hub whose small centre is dominated by office blocks and a couple of shopping malls running down two main streets. With the exception of the market, Manzini itself has limited appeal for the tourist. That said, it's a key transport hub, so you're likely to pass through if you're getting around on public transport.

## Sights

**Manzini Market** MARKET
(cnr Mhlakuvane & Mancishane Sts; 7am-5pm Mon-Sat) Manzini's main drawcard is its colourful market, whose upper section is packed with handicrafts from Swaziland and elsewhere in Africa. Thursday morning is a good time to see the rural vendors and Mozambican traders bringing in their handicrafts and textiles to sell to the retailers.

### CULTURAL EXPERIENCES

**Woza Nawe Tours** (2505 8363; www.swaziculturaltours.com) Headed by proud local Myxo Mdluli, this outfit runs highly recommended village visits (day tour R1210) and overnight stays (adult/child E1450/725) to Kaphunga, 55km southeast of Manzini. The fee includes transport, meals and a guide. Guests join in on whatever activities are going on in the village – including cooking, planting and harvesting.

## Sleeping & Eating

Accommodation is limited; you're best to head to the nearby Malkerns or Ezulwini Valleys.

**George Hotel** BUSINESS HOTEL $$
(2505 2260; www.tgh.co.sz; cnr Ngwane & Du Toit Sts; s/d incl breakfast from E1070/1520; P) Don't be discouraged by this hotel's modest exterior and unspectacular location up the main road. Manzini's fanciest hotel attempts an international atmosphere and features a respectable collection of various-size comfy rooms (tip: ask for a poolside one), two stylish restaurants, a lovely garden with a pool, a small spa and conference facilities.

**Gil Vincente Restaurant** PORTUGUESE $$
(2505 3874; Ngwane St; mains R80-150; 9am-10pm Tue-Sun) Gourmands saunter here for well-prepped Portuguese-inspired dishes with a twist, a respectable wine list, efficient service and smart decor. Sink your teeth into a juicy *bitoque* (beefsteak with fried egg) or a succulent *bacalhau* (cod). Enough protein? Pastas and salads are also available.

## Getting There & Away

The main bus and minibus-taxi park is at the northern end of Louw St, where you can also find some nonshared taxis. A minibus shared-taxi trip up the Ezulwini Valley to Mbabane costs E40 (35 minutes). Minibus taxis to Mozambique (E120) also depart from here.

# MALOLOTJA NATURE RESERVE

One of Swaziland's premier natural attractions, the beautiful **Malolotja Nature Reserve** (2444 3048, mobile 7660 6755; www.sntc.org.sz/reserves/malolotja.asp; adult/child E30/20; 6am-6pm) is a true wilderness area that's rugged and, for the most part, unspoilt. The reserve is laced by streams and cut by three rivers, including the Komati, which flows east through a gorge in a series of falls and rapids until it meets the lowveld. No prizes for guessing that this spectacular area is a fantastic playground for nature-lovers and ornithologists, with more than 280 species of bird.

Don't expect to see plenty of large mammals, though. It's the scenery that's the pull here, rather than the wildlife.

## Activities

Malolotja offers some of the most inspirational **hiking** trails in Swaziland, so pack your sturdy shoes. Walking options range from short walks to multiday hikes. Well-known and much enjoyed walks include the 11.5km Malolotja Falls Trail, with superb views of the Malolotja Valley, and the 8km Komati River Trail.

**Malolotja Canopy Tour** OUTDOORS
(mobile 7660 6755; www.malolotjacanopytour.com; Malolotja Nature Reserve; per person E650; 8am-2pm) This tour is a definite must-do for those wanting to experience the Malolotja Nature Reserve from a different perspective. Here you will make your way across Malolotja's stunning, lush tree canopy on 10 slides (11 wooden platforms) and via a 50m-long suspension bridge. It's very safe and no previous experience is required.

## Sleeping

**Malolotja Cabins** CABIN $
(2444 3048; www.sntc.org.sz/tourism/malolotja.asp; Malolotja Nature Reserve; s/d E400/600; P) These cosy, fully equipped, self-catering wooden cabins, each sleeping a maximum of five, are located near Malolotja Nature Reserve reception and afford lovely mountain views.

If cooking's not your thing, there's a restaurant (also located near reception). Wi-fi is available at reception and costs E25 per hour.

**Malolotja Camping** CAMPGROUND $
(Malolotja Nature Reserve; camping per person E100) Camping is available at the well-equipped main site near reserve reception, with ablutions (hot shower) and braai (barbecue) area, or along the overnight trails (E70; no facilities).

## Information

Go year-round, but expect heavy mist between October and March.

Some stretches of road that are heavily eroded require a 4WD in wet weather.

## Getting There & Away

The entrance gate for Malolotja is about 35km northwest of Mbabane, along the Piggs Peak road (MR1). It's well signposted.

DON'T MISS

### MAGUGA DAM LODGE

**Maguga Dam Lodge** (2437 3975; www.magugalodge.com; Maguga Dam; camping per person E145, s/d incl breakfast E690/1045; P) Scenically positioned east of Malolotja Nature Reserve on the shore of Maguga Dam, this laid-back venture is blessed with commanding views of the dam and surrounding hills. It comprises two well-equipped camping grounds, a clutch of spacious and light-filled rondavels and an excellent restaurant with a deck overlooking the dam. Various activities are on offer, including fishing, cultural tours, hiking and boat cruises.

# NORTHEASTERN SWAZILAND

Within an easy drive of the Mozambique border, this remote corner is the country's top wildlife-watching region: you'll find a duo of excellent wildlife parks – Hlane Royal National Park and Mkhaya Game Reserve – as well as lesser-known Mlawula Rature Reserve that also begs exploration. If it's action you're after, the superb rapids of the Great Usutu River (Lusutfu River) provide an incredible playground.

## Hlane Royal National Park

The country's largest protected area, well-organised **Hlane Royal National Park** (2528 3943; www.biggameparks.org/hlane; E50; 6am-6pm) is home to elephants, lions, leopards, white rhinos and many antelope species, and offers wonderfully low-key wildlife and bird-life watching. And it's so easy to enjoy it: hippos and elephants are found around Ndlovu Camp just metres from your cottage. There's plenty to do, including bush walking, wildlife drives, mountain biking and cultural tours. Go year-round.

### Activities

All activities (mountain biking, bush walking and wildlife drives) can be booked at Ndlovu Camp (p964). You can explore most of the park with a 2WD, with the notable exception of the special lion compound, which can be visited on the wildlife drives only.

DON'T MISS

**PHOPHONYANE FALLS ECOLODGE & NATURE RESERVE**

A little morsel of paradise about 14km north of Piggs Peak, **Phophonyane Falls Ecolodge & Nature Reserve** (☎2431 3429; www.phophonyane.co.sz; s/d safari tent with shared bathroom E915/1310, s/d beehive hut E1525/2190, d cottage E2050; P) is a dream come true for those seeking to get well and truly off the beaten track. It lies on a river in its own nature reserve of lush indigenous forest. Accommodation is in comfortable cottages, stylish beehives or luxury safari tents overlooking cascades.

#### Guided Tours

Growing weary of antelope, rhinos and lions? Bookmark the Ndlovu Camp's 'Umphakatsi Experience' cultural tour (two hours; per person E115, minimum four people), during which you'll visit a chief's village and learn about traditional Swazi culture.

**Swazi Travel** WILDLIFE
(☎2416 2180; www.swazi.travel; day tour from R1850) This company offers day tours to Hlane Royal National Park, collecting from the Ezulwini Valley.

### Sleeping & Eating

**Ndlovu Camp** CAMPGROUND, COTTAGE $$
(☎2528 3943; www.biggameparks.org/hlane; Hlane Royal National Park; camping E115, rondavel s/d E610/870, cottage s/d from E650/930; P) Ndlovu Camp is a delightfully mellow spot, with spacious grounds and an atmospheric restaurant that serves outstanding food. Accommodation is in rondavels and self-catering cottages with no electricity (paraffin lanterns are provided). You can also pitch your tent on a grassy plot. Ndlovu is just inside the main gate, and near a water hole that draws hippos and rhinos.

**Bhubesi Camp** BUNGALOW $$
(☎2528 3943; www.biggameparks/hlane; Hlane Royal National Park; s/d E650/930; P) Set in a pristine setting about 14km from Ndlovu Camp, Bhubesi Camp features tasteful, stone, four-person, self-catering bungalows that overlook a river and green lawns and are surrounded by lush growth. Electricity is available, but there's no restaurant.

### Getting There & Away

The gate to Hlane is about 7km south of Simunye (it's signposted). If you don't have your own transport, you can book a tour through Swazi Travel.

## Mlawula Nature Reserve

The low-key Mlawula Nature Reserve, where the lowveld plains meet the Lubombo Mountains, boasts antelope species and a few spotted hyenas, among others, plus rewarding birdwatching. Keep your expectations in check, though; wildlife is more elusive here than anywhere else in the country and visitor infrastructure is fairly limited. The park's real highlight is its network of walking trails amid beautifully scenic landscapes.

### Sleeping

**Siphiso Campground** CAMPGROUND $
(www.sntc.org.sz; adult/child E100/30) A basic campsite within the Mlawula Nature Reserve, which offers shared ablutions and shady trees.

**Magadzavane Lodge** CHALET $$
(☎2383 8885; magadzavane@sntc.org.sz; Mlawula Nature Reserve; s/d incl breakfast E600/900; P) This great option offers 20 enticing chalets in southern Mlawula, on the edge of the Lubombo escarpment, with magnificent views of the valley below. There's a restaurant and a small infinity pool. From the northern gate, it's a 17km drive on a gravel road; the last kilometres are very steep (but manageable in a standard vehicle in dry weather).

### Getting There & Away

The turn-off for the entrance gates to the Mlawula Nature Reserve is about 10km north of Simunye, from where it's another 4km from the main road. You'll need your own transport to explore the reserve.

## Mkhaya Game Reserve

The crowning glory of Swaziland's parks, the top-notch and stunning **Mkhaya Game Reserve** (☎2528 3943; www.mkhaya.org) is famous for its black and white rhino populations (it boasts that you're more likely to meet rhinos here than anywhere else in Africa and, judging from our experience, this is true). Its other animals include roan and sable antelope, giraffes, tsessebe, buffaloes and elephants, along with a rich diversity of birds. If you're lucky, you might spot the elusive narina trogon and other rare bird species. Note that children under 10 are not allowed in the park.

## Activities

Swaziland's most exclusive safari retreat is good all year-round. Come here for a real sense of wilderness; *really* close encounters with rhinos; atmospheric accommodation; excellent wildlife drives and sensational bush walks run by expert guides.

### Wildlife Drives

Wildlife drives through Mkhaya in an open vehicle are included in Stone Camp's accommodation rates. For overnight guests, they take place in the early morning and late afternoon. As day trips (per person E735), they start at 10am and include lunch.

### Bush Walks

Mkhaya's signature activity, guided bush walks are an ideal way to approach wildlife, especially white rhinos. You periodically disembark from the open vehicle and track rhinos on foot, under the guidance of an experienced ranger. Unforgettable.

Bush walks take place at 11am. Note that they're offered to Stone Camp's overnight guests only.

### White-water Rafting & Caving

One of the highlights of Swaziland is rafting the Great Usutu River (Lusutfu River). The river varies radically from steep creeks to sluggish flats, but in the vicinity of Mkhaya Game Reserve it passes through a gorge, where a perfect mix of rapids can be encountered all year round.

Swazi Trails (p959) is the best contact to organise a rafting trip (it offers full-/half-day trips E1300/1100 per person, including lunch and transport, minimum two people). Abseiling and cliff jumps are added for extra adrenaline in the winter months.

For an off-the-scale challenge rating, the company's adventure-caving trips offer a rare window into the elite world of cave exploration. A few kilometres from Mbabane, the vast Gobholo Cave is 98% unexplored.

## Sleeping

**★ Stone Camp** LODGE $$$
(☎2528 3943; www.mkhaya.org; Mkhaya Game Reserve; s/d with full board & activities from E2620/3940; P) A dream come true for nature-lovers, Stone Camp consists of a series of rustic and luxurious semi-open stone-and-thatch cottages (a proper loo with a view!) located in secluded bush zones. The price includes wildlife drives, walking safaris and meals, and is excellent value compared to many of the private reserves in Southern Africa. Simply arrive, absorb and wonder.

No electricity, but paraffin lanterns are provided.

## Information

You can't visit the reserve without booking in advance, and even then you can't drive in alone; you'll be met at Phuzumoya at a specified pick-up time – either 10am or 4pm – and escorted to the ranger base station, where you'll leave your vehicle.

## Getting There & Away

The Mkhaya Game Reserve is near the hamlet of Phuzumoya, off the Manzini–Big Bend road (it's signposted off the MR8). Rangers meet you at the gate to transfer you to camp. There is secure parking at the ranger base station.

# UNDERSTAND SWAZILAND

## Swaziland Today

Democratic freedom is an issue in Swaziland, where absolute monarch King Mswati III has been accused of silencing opponents. In 2014 the country was excluded from a trade pact giving duty-free access to the US market due to human rights concerns. Despite calls for greater democracy, pride in the monarchy lingers, and some propose a constitutional monarchy. The rural, homogeneous country has many challenges, including widespread poverty, a declining economy reliant on South Africa and the world's highest HIV prevalence at 28.8%. Life expectancy hovers around 50 years – among the lowest in the world.

## History

### Beginnings of a Nation

The area that is now Swaziland has been inhabited for millennia, and human-like remains possibly dating back as far as 100,000 years have been discovered around the Lubombo Mountains in eastern Swaziland. However, today's Swazis trace their ancestors to much more recent arrivals. By around AD 500, various Nguni groups had made their way to the region as part of the great Bantu migrations. One of these groups settled in the area around present-day Maputo (Mozambique), eventually founding the Dlamini dynasty. In the mid-18th century, in response to increasing pressure from other clans in the area, the Dlamini king, Ngwane III, led his people southwest to the Pongola River, in present-day southern Swaziland and northern KwaZulu-Natal. This became the first Swazi heartland.

Ngwane's successor, Sobhuza I, established a base in the Ezulwini Valley, which still remains the centre of Swazi royalty and ritual. Next came King Mswazi (or Mswati), after whom the Swazi take their name. Despite pressure from the neighbouring Zulu, Mswazi succeeded in unifying the whole kingdom.

From the mid-19th century, Swaziland attracted increasing numbers of European farmers in search of land for cattle, as well as hunters, traders and missionaries.

Over the next decades, the Swazis saw their territory whittled away as the British and Boers jostled for power in the area. In 1902, following the second Anglo-Boer War, the Boers withdrew and the British took control of Swaziland as a protectorate.

### Struggle for Independence

Swazi history in the early 20th century centred on the ongoing struggle for independence. Under the leadership of King Sobhuza II (guided by the capable hands of his mother, Lomawa Ndwandwewho, who acted as regent while Sobhuza was a child), the Swazis succeeded in regaining much of their original territory. This was done in part by direct purchase and in part by British government decree. This was a major development, as Swazi kings are considered to hold the kingdom in trust for their subjects, and land ownership is thus more than just a political and economic issue.

Independence was finally achieved – the culmination of a long and remarkably nonviolent path – on 6 September 1968, 66 years after the establishment of the British protectorate.

The first Swazi constitution was largely a British creation, and in 1973 the king suspended it on the grounds that it did not accord with Swazi culture. Four years later parliament reconvened under a new constitution vesting all power in the king.

Sobhuza II died in 1982, at that time the world's longest-reigning monarch. In 1986 the young Mswati III ascended the throne, where he continues today to represent and maintain the traditional Swazi way of life, and to assert his pre-eminence as absolute monarch. Despite an undercurrent of political dissent, political parties are still unable to participate in elections.

## Economy & Culture

Swaziland's economic scene is almost completely wrapped up in that of its larger neighbour. About two-thirds of Swazi exports go to South Africa and more than 90% of goods and services are imported. Overall, some 70% of Swazis live in rural areas and rely on subsistence farming for survival.

Swazi culture is very strong and quite distinct from that of South Africa. The monarchy influences many aspects of life, from cultural ceremonies to politics. While some Swazis are proud of the royal traditions and suspicious of those who call for greater democracy, a growing number of human-rights and opposition activists believe power should be transferred from the king to the people.

## Environment

Swaziland is one of Africa's smallest countries at only 17,364 sq km in area, but with a remarkable diversity of landscapes, climates and ecological zones for its size. These range from low-lying savannah to the east, rolling hills towards the centre, and rainforest and perpetually fog-draped peaks in the northwest. Swaziland has about 120 mammal species, representing one-third of Southern Africa's nonmarine mammal species. Many (including elephants, rhinos and lions) have been introduced, and larger animals are restricted to nature reserves and private wildlife farms.

# SURVIVAL GUIDE

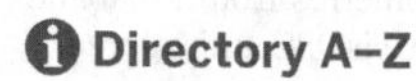


#### ACCOMMODATION

Rates are reasonable in Swaziland and much lower than you would find in Europe or North America. There is a handful of backpackers hostels, and camping is possible on the grounds of many accommodation options.

### Booking Online

**Where to Stay** (www.wheretostay.co.za) Covers a range of accommodation, activities and restaurants in Swaziland and neighbouring countries.

### Backpackers

Backpacker accommodation is found in areas including the Ezulwini Valley. Prices and facilities are similar to those in South Africa.

### Camping

Apart from in Swaziland's national parks, nature reserves and lodges, there are few official campsites. It's usually possible to free-camp, but get permission from elders in the nearest village before setting up, both out of respect for the local community and to minimise security risks. You may be offered a hut for the night; expect to pay a token fee of about E20 for this.

## ACTIVITIES

Swaziland's geographical diversity makes for some fabulous hiking experiences and you'll find short and long trails throughout the country, many within the excellent parks and nature reserves. The terrain can also be explored on horseback, by mountain bike and from the soggy seat of a river raft or canoe.

## DANGERS & ANNOYANCES

Petty crime such as pickpocketing and phone- and bag-snatching can happen in urban areas. Always take common-sense precautions and be vigilant at all times. Never walk around alone at night or flaunt valuables.

Schistosomiasis (bilharzia) and malaria are both present in Swaziland, although Swaziland is taking serious steps to be the first country in sub-Saharan Africa to move to malaria-free status.

## EMBASSIES & CONSULATES

Embassies and consulates are found in Mbabane and the Ezulwini Valley. Missions in South Africa generally have responsibility for Swaziland.

**German Liaison Office** (☎2404 3174; www.southafrica.diplo.de; 3rd fl, Lilunga House, Samhlolo St; ⏲9am-noon Mon-Fri)

**Mozambican High Commission** (☎2404 1296; moz.high@swazi.net; Princess Drive Rd, Highlands View)

**Netherlands Honorary Consul** (☎2404 3547; southafrica.nlembassy.org)

**South African High Commission** (☎2404 4651; www.dfa.gov.za; 2nd fl, the New Mall, Dr Sishayi Rd; ⏲9am-3pm Mon-Fri)

**US Embassy** (☎2417 9000; http://swaziland.usembassy.gov; nr MR103 & Cultural Center Drive, Lobamba; ⏲7.30am-5pm Mon-Thu, to 1.30pm Fri)

## EMERGENCY & IMPORTANT NUMBERS

**Ambulance** ☎977

**Fire** ☎933

**Police** ☎2404 2221, 999

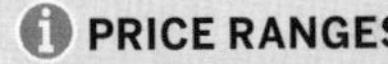

### PRICE RANGES

The following price ranges refer to a double room with bathroom in high season.

**$** less than E700 (US$50)

**$$** E700 to E1400 (US$50 to $100)

**$$$** more than E1400 (US$100)

The following price ranges refer to a standard main course.

**$** less than E75 (US$5)

**$$** E75 to E150 (US$5 to $10)

**$$$** more than E150 (US$10)

## INTERNET ACCESS

Wi-fi is still rare in Swaziland, even in many accommodation establishments. You will find a few (paid-for) wi-fi spots and internet cafes in Mbabane, Manzini and Malkerns Valley.

## LGBTIQ TRAVELERS

Swaziland is one of the most conservative countries in Southern Africa. Male homosexual activities are illegal, and gay relationships are culturally taboo, with homosexuals subjected to discrimination and harassment.

## MONEY

ATMs are common throughout Swaziland. Cards might not be accepted in rural spots so keep a small stash of cash handy.

Swaziland's currency is the lilangeni (plural emalangeni, E), divided into 100 cents. It is fixed at a value equal to the South African rand. Rand are accepted everywhere, though you will invariably be given emalangeni in change.

## OPENING HOURS

**Banks** 8.30am–2.30pm Mon–Fri, 9–11am Sat

**Post offices** 8am–4pm Mon–Fri, 8.30–11am Sat

**Government offices** 8am–4pm Mon–Fri

**Cafes** 8am–5pm

**Restaurants** 11.30am–3pm & 7–10pm (last orders); many open 3–7pm

**Bars** noon–2am

**Businesses and shopping** 8.30am–5pm Mon–Fri, 8.30am–1pm Sat

## PUBLIC HOLIDAYS

**New Year's Day** 1 January

**Good Friday** March/April

**Easter Monday** March/April

**King Mswati III's Birthday** 19 April

**National Flag Day** 25 April

**Workers' Day** 1 May

**King Sobhuza II's Birthday** 22 July

**Umhlanga Reed Dance Festival** August/September

### PRACTICALITIES

- *Times of Swaziland* (www.times.co.sz) and *Swazi Observer* (www.observer.org.sz) carry local news.
- The electricity supply in Swaziland is 220V. Plugs have three large round pins as used in South Africa
- Swaziland uses the metric system.

**Somhlolo (Independence) Day** 6 September
**Christmas Day** 25 December
**Boxing Day** 26 December
**Incwala Ceremony** December/January

### TELEPHONE

- Swaziland has a reasonably good telephone network, operated by SwaziTelecom (www.sptc.co.sz/swazitelecom).
- There are no area codes.
- MTN Swaziland (www.mtn.co.sz) provides the mobile-phone network.
- You can buy SIM cards for a nominal fee and South African SIMs work on roaming.

### TIME

- Swaziland is on SAST (South Africa Standard Time), which is two hours ahead of GMT/UTC.
- There is no daylight-saving period.

### TOURIST INFORMATION

Swaziland has tourist offices in Mbabane and the Ezulwini and Malkerns Valleys; elsewhere they are thin on the ground.

- **Swaziland National Trust Commission** (www.sntc.org.sz)
- **Swaziland Tourism** (www.thekingdomofswaziland.com)
- **Swazi.travel** (www.swazi.travel)

### VISAS

- Visitors from most Western countries don't need a visa to enter Swaziland for up to 30 days.
- To stay for longer than 30 days, apply at the **Ministry of Home Affairs immigration department** (☎2404 2941; www.gov.sz; Home Affairs & Justice Bldg, Mhlambanyatsi Rd, Mbabane; ⏲8am-4pm Mon-Fri).
- Visas cannot be obtained on arrival.
- Visa applications must be accompanied by documents including a letter of invitation.

## Getting There & Away

### AIR

There are Airlink subsidiary **Swaziland Airlink** (☎in South Africa 0861 606 606, in Swaziland 2335 0107; www.flyswaziland.com) flights into Swaziland (King Mswati III International Airport) from Johannesburg (Jo'burg).

Departure tax is E100.

### LAND

Most travellers enter Swaziland overland. Car rental is available from **Avis** (☎2333 5299; www.avis.co.za; King Mswati III International Airport; ⏲7am-6pm) and **Europcar** (☎2518 4393; www.europcar.com; Matshapa Airport; ⏲8am-5pm Mon-Fri, 11am-5pm Sat & Sun), but it's usually cheaper to rent a car in South Africa.

#### Border Crossings

There are 12 Swaziland–South Africa border posts, all of which are hassle-free, including the following. Note that small posts close at 4pm.

**Mhlumeni/Goba** (24hr) To/from Mozambique.

**Lavumisa/Golela** (7am-10pm) En route between Durban and Swaziland's Ezulwini Valley.

**Namaacha/Lomahasha** (7am-10pm) The busy post in extreme northeast Swaziland is the main crossing to/from Mozambique.

**Mahamba** (7am-10pm) The best crossing to use from Piet Retief in Mpumalanga.

**Jeppe's Reef/Matsamo** (8am-8pm) Southwest of Malelane and a possible route to Kruger National Park.

**Ngwenya/Oshoek** (7am-midnight) The busiest crossing (and a good place to pick up lifts), about 360km southeast of Pretoria.

## Getting Around

There is a good network of minibus shared taxis covering Swaziland.

### BUS

Minibus shared taxis are the main form of public transport in Swaziland. They run almost everywhere, with frequent stops en route. They leave when full; no reservations are necessary.

Local buses connect towns and villages throughout the country. Most start and terminate at the main stop in central Mbabane; they are slightly cheaper than minibuses but are slow and often overcrowded.

### CAR & MOTORCYCLE

It usually works out cheaper to rent a vehicle in South Africa and drive it over the Swazi border (you'll need a permission letter from the rental company to cross the border; this costs about R300).

You'll find rentals in Swaziland in Mbabane and **King Mswati III International Airport** (SHO; ☎2518 4390; www.swacaa.co.sz).

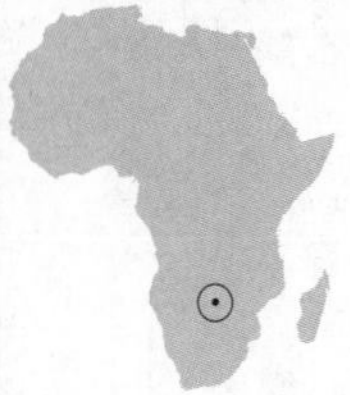

# Victoria Falls

**Includes ➡**



## Best Places to Eat

➡ Cafe Zambezi (p977)

➡ Lola's Tapas & Carnivore Restaurant (p982)

➡ Olga's Italian Corner (p977)

➡ Lookout Cafe (p981)

➡ Boma (p982)

## Best Places to Sleep

➡ Victoria Falls Hotel (p981)

➡ Jollyboys Backpackers (p975)

➡ Stanley Safari Lodge (p977)

➡ Victoria Falls Backpackers (p981)

## Why Go?

Taking its place alongside the Pyramids and the Serengeti, Victoria Falls (*Mosi-oa-Tunya* – the 'smoke that thunders') is one of Africa's original blockbusters. And although Zimbabwe and Zambia share it, Victoria Falls is a place all of its own.

As a magnet for tourists of all descriptions – backpackers, tour groups, thrill seekers, families, honeymooners – Victoria Falls is one of Earth's great spectacles. View it directly as a raging mile-long curtain of water, in all its glory, from a helicopter ride or peek precariously over its edge from Devil's Pools; the sheer power and force of the falls is something that simply does not disappoint.

Whether you're here purely to take in the sight of a natural wonder of the world, or for a serious hit of adrenalin via rafting or bungee jumping into the Zambezi, Victoria Falls is a place where you're sure to tick off numerous items from that bucket list.

## When to Go

➡ There are two main reasons to go to Victoria Falls – to view the falls, and to experience the outdoor activities – and each has its season.

➡ July to December is the season for white-water rafting, especially August for hard-core rapids.

➡ From February to June you'll experience the falls at their full force, so don't forget your raincoat.

➡ From July to September you'll get the best views of the falls, combined with lovely weather and all activities to keep you busy.

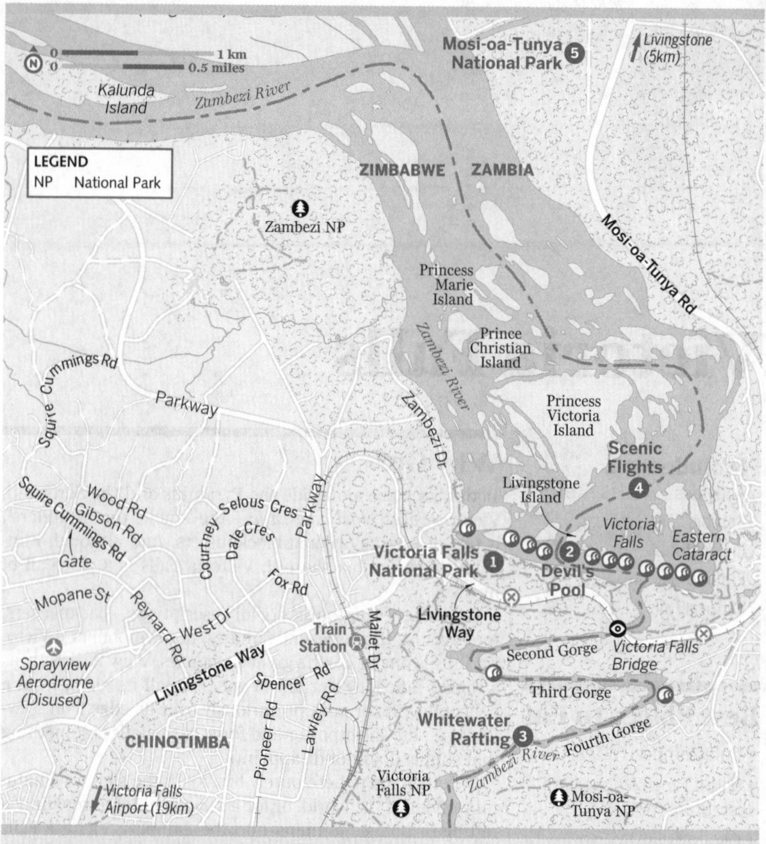

## Victoria Falls Highlights

**1 Victoria Falls National Park** (p979) Taking in the full force of the falls with unobstructed views.

**2 Devil's Pool** (p974) Experiencing the world's most extreme infinity pool.

**3 Whitewater rafting** (p971) Taming Grade-5 rapids along the Zambezi.

**4 Scenic flights** (p972) Taking the 'flight of the angels' helicopter ride over Victoria Falls.

**5 Mosi-oa-Tunya National Park** (p974) Tracking white rhino on foot on a walking safari.

# SEVENTH NATURAL WONDER OF THE WORLD

Victoria Falls is the largest, most beautiful and most majestic waterfall on the planet, and is the Seventh Natural Wonder of the World as well as a Unesco World Heritage Site. A trip to Southern Africa would not be complete without visiting this unforgettable place.

Up to one million litres of water fall – per second – down a 108m drop along a 1.7km wide strip in the Zambezi Gorge; it's an awesome sight. Victoria Falls can be seen, heard, tasted and touched; it is a treat that few other places in the world can offer, a 'must see before you die' spot.

Victoria Falls is spectacular at any time of year, yet varies in the experiences it offers.

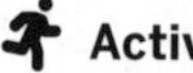

## Activities

While it's the falls that lures travellers to the region, its awesome outdoor adventure scene is what makes them hang around. From world-class whitewater rafting, bungee jumping and high-adrenalin activities, to scenic flights and walking with rhinos, Victoria Falls is undoubtedly one of the world's premier adventure destinations.

### Abseiling

Strap on a helmet, grab a rope and spend the day rappelling down the 54m sheer drop cliff face of Batoka Gorge from US$55.

### Birdwatching

Twitchers will want to bring binoculars to check out 470 species of bird that inhabit the region, including Schalow's turaco, Taita falcon, African finfoot and half-collared kingfisher. Spot them on foot in the parks or on a canoe trip along the Zambezi.

### Bridge Walk

For those not interested in bungee jumping off the bridge, walking along it is a good alternative. Strapped in with a harness, the guided tours take the walkways running just beneath the Victoria Falls Bridge, and offer a good way to learn about this engineering marvel, as well as fantastic photo ops. It's US$65 per person. Don't forget your passport.

### Bungee Jumping & Bridge Swinging

One of the most famous bungee jumps in the world, the leap here is from atop of the iconic Victoria Falls bridge, plunging 111m into the Zambezi River. It's a long way down, but man it's a lot of fun. It costs US$160 per person.

Otherwise there's the bridge swing where you jump feet first, and free fall for four seconds; you'll end up swinging, but not upside down. There are two main spots: one right off the Victoria Falls Bridge, and the other a bit further along the Batoka Gorge. Costs for single/tandem are US$160/240.

Combine bungee with a bridge swing and bridge slide, and it'll cost US$210.

### Canoeing & Kayaking

If whitewater rafting isn't for you, there's more relaxed guided canoe trips along the Upper Zambezi River on two-person inflatable canoes. Options include half (US$110) or whole day (US$125 to US$155) trips, and overnight jaunts (US$250 to US$285) and longer trips are available.

There's even more relaxed three-hour guided sunset river float trips where you can kick back and let someone else do the paddling for US$100, including refreshments.

On the Zambian side, take on the Zambezi's raging rapids in an inflatable kayak on a full-day trip (US$155).

### Crocodile Cage Diving

On the Zimbabwe side of the falls, bring along your bathers for a close encounter with a Nile croc, where you plunge within the safety of a cage into a croc-filled enclosure wearing a mask and breathing apparatus. It costs US$70

### Cultural Activities

Spend an hour in the evening by a campfire drumming under the African sky, which includes a traditional meal, for US$25. On the Zimbabwe side you can visit a local's home for lunch (US$23) or dinner (US$25)

### Hiking

There's a good choice of guided walks in the area. One of the most popular treks is the trek down Batoka Gorge to the Boiling Pot (US$48) where you can get up close and personal with Victoria Falls. You can only do this from late August to December.

### Horse Riding

Indulge in a bit of wildlife spotting from horseback along the Zambezi. Rides for 2½ hours cost US$100, and full-day trips for experienced riders are US$155.

### Jet Boating

This hair-raising trip costs US$120, and is combined with a cable-car ride down into the Batoka Gorge.

### Quadbiking

Discover the spectacular landscape surrounding Livingstone, Zambia, and the Batoka Gorge, spotting wildlife as you go on all-terrain quad bikes. Trips vary from ecotrail riding at Batoka Land to longer-range cultural trips in the African bush. Trips are one hour (US$95) or 2½ hours (US$165).

### Rafting

This is one of the best white-water rafting destinations in the world, both for experienced rafters and newbies. Rafting can be done on either side of the Zambezi River, so it doesn't matter what side of the border you're on – you'll find Grade 5 rapids. Expect very long rides with huge drops and big kicks; it's not for the faint-hearted.

The best time for rafting is between July and mid-February (low water season); peak season is around August to October. Day trips run between rapids 1 and 21 (to rapid 25 on the Zambian side), covering a distance of around 25km.

The river fills up between mid-February and July (high water season), when day trips move downstream from rapids 11 to 25, covering a distance of around 18km. Only half-day trips are offered during this time. The river will usually close for its 'off season' around April or May, depending on the rain pattern for the year.

Trips are cheaper on the Zimbabwe side, costing about US$120 (versus US$160 in Zambia), but Zambia has the benefit of the cable car (and a few additional rapids) as opposed to the steep climb out on the Zimbabwe side.

Overnight and multiday jaunts can also be arranged.

An add-on activity to rafting is **riverboarding**, which is basically lying on a boogie board and careering down the rapids. A package including rafting for a half/full day is US$170/190. Otherwise get in touch with **Bundu Adventures** (☎0213-324406, 0978-203988; www.bunduadventures.com; 1364 Kabompo Rd, Gemstone Restaurant) about its **hydrospeed surfing** trips, where you can ride rapid number 2 on an Anvil board for US$70 for three hours.

### River Cruises

River cruises along the Zambezi range from breakfast cruises to civilised jaunts on the grand *African Queen* and all-you-can-drink sunset booze cruises. Prices range from US$48 to US$85, excluding park fees. They're great for spotting wildlife, though some tourists get just as much enjoyment out of the bottomless drinks. Highly recommended.

### Scenic Flights

Just when you thought the falls couldn't get any more spectacular, discover the 'flight of angels' helicopter ride that flies you right by the drama for the undisputed best views available. Rides aren't cheap, but they're worth it. **Zambezi Helicopter Company** (☎013-43569; www.zambezihelicopters.com; flights 13-/25-min US$150/284, plus US$12 govt fee) and **Bonisair** (☎0776 497888; www.bonisair.com; 15-/22-/25-mins US$150/235/277) in Zimbabwe, and **United Air Charter** (☎0955 204282, 0213-323095; www.uaczam.com; Baobab Ridge, Livingstone; 15/20/30min US$165/235/330) and **Batoka Sky** (☎0213-323589; www.seasonsinafrica.com; 15-min flights from US$155) in Zambia all offer flights. Flights cost from US$150 for 15 minutes over the falls, with longer trips available to take in the surrounding area.

On the Zambian side you can take a microlight flight with Batoka Sky, which offers another way to get fabulous aerial views.

### Steam Train Journeys

To take in the romance of yesteryear, book yourself a ride on a historical steam train on the **Bushtracks Express** (☎013-45176; www.gotothevictoriafalls.com; 205 Courtney Selous Cr),

## THE FALLS VIEWING SEASONS

Though spectacular at any time of year, the falls has a wet and dry season and each brings a distinct experience.

When the river is higher and the falls fuller it's the Wet, and when the river is lower and the falls aren't smothered in spray it's the Dry. Broadly speaking, you can expect the following conditions during the year:

**January to April** The beginning of the rainy season sees the falls begin their transitional period from low to high water, which should give you decent views, combined with experiencing its famous spray.

**May to June** Don't forget your raincoat, as you're gonna get drenched! While the falls will be hard to see through the mist, it'll give you a true sense of its power as 500 million litres of water plummets over the edge. The mist during this time can be seen from 50km away. If you want views, don't despair, this is the best time for aerial views with a chopper flight taking you up and over this incredible sight.

**July to October** The most popular time to visit, as the mist dissipates to unveil the best views and photography options from directly across the falls, while the volume maintains its rage to give you an idea of its sheer force – but only from the Zimbabwe side. However, those on the Zambian side will be able to experience Devil's Pool, which is accessible from August.

**November to January** The least popular time to visit, as temperatures rise and the falls are at their lowest flow. But they're impressive nevertheless, as the curtain of water divides into sections. The advantage of this time of year is you're able to swim right up to the edge of Devil's Pool on the Zambian side.

a 1953 class 14A Garratt steam train that will take you over the iconic Victoria Falls bridge at sunset with gourmet canapés and unlimited drinks. It's US$125 (including transfers, alcohol and snacks), with departures on Tuesday and Friday either at 5pm or 5.30pm; check the website for the latest schedule. Even if you're not booked on a trip it's worth getting along to the station to watch the drama of its departure.

In Zambia the **Royal Livingstone Express** (☎0213-4699300; www.royal-livingstone-express.com; Mosi-oa-Tunya Rd; US$180 incl dinner, drinks & transfers; ⏲4.30pm Wed & Sat) takes you on a 3½-hour ride including five-course dinner and drinks on a 1924 10th-class or 12th-class steam engine. The journey takes you to through Mosi-oa-Tunya National Park on plush leather couches, en route to the Victoria Falls Bridge for a sundowner. It's priced at $180 per person, including return transfers within Livingstone.

### Wildlife Safaris

There are plenty of options for wildlife watching in the area, both in the national park in the immediate area and further afield, as well as private game reserves.

In Zambia the game reserve section of Mosi-oa-Tunya National Park is home to white rhino, and hence a popular spot to tick off that last member from the big five in the wild. You're able to track them on foot for US$80 per person (including park fees), but you can only do this as part of a walking tour. Get in touch with Livingstone Rhino Walks (p975) or Savannah Southern Safaris (p974) for bookings; note that you need to be over 12 years of age.

The Zambezi National Park in Zimbabwe is much bigger in scale and has a greater diversity of wildlife (including a few cats) and some wonderful lodges and campsites along the Zambezi.

On both sides of the border river cruises (from US$48) along the Zambezi River are another popular way to see various wildlife including elephants, hippos and plenty of birdlife.

Another convenient option, only 15km from Victoria Falls town, is the Stanley and Livingstone Private Game Reserve. Set on a 4000-hectare private reserve here you can track the Big Five, including black rhino that have been translocated from Hwange National Park. A standard three-hour game drive costs US$100, or you can do a night drive and a bush dinner (US$137).

**Hwange National Park** (www.zimparks.org; national parks accommodation per day guests/nonguests US$10/20; ⏲main gate 6am-6pm) in Zimbabwe is the other option, with one of the largest number of elephants in the world, as well as good sightings of predators. A day trip will cost around US$220 (minimum four people), or otherwise it's a two-hour bus ride away.

You can travel further afield, with operators arranging day trips to Chobe National Park in Botswana for US$160 (excluding visas). It's only a one-hour drive from Victoria Falls, and includes a breakfast boat cruise, a game drive in Chobe National Park, lunch and transfer back to Victoria Falls by 5pm. Wildlife viewing is excellent: lions, elephants, wild dogs, cheetahs, buffaloes and plenty of antelopes.

### Zipline, Flying Fox & Gorge Swings

Glide at 106km/h along a zipline (single/tandem US$69/111), or soar like a superhero from one country to another (from Zim to Zam) on the 'bridge slide' as you whiz over Batoka Gorge (single/tandem US$45/70). Other similar options are flying-fox rides (US$42).

A *slightly* less terrifying variation of the bungee jump is the gorge swing (US$95), where you take the plunge foot first before swinging across the gorge like a human pendulum.

## ℹ Information

Hands down the best independent advice is from **Backpackers Bazaar** (☎013-45828, 013-44511, 013-42208; www.backpackersbazaarvicfalls.com; off Parkway, Shop 5, Bata Bldg; ⏲8am-5pm Mon-Fri, 9am-4pm Sat & Sun) in the town of Victoria Falls, run by the passionate owner, Joy, who has a wealth of all info and advice for Victoria Falls and beyond. In Livingstone, the folks at Jollyboys Backpackers (p975) are also extremely knowledgeable on all the latest happenings. Both are good places to book activities and onward travel.

# ZAMBIA

☎260

As Zambia continues to ride the wave of tourism generated by the falls, it manages to keep itself grounded, offering a wonderfully low-key destination. The waterfront straddling the falls continues its rapid development and is fast becoming one of the most exclusive destinations in Southern Africa.

### VISAS

You will need a visa to cross between Zimbabwe and Zambia. These are available at the border, open from around 6am to 10pm.

You can't get multi-entry visas at the Victoria Falls crossings; you'll usually need to apply at your home country embassy before travelling.

**Crossing into Zambia** A day visit costs US$20 for 24 hours (but you'll need a Zimbabwean double-entry to return), a single-entry visa costs US$50 and double entry is US$80.

**Crossing into Zimbabwe** A single-entry visa costs US$30 for most nationalities (US$55 for British/Irish and US$75 for Canadian). Double entry is US$45 for most nationalities (US$75 for British/Irish and unavailable for Canadians).

Note that the KAZA Uni-Visa (which formerly allowed travel between the two countries) was suspended in 2016. It's worth checking, though, before you leave to see if it's back in effect.

# Livingstone

POP 136,897 / ☎0213

The relaxed and friendly town of Livingstone, set just 11km from Victoria Falls, is a fantastic base for visiting the Zambian side of the natural world wonder. It attracts travellers not only to experience the falls but also to tackle the thrilling adventure scene, and has taken on the role of a backpacking mecca. Its main thoroughfare, Mosi-oa-Tunya Rd, leads south to a wonderful stretch of the Zambezi River around 7km from town.

## Sights

**★Victoria Falls World Heritage National Monument Site** WATERFALL
(Mosi-au-Tunya National Park; adult/child/guide US$20/10/10; ⏲6am-6pm) This is what you're here for. The mighty Victoria Falls is part of the Mosi-oa-Tunya National Park, located 11km outside town before the Zambia border. From the centre, a network of paths leads through thick vegetation to various viewpoints.

For close-up views of the **Eastern Cataract**, nothing beats the hair-raising (and hair-wetting) walk across the footbridge, through swirling clouds of mist, to a sheer buttress called the **Knife Edge**.

**★Devil's Pool** VIEWPOINT
(www.devilspool.net; Livingstone Island; from US$90) One of the most thrilling experiences, not only at the falls but in all of Africa, is the hair-raising journey to **Livingstone Island**. Here you will bathe in Devil's Pool – nature's ultimate infinity pool, set directly on the edge of Victoria Falls. You can leap into the pool and then poke your head over the edge to get an extraordinary view of the 100m drop. Here also you'll see the plaque marking the spot where David Livingstone first sighted the falls.

**Mosi-oa-Tunya National Park** NATIONAL PARK
(adult/child US$15/7.50; ⏲6am-6pm) This park is divided into two sections: the Victoria Falls area and the wildlife sector. The latter is only 3km southwest of Livingstone, and most famous for its population of white rhino, which you can track on foot. For their protection, the rhino are accompanied by anti-poaching rangers round-the-clock. You can only see them as part of a pre-booked tour (US$80 per person, inclusive of park fees and hotel transfer), booked through Livingstone Rhino Walks or Savannah Southern Safaris.

**Livingstone Museum** MUSEUM
(☎0213-324429; www.museumszambia.org; Mosi-oa-Tunya Rd; adult/child US$ 5/3; ⏲9am-4.30pm) The excellent Livingstone Museum is the oldest, largest and best museum in the country. It's divided into sections covering archaeology, history, ethnography and natural history. Highlights include its collection of original David Livingstone memorabilia (including signed letters), tribal artefacts (from bark cloth to witchcraft exhibits), a life-sized model of an African village, taxidermy displays and coverage of modern-day Zambian history.

## Tours

**Savannah Southern Safaris** WILDLIFE, WALKING
(☎0973 471486; www.savannah-southern-safaris.com) Offers a range of nature tours, but it's best known for its walks to see white rhino in Mosi-au-Tunya National Park. For two or more people it's US$70, or US$80 for individuals, inclusive of transport and park fees. Note you need to be over 12 years of age.

There are also tours to visit local communities, as well as Livingstone walking tours.

**Livingstone Rhino Walks** SAFARI
(0213-322267; www.livingstonerhinosafaris.com; per person US$80) This Livingstone-based tour operator specialises in walking safaris to see white rhino in Mosi-au-Tunya National Park. Visitors must be over 12 years of age. The price is inclusive of park entry fees and transfers in the Livingstone area.

## Sleeping

**★Jollyboys Backpackers** HOSTEL, CAMPGROUND $
(0213-324229; www.backpackzambia.com; 34 Kanyanta Rd; campsite per person US$9, dm US$12-15, d from US$65, d/tr/q with shared bathroom US$45/50/80; ) The clued-in owner knows exactly what backpackers want, making Jollyboys popular for good reason. From its friendly staff, social bar and restaurant to the sunken reading lounge and sparkling pool, it's a great place to hang out. Dorms and bathrooms are spotless (with a flashpacker option, too), while the private rooms comprise A-frame garden cottages or very comfortable rooms with air-con and attached bathroom.

**Rose Rabbit Zambezi River Bushcamp** TENTED CAMP $
(in Zimbabwe 0784 007283, 0773 368608; www.facebook.com/theroserabbit; Rapid 21, Lower Zambezi River; per person campsite/dm/tented camping/treehouse US$10/15/20/40) This riverside beach camp is one for independent travellers looking for a different scene. Right on rapid 21 of the Lower Zambezi, it will suit not only rafting enthusiasts but also a more free-spirited crowd who are into bonfire jamborees, swimming and hanging out by the beach. As well as campsites, there are dorms, tented camps and A-frame treehouse digs.

**Livingstone Backpackers** HOSTEL, CAMPGROUND $
(0213-324730; www.livingstonebackpackers.com; 559 Mokambo Rd; campsite US$7, dm from US$12, d US$45, with shared bathroom US$65; ) Resembling the *Big Brother* household, this place can be a bit 'party central', particularly when the Gen Y volunteer brigade is on holiday. You'll find them lounging by the pool, in the hot tub, at the bar, or in the sandy outdoor cabana, swinging in hammocks, cooking barbecues or tackling the rock-climbing wall. There is also an open-air kitchen and living room. Very friendly staff.

**Fawlty Towers** BACKPACKERS, LODGE $
(0213-323432; www.adventure-africa.com; 216 Mosi-oa-Tunya Rd; dm US$12, r from US$50, with shared bathroom US$45; ) As well as some of the nicest and most spacious dorms we've seen, things have been spruced up here into a guesthouse full of upmarket touches – no longer catering exclusively to backpackers. There's free wi-fi, large well-maintained lawns, a great pool, a bar, a homely lounge, free pancakes for afternoon tea, a self-catering kitchen, and no Basil or Manuel in sight.

**Olga's Guesthouse** GUESTHOUSE $$
(0213-324160; www.olgasproject.com; cnr Mosi-oa-Tunya & Nakatindi Rds; s/d/f incl breakfast US$40/60/80; ) With a good location

### ZIM OR ZAM?

Victoria Falls straddles the border between Zimbabwe and Zambia, and is easily accessible from both countries. However, the big question for most travellers is: do I visit the falls from the town of Victoria Falls, Zimbabwe, or from Livingstone, Zambia? The answer is simple: visit the falls from both sides and, if possible, stay in both towns. You'll need to pay for extra visas, but you've come this far so it's worth it.

From the Zimbabwean side, you're further from the falls, though the overall views are much, much better. From the Zambian side, for daring souls you can literally stand on top of the falls from Devil's Pool, though from here your perspective is narrowed.

The town of Victoria Falls was built for tourists, so it's easily walkable and located right next to the entrance to the Falls. It has a natural African bush beauty. As for whether it's safe given Zimbabwe's ongoing political issues, the answer is a resolute 'yes'.

Livingstone is an attractive town with a relaxed ambience and a proud, historic air. Since the town of Victoria Falls was the main tourist centre for so many years, Livingstone feels more authentic, perhaps because locals earn their livelihood through means other than tourism. Livingstone is bustling with travellers year-round, though the town is fairly spread out, and is located 11km from the falls.

## Livingstone

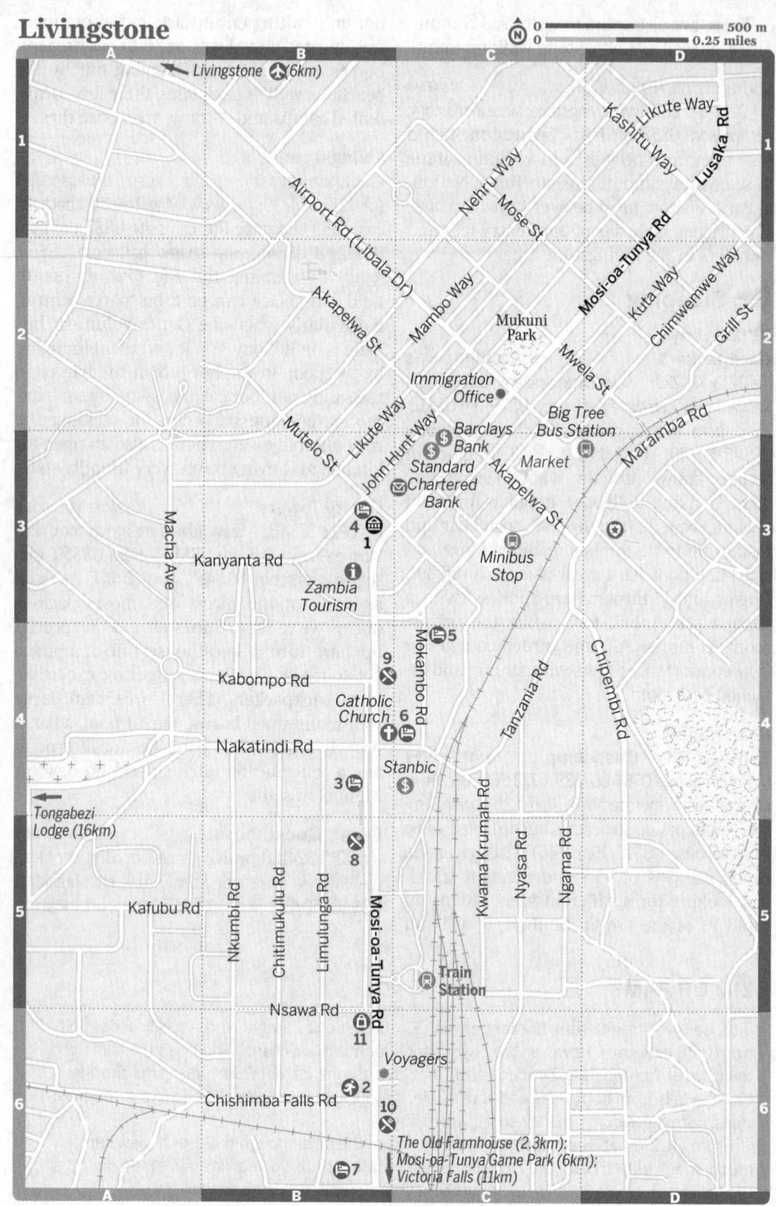


in the centre of town, Olga's offers clean, spacious rooms with cool tiled floors, teak furniture and slick bathrooms just a few feet away. Profits go towards helping an organisation supporting local youth. Another bonus is its on-site Italian restaurant, Olga's Italian Corner.

**ZigZag** GUESTHOUSE **$$**

(☎0213-322814; www.zigzagzambia.com; 693 Linda Rd, off Mosi-oa-Tunya Rd; s/d/tr incl breakfast

## Livingstone

**Sights**
1 Livingstone Museum ........ B3

**Activities, Courses & Tours**
2 Royal Livingstone Express ........ B6

**Sleeping**
3 Fawlty Towers ........ B4
4 Jollyboys Backpackers ........ B3
5 Livingstone Backpackers ........ C4
6 Olga's Guesthouse ........ C4
7 ZigZag ........ B6

**Eating**
8 Cafe Zambezi ........ B5
9 Da Canton ........ B4
10 Golden Leaf ........ B6
Olga's Italian Corner ........ (see 6)
ZigZag ........ (see 7)

**Shopping**
11 Wayawaya ........ B6

US$50/70/90; P ❄ @ ☎ ≋) Don't be deceived by the motel-meets-caravan-park exterior: the rooms here are more boutique B&B with loving touches throughout. Rooms are spotless, and set on a sprawling garden property with an assortment of fruit trees, picnic tables, a plush pool and a playground for kids. Its great restaurant is another drawcard, too.

**Victoria Falls Waterfront** LODGE, CAMPGROUND $$
(☎0213-320606; www.thevictoriafallswaterfront.com; Sichango Dr; campsite per person US$13, s/d tented camping US$36/48, s/d incl breakfast chalet from US$165/215; ❄ ☎ ≋) Sharing space with the luxury resorts along the banks of the Zambezi, this is the only waterfront lodge that caters to budget travellers. For this reason it's a popular place, with a wilderness charm (crocs inhabit a small creek on the property), and a choice of camping, domed tents or alluring riverside chalets. Its pool with decking and bar overlooking the river is unsurprisingly popular at sunset.

★**Stanley Safari Lodge** LODGE $$$
(☎in Malawi 0265-1794491; www.stanleysafaris.com; Stanley Rd; per person with full board & activities from US$510; @ ☎ ≋) Intimate and indulgent, Stanley is a 10km drive from the falls in a peaceful spot surrounded by mopane (woodland). Rooms scattered among the landscaped bush garden are as plush as can be expected at these prices; the standouts are the rustic open-air suites where you can soak up nature from your own private plunge pool. When you tire of that, curl up by the fire in the open-air lounge. Rates are all-inclusive.

**Tongabezi Lodge** LODGE $$$
(☎0979 312766, 0213-327468; www.tongabezi.com; cottage/house per person incl full board & activities from US$775/875; ❄ ☎ ≋) Has sumptuous, spacious cottages, open-faced 'treehouses' and private dining decks. The houses are good for families and have private plunge pools. Guests are invited to spend an evening on nearby Sindabezi Island (from US$595 per person), a luxurious, rustic getaway.

### Eating

★**Da Canton** GELATERIA $
(Mosi-Oa-Tunya Rd; gelato small/large cup ZMW8/24, pizza from ZMW19; ⏲9am-11pm) While all the Italian food here is tasty and authentic, it's the homemade gelato that has locals raving. The Italian owner makes all 18 flavours, including all the classics and some original concoctions.

★**Cafe Zambezi** AFRICAN $$
(☎0978 978578; www.facebook.com/cafezambezi; 217 Mosi-oa-Tunya Rd; mains US$6-10; ⏲7.15am-midnight; ☎ ✎) Head straight through to the courtyard, sunny by day and candlelit by night. Bursting with local flavour, the broad menu covers local favourites of goat meat, smoky crocodile tail and mopane (woodland) caterpillars. Authentic wood-fired pizzas are a winner or sink your teeth into impala or eggplant-and-haloumi burgers.

★**Olga's Italian Corner** ITALIAN $$
(www.olgasproject.con; cnr Mosi-oa-Tunya & Nakatindi Rds; pizza & pasta ZMW35-88; ⏲7am-10pm; ☎ ✎) Olga's does authentic wood-fired thin-crust pizzas, as well as delicious homemade pasta classics all served under a large thatched roof. Great options for vegetarians include the lasagne with its crispy blackened edge served in the dish. All profits go to a community centre to help disadvantaged youth.

**Golden Leaf** INDIAN $$
(☎0213-321266; 1174 Mosi-Oa-Tunya Rd; mains ZMW54-95; ⏲12.30-10pm) As soon as those aromas hit you upon arrival you'll realise Golden Leaf is the real deal when it comes to authentic

Indian food. It's a good option for vegetarians with a lot of choices including house-made paneer dishes, creamy North Indian curries and tandoori dishes in the evenings.

**ZigZag** CAFE $$
(Mango Tree Cafe; www.zigzagzambia.com/the-mango-tree-cafe; 693 Linda Rd, off Mosi-oa-Tunya Rd; mains from ZMW25-62; 7am-9pm; ) ZigZag does drool-inducing homemade muffins, excellent Zambian coffee and smoothies using fresh fruit from the garden. Its changing menu of comfort food is all made from scratch, and you can expect anything from drop scones (pikelets) with bacon and maple syrup to thin-crust pizzas and burgers.

## Drinking & Nightlife

**The Sundeck** BAR
(http://royal-livingstone.anantara.com/the-sun decks; Mosi-au-Tunya Rd; cocktail from ZMW40; 10.30am-7pm; ) Just the spot for a sundowner, this open-air bar within the Royal Livingstone Hotel overlooks a dramatic stretch of the Zambezi. As well as the usual bar drinks there's a choice of old-fashioned cocktails such as the Manhattan, Americano and champagne cocktail. There's also decent burgers, mezze platters and salads. From here it's a 15-minute walk to the falls.

## Shopping

**Wayawaya** FASHION & ACCESSORIES
(www.wayawaya.no; Mosi-oa-Tunya Rd; 9am-5pm) A social enterprise founded by two Norwegian girls, Wayawaya sells quality, contemporary handmade bags put together by local women. Its principles are based on the slow fashion movement, and you can meet all the ladies when visiting. Get in touch if you want to volunteer.

### DANGERS & ANNOYANCES

Don't walk from town to the falls as there have been a number of muggings along this stretch of road – even tourists on bicycles have been targeted. It's a long and not terribly interesting walk anyway, and simply not worth the risk (especially given there are elephants around). Take a taxi or free shuttle from your guesthouse. While Livingstone is generally a very safe town, avoid walking around town once it becomes dark.

### IMMIGRATION

**Immigration Office** (0213-3320648; www.zambiaimmigration.gov.zm; Mosi-oa-Tunya Rd; 8am-1pm & 2-5pm Mon-Fri)

### MEDICAL SERVICES

**SES-Zambia** (www.ses-zambia.com; Mosi-au-Tunya Rd, AVANI Victoria Falls Resort; 8am-5pm) The best medical facility in the area, both for emergency services and general medicine. It's within the **AVANI resort** (0978 777044; www.minorhotels.com/en/avani; Mosi-oa-Tunya Rd).

### MONEY

The following banks accept MasterCard and Visa, but can occasionally go offline during power outages.

**Barclays** in town (cnr Mosi-oa-Tunya Rd & Akapelwa St) and at the AVANI resort.

**Standard Chartered Bank** (Mosi-oa-Tunya Rd) In town.

**Stanbic** (Mosi-oa-Tunya Rd) In town.

### POLICE

**Police** (0213-320116, 0213-323575; Maramba Rd)

### POST

**Post Office** (Mosi-oa-Tunya Rd) Has a poste restante service.

### TOURIST INFORMATION

**Tourist Centre** (0213-321404; www.zambiatourism.com; Mosi-oa-Tunya Rd; 8am-5pm Mon-Fri, 8am-noon Sat) Mildly useful and can help with booking tours and accommodation, but Jollyboys and Fawlty Towers have all the information you need.

## Getting There & Away

### AIR

Livingstone's newly renovated airport – officially known as Harry Mwanga Nkumbula International Airport – is located 6km northwest of town. It has an ATM and free wi-fi. It's around a US$5 taxi ride into town, or US$8 to the waterfront hotels.

**South African Airways** (0213-323031; www.flysaa.com) and **British Airways** (Comair; in South Africa +27 10-3440130; www.britishairways.com) have daily flights to and from Johannesburg (1¾ hours); the cheapest economy fare starts at around US$270 return.

**Proflight Zambia** (0977 335563, in Lusaka 0211-252452; www.proflight-zambia.com) flies daily from Livingstone to Lusaka for around US$210 one way (1¼ hours).

### BUS & MINIBUS

Plenty of minibuses and shared taxis ply the route from the Big Tree Bus Station at Livingstone's town market along Senanga Rd in Livingstone. Note that plans are in place to relocate the bus terminal to Nakatindi Rd. As muggings have been reported, it is best to take a taxi if you arrive at night.

#### CAR & MOTORCYCLE

If you're driving a rented car or motorcycle, be sure to carefully check all info regarding insurance, and that you have all the necessary papers for checks and border crossings such as 'owners' and 'permission to drive' documents, insurance papers and a copy of the carbon tax receipt. Expect to pay around US$100 in various fees when crossing the border into Zimbabwe.

#### TRAIN

While the bus is a much quicker way to get around, the train to Lusaka is for lovers of slow travel or trains. The operative word here is *slow*, taking anywhere from 15 to 20 hours for the trip to Lusaka (economy/business/1st-class sleeper ZMW 70/90/135), via Choma, departing 8pm on Monday and Friday. Bring your own food. Reservations are available at the **train station** (☎0961 195353), which is signed off Mosi-oa-Tunya Rd.

### Getting Around

#### CAR & MOTORCYCLE

**Hemingways** (☎0213-323097; www.hemingwayszambia.com) in Livingstone has new 4WD Toyota Hiluxes for around US$225 per day. Vehicles are fully kitted out with everything you need, including cooking and camping equipment. Drivers must be over 25.

**Voyagers** (☎0213-320517, 0213-323259; www.voyagerszambia.com; 163 Mosi-oa-Tunya Rd) Zambian operator affiliated with Europcar has reasonably priced 4WDs for around US$100 per day.

#### TAXIS

Minibuses run regularly along Mosi-oa-Tunya Rd to Victoria Falls and the Zambian border (ZMW5,15 minutes). Blue taxis cost ZMW60 to ZMW80 from the border to Livingstone. Coming from the border, shared taxis are parked just over from the waiting taxis, and depart when full. The going rate for one day's taxi hire around Livingstone and the falls is about US$25.

# ZIMBABWE

☎263

There may still be a long way to go, but finally things seem to be looking up for Zimbabwe. All the bad news that has kept it in the glare of the spotlight – rampant land reform, hyperinflation and food shortages – fortunately now seem to be a thing of the past. In reality, safety has never been a concern for travellers here and, even during the worst of it, tourists were never targets for political violence. Word of this seems to have spread, as tourists stream back to the Zim side of the falls.

## Victoria Falls

POP 33,360 / ☎013

A genuine bucket-list destination, Victoria Falls remains one of Africa's most famous tourist towns. Not only does it offer the best views of the iconic falls, but it also has a world-class adventure-tourism scene and wildlife safaris.

It's home to the country's tourism industry, and despite Zimbabwe's political issues, it's always been a safe spot for tourists; locals are exceptionally friendly. While for a few years it felt like a resort in off-season, there's no mistake about it now – it's officially reopened for business.

Though built specifically for tourism, it retains a relaxed local feel, and has neat, walkable streets (though not at dark, because of the wild animals) lined with hotels, bars and some of the best crafts you'll find anywhere in Southern Africa.

### Sights

★**Victoria Falls National Park** WATERFALL
(US$30; ⏲6am-6pm) Here on the Zimbabwe side of the falls you're in for a real treat. Some two-thirds of Victoria Falls are located here, including the main falls themselves, which flow spectacularly year-round. The walk is along the top of the gorge, following a path with various viewing points that open up to extraordinary front-on panoramas of these world-famous waterfalls.

★**Jafuta Heritage Centre** CULTURAL CENTRE
(www.elephantswalk.com/heritage.htm; Adam Stander Dr, Elephant's Walk; admission by donation; ⏲8am-5pm) FREE This impressive little museum details the cultural heritage of Zimbabwe's indigenous ethnic groups. There's good background information on the Shona, Ndebele, Tonga and Lozi people, as well as fascinating artefacts, jewellery and costumes.

**Zambezi National Park** NATIONAL PARK
(☎013-42294; www.zimparks.org; day/overnight US$15/23; ⏲6am-6pm) Just 5km from the town centre is this vastly underrated national park, comprising 40km of Zambezi River frontage and a spread of wildlife-rich mopane (woodland) and savannah. It's best known for its herds of sable, elephant, giraffe, zebra and buffalo, plus the occasional (rarely spotted) lion, leopard and cheetah. It's easily accessible by 2WD vehicle.

# Victoria Falls

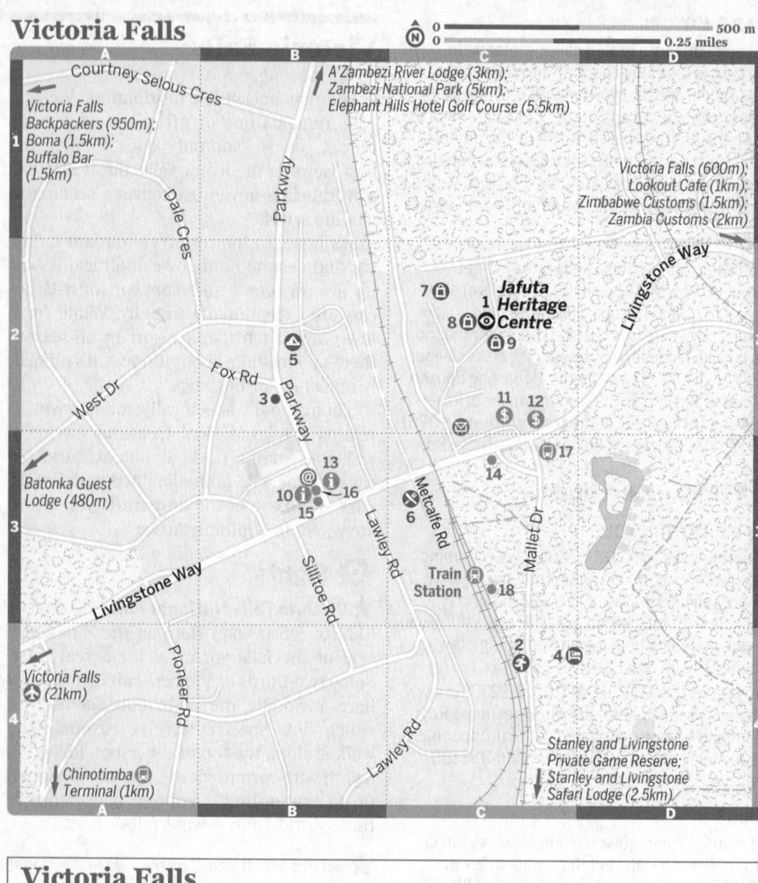


VICTORIA FALLS VICTORIA FALLS

## Victoria Falls

**Top Sights**
1 Jafuta Heritage Centre.......C2

**Activities, Courses & Tours**
2 Bushtracks Express.......C4
3 Wild Horizons.......B2

**Sleeping**
4 Victoria Falls Hotel.......C4
5 Victoria Falls Restcamp & Lodges.......B2

**Eating**
Africa Café.......(see 8)
In Da Belly Restaurant.......(see 5)
6 Lola's Tapas & Carnivore Restaurant.......C3

**Drinking & Nightlife**
Stanley's Terrace.......(see 4)

**Shopping**
7 Big Curio Open Market.......C2
8 Elephant's Walk Shopping & Artist Village.......C2
Matsimela.......(see 8)
Ndau Collection.......(see 8)
Prime Art Gallery.......(see 8)
9 Tshaka's Den Complex.......C2

**Information**
10 Backpackers Bazaar.......B3
11 Barclays Bank.......C2
12 Standard Chartered Bank.......C2
13 Zimbabwe Tourism Authority.......B3

**Transport**
14 Avis.......C3
15 FastJet.......B3
16 Hertz.......B3
17 Intercape Pathfinder.......C3
18 Train Ticket Office.......C3

**Stanley and Livingstone Private Game Reserve** WILDLIFE RESERVE
(Victoria Falls Private Game Reserve; ☎013-44571; www.stanleyandlivingstone.com/activities) This private 4000-hectare game reserve 12km from town has the Big Five, including the critically endangered black rhino, which you're almost guaranteed to see. Game drives are US$100, US$135 for a night drive with a bush dinner.

## Sleeping

**★Victoria Falls Backpackers** HOSTEL, CAMPGROUND $
(☎013-42209; www.victoriafallsbackpackers.com; 357 Gibson Rd; camping/dm per person US$10/18, d US$60, with shared bathroom US$50; @☎≋) One of the best budget choices in town, this long-standing backpackers received a much-needed revamp when the original owners returned. The eclectic mix of rooms are scattered among the well-tended garden property full of quirky touches. Other notable features are its bar, small inviting pool, games room and TV lounge, plus self-catering kitchen, massage and fish spa.

**Victoria Falls Restcamp & Lodges** CAMPGROUND, LODGE $
(☎013-40509; www.vicfallsrestcamp.com; cnr Parkway & West Dr; camping/dm US$16/20, s/d dome tents from US$29/40, s/d chalets without bathroom US$35/46, cottages from US$127; ❄☎≋) A great alternative for independent travellers, it has a relaxed holiday-camp feel, within secure grassy grounds, with a choice of no-frills dorms, lodge-style rooms (or pricier air-con rooms with bathroom) and safari tents. There's a lovely pool and fantastic open-air restaurant, In Da Belly. Wi-fi available (for a fee).

**Zambezi National Park Lodge** CHALETS, CAMPGROUND $$
(☎013-42294; www.zimparks.org; camping $17, cottage $138; ❄) These wonderful two-bedroom cottages are right on the Zambezi river. You'll need to bring your own food, but all come with fridges, full kitchen, couches, TV, bathtubs and even air-con. There's an outdoor barbecue area too. Further into the park are basic bush campsites (firewood US$5), but with no water or ablutions.

**★Victoria Falls Hotel** LUXURY HOTEL $$$
(☎0772 132175, 013-44751; www.victoriafallshotel.com; 1 Mallet Dr; s/d incl breakfast from US$423/455; ❄☎≋) Built in 1904, this historic hotel (the oldest in Zimbabwe) oozes elegance and sophistication. It occupies an impossibly scenic location, looking across manicured lawns (with roaming warthogs) to the gorge and bridge. You can't see the falls as such, but you do see the spray from some rooms. Taking high tea here at Stanley's Terrace is an institution.

**Stanley and Livingstone Safari Lodge** LODGE $$$
(☎013-44571; www.stanleyandlivingstone.com; Stanley & Livingstone Private Game Reserve; r per person incl full board & activities US$436; ❄☎≋) Set on a private game reserve 15km from Victoria Falls, this luxury lodge will suit visitors without the time to visit a national park but who want to be surrounded by wildlife. Rooms on the luxurious grounds feature all the modern comforts combined with Victorian-style bathrooms featuring claw-foot tubs, lounge suite and patio.

**Batonka Guest Lodge** GUESTHOUSE $$$
(☎013-47189/90; www.batonkaguestlodge.com; Reynard Rd; s/d incl breakfast US$195/300; ❄☎≋) Mixing modern comforts with colonial charm, Batonka is an excellent choice for those not wanting a large-scale resort. It has a relaxed ambience, with rooms overlooking a landscaped lawn and inviting pool. Rooms have stylish bathrooms, cable TV and filter coffee. The reception/bar/restaurant is in a homestead-style building with wrap-around veranda and a boutique interior design with original artwork throughout.

**Elephant Camp** LODGE $$$
(☎013-44571; www.theelephantcamp.com; s/d incl full board US$838/1118; @☎≋) One of the best spots to splash out; the luxurious 'tents' have a classic lodge feel and are set on a private concession within the Victoria Falls National Park. Each room has its own outdoor private plunge pool and balcony decking to spot grazing animals or the spray of the falls. You might get to meet Sylvester, the resident cheetah.

## Eating

**★Lookout Cafe** CAFE $$
(☎0782 745112; www.wildhorizons.co.za/the-lookout-cafe; Batoka Gorge; mains US$12-15; ⊙8am-7pm; ☎) A stunning location overlooking Batoka Gorge. Enjoy views of the bridge and the Zambezi river while tucking into a burger or crocodile kebab, or a cold drink on its open-air deck or grassy lawn terrace. It's operated by **Wild Horizons** (☎013-44571, 0712 213721; www.wildhorizons.co.za; 310 Parkway Dr), so you'll get the added

## Victoria Falls & Mosi-oa-Tunya National Parks

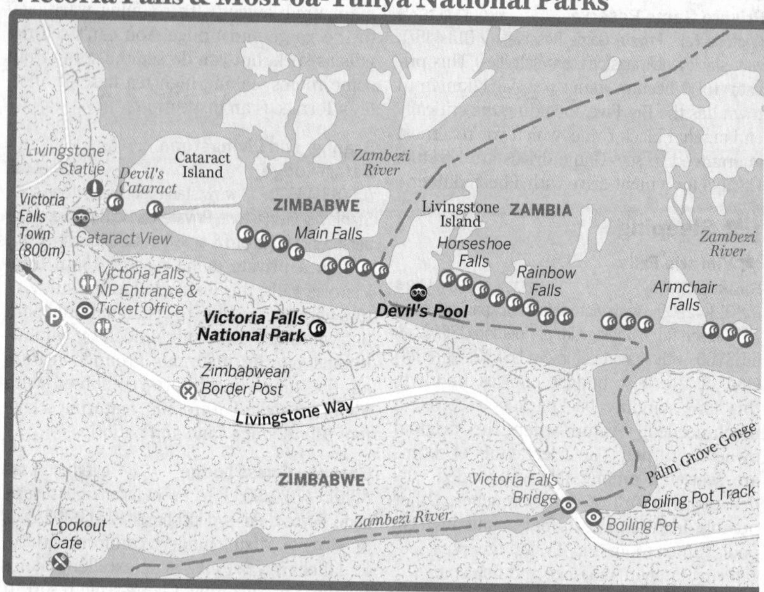




entertainment of watching daredevils take the plunge or soar across the gorge.

**Africa Café** CAFE **$$**

(www.elephantswalk.com/africa_cafe.htm; Adam Stander Dr, Elephant's Walk; breakfast/burgers US$7/11; ⌚8am-5pm; 📶✍) This appealing outdoor cafe does the best coffee in Victoria Falls, made by expert baristas using beans sourced from Zimbabwe's eastern highlands. There's plenty of seating scattered about to enjoy big breakfasts, burgers, vegetarian dishes and desserts such as its signature baobab-powder cheese cake. There's a bar, too.

**★Lola's Tapas & Carnivore Restaurant** SPANISH, AFRICAN **$$**

(☎013-42994; 8B Landela Complex; dishes US$8-20; ⌚8am-10pm; 📶) Run by welcoming host Lola from Barcelona, this popular eatery combines a menu of Mediterranean cuisine with local game meats, with anything from crocodile ravioli to paella with kudu. Other items include zebra burgers, impala meatballs, and more traditional tapas dishes. There's also a full spread of all-you-can-eat game meat for US$30.

**★Boma** AFRICAN **$$**

(☎013-43211; www.victoria-falls-safari-lodge.com; Squire Cummings Rd, Victoria Falls Safari Lodge; buffet US$40; ⌚dinner 7pm, cafe from 7am) Enjoy a taste of Africa at this buffet restaurant set under a massive thatched roof. Here you can dine on smoked crocodile tail, BBQ warthog, guinea fowl stew and wood-fired spit roasts; and the more adventurous can try a mopane worm (you'll get a certificate from the chef for your efforts). There's also traditional dancing (8pm), interactive drumming (8.45pm) and fortune telling by a witch doctor. Bookings essential.

**In Da Belly Restaurant** AFRICAN, INTERNATIONAL **$$**

(☎013-332077; Parkway, Victoria Falls Restcamp & Lodges; meals US$5-15; ⌚7am-9.30pm) Under a large thatched hut, looking out to a sparkling pool, this relaxed open-air eatery has a menu of warthog schnitzel, crocodile curry and impala burgers, as well as one of the best breakfast menus in town. The name is a play on Ndebele, one of the two major population tribes in Zimbabwe.

### 🍷 Drinking & Nightlife

**★Stanley's Terrace** HIGH TEA

(☎013-44751; www.victoriafallshotel.com/stanleys-terrace; Mallet Dr, Victoria Falls Hotel; high tea for 1-/2-people US$15/30; ⌚high tea 3-6pm; 📶) The Terrace at the stately Victoria Falls Hotel just

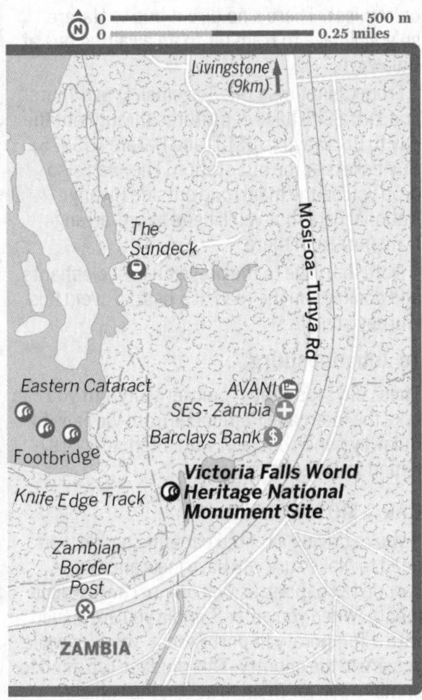


brims with English colonial ambience. High tea is served to a postcard-perfect backdrop of the gardens and Victoria Falls Bridge, with polished silverware, decadent cakes and three-tiered trays of finger sandwiches. (Cucumber? Why yes, of course.) A jug of Pimms makes perfect sense on summer day at US$24. The only thing missing is croquet.

**Buffalo Bar** BAR

(www.victoria-falls-safari-lodge.com; Squire Cummings Rd, Victoria Falls Safari Lodge; 7am-10pm) Unquestionably the best sundowner spot in town; enjoy a gin-and-tonic on its outdoor terrace overlooking distant animals on the plains of Zambezi National Park. Part of the Victoria Falls Safari Lodge, it's a good pre-dinner spot if you've got a booking at the hotel's Boma restaurant. Otherwise come during the day for the 1pm vulture feeding.

## Shopping

**★Elephant's Walk Shopping & Artist Village** SHOPPING CENTRE

(0772 254552; www.elephantswalk.com; Adam Stander Dr; 9am-5pm) A must for those in the market for quality Zimbabwean and African craft, this shopping village is home to boutique stores and galleries owned by a collective that aims to promote and set up local artists.

At the back of Elephant's Walk Village you'll find local vendors at **Big Curio Open Market** (Adam Stander Dr), and the **Tshaka's Den Complex** (7.30am-6pm), both of which sell locally made handicraft and Shona sculpture.

**Matsimela** COSMETICS

(www.matsimela.co.za; Adam Stander Dr, Elephant's Walk; 8am-5pm) South African body-care brand Matsimela has set up shop here with an enticing aroma of natural scented soaps, body scrubs and bath bombs (anything from rose and lychee to baobab-seed oil). They also offer massage treatments (from US$30), manicures and pedicures.

**Prime Art Gallery** ART

(0772 239805; www.primeart-gallery.com; Adam Stander Dr, Elephant's Walk; 8am-5pm) This quality gallery, run by two friendly brothers, represents more than 40 local artists, most notably it has original pieces by Dominic Benhura, Zimbabwe's pre-eminent current-day Shona sculptor whose worked has been exhibited around the world.

**Ndau Collection** JEWELLERY

(013-386221; www.ndaucollectionstore.com; Adam Stander Dr, Elephant's Walk; 8am-6pm) This upmarket showroom stocks handmade individual pieces, including silver bracelets, rings and necklaces, made at its on-site studio. They also sell exquisite antique African trade beads to be incorporated into custom-made jewellery. Its range of organic fragrances made using local ingredients is also popular, as are its croc-skin purses and briefcases.

## Information

### DANGERS & ANNOYANCES

Mugging is not such a problem any more, but at dawn and dusk wild animals such as elephants and warthogs do roam the streets away from the town centre, so take taxis at these times. Although it's perfectly safe to walk to and from the falls, it's advisable to stick to the more tourist areas.

### INTERNET ACCESS

Most lodges and restaurants offer wi-fi; otherwise there are a few internet cafes about town, including **Econet** (Park Way; per 30min/1hr US$1/2; 8am-5pm Mon-Fri, to 1pm Sat & Sun).

#### MONEY

**Barclays Bank** (off Livingstone Way)

**Standard Chartered Bank** (off Livingstone Way)

#### POST

**Post Office** (off Livingstone Way)

#### TOURIST INFORMATION

**Backpackers Bazaar** (p973) Definitive place for all tourist info and bookings.

**Zimbabwe Tourism Authority** (☎0772 225427, 013-44202; zta@vicfalls.ztazim.co.zw; Park Way; ⏰8am-6pm) A few brochures, but not very useful.

## Getting There & Away

#### AIR

Victoria Falls Airport is located 18km southeast of town. Its new international terminal opened in late 2015.

While nothing compared to the heydays of the 1980s and '90s, there's still no shortage of flights arriving at Victoria Falls. Most come from Johannesburg (US$150 to US$500 return). There are also regular flights from Harare with FastJet and Air Zimbabwe for as little as US$20.

Check out www.flightsite.co.za or www.travelstart.co.za, where you can search all the airlines including low-cost carriers (and car-hire companies) for the cheapest flights and then book yourself.

**Air Namibia** (☎0774 011320, 0771 401918; www.airnamibia.com)

**Air Zimbabwe** (☎0712 212121, 013-443168, 013-44665; www.airzimbabwe.aero)

**British Airways** (☎013-2053; www.britishairways.com)

**FastJet** (☎86 7700 6060; www.fastjet.com/zw; cnr Livingstone Way and Parkway Dr; ⏰9am-4pm Mon-Fri, to 1pm Sat)

**South African Airways** (☎04-702702; www.flysaa.com)

#### BUS & SHARED TAXI

Though its standards have dropped in recent years, **Intercape Pathfinder** (☎0778 888880; www.intercapepathfinder.com) easily remains the safest and most comfortable bus company in Zimbabwe.

### To Bulawayo & Harare

Intercape Pathfinder has departures for Hwange National Park (US$10, two hours), Bulawayo (US$15, six hours) and Harare (US$35, 12 hours) on Wednesday, Friday and Sunday at 7.30am from outside the Kingdom Hotel. You can book tickets online. If you're heading to Hwange National Park, you'll need to tell the driver beforehand as it only stops there on request. There's no direct bus to Harare, so you'll have to transfer to an awaiting bus at Bulawayo.

From Chinotimba Bus Terminal, Bravo Tours and Extra City have departures throughout the day to Bulawayo (US$13) and Harare (US$25). Buy tickets at the bus station. They can also drop you on the main road outside Hwange National Park, but you'll need to pre-arrange transport from there.

Note that, due to the prevalence of elephants and donkeys on the road, it's best to avoid this journey at night.

### To Johannesburg

These days it's almost quicker to fly, but you can take the Intercape Pathfinder from Vic Falls to Bulawayo, then connect with Intercaper Greyhound to Johannesburg.

#### CAR & MOTORCYCLE

If you're driving a rented car into Zambia, you need to make sure you have insurance and carbon tax papers, as well original owner documents. When you enter Zambia you are issued with a Temporary Import Permit, valid for while you are in the country. This must be returned to immigration for them to acquit the vehicle.

#### TRAIN

A popular way of getting to/from Victoria Falls is by the overnight *Mosi-oa-Tunya* train that leaves Victoria Falls daily at 7pm for Bulawayo (economy/2nd/1st class US$8/10/12, 12 hours). First class (comprising two-berth compartments) is the only way to go. Be aware that delays of several hours aren't uncommon, and you'll need to bring your own food. Make reservations at the **ticket office** (⏰7am-noon & 2-7pm) inside the train station.

The luxurious **Rovos Rail** (☎in South Africa 012-315 8242; www.rovos.com; from US$1650) to Pretoria also departs from here.

## Getting Around

#### CAR & MOTORCYCLE

**Zimbabwe Car Hire** (☎0783 496253, 09-230306; www.zimbabwecarhire.com; Victoria Falls Airport) gets positive reviews for its good rates, and is a good place for 4WDs. All the big name companies, such as **Hertz** (☎013-47012; www.hertz.co.za; 1 Bata Bldg, Parkway; ⏰8am-5pm Mon-Fri), **Avis** (☎091 2511128; www.avis.com; 251 Livingstone Way) and **Europcar** (☎013-43466; Victoria Falls Airport), have offices in town and at the airport.

#### TAXI

A taxi around town costs about US$10, or slightly more after dark.

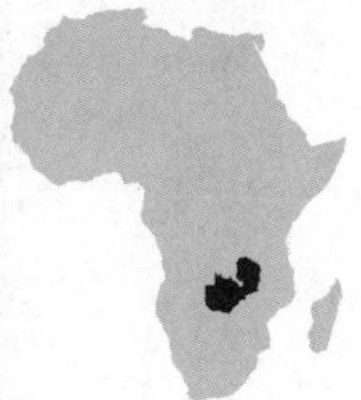

# Zambia

POP 15.5 MILLION

## Includes ➡



## Best Places to Eat

➡ Sugarbush Cafe (p989)

➡ Courtyard Café (p999)

➡ Thorn Tree Guesthouse (p997)

➡ Deli (p989)

## Best Places to Sleep

➡ Chizombo (p993)

➡ Chiawa Camp (p994)

➡ Kapishya Hot Springs Lodge (p997)

➡ Latitude 15 Degrees (p989)

## Why Go?

The rewards of travelling in Zambia are those of exploring remote, mesmerising wilderness as full of an astonishing diversity of wildlife as any part of Southern Africa. Adventures undertaken here will lead you deep into the bush where animals, both predators and prey, wander through unfenced camps, where night-time means swapping stories around the fire and where the human footprint is nowhere to be seen. Where one day you can canoe down a wide, placid river and the next raft through the raging rapids near world-famous Victoria Falls.

Though landlocked, three great rivers – the Kafue, the Luangwa and the Zambezi – flow through Zambia, defining both its geography and the rhythms of life for many of its people. For the independent traveller, however, Zambia is a logistical challenge, because of its size, dilapidated road network and upmarket facilities. For those who do venture here, the relative lack of crowds means an even more satisfying journey.

## When to Go

### Lusaka

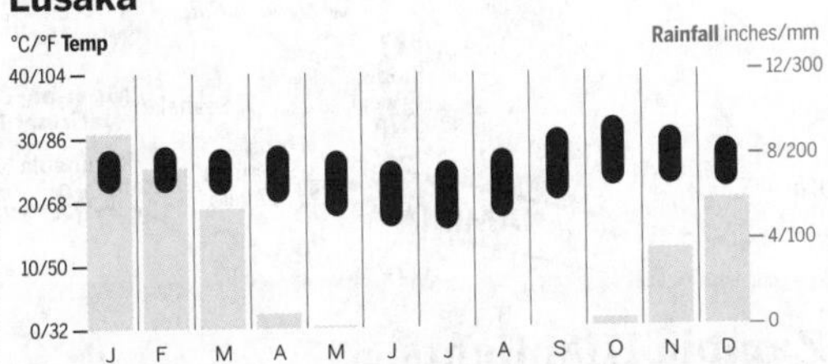


**Late May–early Oct** Dry season, with prime wildlife viewing; tourist high season.

**Jun–Aug** Dry, cooler temperatures and sometimes frosty nights.

**Nov–Apr** Vibrant, blooming landscapes during the rainy ('emerald') season. Wildebeest and bat migration.

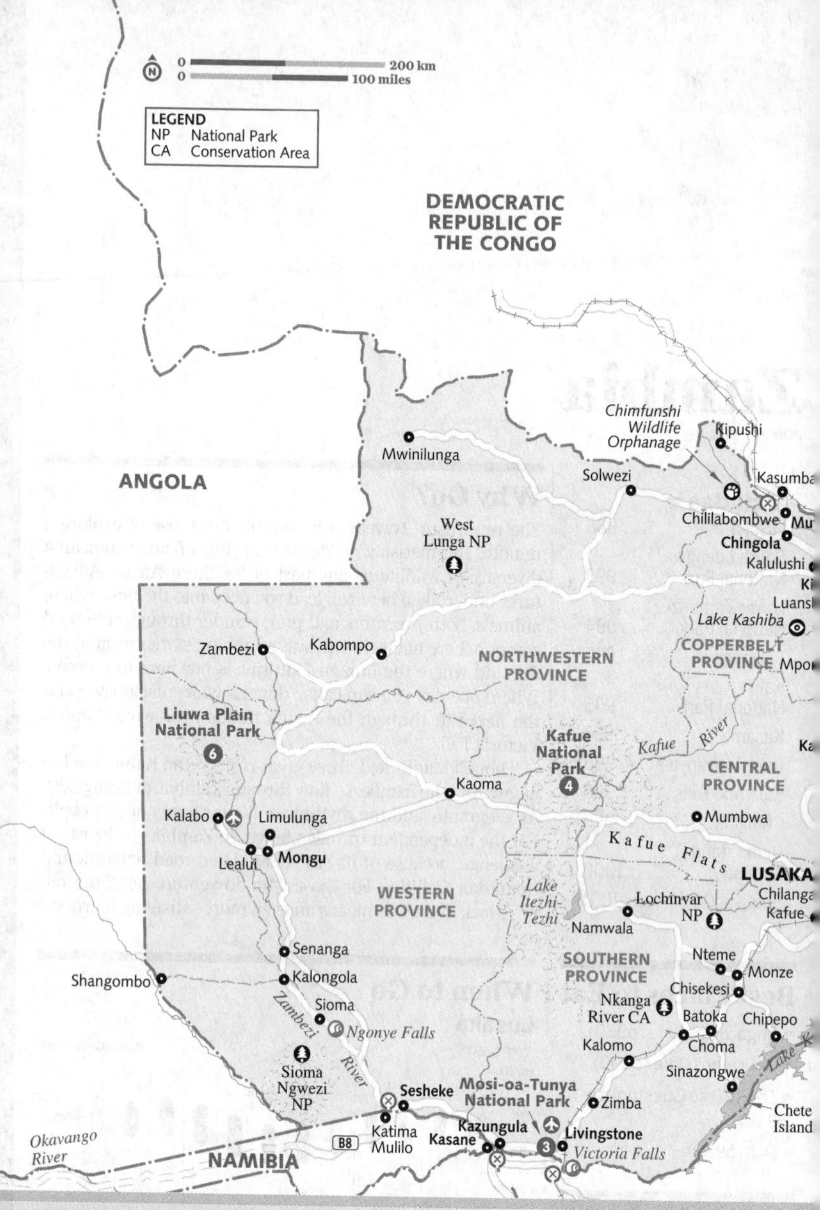


## Zambia Highlights

❶ **South Luangwa National Park** (p993) Bushwalking like a detective following the tracks of wild animals.

❷ **Zambezi River** (p994) Paddling a canoe down this mighty river past pods of hippos, menacing-looking crocs and thirsty elephants.

❸ **Victoria Falls** (p969) Rafting, bungee jumping or getting your adrenaline going in any one of the adventures available at Mosi-oa-Tunya National Park.

❹ **Kafue National Park** (p995) Spotting leopards in this behemoth wilderness area

where wildlife dreams unfold amid stunning landscapes.

**5 Lake Tanganyika** (p998) Lazing on white sandy beaches and snorkelling with tropical fish on this beautiful lake in the country's far north.

**6 Liuwa Plain National Park** (p996) Witnessing the wildebeest migration unfold at Zambia's 'mini Serengeti'.

**7 Shiwa Ng'andu** (p997) Taking a step back in time and a leap to another continent at a remarkably well-preserved English manor estate.

# LUSAKA

POP 2 MILLION / ☎0211 / ELEV 1300M

All roads lead to Lusaka, the geographic, commercial and metaphorical heart of Zambia. Although there are no real attractions, for some the city's genuine African feel, cosmopolitan populace and quality restaurants and accommodation are reason enough to spend a night or two.

## Sights

**Lusaka National Park** NATIONAL PARK

(☎0955 472433; adult/child US$30/15) The idea of seeing a rhino in the wild just 15km from the capital seems absurd, but this new national park (opened in 2015) allows you to do just that. Set over 46 sq km, it's home to eland, zebra, giraffe and wildebeest, among others. But it's the white rhino that brings people here. While you'll be able to tick it off from the list of Big Five, most likely you'll see them in their holding pen, so it can feel more like a zoo than national park.

**Lilayi Elephant Nursery** WILDLIFE RESERVE

(☎0211-840435; www.lilayi.com; adult/child/under 12yr ZMW50/20/free; ⏲elephant feeding 11.30am-1pm) On the southern outskirts of town is this elephant nursery set up by Game Rangers International (a Zambian conservationist NGO), which works with rescuing and rehabilitating orphaned elephants in Kafue National Park. You can see them being fed from 11am to 1.30pm daily; Monday is free entry. You can also do wildlife drives on its 650-hectare property. There's a lovely restaurant and lodge where, if you're staying, you can get a behind-the-scenes look at the elephants.

**Lusaka National Museum** MUSEUM

(Nasser Rd; adult/child US$5/3; ⏲9am-4.30pm) This big square box of a building resembling a Soviet-era Moscow ministry has upstairs galleries displaying exhibits on urban culture and Zambian history as well cultural, ethnographic and archaeological displays. Contemporary Zambian paintings and sculpture are shown downstairs.

**Lusaka City Market** MARKET

(Lumumba Rd; ⏲7am-5pm) Fronted by the chaotic and congested eponymously named bus station, as well as a veritable Maginot Line of sidewalk vendors, reaching the entrance to the Lusaka City Market is an achievement in and of itself. Unfortunately, while large, lively and packed to the rafters, the clothing and housewares sold in the warren of stalls aren't of much interest to the average traveller.

### LIVINGSTONE & VICTORIA FALLS

Historical Livingstone (p974) is Zambia's gateway to thundering Victoria Falls, where adventurous excursions await: serene canoe trips above the falls or white-water rafting the churning Zambezi down below. See the Victoria Falls chapter (p969) for more information.

## Sleeping

★**Natwange Backpackers** HOSTEL $

(☎0977 886240, 0966 303816; www.natwange-backpackers.com; 6808 Kapuka Rd; dm/s/d incl breakfast with shared bathroom US$12/30/40; 📶🏊) In quiet residential street, this lovely and secure home offers a relaxed atmosphere for independent travellers. Rooms are clean, though can be a little cramped, and all share bathrooms. It has plenty of lawn with fruit trees and a nice little pool and gym. There are several lounge areas to hang out, and a fully equipped kitchen for self-caterers.

**Tanuger Travels** HOSTEL $

(☎0972 662588; www.tanuger.com; cnr Sibweni & Chigwilizano Rds; dm US$15, r US$60, with shared bathroom US$40; 📶🏊) Set up by a bunch of local female friends, this funky and vibrant hostel offers a homely, social and relaxed atmosphere. There's plenty of artwork about, including graffiti-splashed walls, plus a swimming pool, firepit, giant chess board and free pool table. Its members-only bar is one of the liveliest in town, and a great place to meet travellers and locals alike.

**Bongwe Barn** GUESTHOUSE $$

(☎0973 589419; www.bongwesafaris.com/guesthouse.html; 609 Zambezi Rd, Roma; r US$55-75; 📶🏊) If you've outgrown the whole backpacker scene, but still want something informal and homely – and social, if inclined – then Bongwe's your place. Run by UK expat Stacey, the staff here are exceptionally friendly and helpful, and rooms (some of which share bathrooms) are spotless and spacious. There's a stocked kitchen, couches in the living room and a sparkling pool to relax by.

**Pioneer Camp** CAMPGROUND, CHALET **$$**
(☎0966 432700; www.pioneercampzambia.com; Palabana Rd, off Great East Rd; camping US$10, chalet with shared/private bathroom from US$88/132; ) An isolated 25-acre camp, surrounded by bird-rich woodland, Pioneer is the accommodation of choice for many expats living outside Lusaka, especially those with an early flight out of the country. Most of the widely dispersed and simply furnished thatch-roofed chalets have flagstone floors, small verandas and large bathrooms. The well-kept facilities for campers are up the front next to the small plunge pool.

★**Latitude 15 Degrees** BOUTIQUE HOTEL **$$$**
(☎0211-268802; http://15.latitudehotels.com; Leopards Lane, Kabulonga; s/d incl breakfast US$244/297; ) Lusaka's best accommodation is this fashionable hotel with an architecturally designed building that resembles a chic contemporary gallery. Its rooms are plush with king-sized beds, standalone tubs, coffee makers, fast wi-fi, cable TV and plenty of art decorating its walls. Guests also have access to the 'Other Side' executive members-only lounge. Its **restaurant** (http://15.latitudehotels.com/lat15-eating-drinking; mains ZMW140-180; 7-10am, noon-3pm & 6-9.30pm) is also very popular. It's just off Leopards Hill Rd.

## Eating

For local meals, try the food stalls at the Town Centre Market off Cairo Rd or restaurants in the Showgrounds off Great East Rd, which serve cheap dishes of *nshima* and grilled meats.

★**Deli** CAFE, BAKERY **$**
(Lunzua Rd, Rhodes Park; mains from ZMW25, coffee ZMW14; 7am-4pm Mon-Fri, 8.30am-12.30pm Sat; ) Boasting the best barista in Lusaka (the winner of an international competition) as well as an enviable garden setting, the Deli is a good place to plant yourself for a few hours. The sophisticated kitchen turns out all-day breakfasts like eggs and French toast, speciality sandwiches like Asian pork meatball and classics like pastrami, wood-fired pizzas and homemade ice cream.

★**Sugarbush Cafe** INTERNATIONAL, ORGANIC **$$**
(☎0967 648761; www.facebook.com/sugarbushcafezam; Leopards Hill Rd, Sugarbush Farm; breakfast ZMW40-75, mains ZMW75-120; 8am-5pm Tue-Sat, 8.30am-4.30pm Sun; ) This picture-postcard idyllic cafe is worth every kwacha of the journey it takes to get here. Chill out for an afternoon at one of the picnic tables munching on homemade bread and pastries, salads made with organic homegrown vegetables, and expertly prepared sandwiches, pasta and meat dishes, as well as a glass of wine, or Pimms by the jug.

**Casa Portico** ITALIAN **$$**
(☎0211-255198; 27 Ngumbo Rd, Longacres; mains from ZMW85; 8am-10pm Mon-Thu, to midnight Fri & Sat) Italian owned and operated, this garden restaurant offers as authentic cuisine as you'll get outside Italy. There's homemade pastas (go the tagliatelle ragu), homebaked panini, and imported Italian cheeses and meats. It's a good spot, too, for a glass of Prosecco or well-made negroni cocktails.

## Drinking & Nightlife

★**Bongwe Pub & Grill** PUB
(www.facebook.com/bongwebarn; 609 Zambezi Rd, Roma; 2pm-late) A favourite watering hole for many locals, expats and tourists (and basically anyone who likes a drink) is this tropical dive bar, set in an open-air shack centred on a palm tree. There's a pool table, sports on the TV and always someone around for a chat. On Fridays it's usually pumping and regularly has local bands and DJs.

## Shopping

**Kabwata Cultural Village** ARTS & CRAFTS
(Burma Rd; 7am-6pm) A popular shopping stop for tourists, this open-air market comprises thatch-roofed huts and stalls selling carvings, baskets, masks, drums, fabrics and more. Prices are cheap because you can buy directly from the workers who live here. There's usually cultural performances (ZMW30) held on weekends around 2pm. It's southeast of the city centre.

**Lightfoot Zambia** FASHION & ACCESSORIES
(Jackal & Hide; www.jackalandhide.net; Leopards Hill Rd; 8am-5pm) For high-quality leather goods, especially purses, travel bags and accessories, head to this spot, which shares an idyllic location with a highly recommended cafe on Sugarbush Farm east of Kabulonga, around 15km from the city centre. They have a smaller branch at Latitude 15 restaurant.

**Sunday Market** MARKET
(Arcades Shopping Centre, Great East Rd; 9am-6pm Sun) This weekly market, held in the car park at the Arcades Shopping Centre, features Lusaka's best range of handicrafts, especially

# Lusaka

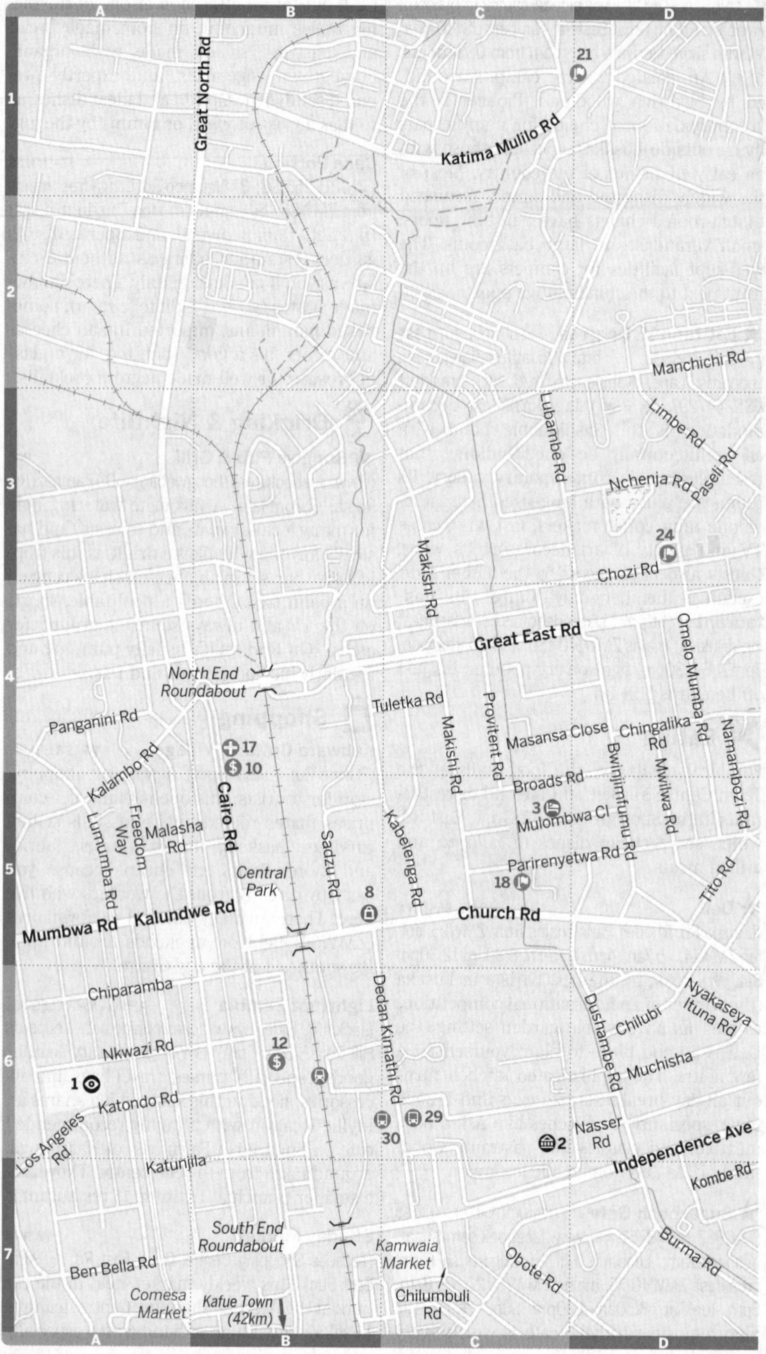

A
B
C
D
1
2
3
4
5
6
7
Great North Rd
21
Katima Mulilo Rd
Manchichi Rd
Lubambe Rd
Limbe Rd
Paseli Rd
Nchenja Rd
24
Chozi Rd
Makishi Rd
Great East Rd
Omelo Mumba Rd
North End Roundabout
Tuletka Rd
Provitent Rd
Makishi Rd
Masansa Close
Chingalika Rd
Namambozi Rd
Panganini Rd
17
10
Kalambo Rd
Cairo Rd
Broads Rd
Bwinjimfumu Rd
Mwilwa Rd
3
Mulombwa Cl
Lumumba Rd
Freedom Way
Malasha Rd
Sadzu Rd
Kabelenga Rd
Parirenyetwa Rd
Central Park
18
Tito Rd
8
Mumbwa Rd
Kalundwe Rd
Church Rd
Chiparamba
Dedan Kimathi Rd
Dushambe Rd
Nyakaseya
Ituna Rd
Chilubi
12
Nkwazi Rd
Muchisha
1
Katondo Rd
29
30
Nasser Rd
2
Independence Ave
Los Angeles Rd
Katunjila
Kombe Rd
South End Roundabout
Kamwaia Market
Obote Rd
Burma Rd
Ben Bella Rd
Comesa Market
Kafue Town (42km)
Chilumbuli Rd

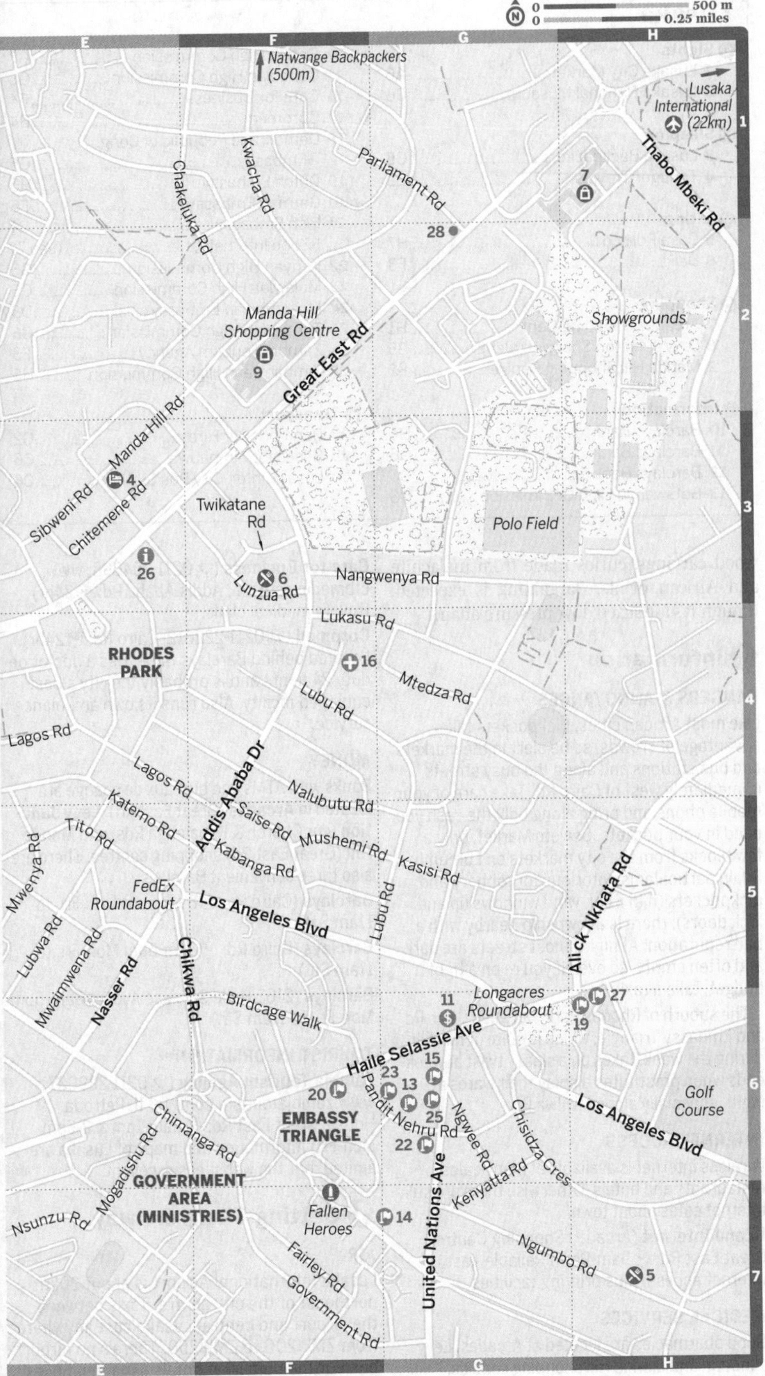

0 500 m
0 0.25 miles
Natwange Backpackers (500m)
Lusaka International (22km)
Thabo Mbeki Rd
Parliament Rd
Kwacha Rd
Chakeluka Rd
7
28
Manda Hill Shopping Centre
9
Great East Rd
Showgrounds
Manda Hill Rd
4
Sibweni Rd
Chitemene Rd
Twikatane Rd
Polo Field
26
6
Lunzua Rd
Nangwenya Rd
Lukasu Rd
RHODES PARK
16
Mtedza Rd
Lubu Rd
Lagos Rd
Addis Ababa Dr
Nalubutu Rd
Katemo Rd
Saise Rd
Tito Rd
Mushemi Rd
Kabanga Rd
Kasisi Rd
Mwenya Rd
FedEx Roundabout
Los Angeles Blvd
Lubu Rd
Alick Nkhata Rd
Lubwa Rd
Mwaimwena Rd
Nasser Rd
Chikwa Rd
Birdcage Walk
11
Longacres Roundabout
27
19
Haile Selassie Ave
15
23
13
20
Pandit Nehru Rd
25
EMBASSY TRIANGLE
22
Ngwee Rd
Chisidza Cres
Golf Course
Los Angeles Blvd
Chimanga Rd
Mogadishu Rd
GOVERNMENT AREA (MINISTRIES)
Kenyatta Rd
United Nations Ave
Fallen Heroes
14
Nsunzu Rd
Fairley Rd
Government Rd
Ngumbo Rd
5

## Lusaka

**Sights**

1 Lusaka City Market ........ A6
2 Lusaka National Museum ........ C6

**Sleeping**

3 Lusaka Backpackers ........ C5
4 Tanuger Travels ........ E3

**Eating**

5 Casa Portico ........ H7
6 Deli ........ F3

**Shopping**

7 Arcades Shopping Centre ........ H1
8 Levy Junction Shopping Centre ........ B5
9 Manda Hill Shopping Centre ........ F2

**Information**

10 Barclays Bank ........ B4
11 Barclays Bank ........ G6
12 Barclays Bank ........ B6
13 Botswanan High Commission ........ G6
14 British High Commission ........ G7
15 Canadian High Commission ........ G6
16 Care for Business ........ F4
17 Corpmed ........ B4
18 Democratic Rebublic of Congo Embassy ........ C5
19 Dutch Embassy ........ H6
20 German Embassy ........ F6
21 Irish Embassy ........ D1
I-Zone Internet ........ (see 7)
22 Kenyan High Commission ........ G6
23 Malawian High Commission ........ G6
24 Mozambican Embassy ........ D3
25 Tanzanian High Commission ........ G6
26 Zambia Tourism Agency ........ E3
27 Zimbabwean High Commission ........ H6

**Transport**

28 Benmark Car Hire ........ G2
29 Buses for Zimbabwe ........ C6
30 Lusaka Inter-City Bus Station ........ C6

wood carvings, curios made from malachite and African prints. Bargaining is expected, though it's a relaxed, low-pressure affair.

## Information

### DANGERS & ANNOYANCES

Like most African cities, pickpockets take advantage of crowds, so be alert in the markets and bus stations and along the busy streets immediately west of Cairo Rd. Take care of your mobile phone and bring along only the cash you need in your pockets. Soweto Market, only a few blocks from the city markets on Lumumba Rd, in particular is notorious for robbery and pickpockets (if in a car, wind windows up and lock doors); there is a township nearby with a bad reputation. At night, most streets are dark and often empty, so even if you're on a tight budget, take a taxi.

The suburb of Rhodes Park, between Cairo Rd and Embassy Triangle, which is quite upmarket during the week, takes on a sleazy twist at weekends when prostitutes display their wares at night, especially along Mwilwa Rd.

### INTERNET ACCESS

Wireless internet is available at many cafes, restaurants and hotels. Otherwise there are still internet cafes about town.

**I-Zone Internet** (Arcades Shopping Centre, Great East Rd; 9am-9pm) Reliable, fast internet access, plus printing facilities.

### MEDICAL SERVICES

Good pharmacies are located at Arcades, Levy Junction and Manda Hill shopping centres.

**Care for Business** (0211-254398; www.cfbmedic.com.zm; Addis Ababa Rd; 24hr) Private medical clinic.

**Corpmed** (0211-222612; Cairo Rd; 24hr) Located behind Barclays Bank. Has a doctor on duty 24 hours and is probably the city's best-equipped facility. Also runs its own ambulance service.

### MONEY

Banks with ATMs and bureaux de change are located in **Arcades** (Great East Rd), **Levy Junction** (cnr Church & Kabalenga Rds) and **Manda Hill** (Great East Rd) shopping centres. There are also three convenient Barclays:

**Barclays** (Cairo Rd; 8am-5pm Mon-Fri, to 11am Sat)

**Barclays** (Cairo Rd; 8am-5pm Mon-Fri, to 11am Sat)

**Barclays** (2162 Haile Selaisse Ave; 8am-5pm Mon-Fri, to 11am Sat)

### TOURIST INFORMATION

**Zambia Tourism Agency** (0211-229087; www.zambiatourism.com; 1st fl, Petroda House, Great East Rd; 8am-1pm & 2-5pm Mon-Fri) Information and maps of Lusaka are limited, but the website is excellent.

## Getting There & Away

### AIR

Lusaka International Airport is about 20km northeast of the city centre. Taxis between the airport and central Lusaka cost anywhere from ZMW200 to ZMW250. There's no airport bus but the upmarket hotels send minibuses (usually for a fee) to meet international flights, so you may be able to arrange a ride into town with the minibus driver (for a negotiable fee).

**BUS & MINIBUS**

From a tourist point of view, the only real bus station you'll need to worry about is the **Lusaka Inter-City Bus Station** (Dedan Kimathi Rd). Here you can find a bus to all long-distance destinations in Zambia and across the border.

Directly opposite the Lusaka Inter-City bus station are buses heading to Zimbabwe via both Chirundu and Siavonga (Lake Kariba). It's US$20 to Harare (eight hours via Chirundu) and US$10 to Siavonga (three hours)

## Getting Around

Local minibuses run along Lusaka's main roads, but there are no route numbers or destination signs, so the system is difficult to work out. There is also a confusing array of bus and minibus stations.

# EASTERN ZAMBIA

## South Luangwa National Park

For scenery, variety and density of animals, **South Luangwa National Park** (per person/self-drive vehicle US$25/30; ⌚6am-6pm) is one of the best parks in Zambia, if not Africa. Impalas, pukus, waterbucks, giraffes and buffaloes wander on the wide-open plains; leopards, of which there are many in the park, hunt in the dense woodlands; herds of elephants wade through the marshes; and hippos munch serenely on Nile cabbage in the Luangwa River. The bird life is a highlight: about 400 species have been recorded – large birds like snake eagles, bateleurs and ground hornbills are normally easy to spot.

Much of the park is inaccessible because of rains between November and April.

### Activities

All lodges/camps run excellent day or night wildlife drives and some have walking safaris (June to November). These activities are included in the rates charged by the upmarket places, while the cheaper lodges/camps can organise things with little notice. A three-hour morning or evening wildlife drive normally costs around US$40, while a wildlife walk is about US$50.

### Sleeping

**★Marula Lodge** LODGE $

(☎0216-246073; www.marulalodgezambia.com; Mfuwe; dm US$10, dome tents per person US$15, r from US$40; ) Occupying a stretch of riverfront with plenty of lawn, Marula offers one of the best choices in the park for budget travellers. Options include waterfront domed tents, upstairs dorm rooms with a view and some charming, comfortable chalets with private bathroom. The shared bathroom for those in the tents and dorms offers a unique experience in a wonderful circular open-air structure built around a lovely mahogany tree.

**★Chizombo** LODGE $$$

(☎0216-246025; www.normancarrsafaris.com/camps/chinzombo; per person all-inclusive US$1300; ) One of the park's most exquisite lodges, Chizombo offers luxury villas done out in designer soft white tones, with spacious, breezy and immaculate areas furnished with a classy vintage decor. Each of the six villas has its own massive decking area with a sofa and private plunge pool overlooking the wildlife-viewing areas.

**★Luwi Bush Camp** LODGE $$$

(☎0216-246025, 0216-246015; www.normancarrsafaris.com/camps/luwi; per person all-inclusive US$840) One of Norman Carr Safari's original remote luxury wilderness camps in South Luangwa, Luwi nails the rustic:luxury ratio with each of its open-plan thatch-and-reed chalets overlooking the plains. It's dismantled at the end of each season to minimise environmental impact.

**★Nkonzi Camp** TENTED CAMP $$$

(☎0966 411320; www.jackalberrysafaris.net; 3 days per person all-inclusive US$610; ⌚1 Jun-31 Oct) Run by Jackalberry Safaris, Nkonzi is a bush camp within the national park that offers a wonderful (and relatively more affordable) wilderness experience; it's excellent value for those looking to spend a few days on safari. The seasonal site offers tented accommodation with double bed and attached open-air bathrooms constructed from reed material. Rates include activities led by experienced owner/guide Gavin Opie.

### Getting There & Away

Many people reach South Luangwa by air. Mfuwe Airport is 20km southeast of Mfuwe Gate and served by Proflight (www.proflight-zambia.com), with several daily flights from Lusaka (from US$150 one way). Almost every lodge meets clients at the airport (the charge is often included in the room rates).

There are several buses from Mfuwe village for Chipata (around ZMW50) and Lusaka (ZMW220); Jonada Bus is probably the most reliable.

# SOUTHERN ZAMBIA

## Lower Zambezi National Park

One of the country's premier wildlife-viewing areas, the **Lower Zambezi National Park** (adult/self-drive vehicle US$25/30; 6am-6pm) covers a large stretch of wilderness area along the northeastern bank of the Zambezi River. Several smaller rivers flow through the park, which is centred on a beautiful flood plain alongside the Zambezi, dotted with acacias and other large trees, and flanked by a steep escarpment on the northern side, covered with thick miombo woodland.

On the opposite bank, in Zimbabwe, is Mana Pools National Park, and together the parks constitute one of Africa's finest wildlife areas.

The best time to visit is May to October; however, temperatures average around 40°C in the latter half of October.

### Sights & Activities

One of the best ways to see the Lower Zambezi is by **canoe safari**. Most of the camps and lodges have canoes, so you can go out with a river guide for a few hours. Longer safaris are even more enjoyable; ask your lodge what is available.

Most lodges are not fenced and offer **wildlife-viewing** activities by boat or by safari vehicle. Keep in mind, however, that while theoretically on offer, most of the lodges in the Game Management Area (GMA), especially those closer to Chirundu than to Chongwe Gate, don't take their wildlife drives in the park proper.

The best time for **tiger fishing** (strictly catch and release) is September to December but it's still possible during other months. Rods, reels and even bait can be supplied by all the lodges and camps.

### Sleeping

**Munyemeshi River Lodge** LODGE $
(0211-231466, 0979 565646; www.munyemeshi.co.zm; r ZMW450; ) An affordable waterfront lodge close to the park, Munyemeshi's stone-and-thatch chalets are rough around the edges, but at these prices you can't be too choosy. It was undergoing renovations at the time of research, so call ahead to see if it's going to remain as a budget lodge. There's no restaurant, so it's one for self-caterers, with a fully equipped kitchen on hand.

**Kiambi Safaris** CAMPGROUND, CHALETS $$
(0977 186106, 0977 876003; www.kiambi.com; camping US$12, tent rental US$28, chalets s/d with full board from US$208/306; ) This well-run and atmospheric operation at the confluence of the Zambezi and Kafue Rivers has a smattering of different, relatively affordable accommodation options. Set in attractive, verdant surrounds, chalets and cottages are comfortable and characterful. Campsites come with a powerpoint and firepit, and a tent if you don't have one. The social restaurant and bar is another highlight.

★ **Chiawa Camp** CHALET $$$
(0211-261588; www.chiawa.com; per person all-inclusive US$1120; mid-Apr–mid-Nov; @) In a spectacular position at the confluence of the Chiawa and Zambezi Rivers, this luxurious lodge inside the park was the first in the Lower Zambezi. As a pioneer in this area, the owner Grant Cummings knows the park intimately and his guiding expertise is highly regarded. The large walk-in canvas-thatch tents feature pine-clad private bathrooms.

★ **Royal Zambezi Lodge** TENTED CAMP $$$
(0979 486618; www.royalzambezilodge.com; per person all-inclusive from US$990; year-round; ) The epitome of luxury bush mixed with a colonial-era vibe, Royal is only a short drive to the eponymous airstrip as well as Chongwe Gate. Despite its understated opulence – think brass fixtures, claw-footed tubs and private day beds on decks overlooking the river – it's unpretentious and exceptionally friendly. Its bar built around the trunk of a sausage tree is a well-received feature.

### Getting There & Away

**Proflight** (0211-271032; www.proflight-zambia.com) has daily flights between Lusaka and Royal Airstrip (30 minutes; in the GMA just a few kilometres west of Chongwe Gate) and Jeki Airstrip (40 minutes; in the heart of the park).

Proflight is also planning to offer flights between Lower Zambezi and Mfuwe in South Luangwa National Park; check the website.

Uncomfortable minibuses run from Lusaka to Chirundu; departures run throughout the morning, but you have to sort out transport from town to your accommodation.

## Siavonga

Siavonga, the main town and resort along the Zambian side of Lake Kariba, has a location to be envied. Set among hills and verdant greenery, just a few kilometres from the massive Kariba Dam, views of the lake pop up from many vantage points, especially from the lodges. The lodges can organise activities in and around the lake, including boat trips to the dam wall, sunset cruises, fishing trips, longer-distance boat trips and one-day to four-night canoe safaris on the Zambezi.

**Eagles Rest** CAMPGROUND, CHALET **$$**
(☎0978 869126, 0967 688617; www.eaglesrestresort.com; camping/tent hire US$1025, s/d/tr incl breakfast US$50/75/90; ❄🏊) While it's all a little bit tired and in need of a refurb, this laid-back beachfront resort is still the best spot for independent travellers. It has its own little sandy area (no swimming, however), pool and beach bar. It's the only campsite around town, and its chalets are spacious with stone floors and great decking outside with patio furniture overlooking the lake.

**Lake Kariba Inns** HOTEL **$$**
(☎0211-511290, 0977 770480; www.karibainns.com; s/d from ZMW825/945; ❄@📶🏊) With a commanding hilltop location with lush gardens (home to some roaming zebra) and lake views, this hotel has relatively luxurious rooms (some with verandas) and is a good choice if you don't mind sharing space with conference attendees. The restaurant (buffet ZMW150) and sports bar overlook the pool area, which is itself perched high above the lake.

### Getting There & Away

Minibuses from Lusaka (ZMW70, three hours, three to five daily) leave when bursting to capacity for Siavonga and the nearby border. Alternatively get a bus towards Chirundu and get dropped off at the Siavonga turn-off; from here take a local pick-up (ZMW15) the rest of the way.

# WESTERN ZAMBIA

## Kafue National Park

Covering more than 22,500 sq km, **Kafue National Park** (adult/vehicle US$20/15; ⏲6am-6pm) is the largest in Zambia and one of the biggest in the world. With terrain ranging from the lush riverine forest of the Kafue River to the vast grassland of the Busanga Plains, the park rewards wildlife enthusiasts with glimpses of various carnivores and their nimble prey. There's a good chance of sighting lions and leopards, and, if you're lucky, cheetahs in the north of the park, plus elephants, zebras and numerous species of antelope. There are some 500 species of birds too.

The main route into the park is via the sealed highway running between Lusaka and Mongu, which loosely divides the park into its northern and southern sectors. Kafue is one of the few parks in Zambia that's easily accessible by public transport, with a handful of camps just off the highway.

For a budget safari into the park, check with **Lusaka Backpackers** (☎0977 805483; www.lusakabackpackers.com; 161 Mulombwa Cl; 4-/8-bed dm US$12/15, r US$55, with shared bathroom US$40; @📶🏊) and Bongwe Barn (p988) in Lusaka, or the **Mobile Safari Company** (☎0963 005937; www.wild-kafue.com; 2 nights/3 days from US$425) based in Livingstone.

### Sleeping

**Chibila Camp** LODGE **$**
(☎0211-251630; www.conservationzambia.org/camps-and-lodges; Southern Sector; r member/non-member ZMW100/150) Just outside the park in the GMA, Chibila offers three basic, bargain-priced rooms that overlook Lake

**KUOMBOKA CEREMONY**

The Kuomboka (literally, 'to move to dry ground') is probably one of the last great Southern African ceremonies. It is celebrated by the Lozi people of western Zambia, and marks the ceremonial journey of the *litunga* (the Lozi king) from his dry-season palace at Lealui, near Mongu, to his wet-season palace on higher ground at Limulunga. It usually takes place in late March or early April, and sometimes ties in with Easter.

Itezhi-tezhi. Rooms come with attached bathroom, and while you need to bring along your own food, the team here is happy to cook it up for you. It's a peaceful spot among woodland and boulders, where plenty of hyrax dart about.

**Hippo Bay Bush Camp** CAMPGROUND, CHALET **$$**
(☎0962 841364; www.hippobaycamp.com; Southern Sector; camping US$20, chalets US$60-100) Hippo Bay is easily one of the best budget options in south Kafue. It has six rustic, well-priced thatched reed chalets with attached bathroom, or a campsite with flush toilets and hot water. There's a braai and firewood to cook meals, but otherwise you can drive to its nearby sister **Konkamoya Lodge** (☎0962 841364; www.konkamoya.com; Southern Sector; per person all-inclusive US$500; ⏲mid-Jun–mid-Nov; 📶) for meals (breakfast/lunch US$15, dinner US$30) and drinks. Wildlife drives cost US$35.

★**KaingU Safari Lodge** CAMPGROUND, TENTED CAMP **$$$**
(☎in Lusaka 0211-256992; www.kaingu-lodge.com; Southern Sector; camping US$20-25, tented camping with full board & 2 activities US$450; ⏲Apr-Dec; 📶) Set on a magical stretch of the Kafue River, this lodge overlooks a primordial stretch of lush islands among the rapids, with delightful birdwatching. The four tastefully furnished Meru-style tents are raised on rosewood platforms with stone bathrooms and large decks to enjoy the view. There are also three campsites, each with its own well-kept thatch ablution and braai facilities.

### ℹ Getting There & Away

Most guests of the top-end lodges/camps fly in on chartered planes. Given there's a sealed road passing through the centre of the park, you can easily catch a Mongu-bound bus here from Lusaka (ZMW120, 3½ hours). On the highway ask to be let off either near Mukambi Safari Lodge or Mayukuyuku (arrange pick-up from the highway for US$35).

## Liuwa Plain National Park

About 100km northwest of Mongu, near the Angolan border, **Liuwa Plain National Park** (☎0964 168394; liuwa@africanparks.co.zm; adult/child US$30/10) is 3600 sq km of true wilderness. The remote park is characterised by expanses of flat, grassy flood plains, and is most famous for the second-largest wildebeest migration in Africa, which takes place in November, turning the park into a 'mini Serengeti'. Although it's often called a migration, in reality the wildebeest are here year round, so it's more a meander from one sector of the park to another. While November is undoubtedly the best time to visit, you can see them at other times in the northern part of the park in large numbers.

The park is also notable for having one of the highest population densities of hyena in the world, as well as a stunning variety of birdlife. Other wildlife include lion, cheetah, wild dog, zebra, buffalo, lechwe, tsessebe and Roan antelope.

For self-sufficient travellers with their own vehicles, there are five well-maintained campsites in the park – including one close to the park headquarters for late arrivals. They are run by local Lozi people in partnership with African Parks, with all proceeds going to the community.

There's also a new luxury lodge, **King Lewanika Lodge** (☎0216-246025; www.normancarrsafaris.com/camps/liuwaplain; per person all-inclusive US$1070), set up by Norman Carr Safaris, which offers all-inclusive rates.

The only option of visiting Liuwa Plain is either by 4WD or to come along on a safari package. While you can get public transport as far as Kalabo at the national park HQ, accessing the park from here isn't possible unless you have a 4WD vehicle. The majority of guests staying at the Norman Carr camp fly in and out from the park's airstrip – which African Parks is aiming to operate year round.

# NORTHERN ZAMBIA

## Kasanka National Park

One of Zambia's least-known wilderness areas and a real highlight of a visit to this part of the country is the privately managed **Kasanka National Park** (☎in South Africa +27 72-298 0777; www.kasankanationalpark.com; adult US$8; ⏲6am-6pm). At just 390 sq km, it's pretty small compared to most African parks, it doesn't have a huge range of facilities and it sees very few visitors – and this is what makes it special. There are no queues of jeeps to get a look at a leopard here; instead, you'll discover great tracts of miombo woodland, evergreen thicket, open grassland and rivers fringed with emerald forest, all by yourself.

Kasanka is most famous for its fruit bat migration in November and December, which sees up to 10 million of the nocturnal creatures arrive. The park is also known for its swampland, and this is the terrain to see the park's shy and retiring star, the sitatunga.

Doubling as the park headquarters, **Wasa Lodge** (☎ in South Africa +27 72-298 0777; www.kasankanationalpark.com; per person self-catering chalets US$70, all-inclusive US$420) accommodation consists of thatched bungalows overlooking Lake Wasa. Larger chalets are airy and cool with wide balconies and lovely stone showers. There are multiple vantage points – including the deck of the large bar and dining area – to look out over the swamp to spot hippos, puku and sometimes even sitatungas.

From Lusaka, take a bus (ZMW130) in the direction of Mansa, or take any bus from Lusaka to Serenje and change onto a minibus (ZMW45) for Mansa. After turning off the Great North Rd, ask the driver to drop you at Kasanka National Park (near Mulembo village), not at Kasanka village, which is much further away.

## Shiwa Ng'andu

Deep in the northern Zambian wilderness sits Shiwa Ng'andu, a grand country estate and labour of love of eccentric British aristocrat Sir Stewart Gore-Brown. The estate's crowning glory is Shiwa Ng'andu manor house, which is a magnificent English-style mansion. Driving up to the house through farm buildings, settlements and workers' houses it almost feels like an old feudal domain: there's a whole community built around it, including a school and a hospital, and many of the people now working at Shiwa Ng'andu are the children and grandchildren of Sir Stewart's original staff. Today Gore-Brown's grandchildren live on and manage the estate, which is a working farm.

The area offers some memorable places to stay, from the historic **Shiwa House mansion** (☎ 0211-229261; www.shiwasafaris.com; per person with full board from US$470) to the picturesque **Kapishya Hot Springs Lodge** (☎ 0976 970444; www.shiwasafaris.com; camping US$15, d from US$75, per person all-inclusive US$165).

To reach Shiwa House, head north along the Great North Rd by bus (or car) from Mpika for about 90km towards Chisoso. Look for the signpost to the west, from where a 20km dirt road leads to the house. Kapishya Hot Springs and the lodge are a further 20km along this track.

You can also get to Shiwa from the Mpika to Kasama road – this time look for the signpost pointing east and it's then 42km down the dirt track to Kapishya. There is no public transport along this last section, but vehicle transfers are available from the Great North Rd turnoff for US$35 per vehicle.

## Kasama

Kasama is the capital of the Northern Province and the cultural centre of the Bemba people. With its wide, leafy streets and handsome, old, tin-roofed colonial houses, it is the most appealing of the northern towns. Kasama's environs are home to ancient rock art and a beautiful waterfall, as well as to the **Kusefya Pangwena festival** (www.zambiatourism.com).

**Kasama Rock Art** HISTORIC SITE
(adult/child US$15/7, camping US$10; ⏲ 6am-6pm) Archaeologists rate the Kasama rock art as one of the largest and most significant collections of ancient art in Southern Africa, though their quality is outdone in Zimbabwe and Namibia. The works are attributed to Stone Age hunter-gatherers (sometimes known as Twa) and are up to 2000 years old. Many are abstract designs, but some of the finest pictographs show human figures and animals, often capturing a remarkable sense of fluidity and movement, despite being stylised with huge bodies and minute limbs.

★ **Thorn Tree Guesthouse** GUESTHOUSE $
(☎ 0214-221615; kansato@iconnect.zm; 612 Zambia Rd; s/d from ZMW210/270, f from ZMW350; ) The Thorn Tree is family-run, homey and very popular, so book ahead to avoid disappointment. Rooms are either in the main house sharing spick-and-span facilities or in larger family rooms, including a three-room cottage. There's a bar and a restaurant serving fresh farm produce; they also roast their own coffee beans on site, so you'll get a decent brew here.

### ℹ Getting There & Away

Buses and minibuses leave for Lusaka (ZMW130, 12 hours) daily. Buses go via Mpika (ZMW80, two hours) and Serenje (ZMW95, four hours).

Northbound buses go to Mbala (ZMW35, two hours) and Mpulungu (ZMW50, three hours). Cheaper local minibuses run to Mpulungu, Mbala and Mpika.

## Lake Tanganyika

Spreading over a massive 34,000 sq km, and reaching almost 1500m deep, cavernous Lake Tanganyika is the second-deepest lake in the world and contains about 15% of the earth's fresh water. Believed to be up to 15 million years old and lying in the Great Rift Valley, the shores of the lake reach Tanzania, Burundi, the Democratic Republic of the Congo and Zambia. The climate here is always very hot, especially at the end of the dry season.

Of most interest to visitors are its white sandy beaches that, along with palm trees and snorkelling in crystal-clear waters with multicoloured tropical fish, can make it feel more like Thailand than Zambia.

**★Mishembe Bay (Luke's Beach)** BUNGALOW, CAMPGROUND **$**
(☎0976 664999; www.facebook.com/mishembebayzambia; camping per person US$10, lodge US$25) With its stunning white sands, palm trees and thatched bungalows, Luke's Beach resembles some secluded Southeast Asian beach paradise. The stilted thatched bungalows are luxurious on the outside, yet remain bare bones within to suit the budget traveller, and feature magnificent views of the water. You'll need to bring along all your own food, but there's a kitchen where you can cook.

**Isanga Bay Lodge** RESORT, CAMPGROUND **$$**
(☎0973 472317; www.isangabay.com; camping US$15, r incl breakfast US$80-100) Lake Tanganyika's most popular all-round choice is fronted by a pure white sandy beach. Undoubtedly the best pick here are the beach-facing bungalows in magnificent thatched structures; however, it's also a popular spot to pitch a tent; campers can access the same facilities including its lovely restaurant.

To get here it's US$100 return boat transfer from Mpulungu, or otherwise a fairly arduous two-hour 4WD journey from Mbala.

### ℹ Getting There & Away

All of the lodges can arrange boat transfers. Otherwise you can try the water taxi service (ZMW25), which departs Monday, Wednesday and Friday – leaving Mpulungu at 3pm, and making the return journey about 5am or 6am. However, be warned: it gets very full. Travel by road is possible, but only with a 4WD.

## Kalambo Falls

At 221m in height **Kalambo Falls** (adult/child/car US$15/7/15, camping US$15) is twice as high as Victoria Falls, and the second-highest single-drop waterfall in Africa (the highest being Tugela Falls in South Africa). From spectacular viewpoints near the top of the falls, you can see the Kalambo River plummeting off a steep V-shaped cliff cut into the Rift Valley escarpment down into a deep valley, which then winds towards Lake Tanganyika.

The best way for travellers without a car to get here is from Mpulungu. A thrice-weekly taxi boat service (ZMW25) stops at villages east of Mpulungu. It's also possible to hire a private boat from Mpulungu harbour, which will cost around US$150 for a return trip. Ask around at the market near the lake in Mpulungu.

# THE COPPERBELT

While the Copperbelt Province is the industrial heartland of Zambia, there are a few interesting spots for tourists too. The most important is the Chimfunshi Wildlife Orphanage, one of the largest chimpanzee sanctuaries in the world. The Copperbelt's major towns – Kitwe, Ndola and Chingola – are nice spots to break up the trip with museums, comfortable hotels and some good restaurants.

The region is home to the country's lucrative copper-mining industry. After a slump during the 1970s, the cost of copper and cobalt went through the roof in the early 21st century and this has once more seen the region prosper as Zambia records impressive economic growth. As you drive through the region, it's a common sight to pass trucks carrying large sheets of stacked copper to take across the borders.

## Ndola

POP 520,000 / ☎0212

Ndola, the capital of the Copperbelt Province (and third largest in Zambia), is a prosperous, sprawling city that makes a good spot to break up the journey or spend the night en route to the Chimfunshi Wildlife Orphanage (p1000). Once you get off its main thoroughfare, and hit its genteel, well-tended residential streets, there is no real evidence of its industrial base. Interestingly it's only 10km from the border with the Democratic Republic of Congo.

## Sights

**Copperbelt Museum** MUSEUM
(0212-617450; Buteko Ave; adult/child US$5/3; 8am-4.30pm) Definitely worth a visit, this museum starts upstairs with its cultural and ethnography galleries exhibiting artefacts used in witchcraft, personal ornaments, smoking and snuffing paraphernalia, and musical instruments such as talking drums. Downstairs it showcases the local mining industry with displays on its history, gemstones and the processing of copper.

## Sleeping & Eating

★ **Katuba Guesthouse** GUESTHOUSE $
(0978 450245, 0212-671341; www.katubaguesthouse.com; 4 Mwabombeni Rd; d incl breakfast ZMW350-450; ) Comfortable, clean and relaxed, this friendly guesthouse is within a secure residential compound in a well-heeled neighbourhood with jacaranda-lined streets. Rooms are spacious and come with fast wi-fi, cable TV and reliable hot water. Meals are available in the evening (ZMW50), along with cold beer, and there's a complimentary continental breakfast in the morning.

**Savoy Hotel** HOTEL $
(0212-611097; www.savoyhotel.co.zm; Buteko Ave; s/d incl breakfast ZMW350/400; ) It's a bit of a hulking concrete block from the outside and the 154 rooms add up to the largest hotel in the Copperbelt; however, inside the Savoy is upholding standards well – old-fashioned, true, but not without a certain charm.

**Michelangelo** ITALIAN $$
(0212-620325; 126 Broadway; pizzas from ZMW50, mains ZMW90-150; 7.30am-9.40pm Mon-Fri, 8am-2pm & 7-10pm Sat; ) Long regarded as one of Ndola's best restaurants, this Italian cafe-terrace under a designer awning does thin-crust pizzas, pastas and Western mains. Coffee, gelato or a home-made pastry round out the meal nicely. There is also a small boutique hotel (rooms from US$130) attached. On Sundays it is only open to hotel guests and local residents.

## Getting There & Away

Ndola is about 320km north of Lusaka, about a 4½-hour drive along a well-maintained but busy stretch of highway.

One of only three cities in Zambia to have an international airport, Ndola's airport is 3.5km south of the public bus station.

Long-distance buses depart from the stand next to the Broadway–Maina Soko roundabout and run to Lusaka (ZMW85, five hours), Kitwe (ZMW20, two hours) and Chingola (ZMW60, 2½ hours). Joldan is a recommended company.

# Kitwe

Zambia's second-largest city and the centre of the country's mining industry, Kitwe seems far larger than quiet Ndola. Business travellers (read mining consultants) stop here for the good selection of accommodation and eating places.

**Mukwa Lodge** (0212-224266; www.mukwalodge.co.zm; 26 Mpezeni Ave; s/d incl breakfast ZMW895/1195; ) has gorgeous stone-floor rooms that are beautifully furnished, and the bathrooms are as good as any in Zambia. It's a delightful place to stay that's well worth the indulgence. There are also suites across the road at its excellent restaurant, the **Courtyard Cafe** (mains ZMW55-70; noon-2pm & 6-9pm; ).

The lodge is in the process of shifting its restaurant across the road to 17 Mpezeni Ave, most likely to be named Cardamom. If you're heading to Chingola, also keep an eye out for its new restaurant there called Cumin, which should be open by the time you read this.

Kitwe is about 60km northwest of Ndola. The public bus station is situated 500m west of Independence Ave, and the **train station** (0212-223078) is at the southern end of Independence Ave. Frequent minibuses and buses run to Lusaka (ZMW90, five hours), Ndola (ZMW17, 45 minutes) and Chingola (ZMW17, 30 minutes).

**Voyagers** (0212-225056; www.voyagerszambia.com/kitwe.php; Enos Chomba Ave) is very helpful and can organise car hire and other travel arrangements.

# Chingola

As the closest town to the Chimfunshi Wildlife Orphanage, Chingola sees its fair share of travellers stopping over for the night. And given it's essentially a huge mine with a settlement wrapped around it, all up it's a surprisingly pleasant and relaxed town. It's more laid back then Ndola or Kitwe, and has some attractive, affluent pockets, a well-tended golf course and some good spots to eat.

Chingola's **bus station** (13th St) is in the centre of town. Frequent buses and minibuses (ZMW16, 30 minutes) run to the station from Kitwe, 50km to the southeast. Those heading to Chimfunshi Wildlife Orphanage, will need to catch any bus heading west to Solwezi, and prearrange a pick-up with the wildlife orphanage from Muchinshi for the last 25km leg off the highway.

## Chimfunshi Wildlife Orphanage

On a farm deep in the African bush, about 65km northwest of Chingola, is this impressive **chimpanzee sanctuary** (www.chimfunshi.de/en; day visit adult/child US$6/3; ⌚8am-4pm) that's undoubtedly the standout highlight in the Copperbelt region. Home to around 120 adult and young chimps, most have been rescued from poachers and traders in the neighbouring Democratic Republic of Congo or other parts of Africa. It's one of the largest sanctuaries of its kind in the world. This is not a natural wildlife experience, but it's still a unique and fascinating opportunity to observe the chimps as they feed, play and socialise.

You can overnight at **self-catering cottages** (www.chimfunshi.de/en; adult/child with shared bathroom US$30/15) or **camp** (☎0212-311293, 0968 568830; www.chimfunshi.de/en; camping US$15).

From Chingola, you'll need to make the slow, bumpy and incredibly dusty journey across the unsealed Chingola–Solwezi road (hopefully construction will be completed by the time you read this) for 50km or so until you see the Chimfunshi Wildlife Orphanage sign. From here it's a further 15km. All up count on a two-hour drive from Chingola.

# UNDERSTAND ZAMBIA

## Zambia Today

Politically speaking it's been a tumultuous few years for Zambia: since late 2014, it's had three presidents (including one who's died), two elections and an overall tense atmosphere characterised by disputed results, riots and violence.

After ruling for three years, President Sata passed away in late 2014 following a long, undisclosed illness, aged 77. He became the second president to die in office within six years, after Levy Mwanawasa passed away in 2008.

In 2015 the defence minister Edgar Lungu was inaugurated as Zambia's sixth president. He won in a narrow victory with 48.4% of the vote, taking over leadership for the remaining one year of Sata's five-year term. The 2016 elections were marred by political violence, opposition arrests and alleged voting fraud. Lungu again emerged victorious with 50.35% of the vote to 47.67% for Hakainde Hichilema (better known as HH). Lungu was sworn in for his five-year term on 13 September 2016.

The 59-year-old President Lungu faces challenges rising from a number of ongoing issues, namely tackling corruption, nationwide power cuts that continue to cripple the economy, wildlife poaching and the influence of Chinese investment in the mining, agriculture and manufacturing sectors.

## History

### The Colonial Era

The first Europeans to arrive were Portuguese explorers in the late 18th century, following routes established many centuries earlier by Swahili-Arab slave traders. The celebrated British explorer David Livingstone travelled up the Zambezi in the early 1850s in search of a route to the interior of Africa. In 1855 he reached the awesome waterfall that he promptly named Victoria Falls.

Close on Livingstone's heels came missionaries, explorers, hunters and prospectors. In 1890 the area became known as Northern Rhodesia and was administered by the British South Africa Company, owned by empire-builder Cecil John Rhodes.

At around the same time, vast deposits of copper were discovered in the area now called the Copperbelt. The main sources of labour were Africans who had to earn money to pay the new 'hut tax'; in any case, most were driven from their land by the European settlers.

In 1924 the colony was put under direct British control, and in 1935 the capital was moved to Lusaka.

## Resistance & Independence

The United National Independence Party (UNIP) was founded in the late 1950s by Dr Kenneth Kaunda, who spoke out against the federation.

Northern Rhodesia became independent in 1964, changing its name to Zambia. Kaunda became president and remained so for the next 27 years. Over the years, government corruption and mismanagement, coupled with civil wars in neighbouring states, left Zambia's economy in dire straits, and violent street protests were quickly transformed into a general demand for multiparty politics.

Full elections were held in October 1991, and Kaunda and UNIP were resoundingly defeated by Frederick Chiluba and the Movement for Multiparty Democracy (MMD). Kaunda bowed out gracefully, and Chiluba became president.

Austerity measures were introduced and food prices soared, inflation was rampant and state industries were privatised or simply closed, leaving many thousands of people out of work. Kaunda tried to re-enter the political arena. He attracted strong support but withdrew from the November 1996 elections in protest at MMD irregularities. Chiluba won a landslide victory and remained in firm control.

## The 21st Century

Chiluba, unable to run for a third presidential term in December 2001, anointed his former vice-president, Levy Mwanawasa, as his successor. Mwanawasa only just beat a coalition of opposition parties, amid allegations of vote rigging. Mwanawasa stripped his predecessor of immunity from prosecution, though Chiluba was eventually cleared of embezzlement charges by Zambia's High Court in August 2009.

Zambia's economy experienced strong growth in the early part of the 21st century, however it plummetted for a time when the price of minerals such as copper fell during the global economic slump of 2008–09. There has been large foreign investment in the mines (especially from China), and South African–owned businesses are multiplying in towns across the country, as there is finally a local demand for their businesses.

## People

Zambia's population is made up of between 70 and 80 different ethnic groups (the final count varies according to your definition of ethnicity, but the Zambian government officially recognises 73 groups). After independence President Kaunda fostered national unity, while still recognising the disparate languages and cultures. Intermarriage among the officially recognised groups is common. Hence Zambia is justifiably proud of its relative lack of ethnic problems, and its official motto on the coat of arms reads: 'One Zambia, One Nation'.

# SURVIVAL GUIDE

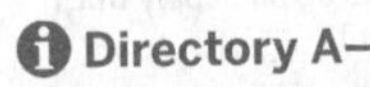


### ACCOMMODATION

Zambia offers an excellent choice of accommodation options to cater for all budgets. National park safari lodges especially provide a memorable stay. During shoulder season prices drop, and offer some good deals.

### ACTIVITIES

Zambia offers an array of activities for the adventurous traveller. Livingstone (and Victoria Falls town in Zimbabwe) are hubs, with adrenaline-pumping options such as white-water rafting and bungee jumping. At the main national parks you can arrange

### PRICE RANGES

These price ranges refer to a double room with bathroom in high season (August to October), based on 'international rates'.

**$** less than ZMW500 (US$50)

**$$** ZMW500 to ZMW1000 (US$50 to $100)

**$$$** more than ZMW1000 (US$100)

These price ranges refer to a standard main course. This is a guide only and prices will be considerably more in many lodges and camps in national parks.

**$** less than ZMW50 (US$5)

**$$** ZMW50 to ZMW100 (US$5 to $10)

**$$$** more than ZMW100 (US$10)

wildlife drives and walks, though you might prefer to safari on water, canoeing downriver alongside basking hippos.

### DANGERS & ANNOYANCES

Zambia is generally very safe, but in the cities and tourist areas there's always a chance of being targeted by muggers or con artists. As always, you can reduce the risk considerably by being sensible.

➡ While civil strife continues in the Democratic Republic of the Congo, avoid areas along the Zambia–Congo border, especially around Lake Mweru.

➡ Due to electricity shortages, load-shedding is now a reality of daily life across the country; however, most tourist lodges will have a back-up generator.

➡ Tsteste flies are an incessant nuisance when driving in many national parks; where problematic, wind the windows up and apply DEET-containing insect repellent.

### ELECTRICITY

Supply is 220V to 240V/50Hz and plugs are of the British three-prong variety.

### EMBASSIES & CONSULATES

Most embassies or high commissions are located in Lusaka. The British High Commission looks after the interests of Aussies and Kiwis.

**Botswanan High Commission** (☎0211-250555; 5201 Pandit Nehru Rd; ⏲8am-1pm & 2-4pm Mon-Fri)

**British High Commission** (☎0211-423200; www.ukinzambia.fco.gov.uk/en; 5210 Independence Ave; ⏲8am-4.30pm Mon-Fri)

**Canadian High Commission** (☎0211-250833; 5119 United Nations Ave; ⏲7.45am-5pm Mon-Thu, to 12.15pm Fri)

**DRC Embassy** (☎0211-235679; 1124 Parirenyetwa Rd; ⏲8.30am-1pm & 2-4pm Mon-Thu, to noon Fri)

**Dutch Embassy** (☎0211-253819; Swedish Embassy, Haile Selassie Ave; ⏲8am-1pm & 2-4pm Mon-Fri)

**French Embassy** (☎0977-110020; www.ambafrance-zm.org; 31F Leopards Hill Close; ⏲8am-12.30pm & 2-6pm Mon-Thu, 8am-12.30pm Fri)

**German Embassy** (☎0211-250644; www.lusaka.diplo.de; 5219 Haile Selassie Ave; ⏲9-11am Mon-Thu)

**Irish Embassy** (☎0211-291298; www.dfa.ie/irish-embassy/zambia; 6663 Katima Mulilo Rd; ⏲8am-4.30pm Mon-Thu, to 12.30pm Fri)

**Kenyan High Commission** (☎0211-250722; 5207 United Nations Ave; ⏲9am-12.30pm Mon-Fri)

**Malawian High Commission** (5202 Pandit Nehru Rd; ⏲8.30am-noon Mon-Thu, to 11am Fri)

**Mozambican Embassy** (☎0211-220339; 9592 Kacha Rd, Northmead; ⏲8am-1pm Mon-Fri)

**Namibian High Commission** (☎0211-260407; 30B Mutende Rd, Woodlands; ⏲8am-1pm & 2-4pm Mon-Fri)

**South African High Commission** (☎0211-260999; 26D Cheetah Rd, Kabulonga; ⏲8.30am-12.30pm Mon-Thu, to 12.30pm Fri)

**Tanzanian High Commission** (☎0211-253323; 5200 United Nations Ave; ⏲8am-4pm, consular 9am-1pm Mon-Fri)

**US Embassy** (☎0211-357000; https://zm.usembassy.gov; Kabulonga Rd, Ibex Hill)

**Zimbabwean High Commission** (☎0211-254006; 11058 Haile Selassie Ave; ⏲8.30am-noon Mon-Thu, to 11am Fri)

### INTERNET ACCESS

Wi-fi is available in many lodges across the country, sometimes for a small fee. You can also get online through inexpensive pre-paid sim card internet data bundles; either MTN or Airtel are recommended. For 1GB expect to pay around US$10, which is valid for 30 days.

You'll need to bring along your passport to the shop to get it activated. Coverage for the most part is fast, but is poor to non-existent within the national parks.

Otherwise there are internet cafes in most large towns.

### LGBTIQ TRAVELLERS

Male homosexual activity is illegal in Zambia. Lesbian activity is not illegal but that's only due to it not being recognised. Public displays of affection, while possibly not being illegal, are insensitive to local attitudes and are very much frowned upon, whatever your orientation.

### MONEY

The unit of currency is the Zambian kwacha. President Sata passed legislation in 2012 that revalued Zambia's currency and prohibits any other currency from being accepted as a form of payment. Prices are sometimes quoted in US$, but you'll pay in local currency.

In the cities and larger towns, you can easily change cash (no commission; photo ID required) and withdraw it (in kwacha) from ATMs at branches of the major banks. Visa is the most readily recognised credit card; a surcharge of between 4% and 7% may be added to your bill.

**Exchange Rates**

| | | |
|---|---|---|
| Australia | A$1 | ZMW7.30 |
| Canada | C$1 | ZMW7.52 |
| Euro zone | €1 | ZMW10.54 |
| Japan | ¥100 | ZMW8.60 |
| New Zealand | NZ$1 | ZMW6.98 |
| South Africa | R1 | ZMW 0.73 |
| UK | £1 | ZMW12.36 |
| US | US$1 | ZMW9.95 |

For current exchange rates, see www.xe.com.

### OPENING HOURS

**Banks** Weekdays from 8am to 3.30pm (or 5pm), and 8am to 11am (or noon) on Saturday.

**Government offices** From 8am or 9am to 4pm or 5pm weekdays, with a one-hour lunch break between noon and 2pm.

**Post offices** From 8am or 9am to 4pm or 4.30pm weekdays.

**Restaurants** Normally open for lunch between 11.30am and 2.30pm and dinner between 6pm and 10.30pm.

**Shops** Keep the same hours as government offices but also open Saturday.

**Supermarkets** Normally open from 8am to 8pm weekdays, and 8am to 6pm weekends; some open later at Lusaka's big shopping centres.

### PUBLIC HOLIDAYS

During public holidays, most businesses and government offices are closed.

**New Year's Day** 1 January

**Youth Day** 2nd Monday in March

**Easter** March/April

**Labour/Workers' Day** 1 May

**Africa (Freedom) Day** 25 May

**Heroes' Day** 1st Monday in July

**Unity Day** 1st Tuesday in July

**Farmers' Day** 1st Monday in August

**Independence Day** 24 October

**Christmas Day** 25 December

### TELEPHONE

MTN and Airtel are the most reliable mobile (cell) phone networks. If you own a GSM phone, you can buy a cheap SIM card without a problem (including at the Lusaka or Livingstone Airport). You'll need to bring along your passport to have it activated.

### TIME

Zambia is in the Central Africa time zone, which is two hours ahead of GMT/UTC. There is no daylight saving.

### TOURIST INFORMATION

The regional tourist office in Livingstone is worth visiting for specific enquiries, but the main office in Lusaka is generally of little use.

The official website of Zambia Tourism Agency (www.zambiatourism.com) is pretty useful, though be aware a lot of information is out of date.

### VISAS

Tourist visas are available at major borders, airports and ports, but it's important to note that you should have a Zambian visa *before* arrival if travelling by train or boat from Tanzania.

All foreign visitors – other than Southern African Development Community (SADC) passport holders who are issued visas free of charge – pay US$50 for single entry (up to one month) and US$80 for double entry (up to three months).

In December 2016 the KAZA visa was reintroduced, which allows most visitors to acquire a single 30-day visa (US$50) for both Zambia and Zimbabwe. As long as you remain within these two countries, you can cross the border multiple times. These visas are available at Livingstone and Lusaka airports, as well as at the Victoria Falls and Kazungula crossings.

## Getting There & Away

### AIR

Given there are very few direct flights into Zambia from outside Africa, many international visitors are likely to transfer to connecting flights in either Johannesburg or Nairobi.

#### Airports & Airlines

Zambia's main international airport is in Lusaka. An increasing number of international airlines also fly to the airport at Livingstone (for Victoria Falls), and a lesser amount to Mfuwe (for South Luangwa National Park) and Ndola.

### LAND

Zambia shares borders with eight countries, so there's a huge number of crossing points. Most are open daily from 6am to 6pm; the border closes at 8pm at Victoria Falls and at 7pm at Chirundu.

### SEA & LAKE

There is an international port at Mpulungu where you can get the MV *Liemba* ferry along Lake Tanganyika to/from Tanzania (p707).

## Getting Around

### AIR

Proflight (p994) is the only domestic airline offering regularly scheduled flights connecting Lusaka to Livingstone (for Victoria Falls), Lower

Zambezi (Jeki and Royal airstrips), Mfuwe (for South Luangwa National Park), Ndola, Kasama and Solwezi.

### BUS

All main routes are served by ordinary public buses, which either run on a fill-up-and-go basis or have fixed departures (these are called 'time buses'). 'Express buses' are faster – often terrifyingly so – and stop less, but cost about 15% more. In addition, several private companies run comfortable European-style express buses along the major routes, eg between Lusaka and Livingstone, Lusaka and Chipata, and Lusaka and the Copperbelt region.

### CAR & MOTORCYCLE

Companies such as **Voyagers** (☎0212-620314; www.europcarzambia.com), **Benmark** (☎0211-292192; ben@benmarkcarhire.com; cnr Parliament & Great East Rds), **Hemingways** (☎0213-323097; www.hemingwayszambia.com), **4x4 Hire Africa** (☎in South Africa +27 21-791 3904; www.4x4hire.co.za) and **Limo Car Hire** (☎0977 743145; www.limohire-zambia.com) rent out Toyota Hiluxes and old-school Land Rover vehicles, unequipped or fully decked out with everything you would need for a trip to the bush (including roof-top tents!); prices vary from US$120 to US$250 per day.

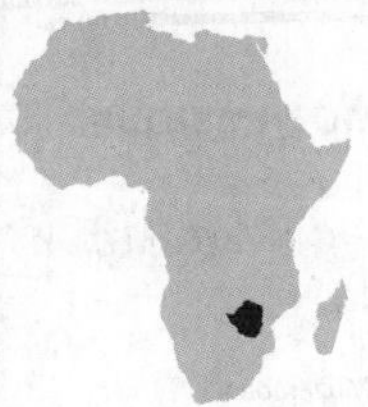

# Zimbabwe

POP 13.1 MILLION / ☎263

**Includes ➡**



## Best Places to Eat

- Amanzi (p1011)
- Portuguese Recreation Club (p1015)
- 26 on Park (p1021)
- Bulawayo Club (p1020)
- 40 Cork Road (p1011)

## Best Places to Sleep

- Camp Amalinda (p1022)
- Jacana Gardens Guest Lodge (p1008)
- Rhino Safari Camp (p1014)
- Chilo Gorge Safari Lodge (p1018)
- Heaven Lodge (p1016)

## Why Go?

While from afar Zimbabwe's plight doesn't paint a rosy picture, the reality is different on the ground for tourists – most insist it's hands down one of the safest, friendliest and most spectacular countries in Africa.

A journey here will take you through an attractive patchwork of landscapes, from highveld, balancing boulders and flaming msasa trees to laid-back towns, lush mountains and lifeblood rivers up north. Here you can spot the Big Five in its national parks, discover World Heritage–listed archaeological sites and stand in awe of one of the natural wonders of the world, Victoria Falls.

Along the way you'll receive a friendly welcome from locals, who are famous for their politeness and resilience in the face of hardship. After almost two decades of political ruin, violence and economic disaster, Zimbabweans continue to hold on to hope that a new dawn will soon rise upon this embattled nation.

## When to Go

### Harare

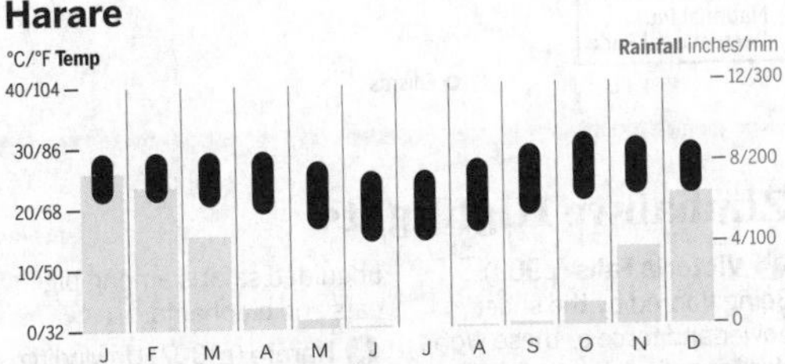


**Apr–Oct** Best time seasonally, with sunny days and cold, clear nights.

**Nov–Apr** The rainy season is beautiful, with generally sporadic rain and dramatic afternoon electrical storms.

**Jul–Sep** Peak season brings prime wildlife viewing, optimal white-water rafting and canoeing the Zambezi.

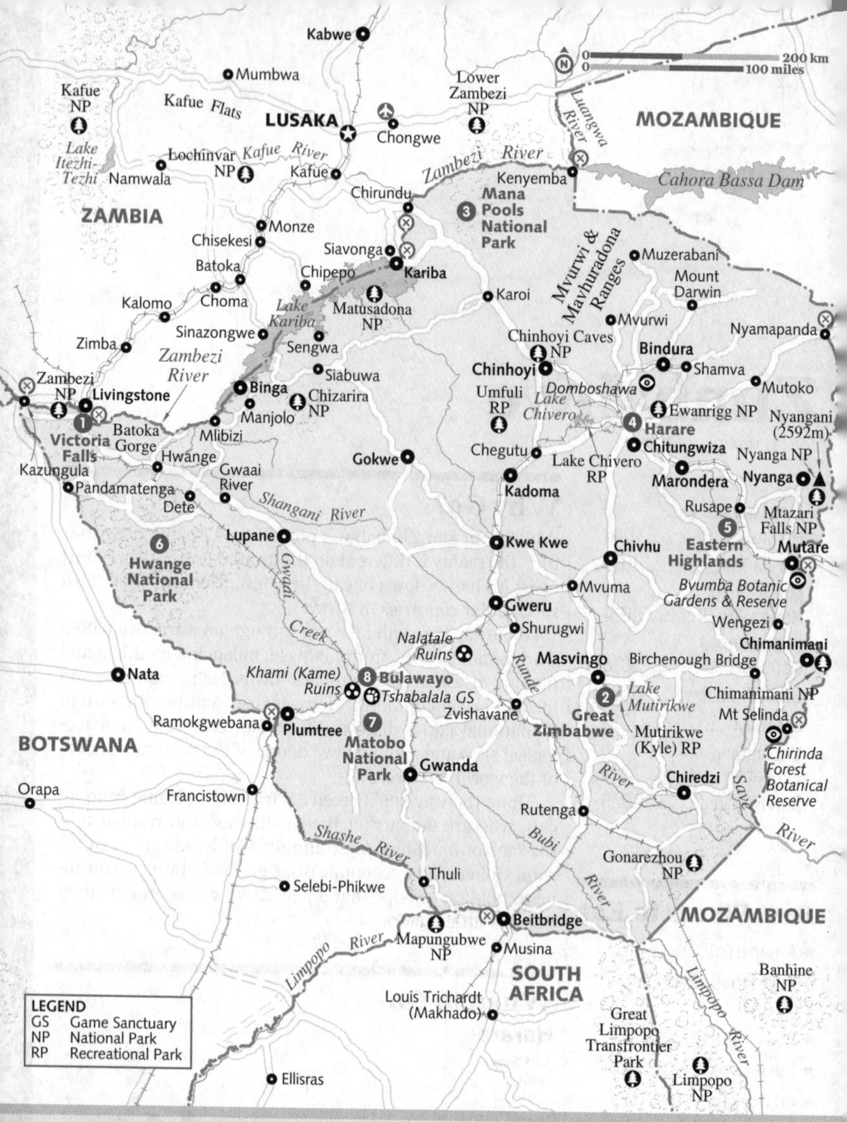


## Zimbabwe Highlights

❶ **Victoria Falls** (p969) Being floored by the sheer power and force of these World Heritage–listed waterfalls.

❷ **Great Zimbabwe** (p1017) Taking the spiritual pulse of Zimbabwe at these atmospheric stone ruins.

❸ **Mana Pools National Park** (p1014) Walking through Africa's only park that allows unguided safaris among big cats and elephants.

❹ **Harare** (p1007) Unwinding in garden restaurants within converted colonial homes.

❺ **Eastern Highlands** (p1015) Breathing in lush pine forests and mountain air.

❻ **Hwange** (p1022) Feeling humbled at Zim's largest national park, home to Africa's biggest elephant population.

❼ **Matobo National Park** (p1021) Tracking rhinos and seeing ancient rock art and superb scenery.

❽ **Bulawayo** (p1018) Soaking up the wonderful architecture, art galleries and history.

# HARARE

POP 1.5 MILLION / ☎04

More attractive than most other Southern African capitals, Harare gets a bad rap and unjustly so. While it's certainly not without its problems, overall it's a safe and laid-back city where wide avenues are lined with dusty red earth, and indigenous plants and blooming jacarandas give it a lovely African summertime feel. While it's tempting to rush off to your safari, it's worth hanging around in Harare to sample its fine dining, museums, craft markets and varied bars.

## Sights

Harare has a good variety of sights: some fantastic art galleries, wildlife encounters and a few offbeat sights unique to the city. Another reason to visit is for the fantastic day trips you can do from here.

**★National Gallery of Zimbabwe** GALLERY

(Map p1010; ☎04-704666; www.nationalgallery.co.zw; cnr Julius Nyerere Way & Park Lane; US$1; 9am-5pm Tue-Sun) In the southeast corner of Harare Gardens, this lovely gallery has multiple spaces exhibiting a mix of contemporary local, African and international artists. Shows change monthly, with a mix of paintings, photography, stone sculptures, masks and carvings. The attached shop is an excellent place to stock up on crafts and books on Zimbabwean art, before coffee and cake in the cafe. There's an open-air Shona sculpture garden outside.

**Wild is Life** WILDLIFE RESERVE

(☎0779 949821; www.wildislife.com; adult/teenager US$95/80; 3.30-6.30pm) A wildlife sanctuary with a difference – sip on afternoon tea and champagne while getting a hands-on experience with the injured, rescued or orphaned animals here. Located near the airport (p1013). You need to book well in advance and children under 12 are not permitted.

**National Heroes' Acre** MONUMENT

(Map p1008; ☎04-277965; 107 Rotten Row; adult/child museum US$10/5; 8am-4.30pm) The grandiose obelisk of Heroes' Acre, overlooking the town, is straight out of Pyongyang, yet lies just 7km from Harare. Designed with the assistance of North Korea, it serves as a sombre memorial to the forces who died during the Second Chimurenga. There's a giant socialist realism statue of the unknown soldier (actually three soldiers), flanked by bronze friezes depicting stirring war victories. Entrance is free, but there's an admission fee for the interesting museum dedicated to the resistance movement.

**Delta Gallery** GALLERY

(☎04-792135; www.gallerydelta.com; 110 Livingstone Ave; 8am-4.30pm Mon-Fri, to 2.30pm Sat) A must for contemporary art lovers is this gallery inside the charming colonial house of eminent Rhodesian painter Robert Paul (1906–79). It showcases wonderful works by contemporary Zimbabwean artists, with shows held monthly. Its small bookshop has some interesting local novels and art books for sale.

**Tobacco Floor** NOTABLE BUILDING

(☎04-666801; www.timb.co.zw; Gleneagles Rd; 7.30am-1pm Mon-Fri Feb-Jul) Not quite the NY stock exchange but certainly fast paced. Get among the action on the floors where farmers on one side sell bales of tobacco to brokers on the other. Tobacco used to be one of Zimbabwe's major foreign-exchange earners and the country produced the best leaf in the world. Auctions only take place from around February to July.

## Festivals & Events

**HIFA – Harare International Festival of Arts** MUSIC

(☎04-300119; www.hifa.co.zw) *The* annual event, held over six days around late April or early May, brings international acts to produce a crammed timetable alongside Zimbabwean artists. Performances include Afrobeat, funk, jazz, soul, opera, classical music, theatre and dance. If you're in the region, don't miss it.

## Sleeping

**★It's a Small World Backpackers Lodge** HOSTEL $

(Map p1008; ☎04-335176; www.smallworldlodge.com; 25 Ridge Rd, Avondale; camping US$9, dm US$12, r US$45-65, r with shared bathroom $20-40; ) Single-handedly flying the flag for backpackers in Harare, It's a Small World does a wonderful job catering to the needs of independent travellers. It knows what backpackers want – clean rooms, fast and free wi-fi, a communal kitchen, pool table, rooftop deck and a sociable, low-key bar. Bikes are also available for hire (US$5 per day).

**★Wavell House** GUESTHOUSE $$

(Map p1008; ☎04-495263, 0772 236626; www.wavell-house.com; 9 Wavell Rd, Highlands; r incl breakfast US$100-150; ) In an attractive

# Harare

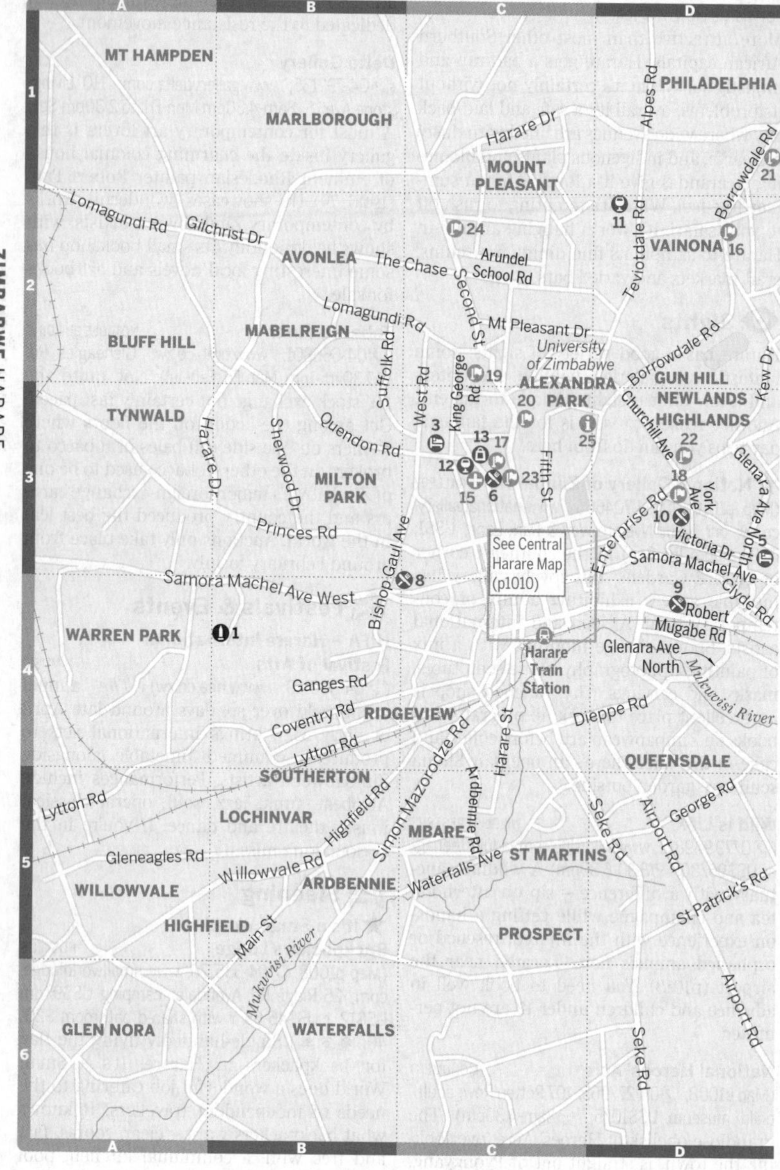


renovated colonial house, refined Wavel House is very much an oasis with over a hectare of gardens and a luxurious swimming pool. Rooms vary in size, but are all comfortable, modern and with individual flair; they're excellent value given the rate includes an impressive breakfast spread. The owners are both well-regarded designers, and will make you feel welcome.

★ **Jacana Gardens Guest Lodge** B&B $$
(Map p1008; ☎0779 715297; www.jacana-gardens.com; 14 Jacana Dr, Borrowdale; s/d incl breakfast

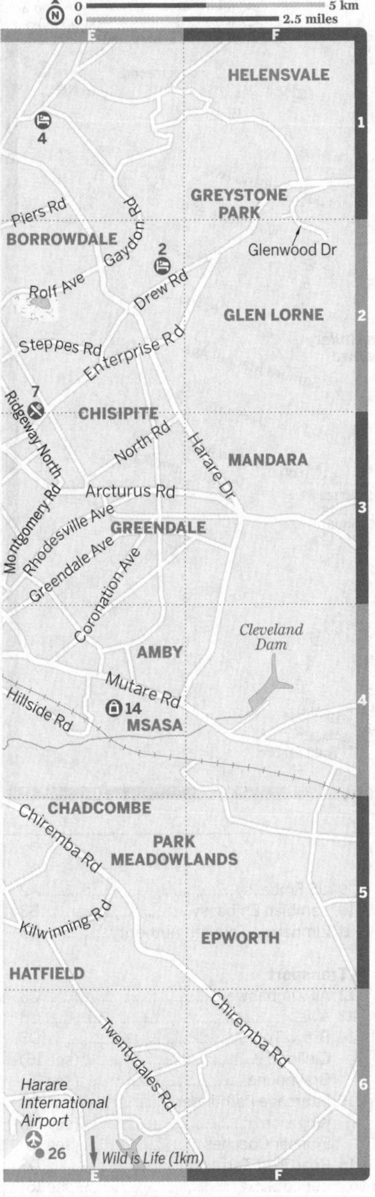


## Harare

**Sights**
1 National Heroes' Acre .......... B4

**Sleeping**
2 Amanzi Lodges .......... E2
3 It's a Small World Backpackers Lodge .......... C3
4 Jacana Gardens Guest Lodge .......... E1
5 Wavell House .......... D3

**Eating**
6 40 Cork Road .......... C3
7 Amanzi .......... E2
8 Bakers .......... C4
9 Garwe .......... D4
Shop Café @ Amanzi .......... (see 7)
10 Victoria 22 .......... D3

**Drinking & Nightlife**
11 Jam Tree .......... D2
12 Pariah State .......... C3

**Shopping**
13 Avondale Shopping Centre .......... C3
14 Chapungu Village .......... E4
Doon Estate .......... (see 14)
KwaMambo .......... (see 6)

**Information**
15 AMI Hospital .......... C3
16 Australian Embassy .......... D2
17 Botswanan Embassy .......... C3
18 French Embassy .......... D3
19 German Embassy .......... C2
Internet Cafe .......... (see 13)
20 Malawian High Commission .......... C3
21 Namibian Embassy .......... D1
22 Netherlands Embassy .......... D3
23 South African Embassy .......... C3
24 UK Embassy .......... C2
25 Zimbabwe Parks & Wildlife Central Reservations Office .......... C3

**Transport**
26 Europcar .......... E6
FastJet .......... (see 17)
Zimbabwe Car Hire .......... (see 26)

from US$95/130; ❄ 📶 🏊) Harare does charming guesthouses as well as anywhere in the world, and Jacana is one of its best. The tasteful interior designed by the friendly Dutch owners incorporates Zimbabwean antiques and colourful local paintings. Renowned Zimbabwean architect Mick Pearce designed the award-winning house using the principles of feng shui – natural light pours into open spaces.

**★Amanzi Lodges** LODGE **$$$**
(Map p1008; ☎0772 367495, 04-499257; www.amanzi.co.zw; 1 Masasa Lane, Kambanji; s/d incl breakfast US$230/280, ste s/d US$280/330; ❄ 📶 🏊) Set among a tropical, flower-filled garden, Amanzi is easily one of Harare's best and most unique choices, offering intimate and classy five-star service. Rooms are

## Central Harare

## Central Harare

**Top Sights**
1 National Gallery of Zimbabwe .............. B2

**Sights**
2 Harare Gardens .............. B2

**Sleeping**
3 It's a Small World (Harare Centre) .............. D1

**Information**
4 Avenues Clinic .............. B1
5 Canadian Embassy .............. A1
6 Kenyan Embassy .............. B2
7 Mozambican Embassy .............. A2
8 Tanzanian Embassy .............. A1
9 US Embassy .............. A2
10 Zambian Embassy .............. B3
11 Zimbabwe Tourism Authority .............. B3

**Transport**
12 Air Zimbabwe .............. C3
13 Avis .............. C3
14 Bravo Tours .............. D3
Citiliner .............. (see 16)
Greyhound .............. (see 16)
15 Intercape Pathfinder .............. D3
King Lion .............. (see 16)
Pioneer Coaches .............. (see 16)
16 Road Port Terminal .............. D3
Zupco .............. (see 16)

individually styled in themes from different African countries; it's worth having a look at a few on its website. There's a gym, pool, tennis court and complimentary coffee and evening snacks at the bar.

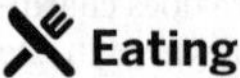

## Eating

Harare has a great choice of eating options, from restaurants doing local dishes to an impressive range of multicultural cuisine. Many of its restaurants are set in charming converted houses surrounded by gardens, which adds to the experience.

For self-caterers and those budgeting, supermarkets are well stocked and also have inexpensive ready-to-eat meals such as *sadza* (maize-meal porridge) and meat dishes.

**Bakers** PORTUGUESE **$**
(Map p1008; www.facebook.com/bakerschickens; 58 Denbeigh Rd, Belvedere; whole chicken US$7; ⌚10am-9pm Mon, Tue & Thu, 5-9pm Wed, 10am-10pm Fri & Sat) A basic no-frills joint in central Harare known for its delicious peri peri charcoal chicken. It also does steaks and burgers etc. It's 100% halal.

**★ 40 Cork Road** CAFE **$$**
(Map p1008; ☎04-253585; 40 Cork Rd, Belgravia; breakfast/lunch from US$6/10, coffee US$3; ⌚8am-4pm Mon-Fri, to 3pm Sat; 📶) An attractive house-turned-restaurant with a relaxed garden setting, 40 Cork serves quality breakfasts and lunches, and does one of the best coffees in Harare. Also here is its **Tutti Gelati**, serving excellent homemade gelato (US$2 a scoop), and the quality **KwaMambo** (Map p1008; 40 Cork Rd; ⌚8.30am-4pm Mon-Sat) craft shop.

**Garwe** AFRICAN **$$**
(Map p1008; ☎04-778992; bookings@garwerestaurant.co.zw; 18637 Donald McDonald Rd, Eastlea; mains from US$5; ⌚11.30am-5pm; 🖉) Highly recommended by locals, this restaurant has traditional Zimbabwean cuisine served under a thatched roof around a large roaring fire. Lunch draws a busy crowd filling up on *sadza* and other dishes, including goat and guinea fowl. Vegetarians are catered for with tasty leaf-vegetable dishes. It's about a US$5 cab ride from town.

**★ Amanzi** FUSION **$$$**
(Map p1008; ☎04-497768; www.amanzi.co.zw/restaurant.php; 158 Enterprise Rd, Highlands; mains $15-25; ⌚noon-2.30pm Tue-Sat, 6.30-10pm Mon-Sat) Don some nice threads as Amanzi is a class act and still *the* special night out. In a stunning colonial house with African decor, local art (for sale) and an amazing garden, it serves delicious international fusion dishes with a great vibe.

The outdoor patio is ridiculously atmospheric with a nearby garden waterfall and crackling fire brazier. Bookings are essential.

## Drinking & Nightlife

**Pariah State** BAR
(Map p1008; www.pariahstate.co.zw; 1 Hilary House, King George Rd, Avondale; beer US$2, cocktails from US$6; ⌚3.30pm-1am) Across the road from Avondale Shopping Centre is this cool little bar that attracts a mixed, friendly crowd of students and professionals. There's a good choice of drinks, including South African wines and beer. Things get lively Thursday and Friday nights with live bands, while Sundays have DJs playing reggae and hip hop. Also has a few other bars across town.

**Jam Tree** BEER GARDEN
(Map p1008; ☎0778 173286; www.facebook.com/thejamtreeharare; 40 Bargate Rd, Mt Pleasant; ⌚9am-midnight) One of Harare's current hot spots, the Jam Tree is all about its outdoor garden space, good choice of drinks (including bottled craft beers), tasty food and coffee, and live music. Check its Facebook page for upcoming events.

## ☆ Entertainment

There's always some sort of theatre, music and sports going on in town. Visit Art Harare's Facebook page to be kept in the loop for the latest art events.

Unfortunately Harare's premier arts venue, the Book Cafe, has closed its doors, but keep an eye out for pop-up events on its Facebook page.

**Harare Sports Club** CRICKET
(www.zimcricket.org; cnr Fifth St & Josiah Tongogara Ave) With Zimbabwe regaining its status as a test-playing nation, cricket fans should try to make it to this scenic ground surrounded by jacaranda trees. There's a **pub** (www.thecenturion.co.zw; Harare Sports Club, cnr Fifth St & Josiah Tongogara Ave; ⌚8am-late) right behind the bowler's arm, which enhances enjoyment when viewing domestic or international T20s, one-dayers or test matches. See the website for upcoming events.

**Theatre in the Park** PERFORMING ARTS
(☎8644 143016; www.theatreinthepark.co.zw; Harare Gardens; tickets from US$3; ⌚from 6pm Wed-Fri) This is a new space in Harare Gardens (p1007) for this long-standing theatre company (on hiatus for four years). Plays are held on Wednesday, Thursday and Friday evenings from 6pm – it can be an interesting way to spend an evening. Check the website

or its Facebook page for the schedule. In summer there's jazz on Sunday evenings.

## Shopping

One of the highlights of visiting Harare is the quality of shopping, and it's a great spot to pick up quality souvenirs. Sculpture and handicrafts are the most popular items, as well as artworks and jewellery – all of which are uniquely Zimbabwean.

**★Patrick Mavros** JEWELLERY
(☎0772 570533; www.patrickmavros.com; Haslemere Lane, Umwinsidale; ⏲8am-5pm Mon-Fri, to 1pm Sat) His clients may include Bruce Springsteen, Kate Middleton and the King of Spain, but Patrick Mavros' stunning handmade silver jewellery is very affordable. The shop has a spectacular setting, overlooking a picture-perfect valley with wildlife. All silver is from Zimbabwe and you can arrange a behind-the-scenes tour in the workshop.

**Chapungu Village** ART
(Map p1008; www.facebook.com/doonestate; Doon Estate, 1 Harrow Rd, Msasa; ⏲8am-5pm) Part of the Doon Estate complex, Chapungu has long been one of Harare's best places for Shona sculpture – one of the best things to buy in Zimbabwe. It comprises a collective of 16 artists, each with their own plot to sell their handiwork.

## Information

### DANGERS & ANNOYANCES

Harare is generally a safe city, but you'll need to be careful as robberies occasionally occur. Take a cab in the evenings and watch for bag snatching and pickpocketing in markets, parks and bus stations. While in no way comparable to South Africa, carjacking is on the rise, so take precautions by always keeping your windows up and your bags in the boot or, if not possible, safely wedged under your feet.

Take care when photographing certain areas in the city centre, particularly government buildings, offices and residential areas.

### Police Stations

**Police** (Map p1010; ☎995; cnr Inez Tce & Kenneth Kaunda Ave)

### INTERNET ACCESS

The town centre, radiating out from First St, has many internet centres. All charge US$1 to US$2 per hour. However, there's free wi-fi internet access at most hotels, restaurants and cafes.

**Internet Cafe** (Map p1008; Avondale Shopping Centre; ⏲8am-7pm) Reliable internet; located above Nando's.

### MEDICAL SERVICES

**Avenues Clinic** (Map p1010; ☎04-251180, 04-251199; www.avenuesclinic.co.zw; cnr Mazowe St & Baines Ave) Hospital recommended by expats.

### BUSES FROM HARARE

| DESTINATION | COMPANY | FARE (US$) | SCHEDULE | TIME (HR) | TERMINAL |
|---|---|---|---|---|---|
| Bulawayo | Intercape Pathfinder | 20 | 7.30am & 2pm | 6 | Intercape Pathfinder |
| Bulawayo | Bravo Tours | 20-25 | 7am & 1.30pm | 6 | Bravo Tours |
| Bulawayo | City Link | 25 | 7.30am & 2pm | 6 | Rainbow Towers Hotel |
| Vic Falls | Intercape Pathfinder | 35 | 7.30am Wed, Fri, Sun | 12 | Intercape Pathfinder |
| Vic Falls | Bravo Tours | 35 | 7.30am Wed, Fri, Sun | 12 | Mbare |
| Hwange National Park | Intercape Pathfinder | 30 | 7.30am Wed, Fri, Sun | 10 | Intercape Pathfinder |
| Masvingo (for Great Zimbabwe) | Local buses and minibuses | 8 | from 6.30am to early afternoon | 4½ | Mbare |
| Mutare (for Eastern Highlands) | Local buses | 8 | times vary | 4½ | Mbare |
| Mutare (for Eastern Highlands) | Combis | 5-8 | regularly | 4 | 4th St Terminal; outside Road Port |
| Kariba | CAG | 10 | times vary | 6½ | Mbare |

**AMI Hospital** (Map p1008; 04-700666; www.ami.co.zw; 15 Lanark Rd; 24hr) Also recommended by expats.

**MONEY**

There were major cash shortages at the time of research, with lengthy waits for most ATMs. Banks accepting international cards include **Barclays** (Map p1010; cnr 1st St & Jason Moyo Ave), Stanbic and Standard Chartered. Visa is the preferred card for ATM cash withdrawals, but MasterCard is becoming more common.

**POST**

**Main Post Office** (Map p1010; 04-783583; www.zimpost.co.zw; cnr Inez Tce & Jason Moyo Ave; 8.30am-4pm Mon-Fri, to 11.30am Sat) Stamp sales and poste-restante facilities are in the arcade, while the parcel office is downstairs.

**TOURIST INFORMATION**

**Zimbabwe Parks & Wildlife Central Reservations Office** (NPWZ; Map p1008; 04-707625, 04-706077; www.zimparks.org; cnr Borrowdale Rd & Sandringham Dr; 8am-4pm Mon-Fri) A good source of information and accommodation-booking assistance for those planning to head into the national parks.

**Zimbabwe Tourism Authority** (Map p1010; 04-758712; www.zimbabwetourism.net; 55 Samora Machel Ave; 8am-4.45pm Mon-Fri) Has a few brochures (but don't expect too much) and an excellent website.

## Getting There & Away

**AIR**

All international and domestic airlines use **Harare International Airport** (Map p1008), located 15km southeast of the city centre. Taxis from the airport cost US$25 into town.

**Air Zimbabwe** (Map p1010; 04-251836, at airport 04-575111; www.airzimbabwe.aero; cnr Speke Ave & Third St) operates flights to/from Bulawayo (one way/return US$176/342, 45 minutes) and Victoria Falls (one way/return US$215/421).

A more popular option these days to get to Victoria Falls is the low-cost carrier **FastJet** (Map p1008; 086-7700 6061; www.fastjet.com; 9 Phillips Ave, Belgravia; 8.30am-4pm Mon-Fri, to noon Sat), with flights starting from as little as US$25.

**BUS**

All bus companies servicing international destinations depart from **Road Port Terminal** (Map p1010; cnr Robert Mugabe Rd & Fifth St).

## Getting Around

**CAR**

**Zimbabwe Car Hire** (Map p1008; 0783 496253, 09-230306; www.zimbabwecarhire.com; Harare International Airport) gets good reviews for reliable, well-priced vehicle rental. Sedans start at around US$40 a day, and 4WDs from US$80 a day, with discounts for longer rentals. There's also **Avis** (Map p1010; 04-796409; www.avis.co.zw; cnr Third St & Jason Moyo Ave) and **Europcar** (Map p1008; 04-581411; www.europcar.co.zw; Harare International Airport).

**TAXI**

Zimbabwe's equivalent to Uber is **GTAXI** (8677 200200; www.gtaxi.net), a well-received taxi-booking app that will get you the best prices around Harare.

Taxis are best arranged through your hotel; try **Rixi Taxi** (04-753080).

# NORTHERN ZIMBABWE

## Kariba Town

POP 27,500 / 061

The sprawling, sleepy lakeside settlement of Kariba is spread out along the steep undulating shore of its namesake lake. There are lovely lake views and elephants often come through town. While self-equipped Zimbabwean and South African families flock here to socialise on houseboats and to fish, most foreign tourists are here as a stop en route to their next destination or just to chill out by the lake.

### Sights

**Kariba Dam Wall** LANDMARK

Forming the border between Zambia (Siavonga) and Zimbabwe is the Kariba dam wall. It's an impressive engineering feat that you can walk the length across; you'll need to leave your passport or ID with the immigration office. At the time of construction, it was the world's biggest dam and today remains one of the largest.

**Dam Observation Point** VIEWPOINT

FREE Head up to Observation Point for excellent sweeping views of the lake and Kariba Dam. The Kariba Publicity Association is based up here and it houses some interesting information on the history of the dam's construction. To get here, head towards the

DON'T MISS

### LAKE KARIBA

Lake Kariba is the nation's Riviera where it's all about houseboats, beer, fishing and amazing sunsets. It's one of the world's largest artificial lakes, covering an area of more than 5000 sq km and holding 180 billion tonnes of water. Its location adjoining the Matusadona National Park means it's home to plenty of wildlife, including the Big Five – lions, leopards, buffaloes, elephants and rhinos.

Swimming in the lake isn't possible due to hippos, big crocs and bilharzia. In Kariba town, avoid walking around at night due to the prevalence of elephants.

border near the dam and take a right at the petrol station.

## Sleeping & Eating

Most of the lodges and hotels have restaurants or self-catering kitchens. Warthogs' pub is a good spot for a meal even if you're not staying there. For supermarkets head into Nyamhunga, Kariba's commercial centre of town.

**★Warthogs Bush Camp** LODGE $

(0775-068406; www.warthogs.co.zw; Kariba; campsite per person US$5, tented camps s/d US$10/15, lodges d US$40, 6-person chalet US$70; ) One of only a handful of places in Zimbabwe catering to the needs of independent budget travellers, Warthogs is doing a fantastic job of it. Accommodation is no-frills, with campsites, domed tents, A-frame huts and thatched cabins, all with piping hot wood-fired showers.

**Hornbill Lodge** LODGE $$

(0772-348565; www.hornbilllodge.com; 797 Mica Point; r per person incl half board US$115; ) A prime spot with a commanding hilltop location, Hornbill's rooms comprise unique open-air design, thatched rondavels that open up to lake views. It's set among landscaped gardens and a small plunge pool.

## Getting There & Away

The CAG bus has daily departures to Harare (US$10, 6½ hours) with the first services from 8am. Taxis are the best way to get to Zambia (Siavonga), 10km from Kariba. Expect to pay US$20 to US$25 for a taxi to take you all the way to the Zambia immigration point.

# Matusadona National Park

Situated on the southern shore of Lake Kariba, the beautiful **Matusadona National Park** (0772-143506; www.zimparks.org; per person US$15) is home to the Big Five, including the endangered black rhino. While poaching has hit the park hard in the past decade, there remains an abundance of elephants, lions and outstanding birdwatching. The best time for wildlife viewing is between July and November.

**Tashinga** CAMPGROUND $

(04-706077; www.zimparks.org; campsite per person from US$17, lodge US$138) Run by Zimparks, this national park campsite offers only basic facilities but a magnificent lakeside location. Accommodation comprises a few tent shelters, a braai stand, showers (including hot water), toilets and firewood; bring plenty of drinking water. There's also a self-catering lodge that sleeps nine. It's only really accessed by 4WD, as there's no boat landing.

**★Rhino Safari Camp** LODGE $$$

(0772-205000, 0772-400021; www.rhinosafaricamp.com; Elephant Point; r per person US$195-340; ) One of the best camps in the country, this is remote, wild and everything you want from a safari experience. Its simplicity in design is genius, blending in beautifully among its surrounds with sandy paths and a rustic charm mixed with subtle luxuries. The thatched, stilted chalets have magnificent views and delightful outdoor bathrooms.

## Getting There & Away

The most common way to arrive to Matusadona is via a speedboat from Kariba (US$70 to US$300 return). Driving is another option, but only if you have a 4WD during the dry season; it's around a 10-hour journey from Harare.

# Mana Pools National Park

This magnificent 2200-sq-km **national park** (63533; www.zimparks.org/index.php/parks-overview/national/mana-pools; adult/child US$20/15; 6am-6pm) is a Unesco World Heritage–listed site and its magic stems from its remoteness and pervading sense of the wild and natural. This is one park in Zimbabwe where you're guaranteed plenty of close encounters with hippos, crocs, zebras and elephants, and are *almost* guaranteed to see lions and possibly wild dogs, leopards and cheetahs.

What sets Mana Pools apart from just about any other park in the world is that you're allowed to walk around on foot without a guide.

## Activities

Game drives and walking safaris (per person, per hour US$30) are the most popular activity in the park. Note you to need to pay a permit (US$15) if you are going to walk without a guide. Canoeing on the Zambezi River provides a breathtaking (read: heart in mouth) experience.

## Sleeping

**National Parks Camping & Lodges** CAMPGROUND $$
(706077; www.zimparks.org; campsites US$70, lodges from US$100) The only semibudget option in Mana Pools are these well-equipped lodges and campsites along the Zambezi River at Nyamepi, which offer prime animal viewing. Campsites are inclusive for six people, so it's not great value unless you're in a group (otherwise you can pay per person rates on arrival).

★**Ruckomechi** TENTED CAMP $$$
(0772-247155, 43371; www.wilderness-safaris.com/camps/ruckomechi-camp; per person US$995; closed mid-Nov–Apr; ) One of Mana's best luxury camps, Ruckomechi has a remote location on its private concession in the northwest of the park. All of its tented chalets overlook the Zambezi and beyond to Zambia and the mountainous backdrop.

**Vundu Camp** TENTED CAMP $$$
(0712-607704; www.bushlifesafaris.com/vunducamp; per person incl full board & activities US$800) Luxury thatch-and-canvas tented chalets with outdoor bathrooms and a prime position overlooking the Zambezi. Its set-up is more like the original style safari camps whereby less is more, which is also a big reason for its popularity.

## Getting There & Away

Mana Pools National Park is only accessible via 4WD, so it's limited to self-drive or those on all-inclusive packages. For those self-driving, Karoi or Makuti are the closest petrol stations (however Makuti often only has diesel). You need to register at the gate before 3pm.

Wet season (November to April) is best avoided as dirt roads turn to sludge and no assisting car service is available. Note that the park mostly closes in the rainy season from January to March.

# EASTERN HIGHLANDS

## Mutare

POP 262,124 / 020

Zimbabwe's fourth largest city, Mutare has a relaxed rural-town atmosphere. It's set in a pretty valley surrounded by hills. There are a few things to see in town, but its real value lies in its proximity to Mozambique.

Mutare is a nice enough place to break up your trip.

### Sleeping & Eating

★**Ann Bruce Backpackers** HOSTEL $
(020-63569, 0772 249089; annbruce@zol.co.zw; cnr Fourth St & Sixth Ave; dm/r US$15/30, r with shared bathroom US$25; ) Homely and welcoming, this long-established guesthouse has been catering to budget travellers for years. It's run by the friendly owner Ann Bruce, along with Emma and her extended family, which gives the place a wonderful homestay atmosphere. There's a cosy TV lounge, kitchen for self-caterers, garden gazebo and a mix of dorms and private rooms, but only some have bathrooms.

**Gordon's** B&B $$$
(020-67200, 0712 231772; www.innsofzimbabwe.co.zw; 125 First St; s/d incl breakfast US$100/160; ) Opening its doors in late 2016, this upmarket B&B is run by Gordon Adams, a local identity long involved in the tourist industry. As an experienced hotelier, he knows exactly what makes a place run well. The B&B has comfortable rooms that will suit business travellers and tourists alike, with air-con, wi-fi, filter coffee and TV.

★**Portuguese Recreation Club** PORTUGUESE $$
(020-61518; 5 Hosgood Ave; chicken & chips US$10; 12.45-3pm & 6.30-9pm Tue-Sat, 12.45-3pm Sun) Given this old-school club was set up for the local Portuguese/Mozambique

community (with an honour board dating from the 1950s), it's not surprising the peri peri chicken here is as good as you'll get anywhere. It has an atmospheric front bar, and busy dining area around the back with gingham tablecloths. It's down an industrial street off Simon Mazorodze Rd.

### Information

**Manicaland Publicity Bureau** (☎020-64711; www.manicalandpublicity.co.zw; cnr Herbert Chitepo St & Robert Mugabe Rd; ⏲8.30am-12.45pm & 2-4pm Mon-Fri) has basic tourist info available, but head to Ann Bruce Backpackers (p1015) for up-to-date travel info.

### Getting There & Away

Regular local and express buses head to Harare (US$7, four hours) from either the town bus terminal, long-distance bus terminal (Railway Ave) or central bus stand (Sakubva market, Masvingo Rd), 3km south of town.

## Chimanimani

POP 2752 / ☎026

Chimanimani, a logging town located 150km south of Mutare, is enclosed by green hills on three sides, and opens on the fourth side to the dramatic wall of the Chimanimani Mountains. It's the gateway town to the national park, offering world-class hiking trails among idyllic surrounds. In the 1990s it was a thriving backpacker centre, and once again eagerly awaits visitors.

### Sights & Activities

Almost all visitors are here for hiking in the area – particularly within the national park – and guides can be arranged through the lodges. **African Wilderness Link** (☎026-2436; http://africanwildernesslink.simdif.com; 162a Haynes St; per person from US$15) can organise a number of hikes in the area.

For cultural events, contact the Chimanimani Tourist Association (www.facebook.com/chimanitourism), which can arrange drumming and *mbira* (thumb piano) performances.

**Bridal Veil Falls** WATERFALL

(US$10) The aptly named Bridal Veil Falls drop 50m in a delicate, fanned manner. It's worth a visit for its tranquil sanctuary location where you can swim at the base of the falls. It's 6km northwest of town, just over an hour's walk. Pay the admission fee before you leave at the parks office in town.

### Sleeping & Eating

★**Heaven Lodge** LODGE $

(☎0775 904679, 0772 752752; www.heavenlodge.com; camping per person US$5, dm US$10, d & cottage US$60, d with shared bathroom US$25; 📶) One of Zimbabwe's original backpackers, Heaven Lodge fell on hard times during the turmoil, but is back as good as ever. It's run by friendly owners, Jacqui and Allen, who are excellent sources of info, and know exactly what backpackers want: cold beer, warm showers and clean rooms. Its common area is a highlight with excellent food, bar and lounge with roaring fireplace.

**Frog & Fern** LODGE $

(☎0775 920440; www.thefrogandfern.com; camping per person US$10, r from US$35; 📶) On a hill above town, backing on to the Pork Pie Eland sanctuary, Frog & Fern is Chimanimani's nicest place to stay. There's a choice of stone cabins or rondavel cottages (the double-storey rondavels are architectural masterpieces), all with cooking facilities, fireplaces and garden views. Breakfast is available for US$10, but otherwise it's self-catering.

### Information

There's no ATM in town that accepts international cards, so ensure you bring enough cash. Mutare is the closest town with a bank.

Headed by Jane High from Frog & Fern cottages, the Chimanimani Tourist Association (☎0775 920440; www.facebook.com/chimanitourism) does a good job of promoting the area. Also check out www.chimanimani.com for useful info.

### Getting There & Away

Transport to Chimanimani is via local buses and combis from either Mutare (US$5, 2½ hours) or Harare (US$15, seven hours); buses/combis arrive at/depart from the bus stop in town.

## Chimanimani National Park

With its pristine wilderness, **Chimanimani National Park** (www.zimparks.org; day fee US$10; ⏲6am-6pm) is a hiker's paradise. Sharing a border with Mozambique, the park is still very wild and unspoiled, with stunning mountainous landscapes, evergreen forest, cascading streams and natural swimming holes.

Most people begin their hikes at Mutekeswane Base Camp, 15km from Chimanimani town, where you must sign in and pay park fees. The road ends here and the park is then only accessible on foot.

While a guide isn't necessary, it's not a bad idea and can be arranged in Chimanimani town through the lodges or African Wilderness Link.

**Mountain Hut** HUT $
(www.zimparks.org; per person US$9) At an elevation of 1630m, the mountain hut is a long and steep half-day walk from the base camp. It's a bit grubby but has running water and cooking facilities.

**Mutekeswane Base Camp** CAMPGROUND $
(☎0775 131072, 0775 475531; www.zimparks.org; campsite per person US$10) At the park's entrance is this well-maintained campsite with showers and toilets. It's a good base from where you can do day hikes.

### Getting There & Away

The park entrance at Mutekeswane Base Camp is 15km from Chimanimani. Unless you have your own vehicle (or you want to walk), it's only reachable by taxi (US$7); you'll need to pre-arrange your return transport with your driver as there's no network signal.

# THE MIDLANDS & SOUTHEASTERN ZIMBABWE

## Great Zimbabwe

☎039

The greatest medieval city in sub-Saharan Africa, the World Heritage–listed **Great Zimbabwe** (☎0776 308755; www.greatzimbabweruins.com; adult/child US$15/8, guide $US3; ⏲6am-6pm) is one of the nation's most treasured sights. These wonderfully preserved ruins of the Bantu civilization and fabled capital of the Queen of Sheba provide evidence that ancient Africa reached a level of civilisation not suspected by earlier scholars. As a religious and political capital, this city of 10,000 to 20,000 dominated a realm that stretched across eastern Zimbabwe and into modern-day Botswana, Mozambique and South Africa. Trade of gold and ivory was rampant, with goods coming from and going to places as far as Arabia and China.

The site is divided into several major ruins with three main areas – Hill Complex, the Valley and the Great Enclosure. Located 30km from Masvingo, the ruins are an essential stop on any visitor's itinerary in Zimbabwe.

### Sights

This elaborately constructed series of stone complexes and enclosures, most of which date back to the 13th and 14th centuries, can be easily explored by yourself. For more info, essential maps and the best routes, duck into the information centre at the site's checkpoint to pick up one of the booklets. While there you can also arrange a two-hour guided tour (about US$12 per person) for a more in-depth experience.

The best time to visit is around dawn and dusk when the sunrise, or sunset, enhances what is already a stunning site and you can beat the heat. Allow at least three hours to explore.

**Great Zimbabwe Museum** MUSEUM
(⏲7.45am-4.45pm) FREE Head to the Great Zimbabwe Museum before you start exploring the site to prep yourself and gain some insight through the informative displays there. They have numerous soapstone bird totems on display, Zimbabwe's national symbol. It's a short walk within the entry, across from the kiosk.

### Sleeping & Eating

Sunset makes for an enchanting time to explore the ruins, so it's recommended you spend a night here. All of the accommodation places in the area provide food.

**Norma Jeane's Lakeview Resort** LODGE $
(☎0712 220397; normajeanes@yoafrica.com; camping per person US$13, r per person US$30, self-catering lodge per person from US$50, hotel r s/d US$110/175; 📶) Located 8km from Great Zimbabwe is this wonderful hilltop lodge overlooking Lake Mutirikwi (Lake Kyle). It's set on a sprawling garden property with rooms catering to all budgets, from grassy campsites popular with Overland trucks to basic rooms and fully self-equipped cottages.

**Great Zimbabwe Family Lodges** CAMPGROUND $
(☎0773 456633, 0775 398917; camping per person US$7, dm US$10, rondavel s/d with shared bathroom US$20/30, lodge s/d/tr/q from US$30/40/78/80) Inside the main gate and within plain sight of the Great Zimbabwe complex, is this very convenient lodge

and campsite. Don't expect too much, but rooms all get the job done and comprise institutional-style dorms, lodges of varying comfort levels (some with TV, kitchen and fridge) and atmospheric rondavels spread out along the hill from reception.

**Norma Jeane's** INTERNATIONAL

Call ahead if you want to drop in for a fantastic set-course dinner (often featuring delicious home-style roasts) served among very British surrounds and magnificent gardens. It's within the homestead of Murray McDougal, who was the brains trust for constructing the Lake Kyle dam (which the restaurant overlooks) in order to irrigate the sugar-cane plantations south from here.

## Information

The **Great Zimbabwe Tourist Information Centre** (⏲6am-6pm) is where you buy entry tickets and organise guides; it also sells various cultural books.

## Getting There & Away

Combis run frequently between Masvingo and Great Zimbabwe (US$2, 30 minutes) and drop off at the Great Zimbabwe Hotel entrance. Walk through the grounds to reach the Great Zimbabwe main gate – about 800m.

# Gonarezhou National Park

Hidden in the southeast corner of the country is the stunning **Gonarezhou National Park** (www.zimparks.org; US$15; ⏲6am-6pm May-Oct), Zimbabwe's second-largest park (5000 sq km) and regarded by many as one of its best-kept secrets. Sharing the border with Mozambique, the park is also virtually an extension of South Africa's Kruger National Park. So, in late 2002, the relevant authorities in Zimbabwe, South Africa and Mozambique created the **Great Limpopo Transfrontier Park**, a 35,000-sq-km park straddling all three countries (with no boundaries).

Here you'll find an abundance of elephants, plus giraffes, buffaloes, zebras, lions, leopards, cheetahs, hyenas, wild dogs and nyala (among the usual antelope species) and an impressive 453 different kinds of bird species.

Don't miss the spectacular red-and-white banded sandstone columns of **Chilojo Cliffs** (Gonarezhou National Park), one of the most photogenic sights in the country. Drive up the top for incredible outlooks to Gonarezhou.

**National Park Campsites & Lodges** CAMPGROUND, LODGE $$

(www.zimparks.org; campsites US$17-90, tented camps d from US$115, lodges d from US$86) Zimparks offers decent sleeping options at various sites across the park. There's tented camping at the park HQ in Chipinda Pools and lodges at Mabalauta and Swimuwini in the southern sector. Campsites are available but rates are geared towards groups rather than individuals; you can keep costs down if you're OK to risk arriving without a reservation (per person US$17).

★**Chilo Gorge Safari Lodge** LODGE $$$

(☎0774-999059; http://chilogorge.com; per person incl meals & activities US$600; ) With its stunning elevated location overlooking the Save River, safari lodges really don't get much better than this. All of its luxurious stilted thatched chalets open up to river views, allowing you to spot game from your balcony. The staff is friendly and features a team of crack guides.

## Getting There & Away

Most people access the park via self-drive 4WD, tour package or charter flight. It's about 300km south of Chimanimani (four hours' drive), along an often pot-holed road, or similar distance from Masvingo on a smooth tarmac through sugar-cane plantations.

# WESTERN ZIMBABWE

# Bulawayo

POP 653,337 / ☎09

Wide tree-lined avenues, parks and charming colonial architecture make Bulawayo, Zimbabwe's second city, an attractive one. It has a lovely historic feel to it, and it's worth spending a night or two, especially given it's a gateway to Matobo National Park, and an ideal staging point for Hwange National Park and Victoria Falls.

## Sights

When you factor in day trips to Matobo and Khami Ruins (p1020), along with beautiful colonial architecture and world-class galleries and museums, it becomes clear that

## Bulawayo

**Top Sights**
1 Bulawayo Railway Museum .......... A3
2 Natural History Museum .......... D2

**Sleeping**
3 Bulawayo Club .......... B2

**Eating**
4 26 on Park .......... D2
Bulawayo Club .......... (see 3)
5 Dickies .......... C2

**Information**
6 Barclays Bank .......... B2
7 Bulawayo & District Publicity Association .......... C2
8 Galen House Casualty .......... C2
9 National Parks & Wildlife Zimbabwe .......... B3
10 Stanbic .......... B2

**Transport**
11 Combis/Local Bus Terminal .......... C2
12 Intercape Pathfinder .......... B2

sightseeing in Bulawayo is as good as you'll find in any African city.

Note that photography of government buildings is prohibited, including the train station.

**★Bulawayo Railway Museum** MUSEUM
(NRZ Museum; ☎09-36245; www.geoffs-trains.com/museum/museumhome.html; cnr Prospect Ave & Crew Rd; adult/child US$2/1; ⊙8.30am-4.30pm Mon-Fri, from 9am Sat & Sun) Whether you're a train enthusiast or not, Bulwayo's Railway Museum rarely disappoints. Its passionate curator, Gordon Murray, will take you on a tour of the place, where you'll get a fascinating insight into the colonial history of the country through Bulawayo's extensive railway network. There are some wonderful Rhodesian Railways steam engines and carriages to clamber aboard, including the *Jack Tar* (1889), the first train to cross the Victoria Falls Bridge.

**★Natural History Museum** MUSEUM
(☎09-250045; www.naturalhistorymuseumzimbabwe.com; Centenary Park; adult/child US$10/5; ⊙9am-5pm) Zimbabwe's largest and best museum is an essential visit. Set over three floors, it offers a great overview of the country's natural, anthropological and geological history. Its highlight is its taxidermy display, which includes a monster elephant, shot

160km south from here. There's also an impressive collection of gemstones, showcasing the country's astounding wealth of natural resources. At its centre is a collection of live snakes, including black mambas and cobras.

**Khami Ruins** ARCHAEOLOGICAL SITE
(Kame, Kami; adult/child US$10/5; ⊙8am-5pm) Just 22km from Bulawayo, the Unesco World Heritage–listed Khami Ruins may not have the grandeur of Great Zimbabwe, but it's an impressive archaeological site nonetheless. The second largest stone monument built in Zimbabwe, Khami was developed between 1450 and 1650 as the capital of the Torwa dynasty, and abandoned in the 19th century with the arrival of Ndebele. It's spread over a 2km site in a peaceful natural setting overlooking the Khami Dam.

**National Art Gallery** GALLERY
(☎09-70721; www.nationalgallerybyo.com; cnr Joshua Nkomo (Main) St & Leopold Takawira Ave; adult/child US$5/3; ⊙9am-5pm Tue-Sat) Set in a beautiful 100-year-old, colonial, double-terrace Edwardian building, the National Art Gallery shows temporary and permanent exhibitions of contemporary Zimbabwean sculpture and paintings. A visit here wouldn't be complete without dropping by the studios of the artists in residence, who you can meet at work and buy from directly.

## Tours

**★Prospector's Pub Crawl** WALKING
(☎0733 781246; hubbardszimtours@gmail.com; half day min 4 people US$65, 1 person US$100) A pub crawl and history lesson rolled into one: archaeologist, historian and local Paul Hubbard will show you Bulawayo's architectural and pioneer gems. Give 48 hours' notice. There's also a range of other themed walks on offer, as well as tours to visit Zimbabwe's ruined cities, from nearby Khami to further afield.

### VICTORIA FALLS

The crowning jewel of Western Zimbabwe is **Victoria Falls National Park**, where the mighty falls are an awe-inspiring sight that's a feast for the senses. Combined with a world-class outdoor adventure scene, it's clear to see why tourists flock en masse to this resort town. See the Victoria Falls chapter (p969) for more information.

## Sleeping

**Burke's Paradise** HOSTEL $
(☎0782 311011, 09-246481; www.burkes-paradise.com; 11 Inverleith Dr, Burnside; campsite per person US$7, dm US$15, s/d with shared bathroom US$25/30; ) Set on a well-maintained, 5-hectare property, Burke's Paradise is hands down Bulawayo's best choice for budget independent travellers. There's a good mix of dorms and private rooms, a lovely pool and an overall relaxed atmosphere. It's on the outskirts of town, but you can catch combis to/from town, or it's a US$10 cab ride.

**★Bulawayo Club** HISTORIC HOTEL $$
(☎09-244109, 09-244990; www.bulawayoclub.com; cnr Eighth Ave & Fort St; s/d incl breakfast from US$70/100; ) Founded in 1895, the BC is still the most exclusive address in town. The opportunity to stay in such an elegant historical place at such a reasonable price is hard to pass up. Both its facade and interior are stunning, with period charm and history at every turn. The recently refurbed rooms are lovely, and offer plenty of historical character.

**★Traveller's Guest House** GUESTHOUSE $$
(☎09-246059; www.travellerszim.net; 2 Banff Rd, Hillside; s/d from US$45/60, ste d/tr US$90/120; ) Charm oozes from this guesthouse where renovated rooms come with blond-wood floors, stainless-steel bathroom fittings and African art. The suites are the pick of the rooms and worthy of an upgrade. The communal designer kitchen is well equipped, while the flower-filled garden and pool setting provide a nice spot to kick back in.

## Eating

**Dickies** AFRICAN $
(cnr Tenth Ave & Josiah Tongogara St; mains US$3-5; ⊙8am-midnight) Try a traditional Zimbabwean meal at this bright and cheery eatery. Follow the locals and plunge your fingers into tasty fish and sticky meat dishes sopped up with filling piles of *sadza* (maize-meal porridge). There are a few branches throughout town. BYO alcohol.

**Bulawayo Club** INTERNATIONAL $$
(Governors' Restaurant; ☎09-244990; www.bulawayoclub.com; cnr Eighth Ave & Fort St; mains from

US$8; ⌚8am-10pm) Chandeliers, silverware, marble pillars and gleaming hardwood floors might have you thinking you need to dust off your blazer. Not to worry chaps: the Bulawayo Club's dining-room surrounds may be decked out for Rhodesian high society, but these days it's welcoming to all. Its retro menu card offers old-world dishes such as pie with gravy, chips and peas, or pavlova for dessert.

**★26 on Park** INTERNATIONAL **$$$**
(☎09-230399; 26 Park Rd; mains US$13-17; ⌚11am-9pm Wed-Sat, 10am-3pm Sun; 📶) Housed in a colonial building with sprawling lawns and a big patio, this casual fine-dining restaurant is one of Bulawayo's best. Its menu changes seasonally, and well-trained chefs cook up the likes of regional Nyanga trout, game venison pie or Zimbabwe dry-aged beef. Its thin-crust pizzas are very popular too, and its cocktail bar makes for a lively drinking spot.

## ℹ Information

### MEDICAL SERVICES

**Galen House Casualty** (☎09-881051; galen@gatorzw.co.uk; cnr Josiah Tongogara St & Ninth Ave) This privately run clinic is better than the central hospital.

### MONEY

**Barclays Bank** (100 Joshua Nkomo (Main) St)

**Stanbic** (cnr Joshua Nkomo (Main) St & Eighth Ave)

### POLICE

**Main Police Station** (☎09-72516; cnr Leopold Takawira Ave & Fife St)

### POST

**Main Post Office** (☎09-62535; Joshua Nkomo (Main) St; ⌚8am-4pm Mon-Fri, to 11.30am Sat) Between Leopold Takawira and Eighth Aves.

### TOURIST INFORMATION

**Bulawayo & District Publicity Association** (☎09-72969, 09-60867; www.bulawayopublicity.com; btwn Eighth & Leopold Takawira Aves; ⌚8.30am-4.45pm Mon-Fri) In the City Hall car park, this is an excellent source of information on accommodation, transport, tours and activities in Bulawayo and around.

**National Parks & Wildlife Zimbabwe** (☎09-63646; Fifteenth Ave, btwn Fort & Main Sts; ⌚8am-4pm Mon-Fri) Takes accommodation bookings for Matobo National Park.

> **GIGA & SONS**
>
> Established in 1932, this fourth-generation family-run menswear **store** (☎09-62631; 93b Robert Mugabe Way; boots US$140-900; ⌚8.30am-5pm Mon-Fri, 8am-1pm Sat) is most famous for its Courtney Boots – a homegrown shoe, sold worldwide. All of its safari boots are handmade, and are produced from a range of materials, including elephant, hippo, buffalo, kudu, ostrich and crocodile leather. There are also leather bags and a good range of khaki safari wear.

## ℹ Getting There & Away

### BUS

Get in touch with the Bulawayo & District Publicity Association for the latest bus and train schedules.

### TRAIN

#### To Victoria Falls

A popular way to get to Victoria Falls is by overnight **train** (☎09-362294; www.nrz.co.zw; ⌚tickets 4-7pm), which departs daily at 7.30pm (1st/2nd class US$12/10). The journey takes you through Hwange National Park, a highlight of the trip.

#### To Botswana

The train to Francistown runs Mondays and Fridays (US$4.50), departing 9am.

## ℹ Getting Around

The city centre is fairly walkable during the day.

A taxi or **combi** (Eighth Ave, btwn Fife St & Robert Mugabe Way) is the best way to reach the outer limits, and take a taxi for travelling anywhere at night. Try **Proline Taxis** (☎09-886686); agree on a price before setting out.

# Matobo National Park

Home to some of the most majestic granite scenery in the world, the **Matobo National Park** (Matopos; www.zimparks.org; US$15, overnight guests US$8, car US$3; ⌚main gate 24hr, game park 6am-6pm) is one of the unsung highlights of Zimbabwe. This Unesco World Heritage Site is a stunning and otherworldly landscape of balancing rocks, or *kopjes* – giant boulders unfeasibly teetering on top of one another. When you see it, it's easy to understand why Matobo is considered the spiritual home of Zimbabwe.

## Sights

**World's View (Malindidzimu Hill)** HISTORIC SITE
(adult/child US$10/5) One of Zimbabwe's most breathtaking sites, the aptly named World's View takes in epic 360-degree views of the park. The peacefulness up here is immense, taking on a spiritual quality that makes it clear why it's so sacred to the Ndebele people. It's also the burial spot of Rhodesia's founder, Cecil Rhodes, whose grave sits, somewhat controversially, atop between two boulders.

**Rock Art Caves** ARCHAEOLOGICAL SITE
(adult/child US$10/5) Dotted around the 425-sq-km Matobo National Park are 3000 officially registered rock-art sites, including one of the best collections in the world of San paintings (estimated to be anywhere from 6000 to 10,000 years old). **White Rhino Shelter**, **Bambata Cave**, **Pomongwe Cave** and **Nswatugi Cave** have some fine examples.

## Tours

**Game Drive** WILDLIFE
The game park at Matobo National Park is a good spot to try your luck at spying white rhinos, and if you're lucky you'll see black rhinos too. Guides can be arranged at the park if you have your own vehicle; otherwise sign up for a tour in Bulawayo or through your lodge.

## Sleeping

**Maleme Rest Camp** CAMPGROUND $
(☎09-63646; www.zimparks.org; campsite per person US$9, chalet US$40-70, lodge US$86-250) Set around boulders and candelabra cacti, this national park's accommodation offers the best option for budget travellers. While a bit on the shabby side, lodges come with kitchens and bathrooms, while camping is down near the dam. There's no restaurant, but it has a kiosk with basic items.

★**Camp Amalinda** LODGE $$$
(☎09-243954; www.campamalinda.com; 45km, Kezi Rd; per person US$255; ) Tucked away in Matobo's granite, the 10 thatched chalets here are carved and seamlessly blended into the boulders and have bulging rocks as in-room features. Each room is unique: some have open bathrooms, claw-foot outdoor baths and even a swing bridge to a private sundeck (room 10). End the day with a sundowner at the stunning lagoon-style pool and bar.

## Getting There & Away

Just 33km from Bulawayo, Matobo National Park can be done as a day trip, although it's recommended to stay at least one night in this beautiful area. If you don't have transfers pre-arranged by your accommodation, take a taxi (around US$40).

# Hwange National Park

☎018

One of the 10 largest national parks in Africa, and the largest in Zimbabwe, at 14,651 sq km, **Hwange National Park** (www.zimparks.org; national parks accommodation per day guests/nonguests US$10/20; ⊙main gate 6am-6pm), pronounced 'Wang-ee', has a ridiculous amount of wildlife. Some 400 species of bird and 107 types of animal can be found in the park, including lions, giraffes, leopards, cheetahs, hyenas and wild dogs. But the elephant is what really defines Hwange, being home to one of the world's largest populations of around 40,000 tuskers.

The best time for wildlife viewing is July to October, when animals congregate around the 60 waterholes or 'pans' (most of which are artificially filled) and the forest is stripped of its greenery.

## Sleeping

**Hwange Main Camp** CAMPGROUND $
(☎018-371, 0783 732479; campsites per person US$17, chalet/cottage/lodge d from US$40/69/86; ⊙office 6am-6pm; ) At the main park entrance, this attractive camp feels a bit like a village, with its lodges, grocery shop, museum, petrol station and restaurant. More importantly, it's also surrounded by wildlife, and the sounds of predators at night – making it a wonderful spot to stay. There's a good mix of self-catering lodges, cottages with communal kitchens, chalets (without bathroom) and campsites.

**Gwango Heritage Resort** LODGE $$
(☎0783 557773; www.gwango.com; campsite per person US$10, d from US$85, lodge incl full board s/d from US$269/378; ) This relaxed lodge, just off the main highway, is a great new affordable, easily accessible addition to Hwange. There's camping and no-frills A-frame chalets, along with upmarket treetop villas overlooking a pan. The owner has put a lot of thought into the place, which

includes an on-site Nambya replica village, complete with interpretive centre and cultural performances.

**Davison's Camp** TENTED CAMP $$$
(☎ in South Africa +27 11 807 1800; www.wilderness-safaris.com/camps/davisons-camp; Linkwasha Concession; per person incl meals & activities US$605; ) Of the several bush camps run by Wilderness Safaris in this private Linkwasha concession, Davison's is the most popular. Here you've a good chance of spotting all animals in the immediate area. All its luxury tents look out to a waterhole, as does the open-air lounge, pool and restaurant.

### Getting There & Away

The park is between Bulawayo and Victoria Falls, 300km and 180km away respectively, making it the most accessible and convenient park for many visitors.

The Intercape Pathfinder (www.intercape.co.za) bus stops at **Hwange Safari Lodge** (☎ 018-750; www.hwangesafarilodge.com; per person incl breakfast from US$87; ). From here Main Camp is a further 10km. It's essential to pre-book the bus otherwise it won't make the detour here.

# UNDERSTAND ZIMBABWE

## Zimbabwe Today

Despite being well into his 90s and plagued by incessant rumours of ongoing health issues, Robert Mugabe shows no intention of relinquishing his grip on the power he's held since 1980. However, in 2016 some cracks were beginning to show as a groundswell of protests spread across the nation in what were the largest anti-government gatherings in almost a decade.

Orchestrated largely through social media, at the forefront was the #ThisFlag movement. Led by activist Pastor Evan Mawarire (who's since fled the country in fear of his safety), Zimbabweans were encouraged to wear the nation's flag as a symbol of peaceful protest, calling for reform and to return pride back to the nation. It was combined with several 'stay away day' protests by government workers and the War Veterans (staunch pro-Mugabe supporters from Zimbabwe's war of independence). Predictably though protests were shut down using heavy-handed tactics by Mugabe. None of the demands for change were met and cash shortages, rampant corruption, incessant police roadblocks and border trade restrictions remain in place, along with currency uncertainty – all factors that will continue to cripple the economy.

Talk continues about who his successor will be. Current vice president Emmerson Mnangagwa, former Zanu PF vice president and founder of the Zimbabwe People First Party, Joyce Mujuru, and Mugabe's highly controversial wife Grace are the most likely contenders. Morgan Tsvangirai remains the other main candidate, however, his diagnosis with bowel cancer in June 2016 has cast doubt upon his future in politics.

## History

### The Shona Kingdoms & the Portuguese

In the 11th century, the city of Great Zimbabwe was wealthy and powerful from trading gold and ivory to Swahili traders for glass, porcelain and cloth from Asia. However, by the 15th century its influence was in decline because of overpopulation, overgrazing, political fragmentation and uprisings.

In the 16th century Portuguese traders arrived in search of riches and golden cities in the vast empire of Mwene Mutapa (or 'Monomatapa' to the Europeans). They hoped to find King Solomon's mines and the mysterious land of Ophir.

A new alliance of Shona was formed – the Rozwi State – which covered over half of present-day Zimbabwe, until 1834 when Ndebele raiders (Those Who Carry Long Shields), under the command of Mzilikazi, invaded from what is now South Africa. They assassinated the Rozwi leader. Upon reaching the Matobo Hills, Mzilikazi established a Ndebele state. After Mzilikazi's death in 1870, his son, Lobengula, ascended the throne and relocated the Ndebele capital to Bulawayo.

In 1888 Cecil Rhodes, the founder of the British South African Company (BSAC), coerced Lobengula into signing the Rudd Concession, which granted foreigners mineral rights in exchange for 10,000 rifles,100,000 rounds of ammunition, a gunboat and £100 each month. Lobengula sent a group of Ndebele raiders to Fort

Victoria (near Masvingo) to stop Shona interference between the British and the Ndebele. The British mistook this as aggression and launched an attack on Matabeleland. Lobengula's kraals (hut villages) were destroyed and Bulawayo was burned. Lobengula died in exile of smallpox.

Without their king, the Ndebele continued to resist the BSAC and foreign rule. In the early 1890s they allied themselves with the Shona, and guerrilla warfare broke out against the BSAC in the Matobo Hills. When Rhodes suggested a negotiated settlement, the Ndebele, with their depleted numbers, couldn't refuse. Meanwhile, finding little gold, the colonists appropriated farmlands on the Mashonaland Plateau. By 1895 the new country was being called Rhodesia, after its heavy-handed founder, and a white legislature was set up. European immigration began in earnest: by 1904 there were some 12,000 settlers in the country, and seven years later the figure had doubled.

## White Nationalism

Conflicts between black and white in Zimbabwe came into sharp focus after the 1922 referendum in which the whites chose to become a self-governing colony rather than join the Union of South Africa. In 1930 white supremacy was legislated in the form of the Land Apportionment Act. Over the decades that followed, two African parties emerged – the Zimbabwe African People's Union (ZAPU) under Joshua Nkomo, and the Zimbabwe African National Union (ZANU).

In 1964 Ian Smith took over the Rhodesian presidency and began pressing for independence. The British prime minister, Harold Wilson, argued for conditions to be met before Britain would agree: guarantee of racial equality, course towards majority rule, and majority desire for independence. Smith realised the whites in Rhodesia would never agree, so in 1965 he made a Unilateral Declaration of Independence.

The war that followed would last for more than a decade.

## Independence

On 10 September 1979, delegations met at Lancaster House, London, to draw up a constitution favourable to both the Patriotic Front (an alliance between ZANU and ZAPU) of Nkomo and Robert Mugabe, and the Zimbabwe-Rhodesian government of Abel Muzorewa and Smith.

Mugabe, who wanted ultimate power, initially refused to make any concessions, but after 14 weeks the Lancaster House Agreement was reached. It guaranteed whites (then 3% of the population) 20 of the 100 parliamentary seats. Soon after, the economy soared, wages increased and basic social programs – notably education and healthcare – were initiated.

However, the initial euphoria, unity and optimism quickly faded: a resurgence of rivalry between ZANU (run mostly by Shona people) and ZAPU (mostly by Ndebele) escalated into armed conflict. Mugabe (elected prime minister in 1980) deployed the North Korean–trained Fifth Brigade in early 1983 to quell the disturbances. Tens of thousands of civilians, sometimes entire villages, were slaughtered.

A world that was eager to revere Mr Mugabe closed its eyes. Nkomo fled to England until Mugabe publicly relented and guaranteed his safe return. Talks resulted in a ZAPU–ZANU confederation (called ZANU PF). Zimbabwe's one-party state had begun.

## Life As the Opposition

In 1999 thousands attended a Zimbabwe Congress of Trade Unions (ZCTU) rally to launch the Movement for Democratic Change (MDC). Morgan Tsvangirai, the secretary general, stated he would lead a social democratic party fighting for workers' interests. The arrival of the MDC brought waves of new hope and real opportunity for the end of Mugabe's era.

Mugabe responded to the threat of defeat with waves of violence, voter intimidation, and a chaotic and destructive land reform program that saw many white farmers evicted from their land. He claimed the next three elections.

In February 2009, Morgan Tsvangirai signed a coalition deal with ZANU-PF: a mutual promise to restore the rule of law and to 'ensure security of tenure to all landholders'. Nonetheless, the violence and evictions continued.

# People of Zimbabwe

Most Zimbabweans are of Bantu origin; 9.8 million belong to various Shona groups and about 2.3 million are Ndebele. The remainder are divided between the Tonga (or Batonga) people of the upper Kariba area, the Shangaan (or Hlengwe) of the lowveld, and the Venda of the far south. Europeans (18,000), Asians (10,000) and mixed Europeans and Africans (25,000) are scattered around the country.

## Environment

The Big Five (that is, lions, leopards, buffaloes, elephants and rhinos) are found in Zimbabwe. There are also cheetahs, hippos, hyenas, wild dogs, giraffes, zebras and a wide range of antelope species such as impala, waterbuck, eland, sable and roan. Sadly, poaching – like in most of Southern Africa – remains a major issue.

Close to 20% of Zimbabwe's surface area is protected, or semiprotected, in national parks, privately protected game parks, nature conservancies and recreational parks.

# SURVIVAL GUIDE

## Directory A–Z

### ACCOMMODATION

Despite its economic woes, Zimbabwe generally has a good standard of accommodation from roughing it in dorms to lapping it up in luxury lodges. In larger towns there's usually one or two backpackers, a few boutique guesthouses and some business hotels. National parks, though, are very much geared towards the two ends of the spectrum, from stunning upmarket safari lodges to rudimentary bush camps, with only a few options inbetween.

### PRICE RANGES

The following price ranges refer to a double room with bathroom in high season.

**$** less than US$75

**$$** US$75 to $150

**$$$** more than US$150

The following price ranges refer to a standard main course.

**$** less than US$5

**$$** US$5 to $10

**$$$** more than US$10

### ACTIVITIES

It's all about natural features in Zimbabwe: wildlife viewing in national parks, hiking in the Eastern Highlands, canoeing safaris along the Zambezi or fishing on Lake Kariba. Victoria Falls is the epicentre of activities in Southern Africa, where you can white-water raft, take helicopter rides and bungee jump.

### DANGERS & ANNOYANCES

Zimbabwe is nowhere near as dangerous as foreign media makes out and all up it's a very safe country to visit. Although the number of incidents and degree of violence are a far cry from that in South Africa, like anywhere in the world the usual theft and crimes occurs. Don't walk around at night; the best option is to take a taxi, which is generally safe. Drivers should take the following precautions: lock all doors, lock all valuables in the boot, keep windows up and avoid stopping at traffic lights at night if it's safe to do so.

It is illegal to criticise the government – and best to avoid talking about the government at all. Avoid antigovernment posts on social media and don't take photographs of 'sensitive' sites, such as government buildings.

### EMBASSIES & CONSULATES

**Australian Embassy** (Map p1008; ☎04-853235; www.zimbabwe.embassy.gov.au; 1 Green Close, Borrowdale; ⏲8am-5pm Mon-Thu, to 2pm Fri)

**Botswanan Embassy** (Map p1008; ☎04-794645; www.botswanaembassy.co.zw; 22 Phillips Ave, Belgravia; ⏲visas 8am-12.30pm Mon, Wed & Fri, enquiries 8am-12.45pm & 2-4.30pm Mon-Fri)

**Canadian Embassy** (Map p1010; ☎04-252181; www.canadainternational.gc.ca/zimbabwe; 45 Baines Ave; ⏲7.30am-4.30pm Mon-Thu, to noon Fri)

**French Embassy** (Map p1008; ☎04-776118; www.ambafrance-zw.org; 3 Princess Dr, Newlands; ⏲9am-1pm & 2-5pm)

**German Embassy** (Map p1008; ☎04-308655; www.harare.diplo.de; 30 Ceres Rd, Avondale; ⏲9-11am & 2-3pm Mon-Fri)

**Kenyan Embassy** (Map p1010; ☎04-704820; www.mfa.go.ke/contacts; 95 Park Lane; ⏲8.30am-4.30pm Mon-Thu, to 1pm Fri)

**Malawian High Commission** (Map p1008; ☎04-798584; malahigh@africaonline.co.zw; 9/11 Duthie Rd, Alexandra Park; ⏲visas 9am-noon Mon-Thu)

**Mozambican Embassy** (Map p1010; ☎04-253871; 152 Herbert Chitepo Ave; ⏲visas 8am-noon Mon-Fri)

**Namibian Embassy** (Map p1008; ☎04-885841; secretary@namibianembassy.co.zw; 69 Borrowdale Rd; ⏰8am-5pm Mon-Fri)

**Netherlands Embassy** (Map p1008; ☎04-776701; http://zimbabwe.nlembassy.org/; 2 Arden Rd, Newlands; ⏰8am-5pm Mon-Thu, to 2pm Fri)

**South African Embassy** (Map p1008; ☎04-251843, 04-251845; admin@saembassy.co.zw; 7 Elcombe Ave; ⏰7.30am-4.30pm Mon-Thu, 7.30am-12.30pm Fri)

**Tanzanian Embassy** (Map p1010; ☎04-792714; tanrep@tanrep.co.zw; Ujamaa House, 23 Baines Ave; ⏰9am-1pm Mon-Fri)

**UK Embassy** (Map p1008; ☎04-85855200; www.ukinzimbabwe.fco.gov.uk/en; 3 Norfolk Rd, Mt Pleasant; ⏰8am-4.30pm Mon-Thu, to 1pm Fri)

**US Embassy** (Map p1010; ☎04-250593; http://harare.usembassy.gov; Arax House, 172 Herbert Chitepo Ave; ⏰11am-noon & 1.30-4pm Mon-Thu, 9-11.30am Fri)

**Zambian Embassy** (Map p1010; ☎04-773777; zambians@africaonline.com; Zambia House, 48 Kwame Nkrumah Ave; ⏰9am-1pm Mon-Fri)

## EMERGENCY & IMPORTANT NUMBERS

| | |
|---|---|
| Zimbabwe's country code | ☎+263 |
| International access code | ☎00 |
| Ambulance | ☎999; 04-771221; 0712-600002 |
| Police | ☎995 |
| Fire | ☎999, 993 |

## INTERNET ACCESS

In the bigger cities, free wi-fi access is widely available in many hotels, restaurants and cafes. It's easy to arrange a local sim card to get data on your phone or a USB dongle for your laptop. Econet and Telecel both have branches at Harare's airport and about town.

Otherwise, there are internet centres in all the main cities and towns that charge around US$2 per hour.

## LGBTIQ TRAVELLERS

Like many African nations, homosexual activities for men are illegal and officially punishable by up to five years in jail (although penalties are invariably not nearly as severe), yet lesbianism is not illegal.

Contact **Gays & Lesbians of Zimbabwe** (☎04-740614, 04-741736; http://galz.org; Colenbrander Rd) for information about LGBTIQ clubs and meeting places in Zimbabwe.

## MONEY

In November 2016, Zimbabwe's reserve bank introduced its own 'bond' money after the country effectively ran out of US dollars. Due to issues in withdrawing cash from banks and uncertainty over the future currency to be used in Zimbabwe, as of 2016 it is recommended to carry enough US dollars to last the entirety of your stay; prepay any accommodation or tours to reduce the amount you need to bring in. Many foreign cards have been limited to withdrawals of US$100 per day, if any – so it's best not to rely on ATMs. Take along plenty of small US dollar notes for tips etc.

## OPENING HOURS

Shops and restaurants are generally open from 8am to 1pm and 2pm to 5pm Monday to Friday, and 8am to noon on Saturday. Very little is open on Sunday.

## PUBLIC HOLIDAYS

**New Year's Day** 1 January
**Good Friday** late March/April
**Easter Monday** late March/April
**Independence Day** 18 April
**Workers' Day** 1 May
**Africa Day** 25 May
**Heroes' Day** 11 August
**Defence Forces' Day** 12 August
**National Unity Day** 22 December
**Christmas Day** 25 December
**Boxing Day** 26 December

## TELEPHONE

Easily the best option for making calls is to purchase a prepaid SIM card (US$1), available on arrival at the airport; these are cheap and easy to arrange. Econet and Telecel are the main operators and have branches throughout the main towns, as well as at Harare airport. Econet has the best phone and data coverage across the country, but in national parks you won't get a signal.

## TIME

Zimbabwe is two hours ahead of Greenwich Mean Time (GMT/UTC). There is no daylight saving.

## TOURIST INFORMATION

The Zimbabwe Tourism Authority (p1013) has general tourist info. There are Publicity Associations in Harare, Bulawayo, Victoria Falls, Kariba, Masvingo and Nyanga. Some are very efficient, helpful and have useful information and advice, but others have little more to offer than a smile.

## VISAS

Single-/double-entry visas cost US$30/45 (and can be issued upon arrival) and multiple-entry visas (valid for six months) cost US$55, but are only issued at Zimbabwean diplomatic missions. British and Irish citizens pay US$55/70 for single/double entry.

In December 2016 the KAZA visa was reintroduced, which allows most visitors to acquire a single 30-day visa (US$50) for both Zimbabwe and Zambia.

## Getting There & Away

### AIR

Several international airlines offer flights into Zimbabwe, arriving in either Harare International Airport or Victoria Falls Airport.

### LAND

#### Botswana

The most popular border crossing into Botswana is from Kazangula near Victoria Falls, which links it to Chobe National Park. Border posts are open 6am to 6pm.

**Zupco** (Map p1010; ☎04-750571, 0772 666530; www.zupco.co.zw; Road Port Terminal, cnr Robert Mugabe Rd & Fifth St) has buses from Harare to Francistown (US$24) at 4pm

#### Malawi

The most direct route between Malawi and Zimbabwe is via Mozambique's Tete Corridor. Zupco has buses from Harare to Blantyre (Malawi) daily (except Saturday) at 7.30am (US$25, 12 hours).

#### Mozambique

There are two border crossings into Mozambique (open from 6am to 8pm). Easily the more popular is from Mutare, which links up to Beira. The other is at Nyamapanda, northeast from Harare, used to get to Malawi.

#### South Africa

Numerous luxury and semiluxury buses ply the route between Harare or Bulawayo to Johannesburg (16 to 20 hours), departing from Road Port Terminal in Harare.

Buses from Harare:

**Citiliner** (Map p1010; ☎in South Africa 011 611 8000; www.citiliner.co.za; Road Port Terminal, cnr Robert Mugabe Rd & Fifth St) Daily departures (from US$33).

**Greyhound** (Map p1010; ☎Bulawayo 09-889078, Harare 04-761463; www.greyhound.co.za; Road Port Terminal, cnr Robert Mugabe Rd & Fifth St) Has an overnight bus departing 8pm Monday to Saturday and 1pm on Sundays (US$37).

**Intercape Pathfinder** (Map p1010; ☎0778 888880; www.intercapepathfinder.com; Cresta Oasis Hotel, 124 Nelson Mandela Ave) Two daily sleeper buses (US$40 to US$70) at 1pm and 7.30pm.

**Pioneer Coaches** (Map p1010; ☎Bulawayo 0783 732721, Harare 0783 732720; www.pioneercoacheszim.co.zw; Road Port Terminal, cnr Robert Mugabe Rd & Fifth St) Has a departure at 2.30pm (US$30).

Buses from Bulawayo:

**Intercape Pathfinder** (www.intercape.co.za; cnr Joshua Nkomo (Main) St & Eleventh Ave) By far the most recommendable company, with a daily departure at 3.30pm ($US42).

Trains are once again running between Zimbabwe and South Africa. **Rovos Rail** (☎in South Africa 012-315 8242; www.rovos.com; from US$1650) runs a three-day/two-night luxury-train journey from Pretoria to Victoria Falls travelling through Zimbabwe via Bulawayo.

#### Zambia

Zimbabwe has three border crossings into Zambia, with Victoria Falls (open 6am to 10pm) by far the most popular. You can also cross via Kariba/Siavonga and Chirundu, which is open 6am to 6pm.

Public transport options from Harare include the following:

**Zupco** Two daily buses depart for Lusaka (US$20, nine hours) at 7.30am and a slower bus via Kariba/Siavonga ($20, 10 hours).

**King Lion** (Map p1010; ☎0772 635472; www.kinglioncoaches.co.zw; Road Port Terminal, cnr Robert Mugabe Rd & Fifth St) Has buses to Lusaka (US$15, 10 hours) at 7.30am and 7.30pm.

## Getting Around

### AIR

Air Zimbabwe (www.airzimbabwe.aero) has flights from Harare to Bulawayo (45 minutes) and Victoria Falls. New to Zimbabwe is FastJet (www.fastjet.com), a popular budget airline offering cheap flights to Victoria Falls from Harare. There's a domestic departure tax of US$15.

### BOAT

**Kariba Ferries** (☎04-614162, 0772 236330; www.karibaferries.com; Andora Harbour, Kariba) runs a ferry service between Kariba at the eastern end of the lake and Mlibizi at the western end.

### BUS

The express or 'luxury' buses operate according to published timetables. Check carefully, however, as most bus companies have both local ('chicken buses' for locals) and luxury coaches. For example, Pioneer and Zupco have both luxury and chicken buses.

**Pathfinder** This luxury '7-star' (it claims to have wi-fi) bus service has started up a daily service linking Harare to Victoria Falls, Bulawayo and even Hwange. It has plans for services to Mutare and Kariba.

**Bravo** (Map p1010; ☎0778 888777; www.bravotours.co.zw; 88 George Silundika Ave) Plies the Harare–Bulawayo–Victoria Falls route.

### CAR & MOTORCYCLE

Many residents make a rule of not driving outside the major towns after dark. Police roadblocks are another inevitable pain of driving in Zimbabwe and you can expect to be waved down multiple times during long journeys. As long as you have all the correct papers and safety equipment, a smile and being courteous should see you waved through without any problems.

### TRAIN

Connecting Harare, Bulawayo, Mutare and Victoria Falls, all major train services travel at night. The most popular route is from Victoria Falls to Bulawayo. Definitely opt for 1st class, which is good value, comfortable and gets you a sleeping compartment.

# Understand Africa

# Africa Today

**Plus ça change. The problems of modern Africa are, in many ways, the same problems that have stalked the continent for much of the past half-century – stubbornly high levels of disease, poverty, corruption and conflict continue in many corners of the continent. Such is the view from afar. But it is only partly true. Look a little closer and a more nuanced take is that things are changing, and very often for the better.**

### Best on Film

**Half of a Yellow Sun** (2013) Stirring love story and evocation of Nigeria's Biafra civil war in the late 1960s.

**Moolaadé** (2005) An important film by Ousmane Sembène, one of West Africa's finest directors.

**A United Kingdom** (2016) Based on the love story of Botswana's first president and his British bride.

**Invictus** (2009) Covers the historic 1995 Rugby World Cup; stars Morgan Freeman and Matt Damon. Clint Eastwood directs.

**The Constant Gardener** (2005) Based on John le Carre's thriller set in Kenya.

### Best in Print

**Shadow of the Sun** (Ryszard Kapuścinski; 1998) Illuminating stories from a veteran foreign correspondent.

**The Tree Where Man Was Born** (Peter Matthiessen; 1972) Lyrical account of East Africa's people, wildlife and landscapes.

**Things Fall Apart** (Chinua Achebe; 1958) Timeless dramatisation of the collision between traditional culture and Europeans in 19th-century Nigeria.

**Disgrace** (JM Coetzee; 1999) Harrowing Booker Prize winner about post-apartheid South Africa.

**Don't Let's Go to the Dogs Tonight – An African Childhood** (Alexandra Fuller; 2001) A stunning memoir of life and loss, and a family's bond with Africa.

## Democracy's March

Not that long ago, the Big Man – the all-powerful ruler, the president for life, the untouchable overlord with friends in Western capitals – was a peculiarly African phenomenon. A few relics remain, it is true, and the world's four longest ruling (non-royal) leaders are in Africa. But Paul Biya (in power in Cameroon since 1975) is facing increasing protests at home, Teodoro Obiang Nguema (Equatorial Guinea, 1979) has retreated to a new capital deep in the rainforest, and Angola's José Eduardo dos Santos (1979) has announced plans to step down in 2018. Even Robert Mugabe (Zimbabwe, 1980) seems a spent force with most discussion centring on who will succeed him. The new reality is perhaps better summed up by what happened in The Gambia in early 2017. When Yahya Jammeh, who once promised to rule for a billion years, tried to cling to power after his unexpected election loss, he was forced from power when Senegalese troops organised by the Economic Community of West African States (Ecowas) moved in. That it was other African states that made sure he went confirms just how much the world has changed.

## Conservation Fights Back

The environmental issues facing Africa make for pretty grim reading. Deserts are on the march, water scarcity is a problem almost everywhere, and habitat destruction and growing human populations are sending numerous signature African species – lions, cheetahs, elephants and mountain gorillas – hurtling towards extinction. But conservationists (and some governments) are fighting back. In Gabon, the setting aside of more than 10% of the country for national parks more than a decade ago has transformed the outlook for a whole raft of species. In East and Southern Africa, conservationists have teamed up with local communities and large landowners to build a future in which growing numbers of people, livestock and wildlife can coexist; the Lion Guardians program (www.lionguardians.org) in southern Kenya is one, while the proliferation of private conservancies is leading conservation in whole new directions. Tourism, too, is an industry where innovations are happening – operators such as Great Plains Conservation, Wilderness Safaris and &Beyond have led the way in putting clever conservation programs at the heart of everything they do.

## War Without End

Despite all of the positive news coming out of Africa, there are some wars that just won't go away. Libya's disintegration continues to ripple out across the Sahara and Sahel – much of the Sahara has become lawless, flooded with guns and with men who are eager to use them. France and the United Nations may have stopped the insurgent march on Bamako in Mali, but chronic instability and regular attacks by Islamist and Tuareg rebels continue to plague the region. Most of Mali, eastern Mauritania, northern Niger, much of Tunisia and southern Algeria are all effectively no-go areas, while the ripples on occasion reach capitals further south with attacks on targets in Ouagadougou, Bamako and Grand Bassam in recent years. Elsewhere, Central African Republic, Somalia and South Sudan seem hell-bent on self-destruction. The rise of Boko Haram has devastated local communities in northern Nigeria and Cameroon. There are few beacons of light from such places, but it was not *that* long ago that peace seemed an impossible dream in Mozambique or that white rule would ever end in South Africa. Hope springs eternal.

## Resource Rich?

Africa could be one of the richest places on earth. But oil in Nigeria, Equatorial Guinea, Gabon and the Republic of Congo, and diamonds in Sierra Leone, have done little to improve the lives of ordinary Africans. Nigeria seems perennially at war with itself and living standards are too often appalling for what is Africa's largest oil producer. In Equatorial Guinea, fabulous oil riches have propped up a brutal dictatorship whose members enjoy great wealth while too many ordinary Equatorial Guineans live as they always have: in abject poverty. It's much the same story further south in Angola. But things are improving on a number of fronts. Sierra Leone became a byword for Africa's resource curse in the 1990s with a vicious war and it remains an economic basket case, but the country is, at least, once again at peace. On paper Equatorial Guinea has a per-capita income higher than its former colonial ruler, Spain. And Equatorial Guinea, Gabon and Republic of Congo have some of the highest adult female literacy rates on the continent. Best of all, diamond-rich Botswana, Namibia and South Africa enjoy living standards and peaceful, democratic political systems that show it really can be done.

POPULATION: **1.216 BILLION**

AREA: **30.22 MILLION SQ KM**

LIFE EXPECTANCY: **62 FOR MEN, 59 FOR WOMEN**

### if Africa were 100 people

**37** would live in West Africa
**22** would live in East Africa
**14** would live in Central Africa
**14** would live in North Africa
**13** would lie in Southern Africa

### belief systems

(% of population)

Muslim

Christian

traditional religions

### population per sq km

AFRICA

USA

UK

≈ 15 people

# History

**African history is a vast and epic tale. The continent has seen pretty much everything; from proto-bacteria and dinosaurs to the colonial 'scramble for Africa' and the Arab Spring that ousted long-time leaders in North Africa. The first humans walked out of the continent about 100,000 years ago to eventually populate the globe. Since then, African empires have come and gone – as have European explorers and colonialists.**

Even covering Africa's post-independence period alone is a monumental task, but Richard Dowden, former Africa editor of the *Economist*, carries it off with aplomb in *Africa – Altered States, Ordinary Miracles* (2008).

## Human Origins & Migrations

Around five to 10 million years ago, a special kind of ape called *Australopithecines* branched off (or rather let go of the branch) and walked on two legs down a separate evolutionary track. This radical move led to the development of various hairy, dim-witted hominids (early humans) – *Homo habilis* around 2.4 million years ago, *Homo erectus* some 1.8 million years ago and finally *Homo sapiens* (modern humans) around 200,000 years ago. Around 50,000 years later, somewhere in Tanzania or Ethiopia, a woman was born who has become known as 'mitochondrial Eve'. All humans today descend from her: at a deep genetic level, we're all Africans.

The first moves away from the nomadic hunter-gatherer way of life came between 14,000 BC and 9500 BC, when rainfall was high and the Sahara and North Africa became verdant. By 2500 BC the rains began to fail and the sandy barrier between North and West Africa became the Sahara we know today. People began to move southwest into the rainforests of Central Africa, most notably a group of people speaking the same family of languages. Known as the Bantu, the group's population grew as it discovered iron-smelting technology and developed new agricultural techniques. By 100 BC, Bantu peoples had reached East Africa; by AD 300 they were living in Southern Africa, and the age of the African empires had begun.

## African Empires Through the Ages

Victorian missionaries liked to think they were bringing the beacon of 'civilisation' to the 'backward' Africa, but the truth is that Africans were developing sophisticated commercial empires and complex urban societies while Europeans were still running after wildlife with clubs.

**TIMELINE**

**200,000 years ago**

The first 'humans' (*Homo sapiens*) begin to definitively diverge from other similar species (such as *Homo erectus*, which persists for millennia), marking Africa as the birthplace of humanity.

**from 5000 BC**

The Sahara begins the millennia-long process of becoming a desert. The drying climate prompts people to settle around waterholes, to rely on agriculture and to move south.

**3100 BC**

Lower Egypt in the Nile's Delta, and Upper Egypt, upstream of the Delta, are unified under Pharaoh Menes. Over the next 3000 years a great African civilisation flourishes.

## Pyramids of Power

Arguably the greatest of the African empires was the first: ancient Egypt. Formed through an amalgamation of already organised states in the Nile Delta around 3100 BC, Egypt achieved an amazing degree of cultural and social sophistication. The Pharaohs, kings imbued with the power of gods, sat at the top of a highly stratified social hierarchy. The annual flooding of the Nile kept the lands of the Pharaohs fertile and fed their legions of slaves and artisans, who in turn worked to produce some of the most amazing public buildings ever constructed. Many of these, like the Pyramids of Giza, are still standing today. Ancient Egypt was eventually overrun by the Nubian Empire, then by the Assyrians, Persians, Alexander the Great and finally the Romans.

Until the Portuguese dispelled the myths, Cape Bojador (along the coast of Moroccan-administered Western Sahara) was considered by sailors as the point of no return, beyond which lay monstrous sea creatures, whirlpools, boiling waters and waterless coastlines.

## Phoenician & Roman North Africa

Established in Tunisia by the Phoenicians (seafaring people with their origins in Tyre, in what is now Lebanon), the city-state of Carthage filled the power vacuum left by the decline of ancient Egypt. By the 6th century BC, Carthage was an empire in its own right and controlled much of the Mediterranean sea trade. Back on land, scholars were busy inventing the Phoenician alphabet, from which Greek, Hebrew and Latin are all thought to derive. It all came to an abrupt end with the arrival of the Romans, who razed Carthage and enslaved its population in 146 BC.

The Romans built some of Africa's most beautiful ancient cities in what are now Libya, Algeria and Morocco, and African-born Septimius Severus (r AD 193–211) went on to become Emperor of Rome. But the Romans, like the Carthaginians before them and the Byzantines who came after, had their control over Africa effectively restricted to the Mediterranean coastal strip. This was swept away by the Arabs who arrived in North Africa, bearing Islam, around AD 670.

## The Kingdom of Sheba

Aksum was the first truly African indigenous state – no conquerors from elsewhere arrived to start this legendary kingdom, which controlled much of Sudan and southern Arabia at the height of its powers between AD 100 and 940. Aksum's heart was the hilly, fertile landscape of northern Ethiopia. The Aksumites traded with Egypt, the eastern Mediterranean and Arabia, developed a written language, produced gold coins and built imposing stone buildings. In the 4th century AD, the Aksumite king converted to Christianity, founding the Ethiopian Orthodox church. Legend has it that Ethiopia was the home of the fabled Queen of Sheba and the last resting place of the mysterious Ark of the Covenant.

**146 BC**

The city-state of Carthage (in modern-day Tunisia) is destroyed by the Romans. Its people are sold into slavery and the site is symbolically sprinkled with salt and damned forever.

**100 BC**

The Bantu people arrive in East Africa from the west and northwest. By the 11th century they reach Southern Africa.

**400 AD**

Christianity is embraced by the East African kingdom of Aksum (in present-day Ethiopia). Three centuries later the trading empire is isolated by the rise of Islam in Arabia.

**670**

Islam sweeps across North Africa, where it remains the dominant religion today. A century later the religion has spread down the East African coast.

### Swahili Sultans

As early as the 7th century AD, the coastal areas of modern-day Tanzania, Kenya and Mozambique were home to a chain of vibrant, well-organised city-states, whose inhabitants lived in stone houses, wore fine silks and decorated their gravestones with artisanal ceramics and glass. Merchants from as far afield as China and India came to the East African coast, then set off again, their holds groaning with trade goods, spices, slaves and exotic beasts. The rulers of these city-states were the Swahili sultans – kings and queens who kept a hold on their domains via their control over magical objects and knowledge of secret religious ceremonies. The Swahili sultans were eventually defeated by Portuguese and Omani conquerors, but the rich cultural melting pot they presided over gave rise to the Swahili language, a fusion of African, Arabic and Portuguese words that still thrives.

Respected African-American scholar Henry Louis Gates Jr has spent a lifetime refuting perceptions of Africa's precolonial backwardness. The result is the compelling *Wonders of the African World* (1999).

### Golden Kingdoms

The area centred on present-day Mali was home to a hugely wealthy series of West African empires that flourished over the course of more than 800 years. The Empire of Ghana lasted from the 4th to 11th centuries AD, and was followed by the fabulously wealthy Empire of Mali (around 1250 to 1500), which once stretched all the way from the coast of Senegal to Niger.

The Songhaï Empire (1000–1591), with its capital at Gao in modern-day Mali, was the last of Africa's golden empires, which at their peak covered areas larger than Western Europe. Their wealth was founded on the salt from Saharan mines, which was traded ounce for ounce with West African gold. Organised systems of government and Islamic centres of scholarship – the most famous of which was Timbuktu – flourished in the kingdoms of West Africa, but conversely, it was Islam that led to their downfall when the forces of Morocco invaded in 1591.

## The Age of the Explorers

By the 15th century, with gold and tales of limitless wealth making their way across the Sahara and the Mediterranean, European royalty became obsessed with Africa.

The Portuguese were first off the block, building a fortified trading post, the earliest European structure in sub-Saharan Africa, along today's Ghanaian coast. By the end of the century their ships had rounded Southern Africa. In the early 16th century French, British and Dutch ships joined the Portuguese along the coast, building forts as they went. But unlike the Carthaginians and Romans, the European powers were never content with mere coastal footholds.

**9th century**

Islam reaches the Sahel via trans-Saharan camel caravans, almost 250 years after it swept across North Africa; it would later become the predominant religion of West Africa.

**1137–1270**

Ethiopia's Zaghwe dynasty builds Lalibela's rock-hewn churches. The dynasty is overthrown by Yekuno Amlak, a self-professed descendant of King Solomon and the Queen of Sheba.

**1498**

Portuguese explorer Vasco da Gama lands at Mozambique Island. Over the next 200 years the Portuguese establish trading enclaves along the coast and several settlements in the interior.

**1650s**

The Dutch East India Company sets up a permanent supply station at Cape Town and the French set up a permanent trading post at Saint-Louis in modern Senegal.

Victorian heroes such as Richard Burton and John Speke captured the public imagination with their hair-raising tales from the East African interior, while Mungo Park and the formidable Mary Wesley battled their way through fever-ridden swamps, and avoided charging animals while 'discovering' various parts of West Africa.

## The European Slave Trade

There has always been slavery in Africa (slaves were common by-products of intertribal warfare, and the Arabs and Shirazis who dominated the East African coast took slaves by the thousands). But the slave trade took on a whole new dimension after the European arrival. The Portuguese in West Africa, the Dutch in South Africa and other Europeans who came after them saw how African slavery worked and, with one eye on their huge American sugar plantations, saw the potential for slavery to fuel agricultural production. They were helped by opportunistic African leaders who used slavery and other trade with Europeans as a means to expand their own power.

To understand the horrors of the European slave trade and its ultimate abolition, look no further than Adam Hochschild's definitive 2006 book, *Bury the Chains*.

Exact figures are impossible to establish, but from the end of the 15th century until around 1870, when the slave trade was fully abolished, up to 20 million Africans were enslaved. Perhaps half died en route to the Americas; millions of others perished in slaving raids. The trans-Atlantic slave trade gave European powers a huge economic boost, while the loss of farmers and tradespeople, as well as the general chaos, made Africa an easy target for colonialism.

## Colonial Africa

Throughout the 19th century, the region-by-region conquest of the continent by European powers gathered pace and became known as the 'Scramble for Africa'. This was formalised at the Berlin Conference of 1884–85, when Europe's governments divided Africa between them. After the conference, Britain's Lord Salisbury told the London *Times* in 1890: 'We have been giving away mountains and rivers and lakes to each other, only hindered by the small impediment that we never knew exactly where the mountains and rivers and lakes were.' That Africans had no say in the matter scarcely seemed to register. France and Britain got the biggest swaths, with Germany, Portugal, Italy, Spain and Belgium picking up the rest. The resulting boundaries, determined more by colonial expediency than the complex realities on the ground, remain largely in place today.

The extravagant, gold-laden pilgrimage to Mecca by Mali's King Kankan Musa in 1324 is often credited with sparking Europe's interest in Africa and its riches. He was accompanied by an entourage of more than 60,000 people and needed 500 slaves to carry all the gold.

Forced labour, heavy taxation, and vengeful violence for any insurrection were all commonplace in colonial Africa. African territories were essentially organised to extract cheap cash crops and natural resources for use by the colonial powers. To facilitate easy administration, tribal

**1807**
Britain makes trade in slaves illegal in its empire. But it will take until the 1870s for other countries to follow suit and the trade to be fully abolished.

**1869**
Suez Canal opens. Discovery of the world's largest diamond deposits in Kimberley and gold in the Transvaal around the same time helps keep Cape Town as Africa's premier port.

**1884–85**
The Berlin Conference gives France almost one-third of the continent (mostly in West and Central Africa), while Britain gets Ghana, Nigeria and much of Southern and East Africa.

**1931**
Apart from Liberia (which became independent in 1847) and Ethiopia (which was never colonised save for an Italian occupation during WWII), South Africa becomes Africa's first independent country.

differences and rivalries were exploited to the full, and industrial development, social welfare and education were rarely policy priorities. The effects of the colonial years, which in some cases only ended a few decades ago, continue to leave their mark on the continent.

A mere 1% increase in world trade from Africa (Mozambique alone loses US$150 million annually due to restrictions on importing into Europe) would be the equivalent of five times the foreign aid currently received by Africa.

## Africa for the Africans

African independence movements existed throughout the colonial period, but organised political resistance gained momentum in the 1950s and '60s. Soldiers who had fought in both world wars on behalf of their colonial masters joined forces with African intellectuals who had gained their education through missionary schools and universities; their catchcry became 'Africa for the Africans'.

Many African countries became independent in the 1960s – some peacefully, others only after years of bloodshed and struggle. The Organisation of African Unity was established with 32 members in 1963 to promote solidarity and act as a collective voice for the continent. By the 1970s most African countries had become masters of their own destinies, at least on paper.

It is impossible to overstate the euphoria that gripped Africa in the post-independence period. The speeches of bright young leaders such as Kwame Nkrumah (Ghana), Jomo Kenyatta (Kenya) and Patrice Lumumba (Congo) had Africans across the continent dreaming of a new African dawn. For the most part, they were disappointed. Most African countries were woefully unprepared for independence, ruled over by an ill-equipped political class. The situation worsened when fledgling African nations became pawns in the Cold War machinations of the US and USSR, and factors such as drought, economic collapse and ethnic resentment led many to spiral down into a mire of corruption, violence and civil war.

Martin Meredith's *The State of Africa* (2013) is a clear and concise run-through of Africa's post-independence history. *The Scramble for Africa* (1992), by Thomas Pakenham, is a scintillating read, full of ruthless and eccentric characters, tracing the European greed for territory that shaped today's continent.

## 21st-Century Africa

The first decade in the 21st century held out hope for the continent. The Human Security Report Project (www.hsrgroup.org) found that between 1999 and 2006 the number of state-based armed conflicts dropped by 46%, while those between rebel groups fell by 54%. The annual number of deaths in battle actually diminished by two-thirds between 2002 and 2006.

Oil discoveries and lessening conflict resulted in more than 30 African countries growing economically at a rate of 4% or more in 2006 and 2007. Also in 2007, the G8 countries pledged US$25 billion aid for Africa and promised to eliminate the outstanding debts of the poorest countries. However, by the end of the decade, shrinking remittances from the diaspora, cuts in exports and falls in tourism earnings had

**1960**

Seventeen African countries gain independence from European colonial rule. Most are former French colonies, but also include Congo (from Belgium), Somalia (from Italy and Britain) and Nigeria (from Britain).

**1975**

Portuguese rule ends in Angola and Mozambique; both countries align themselves with the Soviet Union, intensifying the Cold War between the superpowers on the continent.

**1980**

Rhodesia becomes the last African country to gain independence from European rule; following the Lancaster House agreement it is known as Zimbabwe.

**1990**

Nelson Mandela is released after almost three decades in prison. Four years later he is voted South Africa's president after multiracial elections.

## CHINA IN AFRICA

Despite the fact that the US gets between 10% and 15% of its oil from African sources, Africa's bond with the US is arguably not the one that matters. The key relationship is becoming the one with China, an economic behemoth hungry for Africa's minerals, oils and timbers.

Chinese trade with Africa dates back to the 15th century when Admiral Zheng He's fleet arrived on the continent's east coast. Some 60,000 Chinese joined the South African gold rush at the end of the 19th century, while Chairman Mao sent tens of thousands more workers to assist with the glorious revolutions planned across the continent in the 1960s and '70s. In recent decades, though, Chinese economic involvement in Africa has gone off the scale. Today more than 900 Chinese companies operate on African soil and more than a million Chinese live on the continent.

Beijing's readiness to provide much-needed infrastructure, which Western aid doesn't cover and local governments cannot afford, is already having a transformative impact. Such largesse holds out the potential of a Pax Sinica, as African nation states are finally linked together by modern infrastructure. Others warn that Beijing's relationship with Africa often bears a depressing resemblance to those of the colonial era, despite all the talk of fresh paradigms. There are also concerns that the leverage that came with Western aid being to tied good governance outcomes is now a thing of the past as, so critics say, much of the Chinese aid comes with no such strings attached.

It's a complex topic: for analysis and thoughts beyond the headlines read the blog China in Africa (www.chinaafricarealstory.com) by Professor Deborah Brautigam, author of *The Dragon's Gift: The Real Story of China in Africa* (2011). Other treatments of the subject worth reading are *China's Second Continent: How a Million Migrants Are Building a New Empire in Africa* (2015), by Howard W French, and *China and Africa: A Century of Engagement* (2012), by David H Shinn and Joshua Eisenman.

taken a measurable toll. Above all, the global economic crisis and ongoing uncertainty threatens to dry up the generosity of industrialised nations.

The outbreak of the Ebola virus in Sierra Leone, Guinea and Liberia from 2013 to 2016 rocked the continent to its core. Although there were isolated cases elsewhere, Africa breathed a huge sigh of relief when the epidemic was officially declared to be over, not least because the rest of world had steered clear of the entire continent – it was the equivalent of people not visiting Spain because of a disease outbreak in Norway. The after-effects of the Arab Spring, too, continued to be felt – from Tunisia and Libya to Mali and Niger – even as conflicts ended and democracy continued to deepen its roots in many places.

When Ethiopian rebel forces rolled into Addis Ababa in 1991 they were navigating with photocopies of the Addis Ababa map found in Lonely Planet's *Africa on a Shoestring*!

**2001**

The African Union is established as successor to the Organisation of African Unity. All 54 African nations, except Morocco, are members; its secretariat is based in Addis Ababa.

**2011**

The 'Arab Spring' series of popular uprisings sees long-time leaders Zine el-Abidine Ben Ali in Tunisia, Hosni Mubarak in Egypt and Colonel Muammar Qaddafi in Libya ousted from power.

**2013**

An outbreak of the Ebola virus in Guinea spreads to Sierra Leone and Liberia. The outbreak peaks in 2014 but it is not until 2016 that all countries are declared Ebola-free. More than 11,300 people perish.

**2014**

Militants from Boko Haram kidnap more than 200 girls from a boarding school in Chibok, a town in northern Nigeria. Although some are later freed, many remain in captivity at the time of writing.

# Culture

**It is impossible to talk of Africa as a single entity, but within its diversity lie extraordinary cultural riches. How could it not be so with more than one billion Africans and well over 2000 different languages? Africans of all persuasions and from all corners of the continent have produced (and continue to produce) world-class literature and cinema, traditional crafts and cuisines that together provide so many insights into the ordinary lives of Africans.**

## Daily Life

Africa's peoples have been moving from one part of the continent to the other since the great Bantu migrations of centuries past. But nothing in the modern era has changed African social structures quite like the movement from rural areas to the cities and the ravages of HIV/AIDS.

### Urbanisation

At the beginning of the 20th century, around 5% of Africans lived in cities. Now, over a third of the continent's one billion population is urbanised with the figure set to rise to over half by 2030 according to a 2010 UN report. By some estimates, Africa's rate of urbanisation is the fastest in the world and the population of urban centres is growing at twice the rate of rural areas.

While generalisations can be dangerous, most often the daily lives of ordinary Africans revolve around family and other tightly knit social networks. These pillars of society tend to become a little shaky in urban areas, where traditional networks are often less important than economic and other factors.

Africa's least urbanised countries are Burundi (12%), Uganda (16.1%) and Niger (17.8%), while Gabon (87.2%), Djibouti (77.1%) and Algeria (73%) are way above the African average when it comes to city dwellers.

The reasons for this epochal demographic shift are legion: growing populations due to improved health care, environmental degradation leading to shrinking grazing and agricultural land, and poor rural infrastructure are among the most important.

Unfortunately, urban population growth has far outpaced job creation; unemployment in many African cities is rife. One UN study found that in 38 African countries more than 50% of the urban population lives in slums. At the same time, many African cities have a growing and increasingly influential and sophisticated middle class.

Thanks to urbanisation, a whole generation of Africans is growing up with no connection to the countryside and its lores and traditions, and in many cases urbanisation has led to the breakdown of traditional social values such as respect for elders, and the loosening of family structures. Urbanisation has also caused critical labour shortages in rural areas, and has accelerated the spread of HIV.

In spite of these daunting challenges, rural life remains a pillar of African society, a place where the continent's historical memory survives. Family bonds are still much stronger than in many developed societies, with the concepts of community and shared responsibility deeply rooted. These values retain a strong hold over many Africans, even those who long ago left for the cities.

## HIV/AIDS

According to the UN, there has been some very welcome news: between 2005 and 2013 the number of people dying from AIDS-related causes in sub-Saharan Africa had dropped from 18 million to 1.1 million. The number of new HIV infections had also dipped dramatically, by 25% over the previous decade to a total of 1.5 million in 2013. That's the good news. But the fact is that sub-Saharan Africa still has 24.7 million people living with HIV, or 71% of the global total.

Southern Africa has been the epicentre of the HIV/AIDS catastrophe. At the height of the crisis, more than a third of Botswanans were afflicted. And still 27.4% of Swaziland's adults have the disease, as do 5.9 million South Africans. This is staggeringly high, especially when compared to Senegal (0.5%) and even Kenya (6%).

There are many reasons why HIV/AIDS has taken such a hold in Africa. Collective denial of the problem, migration in search of work and to escape wars and famine, a general lack of adequate health care and prevention programs, and social and cultural factors – in particular the low status of women in many African societies – are all believed to have played a role in the rapid spread of the disease.

The personal, social and economic costs associated with the disease are devastating. HIV/AIDS predominantly hits the most productive members of society – young adults. This has a huge impact on family income, food production and local economies in general, and large parts of Africa face the loss of a significant proportion of entire generations. Employers, schools, factories and hospitals have to train other staff to replace those at the workplace who become too ill to work, setting economic and social development back by decades. The numbers of HIV/AIDS orphans (the UN estimates 11 million, with one in four Zambian children, or 380,000 children, said to be without both parents) is at once an enduring human tragedy and a massive societal problem.

Antiretroviral drug treatments, available in the West to increase the lifespan of AIDS sufferers and reduce the risk of HIV-infected women passing the infection on to their unborn babies, are still out of the reach of most Africans (according to the World Health Organization, Brazil has managed to halve AIDS deaths by making such drugs free). Although things are improving, only 39% of sub-Saharan African adults with HIV are receiving the necessary retroviral treatment.

For all its international prominence, HIV/AIDS is by no means Africa's only killer: WHO reports that malaria kills an African child every minute, with the Democratic Republic of Congo and Nigeria accounting for 40% of the worldwide total of deaths from the infection.

For an exhaustive list of UN socio-economic data (ranging from literacy and life expectancy to income and infant mortality) for African countries, visit the website of the UN Development Programme (www.hdr.undp.org/en/countries).

## Religion

Most Africans are deeply religious, with religious values informing every aspect of their daily life. Generally speaking, a majority of the population in North Africa, West and Central Africa close to the Sahara, together with much of the East African coast, is Islamic; East and Southern Africa, and the rest of the continent, is predominantly Christian.

Accurate figures are hard to come by, but roughly 40% of Africans are Muslim and 40% Christian (including a burgeoning evangelical Christian movement), leaving around 20% who follow other religions or traditional African beliefs. These figures should be taken with a pinch of salt, however, as many Africans see no contradiction at all in combining their traditional beliefs with Islam or Christianity.

Hindus and Sikhs are found in places where immigrants arrived from Asia during the colonial era, particularly in East African countries such

To find out how to listen to the BBC World Service in Africa, visit www.bbc.co.uk/worldserviceradio.

as Kenya, Tanzania and Uganda. Jewish communities, some centuries old, are found mainly in North and Southern Africa.

### Religion African Style

Africa's traditional religions are generally animist, believing that objects such as trees and caves or ritual objects such as gourds or drums are endowed with spiritual powers. Thus a certain natural object may be sacred because it represents, is home to, or simply *is* a spirit or deity. Several traditional religions accept the existence of a supreme being or creator, alongside spirits and deities.

Niger has the lowest female adult literacy rate (11%) in Africa, followed by Guinea (18.1%), Benin (27.3%) and Mali (29.2%). At the other end of the scale are South Africa (93.1%), Equatorial Guinea (93%), Botswana (88.9%), Lesotho (88.3%), Namibia (84.5%) and Gabon (81%).

Most African religions centre on ancestor veneration, the idea that the dead remain influential after passing from the physical into the spiritual world. Ancestors must therefore be honoured in order to ensure that they intervene positively with other spiritual beings on behalf of their relatives on earth.

The practice of traditional medicine is closely intertwined with traditional religion. Practitioners (often derogatorily referred to as 'witch doctors' by foreigners) use divining implements such as bones, prayers, chanting and dance to facilitate communication with the spirit world. Patients are cured with the use of herbal preparations or by exorcist-style interventions to drive out evil spirits that have inhabited the body. Not all magical practitioners are benign – some are suspected of being paid to place curses on people, causing bad luck, sickness or even death.

Although traditional religious practices can be a force for social good within a community, and herbalists are often very skilled in their craft, there's a flip side: some religious practitioners discourage their patients from seeking conventional medical help at hospitals or clinics, and someone who considers themselves cursed will very often give up the will to live entirely. In some parts of Southern and East Africa, killings occasionally take place, in which children or adults are abducted and murdered in order to gain body parts for use in magic rituals. Albinos in Tanzania and Burundi have come under particular threat in recent years.

## Sport

Sport, especially football, is one of Africa's most popular forms of entertainment and important games featuring national or leading club sides can bring daily life to a grinding halt as everyone crowds around communal TV sets. In South Africa, and to a lesser extent Zimbabwe, rugby and cricket are also popular.

### Football

With Cameroon's victory in the 2017 African Cup of Nations, the West African country moved into second place on the all-time table, with five victories, behind Egypt (seven) and ahead of Ghana (four).

Football (soccer) is the most popular of Africa's sports, and you'll never have to go far before you find someone kicking a ball (or a bundle of plastic bags tied together with string) around on a dusty patch of ground.

West African and North African countries are Africa's footballing powerhouses. Ever since Cameroon stormed to the quarter finals of the 1990 World Cup finals in Italy, West Africa has been touted as an emerging world power in the sport. Cameroon built on its success by winning the football gold medal at the 2000 Sydney Olympics. But apart from Senegal reaching the World Cup quarter finals in 2002, and Ghana's team winning the 2009 U-20 World Cup in Cairo, further success has proved elusive.

At the 2010 World Cup in South Africa, the host team was knocked out in the first round; of the other five African nations in the tournament only Ghana made it into the quarter finals.

The African Cup of Nations also stirs great passions across the continent. Almost two years of qualifying rounds culminate in the 16 best teams playing for the crown of African champions. North African sides (Tunisia in 2004, and Egypt in 2006, 2008 and 2010) have dominated the event in recent years, but in 2012 Zambia took the trophy. In January 2013 the tournament switched to being held every odd-numbered year so as not to clash with the World Cup.

West African nations have again dominated in recent years with winners being Nigeria (2013), Côte d'Ivoire (2015) and Cameroon (2017).

But the success or otherwise of national teams is only part of the story. West African footballers in particular have enjoyed phenomenal success in European leagues, in the process becoming the focal point for the aspirations of a generation of West African youngsters dreaming of becoming the next Yaya Touré or Didier Drogba.

And it's not just the kids: every weekend from September to May, Africans crowd around communal TV sets to follow the fortunes of teams in Spain, Italy, the UK and France, especially those games involving African players. There is a sense that the success of Africans in Europe is something in which they can all share with pride, and that reflects well on the continent as a whole.

*Monique and the Mango Rains: Two Years with a Midwife in Mali* (2007), by Kris Holloway, gives a human face to statistics about difficulties faced by women in traditional, rural West Africa. It's a great but sobering read.

### Other Sports

Other popular sports in Africa include marathon running (at which Kenya and Ethiopia dominate the world) and boxing. Basketball is becoming increasingly popular with the arrival of American TV channels. In South Africa rugby is massively popular and has benefited from development programs across the colour divide. South African fans adore their beloved 'Boks', ranked a rather disappointing sixth in the world as of early 2017. Cricket is also widely played, particularly in Southern Africa and Zimbabwe.

## Media

Although no one doubts the potential of mass media such as newspapers, radio stations or TV to be a tool for development in Africa, the media industry on the continent is beset by many problems. Access is one, as many people still live in rural areas, with little or no infrastructure. Many corrupt governments also ruthlessly suppress all but state-controlled media.

A good barometer of press freedom in the region is to be found in the annual Press Freedom Index compiled by Reporters Without Borders (www.rsf.org), which ranks 180 countries according to the freedoms enjoyed by the independent media. In 2016 Eritrea came in last (the only country to lag behind North Korea), while Sudan (174th), Djibouti (172nd), Equatorial Guinea (168th), Somalia (167th), Libya (164th), Rwanda (161st) and Egypt (159th) also fared badly. Namibia (17th) and Ghana (26th) were the best performing mainland African states and finished above both the UK (38th) and USA (41st).

At the same time, many Africans feel that much reporting on the continent by the international media paints an unfair portrait of Africa as a hopeless case, troubled by war, famine and corruption. In one famous example, the 13 May 2000 issue of the *Economist* was entitled simply 'The hopeless continent'.

### Internet

Africans are now using the internet to bypass the often unreliable reporting of the state-funded media, while groups such as rural women, who have in the past been denied access to information on health care and human rights, are empowered by their access to online education resources. Many such grass roots cyber-education projects are still in their infancy, but exciting times are ahead.

The power of the internet, in particular social media, came strongly to the fore in the Arab Spring uprisings across North Africa. Some repressive African governments have since taken precautionary measures to further censor and control internet usage; Ethiopia is one country that consistently blocks access to social media and other internet sites.

## Newspapers & Magazines

There is no shortage of newspapers and current-affairs mags available across Africa, including the monthly *New African* (www.newafricanmagazine.com) and *Africa Today* (www.africatoday.com).

The *East African* (www.theeastafrican.co.ke) is good for an overview of what's happening in Kenya, Tanzania and Uganda. South Africa's weekly newspaper the *Mail & Guardian* (www.mg.co.za) is highly respected and has a good selection of features on the continent. If you're in West Africa and your French is well oiled, *Jeune Afrique* (www.jeuneafrique.com) is a highly regarded weekly news magazine.

For links to a range of websites and local newspapers for most countries in Africa, as well as a handful of pan-African sites, head to World Newspapers (www.world-newspapers.com/africa).

### Websites

- *AllAfrica (www.allafrica.com)*
- *Reuters Africa (www.reuters.com/places/africa)*
- *Afrol News (www.afrol.com)*
- *BBC (www.bbc.com/news/world/africa)*
- *IRINNews (www.irinnews.org/africa)*
- *West Africa News (www.westafricanews.com)*
- *Media Foundation for West Africa (www.mfwa.org)*

## Radio

Radio remains by far the most popular medium of communication in Africa, with even the most remote rural villagers gathering around a crackling radio to listen to the latest news and music. Innovative projects such as the charity Farm Radio International (www.farmradio.org) support rural radio broadcasters in around 40 African countries.

For continental coverage, however, locals and travellers tune into international broadcasters; most have dedicated Africa slots. As well as the trusty BBC World Service (www.bbc.co.uk/worldserviceradio), Voice of America (www.voanews.com) and Radio France Internationale (www.rfi.fr) are perennial favourites. If you'd rather hear African news from Africans, try Channel Africa (www.channelafrica.co.za), the international radio service of the South African Broadcasting Corporation.

## TV

TV ownership in Africa is much lower than elsewhere in the world and televisions mostly remain luxury items, unavailable to most of Africa's poorer inhabitants. Walk around many African towns and villages after dark, however, and you're likely to come across the dim blue glow of a TV set, often set in a doorway so that an audience of 20 or 30 can gather around it to watch the latest episode of a local soap or a football match.

A sign of some African nations' growing affluence is that in 2016, Digital TV Research reported that about 2.24 million homes in sub-Saharan Africa (not including South Africa) received digital TV. It also forecast that digital TV penetration across this area of Africa will rocket to 99.9 per cent by 2021 – with household numbers quadrupling to nearly 75 million.

# Women in Africa

Women form the bedrock of African society, especially in rural areas where they bear the burden of child-rearing and most agricultural work. Their task is made more difficult by the HIV/AIDS epidemic and the absence of men who move to the cities as migrant industrial workers.

In some countries sexual equality is enshrined in law. African women made history in 2005 when a legal protocol came into force that specifically protects women's human rights in the 17 countries that ratified it. These countries have pledged to amend their laws to uphold a raft of women's rights, including the right to property after divorce, the right to abortions after rape or abuse, and the right to equal pay in the workplace, among many others. The reality is, however, somewhat different, and in many places women are treated as second-class citizens. Families

## FEMALE GENITAL MUTILATION IN AFRICA

Female genital mutilation (FGM), often euphemistically termed 'female circumcision' or 'genital alteration' but more accurately called female genital cutting (FGC), is widespread throughout West Africa. The term covers a wide range of procedures, but in West Africa, where the practice is widespread, the procedure usually involves removal of the entire clitoris (called infibulation).

Although outsiders often believe that FGM is associated with Islam, it actually predates the religion (historical records of infibulation date back 6000 years) and has far more to do with longstanding cultural traditions than religious doctrine; in predominantly Muslim northern Mali, FGM prevalence rates are less than 10%. The procedure is usually performed by midwives on girls and young women. They sometimes use modern surgical instruments, but more often it's done with a razor blade or even a piece of glass. If the procedure is done in a traditional setting the girl will not be anaesthetised, although nowadays many families take their daughters to clinics to have the procedure performed by a trained doctor. Complications, especially in the traditional setting, include infection of the wound, leading to death, or scarring, which makes childbirth and urination difficult.

In West Africa, FGM is seen among traditionalists as important for maintaining traditional society. An unaltered woman would dishonour her family and lower its position in society, as well as ruining her own chances for marriage – a circumcised woman is thought to be a moral woman, and more likely a virgin. Many believe that if left, the clitoris can make a woman infertile, or damage and even kill her unborn children.

Some West African countries have enacted laws outlawing FGM, but poor enforcement means that, even where FGM is illegal, the practice continues as before. FGM is illegal in Guinea, for example, and punishable in some cases by life imprisonment with hard labour, yet an estimated 96% of women still undergo the procedure according to the World Health Organization. Laws against FGM are also on the books in Burkina Faso, which nonetheless has a 76% prevalence rate, in Côte d'Ivoire (38%) and in Senegal (26%). The practice is also extremely common in Mali (89%), Sierra Leone (88%), The Gambia (76%), Mauritania (69%), Liberia (66%), Guinea-Bissau (50%) and Nigeria (27%), none of which have laws outlawing FGM. FGM is a particularly common practice among the Fulani.

Beyond West Africa, Somalia (98%), Djibouti (93%), Egypt (91%), Eritrea (89%) and Ethiopia (74%) have particularly high rates of FGC, but progress is being made elsewhere – in Kenya, for example, rates of FGC fell from 41% in 1984 to just 11% in 2015.

NGO Tostan (www.tostan.org) operates throughout West Africa at the village level with a number of long-term projects promoting ending the practice as well as providing maternal health, education and other services.

sometimes deny girls schooling, although education is valued highly by most Africans. More serious still are reports of female infanticide, forced marriages, female genital mutilation and honour killings.

*Moolaadé*, the powerful 2004 film by Senegalese director Ousmane Sembène, is one of the few mass-release artistic endeavours to tackle head-on the taboo issue of female genital mutilation.

# Arts

Traditional African art and craft has stood at the centre of African life for centuries. It is a world of ceremonial masks, figures related to ancestral worship and fetishes (which protect against certain spirits) conceived in the spirit world and cast in wood and in bronze, in textiles and in basketry. Such art forms, along with traditional music, survive into the present, adding depth and richness to modern life alongside more contemporary media, such as literature, art and cinema.

## Contemporary Arts

The art world has its eye on Africa. In March 2011 a painting by South African artist Irma Stern (1894–1966) sold for US$4.94 million at auction in London. Some contemporary African artists such as Ghanaian

## AFRICA'S FILM FESTIVALS

Burkina Faso, as one of the world's poorest countries, may be an unlikely venue for a world-renowned festival of film, but the biennial nine-day Pan-African Film Festival, Fespaco (Festival Pan-Africain du Cinema; www.fespaco.bf), goes from strength to strength.

Fespaco began in 1969, when it was little more than a few African film-makers getting together to show their short films to interested audiences. Hundreds of films from Africa and the diaspora in the Americas and the Caribbean are now viewed every year, with 20 selected to compete for the prestigious Étalon D'Or de Yennenga – Fespaco's equivalent of the Oscar – as well as prizes in other categories (including TV).

Fespaco is held in Ouagadougou every odd year, in the second half of February or early March, and has become an essential pillar of Burkina Faso's cultural life. Since its early days, it has also helped stimulate film production throughout Africa and has become such a major African cultural event that it attracts celebrities from around the world.

East Africa is not known for its film-making, but it does host one of the continent's best film festivals: Zanzibar International Film Festival (ZIFF; www.ziff.or.tz), also known as the Festival of the Dhow Countries. The festival, which has been held annually on Zanzibar island since 1998, continues to be one of the region's premier cultural events. It serves as a venue for artists from the Indian Ocean basin and beyond.

In December, Marrakesh hosts the more mainstream but always worthwhile Marrakesh International Film Festival (www.festivalmarrakech.info).

sculptor El Anatsui, Kenyan ceramicist Magdalene Odunodo and Nigerian sculptor Ben Enwonwu are also securing six-figure sums at auction for their works.

In a bid to bring some of Africa's little-known artists to the world stage and to find the next Stern or Odunodo, the African Arts Trust (www.theafricanartstrust.org) was set up in 2011 to enable artists initially in Botswana, Ethiopia, Kenya, Malawi, Mozambique, Tanzania, Uganda, Zambia and Zimbabwe to buy materials, create works, travel and study.

In recent years recycled art has become popular, with artists from South Africa to West Africa producing sculptures and textiles created entirely from discarded objects such as tin cans and bottle tops.

### Literature

Sub-Saharan Africa's rich, multilayered literary history is almost entirely oral. Folk tales, poems, proverbs, myths, historical tales and (most importantly) ethnic traditions are passed down through generations by word of mouth. Some societies have specific keepers of history and storytelling, such as the *griots* of West Africa, and in many cases stories are sung or tales are performed in a form of theatre. As a result, little of Africa's rich literary history was known to the outside world until relatively recently.

*Gogo Mama: A Journey into the Lives of Twelve African Women* (2007), by Sally Sara, includes illuminating chapters on a Liberian former child soldier, a Zanzibari diva, and a HIV/AIDS-fighting grandmother in South Africa.

Twentieth- and 21st-century African literature has been greatly influenced by colonial education and Western trends. Some African authors have nonetheless made an effort to employ traditional structures and folk tales in their work; others write of the contemporary hardships faced by Africans and their fight to shake off the shackles of colonialism, using Western-influenced narrative methods (and penning their works in English, French or Portuguese).

Nigerian authors are prominent on the English-speaking African literature scene and some, like Amos Tutuola, adapt African folklore into their own works. Penned by Tutuola, *The Palm-Wine Drunkard* is a rather grisly tale of a man who enters the spirit world in order to find his palm-wine supplier! In a 1952 review in London's *Observer* newspaper, Dylan Thomas described the novel as 'brief, thronged, grisly and bewitching' and a 'nightmare of indescribable adventures'. The magical world of Ben Okri, most notably his Azaro trilogy and its spirit-child narrator, shows that such magical storytelling and the enduring power of traditional folklore are very much African specialities.

In March 2013 Chinua Achebe, hailed by Nobel Laureate Nadine Gordimer as the father of African Literature, died. His most famous novel, *Things Fall Apart*, is a deeply symbolic tale about a man's rise and fall at the time colonialism arrived in Africa.

South Africa has also produced many famous writers including Nobel Prize winners JM Coetzee and Nadine Gordimer, as well as André Brink, Alan Paton and Man Booker-prize–nominated Damon Galgut.

Nigeria's 'Nollywood' film industry is the second most prolific in the world (after India), pumping out up to 200 movies for the home market every month. Nigerian director Chico Ejiro (widely known as 'Mr Prolific') is famous for having directed more than 80 films in just five years.

## Traditional Decorative Arts & Crafts

The creation of many African arts and crafts is often the preserve of distinct castes of blacksmiths and weavers who rely almost exclusively on locally found or produced materials. Tourism has, however, greatly affected African art and craft, with considerable effort now going into producing objects for sale rather than traditional use. Some art forms, such as the Tingatinga paintings of Tanzania, evolved entirely out of demand from tourists. Although it causes a departure from art's role in traditional society, tourism can ensure artisans remain employed in their traditional professions, and many pieces retain their power precisely because they still carry meaning for Africa's peoples.

West Africa has arguably Africa's most extraordinary artistic tradition. The mask traditions of Côte d'Ivoire, Mali and the Congos are world famous, and Picasso, Matisse and others found inspiration in the radical approach to the human form. Nigeria and Benin have long been associated with fine bronze sculptures and carvings, and the Ashanti people of Ghana are renowned for fine textiles and gold sculptures.

In North Africa, ancient Arabic and Islamic traditions have produced some beautiful artworks (ceramics and carpets are particularly refined), as well as some phenomenal architecture; in the Sahara, Tuareg silver jewellery is unique and beautiful.

Throughout East and Southern Africa the Makonde people of Mozambique and the Shona of Zimbabwe produce excellent and widely copied sculptures.

## Cinema

West Africa in particular has an acclaimed cinematic tradition – quite an achievement for one of the poorest regions of the planet. North African directors, too, are regulars on the international festival circuit, while South African film has a good reputation..

Senegalese director Ousmane Sembène (1923–2007) is often called the 'father of African film'; his 1966 movie *La Noire de...* was the first movie released by a sub-Saharan African director. His final film *Moolaadé* won awards at Cannes and the premier African film festival Fespaco. Predating Sembène is Egyptian film-maker Youssef Chahine, who made the musical melodrama *Cairo Station* in 1958.

Algeria far outstrips any other African country for Oscar nominations in the category of Best Foreign Language Film, with five nominations, including *Z*, which won the award in 1969.

Sarah Maldoror filmed *Sambizanga* in Congo in the early 1970s, although the movie is set in Angola. *Chronicle of the Year of Embers* won the coveted Palme d'Or at Cannes in 1975 for Algerian director Mohammed Lakhdar-Hamina. Mauritanian director Abderrahmane Sissako's *Waiting for Happiness* gained international attention in 2002.

The continent's most technically accomplished film-makers gather in South Africa – local talent Neill Blomkamp's sci-fi thriller *District 10* was an international hit in 2009. Several major Hollywood productions have been shot at Cape Town Film Studios, including the Cape Town–set thriller *Safe House* (2012).

# African Music

**They don't call Africa the Motherland for nothing. The continent has a musical history that stretches back further than any other, a history as vast and varied as its range of rhythms, melodies and overlapping sources and influences. Here, music – traditional and contemporary – is as vital to communication and storytelling as the written word. It is the lifeblood of communities, the solace of the nomad, the entertainment of choice.**

## Cross-Cultural Influences

Without African music there would be no blues, reggae or – some say – rock, let alone Brazilian samba, Puerto Rican salsa, Trinidadian soca or any of a wide array of genres with roots in Africa's timeless sounds. And it works both ways: colonialism saw European instruments such as saxophone, trumpet and guitars integrated into traditional patterns. Independence ushered in a golden era; a swath of dance bands in 1970s Mali and Guinea spawned West African superstars such as Salif Keita and Mory Kante. Electric guitars fuelled Congolese rumba and *soukous* and innumerable other African genres (including Swahili rumba). Ghana's guitar-based high-life (urban dance music) blended with American hip-hop to become hip-life; current faves include Tic Tac, Sarkodie and prank-rap duo FOKN Bois. Jazz, soul and even classical music helped form the Afrobeat of late Nigerian legend Fela Kuti (which carries on through his sons, Femi and Seun, and a host of others today).

## Music of North Africa

*Sauti za Busara* (Sounds of Wisdom; www.busaramusic.org) Swahili Music Festival in Stonetown, Zanzibar, is one of East Africa's finest annual events: a four-days-in-February extravaganza of music, theatre and dance before a horizon dotted with dhow boats.

Africa's music may have a multiplicity of styles, but even within Africa's regions there's great variety, and that's particularly so in North Africa.

In Algeria it's all about the oft-controversial trad-rock genre *rai* (think Khaled, Messaoud Bellemou, the late grand dame Cheikha Rimitti) and the street-style pop known as *chaabi* (Arabic for 'popular'). Many of Algeria's Paris-based musicians are performing at home again: check out rocker Rachid Taha and folk chanteuse Souad Massi. In Egypt the stern presence of late diva Oum Kalthoum, the Arab world's greatest 20th-century singer, is everywhere; scratch the surface for a thrumming industry that includes pop stars Amr Diab and Samira Said, along with the 'Voice of Egypt' Mohammed Mounir and composer and pianist Omar Khairat.

There is also *chaabi* in Egypt and Morocco, along with the Arabic techno pop called *al-jil* and a wealth of other influences. The Berber shepherdess blues of Cherifa, the Maghreb's very own Aretha, have made her a singer-sheika (or popular artist) to be reckoned with. The pentatonic healing music of the Gnaoua – chants, side drums, metal castanets, the throbbing *guimbri*-lute (long-necked lute) – hijacks Essaouira each June during the huge Gnaoua and World Music Festival.

## Music of East Africa

East Africa may be one of the continent's economic and political powerhouses, but East African music is often overlooked, lacking the name-brand recognition and irresistible rhythms of West or Central Africa.

In the east, *bongo flava* (that's Swahili rap and hip-hop) is thriving; as is *taarab*, the Arab- and Indian-influenced music of Zanzibar and the Tanzanian-Kenyan coastal strip. Hip-hop hybrids are creating musical revivals in countries such as Tanzania and Kenya; Rwanda is nodding along to female hip-hop acts such as Knowless and Allioni.

Ethiopian jazz is enjoying an international renaissance thanks to the likes of Mulatu 'Daddy from Addy' Astatke and pianist and rising star Samuel Yirga.

## Music of Central Africa

If you hear dance music while in Africa, chances are that it comes from the Democratic Republic of Congo. With echoes of the Cuban *son* style, Congoloese rumba, for which the region is best known, was born in the 1940s but came into its own in the decades that followed with the legendary Franco and his TPOK Jazz. Its offshoot, *soukous*, is the quintessentially Congolese sound, with mellifluous beats and rippling guitar riffs that you can shake your booty to. Papa Wemba (who died in 2016 and was performing to the last) was the finest exponent of the art. Koffi Olomide and the late Madilu System are also played across Africa.

For something a little different, Konono No1 has made its name by playing electric thumb pianos to great effect and popular acclaim.

*Sout el Horreya* (I'm Not Turning Around; search www.youtube.com) by Amir Eid and Hany Adel became the anthem for anti-government protestors in Egypt's Tahrir Sq and beyond in November 2011.

## Music of Southern Africa

Down in Zimbabwe they're listening to the *tuku* (swinging, rootsy, self-styled) music of Oliver Mutukudzi or, in secret, the *chimurenga* (struggle) music as created by their self-exiled Lion, Thomas Mapfumo. Mozambique sways to the sound of *marrabenta* – Ghorwane is a roots-based urban dance band and a national institution – and the marimba style known as *timbila*.

In South Africa, where the ever-popular *kwaito* rules supreme (think slowed-down, rapped-over house music), the country's giant recording industry continues to rival that of Europe and America, embracing everything from the Zulu *iscathimiya* call-and-response singing as

### CLASSIC AFRICAN ALBUMS

- *Savane* (Ali Farka Touré; 2006)
- *Zombie* (Fela Kuti; 1976)
- *Specialist in All Styles* (Orchestra Baobab; 2002)
- *In the Heart of the Moon* (Ali Farke Touré and Toumani Diabaté; 2005)
- *Khaled* (Khaled; 1992)
- *Best of Miriam Makeba and the Skylarks* (Miriam Makeba; 1998)
- *The Black President* (Fela Kuti; 1981)
- Soro (Salif Keita; 1987)
- *Bouger Le Monde!* (Staff Benda Bilili; 2009)
- *Father Creeper* (Spoek Mathambo; 2012)
- *Dimanche á Bamako* (Amadou and Mariam; 2004)
- *Worotan* (Oumou Sangare; 1996)
- *Aman Iman: Water is Life* (Tinariwen; 2007)
- *Home is Where the Music Is* (Hugh Masekela; 1972)
- *Shaka Zulu* (Ladysmith Black Mambazo; 1987)
- *The Very Best Of The Rumba Giant Of Zaire* (Franco; 2000)
- *Ethiopiques* (various artists)

### BEST NEW WEST AFRICAN ALBUMS

- *Emmar* (Tinariwen; 2014)
- *Music in Exile* (Songhoy Blues; 2015)
- *Tzenni* (Noura Mint Seymali; 2014)
- *New Era* (Kiss Daniel; 2016)
- *God Over Everything* (Patoranking; 2016)

popularised by Ladysmith Black Mambazo, to jazz, funk, gospel, reggae, soul, pop, rap, Afrofuturism and all points in between.

Once-exiled artists such as Hugh Masekela and Abdullah Ibrahim have returned to South Africa to inspire a new generation of artists who include the likes of R&B soulstress Simphiwe Dana and Afro-fusion popsters Freshlyground.

## Music of West Africa

Across West Africa the haunting vocals of the *griots* and *jalis*, the region's oral historians–cum-minstrels, are ubiquitous. In Mali the *jelimuso* (female *griot*) Babani Koné rules, though *jalis* in the country's north are currently out of work because of Islamic extremism; in Mauritania *griot* Veirouz Mint Seymali is poised to fill the formidable shoes of her late mother, the iconic Dimi Mint Abba.

Mali's Arabic-flavoured *wassoulou* rhythms have their most famous champion in songbird Oumou Sangaré, just as the 21-string *kora*, one of the traditional instruments of *griot* and *jali*, is closely linked to Toumani Diabaté. Others are making their mark: Guinea's electric *kora* master Ba Cissoko is pushing the envelope. *I Speak Fula*, the 2009 album by *ngoni*-player Bassekou Kouyaté, was nominated for a Grammy.

The mighty Youssou N'Dour kick-started Senegal's pervasive *mbalax* rhythms when he mixed traditional percussion with plugged-in salsa, reggae and funk – though today it's Wolof-language rap groups that really appeal to the kids (there's a natural rap vibe to the country's ancient rhythmic poetry, *tasso*). Elsewhere, militant artists such as Côte d'Ivoire reggae star Tiken Jah Fakoly, former Sudanese child soldier-turned-rapper Emmanuel Jal, and Somalia's 'Dusty Foot Philosopher', rapper and poet K'Naan, are telling it like it is.

With the passing of Ali Farka Touré in 2006, his son Vieux Farka Touré is – along with redoubtable Bambara blues guitarist Boubacar Traore – continuing the Malian guitar blues legacy. Guitar heroes abound throughout Africa, the Congo's Diblo Dibala, Malagasy originator Jaojoby and South African axeman Louis Mhlanga among them.

There's nomad desert blues in exile to be had, from Tuareg guitar bands such as Tinariwen, Tamikrest, Terakaft and Etran Finatawa to the so-called 'Jimi Hendrix of Niger' (well, each country's got to have one) Omara 'Bombino' Moctar. In the Côte d'Ivoire, Abidjan remains a hugely influential centre for music production (if you can make it here, you'll probably make it in Paris), while the percussive, melodious and totally vacuous coupé-décale dance music sound fills stadiums. Seek out the likes of reggae legend Alpha Blondy and fusionist Dobet Gnahoré – the latter in charisma and vocal power not unlike Beninese diva Angélique Kidjo.

Over in Cameroon they're whooping it up to the guitar-based *bikutsi* and the brass-heavy sound of *makossa* while the polyphonic voices of that country's pygmies have struck a chord with the Western world. Down in Congo and Gabon, all you''ll hear are the sounds of rumba and soukous, though most comes from the DRC in Central Africa.

### Music Sites

- *Afropop Worldwide (www.afropop.org)*
- *African Music Encyclopedia (www.africanmusic.org)*
- *AfricMusic (www.africmusic.com)*
- *Sterns Music (www.sternsmusic.com)*
- *African Hip Hop (www.africanhiphop.com)*
- *Akwaaba Music (www.akwaabamusic.com)*

# Environment

**Africa is the oldest land mass in the world, but this tells only half the story. Atop a foundation where 97% of what's under your feet has been in place for over 300 million years sits an astonishing breadth of landscapes, from the world's biggest desert to some of the largest rivers, lakes and tracts of rainforests on the planet, and stirring mountains and iconic savannah. Inhabiting these epic landscapes is the richest and largest collection of wildlife anywhere in the world.**

## The Land

Africa is the world's second-largest continent, after Asia, covering 30 million sq km and accounting for 23% of the total land area on earth. From the most northerly point, Cap Blanc (Ra's al Abyad) in Tunisia, to the most southerly point, Cape Agulhas in South Africa, is a distance of approximately 8000km. The distance between Cap Vert in Senegal, the westernmost point in mainland Africa, and Raas Xaafuun in Somalia, the continent's most easterly point, is 7400km. Such are the specs of this vast continent when taken as a whole. But zoom in a little closer and that's when the story really gets interesting.

### Mountains & the Great Rift Valley

East and Southern Africa is where the continent really soars. It's here that you find the great mountain ranges of the Drakensberg in South Africa and Rwenzori (the fabled Mountains of the Moon) that straddle the borders of Uganda and Democratic Republic of Congo (DRC), as well as classic, stand-alone, dormant volcanoes such as Mt Kenya (5199m) and Mt Kilimanjaro (5895m), Africa's highest peak. And then there's Ethiopia, Africa's highest country, which lies on a plateau between 2000m and 3000m above sea level – in the space of a few hundred kilometres, the country rises to the Simien Mountains and Ras Dashen (4543m), then drops to 120m below sea level in the Danakil Depression.

Perfect armchair-travel fodder, BBC Earth's *Africa* series (2013) is simply magnificent, with episodes 'Kalahari', 'Savannah', 'Congo', 'Cape', 'Sahara' and 'The Future'. Also excellent is the earlier *Wild Africa* series (2001), which consists of six documentaries entitled 'Jungle', 'Coasts', 'Mountains', 'Deserts', 'Savannahs' and 'Rivers & Lakes'.

North and West Africa also have plenty of topographical drama to call their own. In the far northwest of the continent, the Atlas Mountains of Morocco – formed by the collision of the African and Eurasian tectonic plates – run like a spine across the land, scaling the heights of Jebel Toubkal (4167m), North Africa's highest peak. In West Africa, Mt Cameroon (4095m) is the highest point, while other notable high-altitude landmarks include the Fouta Djalon plateau of Guinea and the massifs of the Aïr (Niger) and Hoggar (Algeria) in the Sahara.

The African earth deep beneath your feet is being slowly pulled apart by the action of hot currents, resulting in a gap, or rift. This action over thousands of years has formed what's known as the Great Rift Valley, which begins in Syria and winds over 5000km before it peters out in southern Mozambique. The valley is flanked in many places by sheer escarpments and towering cliffs, the most dramatic of which can be seen in Ethiopia, Kenya, and along DRC's border with Uganda and Rwanda. The valley's floor contains the legendary wildlife-watching habitats of the

Serengeti and Masai Mara in Tanzania and Kenya, alkaline lakes such as Bogoria and Turkana, and some of Africa's largest freshwater lakes.

### Deserts

Geologists believe that if the process that created the rift continues, the Horn of Africa may one day break away from the African mainland and become an island, just as Madagascar did in the distant past.

Deserts and arid lands cover 60% of Africa. Much of this is the Sahara, the world's largest desert at over 9 million sq km, which is comparable in size to the continental USA. The Sahara occupies 11 countries, including more than half of Mauritania, Mali and Chad, 80% of Niger and Algeria and 95% of Libya. Contrary to popular misconception, sand covers just 20% of the Sahara's surface and just one-ninth of the Sahara rises as sand dunes. More typical of the Sahara are the vast gravel plains and plateaus such as the Tanezrouft of northeastern Mali and southwestern Algeria. The Sahara's other signature landform is the desert massif: barren mountain ranges of sandstone, basalt and granite such as the Hoggar (or Ahaggar) Mountains in Algeria, Aïr Mountains in Niger and Mali's Adrar des Iforas. By one estimate, the Sahara is home to 1400 plant species, 50 mammal species and 18 bird species.

Another little-known fact about the Sahara is that this is the youngest desert on earth. As recently as 8000 years ago, the Sahara was a fertile land, made up of savannah grasslands, forests and lakes watered by relatively regular rainfall, and home to abundant wildlife. Around 7000 years ago rains became less frequent and by 400 BC the Sahara was the desert we know today, albeit on a smaller scale.

If the Sahara is a relatively recent phenomenon, the Namib Desert in Namibia is one of the world's oldest – a staggering 55 million years old. It was created (and is sustained) by cold-air convection that sucks the moisture from the land and creates an arid landscape of rolling sand dunes with its own unique ecosystem. Even larger than the Namib, the Kalahari Desert spans Botswana, Namibia and South Africa and is around the size of France and Germany combined.

**Diving Wonders**

- *Dahab, Red Sea Coast, Egypt*
- *Aliwal Shoal, South Africa*
- *Ifaty, Madagascar*
- *Zanzibar, Tanzania*
- *Bazaruto Archipelago, Mozambique*
- *Malindi Marine National Park, Kenya*
- *Pemba, Tanzania*
- *São Tomé & Príncipe*
- *Lake Malawi, Malawi*

### Forests

African forests include dry tropical forests in eastern and Southern Africa, humid tropical rainforests in western and central regions, montane forests and subtropical forests in northern Africa, as well as mangroves in the coastal zones.

Despite the myth of the African 'jungle', Africa actually has one of the lowest percentages of rainforest cover in the world – just one-fifth of Africa is covered by forests, with over 90% of what's left found in the Congo basin. Not surprisingly, the countries of West and Central Africa have the highest proportion of their territory covered by forest – Gabon (84.5%), Guinea-Bissau (73.7%), Congo (65.6%), DRC (58.9%) and Equatorial Guinea (58.2%). Mauritania (0.3%) and Niger (1%) have almost no forests left.

The rainforest of the Congo Basin and Madagascar supports the greatest and most specialised biodiversity on the continent: 80% to 90% of species found in these biomes are endemic. The Congo Basin is also one of the last havens for gorilla, chimpanzee and other endangered primates.

Beyond their biodiversity mantle, however, forests are essential to the livelihood of many communities, providing food, fuel, livelihood, medicine and spiritual well-being.

### Savannah

The savannah is a quintessentially African landform, covering an estimated two-thirds of the African land mass. Savannah is usually located in a broad swath surrounding tropical rainforest and its sweeping plains are home to some of the richest concentrations of wildlife on earth, especially in East Africa. The term itself refers to a grasslands ecosystem. While trees may be (and usually are) present, such trees do not, under

## SHRINKING LAKE CHAD

Lake Chad once straddled the borders of Chad, Niger, Nigeria and Cameroon, and its waters are essential to the lives of 20 million people around its shores and in its hinterland. This was once the sixth-largest lake in the world and Africa's second-largest wetland, supporting a rich variety of wildlife. But falling rainfall, a growing population (and hence increased water consumption) and a notoriously shallow average depth of 4.11m have taken their toll: Lake Chad has shrunk by 95% over the past 35 years. Although satellite imagery from the European Space Agency suggests that things may be improving and a few recent years of greater rainfall have sparked a minor recovery, Lake Chad has retreated from Niger and Nigeria, and its extent in Chad and Cameroon is just one-tenth of the lake's original size.

the strict definition of the term, form a closed canopy, while wet and dry seasons (the latter often with regenerating and/or devastating wildfires) are also typical of Africa's savannahs. The Serengeti is probably the continent's most famous savannah region.

### Rivers

Africa's waterways are more than stunning natural phenomena. They also serve as the lifeblood for millions of Africans who rely on them for transport, fishing and water. The Nile (6650km) and Congo (4700km) Rivers dominate Africa's hydrology, but it's the Niger River (4100km), Africa's third-longest, that is the focus of most environmental concern.

The Niger's volume has fallen by 55% since the 1980s because of climate change, drought, pollution and population growth. Fish stocks have fallen, water hyacinth is a recurring problem and the growth of sand bars has made navigation increasingly difficult. Given that an estimated 110 million people live in the Niger's basin, problems for the Niger could cause a catastrophic ripple well beyond the river's shoreline. In 2008 the alarming signs of a river in distress prompted nine West African countries to agree on a US$8 billion, 20-year rescue plan to save the river. In the years since, progress has been slow with already-scarce resources diverted to fighting Islamist insurgencies.

### Lakes & Wetlands

Africa has its share of famous lakes. Lake Victoria, which lies across parts of Uganda, Tanzania and Kenya, is Africa's largest freshwater lake (and the second largest by area in the world after North America's Lake Superior). Lake Tanganyika, with a depth of 1471m, is the world's second-deepest lake after Lake Baikal in Russia, while Lake Malawi, which borders Malawi, Mozambique and Tanzania, is reportedly home to more fish species (over 1000) than any other lake on earth.

Less a lake than one of the world's largest inland deltas, the Okavango Delta is home to a stunning array of wildlife, with over 2000 plant and 450 bird species. The delta's 130,000-strong elephant population is believed to be close to capacity, with increasing conflict between elephants and farmers around the delta's boundaries.

### Coastal Africa

Along the coast of East Africa and the Red Sea, warm currents provide perfect conditions for coral growth, resulting in spectacular coral reefs. Off the west coast, the Benguela current, which shadows Angola, Namibia and South Africa, consists predominantly of nutrient-rich cold water. Whales, sharks and turtles are common all along the African coastline – South Africa and Madagascar in particular are whale-watching hotspots.

#### River Trips

*White-water rafting, Zambezi River, Zimbabwe*

*Cruising on the Nile, Egypt*

*Canoe excursions, Okavango Delta, Botswana*

*Travelling along the Congo River, DRC*

*Canoeing the Orange River, Botswana/ Namibia*

*Rafting the Great Usutu River, Swaziland*

Coral reefs are the most biologically diverse marine ecosystems on earth, rivalled only by tropical rainforests. Corals grow over geologic time – that is, over millennia rather than the decades that mammals live – and have been in existence for about 200 million years. The delicately balanced marine environment of the coral reef relies on the interaction of hard and soft corals, sponges, fish, turtles, dolphins and other life forms.

Coral reefs also rely on mangroves, the salt-tolerant trees with submerged roots that form a nursery and breeding ground for birds and most of the marine life that migrates to the reef. Mangroves trap and produce nutrients for food and habitat, stabilise the shoreline, and filter pollutants from the land base.

## Biodiversity

African wildlife accounts for almost a third of global biodiversity and its statistics alone tell the story – a quarter of the world's 4700 mammal species are found in Africa, as are a fifth of the world's bird species and more fish species than on any other continent. Discoveries in the 1990s in Madagascar alone increased the numbers of the world's known amphibian and reptile species by 25% and 18% respectively.

The continent's highest point is the perpetually (for now) snow-capped Kilimanjaro (5895m) in Tanzania, and the lowest is Lake Assal (153m below sea level) in Djibouti.

The continent is home to eight of the world's 34 biodiversity hotspots, as defined by Conservation International. To qualify, a region must contain at least 1500 species of vascular plants and have lost at least 70% of its original habitat. Three of these touch on South Africa (where 34% of terrestrial ecosystems and 82% of river ecosystems are considered threatened), with others in West Africa, Madagascar, the Horn of Africa, the coastal forests of East Africa and the Great Rift Valley.

## National Parks

Africa's protected areas range from world-class national parks in eastern and Southern Africa to barely discernible wildlife reserves in West Africa.

Southern African countries lead the way in protected area cover, with Zambia and Botswana the only two countries in Africa having put aside more than 30% of their territory for conservation (36% and 31%, respectively). In eastern Africa, Tanzania wins the stakes, with 27% of its surface area registered as protected, against just 12% and 10% in Kenya and Uganda. West Africa is a mixed bag, with countries like Guinea-Bissau, Benin and Senegal all scoring around 25%, while many of their neighbours hover around the 10% mark. All in all, 11.5% of sub-Saharan Africa is protected, but the proportion is much lower in North Africa (4%), which has very few national parks.

Africa has numerous examples of transfrontier national parks that stand out as shining examples of neighbourly cooperation. There are more than a dozen of these spread around the continent; among the ones you're most likely to encounter are the Park Régional du W, which spans Niger, Benin and Burkina Faso; the Masai Mara, which encompasses Kenya's Masai Mara National Reserve and Tanzania's Serengeti

### KILIMANJARO'S MELTING ICE CAP

Glittering white, like a mirage behind its veil of cloud, Mt Kilimanjaro's perfect white cap of ice is one of Africa's most iconic images. It has also become a *cause célèbre* in the debate over global warming. According to the UN, Kilimanjaro's glaciers have shrunk by 80% since the early 20th century and the mountain has lost over a third of its ice in the last 20 years alone. The causes are complex and not solely attributable to rising temperatures, with deforestation also to blame – the upper limit of the mountain's forests has descended significantly and overall forest cover has, thanks to fire, decreased by 15% since 1976. Whatever is to blame, some estimates suggest that Kilimanjaro's ice could disappear completely by 2025.

### AFRICAN PARKS

When it comes to rebuilding some of Africa's most vulnerable national parks, non-profit African Parks (www.african-parks.org) has done an outstanding job. Together with local governments, it takes over the long-term management of national parks and protected areas, focusing on saving wildlife, restoring landscapes and building sustainable futures for local communities. Its funding comes from a range of sources, including governments, philanthropists, conservation organisations and ordinary donors.

In Southern Africa, African Parks is responsible for five parks: Bangweulu Wetlands and Liuwa Plain National Park in Zambia; and Liwonde National Park, Majete Wildlife Reserve and Nkhotakota Wildlife Reserve in Malawi. In some of these areas its work has been nothing short of miraculous.

Beyond Southern Africa, African Parks also counts Rwanda's Akagera National Park within its portfolio, while its remaining four parks inhabit war zones or areas where government or any other control is minimal: Zakouma National Park (Chad), Garamba National Park (DRC), Odzala-Kokoua (Republic of Congo) and Chinka (Central African Republic).

National Park; and the Great Limpopo Transfrontier Park, which links South Africa's Kruger and Mozambique's Limpopo National Parks.

## Environmental Challenges

Africa is the second-most populous continent after Asia, and population growth, although slowing, is still the highest in the world. This, along with poor natural resource management and the increasing effects of climate change, are putting tremendous pressure on the environment.

### Climate Change

Africa, like everywhere else in the world, is grappling with climate change. The irony for the continent is that it has historically contributed little to the greenhouse gas emissions responsible for global warming.

Whatever part Africa played in climate change, the effects are likely to be significant. According to the Intergovernmental Panel on Climate Change (IPCC), Africa will likely experience temperature increases of 2°C to 4°C (more than the global average) over the coming century, which will in turn disrupt rainfall patterns. Although forecast models still produce mixed results, it is thought that northern and Southern Africa will become drier, while equatorial parts of the continent will turn wetter and East Africa more unpredictable.

The impact of this climatic upheaval will be broad-ranging, from disruption to agricultural yields and cropping systems to reduced water availability, changes in ecosystem boundaries and an increase in extreme weather events (such as cyclones, drought and flooding).

> Forty million metric tonnes of Saharan sand reaches the Amazon annually, replenishing mineral nutrients depleted by tropical rains. Half of this dust comes from the Bodele Depression on the Niger–Chad border.

### Deforestation

African forests are under threat: thousands of hectares are being chopped not only for timber, but also for firewood and charcoal, and to be cleared for agriculture.

A recent report by international forest-policy group the Rights and Resources Initiative (www.rightsandresources.org) found that African forests are disappearing at a rate four times faster than forests anywhere else in the world. The reason, according to the study, is that less than 2% of the continent's forests are under the control of local communities – over half of the rainforests of the Congo basin are already under commercial-logging leases – compared to around a third in Latin America and Asia.

East and Central Africa have the most to lose and the signs there aren't good – Burundi is losing around 5% of its forest cover every year, with

## GREEN HEROES

Along with the dozens of well-known conservation organisations, there are many Africans fighting in the environment's corner at the grassroots level.

The Goldman Environmental Prize (www.goldmanprize.org) is an annual award that honours these green heroes on each continent. The prize has been dubbed the 'green Nobel' and many of its recipients have become role models for a generation. Among the most famous African winners are Kenyan Green Belt Movement founder and Nobel Peace Prize laureate Wangari Maathai (1940–2011); Nigerian oil campaigner Ken Saro-Wiwa (1941–95), who was hanged by a military court for his defence of the rights of the Ogoni people in the Niger Delta; and founder of the NGO Brainforest and activist Marc Ona-Essangui, from Gabon, whose advocacy led to a change in the country's environmental legislation.

Other winners may not be as well known but they are just as deserving, their work focusing on anything from poaching to conservation and sustainable development. The prize is awarded in April every year; profiles of all laureates can be found on the Goldman Foundation's website.

massive deforestation issues in Central African Republic, Cameroon, Kenya, Tanzania and Zambia. West Africa is faring little better. Over 90% of West Africa's original forest has been lost, while Nigeria and Ghana in particular are losing forest cover at an alarming rate.

Internationally, these figures raise concern over the effect such large-scale deforestation has on global warming. At a local level major side effects include soil erosion (with its devastating impact on agriculture), loss of biodiversity and an increase in the amount of wildlife hunted for bushmeat as new roads and accompanying settlements penetrate the forests.

### Desertification

As forest cover diminishes, all too often the desert moves in. Desertification is one of the most serious forms of land degradation and it's one to which the countries of the West African Sahel and North Africa are particularly vulnerable. Desertification has reached critical levels in Niger, Chad, Mali and Mauritania, each of which some believe could be entirely consumed by the Sahara within a generation; up to 80% of Morocco is also considered to have a high risk of desertification. The Sahara's southward march is by no means a uniform process (and some scientists even doubt its existence), but the Sahel in particular remains critically vulnerable to short-term fluctuations in rainfall.

Desertification is also a problem for countries beyond the Sahelian danger zone: a high to moderate risk of desertification exists in numerous West African countries, as well as Botswana, Namibia, DRC, Central African Republic, Kenya, Ethiopia, Sudan and Somalia.

In 1950 there were, on average, 13.5 hectares of land for every person in Africa. By 2050 that figure will have shrunk to 1.5 hectares.

The major causes of desertification are easy to identify – drought, deforestation, overgrazing and agricultural practices (such as cash crops, which require intensive farming) that have led to the over-exploitation of fragile soils on the desert margin – and are the result of both human activity and climatic variation. But one of the most significant causes in West Africa is the use of deliberately lit fires. Such fires are sometimes necessary for maintaining soil quality, regenerating savannah grasslands and ecosystems, enabling livestock production and as a form of pest control. But when the interval between fires is insufficient to allow the land to recover, the soil becomes exposed to wind and heavy rains and can be degraded beyond the point of recovery.

## Water

Africa has enormous water resources. The trouble is that they are unevenly distributed and often hard to access: the amount of groundwater stored in aquifers is thought to be 100 times the volume available in surface water. This spatial and temporal inequality is what causes scarcity. The continent also faces quality issues: pollution and increased salinity due to over-extraction of coastal aquifers are growing concerns.

African governments also have a poor track record in water resource management. Urban utilities lose 20% to 50% of the water they produce through leaks in their networks and few irrigation systems use modern, efficient drip-irrigation technology. In Egypt, for example, irrigated agriculture uses 90% of the country's water. And in Libya, prior to the fall of Colonel Qaddafi and the country's descent into civil conflict, vast amounts of non-renewable 'fossil' water (from deep aquifers) were being piped over hundreds of kilometres along the Great Manmande River to provide drinking water to cities along the coast.

Africa only accounts for 3% of carbon credits on the market while CO2 emissions per head in Africa are four times lower than the world average.

## Community-Based Conservation

While the history of environmental protection in Africa is one that often saw Africans evicted from their land to make way for national parks, the future lies in community-based conservation. This local, as opposed to large-scale, approach is based on the tenet that in order for the African environment to be protected, ordinary Africans must have the primary stake in its preservation.

## Poaching

Rhino horn has long been a sought-after commodity in some Asian countries. It is a status symbol and is believed to be a healing agent. By one estimate, rhino horn can sell on the black market in China or Vietnam for US$60,000 per kilo and has been as high as US$100,000. Ivory prices regularly rise above US$2000 per kilo. Both products are now, literally, worth more than their weight in gold.

From the 1970s various factors led to an increase in elephant poaching in many parts of Africa. The real money was made not by poachers – often villagers who were paid a pittance for the valuable tusks – but by dealers. The number of elephants in Africa went from 1.3 million to 625,000 between 1979 and 1989, and in East Africa and some Southern African countries – notably Zambia – elephant populations were reduced by up to 90% in about 15 years. In other Southern African countries, where parks and reserves were well managed, in particular South Africa, Botswana and Namibia, elephant populations were relatively unaffected.

In 1989, in response to the illegal trade and diminishing numbers of elephants, a world body called the Convention on International Trade in Endangered Species (CITES) internationally banned the import and export of ivory. It also increased funding for anti-poaching measures. When the ban was established, world raw ivory prices plummeted by 90%, and the market for poaching and smuggling was radically reduced.

Tanzania has the second-largest network of coral reefs in Africa (after Egypt), at 3580 sq km, and its waters are home to 150 different species of coral.

In 2009 everything changed and poachers again began killing elephants (and rhinos) in great numbers. Perhaps tellingly, a year earlier, in 2008, a number of Southern African countries were allowed to sell their ivory stockpiles to China and Japan, thereby reigniting demand that had shown no signs of growth in decades. Whatever the reason, the killing hasn't stopped since. Most worrying of all, a 2014 study found that Africa's elephants had crossed a critical threshold: poachers now kill more African elephants each year than there are elephants being born.

Governments and park authorities are, of course, fighting back and innovative ways of tracking down poachers are being deployed. But for the moment, the poachers seem to be winning.

# Wildlife

**Africa is home to more than 1100 mammal species and some 2400 bird species. Throughout the continent, wildlife brings drama and life to the beauty of the African landscape. Your first sight of elephants in the wild, chimpanzees high in the forest canopy, or a lion or cheetah on the hunt will rank among the most unforgettable experiences of your trip. Many national parks and reserves across Africa provide refuges for wildlife under threat from changing land use and wars – but even here poaching is a persistent problem and one that conservationists report is getting worse.**

## Elephants

The African elephant, the largest living land animal, are plentiful in many areas of Africa but their survival is not assured.

In 1989, when the trade in ivory was banned under the Convention for International Trade in Endangered Species (CITES), elephant population numbers began to climb again from dangerously low levels. However, illegal poaching continues to feed demand in Asia, particularly in China.

Published in 2016 and the most comprehensive survey of the continent's elephants ever undertaken, the Great Elephant Census (www.greatelephantcensus.com) found that 352,271 African savanna elephants survive in 18 countries. These figures represent a 30% fall in Africa's elephant population over the preceding seven years.

Seeing the 'Big Five' has become a mantra for African wildlife-watchers, but few know it was coined by white hunters for the five species deemed most dangerous to hunt: elephant, lion, leopard, rhino and buffalo.

## Primates

### Gorillas

The last refuges in West and Central Africa of the world's largest living primate have too often occupied war zones. In the Democratic Republic of Congo (DRC), the mountain gorilla's forest habitat has often come under the control of rebel armies; in the first half of 2007, seven gorillas were shot in DRC's Parc National des Virunga. Poaching, the Ebola and Marburg viruses and even the trade in bushmeat have all contributed to the vulnerability of gorillas. The most endangered subspecies is the Cross

**ELEPHANT SPOTTING**

- Chobe National Park, Botswana
- Hwange National Park, Zimbabwe
- Serengeti National Park, Tanzania
- Masai Mara National Reserve, Kenya
- Kruger National Park, South Africa
- Etosha National Park, Namibia
- Damaraland, Namibia
- Addo Elephant National Park, South Africa
- Gorongosa National Park, Mozambique

**GORILLA SPOTTING**

- Bwindi Impenetrable National Park, Uganda
- Volcanoes National Park, Rwanda
- Loango National Park, Gabon
- Parc National d'Odzala, Republic of Congo
- Parc National Nouabalé-Ndoki, Congo
- Monte Alen National Park, Equatorial Guinea

River gorilla living in the highland forests of Cameroon and Nigeria, numbering no more than 300.

It's not all bad news. In recent years the world's population of critically endangered mountain gorillas has risen to a total of 880 (400 in the Bwindi Impenetrable National Park, and 480 in the Virunga Masiff), which is up from the estimate of 786 animals in 2010.

Across the other side of Africa, a staggering 125,000 western lowland gorillas were discovered in 2008 in the swamps of northern Congo, almost doubling previous projections; the WWF puts the current population at 100,000.

### Chimpanzees & Other Primates

Chimpanzees are the animal world's closest living relative to humans, with whom they share 99% of their genetic make-up. You'll find these sometimes playful, sometimes cranky creatures throughout Africa and they're usually more accessible (and cheaper to see) than gorillas.

## Cats

### Lions

The peak cat conservation body Panthera (www.panthera.org) estimates that fewer than 20,000 lions remain in Africa (there is a tiny population of Asian lions in the Gir Forest in Gujarat state in India). While that may seem like a lot, the IUCN classifies the lion as Vulnerable, not least because many lions live in small, fragmented and isolated populations that may not be sustainable beyond the short term.

Only six lion populations in Africa – Botswana's Okavango Delta and the broader ecosystem to which it belongs in Namibia, Zambia and Zimbabwe, along with the Serengeti/Masai Mara, and Tanzania's Ruaha National Park and Selous Game Reserve – are sufficiently protected to hold at least 1000 lions. That's the conservation gold standard that Panthera applies for guaranteeing the long-term survival of the species.

### Leopards

Leopards are present throughout sub-Saharan Africa and, unlike lions, are at home in most African landscapes, from the semidesert to tropical rainforest. In addition to places where lions are found, leopards can be spotted in Kenya's Lake Nakuru and Tsavo West National Parks.

In Southern Africa, try Savuti in Botswana, Zambia's South Luangwa and Kafue National Parks, South Africa's Kruger National Park, Malawi's Nyika National Park and Namibia's Namib-Naukluft National Park. In West Africa, leopards are found in Niger's Parc Regional du W.

Leopards are listed as Vulnerable on the International Union for the Conservation of Nature (IUCN) Red List of Threatened Species.

The status of the world's species is determined by the International Union for the Conservation of Nature (IUCN), which oversees the IUCN Red List of Threatened Species (www.iucnredlist.org). Each species is assessed according to a set of rigorous scientific criteria and classified as Least Concern, Near Threatened, Vulnerable, Endangered, Critically Endangered, Extinct in the Wild or Extinct.

### Cheetahs

The fastest land animal on earth (it can reach speeds of 75km/h in the first two seconds of its pursuit and at full speed may reach 115km/h), the cheetah in full flight is one of the most thrilling sights in the African wild. Cheetahs inhabit mostly open country, from the savannah to the desert, and they're most easily spotted in the major national parks of Kenya, Tanzania, Namibia, Botswana, South Africa and Zambia.

Watching gorillas in the wild doesn't come cheap. In Rwanda, gorilla permits cost US$1500 per person, while it costs around US$600 in Uganda. It's slightly cheaper in Gabon (US$487) and Republic of Congo (around US$267).

At the end of 2016, a scientific study confirmed what many conservationists in the field had long feared – the cheetah is in trouble. The latest estimates suggest that just 7100 cheetahs remain in the wild, all of which live in Africa save for an isolated population of around 50 in the deserts and mountains of central Iran.

Between two-thirds and half of Africa's surviving cheetahs live in Southern Africa, which effectively remains the cheetah's last stronghold. More than three-quarters of Africa's wild cheetahs live outside protected areas.

## Hoofed Animals

### Rhinoceros

Rhinos rank among Africa's most endangered large mammals. These inoffensive vegetarians are armed with impressive horns that have made them the target of both white hunters and poachers – rhino numbers plummeted to the brink of extinction during the 20th century.

There are two species of rhino, black and white, both of which are predominantly found in savannah regions. White rhinos aren't white at all – the name comes from the Dutch word *wijd*, which means wide and refers to the white rhino's wide lip (the black rhino has a pointed lip).

The survival of the white rhino is an environmental-conservation success story, having been brought back from the brink of extinction in South Africa through captive breeding. As a result, it is now off the endangered list. Black rhinos are thought to now number between 5000 and 5500, with small but encouraging gains made in recent years. The

### WILDLIFE WATCHING: THE BASICS

- Most animals are naturally wary of people, so to minimise their distress (or aggression) keep as quiet as possible, avoid sudden movements and wear subdued colours when in the field.
- Avoid direct eye contact, particularly with primates, as this is seen as a challenge and may provoke aggressive behaviour.
- Good binoculars are an invaluable aid to observing wildlife at a distance and are essential for birdwatching.
- When on foot, stay downwind of animals wherever possible – they'll smell you long before they see or hear you.
- Never get out of your vehicle unless it's safe to do so.
- Always obey park regulations, including traffic speed limits; thousands of animals are needlessly killed on African roads every year.
- Follow your guide's instructions at all times – it may mean the difference between life and death on a walking safari.
- Never get between a mother and her young.
- Exercise care when boating or swimming, and be particularly aware of the dangers posed by crocodiles and hippos.
- Never feed wild animals – it encourages scavenging, may adversely affect their health and can cause animals to become aggressive towards each other and humans.

### RHINO SPOTTING

- Ngorongoro Crater, Tanzania
- Liwonde National Park, Malawi
- Ziwa Rhino Sanctuary, Uganda
- Etosha National Park, Namibia
- Damaraland, Namibia
- Khama Rhino Sanctuary, Botswana
- Nairobi National Park, Kenya
- Matobo National Park, Zimbabwe
- Meru National Park, Kenya
- Ol Pejeta Conservancy, Kenya
- Lewa Conservancy, Kenya
- North Luangwa National Park, Zambia

West African black rhino was declared extinct in 2006, while just three Northern white rhinos live in captivity at Kenya's Ol Pejeta Conservancy and all attempts for them to breed have so far proved to be unsuccessful.

Current estimates for white rhinos stand at between 19,682 and 21,077.

Primate conservation is about far more than gorillas and chimps – 37% of primate species in mainland Africa are considered endangered, with the figure at 43% in Madagascar.

## Hippopotamus

Hippos, the third-heaviest land mammal on earth (after the elephant and white rhino), are found throughout sub-Saharan Africa, with the largest numbers in Tanzania, Zambia and Botswana. They're usually seen wallowing in shallow water in lakes, ponds and rivers, although the wave-surfing hippos in Gabon's Loango National Park are international celebrities. They're also one of the most dangerous animals in Africa, thanks to their aggression towards humans and propensity for attacking boats.

## Giraffes

One of the most worrying developments in recent years has been the downgrading of the giraffe by the IUCN from Least Concern in 2010 to Vulnerable in 2016. The world's tallest land mammal remains widespread across Southern and East Africa, but a precipitous 40% decline (from an estimated 151,702 to 163,452 individuals in 1985 to 97,562 in 2015) has brought the species' fate into sharp focus.

The main threats to the giraffe are illegal hunting, habitat loss, increasing human-wildlife conflict and civil conflict.

Africa's rarest hoofed creature is the okapi. Just 20,000 of this zebra-giraffe hybrid survive. You can catch a rare glimpse in the breeding centre in DRC's Okapi Wildlife Reserve.

## Wildebeest

The annual migration of more than a million wildebeest, the largest single movement of herd animals on earth, is one of the grandest wildlife spectacles you could imagine. It all takes place in Kenya's Masai Mara National Reserve and Tanzania's Serengeti National Park from June to October.

## Antelope

Antelope range from the tiny, knee-high dik-dik and duiker, through to the graceful gazelle, impala and springbok, to giants such as the buffalo, eland and kudu. Many of these will be seen on a typical East or Southern African safari.

### MADAGASCAR: A WORLD APART

In any discussion of African wildlife, Madagascar rates a separate mention for its unique treasure trove of endemic wildlife that has remained virtually unchanged since the island split from the mainland 165 million years ago. Most of Madagascar's wildlife exists nowhere else on earth, including 98% of its land mammals, 92% of its reptiles, and 41% of bird species. Most famous are its lemurs, a group of primates that have followed a separate evolutionary path. Lemurs have adapted to nearly every feeding niche, and range in size from tiny pygmy mouse lemurs (at 85g, the world's smallest primate) to the 2.5kg ring-tailed lemur. Perhaps the most curious, however, is the indri, which looks like a cross between a koala and a giant panda, and has a voice like a police siren. The best wildlife-watching in Madagascar is to be found at Réserve Spécial d'Analamazaotra, Parc National de l'Isalo and Parc National de Ranomafana.

West Africa also has its share of antelope species, including bushbucks, reedbucks, waterbucks, kobs, roans, elands, oribis and various gazelles and duikers. The Sahel-dwelling dama gazelle is the largest gazelle species in Africa, but is now close to extinction, and the red-fronted gazelle may still survive in Mali's remote far east. Buffalos in West Africa inhabit forest regions, and are smaller and redder than the East African version.

## Birds

Even if you're not into birdwatching, Africa's abundant and incredibly varied birdlife could turn you into an avid birder. In most sub-Saharan countries, you're likely to see hundreds of different species without looking too hard, and a bit of preparation – there are some excellent field guides – can greatly enhance your visit. Birds reach their highest profusion in the Congo rainforests, but are easier to see in habitats such as rainforest, savannah and wetland. Several bird families, such as the ostrich, secretary bird, touracos, shoebill, hamerkop and mousebird are unique to Africa. Apart from endemic species, hundreds more species flood into the continent on migration during the northern winter.

### Bird Spotting

It is estimated that 500 million birds from Europe and Asia migrate to tropical Africa every year, a journey of up to 11,000km – fewer than half make it home, either dying en route or preferring to remain in Africa.

Any of East Africa's major national parks are good for birdwatching. Kenya has recorded 1200 bird species and, in particular, Kakamega Forest Reserve, Lake Naivasha and the flamingos of Lake Nakuru National Park stand out. Tanzania, with over 1000 species, isn't far behind – Lake Manyara National Park is a good choice. Southern Ethiopia is also prime birding country, especially the Rift Valley Lakes and Bale Mountains National Park.

In Southern Africa, Malawi's Nyika National Park, Liwonde National Park and Vwaza Marsh Wildlife Reserve are prime birders' destinations. Madagascar, too, has plenty of interest, especially in Parc National Ranomafana and Réserve Spécial d'Analamazaotra, as does Namibia at Swakopmund, Caprivi Strip and Etosha National Park. Elsewhere, Botswana's Okavango Delta and Zimbabwe's Hwange National Park won't disappoint.

West Africa lies along one of the busiest bird migratory routes between Europe and Africa, and more than 1000 species have been recorded in the region. Tiny Gambia has a devoted following in the birding community. Good places include Abuko Nature Reserve, Tanji Bird Reserve and Kiang West National Park. Senegal also offers excellent birding, particularly in Parc National des Oiseaux du Djoudj and Parc National de la Langue de Barbarie; both are famous for vast pelican and flamingo flocks. Sierra Leone is also good; notably, Outamba-Kilimi National Park supports more than 250 species, including the spectacular great blue turaco.

# Survival Guide

# Directory A–Z

## Accommodation

### Camping

A tent usually saves you money, and can be vital in some national parks or wilderness areas. However, it's not essential for travel in Africa, as many campsites have simple cabins, with or without bedding and cooking utensils. Official campsites, of varying quality and security, allow you to pitch a tent, as do most backpackers' hostels.

In Southern Africa, especially in Botswana and Namibia, most 4WD rentals come with full camping equipment, including tents (ground or roof), bedding and all cooking equipment. Advance booking for campsites in Southern Africa is essential.

Be cautious about 'wild camping' – you may be trespassing on private land or putting yourself at risk from attack by animals.

In rural areas, if there's no campsite, you're usually better off pitching your tent near a village. Seek permission from the village chief first, and you'll probably be treated as an honoured guest and really get under the skin of Africa.

### Homestays

In rural areas you can sometimes arrange informal 'homestays' simply by politely asking for somewhere to bed down and get a dish of local food, in return for a payment.

Do not get carried away with bargaining – pay a fair fee, normally the cost of a cheap hotel.

### Guesthouses & B&Bs

B&Bs and guesthouses are interchangeable terms in much of Southern Africa.

They range from a simple room in someone's house to well-established B&Bs with five-star ratings and deluxe accommodation.

B&Bs and guesthouses are most prevalent in South Africa, where the standards are high and features such as antique furniture, private verandahs, landscaped gardens and a pool are common.

Indeed some of the finest accommodation on the continent is found in B&Bs along the Garden Route. Breakfast is usually included and almost always involves gut-busting quantities of eggs, bacon, toast and other cooked goodies.

In West Africa (especially Burkina Faso), B&Bs can go by the names of *chambres d'hôtes* or *maisons d'hôtes*. They operate along similar lines to B&Bs, with a more personal or intimate experience than hotels.

### Hostels

Hostels aimed squarely at backpackers line the popular routes from Nairobi to Cape Town, although elsewhere in Africa they're less common. Most have beds in a dorm, as well as double or twin rooms.

Backpackers' hostels are good places to get information on stuff to do or onward transport, and they also offer a range of cheap safaris and tours.

A potential downside is that you'll be surrounded by fellow travellers, rather than the Africans you came to meet.

### Hotels

Africa's hotels range from no-frills establishments to sky's-the-limit dens of luxury. Under the 'hotel' category you could also be bedding down at a guesthouse, B&B, rest house, *pensao* (in Mozambique) or *campement* (in West Africa). The latter is a simple rural hotel, often with a campsite attached. A cheap

**BOOK YOUR STAY ONLINE**

For more accommodation reviews by Lonely Planet authors, check out http://lonelyplanet.com/hotels/. You'll find independent reviews, as well as recommendations on the best places to stay. Best of all, you can book online.

local hotel in East Africa is called a *gesti* or lodgings, while *hoteli* is Swahili for basic eating place.

In cheaper local hotels it's rare to get a private bathroom, and you can forget air-conditioning. Other 'extras' such as a fan or mosquito net usually increase the price. Africa has a huge choice of midrange hotels, and standards can be high, especially in privately run (as opposed to government-run) places.

### Lodges & Tented Camps

Lodges and tented camps are the prestige end of the safari market and it's important to note that 'camp' doesn't necessarily denote a campsite (although it may). A camp sometimes refers to a well-appointed, upmarket option run by a private company. Accommodation is usually in tents or chalets made from natural materials. The contact number for these places will be for their office in a larger town and are for bookings and inquiries only, not for direct contact with the lodge or camp.

In upmarket lodges and camps the rates will typically include accommodation plus full board, activities (wildlife drives, boat trips etc) and perhaps even house wine and beer. It may also include laundry and transfers by air or 4WD (although these are usually extra).

Lodges and tented camps are particularly prevalent in Southern and East Africa, although there are some high-end outposts elsewhere.

## Bargaining

In many parts of Africa, especially in markets and/or craft and curio stalls, items are worth whatever the seller can get. Once you get the hang of bargaining, it's all part of the fun. Hagglers are rarely trying to rip you off, so there's no point getting hot and bothered about it. Decide what price you're prepared to pay and if you can't get it, decline politely and move on.

## Children

Approached sensibly, many families find an African holiday a rewarding and thrilling experience. While some posh hotels, lodges and tented camps ban kids under a certain age, some higher-end safari lodges run special wildlife-watching programs for kids, and babysitting services are available in some midrange and top-end hotels.

On the whole, Africans adore children, and wherever your kids go they will be assured of a warm reception and a host of instant new friends.

### Practicalities

Outside the main cities, you can pretty safely assume that disposable nappies won't be available, so bring everything you need with you. Child car seats, high chairs in restaurants and cots in hotels are rare except in top-end hotels in tourist areas. Hygiene is likely to be a major issue – carry a hand sanitiser with you.

## Customs Regulations

➡ At some borders you may have your bag searched, but serious searches are rare.

➡ Anything made from an endangered animal is likely to land you in trouble. You'll also need a permit from the Ministry of Antiquities or a similar office in the relevant country if you are exporting valuable cultural artefacts (no, not that 'ebony' hippo carving you bought on the beach with the shoe polish that comes off on your hands). It usually applies to artefacts that are more than 100 years old.

➡ Some countries limit the local currency you can take in or out, although small amounts are unlikely to be a problem. You can carry CFA francs between countries in the CFA zones.

➡ A few countries have restrictive exchange regulations, and occasionally you may need to fill in a declaration form with details of your dollars or other 'hard' currencies.

## Dangers & Annoyances

The overwhelming majority of travellers to Africa return home without encountering any of the following problems. That said, be aware of potential issues and keep your wits about you.

➡ Research your destination carefully and make note of any potential trouble spots in advance.

➡ Don't make yourself a target. Carry as little as possible and don't wear jewellery or watches. Keep the bulk of your cash hidden under loose-fitting clothing.

➡ Don't walk city streets after dark. Take a taxi.

➡ Walk purposefully and confidently. Never look like you are lost (even if you are!).

➡ Always be discreet with your possessions.

### Crime

Most Africans are decent, hard-working people who want from you only respect and the chance to make an honest living; given the extreme poverty levels, robbery rates are incredibly low. Even so, you need to be alert on the streets of some cities. Nairobi (Kenya) is often called 'Nairobbery', Lagos (Nigeria) is not for the faint-hearted, while Dakar (Senegal), Abidjan (Côte d'Ivoire) and parts of Johannesburg (South Africa) all have edgy reputations. Snatch-theft and

## GOVERNMENT TRAVEL ADVICE

The following government websites offer travel advisories and information for travellers.

**Australian Department of Foreign Affairs & Trade** (www.smartraveller.gov.au)

**Canadian Department of Foreign Affairs & International Trade** (www.voyage.gc.ca)

**French Ministère des Affaires Étrangères et Européennes** (www.diplomatie.gouv.fr/fr/conseils-aux-voyageurs)

**Italian Ministero degli Affari Esteri** (www.viaggiaresicuri.mae.aci.it)

**New Zealand Ministry of Foreign Affairs & Trade** (www.safetravel.govt.nz)

**UK Foreign & Commonwealth Office** (www.gov.uk/foreign-travel-advice)

**US Department of State** (www.travel.state.gov)

pickpocketing are the most common crimes, but violent muggings can occur, so it pays to heed local warnings.

## Emergencies

Generally speaking, emergency services in most African countries are not what you'd be used to at home. For example, if you're robbed or attacked, don't count on the police to respond quickly (or at all) when you dial an emergency number. However, you'll have to visit the police to report the offence – otherwise your insurance won't be valid – so expect an all-day form-filling process. Likewise, if you're sick or injured, don't waste time phoning an ambulance – get a taxi straight to a hospital or clinic. And if you want a private medical service or an English-speaking doctor, ask for directions at an embassy or a top-end hotel.

## Scams

The main annoyance you'll come across in Africa is the various hustlers, touts, con men and scam merchants who always see tourists as easy prey. Although these guys are not necessarily dangerous, some awareness and suitable precautions are advisable, and should help you deal with them without getting stung.

## War Zones

Going to a war zone as a tourist is, to put it bluntly, bloody stupid. Unless you're there to help out with a recognised aid agency and are qualified to do so, you'll be no help to anyone, and you'll quite likely get yourself kidnapped or killed.

At the time of writing, it was considered unsafe to visit Angola, Burundi, Central African Republic, Chad, Tunisia, Libya, Mali, Niger, Somalia and South Sudan, while there may be some areas within countries (eg Sahara regions of Mauritania) that we recommend you steer clear of for the time being.

# Electricity

Most countries use a 220/240V current, but some mix 110V and 240V. Some (eg Liberia) still use mostly 110V. Generally, in English-speaking countries, sockets are the British type. In Francophone parts of Africa they're the Continental European two-pin variety. South Africa has yet another system. In some countries you'll find whatever people can get hold of. Some countries (such as Botswana) use two different kinds of plugs. If possible, purchase plug adaptors before travelling.

Beware: power cuts and surges are part of life in many African countries.

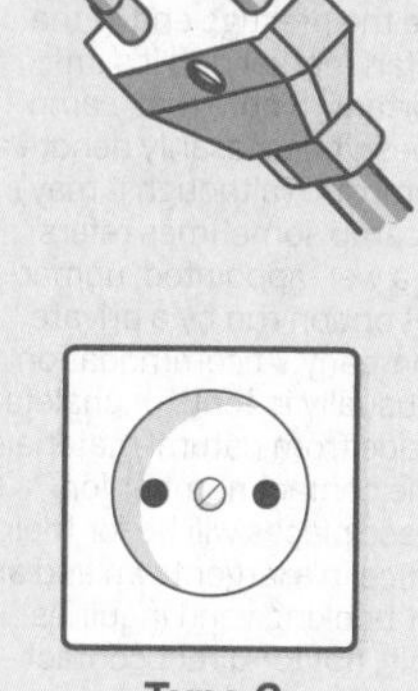

Type C

Type G

## Embassies & Consulates

If you get into trouble on your travels, it's important to realise what your embassy can and can't do to help. Remember that you're bound by the laws of the country you are in, and diplomatic staff won't be sympathetic if you're jailed after committing a crime locally, even if such actions are legal at home.

In genuine emergencies you might get some assistance, but only if other channels have been exhausted. For example, to get home urgently, a free ticket is exceedingly unlikely – the embassy would expect you to have insurance. If all your money and documents are stolen, staff might assist with getting a new passport, but a loan for onward travel is out of the question.

On the more positive side, some embassies (especially US embassies) have notice boards with 'travel advisories' about security or local epidemics. If you're heading for remote or potentially volatile areas, it might be worth registering with your embassy, and 'checking in' when you come back.

## Emergency & Important Numbers

Emergency numbers differ from one country to the next. Some have a general emergency number, others have separate numbers for police, fire and ambulance services.

In most African countries, the prefix to use for dialling international numbers from within Africa is ☎00. The main exception is Nigeria (☎009).

| EMERGENCY NUMBER | COUNTRIES |
|---|---|
| ☎019 | Sierra Leone |
| ☎111 | Côte d'Ivoire |
| ☎112 | Lesotho, South Africa, Benin, Burkina Faso, Cameroon, Nigeria, São Tomé & Príncipe, Angola, DRC, Kenya, Rwanda, Uganda, Tanzania |
| ☎113 | Eritrea, Equatorial Guinea |
| ☎117 | Guinea-Bissau, Republic of Congo, Togo, Burundi, Central African Republic |
| ☎119 | Mozambique |
| ☎10111 | Namibia |
| ☎122 | Guinea, Egypt |
| ☎1515 | Libya |
| ☎17 | Mali, Mauritania, Niger, Chad, Djibouti, Senegal, The Gambia |
| ☎18 | Algeria |
| ☎19 | Morocco |
| ☎177 | Gabon |
| ☎191 | Ghana |
| ☎197 | Tunisia |
| ☎888 | Somalia |
| ☎911 | Liberia, Ethiopia |
| ☎999 | Botswana, Malawi, Swaziland, Zimbabwe, Sudan, South Sudan, Zambia |

## Insurance

Travel insurance to cover theft and illness is essential. Although having your camera stolen by monkeys or your music player eaten by a goat can be a problem, the medical cover is by far the most important aspect because hospitals in Africa are not free, and the good ones aren't cheap. Simply getting to a hospital can be expensive, so ensure you're covered for ambulances (land and air) and flights home.

Some insurance policies forbid unscheduled boat or plane rides, or exclude dangerous activities such as white-water rafting, canoeing or even hiking. Others also don't cover people in countries subject to foreign office warnings. Others are more sensible and understand the realities of travel in Africa. Ask your travel agent or search on the web, but shop around and read the small print to make sure you're fully covered.

Worldwide travel insurance is available at www.lonelyplanet.com/travel-insurance. You can buy, extend and claim online anytime – even if you're already on the road.

## Internet Access

- There are cybercafes in most capitals and major towns, although many of these are disappearing as wi-fi becomes more widespread.
- Many hotels and hostels also offer internet access. Midrange and top-end hotels increasingly offer wi-fi; sometimes you have to pay but most often it's free.
- Although things are improving, many connections (both wi-fi and and in internet cafes) can be excruciatingly slow, meaning that uploading photos to the Cloud or emailing attachments can prove arduous.

## Legal Matters

The buying, selling, possession and use of all recreational drugs is illegal in every country in Africa. In most countries, if you're arrested you have the right to a phone call – this should probably be to your embassy.

Otherwise, the legal situation varies from country to country.

## LGBTIQ Travellers

- African societies are conservative towards gays and lesbians; same-sex relationships are a cultural taboo, and there are very few openly gay communities. Officially, homosexuality (male, female or both) is illegal in many African countries, with homosexual acts risking the death penalty in Mauritania and in parts of Nigeria, Somalia and Sudan.
- Although prosecutions rarely occur, discretion is key and public displays of affection should generally be avoided, advice which applies to both homosexual and heterosexual couples.
- Cape Town is Africa's most gay-friendly city, with a lively club scene and a welcoming vibe.

### Resources

**Afriboyz** (www.afriboyz.com/Homosexuality-in-Africa.html) Worth checking out for (often-dated) links to gay issues around the continent.

**David Travel** (www.davidtravel.com) A US-based tour company offering specialist tours for gay men and women.

**Global Gayz** (www.globalgayz.com/africa/) Links to information about the situation for gays and lesbians in most African countries.

**ILGA** (www.ilga.org) Another good resource with information for many West African countries.

## Maps

Buy Michelin maps of Africa – No 741 *North & West*, No 745 *North-East* and No 746 *Central & South* – before you leave home. Expect a few discrepancies, particularly with regard to roads, as rough tracks get upgraded and smooth highways become potholed disasters. For these and other African maps in the UK, try Stanfords (www.stanfords.co.uk). In France, IGN (www.ign.fr) sells its sheet maps at stores in Paris.

## Money

You can exchange your hard cash or travellers cheques into local currency at banks or foreign-exchange bureaus in cities and tourist areas. For cash, bureaus normally offer the best rates, low (or no) charges and the fastest service, but what you get for travellers cheques can be pitiful – if they're accepted at all.

ATMs are increasingly common but don't rely on them or being able to pay by credit card; always carry sufficient cash.

### ATMs

- In many (but by no means all) African countries you can draw local cash as you go with a credit or debit card. Visa is the most widely accepted card. Charges can be low and exchange rates are usually good, but check with your home bank or card provider before leaving.
- Although ATM numbers are on the rise, most are still located in capitals and major towns, plus there are usually daily withdrawal limits. What's more, due to dodgy phone lines, they frequently malfunction, so you'll still need a pile of hard cash as backup.
- Always keep your wits about you when drawing money out, as ATMs are often targeted by thieves. Try to visit them in busy areas during daylight hours, and stash your money securely before you move away.

### Black Market

In countries with controlled exchange rates, you can get more local money for your hard currency by dealing with unofficial moneychangers on the so-called black market, instead of going to a bank or bureau. This helps with costs, but it's illegal and sometimes dangerous – think twice before you do it.

However, you may have to resort to unofficial methods if you're stuck with no local cash when banks and exchange offices are closed. Hotels or tour companies may help, although rates are lousy. Try shops selling imported items. Be discreet though: 'The banks are closed, do you know anyone who can help?' is better than a blunt 'D'you wanna change money?'.

Even in countries with free exchange rates (and therefore no black market), moneychangers often lurk at borders where there's no bank. Although illegal, they operate in full view of customs officers, so trouble from this angle is unlikely.

There's more chance of trouble from the moneychangers themselves, so make sure you know the exchange rates, and count all local cash carefully, *before* you hand over your money. Watch out for old or folded notes. A calculator ensures you don't miss a zero or two on the transaction. And beware of 'Quick, it's the police' tricks, where you're panicked into handing over money too soon. Use common sense and you'll have no problem, but it's best to change only small amounts to cover what you'll need until you reach a reliable bank or exchange office.

### Credit & Debit Cards

- Credit or debit cards are handy for expensive items such as tours and flights, but most agents add a hefty

10% surcharge. It's therefore often cheaper to use your card to draw cash from an ATM, if one is available.

- If there's no ATM, another option is to withdraw money from a local bank using your card, but be warned – this also incurs a charge of around 5%, and can be an all-day process, so go early.
- Before leaving home, check with your own bank to see which banks in Africa accept your card (and find out about charges). Cards with the Visa logo are most readily recognised, although MasterCard is accepted in many places.
- Whatever card you use, don't rely totally on plastic, as computer or telephone breakdowns can leave you stranded. Always have cash or (less helpful) travellers cheques too.
- To avoid credit-card fraud, always make sure that you watch the transaction closely and destroy any additional transaction slips that are produced, whether innocently or otherwise.

### Currencies

Whether you're carrying cash or travellers cheques, or both, give some thought to the currency you take before you leave home. This will depend on the countries you visit. Whatever currency you decide on, take a mixture of high and low denominations. Smaller denominations can be handy if you need to change money to last just a few days before leaving a country.

### Tipping

The situation with regard to tipping varies across the continent, but as a general rule the following applies:

**Hotels & Restaurants** Usually expected in top-end hotels and restaurants, very rarely in cheaper places.

**Safari Lodges** Count on US$10 per guest per day, plus more for guides.

**Taxis** Rounding up is usually sufficient.

### Travellers Cheques

- Never make travellers cheques your sole source of money.
- The pros are that they're secure – ATMs sometimes don't work and cash, unlike travellers cheques, cannot usually be replaced if lost.
- The cons are that many countries don't accept travellers cheques, and in those that do it's rare to find a bank that will change them outside major cities, commissions can be prohibitive, you'll spend a lot of time waiting and they're often a pain to deal with.
- When exchanging travellers cheques, most banks also check the purchase receipt (the paper you're supposed to keep separate) and your passport, so make sure you have these with you (and keep a copy elsewhere in a secure location).
- You can sometimes pay for items such as safaris and activities directly with travellers cheques, but most operators add a surcharge – usually 10%, but sometimes up to 20%, because that's what banks charge them.

## Opening Hours

Standard opening hours vary from country to country. As a general rule, the working week runs from Monday to Friday; some shops and tourism-related businesses sometimes open on Saturdays, either all day or just in the morning. In some predominantly Muslim countries, some businesses may close on Friday (either all day or just in the morning), and instead open on Sunday.

## Photography

A simple point-and-shoot is fine for mementos of people, landscapes, market scenes and so on, but for better-quality shots, especially of animals, you'll need a zoom lens and maybe an SLR camera with changeable lenses. It's also worth taking a couple of spare batteries with you and charging them whenever you have a reliable electricity source for those times when you're travelling in remote areas. For the same reasons, take extra memory cards and a cleaning kit. Africa's extremes of climate, especially heat, humidity and very fine sand, can also take their toll on your camera, so always take appropriate precautions; changing lenses in a dust-laden wind is, for example, a recipe for disaster.

Other useful photographic accessories might include a small flash, a cable or remote shutter release and a tripod. Absolutely essential is a good padded bag, containing at least one desiccation sac, and sealed to protect your camera from dust and humidity. Avoid leaving your camera on the floor of buses or cars, as the jolting could well destroy the delicate inner workings of the lens.

For more advice, Lonely Planet's *Guide to Travel Photography* is an excellent resource, full of helpful tips for photography while on the road.

## Post

If you want to send a letter, parcel or postcard, it's always better doing this from a capital city. From some countries, the service is remarkably quick (just two or three days to Europe, a week to the USA or Australia). From others it really earns the snail-mail tag, but it's still more reliable than sending stuff from really remote areas.

You can use the poste-restante service at any post office where mail is held for collection. Letters should be addressed clearly with surname underlined and in capitals, to '(Your Name), Poste Restante, General Post

Office, Lusaka, Zambia', for example. In French-speaking countries, send it to 'Poste Restante, PTT', then the name of the city.

To collect mail, you need your passport, and to sometimes pay about US$0.50 per item. Letters sometimes take a few weeks to arrive, so have them sent to a town where you'll be for a while or will be passing through more than once – although in some places mail is only held for a month, then returned to the sender.

The price, quality and speed for parcel post varies massively from place to place; courier companies can sometimes be more reliable than government postal services and not always a lot more expensive.

# Public Holidays

## Christian Holidays

Most countries with significant Christian populations celebrate one or more of the following:

**Good Friday** March or April

**Easter Sunday** March or April

**Easter Monday** March or April

**Christmas Day** 25 December

## Other Holidays

In addition to the Islamic ceremonies, there are many public holidays – either government or religious – when businesses and government offices are closed. Nonreligious public holidays may include New Year's Day (1 January) and Labour or Workers' Day (1 May). Government holidays are often marked with parades, dancing and other such events, while the Christian religious holidays invariably centre on beautiful church services and singing.

# Telephone

In most capital cities and major towns, phone connections are good. Thanks to satellite technology, it's often easier to make an international call than to dial someone 20km up the road. Rates vary from country to country, ranging from US$5 to US$15 for a three-minute call to Europe, the USA or Australia. Many cybercafes now offer dirt-cheap internet-connected phone calls, but the quality of the line depends on the quality of the internet connection – if it's a dial-up connection as opposed to ADSL, it's unlikely to be worth the effort.

## Bureaus

To call long distance or even locally, you're usually better off at a public-phone bureau than a booth in the street. In each city there's normally a bureau at the main post office, plus numerous privately run bureaus where rates can be cheaper and the service faster. At most bureaus you can also send or receive faxes.

## Mobile Phones

Mobile (cell) phones are almost universal in Africa, with connection rates, call rates and coverage improving all the time, although you're unlikely to have coverage in remote rural areas. You can buy local SIM cards just about everywhere where there's mobile coverage. Some local companies also offer rates for international calls that work out cheaper than using landlines.

To check whether your phone will work in the African countries you plan to visit, contact your network provider. Ask about charges as well – and don't forget that if anyone rings you while you're overseas, the bulk of the cost goes on *your* bill.

## Phonecards

In some countries you can buy phonecards that let you dial a local number, enter a PIN, and then make cheap international calls. You can also buy scratchcards to top up mobile phones, and phonecards to use in public booths instead of coins.

# Time

Africa is covered by four time zones, from UTC (formerly GMT) in the west to UTC plus three hours in the east. Crossing from Chad to Sudan there's a two-hour difference, but elsewhere it's one hour or none at all. At borders where there's a one-hour time difference

## ISLAMIC HOLIDAYS

Since the Islamic calendar is based on 12 lunar months totalling 354 or 355 days, holidays are always about 11 days earlier than the previous year. The exact dates depend on the moon and are announced for certain only about a day in advance. Estimated dates for these events are:

| EVENT | 2017 | 2018 | 2019 | 2020 | 2021 |
|---|---|---|---|---|---|
| Ramadan begins | 28 May | 17 May | 6 May | 25 Apr | 14 Apr |
| Eid al-Fitr | 27 Jun | 16 Jun | 5 Jun | 25 May | 14 May |
| Tabaski | 2 Sep | 22 Aug | 11 Aug | 1 Aug | 21 Jul |
| Eid al-Moulid | 12 Dec | 1 Dec | 20 Nov | 9 Nov | 30 Oct |

(eg Malawi–Tanzania), some have their opening and closing hours coordinated to avoid problems, but others don't – try to plan your travels at these crossings to avoid getting caught in no-man's land after you've been stamped out of one side, only to discover that the other side is already closed.

## Toilets

There are two types of toilet in Africa: the Western style, with a bowl and seat (common in most midrange or top-end hotels and restaurants); and the African style, a hole in the floor that you squat over. You might even find a combination of the two, with a Western-style toilet bowl propped over a hole in the floor. Standards vary tremendously, from pristine to those that leave little to the imagination as to the health or otherwise of the previous occupant. In our experience, a non-contact hole in the ground is better than a filthy bowl any day.

In rural areas, squat toilets are built over a deep hole in the ground and called 'long-drops'; the crap just fades away naturally, as long as the hole isn't filled with too much other material (such as tampons – these should be disposed of separately). Toilet paper is OK – although you'll need to carry your own. In Muslim countries, a jug of water or hosepipe arrangement is provided for the same task – use your left hand to wipe, then use the water to wash your hand. This is why it's a breach of etiquette in many countries to shake hands or pass food with the left hand.

Some travellers complain that African toilets are difficult to use, but it only takes a little practice to accomplish a comfortable squatting technique, and you'll soon become adept at assuming the position in one swift move, while nimbly hoiking your trouser hems up at the same time so they don't touch the floor.

## Tourist Information

Much of Africa isn't geared for tourism, and decent tourist offices are rare. Some countries have a tourist-information office in the capital, but apart from a few tatty leaflets and vague advice from the remarkably little-travelled staff, you're unlikely to get much. Tour companies, hotels and hostels are often better sources of information.

## Travellers with Disabilities

There are more people with disabilities per head of population in Africa than in the West, but wheelchair facilities are virtually nonexistent. Don't expect things like wheelchair ramps, signs in Braille, or any other facilities that are available in tourist areas in other parts of the world. Most travellers with disabilities find travel much easier with the assistance of an able-bodied companion, or with an organised tour through an operator that specialises in arranging travel for those with disabilities. Safaris in South Africa and diving holidays in Egypt are both easily arranged with companies like these.

A final factor to remember, which goes some way to making up for the lack of facilities, is the friendliness and accommodating attitude of the African people. In the majority of situations, they will be more than happy to help if you explain to them exactly what you need.

Before setting out for Africa, travellers with disabilities should consider contacting any of the following organisations, which may be able to help you with advice and assistance:

**Access-Able Travel Source** (www.access-able.com) US-based site providing information on disabled-friendly tours and hotels.

**Accessible Travel & Leisure** (www.accessibletravel.co.uk) Claims to be the biggest UK travel agent dealing with travel for people with a disability, and encourages independent travel.

**Endeavour Safaris** (www.endeavour-safaris.com) Focuses on Southern Africa.

**Epic Enabled** (www.epic-enabled.com) Trips in Southern Africa for people with disabilities.

**Mobility International USA** (www.miusa.org) In the US, it advises disabled travellers on mobility issues; it primarily runs educational exchange programs, and some include African travel.

**Society for Accessible Travel & Hospitality** (www.sath.org) In the US; offers assistance and advice.

**Tourism for All** (www.tourismforall.org.uk) Click on its 'Overseas Travel' page for links, although there's little of interest for travellers.

You can also download Lonely Planet's free Accessible Travel guide from http://lptravel.to/AccessibleTravel.

## Visas

For short trips sort out visas before leaving home; for longer ones, arrange as you go. In some countries they're available at borders, others not. Remember that regulations can change, so it's always worth checking before you enter the country.

For a short trip through Africa you might get all your visas before you leave home, which will save considerable hassle while on the road. For a longer trip, it's easier to get them as you go along.

Most countries have an embassy in each neighbouring country, but not all, so careful planning is required. And not all embassies issue visas; getting an Angolan visa in Namibia or an Ethiopian

### WARNING: ISRAELI STAMPS

A final note: if you have Israeli stamps in your passport, they may prove problematic when you enter Algeria, Libya and Sudan. Israeli border officials may stamp a piece of paper, which you can then remove, but, for example, your Egyptian entry-point can still be a giveaway.

visa in Kenya has been problematic in the past, for example.

Remember that some visas are valid from when they are issued, so you may have to enter the country pretty soon after getting them. On other visas you say when you plan to enter the country and arrive within a month of that date. Sometimes it's convenient (and relatively cheap) to get several visas in one place – South Africa or Kenya, for example.

Prices vary widely, but you can expect to pay US$10 to US$50 for standard one-month single-entry visas, and up to US$200 for three-month multiple-entry visas. If you want to stay longer, extensions are usually available for an extra fee, but only once you're in the country in question.

Rules vary for different nationalities: for example, British and Aussie citizens don't need advance visas for some Southern African countries; French citizens don't need them in much of West Africa; Americans need them nearly everywhere. The price of a visa also varies according to nationality (Irish-passport holders seem to be able to get free visas in dozens of countries!) and where you buy it. In some of Africa's more, ahem, informal countries, you'll also be factoring in the mood/corruption level of the person you're buying it from.

Most visas are issued in 24 or 48 hours – and it always helps to go to embassies in the morning – but occasionally the process can take a week or longer (such as for Sudan or Angola).

You may have to show you have enough funds to cover the visit, or prove that you intend to leave the country rather than settle down and build a hut somewhere. (This could be an air ticket home or a letter from your employer stating you're expected to return to work on a specified date.) For most visas you also need two or three passport photos, so take what you'll need, although you can get new supplies from photo booths in most capitals. Some embassies ask for a photocopy of your passport data page, so it's always worth carrying a few spare copies.

A few countries demand a *note verbale* (letter of recommendation) from your own embassy before they issue a visa. This is generally no problem as your embassy will be aware of this, but be prepared to fork out yet more cash. It'll say: 'This letter is to introduce Mr/Ms [name], carrying [British/French] passport No [1234]. He/she is a tourist travelling to [Chad]. Please issue him/her with a tourist visa. All assistance you can give would be most appreciated.' Or: 'Par la présente, nous attestons que Mr/Ms [Name] est titulaire de passport [Britannique/Française] No [1234]. Il doit se rendre au [Tchad] pour faire le tourism. Toute assistance que pourrait lui être accordée serait appréciée.'

Australians travelling in Africa have only eight of their own embassies or consulates on the entire continent, so it's handy to obtain a letter of introduction from the Passports section of the Department of Foreign Affairs & Trade before you leave home.

## Regional Visas

### WEST AFRICA

The Visa des Pays de l'Entente is a multi-country visa that covers travel in Benin, Burkina Faso, Côte d'Ivoire, Niger and Togo. If you've never heard of it, don't be surprised – it's so poorly publicised that most travellers never learn of its existence. Implementation of this relatively new visa is also still patchy, which significantly diminishes its appeal.

In remote border crossings there is also the danger that officials won't recognise the visa and will force travellers to purchase a new individual country visa or, worse still, return to some far-distant capital city to apply for a new one.

Before you go rushing off to your nearest West African embassy to ask for this visa, you need to learn how it works. For a start, it is only obtainable within these five West African countries, which means that you must obtain a visa for the first of these countries and, once there, apply at the immigration or visa extension office (or neighbouring country's embassy) in the capital city. To get the Visa des Pays de l'Entente, which is valid for two months, you'll need to take along CFA15,000 to CFA25,000 depending on the country, and up to two passport photos. It usually takes 24 to 72 hours for the visa to be issued.

Although the Visa des Pays de l'Entente may work out to be more convenient in some cases, it's worth remembering that it's only valid for one entry into each country: ideal for overlanders, less so for those who plan to visit countries more than once.

### EAST AFRICA

There is now an East African tourist visa covering Kenya, Rwanda and Uganda. Visas are issued for 90 days, cost

US$100 and allow for unlimited travel between these countries for the duration. Apply for the visa through the embassy of the first of the three countries you plan to visit.

At the time of writing, Tanzania was yet to sign on to the region visa, although it doesn't actually make a whole lot of difference. If you have a Tanzanian single-entry visa, you can travel to Kenya, Uganda, Burundi and Rwanda and return to Tanzania without having to obtain another visa, provided your visa is still valid and you don't go beyond these other four countries in the meantime.

## Volunteering

There are very few openings for ad-hoc volunteer work in Africa. Unless you've got some expertise, and are prepared to stay for at least a year, you're unlikely to be much use anyway. What Africa needs is people with skills. Just 'wanting to help' isn't enough. In fact, your presence may be disruptive for local staff and management, prevent locals from gaining employment or cause a drain on resources.

For formal volunteer work, which must be arranged in your home country, organisations such as Voluntary Service Overseas (VSO; in the UK) and the Peace Corps (in the US) have programs throughout Africa where people, usually with genuine training (eg teachers, health workers, environmentalists), do two-year stints. Similar schemes for 'gap-year' students (between school and university) tend to be for shorter periods, and focus on community-building projects, teaching or scientific research. Almost all these projects require an additional financial donation, which may be raised by sponsorship and fundraising in your home country.

The following international organisations are good places to start gathering information on volunteering, although they won't necessarily always have projects on the go in Africa.

**African Impact** (www.africanimpact.com)

**African Volunteer Network** (www.african-volunteer.net)

**Australian Volunteers International** (www.australianvolunteers.com)

**Coordinating Committee for International Voluntary Service** (ccivs.org)

**Earthwatch** (www.earthwatch.org)

**Frontier Conservation Expeditions** (www.frontier.ac.uk)

**Idealist** (www.idealist.org)

**International Citizen Service** (ICS; www.volunteerics.org)

**International Volunteer Programs Association** (www.volunteerinternational.org)

**Peace Corps** (www.peacecorps.gov)

**Step Together Volunteering** (www.step-together.org.uk)

**UN Volunteers** (www.unv.org)

**Volunteer Abroad** (www.goabroad.com/volunteer-abroad)

**Volunteer Service Abroad** (www.vsa.org.nz)

**VSO** (www.vso.org.uk)

**Worldwide Experience** (www.worldwideexperience.com)

### SOLO TRAVELLERS

Travelling alone in Africa is, for the most part, an exciting and liberating experience. Being on your own allows unbeatable flexibility and total immersion in the culture of the country you're travelling in.

Africans everywhere are incredibly sociable, so if you're looking for someone to chat to, you'll never be short of new friends eager to make your acquaintance. In some areas, fellow travellers can be easy to find, either at hostels or during those long waits at bus stations, although it depends how far off the beaten track you travel. And it's usually easy to make friends with local guides or hotel staff.

On the downside, prices for single occupancy in many African hotels are often not much less than for a double or twin room, and organised trips such as safaris can be prohibitively expensive if you're doing them on your own – you might have to wait around until a group comes along that you can attach yourself to. Travelling on your own might be regarded as rather bizarre by locals, but it's unlikely to be any more dangerous than being in a couple or group, even for solo women.

Female backpackers may be regarded with a mixture of bewilderment and suspicion in places unused to tourists, especially if alone. You should be at home rearing families or tending the crops, not engaged in frivolous pastimes like travel, the thoughts sometimes go. To show you do have a home life, you could carry photographs of family or friends, or even a mythical husband (unless you've got a real one, of course). Photos of yourself at work sometimes do the same trick.

## Women Travellers

It's no use pretending otherwise – women travelling in Africa (alone or with other women) will occasionally encounter specific problems, most often harassment from men. North Africa can be particularly tiresome from this perspective. And in places where an attack or mugging is a real possibility, women are seen as easy targets, so it pays to keep away from these areas (talk to people on the ground to get the latest situation).

But don't panic. On a day-to-day basis, compared to many places, travel in Africa is relatively safe and unthreatening, and you'll meet friendliness and generosity – not to mention pure old-fashioned gallantry – far more often than hostility or predatory behaviour. Many men are simply genuinely curious as to why on earth a woman is out travelling the world rather than staying at home with the babies, so keep an open mind and try not to be too hostile in the face of endless questions. Remember also that half of the authors who research in Africa for Lonely Planet are women and many of them travelled alone – and lived to tell the tale.

Having said that, when it comes to evening entertainment, Africa is a conservative society and in many countries 'respectable' women don't go to bars, clubs or restaurants without a male companion. However distasteful this may be to post-feminist Westerners, acting as if this isn't the reality may lead to trouble.

Meeting and talking with local women can be problematic. It may require being invited into a home, although since many women have received little education, unless you have learnt some of the local language, communication could be tricky. However, this is changing to some extent because a surprising number of girls go to school while boys are sent away to work. This means that many of the staff in tourist offices, hotels or government departments are educated women, and this can be as good a place as any to try and strike up a conversation. In rural areas, a good starting point might be teachers at local schools, or staff at health centres.

Some expatriates you meet may be appalled at the idea of a female travelling alone and will do their best to discourage you with horror stories, often of dubious accuracy. Others will have a far more realistic attitude. When you are on the road, the best advice on what can and can't be undertaken safely will come from local women. Use your common sense and things should go well. It's also worth remembering that, as a solo female traveller, it might be best to pay a little extra for midrange hotels where the surroundings may make you feel more comfortable – many of the cheapest hotels in African towns rent rooms by the hour.

### Sexual Harassment

Unwanted interest from male 'admirers' is an inevitable aspect of travel in Africa, especially for lone women. This is always unpleasant, but it's worth remembering that although you may encounter a lewd border official or a persistent suitor who won't go away, real harm or rape is very unlikely. If you're alone in an uneasy situation, act cold or uninterested, rather than threatened. Stick your nose in a book, or invent an imaginary husband who will be arriving shortly. If none of this works and you can't shake off a hanger-on, going to the nearest public place, such as the lobby of a hotel, usually works well, or you could try asking for help from local women in a public place. If the problem still persists, asking the receptionist to call the police usually frightens them off.

Part of the reason for the interest is that local women rarely travel long distances alone, and a single foreign female is an unusual sight. And, thanks to imported TV and Hollywood films (and the behaviour of some tourists), Western women are frequently viewed as 'easy'.

What you wear may greatly influence how you're treated. Most African women dress conservatively, in traditional or Western clothes, so when a visitor wears something different from the norm, she will draw attention. In the minds of some men this is provocative. In general, look at what other women are wearing and follow suit. Keep your upper arms, midriff and legs covered.

### Sanitary Protection

You can buy tampons and pads in most cities and major towns from pharmacies or supermarkets. Prices are about the same as in Europe, but you seldom have choice of type or brand. They're rarely found in shops away from the main towns, so you might want to bring supplies if you're spending a lot of time in remote areas.

## Work

It's hard for outsiders to find work in most African countries, as high unemployment means a huge number of local people chase every job vacancy. You will also need a work permit, and these are usually hard to get as priority is rightly given to qualified locals over travellers. You're unlikely to see many jobs advertised, so the best way to find out about them is by asking around among the expatriate community.

Most opportunities are usually in the fields of aid, conservation and tourism (such as working in a lodge or hotel, as a tour guide, as a diving instructor...); the latter sector is the one most likely to be looking for skilled overseas workers at shorter notice.

# Transport

## GETTING THERE & AWAY

Getting yourself into Africa can be as simple as booking a direct-flight ticket from a major European hub, or as adventurous as hitching a lift on a car ferry then jumping onto a cargo truck. However you choose to do it, it pays to do advance research to make sure you don't blow unnecessary bucks or time.

Flights, cars and tours can be booked online at lonelyplanet.com/bookings.

### Entering the Country

Entering African countries varies significantly from country to country – in some places you'll be across the border in no time, in others you'll spend hours waiting to get across. Obtaining visas on arrival at borders is increasingly possible, but by no means universal – research the situation before setting out. A valid passport, usually with at least six months validity remaining, is always required.

### Air

The bulk of air traffic with Africa is to and from Europe, but there are a handful of direct flights between Africa and North and South America, the Middle East and Asia. Many North American travellers pass through a European 'hub' en route to Africa. For Australasian travellers it's often cheaper to pass through a Middle Eastern and/or Asian hub before arriving.

#### Airports & Airlines

Africa's main international gateways:

**Cairo International Airport** (☎flight info phoning from landline 0900 77777, flight info phoning from mobile 27777; www.cairo-airport.com; 📶)

**Léopold Sédar Senghor International Airport** (DKR; ☎24hr info line 33 869 5050; www.aeroport-dakar.com)

**Jomo Kenyatta International Airport** (NBO; ☎0722205061, 020-6822111; www.kaa.go.ke)

**OR Tambo International Airport** (Ortia; ☎011-921 6262; www.airports.co.za)

**Mohammed V International Airport** (☎0522 43 58 58; www.onda.ma)

#### Tickets

Wild climatic variations across Africa, and differing holiday seasons in the northern and southern hemispheres, mean that it's tricky to pin down the cheapest times to fly to Africa – get the low-down on costs from a travel agent well in advance. Using mile-wide brushstrokes, it could be argued that flying from June to September or around Christmas (a 'peak season' that can last from November to March if you're

**CLIMATE CHANGE & TRAVEL**

Every form of transport that relies on carbon-based fuel generates $CO_2$, the main cause of human-induced climate change. Modern travel is dependent on aeroplanes, which might use less fuel per kilometre per person than most cars but travel much greater distances. The altitude at which aircraft emit gases (including $CO_2$) and particles also contributes to their climate change impact. Many websites offer 'carbon calculators' that allow people to estimate the carbon emissions generated by their journey and, for those who wish to do so, to offset the impact of the greenhouse gases emitted with contributions to portfolios of climate-friendly initiatives throughout the world. Lonely Planet offsets the carbon footprint of all staff and author travel.

## BORDER CROSSINGS

There are a lot of borders in Africa, and a whole lot more border posts. And let's be honest, crossing some of Africa's land borders requires the patience of a saint and may provide you with some of your more frustrating and dysfunctional tales from life on the road (even assuming that your visas and paperwork are in order). Endless baggage checks, overworked immigration officers, officials in search of a *cadeau* (gift) and long queues can all be a part of the mix. Others you'll fly through with neither delay nor incident.

Whichever is your experience, at all times remember that patience and politeness will see you through. Getting shirty with a person in uniform is one sure-fire way for 'discrepancies' to be discovered and delays to be even longer – you're the one who will end up paying for your impatience.

There's usually a border post on each side of the border crossing (ie one belonging to each country). Sometimes the border posts are just 100m apart, such as at the Namanga crossing between Kenya and Tanzania; sometimes they can be 100km apart, with a 'no-man's land' in between, such as those on the route between Algeria and Niger. If you're catching a bus 'to the border', check exactly how far it goes. Does it take you just to the first border post, from where you have to walk or take a taxi to the second one? Or does the bus go across the border all the way to the second border post, before you have to change to onward transport?

Although they're rare, it's also worth watching out for new border crossings. For example, the 'Unity Bridge' over the Rovuma River opened in 2010, becoming the main border crossing between Tanzania and Mozambique.

coming from Australasia) is going to hit your budget hardest.

### Departure Tax

Departure tax is usually included in the price of a ticket, but check when making your booking.

## Land

Africa's only land border divides Israel and Egypt in the Sinai – the continuing troubles in Israel and the Palestinian Territories mean that the direct route via Rafah is very often closed to foreigners, so make your way via the Eilat–Taba border crossing on the Gulf of Aqaba. However, note that if your passport has an Israeli stamp in it you won't get into some African countries; if this is going to be a problem, take the (car and passenger) ferry from Jordan.

## Sea

From various ports in southern Europe and the Middle East, towering car ferries, sleek powerful 'fast ferries' and hi-tech catamarans ply the routes across the Mediterranean.

### Egypt

There are daily ferries between Nuweiba in Sinai (Egypt) and Aqaba (Jordan), which is a stone's throw from Eilat (Israel). There are also four sailings per week from Port Said to Iskenderun in Turkey.

### Morocco

Two main companies sail the Spain to Morocco route: **Trasmediterránea** (www.trasmediterranea.es) and **FRS** (www.frs.es). All routes usually take vehicles as well as passengers, and most services increase in frequency during the summer months, when other routes are sometimes added. The two main routes:

- Almería–Nador
- Algeciras–Tangier

Longer-haul ferries that operate as part of the Cemar (www.cemar.it) network also sail between Tangier and Genoa (Italy).

### Algeria

Cemar (www.cemar.it) sails between Marseilles and Algiers, while Trasmediterránea (www.trasmediterranea.es) runs ferries from Almería in southern Spain to Ghazaouet (Algeria). You might also find summer services to Oran (Algeria) from Almería or southern France.

# GETTING AROUND

In Africa, the journey is very often the destination. There's everything from impossibly crowded minibus services along rutted roads to international-standard airlines between major cities.

**Air** Major capitals are reasonably well connected by flights within Africa; smaller capitals may require inconvenient connections.

**Bus & Bush Taxi** Often the only option in rural areas, bush or shared taxis leave when full; buses connect major cities.

**Car & 4WD** Reasonable road infrastructure connects major cities; roads deteriorate elsewhere, and are sometimes impassable after rains so 4WD is often required.

**Train** Trains operate in West Africa and South Africa with limited services elsewhere and very few cross-border operations.

# Air

Africa's internal air network is comprehensive; certainly, flying over the Sahara, Central African Republic and the often difficult South Sudan can be a good idea. Always check flight details carefully, but be prepared for delays and cancellations. Don't expect to be put up in a four-star hotel should your flight get canned.

If you're serious about taking a few African flights, consider sorting it out when booking your main ticket. Any half-decent travel agent should be able to book a host of 'add-on' African flights and possibly find fares that allow a little flexibility.

Airlines with extensive African networks from their hub cities include the following:

**EgyptAir** (www.egyptair.com.eg)

**Ethiopian Airlines** (Map p584; ☎011 551 1540; www.ethiopianairlines.com; Hilton Hotel, Menelik II Ave; ⏰7am-8.30pm Mon-Sat, 8am-noon Sun)

**Interair** (www.interair.co.za)

**Kenya Airways** (☎020-3274747; www.kenya-airways.com)

**Royal Air Maroc** (RAM; ☎0890 00 08 00; www.royalairmaroc.com)

**South African Airways** (SAA; ☎0860 606 606; www.flysaa.com)

## Air Passes

If you're planning to take a few African flights, some 'air pass' schemes offer great value in the long run – the best offer savings of well over 50% on domestic and continental fares.

The Star Alliance 'Africa Airpass' allows flexible travel around sub-Saharan Africa. It covers more than 30 airports in 23 different countries, and you can buy between three and 10 coupons (each coupon representing a single trip, eg Jo'burg to Windhoek). The Airpass allows for substantial savings, and flights are operated by Ethiopian Airlines, South African Airways and EgyptAir – see www.staralliance.com for more.

# Bicycle

Cycling around Africa is predictably tough but rewarding. Long, hot, gruelling journeys are pretty standard, but you'll be in constant close contact with the peoples and environments of the continent and will get to visit small towns and villages that most people just shoot through. In general, the more remote the areas, the better the experience, but you've got to be fully prepared. A tent is standard issue, but remember to ask the village headman where you can pitch a tent when camping near settlements in rural areas.

Touring bikes aren't the best choice for Africa, a continent not blessed with universally smooth tarmac roads. Adapted mountain bikes are your best bet – their smaller 660mm (26in) wheel rims are less likely to be misshaped by rough roads than the 700mm rims of touring bikes, and mountain-bike frames are better suited to the rigours of African travel. Multipurpose hybrid tyres with knobbles on their edges for off-road routes and a smooth central band for on-road cruising are useful in Africa, but your tyre choices (along with the types of components, number of spares and the like) should depend on the terrain you want to tackle.

You may encounter the odd antelope or zebra while cycling, but motorists are more of a threat to cyclists than rampaging wildlife. Cyclists lie just below donkeys on the transport food chain, so if you hear a vehicle coming up from behind, be prepared to bail out onto the verges. That said, many of Africa's roads are fairly quiet. Be very cautious about cycling in busy towns and cities.

The heat can be a killer so carry at least 4L of water and don't discount the possibility of taking a bus, truck or boat across some sections (bikes can easily be transported).

The International Bicycle Fund (www.ibike.org/africaguide) has a handy guide to cycling in Africa by country, although information for some countries is limited and out of date.

### BRINGING YOUR BIKE

You could cycle all the way into Africa or you could save your legs for Africa's rough roads and stick your wheels in the hold of a plane. There are two ways of doing this: you could partially dismantle your bike and stuff it into a large box, or just simply wheel your bike to the check-in desk, where it should be treated as a piece of baggage (although you might need to take the pedals off, turn the handlebars sideways and wrap it in cardboard and/or foam). Don't lose too much sleep about the feather touch of baggage handlers – if your bike doesn't stand up to air travel, it won't last long in Africa.

Some airlines don't include sports equipment in the baggage allowance; others may charge around US$50 extra because your bike is not standard luggage size; others, however, will take it without hassles.

# Boat

Travelling by boat could well rank among your most memorable journeys in Africa.

## Rivers & Lakes

On simple riverboats you'll be sat on mountains of cargo, the bows of the craft sitting just above the water line, but on some major river routes large ferries and barges are used. Generally speaking, 3rd class on all ferries is crammed with people, goods and livestock, making it hot and uncomfortable. Happily there's usually a better way: at a price, cabins (semiluxurious and otherwise) with bar and restaurant access can be yours.

Pirogues (traditional canoes) and *pinasses* (motorised canoes) are staples of travel on remote waterways where small, diesel-powered (and often unreliable), pontoon-style car ferries are not available. They're especially common in the rivers of West Africa. The Southern African equivalent, the *mokoro* (dugout canoe), is more for sightseeing in and around the Okavango Delta than getting from A to B. Not many ferries or boats take vehicles (the river border crossing between Zambia and Botswana is an exception), but you can get a motorbike onto some.

Common routes or lakes with ferry, cargo or some other form of boat service:

- Lake Malawi/Nyasa (Malawi, Mozambique and Tanzania)
- Lake Tanganyika (Tanzania and Zambia)
- Lake Victoria (Tanzania and Kenya)
- Congo River (Democratic Republic of Congo and Republic of Congo)
- Nile (Egypt)
- Senegal River (Senegal)
- Gambia River (The Gambia)
- Zambezi River (Zimbabwe & Zambia)

## Coastal Ferries

The most important coastal ferry service is that between Dar es Salaam and Zanzibar. There are also some services along the West African coast, especially in Sierra Leone and Guinea-Bissau. There are also ferries between Limbe (Cameroon) and Calabar (Nigeria), and between Malabo and Bata in Equatorial Guinea. Coastal ferries are also important in Gabon and São Tomé & Príncipe.

A more romantic alternative is to travel by small Arabic-style dhow sailing vessels that ply the Indian Ocean coast. The easiest place to organise this is in Mozambique, where you can sail to and around the Quirimbas Archipelago. Similar to dhows are feluccas, the ancient sailing boats of the Nile.

## Safety Warning

Travelling by boat can sometimes be hazardous. For the most part you can forget about safety regulations, lifeboats or life jackets, and overloading is very common. To make matters worse, on some ferries the 3rd-class passengers are effectively jammed into the hold with little opportunity for escape.

# Car & Motorcycle

Exploring Africa with your own wheels takes some doing, but is a wonderful way to see the continent.

The easiest way to enter Africa with your own car or motorcycle is to cross from southern Europe to Morocco aboard a car ferry and then take it from there. The obvious main barrier to travelling this way is the Sahara, most of which is problematic at present.

At the time of writing, most trans-Saharan routes were off limits to travellers due to simmering rebellion and banditry, although the Western Sahara route (from Morocco to Mauritania via Dakhla) was considered safe. Other potential barriers to getting around Africa by car or motorcycle include the cost of hiring a barge to transport your vehicle from Egypt into Sudan; and either war or the nonexistent roads of the DRC (or both). For a multitude of other options and inspiring tales from those who've made overland trips present, future and past, check out the website of the Africa Overland Network (www.africa-overland.net) or, for motorcyclists, Horizons Unlimited (www.horizonsunlimited.com).

If you're keen to begin in East or South Africa, it can be expensive to ship your vehicle all the way to Mombasa or Cape Town – it may work out cheaper to fly there and purchase something once you arrive. South Africa in particular is a pretty easy place to purchase a car – either from a dealership or from a fellow traveller who has finished with it. Handily, cars registered in South Africa don't need a *carnet de passage* for travel around Southern Africa, but you will need to have an international driving licence, your home licence, vehicle insurance and registration, and you will have to get a new set of plates made. The AA of South Africa (www.aa.co.za) offers vehicle check-ups, insurance and travel advice.

Travelling around Africa by motorcycle is popular among hard-core motorcyclists, but road conditions vary greatly. Remember also that many drivers (particularly truck drivers) are either unaccustomed or disinclined to taking two-wheeled transport into consideration. Motorcyclists, especially those with newer model bikes, should also, where possible, be self-sufficient in parts.

## Carnets

A *carnet de passage* (sometimes known as a *triptyque*) is required for many countries in Africa, with the nota-

## ROAD TIPS

➡ Watch out for kamikaze cyclists, pedestrians and livestock – and massive potholes.

➡ Night-time road travel is *never* recommended.

➡ Local driving skills are generally nerve-shatteringly poor, especially in rural areas; moderate your speed.

➡ Tree branches placed in the roadway signal a stopped vehicle or other problem ahead.

➡ Reckless overtaking on blind bends, hills and other areas with poor visibility is standard operating procedure; head-on collisions are common.

➡ Keep your fuel tank full and carry a jerry can. Fuel sold on the roadside is unreliable (it's often diluted), and some types of fuel (including diesel) aren't always available in remote areas.

➡ Expect frequent stops at checkpoints: police, customs and border officials will want to see all your documentation. The time taken at these checkpoints is one of the biggest variables of African overland travel. Sometimes it can take two minutes, sometimes hours.

➡ Mechanical knowledge and a collection of spares are essential. A winch and a set of planks can get you out of muddy trouble in the rainy season.

➡ Most trips off the beaten track require a 4WD.

➡ Motorcycles generally aren't permitted in national parks.

ble exceptions of Morocco, Algeria and Tunisia. A *carnet* guarantees that if you take a vehicle into a country, but don't take it out again, then the organisation that issued the *carnet* will accept responsibility for payment of import duties (up to 150% of its value). *Carnets* can only be issued by national motoring organisations; they're only issued if it's certain that if ever duties arose you would reimburse them. This means you have to deposit a bond with a bank or insure yourself against the potential collection of import duties before getting a *carnet*.

You don't need to pre-arrange a *carnet* for many West and Southern African countries (most Southern African countries will issue a Temporary Import Permit at the border, which you must buy), but if you're driving through Africa, you're going to need a *carnet*, which sadly doesn't exempt you from the bureaucratic shenanigans encountered at numerous borders. If you're starting in South Africa, you can get one from AA of South Africa (www.aa.co.za) pretty easily. In the UK, try the RAC (www.rac.co.uk).

Also consider the following:

➡ Motoring organisations' insurance companies can be a little paranoid in their designation of 'war zones' in Africa so watch out; none will insure against the risks of war, thus denying you a *carnet*.

➡ If you intend to sell the vehicle at some point, arrangements have to be made with the customs people in the country in which you plan to sell the car for the *carnet* entry to be cancelled.

➡ If you abandon a vehicle in the Algerian desert, you'll be up for import duties that are twice the value of your car when it was new.

### Hire

Hiring a vehicle is not recommended everywhere but renting a 4WD is an increasingly popular way to get around in Southern Africa, especially Botswana, Namibia and Zambia.

Renting in Africa is usually only an option to travellers aged over 25 years. For the most part, vehicle hire is a fairly expensive option (2WD vehicles commonly cost over US$75 a day in sub-Saharan Africa; you're looking at around US$150 a day for a 4WD) and rental can come with high insurance excesses and bundles of strings.

On a brighter note, car hire in South Africa can be a real bargain (if you hire for a longer period, it can be less than US$30 a day), especially if booked from overseas. Some vehicles can then be taken into Namibia, Mozambique and Botswana. Also consider hiring a car for exploring southern Morocco and taking a 4WD (possibly with driver) to explore Kenya and Tanzania's wildlife parks at your leisure.

In some places it's not possible to rent a car without a local driver being part of the deal. In others (eg Botswana and Namibia) it's impossible to rent one *with* a driver.

### RENTING A 4WD IN SOUTHERN AFRICA

The following companies rent 4WD vehicles in Southern Africa.

**Africamper** (www.africamper.com) 4WD rental from South Africa.

**Avis Safari Rentals** (www.avisvanrental.co.za/avis-safari-rental.aspx) Offices in Botswana, Namibia and South Africa.

**Britz** (in Jo'burg 27 11 230 5200, in Namibia 264-61-219590; www.britz.co.za) 4WD rental with offices in South Africa and Namibia.

**Bushlore** (www.bushlore.com) 4WD rental.

**Drive Botswana** (in Palapye 492 3416; www.drivebotswana.com) Arranges trips and makes bookings for Mozambique, Namibia, South Africa, Zambia and Zimbabwe.

**Safari Drive** (www.safaridrive.com) Expensive but professional and upmarket company with its own fleet of recent-model vehicles.

**Self Drive Adventures** (686 3755; www.selfdriveadventures.com) Guided self-drive expeditions.

### Insurance

Legislation covering third-party insurance varies considerably from one country to another – in some places it isn't even compulsory. Where it is, you generally have to buy insurance at the border (a process fraught with corruption), but the liability limits on these policies are often absurdly low by Western standards; this means if you have any bad accidents, you'll be in serious trouble, so it's a smart plan to insure yourself before heading out. If you're starting from the UK, one company highly recommended for insurance policies and for detailed information on *carnets* is Campbell Irvine (www.campbellirvine.com).

## Hitching

Hitching is never entirely safe in any country, and we don't recommend it. But in some parts of Africa, there is often simply no other option than grabbing lifts on trucks, 4WDs, lorries or whatever vehicle happens to come down the road first. Whatever vehicle you jump on to, you'll generally have to pay. In more developed countries, such as Ghana, Kenya, Morocco, South Africa and Zimbabwe, where there are plenty of private cars on the road, it may be possible to hitch for free.

Travellers who decide to hitch should understand that they are taking a small but potentially serious risk. People who do choose to hitch will be safer if they travel in pairs. Remember that sticking out your thumb in many African countries is an obscene gesture; wave your hand vertically up and down instead.

## Local Transport

### Bus

This is the way to go where there's a good network of sealed roads. International bus services are pretty common across the continent, and in the wealthier African states you may get a choice between 'luxury' air-con buses, with movies (the trashy Hollywood/Bollywood variety) on tap, and rough old European rejects with nonfunctioning air-con and questionable engineering. In some countries you just get the latter. Out in the sticks, where there are very few or no sealed roads, ancient buses tend to be very crowded with people, livestock and goods; these buses tend to stop frequently, either for passengers or because something is broken.

### BUS SURVIVAL TIPS

- Bus station touts are there to drum up business and work on commission; they're occasionally a pain but they can be very helpful.
- When using bush taxis keep your options open; hold on to your money until departure.
- Sitting on a camping mat or towel can ease the pain of African roads.
- Drinking more means peeing more – balance hydration with bladder control.
- When travelling on dirt roads use a scarf to keep dust from your nose and mouth.
- That baby may look cute – but let it onto your lap and it WILL pee...
- Carry your passport at all times – getting through roadblocks without it can be expensive and complicated.
- Try to book your bus or minibus ticket in advance.
- Addressing questions to the driver directly is a social no-no – the conductor is the social hub of the journey, while the driver is the quiet achiever.
- If you have a choice as to your seat (more likely on buses), opt for what will be the shady side.

### Minibus

Small minibuses take up the slack in many African transport systems. All too often they are driven at breakneck speed and crammed with close to 30 people when they were designed for 18 (there's always room for one more), with a tout or conductor leaning out the side door. The front seat is the most comfortable, but thanks to the high number of head-on collisions in Africa, this seat is called the 'death seat': how many old bus-drivers have you seen? (If you do see one, be sure to choose his bus!)

These minibuses are known by different names

across the continent (*matatus* in Kenya, *dalla-dallas* in Tanzania, *tro-tros* in Ghana, *poda-podas* in Sierra Leone), names that are, confusingly, fairly interchangeable for shared taxis and bush taxis.

Minibuses usually only leave when very full (a process that may take hours), and will stop frequently en route to pick up and set down passengers. Minibuses are also the favourite prey of roadblock police, who are not averse to unloading every passenger while they enter into lengthy discussions about paperwork and 'fines' that may need paying.

### Shared Taxi

Shared taxis are usually Peugeot 504s or 505s or old spacious Mercedes saloons (common in North Africa). They should definitely be considered, where available (which is not everywhere). Your average shared taxi is certainly quicker, more comfortable (if a little crowded) and less of a palaver than taking a bus or minibus, although many shared taxis are driven by lunatic speed freaks. They cost a little more than the corresponding bus fare, but in most cases once the vehicle has filled up (usually with nine to 12 people, packed in like sardines) it heads more or less directly to the destination (in most cases), without constant stops for passengers. You should expect to pay an additional fee for your baggage in West Africa, but usually not elsewhere. Motorcycle taxis can also be convenient, if dangerous.

'Bush taxi' is something of a catch-all term and is used slightly differently across the continent. Basically, a bush taxi is any multiperson mode of public transport that isn't a bus.

## Train

Where available, travelling by train is a wonderful way to get around Africa. Even the shortest rail journey can be a classic experience, full of cultural exchange, amazing landscapes and crazy stations where all kinds of food, drinks and goods are hawked at train windows.

Train travel is safer and usually more comfortable than travelling by road, although outside Southern and North Africa the trains are often very slow. Long delays aren't uncommon. Second-class fares weigh in about the same as, or less than, the corresponding bus fare.

More expensive (but still negligible by Western standards) are sleeping compartments and 1st- or 2nd-class carriages, which take the strain out of long journeys and occasionally allow you to travel in style – some high-class train carriages are like little wood-panelled museums of colonialism. It's worth noting that in many countries male and female passengers can only sleep in the same compartment if they buy the tickets for the whole compartment (four or six bunks), and even then you might be asked for evidence that you're married!

The flip side of train travel is that security and sanitation facilities on trains can be poor, especially in 3rd class, which, although novel and entertaining at first, soon becomes simply crowded and uncomfortable. Keep an eye on your baggage at all times and lock carriage doors and windows at night.

Some of Africa's most iconic train journeys:

- Nairobi–Mombasa (Kenya)
- Zouérat–Nouâdhibou (Mauritania)
- Dakar–Bamako (Senegal and Mali)
- Transgabonais (Gabon)
- Windhoek–Swakopmund (Namibia)
- Pretoria–Swakopmund (South Africa and Namibia).

## Truck

In many out-of-the-way places, trucks are the only reliable form of transport. They may primarily carry goods, but drivers are always keen to supplement their income, so there's usually room for paying passengers. Most folks are stuck up on top of the cargo, but a few more expensive spots are often available in the cab.

Sitting high and exposed on top of a truck chugging through the African landscape can be a great experience; just take heavy precautions against the sun, wrap up against dust and bring a carry mat or similar to cushion yourself against uncomfortable cargo – you could find yourself sitting on top of a car engine for hours on end! Also, remember that trucks are even slower than buses.

On many routes you'll be able to wave down a truck, but lifts can often be arranged the night before departure at the 'truck park' – a compound or dust patch that you'll find in almost every African town of note. 'Fares' are pretty much fixed – expect to pay a little less than an equivalent bus fare, and make sure you agree on the price before climbing aboard. If the journey is going to take more than one night or one day, bring your own food and water.

### Overlanding on the Cheap

Because most people prefer to travel north to south, overland truck companies sometimes drive empty trucks back from South Africa's Cape Town, Victoria Falls and Harare, and will sometimes transport travellers back up to Arusha (Tanzania) or Nairobi (Kenya) for negotiable knockdown prices, with a pleasant two-day stop by Lake Malawi sometimes thrown in. Ask around in backpacker hangouts in the departure towns for tips on when these trucks may be leaving.

# Health

As long as you stay up to date with your vaccinations and take some basic preventive measures, you'd have to be pretty unlucky to succumb to any serious health hazards. Africa certainly has an impressive selection of tropical diseases on offer, but you're much more likely to get a bout of diarrhoea (in fact, you should bank on it), a cold or an infected mosquito bite than an exotic disease such as Rift Valley or West Nile fever. When it comes to injuries (as opposed to illness), the most likely reason for needing medical help in Africa is as a result of road accidents – vehicles are rarely well maintained, the roads are potholed and poorly lit, and drink driving is common.

## Before You Go

### Pre-Travel Checklist

➡ Get a check-up from your dentist and from your doctor if you take any regular medication or have a chronic illness, eg high blood pressure or asthma.

➡ Organise spare contact lenses and glasses (and take your optical prescription with you).

➡ Assemble a first-aid and medical kit.

➡ Arrange necessary vaccinations. Don't leave this until the last minute. Many vaccines don't take effect until two weeks after you've been immunised, so visit a doctor four to eight weeks before departure. Ask your doctor for an International Certificate of Vaccination (otherwise known as the yellow booklet), which will list all the vaccinations you've received. This is mandatory for the African countries that require proof of yellow fever vaccination upon entry, but it's a good idea to carry it anyway wherever you travel.

➡ Become a member of the International Association for Medical Advice to Travellers (IAMAT; www.iamat.org), which lists trusted English-speaking doctors.

➡ If you'll be spending significant time in remote areas, you might like to do a first-aid course (contact the Red Cross or St John's Ambulance) or attend a remote medicine first-aid course, such as that offered by the Royal Geographical Society (www.wildernessmedicaltraining.co.uk) or the American Red Cross (www.redcross.org).

➡ Bring medications in their original containers, clearly labelled.

➡ A signed and dated letter from your physician describing all medical conditions and medications, including generic names, is also a good idea.

➡ If carrying syringes or needles, be sure to have a physician's letter documenting their medical necessity.

### Insurance

Find out in advance whether your insurance plan will make payments directly to providers or will reimburse you later for overseas health expenditures (in many countries doctors expect payment in cash). It's vital to ensure that your travel insurance will cover the emergency transport to get you to a hospital in a major city, to better medical facilities elsewhere in Africa, or all the way home, by air and with a medical attendant if necessary. Not all insurance covers this, so check the contract carefully. If you need medical help, your insurance company might be able to help locate the nearest hospital or clinic, or you can ask at your hotel. In an emergency, contact your embassy or consulate.

### Recommended Vaccinations

The World Health Organization (www.who.int/ith) recommends that all travellers be covered for diphtheria, tetanus, measles, mumps, rubella and polio, as well as for hepatitis B, regardless of their destination. Planning to travel is a great time to ensure that all routine vaccination cover is complete. The consequences of these particular diseases can be severe, and outbreaks do occur.

According to the Centers for Disease Control and Prevention (wwwnc.cdc.gov/travel), the following vaccinations are recommended for all parts of Africa: hepatitis A, hepatitis B, meningococcal meningitis, rabies and typhoid, and boosters for tetanus, diphtheria and measles. A yellow-fever vaccination is not necessarily recommended for all parts of Africa, although the certificate is an entry requirement for a number of countries.

## Medical Checklist

Consider packing the following:

- Acetaminophen (paracetamol) or aspirin
- Acetazolamide (Diamox) for altitude sickness (prescription only)
- Adhesive or paper tape
- Antibacterial ointment (eg Bactroban) for cuts and abrasions (prescription only)
- Antibiotics (prescription only), eg ciprofloxacin (Ciproxin) or norfloxacin (Utinor)
- Antidiarrhoeal drugs (eg loperamide)
- Antihistamines (for hay fever and allergic reactions)
- Anti-inflammatory drugs (eg ibuprofen)
- Antimalaria pills
- Bandages, gauze, gauze rolls
- DEET-containing insect repellent for the skin
- Iodine tablets (for water purification)
- Oral rehydration salts
- Permethrin-containing insect spray for clothing, tents and bed nets
- Scissors, safety pins, tweezers, pocket knife
- Sterile needles, syringes and fluids if travelling to remote areas
- Steroid cream or hydrocortisone cream (for allergic rashes)
- Sunblock
- Thermometer

If you are travelling through a malarial area – particularly an area in which falciparum malaria predominates – consider taking a self-diagnostic kit that can identify malaria in the blood from a finger prick.

## Websites

There is a wealth of travel-health advice on the internet. The Lonely Planet website at www.lonelyplanet.com is a good place to start. The World Health Organization publishes the helpful International Travel and Health, available free at www.who.int/ith/. Other useful websites include MD Travel Health (www.mdtravelhealth.com) and Fit for Travel (www.fitfortravel.scot.nhs.uk).

Official government travel health websites:

**Australia** smartraveller.gov.au/guide/all-travellers/health/Pages/default.aspx

**Canada** www.hc-sc.gc.ca/index_e.html

**UK** www.gov.uk/foreign-travel-advice

**USA** wwwnc.cdc.gov/travel

## Further Reading

- *A Comprehensive Guide to Wilderness and Travel Medicine* (Eric A Weiss; 1998)
- *The Essential Guide to Travel Health* (Jane Wilson-Howarth; 2009)
- *Healthy Travel Africa* (Isabelle Young; 2000)
- *How to Stay Healthy Abroad* (Richard Dawood; 2002)
- *Travel in Health* (Graham Fry; 1994)
- *Travel with Children* (Sophie Caupeil et al; 2015)

# In Transit

## Deep Vein Thrombosis (DVT)

Blood clots can form in the legs during flights, chiefly because of prolonged immobility. This formation of clots is known as deep vein thrombosis (DVT), and the longer the flight, the greater the risk. Although most blood clots are reabsorbed uneventfully, some might break off and travel through the blood vessels to the lungs, where they could cause life-threatening complications.

The chief symptom of DVT is swelling or pain of the foot, ankle or calf, usually but not always on just one side. When a blood clot travels to the lungs, it can cause chest pain and breathing difficulty. Travellers with any of these symptoms should immediately seek medical attention.

To prevent the development of DVT on long flights you should walk about the cabin, perform isometric compressions of the leg muscles (ie contract the leg muscles while sitting), drink plenty of fluids, and avoid alcohol.

## Jet Lag & Motion Sickness

If you're crossing more than five time zones you could suffer jet lag, resulting in insomnia, fatigue, malaise or nausea. To avoid jet lag try drinking plenty of fluids (nonalcoholic) and eating light meals. Upon arrival, get exposure to natural sunlight and readjust your schedule (for meals, sleep etc) as soon as possible.

Antihistamines such as dimenhydrinate (Dramamine) and meclizine (Antivert, Bonine) are usually the first choice for treating motion sickness. Their main side effect is drowsiness. A herbal alternative is ginger (in the form of ginger tea, biscuits or crystallised ginger), which works like a charm for some people.

# In Africa

## Availability & Cost of Health Care

Health care in Africa is varied: it can be excellent in the major cities, which generally have well-trained doctors and nurses, but it is often patchy off the beaten track.

Most drugs can be purchased over the counter throughout Africa, without a prescription. Many drugs for sale within Africa might be ineffective – they might be counterfeit or might not have been stored under the right conditions. The most common examples of counterfeit drugs are malaria tablets and expensive antibiotics, such as ciprofloxacin. Most drugs are available in capital cities, but in remote villages you will be lucky to find a couple of paracetamol tablets. It is strongly recommended that all drugs for chronic diseases be brought with you from home. Also, the availability and efficacy of condoms cannot be relied upon – bring all the contraception you'll need. Condoms bought in Africa might not be of the same quality as in Europe, North America or Australia, and they might have been stored in too hot an environment. Keep all condoms as cool as you can.

There is a high risk of contracting HIV from infected blood if you receive a blood transfusion in Africa. The BloodCare Foundation (www.bloodcare.org.uk) is a useful source of safe, screened blood, which can be transported to any part of the world within 24 hours.

The cost of health care might seem very cheap compared to first-world countries, but good care and drugs might be not be available. Evacuation to good medical care can be very expensive indeed. Unfortunately, adequate – let alone good – health care is available only to very few residents of Africa.

## Infectious Diseases

### BILHARZIA (SCHISTOSOMIASIS)

**Present** Throughout Africa with possible exception of Morocco, Algeria and Libya.

**Spread through** Flukes (minute worms) that are carried by a species of freshwater snail. The flukes are carried inside the snail, which sheds them into slow-moving or still water. The parasites penetrate human skin during paddling or swimming and then migrate to the bladder or bowel. They are passed out via stool or urine and could contaminate fresh water, where the cycle starts again.

**Symptoms and effects** There might be no symptoms. There might be a transient fever and rash, and advanced cases might have blood in the stool or urine.

**Prevention and treatment** Avoid paddling or swimming in freshwater lakes or slow-running rivers anywhere. A blood test can detect antibodies if you might have been exposed, and treatment is then possible in specialist travel or infectious disease clinics. If left untreated the infection could cause kidney failure or permanent bowel damage. It is not possible for you to infect others. Self-treatment: none.

### CHOLERA

Cholera is usually only a problem during natural or artificial disasters, eg war, floods or earthquakes, although small outbreaks can also occur at other times. Travellers are rarely affected.

**Spread through** Contaminated drinking water.

**Symptoms and effects** Profuse watery diarrhoea, which causes collapse if fluids are not replaced quickly.

**Prevention and treatment** Most cases could be avoided by close attention to good drinking water and by avoiding potentially contaminated food. Treatment is by fluid replacement (orally or via a drip), but sometimes antibiotics are needed. Self-treatment is not advised.

### DENGUE FEVER (BREAK-BONE FEVER)

**Present** Sudan, Cameroon, Democratic Republic of Congo (DRC), Senegal, Burkina Faso, Guinea, Ethiopia, Djibouti, Somalia, Madagascar, Mozambique and South Africa.

**Spread through** Mosquito bites.

**Symptoms and effects** A feverish illness with headache and muscle pains similar to those experienced with a bad, prolonged attack of influenza. There might be a rash. In rare cases in Africa this becomes Severe Dengue Fever, with worsening symptoms including vomiting, rapid breathing and abdominal pain. Seek medical help, as this can be fatal.

**Prevention and treatment** Mosquito bites should be avoided whenever possible. Self-treatment: paracetamol and rest.

### DIPTHERIA

**Present** Throughout Africa.

**Spread through** Close respiratory contact.

**Symptoms and effects** Usually causes a temperature and a severe sore throat. Sometimes a membrane forms across the throat, and a tracheostomy is needed to prevent suffocation.

**Prevention and treatment** Vaccination is recommended for all travellers, particularly those likely to be in close contact with the local population in infected areas. More important for long stays than for short-term trips. The vaccine is given as an injection alone or with tetanus, and lasts 10 years. Self-treatment: none.

### EBOLA & MARBURG VIRUSES

**Present** Massive outbreak in Sierra Leone, Guinea and Liberia from 2013 to 2016 killed an estimated 11,310 people. Smaller outbreaks in recent decades throughout West and Central Africa (especially Congo, the DRC, the Central African Republic and Sudan) and in Uganda.

**Spread through** Eating bushmeat is considered a common cause of Ebola; spread through bodily fluids.

**Symptoms and effects** Haemorrhagic fever, which is usually fatal.

**Prevention and treatment.** Both diseases are rare in travellers, although at least one traveller in Uganda is believed to have contracted the Marburg virus after visiting caves. Self-treatment: none.

### FILARIASIS

**Present** Most parts of West, Central, East and Southern Africa.

**Spread through** Mosquito bites, then tiny worms migrating in the lymphatic system.

**Symptoms and effects** Can include localised itching and swelling of the legs and/or genitalia.

**Prevention and treatment** Avoid mosquito bites. Treatment is available, but self-treatments are not.

### HEPATITIS A

**Present** Throughout Africa.

**Spread through** Contaminated food (particularly shellfish) and water.

**Symptoms and effects** Jaundice and, although it is rarely fatal, it can cause prolonged lethargy and delayed recovery. If you've had hepatitis A, you shouldn't drink alcohol for up to six months afterwards, but once you've recovered, there won't be any long-term problems. The first symptoms include dark urine and a yellow colour to the whites of the eyes. Sometimes a fever and abdominal pain might be present.

**Prevention and treatment** Hepatitis A vaccine (Avaxim, VAQTA, Havrix) is given as an injection: a single dose will give protection for up to a year, and a booster after a year gives 10-year protection. Hepatitis A and typhoid vaccines can also be given as a single-dose vaccine, hepatyrix or viatim. Self-treatment: none.

### HEPATITIS B

**Present** Thoughout Africa.

**Spread through** Infected blood, contaminated needles and sexual intercourse. It can also be spread from an infected mother to the baby during childbirth.

**Symptoms and effects** Attacks the liver, causing jaundice and occasionally liver failure. Most people recover completely, but some people might be chronic carriers of the virus, which could lead eventually to cirrhosis or liver cancer.

**Prevention and treatment** Those visiting high-risk areas for long periods or at social or occupational risk should be immunised. Many countries now give hepatitis B as part of the routine childhood vaccination. It is given singly or can be given at the same time as hepatitis A. A course will give protection for at least five years. It can be given over four weeks or six months. Self-treatment: none.

### HIV/AIDS

**Present** Throughout Africa.

**Spread through** Infected blood and blood products, by sexual intercourse with an infected partner, and from an infected mother to her baby during childbirth and breastfeeding. It can be spread through 'blood to blood' contacts, such as with contaminated instruments during medical, dental, acupuncture and other body-piercing procedures, and through sharing used intravenous needles.

**Prevention and treatment** At present there is no cure; medication that might keep the disease under control is available, but many countries in Africa do not have access to it for their own citizens, let alone for travellers. If you think you might have put yourself at risk of HIV infection, a blood test is necessary; a three-month gap after the exposure and before testing is required to allow antibodies to appear in the blood. Self-treatment: none.

### LEISHMANIASIS

**Present** North Africa.

**Spread through** Bite of an infected sandfly.

**Symptoms and effects** Can cause a slowly growing skin lump or ulcer (the cutaneous form) and can sometimes develop into a serious life-threatening fever with anaemia and weight loss. Dogs can also be carriers of leishmaniasis.

**Prevention and treatment** Sandfly and dog bites should be avoided whenever possible. Self-treatment: none.

### LEPTOSPIROSIS

**Present** West and Southern Africa; in Chad, Congo, Sudan and DRC in Central Africa; in Algeria and Morocco in North Africa; and in Ethiopia and Somalia in East Africa.

**Spread through** The excreta of infected rodents, especially rats.

**Symptoms and effects** A fever, sometimes jaundice, hepatitus and renal failure.

**Prevention and treatment** It is unusual for travellers to be affected unless living in poor sanitary conditions. Self-treatment: none.

### MALARIA

**Present** Endemic in Central, East, West and Southern Africa; slight risk in North Africa. The risk of malarial transmission at altitudes higher than 2000m is rare.

**Spread through** The bite of the female Anopheles mosquito. There are several types of malaria; falciparum malaria is the most dangerous type and the predominant form in Africa. Infection rates vary with season and climate, so check out the situation before departure. Unlike most other diseases regularly encountered by travellers, there is no vaccination against malaria (yet). However, several different drugs are used to prevent malaria, and new ones are in the pipeline. Up-to-date advice from a travel health clinic is essential, as some medication is more suitable for some travellers than others. The pattern of drug-resistant malaria is changing rapidly, so what was advised several years ago might no longer be the case.

**Symptoms and effects** The early stages include headaches, fevers, generalised aches and pains, and malaise, which could be mistaken for flu. Other symptoms can include abdominal pain, diarrhoea and a cough.

**Prevention and treatment** Anyone who develops a fever in a malarial area should assume malarial infection until a blood test proves negative, even if you have been taking antimalarial medication. If not treated, the next stage could develop within 24 hours (particularly if falciparum malaria is the parasite): jaundice, then reduced consciousness and coma (also known as cerebral malaria) followed by death. Treatment in hospital is essential, though the death rate might still be as high as 10% even in the best intensive-care facilities.

Many travellers are under the impression that malaria is a mild illness, that treatment is always easy and successful, and that taking antimalarial

## Malarial Risk in Africa

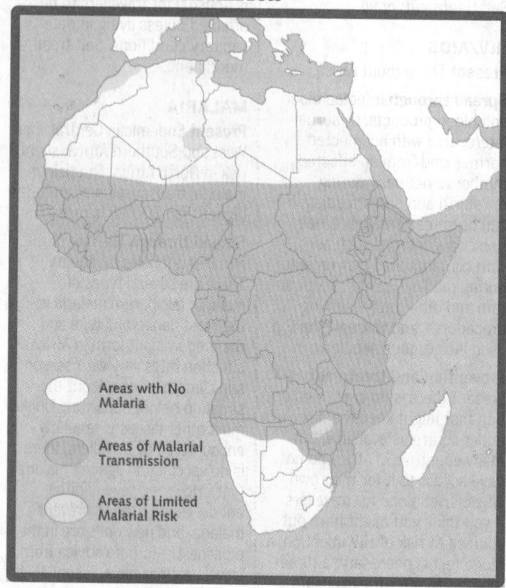


drugs causes more illness through side effects than actually getting malaria. In Africa, this is unfortunately not true. Side effects depend on the drug being taken. Doxycycline can cause heartburn and indigestion; mefloquine (Larium) can cause anxiety attacks, insomnia and nightmares, and (rarely) severe psychiatric disorders; chloroquine can cause nausea and hair loss; and proguanil can cause mouth ulcers. Side effects are not universal, and can be minimised by taking medication correctly, eg with food. Also, some people should not take a particular antimalarial drug, eg people with epilepsy should avoid mefloquine, and doxycycline should not be taken by pregnant women or children younger than 12.

People of all ages can contract malaria, and falciparum malaria causes the most severe illness. Repeated infections might result eventually in less serious illness. Malaria in pregnancy frequently results in miscarriage or premature labour. Adults who have survived childhood malaria have developed immunity and usually only develop mild cases of malaria; most Western travellers have no immunity at all. Immunity wanes after 18 months of nonexposure, so even if you have had malaria in the past and used to live in a malaria-prone area, you might no longer be immune. One million children die annually from malaria in Africa.

If you decide that you really do not wish to take antimalarial drugs, you must understand the risks, and be obsessive about avoiding mosquito bites. Use nets and insect repellent, and report any fever or flulike symptoms to a doctor as soon as possible. Some people advocate homeopathic preparations against malaria, such as Demal200, but as yet there is no conclusive evidence that they are effective, and many homeopaths do not recommend their use.

If you are planning a journey through a malarial area, particularly where falciparum malaria predominates, consider taking stand-by treatment. Emergency stand-by treatment should be seen as emergency treatment aimed at saving the patient's life and not as routine self-medication. It should be advised only if you will be remote from medical facilities and have been advised about the symptoms of malaria and how to use the medication. Medical advice should be sought as soon as possible to confirm whether the treatment has been successful. The type of stand-by treatment used will depend on local conditions, such as drug resistance, and on what antimalarial drugs are being used before stand-by treatment. This is worthwhile because you want to avoid contracting a particularly serious form such as cerebral malaria, which affects the brain and central nervous system and can be fatal in 24 hours. Self-diagnostic kits, which can identify malaria in the blood from a finger prick, are also available in the West.

The risks from malaria to both mother and foetus during pregnancy are considerable. Unless good medical care can be absolutely guaranteed, travel throughout Africa when pregnant – particularly to malarial areas – should be discouraged unless essential. Self-treatment: see stand-by treatment if you are more than 24 hours away from medical help.

### THE ANTIMALARIAL A TO D

**A** Awareness of the risk. No medication is totally effective, but protection of up to 95% is achievable with most drugs, as long as other measures are taken.

**B** Bites – avoid at all costs. Sleep in a screened room, use a mosquito spray or coils, and sleep under a permethrin-impregnated net at night. Cover up at night with long trousers and long sleeves, preferably with permethrin-treated clothing. Apply appropriate repellent to all areas of exposed skin in the evenings.

**C** Chemical prevention (ie antimalarial drugs) is usually needed in malarial areas. Expert advice is needed as resistance patterns can change, and new drugs are in development. Not all antimalarial drugs are suitable for everyone, particularly for children, pregnant women or people with depression or epilepsy. Most antimalarial drugs need to be started at least a week in advance and continued for four weeks after the last possible exposure to malaria.

**D** Diagnosis. If you have a fever or flulike illness within a year of travel to a malarial area, malaria is a possibility, and immediate medical attention is necessary.

### MENINGOCOCCAL MENINGITIS

**Present** Central, West and East Africa; and only in Namibia, Malawi, Mozambique and Zambia in Southern Africa.

**Spread through** Close respiratory contact and is more likely in crowded situations, such as dormitories, buses and clubs. Infection is uncommon in travellers. Vaccination is recommended for long stays and especially towards the end of the dry season, which is normally from June to November.

**Symptoms and effects** Fever, severe headache, neck stiffness and a red rash.

**Prevention and treatment** Immediate medical treatment is necessary. The ACWY vaccine is recommended for all travellers in sub-Saharan Africa. This vaccine is different from the meningococcal meningitis C vaccine given to children and adolescents in some countries, and it is safe to be given both types of vaccine. Self-treatment: none.

### ONCHOCERCIASIS (RIVER BLINDNESS)

**Present** Central, West and East Africa; and Malawi in Southern Africa.

**Spread through** The bite of a small fly.

**Symptoms and effects** Intensely itchy, red, sore eyes.

**Prevention and treatment** Travellers are rarely severely affected. Treatment in a specialised clinic is curative. Self-treatment: none.

### POLIOMYELITIS

**Present** Throughout Africa.

**Spread through** Contaminated food and water.

**Symptoms and effects** Polio can be carried asymptomatically (ie showing no symptoms) and can cause a transient fever. In rare cases it causes weakness or paralysis of one or more muscles, which might be permanent.

**Prevention and treatment** It is one of the vaccines given in childhood and should be boosted every 10 years, either orally (a drop on the tongue) or as an injection. Self-treatment: none.

### RABIES

**Present** Throughout Africa.

**Spread through** The bites or licks of an infected animal on broken skin.

**Symptoms and effects** It is always fatal once the clinical symptoms start (which might be up to several months after an infected bite), so postbite vaccination should be given as soon as possible.

**Prevention and treatment** Avoid contact with animals, particularly dogs. Postbite vaccination (whether or not you've been vaccinated before the bite) prevents the virus from spreading to the central nervous system. Animal handlers should be vaccinated, as should those travelling to remote areas where a reliable source of postbite vaccine is not available within 24 hours. Three preventive injections are needed over a month. If you have not been vaccinated you will need a course of five injections starting 24 hours or as soon as possible after the injury. If you have been vaccinated, you will need fewer postbite injections, and have more time to seek medical help. Self-treatment: none.

### RIFT VALLEY FEVER

**Present** In Kenya.

**Spread through** Mosquito bites – avoiding being bitten is the best preventative tool.

**Symptoms and effects** Fever and flulike illness, and it is rarely fatal.

**Prevention and treatment** Self-treatment: none.

### TRYPANOSOMIASIS (SLEEPING SICKNESS)

**Present** Most of West, Central, East and Southern Africa.

**Spread through** Bite of the tsetse fly.

**Symptoms and effects** Headache, fever and eventually coma.

**Prevention and treatment** There is an effective treatment. Self-treatment: none.

### TUBERCULOSIS

**Present** Throughout Africa.

**Spread through** Close respiratory contact and occasionally through infected milk or milk products.

**Symptoms and effects** Can be asymptomatic, only being picked up on a routine chest X-ray. Alternatively, it can cause a cough, weight loss or fever, sometimes months or even years after exposure.

**Prevention and treatment** BCG vaccination is recommended for those likely to be mixing closely with the local population. It is more important for long stays than for short-term stays. Inoculation with the BCG vaccine is not available in all countries. It is given routinely to many children in developing countries. In some countries, for example the UK, it is given to babies if they will be travelling with their families to areas with a high-risk of TB, and to previously unvaccinated school-age children if they live in areas of higher TB risk (eg multiethnic immigrant populations). The BCG gives a moderate degree of protection against TB. It causes a small permanent scar at the site of injection, and is usually given in a specialised chest clinic. It is a live vaccine and should not be given to pregnant women or immunocompromised individuals. Self-treatment: none.

### TYPHOID

**Present** Throughout Africa.

**Spread through** Food or water contaminated by infected human faeces.

**Symptoms and effects**
Starts usually with a fever or a pink rash on the abdomen. Sometimes septicaemia (blood poisoning) can occur.

**Prevention and treatment**
A typhoid vaccine (typhim Vi, typherix) will give protection for three years. In some countries, the oral vaccine Vivotif is also available. Antibiotics are usually given as treatment, and death is rare unless septicaemia occurs. Self-treatment: none.

### WEST NILE FEVER

**Present** In Egypt.

**Spread through** This rare disease is spread via mosquito bites.

**Symptoms and effects** Fever and flulike illness; it is very occasionally fatal.

**Prevention and treatment**
Self-treatment: none.

### YELLOW FEVER

**Present** West Africa, parts of Central and Eastern Africa. Travellers should carry a certificate as evidence of vaccination if they have recently been in an infected country, to avoid any possible difficulties with immigration. For a full list of these countries visit the Centers for Disease Control and Prevention website (wwwnc.cdc.gov/travel). There is always the possibility that a traveller without a legally required, up-to-date certificate will be vaccinated and detained in isolation at the port of arrival for up to 10 days or possibly repatriated.

**Spread through** Infected mosquitoes.

**Symptoms and effects** Range from a flulike illness to severe hepatitis (liver inflammation), jaundice and death.

**Prevention and treatment** The yellow fever vaccination must be given at a designated clinic and is valid for 10 years. It is a live vaccine and must not be given to immunocompromised or pregnant travellers. Self-treatment: none.

## Yellow Fever Risk in Africa

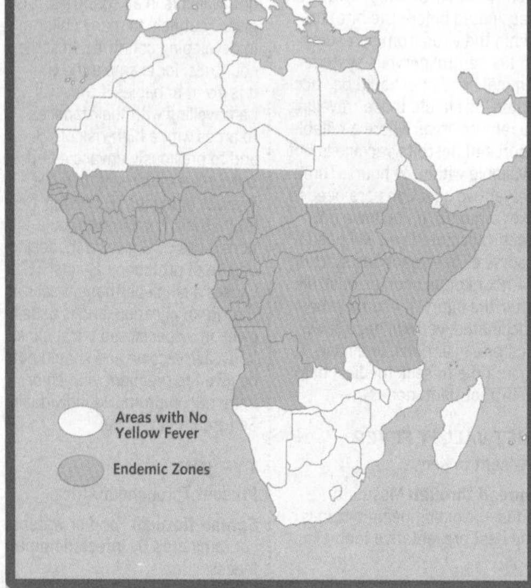


## Traveller's Diarrhoea

**Present** Throughout Africa. Although it's not inevitable that you will get diarrhoea, it's certainly very likely. Diarrhoea is the most common travel-related illness – figures suggest that at least half of all travellers to Africa will get diarrhoea at some stage.

**Spread through** Sometimes caused by dietary changes, such as increased spices or oils.

**Symptoms and effects** A few loose stools don't require treatment, but if you start having more than four or five stools a day, you should start taking an antibiotic (usually a quinoline drug, such as ciprofloxacin or norfloxacin) and an antidiarrheal agent (such as loperamide) if you are not within easy reach of a toilet.

**Prevention and treatment** To help prevent diarrhoea, avoid tap water unless you're sure it's safe to drink. You should also only eat fresh fruits or vegetables if cooked or peeled, and be wary of dairy products that might contain unpasteurised milk. Although freshly cooked food can often be a safe option, plates or serving utensils might be dirty, so you should be highly selective when eating food from street vendors (make sure that cooked food is piping hot all the way through).

If you develop diarrhoea, be sure to drink plenty of fluids, preferably an oral rehydration solution containing water, and salt and sugar. If diarrhoea is bloody, persists for more than 72 hours or is accompanied by fever, shaking chills or severe abdominal pain, you should seek medical attention.

### AMOEBIC DYSENTERY

**Present** Throughout Africa.

**Spread through** Eating/drinking contaminated food and water.

**Symptoms and effects** Amoebic dysentry causes blood and mucus in the faeces. It can be relatively mild and tends to come on gradually.

**Prevention and treatment**
Seek medical advice as soon as possible as it won't clear up without treatment (which is with specific antibiotics). Self-treatment: none.

### GIARDIASIS

Giariasis usually appears a week or more after you have been exposed to the offending parasite. Giardiasis might cause only a short-lived bout of typical travellers' diarrhoea, but it can also cause persistent diarrhoea. Ideally, seek medical advice if you suspect you have giardiasis, but if you are in a remote area you could start a course of antibiotics.

## Environmental Hazards

### HEAT EXHAUSTION

**Causes** Occurs following heavy sweating and excessive fluid loss with inadequate replacement of fluids and salt, and is particularly common in hot climates when taking unaccustomed exercise before full acclimatisation.

**Symptoms and effects** Headache, dizziness and tiredness.

**Prevention** Dehydration is already happening by the time you feel thirsty – aim to drink sufficient water to produce pale, diluted urine.

**Treatment** Fluid replacement with water and/or fruit juice, and cooling by cold water and fans. The treatment of the salt loss component consists of consuming salty fluids, as in soup, and adding a little more table salt to foods than usual.

### HEATSTROKE

**Causes** Heat exhaustion is a precursor to the much more serious condition of heatstroke.

**Symptoms and effects** Damage to the sweating mechanism, with an excessive rise in body temperature; irrational and hyperactive behaviour; and eventually loss of consciousness and death.

**Treatment** Rapid cooling by spraying the body with water and fanning. Emergency fluid and electrolyte replacement is often also required by intravenous drip.

### INSECT BITES & STINGS

Mosquitoes might not always carry malaria or dengue fever, but they (and other insects) can cause irritation and infected bites. To avoid these, take the same precautions you would for avoiding malaria. Use DEET-based insect repellents, although these are not the only effective repellents. Excellent clothing treatments are also available; mosquitoes that land on treated clothing will die.

Bee and wasp stings cause real problems only to those who have a severe allergy to the stings (anaphylaxis). If you are one of these people, make sure you carry an 'epipen' – an adrenaline (epinephrine) injection, which you can give yourself. This could save your life.

Sandflies are found around the Mediterranean beaches. They usually only cause a nasty itchy bite but can carry a rare skin disorder called cutaneous leishmaniasis. Prevention of bites with DEET-based repellents is sensible.

Scorpions are frequently found in arid climates. They can cause a painful sting that is sometimes life-threatening. If stung by a scorpion, take a painkiller. Medical treatment should be sought if collapse occurs.

Bed bugs are often found in hostels and cheap hotels. They lead to very itchy, lumpy bites. Spraying the mattress with crawling insect killer after changing bedding will get rid of them.

Scabies is also frequently found in cheap accommodation. These tiny mites live in the skin, particularly between the fingers. They cause an intensely itchy rash. The itch is easily treated with malathion and permethrin lotion from a pharmacy; other members of the household also need treating to avoid spreading scabies, even if they do not show any symptoms.

### SNAKE BITES

Basically, avoid getting bitten! Do not walk barefoot, or stick your hand into holes or cracks. However, 50% of those bitten by venomous snakes are not actually injected with poison (envenomed). If bitten by a snake, do not panic. Immobilise the bitten limb with a splint (such as a stick) and apply a bandage over the site, with firm pressure – similar to bandaging a sprain. Do not apply a tourniquet, or cut or suck the bite. Get the victim to medical help as soon as possible, where antivenom can be given if needed.

### TRADITIONAL MEDICINE

At least 80% of the African population relies on traditional medicine, either because they can't afford conventional Western-style medicine, because of prevailing cultural attitudes and beliefs, or simply because (in some cases) it works. It might also be because there's often no other choice.

Rather than attempting to entirely stamp out traditional practices, or simply pretend they are not happening, a positive first step taken by some African countries is the regulation of traditional medicine through the creation of healers' associations and by offering courses on such topics as sanitary practices. Although it remains unlikely that even a basic level of conventional Western-style medicine will be made available to all the people of Africa any time soon, traditional medicine will almost certainly continue to be practised widely throughout the continent.

### WATER

- Except in South Africa, never drink tap water unless it has been boiled, filtered or chemically disinfected (such as with iodine tablets).
- Never drink from streams, rivers and lakes.
- Avoid drinking from pumps and wells – some do bring pure water to the surface, but the presence of animals can still contaminate supplies.

# Language

Africa's myriad ethnic groups speak several hundred local languages, many subdivided into numerous distinct dialects. The people of Nigeria, for example, speak around 500 languages and dialects according to the Ethnologue report, while even tiny Guinea-Bissau has around 20 languages. Consequently, common languages are essential, and several are used. These may be the language of the largest group in a particular area or country, such as Hausa, or a language that has spread beyond its original geographical boundaries due to trade, such as Swahili. The former colonial languages (English, French and Portuguese) also serve as common languages and have official status in many African countries. In some areas, the common tongue is a creole – a combination of African and European languages.

This chapter provides the basics in several European and African languages that you'll find most useful when travelling across the continent, as they are either in official use or spoken as regional lingua francas. See also the relevant destination chapter for a list of languages spoken in each country.

## AMHARIC

Amharic is Ethiopia's national language, and it is also widely spoken in Eritrea.

If you read our pronunciation guides as if they were English, you'll be understood. The apostrophe (') before a vowel indicates a glottal stop, which sounds the pause in the middle of 'uh-oh'. Amharic's 'glottalised' consonants (ch', k', p', s' and t' in our pronunciation guides) are pronounced by tightening and releasing the vocal cords, a bit like combining the sound with the glottal stop. Note also that the sound r is trilled.

Amharic word endings vary according to the gender of people you're speaking to, which is indicated in this chapter where relevant by the abbreviations 'm' (for speaking to a male) and 'f' (for addressing a female).

Arabic numerals (ie those used in English) are commonly used in writing. Amharic words are used to refer to numbers in speech.

| | | |
|---|---|---|
| **Hello.** | ሰላም | suh·lam |
| **Goodbye.** | ደህና ሁን | duh·na hun (m) |
| | ደህና ሁኚ | duh·na hun·yee (f) |
| **Yes.** | አዎ | 'a·wo |
| **No.** | አይደለም· | 'ai·duh·luhm |
| **Please.** | እባክህ | 'i·ba·kih (m) |
| | እባክሽ | 'i·ba·kish·(f) |
| **Thank you.** | አመሰግናለሁ | 'a·muh·suh·gi·na·luh·hu |
| **Sorry.** | ይቅር | yi·k'ir·ta |
| **Help!** | እርዳታ | 'ir·da·ta |
| | እርዳታ! | 'ir·da·ta |

**Do you speak English?**
እንግሊዘኛ ትችላለህ/ትችያለሽ? — 'in·glee·zuh·nya ti·chi·la·luh·hi/ti·chia·luhsh (m/f)

**I don't understand.**
አልገባኝም — 'al·guh·bany·mi

**How much is it?**
ዋጋው ስንት ነው? — wa·gow sint nuhw

**Where are the toilets?**
ሽንት ቤት የት ነው? — shint bet yuht nuhw

### WANT MORE?

For in-depth language information and handy phrases, check out Lonely Planet's *Africa Phrasebook*. You'll find it at **shop.lonelyplanet.com**, or you can buy Lonely Planet's iPhone phrasebooks at the Apple App Store.

| | | |
|---|---|---|
| 1 | አንድ | and |
| 2 | ሁለት | hu·luht |
| 3 | ሶስት | sost |
| 4 | አራት | 'ar·at |
| 5 | አምስት | 'am·mist |
| 6 | ስድስት | si·dist |
| 7 | ሰባት | suh·bat |
| 8 | ስምንት | si·mint |
| 9 | ዘጠኝ | zuh·t'uhny |
| 10 | አስር | a·sir |

## AFRIKAANS

Afrikaans is one of the official languages of South Africa. It has about six million speakers and is also spoken in Botswana, Malawi, Namibia and Zambia.

Read our coloured pronunciation guides as if they were English and you'll be understood. The stressed syllables are in italics. Note that kh is pronounced as the 'ch' in the Scottish *loch* and r is trilled.

| | | |
|---|---|---|
| **Hello.** | *Hallo.* | ha·*loh* |
| **Goodbye.** | *Totsiens.* | tot·*seens* |
| **Yes.** | *Ja.* | yaa |
| **No.** | *Nee.* | ney |
| **Please.** | *Asseblief.* | a·si·*bleef* |
| **Thank you.** | *Dankie.* | *dang*·kee |
| **Sorry.** | *Jammer.* | *ya*·min |
| **Help!** | *Help!* | help |

**Do you speak English?**
*Praat jy Engels?* — praat yay *eng*·ils

**I don't understand.**
*Ek verstaan nie.* — ek vir·*staan* nee

**How much is it?**
*Hoeveel kos dit?* — *hu*·fil kos dit

**Where are the toilets?**
*Waar is die toilette?* — vaar is dee toy·*le*·ti

| | | |
|---|---|---|
| 1 | *een* | eyn |
| 2 | *twee* | twey |
| 3 | *drie* | dree |
| 4 | *vier* | feer |
| 5 | *vyf* | fayf |
| 6 | *ses* | ses |
| 7 | *sewe* | *see*·vi |
| 8 | *agt* | akht |
| 9 | *nege* | *ney*·khi |
| 10 | *tien* | teen |

## ARABIC

The following phrases are in MSA (Modern Standard Arabic), which is the official language of the Arab world, used in schools, administration and the media. Note, though, that there are significant differences between MSA and the colloquial Arabic from different countries. Egyptian, Gulf, Levantine, Moroccan and Tunisian Arabic are the most common spoken varieties, sometimes mutually unintelligible and with no official written form.

Arabic is written from right to left in Arabic script. Read our coloured pronunciation guides as if they were English and you should be understood. Note that a is pronounced as in 'act', aa as the 'a' in 'father', aw as in 'law', ay as in 'say', ee as in 'see', i as in 'hit', oo as in 'zoo', u as in 'put', gh is a throaty sound, r is rolled, dh is pronounced as in 'that', th as in 'thin' and kh as the 'ch' in the Scottish *loch*. The apostrophe ( ' ) indicates the glottal stop (like the pause in the middle of 'uh-oh'). The stressed syllables are indicated with italics. Masculine and feminine options are indicated with 'm' and 'f' respectively.

### Basics

| | | |
|---|---|---|
| **Hello.** | السلام عليكم. | as·sa·*laa*·mu 'a·*lay*·kum |
| **Goodbye.** | إلى اللقاء. | *'i*·laa al·li·*kaa'* |
| **Yes.** | نعم. | *na*·'am |
| **No.** | لا. | laa |
| **Excuse me.** | عفواً. | *'af*·wan |
| **Sorry.** | آسف. | *'aa*·sif (m) |
| | آسفة. | *'aa*·si·fa (f) |
| **Please.** | لو سمحتَ. | law sa·*mah*·ta (m) |
| | لو سمحتِ. | law sa·*mah*·ti (f) |
| **Thank you.** | شكراً. | *shuk*·ran |

**What's your name?**
ما اسمكَ؟ — maa *'is*·mu·ka (m)
ما اسمكِ؟ — maa *'is*·mu·ki (f)

**My name is ...**
اسمي ... — *'is*·mee ...

**Do you speak English?**
هل تتكلّمُ/ — hal ta·ta·*kal*·la·mu/
تتكلّمين — ta·ta·kal·la·*mee*·na
الإنجليزية؟ — al·'inj·lee·*zee*·ya (m/f)

**I don't understand.**
أنا لا أفهم. — *'a*·naa laa *'af*·ham

## Accommodation

| | | |
|---|---|---|
| **Where's a ...?** | أين أجدُ ...؟ | *'ay*·na *'a*·ji·du ... |
| **campsite** | مخيم | mu·*khay*·yam |
| **guesthouse** | بيت للضيوف | bayt li·du·*yoof* |
| **hotel** | فندق | *fun*·duk |
| **youth hostel** | فندق شباب | *fun*·duk sha·*baab* |

| | | |
|---|---|---|
| **Do you have** | هل عندكم | hal *'in*·da·kum |
| **a ... room?** | غرفةٌ ...؟ | *ghur*·fa·tun ... |
| **single** | بسريرٍ | bi·sa·*ree*·rin |
| | منفردٍ | *mun*·fa·rid |
| **double** | بسريرٍ | bi·sa·*ree*·rin |
| | مزدوّجٍ | muz·*daw*·waj |

| | | |
|---|---|---|
| **How much is** | كم ثمنه | kam *tha*·ma·nu·hu |
| **it per ...?** | لِـ ...؟ | li ... |
| **night** | ليلةٍ واحدة | *lay*·la·tin *waa*·hid |
| **person** | شخصٍ واحدة | *shakh*·sin *waa*·hid |

## Eating & Drinking

**What would you recommend?**

| | |
|---|---|
| ماذا توصي؟ | *maa*·dhaa *too*·see (m) |
| ماذا توصينَ؟ | *maa*·dhaa too·*see*·na (f) |

**What's the local speciality?**

| | |
|---|---|
| ما الوجبة الخاصّة | maa al·*waj*·ba·tul *khaa*·sa |
| لهذه المنطقة؟ | li·*haa*·dhi·hil *man*·ta·ka |

**Do you have vegetarian food?**

| | |
|---|---|
| هل لديكم | hal la·*day*·ku·mu |
| طعامٌ نباتيّ؟ | ta·*'aa*·mun na·*baa*·tee |

| | | |
|---|---|---|
| **I'd like the** | أريد ...، | 'u·*ree*·du ... |
| **..., please.** | لو سمحت. | law sa·*mah*·ta |
| **bill** | الحساب | hi·*saab* |
| **menu** | قائمة | kaa·*'i*·ma·tu |
| | الطعام | at·ta·*'aam* |

| | | |
|---|---|---|
| **beer** | بيرة | *bee*·ra |
| **bottle** | زجاجة | zu·*jaa*·ja |
| **breakfast** | فطور | fu·*toor* |
| **cafe** | مقهىً | *mak*·han |
| **coffee** | قهوة | *kah*·wa |
| **cold** | بارد | *baa*·rid (m) |
| | باردة | *baa*·ri·da (f) |
| **cup** | فنجان | fin·*jaan* |
| **dinner** | عشاء | 'a·*shaa'* |
| **drink** | مشروب | mash·*roob* |
| **fish** | سمك | *sa*·mak |
| **food** | طعام | ta·*'aam* |
| **fork** | شوكة | *shaw*·ka |
| **fruit** | فاكهة | *faa*·ki·ha |
| **glass** | كأس | ka's |
| **hot** | حار | haar (m) |
| | حارة | *haa*·ra (f) |
| **juice** | عصير | 'a·*see*·ru |
| **knife** | سكين | sik·*keen* |
| **lunch** | غداء | gha·*daa'* |
| **market** | سوق | sook |
| **meat** | لحم | lahm |
| **milk** | حليب | ha·*leeb* |
| **mineral water** | مياه معدنية | mi·*yaah* ma'·da·*nee*·ya |
| **plate** | صحن | sahn |
| **restaurant** | مطعمٌ | *mat*·'am |
| **spoon** | ملعقة | *mal*·'a·ka |
| **vegetable** | خضراوات | khud·raa·*waat* |
| **water** | ماء | maa' |
| **wine** | نبيذ | na·*beedh* |

## Emergencies

| | | |
|---|---|---|
| **Help!** | ساعدني! | saa·*'i*·du·nee (m) |
| | ساعديني! | *saa*·'i·*dee*·nee (f) |
| **Go away!** | اتركني! | 'it·*ruk*·nee (m) |
| | اتركيني! | 'it·ru·*kee*·nee (f) |

| | | |
|---|---|---|
| **Call ...!** | اتّصلْ بـ ...! | *'it*·ta·sil bi ... (m) |
| | اتّصلي بـ ...! | 'it·*ta*·si·lee bi ... (f) |
| **a doctor** | طبيبٍ | ta·*beeb* |
| **the police** | الشرطة | ash·*shur*·ta |

### Numbers – Arabic

| | | | |
|---|---|---|---|
| 1 | ١ | واحد | *waa*·hid |
| 2 | ٢ | اثنان | 'ith·*naan* |
| 3 | ٣ | ثلاثة | tha·*laa*·tha |
| 4 | ٤ | أربعة | *'ar*·ba·'a |
| 5 | ٥ | خمسة | *kham*·sa |
| 6 | ٦ | ستة | *sit*·ta |
| 7 | ٧ | سبعة | *sab*·'a |
| 8 | ٨ | ثمانية | tha·*maa*·ni·ya |
| 9 | ٩ | تسعة | *tis*·'a |
| 10 | ١٠ | عشرة | *'a*·sha·ra |

Note that Arabic numerals, unlike letters, are written from left to right.

**Where are the toilets?**
أينَ دورات المياه؟ *'ay·na daw·raa·tul mee·yaah*

**I'm lost.**
أنا ضائع. *'a·naa daa·'i'* (m)
أنا ضائعة. *'a·naa daa·'i·'a* (f)

**I'm sick.**
أنا مريض. *'a·naa ma·reed*

## Shopping & Services

**I'm looking for ...**
أبحثُ عن ... *'ab·ha·thu 'an ...*

**Can I look at it?**
هل يمكنني أن أراه؟ *hal yum·ki·nu·nee 'an 'a·raa·hu*

**Do you have any others?**
هل عندك غيره؟ *hal 'in·da·kum ghay·ru·hu*

**How much is it?**
كم سعره؟ *kam si'·ru·hu*

**That's too expensive.**
هذا غالٍ جداً. *haa·dhaa ghaa·lin jid·dan*

**Where's an ATM?**
أينَ جهاز الصرافة؟ *'ay·na ji·haaz as·sar·raa·fa*

## Time & Dates

**What time is it?**
كم الساعة الآن؟ *kam as·saa·'a·tul 'aan*

**It's (two) o'clock.**
الساعة(الثانية). *as·saa·'a tu (ath·thaa·nee·ya)*

| | | |
|---|---|---|
| **morning** | صباح | *sa·baah* |
| **afternoon** | بعد الظهر | *ba'·da adh·dhuh·ri* |
| **evening** | مساء | *ma·saa'* |

| | | |
|---|---|---|
| **yesterday** | أمس | *'am·si* |
| **today** | اليوم | *al·yawm* |
| **tomorrow** | غداً | *gha·dan* |

## Transport & Directions

**Is this the ... to (Dubai)?**
هل هذا الـ ... إلى (دبي)؟ *hal haa·dhaa al ... 'i·laa (du·ba·yee)*

| | | |
|---|---|---|
| **boat** | سفينة | *sa·fee·na* |
| **bus** | باص | *baas* |
| **plane** | طائرة | *taa·'i·ra* |
| **train** | قطار | *ki·taar* |

**What time's the ... bus?**
في أيّ ساعةٍ يغادر الباص الـ ...؟ *fee 'ay·yee saa·'a·tin yu·ghaa·di·ru al·baas al ...*

| | | |
|---|---|---|
| **first** | أوّل | *'aw·wal* |
| **last** | آخر | *'aa·khir* |

**One ... ticket, please.**
تذكرة ... واحدة, لو سمحت. *tadh·ka·ra·tu ... waa·hi·da law sa·mah·ta*

| | | |
|---|---|---|
| **one-way** | ذهاب فقط | *dha·haa·bu fa·kat* |
| **return** | ذهاب وإياب | *dha·haa·bu wa·'ee·yaab* |

**How much is it to ...?**
كم الأجرة إلى ...؟ *kam al·'uj·ra·ti 'i·laa ...*

**Please take me to ...**
أوصلني عند ... لو سمحت. *'aw·sal·nee 'ind ... law sa·mah·ta*

**Where's the (market)?**
أين الـ (سوق)؟ *'ay·na al (sook)*

**What's the address?**
ما هو العنوان؟ *maa hu·wa al·'un·waan*

# FRENCH

The sounds used in spoken French can almost all be found in English. There are a couple of exceptions: nasal vowels (represented in our pronunciation guides by o or u followed by an almost inaudible nasal consonant sound m, n or ng), the 'funny' *u* (ew in our guides) and the deep-in-the-throat *r*. Bearing these few points in mind and reading our pronunciation guides below as if they were English, you won't have problems being understood. Note that syllables are for the most part equally stressed in French.

Masculine and feminine forms of words are provided in the following phrases where relevant, indicated with 'm' and 'f' respectively.

## Basics

| | | |
|---|---|---|
| **Hello.** | *Bonjour.* | bon·zhoor |
| **Goodbye.** | *Au revoir.* | o·rer·vwa |
| **Excuse me.** | *Excusez-moi.* | ek·skew·zay·mwa |
| **Sorry.** | *Pardon.* | par·don |
| **Yes.** | *Oui.* | wee |
| **No.** | *Non.* | non |
| **Please.** | *S'il vous plaît.* | seel voo play |
| **Thank you.** | *Merci.* | mair·see |
| **You're welcome.** | *De rien.* | der ree·en |

**How are you?**
*Comment allez-vous?* ko·mon ta·lay·voo

**Fine, and you?**
*Bien, merci. Et vous?* byun mair·see ay voo

**My name is ...**
*Je m'appelle ...* zher ma·pel ...

**What's your name?**
*Comment vous appelez-vous?* ko·mon voo·za·play voo

**Do you speak English?**
*Parlez-vous anglais?* par·lay·voo ong·glay

**I don't understand.**
*Je ne comprends pas.* zher ner kom·pron pa

## Accommodation

| | | |
|---|---|---|
| **campsite** | *camping* | kom·peeng |
| **guesthouse** | *pension* | pon·syon |
| **hotel** | *hôtel* | o·tel |
| **youth hostel** | *auberge de jeunesse* | o·berzh der zher·nes |

| | | |
|---|---|---|
| **a ... room** | *une chambre ...* | ewn shom·brer ... |
| **double** | *avec un grand lit* | a·vek un gron lee |
| **single** | *à un lit* | a un lee |

**How much is it per night/person?**
*Quel est le prix par nuit/personne?* kel ay ler pree par nwee/per·son

**Is breakfast included?**
*Est-ce que le petit déjeuner est inclus?* es·ker ler per·tee day·zher·nay ayt en·klew

## Eating & Drinking

**Can I see the menu, please?**
*Est-ce que je peux voir la carte, s'il vous plaît?* es·ker zher per vwar la kart seel voo play

**What would you recommend?**
*Qu'est-ce que vous conseillez?* kes·ker voo kon·say·yay

**I'm a vegetarian.**
*Je suis végétarien/végétarienne.* (m/f) zher swee vay·zhay·ta·ryun/vay·zhay·ta·ryen

**I don't eat ...**
*Je ne mange pas ...* zher ner monzh pa ...

**Cheers!**
*Santé!* son·tay

**Please bring the bill.**
*Apportez-moi l'addition, s'il vous plaît.* a·por·tay·mwa la·dee·syon seel voo play

### Numbers – French

| | | |
|---|---|---|
| 1 | *un* | un |
| 2 | *deux* | der |
| 3 | *trois* | trwa |
| 4 | *quatre* | ka·trer |
| 5 | *cinq* | sungk |
| 6 | *six* | sees |
| 7 | *sept* | set |
| 8 | *huit* | weet |
| 9 | *neuf* | nerf |
| 10 | *dix* | dees |

| | | |
|---|---|---|
| **beer** | *bière* | bee·yair |
| **bottle** | *bouteille* | boo·tay |
| **bread** | *pain* | pun |
| **breakfast** | *petit déjeuner* | per·tee day·zher·nay |
| **cheese** | *fromage* | fro·mazh |
| **coffee** | *café* | ka·fay |
| **cold** | *froid* | frwa |
| **dinner** | *dîner* | dee·nay |
| **dish** | *plat* | pla |
| **egg** | *œuf* | erf |
| **food** | *nourriture* | noo·ree·tewr |
| **fork** | *fourchette* | foor·shet |
| **glass** | *verre* | vair |
| **grocery store** | *épicerie* | ay·pees·ree |
| **hot** | *chaud* | sho |
| **(orange) juice** | *jus (d'orange)* | zhew (do·ronzh) |
| **knife** | *couteau* | koo·to |
| **local speciality** | *spécialité locale* | spay·sya·lee·tay lo·kal |
| **lunch** | *déjeuner* | day·zher·nay |
| **main course** | *plat principal* | pla prun·see·pal |
| **market** | *marché* | mar·shay |
| **milk** | *lait* | lay |
| **plate** | *assiette* | a·syet |
| **red wine** | *vin rouge* | vun roozh |
| **rice** | *riz* | ree |
| **salt** | *sel* | sel |
| **spoon** | *cuillère* | kwee·yair |
| **sugar** | *sucre* | sew·krer |
| **tea** | *thé* | tay |
| **vegetable** | *légume* | lay·gewm |
| **(mineral) water** | *eau (minérale)* | o (mee·nay·ral) |
| **white wine** | *vin blanc* | vun blong |
| **with/without** | *avec/sans* | a·vek/son |

## Emergencies

| | |
|---|---|
| **Help!** | |
| *Au secours!* | o skoor |
| **I'm lost.** | |
| *Je suis perdu/ perdue.* | zhe swee· pair·dew (m/f) |
| **Leave me alone!** | |
| *Fichez-moi la paix!* | fee·shay·mwa la pay |
| **Call a doctor.** | |
| *Appelez un médecin.* | a·play un mayd·sun |
| **Call the police.** | |
| *Appelez la police.* | a·play la po·lees |
| **I'm ill.** | |
| *Je suis malade.* | zher swee ma·lad |
| **Where are the toilets?** | |
| *Où sont les toilettes?* | oo son lay twa·let |

## Shopping & Services

| | |
|---|---|
| **I'd like to buy ...** | |
| *Je voudrais acheter ...* | zher voo·dray ash·tay ... |
| **Can I look at it?** | |
| *Est-ce que je peux le voir?* | es·ker zher per ler vwar |
| **How much is it?** | |
| *C'est combien?* | say kom·byun |
| **It's too expensive.** | |
| *C'est trop cher.* | say tro shair |
| **Can you lower the price?** | |
| *Vous pouvez baisser le prix?* | voo poo·vay bay·say ler pree |

| | | |
|---|---|---|
| **ATM** | *guichet automatique de banque* | gee·shay o·to·ma·teek der bonk |
| **internet cafe** | *cybercafé* | see·bair·ka·fay |
| **post office** | *bureau de poste* | bew·ro der post |
| **tourist office** | *office de tourisme* | o·fees der too·rees·mer |

## Time & Dates

| | |
|---|---|
| **What time is it?** | |
| *Quelle heure est-il?* | kel er ay til |
| **It's (eight) o'clock.** | |
| *Il est (huit) heures.* | il ay (weet) er |
| **It's half past (10).** | |
| *Il est (dix) heures et demie.* | il ay (deez) er ay day·mee |

| | | |
|---|---|---|
| **morning** | *matin* | ma·tun |
| **afternoon** | *après-midi* | a·pray·mee·dee |
| **evening** | *soir* | swar |
| **yesterday** | *hier* | yair |
| **today** | *aujourd'hui* | o·zhoor·dwee |
| **tomorrow** | *demain* | der·mun |

## Transport & Directions

| | | |
|---|---|---|
| **boat** | *bateau* | ba·to |
| **bus** | *bus* | bews |
| **plane** | *avion* | a·vyon |
| **train** | *train* | trun |

| | | |
|---|---|---|
| **a ... ticket** | *un billet ...* | un bee·yay ... |
| **one-way** | *simple* | sum·pler |
| **return** | *aller et retour* | a·lay ay rer·toor |

| | |
|---|---|
| **I want to go to ...** | |
| *Je voudrais aller à ...* | zher voo·dray a·lay a ... |
| **At what time does it leave/arrive?** | |
| *À quelle heure est-ce qu'il part/arrive?* | a kel er es kil par/a·reev |
| **Does it stop at ...?** | |
| *Est-ce qu'il s'arrête à ...?* | es·kil sa·ret a ... |
| **Can you tell me when we get to ...?** | |
| *Pouvez-vous me dire quand nous arrivons à ...?* | poo·vay·voo mer deer kon noo za·ree·von a ... |
| **I want to get off here.** | |
| *Je veux descendre ici.* | zher ver day·son·drer ee·see |
| **Where's ...?** | |
| *Où est ...?* | oo ay ... |
| **What's the address?** | |
| *Quelle est l'adresse?* | kel ay la·dres |
| **Can you show me (on the map)?** | |
| *Pouvez-vous m'indiquer (sur la carte)?* | poo·vay·voo mun·dee·kay (sewr la kart) |

# HAUSA

Hausa is spoken by around 40 million people. Most native speakers live in northern Nigeria and southern Niger. It's also spoken in parts of Benin, Burkina Faso, Cameroon, Côte d'Ivoire and Ghana.

Hausa's glottalised consonants ( b', d', k', ts' and y'), indicated here by an apostrophe after the letter, are produced by tightening and releasing the space between the vocal cords; for the sounds b' and d', instead of breathing out, you breathe in. The apostrophe before a vowel indicates a glottal stop (like the pause in 'uh-oh').

| | | |
|---|---|---|
| **Hello.** | *Sannu.* | san·nu |
| **Goodbye.** | *Sai wani lokaci.* | say wa·ni law·ka·chee |

| | | |
|---|---|---|
| **Yes.** | *I.* | ee |
| **No.** | *A'a.* | a'a |
| **Please.** | *Don Allah.* | don al·laa |
| **Thank you.** | *Na gode.* | naa gaw·dey |
| **Sorry.** | *Yi hak'uri.* | yi ha·k'u·ree |
| **Help!** | *Taimake ni!* | tai·ma·kyey ni |

**Do you speak English?**
*Kana/Kina jin turanci?* (m/f) — ka·naa/ki·naa jin too·ran·chee

**I don't understand.**
*Ban gane ba.* — ban gaa·ney ba

**How much is it?**
*Kud'insa nawa ne?* — ku·d'in·sa na·wa ney

**Where are the toilets?**
*Ina ban d'aki yake?* — i·naa ban d'aa·kee yak·yey

| | | |
|---|---|---|
| 1 | *d'aya* | d'a·ya |
| 2 | *biyu* | bi·yu |
| 3 | *uku* | u·ku |
| 4 | *hud'u* | hu·d'u |
| 5 | *biyar* | bi·yar |
| 6 | *shida* | shi·da |
| 7 | *bakwai* | bak·wai |
| 8 | *takwas* | tak·was |
| 9 | *tara* | ta·ra |
| 10 | *goma* | gaw·ma |

## MALAGASY

Malagasy has around 18 million speakers and is the official language of Madagascar.

The pronunciation of Malagasy words is not always obvious from their written form. Unstressed syllables can be dropped and words pronounced in different ways depending on where they fall in a sentence. If you read our pronunciation guides as if they were English, you'll be understood. Note that dz is pronounced as the 'ds' in 'adds'. The stressed syllables are indicated with italics.

| | | |
|---|---|---|
| **Hello.** | *Manao ahoana.* | maa·*now* *aa*·hon |
| **Goodbye.** | *Veloma.* | ve·*lum* |
| **Yes./No.** | *Eny./Tsia.* | e·ni/*tsi*·aa |
| **Please.** | *Azafady.* | aa·zaa·*faad* |
| **Thank you.** | *Misaotra.* | mi·*sotr* |
| **Sorry.** | *Miala tsiny.* | mi·*aa*·laa tsin |
| **Help!** | *Vonjeo!* | vun·*dze*·u |

**Do you speak English?**
*Miteny angilisy ve ianao?* — mi·*ten* aan·gi·*lis* ve *i*·aa·now

**I don't understand.**
*Tsy azoko.* — tsi *aa*·zuk

**How much is it?**
*Ohatrinona?* — o·*trin*

**Where are the toilets?**
*Aiza ny trano fivoahana?* — ai·*zaa* ni *traa*·nu fi·vu·*aa*·haan

| | | |
|---|---|---|
| 1 | *isa/iray* | *i*·saa/*i*·rai |
| 2 | *roa* | ru |
| 3 | *telo* | tel |
| 4 | *efatra* | e·faatr |
| 5 | *dimy* | dim |
| 6 | *enina* | e·nin |
| 7 | *fito* | fit |
| 8 | *valo* | vaal |
| 9 | *sivy* | siv |
| 10 | *folo* | ful |

## PORTUGUESE

Most sounds in Portuguese are also found in English. The exceptions are the nasal vowels (represented in our pronunciation guides by ng after the vowel), which are pronounced as if you're trying to make the sound through your nose; and the strongly rolled *r* (represented by rr in our pronunciation guides). Also note that the symbol zh sounds like the 's' in 'pleasure'. The stressed syllables are indicated with italics.

Masculine and feminine forms of words are provided in the following phrases where relevant, indicated with 'm' and 'f' respectively.

### Basics

| | | |
|---|---|---|
| **Hello.** | *Olá.* | o·*laa* |
| **Goodbye.** | *Adeus.* | a·de·*oosh* |
| **Excuse me.** | *Faz favor.* | faash fa·*vor* |
| **Sorry.** | *Desculpe.* | desh·*kool*·pe |
| **Yes./No.** | *Sim./Não.* | seeng/nowng |
| **Please.** | *Por favor.* | poor fa·*vor* |
| **Thank you.** | *Obrigado.* *Obrigada.* | o·bree·*gaa*·doo (m) o·bree·*gaa*·da (f) |
| **You're welcome.** | *De nada.* | de *naa*·da |

**How are you?**
*Como está?* — *ko*·moo shtaa

**Fine, and you?**
*Bem, e você?* — beng e vo·*se*

**What's your name?**
*Qual é o seu nome?* — kwaal e oo *se*·oo *no*·me

**My name is ...**
*O meu nome é ...* oo *me*·oo *no*·me e ...

**Do you speak English?**
*Fala inglês?* *faa*·la eeng·*glesh*

**I don't understand.**
*Não entendo.* nowng eng·*teng*·doo

## Accommodation

| | | |
|---|---|---|
| **campsite** | *parque de campismo* | *paar*·ke de kang·*peezh*·moo |
| **guesthouse** | *casa de hóspedes* | *kaa*·za de *osh*·pe·desh |
| **hotel** | *hotel* | o·*tel* |
| **youth hostel** | *pousada de juventude* | poh·*zaa*·da de zhoo·veng·*too*·de |

**Do you have a single/double room?**
*Tem um quarto de solteiro/casal?* teng oong *kwaar*·too de sol·*tay*·roo/ka·*zal*

**How much is it per night/person?**
*Quanto custa por noite/pessoa?* *kwang*·too *koosh*·ta poor *noy*·te/pe·*so*·a

**Is breakfast included?**
*Inclui o pequeno almoço?* eeng·*kloo*·ee oo pe·*ke*·noo aal·*mo*·soo

## Eating & Drinking

**I'd like (the menu).**
*Queria (um menu).* ke·*ree*·a (oong me·*noo*)

**What would you recommend?**
*O que é que recomenda?* oo ke e ke rre·koo·*meng*·da

**I don't eat ...**
*Eu não como ...* e·oo nowng *ko*·moo ...

**Cheers!**
*Saúde!* sa·*oo*·de

**Please bring the bill.**
*Pode-me trazer a conta.* *po*·de·me tra·*zer* a *kong*·ta

| | | |
|---|---|---|
| **beer** | *cerveja* | ser·*ve*·zha |
| **bottle** | *garrafa* | ga·*rraa*·fa |
| **bread** | *pão* | powng |
| **breakfast** | *pequeno almoço* | pe·*ke*·noo aal·*mo*·soo |
| **cheese** | *queijo* | *kay*·zhoo |
| **coffee** | *café* | ka·*fe* |
| **cold** | *frio* | *free*·oo |
| **dinner** | *jantar* | zhang·*taar* |
| **egg** | *ovo* | *o*·voo |
| **food** | *comida* | koo·*mee*·da |
| **fork** | *garfo* | *gar*·foo |
| **fruit** | *fruta* | *froo*·ta |
| **glass** | *copo* | *ko*·poo |
| **hot (warm)** | *quente* | *keng*·te |
| **juice** | *sumo* | *soo*·moo |
| **knife** | *faca* | *faa*·ka |
| **lunch** | *almoço* | aal·*mo*·soo |
| **main course** | *prato principal* | *praa*·too preeng·see·*paal* |
| **market** | *mercado* | mer·*kaa*·doo |
| **milk** | *leite* | *lay*·te |
| **plate** | *prato* | *praa*·too |
| **red wine** | *vinho tinto* | *vee*·nyoo *teeng*·too |
| **restaurant** | *restaurante* | rresh·tow·*rang*·te |
| **rice** | *arroz* | a·*rrosh* |
| **salt** | *sal* | saal |
| **spicy** | *picante* | pee·*kang*·te |
| **spoon** | *colher* | koo·*lyer* |
| **sugar** | *açúcar* | a·*soo*·kar |
| **tea** | *chá* | shaa |
| **vegetable** | *hortaliça* | or·ta·*lee*·sa |
| **vegetarian food** | *comida vegetariana* | koo·*mee*·da ve·zhe·ta·ree·*aa*·na |
| **(mineral) water** | *água (mineral)* | *aa*·gwa (mee·ne·*raal*) |
| **white wine** | *vinho branco* | *vee*·nyoo *brang*·koo |
| **with/without** | *com/sem* | kong/seng |

### Numbers – Portuguese

| | | |
|---|---|---|
| **1** | *um* | oong |
| **2** | *dois* | doysh |
| **3** | *três* | tresh |
| **4** | *quatro* | *kwaa*·troo |
| **5** | *cinco* | *seeng*·koo |
| **6** | *seis* | saysh |
| **7** | *sete* | *se*·te |
| **8** | *oito* | *oy*·too |
| **9** | *nove* | *no*·ve |
| **10** | *dez* | desh |

## Emergencies

| | | |
|---|---|---|
| **Help!** | *Socorro!* | soo·*ko*·rroo |
| **Go away!** | *Vá-se embora!* | *vaa*·se eng·*bo*·ra |
| **Call ...!** | *Chame ...!* | *shaa*·me ... |
| **a doctor** | *um médico* | oong *me*·dee·koo |
| **the police** | *a polícia* | a poo·*lee*·sya |

**I'm lost.**
*Estou perdido.* shtoh per·*dee*·doo (m)
*Estou perdida.* shtoh per·*dee*·da (f)

**I'm ill.**
*Estou doente.* shtoh doo·*eng*·te

**Where is the toilet?**
*Onde é a casa de banho?* *ong*·de e a *kaa*·za de *ba*·nyoo

## Shopping & Services

**I'd like to buy ...**
*Queria comprar ...* ke·*ree*·a kong·*praar* ...

**Can I look at it?**
*Posso ver?* *po*·soo ver

**How much is it?**
*Quanto custa?* *kwang*·too *koosh*·ta

**It's too expensive.**
*Está muito caro.* shtaa *mweeng*·too *kaa*·roo

**Can you lower the price?**
*Pode baixar o preço?* *po*·de bai·*shaar* oo *pre*·soo

| | | |
|---|---|---|
| **ATM** | *caixa automático* | *kai*·sha ow·too·*maa*·tee·koo |
| **internet cafe** | *café da internet* | ka·*fe* da eeng·ter·*ne*·te |
| **post office** | *correio* | koo·*rray*·oo |
| **tourist office** | *escritório de turismo* | shkree·*to*·ryoo de too·*reezh*·moo |

## Time & Dates

**What time is it?**
*Que horas são?* kee *o*·rash sowng

**It's (10) o'clock.**
*São (dez) horas.* sowng (desh) *o*·rash

**Half past (10).**
*(Dez) e meia.* (desh) e *may*·a

| | | |
|---|---|---|
| **morning** | *manhã* | ma·*nyang* |
| **afternoon** | *tarde* | *taar*·de |
| **evening** | *noite* | *noy*·te |

| | | |
|---|---|---|
| **yesterday** | *ontem* | *ong*·teng |
| **today** | *hoje* | *o*·zhe |
| **tomorrow** | *amanhã* | aa·ma·*nyang* |

## Transport & Directions

| | | |
|---|---|---|
| **boat** | *barco* | *baar*·koo |
| **bus** | *autocarro* | ow·to·*kaa*·roo |
| **plane** | *avião* | a·vee·*owng* |
| **train** | *comboio* | kong·*boy*·oo |

| | | |
|---|---|---|
| **... ticket** | *um bilhete de ...* | oong bee·*lye*·te de ... |
| **one-way** | *ida* | *ee*·da |
| **return** | *ida e volta* | *ee*·da ee *vol*·ta |

**I want to go to ...**
*Queria ir a ...* ke·*ree*·a eer a ...

**What time does it leave/arrive?**
*A que horas sai/chega?* a ke *o*·rash sai/*she*·ga

**Does it stop at ...?**
*Pára em ...?* *paa*·ra eng ...

**Please tell me when we get to ...**
*Por favor avise-me quando chegarmos a ...* poor fa·*vor* a·*vee*·ze·me *kwang*·doo she·*gaar*·moosh a ...

**Please stop here.**
*Por favor pare aqui.* poor fa·*vor* *paa*·re a·*kee*

**Where's (the station)?**
*Onde é (a estação)?* *ong*·de e (a shta·*sowng*)

**What's the address?**
*Qual é o endereço?* kwaal e oo eng·de·*re*·soo

**Can you show me (on the map)?**
*Pode-me mostrar (no mapa)?* *po*·de·me moosh·*traar* (noo *maa*·pa)

# SHONA

Shona is spoken by about 11 million people. The vast majority of its speakers are in Zimbabwe, but it's also used in the southern African countries of Mozambique, Botswana and Zambia.

Shona's glottalised consonants, represented as b' and d' in our pronunciation guides, are made by tightening and releasing the space between the vocal cords when you pronounce them. Both sounds are 'implosive', meaning that instead of breathing out to make the sound, you breathe in. Note also that the r is trilled.

| | | |
|---|---|---|
| **Yes.** | *Hongu.* | ho·ngoo |
| **No.** | *Kwete.* | kwe·te |
| **Please.** | *-wo.* | -wo |
| **Thank you.** | *Mazviita.* | maa·zvee·ta |
| **Sorry.** | *Ndapota.* | nd'aa·po·ta |

**Do you speak English?**
*Munotaura chiNgezi here?* moo·no·taa·oo·raa chee·nge·zee he·re

**I don't understand.**
*Handinzvisisi.* haa·ndee·nzvee·see·see

**How much is it?**
*Inoita marii?* ee·o·ee·taa maa·ree·ee

**Where are the toilets?**
*Zvimbudzi zviri kupi?* — zvee·mboo·dzee zvee·ree koo·pee

**Could you help me, please?**
*Mungandibatsirawo here?* — moo·ngaa·ndee·b'aa·tsee·raa·wo he·re

| | | |
|---|---|---|
| 1 | *-mwe* | -mwe |
| 2 | *-viri* | -vee·ree |
| 3 | *-tatu* | -taa·too |
| 4 | *-na* | -naa |
| 5 | *-shanu* | -shaa·noo |
| 6 | *-tanhatu* | -taa·nhaa·too |
| 7 | *-nomwe* | -no·mwe |
| 8 | *-sere* | -se·re |
| 9 | *-pfumbamwe* | -pfoo·mbaa·mwe |
| 10 | *gumi* | goo·mee |

## SWAHILI

Swahili, the national language of Tanzania and Kenya, is also the key language of communication in the East African region. Although the number of speakers of Swahili throughout East Africa is estimated to be over 50 million, it's the mother tongue of only about 5 million people.

Most sounds in Swahili have equivalents in English. In our pronunciation guides, dh should be read as the 'th' in 'this'. Note also that in Swahili the sound ng can be found at the start of words, and that Swahili speakers make only a slight distinction between the sounds r and l – instead of the hard 'r', try pronouncing a light 'd'. The stressed syllables are indicated with italics.

| | | |
|---|---|---|
| **Hello. (general)** | *Habari?* | ha·*ba*·ree |
| **Goodbye.** | *Tutaonana.* | too·ta·oh·*na*·na |
| **Yes.** | *Ndiyo.* | n·*dee*·yoh |
| **No.** | *Hapana.* | ha·*pa*·na |
| **Please.** | *Tafadhali.* | ta·fa·*dha*·lee |
| **Thank you.** | *Asante.* | a·*san*·tay |
| **Sorry.** | *Pole.* | *poh*·lay |
| **Help!** | *Saidia!* | sa·ee·*dee*·a |

**Do you speak English?**
*Unasema Kiingereza?* — oo·na·*say*·ma kee·een·gay·*ray*·za

**I don't understand.**
*Sielewi.* — see·ay·*lay*·wee

**How much is it?**
*Ni bei gani?* — ni bay *ga*·nee

**Where's the toilet?**
*Choo kiko wapi?* — choh *kee*·koh *wa*·pee

| | | |
|---|---|---|
| 1 | *moja* | *moh*·ja |
| 2 | *mbili* | m·*bee*·lee |
| 3 | *tatu* | *ta*·too |
| 4 | *nne* | *n*·nay |
| 5 | *tano* | *ta*·noh |
| 6 | *sita* | *see*·ta |
| 7 | *saba* | *sa*·ba |
| 8 | *nane* | *na*·nay |
| 9 | *tisa* | *tee*·sa |
| 10 | *kumi* | *koo*·mee |

## WOLOF

Wolof is the lingua franca of Senegal and Gambia, where it's spoken by about eight million people. It's also spoken in the neighbouring countries of Mauritania, Mali and Guinea.

Note that in our pronunciation guides, the stressed syllables are in italics. Also, uh is pronounced as the 'a' in 'ago', kh as the 'ch' in the Scottish *loch* and r is trilled.

| | | |
|---|---|---|
| **Hello.** | *Salaam aleekum.* | sa·*laam* a·*ley*·kum |
| **Goodbye.** | *Mangi dem.* | *maan*·gee dem |
| **Yes.** | *Waaw.* | waaw |
| **No.** | *Déedéet.* | *dey*·deyt |
| **Please.** | *Bu la neexee.* | boo la *ney*·khey |
| **Thank you.** | *Jërejëf.* | *je*·re·jef |
| **Sorry.** | *Baal ma.* | baal ma |
| **Help!** | *Wóoy!* | wohy |

**Do you speak English?**
*Ndax dégg nga angale?* — ndakh deg nguh *an*·ga·ley

**I don't understand.**
*Dégguma.* — *deg*·goo·ma

**How much is it?**
*Ñaata lay jar?* — *nyaa*·ta lai jar

**Where are the toilets?**
*Ana wanag wi?* — a·na *wa*·nak wee

| | | |
|---|---|---|
| 1 | *benn* | ben |
| 2 | *ñaar* | nyaar |
| 3 | *ñett* | nyet |
| 4 | *ñeent* | nyeynt |
| 5 | *juróom* | *joo*·rohm |
| 6 | *juróom benn* | *joo*·rohm ben |
| 7 | *juróom ñaar* | *joo*·rohm nyaar |
| 8 | *juróom ñett* | *joo*·rohm nyet |
| 9 | *juróom ñeent* | *joo*·rohm nyeynt |
| 10 | *fukk* | fuk |

## XHOSA

Xhosa is the most widely distributed indigenous language in South Africa. About six and a half million people speak Xhosa.

In our pronunciation guides, the apostrophe after the consonant (eg k') indicates that the sound is 'spat out' (in Xhosa, only in case of b' the air is sucked in), a bit like combining it with the sound heard in the middle of 'uh-oh'. Xhosa has a series of 'click' sounds as well; they are not distinguished in the following phrases.

| | | |
|---|---|---|
| **Hello.** | *Molo.* | *maw*·law |
| **Goodbye.** | *Usale ngoxolo.* | u·*saa*·le ngaw·*kaw*·law |
| **Yes.** | *Ewe.* | e·*we* |
| **No.** | *Hayi.* | haa·*yee* |
| **Please.** | *Cela.* | *ke*·laa |
| **Thank you.** | *Enkosi.* | e·*nk'aw*·see |
| **Sorry.** | *Uxolo.* | u·*aw*·law |
| **Help!** | *Uncedo!* | u·*ne*·daw |

**Do you speak English?**
*Uyasithetha isingesi?* — u·yaa·see·*te*·taa ee·see·*nge*·see

**I don't understand.**
*Andiqondi.* — aa·ndee·*kaw*·ndee

**How much is it?**
*Yimalini?* — yee·*maa*·li·nee

**Where are the toilets?**
*Ziphi itoylethi?* — zee·*pee* ee·*taw*·yee·le·tee

In Xhosa, numbers borrowed from English are commonly used and will be understood.

| | | |
|---|---|---|
| **1** | *wani* | *waa*·nee |
| **2** | *thu* | tu |
| **3** | *thri* | tree |
| **4** | *fo* | faw |
| **5** | *fayifu* | *faa*·yee·fu |
| **6** | *siksi* | *seek'*·see |
| **7** | *seveni* | se·*ve*·nee |
| **8** | *eyithi* | e·*yee*·tee |
| **9** | *nayini* | *naa*·yee·nee |
| **10** | *teni* | *t'e*·nee |

## YORUBA

Yoruba is spoken by around 25 million people. It is primarily used as a first language in southwestern Nigeria. There are also Yoruba speakers in Benin, eastern Togo and in Sierra Leone.

Yoruba's nasal vowels, indicated in our pronunciation guides with ng after the vowel, are pronounced as if you're trying to force the sound through the nose.

| | | |
|---|---|---|
| **Hello.** | *Pẹ̀lẹ́ ọ.* | kpe·le o |
| **Goodbye.** | *Ọ́ dàbọ̀.* | oh da·bo |
| **Yes.** | *Bẹ́ẹ̀ni.* | be·e·ni |
| **No.** | *Bẹ́ẹ̀kọ́.* | be·e·ko |
| **Please.** | *Jọ̀wọ́.* | jo·wo |
| **Thank you.** | *Ọṣẹ́.* | oh·shay |
| **Sorry.** | *Má bìínú.* | ma bi·i·nu |
| **Help!** | *Ẹ ràn mí lọ́wọ́ ọ!* | e rang mi lo·wo o |

**Do you speak English?**
*Ṣẹ́ ọ ń ṣọ gẹ̀ẹ́ṣì?* — shay o n so ge·e·si

**I don't understand.**
*Ẹ̀mi kọ̀ gbọ́.* — ay·mi koh gbo

**How much is it?**
*Ẹ̀lọ́ ni?* — ay·loh ni

**Where are the toilets?**
*Ibọ ni ilẹ́ ìgbọ̀nṣẹ̀ wà?* — i·boh ni i·lay i·gbong·se wa

| | | |
|---|---|---|
| **1** | *ọ̀kan* | o·kang |
| **2** | *ẹ̀jì* | ay·ji |
| **3** | *ẹ̀ta* | e·ta |
| **4** | *ẹ̀rin* | e·ring |
| **5** | *àrun* | a·rung |
| **6** | *ẹ̀fà* | e·fa |
| **7** | *ẹ̀jẹ* | ay·jay |
| **8** | *ẹ̀jọ* | e·jo |
| **9** | *ẹ̀ṣan* | e·sang |
| **10** | *ẹ̀wá* | e·wa |

## ZULU

About 10 million Africans speak Zulu as a first language, most of them in South Africa. It is also spoken in Lesotho and Swaziland.

In our pronunciation guides, b' indicates that the air is sucked in when you pronounce this sound (in Zulu, some other consonants are 'spat out'), a bit like combining it with the sound in the middle of 'uh-oh'. Note also that hl is pronounced as in the Welsh *llewellyn* and dl is like hl but with the vocal cords vibrating. Xhosa has a series of 'click' sounds as well; they are not distinguished in this section.

**Hello.**
*Sawubona.* (sg) — saa·wu·*b'aw*·naa
*Sanibonani.* (pl) — saa·nee·b'aw·*naa*·nee

**Goodbye.** (if leaving)
*Sala kahle.* (sg) — saa·laa *gaa*·hle
*Salani kahle.* (pl) — saa·laa·nee *gaa*·hle

**Goodbye.** (if staying)

| | |
|---|---|
| *Hamba kahle.* (sg) | haa·mbaa *gaa*·hle |
| *Hambani kahle.* (pl) | haa·mbaa·nee *gaa*·hle |

| | | |
|---|---|---|
| **Yes./No.** | *Yebo./Cha.* | ye·b'aw/kaa |
| **Thank you.** | *Ngiyabonga.* | ngee·yaa·*b'aw*·ngaa |
| **Sorry.** | *Uxolo.* | u·*kaw*·law |

**Do you speak English?**

| | |
|---|---|
| *Uyasikhuluma isiNgisi?* | u·yaa·see·ku·lu·maa ee·see·ngee·see |

**I don't understand.**

| | |
|---|---|
| *Angizwa.* | aa·*ngee*·zwaa |

**How much is it?**

| | |
|---|---|
| *Yimalini?* | yee·maa·lee·nee |

**Where are the toilets?**

| | |
|---|---|
| *Ziphi izindlu zangasese?* | zee·pee ee·zee·ndlu zaa·ngaa·se·se |

**Could you help me, please?**

| | |
|---|---|
| *Ake ungisize/ ningisize.* (sg/pl) | aa·ge u·ngee·see·ze/ nee·ngee·see·ze |

In Zulu, numbers borrowed from English are commonly used and will be understood.

| | | |
|---|---|---|
| **1** | *uwani* | u·*waa*·nee |
| **2** | *uthu* | u·*tu* |
| **3** | *uthri* | u·*three* |
| **4** | *ufo* | u·*faw* |
| **5** | *ufayifi* | u·*faa*·yee·fee |
| **6** | *usiksi* | u·*seek*·see |
| **7** | *usevene* | u·*se*·ve·nee |
| **8** | *u-eyithi* | u·e·yeet |
| **9** | *unayini* | u·*naa*·yee·nee |
| **10** | *utheni* | u·*the*·nee |

# Behind the Scenes

## SEND US YOUR FEEDBACK

We love to hear from travellers – your comments keep us on our toes and help make our books better. Our well-travelled team reads every word on what you loved or loathed about this book. Although we cannot reply individually to your submissions, we always guarantee that your feedback goes straight to the appropriate authors, in time for the next edition. Each person who sends us information is thanked in the next edition – the most useful submissions are rewarded with a selection of digital PDF chapters.

Visit **lonelyplanet.com/contact** to submit your updates and suggestions or to ask for help. Our award-winning website also features inspirational travel stories, news and discussions.

Note: We may edit, reproduce and incorporate your comments in Lonely Planet products such as guidebooks, websites and digital products, so let us know if you don't want your comments reproduced or your name acknowledged. For a copy of our privacy policy visit lonelyplanet.com/privacy.

## OUR READERS

**Many thanks to the travellers who used the last edition and wrote to us with helpful hints, useful advice and interesting anecdotes:**

Adele Hansen, Ane Zugadi, Hans Derveaux, Jonathan Salisbury, Lumir Kunovsky, Martin Willoughby-Thomas, Michael Walti, Peter Wennington, Ron Perrier, Sean McHugh, Tom Mann, Will Rogers

## WRITER THANKS

### Anthony Ham

So many people helped me along the way and brought such wisdom and insight to this book. Special thanks as always to Andy Raggett at Drive Botswana, and to Paul Funston, Lise Hansson, Luke Hunter, Charlotte Pollard, Rob Reid, Eva Meurs, Daan Smit, Jacob Tembo, Induna Mundandwe, Kasia Sliwa, Lara Good and Ying Yi Ho. At Lonely Planet, heartfelt thanks to my editor Matt Phillips – no-one knows Africa like him – and the excellent team of writers. And to Marina, Carlota and Valentina – I loved sharing some of my favourite corners of Africa with you.

### Brett Atkinson

A big *shukran* to the following: Ben and Ollie in Taghazout, Irene in Tamraght, Jane in Taroudannt, Sissi and Mafhoud in Taliouine, Sadat in Tarfaya, Houssine and Liesbeth in Tafraoute, and Sally in Mirleft. Special thanks to Neil, Jackie and the kids in Dakhla. At LP, thanks to Helen Elfer for the opportunity to explore North Africa, my fellow authors and the hardworking editors and cartos, and final thanks to Carol for holding the fort back home in New Zealand.

### James Bainbridge

Believe the hype about Malawian friendliness: this really is the Warm Heart of Africa. *Zikomo,* then, to pretty much everyone for being so awesome, and in particular to the many folk, too numerous to mention, in lodges from Mzuzu to Mulanje. My research trip was considerably more fruitful and fun with your local knowledge and sociable bottles of Green.

### Stuart Butler

Firstly I must thank my wife, Heather, and children, Jake and Grace, for their patience and understanding while I was away in Guinea and Algeria. In Guinea thanks to Patrick Madelaine for the car and Bouba for driving. Big thanks to Christelle Colin and team for a great weekend with the chimps. In Algeria I owe a huge debt of gratitude to Ahcicene from Expert Algeria as well as to the guides at the archaeological sites for their endless enthusiasm.

### Jean-Bernard Carillet

A huge thanks to everyone who helped out and made this trip an enlightenment, especially

Waleed, and all the people I met on the road. At LP I'm grateful to Matt for his trust and support, and to the hard-working editors. At home, a *gros bisou* to Eva and lots of love to Morgane, whose support was essential.

### Paul Clammer

This was my first Morocco update job where I could commute from home, our house in the Fes medina. So, thanks above all to Robyn for her amazing restoration job, and to Monkey the accidentally adopted mosque roof cat, for not smashing ALL the glassware when I was in Tangier. On the roof, my continued *salaams* to petit taxi drivers everywhere who put the meter on without asking.

### Lucy Corne

A huge *enkosi* to all who shared their insider tips, including Heather, Ivor, Eben, Terri, Shae, Meruschka, Megan, Scott, Troye, Matt, Sean, Sal, Tanya, Elmar, Ed and Sylvia. Thanks to Matt, Dianne and Dan at LP and great big hugs to my mum and dad for becoming travelling au pairs during research. High five to Kai, the cutest little LP writer-in-training, for being awesome throughout those long road trips. And above all, this one is for Shawn – I absolutely couldn't have done it without you.

### Emilie Filou

Thank you to Patricia Rajeriarison, Ortana, Jean Robert, Steve McDonald, Orpheu, Patrick Andrianomena and Mad Trekking for patiently answering queries. And thanks as ever to Adolfo, for everything.

### Mary Fitzpatrick

*Asanteni sana, muito obrigada* to the many people who helped me out on the road in Tanzania and Mozambique. Special thanks to Sidney Bliss for his ongoing Mozambique updates; Rafael Holt for the Tofo background; staff at Ngorongoro Conservation Area Authority; the unnamed policeman near Mwanza; and Mama Sara near Mpanda whose outlook continues to inspire. Thank you most of all to Rick, Christopher, Dominic and Gabriel for their company, patience and good humour on the road and back home.

### Michael Grosberg

In Guinea-Bissau, thanks to Adlino Costa for sharing his insights about his homeland; Daniel da Silva for his good-natured help; Mario for getting me to the islands; Solange and Alain on Rubane for their hospitality and assistance when sick; and to the Swiss travellers with whom I shared a beautiful Thanksgiving lunch and who picked me up when sick on the beach after hippo spotting on Orango. And my baby Rosie for her wonderful homecoming hugs. In Mauritania, my gratitude goes to Theresa Eno, Sidi Boidaha, Jimmy Baum, Adam Janssen, Isabelle and Frederic, and Betsy Freeman.

### Trent Holden

First up thanks to Matt Phillips for commissioning me to go to Zimbabwe, one of my all-time favourite countires in the world, as well as all the production staff for putting this together. A huge thanks to Karl Wright and Jenny Nobes from Rhino Safari Camp for all their assistance in getting around Matusadona and for tips and recommendations across the country – an unbelievable help! Also thanks to the following people for all their time and assistance: the team from Chilo Gorge Lodge, Joy from Victoria Falls and Gordon Addams, Ann Bruce, Tempe, Jane, Jacqui and George from the Eastern Highlands. A huge thanks to James S once again for taking time out to go on a road trip – I had a ball! Finally lots of love to my family, especially my partner, Kate, who allows me to travel to such far-flung, exotic places.



## THIS BOOK

This 14th edition of Lonely Planet's *Africa* guide was written by Anthony Ham, Brett Atkinson, James Bainbridge, Stuart Butler, Jean-Bernard Carillet, Paul Clammer, Lucy Corne, Emilie Filou, Mary Fitzpatrick, Michael Grosberg, Trent Holden, Jess Lee, Stephen Lioy, Nana Luckham, Vesna Maric, Tom Masters, Virginia Maxwell, Lorna Parkes, Helen Ranger, Brendan Sainsbury, Caroline Sieg, Helena Smith, Regis St Louis and Paul Stiles. This guidebook was produced by the following:

**Destination Editors** Helen Elfer, Matt Phillips

**Product Editors** Carolyn Boicos, Kate Chapman

**Senior Cartographer** Diana Von Holdt

**Cartographers** Michael Garrett, Alison Lyall

**Book Designers** Gwen Cotter, Wibowo Rusli

**Assisting Editors** Andrew Bain, Imogen Bannister, Pete Cruttenden, Melanie Dankel, Andrea Dobbin, Gabrielle Innes, Jodie Martire, Charlotte Orr, Ross Taylor, Saralinda Turner, Fionnuala Twomey

**Cover Researcher** Naomi Parker

**Thanks to** Hannah Cartmel, Bruce Evans, Paul Harding, Indra Kilfoyle, Catherine Naghten, Claire Naylor, Karyn Noble, Lauren O'Connell, Kirsten Rawlings, Amanda Williamson

### Jessica Lee

A huge *shukron* to Hisham for helping me out with convoluted Cairo microbus routes, Khairy and family for their wonderful hospitality, Khalid for cheerful cynicism, Fatima and Said, Muhammed, Mahmoud, Rania, and Ahmed. Also a big thank you to the staff at Aswan and Luxor tourist offices.

### Stephen Lioy

Wendelin, for the company and the keen questions in frustrating situations. My favourite local friend, for the long chats and positive vibes. Take that girl to Massawa! Tekeste and Sam, for the fantastic tips and honest info. BGI, for dealing in good grace with my long absences. Nan, for keeping me pumped full of coffee in my wing of the house throughout write-up.

### Nana Luckham

Thanks to all who helped me along the way, including Joe Addo, Aboubacar Diédhiou, Melvin Kraan, Richard at the Sleepy Hippo Hotel, Geoffrey Awoonor-Renner at Visit Sierra Leone for his invaluable advice, Fritz and Angela for their company on the road in Sierra Leone, Tapsir and Hannah for their hospitality in Freetown, Elizabeth Yirenchi, George Tenkorang and Zena Ampofo-Tenkorang for putting me up in Accra, Patrick Smith at Africa Confidential for useful pre-departure advice as always, and Yaa Yeboah and Benjamin Swift for minding the fort at home.

### Vesna Maric

I would like to thank Matt Phillips for commissioning me for the project. Additional thanks go to Pascale and Charlotte in Abidjan, Ali in Burkina Faso, and Cheryl in Grand Bassam.

### Tom Masters

Huge thanks to Gabriel Gatehouse, Joe Kellner, Alex Lee, Josa Glück, Nina Mason, Sean Holiday, William Clowes, Aleks Sawyer, Retha Cook, Tessa Mayouya, Adam Nkunda, Roadtrip Uganda, Central Rent-a-Car and the teams at Kivu Travel, Aruba Mara Camp, Nkuringo Gorilla Campsite and Byoona Amagara who all went beyond the expected to help out with my research. Thanks to Matt Phillips for sending me back to Africa and the entire in-house crew at Lonely Planet.

### Virginia Maxwell

Greatest thanks go to my travelling companion, Peter Handsaker. Thanks also to Tine Riera, Marie-Christine Martinet, Mustapha Bouamara, Helen Ranger and Jess Lee.

### Lorna Parkes

Thanks to Helen Elfer, who gave me the best excuse to travel back to one of my favourite cities. To Said at Dar Bensouda, without whom I would have got lost in the Fez medina many more times than I did. Thanks also to Jess Stephens and Liz Campbell for their trusted insights, and to Robert Johnstone for his offerings of food. Biggest thanks of all goes to Rob, for looking after our son, Austin, and to Austin himself, for joining me on part of the adventure.

### Helen Ranger

In Equatorial Guinea, thanks to Ambassador Crisantos Obama Ondo in Morocco who encouraged my trip to his country. In Malabo, Ángel Vañó shared his kaleidoscopic knowledge of Equatorial Guinea with great enthusiasm. To the local inhabitants who were astonished to see a tourist, thank you for a fascinating experience. May you see many more.

### Brendan Sainsbury

Thanks to all the untold bus drivers, chefs, hotel receptionists, tour guides, and innocent bystanders who helped me during this research.

### Caroline Sieg

Thanks to Myriam and Glenn in Cotonou for being such amazing hosts and travel buddies and for getting me sorted when my phone was stolen on Day 2. I owe you both massive beers in Munich. Special thanks to Lara for the pre-trip Liberia info and for being a voice on the phone when I most needed it. Big *bisou* to Lawrence for all the picnic supplies and last but not least, thanks to my Fatima for the endless supply of information and suggestions.

### Helena Smith

Thanks for pre-trip help to Ranx, Segun, Alastair and Helen and Cordelia. In Cameroon: Caesar for excellent driving, Agatha and Ashwu in Limbe, Cyril in Buea for his kind invitation, Ismael in Foumban, Kelvin from Bamenda and Chris in Yaoundé. In Nigeria: Bikiya, Toba, Odunola and Leke for the warmest Lagos welcome, our friends Chike and Edet at Bogobiri, Kunle and his wife at the Jazz Hole, Boma for taking us to the Shrine, Rasheed for fantastic driving, Nike and her team, Doyin for a gracious Yoruba welcome, Puja and Philip in Benin and Zac in Calabar. And to Art, for bringing a guitar and an open heart to Africa.

### Regis St Louis

Countless guides, drivers, boat captains, innkeepers and many others helped along the way – and I am deeply grateful to the warm-hearted people in West Africa and Morocco. Special thanks go to Adama Ba, whose driving skills, humour and patience made the Senegambia journey a success. In Cabo Verde, thanks to Erick on Brava, Fatima on

Fogo, Guillaume on Santo Antão, and Carolyn, Ismael and Bemvindo on Maio. In Morocco, I'm grateful to Abdel Haydar, Lahcen Igdem, Almodhik Aissa, Mohamed El Qasemy and Carolyn, Tahrbilte Rachid, Abdel Jalil, Omar and Ibrahim of Dar Sofian, Rashid and Doreen (and Jack the donkey), Ziad and Amqrane Tair (and family), Vanessa and Xavier, Toufiq Mousaoui, and Abdel Benalila and his family. Thanks to the support of Cassandra and daughters Magdalena and Genevieve, who make this whole endeavour worthwhile.

## Paul Stiles

My great thanks to Matt for this terrific assignment, to Diogo and Luis for helping steer me through the country, and to the many guides I met along the way, particularly Armando, Helton, Yves, Ruben, and Ramos. No leve leve allowed! As usual, I must also thank Sarah for taking care of the home front while I was away, not to mention putting up that Sáo Tomé wood carving in the kitchen.

# ACKNOWLEDGEMENTS

Climate map data adapted from Peel MC, Finlayson BL & McMahon TA (2007) 'Updated World Map of the Köppen-Geiger Climate Classification', *Hydrology and Earth System Sciences*, 11, 163344.

Cover photograph: Detail of wristbands on Samburu woman, Keren Su/Getty ©

# Index



Map Pages **000**
Photo Pages **000**

Map Pages **000**
Photo Pages **000**

Map Pages **000**
Photo Pages **000**

Map Pages **000**
Photo Pages **000**

# Map Legend

## Sights

- Beach
- Bird Sanctuary
- Buddhist
- Castle/Palace
- Christian
- Confucian
- Hindu
- Islamic
- Jain
- Jewish
- Monument
- Museum/Gallery/Historic Building
- Ruin
- Shinto
- Sikh
- Taoist
- Winery/Vineyard
- Zoo/Wildlife Sanctuary
- Other Sight

## Activities, Courses & Tours

- Bodysurfing
- Diving
- Canoeing/Kayaking
- Course/Tour
- Sento Hot Baths/Onsen
- Skiing
- Snorkelling
- Surfing
- Swimming/Pool
- Walking
- Windsurfing
- Other Activity

## Sleeping

- Sleeping
- Camping

## Eating

- Eating

## Drinking & Nightlife

- Drinking & Nightlife
- Cafe

## Entertainment

- Entertainment

## Shopping

- Shopping

## Information

- Bank
- Embassy/Consulate
- Hospital/Medical
- Internet
- Police
- Post Office
- Telephone
- Toilet
- Tourist Information
- Other Information

## Geographic

- Beach
- Gate
- Hut/Shelter
- Lighthouse
- Lookout
- Mountain/Volcano
- Oasis
- Park
- Pass
- Picnic Area
- Waterfall

## Population

- Capital (National)
- Capital (State/Province)
- City/Large Town
- Town/Village

## Transport

- Airport
- Border crossing
- Bus
- Cable car/Funicular
- Cycling
- Ferry
- Metro station
- Monorail
- Parking
- Petrol station
- Subway station
- Taxi
- Train station/Railway
- Tram
- Underground station
- Other Transport

*Note: Not all symbols displayed above appear on the maps in this book*

## Routes

- Tollway
- Freeway
- Primary
- Secondary
- Tertiary
- Lane
- Unsealed road
- Road under construction
- Plaza/Mall
- Steps
- Tunnel
- Pedestrian overpass
- Walking Tour
- Walking Tour detour
- Path/Walking Trail

## Boundaries

- International
- State/Province
- Disputed
- Regional/Suburb
- Marine Park
- Cliff
- Wall

## Hydrography

- River, Creek
- Intermittent River
- Canal
- Water
- Dry/Salt/Intermittent Lake
- Reef

## Areas

- Airport/Runway
- Beach/Desert
- Cemetery (Christian)
- Cemetery (Other)
- Glacier
- Mudflat
- Park/Forest
- Sight (Building)
- Sportsground
- Swamp/Mangrove

**Caroline Sieg**

Benin, Liberia, Togo Caroline began her career producing foreign-language textbooks before hopping over to travel publishing, first as a travel editor at Frommer's Travel in the US and later as a commissioning editor at Lonely Planet in London. She then managed and curated digital marketing content for diverse brands including Travelzoo and Art Basel. She's written about destinations across the globe. For Lonely Planet she's covered the US, Africa and Europe.

**Helena Smith**

Cameroon, Nigeria Helena is an award-winning writer and photographer covering travel and food – she has written guidebooks on destinations from Fiji to northern Norway. Helena is from Scotland but was partly brought up in Malawi, so Africa always feels like home. She also enjoys global travel in her multicultural home borough of Hackney and wrote, photographed and published *Inside Hackney,* the first guide to the borough (insidehackney.com).

**Regis St Louis**

Cabo Verde, The Gambia, Morocco, Senegal Regis grew up in a small town in the American Midwest and developed an early fascination with foreign dialects and world cultures. Regis has contributed to more than 50 Lonely Planet titles, covering destinations across six continents. His travels have taken him from the mountains of Kamchatka to remote island villages in Melanesia, and to many grand urban landscapes. When not on the road, he lives in New Orleans. Follow him on www.instagram.com/regisstlouis.

**Paul Stiles**

São Tomé & Príncipe When he was 21, Paul bought an old motorcycle in London and drove it to Tunisia. That did it for him. Since then he has explored around 60 countries, and covered many adventure destinations for Lonely Planet, including Morocco, Madagascar, São Tomé & Príncipe, Indonesia, the Philippines, Hawaii, Maui, and Kaua'i. In all things, he tries to follow the rocking chair rule: when making key life decisions, assume the perspective of an elderly person sitting in a rocking chair. Because some day that will be you.

**Stephen Lioy**

Eritrea Stephen Lioy is a photographer, writer, hiker, and travel blogger based in Central Asia. A 'once in a lifetime' Eurotrip and post-university move to China set the stage for what would eventually become a semi-nomadic lifestyle based on sharing his experiences with would-be travellers and helping provide that initial push out of comfort zones and into all that the planet has to offer. Follow Stephen's travels at www.monkboughtlunch.com or see his photography at www.stephenlioy.com.

**Nana Luckham**

Ghana, Sierra Leone Nana began writing about travel in 2006, after several years working as a United Nations press officer in New York. She has been all over the world for Lonely Planet including to Malawi, Zambia, Algeria, South Africa, Fiji and Tuvalu. She has also written features for lonelyplanet.com and for other leading publications. Currently based in London, she's lived in New York, France, Ghana, Zimbabwe, Tanzania and Australia.

**Vesna Maric**

Burkina Faso, Côte d'Ivoire Vesna has been a Lonely Planet author for over a decade, covering places as far and wide as Bolivia, Algeria, Sicily, Cyprus, Barcelona, London and Croatia, among others. Her latest work has been updating the Burkina Faso and Ivory Coast chapters for the *West Africa* and *Africa* guides.

**Tom Masters**

Democratic Republic of Congo, Kenya, Republic of Congo, Rwanda, Uganda Dreaming since he could walk of going to the most obscure places on earth, Tom has always had a taste for the unknown. This has led to a writing career that has taken him all over the world, including North Korea, the Arctic, Congo and Siberia. Despite a brief spell living in the English countryside, Tom has always called London, Paris and Berlin home. He currently lives in Berlin and can be found online at www.tommasters.net.

**Virginia Maxwell**

Morocco Although based in Australia, Virginia spends at least half of her year updating Lonely Planet destination coverage in Europe and the Middle East. The Mediterranean is her favourite place to travel, and she has covered Spain, Italy, Turkey, Syria, Lebanon, Israel, Egypt and Morocco for LP guidebooks – there are only eight more countries to go! Virginia also writes about Armenia, Iran and Australia. Follow her @maxwellvirginia on Instagram and Twitter.

**Lorna Parkes**

Morocco Londoner by birth, Melburnian by palate and ex–Lonely Planet staffer in both cities, Lorna has spent more than 10 years exploring the globe in search of the perfect meal, the friendliest B&B, the best-value travel experience, and the most spectacular lookout point. She's discovered she writes best on planes, and has contributed to numerous Lonely Planet books and magazines. Wineries and the tropics (not at the same time!) are her go-to happy places. Follow her @Lorna_Explorer.

**Helen Ranger**

Equatorial Guinea, Gabon Although born and brought up in the UK, Helen left in her early twenties to explore other shores. Cape Town was her home for many years but she now lives in Fez, Morocco. She has contributed to Lonely Planet's *Fez Encounter, South Africa, Lesotho & Swaziland, Cape Town, Africa* and *Morocco* guides. Follow her on Twitter: @helenranger @fezriads @conciergmorocco and on Instagram: helenranger and conciergemorocco.

**Brendan Sainsbury**

Angola, Mozambique Originally from Hampshire, England, Brendan first experienced Africa on a solo cycling trip around Morocco in the early 1990s. He revisited the continent in 1997, when he hitchhiked from Cape Town to Kilimanjaro. Brendan learned Portuguese and became eternally obsessed with the African Lusosphere while teaching at a rural school in Angola in 2001–02, He once directed a Portuguese production of Shakespeare's *Comedy of Errors* at a theatre in war-torn Benguela.

**Paul Clammer**

Morocco Paul Clammer has worked as a molecular biologist, tour leader and travel writer. Since 2003 he has worked as a guidebook author for Lonely Planet, contributing to over 25 LP titles, covering destinations including swathes of South and Central Asia, West and North Africa and the Caribbean. In recent years he's lived in Morocco, Jordan, Haiti and Fiji, as well as his native England. Find him online at paulclammer.com or on Twitter as @paulclammer.

**Lucy Corne**

South Africa, Lesotho, Swaziland Lucy left university with a degree in journalism and a pair of perpetually itchy feet. She taught EFL for eight years in Spain, South Korea, Canada, China and India, while writing freelance features for a range of magazines, newspapers and websites. She joined the Lonely Planet team in 2008 and has since worked on a range of titles including *Africa, Canary Islands, South Africa, Lesotho & Swaziland* and several foodie titles. Lucy lives in Cape Town with her husband and young son, where she writes on travel, food and beer. Her popular blog, www.brewmistress.co.za, documents the South African beer scene.

**Emilie Filou**

Madagascar Emilie is a freelance journalist specialising in business and development issues, with a particular interest in Africa. Born in France, Emilie is now based in London, UK, from where she makes regular trips to Africa. Her work has appeared in publications such as the BBC, *Economist*, *Guardian*, *Africa Report* and *Christian Science Monitor*.

**Mary Fitzpatrick**

Tanzania, Mozambique Originally from the USA, Mary spent her early years dreaming of how to get across an ocean or two to more exotic locales. Following graduate studies, she set off for Europe. Her fascination with languages and cultures soon led her further south to Africa, where she has spent the past two decades living and working as a professional travel writer all around the continent. She focuses particularly on East and Southern Africa, including Mozambique and Tanzania. Mary has authored and co-authored many guidebooks for Lonely Planet, including *Mozambique; Tanzania; South Africa, Lesotho & Swaziland; East Africa; West Africa;* and *Egypt*.

**Michael Grosberg**

Guinea-Bissau, Mauritania Michael has worked on over 45 Lonely Planet guidebooks. Prior to his freelance writing career, other international work included development on the island of Rota in the western Pacific; South Africa where he investigated and wrote about political violence and helped train newly elected government representatives; and Quito, Ecuador, teaching.

**Trent Holden**

Victoria Falls, Zambia, Zimbabwe A writer based in Geelong, just outside Melbourne, Trent has worked for Lonely Planet since 2005. He's covered 30-plus guidebooks across Asia, Africa and Australia. With a penchant for megacities, Trent's in his element when assigned to cover a nation's capital to unearth cool bars, art, street food and underground subculture. On the flipside he also writes guides to tropical islands across Asia, in between going on safari to national parks in Africa and the subcontinent. When not travelling, Trent works as a freelance editor and reviewer and spends all his money catching live gigs. You can catch him on Twitter @hombreholden.

**Jessica Lee**

Egypt, Morocco Jess high-tailed it for the road at the age of 18 and hasn't looked back since. In 2011 she swapped a career as an adventure-tour leader for travel writing and since then her travels for Lonely Planet have taken her across Africa, the Middle East and Asia. She has lived in the Middle East since 2007 and tweets @jessofarabia. Jess has contributed to Lonely Planet's *Egypt*, *Turkey*, *Cyprus*, *Marrakesh*, *Middle East*, *Europe*, *Africa*, *Cambodia*, and *Vietnam* guidebooks and her travel writing has appeared in *Wanderlust* magazine, the *Daily Telegraph*, the *Independent*, BBC Travel and Lonelyplanet.com.

# OUR STORY

A beat-up old car, a few dollars in the pocket and a sense of adventure. In 1972 that's all Tony and Maureen Wheeler needed for the trip of a lifetime – across Europe and Asia overland to Australia. It took several months, and at the end – broke but inspired – they sat at their kitchen table writing and stapling together their first travel guide, *Across Asia on the Cheap*. Within a week they'd sold 1500 copies. Lonely Planet was born.

Today, Lonely Planet has offices in Franklin, London, Melbourne, Oakland, Dublin, Beijing and Delhi, with more than 600 staff and writers. We share Tony's belief that 'a great guidebook should do three things: inform, educate and amuse'.

# OUR WRITERS

**Anthony Ham**

Botswana, Libya, Namibia, Tunisia, Plan Your Trip, Understand Africa, Survival Guide Anthony is a freelance writer and photographer who specialises in Spain, East and Southern Africa, the Arctic and the Middle East. When he's not writing for Lonely Planet, Anthony writes about and photographs Spain, Africa and the Middle East for newspapers and magazines in Australia, the UK and US.

**Brett Atkinson**

Morocco For this new edition, Brett travelled from his New Zealand home to explore the fascinating medinas of Taroudannt and Tiznit, the spectacular Atlantic coastline, and the wild desert vistas of the Sahara. A highlight was the poignant and elegant Spanish Art Deco architecture of Sidi Ifni. Brett's contributed to Lonely Planet guidebooks spanning Europe, Africa, Asia and the Pacific, and covered over 60 countries as a food and travel writer. See www.brett-atkinson.net for his latest adventures.

**James Bainbridge**

Malawi James is a British travel writer and journalist based in Cape Town, South Africa, from where he roams the globe and contributes to publications worldwide. He has been working on Lonely Planet projects for over a decade. He has contributed to several editions of Lonely Planet's *South Africa, Lesotho & Swaziland, Turkey* and *Morocco* guides, and his articles on travel, culture and investment appear in the likes of *BBC Travel*, the UK *Guardian* and *Independent* and *Condé Nast Traveller*.

**Stuart Butler**

Algeria, Burundi, Central African Republic, Chad, Guinea, Mali, Niger, South Sudan Stuart's earliest travel writing was all based on surfing and exploring little-known coastlines for waves. Today, as well as guidebooks, Stuart writes often about conservation and environmental issues, wildlife watching and hiking. He also works as a photographer and was a finalist in both the 2015 and 2016 Travel Photographer of the Year Awards. His website is at www.stuartbutlerjournalist.com.

**Jean-Bernard Carillet**

Djibouti, Ethiopia, Somalia, Sudan Jean-Bernard is a Paris-based freelance writer and photographer who specialises in Africa, France, Turkey, the Indian Ocean, the Caribbean and the Pacific. He loves adventure, remote places, islands, outdoors, archaeological sites and food. His insatiable wanderlust has taken him to 114 countries across six continents. It has inspired lots of articles and photos for travel magazines and some 70 Lonely Planet guidebooks, both in English and in French.

OVER PAGE MORE WRITERS

**Published by Lonely Planet Global Limited**
CRN 554153
14th edition – Nov 2017
ISBN 978 1 78657 152 6

10 9 8 7 6 5 4 3 2 1
Printed in Singapore